Rand McNally

The Explorer World Atlas

Rand McNally
The Explorer World Atlas

Chicago • New York • San Francisco

Rand McNally
Explorer World Atlas

General Manager: Russell L. Voisin
Managing Editor: Jon M. Leverenz
Cartographic Services:
Michael W. Dobson, Ph.D., V. Patrick Healy
Designers: Vito M. DePinto, Robert Palmer
Production Editor: Laura C. Schmidt
Production Manager: Patricia Martin

Rand McNally Explorer World Atlas
Copyright ©1991 by Rand McNally & Company

Printed in the United States of America

Library of Congress Catalog Card Number: 90-53235
ISBN: 0-528-83411-8

Photograph and Illustration Credits

Page I-1: Juan Vespucci World Map, 1526/Courtesy of the Hispanic Society of
America, New York. Page I-2: Ptolemy's world/Vatican Apostolic Library, Vatican
City; Americans/from Winsor, Justin, *Narrative and Cultural History of America*,
Vol. 1, Boston and New York, Houghton Mifflin & Co., 1886; 1400's compass/
©National Geographic Society, courtesy of Casa de Colon. Las Palmas de Gran
Canaria; *Pinta, Santa Maria, Niña*/painting by Richard Schlecht ©National Geo-
graphic Society. Page I-3: Babylonian World Map/By permission of the British
Museum; Page of Columbus's Log/Biblioteca Nacional, Madrid; Martellus world map,
1489/By permission of the British Library. Page I-4: Sea Serpent/Winsor, 1886 (from
Olaus Magnus, 1555); Hecataeus, Herodotus, Strabo maps/from Bunbury, E. H., *A
History of Ancient Geography*, Vol. 2, London, John Murray, 1883. Page I-5:
Phoenician ship/artist unknown. Page I-6: Babylonian world map/By permission of
the British Museum; Ptolemy/Winsor, 1886; Ptolemy world map/Vatican Apostolic
Library. Page I-7: Behaim globe/facsimile reproduction by E. G. Ravenstein, by
permission of George Philip & Son, Ltd.; Pizzigano chart, 1424/courtesy of the
Associates of the James Ford Bell Library, University of Minnesota. Page I-8: Chinese
compass, Beazley, C., *The Dawn of Modern Geography*, London, John Murray, 1897;
Carrack and caraval ships/*The World Atlas of Exploration*, London, Mitchell Beazley
Publishers, Ltd., 1975; *Niña*/painting by Richard Schlecht ©National Geographic
Society. Page I-9: Astrolabe/Ogilvie and Waitley, *Children's Atlas of the World*,
Chicago, Rand McNally & Co., 1985; North Star drawing/National Maritime Museum,
London; 1400's compass/©National Geographic Society, courtesy of Casa de Colon.
Las Palmas de Gran Canaria. Page I-10: 1400's ship/Bernhard von Breydenbach,
1486. Page I-11: St. Brendan/Thacher, John Boyd, *Christopher Columbus, His Life,
His Work, His Remains*, Vol. 3, New York, G. P. Putnam, 1903. Page I-12: 1479
transcript/State Archives, Genoa, Italy; Columbus Portraits: A. Piombo/The Metro-
politan Museum of Art, Gift of J. Pierpont Morgan, 1900. (00.18.2); B. Durlacher/
©Ruth Durlacher-Wolper; C. Lasansky/courtesy of the Associates of the James Ford
Bell Library; D. DeBry/Winsor, 1886; E. Jovian/Thacher, 1903. Page I-13: Coat of
Arms/Winsor, 1886. Page I-14: King Ferdinand/Carta de Colòn, Basel, 1493. Page
I-15: King Ferdinand, after the original portrait at Madrid, from Prescott, William H.,
History of the Reign of Ferdinand and Isabella the Catholic, Philadelphia and
London, J. P. Lippincott Co., 1904; Queen Isabela/by Masson, Madrid, 1865, from
John Fiske, *The Discovery of America*, Vol. 1, Boston and New York, Houghton
Mifflin & Co., 1902; 1400's ship/Honorius Philoponus, *Nova typis transacta
navigatio*, Venezia, 1621. Page I-16: Columbus landing/Winsor, 1866; *Pinta, Santa
Maria, Niña*/painting by Richard Schlecht ©National Geographic Society. Page I-19:
Woodcuts, the New World/courtesy of the Newberry Library, Chicago. Page I-20:
Juan de la Cosa world map/Museo Naval, Madrid; Cantino map/Biblioteca Estense,
Modena, Italy. Page I-21: Waldseemüller map/facsimile courtesy of the Newberry
Library; Contarini map/By permission of the British Library. Page I-22: Pineapple/
Winsor, 1886. Page I-24: Indian club/Winsor, 1886. Page I-25: Americans/Winsor,
1886. Page I-28: Magellan's ship/Kenneth Nebenzahl collection. Page I-30: Greek
vase/The Metropolitan Museum of Art, Harris Brisbane Dick Fund, 1934. (34.11.7);
Caravan/courtesy of the British Museum; Columbus in the New World/courtesy of
the Newberry Library; Amerigo Vespucci/Kenneth Nebenzahl collection; 1500's
ship/Topkapi Saray Museum, Istanbul. Page I-31: Mariner's compass/©National
Geographic Society, courtesy of Casa de Colon. Las Palmas de Gran Canaria; Sir
Francis Drake/Kenneth Nebenzahl collection; Map of North America/©Rand
McNally & Co.; Lewis and Clark/Eide, Ingvard H. *American Odyssey* Chicago, Rand
McNally & Co., 1969. Page I-32: Map of the Grand Canyon/private collection;
Voyager 2, Jet Propulsion Laboratory; Astronaut/NASA; *Columbia*/NASA.

Maps on pages I-10, I-11, I-16, I-17, I-18, I-19, and I-22 compiled by Robert H. Fuson.

Contents

Using the Atlas   vi

Columbus and Beyond

Introduction   I.2

Events Leading to The Great Discovery

Early Perceptions of the World   I.4

Maps and Globes Before Columbus   I.6

Marine Technology of the 1400's   I.8

Voyages Before 1492   I.10

Columbus and His Time

The Years Before Spain   I.12

Columbus in Spain   I.14

The Voyages of Columbus —One and Two   I.16

The Voyages of Columbus —Three and Four   I.18

Impact of The Great Discovery

Landmark Maps Showing the New Discoveries   I.20

Europe Reacts to the Columbian Encounter   I.22

The Discoverers Change the New World   I.24

In the Wake of Columbus, 1493–1519   I.26

Filling in the Features of the Earth, 1519–1600   I.28

Argonauts to Astronauts— Chart of Explorers   I.30

Reference Maps   1–128

Map Symbols   1

The World and Special Regions   2–7

The World   2

Polar Map of the World   4

Atlantic Ocean   5

Pacific Ocean   6

Antarctica   7

Europe   8–29

Europe and Western Asia   8

British Isles   10

Ireland   11

England and Wales   12

Scotland and Northern England   13

Norway, Sweden and Finland   14

Denmark and Northern Germany   15

France and the Low Countries   16

Belgium, Netherlands, Luxembourg and Western Germany   17

Germany, Austria and Switzerland   18

Central Germany   19

Alpine Regions   20

Switzerland   21

Spain and Portugal   22

Italy   23

Yugoslavia, Hungary, Romania and Bulgaria   24

Greece, Albania and Western Turkey   25

Poland and Czechoslovakia   26

Western Soviet Union   27

South Central Soviet Union   28

Soviet Union   29

Asia   30–41

Asia   30

China, Mongolia, Korea, Japan and Taiwan   31

Northeastern China   32

Japan and Korea   33

Indonesia and the Philippines   34

Cambodia (Kampuchea), Laos, Vietnam, Thailand and Malaysia   35

India, Pakistan, Bangladesh, Burma (Myanmar) and Sri Lanka   36

Central India and Nepal   37

Middle East   38

Iran and Afghanistan   39

Turkey, Cyprus, Syria, Jordan, Israel and Lebanon   40

Israel and Northern Egypt   41

Africa   42–49

Africa   42

Northeast Africa   43

Northwest Africa   44

West Africa   45

Equatorial Africa   46

East Africa   47

Central Africa   48

Southern Africa   49

Australia and Oceania   50–52

Australia   50

Southeastern Australia and New Zealand   51

Pacific Islands   52

South America   53–60

South America   53

Central and Southern Argentina and Chile   54

Bolivia, Paraguay, Northern Argentina and Chile   55

Uruguay and Southern Brazil   56

Eastern Brazil   57

Peru and Ecuador   58

Guyana, Suriname, French Guiana and Northern Brazil   59

Colombia and Venezuela   60

North America   61–127

North America   61

Central America   62

Mexico   63

West Indies   64

Caribbean Islands   65

Canada   66

Alberta   68

British Columbia   69

Manitoba   70

Maritime Provinces   71

Newfoundland   72

Ontario   73

Quebec   74

Saskatchewan   75

United States of America   76

Alabama   78

Alaska   79

Arizona   80

Arkansas   81

California   82

Colorado   83

Connecticut   84

Delaware   85

Florida   86

Georgia   87

Hawaii   88

Idaho   89

Illinois   90

Indiana   91

Iowa   92

Kansas   93

Kentucky   94

Louisiana   95

Maine   96

Maryland   97

Massachusetts   98

Michigan   99

Minnesota   100

Mississippi   101

Missouri   102

Montana   103

Nebraska   104

Nevada   105

New Hampshire   106

New Jersey   107

New Mexico   108

New York   109

North Carolina   110

North Dakota   111

Ohio   112

Oklahoma   113

Oregon   114

Pennsylvania   115

Rhode Island   116

South Carolina   117

South Dakota   118

Tennessee   119

Texas   120

Utah   121

Vermont   122

Virginia   123

Washington   124

West Virginia   125

Wisconsin   126

Wyoming   127

North Polar Regions   128

Index to World Reference Maps   129–224

Introduction to the Index and List of Abbreviations   129

Index to World Reference Maps   130

Using the Atlas

Maps and Atlases

Mapmaking appears to have had its origins in the earliest ages of human history. People of all cultures have needed maps, and artifacts show they possessed the skill to draw them. The ease with which almost anyone can sketch simple directions lends credibility to the assumption that maps have been around a long time. They have always played an important and unique role in presenting information about the world — its routes, territories, and the lay of the land.

Some of the earliest maps are those defining territory and ownership. Dating from the second and first millenia B.C., the rock carving map of the Val Camonica, Italy, in figure 1 shows stepped square fields, paths, rivers, and houses. Elegant as well as useful maps have been produced by many cultures. In figure 2, the Mexican map of the Tepetlaoztoc Valley, drawn in 1583, marks hills with wavy lines and roads with footprints between parallel lines. The methods and materials used to create these maps were dependent upon the technology available, and their accuracy suffered considerably, whereas modern maps are highly accurate, benefiting from our ever-increasing technological knowledge. Satellite imagery, shown in figure 3, now furnishes current, highly precise material from which maps such as that in figure 4 may be created or updated.

In the 1500s Gerardus Mercator, a Flemish cartographer, coined the word *atlas* to describe a collection of maps. The atlas is unique among reference publications because only it, with its maps, actually shows *where* things are located in the world. As a dictionary defines words, as an encyclopedia defines things, an atlas graphically defines the world. Only on a map can the countries, cities, roads, rivers, and lakes covering a vast area be simultaneously viewed in their relative locations. Routes between places can be traced, trips planned, boundaries of neighboring states and countries examined, distances between places measured, the meandering of rivers and streams and the sizes of lakes visualized — and remote places imagined.

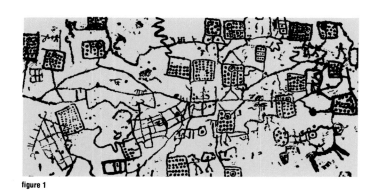

figure 1

figure 3

figure 2

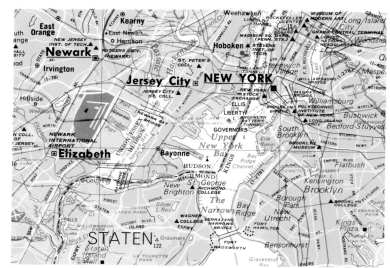

figure 4

Sequence of the Maps

The world is made up of seven major land-masses: the continents of Europe, Asia, Africa, Australia, South America, North America, and Antarctica (figure 5). To allow for the inclusion of detail, each continent is broken down into a series of maps, and this grouping is arranged so that as consecutive pages are turned, a continuous and successive part of the continent is shown. Larger-scale maps are used for regions of greater detail (having many cities, for example) or for areas of global significance.

The continental sequence of the maps is as follows: Europe (traditionally first in atlases), Asia (connected to Europe and forming the Eurasian landmass), Africa, Australia and Oceania, South America, and North America.

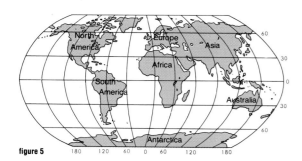

figure 5

Getting the Information

An atlas can be used for many purposes, from planning a trip to finding hot spots in the news and supplementing world knowledge. But to realize the full potential of an atlas, the user must be able to:

1. Find places on the maps
2. Measure distances
3. Determine directions
4. Understand map symbols

Finding Places

One of the most common and important tasks facilitated by an atlas is finding the *location* of a place in the world. A river's name in a book, a city mentioned in the news, or a vacation spot may prompt your need to know where the place is located. The illustrations and text below explain how to find Benguela, Angola.

1. Look up the place-name in the index at the back of the atlas. Benguela, Angola, can be found on the map on page 48, and it can be located on the map by the letter-number key *D1* (figure 6).

Benevento, Italy	D5	23	Benzonia, Mi., U.S.
Benevolence, Ga., U.S.	E2	87	Beo, Indon.
Benewah, co., Id., U.S.	B2	89	Béoumi, I.C.
Benezett, Pa., U.S.	D5	115	Beowawe, Nv., U.S.
Benfeld, Fr.	A3	20	Beppu, Japan
Bengal, Ok., U.S.	C6	113	Beqa, i., Fiji
Bengal, hist reg., Asia	D8	36	Beqa Passage, strt., Fiji
Bengal, Bay of, b., Asia	F8	36	Bequia, i., St. Vin.
Ben Gardane, Tun.	C7	44	Berach, stm., India
Bengbu, China	E8	31	Berati, Alb.
Benghazi (Banghāzī), Libya	C4	43	Berau, F.R.Ger.
Bengkalis, Indon.	E2	34	Berau Bay, b., Indon.
Bengkalis, i., Indon.	L5	35	Berbera, Som.
Bengkulu, Indon.	F2	34	Berbérati, Cen. Afr. Rep.
Bengo, dept., Ang.	C1	48	Berbice, stm., Guy.
Bengough, Sk., Can.	H3	75	Berceto, Italy
Benguela, Ang.	D1	48	Bercher, Switz.
Benguela, dept., Ang.	D1	48	Berchogur, Sov. Un.
Benham, Ky., U.S.	D7	94	Berchtesgaden, F.R.Ger.
Ben Hill, co., Ga., U.S.	E3	87	Berck, Fr.
Beni, Nig.	D7	45	Berclair, Tx., U.S.
Beni, Zaire	A4	48	Berdichev, Sov. Un.
Beni, dept., Bol.	B2	55	Berdsk, Sov. Un.
Beni, stm., Bol.	B2	55	Berdyansk, Sov. Un.
Béni Abbas, Alg.	C4	44	Berea, Ky., U.S.
Benicarló, Spain	B5	22	Beren, Ne., U.S.

figure 6

2. Turn to the map of Central Africa on page 48. Note that the letters A through E and the numbers 1 through 7 appear in the margins of the maps.

3. To find Benguela on the map, place your left index finger on D and your right index finger on 1. Move your left finger across the map and your right finger into the map. Your fingers will meet in the area in which Benguela is located (figure 7).

figure 7

Measuring Distances

In planning trips, determining the distance between two places is essential, and an atlas can help in travel preparation. For instance, to determine the approximate distance between Paris and Rouen, France, follow these three steps:

1. Lay a slip of paper on the map on page 16 so that its edge touches the two cities. Adjust the paper so one corner touches Rouen. Mark the paper directly at the spot where Paris is located (figure 8).

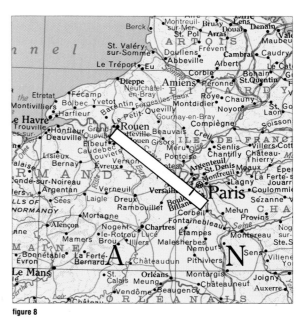

figure 8

2. Place the paper along the scale of statute miles beneath the map. Position the corner at 0 and line up the edge of the paper along the scale. The pencil mark on the paper indicates Rouen is between 50 and 75 miles from Paris (figure 9).

3. To find the exact distance, move the paper to the left so that the pencil mark is at 50 on the scale. The corner of the paper stands in the fourth 5-mile unit on the scale. This means that the two towns are 50 miles plus 15 miles plus 2 miles, or 67 miles, apart (figure 10).

figure 9

figure 10

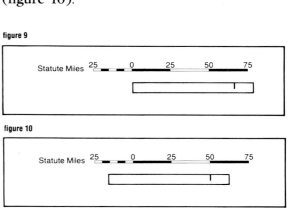

The scale relationship of the map to the earth may also be expressed as a ratio, for example, 1:1,000,000 (one to one million). The map unit in the ratio is always given as one, and the number of similar units the map unit represents on the earth's surface is written after the colon. Thus for a 1:1,000,000 map, 1 inch on the map represents 1,000,000 inches on the earth's surface. In order to determine how many miles on the earth 1 inch on the map represents, divide 63,360 (the number of inches in one mile) into 1,000,000. This results in the written scale for a 1:1,000,000 map being stated as, 1 inch (on the map) = 16 miles (on the earth).

Determining Directions

Most of the maps in the atlas are drawn so that when oriented for normal reading north is at the top of the map, south is at the bottom, west is at the left, and east is at the right. Most maps have a series of lines drawn across them — the lines of latitude and longitude. Lines of latitude, or parallels of latitude, are drawn east and west. Lines of longitude, or meridians of longitude, are drawn north and south (figure 11).

Parallels and meridians appear as either curved or straight lines. For example, in the section of the map of Europe in figure 12, the parallels of latitude appear as curved lines. The meridians of longitude are straight lines that come together toward the top of the map.

Latitude and longitude lines help locate places on maps. Parallels of latitude are numbered in degrees north and south of the *Equator*. Meridians of longitude are numbered in degrees east and west of a line called the *Prime Meridian,* running through Greenwich, England, near London. Any place on earth can be located by the latitude and

longitude lines running through it.

To determine directions or locations on maps, you must use the parallels and meridians. For example, suppose you want to know which city is farther north, Bergen, Norway, or Stockholm, Sweden. The map in figure 12 shows that Stockholm is south of the 60° parallel of latitude and Bergen is north of it. This means that Bergen is farther north than Stockholm. By looking at the meridians of longitude, you can determine which city is farther east. Bergen is approximately 5° east of the 0° meridian (Prime Meridian), and Stockholm is almost 20° east of it. This means that Stockholm is farther east than Bergen.

Understanding Map Symbols

In a very real sense, the whole map is a symbol, representing the world or a part of it. It is a reduced representation of the earth; each of the world's features — cities, rivers, etc. — is represented on the map by a symbol. Map symbols may take the form of points, such as dots or stars (often used for cities, capital cities, or points of interest), or lines (roads, rivers, railroads). Symbols may also occupy an area, showing extent of coverage (states, forests, deserts). They seldom look like the feature they represent and therefore must be identified and interpreted. For instance, the maps in this atlas show and differentiate political units (countries, states) with color. The political units are further defined by a heavy line depicting their boundaries. Neither the colors nor the boundary lines are actually found on the surface of the earth, but because countries and states are such important political components of the world, strong symbols are used to represent them.

The legend on page 1 identifies the symbols used in this atlas.

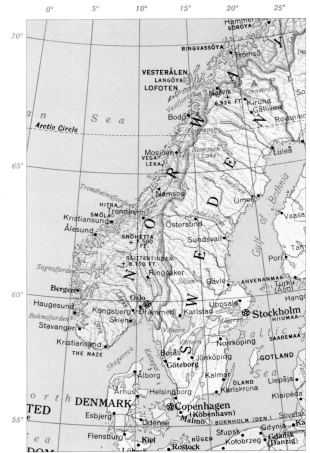

figure 12

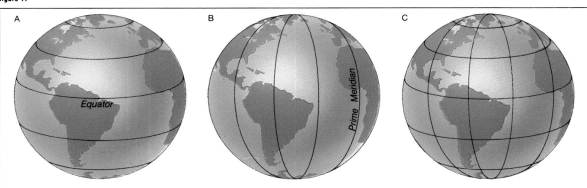

figure 11

Columbus and Beyond

ROBERT H. FUSON, Ph.D.

PROFESSOR EMERITUS OF GEOGRAPHY
UNIVERSITY OF SOUTH FLORIDA

Columbus and

Introduction

The ancient Romans had a word for nearly everything—everything, that is, but for "discovery." In classical Latin, the closest term was *inventio*, invention. We still use this word to describe something created from scratch. The bow and arrow would have been called an invention in Caesar's language just as it is in our own. But no one can "invent" the laws of motion governing an arrow's flight. When you reveal something that already exists, it is called a *discovery*.

Christopher Columbus *discovered* a New World. He reported his finding to others who, once they accepted the new knowledge, had their ideas of the known world radically changed. Such voyages of discovery and their impact are quite different from the Vikings' journeys to Vinland or even from the migration of Asiatic peoples into what is now North America. These unheralded events—regardless of their historical interest—are not discoveries in the true sense of the word.

But Columbus did not make just a discovery. He made a Great Discovery, one that caused immediate and profound changes in the course of history and geography. As with most discoveries, however, there were countless events during the preceding centuries that led to The Great Discovery on the twelfth of October in 1492. The first part of this essay focuses on these events.

Events Leading to the Great Discovery

The first section examines perceptions of the world before 1492. The earliest ideas come from Homer, the Phoenicians, and the Greeks and Romans of the classical period. In the eighth century A.D. the Arab world became the center for science and technology. By the fourteenth and early fifteenth centuries, the Ming Chinese had made significant advances in navigation

and exploration at sea. On the other side of the ocean, northern Europeans such as the Irish and Norse, and southern Europeans, particularly the Genoese, Venetians, and Portuguese, added to the accumulated maritime knowledge. From all this activity came numerous maps and globes, depicting the world as it was then perceived. Though crude, they were the first threads in a fabric that has gradually been woven into the complex map creations we know today. The prevailing technology is also reviewed: the types of vessels and their evolution, and the development of navigation equipment.

A look is taken at some of the more important voyages made before 1492. Whatever the reasons for sailing, everyone agreed on one fact: only one body of water, the Ocean Sea, lay between Africa/Europe and Asia. Before Columbus, no one who attempted to cross this vast sea returned with a map of his exploits. There were no credible charts showing what existed on this ocean, nor how to get back. Popular superstition held that the voyagers who did not return were devoured by sea creatures or fell off the edge of the world. Many people made the same dire predictions for Columbus's three ships.

Ptolemy's world

1400's compass

Americans

EVENTS LEADING TO COLUMBUS'S GREAT DISCOVERY

1000 - 100 BC	100 BC - AD 1000	AD 1000 - 1300
Phoenicians sail to England and Germany (1000 BC).	Eratosthenes accurately measures earth's circumference (276 - 194 BC).	Lief Ericksson reaches North America (1003).
Phoenician/Egyptian ship rounds Cape of Good Hope, Africa (600 BC).	Poseidonius underestimates the earth's circumference (135 BC).	Earliest extant map of China (1137).
Pythagoras perceives earth as a sphere (500 BC).	Strabo preserves early writings and circumnavigation attempts (64 BC - AD 20).	Era of Portolan Charts (1200 - 1500).
Herodotus documents geographical and historical events (484 - 425 BC).	Ptolemy writes *Geographia* source for world maps until 1500s. (AD 75 - 153).	Marco Polo returns to Europe from eastern Asia (1295).
Earliest preserved world map from Babylon (500 BC).	Irish reach Iceland (AD 795); Vikings reach North America (AD 987).	First Genoese voyage into the Atlantic Ocean (1291).

Beyond

Columbus and His Time

The second major portion of this essay provides a glimpse of Columbus—the man, his family, and his benefactors. Topics covered include the navigational tools he used, as well as problems of health on long ocean voyages in the late fifteenth century. Columbus's early travels and associations set the stage for his four Voyages of Discovery. To follow the First Voyage, the story is taken straight from the pages of his *diario de a bordo* (on-board journal).

Impact of the Great Discovery

The third section describes the impact that Columbus's momentous discovery had on the Old and New Worlds. The voyages brought about startling changes in both worlds that continue to this day. From the moment the New World became known, a complex network of trade and immigration sprang up involving first the Americas, Africa, and Europe and shortly afterward, eastern and southeastern Asia.

Along this network, ships ferried plants, animals, and people back and forth across the Atlantic sea. Even fatal diseases passed both ways across the ocean. New commercial and financial institutions arose to manage the traffic in goods and people. The European invasion destroyed Indian societies that had existed for hundreds of years, while radically changing the very landscape of the New World.

Since 1492, explorer after explorer has followed in the wake of Columbus, mapping the seas and lands of the entire world. In modern times, explorers have reached the polar zones, sounded the oceanic depths, and soared into space. At the close of the essay the future of exploration is briefly reviewed. It is interesting to note that when the United States resumed its space program in 1988, the first shuttle launched was named *Discovery*, and its sister ship was christened *Columbia*. As we celebrate the 500-year anniversary of the Great Discovery, the spirit of Christopher Columbus is very much alive.

Babylonian world map

Page of Columbus's log

Pinta, Santa María, Niña

1489 world map

AD 1300 - 1400

Portuguese expedition charts the Canary Islands (1341).

Last Norse visit to North America (1347).

Chinese Ming Dynasty produces maps of the Far East (1368 - 1644).

Catalan Atlas maps coasts and Arabic knowledge of the world (1375).

Scottish/Venetian voyage to North America (1398).

AD 1400 - 1500

Cheng Ho charts Indian Ocean from East Indies to Africa (1405 - 1433).

Portuguese/Danish-Norwegian voyage to North America (1472).

Toscanelli chart shows Asia 3,000 miles west of Canary Islands (1474).

Martin Behaim produces globe showing undersized Atlantic Ocean (1492).

Columbus sets sail (August 3, 1492).
Columbus sights land (October 12, 1492).

Early Perceptions of the World

In ancient Greek mythology, *Oceanus* was the son of Uranus (heaven) and Gaea (earth). His earthly manifestation was a mighty river—swift, deep, and foreboding—that encircled the flat, disk-shaped earth. This flowing water, father of all rivers, became known as the Ocean River.

The Greeks and their neighbors believed that this Ocean River defined the outer limits of the world. All land inhabited by mortals lay snugly within its circular boundary. Beyond the Ocean River—or perhaps on islands within it—dwelled the immortals, including Oceanus himself.

The World of Homer

Perhaps our two best sources to illustrate exploration in those enchanting and mystical times are the *Iliad* and the *Odyssey*. In the latter, Homer (800 B.C.) transports us—through the eyes of Ulysses—on a marvelous voyage into the mysterious Ocean River.

Homer also preserved the tale of an earlier voyage, of Jason and his ship *Argo*,

terranean, holding a virtual monopoly on transport across the inland sea and serving Egypt and Babylon. Phoenician merchants established themselves in every large port city in the Mediterranean basin and had major entrepôt centers at Memphis (Egypt), in Mesopotamia, and in Jerusalem.

How the Phoenicians perceived the earth remains a mystery, but it is clear that the Ocean River held few terrors for them. On the contrary, they may have spread tall tales about maritime conditions beyond the Pillars of Hercules to protect their monopoly. All the while they continued to ply the waters of the eastern Atlantic, adding to their knowledge of navigation, shiplore, and maritime conditions.

Not until the sixth century B.C. did Greek thought catch up with Phoenician practical knowledge of the world. The Greek mathematician Pythagoras (c. 582–500 B.C.) proved the world was round. From that time on, knowledgeable people thought of the world as a sphere.

The circular map reconstructs one by Hecataeus (550 - 475 BC) and reflects the Greek notion of the land surrounded by an Ocean Sea, not an Ocean River. Little detail is shown outside the Mediterranean area.

CALCULATING THE EARTH'S SIZE
Using a method attributed to Eratosthenes (276-194 BC)

1. Assume the earth is a sphere.
2. Know the sun's rays are directly overhead and shine to the bottom of a well at Syene, Egypt.
3. Observe and measure the length of the shadow cast by a wall on the same day in Alexandria, 500 miles north of Syene.
4. Derive the angle "a" as 7°; mathematically determine that angle "b" is 7°; and that it describes the 500-mile segment of the earth between Syene and Alexandria.
5. Calculate there are 50 such segments in the earth's circumference by dividing 7° into 360° (the number of degrees in a circle).
6. Multiply the 500-mile segment by 50 (the number of segments in the circumference) to arrive at 25,000 miles, the approximate circumference of the earth.

Note: Although Eratosthenes made errors in his measurements, arriving at a circumference of 29,000 miles, it was still closer to the earth's size of 24,900 than any other up until that time.

---

that reached the "farthest east" on the banks of the Ocean River. In that land (now known as Soviet Georgia), Jason and the Argonauts found the legendary Golden Fleece. Even in these early times humanity ventured into the unknown in search of knowledge, wealth, and new lands.

Merchant Mariners

The Phoenicians emerged as the first true masters of the Ocean River. They managed to survive the destruction of the Bronze Age and make the best of the dismal period that marked the early centuries of the Iron Age (c. 1200 B.C.). At about that time, Phoenicia broke away from a weakening Egyptian empire.

We know little about these remarkable people. Both Homer and the Old Testament refer to them as Sidonians, a name derived from Sidon, one of the major Phoenician cities; other important centers included Tyre, Aradus, and, later, Carthage.

Far from chasing a mythical Golden Fleece, the Phoenicians sailed for more profitable trade. They were the warehousemen and wholesalers of the Medi-

Greek and Roman Classical Concepts

The Ocean River concept died during the Classical period in Greece. It was replaced by the idea of an Ocean Sea. Not until the time of Columbus were explorers able to determine if the sea was surrounded by land, or the land by sea, or neither. Herodotus (484-425 B.C.) embraced the Ocean Sea concept. Herodotus was an indefatigable traveler and writer, and his works have come down to us virtually intact, giving him a special status for many as the father of geography as well as history.

Despite the fact that his monumental *History* is a classic, its geographical portions leave much to be desired. Herodotus omits vast quantities of material that were known to him and seems to have shaped the world according to certain philosophical notions, particularly the Greek idea of "symmetry." His concept of the earth retained the flat, disk shape but deleted the Ocean River from western and northern Europe. He enclosed the Caspian Sea and placed the Indus River in its approximate true position. It is clear from his work that information from India and beyond was beginning to alter the Mediterranean world view.

The size of the earth occupied Greek thinking very early. Mathematicians associated with Aristotle stated the circumference to be 46,000 miles (74,030 km). Eratosthenes (276–194 B.C.) attempted to correct this figure, using the right equation but the wrong data. Although he erred by roughly 16 percent, his 29,000-mile (46,671 km) circumference was still closer to the earth's true size.

The Earth Takes Shape

Claudius Ptolemaeus, known to the world as Ptolemy (A.D. c. 75–c. 153), passed on the figure of the earth's circumference—20,400 miles (32,830 km), calculated earlier by Poseidonius. Ptolemy's figures dominated geography for the next 1,400 years and were used even by Christopher Columbus. These calculations, however, reduced the actual breadth of the Ocean Sea by about 5,000 miles (8,047 km).

This fact helps explain why Columbus thought he had reached Asia after only thirty-three days at sea. America appeared precisely where Asia should have been. It also explains why cartographers had such difficulty trying to squeeze the new discoveries into the western Ocean Sea. According to their current maps, there simply wasn't enough room for the new continents!

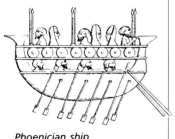

Phoenician ship

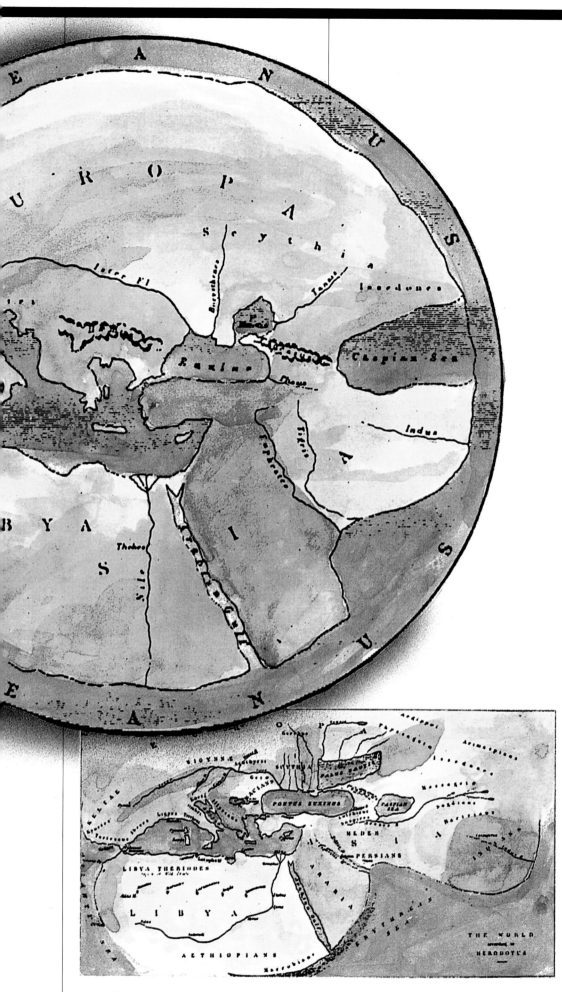

Arabic Influence

Such was not the case in the Arab world. When the Arabs rose to prominence in the seventh century, the sciences flourished once again. The Arab world preserved and translated great scientific and literary works left by the Greeks and carried the knowledge with them westward across North Africa. By A.D. 711 the Moors had invaded Spain and Portugal and re-introduced Greco-Roman learning to Europe. Although these works made numerous contributions to the sciences, they gave Europe no new perception of the world.

In the Americas, only the Eskimos, Aztecs, and Incas drew maps. These were highly localized and offered no hints of a global concept. The same can be said of Africa south of Arab influence. The non-Arab Middle East derived its perception of the globe from the Arabs, and even China was greatly influenced by the Arabic culture.

The Eastern World

The earliest known Chinese map dates from A.D. 1137, although references exist to maps as far back as 227 B.C. During the Ming Dynasty (A.D. 1368–1644) cartographers constructed numerous maps of the Indian Ocean region and the eastern littoral. One pre-Ming map, probably drafted about A.D. 1320, shows marked Arabic influence. In fact, most pilots and navigators on Chinese ships during the early Ming period were Muslims, and probably Arabs.

Sea Serpent

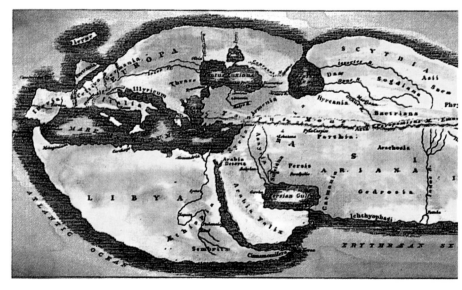

The illustration above shows the world according to the writings of Herodotus (484 - 425 BC). Though sketchy, details of Asia and Africa begin to fill the map as European explorers venture out.

Ancient western geography culminated with Ptolemy. But two important facts had been established: the Ocean Sea had been given the form it was to retain until the Voyages of Discovery, and the earth's spherical shape was no longer debated by any practical navigator.

The Romans added little to the geographical and maritime legacy left by the Greeks.

The Chinese were certainly aware of the Ocean Sea, for they sailed on it and traded over it on occasion. Before and during much of the Ming Dynasty the Chinese viewed the world as a flat disk with China at the center. Surrounding their land was not a vast Ocean River but more land filled with barbarians. Rather than explore these regions, the Chinese preferred to ignore them for much of their history. Therefore, instead of being the discoverers, they were the discovered.

Strabo (64 BC - 20 AD) used early writings and travelers' accounts to furnish explorers with his idea of a more complete world just before the Christian Era, as shown in the map above.

Maps and Globes Before Columbus

The 500 BC, small clay world map from Babylonia shows Mesopotamia girdled by the Ocean River and cut by the Tigris and Euphrates rivers. Its scope reflects the ancient's concept and limited knowledge of the world.

This fifteenth century map was reconstructed from Ptolemy's second century information. Consequently it erroneously portrayed a reduced world and Ocean Sea. Columbus's idea of the earth was likely influenced by the Ptolemaic maps of his generation.

Although maps may have existed since at least the third millennium B.C., the oldest surviving map of the world dates from the fifth century B.C. in Babylon. The map, which can be seen today in the British Museum, is impressed on a clay tablet. Partially defaced, it still clearly depicts the world known to the Babylonians. At first glance, the flat, disk-shaped, world view appears to be essentially the same as that of the pre-Classical Greeks. Because most Greek mathematics, astronomy, and technology came from the Near East, it is logical to assume this to be true.

Yet this flat-earth view of the world may be more a reflection of Babylonian folklore than an indication of their scientific knowledge. Babylonian astronomy as a science dates from about 500 B.C. and may have existed as early as 1000 B.C. Though much of the Mesopotamian record between 1500 B.C. and 300 B.C. has been lost, we do know the Babylonians correctly correlated solar years and lunar months, and predicted with great accuracy solar and lunar eclipses. They gave the world the first *gnomon*, a simple instrument that indicates time. Since these de-

velopments are impossible based on a flat-earth theory, they suggest that the surviving clay tablet in the British Museum does not accurately represent Babylonian cosmography. The people of the Tigris-Euphrates Valley may have been the first to propose a spherical earth.

Geographers and Maps of Ancient Greece

The earliest Greek map of the world was reportedly made of bronze by Anaximander (611–547 B.C.) in the city of Miletus in Ionia (now southwestern Turkey). In about 499 B.C., Aristagorus, the ruler of Miletus, carried it all the way to Sparta in an effort to enlist Spartan help in fighting the Persians. The map depicted rivers, seas, and all that surrounded these areas. Unfortunately for Aristagorus, the map was so well done that the Spartans, after seeing how far Persia was from their homeland, rejected the ruler's appeal!

"Scientific" geography based more on observation than on philosophical thought did not develop until the founding of the great library at Alexandria, Egypt. This occurred two centuries after the spherical shape of the earth had been accepted

throughout the Greek world. The Athenian scholar Demetrius Phalereus planned and organized the library a few years after the death of Alexander the Great, 323 B.C.

Ptolemy's Legacy

Ancient geography culminated with Ptolemy in the second century A.D.. He provided instructions for the most scientific map the ancients had ever seen. These guidelines were to remain the standard until the fifteenth century, although there were many revisions. Even so, some editions of Ptolemy's map were printed as late as 1883.

Ptolemy was the librarian at Alexandria between A.D. 127 and A.D. 150. During that time he drew upon the writings of Eratosthenes, Herodotus, and other scholars that preceded him and assembled the data that were pouring into Alexandria to produce his impressive *Geographia*, composed of seven volumes. Book I presents a general introduction and various astronomical calculations, with the latter part of the book devoted to maps and map projections. Books II–VII mainly list various geographic locations by latitude and longitude. The many maps that ac-

Ptolemy

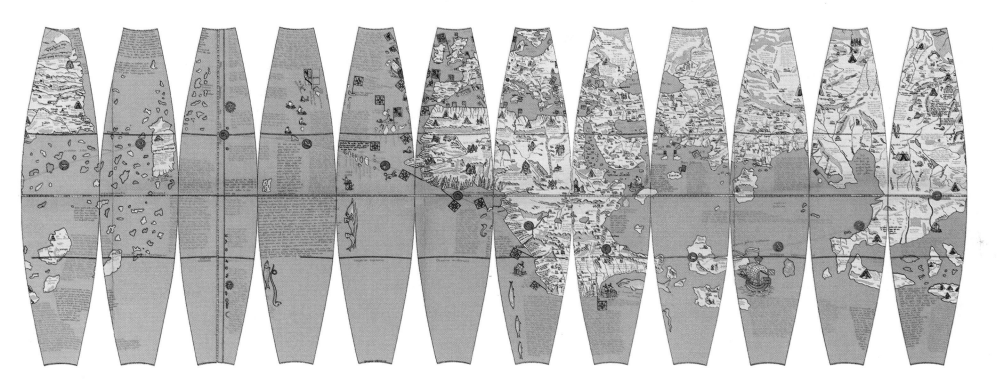

company *Geographia* are sometimes regarded as an eighth volume to Ptolemy's work. Unfortunately, none of his original maps was preserved. Those made later, based on his instructions and data, were used by Columbus and undoubtedly influenced his perception of the world.

Although Ptolemy, and maps based on his perspective, passed along erroneous data about the size of the earth, Ptolemy gave the world its first map with functional parallels of latitude and a prime meridian. He placed the meridian in the western-most part of the Fortunate (Canary) Islands, where it remained for sixteen centuries.

The Portolan Charts
After the death of Ptolemy, during the last three hundred years of the Roman Empire, geography, and mapping in particular, declined steadily. The genius of Ptolemy's work did not reach Florence until it was brought from Constantinople when the Turks overran the city in A.D. 1453.

In the meantime, a new cartographic form had appeared in Europe: the portolan chart. Although thousands of these charts must have been made, only 181 survive from the portolan period, which ended around 1500. Of this number, 60 are in atlas form. These were far more likely to survive intact since they did not suffer the rigors of constant use at sea nor were they discarded as new updated charts appeared. The oldest survivor is the *Carte Pisane*, developed near the end of the thirteenth century. The portolan by *Pizzigano*, shown here, is a representative of these magnificent and practical charts.

The portolans were constructed from the detailed reports of merchants, sailors, and scholars, a technique known from the days of Classical Greece. At first, only the Mediterranean and Black seas were charted. As knowledge of the world grew, the charts included the Baltic and North seas and the British Isles. Later, the West

African discoveries of the Portuguese were added, along with islands in the Atlantic.

Because portolans were designed and used for open-sea navigation, cartographers generalized coastal features. Unlike medieval world maps, which often boasted more art than science, the portolans were extremely conservative. They were never cluttered with sea monsters, mythical beasts, or other extraneous matter. Portolan cartographers did not engage in flights of fancy or mythology, with one possible exception. As with modern nautical charts, navigational hazards that were reported but not necessarily verified were plotted. Thus, a reported island may have been charted even though it did not actually exist. Then, as now, it was better to err on the side of caution.

The First Globe
The concept of the Ocean Sea had been around so many centuries that it did not disappear until after Vasco Núñez de Bal-

boa discovered the South Sea in 1513. It was renamed the Pacific Ocean by Ferdinand Magellan on his voyage around the world (1519–1522). Certainly Columbus believed in the Ocean Sea as he set sail in 1492. By a twist of fate, the oldest known globe, and the last one to depict the Ocean Sea, was constructed in the year of the Great Discovery.

Martin Behaim of Nürnberg, who may have been an acquaintance of Columbus, created the globe from maritime maps. Behaim was in charge of the royal map library in Lisbon and had been a long-time resident of the Azores. The first globe, now housed in the German National History Museum in Nürnberg, is a dramatic reminder of when people believed that only one ocean, on a smaller world sphere, surrounded the land. In time, new knowledge from the Voyages of Discovery changed not only the Old World's concept of geography but its entire world view.

The gores of the 1492 Behaim globe reveal Asia and what is believed to be Japan, to the left, separated from Europe by a reduced Ocean Sea. Observing this diminutive ocean could have encouraged Columbus as he planned his westerly course to reach Asia.

Portolan charts are characterized by intersecting straight lines that define compass or wind directions. Their accurate delineation of coastal features made them indispensible for Columbus and the early explorers. (Chart by Zuane Pizzigano, 1424.)

Marine Technology of the 1400's

Events Leading to the Great Discovery

Early Chinese compass

The large carrack ships had deep holds, a high stern, and square sails, making them suitable for carrying large cargoes while running before the constant trade winds of the open ocean.

The caravel ships were smaller than the carracks. They sat low in the water, had smooth hulls (*carvel-built,* planks laid flush), and usually triangular sails; ideal for coastal sailing and exploration.

The Voyages of Discovery required two categories of maritime technology: reliable vessels for open-ocean sailing and adequate navigational instruments. The need to make the voyages did not create the technology; rather the technology made the voyages possible. By 1400 the evolving marine technology that combined innovations and experience from northern and southern Europe, Asia, and the Middle East made an ocean crossing practical. Such voyages had long been *possible,* but by the fifteenth century there was a reasonable chance of getting back.

Caravels and Carracks

The vessel that became the workhorse of early navigators was known as the caravel (Arabic = *karib),* essentially an improved version of the Arabic *dhow.* The seaworthy little boat had been used for centuries in the Red Sea, Persian Gulf, and Indian Ocean. It may still be seen plying the coastal waters of the Middle East. The Portuguese added one or two masts to carry more sail and a bowsprit, and increased the ship's length to about 65 feet (20 meters). They maintained the ship's

wide hull, which displaced little water while holding ample cargo, and kept the lateen (triangular) sail of the *dhow.*

Both the *Niña* and the *Pinta* of the First Voyage were caravels. The *Pinta* sailed from Spain with square rigging and the *Niña* was re-rigged to square sails in the Canary Islands. Columbus felt that a square-rigged vessel offered more sail than the lateen to take advantage of the prevailing northeast trade winds.

The other mainline vessel was the *nao,* or carrack. The *Santa María* was of the carrack class. These ships were about 80 feet (24 meters) long, with an after-castle and poop-deck, and a forecastle that overhung the bow. They were full-rigged ships with three masts and a minimum of five working sails. *Pinta,* a caravel, carried the same sail arrangements as the *Santa María,* minus the topsail. The *Niña,* on the other hand, was a four-masted caravel.

Small carracks like the *Santa María* were crewed by about 40 men, while the caravels were manned by 20 to 25 seamen. On occasion, however, the sturdy little caravels carried more. *Niña* returned from the First Voyage with as many as ten extra passengers—Indians Columbus

brought with him to Spain. On the Third Voyage, *Niña* also carried colonists, possibly as many as 40 in addition to the normal crew. Each caravel was large enough to also carry a small boat, several anchors, pumps, and cannons, all necessary for the long ocean voyages.

The caravels and carracks were equipped with a central, hinged rudder, fixed to the stern post. This Baltic invention of the middle thirteenth century made steering easier than the oar-like lateral rudder that had been traditional in southern Europe, which it quickly replaced.

Compasses, Quadrants, and Astrolabes

Not only were reliable vessels in existence by the fifteenth century but so were the basic navigational instruments and charts. The single most important navigator's tool was the compass, probably introduced into Europe in the twelfth century by the Arabs, who learned of it from the Chinese.

Originally, the compass was marked with eight principal directions, named for the place in the direction from which a particular wind blew. Europeans had long

The painting details Columbus's *Niña,* a caravel, and among the most practical ships of her day. Columbus modified the standard caravel design by having four masts and square sails. Though only 67 feet long (20 meters), sturdy construction enabled it to carry 50 to 60 tons.

referred to directions as "winds," and the practice continued after the compass came into widespread use.

By the time of Columbus, the directional names we use today had been accepted (north, south, east, west, etc.). Eight intermediate directions, called "half-winds," were added and eventually even "quarter-winds" found their way onto the compass. By 1492, the compass card contained thirty-two directions, with each quarter equal to 11°15'. Assuming that a pilot could sail within the range defined by a "quarter," he could be 5°37'30" on either side of the quarter and still be right on course. This is one of the reasons that it is virtually impossible to re-plot the course of the First Voyage across the Atlantic from the data found in Columbus's log. Every entry could be more than five degrees off, even if each were recorded and reckoned accurately.

Compasses also had to be corrected for magnetic variations in different parts of the world. The magnetic variations in Europe were known in the fifteenth century, and compass corrections were apparent in the portolan charts of the period. But no one knew the variations in the Atlantic or West Indies.

This fact did not bother the Mediterranean pilots, who were not concerned with precise latitudes. For them the compass superseded every other navigational instrument, and they could follow a compass—even if the instrument, were off by a few degrees—and still reach port. The Mediterranean shore is high all around and much of it may be seen from fifty or more miles. As soon as land broke the horizon, the pilots corrected for any error.

Northern sailors, on the other hand, such as the Flemish, were celestial navigators. They actually published manuals on the erroneous magnetic data on the portolan charts and on the disagreement between Flemish and Mediterranean compasses. When Columbus sailed west, he meant west by the compass; according to his log, he did not attempt any magnetic corrections since he wouldn't have known what they were. He knew he was sailing "generally west," and that was good enough. Like the Mediterranean sailors, Columbus sailed by dead reckoning, following the compass.

The Admiral carried at least two different types of celestial instruments for determining his latitudinal position at sea, a quadrant and an astrolabe. He rarely used them and once said that he could not depend on his quadrant. This instrument was a forerunner of the sextant, had no optics, and had to be leveled from a plumb bob. The elevation of a celestial body could then be read from a scale, *if* sighted properly and *if* held perfectly level. One can imagine the degree of error if there were even a slight chop to the sea. The astrolabe provided a measurement of the earth's inclination, relative to the sun, for each day of the year.

Jack-staffs and cross-staffs were in common use in the fifteenth century, both derived from the Arabic *kamal.* These instruments were constructed of one or more perpendicular sticks on a bar held horizontally. The horizontal bar was calibrated, and the elevation of a body could be determined by sliding the perpendicular stick back and forth until the bottom tip was on the horizon and the top touched the body to be measured. The elevation was then read from the calibrated horizontal member. These instruments could be used to maintain a course along a particular latitude to a destination. Sticks of various lengths could be cut for different landfalls.

Fifteenth-century sailors measured time in various ways, none of them very accurate. The basic timepiece was the *ampolleta,* or half-hour sand glass. For short periods, rhymes and chants measured time. This method was used, for example, to calculate speed by measuring the elapsed time of an object floating from bow to stern.

Navigators and pilots also determined time by the stars and sun. At night, they followed the counterclockwise movement of the outer stars of the Little Dipper, the so-called Regiment of the North. The North Star was imagined to be at the center of a man's body. The outer stars then moved from head to elbow, to finger

tip, and so on, 15° every hour. It took twelve hours for the stars to move from the head to the feet.

Shipboard Health

In the fifteenth century, maritime medical science had not kept up with advances in ship design and navigational devices. Health and hygiene on long voyages were deplorable. Atlantic crossings, lasting three to five weeks, were not too physically demanding on the crews. But longer voyages, such as those of the Portuguese around Africa to India and the East Indies or those across the Pacific, had devastating effects on sailors. On many of these voyages, more than half the crew perished, usually from scurvy. Until 1753, no one knew that consuming foods high in vitamin C would prevent the disease. The Dutch were the only sailors who seldom got scurvy because they carried with them food high in vitamin C—sauerkraut.

Typical rations in the fifteenth and sixteenth centuries included only food that could be salted, dried, pickled, or baked. There were, therefore, no green vegetables and no citrus fruits because they would not keep on the long voyages. After the Great Discovery, cassava bread (from manioc) and several varieties of American beans became important staples on board.

Sanitation was virtually nonexistent on ships of the fifteenth and sixteenth centuries. The bilges were floating sewers, and the filth and stench from them permeated the entire vessel. Rats competed with cockroaches in a race for dominance. Toilet facilities did not exist, except for a boatswain's chair (affectionately called the "garden seat") slung over the side. Shipboard survival on these vessels was, to a large degree, survival of the fittest—or the luckiest!

Though marine technology had reached a stage of development making ocean travel practical by the fifteenth century, only the determined, skilled—and lucky—captains ventured out and returned.

The fifteenth-century compass with 32 direction points made it possible to sail within 5 1/2 degrees of a destination. It was the southern European navigator's most important instrument for sailing the Mediterranean and other waters where land was close at hand.

The Regiment of the North was a means of keeping time. The North Star was thought of as the center of the body; the outer stars moved, in regimented fashion, counterclockwise from head to elbow and so on—15 degrees every hour.

The mariner's astrolabe was held by the ring and sighted along the movable arm to measure the height of a celestial body—such as the North Star—above the horizon. The lower the North Star was in the sky, the farther south was the position.

Events Leading to the Great Discovery

Voyages Before 1492

History is spotty in recording early exploration and discovery, especially outside of the Mediterranean region. Nevertheless, information about the earth was building—some reliable, some myth—as each explorer added to the body of knowledge left by those he followed.

The Mysterious Mariners

The Phoenicians were venturing to England for tin and to Germany for amber before 1000 B.C. There is little doubt that these were the first known journeys by Mediterranean sailors beyond the Pillars of Hercules. Unfortunately, details of Phoenician navigation are lacking and almost nothing is known of precise voyages or ports of call.

and to observe that the North Star did not line up precisely over the North Pole.

The Irish and Iceland

The chronicles are usually silent on oceanic voyages from the days of Pytheas until the sixth century A.D.. During that span of almost a millennium the Romans and Carthaginians made numerous coast-hugging excursions. But the first reported adventure in the open Atlantic is attributed to St. Brendan of Ardfert (c. A.D. 484–577). Although Brendan was a historical personage, the voyage he led falls into the realm of legend and for many maritime historians is no more than a myth.

Nevertheless, some factual material is contained in the written accounts of Brendan's voyage, composed before A.D.

Leif Eriksson is usually credited with the discovery of North America, in 987 Bjarni Herjulfsson actually visited the New World before him. Herjulfsson, on his way to visit his father in Erik's Greenland colony, overshot his goal. This appears to have been a common occurrence among Viking navigators in the tenth century!

Leif the Lucky, as he was called, did not reach America until 1003, when he landed somewhere between Cape Cod and Labrador. This was the Vinland of the Norse sagas. After Eriksson, Thorfinn Karsefni led an expedition to Vinland and established a colony. It was defeated by the harsh climate, lack of food, trouble with local Indians, and considerable internal bickering. The Greenland colonies did not fare much better.

Probably other wanderers came to America's shores between the Vikings and Columbus. All that was necessary was poor navigation on the way to Iceland or Greenland. There is some evidence for two voyages, one in 1398 and another in 1472.

A Scot and Venetian Venture

The 1398 voyage, if it occurred, was led by a Scotsman, Henry Sinclair, accompanied by Antonio Zeno, a Venetian sailor. They set out for a western land named *Estotiland*, supposedly visited by fishermen in 1371. Some of the fishermen claimed to have lived in Estotiland for five years before moving south to another region called *Drogio*. From their descriptions of the land, Drogio may have been Nova Scotia. Here Sinclair and Zeno found coal and asphalt combined, the only place on the coast of North America where this remarkable combination occurs.

Mediterranean Sea Routes

The established trade routes of the Mediterranean Sea provided a unique communications network to keep southern European explorers informed about the latest discoveries of the fourteenth and fifteenth centuries.

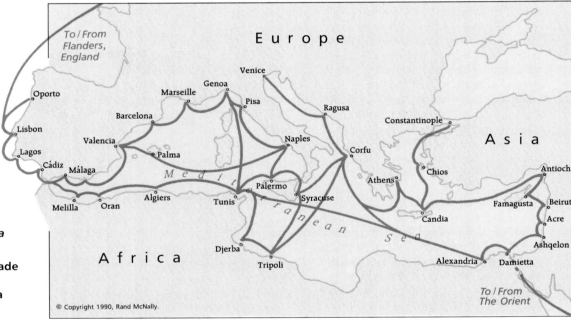

Map labels: To/From Flanders, England · Europe · Venice · Oporto · Genoa · Marseille · Pisa · Ragusa · Barcelona · Constantinople · Lisbon · Valencia · Naples · Asia · Lagos · Palma · Corfu · Cádiz · Málaga · Chios · Athens · Antioch · Melilla · Oran · Algiers · Tunis · Palermo · Syracuse · Famagusta · Beirut · Candia · Acre · Djerba · Ashqelon · Africa · Tripoli · Alexandria · Damietta · To/From The Orient · Mediterranean Sea · © Copyright 1990, Rand McNally.

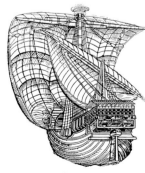

1400's ship

We do know that the object of their explorations was Africa and Europe, not lands beyond the Ocean Sea. According to some writings, the Egyptian king Necho II (610–595 B.C.) sent a fleet manned by Phoenicians to circumnavigate Africa. A few years later, probably between 520 B.C. and 470 B.C., Hanno sailed from the city of Carthage (in modern Tunisia), passed the Pillars of Hercules, and traveled south to at least the latitude of Sierra Leone. Phoenicians may even have reached the Azores and Canary islands. One of the most interesting early voyages beyond the Mediterranean was that of Pytheas of Massilia (Marseilles). Sometime around 275 B.C., he sailed to northern Europe and visited Britain, northern France, Flanders, and possibly northwestern Germany. His most adventuresome voyage was to *Thule,* which most scholars believe to have been Iceland but may have been Norway, the Shetlands, the Orkneys, or the Faeroes.

Pytheas, an excellent astronomer, measured the length of the daylight periods in the northern latitudes. His measurements were used by later geographers, such as Ptolemy, to establish parallels of latitude. He was also one of the first to note the lunar influence on ocean tides

704. This material shows that even before the days of the Vikings, the people of Ireland possessed considerable maritime knowledge. The Irish reached Iceland in 795, before it was inhabited, the same year the Vikings first raided Ireland. The Vikings did not reach Iceland until 860, and it was another fourteen years before they established a colony there.

The Vikings and Vinland

There are legends or myths that the Irish, always a few steps ahead of the Vikings, reached Greenland after their Icelandic colony had been abandoned. This is mostly speculation. Gunnbjörn Ulfsson discovered Greenland in 900 through a navigational error—he missed Iceland. History usually assigns the discovery of Greenland to Erik the Red in 986. If the Irish ever stepped ashore on Greenland, there is no evidence to prove or disprove it.

The Vikings did not confine their voyages to raids on neighboring Ireland, Britain, and other nearby lands or to expeditions to Iceland and Greenland, where they established colonies. Their astonishing voyages to America are well documented, supported by solid archeological evidence. Their discoveries of newfound lands to the west altered many world maps even before Columbus. Although

Three Nations Touch North America

The second expedition of 1472 was a joint undertaking by the Danes, Norwegians, and Portuguese. Afonso V, king of Portugal, proposed the voyage in 1470 to Christian I of Denmark. Led by two Danish captains, Diderik Pining and Hans Pothorst, and accompanied by João Vaz Corte-Real from Portugal, the expedition touched Greenland and North America. The voyage left Portuguese names in the New World: *Labrador, Terra do Bacalhau* (Land of Codfish, the name for Newfoundland used by Mediterranean cartographers for many years), and *Terra de Corte Real* (used for both Greenland and Newfoundland at different times).

Although the northern route to America via the Faeroes, Iceland, and Greenland was traveled repeatedly from the tenth century onward, activity began to increase in the southern latitudes in the thirteenth century. The pioneers were the Genoese.

For God, Gold, and Glory

The first Genoese voyage into the Atlantic occurred in 1291, when Ugolino and Vadino Vivaldi attempted to reach India by rounding Africa. Although the expedition failed, the brothers probably got as far as the Canary Islands.

By 1314, Portugal had emerged from Muslim domination, and its King Dinis began to assemble a navy. A Genoese, Emmanuele Pessagno, was named admiral and put in charge of the fleet. A number of exploratory expeditions sailed from Portugal, including one in 1341 in which the Canary Islands were charted. The Portuguese also translated the Italian-named *Legname* Islands to *Madeira* Islands and re-discovered the Azores islands, probably stumbling upon them when their ships were blown off course.

Three motives drove the fifteenth-century Portuguese to explore Africa and other Old World lands: God, gold, and glory. They wished to re-establish Christian domination in North Africa; to find the legendary kingdom of Prester John, supposedly a Christian land south of the Muslims in Africa; and to discover the Muslims' source of gold to finance these efforts. They had no plans to reach modern India by sailing around Africa or by sailing west.

Despite legends to the contrary, Prince Henry the Navigator did not mastermind Portuguese maritime expansion. This was largely directed by its kings—João I, Duarte, Afonso V, and João II. The accidental re-discovery of the Madeira and Azores islands interrupted Portugal's true goal of conquering North Africa. In fact, the Portuguese were so uninterested in these lands that most of the early colonists came from Flanders.

The Portuguese gradually worked their way down the west coast of Africa, and in 1488, Bartolomeu Dias reached the Cape of Good Hope. Even then, Portuguese sailors did not cross the Indian Ocean; for many years only the Arabs and Chinese sailed this sea. Of special interest were the voyages of a particularly venturesome captain named Cheng Ho.

Exploration in the East

During the reign of the third Ming Emperor, Yung-lo (Ch'eng Tsu) from 1402 until 1424, and for nine years after, Cheng Ho was China's "Admiral of the Ocean Sea." Between 1405 and 1433, Cheng Ho made seven great voyages across the Indian Ocean with a fleet so large no European would have believed it possible.

The first great expedition began in the summer of 1405 at Liuhe, twenty-five miles northwest of Shanghai. The fleet, composed of 317 vessels and manned by 27,800 men, carried silk, fine embroideries, jade work, pepper, and a host of other trade items along with troops, horses, and cannons. The expedition's primary aim, however, was not to conquer other lands but to offer Chinese culture to the world.

The fourth voyage in 1413 reached Kerguelan Islands, not seen by Europeans until the French "discovered" them in 1772. The fifth voyage from 1417 to 1419 brought thirty foreign emissaries to the Ming court. By the end of the seventh voyage, Cheng Ho's fleet had visited every country along China's eastern littoral: Japan, Formosa, and the Philippines. Indonesia had been explored as far east as Timor, as were southeast Asia, India, Sri Lanka, Iran, the Arabian peninsula, Egypt, and eastern Africa as far south as Mozambique.

The Chinese began charting these lands during this period. The first known map of east Africa dates from about 1320, probably based on Arab sources; the Chinese had had contact with Arab geographers since the ninth century.

Sometime before 1424, Chinese information concerning a great chain of islands from Japan to the Philippines reached Venetian sailors and geographers. These islands were duly added to the Venetian portolans in the western Ocean Sea, and

appear on a famous 1424 nautical chart. The name for one of the islands, *Antilia,* was later associated with the West Indies discovered by Columbus.

The confusion of names resulted from the fact that for the Europeans, Arabs, Chinese, and others there was only one ocean. The idea of separate Atlantic and Pacific oceans did not exist before the early sixteenth century. For several hundred years, Antilia defied identification because every Antilia-seeker was looking in the wrong sea!

As it turns out, Antilia on the 1424 chart is none other than the island of Taiwan, located in the western Ocean Sea (the Pacific) not in the western Atlantic Ocean. Taiwan's neighbors, the Pescadores Islands, also appear on the same chart, along with Japan and a portion of the Philippines.

Giant fish carrying St. Brendan

Chinese and Portuguese Exploration

By 1431 Ming Chinese trade (orange) extended to places in italics. By 1500 Portuguese exploration reached East Africa (purple). Names with dates indicate Portugal's progress to reach the Orient. Overlapping routes (blue) enabled them to learn of a rapidly changing world.

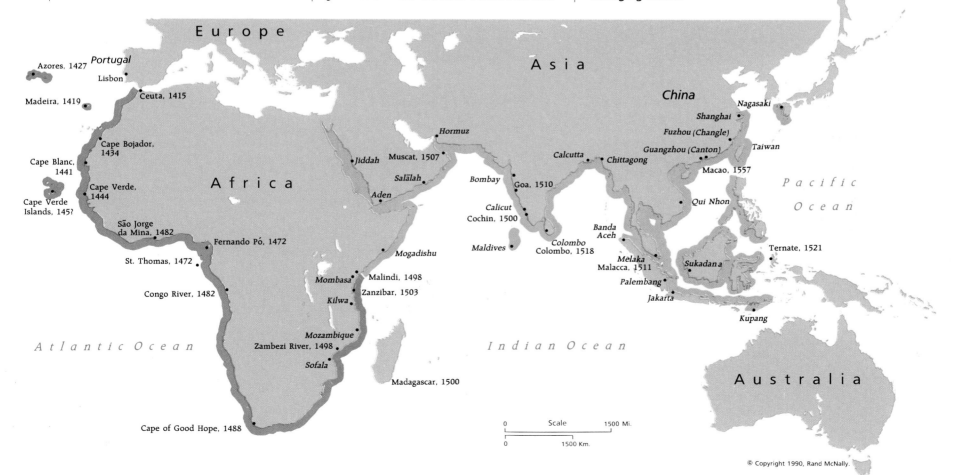

Columbus and His Time

The Years Before Spain

Christopher Columbus is one of the most enigmatic figures of history. Because he was born a commoner, few records were kept of events in his childhood, education, or family life. Once a person such as Columbus attained the fifteenth-century equivalent of stardom, then attempts to reconstruct the vital statistics for his earlier years began. If Columbus, or anyone who knew him, decided to create a fictional biography, it would be difficult for later scholars to correct the record.

Unheralded Beginnings
The first undisputed fact about Christopher Columbus appears on May 5, 1487, when it is recorded that he received a stipend from Alonso de Quintanilla, treasurer to the Spanish sovereigns. Columbus was in Spain at the time and had probably lived there for two years (since 1485). Before that time, all the information we have about Columbus is open to some debate.

He was probably born in the port city of Genoa, Italy, in 1451 as Cristoforo Colombo, the son of Domenico Colombo and Susanna Fontanarossa. In addition to young Cristoforo (Christopher), there were four other known children: Bartolomeo (Bartholomew), Giacomo (Diego or James), Giovanni (John), and Bianchinetta. Giovanni died young and Bianchinetta married a cheesemonger and faded from history. Bartholomew and Diego (as Giacomo is usually known to us) also played important roles in the history of the New World.

The Young Sailor
Christopher went to sea at an early age, perhaps no more than fourteen. He may have made a number of voyages before sailing to the Genoese colony of Chios (now in Greece) in 1474 or 1475. Apparently he was in the employ of one of the Genoese shipping families, Spinola or Di Negro, or may even have worked for both.

In late summer of 1476, a small fleet of five vessels departed Genoa for England, with Columbus in the crew. On August 13, 1476, the fleet was attacked by a French squadron commanded by Vice Admiral Guillame de Casenove. France and Portugal had been at war with the Spanish kingdoms of Castilla and Aragón for over a year. Although the attack was apparently a case of mistaken identity (Genoa was neutral), the French sank the ship carrying Columbus, and the future admiral barely made it to shore. In this manner Christopher Columbus entered Portugal somewhere near Cape St. Vincent.

Eventually the fleet was reassembled in Lisbon and continued on to Britain. Opinion is divided as to whether or not Columbus continued the trip with them; some historians even suggest he sailed all the way to Iceland—a very questionable voyage. By July 1478, however, Columbus did sail for the Madeira Islands to acquire a load of sugar for his Genoese employers.

Some thirteen months later, we learn that on August 25, 1479, Columbus was in Genoa for a judicial hearing. From the documentation of this proceeding, we discover that (a) he was a Genoese citizen,

No known portrait was made of Columbus during his lifetime. The likenesses shown here present only a few of the many artists' varying impressions of a man who must have been multifaceted and extraordinary—a mariner whose drive and determination changed history.

A.

B.

C.

1479 transcript: Columbus, 27, citizen of Genoa

D.

E.

A. The oil painting attributed to Sebastiano del Piombo and dated 1519 is frequently reproduced and, therefore, has become a familiar and traditional image of Columbus.

B. In 1965 Ruth Durlacher painted this portrait on the island of San Salvador. It was based on descriptions of Columbus written by his contemporaries.

C. The color intaglio print by Leonardo Lasansky was created in 1984. It breaks from the traditional images to present other dimensions of Columbus.

D. Theodore DeBry published his engraving of Columbus in 1595. As with the Jovian, this picture has been used by other artists to fashion their impressions of Columbus.

E. In 1575 Tobias Stimmer made a woodcut by copying a portrait, thought to be from the early 1500s, in the collection of Paulus Jovius. The woodcut is known as the Jovian Portrait.

(b) he was about twenty-seven years old, and (c) he was to depart for Lisbon on August 26.

Marriage and Family

Soon after Columbus's return to Lisbon in 1479, he married Felipa Monis. Felipa's great aunt Isabel was the second wife of Bartolomeu Perestrello, a minor nobleman who served as the first governor of Porto Santo.

Felipa was not related to Perestrello, but traditional history has incorrectly made him out to be her father. This error may have been deliberate on the part of Christopher's second son, Fernando, to establish a line of nobility for his father.

Christopher and Felipa probably lived on Porto Santo for a time and then on the island of Madeira, with perhaps a residence in Lisbon. Diego, the first-born son of the Admiral, may have been born on Porto Santo about 1480.

The name of Felipa—the wife of the Discoverer of America—does not appear in any records until March 16, 1509, when she is mentioned by her son, Diego. It is only an educated guess that Felipa died in Portugal in 1485, the year when most scholars believe Columbus left Portugal for Spain, accompanied by his young son Diego.

The Years in Portugal

We have only hearsay reports of what Columbus did while he was in Portugal, or its colony Madeira/Porto Santo, during the years 1476–1485. One popular story goes that he developed his Grand Design for sailing to the East by way of the West during this time, presented his plan to King João II of Portugal in 1484, and had it rejected after consideration by a committee of maritime experts. Few specifics of this are known.

At this time, the Portuguese were at war with the Spanish kingdoms and were concentrating their efforts on securing northern and western Africa. Because Portugal had no intention to reach the East Indies during the time Columbus was in the country, any proposals he might have made to the royal court would have fallen on deaf ears.

It was also during his Portuguese sojourn that Columbus was supposed to have corresponded with the great Florentine physician and cosmographer Paolo del Pozzo Toscanelli. In one of Toscanelli's letters, so the story goes, he sent Columbus a map, clearly pointing out the course to Cathay (China). However, the letters of this supposed correspondence are so woefully inaccurate that they can best be described as clever forgeries, penned *after* the First Voyage and designed to lend a scientific air to an expedition that some felt was tainted. Columbus's brother Bartholomew may have written them to counteract a rumor abroad in the land that Columbus had learned of the western lands from a navigator who had actually been there. Whether the rumor was true or false, it had to be squelched quickly by the Columbus family. A fake correspondence with Toscanelli seemed the best way to do so.

We shall probably never know with any certainty when or why the notion to sail west came to Columbus. Nor is it certain that rejection of his idea by Portugal drove Columbus to seek a more receptive audience in the Spanish kingdoms. There is ample evidence to suggest that he was deeply in debt. It would not be the first time in history that a desire to escape one's creditors served as the motivation for seeking new surroundings! Whatever the reason, Columbus left Portugal and made the fateful journey to Spain in 1485.

Columbus's coat of arms

The importance of noble heritage in the 1400s, and Columbus's lack of it (illustrated here by his family tree), made gaining royal support for his plan a remarkable feat.

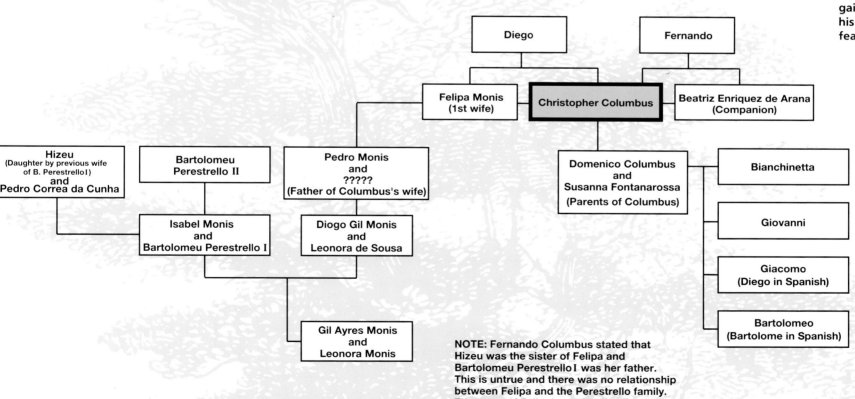

NOTE: Fernando Columbus stated that Hizeu was the sister of Felipa and Bartolomeu Perestrello I was her father. This is untrue and there was no relationship between Felipa and the Perestrello family. The name of Felipa's mother is unknown.

Columbus and His Time

Columbus in Spain

Columbus and his son Diego first came to the Spanish kingdom of Castilla in 1485, entering at the small seaport of Palos. They sought refuge at the nearby Franciscan monastery of La Rábida. It was here that Columbus met Father Antonio Marchena. Father Marchena, an accomplished astronomer, became the first, and for a long while the only, supporter the Admiral had in Castilla.

Petitioning the King and Queen

During the next seven years, Columbus followed the Castilian court as it moved from one residence to another. His first audience with the Catholic sovereigns, King Ferdinand and Queen Isabela, came in the ancient city of Alcalá de Henares in January 1486. Columbus put forth his proposal to reach Asian lands by sailing west, and the king and queen promised to consider the matter. They reminded him, however, that they were currently engaged in the *Reconquista* to expel the Moors from Spanish land.

During the remainder of 1486 and throughout 1488, Columbus spent most of his time in Córdoba, waiting for an answer to his proposal. It was there that he met Beatriz Enríquez de Arana, who gave birth to Columbus's second son, Fernando, in 1488.

In 1487, the king and queen received Columbus in their forward military camp in Málaga and told him they could not accept his plan. Columbus languished in Castilla for another two years before being summoned to a private meeting with Queen Isabela at Jaén in 1489. This time the queen offered Columbus the possibility of support as soon as the Moors were driven from the city of Granada.

Unwilling to wait, the Admiral sought assistance for his expedition from two Andalusian dukes, Enrique de Guzmán and Luis de la Cerda. Although de la Cerda took Columbus into his home for a year during 1490–1491, he could offer no funds for a westward voyage across the Ocean Sea. By autumn of 1491, Columbus had all but given up hope of ever realiz-

ing his goal. He decided to return to La Rábida, pick up his son Diego, and leave Spain.

Father Pérez and the Queen

Columbus's dream might have died at that point, or been carried to France, had it not been for Father Juan Pérez, the Queen's former confessor. Father Pérez heard about Columbus's plan and urged the king and queen to give him one more royal hearing.

Columbus met the sovereigns at Granada and was a witness to the city's fall on January 2, 1492. The Moors had been driven from Spain, and the royal family was free to turn to other matters. Three months later, on April 17, the Catholic king and queen approved Columbus's plan. They even accepted the agreements or *capitulaciónes* that Columbus insisted upon. These included titles, rights, and privileges for Columbus and his heirs. It remains one of the mysteries of the Columbus story why these sovereigns agreed to make any concessions at all to some-

Events in the Life of Columbus

Columbus was about twenty-seven when he lived on Porto Santo, an island 700 miles southwest of Portugal. After reaching Spain at age thirty-five, he sought support for his plan by following the royal court and negotiating for certain titles and rights. He then made four voyages of discovery and finally returned to Spain, where he died at the age of fifty-five in Valladolid.

King Ferdinand

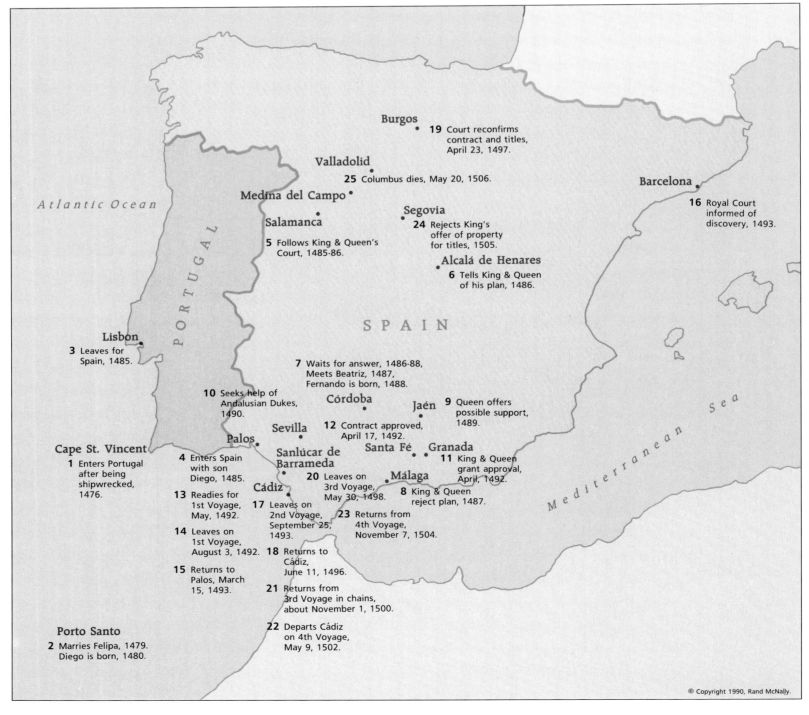

- Burgos • **19** Court reconfirms contract and titles, April 23, 1497.
- Valladolid • **25** Columbus dies, May 20, 1506.
- Barcelona • **16** Royal Court informed of discovery, 1493.
- *Atlantic Ocean*
- Medina del Campo •
- Salamanca • **5** Follows King & Queen's Court, 1485-86.
- Segovia • **24** Rejects King's offer of property for titles, 1505.
- Alcalá de Henares • **6** Tells King & Queen of his plan, 1486.
- *PORTUGAL*
- *SPAIN*
- Lisbon • **3** Leaves for Spain, 1485.
- **7** Waits for answer, 1486-88, Meets Beatriz, 1487, Fernando is born, 1488.
- **10** Seeks help of Andalusian Dukes, 1490.
- Córdoba •
- Jaén • **9** Queen offers possible support, 1489.
- Sevilla •
- **12** Contract approved, April 17, 1492.
- *Mediterranean Sea*
- Cape St. Vincent
- **1** Enters Portugal after being shipwrecked, 1476.
- Palos •
- **4** Enters Spain with son Diego, 1485.
- Sanlúcar de Barrameda
- **20** Leaves on 3rd Voyage, May 30, 1498.
- Santa Fé
- Granada • **11** King & Queen grant approval, April, 1492.
- Málaga • **8** King & Queen reject plan, 1487.
- Cádiz •
- **13** Readies for 1st Voyage, May, 1492.
- **17** Leaves on 2nd Voyage, September 25, 1493.
- **23** Returns from 4th Voyage, November 7, 1504.
- **14** Leaves on 1st Voyage, August 3, 1492.
- **18** Returns to Cádiz, June 11, 1496.
- **15** Returns to Palos, March 15, 1493.
- **21** Returns from 3rd Voyage in chains, about November 1, 1500.
- **22** Departs Cádiz on 4th Voyage, May 9, 1502.
- Porto Santo
- **2** Marries Felipa, 1479. Diego is born, 1480.

© Copyright 1990, Rand McNally.

PEOPLE OF THE FIFTEENTH CENTURY

Population

Census taking is an ancient custom, but few reliable records exist prior to A.D. 1800. In A.D. 14 the population of the Roman Empire numbered 50 million. The Portuguese conducted an accurate census in the mid-1500s. Approximately one million people occupied Portugal, and Lisbon was considered a metropolis with 50,000 people. Modern Spain, as we know it, did not even exist in 1492. Instead, three kingdoms—Castilla, Aragon, and Navarra—divided the Iberian Peninsula. The combined population of these three kingdoms totaled about 6 million people.

Eight centuries of conflict with the Moors between 711 and 1492 took its toll on the entire Iberian population. Besides the expected battlefield deaths, the war also ravaged crops, destroyed irrigation systems, and disrupted vital transport routes.

Before the Industrial Revolution the entire world was at the mercy of starvation and disease. France, for example, between 970 and 1100, suffered through sixty famine years. The dreaded bubonic plague of the fourteenth century swept through Europe and killed one-quarter to one-third of the population.

The influence of war, famine, and infectious diseases acted as a check on population growth in Europe.

Ways of Life

In the fifteenth century, most of the peoples of the Old and New World were either farmers or hunter/gatherers. In the New world, the advanced farming societies of the Aztecs and Incas supported large populations with true urban centers. The Mayas, on the other hand, were nonurban, rural people.

Knowledge of Geography

In Columbus's time, most peoples outside the Old World tended to remain isolated from one another. The American Indians were almost totally unaware of any other peoples on the planet. Central Pacific islands, Australia, and the larger islands of Melanesia were physically and culturally isolated from any neighbors. Africa, on the other hand, was within reach of both Arabs and Europeans. By the 1400's, Arab influence along the east African coast reached as far south as Mozambique. On the west coast, the Portuguese had advanced from Senegal to the Cape of Good Hope between 1460 and 1488.

By the early fifteenth century, the Chinese were thoroughly familiar with all of the important islands to the east. They were making regular excursions to southeast Asia and all the lands fronting the Indian Ocean.

Arabs were by far the most knowledgeable people in the fifteenth century, and their range of influence extended from Morocco to China. They provided information on other lands to the Venetians and Genoese.

European knowledge of the world came largely from three sources: Greek and Roman works some 1500 years old, Arab travelers between the tenth and fifteenth centuries, and occasional tales of northern expeditions to a land called Thule.

There were, however, some direct contacts with other lands made by a few adventurous travelers such as Marco Polo. His account of his eastern journeys made an enormous impact on Europe and served as Columbus's primary source for information concerning Asia and the East Indies.

1400's ships

THE WORLD'S POPULATION, 1492 and 1990

Asia	169,000,000	3,156,100,000
Africa, South of the Sahara	75,000,000	532,438,000
Europe	70,000,000	688,000,000
Middle and South America	25,000,000	440,735,000
United States and Canada	5,000,000	276,565,000
North Africa	5,000,000	115,862,000
Oceania	1,000,000	26,300,000
Total World Population	350,000,000	5,236,000,000

King Ferdinand of Spain

Queen Isabela of Spain

one who was both an outsider and of humble origin. It may be they considered it a reasonable price to pay for the potential rewards that the voyage might bring.

By May 1492 Columbus had returned to Palos, armed with the necessary documents to acquire the ships, crews, and provisions for the long voyage. The *Santa María* was chartered from Juan de la Cosa, who went along as ship's master. The *Pinta* and *Niña* were confiscated by the Crown as a partial payment of fines the town of Palos had incurred during the 1475–79 war with Portugal. The citizens of Palos had consistently refused to abide by the queen's edicts during that war, par-

ticularly those that forbade unauthorized voyages to Africa and the Canaries and those that required payment of royal tithes.

The owners of the two vessels, Martín Alonso and Vicente Yáñez Pinzón, were permitted to make the voyage with Columbus but were not paid for their ships. Further, Queen Isabela decreed that the town of Palos had to provision the ships at its own expense. The crew members who manned the *Pinta* and *Niña* were all volunteers. Seven years after first setting foot on Spanish land, Columbus was ready to set sail for Asia.

The Voyages of Columbus — One and Two

Columbus and His Time

Columbus landing, King Ferdinand overseeing

Christopher Columbus made four voyages to America between 1492 and 1504. In the process, he discovered the Bahamas, most of the Caribbean islands, South America, and portions of Central America.

Did Columbus ever realize that he had failed to reach Asia—that he had discovered a New World? Probably not, to judge by the cartography of the period. After 1492 the size of the earth remained underestimated, and the geographic evidence insufficient to believe a New World could be squeezed between Europe and Asia. The new discoveries were simply mapped as offshore islands, peninsulas, and coastal stretches of eastern Asia.

Cartographers are careful scientists. It took approximately fifty years of further discovery to convince them to properly show two new continents so the world could begin to comprehend the magnitude of Columbus's voyages of discovery.

over the precise identity of this island (one of 723 islands and cays in the Bahamas), the navigational data from Columbus's *Log* of the voyage strongly suggest it was Samana Cay.

The second island was named *Santa María de La Concepción* (modern Acklins-Crooked Island); the third, *Fernandina* (modern Long Island); and the fourth *Isabela* (modern Fortune Island). Another island chain was named but not visited, *Islas de Arena* (modern Ragged Islands), before Columbus sailed on to discover Cuba.

From Cuba the *Santa María* and *Niña* went to Haiti, while the *Pinta* took an unauthorized detour to the Dominican Republic. Columbus named the island that contains Haiti and the Dominican Republic today *La Isla Española*—the Spanish Island.

Then on December 24–25, the *Santa María* foundered on a sandbar and was

the islands facing that continent. Later he was to conclude that Cuba was a peninsula of the Asiatic mainland.

Columbus also recognized that the Lucayan Indians (also called Taino and Arawak) formed one unified cultural group, with a common language and economy. He was aware of the cannibalistic Caribs, but did not see any on this voyage. He found the people to be friendly, shy, and intelligent, living in an earthly paradise—people who did not know the Christian God but who were, nonetheless, children of that God. He had found Eden and innocence.

The Spaniards had also found gold; not a mother lode but enough to whet their appetite. Columbus and his crew were the first Europeans to see tobacco, hammocks, corn, sweet potatoes, cassava, and a host of other native American plants. The Spaniards marveled at the New World's strange animals (such as the iguana), and its spectacular array of colorful tropical birds and fish.

Columbus brought a number of Indians back with him to Spain, along with gold, cotton, and a variety of potentially valuable plants which he thought were spices. This appeared to be sufficient evidence that the admiral had been right all along: Asia could be reached by sailing west. The Spanish king and queen authorized a second voyage almost immediately.

The Second Voyage — September 25, 1493, to June 11, 1496)

The second voyage was the grandest of all four, boasting seventeen ships with a total crew of 1,200 to 1,500 men. Among those on the Second Voyage were Juan de la Cosa (cartographer and master of the *Santa María* on the First Voyage), Juan Ponce de León, the discoverer of Florida, and Friar Antonio de Marchena who had befriended Columbus at La Rábida in 1485.

The fleet departed from Cádiz and followed Columbus's original route to the Canaries. On November 3, they reached Dominica (Lesser Antilles) in the New World, and proceeded northwestward where they discovered and named most of the Leeward Islands from Guadaloupe to Saba. On November 13, the fleet turned westward, with stops in the Virgin Islands and Puerto Rico.

From Puerto Rico, the ships passed through the Mona Passage and reached the province of Xamaná (Samaná) in the northeastern part of what is now the Dominican Republic. From this point the coast was familiar to Columbus and some of the crew who had been on the First Voyage. On November 26, the peak of Monte Cristi came in view, and the fleet anchored offshore near the tiny island of *Isla Cabra*. The next day Columbus was devastated to find that all the men he had left behind had died.

After lingering there for ten days, the fleet turned eastward. At a location about halfway between Monte Cristi and mod-

The Four Voyages of Columbus, 1492 to 1504

[Map: The Four Voyages of Columbus showing North America, South America, Atlantic Ocean, Pacific Ocean, Caribbean Sea, West Indies, Europe, Africa, with voyage routes labeled First Voyage, Second, Third, Fourth. Locations include Azores Islands, Madeira Islands, Canary Islands, Cape Verde Islands, Lisbon, Palos, Cádiz. © Copyright 1990, Rand McNally. Scale 1500 Mi. / 1500 Km.]

The First Voyage — August 3, 1492, to March 15, 1493

The *Santa María*, *Pinta*, and *Niña* departed the Castilian port of Palos, sailing first to Gomera in the Canary Islands (though the *Pinta* had to put in at Gran Canaria for rudder repairs). Westward departure from the Canaries was on September 6, but lack of wind prevented any progress until September 8.

The thirty-three-day crossing was uneventful, blessed by unusually mild weather and few equipment problems. At 2 AM on October 12, as reckoned by the Julian calendar, landfall occurred at an island the Indians called *Guanahaní*. Columbus immediately renamed it *San Salvador* (Holy Savior). Although a debate continues

lost near the modern city of Cap Haitien. Roughly forty of the crew were left behind to establish the first Spanish colony in the New World, Navidad. Unfortunately, none in the colony survived.

The homeward voyage began on January 16, 1493, and nearly ended in tragedy. In mid-Atlantic, a terrible storm forced the *Niña* into the Azores, where Columbus and his crew were almost imprisoned by local authorities. Columbus and the *Niña* stopped in Lisbon and an audience with João II. The *Pinta* struggled on to reach Bayona in northern Spain. On March 15, both vessels reached Palos within an hour of each other.

What had Columbus learned from the voyage and what did he believe he had accomplished? He never wavered in the belief that he had reached Asia, at least

ern Puerto Plata, the admiral founded the town of Isabela. From this base, he and a few crewmen explored the interior of Española (Cibao) in the early part of 1494. He sent some ships back to Spain, but set sail himself for Cuba, eventually stopping short of its western tip where he may then have continued on to discover it was an island. Ironically, it was at this point that he declared Cuba to be part of the Asian continent and sought confirmation of his belief from all of the crew. He then sailed eastward, by way of Jamaica, returning to Isabela on September 29, five months after the Cuba/Jamaica exploration began. Most of the next year, 1495, was spent trying to conquer the Indians of Española and to discover their sources of gold.

On March 10, 1496, Columbus sailed for Spain in the *Niña* and entered the harbor at Cádiz on June 11, 1496.

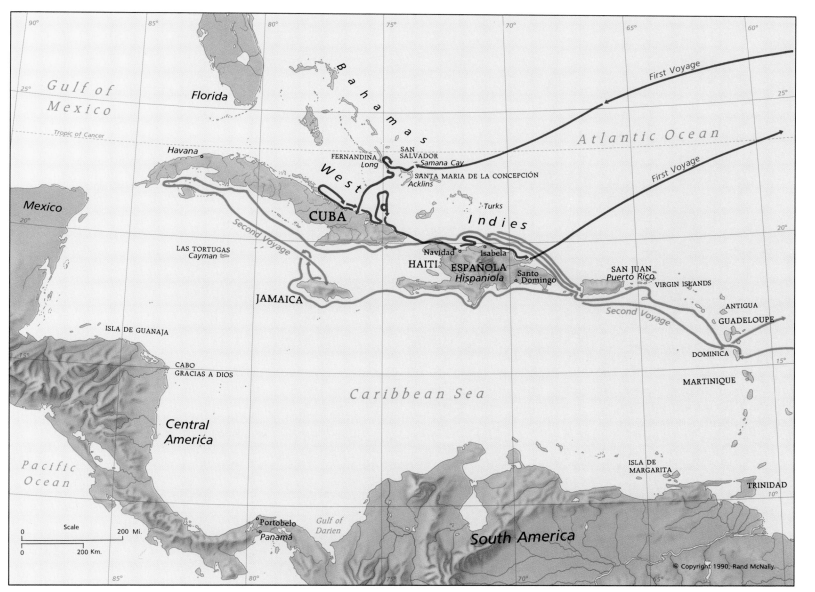

An artist's concept of the *Pinta*, *Santa María*, and *Niña* sailing into the New World. The *Santa María* ran aground in the Caribbean and only the *Pinta* and *Niña* made it back to Spain on the first voyage. The *Niña* made the second and third voyage as well.

First and Second Tracks in the New World

On the first voyage Columbus spent about three months exploring the Caribbean, discovering the Bahamas, Cuba, and Española (Hispaniola). On the second voyage approximately ten months were spent sailing the region, discovering the Lesser Antilles, Puerto Rico, and Jamaica.

I-17

The Voyages of Columbus — Three and Four

Columbus and His Time

The Second Voyage turned out to be the high-water mark for Columbus, Admiral of the Ocean Sea. The coming years witnessed opposition to his leadership, both in Española and in Spain. Columbus was a seaman, not a landsman; he could not navigate through the intrigues of the court, the church, and countless greedy associates. In addition, he was no longer master of the route to the Indies. Other ships were beginning to sail the Atlantic route regularly. Finally, with Spain and France now at war, ships were in short supply. Columbus asked for eight ships but received only three for his Third Voyage. Three additional supply ships were authorized, but only to go to Española and no further.

Sea. Initiating this new southern route was his attempt to locate a continental landmass supposedly known to the Portuguese (Brazil?) and to determine in whose jurisdiction it lay according to treaty.

Columbus sailed from the Cape Verde Islands on July 7, made landfall at Trinidad on July 31, and the next day became the first European to sight South America. For the next two weeks, he and his crew explored the Gulf of Paria (between Trinidad and Venezuela), marveling at the incredible discharge of the Orinoco River. From this region, Columbus possibly sighted Tabago and Grenada before reaching Margarita Island. From there he sailed directly for Santo Domingo but made landfall about one hundred miles to the west

and sent them home to Spain in chains that October. The Admiral of the Ocean Sea, Viceroy and Governor of the Indies, arrived as a common prisoner in Cádiz about November 1, 1500, bringing the Third Voyage to an ignominious end. However, upon seeing the manacled Columbus, a chagrined Queen Isabela freed him, recalled Bobadilla, and authorized another voyage.

The Fourth Voyage — May 9, 1502, to November 7, 1504

The last and most difficult of the voyages began on May 9, 1504, when Columbus's small fleet of four ships departed Cádiz. Only a miraculous discovery on this voyage could restore Columbus to his former

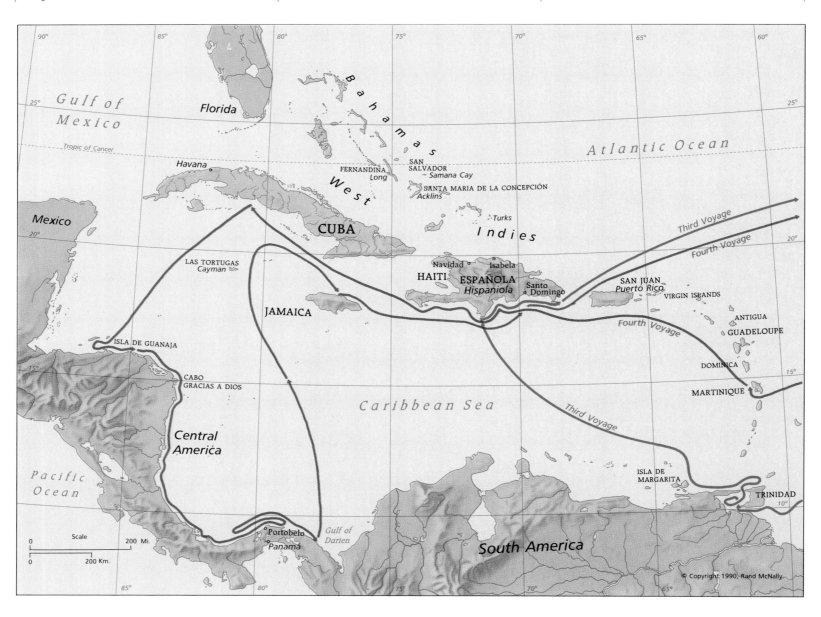

Third and Fourth Tracks in the New World

On the third voyage, Columbus landed on Trinidad and spent about one month discovering and exploring the northern coast of South America before being sent back to Castile in chains. Columbus spent over two years on the fourth voyage exploring Central America and the Cayman Islands. One year of that time was spent marooned on Jamaica.

The Third Voyage — May 30, 1498, to c. November 1, 1500

The six ships departed Sanlúcar de Barrameda to Porto Santo and then on to Madeira Island. Columbus left Madeira on June 16 and arrived at Gomera in the Canary Islands on June 19, just in time to rescue two vessels that had been seized by the French. The three supply ships were sent to Isabela on Española. On June 21, Columbus sailed south to the Cape Verde Islands before crossing the Ocean

because of prevailing currents. Nevertheless, to sail a trans-Atlantic course for the first time, by dead-reckoning navigation, as Columbus did and still to come within a hundred miles of an intended landfall is nothing short of remarkable.

On August 31, 1498, Columbus reached Santo Domingo and was reunited with his brothers Bartholomew and Diego. However, quarrels broke out among the colonists at Santo Domingo and bitter fighting continued throughout 1499. When the new governor, Francisco de Bobadilla, arrived in August 1500 to establish order, he arrested Columbus and his brothers

position, and he came within fifty miles of finding it. Had he crossed the Isthmus of Panama, he would have discovered the Pacific Ocean a decade before Balboa.

The fleet of four ships followed the Canary Island course and arrived at Martinique on June 15, a record time for the ocean crossing. Columbus took along his brother, Bartholomew, and thirteen-year-old Fernando, his youngest son. During much of the trip, the admiral was too ill to command (gout and diabetes?), and young Fernando maintained the log that is our best account of the journey.

From Martinique the fleet sailed to Santo Domingo, on to Jamaica and Cuba, and finally to the Bay Islands of Honduras. Here they met a group of Indians who might have led them to the Mayas of Mexico and the great discovery Columbus needed, but he chose instead to continue along the Honduran coast. Contrary winds off northern Honduras slowed the vessels to a crawl; they managed only 180 miles (290 kilometers) in 70 days! When they finally reached the cape where the coast curves to the south, Columbus said, "Thanks be to God!" The cape still bears that name: *Gracias a Dios.*

Columbus explored the coastline of Nicaragua, Costa Rica, and Panama to the town of Portobelo and spent Christmas of 1502 near the Atlantic entrance of what would one day be the Panama Canal.

From the *Lettera Rarissima,* written in Jamaica and dated July 7, 1503, it is clear that Columbus understood that while he was on the Caribbean coast of Panama he knew that only a narrow isthmus separated him from what he believed to be the Indian Ocean. Had Columbus been physically able he might have marched overland and achieved the miraculous discovery—of the *Pacific* Ocean—he needed so desperately to rescue his waning reputation.

Even Columbus's attempts in 1503 to establish the first Spanish town on the American mainland failed. Work on the settlement at Santa María de Belén, about a hundred miles west of the present Panama Canal, was hampered by terrible storms, an impossible anchorage and defensive position, Columbus's grave illness, and fierce attacks from the Indians. The Spaniards were forced to abandon the colony along with one of their four ships. The survivors sailed for Portobelo and then to the San Blas Islands to the east. After losing another ship they set a course for Española. Battling wind and currents they reached the western end of Cuba, then sailed on to finally anchor at St. Ann's Bay, Jamaica, on June 23. The two remaining ships were beached, for they were completely unseaworthy.

Although messengers were dispatched to Española by canoe, Columbus and his men suffered a year of sickness, death, deprivation, and mutinies before a rescue ship arrived on June 28, 1504. They immediately departed and arrived in Santo Domingo, Española on August 13, 1504. On September 12, Columbus departed the New World for the last time, reaching Sanlúcar de Barrameda on November 7. The Fourth Voyage of Discovery had ended in failure.

Less than three weeks after his return, Queen Isabela died, thus ending any hope that Columbus might have had for restoring his proper authority. Eighteen months later, on May 20, 1506, Columbus himself died in Valladolid, Spain. The death of the Great Discoverer passed almost unnoticed except by a few old friends and family members.

THE LANDFALL PUZZLE

Exactly where did Columbus discover the New World at 2:00 AM on October 12, 1492?

Nine different landfalls have been proposed as the site, but only two islands of the 723 in the Bahamas, Samana Cay and San Salvador (Watlings), fit the description set forth in the log. The numbered items and map below are based upon the navigational data from the abstract of Columbus's log. They track his course if sailed from Samana Cay or San Salvador (Watlings Island) in order to establish the place where Columbus first set foot in the New World.*

1. On October 14, Columbus sailed southwest from Island I, called Guanahani by the inhabitants and renamed San Salvador by Columbus, to Island II. He saw so many islands that he decided to head for the largest. This second island was estimated to be about fifteen to twenty-one miles from the first island. He named it Santa Maria de la Concepcion. If one sails southwest from Samana Cay many islands fill the horizon, and the distance to modern Aklins Island is correct.

If one sails southwest from Watlings then modern Rum Cay is a logical second island. However, Rum Cay is not the correct distance from Watlings, is much too small, and is not one among many, but the only island that breaks the horizon.

2. Island III, named Fernandina by Columbus, lay twenty-four to twenty-seven miles west of Island II.

The "Samana track" leads to southern Fernandina (modern Long Island) and the distance corresponds to that recorded in the log.

Using the "Watlings track" takes us to northern Fernandina, but the distance is too short.

3. Columbus said that the coast of Island IV, which he named Isabela, trended to the west for 12 leagues (36 miles).

This appears to be a mistranscription for twelve miles not leagues. In addition, the coast could not have extended to the west or the fleet would have run aground when it departed to the west-southwest on October 24.

Island IV (modern Fortune Island) of the Samana track has a coast that trends southwest by south for twelve miles.

Island IV (modern Crooked Island) of the Watling track has

a coast that trends south and then southeast.

4. On October 24 the log describes Columbus's location as being west-southwest of his departure point on Isabela and twenty-one miles southeast of Fernandina.

This spot is precisely where the Samana track places Columbus.

The Watling track places the fleet only twelve miles southeast of Fernandina.

5. After this point, the voyage to Cuba is essentially the same for both tracks, but on November 19 and 20, Columbus sailed north-northeast from Cuba, toward the Bahamas.

About seventy-five miles out he stated that Isabela was thirty-six miles away, and that San Salvador was twenty-four miles from Isabela. These figures are approximately correct if Samana Cay is San Salvador.

If we take Watlings as Columbus's San Salvador, there is a one hundred percent error.

If the navigational data in the abstract of the log is correct, then the conclusion from the foregoing is that Samana Cay was the place where Columbus and his crew discovered the New World.

*The on-board log of the Santa Maria has been lost. A copy of that has disappeared. What exists is an abstract of the copy made by Bartolome de Las Casas. Between 1981 and 1986 the National Geographic Society and the author studied all available information and concluded Samana Cay was the landfall.

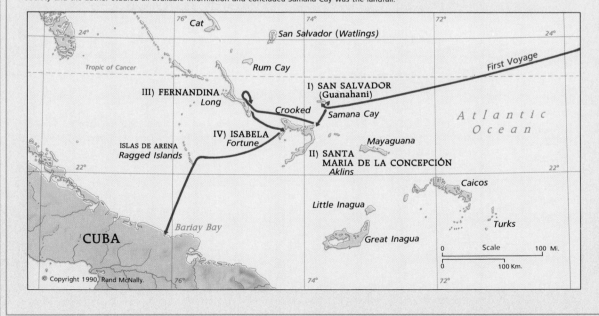

Islands of the New World

Navidad

Columbus in the New World

**Impact
of the
Great
Discovery**

Landmark Maps Showing the New Discoveries

Though the thread may be thin, many events of the past 500 years could be tied to the discovery of the New World. However important the Discovery, it is unfair to burden Columbus with all the vagaries of humankind since 1492. After all, Columbus himself died believing that he had only discovered land attached to the Asian continent—not two *new* continents.

The impact of the new discoveries is reflected on the early maps that charted the explorers' progress. Someone once said that the Voyages of Discovery gave the world its first scientific laboratory, the world itself. This is certainly true for the science of cartography, which for centuries had struggled with the formidable problem of mapping a world only half known.

The Spanish Map the Discoveries
The famous map of Juan de la Cosa, who sailed with Columbus and was one of the greatest navigators of his time, is both the oldest Castilian map and the oldest dated map showing any portion of North and South America. De la Cosa drafted the map in Puerto de Santa María, just across the harbor from the Spanish port of Cádiz, in 1500.

The map places the Tropic of Cancer *south* of both Cuba and Española at about latitude 17° N, an error of some six degrees. The error was probably deliberate, for the Treaty of Alcáçovas (1479) between Portugal and Castilla placed this region on the Portuguese side of the line. For the islands to be on the Castilian (and legal) side, it was necessary for de la Cosa

falls within the Portuguese realm, as does all of Greenland. De la Cosa does not show Newfoundland or Greenland. Cantino also extends further eastward to reveal all of the Asiatic coast as it was then imagined. De la Cosa stops short of the Pacific Ocean on the east.

The most remarkable feature of the Cantino map is the depiction of a landmass at the western edge of the map, northwest of Cuba. This shape has been the source of unending controversy. Most scholars believe it is the southeastern part of the United States. If so, the discovery of Florida may no longer belong to Juan Ponce de León in 1513.

There are, however, many compelling arguments against such a theory. The most obvious, from the Cantino itself, is that Florida is not northwest of Cuba but due north. Its shape is wrong on the map, and the details of its capes and harbors do not match the actual Florida peninsula. This so-called "northwest coast" seems to be a piece of Asia taken from earlier maps and globes such as the one made by Behaim. An almost exact duplicate of this mysterious landmass appears on Behaim's 1492 globe.

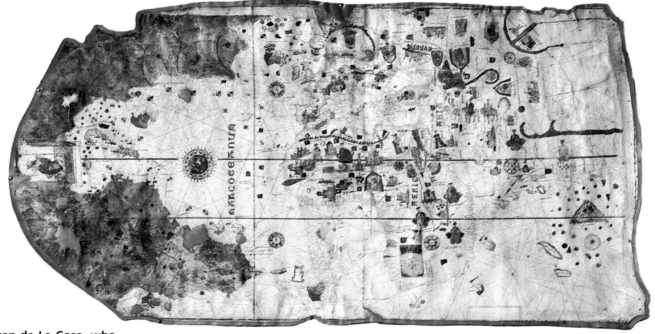

Juan de La Cosa, who sailed with Columbus, drew this map on ox hide in 1500. It is the earliest surviving cartographic record of the voyages of Columbus.

New Maps of the World
After the First Voyage of Columbus, the evolution of a true *mappamundi,* or world map, could begin. The arrival of movable type and the printing press in Europe meant that for the first time, the original work of a cartographer could remain "fixed" until it needed to be amended. Before printing, every hand-drawn copy of a map was unique, subject to copying errors and the idiosyncracies of the copyist. As a result, spellings, coastlines—even geographic locations, shapes, and sizes—changed from map to map.

Surprisingly, few maps were developed in Portugal or Spain after Columbus's voyages. There is only one existing Spanish map detailing any of the Spanish discoveries before 1523. The Portuguese developed only two maps before 1502, both indicating Portugal's discoveries along the coast of West Africa and dated 1471 and 1490, respectively. The few produced in Spain and Portugal were among the landmark maps of the period. Between 1500 and 1523, most of the extant maps were produced in Italy and Germany.

to move them farther north. It was also expedient for Columbus to state that San Salvador was "on an east-west line" with the Canaries, or about latitude 28° N. If he had stated the true position of his landfall Columbus would have been up to six degrees south of that latitude and "illegally" in Portuguese territory.

The Portuguese View of the New World
Another landmark map was constructed between December 1501 and October 1502 in Lisbon. Although known today as the "Cantino map," its compiler and designer remains anonymous. Alberto Cantino was the envoy of Hercules d'Este, Duke of Ferrara, to the Portuguese court. Cantino ordered the map drawn and gave it to the Duke on November 19, 1502.

Cantino, as the map is called, also displaces the West Indies, locating all of the Greater Antilles to the north of the Tropic of Cancer. The map indicates the Treaty of Tordesillas demarcation line of 1494, while de la Cosa gave the earlier Papal demarcation line of 1493. Not only did Cantino depict the 1494 line but also moved Newfoundland eastward so that it

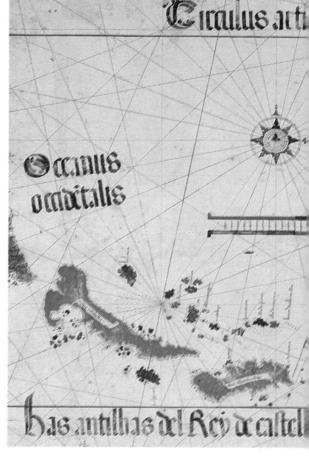

The Cantino map of 1502 shows the world according to the Portuguese. This portion of the 40-by-86-inch map is of the West Indies.

The 53-by-94-inch Waldseemüller world map of 1507. It was the first map to use the name *America* and to show North America separate from Asia.

A Mapmaker Names America

In 1506 the first *printed* map depicting the new discoveries appeared. Designed by Giovanni Matteo Contarini and engraved by Francesco Roselli in Florence, Italy, the map places the West Indies off the coast of Asia and east of Japan.

The following year, Martin Waldseemüller at St. Dié in French Lorraine produced a small globe and world map reflecting the new discoveries. It appears he derived the East Indies from the Cantino and he showed North America separate from Asia. In the descriptive text accompanying the two items, Waldseemüller suggested that the name *America* be applied to the newly discovered lands in honor of Amerigo Vespucci who explored South America. On his map, a woodcut in twelve sheets, he placed the name "America" on the South American land mass. It was the first time the name was used on a dated map. Eventually and probably accidentally the name was used for North America as well. Martin Waldseemüller was the last man to name a continent; by sheer happenstance, he may be credited with naming two.

Then, as now, maps reflected the new information as well as the technology would allow. Maps of the day also show us in graphic form some of the confusion, political jousting, and human error that plagued Europeans competing for a stake in the New World. The impact of the New Discoveries was just beginning to be felt.

This detailed section of the Contarini world map of 1506 shows *terra de cuba* and *hispani* south of Asia, a common perception of Europeans at the time.

**Impact
of the
Great
Discovery**

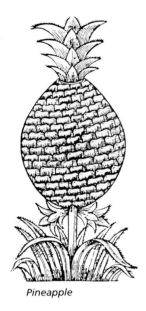

Pineapple

Initially, the discoveries of the First Voyage affected only the highest levels of society. Yet even the Spanish sovereigns did not grasp the full significance of what Columbus had to report. In this light, it is easier to understand some of the policies and mistakes made by the Europeans.

The News and Spanish Action
When Columbus was on his way home from the First Voyage, he wrote a brief letter to Luis de Santangel, a long-time friend and the man most responsible for financing the venture. Santangel was both chief quartermaster of Aragón and chief paymaster of Castilla. Enclosed with the letter was another, addressed to the king and queen.

Upon arriving at Palos on March 15, 1493, Columbus dispatched his letter announcing the Discovery. He learned that the Court was then in Barcelona, and set off to have an audience with King Ferdinand and Queen Isabela. Almost by the time Columbus reached Barcelona in early April, the letter to Santangel had been published. By May the letter was translated into Latin and printed in Rome. At least ten other editions were published before the end of 1493. The only known copy of the first Spanish edition is in the New York Public Library.

This rarest of documents is the first printed notice of the Discovery of America. The rapid dissemination of the *Carta de Colón*, as the letter was called, was a dramatic example of how printing affected European society.

The impact of Columbus's discovery on the Catholic Sovereigns of Aragón and Castilla was immediate. Here, at last, was the means to finance the liberation of the Holy Land and all other Christian lands occupied by the Muslims. Perhaps now Spain could at last wrest control of the East Indian spice trade from Arabic/Turkish domination. The holy fathers would have an unlimited number of new souls to win over, and there might be a little profit for the royal coffers. For these and other reasons, the Admiral of the Ocean Sea was granted immediate authorization for a second, and much more ambitious, return voyage.

England and Portugal Join In
The impact of Columbus's voyage on cosmographers and the educated class must have been devastating. Could it really be possible that this Genoese navigator had been correct all along about the size of the earth? Was the Ocean Sea only some three thousand miles across? Did the Admiral actually reach the mainland of Asia, or did he merely reach a few of the countless islands depicted on the *mappaemundi*? Where was the great Cathay of Marco Polo—the imperial cities, the opulence, the bustling seaports with their huge ships?

At least one man, John Cabot, knew that Columbus had fallen short of his true destination. Some scholars believe that Cabot was in Barcelona the day in 1493 when Columbus delivered his report to the Sovereigns. If so, could he have accepted the primitive Indians Columbus brought with him as subjects of the Great Khan? How could the crude artifacts Columbus displayed possibly compare to the opulence described by Marco Polo? To a puzzled Cabot these sights could only mean that Columbus had not sailed far enough west. Cabot knew that China was more accessible by the shorter Great Circle route in the north. By 1494, Cabot was in England, seeking permission to test his theory.

One of the more puzzling aspects concerning the Discovery was the inaction of the Portuguese in the face of Spain's expeditions. João II had learned of the successful voyage before anyone in Spain. Bad weather had forced Columbus to put into Lisbon harbor on March 4, and the Admiral had told João II of his discoveries. The entries in Columbus's log indicate that João's first concern was whether Columbus had violated Portuguese claims by sailing south of the east-west line established by the 1479 Treaty of Alcáçovas. This parallel, set at roughly 28° N, separated the Portuguese territory to the south from Spanish areas to the north.

But why didn't the Portuguese send a fleet to the Indies Columbus had found? Supposedly, João II did order Francisco de Almeida to find the islands claimed by Columbus and, if they lay south of the treaty line, to seize them. Almeida's fleet was apparently lost at sea. João II then requested a new north-south demarcation line, drawn by the pope in 1493. Why would he fail to pursue a claim on the new Indies? Only one answer seems plausible: João II, like Columbus, believed the new discoveries to be in Asia.

Although the new north-south line gave all the East Indies to Portugal, João II lost far more than he gained. All of Portugal's future Asiatic interests lay south of the 1479 line, along with all of modern Latin America except for a small portion of northern Mexico. Legally, every discovery made by Columbus during his four voyages was in Portuguese territory, as defined by the Treaty of Alcáçovas. By accepting a new north-south division—drawn one hundred leagues west of the Azores—Portugal had surrendered the entire western hemisphere to Spain.

In 1494, Spain and Portugal negotiated the Treaty of Tordesillas that moved the demarcation line further west to a meridian 370 leagues beyond the Cape Verde Islands. The line sliced through Brazil, giving Portugal legal authority in a land not yet discovered. Thus, one impact of the Discovery was an emerging political perception of the world as a prize to be fought over by rival European nations.

Changing Economics
The economic consequences of the Discovery for Spain and the rest of Europe were not as immediate as the political impact and are still a subject of debate among historians. Everyone agrees that in the sixteenth century, Spain and most of western Europe experienced a staggering rise in inflation, reaching 300 to 400 percent in Spain. There is no general agreement as to the cause. The obvious reason would seem to be the influx of silver and gold from the New World, which greatly in-

---

***Spain and Portugal
Divide the
World — Three Times***

1479 Treaty of Alcáçovas:
Spain (Castile) and Portugal retained their former holdings. South of 28 N. latitude the new lands became open to Portugal. Spain had reign north of that line.
1493 Papal Demarcation Line:
Spanish Pope Alexander VI drew a N-S line because Portugal correctly believed Columbus sailed south of the 1479 treaty line. Spain gained rights to the west-

ern, and Portugal to the eastern, hemisphere. The line's imprecise location in the Pacific allowed Spanish intrusion in that area.
1494 Treaty of Tordesillas:
Negotiations moved the line to a meridian 1,110 miles west of the Cape Verdes giving Portugal a piece of Brazil. The line's imprecision in the east led to further encroachment by Spain in SE Asia.

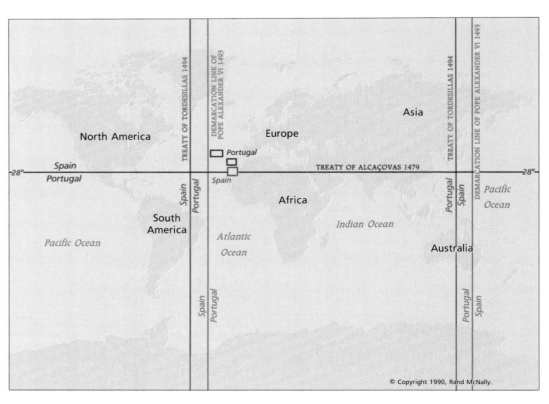

creased the European money supply. As the money supply increases, prices rise. But the inflation of the sixteenth century may not be that simple to explain.

Europe had been in the throes of a gold shortage since the middle of the fourteenth century. This had caused all governments to devalue their coinage; one of the results was a staggering rise in the price of gold. In Portugal, for example, the price rose one thousand percent between 1375 and 1435. One of the principal motives behind Portugal's African expeditions was a quest for the source of the Arabs' gold supply. But the amount of gold that entered Portugal after the 1470s did not have any noticeable effect on prices. In fact, the price revolution did not occur until the mid-1500s, when gold and silver from the Spanish colonies began pouring into the peninsula; the population began to increase; the India trade became established; and silver ore was found in Bolivia, Peru, and Mexico. A new method of extracting silver caused an additional increase in the precious metal.

Unlike Portugal, however, Spain was not as dependent on gold. For one thing, Spain's American colonies produced more silver than gold, and silver was the local currency used in the Indies. Spanish currency was so well regulated that it served as the international currency for over three hundred years.

The inflation of the sixteenth century was not uniform, either in time or place. Nor was there any consistency in the commodities affected. For example, food prices rose faster than the value of precious metals. The post-Discovery inflation seems to have been the product of many forces. Increased gold and silver supply, rising demand from a growing population, general expansion at home and abroad, increased capital investment and government expenditures, and debasement of coinage all played a role in this economic consequence of the Great Discovery.

Bureaucracy Grows

Numerous institutional changes can be tied directly to the Discovery. All these new territories needed to be managed—politically, economically, socially, and theologically. In such matters, the Sovereigns were absolute, but how well could they rule from thousands of miles away? Bureaucratic institutions—ponderous, clumsy, and costly—were created to govern the Indies.

After 1503, the economic affairs of the Indies were controlled by the *Casa de Contratación* (Board of Trade). This body had authority over all commerce to and from the Indies, immigration, commercial litigation, and maritime activities. By 1524 another government body, the *Consejo de Indias* (Council of the Indies), was established to manage all non-economic matters in the Indies. Both these organizations grew into large, cumbersome bureaucracies that spawned numerous subsidiary offices, populated by nobles and their friends and relatives. These organizations not only complicated trade and other matters, but in some instances their petty

---

EUROPEAN NOTIONS OF THE NEW WORLD

During his voyage along the coast of northern South America on August 13, 1498, Columbus made this entry in his log: *"I have come to believe that this is a great continent that was unknown until now."* A few days before this entry, he had written, *"...Your Highnesses have gained these vast lands, which are another world..."* In October 1500, while being returned to Spain in chains, Columbus wrote a letter in which he said, *"...I undertook a new voyage to the new Heaven and world, which had been hidden until now."*

Columbus did not abandon his faith in a Ptolemaic world. That is, a large continent located to the south of the Malay Peninsula and Indo-China that enclosed the Indian Ocean. And that a connecting isthmus might have a passageway from the Ocean Sea to that ocean.

By the Third Voyage Columbus concluded that he had discovered a large land mass that had been a hidden part of the world. However, Columbus continued to believe that the new lands were close to Asia and probably connected to it. This belief was shared by many Europeans.

The "Old World" View

The First Voyage of Discovery had very little effect on the average European. Had it not been for the recent invention of printing, it would have taken months, perhaps years, for news of this event to reach beyond the Spanish court in Barcelona.

For most fifteenth-century Europeans the planet was inhabited by Christians like themselves, with heathens in the periphery. In the view of most there were no American Indians, no Polynesians, no Eskimos—no inhabitants at all south of the equator, and there was only one ocean, the vast and mysterious Ocean Sea.

However, for the educated few the First Voyage confirmed what the ancients had taught; everything was where they had said it would be. But, of course, the ancients knew nothing about the lands Columbus had discovered.

Lure of the New Lands

Columbus wrote poetically in his February 21, 1493, log entry that he had discovered a virtual paradise, but there was no mass exodus from Europe to populate it. As news of New World riches slowly spread, more people sailed in search of excitement and fame; and for the fabled wealth of the Orient. The Church envisioned souls to save, while others saw these souls as a cheap labor supply.

The New World Revealed

The notion of a *new* world, as opposed to *another* world such as Cathay, did not begin to take hold until Balboa discovered the South Sea in 1513. In 1520, when Magellan threaded his way through the straits that now bears his name, he expected to reach the Spice Islands in three or four days. Instead, it took four months.

The Columbus-Balboa-Magellan voyages showed that Europe was not the *only* world, nor was the Ocean Sea the *only* sea. At long last, a New World had been revealed.

---

jealousies and favoritism led to tragedy. In the case of Magellan's ill-fated voyage around the world, for example, the *Casa de Contratación* succeeded in placing its own people on most of Magellan's ships and, through bureaucratic bumbling, loaded only half the necessary supplies on board.

New Diseases, New Plants

Columbus and his crew unknowingly brought back more than Indians, plants, and a variety of artifacts. They also carried syphilis with them, a disease to which New World populations were immune. The disease was unknown in Europe and gradually spread across the continent, causing untold misery and death among the population for centuries.

On a brighter note, Spanish and European farmers benefitted greatly from the Discovery. In the first decade of the sixteenth century, new plants and animals began to enter the Old World. Although America had little to offer in the way of domestic animals, except for the turkey, it was a virtual cornucopia of new plant species. Corn (maize), beans, squashes of all kinds, and sweet potatoes were among the first to make the trip. Later, tomatoes came from Mexico and white potatoes from the Andean region. With the food plants came other products such as fibers and medicines (quinine and ipecac). A vast new agricultural inventory was appearing on the European landscape.

SELECTED NEW WORLD PLANTS UNKNOWN TO EUROPEANS BEFORE 1492

Achiote *(yields a red dye)*	**Cranberry** *(large)*	**Peanut**
Avocado	**Curare**	**Pecan**
Balsa *(exceedingly light wood)*	**Guava**	**Pineapple**
Bean *(string, snap, red, kidney, black, lima)*	**Indigo**	**Plantain** *(cooking banana)*
Brazil nut	**Ipecac** *(emetic, purgative)*	**Potato** *(all varieties)*
Cacao *(chocolate)*	**Kapok** *(tree cotton)*	**Rubber**
Cashew nut	**Lignum vitae** *(exceedingly heavy wood)*	**Sisal**
Chicle *(base for chewing gum)*	**Mahogany**	**Squash** *(including pumpkin)*
Chile pepper	**Mamey** *(fruit)*	**Sunflower**
Cinchona *(bark yields quinine)*	**Manioc** *(yuca; yields cassava bread and tapioca)*	**Sweet Potato**
Coca *(base for cocaine)*	**Papaya**	**Tobacco**
Corn *(maize; including popcorn)*		**Tomato**
		Vanilla

The Discoverers Change the New World

Indian club

*European Influence
after
the Great Discovery*

**European settlement
and the associated culture
ture had its most dramatic extension in North
and South America. Europe's influence and
control, however,
touched most areas of
the world. Only China
and Japan remained
outside the main sphere
of influence until the
late 19th century.**

October 12, 1492, marked the beginning of the end for most of the civilizations and cultures of the Americas. Within one generation, most indigenous peoples of the Bahamas and Caribbean region were either killed or had died from disease. They were replaced by Europeans, Africans, and a new race called *mestizo,* a blend of European and Indian genes. This pattern of replacement was duplicated time and again, until today only a few descendants of the original peoples survive.

A People Lose Their Paradise
The destruction of the Indians that Columbus encountered was not intentional. It began with the accidental introduction of two diseases: smallpox and measles. Unknown in the New World, these diseases decimated Indian populations, who had no resistance to the exotic strains of virus and bacteria.

The Spanish also introduced their own system of forced labor, or slavery, into the New World. By 1503 the system was institutionalized as the *encomienda,* whereby Indians were "commended" to deserving Spaniards for protection and for instruction in the Christian faith. For these services, the Indians were to provide labor, supposedly for pay. In many ways this was a New World version of the Old World feudal system. The line separating slaves from serfs has always been thin.

Regimented labor was completely alien to all but a few American Indian groups. It did occur among some advanced civilizations, such as the Aztec and Incas, who also used slaves for much of their heavy labor. But for the other peoples of the Caribbean region, the work demands of the Europeans were unbearable, especially working in the gold and silver mines. The lust for gold turned many of the Spaniards on Española into tyrants. The death toll among Indians from overwork and disease took on the aspects of a plague. Uprisings, or even resistance to work demands, brought swift, violent retaliation from the Spanish with their European weapons.

It is difficult to estimate the pre-Columbian population of Española, but it may have been one million. Twenty years after the First Voyage, the Bahamas were being scoured for fresh workers. Within another decade, every inhabitant of the Bahamas had disappeared. By that time, most of Española's Indians had perished. The Spanish found another answer to their labor problem: import slaves from Africa. Only thirty years after Columbus found his "paradise," the new Eden had already been corrupted.

The Hacienda System
The hacienda system developed in the New World was a direct carryover from the feudal estates in Spain. The system was a family-run operation, incorporating farming, livestock production, primitive manufacturing, and a resident labor force. It was a perfect arrangement for the *encomienda* system.

The hacienda should not be confused with the plantation, even in the early sixteenth century. The plantation usually produced only one cash crop, such as sugar. Production of sugarcane became dominant in the Caribbean. The hacienda, on the other hand, depended on a variety of activities to maintain itself.

Both the hacienda and early plantation depended to a great extent on European, African, and Asian plants and animals, not just American varieties. Cattle, horses, goats, sheep, and pigs were brought into the Caribbean before 1500. Settlers introduced sugarcane and bananas, while the better coconut trees came later from the Philippines. Although cotton was native to America, the Old World varieties improved the indigenous plants. Rice was introduced first to Panama, but became a major New World crop only in Cuba, Brazil, and the English Carolina colonies. It never became a dominant crop where corn had been established first.

Old Imprints on the New Land
The European settlement produced profound changes in the landscape of the New World. On the surface, Indian settle-

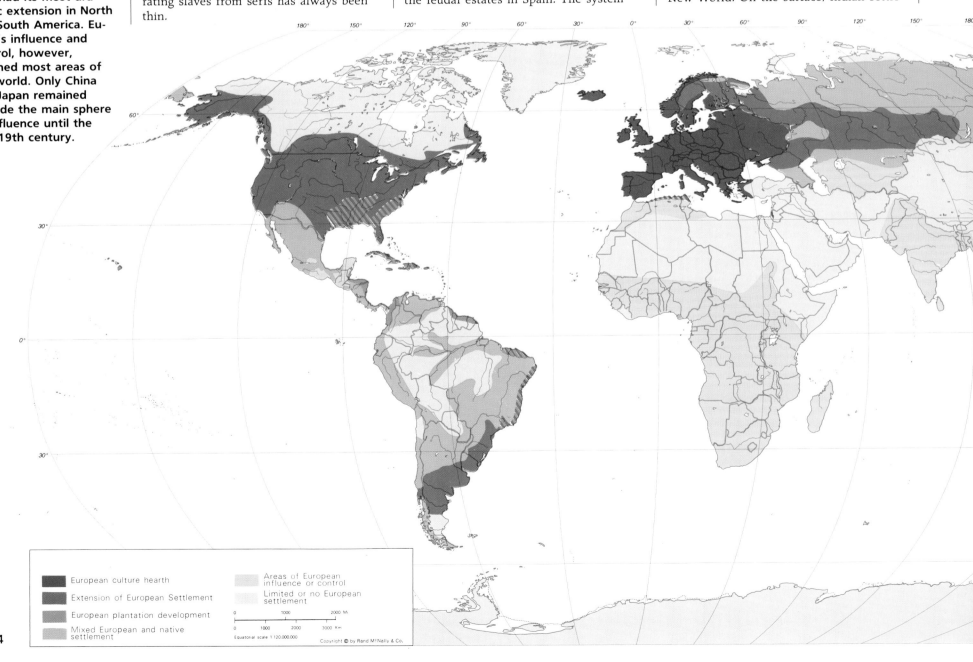

European culture hearth

Extension of European Settlement

European plantation development

Mixed European and native settlement

Areas of European influence or control

Limited or no European settlement

Equatorial scale 1:120,000,000

Copyright © by Rand M?Nally & Co.

ment patterns were not greatly affected by the conquest. In many instances, Spanish settlement merely meant the occupation of an Indian village or, in the case of central Mexico, an Indian city. Most of the major urban areas of modern Latin America were once Indian villages and farming communities. Even the hacienda owner typically maintained a residence in the nearest town.

What did occur, however, was the wholesale flight of many Indians to the mountains, swamps, or nearby islands to escape Spanish enslavement of the encomienda. Some of these refugees were hunted, captured, and returned to their villages. Others were killed to set an example for anyone harboring thoughts of escape. The Indians were faced with two equally difficult choices: escape and attempt to survive on their own or remain among the Spaniards and die of disease or overwork.

Those Indian groups who stayed with the Spaniards saw their race gradually die out as Indians and Europeans mixed, creating a new race, the *mestizo*. In other regions, where African slaves were brought in, blacks and Afro-Europeans (*mulattoes*) became dominant as the native Indian population slowly vanished.

The Spaniards also brought their architecture and urban and agrarian designs with them. All formal buildings conformed to Spanish patterns, which by this time had a decidedly Moorish influence. After 1510, towns were laid out in the typical grid pattern built around a central plaza. The finer homes were constructed in the European manner. Rural homes, however, even in *mestizo* areas, continued to follow the traditional ways, constructed either of cane and thatch or wattle-daub and thatch. Although the Spaniards introduced their own system of land distribution and field patterns, they were quite willing to borrow from the Indians when it suited them. Because European crops would not grow in tropical conditions, Indian foods became as important as the imported European crops. In non-tropical areas, such as the Mexican plateau, the Spaniards had more success with familiar crops like wheat.

Indian root crops—manioc and sweet potatoes—were so basic to the Spanish colonial economy in Española that on the island (and later in Panama), land was distributed in *montones,* or large mounds, in which the plants grew. An area of 200,000 *montones* was equal to about ninety acres. Such a parcel was called a *caballería,* and as many as three units of this size may have been given to a calvary soldier (*caballero*). An area of 100,000 *montones,* or forty-five acres was called a *peonía.* Five of these units might be given to a foot soldier (*peón*). Other individuals—nobles or those who had the favor of the church or crown—were given land grants in the Indies even before they left Spain.

A Model of Conquest and Rule

One surprising fact about the Spanish occupation and settlement of the New World—and a fact universally ignored by historians—is that it had its precedent in the Old World. For over a century, the Canary Islands had been a training school for future *conquistadores* of the New World.

The Canaries, from which Columbus had launched all four of his voyages, had been under some form of Spanish jurisdiction since the fourteenth century. Although Castilla did not totally subdue the region until after the First Voyage, the Spanish kingdom had a firm foothold in six of the seven islands. Nearby, in the Portuguese islands of Madeira and Porto Santo, a comparable "school" existed for Portuguese explorers. Historians have yet to examine the influence of the Canary/Madeira models on the conquest and settlement of the New World.

The first written account of an expedition to the Canaries in 1341, reported by Giovanni Boccaccio who also wrote the *Decameron,* reads like the log of Columbus on Discovery Day. The subsequent development of both the Canaries and Madeira in the fifteenth century foreshadows what was to happen in the West Indies.

In both cases, a group of fertile, volcanic islands, with rugged natural beauty and dense populations, were completely changed by such institutions as sugarcane plantations, feudalism, absentee landownership, and slavery. Taxes and royal tithes soon followed, along with free land grants for the conquerors or royal favorites. All of these elements were in place in the Canary and Madeira islands before 1492. The Canary Islands were the last land seen by most Spaniards before arriving in the Indies. Surely they did not forget in three or four weeks the settlement model that history and geography had provided.

IN HONOR OF COLUMBUS

Places named for the Great Discoverer are almost all in the New World. This very abbreviated listing shows how widespread has been the use of Columbus's name or derivatives.

Country
Colombia, *South America*

Province
Archipiélago de Colón, *Ecuador*
British Columbia, *Canada*
Colón, *Honduras*
Colón, *Panama*

Federal District
District of Columbia, *United States*

United States Cities
Columbus, *AR, GA, IL, IN, KS, KY, MS, MT, NE, NJ, NM, NC, ND, OH, PA, TX, WI*
Columbus City and Columbus Junction, *IA*
Columbus Grove, and Columbus Park, *OH*
Columbia, *AL, CA, CT, IL, IA, KY, LA, MD, MS, MO, NJ, NC, PA, SC, SD, TN, VA*
Columbia City, *IN, OR;* **C. Crossroads,** *PA;* **C. Falls,** *ME, MT;* **C. Heights,** *LA, MN, WA;* **C. Park,** *MD;* **C. Station,** *OH*
Columbiana, *AL, OH*
Columbiaville, *MI, NY*
West Columbia, *SC, TX, WV*

United States Counties
Columbus County, *NC*
Columbia County, *AR, FL, GA, NY, OR, PA, WA, WI*

Other United States Features
Columbus Salt Marsh, *NV*
Columbia Basin, *WA*
Columbia Plateau, *WA-OR-ID*
Columbia River, *WA-OR-Canada*

Canadian Features
Cape Columbia, *Northwest Territories*
Columbia Lake, *British Columbia*
Columbia Mountains, *British Columbia*

Oceanic and Lunar Names
Colombian Abyssal Plain, *Atlantic Ocean*
Colombian Basin, *Caribbean Sea*
Columbia Seamount, *east of Brazil*
Colombo, *lunar crater*

Americans

In the Wake of Columbus, 1493-1519

Impact of the Great Discovery

The successful return of Christopher Columbus from the First Voyage in March 1493 and the publication of his famous letter announcing the Discovery marked the beginning of what is known as the Age of Discovery. In many ways the period has not been concluded, only redirected and specialized.

The western segment of the post Columbian maritime exploration involved the Spanish, Portuguese, English, and French. The eastern segment was basically a Portuguese monopoly in Africa and India. The Dutch did not enter the race until the seventeenth century, largely because of Spanish domination.

Other than the Columbus voyages only one significant Atlantic crossing took place between 1492 and 1499. The Venetian, John Cabot, sailing for England, may have been spurred by Columbus's Discov-

ery to make his own voyage. The first expedition in 1496 got no farther west than Ireland before Cabot was forced to turn back. The second expedition in 1497, however, reached Canada.

The Efficient Portuguese

The post-Columbian Portuguese expedition to India led by Vasco da Gama departed Lisbon in July, 1497, a month after Cabot sailed west from Bristol. This was another voyage in the Portuguese exploration to the south and east that had begun in 1415. It ranks with Columbus's First Voyage. Da Gama was out of sight of land for three months compared to 33 days for Columbus and ultimately landed in Calicut, India, a journey of over 12,000 miles (19,320 kilometers).

Upon da Gama's return to Lisbon in 1499, a second expedition was assembled.

In March 1500, Pedro Álvares Cabral departed, and following the westward arc taken by da Gama, reached Brazil on April 22 at a place he named *Terra da Vera Cruz.* The Portuguese maintain this was the discovery of that great land. Cabral then proceeded eastward and reached India in August, 1500.

Within fifteen years after the First Voyage of Columbus the Portuguese had visited most of the islands in the South Atlantic, investigated all of the Indian Ocean's shores, and made thrusts into the Pacific. The Spanish had not yet revealed the coasts of the Caribbean Sea and Gulf of Mexico.

Columbus's Crew Sets Sail

Fourteen ninety-nine marked the year that post-Columbian Spanish voyages of discovery really began. Up until that time jour-

The Age of Discovery

Columbus triggered a chain reaction of maritime exploration and discovery. For more than a century there were only four important participants—Spain, Portugal, England, and France. These four concentrated on the Americas. Portugal monopolized Africa, India, and SE Asia, though Spain challenged this monopoly in the Philippines and Moluccas. After 1600 the French, English, and Dutch offered competition in Africa and Asia while the Dutch entered the New World arena.

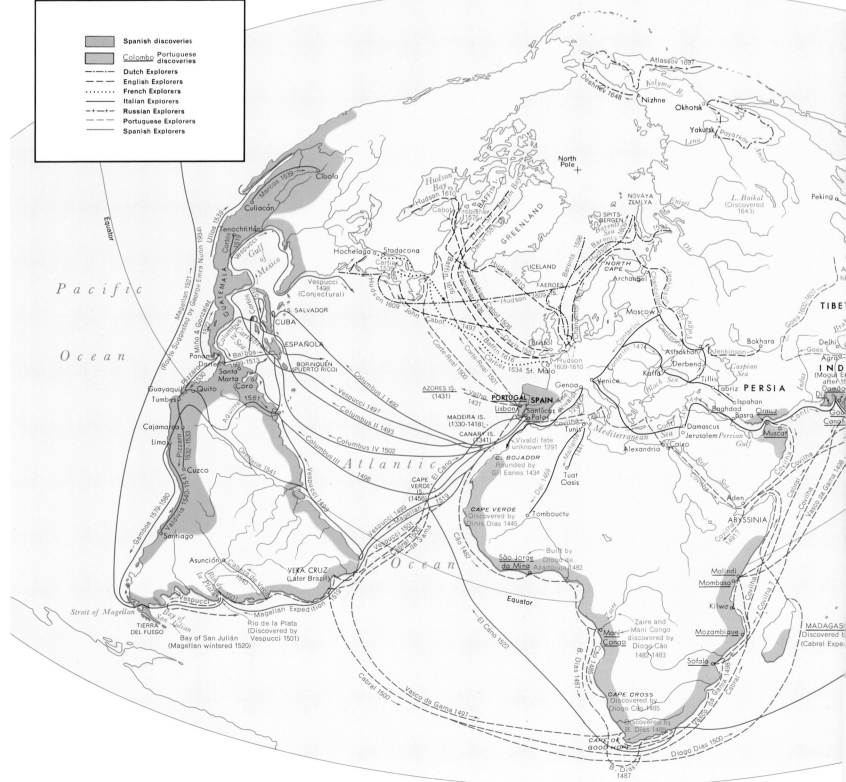

neys were to re-supply and bring colonists primarily to Española. As might be expected, men who sailed on the Voyages of Discovery were the first to initiate their own "voyages of discovery" to the New World.

Alonso de Ojeda, a companion of Columbus on the Second Voyage, sailed from Cádiz for Venezuela in May 1499. With him was Juan de la Cosa, a shipmate of Columbus on the First Voyage, and Amerigo Vespucci, who knew Columbus. They crossed from the Canaries to Suriname, coasted South America, and discovered the great pearl fisheries of Margarita Island—something Columbus had missed.

After his return, the Italian, Vespucci, an excellent navigator, transferred his services from Spain to Portugal and in 1501 sailed for South America. He arrived at Cape de São Roque and, according to unsubstantiated reports, sailed as far south as South Georgia Island before returning to Lisbon in 1502. Accounts of these and other voyages led Waldseemüller to place the name, America, on his famous map of 1507, in honor of Vespucci—instead of the discoverer of the continent, Columbus.

Pedro Alonso Niño, a First Voyage pilot, left Spain in 1499, a month after Ojeda. He went to Venezuela, traded for pearls and gold, and was back in Spain by April 1500, well before Ojeda.

In December 1499, Vicente Yáñez Pinzón, captain of the *Niña* on the first crossing, sailed directly for South America, where the Spanish believe he discovered Brazil and the Amazon River in January 1500. He, too, traded for gold and pearls and returned.

Another Spanish expedition sailed from Palos in early 1500 under the command of Diego de Lepe. After reaching South America, de Lepe turned south and may have gotten to the Rio de la Plata in what is now Argentina, the farthest south any European had been in the New World to that time.

In October 1500, yet another expedition, under the command of Rodrigo de Bastidas, left Cádiz on what was becoming a well-travelled route to Venezuela, via Gomera in the Canary Islands. Juan de la Cosa, on his fourth trip, and Vasco Núñez de Balboa, accompanied Bastidas. This was the first expedition to reach the Gulf of Darién and Panama, early in 1501. Balboa learned that the Indians on the western side of the gulf were friendly. Later, he used this fact and other knowledge he gained to help establish a foothold on the mainland in 1510, and discover the Pacific Ocean in 1513.

Settlements in the New World

In 1509, seventeen years after the Great Discovery, there was still no mainland settlement in the New World. There had been only two feeble attempts earlier to establish a colony. Much of the Central American coast north of Honduras and the shores of the Gulf of Mexico were still unexplored, although Cuba was finally circumnavigated in 1508 by Sebastián Ocampo. It seems that Spain was more interested in exploitation than exploration. But 1509 marked an important new stage in the Spanish conquest of America.

In that year King Ferdinand divided the mainland into two regions. The area east of the Gulf of Darién to Cape Vela (Colombia), named *Nueva Andalucía,* was assigned to the explorer Alonso de Ojeda, who was to become the first governor of South America. The region to the west and north, up to Honduras, named *Castilla del Oro,* went to Diego de Nicuesa. As preparations began for expeditions to these areas, Juan Ponce de León was conquering Puerto Rico, then called the *Isla de San Juan,* while Juan de Esquivel was settling Jamaica.

The race for the mainland began on November 10, 1509, when Ojeda sailed for Colombia, taking with him Juan de la Cosa and a newcomer, Francisco Pizarro. Nicuesa was delayed in Santo Domingo, and one of his crew, Hernán Cortés, became ill and had to be left behind. Fate had spared him for a future assignment.

Ojeda and his party encountered fierce resistance from the Carib Indians when they landed in Colombia. Eventually Ojeda was forced to return to Española to seek help, leaving Pizarro in charge of the encampment near modern Cartagena. Vasco Núñez de Balboa arrived in Colombia as a stowaway and offered to lead the men to the safer west side of the Gulf of Darién. They reached an Indian village there about September 10 and named it *Nuestra Señora de la Antigua del Darién.* It became the first Spanish settlement on the mainland of the New World.

In the meantime, Diego de Nicuesa had sailed along the coast to Belén in Panama, where Columbus had stayed briefly in 1503. It proved impossible to establish an outpost at Belén, and Nicuesa finally landed his men at a spot that in his desperation he named *Nombre de Dios* ("Let's stop here, in the name of God."). Although Nicuesa was the legal governor of Antigua, he was so unpopular that he was not allowed to land at the village and govern. Nicuesa was sent home to Española in a leaking ship in March 1511 and was lost at sea.

In the spring of that year there were many Spaniards on the Caribbean islands, but only 200 on the mainland of America, and those were all at Antigua. They had not uncovered or settled much mainland territory. Two years later, Balboa was named Governor of Darién and in September 1513 discovered the Pacific Ocean. In 1514, a new governor, Pedro Arias de Ávila (Pedrarias) arrived with eighteen ships and 1,500 colonists. A roster of the men would have read like a *Who's Who* of the Conquest. Within a year, however, half the colonists had perished and another hundred had sailed to Cuba where the city of Santiago was founded by Diego Velásquez de León. Still, the Spanish had not established a solid settlement on the mainland.

The year 1519—exactly one decade after the revitalized exploration and conquest began—witnessed a flurry of momentous events. Balboa was executed by Pedrarias on trumped-up charges, thus ending the life of one of Spain's greatest explorers. Alonso de Piñeda explored the Gulf of Mexico and the mouth of the Mississippi River, thereby becoming its true discoverer. Pedrarias established Panama City, the first European settlement on the Pacific Ocean. Hernán Cortés, who at last had reached the mainland, landed at the site of present-day Vera Cruz and launched his conquest of Mexico.

From Panama City, the Spaniards set out to explore the Pacific littoral, ranging north to Mexico and south to Peru. From Panama, Mexico City, and Santo Domingo, the Spanish conquest could proceed beyond its starting phase, which had taken a whole generation, from 1492 to 1519.

Two Realms

Spanish exploration of the New World accelerated after King Ferdinand divided the mainland in 1509.

Filling in the Features of the Earth, 1519-1600

The post-1519 era of exploration began with three significant events: Cortés completed his conquest of the Aztecs (1521); Ponce de León returned to Florida with two hundred men to attempt the first European settlement of what is now the United States (1521); and Magellan's ship returned from the first circumnavigation of the world (1522). Although Magellan and Ponce de León both perished in these ventures, along with hundreds of their followers, Europe now realized the wealth of the new lands, the true size of the earth, and the vast expanse of land north of the Gulf of Mexico waiting to be explored.

French Sail into Spanish Waters

In 1524 France entered the race to explore the New World. A Florentine, Giovanni Verrazzano, sailed from Le Havre to North America, where he discovered the Outer Banks of North Carolina. Verrazzano was looking for China, and when he peered over the low, sandy barrier islands separating the Atlantic Ocean from Pamlico Sound he concluded that he had found the Pacific Ocean! A second voyage in 1527 took Verrazzano to Brazil, but the third voyage to the Caribbean in 1528 ended with the Florentine being eaten by the Carib Indians. The only contribution Verrazzano made from these voyages was the distorted cartography that resulted from his notion that the Pacific lay just beyond Cape Hatteras.

France later sent Jacques Cartier on three voyages in 1534, 1535, and 1541, all to the same general area of the St. Lawrence River. His expeditions set the stage for the French colonization of Canada.

Although overland exploration began in North America as early as 1513, South America did not become of major interest to the Spaniards until Francisco Pizarro conquered the Incan Empire in the 1530s. The fabulous wealth yielded by this conquest enticed the Spanish sovereigns to support expeditions to Argentina and Paraguay to establish colonies.

Between 1526 and 1528, the Spanish also attempted to found a colony on the eastern seaboard of the United States. They tried twice more to settle Florida, once in 1539 and again in 1559, before King Felipe II ordered that no more effort be wasted on this region of the New World.

The failure of Spain to colonize Florida was probably welcome news to the French, who were interested in colonizing the New World themselves. Jean Ribault, leading a group of French Huguenots, landed on the shore of Port Royal in present-day South Carolina in 1562. They constructed a small fort, named Charlesfort in honor of the twelve-year-old monarch, Charles IX. The colony did not prosper, however, and a second expedition reached the St. John's River, Florida, in 1564, where the colonists built Fort Caroline. This settlement of three hundred French Protestants alarmed the Spanish, who felt

the fort was a threat to the Gulf Stream sealane used by their ships on the return voyage to Europe.

In 1565, Pedro Menéndez de Avilés attacked the French colony and killed most of its inhabitants. The Spanish then founded a town nearby, naming it St. Augustine. The site is still the oldest town in the United States. The French did not establish a lasting colony until the founding of Québec in 1608.

English and Dutch Sail Northwest

England's main purpose in sailing the Atlantic after Cabot was to discover a northwest passage to the Pacific Ocean and to raid Spanish and French vessels bearing wealth from the New World. Humphrey Gilbert made the first attempt at colonization in 1583, but his five ships were lost

at sea. Sir Walter Raleigh succeeded in establishing a colony at Roanoke, Virginia, in 1587, but the settlement disappeared in 1591. England made no other attempts to colonize the New World until 1607 when Jamestown, Virginia, was founded.

The Dutch were the last of the four principal nations to participate in exploring the western hemisphere. Hendrik Hudson sailed into New York harbor in 1609, having crossed the Atlantic by the northern route. By 1614 the Dutch had created a small colony near Albany, and in 1626 made their famous "purchase" of Manhattan Island from the native Indians.

Although the Dutch still maintained a presence in the Caribbean islands, most of their colonial activity took place in Sri

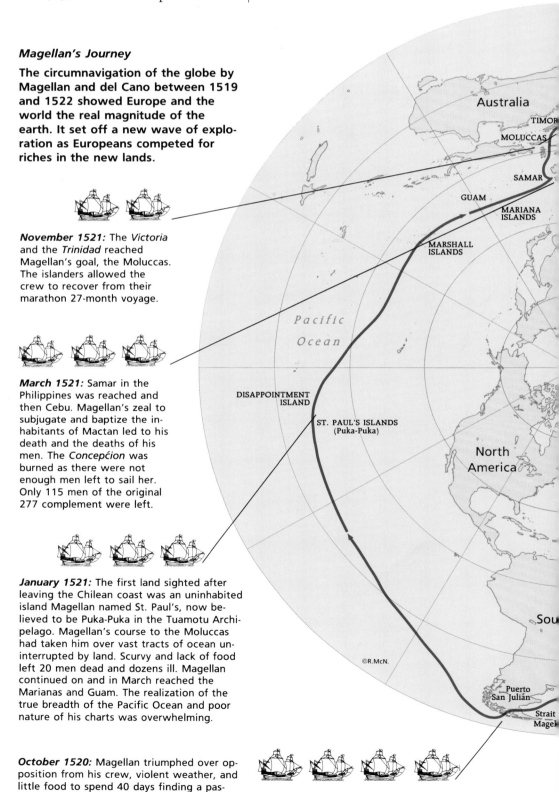

Magellan's Journey

The circumnavigation of the globe by Magellan and del Cano between 1519 and 1522 showed Europe and the world the real magnitude of the earth. It set off a new wave of exploration as Europeans competed for riches in the new lands.

November 1521: The *Victoria* and the *Trinidad* reached Magellan's goal, the Moluccas. The islanders allowed the crew to recover from their marathon 27-month voyage.

March 1521: Samar in the Philippines was reached and then Cebu. Magellan's zeal to subjugate and baptize the inhabitants of Mactan led to his death and the deaths of his men. The *Concepción* was burned as there were not enough men left to sail her. Only 115 men of the original 277 complement were left.

January 1521: The first land sighted after leaving the Chilean coast was an uninhabited island Magellan named St. Paul's, now believed to be Puka-Puka in the Tuamotu Archipelago. Magellan's course to the Moluccas had taken him over vast tracts of ocean uninterrupted by land. Scurvy and lack of food left 20 men dead and dozens ill. Magellan continued on and in March reached the Marianas and Guam. The realization of the true breadth of the Pacific Ocean and poor nature of his charts was overwhelming.

October 1520: Magellan triumphed over opposition from his crew, violent weather, and little food to spend 40 days finding a passage through the straits to the Pacific Ocean. The *San Antonio* defected and returned to Spain with most of the stores.

Lanka (Ceylon), and the East Indies (Indonesia). The Dutch played only a minor role in exploration and colonization of the New World, but they were active economically. During the latter part of the seventeenth century, the Dutch posssessed the world's largest merchant fleet. In many ways they were the "Venetians" of the ocean: shippers, wholesalers, processors, and so on. Much of the growing slave trade was controlled by the Dutch, and Dutch pirates operated openly from ports in the Netherlands.

1600 and into the Future

By mid-1600 the general outlines of continents and major island chains were located, and world maps created in Europe began to resemble their modern counterparts more closely. Even Australia was making a tentative appearance on some charts. The inland and overland exploration of the new regions was just beginning, and the voyages of James Cook and many others were still to come. Not until the nineteenth century did the great scientific voyages of the *Beagle* and *Challenger* set the stage for the twentieth century and our own Age of Discovery.

The discovery of new lands and seas on this planet has come nearly to an end. Many details remain to be filled in and much remains to probe and ponder. But for seekers of new worlds, the future lies in outer space. Yet as dramatic as such voyages will be, there will never be another expedition analogous to the voyages of the sixteenth century and earlier.

The exploration of space is too complex and expensive for a handful of individuals, such as Columbus and his crew, to go it alone. Even if such a venture were possible, space-age explorers would travel in a spacecraft filled with data from dozens of automated and unmanned probes launched before them. No one on Columbus's ships knew with any certainty what lay beyond the Ocean Sea; they had only hearsay reports and the speculations of ancient geographers.

We have come a long way from that distant time when one could climb a hill and believe that the entire world lay below. It was not until 1961 that Yuri Gagarin ascended high enough to catch a glimpse of what that totality really was. And it was not until Christmastime, 1968, that the American astronauts Borman, Lovell, and Anders viewed our world while orbiting another. A lunar base is just as much a certainty as the first colonies in sixteenth-century America. And the trip to Mars is that next step, not unlike Magellan's voyage across the Pacific Ocean.

It has taken humanity fifty centuries to explore the world, and most of the discoveries have been accomplished during the past 500 years. The chart of discoverers, "Argonauts to Astronauts," on the following pages summarizes the exploration before and since Columbus. We have no way of imagining the itineraries or timetables for the next 500 years. It is clear, however, that as distances have increased so has our technology, and the faster we have learned to travel, the more we have compressed time. We can now circumnavigate the world in ninety minutes; a trip to the moon requires fewer days than it took Columbus to sail from Spain to the Canary Islands. Our conquest of space may well mean the conquest of time.

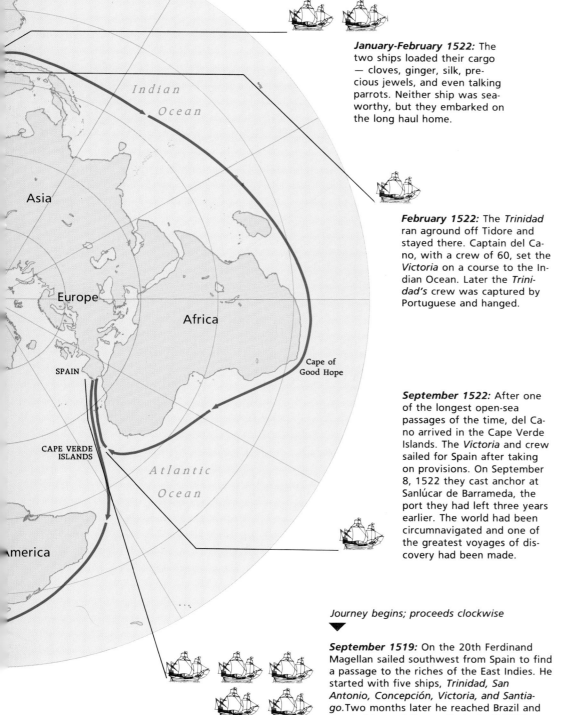

January-February 1522: The two ships loaded their cargo — cloves, ginger, silk, precious jewels, and even talking parrots. Neither ship was seaworthy, but they embarked on the long haul home.

February 1522: The *Trinidad* ran aground off Tidore and stayed there. Captain del Cano, with a crew of 60, set the *Victoria* on a course to the Indian Ocean. Later the *Trinidad's* crew was captured by Portuguese and hanged.

September 1522: After one of the longest open-sea passages of the time, del Cano arrived in the Cape Verde Islands. The *Victoria* and crew sailed for Spain after taking on provisions. On September 8, 1522 they cast anchor at Sanlúcar de Barrameda, the port they had left three years earlier. The world had been circumnavigated and one of the greatest voyages of discovery had been made.

Journey begins; proceeds clockwise

▼

September 1519: On the 20th Ferdinand Magellan sailed southwest from Spain to find a passage to the riches of the East Indies. He started with five ships, *Trinidad, San Antonio, Concepción, Victoria, and Santiago.* Two months later he reached Brazil and coasted toward the south. In April 1520 captains Quesada and Mendoza were killed because of mutinies. Four months later the *Santiago* was lost.

Magellan's flagship, Trinidad

Someday, somewhere, another Columbus will discover another new world. There is no question but that the technology of the future will make travel in deep space a reality. The question that will confront those explorers and discoverers of the future is whether we have learned anything during the centuries of earth-bound exploration—not lessons in technology, but those concerned with tolerance, compassion, and the human spirit.

Argonauts to Astronauts

1300 BC

Date: 1300 B.C.
Explorer: Jason and the Argonauts
Explored for: Thessaly
Area Explored: Black Sea

Date: 1250
Explorer: Ulysses (Odysseus)
Explored for: Ithaca
Area Explored: Mediterranean

Date: 500
Explorer: Anonymous (for Necho II)
Explored for: Egypt
Area Explored: Sailed around Africa

Greek vase showing Jason and the Argonauts, 470 BC

Date: 500
Explorer: Hanno
Explored for: Carthage
Area Explored: Sierra Leone

Date: 460
Explorer: Herodotus
Explored for: Caria/Ionia
Area Explored: Middle East, Danube, Don River, Egypt

Date: 334-324
Explorer: Alexander the Great
Explored for: Macedonia
Area Explored: Middle East, Indus

Date: 325-310
Explorer: Pytheas
Explored for: Massilia
Area Explored: Thule, Great Britian

Caravan in Asia from early map

AD 500

Date: A.D. 570
Explorer: St. Brendan
Explored for: Ireland
Area Explored: Atlantic Ocean

Date: 900
Explorer: Gunnbjörn Ulfsson
Explored for: Denmark/Norway
Area Explored: Greenland

Date: 900
Explorer: Al-Masudi
Explored for: Baghdad
Area Explored: India, Sri Lanka, China, East Africa, Madagascar

Date: 987
Explorer: Bjarni Herjulfsson
Explored for: Denmark/Norway
Area Explored: Northeast North America

Date: 1003
Explorer: Leif Eriksson
Explored for: Denmark/Norway
Area Explored: Northeast North America

Date: 1271-95
Explorer: Marco Polo
Explored for: Venice
Area Explored: China, India, Middle East

Date: 1325-53
Explorer: Ibn-Batutah
Explored for: Morocco
Area Explored: North Africa, Sahara, India, China, Sri Lanka, Indus Valley, Afghanistan, Middle East, Sumatra

1400

Date: 1402-05
Explorer: Jean de Béthencourt and Gadiffer de la Salle
Explored for: France
Area Explored: Canary Islands

Date: 1404-33
Explorer: Cheng Ho
Explored for: China
Area Explored: Tiawan, Philippines, Indonesia, SE Asia, India, SW Asia, East Africa

Date: 1419-20
Explorer: João Gonçalves Zarco and Tristão Vaz Teixeira
Explored for: Portugal
Area Explored: Madeira Islands

Date: 1423
Explorer: Gonçalo Velho Cabral
Explored for: Portugal
Area Explored: Azores Islands

Date: 1427
Explorer: Diogo de Silves
Explored for: Portugal
Area Explored: Azores Islands

Date: 1434
Explorer: Gil Eanes
Explored for: Portugal
Area Explored: Cape Bojador

Date: 1460
Explorer: Diogo Gomes, Antonio da Nola
Explored for: Portugal
Area Explored: Cape Verde Islands

Date: 1472-73
Explorer: Diderik Pining and Hans Pothorst; João Vaz Corte-Real and Alvaro Martins Homen (observers)
Explored for: Denmark/Norway
Area Explored: Newfoundland

Date: 1475
Explorer: Fernão Teles
Explored for: Portugal
Area Explored: Searched for Island of Seven Cities

Date: 1480
Explorer: John Lloyd
Explored for: England
Area Explored: Searched for Island of Brazil

Date: 1481
Explorer: Thomas Croft
Explored for: England
Area Explored: Newfoundland (?)

Date: 1486
Explorer: Fernão Dulmo
Explored for: Portugal
Area Explored: Searched for Island of Seven Cities

Date: 1488
Explorer: Bartolomeu Dias
Explored for: Portugal
Area Explored: Cape of Good Hope

Columbus in the New World

Date: 1492-1504
Explorer: Christopher Columbus
Explored for: Castilla/Aragón
Area Explored: Bahamas, West Indies, Honduras to Panama, Venezuela

Date: 1493-1503
Explorer: Vasqueanos, Gaspar, and Miguel Corte-Real
Explored for: Portugal
Area Explored: Northwest Passage

Date: 1497
Explorer: John Cabot
Explored for: England
Area Explored: Newfoundland/Nova Scotia

Date: 1497-98
Explorer: Vasco da Gama and Ahmad Ibn Madjid (pilot)
Explored for: Portugal
Area Explored: East Africa and India

Date: 1499
Explorer: Alonso de Ojeda, Juan de la Cosa, and Amerigo Vespucci
Explored for: Castilla/Aragón
Area Explored: Venezuela

Amerigo Vespucci

Date: 1499
Explorer: Pedro Alonso Niño
Explored for: Castilla/Aragón
Area Explored: Venezuela

Date: 1499
Explorer: Vicente Yáñez Pinzón
Explored for: Castilla/Aragón
Area Explored: NE South America, Amazon River

1500

Date: 1500
Explorer: Pedro Álvares Cabral
Explored for: Portugal
Area Explored: Brazil

Date: 1500
Explorer: Diego de Lepe
Explored for: Castilla/Aragón
Area Explored: Argentina

Date: 1500-02
Explorer: Rodrigo de Bastidas, Juan de la Cosa, Vasco Núñez de Balboa
Explored for: Castilla/Aragón
Area Explored: Venezuela, Colombia, Panama

Date: 1502
Explorer: Alonso de Ojeda
Explored for: Castilla/Aragón
Area Explored: Venezuela

Date: 1509-11
Explorer: Alonso de Ojeda, Juan de la Cosa, Francisco Pizarro
Explored for: Castilla/Aragón
Area Explored: Colombia

Date: 1509-11
Explorer: Diego de Nicuesa
Explored for: Castilla/Aragón
Area Explored: Panama

Ship, 1500s

Date: 1510-11
Explorer: Martín Fernández de Enciso and Vasco Núñez de Balboa
Explored for: Castilla/Aragón
Area Explored: Colombia

Date: 1510-19
Explorer: Vasco Núñez de Balboa
Explored for: Castilla/Aragón
Area Explored: Colombia, Panama, Pacific Ocean

Date: 1513
Explorer: Juan Ponce de León
Explored for: Castilla/Aragón
Area Explored: Florida

Date: 1513
Explorer: Jorge Álvares
Explored for: Portugal
Area Explored: China

Date: 1515
Explorer: Diego Velásquez de León
Explored for: Castilla/Aragón
Area Explored: Cuba

Date: 1517
Explorer: Francisco Hernández de Córdoba
Explored for: Spain
Area Explored: Yucatan Peninsula

Date: 1519
Explorer: Alonso de Pineda
Explored for: Spain
Area Explored: Gulf of Mexico, Mississippi River

Date: 1519-21
Explorer: Hernán Cortés
Explored for: Spain
Area Explored: Vera Cruz, Mexico City

Date: 1519-22
Explorer: Ferdinand Magellan and Juan Sebastián del Cano
Explored for: Spain
Area Explored: Circumnavigation of the world

Chart of Explorers

Date: 1521
Explorer: Juan Ponce de León
Explored for: Spain
Area Explored: Florida

Date: 1524
Explorer: Giovanni Verrazzano
Explored for: France
Area Explored: North Carolina to Newfoundland

Date: 1528
Explorer: Pánfilo de Narváez and Álvar Núñez Cabeza de Vaca
Explored for: Spain
Area Explored: Florida

Date: 1528-36
Explorer: Álvar Núñez Cabeza de Vaca
Explored for: Spain
Area Explored: Florida to Mexico

Date: 1531-41
Explorer: Francisco Pizarro
Explored for: Spain
Area Explored: Peru

Date: 1534
Explorer: Jacques Cartier
Explored for: France
Area Explored: Québec

Date: 1539-40
Explorer: Hernán Cortés
Explored for: Spain
Area Explored: Baja California

Date: 1539-42
Explorer: Hernando de Soto
Explored for: Spain
Area Explored: Florida, SE United States, Mississippi River

Date: 1540
Explorer: Fernão Mendes Pinto
Explored for: Portugal
Area Explored: Japan

Date: 1540-42
Explorer: Francisco Vásquez de Coronado
Explored for: Spain
Area Explored: SW United States

Mariner's compass, 1400s

Date: 1542-49
Explorer: Francis Xavier
Explored for: Portugal
Area Explored: India, Japan

Date: 1559-61
Explorer: Tristán de Luna
Explored for: Spain
Area Explored: Florida

Date: 1562
Explorer: Jean Ribault
Explored for: France
Area Explored: Florida, Georgia, South Carolina

Date: 1564
Explorer: René de Goulaine de Laudonnière
Explored for: France
Area Explored: Florida

Date: 1565
Explorer: Pedro Menéndez de Avilés
Explored for: Spain
Area Explored: Florida

Date: 1576-78
Explorer: Martin Frobisher
Explored for: England
Area Explored: Northwest Passage

Date: 1577-80
Explorer: Francis Drake
Explored for: England
Area Explored: Circumnavigation of the world

Sir Francis Drake

Date: 1578-1610
Explorer: Matteo Ricci
Explored for: Portugal
Area Explored: India, China

Date: 1579-85
Explorer: Timofeyevich Yermak
Explored for: Russia
Area Explored: Ural region

Date: 1583
Explorer: Humphrey Gilbert
Explored for: England
Area Explored: First colony attempt by the English

Date: 1587-91
Explorer: John White (for Walter Raleigh)
Explored for: England
Area Explored: Roanoke Island ('Lost Colony')

Date: 1595-97
Explorer: Álvaro de Mendaña and Pedro Fernández de Quirós
Explored for: Spain
Area Explored: Pacific and Philippines

Date: 1596-97
Explorer: Willem Barents
Explored for: Netherlands
Area Explored: Northeast passage, Svalbard, Novaya Zemlya

1600

Date: 1603-15
Explorer: Samuel de Champlain
Explored for: France
Area Explored: Canada, Québec

Date: 1605-06
Explorer: Pedro Fernández de Quirós and Luis Váez de Torres
Explored for: Spain
Area Explored: South Pacific, Indonesia, Melanesia, Australia (?)

Date: 1607
Explorer: Christopher Newport
Explored for: England
Area Explored: Jamestown, Virginia

Date: 1608
Explorer: Samuel de Champlain
Explored for: France
Area Explored: Québec (city)

Date: 1609
Explorer: Hendrik (Henry) Hudson
Explored for: Netherlands
Area Explored: New York

Date: 1612-16
Explorer: William Baffin
Explored for: England
Area Explored: Northwest Passage

Date: 1642-44
Explorer: Abel Janszoon Tasman
Explored for: Netherlands
Area Explored: Fiji, New Zealand, Australia

Date: 1673
Explorer: Louis Jolliet and Jacques Marquette
Explored for: France
Area Explored: Great Lakes, Mississippi River

Date: 1682
Explorer: René-Robert Cavelier de La Salle
Explored for: France
Area Explored: Mississippi Valley

1700

Date: 1741
Explorer: Vitus Bering
Explored for: Russia
Area Explored: Alaska, Aleutian Islands

Date: 1766-69
Explorer: Louis-Antoine de Bougainville
Explored for: France
Area Explored: South Pacific, circled the world

Date: 1768-80
Explorer: James Cook
Explored for: Great Britain
Area Explored: Pacific Ocean, Hawaii, (Australia ?)

Date: 1789-93
Explorer: Alexander Mackenzie
Explored for: Great Britain
Area Explored: Canada, crossed North America E to W

Date: 1795-1806
Explorer: Mungo Park
Explored for: Great Britain/United Kingdom
Area Explored: West Africa

Date: 1799-1804
Explorer: Alexander von Humboldt and Aimé Bonpland
Explored for: Germany
Area Explored: Orinoco River, Peru, Mexico, Cuba, Colombia, Ecuador

Map of North America

1800

Date: 1804-05
Explorer: Meriwether Lewis and William Clark
Explored for: United States
Area Explored: Crossed United States E to W

Lewis and Clark

Date: 1818-27
Explorer: John Franklin
Explored for: United Kingdom
Area Explored: Northwest Passage

Date: 1819-21
Explorer: Fabian G. von Bellingshausen
Explored for: Russia
Area Explored: Antarctic

Date: 1820
Explorer: Nathaniel Palmer
Explored for: United States
Area Explored: Antarctic

Date: 1826-29
Explorer: Jedediah Smith
Explored for: United States
Area Explored: California

Date: 1831
Explorer: John Ross, James Clark Ross
Explored for: United Kingdom
Area Explored: North magnetic pole

Date: 1831-36
Explorer: Charles Darwin
Explored for: United Kingdom
Area Explored: Voyage of Beagle

Date: 1841-73
Explorer: David Livingstone
Explored for: United Kingdom
Area Explored: Southern Africa

Date: 1842-47
Explorer: John C. Frémont
Explored for: United States
Area Explored: Oregon Trail, Rocky Mountains, California

Date: 1845-47
Explorer: John Franklin
Explored for: United Kingdom
Area Explored: Northwest Passage

Date: 1849
Explorer: Matthew F. Maury
Explored for: United States
Area Explored: Atlantic Ocean floor

Date: 1860-63
Explorer: John H. Speke, James A. Grant
Explored for: United Kindom
Area Explored: East Africa, White Nile

Date: 1867-88
Explorer: Nikolay Przhevalsky
Explored for: Russia
Area Explored: Central Asia

Date: 1867-92
Explorer: John Wesley Powell
Explored for: United States
Area Explored: American West, Grand Canyon

Map of the Grand Canyon

Date: 1871-89
Explorer: Henry M. Stanley
Explored for: United States/Belgium
Area Explored: East Africa, Congo, Lake Victoria, Lake Tanganyika

Date: 1872-77
Explorer: Scientists of survey ships: *Challenger, Tuscarora, Gazelle*
Explored for: United Kingdom/United States/Germany
Area Explored: Worldwide ocean survey

Date: 1888-96
Explorer: Fridtjof Nansen
Explored for: Norway
Area Explored: Greenland, North Pole

1900

Date: 1908-09
Explorer: Ernest Shackleton
Explored for: United Kingdom
Area Explored: Antarctic

Date: 1909
Explorer: Robert Peary, Matthew Henson
Explored for: United States
Area Explored: North Pole (?)

Date: 1910-11
Explorer: Roald Amundsen
Explored for: Norway
Area Explored: South Pole

Date: 1910-12
Explorer: Robert Scott
Explored for: United Kingdom
Area Explored: South Pole

Date: 1921-24
Explorer: Alexandra David-Néel
Explored for: France
Area Explored: Tibet

Date: 1926
Explorer: Richard Byrd
Explored for: United States
Area Explored: North Pole, by air

Date: 1929
Explorer: Richard Byrd
Explored for: United States
Area Explored: South Pole

Date: 1931
Explorer: Auguste Piccard
Explored for: Switzerland
Area Explored: Stratosphere

Date: 1934
Explorer: C. William Beebe
Explored for: United States
Area Explored: Atlantic Ocean depths in bathysphere

Date: 1950-to present
Explorer: Jacques-Yves Cousteau
Explored for: France
Area Explored: Worldwide research in *Calypso*

Date: 1953
Explorer: Edmund Hillary and Tenzing Norgay
Explored for: United Kingdom
Area Explored: Mount Everest

Date: 1960
Explorer: Don Walsh, Jacques Piccard
Explored for: United States
Area Explored: Mariana Trench in the *Trieste*

Date: 1961
Explorer: Yuri Gagarin
Explored for: USSR
Area Explored: Earth orbit; first manned flight

Date: 1961
Explorer: Alan B. Shepard, Jr.
Explored for: United States
Area Explored: First American in space

Date: 1962
Explorer: John H. Glenn, Jr.
Explored for: United States
Area Explored: First American in orbit

Date: 1963
Explorer: Valentina V. Tereshkova
Explored for: USSR
Area Explored: First woman in space

Date: 1965
Explorer: Frank Borman and James A. Lovell, Jr. (*Gemini 7*); Walter M. Schirra, Jr. and Thomas P. Stafford (*Gemini 6-A*)
Explored for: United States
Area Explored: First space rendezvous

Voyager 2 space probe

Date: 1967
Explorer: *Mariner 5* (Unmanned)
Explored for: United States
Area Explored: Passed Venus

Date: 1968
Explorer: Ralph Plaisted
Explored for: United States
Area Explored: First confirmed surface arrival at North Pole

Date: 1968
Explorer: Frank Borman, James A. Lovell, Jr., and William A. Anders
Explored for: United States
Area Explored: First lunar flight (no landing), *Apollo 8*

Astronaut on the moon

Date: 1969
Explorer: Neil Armstrong, Edwin E. Aldrin, Jr., and Michael Collins
Explored for: United States
Area Explored: First lunar landing, *Apollo 11*

Date: 1975
Explorer: Vance Brand, Thomas P. Stafford, and Donald K. Slayton (*Apollo 18*); Alexi Leonov, and Valeri Kubason (*Soyuz 19*)
Explored for: United States/USSR
Area Explored: United States/USSR joint project; docked in space

Date: 1977-1989
Explorer: *Voyager 1 and 2* (Unmanned)
Explored for: United States
Area Explored: Passed Jupiter 1979, Saturn 1981, Uranus 1986, Neptune 1989

Date: 1981
Explorer: Robert L. Crippen and John W. Young
Explored for: United States
Area Explored: First space shuttle flight (*Columbia*)

Date: 1986
Explorer: Francis R. Scobee, Michael J. Smith, Ronald E.McNair, Ellison S. Onizuka, Judith A. Resnick, Gregory B. Jarvis, Sharon Crista McAuliffe
Explored for: United States
Area Explored: *Challenger* (exploded after liftoff; all aboard perished; McAuliffe was to have been the first teacher in space)

Date: 1988
Explorer: Fredrick H. Hauck, Richard O. Covey, David C. Hilmers, George D. Nelson, John M. Lounge
Explored for: United States
Area Explored: *Discovery* (resumption of U.S. shuttle program after two-year delay brought on by *Challenger* tragedy)

Date: 1990
Explorer: Loren Shriver, Charles F. Bolden, Kathryn D. Sullivan, Bruce McCandless, Steven A. Hawley
Explored for: United States
Area Explored: *Discovery* (launch of Hubble Space Telescope)

Launch of space shuttle, Columbia

Reference Maps

MAP SYMBOLS

CULTURAL FEATURES

Political Boundaries

═══════ International

─────── Secondary (State, province, etc.)

─────── County

Populated Places

Cities, towns, and villages

• • • • • ● Symbol size represents population of the place

Chicago
Gary
Racine
Glenview
Edgewood

Type size represents relative importance of the place.

 Corporate area of large U.S. and Canadian cities and urban area of other foreign cities

Major Urban Area
Area of continuous commercial, industrial, and residential development in and around a major city

○ Community within a city

⊛ Capital of major political unit

☆ Capital of secondary political unit

◉ Capital of U.S. state or Canadian province

● County Seat

▲ Military Installation

⊙ Scientific Station

Miscellaneous

National Park

National Monument

Provincial Park

Indian Reservation

△ Point of Interest

∴ Ruins

■ ⚓ Buildings

⬭ Race Track

─── Railroad – International Maps

─┤├─ Tunnel

- - - - - Underground or Subway

 Dam

Bridge

Dike

─── Highway – U.S. and Canadian Maps

─── Railroad – U.S. and Canadian Maps

LAND FEATURES

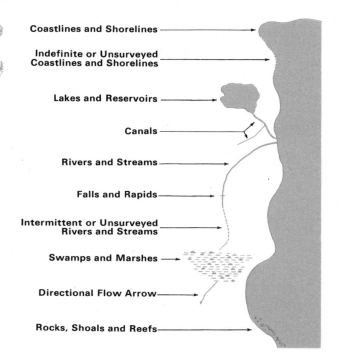

Ranges →

Peaks →

Passes → *LITTLE PASS*

Point of Elevation above sea level — *8,520 FT.* +

Escarpments, Bluffs, Cliffs, and Plateaus — *PLATEAU*

Glaciers →

Volcanoes →

Lava Flows →

Sand Dunes →

Deserts →

WATER FEATURES

Coastlines and Shorelines ────────→

Indefinite or Unsurveyed Coastlines and Shorelines ──→

Lakes and Reservoirs ──→

Canals →

Rivers and Streams →

Falls and Rapids →

Intermittent or Unsurveyed Rivers and Streams →

Swamps and Marshes →

Directional Flow Arrow →

Rocks, Shoals and Reefs →

TYPE STYLES USED TO NAME FEATURES

A S I A	Continent	PANTELLERIA (ITALY)	Country of which unit is a dependency in parentheses
DENMARK CANADA	Country, State, or Province	SRI LANKA (CEYLON)	Former or alternate name
		Rome (Roma)	Local or alternate city name
BÉARN	Region, Province, or Historical Region	Naval Air Station	Military Installation
CROCKETT	County	MESA VERDE SAN XAVIER	National Park or Monument, Provincial Park, Indian Res.,

UINTA DESERT	Major Terrain Features
MT. MORIAH	Individual Mountain
STROMBOLI NUNIVAK	Island or Coastal Feature
Ocean Lake River Canal	Hydrographic Features

Note: Size of type varies according to importance and available space. Letters for names of major features are spread across the extent of the feature.

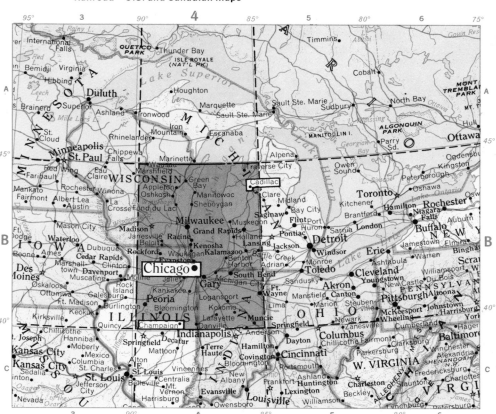

THE INDEX REFERENCE SYSTEM

Place	Location	Index Key	Page
Cadillac, Que., Can	*h11		73
Cadillac, Sask., Can	H2		70
Cadillac, Fr	E3		14
Cadillac, Wexford, Mich	B4		90
Cadiz, San Bernardino, Calif.	E6		82
Cadiz, Trigg, Ky	D2		94
Cadron, creek, Ark	B3		81
Caen, Fr	C3		14
Caetité, Braz.	D2		57
Calcutta, India	D8		39
Cambridge, Eng.	B8		12
Catania, It	F5		21
Ceará, state, Braz	C3		57
Chamblee, DeKalb, Ga.	h8		87
Chambly, Que., Can	D4		73
Chambord, Que., Can	A5		73
Champagne, former prov., Fr.	C5		14
Champaign, Champaign, Ill.	B4		90
Champdore, lake, Que., Can	g8		75
Champerico, Guat	C2		62
Champéry, Switz	D2		19
Champex, Switz	D3		19
Champigneulles, Fr	F6		15
Champion, Chase, Nebr	D4		103
Champlain, co., Que., Can	B4		73
Champlain, lake, N.Y., Vt.	B2		120
Champotón, Mex	D6		63
Changchou, China	E8		34
Chanthaburi, Thai	F5		38
Chaparral, Col	C2		60
Charleville-Mézières, Fr.	C6		14
Chatham, Eng.	C8		12
Chiapa de Corzo, Mex	D6		63
Chiapas, state, Mex	D6		63
Chiba, Jap.	I10, n19		37
Chiba, pref., Jap.	*I10		37
Chibemba, Ang	E1		48
Chibougamau, Que., Can.	k12		73
Chicago, Cook, Ill.	B4		90
Chicahoua, Mor	C3		44
Chichen Itzá, ruins, Mex.	C7		63
Chichester, Eng.	D7		12
Chickasaw, co., Iowa	A5		92
Chiclana, Sp.	D2		20
Chiclayo, Peru	C2		58
Columbus, Franklin, Ohio	C3		111

The indexing system used in this atlas is based upon the conventional pattern of parallels and meridians used to indicate latitude and longitude. The index samples beside the map indicate that the cities of *Chicago, Cadillac,* and *Champaign* are all located in *B4.* Each index key letter, *in this case "B,"* is placed between corresponding degree numbers of latitude in the vertical borders of the map. Each index key number, *in this case "4,"* is placed between corresponding degree numbers of longitude in the horizontal borders of the map. Crossing of the parallels above and below the index letter with the meridians on each side of the index number forms a confining "box" in which the given place is certain to be located. It is important to note that location of the place may be anywhere in this confining "box."

Insets on many foreign maps are indexed independently of the main maps by separate index key letters and figures. All places indexed to these insets are identified by the lower case reference letter in the index key. A diamond-shaped symbol in the margin of the map is used to separate the insets from the main map and also to separate key letters and numbers where the spacing of the parallels and meridians is great.

Place-names are indexed to the location of the city symbol. Political divisions and physical features are indexed to the location of their names on the map.

1

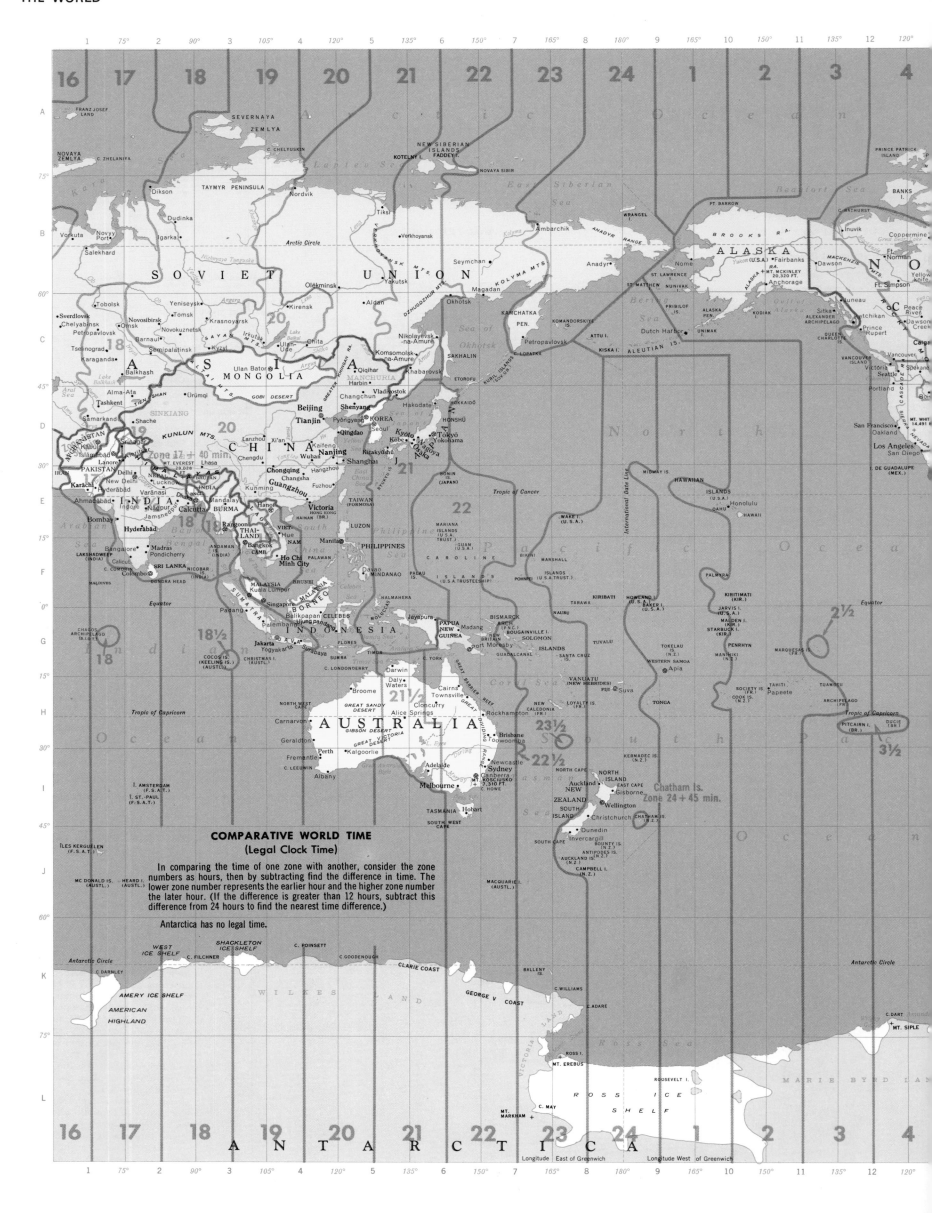

COMPARATIVE WORLD TIME
(Legal Clock Time)

In comparing the time of one zone with another, consider the zone numbers as hours, then by subtracting find the difference in time. The lower zone number represents the earlier hour and the higher zone number the later hour. (If the difference is greater than 12 hours, subtract this difference from 24 hours to find the nearest time difference.)

Antarctica has no legal time.

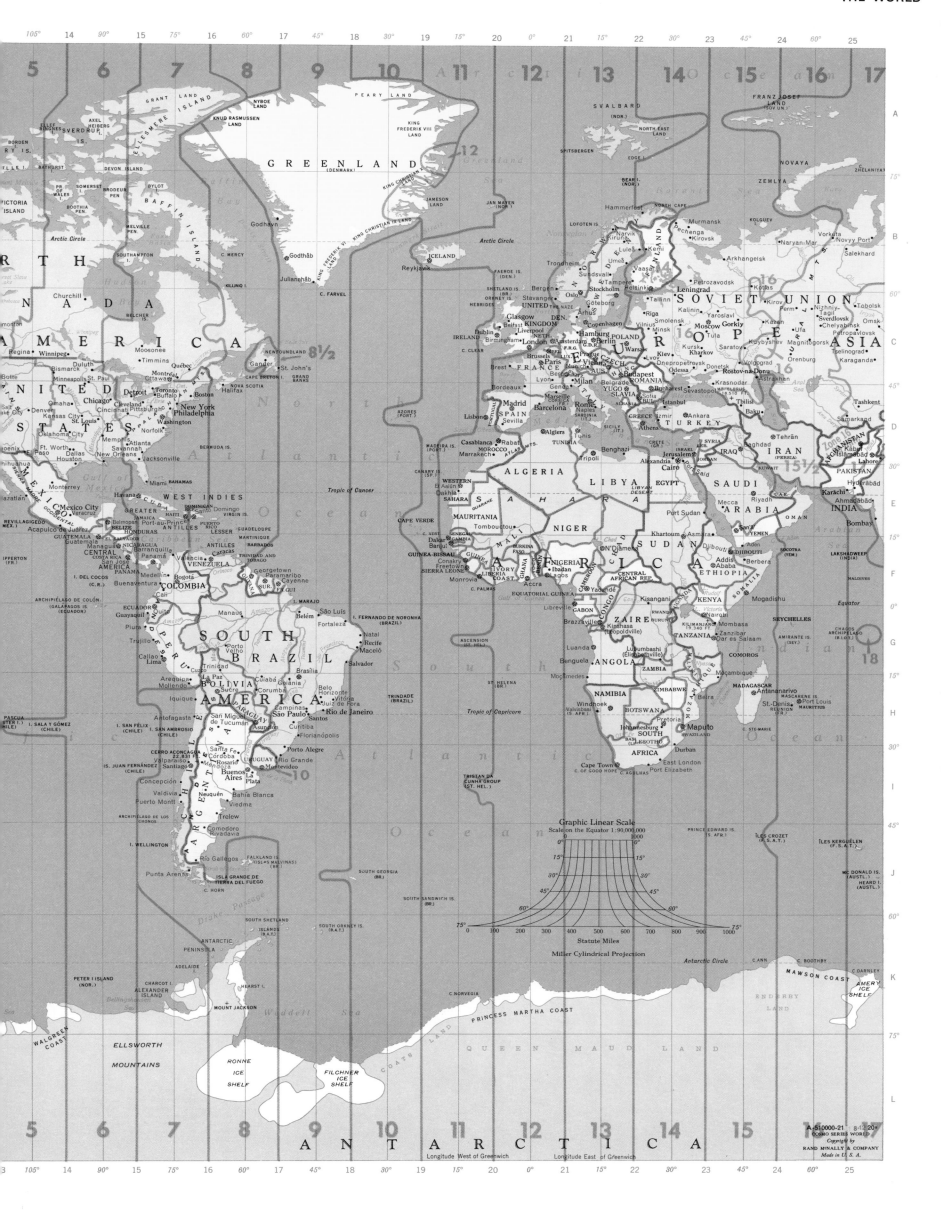

Graphic Linear Scale
Scale on the Equator 1:90,000,000
Statute Miles
Miller Cylindrical Projection

Longitude West of Greenwich · Longitude East of Greenwich

A-510000-21 8-12-20¢
COSMO SERIES WORLD
Copyright by
RAND McNALLY & COMPANY
Made in U.S.A.

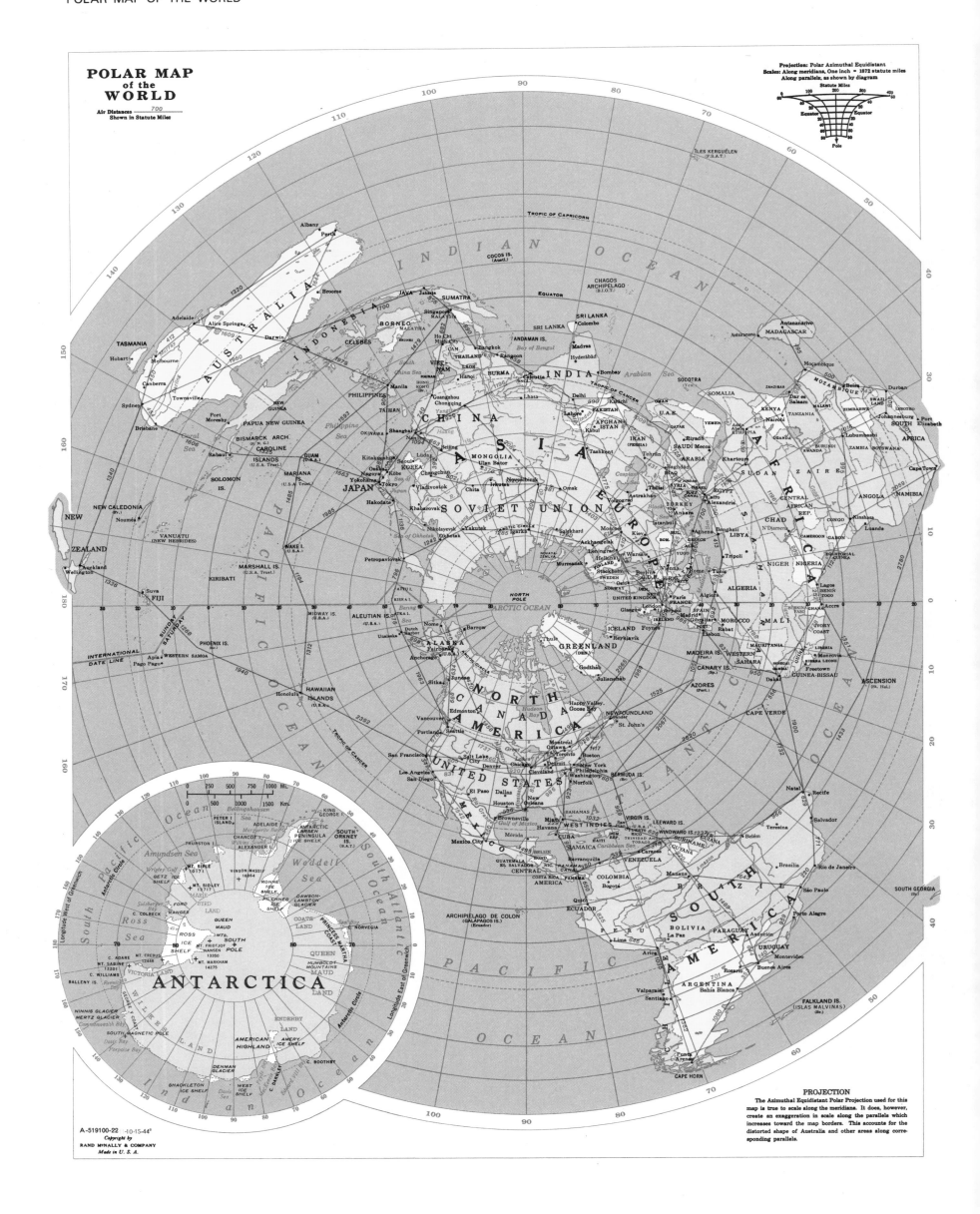

POLAR MAP of the WORLD

Air Distances ——— 700
Shown in Statute Miles

Projection: Polar Azimuthal Equidistant
Scales: Along meridians, One inch = 1872 statute miles
Along parallels, as shown by diagram

PROJECTION

The Azimuthal Equidistant Polar Projection used for this map is true to scale along the meridians. It does, however, create an exaggeration in scale along the parallels which increases toward the map borders. This accounts for the distorted shape of Australia and other areas along corresponding parallels.

A-519100-22 -10-15-44⁰
Copyright by
RAND McNALLY & COMPANY
Made in U.S.A.

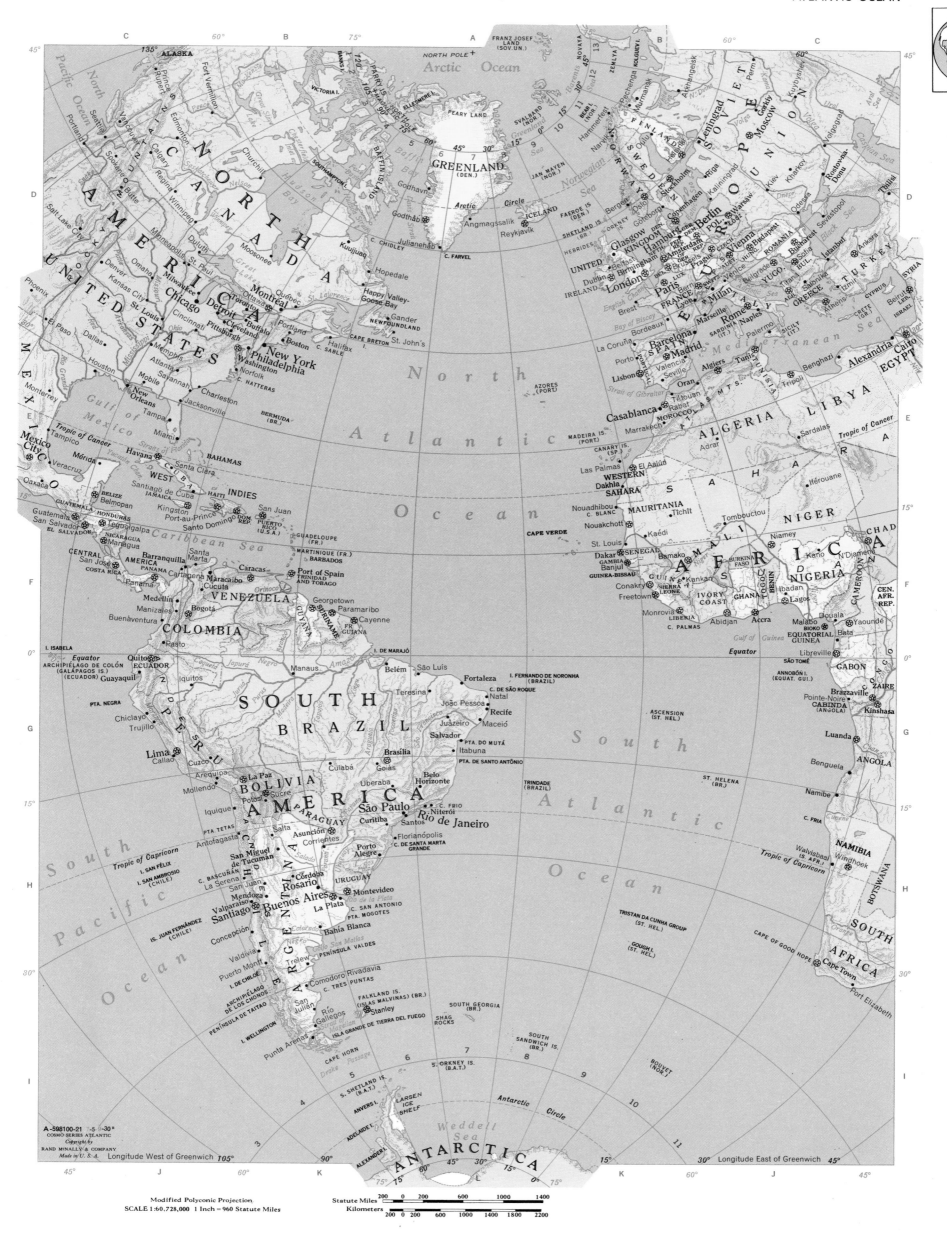

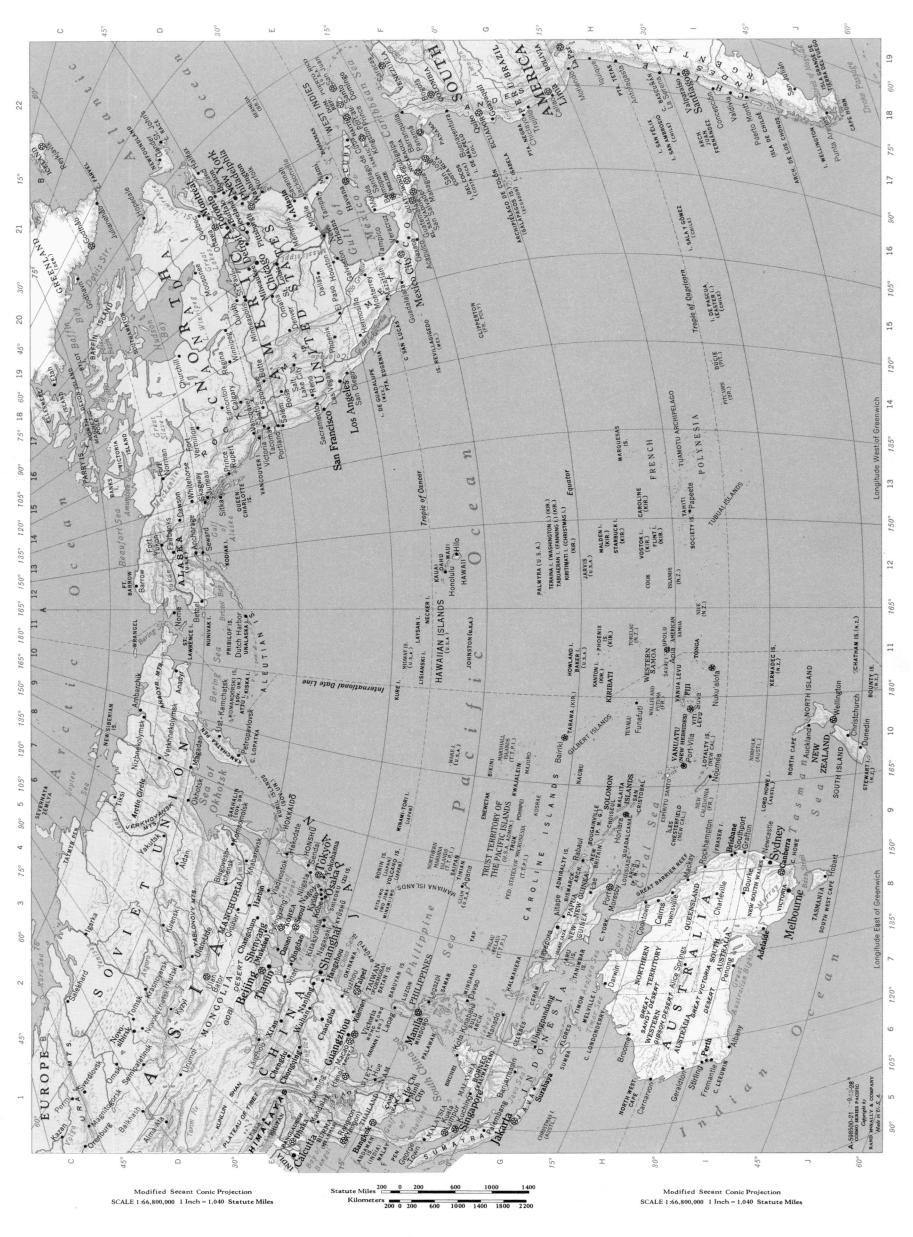

Modified Secant Conic Projection
SCALE 1:66,800,000 1 Inch = 1,040 Statute Miles

Statute Miles 200 0 200 600 1000 1400
Kilometers 200 0 200 600 1000 1400 1800 2200

Modified Secant Conic Projection
SCALE 1:66,800,000 1 Inch = 1,040 Statute Miles

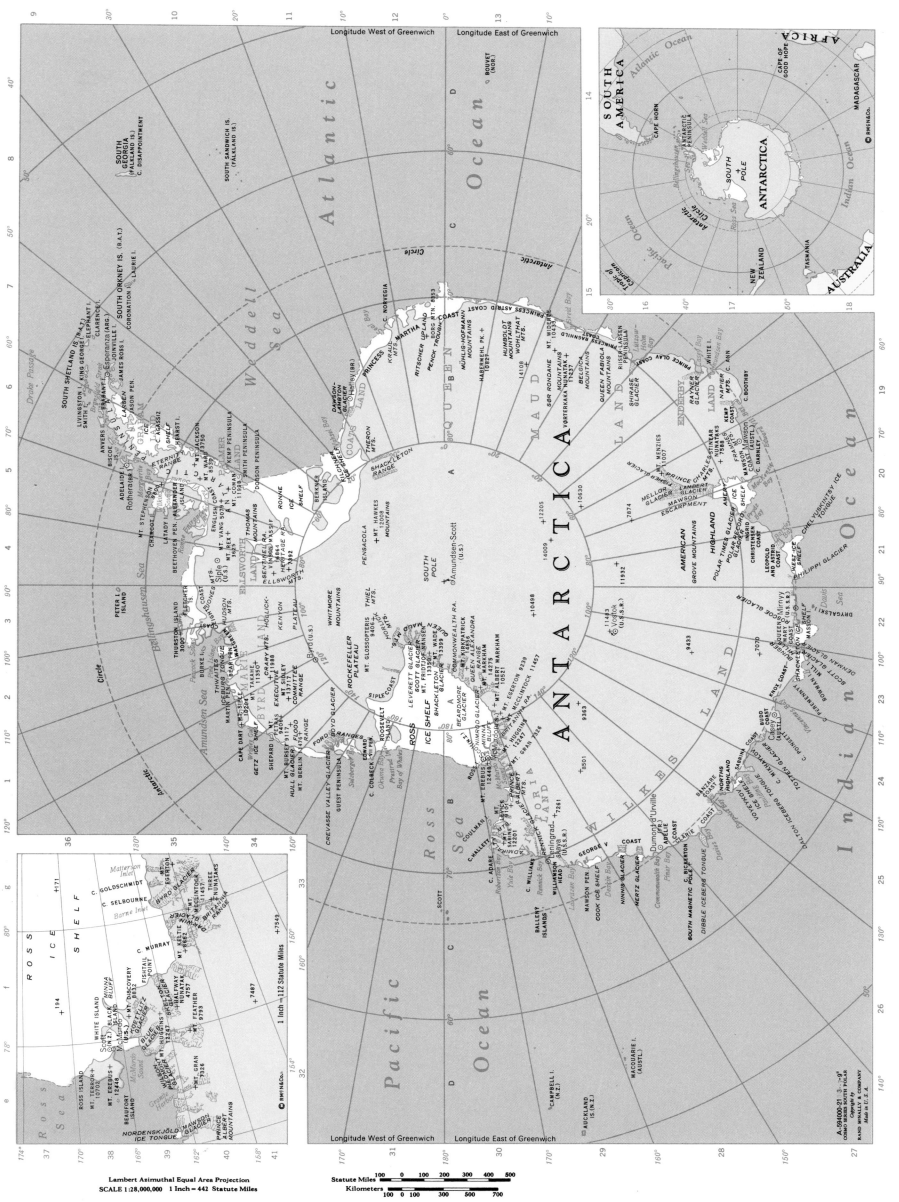

Lambert Azimuthal Equal Area Projection
SCALE 1:28,000,000 1 Inch = 442 Statute Miles

Longitude West of Greenwich

ICELAND

Arctic Circle

Norwegian Sea

Atlantic Ocean

IRELAND

Glasgow

Dublin

UNITED KINGDOM

London

DENMARK

Copenhagen (København)

NORWAY

Oslo

Stockholm

SWEDEN

FINLAND

Helsinki

Leningrad

NETH. FED. REP.

Hamburg

Berlin

POLAND

Warsaw (Warszawa)

W. GER.

CZECHOSLOVAKIA

Prague (Praha)

FRANCE

Paris

SWITZERLAND

AUSTRIA

Vienna (Wien)

HUNGARY

Budapest

ROMANIA

Bucharest

PORTUGAL

Lisbon (Lisboa)

SPAIN

Madrid

Barcelona

YUGOSLAVIA

BULGARIA

Sofia

CORSICA

ITALY

Rome (Roma)

Naples

SARDINIA

GREECE

Athens

Istanbul

SICILY

MALTA Valletta

MOROCCO

ALGERIA

TUNISIA

SAHARA

LIBYA

Tripoli (Tarābulus)

Benghazi (Banghāzī)

EGYPT

Alexandria (Al Iskandarīyah)

Cairo

CRETE

CYPRUS

A-519697-21 J1H143
COSMO SERIES EUROPE
Copyright by
RAND McNALLY & COMPANY
Made in U.S.A.

Statute Miles
100 0 100 200 300
Kilometers
100 0 100 200 300 400

Conic Projection
SCALE 1:16,000,000 1 Inch = 252 Statute Miles

Longitude East of Greenwich

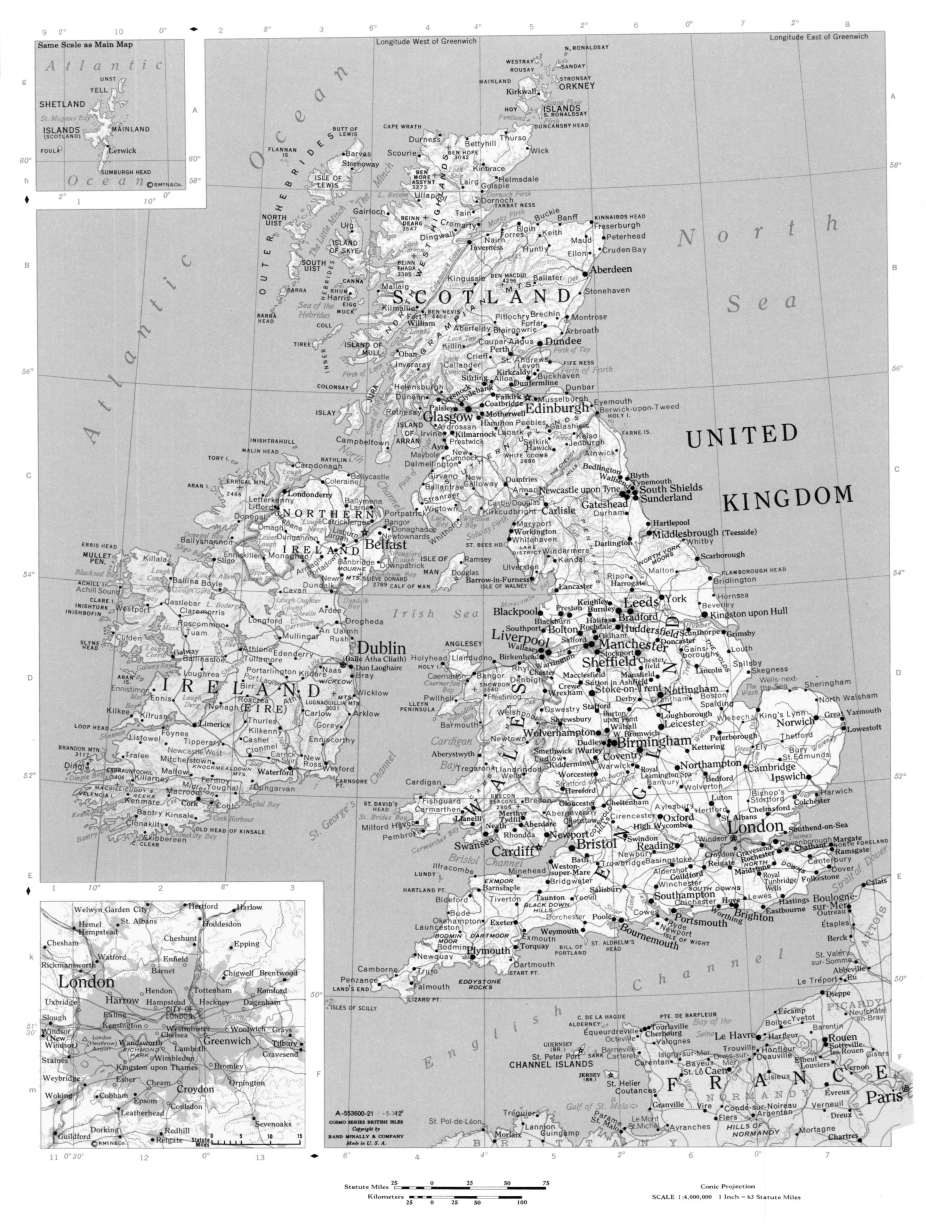

BRITISH ISLES

Same Scale as Main Map

Atlantic

UNST
YELL
SHETLAND
St. Magnus Bay
ISLANDS
(SCOTLAND)   MAINLAND
FOULA   Lerwick
SUMBURGH HEAD

Ocean

© RM°N&Co.

London

Welwyn Garden City
Hertford   Harlow
Hemel   St. Albans
Hempstead   Hoddesdon
Chesham   Cheshunt
Rickmansworth   Watford   Enfield   Epping
Chesham   Chigwell   Brentwood
Uxbridge   Barnet   Romford
Slough   Hendon   Tottenham   Dagenham
London   Harrow   Hampstead   Hackney
(New   Ealing   CITY OF
Windsor)   Kensington   LONDON
Staines   Westminster   Woolwich   Grays
Windsor   Wandsworth   Chelsea   Lambeth   Greenwich   Tilbury
Weybridge   Richmond   Wimbledon   Gravesend
Kingston upon Thames   Bromley
Woking   Esher   Cheam   Orpington
Cobham   Croydon
Epsom   Coulsdon
Leatherhead
Dorking   Sevenoaks
Guildford   Redhill
Reigate

© RM°N&Co.

SCOTLAND

IRELAND (EIRE)

NORTHERN IRELAND

WALES

ENGLAND

UNITED KINGDOM

North Sea

Atlantic Ocean

Irish Sea

English Channel

FRANCE

NORMANDY

PICARDY

BRITTANY

London

Dublin (Baile Atha Cliath)

Belfast

Edinburgh

Glasgow

Aberdeen

Birmingham

Manchester

Liverpool

Paris

A-553600-21   -5-42
COSMO SERIES BRITISH ISLES
Copyright by
RAND McNALLY & COMPANY
Made in U.S.A.

Statute Miles   25   0   25   50   75
Kilometers   25   0   25   50   100

Conic Projection
SCALE 1:4,000,000   1 Inch = 63 Statute Miles

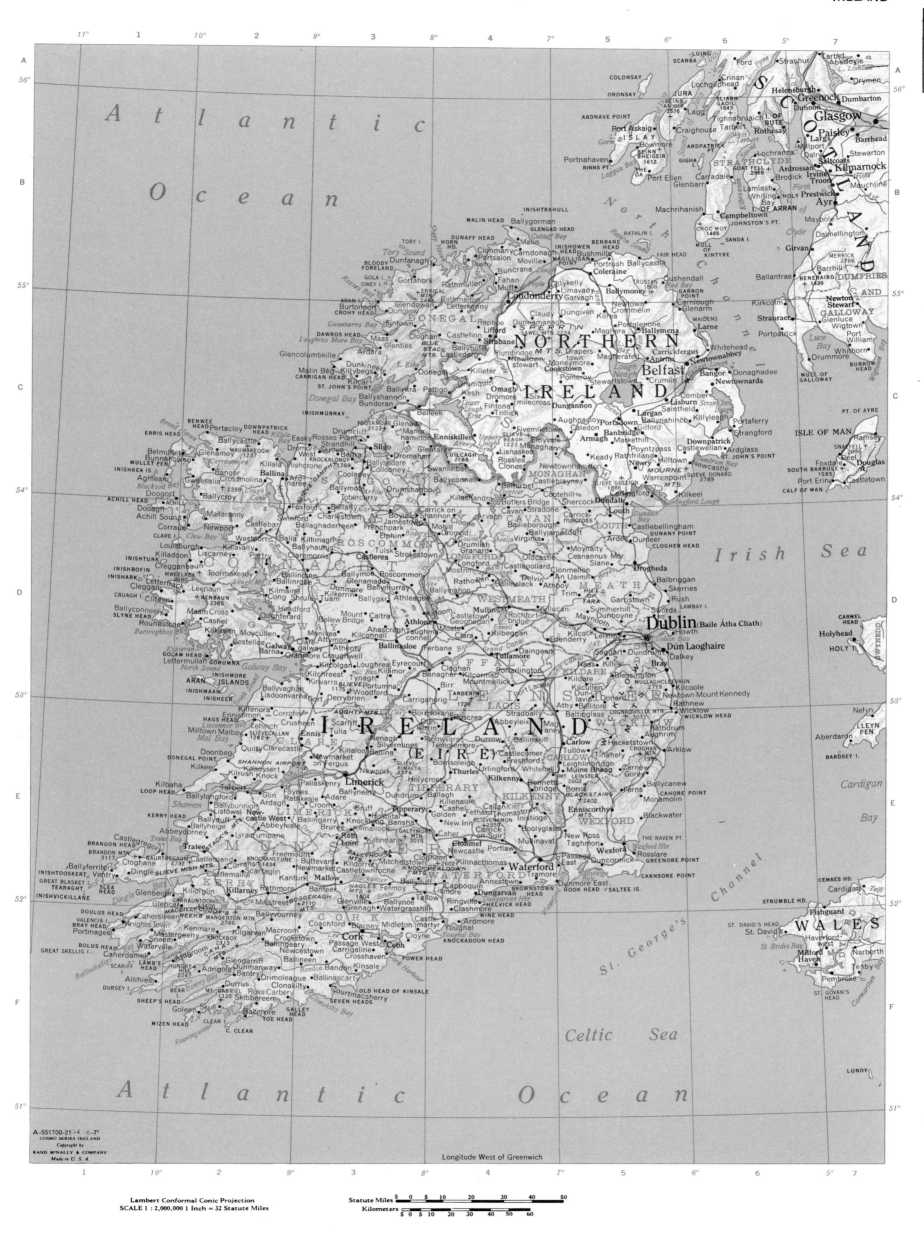

Lambert Conformal Conic Projection
SCALE 1 : 2,000,000 1 Inch = 32 Statute Miles

Statute Miles
Kilometers

Longitude West of Greenwich

A-551700-21-4-6-7°
COSMO SERIES IRELAND
Copyright by
RAND MℭNALLY & COMPANY
Made in U. S. A.

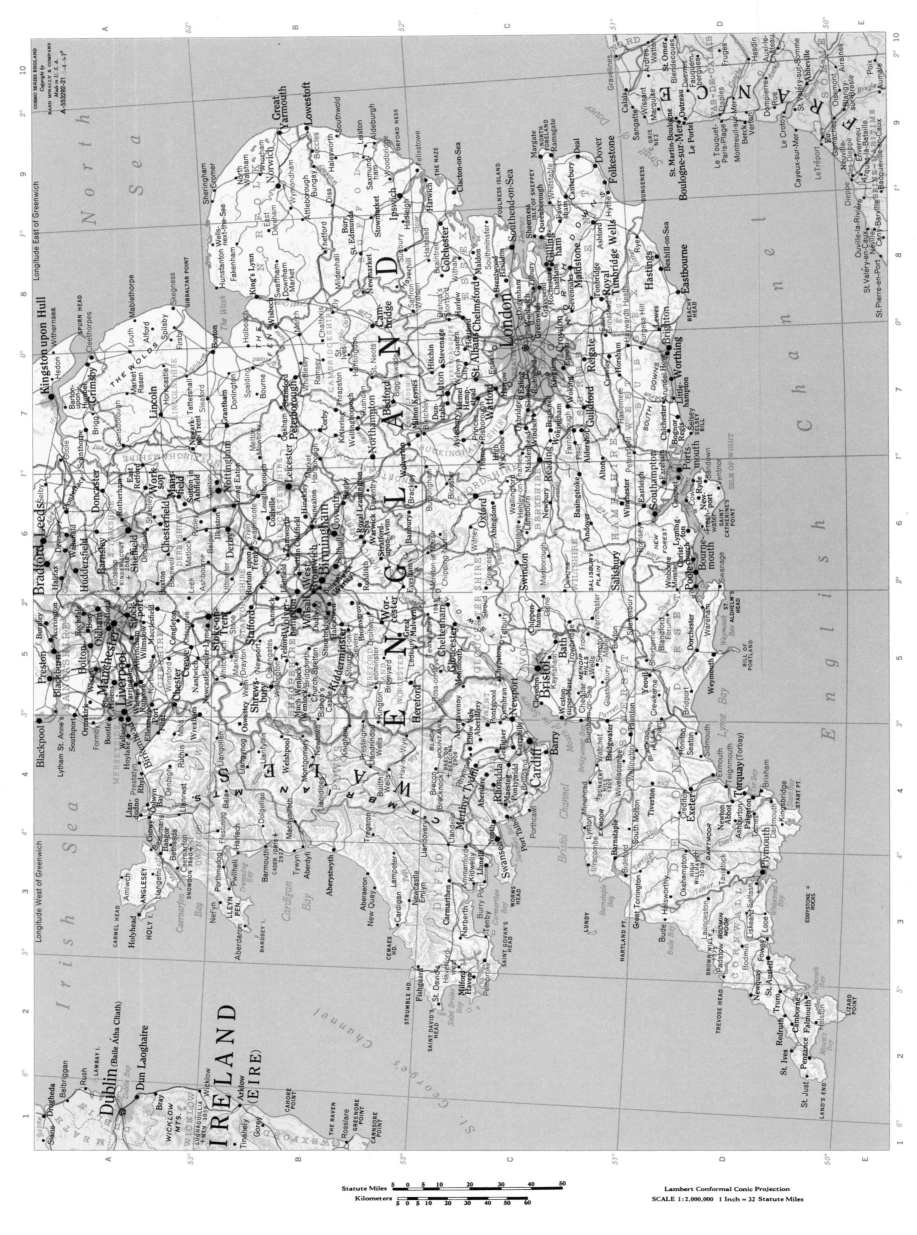

Statute Miles 5 0 5 10 20 30 40 50

Kilometers 5 0 5 10 20 30 40 50 60

Lambert Conformal Conic Projection
SCALE 1:2,000,000   1 Inch = 32 Statute Miles

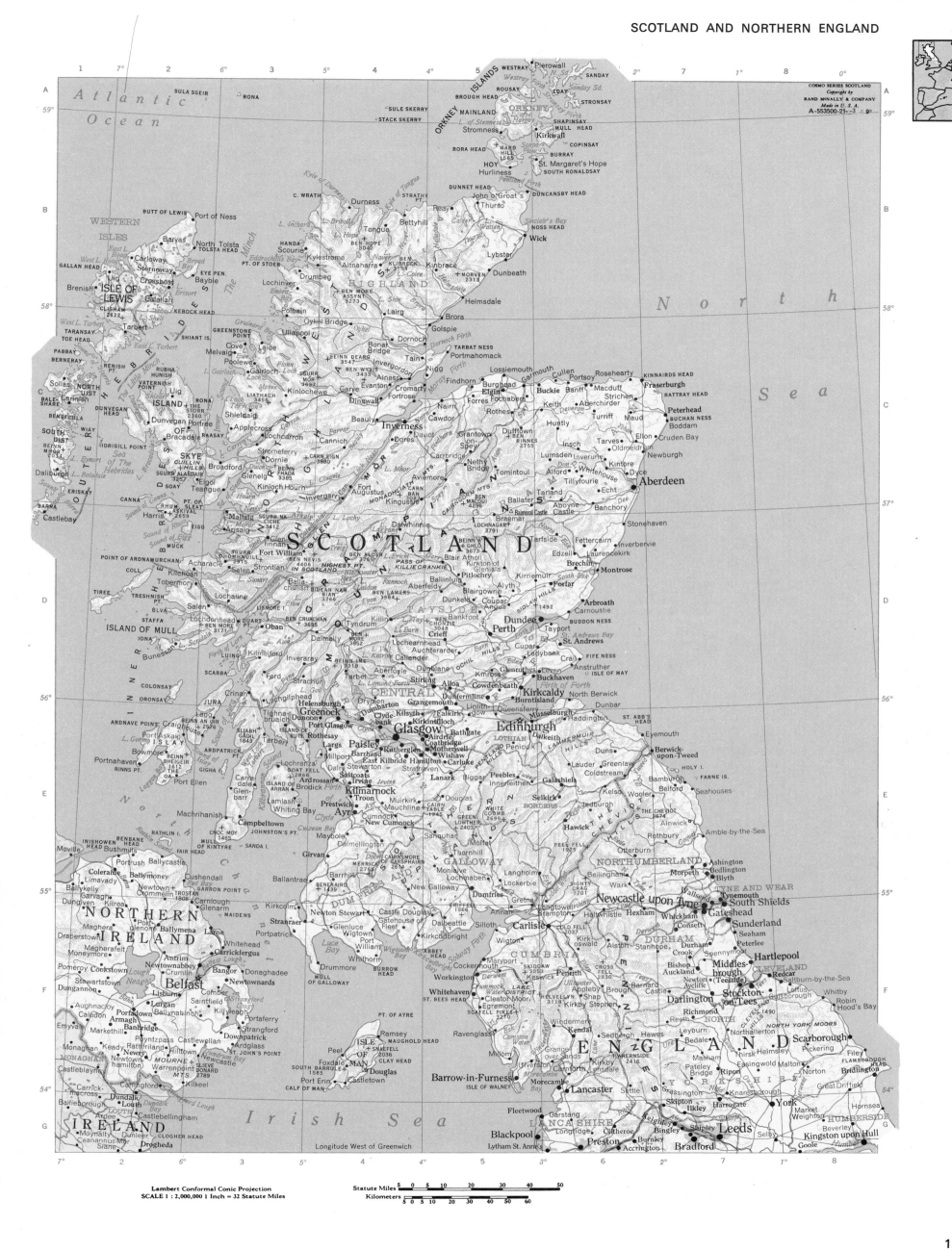

COSMO SERIES SCOTLAND
Copyright by
RAND McNALLY & COMPANY
Made in U.S.A.
A-553500-21--3

Lambert Conformal Conic Projection
SCALE 1 : 2,000,000 1 Inch = 32 Statute Miles

Statute Miles

Kilometers

Longitude West of Greenwich

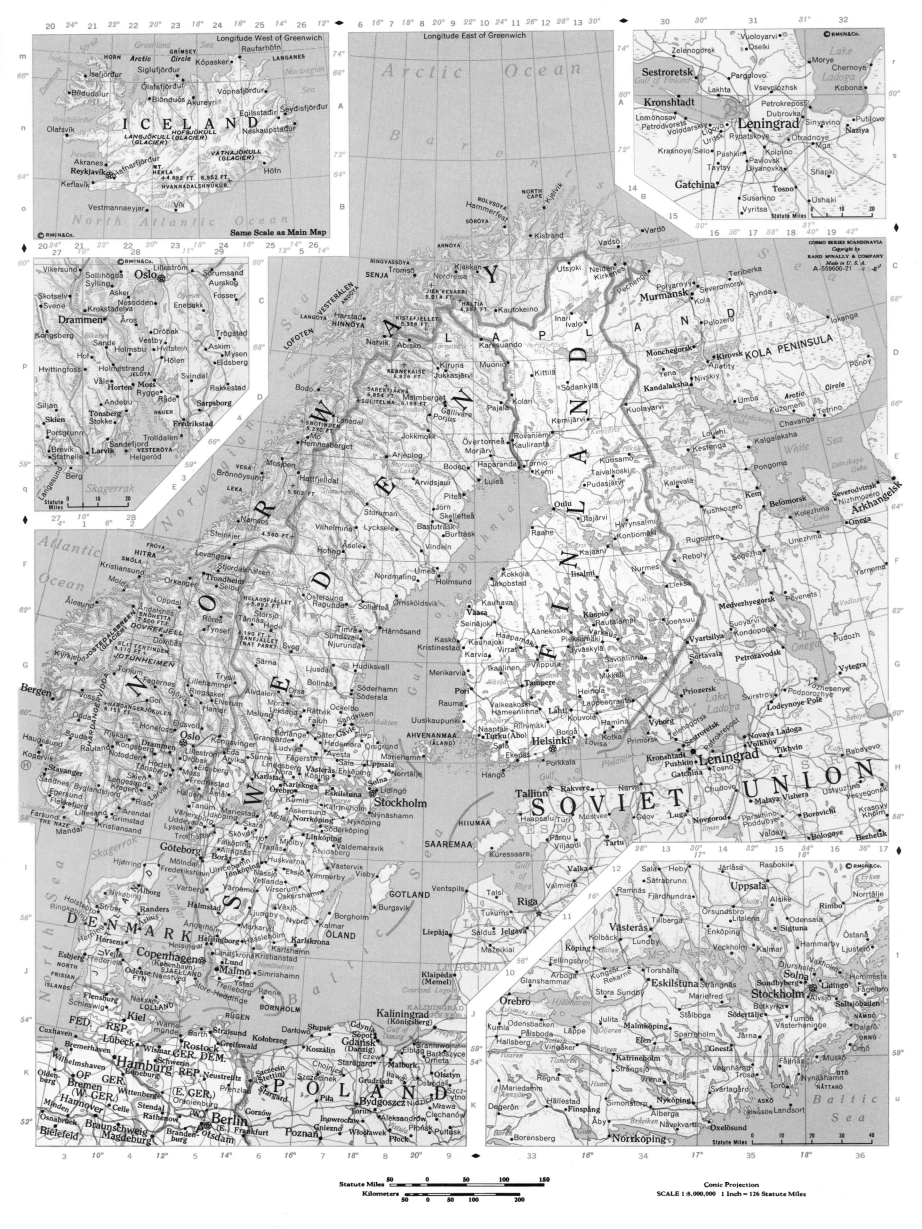

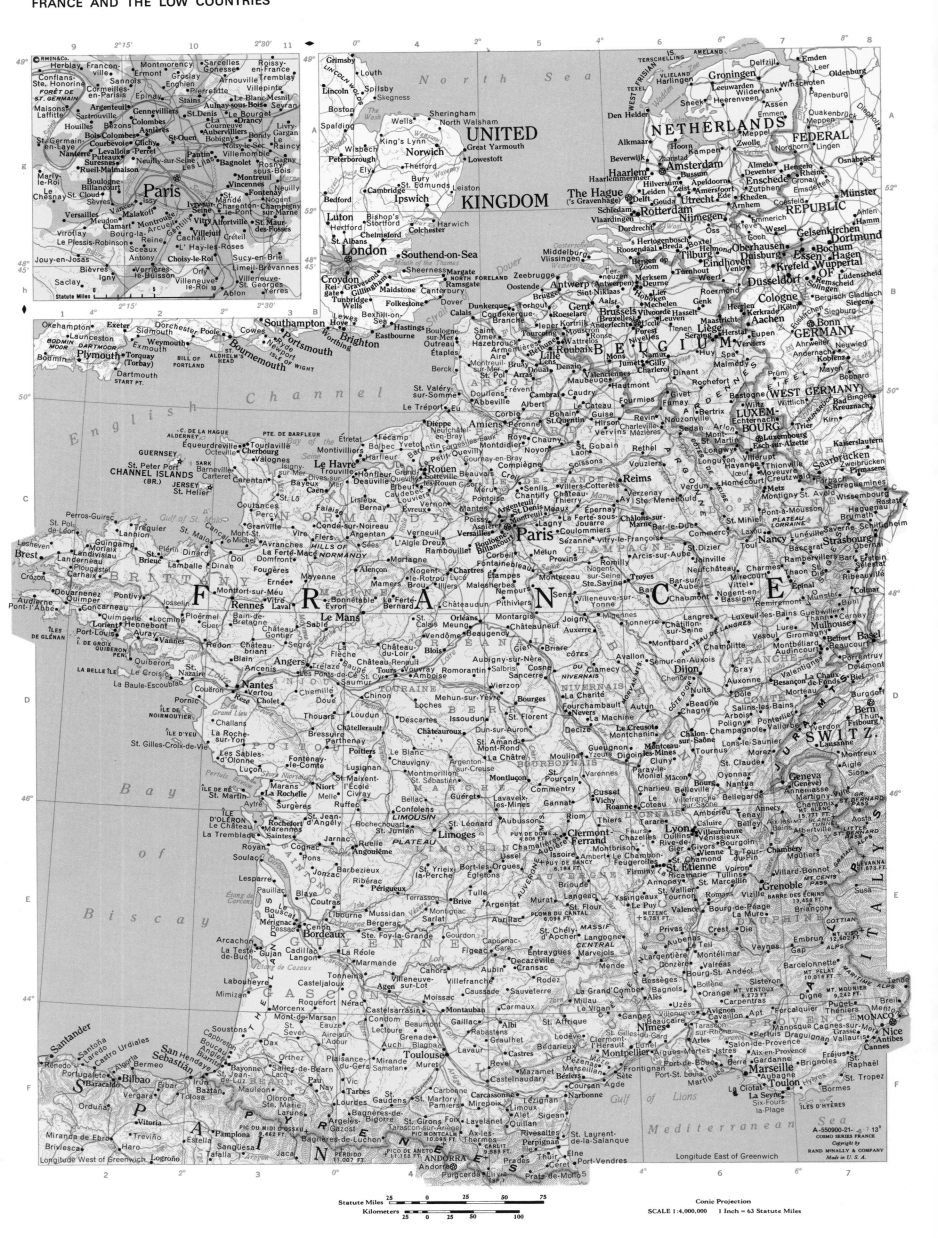

Longitude East of Greenwich

COSMO SERIES BELGIUM NETH.
Copyright by
RAND M^cNALLY & COMPANY
Made in U. S. A.
A-559199-21

Lambert Conformal Conic Projection
SCALE 1:2,000,000   1 Inch = 32 Statute Miles

Statute Miles
Kilometers

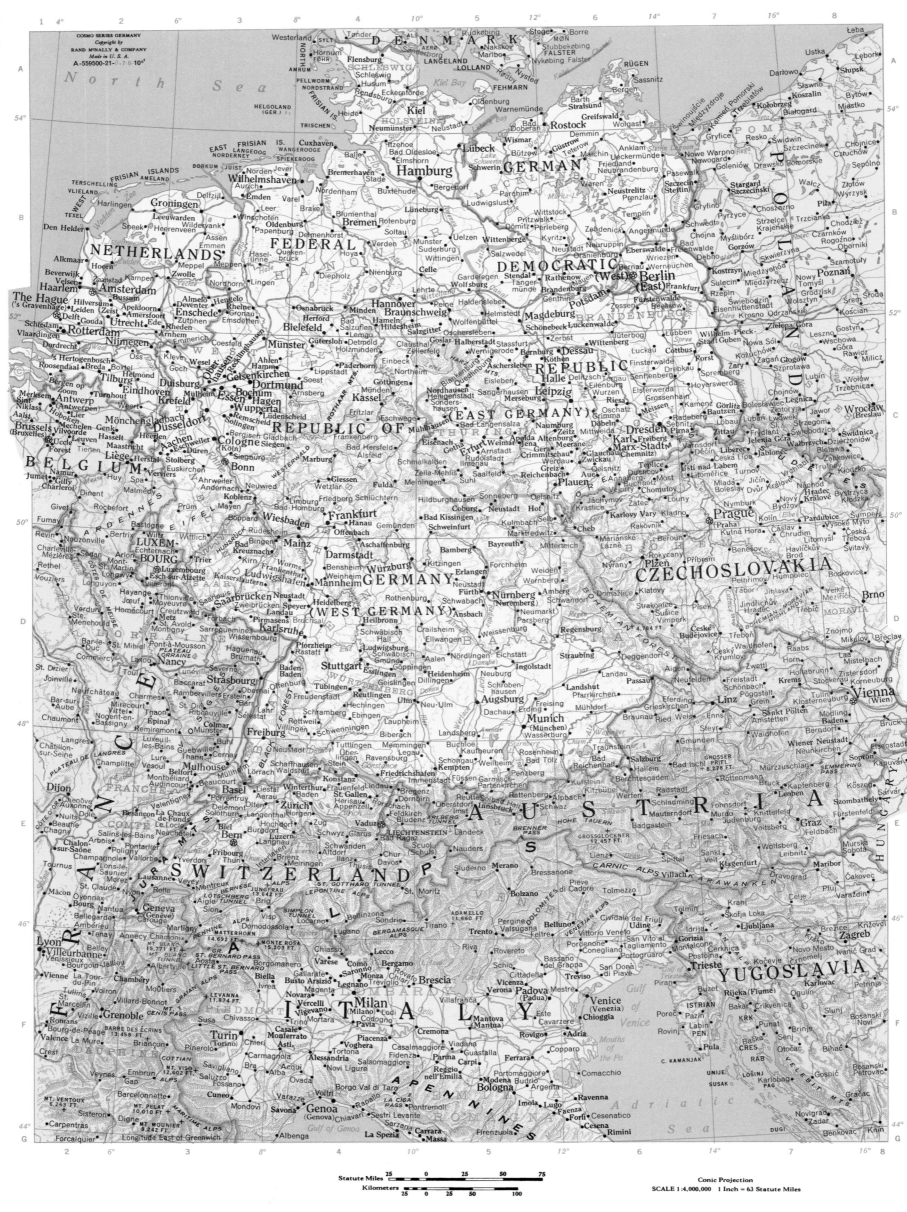

Lambert Conformal Conic Projection
SCALE 1:2,000,000 1 Inch = 32 Statute Miles

Statute Miles
5 0 5 10   20   30   40   50

Kilometers
5 0 5 10   20   30   40   50   60

Statute Miles 5 0 5 10 20 30 40 50
Kilometers 5 0 5 10 20 30 40 50 60

Lambert Conformal Conic Projection
SCALE 1:2,000,000   1 Inch = 32 Statute Miles

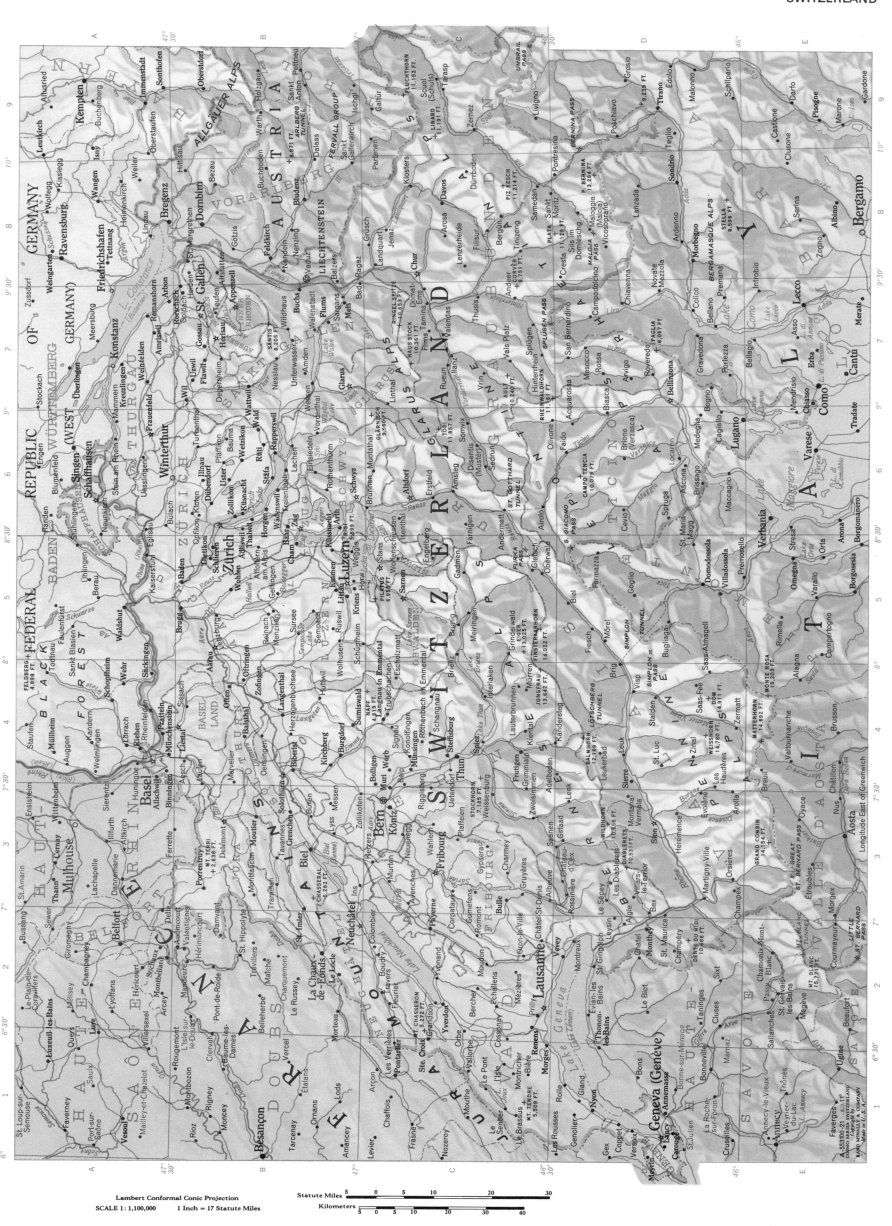

Lambert Conformal Conic Projection

SCALE 1 : 1,100,000   1 Inch = 17 Statute Miles

Statute Miles

Kilometers

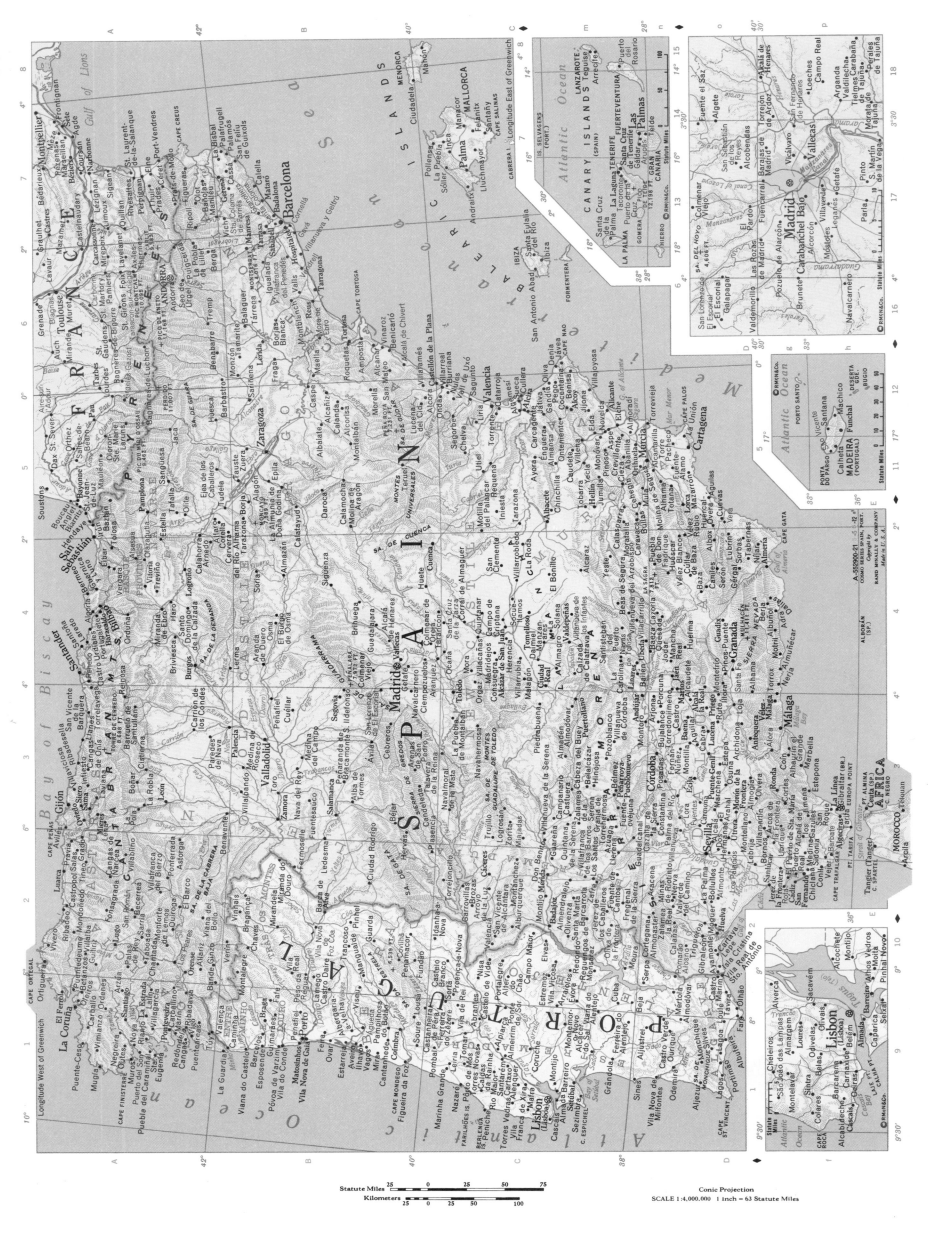

Conic Projection
SCALE 1:4,000,000 1 inch = 63 Statute Miles

Statute Miles 25 0 25 50 75
Kilometers 25 0 25 50 100

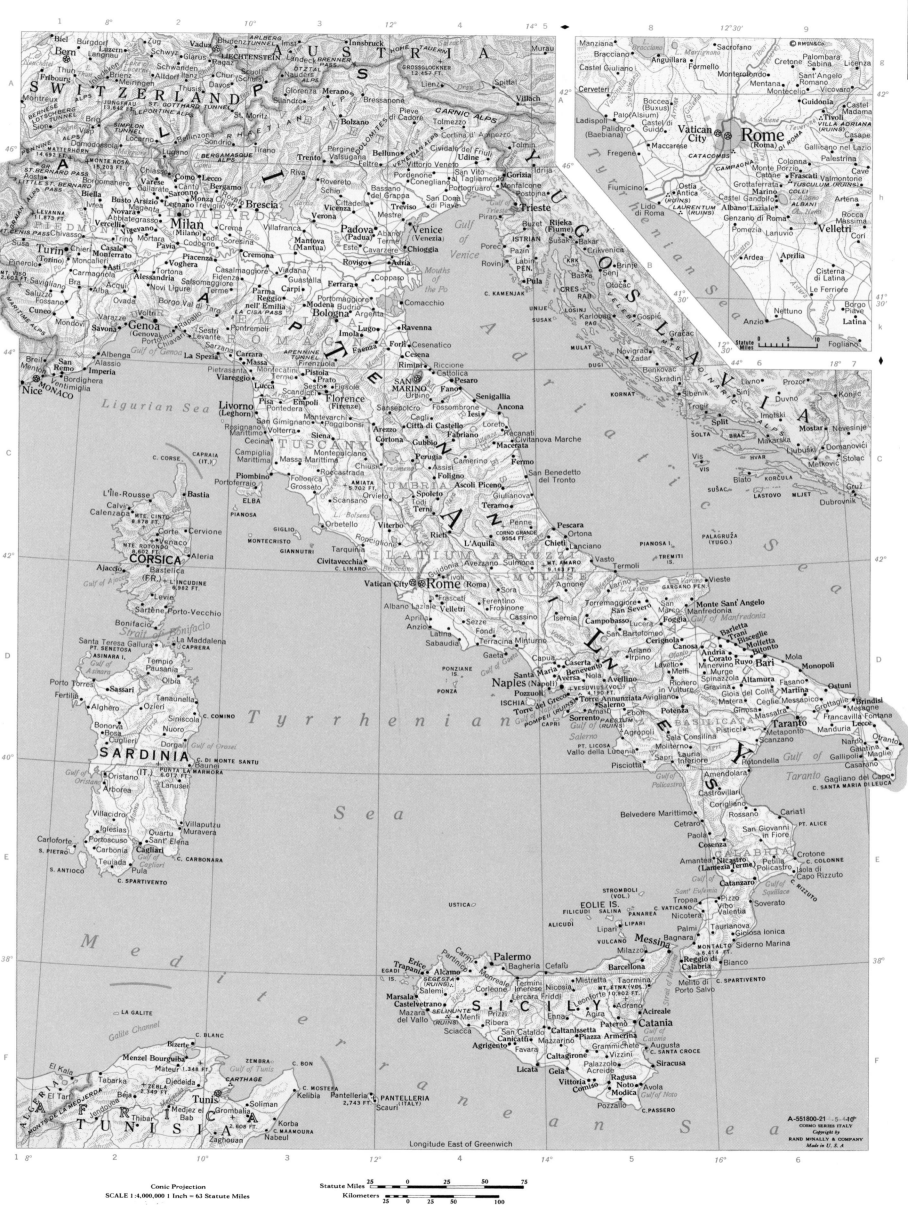

Statute Miles 25 0 25 50 75

Kilometers 25 0 25 50 100

Conic Projection

SCALE 1:4,000,000 1 Inch = 63 Statute Miles

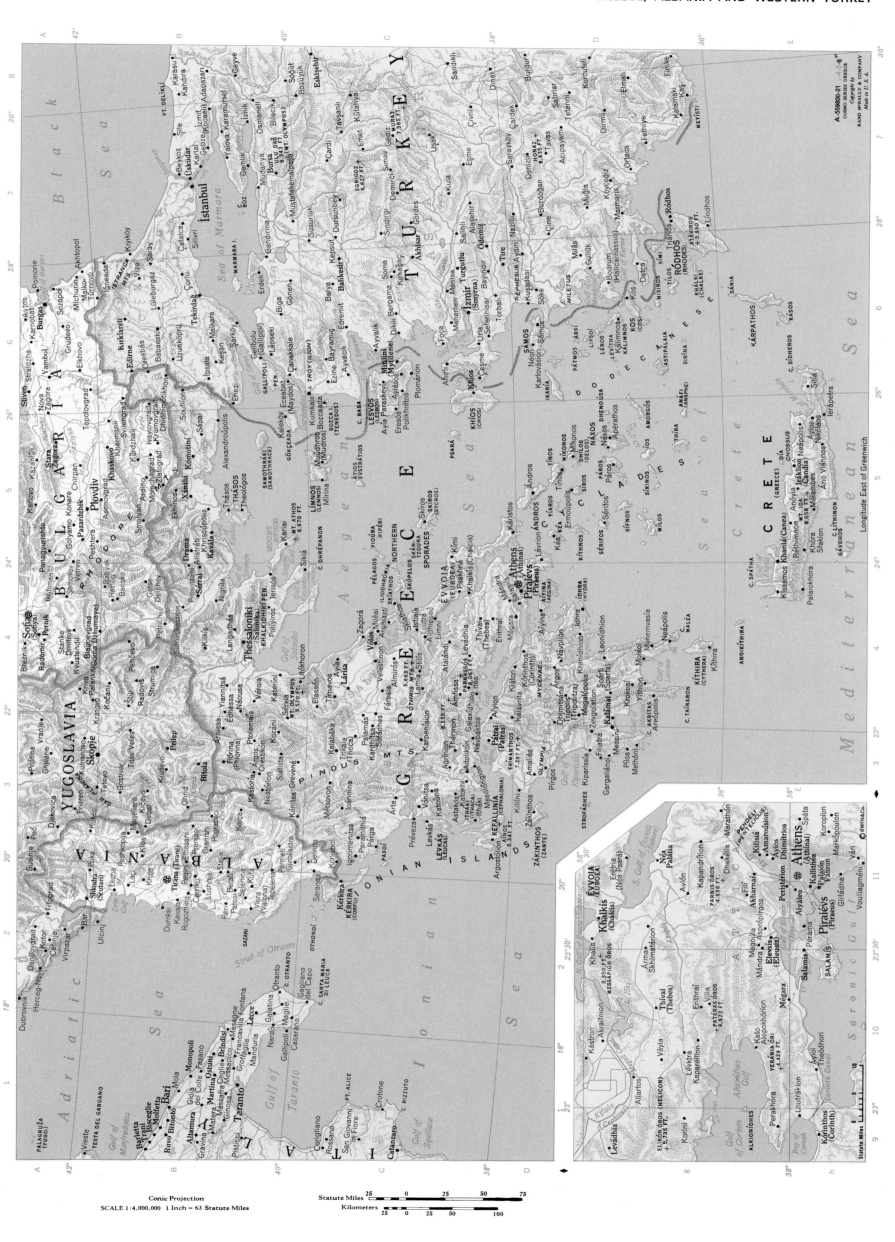

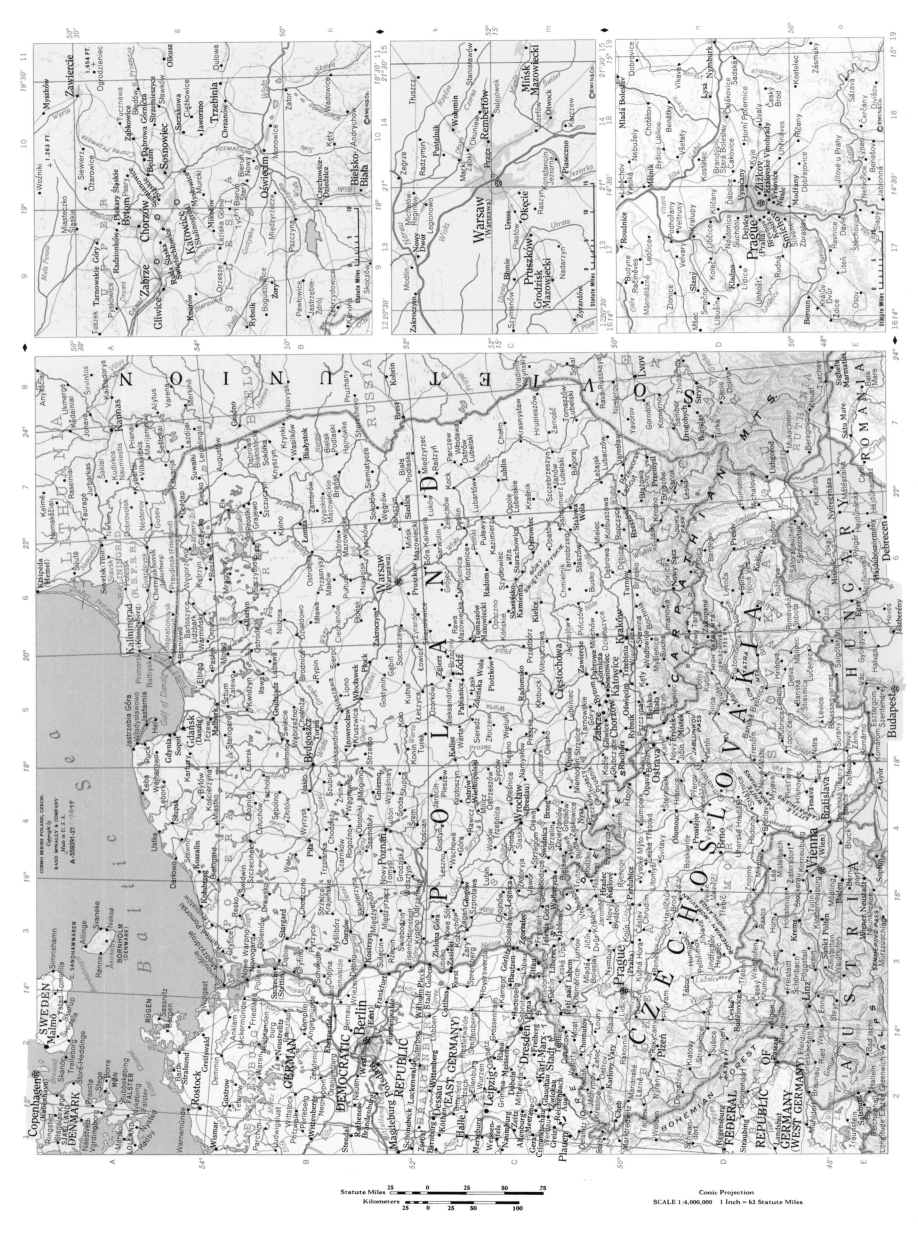

Statute Miles 25 0 25 50 75

Kilometers 25 0 25 50 100

Conic Projection

SCALE 1:4,000,000 1 Inch = 63 Statute Miles

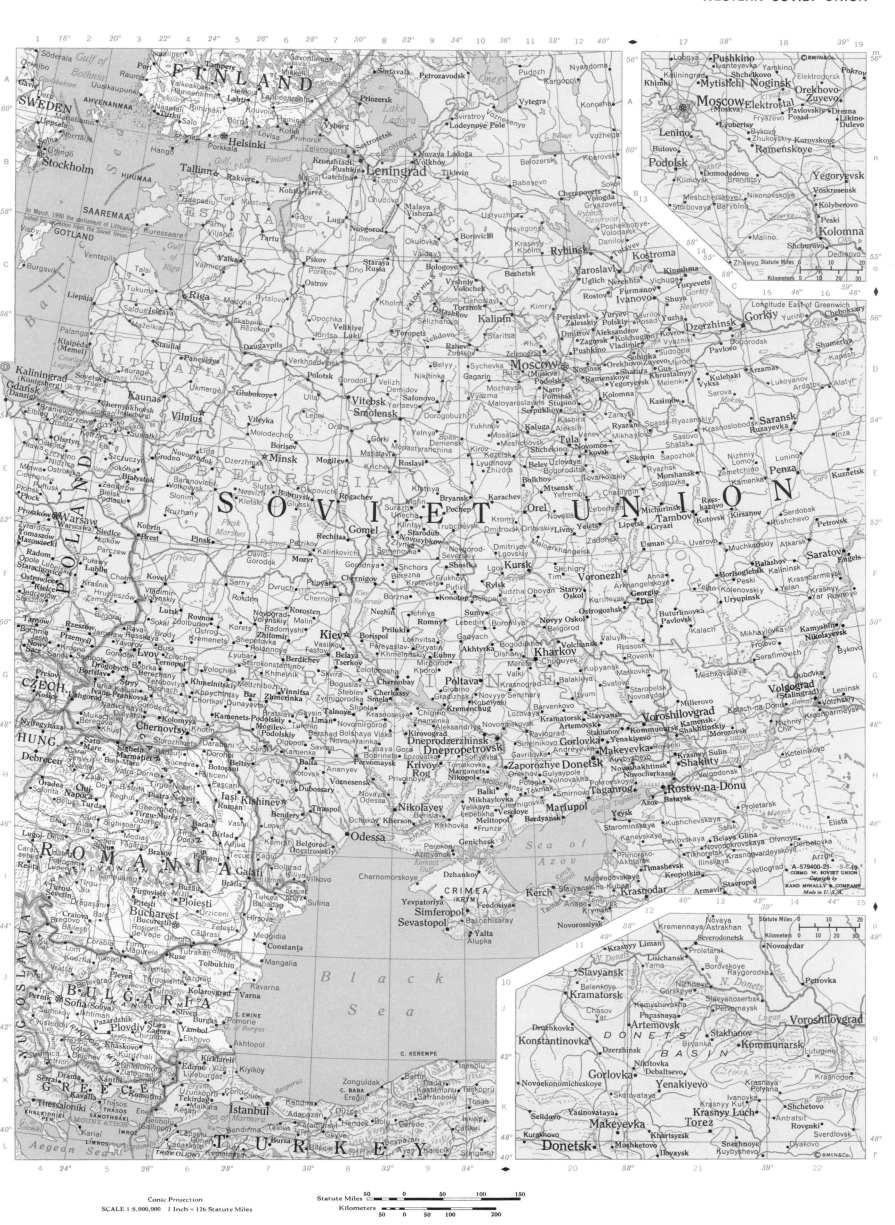

Statute Miles 50 0 50 100 150 200 250

Kilometers 50 0 50 100 150 200 250 300

Sinusoidal Projection

SCALE 1 : 11,400,000   1 Inch = 180 Statute Miles

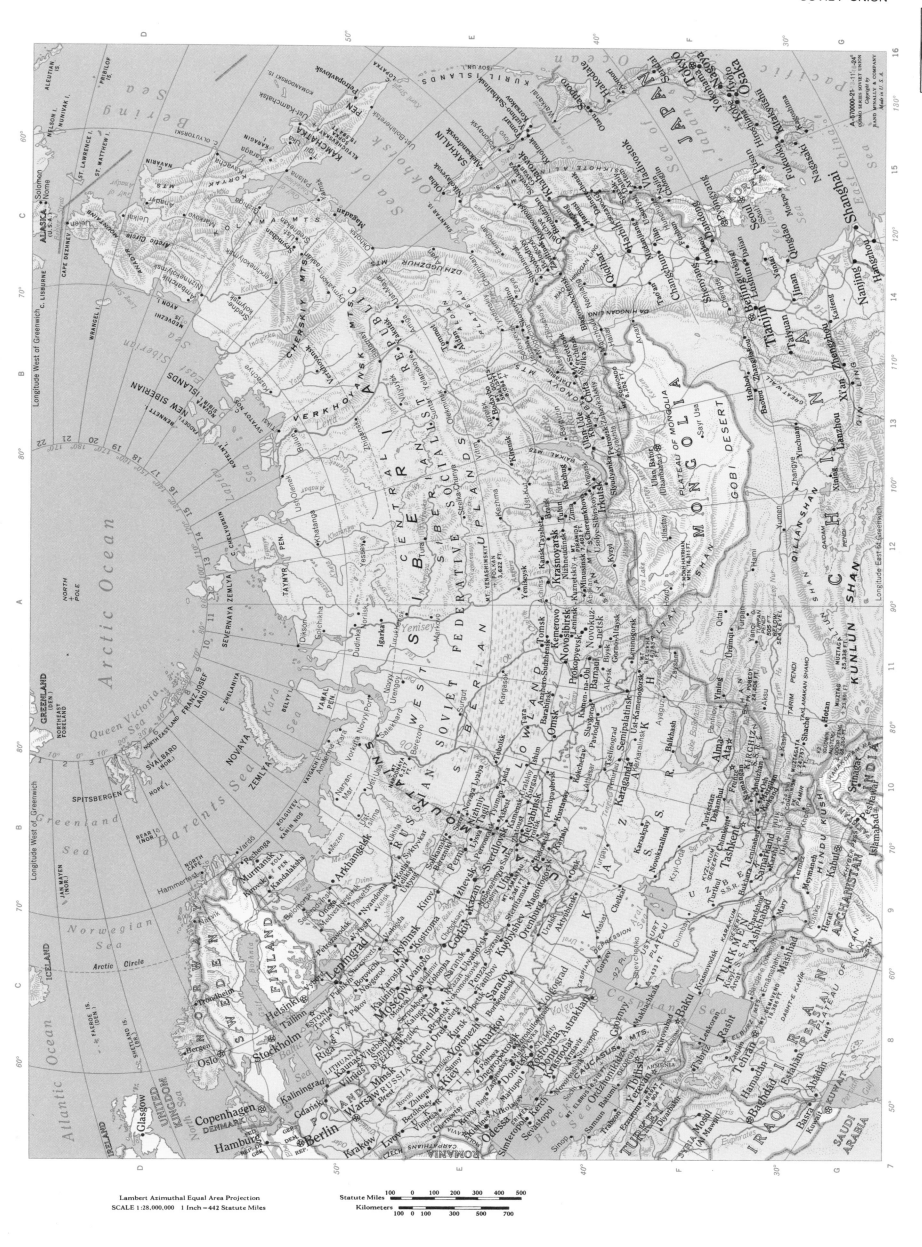

Lambert Azimuthal Equal Area Projection
SCALE 1:28,000,000   1 Inch = 442 Statute Miles

Statute Miles
100 0 100 200 300 400 500

Kilometers
100 0 100 300 500 700

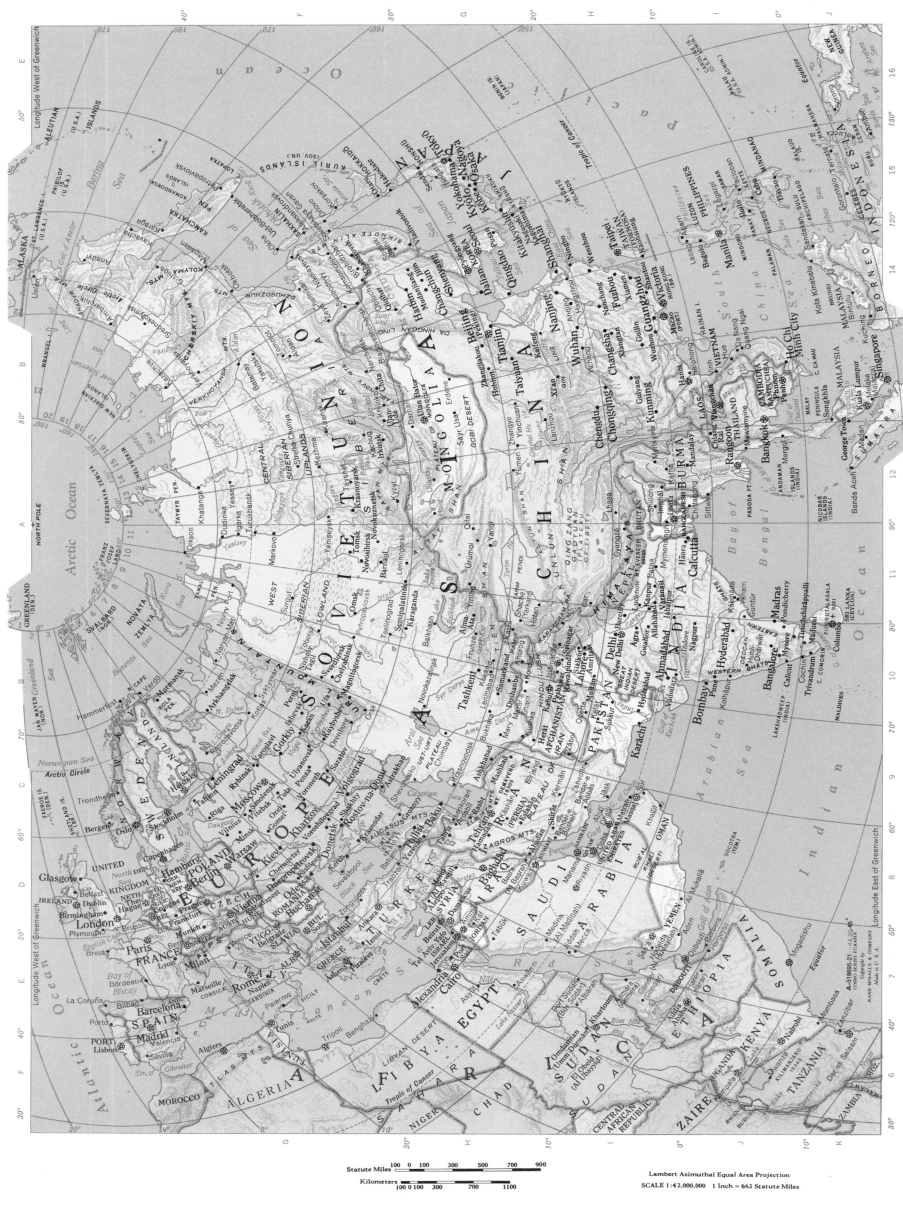

Statute Miles 100 0 100 300 500 700 900

Kilometers 100 0 100 300 700 1100

Lambert Azimuthal Equal Area Projection

SCALE 1:42,000,000 1 Inch = 663 Statute Miles

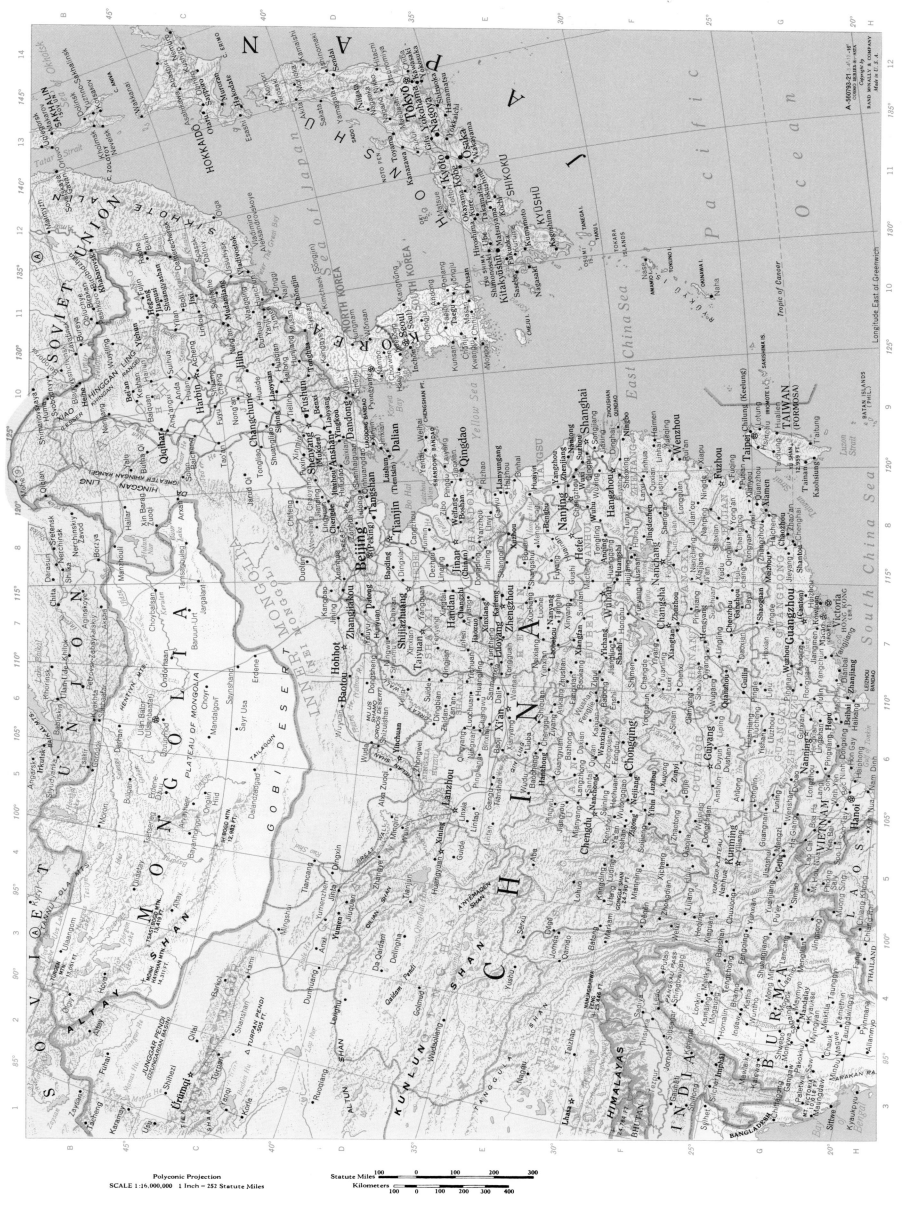

Polyconic Projection
SCALE 1:16,000,000   1 Inch = 252 Statute Miles

Statute Miles

Kilometers

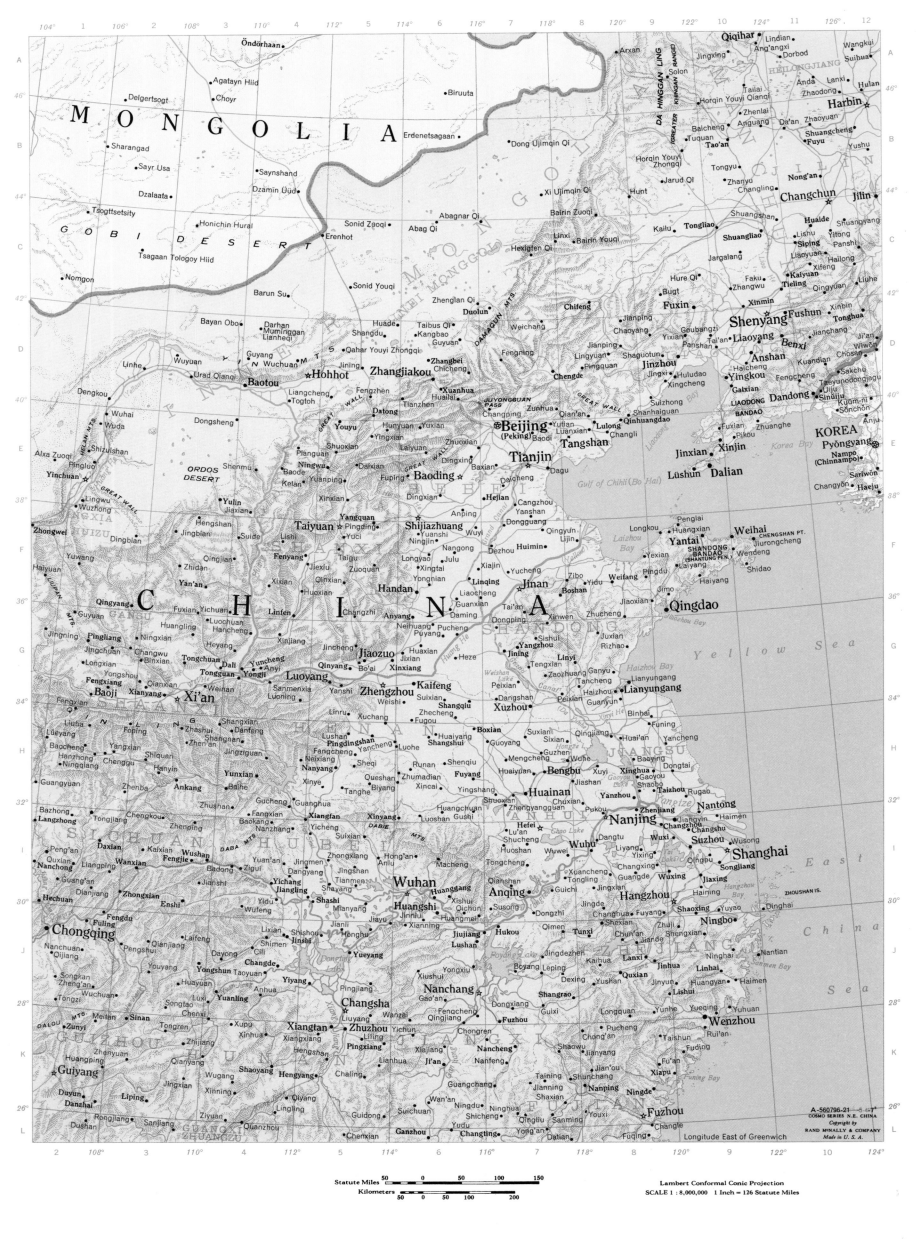

MONGOLIA

GOBI DESERT

C H I N A

MONGOLIA

HEILONGJIANG

Qiqihar

Harbin

Changchun Jilin

Shenyang Fushun

KOREA
Pyŏngyang
Nampo
(Chinnampo)

Beijing
(Peking)

Tianjin

Tangshan

Baoding

Taiyuan Shijiazhuang

Jinan

Qingdao

Yellow Sea

Xi'an

Luoyang Zhengzhou Kaifeng

Xuzhou

Nanjing

Shanghai

Wuhan

Hangzhou

Chongqing

East China Sea

Changsha

Nanchang

Ningbo

Wenzhou

Guiyang

Fuzhou

A-560796-21
COSMO SERIES N.E. CHINA
Copyright by
RAND McNALLY & COMPANY
Made in U.S.A.

Longitude East of Greenwich

Statute Miles   50   0   50   100   150
Kilometers   50   0   50   100   200

Lambert Conformal Conic Projection
SCALE 1 : 8,000,000   1 Inch = 126 Statute Miles

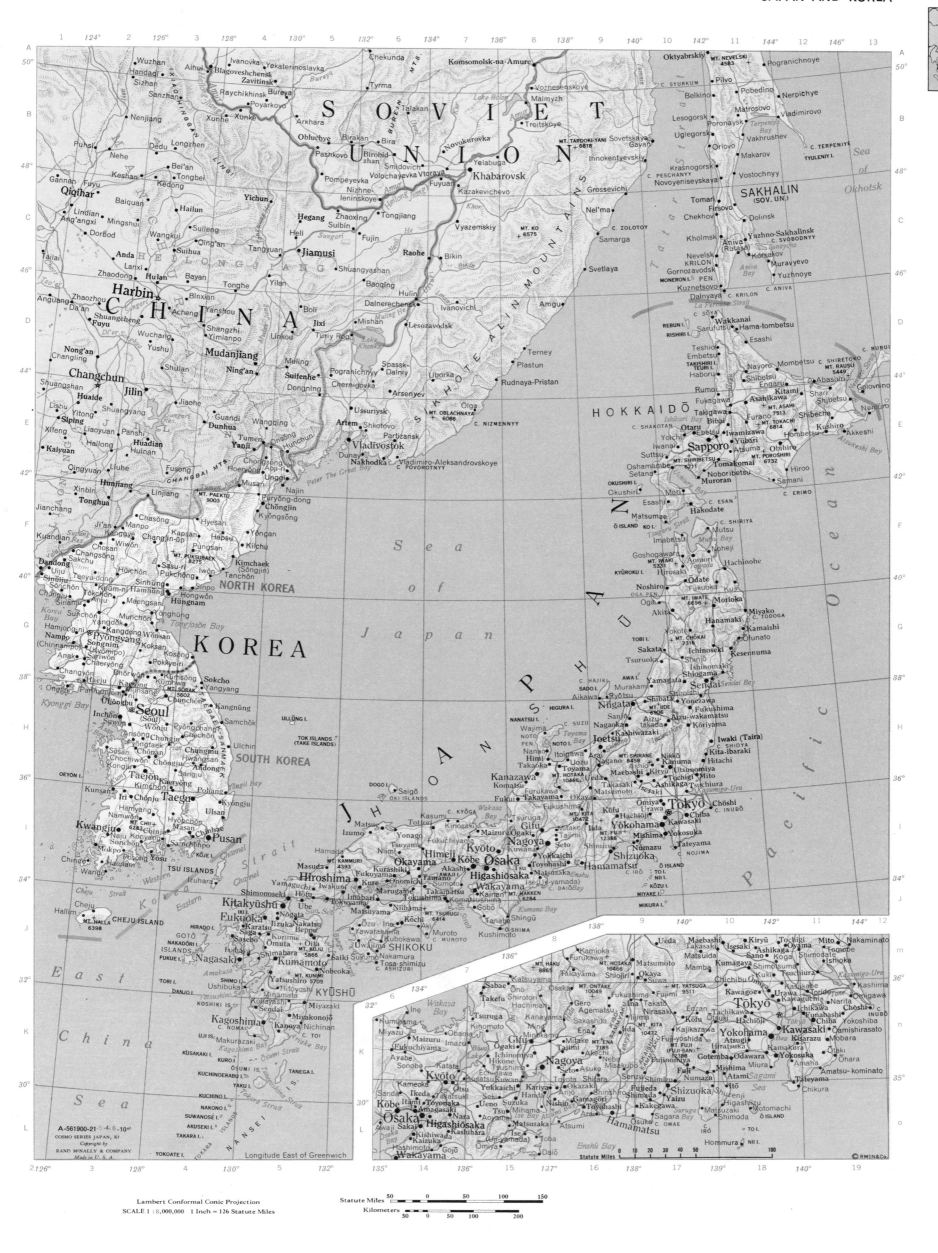

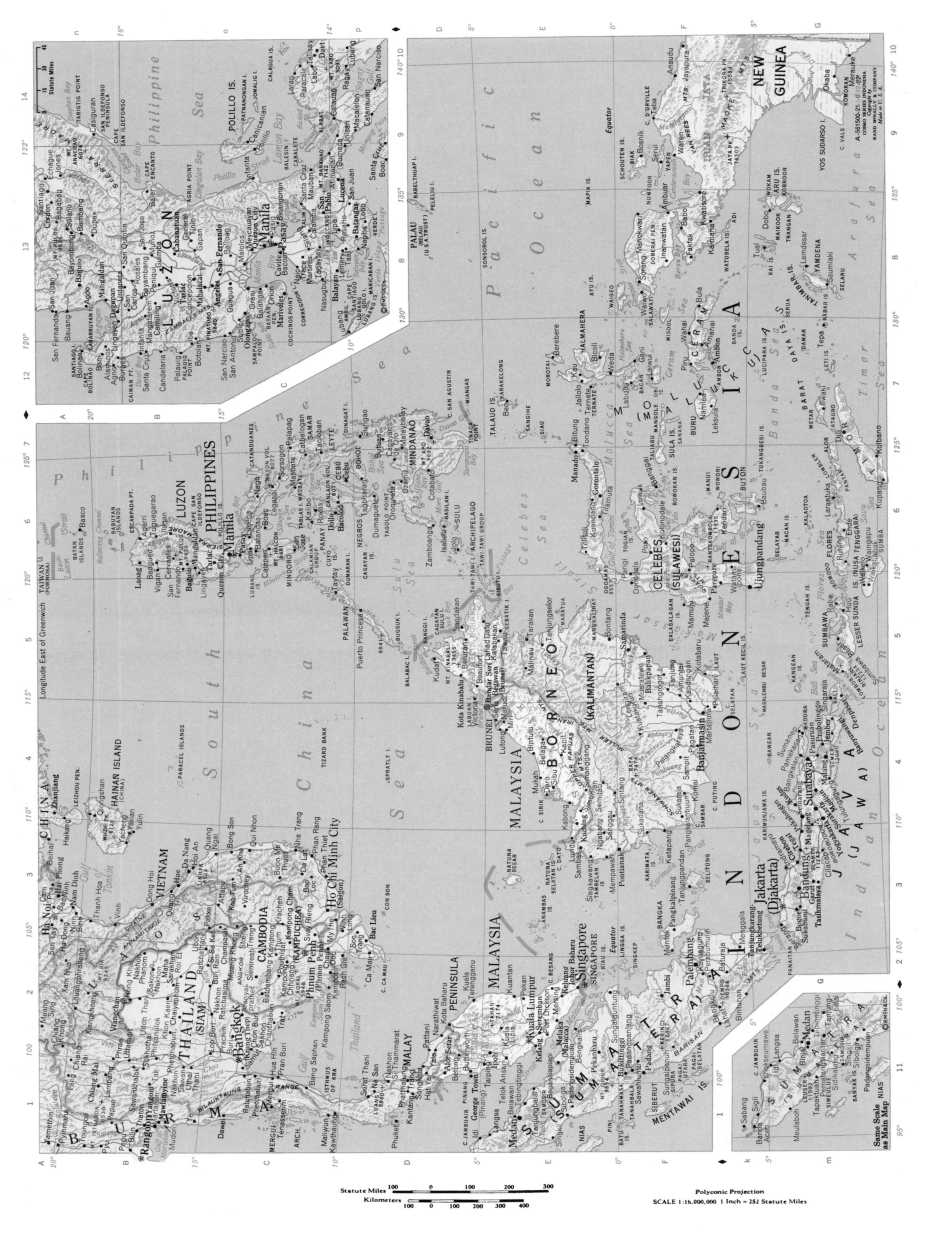

Statute Miles 100 0 100 200 300
Kilometers 100 0 100 200 300 400

Polyconic Projection
SCALE 1:16,000,000 1 Inch = 252 Statute Miles

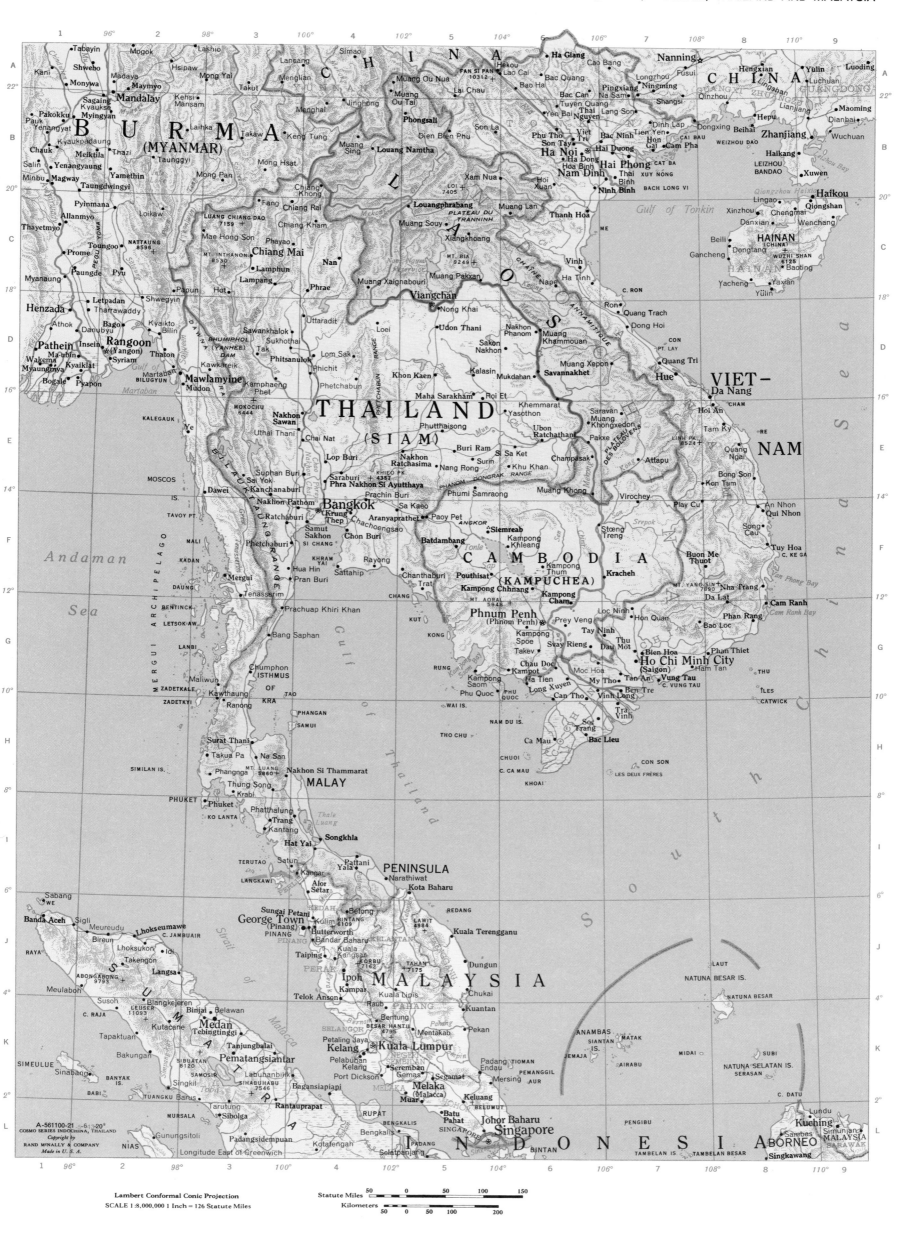

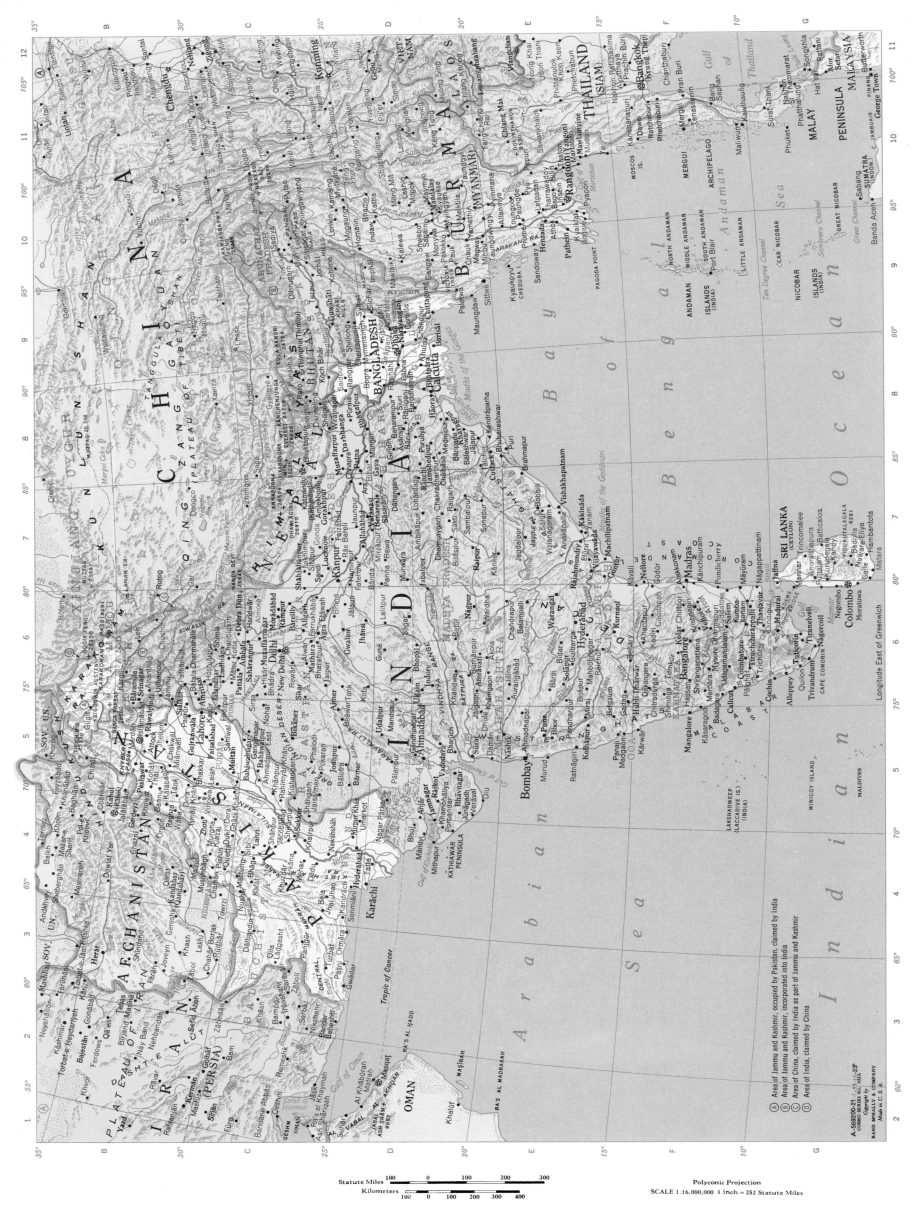

Statute Miles 100 0 100 200 300

Kilometers 100 0 100 200 300 400

Polyconic Projection

SCALE 1:16,000,000 1 inch = 252 Statute Miles

Ⓐ Area of Jammu and Kashmir, occupied by Pakistan, claimed by India
Ⓑ Area of Jammu and Kashmir, incorporated into India
Ⓒ Area, claimed by India as part of Jammu and Kashmir
Ⓓ Area of China, claimed by India

A-569000-21 23° ASIA
COSMO SERIES SO. ASIA
Copyright by
RAND M℞NALLY & COMPANY
Made in U.S.A.

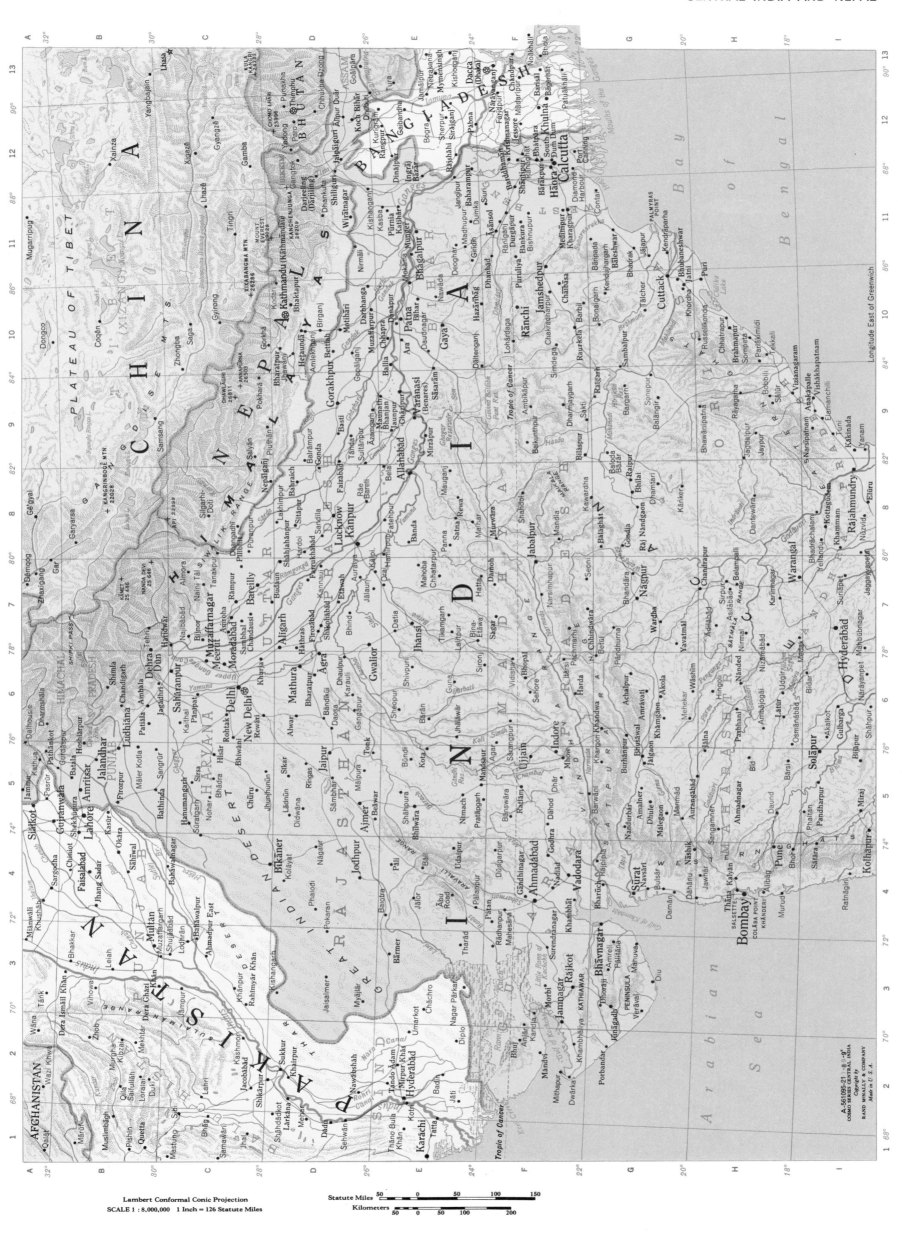

Lambert Conformal Conic Projection

SCALE 1 : 8,000,000   1 Inch = 126 Statute Miles

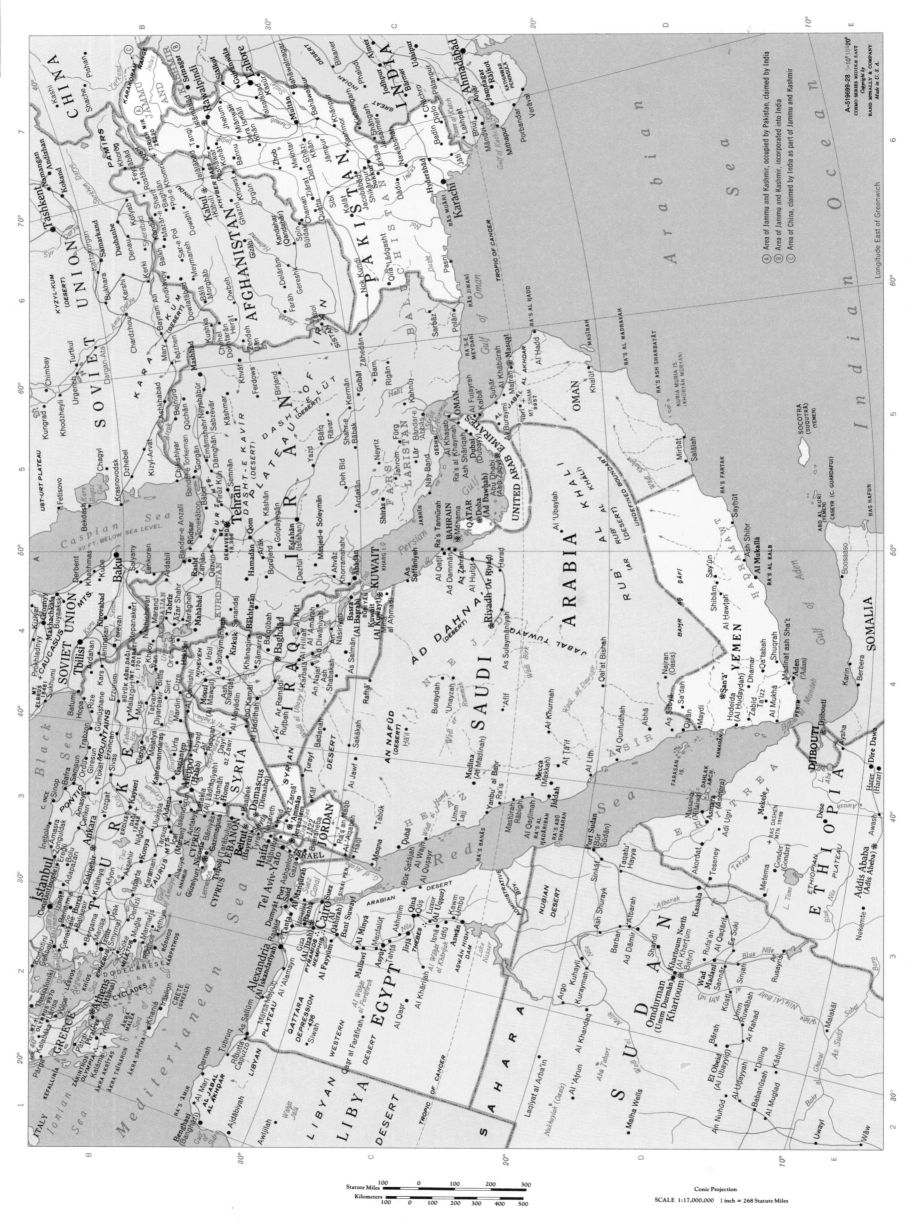

Lambert Conformal Conic Projection
SCALE 1 : 8,000,000 1 Inch = 126 Statute Miles

Statute Miles
Kilometers

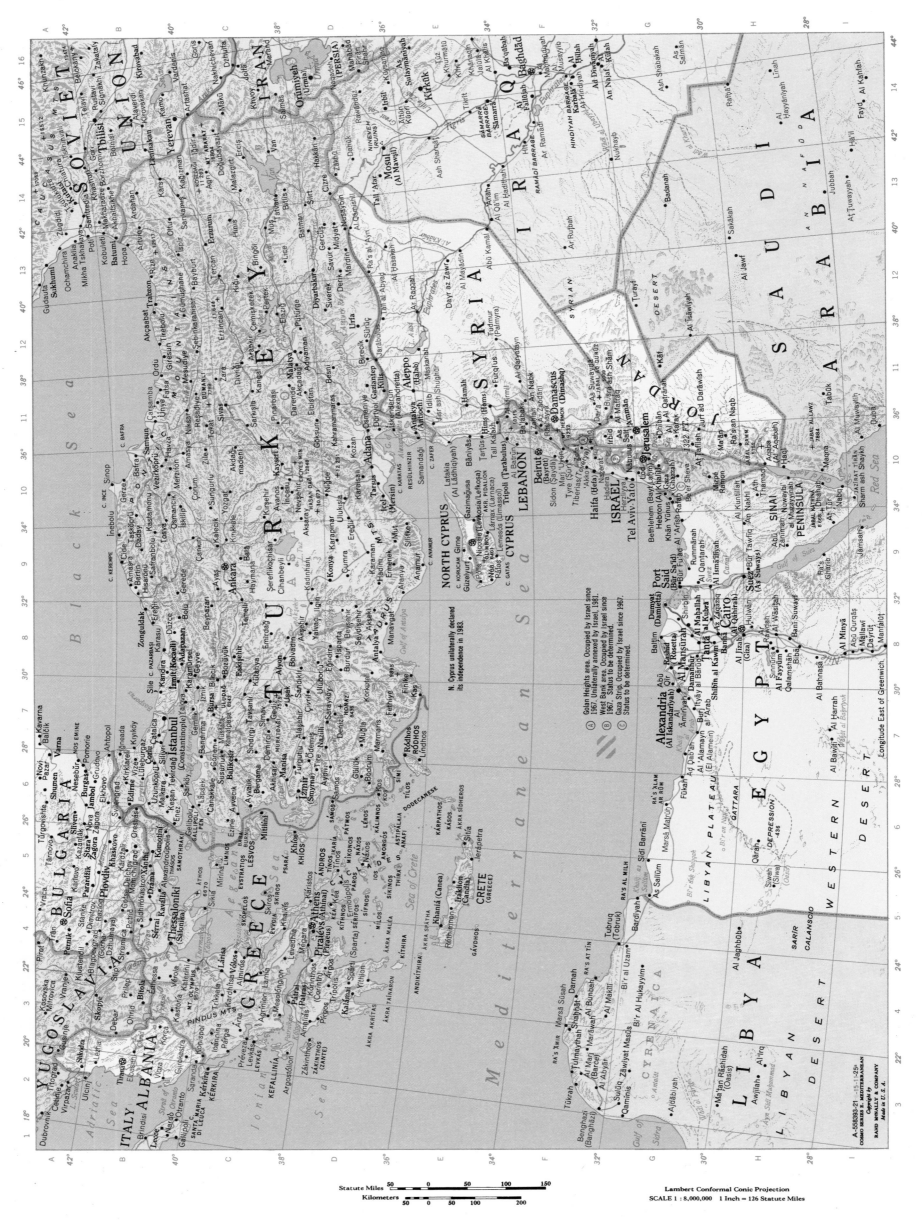

Golan Heights area. Occupied by Israel since 1967. Unilaterally annexed by Israel 1981.
West Bank area. Occupied by Israel since 1967. Status to be determined.
Gaza Strip. Occupied by Israel since 1967. Status to be determined.

Statute Miles 50 0 50 100 150
Kilometers 50 0 50 100 200

Lambert Conformal Conic Projection
SCALE 1 : 8,000,000   1 Inch = 126 Statute Miles

A-558393-21 COSMO SERIES E. MEDITERRANEAN
Copyright by
RAND M?NALLY & COMPANY
Made in U.S.A.

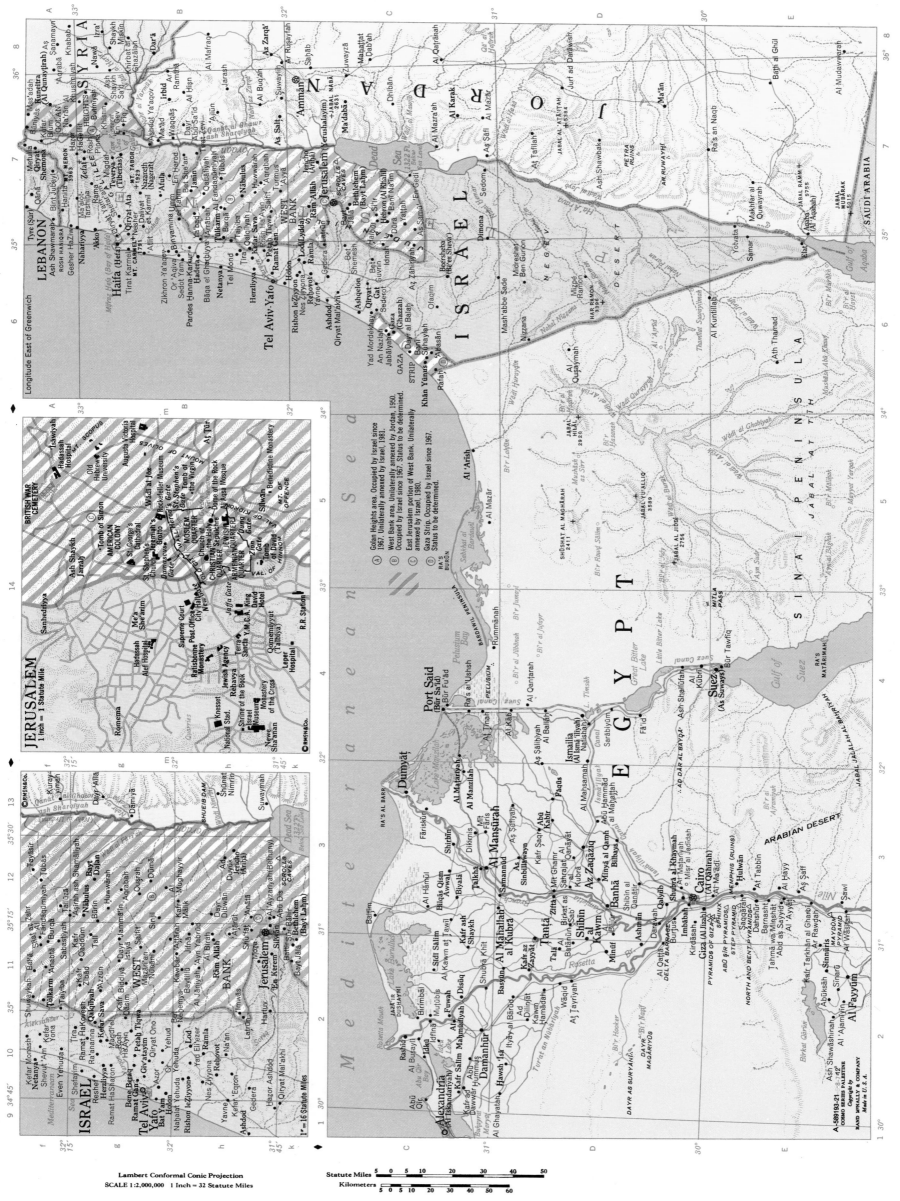

AFRICA

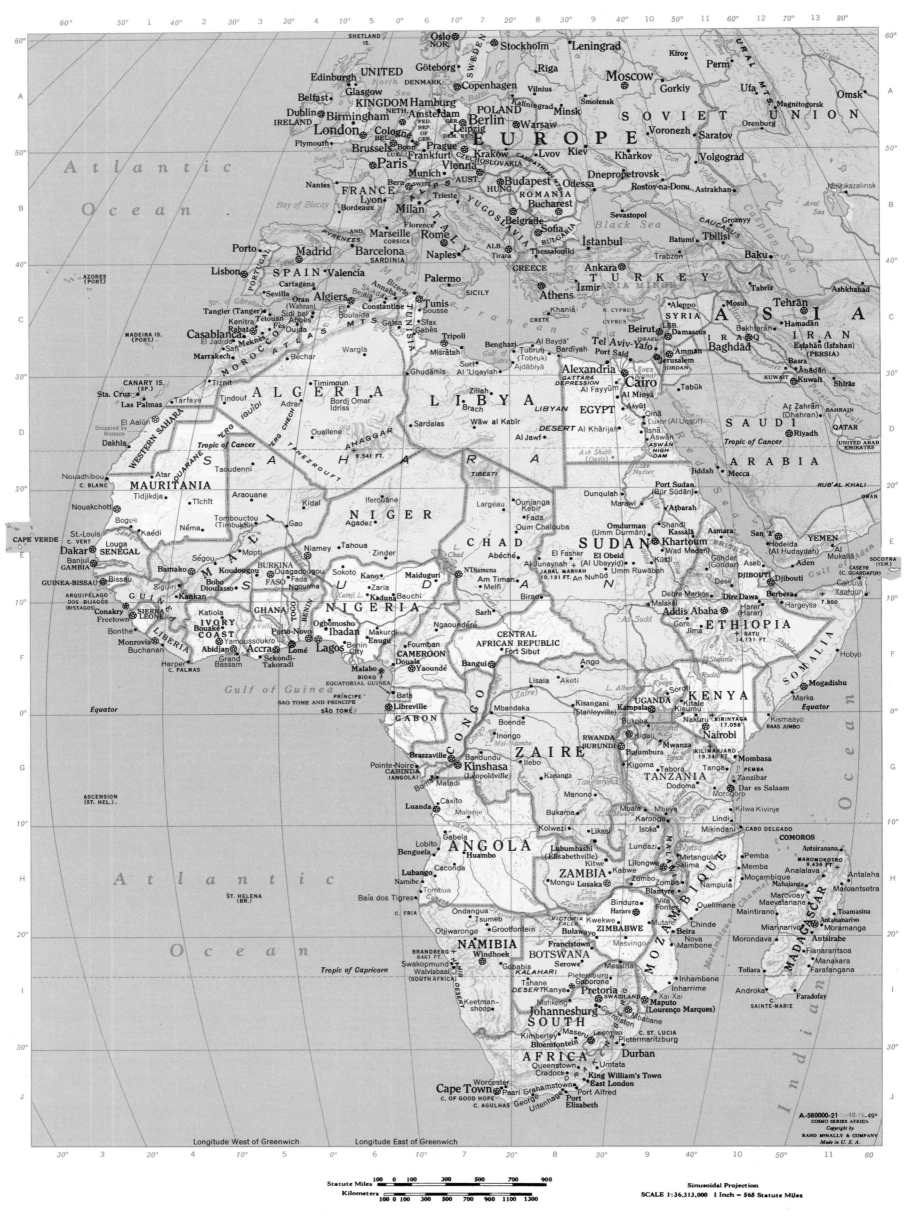

SHETLAND IS.

Oslo NOR.

Stockholm

Leningrad

Kirov Perm

Moscow

Gorkiy Ufa

Magnitogorsk

Omsk

Edinburgh UNITED Göteborg

Riga

Kalinin Smolensk Omsk

Belfast KINGDOM Hamburg Copenhagen Vilnius Minsk

S O V I E T U N I O N

Dublin Birmingham Amsterdam Berlin Warsaw Smolensk Voronezh Saratov

IRELAND London Cologne FED. Leipzig POLAND Kiev Kharkov Volgograd

Plymouth Brussels Bonn Frankfurt Prague CZECH E U R O P E Dnepropetrovsk Rostov-na-Donu

Paris Munich Vienna CHOSLOVAKIA Budapest Odessa Novokazalinsk

Nantes FRANCE Bern Trieste HUNG. ROMANIA Astrakhan

Lyon Milan YUGOSLAVIA Bucharest Sevastopol

Bordeaux Florence Belgrade Sofia Black Sea Batumi Tbilisi

Marseille Rome BULGARIA İstanbul CAUCASUS Groznyy

Porto CORSICA Naples ALB. Tirana Thessaloniki TURKEY Trabzon Baku

Madrid Barcelona SARDINIA GREECE Ankara İzmir ASIA MINOR Tehrān Tabrīz Ashkhabad

Lisbon SPAIN Valencia Palermo Athens Aleppo Mosul Tehrān

Cartagena SICILY CRETE N. CYPRUS Khaniá SYRIA Bakhtaran Hamadān IRAN

Algiers Tunis CYPRUS Beirut ISRAEL Damascus IRAQ Eşlahān (Isfahan) (PERSIA)

Tangier (Tanger) Constantine Sousse Tel Aviv-Yafo Amman Baghdād Basra Ābādān Shīrāz

Casablanca Fès Oujda Tripoli Benghazi Tübruq Bardīyah Port Said JORDAN Jerusalem KUWAIT Kuwait

Marrakech Béchar Ghudāmis Surt Ajdābiyā Alexandria Cairo Az Zahrān (Dhahran) QATAR

CANARY IS. (SP.) ALGERIA LIBYA QATTARA DEPRESSION Al Fayyūm EGYPT Al Minyā Tabūk SAUDI UNITED ARAB EMIRATES

Las Palmas Timimoun DESERT Al Khārijah Asyūt Tropic of Cancer ARABIA

WESTERN SAHARA MAURITANIA SAHARA NIGER CHAD SUDAN Khartoum ETHIOPIA SOMALIA

Nouakchott MALI Omdurman Kassala Asmara YEMEN

Dakar SENEGAL BURKINA FASO NIGERIA Kano N'Djamena Addis Ababa DJIBOUTI

GUINEA IVORY COAST GHANA Lagos CAMEROON CENTRAL AFRICAN REPUBLIC KENYA Mogadishu

Freetown LIBERIA Accra GABON CONGO ZAIRE Nairobi

Monrovia Gulf of Guinea SAO TOME AND PRINCIPE Kinshasa UGANDA TANZANIA Dar es Salaam

Luanda ANGOLA ZAMBIA Lusaka MALAWI MOZAMBIQUE COMOROS

NAMIBIA Windhoek BOTSWANA ZIMBABWE Harare MADAGASCAR Antananarivo

Walvisbaai Gaborone Pretoria SWAZILAND Maputo

Johannesburg SOUTH AFRICA LESOTHO Durban

Cape Town Port Elizabeth

Atlantic Ocean

Indian Ocean

42

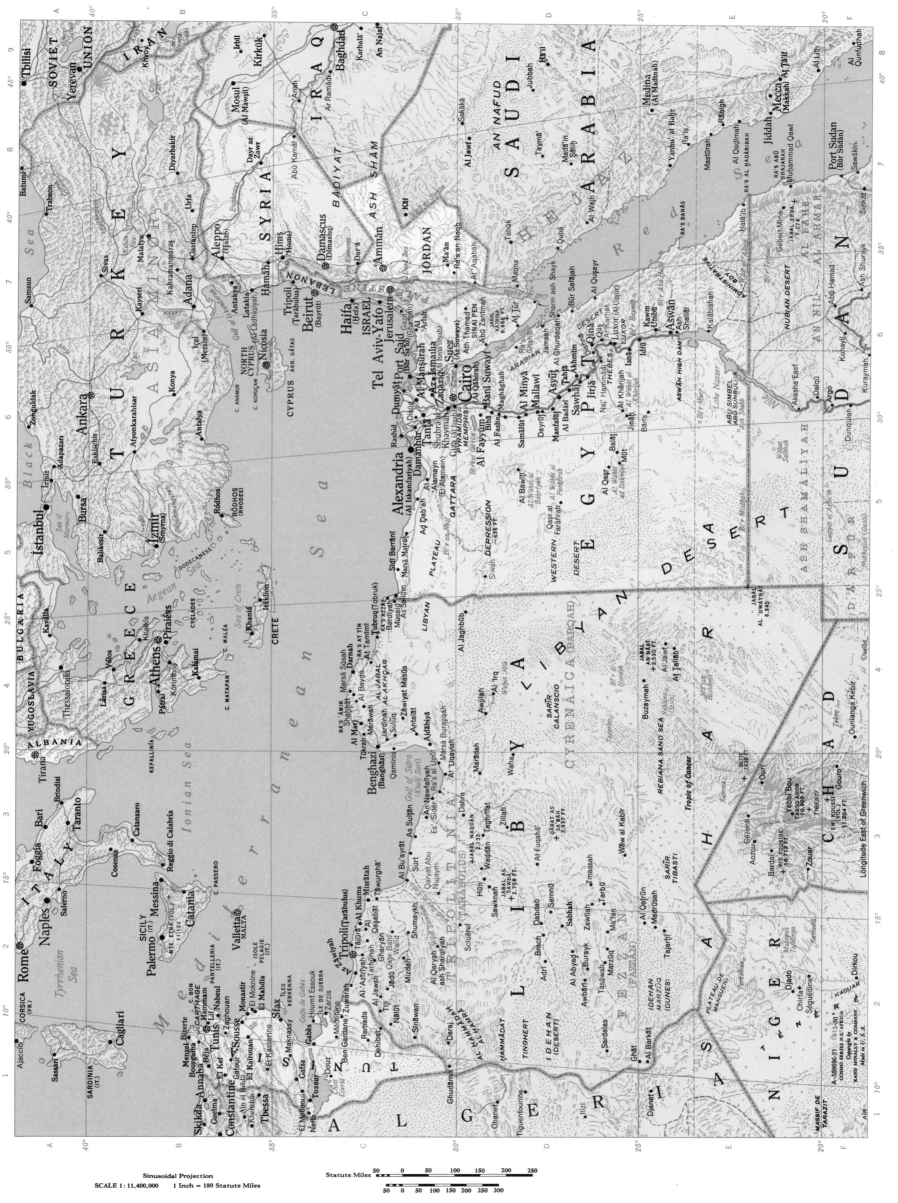

Sinusoidal Projection
SCALE 1: 11,400,000   1 Inch = 180 Statute Miles

Statute Miles
50 0 50 100 150 200 250
50 0 50 100 150 200 250 300

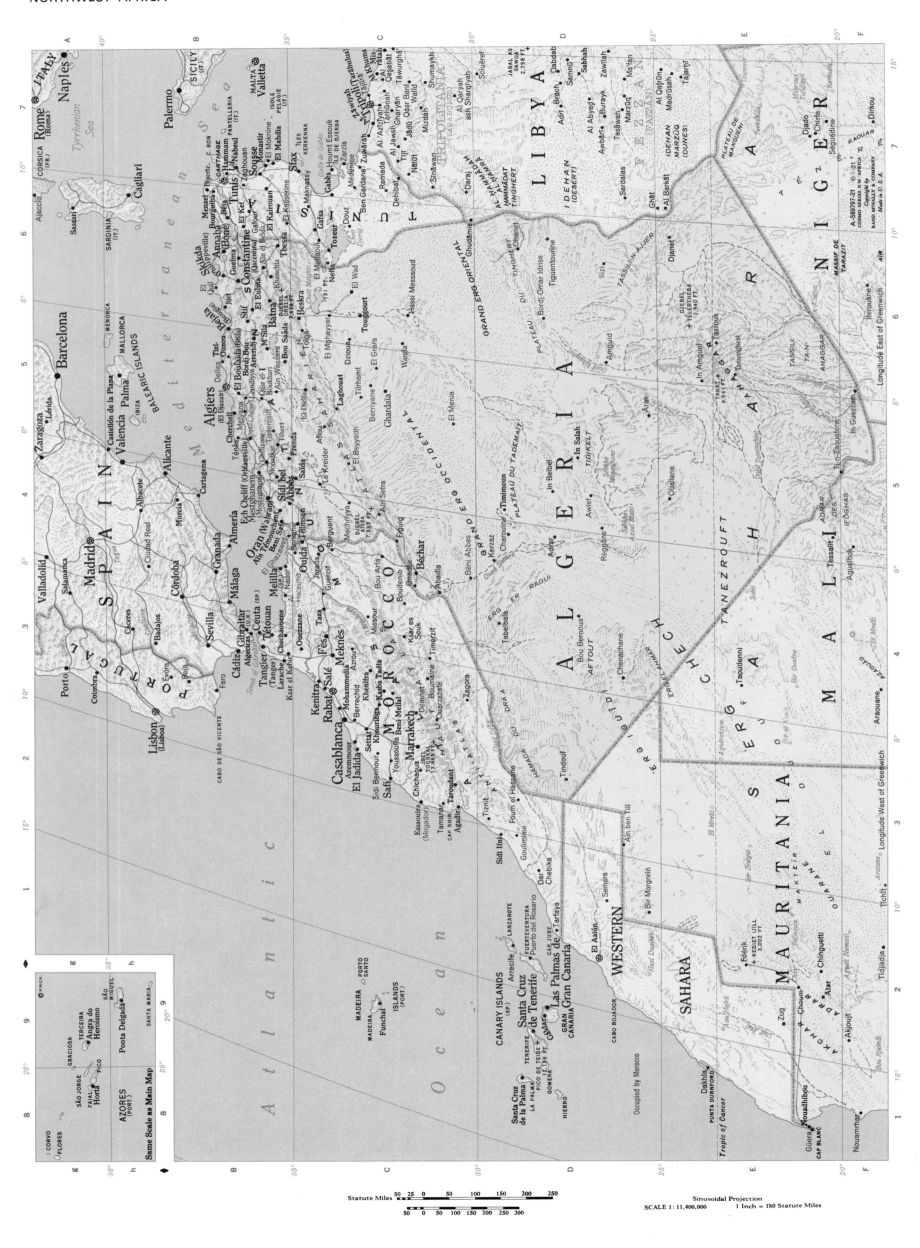

Statute Miles 50 25 0   50   100   150   200   250

50 0 50 100 150 200 250 300

Sinusoidal Projection

SCALE 1: 11,400,000   1 Inch = 180 Statute Miles

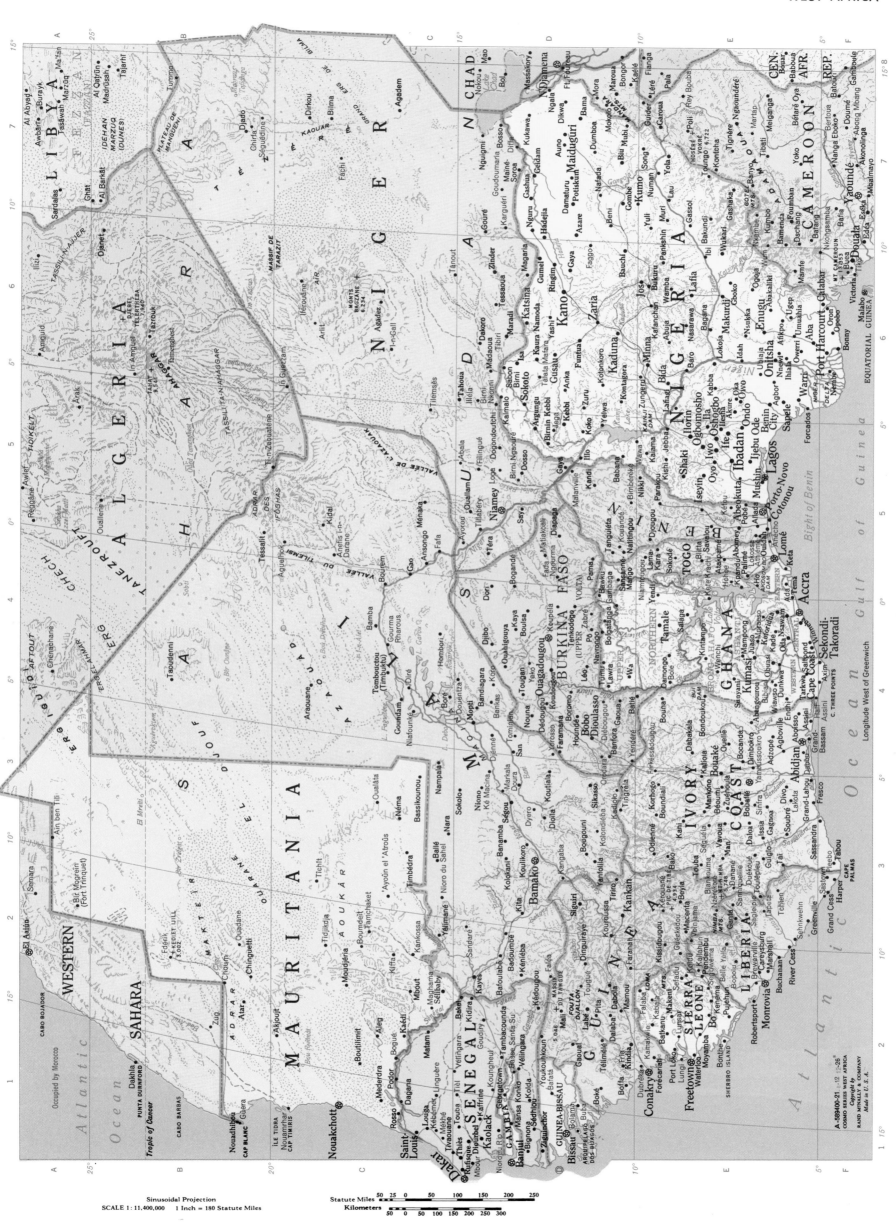

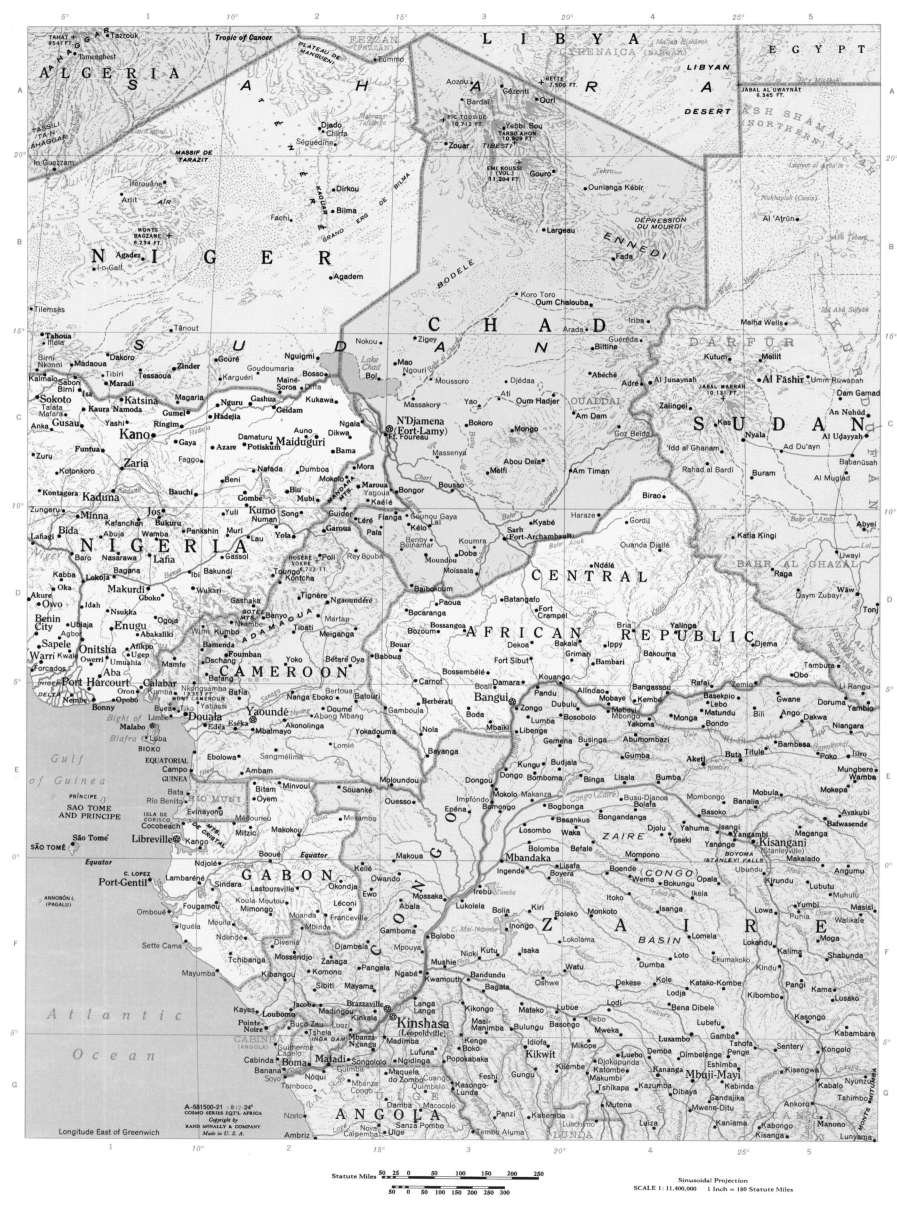

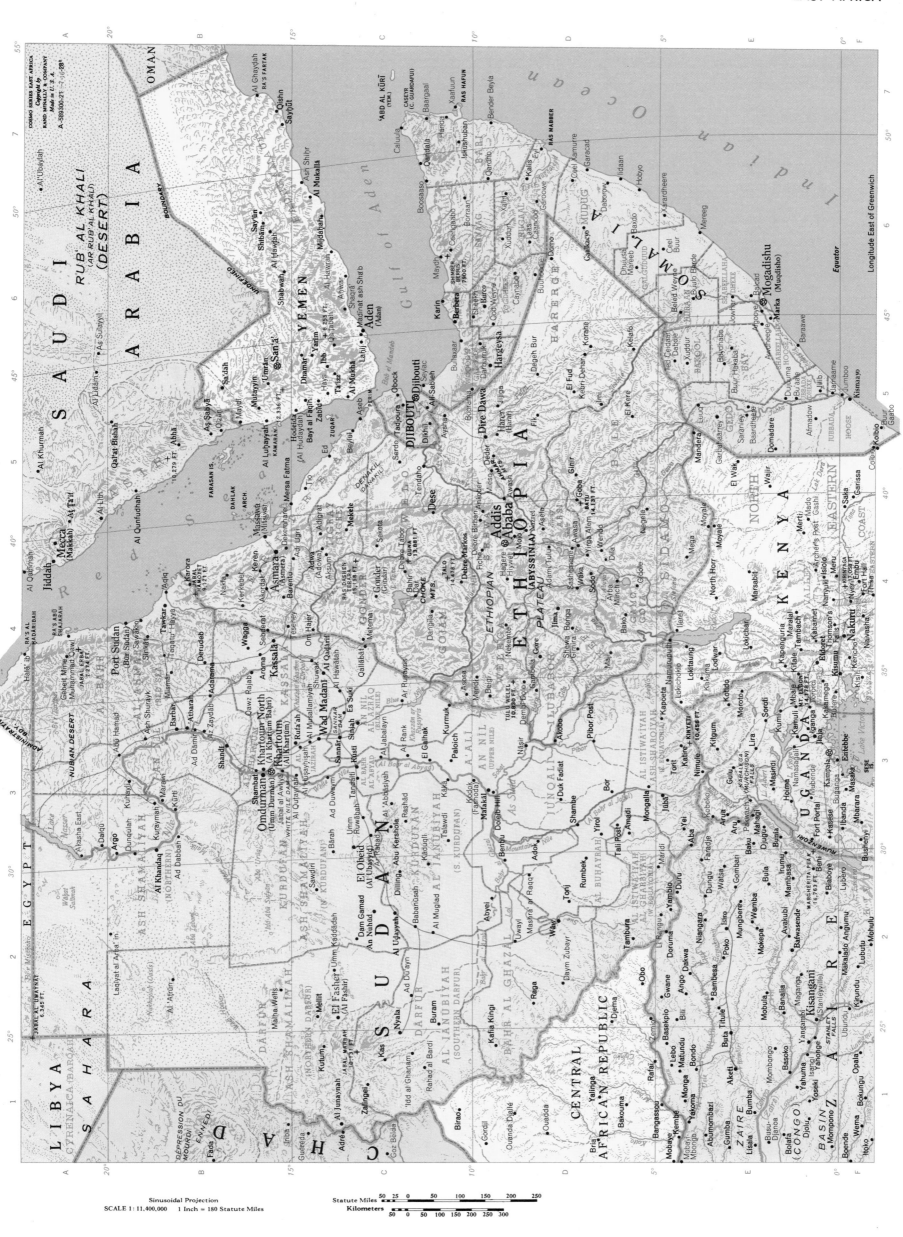

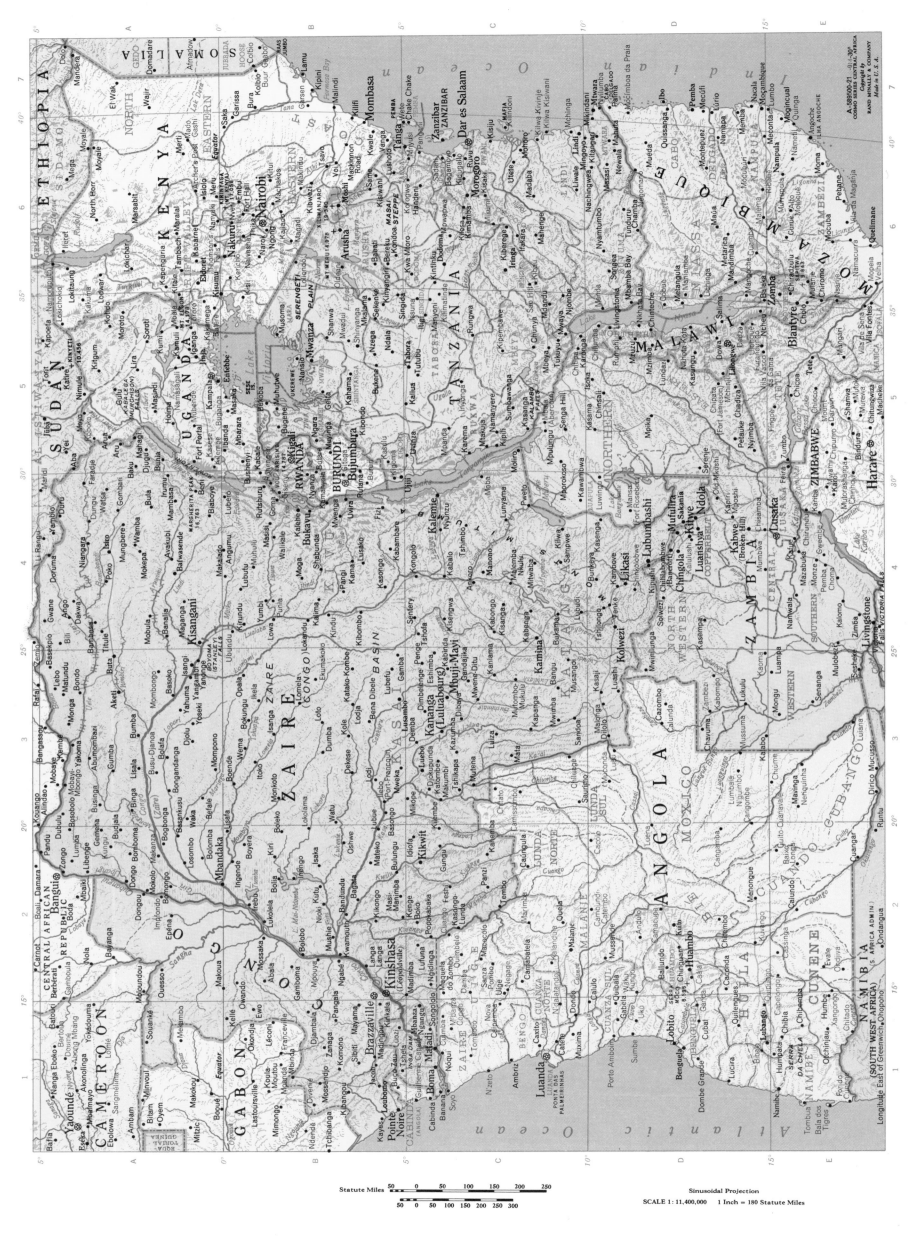

Statute Miles 50 0 50 100 150 200 250

50 0 50 100 150 200 250 300

Sinusoidal Projection

SCALE 1:11,400,000   1 Inch = 180 Statute Miles

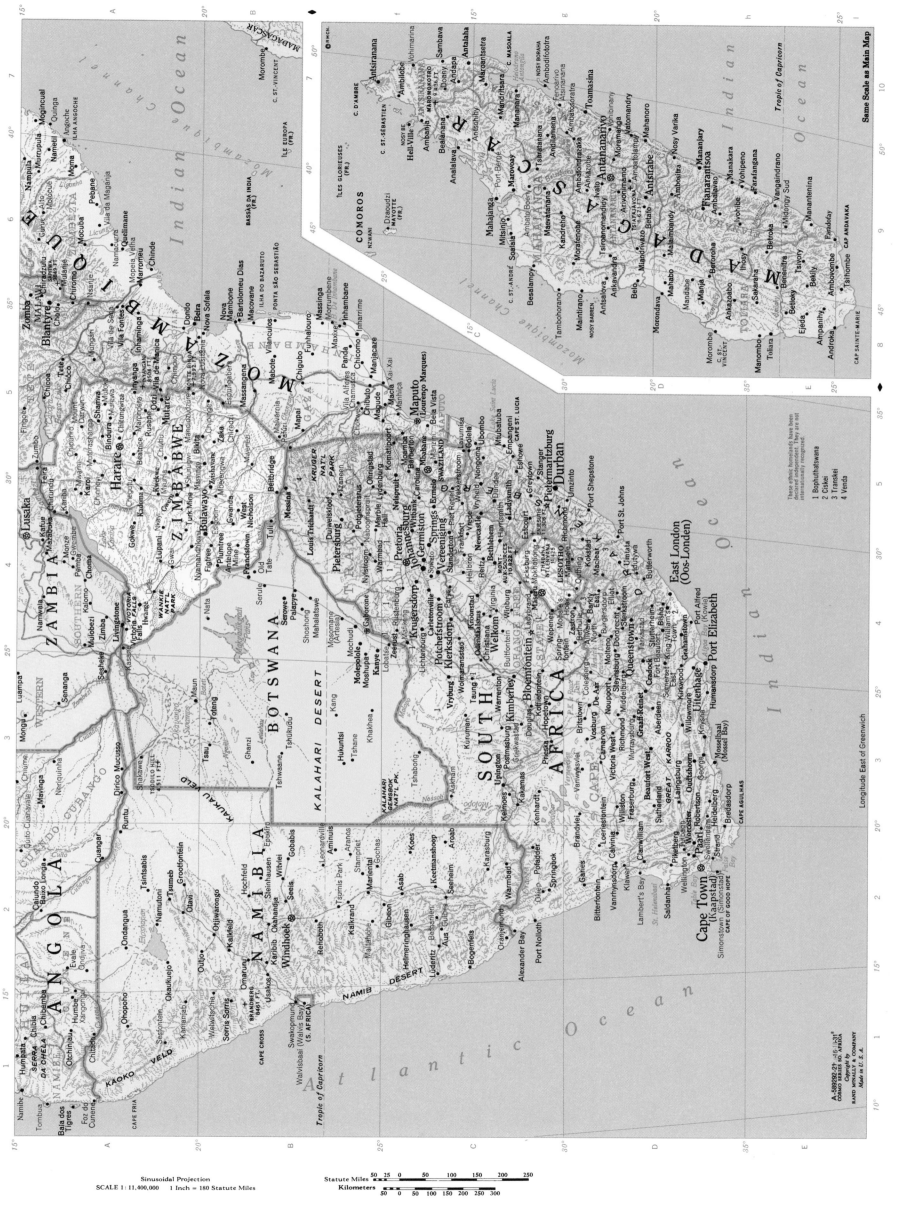

Sinusoidal Projection
SCALE 1 : 11,400,000   1 Inch = 180 Statute Miles

Statute Miles
Kilometers

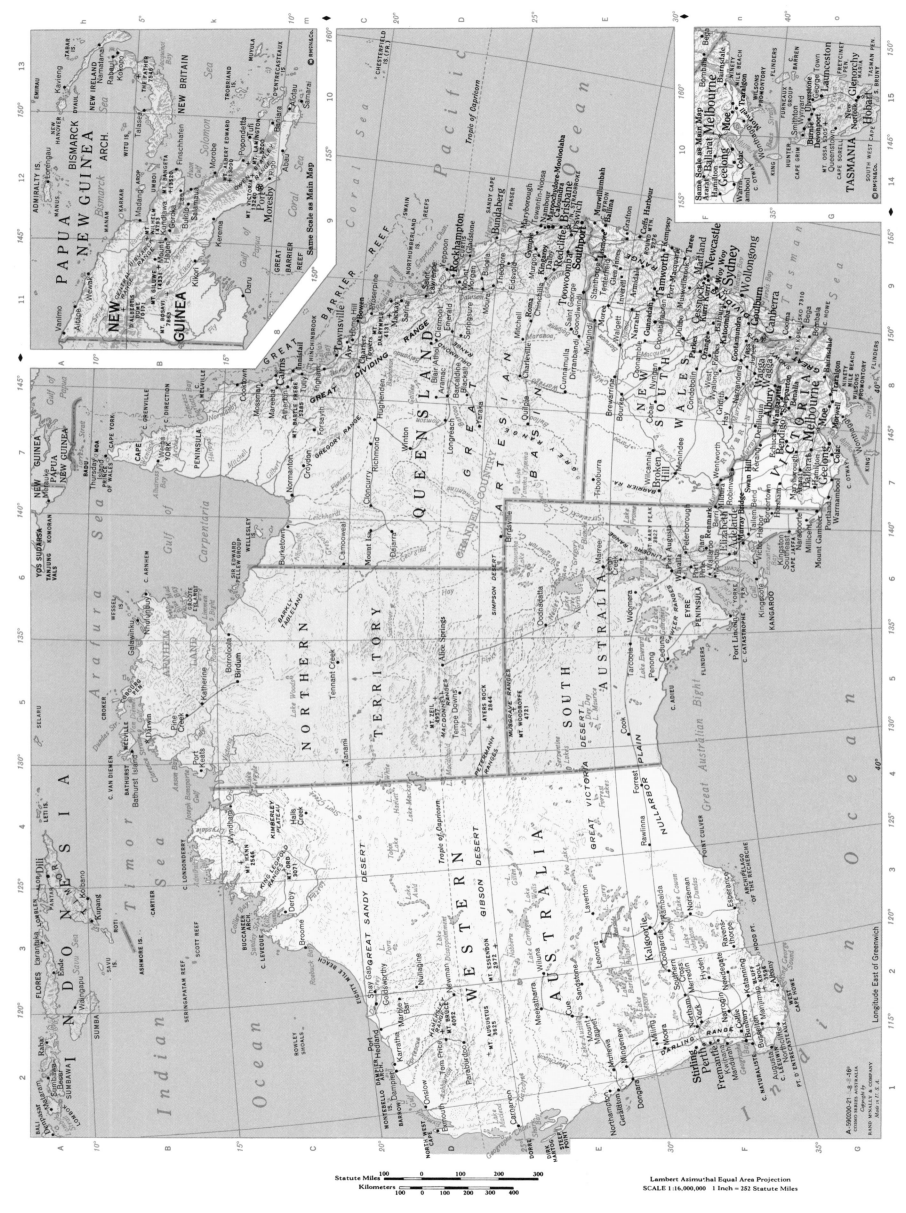

Statute Miles

Kilometers

Lambert Azimuthal Equal Area Projection
SCALE 1:16,000,000   1 Inch = 252 Statute Miles

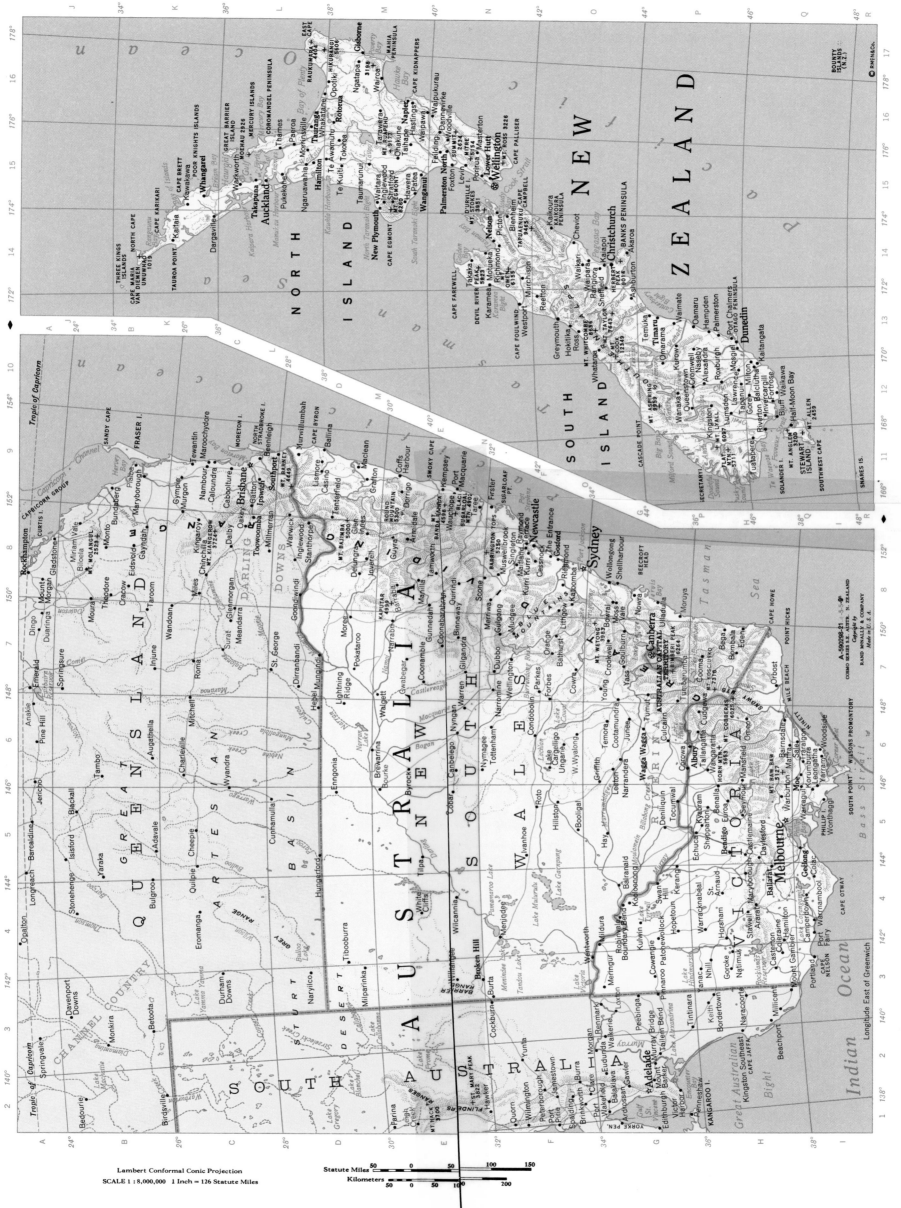

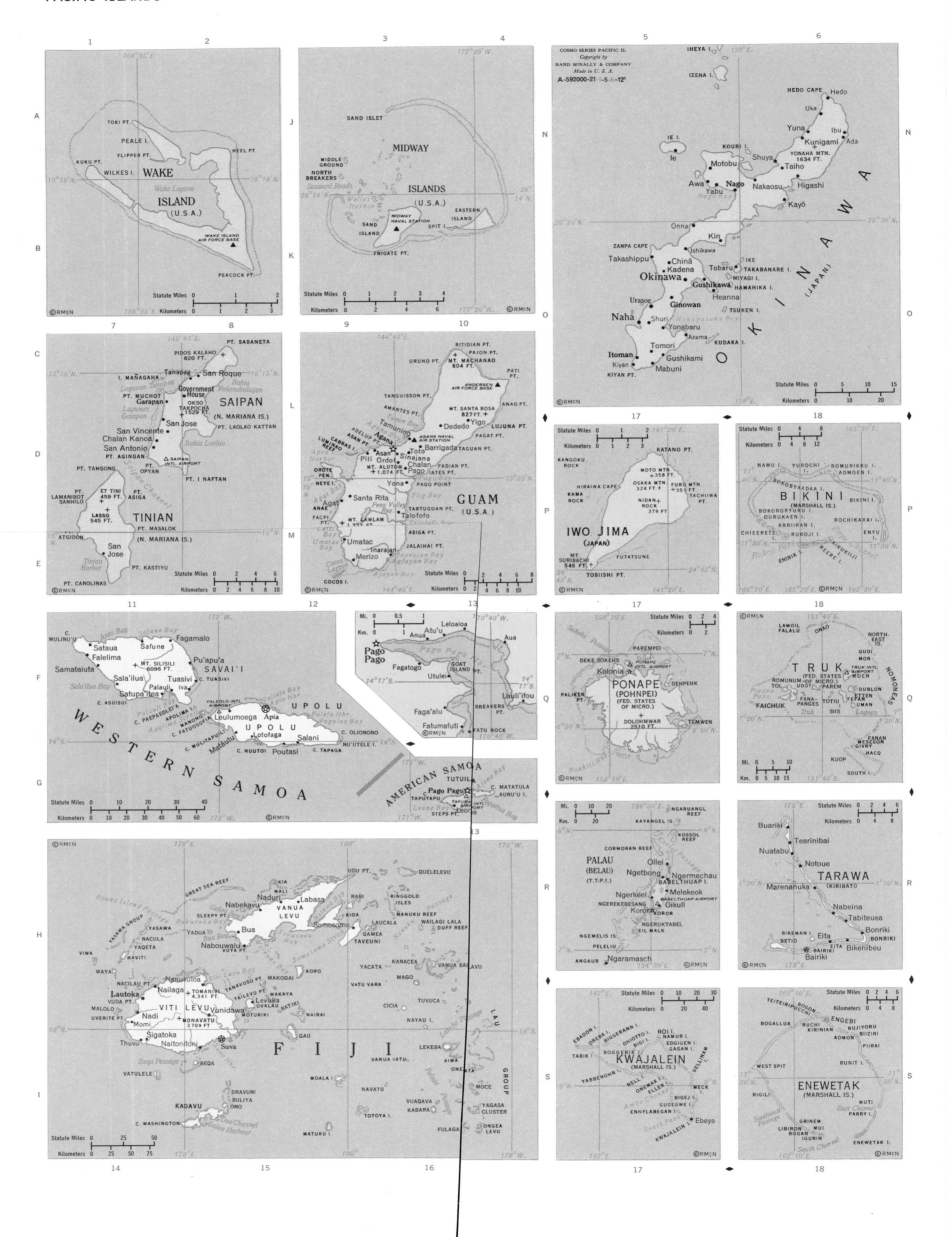

WAKE ISLAND (U.S.A.)

TOKI PT.
PEALE I.
FLIPPER PT.
HEEL PT.
KUKU PT.
WILKES I.
WAKE
10°18' N.
Wake Lagoon
19°18' N.
WAKE ISLAND
AIR FORCE BASE
PEACOCK PT.

Statute Miles 0 1 2
Kilometers 0 1 2 3
©RMCN
166°35' E.

MIDWAY ISLANDS (U.S.A.)

SAND ISLET
MIDDLE GROUND
NORTH BREAKERS
Seaward Roads
28°14' N.
Welles Harbor
SAND ISLAND
MIDWAY NAVAL STATION
EASTERN ISLAND
SPIT I.
FRIGATE PT.
28° 14' N.
177°20' W.

Statute Miles 0 1 2 3 4
Kilometers 0 1 2 3 4 5
177°20' W. ©RMCN

COSMO SERIES PACIFIC IS.
Copyright by
RAND MCNALLY & COMPANY
Made in U.S.A.
A-592000-21—5-6-12°

OKINAWA (JAPAN)

IHEYA I.
IZENA I.
HEDO CAPE Hedo
Uka
IE I. KOURI I. Yuna Ibu Ada
Kunigami
Ie Motobu Shuya YONAHA MTN. 1634 FT.
Awa Yabu Nago Nakaosu Taiho Higashi
Nago Bay Kayō
Onna Kin
ZANPA CAPE Ishikawa IKE
Takashippu Chinā TAKABANARE I.
Kadena Tobaru MIYAGI I. HAMAHIKA I.
Okinawa Gushikawa
Urasoe Ginowan Heanna
Naha Shuri TSUKEN I.
Yonabaru KUDAKA I.
Itoman Azama
Tomori Gushikami
Kiyan Mabuni
KIYAN PT.

Statute Miles 0 5 10 15
Kilometers 0 10 20
128° E. ©RMCN

SAIPAN (N. MARIANA IS.)

PT. SABANETA
PIDOS KALAHO 820 FT.
I. MAÑAGAHA Tanapag San Roque
15°15' N.
Laguna Tanapag Government House
PT. MUCHOT Garapan OKSO TAKPOCHA 1529 FT.
SAIPAN
San Vincente
Lagunan Garapan San Jose
Chalan Kanoa PT. LAOLAO KATTAN
San Antonio
PT. AGINGAN
PT. TAHGONG SAIPAN INTL. AIRPORT
OPYAN
Bahia Laolao
PT. I NAFTAN

TINIAN (N. MARIANA IS.)

ET TINI 459 FT. PT. ASIGA
PT. LAMANIBOT SANHILO
LASSO 545 FT.
ATGIDON
PT. MASALOK
San Jose
Tinian Harbor
PT. KASTIYU
PT. CAROLINAS

Statute Miles 0 2 4 6
Kilometers 0 2 4 6 8 10
©RMCN

GUAM (U.S.A.)

RITIDIAN PT.
URUNO PT. PAJON PT.
MT. MACHANAO 604 FT. PATI PT.
TANGUISSON PT. ANDERSEN AIR FORCE BASE
AMANTES PT. ANAO PT.
MT. SANTA ROSA 827 FT.
Tamuning Dededo Yigo LUJUNA PT.
Tagua Bay Agana PAGAT PT.
ADELUP PT. Agana AGANA NAVAL AIR STATION Barrigada Taguan PT.
CABRAS I. Asan Toto FADIAN PT.
LUMUNA REEF Ordot Sinajana IATES PT.
Piti MT. ALUTOM 1,074 FT. Chalan
OROTE PEN. Yona PAGO POINT
NEYE I. Santa Rita Pago
Apra Harbor Agat Talofofo TARTUGUAN PT.
FACPI PT. MT. LAMLAM Feng Valley Res.
ASIGA PT. Inarajan
Umatac JALAIHAI PT.
Merizo Inarajan Bay
COCOS I.

Statute Miles 0 2 4 6 8
Kilometers 0 2 4 6 8 10
144°45' E. ©RMCN

IWO JIMA (JAPAN)

KATANO PT.
KANGOKU ROCK
HIRAIWA CAPE MOTO MTN. 358 FT.
OSAKA MTN. 324 FT. FURO MTN. 351 FT.
KAMA ROCK NIDAN ROCK 379 FT. TACHIIWA PT.
MT. SURIBACHI 545 FT. FUTATSUNE
TOBIISHI PT.

Statute Miles 0 1 2
Kilometers 0 1 2 3
141°20' E. ©RMCN

BIKINI (MARSHALL IS.)

NAMU I. YUROCHI ROMURIKKU I. AOMOEN I.
BOKOBYAADAA I. Bikini I.
BOKORORYURU I. OURUKAEN I.
ROCHIKARAI I.
CHIEERETE RUKOJI I. ENYU
ENIRIK REERE I.

Statute Miles 0 4 8
Kilometers 0 4 8 12
165°30' E. ©RMCN

PAGO PAGO / AMERICAN SAMOA

Leloaloa
Anua Atu'u
Pago Pago Aua
Fagatogo GOAT ISLAND
Utulei BREAKERS PT.
Faga'alu
Fatumafuti FATU ROCK

Mi. 0 0.5 1
Km. 0 1
170°40' W. ©RMCN

PONAPE (POHNPEI) (FED. STATES OF MICRO.)

Sokehs Passage
PAREMPEI
DEKE SOKEHS PONAPE INTL. AIRPORT
Kolonia DEHPEHK
PALIKER PT.
PONAPE (POHNPEI) (FED. STATES OF MICRO.)
DOLOHMWAR 2510 FT. TEMWEN

Statute Miles 0 2 4
Kilometers 0 2 4
158°10' E. ©RMCN

TRUK (FED. STATES OF MICRO.)

LAMOIL FALALU
ONAO NORTHEAST
QUOI MOR
TRUK INTL. AIRPORT MOEN
ROMUNUM (OF MICRO.) PAREM
TOL UDOT FEFAN
FAICHUK TOTIU FITTEN UMAN
SIIS
FANAN GIVRY
MESEGGON HACO
KUOP
SOUTH I.

Mi. 0 5 10
Km. 0 5 10 15
151°45' E. ©RMCN

PALAU (BELAU) (T.T.P.I.)

NGARUANGL REEF
KAYANGEL IS.
KOSSOL REEF
CORMORAN REEF
Ollei
Ngermechau BABELTHUAP I.
Ngetbong Melekeok
Ngerkeel BABELTHUAP AIRPORT
NGEREKEBESANG Koror Oikull
PELELIU Koror
NGEMELIS IS. EIL MALK
ANGAUR Ngaramasch

Mi. 0 10 20
Km. 0 20 40
134°30' E. ©RMCN

TARAWA (KIRIBATI)

Buariki
Tearinibai
Nuatabu
Notoue
Marenanuka Nabeina
Tabiteuea
BIKEMAN I. Eita Bonriki
BETIO Bairiki EITA Bikenibeu
Bairiki BONRIKI

Statute Miles 0 2 4 6
Kilometers 0 4 8
173° E. ©RMCN

KWAJALEIN (MARSHALL IS.)

EBADON I. ORESA I.
ROI I. BIGGERANN I.
ONIOTTO I. NAMUR I.
BIGI I. EDGIGEN I.
TABIK I. GAGAN I.
BOGGERIK I. SELLMAN
NELL I. GELLINAM
YABBENOHR I. OMELEK MECK
ONEMAK
ELLER I. BIGEJ I.
GUGEGWE I.
ENNYLABEGAN I. Ebeye
KWAJALEIN I.

Statute Miles 0 10 20 30
Kilometers 0 20 40
162° E. ©RMCN

ENEWETAK (MARSHALL IS.)

TEITEIRIPUCCHI BOGON
BOGALLUA RUCHI ENGEBI
KIRINIAN RUJIYORU
BIZIRI
WEST SPIT AOMON PIIRAI
RUNIT I.
RIGILI
GRINEM
LIBIRON MUI
BOGAN IGURIN PARRY I.
MUTI
ENEWETAK I.

Statute Miles 0 2 4 6
Kilometers 0 4 8
162°16' E. ©RMCN

WESTERN SAMOA

C. MULINU'U Asau Bay Safune Bay
Sataua Safune Fagamalo
Falelima
Samataiuta MT. SILISILI 6096 FT. SAVAI'I Pu'apu'a
Sala'ilua Tuasivi
Satupa'itea Palauli Iva
C. ASUISUI Sala'ilua Bay PT. TUASIVI
Pisanga Point Apolima Strait UPOLU
C. PAEPAEOLE'A FALEOLO INTL. AIRPORT
APOLIMA I. Leulumoega Apia
Manono Apolima Tuutuo I. UPOLU
C. FATUOSOFIA Lotofaga Salani
Matautu Falefa Hbr.
C. MULITAPUILI Fagaloa Bay
Matatula C. OLIONONO
C. NUUTOI Poutasi
NU'UTELE I.
C. TAPAGA

Statute Miles 0 10 20 30 40
Kilometers 0 10 20 30 40 50 60
172° W. ©RMCN

AMERICAN SAMOA

TUTUILA
Pago Pago TAPUTAPU TAFUNA INTL. AIRPORT C. MATATULA
AUNU'U I.
Leone STEPS PT.
Leone Bay

171° W.

FIJI

Round Island Passage
GREAT SEA REEF
UDU PT. QUELELEVU
KIA
MALI
Nabekavu Naduri Labasa RABI RINGGOLD ISLES
YASAWA GROUP YASAWA SLEEPY PT. VANUA LEVU KIOA NANUKU REEF
NACULA YADUA Bua LAUCALA WAILAGI LALA DUFF REEF
YAQETA Nabouwalu SOMOSOMO QAMEA
VIWA WAYA Somosomo Bay TAVEUNI VANUA BALAVU
NAVITI KORO YACATA KANACEA MAGO
NACILAU PT. Nanukuloa BUA Bay MAKOGAI VATU VARA
Nailaga TAILEVU PT. WAKAYA CICIA TUVUCA
Lautoka TOMANIVI 4,341 FT. Levuka OVALAU MOTURIKI NAIRAI NAYAU I. LAU
VUDA PT. Vunidawa Ovalau GROUP
MALOLO Nadi MONAVATU 3709 FT. GAU
UVERITE PT. Momi Suva LEKEBA
Sigatoka AIWA VANUA VATU
Thuvu Naitonitoni MOALA I. ONEATA
18° S. Bega Passage BEQA NAVATU MOCE
VATULELE VUAQAVA KABARA
DRAVUNI FULAGA
BULIYA
KADAVU ONO MATUKU I. TOTOYA I. YAGASA CLUSTER ONGEA LEVU
C. WASHINGTON
Galoa Harbour

Statute Miles 0 25 50
Kilometers 0 25 50 75
178° E. ©RMCN

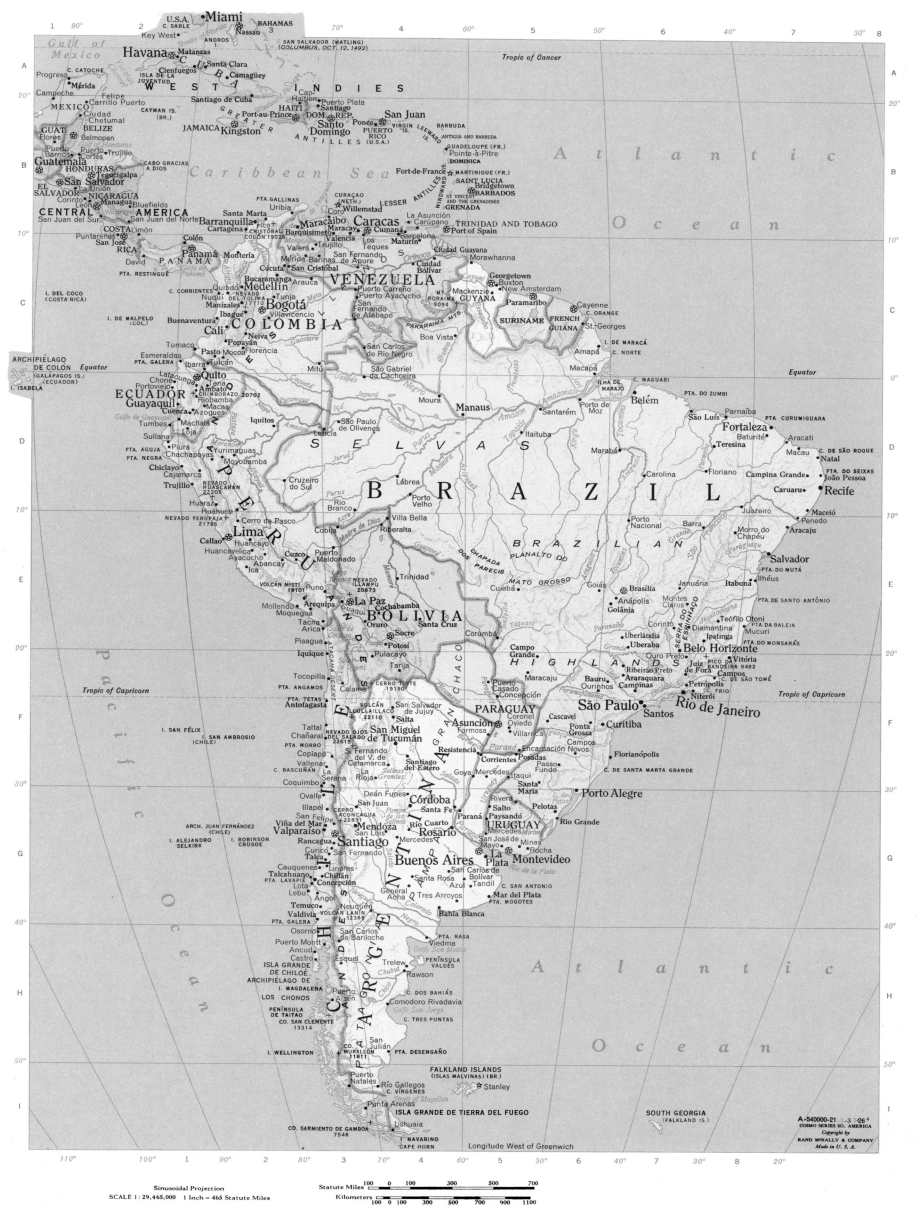

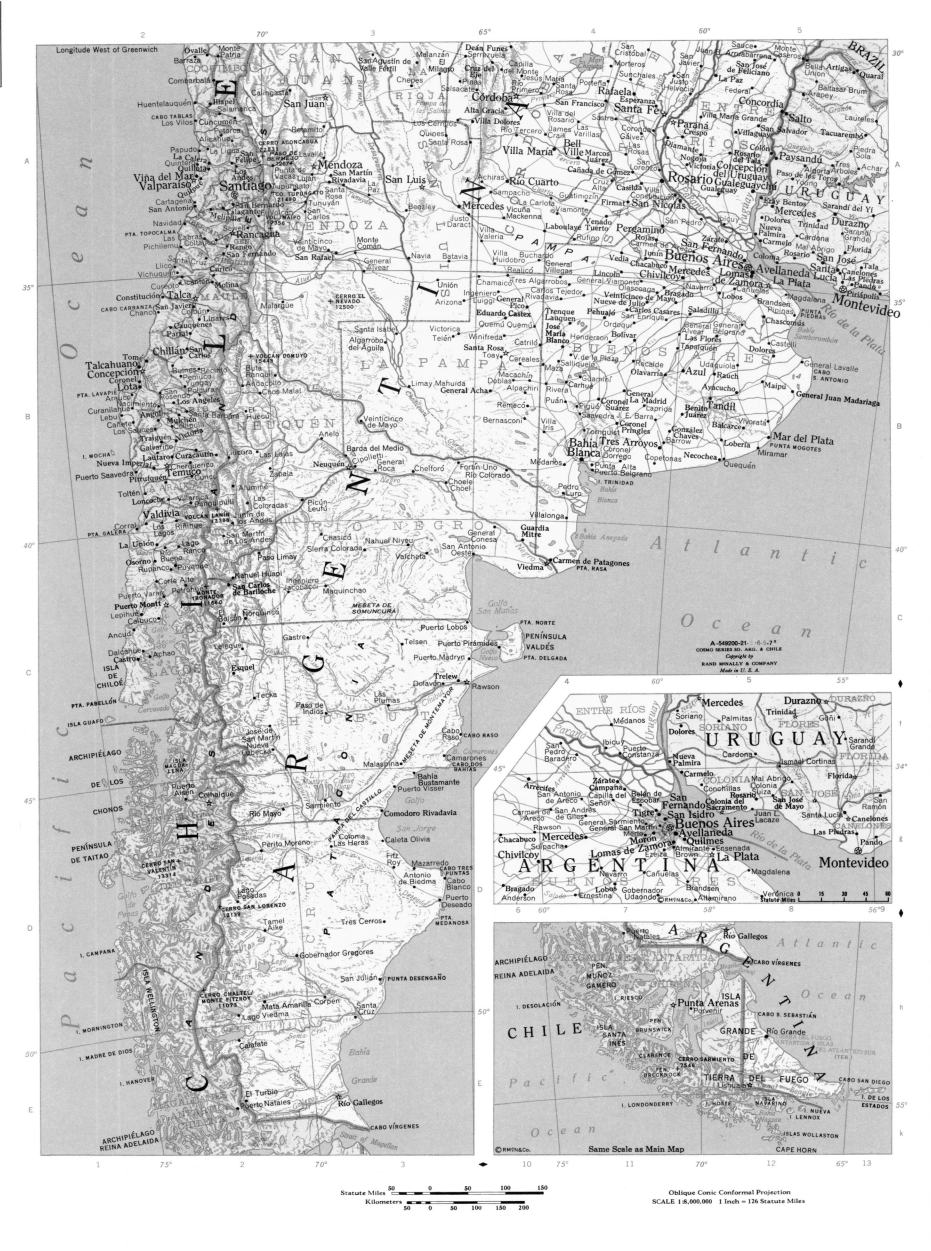

Longitude West of Greenwich

Pacific Ocean

Atlantic Ocean

A-549200-21-'-6-5-7⁸
COSMO SERIES SO. ARG. & CHILE
Copyright by
RAND MCNALLY & COMPANY
Made in U.S.A.

URUGUAY

ARGENTINA

Montevideo

4   60°   7   58°   8   56°9
Statute Miles

CHILE

TIERRA DEL FUEGO

Same Scale as Main Map

CAPE HORN

Statute Miles 50 0 50 100 150
Kilometers 50 0 50 100 150 200

Oblique Conic Conformal Projection
SCALE 1:8,000,000   1 Inch = 126 Statute Miles

54

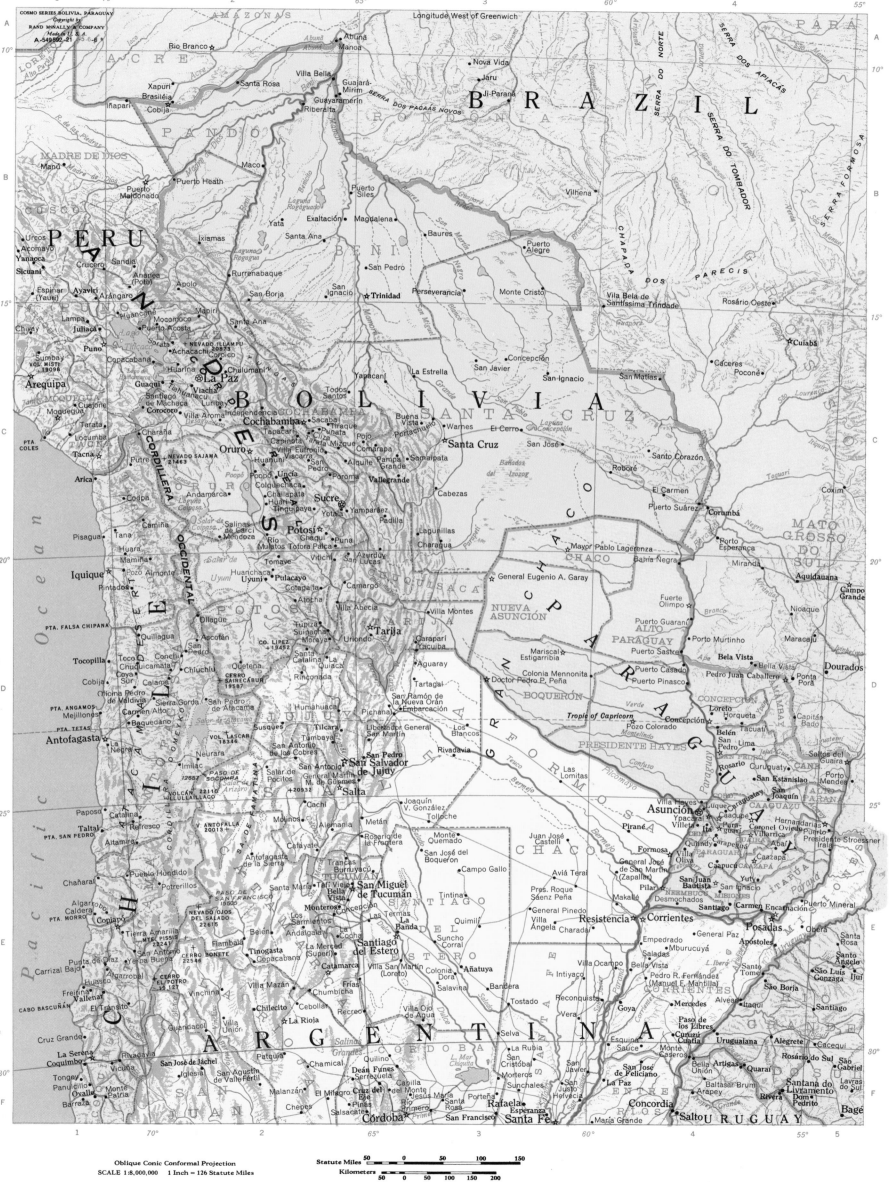

Oblique Conic Conformal Projection
SCALE 1:8,000,000   1 Inch = 126 Statute Miles

Statute Miles
50   0   50   100   150

Kilometers
50   0   50   100   150   200

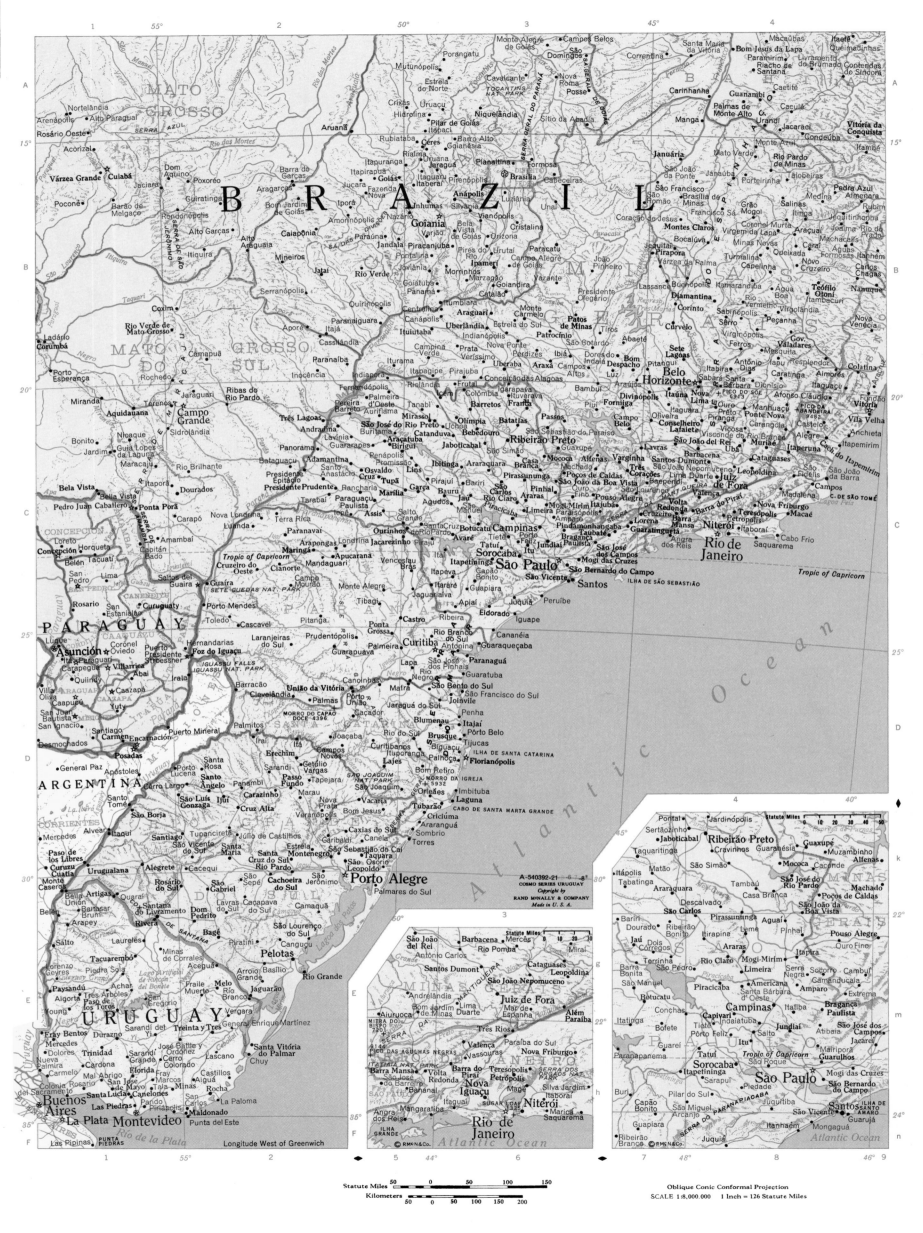

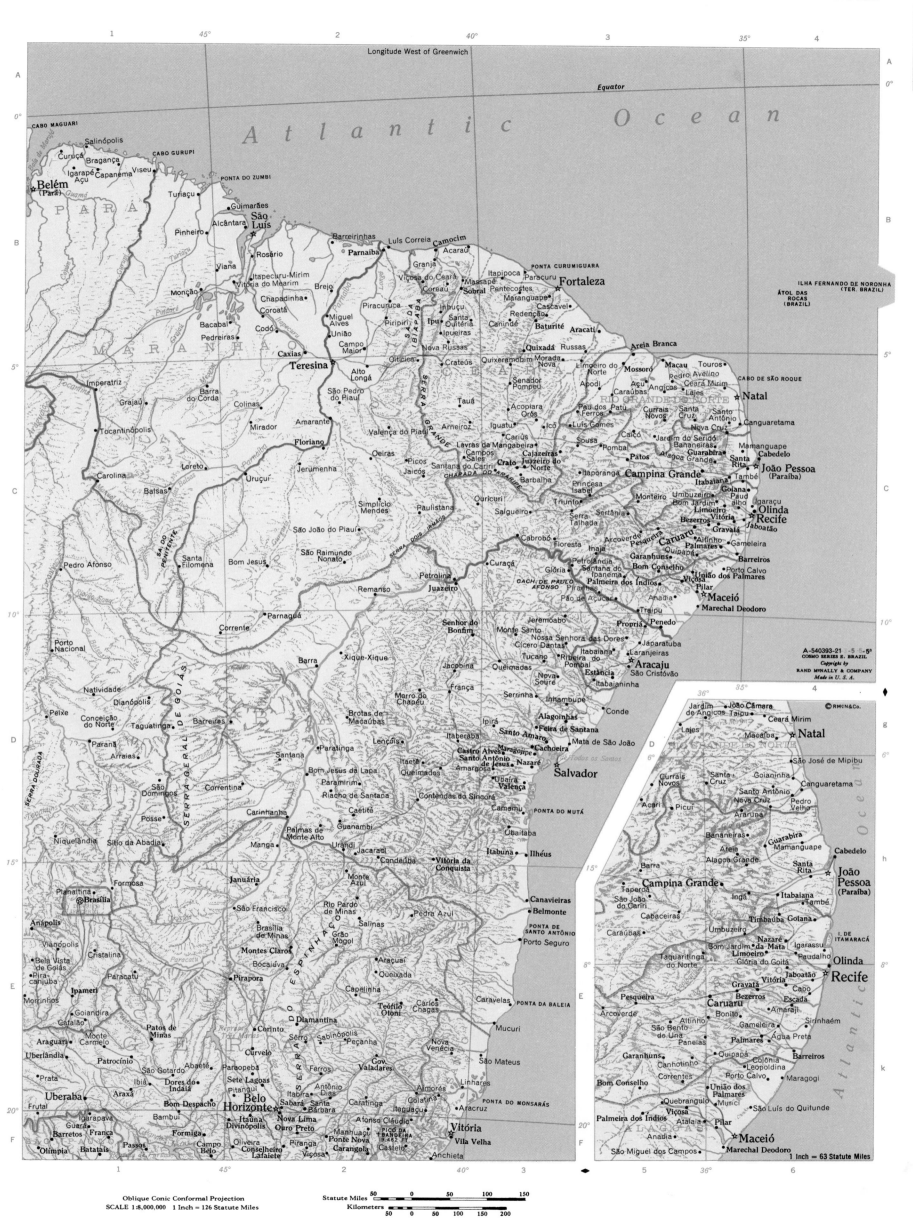

Longitude West of Greenwich

Equator

A t l a n t i c   O c e a n

CABO MAGUARI

Belém
(Pará)

PARÁ

MARANHÃO

São Luís

Teresina

Fortaleza

ILHA FERNANDO DE NORONHA
(TER. BRAZIL)
ÁTOL DAS ROCAS
(BRAZIL)

CABO DE SÃO ROQUE

Natal

RIO GRANDE DO NORTE

João Pessoa
(Paraíba)

Campina Grande

Olinda
Recife

Caruaru

Maceió
Marechal Deodoro

Aracaju
São Cristóvão

Salvador

Brasília

Belo Horizonte

Vitória
Vila Velha

PICO DA BANDEIRA
9,462 FT

PONTA DO MONSARÁS

SERRA GERAL DE GOIAS

SERRA DO ESPINHAÇO

MINAS GERAIS

Natal

João Pessoa
(Paraíba)

Campina Grande

Olinda
Recife

Caruaru

Maceió
Marechal Deodoro

I. DE ITAMARACÁ

A t l a n t i c   O c e a n

1 Inch = 63 Statute Miles

Oblique Conic Conformal Projection
SCALE 1:8,000,000   1 Inch = 126 Statute Miles

Statute Miles
50   0   50   100   150

Kilometers
50   0   50   100   150   200

A-540393-21   -5-5-5ª
COSMO SERIES E. BRAZIL
Copyright by
RAND McNALLY & COMPANY
Made in U.S.A.

57

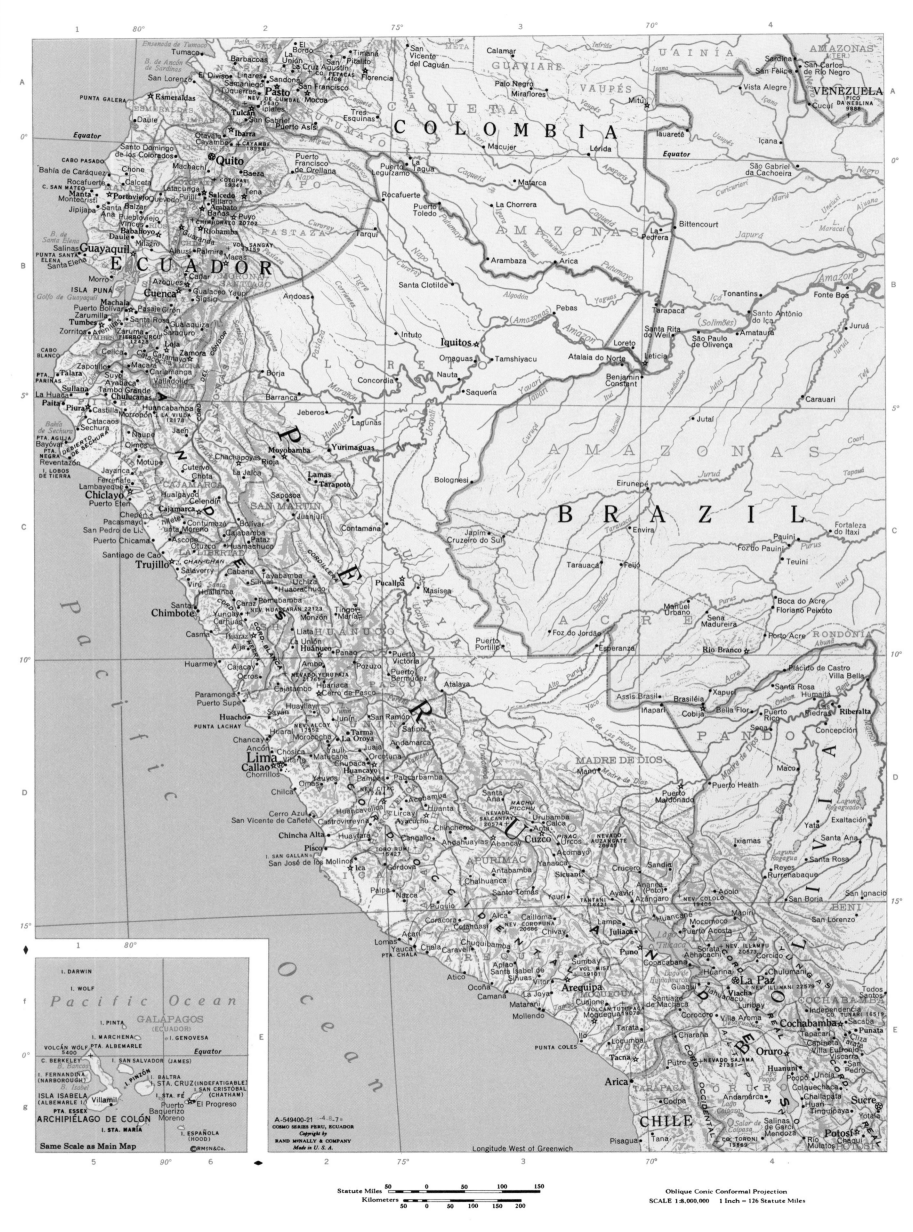

A-549400-21   4-8-7°
COSMO SERIES PERU, ECUADOR
Copyright by
RAND McNALLY & COMPANY
Made in U.S.A.

Longitude West of Greenwich

Oblique Conic Conformal Projection
SCALE 1:8,000,000   1 Inch = 126 Statute Miles

Statute Miles   50   0   50   100   150
Kilometers   50   0   50   100   150   200

Pacific Ocean

ISLA PUNÁ
Golfo de Guayaquil

GALÁPAGOS
(ECUADOR)
I. DARWIN
I. WOLF
I. PINTA
I. MARCHENA
I. GENOVESA
VOLCÁN WOLF 5400
PTA. ALBEMARLE
C. BERKELEY
I. SAN SALVADOR (JAMES)
I. FERNANDINA (NARBOROUGH)
B. Isabel
BALTRA
STA. CRUZ (INDEFATIGABLE)
I. SAN CRISTÓBAL (CHATHAM)
I. PINZÓN
I. SANTA FÉ
I. ISABELA (ALBEMARLE)
Villamil
Puerto Baquerizo Moreno
El Progreso
PTA. ESSEX
ARCHIPIÉLAGO DE COLÓN
I. SANTA MARÍA
I. ESPAÑOLA (HOOD)

Same Scale as Main Map
©RMcN&Co.

COLOMBIA

ECUADOR

VENEZUELA
PICO DA NEBLINA 9888

BRAZIL

AMAZONAS

ACRE

RONDÔNIA

PERU

BOLIVIA

CHILE

Equator

Quito
Guayaquil
Cuenca
Iquitos
Lima
Callao
Cuzco
Arequipa
Trujillo
Chiclayo
Chimbote
La Paz
Cochabamba
Oruro
Sucre
Potosí

58

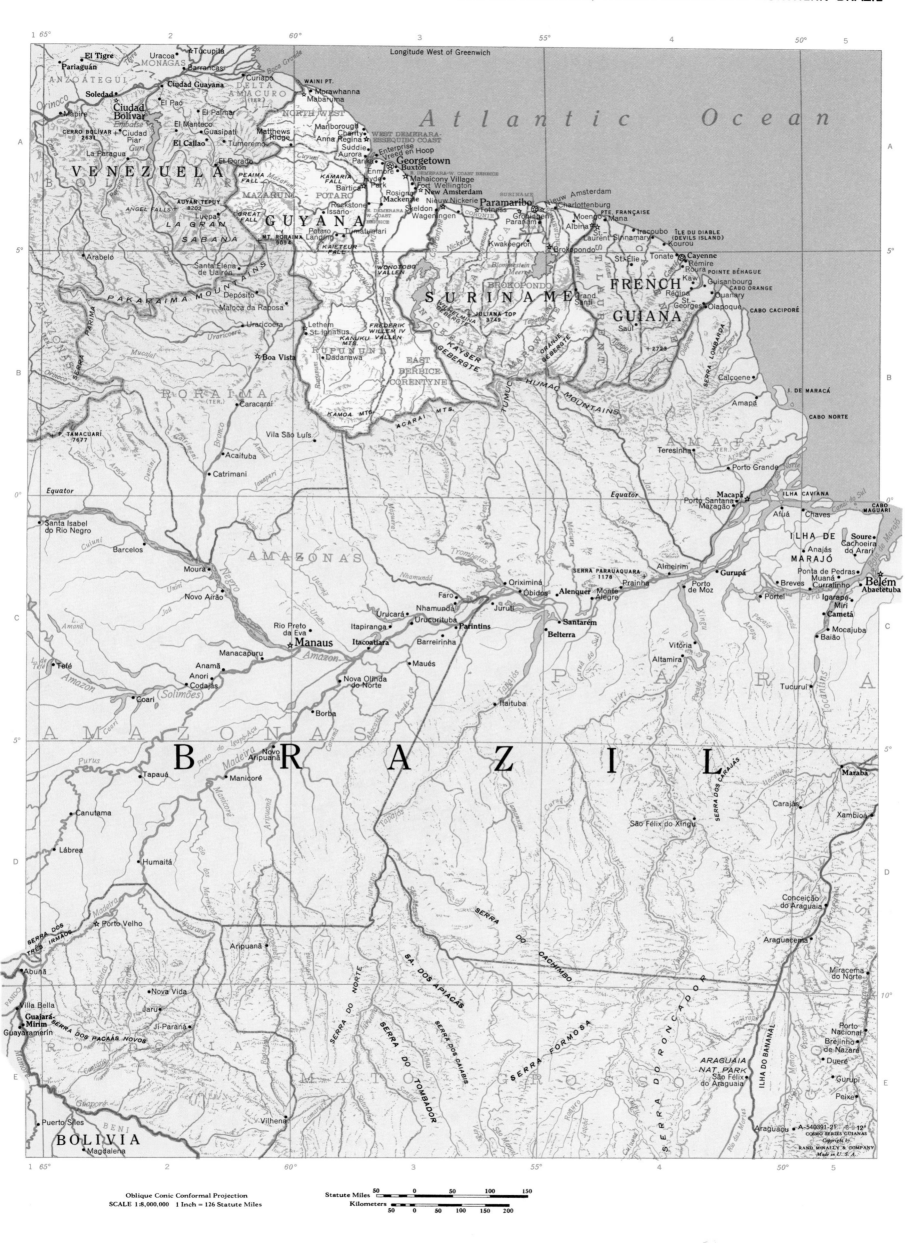

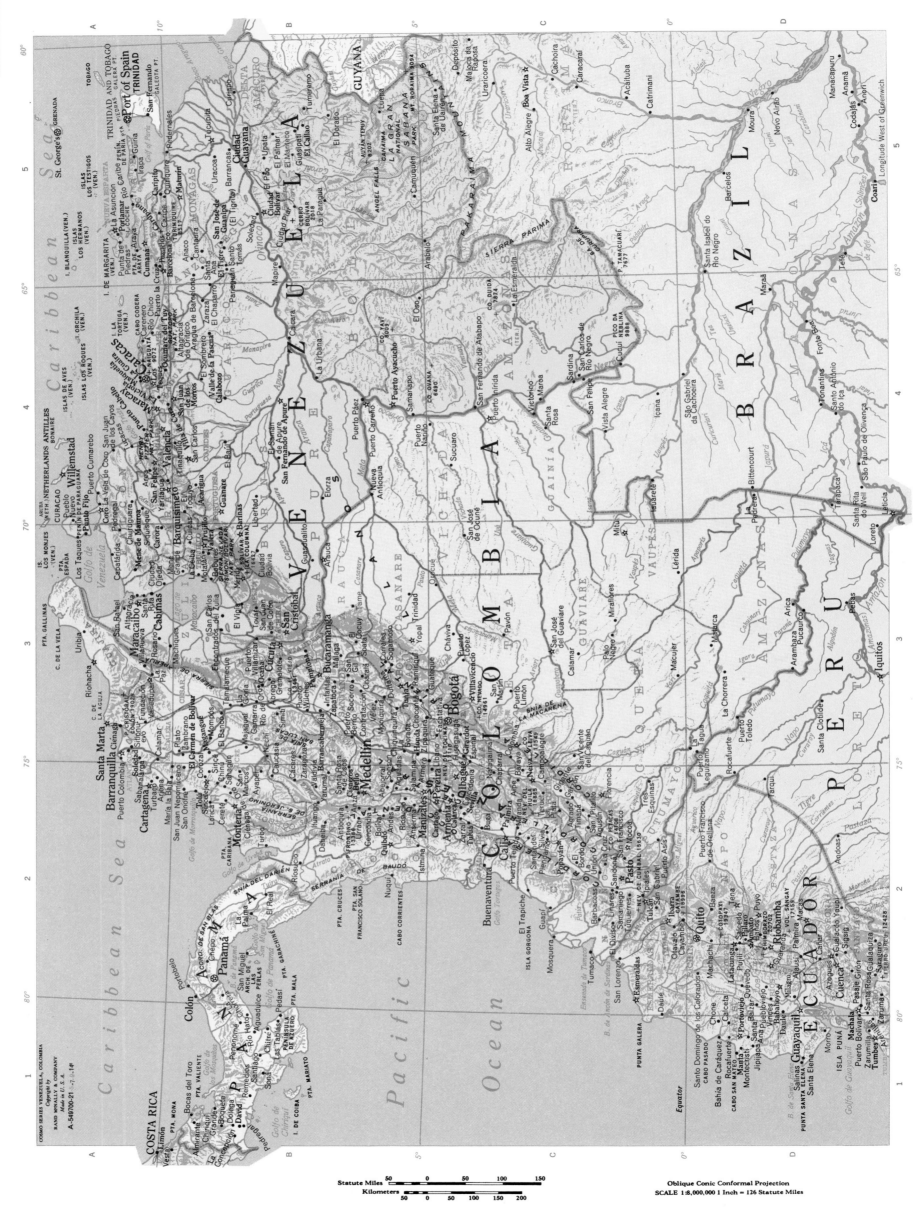

COLOMBIA AND VENEZUELA

Statute Miles
50   0   50   100   150

Kilometers
50   0   50   100   150   200

Oblique Conic Conformal Projection
SCALE 1:8,000,000 1 Inch = 126 Statute Miles

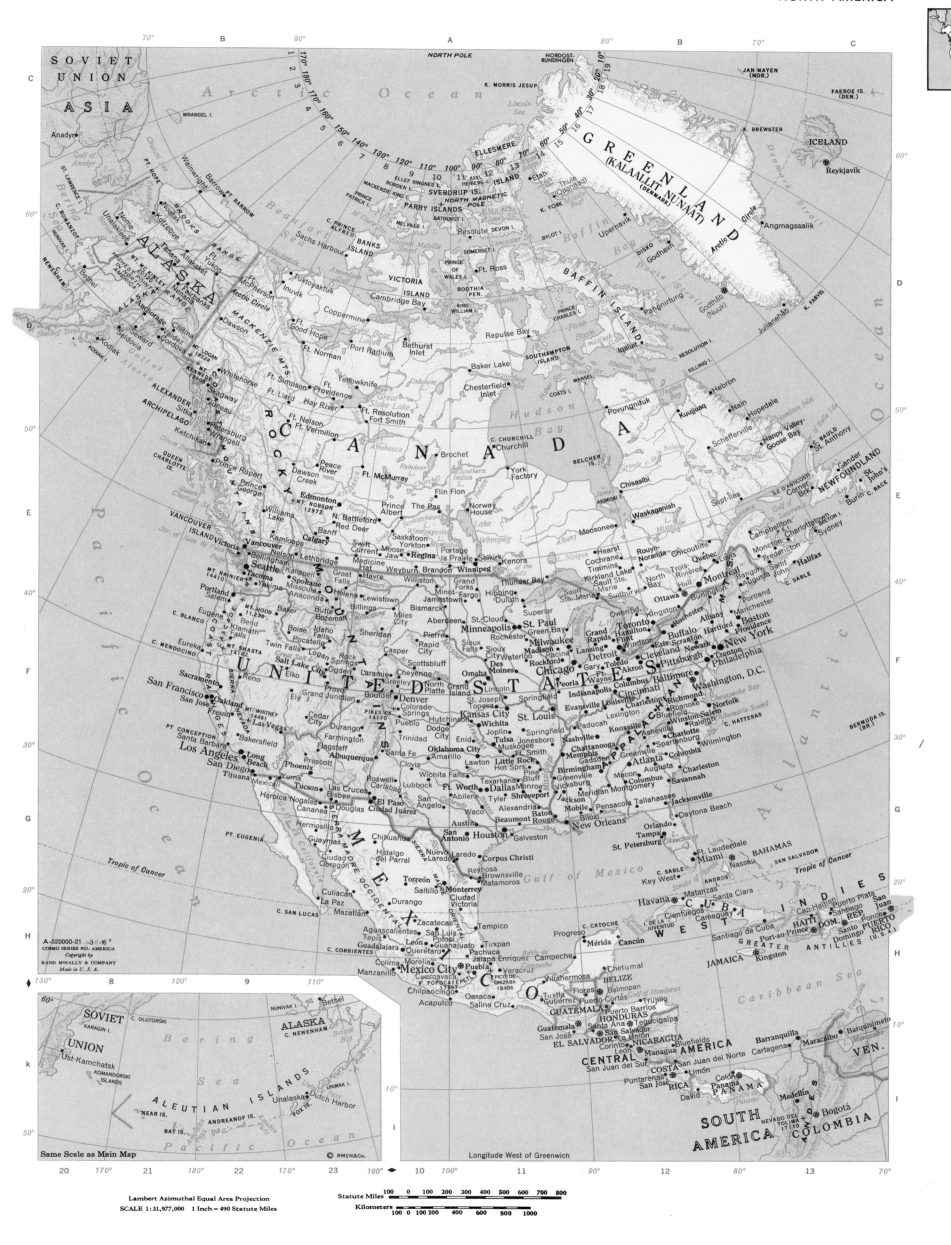

SOVIET UNION

ASIA

Arctic Ocean

NORTH POLE

NORDOST-RUNDINGEN

JAN MAYEN (NOR.)

FAEROE IS. (DEN.)

K. MORRIS JESUP

G R E E N L A N D
(KALAALLIT NUNAAT)
(DENMARK)

ICELAND

Reykjavik

Angmagssalik

ELLESMERE

BAFFIN ISLAND

Baffin Bay

A L A S K A

BROOKS RANGE

MACKENZIE MTS

C A N A D A

R O C K Y   M O U N T A I N S

Hudson Bay

NEWFOUNDLAND

ALEXANDER ARCHIPELAGO

QUEEN CHARLOTTE IS.

VANCOUVER ISLAND

Great Bear Lake

Great Slave Lake

U N I T E D   S T A T E S

Seattle
Portland
San Francisco
Los Angeles
San Diego

Denver
Chicago
Minneapolis
St. Paul

New York
Boston
Washington, D.C.

Pacific Ocean

Atlantic Ocean

Gulf of Mexico

M E X I C O

Mexico City

Tropic of Cancer

C U B A

W E S T   I N D I E S

JAMAICA

HAITI
DOM. REP.
PUERTO RICO (U.S.A.)

GREATER ANTILLES

Caribbean Sea

C E N T R A L   A M E R I C A

GUATEMALA
BELIZE
HONDURAS
EL SALVADOR
NICARAGUA
COSTA RICA
PANAMA

S O U T H   A M E R I C A

COLOMBIA

VEN.

SOVIET UNION

ALASKA

ALEUTIAN ISLANDS

Bering Sea

Pacific Ocean

Same Scale as Main Map

Longitude West of Greenwich

Lambert Azimuthal Equal Area Projection
SCALE 1:31,977,000   1 Inch = 490 Statute Miles

Statute Miles

Kilometers

61

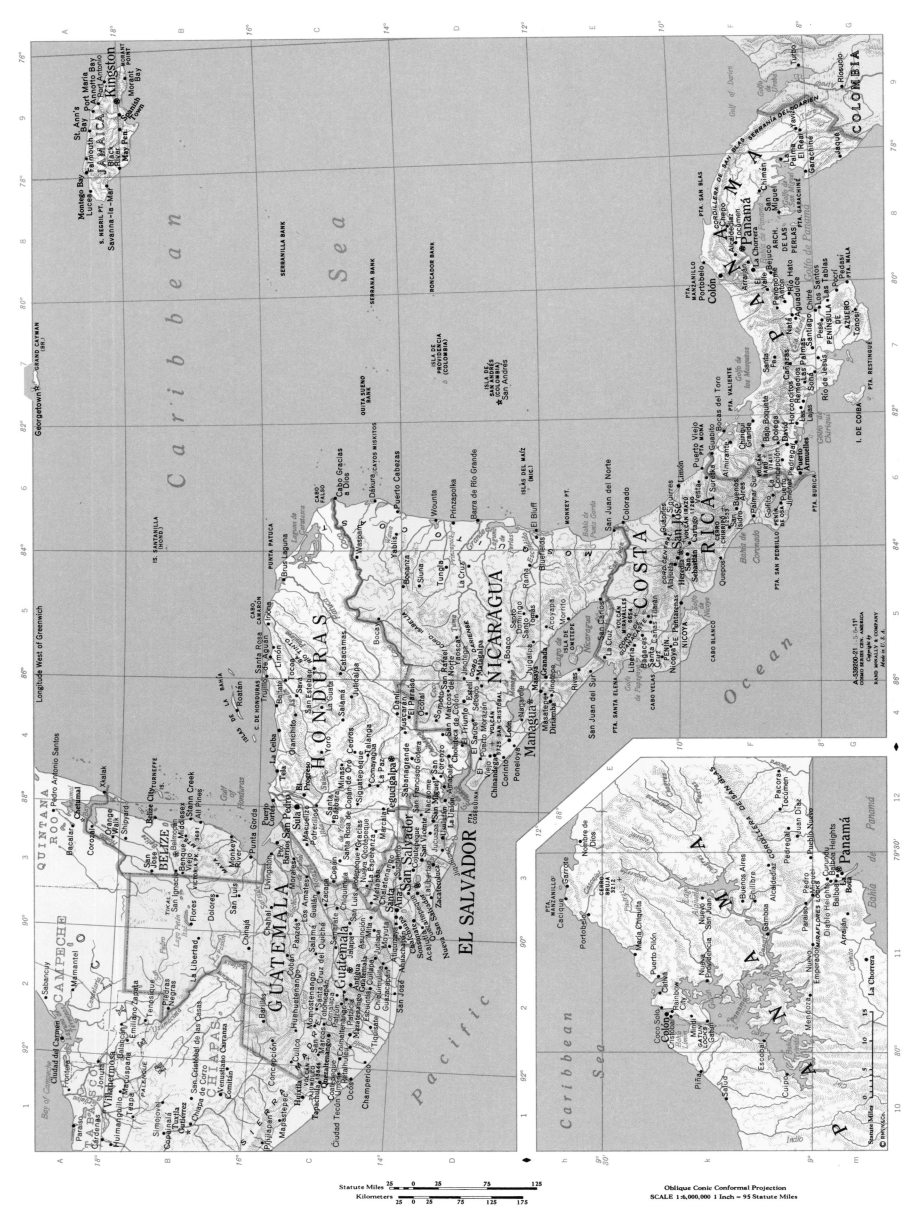

Statute Miles 25 0 25 75 125

Kilometers 25 0 25 75 125 175

Oblique Conic Conformal Projection
SCALE 1:6,000,000 1 Inch = 95 Statute Miles

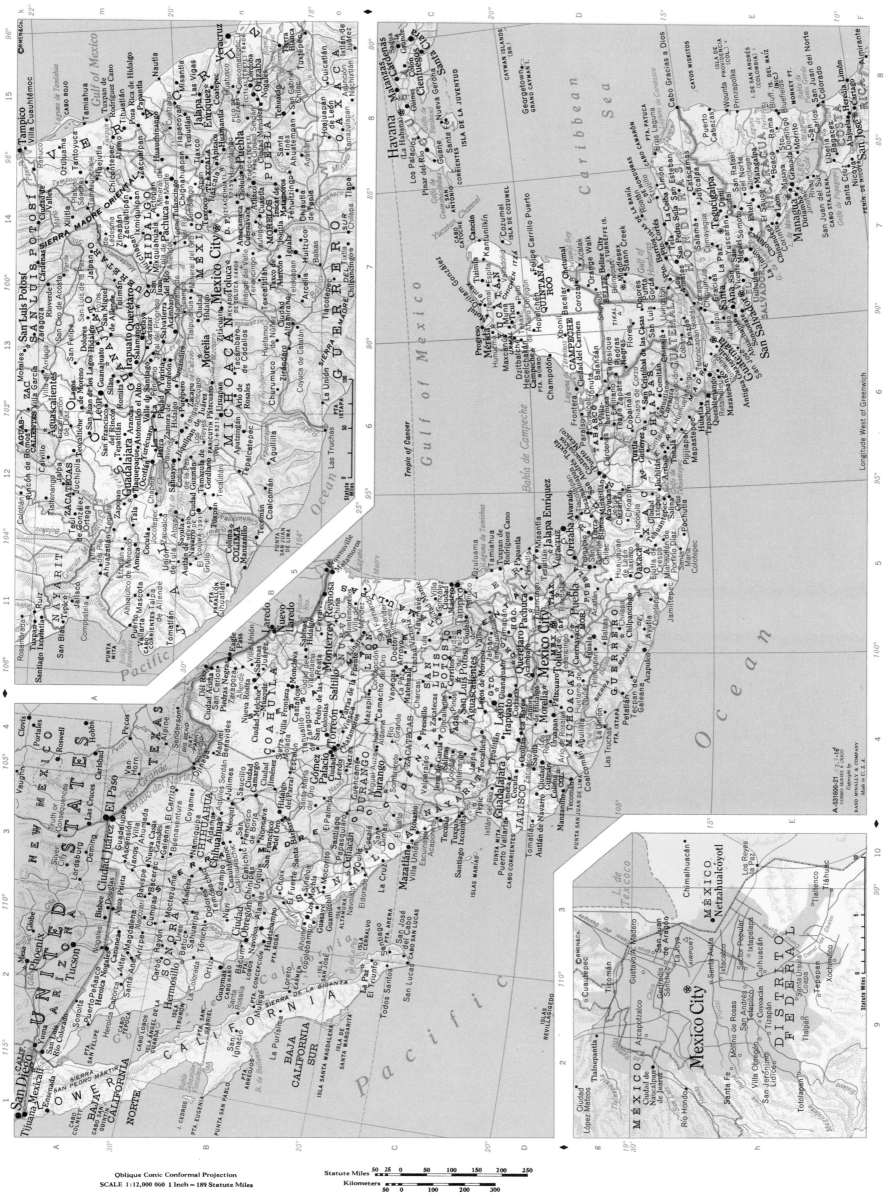

Oblique Conic Conformal Projection
SCALE 1:12,000,000 1 Inch = 189 Statute Miles

Statute Miles 50 25 0 50 100 150 200 250

Kilometers
50 0 100 200 300

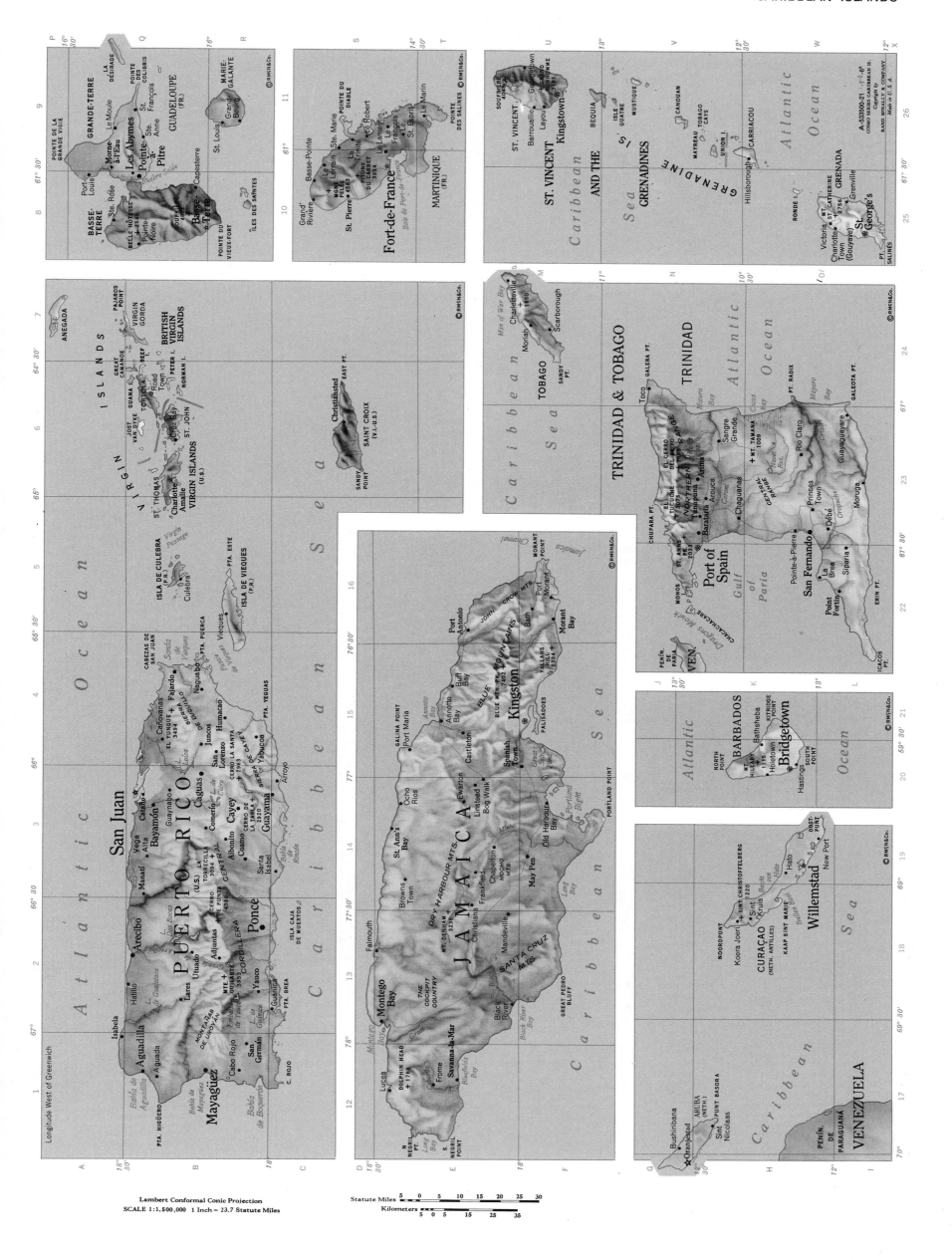

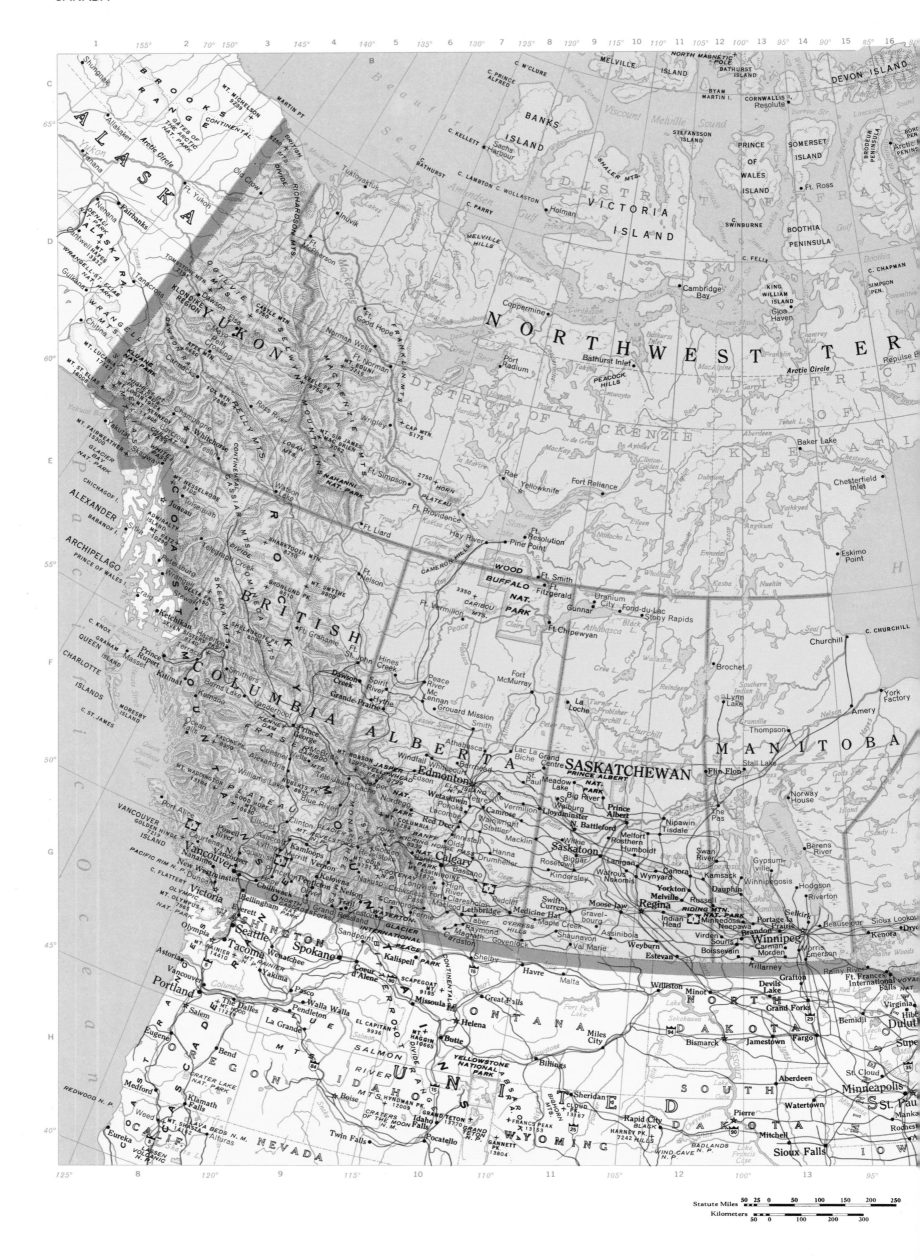

GREENLAND (DENMARK)

QUEEN ELIZABETH ISLANDS

CAPE STALLWORTHY

AXEL HEIBERG ISLAND

SVERDRUP IS.

ELLEF RINGNES ISLAND AMUND RINGNES ISLAND

BORDEN ISLAND

BROCK I.

MACKENZIE KING ISLAND

LOUGHEED I.

CORNWALL GRAHAM

PRINCE PATRICK ISLAND

CAMERON I.

EGLINTON I.

Mould Bay

PARRY ISLANDS

NORTH MAGNETIC POLE

GRINNELL PEN.

BATHURST ISLAND

MELVILLE ISLAND

BYAM MARTIN I.

CORNWALLIS ISLAND

Resolute

BANKS ISLAND

DEVON ISLAND

STEFANSSON ISLAND

PRINCE OF WALES ISLAND

SOMERSET ISLAND

BAFFIN ISLAND

VICTORIA ISLAND

Grise Fiord

COBURG I.

BRODEUR PEN.

BORDEN PEN.

BYLOT ISLAND

Eureka

C. COLUMBIA

BARBEAU PK. 8544

Alert

ELLESMERE ISLAND

GREENLAND (DENMARK)

Same Scale as Main Map ©RM℅N&Co.

ITORIES

BAFFIN ISLAND

C. WALTER BATHURST

C. MacCULLOCH

C. HUNTER

Pond Inlet

Clyde

C. HENRY KATER

AUYUITTUQ NATIONAL PARK

Arctic Circle

Godhavn

DISKO

GREENLAND (DENMARK)

NORTH SPICER I.

SOUTH SPICER I.

PRINCE CHARLES ISLAND

AIR FORCE ISLAND

FOLEY I.

CUMBERLAND PENINSULA

C. WALSINGHAM

C. PENRHYN

C. DOMINION

C. MERCY

C. DORCHESTER

C. QUEEN PENINSULA

Cape Dorset

HALL PENINSULA

META INCOGNITA PENINSULA

Iqaluit

Lake Harbour

FOXE PENINSULA

SALISBURY ISLAND

BIG I.

C. DE NOUVELLE-FRANCE

RESOLUTION ISLAND

NOTTINGHAM ISLAND

Ivujivik

Kangiqsujuaq

C. HOPES ADVANCE

AKPATOK ISLAND

C. CHIDLEY

COATS ISLAND

Kangirsuk

MANSEL ISLAND

Povungnituk

Kuujjuaq

Hebron

NEWFOUNDLAND

C. BAULD

St. Anthony

Nain

Hopedale

Rigolet

Cartwright

Battle Harbour

Happy Valley Goose Bay

Twillingate

C. FREELS

TERRA NOVA NAT. PARK

Gander

Grand Falls

Bishop's Falls

Botwood

Carbonear

Bonavista

Wabana

St. John's

Trepassey

C. RACE

Schefferville

GROS MORNE NAT. PARK

GROS MORNE RANGE MTS. 2644

Deer Lake

Corner Brook

Stephenville

St. George's

NEWFOUNDLAND

Grand Bank

Harbour Grace

Bay Roberts

Burin

Channel-Port aux Basques

ST. PIERRE AND MIQUELON (FR.)

Inukjuak

QUEBEC

Labrador City

Gagnon

Mingan Natashquan

ILE D'ANTICOSTI

Clarke City

Sept-Îles (Seven Islands)

Port-Cartier

CAP GASPÉ

PARC NAT. DE FORILLON

Gaspé

New Carlisle

Chandler

ÎLES DE LA MADELEINE (QUEBEC)

Matane

Mont-Joli

Campbellton

CAPE BRETON ISLAND

HIGHLANDS NAT. PARK

CAPE BRETON

Sydney Mines

North Sydney

Glace Bay

Louisbourg

New Waterford

ONTARIO

Fort Severn

C. HENRIETTA MARIA

PTE. LOUIS-XIV

Fort Albany

Moosonee

Moose Factory

AKIMISKI ISLAND

Eastmain

Waskaganish

Chisasibi

James Bay

Chibougamau

Dolbeau

St. Félicien

Roberval

Chambord

Alma

Jonquière

La Malbaie

La Baie

St. Paul

Baie-St-Paul

Tadoussac

Les Escoumins

Rimouski

Mont-Joli

Rivière-du-Loup

Edmundston

NEW BRUNSWICK

Bathurst

Caraquet

Newcastle

Chatham

Fredericton

Moncton

Sackville

Amherst

Springhill

Truro

New Glasgow

Stellarton

Port Hawkesbury

Canso

SABLE ISLAND

NOVA SCOTIA

Halifax

Dartmouth

Lunenburg

Bridgewater

Liverpool

KEJIMKUJIK NAT. PARK

Shelburne

Yarmouth

C. SABLE

Armstrong Station

Nakina

Longlac

Geraldton

Beardmore

Terrace Bay

Marathon

Nipigon

Schreiber

Thunder Bay

ISLE ROYALE NAT. PARK

PUKASKWA NAT. PARK

Wawa

Chapleau

Hearst

Kapuskasing

Cochrane

Iroquois Falls

Ansonville

Timmins

Kirkland Lake

New Liskeard

Cobalt

Englehart

La Sarre

Amos

Val-d'Or

Rouyn-Noranda

Malartic

Senneterre

Parent

RÉS. GOUIN

PARC DE LA VÉRENDRYE

RÉS. CABONGA

La Tuque

Shawinigan

Grand-Mère

Trois-Rivières

PARC NAT. DE LA MAURICIE

Joliette

North Bay

Mattawa

Sturgeon Falls

Sudbury

Espanola

Blind River

Thessalon

Sault Ste. Marie

MANITOULIN ISLAND

Little Current

Parry Sound

Huntsville

Bracebridge

Gravenhurst

Pembroke

Renfrew

Arnprior

Smiths Falls

Brockville

Ottawa

Hull

Maniwaki

Mont-Laurier

Ste-Agathe

St-Jérôme

Montreal

Sorel

Drummondville

Victoriaville

Granby

St-Jean

St-Hyacinthe

Valleyfield

Quebec

Lévis

Lac-Mégantic

Thetford Mines

Sherbrooke

Magog

Windsor

MAINE

Augusta

Bangor

VT.

Montpelier

N.H.

Concord

Manchester

WHITE MTS.

MT. WASHINGTON 6288

GREEN MTS.

ADIRONDACK MTS.

Portland

MASS.

Boston

C. COD

Providence

CONN.

Hartford

New Haven

Springfield

Worcester

NEW YORK

Watertown

Kingston

Utica

Syracuse

Rochester

Buffalo

Binghamton

Albany

Schenectady

Newburgh

New York

Newark

LONG ISLAND

PENNSYLVANIA

Scranton

Williamsport

Harrisburg

Philadelphia

Trenton

N.J.

WISCONSIN

La Crosse

Madison

Oshkosh

Sheboygan

Milwaukee

Racine

Green Bay

Manistee

Oshkosh

MICHIGAN

Ironwood

Marquette

Escanaba

Sault Ste. Marie

Cheboygan

Alpena

Traverse City

Saginaw

Muskegon

Grand Rapids

Lansing

Flint

Detroit

Windsor

Kalamazoo

ILL.

Chicago

Gary

IND.

OHIO

Toledo

Cleveland

Youngstown

Lake Michigan

Lake Huron

Lake Superior

Lake Erie

Lake Ontario

Keweenaw

Hancock

ONTARIO

Owen Sound

Wiarton

Kincardine

Wingham

Goderich

Toronto

Brampton

Hamilton

Brantford

Woodstock

London

St. Thomas

Chatham

Leamington

Port Huron

Sarnia

Simcoe

Barrie

Orillia

Midland

Collingwood

Lindsay

Peterborough

Cobourg

Oshawa

Whitby

Trenton

Belleville

Niagara Falls

Port Hope

Rhinelander

Winona

Atlantic Ocean

Gulf of St. Lawrence

St. Lawrence

Hudson Bay

Ungava Bay

Hudson Strait

Davis Strait

Baffin Bay

Arctic Ocean

A-52020072 7-8-8 12°

COSMO SERIES CANADA

Copyright by

RAND M℅NALLY & COMPANY

Made in U.S.A.

Longitude West of Greenwich

Lambert Conformal Conic Projection

SCALE 1:12,000,000   1 Inch = 189 Statute Miles

67

Oblique Cylindrical Projection
SCALE 1:4,255,000 1 Inch = 67 Statute Miles

Statute Miles 10 0 10 20 30 40 50 60 70 80 90 100

Kilometers
10 0 10 20   40   60   80   100   120   140

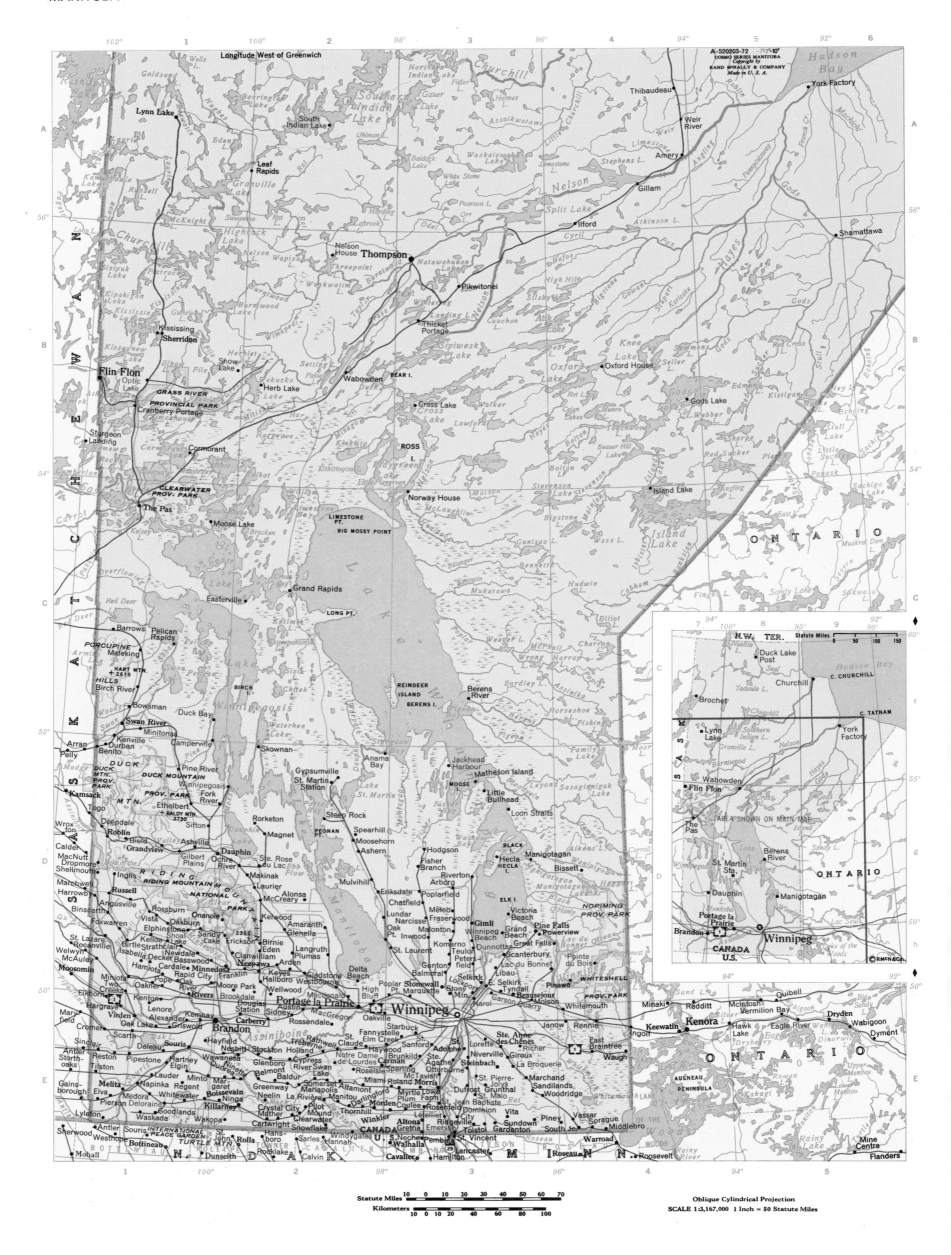

Oblique Cylindrical Projection
SCALE 1:3,167,000 1 Inch = 50 Statute Miles

Statute Miles
Kilometers

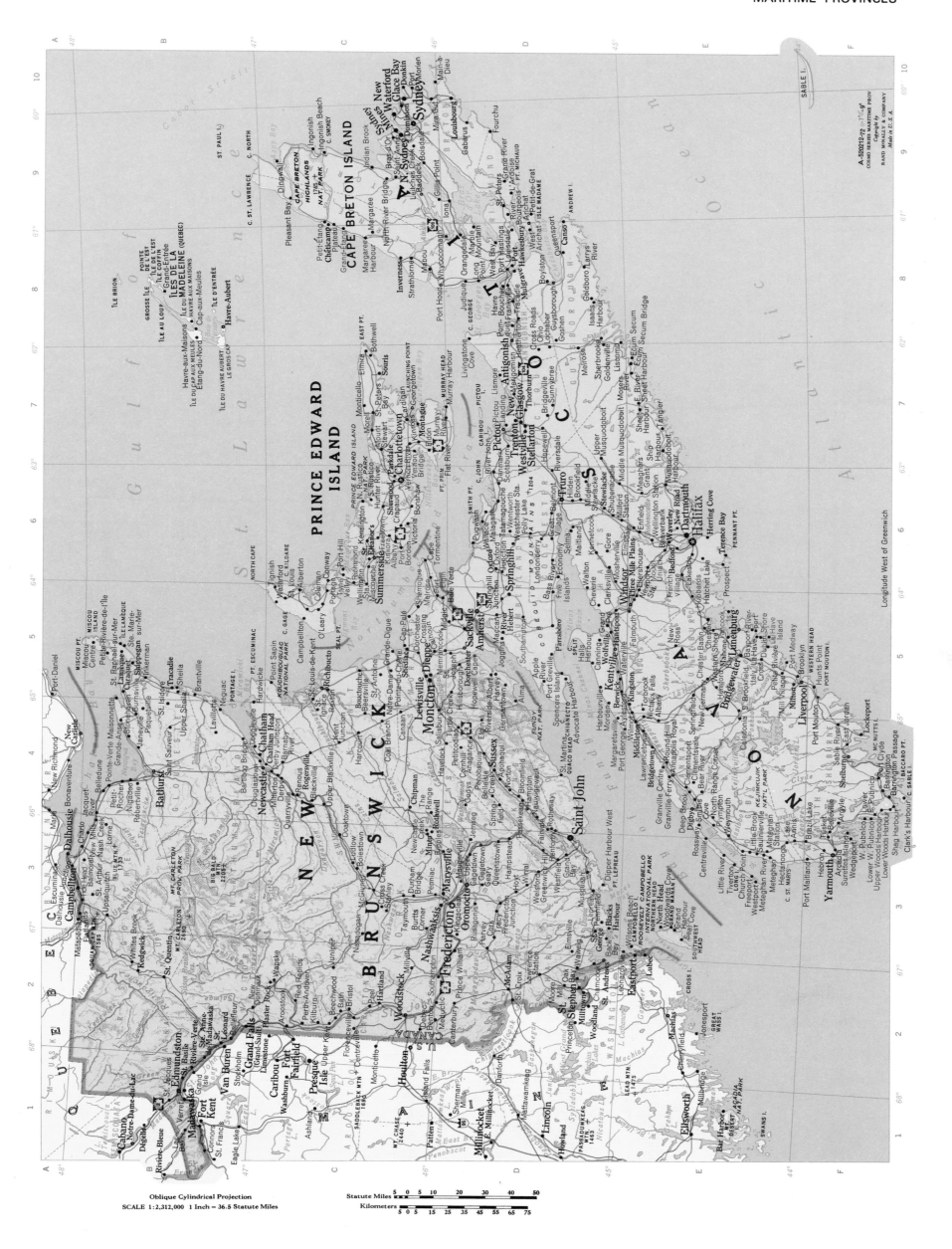

Oblique Cylindrical Projection
SCALE 1:2,312,000   1 Inch = 36.5 Statute Miles

Statute Miles   5 0 5   10   20   30   40   50
Kilometers   5 0 5   15   25   35   45   55   65   75

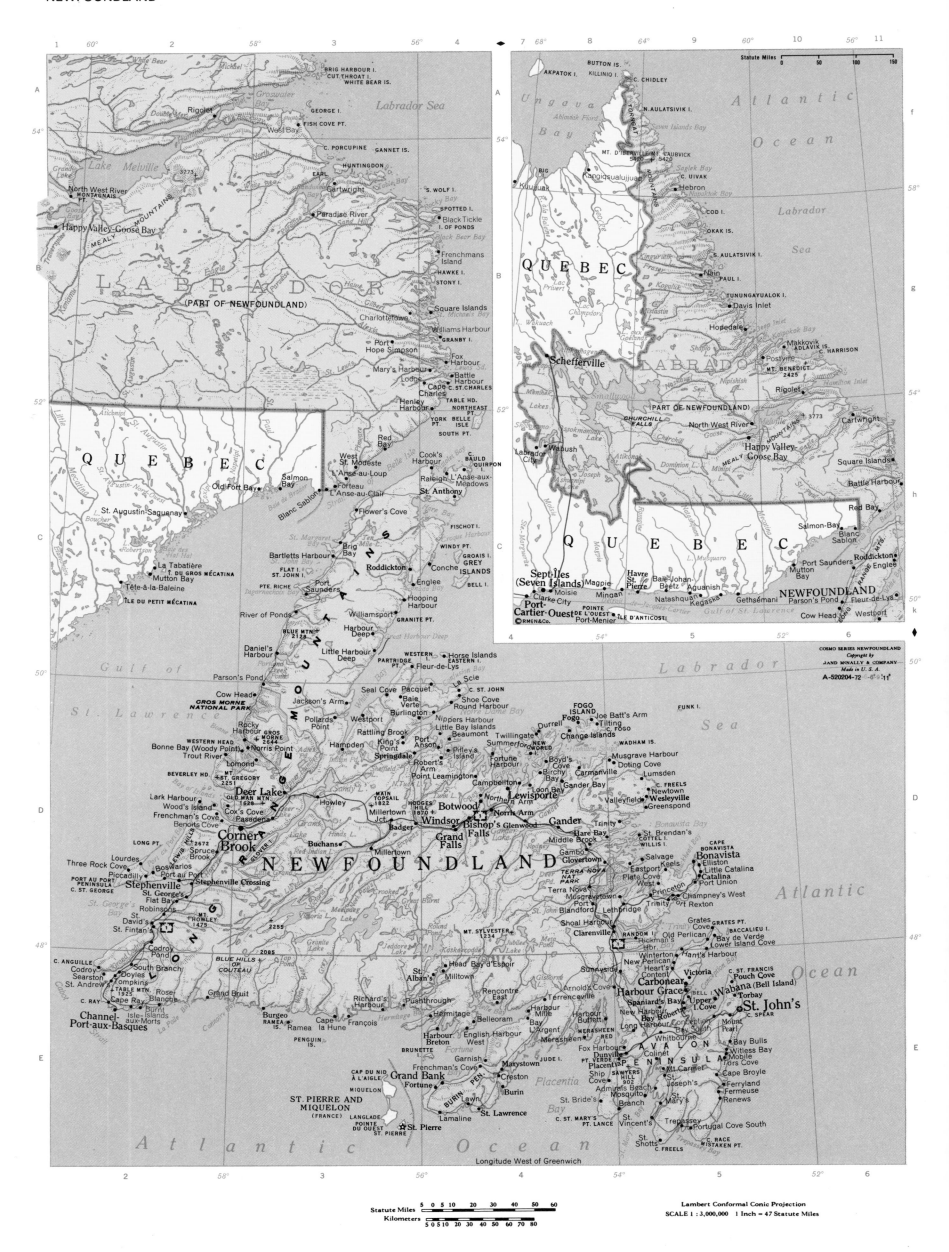

Statute Miles
0   50   100   150

COSMO SERIES NEWFOUNDLAND
Copyright by
RAND McNALLY & COMPANY
Made in U.S.A.
A-520204-72

Statute Miles
5 0 5 10   20   30   40   50 60
Kilometers
5 0 5 10 20 30 40 50 60 70 80

Lambert Conformal Conic Projection
SCALE 1 : 3,000,000   1 Inch = 47 Statute Miles

Longitude West of Greenwich

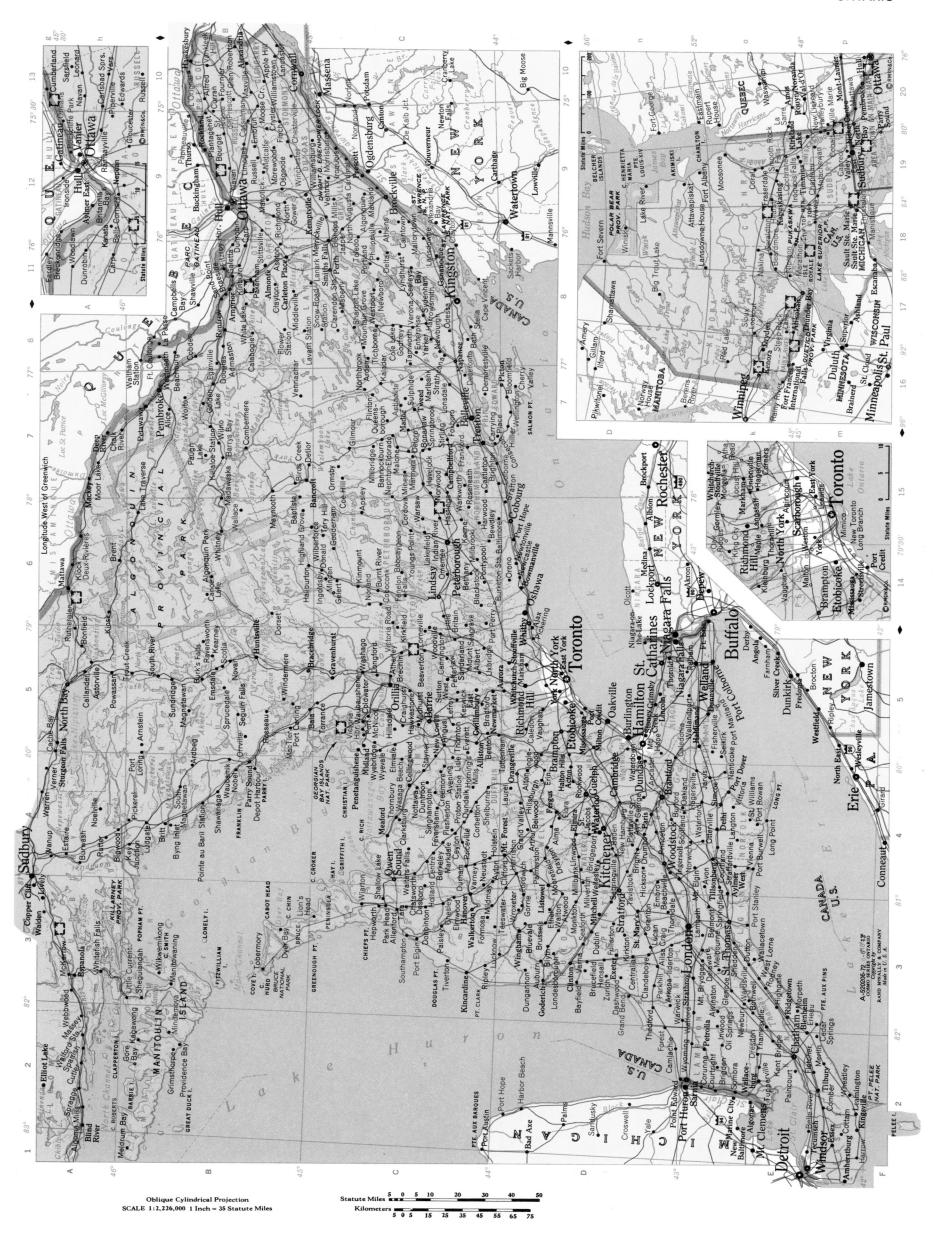

Oblique Cylindrical Projection
SCALE 1:2,226,000   1 Inch = 35 Statute Miles

Statute Miles
Kilometers

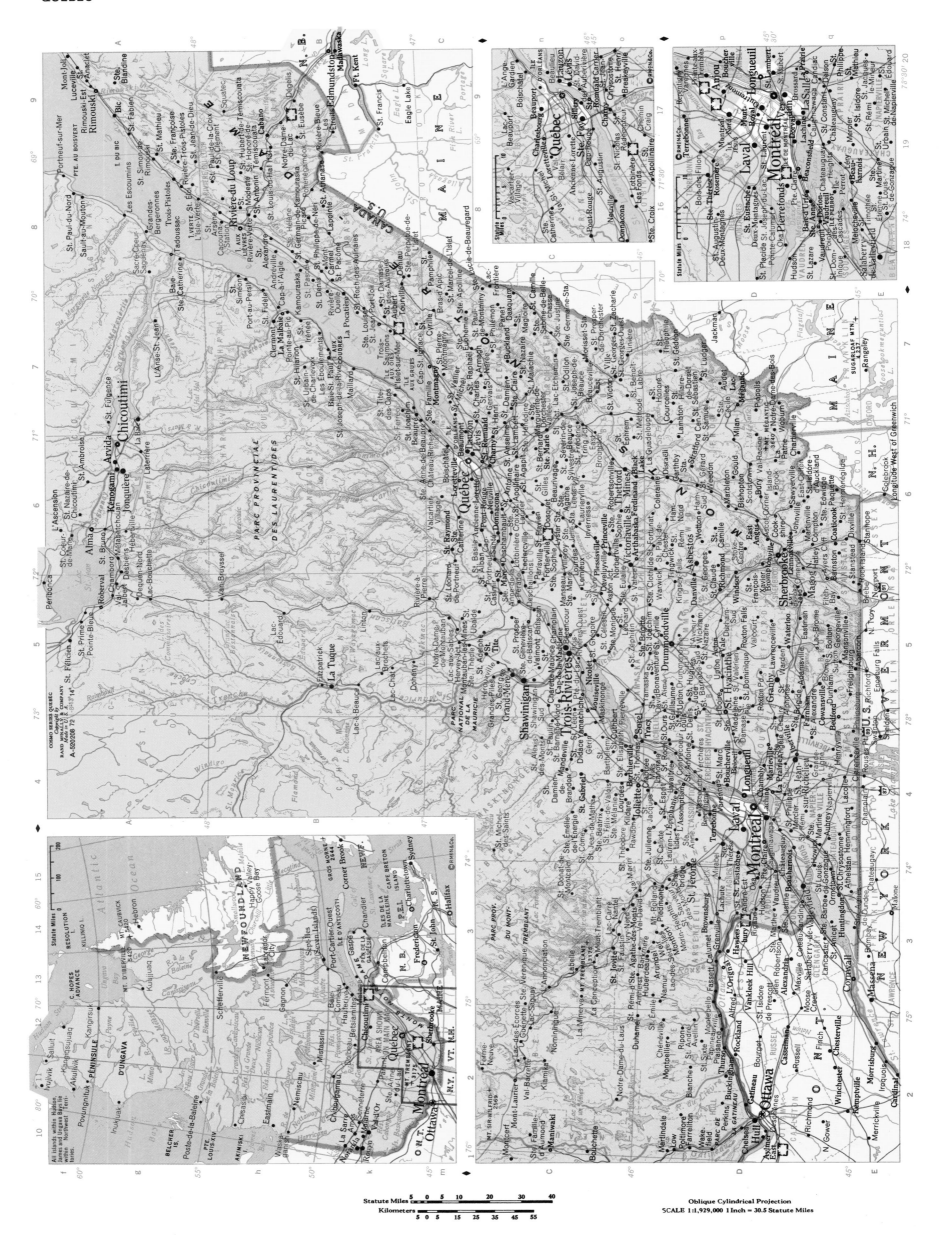

Oblique Cylindrical Projection
SCALE 1:1,929,000 1 Inch = 30.5 Statute Miles

Statute Miles
Kilometers

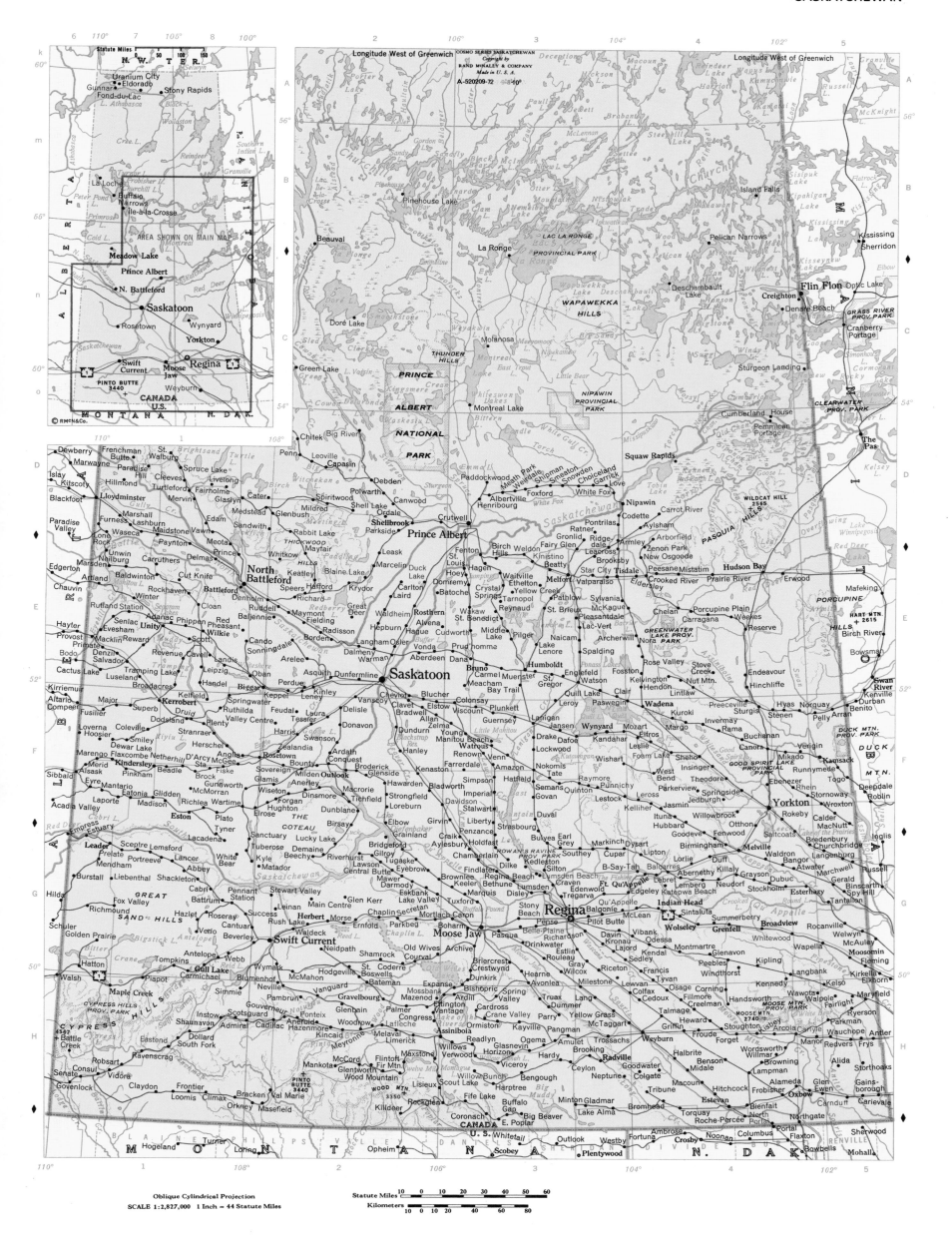

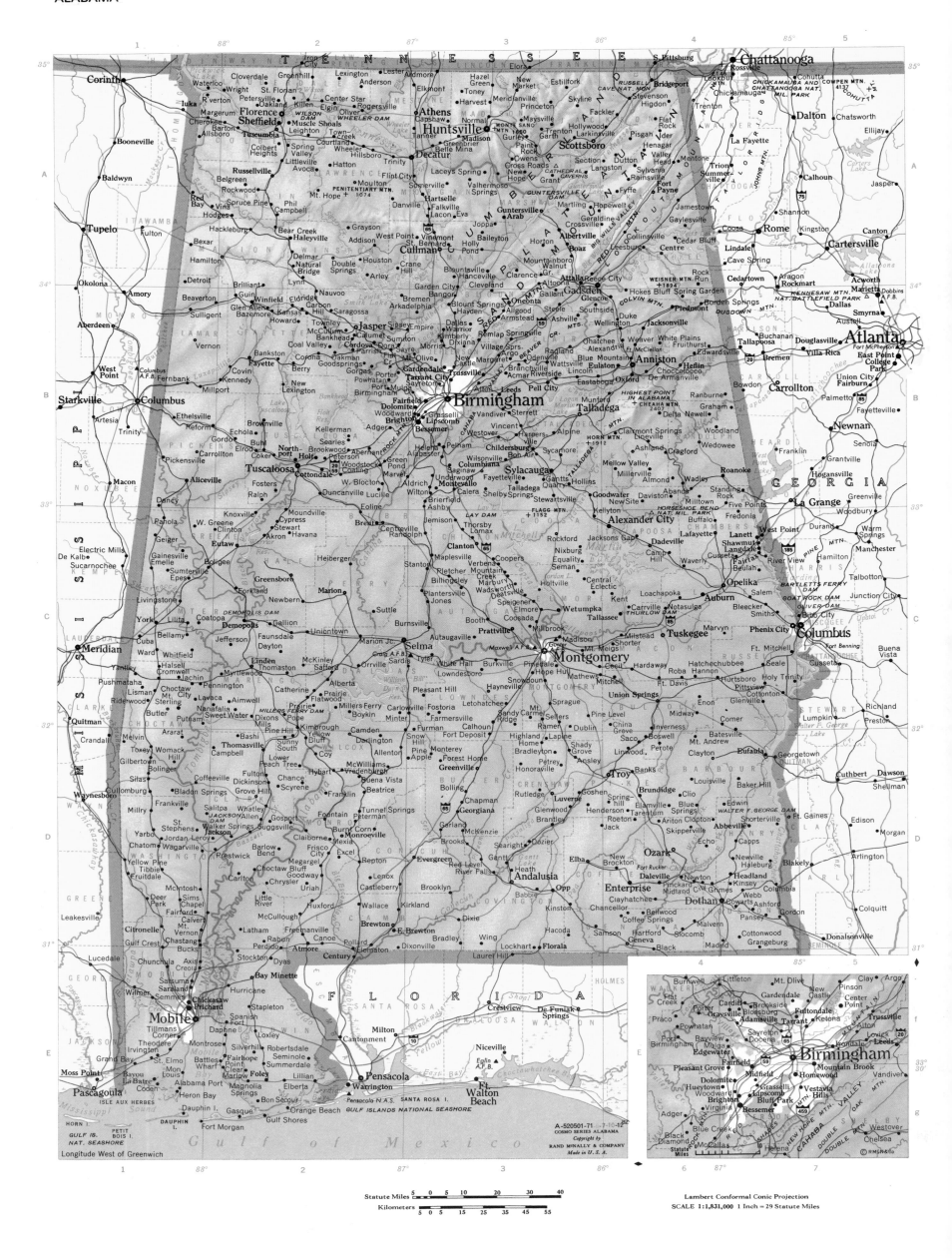

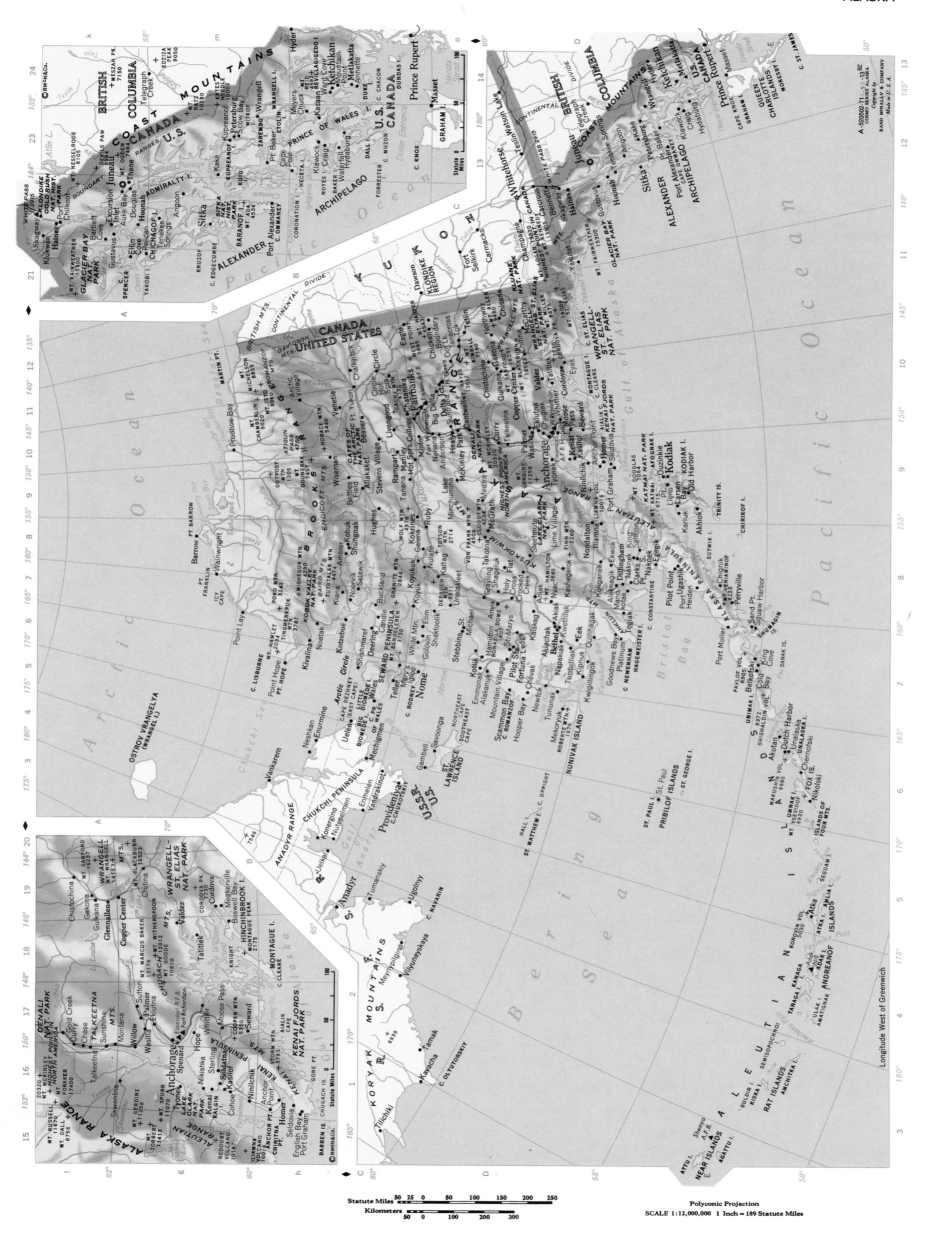

Statute Miles
50 25 0   50   100   150   200   250
Kilometers
50 0   100   200   300

Polyconic Projection
SCALE 1:12,000,000   1 Inch = 189 Statute Miles

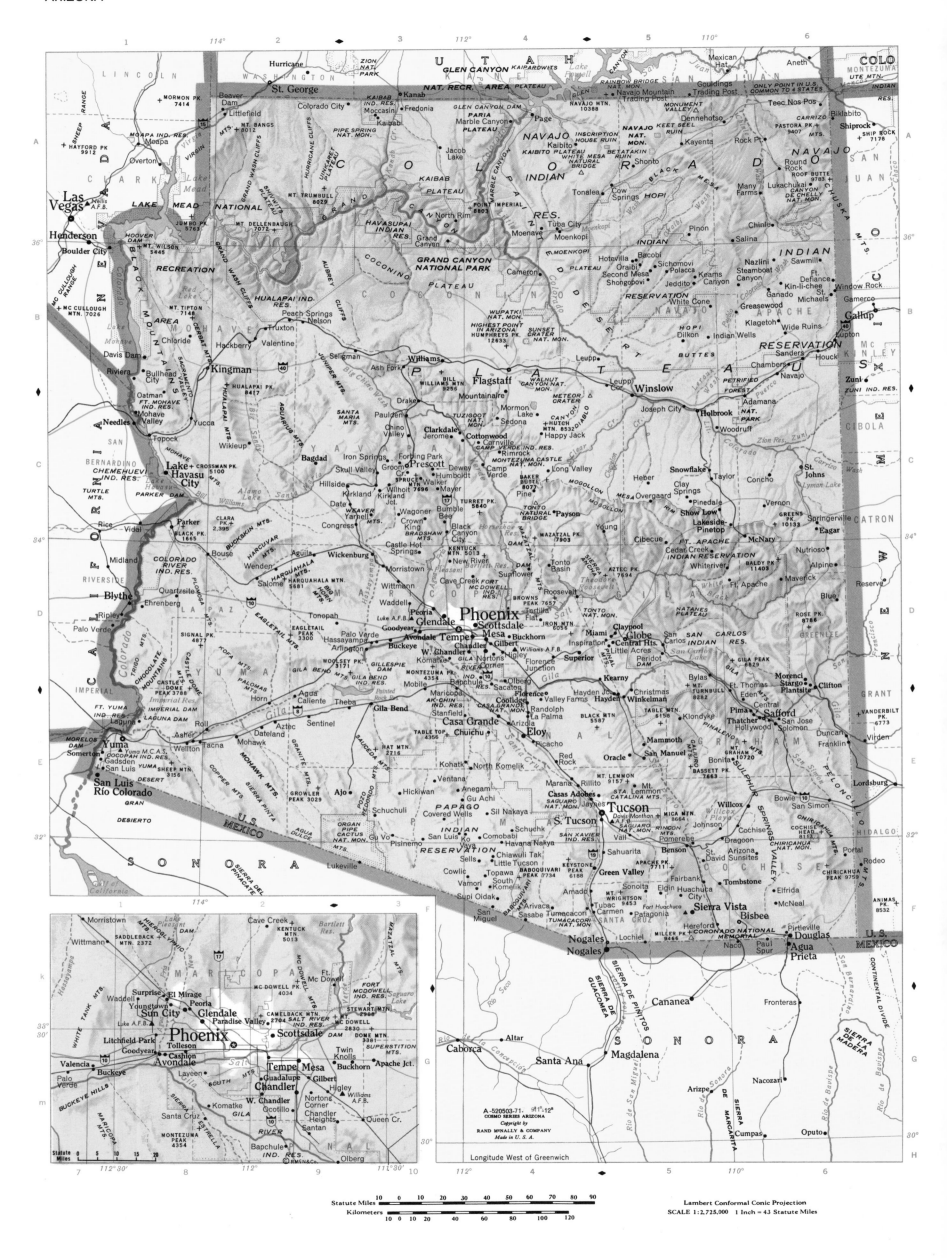

Statute Miles
Kilometers

Lambert Conformal Conic Projection
SCALE 1:2,725,000   1 Inch = 43 Statute Miles

A-520503-71-
COSMO SERIES ARIZONA
Copyright by
RAND McNALLY & COMPANY
Made in U.S.A.

Longitude West of Greenwich

Statute Miles 5 0 5 10 20 30 40
Kilometers 5 0 5 15 25 35 45 55

Lambert Conformal Conic Projection
SCALE 1:1,832,000 1 Inch = 29 Statute Miles

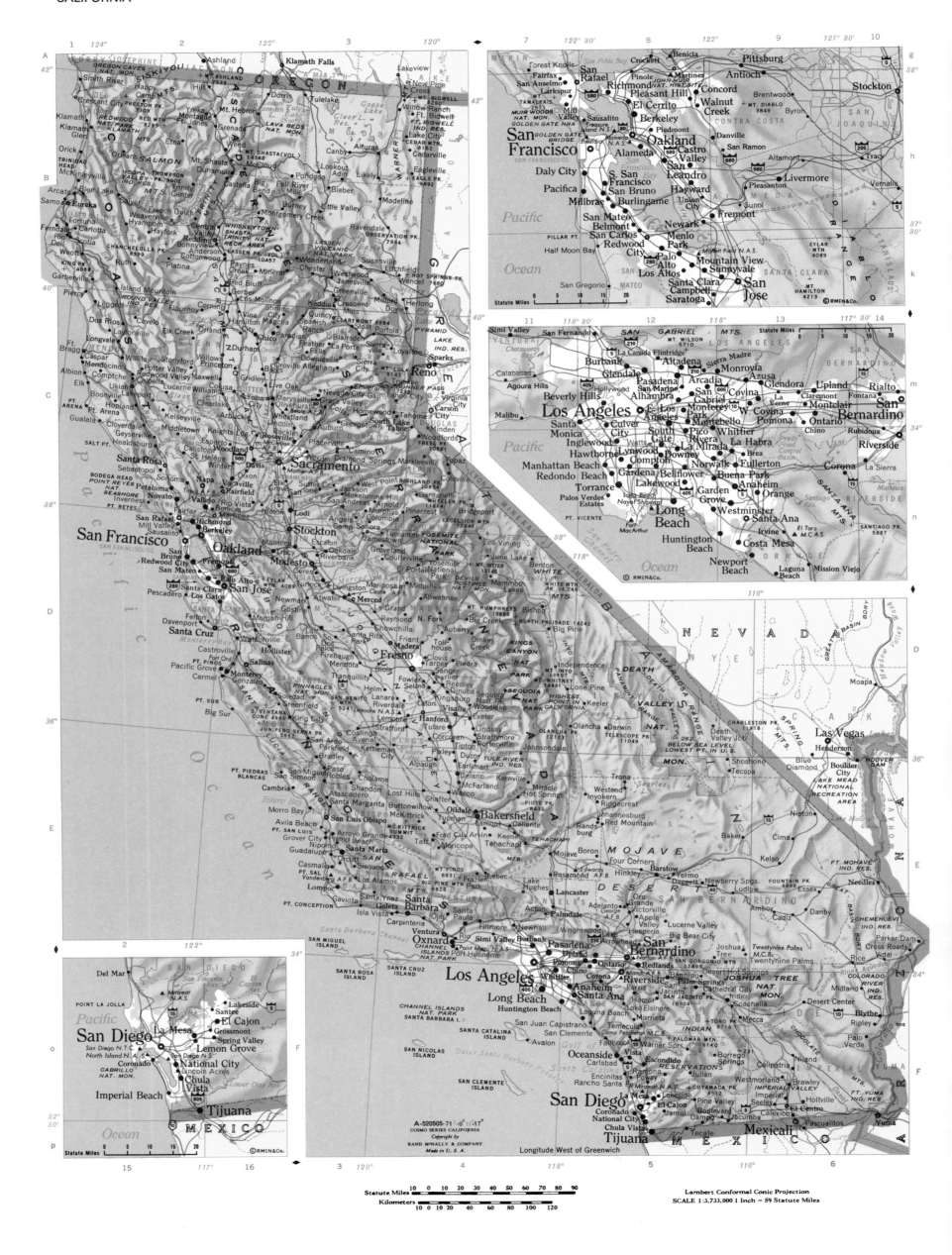

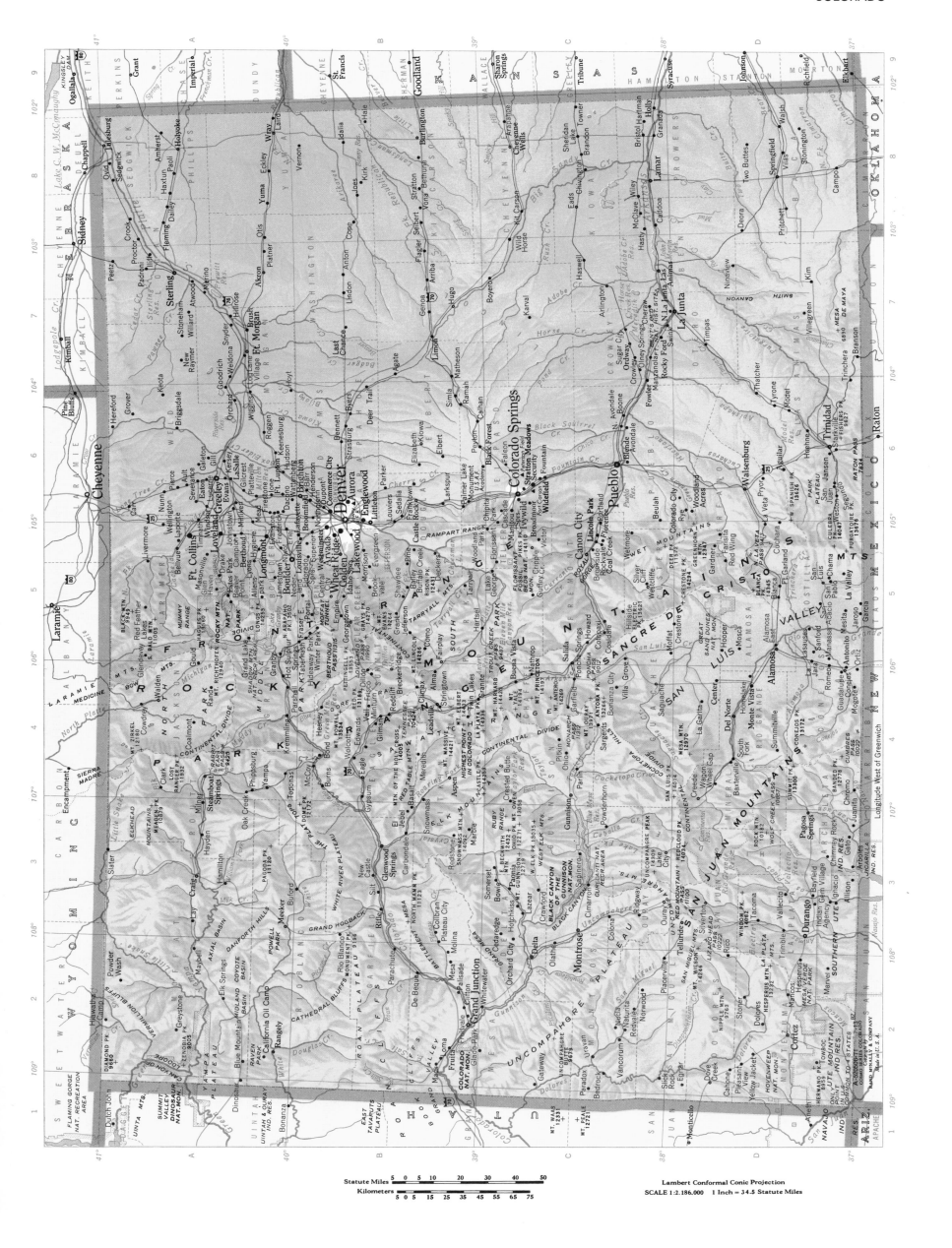

Statute Miles 5 0 5 10 20 30 40 50
Kilometers 5 0 5 15 25 35 45 55 65 75

Lambert Conformal Conic Projection
SCALE 1:2.186.000   1 Inch = 34.5 Statute Miles

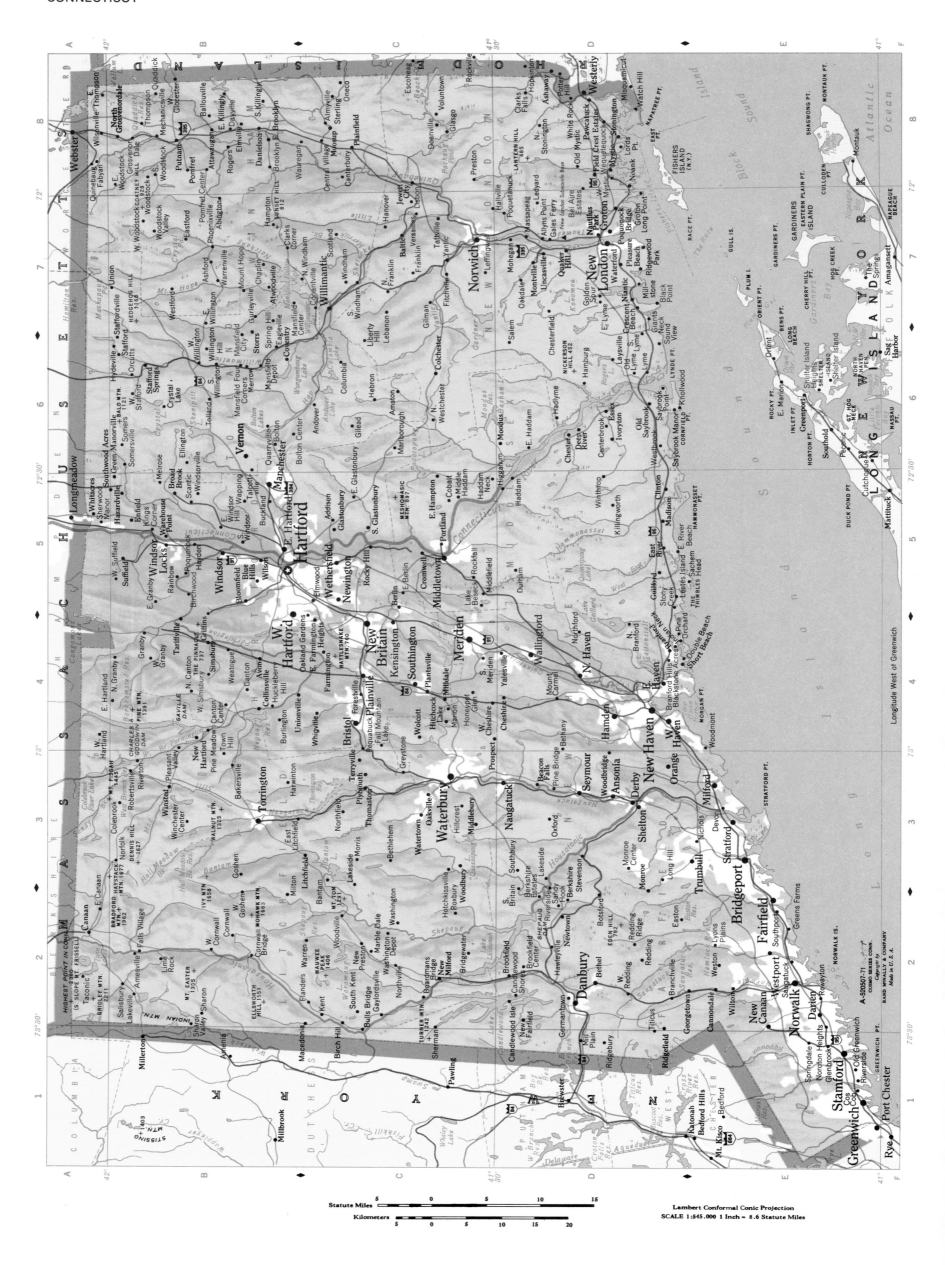

Statute Miles

Kilometers

Lambert Conformal Conic Projection
SCALE 1:545,000 1 Inch = 8.6 Statute Miles

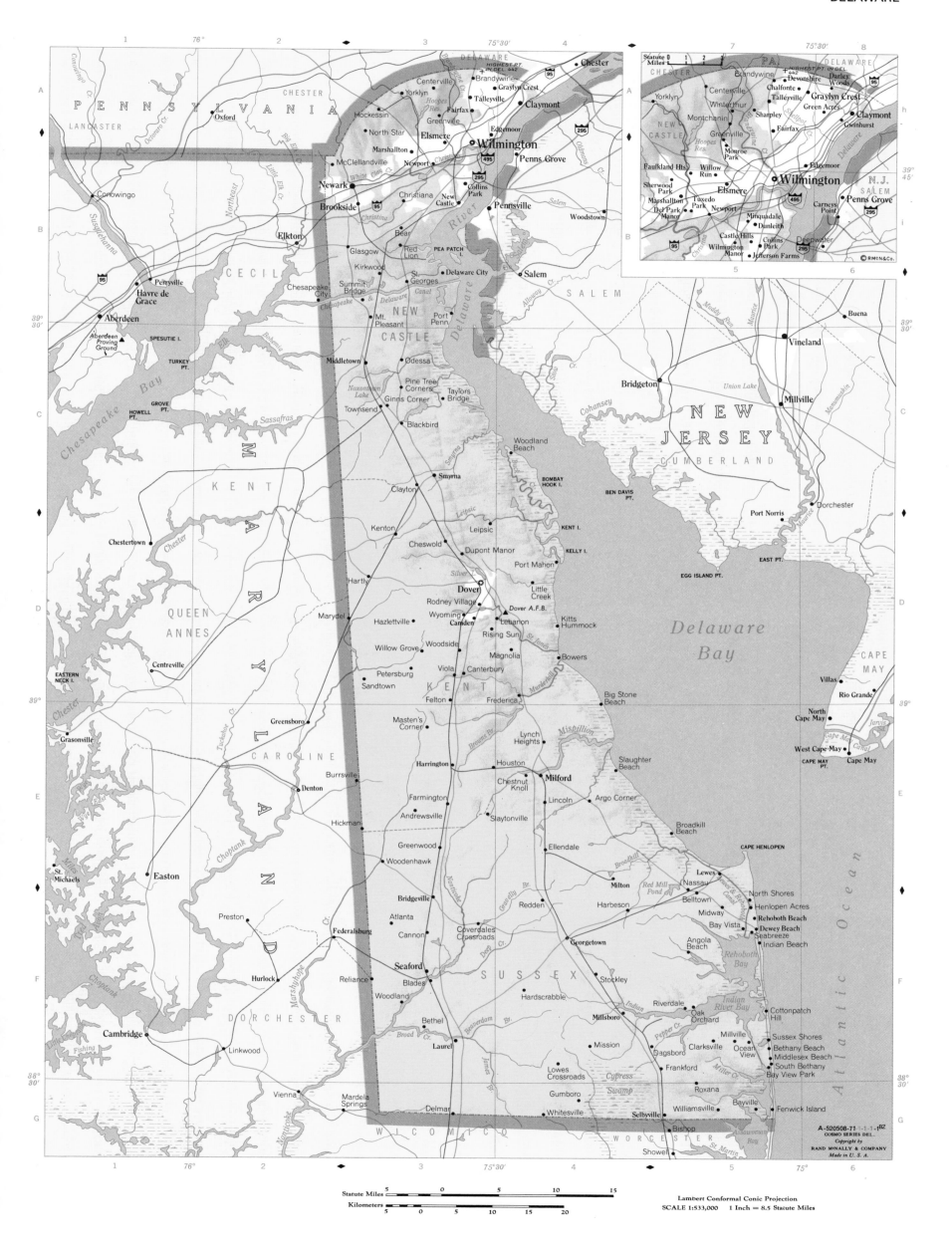

Statute Miles 0 1 2 3

Lambert Conformal Conic Projection
SCALE 1:533,000   1 Inch = 8.5 Statute Miles

Statute Miles 5 0 5 10 15
Kilometers 5 0 5 10 15 20

A-520508-71-1-1-1^BZ
COSMO SERIES DEL.
Copyright by
RAND McNALLY & COMPANY
Made in U.S.A.

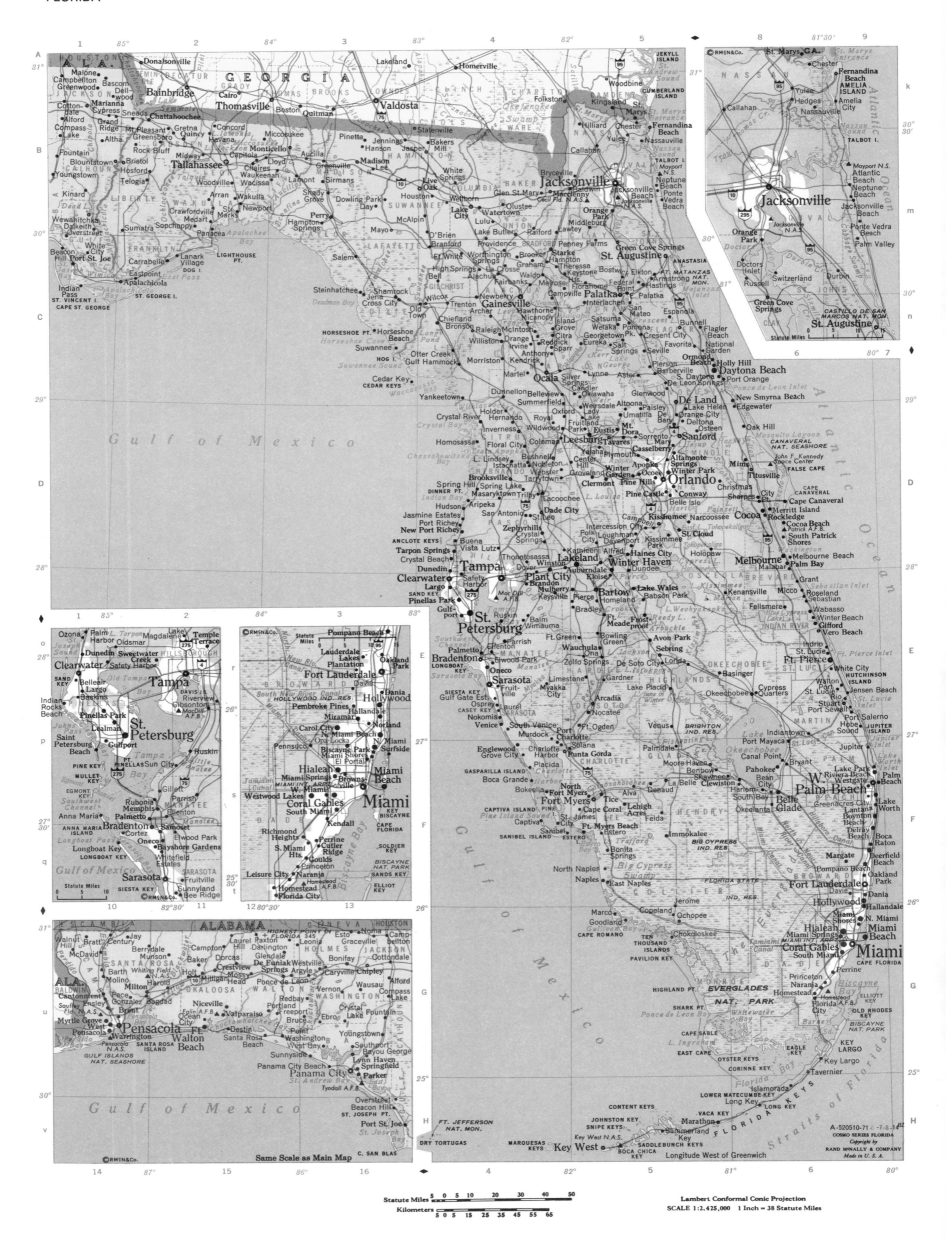

Statute Miles 5 0 5 10 20 30 40 50
Kilometers 5 0 5 15 25 35 45 55 65

Lambert Conformal Conic Projection
SCALE 1:2,425,000   1 Inch = 38 Statute Miles

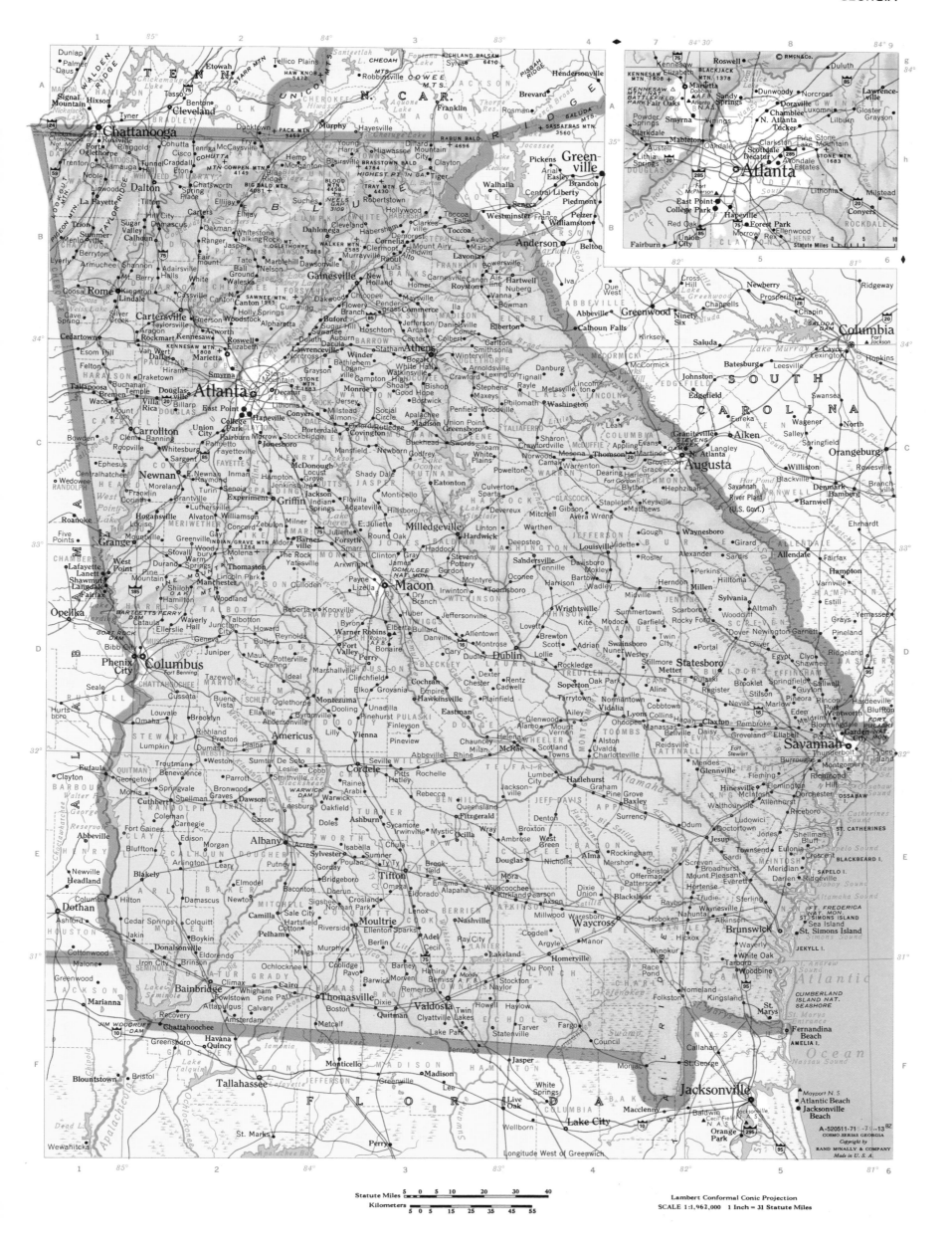

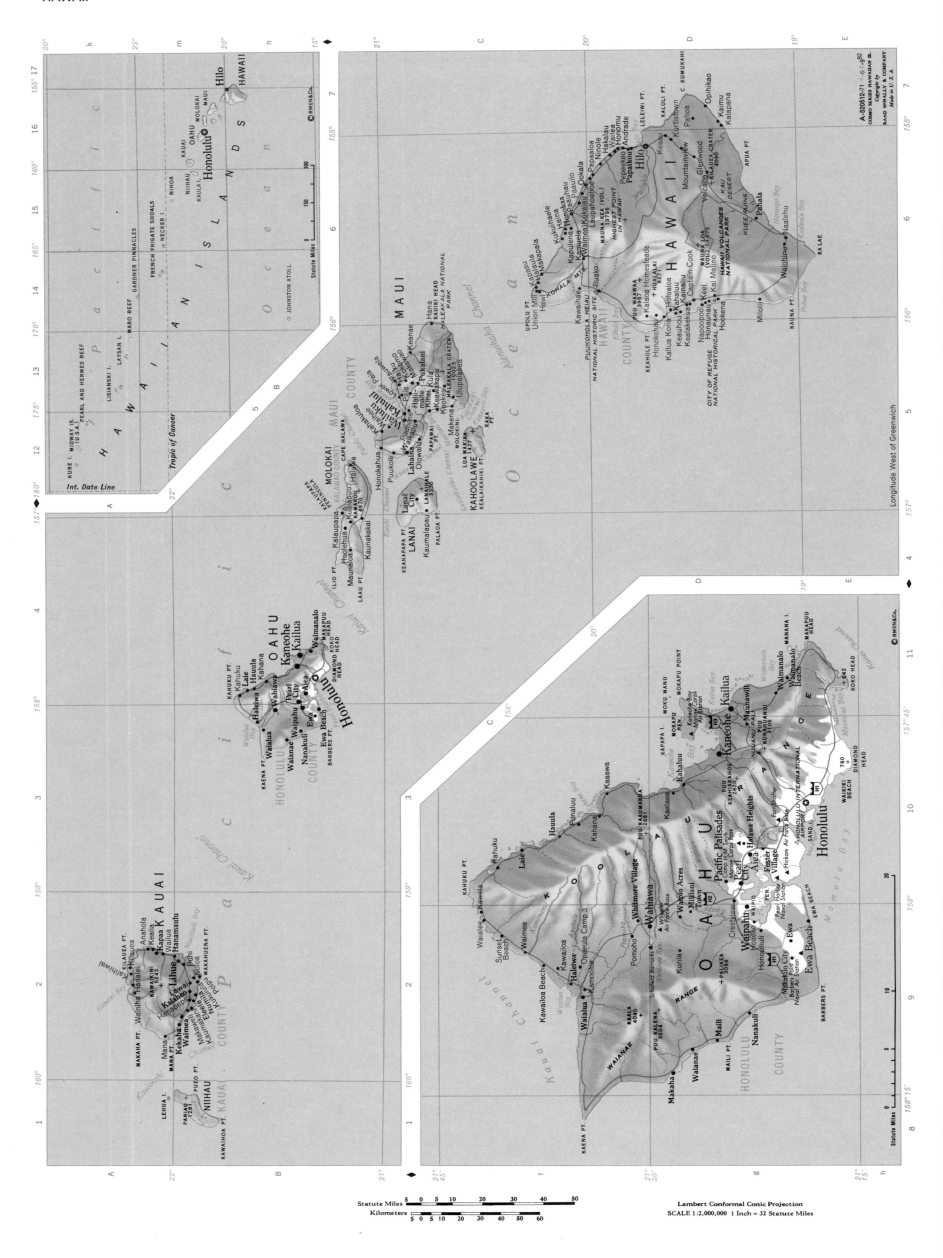

Lambert Conformal Conic Projection
SCALE 1:2,000,000 1 Inch = 32 Statute Miles

Statute Miles

Kilometers

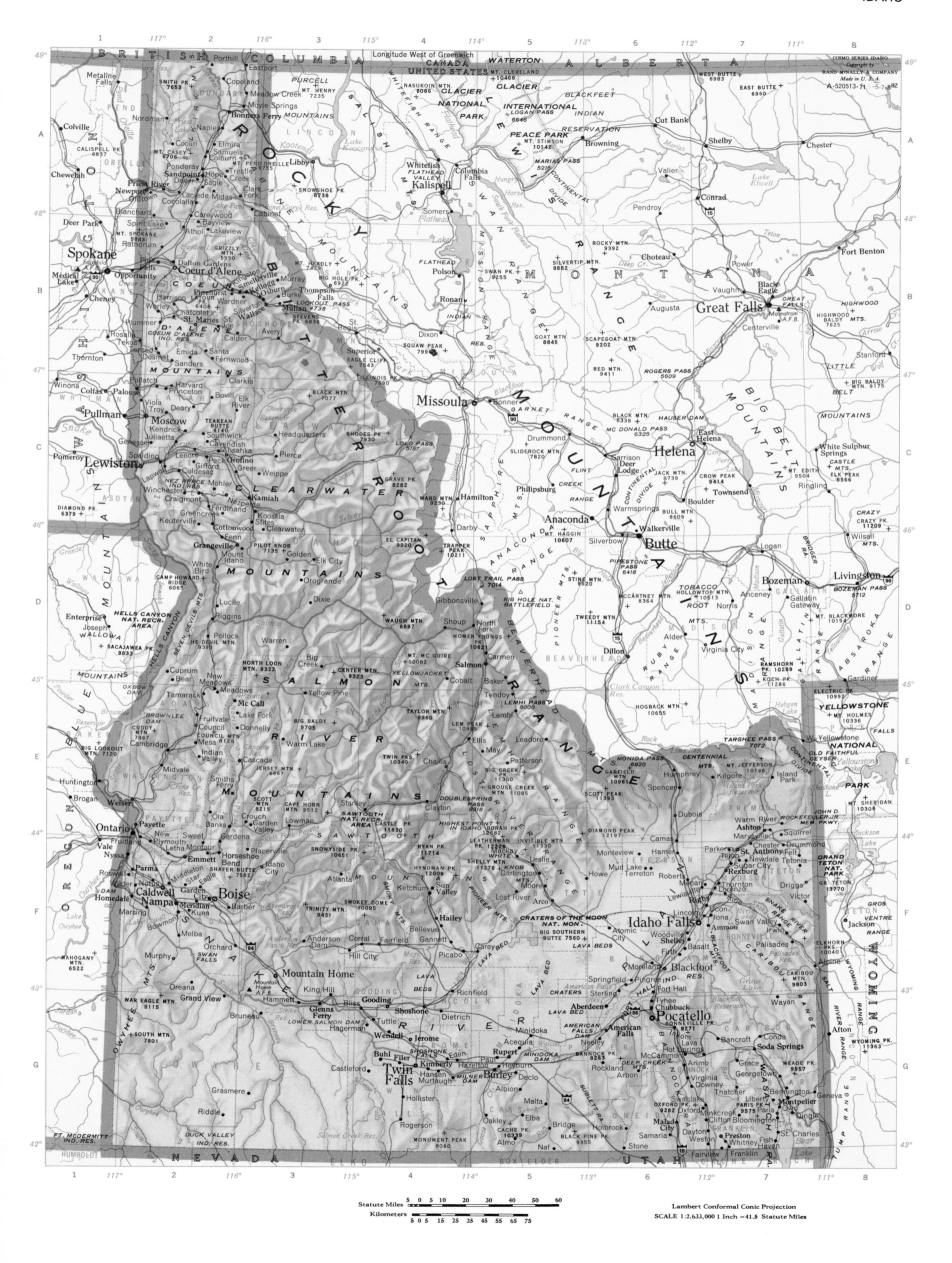

Statute Miles 5 0 5 10   20   30   40   50   60
Kilometers 5 0 5   15   25   35   45   55   65   75

Lambert Conformal Conic Projection
SCALE 1:2,633,000 1 Inch = 41.5 Statute Miles

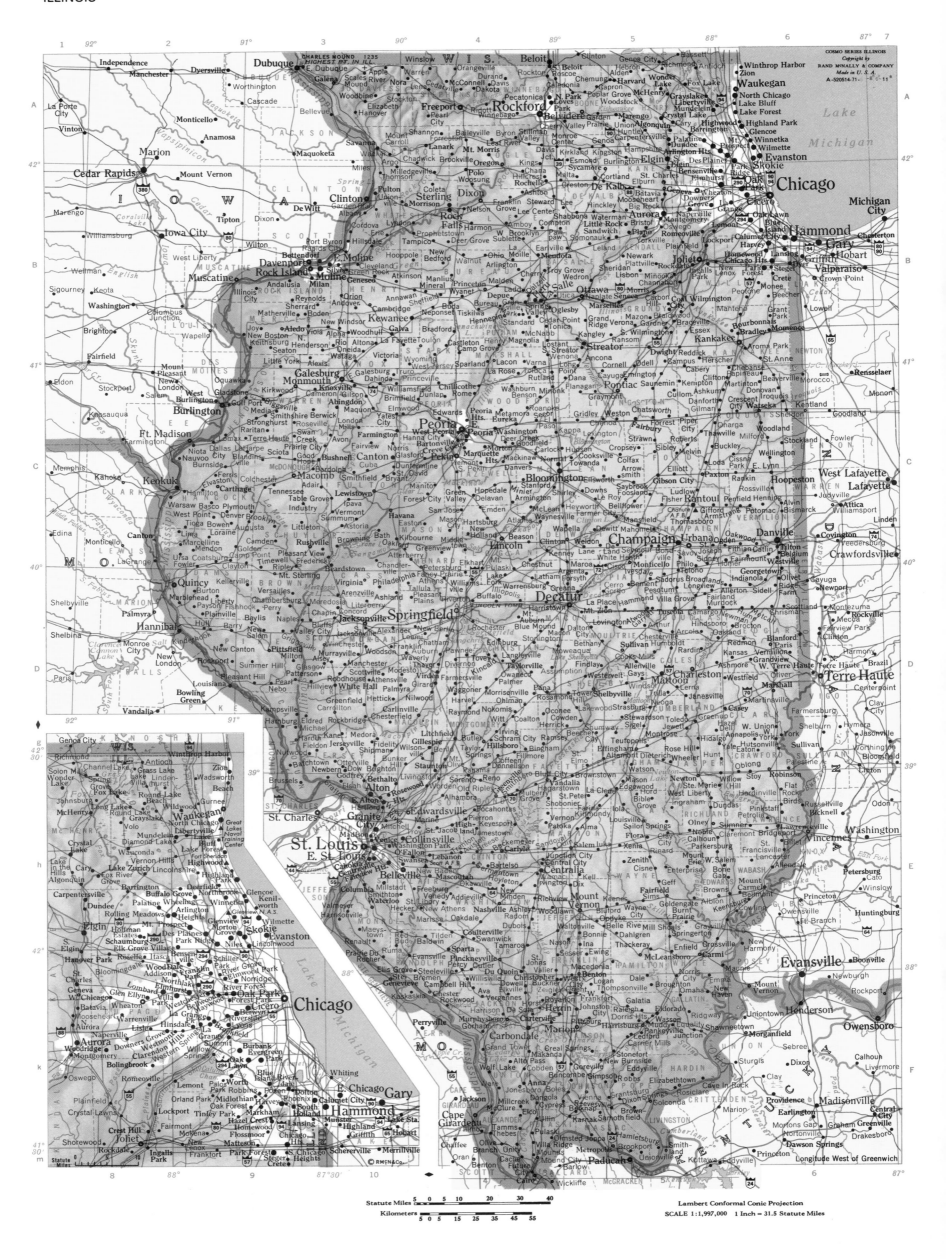

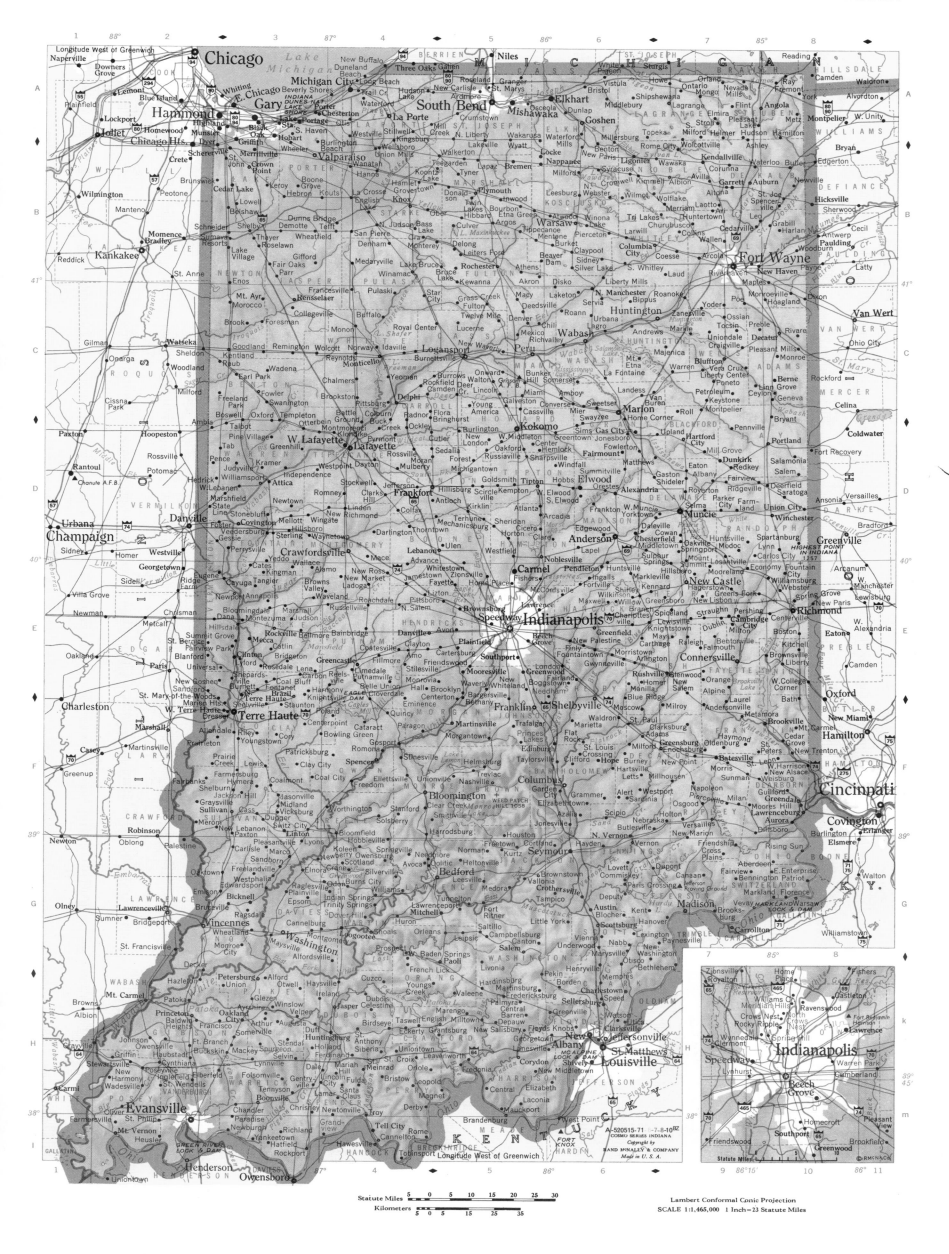

Statute Miles
Kilometers

Lambert Conformal Conic Projection
SCALE 1:1,465,000   1 Inch = 23 Statute Miles

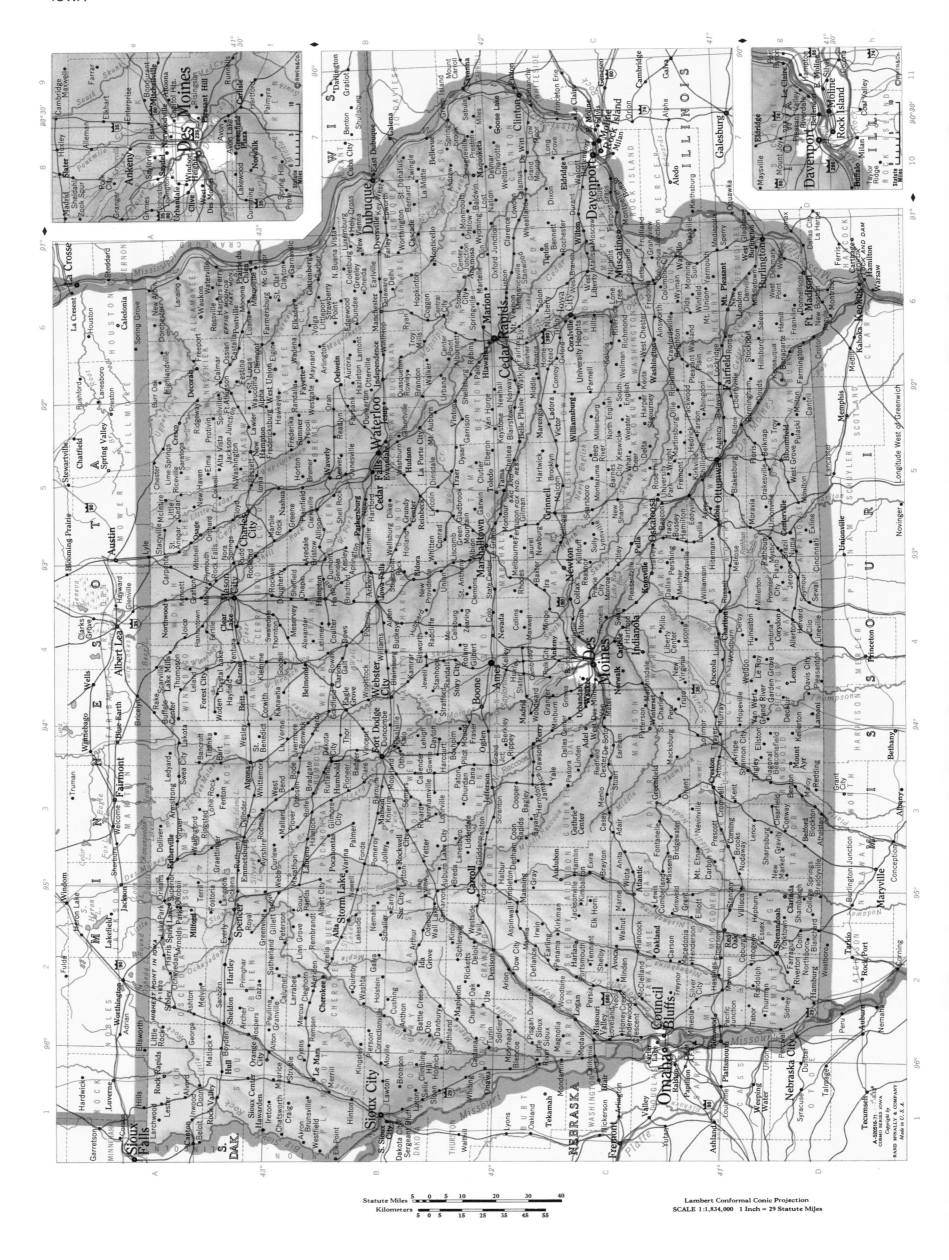

Statute Miles 5 0 5 10 20 30 40
Kilometers 5 0 5 15 25 35 55

Lambert Conformal Conic Projection
SCALE 1:1,834,000   1 Inch = 29 Statute Miles

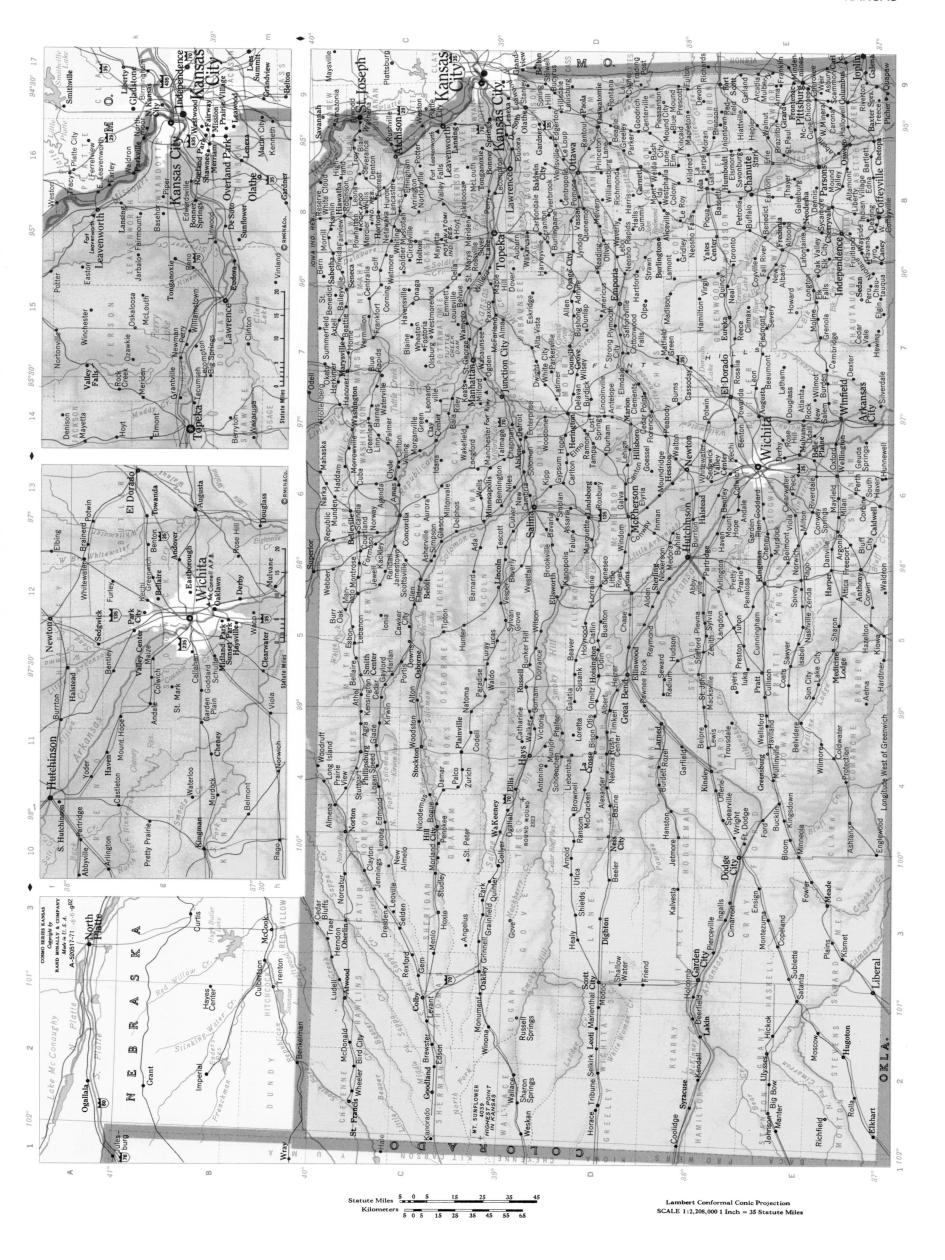

Statute Miles 5 0 5 15 25 35 45
Kilometers 5 0 5 15 25 35 45 55 65

Lambert Conformal Conic Projection
SCALE 1:2,208,000 1 Inch = 35 Statute Miles

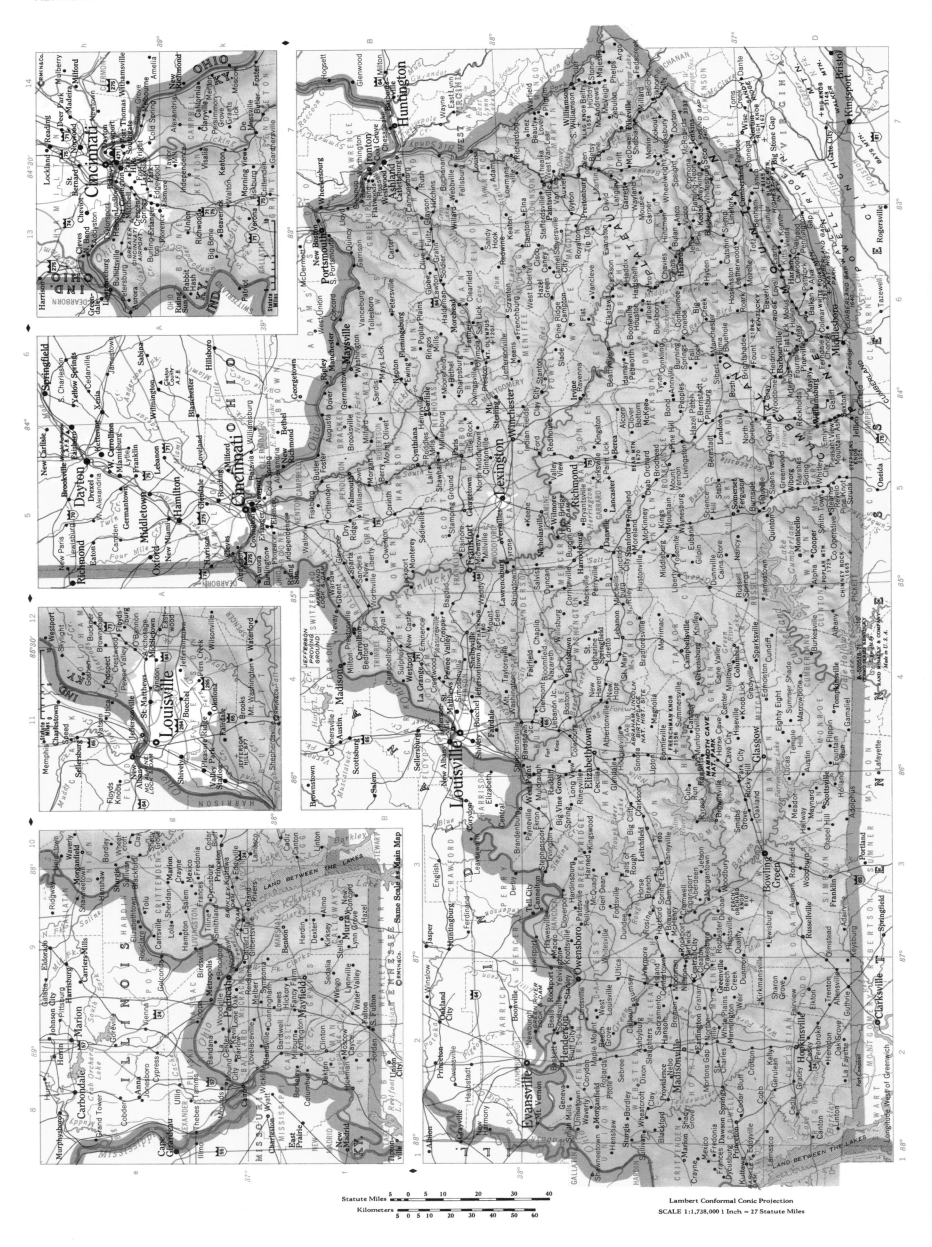

Statute Miles 5 0 5 10 20 30 40
Kilometers 5 0 5 10 20 30 40 50 60

Lambert Conformal Conic Projection
SCALE 1:1,738,000 1 Inch = 27 Statute Miles

Statute Miles 5 0 5 10 20 30 40
Kilometers 5 0 5 15 25 35 45 55

Lambert Conformal Conic Projection
SCALE 1:2,083,000   1 Inch = 33 Statute Miles

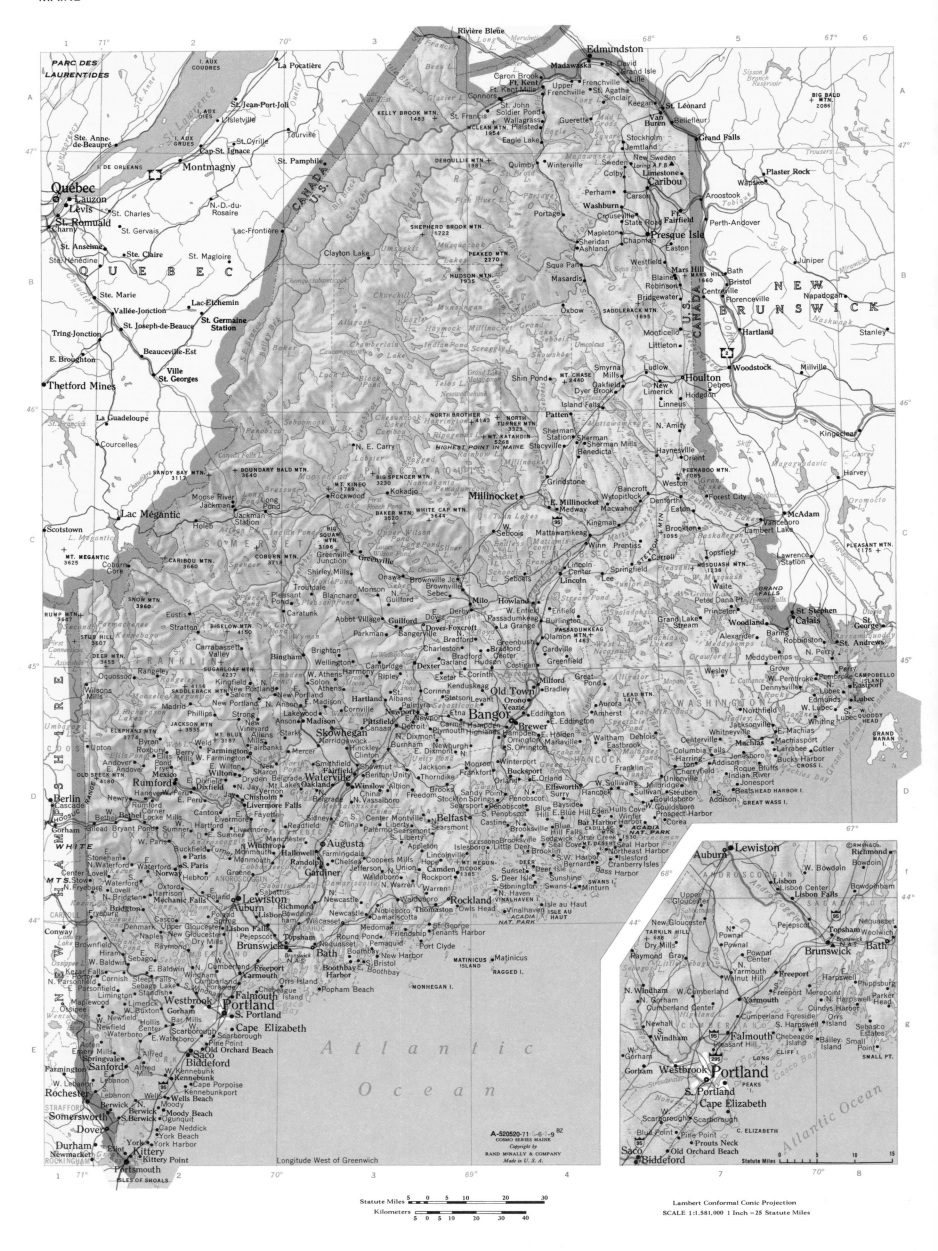

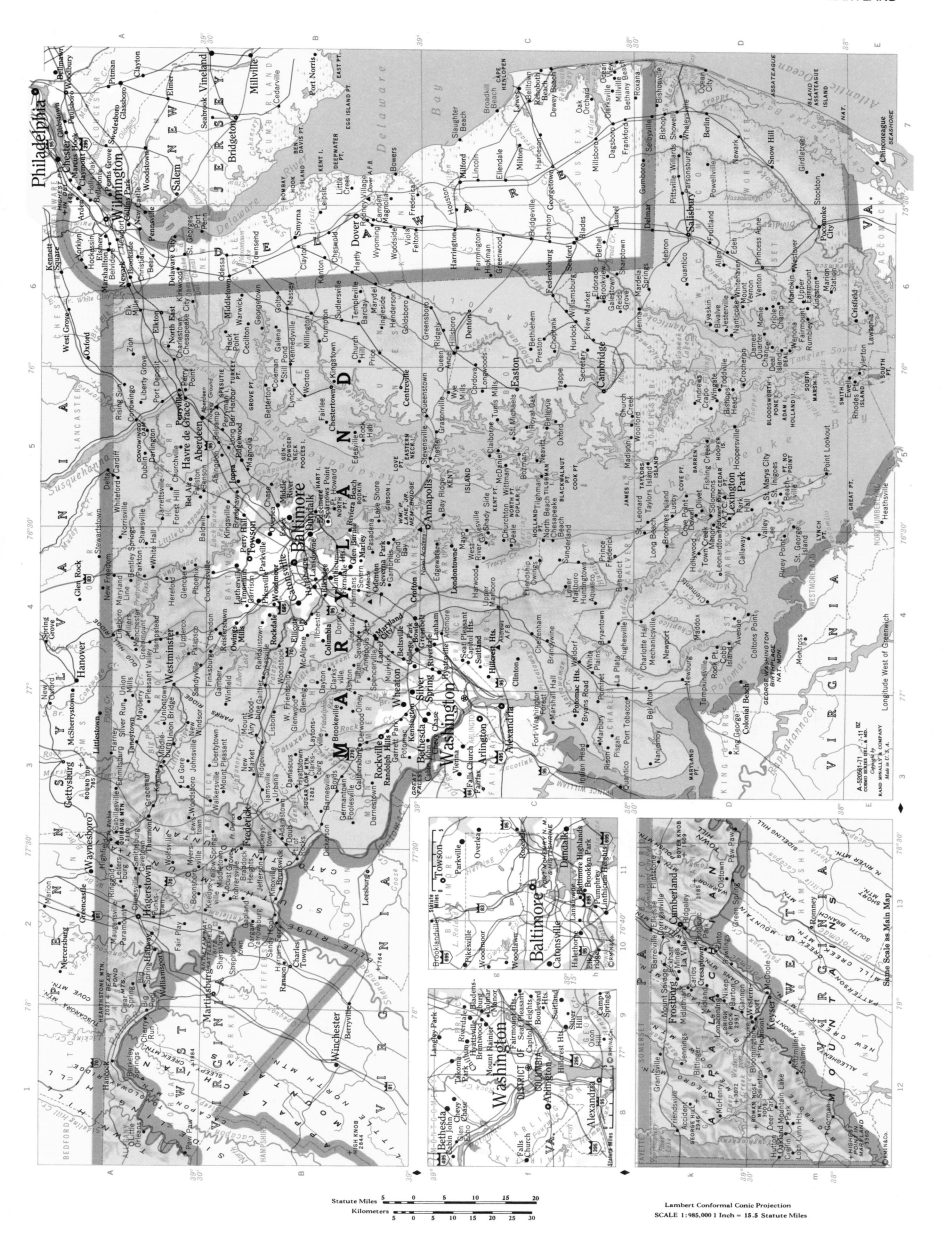

Statute Miles 5 0 5 10 15 20
Kilometers 5 0 5 10 15 20 25 30

Lambert Conformal Conic Projection
SCALE 1:985,000 1 Inch = 15.5 Statute Miles

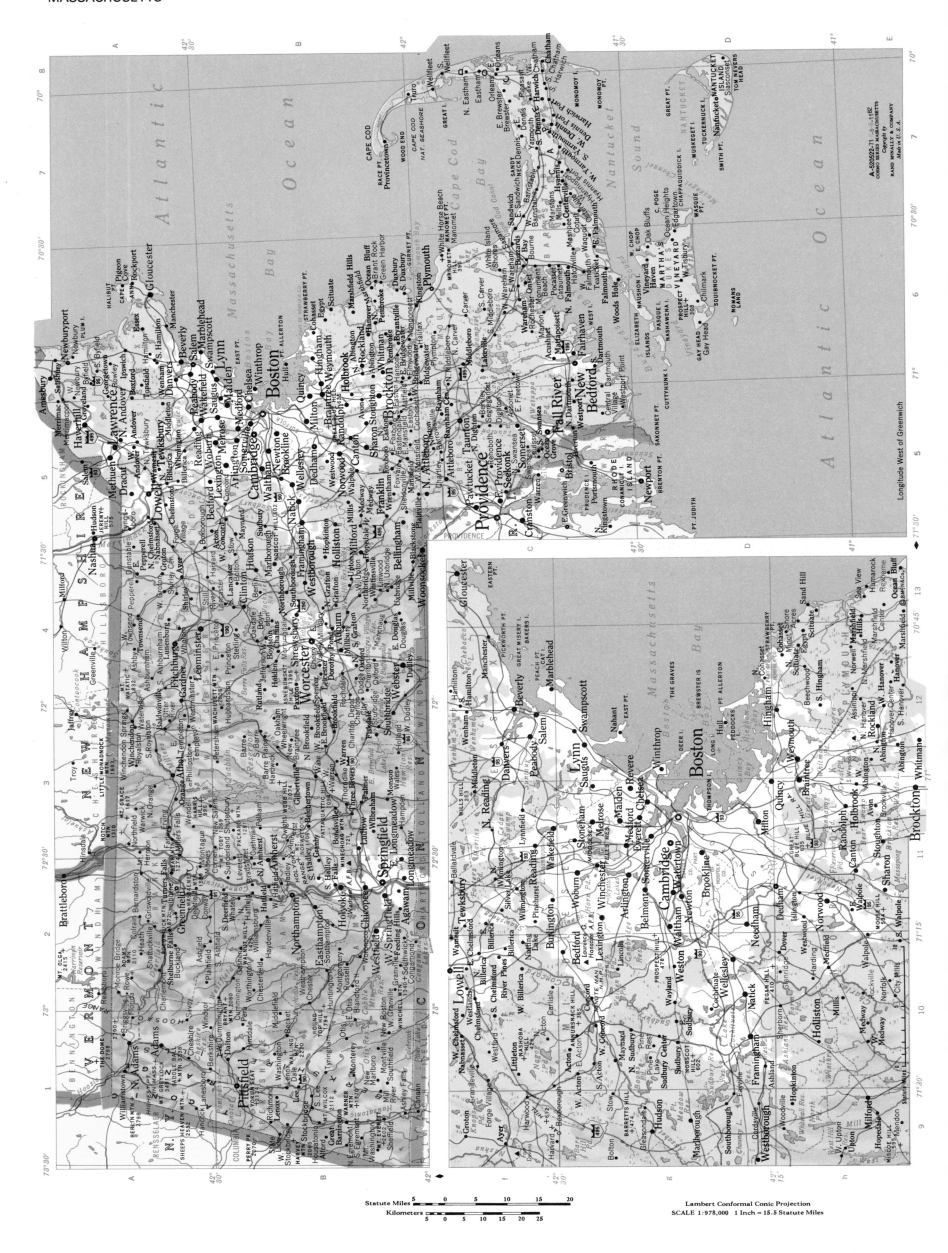

Statute Miles
Kilometers

Lambert Conformal Conic Projection
SCALE 1:978,000 1 Inch = 15.5 Statute Miles

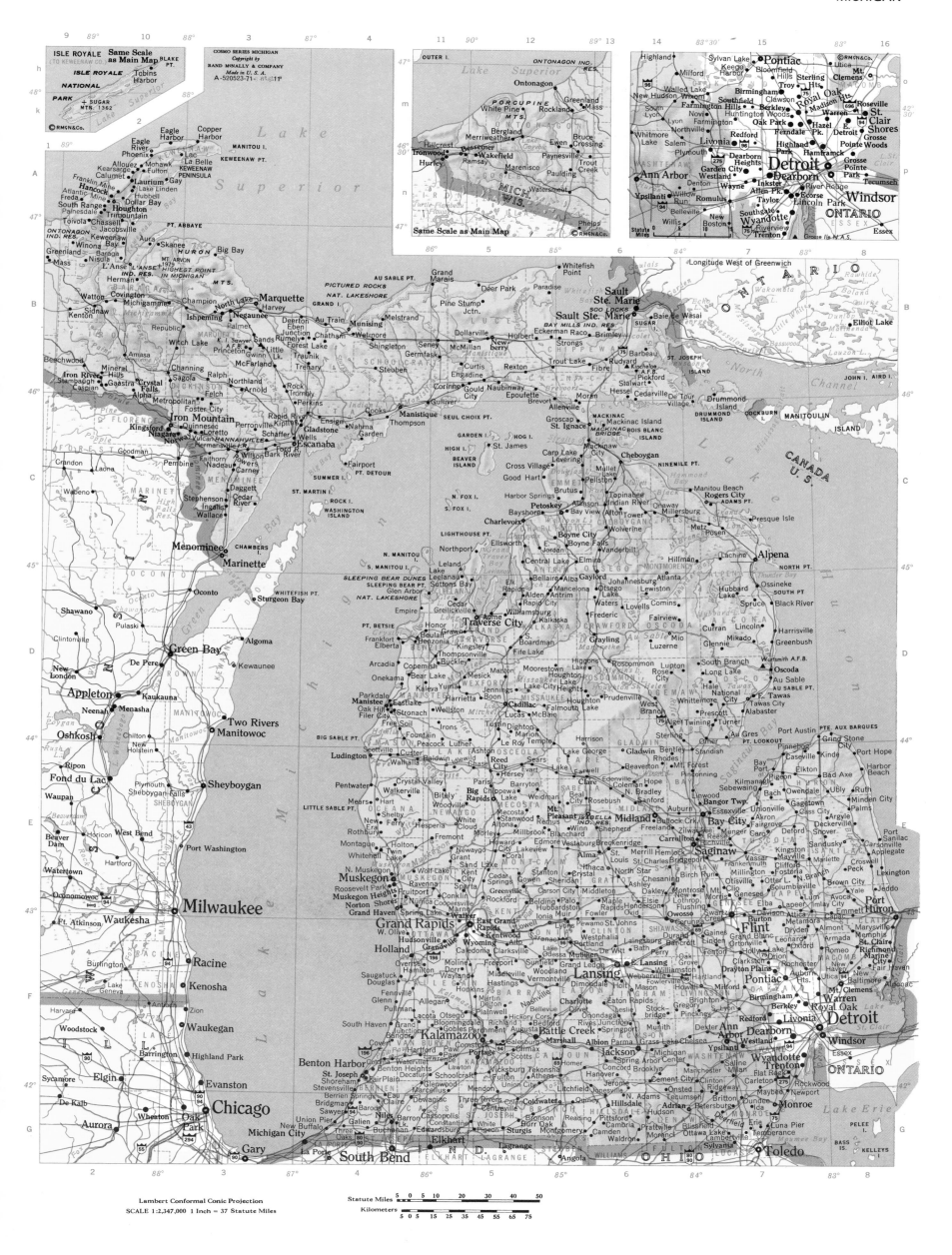

ISLE ROYALE
Same Scale as Main Map
ISLE ROYALE NATIONAL PARK

COSMO SERIES MICHIGAN
Copyright by
RAND McNALLY & COMPANY
Made in U.S.A.
A-520523-71

OUTER I.
Lake Superior
ONTONAGON IND. RES.

Same Scale as Main Map

Lambert Conformal Conic Projection
SCALE 1:2,347,000 1 Inch = 37 Statute Miles

Statute Miles 5 0 5 10   20   30   40   50

Kilometers 5 0 5 15 25 35 45 55 65 75

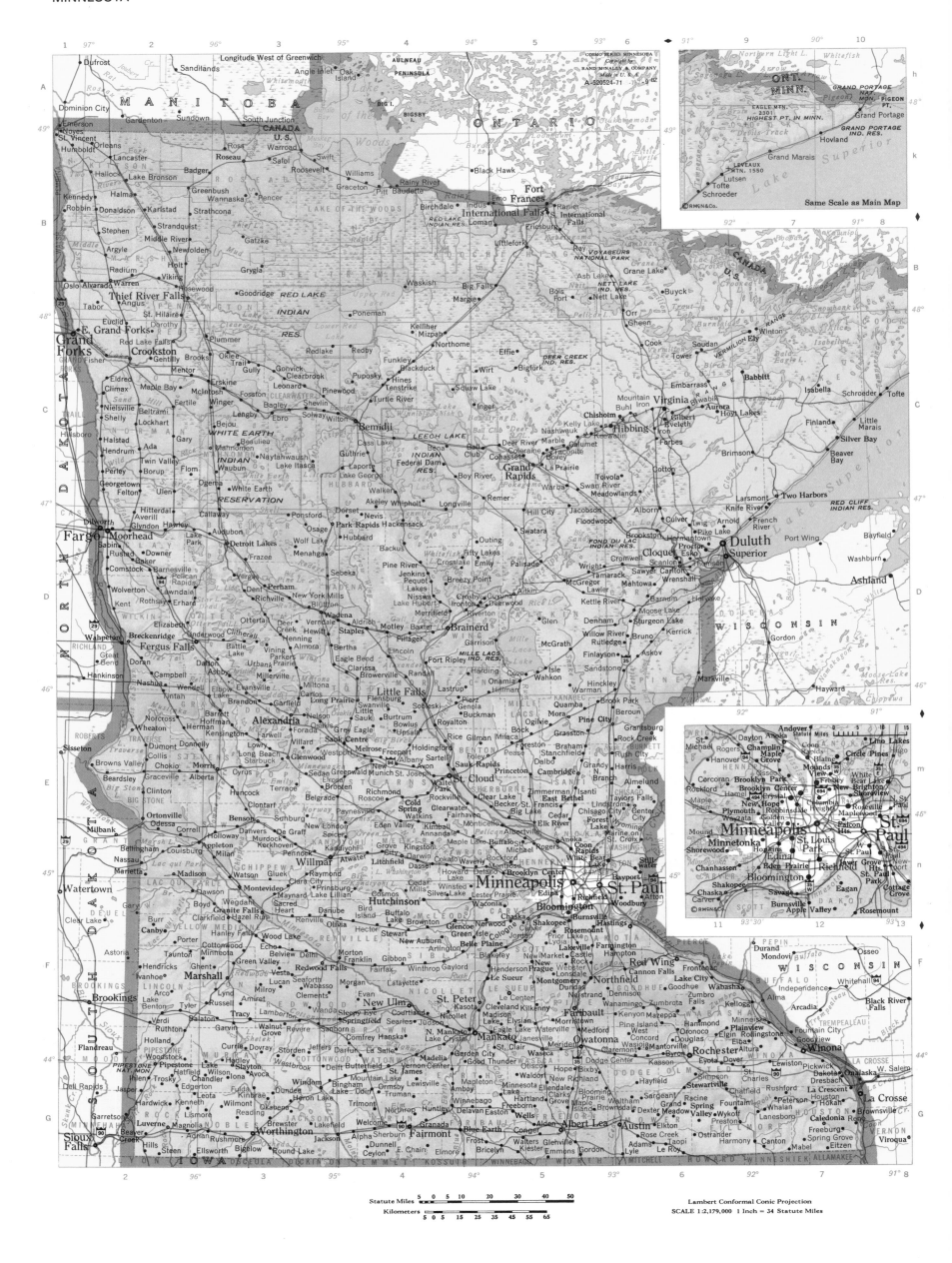

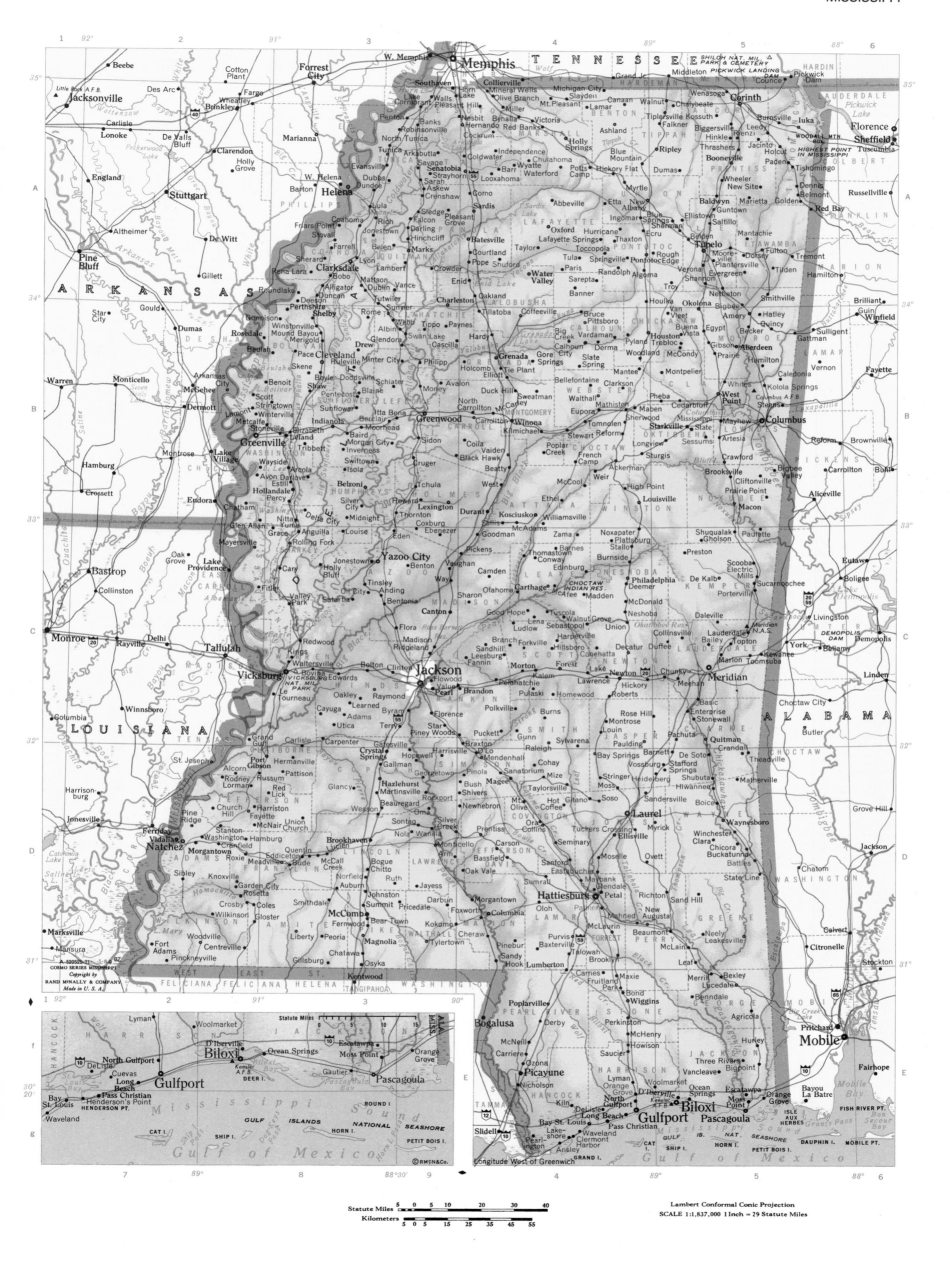

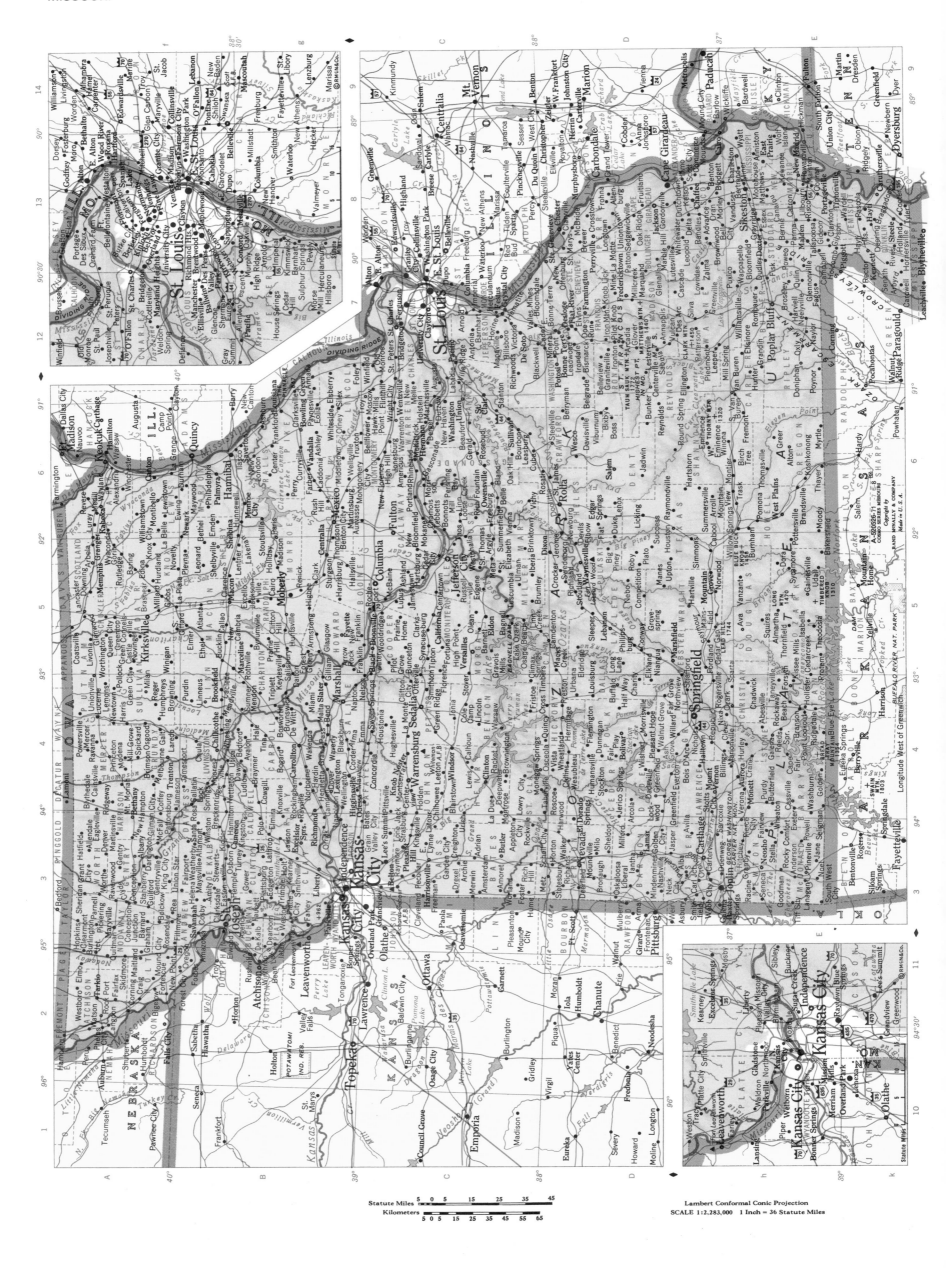

Statute Miles

Kilometers

Lambert Conformal Conic Projection
SCALE 1:2,283,000   1 Inch = 36 Statute Miles

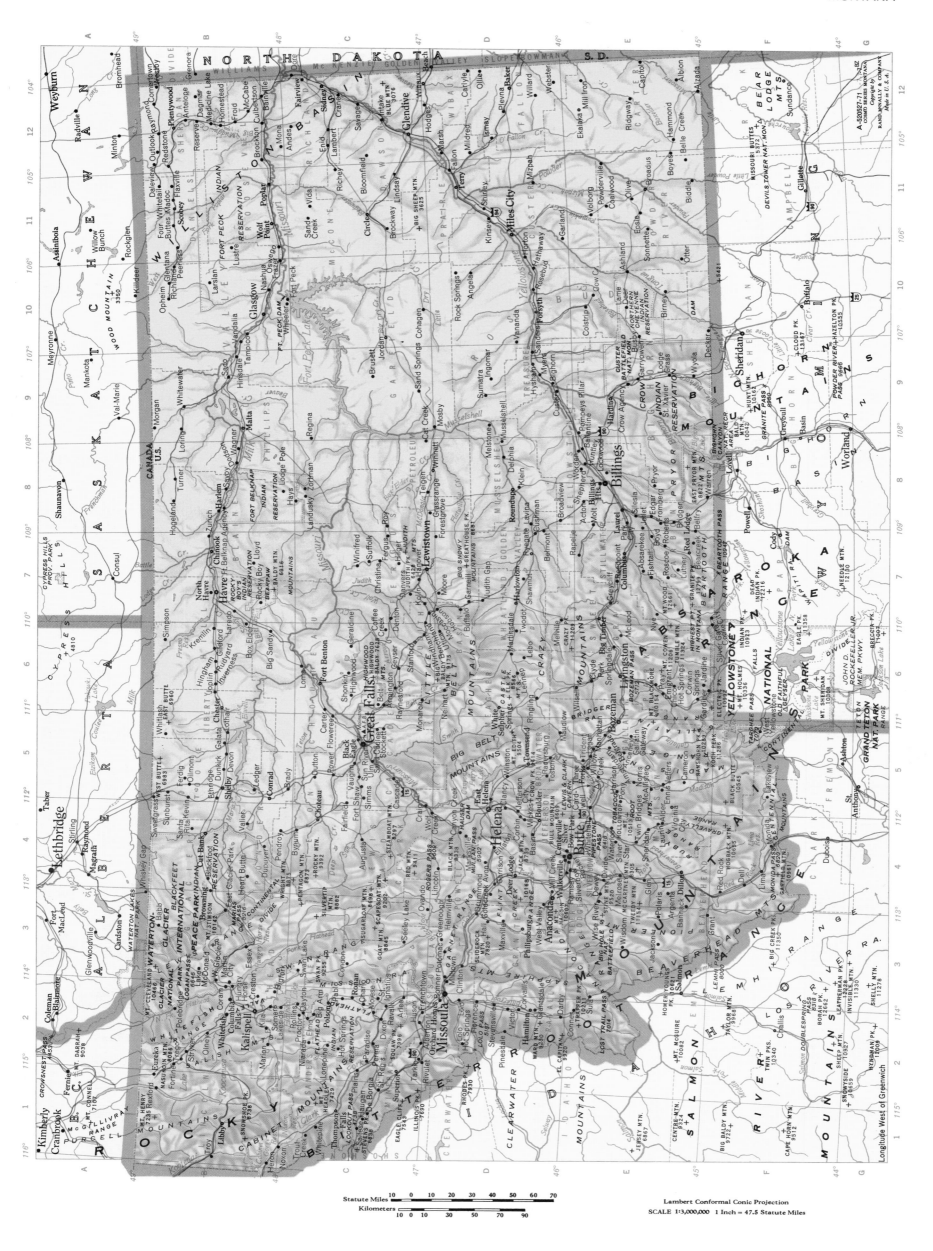

Statute Miles 10 0 10 20 30 40 50 60 70
Kilometers 10 0 10 30 50 70 90

Lambert Conformal Conic Projection
SCALE 1:3,000,000 1 Inch = 47.5 Statute Miles

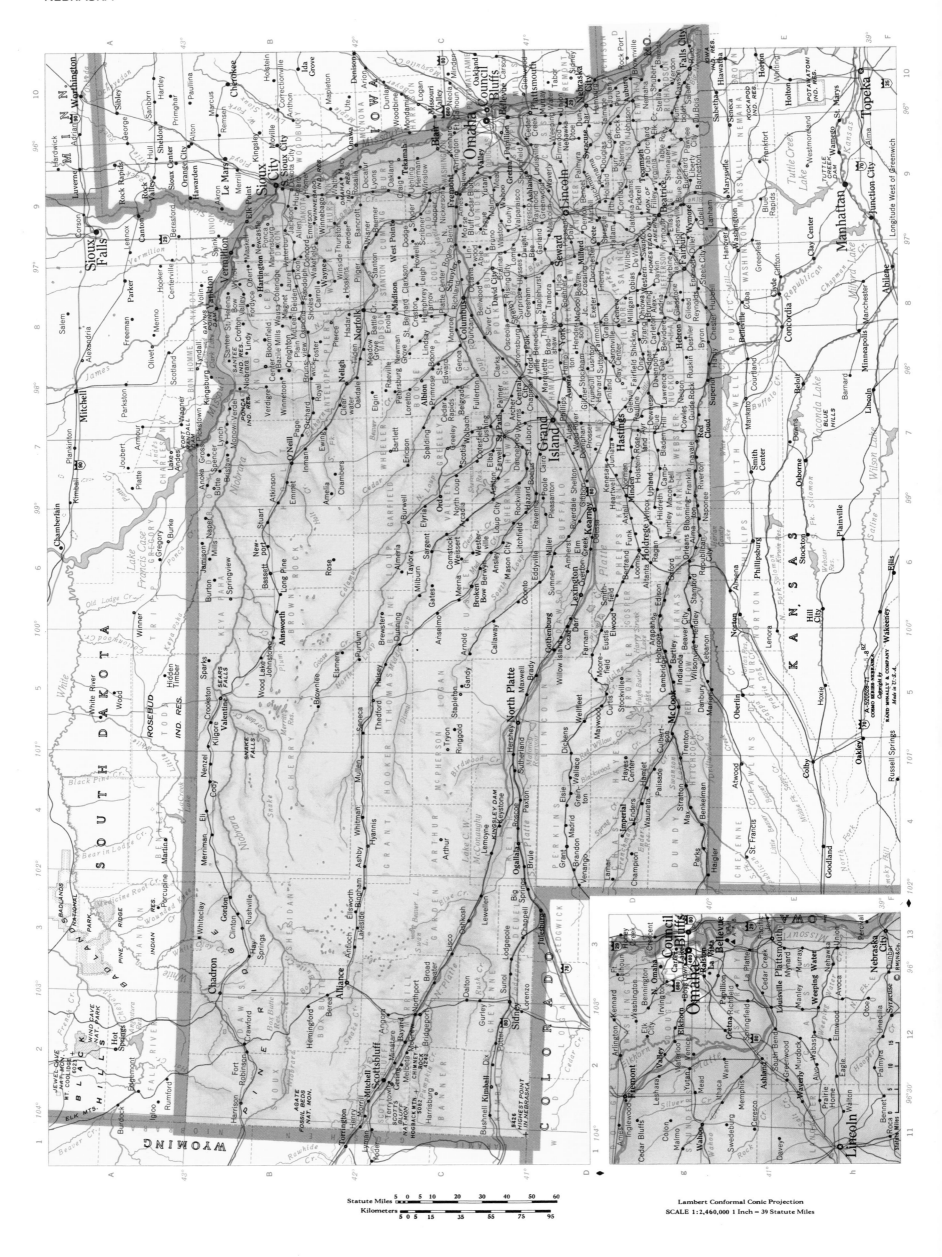

Statute Miles 5 0 5 10   20   30   40   50   60
Kilometers 5 0 5   15   35   55   75   95

Lambert Conformal Conic Projection
SCALE 1:2,460,000 1 Inch = 39 Statute Miles

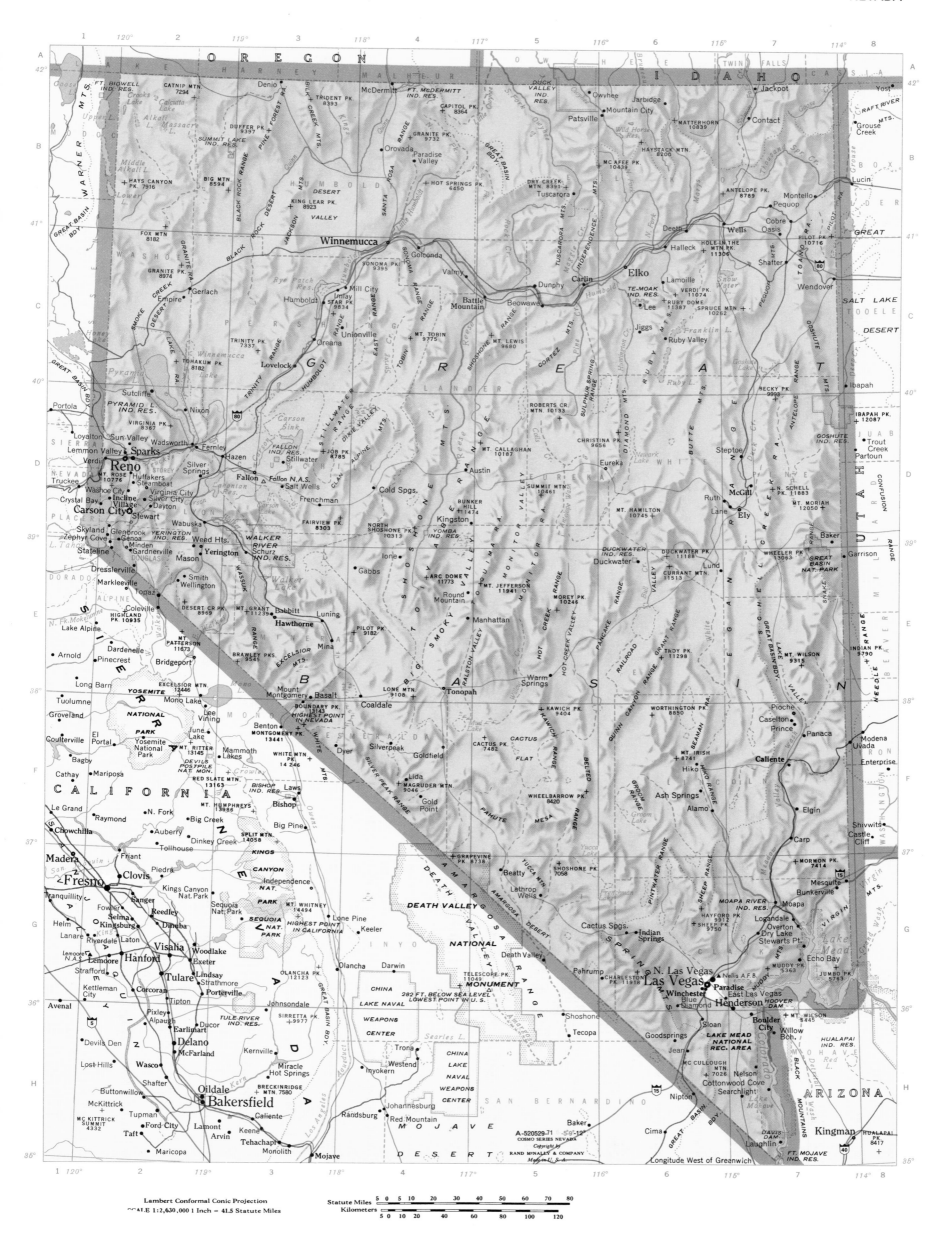

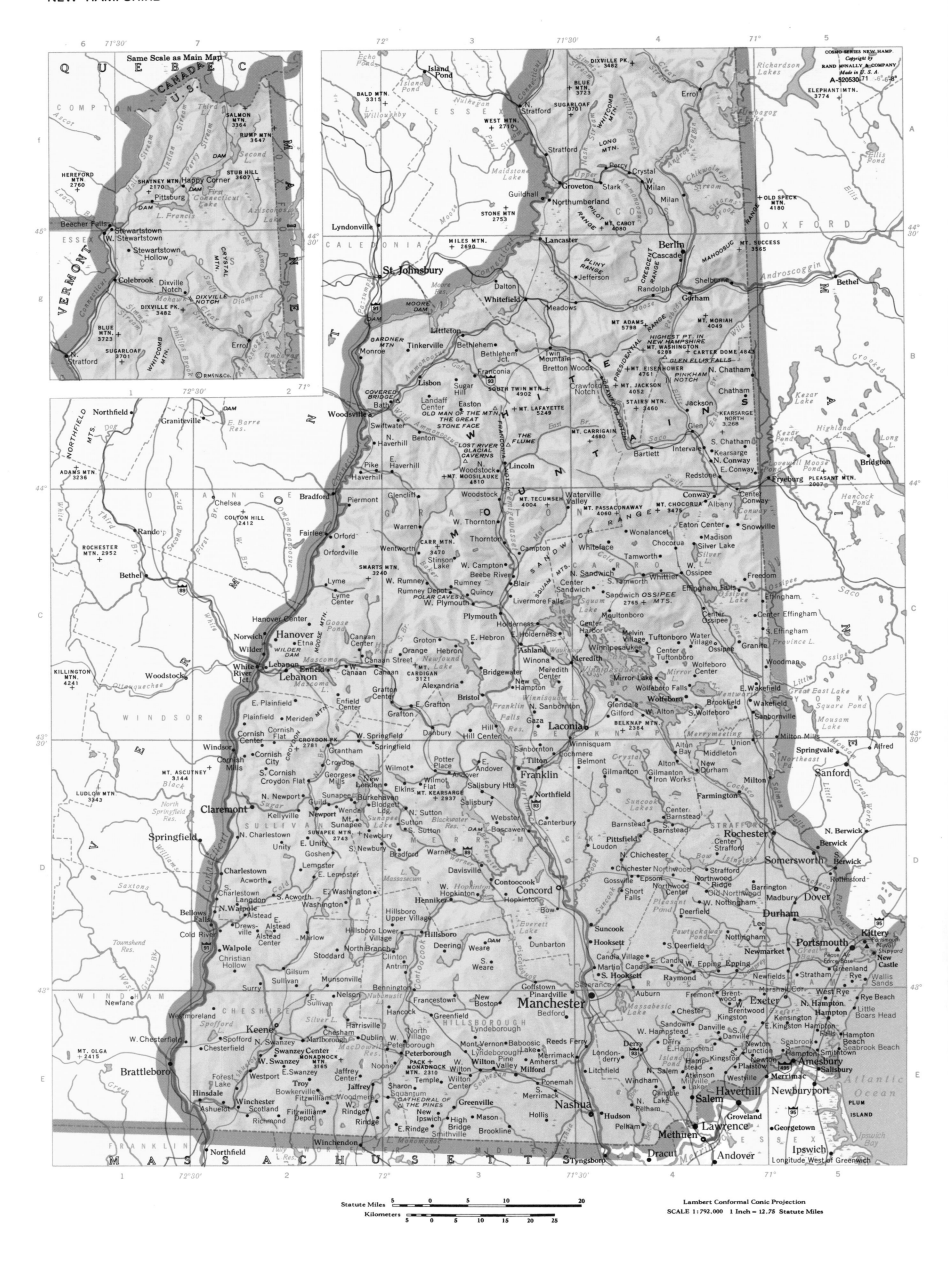

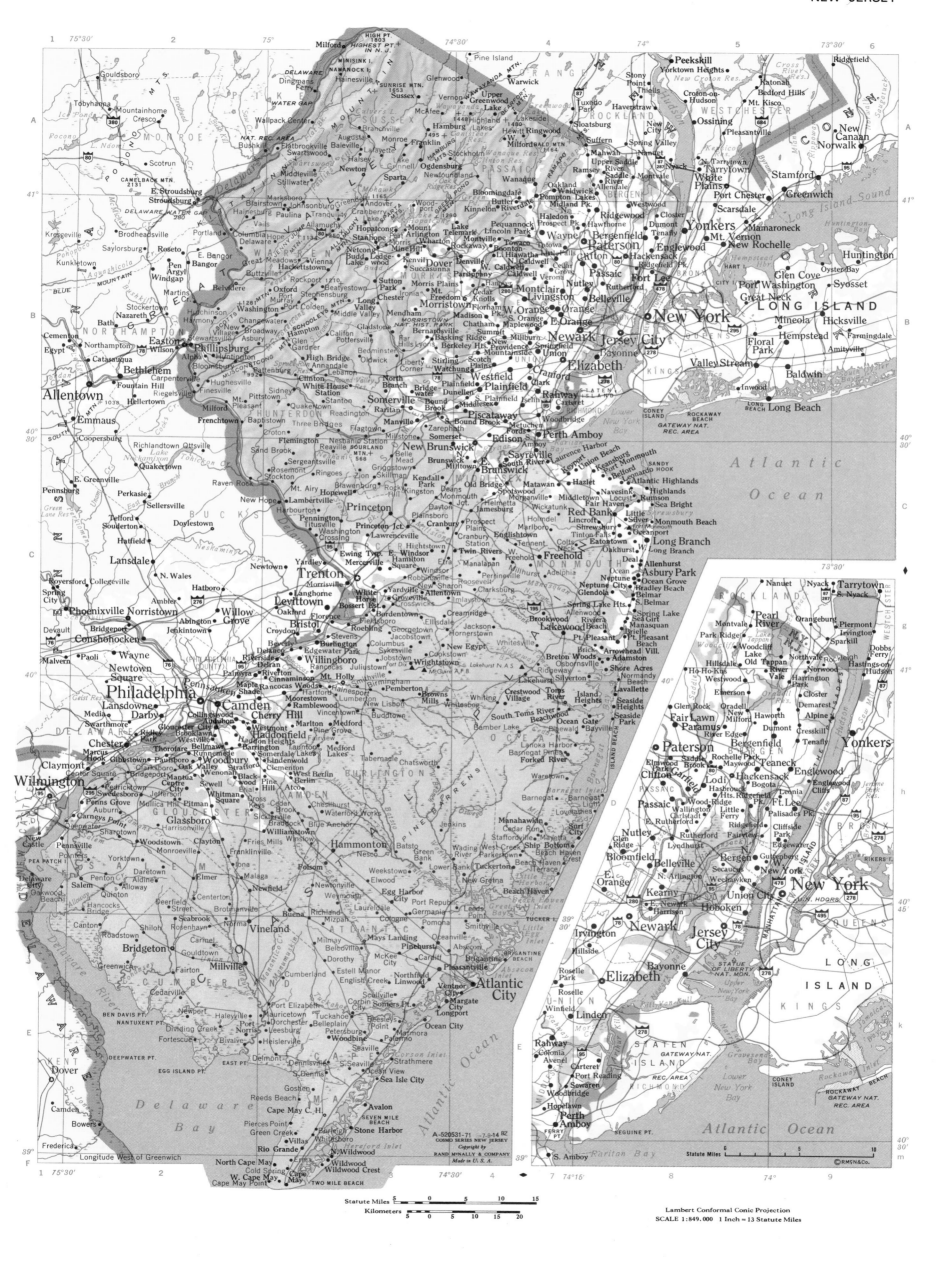

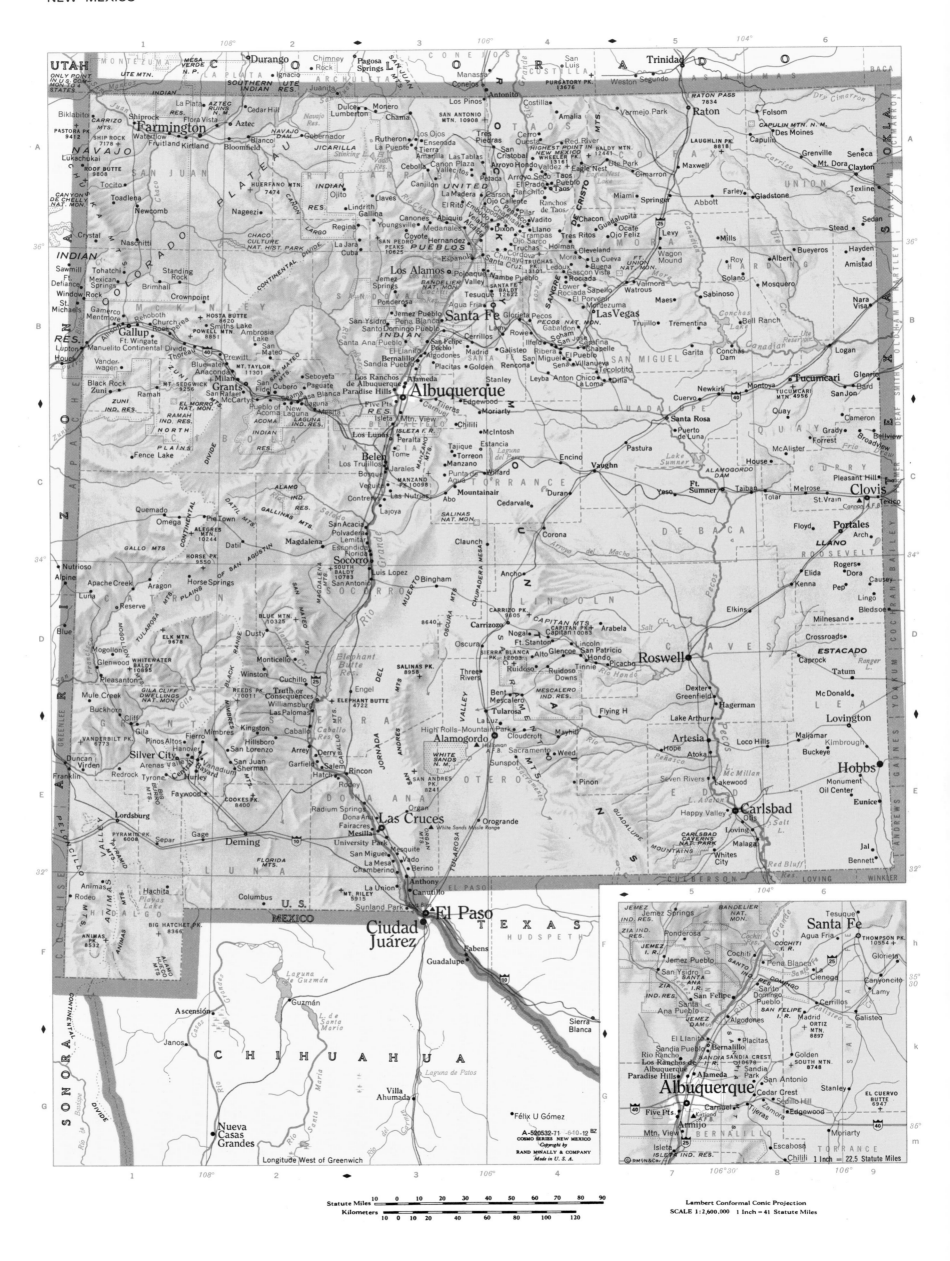

Statute Miles
10 0 10 20 30 40 50 60 70 80 90

Kilometers
10 0 10 20 40 60 80 100 120

Lambert Conformal Conic Projection
SCALE 1:2,600,000   1 Inch = 41 Statute Miles

1 Inch = 22.5 Statute Miles

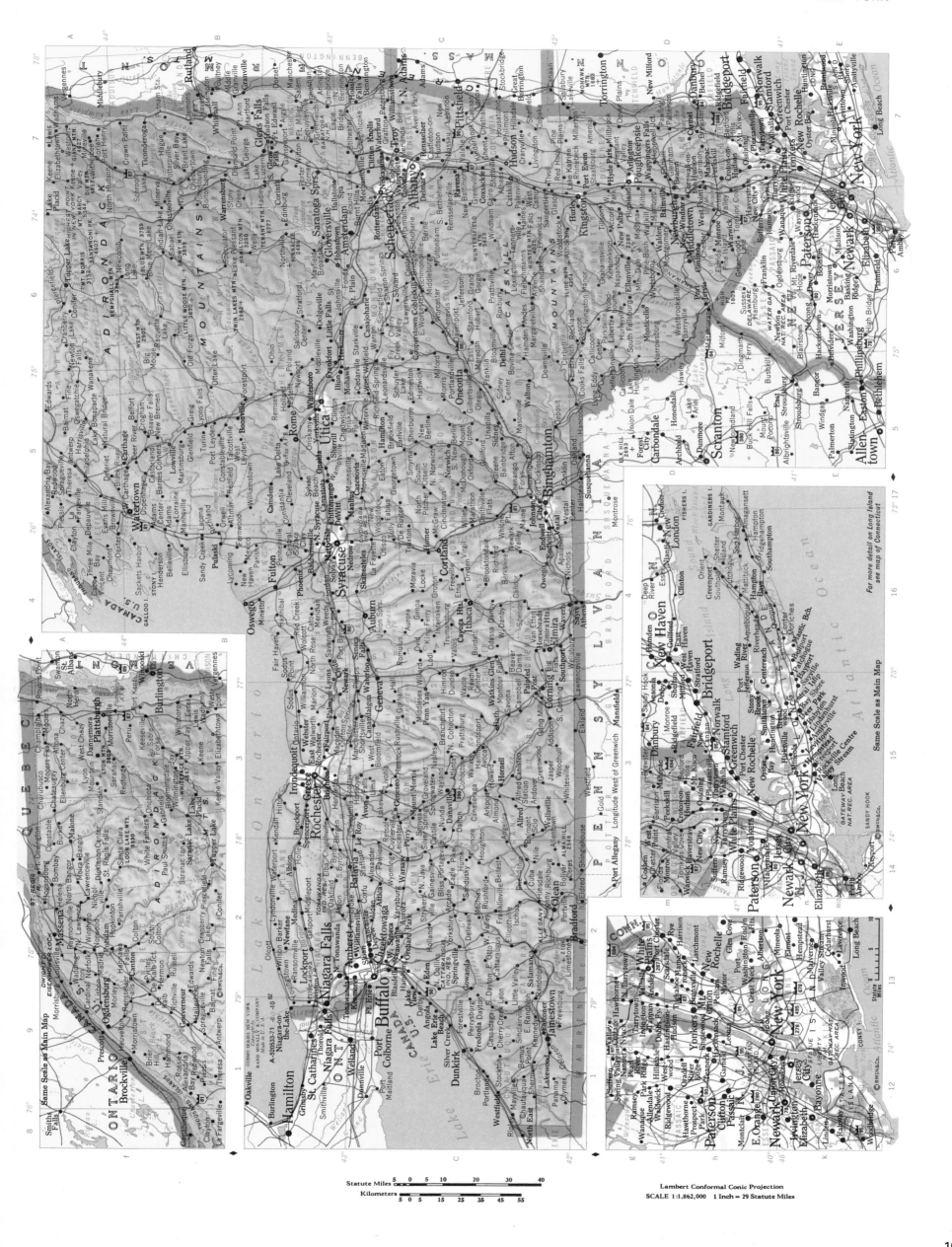

Statute Miles 5 0 5 10   20   30   40
Kilometers 5 0 5 15 25 35 45 55

Lambert Conformal Conic Projection
SCALE 1:1,862,000   1 Inch = 29 Statute Miles

109

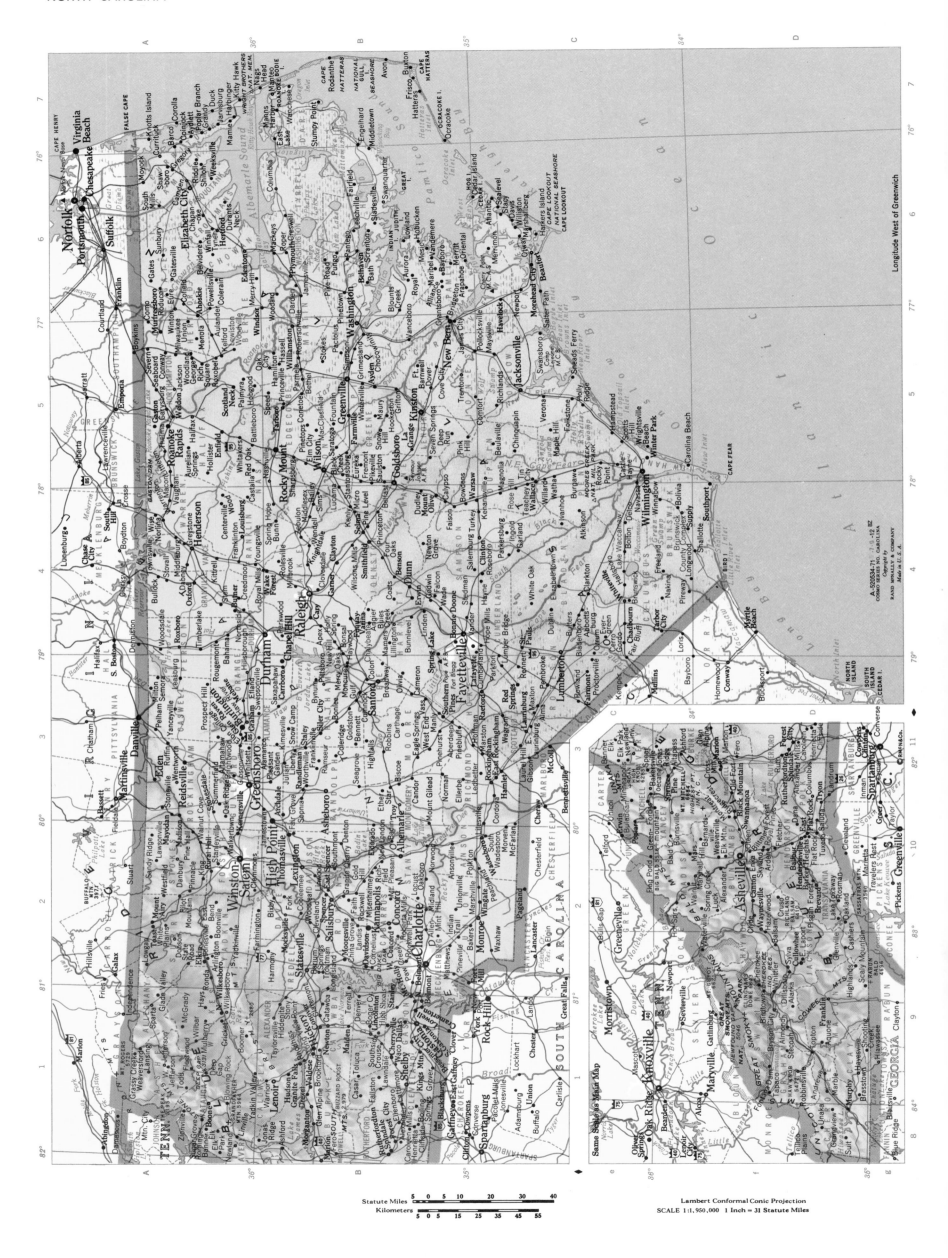

Statute Miles 5 0 5 10 20 30 40
Kilometers 5 0 5 15 25 35 45 55

Lambert Conformal Conic Projection
SCALE 1:1,950,000   1 Inch = 31 Statute Miles

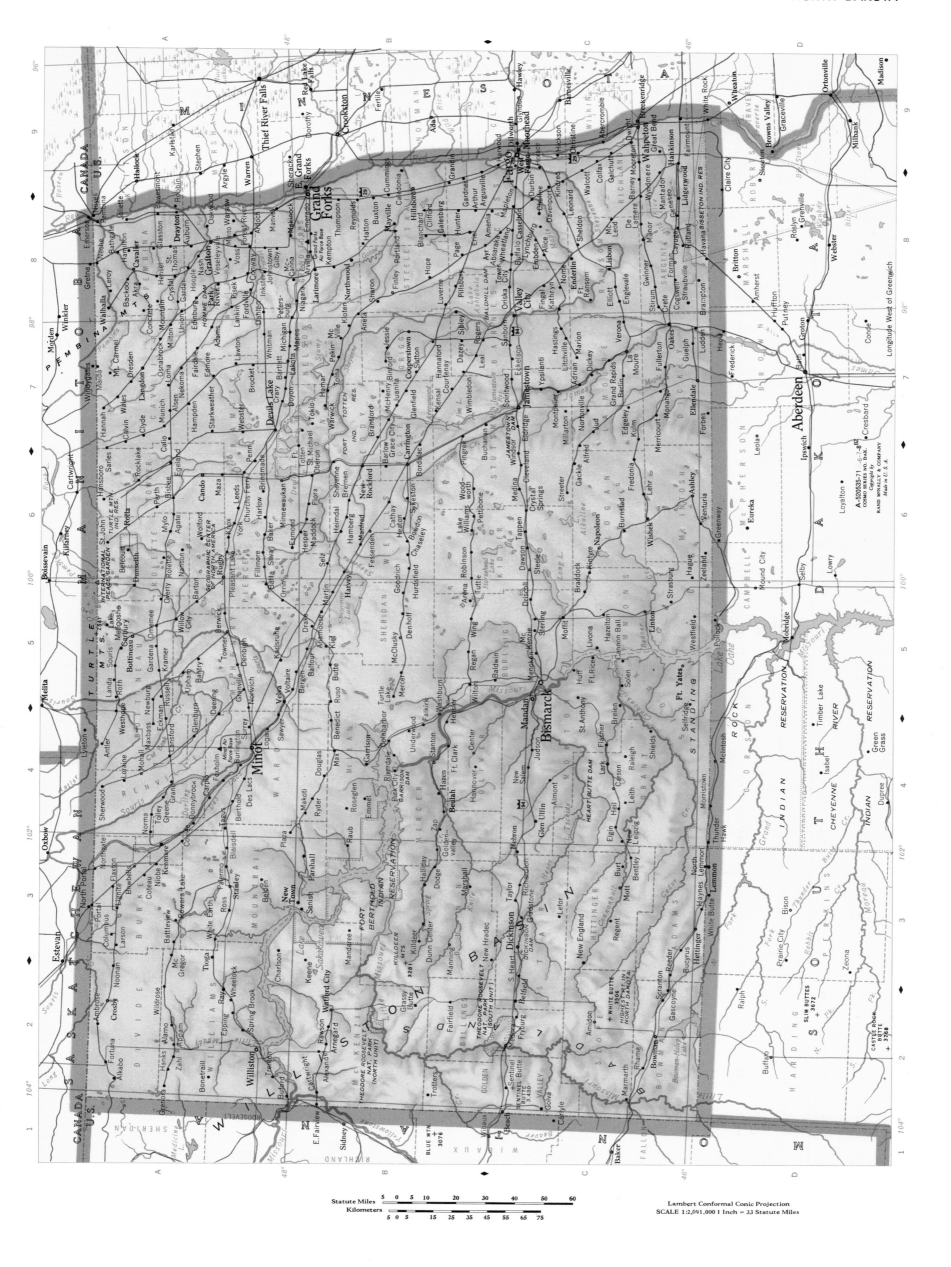

Statute Miles
Kilometers

Lambert Conformal Conic Projection
SCALE 1:2,091,000 1 Inch = 33 Statute Miles

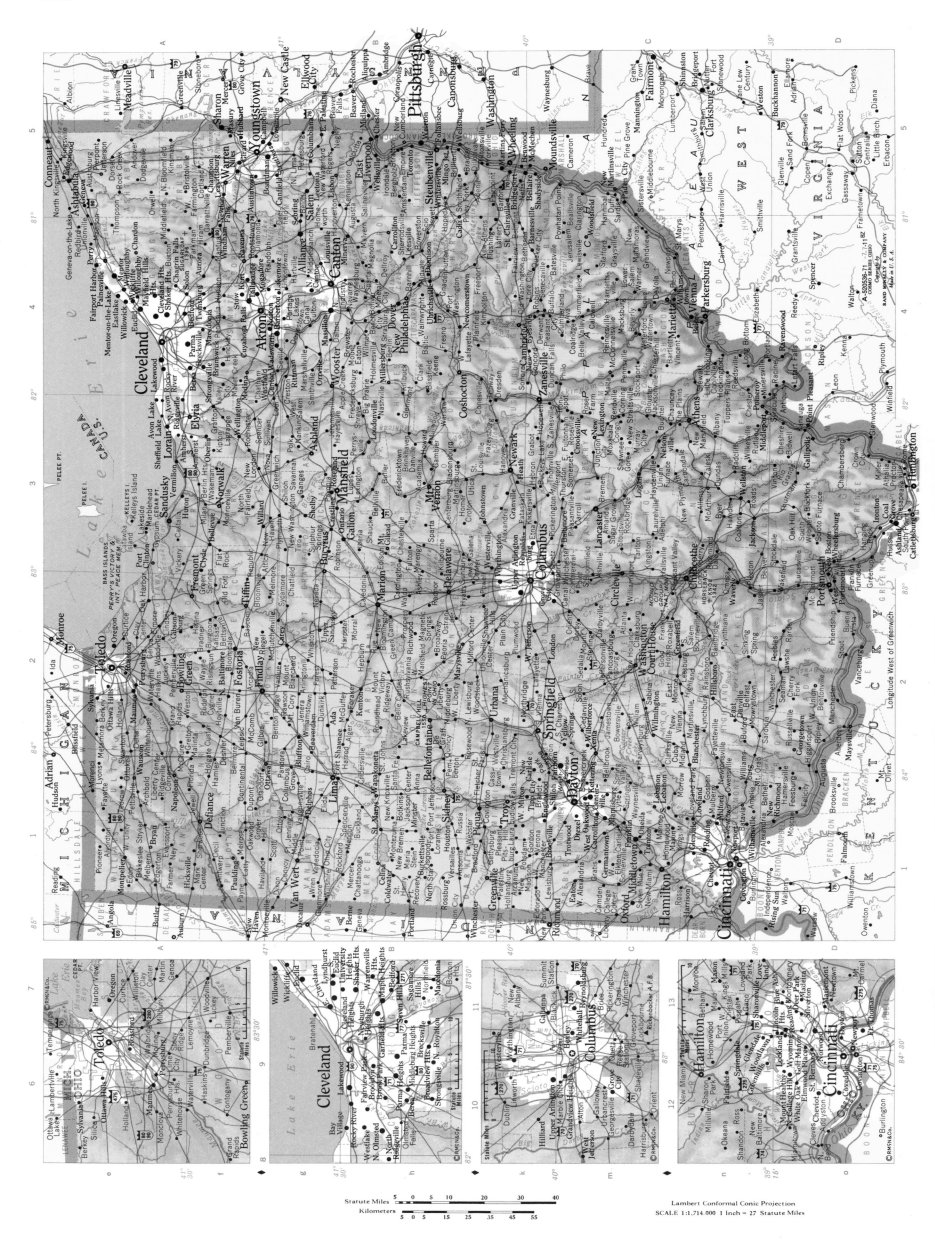

Statute Miles 5 0 5 10 20 30 40
Kilometers 5 0 5 15 25 35 45 55

Lambert Conformal Conic Projection
SCALE 1:1,714,000 1 Inch = 27 Statute Miles

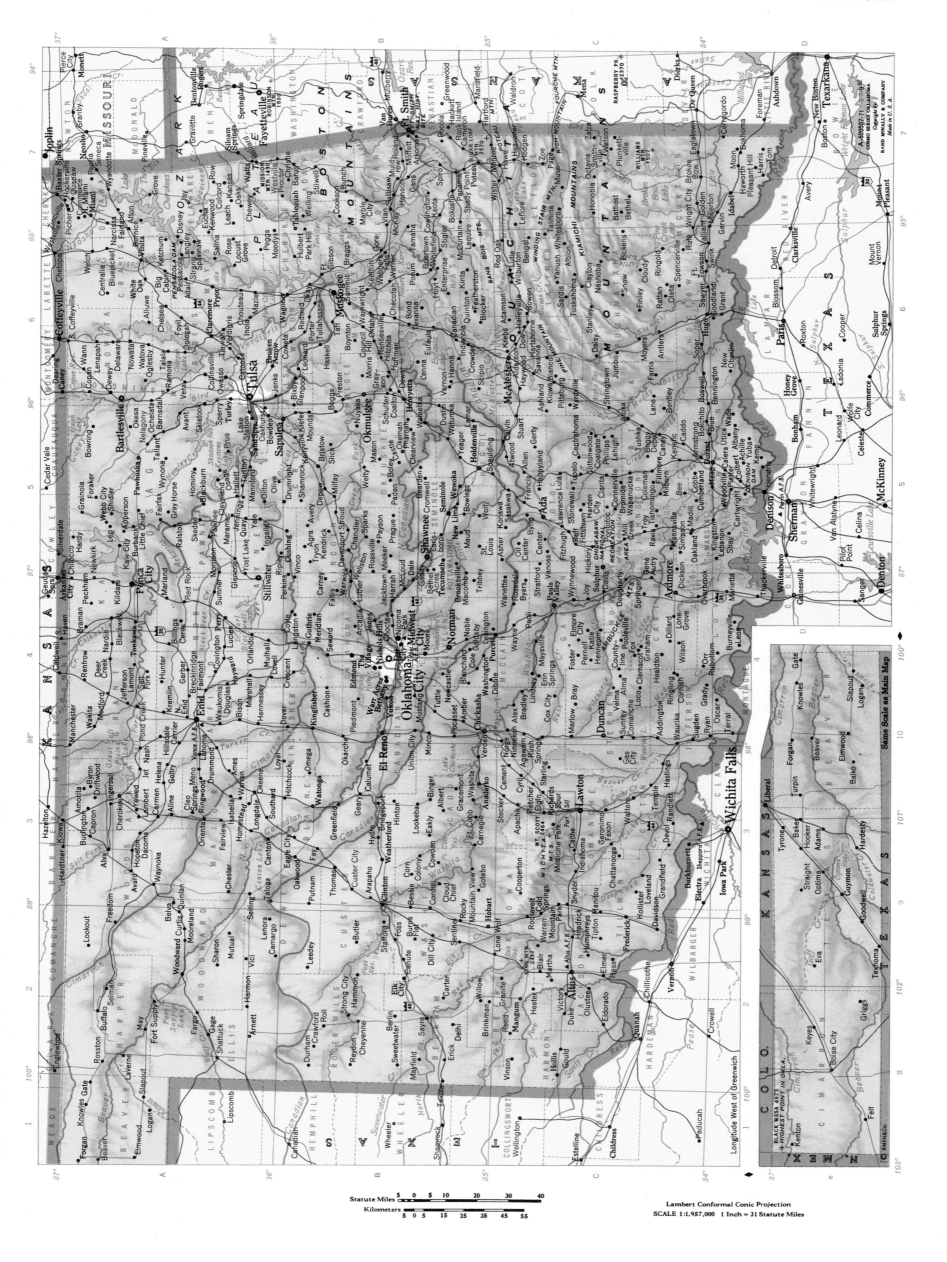

Statute Miles 5 0 5 10 20 30 40
Kilometers 5 0 5 15 25 35 45 55

Lambert Conformal Conic Projection
SCALE 1:1,957,000   1 Inch = 31 Statute Miles

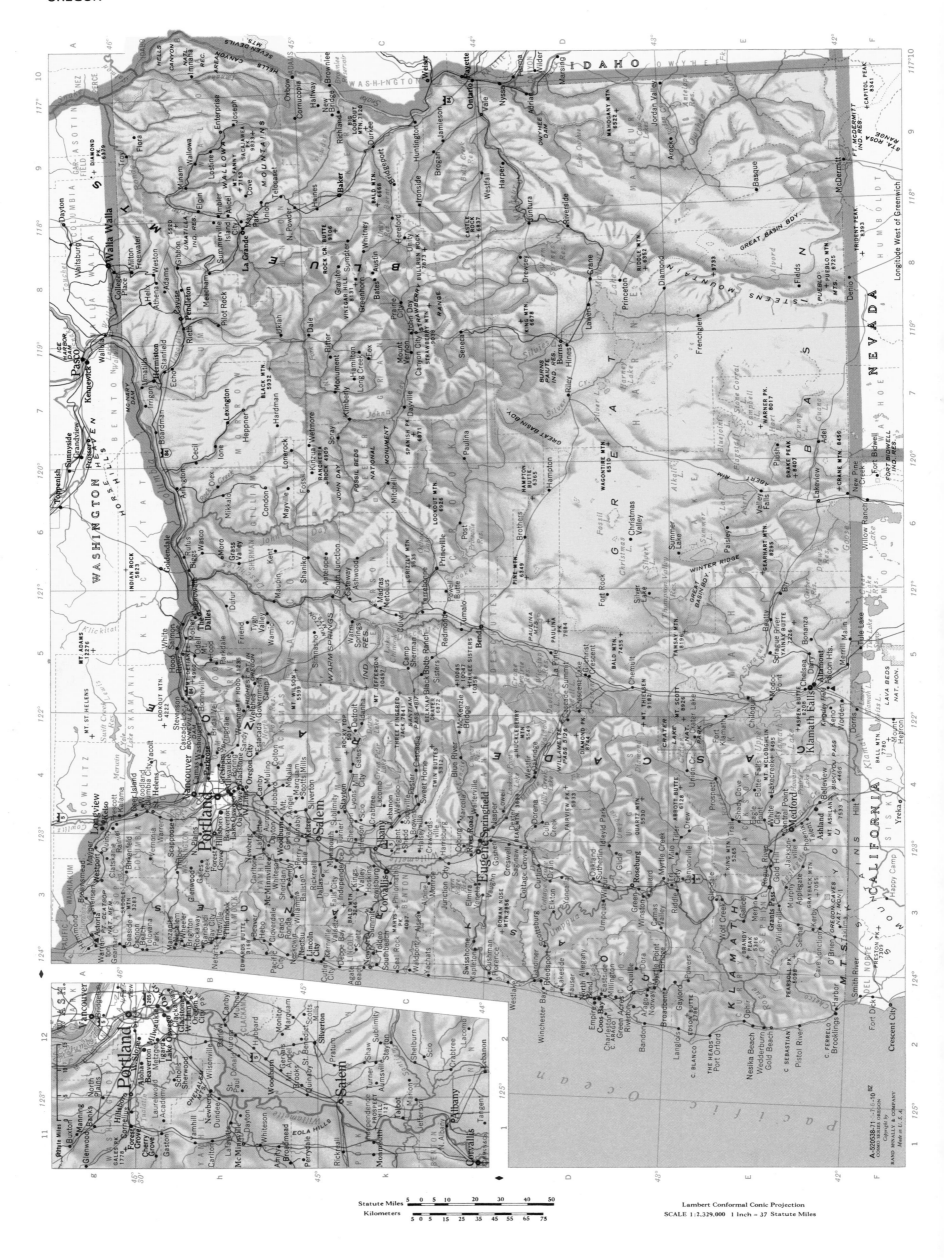

Statute Miles
Kilometers

Lambert Conformal Conic Projection
SCALE 1:2,329,000   1 Inch = 37 Statute Miles

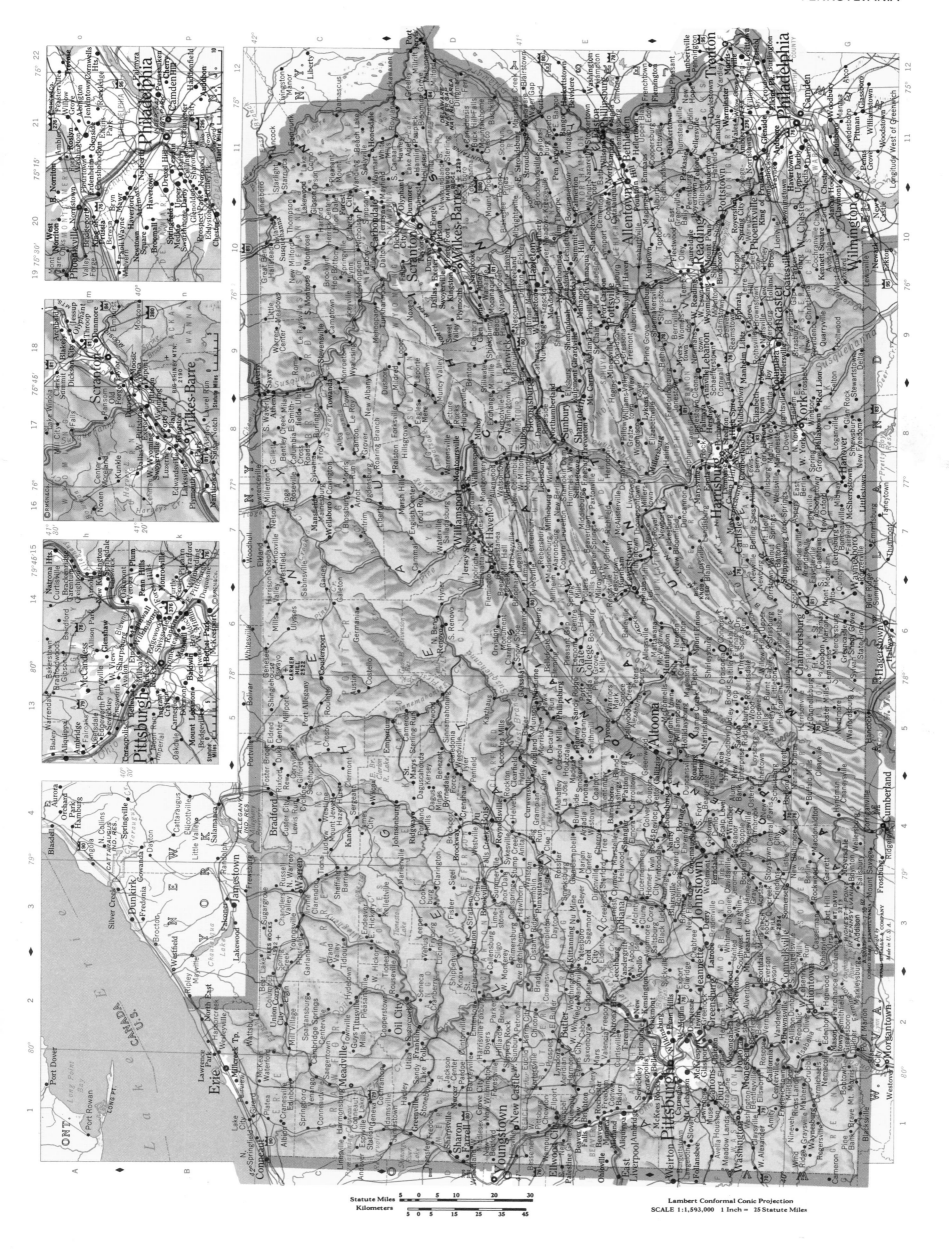

Statute Miles
Kilometers

Lambert Conformal Conic Projection
SCALE 1:1,593,000   1 Inch = 25 Statute Miles

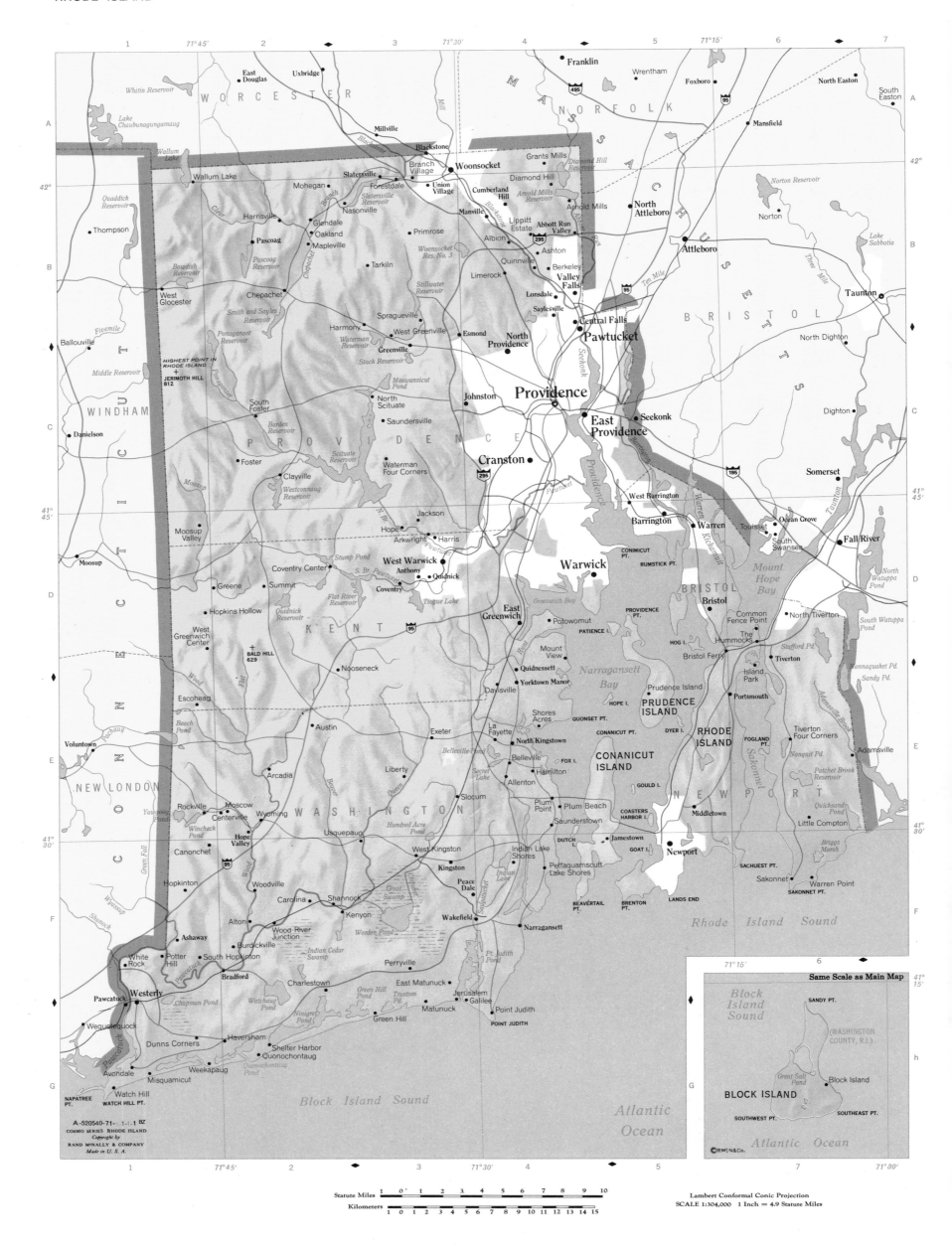

RHODE ISLAND

A | **B** | **C** | **D** | **E** | **F** | **G**

WORCESTER

MASS

NORFOLK

Franklin
Wrentham
Foxboro
North Easton
South Easton
Mansfield

Whitin Reservoir
East Douglas
Uxbridge

Lake Chaubunagungamaug
Millville

Wallum Lake
Blackstone
Grants Mills
Diamond Hill Reservoir

Quaddick Reservoir
Woonsocket
Branch Village
Slatersville
Diamond Hill

Thompson
Mohegan
Forestdale
Union Village
Cumberland Hill
Arnold Mills Reservoir
Arnold Mills
North Attleboro
Norton

Harrisville
Nasonville
Manville
Lippitt Estate
Abbott Run Valley

Glendale
Oakland
Mapleville
Primrose
Albion
Ashton
Berkeley
Attleboro
Lake Sabbatia

Pascoag
Tarkiln
Quinnville
Valley Falls

Bowdish Reservoir
Limerock
Lonsdale
Saylesville

West Glocester
Chepachet
Stillwater Reservoir
North Providence
Central Falls
Pawtucket
Taunton

Ballouville
Smith and Sayles Reservoir
Spragueville
West Greenville
Esmond
North Dighton

Fivemile
Harmony
Waterman Reservoir
Greenville
BRISTOL

Middle Reservoir
Ponaganset Reservoir
Stack Reservoir
North Dighton

HIGHEST POINT IN RHODE ISLAND
JERIMOTH HILL 812

South Foster
North Scituate
Johnston
Providence
Dighton

Danielson
Barden Reservoir
Saundersville
East Providence
Seekonk

Foster
Scituate Reservoir
Cranston
Somerset

Clayville
Waterman Four Corners
West Barrington

Moosup Valley
Westconnaug Reservoir
Jackson
Barrington
Warren
Ocean Grove

Moosup
Hope
Arkwright
Harris
Warwick
South Swansea
Fall River

West Warwick
Anthony
Quidnick
CONIMICUT PT.
RUMSTICK PT.

Greene
Coventry Center
Coventry
PROVIDENCE PT.

Summit
S. Br. Pawtuxet
Flat River Reservoir
Tiogue Lake

Hopkins Hollow
Quidnick Reservoir
East Greenwich
Bristol

West Greenwich Center
BALD HILL 629
Nooseneck
Potowomut
PATIENCE I.
North Tiverton
South Watuppa Pond

Mount View
HOG I.
The Hummocks
Tiverton

Escoheag
Beach Pond
Quidnessett
Bristol Ferry
Island Park

Voluntown
Austin
Exeter
Belleville Pond
Yorktown Manor
Narragansett Bay
PRUDENCE ISLAND
Portsmouth
Tiverton Four Corners

Arcadia
Liberty
La Fayette
Shores Acres
QUONSET PT.
CONANICUT PT.
DYER I.
RHODE ISLAND
Adamsville

North Kingstown
FOX I.
CONANICUT ISLAND
FOGLAND PT.

Rockville
Moscow
Centerville
Wyoming
Usquepaug
Belleville
Hamilton
Allenton
GOULD I.
NEWPORT

Hope Valley
Hundred Acre Pond
Slocum
Plum Point
Plum Beach
COASTERS HARBOR I.
Middletown
Little Compton

Canonchet
West Kingston
Saunderstown
DUTCH I.
Jamestown
GOAT I.
Newport
Quicksand Pond

Hopkinton
Kingston
Indian Lake Shores
Pettaquamscutt Lake Shores
SACHUEST PT.
Briggs Marsh

Woodville
Shannock
Peace Dale
BEAVERTAIL PT.
BRENTON PT.
LANDS END
Warren Point

Alton
Kenyon
Wakefield
Narragansett
SAKONNET PT.

Ashaway
Carolina
Wood River Junction
Great Swamp
Indian Cedar Swamp
Rhode Island Sound

White Rock
Burdickville
Perryville
Pt. Judith Pond

Potter Hill
South Hopkinton
Bradford
East Matunuck
Jerusalem
Galilee

Westerly
Charlestown
Green Hill Pond
Matunuck
Point Judith
POINT JUDITH

Pawcatuck
Green Hill
Weequapaug

Dunns Corners
Haversham
Shelter Harbor
Quonochontaug

Avondale
Misquamicut
Weekapaug

NAPATREE PT.
Watch Hill
WATCH HILL PT.

Block Island Sound
Atlantic Ocean

Statute Miles 1 0 1 2 3 4 5 6 7 8 9 10
Kilometers 1 0 1 2 3 4 5 6 7 8 9 10 11 12 13 14 15

A-520540-71- 1-1-1 82
COSMO SERIES RHODE ISLAND
Copyright by
RAND McNALLY & COMPANY
Made in U.S.A.

Lambert Conformal Conic Projection
SCALE 1:304,000   1 Inch = 4.9 Statute Miles

Inset: BLOCK ISLAND

Same Scale as Main Map

Block Island Sound
SANDY PT.
(WASHINGTON COUNTY, R.I.)
Great Salt Pond
Block Island
BLOCK ISLAND
SOUTHWEST PT.
SOUTHEAST PT.
Atlantic Ocean
©RM&N&Co.

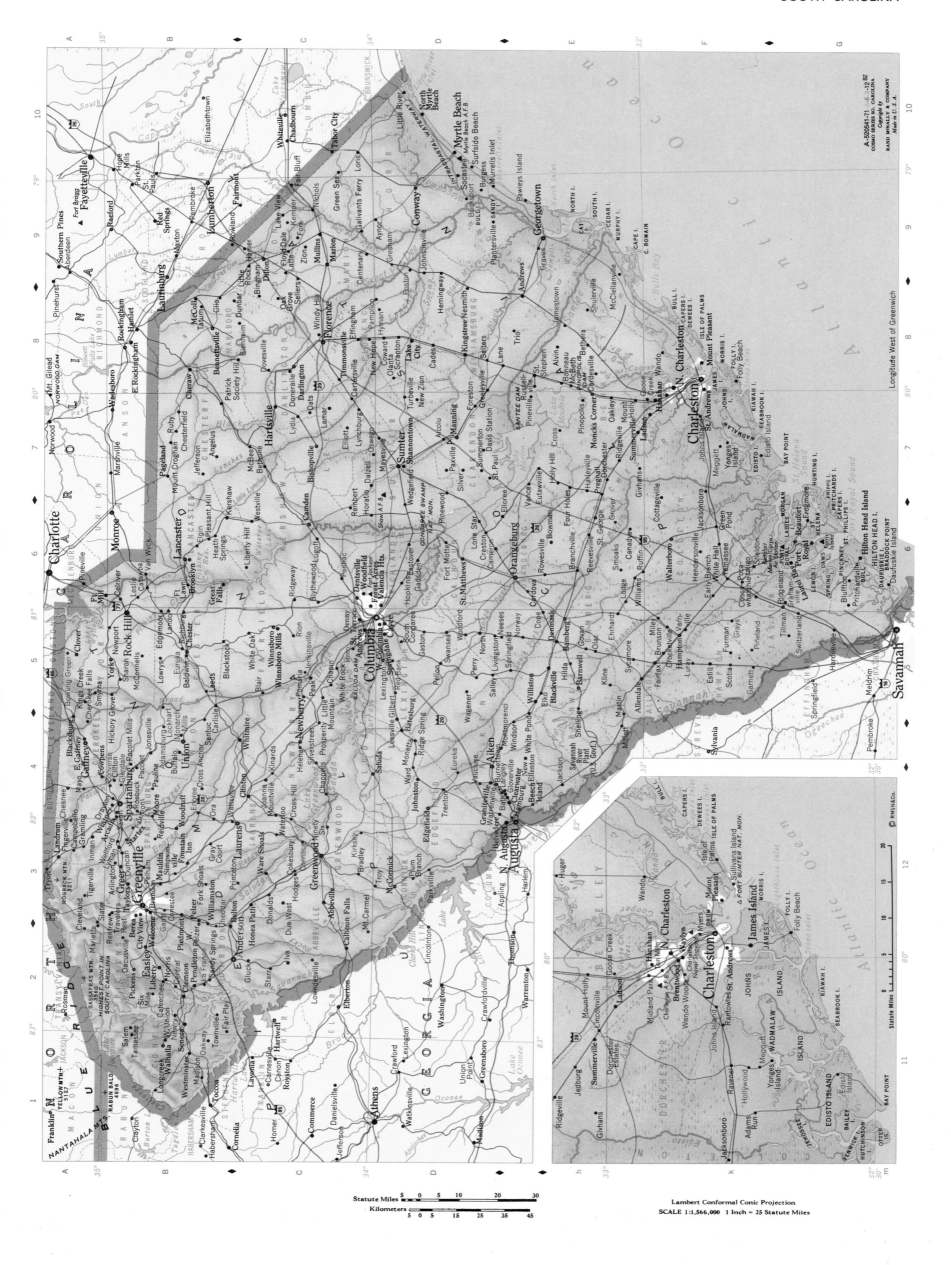

Lambert Conformal Conic Projection
SCALE 1:1,566,000   1 Inch = 25 Statute Miles

Statute Miles
Kilometers

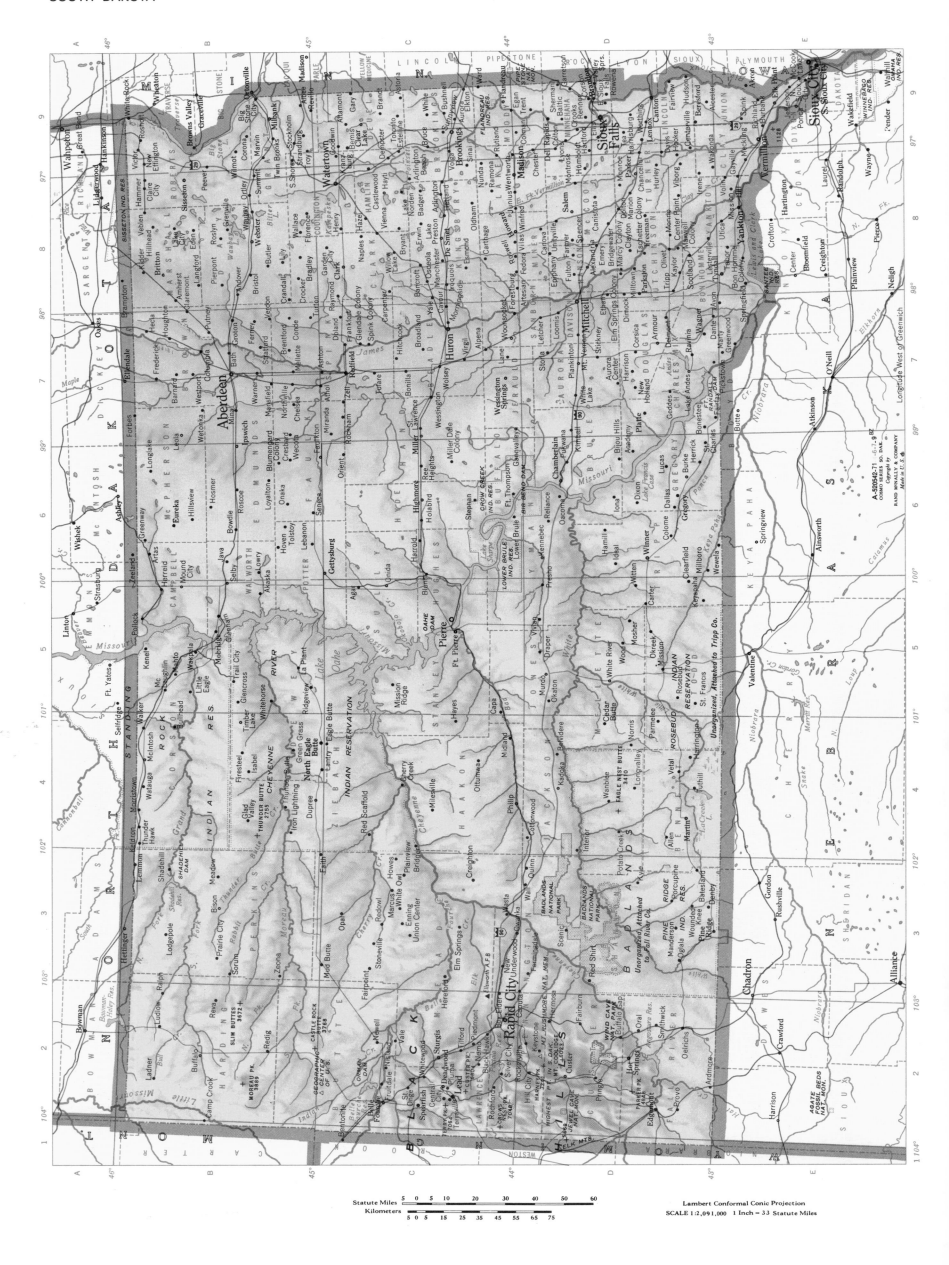

Statute Miles 5 0 5 10 20 30 40 50 60
Kilometers 5 0 5 15 25 35 45 55 65 75

Lambert Conformal Conic Projection
SCALE 1:2,091,000   1 Inch = 33 Statute Miles

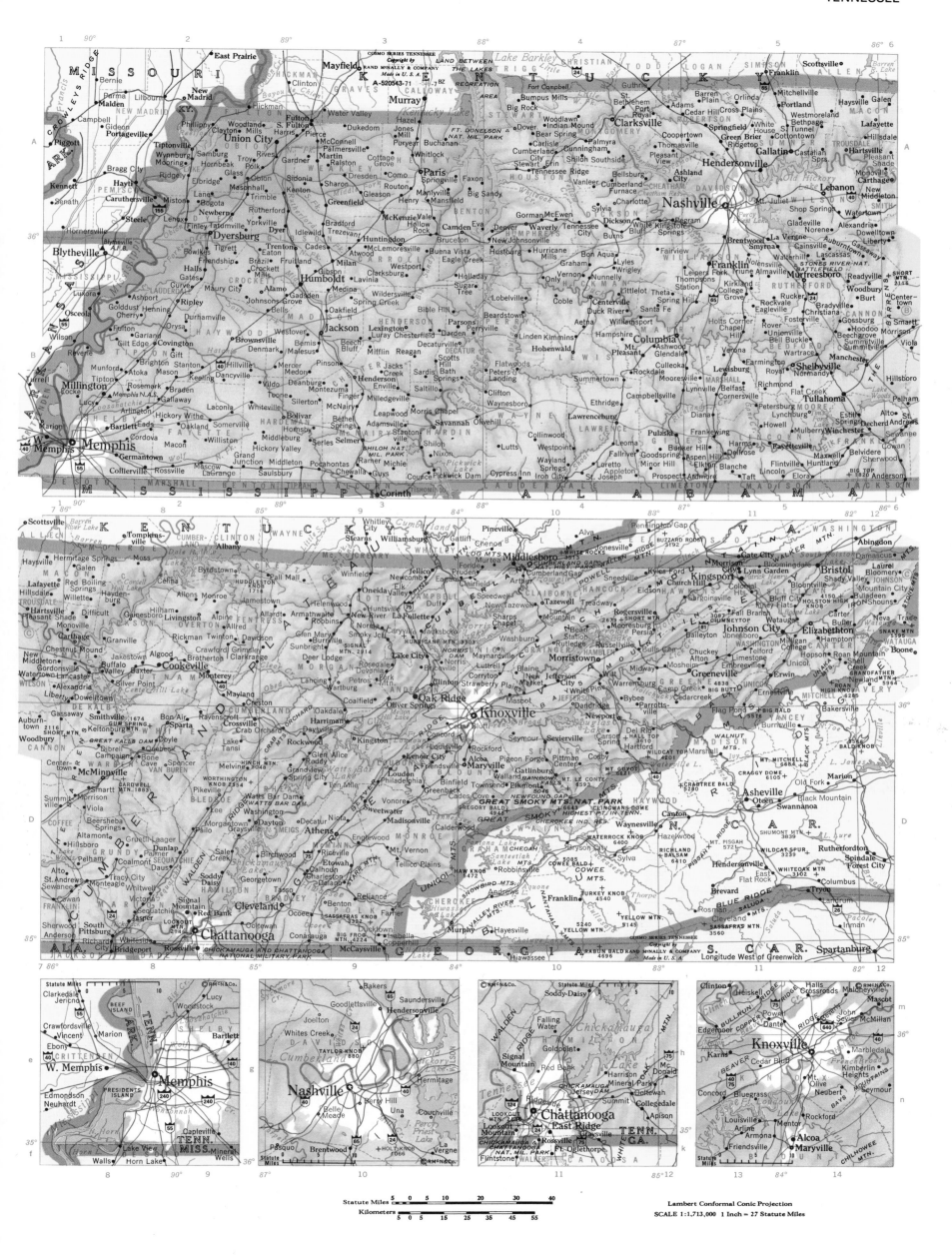

Statute Miles
5 0 5 10 20 30 40

Kilometers
5 0 5 15 25 35 45 55

Lambert Conformal Conic Projection
SCALE 1:1,713,000 1 Inch = 27 Statute Miles

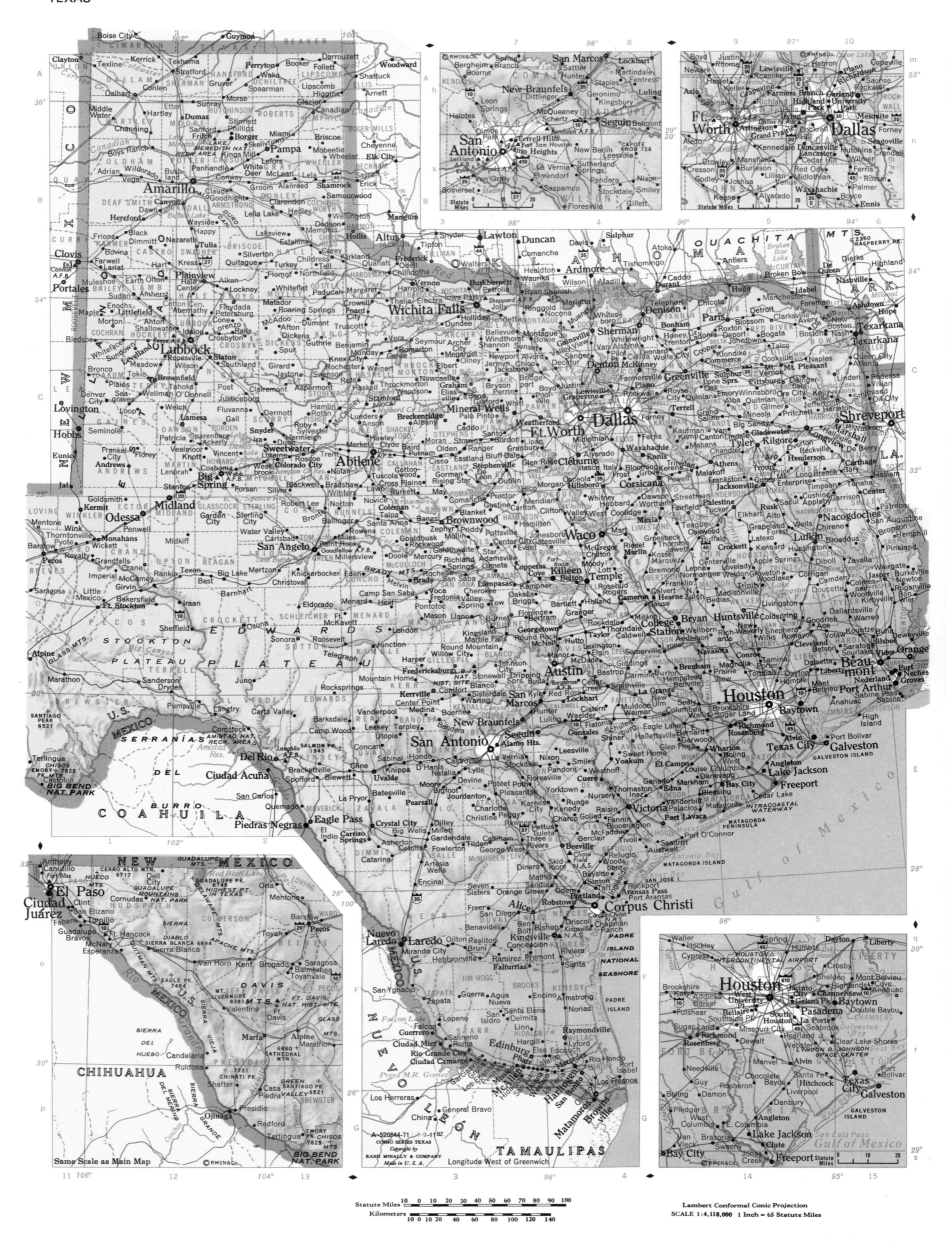

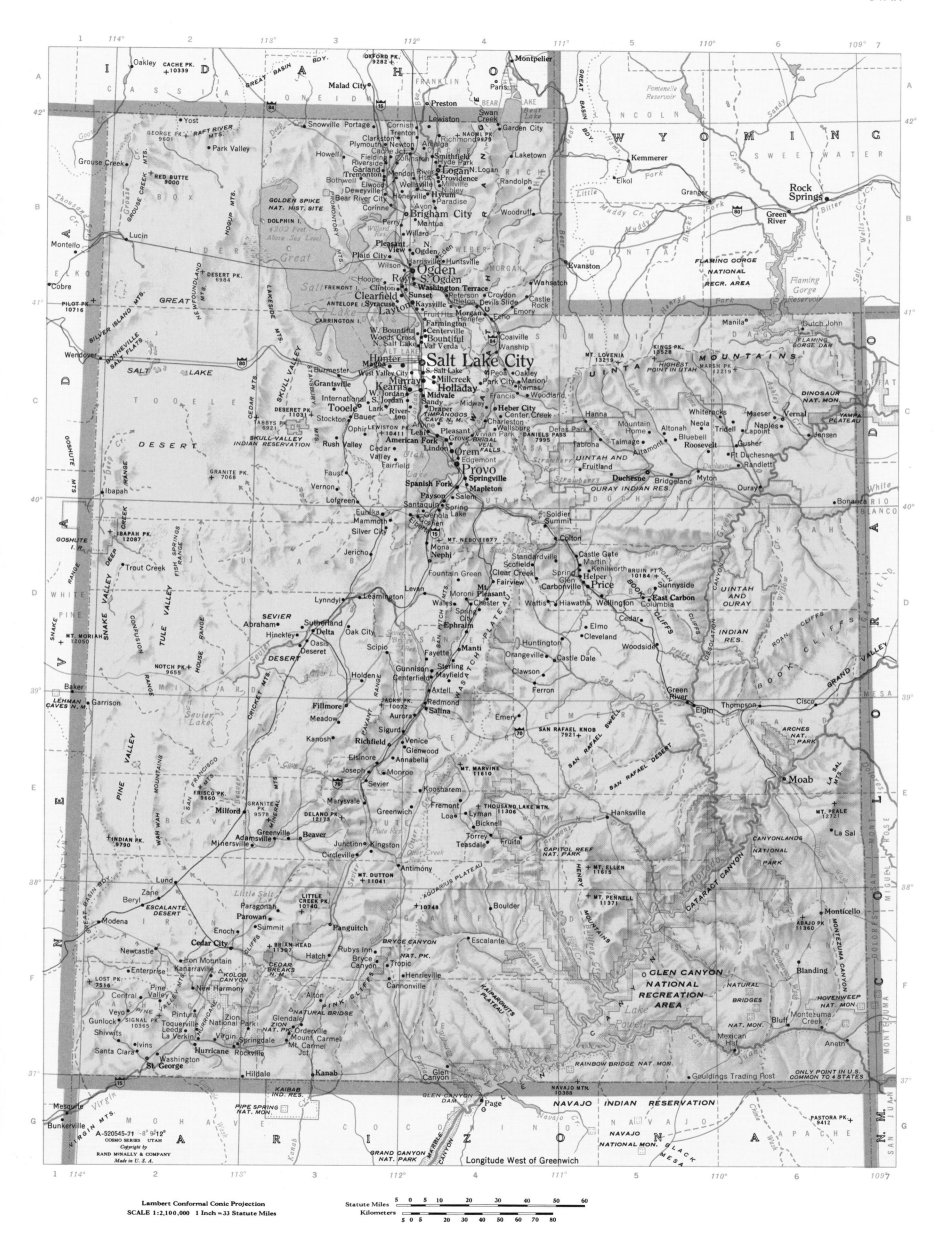

Lambert Conformal Conic Projection
SCALE 1:2,100,000   1 Inch ≈ 33 Statute Miles

Statute Miles
Kilometers

A-520545-71 -8°-12°
COSMO SERIES UTAH
Copyright by
RAND M℀NALLY & COMPANY
Made in U.S.A.

VERMONT

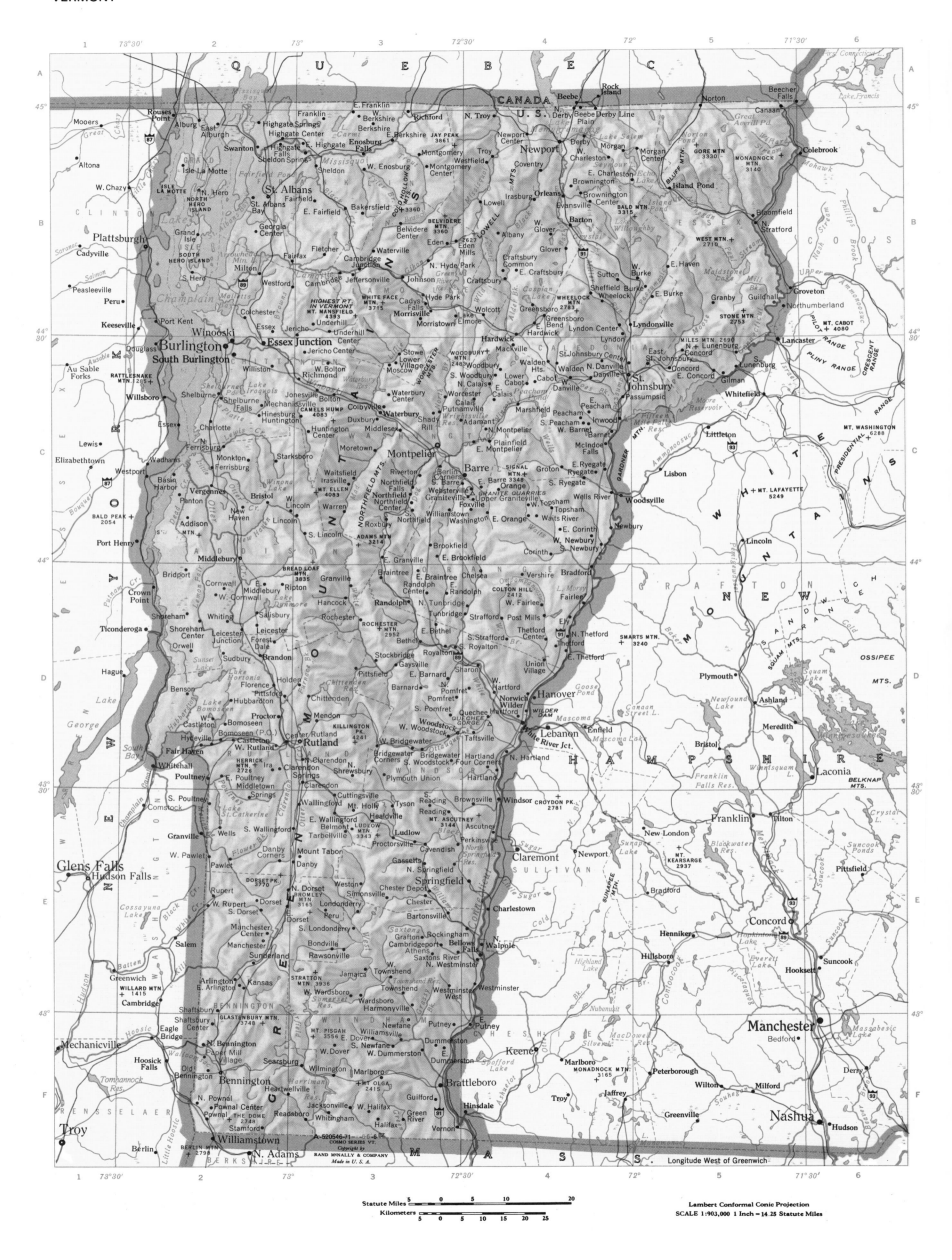

Statute Miles 5 0 5 10 20
Kilometers 5 0 5 10 15 20 25

Lambert Conformal Conic Projection
SCALE 1:903,000 1 Inch = 14.25 Statute Miles

Longitude West of Greenwich

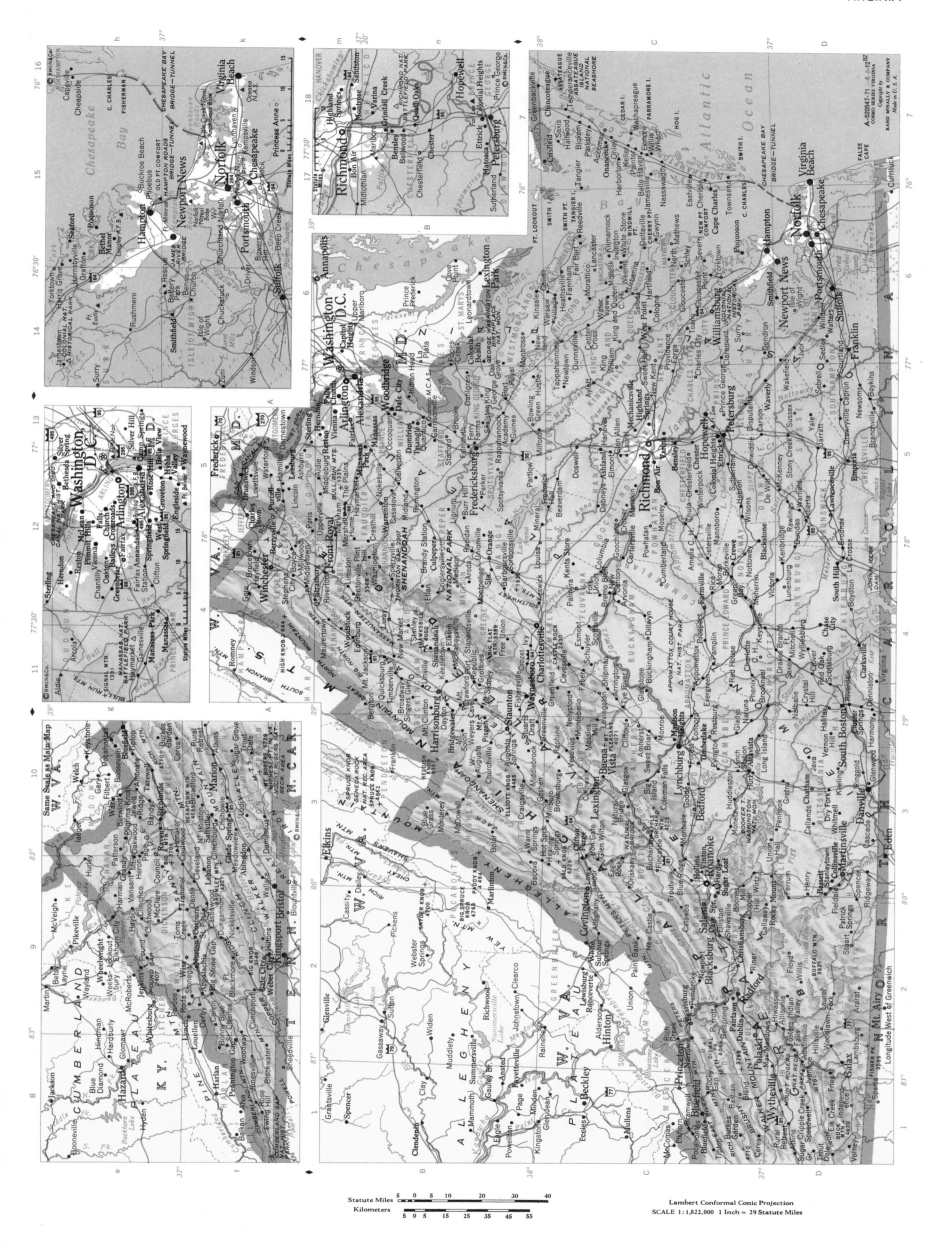

Statute Miles
Kilometers

Lambert Conformal Conic Projection
SCALE 1 : 1,822,000   1 Inch = 29 Statute Miles

Statute Miles 5 0 5 10 20 30 40 50
Kilometers 5 0 5 15 25 35 45 55 65

Lambert Conformal Conic Projection
SCALE 1:2,091,000 1 Inch = 33 Statute Miles

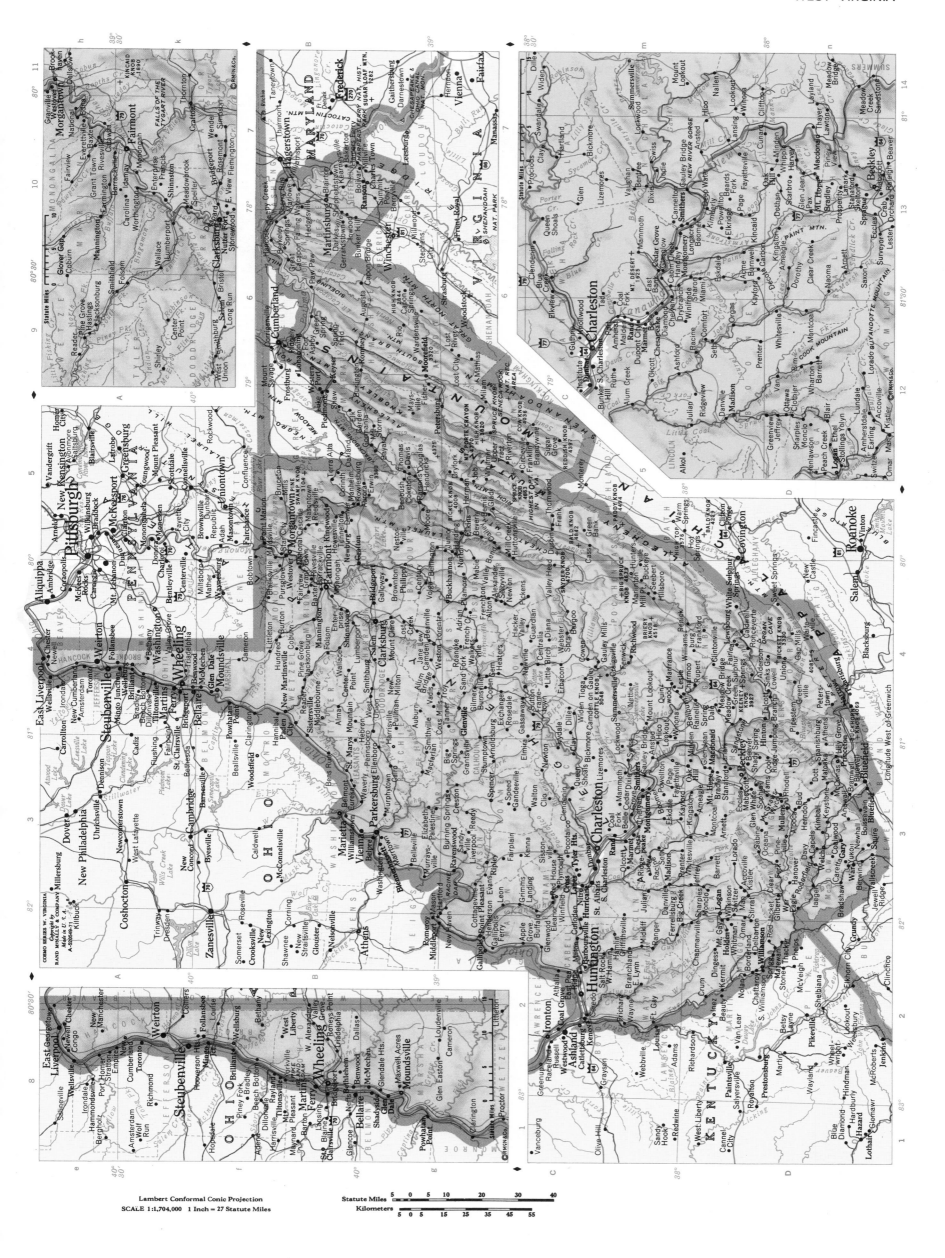

Lambert Conformal Conic Projection
SCALE 1:1,704,000   1 Inch = 27 Statute Miles

Statute Miles
Kilometers

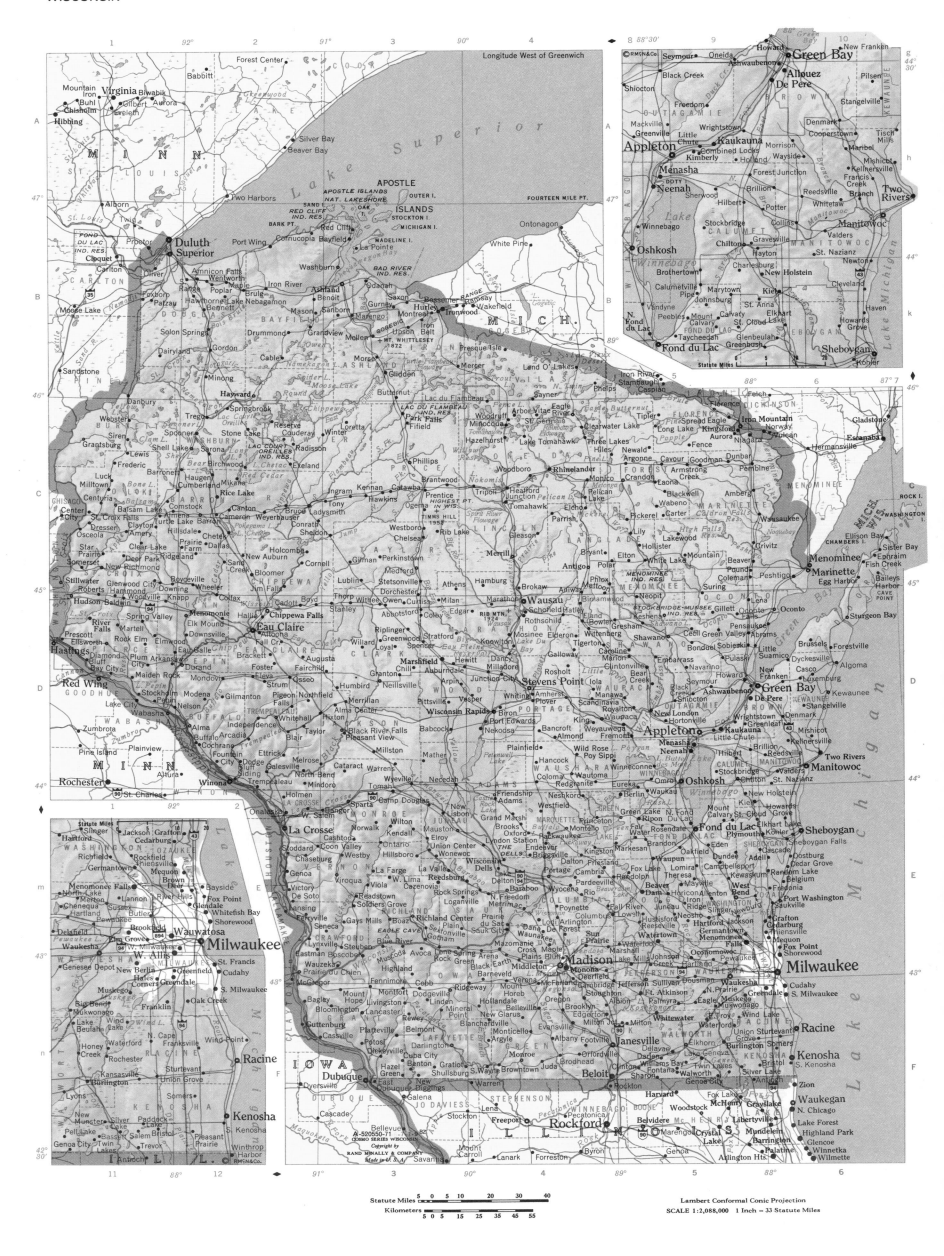

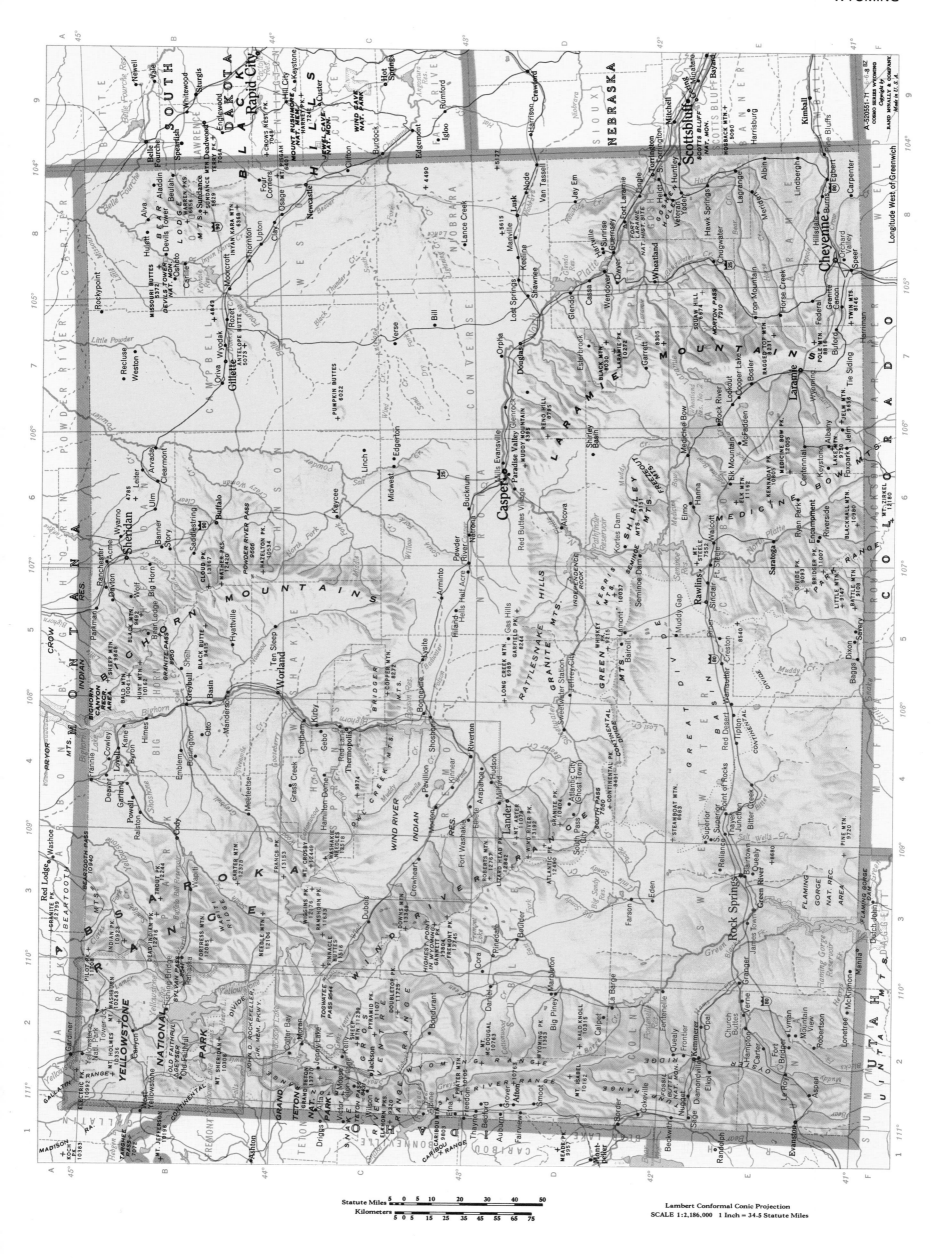

Statute Miles
Kilometers

Lambert Conformal Conic Projection
SCALE 1:2,186,000   1 Inch = 34.5 Statute Miles

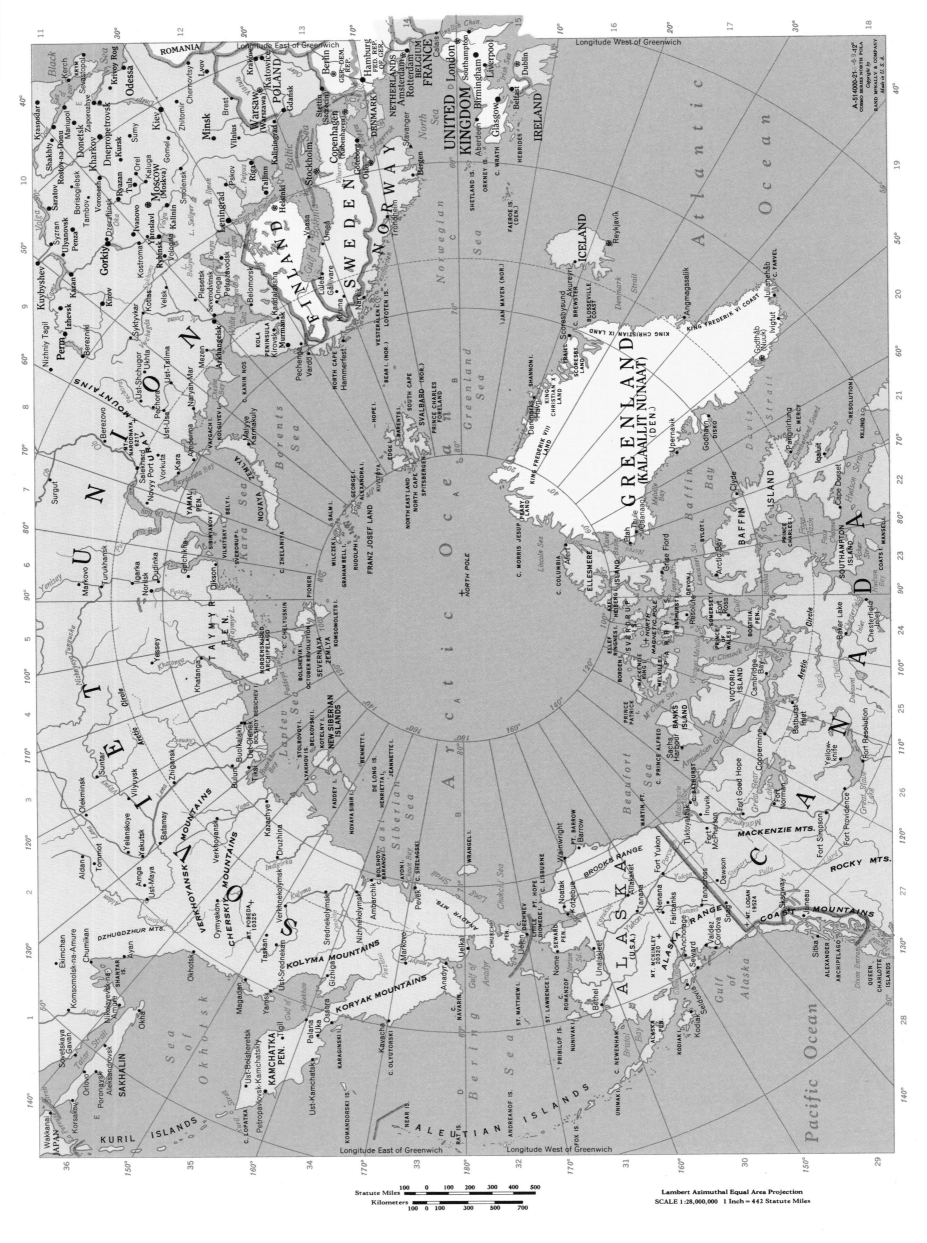

Lambert Azimuthal Equal Area Projection
SCALE 1:28,000,000   1 Inch = 442 Statute Miles

Statute Miles   100 0 100 200 300 400 500
Kilometers   100 0 100 300 500 700

INDEX TO WORLD REFERENCE MAPS

INTRODUCTION TO THE INDEX

This universal index includes in a single alphabetical list approximately 78,000 names of features that appear on the reference maps. Each name is followed by the name of the country or continent in which it is located, a map-reference key and a page reference.

Names The names of cities appear in the index in regular type. The names of all other features appear in *italics*, followed by descriptive terms (hill, mtn., state) to indicate their nature.

Names that appear in shortened versions on the maps due to space limitations are spelled out in full in the index. The portions of these names omitted from the maps are enclosed in brackets — for example, Acapulco [de Juárez].

Abbreviations of names on the maps have been standardized as much as possible. Names that are abbreviated on the maps are generally spelled out in full in the index.

Country names and names of features that extend beyond the boundaries of one country are followed by the name of the continent in which each is located. Country designations follow the names of all other places in the index. The locations of places in the United States, Canada, and the United Kingdom are further defined by abbreviations that indicate the state, province, or political division in which each is located.

All abbreviations used in the index are defined in the List of Abbreviations below.

Alphabetization Names are alphabetized in the order of the letters of the English alphabet. Spanish *ll* and *ch*, for example, are not treated as distinct letters. Furthermore, diacritical marks are disregarded in alphabetization — German or Scandinavian *ä* or *ö* are treated as *a* or *o*.

The names of physical features may appear inverted, since they are always alphabetized under the proper, not the generic, part of the name, thus: 'Gibraltar, Strait of'. Otherwise every entry, whether consisting of one word or more, is alphabetized as a single continuous entity. 'Lakeland', for example, appears after 'La Crosse' and before 'La Salle'. Names beginning with articles (Le Havre, Den Helder, Al Manşūrah) are not inverted. Names beginning 'St.', 'Ste.' and 'Sainte' are alphabetized as though spelled 'Saint'.

In the case of identical names, towns are listed first, then political divisions, then physical features. Entries that are completely identical are listed alphabetically by country name.

Map-Reference Keys and Page References The map-reference keys and page references are found in the last two columns of each entry.

Each map-reference key consists of a letter and number. The letters appear along the sides of the maps. Lowercase letters indicate reference to inset maps. Numbers appear across the tops and bottoms of the maps.

Map reference keys for point features, such as cities and mountain peaks, indicate the locations of the symbols. For extensive areal features, such as countries or mountain ranges, locations are given for the approximate centers of the features. Those for linear features, such as canals and rivers, are given for the locations of the names.

Names of some important places or features that are omitted from the maps due to space limitations are included in the index. Each of these places is identified by an asterisk (*) preceding the map-reference key.

The page number generally refers to the main map for the country in which the feature is located. Page references to two-page maps always refer to the left-hand page.

LIST OF ABBREVIATIONS

Afg.	Afghanistan	De., U.S.	Delaware, U.S.	Ks., U.S.	Kansas, U.S.	Nmb.	Namibia	St. Luc.	St. Lucia
Afr.	Africa	Den.	Denmark	Kuw.	Kuwait	Nor.	Norway	*stm.*	stream (river, creek)
Ak., U.S.	Alaska, U.S.	*dep.*	dependency, colony	Ky., U.S.	Kentucky, U.S.	Norf. I.	Norfolk Island	S. Tom./P.	Sao Tome and Principe
Al., U.S.	Alabama, U.S.	*depr.*	depression	*l.*	lake, pond	N.S.	Nova Scotia, Can.	St. P./M.	St. Pierre and Miquelon
Alb.	Albania	*dept.*	department, district	La., U.S.	Louisiana, U.S.	Nv., U.S.	Nevada, U.S.	*strt.*	strait, channel, sound
Alg.	Algeria	*des.*	desert	Leb.	Lebanon	N.W. Ter.	Northwest Territories, Can.	St. Vin.	St. Vincent and the Grenadines
Alta.	Alberta, Can.	Dji.	Djibouti	Leso.	Lesotho	N.Y., U.S.	New York, U.S.		
Am. Sam.	American Samoa	Dom.	Dominica	Lib.	Liberia	N.Z.	New Zealand		
anch.	anchorage	Dom. Rep.	Dominican Republic	Liech.	Liechtenstein	Oc.	Oceania	Sud.	Sudan
And.	Andorra	Ec.	Ecuador	Lux.	Luxembourg	Oh., U.S.	Ohio, U.S.	Sur.	Suriname
Ang.	Angola	Eg.	Egypt	Ma., U.S.	Massachusetts, U.S.	Ok., U.S.	Oklahoma, U.S.	*sw.*	swamp, marsh
Ant.	Antarctica	E. Ger.	German Democratic Republic			Ont.	Ontario, Can.	Swaz.	Swaziland
Antig.	Antigua and Barbuda			Madag.	Madagascar	Or., U.S.	Oregon, U.S.	Swe.	Sweden
		El Sal.	El Salvador	Malay.	Malaysia	Pa., U.S.	Pennsylvania, U.S.	Switz.	Switzerland
Ar., U.S.	Arkansas, U.S.	Eng., U.K.	England, U.K.	Mald.	Maldives	Pak.	Pakistan	Tai.	Taiwan
Arg.	Argentina	Eq. Gui.	Equatorial Guinea	Man.	Manitoba, Can.	Pan.	Panama	Tan.	Tanzania
Aus.	Austria	*est.*	estuary	Marsh. Is.	Marshall Islands	Pap. N. Gui.	Papua New Guinea	T./C. Is.	Turks and Caicos Islands
Austl.	Australia	Eth.	Ethiopia	Mart.	Martinique	Para.	Paraguay		
Az., U.S.	Arizona, U.S.	Eur.	Europe	Maur.	Mauritania	P.E.I.	Prince Edward Island, Can.	*ter.*	territory
b.	bay, gulf, inlet, lagoon	Faer. Is.	Faeroe Islands	May.	Mayotte			Thai.	Thailand
		Falk. Is.	Falkland Islands	Md., U.S.	Maryland, U.S.	*pen.*	peninsula	Tn., U.S.	Tennessee, U.S.
Bah.	Bahamas	Fin.	Finland	Me., U.S.	Maine, U.S.	Phil.	Philippines	Tok.	Tokelau
Bahr.	Bahrain	Fl., U.S.	Florida, U.S.	Mex.	Mexico	Pit.	Pitcairn	Trin.	Trinidad and Tobago
Barb.	Barbados	*for.*	forest, moor	Mi., U.S.	Michigan, U.S.	*pl.*	plain, flat		
B.A.T.	British Antarctic Territory	Fr.	France	Micron.	Federated States of Micronesia	*plat.*	plateau, highland	T.T.P.I.	Trust Territory of the Pacific Islands
		Fr. Gu.	French Guiana			Pol.	Poland		
B.C.	British Columbia, Can.	Fr. Poly.	French Polynesia	Mid. Is.	Midway Islands	Port.	Portugal	Tun.	Tunisia
		F.S.A.T.	French Southern and Antarctic Territory	*mil.*	military installation	P.R.	Puerto Rico	Tur.	Turkey
Bdi.	Burundi			Mn., U.S.	Minnesota, U.S.	*prov.*	province, region	Tx., U.S.	Texas, U.S.
Bel.	Belgium			Mo., U.S.	Missouri, U.S.	Que.	Quebec, Can.	U.A.E.	United Arab Emirates
Ber.	Bermuda	Ga., U.S.	Georgia, U.S.	Mon.	Monaco	*reg.*	physical region		
Bhu.	Bhutan	Gam.	Gambia	Mong.	Mongolia	*res.*	reservoir	Ug.	Uganda
B.I.O.T.	British Indian Ocean Territory	Gib.	Gibraltar	Monts.	Montserrat	Reu.	Reunion	U.K.	United Kingdom
		Grc.	Greece	Mor.	Morocco	*rf.*	reef, shoal	Ur.	Uruguay
Bngl.	Bangladesh	Gren.	Grenada	Moz.	Mozambique	R.I., U.S.	Rhode Island, U.S.	U.S.	United States
Bol.	Bolivia	Grnld.	Greenland	Mrts.	Mauritius	Rom.	Romania	Ut., U.S.	Utah, U.S.
Boph.	Bophuthatswana	Guad.	Guadeloupe	Ms., U.S.	Mississippi, U.S.	Rw.	Rwanda	Va., U.S.	Virginia, U.S.
Bots.	Botswana	Guat.	Guatemala	Mt., U.S.	Montana, U.S.	S.A.	South America	*val.*	valley, watercourse
Braz.	Brazil	Gui.	Guinea	*mth.*	river mouth or channel	S. Afr.	South Africa	Vat.	Vatican City
Bru.	Brunei	Gui.-B.	Guinea-Bissau			Sask.	Saskatchewan, Can.	Ven.	Venezuela
Bul.	Bulgaria	Guy.	Guyana	*mtn.*	mountain			V.I., Br.	Virgin Islands, British
Burkina	Burkina Faso	Hi., U.S.	Hawaii, U.S.	*mts.*	mountains	Sau. Ar.	Saudi Arabia		
c.	cape, point	*hist.*	historic site, ruins	Mwi.	Malawi	S.C., U.S.	South Carolina, U.S.	Viet.	Vietnam
Ca., U.S.	California, U.S.	*hist. reg.*	historic region	N.A.	North America	*sci.*	scientific station	V.I.U.S.	Virgin Islands (U.S.)
Cam.	Cameroon	H.K.	Hong Kong	N.B.	New Brunswick, Can.	Scot., U.K.	Scotland, U.K.	*vol.*	volcano
Camb.	Cambodia	Hond.	Honduras			S.D., U.S.	South Dakota, U.S.	Vt., U.S.	Vermont, U.S.
Can.	Canada	Hung.	Hungary	N.C., U.S.	North Carolina, U.S.	Sen.	Senegal	Wa., U.S.	Washington, U.S.
Cay. Is.	Cayman Islands	*i.*	island	N. Cal.	New Caledonia	Sey.	Seychelles	Wal./F.	Wallis and Futuna
Cen. Afr. Rep.	Central African Republic	Ia., U.S.	Iowa, U.S.	N. Cyp.	North Cyprus	Sing.	Singapore	W. Ger.	Federal Republic of Germany
		I.C.	Ivory Coast	N.D., U.S.	North Dakota, U.S.	S. Kor.	South Korea		
Christ. I.	Christmas Island	Ice.	Iceland	Ne., U.S.	Nebraska, U.S.	S.L.	Sierra Leone	Wi., U.S.	Wisconsin, U.S.
clf.	cliff, escarpment	Id., U.S.	Idaho, U.S.	Neth.	Netherlands	S. Mar.	San Marino	W. Sah.	Western Sahara
co.	county, parish	Il., U.S.	Illinois, U.S.	Neth. Ant.	Netherlands Antilles	Sol. Is.	Solomon Islands	W. Sam.	Western Samoa
Co., U.S.	Colorado, U.S.	In., U.S.	Indiana, U.S.	Newf.	Newfoundland, Can.	Som.	Somalia	*wtfl.*	waterfall
Col.	Colombia	Indon.	Indonesia	N.H., U.S.	New Hampshire, U.S.	Sov. Un.	Soviet Union	W.V., U.S.	West Virginia, U.S.
Com.	Comoros	I. of Man	Isle of Man			Sp. N. Afr.	Spanish North Africa	Wy., U.S.	Wyoming, U.S.
cont.	continent	Ire.	Ireland	Nic.	Nicaragua			Yugo.	Yugoslavia
C.R.	Costa Rica	*is.*	islands	Nig.	Nigeria	Sri L.	Sri Lanka	Yukon	Yukon Territory, Can.
crat.	crater	Isr.	Israel	N. Ire., U.K.	Northern Ireland, U.K.	*state*	state, republic, canton		
Ct., U.S.	Connecticut, U.S.	Isr. Occ.	Israeli Occupied Territories					Zam.	Zambia
ctry.	country			N.J., U.S.	New Jersey, U.S.	St. C.-N.	St. Christopher-Nevis	Zimb.	Zimbabwe
C.V.	Cape Verde	Jam.	Jamaica	N. Kor.	North Korea				
Cyp.	Cyprus	Jord.	Jordan	N.M., U.S.	New Mexico, U.S.				
Czech.	Czechoslovakia	Kir.	Kiribati	N. Mar. Is.	Northern Mariana Islands	St. Hel.	St. Helena		
D.C., U.S.	District of Columbia, U.S.								

129

INDEX

A

Name	Map Ref.	Page
Aachen, W. Ger.	C3	18
Aalen, W. Ger.	D5	18
A'ali an Nil (Upper Nile), prov., Sud.	D3	47
Aalsmeer, Neth.	B4	17
Aalst (Alost), Bel.	B6	16
Aalten, Neth.	C6	17
Äänekoski, Fin.	F11	14
Aarau, Switz.	E4	18
Aare, stm., Switz.	E3	18
Aargau, state, Switz.	B4	20
Aaronsburg, Pa., U.S.	E7	115
Aarschot, Bel.	D4	17
Aba, China	E5	31
Aba, Nig.	E6	45
Aba, Zaire	A5	48
Abacaxis, stm., Braz.	C3	59
Abādān, Iran	B4	38
Ābādeh, Iran	F6	39
Abadla, Alg.	C4	44
Abaeté, Braz.	B3	56
Abaetetuba, Braz.	C5	59
Abag Qi, China	C6	32
Abai, Para.	C4	55
Abajo Peak, mtn., Ut., U.S.	F6	121
Abakaliki, Nig.	E12	29
Abakan, Sov. Un.	D12	29
Abala, Congo	B2	48
Abala, Niger	D5	45
Abancay, Peru	D3	58
Abanda, Al., U.S.	B4	78
Abanilla, Spain	C5	22
Abano Terme, Italy	B3	23
Abar Kūh, Iran	F6	39
'Abasān, Isr. Occ.	C6	41
Abashiri, Japan	C13	31
Abau, Pap. N. Gui.	m12	50
Abaya, L., Afr.	D4	47
Abaya, Point, c., Mi., U.S.	B2	99
Abbaye, Point, c., Mi., U.S.	B2	99
Abbeville, Fr.	B4	16
Abbeville, Al., U.S.	D4	78
Abbeville, Ga., U.S.	E3	87
Abbeville, La., U.S.	E3	95
Abbeville, Ms., U.S.	A4	101
Abbeville, S.C., U.S.	C3	117
Abbeville, co., S.C., U.S.	C2	117
Abbey, Sask.	G1	75
Abbeydorney, Ire.	E2	11
Abbeyfeale, Ire.	E2	11
Abbey Head, c., Scot., U.K.	F5	13
Abbeyleix, Ire.	E4	11
Abbiategrasso, Italy	B2	23
Abbotsford, B.C.	f13	69
Abbotsford, Wi., U.S.	D3	126
Abbott, Ar., U.S.	B1	81
Abbott Butte, mtn., Or., U.S.	E4	114
Abbott Run, stm., U.S.	B4	116
Abbott Run Valley, R.I., U.S.	B4	116
Abbottsburg, N.C., U.S.	C4	110
Abbottstown, Pa., U.S.	G7	115
Abbyville, Ks., U.S.	E5	93
'Abd al Kūrī, i., Yemen	D5	38
Abdulino, Sov. Un.	E19	8
Abe, Lake, l., Afr.	C5	47
Abéché, Chad	C4	46
Abee, Alta.	B4	68
Abejorral, Col.	B2	60
Abengourou, I.C.	E4	45
Åbenrå, Den.	C3	15
Abeokuta, Nig.	E5	45
Aberaeron, Wales, U.K.	B3	12
Abercorn, Que.	D5	74
Abercrombie, N.D., U.S.	C9	111
Aberdare, Wales, U.K.	E5	10
Aberdaron, Wales, U.K.	B3	12
Aberdeen, Sask.	E2	75
Aberdeen, S. Afr.	D3	49
Aberdeen, Scot., U.K.	B5	10
Aberdeen, Id., U.S.	G6	89
Aberdeen, In., U.S.	G8	91
Aberdeen, Ky., U.S.	A3	97
Aberdeen, Md., U.S.	A5	97
Aberdeen, Ms., U.S.	B5	101
Aberdeen, N.C., U.S.	B3	110
Aberdeen, Oh., U.S.	D2	112
Aberdeen, S.D., U.S.	B7	118
Aberdeen, Wa., U.S.	C2	124
Aberdeen Lake, l., N.W. Ter.	D13	66
Aberdeen Proving Ground, mil., Md., U.S.	A5	97
Aberdeen Township, N.J., U.S.	*C4	107
Aberfeldy, Scot., U.K.	B5	10
Aberfoyle, Scot., U.K.	D4	13
Abergavenny, Wales, U.K.	E5	10
Abernant, Al., U.S.	B2	78
Abernethy, Sask.	G4	75
Abert, Lake, l., Or., U.S.	E6	114
Abert Rim, clf., Or., U.S.	E6	114
Aberystwyth, Wales, U.K.	E4	10
Abesville, Or., U.S.	E4	102
Abhā, Sau. Ar.	D3	38
Abhar, Iran	C4	39
Abidjan, I.C.	E4	45
Abie, Ne., U.S.	C9	104
Abilene, Ks., U.S.	D6	93
Abilene, Tx., U.S.	C3	120
Abingdon, Eng., U.K.	C6	12
Abingdon, Il., U.S.	C3	90
Abingdon, Ia., U.S.	C5	92
Abingdon, Md., U.S.	B5	97
Abingdon, Va., U.S.	f10	123
Abington, Ct., U.S.	B7	84
Abington, Ma., U.S.	B6	98
Abington [Township], Pa., U.S.	o21	115
Abiquiu, N.M., U.S.	A3	108
Abisko, Swe.	C8	14
Abita Springs, La., U.S.	D5	95
Abitibi, stm., Ont.	o19	73
Abitibi, Lake, l., Can.	G16	66
Ablon, Fr.	h10	16
Abloviak Fiord, Que.	f8	72
Aboisso, I.C.	E4	45
Abomey, Benin	E5	45
Abongabong, mtn., Indon.	J2	35
Abony, Hung.	B5	24
Abou Deïa, Chad	C3	46
Aboyne, Scot., U.K.	C6	13
Abraham Lake, res., Alta.	C2	68
Abraham Lincoln Birthplace National Historic Site, hist., Ky., U.S.	C4	94
Abrams, Wi., U.S.	D5	126
Abrantes, Port.	C1	22
Ābrego, Col.	B3	60
Abreojos, Punta, c., Mex.	B2	63
Abruzzi, prov., Italy	C4	23
Absaraka, N.D., U.S.	C8	111
Absaroka Range, mts., U.S.	F7	127
Absarokee, Mt., U.S.	E7	103
Absecon, N.J., U.S.	E4	107
Absecon Inlet, b., N.J., U.S.	E4	107
Abū 'Alī, i., Sau. Ar.	H4	39
Abu Dhabi (Abū Ẓaby), U.A.E.	C5	38
Abū Dīs, Isr. Occ.	h12	41
Abū Ḥadd, Bi'r, well, Eg.	E6	43
Abū Ḥamad, Sud.	B3	47
Abū Ḥammād al Maḥaṭṭah, Eg.	D3	41
Abū Ḥummuṣ, Eg.	C2	41
Abuja, Nig.	E6	45
Abū Kabīr, Eg.	C2	41
Abū Kamāl, Syria	B4	38
Abū Kershola, Sud.	C3	47
Abū Khawf, Mushāsh, well, Eg.	E6	43
Abūksāh, Eg.	E2	41
Abumombazi, Zaire	A3	48
Abū Mūsā, i., U.A.E.	I7	39
Abunã, Braz.	A2	55
Abunã (Abuná), stm., S.A.	A2	55
Abunã (Abuná), stm., S.A.	A2	55
Abū Qīr, Eg.	C2	41
Abu Qir Bay, b., Eg.	C2	41
Abū Qurqāṣ, Eg.	I8	40
Abū Road, India	E4	37
Abū Shajarah, Ra's, c., Sud.	A4	47
Abu Simbel (Abū Sunbul), hist., Eg.	E6	43
Abū Sufyān, 'Idd, well, Sud.	B2	47
Abū Ṭabarī, well, Sud.	B2	47
Abū 'Urūq, well, Sud.	B2	47
Abū Zanīmah, Eg.	D6	43
Åby (part of Norrköping), Swe.	u34	14
Åbybro, Den.	A3	15
Abyei, Sud.	D2	47
Abyssinia see Ethiopia, ctry., Afr.	F2	11
Academia, Oh., U.S.	B3	112
Academy, S.D., U.S.	D6	118
Acadia, co., La., U.S.	D3	95
Acadia National Park, Me., U.S.	D4	96
Acadia Valley, Alta.	D5	68
Acaitsuba, Braz.	B2	59
Acajutla, El Sal.	D3	62
Acámbaro, Mex.	C4	63
Acaponeta, Mex.	C3	63
Acapulco [de Juárez], Mex.	D4	63
Acaraí Mountains, mts., S.A.	B3	59
Acaraú, Braz.	B3	59
Acaray, stm., Para.	E5	55
Acari, Braz.	B4	59
Acari, Peru	h5	57
Acarigua, Ven.	B4	60
Acatlán [de Osorio], Mex.	D5	63
Acayucan, Mex.	D6	63
Accident, Md., U.S.	k12	97
Accomac, Va., U.S.	C7	123
Accomack, co., Va., U.S.	C7	123
Accord, N.Y., U.S.	D6	109
Accord Pond, l., Ma., U.S.	h12	98
Accoville, W.V., U.S.	D3	125
Accra, Ghana	E4	45
Accrington, Eng., U.K.	A5	12
Ace, Tx., U.S.	D5	120
Aceguá, Ur.	E2	56
Acequia, Id., U.S.	G5	89
Achacachi, Bol.	C2	55
Achalpur, India	G6	37
Achao, Chile	C2	54
Achar, Ur.	E1	56
Acharacle, Scot., U.K.	D3	13
Acheng, China	B10	31
Achenkirch, Aus.	B7	20
Achen Lake, l., Aus.	B7	20
Achern, W. Ger.	E3	19
Achicourt, Fr.	D2	17
Achill Head, c., Ire.	D1	11
Achill Island, i., Ire.	D1	10
Achill Sound, Ire.	D2	10
Achinsk, Sov. Un.	D7	29
Achiras, Arg.	A4	54
Achisay, Sov. Un.	E7	28
Achtubinsk, Sov. Un.	D3	28
Acireale, Italy	F5	23
Ackerly, Tx., U.S.	C2	120
Ackerman, Ms., U.S.	B4	101
Ackley, Ia., U.S.	B4	92
Acklins Island, i., Bah.	C6	64
Acmar, Al., U.S.	B3	78
Acme, Alta.	D4	68
Acme, La., U.S.	C3	95
Acme, Mi., U.S.	D5	99
Acme, Wa., U.S.	A3	124
Acme, W.V., U.S.	m13	125
Acme, Tx., U.S.	B6	127
Acobamba, Peru	D3	58
Acoma Indian Reservation, N.M., U.S.	C2	108
Acomayo, Peru	D3	58
Aconcagua, Cerro, mtn., Arg.	A3	54
Acopiara, Braz.	B1	56
Acorizal, Braz.	B1	56
Acosta, Pa., U.S.	F3	115
Acoyapa, Nic.	E5	62
Acquarossa, Switz.	D2	20
Acqui [Terme], Italy	B2	23
Acre, state, Braz.	C4	58
Acre, stm., S.A.	C4	58
Acree, Ga., U.S.	E2	87
Actinolite, Ont.	C7	73
Acton, Ont.	D4	73
Acton, Ca., U.S.	E4	82
Acton, Ma., U.S.	B5	98
Acton, Me., U.S.	E2	96
Acton, Mt., U.S.	D6	103
Acton Vale, Que.	D5	74
Actopan, Mex.	C5	63
Açu, Braz.	C3	57
Acushnet, Ma., U.S.	C6	98
Acworth, Ga., U.S.	B2	87
Acworth, N.H., U.S.	D2	106
Ada, Ghana	E5	45
Ada, Mn., U.S.	C2	100
Ada, Oh., U.S.	B2	112
Ada, Ok., U.S.	C5	113
Ada, Yugo.	C5	24
Ada, co., Id., U.S.	F2	89
Ada, Cape, c., Sov. Un.	G19	8
Ada, Mount, mtn., Ak., U.S.	m22	79
Adair, Il., U.S.	C3	90
Adair, Ia., U.S.	C3	92
Adair, Ok., U.S.	A6	113
Adair, co., Ia., U.S.	C3	92
Adair, co., Ky., U.S.	C4	94
Adair, co., Mo., U.S.	A5	102
Adair, co., Ok., U.S.	B7	113
Adairsville, Ga., U.S.	B2	87
Adairville, Ky., U.S.	D3	94
Adak Island, i., Ak., U.S.	E4	79
Adak Naval Station, mil., Ak., U.S.	E4	79
Adamant, Vt., U.S.	C3	122
Adamantina, Braz.	C2	56
Adamaoua, mts., Afr.	D2	46
Adami Tulu, Eth.	D4	47
Adams, In., U.S.	F6	91
Adams, Ky., U.S.	B7	94
Adams, Ma., U.S.	A1	98
Adams, Mn., U.S.	G6	100
Adams, Ne., U.S.	D9	104
Adams, N.Y., U.S.	B4	109
Adams, N.D., U.S.	A7	111
Adams, Ok., U.S.	e9	113
Adams, Or., U.S.	B8	114
Adams, Tn., U.S.	A4	119
Adams, Wi., U.S.	E4	126
Adams, co., Co., U.S.	B6	83
Adams, co., Id., U.S.	E2	89
Adams, co., Il., U.S.	D2	90
Adams, co., In., U.S.	C8	91
Adams, co., Ia., U.S.	C3	92
Adams, co., Ms., U.S.	D2	101
Adams, co., Ne., U.S.	D7	104
Adams, co., N.D., U.S.	C3	111
Adams, co., Oh., U.S.	D2	112
Adams, co., Pa., U.S.	G7	115
Adams, co., Wa., U.S.	B7	124
Adams, co., Wi., U.S.	D4	126
Adams, Mount, mtn., N.H., U.S.	B4	106
Adams, Mount, mtn., Wa., U.S.	C4	124
Adams, Mount, mtn., Vt., U.S.	C3	122
Adams Bridge, rf., Asia	G6	36
Adams Center, N.Y., U.S.	B5	109
Adams City, Co., U.S.	*B6	83
Adams Lake, l., B.C.	D8	69
Adams Mountain, mtn., Ma., U.S.	A2	98
Adams Run, S.C., U.S.	k11	117
Adamstown, N.J., U.S.	C4	107
Adamstown, Md., U.S.	B3	97
Adamstown, Pa., U.S.	F9	115
Adamsville, Que.	D5	74
Adamsville, Al., U.S.	f7	78
Adamsville, R.I., U.S.	E6	116
Adamsville, Tn., U.S.	B3	119
Adamsville, Tx., U.S.	D3	120
Adamsville, Ut., U.S.	E3	121
Adamsville Brook, stm., R.I., U.S.	E6	116
Adana, Tur.	D10	40
Adanac, Sask.	E1	75
Adapazarı, Tur.	B8	40
Adarama, Sud.	B4	47
Adare, Ire.	E3	11
Adare, Cape, c., Ant.	B30	7
Adavale, Austl.	B5	51
Adda, stm., Italy	B2	23
Aḍ Ḍab'ah, Eg.	C5	43
Ad Dabbah, Sud.	B3	47
Ad Dahnā', des., Sau. Ar.	C4	38
Ad Dāmir, Sud.	B3	47
Ad Dammām, Sau. Ar.	C5	38
Ad Dibdibah, pl., Sau. Ar.	G3	39
Addicks Barker, Tx., U.S.	r14	120
Addieville, Il., U.S.	E4	90
Ad Dilinjāt, Eg.	D2	41
Addington, Ok., U.S.	C4	113
Addis, La., U.S.	D4	95
Addis Ababa (Adis Abeba), Eth.	D4	47
Addison, Al., U.S.	A2	78
Addison, Ct., U.S.	C5	84
Addison, Il., U.S.	k8	90
Addison, Me., U.S.	D5	96
Addison, N.Y., U.S.	C3	109
Addison, Tx., U.S.	*n10	120
Addison, Vt., U.S.	C2	122
Addison, co., Vt., U.S.	C2	122
Addy, Wa., U.S.	A8	124
Addyston, Oh., U.S.	o12	112
Adel, Ga., U.S.	E3	87
Adel, Ia., U.S.	C3	92
Adel, Or., U.S.	E7	114
Adelaide, Austl.	F6	50
Adelaide, Bah.	m17	64
Adelaide Island, i., Ant.	C6	7
Adelanto, Ca., U.S.	E5	82
Adelboden, Switz.	D2	21
Adélie Coast, Ant.	C26	7
Adelphi, Md., U.S.	*B4	97
Adelphia, N.J., U.S.	C4	107
Aden ('Adan), Yemen	D4	38
Aden, Gulf of, b.	D4	38
Adena, Oh., U.S.	B5	112
Adgateville, Ga., U.S.	C3	87
Adi, i., Indon.	F8	34
Adieu, Cape, c., Austl.	F5	50
Adige, stm., Italy	B3	23
Adigrat, Eth.	C4	47
Adilābād, India	H7	37
Adin, Ca., U.S.	B3	82
Adirondack Mountains, mts., N.Y., U.S.	A6	109
Adi Ugri, Eth.	C4	47
Adıyaman, Tur.	C12	40
Adjuntas, P.R.	B2	65
Adliswil, Switz.	B6	21
Admaston, Ont.	B8	73
Admiral, Sask.	H1	75
Admirals Beach, Newf.	E5	72
Admiralty Bay, b., Ak., U.S.	A9	79
Admiralty Gulf, b., Austl.	B4	50
Admiralty Inlet, b., N.W. Ter.	B15	66
Admiralty Island, i., Ak., U.S.	m22	79
Admiralty Islands, is., Pap. N. Gui.	h12	50
Admiralty Mountains, mts., Ant.	B29	7
Admire, Ks., U.S.	D7	93
Adobe Acres, N.M., U.S.	B3	108
Adobe Creek, stm., Co., U.S.	C7	83
Adobe Creek Reservoir, res., Co., U.S.	C7	83
Ado-Ekiti, Nig.	*E6	45
Adok, Sud.	D3	47
Adolphus, Ky., U.S.	D3	94
Adona, Ar., U.S.	B3	81
Adoni, India	*E6	36
Adony, Hung.	B4	24
Adorf, E. Ger.	C7	19
Adour, stm., Fr.	F3	16
Adowa see Adwa, Eth.	C4	47
Adra, Spain	D4	22
Adrano, Italy	F5	23
Adrar, Alg.	D4	44
Adrar, reg., Maur.	B2	45
Adré, Chad	C4	46
Adrī, Libya	D2	43
Adria, Italy	B4	23
Adrian, Ga., U.S.	D4	87
Adrian, Mi., U.S.	G6	99
Adrian, Mn., U.S.	G3	100
Adrian, Mo., U.S.	C3	102
Adrian, N.D., U.S.	C7	111
Adrian, Or., U.S.	D9	114
Adrian, Tx., U.S.	B1	120
Adrian, W.V., U.S.	C4	125
Adriatic Sea, Eur.	G12	8
Adrigole, Ire.	F2	11
Advance, In., U.S.	D4	91
Advance, Mo., U.S.	D8	102
Advance, N.C., U.S.	B2	110
Advocate Harbour, N.S.	D5	71
Adwa (Adowa), Eth.	C4	47
Adzopé, I.C.	E4	45
Æbelø, i., Den.	C4	15
Aegean Sea, Eur.	C5	40
Aegeri, Lake, l., Switz.	B4	20
Aegina see Aíyina, i., Grc.	D4	25
Ærø, i., Den.	D4	15
Ærøskøbing, Den.	D4	15
Aesch, Switz.	B4	21
Aetna, Alta.	E4	68
Aetna, Tn., U.S.	B4	119
Afars and Issas see Djibouti, ctry., Afr.	C5	47
Affoltern am Albis, Switz.	B5	21
Afghanistan, ctry., Asia	B3	36
Afgooye, Som.	E6	47
'Afif, Sau. Ar.	C4	38
Afikpo, Nig.	E6	45
Aflou, Alg.	C5	44
Afognak Island, i., Ak., U.S.	D9	79
Afonso Cláudio, Braz.	C4	56
Africa, cont.	C4	42
Afton, De., U.S.	*A4	85
Afton, Ia., U.S.	C3	92
Afton, Mi., U.S.	C6	99
Afton, Mn., U.S.	F6	100
Afton, N.Y., U.S.	C5	109
Afton, Ok., U.S.	A7	113
Afton, Tn., U.S.	C11	119
Afton, Wy., U.S.	D2	127
Aftout, reg., Alg.	D4	44
Afuá, Braz.	C4	59
'Afula, Isr.	B7	41
Afyon, Tur.	C8	40
Agadem, Niger	C7	45
Agadez, Niger	C6	45
Agadir, Mor.	C3	44
Agana, Guam	L9	52
Agana Bay, b., Guam	L9	52
Agana Heights, Guam	*L9	52
Agana Naval Air Station, mil., Guam	L10	52
Agar, India	F5	37
Agar, S.D., U.S.	C5	118
Agartala, India	D9	36
Agassiz, B.C.	E7	69
Agassiz, Cape, c., Ant.	C6	7
Agat, Guam	M9	52
Agate, Co., U.S.	B7	83
Agate, N.D., U.S.	A6	111
Agate Beach, Or., U.S.	C2	114
Agate Fossil Beds National Monument, Ne., U.S.	B2	104
Agattu Island, i., Ak., U.S.	E2	79
Agawam, Mt., U.S.	B2	98
Agawam, Ma., U.S.	B2	98
Agbor, Nig.	E6	45
Agde, Fr.	F5	16
Agege, Nig.	*E5	45
Agematsu, Japan	n16	33
Agen, Fr.	E4	16
Agency, Ia., U.S.	D5	92
Agency, Mo., U.S.	B3	102
Agenda, Ks., U.S.	C6	93
Ageri, Lake, l., Switz.	B4	20
Agersø, i., Den.	C5	15
Ageo, Japan	*I9	33
Aghā Jārī, Iran	F4	39
Aghleam, Ire.	C1	11
Agincourt (part of Scarborough), Ont.	k15	73
Aginan, Puntan, c. N. Mar. Is.	D7	52
Aginskoye, Sov. Un.	A7	31
Agira, Italy	F5	23
Agno, Phil.	n12	34
Agno, stm., Phil.	o13	34
Agnone, Italy	C5	23
Agogna, stm., Italy	A4	81
Agogo, Ghana	E4	45
Agordo, Italy	C8	20
Agoura Hills, Ca., U.S.	m11	82
Āgra, India	C6	36
Agra, Ks., U.S.	B5	93
Agra, Ok., U.S.	B5	113
Agri, stm., Italy	D5	23
Ağrı (Karaköse), Tur.	*C14	40
Agria Point, c., Phil.	o13	34
Agricola, Ms., U.S.	E5	101
Agrigento, Italy	F4	23
Agrínion, Grc.	C3	40
Agripoli, Italy	D5	23
Agryz, Sov. Un.	D19	8
Água Boa, Braz.	B4	56
Aguachica, Col.	B3	60
Aguada, P.R.	B1	65
Aguadas, Col.	B2	60
Aguadilla, P.R.	G11	64
Aguadilla, P.R.	B1	65
Aguadilla, Bahía de b., P.R.	B1	65
Aguadulce, Pan.	F7	62
Agua Dulce Mountains, mts., Az., U.S.	E2	80
Agua Fria, N.M., U.S.	B3	108
Agua Fria, stm., Az., U.S.	D3	80
Aguaí, Braz.	m8	56
Aguán, stm., Hond.	C4	62
Agua Nueva, Tx., U.S.	F3	120
Aguapey, stm., Arg.	E4	55
Agua Preta, Braz.	k6	57
Agua Prieta, Mex.	A3	63
Aguaray, Arg.	D3	55
Aguarico, stm., S.A.	B2	58
Aguascalientes, Mex.	C4	63
Aguascalientes, state, Mex.	C4	63
Águas Formosas, Braz.	B4	56
Agudos, Braz.	C3	56
Águeda, Port.	B1	22
Águeda, stm., Eur.	B2	22
Aguelhok, Mali	C5	45
Aguêraktem, well, Mali	B4	45
Aguila, Az., U.S.	D2	80
Aguilar, Spain	D3	22
Aguilar, Co., U.S.	D6	83
Águilas, Spain	D5	22
Aguililla, Mex.	D4	63
Aguja, Cabo de la, c., Col.	A3	60
Aguja, Punta, c., Peru	C1	58
Agulhas, Cape, c., S. Afr.	D3	49
Agulhas Negras, Pico das, mtn., Braz.	h5	56
Agusan, stm., Phil.	D7	34
Aha, Japan	J6	33
Ahaggar, mts., Afr.	E6	44
Ahaggar, Tassili ta-n-, plat., Alg.	E6	44
Ahar, Iran	B3	39
Ahaus, W. Ger.	A2	19
Ahascragh, Ire.	D3	11
Ahlen, W. Ger.	C3	18
Ahlhorn, W. Ger.	F2	15
Ahmadābād (Ahmedabad), India	E5	36
Ahmadnagar, India	E5	36
Ahmar, 'Erg el, des., Afr.	E4	44
Ahmar Mountains, mts., Eth.	D5	47
Ahmic Lake, l., Ont.	B5	73
Ahome, Som.	E6	47
Ahon, Tarso, mtn., Chad	A3	46
Ahoskie, N.C., U.S.	A6	110
Ahousat, B.C.	E4	69
Ahrensbök, W. Ger.	D4	15
Ahrweiler, W. Ger.	C3	18
Ahtanum Creek, stm., Wa., U.S.	C5	124
Ahuacatlán, Mex.	m11	63
Ahuachapán, El Sal.	D2	62
Ahualulco de Mercado, Mex.	m11	63
Āhus, Swe.	C8	15
Ahvāz (Nāsiri), Iran	B4	38
Ahvenanmaa (Åland), is., Fin.	G4	14
Ahwahnee, Ca., U.S.	D4	82
Aḥwar, Yemen	C6	47
Aialik, Cape, c., Ak., U.S.	D10	79
Aibonito, P.R.	C2	65
Aichach, W. Ger.	E6	19
Aiea, Hi., U.S.	B4	88
Aigen [in Mühlkreis], Aus.	D6	18
Aigle, Switz.	E2	56
Aiguá, Ur.	E2	56
Aigues-Mortes, Fr.	F6	16
Aiguilles, Fr.	E2	56
Aija, Peru	C2	58
Aikawa, Japan	G9	33
Aiken, S.C., U.S.	D4	117
Aiken, Tx., U.S.	B2	120
Aiken, co., S.C., U.S.	D4	117
Aikens Lake, l., Man.	D4	70
Ailey, Ga., U.S.	D4	87
Ailsa Craig, Ont.	D3	73
Aimorés, Braz.	B4	56
Ain, dept., Fr.	C1	20
Ain, stm., Fr.	F6	16
Aïn ben Tili, Maur.	A3	44
Aïn el Beïda, Alg.	B6	44
Aïn Sefra, Alg.	C4	44
Aïn Témouchent, Alg.	B4	44
Aïn Wessara, Alg.	B5	44
Aipe, Col.	C2	60
Aïr, mts., Niger	C6	45
Airabu, i., Indon.	K7	35
Airaines, Fr.	E1	17
Airdrie, Alta.	D3	68
Airdrie, Scot., U.K.	E5	13
Aire, stm., Fr.	B6	16
Aire, stm., Eng., U.K.	A6	12
Aire [-sur-la-Lys], Fr.	B5	16
Aire-sur-l'Adour, Fr.	E3	16
Air Force Island, i., N.W. Ter.	C18	66
Airline, Ga., U.S.	B3	87
Air Park West, Ne., U.S.	D9	104
Aisch, stm., W. Ger.	D5	19
Aisén del General Carlos Ibáñez del Campo, prov., Chile	D7	52
Aishihik Lake, l., Yukon	D5	66
Aisne, dept., Fr.	C6	16
Aisne, stm., Fr.	C6	16
Aitape, Pap. N. Gui.	h11	50
Aitkin, Mn., U.S.	D5	100
Aitkin, co., Mn., U.S.	D5	100
Aiud, Rom.	B6	24
Aiuruoca, stm., Braz.	g5	56
Aix, Mount, mtn., Wa., U.S.	C4	124
Aix-en-Provence, Fr.	F6	16
Aix-les-Bains, Fr.	E6	16
Aiyáleo, Grc.	h11	25
Aíyina (Aegina), i., Grc.	D4	25
Aíyion, Grc.	C4	25
Aizu-takada, Japan	H9	33
Aizu-wakamatsu, Japan	H9	33
Ajaccio, Fr.	D2	23
Ajaccio, Gulf of, b., Fr.	D2	23
Ajax, Ont.	D6	73
Ajayan Bay, b., Guam	M9	52
Ajdābiyā, Libya	C4	43
Ajjer, Tassili-n-, plat., Alg.	B6	44
'Ajlūn, Jord.	B7	41
Ajmer, India	C5	36
Ajo, Az., U.S.	E3	80
'Ajramīyah, Bi'r al, well, Eg.	E3	41
Akaishi-sammyaku, mts., Japan	n17	33
Akaki Beseka, Eth.	*D4	47
Akalkot, India	I6	37
Akaroa, N.Z.	O14	51
'Akasha East, Sud.	A3	47
Akashi, Japan	I7	33
Akaska, S.D., U.S.	B5	118
Akbulak, Sov. Un.	E20	8
Akçaabat, Tur.	B12	40
Akçadağ, Tur.	C11	40
Ak-Chin Indian Reservation, Az., U.S.	E3	80
Akdağmadeni, Tur.	C10	40
Akechi, Japan	n16	33
Akeley, Mn., U.S.	C4	100
Aken, E. Ger.	B7	19
Akers, La., U.S.	D5	95
Aketi, Zaire	A3	48
Akhaltsikhe, Sov. Un.	B14	40
Akharnaí, Grc.	g11	25
Akhḍar, Al Jabal al, mts., Libya	C4	43
Akhḍar, Al Jabal al, mts., Oman	C5	38
Akhelóös, stm., Grc.	C3	40
Akhiok, Ak., U.S.	D9	79
Akhisar, Tur.	C6	40
Akhmīm, Eg.	C3	38
Akhtopol, Bul.	D8	24
Akhtyrka, Sov. Un.	F10	27
Aki, Japan	J6	33
Akiachak, Ak., U.S.	C7	79
Akiak, Ak., U.S.	C7	79
Akimiski Island, i., N.W. Ter.	F16	66
Akita, Japan	E12	33
Akjoujt, Maur.	C2	45
'Akko, Isr.	F10	41
Akobo, Sud.	D3	47
Akobo, stm., Afr.	D3	47
Akola, India	D6	36
Akonolinga, Cam.	E2	45
Akordat, Eth.	B4	47
Akosombo Dam, Ghana	E5	45
Akpatok Island, i., N.W. Ter.	D19	66
Akra, N.D., U.S.	A8	111
Akraífnion, Grc.	g10	25
Akranes, Ice.	n21	14
Akritas, Ákra, c., Grc.	D3	40
Akron, Al., U.S.	C2	78
Akron, Co., U.S.	A7	83
Akron, In., U.S.	B5	91
Akron, Ia., U.S.	B1	92
Akron, Mi., U.S.	E7	99
Akron, N.Y., U.S.	B2	109
Akron, Oh., U.S.	A4	112
Akron, Pa., U.S.	F9	115
Aksaray, Tur.	C10	40
Akşehir, Tur.	C8	40
Akşehir, Lake, l., Tur.	C8	40
Akseki, Tur.	D8	40
Aksenovo-Zilovskoye, Sov. Un.	D14	29
Aksha, Sov. Un.	A7	31
Akshimrau, Sov. Un.	E4	28
Aksoran, Mount, mtn., Sov. Un.	F24	8
Aksu, China	E11	29
Aksum, Eth.	C4	47
Aktogay, Sov. Un.	D9	28
Aktumsyk, Sov. Un.	D5	28
Aktyubinsk, Sov. Un.	D8	29
Akulivik, Que.	f11	74
Akure, Nig.	E6	45
Akureyri, Ice.	n23	14
Akuseki Island, i., Japan	L4	33
Akutan, Ak., U.S.	E6	79
Akyab see Sittwe, Burma	D9	36
Alabama, state, U.S.	C3	78
Alabama, stm., Al., U.S.	D2	78
Alabama Port, Al., U.S.	E1	78
Alabaster, Al., U.S.	B3	78
Alabaster, Mi., U.S.	D7	99
Alabat, i., Phil.	o14	34
Al 'Abbāsīyah, Sud.	C3	47
Al Abyaḍ, Libya	D2	43
Al Abyār, Libya	F3	40
Alachua, Fl., U.S.	C4	86
Alachua, co., Fl., U.S.	C4	86
Aladdin, Wy., U.S.	B8	127
Alagna [Valsesia], Italy	D2	20
Alagoa Grande, Braz.	D3	57
Alagoas, state, Braz.	D3	57
Alagoinhas, Braz.	B5	57
Alagón, Spain	B5	22
Alagón, stm., Spain	B2	22
Al 'Ajamiyīn, Eg.	D6	41
Al 'Ajrūd, well, Eg.	D6	41
Alajuela, Lago, res., Pan.	k11	62
Alakanuk, Ak., U.S.	C7	79
Alakol, Lake, l., Sov. Un.	D10	29
Alalakeiki Channel, strt., Hi., U.S.	C5	88
Al 'Alamayn, Eg.	B2	38
Alalaú, Braz.	B2	59
Alamance, N.C., U.S.	A3	110
Alamance, co., N.C., U.S.	A3	110
Alamance Creek, stm., N.C., U.S.	A3	110
'Alam ar Rūm, Ra's, c., Egypt	G6	43
Alameda, Sask.	H4	75
Alameda, Ca., U.S.	h8	82
Alameda, co., Ca., U.S.	D3	82
Alameda Naval Air Station, mil., Ca., U.S.	h8	82
Alaminos, Phil.	n12	34
Al 'Āmirīyah, Eg.	G7	43
Alamitos Creek, stm., Tx., U.S.	p12	120
Alamo, Mex.	*D2	82
Alamo, Ga., U.S.	D4	87
Alamo, Nv., U.S.	F6	105
Alamo, N.D., U.S.	A2	111
Alamo, Tn., U.S.	B2	119
Alamo, Tx., U.S.	F3	120
Alamo, stm., Ca., U.S.	F6	82
Alamogordo, N.M., U.S.	E4	108
Alamogordo Dam, N.M., U.S.	C5	108
Alamo Heights, Tx., U.S.	E3	120

Name	Map Ref.	Page

Alamo Hueco Mountains, mts., N.M., U.S. — F1 108
Alamo Indian Reservation, N.M., U.S. — C2 108
Alamo Lake, res., Az., U.S. — C2 80
Alamos, Mex. — B3 63
Alamosa, Co., U.S. — D5 83
Alamosa, co., Co., U.S. — D5 83
Alamosa, stm., Co., U.S. — D4 83
Alamosa Creek, stm., N.M., U.S. — D2 108
Alamosa East, Co., U.S. — D5 83
Åland see Ahvenanmaa, is., Fin. — G9 14
Alanreed, Tx., U.S. — B2 120
Alanson, Mi., U.S. — C6 99
Alanya, Tur. — D9 40
Alaotra, Lac, l., Madag. — g9 49
Alapaha, Ga., U.S. — E3 87
Alapaha, stm., U.S. — E3 87
Alapayevsk, Sov. Un. — B6 28
Al 'Aqabah, Jord. — C3 38
Al 'Arīsh, Eg. — m14 41
Alasdair, Sgurr, mtn., Scot., U.K. — C2 13
Alaşehir, Tur. — C7 40
Alaska, state, U.S. — C9 79
Alaska, Gulf of, b., Ak., U.S. — D10 79
Alaska Peninsula, pen., Ak., U.S. — D8 79
Alaska Range, mts., Ak., U.S. — C9 79
Alassio, Italy — C2 23
Alatna, stm., Ak., U.S. — B9 79
Al 'Aṭrūn, Sud. — B2 47
Alatyr, Sov. Un. — D16 27
Alausí, Ec. — B2 58
Alava, Cape, c., Wa., U.S. — A1 124
Alaverdi, Sov. Un. — B15 40
Al 'Ayyāṭ, Eg. — E3 41
Al 'Ayzarīyah (Bethany), Isr. Occ. — h12 41
Al 'Azīzīyah, Libya — C2 43
Alb, stm., W. Ger. — A5 21
Alba, Italy — B2 23
Alba, Mi., U.S. — D6 99
Alba, Mo., U.S. — D3 102
Alba, Pa., U.S. — C8 115
Alba, Tx., U.S. — E5 120
Albacete, Spain — C5 22
Al Badārī, Eg. — D6 43
Alba de Tormes, Spain — B3 22
Ålbæk, Den. — A4 15
Albæk Bugt, b., Den. — A4 15
Al Bahnasā, Eg. — H8 40
Al Baḥr al Abyaḍ, prov., Sud. — C3 47
Al Baḥr al Aḥmar (Red Sea), prov., Sud. — B4 47
Alba Iulia, Rom. — B6 24
Al Bājūr, Eg. — D3 41
Albalate [del Arzobispo], Spain — B5 22
Al Ballaḥ, Eg. — D4 41
Albanel, Lac, l., Que. — F18 66
Albani, Colli, hills, Italy — h9 23
Albania, ctry., Eur. — B2 40
Albano, Lake, l., Italy — h9 23
Albano Laziale, Italy — D4 23
Albany, Austl. — F2 50
Albany, N.S. — E4 71
Albany, P.E.I. — C6 71
Albany, Ca., U.S. — *h8 82
Albany, Ga., U.S. — E2 87
Albany, Il., U.S. — B3 90
Albany, In., U.S. — D7 91
Albany, Ky., U.S. — D4 94
Albany, La., U.S. — g10 95
Albany, Mn., U.S. — E4 100
Albany, Mo., U.S. — A3 102
Albany, N.H., U.S. — C4 106
Albany, N.Y., U.S. — C7 109
Albany, Oh., U.S. — C3 112
Albany, Ok., U.S. — D5 113
Albany, Or., U.S. — C3 114
Albany, Tx., U.S. — C3 120
Albany, Vt., U.S. — B4 122
Albany, Wi., U.S. — F4 126
Albany, Wy., U.S. — E6 127
Albany, co., N.Y., U.S. — C6 109
Albany, co., Wy., U.S. — E7 127
Albany, stm., Ont. — o18 73
Al Barkāt, Libya — E2 43
Al Batānūn, Eg. — D2 41
Albatross Bay, b., Austl. — B7 50
Al Batrūn, Leb. — E10 40
Al Bayḍā, Libya — C4 43
Albee, S.D., U.S. — B9 118
Albemarle, N.C., U.S. — B2 110
Albemarle, co., Va., U.S. — C4 123
Albemarle, Punta, c., Ec. — f5 58
Albemarle Lake, l., Ms., U.S. — C2 101
Albemarle Sound, strt., N.C., U.S. — A6 110
Albenga, Italy — B2 23
Alberche, stm., Spain — B3 22
Ålberga (part of Eskilstuna), Swe. — u34 14
Albergaria-a-Velha, Port. — B1 22
Albersdorf, W. Ger. — D3 15
Albert, Fr. — B5 16
Albert, Ks., U.S. — D4 93
Albert, N.M., U.S. — B6 108
Albert, Ok., U.S. — B3 113
Albert, co., N.B. — D5 71
Albert, Lake, l., Afr. — A5 48
Alberta, Al., U.S. — C2 78
Alberta, Mn., U.S. — E2 100
Alberta, Va., U.S. — D5 123
Alberta, prov., Can. — C4 68
Alberta, Mount, mtn., Alta. — C2 68
Albert Canyon, B.C. — D9 69
Albert City, Ia., U.S. — B3 92
Albert Edward, Mount, mtn., Pap. N. Gui. — k12 50
Albert Lea, Mn., U.S. — G5 100
Albert Markham, Mount, mtn., Ant. — A28 7
Albert Nile, stm., Ug. — A5 48
Alberton, P.E.I. — C5 71
Alberton, Mt., U.S. — C2 103
Albertson, N.Y., U.S. — *k13 109
Albertville, Sask. — D3 75
Albertville, Fr. — E7 16
Albertville, Al., U.S. — A3 78
Albertville, Mn., U.S. — E5 100
Albeuve, Switz. — C3 21
Albi, Fr. — F5 16
Albia, Ia., U.S. — C5 92
Albin, Wy., U.S. — E8 127
Albina, Sur. — A4 59
Albino, Italy — E8 21
Albion, Ca., U.S. — C2 82
Albion, Id., U.S. — G5 89
Albion, Il., U.S. — E5 90
Albion, In., U.S. — B7 91

Albion, Ia., U.S. — B5 92
Albion, Me., U.S. — D3 96
Albion, Mi., U.S. — F6 99
Albion, Ne., U.S. — C7 104
Albion, N.Y., U.S. — B2 109
Albion, Ok., U.S. — C6 113
Albion, Pa., U.S. — C1 115
Albion, R.I., U.S. — B4 116
Albion, Wa., U.S. — C8 124
Albion, Wi., U.S. — F4 126
Alborán, i., Spain — E4 22
Ålborg, Den. — I3 14
Ålborg Bugt, b., Den. — B4 15
Alborn, Mn., U.S. — D6 100
Albox, Spain — D4 22
Albreda, B.C. — C8 69
Albrightsville, Pa., U.S. — D10 115
Albufeira, Port. — D1 22
Al Buḥayrah, prov., Sud. — D2 47
Al Bunbah, Libya — F4 40
Albuñol, Spain — D4 22
Al Buq'ayrāt, Libya — C3 43
Albuquerque, N.M., U.S. — B3 108
Al Buraymi, Oman — C5 38
Alburg, Vt., U.S. — B2 122
Alburnett, Ia., U.S. — B6 92
Alburquerque, Spain — C2 22
Alburtis, Pa., U.S. — F10 115
Albury, Austl. — G8 50
Alca, Peru — E3 58
Alcabideche, Port. — f9 22
Alcácer do Sal, Port. — C1 22
Alcalá de Chivert, Spain — B6 22
Alcalá [de Guadaira], Spain — D3 22
Alcalá de Henares, Spain — B4 22
Alcalá de los Gazules, Spain — D3 22
Alcalá la Real, Spain — D4 22
Alcalde, N.M., U.S. — A3 108
Alcaldedíaz, Pan. — F8 62
Alcamo, Italy — F4 23
Alcanadre, stm., Spain — B5 22
Alcanar, Spain — B6 22
Alcañiz, Spain — B5 22
Alcântara, Braz. — B2 57
Alcantarilla, Spain — D5 22
Alcaraz, Spain — C4 22
Alcaudete, Spain — D3 22
Alcázar de San Juan, Spain — C4 22
Alcester, S.D., U.S. — D9 118
Alcira, Spain — C5 22
Alco, Ar., U.S. — B3 81
Alco, La., U.S. — C2 95
Alcoa, Tn., U.S. — D10 119
Alcobendas, Spain — o17 22
Alcochete, Port. — f10 22
Alcolu, S.C., U.S. — D7 117
Alcomdale, Alta. — C4 68
Alcona, co., Mi., U.S. — D7 99
Alcora, Spain — B5 22
Alcorcón, Spain — p17 22
Alcorisa, Spain — B5 22
Alcorn, Ms., U.S. — D2 101
Alcorn, co., Ms., U.S. — A5 101
Alcova, Wy., U.S. — D6 127
Alcovy, stm., Ga., U.S. — C3 87
Alcoy, Spain — C5 22
Alcoy, Nevado, mtn., Peru — D2 58
Alda, Ne., U.S. — D7 104
Aldama, Mex. — B3 63
Aldan, Sov. Un. — D15 29
Aldan, stm., Sov. Un. — C16 29
Aldan Plateau, plat., Sov. Un. — D15 29
Al Dār al Bayḍā', hist., Eg. — D3 41
Aldeburgh, Eng., U.K. — B9 12
Alden, Il., U.S. — A5 90
Alden, Ia., U.S. — B4 92
Alden, Ks., U.S. — D5 93
Alden, Mi., U.S. — D5 99
Alden, Mn., U.S. — G5 100
Alden, N.Y., U.S. — C2 109
Alden, Pa., U.S. — D9 115
Alder, Mt., U.S. — E5 103
Alder, Ben, mtn., Scot., U.K. — D4 13
Alder Brook, stm., Vt., U.S. — B4 122
Alderney, i., Guernsey — F5 10
Aldershot, Eng., U.K. — J12 12
Alderson, Ok., U.S. — C6 113
Alderson, W.V., U.S. — D4 125
Aldersyde, Alta. — D4 68
Alderwood Manor, Wa., U.S. — *B3 124
Aldie, Va., U.S. — B5 123
Aldine, N.J., U.S. — D2 107
Aldora, Ga., U.S. — C2 87
Aldrich, Al., U.S. — B3 78
Aldrich, Mn., U.S. — D4 100
Aledo, Il., U.S. — B3 90
Aledo, Tx., U.S. — n9 120
Aleg, Maur. — C3 44
Alegre, Braz. — C4 56
Alegrete, Braz. — D1 56
Alegros Mountain, mtn., N.M., U.S. — C2 108
Alejandro Selkirk, Isla, i., Chile — G2 53
Aleknagik, Ak., U.S. — D8 79
Aleksandriya, Sov. Un. — G9 27
Aleksandrov, Sov. Un. — C12 27
Aleksandrov-Gay, Sov. Un. — C3 28
Aleksandrovsk [-Sakhalinskiy], Sov. Un. — D17 29
Aleksandrów [Kujawski], Pol. — B5 26
Aleksandrów [Łódzki], Pol. — C5 26
Aleksin, Sov. Un. — D11 27
Aleksinac, Yugo. — D5 24
Alemania, Arg. — E2 55
Além Paraíba, Braz. — g6 56
Alençon, Fr. — C4 16
Alenquer, Braz. — C4 59
Alenquer, Port. — C1 22
Alentejo, hist. reg., Port. — C2 22
Alenuihaha Channel, strt., Hi., U.S. — C5 88
Aleppo (Ḥalab), Syria — B3 38
Aléria, Fr. — C2 23
Alert, N.W. Ter. — k39 66
Alert Bay, B.C. — D4 69
Alès, Fr. — E6 16
Alessandria, Italy — B2 23
Ålestrup, Den. — B3 15
Ålesund, Nor. — F2 14
Aleutian Islands, is., Ak., U.S. — E3 79
Aleutian Range, mts., Ak., U.S. — D9 79
Alex, Ok., U.S. — C4 113
Alexander, Man. — E1 70
Alexander, Ar., U.S. — C3 81
Alexander, Il., U.S. — D4 90
Alexander, Ks., U.S. — D4 93

Alexander, Me., U.S. — C5 96
Alexander, N.Y., U.S. — C2 109
Alexander, N.C., U.S. — f10 110
Alexander, N.D., U.S. — B2 111
Alexander, W.V., U.S. — C4 125
Alexander, co., Il., U.S. — F4 90
Alexander, co., N.C., U.S. — B1 110
Alexander Archipelago, is., Ak., U.S. — D12 79
Alexander Bay, S. Afr. — C2 49
Alexander City, Al., U.S. — C4 78
Alexander Island, i., Ant. — B5 7
Alexander Mills, N.C., U.S. — B1 110
Alexandra, N.Z. — P12 51
Alexandra, i., Sov. Un. — B10 128
Alexandretta see İskenderun, Tur. — D11 40
Alexandria, B.C. — C6 69
Alexandria, Ont. — B10 73
Alexandria (Al Iskandarīyah), Eg. — B2 38
Alexandria, Rom. — D7 24
Alexandria, Al., U.S. — B4 78
Alexandria, In., U.S. — D6 91
Alexandria, Ky., U.S. — B5 94
Alexandria, La., U.S. — C3 95
Alexandria, Mn., U.S. — E3 100
Alexandria, Mo., U.S. — A6 102
Alexandria, Ne., U.S. — D8 104
Alexandria, N.H., U.S. — C3 106
Alexandria, Oh., U.S. — B3 112
Alexandria, Pa., U.S. — E5 115
Alexandria, S.D., U.S. — D8 118
Alexandria, Tn., U.S. — A5 119
Alexandria, Va., U.S. — B5 123
Alexandria Bay, N.Y., U.S. — A5 109
Alexandrina, Lake, l., Austl. — G2 51
Alexandroúpolis, Grc. — B5 40
Alexis, Il., U.S. — B3 90
Alexis, stm., Newf. — B3 72
Alexis Creek, B.C. — C6 69
Aley, stm., Sov. Un. — E25 8
Aleysk, Sov. Un. — D11 29
Alfalfa, co., Ok., U.S. — A3 113
Al Fallūjah, Iraq — F14 40
Al Fandaqūmīyah, Isr. Occ. — B7 41
Alfaro, Spain — A5 22
Al Fashn, Eg. — D6 43
Alfatar, Bul. — B3 24
Al Fāw, Iraq — G4 39
Al Fayyūm, Eg. — C3 38
Alfeld, W. Ger. — B4 19
Alfenas, Braz. — C3 56
Alfiós (Alpheus), stm., Grc. — D3 25
Alfonsine, Italy — E8 21
Alford, Eng., U.K. — A8 12
Alford, Scot., U.K. — C6 13
Alford, Fl., U.S. — B1 86
Alford, In., U.S. — H3 91
Alford, Ma., U.S. — B1 98
Alfordsville, In., U.S. — G4 91
Alfred, Ont. — B10 73
Alfred, Me., U.S. — E2 96
Alfred, N.Y., U.S. — C3 109
Alfred, N.D., U.S. — C6 111
Alfred Mills, Me., U.S. — E2 96
Alfred Station, N.Y., U.S. — C3 109
Al Fujayrah, U.A.E. — C5 38
Al Fuqahā', Libya — D3 43
Algarroba, Chile — E1 55
Algarrobo, Chile — E1 55
Algarrobo del Águila, Arg. — B3 54
Algarve, hist. reg., Port. — D1 22
Algeciras, Spain — D3 22
Algemesí, Spain — C5 22
Alger, Mi., U.S. — D6 99
Alger, Oh., U.S. — B2 112
Alger, co., Mi., U.S. — B4 99
Algeria, ctry., Afr. — D5 44
Algete, Spain — o18 22
Al Ghayatah, Eg. — D2 41
Al Ghaydah, Yemen — B7 47
Alghero, Italy — D2 23
Al Ghurdaqah, Eg. — D6 43
Algiers (El Djazair), Alg. — B5 44
Algoa, Ar., U.S. — *B4 81
Algoa Bay, b., S. Afr. — D4 49
Algodón, stm., Peru — B3 58
Algodones, N.M., U.S. — B3 108
Algoma, Ms., U.S. — A4 101
Algoma, Wi., U.S. — D6 126
Algoma, dept., Ont. — A2 73
Algoma Mills, Ont. — A2 73
Algona, Ia., U.S. — A3 92
Algonac, Mi., U.S. — F8 99
Algonquin, Ont. — C9 73
Algonquin, Il., U.S. — A5 90
Algonquin Park, Ont. — B6 73
Algonquin Provincial Park, Ont. — B6 73
Algood, Tn., U.S. — C8 119
Algorta (Guecho), Spain — A4 22
Algorta, Ur. — E1 56
Algrange, Fr. — C6 17
Al Ḥadd, Oman — C5 38
Al Ḥadīthah, Iraq — A9 28
Alhama [de Granada], Spain — D4 22
Alhama [de Murcia], Spain — D5 22
Alhambra, Ca., U.S. — m12 82
Alhambra, Il., U.S. — E4 90
Al Ḥāmūl, Eg. — C3 41
Al Ḥarrah, Egypt — H7 40
Al Ḥasakah, Syria — D13 40
Alhaurín el Grande, Spain — D3 22
Al Ḥawātah, Sud. — C4 47
Al Ḥawrah, Yemen — B7 47
Al Ḥawtah, Yemen — D4 38
Al Ḥayy, Eg. — E3 41
Al Ḥayy, Iraq — E3 39
Al Ḥayyānīyah, Sau. Ar. — H14 40
Al Ḥillah (Hilla), Iraq — B4 38
Al Ḥindīyah, Iraq — F15 40
Al Ḥişn, Jord. — E11 40
Al Hoceïma, Mor. — B4 44
Alhos Vedros, Port. — f9 22
Al Hufūf (Hofuf), Sau. Ar. — C4 38
Al Ḥuṣayḥiṣah, Sud. — C4 47
'Alī al Gharbī, Iraq — B5 38
Aliartos, Grc. — g10 25
Alībāg, India — H4 37
Alicahue, Chile — A2 54
Alicante, Spain — C5 22
Alicante, Gulf of, b., Spain — C5 22
Alice, Ont. — B7 73
Alice, N.D., U.S. — C8 111
Alice, Tx., U.S. — F3 120
Alice, Point, c., Italy — E6 23
Alice Lake, l., Mn., U.S. — C7 100

Alice Springs, Austl. — D5 50
Aliceville, Al., U.S. — B1 78
Aliceville, Ks., U.S. — D8 93
Alicia, Ar., U.S. — B4 81
Alicudi, i., Italy — E5 23
Alida, Sask. — H5 75
Aligarh, India — C6 36
Alindao, Cen. Afr. Rep. — E4 46
Aline, Ok., U.S. — A3 113
'Alipur Duār, India — D12 37
Al 'Irq, Libya — D4 43
Al Istiwa'iyah al Gharbīyah (Western Equatoria), prov., Sud. — D2 47
Al Istiwa'iyah ash Sharqīyah (Eastern Equatoria), prov., Sud. — E3 47
Alistráti, Grc. — B4 25
Aliwal North, S. Afr. — D4 49
Alix, Alta. — C4 68
Alix, Ar., U.S. — B2 81
Al Jabalayn, Sud. — C3 47
Al Jāfūrah, des., Sau. Ar. — I5 39
Al Jaghbūb, Libya — D4 43
Al Jahrah, Kuw. — G3 39
Al Jānīyah, Isr. Occ. — h11 41
Al Jawf, Libya — E4 43
Al Jawf, Sau. Ar. — C3 38
Al Jawsh, Libya — C2 43
Al Jazīrah, prov., Sud. — C3 47
Aljezur, Port. — D1 22
Al Jubayl, Sau. Ar. — H4 39
Aljustrel, Port. — D1 22
Al Kāb, Eg. — D4 41
Alkabo, N.D., U.S. — A2 111
Al Kahfah, Sau. Ar. — I14 40
Alkali Lake, l., Nv., U.S. — B2 105
Alkaline Lake, l., N.D., U.S. — C6 111
Al Karak, Jord. — G10 40
Al Karnak, Eg. — C3 41
Al Khābir, stm., Syria — B4 38
Al Khābūrah, Oman — C5 38
Al Khālis, Iraq — E15 40
Al Khandaq, Sud. — B3 47
Al Khārijah, Eg. — C3 38
Al Khartūm, prov., Sud. — B4 47
Al Khasab, Oman — C5 38
Al Khums, Libya — C2 43
Al Khurmah, Sau. Ar. — C4 38
Al Khushnīyah, Isr. Occ. — A7 41
Alkionídhes, Grc. — g9 25
Alkionídhes Gulf, b., Grc. — g10 25
Alkmaar, Neth. — A6 16
Alkol, W.V., U.S. — m12 125
Al Kūbrī, Eg. — D4 41
Al Kūfah, Iraq — G15 40
Al Kuntillah, Eg. — E6 41
Al Kūt, Iraq — B4 38
Allada, Benin — E5 45
Allagash, Me., U.S. — B3 96
Allagash, stm., Me., U.S. — B3 96
Allagash Lake, l., Me., U.S. — B3 96
Allahābād, India — C7 36
Allakaket, Ak., U.S. — B9 79
Allamakee, co., Ia., U.S. — A6 92
Allamuchy Mountain, mtn., N.J., U.S. — B3 107
Allan, Sask. — F2 75
Allanmyo, Burma — E10 36
Allardt, Tn., U.S. — C9 119
Allariz, Spain — A2 22
Al Mansūrah, Eg. — B3 38
Alleene, Ar., U.S. — D1 81
Allegan, Mi., U.S. — F5 99
Allegan, co., Mi., U.S. — F5 99
Allegany, N.Y., U.S. — C2 109
Allegany, Or., U.S. — D2 114
Allegany, co., Md., U.S. — k13 97
Allegany, co., N.Y., U.S. — C2 109
Allegany Indian Reservation, N.Y., U.S. — C2 109
Alleghany, Ca., U.S. — C3 82
Alleghany, Va., U.S. — C2 123
Alleghany, co., N.C., U.S. — A1 110
Alleghany, co., Va., U.S. — C2 123
Allegheny, co., Pa., U.S. — E2 115
Allegheny, stm., U.S. — E2 115
Allegheny Front, mtn., W.V., U.S. — B5 125
Allegheny Mountain, mts., U.S. — B5 123
Allegheny Plateau, plat., U.S. — E11 115
Allegheny Reservoir, res., U.S. — B4 115
Allemands, Bayou Des, stm., La., U.S. — k11 95
Allemands, Lac Des, l., La., U.S. — E5 95
Allen, Al., U.S. — D2 78
Allen, Ks., U.S. — D7 93
Allen, Ky., U.S. — C7 94
Allen, Md., U.S. — D6 97
Allen, Ne., U.S. — B9 104
Allen, Ok., U.S. — C5 113
Allen, Pa., U.S. — F7 115
Allen, S.D., U.S. — D4 118
Allen, Tx., U.S. — *C4 120
Allen, co., In., U.S. — B7 91
Allen, co., Ks., U.S. — E8 93
Allen, co., Ky., U.S. — D3 94
Allen, co., La., U.S. — D3 95
Allen, co., Oh., U.S. — B1 112
Allen, Lough, l., Ire. — C2 10
Allen, Mount, mtn., Ak., U.S. — C11 79
Allendale, Il., U.S. — E6 90
Allendale, N.J., U.S. — A4 107
Allendale, S.C., U.S. — F5 117
Allendale, Wy., U.S. — *D6 127
Allende, Mex. — B4 63
Allenhurst, Ga., U.S. — E5 87
Allenhurst, N.J., U.S. — C4 107
Allen Park, Mi., U.S. — p15 99
Allens Mills, Me., U.S. — D2 96
Allenspark, Co., U.S. — A5 83
Allenstein see Olsztyn, Pol. — B6 26
Allensville, Oh., U.S. — C3 112
Allensville, Pa., U.S. — E6 115
Allenton, Wi., U.S. — E5 126
Allentown, Ga., U.S. — D3 87

Allentown, Mo., U.S. — f12 102
Allentown, N.J., U.S. — C3 107
Allentown, N.Y., U.S. — C2 109
Allentown, Pa., U.S. — E11 115
Allenville, Il., U.S. — D5 90
Allenwood, N.J., U.S. — C4 107
Allenwood, Pa., U.S. — D8 115
Alleppey, India — G6 36
Aller, stm., Eur. — B4 18
Allerton, Il., U.S. — D6 90
Allerton, Ia., U.S. — D4 92
Allerton, Point, c., Ma., U.S. — B6 98
Allgäuer Alps, mts., Eur. — B9 21
Allgood, Al., U.S. — B3 78
Alliance, Alta. — C5 68
Alliance, Ne., U.S. — B3 104
Alliance, N.C., U.S. — B6 110
Alliance, Oh., U.S. — B4 112
Allier, stm., Fr. — F10 16
Alligator, Ms., U.S. — B3 101
Alligator, stm., N.C., U.S. — B6 110
Alligator Lake, l., Me., U.S. — D4 96
Allihies, Ire. — F1 10
Allingåbro, Den. — B4 15
Allinge [-Sandvig], Den. — D3 15
Allison, Co., U.S. — D3 83
Allison, Ia., U.S. — B5 92
Allison, N.M., U.S. — B1 108
Allison, Pa., U.S. — G2 115
Allisonia, Va., U.S. — D2 123
Allison Park, Pa., U.S. — h14 115
Alliston, Ont. — C5 73
Al Līth, Sau. Ar. — D3 38
Alloa, Scot., U.K. — B5 13
Allons, Tn., U.S. — C8 119
Allouez, Mi., U.S. — A2 99
Allouez, Wi., U.S. — h9 126
Alloway, N.J., U.S. — D2 107
Alloway Creek, stm., N.J., U.S. — D2 107
Allyn, Wa., U.S. — B3 124
Alma, N.B. — D5 71
Alma, Ont. — D4 73
Alma, Que. — A6 74
Alma, Ar., U.S. — B1 81
Alma, Co., U.S. — B4 83
Alma, Ga., U.S. — E4 87
Alma, Il., U.S. — E5 90
Alma, Ks., U.S. — C7 93
Alma, Mi., U.S. — E6 99
Alma, Mo., U.S. — B4 102
Alma, Ne., U.S. — D6 104
Alma, N.C., U.S. — C3 110
Alma, Ok., U.S. — C4 113
Alma, W.V., U.S. — B4 125
Alma, Wi., U.S. — D1 126
Alma Center, Wi., U.S. — D3 126
Almada, Port. — C1 22
Almadén, Spain — C3 22
Almagro, Spain — C4 22
Al Mafraq, Jord. — F11 40
Al Maḥallah al Kubrá, Eg. — D3 41
Alma Hill, hill, N.Y., U.S. — C3 109
Al Maḥmūdīyah, Eg. — C2 41
Al Maḥmūdīyah, Iraq — F15 40
Al Maḥsamah, Eg. — D4 41
Al Maṭarīyah, Eg. — C4 41
Almanor, Lake, l., Ca., U.S. — B3 82
Almansa, Spain — C5 22
Al Mansūrah, Eg. — B3 38
Almanzora, stm., Spain — D4 22
Almargem, Port. — f9 22
Al Marj, Libya — C4 43
Almartha, Mo., U.S. — E5 102
Al Maṭarīyah, Eg. — C4 41
Almaville, Tn., U.S. — B5 119
Al Mayādīn, Syria — B4 38
Al Mazār, Jord. — D3 41
Al Mazār, Jord. — G10 40
Al Mazra'ah, Jord. — C7 41
Almeirim, Braz. — C4 59
Almeirim, Port. — C1 22
Almelo, Neth. — A7 16
Almelund, Mn., U.S. — E6 100
Almena, Ks., U.S. — C4 93
Almena, Wi., U.S. — C1 126
Almenara, Braz. — B4 56
Almendralejo, Spain — C2 22
Almería, Spain — D4 22
Almería, Ne., U.S. — C6 104
Almería, Gulf of, b., Spain — D4 22
Almetyevsk, Sov. Un. — *D8 29
Ålmhult, Swe. — B8 15
Al Minyā, Eg. — C3 38
Al Miqdādīyah, Iraq — E2 39
Almira, Wa., U.S. — B7 124
Almiradí, stm., Spain — D4 22
Almirante, Pan. — F6 62
Almirante Brown, Arg. — g7 54
Almirós, Grc. — C4 40
Almo, Id., U.S. — G5 89
Almo, Ky., U.S. — f9 94
Almodóvar, Port. — D1 22
Almodóvar [del Campo], Spain — C3 22
Almogía, Spain — D3 22
Almon, Ga., U.S. — C3 87
Almonaster [la Real], Spain — C2 22
Almond, N.C., U.S. — f9 110
Almond, N.Y., U.S. — C3 109
Almond, Wi., U.S. — D4 126
Almonte, Ont. — B8 73
Almonte, Spain — D2 22
Almonte, stm., Spain — C3 22
Almora, India — C7 36
Almora, Mn., U.S. — D3 100
Al Mubarraz, Sau. Ar. — C4 38
Al Mudawwarah, Jord. — E8 41
Al Mughayyir, Isr. Occ. — g12 41
Al Muglad, Sud. — C2 47
Al Mukalla, Yemen — D4 38
Al Mukhā, Yemen — D4 38
Almuñécar, Spain — D4 22
Al Musallamīyah, Sud. — C4 47
Al Musayyib, Iraq — F15 40
Al Muwaylih, Sau. Ar. — I10 40
Al Marj, Libya — C4 43
Almira, Wa., U.S. — B7 124
Almville, Ct., U.S. — C8 84
Almyville, Tn., U.S. — B5 119
Almena, Ks., U.S. — C4 93

Alondra, Ca., U.S. — *n12 82
Alonsa, Man. — D2 70
Alor, i., Indon. — G6 34
Álora, Spain — D3 22
Alor Setar, Malay. — D2 34
Alosno, Spain — D2 22
Alost see Aalst, Bel. — B6 16
Alotau, Pap. N. Gui. — m13 50
Alpachiri, Arg. — B4 54
Alpaugh, Ca., U.S. — E4 82
Alpena, Ar., U.S. — A2 81
Alpena, Mi., U.S. — C7 99
Alpena, S.D., U.S. — C7 118
Alpena, co., Mi., U.S. — D7 99
Alpha, Il., U.S. — B3 90
Alpha, Ky., U.S. — D4 94
Alpha, Mi., U.S. — B2 99
Alpha, Mn., U.S. — G4 100
Alpharetta, Ga., U.S. — B2 87
Alphen aan den Rijn, Neth. — B4 17
Alpheus see Alfiós, stm., Grc. — D3 25
Alpiarça, Port. — C1 22
Alpine, Al., U.S. — B3 78
Alpine, Az., U.S. — D6 80
Alpine, Ca., U.S. — *F5 82
Alpine, N.J., U.S. — h9 107
Alpine, Or., U.S. — C3 114
Alpine, Tn., U.S. — C8 119
Alpine, Tx., U.S. — D1 120
Alpine, Ut., U.S. — C4 121
Alpine, Wy., U.S. — C2 127
Alpine, co., Ca., U.S. — C4 82
Alpine Junction, Wy., U.S. — *C1 127
Alpoca, W.V., U.S. — D3 125
Alps, mts., Eur. — E4 18
Al Qadārif, Sud. — C4 47
Al Qadīmah, Sau. Ar. — C3 38
Al Qā'im, Iraq — E13 40
Al Qāmishlī, Syria — B4 38
Al Qanāyāt, Eg. — D3 41
Al Qantarah, Eg. — D4 41
Al Qaryah ash Sharqīyah, Libya — C2 43
Al Qaryatayn, Syria — E11 40
Al Qaşabāt, Libya — C2 43
Al Qaşr, Eg. — C2 38
Al Qaţif, Sau. Ar. — C4 38
Al Qaţrānah, Jord. — G11 40
Al Qaţrūn, Libya — E2 43
Al Qattā, Eg. — D2 41
Al Qunfudhah, Sau. Ar. — D3 38
Al Qurnah, Iraq — F3 39
Al Quşaymah, Eg. — D6 41
Al Quşayr, Eg. — C3 41
Al Quţaynah, Sud. — C4 47
Alrø, Den. — C4 15
Als, Den. — B4 15
Als, i., Den. — D3 15
Alsace, hist. reg., Fr. — C7 16
Alsask, Sask. — F1 75
Alsasua, Spain — A4 22
Alsdorf, W. Ger. — D6 19
Alsea, Or., U.S. — C3 114
Alsen, N.D., U.S. — A7 111
Alsenbrück-Langmeil, W. Ger. — D7 19
Alsey, Il., U.S. — D3 90
Alsfeld, W. Ger. — C4 18
Alsike (part of Uppsala), Swe. — t35 14
Alsip, Il., U.S. — *k9 90
Alstead, N.H., U.S. — D2 106
Alstead, stm., Sask. — B2 75
Alstead Center, N.H., U.S. — D2 106
Alston, Eng., U.K. — F6 11
Alta, Ia., U.S. — B2 92
Alta, Ut., U.S. — *C4 121
Alta, Wy., U.S. — C1 127
Altadena, Ca., U.S. — m12 82
Alta Gracia, Arg. — A4 54
Altagracia, Ven. — A3 60
Altagracia de Orituco, Ven. — B4 60
Altamaha, stm., Ga., U.S. — E5 87
Altamaha Sound, strt., Ga., U.S. — E5 87
Altamahaw, N.C., U.S. — A3 110
Altamira, Braz. — C4 59
Altamira, Chile — E2 55
Altamirano, Arg. — g7 54
Altamont, Man. — E2 70
Altamont, Il., U.S. — D5 90
Altamont, Ks., U.S. — E8 93
Altamont, Mo., U.S. — B3 102
Altamont, N.Y., U.S. — C6 109
Altamont, Or., U.S. — E5 114
Altamont, S.D., U.S. — C9 118
Altamont, Tn., U.S. — D8 119
Altamont, Ut., U.S. — C5 121
Altamonte Springs, Fl., U.S. — D5 86
Altamura, Italy — D6 23
Altamura, Isla, i., Mex. — C3 63
Altapass, N.C., U.S. — f10 110
Altar, Mex. — A2 63
Altario, Alta. — D5 68
Alta Vista, Ia., U.S. — A5 92
Altavista, Va., U.S. — C3 123
Altay, China — B3 31
Altay, Mong. — B4 31
Altay Shan, mts., Asia — B3 31
Altdorf, Switz. — E4 18
Altdorf [bei Nürnberg], W. Ger. — D6 19
Altefähr, E. Ger. — E8 15
Altenberg, E. Ger. — C8 19
Altenbruch, W. Ger. — E8 15
Altenburg, E. Ger. — C2 19
Altenburg, Mo., U.S. — D8 102
Altenkirchen, E. Ger. — D2 15
Altenkirchen, W. Ger. — C2 19
Altenmarkt [an der Alz], W. Ger. — A8 20
Altentreptow, E. Ger. — E7 15
Alter do Chão, Port. — C2 22
Altha, Fl., U.S. — B1 86
Altheim, Aus. — A9 20
Altinho, Braz. — D3 57
Altkirch, Fr. — D7 16
Altman, Ar., U.S. — n5 87
Altmar, N.Y., U.S. — B4 109
Altmühl, stm., W. Ger. — D5 19
Altnaharra, Scot., U.K. — B4 13
Alto, Ga., U.S. — B3 87
Alto, La., U.S. — B4 95
Alto, Mi., U.S. — F5 99
Alto, N.M., U.S. — D4 108
Alto, Tn., U.S. — D8 119
Alto, Tx., U.S. — D5 120
Alto Araguaia, Braz. — B2 56
Alto Cedro, Cuba — D5 64

Index

Name	Map Ref.	Page
Alto Garças, Braz.	B2	56
Alto Longá, Braz.	C2	57
Alto Molócuè, Moz.	A6	49
Altomünster, W. Ger.	A7	20
Alton, Ont.	D4	73
Alton, Eng., U.K.	C7	12
Alton, Al., U.S.	B3	78
Alton, Il., U.S.	E3	90
Alton, Ia., U.S.	B2	92
Alton, Ks., U.S.	C5	93
Alton, La., U.S.	h12	95
Alton, Mo., U.S.	E6	102
Alton, N.H., U.S.	D4	106
Alton, Oh., U.S.	m10	112
Alton, R.I., U.S.	F2	116
Alton, Ut., U.S.	F3	121
Alton, W.V., U.S.	C4	125
Altona, Man.	E3	70
Altona (part of Hamburg), W. Ger.	E3	15
Altona, Il., U.S.	B3	90
Altona, N.Y., U.S.	f11	109
Altonah, Ut., U.S.	C5	121
Alton Bay, N.H., U.S.	D4	106
Altoona, Al., U.S.	A3	78
Altoona, Fl., U.S.	D5	86
Altoona, Ia., U.S.	C4	92
Altoona, Ks., U.S.	E8	93
Altoona, Pa., U.S.	E5	115
Altoona, Wi., U.S.	D2	126
Alto Paraguai, Braz.	A1	56
Alto Paraguay, dept., Para.	D4	55
Alto Paraná, dept., Para.	D5	55
Alto Pass, Il., U.S.	F4	90
Alto Purus, stm., Peru	D3	58
Altötting, W. Ger.	A8	20
Altrincham, Eng., U.K.	A5	12
Altro, Ky., U.S.	C6	94
Altstätten, Switz.	B5	20
Āltūn Kūprī, Iraq	E15	40
Altun Shan, mts., China	D2	31
Altura, Mn., U.S.	F7	100
Alturas, Ca., U.S.	B3	82
Altus, Ar., U.S.	B2	81
Altus, Ok., U.S.	C2	113
Altus Air Force Base, mil., Ok., U.S.	C2	113
Altus Reservoir, res., Ok., U.S.	C2	113
Altusried, W. Ger.	A9	21
Alt Zachun, E. Ger.	E5	15
Al 'Ubaylah, Sau. Ar.	C5	38
Al Uḍayyah, Sud.	C2	47
Alum Bank, Pa., U.S.	F4	115
Alum Bridge, W.V., U.S.	B4	125
Alum Creek, W.V., U.S.	m12	125
Alum Creek, stm., Oh., U.S.	k11	112
Aluminé, Arg.	D2	56
Alum Rock, Ca., U.S.	*k9	82
'Aluqa, Sov. Un.	I10	27
Al 'Uqaylah, Libya	C3	43
Al 'Uqayr, Sau. Ar.	I5	39
Alutom, Mount, hill, Guam	L9	52
Alva, Fl., U.S.	F5	86
Alva, Ky., U.S.	D6	94
Alva, Ok., U.S.	A3	113
Alva, Wy., U.S.	B8	127
Alvarado, Mex.	D5	63
Alvarado, Mn., U.S.	B2	100
Alvarado, Tx., U.S.	C4	120
Alvaton, Ga., U.S.	C2	87
Älvdalen, Swe.	G6	14
Alvear, Arg.	E4	55
Alvena, Sask.	E2	75
Alverca, Port.	f9	22
Alverton, Pa., U.S.	F2	115
Alvesta, Swe.	B8	15
Alvin, Il., U.S.	C6	90
Alvin, S.C., U.S.	E8	117
Alvin, Tx., U.S.	E5	120
Alvinston, Ont.	E3	73
Alvo, Ne., U.S.	h12	104
Alvord, Ia., U.S.	A1	92
Alvord, Tx., U.S.	C4	120
Alvord Lake, l., Or., U.S.	E8	114
Alvordton, Oh., U.S.	A1	112
Älvsborg, co., Swe.	A6	15
Älvsered, Swe.	A6	15
Älvsjö (part of Stockholm), Swe.	t36	14
Al Wajh, Sau. Ar.	C3	38
Alwar, India	C6	36
Al Wāsiṭah, Eg.	E3	41
Alxa Zuoqi, China	D6	31
Alyat, Sov. Un.	F3	28
Alyth, Scot., U.K.	D5	13
Alytus, Sov. Un.	A8	26
Alz, stm., W. Ger.	A8	20
Alzada, Mt., U.S.	E12	103
Alzey, W. Ger.	D3	18
Ama, La., U.S.	k11	95
Amacuzac, stm., Mex.	n14	63
Amadeus, Lake, l., Austl.	D5	50
Amadi, Sud.	D3	47
Amadjuak Lake, l., N.W. Ter.	C18	66
Amado, Az., U.S.	F4	80
Amador, co., Ca., U.S.	C3	82
Amagansett, N.Y., U.S.	n16	109
Amagasaki, Japan	o14	33
Amager, i., Den.	C6	15
Amagon, Ar., U.S.	B4	81
Amaha, Japan	n18	33
Amahai, Indon.	F7	34
Amai, Indon.	J4	34
Amakusa Sea, Japan	J4	33
Åmål, Swe.	H5	14
Amalfi, Italy	D5	23
Amalga, Ut., U.S.	B4	121
Amalia, N.M., U.S.	A4	108
Amaliás, Grc.	D3	40
Amalner, India	G5	37
Amambaí, Braz.	C1	56
Amambaí, Serra de, mts., S.A.	C1	56
Amambay, dept., Para.	C1	56
Amamio Island, i., Japan	F10	31
Amana, Ia., U.S.	C6	92
Amaná, Lago, l., Braz.	C2	59
Amancey, Fr.	B1	21
Amanda, Oh., U.S.	C3	112
Amangeldy, Sov. Un.	C7	28
Amantea, Italy	E6	23
Amantes Point, c., Guam	L10	52
Amapá, Braz.	B4	59
Amapá, ter., Braz.	B4	59
Amapala, Hond.	D4	62
Amaraji, Braz.	k6	57
Amarante, Braz.	C2	57
Amaranth, Man.	D2	70
Amargosa, Braz.	D3	57
Amargosa, stm., U.S.	D5	82
Amargosa Desert, des., U.S.	G5	105
Amargosa Range, mts., U.S.	G5	105
Amarillo, Tx., U.S.	B2	120
Amaro, Mount, mtn., Italy	C5	23
Amaroúsion, Grc.	g11	25
Amasa, Mi., U.S.	B2	99
Amasra, Tur.	B9	40
Amasya, Tur.	B10	40
Amataurá, Braz.	B4	58
Amatignak Island, i., Ak., U.S.	E4	79
Amatsu-kominato, Japan	n19	33
Amazon, Sask.	F3	75
Amazon (Solimões) (Amazonas), stm., S.A.	D5	53
Amazonas, state, Braz.	C2	59
Amazonas, dept., Col.	D3	60
Amazonas, dept., Peru	C2	58
Amazonas, ter., Ven.	C4	60
Amazonia, Mo., U.S.	B3	102
Ambājōgāi, India	H6	37
Ambāla, India	B6	36
Ambalavao, Madag.	h9	49
Ambam, Cam.	E2	46
Ambanja, Madag.	f9	49
Ambarchik, Sov. Un.	C19	29
Ambato, Ec.	B2	58
Ambato Boeny, Madag.	g9	49
Ambatolampy, Madag.	g9	49
Ambatondrazaka, Madag.	g9	49
Ambatosoratra, Madag.	g9	49
Amber, Ok., U.S.	B4	113
Amberg, W. Ger.	D5	18
Amberg, Wi., U.S.	C6	126
Ambérieu [-en-Bugey], Fr.	E6	16
Amberson, Pa., U.S.	F6	115
Ambert, Fr.	E5	16
Ambia, In., U.S.	D2	91
Ambikāpur, India	D7	36
Ambil Island, i., Phil.	p13	34
Ambilobe, Madag.	f9	49
Amble-by-the-Sea, Eng., U.K.	B8	12
Ambler, Ak., U.S.	B7	79
Ambler, Pa., U.S.	F11	115
Ambo, Peru	D3	58
Ambo Channel, strt., Marsh Is.	S17	52
Ambodifototra, Madag.	g9	49
Amboina see Ambon, Indon.	F7	34
Amboise, Fr.	D4	16
Ambon, Indon.	F7	34
Ambon, i., Indon.	F7	34
Ambositra, Madag.	h9	49
Ambovombe, Madag.	h9	49
Amboy, Ca., U.S.	E6	82
Amboy, Il., U.S.	B4	90
Amboy, In., U.S.	C6	91
Amboy, Mn., U.S.	G4	100
Amboy, Wa., U.S.	D3	124
Ambridge, Pa., U.S.	E1	115
Ambriz, Ang.	C1	48
Ambrose, Ga., U.S.	E3	87
Ambrose, N.D., U.S.	A2	111
Ambrosia Lake, N.M., U.S.	B2	108
Ambur, Indon.	F8	34
Amchitka Island, i., Ak., U.S.	E3	79
Amchitka Pass, strt., Ak., U.S.	E3	79
Am Dam, Chad	C4	46
Amden, Switz.	B7	21
Amderma, Sov. Un.	C9	29
Ameagle, W.V., U.S.	D3	125
Ameca, Mex.	C4	63
Ameca, stm., Mex.	m11	63
Amecameca [de Juárez], Mex.	n14	63
Ameland, i., Neth.	A6	16
Amelia, La., U.S.	E4	95
Amelia, Ne., U.S.	B7	104
Amelia, Oh., U.S.	C1	112
Amelia, Va., U.S.	C4	123
Amelia City, Fl., U.S.	k9	86
Amelia Court House, Va., U.S.	C5	123
Amelia Island, i., Fl., U.S.	k9	86
Amelinghausen, W. Ger.	E4	15
Amendolara, Italy	E6	23
Amenia, N.Y., U.S.	D7	109
Amenia, N.D., U.S.	B8	111
American, stm., Ca., U.S.	C3	82
American, South Fork, stm., Ca., U.S.	C3	82
Americana, Braz.	m8	56
American Canyon, Ca., U.S.	*C2	82
American Falls, Id., U.S.	G6	89
American Falls Dam, Id., U.S.	G6	89
American Falls Reservoir, res., Id., U.S.	F5	89
American Fork, Ut., U.S.	C4	121
American Highland, plat., Ant.	B20	7
American Samoa, dep., Oc.	G11	6
Americus, Ga., U.S.	D2	87
Americus, Ks., U.S.	D7	93
Americus, Mo., U.S.	C6	102
Amersfoort, Neth.	A6	16
Amery, Man.	A4	70
Amery, Wi., U.S.	C1	126
Amery Ice Shelf, ice, Ant.	C20	7
Ames, Ia., U.S.	B4	92
Ames, Ks., U.S.	C5	93
Ames, Ne., U.S.	C9	104
Ames, Ok., U.S.	A3	113
Amesbury, Ma., U.S.	A5	98
Amesville, Oh., U.S.	C3	112
Amfissa, Grc.	C4	25
Amga, Sov. Un.	C16	29
Amgu, Sov. Un.	D8	29
Amguid, Alg.	D6	44
Amgun, stm., Sov. Un.	D16	29
Amherst, N.S.	D5	71
Amherst, Co., U.S.	A8	83
Amherst, Ma., U.S.	B2	98
Amherst, Ne., U.S.	D6	104
Amherst, N.H., U.S.	E3	106
Amherst, N.Y., U.S.	C2	109
Amherst, Oh., U.S.	A3	112
Amherst, S.D., U.S.	B8	118
Amherst, Tx., U.S.	B1	120
Amherst, Va., U.S.	C3	123
Amherst, co., Va., U.S.	C3	123
Amherstburg, Ont.	E1	73
Amherstdale, W.V., U.S.	n12	125
Amiata, mts., Italy	C3	23
Amidon, N.D., U.S.	C2	111
Amiens, Fr.	C4	16
Aminuis, Nmb.	B2	49
'Āmir, Ra's, c., Libya	C4	43
Amirante Islands, is., Sey.	G24	2
Amir Kabir Dam, Iran	C5	39
Amisk Lake, l., Sask.	C4	75
Amistad National Recreation Area, Tx., U.S.	E2	120
Amistad Reservoir, res., N.A.	E2	120
Amite, La., U.S.	D5	95
Amite, co., Ms., U.S.	D3	101
Amite, stm., La., U.S.	D5	95
Amity, Ar., U.S.	C2	81
Amity, Mo., U.S.	B3	102
Amity, Or., U.S.	B3	114
Amity, Pa., U.S.	F1	115
Amityville, N.Y., U.S.	E7	109
Amlekhganj, Nepal	C7	36
Amli Island, i., Ak., U.S.	E5	79
Amlwch, Wales, U.K.	A3	12
'Ammān, Jord.	B3	38
Ammanford, Wales, U.K.	A1	19
Ammeloe, W. Ger.	B6	19
Ammendorf, E. Ger.	D5	18
Ammer Lake, l., W. Ger.	D5	18
Ammon, Id., U.S.	F7	89
Ammonoosuc, stm., N.H., U.S.	B3	106
Amne Machin Shan see A'nyêmaqên Shan, mts., China		
Amnicon Falls, Wi., U.S.	B2	126
Amo, In., U.S.	E4	91
Āmol, Iran	C6	39
Amonate, Va., U.S.	e10	123
Amoret, Mo., U.S.	C3	102
Amorgós, i., Grc.	D5	40
Amorinópolis, Braz.	B2	56
Amorita, Ok., U.S.	A3	113
Amory, Ms., U.S.	B5	101
Amos, Que.	k11	74
Amoy see Xiamen, China	G8	31
Ampanihy, Madag.	h8	49
Amparo, Braz.	C3	56
Ampelókipoi, Grc.	*B4	25
Amper, stm., W. Ger.	E6	19
Ampezzo, Italy	C8	23
Amposta, Spain	B6	22
Amrāvati (Amraoti), India	D6	36
Amreli, India	J3	37
Amriswil, Switz.	A7	21
Amritsar, India	B5	36
Amroha, India	C7	37
Amrum, i., W. Ger.	A4	18
Amsteg, Switz.	C6	21
Amstelveen, Neth.	*B4	17
Amsterdam, Neth.	A6	16
Amsterdam, Mo., U.S.	C3	102
Amsterdam, Mt., U.S.	E5	103
Amsterdam, N.Y., U.S.	C6	109
Amsterdam, Oh., U.S.	B5	112
Amsterdam, Île, i., F.S.A.T.	I2	2
Amstetten, Aus.	D7	18
Amston, Ct., U.S.	C6	84
Am Timan, Chad	C4	46
Amu Darya, stm., Asia	F9	29
Amukta Pass, strt., Ak., U.S.	E4	79
Amulet, Sask.	H3	75
Amund Ringnes Island, i., N.W. Ter.	m32	66
Amundsen Bay, b., Ant.	C17	7
Amundsen Gulf, b., N.W. Ter.	B8	66
Amundsen-Scott, sci., Ant.	A17	7
Amundsen Sea, Ant.	B36	7
Amuntai, Indon.	F5	34
Amur (Heilong Jiang), stm., Asia	E16	29
Amvrakía, Gulf of, b., Grc.	C3	25
Amy, Ar., U.S.	D3	81
Amzi, Oued ti-n-, val., Afr.	E5	44
Anabar, stm., Sov. Un.	B14	29
'Anābtā, Isr. Occ.	f11	41
Anaco, Ven.	B5	60
Anacoco, La., U.S.	C2	95
Anacoco, Bayou, stm., La., U.S.	D2	95
Anaconda, Mt., U.S.	D4	103
Anaconda, N.M., U.S.	B2	108
Anaconda Range, mts., Mt., U.S.	E3	103
Anacortes, Wa., U.S.	A3	124
Anacostia, stm., U.S.	C4	97
Anacostia, Northwest Branch, stm., Md., U.S.	B3	97
Anacuao, Mount, mtn., Phil.	n13	34
Anadarko, Ok., U.S.	B3	113
Anadia, Braz.	C3	57
Anadyr, Sov. Un.	C20	29
Anadyr, stm., Sov. Un.	C20	29
Anadyr, Gulf of, b., Sov. Un.	C21	29
Anadyr Mountains, mts., Sov. Un.	C20	14
Anae, i., Guam	M9	52
Anáfi (Anaphe), i., Grc.	D5	40
Anagance, N.B.	D4	71
Anaheim, Ca., U.S.	F5	82
Anahim Lake, B.C.	C5	69
Anahola, Hi., U.S.	A2	88
Anahuac, Tx., U.S.	E5	120
Anahulu, stm., Hi., U.S.	f9	88
Anajás, Braz.	C5	59
Anak, N. Kor.	G2	33
Anakāpalle, India	E7	36
Anakie, Austl.	A13	40
Anakalava, Madag.	f9	49
Anama, Braz.	C2	59
Anama Bay, Man.	D2	70
Ana Maria, Golfo de, b., Cuba	D4	64
Anambas Islands, is., Indon.	E3	34
Anamoose, N.D., U.S.	B5	111
Anamosa, Ia., U.S.	B6	92
Anamur, Tur.	D9	40
Anamur, Cape, c., Tur.	D9	40
Anandale, La., U.S.	*C3	95
Ananea (Poto), Peru	D4	58
Anantapur, India	E4	36
Anantnāg, India	B6	36
Anānyev, Sov. Un.	H9	27
Anao Point, c., Guam	L10	52
Anapa, Sov. Un.	I11	27
Anaphe see Anáfi, i., Grc.	D5	40
Anápolis, Braz.	C4	59
Anapu, stm., Braz.	C5	59
Anār, Iran	E6	39
Anārak, Iran	E10	39
Anār Darreh, Afg.	C5	36
Anastasia Island, i., Fl., U.S.	F6	121
'Anātā, Isr. Occ.	h12	41
Anatone, Wa., U.S.	C8	124
Añatuya, Arg.	B2	55
Anauá, stm., Braz.	B2	55
Anawalt, W.V., U.S.	D2	125
Ancash, dept., Peru	C2	58
Ancaster, Ont.	D4	73
Ancenis, Fr.	D3	16
Ancha, Sierra, mts., Az., U.S.	C4	80
Anchieta, Braz.	C4	56
Anching see Anqing, China	E8	31
Anchorage, Ak., U.S.	C10	79
Anchorage, Ky., U.S.	g11	94
Anchor Point, Ak., U.S.	D9	79
Anchor Point, c., Ak., U.S.	h15	79
Ancienne-Lorette, Que.	C6	74
Anclote Keys, is., Fl., U.S.	*D4	86
Anco, Ky., U.S.	C6	94
Ancón, Peru	B7	117
Ancona, Italy	C4	23
Ancona, Il., U.S.	B5	90
Ancón de Sardinas, Bahía de, b., S.A.	C2	60
Ancud, Chile	D2	54
Ancud, Golfo de, b., Chile	D2	54
Anda, China	B10	31
Andacollo, Arg.	B2	54
Andahuaylas, Peru	D3	58
Andale, Ks., U.S.	E6	93
Andalgalá, Arg.	E2	55
Åndalsnes, Nor.	F2	14
Andalusia, Al., U.S.	D3	78
Andalusia, Il., U.S.	B3	90
Andalusia, hist. reg., Spain	D3	22
Andaman and Nicobar Islands, ter., India	*F9	36
Andaman Islands, is., India	F9	36
Andaman Sea, Asia	F10	36
Andamarca, Bol.	C2	55
Andamarca, Peru	D3	58
Andapa, Madag.	f9	49
Andava, Cap, c., Madag.	i9	49
Andebu, Nor.	p28	21
Andeer, Switz.	C7	21
Andenne, Bel.	D5	17
Anderlecht, Bel.	B6	16
Andermatt, Switz.	C4	20
Andernach, W. Ger.	C3	18
Anderson Air Force Base, mil., Guam	L10	52
Anderslöv, Swe.	C7	15
Anderson, Arg.	g6	54
Anderson, Al., U.S.	A2	78
Anderson, Ak., U.S.	C10	79
Anderson, Ca., U.S.	B2	82
Anderson, In., U.S.	D6	91
Anderson, Mo., U.S.	E3	102
Anderson, S.C., U.S.	B2	117
Anderson, Tn., U.S.	D8	119
Anderson, Tx., U.S.	D4	120
Anderson, co., Ks., U.S.	D8	93
Anderson, co., S.C., U.S.	B2	117
Anderson, co., Ky., U.S.	C4	94
Anderson, co., Tn., U.S.	C9	119
Anderson, co., Tx., U.S.	D5	120
Anderson, stm., N.W. Ter.	C7	66
Anderson, stm., In., U.S.	H4	91
Anderson, Mount, mtn., Wa., U.S.	B2	124
Anderson Ranch Reservoir, res., Id., U.S.	F3	89
Andersonville, Ga., U.S.	D2	87
Andersonville, In., U.S.	F7	91
Andes, Col.	B2	60
Andes, N.Y., U.S.	C6	109
Andes, mts., S.A.	E4	53
Andes, Lake, l., S.D., U.S.	D7	118
Andfjorden, strt., Nor.	C7	14
Andhra Pradesh, state, India	E6	36
Andīkíthira, i., Grc.	E4	40
Andilamena, Madag.	g9	49
Andīmeshk, Iran	E4	39
Andizhan, Sov. Un.	E10	29
Andkhvoy, Afg.	A4	36
Andoas, Peru	A4	58
Andong, S. Kor.	D10	31
Andorra, And.	A6	22
Andorra, ctry., Eur.	A6	22
Andover, Eng., U.K.	C6	12
Andover, Ct., U.S.	C6	84
Andover, Il., U.S.	B3	90
Andover, Ks., U.S.	g12	93
Andover, Me., U.S.	D2	96
Andover, Ma., U.S.	A5	98
Andover, Mn., U.S.	m12	100
Andover, N.H., U.S.	D3	106
Andover, N.Y., U.S.	C3	109
Andover, Oh., U.S.	A5	112
Andover, S.D., U.S.	B8	118
Andøya, i., Nor.	C6	14
Andøya, i., Nor.	C6	14
Andrade, Hi., U.S.	D6	88
Andradina, Braz.	C2	56
Andraitx, Spain	C7	22
Andreanof Islands, is., Ak., U.S.	E4	79
Andrelândia, Braz.	g5	56
Andréville, Que.	B8	74
Andrew, Alta.	C4	68
Andrew, co., Mo., U.S.	B3	102
Andrew Island, i., N.S.	D9	71
Andrews, In., U.S.	C6	91
Andrews, N.C., U.S.	f9	110
Andrews, S.C., U.S.	E8	117
Andrews, Tx., U.S.	C1	120
Andrews Air Force Base, mil., Md., U.S.	C4	97
Andrewsville, De., U.S.	E3	85
Andreyevka, Sov. Un.	G11	27
Andriba, Madag.	D2	23
Androka, Madag.	h8	49
Andros, Grc.	D5	40
Ándros, i., Grc.	D5	40
Androscoggin, stm., Me., U.S.	D2	96
Androscoggin, co., Me., U.S.	D2	96
Androscoggin Lake, l., Me., U.S.	D2	96
Andros Island, i., Bah.	B5	64
Andújar, Spain	C3	22
Andulo, Ang.	D2	48
Anduze, Togo	G5	45
Anegada, i., V.I., Br.	G12	64
Anegada, Bahía, b., Arg.	E4	54
Anegada Passage, strt., N.A.	G13	64
Anegam, Az., U.S.	E3	80
Añelo, Arg.	B3	54
Anerley, Sask.	F2	75
Aneroid, Sask.	H2	75
Aneta, N.D., U.S.	B8	111
Aneth, Ut., U.S.	F6	121
Aneto, Pico de, mtn., Spain	A6	22
Añewetak, Puntas, c., Chile	D1	55
Ang'angxi, China	B9	31
Angarsk, Sov. Un.	D12	29
Angaur, i., Palau	R17	52
Angela, Mt., U.S.	D10	103
Angela, Isla de la Guarda, Isla, i., Mex.	B2	63
Angeles, Phil.	o13	34
Angeles Point, c., Wa., U.S.	A2	124
Ángelholm, Swe.	I5	14
Angelina, co., Tx., U.S.	D5	120
Angelina, stm., Tx., U.S.	D5	120
Angels Camp, Ca., U.S.	C3	82
Angelus, S.C., U.S.	C8	93
Ang'angxi, China	B7	117
Angermanälven, stm., Swe.	F7	14
Angermünde, E. Ger.	B6	18
Angers, Fr.	D3	16
Angicos, Braz.	C3	57
Angie, La., U.S.	D6	95
Angikuni Lake, l., N.W. Ter.	D13	66
Angle Inlet, Mn., U.S.	A3	100
Angle Lake, Wa., U.S.	*B3	124
Anglem, Mount, mtn., N.Z.	Q11	51
Anglesey, i., Wales, U.K.	D4	10
Angleton, Tx., U.S.	E5	120
Angliers, Que.	G17	66
Angling, stm., Man.	A5	70
Angling Lake, l., Man.	A5	70
Angmagssalik, Grnld.	C17	61
Angoche, Moz.	A6	49
Angoche, Ilha, i., Moz.	A6	49
Angol, Chile	B2	54
Angola, In., U.S.	A8	91
Angola, N.Y., U.S.	C1	109
Angola, ctry., Afr.	D2	48
Angola Beach, De., U.S.	F5	85
Angola Swamp, sw., N.C., U.S.	C5	110
Angora, Ak., U.S.	D13	79
Angora, Ne., U.S.	C2	104
Angora see Ankara, Tur.	C9	40
Angostura Reservoir, res., S.D., U.S.	D2	118
Angoulême, Fr.	E4	16
Angra do Heroísmo, Port.	g9	44
Angra dos Reis, Braz.	C4	56
Angren, Sov. Un.	E7	28
Anguang, China	B10	32
Anguilla, Ms., U.S.	C3	101
Anguilla, ctry., N.A.	G13	64
Anguillara [Sabazia], Italy	g8	23
Anguille, Cape, c., Newf.	E2	72
Angumu, Zaire	B4	48
Angus, Ont.	C5	73
Angus, Mn., U.S.	B2	100
Angusville, Man.	D1	70
Anholt, i., Den.	B5	15
Anholt, W. Ger.	B5	19
Anhua, China	J4	32
Anhui, prov., China	E8	31
Anhwei see Anhui, prov., China	E8	31
Aniak, Ak., U.S.	C8	79
Aniche, Fr.	D3	17
Aniene (Teverone), stm., Italy	h9	23
Animas, N.M., U.S.	F1	108
Animas, stm., U.S.	D3	83
Animas Mountains, mts., N.M., U.S.	F1	108
Animas Peak, mtn., N.M., U.S.	F2	108
Animas Valley, val., N.M., U.S.	F1	108
Anina, Rom.	C5	24
Anita, Ia., U.S.	C3	92
Anita, Pa., U.S.	D4	115
Aniva, Sov. Un.	C11	33
Aniva, Cape, c., Sov. Un.	B13	31
Aniva Bay, b., Sov. Un.	C11	33
Aniwa, Wi., U.S.	C4	126
Anizy-le-Château, Fr.	E3	17
Anjār, India	D5	36
Anjō, Japan	o16	33
Anjou, Que.	p19	74
Anjou, hist. reg., Fr.	D3	16
Anju, N. Kor.	G2	33
Anjuman, Neth.	A6	17
Anka, Nig.	D6	45
Ankang, China	E6	31
Ankara, Tur.	C9	40
Ankavandra, Madag.	g9	49
Ankazoabo, Madag.	h8	49
Ankazobe, Madag.	g9	49
Ankeny, Ia., U.S.	C4	92
An Khe, Viet.	C3	34
Anklam, E. Ger.	B6	18
Ankober, Eth.	D4	47
Ankoro, Zaire	C4	48
Anlong, China	F6	31
Anlu, China	I5	32
Ann, Cape, c., Ant.	C18	7
Ann, Cape, c., Ma., U.S.	A6	98
Anna, Sov. Un.	F13	27
Anna, Il., U.S.	F4	90
Anna, Oh., U.S.	B1	112
Anna, Lake, res., Va., U.S.	B5	123
Annaba (Bône), Alg.	B6	44
Annabella, Ut., U.S.	E3	121
Annaberg-Buchholz, E. Ger.	C6	18
An Nabk, Syria	E11	40
Annandale, Mn., U.S.	E4	100
Annandale, N.J., U.S.	B3	107
Annandale, Va., U.S.	*B5	123
An Nafūd, des., Sau. Ar.	C4	38
An Najaf, Iraq	E3	39
An Nakhl, Eg.	H9	40
Annalee Heights, Va., U.S.	*B5	123
Annam, hist. reg., Viet.	F7	35
An Nakhl, Eg.	H9	40
Annam, hist. reg., Viet.	F7	35
Annamitique, Chaîne, mts., Asia	B3	34
Annan, Scot., U.K.	C5	10
Annan, stm., Scot., U.K.	E5	13
Annapolis, Il., U.S.	D6	90
Annapolis, Md., U.S.	C5	97
Annapolis, Mo., U.S.	D7	102
Annapolis, co., N.S.	E4	71
Annapolis Junction, Md., U.S.	B4	97
Annapolis Royal, N.S.	E4	71
Annapūrna, mtn., Nepal	C7	36
Anna Regina, Guy.	A3	59
Annawan, Il., U.S.	B4	90
An Nāṣirīyah, Iraq	F7	121
Annecy, Fr.	E7	16
Annecy-le-Vieux, Fr.	E1	21
Annemasse, Fr.	E7	16
Annestown, Ire.	D4	11
An Nhon, Viet.	F8	35
An Nîl, prov., Sud.	B3	47
An Nîl al Azraq (Blue Nile), prov., Sud.	C3	47
Anniston, Al., U.S.	B4	78
Annobón Island (Pagalu), i., Eq. Gui.	F1	46
Annonay, Fr.	E6	16
Annone, Lago di, l., Italy	E7	21
Annotto Bay, Jam.	E5	64
Annotto Bay, b., Jam.	E15	65
Annsjön, l., Swe.	u33	14
An Nuhūd, Sud.	C2	47
Annursnack Hill, hill, Ma., U.S.	g10	98
Annville, Ky., U.S.	C6	94
Annville, Pa., U.S.	F8	115
Anoka, Mn., U.S.	E5	100
Anoka, Ne., U.S.	B7	104
Anoka, co., Mn., U.S.	E5	100
Anori, Braz.	C2	59
Áno Viánnos, Grc.	E5	25
Anóyia, Grc.	E5	25
Anping, China	E6	32
Anqing, China	E8	31
Ansbach, W. Ger.	D5	18
Anse d'Hainault, Haiti	E6	64
Anselmo, Ne., U.S.	C6	104
Anserma, Col.	B2	60
Anshan, China	C9	31
Anshun, China	F6	31
Ansley, Al., U.S.	D3	78
Ansley, Ms., U.S.	E4	101
Ansley, Ne., U.S.	C6	104
Anson, Me., U.S.	D3	96
Anson, Tx., U.S.	C3	120
Anson, co., N.C., U.S.	B2	110
Anson Bay, b., Austl.	B5	50
Ansong see Anseong, S. Kor.	H3	33
Ansongo, Mali	C5	45
Ansonia, Ct., U.S.	D3	84
Ansonia, Oh., U.S.	B1	112
Ansonville, N.C., U.S.	B2	110
Ansted, W.V., U.S.	C3	125
Anstruther, Scot., U.K.	D6	13
Ansudu, Indon.	F9	34
Anta, Peru	D3	58
Antabamba, Peru	D3	58
Antakya (Antioch), Tur.	D11	40
Antalaha, Madag.	f10	49
Antalāt, Libya	C4	43
Antalāt, well, Libya	G3	40
Antalya, Tur.	D8	40
Antalya, Gulf of, b., Tur.	D8	40
Antananarivo, Madag.	g9	49
Antananarivo, prov., Madag.	g9	49
Antarctica, cont.	A19	7
Antarctic Peninsula, pen., Ant.	A19	7
Antelope, Sask.	G1	75
Antelope, Ks., U.S.	D7	93
Antelope, Mt., U.S.	B12	103
Antelope, Or., U.S.	*C6	114
Antelope, S.D., U.S.	*D5	118
Antelope Butte, mtn., Wy., U.S.	B7	127
Antelope Creek, stm., Wy., U.S.	C7	127
Antelope Island, i., Ut., U.S.	B3	121
Antelope Lake, l., Sask.	G1	75
Antelope Mine, Zimb.	B4	49
Antelope Peak, mtn., Nv., U.S.	D7	105
Antelope Range, mts., U.S.	D7	105
Antelope Reservoir, res., Or., U.S.	E9	114
Antelope Wash, val., Nv., U.S.	D5	105
Antero, Mount, mtn., Co., U.S.	C4	83
Antero Reservoir, res., Co., U.S.	C5	83
Antes Fort, Pa., U.S.	D7	115
Anthon, Ia., U.S.	B2	92
Anthony, Fl., U.S.	C4	86
Anthony, Ks., U.S.	E5	93
Anthony, N.M., U.S.	F3	108
Anthony, R.I., U.S.	D3	116
Anthony Creek, stm., W.V., U.S.	D4	125
Anti-Atlas, mts., Mor.	C3	44
Antibes, Fr.	F7	16
Anticosti, Île d', i., Que.	k14	74
Antietam Creek, stm., Md., U.S.	B2	97
Antietam National Battlefield Site, hist., Md., U.S.	B2	97
Antigo, Wi., U.S.	C4	126
Antigonish, N.S.	D8	71
Antigonish, co., N.S.	H14	64
Antigua, i., Antig.	H14	64
Antigua and Barbuda, ctry., N.A.	H14	64
Antigua Guatemala, Guat.	E6	63
Antilla, Cuba	D6	64
Antimony, Ut., U.S.	E4	121
Antioch, Ca., U.S.	h9	82
Antioch, Il., U.S.	A5	90
Antioch, Ne., U.S.	B3	104
Antioch see Antakya, Tur.	D11	40
Antioquia, Col.	B2	60
Antioquia, dept., Col.	B2	60
Antipodes Islands, is., N.Z.	J8	2
Antler, Sask.	H5	75
Antler, N.D., U.S.	A4	111
Antler, stm., N.A.	E1	70
Antlers, Ok., U.S.	C6	113
Antofagasta, Chile	D1	55
Antofagasta, prov., Chile	D1	55
Antofagasta de la Sierra, Arg.	E2	55
Antofalla, Volcán, vol., Arg.	E2	55
Antoine, Ar., U.S.	C2	81
Antón, Pan.	F7	64
Anton, Co., U.S.	B7	83
Anton, Tx., U.S.	C1	120
Anton Chico, N.M., U.S.	B4	108
Antongila, Helodrano, b., Madag.	g9	49
Antonia, Mo., U.S.	C7	102
Antonina, Braz.	D3	56
Antônio Carlos, Braz.	g6	56
Antônio de Biedma, Arg.	E3	54
Antônio Dias, Braz.	D5	57
Antonito, Co., U.S.	D5	83
Antony, Fr.	g10	16
Antora Peak, mtn., Co., U.S.	C4	83
Antratsit, Sov. Un.	q22	27
Antrim, N. Ire., U.K.	C5	11
Antrim, N.H., U.S.	D3	106
Antrim, co., Mi., U.S.	C5	99
Antrim, co., N. Ire., U.K.	C5	11
Antsirabe, Madag.	g9	49
Antsiranana, Madag.	f9	49
Antsiranana, prov., Madag.	f9	49
Antsohihy, Madag.	f9	49
Antwerp (Antwerpen), Bel.	B5	16
Antwerp, N.Y., U.S.	A5	109
Antwerp, Oh., U.S.	A1	112
Antwerp, prov., Bel.	C4	17

Name Map Ref. Page

Antwerpen see Antwerp, Bel. B5 16
Anua, Am. Sam. F13 52
An Uaimh (Navan), Ire. D3 10
Anuradhapura, Sri L. G7 36
Anvers Island, i., Ant. C6 7
Anvik, Ak., U.S. C7 79
Anxi, China F8 31
Anxi, China C4 31
Anyang, China D7 31
Anyang, S. Kor. *H3 33
A'nyêmaqên Shan, mts., China D4 31
Anyi, China G4 32
Anykščiai, Sov. Un. A8 26
Anzá, Col. B2 60
Anza, stm., Italy E5 21
Anzac, Alta. A5 68
Anzhero-Sudzhensk, Sov. Un. D11 29
Anzin, Fr. D3 17
Anzio, Italy D4 23
Anzoátegui, state, Ven. B5 60
Aoji-ri, N. Kor. E5 33
Aomoen Island, i., Marsh Is. P18 52
Aomon, i., Marsh Is. S18 52
Aomori, Japan C13 31
Aoral, Mount, mtn., Camb. C2 34
Aosta, Italy B1 23
Aou Hofrit, well, W. Sah. E2 44
Aouk, Bahr, stm., Afr. D3 46
Aoukâr, reg., Maur. C2 45
Aoyama, Japan o15 33
Aozou, Chad A3 46
Apa, stm., S.A. D4 55
Apache, Ok., U.S. C3 113
Apache, co., Az., U.S. B6 80
Apache Creek, N.M., U.S. D1 108
Apache Junction, Az., U.S. m9 80
Apache Peak, mtn., Az., U.S. F5 80
Apalachee, Ga., U.S. C3 87
Apalachee Bay, b., Fl., U.S. B2 86
Apalachicola, Fl., U.S. C2 86
Apalachicola, stm., Fl., U.S. B1 86
Apalachicola Bay, b., Fl., U.S. C2 86
Apalachin, N.Y., U.S. C4 109
Apan, Mex. n14 63
Apaporis, stm., S.A. D3 60
Aparri, Phil. B6 34
Apatin, Yugo. C4 24
Apatity, Sov. Un. D15 14
Apatzingán [de la Constitución], Mex. n12 63
Apeldoorn, Neth. A6 16
Apennines, mts., Italy C4 23
Apennine Tunnel, Italy B3 23
Apérathos, Grc. D5 25
Apex, N.C., U.S. B4 110
Apex Mountain, mtn., Yukon D5 66
Api, mtn., Nepal C8 37
Apia, W. Sam. F12 52
Apiacás, Serra dos, plat., Braz. E3 59
Apia Harbour, b., W. Sam. F12 52
Apiaí, Braz. C3 56
Apishapa, stm., Co., U.S. D6 83
Apison, Tn., U.S. h11 119
Apizaco, Mex. n14 63
Aplao, Peru E3 58
Aplin, Ar., U.S. C3 81
Aplington, Ia., U.S. B5 92
Apo, Mount, mtn., Phil. D7 34
Apodi, Braz. C3 57
Apohaqui, N.B. D4 71
Apolda, E. Ger. C5 18
Apolima Island, i., W. Sam. F11 52
Apolima Strait, strt., W. Sam. F11 52
Apollo, Pa., U.S. E2 115
Apolo, Bol. B2 55
Apopka, Fl., U.S. D5 86
Apopka, Lake, l., Fl., U.S. D5 86
Aporé, Braz. B2 56
Aporé, stm., Braz. B2 56
Apostle Islands, is., Wi., U.S. A3 126
Apostle Islands National Lakeshore, Wi., U.S. A3 126
Apóstoles, Arg. E4 55
Appalachia, Va., U.S. f9 123
Appalachian Mountains, mts., N.A. C11 76
Appam, N.D., U.S. A2 111
Appanoose, co., Ia., U.S. D5 92
Appenzell, Switz. E4 18
Appenzell-Ausser Rhoden, state, Switz. B5 20
Appenzell-Inner Rhoden, state, Switz. B5 20
Apperson, Ok., U.S. A5 113
Appingedam, Neth. A6 17
Apple, stm., Wi., U.S. C1 126
Appleby, Eng., U.K. F6 13
Appleby, Tx., U.S. D5 120
Apple Creek, Oh., U.S. B4 112
Applecross, Scot., U.K. C3 13
Applegate, Mi., U.S. E8 99
Applegate, Or., U.S. E3 114
Applegate, stm., Or., U.S. E3 114
Apple Grove, W.V., U.S. C2 125
Apple Hill, Ont. B10 73
Apple Orchard Mountain, mtn., Va., U.S. C3 123
Apple River, N.S. D5 71
Apple River, Il., U.S. A3 90
Apple Springs, Tx., U.S. D5 120
Appleton, Ar., U.S. B3 81
Appleton, Me., U.S. D3 96
Appleton, Mn., U.S. E2 100
Appleton, Tn., U.S. B4 119
Appleton, Wa., U.S. D4 124
Appleton, Wi., U.S. D5 126
Appleton City, Mo., U.S. C3 102
Apple Valley, Ca., U.S. E5 82
Apple Valley, Mn., U.S. n12 100
Apple Valley, N.D., U.S. *C5 111
Applewood, Co., U.S. B5 83
Appleyard, Wa., U.S. B5 124
Appling, Ga., U.S. C4 87
Appling, co., Ga., U.S. E4 87
Appomattox, Va., U.S. C4 123
Appomattox, co., Va., U.S. C4 123
Appomattox, stm., Va., U.S. C4 123
Appomattox Court House National Historical Park, Va., U.S. C4 123
Apra Harbor, b., Guam L9 52
Aprelsk, Sov. Un. D14 29
Aprilia, Italy D4 23
Apsheron Peninsula, pen., Sov. Un. G19 8
Apsley, Ont. C6 73
Apt, Fr. F6 16
Aptos, Ca., U.S. *D3 82
Apua Point, c., Hi., U.S. D6 88
Apucarana, Braz. C2 56
Apulia (Puglia), prov., Italy D6 23
Apure, state, Ven. B4 60
Apure, stm., Ven. B4 60
Apurímac, dept., Peru D3 58
Apurímac, stm., Peru D3 58
Aqaba, Gulf of, b. C3 38
'Aqīq, Sud. B4 47
'Aqrabā, Syria A8 41
'Aqrabah, Isr. Occ. B7 41
Aquarius Mountains, mts., Az., U.S. C2 80
Aquarius Plateau, plat., Ut., U.S. E4 121
Aquasco, Md., U.S. C4 97
Aquebogue, N.Y., U.S. n16 109
Aquidauana, Braz. C1 56
Aquila see L'Aquila, Italy C4 23
Aquileia, Italy D9 20
Aquiles Serdán, Mex. B3 63
Aquin, Haiti E7 64
Aquone, N.C., U.S. f9 110
Ara, India C7 36
Arab, Al., U.S. A3 78
'Arab, Baḥr al, stm., Sud. D2 47
Arab, Khalīj al, b., Egypt G7 40
Arab, Shatt al, stm., Iraq B4 38
Arabelo, Ven. C5 60
Arabi, Ga., U.S. E3 87
Arabi, La., U.S. k11 95
Arabian Desert, des., Eg. C3 38
Arabian Sea H9 30
Araçá, stm., Braz. B2 59
Aracaju, Braz. D3 57
Aracati, Braz. B3 57
Araçatuba, Braz. C2 56
Aracena, Spain D2 22
Aracruz, Braz. B4 56
Araçuaí, Braz. B4 56
Arad, Rom. B5 24
Arada, Chad B4 46
Arafura Sea G7 6
Aragarças, Braz. B2 56
Arago, Or., U.S. D2 114
Arago, Cape, c., Or., U.S. D2 114
Aragon, Ga., U.S. B1 87
Aragon, N.M., U.S. D1 108
Aragon, hist. reg., Spain B5 22
Aragón, stm., Spain A5 22
Aragua, state, Ven. A4 60
Araguacema, Braz. D5 59
Araguaçu, Braz. E5 59
Aragua de Barcelona, Ven. B5 60
Araguaia, stm., Braz. D6 53
Araguaia, Braço Menor, stm., Braz. E5 59
Araguaia National Park, Braz. E4 59
Araguao, Boca, mth., Ven. B5 60
Araguari, Braz. B3 56
Araguari, stm., Braz. B4 59
Arai, Japan H9 33
Arai, Japan o16 33
Arāk, Alg. D5 44
Arāk, Iran B4 38
Arakan Range, mts., Burma E9 36
Árakhthos, stm., Grc. C3 25
Arakkonam, India F6 36
Araks, stm., Asia B3 39
Aral Sea, Sov. Un. E9 29
Aralsk, Sov. Un. D6 28
Aramac, Austl. D8 50
Arambaza, Col. D3 60
Ārān, Iran D5 39
Aranda de Duero, Spain B4 22
Arandas, Mex. m12 63
Aran Island, i., Ire. C2 10
Aran Islands, is., Ire. D2 10
Aranjuez, Spain B4 22
Aranos, Nmb. B2 49
Aransas, co., Tx., U.S. E4 120
Aransas Bay, b., Tx., U.S. E4 120
Aransas Pass, Tx., U.S. F4 120
Aranyaprathet, Thai. C2 34
Araouane, Mali C4 45
Arapaho, Ok., U.S. B3 113
Arapahoe, Co., U.S. C8 83
Arapahoe, Ne., U.S. D6 104
Arapahoe, N.C., U.S. B6 110
Arapahoe, Wy., U.S. D4 127
Arapahoe, co., Co., U.S. B6 83
Arapey, Ur. E1 56
Arapey Grande, stm., Ur. E1 56
Arapkir, Tur. C12 40
Araponga, Braz. C2 56
Araranguá, Braz. D3 56
Araraquara, Braz. C3 56
Araras, Braz. C3 56
Ararat, Austl. G7 50
Ararat, Va., U.S. D2 123
Ararat, Mount, mtn., Tur. C15 40
Araripe, Chapada do, plat., Braz. C3 57
Araruna, Braz. h6 57
Arauca, Col. B3 60
Arauca, dept., Col. B3 60
Arauca, stm., S.A. B3 60
Arauco, Chile B2 54
Araújos, Braz. B3 56
Arāvalli Range, mts., India D5 36
Araxá, Braz. B3 56
Araya, Ven. A5 60
Araya, Punta de, c., Ven. A5 60
Arba Minch, Eth. D4 47
Arbela, Mo., U.S. A5 102
Arboga, Swe. t33 14
Arbois, Fr. D6 16
Arboles, Co., U.S. D3 83
Arbon, Switz. B5 20
Arbon, Id., U.S. G6 89
Arborea (Mussolinia), Italy E2 23
Arborfield, Sask. D4 75
Arborg, Man. D3 70
Arbor Vitae, Wi., U.S. C4 126
Arbroath, Scot., U.K. B5 10
Arbuckle, Ca., U.S. C2 82
Arbuckle, Lake, l., Fl., U.S. E5 86
Arbuckle Mountains, mts., Ok., U.S. C4 113
Arbuckles, Lake of the, res., Ok., U.S. C5 113
Arbyrd, Mo., U.S. E7 102
Arc, Bayou des, stm., Ar., U.S. B4 81
Arcachon, Fr. E3 16
Arcade, Ca., U.S. c3 82
Arcade, Ga., U.S. B3 87
Arcade, N.Y., U.S. C2 109
Arcadia, N.S. F3 71
Arcadia, Ca., U.S. m12 82
Arcadia, Fl., U.S. E5 86
Arcadia, In., U.S. D5 91
Arcadia, Ia., U.S. B2 92
Arcadia, Ks., U.S. E9 93
Arcadia, La., U.S. B3 95
Arcadia, Mi., U.S. D4 99
Arcadia, Mo., U.S. D7 102
Arcadia, Ne., U.S. C6 104
Arcadia, Oh., U.S. A2 112
Arcadia, Ok., U.S. B4 113
Arcadia, Pa., U.S. E4 115
Arcadia, R.I., U.S. E2 116
Arcadia, S.C., U.S. B4 117
Arcadia, Wi., U.S. D2 126
Arcanum, Oh., U.S. C1 112
Arcata, Ca., U.S. B1 82
Arc Dome, mtn., Nv., U.S. E4 105
Arcelia, Mex. n13 63
Arcey, Fr. A2 21
Archambault, Lac, l., Que. C3 74
Archbald, Pa., U.S. m18 115
Archbold, Oh., U.S. A1 112
Archdale, N.C., U.S. B3 110
Archer, Fl., U.S. C4 86
Archer, Ia., U.S. A2 92
Archer, Ne., U.S. C7 104
Archer, co., Tx., U.S. C3 120
Archer, stm., Austl. B7 50
Archer City, Tx., U.S. C3 120
Archer's Post, Kenya A6 48
Archerwill, Sask. E4 75
Arches National Park, Ut., U.S. E6 121
Archidona, Spain D3 22
Archie, Mo., U.S. C3 102
Archive, Sask. G3 75
Archuleta, co., Co., U.S. D3 83
Arcis-sur-Aube, Fr. C6 16
Arco, Id., U.S. F5 89
Arco, Mn., U.S. F2 100
Arcola, Sask. H4 75
Arcola, Il., U.S. D5 90
Arcola, In., U.S. B7 91
Arcola, Ms., U.S. B3 101
Arcola, Mo., U.S. D4 102
Arcola, Va., U.S. g11 123
Arçon, Fr. C1 21
Arcos de la Frontera, Spain D3 22
Arcot, India F6 36
Arcoverde, Braz. C3 57
Arctic Bay, N.W. Ter. B16 66
Arctic Ocean A1 128
Arctic Village, Ak., U.S. B10 79
Arcueil, Fr. g10 16
Arda, stm., Eur. E7 24
Ardabīl (Ardebil), Iran B4 38
Ardagh, Ire. E2 11
Ardahan, Tur. B14 40
Ardakān, Iran B5 38
Ardakān, Iran E6 39
Ardara, Ire. C3 11
Ardath, Sask. F2 75
Ardatov, Sov. Un. D16 27
Ardbeg, Ont. B4 73
Ardea, Italy h9 23
Ardebil see Ardabīl, Iran B4 38
Ardee, Ire. E2 10
Arden, Man. D2 70
Arden, Ont. C8 73
Arden, Den. B3 15
Arden, Ar., U.S. D1 81
Arden, Ca., U.S. *C2 82
Arden, N.C., U.S. f10 110
Arden Hills, Mn., U.S. *m12 100
Ardennes, dept., Fr. E4 17
Ardennes, reg., Eur. B6 16
Ardenno, Italy C5 20
Ardenvoir, Wa., U.S. B5 124
Arderin, mtn., Ire. D4 11
Ardestān, Iran E6 39
Ardglass, N. Ire., U.K. C6 11
Ardgroom, Ire. F2 11
Ardila, stm., Eur. C2 22
Ardill, Sask. H3 75
Ardino, Bul. E7 24
Ardley, Alta. C4 68
Ardmore, Alta. B5 68
Ardmore, Ire. F4 11
Ardmore, Al., U.S. A3 78
Ardmore, In., U.S. A5 91
Ardmore, Md., U.S. C4 97
Ardmore, Ok., U.S. C4 113
Ardmore, Pa., U.S. F11 115
Ardmore, S.D., U.S. D2 118
Ardmore, Tn., U.S. B5 119
Ardnamurchan, Point of, c., Scot., U.K. D2 13
Ardnaree, Ire. C2 11
Ardnave Point, c., Scot., U.K. E2 13
Ardoch, N.D., U.S. A8 111
Ardpatrick Point, c., Scot., U.K. E3 13
Ardres, Fr. D1 17
Ardrossan, Austl. G1 51
Ardrossan, Alta. C4 68
Ardrossan, Scot., U.K. C4 10
Ardsley, N.Y., U.S. g13 109
Arecibo, P.R. G11 64
Aredale, Ia., U.S. B5 92
Areia, Braz. h6 57
Areia Branca, Braz. B3 57
Arelee, Sask. E2 75
Arena, N.D., U.S. B5 111
Arena, Wi., U.S. E4 126
Arena, Point, c., Ca., U.S. C2 82
Arena, Punta, c., Mex. C3 63
Arenac, co., Mi., U.S. D7 99
Arenápolis, Braz. A1 56
Arenas de San Pedro, Spain B3 22
Arenas Valley, N.M., U.S. E1 108
Arendal, Nor. H3 14
Arendonk, Bel. C5 17
Arendsee, E. Ger. B5 18
Arendtsville, Pa., U.S. G7 115
Arenillas, Ec. B1 58
Arenzville, Il., U.S. D3 90
Areópolis, Grc. D4 25
Arequipa, Peru E3 58
Arequipa, dept., Peru E3 58
Arezzo, Italy C3 23
Arga, stm., Spain A5 22
Argalastí, Grc. C4 25
Arganda, Spain p18 22
Argelès-Gazost, Fr. F3 16
Argen, stm., W. Ger. A1 21
Argenta, Italy B3 23
Argenta, Il., U.S. D5 90
Argentan, Fr. C4 16
Argentat, Fr. E4 16
Argenteuil, Fr. C5 16
Argenteuil, co., Que. D3 74
Argentina, ctry., S.A. G4 53
Argentino, Lago, l., Arg. E2 54
Argenton-sur-Creuse, Fr. D4 16
Argeș, stm., Rom. C7 24
Arghandāb, stm., Afg. E13 39
Arghandāb, Band-e, res., Afg. F13 39
Argo, Sud. B3 47
Argo, Al., U.S. B3 78
Argo, Il., U.S. A3 90
Argo, Ky., U.S. C7 94
Argo Corner, De., U.S. E4 85
Argolis, Gulf of, b., Grc. D4 25
Argonia, Ks., U.S. E6 93
Argonne, Wi., U.S. C5 126
Argonne, reg., Fr. C6 16
Argonne, Forêt d', for., Fr. E4 17
Árgos, Grc. D4 40
Argos, In., U.S. B5 91
Árgos Orestikón, Grc. B3 25
Argostólion, Grc. C3 40
Argun, stm., Asia D14 29
Argungu, Nig. D5 45
Argusville, N.D., U.S. B9 111
Argyle, N.S. F4 71
Argyle, Fl., U.S. u15 86
Argyle, Ga., U.S. E4 87
Argyle, Ia., U.S. D6 92
Argyle, Mi., U.S. E8 99
Argyle, Mn., U.S. B2 100
Argyle, Mo., U.S. C5 102
Argyle, N.Y., U.S. B7 109
Argyle, Wi., U.S. F4 126
Argyle, Lake, res., Austl. C4 50
Århus, Den. I4 14
Århus, co., Den. B4 15
Århus Bugt, b., Den. B4 15
Ari, In., U.S. B7 91
Ariake Bay, b., Japan K5 33
Ariano Irpino, Italy D5 23
Ariano nel Polesine, Italy E8 20
Ariari, stm., Col. C3 60
Arica, Chile C1 55
Arica, Col. D3 60
Arichat, N.S. D8 71
Ariège, stm., Fr. F4 16
Ariel, Wa., U.S. D3 124
Arieș, stm., Rom. B6 24
Arikaree, stm., U.S. B8 83
Arima, Trin. K14 64
Arimo, Id., U.S. G6 89
Arinos, stm., Braz. B4 55
Ario de Rosales, Mex. D4 63
Arion, Ia., U.S. C2 92
Aripeka, Fl., U.S. D4 86
Aripo, El Cerro del, mtn., Trin. K14 64
Aripuanã, Braz. D2 59
Aripuanã, stm., Braz. D2 59
Arisaig, Scot., U.K. D3 13
'Arīsh, Wādī al, val., Eg. D6 41
Arispe, Ia., U.S. D3 92
Aristazabal Island, i., B.C. C3 69
Ariton, Al., U.S. D4 78
Arivaca, Az., U.S. F4 80
Arivonimamo, Madag. g9 49
Arizaro, Salar de, pl., Arg. D2 55
Arizona, Arg. B3 54
Arizona, state, U.S. C4 80
Arizona Sunsites, Az., U.S. F6 80
Arizpe, Mex. A2 63
Arjay, Ky., U.S. D6 94
Arjeplog, Swe. D8 14
Arjona, Col. A2 60
Arjona, Spain D3 22
Arkabutla, Ms., U.S. A3 101
Arkabutla Lake, res., Ms., U.S. A4 101
Arkadelphia, Al., U.S. B3 78
Arkadelphia, Ar., U.S. C2 81
Arkaig, Loch, l., Scot., U.K. D3 13
Arkalyk, Sov. Un. D7 28
Arkansas, co., Ar., U.S. C4 81
Arkansas, state, U.S. C3 81
Arkansas, stm., U.S. C9 76
Arkansas, Salt Fork, stm., U.S. A3 113
Arkansas City, Ar., U.S. D4 81
Arkansas City, Ks., U.S. E6 93
Arkansaw, Wi., U.S. D1 126
Arkelstorp, Swe. B8 15
Arkhangelsk, Sov. Un. C7 29
Arkhangelskoye, Sov. Un. F13 27
Arkhara, Sov. Un. B5 33
Árki, i., Grc. D6 25
Arkinda, Ar., U.S. D1 81
Arklow, Ire. D3 10
Arkoma, Ok., U.S. B7 113
Arkona, Ont. D3 73
Arkona, Kap (The Skaw), c., E. Ger. D7 15
Arkport, N.Y., U.S. C3 109
Arkville, N.Y., U.S. C6 109
Arkwright, Ga., U.S. D3 87
Arkwright, R.I., U.S. D3 116
Arlanza, stm., Spain A4 22
Arlanzón, stm., Spain A4 22
Arlberg Tunnel, Aus. E5 18
Arlee, Mt., U.S. C2 103
Arles, Fr. F6 16
Arley, Al., U.S. A2 78
Arlington, Az., U.S. D3 80
Arlington, Co., U.S. C7 83
Arlington, Ga., U.S. E2 87
Arlington, Il., U.S. B4 90
Arlington, In., U.S. E6 91
Arlington, Ia., U.S. B6 92
Arlington, Ks., U.S. E5 93
Arlington, Ky., U.S. f9 94
Arlington, La., U.S. h9 95
Arlington, Ma., U.S. B5 98
Arlington, Mn., U.S. F4 100
Arlington, Ne., U.S. C9 104
Arlington, N.Y., U.S. D7 109
Arlington, N.C., U.S. A2 110
Arlington, Oh., U.S. B2 112
Arlington, Or., U.S. B6 114
Arlington, S.C., U.S. B3 117
Arlington, S.D., U.S. C8 118
Arlington, Tn., U.S. B2 119
Arlington, Tx., U.S. n9 120
Arlington, Vt., U.S. E2 122
Arlington, Va., U.S. B5 123
Arlington, Wa., U.S. A3 124
Arlington, Wi., U.S. E4 126
Arlington, co., Va., U.S. g12 123
Arlington, Lake, res., Tx., U.S. n9 120
Arlington Beach, S.D., U.S. C8 118
Arlington Heights, Il., U.S. A5 90
Arlit, Niger C6 45
Arlon, Bel. C6 16
Arly, stm., Fr. D2 20
Arm, Ms., U.S. D3 101
Arm, stm., Sask. F3 75
Arma, Ks., U.S. E9 93
Armada, Mi., U.S. F8 99
Armagh, Que. C7 74
Armagh, N. Ire., U.K. C3 10
Armagh, Pa., U.S. F3 115
Armathwaite, Tn., U.S. C9 119
Armavir, Sov. Un. E7 29
Armenia, Col. C2 60
Armenia, state, Sov. Un. E7 29
Armentières, Fr. B5 16
Armería, stm., Mex. n12 63
Armero, Col. B3 60
Armidale, Austl. F9 50
Armijo, N.M., U.S. k7 108
Armington, Il., U.S. C4 90
Armington, Mt., U.S. C6 103
Arminto, Wy., U.S. C5 127
Armit Lake, l., Can. C1 70
Armley, Sask. D3 75
Armonk, N.Y., U.S. *g13 109
Armorel, Ar., U.S. B6 81
Armour, S.D., U.S. D7 118
Armstead, Al., U.S. B3 78
Armstrong, B.C. D8 69
Armstrong, Fl., U.S. C5 86
Armstrong, Il., U.S. C6 90
Armstrong, Ia., U.S. A3 92
Armstrong, Mo., U.S. B5 102
Armstrong, Ok., U.S. C5 113
Armstrong, Tx., U.S. F4 120
Armstrong, co., Pa., U.S. E2 115
Armstrong, co., Tx., U.S. B2 120
Armstrong Creek, Wi., U.S. C5 126
Armstrong Creek, stm., W.V., U.S. m13 125
Armstrong Station, Ont. F15 66
Armuchee, Ga., U.S. B1 87
Armyansk, Sov. Un. H9 27
Arnaud, stm., Que. E18 66
Arnaudville, La., U.S. D4 95
Arneburg, E. Ger. F5 15
Arnedo, Spain A4 22
Arnegard, N.D., U.S. B2 111
Arneiroz, Braz. C2 57
Arnett, Ok., U.S. A2 113
Arnett, W.V., U.S. D3 125
Arney, stm., N. Ire., U.K. C4 11
Arnhem, Neth. B6 16
Arnhem, Cape, c., Austl. B6 50
Arnhem Land, reg., Austl. B5 50
Árnissa, Grc. B3 25
Arno, stm., Italy C3 23
Arnold, Ca., U.S. C3 82
Arnold, Ks., U.S. D3 93
Arnold, Md., U.S. *B4 97
Arnold, Mi., U.S. B3 99
Arnold, Mn., U.S. D6 100
Arnold, Mo., U.S. C7 102
Arnold, Ne., U.S. C5 104
Arnold, Pa., U.S. h14 115
Arnold Mills, R.I., U.S. B4 116
Arnold Mills Reservoir, res., R.I., U.S. B4 116
Arnoldsburg, W.V., U.S. C3 125
Arnold's Cove, Newf. E4 72
Arnolds Park, Ia., U.S. A2 92
Arnoldsville, Ga., U.S. C3 87
Arnot, Pa., U.S. C7 115
Arnouville, Fr. g10 16
Arnöya, i., Nor. B9 14
Arnprior, Ont. B8 73
Arnsberg, W. Ger. C4 18
Arnstadt, E. Ger. C5 18
Arnstein, Ont. B5 73
Ærø, i., Den. C3 15
Aroa, Ven. A4 60
Aroab, Nmb. C2 49
Arock, Or., U.S. E9 114
Aroda, Va., U.S. B4 123
Arolla, Switz. D3 21
Arolsen, W. Ger. B4 19
Aroma, Sud. B4 47
Aroma Park, Il., U.S. B6 90
Arona, Italy E6 21
Aroostook, N.B. C2 71
Aroostook, co., Me., U.S. B4 96
Aroostook, stm., N.A. B4 96
Arop, i., Pap. N. Gui. k12 50
Åros, Nor. p28 14
Arosa, Switz. C5 20
Arouca, Trin. N23 65
Arp, Tx., U.S. C5 120
Arpajon, Fr. F2 17
Arpin, Wi., U.S. D3 126
Arques, Fr. D2 17
Arques-la-Bataille, Fr. E9 12
'Arrābah, Isr. Occ. B7 41
Ar Rahad, Sud. C3 47
Arraias, Braz. D1 57
Arraiján, Pan. F8 62
Arraiolos, Port. C2 22
Ar Ramādī, Iraq B4 38
Ar Ramthā, Jord. B7 41
Arran, Sask. F5 75
Arran, Fl., U.S. B2 86
Arran, Island of, i., Scot., U.K. C4 10
Ar Rank, Sud. C3 47
Ar Raqqah, Syria B3 38
Arras, Fr. B5 16
Ar Rawḍah, Eg. E3 41
Arrecife, Spain m15 22
Arrecifes, Arg. g6 54
Arrecifes, stm., Arg. g7 54
Arrey, N.M., U.S. E2 108
Arriaga, Mex. D6 63
Arriba, Co., U.S. B7 83
Arriikan Island, i., Marsh Is. P18 52
Arrington, Ks., U.S. C8 93
Arrington, Va., U.S. C4 123
Arroio Grande, Braz. E2 56
Arroll, Mo., U.S. D6 102
Arrone, stm., Italy h8 23
Arrow, Lough, l., Ire. C3 11
Arrow Creek, stm., Mt., U.S. C6 103
Arrow Head Lodge, Wy., U.S. *B5 127
Arrowhead Mountain Lake, res., Vt., U.S. B2 122
Arrowhead Village, N.J., U.S. C4 107
Arrow Rock, Mo., U.S. B5 102
Arrowrock Reservoir, res., Id., U.S. F3 89
Arrowsmith, Il., U.S. C5 90
Arrowwood, Alta. D4 68
Arrowwood Lake, res., N.D., U.S. B7 111
Arroyo, P.R. C3 65
Arroyo de la Luz, Spain C2 22
Arroyo Grande, Ca., U.S. E3 82
Arroyo Hondo, N.M., U.S. A4 108
Arroyo Seco, N.M., U.S. A4 108
Ar Rumaythah, Iraq F2 39
Ar Ruṣayfah, Jord. B8 41
Ar Ruşayriş, Sud. C3 47
Ar Ruṭbah, Iraq B4 38
Ar Ruwayḩī, hist., Jord. D7 41
Års, Den. B3 15
Arsenyev, Sov. Un. D6 33
Arsi, prov., Eth. D4 47
Årstad, Swe. B6 15
Árta, Grc. C3 40
Árta, dept., Grc. *C3 25
Artas, S.D., U.S. B6 118
Artashat, Sov. Un. B2 39
Arṭayyān, well, Sau. Ar. H13 40
Artem, Sov. Un. E16 29
Artemisa, Cuba C2 64
Artemovsk, Sov. Un. E27 8
Artemovsk, Sov. Un. G11 27
Artemovskiy, Sov. Un. B6 28
Artemus, Ky., U.S. D6 94
Artena, Italy h9 23
Arter, Mount, mtn., Wy., U.S. D4 127
Artern, E. Ger. B6 19
Artesia, Ca., U.S. *n12 82
Artesia, Ms., U.S. B5 101
Artesia, N.M., U.S. E5 108
Artesian, S.D., U.S. C8 118
Artesia Wells, Tx., U.S. E3 120
Arth, Switz. B4 20
Arthabaska, Que. C6 74
Arthabaska, co., Que. C5 74
Arthur, Ont. D4 73
Arthur, Il., U.S. D5 90
Arthur, In., U.S. H3 91
Arthur, Ia., U.S. B2 92
Arthur, Ne., U.S. C4 104
Arthur, N.D., U.S. B8 111
Arthur, Tn., U.S. C10 119
Arthur, co., Ne., U.S. C4 104
Arthur, Lake, l., La., U.S. D3 95
Arthur, Lake, res., Pa., U.S. E1 115
Arthur Kill, stm., N.J., U.S. k8 107
Arthurs Town, Bah. B6 64
Artibonite, stm., Haiti E7 64
Artigas, Ur. E1 56
Artland, Sask. E1 75
Artois, hist. reg., Fr. B5 16
Artois, Collines de l', hills, Fr. D2 17
Artvin, Tur. B13 40
Aru, Zaire A5 48
Arua, Ug. A5 48
Aruanã, Braz. A2 56
Aruba, ctry., N.A. H17 65
Arucas, Spain m14 22
Aru Islands, is., Indon. G8 34
Arun, stm., Eng., U.K. D7 12
Arunachal Pradesh, state, India C10 36
Arundel, Que. D3 74
Arundel, Eng., U.K. D7 12
Arundel Village, Md., U.S. *h11 97
Arusha, Tan. B6 48
Arusha, prov., Tan. B6 48
Aruwimi, stm., Zaire A4 48
Arvada, Co., U.S. B5 83
Arvada, Wy., U.S. B6 127
Arvagh, Ire. D4 11
Arvayheer, Mong. B5 31
Arve, stm., Eur. D2 20
Arvida, Que. A6 74
Arvidsjaur, Swe. E8 14
Arvigo, Switz. D7 21
Arvika, Swe. H5 14
Arvilla, N.D., U.S. B8 111
Arvin, Ca., U.S. E4 82
Arvon, Mount, mtn., Mi., U.S. B2 99
Arvonia, Va., U.S. C4 123
Arxan, China B8 31
Arys, Sov. Un. E7 28
Arzamas, Sov. Un. D14 27
Arzgir, Sov. Un. I15 27
Arzúa, Spain A1 22
Aš, Czech. C2 26
Aså, Den. A4 15
Asab, Nmb. C2 49
Asad, Lake, res., Syria B12 40
Asahi, Mount, mtn., Japan E11 33
Asahikawa, Japan C13 31
Asan, Guam L9 52
Asan Bay, b., S. Kor. H3 33
Asan Point, c., Guam L9 52
Āsānsol, India D8 36
Asau Bay, b., W. Sam. F11 52
Asbach, W. Ger. C2 19
Asbest, Sov. Un. D9 29
Asbestos, Que. D6 74
Asbury, Mo., U.S. D3 102
Asbury Park, N.J., U.S. C4 107
Ascensión, Mex. A3 63
Ascension, co., La., U.S. D5 95
Ascension, i., St. Hel. G4 42
Aschaffenburg, W. Ger. D4 18
Aschersleben, E. Ger. C5 18
Ascoli Piceno, Italy C4 23
Ascona, Switz. D6 21
Ascope, Peru C2 58
Ascotán, Chile D2 55
Ascot-Corner, Que. D6 74
Ascutney, Vt., U.S. E4 122
Ascutney, Mount, mtn., Vt., U.S. E4 122
Aseb, Eth. C5 47
Asela, Eth. D4 47
Åsele, Swe. E7 14
Asenovgrad, Bul. E7 24
Asha, Sov. Un. B5 28
Ashanti, prov., Ghana E4 45
Ashaway, R.I., U.S. F1 116
Ashbourne, Eng., U.K. A6 12
Ashburn, Ga., U.S. E3 87
Ashburn, Mo., U.S. B6 102
Ashburn, Va., U.S. A5 123
Ashburnham, Ma., U.S. A4 98
Ashburton, N.Z. O13 51
Ashburton, Eng., U.K. D4 12
Ashburton, stm., Austl. D2 50
Ashby, Al., U.S. B3 78
Ashby, Ma., U.S. A4 98
Ashby, Mn., U.S. D3 100
Ashby, Ne., U.S. B4 104
Ashbyburg, Ky., U.S. C2 94
Ashcroft, B.C. D7 69
Ashdod, Isr. C6 41
Ashdot Ya'aqov, Isr. B7 41
Ashdown, Ar., U.S. D1 81
Ashe, co., N.C., U.S. A1 110
Asheboro, N.C., U.S. B3 110
Ashepoo, stm., S.C., U.S. F6 117
Asher, Ok., U.S. C5 113
Ashern, Man. D2 70
Asherton, Tx., U.S. E3 120
Asherville, Ks., U.S. C6 93
Asheville, N.C., U.S. f10 110
Ashfield, Ma., U.S. A2 98
Ash Flat, Ar., U.S. A4 81
Ashford, Eng., U.K. C8 12
Ashford, Al., U.S. D4 78
Ashford, Ct., U.S. B7 84
Ashford, W.V., U.S. m12 125
Ash Fork, Az., U.S. B3 80
Ash Grove, Mo., U.S. D4 102
Ashiaman, Ghana *E4 45
Ashikaga, Japan H9 33
Ashington, Eng., U.K. E7 13
Ashio, Japan H9 33
Ashizuri, Cape, c., Japan J6 33
Ashkhabad, Sov. Un. F8 29
Ashkum, Il., U.S. C6 90
Ash Lake, Mn., U.S. B6 100
Ashland, Al., U.S. B4 78
Ashland, Ca., U.S. *h8 82
Ashland, Il., U.S. D3 90
Ashland, Ks., U.S. E4 93
Ashland, Ky., U.S. B7 94
Ashland, La., U.S. B2 95
Ashland, Me., U.S. B4 96
Ashland, Ma., U.S. g10 98
Ashland, Ms., U.S. A4 101

Name	Map Ref.	Page
Ashland, Mo., U.S.	C5	102
Ashland, Mt., U.S.	E10	103
Ashland, Ne., U.S.	C9	104
Ashland, N.H., U.S.	C3	106
Ashland, Oh., U.S.	B3	112
Ashland, Ok., U.S.	C5	113
Ashland, Or., U.S.	E4	114
Ashland, Pa., U.S.	E9	115
Ashland, Va., U.S.	C5	123
Ashland, Wi., U.S.	B3	126
Ashland, co., Oh., U.S.	B3	112
Ashland, co., Wi., U.S.	B3	126
Ashland, Mount, mtn., Or., U.S.	E4	114
Ashland City, Tn., U.S.	A4	119
Ashland Reservoir, res., Ma., U.S.	h10	98
Ashley, Il., U.S.	E4	90
Ashley, In., U.S.	A7	91
Ashley, Mi., U.S.	E6	99
Ashley, Mo., U.S.	B6	102
Ashley, N.D., U.S.	C6	111
Ashley, Oh., U.S.	B3	112
Ashley, Pa., U.S.	n17	115
Ashley, co., N.C., U.S.	D4	81
Ashley, stm., S.C., U.S.	F7	117
Ashley Creek, stm., Ut., U.S.	C6	121
Ashley Falls, Ma., U.S.	B1	98
Ashmont, Alta.	B5	68
Ashmore, Il., U.S.	D5	90
Ashmore Islands, is., Austl.	B3	50
Ashmūn, Eg.	D2	41
Ashnola, stm., N.A.	A5	124
Ashokan, N.Y., U.S.	D6	109
Ashokan Reservoir, res., N.Y., U.S.	D6	109
Ashport, Tn., U.S.	B2	119
Ashqelon, Isr.	D3	38
Ash Shabakah, Iraq	B3	38
Ash Shabb, well, Eg.	E5	43
Ash Shallāl, Eg.	E6	43
Ash Shallūfah, Eg.	D4	41
Ash Shamālīyah (Northern), prov., Sud.	B2	47
Ash Shāriqah, U.A.E.	C5	38
Ash Shāriqah, Iraq	B4	38
Ash Shaṭrah, Iraq	F3	39
Ash Shawbānah, Eg.	E2	41
Ash Shawbak, Jord.	D7	41
Ash Shawmarah, Leb.	A7	41
Ash Shaykh Jarrāḥ (part of Jerusalem), Isr. Occ.	m14	41
Ash Shaykh Sa'd, Syria	B7	41
Ash Shiḥr, Yemen	D4	38
Ash Shumlul, Sau. Ar.	H3	39
Ash Shurayk, Sud.	B3	47
Ash Springs, Nv., U.S.	F6	105
Ashtabula, Oh., U.S.	A5	112
Ashtabula, co., Oh., U.S.	A5	112
Ashtabula, Lake, res., N.D., U.S.	B8	111
Ashton, Ont.	B8	73
Ashton, Id., U.S.	E7	89
Ashton, Il., U.S.	B4	90
Ashton, Ia., U.S.	A2	92
Ashton, Md., U.S.	B3	97
Ashton, Mi., U.S.	E5	99
Ashton, Ne., U.S.	C7	104
Ashton, R.I., U.S.	B4	116
Ashton, S.D., U.S.	C7	118
Ashuanipi Lake, l., Newf.	h8	72
Ashuelot, N.H., U.S.	E2	106
Ashuelot, stm., N.H., U.S.	E2	106
Ashville, Man.	D1	70
Ashville, Al., U.S.	B3	78
Ashville, Oh., U.S.	C3	112
Ashwaubenon, Wi., U.S.	D5	126
Ashwood, Or., U.S.	C6	114
Ashwood, Tn., U.S.	B4	119
Asia, cont.	E11	30
Asiago, Italy	D7	20
Asia Minor, reg., Tur.	C10	40
Asifābād, India	H7	37
Asiga, Puntan, c., N. Mar. Is.	D7	52
Asiga Point, c., Guam	M10	52
Asinara, Gulf of, b., Italy	D2	23
Asinara Island, i., Italy	D2	23
Asino, Sov. Un.	B11	28
'Asīr, reg., Sau. Ar.	D4	38
'Aṣīrah ash Shamālīyah, Isr. Occ.	g12	41
Asker, Nor.	p28	14
Askersund, Swe.	H6	14
Askew, Ms., U.S.	A3	101
Askham, S. Afr.	C3	49
Askim, Nor.	p29	14
Askim, Swe.	—	—
Askival, mtn., Scot., U.K.	D2	13
Askö, i., Swe.	u35	14
Askov, Mn., U.S.	D6	100
Åsmār, Afg.	D15	39
Asmera (Asmara), Eth.	B4	47
Asnæs, Den.	C5	15
Asnebumskit Hill, hill, Ma., U.S.	B4	98
Åsnen, l., Swe.	B8	15
Asnières [-sur-Seine], Fr.	C5	16
Asopós, stm., Grc.	g11	25
Asosa, Eth.	C3	47
Asotin, Wa., U.S.	C8	124
Asotin, co., Wa., U.S.	C8	124
Asotin Creek, stm., Wa., U.S.	C8	124
Aspe, Spain	C5	22
Aspen, Co., U.S.	B4	83
Aspen Butte, mtn., Or., U.S.	E4	114
Aspen Hill, Md., U.S.	*B3	97
Aspen Hill, U.S.	B4	119
Asperg, W. Ger.	E4	19
Aspermont, Tx., U.S.	C2	120
Aspers, Pa., U.S.	G7	115
Aspinwall, Ia., U.S.	C2	92
Aspinwall, Pa., U.S.	k14	115
Aspiring, Mount, mtn., N.Z.	P12	51
Aspres [-sur-Buëch], Fr.	E1	20
Asprópirgos, Grc.	g11	25
Aspy Bay, b., N.S.	C9	71
Asquith, Sask.	E2	75
Assabet, stm., Ma., U.S.	g9	98
Aş Şabya, Sau. Ar.	D4	38
Aş Şaff, Eg.	E3	41
Aş Şaffānīyeh, Sau. Ar.	C4	38
Aş Şāfī, Jord.	C7	41
Assaikwatamo, stm., Man.	A3	70
Aş Şāliḥīyah, Eg.	D4	41
Aş Şallūm, Eg.	B2	38
As Salmān, Iraq	B4	38
Aş Şalṭ, Jord.	F10	40
Assam, state, India	C9	36
Aş Şamū', Isr. Occ.	C7	41
Aş Şanamayn, Syria	A8	41
Assaria, Ks., U.S.	D6	93
Assateague Island, i., U.S.	D7	97
Assateague Island National Seashore, U.S.	D7	97
Assawoman Bay, b., Md., U.S.	D7	97
Assawompset Pond, l., Ma., U.S.	C6	98
Assen, Neth.	A7	16
Assens, Den.	C3	15
Assens, Den.	B4	15
As Sinbillāwayn, Eg.	D3	41
Assini, I.C.	E4	45
Assiniboia, Sask.	H2	75
Assiniboine, stm., Can.	E2	70
Assiniboine, Mount, mtn., Can.	D3	68
Assiniboine Lake, l., Man.	A4	70
Assinika, stm., Man.	C4	70
Assinippi, Ma., U.S.	h12	98
Assis, Braz.	C2	56
Assis Brasil, Braz.	D4	58
Assisi, Italy	C4	23
Asso, Italy	E7	21
Assonet, Ma., U.S.	C5	98
As Sudd, reg., Sud.	D3	47
Aş Şūfīyah, Eg.	D3	41
As Sulaymānīyah, Iraq	B4	38
As Sulaymānīyah, Sau. Ar.	C4	38
As Sulayyil, Sau. Ar.	A6	47
As Sulṭān, Libya	C3	43
As Suwaydā, Syria	F11	40
As Suwayda', Syria	—	—
Astakós, Grc.	C3	25
Āstārā, Iran	B4	39
Asten, Neth.	C5	17
Asterābād see Gorgān, Iran	B5	38
Asti, Italy	B2	23
Astipálaia, i., Grc.	D6	40
Astola, i., Pak.	I11	39
Aston, Pa., U.S.	*p20	115
Aston Jonction, Que.	C5	74
Astor, Fl., U.S.	C5	86
Astorga, Spain	A2	22
Astoria, Il., U.S.	C3	90
Astoria, Or., U.S.	A3	114
Astoria, S.D., U.S.	C9	118
Astorville, Ont.	A5	73
Astrakhan, Sov. Un.	E7	29
Astura, stm., Italy	h9	23
Asturias, hist. reg., Spain	A2	22
Asuisui, Cape, c., W. Sam.	F11	52
Asuke, Japan	n16	33
Asunción, Para.	C3	56
Asunción Mita, Guat.	C3	62
Asunción Nochixtlán, Mex.	o15	63
Ásunden, l., Swe.	A7	15
Aswān, Eg.	C3	38
Aswān High Dam, Eg.	C3	38
Asyūṭ, Eg.	C3	38
Atacama, prov., Chile	E2	55
Atacama, Salar de, pl., Chile	D2	55
Atacama Desert, des., Chile	D2	55
'Aṭā'iṭah, Jabal al, mtn., Jord.	D7	41
Atakpamé, Togo	E5	45
Atalaia, Braz.	k5	57
Atalaia do Norte, Braz.	B3	58
Atalándi, Grc.	C4	25
Atalaya, Peru	D3	58
Atalissa, Ia., U.S.	C6	92
Atami, Japan	n18	33
Atar, Maur.	B2	45
'Aṭārūt, Isr. Occ.	h11	41
Atascadero, Ca., U.S.	E3	82
Atascosa, co., Tx., U.S.	E3	120
Atasu, Sov. Un.	D8	28
Atauro, i., Indon.	G7	34
Atáviros, mtn., Grc.	D6	25
Aṭbarah, Sud.	B3	47
'Aṭbarah, stm., Afr.	B4	47
Atbasar, Sov. Un.	D9	29
Atchafalaya, stm., La., U.S.	D4	95
Atchafalaya Bay, b., La., U.S.	E4	95
Atchison, Ks., U.S.	C8	93
Atchison, co., Ks., U.S.	C8	93
Atchison, co., Mo., U.S.	A2	102
Atco, N.J., U.S.	D3	107
Atgidon, Puntan, c., N. Mar. Is.	E7	52
Ath, Bel.	D3	17
Athabasca, Alta.	B4	68
Athabasca, stm., Alta.	f8	68
Athabasca, Lake, l., Can.	m7	75
Athalia, Oh., U.S.	D3	112
Athalmer, B.C.	D10	69
Athapapuskow Lake, l., Man.	B1	70
Atha Road (part of Pickering), Ont.	k15	73
Athboy, Ire.	D5	11
Athelstan, Que.	D3	74
Athena, Or., U.S.	B8	114
Athenry, Ire.	D3	11
Athens (Athinai), Grc.	C9	73
Athens, Al., U.S.	A3	78
Athens, Ga., U.S.	C3	87
Athens, Il., U.S.	D4	90
Athens, In., U.S.	C5	91
Athens, La., U.S.	B2	95
Athens, Me., U.S.	D3	96
Athens, N.Y., U.S.	C7	109
Athens, Oh., U.S.	C3	112
Athens, Pa., U.S.	C8	115
Athens, Tn., U.S.	D9	119
Athens, Tx., U.S.	C5	120
Athens, Vt., U.S.	E3	122
Athens, W.V., U.S.	D3	125
Athens, co., Oh., U.S.	C3	112
Athensville, Il., U.S.	D3	90
Atherley, Ont.	C5	73
Atherton, Austl.	C8	50
Atherton, Ca., U.S.	*k8	82
Athertonville, Ky., U.S.	C4	94
Athi, stm., Kenya	B6	48
Athiémé, Benin	E5	45
Athleague, Ire.	D3	11
Athlone, Ire.	D3	11
Athok, Burma	E10	36
Athol, Id., U.S.	B2	89
Athol, Ks., U.S.	C5	93
Athol, Ma., U.S.	A3	98
Athol, S.D., U.S.	C7	118
Athol Island, i., Bah.	m18	64
Áthos, mtn., Grc.	B5	40
Ath Thamad, Eg.	D6	41
Athy, Ire.	D3	11
Ati, Chad	C3	46
Atibaia, Braz.	m8	56
Atico, Peru	E3	58
Aticonipi, Lac, l., Que.	C2	72
Atikameg, Alta.	B3	68
Atik Lake, l., Man.	B4	70
Atikokan, Ont.	o17	73
Atikonak Lake, l., Newf.	h8	72
Atimonan, Phil.	p13	34
Atiquizaya, El Sal.	D3	62
Atka, Ak., U.S.	E5	79
Atka Island, i., Ak., U.S.	E5	79
Atkarsk, Sov. Un.	F15	27
Atkins, Ar., U.S.	B3	81
Atkins, Va., U.S.	D1	123
Atkinson, Ga., U.S.	E5	87
Atkinson, Il., U.S.	B3	90
Atkinson, Ne., U.S.	B7	104
Atkinson, N.H., U.S.	E4	106
Atkinson, N.C., U.S.	C4	110
Atkinson, co., Ga., U.S.	E4	87
Atlanta, Ar., U.S.	D2	81
Atlanta, Ga., U.S.	C2	87
Atlanta, Id., U.S.	F3	89
Atlanta, Il., U.S.	C4	90
Atlanta, In., U.S.	D5	91
Atlanta, Ks., U.S.	E7	93
Atlanta, La., U.S.	C3	95
Atlanta, Mi., U.S.	C6	99
Atlanta, Mo., U.S.	B5	102
Atlanta, Ne., U.S.	D6	104
Atlanta, N.Y., U.S.	C3	109
Atlanta, Oh., U.S.	C2	112
Atlanta, Tx., U.S.	C5	120
Atlantic, Ia., U.S.	C2	92
Atlantic, N.C., U.S.	C6	110
Atlantic, co., N.J., U.S.	E3	107
Atlantic Beach, Fl., U.S.	m9	86
Atlantic City, N.J., U.S.	E4	107
Atlantic City, Wy., U.S.	D4	127
Atlantic Highlands, N.J., U.S.	C4	107
Atlantic Mine, Mi., U.S.	A2	99
Atlantic Ocean	—	—
Atlántico, dept., Col.	G8	5
Atlantic Ocean	—	—
Atlantic Peak, mtn., Wy., U.S.	D3	127
Atlas Mountains, mts., Afr.	C4	44
Atlas Saharien, mts., Alg.	C5	44
Atlee, Alta.	D5	68
Atlin, B.C.	m16	69
Atlin Lake, l., Can.	E6	66
Atlit, Isr.	B6	41
Atlixco, Mex.	n14	63
Atmore, Al., U.S.	D2	78
Atna Peak, mtn., B.C.	C3	69
Atocha, Bol.	D2	55
Atoka, N.M., U.S.	E5	108
Atoka, Ok., U.S.	C5	113
Atoka, Tn., U.S.	B2	119
Atoka, co., Ok., U.S.	C5	113
Atoka Reservoir, res., Ok., U.S.	C5	113
Atomic City, Id., U.S.	F6	89
Atotonilco el Alto, Mex.	m12	63
Atoyac, Mex.	m12	63
Atoyac, stm., Mex.	n14	63
Atrak, stm., Asia	B5	38
Åtran, stm., Swe.	B6	15
Atrato, stm., Col.	B2	60
Atrek (Atrak), stm., Asia	C7	39
Atsugi, Japan	n18	33
Atsukeshi Bay, b., Japan	E12	33
Atsuma, Japan	E10	33
Atsumi, Japan	o16	33
Atsumi Bay, b., Japan	o16	33
Aṭ Ṭabbīn, Eg.	E3	41
Aṭ Ṭafīlah, Jord.	G10	40
Aṭ Ṭā'if, Sau. Ar.	C4	38
Aṭ Ṭallāb, Libya	E4	43
Aṭ Ṭamīmī, Libya	C4	43
Attapu, Laos	C3	34
Attapulgus, Ga., U.S.	F2	87
'Aṭṭārah, Isr. Occ.	h11	41
Attawapiskat, Ont.	n19	73
Attawapiskat, stm., Ont.	n18	73
Aṭ Ṭayrīyah, Eg.	D2	41
Attean Pond, l., Me., U.S.	C2	96
Atterberry, Il., U.S.	C4	90
Attica, In., U.S.	D3	91
Attica, Ks., U.S.	E5	93
Attica, Mi., U.S.	E7	99
Attica, N.Y., U.S.	C2	109
Attica, Oh., U.S.	A3	112
Attica, hist. reg., Grc.	g11	25
Attigny, Fr.	E4	17
Attikamagen Lake, l., Newf.	g8	72
Aṭ Ṭīnah, Eg.	D4	41
Attleboro, Ma., U.S.	C5	98
Attleborough, Eng., U.K.	B9	12
Attock, Pak.	B5	36
Attu Island, i., Ak., U.S.	E2	79
Aṭ Ṭūr, Eg.	D6	43
Aṭ Ṭūr, Isr. Occ.	m14	41
Aṭ Ṭuwayrah, Sau. Ar.	I13	40
Attymon, Ire.	D3	11
Atuel, stm., Arg.	B3	54
Aṭu'u, Am. Sam.	F13	52
Åtvidaberg, Swe.	H6	14
Atwater, Ca., U.S.	D3	82
Atwater, Mn., U.S.	E4	100
Atwood, Ont.	D3	73
Atwood, Co., U.S.	A7	83
Atwood, Il., U.S.	D5	90
Atwood, Ks., U.S.	C2	93
Atwood, Ok., U.S.	C5	113
Atwood, Tn., U.S.	B3	119
Atwood Lake, res., Oh., U.S.	B4	112
Atwoodville, Ct., U.S.	B7	84
Aua, Am. Sam.	F13	52
Auau Channel, strt., Hi., U.S.	C5	88
Aubagne, Fr.	F6	16
Aube, dept., Fr.	F4	17
Aube, stm., Fr.	F4	17
Aubenas, Fr.	E6	16
Aubière, Fr.	E5	16
Aubigny-sur-Nère, Fr.	D5	16
Aubin, Fr.	E5	16
Aubrey, Que.	D3	74
Aubrey, Ar., U.S.	C5	81
Aubrey, Tx., U.S.	C4	120
Aubrey Cliffs, clf., Az., U.S.	B2	80
Auburn, Ont.	D3	73
Auburn, Al., U.S.	C4	78
Auburn, Ca., U.S.	C3	82
Auburn, Ga., U.S.	B3	87
Auburn, Il., U.S.	D4	90
Auburn, In., U.S.	B7	91
Auburn, Ks., U.S.	D8	93
Auburn, Ky., U.S.	D3	94
Auburn, Me., U.S.	D2	96
Auburn, Ma., U.S.	B4	98
Auburn, Mi., U.S.	E6	99
Auburn, Ne., U.S.	D10	104
Auburn, N.H., U.S.	E4	106
Auburn, N.Y., U.S.	C4	109
Auburn, Pa., U.S.	E9	115
Auburn, Wa., U.S.	B3	124
Auburn, W.V., U.S.	B4	125
Auburndale, Fl., U.S.	D5	86
Auburndale, Wi., U.S.	D3	126
Auburn Heights, Mi., U.S.	F7	99
Auburntown, Tn., U.S.	B5	119
Aubusson, Fr.	E5	16
Auch, Fr.	F4	16
Auchel, Fr.	D2	17
Auckland, N.Z.	L15	51
Auckland Islands, is., N.Z.	J8	2
Aude, stm., Fr.	F5	16
Audet, Que.	D7	74
Audierne, Fr.	C1	16
Audincourt, Fr.	D7	16
Audrain, co., Mo., U.S.	B6	102
Audubon, Ia., U.S.	C3	92
Audubon, Mn., U.S.	D2	100
Audubon, N.J., U.S.	D2	107
Audubon, Pa., U.S.	*F11	115
Audubon, co., Ia., U.S.	C2	92
Audun-le-Roman, Fr.	C6	18
Aue, E. Ger.	C7	19
Auerbach, E. Ger.	C7	19
Augathella, Austl.	A4	21
Auggen, W. Ger.	C5	11
Aughnacloy, N. Ire., U.K.	E5	11
Aughrim, Ire.	B1	112
Auglaize, co., Oh., U.S.	A1	112
Auglaize, stm., Oh., U.S.	A1	112
August, Ca., U.S.	*D3	82
Augsburg, W. Ger.	D5	19
Augusta, Austl.	F2	50
Augusta, Italy	F5	23
Augusta, Ar., U.S.	B4	81
Augusta, Ga., U.S.	C5	87
Augusta, Il., U.S.	C3	90
Augusta, Ks., U.S.	E7	93
Augusta, Ky., U.S.	B6	94
Augusta, Me., U.S.	D3	96
Augusta, Mo., U.S.	F5	99
Augusta, Mt., U.S.	C4	103
Augusta, Oh., U.S.	B4	112
Augusta, W.V., U.S.	B6	125
Augusta, Wi., U.S.	D2	126
Augusta, co., Va., U.S.	B3	123
Augusta Springs, Va., U.S.	B3	123
Augusta Victoria Hospital, Isr. Occ.	m14	41
Augustenborg, Den.	D3	15
Augustów, Pol.	B7	26
Augustus, Mount, mtn., Austl.	D2	50
Aulander, N.C., U.S.	A5	110
Auld, Lake, l., Austl.	D3	50
Aulendorf, W. Ger.	B5	20
Aulnay-sous-Bois, Fr.	g11	16
Aulne, stm., Fr.	C2	16
Aulneau Peninsula, pen., Ont.	E4	70
Aulnoye [-Aymeries], Fr.	D3	17
Ault, Co., U.S.	A6	83
Ault, Piz, mtn., Switz.	C7	21
Aumale, Fr.	E2	17
Aumsville, Or., U.S.	k12	114
Auneuil, Fr.	B2	16
Auning, Den.	B4	15
Aup, Alta.	D7	45
Aur, i., Malay.	N5	34
Aura, Mi., U.S.	B2	99
Auraiya, India	D7	37
Aurangābād, India	E6	36
Auray, Fr.	D2	16
Aurelia, Ia., U.S.	B2	92
Aurelius, Mi., U.S.	—	—
Aurillaga, Braz.	—	—
Aurich, W. Ger.	B3	18
Aurillac, Fr.	E5	16
Aurora, Ont.	C5	73
Aurora, Guy.	A3	59
Aurora, Co., U.S.	B6	83
Aurora, Il., U.S.	B5	90
Aurora, In., U.S.	F8	91
Aurora, Ks., U.S.	C6	93
Aurora, Me., U.S.	D4	96
Aurora, Mn., U.S.	C6	100
Aurora, Mo., U.S.	E4	102
Aurora, Ne., U.S.	D7	104
Aurora, N.Y., U.S.	C4	109
Aurora, N.C., U.S.	B6	110
Aurora, Oh., U.S.	A4	112
Aurora, Or., U.S.	B4	114
Aurora, S.D., U.S.	C9	118
Aurora, Ut., U.S.	E4	121
Aurora, W.V., U.S.	B5	125
Aurora, co., S.D., U.S.	D7	118
Aurora Center, S.D., U.S.	D7	118
Aurskog, Nor.	p29	14
Aus, Nmb.	C2	49
Au Sable, Mi., U.S.	D7	99
Au Sable, stm., Mi., U.S.	D6	99
Ausable, stm., N.Y., U.S.	f11	109
Au Sable, North Branch, stm., Mi., U.S.	D6	99
Au Sable Forks, N.Y., U.S.	f11	109
Au Sable Point, c., Mi., U.S.	B4	99
Au Sable Point, c., Mi., U.S.	D7	99
Auschwitz see Oświęcim, Pol.	C5	26
Aussa, stm., Italy	D9	20
Austell, Ga., U.S.	h7	87
Austin, Man.	E2	70
Austin, Ar., U.S.	B4	81
Austin, In., U.S.	G6	91
Austin, Ky., U.S.	D3	94
Austin, Mn., U.S.	G6	100
Austin, Nv., U.S.	D4	105
Austin, Pa., U.S.	C5	115
Austin, Tx., U.S.	D4	120
Austin, co., Tx., U.S.	E4	120
Austin, Lake, l., Austl.	E2	50
Austinburg, Oh., U.S.	A5	112
Austintown, Oh., U.S.	A5	112
Austinville, Va., U.S.	D2	123
Australia, ctry., Oc.	—	—
Australian Capital Territory, ter., Austl.	G7	51
Austria, ctry., Eur.	E7	18
Austwell, Tx., U.S.	E4	120
Auther, Ca., U.S.	C3	78
Autlán de Navarro, Mex.	D4	63
Autun, Fr.	B6	16
Auvergne, Ar., U.S.	B4	81
Auvergne, hist. reg., Fr.	E5	16
Auvergne Mountains, mts., Fr.	E5	16
Auvers [-sur-Oise], Fr.	D5	16
Auxerre, Fr.	C7	94
Auxier, Ky., U.S.	D2	17
Auxi-le-Château, Fr.	D6	16
Auxonne, Fr.	—	—
Auxvasse, Mo., U.S.	B6	102
Auyán Tepuy, mtn., Ven.	B5	60
Auyuittuq National Park, N.W. Ter.	C19	66
Auzangate, Nevado, mtn., Peru	D3	58
Ava, Il., U.S.	F4	90
Ava, Mo., U.S.	E5	102
Ava, Oh., U.S.	C4	112
Avallon, Fr.	E5	16
Avalon, Ca., U.S.	F4	82
Avalon, Ms., U.S.	B3	101
Avalon, Mo., U.S.	B4	102
Avalon, N.J., U.S.	E3	107
Avalon, Lake, res., N.M., U.S.	E5	108
Avalon Peninsula, pen., Newf.	E5	72
Avanos, Tur.	C10	40
Avard, Ok., U.S.	A3	113
Avaré, Braz.	C3	56
Aveiro, Port.	B1	22
Avella, Pa., U.S.	F1	115
Avellaneda, Arg.	A5	54
Avellino, Italy	D5	23
Avenal, Ca., U.S.	E3	82
Avenches, Switz.	C3	21
Avenel, Md., U.S.	*B4	97
Avenel, N.J., U.S.	k7	107
Avenue, Md., U.S.	D4	97
Avenwedde, W. Ger.	B3	19
Avera, Ga., U.S.	C4	87
Averill, Vt., U.S.	B5	122
Averill Park, N.Y., U.S.	C7	109
Avesnes, Fr.	D3	17
Avesta, Swe.	G7	14
Avezzano, Italy	C4	23
Aviá Terai, Arg.	B4	56
Aviano, Italy	D7	20
Aviemore, Scot., U.K.	C5	13
Avigliano, Italy	D5	23
Avignon, Fr.	F6	16
Ávila, Spain	B3	22
Avila Beach, Ca., U.S.	E3	82
Avilés, Spain	A3	22
Avilla, In., U.S.	B7	91
Avilla, Mo., U.S.	D3	102
Avis, Pa., U.S.	D7	115
Avisio, stm., Italy	C7	20
Aviston, Il., U.S.	E4	90
Avize, Fr.	F4	17
Avlón, Grc.	g11	25
Avlum, Den.	B2	15
Avoca, Ar., U.S.	A1	81
Avoca, In., U.S.	G4	91
Avoca, Ia., U.S.	C2	92
Avoca, Mn., U.S.	G3	100
Avoca, Ne., U.S.	h12	104
Avoca, N.Y., U.S.	C3	109
Avoca, Pa., U.S.	m18	115
Avoca, Tx., U.S.	C3	120
Avon, Ct., U.S.	B4	84
Avon, Il., U.S.	C3	90
Avon, Ma., U.S.	B5	98
Avon, Mn., U.S.	E4	100
Avon, N.Y., U.S.	C3	109
Avon, N.C., U.S.	B7	110
Avon, Oh., U.S.	A3	112
Avon, S.D., U.S.	D8	118
Avon, co., Eng., U.K.	E5	12
Avon, stm., Austl.	F2	50
Avon, stm., Eng., U.K.	B5	12
Avon, stm., Eng., U.K.	E6	10
Avon, stm., Eng., U.K.	E5	12
Avon, stm., Scot., U.K.	C5	13
Avon by the Sea, N.J., U.S.	*C4	107
Avondale, Az., U.S.	D3	80
Avondale, Co., U.S.	C6	83
Avondale, La., U.S.	k11	95
Avondale, Mo., U.S.	h10	102
Avondale, Oh., U.S.	*C1	112
Avondale, Pa., U.S.	G10	115
Avondale, R.I., U.S.	G1	116
Avondale Estates, Ga., U.S.	h8	87
Avon Lake, Oh., U.S.	e8	92
Avon Lake, Oh., U.S.	A3	112
Avonlea, Sask.	G3	75
Avonmore, Pa., U.S.	E3	86
Avon Park, Fl., U.S.	E5	86
Avoyelles, co., La., U.S.	C3	95
Avranches, Fr.	E3	16
Awa, Japan	G6	100
Awa Island, i., Japan	G9	33
Awaji, Japan	o14	33
Awaji Island, i., Japan	I7	33
Awasa, Eth.	D5	47
Awash, Eth.	C5	47
Awash, stm., Eth.	C5	47
Awbārī, Libya	D2	43
Awdheegle, Som.	D4	47
Awe, Loch, l., Scot., U.K.	D3	13
Awjilah, Libya	C4	43
Awka, Nig.	*E6	45
Axel, Neth.	C3	17
Axel Heiberg Island, i., N.W. Ter.	m33	66
Axim, Ghana	F4	45
Axiós (Vardar), stm., Grc.	B4	25
Axis, Al., U.S.	E1	78
Axminster, Eng., U.K.	D7	99
Axson, Ga., U.S.	E4	87
Au Train, Mi., U.S.	B4	99
Axtell, Ks., U.S.	C7	93
Axtell, Ne., U.S.	D6	104
Axtell, Ut., U.S.	D4	121
Aÿ, Fr.	C5	16
Ay, stm., Sov. Un.	B5	28
Ayabaca, Peru	B2	58
Ayabe, Japan	n14	33
Ayacucho, Arg.	B5	54
Ayacucho, Peru	D3	58
Ayacucho, dept., Peru	D3	58
Ayaguz, Sov. Un.	E11	29
Ayamonte, Spain	D2	22
Ayan, Sov. Un.	D16	29
Ayapel, Col.	B2	60
Ayas, Tur.	B9	40
Ayaş, Tur.	—	—
Ayaviri, Peru	D3	58
Aydar, stm., Sov. Un.	G12	27
Ayden, N.C., U.S.	B5	110
Aydin, Tur.	D6	40
Aydlett, N.C., U.S.	A7	110
Ayer, Ma., U.S.	A4	98
Ayers Cliff, Que.	D5	74
Ayers Rock, mtn., Austl.	E5	50
Ayeyarwady, stm., Burma	D10	36
Ayía, Grc.	C4	25
Ayía Paraskeví, Grc.	C6	25
Ayiásos, Grc.	C6	25
Ayioi Theódhoroi, Grc.	h10	25
Áyios Dhimítrios, Grc.	g11	25
Áyios Evstrátios, i., Grc.	C5	25
Áyios Nikólaos, Grc.	E5	72
Aylen Lake, l., Ont.	B7	73
Aylesbury, Sask.	G3	75
Aylesbury, Eng., U.K.	E6	10
Aylesford, N.S.	D5	71
Aylett, Va., U.S.	C5	123
Aylmer, Mount, mtn., Alta.	D2	68
Aylmer East, Ont.	D2	73
Aylmer Lake, l., N.W. Ter.	D11	66
Aylmer West, Ont.	E4	73
Aylsham, Sask.	D4	75
Aynor, S.C., U.S.	D9	117
'Ayn Yabrūd, Isr. Occ.	h11	41
Ayon Island, i., Sov. Un.	B9	29
Ayora, Spain	C5	22
Ayorou, Niger	D5	45
'Ayoûn el 'Atroûs, Maur.	C3	45
Ayr, Austl.	C8	50
Ayr, Ont.	D4	73
Ayr, Scot., U.K.	C4	10
Ayr, Ne., U.S.	D7	104
Ayr, N.D., U.S.	B8	111
Ayr, stm., Scot., U.K.	C4	10
Ayre, Point of, c., I. of Man	F4	13
Ayrshire, In., U.S.	H3	91
Ayrshire, Ia., U.S.	A3	92
Aysary, Sov. Un.	C8	28
Aysha, Eth.	C5	47
Ayton, Ont.	C4	73
Aytos, Bul.	D8	24
Aytré, Fr.	C3	16
Ayu Islands, is., Indon.	E8	34
Ayutla [de los Libres], Mex.	D5	63
Ayvacık, Tur.	C6	40
Ayvalık, Tur.	C6	40
Azalea Park, Fl., U.S.	*D5	86
Azalia, In., U.S.	F6	91
Azama, Japan	O5	52
Āzamgarh, India	D9	36
Azángaro, Peru	D3	58
Azaouâd, reg., Mali	C4	45
Azaouak, Vallée de l', val., Afr.	C5	45
Azare, Nig.	D7	45
Āzar Shahr, Iran	B4	38
Azcapotzalco (part of Mexico City), Mex.	h9	63
Azemmour, Mor.	C3	44
Azerbaijan, hist. reg., Iran	B4	38
Azerbaijan S.S.R., state, Sov. Un.	E7	29
Aziscohos Lake, l., Me., U.S.	C1	96
Azle, Tx., U.S.	n9	120
Azogues, Ec.	B2	58
Azor, Isr.	g10	41
Azores, is., Port.	g9	44
Azov, Sov. Un.	H12	27
Azov, Sea of, Sov. Un.	C3	44
Azrou, Mor.	C3	44
Aztec, Az., U.S.	E2	80
Aztec, N.M., U.S.	A2	108
Aztec Peak, mtn., Az., U.S.	D5	80
Aztec Ruins National Monument, N.M., U.S.	A1	108
Azua, Dom. Rep.	E8	64
Azuaga, Spain	C3	22
Azuay, prov., Ec.	B2	58
Azuero, Peninsula de, pen., Pan.	G7	62
Azul, Arg.	B5	54
Azul, Cordillera, mts., Peru	C2	58
Azul, Serra, plat., Braz.	A2	56
Azurduy, Bol.	D3	58
Azusa, Ca., U.S.	m13	82
Az Zabdānī, Syria	F11	40
Az Zāhirīyah, Isr. Occ.	C6	41
Az Zahrān (Dhahran), Sau. Ar.	C4	38
Az Zaqāzīq, Eg.	B3	38
Az Zarqā', Jord.	B3	38
Az Zāwiyah, Libya	B3	43
Az Zaydāb, Sud.	B3	47
'Azzāz, Ra's, c., Libya	C4	43
Azzel Matti, Sebkha, pl., Alg.	D5	44
Az Zubayr, Iraq	F3	39
'Azzūn, Isr. Occ.	g11	41

B

Name	Map Ref.	Page
Baal, W. Ger.	C6	17
Baalbek, Leb.	B3	38
Baar, Switz.	B6	21
Baardheere, Som.	C5	47
Baargaal, Som.	C7	47
Baarle-Hertog, Bel.	C4	17
Baba Burnu, c., Tur.	C6	40
Babadag, Rom.	C9	24
Babaeski, Tur.	B6	25
Babahoyo, Ec.	B2	58
Babana, Nig.	D5	45
Babanūsah, Sud.	C3	47
Babar Islands, is., Indon.	G7	34
Babati, Tan.	B6	48
Babayevo, Sov. Un.	B11	27
Babb Creek, stm., Pa., U.S.	B7	115
Babbie, Al., U.S.	D3	78
Babbitt, Mn., U.S.	C7	100
Babbitt, Nv., U.S.	E3	105
Babcock, Wi., U.S.	D3	126
Babelthuap International Airport, Palau	R17	52
Babelthuap Island, i., Palau	R17	52
Babenhausen, W. Ger.	A6	20
Babi, i., Indon.	K2	35
Babine, stm., B.C.	B4	69
Babine Lake, l., B.C.	B4	69
Babine Range, mts., B.C.	B4	69
Babo, Indon.	F8	34

Name	Map Ref.	Page
Bābol, Iran	B5	38
Bābol Sar, Iran	C6	39
Baboosic Lake, N.H., U.S.	E3	106
Baboquivari Mountains, mts., Az., U.S.	F4	80
Baboquivari Peak, mtn., Az., U.S.	F4	80
Baboua, Cen. Afr. Rep.	D2	46
Babson Park, Fl., U.S.	E5	86
Babuskin, Sov. Un.	A6	31
Babuyan Islands, is., Phil.	B6	34
Babyak, Bul.	E6	24
Babylon, N.Y., U.S.	n15	109
Baca, co., Co., U.S.	D8	83
Bacabal, Braz.	B2	57
Bacajá, stm., Braz.	C4	59
Bacalar, Mex.	D7	63
Bacan, i., Indon.	F7	34
Bacău, Rom.	B8	24
Bacalieu Island, i., Newf.	D5	72
Bac Can, Viet.	A6	35
Baccarat, Fr.	C7	16
Baccaro Point, c., N.S.	F5	71
Bacerac, Mex.	A3	63
Bach, Mi., U.S.	E7	99
Bacharach, W. Ger.	C2	19
Bach Long Vi, i., Viet.	B7	35
Back, stm., N.W. Ter.	C12	66
Back, stm., S.C., U.S.	h12	117
Bačka Palanka, Yugo.	C4	24
Bačka Topola, Yugo.	C4	24
Back Bay, N.B.	D3	71
Backbone Mountain, mtn., U.S.	m12	97
Backnang, W. Ger.	E4	19
Backoo, N.D., U.S.	A8	111
Backus, Mn., U.S.	D4	100
Bac Lieu, Viet.	D3	34
Bac Ninh, Viet.	A3	34
Bacobi, Az., U.S.	B5	80
Bacolod, Phil.	C6	34
Bacon, co., Ga., U.S.	E4	87
Baconton, Ga., U.S.	E2	87
Bacoor, Phil.	o13	34
Bacova, Va., U.S.	B3	123
Bac Quang, Viet.	A6	35
Bacqueville-en-Caux, Fr.	E9	12
Bácsalmás, Hung.	B4	24
Bácum, Mex.	B2	63
Bad, stm., S.D., U.S.	C5	118
Bad, stm., Wi., U.S.	B3	126
Badagara, India	F6	36
Bad Aibling, W. Ger.	B7	20
Badajoz, Spain	C2	22
Badalona, Spain	B7	22
Badanah, Sau. Ar.	B4	38
Bad Axe, Mi., U.S.	E8	99
Bad Bergzabern, W. Ger.	D2	19
Bad Berneck, W. Ger.	C6	19
Bad Bramstedt, W. Ger.	E3	15
Baddeck, N.S.	C9	71
Bad Doberan, E. Ger.	A5	18
Bad Düben, E. Ger.	B7	19
Baden, Ont.	D4	73
Baden, Switz.	E4	18
Baden, Pa., U.S.	E1	115
Baden, hist. reg., W. Ger.	D4	19
Baden-Baden, W. Ger.	D4	18
Baden [bei Wien], Aus.	D8	18
Baden-Württemberg, state, W. Ger.	D4	19
Bad Freienwalde, E. Ger.	B7	18
Bad Friedrichshall, W. Ger.	D4	19
Badgastein, Aus.	E6	18
Badger, Newf.	D3	72
Badger, Ia., U.S.	B3	92
Badger, Mn., U.S.	B2	100
Badger, S.D., U.S.	C8	118
Badger Creek, stm., Co., U.S.	B7	83
Bad Godesberg, W. Ger.	C2	19
Bad Hersfeld, W. Ger.	C4	19
Bad Homburg [vor der Höhe], W. Ger.	C4	18
Bad Honnef, W. Ger.	C2	19
Bad Hönningen, W. Ger.	C2	19
Badia Polesine, Italy	D7	20
Badín, Pak.	E2	37
Badin, N.C., U.S.	B2	110
Badin Lake, res., N.C., U.S.	B2	110
Bad Ischl, Aus.	E6	18
Bad Kissingen, W. Ger.	C5	19
Bad Kreuznach, W. Ger.	D2	18
Badlands, hills, S.D., U.S.	D3	118
Badlands, reg., U.S.	C2	111
Badlands National Park, S.D., U.S.	D3	118
Bad Langensalza, E. Ger.	C5	18
Bad Lauterberg, E. Ger.	B5	19
Bad Leonfelden, Aus.	E9	19
Bad Liebenwerda, E. Ger.	B8	19
Bad Lippspringe, W. Ger.	B3	19
Bad Mergentheim, W. Ger.	D4	19
Bad Münstereifel, W. Ger.	C1	19
Bad Muskau, E. Ger.	B9	19
Bad Nauheim, W. Ger.	C3	19
Bad Neustadt [an der Saale], W. Ger.	C5	19
Bad Oeynhausen, W. Ger.	A3	19
Bad Oldesloe, W. Ger.	B5	18
Badong, China	E7	31
Bad Orb, W. Ger.	C4	19
Badoumbé, Mali	D2	45
Bad Pyrmont, W. Ger.	B4	19
Bad Ragaz, Switz.	E4	18
Bad Reichenhall, W. Ger.	E6	19
Bad River Indian Reservation, Wi., U.S.	B3	126
Bad Salzuflen, W. Ger.	C4	19
Bad Salzungen, E. Ger.	C5	19
Bad Schandau, E. Ger.	C9	19
Bad Segeberg, W. Ger.	E4	15
Bad Sülze, E. Ger.	D6	15
Bad Tennstedt, E. Ger.	B5	19
Bad Tölz, W. Ger.	E5	19
Badu, i., Austl.	A7	50
Badulla, Sri L.	G7	36
Badwater Creek, stm., Wy., U.S.	C5	127
Bad Wildungen, W. Ger.	B4	19
Bad Windsheim, W. Ger.	D5	19
Bad Wörishofen, W. Ger.	E5	20
Bad Wurzach, W. Ger.	B5	20
Baena, Spain	D3	22
Baependi, Braz.	C4	56
Baeza, Ec.	B2	58
Baeza, Spain	D4	22
Bafang, Cam.	D2	46
Bafatá, Gui.-B.	D2	45
Baffin Bay, b., N.A.	B14	61
Baffin Bay, b., Tx., U.S.	E4	120
Baffin Island, i., N.W. Ter.	C18	66
Bafia, Cam.	E2	46
Bafoulabé, Mali	D2	45
Bafoussam, Cam.	*D2	46
Bāfq, Iran	B5	38
Bafra, Tur.	B10	40
Bafra, Cape, c., Tur.	B11	40
Bäft, Iran	G8	39
Bafwasende, Zaire	A4	48
Bagabag, Phil.	n13	34
Bagaces, C.R.	E7	63
Bagamoyo, Tan.	C6	48
Bagana, Nig.	E6	45
Bagansiapiapi, Indon.	E2	34
Bagata, Zaire	B2	48
Bagdad, Fl., U.S.	u14	86
Bagdad, Ky., U.S.	B4	94
Bagé, Braz.	E2	56
Bagenkop, Den.	D4	15
Bägerhät, Bngl.	F12	37
Baggs, Wy., U.S.	E5	127
Baghdad, Iraq	B4	38
Bagheria, Italy	E4	23
Baghlān, Afg.	A4	36
Bagley, Ia., U.S.	C3	92
Bagley, Mn., U.S.	C3	100
Bagley, Wi., U.S.	F2	126
Bagnacavallo, Italy	E7	20
Bagnara [Calabra], Italy	E5	23
Bagnell, Mo., U.S.	C5	102
Bagnell Dam, Mo., U.S.	C5	102
Bagnères-de-Bigorre, Fr.	F4	16
Bagnères-de-Luchon, Fr.	F4	16
Bagnolet, Fr.	g10	16
Bagnols, Fr.	E6	16
Bago, Burma	E10	36
Bagoé, stm., Afr.	C3	45
Bagolino, Italy	D6	20
Bagot, co., Que.	D5	74
Bagrationovsk, Sov. Un.	A4	26
Baguio, Phil.	B6	34
Bagzane, Monts, mts., Niger.	C6	45
Bahama, N.C., U.S.	A4	110
Bahamas, ctry., N.A.	B5	64
Bahār, Iran	D8	36
Bahārampur, India	D8	37
Bahāwalnagar, Pak.	C5	36
Bahāwalpur, Pak.	C5	36
Bahia, state, Braz.	D2	57
Bahía, Islas de la, is., Hond.	D7	63
Bahía Blanca, Arg.	B4	54
Bahía Bustamante, Arg.	D3	54
Bahía de Caráquez, Ec.	B1	58
Bahia Negra, Para.	D4	55
Bahir Dar, Eth.	C4	47
Bahraich, India	D8	37
Bahrain, ctry., Asia	C5	38
Bahr al Ghazāl, prov., Sud.	D2	47
Bahr aş Şāfī, des., Asia	D4	38
Baḩrīyah, Al Wāḩāt al, well, Eg.	D5	43
Bāhū Kalāt, Iran	I10	39
Baia dos Tigres, Ang.	E1	48
Baia-Mare, Rom.	B6	24
Baião, Braz.	C5	59
Baïbokoum, Chad	D3	46
Baicheng, China	B9	31
Baie-Comeau, Que.	k13	74
Baie de Wasai, Mi., U.S.	B6	99
Baie-d'Urfé, Que.	q19	74
Baie-Johan-Beetz, Que.	h9	72
Baiersbronn, W. Ger.	E3	19
Baie-Sainte-Catherine, Que.	A8	74
Baie-Saint-Paul, Que.	B7	74
Baie Verte, N.B.	C5	71
Baie Verte, Newf.	D3	72
Baihe, China	H4	32
Baikal, Lake, l., Sov. Un.	D13	29
Baikal Mountains, mts., Sov. Un.	D13	29
Baikunthpur, India	F9	37
Bailén, Spain	C4	22
Băileşti, Rom.	C6	24
Bailey, Co., U.S.	B5	83
Bailey, Ms., U.S.	C5	101
Bailey, N.C., U.S.	B4	110
Bailey, co., Tx., U.S.	B1	120
Bailey Brook, stm., Me., U.S.	B2	96
Bailey Island, Me., U.S.	g8	96
Baileys Crossroads, Va., U.S.	g12	123
Baileys Harbor, Wi., U.S.	C6	126
Baileyton, Al., U.S.	A3	78
Baileyton, Tn., U.S.	C11	119
Baileyville, Il., U.S.	A4	90
Baileyville, Ks., U.S.	C7	93
Bailieborough, Ire.	D5	11
Bailundo, Ang.	D2	48
Bainbridge, Ga., U.S.	F2	87
Bainbridge, In., U.S.	E4	91
Bainbridge, N.Y., U.S.	C5	109
Bainbridge, Oh., U.S.	C2	112
Bainbridge Island, i., Wa., U.S.	e10	124
Bain-de-Bretagne, Fr.	D3	16
Bains, La., U.S.	D4	95
Bainville, Mt., U.S.	B12	103
Baiquan, China	B10	31
Baird, Ms., U.S.	B3	101
Baird, Tx., U.S.	C3	120
Bairdford, Pa., U.S.	h14	115
Baird Inlet, b., Ak., U.S.	C7	79
Baird Mountains, mts., Ak., U.S.	B7	79
Bairiki, Kir.	R18	52
Bairiki, i., Kir.	R18	52
Bairin Youqi, China	C8	32
Bairin Zuoqi, China	B8	32
Bairnsdale, Austl.	G8	50
Bairoil, Wy., U.S.	D5	127
Baïse, stm., Fr.	F4	16
Baixo Longa, Ang.	E2	48
Baja, Hung.	B4	24
Baja California Norte, state, Mex.	A1	63
Baja California Sur, state, Mex.	B2	63
Bajestan, Iran	D9	39
Bajimba, Mount, mtn., Austl.	D8	51
Bajo Boquete, Pan.	F6	62
Bajram-Ali, Sov. Un.	C11	39
Bakala, Cen. Afr. Rep.	D4	46
Bakar, Yugo.	D9	20
Bakel, Sen.	D2	45
Baker, Ca., U.S.	E5	82
Baker, Fl., U.S.	u15	86
Baker, La., U.S.	D4	95
Baker, Mn., U.S.	D6	100
Baker, Nv., U.S.	D7	105
Baker, Or., U.S.	C9	114
Baker, co., Fl., U.S.	B4	86
Baker, co., Ga., U.S.	E2	87
Baker, co., Or., U.S.	C9	114
Baker, stm., N.H., U.S.	C3	106
Baker, Mount, mtn., Wa., U.S.	A4	124
Baker Butte, mtn., Az., U.S.	C4	80
Baker Hill, Al., U.S.	D4	78
Baker Island, i., Oc.	F11	6
Baker Island, i., Ak., U.S.	n22	79
Baker Lake, N.W. Ter.	D13	66
Baker Lake, l., N.W. Ter.	D13	66
Baker Lake, l., Me., U.S.	B3	96
Baker Lake, res., Wa., U.S.	A4	124
Baker Mountain, mtn., Me., U.S.	C3	96
Bakers, N.C., U.S.	B2	110
Bakers Bayou, stm., Ar., U.S.	k11	81
Bakersfield, Ca., U.S.	E4	82
Bakersfield, Mo., U.S.	E5	102
Bakersfield, Vt., U.S.	B3	122
Bakers Island, i., Ma., U.S.	f12	98
Bakers Mill, Fl., U.S.	B4	86
Bakerstown, Pa., U.S.	h14	115
Bakersville, Ct., U.S.	B3	84
Bakersville, N.C., U.S.	e10	110
Bakerton, W.V., U.S.	B7	125
Bakewell, Eng., U.K.	A6	12
Bakhchisaray, Sov. Un.	I9	27
Bakhmut, stm., Sov. Un.	q21	27
Bākhtarān (Kermānshāh), Iran	B4	38
Bakr, stm., Tur.	C6	25
Bako, Eth.	D4	47
Bako, I.C.	E3	45
Bakony Mountains, mts., Hung.	B3	24
Bakool, prov., Som.	E5	47
Bakouma, Cen. Afr. Rep.	D4	46
Bakoye, stm., Afr.	D3	45
Baku, Sov. Un.	E7	29
Baku, Zaire	A5	48
Bakundi, Nig.	E7	45
Bakungan, Indon.	K2	35
Bal'ā, Isr. Occ.	f11	41
Balā, Tur.	C9	40
Bala, Wales, U.K.	B4	12
Bala, Ks., U.S.	C7	93
Balabac Island, i., Phil.	D5	34
Balabac Strait, strt., Asia	D5	34
Balabalagan Islands, is., Indon.	F5	34
Balad, Iraq	B4	38
Bālāghāt, India	G8	37
Balaguer, Spain	B6	22
Balaka, Mwi.	D6	48
Balakhna, Sov. Un.	D17	8
Balakhta, Sov. Un.	D27	8
Balaklava, Austl.	G2	51
Balaklava, Sov. Un.	G11	27
Balakovo, Sov. Un.	*D7	29
Balallan, Scot., U.K.	B2	13
Bālā Morghāb, Afg.	D11	39
Balancán [de Domínguez], Mex.	D6	63
Balanga, Phil.	o13	34
Balāngīr, India	G9	37
Balashov, Sov. Un.	F14	27
Balassagyarmat, Hung.	A4	24
Balāt, Eg.	D5	43
Balaton, Mn., U.S.	F3	100
Balaton, Lake, l., Hung.	B3	24
Balayan, Phil.	p13	34
Balayan Bay, b., Phil.	p13	34
Balbi, mtn., Pap. N. Gui.	*G9	6
Balboa, Pan.	m11	62
Balboa Heights, Pan.	m11	62
Balbriggan, Ire.	D5	11
Balcad, Som.	E6	47
Balcarce, Arg.	B5	54
Balcarres, Sask.	G4	75
Balch, Ar., U.S.	B5	81
Balchik, Bul.	D9	24
Balch Springs, Tx., U.S.	*n10	120
Balclutha, N.Z.	Q12	51
Bald Creek, N.C., U.S.	f10	110
Bald Eagle Lake, l., Mn., U.S.	m12	100
Balde, Co., U.S.	B5	83
Bald Eagle Lake, l., Mn., U.S.	C7	100
Bald hill, R.I., U.S.	D2	116
Baldhill Dam, N.D., U.S.	B7	111
Bald Knob, Ar., U.S.	B4	81
Bald Knob, mtn., Va., U.S.	c3	123
Bald Knob, mtn., W.V., U.S.	C5	125
Bald Knoll, mtn., Wy., U.S.	D2	127
Bald Mountain, mtn., Ct., U.S.	B2	84
Bald Mountain, mtn., N.J., U.S.	A4	107
Bald Mountain, mtn., Or., U.S.	D5	114
Bald Mountain, mtn., Or., U.S.	C9	114
Bald Mountain, mtn., Vt., U.S.	B5	122
Bald Mountain, mtn., Wy., U.S.	B5	127
Bald Mountains, mts., N.C., U.S.	f10	110
Baldock Lake, l., Man.	A3	70
Baldur, Man.	E2	70
Baldwin, Fl., U.S.	B5	86
Baldwin, Ga., U.S.	B3	87
Baldwin, Il., U.S.	E4	90
Baldwin, La., U.S.	E4	95
Baldwin, Md., U.S.	B5	97
Baldwin, Mi., U.S.	E5	99
Baldwin, N.Y., U.S.	*E7	109
Baldwin, N.D., U.S.	C5	111
Baldwin, Pa., U.S.	k13	115
Baldwin, Wi., U.S.	D1	126
Baldwin, co., Al., U.S.	E2	78
Baldwin, co., Ga., U.S.	C3	87
Baldwin City, Ks., U.S.	D8	93
Baldwin Heights, Wi., U.S.	C1	126
Baldwin Park, Ca., U.S.	*E4	82
Baldwinsville, N.Y., U.S.	B4	109
Baldwinton, Sask.	E1	75
Baldwinville, Ma., U.S.	A3	98
Baldwyn, Ms., U.S.	A5	101
Baldy Mountain, mtn., Man.	D1	70
Baldy Mountain, mtn., Mt., U.S.	B7	103
Baldy Mountain, mtn., N.M., U.S.	A4	108
Baldy Peak, mtn., Az., U.S.	D6	80
Bali, i., Indon.	G5	34
Balıkesir, Tur.	C6	40
Balıkpapan, Indon.	F5	34
Balintang Channel, strt., Phil.	B6	34
Bali Sea, Indon.	G5	34
Baliuag, Phil.	o13	34
Balje, W. Ger.	B4	18
Baljennie, Sask.	E2	75
Balkan, Ky., U.S.	D6	94
Balkan Mountains, mts., Eur.	D7	24
Balkh, Afg.	A4	36
Balkhash, Sov. Un.	E10	29
Balkhash, Lake, l., Sov. Un.	E10	29
Balki, Sov. Un.	H10	27
Balko, Ok., U.S.	e10	113
Balla, La., U.S.	C3	95
Ballachulish, Scot., U.K.	D3	13
Ballaghaderreen, Ire.	D3	11
Ballantine, Mt., U.S.	E8	103
Ballantrae, Scot., U.K.	C4	10
Ballarat (Ballaarat), Austl.	G7	50
Ballard, Ok., U.S.	A7	113
Ballard, co., Ky., U.S.	e8	94
Ballard, Lake, l., Austl.	E3	50
Ballardvale, Ma., U.S.	f11	98
Ball Club, Mn., U.S.	C5	100
Ball Club Lake, l., Mn., U.S.	C5	100
Ballé, Mali	C3	45
Ballenas, Bahía de, b., Mex.	B2	63
Ballenstedt, E. Ger.	B6	19
Balleny Islands, is., Ant.	C29	7
Ballerup [-Måløv], Den.	C6	15
Ball Ground, Ga., U.S.	B2	87
Ballia, India	E10	37
Ballina, Austl.	E9	50
Ballina, Ire.	C2	10
Ballina, Ire.	E3	11
Ballinafad, Ire.	E4	11
Ballinakill, Ire.	D4	11
Ballinalack, Ire.	D4	11
Ballinascarty, Ire.	F3	11
Ballinasloe, Ire.	D2	10
Ballindine, Ire.	D3	11
Ballingarry, Ire.	F2	11
Ballingeary, Ire.	F2	11
Ballinger, Tx., U.S.	D3	120
Ballinrobe, Ire.	D2	11
Ballinskellig Bay, b., Ire.	F1	11
Ballintra, Ire.	C3	11
Ballitore, Ire.	E5	11
Ballouville, Ct., U.S.	B8	84
Ballston, Or., U.S.	B3	114
Ballston Spa, N.Y., U.S.	B7	109
Ballwin, Mo., U.S.	f12	102
Bally, Pa., U.S.	F10	115
Ballybofey, Ire.	C4	11
Ballybunnion, Ire.	E2	11
Ballycanew, Ire.	E5	11
Ballycastle, Ire.	C2	11
Ballycastle, N. Ire., U.K.	C3	10
Ballyconnely, Ire.	D1	11
Ballyconnell, Ire.	D4	11
Ballycroy, Ire.	C2	11
Ballyduff, Ire.	E3	11
Ballyduff, Ire.	E2	11
Ballyferriter, Ire.	E1	11
Ballygar, Ire.	D3	11
Ballygorman, Ire.	B4	11
Ballyhaunis, Ire.	D3	11
Ballyheige, Ire.	E2	11
Ballyhoura Mountains, mts., Ire.	E3	11
Ballyjamesduff, Ire.	D4	11
Ballykelly, N. Ire., U.K.	C4	11
Ballylongford, Ire.	E2	11
Ballymahon, Ire.	D4	11
Ballymena, N. Ire., U.K.	C3	10
Ballymoe, Ire.	D3	11
Ballymoney, N. Ire., U.K.	B5	11
Ballymote, Ire.	C3	11
Ballymurray, Ire.	D3	11
Ballynahinch, N. Ire., U.K.	C6	11
Ballyneety, Ire.	E3	11
Ballynoe, Ire.	E3	11
Ballysadare, Ire.	C3	11
Ballyshannon, Ire.	C3	11
Ballyteige Bay, b., Ire.	E5	11
Ballyvaghan, Ire.	D2	11
Ballyvourney, Ire.	F2	11
Balm, Fl., U.S.	E4	86
Balmat, N.Y., U.S.	A5	109
Balmoral, Man.	D3	70
Balmorhea, Tx., U.S.	o13	120
Balmville, N.Y., U.S.	D6	109
Baloda Bāzār, India	G9	37
Balonne, stm., Austl.	E8	50
Bālotra, India	H5	37
Balrāmpur, India	D9	37
Balranald, Austl.	G4	51
Bals, Rom.	C7	24
Balsam, N.C., U.S.	f9	110
Balsam Lake, Wi., U.S.	C1	126
Balsam Lake, l., Ont.	C6	73
Balsas, Braz.	C5	57
Balsas, Mex.	D5	63
Balsas, stm., Braz.	C1	57
Balsas, stm., Mex.	D4	63
Balsas, Rio das, stm., Braz.	D1	57
Balsthal, Switz.	B4	21
Balta, Sov. Un.	H7	27
Balta, N.D., U.S.	A5	111
Baltasar Brum, Ur.	E1	56
Baltic, Ct., U.S.	C7	84
Baltic, S.D., U.S.	D9	118
Baltic Sea, Eur.	I8	14
Baltīm, Eg.	C3	41
Baltimore, Ire.	F2	11
Baltimore, Md., U.S.	B4	97
Baltimore, Oh., U.S.	C3	112
Baltimore, co., Md., U.S.	B4	97
Baltimore Highlands, Md., U.S.	h11	97
Baltra, Isla, i., Ec.	g5	58
Baltrum, i., W. Ger.	A7	17
Baluchistan, hist. reg., Asia	C3	36
Balya, Tur.	C6	25
Balzac, Alta.	D3	68
Bāli, India	E4	37
Balzers, Liech.	B8	21
Bam, Iran	C5	38
Bama, Nig.	D7	45
Bamako, Mali	D3	45
Bambang, Phil.	n13	34
Bambari, Cen. Afr. Rep.	D4	46
Bamberg, W. Ger.	D5	18
Bamberg, S.C., U.S.	E5	117
Bamberg, co., S.C., U.S.	E5	117
Bamber Lake, N.J., U.S.	D4	107
Bambesa, Zaire	A4	48
Bambuí, Braz.	C6	56
Bamburgh, Eng., U.K.	E7	13
Bamenda, Cam.	D2	46
Bampūr, Iran	H10	39
Bampūr, stm., Iran	H9	39
Ban, Carn, mtn., Scot., U.K.	C4	13
Banagher, Ire.	D4	11
Banahao, Mount, mtn., Phil.	o13	34
Banalia, Zaire	A4	48
Banamba, Mali	D3	45
Banana, Zaire	C1	48
Bananal, Braz.	h5	56
Bananal, Ilha do, i., Braz.	E4	59
Banana River, b., Fl., U.S.	D6	86
Bananeiras, Braz.	C3	57
Banas, stm., India	E4	37
Banās, Ra's, c., Eg.	C3	38
Banbridge, N. Ire., U.K.	C3	10
Banbury, Eng., U.K.	D6	10
Banchory, Scot., U.K.	C6	13
Bancroft, Ont.	B7	73
Bancroft, Id., U.S.	G7	89
Bancroft, Ia., U.S.	A3	92
Bancroft, Me., U.S.	C4	96
Bancroft, Mi., U.S.	F6	99
Bancroft, Ne., U.S.	B9	104
Bancroft, S.D., U.S.	C8	118
Bancroft, Wi., U.S.	D4	126
Bānda, India	C7	36
Banda Aceh, Indon.	k11	34
Banda Banda, Mount, mtn., Austl.	E9	51
Banda Islands, is., Indon.	F7	34
Bandana, Ky., U.S.	e9	94
Bandar see Machilipatnam, India	E7	36
Bandar Baharu, Malay.	J4	35
Bandar Beheshtī, Iran	I10	39
Bandar-e 'Abbās, Iran	C5	38
Bandar-e Anzalī (Bandar-e Pahlavī), Iran	B4	38
Bandar-e Büshehr, Iran	G5	39
Bandar-e Deylam, Iran	F5	39
Bandar-e Khomeynī (Bandar-e Shāhpūr), Iran	F4	39
Bandar-e Lengeh, Iran	H7	39
Bandar-e Māhshahr, Iran	*F4	39
Bandar-e Pahlavī see Bandar-e Anzalī, Iran	B4	38
Bandar-e Rīg, Iran	G5	39
Bandar-e Shāh see Bandar-e Torkeman, Iran	B5	38
Bandar-e Shāhpūr see Bandar-e Khomeynī, Iran	F4	39
Bandar-e Torkeman (Bandar-e Shāh), Iran	B5	38
Bandar Maharani see Muar, Malay.	K5	35
Bandar Seri Begawan (Brunei), Bru.	E5	34
Banda Sea, Indon.	G7	34
Bande, Spain	A2	22
Banded Peak, mtn., Co., U.S.	D4	83
Bandeira, Pico da, mtn., Braz.	C4	56
Bandelier National Monument, N.M., U.S.	B3	108
Bandera, Arg.	A4	55
Bandera, Tx., U.S.	E3	120
Bandera, co., Tx., U.S.	E3	120
Banderas, Bahía de, b., Mex.	m11	63
Bandholm, Den.	D5	15
Bandiagara, Mali	D4	45
Bāndīkūi, India	D6	37
Bandırma, Tur.	B7	40
Bandon, Ire.	F3	11
Bandon, Or., U.S.	D2	114
Bandon, stm., Ire.	F3	11
Bandundu, Zaire	B2	48
Bandung, Indon.	G3	34
Bandy, Va., U.S.	e10	123
Bāneh, Iran	D6	42
Banes, Cuba	D6	64
Banff, Alta.	D3	68
Banff, Scot., U.K.	C6	13
Banff National Park, Alta.	D2	68
Banfora, Burkina	D4	45
Bangalore, India	F5	36
Bangassou, Cen. Afr. Rep.	D4	46
Bangeta, Mount, mtn., Pap. N. Gui.	k12	50
Banggai, Indon.	F6	34
Banggong Co, l., China	B6	36
Bangkalan, Indon.	G4	34
Bangka, i., Indon.	F3	34
Bangkok (Krung Thep), Thai.	G4	35
Bangladesh, ctry., Asia	D9	36
Bangor, Sask.	G4	75
Bangor, Ire.	C2	11
Bangor, N. Ire., U.K.	C4	10
Bangor, Wales, U.K.	B3	12
Bangor, Al., U.S.	A3	78
Bangor, Me., U.S.	D4	96
Bangor, Mi., U.S.	F4	99
Bangor, N.Y., U.S.	f10	109
Bangor, Pa., U.S.	E11	115
Bangor, Wi., U.S.	E3	126
Bangor Township, Mi., U.S.	E7	99
Bangs, Tx., U.S.	D3	120
Bangs, Mount, mtn., Az., U.S.	A2	80
Bang Saphan, Thai.	C1	34
Bangu, Zaire	C3	48
Bangued, Phil.	B6	34
Bangweulu, Lake, l., Zam.	D4	48
Banhā, Eg.	h12	43
Ban Hat Yai see Hat Yai, Thai.	K6	35
Baní, Dom. Rep.	E8	64
Bani, Phil.	n12	34
Bani, stm., Mali	D3	45
Banī Na'īm, Isr. Occ.	C7	41
Banister, stm., Va., U.S.	D4	123
Banī Suhaylah, Isr. Occ.	C6	41
Banī Suwayf, Eg.	C3	43
Bāniyās, Isr. Occ.	B4	41
Banja Luka, Yugo.	B2	24
Banjarmasin, Indon.	F4	34
Banjul, Gam.	D1	45
Bankas, Mali	D4	45
Bankeryd, Swe.	A8	15
Bankfoot, Scot., U.K.	D5	13
Bankhead, Al., U.S.	A2	78
Bankhead Lake, res., Al., U.S.	B2	78
Banks, Al., U.S.	D4	78
Banks, Ar., U.S.	D3	81
Banks, Id., U.S.	E2	89
Banks, Ms., U.S.	A3	101
Banks, Or., U.S.	g11	114
Banks, co., Ga., U.S.	B3	87
Banksian, stm., Can.	C4	70
Banks Island, i., B.C.	C2	69
Banks Island, i., N.W. Ter.	B8	66
Banks Lake, res., Wa., U.S.	B6	124
Banks Peninsula, pen., N.Z.	O14	51
Bankston, Austl.	*F9	50
Bānkura, India	D4	36
Bann, stm., N. Ire., U.K.	C4	13
Bannack, Mt., U.S.	E4	103
Banner, Ms., U.S.	A4	101
Banner, Wy., U.S.	B6	127
Banner, co., Ne., U.S.	C2	104
Banner Elk, N.C., U.S.	A1	110
Banning, Ca., U.S.	F5	82
Bannock, co., Id., U.S.	G6	89
Bannockburn, Ont.	C7	73
Bannock Peak, mtn., Id., U.S.	F6	89
Bannock Range, mts., Id., U.S.	G6	89
Bannu, Pak.	B5	36
Bañolas, Spain	A7	22
Baños, Ec.	B2	58
Bansha, Ire.	E3	11
Banská Bystrica, Czech.	D5	26
Banská Štiavnica, Czech.	D5	26
Bansko, Bul.	E6	24
Bānswāra, India	F5	37
Bantam, Ct., U.S.	C3	84
Bantam, stm., Ct., U.S.	C3	84
Bantam Lake, l., Ct., U.S.	C3	84
Banteer, Ire.	E3	11
Bantry, Ire.	E2	10
Bantry, N.D., U.S.	A5	111
Bantry Bay, b., Ire.	E2	10
Banyak Islands, is., Indon.	m11	34
Banyo, Cam.	D2	46
Banyuwangi, Indon.	G4	34
Banzare Coast, Ant.	C25	7
Baocheng, China	E4	32
Baode, China	E4	32
Baodi, China	E7	32
Baoding, China	D8	31
Bao Ha, Viet.	A6	35
Baoji, China	E6	31
Bao Loc, Viet.	C3	34
Baoqing, China	B13	31
Baoshan, China	C8	35
Baoting, China	C3	31
Baotou, China	C6	31
Baoulé, stm., Afr.	D3	45
Baoulé, stm., Mali	C3	45
Bapaume, Fr.	C5	16
Bapchule, Az., U.S.	D4	80
Baptiste, Ont.	B6	73
Baptiste Lake, l., Ont.	B6	73
Baptistown, N.J., U.S.	B2	107
Bāqa al Gharbiyya, Isr. Occ.	B4	38
Ba'qūbah, Iraq	B4	38
Baquedano, Chile	D2	55
Bar, Fr.	C6	16
Bar, Sov. Un.	G7	27
Bar, Yugo.	D4	24
Baraawe, Som.	C6	47
Barabinsk, Sov. Un.	D10	29
Baraboo, Wi., U.S.	E4	126
Baraboo, stm., Wi., U.S.	E3	126
Baracaldo, Spain	A4	22
Baracoa, Cuba	D6	64
Barada, Ne., U.S.	D10	104
Baradero, Arg.	f7	54
Baraga, Mi., U.S.	B2	99
Baraga, co., Mi., U.S.	B2	99
Bārah, Sud.	C3	47
Barahona, Dom. Rep.	E8	64
Barajas de Madrid, Spain	p17	22
Bārākpur, India	F12	37
Bārāmūla, India	C5	36
Bārān, India	E6	37
Baranagar, India	*D8	36
Baranof Island, i., Ak., U.S.	m22	79
Baranovichi, Sov. Un.	E5	27
Barão de Melgaço, Braz.	B1	56
Barão, Trin.	N23	65
Barataria, La., U.S.	E5	95
Barataria, Bayou, stm., La., U.S.	k11	95
Barataria Bay, b., La., U.S.	E6	95
Barat Daya Islands, is., Indon.	G7	34
Baraya, Col.	C2	60
Barbacena, Braz.	C4	56
Barbacoas, Col.	C2	60
Barbado, stm., Braz.	C2	56
Barbados, ctry., N.A.	J15	64
Barbalha, Braz.	B3	57
Barbar, Sud.	B3	47
Barbastro, Spain	A6	22
Barbate [de Franco], Spain	D3	22
Barbeau Peak, mtn., N.W. Ter.	k37	66
Barber, Ar., U.S.	B1	81
Barber, co., Ks., U.S.	E5	93
Barbers Point, c., Hi., U.S.	B3	88
Barbers Point Naval Air Station, mil., Hi., U.S.	g9	88
Barberton, S. Afr.	C5	49
Barberton, Oh., U.S.	A4	112
Barberville, Fl., U.S.	C5	86
Barbezieux, Fr.	E3	16
Barbil, India	F10	37
Barbour, co., Al., U.S.	D4	78
Barbour, co., W.V., U.S.	B4	125
Barboursville, W.V., U.S.	C2	125
Barbourville, Ky., U.S.	D6	94
Barbuda, i., Antig.	H14	64
Barca de Alva, Port.	B2	22
Barcaldine, Austl.	D8	50
Barcarena, Port.	f9	22
Barcellona [Pozzo di Gotto], Italy	E5	23
Barcelona, Spain	B7	22
Barcelona, Ven.	A5	60
Barcelonnette, Fr.	E7	16
Barcelos, Braz.	D5	59
Barcelos, Port.	B1	22
Barclay, Md., U.S.	B6	97

Name	Map Ref.	Page
Barco, N.C., U.S.	A7	110
Barcoo, stm., Austl.	D7	50
Barcroft, Lake, res., Va., U.S.	g12	123
Bard, N.M., U.S.	B6	108
Barda del Medio, Arg.	B3	54
Bardaï, Chad	A3	46
Bardawīl, Sabkhat al, sw., Eg.	C5	41
Bardawil Peninsula, spit, Eg.	C4	41
Barddhamān, India	D8	36
Bardejov, Czech.	D6	26
Barden Reservoir, res., R.I., U.S.	C2	116
Bardi, Italy	E5	20
Bardīyah, Libya	C5	43
Bardolph, Il., U.S.	C3	90
Bardonecchia, Italy	D2	20
Bardsey Island, i., Wales, U.K.	B3	12
Bardstown, Ky., U.S.	C4	94
Bardstown Junction, Ky., U.S.	C4	94
Bardswell Group, is., B.C.	C3	69
Bardwell, Ky., U.S.	f9	94
Bardwell Lake, res., Tx., U.S.	C4	120
Bare Hill Pond, l., Ma., U.S.	g9	98
Bareilly, India	C6	36
Barenburg, W. Ger.	F2	15
Barentin, Fr.	C4	16
Barents, i., Nor.	B12	128
Barents Sea, Eur.	B6	29
Barentu, Eth.	B4	47
Barfleur, Pointe de, c., Fr.	C3	16
Bargarh, India	G9	37
Bargersville, In., U.S.	E5	91
Barguzin, Sov. Un.	D13	29
Bar Harbor, Me., U.S.	D4	96
Bari, Italy	D6	23
Bari, prov., Som.	D6	47
Barillas, Guat.	C2	62
Barinas, Ven.	B3	60
Barinas, state, Ven.	B4	60
Baring, Me., U.S.	C5	96
Baring, Mo., U.S.	A5	102
Bāripada, India	D8	36
Bariri, Braz.	C3	56
Bārīs, Eg.	E6	43
Barisāl, Bngl.	D9	36
Barisan Mountains, mts., Indon.	F2	34
Barito, stm., Indon.	F4	34
Barium Springs, N.C., U.S.	B2	110
Barker, N.Y., U.S.	B2	109
Barker Heights, N.C., U.S.	f10	110
Barkerville, B.C.	C7	69
Barkeyville, Pa., U.S.	D2	115
Barkhamsted Reservoir, res., Ct., U.S.	B3	84
Bark Lake, l., Ont.	B7	73
Barkley, Ia., U.S.	f10	94
Barkley Dam, Ky., U.S.	e9	94
Barkley Sound, strt., B.C.	E5	69
Barkly East, S. Afr.	D4	49
Barkly Tableland, plat., Austl.	C6	50
Barkmere, Que.	C3	74
Barkol, China	C3	31
Bark Point, c., Wi., U.S.	B2	126
Bark River, Mi., U.S.	C3	99
Barksdale, Tx., U.S.	E2	120
Barksdale Air Force Base, mil., La., U.S.	B2	95
Bar Lake, l., Sask.	B2	75
Bar-le-Duc, Fr.	C6	16
Barlee, Lake, l., Austl.	E2	50
Barletta, Italy	D6	23
Barling, Ar., U.S.	B1	81
Barlow, Ky., U.S.	e8	94
Barlow, N.D., U.S.	B6	111
Barlow, Or., U.S.	h12	114
Bārmer, India	E2	36
Bar Mills, Me., U.S.	E2	96
Barmouth, Wales, U.K.	D4	10
Barna, Ire.	D2	11
Barnaby River, N.B.	C4	71
Barnard, Ks., U.S.	C5	93
Barnard, Mo., U.S.	A3	102
Barnard, S.D., U.S.	B7	118
Barnard, Vt., U.S.	D3	122
Barnard Castle, Eng., U.K.	F7	13
Barnardsville, N.C., U.S.	f10	110
Barnasht, Eg.	E3	41
Barnaul, Sov. Un.	D11	29
Barnegat, N.J., U.S.	D4	107
Barnegat Bay, b., N.J., U.S.	D4	107
Barnegat Inlet, b., N.J., U.S.	D4	107
Barnegat Light, N.J., U.S.	D4	107
Barnegat Pines, N.J., U.S.	D4	107
Barne Inlet, b., Ant.	g40	7
Barnes, Ks., U.S.	C7	93
Barnes, Pa., U.S.	C3	115
Barnes, co., N.D., U.S.	B7	111
Barnesboro, Pa., U.S.	E4	115
Barnes City, Ia., U.S.	C5	92
Barnes Corners, N.Y., U.S.	B5	109
Barnes Creek, stm., La., U.S.	D2	95
Barnes Sound, strt., Fl., U.S.	G6	86
Barneston, Ne., U.S.	D9	104
Barnesville, Ga., U.S.	C2	87
Barnesville, Md., U.S.	B3	97
Barnesville, Mn., U.S.	D2	100
Barnesville, Oh., U.S.	C4	112
Barnet (part of London), Eng., U.K.	k12	10
Barnet, Vt., U.S.	C4	122
Barnett, Mo., U.S.	C5	102
Barneveld, Neth.	B5	17
Barneveld, Wi., U.S.	E4	126
Barneville-Carteret, Fr.	F6	10
Barney, Ga., U.S.	F3	87
Barney, N.D., U.S.	C8	111
Barney, Mount, mtn., Austl.	D9	51
Barnhart, Mo., U.S.	C7	102
Barnhart, Tx., U.S.	D2	120
Barnhill, Oh., U.S.	B4	112
Barnsdall, Ok., U.S.	A5	113
Barnsley, Eng., U.K.	A6	12
Barnstable, Ma., U.S.	C7	98
Barnstable, co., Ma., U.S.	C7	98
Barnstaple, Eng., U.K.	C3	12
Barnstaple Bay, b., Eng., U.K.	C3	12
Barnstead, N.H., U.S.	D4	106
Barnum, Ia., U.S.	B3	92
Barnum, Mn., U.S.	D6	100
Barnwell, Al., U.S.	H2	78
Barnwell, S.C., U.S.	E5	117
Baro, Nig.	E6	45
Baro, stm., Afr.	D3	47
Baroda, Mi., U.S.	G4	99
Baroda see Vadodara, India	D5	36
Baron, Ok., U.S.	B7	113
Barons, Alta.	E4	68
Barques, Pointe aux, c., Mi., U.S.	D8	99
Barquisimeto, Ven.	A4	60
Barr, Co., U.S.	B6	83
Barr, Ra's al, c., Eg.	C3	41
Barra, Braz.	h5	57
Barra, Braz.	D2	57
Barra, i., Scot., U.K.	B3	10
Barra, Sound of, strt., Scot., U.K.	C1	13
Barraba, Austl.	E8	51
Barra Bonita, Braz.	m7	56
Barracão, Braz.	D2	56
Barrackville, W.V., U.S.	B4	125
Barra de Río Grande, Nic.	D6	62
Barra do Corda, Braz.	C1	57
Barra do Garças, Braz.	B2	56
Barra do Piraí, Braz.	C4	56
Barra Head, c., Scot., U.K.	B3	10
Barra Mansa, Braz.	C4	56
Barranca, Peru	B2	58
Barranca, N.M., U.S.	*A3	108
Barrancabermeja, Col.	B3	60
Barrancas, Ven.	B5	60
Barranco, Peru	*D2	58
Barranquilla, Col.	A3	60
Barraza, Chile	A2	54
Barre, Ma., U.S.	B3	98
Barre, Vt., U.S.	C4	122
Barre, Lake, l., La., U.S.	E5	95
Barre des Écrins, mtn., Fr.	E7	16
Barreiras, Braz.	D2	57
Barreirinha, Braz.	C3	59
Barreirinhas, Braz.	B2	57
Barreiro, Port.	C1	22
Barreiros, Braz.	C3	57
Barrelville, Md., U.S.	k13	97
Barren, co., Ky., U.S.	D4	94
Barren, stm., Ky., U.S.	C3	94
Barren, Nosy, is., Madag.	g8	49
Barren Island, i., Md., U.S.	D5	97
Barren Islands, is., Ak., U.S.	h15	79
Barren Plain, Tn., U.S.	A5	119
Barren River Lake, res., Ky., U.S.	D3	94
Barre Plains, Ma., U.S.	B3	98
Barretos, Braz.	C3	56
Barrett, Mn., U.S.	E3	100
Barrett, W.V., U.S.	D3	125
Barrhead, Alta.	B3	68
Barrhead, Scot., U.K.	E4	13
Barrhill, Scot., U.K.	E4	13
Barrie, Ont.	C5	73
Barrie Island, i., Ont.	B2	73
Barrier Bay, b., Ant.	C21	7
Barrière, B.C.	D7	69
Barrier Lake, l., Sask.	E4	75
Barrier Range, mts., Austl.	F7	50
Barrigada, Guam	L10	52
Barrington, Il., U.S.	A5	90
Barrington, N.H., U.S.	D4	106
Barrington, R.I., U.S.	D5	116
Barrington, stm., R.I., U.S.	C5	116
Barrington Lake, l., Man.	A1	70
Barrington Passage, N.S.	F4	71
Barrington Tops, mts., Austl.	F8	51
Barrio Obrero Industrial, Peru	*D2	58
Barro Alto, Braz.	B3	56
Barron, Wi., U.S.	C2	126
Barron, co., Wi., U.S.	C2	126
Barronett, Wi., U.S.	C2	126
Barron Lake, Mi., U.S.	G4	99
Barrouallie, St. Vin.	U26	65
Barrow, Arg.	B4	54
Barrow, Ak., U.S.	A8	79
Barrow, i., Austl.	D2	50
Barrow, stm., Ire.	D3	10
Barrow, Point, c., Ak., U.S.	A8	79
Barrow-in-Furness, Eng., U.K.	C5	10
Barrows, Man.	C1	70
Barrow Strait, strt., N.W. Ter.	B14	66
Barrowsville, Ma., U.S.	C5	98
Barruelo de Santullán, Spain	A3	22
Barry (Vale of Glamorgan), Wales, U.K.	C4	12
Barry, Il., U.S.	D2	90
Barry, co., Mi., U.S.	F5	99
Barry, co., Mo., U.S.	E4	102
Barrys Bay, Ont.	B7	73
Barryton, Mi., U.S.	E5	99
Barryville, N.Y., U.S.	D6	109
Bārsi, India	B4	36
Barsinghausen, W. Ger.	A4	19
Barsø, i., Den.	C3	15
Barstow, Ca., U.S.	E5	82
Barstow, Tx., U.S.	D1	120
Bartelso, Il., U.S.	E4	90
Barth, E. Ger.	A6	18
Barth, Fl., U.S.	u14	86
Bartholomew, co., In., U.S.	F6	91
Bartholomew, Bayou, stm., U.S.	D4	81
Bartibog Bridge, N.B.	B4	71
Bartica, Guy.	A3	59
Bartin, Tur.	B9	40
Bartle Frere, Mount, mtn., Austl.	C8	50
Bartlesville, Ok., U.S.	A6	113
Bartlett, Il., U.S.	*k8	90
Bartlett, Ks., U.S.	E8	93
Bartlett, Ne., U.S.	C7	104
Bartlett, N.H., U.S.	B4	106
Bartlett, N.D., U.S.	A7	111
Bartlett, Oh., U.S.	C4	112
Bartlett, Tn., U.S.	B2	119
Bartlett, Tx., U.S.	D4	120
Bartlett Cove, Ak., U.S.	k22	79
Bartlett Reservoir, res., Az., U.S.	C4	80
Bartletts Ferry Dam, U.S.	C4	78
Bartletts Harbour, Newf.	C3	72
Bartley, Ne., U.S.	D5	104
Bartolomeu Dias, Moz.	B6	49
Barton, Al., U.S.	A2	78
Barton, Md., U.S.	k12	97
Barton, N.D., U.S.	A5	111
Barton, Oh., U.S.	B5	112
Barton, Vt., U.S.	B4	122
Barton, co., Ks., U.S.	D5	93
Barton, co., Mo., U.S.	D3	102
Barton, Vt., U.S.	B4	122
Bartonsville, Vt., U.S.	E3	122
Barton-upon-Humber, Eng., U.K.	A7	12
Bartonville, Il., U.S.	C4	90
Bartoszyce, Pol.	A6	26
Bartow, Fl., U.S.	E5	86
Bartow, Ga., U.S.	C4	87
Bartow, co., Ga., U.S.	B2	87
Barú, Volcán, vol., Pan.	F6	62
Barun Su, China	C4	32
Barus, Indon.	K3	35
Baruth, E. Ger.	A8	19
Baruun-Urt, Mong.	B7	31
Barvas, Scot., U.K.	A3	10
Barvenkovo, Sov. Un.	G11	27
Barview, Or., U.S.	*D2	114
Barwāni, India	F5	37
Barwick, Ga., U.S.	F3	87
Barwon, stm., Austl.	E8	50
Barybino, Sov. Un.	n17	27
Barycz, stm., Pol.	C4	26
Basalt, Co., U.S.	B3	83
Basalt, Id., U.S.	F6	89
Basalt, Nv., U.S.	E3	105
Basankusu, Zaire	A2	48
Basbulak, Sov. Un.	E6	28
Basco, Phil.	A6	34
Basco, Il., U.S.	C2	90
Bascom, Fl., U.S.	B1	86
Bascom, Oh., U.S.	A2	112
Bascuñán, Cabo, c., Chile	B2	54
Basehor, Ks., U.S.	k16	93
Basekpio, Zaire	A3	48
Basel, Switz.	E3	18
Basel-Land, state, Switz.	B3	20
Basel-Stadt, state, Switz.	B3	20
Bashan Lake, l., Ct., U.S.	D6	84
Bashaw, Alta.	C4	68
Bashi, Al., U.S.	D2	78
Bashi Channel, strt., Asia	A6	34
Basiad Bay, b., Phil.	o14	34
Basilan Island, i., Phil.	D6	34
Basildon, Eng., U.K.	C8	12
Basile, La., U.S.	D3	95
Basilicata (Lucania), prov., Italy	D6	23
Basilio, Braz.	E2	56
Basin, Mt., U.S.	D4	103
Basin, Wy., U.S.	B4	127
Basinger, Fl., U.S.	E5	86
Basingstoke, Eng., U.K.	E6	10
Basin Harbor, Vt., U.S.	C2	122
Basin Lake, l., Sask.	E3	75
Baška, Yugo.	C2	24
Baskahegan Lake, l., Me., U.S.	C5	96
Baskatong, Réservoir, res., Que.	k11	74
Baskett, Ky., U.S.	C2	94
Baskin, Fl., U.S.	p10	86
Baskin, La., U.S.	B4	95
Basking Ridge, N.J., U.S.	B3	107
Basoko, Zaire	A3	48
Basongo, Zaire	B3	48
Basora, Punt, c., Neth. Ant.	H17	65
Basque Provinces, hist. reg., Spain	A4	22
Basra (Al Başrah), Iraq	B4	39
Bas-Rhin, dept., Fr.	F7	17
Bassano, Alta.	D4	68
Bassano del Grappa, Italy	B3	23
Bassas da India, rf., Reu.	F1	34
Basse-Pointe, Mart.	S10	65
Basse Santa Su, Gam.	D2	45
Basse-Terre, Guad.	I14	64
Basseterre, St. C.-N.	H13	64
Basse-Terre, i., Guad.	Q8	65
Bassett, Ar., U.S.	B5	81
Bassett, Ks., U.S.	E8	93
Bassett, Ne., U.S.	B6	104
Bassett, Va., U.S.	D3	123
Bassett, Wi., U.S.	n11	126
Bassett Creek, stm., Al., U.S.	D2	78
Bassett Peak, mtn., Az., U.S.	E5	80
Bassfield, Ms., U.S.	D4	101
Bass Harbor, Me., U.S.	D4	96
Bassikounou, Maur.	C3	45
Bass Islands, is., Oh., U.S.	A3	112
Bass Lake, In., U.S.	B4	91
Bass River, N.S.	D6	71
Bass Strait, strt., Austl.	n15	50
Bassum, W. Ger.	F2	15
Bastak, Iran	H7	39
Bastelica, Fr.	D2	23
Basti, India	D9	37
Bastia, Fr.	C2	23
Bastia, i., Fr.	C13	23
Bastogne, Bel.	B6	16
Bastrop, La., U.S.	B4	95
Bastrop, Tx., U.S.	D4	120
Bastrop, co., Tx., U.S.	D4	120
Bastuträsk, Swe.	E9	14
Baxdo, Som.	D2	41
Bata, Eq. Gui.	E1	45
Bataan Peninsula, pen., Phil.	o13	34
Batabanó, Cuba	C2	64
Batabanó, Golfo de, b., Cuba	C2	64
Bataguaçu, Braz.	C2	56
Batala, India	B6	36
Batamay, Sov. Un.	C15	29
Batang, China	E4	31
Batangafo, Cen. Afr. Rep.	D3	46
Batangas, Phil.	C6	34
Batan Islands, is., Phil.	A6	34
Bátaszék, Hung.	B4	24
Batatais, Braz.	C3	56
Batavia, Arg.	A3	54
Batavia, Il., U.S.	B5	90
Batavia, N.Y., U.S.	C2	109
Batavia, Oh., U.S.	C1	112
Bataysk, Sov. Un.	H12	27
Batchelor, La., U.S.	D4	95
Batchelor Bay, b., N.C., U.S.	B6	110
Batchtown, Il., U.S.	D3	90
Batdambang, Camb.	C2	35
Bateman, Sask.	G2	75
Bates, Ar., U.S.	C1	81
Bates, co., Mo., U.S.	C3	102
Batesburg, S.C., U.S.	D4	117
Bates City, Mo., U.S.	C3	102
Batesland, S.D., U.S.	D3	118
Batesville, Ar., U.S.	B4	81
Batesville, In., U.S.	F7	91
Batesville, Ms., U.S.	A4	101
Batesville, Oh., U.S.	C4	112
Batesville, Tx., U.S.	E3	120
Bath, N.B.	C2	73
Bath, Jam.	F16	65
Bath, Eng., U.K.	E5	10
Bath, Il., U.S.	C3	90
Bath, In., U.S.	E8	91
Bath, Me., U.S.	E3	96
Bath, Mi., U.S.	F6	99
Bath, N.H., U.S.	B3	106
Bath, N.Y., U.S.	C3	109
Bath, N.C., U.S.	B6	110
Bath, Pa., U.S.	E11	115
Bath, S.C., U.S.	D4	117
Bath, S.D., U.S.	B7	118
Bath, co., Ky., U.S.	B6	94
Bath, co., Va., U.S.	B3	123
Bathgate, Scot., U.K.	E5	13
Bathgate, N.D., U.S.	A8	111
Bathinda, India	E6	36
Bathsheba, Barb.	J15	64
Bath Springs, Tn., U.S.	B3	119
Bathurst, Austl.	F8	50
Bathurst, N.B.	B4	71
Bathurst see Banjul, Gam.	D1	45
Bathurst, i., Austl.	B5	50
Bathurst, Cape, c., N.W. Ter.	B7	66
Bathurst Inlet, N.W. Ter.	C11	66
Bathurst Inlet, b., N.W. Ter.	C11	66
Bathurst Island, Austl.	B5	50
Bathurst Island, i., N.W. Ter.	m31	66
Batié, Burkina	E4	45
Batikı, i., Fiji	H15	52
Batiscan, Que.	C5	74
Batiscan, stm., Que.	B5	74
Batkanu, S.L.	E2	45
Batman, Tur.	D13	40
Batna, Alg.	B6	44
Batoche, Sask.	E2	75
Baton Rouge, La., U.S.	D4	95
Batouri, Cam.	E2	46
Batroûn, Leb.	D5	41
Batson, Tx., U.S.	D5	120
Batsto, N.J., U.S.	D3	107
Batsto, stm., N.J., U.S.	D3	107
Batten Kill, stm., U.S.	E2	122
Battery Park, Va., U.S.	k14	123
Battiest, Ok., U.S.	C7	113
Batticaloa, Sri L.	G7	36
Battle, Can.	F11	66
Battleboro, N.C., U.S.	A5	110
Battle Creek, Sask.	H1	75
Battle Creek, Ia., U.S.	B2	92
Battle Creek, Mi., U.S.	F5	99
Battle Creek, Ne., U.S.	C8	104
Battle Creek, stm., N.A.	B7	103
Battleford, Sask.	E1	75
Battle Ground, In., U.S.	C4	91
Battle Ground, Wa., U.S.	D3	124
Battle Harbour, Newf.	B4	72
Battle Mountain, Nv., U.S.	C5	105
Battle Mountain, mtn., Wy., U.S.	E5	127
Battles, Ms., U.S.	D5	101
Battles Wharf, Al., U.S.	E2	78
Battleview, N.D., U.S.	A3	111
Battonya, Hung.	B5	24
Battrum, Sask.	G1	75
Batu, mtn., Eth.	D4	47
Batu, Mex.	D2	63
Batu Islands, is., Indon.	F1	34
Batu Pahat, Malay.	L5	35
Baturaja, Indon.	F2	34
Baturino, Sov. Un.	B11	28
Baturité, Braz.	B3	57
Bat Yam, Isr.	g9	41
Baubau, Indon.	G6	34
Bauchi, Nig.	D6	45
Baudette, Mn., U.S.	B4	100
Baudó, Serranía de, mts., Col.	C3	121
Bauer, Ut., U.S.	B7	124
Bauer Coulee, val., Wa., U.S.	B7	124
Baugé, Fr.	D3	16
Bauld, Cape, c., Newf.	C4	72
Bauma, Switz.	B6	21
Baume-les-Dames, Fr.	B2	20
Baunei, Italy	D2	23
Baunes, Bol.	B3	55
Baures, stm., Bol.	B3	55
Baurtregaum, mtn., Ire.	E2	11
Bauru, Braz.	C3	56
Bautzen, E. Ger.	C7	18
Bauxite, Ar., U.S.	C3	81
Bavaria, Ks., U.S.	D6	93
Bavaria, hist. reg., W. Ger.	D5	18
Bavarian Alps, mts., Eur.	B7	20
Bavay, Fr.	D3	17
Bavispe, Mex.	A3	63
Baw Baw, Mount, mtn., Austl.	H6	51
Bawcomville, La., U.S.	*B3	95
Bawean, i., Indon.	G4	34
Bawku, Ghana	D4	45
Baxdo, Som.	D6	47
Baxian, China	E7	32
Baxley, Ga., U.S.	E4	87
Baxter, Mn., U.S.	D4	100
Baxter, Tn., U.S.	C8	119
Baxter, W.V., U.S.	B4	125
Baxter, co., Ar., U.S.	A3	81
Baxter Springs, Ks., U.S.	E9	93
Baxterville, Ms., U.S.	D4	101
Bay, Ar., U.S.	B5	81
Bay, prov., Som.	E5	47
Bay, co., Fl., U.S.	u16	86
Bay, co., Mi., U.S.	E6	99
Bay, Laguna de, l., Phil.	o13	34
Bay al Kabīr, Wādī, val., Libya	C2	43
Bayambang, Phil.	o13	34
Bayamo, Cuba	D5	64
Bayamón, P.R.	G11	64
Bayan, China	C3	33
Bayana, India	E3	46
Bayanga, Cen. Afr. Rep.	E3	46
Bayanhongor, Mong.	B5	31
Bayan Obo, China	D3	32
Bayard, Ia., U.S.	C3	92
Bayard, Ne., U.S.	C2	104
Bayard, N.M., U.S.	E1	108
Bayard, W.V., U.S.	B5	125
Bayberry, N.Y., U.S.	B4	109
Bayboro, N.C., U.S.	B6	110
Bay Bulls, Newf.	E5	72
Bay Center, Wa., U.S.	C2	124
Bay City, Mi., U.S.	E7	99
Bay City, Or., U.S.	B3	114
Bay City, Tx., U.S.	E5	120
Bay City, Wi., U.S.	D1	126
Baydaratta Bay, b., Sov. Un.	B22	8
Bay de Verde, Newf.	D5	72
Baydhabo, Som.	E5	47
Baydrag, stm., Mong.	B4	31
Bayeux, Fr.	C6	16
Bayfield, Ont.	D3	73
Bayfield, Wi., U.S.	B3	126
Bayfield, co., Wi., U.S.	B3	126
Bay Head, N.J., U.S.	*C4	107
Bayındır, Tur.	C6	25
Baykonyr, Sov. Un.	D7	28
Bay L'Argent, Newf.	E4	72
Baylis, Il., U.S.	D3	90
Baylor, co., Tx., U.S.	C3	120
Baymak, Sov. Un.	C5	28
Bay Mills Indian Reservation, Mi., U.S.	B6	99
Bay Minette, Al., U.S.	E2	78
Bayombong, Phil.	n13	34
Bayonet Point, Fl., U.S.	*D4	86
Bayonne, Fr.	F3	16
Bayonne, N.J., U.S.	B4	107
Bayou Bodcau Reservoir, res., La., U.S.	B2	95
Bayou Cane, La., U.S.	*E5	95
Bayou D'Arbonne Lake, res., La., U.S.	B3	95
Bayou George, Fl., U.S.	u16	86
Bayou Goula, La., U.S.	D4	95
Bayóvar, Peru	C1	58
Bay Pines, Fl., U.S.	*E4	86
Bay Point, c., S.C., U.S.	G7	117
Bayport, Mn., U.S.	E6	100
Bayport, N.S.	E5	71
Bay Port, Mi., U.S.	E7	99
Bayport, N.Y., U.S.	n15	109
Bayramiç, Tur.	C6	25
Bayreuth, W. Ger.	D5	18
Bay Ridge, Md., U.S.	C5	97
Bayrischzell, W. Ger.	B7	20
Bay Roberts, Newf.	E5	72
Bays, Lake of, l., Ont.	B5	73
Bay Saint Louis, Ms., U.S.	E4	101
Bayshore, Mi., U.S.	C5	99
Bay Shore, N.Y., U.S.	E7	109
Bayside Gardens, Fl., U.S.	q10	86
Bayside, Tx., U.S.	E4	120
Bayside, Wi., U.S.	m12	126
Bays Mountains, mtn., Tn., U.S.	n14	119
Bays Mountains, mtn., Tn., U.S.	C10	119
Baysun, Sov. Un.	B13	29
Bayt Dajan, Isr. Occ.	g12	41
Baytillū, Isr. Occ.	h11	41
Bayt Jālā, Isr. Occ.	C7	41
Baytown, Tx., U.S.	E5	120
Bay Trail, Sask.	E3	75
Bayview, Al., U.S.	f7	78
Bayview, Id., U.S.	A2	89
Bay View, Mi., U.S.	C6	99
Bay View Park, Oh., U.S.	A3	111
Bay Village, Ar., U.S.	B5	81
Bay Village, Oh., U.S.	h9	112
Bayville, N.J., U.S.	D4	107
Bayville, N.Y., U.S.	*E7	109
Baza, Spain	D4	22
Bazaruto, Ilha do, i., Moz.	C6	49
Bazhong, China	E6	31
Bazile Mills, Ne., U.S.	B8	104
Bazine, Ks., U.S.	D4	93
Bazmān, Kūh-e, mtn., Iran	G10	39
Baztán, Spain	A5	22
Be, Nosy, i., Madag.	f9	49
Beach, N.D., U.S.	B2	111
Beach City, Oh., U.S.	B4	112
Beach Haven, N.J., U.S.	D4	107
Beach Haven Crest, N.J., U.S.	D4	107
Beach Haven Inlet, b., N.J., U.S.	D4	107
Beach Haven Terrace, N.J., U.S.	D4	107
Beach Lake, Pa., U.S.	C11	115
Beach Pond, l., U.S.	C8	84
Beachville, Ont.	D4	73
Beachwood, N.J., U.S.	D4	107
Beachwood, Oh., U.S.	*h10	112
Beachy Head, c., Eng., U.K.	E8	12
Beacon, Ia., U.S.	C5	92
Beacon, N.Y., U.S.	D7	109
Beacon Falls, Ct., U.S.	D3	84
Beacon Hill, Fl., U.S.	v16	86
Beaconsfield, Que.	q19	74
Beacon Square, Fl., U.S.	*D4	86
Beadle, Sask.	F1	75
Beadle, co., S.D., U.S.	C7	118
Beagh, Slieve, hill, N. Ire., U.K.	C4	11
Beagle, Ks., U.S.	D8	93
Beagle, Canal, strt., S.A.	h12	54
Bealanana, Madag.	f9	49
Beale City, Mi., U.S.	E6	99
Beale Air Force Base, mil., Ca., U.S.	C3	82
Beallsville, Oh., U.S.	C4	112
Beals, Ky., U.S.	C3	94
Beals, Me., U.S.	D5	96
Bean Lake, Mo., U.S.	o13	34
Bean Station, Tn., U.S.	C10	119
Bear, i., Nor.	B13	128
Bear, stm., Al., U.S.	A2	78
Bear, stm., U.S.	A1	78
Bearcreek, Mt., U.S.	E7	103
Bear Creek, Al., U.S.	A2	78
Bear Creek, Wi., U.S.	D5	126
Bear Creek, stm., Al., U.S.	A1	78
Bear Creek, stm., Wy., U.S.	E8	127
Bearden, Ar., U.S.	D3	81
Bearden, Ok., U.S.	B5	113
Beardmore, Ont.	o18	73
Beardmore Glacier, ice, Ant.	A30	7
Beards Fork, W.V., U.S.	m13	125
Beardsley, Mn., U.S.	E2	100
Beardstown, Tn., U.S.	B4	119
Beaufort Inlet, b., N.C., U.S.	A4	107
Bear Inlet, b., N.C., U.S.	C5	110
Bear Island, i., Ire.	F2	11
Bear Lake, Mi., U.S.	D4	99
Bear Lake, Pa., U.S.	C2	115
Bear Lake, l., Alta.	B1	68
Bear Lake, l., Man.	A4	70
Bear Lake, l., Wi., U.S.	A2	126
Bear Lake, co., Id., U.S.	G7	89
Bear Lodge Mountains, mts., Wy., U.S.	B8	127
Bear Mountain, mtn., Ar., U.S.	f7	81
Bear Mountain, mtn., Ky., U.S.	C5	94
Bear Mountain, mtn., Ma., U.S.	A3	98
Bear Mountain, mtn., Or., U.S.	D4	114
Béarn, hist. reg., Fr.	F3	16
Bearpaw Mountains, mts., Mt., U.S.	B7	103
Bear Peninsula, pen., Ant.	B1	7
Bear Pond Mountains, mts., Md., U.S.	A2	97
Bear River, N.S.	E4	71
Bear River City, Ut., U.S.	B3	121
Bear Spring, Tn., U.S.	A4	119
Bear Swamp, sw., Ma., U.S.	h11	98
Bear Tooth Pass, Wy., U.S.	E7	103
Beartooth Range, mts., U.S.	E7	103
Bear Town, Ms., U.S.	D3	101
Beartown Mountain, mtn., Va., U.S.	f10	123
Beas de Segura, Spain	C4	22
Beason, Il., U.S.	C4	90
Beata, Cabo, c., Dom. Rep.	F8	64
Beaton, B.C.	D9	69
Beatrice, Al., U.S.	D2	78
Beatrice, Ne., U.S.	D9	104
Beatrice, Zimb.	A5	49
Beattie, Ks., U.S.	C7	93
Beatton, stm., B.C.	A7	69
Beatty, Sask.	E3	75
Beatty, Nv., U.S.	G5	105
Beatty, Or., U.S.	E5	114
Beattyville, Ky., U.S.	C6	94
Beatyestown, N.J., U.S.	B3	107
Beaucaire, Fr.	F6	16
Beauce, co., Que.	C7	74
Beauceville-Est, Que.	C7	74
Beaucoup Creek, stm., La., U.S.	B3	95
Beaucourt, Fr.	D7	16
Beaufort, Fr.	E2	21
Beaufort, Malay.	D6	34
Beaufort, Mo., U.S.	C6	102
Beaufort, N.C., U.S.	C6	110
Beaufort, S.C., U.S.	G6	117
Beaufort, co., N.C., U.S.	B5	110
Beaufort, co., S.C., U.S.	G6	117
Beaufort Island, i., Ant.	e38	7
Beaufort Marine Corps Air Station, mil., S.C., U.S.	F6	117
Beaufort Sea, N.A.	B7	61
Beaufort West, S. Afr.	D3	49
Beaugency, Fr.	D4	16
Beauharnois, Que.	D4	74
Beauharnois, co., Que.	D4	74
Beau Lake, l., Me., U.S.	A3	96
Beaulieu, Que.	n17	74
Beaulieu, Mn., U.S.	C3	100
Beauly, Scot., U.K.	D4	13
Beauly, stm., Scot., U.K.	D4	13
Beaumaris, Wales, U.K.	A3	12
Beaumont, Alta.	C4	68
Beaumont, Newf.	D4	72
Beaumont, Que.	C7	74
Beaumont, Fr.	F4	16
Beaumont, Ca., U.S.	*F5	82
Beaumont, Ks., U.S.	E7	93
Beaumont, Ms., U.S.	D5	101
Beaumont, Tx., U.S.	D5	120
Beaumont [-sur-Oise], Fr.	E2	17
Beaune, Fr.	D6	16
Beauport, Que.	n17	74
Beaupré, Que.	B7	74
Beauraing, Bel.	A4	17
Beauregard, Ms., U.S.	D3	101
Beauregard, co., La., U.S.	D2	95
Beaurivage, Que.	D6	74
Beausejour, Man.	D3	70
Beauty, Ky., U.S.	C7	94
Beauvais, Fr.	E2	16
Beauval, Sask.	B2	75
Beauvallon, Alta.	C5	68
Beaver, Ak., U.S.	B10	79
Beaver, Ia., U.S.	B3	92
Beaver, Ks., U.S.	C8	92
Beaver, Ok., U.S.	e10	113
Beaver, Or., U.S.	B3	114
Beaver, Pa., U.S.	E1	115
Beaver, Ut., U.S.	E3	121
Beaver, W.V., U.S.	D3	125
Beaver, Wi., U.S.	D5	126
Beaver, co., Ok., U.S.	e10	113
Beaver, co., Pa., U.S.	E1	115
Beaver, co., Ut., U.S.	E2	121
Beaver, stm., Can.	B2	75
Beaver, stm., N.Y., U.S.	B6	109
Beaver, stm., R.I., U.S.	E2	116
Beaver, stm., U.S.	E1	113
Beaver, stm., Ut., U.S.	E2	121
Beaver Brook, stm., N.H., U.S.	E4	106
Beaver City, Ne., U.S.	D6	104
Beaver Creek, B.C.	C5	69
Beaver Creek, Mn., U.S.	G2	100
Beavercreek, Oh., U.S.	C1	112
Beaver Creek, stm., Sask.	F2	75
Beaver Creek, stm., Ak., U.S.	E4	104
Beaver Creek, stm., Ky., U.S.	A2	94
Beaver Creek, stm., Md., U.S.	A2	97
Beaver Creek, stm., Mt., U.S.	B9	103
Beaver Creek, stm., N.D., U.S.	C5	111
Beaver Creek, stm., Wy., U.S.	D4	127
Beaver Creek Mountains, mts., Al., U.S.	B3	78
Beaver Crossing, Ne., U.S.	D8	104
Beaverdale, Pa., U.S.	F4	115
Beaver Dam, Az., U.S.	A2	80
Beaver Dam, Ky., U.S.	C3	94
Beaverdam, Oh., U.S.	B2	112
Beaver Dam, Wi., U.S.	E5	126
Beaver Dam, stm., De., U.S.	F3	85
Beaverdam Branch, stm., De., U.S.	F3	85
Beaver Dams, N.Y., U.S.	C4	109
Beaverdell, B.C.	E8	69
Beaver Falls, N.Y., U.S.	B5	109
Beaver Falls, Pa., U.S.	E1	115
Beaverhead, co., Mt., U.S.	E4	103
Beaverhead, stm., Mt., U.S.	E4	103

Name	Map Ref.	Page
Beaverhead Mountains, mts., U.S.	D5	89
Beaverhill Lake, l., Alta.	C4	68
Beaver Hill Lake, l., Man.	B4	70
Beaver Island, i., Mi., U.S.	C5	99
Beaver Island, l., Alta.	B5	68
Beaver Lake, res., Ar., U.S.	A2	81
Beaverlick, Ky., U.S.	k13	94
Beaverlodge, Alta.	B1	68
Beaver Meadows, Pa., U.S.	E10	115
Beaver Point, Co., U.S.	A5	83
Beaver Ridge, mtn., Tn., U.S.	D9	119
Beaver Run Reservoir, res., Pa., U.S.	F2	115
Beaver Springs, Que.	E7	115
Beavertail Point, c., R.I., U.S.	F4	116
Beaverton, Ont.	C5	73
Beaverton, Al., U.S.	B1	78
Beaverton, Mi., U.S.	E6	99
Beaverton, Or., U.S.	B4	114
Beavertown, Pa., U.S.	E7	115
Beaverville, Il., U.S.	C6	90
Beāwar, India	C5	36
Beazley, Arg.	A3	54
Bebedouro, Braz.	C3	56
Bebra, W. Ger.	C4	19
Bécancour, Que.	C5	74
Bécancour, stm., Que.	C6	74
Beccles, Eng., U.K.	B9	12
Bečej, Yugo.	C5	24
Becerreá, Spain	A2	22
Béchar, Alg.	C4	44
Becharof Lake, l., Ak., U.S.	D8	79
Bechyně, Czech.	D9	19
Beckemeyer, Il., U.S.	E4	90
Becker, Mn., U.S.	E5	100
Becker, Ms., U.S.	B5	101
Becker, co., Mn., U.S.	D3	100
Becket, Ma., U.S.	B1	98
Beckham, co., Ok., U.S.	B2	113
Beckley, W.V., U.S.	D3	125
Beckum, W. Ger.	B3	19
Beckville, Tx., U.S.	C5	120
Beckwith Creek, stm., La., U.S.	D2	95
Becky Peak, mtn., Nv., U.S.	D7	105
Bedale, Eng., U.K.	F7	13
Bédarieux, Fr.	F5	16
Bedburg, W. Ger.	C1	19
Bederkesa, W. Ger.	E2	15
Bedford, N.S.	E6	71
Bedford, Que.	D5	74
Bedford, Eng., U.K.	D6	10
Bedford, In., U.S.	G5	91
Bedford, Ia., U.S.	D3	92
Bedford, Ky., U.S.	B4	94
Bedford, Ma., U.S.	B5	98
Bedford, Mi., U.S.	F5	99
Bedford, Mo., U.S.	B4	102
Bedford, N.H., U.S.	E3	106
Bedford, Oh., U.S.	A4	112
Bedford, Pa., U.S.	F4	115
Bedford, Tx., U.S.	*n9	120
Bedford, Va., U.S.	C3	123
Bedford, Wy., U.S.	D2	127
Bedford, co., Pa., U.S.	G4	115
Bedford, co., Tn., U.S.	B5	119
Bedford, co., Va., U.S.	C3	123
Bedford Heights, Oh., U.S.	*h9	112
Bedford Hills, N.Y., U.S.	D7	109
Bedfordshire, co., Eng., U.K.	B7	12
Bedias, Tx., U.S.	D5	120
Bedlington, Eng., U.K.	C6	10
Bedminster, N.J., U.S.	B3	107
Bedourie, Austl.	B2	51
Bedrock, Co., U.S.	C2	83
Będzin, Pol.	g10	26
Bee, Ne., U.S.	C8	104
Bee, Ok., U.S.	C5	113
Bee, co., Tx., U.S.	E4	120
Beebe, Que.	D5	74
Beebe, Ar., U.S.	B4	81
Beebe Plain, Vt., U.S.	A4	122
Beebe River, N.H., U.S.	C3	106
Bee Branch, Ar., U.S.	B3	81
Beech Bluff, Tn., U.S.	B3	119
Beech Bottom, W.V., U.S.	f8	125
Beech Creek, Ky., U.S.	C2	94
Beech Creek, Pa., U.S.	D6	115
Beecher, Il., U.S.	B6	90
Beecher, Mi., U.S.	E7	99
Beecher City, Il., U.S.	D5	90
Beechey Head, c., B.C.	h12	69
Beech Fork, stm., Ky., U.S.	C4	94
Beech Grove, Ar., U.S.	A5	81
Beech Grove, In., U.S.	E5	91
Beech Grove, Ky., U.S.	C2	94
Beechgrove, Tn., U.S.	B5	119
Beech Island, S.C., U.S.	E4	117
Beechwood, N.B.	C2	71
Beechwood, Ma., U.S.	h12	98
Beechwood, Mi., U.S.	B2	99
Beechy, Sask.	G2	75
Beecroft Head, c., Austl.	G8	51
Beedeville, Ar., U.S.	B4	81
Beef Island, i., V.I., Br.	e8	119
Beek, Neth.	D5	17
Beeler, Ks., U.S.	D3	93
Beelitz, E. Ger.	A7	19
Beemer, Ne., U.S.	C9	104
Beenleigh, Austl.	C9	51
Bee Ridge, Fl., U.S.	q11	86
Beersheba (Be'er Sheva'), Isr.	B3	38
Beersheba Springs, Tn., U.S.	D8	119
Beersville, N.B.	C4	71
Beeskow, E. Ger.	B7	18
Beesleys Point, N.J., U.S.	E3	107
Beethoven Peninsula, pen., Ant.	B5	7
Beeton, Ont.	C5	73
Beetzendorf, E. Ger.	F5	15
Beeville, Tx., U.S.	E4	120
Befale, Zaire	A3	48
Beg, Lough, l., N. Ire., U.K.	C5	11
Beggs, Ok., U.S.	B5	113
Begichevo, i., Sov. Un.	B28	128
Béhague, Pointe, c., Fr. Gu.	B4	59
Behāla (South Suburban), India	*D8	36
Behbahān, Iran	F5	39
Behm Canal, strt., Ak., U.S.	n24	79
Behshahr, Iran	C6	39
Bei'an, China	B10	31
Beigi, Eth.	D3	47
Beihai, China	G6	31
Beijing (Peking), China	D8	31
Beili, China	C8	35
Beilngries, W. Ger.	D6	19
Beinamar, Chad	D3	46
Beipiao, China	*C9	31
Beira, Moz.	C4	49
Beira, hist. reg., Port.	B2	22
Beirne, Ar., U.S.	D2	81
Beirut (Bayrūt), Leb.	B3	38
Beiseker, Alta.	D4	68
Beitbridge, Zimb.	B5	49
Beiuş, Rom.	B6	24
Beja, Port.	C2	22
Béja, Tun.	B6	44
Béjaïa (Bougie), Alg.	B6	44
Béjar, Spain	B3	22
Bejou, Mn., U.S.	C3	100
Bejuco, Pan.	F8	62
Bekabad, Sov. Un.	G22	8
Bekdash, Sov. Un.	E4	28
Békés, Hung.	B5	24
Békéscsaba, Hung.	B5	24
Bekily, Madag.	h9	49
Bela, India	E8	37
Bela, Pak.	C4	36
Bela Crkva, Yugo.	C5	24
Belaga, Malay.	E4	34
Bel Air, Md., U.S.	A5	97
Bel Aire Estates, Ct., U.S.	D7	84
Belalcázar, Spain	C3	22
Bel Alton, Md., U.S.	D4	97
Belampalli, India	E6	36
Bélanger, stm., Man.	C3	70
Belanger, stm., Sask.	C2	75
Belas, Port.	f9	22
Bela Vista, Braz.	C1	56
Bela Vista, Moz.	C5	49
Bela Vista de Goiás, Braz.	B5	56
Belawan, Indon.	E1	34
Belaya, stm., Sov. Un.	B4	28
Belaya Glina, Sov. Un.	H13	27
Belaya Tserkov, Sov. Un.	G8	27
Belcamp, Md., U.S.	B5	97
Belcher, Ky., U.S.	C7	94
Belcher, La., U.S.	B2	95
Belcherāgh, Afg.	D12	39
Belcher Islands, is., N.W. Ter.	E17	66
Belchertown, Ma., U.S.	B3	98
Belcourt, N.D., U.S.	A6	111
Belcoville, N.J., U.S.	E3	107
Belden, Ms., U.S.	A5	101
Belden, Ne., U.S.	B8	104
Belden, N.D., U.S.	A3	111
Belding, Mi., U.S.	F5	99
Belecke, W. Ger.	B3	19
Beled Weyne, Som.	E6	47
Belém (Pará), Braz.	B1	57
Belén, Arg.	E2	55
Belen, Para.	A3	54
Belen, Ms., U.S.	A3	101
Belen, N.M., U.S.	C3	108
Belén, Ur.	E1	56
Belén de Escobar, Arg.	g7	54
Belenkoye, Sov. Un.	q20	27
Belev, Sov. Un.	E11	27
Belfair, Wa., U.S.	B3	124
Belfast, N. Ire., U.K.	C4	10
Belfast, Me., U.S.	D3	96
Belfast, N.Y., U.S.	C2	109
Belfast, N.C., U.S.	B5	110
Belfast, Oh., U.S.	C2	112
Belfast, Tn., U.S.	B5	119
Belfast Lough, b., N. Ire., U.K.	C6	11
Belfield, N.D., U.S.	C2	111
Belford, Eng., U.K.	E7	13
Belford, N.J., U.S.	C4	107
Belfort, Fr.	D7	16
Belfort, N.Y., U.S.	B5	109
Belfort, ter., Fr.	B2	20
Belfry, Ky., U.S.	C7	94
Belfry, Mt., U.S.	E8	103
Belgaum, India	D2	36
Belgica Mountains, mts., Ant.	B16	7
Belgium, Il., U.S.	C6	90
Belgium, Wi., U.S.	E6	126
Belgium, ctry., Eur.	B6	16
Belgorod, Sov. Un.	F11	27
Belgorod-Dnestrovskiy, Sov. Un.	H8	27
Belgrade, Me., U.S.	D3	96
Belgrade, Mo., U.S.	D7	102
Belgrade, Mt., U.S.	E5	103
Belgrade, Ne., U.S.	C7	104
Belgrade (Beograd), Yugo.	C5	24
Belgrade Lakes, Me., U.S.	D3	96
Belgreen, Al., U.S.	A2	78
Belhaven, N.C., U.S.	B6	110
Belice, stm., Italy	F4	23
Beli Lom, stm., Bul.	D8	24
Belington, W.V., U.S.	B5	125
Belitung, i., Indon.	F3	34
Belize, ctry., N.A.	D7	63
Belize, stm., Belize	B3	62
Belize City, Belize	D7	63
Belkino, Sov. Un.	B11	28
Belknap, Il., U.S.	F5	90
Belknap, Ia., U.S.	D5	92
Belknap, co., N.H., U.S.	C3	106
Belknap Crater, crat., Or., U.S.	C5	114
Belknap Mountain, mtn., N.H., U.S.	C4	106
Belkovski, stm., Sov. Un.	B11	128
Bell, Ca., U.S.	*E4	82
Bell, Fl., U.S.	C4	86
Bell, co., Ky., U.S.	D6	94
Bell, co., Tx., U.S.	D4	120
Bella Bella, B.C.	C3	69
Bellac, Fr.	D4	16
Bella Coola, B.C.	C4	69
Bella Coola, stm., B.C.	C4	69
Bellagio, Italy	D5	20
Bellahy, Ire.	D3	11
Bellair, Fl., U.S.	*m8	86
Bellaire, Ks., U.S.	C5	93
Bellaire, Mi., U.S.	D5	99
Bellaire, Oh., U.S.	B5	112
Bellaire, Tx., U.S.	r14	120
Bellamy, Al., U.S.	C1	78
Bellary, India	E4	36
Bella Unión, Ur.	E2	55
Bella Vista, Arg.	D4	55
Bella Vista, Arg.	B1	54
Bella Vista, Para.	A4	54
Bellbrook, Oh., U.S.	C1	112
Bell Buckle, Tn., U.S.	B5	119
Bell City, La., U.S.	D3	95
Bell City, Mo., U.S.	D8	102
Belle, Mo., U.S.	C6	102
Belle, W.V., U.S.	C3	125
Belleair, Fl., U.S.	p10	86
Belle-Anse, Haiti	E7	64
Belle Bay, b., Newf.	E4	72
Belle Center, Oh., U.S.	B2	112
Belle Chasse, La., U.S.	E5	95
Bellechasse, co., Que.	C7	74
Belle Creek, Mt., U.S.	E11	103
Belledune, N.B.	B4	71
Belleek, N. Ire., U.K.	C3	11
Bellefleur, N.B.	B2	71
Bellefontaine, Ms., U.S.	B4	101
Bellefontaine, Oh., U.S.	B2	112
Bellefontaine Neighbors, Mo., U.S.	*f13	102
Bellefonte, Ar., U.S.	A2	81
Bellefonte, De., U.S.	*A3	85
Bellefonte, Pa., U.S.	E6	115
Belle Fourche, S.D., U.S.	C2	118
Belle Fourche, stm., U.S.	C3	118
Belle Fourche Reservoir, res., S.D., U.S.	C2	118
Belle Glade, Fl., U.S.	F6	86
Belle Haven, Va., U.S.	C7	123
Belleherbe, Fr.	B2	21
Belle Hôtesse, mtn., Guad.	Q8	65
Belle Isle, Fl., U.S.	D5	86
Belle Isle, i., Newf.	g12	89
Belle Isle, Strait of, strt., Newf.	C3	72
Belleisle Creek, N.B.	D4	71
Belle Mead, N.J., U.S.	C3	107
Belle Meade, Tn., U.S.	g10	119
Belle Mina, Al., U.S.	*A3	78
Belleoram, Newf.	E4	72
Belle-Plaine, Sask.	G3	75
Belle Plaine, Ia., U.S.	C5	92
Belle Plaine, Ks., U.S.	E6	93
Belle Plaine, Mn., U.S.	F5	100
Belle Rive, Il., U.S.	E5	90
Belle River, Ont.	E2	73
Belle Rose, La., U.S.	D4	95
Belleu, Fr.	E3	17
Belle Union, In., U.S.	E4	91
Belle Valley, Oh., U.S.	C4	112
Belle Vernon, Pa., U.S.	F2	115
Belleview, Fl., U.S.	C4	86
Belleview, Mo., U.S.	D7	102
Belle View, Va., U.S.	g12	123
Belleville, N.S.	F4	71
Belleville, Ont.	C7	73
Belleville, Fr.	D6	16
Belleville, Ar., U.S.	B2	81
Belleville, Il., U.S.	E4	90
Belleville, Ks., U.S.	C6	93
Belleville, Mi., U.S.	p15	99
Belleville, N.J., U.S.	B4	107
Belleville, N.Y., U.S.	B4	109
Belleville, Pa., U.S.	E6	115
Belleville, R.I., U.S.	E4	116
Belleville, Wi., U.S.	F4	126
Belleville Pond, l., R.I., U.S.	E4	116
Belleville [-sur-Meuse], Fr.	E5	17
Bellevue, Ia., U.S.	B7	92
Bellevue, Id., U.S.	F4	89
Bellevue, Ky., U.S.	h13	94
Bellevue, Mi., U.S.	F6	99
Bellevue, Ne., U.S.	C10	104
Bellevue, Oh., U.S.	A3	112
Bellevue, Pa., U.S.	F1	115
Bellevue, Wa., U.S.	e11	124
Belley, Fr.	E6	16
Belle Yella, Lib.	E3	45
Bellflower, Ca., U.S.	n12	82
Bellflower, Il., U.S.	C5	90
Bellflower, Mo., U.S.	B6	102
Bell Gardens, Ca., U.S.	*n12	82
Bellingham, Eng., U.K.	C6	10
Bellingham, Ma., U.S.	B5	98
Bellingham, Mn., U.S.	E2	100
Bellingham, Wa., U.S.	A3	124
Bellingshausen Sea, Ant.	B3	7
Bell-Irving, stm., B.C.	A3	69
Bellis, Alta.	B4	68
Bell Island, i., Newf.	E5	72
Bell Island, i., Newf.	C4	72
Bellmawr, N.J., U.S.	D2	107
Bellmead, Tx., U.S.	*D4	120
Bellmore, In., U.S.	E3	91
Bellmore, N.Y., U.S.	*n15	109
Bello, Col.	B2	60
Bellows Falls, Vt., U.S.	E4	122
Bellport, N.Y., U.S.	n16	109
Bell Ranch, N.M., U.S.	B5	108
Bells, Tn., U.S.	B2	119
Bells, Tx., U.S.	C4	120
Bells Corners, Ont.	h12	73
Bells Creek, stm., W.V., U.S.	m13	125
Bellshill, Scot., U.K.	*E4	13
Belluno, Italy	A4	23
Bellvale, N.Y., U.S.	D6	109
Bellville, Ga., U.S.	D5	87
Bellville, Oh., U.S.	B3	112
Bellville, Tx., U.S.	E4	120
Bellvue, Co., U.S.	A5	83
Bellwood, Al., U.S.	D4	78
Bellwood, Ne., U.S.	C8	104
Bellwood, Pa., U.S.	E5	115
Bellwood, Va., U.S.	n18	123
Belly, stm., N.A.	E4	68
Belmar, N.J., U.S.	C4	107
Bélmez, Spain	C5	22
Belmond, Ia., U.S.	B4	92
Belmont, Man.	E2	70
Belmont, N.S.	D6	71
Belmont, Ont.	E3	73
Belmont, Ca., U.S.	h8	82
Belmont, Ma., U.S.	g11	98
Belmont, Ms., U.S.	A5	101
Belmont, N.H., U.S.	D4	106
Belmont, N.Y., U.S.	C2	109
Belmont, N.C., U.S.	B1	110
Belmont, Tx., U.S.	k8	120
Belmont, Vt., U.S.	E3	122
Belmont, Wa., U.S.	B8	124
Belmont, Wi., U.S.	F3	126
Belmont, co., Oh., U.S.	C5	112
Belmonte, Braz.	C9	57
Belmont Heights, Ut., U.S.	*C4	121
Belmopan, Belize	D7	63
Belmullet, Ire.	C1	11
Bel-Nor, Mo., U.S.	*f13	102
Belo, Madag.	g8	49
Beloeil, Que.	D4	74
Belogorsk, Sov. Un.	D15	29
Belo Horizonte, Braz.	B4	56
Beloit, Ia., U.S.	A1	92
Beloit, Ks., U.S.	C5	93
Beloit, Oh., U.S.	B5	112
Beloit, Wi., U.S.	F4	126
Beloit North, Wi., U.S.	F4	126
Belokany, Sov. Un.	B16	40
Belomorsk, Sov. Un.	C6	29
Belopolye, Sov. Un.	F10	27
Beloretsk, Sov. Un.	D8	29
Belovo, Sov. Un.	E26	8
Beloye, Lake, l., Sov. Un.	A11	27
Belozersk, Sov. Un.	B11	27
Belp, Switz.	C4	21
Belper, Eng., U.K.	A6	12
Belpre, Ks., U.S.	E4	93
Belpre, Oh., U.S.	C4	112
Belshaw, In., U.S.	B3	91
Belspring, Va., U.S.	C2	123
Belt, Mt., U.S.	C6	103
Belt Creek, stm., Mt., U.S.	C6	103
Belted Range, mts., Nv., U.S.	F5	105
Belterra, Braz.	C4	59
Belton, Mo., U.S.	C3	102
Belton, S.C., U.S.	B3	117
Belton, Tx., U.S.	D4	120
Belton Lake, res., Tx., U.S.	D4	120
Beltra, Ire.	C3	11
Beltrami, Mn., U.S.	C2	100
Beltrami, co., Mn., U.S.	B3	100
Beltsville, Md., U.S.	B4	97
Beltsy, Sov. Un.	H6	27
Belturbet, Ire.	C4	11
Belukha, Mount, mtn., Sov. Un.	E11	29
Belview, Mn., U.S.	F3	100
Belvedere, Ga., U.S.	*C2	87
Belvedere, S.C., U.S.	D4	117
Belvedere Marittimo, Italy	E5	23
Belvedere Park, Ga., U.S.	*h8	87
Belvidere, De., U.S.	*B3	85
Belvidere, Il., U.S.	A5	90
Belvidere, Ks., U.S.	E4	93
Belvidere, Ne., U.S.	D8	104
Belvidere, N.J., U.S.	B2	107
Belvidere, N.C., U.S.	A6	110
Belvidere, S.D., U.S.	D4	118
Belvidere, Tn., U.S.	B5	119
Belvidere Center, Vt., U.S.	B3	122
Belvidere Mountain, mtn., Vt., U.S.	B3	122
Belview, Mn., U.S.	F3	100
Belvue, Ks., U.S.	C7	93
Belwood, Ont.	D4	73
Belyando, stm., Austl.	D8	50
Belyy, Sov. Un.	D9	27
Belyy Bom, Sov. Un.	E26	8
Belyy Island, i., Sov. Un.	B9	29
Belyy Yar, Sov. Un.	B11	28
Belzig, E. Ger.	A7	19
Belzoni, Ms., U.S.	B3	101
Bembézar, stm., Spain	C3	22
Bement, Il., U.S.	D5	90
Bemidji, Lake, l., Mn., U.S.	C4	100
Bemis, Tn., U.S.	B3	119
Bemis, W.V., U.S.	C5	125
Bemiss, Ga., U.S.	F3	87
Bemus Point, N.Y., U.S.	C1	109
Bena, Mn., U.S.	C4	100
Benāb, Iran	C3	39
Benabarre, Spain	A6	22
Bena Dibele, Zaire	B4	48
Benalla, Austl.	G8	50
Benalto, Alta.	C3	68
Benares see Vārānasi, India	C7	36
Benátky [nad Jizerou], Czech.	n18	26
Benavente, Spain	A3	22
Benavides, Tx., U.S.	F3	120
Benban, mtn., Ire.	D2	11
Benbecula, i., Scot., U.K.	C1	13
Ben Bolt, Tx., U.S.	F3	120
Benbow, Fl., U.S.	F5	86
Benbrook Lake, res., Tx., U.S.	*n9	120
Benchland, Mt., U.S.	C7	103
Ben Davis Point, c., N.J., U.S.	E2	107
Bendeleben, Mount, mtn., Ak., U.S.	B7	79
Bender Beyla, Som.	D7	47
Bendersville, Pa., U.S.	G7	115
Bendigo, Austl.	G7	50
Bendorf, W. Ger.	E3	19
Bené Beraq, Isr.	g10	41
Benedict, Ks., U.S.	E8	93
Benedict, Md., U.S.	C4	97
Benedict, Ne., U.S.	C8	104
Benedict, N.D., U.S.	B4	111
Benedict, Mount, mtn., Newf.	g10	72
Benedicta, Me., U.S.	C4	96
Benenitra, Madag.	h9	49
Beneraird, hill, Scot., U.K.	A6	13
Benešov, Czech.	D3	26
Bénestroff, Fr.	F6	17
Benevento, Italy	D5	23
Benevolence, Ga., U.S.	E2	87
Benewah, co., Id., U.S.	B2	89
Benezett, Pa., U.S.	D5	115
Benfeld, Fr.	A3	20
Bengal, Ok., U.S.	C6	113
Bengal, Bay of, b., Asia	F8	36
Ben Gardane, Tun.	C7	44
Bengbu, China	E8	31
Benghazi (Banghāzī), Libya	*C4	44
Bengkalis, Indon.	E2	34
Bengkalis, i., Indon.	L5	35
Bengkulu, Indon.	F2	34
Bengo, dept., Ang.	C1	48
Bengough, Sask.	H3	75
Benguela, Ang.	D1	48
Benguela, dept., Ang.	D1	48
Ben Hill, co., Ga., U.S.	E3	87
Beni, Zaire	A4	48
Beni, stm., Bol.	B2	55
Beni Abbas, Alg.	C4	44
Benicarló, Spain	B6	22
Benicia, Ca., U.S.	C2	82
Benicito, stm., Bol.	B2	55
Beni Mellal, Mor.	C4	44
Benin, ctry., Afr.	E5	45
Benin, Bight of, Afr.	E6	45
Benin City, Nig.	E6	45
Beni Saf, Alg.	B4	44
Benito Juárez, Arg.	B5	54
Benjamin, Tx., U.S.	C3	120
Benkelman, Ne., U.S.	D4	104
Benkovac, Yugo.	C2	24
Ben Lomond, Ar., U.S.	D1	81
Ben Lomond, Ca., U.S.	*D2	82
Benmore, Lake, res., N.Z.	P12	51
Bennet, Ne., U.S.	D9	104
Bennett, Co., U.S.	B6	83
Bennett, Ia., U.S.	C7	92
Bennett, N.C., U.S.	B3	110
Bennett, Wi., U.S.	B2	126
Bennett, co., S.D., U.S.	D4	118
Bennett Creek, stm., Md., U.S.	B3	97
Bennett Island, i., Sov. Un.	B18	29
Bennett Lake, l., Man.	D4	70
Bennettsbridge, Ire.	E4	11
Bennettsville, S.C., U.S.	B8	117
Bennington, Id., U.S.	G7	89
Bennington, In., U.S.	G7	91
Bennington, Ks., U.S.	C6	93
Bennington, Ne., U.S.	g12	104
Bennington, N.H., U.S.	D3	106
Bennington, Ok., U.S.	C5	113
Bennington, Vt., U.S.	F2	122
Bennington, co., Vt., U.S.	E2	122
Bennion, Ut., U.S.	*C4	121
Benns Church, Va., U.S.	k14	123
Benoit, Ms., U.S.	B2	101
Benoit, Wi., U.S.	B2	126
Benoits Cove, Newf.	D2	72
Bénoué (Benue), stm., Afr.	E7	45
Benoy, Chad	D3	46
Bensalem, Pa., U.S.	*F12	115
Bensberg, W. Ger.	C2	19
Bensenville, Il., U.S.	B6	90
Bensheim, W. Ger.	D4	18
Bensley, Va., U.S.	C5	123
Benson, Az., U.S.	F5	80
Benson, Il., U.S.	C4	90
Benson, La., U.S.	C3	95
Benson, Md., U.S.	A5	97
Benson, Mn., U.S.	E3	100
Benson, N.C., U.S.	B4	110
Benson, Vt., U.S.	D2	122
Benson, co., N.D., U.S.	A6	111
Bens Run, W.V., U.S.	B3	125
Bent, N.M., U.S.	C4	108
Bent, co., Co., U.S.	D7	83
Bentheim, W. Ger.	A2	19
Bentinck, i., Burma	G2	35
Bentiu, Sud.	D2	47
Bentley, Alta.	C3	68
Bentley, Ks., U.S.	E6	93
Bentley, La., U.S.	C3	95
Bentley, Mi., U.S.	E6	99
Bentley, N.D., U.S.	C3	111
Bentley, Ok., U.S.	C5	113
Bentley Creek, Pa., U.S.	C8	115
Bentley Springs, Md., U.S.	A4	97
Bentleyville, Pa., U.S.	F1	115
Benton, N.B.	D2	71
Benton, Ar., U.S.	C3	81
Benton, Ca., U.S.	D4	82
Benton, Il., U.S.	E5	90
Benton, Ks., U.S.	E6	93
Benton, Ky., U.S.	f9	94
Benton, La., U.S.	B2	95
Benton, Me., U.S.	D3	96
Benton, Ms., U.S.	C3	101
Benton, Mo., U.S.	D8	102
Benton, Pa., U.S.	D9	115
Benton, Tn., U.S.	D9	119
Benton, Wi., U.S.	F3	126
Benton, co., Ar., U.S.	A1	81
Benton, co., In., U.S.	C3	91
Benton, co., Ia., U.S.	B5	92
Benton, co., Ms., U.S.	A4	101
Benton, co., Mo., U.S.	C4	102
Benton, co., Or., U.S.	C3	114
Benton, co., Tn., U.S.	A3	119
Benton, co., Wa., U.S.	C6	124
Benton City, Mo., U.S.	B6	102
Benton City, Wa., U.S.	C6	124
Benton Harbor, Mi., U.S.	F4	99
Benton Heights, Mi., U.S.	F4	99
Bentonia, Ms., U.S.	C3	101
Benton Ridge, Oh., U.S.	A2	112
Bentonville, Ar., U.S.	A1	81
Bentonville, Oh., U.S.	D2	112
Ben Tre, Viet.	G7	35
Bentung, Malay.	K4	35
Benue (Bénoué), stm., Afr.	E6	45
Benwee Head, c., Ire.	C2	11
Benwood, W.V., U.S.	f8	125
Benxi, China	C9	31
Benzie, co., Mi., U.S.	D4	99
Benzonia, Mi., U.S.	D4	99
Beo, Indon.	E7	34
Béoumi, I.C.	E3	45
Beowawe, Nv., U.S.	C5	105
Beppu, Japan	J5	33
Beqa, Fiji	I15	52
Beqa Passage, strt., Fiji	I14	52
Berach, stm., India	H6	37
Berati, Alb.	D3	24
Berau, W. Ger.	A5	21
Berau Bay, b., Indon.	F9	35
Berbera, Som.	C6	47
Berbérati, Cen. Afr. Rep.	B3	48
Berbice, stm., Guy.	B3	59
Berceto, Italy	E5	20
Bercher, Switz.	C2	21
Berchtesgaden, W. Ger.	E6	18
Berck, Fr.	B8	16
Berclair, Tx., U.S.	E4	120
Berdsk, Sov. Un.	C10	28
Berdyansk, Sov. Un.	H11	27
Berea, Ky., U.S.	C5	94
Berea, Ne., U.S.	B3	104
Berea, Oh., U.S.	A4	112
Berea, S.C., U.S.	B3	117
Berebere, Indon.	E7	34
Beregovo, Sov. Un.	G4	27
Bereku, Tan.	B6	48
Berens, stm., Can.	C3	70
Berens Island, i., Man.	C2	70
Berens River, Man.	C3	70
Beresford, S.D., U.S.	D9	118
Berettyóújfalu, Hung.	B5	24
Berezhany, Sov. Un.	G5	27
Berezna, stm., Sov. Un.	E7	27
Bereznik, Sov. Un.	F8	27
Berezniki, Sov. Un.	D8	29
Berezovo, Sov. Un.	C9	28
Berg, Nor.	q27	14
Berga, Spain	A6	22
Berga, Swe.	B8	15
Berga, E. Ger.	C5	25
Bergamasque Alps, mts., Italy	A2	23
Bergamo, Italy	B2	23
Bergedorf, W. Ger.	B5	18
Bergen, W. Ger.	F3	15
Bergen, Nor.	G1	14
Bergen, N.Y., U.S.	B3	109
Bergen, N.D., U.S.	A5	111
Bergen, co., N.J., U.S.	A4	107
Bergen aan Zee, Neth.	B4	17
Bergen [auf Rügen], E. Ger.	A6	18
Bergen see Mons, Bel.	B5	16
Bergenfield, N.J., U.S.	B4	107
Bergen op Zoom, Neth.	C6	16
Bergerac, Fr.	E4	16
Bergheim, Tx., U.S.	h7	120
Bergholz, Oh., U.S.	B5	112
Bergisch Gladbach, W. Ger.	C2	19
Bergkamen, W. Ger.	B2	19
Bergland, Mi., U.S.	m12	99
Bergman, Ar., U.S.	A2	81
Bergoo, W.V., U.S.	C4	125
Bergstrom Air Force Base, mil., Tx., U.S.	D4	120
Bergton, Va., U.S.	B4	123
Bergün, Switz.	C8	21
Bering Sea	D32	128
Bering Strait, strt.	C6	79
Berino, N.M., U.S.	E3	108
Berislav, Sov. Un.	H9	27
Berja, Spain	D4	22
Berkane, Mor.	C4	44
Berkeley, Ont.	C4	73
Berkeley, Ca., U.S.	*k9	90
Berkeley, Il., U.S.	f8	94
Berkeley, Ky., U.S.	f13	102
Berkeley, Mo., U.S.	B4	116
Berkeley, co., S.C., U.S.	E8	117
Berkeley, co., W.V., U.S.	B6	125
Berkeley, Cabo, c., Ec.	f5	58
Berkeley Heights, N.J., U.S.	B4	107
Berkeley Springs, W.V., U.S.	B6	125
Berkley, Ia., U.S.	C3	92
Berkley, Ma., U.S.	C5	98
Berkley, Mi., U.S.	F7	99
Berkner Island, i., Ant.	B7	7
Berkovitsa, Bul.	D6	24
Berks, co., Pa., U.S.	F9	115
Berkshire, Ma., U.S.	A1	98
Berkshire, N.Y., U.S.	C4	109
Berkshire, Vt., U.S.	B3	122
Berkshire, co., Ma., U.S.	B1	98
Berkshire Estates, Ct., U.S.	D2	84
Berkshire Hills, hills, Ma., U.S.	B1	98
Berland, Alta.	C1	68
Berleburg, W. Ger.	B3	19
Berlin (East), E. Ger.	B6	18
Berlin (West), W. Ger.	B6	18
Berlin, Ct., U.S.	C5	84
Berlin, Ga., U.S.	E3	87
Berlin, Md., U.S.	D7	97
Berlin, Ma., U.S.	B4	98
Berlin, N.H., U.S.	B4	106
Berlin, N.J., U.S.	D3	107
Berlin, N.Y., U.S.	C7	109
Berlin, Oh., U.S.	B4	112
Berlin, Pa., U.S.	G4	115
Berlin, Wi., U.S.	E5	126
Berlin, Mount, mtn., Ant.	B35	7
Berlin Corners, Ct., U.S.	C3	122
Berlin Heights, Oh., U.S.	A3	112
Berlin Lake, res., Oh., U.S.	B4	112
Berlin Mountain, mtn., Ma., U.S.	A1	98
Berlin [West], state, W. Ger.	F7	15
Bermejo, stm., S.A.	A5	54
Bermejo, stm., S.A.	A4	54
Bermeo, Spain	A4	22
Bermuda, dep., N.A.	F14	61
Bermuda, i., Ber.	p20	64
Bern, Switz.	C3	21
Bern, Ks., U.S.	C8	93
Bern, state, Switz.	C3	21
Bernalillo, N.M., U.S.	B3	108
Bernalillo, co., N.M., U.S.	C3	108
Bernam, stm., Malay.	K4	35
Bernard, Ia., U.S.	B7	92
Bernard Lake, l., Ont.	B5	73
Bernardsville, N.J., U.S.	B3	107
Bernasconi, Arg.	B4	54
Bernau [am Chiemsee], W. Ger.	B8	20
Bernau [bei Berlin], E. Ger.	B6	18
Bernay, Fr.	C4	16
Bernburg, E. Ger.	C5	18
Berndorf, Aus.	C8	19
Berne, In., U.S.	C8	91
Berne, N.Y., U.S.	C6	109
Bernese Alps, mts., Switz.	E3	21
Bernice, La., U.S.	B3	95
Bernie, Mo., U.S.	E8	102
Bernina, Piz, mtn., Eur.	C5	20
Bernina Pass, Switz.	C6	21
Bernville, Pa., U.S.	F9	115
Beroroha, Madag.	h9	49
Beroun, Czech.	C4	26
Beroun, Mn., U.S.	E6	100
Berounka, stm., Czech.	C3	26
Berrechid, Mor.	C3	44
Berri, Austl.	F7	50
Berriane, Alg.	C5	44
Berrien, co., Ga., U.S.	E3	87
Berrien, co., Mi., U.S.	F4	99
Berrien Springs, Mi., U.S.	G4	99
Berry, Al., U.S.	B2	78
Berry, Ky., U.S.	B5	94
Berry, hist. reg., Fr.	E5	16
Berry Creek, stm., Alta.	D5	68
Berrydale, Fl., U.S.	u14	86
Berryessa, Lake, res., Ca., U.S.	C2	82
Berry Hill, Tn., U.S.	g10	119
Berryman, Mo., U.S.	D6	102
Berryton, Ga., U.S.	B1	87

Index

Name — Map Ref. — Page

Berryton, Ks., U.S. m14 93
Berryville, Ar., U.S. A2 81
Berryville, Va., U.S. A5 123
Bersenbrück, W. Ger. B7 17
Bershad, Sov. Un. G7 27
Bertha, Mn., U.S. D3 100
Berthier, co., Que. C4 74
Berthierville, Que. C4 74
Berthold, N.D., U.S. A4 111
Berthoud, Co., U.S. A5 83
Berthoud Pass, Co., U.S. B5 83
Bertie, co., N.C., U.S. A5 110
Bertoua, Cam. E2 46
Bertraghboy Bay, b., Ire. D2 11
Bertram, Tx., U.S. D4 120
Bertrand, Mi., U.S. *G5 99
Bertrand, Mo., U.S. E8 102
Bertrand, Ne., U.S. D6 104
Bertrandville, La., U.S. E5 95
Bertrix, Bel. C6 16
Berwick, N.S. D5 71
Berwick, Il., U.S. C3 90
Berwick, Ia., U.S. e8 92
Berwick, La., U.S. E4 95
Berwick, Me., U.S. E2 96
Berwick, N.D., U.S. A5 111
Berwick, Pa., U.S. D9 115
Berwick-upon-Tweed, Eng., U.K. C6 10
Berwind, W.V., U.S. D3 125
Berwyn, Alta. A2 68
Berwyn, Il., U.S. k9 90
Berwyn, Ne., U.S. C6 104
Berwyn, Pa., U.S. o20 115
Beryl, Ut., U.S. F2 121
Besalampy, Madag. g8 49
Besançon, Fr. D7 16
Besar Hantu, mtn., Malay. K4 35
Beskid Mountains, mts., Eur. D5 26
Beskra, Alg. C6 44
Besnard Lake, l., Sask. B2 75
Besni, Tur. D11 40
Bessèges, Fr. E6 16
Bessemer, Al., U.S. B3 78
Bessemer, Mi., U.S. n11 99
Bessemer, Pa., U.S. E1 115
Bessemer City, N.C., U.S. B1 110
Bessie, Ok., U.S. B3 113
Best, Tx., U.S. D2 120
Bestfield, De., U.S. *B3 85
Bestobe, Sov. Un. C8 28
Betafo, Madag. g9 49
Betanzos, Spain A1 22
Bétaré Oya, Cam. D2 46
Betatakin Ruin, hist., Az., U.S. A5 80
Bet Guvrin, Isr. C6 41
Bethalto, Il., U.S. E3 90
Bethanien, Nmb. C2 49
Bethany, Ont. C6 73
Bethany, Ct., U.S. D4 84
Bethany, Il., U.S. D5 90
Bethany, In., U.S. F5 91
Bethany, La., U.S. B1 95
Bethany, Mo., U.S. A3 102
Bethany, Oh., U.S. n13 112
Bethany, Ok., U.S. B4 113
Bethany, W.V., U.S. A4 125
Bethany see Al 'Ayzarīyah, Isr. Occ. h12 41
Bethany Beach, De., U.S. F5 85
Bethel, Ak., U.S. C7 79
Bethel, Ct., U.S. D2 84
Bethel, De., U.S. F3 85
Bethel, Ky., U.S. B6 94
Bethel, Me., U.S. D2 96
Bethel, Mo., U.S. B5 102
Bethel, N.C., U.S. B5 110
Bethel, Oh., U.S. D1 112
Bethel, Ok., U.S. C7 113
Bethel, Pa., U.S. F9 115
Bethel, Vt., U.S. D3 122
Bethel Acres, Ok., U.S. #C2 113
Bethel Park, Pa., U.S. k14 115
Bethel Springs, Tn., U.S. B3 119
Bethera, S.C., U.S. E8 117
Bethesda, Wales, U.K. A3 12
Bethesda, Ar., U.S. B4 81
Bethesda, Md., U.S. C3 97
Bethesda, Oh., U.S. B4 112
Bethlehem (Bayt Laḥm), Isr. Occ. G10 40
Bethlehem, S. Afr. C4 49
Bethlehem, Ct., U.S. C3 84
Bethlehem, Ga., U.S. C3 87
Bethlehem, In., U.S. G7 91
Bethlehem, Md., U.S. C6 97
Bethlehem, N.H., U.S. B3 106
Bethlehem, Pa., U.S. E11 115
Bethlehem, W.V., U.S. f8 125
Bethlehem Junction, N.H., U.S. B3 106
Bethpage, N.Y., U.S. *E7 109
Bethpage, Tn., U.S. A5 119
Bethulie, S. Afr. D4 49
Bethune, Sask. G3 75
Béthune, Fr. B5 16
Bethune, Co., U.S. B8 83
Bethune, S.C., U.S. C7 117
Betio, i., Kir. R18 52
Betioky, Madag. h8 49
Bet Neḥemya, Isr. h10 41
Betong, Thai. D2 34
Betoota, Austl. B3 51
Betpak-Dala, des., Sov. Un. D7 28
Betroka, Madag. h9 49
Bet Sh'ean, Isr. B7 41
Bet Shemesh, Isr. C6 41
Betsiamites, Que. k13 74
Betsiboka, stm., Madag. g9 49
Betsie, Point, c., Mi., U.S. D4 99
Betsy Layne, Ky., U.S. C7 94
Bette, mtn., Libya E3 43
Bettendorf, Ia., U.S. C7 92
Betterton, Md., U.S. B5 97
Bettiah, India D10 37
Bettles Field, Ak., U.S. B9 79
Bettsville, Oh., U.S. A2 112
Bettyhill, Scot., U.K. A4 10
Betūl, India D6 36
Betwa, stm., India D6 36
Betzdorf, W. Ger. C2 19
Beulah, Al., U.S. C4 78
Beulah, Co., U.S. C6 83
Beulah, Mi., U.S. D4 99
Beulah, Ms., U.S. B3 101
Beulah, N.D., U.S. B4 111
Beulah, Wy., U.S. B8 127
Beulah, Lake, l., Ms., U.S. B3 101
Beulaville, N.C., U.S. C5 110
Beuthen see Bytom, Pol. C5 26
B. Everett Jordan Lake, res., N.C., U.S. B3 110
Beverley, Sask. G1 75
Beverley, Eng., U.K. D6 10
Beverley Head, c., Newf. D2 72
Beverly, Ks., U.S. C6 93
Beverly, Ky., U.S. D6 94
Beverly, Ma., U.S. A6 98
Beverly, N.J., U.S. C3 107
Beverly, Oh., U.S. C4 112
Beverly, Tn., U.S. m14 119
Beverly, W.V., U.S. C5 125
Beverly Hills, Ca., U.S. m12 82
Beverly Hills, Mi., U.S. *o15 99
Beverly Shores, In., U.S. A4 91
Beverstedt, W. Ger. E2 15
Beverwijk, Neth. A6 16
Bewdley, Ont. C6 73
Bex, Switz. D3 21
Bexar, co., Tx., U.S. E3 120
Bexhill-on-Sea, Eng., U.K. D8 12
Bexley, Ms., U.S. E5 101
Bexley, Oh., U.S. m11 112
Beya, Sov. Un. E27 8
Beyer, Pa., U.S. E3 115
Beykoz, Tur. B7 25
Beyla, Gui. E3 45
Beylul, Eth. C5 47
Beypazarı, Tur. B8 40
Beyşehir, Tur. D8 40
Beyşehir, Lake, l., Tur. D8 40
Bezau, Aus. B5 20
Bezerros, Braz. C3 57
Bezhetsk, Sov. Un. C11 27
Béziers, Fr. F5 16
Bezmer, Bul. D8 24
Bezons, Fr. g9 16
Bhādra, India C6 36
Bhadrāchalam, India I8 37
Bhadrak, India G11 37
Bhāg, Pak. C4 36
Bhāgalpur, India C8 36
Bhakkar, Pak. B5 36
Bhaktapur, Nepal C8 36
Bhamo, Burma D10 36
Bhandāra, India C6 36
Bharatpur, India C6 36
Bharatpur, Nepal D10 37
Bharūch, India D5 36
Bhātpāra, India D8 36
Bhāvnagar, India D5 36
Bhawānipatna, India H9 37
Bheigeir, Beinn, hill, Scot., U.K. E2 13
Bhilai (Bhilainagar), India *D7 36
Bhilai, India G8 37
Bhīlwāra, India E5 37
Bhīma, stm., India E6 36
Bhind, India C6 36
Bhiwāni, India C6 37
Bhola, Bngl. F13 37
Bhopāl, India D6 36
Bhor, India E5 36
Bhubaneshwar, India D8 36
Bhuj, India D4 36
Bhumiphol (Yanhee) Dam, Thai. D3 35
Bhusāwal, India G5 37
Bhutan, ctry., Asia C9 36
Bia, Mount, mtn., Laos B2 34
Biaboye, Zaire A4 48
Biafra, Bight of, Afr. E1 46
Biak, i., Indon. F9 34
Biała, stm., Pol. h10 26
Biała Podlaska, Pol. B7 26
Biała Przemsza, stm., Pol. g11 26
Białogard (Belgard), Pol. A4 26
Białystok, Pol. B7 26
Bian, Bidean nam, mtn., Scot., U.K. D4 13
Bianco, Italy E6 23
Biankouma, I.C. E3 45
Biarritz, Fr. F3 16
Biasca, Switz. C4 20
Bibā, Eg. D6 43
Bibai, Japan E10 33
Bibala, Ang. D1 48
Bibb, co., Al., U.S. C2 78
Bibb, co., Ga., U.S. D3 87
Bibb City, Ga., U.S. D2 87
Biberach, W. Ger. D4 18
Biberist, Switz. B4 21
Bibiani, Ghana E4 45
Bible Grove, Il., U.S. E5 90
Bible Hill, Tn., U.S. B3 119
Bic, Que. A9 74
Bic, Île du, i., Que. A9 74
Bicaz, Lake, res., Rom. B8 24
Bicester, Eng., U.K. C6 12
Biche, Lac la, l., Alta. B4 68
Bichl, W. Ger. B7 20
Bickerton, Cape, c., Ant. C26 7
Bickett Knob, mtn., W.V., U.S. D4 125
Bickle Knob, mtn., W.V., U.S. C5 125
Bickleton, Wa., U.S. C5 124
Bickmore, W.V., U.S. C3 125
Bicknell, In., U.S. G3 91
Bicknell, Ut., U.S. E4 121
Bicoli, Indon. E7 34
Bicske, Hung. B4 24
Bīd, India H5 37
Bida, Nig. E6 45
Bīdar, India E6 36
Biddeford, Me., U.S. E2 96
Biddiyā, Isr. Occ. g11 41
Biddle, Mt., U.S. E11 103
Bideford, Eng., U.K. E4 10
Bidwell, Oh., U.S. D3 112
Bidwell, Mount, mtn., Ca., U.S. B3 82
Bié, dept., Ang. D2 48
Bieber, Ca., U.S. B3 82
Biebrza, stm., Pol. B7 26
Biedenkopf, W. Ger. C3 19
Biel, Switz. E3 18
Biel, Switz. B3 21
Biel (Bienne), Lake, l., Switz. B3 20
Bielawa, Pol. C4 26
Bield, Man. D1 70
Bielefeld, W. Ger. B4 18
Biella, Italy B2 23
Bielsko-Biała, Pol. D5 26
Bielsk Podlaski, Pol. B7 26
Bienfait, Sask. H4 75
Bien Hoa, Viet. G7 35
Bienville, La., U.S. B3 95
Bienville, co., La., U.S. B2 95
Bienville, Lac, l., Que. g12 74
Bierawka, stm., Pol. g9 26
Bière, Switz. C1 21
Bieruń Nowy, Pol. g10 26
Bieruń Stary, Pol. g10 26
Biese, stm., E. Ger. F5 15
Bietigheim, W. Ger. E4 19
Bièvre, stm., Fr. g9 16
Bièvres, Fr. h9 16
Biferno, stm., Italy D5 23
Big, stm., Sask. D2 75
Big, stm., Mo., U.S. c7 102
Biga, Tur. B6 25
Big A Mountain, mtn., Va., U.S. e9 123
Big Arm, Mt., U.S. C2 103
Big Bald, mtn., U.S. f10 110
Big Bald, mtn., Ga., U.S. B2 87
Big Bald Mountain, mtn., N.B. B3 71
Big Baldy, mtn., Id., U.S. E3 89
Big Baldy Mountain, mtn., Mt., U.S. D6 103
Big Bay, Mi., U.S. B3 99
Big Bay, b., N.Z. P11 51
Big Bay De Noc, b., Mi., U.S. C4 99
Big Bayou, stm., Ar., U.S. D4 81
Big Bear, Ca., U.S. *E5 82
Big Bear City, Ca., U.S. E5 82
Big Beaver, Sask. H3 75
Bigbee Valley, Ms., U.S. B5 101
Big Belt Mountains, mts., Mt., U.S. D5 103
Big Bend, Ca., U.S. B3 82
Big Bend, La., U.S. C4 95
Big Bend, Wi., U.S. n11 126
Big Bend Dam, S.D., U.S. C6 118
Big Bend National Park, Tx., U.S. E1 120
Big Bend Reservoir, res., Alta. C3 68
Big Birch Lake, l., Mn., U.S. E4 100
Big Black, stm., Me., U.S. B3 96
Big Black, stm., Ms., U.S. C3 101
Big Blue, stm., In., U.S. E6 91
Big Bone, Ky., U.S. k13 94
Big Bow, Ks., U.S. E2 93
Big Burro Mountains, mts., N.M., U.S. E1 108
Big Butt, mtn., Tn., U.S. C11 119
Big Cabin, Ok., U.S. A6 113
Big Cabin Creek, stm., Ok., U.S. A6 113
Big Canyon, val., Tx., U.S. D1 120
Big Chino Wash, val., Az., U.S. B3 80
Big Clifty, Ky., U.S. C3 94
Big Coal, stm., W.V., U.S. C3 125
Big Corney Bayou, stm., U.S. D3 81
Big Costilla Peak, mtn., N.M., U.S. A4 108
Big Creek, B.C. D6 69
Big Creek, Ca., U.S. D4 82
Big Creek, Id., U.S. D3 89
Big Creek, Ky., U.S. C6 94
Big Creek, Ms., U.S. B4 101
Big Creek, W.V., U.S. C2 125
Big Creek, stm., B.C. D6 69
Big Creek, stm., Ar., U.S. C5 81
Big Creek, stm., In., U.S. H2 91
Big Creek, stm., In., U.S. G7 91
Big Creek, stm., Ks., U.S. D4 93
Big Creek, stm., La., U.S. B4 95
Big Creek, stm., Ms., U.S. D5 101
Big Creek, stm., Mo., U.S. C3 102
Big Creek, stm., Tn., U.S. e8 119
Big Creek Lake, res., Al., U.S. E1 78
Big Creek Peak, mtn., Id., U.S. E5 89
Big Cypress Indian Reservation, Fl., U.S. F5 86
Big Cypress Swamp, sw., Fl., U.S. F5 86
Big Darby Creek, stm., Oh., U.S. C2 112
Big Delta, Ak., U.S. C10 79
Big Dry Creek, stm., Mt., U.S. C10 103
Big Duke Dam, N.C., U.S. B2 110
Big Eau Pleine, stm., Wi., U.S. D3 126
Big Eau Pleine Reservoir, res., Wi., U.S. D4 126
Bigej Island, i., Marsh Is. S17 52
Big Elk Creek, stm., Md., U.S. A6 97
Bigelow, Ar., U.S. B3 81
Bigelow, Mn., U.S. G3 100
Bigelow, Mo., U.S. A2 102
Bigelow, Mount, mtn., Me., U.S. C2 96
Big Escambia Creek, stm., U.S. D2 78
Big Falls, Mn., U.S. B5 100
Big Flat, Ar., U.S. A3 81
Big Flat Mountain, mtn., Va., U.S. B4 123
Big Flats, N.Y., U.S. C4 109
Bigfoot, Tx., U.S. E3 120
Bigfork, Mn., U.S. C5 100
Bigfork, Mt., U.S. B2 103
Big Fork, stm., Mn., U.S. B5 100
Big Frog Mountain, mtn., Tn., U.S. D9 119
Biggar, Sask. E1 75
Biggar, Scot., U.K. E5 13
Biggerann Island, i., Marsh Is. S17 52
Biggers, Ar., U.S. A5 81
Biggersville, Ms., U.S. A5 101
Biggleswade, Eng., U.K. B7 12
Biggs, Ca., U.S. C3 82
Biggs, Or., U.S. B6 114
Biggsville, Il., U.S. C3 90
Big Gull Lake, l., Ont. C8 73
Big Gully Creek, stm., Sask. D1 75
Big Hatchet Peak, mtn., N.M., U.S. F1 108
Big Hole, stm., Mt., U.S. E4 103
Big Hole National Battlefield, hist., Mt., U.S. E3 103
Bighorn, Mt., U.S. D9 103
Big Horn, Wy., U.S. B5 127
Big Horn, co., Mt., U.S. E9 103
Big Horn, co., Wy., U.S. B4 127
Bighorn, stm., U.S. B6 76
Bighorn Canyon National Recreation Area, U.S. F8 103
Bighorn Lake, res., U.S. E8 103
Bighorn Mountains, mts., U.S. B5 127
Big Horn Mountains, mts., Az., U.S. D2 80
Bigi Island, i., Marsh Is. S17 52
Big Island, Va., U.S. C3 123
Big Island, i., N.W. Ter. D18 66
Big Island, i., N.W. Ter. f8 72
Big Kandiyohi Lake, l., Mn., U.S. F4 100
Big Knob, mtn., Pa., U.S. F6 115
Big Knob, mtn., Va., U.S. f9 123
Big Lake, Mn., U.S. E5 100
Big Lake, Tx., U.S. D2 120
Big Lake, l., Me., U.S. C5 96
Bigler, Pa., U.S. E5 115
Biglerville, Pa., U.S. G7 115
Big Lookout Mountain, mtn., Or., U.S. C9 114
Big Lost, stm., Id., U.S. F5 89
Big Moose, N.Y., U.S. B6 109
Big Mossy Point, c., Man. C2 70
Big Mountain, mtn., Nv., U.S. B2 105
Big Muddy, stm., Il., U.S. F4 90
Big Muddy Creek, stm., Mt., U.S. B12 103
Big Muddy Lake, l., Sask. H3 75
Big Nemaha, stm., Ne., U.S. D10 104
Bignona, Sen. D1 45
Big North Mountain, mts., Va., U.S. B4 123
Bigonville, Lux. E5 17
Big Otter, stm., Va., U.S. C3 123
Big Pine, Ca., U.S. D4 82
Big Pine Creek, stm., In., U.S. D3 91
Big Pine Lake, l., Mn., U.S. D3 100
Big Pine Mountain, mtn., Ca., U.S. E4 82
Big Piney, Mo., U.S. D5 102
Big Piney, Wy., U.S. D2 127
Big Piney, stm., Mo., U.S. D5 102
Big Piney Creek, stm., Ar., U.S. B2 81
Big Pipe Creek, stm., Md., U.S. A3 97
Bigpoint, Ms., U.S. E5 101
Big Pool, Md., U.S. A1 97
Big Prairie, Oh., U.S. B3 112
Big Quill Lake, l., Sask. F3 75
Big Raccoon Creek, stm., In., U.S. E4 91
Big Rapids, Mi., U.S. E5 99
Big Rib, stm., Wi., U.S. C3 126
Big River, Sask. D2 75
Big Rock, Il., U.S. B5 90
Big Rock, Tn., U.S. A4 119
Big Rock Mountain, mtn., Ar., U.S. h10 81
Big Run, Pa., U.S. E4 115
Big Sable Point, c., Mi., U.S. D4 99
Big Sandy, Mt., U.S. B6 103
Big Sandy, Tn., U.S. A3 119
Big Sandy, Tx., U.S. C5 120
Big Sandy, stm., U.S. C2 125
Big Sandy, stm., Az., U.S. C2 80
Big Sandy, stm., Tn., U.S. B3 119
Big Sandy, stm., Wy., U.S. D3 127
Big Sandy Creek, stm., Co., U.S. C8 83
Big Sandy Creek, stm., Mt., U.S. B6 103
Big Sandy Creek, stm., W.V., U.S. C3 125
Big Sandy Lake, l., Ont. E5 70
Big Sandy Lake, l., Sask. C3 75
Big Sandy Lake, l., Mn., U.S. D5 100
Big Sandy Reservoir, res., Wy., U.S. D3 127
Big Satilla Creek, stm., Ga., U.S. E4 87
Big Savage Mountain, mtn., U.S. k12 97
Big Sheep Mountain, mtn., Mt., U.S. C11 103
Big Shiney Mountian, mtn., Pa., U.S. n18 115
Big Sioux, stm., U.S. E9 118
Big Slough, stm., Ga., U.S. F2 87
Big Smoky Valley, val., Nv., U.S. E4 105
Big Snowy Mountains, mts., Mt., U.S. D7 103
Big Southern Butte, mtn., Id., U.S. F5 89
Big South Fork, stm., Ky., U.S. k13 94
Big Spencer Mountain, mtn., Me., U.S. C3 96
Big Spring, Ky., U.S. C3 94
Big Spring, Md., U.S. A2 97
Big Spring, Tx., U.S. C2 120
Big Springs, Ks., U.S. k15 93
Big Springs, Ne., U.S. C3 104
Big Springs, W.V., U.S. C3 125
Big Spruce Knob, mtn., W.V., U.S. C4 125
Big Squaw Mountain, mtn., Me., U.S. C3 96
Bigstick Lake, l., Sask. G1 75
Big Stone, co., Mn., U.S. E2 100
Bigstone, stm., Man. B4 70
Big Stone Beach, Ct., U.S. D4 85
Big Stone City, S.D., U.S. B9 118
Big Stone Gap, Va., U.S. f9 123
Bigstone Lake, l., Man. C4 70
Bigstone Lake, l., Sask. C4 75
Big Stone Lake, l., U.S. E2 100
Big Sunflower, stm., Ms., U.S. B3 101
Big Sur, Ca., U.S. D3 82
Big Thompson, stm., Co., U.S. A5 83
Big Timber, Mt., U.S. E7 103
Big Top, mtn., Tn., U.S. B5 119
Big Trout Lake, Ont. n17 73
Big Trout Lake, l., Ont. n17 73
Biguaçu, Braz. D3 56
Big Valley, Alta. C4 68
Big Walnut Creek, stm., Oh., U.S. m11 112
Big Wells, Tx., U.S. E3 120
Big Wills Creek, stm., Al., U.S. A3 78
Big Wills Valley, val., Al., U.S. A4 78
Bigwood, Ont. A4 73
Big Wood, stm., Id., U.S. F4 89
Bihać, Yugo. C2 24
Bihār, India C8 36
Bihār, state, India D8 36
Biiziri, i., Marsh Is. S18 52
Bijagós, Arquipélago dos, is., Gui.-B. D1 45
Bijāpur, India E6 36
Bījār, Iran D3 39
Bijeljina, Yugo. C4 24
Bijelo Polje, Yugo. D4 24
Bijie, China F6 31
Bijnor, India C7 37
Bijou Creek, stm., Co., U.S. B6 83
Bijou Hills, S.D., U.S. D6 118
Bīkāner, India C5 36
Bikeman Island, i., Kir. R18 52
Bikenibeu, Kir. R18 52
Bikin, Sov. Un. B11 31
Bikin, stm., Sov. Un. C7 33
Bikini, atoll, Marsh Is. F10 6
Bikini Island, i., Marsh Is. P18 52
Bikita, Zimb. B5 49
Bilāspur, India D7 36
Bilauktaung Range, mts., Asia C1 34
Bilbao, Spain A4 22
Bilbays, Eg. D3 41
Bíldudalur, Ice. n21 14
Bileća, Yugo. D4 24
Bilecik, Tur. B7 40
Biłgoraj, Pol. C7 26
Bili, Zaire A4 48
Bilin, Burma E10 36
Bílina, Czech. C8 19
Bilk Creek Mountains, mts., Nv., U.S. B3 105
Bill, Wy., U.S. C7 127
Billarp, Ga., U.S. C2 87
Billerica, Ma., U.S. A5 98
Billet, Il., U.S. E6 90
Billings, Mo., U.S. D4 102
Billings, Mt., U.S. E8 103
Billings, Ok., U.S. A4 113
Billings, co., N.D., U.S. B2 111
Billings Heights, Mt., U.S. E8 103
Billingsley, Al., U.S. C3 78
Bill Williams, stm., Az., U.S. C1 80
Bill Williams Mountain, mtn., Az., U.S. B3 80
Bilma, Niger C7 45
Biloela, Austl. D9 50
Biloxi, Ms., U.S. E5 101
Biloxi, stm., Ms., U.S. E4 101
Biloxi Bay, b., Ms., U.S. f8 101
Bilqās Qism Awwal, Eg. C3 41
Biltine, Chad C4 46
Biltmore Forest, N.C., U.S. f10 110
Bilugyun, i., Burma D2 35
Bilzen, Bel. D5 17
Bim, W.V., U.S. n12 125
Bimbéréké, Benin D5 45
Bimberi Peak, mtn., Austl. G7 51
Bimini Islands, is., Bah. B4 64
Bīna-Etāwa, India E7 37
Binangonan, Phil. o13 34
Bindloss, Alta. D5 68
Bindura, Zimb. A5 49
Binfield, Tn., U.S. D9 119
Binford, N.D., U.S. B7 111
Binga, Zaire A3 48
Binga, Monte, mtn., Afr. A5 49
Bingamon Creek, stm., W.V., U.S. k10 125
Bingen, W. Ger. D3 18
Bingen, Wa., U.S. D4 124
Binger, Ok., U.S. B3 113
Bingham, Il., U.S. D4 90
Bingham, Me., U.S. C3 96
Bingham, Ne., U.S. B3 104
Bingham, N.M., U.S. D3 108
Bingham, co., Id., U.S. F6 89
Bingham Lake, Mn., U.S. G3 100
Binghamton, N.Y., U.S. C5 109
Bingley, Eng., U.K. G7 13
Bingöl, Tur. C13 40
Binhai, China E8 31
Binjai, Indon. m11 34
Binnaway, Austl. E7 51
Binningen, Switz. A4 21
Binscarth, Man. D1 70
Bintan, i., Indon. L6 35
Bintang, mtn., Malay. J4 35
Bint Jubayl, Leb. A7 41
Bintuhan, Indon. F2 34
Bintulu, Malay. E4 34
Binxian, China D6 31
Binxian, China D3 33
Binyamina, Isr. B6 41
Biobío, prov., Chile B2 54
Biobío, stm., Chile B2 54
Bioko, i., Eq. Gui. E1 46
Biola, Ca., U.S. D3 82
Bippus, In., U.S. C6 91
Bira, Sov. Un. B6 33
Birakan, Sov. Un. B11 31
Bi'r al Uzam, Libya G4 40
Birao, Cen. Afr. Rep. C4 46
Birch, stm., Can. D4 75
Birch, stm., W.V., U.S. C4 125
Birchdale, Mn., U.S. B4 100
Birch Hill, Ct., U.S. C2 84
Birch Hills, Sask. E3 75
Birch Island, B.C. D8 69
Birch Island, i., Man. C2 70
Birch Lake, l., Alta. C5 68
Birch Lake, l., Sask. D1 75
Birch Lake, l., Mn., U.S. C7 100
Birch River, Man. C1 70
Birch Rock Hill, mtn., Pa., U.S. F3 115
Birch Run, Mi., U.S. E7 99
Birch Tree, Mo., U.S. E6 102
Birchwood, Ct., U.S. B5 84
Birchwood, Tn., U.S. D9 119
Birchwood, Wi., U.S. C2 126
Birchwood City, Md., U.S. f9 97
Birchwood Park, De., U.S. *B3 85
Birchy Bay, Newf. D4 72
Bird City, Ks., U.S. C2 93
Bird Creek, stm., Ok., U.S. A6 113
Bird Island, Mn., U.S. F4 100
Bird Island, i., N.C., U.S. D4 110
Birds, Il., U.S. E6 90
Birdsboro, Pa., U.S. F10 115
Birds Creek, Ont. B7 73
Birdseye, In., U.S. H4 91
Birdsong, Ar., U.S. B5 81
Birdsville, Austl. E6 50
Birdsville, Ky., U.S. e9 94
Birdtail Creek, stm., Man. D1 70
Birdtown, N.C., U.S. f9 110
Birdum, Austl. C5 50
Birdwood Creek, stm., Ne., U.S. C4 104
Birecik, Tur. D11 40
Bireun, Indon. J2 35
Bīrganj, Nepal D10 37
Birigui, Braz. C2 56
Birimbāl, Eg. C2 41
Bīrjand, Iran B5 38
Birk, Wādī, val., Sau. Ar. C4 38
Birkat as Sab', Eg. D3 41
Birkenfeld, W. Ger. D2 19
Birkenfeld, Or., U.S. B3 114
Birkenhead, Eng., U.K. D5 10
Bîrlad, Rom. B8 24
Bîrlad, stm., Rom. B8 24
Birmingham, Sask. G4 75
Birmingham, Eng., U.K. D6 10
Birmingham, Al., U.S. B3 78
Birmingham, Ia., U.S. D6 92
Birmingham, Mi., U.S. F7 99
Birmingham, Mo., U.S. h11 102
Birmingham, N.J., U.S. D3 107
Bir Mogreïn (Fort Trinquet), Maur. A2 45
Birnamwood, Wi., U.S. D4 126
Birney, Mt., U.S. E10 103
Birnie, Man. D2 70
Birni Ngaouré, Niger D5 45
Birnin Kebbi, Nig. D5 45
Birni Nkonni, Niger D6 45
Birobidzhan, Sov. Un. E16 29
Biron, Wi., U.S. D4 126
Birr, Ire. D3 10
Birs, stm., Switz. B3 20
Birsay, Sask. F2 75
Birsk, Sov. Un. D20 8
Birta, Ar., U.S. B2 81
Birtle, Man. D1 70
Biruuta, Mong. A6 32
Bisbee, Az., U.S. F6 80
Bisbee, N.D., U.S. A6 111
Biscay, Bay of, b., Eur. G8 8
Biscayne, Key, i., Fl., U.S. s13 86
Biscayne Bay, b., Fl., U.S. G6 86
Biscayne Gardens, Fl., U.S. *s13 86
Biscayne National Monument, Fl., U.S. G6 86
Biscayne Park, Fl., U.S. s13 86
Bisceglie, Italy D6 23
Bischheim, Fr. F7 17
Bischofshofen, Aus. B9 20
Bischofswerda, E. Ger. B9 19
Bischwiller, Fr. F7 17
Biscoe, Ar., U.S. C4 81
Biscoe, N.C., U.S. B3 110
Biscoe Islands, is., Ant. C6 7
Biševo, i., Yugo. D3 24
Bishārah, Ma'ṭan, well, Libya E4 43
Bishnupur, India F11 37
Bisho, Ciskei D4 49
Bishop, Ca., U.S. D4 82
Bishop, Ga., U.S. C3 87
Bishop, Md., U.S. D7 97
Bishop, Tx., U.S. F4 120
Bishop Auckland, Eng., U.K. F7 13
Bishopric, Sask. H3 75
Bishop's Castle, Eng., U.K. B5 12
Bishop's Falls, Newf. D4 72
Bishops Head, Md., U.S. D5 97
Bishops Mills, Ont. C9 73
Bishop's Stortford, Eng., U.K. E7 10
Bishopton, Que. D6 74
Bishopville, Md., U.S. D7 97
Bishopville, S.C., U.S. C7 117
Bismarck, Ar., U.S. C2 81
Bismarck, Il., U.S. C6 90
Bismarck, Mo., U.S. D7 102
Bismarck, N.D., U.S. C5 111
Bismarck, Cape, c., Grnld. A16 128
Bismarck Archipelago, is., Pap. N. Gui. h12 50
Bismarck Range, mts., Pap. N. Gui. k11 50
Bismarck Sea, Pap. N. Gui. h12 50
Bismark, E. Ger. F5 15
Bison, Ks., U.S. D4 93
Bison, Ok., U.S. A4 113
Bison, S.D., U.S. B3 118
Bison Lake, l., Alta. A2 68
Bison Peak, mtn., Co., U.S. B5 83
Bissau, Gui.-B. D1 45
Bissett, Man. D4 70
Bistineau, Lake, res., La., U.S. B2 95
Bistrița, Rom. B7 24
Bistrița, stm., Rom. B7 24
Bitam, Gabon E2 46
Bitburg, W. Ger. E6 17
Bitche, Fr. E7 17
Bitely, Mi., U.S. E5 99
Bitlis, Tur. C14 40
Bitola, Yugo. E5 24
Bitonto, Italy D6 23
Bittencourt, Braz. B4 58
Bitter Creek, stm., Wy., U.S. E4 127
Bitterfeld, E. Ger. B7 19
Bitterfontein, S. Afr. D2 49
Bitter Lake, l., Sask. G1 75
Bitter Lake, l., S.D., U.S. B8 118
Bittern Lake, Alta. C4 68
Bittern Lake, l., Sask. D3 75
Bitterroot, stm., Mt., U.S. D2 103
Bitterroot Range, mts., U.S. B3 89
Bittinger, Md., U.S. k12 97
Bitung, Indon. E7 34
Bityug, stm., Sov. Un. F13 27
Biu, Nig. D7 45
Bivalve, Md., U.S. D6 97
Bivalve, N.J., U.S. E2 107
Biwabik, Mn., U.S. C6 100
Biwa Lake, l., Japan n15 33
Bixby, Mn., U.S. G5 100
Bixby, Mo., U.S. D6 102
Bixby, N.C., U.S. B2 110
Bixby, Ok., U.S. B6 113
Biya, stm., Sov. Un. E26 8
Biyalā, Eg. C3 41
Biyang, China H5 32
Biysk, Sov. Un. D11 29
Bizerte, Tun. B6 44
Bjelovar, Yugo. C3 24
Bjerringbro, Den. B3 15
Bjork Lake, l., Sask. E4 75
Black, Al., U.S. D4 78
Black, Tx., U.S. B1 120
Black, stm., Asia B5 35
Black, stm., Man. D4 70
Black, stm., Jam. E13 65
Black, stm., N.A. B3 96
Black, stm., Az., U.S. D5 80
Black, stm., Ar., U.S. B4 81
Black, stm., La., U.S. C4 95
Black, stm., Mi., U.S. E8 99
Black, stm., N.Y., U.S. B4 109
Black, stm., N.C., U.S. C4 110
Black, stm., S.C., U.S. D8 117
Black, stm., Vt., U.S. E3 122
Black, stm., Vt., U.S. B4 122
Black, stm., Wi., U.S. D3 126
Black, Bayou, stm., La., U.S. E5 95
Blackall, Austl. D8 50
Black Bear Bay, b., Newf. B4 72
Black Bear Creek, stm., Ok., U.S. A4 113
Blackbeard Island, i., Ga., U.S. E5 87
Black Bear Island Lake, l., Sask. B3 75
Blackbird, De., U.S. C3 85
Blackburn, Eng., U.K. D5 10
Blackburn, Mo., U.S. B4 102
Blackburn, Ok., U.S. A5 113
Blackburn, Mount, mtn., Ak., U.S. C11 79
Black Butte, mtn., Mt., U.S. F5 103
Black Butte, mtn., Wy., U.S. B5 127
Black Butte Lake, res., Ca., U.S. C2 82
Black Butte Ranch, Or., U.S. C5 114
Black Canyon, val., Co., U.S. C3 83
Black Canyon City, Az., U.S. C3 80
Black Canyon of the Gunnison National Monument, Co., U.S. C3 83
Black Creek, B.C. E5 69
Black Creek, N.C., U.S. B5 110
Black Creek, Wi., U.S. D5 126
Black Creek, stm., U.S. B1 108
Black Creek, stm., Ms., U.S. D4 101
Black Creek, stm., S.C., U.S. B7 117
Black Diamond, Alta. D3 68
Black Diamond, Al., U.S. g6 78
Black Diamond, Wa., U.S. B4 124
Black Down Hills, hills, Eng., U.K. E5 10
Blackduck, Mn., U.S. C4 100
Black Eagle, Mt., U.S. C5 103
Black Earth, Wi., U.S. E4 126
Blackey, Ky., U.S. C7 94
Blackfalds, Alta. C4 68

Name | Map Ref. | Page

Blackfeet Indian Reservation, Mt., U.S. B4 103
Blackfoot, Alta. C5 68
Blackfoot, Id., U.S. F6 89
Blackfoot, Mt., U.S. B4 103
Blackfoot, stm., Mt., U.S. C3 103
Blackfoot Mountains, mts., Id., U.S. F7 89
Blackfoot Reservoir, res., Id., U.S. G7 89
Blackford, Ky., U.S. C2 94
Blackford, co., In., U.S. D7 91
Black Forest, Co., U.S. C6 83
Black Forest, mts., W. Ger. D4 18
Blackfork, Oh., U.S. D3 112
Blackhall Mountain, mtn., Wy., U.S. E6 127
Black Hawk, Ms., U.S. B3 101
Black Hawk, S.D., U.S. C2 118
Black Hawk, co., Ia., U.S. B5 92
Blackhead Bay, b., Newf. D5 72
Black Hills, mts., U.S. C2 118
Blackie, Alta. D4 68
Black Island, i., Ant. f38 7
Black Island, i., Man. D3 70
Black Jack, Mo., U.S. *f13 102
Blackjack Mountain, mtn., Ga., U.S. h7 87
Black Lake, Que. C6 74
Black Lake, l., Sask. m7 75
Black Lake, l., Mi., U.S. C6 99
Black Lake, l., N.Y., U.S. f9 109
Black Lake Bayou, stm., La., U.S. B2 95
Blacklick, Oh., U.S. m11 112
Black Lick, Pa., U.S. F3 115
Blacklick Estates, Oh., U.S. m11 112
Black Mesa, mtn., Az., U.S. A5 80
Black Mesa, mtn., Ok., U.S. e8 113
Black Mingo Creek, stm., S.C., U.S. D9 117
Blackmore, Mount, mtn., Mt., U.S. E6 103
Black Mountain, N.C., U.S. f10 110
Black Mountain, mtn., U.S. D7 94
Black Mountain, mtn., Az., U.S. E4 80
Black Mountain, mtn., Co., U.S. A5 83
Black Mountain, mtn., Id., U.S. C3 89
Black Mountain, mtn., Mt., U.S. D4 103
Black Mountain, mtn., Or., U.S. B7 114
Black Mountain, mtn., Wy., U.S. D7 127
Black Mountain, mtn., Wy., U.S. B5 127
Black Mountains, mts., Wales, U.K. C4 12
Black Mountains, mts., Az., U.S. B1 80
Black Oak, Ar., U.S. B5 81
Black Oak, In., U.S. A3 91
Black Peak, mtn., Az., U.S. C1 80
Black Pine Peak, mtn., Id., U.S. G5 89
Black Point, Ct., U.S. D7 84
Black Point Beach Club, Ct., U.S. *D7 84
Black Pond, l., Me., U.S. B3 96
Blackpool, Eng., U.K. D5 10
Black Range, mts., N.M., U.S. D2 108
Black River, Jam. E5 64
Black River, Mi., U.S. D7 99
Black River, N.Y., U.S. A5 109
Black River Bay, b., Jam. F13 65
Black River Falls, Wi., U.S. D3 126
Black Rock, Ar., U.S. A4 81
Black Rock, N.M., U.S. B1 108
Black Rock Desert, des., Nv., U.S. B3 105
Black Rock Range, mts., Nv., U.S. B3 105
Blacksburg, S.C., U.S. A4 117
Blacksburg, Va., U.S. C2 123
Black Sea G15 8
Blacks Fork, stm., U.S. E3 127
Blacks Harbour, N.B. D3 71
Blackshear, Ga., U.S. E4 87
Blackshear, Lake, res., Ga., U.S. E2 87
Blacksod Bay, b., Ire. C1 10
Black Springs, Ar., U.S. C2 81
Black Springs, Nv., U.S. *D2 105
Black Squirrel Creek, stm., Co., U.S. C6 83
Blackstock, Ont. C6 73
Blackstock, S.C., U.S. B5 117
Blackstone, Ma., U.S. B4 98
Blackstone, Va., U.S. C5 123
Blackstone, stm., Alta. C2 68
Blackstone, stm., R.I., U.S. B4 116
Blackstrap Reservoir, res., Sask. F2 75
Black Sugarloaf Mountain, mtn., Austl. E9 51
Blacksville, W.V., U.S. B4 125
Black Thunder Creek, stm., Wy., U.S. C8 127
Black Tickle, Newf. B4 72
Blacktown, Austl. *F9 50
Blackville, N.B. C4 71
Blackville, S.C., U.S. E5 117
Black Volta (Volta Noire), stm., Afr. E4 45
Blackwalnut Point, c., Md., U.S. C5 97
Black Warrior, stm., Al., U.S. C2 78
Blackwater, Ire. E5 11
Blackwater, Mo., U.S. C5 102
Blackwater, Va., U.S. f8 123
Blackwater, stm., Ire. E3 11
Blackwater, stm., Fl., U.S. u15 86
Blackwater, stm., Md., U.S. D5 97
Blackwater, stm., N.H., U.S. D3 106
Blackwater, stm., Va., U.S. D6 123
Blackwater Reservoir, res., Scot., U.K. D4 13
Blackwater Reservoir, res., N.H., U.S. D3 106
Blackwell, Ar., U.S. B3 81
Blackwell, Mo., U.S. C7 102
Blackwell, Ok., U.S. A4 113
Blackwell, Tx., U.S. C2 120
Blackwell, Wi., U.S. C5 126
Blackwood, N.J., U.S. D2 107
Blackwood Creek, stm., Ne., U.S. D4 104
Bladen, Ne., U.S. D7 104
Bladen, co., N.C., U.S. C4 110
Bladenboro, N.C., U.S. C4 110
Bladensburg, Md., U.S. f9 97
Bladensburg, Oh., U.S. B3 112
Blades, De., U.S. F3 85
Bladon Springs, Al., U.S. D1 78
Bladworth, Sask. F2 75
Blaeberry, stm., B.C. D2 68
Blagnac, Fr. F4 16
Blagodarnoye, Sov. Un. D2 28
Blagoevgrad (Gorna Dzhumaya), Bul. D6 24
Blagoveshchensk, Sov. Un. D20 8
Blagoveshchensk, Sov. Un. D15 29
Blain, Fr. D3 16
Blain, Pa., U.S. F7 115
Blaine, Ks., U.S. C7 93
Blaine, Me., U.S. B5 96
Blaine, Mn., U.S. m12 100
Blaine, Ms., U.S. B3 101
Blaine, Tn., U.S. C10 119
Blaine, Wa., U.S. A3 124
Blaine, co., Id., U.S. F4 89
Blaine, co., Mt., U.S. B7 103
Blaine, co., Ne., U.S. C6 104
Blaine, co., Ok., U.S. B3 113
Blaine Creek, stm., Ky., U.S. B7 94
Blaine Lake, Sask. E2 75
Blainville-sur-l'Eau, Fr. F6 17
Blair, Ks., U.S. C8 93
Blair, Ne., U.S. C9 104
Blair, Ok., U.S. C2 113
Blair, S.C., U.S. C5 117
Blair, W.V., U.S. n12 125
Blair, Wi., U.S. D2 126
Blair, co., Pa., U.S. E5 115
Blair Athol, Austl. D8 50
Blair Athol, Scot., U.K. D5 13
Blairgowrie, Scot., U.K. B5 10
Blairsburg, Ia., U.S. B4 92
Blairsden, Ca., U.S. C3 82
Blairstown, Ia., U.S. C5 92
Blairstown, Mo., U.S. C4 102
Blairsville, Ga., U.S. B3 87
Blairsville, Pa., U.S. F3 115
Blairton, W.V., U.S. B7 125
Blaisdell, N.D., U.S. A3 111
Blaj, Rom. B6 24
Blake Island, i., Wa., U.S. e11 124
Blakeley, Mn., U.S. F5 100
Blakely, Ar., U.S. C2 81
Blakely, Ga., U.S. E2 87
Blakely, Pa., U.S. m18 115
Blake Point, c., Mi., U.S. h10 99
Blakesburg, Ia., U.S. D5 92
Blakeslee, Oh., U.S. A1 112
Blakeslee, Pa., U.S. D10 115
Blâmont, Fr. F6 17
Blanc, Cap, c., Afr. B1 45
Blanc, Cap, c., Tun. F2 23
Blanc, Mont, mtn., Eur. E7 16
Blanca, Co., U.S. D5 83
Blanca, Bahía, b., Arg. B4 54
Blanca, Cordillera, mts., Peru C2 58
Blanca, Sierra, mtn., Tx., U.S. o12 120
Blanca Peak, mtn., Co., U.S. D5 83
Blanchard, Id., U.S. A2 89
Blanchard, Ia., U.S. D2 92
Blanchard, La., U.S. B2 95
Blanchard, Me., U.S. C3 96
Blanchard, Mi., U.S. E5 99
Blanchard, N.D., U.S. B8 111
Blanchard, Ok., U.S. B4 113
Blanchard, Pa., U.S. D6 115
Blanchard, Wa., U.S. A3 124
Blanchard, stm., Oh., U.S. A1 112
Blanchardville, Wi., U.S. F4 126
Blanche, Que. D2 74
Blanche, Tn., U.S. B5 119
Blanche, Lake, l., Austl. E6 50
Blanchester, Oh., U.S. C2 112
Blanco, N.M., U.S. A2 108
Blanco, Ok., U.S. C6 113
Blanco, Tx., U.S. D3 120
Blanco, co., Tx., U.S. D3 120
Blanco, stm., Arg. E2 55
Blanco, stm., Mex. n15 63
Blanco, Cabo, c., C.R. C5 62
Blanco, Cabo, c., Peru B1 58
Blanco, Cape, c., Or., U.S. E2 114
Blanc-Sablon, Que. C3 72
Bland, Mo., U.S. C6 102
Bland, Va., U.S. C1 123
Bland, co., Va., U.S. C1 123
Blandburg, Pa., U.S. E5 115
Blandford, Ma., U.S. B2 98
Blandford Forum, Eng., U.K. D5 12
Blanding, Ut., U.S. F6 121
Blandinsville, Il., U.S. C3 90
Blandville, Ky., U.S. f9 94
Blanford, In., U.S. E2 91
Blangkejeren, Indon. K2 35
Blangy-sur-Bresle, Fr. C3 17
Blankenberge, Bel. C3 17
Blankenburg, E. Ger. C5 18
Blankenfelde, E. Ger. A8 19
Blankenheim, W. Ger. C3 18
Blanket, Tx., U.S. D3 120
Blanquilla, Isla, i., Ven. A5 60
Blantyre, Mwi. E5 48
Blarney, Ire. F3 11
Blasdell, N.Y., U.S. C2 109
Blatná, Czech. D3 19
Blato, Yugo. D3 24
Blaubeuren, W. Ger. E4 19
Blauvelt, N.Y., U.S. *g13 109
Blåvands Huk, c., Den. C2 15
Blawenburg, N.J., U.S. C3 107
Blawnox, Pa., U.S. k14 115
Blaye, Fr. E3 16
Błażowa, Pol. D7 26
Bleckede, W. Ger. E4 15
Bleckley, co., Ga., U.S. D3 87
Bled, Yugo. B2 24
Błędów, Pol. g10 26
Bledsoe, Tx., U.S. C1 120
Bledsoe, co., Tn., U.S. D8 119
Bleecker, Al., U.S. C4 78
Bleicherode, E. Ger. C5 18
Blekinge, co., Swe. B8 15
Blencoe, Ia., U.S. C1 92
Blende, Co., U.S. C6 83
Blendecques, Fr. B2 17
Blenheim, Ont. E3 73
Blenheim, N.Z. N14 51
Blenheim, S.C., U.S. B8 117
Blennerhassett, W.V., U.S. B3 125
Blessing, Tx., U.S. E4 120
Blessington, Ire. D5 11
Bletchley, Eng., U.K. C7 12
Blevins, Ar., U.S. D2 81
Blija, Neth. A5 17
Blind, stm., La., U.S. h10 95
Blind River, Ont. A2 73
Bliss, Id., U.S. G4 89
Bliss, N.Y., U.S. C2 109
Blissfield, Mi., U.S. G7 99
Blissfield, Oh., U.S. B4 112
Blitar, Indon. *G4 34
Blitta, Togo E5 45
Blocher, In., U.S. G6 91
Blocker, Ok., U.S. B6 113
Block Island, R.I., U.S. h7 116
Block Island, i., R.I., U.S. h7 116
Block Island Sound, strt., U.S. G2 116
Blockton, Ia., U.S. D3 92
Blodgett, Mo., U.S. D8 102
Blodgett Landing, N.H., U.S. D2 106
Bloedel, B.C. D5 69
Bloemfontein, S. Afr. C4 49
Blois, Fr. D4 16
Blokhus, Den. A3 15
Blomberg, W. Ger. B4 19
Blommestein Meer, res., Sur. B3 59
Blönduós, Ice. n22 14
Błonie, Pol. m13 26
Blood Mountain, mtn., Ga., U.S. B3 87
Bloodsworth Island, i., Md., U.S. D5 97
Bloodvein, stm., Can. D3 70
Bloody Foreland, c., Ire. B3 11
Bloom, Ks., U.S. E4 93
Bloom, Slieve, mts., Ire. D4 11
Bloomdale, Oh., U.S. A2 112
Bloomer, Ar., U.S. B1 81
Bloomer, Wi., U.S. C2 126
Bloomfield, N.B. D4 71
Bloomfield, Ont. D7 73
Bloomfield, Ct., U.S. B5 84
Bloomfield, In., U.S. F4 91
Bloomfield, Ia., U.S. D5 92
Bloomfield, Ky., U.S. C4 94
Bloomfield, Mo., U.S. E8 102
Bloomfield, Mt., U.S. C12 103
Bloomfield, Ne., U.S. B8 104
Bloomfield, N.J., U.S. h8 107
Bloomfield, N.M., U.S. A2 108
Bloomfield, Vt., U.S. B5 122
Bloomfield Hills, Mi., U.S. o15 99
Bloomfield Township, Mi., U.S. *F7 99
Bloomingburg, Oh., U.S. C2 112
Bloomingdale, Ga., U.S. D5 87
Bloomingdale, Il., U.S. k8 90
Bloomingdale, In., U.S. E3 91
Bloomingdale, Mi., U.S. F5 99
Bloomingdale, N.J., U.S. A4 107
Bloomingdale, N.Y., U.S. f10 109
Bloomingdale, Tn., U.S. C11 119
Blooming Grove, Pa., U.S. D11 115
Blooming Grove, Tx., U.S. C4 120
Blooming Prairie, Mn., U.S. G6 100
Bloomington, Ca., U.S. *m14 82
Bloomington, Id., U.S. G7 89
Bloomington, Il., U.S. C4 90
Bloomington, In., U.S. F4 91
Bloomington, Md., U.S. m12 97
Bloomington, Mn., U.S. F5 100
Bloomington, Ne., U.S. D6 104
Bloomington, Tx., U.S. E4 120
Bloomington, Ut., U.S. *F2 121
Bloomington, Wi., U.S. F3 126
Bloomington, Lake, res., Il., U.S. C5 90
Bloomsburg, Pa., U.S. E9 115
Bloomsbury, N.J., U.S. B2 107
Bloomsdale, Mo., U.S. C7 102
Bloomville, N.Y., U.S. C6 109
Bloomville, Oh., U.S. A2 112
Blossburg, Al., U.S. f7 78
Blossburg, Pa., U.S. C7 115
Blosseville Coast, Grnld. C17 128
Blossom, Tx., U.S. C5 120
Blount, co., Al., U.S. B3 78
Blount, co., Tn., U.S. D10 119
Blounts Creek, N.C., U.S. B6 110
Blount Springs, Al., U.S. A3 78
Blountstown, Fl., U.S. B1 86
Blountsville, Al., U.S. A3 78
Blountville, Tn., U.S. C11 119
Blovice, Czech. D8 19
Blowing Rock, N.C., U.S. A1 110
Bloxom, Va., U.S. C7 123
Blucher, Sask. E2 75
Bludenz, Aus. E4 18
Blue, Az., U.S. D6 80
Blue, Ok., U.S. C5 113
Blue, stm., Co., U.S. B4 83
Blue, stm., In., U.S. H5 91
Blue, stm., Mo., U.S. k10 102
Blue, stm., Ok., U.S. C5 113
Blue, Bayou, stm., La., U.S. E5 95
Blue, Mount, mtn., Me., U.S. D2 96
Blue Anchor, N.J., U.S. D3 107
Blue Ash, Oh., U.S. o13 112
Bluebell, Ut., U.S. C5 121
Blueberry, stm., B.C. A7 69
Blue Buck Knob, hill, Mo., U.S. E5 102
Blue Buck Point, c., La., U.S. E2 95
Blue Creek, Al., U.S. g6 78
Blue Creek, Wa., U.S. A8 124
Blue Creek, W.V., U.S. m13 125
Blue Creek, stm., Ne., U.S. C3 104
Blue Creek, stm., W.V., U.S. m13 125
Blue Cypress Lake, l., Fl., U.S. E6 86
Blue Diamond, Nv., U.S. G6 105
Blue Earth, Mn., U.S. G4 100
Blue Earth, co., Mn., U.S. G4 100
Blue Earth, stm., Mn., U.S. G4 100
Bluefield, Va., U.S. C1 123
Bluefield, W.V., U.S. D3 125
Bluefields, Nic. E8 63
Bluefields Bay, b., Jam. E12 65
Blue Glacier, ice, Ant. e39 7
Blue Grass, Ia., U.S. C7 92
Blue Grass, Va., U.S. B3 123
Blue Hill, Me., U.S. D4 96
Blue Hill, Ne., U.S. D7 104
Blue Hill Falls, Me., U.S. D4 96
Blue Hill Range, hills, Ma., U.S. h11 98
Blue Hills, Ct., U.S. B5 84
Blue Hills of Couteau, hills, Newf. E3 72
Bluehole, Ky., U.S. C6 94
Blue Island, Il., U.S. B6 90
Bluejacket, Ok., U.S. A6 113
Bluejoint Lake, l., Or., U.S. E7 114
Blue Knob, mtn., Pa., U.S. F4 115
Blue Lake, Ca., U.S. B2 82
Blue Mesa Reservoir, res., Co., U.S. C3 83
Blue Mound, Il., U.S. D4 90
Blue Mound, Ks., U.S. D8 93
Blue Mountain, Al., U.S. B4 78
Blue Mountain, Ar., U.S. B2 81
Blue Mountain, Co., U.S. A2 83
Blue Mountain, Ms., U.S. A4 101
Blue Mountain, mtn., N.B. B3 71
Blue Mountain, mtn., Newf. C3 72
Blue Mountain, mtn., Ar., U.S. C1 81
Blue Mountain, mtn., Mt., U.S. C12 103
Blue Mountain, mtn., N.H., U.S. A4 106
Blue Mountain, mtn., N.M., U.S. D2 108
Blue Mountain, mtn., N.Y., U.S. B6 109
Blue Mountain, mtn., Pa., U.S. F6 115
Blue Mountain Lake, N.Y., U.S. B6 109
Blue Mountain Lake, res., Ar., U.S. B2 81
Blue Mountain Peak, mtn., Jam. E5 64
Blue Mountains, mts., Austl. F8 51
Blue Mountains, mts., Jam. E15 65
Blue Mountains, mts., U.S. A4 76
Blue Mud Bay, b., Austl. B6 50
Blue Nile, stm., Afr. C3 47
Bluenose Lake, l., N.W. Ter. C9 66
Blue Point, Me., U.S. g7 96
Blue Rapids, Ks., U.S. C7 93
Blue Ridge, Alta. B3 68
Blue Ridge, Ga., U.S. B2 87
Blue Ridge, In., U.S. E6 91
Blue Ridge, Va., U.S. C3 123
Blue Ridge, mtn., U.S. C11 76
Blue Ridge Lake, res., Ga., U.S. B2 87
Blue Ridge Summit, Pa., U.S. G7 115
Blue River, B.C. C8 69
Blue River, Or., U.S. C4 114
Blue River, Wi., U.S. E3 126
Bluesky, Alta. A1 68
Blue Springs, Al., U.S. D4 78
Blue Springs, Ms., U.S. A5 101
Blue Springs, Mo., U.S. h11 102
Blue Springs, Ne., U.S. D9 104
Blue Stack Mountains, mts., Ire. C3 11
Bluestone, stm., W.V., U.S. D3 125
Bluestone Lake, res., U.S. D4 125
Bluevale, Ont. D3 73
Bluewater, N.M., U.S. B2 108
Bluewell, W.V., U.S. D3 125
Bluff, N.Z. Q12 51
Bluff, Ut., U.S. F6 121
Bluff City, Ar., U.S. D2 81
Bluff City, Il., U.S. E4 90
Bluff City, Ks., U.S. E6 93
Bluff City, Ky., U.S. C2 94
Bluff City, Tn., U.S. C11 119
Bluff Creek, stm., Ks., U.S. E4 93
Bluff Creek, stm., Ok., U.S. A4 113
Bluff Dale, Tx., U.S. C3 120
Bluffdale, Ut., U.S. *C4 121
Bluff Knoll, mtn., Austl. F2 50
Bluff Lake, res., Ms., U.S. B5 101
Bluff Mountain, mtn., Vt., U.S. B5 122
Bluff Park, Al., U.S. g7 78
Bluffs, Il., U.S. D3 90
Bluffton, Ar., U.S. C2 81
Bluffton, Ga., U.S. E2 87
Bluffton, In., U.S. C7 91
Bluffton, Mn., U.S. D3 100
Bluffton, Oh., U.S. B2 112
Bluffton, S.C., U.S. G6 117
Bluford, Il., U.S. E5 90
Blumenau, Braz. D3 56
Blumenfeld, W. Ger. A6 21
Blumengard Colony, S.D., U.S. B6 118
Blumenhof, Sask. G2 75
Blumenthal (part of Bremen), W. Ger. B4 18
Blunt, S.D., U.S. C6 118
Bly, Or., U.S. E5 114
Blying Sound, strt., Ak., U.S. h17 79
Blyth, Ont. D3 73
Blyth, Eng., U.K. C6 10
Blythe, Ca., U.S. F6 82
Blythe, Ga., U.S. C4 87
Blythedale, Mo., U.S. A4 102
Blytheville, Ar., U.S. B6 81
Blytheville Air Force Base, mil., Ar., U.S. B6 81
Blythewood, S.C., U.S. C6 117
Bo, S.L. E2 45
Boac, Phil. C6 34
Boaco, Nic. E7 63
Bo'ai (Qinghua), China G5 32
Boali, Cen. Afr. Rep. E3 46
Boalsburg, Pa., U.S. E6 115
Board Camp, Ar., U.S. C1 81
Boardman, Oh., U.S. A5 112
Boardman, Or., U.S. B7 114
Boa Vista, Braz. B2 59
Boaz, Al., U.S. A3 78
Boaz, Wi., U.S. E3 126
Bobbili, India E7 36
Bobbio, Italy E5 20
Bobcaygeon, Ont. C6 73
Bobigny, Fr. g10 16
Böblingen, W. Ger. E4 19
Bobo, Ms., U.S. A3 101
Bobo Dioulasso, Burkina D4 45
Bobov Dol, Bul. D6 24
Bóbr, stm., Pol. C3 26
Bobrinets, Sov. Un. G9 27
Bobrka, Sov. Un. G5 27
Bobruysk, Sov. Un. E7 27
Bobtown, Pa., U.S. G2 115
Bobures, Ven. B3 60
Boca Chica Key, i., Fl., U.S. H5 86
Boca Ciega Bay, b., Fl., U.S. p10 86
Bôca do Acre, Braz. C4 58
Boca Grande, Fl., U.S. F4 86
Bocaiúva, Braz. B4 56
Bocanda, I.C. E4 45
Bocaranga, Cen. Afr. Rep. D3 46
Boca Raton, Fl., U.S. F6 86
Bocas del Toro, Pan. F6 62
Bocay, Nic. C5 62
Boccea (Buxus), Italy h8 23
Bochnia, Pol. D6 26
Bocholt, W. Ger. B1 19
Bochov, Czech. C8 19
Bochum, W. Ger. C3 18
Bock, Mn., U.S. E5 100
Bockhorn, W. Ger. E2 15
Bockum-Hövel, W. Ger. B2 19
Boda, Cen. Afr. Rep. E3 46
Bodafors, Swe. A8 15
Bodaybo, Sov. Un. D14 29
Bodcau Creek, stm., Ar., U.S. D2 81
Bodcaw, Ar., U.S. D2 81
Boddam, Scot., U.K. C7 13
Bode, Ia., U.S. B3 92
Bode, stm., E. Ger. B6 19
Bodega Head, c., Ca., U.S. C2 82
Bodele, reg., Chad B3 46
Boden, Swe. E9 14
Boden, Il., U.S. B3 90
Boderg, Lough, l., Ire. D2 10
Bodie Island, i., N.C., U.S. B7 110
Bodine, Mount, mtn., B.C. B5 69
Bodkin Point, c., Md., U.S. B5 97
Bodmin, Eng., U.K. E4 10
Bodmin Moor, for., Eng., U.K. E4 10
Bodo, Alta. C5 68
Bodö, Nor. D6 14
Bodrog, stm., Eur. A5 24
Bodrum, Tur. D6 40
Bödva, stm., Eur. A5 24
Boelus, Ne., U.S. C7 104
Boende, Zaire B3 48
Boerne, Tx., U.S. E3 120
Boeuf, stm., La., U.S. C4 95
Boeuf, Bayou, stm., La., U.S. D3 95
Boeuf, Lake, l., La., U.S. k10 95
Bofete, Braz. m7 56
Boffa, Gui. D2 45
Bogale, Burma E10 36
Bogallua, i., Marsh Is. S18 52
Bogalusa, La., U.S. D6 95
Bogan, i., Marsh Is. S18 52
Bogan, stm., Austl. E6 51
Bogandé, Burkina D4 45
Bogard, Mo., U.S. B4 102
Bogart, Ga., U.S. C3 87
Bogata, Tx., U.S. C5 120
Bogatynia, Pol. *C4 26
Bogatynia, Pol. C9 19
Bogbonga, Zaire A2 48
Bogen, W. Ger. E7 19
Bogenfels, Nmb. C2 49
Bogense, Den. C4 15
Boger City, N.C., U.S. B1 110
Boggeragh Mountains, mts., Ire. E3 11
Boggerik Island, i., Marsh Is. S17 52
Boggstown, In., U.S. E6 91
Bogno, Switz. E6 21
Bognor Regis, Eng., U.K. D7 12
Bogodukhov, Sov. Un. F10 27
Bogon, i., Marsh Is. S18 52
Bogor, Indon. G3 34
Bogor (Buitenzorg), Indon. G3 34
Bogoroditsk, Sov. Un. E12 27
Bogorodsk, Sov. Un. C14 27
Bogotá, Col. C3 60
Bogota, N.J., U.S. h8 107
Bogota, Tn., U.S. A2 119
Bogotol, Sov. Un. D26 8
Bogra, Bngl. D8 36
Boguchany, Sov. Un. D28 8
Bogué, Maur. C2 45
Bogue, Ks., U.S. C4 93
Bogue Chitto, Ms., U.S. D3 101
Bogue Chitto, stm., U.S. D5 95
Bogue Inlet, b., N.C., U.S. C5 110
Bogue Phalia, stm., Ms., U.S. B3 101
Boguslav, Sov. Un. G8 27
Bog Walk, Jam. E14 65
Bo Hai, b., China D8 31
Bohain[-en-Vermandois], Fr. C5 16
Boharm, Sask. G3 75
Bohemia, La., U.S. E6 95
Bohemia, N.Y., U.S. *n15 109
Bohemia, hist. reg., Czech. D3 26
Bohemian Forest, mts., Eur. D6 18
Bohemian-Moravian Highlands, plat., Czech. D3 26
Böhme, stm., W. Ger. F3 15
Bohmte, W. Ger. A3 19
Bohol, i., Phil. D6 34
Bohol Sea, Phil. D6 34
Boiestown, N.B. C3 71
Boiling Springs, N.C., U.S. B1 110
Boiling Springs, Pa., U.S. F7 115
Bois, Lac des, l., N.W. Ter. C7 66
Bois, Rio dos, stm., Braz. B2 56
Bois Blanc Island, i., Mi., U.S. C6 99
Bois Brule, stm., Wi., U.S. B2 126
Boischâtel, Que. C6 74
Bois-Colombes, Fr. g10 16
Boisdale, N.S. C9 71
Boisdale, Loch, b., Scot., U.K. C1 13
Bois D'Arc, Mo., U.S. D4 102
Bois-des-Filion, Que. p19 74
Bois de Sioux, stm., Mn., U.S. E2 100
Boise, Id., U.S. F2 89
Boise, co., Id., U.S. F3 89
Boise City, Ok., U.S. e8 113
Bois Fort, Mn., U.S. B5 100
Boissevain, Man. E1 70
Boissevain, Va., U.S. e10 123
Boistfort Peak, mtn., Wa., U.S. C2 124
Boisvert, Pointe au, c., Que. A8 74
Boizenburg, E. Ger. E4 15
Bojador, Cabo, c., W. Sah. D2 44
Bojnūrd, Iran B5 38
Bokchito, Ok., U.S. C5 113
Boké, Gui. D2 45
Bokeelia, Fl., U.S. F4 86
Bokhoma, Ok., U.S. D7 113
Boko, Zaire C2 48
Bokobyaadaa Island, i., Marsh Is. P18 52
Bokoro, Chad C3 46
Bokororyuru Island, i., Marsh Is. P18 52
Bokoshe, Ok., U.S. B7 113
Bokungu, Zaire B3 48
Bol, Chad C2 46
Bolafa, Zaire A3 48
Bolama, Gui.-B. D1 45
Bolaños, stm., Mex. m12 63
Bolar, Va., U.S. B3 123
Bolbec, Fr. C4 16
Bolckow, Mo., U.S. A3 102
Bole, Ghana E4 45
Boleko, Zaire B2 48
Boles, Ar., U.S. C1 81
Boles, Il., U.S. F5 90
Boles, N.M., U.S. *E4 108
Bolesławiec, Pol. C3 26
Boley, Ok., U.S. B5 113
Bolgatanga, Ghana D4 45
Bolgrad, Sov. Un. I7 27
Boli, China B11 31
Bolia, Zaire B2 48
Boligee, Al., U.S. C1 78
Bolinao, Phil. n12 34
Bolinao, Cape, c., Phil. n12 34
Boling, Tx., U.S. E5 120
Bolingbrook, Il., U.S. k8 90
Bolinger, Al., U.S. D1 78
Bolívar, Arg. B4 54
Bolívar, Col. B2 60
Bolívar, Peru C2 58
Bolivar, Mo., U.S. D4 102
Bolivar, N.Y., U.S. C2 109
Bolivar, Oh., U.S. B4 112
Bolivar, Pa., U.S. F3 115
Bolivar, Tn., U.S. B3 119
Bolivar, W.V., U.S. B7 125
Bolívar, state, Ven. B5 60
Bolívar, prov., Ec. B2 58
Bolívar, dept., Col. B3 60
Bolivar, co., Ms., U.S. B3 101
Bolívar, Cerro, mtn., Ven. B5 60
Bolivar, Lake, l., Ms., U.S. B3 101
Bolívar, Pico, mtn., Ven. B3 60
Bolivia, N.C., U.S. C4 110
Bolivia, ctry., S.A. C2 55
Bolkhov, Sov. Un. E11 27
Bollebygd, Swe. A6 15
Bollène, Fr. E6 16
Bolligen, Switz. C4 21
Bolling, Al., U.S. D3 78
Bollinger, co., Mo., U.S. D7 102
Bollnäs, Swe. G7 14
Bollullos [par del Condado], Spain D2 22
Bolmen, l., Swe. B7 15
Bolnisi, Sov. Un. B15 40
Bolobo, Zaire B2 48
Bologna, Italy B3 23
Bolognesi, Peru C3 58
Bologoye, Sov. Un. C10 27
Bolomba, Zaire A2 48
Bolon, Lake, l., Sov. Un. B8 33
Bolotnoye, Sov. Un. B10 28
Bolovens, Plateau des, plat., Laos E7 35
Bolsena, Lake, l., Italy C3 23
Bolshaya Kamenka, stm., Sov. Un. q22 27
Bolshaya Viska, Sov. Un. G8 27
Bolshevik, i., Sov. Un. B4 128
Bolshoy Irgiz, stm., Sov. Un. C3 28
Bolshoy Uzen, stm., Sov. Un. D3 28
Bolshoy Yugan, stm., Sov. Un. B8 28
Bolsward, Neth. A5 17
Bolton, Eng., U.K. D5 10
Bolton, Ct., U.S. B6 84
Bolton, Ma., U.S. B4 98
Bolton, Ms., U.S. C3 101
Bolton, N.C., U.S. C4 110
Bolton, Vt., U.S. C3 122
Bolton, stm., Man. B4 70
Bolton Center, Ct., U.S. B6 84
Bolton Lake, l., Man. B4 70
Bolton Lakes, l., Ct., U.S. B6 84
Bolton Landing, N.Y., U.S. B7 109
Bolu, Tur. B8 40
Bolus Head, c., Ire. F1 11
Bolvadin, Tur. C8 40
Bolzano, Italy A3 23
Boma, Zaire C1 48
Bomarton, Tx., U.S. C3 120
Bombala, Austl. G8 50
Bombay, India E5 36
Bombay Hook Island, i., De., U.S. C4 85
Bomboma, Zaire A2 48
Bom Conselho, Braz. C3 57
Bom Despacho, Braz. B3 56
Bom Jardim, Braz. C3 57
Bom Jardim de Goiás, Braz. B2 56
Bom Jardim de Minas, Braz. g5 56
Bom Jesus, Braz. D2 56
Bom Jesus, Braz. C2 57
Bom Jesus da Lapa, Braz. A4 56
Bomokandi, stm., Zaire A4 48
Bomongo, Zaire A2 48
Bomoseen, Vt., U.S. D2 122
Bomoseen, Lake, l., Vt., U.S. D2 122
Bom Retiro, Braz. D3 56
Bomu, stm., Afr. E4 46
Bon, Cap, c., Tun. B7 44
Bon Accord, Alta. C4 68
Bonaigarh, India G10 37
Bon Air, Al., U.S. B3 78
Bon Air, Tn., U.S. D8 119
Bon Air, Va., U.S. C5 123
Bonaire, Ga., U.S. D3 87
Bonaire, i., Neth. Ant. A4 60
Bonanza, Nic. D5 62
Bonanza, Ar., U.S. B1 81
Bonanza, Or., U.S. E5 114
Bonanza, Ut., U.S. C6 121
Bonanza City, Co., U.S. C4 83
Bonanza Peak, mtn., Wa., U.S. A5 124
Bonaparte, Ia., U.S. D6 92
Bonaparte, stm., B.C. D7 69
Bonaparte, Mount, mtn., Wa., U.S. A6 124
Bonaparte Lake, l., B.C. D7 69
Bon Aqua, Tn., U.S. B4 119
Boñar, Spain A3 22
Bonar Bridge, Scot., U.K. C4 13
Bonarlaw, Ont. C7 73
Bonasila Dome, mtn., Ak., U.S. C7 79
Bonaventure, Que. A4 71
Bonaventure, Fl., U.S. *F6 86
Bonavista, Newf. D5 72
Bonavista, Cape, c., Newf. D5 72
Bonavista Bay, b., Newf. D5 72
Bond, Co., U.S. B4 83
Bond, Ky., U.S. C5 94
Bond, Ms., U.S. E4 101
Bond, Ok., U.S. B6 113
Bond, co., Il., U.S. E4 90
Bondeno, Italy E7 20
Bondo, Zaire A3 48
Bondoukou, I.C. E4 45
Bondsville, Ma., U.S. B3 98
Bonduel, Wi., U.S. D5 126
Bondurant, Ia., U.S. C4 92
Bondurant, Wy., U.S. C2 127
Bondville, Il., U.S. C5 90
Bondville, Vt., U.S. E3 122
Bondy, Fr. g10 16
Bone, Gulf of, b., Indon. F6 34
Bone Cave, Tn., U.S. D8 119
Bone Gap, Il., U.S. E6 90
Bone Lake, l., Wi., U.S. C1 126
Bonesteel, S.D., U.S. D7 118
Bonete, Cerro, mtn., Arg. E2 55
Bonetraill, N.D., U.S. A2 111
Bonfield, Ont. A5 73
Bonfouca, La., U.S. h12 95
Bonga, Eth. D4 47
Bongandanga, Zaire A3 48
Bongor, Chad C3 46
Bong Son, Viet. C3 34
Bonham, Tx., U.S. C4 120
Bon Homme, co., S.D., U.S. D8 118
Bon Homme Colony, S.D., U.S. E8 118
Bonifacio, Fr. D2 23
Bonifacio, Strait of, strt., Eur. D2 23
Bonifay, Fl., U.S. u16 86
Bonilla, S.D., U.S. C7 118
Bonin Islands, is., Japan E8 6
Bonita, Ca., U.S. *F5 82
Bonita, La., U.S. B4 95
Bonita Springs, Fl., U.S. F5 86
Bonito, Braz. C1 56
Bonito, Braz. k6 57
Bonlee, N.C., U.S. B3 110
Bonn, W. Ger. C3 18
Bonneau, S.C., U.S. E8 117
Bonneauville, Pa., U.S. G7 115

Name	Map Ref.	Page
Bonne Bay (Woody Point), Newf.	D3	72
Bonne Bay, b., Newf.	D3	72
Bonne Idee, Bayou, stm., La., U.S.	B4	95
Bonner, Mt., U.S.	D3	103
Bonner, co., Id., U.S.	A2	89
Bonnerdale, Ar., U.S.	C2	81
Bonners Ferry, Id., U.S.	A2	89
Bonner Springs, Ks., U.S.	C9	93
Bønnerup Strand, Den.	B4	15
Bonne-sur-Ménoge, Fr.	D1	21
Bonnet, Lac du, l., Man.	A4	70
Bonnétable, Fr.	C4	16
Bonnet Clare Floodway, La., U.S.	h11	95
Bonne Terre, Mo., U.S.	D7	102
Bonneville, Fr.	C2	20
Bonneville, Or., U.S.	B5	114
Bonneville, co., Id., U.S.	F7	89
Bonneville Dam, U.S.	B4	114
Bonneville Peak, mtn., Id., U.S.	F6	89
Bonneville Salt Flats, pl., Ut., U.S.	C2	121
Bonnevoie-Sud, Lux.	*E6	17
Bonney Lake, Wa., U.S.	B3	124
Bonnie, Il., U.S.	E5	90
Bonnie Doone, N.C., U.S.	B4	110
Bonnieville, Ky., U.S.	C4	94
Bonnots Mill, Mo., U.S.	C6	102
Bonny, Nig.	F6	45
Bonny Blue, Va., U.S.	f8	123
Bonny Reservoir, res., Co., U.S.	B8	83
Bonnyville, Alta.	B5	68
Bono, Ar., U.S.	B5	81
Bono, Oh., U.S.	*A2	112
Bonorva, Italy	D2	23
Bonriki, Kir.	R18	52
Bonriki, i., Kir.	R18	52
Bons, Fr.	D1	21
Bonsal, N.C., U.S.	B4	110
Bon Secour, Al., U.S.	E2	78
Bonshaw, P.E.I.	C6	71
Bontang, Indon.	E5	34
Bonthe, S.L.	E2	45
Bon Wier, Tx., U.S.	D6	121
Book Cliffs, clf., U.S.	D6	121
Booker, Tx., U.S.	A2	120
Booker T. Washington National Monument, Va., U.S.	C3	123
Booligal, Austl.	F5	51
Boolyglass, Ire.	E4	11
Boomer, N.C., U.S.	A1	110
Boomer, W.V., U.S.	C3	125
Boon, Mi., U.S.	D5	99
Boone, Co., U.S.	C6	83
Boone, Ia., U.S.	B4	92
Boone, N.C., U.S.	A1	110
Boone, Ne., U.S.	C8	104
Boone, co., Ar., U.S.	A2	81
Boone, co., Il., U.S.	A5	90
Boone, co., In., U.S.	D4	91
Boone, co., Ia., U.S.	B3	92
Boone, co., Ky., U.S.	B5	94
Boone, co., Mo., U.S.	B5	102
Boone, co., Ne., U.S.	C7	104
Boone, co., W.V., U.S.	C3	125
Boone, stm., Ia., U.S.	B4	92
Boone Grove, In., U.S.	B3	91
Boone Lake, res., Tn., U.S.	C11	119
Boones Mill, Va., U.S.	C3	123
Booneville, Ar., U.S.	B2	81
Booneville, Ky., U.S.	C6	94
Booneville, Ms., U.S.	A5	101
Boonsboro, Md., U.S.	A2	97
Boons Pond, l., Ma., U.S.	g10	98
Boonton, N.J., U.S.	B4	107
Boonville, Ca., U.S.	C2	82
Boonville, In., U.S.	H3	91
Boonville, Mo., U.S.	C5	102
Boonville, N.Y., U.S.	B5	109
Boonville, N.C., U.S.	A2	110
Boorama, Som.	C5	47
Booth, Al., U.S.	C3	78
Boothbay, Me., U.S.	E3	96
Boothbay Harbor, Me., U.S.	E3	96
Boothby, Cape, c., Ant.	C18	7
Boothia, Gulf of, b., N.W. Ter.	B14	66
Boothia Peninsula, pen., N.W. Ter.	B14	66
Booths Creek, stm., W.V., U.S.	h11	125
Boothville, La., U.S.	E6	95
Bootle, Eng., U.K.	A4	12
Booué, Gabon	F2	46
Bophuthatswana, ctry., Afr.	C4	49
Bopolu, Lib.	E2	45
Boppard, W. Ger.	C4	16
Boquerón, dept., Para.	D3	55
Boquerón, Pan.	k11	62
Boquerón, Bahía de, b., P.R.	B1	65
Bor, Sud.	D3	47
Bor, Yugo.	C6	24
Boraha, Nosy, i., Madag.	g10	49
Borah Peak, mtn., Id., U.S.	E5	89
Borås, Swe.	I5	14
Borāzjān, Iran	G5	39
Borba, Braz.	C3	59
Borculo, Neth.	B6	17
Bordeaux, Fr.	E3	16
Bordelonville, La., U.S.	C4	95
Borden, Sask.	E2	75
Borden, co., Tx., U.S.	C2	120
Borden Island, i., N.W. Ter.	m29	66
Borden Peninsula, pen., N.W. Ter.	B16	66
Borden Springs, Al., U.S.	B4	78
Bordentown, N.J., U.S.	C3	107
Borderland, W.V., U.S.	D2	125
Borders, prov., Scot., U.K.	E5	13
Bordertown, Austl.	G7	50
Bordighera, Italy	C1	23
Bordj Bou Arreridj, Alg.	B5	44
Bordj Omar Idriss, Alg.	D6	44
Bordley, Ky., U.S.	C2	94
Bordulac, N.D., U.S.	B7	111
Boré, Mali	C4	45
Boren, i., Swe.	u33	14
Borensberg, Swe.	u33	14
Borgå, Fin.	G11	14
Börger, W. Ger.	B7	17
Borger, Neth.	B6	17
Borger, Tx., U.S.	B2	120
Borgholm, Swe.	I7	14
Borghorst, W. Ger.	A2	19
Borg Mountain, mtn., Ant.	B12	7
Borgne, stm., Switz.	D3	21
Borgne, Lac, b., La., U.S.	D6	95
Borgomanero, Italy	B2	23
Borgo Piave, Italy	k9	23
Borgosesia, Italy	E5	21
Borgo Val di Taro, Italy	B2	23
Borgo Val Sugana, Italy	C7	20
Boring, Or., U.S.	B4	114
Borislav, Sov. Un.	G4	27
Borisoglebsk, Sov. Un.	D7	29
Borisov, Sov. Un.	D7	27
Borispol, Sov. Un.	F8	27
Borja, Peru	B2	58
Borja, Spain	B5	22
Borjas Blancas, Spain	B6	22
Borken, W. Ger.	B1	19
Borken, E. Ger.	B4	19
Børkop, Den.	C3	15
Borkou, hist. reg., Chad	B3	46
Borkum, i., W. Ger.	A6	17
Borkum, W. Ger.	B3	18
Borna, E. Ger.	B7	19
Borne, Neth.	B6	17
Bornheim, W. Ger.	C1	19
Bornholm, co., Den.	C8	15
Bornholm, i., Den.	J6	14
Bornholmsgat, strt., Eur.	C8	15
Bornos, Spain	D3	22
Borobudur, hist., Indon.	G4	34
Boromlya, Sov. Un.	F10	27
Boromo, Burkina	D4	45
Boron, Ca., U.S.	E5	82
Borovan, Bul.	D6	24
Borovichi, Sov. Un.	D6	29
Borovskoye, Sov. Un.	q21	27
Borraan, Som.	C6	47
Borrby, Swe.	C8	15
Borre, Den.	D6	15
Borrego Springs, Ca., U.S.	F5	82
Borris, Ire.	E5	11
Borrisokane, Ire.	E3	11
Borrisoleigh, Ire.	E4	11
Borroloola, Austl.	C6	50
Borşa, Rom.	B7	24
Bort-les-Orgues, Fr.	E5	16
Borūjen, Iran	F5	39
Borūjerd, Iran	B4	38
Borzhomi, Sov. Un.	B14	40
Borzna, Sov. Un.	F9	27
Borzonasca, Italy	A8	31
Borzya, Sov. Un.	A8	31
Bosa, Italy	D2	23
Bosanska Dubica, Yugo.	C3	24
Bosanska Gradiška, Yugo.	C3	24
Bosanska Kostajnica, Yugo.	C3	24
Bosanski Novi, Yugo.	C3	24
Bosanski Petrovac, Yugo.	C3	24
Bosanski Šamac, Yugo.	C4	24
Bosavi, Mount, mtn., Pap. N. Gui.	k11	34
Boscawen, N.H., U.S.	D3	106
Boscobel, Wi., U.S.	E3	126
Boshan, China	D8	31
Boshrūyeh, Iran	E8	39
Boskovice, Czech.	D4	26
Bosler, Wy., U.S.	E7	127
Bosna, stm., Yugo.	C3	24
Bosnia, hist. reg., Yugo.	C3	24
Bosnik, Indon.	F9	34
Bosobolo, Zaire	A2	48
Bosporus, strt.	B7	40
Bosque, N.M., U.S.	C3	108
Bosque, co., Tx., U.S.	D4	120
Boss, Mo., U.S.	D6	102
Bossangoa, Cen. Afr. Rep.	D3	46
Bossembélé, Cen. Afr. Rep.	D3	46
Bossert Estates, N.J., U.S.	C3	107
Bossier, co., La., U.S.	B2	95
Bossier City, La., U.S.	B2	95
Bosso, Niger	D7	45
Bosten Lake, l., China	C2	31
Boston, Eng., U.K.	D6	12
Boston, Ga., U.S.	F3	87
Boston, In., U.S.	E8	91
Boston, Ky., U.S.	C4	94
Boston, Ma., U.S.	B5	98
Boston Bar, B.C.	E7	69
Boston Bay, b., Ma., U.S.	B6	98
Boston Heights, Oh., U.S.	h9	112
Boston Mountains, mts., Ar., U.S.	B2	81
Bostonnais, stm., Que.	B5	74
Bostwick, Fl., U.S.	C5	86
Bostwick, Ga., U.S.	C3	87
Boswarlos, Newf.	D2	72
Boswell, B.C.	E9	69
Boswell, Al., U.S.	D4	78
Boswell, In., U.S.	C3	91
Boswell, Ok., U.S.	C6	113
Boswell, Pa., U.S.	F3	115
Bosworth, Mo., U.S.	B4	102
Botany Bay, b., Austl.	F9	50
Boteti, stm., Bots.	B3	49
Botetourt, co., Va., U.S.	C3	123
Botev, mtn., Bul.	D7	24
Botevgrad, Bul.	D6	24
Botha, Alta.	C4	68
Bothell, Wa., U.S.	B3	124
Bothnia, Gulf of, b., Eur.	F9	14
Bothwell, P.E.I.	E3	73
Botkins, Oh., U.S.	B1	112
Botkyrka, Swe.	t35	14
Botolan, Phil.	o13	34
Botoşani, Rom.	B8	24
Botsford, Ct., U.S.	D2	84
Botswana, ctry., Afr.	B3	49
Bottineau, N.D., U.S.	A5	111
Bottineau, co., N.D., U.S.	A4	111
Bottrop, W. Ger.	B1	19
Botucatu, Braz.	C5	56
Botwood, Newf.	D4	72
Bouaflé, I.C.	E3	45
Bouaké, I.C.	E3	45
Bouar, Cen. Afr. Rep.	D3	46
Bou Arfa, Mor.	C4	44
Boucau, Fr.	F3	16
Boucher, Lac, l., Que.	C4	74
Boucherville, Que.	D4	74
Bouchette, Que.	C2	74
Boudenib, Mor.	C4	44
Boudry, Switz.	C5	21
Boû Djébéha, well, Mali	C4	45
Boudreaux, Lake, l., La., U.S.	E5	95
Bougainville, i., Pap. N. Gui.	G9	6
Bougouni, Mali	D3	45
Bouillon, Bel.	E5	17
Boulder, Co., U.S.	A5	83
Boulder, Mt., U.S.	D4	103
Boulder, Ut., U.S.	F4	121
Boulder, Wy., U.S.	D3	127
Boulder City, Nv., U.S.	H7	105
Boulder Creek, Ca., U.S.	*D2	82
Boulder Hill, Il., U.S.	*B5	90
Boulevard, Ca., U.S.	F5	82
Boulevard Heights, Md., U.S.	f9	97
Boulevard Park, Wa., U.S.	*B3	124
Bouligny, Fr.	C6	16
Boulogne-Billancourt, Fr.	g10	16
Boulogne-sur-Mer, Fr.	B4	16
Boumalne, Mor.	C3	44
Boumdeït, Maur.	C2	45
Bouna, I.C.	E4	45
Boundary, Ak., U.S.	C11	79
Boundary, co., Id., U.S.	A2	89
Boundary Bald Mountain, mtn., Me., U.S.	C2	96
Boundary Bay, b., Wa., U.S.	A3	124
Boundary Bend, Austl.	G4	51
Boundary Peak, mtn., Nv., U.S.	F3	105
Boundary Ranges, mts., N.A.	k22	79
Bound Brook, N.J., U.S.	B3	107
Boundiali, I.C.	E3	45
Bountiful, Ut., U.S.	C4	121
Bounty, Sask.	F2	75
Bounty Islands, is., N.Z.	Q17	51
Bourbeuse, stm., Mo., U.S.	C6	102
Bourbon, In., U.S.	B5	91
Bourbon, Mo., U.S.	C6	102
Bourbon, co., Ks., U.S.	E9	93
Bourbon, co., Ky., U.S.	B5	94
Bourbonnais, Il., U.S.	B6	90
Bourbonnais, hist. reg., Fr.	D5	16
Bourbonne-les-Bains, Fr.	B1	20
Bourem, Mali	C4	45
Bourg, La., U.S.	E5	95
Bourg-de-Péage, Fr.	E6	16
Bourg [-en-Bresse], Fr.	D6	16
Bourges, Fr.	D5	16
Bourget, Ont.	B9	73
Bourget, Lake, l., Fr.	D1	20
Bourg-la-Reine, Fr.	g10	16
Bourgoin [-Jallieu], Fr.	E6	16
Bourg-Saint-Andéol, Fr.	E6	16
Bourg-Saint-Maurice, Fr.	D7	16
Bou Rjeïmat, well, Maur.	C2	45
Bourke, Austl.	F8	50
Bourne, Eng., U.K.	B7	12
Bourne, Ma., U.S.	C6	98
Bournemouth, Eng., U.K.	E6	10
Bourneville, Oh., U.S.	C2	112
Bou Saâda, Alg.	B5	44
Bouse, Az., U.S.	D2	80
Bousso, Chad	C3	46
Boutilimit, Maur.	C2	45
Boutte, La., U.S.	k11	95
Bouvet, i., Ant.	D13	7
Bovey, Mn., U.S.	C5	100
Bovill, Id., U.S.	C2	89
Bovina, Ms., U.S.	C3	101
Bovina, Tx., U.S.	B1	120
Bovina Center, N.Y., U.S.	C6	109
Bow, N.H., U.S.	D3	106
Bow, Wa., U.S.	A3	124
Bow, stm., Alta.	D4	68
Bowbells, N.D., U.S.	A3	111
Bowden, Alta.	D4	68
Bowden, Ok., U.S.	A5	113
Bowdle, S.D., U.S.	B6	118
Bowdoin, Me., U.S.	f8	96
Bowdoinham, Me., U.S.	D3	96
Bowdon, Ga., U.S.	C1	87
Bowdon, N.D., U.S.	B6	111
Bowen, Austl.	C8	50
Bowen, Il., U.S.	C2	90
Bowers, De., U.S.	D4	85
Bowerston, Oh., U.S.	B4	112
Bowersville, Ga., U.S.	B3	87
Bowersville, Oh., U.S.	C2	112
Bowesmont, N.D., U.S.	A8	111
Bowie, Az., U.S.	E6	80
Bowie, Co., U.S.	C3	83
Bowie, Md., U.S.	B4	97
Bowie, co., Tx., U.S.	C5	120
Bowie, stm., Ms., U.S.	D4	101
Bow Island, Alta.	E5	68
Bowling Green, Fl., U.S.	E5	86
Bowling Green, In., U.S.	F4	91
Bowling Green, Ky., U.S.	D3	94
Bowling Green, Mo., U.S.	B6	102
Bowling Green, Oh., U.S.	A2	112
Bowling Green, S.C., U.S.	A5	117
Bowling Green, Va., U.S.	B5	123
Bowman, Ga., U.S.	B3	87
Bowman, N.D., U.S.	C2	111
Bowman, S.C., U.S.	E6	117
Bowman, co., N.D., U.S.	C2	111
Bowman Creek, stm., Pa., U.S.	m16	115
Bowman-Haley Lake, res., N.D., U.S.	C2	111
Bowmanstown, Pa., U.S.	E10	115
Bowmanville (part of Newcastle), Ont.	D6	73
Bow Mar, Co., U.S.	*B5	83
Bowmont, Id., U.S.	F2	89
Bowmore, Scot., U.K.	F6	13
Bowokan Islands, is., Indon.	F6	34
Bowral, Austl.	G8	51
Bowring, Ok., U.S.	A5	113
Bowron, stm., B.C.	C7	69
Bowron Lake Provincial Park, B.C.	C7	69
Bowser Lake, l., B.C.	A2	69
Bowsman, Man.	C1	70
Bowstring Lake, l., Mn., U.S.	C5	100
Bow Valley, Ne., U.S.	B8	104
Boxborough, Ma., U.S.	A5	98
Box Butte, co., Ne., U.S.	B2	104
Box Butte Creek, stm., Ne., U.S.	B3	104
Box Butte Reservoir, res., Ne., U.S.	B2	104
Box Elder, Mt., U.S.	B7	103
Box Elder, S.D., U.S.	C2	118
Box Elder, co., Ut., U.S.	B2	121
Box Elder Creek, stm., Co., U.S.	A6	83
Boxelder Creek, stm., Mt., U.S.	E12	103
Box Elder Creek, stm., Mt., U.S.	C8	103
Boxford, Ma., U.S.	A6	98
Boxholm, Ia., U.S.	B3	92
Boxian, China	E8	31
Boxmeer, Neth.	C5	17
Boxtel, Neth.	B6	16
Boyacá, dept., Col.	B3	60
Boyang, China	J7	32
Boyce, La., U.S.	C3	95
Boyce, Va., U.S.	A4	123
Boyceville, Wi., U.S.	n10	126
Boyd, Mn., U.S.	F2	100
Boyd, Mt., U.S.	E7	103
Boyd, Tx., U.S.	C4	120
Boyd, Wi., U.S.	D2	126
Boyd, co., Ky., U.S.	B7	94
Boyd, co., Ne., U.S.	B7	104
Boydell, Ar., U.S.	D4	81
Boyden, Ia., U.S.	A2	92
Boyd Glacier, ice, Ant.	B34	7
Boyd Lake, l., Me., U.S.	C4	96
Boyds, Md., U.S.	B3	97
Boyd's Cove, Newf.	D4	72
Boydsville, Ar., U.S.	A5	81
Boydton, Va., U.S.	D4	123
Boyer, stm., Ia., U.S.	C2	92
Boyera, Zaire	B2	48
Boyer Knob, mtn., Md., U.S.	k13	97
Boyero, Co., U.S.	C7	83
Boyers, Pa., U.S.	D2	115
Boyertown, Pa., U.S.	F10	115
Boyes, Mt., U.S.	E11	103
Boykin, Al., U.S.	C2	78
Boykins, Va., U.S.	D5	123
Boyle, Alta.	B4	68
Boyle, Ire.	C2	10
Boyle, Ms., U.S.	B3	101
Boyle, co., Ky., U.S.	C5	94
Boylston, N.S.	D8	71
Boylston, Ma., U.S.	B4	98
Boyne, stm., Ire.	C5	11
Boyne City, Mi., U.S.	C6	99
Boyne Falls, Mi., U.S.	C6	99
Boynton, Ok., U.S.	B6	113
Boynton, Pa., U.S.	G3	115
Boynton Beach, Fl., U.S.	F6	86
Boyoma Falls (Stanley Falls), wtfl., Zaire	A4	48
Boy River, Mn., U.S.	C4	100
Boys Ranch, Tx., U.S.	B1	120
Boys Town, Ne., U.S.	g12	104
Boz, Cape, c., Tur.	B7	25
Bozcaada, Tur.	C6	25
Bozca Island (Tenedos), i., Tur.	C6	25
Bozdoğan, Tur.	D7	25
Bozeman, Mt., U.S.	E5	103
Bozeman Pass, Mt., U.S.	E6	103
Bozman, Md., U.S.	C5	97
Bozoum, Cen. Afr. Rep.	D3	46
Bozovici, Rom.	C5	24
Bozqūsh, Kūh-e, mts., Iran	C3	39
Bozüyük, Tur.	C4	40
Bra, Italy	B1	23
Brabant, prov., Bel.	D4	17
Brabant, i., Ant.	C6	7
Brabant Lake, l., Sask.	A4	75
Brač, i., Yugo.	D3	24
Bracadale, Scot., U.K.	C2	13
Bracadale, Loch, b., Scot., U.K.	C2	13
Bracciano, Italy	g8	23
Bracciano, Lake, l., Italy	g8	23
Bracebridge, Ont.	B5	73
Braceville, Il., U.S.	B5	90
Brach, Libya	D2	43
Bracken, Sask.	H1	75
Bracken, co., Ky., U.S.	B5	94
Brackenridge, Pa., U.S.	h15	115
Brackett, Wi., U.S.	D2	126
Brackettville, Tx., U.S.	E2	120
Brackley, Eng., U.K.	C6	12
Bracknell, Eng., U.K.	C7	12
Brackwede, W. Ger.	B3	19
Brad, Rom.	B6	24
Bradano, stm., Italy	D6	23
Braddock, N.J., U.S.	D3	107
Braddock, N.D., U.S.	C5	111
Braddock Heights, Md., U.S.	B2	97
Braddock Point, c., S.C., U.S.	G6	117
Braddyville, Ia., U.S.	D2	92
Braden, Tn., U.S.	B2	119
Bradenton, Fl., U.S.	E4	86
Bradenville, Pa., U.S.	F3	115
Bradford, Ont.	C5	73
Bradford, Eng., U.K.	D6	10
Bradford, Ar., U.S.	B4	81
Bradford, Il., U.S.	B4	90
Bradford, Me., U.S.	C4	96
Bradford, Oh., U.S.	B1	112
Bradford, Pa., U.S.	C4	115
Bradford, R.I., U.S.	F2	116
Bradford, Tn., U.S.	A3	119
Bradford, Vt., U.S.	D4	122
Bradford, co., Fl., U.S.	C4	86
Bradford, co., Pa., U.S.	C8	115
Bradford Mountain, mtn., Ct., U.S.	B2	84
Bradfordsville, Ky., U.S.	C4	94
Bradfordwoods, Pa., U.S.	h13	115
Bradgate, Ia., U.S.	B3	92
Bradley, Al., U.S.	D2	78
Bradley, Ar., U.S.	D2	81
Bradley, Ca., U.S.	E3	82
Bradley, Fl., U.S.	E5	86
Bradley, Il., U.S.	B6	90
Bradley, Me., U.S.	D4	96
Bradley, Oh., U.S.	B5	112
Bradley, S.C., U.S.	C3	117
Bradley, S.D., U.S.	B8	118
Bradley, W.V., U.S.	D3	125
Bradley, co., Ar., U.S.	D3	81
Bradley, co., Tn., U.S.	D9	119
Bradley Beach, N.J., U.S.	C4	107
Bradleyton, Al., U.S.	D3	78
Bradner, Oh., U.S.	A2	112
Bradore Bay, b., Que.	C3	72
Bradshaw, Md., U.S.	B5	97
Bradshaw, Ne., U.S.	D8	104
Bradshaw, Tx., U.S.	C3	120
Bradshaw, W.V., U.S.	D3	125
Bradshaw Mountains, mts., Az., U.S.	C3	80
Bradstreet, Ma., U.S.	B2	98
Bradwell, Sask.	F2	75
Brady, Mt., U.S.	B5	103
Brady, Ne., U.S.	C5	104
Brady, Tx., U.S.	D3	120
Bradyville, Tn., U.S.	B5	119
Brædstrup, Den.	C3	15
Braemar, Scot., U.K.	D5	13
Braeside, Ont.	B8	73
Braga, Port.	B2	22
Bragado, Arg.	B1	57
Bragança, Braz.	B4	54
Bragança, Port.	C2	22
Bragança Paulista, Braz.	G5	57
Braggadocio, Mo., U.S.	E8	102
Braggs, Ok., U.S.	B6	113
Braham, Mn., U.S.	E5	100
Brāhmani, stm., India	D7	36
Brahmapur, India	E7	36
Brahmaputra (Yarlung Zangbo Jiang), stm., Asia	C9	36
Braidwood, Il., U.S.	B5	90
Braila, Rom.	C8	24
Brainard, Ne., U.S.	C9	104
Brainerd, Mn., U.S.	D4	100
Brainerd, Ks., U.S.	C8	12
Braintree, Eng., U.K.	C8	12
Braintree, Ma., U.S.	B5	98
Braintree, Vt., U.S.	D3	122
Braithwaite, La., U.S.	k12	95
Brake, W. Ger.	B4	19
Brakel, W. Ger.	B4	19
Brakpan, S. Afr.	*C4	49
Bralorne, B.C.	D6	69
Braman, Ok., U.S.	A4	113
Brampton, Ont.	D5	73
Brampton, Eng., U.K.	F6	13
Bramsche, W. Ger.	B7	17
Bramwell, W.V., U.S.	D3	125
Branch, Newf.	E5	72
Branch, Ar., U.S.	B2	81
Branch, La., U.S.	D3	95
Branch, Wi., U.S.	h10	126
Branch, co., Mi., U.S.	G5	99
Branch, stm., R.I., U.S.	B3	116
Branch, stm., Wi., U.S.	h10	126
Branchland, W.V., U.S.	C2	125
Branchville, Al., U.S.	B3	78
Branchville, Ct., U.S.	D2	84
Branchville, S.C., U.S.	E6	117
Branchville, Va., U.S.	D5	123
Branco, stm., Braz.	B3	55
Branco, stm., Braz.	D4	55
Brandberg, mtn., Nmb.	B1	49
Brandbu, Nor.	C3	15
Brandenburg, E. Ger.	B6	18
Brandenburg, Ky., U.S.	C3	94
Brandenburg, hist. reg., E. Ger.	B6	18
Brandon, Man.	E2	70
Brandon, Co., U.S.	C8	83
Brandon, Fl., U.S.	E4	86
Brandon, Ia., U.S.	B6	92
Brandon, Mn., U.S.	E3	100
Brandon, Ms., U.S.	C4	101
Brandon, Ne., U.S.	D4	104
Brandon, S.C., U.S.	B3	117
Brandon, S.D., U.S.	D9	118
Brandon, Vt., U.S.	D2	122
Brandon, Wi., U.S.	E5	126
Brandon Head, c., Ire.	E1	11
Brandon Mountain, mtn., Ire.	D1	11
Brandsen, Arg.	B5	57
Brandsville, Mo., U.S.	E6	102
Brandt, Oh., U.S.	C1	112
Brandt, S.D., U.S.	C9	118
Brandvlei, S. Afr.	D3	49
Brandy Peak, mtn., Or., U.S.	E3	114
Brandy Station, Va., U.S.	B5	123
Brandywine, Md., U.S.	C4	97
Brandywine, W.V., U.S.	C5	125
Brandywine Creek, stm., U.S.	A3	85
Branford, Ct., U.S.	D4	84
Branford, Fl., U.S.	C4	86
Branford Hills, Ct., U.S.	D4	84
Braniewo, Pol.	A5	26
Brańsk, Pol.	B7	26
Branson, Co., U.S.	D6	83
Branson, Mo., U.S.	E4	102
Brant, Alta.	D4	68
Brant, co., Ont.	D4	73
Brantford, Ont.	D4	73
Brantford, N.D., U.S.	B7	111
Brant Lake, N.Y., U.S.	B7	109
Brantley, Al., U.S.	D3	78
Brantley, co., Ga., U.S.	E4	87
Brant Rock, Ma., U.S.	B6	98
Brantville, N.B.	B5	71
Brantwood, Wi., U.S.	C3	126
Bras-d'Apic, Que.	C7	74
Bras-d'Or, Que.	C9	71
Bras d'Or Lake, l., N.S.	D9	71
Brasfield, Ar., U.S.	C4	81
Brashear, Mo., U.S.	A5	102
Brasília, Braz.	B2	55
Brasília de Minas, Braz.	B4	56
Brasov (Orașul-Stalin), Rom.	C7	24
Brasstown, N.C., U.S.	f9	110
Brasstown Bald, mtn., Ga., U.S.	B3	87
Brassua Lake, res., Me., U.S.	C3	96
Bratenahl, Oh., U.S.	g9	112
Bratislava, Sov. Un.	D4	26
Bratsk, Sov. Un.	D13	29
Bratsk Reservoir, res., Sov. Un.	D13	29
Bratt, Fl., U.S.	u14	86
Brattleboro, Vt., U.S.	F3	122
Braunau [am Inn], Aus.	D6	18
Braunfels, W. Ger.	B5	18
Braunschweig, W. Ger.	B5	18
Bråviken, b., Swe.	u34	14
Brawley, Ca., U.S.	F6	82
Brawley Peaks, mts., Nv., U.S.	E3	105
Braxton, Ms., U.S.	C4	101
Braxton, co., W.V., U.S.	C4	125
Bray, Ire.	D5	11
Bray, Ok., U.S.	C4	113
Bray Head, c., Ire.	F1	11
Braymer, Mo., U.S.	B4	102
Brazeau, stm., Alta.	C2	68
Brazeau, Mount, mtn., Alta.	C2	68
Brazil, In., U.S.	E3	91
Brazil, Ia., U.S.	D5	92
Brazil, Tn., U.S.	B2	119
Brazil, ctry., S.A.	D5	53
Brazilian Highlands, plat., Braz.	E5	53
Brazil Lake, N.S.	F4	71
Brazilton, Ks., U.S.	E9	93
Brazoria, Tx., U.S.	r14	120
Brazoria, co., Tx., U.S.	E5	120
Brazos, co., Tx., U.S.	D4	120
Brazos, stm., Tx., U.S.	D4	120
Brazzaville, Congo	B2	48
Brčko, Yugo.	C4	24
Brda, stm., Pol.	B4	26
Brea, Ca., U.S.	n13	82
Brea, Punta, c., P.R.	C2	65
Bread Loaf Mountain, mtn., Vt., U.S.	D3	122
Breakenridge, Mount, mtn., B.C.	E7	69
Breakers Point, c., Am. Sam.	F13	52
Breakeyville, Que.	o17	74
Bream Bay, b., N.Z.	K15	51
Breared, Swe.	B7	15
Breathitt, co., Ky., U.S.	C6	94
Breaux Bridge, La., U.S.	D4	95
Brechin, Ont.	C5	73
Brechin, Scot., U.K.	B5	10
Breckenridge, Que.	h12	73
Breckenridge, Co., U.S.	B4	83
Breckenridge, Mi., U.S.	E6	99
Breckenridge, Mn., U.S.	D2	100
Breckenridge, Mo., U.S.	B4	102
Breckenridge, Ok., U.S.	A4	113
Breckenridge, Tx., U.S.	C3	120
Breckenridge Hills, Mo., U.S.	*f13	102
Breckinridge, co., Ky., U.S.	C3	94
Brecknock, Peninsula, pen., Chile	h11	54
Brecksville, Oh., U.S.	A4	112
Břeclav, Czech.	D4	26
Brecon (Brecknock), Wales, U.K.	E5	10
Breda, Neth.	B6	16
Breda, Ia., U.S.	B3	92
Bredasdorp, S. Afr.	D3	49
Bredenbury, Sask.	G4	75
Bredstedt, W. Ger.	D2	15
Bredy, Sov. Un.	E21	8
Bree, Bel.	C5	17
Breese, Il., U.S.	E4	90
Breezy Point, Mn., U.S.	D4	100
Bregalnica, stm., Yugo.	E4	18
Bregenz, Aus.	B8	21
Bregenzerach, stm., Aus.	B8	21
Bregovo, Bul.	C5	24
Breidafjördur, b., Ice.	n21	14
Breid Bay, b., Ant.	B15	7
Breien, N.D., U.S.	C5	111
Breil, Fr.	F7	16
Breisach, W. Ger.	A3	20
Brejinho de Nazaré, Braz.	B2	57
Brejo, Braz.	B4	54
Bremen, W. Ger.	B2	18
Bremen, Al., U.S.	B2	78
Bremen, Ga., U.S.	C1	87
Bremen, In., U.S.	B5	91
Bremen, Ky., U.S.	C2	94
Bremen, N.D., U.S.	B6	111
Bremen, Oh., U.S.	C3	112
Bremen, state, W. Ger.	B2	18
Bremer, Ia., U.S.	B5	92
Bremer, co., Ia., U.S.	B5	92
Bremerhaven (Wesermünde), W. Ger.	B4	18
Bremerton, Wa., U.S.	B3	124
Bremervörde, W. Ger.	B5	18
Bremo Bluff, Va., U.S.	C4	123
Bremond, Tx., U.S.	*D2	58
Breña, Peru	D4	120
Brenham, Tx., U.S.	D4	120
Brenish, Scot., U.K.	B1	13
Brenner Pass, Eur.	A3	23
Brent, Ont.	A6	73
Brent, Al., U.S.	C2	78
Brent, Fl., U.S.	u14	86
Brenta, stm., Italy	D7	20
Brentford, S.D., U.S.	B7	118
Brenton, W.V., U.S.	*D3	125
Brenton Point, c., R.I., U.S.	F5	116
Brentwood, Eng., U.K.	k13	10
Brentwood, Ca., U.S.	h9	82
Brentwood, Md., U.S.	f9	97
Brentwood, Mo., U.S.	f13	102
Brentwood, N.H., U.S.	E4	106
Brentwood, N.Y., U.S.	E7	109
Brentwood, Oh., U.S.	*o12	112
Brentwood, Pa., U.S.	k14	115
Brentwood, S.C., U.S.	k11	117
Brentwood, Tn., U.S.	A5	119
Brescia, Italy	B3	23
Breskens, Neth.	C3	17
Breslau see Wrocław, Pol.	C4	26
Bresle, stm., Fr.	E9	12
Bressanone, Italy	A3	23
Bressuire, Fr.	C1	16
Brest, Fr.	C1	16
Brest (Brest-Litovsk), Sov. Un.	D5	27
Breteuil, Fr.	C4	16
Brétigny [-Notre-Dame], Fr.	C3	68
Breton, Alta.	C3	68
Breton, Pertuis, strt., Fr.	C2	16
Breton Islands, is., La., U.S.	E6	95
Breton Sound, strt., La., U.S.	E6	95
Breton Woods, N.J., U.S.	C4	107
Bretton Woods, N.H., U.S.	B4	106
Breuil, Italy	D3	20
Brevard, N.C., U.S.	f10	110
Brevard, co., Fl., U.S.	D6	86
Breves, Braz.	C4	59
Brevik (part of Porsgrunn), Nor.	p27	14
Březnov (part of Prague), Czech.	n17	26
Brevort Lake, l., Mi., U.S.	B5	99
Brevort, Mi., U.S.	B5	99
Brewarrina, Austl.	D4	51
Brewer, Me., U.S.	D4	96
Brewerville, Lib.	E2	45
Brewster, Ks., U.S.	C2	93
Brewster, Ma., U.S.	C7	98
Brewster, Ne., U.S.	C6	104
Brewster, N.Y., U.S.	D7	109
Brewster, Oh., U.S.	B4	112
Brewster, Wa., U.S.	A6	124
Brewster, co., Tx., U.S.	E1	120
Brewster, Kap, c., Grnld.	B18	61

Name	Map Ref.	Page
Brewster Islands, is., Ma., U.S.	g12	98
Brewton, Al., U.S.	D2	78
Brewton, Ga., U.S.	D4	87
Brezhnev see Naberezhnyye Chelny, Sov. Un.	D8	29
Brežice, Yugo.	C2	24
Březnice, Czech.	D8	19
Breznik, Bul.	D6	24
Brezno, Czech.	D5	26
Bria, Cen. Afr. Rep.	D4	46
Brian Boru Peak, mtn., B.C.	B4	69
Briançon, Fr.	E7	16
Brian Head, mtn., Ut., U.S.	F3	121
Briarcliff, Pa., U.S.	p20	115
Briarcliff Manor, N.Y., U.S.	*D7	109
Briare, Fr.	D5	16
Briartown, Ok., U.S.	B6	113
Brice, Oh., U.S.	m11	112
Bricelyn, Mn., U.S.	G5	100
Briceville, Tn., U.S.	C9	119
Brickeys, Ar., U.S.	C5	81
Brick [Township], N.J., U.S.	C4	107
Bridal Veil, Or., U.S.	B4	114
Bridal Veil Falls, wtfl, Ut., U.S.	C4	121
Bride, stm., Ire.	E3	11
Bridesville, B.C.	E8	69
Bridge, stm., B.C.	D6	69
Bridgeboro, Ga., U.S.	E3	87
Bridge City, La., U.S.	*E5	95
Bridge City, Tx., U.S.	*D6	120
Bridge Creek, stm., Sask.	H1	75
Bridgeford, Sask.	G2	75
Bridgehampton, N.Y., U.S.	n16	109
Bridge Lake, B.C.	D7	69
Bridgeland, Ut., U.S.	C5	121
Bridgend, Wales, U.K.	C4	12
Bridgeport (part of Kitchener), Ont.	D4	73
Bridgeport, Al., U.S.	A4	78
Bridgeport, Ca., U.S.	C4	82
Bridgeport, Ct., U.S.	E3	84
Bridgeport, Il., U.S.	E6	90
Bridgeport, Mi., U.S.	E7	99
Bridgeport, Ne., U.S.	C2	104
Bridgeport, N.J., U.S.	D2	107
Bridgeport, Oh., U.S.	B5	112
Bridgeport, Ok., U.S.	B3	113
Bridgeport, Or., U.S.	C9	114
Bridgeport, Pa., U.S.	o20	115
Bridgeport, Tx., U.S.	C4	120
Bridgeport, Wa., U.S.	B6	124
Bridgeport, W.V., U.S.	B4	125
Bridger, Mt., U.S.	E8	103
Bridger, S.D., U.S.	C4	118
Bridger Mountains, mts., Wy., U.S.	C5	127
Bridger Peak, mtn., Wy., U.S.	E5	127
Bridger Range, mts., Mt., U.S.	E6	103
Bridgeton, In., U.S.	E3	91
Bridgeton, Mo., U.S.	C7	102
Bridgeton, N.J., U.S.	E2	107
Bridgeton, N.C., U.S.	B5	110
Bridgetown, Barb.	J15	64
Bridgetown, N.S.	E4	71
Bridgetown, Oh., U.S.	*o12	112
Bridgeview, Il., U.S.	*k9	90
Bridgeville, N.S.	D7	71
Bridgeville, De., U.S.	F3	85
Bridgeville, Pa., U.S.	k13	115
Bridgewater, N.S.	E5	71
Bridgewater, Ct., U.S.	C2	84
Bridgewater, Ia., U.S.	C3	92
Bridgewater, Me., U.S.	B5	96
Bridgewater, Ma., U.S.	C6	98
Bridgewater, N.H., U.S.	C3	106
Bridgewater, N.J., U.S.	B3	107
Bridgewater, S.D., U.S.	D8	118
Bridgewater, Vt., U.S.	D3	122
Bridgewater, Va., U.S.	B4	123
Bridgewater Corners, Vt., U.S.	D3	122
Bridgman, Mi., U.S.	G4	99
Bridgnorth, Eng., U.K.	B5	12
Bridgton, Me., U.S.	D2	96
Bridgwater, Eng., U.K.	E5	10
Bridgwater Bay, b., Eng., U.K.	C4	12
Bridlington, Eng., U.K.	C6	10
Bridport, Eng., U.K.	D5	12
Bridport, Vt., U.S.	D2	122
Brielle, N.J., U.S.	C4	107
Brienz, Switz.	E4	18
Brienz, Lake, l., Switz.	C3	20
Brier Creek, stm., Ga., U.S.	C5	87
Briercrest, Sask.	G3	75
Brierfield, Alta.	B5	68
Brierfield, Al., U.S.	B3	78
Brier Hill, N.Y., U.S.	f9	109
Briery Knob, mtn., W.V., U.S.	C4	125
Briey, Fr.	E5	17
Brig, Switz.	E3	18
Brigantine, N.J., U.S.	E4	107
Brigantine Beach, N.J., U.S.	E4	107
Brig Bay, Newf.	C3	72
Brigden, Ont.	E2	73
Brigg, Eng., U.K.	A7	12
Briggs, Ne., U.S.	*C10	104
Briggs, Tx., U.S.	D4	120
Briggsdale, Co., U.S.	A6	83
Briggs Marsh, sw., R.I., U.S.	F6	116
Briggsville, Ar., U.S.	C2	81
Briggsville, Ma., U.S.	A1	98
Briggsville, Wi., U.S.	E4	126
Brigham City, Ut., U.S.	B3	121
Brig Harbour Island, i., Newf.	A3	72
Bright, Ont.	D4	73
Brighton, Ont.	C7	73
Brighton, Eng., U.K.	E6	10
Brighton, Al., U.S.	B3	78
Brighton, Co., U.S.	B6	83
Brighton, Il., U.S.	D3	90
Brighton, Ia., U.S.	C6	92
Brighton, Me., U.S.	C3	96
Brighton, Mi., U.S.	F7	99
Brighton, N.Y., U.S.	B3	109
Brighton, Or., U.S.	B3	114
Brighton, Tn., U.S.	B2	119
Brighton, Ut., U.S.	*C4	121
Brighton Indian Reservation, Fl., U.S.	E5	86
Brightsand Lake, l., Sask.	D1	75
Brightshade, Ky., U.S.	C6	94
Brignoles, Fr.	F7	16
Brihuega, Spain	B4	22
Brillante, stm., Braz.	C1	56
Brilliant, B.C.	E9	69
Brilliant, Al., U.S.	A2	78
Brilliant, Oh., U.S.	B5	112
Brillion, Wi., U.S.	D5	126
Brilon, W. Ger.	B3	19
Brimfield, Il., U.S.	C4	90
Brimfield, Ma., U.S.	*B3	98
Brimhall, N.M., U.S.	B1	108
Brimley, Mi., U.S.	B6	99
Brimson, Mn., U.S.	C7	100
Brimson, Mo., U.S.	A4	102
Brindisi, Italy	D6	23
Bringhurst, In., U.S.	C5	91
Brinje, Yugo.	C2	24
Brinkhaven, Oh., U.S.	B3	112
Brinkley, Ar., U.S.	C4	81
Brinkman, Ok., U.S.	B2	113
Brinktown, Mo., U.S.	C5	102
Brinkworth, Austl.	F2	51
Brinnon, Wa., U.S.	B3	124
Brinsmade, N.D., U.S.	A6	111
Brinson, Ga., U.S.	F2	87
Brion, Île, i., Que.	B8	71
Brione (Verzasca), Switz.	D6	21
Brioude, Fr.	E5	16
Brisbane, Austl.	E9	50
Briscoe, Tx., U.S.	B2	120
Briscoe, co., Tx., U.S.	B2	120
Brissago, Switz.	D6	21
Bristol, N.B.	C2	71
Bristol, Eng., U.K.	E5	10
Bristol, Co., U.S.	C8	83
Bristol, Ct., U.S.	C4	84
Bristol, Fl., U.S.	B2	86
Bristol, Ga., U.S.	E4	87
Bristol, Il., U.S.	B5	90
Bristol, In., U.S.	A6	91
Bristol, Me., U.S.	*E3	96
Bristol, N.H., U.S.	C3	106
Bristol, R.I., U.S.	D5	116
Bristol, S.D., U.S.	B8	118
Bristol, Tn., U.S.	C11	119
Bristol, Vt., U.S.	C2	122
Bristol, Va., U.S.	f9	123
Bristol, W.V., U.S.	k9	125
Bristol, Wi., U.S.	F5	126
Bristol, co., Ma., U.S.	C5	98
Bristol, co., R.I., U.S.	D5	116
Bristol Bay, b., Ak., U.S.	D7	79
Bristol Channel, strt., U.K.	E4	10
Bristol Ferry, R.I., U.S.	D5	116
Bristol [Township], Pa., U.S.	F12	115
Bristolville, Oh., U.S.	A5	112
Bristow, In., U.S.	H4	91
Bristow, Ia., U.S.	B5	92
Bristow, Ne., U.S.	B7	104
Bristow, Ok., U.S.	B5	113
Britannia Bay (part of Ottawa), Ont.	h12	73
Britannia Beach, B.C.	E6	69
Britannia Range, mts., Ant.	B28	7
British Antarctic Territory, dep., S.A.	*C7	7
British Columbia, prov., Can.	C6	69
British Indian Ocean Territory, dep., Afr.	*G25	2
British Mountains, mts., N.A.	B12	79
British Virgin Islands, dep., N.A.	G12	64
Britstown, S. Afr.	D3	49
Britt, Ont.	B4	73
Britt, Ia., U.S.	A4	92
Brittany, hist. reg., Fr.	C2	16
Britton, Mi., U.S.	G7	99
Britton, S.D., U.S.	B8	118
Brive [-la-Gaillarde], Fr.	E4	16
Briviesca, Spain	A4	22
Brixham, Eng., U.K.	D4	12
Brno, Czech.	D4	26
Broa, Ensenada de la, b., Cuba	C3	64
Broad, stm., Ga., U.S.	B4	87
Broad, stm., S.C., U.S.	C5	117
Broadacres, Sask.	E1	75
Broadalbin, N.Y., U.S.	B6	109
Broadback, stm., Que.	F17	66
Broad Bay, b., Scot., U.K.	B2	13
Broadbent, Or., U.S.	E2	114
Broad Brook, Ct., U.S.	B5	84
Broad Creek, stm., De., U.S.	F3	85
Broaddus, Tx., U.S.	D5	120
Broadford, Scot., U.K.	C3	13
Broad Top, Pa., U.S.	F5	115
Broadus, Mt., U.S.	E11	103
Broadview, Sask.	G4	75
Broadview, Il., U.S.	*k9	90
Broadview, Mt., U.S.	D8	103
Broadview, N.M., U.S.	C6	108
Broadview Heights, Oh., U.S.	h9	112
Broadwater, Fl., U.S.	F6	86
Broadwater, Ne., U.S.	C3	104
Broadwater, co., Mt., U.S.	D5	103
Broadway, N.J., U.S.	B2	107
Broadway, Oh., U.S.	B2	112
Broadway, Va., U.S.	B4	123
Broager, Den.	D3	15
Brochet, Man.	f7	70
Brock, Sask.	F1	75
Brock, Ne., U.S.	D10	104
Brocken, mtn., E. Ger.	B5	19
Brocket, Alta.	E4	68
Brocket, N.D., U.S.	A7	111
Brock Island, i., N.W. Ter.	m29	66
Brockport, N.Y., U.S.	B3	109
Brockport, Pa., U.S.	D4	115
Brockton, Ma., U.S.	B5	98
Brockton Reservoir, res., Ma., U.S.	h11	98
Brockville, Ont.	C9	73
Brockway, Mt., U.S.	C11	103
Brockway, Pa., U.S.	D4	115
Brockwell, Ar., U.S.	A4	81
Brocton, Il., U.S.	D6	90
Brocton, N.Y., U.S.	C1	109
Broderick, Sask.	F2	75
Brodeur Peninsula, pen., N.W. Ter.	B15	66
Brodhead, Ky., U.S.	C5	94
Brodhead, Wi., U.S.	F4	126
Brodheadsville, Pa., U.S.	E11	115
Brodick, Scot., U.K.	E3	13
Brodnax, Va., U.S.	D4	123
Brodnica, Pol.	B5	26
Brody, Sov. Un.	F5	27
Brogan, Or., U.S.	C9	114
Brokaw, Wi., U.S.	D4	126
Broken Arrow, Ok., U.S.	A6	113
Broken Bow, Ne., U.S.	C6	104
Broken Bow, Ok., U.S.	C7	113
Broken Bow Lake, res., Ok., U.S.	C7	113
Broken Hill, Austl.	F7	50
Brokopondo, Sur.	A3	59
Brokopondo, dept., Sur.	B3	59
Brome, Que.	D5	74
Brome, W. Ger.	F4	15
Brome, Lac, l., Que.	D5	74
Brome, co., Que.	D5	74
Bromhead, Sask.	H4	75
Bromide, Ok., U.S.	C5	113
Bromley (part of London), Eng., U.K.	m13	10
Bromley Mountain, mtn., Vt., U.S.	E3	122
Bromptonville, Que.	D6	74
Bromsgrove, Eng., U.K.	B5	12
Bromyard, Eng., U.K.	B5	12
Bronaugh, Mo., U.S.	D3	102
Bronco, Tx., U.S.	C1	120
Brønderslev, Den.	A3	15
Brong-Ahafo, prov., Ghana	E4	45
Bronlund Peak, mtn., B.C.	E7	66
Bronnitsy, Sov. Un.	n18	27
Brönnöysund, Nor.	E5	14
Bronson, Fl., U.S.	C4	86
Bronson, Ia., U.S.	B1	92
Bronson, Ks., U.S.	E8	93
Bronson, Mi., U.S.	G5	99
Bronson, Tx., U.S.	D6	120
Bronte, Tx., U.S.	D2	120
Bronwood, Ga., U.S.	E2	87
Bronx, co., N.Y., U.S.	E7	109
Bronxville, N.Y., U.S.	h13	109
Brook, In., U.S.	C3	91
Brookdale, Man.	D2	70
Brooke, Va., U.S.	B5	123
Brooke, co., W.V., U.S.	A4	125
Brooker, Fl., U.S.	C4	86
Brookeville, Md., U.S.	B3	97
Brookfield, N.S.	D6	71
Brookfield, Ct., U.S.	D2	84
Brookfield, Ga., U.S.	E3	87
Brookfield, Il., U.S.	k9	90
Brookfield, Ma., U.S.	B3	98
Brookfield, Mo., U.S.	B4	102
Brookfield, N.H., U.S.	C4	106
Brookfield, N.Y., U.S.	C5	109
Brookfield, Vt., U.S.	C3	122
Brookfield, Va., U.S.	B5	123
Brookfield, Wi., U.S.	m11	126
Brookfield Center, Ct., U.S.	D2	84
Brookford, N.C., U.S.	B1	110
Brookhaven, Ms., U.S.	D3	101
Brookhaven, Pa., U.S.	*p20	115
Brookhaven, W.V., U.S.	h11	125
Brooking, Sask.	H3	75
Brookings, Or., U.S.	E2	114
Brookings, S.D., U.S.	C9	118
Brookings, co., S.D., U.S.	C9	118
Brookland, Ar., U.S.	B5	81
Brooklandville, Md., U.S.	g10	97
Brooklawn, N.J., U.S.	D2	107
Brooklet, Ga., U.S.	D5	87
Brooklin, Me., U.S.	D4	96
Brookline, Ma., U.S.	B5	98
Brookline, N.H., U.S.	E3	106
Brooklyn, N.S.	E5	71
Brooklyn, N.S.	D3	71
Brooklyn, Ct., U.S.	B8	84
Brooklyn, Ga., U.S.	D2	87
Brooklyn, Il., U.S.	C3	90
Brooklyn, In., U.S.	E5	91
Brooklyn, Ia., U.S.	C5	92
Brooklyn, Mi., U.S.	F6	99
Brooklyn, Ms., U.S.	D4	101
Brooklyn, Oh., U.S.	h9	112
Brooklyn, Pa., U.S.	C10	115
Brooklyn, S.C., U.S.	B6	117
Brooklyn, Wi., U.S.	F4	126
Brooklyn Center, Mn., U.S.	E5	100
Brooklyn Park, Md., U.S.	h11	97
Brooklyn Park, Mn., U.S.	m12	100
Brookmere, B.C.	E7	69
Brookneal, Va., U.S.	C4	123
Brook Park, Mn., U.S.	E5	100
Brook Park, Oh., U.S.	h9	112
Brookport, Il., U.S.	F5	90
Brookridge, Co., U.S.	*B6	83
Brooks, Alta.	D5	68
Brooks, Ia., U.S.	D3	92
Brooks, Ky., U.S.	g11	94
Brooks, Me., U.S.	D3	96
Brooks, Or., U.S.	C2	100
Brooks, Wi., U.S.	E4	126
Brooks, co., Ga., U.S.	F3	87
Brooks, co., Tx., U.S.	F3	120
Brooks Air Force Base, mil., Tx., U.S.	k7	120
Brooksburg, In., U.S.	G7	91
Brooksby, Sask.	E3	75
Brookshire, Tx., U.S.	E5	120
Brookside, Al., U.S.	f7	78
Brookside, De., U.S.	B3	85
Brooks Peninsula, pen., B.C.	D4	69
Brookston, In., U.S.	C4	91
Brookston, Mn., U.S.	D6	100
Brooksville, Fl., U.S.	D4	86
Brooksville, Ky., U.S.	B5	94
Brooksville, Me., U.S.	D4	96
Brooksville, Ms., U.S.	B5	101
Brooksville, Ok., U.S.	B5	113
Brooktondale, N.Y., U.S.	C4	109
Brookview, Md., U.S.	C6	97
Brookville, In., U.S.	F8	91
Brookville, Ks., U.S.	D6	93
Brookville, Ma., U.S.	h11	98
Brookville, N.Y., U.S.	*E7	109
Brookville, Oh., U.S.	C1	112
Brookville, Pa., U.S.	D3	115
Brookville Lake, res., In., U.S.	E7	91
Brookwood, Al., U.S.	B2	78
Brookwood, N.J., U.S.	C4	107
Broom, Loch, b., Scot., U.K.	A10	—
Broomall, Pa., U.S.	p20	115
Broome, Austl.	C3	50
Broome, co., N.Y., U.S.	C5	109
Broomes Island, Md., U.S.	C4	97
Broomfield, Co., U.S.	B5	83
Brooten, Mn., U.S.	E3	100
Brora, Scot., U.K.	C5	13
Brora, stm., Scot., U.K.	C5	13
Brösarp, Swe.	C8	15
Broseley, Mo., U.S.	E7	102
Brosna, stm., Ire.	D4	11
Brossard, Que.	q20	74
Brotas de Macaúbas, Braz.	D2	57
Brothers, Or., U.S.	D6	114
Brotherton, Tn., U.S.	C8	119
Brothertown, Wi., U.S.	k9	126
Brotmanville, N.J., U.S.	D2	107
Brou, Fr.	C4	16
Brough, Eng., U.K.	F6	13
Brough Head, c., Scot., U.K.	A5	13
Broughton, Il., U.S.	F5	90
Broussard, La., U.S.	D4	95
Browder, Ky., U.S.	C2	94
Browerville, Mn., U.S.	D4	100
Brown, co., Il., U.S.	D3	90
Brown, co., In., U.S.	F5	91
Brown, co., Ks., U.S.	C8	93
Brown, co., Mn., U.S.	F4	100
Brown, co., Ne., U.S.	B6	104
Brown, co., Oh., U.S.	D2	112
Brown, co., S.D., U.S.	B7	118
Brown, co., Tx., U.S.	D3	120
Brown, co., Wi., U.S.	D6	126
Brown City, Mi., U.S.	E8	99
Brown Deer, Wi., U.S.	m12	126
Brownell, Ks., U.S.	D4	93
Brownfield, Il., U.S.	F5	90
Brownfield, Me., U.S.	E2	96
Brownfield, Tx., U.S.	C1	120
Brownfields, La., U.S.	*D4	95
Browning, Il., U.S.	C3	90
Browning, Mo., U.S.	A4	102
Browning, Mt., U.S.	B3	103
Browning Entrance, strt., B.C.	C2	69
Brownington, Mo., U.S.	C4	102
Brownington, Vt., U.S.	B4	122
Brownington Center, Vt., U.S.	B4	122
Brownlee, Sask.	G2	75
Brownlee, Ne., U.S.	B5	104
Brownlee Dam, U.S.	E2	89
Brownlee Reservoir, res., U.S.	C10	114
Browns, Il., U.S.	E6	90
Browns, stm., Vt., U.S.	B2	122
Browns Branch, stm., De., U.S.	E3	85
Brownsboro, Ky., U.S.	g11	94
Brownsburg, In., U.S.	E5	91
Brownsburg, Va., U.S.	C3	123
Brownsdale, Mn., U.S.	G6	100
Browns Inlet, b., N.C., U.S.	C5	110
Browns Mills, N.J., U.S.	D3	107
Browns Peak, mtn., Az., U.S.	D4	80
Browns Town, Jam.	E14	65
Brownstown, Il., U.S.	E5	90
Brownstown, In., U.S.	G5	91
Brownstown, Pa., U.S.	F9	115
Brownstown, Wa., U.S.	C5	124
Brownstown, hist. loc., Ire.	E4	11
Browns Valley, In., U.S.	E4	91
Browns Valley, Mn., U.S.	E2	100
Brownsville, Fl., U.S.	s13	86
Brownsville, In., U.S.	E8	91
Brownsville, Ky., U.S.	C3	94
Brownsville, La., U.S.	B3	95
Brownsville, Mn., U.S.	G7	100
Brownsville, Or., U.S.	C4	114
Brownsville, Pa., U.S.	F2	115
Brownsville, Tn., U.S.	B2	119
Brownsville, Tx., U.S.	G4	120
Brownsville, Vt., U.S.	E4	122
Brownsville, Wi., U.S.	E5	126
Brownsville, W.V., U.S.	B4	125
Browntown, Mn., U.S.	E4	100
Browntown, W.V., U.S.	B4	125
Browntown, Wi., U.S.	F4	126
Brownvale, Alta.	A2	68
Brownville, Al., U.S.	B2	78
Brownville, Me., U.S.	C3	96
Brownville, Ne., U.S.	D10	104
Brownville, N.Y., U.S.	A5	109
Brownville Junction, Me., U.S.	C3	96
Brown Willy, hill, Eng., U.K.	D3	12
Brownwood, Mo., U.S.	D8	102
Brownwood, Tx., U.S.	D3	120
Brownwood, Lake, res., Tx., U.S.	D3	120
Broxton, Ga., U.S.	E4	87
Broye, stm., Switz.	C2	20
Broyhill Park, Va., U.S.	*B5	123
Brozas, Spain	C2	22
Bruay [-en-Artois], Fr.	B5	16
Bruce, Alta.	C4	68
Bruce, Fl., U.S.	u16	86
Bruce, Ms., U.S.	B4	101
Bruce, S.D., U.S.	C9	118
Bruce, Wi., U.S.	C2	126
Bruce, co., Ont.	C3	73
Bruce, Mount, mtn., Austl.	D2	50
Bruce Crossing, Mi., U.S.	m12	99
Brucefield, Ont.	D3	73
Bruce Lake, In., U.S.	B5	91
Bruce National Park, Ont.	B3	73
Bruce Peninsula, pen., Ont.	B3	73
Bruceton, Tn., U.S.	A3	119
Bruceton Mills, W.V., U.S.	B5	125
Brucetown, Va., U.S.	A4	123
Bruceville, In., U.S.	G3	91
Bruchsal, W. Ger.	C4	18
Bruck, Aus.	B8	20
Brück, E. Ger.	A7	19
Bruck [an der Leitha], Aus.	D8	18
Bruck [an der Mur], Aus.	E7	18
Brückenau, W. Ger.	C4	19
Bruderheim, Alta.	C4	68
Bruff, Ire.	E3	11
Bruges see Brugge, Bel.	B5	16
Brugg, Switz.	B5	21
Brugge (Bruges), Bel.	C1	19
Brühl, W. Ger.	C1	19
Bruin Point, mtn., Ut., U.S.	D5	121
Bruja, Cerro, mtn., Pan.	k11	62
Brule, Ne., U.S.	C4	104
Brule, Wi., U.S.	B2	126
Brule, co., S.D., U.S.	D6	118
Brule, stm., U.S.	C5	126
Brûlé Lake, l., Alta.	C2	68
Brule Lake, l., Mn., U.S.	k9	100
Brumath, Fr.	C7	16
Brumley, Mo., U.S.	C5	102
Brumley Mountain, mtn., Va., U.S.	f9	123
Brundidge, Al., U.S.	D4	78
Bruneau, Id., U.S.	G3	89
Bruneau, stm., U.S.	G3	89
Brunei, ctry., Asia	E4	34
Brunei Bay, b., Asia	D5	34
Brunete, Spain	p16	22
Brunette Island, i., Newf.	E4	72
Bruni, Tx., U.S.	F3	120
Brunico, Italy	C7	20
Brünig, Switz.	C5	21
Bruning, Ne., U.S.	D8	104
Brunkild, Man.	E3	70
Brunnen, Switz.	C5	21
Brunner, Lake, l., N.Z.	O13	51
Bruno, Sask.	E3	75
Bruno, Mn., U.S.	D6	100
Bruno, Ne., U.S.	C9	104
Brunson, S.C., U.S.	F5	117
Brunsville, Ia., U.S.	B1	92
Brunswick, Ga., U.S.	E5	87
Brunswick, Me., U.S.	E3	96
Brunswick, Md., U.S.	B2	97
Brunswick, Mo., U.S.	B4	102
Brunswick, Ne., U.S.	B8	104
Brunswick, N.C., U.S.	C4	110
Brunswick, Oh., U.S.	A4	112
Brunswick, co., N.C., U.S.	C4	110
Brunswick, co., Va., U.S.	D5	123
Brunswick, Península, pen., Chile	h11	54
Brunswick see Braunschweig, W. Ger.	B5	18
Brunswick Naval Air Station, mil., Me., U.S.	E3	96
Brus Laguna, Hond.	D8	63
Brusly, La., U.S.	D4	95
Brusque, Braz.	D3	56
Brussels, Ont.	D3	73
Brussels (Bruxelles), Bel.	B6	16
Brussels, Wi., U.S.	D6	126
Brusson, Italy	E4	21
Bruton, Eng., U.K.	C5	12
Brutus, Mi., U.S.	C6	99
Bruyères, Fr.	A2	20
Bryan, Oh., U.S.	A1	112
Bryan, Tx., U.S.	D4	120
Bryan, co., Ga., U.S.	D5	87
Bryan, co., Ok., U.S.	D5	113
Bryanka, Sov. Un.	q21	27
Bryans Road, Md., U.S.	C3	97
Bryant, Ar., U.S.	C3	81
Bryant, Fl., U.S.	F6	86
Bryant, Il., U.S.	C3	90
Bryant, In., U.S.	C8	91
Bryant, S.D., U.S.	C8	118
Bryant, Wi., U.S.	C4	126
Bryant Creek, stm., Mo., U.S.	E5	102
Bryant Mountain, mtn., Ma., U.S.	B2	98
Bryant Pond, Me., U.S.	D2	96
Bryantown, Md., U.S.	C4	97
Bryantsville, Ky., U.S.	C5	94
Bryantville, Ma., U.S.	B6	98
Bryce Canyon, Ut., U.S.	F3	121
Bryce Canyon National Park, Ut., U.S.	F3	121
Bryceland, La., U.S.	B3	95
Bryceville, Fl., U.S.	B5	86
Brynica, stm., Pol.	g9	26
Bryn Mawr, Pa., U.S.	o20	115
Bryn Mawr, Wa., U.S.	e11	124
Bryson, Tx., U.S.	C3	120
Bryson City, N.C., U.S.	f9	110
Brzeg, Pol.	C4	26
Brzesko, Pol.	D6	26
Brzeziny, Pol.	C5	26
Brzozów, Pol.	D7	26
B-Say-Tah, Sask.	G4	75
Bua, Fiji	H15	52
Bu'aale, Som.	E5	47
Bua Bay, b., Fiji	H15	52
Buariki, Kir.	R18	52
Bubīyān, i., Kuw.	C4	38
Buccaneer Archipelago, is., Austl.	C3	50
Buchach, Sov. Un.	G5	27
Buchanan, Sask.	F4	75
Buchanan, Lib.	E2	45
Buchanan, Ga., U.S.	C1	87
Buchanan, Mi., U.S.	G4	99
Buchanan, N.D., U.S.	B7	111
Buchanan, Tn., U.S.	A3	119
Buchanan, Va., U.S.	C3	123
Buchanan, co., Ia., U.S.	B6	92
Buchanan, co., Mo., U.S.	B3	102
Buchanan, co., Va., U.S.	e9	123
Buchanan, Lake, l., Austl.	D8	50
Buchanan, Lake, res., Tx., U.S.	D3	120
Buchan Ness, c., Scot., U.K.	C7	13
Buchans, Newf.	D3	72
Bucharest (București), Rom.	C8	24
Buchholz, W. Ger.	B4	19
Buchloe, W. Ger.	E5	18
Buchs, Switz.	B5	20
Buckatunna, Ms., U.S.	D5	101
Buck Creek, In., U.S.	D4	91
Buck Creek, stm., Ga., U.S.	D2	87
Buck Creek, stm., In., U.S.	m11	91
Buck Creek, stm., Ky., U.S.	C5	94
Buckeye, Az., U.S.	D3	80
Buckeye, W.V., U.S.	C4	125
Buckeye Hills, hills, Az., U.S.	m7	80
Buckeye Lake, Oh., U.S.	C3	112
Buckeystown, Md., U.S.	B3	97
Buckfield, Me., U.S.	D2	96
Buckhannon, W.V., U.S.	C4	125
Buckhannon, stm., W.V., U.S.	k9	125
Buckhaven, Scot., U.K.	B5	10
Buck Hill Falls, Pa., U.S.	D11	115
Buckholts, Tx., U.S.	D4	120
Buckhorn, Ky., U.S.	C6	94
Buckhorn, N.M., U.S.	k9	108
Buckhorn Knob, mtn., W.V., U.S.	C7	16
Buckhorn Lake, res., Ky., U.S.	C6	94
Buckie, Scot., U.K.	B5	10
Buckingham, Que.	D2	74
Buckingham, co., Va., U.S.	C4	123
Buckingham, Eng., U.K.	C5	12
Buckinghamshire, co., Eng., U.K.	C6	12
Buckland, Que.	C7	74
Buckland, Ak., U.S.	B7	79
Buckland, Oh., U.S.	B1	112
Buckley, Il., U.S.	C5	90
Buckley, Mi., U.S.	D5	99
Buckley, Wa., U.S.	B3	124
Bucklin, Ks., U.S.	E4	93
Bucklin, Mo., U.S.	B5	102
Buckman, Mn., U.S.	E4	100
Buck Mountain, mtn., Va., U.S.	D1	123
Buck Mountain, mtn., Wa., U.S.	A6	124
Bucknell Manor, Va., U.S.	*B5	123
Buckner, Ar., U.S.	D2	81
Buckner, Il., U.S.	F4	90
Buckner, Ky., U.S.	g12	94
Buckner, Mo., U.S.	h11	102
Bucks, Al., U.S.	D1	78
Bucks, co., Pa., U.S.	F11	115
Bucks Harbor, Me., U.S.	D5	96
Buckskin, In., U.S.	H3	91
Buckskin Mountains, mts., Az., U.S.	C2	80
Bucksport, Me., U.S.	D4	96
Bucksport, S.C., U.S.	D9	117
Buckville, Ar., U.S.	C2	81
Bucoda, Wa., U.S.	C3	124
Buco Zau, Ang.	B1	48
Bucyrus, Ks., U.S.	D9	93
Bucyrus, N.D., U.S.	C3	111
Bucyrus, Oh., U.S.	B3	112
Bud, W.V., U.S.	D3	125
Buda, Il., U.S.	B4	90
Buda, Tx., U.S.	D4	120
Budapest, Hung.	B4	24
Budaun, India	C7	37
Budd Coast, Ant.	C24	7
Budd Lake, l., N.J., U.S.	B3	107
Buddon Ness, c., Scot., U.K.	D6	13
Buddonovsk, Sov. Un.	G17	8
Bude, Eng., U.K.	E4	10
Bude, Ms., U.S.	D3	101
Bude Bay, b., Eng., U.K.	D3	12
Budjala, Zaire	A2	48
Budrio, Italy	B3	23
Budyně [nad Ohří], Czech.	n17	26
Buea, Cam.	E1	46
Buechel, Ky., U.S.	B4	94
Buena, Wa., U.S.	C5	124
Buena Park, Ca., U.S.	n12	82
Buenaventura, Col.	C2	60
Buenaventura, Mex.	B3	63
Buena Vista, Bol.	C3	55
Buena Vista, Ar., U.S.	D3	81
Buena Vista, Co., U.S.	C4	83
Buena Vista, Fl., U.S.	C4	86
Buena Vista, Ga., U.S.	D2	87
Buena Vista, Ms., U.S.	B5	101
Buena Vista, N.M., U.S.	A4	108
Buena Vista, Oh., U.S.	D2	112
Buena Vista, Tn., U.S.	C3	123
Buena Vista, Va., U.S.	C3	123
Buena Vista, co., Ia., U.S.	B2	92
Buena Vista, stm., Ar., U.S.	B3	81
Buenaventura, Lago (Lago General Carrera), l., S.A.	D2	54
Bueno, stm., Chile	C2	54
Buenópolis, Braz.	B4	56
Buenos Aires, Arg.	A5	54
Buenos Aires, C.R.	F6	62
Buenos Aires, Pan.	k11	62
Buenos Aires, prov., Arg.	B4	54
Buenos Aires, Lago (Lago General Carrera), l., S.A.	D2	54
Bueyeros, N.M., U.S.	B6	108
Buffalo, Alta.	D5	68
Buffalo, Al., U.S.	C4	78
Buffalo, Il., U.S.	D4	90
Buffalo, In., U.S.	C4	91
Buffalo, Ia., U.S.	C7	92
Buffalo, Ks., U.S.	E8	93
Buffalo, Mn., U.S.	E5	100
Buffalo, Mo., U.S.	D4	102
Buffalo, N.Y., U.S.	C2	109
Buffalo, Oh., U.S.	C4	112
Buffalo, Ok., U.S.	A2	113
Buffalo, S.C., U.S.	B4	117
Buffalo, S.D., U.S.	B2	118
Buffalo, Tx., U.S.	D5	120
Buffalo, W.V., U.S.	C3	125
Buffalo, Wi., U.S.	D2	126
Buffalo, Wy., U.S.	B6	127
Buffalo, co., Ne., U.S.	D6	104
Buffalo, co., S.D., U.S.	C6	118
Buffalo, co., Wi., U.S.	D2	126
Buffalo, stm., Mn., U.S.	D2	100
Buffalo, stm., Tn., U.S.	B4	119
Buffalo, stm., Wi., U.S.	D2	126
Buffalo Bill Reservoir, res., Wy., U.S.	B3	127
Buffalo Center, Ia., U.S.	A4	92
Buffalo Creek, Co., U.S.	B5	83
Buffalo Creek, stm., U.S.	f8	125
Buffalo Creek, stm., W.V., U.S.	h10	125
Buffalo Creek, stm., W.V., U.S.	n12	125
Buffalo Gap, Sask.	H3	75
Buffalo Gap, S.D., U.S.	D2	118
Buffalo Grove, Il., U.S.	h9	90
Buffalo Lake, Alta.	C4	68
Buffalo Lake, l., N.W. Ter.	D9	66
Buffalo Lake, res., Tx., U.S.	B1	120
Buffalo Lake, res., Wi., U.S.	E4	126
Buffalo Mills, Pa., U.S.	G4	115
Buffalo Mountain, mtn., Va., U.S.	D2	123
Buffalo Narrows, Sask.	m7	75
Buffalo Pound Lake, l., Sask.	G3	75
Buffalo Valley, Tn., U.S.	C8	119
Buff Bay, Jam.	E15	65
Buffer Lake, l., Sask.	E2	75
Buffumville Lake, res., Ma., U.S.	B4	98
Buford, Ga., U.S.	B3	87
Buford, Oh., U.S.	C2	112
Buford, Wy., U.S.	E7	127
Buga, Col.	C2	60
Buganga, Ug.	B5	48
Bugene, Tan.	B5	48
Bugio, i., Port.	h12	22
Bugliaga, Italy	D5	21
Bugojno, Yugo.	C3	24
Bugsuk Island, i., Phil.	D5	34
Bugt, China	C9	32
Buguma, Nig.	C4	28
Buguruslan, Sov. Un.	D7	16
Buhl, Fr.	C7	74
Bühl, W. Ger.	E3	19
Buhl, Al., U.S.	B2	78
Buhl, Id., U.S.	G4	89
Buhl, Mn., U.S.	C6	100
Buhler, Ks., U.S.	D6	93
Bühlertal, W. Ger.	E3	19
Buhuşi, Rom.	B8	24
Bui Dam, Ghana	E4	45
Buies Creek, N.C., U.S.	B4	110

Name	Map Ref.	Page
Builth Wells, Wales, U.K.	B4	12
Buitenpost, Neth.	A6	17
Bujalance, Spain	D3	22
Bujumbura, Bdi.	B4	48
Bukama, Zaire	C4	48
Bukene, Tan.	B5	48
Bukhara, Sov. Un.	F9	29
Bukittinggi, Indon.	F2	34
Bukoba, Tan.	B5	48
Bukovina, hist. reg., Eur.	B7	24
Bukuru, Nig.	E6	45
Bula, Indon.	F8	34
Bula, Zaire	A4	48
Bülach, Switz.	A6	21
Buladean, N.C., U.S.	e10	110
Buladeen, Tn., U.S.	C11	119
Bulan, Ky., U.S.	C6	94
Bulawayo, Zimb.	B4	49
Buldir Island, i., Ak., U.S.	E3	79
Bulgan, Mong.	B5	31
Bulgaria, ctry., Eur.	D7	24
Bulgroo, Austl.	D4	51
Buliya, i., Fiji	I15	52
Bulkley, stm., B.C.	B4	69
Bulkley Ranges, mts., B.C.	B4	69
Bull, stm., B.C.	E3	68
Bullange see Büllingen, Bel.	D6	17
Bullaue, stm., Spain	C3	22
Bullard, Ga., U.S.	D3	87
Bullas, Spain	C5	22
Bullaxaar, Som.	C5	47
Bullay, W. Ger.	C2	19
Bull Creek, stm., Nv., U.S.	E6	105
Bull Creek, stm., S.D., U.S.	B2	118
Bulle, Switz.	D6	21
Bullen Baai, b., Neth. Ant.	H18	65
Bullfrog Creek, stm., Ut., U.S.	F5	121
Bullhead, S.D., U.S.	B4	118
Bullhead City, Az., U.S.	B1	80
Büllingen (Bullange), Bel.	D6	17
Bull Island, i., S.C., U.S.	G6	117
Bull Island, i., S.C., U.S.	F8	117
Bull Island, i., S.C., U.S.	D9	117
Bullitt, co., Ky., U.S.	C4	94
Bullittsville, Ky., U.S.	h13	94
Bull Mountain, mtn., Mt., U.S.	D4	103
Bulloch, co., Ga., U.S.	D5	87
Bullock, N.C., U.S.	A4	110
Bullock, co., Al., U.S.	C4	78
Bullock Creek, Mi., U.S.	E6	99
Bulloo, stm., Austl.	E7	50
Bulloo Lake, l., Austl.	D4	51
Bull Run, stm., Va., U.S.	g11	123
Bullrun Ridge, mtn., Tn., U.S.	m13	119
Bullrun Rock, mtn., Or., U.S.	C8	114
Bulls Bay, b., S.C., U.S.	F8	117
Bulls Bridge, Ct., U.S.	C1	84
Bulls Gap, Tn., U.S.	C10	119
Bull Shoals, Ar., U.S.	A3	81
Bull Shoals Lake, res., U.S.	A3	81
Bull Sluice Lake, res., Ga., U.S.	h8	87
Bully Creek Reservoir, res., Or., U.S.	C9	114
Bulnes, Chile	B2	56
Bulolo, Pap. N. Gui.	k12	50
Bulsār, India	G4	37
Bultfontein, S. Afr.	C4	49
Bulun, Sov. Un.	B15	29
Bulungu, Zaire	B2	48
Bulwark, Alta.	C5	68
Bulyea, Sask.	G3	75
Bumba, Zaire	A3	48
Bumping, stm., Wa., U.S.	C4	124
Bumpus Mills, Tn., U.S.	A4	119
Buna, Tx., U.S.	D6	120
Bunbury, Austl.	F2	50
Bunceton, Mo., U.S.	C5	102
Bunch, Ok., U.S.	B7	113
Bunche Park, Fl., U.S.	*s13	86
Buncombe, Il., U.S.	F5	90
Buncombe, co., N.C., U.S.	f10	110
Buncrana, Ire.	B4	11
Bundaberg, Austl.	D9	50
Bünde, W. Ger.	A3	19
Bündi, India	E5	37
Bundick Creek, stm., La., U.S.	D2	95
Bundoran, Ire.	C3	11
Bunessan, Scot., U.K.	D2	13
Bungay, Eng., U.K.	B9	12
Bunger Hills, hills, Ant.	C23	7
Bungo Strait, strt., Japan	J6	33
Bunia, Zaire	A5	48
Bunker, Mo., U.S.	D6	102
Bunker Hill, Il., U.S.	D4	90
Bunker Hill, In., U.S.	C5	91
Bunker Hill, Ks., U.S.	D5	93
Bunker Hill, Or., U.S.	*D2	114
Bunker Hill, Tn., U.S.	B5	119
Bunker Hill, W.V., U.S.	B6	125
Bunker Hill, mtn., Nv., U.S.	m12	125
Bunkerville, Nv., U.S.	G7	105
Bunkeya, Zaire	D4	48
Bunkie, La., U.S.	D3	95
Bunn, N.C., U.S.	B4	110
Bunnahowen, Ire.	C2	11
Bunnell, Fl., U.S.	C5	86
Bunnlevel, N.C., U.S.	B4	110
Buolkalakh, Sov. Un.	B2	128
Buon Me Thuot, Viet.	C3	34
Buor-Khaya Bay, b., Sov. Un.	B1	128
Bura, Kenya	B7	48
Buram, Sud.	C2	47
Buras, La., U.S.	E6	95
Buraydah, Sau. Ar.	C4	38
Burayk, Libya	D2	43
Burbank, Ca., U.S.	E4	82
Burbank, Il., U.S.	k9	90
Burbank, Ok., U.S.	A5	113
Burbank, S.D., U.S.	E9	118
Burbank, Wa., U.S.	C7	124
Burchard, Ne., U.S.	D9	104
Burco, Som.	D6	47
Burdekin, stm., Austl.	C8	50
Burden, Ks., U.S.	E7	93
Burdett, Alta.	E5	68
Burdett, Ks., U.S.	D4	93
Burdett, N.Y., U.S.	C4	109
Burdette, Ar., U.S.	B6	81
Burdickville, R.I., U.S.	F2	116
Burdur, Tur.	D8	40
Bureau, Il., U.S.	B4	90
Bureau, co., Il., U.S.	B4	90
Burein Mountains, mts., Sov. Un.	B6	33
Büren, W. Ger.	B3	19
Büren [an der Aare], Switz.	B3	21
Bureya, Sov. Un.	B10	31
Bureya, stm., Sov. Un.	A5	33
Burford, Ont.	D4	73
Bür Fu'ād, Eg.	C4	41
Burg, E. Ger.	A6	19
Burg, W. Ger.	D5	15
Burgas, Bul.	D8	24
Burgas, Gulf of, b., Bul.	D8	24
Burgaw, N.C., U.S.	C5	110
Burgdorf, Switz.	E3	21
Burgdorf, W. Ger.	E3	18
Burgeo, Newf.	E4	72
Burgersdorp, S. Afr.	D4	49
Burgess, S.C., U.S.	D9	117
Burgettstown, Pa., U.S.	F1	115
Burghausen, W. Ger.	D7	19
Burghead, Scot., U.K.	C5	13
Burgin, Ky., U.S.	C5	94
Burglengenfeld, W. Ger.	D7	19
Burgoon, Oh., U.S.	A2	112
Burgos, Phil.	n12	34
Burgos, Spain	A4	22
Burgstädt, E. Ger.	C7	19
Burgsteinfurt, W. Ger.	A2	19
Burgsvik, Swe.	I8	14
Burgundy, hist. reg., Fr.	D6	16
Burhānpur, India	D6	36
Burhave, W. Ger.	E2	15
Burhi Gandak, stm., India	E10	37
Buri, Braz.	m7	56
Burica, Punta, c., N.A.	F6	62
Burien, Wa., U.S.	*f11	124
Bürin, Isr. Occ.	E4	41
Burin, Newf.	E4	72
Burin Peninsula, pen., Newf.	E4	72
Buritama, Braz.	C2	56
Burj al 'Arab, Eg.	G7	40
Burkburnett, Tx., U.S.	B3	120
Burke, Id., U.S.	B3	89
Burke, N.Y., U.S.	f10	109
Burke, S.D., U.S.	D6	118
Burke, Vt., U.S.	B5	122
Burke, Va., U.S.	*B5	123
Burke, co., Ga., U.S.	C4	87
Burke, co., N.C., U.S.	B1	110
Burke, co., N.D., U.S.	A3	111
Burke Channel, strt., B.C.	C4	69
Burke City, Mo., U.S.	f13	102
Burkehaven, N.H., U.S.	D2	106
Burke Island, i., Ant.	B2	7
Burkes Garden, Va., U.S.	C1	123
Burkesville, Ky., U.S.	D4	94
Burketon Station (part of Newcastle), Ont.	C6	73
Burkett, Tx., U.S.	C3	120
Burkettsville, Oh., U.S.	B1	112
Burkeville, Tx., U.S.	D6	120
Burkeville, Va., U.S.	C4	123
Burkina Faso, ctry., Afr.	F5	45
Burk's Falls, Ont.	B5	73
Burkville, Al., U.S.	C3	78
Burleigh, N.J., U.S.	E3	107
Burleigh, co., N.D., U.S.	C5	111
Burleson, Tx., U.S.	n9	120
Burleson, co., Tx., U.S.	D4	120
Burley, Id., U.S.	G5	89
Burley, Wa., U.S.	f10	124
Burlingame, Ca., U.S.	h8	82
Burlingame, Ks., U.S.	D8	93
Burlington, Ont.	D5	73
Burlington, Co., U.S.	B8	83
Burlington, Ct., U.S.	B4	84
Burlington, Il., U.S.	A5	90
Burlington, In., U.S.	D5	91
Burlington, Ia., U.S.	D6	92
Burlington, Ks., U.S.	D8	93
Burlington, Ky., U.S.	A5	94
Burlington, Me., U.S.	C4	96
Burlington, Ma., U.S.	f11	98
Burlington, N.J., U.S.	C3	107
Burlington, N.C., U.S.	A3	110
Burlington, N.D., U.S.	A4	111
Burlington, Oh., U.S.	A3	113
Burlington, Pa., U.S.	C8	115
Burlington, Vt., U.S.	C2	122
Burlington, Wa., U.S.	A3	124
Burlington, W.V., U.S.	B6	125
Burlington, Wi., U.S.	F5	126
Burlington, Wy., U.S.	B4	127
Burlington, co., N.J., U.S.	D3	107
Burlington Beach, In., U.S.	B3	91
Burlington Junction, Mo., U.S.	A2	102
Burlyu-Tobe, Sov. Un.	D9	28
Burma (Myanmar), ctry., Asia	D10	36
Burnaby, B.C.	E6	69
Burnaby Island, i., B.C.	C2	69
Burnet, Tx., U.S.	D3	120
Burnet, co., Tx., U.S.	D3	120
Burnett, stm., Austl.	E9	50
Burnett, co., Wi., U.S.	C1	126
Burnettsville, In., U.S.	C4	91
Burney, Ca., U.S.	B3	82
Burney, In., U.S.	F6	91
Burneyville, Ok., U.S.	D4	113
Burnham, Me., U.S.	D3	96
Burnham, Pa., U.S.	E6	115
Burnham-on-Sea / Highbridge, Eng., U.K.	C5	12
Burnie, Austl.	o15	50
Burning Springs, Ky., U.S.	C6	94
Burning Springs, W.V., U.S.	C3	125
Burnley, Eng., U.K.	D5	10
Burns, Co., U.S.	B4	83
Burns, Ks., U.S.	D7	93
Burns, Or., U.S.	D7	114
Burns, Tn., U.S.	A4	119
Burns, Wy., U.S.	E8	127
Burns City, In., U.S.	G4	91
Burns Flat, Ok., U.S.	B2	113
Burnside, Il., U.S.	D3	90
Burnside, Ky., U.S.	D5	94
Burnside, La., U.S.	h10	95
Burnside, Pa., U.S.	E4	115
Burnside, co., Ia., U.S.	B3	92
Burns Lake, B.C.	B5	69
Burns Paiute Indian Reservation, res., U.S.	D7	114
Burnstad, N.D., U.S.	C6	111
Burnsville, Al., U.S.	C3	78
Burnsville, Mn., U.S.	F5	100
Burnsville, Ms., U.S.	A5	101
Burnsville, N.C., U.S.	f10	110
Burnsville, W.V., U.S.	C4	125
Burnsville Lake, res., W.V., U.S.	C4	125
Burnt Cabins, Pa., U.S.	F6	115
Burnt Corn, Al., U.S.	D2	78
Burnt Hills, N.Y., U.S.	C7	109
Burntisland, Scot., U.K.	D5	13
Burnt Islands, Newf.	E2	72
Burnt Mills, Lake, l., Va., U.S.	k14	123
Burnt Prairie, Il., U.S.	E5	90
Burnt River, Ont.	C6	73
Burntside Lake, l., Mn., U.S.	C6	100
Burntwood, stm., Man.	B1	70
Burntwood Lake, l., Man.	B1	70
Burnwell, Al., U.S.	f6	78
Burnwell, W.V., U.S.	m13	125
Burqā, Isr. Occ.	b7	41
Burr, Mn., U.S.	F2	100
Burr, Ne., U.S.	D9	104
Burra, Austl.	F2	51
Burragorang, Lake, l., Austl.	G8	51
Burray, i., Scot., U.K.	B6	13
Burrendong Reservoir, res., Austl.	F7	51
Burr Ferry, La., U.S.	C2	95
Burr Hill, Va., U.S.	B5	123
Burriana, Spain	E11	22
Burr Oak, Ia., U.S.	A6	92
Burr Oak, Ks., U.S.	C5	93
Burr Oak, Mi., U.S.	G5	99
Burr Oak Reservoir, res., Oh., U.S.	C3	112
Burroughs, Ga., U.S.	E5	87
Burrow Head, c., Scot., U.K.	F4	13
Burrows, In., U.S.	C5	91
Burr Ridge, Il., U.S.	*B6	89
Burrton, Ks., U.S.	D6	93
Burruyacú, Arg.	E3	55
Burrville, Tn., U.S.	C9	119
Burrwood, La., U.S.	F6	95
Burry Port, Wales, U.K.	C3	12
Bursa, Tur.	B7	40
Bür Safājah, Eg.	C3	38
Bursey, Mount, mtn., Ant.	B35	7
Burstall, Sask.	G1	75
Burt, Ia., U.S.	A3	92
Burt, N.D., U.S.	C3	111
Burt, co., Ne., U.S.	C9	104
Burta, Austl.	F3	51
Bür Tawfiq, Eg.	C6	41
Burt Lake, l., Mi., U.S.	C6	99
Burton, B.C.	D9	69
Burton, Il., U.S.	D2	90
Burton, Mi., U.S.	E7	99
Burton, Ne., U.S.	B6	104
Burton, Oh., U.S.	A4	112
Burton, Tx., U.S.	D4	120
Burton, Wa., U.S.	f11	124
Burton, W.V., U.S.	B4	125
Burton, Lake, res., Ga., U.S.	B3	87
Burtonport, Ire.	B4	11
Burton upon Trent, Eng., U.K.	D6	10
Burträsk, Swe.	E9	14
Burtrum, Mn., U.S.	E4	100
Burtts Corner, N.B.	C3	71
Burțu, Eg.	D3	41
Buru, i., Indon.	F7	34
Burūk, Wādī al, val., Eg.	D5	41
Burullus, Lake, l., Eg.	C2	41
Burūn, Ra's, c., Eg.	C5	41
Burundi, ctry., Afr.	B5	48
Bururi, Bdi.	B4	48
Burwash, Ont.	A4	73
Burwell, Ne., U.S.	C6	104
Bury, Que.	D6	74
Bury, Eng., U.K.	A5	12
Burynshik, Sov. Un.	D4	28
Bury Saint Edmunds, Eng., U.K.	D7	10
Busby, Alta.	C4	68
Busby, Mt., U.S.	E10	103
Büschfeld, W. Ger.	D1	19
Bush, Ky., U.S.	C6	94
Bush, La., U.S.	D6	95
Bush City, Ks., U.S.	D8	93
Bushenyi, Ug.	B5	48
Bushimaie, stm., Zaire	C3	48
Bushiribana, Aruba	G17	65
Bushkill, Pa., U.S.	D11	115
Bushland, Tx., U.S.	B1	120
Bushmills, N. Ire., U.K.	B6	11
Bushnell, Fl., U.S.	D4	86
Bushnell, Il., U.S.	C3	90
Bushnell, Ne., U.S.	C9	104
Bushnell, S.D., U.S.	C9	118
Bushong, Ks., U.S.	D7	93
Bush River, stm., Md., U.S.	B5	97
Bushton, Ks., U.S.	D5	93
Businga, Zaire	A4	48
Busk, Sov. Un.	G5	27
Busko [Zdrój], Pol.	F11	27
Buşrá ash Shām, Syria	A2	41
Bussang, Fr.	F2	50
Busselton, Austl.	F2	50
Busseto, Italy	E6	20
Bussey, Ia., U.S.	C4	92
Bussum, Neth.	A6	16
Busto Arsizio, Italy	B2	20
Busu-Djanoa, Zaire	A4	48
Büsum, W. Ger.	D2	15
Buta, Zaire	A3	48
Buta Ranquil, Arg.	B3	56
Butare, Rw.	B5	48
Bute, Island of, i., Scot., U.K.	E3	13
Butedale, B.C.	C3	69
Bute Inlet, b., B.C.	D5	69
Butere, Kenya	A5	48
Butha Qi, China	B9	31
Buthier, stm., Italy	D3	20
Butler, Al., U.S.	C1	78
Butler, Ga., U.S.	D2	87
Butler, Il., U.S.	D4	90
Butler, In., U.S.	B8	91
Butler, Ky., U.S.	B5	94
Butler, Mo., U.S.	C3	102
Butler, N.J., U.S.	B4	107
Butler, Oh., U.S.	B3	112
Butler, Ok., U.S.	B2	113
Butler, Pa., U.S.	E2	115
Butler, S.D., U.S.	C8	118
Butler, Tn., U.S.	C11	119
Butler, Wi., U.S.	m11	126
Butler, co., Al., U.S.	D3	78
Butler, co., Ia., U.S.	B5	92
Butler, co., Ks., U.S.	E7	93
Butler, co., Ky., U.S.	C3	94
Butler, co., Mo., U.S.	E7	102
Butler, co., Ne., U.S.	C8	104
Butler, co., Oh., U.S.	C1	112
Butler, co., Pa., U.S.	E2	115
Butlers Bridge, Ire.	C4	11
Butlerville, In., U.S.	F6	91
Butmīyah, Isr. Occ.	C6	73
Butner, N.C., U.S.	A4	110
Buton, i., Indon.	F6	34
Butovo, Sov. Un.	n17	27
Buttahatchee, stm., U.S.	B5	101
Butte, Mt., U.S.	D4	103
Butte, Ne., U.S.	B7	104
Butte, N.D., U.S.	B5	111
Butte, co., Ca., U.S.	C3	82
Butte, co., Id., U.S.	F5	89
Butte, co., S.D., U.S.	C2	118
Butte des Morts, Lake, l., Wi., U.S.	D5	126
Butte Falls, Or., U.S.	E4	114
Butte Mountains, mts., Nv., U.S.	D6	105
Butterfield, Mn., U.S.	G4	100
Butterfield, Mo., U.S.	E4	102
Butternut, Wi., U.S.	B3	126
Butternut Lake, l., Wi., U.S.	C5	126
Butters, N.C., U.S.	C4	110
Butterworth, Malay.	D2	34
Butterworth, Transkei	D4	49
Buttevant, Ire.	E3	11
Button Islands, is., N.W. Ter.	f8	72
Button Islands, is., N.W. Ter.	f8	72
Buttonwillow, Ca., U.S.	E4	82
Butts, co., Ga., U.S.	C3	87
Butuan, Phil.	D7	34
Butzbach, W. Ger.	C3	19
Bützow, E. Ger.	B5	18
Buuhoodle, Som.	D6	47
Buur Gaabo, Som.	F5	47
Buur Hakaba, Som.	E5	47
Buxtehude, W. Ger.	B4	18
Buxton, Guy.	A3	59
Buxton, Eng., U.K.	A6	12
Buxton, N.C., U.S.	B7	110
Buxton, N.D., U.S.	B8	111
Buxton, Or., U.S.	g11	114
Buxton, Mount, mtn., B.C.	D3	69
Buxton Center, Me., U.S.	*E2	96
Buy, Sov. Un.	B6	28
Buyck, Mn., U.S.	B6	100
Buynaksk, Sov. Un.	E4	28
Buyr Lake, l., Asia	B8	31
Büyükliman see Vakfikebir, Tur.	B12	40
Büyükmenderes, stm., Tur.	D7	40
Buzachi Peninsula, pen., Sov. Un.	E4	28
Buzancy, Fr.	E4	17
Buzău, Rom.	C8	24
Buzău, stm., Rom.	C8	24
Buzaymah, Libya	E4	43
Buzet, Yugo.	C1	24
Buzuluk, Sov. Un.	C4	28
Buzzards Bay, Ma., U.S.	C6	98
Buzzards Bay, b., Ma., U.S.	C6	98
Buzzard Roost, mtn., N.C., U.S.	B1	110
Byala, Bul.	D7	24
Byala Slatina, Bul.	D6	24
Byam Martin Island, i., N.W. Ter.	m31	66
Byars, Ok., U.S.	C4	113
Bybee, Tn., U.S.	C10	119
Bydgoszcz, Pol.	B5	26
Byelorussia (White Russia), state, Sov. Un.	D5	29
Byemoor, Alta.	D4	68
Byer, Oh., U.S.	C3	112
Byers, Co., U.S.	B6	83
Byers, Ks., U.S.	E5	93
Byers, Tx., U.S.	B4	120
Byesville, Oh., U.S.	C4	112
Byfield, Ma., U.S.	A6	98
Byglandsfjord, Nor.	H2	14
Byhalia, Ms., U.S.	A4	101
Bykovo, Sov. Un.	n18	27
Bykovo, Sov. Un.	G15	27
Bylas, Az., U.S.	D5	80
Bylot Island, i., N.W. Ter.	B17	66
Byng, Ok., U.S.	C5	113
Byng Inlet, Ont.	B4	73
Bynum, Al., U.S.	B4	78
Bynum, Mt., U.S.	C4	103
Bynumville, Mo., U.S.	B5	102
Byram, Ms., U.S.	C3	101
Byrd, sci., Ant.	A36	7
Byrd Glacier, ice, Ant.	g40	7
Byrdstown, Tn., U.S.	C8	119
Byrnedale, Pa., U.S.	D5	115
Byrock, Austl.	E6	51
Byromville, Ga., U.S.	D3	87
Byron, Ga., U.S.	h9	82
Byron, Il., U.S.	A4	90
Byron, Me., U.S.	D2	96
Byron, Mn., U.S.	F6	100
Byron, Ne., U.S.	D8	104
Byron, N.Y., U.S.	B2	109
Byron, Ok., U.S.	A3	113
Byron, Wy., U.S.	B4	127
Byron, Cape, c., Austl.	E9	50
Byrum, Den.	A5	15
Byšice-Liblice, Czech.	n18	26
Bystrzyca [Kłodzka], Pol.	C4	26
Bytom (Beuthen), Pol.	C5	26
Bytów, Pol.	B5	26
Byzantium see İstanbul, Tur.	B7	40

C

Name	Map Ref.	Page
Ca, stm., Asia	C6	35
Caacupé, Para.	E4	55
Caaguazú, dept., Para.	E4	55
Čaák, Yugo.	D5	24
Caála, Ang.	D2	48
Caamaño Sound, strt., B.C.	C3	69
Caapucú, Para.	E4	55
Caazapá, Para.	E4	55
Caazapá, dept., Para.	E4	55
Cabaceiras, Braz.	h5	57
Cabalete, i., Phil.	o13	34
Caballo, N.M.	E2	108
Caballo Mountains, mts., N.M., U.S.	E2	108
Caballo Reservoir, res., N.M., U.S.	E2	108
Cabana, Peru	C2	58
Cabanatuan, Phil.	o13	34
Cabano, Que.	B9	74
Cabarita, stm., Jam.	E12	65
Cabell, co., W.V., U.S.	C2	125
Cabery, Il., U.S.	C5	90
Cabeza del Buey, Spain	C3	22
Cabezas, Bol.	C3	55
Cabimas, Ven.	A3	60
Cabin Creek, W.V., U.S.	m13	125
Cabin Creek, stm., W.V., U.S.	m13	125
Cabinda, Ang.	C1	48
Cabinda, prov., Ang.	C1	48
Cabinet Gorge Reservoir, res., U.S.	B1	103
Cabinet Mountains, mts., Mt., U.S.	B1	103
Cabin John, Md., U.S.	C3	97
Cable, Wi., U.S.	B2	126
Cabo, Braz.	k6	57
Cabo Blanco, Arg.	D3	54
Cabo Delgado, dept., Moz.	D6	48
Cabo Frio, Braz.	C4	56
Cabo Gracias a Dios, Nic.	D8	63
Cabonga, Réservoir, res., Que.	k11	74
Cabool, Mo., U.S.	D5	102
Caboolture, Austl.	C9	51
Cabora Bassa Lake, res., Moz.	A5	49
Cabot, Ar., U.S.	C3	81
Cabot, Pa., U.S.	E2	115
Cabot, Vt., U.S.	C4	122
Cabot, Mount, mtn., N.H., U.S.	A4	106
Cabot Head, c., Ont.	B3	73
Cabot Strait, strt., Can.	G20	67
Cabra, Spain	D3	22
Cabras Island, i., Guam	L9	52
Cabrera Baja, Sierra de la, mts., Spain	A2	22
Cabrera Island, i., Spain	C7	22
Cabri, Sask.	G1	75
Cabriel, stm., Spain	C5	22
Cabri Lake, l., Sask.	F1	75
Cabrillo National Monument, Ca., U.S.	o15	82
Cabrobó, Braz.	C3	57
Caçador, Braz.	D2	56
Caçapava do Sul, Braz.	E2	56
Cacapon, stm., W.V., U.S.	B6	125
Cacequi, Braz.	D2	56
Cáceres, Braz.	C4	55
Cáceres, Col.	B2	60
Cáceres, Spain	C2	22
Cachan, Fr.	g10	16
Cache, Il., U.S.	F4	90
Cache, Ok., U.S.	C3	113
Cache, co., Ut., U.S.	B4	121
Cache, stm., Ar., U.S.	C4	81
Cache Bay, Ont.	A5	73
Cache Creek, B.C.	D7	69
Cache Creek, stm., Ca., U.S.	C2	82
Cache Junction, Ut., U.S.	B3	121
Cache la Poudre, stm., Co., U.S.	A5	83
Cache la Poudre, North Fork, stm., Co., U.S.	A5	83
Cache Mountain, mtn., Ak., U.S.	B10	79
Cache Peak, mtn., Id., U.S.	G5	89
Cachi, Arg.	E2	55
Cachimbo, Serra do, mts., Braz.	D4	57
Cachoeira, Braz.	D3	57
Cachoeira do Arari, Braz.	C5	57
Cachoeira do Sul, Braz.	E2	56
Cachoeira do Itapemirim, Braz.	C4	56
Caçiporé, Braz.	B4	59
Caçiporé, Cabo, c., Braz.	B4	59
Cacique, Pan.	h11	62
Cacólo, Ang.	D3	48
Caconda, Braz.	D2	48
Cacouna-Station, Que.	B8	74
Cactus, Tx., U.S.	B1	120
Cactus Flat, pl., Nv., U.S.	F5	105
Cactus Peak, mtn., Nv., U.S.	F5	105
Cactus Springs, Nv., U.S.	G6	105
Caçu, Braz.	A4	56
Caculé, Braz.	C3	57
Caddo, Ok., U.S.	C5	113
Caddo, Tx., U.S.	C3	120
Caddo, co., Ok., U.S.	B3	113
Caddo, par., La., U.S.	B2	95
Caddo, stm., Ar., U.S.	C2	81
Caddo Creek, stm., Ok., U.S.	C4	113
Caddo Gap, Ar., U.S.	C2	81
Caddo Lake, res., U.S.	B2	95
Caddo Mountains, mts., Ar., U.S.	C2	81
Cade, La., U.S.	D4	95
Cader Idris, mtn., Wales, U.K.	A4	90
Cades, S.C., U.S.	D8	117
Cades Cove, Tn., U.S.	D10	119
Cadet, Mo., U.S.	C7	102
Cadillac, Sask.	H2	75
Cadillac, Fr.	E3	16
Cadillac, Mi., U.S.	D5	99
Cadillac Mountain, mtn., Me., U.S.	D4	96
Cadiz, Ky., U.S.	D2	94
Cadiz, Oh., U.S.	B4	112
Cádiz, Spain	D2	22
Cadiz, Gulf of, b., Eur.	D2	22
Cadogan, Alta.	C5	68
Cadott, Wi., U.S.	D2	126
Cadron Creek, stm., Ar., U.S.	B3	81
Cadwell, Ga., U.S.	D3	87
Cadyville, N.Y., U.S.	f11	109
Caen, Fr.	C6	16
Caernarfon, Wales, U.K.	D4	10
Caernarfon Bay, b., Wales, U.K.	D4	10
Caerphilly, Wales, U.K.	C4	12
Caesar Creek Lake, res., Oh., U.S.	C2	112
Caetité, Braz.	C4	56
Cafayate, Arg.	B3	56
Cagayan, stm., Phil.	B6	34
Cagayan de Oro, Phil.	D6	34
Cagayan Islands, is., Phil.	D6	34
Cagayan Sulu Island, i., Phil.	D6	21
Cagli, Italy	F7	20
Cagliari, Italy	E2	23
Cagliari, Gulf of, b., Italy	E2	23
Cagnes-sur-Mer, Fr.	F7	16
Caguas, P.R.	G11	64
Caha Mountains, mts., Ire.	F2	11
Caher, Ire.	E3	11
Caherdaniel, Ire.	F1	11
Cahersiveen, Ire.	F1	11
Cahokia, Il., U.S.	E3	90
Cahore Point, c., Ire.	E5	11
Cahuinari, stm., Col.	D3	60
Caiabis, Serra dos, plat., Braz.	E3	59
Caiapônia, Braz.	B2	56
Cai Bau, i., Viet.	B7	35
Caicara, Ven.	B4	60
Caicedonia, Col.	C2	60
Caicó, Braz.	D3	57
Caicos Islands, is., T./C. Is.	D8	64
Caicos Passage, strt., N.A.	C7	64
Cailloma, Peru	E3	58
Caillou Bay, b., La., U.S.	E5	95
Caillou Lake, l., La., U.S.	E5	95
Caimanera, Cuba	E6	64
Caiman Point, c., Phil.	o12	34
Caimito, stm., Pan.	m11	62
Cains, stm., N.B.	C4	71
Cains Store, Ky., U.S.	C5	94
Cainsville, Mo., U.S.	A4	102
Cainsville, Tn., U.S.	B5	119
Caintown, Ont.	C9	73
Cairnbrook, Pa., U.S.	F4	115
Cairngorm Mountains, mts., Scot., U.K.	C5	13
Cairns, Austl.	C8	50
Cairnsmore of Carsphairn, mtn., Scot., U.K.	E4	13
Cairn Table, mtn., Scot., U.K.	E5	13
Cairo (Al Qāhirah), Eg.	B3	38
Cairo, Ga., U.S.	F2	87
Cairo, Il., U.S.	F4	90
Cairo, Mo., U.S.	B5	102
Cairo, Ne., U.S.	D7	104
Cairo, N.Y., U.S.	C6	109
Cairo, Oh., U.S.	B1	112
Cairo, W.V., U.S.	B3	125
Caiundo, Ang.	E2	48
Cajabamba, Peru	C2	58
Cajamarca, Peru	C2	58
Cajamarca, dept., Peru	C2	58
Cajapió, Braz.	C3	57
Cajazeiras, Braz.	C3	57
Cajatambo, Peru	C2	58
Čajniče, Yugo.	D4	24
Čakovec, Yugo.	B3	24
Čakovice, Czech.	n18	26
Calabar, Nig.	F6	45
Calabasas, Ca., U.S.	m11	82
Calabogie, Ont.	B8	73
Calabogie Lake, l., Ont.	B8	73
Calabozo, Ven.	B4	60
Calabria, prov., Italy	E6	23
Calafat, Rom.	D6	24
Calafate, Arg.	E2	54
Calagua Islands, is., Phil.	o14	34
Calahorra, Spain	A5	22
Calais, Fr.	B4	16
Calais, Me., U.S.	C5	96
Calais, Vt., U.S.	C4	122
Calama, Chile	D2	55
Calamar, Col.	C3	60
Calamar, Col.	C3	60
Calamba, Phil.	o13	34
Calamian Group, is., Phil.	B5	34
Calamocha, Spain	C7	22
Calamus, stm., Ne., U.S.	B6	104
Calañas, Spain	D2	22
Calanda, Spain	C7	22
Calanscio, Sarīr, des., Afr.	H5	40
Calanscio, Sarīr, des., Libya	D4	43
Calapan, Phil.	C6	34
Calarca, Col.	C2	60
Calasparra, Spain	E1	22
Calatafimi, Italy	F5	105
Calatayud, Spain	G6	105
Calau, E. Ger.	B8	18
Calauag, Phil.	p14	34
Calauag Bay, b., Phil.	o14	34
Calaveras, co., Ca., U.S.	C3	82
Calavo Gardens, Ca., U.S.	*o16	82
Calbe, E. Ger.	B6	19
Calbuco, Chile	D3	58
Calca, Peru	E4	58
Calcasieu, co., La., U.S.	D3	95
Calcasieu, stm., La., U.S.	D2	95
Calcasieu Lake, l., La., U.S.	E2	95
Calcasieu Pass, strt., La., U.S.	E2	95
Calceta, Ec.	B1	58
Calchaquí, Arg.	B4	56
Calçoene, Braz.	B4	59
Calcutta, India	D8	36
Calcutta, Oh., U.S.	B5	112
Calcutta Lake, l., Nv., U.S.	B2	105
Caldaro, Italy	C2	20
Caldas, dept., Col.	E2	60
Caldas da Rainha, Port.	C1	22
Calder, Sask.	F5	75
Calder, Id., U.S.	B2	89
Calder, stm., Eng., U.K.	A6	12
Caldera, Chile	E1	55
Calderwood, Tn., U.S.	D10	119
Caldron Falls Reservoir, res., Wi., U.S.	C5	126
Caldwell, Ar., U.S.	B5	81
Caldwell, Id., U.S.	F2	89
Caldwell, Ks., U.S.	E6	93
Caldwell, N.J., U.S.	B4	107
Caldwell, Oh., U.S.	C4	112
Caldwell, Tx., U.S.	D4	120
Caldwell, W.V., U.S.	D4	125
Caldwell, co., Ky., U.S.	C2	94
Caldwell, co., Mo., U.S.	B3	102
Caldwell, co., N.C., U.S.	B1	110
Caldwell, co., Tx., U.S.	E4	120
Cale, Ar., U.S.	D2	81
Caledon, Ont.	D5	73
Caledon, N. Ire., U.K.	E4	11
Caledonia, Ont.	D5	73
Caledonia, Ms., U.S.	B5	101
Caledonia, Mn., U.S.	G7	100
Caledonia, N.Y., U.S.	C3	109
Caledonia, Oh., U.S.	B3	112
Caledonia, co., Vt., U.S.	C4	122
Caledonian Canal, Scot., U.K.	B7	12
Calella, Spain	B7	22
Calenzana, Fr.	F2	23
Calera, Al., U.S.	B3	78
Calera, Ok., U.S.	D5	113
Caleta Olivia, Arg.	D3	54
Calexico, Ca., U.S.	F6	82
Calf of Man, i., I. of Man	G8	10
Calgary, Alta.	D3	68
Calhan, Co., U.S.	B6	83
Calheta, Port.	h11	22
Calhoun, Ga., U.S.	B2	87
Calhoun, Il., U.S.	E5	90

Name	Map Ref.	Page
Calhoun, Ky., U.S.	C2	94
Calhoun, La., U.S.	B3	95
Calhoun, Mo., U.S.	C4	102
Calhoun, Tn., U.S.	D9	119
Calhoun, co., Al., U.S.	B4	78
Calhoun, co., Ar., U.S.	D3	81
Calhoun, co., Fl., U.S.	B1	86
Calhoun, co., Ga., U.S.	E2	87
Calhoun, co., Il., U.S.	D3	90
Calhoun, co., Ia., U.S.	B3	92
Calhoun, co., Mi., U.S.	F5	99
Calhoun, co., Ms., U.S.	B4	101
Calhoun, co., S.C., U.S.	D6	117
Calhoun, co., Tx., U.S.	E4	120
Calhoun, co., W.V., U.S.	C3	125
Calhoun City, Ms., U.S.	B4	101
Calhoun Falls, S.C., U.S.	C2	117
Cali, Col.	C2	60
Calico Rock, Ar., U.S.	A3	81
Calicut (Kozhikode), India	F6	36
Caliente, Ca., U.S.	E4	82
Caliente, Nv., U.S.	F7	105
Califon, N.J., U.S.	B3	107
California, Mo., U.S.	k14	94
California, Mo., U.S.	*D4	97
California, Mo., U.S.	C5	102
California, Pa., U.S.	F2	115
California, state, U.S.	D4	82
California, Golfo de, b., Mex.	B2	63
California Aqueduct, Ca., U.S.	E4	82
California Junction, Ia., U.S.	C1	92
California Oil Camp, Co., U.S.	A2	83
Calingasta, Arg.	A3	54
Calio, N.D., U.S.	A7	111
Calion, Ar., U.S.	D3	81
Calipatria, Ca., U.S.	F6	82
Calispell Peak, mtn., Wa., U.S.	A8	124
Calistoga, Ca., U.S.	C2	82
Callabonna, stm., Austl.	D3	51
Callabonna, Lake, l., Austl.	D3	51
Callaghan, Mount, mtn., Nv., U.S.	D5	105
Callahan, Fl., U.S.	B5	86
Callahan, Ks., U.S.	g12	93
Callahan, co., Tx., U.S.	C3	120
Callan, Ire.	E4	11
Callander, Ont.	A5	73
Callander, Scot., U.K.	B4	10
Callands, Va., U.S.	D3	123
Callao, Peru	D2	58
Callao, Mo., U.S.	B5	102
Callao, Va., U.S.	C6	123
Callao, dept., Peru	*D2	58
Callaway, Fl., U.S.	*u16	86
Callaway, Md., U.S.	D4	97
Callaway, Mn., U.S.	D3	100
Callaway, Ne., U.S.	C6	104
Callaway, co., Mo., U.S.	C2	123
Callender, Ia., U.S.	B3	92
Callensburg, Pa., U.S.	D2	115
Callery, Pa., U.S.	E1	115
Callicoon, N.Y., U.S.	D5	109
Callicoon Center, N.Y., U.S.	D6	109
Calliham, Tx., U.S.	E3	120
Calling Lake, Alta.	B4	68
Calling Lake, l., Alta.	B4	68
Calloway, co., Ky., U.S.	f9	94
Calmar, Alta.	C4	68
Calmar, Ia., U.S.	A6	92
Calne, Eng., U.K.	C5	12
Caloosahatchee, stm., Fl., U.S.	F5	86
Caloundra, Austl.	E9	50
Calpella, Ca., U.S.	C2	82
Calpet, Wy., U.S.	D2	127
Caltagirone, Italy	F5	23
Caltanissetta, Italy	F5	23
Caltra, Ire.	D3	11
Caluire [-et-Cuire], Fr.	E6	16
Calulo, Ang.	D1	48
Calumet, Que.	D3	74
Calumet, Al., U.S.	B2	78
Calumet, Ia., U.S.	B2	92
Calumet, Mi., U.S.	A2	99
Calumet, Mn., U.S.	C5	100
Calumet, Ok., U.S.	B3	113
Calumet, co., Wi., U.S.	D5	126
Calumet, Lake, l., Il., U.S.	k9	90
Calumet City, Il., U.S.	B6	90
Calumet Park, Il., U.S.	*k9	90
Calumet Sag Channel, Il., U.S.	k9	90
Calumetville, Wi., U.S.	k9	126
Calunda, Ang.	D3	48
Caluula, Som.	C7	47
Calvary, Ga., U.S.	F2	87
Calvary, Wi., U.S.	k9	126
Calvert, Al., U.S.	D1	78
Calvert, Tx., U.S.	D4	120
Calvert, co., Md., U.S.	C4	97
Calvert City, Ky., U.S.	e9	94
Calvert Island, i., B.C.	D3	69
Calverton, Md., U.S.	B4	97
Calverton, Va., U.S.	B5	123
Calverton Park, Mo., U.S.	f13	102
Calvi, Fr.	C2	23
Calvillo, Mex.	m12	63
Calvin, La., U.S.	C3	95
Calvin, N.D., U.S.	A7	111
Calvin, Ok., U.S.	C5	113
Calvinia, S. Afr.	D2	49
Calvörde, E. Ger.	A6	19
Calw, W. Ger.	E3	19
Calwa, Ca., U.S.	*D4	82
Calypso, N.C., U.S.	B4	110
Calzada de Calatrava, Spain	C4	22
Cam, stm., Eng., U.K.	D7	10
Camabatela, Ang.	C2	48
Camacho, Mex.	C4	63
Camacupa, Ang.	D2	48
Camagüey, Cuba	D5	64
Camagüey, prov., Cuba	D5	64
Camajuani, Cuba	C4	64
Camak, Ga., U.S.	C4	87
Camamu, Braz.	D3	57
Camana, Peru	E3	58
Camanducaia, Braz.	m8	56
Camano Island, i., Wa., U.S.	A3	124
Camapuã, Braz.	B2	56
Camaquã, Braz.	E2	56
Camaquã, stm., Braz.	E2	56
Camararé, stm., Braz.	E3	59
Camargo, Bol.	D2	55
Camargo, Ok., U.S.	D5	90
Camarillo, Ca., U.S.	*E4	82
Camarón, Cabo, c., Hond.	D7	63
Camarones, Arg.	C3	54
Camarones, Bahía, b., Arg.	C3	54
Camas, Wa., U.S.	D3	124
Camas, co., Id., U.S.	F4	89
Camas Valley, Or., U.S.	D3	114
Ca Mau, Viet.	D3	34
Ca Mau, Cape, c., Viet.	D2	34
Camberwell, Austl.	*G8	50
Cambodia, ctry., Asia	C3	34
Camborne [-Redruth], Eng., U.K.	E4	10
Cambra, Pa., U.S.	D9	115
Cambrai, Fr.	B5	16
Cambria, Ca., U.S.	E3	82
Cambria, Ia., U.S.	D4	92
Cambria, Mi., U.S.	G6	99
Cambria, Wi., U.S.	E4	126
Cambria, co., Pa., U.S.	E4	115
Cambrian Mountains, mts., Wales, U.K.	D5	10
Cambrian Park, Ca., U.S.	*D3	82
Cambridge, Ont.	D4	73
Cambridge, Eng., U.K.	D7	10
Cambridge, Id., U.S.	E2	89
Cambridge, Il., U.S.	B3	90
Cambridge, Ia., U.S.	C4	92
Cambridge, Ks., U.S.	E7	93
Cambridge, Me., U.S.	C3	96
Cambridge, Md., U.S.	C5	97
Cambridge, Mn., U.S.	B5	100
Cambridge, Ne., U.S.	D5	104
Cambridge, N.Y., U.S.	B7	109
Cambridge, Oh., U.S.	B4	112
Cambridge, Vt., U.S.	B3	122
Cambridge, Wi., U.S.	E4	126
Cambridge Bay, N.W. Ter.	C12	66
Cambridge City, In., U.S.	E7	91
Cambridge Junction, Vt., U.S.	B3	122
Cambridgeport, Vt., U.S.	E3	122
Cambridge Reservoir, res., Ma., U.S.	g10	98
Cambridgeshire, co., Eng., U.K.	B7	12
Cambridge Springs, Pa., U.S.	C1	115
Cambuí, Braz.	m8	56
Cambundi-Catembo (Nova Gaia), Ang.	D2	48
Camden, Al., U.S.	D2	78
Camden, Ar., U.S.	D3	81
Camden, De., U.S.	D3	85
Camden, In., U.S.	C4	91
Camden, Me., U.S.	D3	96
Camden, Mi., U.S.	G6	99
Camden, Ms., U.S.	C4	101
Camden, N.J., U.S.	D2	107
Camden, N.Y., U.S.	B5	109
Camden, N.C., U.S.	A6	110
Camden, Oh., U.S.	C1	112
Camden, S.C., U.S.	C6	117
Camden, Tn., U.S.	A3	119
Camden, Tx., U.S.	D5	120
Camden, W.V., U.S.	B4	125
Camden, co., Ga., U.S.	F5	87
Camden, co., Mo., U.S.	C5	102
Camden, co., N.J., U.S.	D3	107
Camden, co., N.C., U.S.	A6	110
Camden on Gauley, W.V., U.S.	C4	125
Camdenton, Mo., U.S.	D5	102
Camelback Mountain, mtn., Az., U.S.	k9	80
Camelot, Wa., U.S.	*B3	124
Camels Hump, mtn., Vt., U.S.	C3	122
Camerino, Italy	C4	23
Cameron, Az., U.S.	B4	80
Cameron, Il., U.S.	C3	90
Cameron, La., U.S.	E2	95
Cameron, Mo., U.S.	B3	102
Cameron, Mt., U.S.	E5	103
Cameron, N.C., U.S.	B3	110
Cameron, Ok., U.S.	B7	113
Cameron, Pa., U.S.	D5	115
Cameron, S.C., U.S.	D6	117
Cameron, Tx., U.S.	D4	120
Cameron, W.V., U.S.	B4	125
Cameron, co., La., U.S.	E2	95
Cameron, co., Pa., U.S.	D5	115
Cameron, co., Tx., U.S.	F4	120
Cameron Hills, hills, Can.	f30	66
Cameron Island, i., N.W. Ter.	m31	66
Cameron Park, Ca., U.S.	*C3	82
Cameroon, ctry., Afr.	D2	46
Cameroon, Mont, mtn., Cam.	E1	46
Cametá, Braz.	C5	59
Camiling, Phil.	o13	34
Camilla, Ga., U.S.	E2	87
Camiña, Chile	G7	58
Caminha, Port.	B1	22
Camino, Ca., U.S.	C3	82
Camissombo (Verísimo Sarmento), Ang.	C3	48
Camlachie, Ont.	D2	73
Cammack Village, Ar., U.S.	C3	81
Cammal, Pa., U.S.	D7	115
Camocim, Braz.	B2	57
Camooweal, Austl.	C6	50
Camopi, stm., Fr. Gu.	B4	59
Camp, co., Tx., U.S.	C5	120
Campagna di Roma, reg., Italy	h9	23
Campaign, Tn., U.S.	D8	119
Campana, Arg.	g7	54
Campana, Isla, i., Chile	D1	54
Campanario, Arg.	C3	22
Campania, prov., Italy	D5	23
Campania Island, i., B.C.	C3	69
Campbell, Al., U.S.	D2	78
Campbell, Ca., U.S.	k8	82
Campbell, Fl., U.S.	D5	86
Campbell, Mn., U.S.	D2	100
Campbell, Ne., U.S.	E7	104
Campbell, N.Y., U.S.	C3	109
Campbell, Oh., U.S.	A5	112
Campbell, co., Ky., U.S.	B5	94
Campbell, co., S.D., U.S.	B5	118
Campbell, co., Tn., U.S.	C9	119
Campbell, co., Wy., U.S.	B7	127
Campbell, Cape, c., N.Z.	N15	51
Campbellford, Ont.	C7	73
Campbell Hill, hill, Oh., U.S.	B2	112
Campbell Island, B.C.	C3	69
Campbell Island, i., B.C.	C3	69
Campbell Island, i., B.C.	J8	2
Campbell Lake, l., Or., U.S.	E7	114
Campbell River, B.C.	D5	69
Campbells Bay, Que.	B8	73
Campbellsburg, In., U.S.	G5	91
Campbellsburg, Ky., U.S.	B4	94
Campbells Creek, stm., W.V., U.S.	m13	125
Campbellsville, Ky., U.S.	C4	94
Campbellton, Tn., U.S.	B4	119
Campbellton, N.B.	A3	71
Campbellton, Newf.	D4	72
Campbellton, P.E.I.	C5	71
Campbellton, Fl., U.S.	B1	86
Campbelltown, Austl.	*F9	50
Campbeltown, Scot., U.K.	C4	10
Camp Creek, Tn., U.S.	C11	119
Camp Crook, S.D., U.S.	B2	118
Camp Douglas, Wi., U.S.	E3	126
Campeche, Mex.	D6	63
Campeche, state, Mex.	D6	63
Campeche, Bahía de, b., Mex.	C6	63
Campechuela, Cuba	D5	64
Camperdown, Austl.	I4	51
Campertogno, Italy	E5	21
Camp Grove, Il., U.S.	B4	90
Cam Pha, Viet.	A3	34
Camp Hill, Al., U.S.	C4	78
Camp Hill, Pa., U.S.	F8	115
Camp H. M. Smith Marine Corps Base, mil., Hi., U.S.	g10	88
Camp Howard Ridge, mtn., Id., U.S.	D2	89
Campiglia Marittima, Italy	C3	23
Campina Grande, Braz.	C3	57
Campinas, Braz.	C3	56
Campina Verde, Braz.	B3	56
Campion, Co., U.S.	A5	83
Campione d'Italia, Italy	D4	21
Camp Lejeune Marine Corps Base, mil., N.C., U.S.	C5	110
Campo, Cam.	E1	46
Campo, Ca., U.S.	F5	82
Campo, Co., U.S.	D8	83
Campoalegre, Col.	C2	60
Campo Alegre de Goiás, Braz.	B5	56
Campobasso, Italy	D5	23
Campo Belo, Braz.	C3	56
Campo de Criptana, Spain	C4	22
Campodolcino, Italy	D7	21
Campo Gallo, Arg.	E3	55
Campo Grande, Braz.	C2	56
Campo Maior, Braz.	B2	57
Campo Maior, Port.	C2	22
Campo Mourão, Braz.	C2	56
Campo Real, Spain	p18	22
Campos, Braz.	C4	56
Campos Altos, Braz.	B3	56
Camposampiero, Italy	D7	20
Campos Belos, Braz.	A3	56
Campos Novos, Braz.	D2	56
Campos Sales, Braz.	C2	57
Campo Tencia, mtn., Switz.	D6	21
Campo Tures, Italy	C7	20
Camp Pendleton Marine Corps Base, mil., Ca., U.S.	F5	82
Camp San Saba, Tx., U.S.	D3	120
Camp Sherman, Or., U.S.	C5	114
Camp Springs, Md., U.S.	f9	97
Campti, La., U.S.	C2	95
Campton, Fl., U.S.	v15	86
Compton, Ga., U.S.	C3	87
Campton, Ky., U.S.	C6	94
Campton, N.H., U.S.	C3	106
Camptown, Pa., U.S.	C9	115
Campus, Il., U.S.	B5	90
Camp Verde, Az., U.S.	C4	80
Camp Verde Indian Reservation, Az., U.S.	C4	80
Campville, Fl., U.S.	C4	86
Camp Wood, Tx., U.S.	E2	120
Cam Ranh, Viet.	G8	35
Cam Ranh Bay, b., Viet.	G8	35
Camrose, Alta.	C4	68
Camuquén, Ven.	B5	60
Canaan, N.B.	C4	71
Canaan, Ct., U.S.	A2	84
Canaan, In., U.S.	G7	91
Canaan, Me., U.S.	D3	96
Canaan, N.H., U.S.	C2	106
Canaan, N.Y., U.S.	C7	109
Canaan, Vt., U.S.	A5	122
Canaan, stm., N.B.	C4	71
Canaan Center, N.H., U.S.	C2	106
Canaan Street, N.H., U.S.	C2	106
Canada, Ky., U.S.	*C7	94
Canada, ctry., N.A.	E13	66
Canada Bay, b., Newf.	D3	72
Cañada de Gómez, Arg.	A4	54
Canada Falls Lake, res., Me., U.S.	C2	96
Canadensis, Pa., U.S.	D11	115
Canadian, Ok., U.S.	B6	113
Canadian, Tx., U.S.	B2	120
Canadian, co., Ok., U.S.	B3	113
Canadian, stm., U.S.	C7	76
Canadys, S.C., U.S.	E6	117
Canajoharie, N.Y., U.S.	C6	109
Çanakkale, Tur.	A3	40
Canale, Italy	E3	21
Canal Flats, B.C.	D10	69
Canal Fulton, Oh., U.S.	B4	112
Canalou, Mo., U.S.	E8	102
Canal Point, Fl., U.S.	F6	86
Canal Winchester, Oh., U.S.	C3	112
Canandaigua, N.Y., U.S.	C3	109
Canandaigua Lake, l., N.Y., U.S.	C3	109
Cananea, Mex.	A2	63
Cananéia, Braz.	D3	56
Canápolis, Braz.	B3	56
Cañar, Ec.	B2	60
Cañar, prov., Ec.	B2	60
Canary Islands, is., Spain	m14	22
Cañas, C.R.	E5	62
Canaseraga, N.Y., U.S.	C3	109
Canastota, N.Y., U.S.	B5	109
Canaveral, Cape, c., Fl., U.S.	D6	86
Canaveral National Seashore, Fl., U.S.	D6	86
Canavieiras, Braz.	D3	57
Cañazas, Pan.	F7	62
Canazei, Italy	C6	20
Canbelego, Austl.	E6	51
Canberra, Austl.	G8	50
Canby, Ca., U.S.	B3	82
Canby, Mn., U.S.	F2	100
Canby, Or., U.S.	B4	114
Cancale, Fr.	D1	17
Canche, stm., Fr.	B8	16
Cancún, Mex.	C7	63
Candeias, stm., Braz.	D2	59
Candelaria, Cuba	C2	64
Candelaria, Phil.	o12	34
Candelaria, stm., Mex.	A2	62
Candeleda, Spain	B3	22
Candia see Iráklion, Grc.	E5	40
Candia, N.H., U.S.	D4	106
Candiac, Que.	q19	74
Candle Village, N.H., U.S.	D4	106
Candle, Ak., U.S.	B7	79
Candle Lake, l., Sask.	D3	75
Candler, Fl., U.S.	C5	86
Candler, co., Ga., U.S.	D5	87
Candlewood, Lake, l., Ct., U.S.	D1	84
Candlewood Isle, Ct., U.S.	D2	84
Candlewood Knolls, Ct., U.S.	*D2	84
Candlewood Shores, Ct., U.S.	D2	84
Candlewood Trails, Ct., U.S.	*C2	84
Cando, Sask.	E1	75
Cando, N.D., U.S.	A6	111
Candor, N.Y., U.S.	C4	109
Candor, N.C., U.S.	B3	110
Cane, stm., La., U.S.	C2	95
Canea see Khaniá, Grc.	E5	40
Canehill, Ar., U.S.	B1	81
Canelas, Braz.	D2	56
Canelones, Ur.	C5	56
Canelones, dept., Ur.	g8	54
Canendiyu, dept., Para.	D4	55
Cañete, Chile	D2	54
Cane Valley, Ky., U.S.	C4	94
Caney, Ks., U.S.	E8	93
Caney, Ky., U.S.	C6	94
Caney, Ok., U.S.	C5	113
Caney, stm., Ok., U.S.	A5	113
Caney Creek, stm., Tx., U.S.	r14	120
Caney Fork, stm., Tn., U.S.	C8	119
Caneyville, Ky., U.S.	C3	94
Canfield, Ar., U.S.	D2	81
Canfield, Oh., U.S.	A5	112
Cangallo, Peru	D3	58
Cangamba, Ang.	D2	48
Cangas, Spain	A1	22
Cangas de Narcea, Spain	A2	22
Cangas de Onís, Spain	A3	22
Cangombe, Ang.	D3	48
Canguaretama, Braz.	C3	57
Canguçu, Braz.	E2	56
Cangzhou, China	D8	31
Canhotinho, Braz.	k5	57
Caniapiscau, stm., Que.	g13	74
Caniapiscau, Lac, l., Que.	h12	74
Canicanian, Phil.	o14	34
Canicattì, Italy	F4	23
Caniles, Spain	D4	22
Canim Lake, B.C.	D7	69
Canim Lake, l., B.C.	D7	69
Canindé, Braz.	B3	57
Canindé, stm., Braz.	C2	57
Canistear Reservoir, res., N.J., U.S.	A4	107
Canisteo, N.Y., U.S.	C3	109
Canisteo, stm., N.Y., U.S.	C3	109
Canistota, S.D., U.S.	D8	118
Canjilon, N.M., U.S.	A3	108
Çankırı, Tur.	B9	40
Canlaon Volcano, vol., Phil.	C6	34
Canmer, Ky., U.S.	C4	94
Canmore, Alta.	D3	68
Canna, i., Scot., U.K.	B3	10
Canna, Sound of, strt., Scot., U.K.	C3	13
Cannelburg, In., U.S.	G5	91
Cannelton, In., U.S.	I4	91
Cannelton, W.V., U.S.	m13	125
Cannes, Fr.	F7	16
Cannes, Bayou des, stm., La., U.S.	D3	95
Cannich, Scot., U.K.	C4	13
Canning, Austl.	*F2	50
Canning, N.S.	D5	71
Cannington, Ont.	C5	73
Cannock, Eng., U.K.	B5	12
Cannon, De., U.S.	F3	85
Cannon, co., Tn., U.S.	B5	119
Cannon Air Force Base, mil., N.M., U.S.	F5	100
Cannonball, N.D., U.S.	C6	111
Cannonball, stm., N.D., U.S.	C5	111
Cannon Beach, Or., U.S.	B3	114
Cannondale, Ct., U.S.	E2	84
Cannon Falls, Mn., U.S.	F6	100
Cannonsburg, Ky., U.S.	B7	94
Cannonsville Reservoir, res., N.Y., U.S.	C5	109
Cannonville, Ut., U.S.	F3	121
Canoas, stm., Braz.	D2	56
Canoe, B.C.	D8	69
Canoe, Al., U.S.	D2	78
Canoe, stm., B.C.	C8	69
Canoinhas, Braz.	D2	56
Canon, Ga., U.S.	B3	87
Canon City, Co., U.S.	C5	83
Canones, Point, c., Phil.	F11	116
Canon Plaza, N.M., U.S.	A3	108
Canon Plaza, N.M., U.S.	F11	115
Canoochee, stm., Ga., U.S.	D5	87
Canosa [di Puglia], Italy	D6	23
Canouan, i., St. Vin.	V26	65
Canova, S.D., U.S.	D8	118
Canóvanas, P.R.	B4	65
Canso, N.S.	D8	71
Cantabrian Mountains, mts., Spain	A3	22
Cantanhede, Port.	B1	22
Cantário, stm., Braz.	E2	59
Cantaura, Ven.	D4	60
Canterbury, Austl.	*F9	50
Canterbury, N.B.	D2	71
Canterbury, Eng., U.K.	E7	10
Canterbury, Ct., U.S.	C8	84
Canterbury, De., U.S.	D3	85
Canterbury, N.H., U.S.	D3	106
Canterbury Bight, N.Z.	P13	51
Can Tho, Viet.	G6	35
Canton, Ct., U.S.	B4	84
Canton, Ga., U.S.	B2	87
Canton, Il., U.S.	C3	90
Canton, Ks., U.S.	D6	93
Canton, Ky., U.S.	D2	96
Canton, Me., U.S.	D2	96
Canton, Ma., U.S.	*p15	99
Canton, Ms., U.S.	G7	100
Canton, Mo., U.S.	A6	102
Canton, N.J., U.S.	E2	107
Canton, N.Y., U.S.	f9	109
Canton, N.C., U.S.	f10	110
Canton, Oh., U.S.	B4	112
Canton, Ok., U.S.	A3	113
Canton, S.D., U.S.	D9	118
Canton, Tx., U.S.	C5	120
Canton, Wi., U.S.	C2	126
Canton Center, Ct., U.S.	B4	84
Canton see Guangzhou, China	G7	31
Canton Lake, res., Ok., U.S.	A3	113
Cantonment, Fl., U.S.	u14	86
Cantril, Ia., U.S.	D5	92
Cantù, Italy	B2	23
Cantuar, Sask.	G1	75
Cantwell, Ak., U.S.	C10	79
Canumã, stm., Braz.	C3	59
Canutama, Braz.	D2	59
Canute, Ok., U.S.	B2	113
Canutillo, Tx., U.S.	o11	120
Canwood, Sask.	D2	75
Cany-Barville, Fr.	C8	12
Canyon, Tx., U.S.	B2	120
Canyon, co., Id., U.S.	F2	89
Canyon, N.M., U.S.	h9	108
Canyon City, Or., U.S.	C8	114
Canyon Country, Ca., U.S.	*E4	82
Canyon Creek, Alta.	B3	68
Canyon Creek, Mt., U.S.	D4	103
Canyon de Chelly National Monument, Az., U.S.	A6	80
Canyon Ferry Lake, res., Mt., U.S.	D5	103
Canyon Lake, Tx., U.S.	E3	120
Canyon Lake, res., Tx., U.S.	E3	120
Canyonlands National Park, Ut., U.S.	E6	121
Canyonville, Or., U.S.	E3	114
Cao Bang, Viet.	A7	35
Caonao, stm., Cuba	D4	64
Caorle, Italy	D8	20
Capac, Mi., U.S.	F8	99
Capanaparo, stm., S.A.	B4	60
Capanema, Braz.	B1	57
Capão Bonito, Braz.	C3	56
Capão Doce, Morro do, mtn., Braz.	D2	56
Caparica, Port.	f9	22
Caparo, stm., Ven.	B3	60
Capasin, Sask.	D2	75
Capatárida, Ven.	A3	60
Cap-aux-Meules, Que.	B8	71
Cap aux Meules, Île du, i., Que.	B8	71
Capbreton, Fr.	F3	16
Cap-Chat, Que.	G19	66
Cap-de-la-Madeleine, Que.	C5	74
Capdenac-Gare, Fr.	E5	16
Cape, prov., S. Afr.	D3	49
Cape Barren, i., Austl.	o15	50
Cape Breton, co., N.S.	C9	71
Cape Breton Highlands National Park, N.S.	C9	71
Cape Breton Island, i., N.S.	C9	71
Cape Broyle, Newf.	E5	72
Cape Canaveral, Fl., U.S.	D6	86
Cape Charles, Newf.	B4	72
Cape Charles, Va., U.S.	C6	123
Cape Coast, Ghana	E4	45
Cape Cod Bay, b., Ma., U.S.	C6	98
Cape Cod Canal, Ma., U.S.	C6	98
Cape Cod National Seashore, Ma., U.S.	C7	98
Cape Coral, Fl., U.S.	F5	86
Cape Dorset, N.W. Ter.	D17	66
Cape Elizabeth, Me., U.S.	E2	96
Cape Fair, Mo., U.S.	E4	102
Cape Fear, stm., N.C., U.S.	C4	110
Cape Girardeau, Mo., U.S.	D8	102
Cape Girardeau, co., Mo., U.S.	D8	102
Cape Hatteras National Seashore, N.C., U.S.	B7	110
Cape Horn Mountain, mtn., Id., U.S.	E3	89
Cape Island, i., S.C., U.S.	E9	117
Cape la Hune, Newf.	E3	72
Capelinha, Braz.	B4	56
Capelongo, Ang.	E2	48
Cape Lookout National Seashore, N.C., U.S.	C6	110
Capels, W.V., U.S.	D3	125
Cape May, N.J., U.S.	F3	107
Cape May, co., N.J., U.S.	E3	107
Cape May Court House, N.J., U.S.	E3	107
Cape May Point, N.J., U.S.	F3	107
Cape Neddick, Me., U.S.	E2	96
Cape Pole, Ak., U.S.	n23	79
Cape Porpoise, Me., U.S.	E2	96
Cape Ray, Newf.	E2	72
Capers Inlet, b., S.C., U.S.	k12	117
Capers Island, i., S.C., U.S.	G6	117
Capers Island, i., S.C., U.S.	F8	117
Cape Sable Island, i., N.S.	F4	71
Cape Saint Claire, Md., U.S.	*B5	97
Capesterre, Guad.	H14	64
Cape Tormentine, N.B.	C6	71
Cape Town (Kaapstad), S. Afr.	D2	49
Cape Verde, ctry., Afr.	B3	42
Capeville, Va., U.S.	h16	123
Cape Vincent, N.Y., U.S.	A4	109
Cape York Peninsula, pen., Austl.	B7	50
Cap-Haïtien, Haiti	E7	64
Capibaribe, stm., Braz.	k5	57
Capim, stm., Braz.	B1	57
Capinota, Bol.	C2	55
Capira, Pan.	J7	62
Capistrano, Braz.	A3	57
Capitan, N.M., U.S.	D4	108
Capitan Bado, Para.	D4	55
Capitan Mountains, mts., N.M., U.S.	D4	108
Capitan Peak, mtn., N.M., U.S.	D4	108
Capitol, Mt., U.S.	E12	103
Capitola, Ca., U.S.	*D3	82
Capitol Heights, Ia., U.S.	e8	92
Capitol Heights, Md., U.S.	C4	97
Capitol Peak, mtn., Nv., U.S.	B4	105
Capitol Reef National Park, Ut., U.S.	E4	121
Capitol View, S.C., U.S.	*D6	117
Capivari, Braz.	m8	56
Cap Mountain, mtn., N.W. Ter.	D8	66
Capon Bridge, W.V., U.S.	B6	125
Capon Springs, W.V., U.S.	B6	125
Capote Knob, mtn., Tx., U.S.	k8	120
Cappoquin, Ire.	E4	11
Capraia, i., Italy	C2	23
Caprara, Point, c., Italy	A3	113
Capreol, Ont.	p19	73
Capri, i., Italy	D5	23
Capricorn Channel, strt., Austl.	D10	50
Capricorn Group, is., Austl.	A8	51
Caprock, N.M., U.S.	D6	108
Capron, Il., U.S.	A5	90
Capron, Ok., U.S.	A3	113
Capron, Va., U.S.	D5	123
Cap-Rouge, Que.	n17	74
Cap-Saint-Ignace, Que.	B7	74
Cap-Santé, Que.	C6	74
Capshaw, Al., U.S.	A3	78
Capitan Cook, Hi., U.S.	D6	88
Captiva, Fl., U.S.	F4	86
Captiva Island, i., Fl., U.S.	F4	86
Capua, Italy	D5	23
Capulin, N.M., U.S.	A6	108
Capulin Mountain National Monument, N.M., U.S.	A6	108
Caputa, S.D., U.S.	D3	118
Caquetá, dept., Col.	C3	60
Caquetá (Japurá), stm., S.A.	p18	22
Carabanchel Bajo, Spain	p17	22
Carabaña, Spain	A4	60
Carabinani, stm., Braz.	D5	60
Carabobo, state, Ven.	C7	24
Caracal, Rom.	B2	59
Caracaraí, Braz.	A4	60
Caracas, Ven.	C3	60
Caraguatay, Para.	E4	55
Carai, Braz.	B4	56
Carajás, Braz.	D5	59
Carajás, Serra dos, mts., Braz.	D4	59
Carangola, Braz.	C4	56
Caransebeș, Rom.	C6	24
Carapari, Bol.	D3	55
Carapeguá, Para.	E4	55
Carapó, Braz.	C1	56
Caraquet, N.B.	B5	71
Caratasca, Laguna de, b., Hond.	D8	63
Caratinga, Braz.	B4	56
Caratunk, Me., U.S.	C3	96
Carauari, Braz.	D4	59
Caraúbas, Braz.	h5	57
Caraúbas, Braz.	C3	57
Caravaca, Spain	C5	22
Caravelas, Braz.	D3	57
Caravelí, Peru	E3	58
Caraway, Ar., U.S.	B5	81
Caraz, Peru	C2	58
Carazinho, Braz.	D2	56
Carballino, Spain	A1	22
Carballo, Spain	A1	22
Carberry, Man.	E2	70
Carbet, Pitons du, mts., Mart.	S10	65
Carbó, Mex.	B2	63
Carbon, Alta.	D4	68
Carbon, In., U.S.	E3	91
Carbon, Ia., U.S.	C3	92
Carbon, W.V., U.S.	m13	125
Carbon, co., Mt., U.S.	E7	103
Carbon, co., Pa., U.S.	E10	115
Carbon, co., Ut., U.S.	D5	121
Carbon, co., Wy., U.S.	E5	127
Carbonara, Cape, c., Italy	E2	23
Carbondale, Alta.	C4	68
Carbondale, Co., U.S.	B3	83
Carbondale, Il., U.S.	F4	90
Carbondale, Ks., U.S.	D8	93
Carbondale, Oh., U.S.	C3	112
Carbondale, Pa., U.S.	C10	115
Carbonear, Newf.	E5	72
Carbon Hill, Al., U.S.	B2	78
Carbon Hill, Il., U.S.	B5	90
Carbonia, Italy	E2	23
Carbonne, Fr.	F4	16
Carbonville, Ut., U.S.	D5	121
Carbury, N.D., U.S.	A5	111
Carcagente, Spain	C5	22
Carcans, Étang de, b., Fr.	F3	16
Carcassonne, Fr.	F5	16
Carchi, prov., Ec.	A2	58
Carcross, Yukon	D6	66
Çardak, Tur.	D7	25
Cardale, Man.	D1	70
Cárdenas, Cuba	C3	64
Cárdenas, Mex.	m14	63
Cárdenas, Mex.	D6	63
Çardi, Tur.	C7	25
Cardiel, Lago, l., Arg.	D2	54
Cardiff, Wales, U.K.	E5	10
Cardiff, Al., U.S.	f7	78
Cardiff, Md., U.S.	A5	97
Cardiff, N.J., U.S.	E3	107
Cardigan, P.E.I.	C7	71
Cardigan, Wales, U.K.	D4	10
Cardigan, Mount, mtn., N.H., U.S.	C3	106
Cardigan Bay, b., P.E.I.	C7	71
Cardigan Bay, b., Wales, U.K.	D4	10
Cardinal, Ont.	C9	73
Cardinal Lake, l., Alta.	A2	68
Cardington, Oh., U.S.	B3	112
Cardona, Ur.	E1	56
Cardross, Sask.	H3	75
Cardston, Alta.	E4	68
Cardville, Me., U.S.	C4	96
Cardwell, Mo., U.S.	E7	102
Cardwell, Mt., U.S.	E5	103
Cardwell Mountain, mtn., Tn., U.S.	D8	119
Carega, mtn., Italy	D7	20
Carei, Rom.	B6	24
Carencro, La., U.S.	D3	95
Carenero, Ven.	A4	60
Carentan, Fr.	C5	16
Caretta, W.V., U.S.	D3	125
Carey, Id., U.S.	F5	89
Carey, Oh., U.S.	B2	112
Carey, Tx., U.S.	B2	120
Carey, Lake, l., Austl.	E3	50
Careysburg, Lib.	G3	42
Careywood, Id., U.S.	A2	89
Carhaix, Fr.	C2	16
Carhué, Arg.	B4	54
Cariamanga, Ec.	B2	58
Cariati, Italy	E6	23
Caribana, Punta, c., Col.	B3	60
Caribbean Sea		
Cariboo Mountains, mts., B.C.	C7	69
Caribou, Me., U.S.	B5	96
Caribou, co., Id., U.S.	G7	89
Caribou Island, i., N.S.	D7	71
Caribou Mountain, mtn., Id., U.S.	G7	89
Caribou Mountain, mtn., Me., U.S.	C2	96
Caribou Mountains, mts., Alta.	f7	68
Caribou Range, mts., Id., U.S.	F7	89
Carichic, Mex.	B3	63
Carievale, Sask.	H5	75
Carignan, Fr.	C6	16
Carinhanha, Braz.	A4	56
Carini, Italy	E4	23
Carinish, Scot., U.K.	C1	13
Carinthia, hist. reg., Aus.	E6	18

Name	Map Ref.	Page
Caripe, Ven.	A5	60
Caripito, Ven.	A5	60
Cariús, Braz.	C3	57
Carl Blackwell, Lake, res., Ok., U.S.	A4	113
Carle Place, N.Y., U.S.	*n15	109
Carleton, Mi., U.S.	F7	99
Carleton, Ne., U.S.	D8	104
Carleton, co., N.B.	C2	71
Carleton, Mount, mtn., N.B.	B3	71
Carleton Place, Ont.	B8	73
Carletonville, S. Afr.	C4	49
Carlile, Wy., U.S.	B8	127
Carlin, Nv., U.S.	C5	105
Carlinford Lough, b., Eur.	C5	11
Carlinville, Il., U.S.	D4	90
Carlisle, Eng., U.K.	C5	10
Carlisle, Ar., U.S.	C4	81
Carlisle, In., U.S.	G3	91
Carlisle, Ia., U.S.	C4	92
Carlisle, Ky., U.S.	B5	94
Carlisle, Ma., U.S.	f10	98
Carlisle, Ms., U.S.	C3	101
Carlisle, Oh., U.S.	C1	112
Carlisle, Pa., U.S.	F7	115
Carlisle, S.C., U.S.	B5	117
Carlisle, Tn., U.S.	A4	119
Carlisle, co., Ky., U.S.	f8	94
Carlit, Pic, mtn., Fr.	F4	16
Carl Junction, Mo., U.S.	D3	102
Carlock, Il., U.S.	C4	90
Carloforte, Italy	E2	23
Carlos, Md., U.S.	k13	97
Carlos, Mn., U.S.	E3	100
Carlos Casares, Arg.	B4	54
Carlos Chagas, Braz.	B4	56
Carlos City, In., U.S.	D7	91
Carlos Tejedor, Arg.	B4	54
Carlotta, Ca., U.S.	B1	82
Carlow, Ire.	D3	10
Carlow, co., Ire.	E5	11
Carloway, Scot., U.K.	B2	13
Carlowville, Al., U.S.	C2	78
Carlsbad, Ca., U.S.	F5	82
Carlsbad, N.M., U.S.	E5	108
Carlsbad, Tx., U.S.	D2	120
Carlsbad Caverns National Park, N.M., U.S.	E5	108
Carlsbad Springs, Ont.	h13	73
Carlsborg, Wa., U.S.	A2	124
Carlstadt, N.J., U.S.	h8	107
Carlton, Sask.	E2	75
Carlton, Eng., U.K.	B6	12
Carlton, Al., U.S.	D2	78
Carlton, Ga., U.S.	B3	87
Carlton, Ks., U.S.	D6	93
Carlton, Mn., U.S.	D6	100
Carlton, Or., U.S.	B3	114
Carlton, Tx., U.S.	D3	120
Carlton, co., Mn., U.S.	D6	100
Carluke, Scot., U.K.	E5	13
Carlyle, Sask.	H4	75
Carlyle, Il., U.S.	E4	90
Carlyle, Mt., U.S.	D12	103
Carlyle Lake, res., Il., U.S.	E4	90
Carmacks, Yukon	D5	66
Carmagnola, Italy	B1	23
Carman, Man.	E2	70
Carmangay, Alta.	D4	68
Carmanville, Newf.	D4	72
Carmarthen, Wales, U.K.	E4	10
Carmarthen Bay, b., Wales, U.K.	E4	10
Carmaux, Fr.	E5	16
Carmel, Sask.	E3	75
Carmel, Ca., U.S.	D3	82
Carmel, In., U.S.	E5	91
Carmel, La., U.S.	B2	95
Carmel, Me., U.S.	D3	96
Carmel, N.J., U.S.	E2	107
Carmel, N.Y., U.S.	D7	109
Carmel, Mount, mtn., Isr.	B7	41
Carmel Head, c., Wales, U.K.	A3	12
Carmelo, Ur.	E1	56
Carmen, Az., U.S.	F4	80
Carmen, Id., U.S.	D5	89
Carmen, Ok., U.S.	A3	113
Carmen, Isla i., Mex.	B2	63
Carmen, Río del, stm., Chile	E1	55
Carmen Alto, Chile	D2	55
Carmen de Areco, Arg.	A5	54
Carmen [del Paraná], Para.	E4	55
Carmen de Patagones, Arg.	C4	54
Carmer Hill, Pa., U.S.	C6	115
Carmi, Il., U.S.	E5	90
Carmi, Lake, l., Vt., U.S.	B3	122
Carmichael, Bah.	m17	64
Carmichael, Sask.	G1	75
Carmichael, Ca., U.S.	*C3	82
Carmichaels, Pa., U.S.	G2	115
Carmine, Tx., U.S.	D4	120
Carmona, Spain	D3	22
Carnarvon, Austl.	D1	50
Carnarvon, S. Afr.	D3	49
Carnarvon, Ia., U.S.	B2	92
Carnation, Wa., U.S.	B4	124
Carnaxide, Port.	f9	22
Carndonagh, Ire.	B4	11
Carnduff, Sask.	H5	75
Carnegie, Pa., U.S.	E2	87
Carnegie, Ga., U.S.	B3	113
Carnegie, Ok., U.S.	F1	115
Carnegie, Lake, l., Austl.	E3	50
Carnes, Ms., U.S.	E4	101
Carnesville, Ga., U.S.	B3	87
Carnew, Ire.	E5	11
Carney, Md., U.S.	*B4	97
Carney, Mi., U.S.	C3	99
Carney, Ok., U.S.	B4	113
Carneys Point, N.J., U.S.	D2	107
Carnforth, Eng., U.K.	F6	13
Carnic Alps, mts., Eur.	A4	23
Car Nicobar, i., India	G9	36
Carnlough, N. Ire., U.K.	C6	11
Carnot, Cen. Afr. Rep.	*F1	115
Carnoustie, Scot., U.K.	D6	13
Carnsore Point, c., Ire.	D3	10
Carnuel, N.M., U.S.	B3	108
Caro, Mi., U.S.	E7	99
Carol City, N.Y., U.S.	s13	86
Caroleen, N.C., U.S.	B1	110
Carolina, Braz.	C1	57
Carolina, P.R.	*B4	65
Carolina, S. Afr.	C5	49
Carolina, R.I., U.S.	F2	116
Carolina, N.C., U.S.	k10	125
Carolina Beach, N.C., U.S.	C5	110
Carolinas, Puntan a, N. Mar. Is.	E7	52
Caroline, Alta.	C3	68
Caroline, Wi., U.S.	D5	126
Caroline, co., Md., U.S.	C6	97
Caroline, co., Va., U.S.	C5	123
Caroline, atoll, Kir.	G13	6
Caroline Islands, is., T.T.P.I.	F8	6
Carol Stream, Il., U.S.	*k8	90
Caron, Sask.	G3	75
Carona, Il., U.S.	E9	93
Caroní, stm., Trin.	N23	65
Caroní, stm., Ven.	B5	60
Carora, Ven.	A3	60
Carouge, Switz.	E3	18
Carp, Ont.	B8	73
Carpathian Mountains, mts., Eur.	F13	8
Carpentaria, Gulf of, b., Austl.	B6	50
Carpenter, Ia., U.S.	A4	92
Carpenter, S.D., U.S.	C8	118
Carpenter, Wy., U.S.	E8	127
Carpenter Dam, Ar., U.S.	g7	81
Carpentersville, Il., U.S.	A5	90
Carpenterville, N.J., U.S.	B2	107
Carpentras, Fr.	E6	16
Carpi, Italy	B3	23
Carpinteria, Ca., U.S.	E4	82
Carpio, N.D., U.S.	A4	111
Carp Lake, Mi., U.S.	C6	99
Carp Lake, l., B.C.	B6	69
Carr, Co., U.S.	A6	83
Carrabassett Valley, Me., U.S.	C2	96
Carrabelle, Fl., U.S.	C2	86
Carradale, Scot., U.K.	E3	13
Carragana, Sask.	E4	75
Carrara, Italy	B3	23
Carrauntoohil, mtn., Ire.	D2	10
Carrboro, N.C., U.S.	B3	110
Carrbridge, Scot., U.K.	C5	13
Carrcroft Crest, De., U.S.	*A3	85
Carriacou, i., Gren.	W26	65
Carrick, Mount, mtn., Wa., U.S.	B2	124
Carrickfergus, N. Ire., U.K.	C4	10
Carrickmacross, Ire.	D5	11
Carrick on Shannon, Ire.	D3	11
Carrick on Suir, Ire.	E4	11
Carrie, Mount, mtn., Wa., U.S.	B2	124
Carrier, Que.	o17	74
Carrier, Ok., U.S.	A3	113
Carriere, Ms., U.S.	E4	101
Carrier Mills, Il., U.S.	F5	90
Carrigahorig, Ire.	D3	11
Carrigaline, Ire.	F3	11
Carrigan, Mount, mtn., N.H., U.S.	B4	106
Carrigan Head, c., Ire.	C3	11
Carrington, N.D., U.S.	B6	111
Carrington Island, i., Ut., U.S.	C3	121
Carrión, stm., Spain	A3	22
Carrión de los Condes, Spain	A3	22
Carrizal Bajo, Chile	E1	55
Carrizo Creek, stm., U.S.	A1	120
Carrizo Mountain, mtn., N.M.		
U.S.	D4	108
Carrizo Mountains, mts., U.S.	A6	80
Carrizo Springs, Tx., U.S.	E3	120
Carrizo Wash, val., U.S.	C6	80
Carrizozo, N.M., U.S.	D4	108
Carroll, Ia., U.S.	B3	92
Carroll, Ne., U.S.	C4	96
Carroll, Oh., U.S.	C3	112
Carroll, co., Ar., U.S.	A2	81
Carroll, co., Ga., U.S.	C1	87
Carroll, co., Il., U.S.	A4	90
Carroll, co., In., U.S.	C4	91
Carroll, co., Ia., U.S.	B3	92
Carroll, co., Ky., U.S.	B4	94
Carroll, co., Md., U.S.	A3	97
Carroll, co., Ms., U.S.	B4	101
Carroll, co., Mo., U.S.	B4	102
Carroll, co., N.H., U.S.	C4	106
Carroll, co., Oh., U.S.	B4	112
Carroll, co., Tn., U.S.	B3	119
Carroll, co., Va., U.S.	D2	123
Carroll Lake, l., Can.	D4	70
Carrolls, Wa., U.S.	C3	124
Carrollton, Al., U.S.	B1	78
Carrollton, Ga., U.S.	C1	87
Carrollton, Il., U.S.	D3	90
Carrollton, Ky., U.S.	B4	94
Carrollton, Mi., U.S.	E7	99
Carrollton, Ms., U.S.	B4	101
Carrollton, Mo., U.S.	B4	102
Carrollton, Oh., U.S.	B4	112
Carrollton, Tx., U.S.	*n10	120
Carrolltown, Pa., U.S.	E4	115
Carrollwood, Fl., U.S.	*E4	86
Carron, Loch, b., Scot., U.K.	C3	13
Carrot, stm., Can.	D4	75
Carrot River, Sask.	D4	75
Carrowmore, Lake, l., Ire.	C2	11
Carrsville, Ky., U.S.	e9	94
Carruthers, Sask.	E1	75
Carrville, Al., U.S.	C4	78
Carry Falls Reservoir, res., N.Y., U.S.	f10	109
Carrying Place, Ont.	C7	73
Çarşamba, Tur.	B11	40
Carseland, Alta.	D4	68
Carson, Ca., U.S.	*E4	82
Carson, Ia., U.S.	C2	92
Carson, Me., U.S.	B4	96
Carson, Ms., U.S.	D4	101
Carson, N.M., U.S.	A4	108
Carson, N.D., U.S.	C4	111
Carson, Wa., U.S.	D4	124
Carson, co., Tx., U.S.	B2	120
Carson, co., Nv., U.S.	D2	105
Carson City, Mi., U.S.	E6	99
Carson City, Nv., U.S.	D2	105
Carson Lake, l., Nv., U.S.	D3	105
Carson Sink, l., Nv., U.S.	D3	105
Carson Spring, Tn., U.S.	D10	119
Carsonville, Mi., U.S.	E8	99
Carstairs, Alta.	D3	68
Carswell Air Force Base, mil., Tx., U.S.	n9	120
Cartagena, Chile	A2	54
Cartagena, Col.	A2	60
Cartagena, Spain	D5	22
Cartago, Col.	C2	60
Cartago, C.R.	F8	63
Carta Valley, Tx., U.S.	E2	120
Cartaxo, Port.	C1	22
Cartaya, Spain	D2	22
Carter, Ky., U.S.	*k8	94
Carter, Mt., U.S.	C6	103
Carter, Ok., U.S.	B2	113
Carter, S.D., U.S.	D5	118
Carter, Tn., U.S.	C11	119
Carter, Wi., U.S.	C5	126
Carter, Wy., U.S.	E2	127
Carter, co., Ky., U.S.	B6	94
Carter, co., Mo., U.S.	E7	102
Carter, co., Mt., U.S.	E12	103
Carter, co., Ok., U.S.	C4	113
Carter, co., Tn., U.S.	C11	119
Carter Dome, mtn., N.H., U.S.	B4	106
Carteret, N.J., U.S.	k8	107
Carteret, co., N.C., U.S.	C6	110
Carter Lake, Ia., U.S.	C2	92
Carter Mountain, mtn., Wy., U.S.	B3	127
Carters, Ga., U.S.	B2	87
Cartersburg, In., U.S.	E5	91
Carters Lake, res., Ga., U.S.	B2	87
Cartersville, Ga., U.S.	B2	87
Cartersville, S.C., U.S.	C7	117
Cartersville, Va., U.S.	C4	123
Carterville, Il., U.S.	F4	90
Carterville, Mo., U.S.	D3	102
Carthage, Ar., U.S.	C3	81
Carthage, Il., U.S.	C2	90
Carthage, In., U.S.	E6	91
Carthage, Ms., U.S.	C4	101
Carthage, Mo., U.S.	D3	102
Carthage, N.Y., U.S.	A5	109
Carthage, N.C., U.S.	B3	110
Carthage, S.D., U.S.	C8	118
Carthage, Tn., U.S.	C8	119
Carthage, Tx., U.S.	C5	120
Carthage, hist., Tun.	B7	44
Cartier, i., Austl.	B5	50
Cartwright, Man.	E2	70
Cartwright, Newf.	B3	72
Cartwright, N.D., U.S.	B2	111
Cartwright, Ok., U.S.	D5	113
Caruaru, Braz.	C3	57
Carúpano, Ven.	A5	60
Caruthers, Ca., U.S.	D3	82
Caruthersville, Mo., U.S.	E8	102
Carver, Ma., U.S.	C6	98
Carver, co., Mn., U.S.	F5	100
Carver Ranch Estates, Fl., U.S.	*r13	86
Carville, La., U.S.	h9	95
Carvin, Fr.	D2	17
Cary, Ga., U.S.	D2	87
Cary, Il., U.S.	A5	90
Cary, Ms., U.S.	C3	101
Cary, N.C., U.S.	B4	110
Caryville, Fl., U.S.	u16	86
Caryville, Tn., U.S.	C9	119
Casa, Ar., U.S.	B3	81
Casablanca, Mor.	C3	44
Casa Blanca, N.M., U.S.	B2	108
Casa Branca, Braz.	C3	56
Casa de Oro, Ca., U.S.	*F5	82
Casa Grande, Az., U.S.	E4	80
Casa Grande National Monument, Az., U.S.	E4	80
Casale Monferrato, Italy	B2	23
Casalmaggiore, Italy	B3	23
Casanare, dept., Col.	B3	60
Casanare, stm., Col.	B3	60
Casanova, Va., U.S.	B5	123
Casape, Italy	h9	23
Casa Piedra, Tx., U.S.	p12	120
Casar, N.C., U.S.	B1	110
Casarano, Italy	D7	23
Casas Adobes, Az., U.S.	E5	80
Casa, Il., U.S.	B3	81
Cascade, B.C.	E8	69
Cascade, Co., U.S.	C6	83
Cascade, Id., U.S.	E2	89
Cascade, Ia., U.S.	B6	92
Cascade, Mo., U.S.	D7	102
Cascade, Mt., U.S.	C5	103
Cascade, Va., U.S.	D3	123
Cascade, Wi., U.S.	E5	126
Cascade, co., Mt., U.S.	C5	103
Cascade Locks, Or., U.S.	B5	114
Cascade Point, c., N.Z.	O12	51
Cascade Range, mts., N.A.	B3	76
Cascade Reservoir, res., Id., U.S.	E3	89
Cascade Summit, Or., U.S.	D4	114
Cascade Tunnel, Wa., U.S.	B4	124
Cascade Vista, Wa., U.S.	*B3	124
Cascadia, Or., U.S.	C4	114
Cascais, Port.	C1	22
Cascais Bay, b., Port.	f9	22
Cascajal, stm., Pan.	h11	62
Cascavel, Braz.	C2	56
Cascavel, Braz.	B3	57
Cascilla, Ms., U.S.	B3	101
Casco, Me., U.S.	D2	96
Casco, Wi., U.S.	D6	126
Casco Bay, b., Me., U.S.	E3	96
Caselton, Nv., U.S.	F7	105
Caseville, Mi., U.S.	E7	99
Casey, Il., U.S.	D6	90
Casey, Ia., U.S.	C3	92
Casey, co., Ky., U.S.	C5	94
Casey, sci., Ant.	C24	7
Casey, Mount, mtn., Id., U.S.	A2	89
Casey Bay, b., Ant.	C17	7
Casey Key, i., Fl., U.S.	E4	86
Caseyr (Cape Guardafui), c., Som.	C7	47
Cash, Ar., U.S.	B5	81
Cashel, Ire.	D3	10
Cashel, Ire.	D2	11
Cashiers, N.C., U.S.	f9	110
Cashion, Az., U.S.	m8	80
Cashion, Ok., U.S.	B4	113
Cashmere, Wa., U.S.	B5	124
Cashton, Wi., U.S.	E3	126
Cashtown, Pa., U.S.	G7	115
Casiguran, Phil.	n14	34
Casiguran Sound, strt., Phil.	n13	34
Casilda, Arg.	A4	54
Casilda, Cuba	D3	64
Casino, Austl.	D9	51
Casiquiare, stm., Ven.	C4	60
Casky, Ky., U.S.	D2	94
Čáslav, Czech.	D3	26
Casma, Peru	C2	58
Casmalia, Ca., U.S.	E3	82
Caspar, Ca., U.S.	C2	82
Caspe, Spain	B2	22
Casper, Wy., U.S.	D6	127
Caspian, Mi., U.S.	B2	99
Caspiana, La., U.S.	B2	95
Caspian Depression, pl., Sov. Un.	E8	29
Caspian Sea	E8	29
Caspian Sea	E8	29
Cass, Il., U.S.	F3	91
Cass, W.V., U.S.	C5	125
Cass, co., Il., U.S.	D3	90
Cass, co., In., U.S.	C5	91
Cass, co., Ia., U.S.	C3	92
Cass, co., Mi., U.S.	G4	99
Cass, co., Mn., U.S.	D4	100
Cass, co., Mo., U.S.	C3	102
Cass, co., Ne., U.S.	D9	104
Cass, co., N.D., U.S.	C8	111
Cass, co., Tx., U.S.	C5	120
Cass, stm., Mi., U.S.	E7	99
Cassadaga, N.Y., U.S.	C1	109
Cassá [de la Selva], Spain	B7	22
Cassai (Kasai), stm., Afr.	D3	48
Casselberry, Fl., U.S.	D5	86
Cassel see Kassel, W. Ger.	C4	18
Casselman, Ont.	B9	73
Casselman, Pa., U.S.	G3	115
Casselman, stm., U.S.	k12	97
Casselton, N.D., U.S.	C8	111
Cassia, co., Id., U.S.	G5	89
Cassiar, B.C.	f12	69
Cassiar Mountains, mts., Can.	E6	66
Cassilândia, Braz.	B2	56
Cassinga, Ang.	E2	48
Cassino, Italy	D4	23
Cass Lake, Mn., U.S.	C4	100
Cass Lake, l., Mn., U.S.	C4	100
Cassoday, Ks., U.S.	D7	93
Cassopolis, Mi., U.S.	G4	99
Casstown, Oh., U.S.	B1	112
Cassville, Ga., U.S.	B2	87
Cassville, Mo., U.S.	E4	102
Cassville, Wi., U.S.	F3	126
Castaic, Ca., U.S.	E4	82
Castalia, Ia., U.S.	A6	92
Castalia, N.C., U.S.	A4	110
Castalia, Oh., U.S.	A3	112
Castalian Springs, Tn., U.S.	A5	119
Castana, Ia., U.S.	B2	92
Castanheira de Pêra, Port.	C1	22
Castaños, Mex.	B4	63
Castel di Guido, Italy	h8	23
Castelfranco Emilia, Italy	E7	20
Castelfranco Veneto, Italy	D7	20
Castel Gandolfo, Italy	h9	23
Castel Giuliano, Italy	g8	23
Casteljaloux, Fr.	E4	16
Castella, Ca., U.S.	B2	82
Castellamonte, Italy	D3	20
Castelli, Arg.	B5	54
Castellón de la Plana, Spain	C5	22
Castel Madama, Italy	h9	23
Castelnaudary, Fr.	F4	16
Castelo, Braz.	C4	56
Castelo Branco, Port.	C2	22
Castelo de Vide, Port.	C2	22
Castel San Pietro dell'Emilia, Italy	E7	20
Castelsarrasin, Fr.	E4	16
Castelvetrano, Italy	F4	23
Casterton, Austl.	H3	51
Castile, N.Y., U.S.	C2	109
Castle, Braz.	B5	113
Castleberry, Al., U.S.	D2	78
Castlebar, Ire.	D2	10
Castlebay, Scot., U.K.	D1	13
Castlebellingham, Ire.	D5	11
Castleberry, Al., U.S.	D2	78
Castleblayney, Ire.	C5	11
Castlecomer, Ire.	E4	11
Castle Dale, Ut., U.S.	D4	121
Castlederg, N. Ire., U.K.	C4	11
Castle Dome Mountains, mts., Az., U.S.	D1	80
Castle Dome Peak, mtn., Az., U.S.	D1	80
Castle Douglas, Scot., U.K.	C5	10
Castlefinn, Ire.	C4	11
Castleford, Id., U.S.	G4	89
Castlegar, B.C.	E9	69
Castlegregory, Ire.	E1	11
Castle Harbour, b., Ber.	o20	64
Castle Hayne, N.C., U.S.	C5	110
Castle Hills, De., U.S.	i7	85
Castle Hot Springs, Az., U.S.	D3	80
Castleisland, Ire.	E2	11
Castlemaine, Austl.	H5	51
Castlemaine, Ire.	E2	11
Castlemartyr, Ire.	F3	11
Castle Mountain, mtn., Yukon	D6	103
Castle Mountains, mts., Mt., U.S.	D6	103
Castle Park, Ca., U.S.	*o15	82
Castle Peak, mtn., Co., U.S.	B4	83
Castle Peak, mtn., Id., U.S.	E4	89
Castle Point, Mo., U.S.	f13	102
Castlepollard, Ire.	D4	11
Castlerea, Ire.	D3	11
Castlereagh, N. Ire., U.K.	*C6	11
Castlereagh, stm., Austl.	E7	51
Castle Rock, Co., U.S.	B6	83
Castle Rock, Mn., U.S.	F5	100
Castle Rock, Wa., U.S.	C3	124
Castle Rock, mtn., Or., U.S.	C8	114
Castle Rock, mtn., Or., U.S.	C4	123
Castle Rock Butte, mtn., S.D., U.S.	B2	118
Castle Rock Lake, res., Wi., U.S.	E3	126
Castle Shannon, Pa., U.S.	*k13	115
Castleton, Ont.	C7	73
Castleton, Jam.	E15	64
Castleton, Il., U.S.	B4	90
Castleton, Ks., U.S.	g11	93
Castleton, Vt., U.S.	D2	122
Castleton on Hudson, N.Y., U.S.	C7	109
Castletown, I. of Man	F4	13
Castletown Geoghegan, Ire.	D4	11
Castletownroche, Ire.	E3	11
Castletownshend, N. Ire., U.K.	C6	11
Castlewood, S.D., U.S.	C8	118
Castlewood, Va., U.S.	f9	123
Castolon, N.M., U.S.	C5	108
Castor, Alta.	C5	68
Castor, stm., Mo., U.S.	D7	102
Castor Creek, stm., La., U.S.	B3	95
Castorland, N.Y., U.S.	B5	109
Castres, Fr.	E5	16
Castries, St. Luc.	J14	64
Castro, Braz.	C3	56
Castro, Chile	C2	54
Castro Alves, Braz.	D3	57
Castro Daire, Port.	D2	22
Castro [del Río], Spain	D4	100
Castro Marim, Port.	D2	22
Castropol, Spain	A2	22
Castrop-Rauxel, W. Ger.	*C3	18
Castro Urdiales, Spain	A4	22
Castro Valley, Ca., U.S.	h8	82
Castro Verde, Port.	D1	22
Castrovillari, Italy	E6	23
Castroville, Ca., U.S.	D3	82
Castroville, Tx., U.S.	E3	120
Castrovirreyna, Peru	D2	58
Castuera, Spain	C3	22
Caswell, co., N.C., U.S.	A3	110
Catacamas, Hond.	E7	63
Catacaos, Peru	C1	58
Catacocha, Ec.	B2	58
Cataguases, Braz.	C4	56
Catahoula, co., La., U.S.	C4	95
Catahoula Lake, l., La., U.S.	C3	95
Catalão, Braz.	B3	56
Çatalca, Tur.	B7	40
Catalina, Newf.	D5	72
Catalina, Chile	E2	55
Catalina Foothills, Az., U.S.	*E5	80
Catalonia, hist. reg., Spain	B6	22
Catamarca, Arg.	E2	55
Catamarca, prov., Arg.	E2	55
Catamayo, Ec.	B2	58
Catanauan, Phil.	p14	34
Catanduanes, i., Phil.	C6	34
Catanduva, Braz.	C3	56
Catania, Italy	F5	23
Catania, Gulf of, b., Italy	F5	23
Catanzaro, Italy	E6	23
Cataouatche, Lake, l., La., U.S.	k11	95
Cataract, In., U.S.	F4	91
Cataract Canyon, val., Ut., U.S.	F5	121
Catarina, Tx., U.S.	E3	120
Catarroja, Spain	C5	22
Catasauqua, Pa., U.S.	E11	115
Catastrophe, Cape, c., Austl.	F6	50
Cataula, Ga., U.S.	D2	87
Cataumet, Ma., U.S.	C6	98
Catawba, N.C., U.S.	B1	110
Catawba, S.C., U.S.	B6	117
Catawba, Va., U.S.	C2	123
Catawba, Wi., U.S.	C3	126
Catawba, W.V., U.S.	h10	125
Catawba, co., N.C., U.S.	B1	110
Catawba, stm., S.C., U.S.	B6	117
Catawba, South Fork, stm., N.C., U.S.	B1	110
Catawba Island, Oh., U.S.	A3	112
Catawissa, Pa., U.S.	E9	115
Cat Ba, i., Viet.	B7	35
Catbalogan, Phil.	C6	34
Cat Creek, Mt., U.S.	C8	103
Cateechee, S.C., U.S.	B2	117
Cater, Sask.	D1	75
Cates, In., U.S.	E3	91
Cathance, Lake, l., Me., U.S.	D5	96
Catharine, Ks., U.S.	D4	93
Cathay, N.D., U.S.	B6	111
Cathedral Bluffs, clf., Co., U.S.	B2	83
Cathedral Caverns, Al., U.S.	A3	87
Cathedral City, Ca., U.S.	F5	82
Cathedral Mountain, mtn., Tx., U.S.	o13	120
Cathedral of the Pines, N.H., U.S.	E3	106
Cecil Field Naval Air Station, mil., Fl., U.S.	B5	86
Cecilia, Ky., U.S.	C4	94
Ceciliton, Md., U.S.	B6	97
Cecina, Italy	C3	23
Cedar, Ks., U.S.	C5	93
Cedar, Mi., U.S.	D5	99
Cedar, Mn., U.S.	A5	100
Cedar, co., Ia., U.S.	C6	92
Cedar, co., Mo., U.S.	D4	102
Cedar, co., Ne., U.S.	B8	104
Cedar, stm., Ne., U.S.	B7	104
Cedar, stm., Wa., U.S.	B4	124
Cedar Bluff, Al., U.S.	A4	78
Cedar Bluff, Va., U.S.	C2	94
Cedarbluff, Ms., U.S.	B5	101
Cedar Bluff Reservoir, res., Ks., U.S.	C4	93
Cedar Bluffs, Ks., U.S.	C3	93
Cedar Bluffs, Ne., U.S.	C9	104
Cedar Breaks National Monument, Ut., U.S.	E8	102
Cedarburg, Wi., U.S.	E6	126
Cedarbutte, S.D., U.S.	D4	118
Cedar City, Mo., U.S.	C5	102
Cedar City, Ut., U.S.	F2	121
Cedar Creek, Az., U.S.	D5	80
Cedarcreek, Mo., U.S.	E5	102
Cedar Creek, Tn., U.S.	C9	104
Cedar Creek, stm., Co., U.S.	A7	83
Cedar Creek, stm., In., U.S.	B7	91
Cedar Creek, stm., Ia., U.S.	D6	92
Cedar Creek, stm., Mo., U.S.	C5	102
Cedar Creek, stm., N.J., U.S.	D4	107
Cedar Creek, stm., N.D., U.S.	C3	111
Cedar Creek, stm., Oh., U.S.	e7	112
Cedar Creek Lake, res., Tx., U.S.	C4	120
Cedar Crest, N.M., U.S.	k8	108
Cedaredge, Co., U.S.	C3	83
Cedar Falls, Ia., U.S.	B5	92
Cedar Gap, Mo., U.S.	D5	102
Cedar Grove, In., U.S.	F8	91
Cedar Grove, N.J., U.S.	B4	107
Cedar Grove, W.V., U.S.	C3	125
Cedar Grove, Wi., U.S.	E6	126
Cedar Hill, Mo., U.S.	g12	102
Cedar Hill, Tn., U.S.	A5	119
Cedar Hill, Tx., U.S.	n10	120
Cedar Hills, Or., U.S.	*h12	114
Cedarhurst, N.Y., U.S.	k13	109
Cedar Island, N.C., U.S.	C6	110
Cedar Island, i., N.C., U.S.	C6	110
Cedar Island, i., S.C., U.S.	E9	117
Cedar Island, i., Va., U.S.	C7	123
Cedar Key, Fl., U.S.	C3	86
Cedar Keys, is., Fl., U.S.	C3	86
Cedar Knolls, N.J., U.S.	B4	107
Cedar Lake, In., U.S.	B3	91
Cedar Lake, l., Ont.	A6	73
Cedar Lake, res., Man.	C1	70
Cedar Lake, res., Il., U.S.	F4	90
Cedar Lake, l., Mn., U.S.	F4	100
Cedar Mountain, mtn., Ca., U.S.	B3	82
Cedar Mountains, mts., Ut., U.S.	C2	121
Cedar Point, Il., U.S.	B4	90

Name	Map Ref.	Page
Cedar Point, Ks., U.S.	D7	93
Cedar Point, c, Md., U.S.	D5	97
Cedar Point, c, Oh., U.S.	A3	112
Cedar Point, c, Oh., U.S.	e7	112
Cedar Rapids, Ia., U.S.	C6	92
Cedar Rapids, Ne., U.S.	C7	104
Cedar River, Mi., U.S.	C3	99
Cedar Run, N.J., U.S.	D4	107
Cedar Springs, Ont.	E2	73
Cedar Springs, Ga., U.S.	E1	87
Cedar Springs, Mi., U.S.	E5	99
Cedar Swamp, sw., Ma., U.S.	f11	98
Cedartown, Ga., U.S.	B1	87
Cedarvale, B.C.	B3	69
Cedarvale, N.M., U.S.	C4	108
Cedar Valley, Ut., U.S.	C3	121
Cedarville, Ar., U.S.	B1	81
Cedarville, Ca., U.S.	B3	82
Cedarville, Il., U.S.	A4	90
Cedarville, In., U.S.	B7	91
Cedarville, Ma., U.S.	*C6	98
Cedarville, N.J., U.S.	E2	107
Cedarville, N.Y., U.S.	C5	109
Cedarville, Oh., U.S.	C2	112
Cedoux, Sask.	H4	75
Cedros, Hond.	C4	62
Cedros, Isla, i., Mex.	B1	63
Ceduna, Austl.	F5	50
Ceel Buur, Som.	E6	47
Ceel Xamurre, Som.	D6	47
Ceepeecee, B.C.	E4	69
Ceerigaabo, Som.	C6	47
Cefalù, Italy	E5	23
Cega, stm., Spain	B3	22
Cegléd, Hung.	B4	24
Ceglie Messapico, Italy	D6	23
Çehegín, Spain	C5	22
Čelákovice, Czech.	n18	26
Celaya, Mex.	m13	63
Celebes (Sulawesi), i., Indon.	F6	34
Celebes Sea, Asia	E6	34
Celendín, Peru	C2	58
Celestine, In., U.S.	H4	91
Celica, Ec.	B2	58
Celina, Oh., U.S.	B1	112
Celina, Tn., U.S.	C8	119
Celina, Tx., U.S.	C4	120
Celje, Yugo.	B2	24
Celle, W. Ger.	B5	18
Cellina, stm., Italy	C8	20
Celoron, N.Y., U.S.	C1	109
Celriver, S.C., U.S.	B6	117
Celtic Sea, Eur.	F5	11
Cemaes Head, c., Wales, U.K.	B3	12
Cement, Ok., U.S.	C3	113
Cement City, Mi., U.S.	F6	99
Cementon, Pa., U.S.	E10	115
Çemişgezek, Tur.	C12	40
Cenderawasih Bay, b., Indon.	F9	34
Cenon, Fr.	E3	16
Centenary, S.C., U.S.	C9	117
Centennial, Wy., U.S.	E6	127
Centennial Lake, res., Ont.	B7	73
Centennial Mountains, mts., Id., U.S.	E7	89
Center, Co., U.S.	D4	83
Center, Ga., U.S.	D2	87
Center, In., U.S.	D5	91
Center, Ky., U.S.	C4	94
Center, Mo., U.S.	B6	102
Center, Ne., U.S.	B8	104
Center, N.D., U.S.	B4	111
Center, Ok., U.S.	C5	113
Center, Tx., U.S.	D5	120
Center Barnstead, N.H., U.S.	D4	106
Centerbrook, Ct., U.S.	D6	84
Centerburg, Oh., U.S.	B3	112
Center City, Mn., U.S.	E6	100
Center City, Tx., U.S.	D3	120
Center Conway, N.H., U.S.	C4	106
Center Creek, Ut., U.S.	C4	121
Center Cross, Va., U.S.	C6	123
Centereach, N.Y., U.S.	n15	109
Center Effingham, N.H., U.S.	C4	106
Centerfield, Ut., U.S.	D4	121
Center Harbor, N.H., U.S.	C4	106
Center Hill, Ar., U.S.	B4	81
Center Hill, Fl., U.S.	D5	86
Center Hill Lake, res., Tn., U.S.	C8	119
Center Junction, Ia., U.S.	B6	92
Center Line, Mi., U.S.	*p15	99
Center Lovell, Me., U.S.	D2	96
Center Montville, Me., U.S.	D3	96
Center Moreland, Pa., U.S.	m17	115
Center Moriches, N.Y., U.S.	n16	109
Center Mountain, mtn., Id., U.S.	D3	89
Center Ossipee, N.H., U.S.	C4	106
Center Point, Al., U.S.	f7	78
Centerpoint, In., U.S.	F3	91
Center Point, Ia., U.S.	B6	92
Center Point, La., U.S.	C3	95
Center Point, S.D., U.S.	D8	118
Center Point, Tx., U.S.	E3	120
Center Point, W.V., U.S.	B4	125
Center Ridge, Ar., U.S.	B3	81
Center Rutland, Vt., U.S.	D2	122
Center Sandwich, N.H., U.S.	C4	106
Center Square, N.J., U.S.	D2	107
Center Star, Al., U.S.	A2	78
Center Strafford, N.H., U.S.	D4	106
Centerton, Ar., U.S.	A1	81
Centerton, In., U.S.	E5	91
Centerton, N.J., U.S.	D2	107
Centertown, Ky., U.S.	C3	94
Centertown, Mo., U.S.	C5	102
Centertown, Tn., U.S.	D8	119
Center Tuftonboro, N.H., U.S.	C4	106
Centerview, Mo., U.S.	C4	102
Centerville, De., U.S.	A3	85
Centerville, Ia., U.S.	E8	91
Centerville, Ia., U.S.	D5	92
Centerville, Ks., U.S.	D8	93
Centerville, La., U.S.	E4	95
Centerville, Me., U.S.	D5	96
Centerville, Ma., U.S.	C7	98
Centerville, Nv., U.S.	*E2	105
Centerville, N.C., U.S.	A4	110
Centerville, Oh., U.S.	C1	112
Centerville, Pa., U.S.	F2	115
Centerville, Pa., U.S.	C2	115
Centerville, R.I., U.S.	E2	116
Centerville, S.D., U.S.	D9	118
Centerville, Tn., U.S.	B4	119
Centerville, Tx., U.S.	D5	120
Centerville, Ut., U.S.	C4	121
Centerville, Wa., U.S.	D5	124
Cento, Italy	E7	20
Centrahoma, Ok., U.S.	C5	113
Central, Al., U.S.	C3	78
Central, Az., U.S.	E6	80
Central, In., U.S.	H5	91
Central, N.M., U.S.	E1	108
Central, S.C., U.S.	B2	117
Central, prov., Ghana	E4	45
Central, prov., Kenya	B6	48
Central, prov., Mwi.	D5	48
Central, prov., Scot., U.K.	D4	13
Central, prov., Zam.	E4	48
Central, dept., Para.	D3	55
Central, Cordillera, mts., Col.	C2	60
Central, Cordillera, mts., C.R.	E5	62
Central, Cordillera, mts., Dom. Rep.	E8	64
Central, Cordillera, mts., P.R.	B2	65
Central Massif, mts., Fr.	E5	16
Central African Republic, ctry., Afr.	D4	46
Central Barren, In., U.S.	H5	91
Central Bridge, N.Y., U.S.	C6	109
Central Butte, Sask.	G2	75
Central City, Co., U.S.	B5	83
Central City, Il., U.S.	E4	90
Central City, Ia., U.S.	B6	92
Central City, Ky., U.S.	C2	94
Central City, Ne., U.S.	C7	104
Central City, Pa., U.S.	F4	115
Central City, S.D., U.S.	C2	118
Central Falls, R.I., U.S.	B4	116
Central Heights, Az., U.S.	D5	80
Centralia, Ont.	D3	73
Centralia, Il., U.S.	E4	90
Centralia, Ks., U.S.	C7	93
Centralia, Mo., U.S.	B5	102
Centralia, Ok., U.S.	A6	113
Centralia, Wa., U.S.	C3	124
Centralia, W.V., U.S.	C4	125
Centralina, Braz.	B3	56
Central Islip, N.Y., U.S.	n15	109
Central Lake, Mi., U.S.	C5	99
Central Makrān Range, mts., Pak.	C3	36
Central Park, Wa., U.S.	C2	124
Central Point, Or., U.S.	E4	114
Central Range, mts., Pap. N. Gui.	h11	50
Central Range, hills, Trin.	O23	65
Central Siberian Uplands, plat., Sov. Un.	C13	29
Central Square, N.Y., U.S.	B4	109
Central Valley, Ca., U.S.	B2	82
Central Valley, N.Y., U.S.	D6	109
Central Village, Ct., U.S.	C8	84
Central Village, Ma., U.S.	C5	98
Centre, Al., U.S.	A4	78
Centre, co., Pa., U.S.	E6	115
Centre City, N.J., U.S.	D2	107
Centre Hall, Pa., U.S.	E6	115
Centre Peak, mtn., B.C.	B4	69
Centreville, N.B.	C2	71
Centreville, N.S.	E3	71
Centreville, Al., U.S.	C2	78
Centreville, Md., U.S.	B5	97
Centreville, Mi., U.S.	G5	99
Centreville, Ms., U.S.	D2	101
Centreville, Va., U.S.	*B5	123
Centropolis, Ks., U.S.	D8	93
Centuria, Wi., U.S.	C1	126
Century, Fl., U.S.	u14	86
Century, W.V., U.S.	B4	125
Century Village, Fl., U.S.	*F6	86
Cephalonia see Kefallinía, i., Grc.	C3	40
Cephisus see Kifisós, stm., Grc.	g9	25
Ceram, i., Indon.	F7	34
Ceram Sea, Indon.	F7	34
Cerbat Mountains, mts., Az., U.S.	B1	80
Čerčany, Czech.	o18	26
Cereal, Alta.	D5	68
Ceredo, W.V., U.S.	C2	125
Ceres, Braz.	B3	56
Ceres, Italy	D3	20
Ceres, Ca., U.S.	D3	82
Ceres, N.Y., U.S.	C2	109
Ceres, Ok., U.S.	A4	113
Ceres, Va., U.S.	C1	123
Ceresco, Ne., U.S.	C9	104
Cereté, Col.	B2	60
Cerignola, Italy	D5	23
Cerknica, Yugo.	C9	24
Cernavodă, Rom.	C9	24
Cernay, Fr.	D7	16
Cerralvo, Mex.	B5	63
Cerralvo, Isla, i., Mex.	C3	63
Çerrikú, Alb.	B2	25
Cerrillos, N.M., U.S.	B3	108
Cerritos, Mex.	C3	95
Cerritos, Ca., U.S.	*E4	82
Cerro, N.M., U.S.	A4	108
Cerro Alto Mountain, mtn.,	o12	120
Cerro Azul, Peru	D2	58
Cerro Colorado, Ur.	E1	56
Cerro de Pasco, Peru	D2	58
Cerro Gordo, Il., U.S.	D5	90
Cerro Gordo, N.C., U.S.	C4	110
Cerro Gordo, co., Ia., U.S.	A4	92
Cerro Largo, Braz.	D2	56
Cervantes, Phil.	B6	34
Cervera del Río Alhama, Spain	A5	22
Cerveteri, Italy	g8	23
Cervignano del Friuli, Italy	D9	20
Cesar, dept., Col.	B3	60
Cesena, Italy	E7	20
Cesenatico, Italy	E7	20
České Kamenice, Czech.	C9	19
Česká Lípa, Czech.	C3	26
Česká Třebová, Czech.	D3	26
České Budějovice, Czech.	D3	26
Český Brod, Czech.	n18	26
Český Krumlov, Czech.	D3	26
Çeşme, Tur.	C3	40
Cessnock, Austl.	F9	50
Cestos, stm., Lib.	E3	45
Cetina, stm., Yugo.	C3	24
Cetinje, Yugo.	D4	24
Cetraro, Italy	E5	23
Cetti Bay, b., Guam	M9	52
Ceuta, Sp. N. Afr.	B3	44
Cévennes, reg., Fr.	E5	16
Cevio, Switz.	C4	20
Ceyhan, Tur.	*D10	40
Ceyhan, stm., Tur.	C6	25
Ceylon, Ont.	C4	73
Ceylon, Sask.	H3	75
Ceylon, In., U.S.	C8	91
Ceylon, Mn., U.S.	G4	100
Ceylon see Sri Lanka, ctry., Asia	G7	36
Chabařovice, Czech.	C8	19
Chacabuco, Arg.	A4	54
Chacachacare, i., Trin.	N22	65
Chacahoula, La., U.S.	E5	95
Chachapoyas, Peru	C2	58
Chachoengsao, Thai.	F4	35
Chāchro, Pak.	E3	37
Chaco, prov., Arg.	E3	55
Chaco, dept., Para.	D3	55
Chaco, Cape, c., N.M., U.S.	A1	108
Chaco Culture National Historic Park, N.M., U.S.	A2	108
Chacon, N.M., U.S.	A4	108
Chacon, Cape, c., Ak., U.S.	n24	79
Chacuaco Creek, stm., Co., U.S.	D7	83
Chad, ctry., Afr.	B3	46
Chad, Lake, l., Afr.	C2	46
Chadbourn, N.C., U.S.	C4	110
Chadds Ford, Pa., U.S.	G10	115
Chadileuvu, stm., Arg.	B3	54
Chadiza, Zam.	D5	48
Chadron, Ne., U.S.	B3	104
Chadwick, Il., U.S.	A4	90
Chadwick, Mo., U.S.	E4	102
Chadwicks, N.Y., U.S.	B5	109
Chaeryŏng, N. Kor.	G2	33
Chaffee, Mo., U.S.	D8	102
Chaffee, N.D., U.S.	C8	111
Chaffee, co., Co., U.S.	C4	83
Chaffin, Ma., U.S.	B4	98
Chaffois, Fr.	C1	21
Chāgai Hills, mts., Asia	G11	39
Chaghcharan, Afg.	D12	39
Chagny, Fr.	D6	16
Chagodoshcha, stm., Sov. Un.	B10	27
Chagos Archipelago, is., B.I.O.T.	G25	2
Chagres, stm., Pan.	k11	62
Chagrin Falls, Oh., U.S.	A4	112
Chaguanas, Trin.	N23	65
Chagyl, Sov. Un.	E5	28
Chahal, Guat.	C3	62
Chahar Borjak, Afg.	B3	36
Chāībāsa, India	D8	36
Chai Nat, Thai.	E4	35
Chaiyaphum, Thai.	B2	34
Chakachamna Lake, l., Ak., U.S.	g15	79
Chake Chake, Tan.	C6	48
Chakradharpur, India	D8	36
Chakwāl, Pak.	B5	36
Chala, Peru	E3	58
Chala, Punta, c., Peru	E3	58
Chalan Kanoa, N. Mar. Is.	D7	52
Chalan Pago, Guam	L10	52
Chalatenango, El Sal.	C3	62
Chalchuapa, El Sal.	D3	62
Chalcis see Khalkís, Grc.	C4	40
Chalco, Canal de, Mex.	h9	63
Chaleur Bay, b., Can.	B4	71
Chalhuanca, Peru	D3	58
Chaling, China	K5	32
Chalke see Khálki, i., Grc.	C4	40
Chalk River, Ont.	A7	73
Chalkyitsik, Ak., U.S.	B11	79
Challans, Fr.	D3	16
Challapata, Bol.	G5	54
Challis, Id., U.S.	E4	89
Chalmers, In., U.S.	C4	91
Chalmette, La., U.S.	E6	95
Châlons-sur-Marne, Fr.	C6	16
Chalon-sur-Saône, Fr.	D6	16
Chaltel, Cerro see Fitzroy, Monte, mtn., S.A.	D2	54
Chālūs, Iran	C5	39
Chalybeate, Ms., U.S.	A5	101
Chalybeate, N.C., U.S.	B4	110
Cham, W. Ger.	D7	19
Cham, Switz.	B5	21
Cham, i., Viet.	E8	35
Chama, Co., U.S.	D5	83
Chama, N.M., U.S.	A3	108
Chama, Rio, stm., N.M., U.S.	A3	108
Chamaicó, Arg.	B4	54
Chamalières, Fr.	E5	16
Chaman, Pak.	B4	36
Chamba, Tan.	D6	48
Chambal, stm., India	C6	36
Chamberino, N.M., U.S.	E3	108
Chamberlain, Sask.	G3	75
Chamberlain, S.D., U.S.	D6	118
Chamberlain Lake, l., Me., U.S.	B3	96
Chamberlin, Mount, mtn., Ak., U.S.	B10	79
Chambers, Az., U.S.	B6	80
Chambers, La., U.S.	C3	95
Chambers, Ne., U.S.	B7	104
Chambers, co., Al., U.S.	C4	78
Chambers, co., Tx., U.S.	E5	120
Chambersburg, Il., U.S.	D3	90
Chambersburg, Pa., U.S.	G6	115
Chambers Island, i., Wi., U.S.	C6	126
Chambéry, Fr.	E6	16
Chambeshi, stm., Zam.	D5	48
Chamblee, Ga., U.S.	h8	87
Chambly, Que.	D4	74
Chambly, co., Que.	D4	74
Chambord, Que.	A5	74
Chamcook, N.B.	D2	71
Chamical, Arg.	F2	55
Chamisal, N.M., U.S.	A4	108
Chamois, Mo., U.S.	C6	102
Chamonix [-Mont-Blanc], Fr.	E7	16
Champ, Md., U.S.	D6	97
Champagne, Yukon	D5	66
Champagne, hist. reg., Fr.	C5	16
Champagney, Fr.	A2	21
Champagnole, Fr.	D6	16
Champaign, Il., U.S.	C5	90
Champaign, co., Il., U.S.	C5	90
Champaign, co., Oh., U.S.	B2	112
Champasak, Laos	D4	34
Champdoré, Lac, l., Que.	g8	71
Champerico, Guat.	C2	62
Champex, Switz.	C3	21
Champigneulles, Fr.	F6	17
Champion, Alta.	D4	68
Champion, Mi., U.S.	B2	99
Champion, Ne., U.S.	D4	104
Champion, Oh., U.S.	A5	112
Champion Creek Reservoir, res., Tx., U.S.	C2	120
Champions, Tx., U.S.	*E5	120
Champlain, Que.	C5	74
Champlain, N.Y., U.S.	f11	109
Champlain, Lake, l., N.A.	B2	122
Champlain, Mn., U.S.	m12	100
Champlitte [-et-le-Prélot], Fr.	D16	16
Champney's West, Newf.	D5	72
Champotón, Mex.	D6	63
Chana, Il., U.S.	A4	90
Chañaral, Chile	E1	55
Chança, stm., Eur.	D2	22
Chancay, Peru	D2	58
Chance, Md., U.S.	D6	97
Chancellor, Al., U.S.	D4	78
Chancellor, S.D., U.S.	D8	118
Chan Chan, hist., Peru	C2	58
Chanchelulla Peak, mtn., Ca., U.S.	B2	82
Chanco, Chile	B2	54
Chandalar, stm., Ak., U.S.	B10	79
Chandausi, India	C7	37
Chandeleur Islands, is., La., U.S.	E7	95
Chandeleur Sound, strt., La., U.S.	E6	95
Chandīgarh, India	B6	36
Chandīgarh, ter., India	*B6	36
Chandler, Que.	k14	74
Chandler, Az., U.S.	D4	80
Chandler, In., U.S.	H3	91
Chandler, Mn., U.S.	G3	100
Chandler, Ok., U.S.	B5	113
Chandler, Tx., U.S.	C5	120
Chandler Heights, Az., U.S.	m9	80
Chandlers Valley, Pa., U.S.	C3	115
Chandlerville, Il., U.S.	C3	90
Chandos Lake, l., Ont.	C6	73
Chāndpur, Bngl.	D9	36
Chandrapur, India	E6	36
Chaneysville, Pa., U.S.	G5	115
Chang, i., Thai.	F5	35
Changane, stm., Moz.	B5	49
Changbai Mountains, mts., Asia	E3	33
Changchou see Zhangzhou, China	G8	31
Changchun, China	C10	31
Changde, China	F7	31
Change Islands, Newf.	D4	72
Changewater, N.J., U.S.	B3	107
Changhua, China	I8	32
Chang Jiang see Yangtze, stm., China	E8	31
Changjin-ŭp, N. Kor.	F3	33
Changle, China	L8	32
Changli, China	E8	32
Changling, China	B10	31
Changping, China	D7	32
Changsha, China	F7	31
Changshu, China	I9	32
Changsŏng, N. Kor.	F2	33
Changwu, China	D6	31
Changxing, China	I9	32
Changyŏn, N. Kor.	G2	33
Changzhi, China	D7	31
Changzhou, China	E8	31
Chanhassen, Mn., U.S.	n11	100
Channahon, Il., U.S.	B5	90
Channel Country, reg., Austl.	D6	50
Channel Islands, is., Eur.	F5	10
Channel Islands National Park, Ca., U.S.	F4	82
Channel Lake, Il., U.S.	H8	90
Channel-Port-aux-Basques, Newf.	E2	72
Channelview, Tx., U.S.	r14	120
Channing, Mi., U.S.	B2	99
Channing, Tx., U.S.	B1	120
Chantada, Spain	A2	22
Chanthaburi, Thai.	C3	34
Chantilly, Fr.	C5	16
Chantilly, Va., U.S.	g12	123
Chantrey Inlet, b., N.W. Ter.	C13	66
Chanute, Ks., U.S.	E8	93
Chanute Air Force Base, mil., Il., U.S.	C5	90
Chany, Lake, l., Sov. Un.	D10	29
Chao'an, China	G8	31
Chao Lake, l., China	I7	32
Chao Phraya, stm., Thai.	C2	34
Chaor He, stm., China	B9	31
Chaoyang, China	C9	31
Chaoyang, China	*G8	31
Chapadinha, Braz.	B2	57
Chapala, Mex.	m12	63
Chapala, Lago de, l., Mex.	m12	63
Chaparral, Col.	C2	60
Chapayevsk, Sov. Un.	C3	28
Chapel Hill, De., U.S.	*B3	85
Chapel Hill, Ky., U.S.	D3	94
Chapel Hill, N.C., U.S.	B3	110
Chapel Hill, Tn., U.S.	B5	119
Chapelle, N.M., U.S.	B4	108
Chapel Square, Va., U.S.	*B5	123
Chapelton, Jam.	E14	65
Chapin, Il., U.S.	D3	90
Chapin, S.C., U.S.	C5	117
Chapleau, Ont.	p19	73
Chaplin, Sask.	G2	75
Chaplin, Ct., U.S.	B7	84
Chaplin, stm., Ky., U.S.	C4	94
Chaplin Lake, l., Sask.	G2	75
Chaplygin, Sov. Un.	E12	27
Chapman, Al., U.S.	D3	78
Chapman, Ks., U.S.	D6	93
Chapman, Ne., U.S.	C7	104
Chapman, Cape, c., N.W. Ter.	C15	66
Chapman Pond, l., R.I., U.S.	F1	116
Chapman Ranch, Tx., U.S.	F4	120
Chapmanville, W.V., U.S.	D2	125
Chappaqua, N.Y., U.S.	*D7	109
Chappaquiddick Island, i., Ma., U.S.	D7	98
Chappell, Ne., U.S.	C3	104
Chappells, S.C., U.S.	C4	117
Chaptico Creek, stm., Md., U.S.	D4	97
Chaqui, Bol.	C2	55
Char, well, Maur.	B2	45
Charadai, Arg.	E4	55
Charagua, Bol.	C3	55
Charalá, Col.	B3	60
Charanā, Bol.	A2	55
Charcas, Mex.	C4	63
Charco, Tx., U.S.	E4	120
Charcot Island, i., Ant.	C5	7
Chard, Eng., U.K.	D5	12
Chardarinsk Reservoir, res., Sov. Un.	E7	28
Chardon, Oh., U.S.	A4	112
Chardzhou, Sov. Un.	F9	29
Charente, stm., Fr.	E3	16
Charenton-le-Pont, Fr.	g10	16
Charette, Que.	C5	74
Chari, stm., Afr.	C3	46
Chārīkār, Afg.	A4	36
Chāring, Ga., U.S.	D2	87
Chariton, Ia., U.S.	C4	92
Chariton, co., Mo., U.S.	B4	102
Chariton, stm., U.S.	A5	102
Charity, Guy.	A3	59
Charity, Mo., U.S.	D4	102
Charlemont, Ma., U.S.	A2	98
Charleroi, Bel.	B6	16
Charleroi, Pa., U.S.	F2	115
Charles, co., Md., U.S.	C3	97
Charles, stm., Ma., U.S.	B5	98
Charles, Cape, c., Va., U.S.	C6	123
Charles A. Goodwin Dam, Ct., U.S.	B3	84
Charlesbourg, Que.	n17	74
Charlesburg, Wi., U.S.	k9	126
Charles City, Ia., U.S.	A5	92
Charles City, Va., U.S.	C5	123
Charles City, co., Va., U.S.	C5	123
Charles Mill Lake, res., Oh., U.S.	B3	112
Charles Mix, co., S.D., U.S.	D7	118
Charles Mound, hill, Il., U.S.	A3	90
Charleston, Ar., U.S.	B1	81
Charleston, Il., U.S.	D5	90
Charleston, Me., U.S.	C3	96
Charleston, Ms., U.S.	A3	101
Charleston, Mo., U.S.	E8	102
Charleston, Or., U.S.	D2	114
Charleston, S.C., U.S.	F8	117
Charleston, Tn., U.S.	D9	119
Charleston, Ut., U.S.	C4	121
Charleston, W.V., U.S.	C3	125
Charleston, co., S.C., U.S.	F8	117
Charleston Air Force Base, mil., S.C., U.S.	k11	117
Charleston Naval Shipyard, mil., S.C., U.S.	k12	117
Charleston Park, Nv., U.S.	*G6	105
Charleston Peak, mtn., Nv., U.S.	G6	105
Charlestown, Ire.	D3	11
Charlestown, St. C.-N.	H13	64
Charlestown, In., U.S.	H6	91
Charlestown, Md., U.S.	A6	97
Charlestown, N.H., U.S.	D2	106
Charlestown, R.I., U.S.	F2	116
Charles Town, W.V., U.S.	B7	125
Charleville, Austl.	E8	50
Charleville-Mézières, Fr.	C6	16
Charlevoix, Mi., U.S.	C5	99
Charlevoix, co., Mi., U.S.	C5	99
Charlevoix, Lake, l., Mi., U.S.	C5	99
Charlevoix-Est, co., Que.	B7	74
Charlevoix-Ouest, co., Que.	B7	74
Charlie Lake, B.C.	A7	69
Charlo, Mt., U.S.	C2	103
Charlotte, Mi., U.S.	F6	99
Charlotte, N.C., U.S.	B2	110
Charlotte, Tn., U.S.	A4	119
Charlotte, Tx., U.S.	E3	120
Charlotte, Vt., U.S.	C2	122
Charlotte, co., Fl., U.S.	F5	86
Charlotte, co., N.B.	D2	71
Charlotte, co., Va., U.S.	C4	123
Charlotte Amalie, V.I.U.S.	G12	64
Charlotte Court House, Va., U.S.	C4	123
Charlotte Hall, Md., U.S.	D4	97
Charlotte Harbor, Fl., U.S.	F4	86
Charlotte Harbor, b., Fl., U.S.	F4	86
Charlotte Lake, l., B.C.	C5	69
Charlottenburg, Sur.	A4	59
Charlottesville, In., U.S.	E6	91
Charlottesville, Va., U.S.	B4	123
Charlottetown, P.E.I.	C6	71
Charlottetown (Gouyave), Gren.	W25	65
Charlotteville, Trin.	M24	65
Charlton, Ma., U.S.	B4	98
Charlton, N.D., U.S.	A3	111
Charlton, co., Ga., U.S.	F4	87
Charlton City, Ma., U.S.	B4	98
Charlton Depot, Ma., U.S.	B4	98
Charlton Island, i., N.W. Ter.	n20	73
Charly [-sur-Marne], Fr.	F3	17
Charmco, W.V., U.S.	C4	125
Charmes, Fr.	C7	16
Charmey, Switz.	C6	21
Charny, Que.	C6	74
Charouine, Alg.	C4	44
Charquemont, Fr.	B2	21
Charron Lake, l., Man.	C4	70
Charsov, Sov. Un.	D10	28
Charter Oak, Ca., U.S.	*E5	82
Charter Oak, Ia., U.S.	B2	92
Charters Towers, Austl.	D8	50
Chartierville, Que.	D6	74
Chartley, Ma., U.S.	C5	98
Chartres, Fr.	C5	16
Charysh, stm., Sov. Un.	C10	28
Chascomús, Arg.	B5	54
Chase, B.C.	D8	69
Chase, Ks., U.S.	D5	93
Chase, Md., U.S.	B5	97
Chase, Mi., U.S.	E5	99
Chase, co., Ks., U.S.	D7	93
Chase, co., Ne., U.S.	D4	104
Chase, Mount, mtn., Me., U.S.	B4	96
Chaseburg, Wi., U.S.	E2	126
Chase City, Va., U.S.	D4	123
Chase Field Naval Air Station, mil., Tx., U.S.	E4	120
Chaseley, N.D., U.S.	B6	111
Chase River, B.C.	f12	69
Chasicó, Arg.	D4	54
Chaska, Mn., U.S.	F5	100
Chasov Yar, Sov. Un.	q20	27
Chassahowitzka Bay, b., Fl., U.S.	D4	86
Chassell, Mi., U.S.	A2	99
Chasseral, mtn., Switz.	B3	20
Chasseron, Mont, mtn., Switz.	C2	21
Chataignier, La., U.S.	D3	95
Chatanika, Ak., U.S.	B10	79
Chatawa, Ms., U.S.	D3	101
Châteaubriant, Fr.	D3	16
Château-d'Oex, Switz.	C3	21
Château-du-Loir, Fr.	D4	16
Châteaudun, Fr.	C5	16
Chateaugay, N.Y., U.S.	f10	109
Château-Gontier, Fr.	D3	16
Châteauguay, Que.	D4	74
Châteauguay, co., Que.	D4	74
Châteauguay Heights, Que.	q19	74
Châteauneuf, Fr.	D5	16
Château-Renault, Fr.	D4	16
Château-Richer, Que.	C6	74
Châteauroux, Fr.	D4	16
Château-Salins, Fr.	F6	17
Château-Thierry, Fr.	C5	16
Châtel, Fr.	D2	21
Châtellerault, Fr.	D4	16
Châtel-Saint-Denis, Switz.	C2	21
Chatfield, Man.	D3	70
Chatfield, Ar., U.S.	B5	81
Chatfield, Mn., U.S.	G6	100
Chatfield, Oh., U.S.	B3	112
Chatham, N.B.	B4	71
Chatham, Ont.	E2	73
Chatham, Eng., U.K.	E7	10
Chatham, Il., U.S.	D4	90
Chatham, La., U.S.	B3	95
Chatham, Ma., U.S.	C8	98
Chatham, Mi., U.S.	B4	99
Chatham, N.J., U.S.	B4	107
Chatham, N.Y., U.S.	C7	109
Chatham, Oh., U.S.	A3	112
Chatham, Va., U.S.	D3	123
Chatham, co., Ga., U.S.	E5	87
Chatham, co., N.C., U.S.	B3	110
Chatham Head, N.B.	C4	71
Chatham Islands, is., N.Z.	I11	6
Chatham Sound, strt., B.C.	B2	69
Chatham Strait, strt., Ak., U.S.	m22	79
Châtillon, Italy	D2	20
Châtillon-sur-Seine, Fr.	D6	16
Chatkal Range, mts., Sov. Un.	E8	28
Chatom, Al., U.S.	D1	78
Chatsworth, Ont.	C4	73
Chatsworth, Ga., U.S.	B2	87
Chatsworth, Il., U.S.	C5	90
Chatsworth, N.J., U.S.	D3	107
Chatsworth Reservoir, res., Ca., U.S.	m11	82
Chattahoochee, Fl., U.S.	B2	86
Chattahoochee, co., Ga., U.S.	D2	87
Chattahoochee, stm., U.S.	E1	87
Chattanooga, Oh., U.S.	B1	112
Chattanooga, Tn., U.S.	D8	119
Chattaroy, Wa., U.S.	B8	124
Chattaroy, W.V., U.S.	D2	125
Chatteris, Eng., U.K.	B8	12
Chattooga, co., Ga., U.S.	B1	87
Chattooga, stm., U.S.	B1	110
Chatuge Lake, res., U.S.	g9	110
Chaudière, stm., Que.	C7	74
Chau Doc, Viet.	C3	34
Chauk, Burma	D9	36
Chaumont, Fr.	C6	16
Chaumont, N.Y., U.S.	A4	109
Chaun Bay, b., Sov. Un.	B34	128
Chauncey, Ga., U.S.	D3	87
Chauncey, Oh., U.S.	C3	112
Chauncy Lake, l., Ma., U.S.	g9	98
Chauny, Fr.	C5	16
Chautauqua, Ks., U.S.	E7	93
Chautauqua, N.Y., U.S.	C1	109
Chautauqua, co., Ks., U.S.	E7	93
Chautauqua, co., N.Y., U.S.	C1	109
Chautauqua Lake, l., N.Y., U.S.	C1	109
Chauvigny, Fr.	D4	16
Chauvin, Alta.	C5	68
Chauvin, La., U.S.	E5	95
Chavanga, Sov. Un.	D17	14
Chaves, Braz.	C5	57
Chaves, Port.	B2	22
Chaves, co., N.M., U.S.	D5	108
Chavies, Ky., U.S.	C6	94
Chavinda, Mex.	m12	63
Cháviva, Col.	C3	60
Chavuma, Zam.	D3	48
Chazelles, Fr.	E6	16
Chazy, N.Y., U.S.	f11	109
Cheadle, Alta.	D4	68
Cheaha Mountain, mtn., Al., U.S.	B4	78
Cheam (part of London), Eng., U.K.	m12	10
Cheapside, Va., U.S.	h16	123
Cheat, Shavers Fork, stm., W.V., U.S.	B5	125
Cheatham, co., Tn., U.S.	A4	119
Cheatham Reservoir, res., Tn., U.S.	A4	119
Cheat Mountain, mtn., W.V., U.S.	C5	125
Cheb, Czech.	C2	26
Chebacco Lake, l., Ma., U.S.	f12	98
Chebanse, Il., U.S.	C6	90
Chebeague Island, Me., U.S.	E2	96
Cheboksary, Sov. Un.	D7	28
Cheboygan, Mi., U.S.	C6	99
Cheboygan, co., Mi., U.S.	C6	99
Chech, 'Erg, des., Afr.	E4	44
Chechaouene, Mor.	B3	44
Chechŏn, S. Kor.	H4	33
Chechotah, Ok., U.S.	B6	113
Chedabucto Bay, b., N.S.	D8	71
Cheddar, S.C., U.S.	B3	117
Cheduba Island, i., Burma	E9	36
Cheecham Hills, hills, Alta.	B5	68
Cheektowaga, N.Y., U.S.	C2	109
Cheepie, Austl.	C5	51
Cheeseman Lake, res., Co., U.S.	B5	83
Chegutu, Zimb.	A5	49
Chehalem Mountains, mts., Or., U.S.	h12	114
Chehalis, Wa., U.S.	C3	124
Chehalis, stm., Wa., U.S.	C3	124
Cheju, S. Kor.	J3	33
Cheju Strait, strt., S. Kor.	J3	33
Chekhov, Sov. Un.	C10	33
Chekiang see Zhejiang, prov., China	F9	31
Chekunda, Sov. Un.	A6	33
Chelan, Sask.	E4	75
Chelan, Wa., U.S.	B5	124
Chelan, co., Wa., U.S.	B4	124
Chelan, Lake, l., Wa., U.S.	A5	124
Chelan Falls, Wa., U.S.	B5	124
Chelan Mountains, mts., Wa., U.S.	A5	124
Cheleiros, Port.	f9	22
Cheleken, Sov. Un.	B6	39

Name	Map Ref.	Page

Cheleken Peninsula, pen., Sov. Un. — B6 39
Chelforó, Arg. — B3 54
Chélia, Djebel, mtn., Alg. — B6 44
Chéliff, Oued, stm., Alg. — B5 44
Chelkar, Sov. Un. — E8 29
Chelles, Fr. — F2 17
Chelm, Pol. — C7 26
Chelmno, Pol. — B5 26
Chelmsford, Eng., U.K. — E7 10
Chelmsford, Ma., U.S. — A5 98
Chelmza, Pol. — B5 26
Chelsea, Que. — D2 74
Chelsea (part of London), Eng., U.K. — m12 10
Chelsea, Al., U.S. — g7 78
Chelsea, Ia., U.S. — C5 92
Chelsea, Me., U.S. — D3 96
Chelsea, Ma., U.S. — B5 98
Chelsea, Mi., U.S. — F6 99
Chelsea, Ok., U.S. — A6 113
Chelsea, S.D., U.S. — B7 118
Chelsea, Wi., U.S. — C3 126
Chelsea Estates, De., U.S. — *B3 85
Cheltenham, Eng., U.K. — E5 10
Cheltenham, Md., U.S. — C4 97
Cheltenham Township, Pa., U.S. — *o21 115
Chelva, Spain — C5 22
Chelyabinsk, Sov. Un. — D9 29
Chelyan, W.V., U.S. — C3 125
Chelyuskin, Cape, c., Sov. Un. — B13 29
Chelyuskintsy Ice Tongue, ice, Ant. — C21 7
Chemainus, B.C. — E6 69
Chemal, Sov. Un. — E26 8
Chemehuevi Indian Reservation, Ca., U.S. — E6 82
Chemillé, Fr. — D3 16
Chemin Craig, Que. — o17 74
Chemnitz see Karl-Marx-Stadt, E. Ger. — C6 18
Chemquasabamticook Lake (Ross Lake), l., Me., U.S. — B3 96
Chemult, Or., U.S. — D5 114
Chemung, Il., U.S. — A5 90
Chemung, co., N.Y., U.S. — C4 109
Chemung, stm., N.Y., U.S. — C8 115
Chemung Lake, l., Ont. — C6 73
Chenāb, stm., Asia — B5 36
Chenango, co., N.Y., U.S. — C5 109
Chenango, stm., N.Y., U.S. — C5 109
Chenango Bridge, N.Y., U.S. — C5 109
Chenango Forks, N.Y., U.S. — C5 109
Chenārān, Iran — C9 39
Chene, Bayou, stm., La., U.S. — k9 95
Chenequa, Wi., U.S. — m11 126
Chenes, River Aux, b., La., U.S. — k12 95
Chénéville, Que. — D2 74
Cheney, Ks., U.S. — E6 93
Cheney, Wa., U.S. — B8 124
Cheney Reservoir, res., Ks., U.S. — E6 93
Cheneyville, La., U.S. — C3 95
Chengchou see Zhengzhou, China — E7 31
Chengde, China — C8 31
Chengdu (Chengtu), China — E5 31
Chenggu, China — G8 31
Chenghai, China — I3 32
Chengkou, China — I3 32
Chengmai, China — G8 31
Chengshan Point, c., China — D9 31
Chengtu see Chengdu, China — E5 31
Chenoa, Il., U.S. — C5 90
Chenoa, Ky., U.S. — D6 94
Chenôve, Fr. — D6 16
Chenoweth, Or., U.S. — B5 114
Chenxi, China — F7 31
Chenzhou, China — F7 31
Chepachet, R.I., U.S. — B2 116
Chepachet, stm., R.I., U.S. — B2 116
Chepén, Peru — C2 58
Chepes, Arg. — A3 54
Chepo, Pan. — F8 62
Chepstow, Wales, U.K. — E5 10
Cheptsa, stm., Sov. Un. — D19 8
Chequamegon Bay, b., Wi., U.S. — B3 126
Cher, stm., Fr. — D4 16
Cheraw, Co., U.S. — C7 83
Cheraw, S.C., U.S. — B8 117
Cherbourg, Fr. — C3 16
Cherchell, Alg. — B5 44
Cherdyn, Sov. Un. — A5 29
Cheremkhovo, Sov. Un. — D13 29
Cherepanovo, Sov. Un. — C10 28
Cherepovets, Sov. Un. — D6 29
Cherhill, Alta. — C3 68
Cheriton, Va., U.S. — C7 123
Cherkassy, Sov. Un. — G9 27
Cherkessk, Sov. Un. — G17 8
Cherlakskiy, Sov. Un. — C8 28
Chernigov, Sov. Un. — D6 29
Chernigovka, Sov. Un. — H11 27
Chernigovka, Sov. Un. — D6 33
Chernobay, Sov. Un. — G9 27
Chernobyl, Sov. Un. — F8 27
Chernogorsk, Sov. Un. — E27 8
Chernomorskoye, Sov. Un. — I9 27
Chernovtsy, Sov. Un. — E5 29
Chernoye, Sov. Un. — r32 14
Chernyakhovsk (Insterburg), Sov. Un. — D3 27
Cherokee, Al., U.S. — A2 78
Cherokee, Ia., U.S. — B2 92
Cherokee, Ks., U.S. — E9 93
Cherokee, N.C., U.S. — f9 110
Cherokee, Ok., U.S. — A3 113
Cherokee, Tx., U.S. — D3 120
Cherokee, co., Al., U.S. — A4 78
Cherokee, co., Ga., U.S. — B2 87
Cherokee, co., Ia., U.S. — B2 92
Cherokee, co., Ks., U.S. — E9 93
Cherokee, co., N.C., U.S. — f8 110
Cherokee, co., Ok., U.S. — B6 113
Cherokee, co., S.C., U.S. — A4 117
Cherokee, co., Tx., U.S. — C5 120
Cherokee Falls, S.C., U.S. — A4 117
Cherokee Indian Reservation, N.C., U.S. — f9 110
Cherokee Lake, res., Tn., U.S. — C10 119
Cherokees, Lake O' The, res., Ok., U.S. — A7 113
Cherokee Sound, Bah. — A5 64
Cherokee Village, Ar., U.S. — *A4 81
Cherquenco, Chile — B2 54
Cherrapunji, India — C9 36
Cherry, Il., U.S. — B4 90
Cherry, Tn., U.S. — B5 119
Cherry, co., Ne., U.S. — B4 104
Cherry Creek, N.Y., U.S. — C1 109

Cherry Creek, S.D., U.S. — C4 118
Cherry Creek, stm., Co., U.S. — B6 83
Cherry Creek, stm., S.D., U.S. — C3 118
Cherryfield, Me., U.S. — D5 96
Cherry Fork, Oh., U.S. — D2 112
Cherry Grove, Or., U.S. — g11 114
Cherry Hill, N.J., U.S. — D2 107
Cherry Hills Village, Co., U.S. — *B6 83
Cherryland, Ca., U.S. — *D2 82
Cherry Point, c., Va., U.S. — C6 123
Cherry Point Marine Corps Air Station, mil., N.C., U.S. — C6 110
Cherry Run, W.V., U.S. — B6 125
Cherry Tree, Pa., U.S. — E4 115
Cherryvale, Ks., U.S. — E8 93
Cherry Valley, Ont. — D7 73
Cherry Valley, Ar., U.S. — B5 81
Cherry Valley, Ca., U.S. — *F5 82
Cherry Valley, Il., U.S. — A5 90
Cherry Valley, Ma., U.S. — B4 98
Cherry Valley, N.Y., U.S. — C6 109
Cherryville, N.C., U.S. — B1 110
Cherskiy Mountains, mts., Sov. Un. — C17 29
Chesaning, Mi., U.S. — E6 99
Chesapeake, Oh., U.S. — D3 112
Chesapeake, Va., U.S. — D6 123
Chesapeake, W.V., U.S. — C3 125
Chesapeake and Delaware Canal, U.S. — B3 85
Chesapeake Bay, b., U.S. — C12 76
Chesapeake Bay Bridge-Tunnel, U.S. — D7 123
Chesapeake Beach, Md., U.S. — C4 97
Chesapeake City, Md., U.S. — A6 97
Chesaw, Wa., U.S. — A6 124
Chesdin, Lake, res., Va., U.S. — C5 123
Chesha Bay, b., Sov. Un. — B18 8
Chesham, Eng., U.K. — k11 10
Chesham, N.H., U.S. — E2 106
Cheshire, Ct., U.S. — D4 84
Cheshire, Ma., U.S. — A1 98
Cheshire, Oh., U.S. — D3 112
Cheshire, co., Eng., U.K. — A5 12
Cheshire, co., N.H., U.S. — E2 106
Cheshire Reservoir, res., Ma., U.S. — A1 98
Cheshunt, Eng., U.K. — k12 10
Chesilhurst, N.J., U.S. — D3 107
Chesley, Ont. — C3 73
Chesnee, S.C., U.S. — A4 117
Chester, N.S. — E5 71
Chester, Eng., U.K. — D5 10
Chester, Ar., U.S. — B1 81
Chester, Ca., U.S. — B3 82
Chester, Ct., U.S. — D6 84
Chester, Fl., U.S. — B5 86
Chester, Ga., U.S. — D3 87
Chester, Id., U.S. — F7 89
Chester, Il., U.S. — F4 90
Chester, Ia., U.S. — A5 92
Chester, Md., U.S. — C5 97
Chester, Ma., U.S. — B2 98
Chester, Mt., U.S. — B6 103
Chester, Ne., U.S. — D8 104
Chester, N.H., U.S. — E4 106
Chester, N.J., U.S. — B3 107
Chester, N.Y., U.S. — D6 109
Chester, Oh., U.S. — C4 112
Chester, Pa., U.S. — G11 115
Chester, S.C., U.S. — B5 117
Chester, S.D., U.S. — D9 118
Chester, Vt., U.S. — E3 122
Chester, Va., U.S. — C5 123
Chester, W.V., U.S. — A4 125
Chester, co., Pa., U.S. — G10 115
Chester, co., S.C., U.S. — B5 117
Chester, co., Tn., U.S. — B3 119
Chester, stm., Md., U.S. — B5 97
Chester Basin, N.S. — E5 71
Chester Depot, Vt., U.S. — E3 122
Chesterfield, Eng., U.K. — D6 10
Chesterfield, Il., U.S. — D3 90
Chesterfield, In., U.S. — D6 91
Chesterfield, Ma., U.S. — B2 98
Chesterfield, N.H., U.S. — E2 106
Chesterfield, S.C., U.S. — B7 117
Chesterfield, Tn., U.S. — B3 119
Chesterfield, co., S.C., U.S. — B7 117
Chesterfield, co., Va., U.S. — C5 123
Chesterfield, Îles, is, N. Cal. — H9 6
Chesterfield Inlet, N.W. Ter. — D14 66
Chesterfield Inlet, b., N.W. Ter. — D14 66
Chesterhill, Oh., U.S. — C4 112
Chesterton, In., U.S. — A3 91
Chestertown, Md., U.S. — B5 97
Chestertown, N.Y., U.S. — B7 109
Chester Township, Pa., U.S. — *p20 115
Chesterville, Ont. — B9 73
Chesterville, Oh., U.S. — B3 112
Chestnut, Il., U.S. — C4 90
Chestnut, La., U.S. — B2 95
Chestnut Hill Estates, De., U.S. — *B3 85
Chestnut Knoll, De., U.S. — E4 85
Chestnut Mound, Tn., U.S. — C8 119
Chestnut Ridge, N.Y., U.S. — *D6 109
Chesuncook Lake, l., Me., U.S. — C3 96
Cheswick, Pa., U.S. — h14 115
Cheswold, De., U.S. — D3 85
Chetac, Lake, l., Wi., U.S. — C2 126
Chetco, Lake, l., Or., U.S. — E2 114
Chetek, Wi., U.S. — C2 126
Chetek Lake, l., Wi., U.S. — C2 126
Chéticamp, N.S. — C8 71
Chetopa, Ks., U.S. — E8 93
Chetumal, Mex. — D7 63
Chetumal Bay, b., N.A. — D7 63
Chetwynd, B.C. — B7 69
Chevak, Ak., U.S. — C6 79
Chevelon Creek, stm., Az., U.S. — C5 80
Cheverie, N.S. — D5 71
Cheverly, Md., U.S. — *C4 97
Cheviot, Oh., U.S. — o12 112
Cheviot, Sask. — E2 75
Cheviot, N.Z. — O14 51
Cheviot, Oh., U.S. — C1 112
Chevreuil, Bayou, stm., La., U.S. — k10 95
Chevreuil, Point, c., La., U.S. — E4 95
Chevy Chase, Md., U.S. — C3 97
Chewack, stm., Wa., U.S. — A5 124
Chewalla, Tn., U.S. — B3 119
Chewelah, Wa., U.S. — A8 124
Chewsville, Md., U.S. — A2 97
Chewton, Pa., U.S. — E1 115
Cheyenne, Ok., U.S. — B2 113
Cheyenne, Wy., U.S. — E8 127
Cheyenne, co., Co., U.S. — C8 83

Cheyenne, co., Ks., U.S. — C2 93
Cheyenne, co., Ne., U.S. — C2 104
Cheyenne, stm., U.S. — C4 118
Cheyenne, Dry Fork, stm., Wy., U.S. — C7 127
Cheyenne River Indian Reservation, S.D., U.S. — B4 118
Cheyenne Wells, Co., U.S. — C8 83
Chhapra, India — C7 36
Chhatarpur, India — E7 37
Chhatrapur, India — H10 37
Chhindwāra, India — H7 37
Chhukha Dzong, Bhu. — D12 37
Chi, stm., Thai. — E6 35
Chiai, Tai. — *G9 31
Chiang Kham, Thai. — C4 35
Chiang Khong, Thai. — A2 34
Chiang Mai, Thai. — B1 34
Chiang Rai, Thai. — B1 34
Chiapa de Corzo, Mex. — D6 63
Chiapas, state, Mex. — D6 63
Chiari, Italy — B2 23
Chiasso, Switz. — E7 21
Chiatura, Sov. Un. — A14 40
Chiautla de Tapia, Mex. — n14 63
Chiavari, Italy — B2 23
Chiavenna, Italy — C5 20
Chiawuli Tak, Az., U.S. — F4 80
Chiba, Japan — D13 31
Chibemba, Ang. — E1 48
Chibia, Ang. — E1 48
Chiblow Lake, l., Ont. — A1 73
Chibougamau, Que. — k12 74
Chibuto, Moz. — B5 49
Chicago, Il., U.S. — B6 90
Chicago Heights, Il., U.S. — B6 90
Chicago Ridge, Il., U.S. — *k9 90
Chicago Sanitary and Ship Canal, Il., U.S. — k8 90
Chicamacomico, stm., Md., U.S. — D6 97
Chicapa, stm., Afr. — C3 48
Chichagof Island, i., Ak., U.S. — m22 79
Chichaoua, Mor. — C3 44
Chicheng, China — D6 32
Chichén Itzá, hist., Mex. — C7 63
Chichester, Eng., U.K. — E6 10
Chichester, N.H., U.S. — D4 106
Chichibu, Japan — n18 31
Chickahominy, stm., Va., U.S. — C5 123
Chickamauga, Ga., U.S. — B1 87
Chickamauga and Chattanooga National Military Park, U.S. — k11 119
Chickamauga Dam, Tn., U.S. — h11 119
Chickamauga Lake, res., Tn., U.S. — D8 119
Chickasaw, Al., U.S. — E1 78
Chickasaw, co., Ia., U.S. — A5 92
Chickasaw, co., Ms., U.S. — B5 101
Chickasawhay, stm., Ms., U.S. — D5 101
Chickasaw National Recreation Area, Ok., U.S. — C5 113
Chickasha, Ok., U.S. — B4 113
Chickasha, Lake, res., Ok., U.S. — B3 113
Chickwolnepy Stream, stm., N.H., U.S. — A4 106
Chiclana [de la Frontera], Spain — D2 22
Chiclayo, Peru — C2 58
Chico, Ca., U.S. — C3 82
Chico, Tx., U.S. — C4 120
Chico, Wa., U.S. — B3 124
Chico, stm., Arg. — C3 54
Chico, stm., Arg. — D3 54
Chico, stm., Mex. — h9 63
Chicoa, Moz. — A5 49
Chico Creek, stm., Co., U.S. — C6 83
Chico Hot Springs, Mt., U.S. — E6 103
Chicomo, Moz. — B5 49
Chicontepec, Mex. — m14 63
Chicopee, Ga., U.S. — B3 87
Chicopee, Ma., U.S. — B2 98
Chicora, Ms., U.S. — D5 101
Chicot, co., Ar., U.S. — D4 81
Chicot, Lake, l., Ar., U.S. — D4 81
Chicota, Tx., U.S. — C5 120
Chicot Island, i., La., U.S. — E6 95
Chicoutimi, Que. — A6 74
Chicoutimi, co., Que. — A6 74
Chicoutimi, stm., Que. — A6 74
Chico West, Ca., U.S. — *C3 82
Chidester, Ar., U.S. — D3 81
Chidley, Cape, c., Can. — f8 72
Chiefland, Fl., U.S. — C4 86
Chiefs Point, c., Ont. — C3 73
Chiem Lake, l., W. Ger. — E6 18
Chien, Bayou de, stm., Ky., U.S. — f8 94
Chieri, Italy — B1 23
Chiers, stm., Eur. — E5 17
Chiese, stm., Italy — D6 20
Chieti, Italy — C5 23
Chifeng, China — C8 31
Chigasaki, Japan — *l9 31
Chignahuapan, Mex. — n14 63
Chignecto, Cape, c., N.S. — D5 71
Chignecto Bay, b., Can. — D5 71
Chignik, Ak., U.S. — D8 79
Chigubo, Moz. — B5 49
Chigwell, Eng., U.K. — k13 10
Chihli, Gulf of see Bo Hai, b., China — D8 31
Chihuahua, Mex. — B3 63
Chihuahua, state, Mex. — B3 63
Chii, Mount, mtn., S. Kor. — I3 33
Chikaskia, stm., U.S. — A4 113
Chilapa [de Alvarez], Mex. — o18 63
Chilca, Peru — D2 58
Chilcotin, stm., B.C. — D6 69
Chilcoot, Ca., U.S. — C3 82

Chililabombwe (Bancroft), Zam. — D4 48
Chilili, N.M., U.S. — C3 108
Chilkat Pass, B.C. — E5 66
Chilko, stm., B.C. — D6 69
Chilko Lake, l., B.C. — D5 69
Chillán, Chile — B2 54
Chilli, Sov. Un. — E7 28
Chillicothe, Il., U.S. — C4 90
Chillicothe, Ia., U.S. — C5 92
Chillicothe, Mo., U.S. — B4 102
Chillicothe, Oh., U.S. — C3 112
Chillicothe, Tx., U.S. — B3 120
Chilliwack, B.C. — E7 69
Chilliwack, stm., N.A. — A4 124
Chillum, Md., U.S. — f9 97
Chilmark, Ma., U.S. — D6 98
Chilocco, Ok., U.S. — A4 113
Chiloé, Isla de, i., Chile — C2 54
Chiloquin, Or., U.S. — E5 114
Chilpancingo [de los Bravos], Mex. — D5 63
Chilton, Tx., U.S. — D4 120
Chilton, Wi., U.S. — D5 126
Chilton, co., Al., U.S. — C3 78
Chiluage, Ang. — C3 48
Chilumba, Mwi. — D5 48
Chilung (Keelung), Tai. — F9 31
Chilwa, Lake, l., Afr. — E6 48
Chimacum, Wa., U.S. — A3 124
Chimaltenango, Guat. — C2 62
Chimán, Pan. — F8 62
Chimay, Bel. — D4 17
Chimayo, N.M., U.S. — A4 108
Chimbay, Sov. Un. — E8 29
Chimborazo, prov., Ec. — B2 58
Chimborazo, vol., Ec. — B2 58
Chimbote, Peru — C2 58
Chimkent, Sov. Un. — E9 29
Chimney Rock, Co., U.S. — D3 83
Chimney Rock, mtn., Ky., U.S. — D5 94
Chimney Rock, mtn., Ne., U.S. — C2 104
Chimneytop, mtn., Tn., U.S. — C11 119
Chimoio, Moz. — A5 49
Chin, Alta. — E4 68
Chin, Cape, c., Ont. — B3 73
Chinā, Japan — O5 52
China, Mex. — B5 63
China, U.S. — D3 96
China, ctry., Asia — E6 31
China Grove, N.C., U.S. — B2 110
China Lake, l., Me., U.S. — D3 96
Chinan see Jinan, China — D8 31
Chinati Peak, mtn., Tx., U.S. — p12 120
Chincha Alta, Peru — D2 58
Chincheros, Peru — D3 58
Chinchilla, Austl. — E9 50
Chinchilla [de Monte Aragón], Spain — C5 22
Chincoteague, Va., U.S. — C7 123
Chincoteague Bay, b., U.S. — D7 97
Chinde, Moz. — A6 49
Chindo, S. Kor. — I3 33
Chindwinn, stm., Burma — C10 36
Chingola, Zam. — D4 48
Chinguar, Ang. — D2 48
Chinguetti, Maur. — B2 45
Chinhae, S. Kor. — I4 33
Chinhoyi, Zimb. — A5 49
Chiniot, Pak. — B4 37
Chinipas, Mex. — B3 63
Chinit, stm., Camb. — F6 35
Chinitna Point, c., Ak., U.S. — h15 79
Chinju, S. Kor. — D10 31
Chinko, stm., Cen. Afr. Rep. — D4 46
Chinle, Az., U.S. — A6 80
Chinle Wash, val., U.S. — A6 80
Chinnampo see Nampo, N. Kor. — D10 31
Chino, Ca., U.S. — F5 82
Chinon, Fr. — D4 16
Chinook, Alta. — D5 68
Chinook, Mt., U.S. — B7 103
Chinook, Lake, res., Or., U.S. — C5 114
Chinook Cove, B.C. — D7 69
Chino Valley, Az., U.S. — C3 80
Chinquapin, N.C., U.S. — C5 110
Chinsali, Zam. — D5 48
Chinteche, Mwi. — D5 48
Chinú, Col. — B2 60
Chioggia, Italy — B4 23
Chios see Khíos, i., Grc. — C5 40
Chipata (Fort Jameson), Zam. — D5 48
Chipewyan, stm., Alta. — A4 68
Chipinge, Zimb. — B5 49
Chipley, Fl., U.S. — u16 86
Chipman, Alta. — C4 68
Chipman, N.B. — C4 71
Chippenham, Eng., U.K. — E5 10
Chippewa, co., Mi., U.S. — B6 99
Chippewa, co., Mn., U.S. — E3 100
Chippewa, co., Wi., U.S. — C2 126
Chippewa, stm., Mn., U.S. — E3 100
Chippewa, stm., Wi., U.S. — D2 126
Chippewa, East Branch, stm., Mn., U.S. — E3 100
Chippewa, East Fork, stm., Wi., U.S. — C3 126
Chippewa Falls, Wi., U.S. — D2 126
Chippewa Lake, l., Wi., U.S. — C2 126
Chipping Norton, Eng., U.K. — C6 12
Chipola, stm., Fl., U.S. — B1 86
Chipuxet, stm., R.I., U.S. — F3 116
Chiputneticook Lakes, l., N.A. — C4 71
Chiquimula, Guat. — C2 62
Chiquinquirá, Col. — B3 60
Chira, stm., S.A. — B1 58
Chiradzulu, Mwi. — E6 48
Chirchik, Sov. Un. — E9 29
Chiredzi, Zimb. — B5 49
Chireno, Tx., U.S. — D5 120
Chiricahua Mountains, mts., Az., U.S. — F6 80
Chiricahua National Monument, Az., U.S. — F6 80
Chiricahua Peak, mtn., Az., U.S. — F6 80
Chirikof Island, i., Ak., U.S. — D8 79
Chiriquí, Golfo de, b., Pan. — G6 62
Chiriquí Grande, Pan. — F6 62
Chiriquí, prov., Pan. — F6 62
Chiromo, Mwi. — E6 48
Chirpan, Bul. — D7 24
Chirripó, Cerro, mtn., C.R. — F6 62

Chirundu, Zimb. — A4 49
Chisago, co., Mn., U.S. — E6 100
Chisago City, Mn., U.S. — E6 100
Chisamba, Zam. — D4 48
Chisana, Ak., U.S. — C11 79
Chisasibi, Que. — h11 74
Chisholm, Alta. — B3 68
Chisholm, Me., U.S. — D2 96
Chisholm, Mn., U.S. — C6 100
Chisineu-Criş, Rom. — B5 24
Chisos Mountains, mts., Tx., U.S. — E1 120
Chistochina, Ak., U.S. — C11 79
Chistopol, Sov. Un. — B4 28
Chita, Sov. Un. — D14 29
Chitado, Ang. — E1 48
Chitato, Ang. — C3 48
Chitek, Sask. — D2 75
Chitek Lake, l., Man. — C2 70
Chitembo, Ang. — D2 48
Chitina, Ak., U.S. — C11 79
Chitina, stm., Ak., U.S. — g19 79
Chitipa, Mwi. — C5 48
Chitose, Japan — *E10 31
Chitradurga, India — F6 36
Chitrāl, Pak. — A5 36
Chitré, Pan. — G7 62
Chittagong, Bngl. — D9 36
Chittenango, N.Y., U.S. — B5 109
Chittenden, Vt., U.S. — D3 122
Chittenden, co., Vt., U.S. — C2 122
Chittenden Reservoir, res., Vt., U.S. — D3 122
Chittoor, India — F6 36
Chitungwiza, Zimb. — A5 49
Chiúchiu, Chile — D2 55
Chiume, stm., Afr. — C3 48
Chiúme, Ang. — E3 48
Chiusi, Italy — C3 23
Chivasso, Italy — B1 23
Chivay, Peru — D3 58
Chivhu, Zimb. — A5 49
Chivilcoy, Arg. — A4 54
Chivington, Co., U.S. — C8 83
Chixoy, stm., Guat. — C2 62
Chizhapka, stm., Sov. Un. — B9 28
Chloride, Az., U.S. — B1 80
Chmielnik, Pol. — C6 26
Choapa, stm., Chile — A2 54
Choapan, Mex. — D5 63
Chobe, stm., Afr. — A3 49
Chochiwŏn, S. Kor. — H3 33
Chocó, dept., Col. — B2 60
Chocolate Mountains, mts., U.S. — F6 82
Chocontá, Col. — B3 60
Chocorua, N.H., U.S. — C4 106
Chocorua, Mount, mtn., N.H., U.S. — C4 106
Chocowinity, N.C., U.S. — B5 110
Choctaw, Ar., U.S. — B3 81
Choctaw, Ok., U.S. — B4 113
Choctaw, co., Al., U.S. — C1 78
Choctaw, co., Ms., U.S. — B4 101
Choctaw, co., Ok., U.S. — C6 113
Choctawhatchee, East Fork, stm., Al., U.S. — D4 78
Choctawhatchee, West Fork, stm., Al., U.S. — D4 78
Choctawhatchee Bay, b., Fl., U.S. — u15 86
Choctaw Indian Reservation, Ms., U.S. — C4 101
Choele Choel, Arg. — B3 54
Chofu, Japan — *l9 31
Choiceland, Sask. — D3 75
Choiseul, i., Sol.Is. — G9 6
Choisy-le-Roi, Fr. — g10 16
Choix, Mex. — B3 63
Chojna, Pol. — B2 26
Chojnice, Pol. — B4 26
Chojnów, Pol. — C3 26
Chŏkai, Mount, mtn., Japan — G10 33
Choke Mountains, mts., Eth. — C4 47
Chokio, Mn., U.S. — E2 100
Chokoloskee, Fl., U.S. — G5 86
Chokwé, Moz. — B5 49
Cholame, Ca., U.S. — E3 82
Cholet, Fr. — D3 16
Cholo, Mwi. — E6 48
Cholula [de Rivadabia], Mex. — n14 63
Choluteca, Hond. — D4 62
Choluteca, stm., Hond. — D4 62
Choma, Zam. — E4 48
Chomo Lhāri, mtn., Asia — D12 37
Chomutov, Czech. — C2 26
Chonan, S. Kor. — H3 33
Chon Buri, Thai. — F6 35
Chone, Ec. — B1 58
Chong'an, China — K8 32
Chŏngjin, N. Kor. — C10 31
Chŏngju, N. Kor. — G2 33
Chŏngju, S. Kor. — *l3 33
Chongqing (Chungking), China — F6 31
Chongren, China — K5 32
Chŏngsŏng, N. Kor. — E4 33
Chŏnju, S. Kor. — D10 31
Chonos, Archipiélago de los, is., Chile — C2 54
Chopim, stm., Braz. — D2 56
Choptank, stm., Md., U.S. — C6 97
Chorrillos, Peru — D2 58
Chortkov, Sov. Un. — D10 31
Chorwŏn, N. Kor. — G3 33
Chorwŏn, S. Kor. — G3 33
Chorzów, Pol. — C5 26
Chosan, N. Kor. — F2 33
Chōshi, Japan — I10 33
Chosica, Peru — D2 58
Chos Malal, Arg. — B2 54
Choszczno, Pol. — B3 26
Chota, Peru — C2 58
Choteau, Mt., U.S. — C4 103
Chotěboř, Czech. — n18 21
Choudrant, Bayou, stm., La., U.S. — B3 95
Choum, Maur. — B2 45
Choushan Islands see Zhoushan Islands, is., China — E9 31
Chouteau, Ok., U.S. — A6 113
Chouteau, co., Mt., U.S. — C6 103
Chowan, co., N.C., U.S. — A6 110
Chowan, stm., N.C., U.S. — A6 110
Chowchilla, Ca., U.S. — D3 82
Choybalsan, Mong. — B7 31
Choyr, Mong. — B6 31

Chrisman, Il., U.S. — D6 90
Chrisney, In., U.S. — H3 91
Christchurch, N.Z. — O14 51
Christchurch, Eng., U.K. — D6 12
Christian, co., Il., U.S. — D4 90
Christian, co., Ky., U.S. — D2 94
Christian, co., Mo., U.S. — E4 102
Christiana, Jam. — E14 65
Christiana, S. Afr. — C4 49
Christiana, De., U.S. — B3 85
Christiana, Pa., U.S. — G9 115
Christiana, Tn., U.S. — B5 119
Christian Hollow, N.H., U.S. — D2 106
Christian Island, i., Ont. — C4 73
Christiansburg, Oh., U.S. — B2 112
Christiansburg, Va., U.S. — C2 123
Christiansfeld, Den. — C3 15
Christian Sound, strt., Ak., U.S. — n22 79
Christiansted, V.I.U.S. — H12 64
Christina, Mt., U.S. — C7 103
Christina, stm., Alta. — A5 68
Christina, stm., De., U.S. — B3 85
Christina, Lake, l., Mn., U.S. — D3 100
Christina, Lake, l., Alta. — B5 68
Christina Peak, mtn., Nv., U.S. — D6 105
Christine, N.D., U.S. — C9 111
Christine, Tx., U.S. — E3 120
Christmas, Fl., U.S. — D5 86
Christmas Island, dep., Oc. — G6 6
Christmas Island see Kiritimati Island, i., Kir. — F12 6
Christmas Lake, l., Or., U.S. — D6 114
Christmas Valley, Or., U.S. — D6 114
Christopher, Il., U.S. — F4 90
Christoval, Tx., U.S. — D2 120
Chromo, Co., U.S. — D3 83
Chrudim, Czech. — D3 26
Chrysler, Al., U.S. — D1 78
Chrzanów, Pol. — g10 26
Chu, Sov. Un. — E10 29
Chu, stm., Sov. Un. — G23 8
Chubbuck, Id., U.S. — G6 89
Chubut, prov., Arg. — C3 54
Chubut, stm., Arg. — C3 54
Chu Chua, B.C. — D7 69
Chuckey, Tn., U.S. — C11 119
Chudovo, Sov. Un. — B8 27
Chugach Islands, is., Ak., U.S. — h16 79
Chugach Mountains, mts., Ak., U.S. — g18 79
Chuguyev, Sov. Un. — G11 27
Chugwater, Wy., U.S. — E8 127
Chugwater Creek, stm., Wy., U.S. — E8 127
Chuichu, Az., U.S. — E4 80
Chuius Mountain, mtn., B.C. — B5 69
Chukai (Kemaman), Malay. — J5 35
Chukchi Sea — C32 128
Chukotsk Peninsula, pen., Sov. Un. — C32 128
Chula, Ga., U.S. — E3 87
Chula, Mo., U.S. — B4 102
Chula, Va., U.S. — C5 123
Chula Vista, Ca., U.S. — F5 82
Chulucanas, Peru — C1 58
Chulumani, Bol. — C2 55
Chulym, Sov. Un. — B10 28
Chulym, stm., Sov. Un. — D11 29
Chumbicha, Arg. — E2 55
Chumikan, Sov. Un. — D16 29
Chumphon, Thai. — G3 35
Chumysh, stm., Sov. Un. — C10 28
Chun'an, China — J8 32
Chunchŏn, S. Kor. — H3 33
Chunchula, Al., U.S. — E1 78
Chungju, S. Kor. — H3 33
Chungking see Chongqing, China — F6 31
Chungmu, S. Kor. — H4 33
Chunky, Ms., U.S. — C5 101
Chunya, Tan. — G3 35
Chuoi, i., Viet. — H6 35
Chupaca, Peru — D2 58
Chupadera Mesa, mtn., N.M., U.S. — D3 108
Chupadero, N.M., U.S. — *B4 108
Chupara Point, c., Trin. — N23 65
Chuquibamba, Peru — E3 58
Chuquicamata, Chile — D3 55
Chuquisaca, dept., Bol. — D3 55
Chur, Switz. — E4 18
Churchbridge, Sask. — G5 75
Church Creek, Md., U.S. — C5 97
Church Hill, Md., U.S. — B6 97
Church Hill, Tn., U.S. — C11 119
Churchill, Man. — f9 70
Churchill, Oh., U.S. — *A5 112
Churchill, co., Nv., U.S. — D3 105
Churchill, stm., Can. — E13 66
Churchill, Newf. — h9 72
Churchill, Cape, c., Man. — f9 70
Churchill, Mount, mtn., B.C. — E6 69
Churchill Falls, wtfl., Newf. — h8 72
Churchill Lake, l., Sask. — m7 75
Churchill Lake, l., Me., U.S. — B3 96
Churchill Peak, mtn., B.C. — E3 71
Church Point, La., U.S. — D3 95
Church Point, c., N.S. — E3 71
Church Rock, N.M., U.S. — B1 108
Churchs Ferry, N.D., U.S. — A6 111
Church Stretton, Eng., U.K. — B5 12
Churchton, Md., U.S. — C4 97
Churchville, Md., U.S. — A5 97
Churchville, N.Y., U.S. — B3 109
Churchville, Va., U.S. — B3 123
Churdan, Ia., U.S. — B3 92
Chūru, India — C5 37
Churubusco, In., U.S. — B7 91
Churubusco, N.Y., U.S. — f11 109
Churuguara, Ven. — A4 60
Churumuco, Mex. — n13 63
Chushul, India — B6 36
Chuska Mountains, mts., Az., U.S. — A6 80
Chusovaya, stm., Sov. Un. — D20 8
Chusovoy, Sov. Un. — B5 29
Chust, Sov. Un. — G23 8
Chuxian, China — H8 32
Chuxiong, China — F5 31
Chuy, Ur. — *G3 54
Cianjur, Indon. — m13 35
Ciano d'Enza, Italy — E6 20
Cianorte, Braz. — C2 56
Cibecue, Az., U.S. — C5 80
Cibola, co., N.M., U.S. — C1 108
Cibolo, Tx., U.S. — h7 120
Cibolo Creek, stm., Tx., U.S. — h7 120
Cicero, Il., U.S. — B6 90
Cicero, In., U.S. — D5 91
Cicero Dantas, Braz. — D3 57
Ciche, Sgurr na, mtn., Scot., U.K. — D3 13
Cicia, i., Fiji — H16 52
Cide, Tur. — B9 40

Name — Map Ref. — Page

Cidra, Lago de, res., P.R. B3 65
Ciechanów, Pol. B6 26
Ciego de Avila, Cuba D4 64
Ciego de Avila, prov., Cuba C4 64
Ciempozuelos, Spain B4 22
Ciénaga, Col. A3 60
Ciénaga de Oro, Col. B2 60
Cienfuegos, Cuba C3 64
Cienfuegos, prov., Cuba C3 64
Cieszyn, Pol. D5 26
Cieza, Spain C5 22
Ciężkowice, Pol. g10 26
Cigüela, stm., Spain C4 22
Cihanbeyli, Tur. C9 40
Cihuatlán, Mex. n11 63
Cilacap, Indon. G3 34
Cili, China J4 32
Cima, Ca., U.S. E6 82
Cimarron, Co., U.S. C3 83
Cimarron, Ks., U.S. E3 93
Cimarron, N.M., U.S. A5 108
Cimarron, co., Ok., U.S. e8 113
Cimarron, stm., U.S. C8 76
Cimarron, North Fork, stm., U.S. E2 93
Cimarron Hills, Co., U.S. *C6 83
Cîmpina, Rom. C7 24
Cîmpulung, Rom. C7 24
Cîmpulung Moldovenesc, Rom. B7 24
Cincinnati, Ia., U.S. D5 92
Cincinnati, Oh., U.S. C1 112
Cincinnatus, N.Y., U.S. C5 109
Cinconsine, Lac, l., Que. B4 74
Çine, Tur. D7 25
Cinnaminson, N.J., U.S. D3 107
Cintalapa [de Figueroa], Mex. D6 63
Cinto, Monte, mtn., Fr. C2 23
Cipolletti, Arg. B3 54
Circle, Ak., U.S. B11 79
Circle, Mt., U.S. C11 103
Circle Hot Springs, Ak., U.S. B11 79
Circle Pines, Mn., U.S. m12 100
Circleville, Ks., U.S. C8 93
Circleville, Oh., U.S. C3 112
Circleville, Ut., U.S. E3 121
Circleville, W.V., U.S. C5 125
Cirebon, Indon. G3 34
Cirencester, Eng., U.K. E6 10
Cirí, stm., Pan. m10 62
Cisco, Ga., U.S. B2 87
Cisco, Il., U.S. C5 90
Cisco, Ky., U.S. C6 94
Cisco, Tx., U.S. C3 120
Cisco, Ut., U.S. E6 121
Ciskei, ctry., Afr. D4 49
Cisne, Il., U.S. E5 90
Cisneros, Col. B2 60
Cisnes, stm., Chile C2 54
Cispus, stm., Wa., U.S. C4 124
Cissna Park, Il., U.S. C6 90
Cistern, Tx., U.S. E4 120
Cisterna di Latina, Italy h9 23
Cistierna, Spain A3 22
Citac, Nevado, mtn., Peru D2 58
Citra, Fl., U.S. C4 86
Citronelle, Al., U.S. D1 78
Citrus, Ca., U.S. *E5 82
Citrus, co., Fl., U.S. D4 86
Citrus Heights, Ca., U.S. *C3 82
Cittadella, Italy B3 23
Città di Castello, Italy C4 23
City Mills, Ma., U.S. h10 98
City of Commerce, Ca., U.S. n12 82
City of Refuge National Historical Park, Hi., U.S. D5 88
City Point, Fl., U.S. D6 86
City View, S.C., U.S. B3 117
Ciudad Acuña, Mex. B4 63
Ciudad Altamirano, Mex. n13 63
Ciudad Bolívar, Ven. B5 60
Ciudad Bolivia, Ven. B3 60
Ciudad Camargo, Mex. B3 63
Ciudad de la Habana, prov., Cuba C2 64
Ciudad del Carmen, Mex. D6 63
Ciudad del Maíz, Mex. C5 63
Ciudad de Naucalpan de Juárez, Mex. h9 63
Ciudad de Valles, Mex. C5 63
Ciudad de Villaldama, Mex. B4 63
Ciudadela, Spain B7 22
Ciudad Guayana, Ven. B5 60
Ciudad Guzmán, Mex. D4 63
Ciudad Hidalgo, Mex. n13 63
Ciudad Ixtepec, Mex. D5 63
Ciudad Jiménez, Mex. B4 63
Ciudad Juárez, Mex. A3 63
Ciudad Lerdo, Mex. B4 63
Ciudad López Mateos, Mex. g9 63
Ciudad Madero, Mex. C5 63
Ciudad Mante, Mex. C5 63
Ciudad Melchor Múzquiz, Mex. B4 63
Ciudad Mendoza, Mex. n15 63
Ciudad Obregón, Mex. B3 63
Ciudad Ojeda, Ven. A3 60
Ciudad Piar, Ven. B5 60
Ciudad Real, Spain C4 22
Ciudad Rodrigo, Spain B2 22
Ciudad Serdán, Mex. n15 63
Ciudad Tecún Umán, Guat. C1 62
Ciudad Victoria, Mex. C5 63
Cividale del Friuli, Italy A4 23
Civitanova Marche, Italy C4 23
Civitavecchia, Italy C3 23
Civray, Fr. D4 16
Çivril, Tur. C7 40
Cizre, Tur. D14 40
C.J. Strike Reservoir, res., Id., U.S. G3 89
Clackamas, Or., U.S. h12 114
Clackamas, co., Or., U.S. B4 114
Clacton-on-Sea, Eng., U.K. C9 12
Claflin, Ks., U.S. D5 93
Claiborne, Al., U.S. D2 78
Claiborne, La., U.S. *B3 95
Claiborne, Md., U.S. C5 97
Claiborne, co., La., U.S. B2 95
Claiborne, co., Ms., U.S. D3 101
Claiborne, co., Tn., U.S. C10 119
Claiborne, Lake, res., La., U.S. B3 95
Clair, N.B. B1 71
Clair, Sask. E3 75
Claire, Lake, l., Alta. f8 68
Claire City, S.D., U.S. B8 118
Clair Engle Lake, res., Ca., U.S. B2 82
Clairfield, Tn., U.S. C10 119
Clair-Mel City, Fl., U.S. *E4 86
Clairmont, Alta. B1 68
Clairton, Pa., U.S. F2 115
Clallam, co., Wa., U.S. B1 124
Clallam Bay, Wa., U.S. A1 124
Clamart, Fr. g10 16
Clamecy, Fr. D5 16
Clam Lake, l., Sask. B3 75
Clam Lake, l., Wi., U.S. C1 126
Clan Alpine Mountains, mts., Nv., U.S. D4 105
Clancy, Mt., U.S. D5 103
Clandeboye, Ont. D3 73
Clandonald, Alta. C5 68
Clanton, Al., U.S. C3 78
Clanwilliam, Man. D2 70
Clanwilliam, S. Afr. D2 49
Clapperton Island, i., Ont. A2 73
Clara, Ire. D4 11
Clara, Ms., U.S. D5 101
Clara City, Mn., U.S. F3 100
Clara Peak, mtn., Az., U.S. C2 80
Clare, Austl. F6 50
Clare, In., U.S. D6 91
Clare, Ia., U.S. B3 92
Clare, Mi., U.S. E6 99
Clare, co., Ire. E3 11
Clare, co., Mi., U.S. E6 99
Clare, stm., Ire. D3 11
Clarecastle (Clare), Ire. E3 11
Claregalway, Ire. D3 11
Clare Island, i., Ire. D1 10
Claremont, Ca., U.S. m13 82
Claremont, Il., U.S. E6 90
Claremont, Mn., U.S. F6 100
Claremont, N.H., U.S. D2 106
Claremont, N.C., U.S. B1 110
Claremont, S.D., U.S. B7 118
Claremont, Va., U.S. C6 123
Claremont, mtn., Ca., U.S. C3 82
Claremore, Ok., U.S. A6 113
Claremorris, Ire. D2 10
Clarence, Al., U.S. A3 78
Clarence, Ia., U.S. C6 92
Clarence, La., U.S. C2 95
Clarence, Mo., U.S. B5 102
Clarence, Pa., U.S. D6 115
Clarence, stm., N.Z. O14 51
Clarence, Isla, i., Chile h11 54
Clarence Cannon Lake, res., Mo., U.S. B6 102
Clarence Island, i., B.A.T. C7 7
Clarence Strait, strt., Austl. B5 50
Clarence Strait, strt., Ak., U.S. n23 79
Clarence Town, Bah. C6 64
Clarenceville, Que. D4 74
Clarendon, Ar., U.S. C4 81
Clarendon, Pa., U.S. C3 115
Clarendon, Tx., U.S. B2 120
Clarendon, Vt., U.S. D3 122
Clarendon, co., S.C., U.S. D7 117
Clarendon, stm., Vt., U.S. E2 122
Clarendon Hills, Il., U.S. k9 90
Clarendon Springs, Vt., U.S. D2 122
Clarendon Station, Ont. C8 73
Clarenville, Newf. D4 72
Claresholm, Alta. D4 68
Claridge, Pa., U.S. F2 115
Clarie Coast, Ant. C26 7
Clarinda, Ia., U.S. D2 92
Clarington, Oh., U.S. C5 112
Clarington, Pa., U.S. D3 115
Clarion, Ia., U.S. B4 92
Clarion, Pa., U.S. D3 115
Clarion, co., Pa., U.S. D3 115
Clarion, stm., Pa., U.S. D3 115
Clarissa, Mn., U.S. D4 100
Clarita, Ok., U.S. C5 113
Clark, Co., U.S. A4 83
Clark, Mo., U.S. B5 102
Clark, N.J., U.S. B4 107
Clark, Oh., U.S. B4 112
Clark, S.D., U.S. C8 118
Clark, co., Ar., U.S. C2 81
Clark, co., Id., U.S. E6 89
Clark, co., Il., U.S. D6 90
Clark, co., In., U.S. H6 91
Clark, co., Ks., U.S. E4 93
Clark, co., Ky., U.S. C5 94
Clark, co., Mo., U.S. A6 102
Clark, co., Nv., U.S. G6 105
Clark, co., Oh., U.S. C2 112
Clark, co., S.D., U.S. C8 118
Clark, co., Wa., U.S. D3 124
Clark, co., Wi., U.S. D3 126
Clark, Lake, l., Ak., U.S. C9 79
Clark, Point, c., Ont. C3 73
Clark Colony, S.D., U.S. *C8 118
Clarkdale, Az., U.S. C3 80
Clarkdale, Ga., U.S. h7 87
Clarke, co., Al., U.S. D2 78
Clarke, co., Ga., U.S. C3 87
Clarke, co., Ia., U.S. D4 92
Clarke, co., Ms., U.S. C5 101
Clarke, co., Va., U.S. A4 123
Clarke City, Que. h8 72
Clarke Lake, l., Sask. C2 75
Clarkesville, Ga., U.S. B3 87
Clarkfield, Mn., U.S. F3 100
Clark Fork, Id., U.S. A2 89
Clark Fork, stm., U.S. C1 103
Clarkia, Id., U.S. B2 89
Clark Mountain, mtn., Mo., U.S. D7 102
Clarkrange, Tn., U.S. C8 119
Clarks, La., U.S. B3 95
Clarks, Ne., U.S. C8 104
Clarks, stm., Ky., U.S. f9 94
Clarks, West Fork, stm., Ky., U.S. f9 94
Clarksboro, N.J., U.S. D2 107
Clarksburg, Ont. C4 73
Clarksburg, In., U.S. F7 91
Clarksburg, Md., U.S. B3 97
Clarksburg, Mo., U.S. C5 102
Clarksburg, N.J., U.S. C4 107
Clarksburg, Oh., U.S. C2 112
Clarksburg, Tn., U.S. B3 119
Clarksburg, W.V., U.S. B4 125
Clarksdale, Ms., U.S. A3 101
Clarksdale, Mo., U.S. B3 102
Clarks Falls, Ct., U.S. D8 84
Clarks Grove, Mn., U.S. G5 100
Clark's Harbour, N.S. F4 71
Clarks Hill, In., U.S. D4 91
Clarkson, Ky., U.S. C3 94
Clarkson, Ne., U.S. C8 104
Clarks Point, Ak., U.S. D8 79
Clarks Summit, Pa., U.S. m18 115
Clarkston, Ga., U.S. h8 87
Clarkston, Mi., U.S. F7 99
Clarkston, Ut., U.S. B3 121
Clarkston, Wa., U.S. C8 124
Clarksville, N.S. D6 71
Clarksville, Ar., U.S. B2 81
Clarksville, De., U.S. F5 85
Clarksville, In., U.S. H6 91
Clarksville, Ia., U.S. B5 92
Clarksville, Md., U.S. B4 97
Clarksville, Mi., U.S. F5 99
Clarksville, Mo., U.S. B7 102
Clarksville, Oh., U.S. C2 112
Clarksville, Tn., U.S. A4 119
Clarksville, Tx., U.S. C5 120
Clarksville, Va., U.S. D4 123
Clarkton, Mo., U.S. E8 102
Clarkton, N.C., U.S. C4 110
Claryville, Ky., U.S. k14 94
Claryville, Mo., U.S. D8 102
Clashmore, Ire. E4 11
Clatonia, Ne., U.S. D9 104
Clatskanie, Or., U.S. A3 114
Clatsop, co., Or., U.S. A3 114
Claude, Tx., U.S. B2 120
Claudy, N. Ire., U.K. C4 11
Claunch, N.M., U.S. C3 108
Clausthal-Zellerfeld, W. Ger. C5 18
Clavet, Sask. F2 75
Clawson, Mi., U.S. o15 99
Clawson, Ut., U.S. D4 121
Claxton, Ga., U.S. D5 87
Clay, Al., U.S. f7 78
Clay, Ky., U.S. C2 94
Clay, La., U.S. B3 95
Clay, N.Y., U.S. B4 109
Clay, W.V., U.S. C3 125
Clay, Wy., U.S. B8 127
Clay, co., Al., U.S. B4 78
Clay, co., Ar., U.S. A5 81
Clay, co., Fl., U.S. B5 86
Clay, co., Ga., U.S. E2 87
Clay, co., Il., U.S. E5 90
Clay, co., In., U.S. F3 91
Clay, co., Ia., U.S. A2 92
Clay, co., Ks., U.S. C6 93
Clay, co., Ky., U.S. C6 94
Clay, co., Mn., U.S. D2 100
Clay, co., Ms., U.S. B5 101
Clay, co., Mo., U.S. B3 102
Clay, co., Ne., U.S. D7 104
Clay, co., N.C., U.S. f9 110
Clay, co., S.D., U.S. E8 118
Clay, co., Tn., U.S. C8 119
Clay, co., Tx., U.S. C3 120
Clay, co., W.V., U.S. C3 125
Clay Center, Ks., U.S. C6 93
Clay Center, Ne., U.S. D7 104
Clay Center, Oh., U.S. A2 112
Clay City, Il., U.S. E5 90
Clay City, In., U.S. F3 91
Clay City, Ky., U.S. C6 94
Clay Creek, stm., Co., U.S. D8 83
Clay Creek, stm., S.D., U.S. H8 118
Claydon, Sask. H1 75
Clayhatchee, Al., U.S. D4 78
Clay Head, c., I. of Man F4 13
Claymont, De., U.S. A4 85
Clayoquot Sound, strt., B.C. E4 69
Claypool, Az., U.S. D5 80
Claypool, In., U.S. B6 91
Claysburg, Pa., U.S. F5 115
Clay Springs, Az., U.S. C5 80
Claysville, Pa., U.S. F1 115
Clayton, Ont. B8 73
Clayton, Al., U.S. D4 78
Clayton, De., U.S. C3 85
Clayton, Ga., U.S. B3 87
Clayton, Id., U.S. E4 89
Clayton, Il., U.S. C3 90
Clayton, In., U.S. E4 91
Clayton, Ia., U.S. B6 92
Clayton, Ks., U.S. C3 93
Clayton, La., U.S. C4 95
Clayton, Mo., U.S. C7 102
Clayton, N.J., U.S. D2 107
Clayton, N.M., U.S. A6 108
Clayton, N.Y., U.S. A4 109
Clayton, N.C., U.S. B4 110
Clayton, Ok., U.S. C6 113
Clayton, S.D., U.S. D8 118
Clayton, Tn., U.S. A2 119
Clayton, Wa., U.S. B8 124
Clayton, Wi., U.S. C1 126
Clayton, co., Ga., U.S. C2 87
Clayton, co., Ia., U.S. B6 92
Clayton Lake, Me., U.S. B3 96
Claytor Lake, res., Va., U.S. C2 123
Clayville, R.I., U.S. C2 116
Clear, stm., Alta. A1 68
Clear, stm., R.I., U.S. B2 116
Clear, Cape, c., Ire. E2 10
Clear, Lake, l., Ont. B7 73
Clear Boggy Creek, stm., Ok., U.S. C5 113
Clearbrook, Mn., U.S. C3 100
Clear Creek, In., U.S. F4 91
Clear Creek, Ut., U.S. D4 121
Clear Creek, W.V., U.S. n13 125
Clear Creek, co., Co., U.S. B5 83
Clear Creek, stm., Az., U.S. C4 80
Clear Creek, stm., Ne., U.S. C6 104
Clear Creek, stm., Tn., U.S. C9 119
Clear Creek, stm., Wy., U.S. B6 127
Cleare, Cape, c., Ak., U.S. D10 79
Clearfield, Ia., U.S. D3 92
Clearfield, Ky., U.S. B6 94
Clearfield, Pa., U.S. D5 115
Clearfield, S.D., U.S. D5 118
Clearfield, Ut., U.S. B3 121
Clearfield, co., Pa., U.S. D5 115
Clear Fork, W.V., U.S. D3 125
Clear Fork, stm., W.V., U.S. n13 125
Clear Fork, stm., W.V., U.S. D3 125
Clear Island, i., Ire. F2 11
Clearlake, Ca., U.S. C2 82
Clear Lake, Ia., U.S. A4 92
Clear Lake, Mn., U.S. E5 100
Clear Lake, S.D., U.S. C9 118
Clearlake, Wa., U.S. A3 124
Clear Lake, Wi., U.S. C1 126
Clear Lake, l., Man. D1 70
Clear Lake, l., Ia., U.S. A4 92
Clear Lake, l., Ut., U.S. D3 121
Clear Lake, res., Ca., U.S. C2 82
Clear Lake City, Tx., U.S. r14 120
Clear Lake Reservoir, res., Ca., U.S. B3 82
Clear Lake Shores, Tx., U.S. r15 120
Clearmont, Mo., U.S. A2 102
Clearmont, Wy., U.S. B6 127
Clear Spring, Md., U.S. A2 97
Clear Stream, stm., N.H., U.S. g7 106
Clearview, Ok., U.S. B5 113
Clearview City, Ks., U.S. g12 93
Clearville, Pa., U.S. G5 115
Clearwater, B.C. D7 69
Clearwater, Man. E2 70
Clearwater, Fl., U.S. E4 86
Clearwater, Id., U.S. C3 89
Clearwater, Ks., U.S. E6 93
Clearwater, Mn., U.S. E4 100
Clearwater, Ne., U.S. B7 104
Clearwater, S.C., U.S. E4 117
Clearwater, Wa., U.S. B1 124
Clearwater, co., Id., U.S. C3 89
Clearwater, co., Mn., U.S. C3 100
Clearwater, stm., Alta. D3 68
Clearwater, stm., Can. A5 68
Clearwater, stm., B.C. C7 69
Clearwater, stm., Id., U.S. C2 89
Clearwater, stm., Mn., U.S. C3 100
Clearwater Lake, Wi., U.S. C4 126
Clearwater Lake, l., B.C. C7 69
Clearwater Lake, l., Man. B1 70
Clearwater Lake, res., Mo., U.S. D7 102
Clearwater Mountains, mts., Id., U.S. C2 89
Clearwater Provincial Park, Man. C1 70
Cleaton, Ky., U.S. C2 94
Cleator Moor, Eng., U.K. F5 13
Cleburne, Tx., U.S. C4 120
Cleburne, co., Al., U.S. B4 78
Cleburne, co., Ar., U.S. B3 81
Cle Elum, Wa., U.S. B5 124
Cle Elum, stm., Wa., U.S. B4 124
Cle Elum Lake, res., Wa., U.S. B4 124
Cleethorpes, Eng., U.K. A7 12
Cleeves, Sask. D1 75
Cleggan, Ire. D1 11
Cleghorn, Ia., U.S. B2 92
Cleland Heights, De., U.S. *B3 85
Clem, Ga., U.S. C1 87
Clementon, N.J., U.S. D3 107
Clements, Ks., U.S. D7 93
Clements, Md., U.S. D4 97
Clements, Mn., U.S. F3 100
Clementsport, N.S. E4 71
Clementsvale, N.S. E4 71
Clemmons, N.C., U.S. A2 110
Clemons, Ia., U.S. B4 92
Clemons, N.Y., U.S. B7 109
Clemscot, Ok., U.S. C4 113
Clemson, S.C., U.S. B2 117
Clendenin, W.V., U.S. C3 125
Clendening Lake, res., Oh., U.S. B4 112
Cleona, Pa., U.S. F9 115
Cleo Springs, Ok., U.S. A3 113
Clermont, Austl. D8 50
Clermont, Que. B7 74
Clermont, Fr. E2 17
Clermont, Fl., U.S. D5 86
Clermont, Ga., U.S. B3 87
Clermont, Ia., U.S. A6 92
Clermont, Ky., U.S. C4 94
Clermont, Pa., U.S. C4 115
Clermont, co., Oh., U.S. C1 112
Clermont-Ferrand, Fr. E5 16
Clermont Harbor, Ms., U.S. E4 101
Clermont-l'Hérault, Fr. F5 16
Clerval, Fr. B1 21
Clervaux, Lux. D6 17
Clevedon, Eng., U.K. C5 12
Cleveland, Al., U.S. A3 78
Cleveland, Ar., U.S. B3 81
Cleveland, Ga., U.S. B3 87
Cleveland, Il., U.S. B3 90
Cleveland, Mn., U.S. F5 100
Cleveland, Ms., U.S. B3 101
Cleveland, Mo., U.S. C3 102
Cleveland, N.M., U.S. A4 108
Cleveland, N.Y., U.S. B5 109
Cleveland, N.C., U.S. B2 110
Cleveland, N.D., U.S. C6 111
Cleveland, Oh., U.S. A4 112
Cleveland, Ok., U.S. A5 113
Cleveland, S.C., U.S. A2 117
Cleveland, Tn., U.S. D9 119
Cleveland, Tx., U.S. D5 120
Cleveland, Ut., U.S. D5 121
Cleveland, Va., U.S. f9 123
Cleveland, Wi., U.S. k10 126
Cleveland, co., Eng., U.K. F7 13
Cleveland, co., Ar., U.S. D3 81
Cleveland, co., N.C., U.S. B1 110
Cleveland, co., Ok., U.S. B4 113
Cleveland, Mount, mtn., Mt., U.S. B3 103
Cleveland Heights, Oh., U.S. A4 112
Cleveland Hills, hills, Eng., U.K. F7 13
Clevelândia, Braz. D2 56
Clever, Mo., U.S. D4 102
Cleves, Oh., U.S. o12 112
Cleves see Kleve, W. Ger. C3 18
Clew Bay, b., Ire. D2 10
Clewiston, Fl., U.S. F6 86
Clichy, Fr. g10 16
Clifden, Ire. D1 10
Cliff, N.M., U.S. E1 108
Cliff Island, i., Me., U.S. g7 96
Clifford, Ont. D4 73
Clifford, In., U.S. F6 91
Clifford, Mi., U.S. E7 99
Clifford, N.D., U.S. B8 111
Clifford, Pa., U.S. C10 115
Clifford, Va., U.S. C3 123
Cliffside, N.C., U.S. B1 110
Cliffside Park, N.J., U.S. h9 107
Clifftop, W.V., U.S. m14 125
Clifton, Az., U.S. D6 80
Clifton, Co., U.S. B2 83
Clifton, Id., U.S. G7 89
Clifton, Il., U.S. C6 90
Clifton, Ks., U.S. C6 93
Clifton, N.J., U.S. B4 107
Clifton, S.C., U.S. B4 117
Clifton, Tn., U.S. B4 119
Clifton, Tx., U.S. D4 120
Clifton, Va., U.S. g12 123
Clifton City, Mo., U.S. C4 102
Clifton Forge, Va., U.S. C3 123
Clifton Heights, Pa., U.S. *p20 115
Clifton Hill, Mo., U.S. B5 102
Clifton Knolls, N.Y., U.S. C7 109
Clifton Springs, N.Y., U.S. C3 109
Cliftonville, Ms., U.S. B5 101
Climax, Sask. H1 75
Climax, Co., U.S. B4 83
Climax, Ga., U.S. F2 87
Climax, Ks., U.S. E7 93
Climax, Mi., U.S. F5 99
Climax, Mn., U.S. C2 100
Climax Springs, Mo., U.S. C4 102
Climbing Hill, Ia., U.S. B1 92
Clinch, co., Ga., U.S. F4 87
Clinch, stm., U.S. D9 119
Clinchburg, Va., U.S. f10 123
Clinchco, Va., U.S. e9 123
Clinchfield, Ga., U.S. D3 87
Clinch Mountain, mtn., U.S. C10 119
Clinchport, Va., U.S. f9 123
Clingmans Dome, mtn., U.S. D10 119
Clint, Tx., U.S. o11 120
Clinton, B.C. D7 69
Clinton, Ont. D3 73
Clinton, Al., U.S. C2 78
Clinton, Ar., U.S. B3 81
Clinton, Ct., U.S. D5 84
Clinton, Ga., U.S. D3 87
Clinton, Il., U.S. C5 90
Clinton, In., U.S. E3 91
Clinton, Ia., U.S. C7 92
Clinton, Ks., U.S. m15 93
Clinton, Ky., U.S. f9 94
Clinton, La., U.S. D4 95
Clinton, Me., U.S. D3 96
Clinton, Md., U.S. C4 97
Clinton, Ma., U.S. B4 98
Clinton, Mi., U.S. F7 99
Clinton, Mn., U.S. E2 100
Clinton, Ms., U.S. C3 101
Clinton, Mo., U.S. C4 102
Clinton, Mt., U.S. D3 103
Clinton, Ne., U.S. B3 104
Clinton, N.H., U.S. D3 106
Clinton, N.J., U.S. B3 107
Clinton, N.Y., U.S. B5 109
Clinton, N.C., U.S. C4 110
Clinton, Ok., U.S. B3 113
Clinton, S.C., U.S. C4 117
Clinton, Tn., U.S. C9 119
Clinton, Ut., U.S. B3 121
Clinton, Wa., U.S. B3 124
Clinton, Wi., U.S. F5 126
Clinton, co., Il., U.S. E4 90
Clinton, co., In., U.S. D4 91
Clinton, co., Ia., U.S. C7 92
Clinton, co., Ky., U.S. D4 94
Clinton, co., Mi., U.S. F6 99
Clinton, co., Mo., U.S. B3 102
Clinton, co., N.Y., U.S. f11 109
Clinton, co., Oh., U.S. C2 112
Clinton, co., Pa., U.S. D6 115
Clinton, Lake, res., Il., U.S. C5 90
Clinton-Colden Lake, l., N.W. Ter. D11 66
Clinton Lake, res., Ks., U.S. m15 93
Clinton Reservoir, res., N.J., U.S. A4 107
Clinton Township, Mi., U.S. *F8 99
Clintonville, Ky., U.S. B5 94
Clintonville, Pa., U.S. D2 115
Clintonville, W.V., U.S. D4 125
Clintonville, Wi., U.S. D5 126
Clintwood, Va., U.S. e9 123
Clio, Al., U.S. D4 78
Clio, Ia., U.S. D4 92
Clio, Mi., U.S. E7 99
Clio, S.C., U.S. B8 117
Clio, W.V., U.S. C3 125
Clipperton, atoll, Fr. Poly. F15 6
Clisham, mtn., Scot., U.K. C2 13
Clitherall, Mn., U.S. D3 100
Clitheroe, Eng., U.K. G6 13
Clive, Alta. C4 68
Clive, Ia., U.S. e8 92
Cliza, Bol. C2 55
Cloan, Sask. E1 75
Cloe, Pa., U.S. E4 115
Cloghan, Ire. C4 11
Cloghan, Ire. D4 11
Cloghane, Ire. E1 11
Clogheen, Ire. E3 11
Clogher Head, c., Ire. D5 11
Clonakilty, Ire. E2 10
Clonakilty Bay, b., Ire. E3 10
Cloncurry, Austl. D7 50
Clones, Ire. C4 11
Clonmany, Ire. B4 11
Clonmel, Ire. D3 10
Clonmellon, Ire. D4 11
Clontarf, Mn., U.S. E3 100
Cloone, Ire. D4 11
Clo-oose, B.C. E5 69
Cloppenburg, W. Ger. F2 15
Clopton, Al., U.S. D4 78
Cloquet, Mn., U.S. D6 100
Cloquet, stm., Mn., U.S. C6 100
Closter, N.J., U.S. B5 107
Clothier, W.V., U.S. n12 125
Cloud, co., Ks., U.S. C6 93
Cloud Chief, Ok., U.S. B3 113
Cloudcroft, N.M., U.S. E4 108
Cloud Peak, mtn., Wy., U.S. B5 127
Cloudy, Ok., U.S. C6 113
Cloudy Bay, b., N.Z. N15 51
Cloudy Mountain, mtn., Ar., U.S. C8 79
Cloutierville, La., U.S. C3 95
Clover, S.C., U.S. A5 117
Clover, Va., U.S. D4 123
Clover Bottom, Ky., U.S. C5 94
Cloverdale, B.C. f13 69
Cloverdale, Al., U.S. A2 78
Cloverdale, Ca., U.S. C2 82
Cloverdale, In., U.S. E4 91
Cloverdale, Or., U.S. B3 114
Cloverdale, Va., U.S. *C3 123
Cloverleaf, Tx., U.S. *r14 120
Cloverport, Ky., U.S. C3 94
Clovis, Ca., U.S. D4 82
Clovis, N.M., U.S. C6 108
Clow, Ar., U.S. D2 81
Cloyne, Ire. F3 11
Cluanie, Loch, l., Scot., U.K. C3 13
Cluj-Napoca, Rom. B6 24
Clune, Pa., U.S. E3 115
Cluny, Alta. D4 68
Cluny, Fr. D6 16
Cluses, Fr. D2 21
Clusone, Italy D5 20
Cluster Springs, Va., U.S. D4 123
Clute, Tx., U.S. r14 120
Clutha, stm., N.Z. P12 51
Clutier, Ia., U.S. B5 92
Clwyd, co., Wales, U.K. A4 12
Clyattville, Ga., U.S. F3 87
Clyde, Alta. B4 68
Clyde, N.W. Ter. B19 66
Clyde, Ks., U.S. C6 93
Clyde, Mo., U.S. A3 102
Clyde, N.Y., U.S. B4 109
Clyde, N.C., U.S. f10 110
Clyde, N.D., U.S. A7 111
Clyde, Oh., U.S. A3 112
Clyde, Tx., U.S. C3 120
Clyde, stm., N.S. E4 71
Clyde, stm., Scot., U.K. E4 13
Clyde, Firth of, est., Scot., U.K. C4 10
Clydebank, Scot., U.K. C4 10
Clyde Park, Mt., U.S. E6 103
Clymer, N.Y., U.S. C1 109
Clymer, Pa., U.S. E3 115
Clyo, Ga., U.S. D5 87
Cnossus, hist., Grc. E5 25
Côa, stm., Port. B2 22
Coachella, Ca., U.S. F5 82
Coachella Canal, Ca., U.S. F6 82
Coachford, Ire. F3 11
Coahoma, Ms., U.S. A3 101
Coahoma, Tx., U.S. C2 120
Coahoma, co., Ms., U.S. A3 101
Coahuayana, stm., Mex. n12 63
Coahuila, state, Mex. B4 63
Coal, co., Ok., U.S. C5 113
Coal, stm., W.V., U.S. C3 125
Coal Bluff, In., U.S. E3 91
Coal Branch, N.B. C4 71
Coal City, Il., U.S. B5 90
Coal City, In., U.S. F3 91
Coalcomán [de Matamoros], Mex. D4 63
Coal Creek, Co., U.S. C5 83
Coal Creek, stm., In., U.S. E3 91
Coal Creek, stm., Ok., U.S. B6 113
Coaldale, Alta. E4 68
Coaldale, Co., U.S. C5 83
Coaldale, Nv., U.S. E4 105
Coaldale, Pa., U.S. E10 115
Coalfield, Tn., U.S. C9 119
Coal Fork, W.V., U.S. C3 125
Coal Fork, stm., W.V., U.S. m13 125
Coalgate, Ok., U.S. C5 113
Coalgood, Ky., U.S. D6 94
Coal Grove, Oh., U.S. D3 112
Coal Harbour, B.C. D4 69
Coal Hill, Ar., U.S. B2 81
Coalhurst, Alta. E4 68
Coaling, Al., U.S. B2 78
Coalinga, Ca., U.S. D3 82
Coalmont, B.C. E7 69
Coalmont, Co., U.S. A4 83
Coalmont, In., U.S. F3 91
Coalmont, Tn., U.S. D8 119
Coalport, Pa., U.S. E4 115
Coalridge, Oh., U.S. C4 112
Coalspur, Alta. C2 68
Coalton, Il., U.S. D4 90
Coalton, Oh., U.S. C3 112
Coalville, Eng., U.K. B6 12
Coalville, Ia., U.S. B3 92
Coalville, Ut., U.S. C4 121
Coalwood, W.V., U.S. D3 125
Coamo, P.R. B3 65
Coari, Braz. C2 59
Coari, stm., Braz. C2 59
Coast, prov., Kenya B6 48
Coasters Harbor Island, i., R.I., U.S. E5 116
Coast Mountains, mts., N.A. E6 66
Coast Ranges, mts., U.S. B3 76
Coatbridge, Scot., U.K. C5 10
Coatepec, Mex. n15 63
Coatepeque, Guat. C2 62
Coatesville, In., U.S. E4 91
Coatesville, Pa., U.S. G10 115
Coaticook, Que. D6 74
Coatney Hill, mtn., Ct., U.S. B7 84
Coatopa, Al., U.S. C1 78
Coats, Ks., U.S. E5 93
Coats, N.C., U.S. B4 110
Coatsburg, Il., U.S. C2 90
Coats Island, i., N.W. Ter. D16 66
Coats Land, reg., Ant. B9 7
Coatsville, Mo., U.S. A5 102
Coatzacoalcos (Puerto México), Mex. D6 63
Cobalt, Ont. p19 73
Cobalt, Ct., U.S. C5 84
Cobalt, Id., U.S. D4 89
Cobán, Guat. D6 63
Cobar, Austl. F8 50
Cobb, Ga., U.S. E3 87
Cobb, Ky., U.S. D2 94
Cobb, Ok., U.S. C5 113
Cobb, Wi., U.S. F3 126
Cobb, co., Ga., U.S. C2 87
Cobb, stm., Mn., U.S. G5 100
Cobberas, Mount, mtn., Austl. H7 51
Cobb Island, Md., U.S. D4 97
Cobble Hill, B.C. g12 69
Cobble Mountain Reservoir, res., Ma., U.S. B2 98
Cobbosseecontee Lake, l., Me., U.S. D3 96
Cobbtown, Ga., U.S. D4 87
Cobden, Ont. B8 73
Cobden, Il., U.S. F4 90
Cobequid Mountains, mts., N.S. D5 71
Cobh, Ire. E2 10
Cobham, Eng., U.K. m12 10
Cobham, stm., Can. C4 70
Cobija, Bol. B2 55
Cobija, Chile D2 55
Coble, Tn., U.S. B4 119
Coblence see Koblenz, W. Ger. C3 18
Cobleskill, N.Y., U.S. C6 109
Coboconk, Ont. C6 73
Cobourg, Ont. D6 73
Cobourg Peninsula, pen., Austl. B5 50
Cobre, Nv., U.S. B7 105
Cóbuè, Moz. D5 48
Cobun Creek, stm., W.V., U.S. h11 125
Coburg, Austl. *G7 50
Coburg, W. Ger. C5 18
Coburg, Ia., U.S. D2 92
Coburg, Or., U.S. C3 114
Coburg Island, i., N.W. Ter. m36 66
Coburn, Pa., U.S. E7 115
Coburn Gore, Me., U.S. C2 96
Coburn Mountain, mtn., Me., U.S. C2 96
Cocentaina, Spain C5 22
Cochabamba, Bol. C2 55
Cochabamba, dept., Bol. C2 55
Coche, Isla, i., Ven. A5 60
Cocheco, stm., N.H., U.S. D5 106
Cochem, W. Ger. C2 19
Cochesett, Ma., U.S. B5 98
Cochetopa Creek, stm., Co., U.S. C4 83
Cochetopa Hills, mts., Co., U.S. C4 83
Cochin, India G6 36
Cochin China, hist. reg., Viet. H6 35
Cochinos Point, c., Phil. o13 34
Cochise, Az., U.S. E6 80
Cochise, co., Az., U.S. F5 80
Cochise Head, mtn., Az., U.S. E6 80
Cochiti, N.M., U.S. h8 108
Cochiti Indian Reservation, N.M., U.S. h8 108
Cochiti Reservoir, res., N.M., U.S. B3 108
Cochituate, Ma., U.S. g10 98
Cochituate, Lake, l., Ma., U.S. g10 98
Cochran, Ga., U.S. D3 87
Cochran, co., Tx., U.S. C1 120
Cochrane, Alta. D3 68
Cochrane, Ont. o19 73
Cochrane, Wi., U.S. D2 126
Cochrane, dept., Ont. o19 73
Cochranton, Pa., U.S. C1 115
Cochranville, Pa., U.S. G10 115

Name	Map Ref.	Page
Cockburn, Austl.	F3	51
Cocke, co., Tn., U.S.	D10	119
Cockermouth, Eng., U.K.	F5	13
Cockeysville, Md., U.S.	B4	97
Cockpit Country, reg., Jam.	E13	65
Cockrell Hill, Tx., U.S.	n10	120
Cockrum, Ms., U.S.	A4	101
Coco, stm., N.A.	E8	63
Coco, Isla del, i., C.R.	C2	53
Cocoa, Fl., U.S.	D6	86
Cocoa Beach, Fl., U.S.	D6	86
Cocoa West, Fl., U.S.	*D6	86
Cocobeach, Gabon	E1	46
Cocolalla, Al., U.S.	A2	89
Coconino, co., Az., U.S.	B3	80
Coconino Plateau, plat., Az., U.S.	B3	80
Coconut Creek, Fl., U.S.	*F6	86
Cocopah Indian Reservation, Az., U.S.	E1	80
Cocos Bay, b., Trin.	O23	65
Cocos Island, i., Guam	M9	52
Cocos Islands (Keeling Islands), is., Oc.	G3	2
Cocos Lagoon, b., Guam	M9	52
Coco Solo, Pan.	k11	62
Cocula, Mex.	C4	63
Cod, Cape, c., Ma., U.S.	C7	98
Codajás, Braz.	C2	59
Codell, Ks., U.S.	C4	93
Coden, Al., U.S.	E1	78
Codera, Cabo, c., Ven.	A4	60
Coderre, Sask.	G2	75
Codesa, Alta.	B1	68
Codette, Sask.	D3	75
Codigoro, Italy	E8	20
Codington, co., S.D., U.S.	C8	118
Cod Island, i., Newf.	g9	72
Codó, Braz.	B2	57
Codogno, Italy	B2	23
Codpa, Chile	C2	55
Codroipo, Italy	D8	20
Codroy, Newf.	E2	72
Codroy Pond, Newf.	D2	72
Cody, Ne., U.S.	B4	104
Cody, Wy., U.S.	B3	127
Codys, N.B.	D4	71
Coe Hill, Ont.	C7	73
Coesfeld, W. Ger.	C3	18
Coesse, In., U.S.	B7	91
Coeur d'Alene, Id., U.S.	B2	89
Coeur d'Alene, stm., Id., U.S.	B2	89
Coeur d'Alene Indian Reservation, Id., U.S.	B2	89
Coeur d'Alene Lake, res., Id., U.S.	B2	89
Coeur d'Alene Mountains, mts., Id., U.S.	B2	89
Coevorden, Neth.	B6	17
Coffee, co., Al., U.S.	D3	78
Coffee, co., Ga., U.S.	E4	87
Coffee, co., Tn., U.S.	B5	119
Coffee Creek, Mt., U.S.	C6	103
Coffeen, Il., U.S.	D4	90
Coffee Springs, Al., U.S.	D4	78
Coffeeville, Al., U.S.	D1	78
Coffeeville, Ms., U.S.	B4	101
Coffey, Mo., U.S.	A3	102
Coffey, co., Ks., U.S.	D8	93
Coffeyville, Ks., U.S.	E8	93
Coffin, Île, i., Que.	F9	50
Coffs Harbour, Austl.	F9	50
Cofield, N.C., U.S.	A6	110
Cogdell, Ga., U.S.	E4	87
Coggon, Ia., U.S.	B6	92
Coghinas, stm., Italy	D2	23
Cognac, Fr.	E3	16
Cogswell, N.D., U.S.	C8	111
Cohagen, Mt., U.S.	C10	103
Cohansey, stm., N.J., U.S.	E2	107
Cohasset, Ma., U.S.	B6	98
Cohasset, Mn., U.S.	C5	100
Cohocton, N.Y., U.S.	C3	109
Cohocton, stm., N.Y., U.S.	C3	109
Cohoe, Ak., U.S.	g16	79
Cohoes, N.Y., U.S.	C7	109
Cohoon, Lake, res., Va., U.S.	k14	123
Cohutta, Ga., U.S.	B2	87
Cohutta Mountain, mtn., Ga., U.S.	B2	87
Coiba, Isla, i., Pan.	G7	62
Coig, stm., Arg.	E2	54
Coihaique, Chile	D2	54
Coila, Ms., U.S.	B4	101
Coils Creek, stm., Nv., U.S.	D5	105
Coimbatore, India	F6	36
Coimbra, Port.	B1	22
Coín, Spain	D3	22
Coin, Ia., U.S.	D2	92
Coinjock, N.C., U.S.	A7	110
Coipasa, Laguna, l., Bol.	C2	55
Coipasa, Salar de, pl., S.A.	C2	55
Coire, Loch, l., Scot., U.K.	B4	13
Cojedes, state, Ven.	B4	60
Cojutepeque, El Sal.	D3	62
Cokato, Mn., U.S.	E4	100
Coke, co., Tx., U.S.	D2	120
Coker, Al., U.S.	B2	78
Cokesbury, S.C., U.S.	C3	117
Coketon, W.V., U.S.	B5	125
Cokeville, Wy., U.S.	D2	127
Coläba Point, c., India	H4	37
Colac, Austl.	G7	50
Colares, Port.	f9	22
Colatina, Braz.	A4	56
Colbeck, Cape, c., Ant.	B33	7
Colbert, Ok., U.S.	D5	113
Colbert, co., Al., U.S.	A2	78
Colbert Heights, Al., U.S.	A2	78
Colbio, Som.	F5	47
Colborne, Ont.	C7	73
Colburn, Chile	B2	54
Colburn, In., U.S.	A2	89
Colby, Ks., U.S.	C2	93
Colby, Me., U.S.	B4	96
Colby, Wi., U.S.	D3	126
Colbyville, Vt., U.S.	C3	122
Colchester, Eng., U.K.	E7	10
Colchester, Ct., U.S.	C6	84
Colchester, Il., U.S.	C3	90
Colchester, Vt., U.S.	B2	122
Colchester, co., N.S.	D6	71
Colcord, Ok., U.S.	A7	113
Cold, stm., N.H., U.S.	C4	106
Cold, stm., N.H., U.S.	B4	106
Cold Bay, Ak., U.S.	E7	79
Cold Fell, mtn., Eng., U.K.	F6	13
Cold Hollow Mountains, mts., Vt., U.S.	B3	122
Colditz, E. Ger.	B7	19
Cold Lake, Alta.	B5	68
Cold Lake, l., Can.	B5	68
Cold River, N.H., U.S.	D2	106
Cold Spring, Ky., U.S.	A5	94
Cold Spring, Mn., U.S.	E4	100
Cold Spring, N.J., U.S.	F3	107
Coldspring, Tx., U.S.	D5	120
Cold Spring Harbor, N.Y., U.S.	*n15	109
Cold Spring, Nv., U.S.	D4	105
Cold Stream Pond, l., Me., U.S.	C4	96
Coldwater, Ont.	C5	73
Coldwater, Ks., U.S.	E4	93
Coldwater, Mi., U.S.	G5	99
Coldwater, Ms., U.S.	A4	101
Coldwater, Oh., U.S.	B1	112
Coldwater, stm., Ms., U.S.	A3	101
Coldwater Creek, stm., U.S.	e9	113
Cole, Ok., U.S.	B4	113
Cole, co., Mo., U.S.	C5	102
Colebrook, Ct., U.S.	B3	84
Colebrook, N.H., U.S.	g7	106
Colebrook River Lake, res., Ct., U.S.	A3	84
Cole Camp, Mo., U.S.	C4	102
Coleen, stm., Ak., U.S.	B11	79
Coleharbor, N.D., U.S.	B4	111
Cole Lake, Ont.	C8	73
Coleman, Fl., U.S.	D4	86
Coleman, Ga., U.S.	E2	87
Coleman, Md., U.S.	B5	97
Coleman, Mi., U.S.	E6	99
Coleman, Tx., U.S.	D3	120
Coleman, Wi., U.S.	C5	126
Coleman, co., Tx., U.S.	D3	120
Coleman Falls, Va., U.S.	C3	123
Colerain, N.C., U.S.	A6	110
Coleraine, Austl.	H3	51
Coleraine, Que.	D6	74
Coleraine, N. Ire., U.K.	C3	10
Coleraine, Mn., U.S.	C5	100
Coleridge, Ne., U.S.	B8	104
Coleridge, N.C., U.S.	B3	110
Coles, co., Il., U.S.	D5	90
Coles, Punta, c., Peru	E3	58
Coles Hill, Ont.	C7	73
Colesberg, S. Afr.	D4	49
Colesburg, Ia., U.S.	B6	92
Colesburg, Ky., U.S.	C4	94
Coleta, Il., U.S.	B4	90
Coleville, Sask.	F1	75
Coleville, Ca., U.S.	C4	82
Colfax, Sask.	H4	75
Colfax, Ca., U.S.	C3	82
Colfax, Il., U.S.	C5	90
Colfax, In., U.S.	D4	91
Colfax, Ia., U.S.	C4	92
Colfax, La., U.S.	C3	95
Colfax, N.D., U.S.	C9	111
Colfax, Wi., U.S.	D2	126
Colfax, co., Ne., U.S.	C8	104
Colfax, co., N.M., U.S.	A5	108
Colgate, Sask.	H4	75
Colhué Huapi, Lago, l., Arg.	D3	54
Colibris, Pointe des, c., Guad.	Q9	65
Colico, Italy	C5	20
Colijnsplaat, Neth.	C3	17
Colima, Mex.	D4	63
Colima, state, Mex.	D4	63
Colima, Nevado de, mtn., Mex.	n12	63
Colinas, Braz.	C2	57
Colinet, Newf.	E5	72
Colinton, Alta.	B4	68
College, Ak., U.S.	B10	79
College City, Ar., U.S.	*A5	81
College Corner, Oh., U.S.	C1	112
Collegedale, Tn., U.S.	h11	119
College Grove, Tn., U.S.	B5	119
College Park, Ga., U.S.	C2	87
College Park, Md., U.S.	C4	97
College Place, Wa., U.S.	C7	124
College Springs, Ia., U.S.	D2	92
College Station, Ar., U.S.	C3	81
College Station, Tx., U.S.	D4	120
Collegeville, Ar., U.S.	*C3	81
Collegeville, In., U.S.	C3	91
College Ward, Ut., U.S.	*B4	121
Colleton, co., S.C., U.S.	F6	117
Colleyville, Tx., U.S.	*n9	120
Collie, Austl.	F2	50
Collier, co., Fl., U.S.	F5	86
Collier Bay, b., Austl.	C3	50
Collier City, Fl., U.S.	*F6	86
Colliers, W.V., U.S.	f8	125
Collierville, Tn., U.S.	B2	119
Collin, co., Tx., U.S.	C4	120
Collingdale, Pa., U.S.	p20	115
Collingswood, N.J., U.S.	D2	107
Collingsworth, co., Tx., U.S.	B2	120
Collingwood, Ont.	C4	73
Collins, Ar., U.S.	D4	81
Collins, Ga., U.S.	D4	87
Collins, Ia., U.S.	C4	92
Collins, Ms., U.S.	D4	101
Collins, Mo., U.S.	D4	102
Collins, Wi., U.S.	h10	126
Collins Park, De., U.S.	B3	85
Collinston, La., U.S.	B4	95
Collinsville, Al., U.S.	A4	78
Collinsville, Ct., U.S.	B4	84
Collinsville, Il., U.S.	E4	90
Collinsville, Ms., U.S.	C5	101
Collinsville, Ok., U.S.	A6	113
Collinsville, Tx., U.S.	C4	120
Collinsville, Va., U.S.	D3	123
Collinwood, Tn., U.S.	B4	119
Collipulli, Chile	D2	54
Collis, Mn., U.S.	E2	100
Collooney, Ire.	G4	11
Collyer, Ks., U.S.	C3	93
Colman, S.D., U.S.	D9	118
Colmar, Fr.	D7	16
Colmar, Ky., U.S.	D6	94
Colmar Manor, Md., U.S.	f9	97
Colmenar de Oreja, Spain	E4	22
Colmenar Viejo, Spain	B4	22
Colmesneil, Tx., U.S.	D5	120
Colnett, Cabo, c., Mex.	A1	63
Colo, Ia., U.S.	B4	92
Cologne (Köln), W. Ger.	C6	18
Cologne, Mn., U.S.	F5	100
Cologne, N.J., U.S.	E3	107
Coloma, Mi., U.S.	F4	99
Coloma, Wi., U.S.	D4	126
Colombes, Fr.	g10	16
Colômbia, Braz.	C3	56
Colombia, Col.	C3	60
Colombia, ctry., S.A.	C3	60
Colombo, Sri L.	G6	36
Colome, S.D., U.S.	D6	118
Colón, Arg.	A5	54
Colón, Cuba	C3	64
Colón, Pan.	F8	62
Colon, Mi., U.S.	G5	99
Colon, Ne., U.S.	g11	104
Colon, N.C., U.S.	B3	110
Colón, Archipiélago de (Galapagos Islands), is., Ec.	g5	58
Colona, Co., U.S.	C3	83
Colonia, N.J., U.S.	k7	107
Colonia, dept., Ur.	g8	54
Colonia del Sacramento, Ur.	C5	56
Colonia Dora, Arg.	E3	54
Colonia Las Heras, Arg.	D3	54
Colônia Leopoldina, Braz.	k6	57
Colonial Beach, Va., U.S.	B6	123
Colonial Heights, Tn., U.S.	C11	119
Colonial Heights, Va., U.S.	C5	123
Colonial National Historical Park, Va., U.S.	C6	123
Colonial Park, Pa., U.S.	*F8	115
Colonia Mennonita, Para.	D5	55
Colonia Suiza, Ur.	g8	54
Colonie, N.Y., U.S.	C7	109
Colonna, Italy	h9	23
Colonne, Cape, c., Italy	E6	23
Colonsay, Sask.	F3	75
Colonsay, i., Scot., U.K.	B3	10
Colony, N. Ire., U.K.	C6	11
Colony, Ok., U.S.	B3	113
Colorado, C.R.	E8	63
Colorado, co., Tx., U.S.	E4	120
Colorado, state, U.S.	B5	83
Colorado, stm., Arg.	B4	54
Colorado, stm., N.A.	D5	76
Colorado, stm., Tx., U.S.	D3	120
Colorado City, Az., U.S.	A3	80
Colorado City, Co., U.S.	D6	83
Colorado City, Tx., U.S.	C2	120
Colorado City, Lake, res., Tx., U.S.	C2	120
Colorado National Monument, Co., U.S.	B2	83
Colorado Plateau, plat., U.S.	D4	80
Colorado River Aqueduct, Ca., U.S.	F6	82
Colorado River Indian Reservation, U.S.	D1	80
Colorados, Archipiélago de los, is., Cuba	C1	64
Colorado Springs, Co., U.S.	C6	83
Colotlán, Mex.	C4	63
Colquechaca, Bol.	C2	55
Colquitt, Ga., U.S.	E2	87
Colquitt, co., Ga., U.S.	E3	87
Colrain, Ma., U.S.	A2	98
Colstrip, Mt., U.S.	E10	103
Colt, Ar., U.S.	B5	81
Coltauco, Chile	A2	54
Colter Bay, Wy., U.S.	C2	127
Colton, Ca., U.S.	*E5	82
Colton, N.Y., U.S.	f10	109
Colton, Or., U.S.	B4	114
Colton, S.D., U.S.	D9	118
Colton, Wa., U.S.	C8	124
Colton Hill, mtn., Vt., U.S.	D4	122
Coltons Point, Md., U.S.	D4	97
Colts Neck, N.J., U.S.	C4	107
Columbia, Al., U.S.	D4	78
Columbia, Ca., U.S.	C3	82
Columbia, Ct., U.S.	C6	84
Columbia, Il., U.S.	E3	90
Columbia, Ky., U.S.	C4	94
Columbia, La., U.S.	B3	95
Columbia, Md., U.S.	B4	97
Columbia, Ms., U.S.	D4	101
Columbia, Mo., U.S.	C5	102
Columbia, N.C., U.S.	B6	110
Columbia, Pa., U.S.	F9	115
Columbia, S.C., U.S.	C5	117
Columbia, S.D., U.S.	B7	118
Columbia, Tn., U.S.	B4	119
Columbia, Va., U.S.	C4	123
Columbia, co., Ar., U.S.	D2	81
Columbia, co., Fl., U.S.	B4	86
Columbia, co., Ga., U.S.	C4	87
Columbia, co., N.Y., U.S.	C7	109
Columbia, co., Or., U.S.	B3	114
Columbia, co., Pa., U.S.	D9	115
Columbia, co., Wa., U.S.	C7	124
Columbia, co., Wi., U.S.	E4	126
Columbia, stm., N.A.	A3	76
Columbia, Cape, c., N.W. Ter.	k37	66
Columbia, Mount, mtn., Can.	C2	68
Columbia Basin, U.S.	C6	124
Columbia City, In., U.S.	B7	91
Columbia City, Or., U.S.	B4	114
Columbia Cross Roads, Pa., U.S.	C7	115
Columbia Falls, Me., U.S.	D5	96
Columbia Falls, Mt., U.S.	B2	103
Columbia Heights, Mn., U.S.	m12	100
Columbia Lake, res., Ct., U.S.	C6	84
Columbia Lake, l., B.C.	D10	69
Columbia Mountains, mts., B.C.	C7	69
Columbiana, Al., U.S.	B3	78
Columbiana, Oh., U.S.	B5	112
Columbiana, co., Oh., U.S.	B5	112
Columbiaville, Mi., U.S.	E7	99
Columbine, Co., U.S.	A5	83
Columbus, Ga., U.S.	D2	87
Columbus, In., U.S.	F6	91
Columbus, Ks., U.S.	E9	93
Columbus, Ms., U.S.	B5	101
Columbus, Mt., U.S.	E7	103
Columbus, Ne., U.S.	C8	104
Columbus, N.M., U.S.	F2	108
Columbus, N.C., U.S.	f10	110
Columbus, N.D., U.S.	A3	111
Columbus, Oh., U.S.	C2	112
Columbus, Tx., U.S.	E4	120
Columbus, Wi., U.S.	E4	126
Columbus, co., N.C., U.S.	C4	110
Columbus Air Force Base, mil., Ms., U.S.	B5	101
Columbus City, Ia., U.S.	C6	92
Columbus Grove, Oh., U.S.	B1	112
Columbus Junction, Ia., U.S.	C6	92
Columbus Lake, res., Ms., U.S.	B5	101
Colusa, Ca., U.S.	C2	82
Colusa, co., Ca., U.S.	C2	82
Colver, Pa., U.S.	E4	115
Colville, Wa., U.S.	A8	124
Colville, stm., Ak., U.S.	B9	79
Colville, stm., Wa., U.S.	A8	124
Colville Indian Reservation, Wa., U.S.	A6	124
Colville Lake, l., N.W. Ter.	C7	66
Colvin Mountain, mtn., Al., U.S.	B4	78
Colvos Passage, strt., Wa., U.S.	f10	124
Colwell, Ia., U.S.	A5	92
Colwich, Ks., U.S.	E6	93
Colwood, B.C.	h12	69
Colwyn Bay, Wales, U.K.	A4	12
Colyell Creek, stm., La., U.S.	h10	95
Comabbio, Lago di, l., Italy	E6	21
Comacchio, Italy	B4	23
Comacchio, Valli di, b., Italy	E8	20
Comal, co., Tx., U.S.	E3	120
Comalapa, Guat.	E6	63
Comalcalco, Mex.	D6	63
Coman, Mount, mtn., Ant.	B6	7
Comanche, Ok., U.S.	C4	113
Comanche, Tx., U.S.	D3	120
Comanche, co., Ks., U.S.	E4	93
Comanche, co., Ok., U.S.	C3	113
Comanche, co., Tx., U.S.	D3	120
Comarapa, Bol.	C5	55
Comayagua, Hond.	E7	63
Combahee, stm., S.C., U.S.	F6	117
Combarbalá, Chile	A2	54
Combeaufontaine, Fr.	B1	20
Combee Settlement, Fl., U.S.	*D5	86
Comber, Ont.	E2	73
Comber, N. Ire., U.K.	C6	11
Combermere, Ont.	B7	73
Combined Locks, Wi., U.S.	h9	126
Combs, Ar., U.S.	B2	81
Combs, Ky., U.S.	C6	94
Comer, Al., U.S.	C4	78
Comer, Ga., U.S.	B3	87
Comerío, P.R.	B3	65
Comet, stm., Austl.	B7	51
Comfort, N.C., U.S.	B5	110
Comfort, Tx., U.S.	E3	120
Comfort, W.V., U.S.	m12	125
Comfrey, Mn., U.S.	F4	100
Comilla, Bngl.	D9	36
Comines, Bel.	D2	17
Comino, Cape, c., Italy	D2	23
Comins, Mi., U.S.	D6	99
Cominto, Ar., U.S.	D4	81
Comiso, Italy	F5	23
Comitán [de Dominguez], Mex.	D6	63
Comite, stm., La., U.S.	D4	95
Commack, N.Y., U.S.	*n15	109
Commentry, Fr.	D5	16
Commerce, Ga., U.S.	B3	87
Commerce, Mo., U.S.	D8	102
Commerce, Ok., U.S.	A7	113
Commerce, Tx., U.S.	C5	120
Commerce City, Co., U.S.	B6	83
Commercial Point, Oh., U.S.	C2	112
Commercy, Fr.	D6	16
Commewijne, dept., Sur.	A4	59
Commiskey, In., U.S.	G6	91
Commissaires, Lac des, l., Que.	A5	74
Committee Bay, b., N.W. Ter.	C15	66
Common Fence Point, R.I., U.S.	D6	116
Commonwealth Bay, b., Ant.	C27	7
Commonwealth Range, mts., Ant.	A30	7
Communism Peak, mtn., Sov. Un.	F10	29
Como, Italy	B2	23
Como, Co., U.S.	B5	83
Como, Ms., U.S.	A4	101
Como, N.C., U.S.	A5	110
Como, Tn., U.S.	A3	119
Como, Lake, l., Italy	B2	23
Comobabi, Az., U.S.	E4	80
Comodoro Rivadavia, Arg.	D3	54
Comorin, Cape, c., India	H6	36
Comoros, ctry., Afr.	H10	42
Comox, B.C.	E5	69
Compass Lake, Fl., U.S.	B1	86
Compeer, Alta.	D5	68
Competition, Mo., U.S.	D5	102
Compiègne, Fr.	C5	16
Compostela, Mex.	m11	63
Comptche, Ca., U.S.	C2	82
Compton, Que.	D6	74
Compton, Ca., U.S.	n12	82
Compton, Il., U.S.	B4	90
Compton, co., Que.	D6	74
Comstock, Mi., U.S.	F5	99
Comstock, Ne., U.S.	C6	104
Comstock, Tx., U.S.	D2	120
Comstock, Wi., U.S.	C1	126
Comstock Park, Mi., U.S.	E5	99
Comté, stm., Fr. Gu.	B4	59
Con, i., Viet.	D7	35
Conakry, Gui.	E2	45
Conanicut Island, i., R.I., U.S.	E5	116
Conanicut Point, c., R.I., U.S.	E5	116
Conasauga, Tn., U.S.	D9	119
Concan, Tx., U.S.	E3	120
Concarneau, Fr.	D2	16
Conceição das Alagoas, Braz.	B5	56
Conceição do Araguaia, Braz.	D5	59
Conceição do Norte, Braz.	D1	57
Concepción, Arg.	E2	55
Concepción, Bol.	C2	55
Concepción, Chile	B2	54
Concepción, Para.	D6	55
Concepción, Phil.	o13	34
Concepción, Tx., U.S.	F3	120
Concepción, dept., Para.	D5	55
Concepción, Laguna, l., Bol.	B2	55
Concepción, Punta, c., Mex.	B2	63
Concepción del Oro, Mex.	C4	63
Concepción del Uruguay, Arg.	A5	54
Conception, Mo., U.S.	A3	102
Conception, Point, c., U.S.	E3	82
Conception Bay, b., Newf.	E5	72
Conception Bay South, Newf.	E5	72
Conception Island, i., Bah.	C6	64
Conception Junction, Mo., U.S.	A3	102
Conchas, Braz.	m7	56
Conchas Dam, N.M., U.S.	B5	108
Conchas Lake, res., N.M., U.S.	B5	108
Conche, Newf.	C4	72
Conchi, Chile	D2	55
Conchillas, Ur.	g7	54
Concho, Az., U.S.	C6	80
Concho, co., Tx., U.S.	D3	120
Concho, stm., Tx., U.S.	D2	120
Conchos, stm., Mex.	B4	63
Conconully, Wa., U.S.	A6	124
Concord, Ar., U.S.	B3	81
Concord, Fl., U.S.	B2	86
Concord, Il., U.S.	D3	90
Concord, Ky., U.S.	B6	94
Concord, Ma., U.S.	B5	98
Concord, Mi., U.S.	F6	99
Concord, Mo., U.S.	g13	102
Concord, Ne., U.S.	B9	104
Concord, N.H., U.S.	D3	106
Concord, N.C., U.S.	B2	110
Concord, Tn., U.S.	D9	119
Concord, Vt., U.S.	C5	122
Concord, Va., U.S.	C4	123
Concord, stm., Ma., U.S.	A5	98
Concordia, Arg.	A5	54
Concordia, Col.	B2	60
Concordia, Peru	B3	58
Concordia, Ks., U.S.	C6	93
Concordia, Mo., U.S.	C4	102
Concordia, co., La., U.S.	C4	95
Concordia, Peru	C2	58
Concrete, N.D., U.S.	A8	111
Concrete, Wa., U.S.	A4	124
Condamine, stm., Austl.	E9	50
Conde, Braz.	D7	57
Conde, S.D., U.S.	B7	118
Condé [-sur-l'Escaut], Fr.	D3	17
Condé-sur-Marne, Fr.	E4	17
Condé-sur-Noireau, Fr.	C3	16
Condeúba, Braz.	A4	56
Condino, Italy	D6	20
Condobolin, Austl.	F8	50
Condom, Fr.	F4	16
Condon, Mt., U.S.	C3	103
Condon, Or., U.S.	B6	114
Cóndor, Cordillera del, mts., S.A.	B2	58
Cone, Tx., U.S.	C2	120
Conecuh, co., Al., U.S.	D2	78
Conecuh, stm., U.S.	D3	78
Conegliano [Veneto], Italy	B4	23
Conehatta, Ms., U.S.	C4	101
Conejos, co., Co., U.S.	D4	83
Conejos, stm., Co., U.S.	D4	83
Conejos Peak, mtn., Co., U.S.	D4	83
Conemaugh, Pa., U.S.	F4	115
Conemaugh River Lake, res., Pa., U.S.	F3	115
Conestee, S.C., U.S.	B3	117
Conesville, Ia., U.S.	C6	92
Conesville, Oh., U.S.	B4	112
Conetoe, N.C., U.S.	B5	110
Coney Island (part of New York), N.Y., U.S.	k13	109
Confluence, Ky., U.S.	C6	94
Confluence, Pa., U.S.	G3	115
Confolens, Fr.	D4	16
Confusion Bay, b., Newf.	D4	72
Confusion Range, mts., Ut., U.S.	D2	121
Confuso, stm., Para.	D4	55
Cong, Ire.	D2	11
Congamond Lakes, l., U.S.	A4	84
Congaree, stm., S.C., U.S.	D6	117
Congaree Swamp National Monument, S.C., U.S.	D6	117
Conger, Mn., U.S.	G5	100
Congers, N.Y., U.S.	*D7	109
Congleton, Eng., U.K.	A5	12
Congo, Oh., U.S.	C3	112
Congo, W.V., U.S.	e8	125
Congo, ctry., Afr.	B2	48
Congo (Zaire), stm., Afr.	B2	48
Congress, Sask.	H2	75
Congress, Az., U.S.	C3	80
Conil [de la Frontera], Spain	D2	22
Coniston, Alta.	B5	68
Coniston Water, l., Eng., U.K.	F5	13
Conklin, Alta.	B5	68
Conklin, Mi., U.S.	E5	99
Conklin, N.Y., U.S.	C5	109
Conlen, Tx., U.S.	A1	120
Conley, Ga., U.S.	*C2	87
Conn, Lough, l., Ire.	D2	11
Connacht (Connaught), hist. reg., Ire.	D2	11
Connaught see Connacht, hist. reg., Ire.	D2	11
Conneaut, Oh., U.S.	A5	112
Conneaut Creek, stm., Oh., U.S.	A5	112
Conneaut Lake, Pa., U.S.	C1	115
Conneaut Lake, l., Pa., U.S.	C1	115
Conneautville, Pa., U.S.	C1	115
Connecticut, state, U.S.	C5	84
Connecticut, stm., U.S.	C5	84
Connell, Wa., U.S.	C7	124
Connellsville, Pa., U.S.	F2	115
Connemara, reg., Ire.	A3	102
Conner, Mt., U.S.	E2	103
Connersville, In., U.S.	E7	91
Connerville, Ok., U.S.	C5	113
Connors, N.B.	B1	71
Conococheague Creek, stm., Md., U.S.	A2	97
Conover, N.C., U.S.	B1	110
Conowingo, Md., U.S.	A5	97
Conowingo Dam, Md., U.S.	A5	97
Conquest, Sask.	F2	75
Conrad, Ia., U.S.	B5	92
Conrad, Mt., U.S.	B5	103
Conrath, Wi., U.S.	C2	126
Conroe, Tx., U.S.	D5	120
Conroy, Ia., U.S.	C6	92
Consecon, Ont.	C7	73
Conselheiro Lafaiete, Braz.	C4	56
Conshohocken, Pa., U.S.	F11	115
Consolación del Sur, Cuba	C2	64
Con Son, is., Viet.	D4	34
Consort, Alta.	D5	68
Constable, N.Y., U.S.	f10	109
Constableville, N.Y., U.S.	B5	109
Constance, Ky., U.S.	*A5	94
Constance, Lake, l., Eur.	E4	18
Constance see Konstanz, W. Ger.	E4	18
Constanța, Rom.	C9	24
Constantia, N.Y., U.S.	B5	109
Constantina, Spain	C3	22
Constantine (Qacentina), Alg.	B4	44
Constantine, Mi., U.S.	G5	99
Constantine, Cape, c., Ak., U.S.	D8	79
Constantinople see İstanbul, Tur.	B7	40
Constitución, Chile	B2	54
Consul, Sask.	H1	75
Contact, Nv., U.S.	B7	105
Contai, India	G11	37
Contamana, Peru	C3	58
Contas, Rio de, stm., Braz.	D3	57
Contendas do Sincorá, Braz.	A4	56
Content Keys, is., Fl., U.S.	H5	86
Continental, Oh., U.S.	A1	112
Continental Divide, N.M., U.S.	B1	108
Continental Peak, mtn., Wy., U.S.	D4	127
Continental Reservoir, res., Co., U.S.	D3	83
Contoocook, N.H., U.S.	D3	106
Contoocook, stm., N.H., U.S.	D3	106
Contra Costa, co., Ca., U.S.	D3	82
Contratación, Col.	B3	60
Contrecoeur, Que.	D4	74
Contreras, N.M., U.S.	C3	108
Contrexéville, Fr.	A1	20
Contumazá, Peru	C2	58
Contwoyto Lake, l., N.W. Ter.	C10	66
Convent, La., U.S.	D5	95
Converse, In., U.S.	C6	91
Converse, La., U.S.	C2	95
Converse, S.C., U.S.	B4	117
Converse, Tx., U.S.	*E3	120
Converse, co., Wy., U.S.	C7	127
Convoy, Oh., U.S.	B1	112
Conway, Ar., U.S.	B3	81
Conway, Fl., U.S.	D5	86
Conway, Ia., U.S.	D3	92
Conway, Ks., U.S.	D6	93
Conway, Ma., U.S.	A2	98
Conway, Mo., U.S.	D5	102
Conway, N.H., U.S.	C4	106
Conway, N.C., U.S.	A5	110
Conway, N.D., U.S.	A8	111
Conway, Pa., U.S.	E1	115
Conway, S.C., U.S.	D9	117
Conway, co., Ar., U.S.	B3	81
Conway, Lake, res., Ar., U.S.	B3	81
Conway, Lake, l., N.H., U.S.	C4	106
Conway Springs, Ks., U.S.	E6	93
Conwy, Wales, U.K.	A4	12
Conyers, Ga., U.S.	C2	87
Cook, Austl.	F5	50
Cook, Mn., U.S.	C6	100
Cook, Ne., U.S.	D9	104
Cook, co., Ga., U.S.	E3	87
Cook, co., Il., U.S.	B6	90
Cook, co., Mn., U.S.	k9	100
Cook, Cape, c., B.C.	D4	69
Cook, Mount, mtn., N.Z.	O13	51
Cooke, co., Tx., U.S.	C4	120
Cooke City, Mt., U.S.	E7	103
Cookes Peak, mtn., N.M., U.S.	E2	108
Cookeville, Tn., U.S.	C8	119
Cook Ice Shelf, ice, Ant.	C28	7
Cooking Lake, l., Alta.	C4	68
Cook Inlet, b., Ak., U.S.	D9	79
Cook Islands, ctry., Oc.	G12	6
Cook Mountain, mtn., W.V., U.S.	n12	125
Cook Point, c., Md., U.S.	C5	97
Cooks, Mi., U.S.	C4	99
Cooksburg, Pa., U.S.	D3	115
Cooks Falls, N.Y., U.S.	D6	109
Cook's Harbour, Newf.	C4	72
Cookshire, Que.	D6	74
Cooks Mills, Il., U.S.	D5	90
Cookson, Ok., U.S.	B7	113
Cookstown, N. Ire., U.K.	C5	11
Cookstown, N.J., U.S.	C3	107
Cooktown, Austl.	C8	50
Cookville, Tx., U.S.	C5	120
Coolah, Austl.	C3	11
Coolamon, Austl.	F9	50
Coolangatta, Austl.	E10	51
Coolgardie, Austl.	F3	50
Coolidge, Az., U.S.	E4	80
Coolidge, Ga., U.S.	E3	87
Coolidge, Ks., U.S.	E2	93
Coolidge, Tx., U.S.	D4	120
Coolidge, Mount, mtn., S.D., U.S.	D2	118
Coolin, Id., U.S.	A2	89
Cool Ridge, W.V., U.S.	D3	125
Coolspring, Pa., U.S.	D3	115
Coolville, Oh., U.S.	C4	112
Cooma, Austl.	G8	50
Coonabarabran, Austl.	F8	50
Coonamble, Austl.	F8	50
Coon Rapids, Ia., U.S.	C3	92
Coon Rapids, Mn., U.S.	E5	100
Coon Valley, Wi., U.S.	E2	126
Cooper, Tx., U.S.	C5	120
Cooper, co., Mo., U.S.	C5	102
Cooper, co., S.C., U.S.	F8	117
Cooper, East Branch, stm., S.C., U.S.	E8	117
Cooper, West Branch, stm., S.C., U.S.	E8	117
Co Operative, Ky., U.S.	C6	94
Cooper City, Fl., U.S.	*F6	86
Cooper Creek, stm., Austl.	E7	50
Cooper Mountain, mtn., Ak., U.S.	g17	79
Cooper Road, stm., La., U.S.	*B2	95
Coopers, Al., U.S.	C3	78
Coopersburg, Pa., U.S.	F11	115
Coopers Mills, Me., U.S.	D3	96
Cooperstown, N.Y., U.S.	C6	109
Cooperstown, N.D., U.S.	B7	111
Cooperstown, Pa., U.S.	D2	115
Cooperstown, Wi., U.S.	h10	126
Coopersville, Mi., U.S.	E5	99
Cooperton, Ok., U.S.	C2	113
Coopertown, Tn., U.S.	A5	119
Coos, co., N.H., U.S.	A4	106
Coos, co., Or., U.S.	D2	114
Coos Bay, Or., U.S.	D2	114
Cootamundra, Austl.	F9	50
Cootehill, Ire.	C4	11
Cooter, Mo., U.S.	E8	102
Copacabana, Arg.	E2	55
Copacabana, Bol.	C2	55
Copainalá, Mex.	D6	63
Copake, N.Y., U.S.	C7	109
Copalis Beach, Wa., U.S.	B1	124
Copalis Crossing, Wa., U.S.	C1	124
Copán, Hond.	C3	62

Name	Map Ref.	Page
Copan, Ok., U.S.	A6	113
Copan Reservoir, res., Ok., U.S.	A6	113
Cope, Co., U.S.	B8	83
Cope, S.C., U.S.	E5	117
Copeland, Fl., U.S.	G5	86
Copeland, Ks., U.S.	E3	93
Copemish, Mi., U.S.	D5	99
Copen, W.V., U.S.	C4	125
Copenhagen (København), Den.	J5	14
Copenhagen, N.Y., U.S.	B5	109
Copetonas, Arg.	B4	54
Copeville, Tx., U.S.	m10	120
Copiague, N.Y., U.S.	*n15	109
Copiah, co., Ms., U.S.	D3	101
Copiapó, Chile	E1	55
Copiapó, stm., Chile	E1	55
Copinsay, i., Scot., U.K.	B6	13
Coplay, Pa., U.S.	E10	115
Copparo, Italy	B3	23
Coppename, stm., Sur.	A3	59
Copper, stm., Ak., U.S.	C11	79
Copperas Cove, Tx., U.S.	D4	120
Copperbelt, prov., Zam.	D4	48
Copper Butte, mtn., Wa., U.S.	A7	124
Copper Center, Ak., U.S.	C10	79
Copper Cliff (part of Sudbury), Ont.	A3	73
Copper Harbor, Mi., U.S.	A3	99
Copperhill, Tn., U.S.	D9	119
Copper Hill, Va., U.S.	C2	123
Coppermine, N.W. Ter.	C9	66
Coppermine, stm., N.W. Ter.	C10	66
Copper Mountain, mtn., Wy., U.S.	C5	127
Copper Mountains, mts., Az., U.S.	E2	80
Copper Ridge, mtn., Tn., U.S.	m13	119
Copper Ridge, mtn., Va., U.S.	f9	123
Copperton, Ut., U.S.	*C3	121
Coppet, Switz.	D1	21
Copton Creek, stm., Alta.	B1	68
Coqên, China	B10	37
Coquet, stm., Eng., U.K.	E7	13
Coquille, Or., U.S.	D2	114
Coquimbo, Chile	E1	55
Coquimbo, prov., Chile	F1	55
Cora, Wy., U.S.	D3	127
Corabia, Rom.	D7	24
Coração de Jesus, Braz.	B4	56
Coracora, Peru	E3	58
Coral, Ont.	o19	73
Coral, Mi., U.S.	E5	99
Coral, Pa., U.S.	F3	115
Coral Gables, Fl., U.S.	G6	86
Coral Hills, Md., U.S.	*C4	97
Coral Sea, Oc.	G9	6
Coral Springs, Fl., U.S.	*F6	86
Coral Terrace, Fl., U.S.	*G6	86
Coralville, Ia., U.S.	C5	92
Coralville Lake, res., Ia., U.S.	C5	92
Coral Way Village, Fl., U.S.	*G6	86
Coram, Mt., U.S.	B2	103
Coram, N.Y., U.S.	*n15	109
Corangamite, Lake, l., Austl.	I4	51
Coraopolis, Pa., U.S.	E1	115
Corato, Italy	D6	23
Corbeil [-Essonnes], Fr.	C5	16
Corbeny, Fr.	E3	17
Corbett, N.Y., U.S.	C5	109
Corbetton, Ont.	C4	73
Corbie, Fr.	C5	16
Corbin, Ks., U.S.	E6	93
Corbin, Ky., U.S.	D5	94
Corbin, N.J., U.S.	D4	103
Corbin City, N.J., U.S.	E3	107
Corby, Eng., U.K.	B7	12
Corcoran, Ca., U.S.	D4	82
Corcoran, Mn., U.S.	m11	100
Corcovado, Golfo, b., Chile	C2	54
Cord, Ar., U.S.	B4	81
Cordaville, Ma., U.S.	g9	98
Cordele, Ga., U.S.	E3	87
Cordell, Ok., U.S.	B3	113
Cordell Hull Lake, res., Tn., U.S.	C8	119
Corder, Mo., U.S.	B4	102
Cordesville, S.C., U.S.	E8	117
Cordillera, dept., Para.	D4	55
Córdoba, Arg.	A4	54
Córdoba, Mex.	n15	63
Córdoba, Spain	D3	22
Córdoba, prov., Arg.	A4	54
Córdoba, dept., Col.	B2	60
Cordon, Phil.	n13	34
Córdova, Peru	D2	58
Cordova, Al., U.S.	B2	78
Cordova, Ak., U.S.	C10	79
Cordova, Il., U.S.	B3	90
Cordova, Md., U.S.	C6	97
Cordova, Ne., U.S.	*D8	104
Cordova, N.M., U.S.	A4	108
Cordova, N.C., U.S.	C3	110
Cordova, S.C., U.S.	E6	117
Cordova, Tn., U.S.	B2	119
Cordova Mines, Ont.	C7	73
Cordova Peak, mtn., Ak., U.S.	C10	79
Corea, Me., U.S.	D5	96
Coreaú, Braz.	B2	57
Corella, Spain	A5	22
Corfu, N.Y., U.S.	C2	109
Corfu see Kérkira, i., Grc.	C2	40
Cori, Italy	h9	23
Corigliano, Italy	E6	23
Corinna, Me., U.S.	D3	96
Corinne, Mi., U.S.	B5	99
Corinne, Ut., U.S.	B3	121
Corinne, W.V., U.S.	*D3	125
Corinne Key, Fl., U.S.	G6	86
Corinth see Kórinthos, Grc.		
Corinth, Ms., U.S.	A5	101
Corinth, N.Y., U.S.	B7	109
Corinth, Vt., U.S.	C4	122
Corinth, W.V., U.S.	B5	125
Corinth, Bay of, b., Grc.	h9	25
Corinth, Gulf of, b., Grc.	h9	25
Corinth Canal, Grc.	h10	25
Corinto, Braz.	B4	56
Corinto, Nic.	E7	63
Corisco, Isla de, i., Eq. Gui.	I4	46
Cork, Ire.	D3	71
Cork, co., Ire.	E3	11
Cork Harbour, b., Ire.	E2	10
Corleone, Italy	F4	23
Çorlu, Tur.	B6	40
Cormeilles-en-Parisis, Fr.	g9	16
Cormorant, Man.	B1	70
Cormorant Lake, l., Man.	B1	70
Corn, Ok., U.S.	B3	113
Cornaca, S.C., U.S.	C3	117
Cornelia, Ga., U.S.	B3	87
Cornelius, N.C., U.S.	B2	110
Cornelius, Or., U.S.	g11	114
Cornell, Il., U.S.	C5	90
Cornell, Wi., U.S.	C2	126
Cornellà, Spain	B7	22
Corner Brook, Newf.	D3	72
Corner Inlet, b., Austl.	I6	51
Cornerstone, Ar., U.S.	C4	81
Cornersville, Tn., U.S.	B5	119
Corneville, Ar., U.S.	D4	81
Cornhill, N.B.	D4	71
Cornimont, Fr.	B2	20
Corning, Ar., U.S.	A5	81
Corning, Ca., U.S.	C2	82
Corning, Ia., U.S.	D3	92
Corning, Ks., U.S.	C7	93
Corning, Mo., U.S.	A2	102
Corning, N.Y., U.S.	C3	109
Corning, Oh., U.S.	C3	112
Cornish, Me., U.S.	E2	96
Cornish, Ok., U.S.	C4	113
Cornish, Ut., U.S.	B4	121
Cornish Center, N.H., U.S.	D2	106
Cornish Flat, N.H., U.S.	D2	106
Cornish Mills, N.H., U.S.	D2	106
Cornishville, Ky., U.S.	C5	94
Corno Grande, mtn., Italy	C4	23
Cornucopia, Wi., U.S.	B2	126
Cornville, Az., U.S.	C4	80
Cornville, Me., U.S.	D3	96
Cornwall, Ont.	B10	73
Cornwall, Ct., U.S.	B2	84
Cornwall, Pa., U.S.	F9	115
Cornwall, Vt., U.S.	D2	122
Cornwall, co., Eng., U.K.	D3	12
Cornwall Bridge, Ct., U.S.	B2	84
Cornwallis Island, i., N.W. Ter.	m33	66
Cornwall Island, i., N.W. Ter.	m32	66
Cornwall-on-Hudson, N.Y., U.S.	D6	109
Cornwells Heights, Pa., U.S.	o22	115
Coro, Ven.	A4	60
Coroatá, Braz.	B2	57
Corocoro, Bol.	C2	55
Coroico, Bol.	C2	55
Corolla, N.C., U.S.	A7	110
Coromandel Coast, India	F7	36
Coromandel Peninsula, pen., N.Z.	L15	51
Corona, Al., U.S.	B2	78
Corona, Ca., U.S.	F5	82
Corona, N.M., U.S.	C4	108
Corona, S.D., U.S.	B9	118
Coronach, Sask.	H3	75
Coronado, Ca., U.S.	F5	82
Coronado, Co., U.S.	*B6	83
Coronado, Bahía de, b., C.R.	F6	62
Coronado National Memorial, Az., U.S.	F5	80
Coronation, Alta.	C5	68
Coronation Gulf, b., N.W. Ter.	C10	66
Coronation Island, i., B.A.T.	C8	7
Coronation Island, i., Ak., U.S.	n22	79
Coronda, Arg.	A4	54
Coronel, Chile	B2	54
Coronel Dorrego, Arg.	B4	54
Coronel Murta, Braz.	B4	56
Coronel Oviedo, Para.	A4	55
Coronel Pringles, Arg.	B4	54
Coronel Suárez, Arg.	B4	54
Coronie, dept., Sur.	A3	59
Coropuna, Nevado, mtn., Peru	E3	58
Corowa, Austl.	G6	51
Corozal, Belize	D7	63
Corozal, Col.	B2	60
Corpataux, Switz.	C3	21
Corpen, Arg.	D3	54
Corps, Fr.	E1	20
Corpus Christi, Tx., U.S.	F4	120
Corpus Christi Naval Air Station, mil., Tx., U.S.	F4	120
Corral, Chile	B2	54
Corral, Id., U.S.	F4	89
Corral de Almaguer, Spain	C4	22
Corrales, Col.	B3	60
Corralillo, Cuba	C3	64
Corraun, Ire.	B2	11
Corravillers, Fr.	B2	20
Correctionville, Ia., U.S.	B2	92
Corregidor Island, i., Phil.	o13	34
Correll, Mn., U.S.	E2	100
Corrente, Braz.	D1	57
Correntes, Braz.	k5	57
Correntina, Braz.	A4	56
Corrib, Lough, l., Ire.	B2	11
Corrientes, Arg.	E4	55
Corrientes, prov., Arg.	E4	55
Corrientes, stm., Arg.	E4	55
Corrientes, stm., S.A.	B2	60
Corrientes, Cabo, c., Col.	B2	60
Corrientes, Cabo, c., Cuba	D1	64
Corrientes, Cabo, c., Mex.	C3	63
Corrientes, Ensenada de, b., Cuba	D1	64
Corrigan, Tx., U.S.	D5	120
Corriganville, Md., U.S.	k13	97
Corrofin, Ire.	E2	11
Corry, Pa., U.S.	C2	115
Corryton, Tn., U.S.	C10	119
Corse, Cap, c., Fr.	C2	23
Corsica, Pa., U.S.	D3	115
Corsica, S.D., U.S.	D7	118
Corsica, i., Fr.	C2	23
Corsicana, Tx., U.S.	C4	120
Corson, co., S.D., U.S.	B4	118
Corson Inlet, b., N.J., U.S.	E3	107
Cortazar, Mex.	C4	63
Corte, Fr.	C2	23
Corte Alto, Chile	C2	54
Cortegana, Spain	D2	22
Corte Madera, Ca., U.S.	*h7	82
Cortes [de la Frontera], Spain	D3	22
Cortez, Co., U.S.	D2	83
Cortez, Fl., U.S.	q10	86
Cortez Mountains, mts., Nv., U.S.	C5	105
Cortina d'Ampezzo, Italy	A4	23
Cortland, Il., U.S.	B5	90
Cortland, In., U.S.	G6	91
Cortland, Ne., U.S.	D9	104
Cortland, N.Y., U.S.	C4	109
Cortland, Oh., U.S.	A5	112
Cortland, co., N.Y., U.S.	C4	109
Cortona, Italy	C3	23
Coruche, Port.	C1	22
Çoruh, stm., Asia	B13	40
Çorum, Tur.	B10	40
Corumbá, Braz.	B1	56
Corumbá, stm., Braz.	B3	56
Corunna, Ont.	E2	73
Corunna, In., U.S.	B7	91
Corunna, Mi., U.S.	F6	99
Corvallis, Mt., U.S.	D2	103
Corvallis, Or., U.S.	C3	114
Corvo, i., Port.	g8	44
Corwin, Ia., U.S.	E5	93
Corwin Springs, Mt., U.S.	E6	103
Corwith, Ia., U.S.	B4	92
Cory, In., U.S.	F3	91
Corydon, In., U.S.	H5	91
Corydon, Ia., U.S.	D4	92
Corydon, Ky., U.S.	C2	94
Coryell, co., Tx., U.S.	D4	120
Cos see Kos, i., Grc.	D6	40
Cosalá, Mex.	C3	63
Cosamaloapan [de Carpio], Mex.	D5	63
Cosby, Mo., U.S.	A3	102
Cosby, Tn., U.S.	D10	119
Coscomatepec [de Bravo], Mex.	n15	63
Coseguina, Punta, c., Nic.	D4	62
Cosenza, Italy	E6	23
Coshocton, Oh., U.S.	B4	112
Coshocton, co., Oh., U.S.	B4	112
Cosmopolis, Wa., U.S.	C2	124
Cosmos, Mn., U.S.	F4	100
Cosne, Fr.	D5	16
Cossatot, stm., Ar., U.S.	C1	81
Cossatot Mountains, mtn., Ar., U.S.	C2	81
Cossonay, Switz.	C2	20
Costa Mesa, Ca., U.S.	n13	82
Costa Rica, ctry., N.A.	F6	62
Costello, Pa., U.S.	C5	115
Costelloe, Ire.	D2	11
Costigan, Me., U.S.	C4	96
Costilla, N.M., U.S.	A4	108
Costilla, co., Co., U.S.	D5	83
Coswig, E. Ger.	B8	19
Coswig, E. Ger.	B7	19
Cotabato, Phil.	D7	34
Cotagaita, Bol.	D2	55
Cotahuasi, Peru	E3	58
Coteau, N.D., U.S.	A3	111
Coteau-Landing, Que.	D3	74
Coteaux, Haiti	E6	64
Côte d'Or, reg., Fr.	D6	16
Côtes de Fer, Haiti	E7	64
Cotesfield, Ne., U.S.	C7	104
Cotija de la Paz, Mex.	n12	63
Cotingo, stm., Braz.	B2	59
Cotonou, Benin	E5	45
Cotopaxi, Co., U.S.	C5	83
Cotopaxi, prov., Ec.	B2	58
Cotopaxi, vol., Ec.	B2	58
Cotswold Hills, hills, Eng., U.K.		
Cottage Grove, Mn., U.S.	n13	100
Cottage Grove, Or., U.S.	D3	114
Cottage Grove, Tn., U.S.	A3	119
Cottage Grove Reservoir, res., Or., U.S.	D3	114
Cottageville, S.C., U.S.	F7	117
Cottageville, W.V., U.S.	C3	125
Cottam, Ont.	E2	73
Cottbus, E. Ger.	C7	18
Cottel Island, i., Newf.	D5	72
Cotter, Ar., U.S.	A3	81
Cottian Alps, mts., Eur.	E7	16
Cottle, co., Tx., U.S.	B2	120
Cottleville, Mo., U.S.	f12	102
Cotton, Ga., U.S.	E2	87
Cotton, Mn., U.S.	C6	100
Cotton, co., Ok., U.S.	C3	113
Cotton Center, Tx., U.S.	B1	120
Cottondale, Al., U.S.	B2	78
Cottondale, Fl., U.S.	B1	86
Cottonpatch Hill, De., U.S.	F5	85
Cotton Plant, Ar., U.S.	B4	81
Cottonport, La., U.S.	C3	95
Cottonton, Al., U.S.	C4	78
Cottontown, Tn., U.S.	A5	119
Cotton Valley, La., U.S.	B2	95
Cottonwood, Al., U.S.	D4	78
Cottonwood, Az., U.S.	C3	80
Cottonwood, Ca., U.S.	B2	82
Cottonwood, Id., U.S.	C2	89
Cottonwood, Mn., U.S.	F3	100
Cottonwood, co., Mn., U.S.	F3	100
Cottonwood, stm., Ks., U.S.	D7	93
Cottonwood, stm., Mn., U.S.	F3	100
Cottonwood Cove, Nv., U.S.	H7	105
Cottonwood Creek, stm., Wy., U.S.	D2	127
Cottonwood Creek, stm., Wy., U.S.	C4	127
Cottonwood Falls, Ks., U.S.	D7	93
Cottonwood Heights, Ut., U.S.	*C4	121
Cottonwood Wash, val., Ut., U.S.	F6	121
Cotuit, Ma., U.S.	C7	98
Cotulla, Tx., U.S.	E3	120
Couchiching, Lake, l., Ont.	C5	73
Couchwood, La., U.S.	B2	95
Coudekerque-Branche, Fr.	B5	16
Couderay, Wi., U.S.	C2	126
Coudersport, Pa., U.S.	C5	115
Coudres, Île aux, i., Que.	B7	74
Couëron, Fr.	D3	16
Cougar, Wa., U.S.	C3	124
Cougar Reservoir, res., Or., U.S.	C4	114
Coulee, N.D., U.S.	A3	111
Coulee City, Wa., U.S.	B6	124
Coulee Creek, stm., Wa., U.S.	g13	124
Coulee Dam, Wa., U.S.	B7	124
Coulee Dam National Recreation Area, Wa., U.S.	A7	124
Coulman Island, i., Ant.	B29	7
Coulommiers, Fr.	C5	16
Coulsdon (part of London), Eng., U.K.	m12	10
Coulter, Ia., U.S.	B4	92
Coulterville, Ca., U.S.	D3	82
Coulwood, Va., U.S.	f9	123
Counce, Tn., U.S.	B3	119
Council, Id., U.S.	E2	89
Council, N.C., U.S.	C4	110
Council Bluffs, Ia., U.S.	C2	92
Council Grove, Ks., U.S.	D7	93
Council Grove Lake, res., Ks., U.S.	D7	93
Council Mountain, mtn., Id., U.S.	E2	89
Country Club Hills, Il., U.S.	*k9	90
Country Homes, Wa., U.S.	B8	124
Countryside, Il., U.S.	*k9	90
Countyline, Ok., U.S.	C4	113
Coupar Angus, Scot., U.K.	B5	10
Coupeville, Wa., U.S.	A3	124
Coupon, Pa., U.S.	E4	115
Courantyne, stm., S.A.	A3	59
Courbevoie, Fr.	g10	16
Courcelles, Que.	D7	74
Courland Lagoon, b., Sov. Un.	D3	27
Courmayeur, Italy	D2	20
Coursan, Fr.	F5	16
Courtenay, B.C.	E5	69
Courtenay, N.D., U.S.	B7	111
Courte Oreilles, Lac, l., Wi., U.S.	C2	126
Courtland, Ont.	E4	73
Courtland, Al., U.S.	A2	78
Courtland, Ks., U.S.	C6	93
Courtland, Mn., U.S.	F4	100
Courtland, Ms., U.S.	A4	101
Courtland, Va., U.S.	D5	123
Courtmacsherry, Ire.	F3	11
Courtrai see Kortrijk, Bel.	B5	16
Courtright, Ont.	E2	73
Courval, Sask.	G2	75
Coushatta, La., U.S.	B2	95
Coutances, Fr.	C3	16
Coutras, Fr.	E3	16
Coutts, Alta.	E5	68
Couvin, Bel.	D4	17
Cove, Ar., U.S.	C1	81
Cove, Or., U.S.	B9	114
Cove City, N.C., U.S.	B5	110
Cove Creek, stm., Ut., U.S.	E3	121
Covedale, Oh., U.S.	o12	112
Cove Island, i., Ont.	B3	73
Covelo, Ca., U.S.	C2	82
Coventry, Ct., U.S.	B6	84
Coventry, Eng., U.K.	D6	10
Coventry, De., U.S.	*B3	85
Coventry, R.I., U.S.	D3	116
Coventry, Vt., U.S.	B4	122
Cove Point, Md., U.S.	D5	97
Coverdales Crossroads, De., U.S.		
Covert, Mi., U.S.	F4	99
Covesville, Va., U.S.	C4	123
Covina, Ca., U.S.	m13	82
Covington, Ga., U.S.	C3	87
Covington, In., U.S.	D3	91
Covington, Ky., U.S.	A5	94
Covington, La., U.S.	D5	95
Covington, Mi., U.S.	B2	99
Covington, Oh., U.S.	B1	112
Covington, Ok., U.S.	A4	113
Covington, Tn., U.S.	B2	119
Covington, Va., U.S.	C2	123
Covington, co., Al., U.S.	D3	78
Covington, co., Ms., U.S.	D4	101
Cowal, Lake, l., Austl.	F6	51
Cowan, In., U.S.	D7	91
Cowan, Tn., U.S.	B5	119
Cowan, stm., Sask.	C2	75
Cowan, Lake, l., Austl.	F3	50
Cowangie, Austl.	G3	51
Cowan Knob, mtn., Ar., U.S.	B2	81
Cowansville, Que.	D5	74
Cowansville, Pa., U.S.	E2	115
Coward, S.C., U.S.	D8	117
Cowarts, Al., U.S.	D4	78
Cowden, Il., U.S.	D5	90
Cowdenbeath, Scot., U.K.	B5	13
Cowdrey, Co., U.S.	A4	83
Cowee Mountains, mts., N.C., U.S.	f9	110
Cowen, W.V., U.S.	C4	125
Cowen, Mount, mtn., Mt., U.S.	E6	103
Coweta, Ok., U.S.	B6	113
Coweta, co., Ga., U.S.	C2	87
Cowgill, Mo., U.S.	B4	102
Cow Head, Newf.	D3	72
Cowiche, Wa., U.S.	C5	124
Cowichan Bay, B.C.	g12	69
Cowichan Lake, l., B.C.	E5	69
Cow Knob, mtn., W.V., U.S.	C5	125
Cow Lakes, l., Or., U.S.	D9	114
Cowles, Ne., U.S.	D7	104
Cowley, Alta.	E3	68
Cowley, Wy., U.S.	B4	127
Cowley, co., Ks., U.S.	E7	93
Cowley, Az., U.S.	F4	80
Cowling, Il., U.S.	E6	90
Cowlington, Ok., U.S.	B7	113
Cowlitz, co., Wa., U.S.	C3	124
Cowlitz, stm., Wa., U.S.	C3	124
Cowpasture, stm., Va., U.S.	B3	123
Cowpen Mountain, mtn., Ga., U.S.	B2	87
Cowpens, S.C., U.S.	A4	117
Cowra, Austl.	F7	51
Cowskin Creek, stm., Ks., U.S.	g11	93
Cow Springs, Az., U.S.	A5	80
Coxburg, Ms., U.S.	B3	101
Coxim, Braz.	B2	56
Coxipi, stm., Can.	C2	72
Coxsackie, N.Y., U.S.	C7	109
Cox's Cove, Newf.	D3	72
Coxs Mills, W.V., U.S.	B4	125
Coy, Al., U.S.	C2	78
Coy, Ar., U.S.	C4	81
Coyame, Mex.	B3	63
Coyanosa Draw, val., Tx., U.S.	D1	120
Coya Sur, Chile	A3	54
Coyle, Ok., U.S.	B4	113
Coyoacán (part of Mexico City), Mex.	h9	63
Coyote, N.M., U.S.	A3	108
Coyote Basin, Co., U.S.	A2	83
Coyuca de Catalán, Mex.	*E8	93
Cozad, Ne., U.S.	D6	104
Cozahome, Ar., U.S.	A3	81
Cozumel, Mex.	C7	63
Cozumel, Isla de, i., Mex.	C7	63
Crab Creek, stm., Wa., U.S.	B7	124
Crab Creek, stm., Wa., U.S.	C6	124
Crab Orchard, Ky., U.S.	C5	94
Crab Orchard, Ne., U.S.	D9	104
Crab Orchard, Tn., U.S.	D9	119
Crab Orchard, W.V., U.S.	n13	125
Crab Orchard Lake, res., Il., U.S.	F4	90
Crab Orchard Mountains, mts., Tn., U.S.	D9	119
Crabtree, Or., U.S.	C4	114
Crabtree, Pa., U.S.	F3	115
Crabtree Mills, Que.	D4	74
Cracking, stm., Sask.	D4	75
Cracow, Austl.	D8	51
Cradock, S. Afr.	D4	49
Crafton, Pa., U.S.	k13	115
Craftsbury Common, Vt., U.S.	B4	122
Cragford, Al., U.S.	B4	78
Craig, Ak., U.S.	D13	79
Craig, Co., U.S.	A3	83
Craig, Ia., U.S.	B1	92
Craig, Mo., U.S.	A2	102
Craig, Ne., U.S.	C9	104
Craig, co., Ok., U.S.	A6	113
Craig, co., Va., U.S.	C2	123
Craig Air Force Base, mil., Al., U.S.	C3	78
Craigellachie, B.C.	D8	69
Craighead, co., Ar., U.S.	B5	81
Craighouse, Scot., U.K.	B5	13
Craighurst, Ont.	C5	73
Craigmont, Id., U.S.	C2	89
Craigmyle, Alta.	D4	68
Craigsville, Va., U.S.	B3	123
Craigsville, W.V., U.S.	C4	125
Craigville, In., U.S.	C7	91
Craik, Sask.	F3	75
Crail, Scot., U.K.	D6	13
Crailsheim, W. Ger.	D5	18
Craiova, Rom.	C6	24
Cramerton, N.C., U.S.	B1	110
Cranberry, Pa., U.S.	D2	115
Cranberry Isles, Me., U.S.	D4	96
Cranberry Lake, N.Y., U.S.	A6	109
Cranberry Lake, l., N.Y., U.S.	A6	109
Cranberry Portage, Man.	B1	70
Cranbrook, B.C.	E10	69
Cranbury, N.J., U.S.	C3	107
Crandall, Ga., U.S.	B2	87
Crandall, S.D., U.S.	B8	118
Crandall, Tx., U.S.	n10	120
Crandon, Wi., U.S.	C5	126
Crane, Az., U.S.	E1	80
Crane, In., U.S.	G4	91
Crane, Mo., U.S.	E4	102
Crane, Or., U.S.	D8	114
Crane, Tx., U.S.	D1	120
Crane, co., Tx., U.S.	D1	120
Crane Creek, stm., Oh., U.S.	e7	112
Crane Creek Reservoir, res., Id., U.S.	E2	89
Crane Hill, Al., U.S.	A2	78
Crane Lake, Mn., U.S.	B6	100
Crane Lake, l., Sask.	G1	75
Crane Lake, l., Il., U.S.	C3	90
Crane Lake, l., Mn., U.S.	B6	100
Crane Mountain, mtn., Or., U.S.	E6	114
Crane Prairie Reservoir, res., Or., U.S.	D5	114
Cranesville, Pa., U.S.	C1	115
Crane Valley, Sask.	H3	75
Cranfield, Ms., U.S.	D2	101
Cranford, N.J., U.S.	B4	107
Cransac, Fr.	E5	16
Cranston, R.I., U.S.	C5	116
Crapaud, P.E.I.	C6	71
Crapo, Md., U.S.	D5	97
Crary, N.D., U.S.	A7	111
Crary Mountains, mts., Ant.	B1	7
Craryville, N.Y., U.S.	C7	109
Crasna, stm., Eur.	B6	24
Crater Lake, Or., U.S.	E4	114
Crater Lake, l., St. Vin.	U26	65
Crater Lake National Park, Or., U.S.	E4	114
Craters of the Moon National Monument, Id., U.S.	F5	89
Cratéus, Braz.	C2	57
Crato, Braz.	C3	57
Craughwell, Ire.	D3	11
Craven, Sask.	G3	75
Craven, co., N.C., U.S.	B5	110
Crawford, Co., U.S.	C3	83
Crawford, Ga., U.S.	C3	87
Crawford, Ms., U.S.	B5	101
Crawford, Ne., U.S.	B2	104
Crawford, Tn., U.S.	C8	119
Crawford, co., Ar., U.S.	B1	81
Crawford, co., Ga., U.S.	D3	87
Crawford, co., Il., U.S.	D6	90
Crawford, co., In., U.S.	H4	91
Crawford, co., Ia., U.S.	B2	92
Crawford, co., Ks., U.S.	E9	93
Crawford, co., Mi., U.S.	D6	99
Crawford, co., Mo., U.S.	D6	102
Crawford, co., Oh., U.S.	B3	112
Crawford, co., Pa., U.S.	C1	115
Crawford, co., Wi., U.S.	E3	126
Crawford Bay, B.C.	E9	69
Crawford Lake, l., Me., U.S.	C5	96
Crawford Notch, N.H., U.S.	B4	106
Crawford Notch State Park, N.H., U.S.	B4	106
Crawfordsville, Ar., U.S.	B5	81
Crawfordsville, In., U.S.	D4	91
Crawfordsville, Or., U.S.	C4	114
Crawfordville, Fl., U.S.	B2	86
Crawfordville, Ga., U.S.	C4	87
Crawley, Eng., U.K.	C7	12
Crayne, Ky., U.S.	e9	94
Crazy Mountains, mts., Mt., U.S.	D6	103
Crazy Peak, mtn., Mt., U.S.	D6	103
Crazy Woman Creek, stm., Wy., U.S.	B6	127
Creal Springs, Il., U.S.	F5	90
Creamridge, N.J., U.S.	C3	107
Crean Lake, l., Sask.	C2	75
Crediton, Eng., U.K.	K9	12
Cree, stm., Sask.	E11	66
Creedmoor, N.C., U.S.	A4	110
Creekside, Pa., U.S.	E3	115
Cree Lake, l., Sask.	E11	66
Creelman, Sask.	H4	75
Creemore, Ont.	C4	73
Cregganbaun, Ire.	B2	11
Creighton, Sask.	C5	75
Creighton, Mo., U.S.	C3	102
Creighton, Ne., U.S.	B8	104
Creighton, Pa., U.S.	h14	115
Creighton, S.D., U.S.	C3	118
Creil, Fr.	C5	16
Crellin, Md., U.S.	m12	97
Crema, Italy	B2	23
Cremona, Alta.	D3	68
Cremona, Italy	B3	23
Crenshaw, Ms., U.S.	A3	101
Crenshaw, co., Al., U.S.	D3	78
Creola, Al., U.S.	E1	78
Creole, La., U.S.	E2	95
Crépy-en-Valois, Fr.	E2	17
Cres, i., Yugo.	C2	24
Cresaptown, Md., U.S.	k13	97
Cresbard, S.D., U.S.	B7	118
Crescent, Ga., U.S.	E5	87
Crescent, Ia., U.S.	C2	92
Crescent, Mo., U.S.	f12	102
Crescent, Ok., U.S.	B4	113
Crescent, Or., U.S.	D5	114
Crescent, Lake, l., Wa., U.S.	A2	124
Crescent City, Ca., U.S.	B1	82
Crescent City, Fl., U.S.	C5	86
Crescent City, Il., U.S.	C6	90
Crescent Lake, l., Fl., U.S.	C5	86
Crescent Lake, l., Or., U.S.	D5	114
Crescent Mills, Ca., U.S.	B3	82
Crescent Range, mtn., N.H., U.S.	B4	106
Crescent Springs, Ky., U.S.	h13	94
Crescent Spur, B.C.	C7	69
Cresco, Ia., U.S.	A5	92
Cresco, Pa., U.S.	D11	115
Crespo, Arg.	A4	54
Cresskill, N.J., U.S.	h9	107
Cresson, Pa., U.S.	F4	115
Cresson, Tx., U.S.	n9	120
Cressona, Pa., U.S.	E9	115
Crest, Fr.	E6	16
Cresta, Switz.	D8	21
Crested Butte, Co., U.S.	C4	83
Cresthaven, Fl., U.S.	*F6	86
Crest Hill, Il., U.S.	k8	90
Crestline, Ca., U.S.	*E5	82
Crestline, Oh., U.S.	B3	112
Creston, B.C.	E9	69
Creston, Newf.	E4	72
Creston, Il., U.S.	B5	90
Creston, Ia., U.S.	C3	92
Creston, La., U.S.	C2	95
Creston, Mt., U.S.	B2	103
Creston, Ne., U.S.	C8	104
Creston, Oh., U.S.	B4	112
Creston, S.C., U.S.	D6	117
Creston, Tn., U.S.	C8	119
Creston, Wa., U.S.	B7	124
Creston, W.V., U.S.	C3	125
Creston, Wy., U.S.	E5	127
Crestone, Co., U.S.	D5	83
Crestone Peak, mtn., Co., U.S.	D5	83
Crestview, Fl., U.S.	u15	86
Crestview, Hi., U.S.	g10	88
Crestwood, Il., U.S.	*k9	90
Crestwood, Ky., U.S.	B4	94
Crestwood, Mo., U.S.	*f13	102
Crestwood Village, N.J., U.S.	D4	107
Crestwynd, Sask.	G3	75
Creswell, N.C., U.S.	B6	110
Creswell, Or., U.S.	D3	114
Crete, Il., U.S.	B6	90
Crete, Ne., U.S.	D9	104
Crete, N.D., U.S.	C8	111
Crete, i., Grc.	E5	40
Crete, Sea of, Grc.	D5	40
Créteil, Fr.	g10	16
Cretone, Italy	g9	23
Creus, Cape, c., Spain	A7	22
Creuse, Fr.	C7	16
Creutzwald, Fr.	C7	16
Crevasse Valley Glacier, ice, Ant.	B34	7
Creve Coeur, Il., U.S.	C4	90
Creve Coeur, Mo., U.S.	*f13	102
Crèvecoeur-le-Grand, Fr.	E2	17
Crevillente, Spain	D5	10
Crewe, Eng., U.K.	D5	12
Crewe, Va., U.S.	C4	123
Crewkerne, Eng., U.K.	D5	12
Criciúma, Braz.	D3	56
Cricket, N.C., U.S.	A1	110
Cricket Mountains, mts., Ut., U.S.	E3	121
Cridersville, Oh., U.S.	B1	112
Crieff, Scot., U.K.	B5	10
Criffell, mtn., Scot., U.K.	F5	13
Criglersville, Va., U.S.	B4	123
Crikvenica, Yugo.	C2	24
Crimea, pen., Sov. Un.	E6	29
Crimmitschau, E. Ger.	C7	18
Crimson Lake Provincial Park, Alta.	C3	68
Crinan, Scot., U.K.	D3	13
Cripple Creek, Co., U.S.	C5	83
Cripple Creek, Va., U.S.	D1	123
Crișana-Maramureș, hist. reg., Rom.	B6	24
Crisfield, Md., U.S.	E6	97
Crisp, co., Ga., U.S.	E3	87
Criss Creek, B.C.	D7	69
Crissolo, Italy	D1	23
Cristal, Monts de, mts., Gabon	A2	46
Cristalina, Braz.	B3	56
Cristóbal, Pan.	k11	62
Cristóbal Colón, Pico, mtn., Col.	A3	60
Criș Alb, stm., Eur.	B5	24
Crittenden, Ky., U.S.	B5	94
Crittenden, co., Ar., U.S.	B5	81
Crittenden, co., Ky., U.S.	e9	94
Crivitz, E. Ger.	E5	15
Crivitz, Wi., U.S.	C6	126
Crna, stm., Yugo.	C2	24
Crnomelj, Yugo.	C2	24
Croatia, hist. reg., Yugo.	C2	24
Croche, stm., Que.	A5	74
Crocheron, Md., U.S.	D5	97
Crocker, Mo., U.S.	D5	102
Crocker, S.D., U.S.	B8	118
Crockett, Ca., U.S.	g8	82
Crockett, Tx., U.S.	D5	120
Crockett, co., Tn., U.S.	B2	119
Crockett, co., Tx., U.S.	D2	120
Crockett Mills, Tn., U.S.	B2	119
Crocketts Bluff, Ar., U.S.	C4	81
Crocketville, S.C., U.S.	F5	117
Crofton, Ky., U.S.	C2	94
Crofton, Md., U.S.	B4	97
Crofton, Ne., U.S.	B8	104
Croghan, N.Y., U.S.	B5	109

Name	Map Ref.	Page
Croghan Mountain, mtn., Ire..	E5	11
Crohy Head, c., Ire.	C3	11
Croix, Fr.	D3	17
Croix, Lac la, l., Mn., U.S.	B6	100
Croker, i., Austl.	B5	50
Croker, Cape, c., Ont.	C4	73
Cromarty, Scot., U.K.	B4	10
Cromer, Man.	E1	70
Cromer, Eng., U.K.	B9	12
Cromona, Ky., U.S.	C7	94
Cromwell, N.Z.	P12	51
Cromwell, Al., U.S.	C1	78
Cromwell, Ct., U.S.	C5	84
Cromwell, In., U.S.	B6	91
Cromwell, Ia., U.S.	C3	92
Cromwell, Ky., U.S.	C3	94
Cromwell, Mn., U.S.	D6	100
Cromwell, Ok., U.S.	B5	113
Crook, Eng., U.K.	F7	13
Crook, Co., U.S.	A8	83
Crook, co., Or., U.S.	C6	114
Crook, co., Wy., U.S.	B8	127
Crooked, stm., B.C.	B6	69
Crooked, stm., Or., U.S.	C6	114
Crooked Creek, Ak., U.S.	C8	79
Crooked Creek, stm., U.S.	E3	93
Crooked Creek, stm., Ar., U.S.	A3	81
Crooked Creek, stm., In., U.S.	k10	91
Crooked Creek, stm., Pa., U.S.	C7	115
Crooked Creek Lake, res., Pa., U.S.	E3	115
Crooked Island, i., Bah.	C6	64
Crooked Island Passage, strt., Bah.	C6	64
Crooked Lake, l., Newf.	D3	72
Crooked Lake, l., Sask.	G4	75
Crooked Lake, l., Fl., U.S.	E5	86
Crooked Lake, l., Mn., U.S.	B7	100
Crooked River, Sask.	E4	75
Crooks, S.D., U.S.	D9	118
Crooks Lake, l., Nv., U.S.	B2	105
Crookston, Mn., U.S.	C2	100
Crookston, Ne., U.S.	B5	104
Crookstown, Ire.	F3	11
Crooksville, Oh., U.S.	C3	112
Crookwell, Austl.	G7	51
Croom, Ire.	E3	11
Cropper, Ky., U.S.	B4	94
Cropsey, Il., U.S.	C5	90
Croque Harbour, b., Newf.	C4	72
Crosby, Mn., U.S.	D5	100
Crosby, Ms., U.S.	D2	101
Crosby, N.D., U.S.	A2	111
Crosby, Tx., U.S.	r14	120
Crosby, co., Tx., U.S.	C2	120
Crosby, Mount, mtn., Wy., U.S.	C3	127
Crosbyton, Tx., U.S.	C2	120
Crosland, Ga., U.S.	E3	87
Cross, S.C., U.S.	E7	117
Cross, co., Ar., U.S.	B5	81
Cross, stm., Afr.	H8	42
Cross, Cape, c., Nmb.	B1	49
Cross Anchor, S.C., U.S.	B4	117
Cross Bay, b., Man.	C2	70
Crossbost, Scot., U.K.	B2	13
Cross City, Fl., U.S.	C3	86
Cross Creek, N.B.	C3	71
Cross Creek, stm., W.V., U.S.	f8	125
Crossett, Ar., U.S.	D4	81
Cross Fell, mtn., Eng., U.K..	F6	13
Crossfield, Alta.	D3	68
Crosshaven, Ire.	F3	11
Cross Hill, S.C., U.S.	C4	117
Cross Island, i., Me., U.S.	D5	96
Cross Keys, N.J., U.S.	D2	107
Cross Lake, Man.	B3	70
Crosslake, Mn., U.S.	D4	100
Cross Lake, l., Man.	B3	70
Cross Lake, res., La., U.S.	B2	95
Cross Lanes, W.V., U.S.	C3	125
Crossman Peak, mtn., Az., U.S.	C1	80
Cross Mill, N.C., U.S.	f10	110
Crossmolina, Ire.	C2	11
Cross Mountains, mtn., Ar., U.S.	C1	81
Cross Plains, In., U.S.	G7	91
Cross Plains, Tn., U.S.	A5	119
Cross Plains, Tx., U.S.	C3	120
Cross Plains, Wi., U.S.	E4	126
Crossroads, N.M., U.S.	D6	108
Cross Roads Ohio, N.S.	D7	71
Crosstown, Mo., U.S.	D8	102
Cross Village, Mi., U.S.	C5	99
Crossville, Al., U.S.	A4	78
Crossville, Il., U.S.	E5	90
Crossville, Tn., U.S.	D8	119
Crosswicks, N.J., U.S.	C3	107
Croswell, Mi., U.S.	E8	99
Crothersville, In., U.S.	G6	91
Croton, Ia., U.S.	D6	92
Croton, N.J., U.S.	B3	107
Croton, Oh., U.S.	B3	112
Crotone (Croton), Italy	E6	23
Croton-on-Hudson, N.Y., U.S.	D7	109
Crottendorf, E. Ger.	C7	19
Crouch, Id., U.S.	E3	89
Crouse, N.C., U.S.	B1	110
Crouseville, Me., U.S.	B4	96
Crow, stm., Mn., U.S.	F4	100
Crow, North Fork, stm., Mn., U.S.	E4	100
Crow Agency, Mt., U.S.	E9	103
Crow Creek, stm., U.S.	A6	83
Crow Creek Indian Reservation, S.D., U.S.	C6	118
Crowder, Ms., U.S.	A3	101
Crowder, Ok., U.S.	B6	113
Crowduck Lake, l., Man.	D4	70
Crowell, Tx., U.S.	C3	120
Crowheart, Wy., U.S.	C3	127
Crow Indian Reservation, Mt., U.S.	E9	103
Crowley, Co., U.S.	C7	83
Crowley, La., U.S.	D3	95
Crowley, Tx., U.S.	n9	120
Crowley, co., Co., U.S.	C7	83
Crowley, Lake, res., Ca., U.S.	D4	82
Crowleys Ridge, mtn., U.S.	B5	81
Crown City, Oh., U.S.	D3	112
Crown King, Az., U.S.	C3	80
Crown Point, In., U.S.	B3	91
Crown Point, La., U.S.	k11	95
Crownpoint, N.M., U.S.	B1	108
Cruglieri, Italy	D2	23
Crow Peak, mtn., Mt., U.S.	D5	103
Crowsnest, B.C.	E10	69
Crowsnest Pass, Alta.	E3	68
Crowsnest Pass, Can.	E3	68
Crows Nest Peak, mtn., S.D., U.S.	C2	118
Crowville, La., U.S.	B4	95
Cuillin Hills, hills, Scot., U.K. .	B1	13
Crow Wing, co., Mn., U.S.	D4	100
Crow Wing, stm., Mn., U.S.	D4	100
Croydon, Austl.	C7	50
Croydon (part of London), Eng., U.K.	E6	10
Croydon, N.H., U.S.	D2	106
Croydon, Pa., U.S.	F12	115
Croydon, Ut., U.S.	B4	121
Croydon Flat, N.H., U.S.	D2	106
Croydon Peak, mtn., N.H., U.S.	D2	106
Crozet, Va., U.S.	B4	123
Crozet, Îles, is., F.S.A.T.	J24	2
Crozier, Va., U.S.	C5	123
Crozon, Fr.	C1	16
Cruachan, Ben, mtn., Scot., U.K.	D3	13
Cruagh Island, i., Ire.	D1	11
Crucero, Peru	D3	58
Cruces, Cuba	C3	64
Cruces, Punta, c., Col.	B2	60
Crucible, Pa., U.S.	G1	115
Cruden Bay, Scot., U.K.	B6	10
Cruger, Ms., U.S.	B3	101
Crum, W.V., U.S.	D2	125
Crumlin, N. Ire., U.K.	C5	11
Crummock Water, l., Eng., U.K.	F5	13
Crump Lake, l., Or., U.S.	E7	114
Crumpton, Md., U.S.	B6	97
Crumrod, Ar., U.S.	C5	81
Crumstown, In., U.S.	A5	91
Cruseilles, Fr.	C2	20
Crusheen, Ire.	E3	11
Cruso, N.C., U.S.	f10	110
Crutwell, Sask.	D2	75
Cruz, Cabo, c., Cuba	E5	64
Cruz Alta, Arg.	A4	54
Cruz Alta, Braz.	D2	56
Cruz Bay, V.I.U.S.	B6	65
Cruz del Eje, Arg.	A4	54
Cruzeiro, Braz.	C4	56
Cruzeiro do Oeste, Braz.	C2	56
Cruzeiro do Sul, Braz.	C3	58
Cruz Grande, Chile	E1	55
Crysler, Ont.	B9	73
Crystal, Mi., U.S.	E6	99
Crystal, Mn., U.S.	m12	100
Crystal, N.D., U.S.	A8	111
Crystal, stm., Co., U.S.	B3	83
Crystal Bay, b., Fl., U.S.	D4	86
Crystal Beach, Fl., U.S.	D4	86
Crystal City, Man.	E2	70
Crystal City, Mo., U.S.	C7	102
Crystal City, Tx., U.S.	E3	120
Crystal Falls, Mi., U.S.	B2	99
Crystal Hill, Va., U.S.	D4	123
Crystal Lake, Ct., U.S.	B6	84
Crystal Lake, Fl., U.S.	u16	86
Crystal Lake, Il., U.S.	A5	90
Crystal Lake, l., Ct., U.S.	B6	84
Crystal Lake, l., Ia., U.S.	A4	92
Crystal Lake, l., Mi., U.S.	D4	99
Crystal Lake, l., N.H., U.S.	D4	106
Crystal Lake, l., Vt., U.S.	B4	122
Crystal Lawns, Il., U.S.	k8	90
Crystal Manor, Il., U.S.	k8	90
Crystal Mountain, mtn., N.H., U.S.	g7	106
Crystal Pond, res., Ct., U.S.	B7	84
Crystal River, Fl., U.S.	D4	86
Crystal Springs, Sask.	E3	75
Crystal Springs, Ar., U.S.	C2	81
Crystal Springs, Fl., U.S.	D4	86
Crystal Springs, Ms., U.S.	D3	101
Crystal Springs, N.D., U.S.	C6	111
Crystal Valley, Mi., U.S.	E4	99
Csongrád, Hung.	B5	24
Csorna, Hung.	B3	24
Cuajone, Peru	G4	58
Cuamba, Moz.	D6	48
Cuando, stm., Afr.	H8	42
Cuando Cubango, dept., Ang.	E3	48
Cuangar, Ang.	E3	48
Cuango, Ang.	C2	48
Cuango (Kwango), stm., Afr.	C2	48
Cuanza, stm., Ang.	C2	48
Cuanza-Norte, dept., Ang.	A5	119
Cuanza-Sul, dept., Ang.	D1	48
Cuarto, stm., Arg.	A4	54
Cuauhtémoc, Mex.	B3	63
Cuauhtepec (part of Mexico City), Mex.	g9	63
Cuautla [Morelos], Mex.	n14	63
Cuba, Port.	C2	22
Cuba, Al., U.S.	C1	78
Cuba, Il., U.S.	C3	90
Cuba, Ks., U.S.	C6	93
Cuba, Mo., U.S.	C6	102
Cuba, N.M., U.S.	A3	108
Cuba, N.Y., U.S.	C2	109
Cuba, Oh., U.S.	C2	112
Cuba, ctry., N.A.	C4	64
Cuba City, Wi., U.S.	F3	126
Cubal, Ang.	D1	48
Cuballing, Austl.	D2	108
Cubango, stm., Afr.	E3	48
Cub Run, Ky., U.S.	C4	94
Cucamonga, Ca., U.S.	*m13	82
Cuchara, stm., Co., U.S.	D5	83
Cucharas, stm., Co., U.S.	D5	83
Cuchillo, N.M., U.S.	D2	108
Cuchivero, stm., Ven.	B4	60
Cucuí, Braz.	A3	60
Cúcuta, Col.	B3	60
Cudahy, Ca., U.S.	*E4	82
Cudahy, Wi., U.S.	F6	126
Cuddalore, India	F6	36
Cuddapah, India	F6	36
Cuddy Mountain, mtn., Id., U.S.	E2	89
Cudgewa, Austl.	H6	51
Cudworth, Sask.	E3	75
Cue, Austl.	E2	50
Cuéllar, Spain	B3	22
Cuenca, Ec.	D3	60
Cuenca, Spain	B4	22
Cuenca, Sierra de, mts., Spain	B4	22
Cuencamé [de Ceniceros], Mex.	C4	63
Cuernavaca, Mex.	D5	63
Cuero, Tx., U.S.	E4	120
Cuervo, N.M., U.S.	B5	108
Cuetzalan, Mex.	m15	63
Cuevas, Ms., U.S.	f7	101
Cuevas [del Almanzora], Spain	D3	23
Cuglieri, Italy	D2	23
Cuiabá, Braz.	B1	56
Cuiabá, stm., Braz.	B1	56
Cuicas, Ven.	B3	60
Cuicatlán, Mex.	o15	63
Cuilapa, Guat.	C2	62
Cuilcagh, mtn., Eur.	C4	11
Cuilco, Guat.	C2	62
Cuillin Hills, hills, Scot., U.K.	B1	13
Cuimba, Ang.	C1	48
Cuipo, Pan.	k10	62
Cuíto, stm., Ang.	E2	48
Cuito-Cuanavale, Ang.	E2	48
Cuitzeo, Lago de, l., Mex.	n13	63
Cuiuni, stm., Braz.	C2	59
Cuivre, West Fork, stm., Mo., U.S.	B6	102
Culberson, co., Tx., U.S.	o12	120
Culbertson, Mt., U.S.	B12	103
Culbertson, Ne., U.S.	D5	104
Culcairn, Austl.	G6	51
Culdaff Bay, b., Ire.	B4	11
Culdesac, Id., U.S.	C2	89
Culebra, P.R.	B5	65
Culebra, Isla de, i., P.R.	G12	64
Culebra Peak, mtn., Co., U.S.	D5	83
Culgoa, stm., Austl.	E8	50
Culhuacán (part of Mexico City), Mex.	h9	63
Culiacán, Mex.	C3	63
Cúllar de Baza, Spain	D4	22
Cullen, Scot., U.K.	C6	13
Cullen, La., U.S.	B2	95
Culleoka, Tn., U.S.	B5	119
Cullera, Spain	C5	22
Cullison, Ks., U.S.	E5	93
Cullman, Al., U.S.	A3	78
Cullman, co., Al., U.S.	A3	78
Culloden, Ga., U.S.	D2	87
Culloden, W.V., U.S.	C2	125
Cullom, Il., U.S.	C5	90
Cullowhee, N.C., U.S.	f9	110
Culoz, Fr.	D1	20
Culp Creek, Or., U.S.	D4	114
Culpeper, Va., U.S.	B5	123
Culpeper, co., Va., U.S.	B5	123
Cultus Lake, B.C.	f14	69
Culuene, stm., Braz.	A2	56
Culver, In., U.S.	B5	91
Culver, Ks., U.S.	D6	93
Culver, Mn., U.S.	D6	100
Culver, Or., U.S.	C5	114
Culver, Point, c., Austl.	F3	50
Culver City, Ca., U.S.	m12	82
Culvers Lake, l., N.J., U.S.	A3	107
Culverton, Ga., U.S.	C4	87
Culzean Bay, b., Scot., U.K.	E4	13
Cumaná, Ven.	A5	60
Cumbal, Nevado de, mtn., Col.	C2	60
Cumberland, B.C.	E5	69
Cumberland, Ont.	g13	73
Cumberland, Ia., U.S.	D7	94
Cumberland, Ky., U.S.	k13	97
Cumberland, Md., U.S.	E3	107
Cumberland, N.J., U.S.	C4	112
Cumberland, Oh., U.S.	C4	123
Cumberland, Va., U.S.	C5	113
Cumberland, Wa., U.S.	f12	124
Cumberland, Wi., U.S.	C1	126
Cumberland, co., N.S.	D5	71
Cumberland, co., Il., U.S.	D5	90
Cumberland, co., Ky., U.S.	D4	94
Cumberland, co., Me., U.S.	E2	96
Cumberland, co., N.J., U.S.	E2	107
Cumberland, co., N.C., U.S.	B4	110
Cumberland, co., Pa., U.S.	F7	115
Cumberland, co., Tn., U.S.	D8	119
Cumberland, co., Va., U.S.	C4	123
Cumberland, stm., U.S.	C11	76
Cumberland, Lake, res., Ky., U.S.	D5	94
Cumberland, South Fork, stm., U.S.	D5	94
Cumberland Center, Me., U.S.	g7	96
Cumberland City, Tn., U.S.	A4	119
Cumberland Foreside, Me., U.S.	E2	96
Cumberland Furnace, Tn., U.S.	A4	119
Cumberland Gap, Tn., U.S.	C10	119
Cumberland Gap, U.S.	D6	94
Cumberland Gap National Historical Park, U.S.	D6	94
Cumberland Hill, R.I., U.S.	B4	116
Cumberland House, Sask.	D4	75
Cumberland Island National Seashore, Ga., U.S.	F5	87
Cumberland Lake, l., Sask.	C4	75
Cumberland Mountain, mtn., Tn., U.S.	C9	119
Cumberland Peninsula, pen., N.W. Ter.	C20	66
Cumberland Plateau, plat., U.S.	D8	119
Cumberland Sound, strt., N.W. Ter.	C19	66
Cumbernauld, Scot., U.K.	*E5	13
Cumbres Pass, Co., U.S.	D4	83
Cumbria, co., Eng., U.K.	F6	13
Cuming, co., Ne., U.S.	C9	104
Cumming, Ga., U.S.	B2	87
Cumming, Ia., U.S.	f8	92
Cummings, N.D., U.S.	B8	111
Cummington, Ma., U.S.	B2	98
Cumnock, N.C., U.S.	B3	110
Cumnock [and Holmhead], Scot., U.K.	E4	13
Cumpas, Mex.	A3	63
Cumra, Tur.	D9	40
Cunard, W.V., U.S.	m13	125
Cunco, Chile	B2	54
Cuncumén, Chile	A2	54
Cundiff, Ky., U.S.	D4	94
Cundinamarca, dept., Col.	C6	34
Cundiyo, N.M., U.S.	*B4	108
Cunene, dept., Ang.	g8	94
Cunene, stm., Afr.	E1	48
Cuneo, Italy	B1	23
Cuney, Tx., U.S.	C5	120
Cunnamulla, Austl.	E8	50
Cunningham, Ks., U.S.	E5	93
Cunningham, Tn., U.S.	f9	94
Cupar, Sask.	G3	75
Cupar, Scot., U.K.	D5	13
Cupertino, Ca., U.S.	*k8	82
Curaçá, Braz.	E11	57
Curaçao, i., Neth. Ant.	H18	65
Curacautin, Chile	B2	54
Curacó, stm., Arg.	B3	54
Curanilahue, Chile	B2	54
Curaray, stm., S.A.	C3	58
Curcubáta, mtn., Rom.	B6	24
Curdsville, Ky., U.S.	C2	94
Curecanti National Recreation Area, Co., U.S.	C3	83
Curepto, Chile	B2	54
Curiapo, Ven.	B5	60
Curicuriari, stm., Braz.	D6	60
Curicó, Chile	A2	54
Curimatáu, stm., Braz.	h6	57
Curitiba, Braz.	D2	56
Curitibanos, Braz.	D2	56
Curlew, Ia., U.S.	B3	92
Curlew, Wa., U.S.	A7	124
Curlew Creek, stm., Wa., U.S.	A7	124
Curlew Lake, l., Wa., U.S.	A7	124
Curllsville, Pa., U.S.	C2	115
Currais Novos, Braz.	C3	57
Curralinho, Braz.	C5	59
Curran, Ont.	B10	73
Curran, Mi., U.S.	D7	99
Currans, Ire.	E2	11
Currant, Nv., U.S.	*D7	105
Currant Creek, stm., Co., U.S.	C5	83
Currant Mountain, mtn., Nv., U.S.	E6	105
Current, stm., U.S.	A5	81
Currie, Mn., U.S.	F3	100
Currie, Nv., U.S.	A6	110
Currituck, N.C., U.S.	A6	110
Currituck, co., N.C., U.S.	A6	110
Curry, co., N.M., U.S.	C6	108
Curry, co., Or., U.S.	E2	114
Curryville, Mo., U.S.	B6	102
Curtea-de-Argeş, Rom.	C7	24
Curtici, Rom.	B5	24
Curtin, Or., U.S.	D3	114
Curtis, Ar., U.S.	D2	81
Curtis, Mi., U.S.	B5	99
Curtis, Ne., U.S.	D5	104
Curtiss, Wi., U.S.	D3	126
Curtis, i., Austl.	E2	115
Curuá, stm., Braz.	C4	59
Curuá, stm., Braz.	D4	59
Curuá do Sul, stm., Braz.	C4	59
Curuçá, Braz.	B1	57
Curuçá, stm., Braz.	C3	58
Curug, Yugo.	C5	24
Curuguaty, Para.	D4	55
Curumiguara, Ponta, c., Braz.	B3	57
Curundu, Pan.	m11	62
Curupira, Sierra de, mts., S.A.	C5	60
Curuzú Cuatiá, Arg.	E4	55
Curvelo, Braz.	B4	56
Curvër, mtn., Switz.	C8	21
Curwensville, Pa., U.S.	E4	115
Curwensville Lake, res., Pa., U.S.	E4	115
Curwood, Mount, mtn., Mi., U.S.	B2	99
Cusco see Cuzco, Peru	A8	124
Cushendall, N. Ire., U.K.	B5	11
Cushing, Ia., U.S.	B2	92
Cushing, Ne., U.S.	C7	104
Cushing, Ok., U.S.	B5	113
Cushing, Tx., U.S.	D5	120
Cushman, Ar., U.S.	B4	81
Cushman, Ma., U.S.	B2	98
Cushman, Lake, res., Wa., U.S.	B2	124
Cusick, Wa., U.S.	A8	124
Cusihuiriáchic, Mex.	B3	63
Cusseta, Sen.	C1	45
Cusset, Fr.	C4	16
Cusseta, Ga., U.S.	D2	87
Cusseta, Ga., U.S.	A2	102
Custer, Oh., U.S.	C3	99
Custer, S.D., U.S.	D2	118
Custer, Wa., U.S.	A3	124
Custer, co., Co., U.S.	C5	83
Custer, co., Id., U.S.	E4	89
Custer, co., Mt., U.S.	D11	103
Custer, co., Ne., U.S.	C6	104
Custer, co., Ok., U.S.	B2	113
Custer, co., S.D., U.S.	D2	118
Custer Battlefield National Monument, Mt., U.S.	E9	103
Custer City, Ok., U.S.	B3	113
Custer City, Pa., U.S.	C4	115
Custer Peak, mtn., S.D., U.S.	C2	118
Cut Bank, Mt., U.S.	B4	103
Cut Bank Creek, stm., N.D., U.S.	A4	111
Cutbank, stm., Alta.	B1	68
Cut Beaver Lake, l., Sask.	A4	111
Cutchogue, N.Y., U.S.	m16	109
Cutervo, Peru	E2	58
Cuthbert, Ga., U.S.	E1	87
Cut Knife, Sask.	E1	75
Cutler, Ont.	A2	73
Cutler, Fl., U.S.	*G6	86
Cutler, Il., U.S.	E4	90
Cutler, In., U.S.	C5	91
Cutler, Me., U.S.	D5	96
Cutler Ridge, Fl., U.S.	s13	86
Cutlerville, Mi., U.S.	*F5	99
Cut Off, La., U.S.	E5	95
Cutshin, Ky., U.S.	C6	94
Cut Throat Island, i., Newf.	A3	72
Cuttack, India	E3	122
Cuttingsville, Vt., U.S.	D6	98
Cuttyhunk Island, i., Ma., U.S.	n13	63
Cutzamalá, stm., Mex.	D1	48
Cuvo, stm., Ang.	B4	18
Cuxhaven, W. Ger.	A4	112
Cuyahoga, co., Oh., U.S.	A4	112
Cuyahoga, stm., Oh., U.S.	A4	112
Cuyahoga Falls, Oh., U.S.	E4	82
Cuyama, stm., Ca., U.S.	F5	82
Cuyamaca Peak, mtn., Ca., U.S.	*B4	108
Cuyamungue, N.M., U.S.	C3	109
Cuyler, N.Y., U.S.	D5	100
Cuyo Islands, is., Phil.	A3	59
Cuyuna, Mn., U.S.	A3	58
Cuyuni, stm., S.A.	D3	58
Cuzco, Peru	C2	91
Cuzco, In., U.S.	D3	58
Cuzco, dept., Peru	C5	12
C.W. McConaughy, Lake, res., U.S.	C4	104
Cybinka, Pol.	A9	19
Cyclades, is., Grc.	t36	11
Cyclone, Pa., U.S.	C4	115
Cylinder, Ia., U.S.	A3	92
Cynthiana, In., U.S.	H2	91
Cynthiana, Ky., U.S.	B5	94
Cynthiana, Oh., U.S.	C2	112
Cypress, Al., U.S.	*n12	82
Cypress, Ca., U.S.	J1	86
Cypress, Fl., U.S.	F4	90
Cypress, Tx., U.S.	r14	120
Cypress Bayou, stm., U.S.	r14	120
Cypress Creek, stm., Tx., U.S.	r14	120
Cypress Hills, hills, Can.	G10	66
Cypress Hills Provincial Park, Alta.	E5	68
Cypress Hills Provincial Park, Sask.	H1	75
Cypress Inn, Tn., U.S.	B3	119
Cypress Lake, Fl., U.S.	*F6	86
Cypress Lake, l., Sask.	H1	75
Cypress Lake, l., Fl., U.S.	D5	86
Cypress Quarters, Fl., U.S.	E6	86
Cypress River, Man.	E2	70
Cypress Swamp, sw., U.S.	F4	85
Cyprus, ctry., Asia	E9	40
Cyprus, North (ctry.), Asia	E9	40
Cyrenaica (Barqah), hist. reg., Libya	D4	43
Cyril, Ok., U.S.	C3	113
Cyril, stm., Man.	B4	70
Cyrus, Mn., U.S.	E3	100
Cythera see Kíthira, i., Grc.	D4	40
Czar, Alta.	C5	68
Czarna, stm., Pol.	k14	26
Czarna Przemsza, stm., Pol.	g10	26
Czarnków, Pol.	B4	26
Czechoslovakia, ctry., Eur.	D4	26
Czechowice-Dziedzice, Pol.	h10	26
Czersk, Pol.	B4	26
Częstochowa, Pol.	C5	26
Człuchów, Pol.	B4	26

D

Name	Map Ref.	Page
Da'an, China	B11	32
Daaquam, Que.	C7	74
Dabakala, I.C.	E4	45
Daba Mountains, mts., China	I4	32
Dabdab, Libya	D2	43
Dabeiba, Col.	B3	26
Dabie (part of Szczecin), Pol.	B3	26
Dabie Mountains, mts., China	I5	32
Ďáblice, Czech.	n18	26
Dabneys, Va., U.S.	D2	45
Dabola, Gui.	D4	45
Daborow, Som.	E4	45
Dabrowa Białostocka, Pol.	B7	26
Dabrowa Górnicza, Pol.	C5	26
Dabrowa [Tarnowska], Pol.	D9	36
Dacca see Dhaka, Bngl.	D5	18
Dachau, W. Ger.	A3	113
Dacoma, Ok., U.S.	A6	83
Dacono, Co., U.S.	C3	87
Dacula, Ga., U.S.	B3	59
Dadanawa, Guy.	B9	40
Daday, Tur.	B1	87
Dade, co., Fl., U.S.	B1	87
Dade, co., Ga., U.S.	D4	102
Dade, co., Mo., U.S.	D4	86
Dade City, Fl., U.S.	C4	78
Dadeville, Al., U.S.	D4	102
Dadeville, Mo., U.S.	*D5	36
Dādra and Nagar Haveli, ter., India	C4	36
Dadu, Pak.	o14	34
Daet, Phil.	F3	75
Dafoe, Sask.	B4	70
Dafoe, stm., Man.	C1	45
Dagana, Sen.	k13	10
Dagenham (part of London), Eng., U.K.	E5	82
Daggett, Ca., U.S.	C3	99
Daggett, Mi., U.S.	C6	121
Daggett, co., Ut., U.S.	B12	103
Dagmar, Mt., U.S.	F5	85
Dagsboro, De., U.S.	E7	32
Dagu, China	n13	34
Dagupan, Phil.	D4	115
Daguscahona, Pa., U.S.	D4	115
Dagus Mines, Pa., U.S.	E9	103
Dahlak Archipelago, is., Eth.	A8	111
Dahlen, N.D., U.S.	E5	90
Dahlgren, Il., U.S.	B5	123
Dahlgren, Va., U.S.	B3	87
Dahlonega, Ga., U.S.	B8	19
Dahme, E. Ger.	E5	45
Dahomey see Benin, ctry., Afr.	E3	41
Dahra, Libya	B3	41
Dahshūr, Eg.	D14	40
Dahūk, Iraq	E7	32
Daicheng, China	C5	125
Dailey, W.V., U.S.	C4	22
Daimiel, Spain	D4	11
Daingean, Ire.	C5	120
Daingerfield, Tx., U.S.	o15	33
Daiō, Japan	I8	33
Daiō, Cape, c., Japan	D9	31
Dairen see Dalian, China	E5	114
Dairy, Or., U.S.	*F5	99
Daisetta, Tx., U.S.	C2	81
Daisy, Ar., U.S.	D5	87
Daisy, Ga., U.S.	C6	113
Daisy, Ok., U.S.	E8	64
Daixian, China	E8	64
Dajabón, Dom. Rep.	D1	50
Dajarra, Austl.	D1	45
Dakar, Sen.	D5	43
Dākhilah, Al Wāḥāt ad, well, Eg.	D6	44
Dakhla, W. Sah.	A4	90
Dakoro, Niger	G7	100
Dakota, Mn., U.S.	F5	100
Dakota, co., Mn., U.S.	B9	104
Dakota, co., Ne., U.S.	B3	92
Dakota City, Ia., U.S.	B9	104
Dakota City, Ne., U.S.	A5	64
Dākura, Nic.	A4	48
Dakwa, Zaire	D2	58
Dalaas, Aus.	D2	45
Dalaba, Gui.	G6	14
Dalälven, stm., Swe.	D7	25
Dalaman, stm., Tur.	C3	31
Dalandzadgad, Mong.	C3	81
Dalark, Ar., U.S.	A9	104
Dalbandin, Pak.	H2	91
Dalbo, Mn., U.S.	E9	50
Dalby, Austl.	E9	14
Dalby, Swe.	*C2	54
Dalcahue, Chile	D4	78
Dale, In., U.S.	H4	91
Dale, Ok., U.S.	B4	113
Dale, Or., U.S.	C8	114
Dale, co., Al., U.S.	D4	78
Dale City, Va., U.S.	B5	123
Dale Hollow Lake, res., U.S.	C8	119
Dalemead, Alta.	D4	68
Daleville, Al., U.S.	D4	78
Daleville, In., U.S.	D6	91
Daleville, Ms., U.S.	C5	101
Dalhart, Tx., U.S.	A1	120
Dalhousie, N.B.	A3	71
Dalhousie, India	A5	37
Dalhousie Junction, N.B.	A3	71
Dali, India	E6	31
Dalian (Lüda), China	D9	31
Dalías, Spain	D4	22
Daliburgh, Scot., U.K.	C1	13
Daliyat el Karmil, Isr.	B7	41
Dalkeith, Scot., U.K.	E5	13
Dalkeith, Fl., U.S.	B1	86
Dalkena, Wa., U.S.	A8	124
Dall, Mount, mtn., Ak., U.S.	f15	79
Dallam, co., Tx., U.S.	A1	120
Dallardsville, Tx., U.S.	D5	120
Dallas, Ga., U.S.	B3	78
Dallas, Ga., U.S.	C2	87
Dallas, N.C., U.S.	B1	110
Dallas, Or., U.S.	C3	114
Dallas, Pa., U.S.	D10	115
Dallas, S.D., U.S.	D6	118
Dallas, Tx., U.S.	C4	120
Dallas, Wi., U.S.	f8	125
Dallas, co., Al., U.S.	C2	126
Dallas, co., Al., U.S.	C2	78
Dallas, co., Ar., U.S.	D3	81
Dallas, co., Ia., U.S.	C3	92
Dallas, co., Mo., U.S.	D4	102
Dallas, co., Tx., U.S.	C4	120
Dallas Center, Ia., U.S.	C4	92
Dallas Naval Air Station, mil., Tx., U.S.	n9	120
Dallastown, Pa., U.S.	G8	115
Dall Island, i., Ak., U.S.	n23	79
Dalmally, Scot., U.K.	D4	13
Dalmatia, Pa., U.S.	E8	115
Dalmatia, hist. reg., Yugo.	C4	24
Dalmellington, Scot., U.K.	C4	10
Dalmeny, Sask.	E2	75
Dalnerechensk, Sov. Un.	E16	27
Dalnyaya, Sov. Un.	D11	33
Daloa, I.C.	E3	45
Dalou Mountains, mts., China	K2	32
Dalqū, Sud.	A3	47
Dalroy, Alta.	D4	68
Dalry, Scot., U.K.	E4	13
Dalrymple, Mount, mtn., Austl.	D8	50
Dalton, Ga., U.S.	B2	87
Dalton, Ma., U.S.	B1	98
Dalton, Mn., U.S.	D3	100
Dalton, Mo., U.S.	B5	102
Dalton, Ne., U.S.	C3	104
Dalton, N.H., U.S.	B3	106
Dalton, N.Y., U.S.	C3	109
Dalton, Oh., U.S.	B4	112
Dalton, Pa., U.S.	C10	115
Dalton, Wi., U.S.	E4	126
Dalton City, Il., U.S.	D5	90
Dalton Gardens, Id., U.S.	B2	89
Dalton Iceberg Tongue, ice, Ant.	C25	7
Dalwhinnie, Scot., U.K.	D4	13
Daly, stm., Austl.	B5	50
Daly City, Ca., U.S.	h8	82
Dalzell, Il., U.S.	B4	90
Dalzell, S.C., U.S.	C7	117
Damān, India	*D5	36
Damān and Diu, ter., India	*D5	36
Damanhūr, Eg.	C6	43
Damaqun Mountains, mts., China	D7	32
Damar, Ks., U.S.	C4	93
Damar, i., Indon.	G7	34
Damara, Cen. Afr. Rep.	D3	48
Damariscotta, Me., U.S.	D3	96
Damariscotta Lake, l., Me., U.S.	D3	96
Damascus, Ar., U.S.	B3	81
Damascus, Ga., U.S.	E2	87
Damascus, Md., U.S.	B3	97
Damascus, Va., U.S.	f10	123
Damascus (Dimashq), Syria	B3	41
Damascus Gate, hist., Isr.	m14	41
Damaturu, Nig.	D7	45
Damba, Ang.	C2	48
Dame Marie, Cap, c., Haiti	E6	64
Dames Quarter, Md., U.S.	D6	97
Damghan, Iran	B5	38
Damietta Branch, stm., Eg.	B3	41
Damietta see Dumyāṭ, Eg.	F6	32
Daming, China	g13	41
Dāmiyā, Jord.	B8	17
Damme, W. Ger.	F10	37
Dāmodar, stm., India	F7	37
Damoh, India	r14	120
Damon, Tx., U.S.	E4	45
Damongo, Ghana	D2	50
Dampier, Austl.	D2	50
Dampier Archipelago, is., Austl.	F8	34
Dampier Strait, strt., Indon.	A4	90
Damvant, Switz.	B3	21
Dana, Sask.	E3	75
Dana, In., U.S.	E3	91
Dana, Ia., U.S.	B3	92
Dana, N.C., U.S.	f10	110
Danané, I.C.	B3	34
Da Nang, Viet.	*F5	82
Dana Point, Ca., U.S.	E10	37
Dānāpur, India	D2	84
Danbury, Ct., U.S.	B2	92
Danbury, Ia., U.S.	D3	106
Danbury, N.H., U.S.	A2	110
Danbury, N.C., U.S.	r14	120
Danbury, Tx., U.S.	B1	126
Danbury, Wi., U.S.	E6	82
Danby, Ca., U.S.	C4	109
Danby, N.Y., U.S.	B1	78
Dancy, Al., U.S.	B2	119
Dancyville, Tn., U.S.	C1	48
Dande, stm., Ang.	*G8	50
Dandenong, Austl.	C9	31
Dandong, China	C10	119
Dandridge, Tn., U.S.	C10	119

Name	Map Ref.	Page

Dane, Wi., U.S. — E4 126
Dane, co., Wi., U.S. — E4 126
Danevang, Tx., U.S. — E4 120
Danfeng, China — H4 32
Danforth, Il., U.S. — C6 90
Danforth, Me., U.S. — C5 96
Danforth Hills, mts., Co., U.S. — A2 83
Dangila, Eth. — C4 47
Dangshan, China — G7 32
Dangtu, China — I8 32
Dangyang, China — I4 32
Dania, Fl., U.S. — F6 86
Daniel, Ut., U.S. — *C4 121
Daniel, Wy., U.S. — D2 127
Daniels, co., Mt., U.S. — B11 103
Daniel's Harbour, Newf. — C3 72
Danielson, Ct., U.S. — B8 84
Daniels Pass, Ut., U.S. — C4 121
Danielsville, Ga., U.S. — B3 87
Danilov, Sov. Un. — B13 27
Danilovgrad, Yugo. — D4 24
Danjo Island, i., Japan — J4 33
Danli, Hond. — E7 63
Dannebrog, Ne., U.S. — C7 104
Dannemarie, Fr. — A3 21
Dannemora, N.Y., U.S. — f11 109
Dannenberg, W. Ger. — E5 15
Dannevirke, N.Z. — N16 51
Dannike, Swe. — A7 15
Dans Mountain, mtn., Md., U.S. — k13 97
Dansville, N.Y., U.S. — C3 109
Dante, S.D., U.S. — D7 118
Dante, Tn., U.S. — m14 119
Dante, Tn., U.S. — f9 123
Dantewāra, India — H8 37
Danube, Mn., U.S. — F3 100
Danube, stm., Eur. — G14 8
Danube Delta, Eur. — I7 27
Danubyu, Burma — D1 35
Danvers, Il., U.S. — C4 90
Danvers, Ma., U.S. — A6 98
Danvers, Mn., U.S. — E3 100
Danvers, Mt., U.S. — C7 103
Danville, Que. — D5 74
Danville, Al., U.S. — A2 78
Danville, Ar., U.S. — B2 81
Danville, Ca., U.S. — h9 82
Danville, Ga., U.S. — D3 87
Danville, Il., U.S. — C6 90
Danville, In., U.S. — E4 91
Danville, Ia., U.S. — D6 92
Danville, Ks., U.S. — E6 93
Danville, Ky., U.S. — C5 94
Danville, La., U.S. — B3 95
Danville, N.H., U.S. — E4 106
Danville, Oh., U.S. — B3 112
Danville, Pa., U.S. — E8 115
Danville, Vt., U.S. — C4 122
Danville, Va., U.S. — D3 123
Danville, Wa., U.S. — A7 124
Danville, W.V., U.S. — C3 125
Danxian, China — C8 35
Danzhai, China — K2 32
Danzig, Gulf of, b., Eur. — A5 26
Danzig see Gdańsk, Pol. — A5 26
Daosa, India — D6 37
Daoxian, China — F7 31
Daphne, Al., U.S. — E2 78
Dapp, Alta. — B4 68
Da Qaidam, China — D4 31
Daqing (Anda), China — *B10 31
Dar'ā, Syria — F11 40
Dārāb, Iran — G7 39
Darabani, Rom. — A8 24
Daraj, Libya — C11 43
Darasun, Sov. Un. — D14 29
Darawah, Eg. — D3 41
Darbandi Khan Dam, Iraq — D2 39
Darbhanga, India — C8 36
D'Arbonne, Bayou, stm., La., U.S. — B3 95
Darburruk, Som. — D5 47
Darby, Mt., U.S. — F6 62
Darby, Pa., U.S. — G11 115
Darbydale, Oh., U.S. — m10 112
Darby Township, Pa., U.S. — *G11 115
Darbyville, Oh., U.S. — C2 112
Dar Chebika, Mor. — D2 44
D'Arcy Station, Sask. — F1 75
Dardanelle, Ar., U.S. — B2 81
Dardanelle, Ca., U.S. — C4 82
Dardanelle Lake, res., Ar., U.S. — B2 81
Dardanelles, strt. — B5 40
Darden, N.C., U.S. — B6 110
Darden, Tn., U.S. — B3 119
Dardenne Creek, stm., Mo., U.S. — f12 102
Dare, co., N.C., U.S. — B7 110
Darende, Tur. — C11 40
Dar es Salaam, Tan. — C6 48
Daretown, N.J., U.S. — D2 107
Darfo, Italy — D6 20
Darfur, Mn., U.S. — F4 100
Dārfūr al Janūbīyah (Southern Darfur), prov., Sud. — C1 47
Dārfūr ash Shamālīyah (Northern Darfur), prov., Sud. — B2 47
Dargan, Md., U.S. — B2 97
Dargan-Ata, Sov. Un. — A11 39
Dargaville, N.Z. — K14 51
Darhan, Mong. — B6 31
Darhan Mumminggan Lianheqi, China — D4 32
Darien, Ct., U.S. — E2 84
Darien, Ga., U.S. — E5 87
Darien, Il., U.S. — *k9 90
Darien, Wi., U.S. — F5 126
Darién, Gulf of, b. — F9 62
Darién, Serranía del, mts. — F9 62
Dariense, Cordillera, mts., Nic. — D5 62
Darjeeling, India — C8 36
Darke, co., Oh., U.S. — B1 112
Darkesville, W.V., U.S. — B6 125
Darley Woods, De., U.S. — h8 85
Darling, Ms., U.S. — A3 101
Darling, stm., Austl. — F7 50
Darling, Lake, res., N.D., U.S. — A4 111
Darling Downs, reg., Austl. — C8 51
Darlingford, Man. — E2 70
Darling Range, mts., Austl. — F2 50
Darlington, Eng., U.K. — C6 10
Darlington, Ct., U.S. — v15 86
Darlington, Fl., U.S. — v15 86
Darlington, Id., U.S. — F5 89
Darlington, In., U.S. — D4 91
Darlington, Md., U.S. — A5 97
Darlington, Mo., U.S. — A3 102
Darlington, S.C., U.S. — C8 117
Darlington, Wi., U.S. — F3 126
Darlington, co., S.C., U.S. — C8 117
Darłowo, Pol. — A4 26
Darmody, Sask. — G2 75

Darmstadt, W. Ger. — D4 18
Darnah, Libya — C4 43
Darnell, La., U.S. — B4 95
Darnestown, Md., U.S. — B3 97
Darney, Fr. — A2 20
Darnley, Cape, c., Ant. — C19 7
Daro, Malay. — E4 34
Daroca, Spain — B5 22
Darr, Ne., U.S. — D6 104
Darrah, Mount, mtn., Can. — E3 68
Darreh Gaz, Iran — C9 39
Darrington, Wa., U.S. — A4 124
Darrow, La., U.S. — h10 95
Darsser Ort, c., E. Ger. — D6 15
Dart, stm., Eng., U.K. — D4 12
Dart, Cape, c., Ant. — B36 7
Dartmoor, for., Eng., U.K. — E5 10
Dartmouth, N.S. — E6 71
Dartmouth, Eng., U.K. — E5 10
Dartmouth, Ga., U.S. — C5 98
Dartmouth Woods, De., U.S. — *A3 85
Daru, Pap. N. Gui. — k11 50
Daruvar, Yugo. — C3 24
Darvel Bay, b., Malay. — E5 34
Darwin, Austl. — B5 50
Darwin, Ca., U.S. — D5 82
Darwin, Mn., U.S. — E4 100
Darwin, Isla, i., Ec. — f5 58
Darwin Glacier, ice, Ant. — f41 7
Dasht, stm., Pak. — C3 36
Dashwood, Ont. — D3 73
Dasol Bay, b., Phil. — o12 34
Dassel, Mn., U.S. — E4 100
Datça, Tur. — D6 25
Dateland, Az., U.S. — E2 80
Datia, India — E7 37
Datian, China — L7 32
Datil, N.M., U.S. — C2 108
Datil Mountains, mts., N.M., U.S. — C2 108
Datong, China — C7 31
Datto, Ar., U.S. — A5 81
Datu, Cape, c., Asia — E3 34
Datze, stm., E. Ger. — E7 15
Daudnagar, India — E10 37
Daufuskie Island, S.C., U.S. — G6 117
Daufuskie Island, i., S.C., U.S. — G6 117
Daugava (Western Dvina), stm., Sov. Un. — C5 27
Daugavpils (Dvinsk), Sov. Un. — D6 27
Daule, Ec. — A2 58
Daule, stm., Ec. — A2 58
Daun, W. Ger. — B2 58
Daund, India — C1 19
Daung, i., Burma — H5 37
Dauphin, Man. — F3 35
Dauphin, Pa., U.S. — D1 70
Dauphin, co., Pa., U.S. — F8 115
Dauphin, stm., Man. — F8 115
Dauphiné, hist. reg., Fr. — D2 70
Dauphin Island, Al., U.S. — E6 16
Dauphin Island, i., Al., U.S. — E1 78
Dauphin Lake, l., Man. — E1 78
Daus, Tn., U.S. — D2 70
Dāvangere, India — D8 119
Davant, La., U.S. — F6 36
Davao, Phil. — E6 95
Davao Gulf, b., Phil. — D7 34
Davenport, Ca., U.S. — D7 34
Davenport, Fl., U.S. — D2 82
Davenport, Ia., U.S. — D5 86
Davenport, Ne., U.S. — C7 92
Davenport, N.Y., U.S. — D8 104
Davenport, N.D., U.S. — C6 109
Davenport, Ok., U.S. — C8 111
Davenport, Wa., U.S. — B5 113
Davenport Downs, Austl. — B7 124
Daventry, Eng., U.K. — B3 51
Davey, Ne., U.S. — B6 12
David, Pan. — h11 104
David, Ky., U.S. — F6 62
David City, Ne., U.S. — C7 94
David-Gorodok, Sov. Un. — C8 104
Davidson, Sask. — E6 27
Davidson, N.C., U.S. — F3 75
Davidson, Ok., U.S. — B2 110
Davidson, Tn., U.S. — C2 113
Davidson, co., N.C., U.S. — C8 119
Davidson, co., Tn., U.S. — B2 110
Davidson Mountains, mts., Ak., U.S. — A5 119
Davidsville, Pa., U.S. — B11 79
Davie, Fl., U.S. — F4 115
Davie, co., N.C., U.S. — F6 86
Daviess, co., In., U.S. — B2 110
Daviess, co., Ky., U.S. — G3 91
Daviess, co., Mo., U.S. — C2 94
Davin, Sask. — B3 102
Davis, Ca., U.S. — G3 75
Davis, Il., U.S. — C3 82
Davis, N.C., U.S. — A4 90
Davis, Ok., U.S. — C6 110
Davis, S.D., U.S. — C4 113
Davis, W.V., U.S. — D9 118
Davis, co., Ia., U.S. — B5 125
Davis, co., Ut., U.S. — D5 92
Davis, Mount, mtn., Pa., U.S. — C3 121
Davisboro, Ga., U.S. — G3 115
Davis City, Ia., U.S. — D4 87
Davis Creek, stm., W.V., U.S. — D4 92
Davis Dam, Az., U.S. — m12 125
Davis Islands, is., Fl., U.S. — B1 80
Davis Junction, Il., U.S. — p11 86
Davis Lake, l., Or., U.S. — A4 90
Davis-Monthan Air Force Base, mil., Az., U.S. — E5 114
Davis Mountains, mts., Tx., U.S. — E5 80
Davison, Mi., U.S. — o12 120
Davison, co., S.D., U.S. — E7 99
Davis Sea, Ant. — D7 118
Davis Station, S.C., U.S. — C22 7
Davis Strait, strt., N.A. — D7 117
Daviston, Al., U.S. — C15 61
Davisville, N.H., U.S. — B4 78
Davisville, R.I., U.S. — D3 106
Davle, Czech. — E4 116
Davos, Switz. — o17 26
Davy, W.V., U.S. — E4 18
Dawa, China — D3 125
Dawa, stm., Afr. — *C9 31
Dawasir, Wādī ad, val., Sau. Ar. — E5 47
Dawei, Burma — D4 38
Dawes, co., Ne., U.S. — F10 36
Debre Tabor, Eth. — B2 104
Dawn, Mo., U.S. — B4 102
Dawna Range, mts., Burma — D3 35
Dawros Head, c., Ire. — C3 11

Daws Island, i., S.C., U.S. — G6 117
Dawson, Yukon — D5 66
Dawson, Ga., U.S. — E2 87
Dawson, Ia., U.S. — C3 92
Dawson, Mn., U.S. — F2 100
Dawson, N.D., U.S. — C6 111
Dawson, Pa., U.S. — F2 115
Dawson, Tx., U.S. — D4 120
Dawson, co., Ga., U.S. — B2 87
Dawson, co., Mt., U.S. — C11 103
Dawson, co., Ne., U.S. — D6 104
Dawson, co., Tx., U.S. — C1 120
Dawson, stm., Austl. — D8 50
Dawson, Mount, mtn., B.C. — D9 69
Dawson Creek, B.C. — B7 69
Dawson-Lambton Glacier, ice, Ant. — B10 7
Dawson Range, mts., Yukon — D5 66
Dawson Springs, Ky., U.S. — C2 94
Dawsonville, Ga., U.S. — B2 87
Dax, Fr. — F3 16
Daxian, China — E6 31
Day, Fl., U.S. — B3 86
Day, co., S.D., U.S. — B8 118
Daykin, Ne., U.S. — D8 104
Daylesford, Austl. — H5 51
Dayong, China — J4 32
Dayr Abū Sa'īd, Jord. — B7 41
Dayr al Balaḥ, Isr. Occ. — C6 41
Dayr 'Allā, Jord. — g13 41
Dayr az Zawr, Syria — B4 38
Dayr Dibwān, Isr. Occ. — h12 41
Dayr Istiyā, Isr. Occ. — g11 41
Dayrūṭ, Eg. — D6 43
Daysland, Alta. — C4 68
Daysville, Tn., U.S. — D9 119
Dayton, Al., U.S. — C2 78
Dayton, Id., U.S. — G7 89
Dayton, In., U.S. — D4 91
Dayton, Ia., U.S. — B3 92
Dayton, Ky., U.S. — h14 94
Dayton, Md., U.S. — B4 97
Dayton, Mn., U.S. — m12 100
Dayton, Nv., U.S. — D2 105
Dayton, N.J., U.S. — C3 107
Dayton, N.Y., U.S. — C2 109
Dayton, Oh., U.S. — C1 112
Dayton, Or., U.S. — B3 114
Dayton, Pa., U.S. — E3 115
Dayton, Tn., U.S. — D8 119
Dayton, Tx., U.S. — D5 120
Dayton, Va., U.S. — B4 123
Dayton, Wa., U.S. — C8 124
Dayton, Wy., U.S. — B5 127
Daytona Beach, Fl., U.S. — C5 86
Dayu, China — F7 31
Dayville, Ct., U.S. — B8 84
Dayville, Or., U.S. — C7 114
Dazey, N.D., U.S. — B7 111
De Aar, S. Afr. — D3 49
Dead, North Branch, stm., Me., U.S. — C2 96
Dead, South Branch, stm., Me., U.S. — C2 96
Dead, stm., Vt., U.S. — C2 122
Dead Diamond, stm., N.H., U.S. — g7 106
Dead Indian Peak, mtn., Wy., U.S. — B3 127
Dead Lake, l., Mn., U.S. — D3 100
Dead Lake, res., Fl., U.S. — B1 86
Deadman Bay, b., Fl., U.S. — C3 86
Deadman Creek, stm., Wa., U.S. — g14 124
Dead Sea, l., Asia — B3 38
Deadwood, S.D., U.S. — C2 118
Deadwood Reservoir, res., Id., U.S. — E3 89
Deaf Smith, co., Tx., U.S. — B1 120
Deakin Bay, b., Ant. — C28 7
Deal, Eng., U.K. — C9 12
Deal, N.J., U.S. — C4 107
Deale, Md., U.S. — C4 97
Deal Island, Md., U.S. — D6 97
Deal Island, i., Md., U.S. — D6 97
Dean, stm., B.C. — C4 69
Deanburg, Tn., U.S. — B3 119
Dean Channel, strt., B.C. — C4 69
Deán Funes, Arg. — A4 54
Deans, N.J., U.S. — C3 107
Deanville, W.V., U.S. — B4 125
Dearborn, Mi., U.S. — F7 99
Dearborn, Mo., U.S. — B3 102
Dearborn, co., In., U.S. — F7 91
Dearborn Heights, Mi., U.S. — p15 99
Dearg, Beinn, mtn., Scot., U.K. — B4 10
Dearing, Ga., U.S. — C4 87
Dearing, Ks., U.S. — E8 93
De Armanville, Al., U.S. — B4 78
Deary, Id., U.S. — C2 89
Dease Arm, b., N.W. Ter. — C8 66
Dease Lake, B.C. — m16 69
Dease Strait, strt., N.W. Ter. — C11 66
Death Valley, val., Ca., U.S. — D5 82
Death Valley Junction, Ca., U.S. — D5 82
Death Valley National Monument, U.S. — D5 82
Deatsville, Al., U.S. — C3 78
Deauville, Fr. — C3 16
Deaver, Wy., U.S. — B4 127
Deba, Nig. — *D6 45
De Baca, co., N.M., U.S. — C5 108
Debaltsevo, Sov. Un. — q21 27
Debao, China — G6 31
Debar, Yugo. — E5 24
De Bary, Fl., U.S. — D5 86
Debauch Mountain, mtn., Ak., U.S. — C8 79
Debden, Sask. — D2 75
Dêbê, Trin. — O23 65
Debec, N.B. — C2 71
De Beque, Co., U.S. — B2 83
De Berry, Tx., U.S. — C5 120
Debica, Pol. — E6 26
Deblin, Pol. — D6 26
Deblois, Me., U.S. — D5 96
Debno, Pol. — B3 26
Debo, Lac, l., Mali — C4 45
De Borgia, Mt., U.S. — C1 103
Deboullie Mountain, mtn., Me., U.S. — B4 96
Debovo, Bul. — D5 47
Debre Birhan, Eth. — D4 47
Debrecen, Hung. — C4 47
Debre Markos, Eth. — C4 47
Debre Tabor, Eth. — C4 47
Debre Zeyit, Eth. — *D4 47
De Cade, Lake, l., La., U.S. — E5 95
Decatur, Ar., U.S. — A1 81

Decatur, Ga., U.S. — C2 87
Decatur, Il., U.S. — D5 90
Decatur, In., U.S. — C8 91
Decatur, Ia., U.S. — D4 92
Decatur, Mi., U.S. — F5 99
Decatur, Ms., U.S. — C4 101
Decatur, Ne., U.S. — B9 104
Decatur, Tn., U.S. — D9 119
Decatur, Tx., U.S. — C4 120
Decatur, co., Ga., U.S. — F2 87
Decatur, co., In., U.S. — F6 91
Decatur, co., Ia., U.S. — D4 92
Decatur, co., Ks., U.S. — C3 93
Decatur, co., Tn., U.S. — B3 119
Decatur, Lake, res., Il., U.S. — D5 90
Decaturville, Tn., U.S. — B3 119
Decazeville, Fr. — E5 16
Deccan, plat., India — E6 36
Deception, Mount, mtn., Wa., U.S. — B2 124
Dechard, Tn., U.S. — B5 119
Decherd, Tn., U.S. — C3 26
Decize, Fr. — D5 16
Decker, Man. — D1 70
Decker, In., U.S. — G2 91
Decker, Mt., U.S. — E10 103
Decker Lake, B.C. — B5 69
Deckers, Co., U.S. — B5 83
Deckerville, Mi., U.S. — E8 99
De Kalb, Il., U.S. — B5 90
De Kalb, Ms., U.S. — C5 101
De Kalb, Mo., U.S. — B3 102
De Kalb, N.Y., U.S. — f9 109
De Kalb, Tx., U.S. — C5 120
De Kalb, co., Al., U.S. — A4 78
De Kalb, co., Ga., U.S. — C2 87
De Kalb, co., Il., U.S. — B5 90
De Kalb, co., In., U.S. — B7 91
De Kalb, co., Mo., U.S. — B3 102
De Kalb, co., Tn., U.S. — D8 119
De Kalb Junction, N.Y., U.S. — f9 109
Dekemhare, Eth. — B4 47
Dekese, Zaire — C3 48
Deke Sokehs, i., Micron. — Q17 52
Dekoa, Cen. Afr. Rep. — D3 46
Dédougou, Burkina — D4 45
Dedu, China — B3 33
Dedza, Mwi. — D5 48
Dee, stm., U.K. — D5 10
Dee, stm., Scot., U.K. — B5 10
Deedsville, In., U.S. — C5 91
Deel, stm., Ire. — E3 11
Deemer, Ms., U.S. — C4 101
Deep, stm., N.C., U.S. — B3 110
Deep Brook, N.S. — E4 71
Deep Creek, stm., De., U.S. — F3 85
Deep Creek, stm., Mt., U.S. — C4 103
Deep Creek, stm., Ut., U.S. — B3 121
Deep Creek, stm., Ut., U.S. — C2 121
Deep Creek, stm., Va., U.S. — F3 121
Deep Creek, stm., Wa., U.S. — g13 124
Deep Creek Lake, res., Md., U.S. — K12 97
Deep Creek Mountains, mts., Id., U.S. — G6 89
Deep Creek Range, mts., Ut., U.S. — D2 121
Deepdale, Man. — D1 70
Deep Fork, stm., Ok., U.S. — B5 113
Deep Gap, N.C., U.S. — A1 110
Deep Gap, N.C., U.S. — A1 110
Deep Inlet, b., Newf. — g10 72
Deep Red Creek, stm., Ok., U.S. — C3 113
Deep River, Ont. — A7 73
Deep River, Ct., U.S. — D6 84
Deep River, Ia., U.S. — C5 92
Deep Run, N.C., U.S. — B5 110
Deepstep, Ga., U.S. — C4 87
Deepwater, Mo., U.S. — C4 102
Deep Water, N.J., U.S. — D2 107
Deep Water, W.V., U.S. — m13 125
Deer, stm., Ar., U.S. — B2 81
Deer Creek, Il., U.S. — C4 90
Deer Creek, In., U.S. — C5 91
Deer Creek, Mn., U.S. — D3 100
Deer Creek, Ok., U.S. — A4 113
Deer Creek, stm., In., U.S. — C5 91
Deer Creek, stm., Md., U.S. — A5 97
Deer Creek, stm., Ms., U.S. — B3 101
Deer Creek, stm., Oh., U.S. — C2 112
Deer Creek Indian Reservation, Mn., U.S. — C5 100
Deerfield, Il., U.S. — h9 90
Deerfield, Ks., U.S. — D8 91
Deerfield, Mi., U.S. — G7 99
Deerfield, N.H., U.S. — D4 106
Deerfield, Wi., U.S. — E4 126
Deerfield Beach, Fl., U.S. — F6 86
Deerfield Street, N.J., U.S. — D2 107
Deer Grove, Il., U.S. — B4 90
Deering, Ak., U.S. — B7 79
Deering, Mo., U.S. — E8 102
Deering, N.H., U.S. — D3 106
Deering, N.D., U.S. — A4 111
Deer Island, pen., Ma., U.S. — g12 98
Deer Island, i., Ms., U.S. — f8 101
Deer Isle, Me., U.S. — D4 96
Deer Lake, Newf. — D3 72
Deer Lake, l., Mn., U.S. — C5 100
Deer Lodge, Mt., U.S. — D4 103
Deer Lodge, Tn., U.S. — C9 119
Deer Lodge, co., Mt., U.S. — E3 103
Deer Mountain, mtn., Me., U.S. — C2 96
Deer Park, Al., U.S. — D1 78
Deer Park, Md., U.S. — m12 97
Deer Park, Mi., U.S. — B5 99
Deer Park, N.Y., U.S. — n15 109
Deer Park, Oh., U.S. — o13 112
Deer Park, Tx., U.S. — *r14 120
Deer Park, Wa., U.S. — B8 124
Deer Peak, mtn., Co., U.S. — C5 83
Deer Pond, l., Newf. — D4 72
Deer River, Mn., U.S. — C5 100
Deer River, stm., N.Y., U.S. — B5 109
Deer Trail, Co., U.S. — B6 83
Deerwood, Mn., U.S. — D5 100
Deeth, Nv., U.S. — B6 105
Deex Nugaaleed, stm., Som. — D6 47
Defeter, N.Y., U.S. — A5 109
Defiance, Ia., U.S. — C2 92
Defiance, Mo., U.S. — f12 102
Defiance, Oh., U.S. — A1 112
Defiance, co., Oh., U.S. — A1 112
Defiance, Mount, mtn., Or., U.S. — B5 114
Deford, Mi., U.S. — E7 99

De Forest, Wi., U.S. — E4 126
Dêgê, China — E4 31
Degeberga, Swe. — C8 15
Degeh Bur, Eth. — D5 47
Dégelis, Que. — B9 74
Degerön, Swe. — u33 14
Degersheim, Switz. — B7 21
Deggendorf, W. Ger. — D6 18
De Graff, Mn., U.S. — E3 100
De Graff, Oh., U.S. — B2 112
De Gray Lake, res., Ar., U.S. — C2 81
De Grey, stm., Austl. — D2 50
Dehibat, Tun. — C7 44
Dehiwala-Mount Lavinia, Sri L. — *G6 36
Dehlorān, Iran — E3 39
Dehpehk, i., Micron. — Q17 52
Dehra Dūn, India — B6 36
Deh Shū, Afg. — F11 39
Deinze, Bel. — D3 17
Dej, Rom. — B6 24
Dejvice (part of Prague), Czech. — n17 26
De Kalb, Il., U.S. — B5 90
Decker, Man. — D1 70
Delamere, N.D., U.S. — C8 111
Delancó, N.J., U.S. — C3 107
De Land, Fl., U.S. — C5 86
De Land, Il., U.S. — C5 90
Delano, Ca., U.S. — E4 82
Delano, Mn., U.S. — E5 100
Delano, Tn., U.S. — D9 119
Delano Peak, mtn., Ut., U.S. — E3 121
Delanson, N.Y., U.S. — C6 109
Delaplaine, Ar., U.S. — A5 81
Delārām, Afg. — E11 39
Delaronde Lake, l., Sask. — C2 75
Delavan, Il., U.S. — C4 90
Delavan, Mn., U.S. — G4 100
Delavan, Wi., U.S. — F5 126
Delavan Lake, Wi., U.S. — *F5 126
Delaware, Ont. — E3 73
Delaware, Ar., U.S. — B2 81
Delaware, Oh., U.S. — B2 112
Delaware, co., In., U.S. — D7 91
Delaware, co., N.Y., U.S. — C5 109
Delaware, co., Oh., U.S. — B2 112
Delaware, co., Ok., U.S. — A7 113
Delaware, state, U.S. — D3 85
Delaware, stm., U.S. — E2 107
Delaware, stm., Ks., U.S. — C8 93
Delaware, East Branch, stm., N.Y., U.S. — C5 109
Delaware, West Branch, stm., N.Y., U.S. — C5 109
Delaware Bay, b., U.S. — C12 76
Delaware City, De., U.S. — B3 85
Delaware Lake, res., Oh., U.S. — B3 112
Delaware Mountains, mts., Tx., U.S. — o12 120
Delaware Water Gap, Pa., U.S. — E11 115
Delaware Water Gap, N.J., U.S. — B2 107
Delaware Water Gap National Recreation Area, U.S. — B2 107
Delburne, W.V., U.S. — D2 125
Delburne, Alta. — C4 68
Delcambre, La., U.S. — E4 95
Del City, Ok., U.S. — B4 113
Deleau, Man. — E1 70
Delémont, Switz. — E3 18
De Leon, Tx., U.S. — C3 120
De Leon Springs, Fl., U.S. — C5 86
Delevan, N.Y., U.S. — C2 109
Delft, Neth. — A6 16
Delft, Neth. — C4 17
Delfzijl, Neth. — A7 16
Delgada, Punta, c., Arg. — C4 54
Delgado, Cabo, c., Moz. — C7 48
Delgertsogt, Mong. — A2 32
Delhi, India — C6 36
Delhi, Ca., U.S. — D3 82
Delhi, La., U.S. — B4 95
Delhi, N.Y., U.S. — C6 109
Delhi, Oh., U.S. — o12 112
Delhi, ter., India — *C6 36
Delhi Hills, Oh., U.S. — *o12 112
Delia, Alta. — C4 68
Delia, Ks., U.S. — C8 93
Delicias, Mex. — *B3 63
Delingha, China — D4 31
De Lisle, Ms., U.S. — E4 101
Delitzsch, E. Ger. — C6 18
Dell, Ar., U.S. — B5 81
Dell, Mt., U.S. — F4 103
Dell City, Tx., U.S. — o12 120
Delle, Ut., U.S. — C3 121
Dellenbaugh, Mount, mtn., Az., U.S. — A2 80
Delleker, Ca., U.S. — B3 82
Dell Rapids, S.D., U.S. — D9 118
Dellroy, Oh., U.S. — B4 112
Dellwood, Fl., U.S. — B1 86
Dellwood, Mo., U.S. — *f13 102
Delmar, De., U.S. — F4 103
Delmar, Ia., U.S. — B7 92
Delmar, Md., U.S. — D6 97
Delmar, N.Y., U.S. — C7 109
Delmas, Sask. — E1 75
Delmenhorst, W. Ger. — B4 18

Delmita, Tx., U.S. — F3 120
Delmont, N.J., U.S. — E3 107
Delmont, S.D., U.S. — D7 118
Del Norte, Co., U.S. — D4 83
Del Norte, co., Ca., U.S. — B2 82
Deloit, Ia., U.S. — B2 92
Delong, Mn., U.S. — B5 91
De Long Islands, is., Sov. Un. — B35 128
Deloraine, Man. — E1 70
Delorme, Lac, l., Que. — F18 66
Deloro, Ont. — C7 73
Delos see Dhílos, i., Grc. — D5 25
Del Park Manor, De., U.S. — i7 85
Delphi, In., U.S. — C4 91
Delphia, Mt., U.S. — D8 103
Delphos, Ks., U.S. — C6 93
Delphos, Oh., U.S. — B1 112
Delran, N.J., U.S. — C3 107
Delray Beach, Fl., U.S. — F6 86
Del Rio, Fl., U.S. — *D4 86
Del Rio, Tn., U.S. — D10 119
Del Rio, Tx., U.S. — E2 120
Delson, Que. — q19 74
Delta, Ont. — C8 73
Delta, Al., U.S. — B4 78
Delta, Co., U.S. — C2 83
Delta, Ia., U.S. — C5 92
Delta, La., U.S. — B5 95
Delta, Mo., U.S. — D8 102
Delta, Oh., U.S. — A1 112
Delta, Pa., U.S. — G9 115
Delta, Ut., U.S. — D3 121
Delta, co., Co., U.S. — C3 83
Delta, co., Mi., U.S. — C3 99
Delta, co., Tx., U.S. — C5 120
Delta, reg., Ms., U.S. — B3 101
Delta Amacuro, terr., Ven. — B5 60
Delta Barrage, Eg. — D3 41
Delta Beach, Man. — D2 70
Delta City, Ms., U.S. — B3 101
Delta Junction, Ak., U.S. — C10 79
Delta Peak, mtn., B.C. — A3 69
Delta Reservoir, res., N.Y., U.S. — B5 109
Deltaville, Va., U.S. — C6 123
Delton, Mi., U.S. — F5 99
Deltona, Fl., U.S. — D5 86
Delungra, Austl. — D8 51
Delvin, Ire. — D4 11
Delvina, Alb. — C3 25
Delyatin, Sov. Un. — G5 27
Demaine, Sask. — G2 75
Demanda, Sierra de la, mtn., Spain — A4 22
Demarest, N.J., U.S. — h9 107
Demavend, Mount, mtn., Iran — B5 38
Demba, Zaire — C3 48
Dembi Dolo, Eth. — D3 47
Demerara, stm., Guy. — A3 59
Demidov, Sov. Un. — D8 27
Deming, N.M., U.S. — E2 108
Deming, Wa., U.S. — A3 124
Demini, stm., Braz. — B2 59
Demirci, Tur. — C7 40
Demir Kapija, Yugo. — E6 24
Demmin, E. Ger. — B6 18
Demmitt, Alta. — B1 68
Demnat, Mor. — C3 44
Demopolis, Al., U.S. — C2 78
Demopolis Dam, Al., U.S. — C2 78
Demorest, Ga., U.S. — B3 87
Demoresville, Ont. — C7 73
De Mossville, Ky., U.S. — k14 94
Demotte, In., U.S. — B3 91
Dempo, mtn., Indon. — F2 34
Dempster, S.D., U.S. — C9 118
Demyanka, stm., Sov. Un. — A7 37
Demyansk, Sov. Un. — C5 109
Denain, Fr. — B5 16
Denakil (Danakil), plat., Afr. — C5 47
Denali National Park, Ak., U.S. — C9 79
Denare Beach, Sask. — C4 75
Denau, Sov. Un. — H22 8
Denaud, Fl., U.S. — F5 86
Denbigh, Wales, U.K. — D5 10
Denbigh, N.D., U.S. — A5 111
Den Burg, Neth. — A4 17
Denby, S.D., U.S. — C3 118
Dendermonde, Bel. — C4 17
Denezhkin Kamen, Mount, mtn., Sov. Un. — A5 28
Dengkou, China — D2 32
Denham, In., U.S. — B4 91
Denham, Mount, mtn., Jam. — E13 64
Denham Springs, La., U.S. — D5 95
Den Helder, Neth. — A6 16
Denhoff, N.D., U.S. — B5 111
Den Hoorn, Neth. — A4 17
Denia, Spain — C6 22
Deniau, Que. — B8 74
Deniliquin, Austl. — G8 51
Denio, Nv., U.S. — B3 105
Denison, Ks., U.S. — k14 93
Denison, Tx., U.S. — C4 120
Denison Dam, U.S. — D5 113
Denizli, Tur. — H13 8
Denman Glacier, ice, Ant. — C22 7
Denmark, N.S. — D6 71
Denmark, Ia., U.S. — D6 92
Denmark, Me., U.S. — E2 96
Denmark, S.C., U.S. — E5 117
Denmark, Wi., U.S. — D6 126
Denmark, ctry., Eur. — I3 14
Denmark Strait, strt. — C17 128
Dennehotso, Az., U.S. — A6 80
Denning, Ar., U.S. — B2 81
Dennis, Ks., U.S. — E8 93
Dennis, Ma., U.S. — A5 101
Dennis, Ms., U.S. — C7 98
Dennis Hill, mtn., Ct., U.S. — B3 84
Dennison, Il., U.S. — D6 90
Dennison, Mn., U.S. — p14 99
Dennison, Oh., U.S. — B4 112
Dennis Port, Ma., U.S. — C7 98
Dennysville, Me., U.S. — D5 96
Denny, Scot., U.K. — *D5 13
Dennysville, Me., U.S. — D9 104
Denny Terrace, S.C., U.S. — D5 117
Den Oever, Neth. — B5 17
Denpasar, Indon. — G5 34
Dent, co., Mo., U.S. — D6 102
Denton, Ga., U.S. — E4 87
Denton, Ks., U.S. — C8 93
Denton, Md., U.S. — C6 97
Denton, Mt., U.S. — C7 103
Denton, N.C., U.S. — B2 110
Denton, Tx., U.S. — C4 120

151

Name	Map Ref.	Page
Denton, co., Tx., U.S.	C4	120
D'Entrecasteaux, Point, c., Austl.	F2	50
D'Entrecasteaux Islands, is., Pap. N. Gui.	k13	50
Dents Du Midi, mts., Switz.	D2	21
Dentsville, S.C., U.S.	C6	117
Denver, Ar., U.S.	A2	81
Denver, Co., U.S.	B6	83
Denver, Il., U.S.	C2	90
Denver, In., U.S.	C5	91
Denver, Ia., U.S.	B5	92
Denver, Mo., U.S.	A3	102
Denver, N.C., U.S.	B1	110
Denver, Pa., U.S.	F9	115
Denver, Tn., U.S.	A4	119
Denver, W.V., U.S.	B5	125
Denver, co., Co., U.S.	B6	83
Denver City, Tx., U.S.	C1	120
Denville, N.J., U.S.	B4	107
Denzil, Sask.	E1	75
Deoghar, India	E11	37
De Panne, Bel.	C2	17
Departure Bay, B.C.	f12	69
Depauville, N.Y., U.S.	A4	109
Depauw, In., U.S.	H5	91
De Pere, Wi., U.S.	D5	126
Depew, N.Y., U.S.	C2	109
Depew, Ok., U.S.	B5	113
Depoe Bay, Or., U.S.	C2	114
Depok, Indon.	*G3	34
Deport, Tx., U.S.	C5	120
Deposit, N.Y., U.S.	C5	109
Depósito, Braz.	B2	59
Depot Harbour, Ont.	B4	73
Depue, Il., U.S.	B4	90
Deputy, In., U.S.	G6	91
Dêqên, China	F4	31
De Queen, Ar., U.S.	C1	81
De Queen Lake, res., Ar., U.S.	C1	81
Dequen-Nord, Que.	A5	74
De Quincy, La., U.S.	D2	95
Dera, al., stm., Afr.	E5	47
Dera Ghāzi Khān, Pak.	B5	36
Dera Ismāīl Khān, Pak.	B5	36
Derbent, Sov. Un.	E3	28
Derbetovka, Sov. Un.	I14	27
Derby, Austl.	C3	50
Derby, N.B.	C4	71
Derby, Eng., U.K.	D6	10
Derby, Ct., U.S.	D3	84
Derby, In., U.S.	H4	91
Derby, Ia., U.S.	D4	92
Derby, Ks., U.S.	E6	93
Derby, Me., U.S.	C4	96
Derby, Ms., U.S.	E4	101
Derby, N.Y., U.S.	C2	109
Derby, Oh., U.S.	C2	112
Derby, Va., U.S.	f9	123
Derby Junction, N.B.	C4	71
Derby Line, Vt., U.S.	A4	122
Derbyshire, co., Eng., U.K.	A6	12
Derecske, Hung.	B5	24
Derg, Lough, l., Ire.	D2	10
Der Grabow, b., E. Ger.	D6	15
De Ridder, La., U.S.	D2	95
Derik, Tur.	D13	40
Derma, Ms., U.S.	B4	101
Dermott, Ar., U.S.	D4	81
Dernieres, Isles, is., La., U.S.	E5	95
Derravaragh, Lough, l., Ire.	D3	10
Derrieusseaux Creek, stm., Ar., U.S.	C3	81
Derry, La., U.S.	C3	95
Derry, N.H., U.S.	E4	106
Derry, N.M., U.S.	E2	108
Derry, Pa., U.S.	F3	115
Derrybrien, Ire.	D3	11
Derry see Londonderry, N. Ire., U.K.	C3	10
Derudeb, Sud.	B4	47
De Ruyter, N.Y., U.S.	C5	109
Derventa, Yugo.	C3	24
Derwent, Alta.	C5	68
Derwent, Oh., U.S.	C4	112
Derwent, stm., Eng., U.K.	F8	13
Derwent, stm., Eng., U.K.	F6	13
Derwent, stm., Eng., U.K.	A7	13
Derwood, Md., U.S.	B3	97
Derzhavinsk, Sov. Un.	C7	28
Desaguadero, stm., Arg.	A3	54
Desaguadero, stm., Bol.	C5	55
Des Allemands, La., U.S.	E5	95
Desamparados, C.R.	*F5	62
Des Arc, Ar., U.S.	C4	81
Des Arc, Mo., U.S.	D7	102
Desbiens, Que.	A6	74
Desboro, Ont.	C3	73
Descalvado, Braz.	k8	56
Descartes, Fr.	D4	16
Deschaillons [-sur-Saint-Laurent], Que.	C5	74
Deschambault, Que.	C6	74
Deschambault Lake, Sask.	C4	75
Deschambault Lake, l., Sask.	C4	75
Deschênes, Que.	D3	74
Deschutes, co., Or., U.S.	D5	114
Deschutes, stm., Or., U.S.	B6	114
Dese, Eth.	C4	47
Deseado, stm., Arg.	D3	54
Desengaño, Punta, c., Arg.	D3	54
Desenzano del Garda, Italy	D6	22
Deseret, Ut., U.S.	D3	121
Deseret Peak, mtn., Ut., U.S.	*C3	121
Deseronto, Ont.	C7	73
Desert, Mount, mtn., N.W., U.S.	m13	125
Deserta Grande, i., Port.	h12	22
Desert Center, Ca., U.S.	F6	82
Desert Creek Peak, mtn., Nv., U.S.	E2	105
Desert Hot Springs, Ca., U.S.	F5	82
Desert Peak, mtn., Ut., U.S.	B2	121
Desert Valley, val., Nv., U.S.	B3	105
Desha, Ar., U.S.	B4	81
Desha, co., Ar., U.S.	D4	81
Deshler, Ne., U.S.	D8	104
Deshler, Oh., U.S.	A2	112
Desio, Italy	D5	20
Des Lacs, N.D., U.S.	A4	111
Des Lacs, stm., N.D., U.S.	A4	111
Desloge, Mo., U.S.	D7	102
Desmarais, Alta.	B4	68
Desmet, Id., U.S.	B2	89
De Smet, S.D., U.S.	C8	118
Desmochados, Para.	E4	55
Des Moines, Ia., U.S.	C4	92
Des Moines, N.M., U.S.	A6	108
Des Moines, Wa., U.S.	B3	124
Des Moines, co., Ia., U.S.	D6	92
Des Moines, stm., U.S.	D5	92
Des Moines, East Fork, stm.,	A3	92
Desna, stm., Sov. Un.	F8	27
Desolación, Isla, i., Chile	h11	54
Desolation Canyon, val., Ut., U.S.	D5	121
De Soto, Ga., U.S.	E2	87
De Soto, Il., U.S.	F4	90
De Soto, Ia., U.S.	C3	92
De Soto, Ks., U.S.	D9	93
De Soto, Ms., U.S.	D5	101
De Soto, Mo., U.S.	C7	102
De Soto, Tx., U.S.	*n10	120
De Soto, Wi., U.S.	E2	126
De Soto, co., Fl., U.S.	E5	86
De Soto, co., La., U.S.	B2	95
De Soto, co., Ms., U.S.	A3	101
De Soto City, Fl., U.S.	E5	86
Despard, W.V., U.S.	k10	125
Des Peres, Mo., U.S.	f13	102
Des Plaines, Il., U.S.	A6	90
Des Plaines, stm., U.S.	k8	90
Dessau, E. Ger.	C6	18
Destin, Fl., U.S.	u15	86
Destrehan, La., U.S.	E5	95
Desvres, Fr.	D1	17
Dete, Zimb.	A4	49
Detlor, Ont.	B7	73
Detmold, W. Ger.	C4	18
Detour, Point, c., Mi., U.S.	C4	99
De Tour Village, Mi., U.S.	C7	99
Detroit, Al., U.S.	A1	78
Detroit, Ks., U.S.	D6	93
Detroit, Me., U.S.	D3	96
Detroit, Mi., U.S.	F7	99
Detroit, Or., U.S.	C4	114
Detroit, Tx., U.S.	C5	120
Detroit, stm., N.A.	F7	99
Detroit Lake, res., Or., U.S.	C4	114
Detroit Lakes, Mn., U.S.	D3	100
Detva, Czech.	D5	26
Deuel, co., Ne., U.S.	C3	104
Deuel, co., S.D., U.S.	C9	118
Deurne (part of Antwerp), Bel.	B6	16
Deux Frères, Les, is., Viet.	H7	35
Deux-Montagnes, Que.	p19	74
Deux-Montagnes, co., Que.	D3	74
Deux Montagnes, Lac des, l., Que.	q19	74
Deux-Rivières, Ont.	A6	73
Deva, Rom.	C6	24
De Valls Bluff, Ar., U.S.	C4	81
Dévaványa, Hung.	B5	24
Deventer, Neth.	A7	16
Devereux, Ga., U.S.	C3	87
Deveron, stm., Scot., U.K.	C6	13
DeView, Bayou, stm., Ar., U.S.	B4	81
Devil River Peak, mtn., N.Z.	N14	51
Devils Elbow, Mo., U.S.	D5	102
Devils Island see Diable, Île du, i., Fr. Gu.	A4	59
Devils Lake, N.D., U.S.	A7	111
Devils Lake, l., N.D., U.S.	A6	111
Devils Paw, mtn., Ak., U.S.	k23	79
Devils Postpile National Monument, Ca., U.S.	D4	82
Devils Slide, Ut., U.S.	B4	121
Devils Tower, Wy., U.S.	B8	127
Devils Tower National Monument, Wy., U.S.	B8	127
Devil Track Lake, l., Mn., U.S.	k9	100
Devin, Bul.	E7	24
Devine, Tx., U.S.	E3	120
Devizes, Eng., U.K.	C6	12
Devol, Ok., U.S.	C3	113
Devola, Oh., U.S.	C4	112
Devoll, stm., Alb.	B3	25
Devon, Alta.	C4	68
Devon, Ks., U.S.	E9	93
Devon, Mt., U.S.	B5	103
Devon, Pa., U.S.	*o20	115
Devon, co., Eng., U.K.	D4	12
Devonia, Tn., U.S.	C9	119
Devon Island, i., N.W. Ter.	m34	66
Devonport, Austl.	o15	50
Devonshire, co.,	h7	85
Dewalt, Tx., U.S.	r14	120
Dewar, Ok., U.S.	B6	113
Dewar Lake, Sask.	F1	75
Dewberry, Alta.	C5	68
Dewdney, B.C.	f8	69
Deweese, Ne., U.S.	D7	104
Dewees Inlet, b., S.C., U.S.	k12	117
Dewees Island, i., S.C., U.S.	F8	117
Dewey, Az., U.S.	C3	80
Dewey, Mt., U.S.	E4	103
Dewey, Ok., U.S.	A6	113
Dewey, co., Ok., U.S.	B2	113
Dewey, co., S.D., U.S.	B4	118
Dewey Beach, De., U.S.	F5	85
Dewey Lake, res., Ky., U.S.	C7	94
Deweyville, Tx., U.S.	D6	120
Deweyville, Ut., U.S.	B3	121
De Winton, Alta.	D3	68
Dewitt, Ar., U.S.	C4	81
DeWitt, Il., U.S.	C5	90
De Witt, Ia., U.S.	C7	92
De Witt, Mi., U.S.	F6	99
De Witt, Mo., U.S.	B4	102
De Witt, N.Y., U.S.	B4	109
DeWitt, Va., U.S.	C5	123
De Witt, co., Il., U.S.	C5	90
De Witt, co., Tx., U.S.	E4	120
Dewsbury, Eng., U.K.	A6	12
Dexing, China	J7	32
Dexter, Ga., U.S.	D3	87
Dexter, Ia., U.S.	C3	92
Dexter, Ks., U.S.	E7	93
Dexter, Ky., U.S.	f9	94
Dexter, Me., U.S.	C3	96
Dexter, Mi., U.S.	F7	99
Dexter, Mn., U.S.	G6	100
Dexter, Mo., U.S.	E8	102
Dexter, N.M., U.S.	D5	108
Dexter, N.Y., U.S.	A4	109
Dexter, Or., U.S.	D4	114
Dexter, Lake, l., Fl., U.S.	C5	86
Dey-Dey, Lake, l., Austl.	E5	50
Deyhūk, Iran	B4	38
Deyyer, Iran	H6	39
Dez, stm., Iran	E4	39
Dezfūl, Iran	B4	38
Dezhnev, Cape, c., Sov. Un.	C21	29
Dezhou, China	D8	31
Dhahab, Eg.	H10	40
Dhahran see Az Zahrān, Sau. Ar.	C4	38
Dhaka (Dacca), Bngl.	D9	36
Dhamār, Yemen	F4	38
Dhamtari, India	G8	37
Dhangadhī, Nepal	C8	36
D'Hanis, Tx., U.S.	E3	120
Dhankuta, Nepal	D11	36
Dhār, India	F5	37
Dharmapuri, India	F6	36
Dharmjaygarh, India	D7	36
Dharmshāla, India	B6	36
Dhaulpur, India	D6	37
Dhawlāgiri, mtn., Nepal	C7	36
Dhekélia, Grc.	g11	25
Dhenoúsa, i., Grc.	D5	25
Dhíbān, Jord.	G10	40
Dhidhimótikhon, Grc.	B6	25
Dhílos (Delos), i., Grc.	D5	25
Dhimitsána, Grc.	D4	25
Dhomhnuill, Sgurr, mtn., Scot., U.K.	D3	13
Dhorāji, India	G3	37
Dhrépanon, Cape, c., Grc.	C4	25
Dhuburi, India	D12	37
Dhule, India	D5	36
Dhuusa Mareeb, Som.	D6	47
Día, i., Grc.	E5	25
Diable, Pointe du, c., Mart.	S11	65
Diablerets, mtn., Switz.	C3	20
Diablo, Canyon, val., Az., U.S.	C4	80
Diablo, Mount, mtn., Ca., U.S.	h9	82
Diablo Dam, Wa., U.S.	A4	124
Diablo Heights, Pan.	m11	62
Diablo Lake, res., Wa., U.S.	A4	124
Diablo Range, mts., Ca., U.S.	D3	82
Diamante, Arg.	A4	54
Diamantina, Braz.	B4	56
Diamantina, stm., Austl.	D7	50
Diamond, Oh., U.S.	A4	112
Diamond, W.V., U.S.	m12	125
Diamond Bar, Ca., U.S.	*n13	82
Diamond Bluff, Wi., U.S.	D1	126
Diamond City, Alta.	E4	68
Diamond Harbour, India	F12	37
Diamond Head, crat., Hi., U.S.	B4	88
Diamond Hill, R.I., U.S.	B4	116
Diamond Hill Reservoir, res., R.I., U.S.	A4	116
Diamond Lake, Il., U.S.	h9	90
Diamond Lake, l., Or., U.S.	D4	114
Diamond Mountains, mts., Nv., U.S.	D6	105
Diamond Peak, mtn., Co., U.S.	A2	83
Diamond Peak, mtn., Id., U.S.	E5	89
Diamond Peak, mtn., Or., U.S.	D4	114
Diamond Peak, mtn., Wa., U.S.	C8	124
Diamond Point, N.Y., U.S.	B7	109
Diamond Springs, Ca., U.S.	C3	82
Diamondville, Wy., U.S.	E2	127
Diana, Tn., U.S.	B5	119
Diana, W.V., U.S.	C4	125
Dianalund, Den.	C5	15
Dianbai, China	G7	31
Dianjiang, China	I2	32
Dianópolis, Braz.	D1	57
Diapaga, Burkina	D5	45
Diapitan Bay, b., Phil.	n14	34
Diaz, Ar., U.S.	B4	81
Dibaya, Zaire	C3	48
Dibble Iceberg Tongue, ice, Ant.	C26	7
D'Iberville, Ms., U.S.	E5	101
D'Iberville, Lac, l., Que.	g12	74
Diboll, Tx., U.S.	D5	120
Dibrell, Tn., U.S.	D8	119
Dibrugarh, India	C9	36
Dickens, Ia., U.S.	A2	92
Dickens, Ne., U.S.	D5	104
Dickens, Tx., U.S.	C2	120
Dickens, co., Tx., U.S.	C2	120
Dickerson, Md., U.S.	B3	97
Dickey, N.D., U.S.	C7	111
Dickey, co., N.D., U.S.	C7	111
Dickeyville, Wi., U.S.	F3	126
Dickinson, Al., U.S.	D2	78
Dickinson, N.D., U.S.	C3	111
Dickinson, Tx., U.S.	*r14	120
Dickinson, co., Ia., U.S.	A2	92
Dickinson, co., Ks., U.S.	D6	93
Dickinson, co., Mi., U.S.	B3	99
Dickinson Center, N.Y., U.S.	f10	109
Dickson, Ok., U.S.	C5	113
Dickson, Tn., U.S.	A4	119
Dickson, co., Tn., U.S.	A4	119
Dickson City, Pa., U.S.	D10	115
Dicle (Tigris), stm., Asia	D13	40
Didsbury, Alta.	D3	68
Dīdwāna, India	D5	37
Die, Fr.	E6	16
Diébougou, Burkina	D4	45
Dieburg, W. Ger.	D3	19
Diefenbaker, Lake, res., Sask.	F2	75
Diégo-Suarez see Antsiranana, Madag.	f9	49
Diekirch, Lux.	E6	17
Diemel, stm., W. Ger.	B3	19
Dien Bien Phu, Viet.	B5	35
Diepholz, W. Ger.	B4	18
Dieppe, N.B.	C5	71
Dieppe, Fr.	C4	16
Dierks, Ar., U.S.	C1	81
Di'er Songhua, stm., China	D2	33
Diessen, W. Ger.	B7	20
Diest, Bel.	D5	17
Dieterich, Il., U.S.	D5	90
Dietikon, Switz.	C3	20
Dietrich, Id., U.S.	G4	89
Dieuze, Fr.	F7	17
Diever, Neth.	B6	16
Diez, W. Ger.	C2	19
Diffa, Niger	D7	45
Differdange, Lux.	E5	17
Difficult, Tn., U.S.	C8	119
Digboi, India	C10	36
Digby, N.S.	E4	71
Digby, co., N.S.	E4	71
Dighton, Ks., U.S.	D3	93
Dighton, Ma., U.S.	C5	98
Dighton, Mi., U.S.	D5	99
Digoin, Fr.	D5	16
Digul, stm., Indon.	G8	34
Dijon, Fr.	D6	16
Dike, Ia., U.S.	B5	92
Dikhil, Dji.	D5	47
Dikili, Tur.	C6	25
Dikirnis, Eg.	C3	41
Diksmuide, Bel.	C2	17
Dikson, Sov. Un.	B11	29
Dikwa, Nig.	D7	45
Dila, Eth.	D4	47
Dili, Indon.	G7	34
Dilke, Sask.	G3	75
Dilkon, Az., U.S.	B5	80
Dillard, Ga., U.S.	B3	87
Dillard, Or., U.S.	D2	114
Dill City, Ok., U.S.	B2	113
Dille, W.V., U.S.	C4	125
Dillenburg, W. Ger.	C3	19
Diller, Ne., U.S.	D9	104
Dilley, Tx., U.S.	E3	120
Dilliner, Pa., U.S.	G2	115
Dilling, Sud.	C2	47
Dillingen, W. Ger.	D1	19
Dillingen [an der Donau], W. Ger.	D5	18
Dillingham, Ak., U.S.	D8	79
Dillon, Co., U.S.	B4	83
Dillon, Mt., U.S.	E4	103
Dillon, S.C., U.S.	C9	117
Dillon, co., S.C., U.S.	C9	117
Dillon, stm., Can.	B5	68
Dillon Lake, l., Sask.	B6	68
Dillon Lake, res., Oh., U.S.	B3	112
Dillon Reservoir, res., Co., U.S.	B4	83
Dillonvale, Oh., U.S.	B5	112
Dillsboro, In., U.S.	F7	91
Dillsboro, N.C., U.S.	f9	110
Dillsburg, Pa., U.S.	F7	115
Dilolo, Zaire	D3	48
Dilworth, Mn., U.S.	D2	100
Dimbelenge, Zaire	C3	48
Dimbokro, I.C.	E4	45
Dimitrovgrad, Bul.	D7	24
Dimitrovgrad, Yugo.	D6	24
Dîmbovita, stm., Rom.	C7	24
Dimmit, co., Tx., U.S.	E3	120
Dimmitt, Tx., U.S.	B1	120
Dimock, S.D., U.S.	D8	118
Dimona, Isr.	C7	41
Dimondale, Mi., U.S.	F6	99
Dinagat Island, i., Phil.	C7	34
Dināpur, Bngl.	E12	37
Dinan, Fr.	C2	16
Dinant, Bel.	B6	16
Dinar, Tur.	C8	25
Dinard, Fr.	C2	16
Dinaric Alps, mts., Yugo.	C3	24
Dindigul, India	F6	36
Dinero, Tx., U.S.	E4	120
Dingalan Bay, b., Phil.	o13	34
Dingbian, China	D6	31
Dingelstädt, E. Ger.	B5	19
Dingess, W.V., U.S.	D2	125
Dinghai, China	E9	31
Dingle, Ire.	D1	10
Dingle, Id., U.S.	G7	89
Dingle Bay, b., Ire.	D1	10
Dingmans Ferry, Pa., U.S.	D12	115
Dingo, Austl.	A7	51
Dingolfing, W. Ger.	E7	19
Dinguiraye, Gui.	D2	45
Dingwall, N.S.	C9	71
Dingwall, Scot., U.K.	B4	10
Dingxian, China	D8	31
Dingxing, China	D8	31
Dinh Lap, Viet.	B5	35
Dinkelsbühl, W. Ger.	D5	19
Dinklage, W. Ger.	F2	15
Dinorwic Lake, l., Ont.	E5	70
Dinosaur, Co., U.S.	A2	83
Dinosaur National Monument, U.S.	C6	121
Dinosaur Provincial Park, Alta.	D5	68
Dinsdale, Ia., U.S.	B5	92
Dinslaken, W. Ger.	B1	19
Dinsmore, Sask.	F2	75
Dinuba, Ca., U.S.	D4	82
Dinwiddie, Va., U.S.	C5	123
Dinwiddie, co., Va., U.S.	C5	123
Dioila, Mali	D3	45
Diourbel, Sen.	D1	45
Diphu Pass, Asia	C10	36
Diplo, Pak.	E2	37
Dipper Harbour West, N.B.	D3	71
Dippoldiswalde, E. Ger.	C8	19
Diré, Mali	D4	45
Direction, Cape, c., Austl.	B7	50
Dire Dawa, Eth.	C4	47
Dirico, Ang.	E3	48
Dirk Hartog, i., Austl.	E1	50
Dirkou, Niger	C7	45
Dirmil, Tur.	D7	25
Dirranbandi, Austl.	E8	50
Dirty Devil, stm., Ut., U.S.	E5	121
Disappointment, Cape, c., Falk. Is.	D9	7
Disappointment, Cape, c., Wa., U.S.	C1	124
Disappointment, Lake, l., Austl.	D3	50
Disappointment Creek, stm., Co., U.S.	D2	83
Discovery, Mount, mtn., Ant.	f39	7
Disentis (Mustér), Switz.	C4	20
Dishman, Wa., U.S.	g14	124
Dishnā, Eg.	D6	43
Disko, i., Grnld.	C15	61
Disley, Que.	G3	75
Dismal, stm., Ne., U.S.	C5	104
Dismal Peak, mtn., Va., U.S.	C22	123
Disney, Ok., U.S.	A6	113
Disputanta, Va., U.S.	C5	123
Disraëli, Que.	D6	74
Diss, Eng., U.K.	B9	12
Distant, Pa., U.S.	E3	115
District Heights-Forestville, Md., U.S.	*C4	97
District of Columbia, dept., U.S.	f8	97
Distrito Especial (Bogotá), dept., Col.	C3	60
Distrito Federal (Federal District), state, Mex.	D5	63
Distrito Federal, dept., Arg.	g7	54
Distrito Federal, dept., Braz.	B3	56
Distrito Federal, dept., Ven.	A4	60
Disūq, Eg.	C6	43
Ditzum, W. Ger.	A7	17
Diu, India	D5	36
Divernon, Il., U.S.	D4	90
Divide, co., N.D., U.S.	A2	111
Divide Peak, mtn., Wy., U.S.	E5	127
Dividing Creek, N.J., U.S.	E2	107
Dividing Creek, stm., Md., U.S.	D6	97
Divinópolis, Braz.	C4	56
Divisões, Serra das, hills, Braz.	B2	56
Divišov, Czech.	o18	26
Divnoye, Sov. Un.	I14	27
Divo, I.C.	E3	45
Divrigi, Tur.	C12	40
Dix, Il., U.S.	E5	90
Dix, Ne., U.S.	C2	104
Dix, stm., Ky., U.S.	C5	94
Dix Dam, Ky., U.S.	C5	94
Dixence, stm., Switz.	D3	21
Dixfield, Me., U.S.	D2	96
Dix Hills, N.Y., U.S.	*n15	109
Dixiana, Al., U.S.	D3	78
Dixie, Ga., U.S.	F3	87
Dixie, Id., U.S.	D3	89
Dixie, La., U.S.	C2	95
Dixie, Wa., U.S.	C7	124
Dixie, co., Fl., U.S.	C3	86
Dixie Union, Ga., U.S.	E4	87
Dixie Valley, val., Nv., U.S.	D4	105
Dix Mountain, mtn., N.Y., U.S.	A7	109
Dixon, Ca., U.S.	C3	82
Dixon, Il., U.S.	B4	90
Dixon, In., U.S.	C8	91
Dixon, Ia., U.S.	C7	92
Dixon, Ky., U.S.	C2	94
Dixon, Mo., U.S.	C5	102
Dixon, Mt., U.S.	C2	103
Dixon, Ne., U.S.	B9	104
Dixon, N.M., U.S.	A4	108
Dixon, Oh., U.S.	C1	112
Dixon, S.D., U.S.	D6	118
Dixon, Wy., U.S.	E5	127
Dixon, co., Ne., U.S.	B9	104
Dixons Mills, Al., U.S.	C2	78
Dixon Springs, Il., U.S.	F5	90
Dixonville, Alta.	A2	68
Dixonville, Pa., U.S.	E3	115
Dixville Notch, N.H., U.S.	g7	106
Dixville Notch, N.H., U.S.	g7	106
Dixville Peak, mtn., N.H., U.S.	g7	106
Diyarbakır, Tur.	D13	40
Dizy-le-Gros, Fr.	E3	17
Dizy-Magenta, Fr.	E3	17
Dja, stm., Afr.	B7	45
Djado, Niger	B7	45
Djakarta see Jakarta, Indon.	G3	34
Djakovica, Yugo.	D5	24
Djakovo, Yugo.	C4	24
Djambala, Congo	B1	48
Djanet, Alg.	E6	44
Djaravica, mtn., Yugo.	D5	24
Djédaa, Chad	C3	47
Djedeida, Tun.	C4	44
Djema, Cen. Afr. Rep.	D4	45
Djénné, Mali	D4	45
Djerba, Île de, i., Tun.	C7	44
Djerid, Chott, sw., Tun.	C6	44
Djibo, Burkina	D4	45
Djibouti, Dji.	C5	47
Djibouti, ctry., Afr.	C5	47
Djokupunda, Zaire	C3	48
Djolu, Zaire	A3	48
Djoua, stm., Afr.	E2	46
Djougou, Benin	E5	45
Djugu, Zaire	A5	48
Djurdjevac, Yugo.	B3	24
Djursholm, Swe.	t36	14
D'Lo, Ms., U.S.	D4	101
Długa, stm., Pol.	k14	26
Dmitriyev-Lgovskiy, Sov. Un.	E10	27
Dmitrov, Sov. Un.	C11	27
Dmitrovsk-Orlovskiy, Sov. Un.	E10	27
Dnepr, stm., Sov. Un.	D5	29
Dneprodzerzhinsk, Sov. Un.	H9	28
Dnepropetrovsk, Sov. Un.	E6	29
Dnestr, stm., Sov. Un.	H7	27
Dnieper see Dnepr, stm., Sov. Un.	D5	29
Dno, Sov. Un.	C7	27
Doaktown, N.B.	C3	71
Doany, Madag.	f9	49
Doba, Chad	D3	49
Dobbins Air Force Base, mil., Ga., U.S.	h7	87
Dobbinton, Ont.	C3	73
Dobbs Ferry, N.Y., U.S.	g13	109
Döbeln, E. Ger.	C6	18
Doberai Peninsula, pen., Indon.	F9	34
Doberlug-Kirchhain, E. Ger.	B8	19
Doblas, Arg.	A4	54
Dobo, Indon.	G8	34
Doboj, Yugo.	C4	24
Doboy Sound, b., Ga., U.S.	E5	87
Dobřejovice, Czech.	o18	26
Dobříš, Czech.	D5	26
Dobrovice, Czech.	n18	26
Dobrovolsk, Sov. Un.	A7	26
Dobruja, reg., Eur.	C12	24
Dobson, N.C., U.S.	A2	110
Doce, stm., Braz.	E2	57
Docena, Al., U.S.	f7	78
Dock Junction, Ga., U.S.	E5	87
Dockton, Wa., U.S.	f11	124
Doctor Arroyo, Mex.	C4	63
Doctor Pedro P. Peña, Para.	A4	54
Doctors Inlet, Fl., U.S.	m8	86
Doctors Lake, l., Fl., U.S.	m8	86
Doctortown, Ga., U.S.	E5	87
Doddridge, Ar., U.S.	D1	81
Doddridge, co., W.V., U.S.	B4	125
Dodds, Alta.	C5	68
Doddsville, Ms., U.S.	B3	101
Dodecanese, is., Grc.	D6	25
Dodge, Ne., U.S.	C9	104
Dodge, N.D., U.S.	B3	111
Dodge, Wi., U.S.	D1	126
Dodge, co., Ga., U.S.	D3	87
Dodge, co., Mn., U.S.	G6	100
Dodge, co., Ne., U.S.	C9	104
Dodge, co., Wi., U.S.	E5	126
Dodge Center, Mn., U.S.	F6	100
Dodge City, Ks., U.S.	E3	93
Dodge Park, Md., U.S.	*C4	97
Dodgeville, Wi., U.S.	F3	126
Dodoma, Tan.	C6	48
Dodoma, prov., Tan.	C6	48
Dodsland, Sask.	F1	75
Dodson, La., U.S.	B3	95
Dodson, Mt., U.S.	B8	103
Dodson, Tx., U.S.	B2	120
Dodson Peninsula, pen., Ant.	B7	7
Doe River, B.C.	A7	69
Doerun, Ga., U.S.	E3	87
Doe Run, Mo., U.S.	D7	102
Doetinchem, Neth.	A7	16
Dog, stm., Vt., U.S.	C3	122
Dogai Coring, l., China	D10	36
Dog Island, i., Fl., U.S.	C2	86
Dog Keys Pass, strt., Ms., U.S.	g8	101
Dog Lake, l., Man.	D2	70
Dōgo Island, i., Japan	H6	33
Do Gonbadān, Iran	*F5	39
Dogondoutchi, Niger	D5	45
Doğubayazit, Tur.	C15	40
Doha (Ad Dawhah), Qatar	C5	38
Doheny, Que.	B5	74
Doiran, Lake, l., Eur.	E6	24
Dois Córregos, Braz.	m7	56
Dokkum, Neth.	A6	17
Doksy, Czech.	C9	19
Dol, Fr.	C3	16
Doland, S.D., U.S.	C7	118
Dolavón, Arg.	C3	54
Dôle, Fr.	D6	16
Dolega, Pan.	F6	62
Doleib Hill, Sud.	D3	47
Doles, Ga., U.S.	E3	87
Dolgellau, Wales, U.K.	B4	12
Dolgeville, N.Y., U.S.	B6	109
Dolina, Sov. Un.	D8	26
Dolinsk, Sov. Un.	B13	31
Dolinskoye, Sov. Un.	B9	24
Dollar Bay, Mi., U.S.	A2	99
Dollard, Sask.	H1	75
Dollart, b., Eur.	A7	17
Dollarville, Mi., U.S.	B5	99
Dolliver, Ia., U.S.	A3	92
Dolný Kubín, Czech.	D5	26
Dolomi, Ak., U.S.	B3	78
Dolomite, Al., U.S.	g7	78
Dolomites, mts., Italy	A3	23
Dolores, Arg.	B5	54
Dolores, Guat.	D7	63
Dolores, Mex.	B3	63
Dolores, Co., U.S.	D2	83
Dolores, Ur.	E1	56
Dolores, co., Co., U.S.	D2	83
Dolores Hidalgo, Mex.	m13	63
Dolphin and Union Strait, strt., N.W. Ter.	C9	66
Dolphin Head, mtn., Jam.	E12	65
Dolphin Island, i., Ut., U.S.	B3	121
Dolton, Il., U.S.	k9	90
Dolton, S.D., U.S.	D8	118
Dom, mtn., Switz.	D4	21
Domadare, Som.	E5	47
Dom Aquino, Braz.	B2	56
Domat-Ems, Switz.	C7	21
Domažlice, Czech.	D2	26
Dombarovskiy, Sov. Un.	C5	28
Dombås, Nor.	F3	14
Dombasle[-sur-Meurthe], Fr.	F6	17
Dombe Grande, Ang.	D1	48
Domburg, Neth.	C3	17
Dôme, Puy de, mtn., Fr.	E5	16
Dôme Mountain, mtn., Az., U.S.	k9	80
Dome of the Rock, Isr. Occ.	m14	41
Dome Peak, mtn., Co., U.S.	B3	83
Domeyko, Cordillera, mts., Chile	D2	54
Domfront, Fr.	C3	16
Dominica, ctry., N.A.	i14	64
Dominica Passage, strt., N.A.	I14	64
Dominion, N.S.	C9	71
Dominion, Cape, c., N.W. Ter.	C18	66
Dominion City, Man.	E3	70
Dominion Lake, l., Newf.	h9	72
Dömitz, E. Ger.	C5	17
Dommel, stm., Eur.	D6	47
Domo, Eth.	C6	47
Domodedovo, Sov. Un.	n17	27
Domodossola, Italy	A2	23
Dom Pedrito, Braz.	E2	56
Dompierre [-sur-Authie], Fr.	D1	17
Domremy, Sask.	E3	75
Domuyo, Volcán, vol., Arg.	H13	29
Don, stm., Scot., U.K.	C6	13
Dona Ana, N.M., U.S.	E3	108
Dona Ana, co., N.M., U.S.	E2	108
Donaghadee, N. Ire., U.K.	C4	10
Donald, Ont.	h12	114
Donalda, Alta.	C4	68
Donalds, S.C., U.S.	C3	117
Donaldson, In., U.S.	B5	91
Donaldson, Mn., U.S.	B2	100
Donaldsonville, La., U.S.	D4	95
Donalsonville, Ga., U.S.	E2	87
Donard, Slieve, mtn., N. Ire., U.K.	D5	11
Donaueschingen, W. Ger.	B4	20
Donauwörth, W. Ger.	F2	75
Donavon, Sask.	F2	75
Don Benito, Spain	C3	22
Doncaster, Eng., U.K.	D6	10
Doncaster and Templestowe, Austl.	*G8	50
Dondo, Ang.	C1	48
Dondo, Moz.	A5	49
Donegal, Ire.	C2	10
Donegal, co., Ire.	C4	11
Donegal Bay, b., Ire.	E2	11
Donegal Point, c., Ire.	E2	11
Doneraile, S.C., U.S.	C8	117
Donets Basin, Sov. Un.	q21	29
Donetsk, Sov. Un.	E6	29
Dongara, Austl.	E1	50
Dongchuan, China	F5	31
Dongfang, China	B7	36
Donggala, Indon.	F6	34
Dongguan, China	C8	35
Dong Hoi, Viet.	B3	35
Dongola, Il., U.S.	F4	90
Dongou, Congo	A2	48
Dongsheng, China	D6	31
Dongting Hu, l., China	F7	31
Dongxiang, China	J7	32
Dongzhi, China	I?	32
Doniphan, Mo., U.S.	E7	102
Doniphan, Ne., U.S.	D7	104
Doniphan, co., Ks., U.S.	C8	93
Donji Vakuf, Yugo.	C3	24
Donkey Creek, stm., Wy., U.S.	B7	127

Name	Map Ref.	Page
Donkin, N.S.	C10	71
Donley, co., Tx., U.S.	B2	120
Donna, Tx., U.S.	F3	120
Donnacona, Que.	C6	74
Donnellson, Il., U.S.	D4	90
Donnellson, Ia., U.S.	D6	92
Donnelly, Alta.	B2	68
Donnelly, Id., U.S.	E2	89
Donnelly, Mn., U.S.	E2	100
Donner, La., U.S.	E5	95
Donner Pass, Ca., U.S.	C3	82
Donora, Pa., U.S.	F2	115
Donovan, Il., U.S.	C6	90
Don Peninsula, pen., B.C.	C3	69
Donzère, Fr.	E6	16
Dooagh, Ire.	D1	11
Doogort, Ire.	C1	11
Doole, Tx., U.S.	D3	120
Dooling, Ga., U.S.	D3	87
Doolittle, Mo., U.S.	D6	102
Dooly, co., Ga., U.S.	D3	87
Doon, Ia., U.S.	A1	92
Doon, Loch, l., Scot., U.K.	E4	13
Doonbeg, Ire.	E2	11
Doonerak, Mount, mtn., Ak., U.S.	B9	79
Door, co., Wi., U.S.	D6	126
Doornik see Tournai, Bel.	D3	17
Dora, Al., U.S.	B2	78
Dora, Mo., U.S.	E5	102
Dora, N.M., U.S.	D6	108
Dora, Lake, l., Austl.	D3	50
Dora Baltea, stm., Italy	B1	23
Doran, Mn., U.S.	D2	100
Doraville, Ga., U.S.	h8	87
Dorbod, China	A11	32
Dorcas, Fl., U.S.	u15	86
Dorcheat, Bayou, stm., U.S.	B2	95
Dorchester, N.B.	D5	71
Dorchester, Eng., U.K.	E5	10
Dorchester, Ga., U.S.	E5	87
Dorchester, Ia., U.S.	A6	92
Dorchester, Ne., U.S.	D8	104
Dorchester, N.J., U.S.	E3	107
Dorchester, S.C., U.S.	E7	117
Dorchester, Wi., U.S.	C3	126
Dorchester, co., Eng., U.K.	C7	74
Dorchester, co., Md., U.S.	D5	97
Dorchester, co., S.C., U.S.	E7	117
Dorchester, Cape, c., N.W. Ter.	C17	66
Dorchester Crossing, N.B.	C5	71
Dorchester Estates, S.C., U.S.	k11	117
Dorcyville, La., U.S.	h9	95
Dordogne, stm., Fr.	E4	16
Dordrecht, Neth.	B6	16
Dordrecht, S. Afr.	D4	49
Doré, stm., Sask.	C2	75
Doré Lake, l., Ont.	B7	73
Doré Lake, Sask.	C2	75
Doré Lake, l., Sask.	C2	75
Dorena, Or., U.S.	D4	114
Dorena Lake, res., Or., U.S.	D3	114
Dorenlee, Alta.	C4	68
Dores, Scot., U.K.	C4	13
Dores do Indaiá, Braz.	B3	56
Dorfen, W. Ger.	A8	20
Dorgali, Italy	D2	23
Dörgön Lake, l., Mong.	B3	31
Dori, Burkina	D4	45
Dorion-Vaudreuil, Que.	q18	74
Dorking, Eng., U.K.	m12	10
Dormagen, W. Ger.	*C3	18
Dormans, Fr.	E3	17
Dormont, Pa., U.S.	k13	115
Dornbirn, Aus.	E4	18
Dornie, Scot., U.K.	C3	13
Dornoch, Scot., U.K.	B4	10
Dornoch Firth, est., Scot., U.K.	B5	10
Dorogobuzh, Sov. Un.	D9	27
Dorohoi, Rom.	B8	24
Dorothy, Alta.	D4	68
Dorothy, Mn., U.S.	C2	100
Dorothy, N.J., U.S.	E3	107
Dorothy, W.V., U.S.	n13	125
Dorothy Pond, Ma., U.S.	B4	98
Dorr, Mi., U.S.	F5	99
Dorrance, Ks., U.S.	D5	93
Dorre, i., Austl.	E1	50
Dorrigo, Austl.	E9	51
Dorris, Ca., U.S.	B3	82
Dorris Heights, Il., U.S.	F5	90
Dorset, Ont.	B6	73
Dorset, Mn., U.S.	D4	100
Dorset, Oh., U.S.	A5	112
Dorset, Vt., U.S.	E2	122
Dorset, co., Eng., U.K.	D5	12
Dorset Peak, mtn., Vt., U.S.	E2	122
Dorsey, Il., U.S.	B4	97
Dorsey, Ms., U.S.	A5	101
Dorsten, W. Ger.	B1	19
Dortmund, W. Ger.	B7	17
Dortmund Ems Canal, W. Ger.	B7	17
Dorton, Ky., U.S.	C7	94
Dörtyol, Tur.	D11	40
Do Rūd, Iran	E4	39
Dorum, W. Ger.	E2	15
Doruma, Zaire	A4	48
Dorval, Que.	q19	74
Dos Bahías, Cabo, c., Arg.	E3	56
Dos Bocas, Lago, res., P.R.	B2	65
Dosquet, Que.	C6	74
Dos Hermanas, Spain	D3	22
Dos Quebradas, Col.	*C2	60
Dos Rios, Ca., U.S.	C2	82
Dosse, stm., E. Ger.	E6	15
Dosso, Niger	D5	45
Dossor, Sov. Un.	D4	28
Doswell, Va., U.S.	C5	123
Dothan, Al., U.S.	D4	78
Dothan, W.V., U.S.	n13	125
Doting Cove, Newf.	D5	72
Dot Lake, Ak., U.S.	C11	79
Dott, W.V., U.S.	D3	125
Doty, Wa., U.S.	C2	124
Douai, Fr.	B5	16
Douala, Cam.	E1	46
Douarnenez, Fr.	C1	16
Double Bayou, Tx., U.S.	r15	120
Double Beach, Ct., U.S.	D4	84
Double Mer, b., Newf.	A2	72
Double Mountain, mtn., Al., U.S.	g7	78
Double Oak Mountain, mtn., Al., U.S.	g7	78
Doublespring Pass, Id., U.S.	E5	89
Double Springs, Al., U.S.	A2	78
Doubletop Peak, mtn., Wy., U.S.	C2	127
Doubs, Md., U.S.	B3	97
Doubs, dept., Fr.	B2	20
Doubs, stm., Eur.	D7	16
Doubtful Sound, strt., N.Z.	P11	51
Doucette, Tx., U.S.	D5	120
Douds, Ia., U.S.	D5	92
Doué, Fr.	D3	16
Douentza, Mali	D4	45
Dougherty, Ia., U.S.	B4	92
Dougherty, Ok., U.S.	C4	113
Dougherty, co., Ga., U.S.	E2	87
Douglas, Ont.	B8	73
Douglas, I. of Man	C4	10
Douglas, S. Afr.	C3	49
Douglas, Scot., U.K.	E5	13
Douglas, Az., U.S.	F6	80
Douglas, Ga., U.S.	E4	87
Douglas, Ma., U.S.	B4	98
Douglas, Mi., U.S.	F4	99
Douglas, Mn., U.S.	F6	100
Douglas, Ne., U.S.	D9	104
Douglas, N.D., U.S.	B4	111
Douglas, Ok., U.S.	A4	113
Douglas, W.V., U.S.	B5	125
Douglas, Wy., U.S.	D7	127
Douglas, co., Co., U.S.	B6	83
Douglas, co., Ga., U.S.	C2	87
Douglas, co., Il., U.S.	D5	90
Douglas, co., Ks., U.S.	D8	93
Douglas, co., Mn., U.S.	E3	100
Douglas, co., Mo., U.S.	E5	102
Douglas, co., Ne., U.S.	C9	104
Douglas, co., Nv., U.S.	E2	105
Douglas, co., Or., U.S.	D3	114
Douglas, co., S.D., U.S.	D7	118
Douglas, co., Wa., U.S.	B6	124
Douglas, co., Wi., U.S.	B2	126
Douglas, Mount, mtn., Ak., U.S.	D9	79
Douglas Channel, strt., B.C.	C3	69
Douglas Creek, stm., Co., U.S.	B2	83
Douglas Lake, B.C.	D7	69
Douglas Lake, l., Mi., U.S.	C6	99
Douglas Lake, res., Tn., U.S.	D10	119
Douglas Point, c., Ont.	C3	73
Douglass, Ks., U.S.	E7	93
Douglas Station, Man.	E2	70
Douglastown, N.B.	B4	71
Douglasville, Ga., U.S.	C2	87
Doullens, Fr.	B5	16
Doulus Head, c., Ire.	F1	11
Doumé, Cam.	E2	46
Dour, Bel.	D3	17
Doura, Mali	m7	56
Dourado, Braz.	C2	56
Dourados, Braz.	C2	56
Dourdan, Fr.	F2	17
Douro (Duero), stm., Eur.	B1	22
Dousman, Wi., U.S.	E5	126
Douz, Tun.	C6	44
Dove Creek, Co., U.S.	D2	83
Dover, Eng., U.K.	E7	10
Dover, Ar., U.S.	B2	81
Dover, De., U.S.	D3	85
Dover, Fl., U.S.	D4	86
Dover, Id., U.S.	A2	89
Dover, Ks., U.S.	D8	93
Dover, Ky., U.S.	B6	94
Dover, Ma., U.S.	h10	98
Dover, Mo., U.S.	B4	102
Dover, N.H., U.S.	D5	106
Dover, N.J., U.S.	B3	107
Dover, N.C., U.S.	B5	110
Dover, Oh., U.S.	B4	112
Dover, Tn., U.S.	A4	119
Dover, stm., Alta.	F8	115
Dover, Strait of, strt., Eur.	B5	16
Dover Air Force Base, mil., De., U.S.	D4	85
Dover-Foxcroft, Me., U.S.	C3	96
Dover Hill, In., U.S.	G4	91
Dover Plains, N.Y., U.S.	D7	109
Dovesville, S.C., U.S.	C8	117
Dovray, In., U.S.	F3	100
Dovrefjell, mts., Nor.	F3	14
Dow, Il., U.S.	D3	90
Dow, Ok., U.S.	C6	113
Dowa, Mwi.	D5	48
Dowagiac, Mi., U.S.	G4	99
Dow City, Ia., U.S.	C2	92
Dowell, Il., U.S.	F4	90
Dowell, Md., U.S.	D5	97
Dowelltown, Tn., U.S.	C8	119
Dowlatābād, Afg.	C13	39
Dowlat Yar, Afg.	B4	36
Dowling Lake, l., Alta.	D4	68
Dowling Park, Fl., U.S.	B3	86
Downer, Mn., U.S.	D2	100
Downers Grove, Il., U.S.	B5	90
Downey, Ca., U.S.	n12	82
Downey, Id., U.S.	G6	89
Downham Market, Eng., U.K.	B8	12
Downieville, Ca., U.S.	C3	82
Downing, Mo., U.S.	A5	102
Downing, Wi., U.S.	C1	126
Downingtown, Pa., U.S.	F10	115
Downpatrick, N. Ire., U.K.	C4	10
Downpatrick Head, c., Ire.	C2	11
Downs, Il., U.S.	C5	90
Downs, Ks., U.S.	C5	93
Downs Mountain, mtn., Wy., U.S.	C3	127
Downsville, La., U.S.	B3	95
Downsville, N.Y., U.S.	C6	109
Downsville, Wi., U.S.	D2	126
Downton, Mount, mtn., B.C.	C5	69
Dows, Ia., U.S.	B4	92
Dowshī, Afg.	D14	39
Doyle, Ca., U.S.	B3	82
Doyle, Tn., U.S.	D8	119
Doyles, Newf.	E2	72
Doylestown, Oh., U.S.	B4	112
Doylestown, Pa., U.S.	F11	115
Doyline, La., U.S.	B2	95
Doyon, N.D., U.S.	A7	111
Dozier, Al., U.S.	D3	78
Dra'a, Hamada du, des., Alg.	D3	44
Drabenderhöhe, W. Ger.	*C3	18
Drachten, Neth.	A6	17
Dracut, Me., U.S.	A5	98
Drăgăneşti-Vlaşca, Rom.	C7	24
Draganovo, Bul.	C7	24
Drăgăşani, Rom.	C7	24
Dragons Mouth, strt.	N22	65
Dragoon, Az., U.S.	E5	80
Dragør, Den.	C6	15
Draguignan, Fr.	F7	16
Dragwiosa, Yugo.	B2	24
Drain, Or., U.S.	D3	114
Drake, Sask.	F3	75
Drake, Az., U.S.	C3	80
Drake, Co., U.S.	A5	83
Drake, N.D., U.S.	B5	111
Drakensberg, mts., Afr.	D4	49
Drake Passage, strt.	J16	2
Drake Peak, mtn., Or., U.S.	E6	114
Drakesboro, Ky., U.S.	C2	94
Drakes Branch, Va., U.S.	D4	123
Drakes Creek, Ar., U.S.	D3	94
Drakes Creek, West Fork, stm., Ky., U.S.	D3	94
Drakesville, Ia., U.S.	D5	92
Draketown, Ga., U.S.	C1	87
Dráma, Grc.	B5	40
Drammen, Nor.	H4	14
Dramselva, stm., Nor.	p27	14
Drancy, Fr.	g10	16
Dranse, stm., Fr.	C2	20
Draper, S.D., U.S.	D5	118
Draper, Ut., U.S.	C4	121
Draperstown, N. Ire., U.K.	C5	11
Drasco, Ar., U.S.	B4	81
Drava (Drau), stm., Eur.	C4	24
Dravosburg, Pa., U.S.	k14	115
Dravuni, i., Fiji	I15	52
Drawsko [Pomorskie], Pol.	B3	26
Drayton, Ont.	D4	73
Drayton, N.D., U.S.	A8	111
Drayton, S.C., U.S.	B4	117
Drayton Plains, Mi., U.S.	F7	99
Drayton Valley, Alta.	C3	68
Dreamland Villa, Az., U.S.	*D4	80
Drebkau, E. Ger.	C7	18
Dreisdorf, W. Ger.	D3	15
Drenthe, prov., Neth.	B6	17
Dresbach, Mn., U.S.	G7	100
Dresden, Ont.	E2	73
Dresden, E. Ger.	C6	18
Dresden, Ks., U.S.	C3	93
Dresden, Oh., U.S.	B3	112
Dresden, Tn., U.S.	A3	119
Dresser, In., U.S.	F3	91
Dresser, Wi., U.S.	C1	126
Dresslerville, Nv., U.S.	E2	105
Dreux, Fr.	C4	16
Drew, Ms., U.S.	B3	101
Drew, co., Ar., U.S.	D4	81
Drewryville, Va., U.S.	D5	123
Drewsey, Or., U.S.	D8	114
Drews Reservoir, res., Or., U.S.	E6	114
Drexel, N.H., U.S.	D2	106
Drexel, Mo., U.S.	C3	102
Drexel, Oh., U.S.	B1	110
Drexel Hill, Pa., U.S.	p20	115
Drezna, Sov. Un.	n18	27
Drift, Ky., U.S.	C7	94
Drifton, Pa., U.S.	D10	115
Driftpile, Alta.	B3	68
Driftwood, Ok., U.S.	A3	113
Driftwood, Pa., U.S.	D5	115
Driftwood Creek, stm., Ne., U.S.	D4	104
Driggs, Id., U.S.	F7	89
Drimoleague, Ire.	F2	11
Drina, stm., Yugo.	C4	24
Drin Gulf, b., Alb.	B2	25
Drini, stm., Alb.	A3	25
Drinkwater, Sask.	G3	75
Dripping Springs, Tx., U.S.	D3	120
Driscoll, N.D., U.S.	C5	111
Driscoll, Tx., U.S.	F4	120
Driskill Mountain, hill, La., U.S.	B3	95
Driver, Ar., U.S.	B5	81
Drobeta-Turnu-Severin, Rom.	C6	24
Drogheda, Ire.	D3	10
Drogobych, Sov. Un.	G4	27
Droitwich, Eng., U.K.	B5	12
Dromahair, Ire.	C3	11
Drôme, stm., Fr.	E6	16
Dromod, Ire.	D4	11
Dromore, N. Ire., U.K.	C4	11
Dromore West, Ire.	C3	11
Dronfield, Eng., U.K.	A6	12
Dronninglund, Den.	A4	15
Dropmore, Man.	D1	70
Druid, Sask.	F1	75
Druid Hills, Ga., U.S.	*C2	87
Drulingen, Fr.	E2	19
Drumbeg, Scot., U.K.	B3	13
Drumbo, Ont.	D4	73
Drumcliff, Ire.	C3	11
Drumheller, Alta.	C4	68
Drum Island, i., S.C., U.S.	k12	117
Drumlish, Ire.	D4	11
Drummond, Id., U.S.	F7	89
Drummond, Mt., U.S.	D3	103
Drummond, Ok., U.S.	A3	113
Drummond, Wi., U.S.	B2	126
Drummond, co., Que.	D5	74
Drummond, Lake, l., Va., U.S.	D6	123
Drummond Island, Mi., U.S.	B7	99
Drummond Island, i., Mi., U.S.	C7	99
Drummond Range, mts., Austl.	D9	51
Drummondville, Que.	D5	74
Drummondville-Sud, Que.	D5	74
Drummore, Scot., U.K.	F4	13
Drumquin, N. Ire., U.K.	C4	11
Drumright, Ok., U.S.	B5	113
Drumshanbo, Ire.	C3	11
Druzhina, Sov. Un.	C36	128
Druzhkovka, Sov. Un.	q20	26
Drweca, stm., Pol.	B4	26
Dryad, Wa., U.S.	C2	124
Dry Branch, Ga., U.S.	D3	87
Dry Cimarron, stm., U.S.	A6	108
Dry Creek, La., U.S.	D2	95
Dry Creek, La., U.S.	g12	95
Dry Creek Mountain, mtn., Nv., U.S.	B3	105
Dryden, Ont.	o16	73
Dryden, Ar., U.S.	*B5	81
Dryden, Me., U.S.	D2	96
Dryden, Mi., U.S.	F7	99
Dryden, N.Y., U.S.	C4	109
Dryden, Tx., U.S.	D1	120
Dryden, Wa., U.S.	B5	124
Dry Fork, La., U.S.	A3	119
Dry Fork, W.V., U.S.	D6	98
Dry Fork, stm., Mo., U.S.	D6	102
Dry Fork, stm., W.V., U.S.	D3	125
Drygalski Island, i., Ant.	C22	7
Dry Harbour Mountains, mts., Jam.	E14	65
Dry Mills, Me., U.S.	E2	96
Dry Prong, La., U.S.	C3	95
Dry Ridge, Ky., U.S.	B5	94
Dry Run, Pa., U.S.	F6	115
Drysdale, stm., Austl.	B4	50
Dry Tortugas, is., Fl., U.S.	H5	86
Drywood, Alta.	E4	68
Dschang, Cam.	D2	46
Duaiheb, Hasi, well, W. Sah.	A7	51
Duaringa, Austl.	A7	51
Duarte, Pico, mtn., Dom. Rep.	E8	64
Duart Point, c., Scot., U.K.	D3	13
Dubā, Sau. Ar.	C3	38
Dubach, La., U.S.	B3	95
Dubai (Dubayy), U.A.E.	C5	38
Dubawnt, stm., N.W. Ter.	D12	66
Dubawnt Lake, l., N.W. Ter.	D12	66
Du Bay, Lake, res., Wi., U.S.	D4	126
Dubberly, La., U.S.	B2	95
Dubbo, Austl.	F8	50
Dübendorf, Switz.	B6	21
Dumka, India	E11	37
Dummer, Sask.	H3	75
Dümmer, l., W. Ger.	F2	15
Dumont, Ia., U.S.	B4	92
Dumont, Mn., U.S.	E2	100
Dumont, N.J., U.S.	B5	107
Dumont, Tx., U.S.	C2	120
Dumont d'Urville, sci., Ant.	C27	7
Dumyāṭ (Damietta), Eg.	B3	38
Dunaff Head, c., Ire.	A4	11
Dunaföldvár, Hung.	B4	24
Dunaire, Ga., U.S.	*h8	87
Dunajec, stm., Eur.	D6	26
Dunajská Streda, Czech.	D4	24
Dunany Point, c., Ire.	D5	11
Dunapataj, Hung.	B3	24
Dunaújváros, Hung.	B4	24
Dunay, Sov. Un.	D5	26
Dunayevtsy, Sov. Un.	G6	27
Dunbar, Scot., U.K.	B5	10
Dunbar, Ky., U.S.	C3	94
Dunbar, Ne., U.S.	D9	104
Dunbar, Pa., U.S.	G2	115
Dunbar, S.C., U.S.	B8	117
Dunbar, W.V., U.S.	C3	125
Dunbarton, Scot., U.K.	C5	13
Dunbarton, N.H., U.S.	D3	106
Dunbeath, Scot., U.K.	B5	10
Dunblane, Sask.	F2	75
Dunblane, Scot., U.K.	D5	13
Dunboyne, Ire.	D5	11
Dunbridge, Oh., U.S.	f6	112
Duncan, B.C.	E6	69
Duncan, Az., U.S.	E6	80
Duncan, Ky., U.S.	C5	94
Duncan, Ms., U.S.	A3	101
Duncan, Ok., U.S.	C4	113
Duncan, S.C., U.S.	B3	117
Duncan, co., B.C.	D9	69
Duncan Falls, Oh., U.S.	C4	112
Duncan Lake, res., B.C.	D9	69
Duncannon, Pa., U.S.	F7	115
Duncansby Head, c., Scot., U.K.	A5	10
Duncansville, Pa., U.S.	F5	115
Duncanville, Al., U.S.	B2	78
Duncanville, Tx., U.S.	n10	120
Duncombe, Ia., U.S.	B4	92
Duncormick, Ire.	E5	11
Dundalk, Ont.	C4	73
Dundalk, Ire.	C5	11
Dundalk, Md., U.S.	B4	97
Dundalk Bay, b., Ire.	D3	10
Dundas, Ont.	D5	73
Dundas, Il., U.S.	E5	90
Dundas, Mn., U.S.	F5	100
Dundas, co., Ont.	B9	73
Dundas, Lake, l., Austl.	F4	50
Dundas Island, i., B.C.	B2	69
Dundas Strait, strt., Austl.	B6	50
Dundee, S. Afr.	C5	49
Dundee, Scot., U.K.	D5	10
Dundee, Fl., U.S.	D5	86
Dundee, Ia., U.S.	B6	92
Dundee, Ky., U.S.	C3	94
Dundee, Mi., U.S.	G7	99
Dundee, Ms., U.S.	A3	101
Dundee, N.Y., U.S.	C4	109
Dundee, Oh., U.S.	B4	112
Dundee, Or., U.S.	h11	114
Dundee, Wi., U.S.	E5	126
Dundrum, Ire.	E2	11
Dundrum, N. Ire., U.K.	D5	11
Dundrum Bay, b., N. Ire., U.K.	C4	11
Dundurn, Sask.	F2	75
Dunean, Pa., U.S.	*D4	117
Dunedin, N.Z.	P13	51
Dunedin, Fl., U.S.	D4	86
Dunedin, stm., B.C.	B2	69
Dunellen, N.J., U.S.	B4	107
Dunfanaghy, Ire.	B4	11
Dunfermline, Sask.	F2	75
Dunfermline, Il., U.S.	C3	90
Dunfermline, Scot., U.K.	B5	10
Dungannon, Ont.	D3	73
Dungannon, Va., U.S.	f9	123
Dungarpur, India	F4	37
Düngarvan, India	F4	37
Dungarvan, Ire.	E4	11
Dungarvon, stm., N.B.	C3	71
Dungeness, c., Eng., U.K.	D8	12
Dungeness, stm., Wa., U.S.	A2	124
Dung Gate, hist., Isr. Occ.	m14	41
Dungiven, N. Ire., U.K.	C3	11
Dunglow, Ire.	B4	11
Dungu, Zaire	A5	48
Dungun, Malay.	J5	35
Dunham, Col.	B3	60
Dunhua, China	*C10	31
Dunhuang, China	C8	31
Dunkard Creek, stm., U.S.	B4	125
Dunkeld, Scot., U.K.	B5	10
Dunkerque, Fr.	B5	16
Dunkerton, Ia., U.S.	B5	92
Dunkineely, Ire.	C3	11
Dunkirk, In., U.S.	D7	91
Dunkirk, N.Y., U.S.	C1	109
Dunkirk, Oh., U.S.	B2	112
Dunklin, co., Mo., U.S.	E7	102
Dunkwa, Ghana	E4	45
Dún Laoghaire, Ire.	C4	10
Dunlap, Il., U.S.	C4	90
Dunlap, Ia., U.S.	A6	91
Dumāʼ, Isr. Occ.	g12	41
Dūmā, Syria	*F11	40
Dumaguete, Phil.	D6	34
Dumanlı, mtn., Tur.	B11	40
Dumaran Island, i., Phil.	C5	34
Dumas, Ar., U.S.	D4	81
Dumas, Ga., U.S.	D2	87
Dumas, Ms., U.S.	A5	101
Dumas, Tx., U.S.	B2	120
Dumba, Zaire	B3	48
Dumbarton, Scot., U.K.	D7	45
Dumboa, Nig.	D7	45
Dumfries, Va., U.S.	B5	123
Dumfries, Scot., U.K.	E4	13
Dumfries and Galloway, prov., Scot., U.K.	E4	13
Dunleer, Ire.	D5	11
Dunleith, De., U.S.	i7	85
Dunlo, Pa., U.S.	F4	115
Dunloup Creek, stm., W.V., U.S.	n13	125
Dunmanway, Ire.	F2	11
Dunmor, Ky., U.S.	C2	94
Dunmore, Ire.	D3	11
Dunmore, Pa., U.S.	D10	115
Dunmore, Lake, l., Vt., U.S.	D2	122
Dunmore East, Ire.	E5	11
Dunn, N.C., U.S.	B4	110
Dunn, Tx., U.S.	C2	120
Dunn, co., N.D., U.S.	B3	111
Dunn, co., Wi., U.S.	D2	126
Dunnamanagh, N. Ire., U.K.	C4	11
Dunn Center, N.D., U.S.	B3	111
Dunnegan, Mo., U.S.	D4	102
Dunnellon, Fl., U.S.	C4	86
Dünnern, stm., Switz.	B4	21
Dunnet Head, c., Scot., U.K.	B5	13
Dunn Loring Woods, Va., U.S.	*B5	123
Dunnottar, Man.	D3	70
Dunns Bridge, In., U.S.	B4	91
Dunns Corners, R.I., U.S.	G1	116
Dunnsville, Va., U.S.	C6	123
Dunnville, Ont.	E5	73
Dunnville, Ky., U.S.	C5	94
Dunoon, Scot., U.K.	C4	10
Dunphy, Nv., U.S.	C5	105
Dunqulah, Sud.	B3	47
Dunrea, Man.	E2	70
Dunrobin, Ont.	B8	73
Duns, Scot., U.K.	E6	13
Dunseith, N.D., U.S.	A5	111
Dunsmuir, Ca., U.S.	B2	82
Dunstable, Ma., U.S.	A5	98
Dun-sur-Auron, Fr.	D5	16
Dun [-sur-Meuse], Fr.	E5	17
Duntroon, Ont.	C4	73
Dunvegan, Scot., U.K.	C2	13
Dunvegan, Loch, b., Scot., U.K.	C2	13
Dunvegan Head, c., Scot., U.K.	C2	13
Dunville, Newf.	E5	72
Dunwoody, Ga., U.S.	h8	87
Duolun, China	C8	31
Du Page, co., Il., U.S.	B5	90
Du Page, stm., Il., U.S.	k8	90
Dupax, Phil.	n13	34
Duplessis, La., U.S.	h10	95
Duplin, co., N.C., U.S.	C5	110
Dupont, Ga., U.S.	F4	87
Dupont, In., U.S.	G6	91
Dupont, La., U.S.	*D4	95
Dupont, Oh., U.S.	A1	112
Dupont, Pa., U.S.	n18	115
Dupont, Bayou, stm., La., U.S.	k11	95
Dupont City, W.V., U.S.	m12	125
Dupont Manor, De., U.S.	D3	85
Dupree, S.D., U.S.	B4	118
Dupuyer, Mt., U.S.	B4	103
Duquesne, Pa., U.S.	k14	115
Du Quoin, Il., U.S.	E4	90
Dūrā, Isr. Occ.	C7	41
Duran, N.M., U.S.	C4	108
Durance, stm., Fr.	F6	16
Durand, Ga., U.S.	D2	87
Durand, Il., U.S.	A4	90
Durand, Mi., U.S.	F6	99
Durand, Wi., U.S.	D2	126
Durango (Victoria de Durango), Mex.	C4	63
Durango, Co., U.S.	D3	83
Durango, state, Mex.	C4	63
Durant, Ia., U.S.	C7	92
Durant, Ms., U.S.	B4	101
Durant, Ok., U.S.	D5	113
Durants Neck, N.C., U.S.	A6	110
Duraton, stm., Spain	B3	22
Durazno, Ur.	E1	56
Durazno, dept., Ur.	f8	54
Durban, Man.	D1	70
Durban, S. Afr.	C5	49
Durbin, N.D., U.S.	C8	111
Durbin, W.V., U.S.	C5	125
Durbin Creek, stm., Fl., U.S.	m8	86
Düren, W. Ger.	C3	18
Durg, India	*D7	36
Durgāpur, India	F11	37
Durham, Ont.	C4	73
Durham, Eng., U.K.	C6	10
Durham, co., Eng., U.K.	A4	110
Durham, Ct., U.S.	C5	84
Durham, Ks., U.S.	D6	93
Durham, Mo., U.S.	B6	102
Durham, N.H., U.S.	D5	106
Durham, N.C., U.S.	B4	110
Durham, Ok., U.S.	B2	113
Durham (Regional Municipality), co., Ont.	C6	73
Durham, co., Eng., U.K.	F7	73
Durham, co., N.C., U.S.	A4	110
Durham Bridge, N.B.	C3	71
Durham Downs, Austl.	C3	51
Durham-Sud, Que.	D5	74
Durhamville, Tn., U.S.	B2	119
Durkee, Or., U.S.	C9	114
Durmersheim, W. Ger.	E3	19
Durmitor, mtn., Yugo.	A3	24
Durness, Scot., U.K.	B4	13
Durness, Kyle of, b., Scot., U.K.	B4	13
Durnford, Punta, c., W. Sah.	E1	44
Dürrboden, Switz.	C8	21
Durrell, Newf.	D4	72
Durrësi, Alb.	B2	25
Durrow, Ire.	E4	11
Durrus, Ire.	F2	11
Dursey Island, i., Ire.	F1	11
Dursunbey, Tur.	G13	24
Duru, Zaire	A4	48
D'Urville, Cape, c., Indon.	F9	34
D'Urville Island, i., N.Z.	N14	51
Duryea, Pa., U.S.	D10	115
Dushan, China	F8	31
Dushanbe, Sov. Un.	F9	29
Dushaymī, Jazāʼir, is., Eg.	C9	115
Dushore, Pa., U.S.	D8	115
Dusky Sound, strt., N.Z.	P11	51
Duson, La., U.S.	D3	95
Düsseldorf, W. Ger.	B5	113
Dustin, Ok., U.S.	B5	113
Dusty, N.M., U.S.	D2	108
Dutch Creek, stm., Ar., U.S.	C2	81
Dutchess, co., N.Y., U.S.	D6	79
Dutch Harbor, Ak., U.S.	E6	79
Dutch Island, i., R.I., U.S.	F4	116

Name	Map Ref.	Page

Name	Map Ref.	Page
Dutch John, Ut., U.S.	C6	121
Dutchtown, Mo., U.S.	D8	102
Dutton, Ont.	E3	73
Dutton, Al., U.S.	A4	78
Dutton, Mt., U.S.	C5	103
Dutton, Mount, mtn., Ut., U.S.	E3	121
Dutzow, Mo., U.S.	C7	102
Duval, co., Fl., U.S.	B5	86
Duval, co., Tx., U.S.	F3	120
Duvergé, Dom. Rep.	E8	64
Duvno, Yugo.	D3	24
Duxbury, Ma., U.S.	B6	98
Duxbury, Vt., U.S.	C3	122
Duyun, China	F6	31
Düzce, Tur.	B8	40
Dvina Bay, b., Sov. Un.	C16	8
Dvůr Králové [nad Labem], Czech.	C3	26
Dwarka, India	F2	37
Dwight, Il., U.S.	B5	90
Dwight, Ks., U.S.	D7	93
Dwight, Ne., U.S.	C8	104
Dwight, N.D., U.S.	C9	111
Dwight D. Eisenhower Lock, N.Y., U.S.	f9	109
Dworshak Reservoir, res., Id., U.S.	C3	89
Dwyer, Wy., U.S.	D8	127
Dyakova, Sov. Un.	r22	27
Dyakovo, Sov. Un.	E10	27
Dyatkovo, Sov. Un.	E10	27
Dyaul, i., Pap. N. Gui.	h13	51
Dyce, Scot., U.K.	C6	13
Dyckesville, Wi., U.S.	D6	126
Dycusburg, Ky., U.S.	e9	94
Dyer, Ar., U.S.	B1	81
Dyer, In., U.S.	A2	91
Dyer, Nv., U.S.	F3	105
Dyer, Tn., U.S.	A3	119
Dyer, co., Tn., U.S.	A2	119
Dyer Bay, Ont.	B3	73
Dyer Bay, b., Ont.	B3	73
Dyer Brook, Me., U.S.	B4	96
Dyer Island, i., R.I., U.S.	E5	116
Dyero, Mali	D3	45
Dyersburg, Tn., U.S.	A2	119
Dyersville, Ia., U.S.	B6	92
Dyess, Ar., U.S.	B5	81
Dyess Air Force Base, mil., Tx., U.S.	C3	120
Dyfed, co., Wales, U.K.	C3	12
Dyje, stm., Eur.	D3	26
Dykh-Tau, Mount, mtn., Sov. Un.	*E7	29
Dyment, Ont.	E5	70
Dysart, Sask.	G3	75
Dysart, Ia., U.S.	B5	92
Dzalaata, Mong.	B2	32
Dzamïn Üüd, Mong.	B4	32
Dzaoudzi, May.	f9	49
Dzaudzhikau see Ordzhonikidze, Sov. Un.	E7	29
Dzavhan, stm., Mong.	B3	31
Dzerzhinsk, Sov. Un.	q20	27
Dzerzhinsk, Sov. Un.	C14	27
Dzerzhinsk, Sov. Un.	E6	27
Dzhalal-Abad, Sov. Un.	E8	28
Dzhambul, Sov. Un.	E10	28
Dzhankoy, Sov. Un.	I10	27
Dzhebel, Sov. Un.	B7	39
Dzhetygara, Sov. Un.	C6	28
Dzhezkazgan, Sov. Un.	C6	28
Dzhizak, Sov. Un.	G22	8
Dzhugdzhur Mountains, mts., Sov. Un.	D16	29
Dzhungarian Alatau Mountains, mts., Asia	D9	28
Dzhusaly, Sov. Un.	D6	28
Działdowo, Pol.	B6	26
Działoszyce, Pol.	C6	26
Dzierżoniów, Pol.	C4	26
Dzilam González, Mex.	C7	63
Dzioua, Alg.	C6	44
Dzitbalché, Mex.	C6	63
Dzulfa, Sov. Un.	C15	40
Dzungarian Basin see Junggar Pendi, China	B2	31
Dzuunmod, Mong.	B6	31

E

Name	Map Ref.	Page
Eads, Co., U.S.	C8	83
Eads, Tn., U.S.	B2	119
Eagan, Mn., U.S.	n12	100
Eagan, Tn., U.S.	C10	119
Eagar, Az., U.S.	C6	80
Eagle, Ak., U.S.	C11	79
Eagle, Co., U.S.	B4	83
Eagle, Id., U.S.	F2	89
Eagle, Ne., U.S.	h12	104
Eagle, N.Y., U.S.	C2	109
Eagle, Wi., U.S.	F5	126
Eagle, co., Co., U.S.	B4	83
Eagle, stm., Newf.	B2	72
Eagle Bend, Mn., U.S.	D3	100
Eagle Bridge, N.Y., U.S.	C7	109
Eagle Butte, S.D., U.S.	C4	118
Eagle Cave, Wi., U.S.	E3	126
Eagle City, Ok., U.S.	B3	113
Eagle Cliff, mtn., U.S.	B3	89
Eagle Creek, Tn., U.S.	B4	119
Eagle Creek, stm., Sask.	F2	75
Eagle Creek, stm., In., U.S.	D5	91
Eagle Creek, stm., Ky., U.S.	B5	94
Eagle Creek Reservoir, res., In., U.S.	E5	91
Eagle Dam, In., U.S.	E4	91
Eagle Grove, Ia., U.S.	B4	92
Eagle Harbor, Mi., U.S.	A2	99
Eagle Key, i., Fl., U.S.	G6	86
Eagle Lake, Me., U.S.	A4	96
Eagle Lake, Mn., U.S.	F5	100
Eagle Lake, Tx., U.S.	E4	120
Eagle Lake, Wi., U.S.	*F5	126
Eagle Lake, l., Ont.	E5	70
Eagle Lake, l., Ca., U.S.	B3	82
Eagle Lake, l., Me., U.S.	A4	96
Eagle Lake, l., Me., U.S.	B3	96
Eagle Lake, l., Me., U.S.	C3	96
Eagle Lake, l., Wi., U.S.	C4	126
Eagle Mills, Ar., U.S.	D3	81
Eagle Mountain, mtn., Mn., U.S.	k9	100
Eagle Mountain Lake, res., Tx., U.S.	m9	120
Eagle Nest, N.M., U.S.	A4	108
Eagle Nest Butte, mtn., S.D., U.S.	D4	118
Eaglenest Lake, l., Can.	D4	70
Eagle Nest Lake, l., N.M., U.S.	A4	108
Eagle Pass, Tx., U.S.	E2	120
Eagle Peak, mtn., Ca., U.S.	B3	82
Eagle Peak, mtn., Tx., U.S.	o12	120

Name	Map Ref.	Page
Eagle Point, Or., U.S.	E4	114
Eagle River, Ont.	E5	70
Eagle River, Mi., U.S.	A2	99
Eagle River, Wi., U.S.	C4	126
Eagle Rock, Va., U.S.	C3	123
Eaglesham, Alta.	B2	68
Eagles Mere, Pa., U.S.	D8	115
Eagle Springs, N.C., U.S.	B3	110
Eagletail Mountains, mts., Az., U.S.	D2	80
Eagletail Peak, mtn., Az., U.S.	D2	80
Eagleton Village, Tn., U.S.	*D10	119
Eagleton, Ok., U.S.	C7	113
Eagleville, Ca., U.S.	B3	82
Eagleville, Ct., U.S.	B6	84
Eagleville, Mo., U.S.	A4	102
Eagleville, Tn., U.S.	B5	119
Eakly, Ok., U.S.	B3	113
Ealing (part of London), Eng., U.K.	k12	10
Eardley, Que.	g11	73
Eardley Lake, l., Man.	C3	70
Earl Grey, Sask.	G3	75
Earl Island, i., Newf.	B3	72
Earl Park, In., U.S.	C3	91
Earle, Ar., U.S.	B5	81
Earlham, Ia., U.S.	C3	92
Earlimart, Ca., U.S.	E4	82
Earling, Ia., U.S.	C2	92
Earlington, Ky., U.S.	C2	94
Earlton, W.V., U.S.	n12	125
Earling, W.V., U.S.	n12	125
Earlsboro, Ok., U.S.	B5	113
Earlton, Ks., U.S.	E8	93
Earlville, Il., U.S.	B5	90
Earlville, Ia., U.S.	B6	92
Earlville, N.Y., U.S.	C5	109
Early, Ia., U.S.	B2	92
Early, co., Ga., U.S.	E2	87
Early Branch, S.C., U.S.	F6	117
Earn, stm., Scot., U.K.	D5	13
Earn, Loch, l., Scot., U.K.	D4	13
Earth, Tx., U.S.	B1	120
Easky, Ire.	C3	11
Easley, S.C., U.S.	B2	117
Eassley, Ct., U.S.	D5	84
East, stm., Ont.	B5	73
East, stm., Ct., U.S.	C3	90
East, stm., N.Y., U.S.	k13	109
East, stm., Wi., U.S.	h9	126
Eastaboga, Al., U.S.	B3	78
Eastabuchie, Ms., U.S.	D4	101
East Acton, Ma., U.S.	g10	98
East Alburgh, Vt., U.S.	B2	122
East Alstead, N.H., U.S.	D2	106
East Alton, Il., U.S.	E3	90
East Andover, Me., U.S.	D2	96
East Andover, N.H., U.S.	D3	106
East Angus, Que.	D6	74
East Arlington, Vt., U.S.	E2	122
East Aurora, N.Y., U.S.	C2	109
East Baldwin, Me., U.S.	E2	96
East Bangor, Pa., U.S.	E11	115
East Bank, W.V., U.S.	m13	125
East Barnard, Vt., U.S.	D3	122
East Barre, Vt., U.S.	C4	122
East Baton Rouge, co., La., U.S.	D4	95
East Bay, b., Fl., U.S.	u16	86
East Bay, b., Tx., U.S.	R15	120
East Beckwith Mountain, mtn., Co., U.S.	C3	83
East Bend, N.C., U.S.	A2	110
East Berbice-Corentyne, dept., Guy.	B3	59
East Berlin, Ct., U.S.	C5	84
East Berlin, Pa., U.S.	G8	115
East Bernard, Tx., U.S.	E4	120
East Bernstadt, Ky., U.S.	C5	94
East Bethel, Mn., U.S.	E5	100
East Bethel, Vt., U.S.	D3	122
East Billerica, Ma., U.S.	f11	98
East Blue Hill, Me., U.S.	D4	96
East Bonne Terre, Mo., U.S.	D7	102
East Boothbay, Me., U.S.	E3	96
Eastborough, Ks., U.S.	g12	93
Eastbourne, Eng., U.K.	E7	10
East Brady, Pa., U.S.	E2	115
East Braintree, Man.	E4	70
East Braintree, Vt., U.S.	D3	122
East Branch, N.Y., U.S.	D5	109
East Branch Clarion River Lake, res., Pa., U.S.	C4	115
East Brewster, Ma., U.S.	C7	98
East Brewton, Al., U.S.	D2	78
East Bridgewater, Ma., U.S.	B6	98
East Brimfield Lake, res., Ma., U.S.	B3	98
Eastbrook, Me., U.S.	D4	96
East Brookfield, Ma., U.S.	B3	98
East Brookfield, Vt., U.S.	C3	122
East Brooklyn, Ct., U.S.	B8	84
East Broughton, Que.	C6	74
East Brunswick, N.J., U.S.	C4	107
East Burke, Vt., U.S.	B5	122
East Butler, Pa., U.S.	E2	115
East Cache Creek, stm., Ok., U.S.	C3	113
East Calais, Vt., U.S.	C4	122
East Canaan, Ct., U.S.	A2	84
East Candia, N.H., U.S.	D4	106
East Cape, c., N.Z.	L17	51
East Cape, c., Fl., U.S.	G5	86
East Carbon, Ut., U.S.	D5	121
East Carroll, co., La., U.S.	B4	95
East Chain, Mn., U.S.	G3	100
East Channel, strt., Marsh Is.	S18	52
East Charleston, Vt., U.S.	B5	122
East Chelmsford, Ma., U.S.	f10	98
Eastchester, N.Y., U.S.	*n15	109
East Chicago, In., U.S.	A3	91
East Chicago Heights, Il., U.S.	*k9	90
East Chop, c., Ma., U.S.	D6	98
East China Sea, Asia	F10	31
East Cleveland, Oh., U.S.	g9	112
East-Clifton, Que.	D6	74
East Columbia, Tx., U.S.	r14	120
East Compton, Ca., U.S.	*F4	82
East Concord, Vt., U.S.	C5	122
East Corinth, Me., U.S.	D3	96
East Corinth, Vt., U.S.	C4	122
East Cote Blanche Bay, b., La., U.S.	E4	95
East Coulee, Alta.	D4	68
East Danville, Oh., U.S.	C2	112
East Demerara-West Coast Berbice, dept., Guy.	A3	59
East Dennis, Ma., U.S.	C7	98
East Dereham, Eng., U.K.	B8	12
East Derry, N.H., U.S.	E4	106
East Detroit, Mi., U.S.	p16	99
East Dixmont, Me., U.S.	D3	96
East Dorset, Vt., U.S.	E2	122

Name	Map Ref.	Page
East Douglas, Ma., U.S.	B4	98
East Dover, Me., U.S.	C3	96
East Dover, Vt., U.S.	F3	122
East Dubuque, Il., U.S.	A3	90
East Dummerston, Vt., U.S.	F3	122
East Eddington, Me., U.S.	D4	96
East Ellijay, Ga., U.S.	B2	87
Eastend, Sask.	H1	75
East End Point, c., Bah.	m18	64
East Enterprise, In., U.S.	G8	91
Easter Island see Pascua, Isla de, i., Chile	H15	6
Eastern, prov., Ghana	E6	45
Eastern, prov., Kenya	B6	48
Eastern, prov., Zam.	D5	49
Eastern Bay, b., Md., U.S.	C5	97
Eastern Channel, strt., Japan	J4	33
Eastern Ghāts, mts., India	E7	36
Eastern Island, i., Newf.	C4	72
Eastern Island, i., Mid. Is.	K4	52
Eastern Neck Island, i., Md., U.S.	B5	97
Eastern Point, c., Ma., U.S.	f13	98
Easterville, Man.	C2	70
East Fairfield, Vt., U.S.	B3	122
East Fairview, N.D., U.S.	B1	111
East Falmouth, Ma., U.S.	C6	98
East Farmingdale, N.Y., U.S.	*E7	109
East Farmington Heights, Ct., U.S.	C4	84
East Feliciana, co., La., U.S.	D4	95
East Flanders, prov., Bel.	C3	17
East Flat Rock, N.C., U.S.	f10	110
East Flevoland, reg., Neth.	B5	17
Eastford, Ct., U.S.	B7	84
East Fork, stm., Wy., U.S.	D3	127
East Fork Lake, res., Oh., U.S.	C1	112
East Foxboro, Ma., U.S.	B5	98
East Franklin, Vt., U.S.	B3	122
East Freetown, Ma., U.S.	C6	98
East Frisian Islands, is., W. Ger.	B3	18
East Fultonham, Oh., U.S.	C3	112
East Gaffney, S.C., U.S.	A4	117
East Galesburg, Il., U.S.	C3	90
Eastgate, Wa., U.S.	*e11	124
East Germany see German Democratic Republic, ctry., Eur.	B6	18
East Glacier Park, Mt., U.S.	B3	103
East Glastonbury, Ct., U.S.	C5	84
East Glenville, N.Y., U.S.	*C7	109
East Grafton, N.H., U.S.	C3	106
East Granby, Ct., U.S.	B5	84
East Grand Forks, Mn., U.S.	C2	100
East Grand Rapids, Mi., U.S.	F5	99
East Granville, Vt., U.S.	C3	122
East Greenville, Pa., U.S.	F10	115
East Greenwich, R.I., U.S.	D4	116
East Grinstead, Eng., U.K.	C8	12
East Gwillimbury, Ont.	C5	73
East Haddam, Ct., U.S.	D6	84
East Half Hollow Hills, N.Y., U.S.	*n15	109
Eastham, Ma., U.S.	C8	98
East Hampden, Me., U.S.	*D4	96
East Hampstead, N.H., U.S.	E4	106
East Hampton, Ct., U.S.	C5	84
Easthampton, Ma., U.S.	B2	98
East Hampton, N.Y., U.S.	n16	109
East Hanover, N.J., U.S.	*B4	107
East Hardwick, Vt., U.S.	B4	122
East Harpswell, Me., U.S.	g8	96
East Hartford, Ct., U.S.	B5	84
East Haven, Ct., U.S.	D4	84
East Haven, Vt., U.S.	B5	122
East Haverhill, N.H., U.S.	B3	106
East Hebron, N.H., U.S.	C3	106
East Helena, Mt., U.S.	D5	103
East Hemet, Ca., U.S.	*F5	82
East Hickory, Pa., U.S.	C3	115
East Highgate, Vt., U.S.	B3	122
East Hills, N.Y., U.S.	*E7	109
East Holden, Me., U.S.	D4	96
East Holderness, N.H., U.S.	C3	106
East Islip, N.Y., U.S.	*n15	109
East Jordan, Mi., U.S.	C5	99
East Jordan, N.S.	F4	71
East Juliette, Ga., U.S.	C3	87
East Kelowna, B.C.	E8	69
East Kilbride, Scot., U.K.	E4	13
East Killingly, Ct., U.S.	B8	84
East Kingston, N.H., U.S.	E4	106
Eastlake, N.C., U.S.	B7	110
Eastlake, Oh., U.S.	A4	112
East Lake, l., Ont.	C5	70
East Lake Tohopekaliga, l., Fl., U.S.	D5	86
East La Mirada, Ca., U.S.	*F5	82
Eastland, Tx., U.S.	C3	120
Eastland, co., Tx., U.S.	C3	120
Eastland Township, Ut., U.S.	*F6	121
East Lansing, Mi., U.S.	F6	99
East Laport, N.C., U.S.	f9	110
East Las Vegas, Nv., U.S.	G6	105
East Laurinburg, N.C., U.S.	C3	110
East Lebanon, Me., U.S.	E2	96
Eastleigh, Eng., U.K.	D6	12
East Lempster, N.H., U.S.	D2	106
East Liberty, Oh., U.S.	B2	112
East Livermore, Me., U.S.	D2	96
East Liverpool, Oh., U.S.	B5	112
East Loch Roag, b., Scot., U.K.	B2	13
East Loch Tarbert, b., Scot., U.K.	C2	13
East London (Oos-Londen), S. Afr.	D4	49
East Longmeadow, Ma., U.S.	B2	98
East Los Angeles, Ca., U.S.	m12	82
East Lyme, Ct., U.S.	D7	84
East Lynn, Il., U.S.	C6	90
East Lynn, W.V., U.S.	C2	125
East Lynn Lake, res., W.V., U.S.		
East Machias, Me., U.S.	D5	96
East Madison, Me., U.S.	D3	96
Eastmain, Que.	h11	74
Eastmain-Opinaca, Réservoir, res., Que.	h11	74
Eastman, Que.	D5	74
Eastman, Ga., U.S.	D3	87
Eastman, Wi., U.S.	E2	126
East Mansfield, Ma., U.S.	B5	98
East Marietta, Ga., U.S.	*C2	87
East Marion, Ma., U.S.	*C6	98
East Marion, N.Y., U.S.	*m16	109
East Matunuck, R.I., U.S.	F3	116
East Meadow, N.Y., U.S.	*n15	109

Name	Map Ref.	Page
East Meredith, N.Y., U.S.	C6	109
East Middlebury, Vt., U.S.	D2	122
East Midvale, Ut., U.S.	*C4	121
East Millbury, Ma., U.S.	B4	98
East Millinocket, Me., U.S.	C4	96
East Moline, Il., U.S.	B3	90
East Monroe, Oh., U.S.	C2	112
East Montpelier, Vt., U.S.	C4	122
East Naples, Fl., U.S.	F5	86
East Newark, N.J., U.S.	k8	107
East New Market, Md., U.S.	C6	97
East Newnan, Ga., U.S.	C2	87
East Newport, Me., U.S.	D3	96
East New Portland, Me., U.S.	D2	96
East Nishnabotna, stm., Ia., U.S.	C2	92
East Norriton, Pa., U.S.	o20	115
East Northport, N.Y., U.S.	*n15	109
East Olympia, Wa., U.S.	C3	124
East Orange, N.J., U.S.	B4	107
East Orange, Vt., U.S.	C4	122
East Orland, Me., U.S.	D4	96
East Orleans, Ma., U.S.	C8	98
East Otis, Ma., U.S.	B1	98
East Otto, N.Y., U.S.	C2	109
East Palatka, Fl., U.S.	C5	86
East Palestine, Oh., U.S.	B5	112
East Palo Alto, Ca., U.S.	*D2	82
East Parsonfield, Me., U.S.	E2	96
East Pass, strt., Fl., U.S.	C2	86
East Patchogue, N.Y., U.S.	*n16	109
East Peacham, Vt., U.S.	C4	122
East Pea Ridge, W.V., U.S.	C2	125
East Peoria, Il., U.S.	C4	90
East Pepperell, Ma., U.S.	A4	98
East Peru, Me., U.S.	D2	96
East Petersburg, Pa., U.S.	F9	115
East Pine, B.C.	B7	69
East Pittsburgh, Pa., U.S.	k14	115
Eastpoint, Fl., U.S.	C2	86
East Point, Ga., U.S.	C2	87
East Point, La., U.S.	C3	95
East Point, c., P.E.I.	C8	71
East Point, c., Ma., U.S.	B6	98
East Point, c., N.J., U.S.	E2	107
East Point, c., V.I.U.S.	C6	65
East Poland, Me., U.S.	D2	96
East Poplar, Sask.	H3	75
Eastport, Newf.	D5	72
Eastport, Id., U.S.	A2	89
Eastport, Me., U.S.	D6	96
East Portal, Co., U.S.	B5	83
East Porterville, Ca., U.S.	*D5	82
East Poultney, Vt., U.S.	D2	122
East Prairie, Mo., U.S.	E8	102
East Princeton, Ma., U.S.	B4	98
East Prospect, Pa., U.S.	G8	115
East Providence, R.I., U.S.	C4	116
East Pryor Mountain, mtn., Mt., U.S.	E8	103
East Quogue, N.Y., U.S.	n16	109
East Randolph, N.Y., U.S.	C2	109
East Randolph, Vt., U.S.	D3	122
East Range, mts., Nv., U.S.	C4	105
East Retford, Eng., U.K.	A7	12
East Ridge, Tn., U.S.	h11	119
East Ridge, Ct., U.S.	D2	84
East Ringe, N.H., U.S.	E3	106
East River, Ct., U.S.	D5	84
East River Mountain, mtn., U.S.	C1	123
East River Sheet Harbour, N.S.	E7	71
East Rochester, N.Y., U.S.	B3	109
East Rockaway, N.Y., U.S.	*k13	109
East Rockingham, N.C., U.S.	C3	110
East Rutherford, N.J., U.S.	h8	107
East Ryegate, Vt., U.S.	C4	122
East Saint Johnsbury, Vt., U.S.	C5	122
East Saint Louis, Il., U.S.	E3	90
East Salt Creek, stm., Co., U.S.	B2	83
East Sandwich, Ma., U.S.	C7	98
East Sebago, Me., U.S.	E2	96
East Selkirk, Man.	D3	70
East Siberian Sea, Sov. Un.	B18	29
Eastside, Or., U.S.	D2	114
East Sioux Falls, S.D., U.S.	D9	118
East Smithfield, Pa., U.S.	C8	115
Eastsound, Wa., U.S.	A3	124
East Sparta, Oh., U.S.	B4	112
East Spencer, N.C., U.S.	B2	110
East Springfield, N.Y., U.S.	C6	109
East Stoneham, Me., U.S.	D2	96
East Stroudsburg, Pa., U.S.	D11	115
East Sudbury, Ma., U.S.	g10	98
East Sullivan, Ma., U.S.	D4	96
East Sullivan, N.H., U.S.	D2	106
East Sumner, Me., U.S.	D2	96
East Sussex, co., Eng., U.K.	D7	12
East Swanzey, N.H., U.S.	E2	106
East Tawas, Mi., U.S.	D7	99
East Templeton, Ma., U.S.	A3	98
East Thermopolis, Wy., U.S.	*C4	127
East Thetford, Vt., U.S.	D4	122
East Thompson, Ct., U.S.	A8	84
East Trout Lake, l., Sask.	C3	75
East Troy, Wi., U.S.	F5	126
East Tustin, Ca., U.S.	*n13	82
East Unity, N.H., U.S.	D2	106
East Vestal, N.Y., U.S.	C5	109
East View, W.V., U.S.	k10	125
Eastville, Va., U.S.	C7	123
East Wakefield, N.H., U.S.	C4	106
East Walker, stm., U.S.	E2	105
East Wallingford, Vt., U.S.	E3	122
East Walpole, Ma., U.S.	h11	98
East Wareham, Ma., U.S.	C6	98
East Washington, Pa., U.S.	F1	115
East Waterboro, Me., U.S.	E2	96
East Waterford, Pa., U.S.	F7	115
East Wenatchee, Wa., U.S.	B6	124
East Wilton, Me., U.S.	D2	96
East Windsor, N.J., U.S.	C3	107
East Windsor Hill, Ct., U.S.	B5	84
Eastwood, Mi., U.S.	*F5	99
Eastwood, Ky., U.S.	g12	94
East Woodstock, Ct., U.S.	B8	84

Name	Map Ref.	Page
East Worcester, N.Y., U.S.	C6	109
East York, Ont.	D5	73
Eaton, Co., U.S.	A6	83
Eaton, Il., U.S.	D6	90
Eaton, In., U.S.	D7	91
Eaton, Me., U.S.	C5	96
Eaton, N.Y., U.S.	C5	109
Eaton, Oh., U.S.	C1	112
Eaton, Tn., U.S.	B2	119
Eaton, co., Mi., U.S.	F6	99
Eaton Center, N.H., U.S.	C4	106
Eaton Rapids, Mi., U.S.	F6	99
Eatonia, Sask.	F1	75
Eatonton, Ga., U.S.	C3	87
Eatontown, N.J., U.S.	C4	107
Eatonville, Wa., U.S.	C3	124
Eau Claire, Mi., U.S.	G4	99
Eau Claire, Wi., U.S.	D2	126
Eau Claire, co., Wi., U.S.	D2	126
Eau Claire, Lac à l', l., Que.	g11	74
Eau Galle, Wi., U.S.	D1	126
Eauze, Fr.	F4	16
Ebadon Island, i., Marsh Is.	S17	52
Ebb and Flow Lake, l., Man.	D2	70
Ebeleben, E. Ger.	B5	19
Ebeltoft, Den.	B4	15
Ebenezer, Sask.	F4	75
Ebenezer, Ms., U.S.	C3	101
Ebenezer, Oh., U.S.	A1	112
Eben Junction, Mi., U.S.	B4	99
Ebensburg, Pa., U.S.	F4	115
Eberbach, W. Ger.	D3	19
Ebermannstadt, W. Ger.	D6	19
Ebersbach, E. Ger.	B9	19
Ebersbach, W. Ger.	D5	19
Eberswalde [-Finow], E. Ger.	B6	18
Ebetsu, Japan	E10	33
Ebeye, Marsh Is.	S17	52
Ebingen, W. Ger.	D4	18
Eboli, Italy	D5	23
Ebolowa, Cam.	B2	46
Ebro, Fl., U.S.	u16	86
Ebro, Mn., U.S.	C3	100
Ebro, stm., Spain	B6	22
Eccles, W.V., U.S.	n13	125
Eccles, Phil.	A5	112
Echague, Phil.	B7	34
Echallens, Switz.	C2	21
Echeconnee Creek, stm., Ga., U.S.	D3	87
Echigawa, Japan	n15	33
Édhessa, Grc.	B4	40
Echo, Al., U.S.	D4	78
Echo, La., U.S.	C3	95
Echo, Mn., U.S.	F3	100
Echo, Or., U.S.	B7	114
Echo, Ut., U.S.	C4	121
Echo Bay, Nv., U.S.	G7	105
Echo Bay, Ont.	B7	70
Echoing Lake, l., Ont.	B5	70
Echo Lake, l., Me., U.S.	D3	96
Echo Lake, l., Vt., U.S.	B5	122
Echols, co., Ga., U.S.	F4	87
Echt, Neth.	C5	17
Echt, Scot., U.K.	C6	13
Echternach, Lux.	C7	16
Echuca, Austl.	G7	50
Écija, Spain	D3	22
Eckelson, N.D., U.S.	C7	111
Eckerman, Mi., U.S.	B5	99
Eckernförde, W. Ger.	A4	18
Eckernförder Bucht, b., W. Ger.	D4	15
Eckerty, In., U.S.	H4	91
Eckhart Mines, Md., U.S.	k13	97
Eckley, Co., U.S.	A8	83
Eckley, Pa., U.S.	E10	115
Eckman, N.D., U.S.	A4	111
Eckman, W.V., U.S.	*D3	125
Eckville, Alta.	C3	68
Eclectic, Al., U.S.	C3	78
Eclipse Sound, strt., N.W. Ter.	B17	66
Econfina, stm., Fl., U.S.	B3	86
Economy, N.S.	D6	71
Economy, In., U.S.	E7	91
Economy, Pa., U.S.	h13	115
Écorces, Rivière aux, stm., Que.	A6	74
Ecorse, Mi., U.S.	p15	99
Ecru, Ms., U.S.	A4	101
Ecuador, ctry., S.A.	B2	58
Ecum Secum, N.S.	E7	71
Ecum Secum Bridge, N.S.	E7	71
Ed, Eth.	F3	47
Eda, Swe.	H5	14
Edam, Sask.	D1	75
Edam, Neth.	B5	17
Eday, i., Scot., U.K.	A6	13
Edberg, Alta.	C4	68
Edcouch, Tx., U.S.	F4	120
Eddiceton, Ms., U.S.	D3	101
Eddington, Me., U.S.	D4	96
Eddrachillis Bay, b., Scot.	B3	13
Eddy, co., N.M., U.S.	E5	108
Eddy, co., N.D., U.S.	B7	111
Eddy, Lake, l., Afr.	B4	48
Eddystone Rocks, Eng., U.K.	E4	10
Eddyville, Ia., U.S.	C5	92
Eddyville, Ky., U.S.	e9	94
Eddyville, Ne., U.S.	C6	104
Ede, Neth.	A6	17
Ede, Nig.	*E5	45
Edéa, Cam.	B2	46
Eden, Austl.	H7	51
Eden, Mn., U.S.	D2	98
Eden, Az., U.S.	E6	80
Eden, Id., U.S.	G5	89
Eden, Md., U.S.	D6	97
Eden, Ms., U.S.	C3	101
Eden, N.C., U.S.	A3	110
Eden, N.Y., U.S.	C2	109
Eden, S.D., U.S.	B8	118
Eden, Tx., U.S.	D3	120
Eden, Vt., U.S.	B3	122
Eden, Wi., U.S.	E5	126
Eden, Wy., U.S.	D3	127
Eden, stm., Eng., U.K.	C5	10
Eden, stm., Scot., U.K.	D5	13
Eden Lake, l., Man.	A1	70
Eden Mills, Vt., U.S.	B3	122
Eden Prairie, Mn., U.S.	n12	100
Eden Valley, Mn., U.S.	E4	100

Name	Map Ref.	Page
Edenville, Mi., U.S.	E6	99
Edenwold, Sask.	G3	75
Eder, stm., W. Ger.	C4	18
Edesville, Md., U.S.	B5	97
Edgar, Ne., U.S.	D8	104
Edgar, Wi., U.S.	D4	126
Edgar, co., Il., U.S.	D6	90
Edgard, La., U.S.	D5	95
Edgar Springs, Mo., U.S.	D6	102
Edgartown, Ma., U.S.	D6	98
Edge, i., Nor.	B12	128
Edgecombe, co., N.C., U.S.	B5	110
Edgecumbe, Cape, c., Ak., U.S.	m21	79
Edgefield, S.C., U.S.	D4	117
Edgefield, co., S.C., U.S.	D4	117
Edgeley, Sask.	G4	75
Edgeley, N.D., U.S.	C7	111
Edgemere, Md., U.S.	B5	97
Edgemont, Ar., U.S.	*B3	81
Edgemont, Ca., U.S.	*F5	82
Edgemont, S.D., U.S.	D2	118
Edgemoor, De., U.S.	A3	85
Edgemoor, S.C., U.S.	B5	117
Edgemoor, Tn., U.S.	m13	119
Edgerly, La., U.S.	D2	95
Edgerton, Alta.	C5	68
Edgerton, Ks., U.S.	D8	93
Edgerton, Mn., U.S.	G2	100
Edgerton, Mo., U.S.	B3	102
Edgerton, Oh., U.S.	A1	112
Edgerton, Wi., U.S.	F4	126
Edgerton, Wy., U.S.	C6	127
Edgewater, Al., U.S.	f7	78
Edgewater, Co., U.S.	*B5	83
Edgewater, Fl., U.S.	D6	86
Edgewater, Md., U.S.	C4	97
Edgewater, N.J., U.S.	h9	107
Edgewater Park, N.J., U.S.	C3	107
Edgewood, B.C.	E8	69
Edgewood, Il., U.S.	E5	90
Edgewood, In., U.S.	D6	91
Edgewood, Ia., U.S.	B6	92
Edgewood, Ky., U.S.	h13	94
Edgewood, Md., U.S.	B5	97
Edgewood, N.M., U.S.	B3	108
Edgewood, Oh., U.S.	A5	112
Edgewood, Pa., U.S.	k14	115
Edgewood, Tx., U.S.	C5	120
Edgeworth, Pa., U.S.	h13	115
Edgeworthstown see Mostrim, Ire.	D4	11
Édgiggen Island, i., Marsh Is.	S17	52
Edina, Mo., U.S.	A5	102
Edina, Mn., U.S.	F5	100
Edinboro, Pa., U.S.	C1	115
Edinburg, Il., U.S.	D4	90
Edinburg, Ms., U.S.	C4	101
Edinburg, N.D., U.S.	A8	111
Edinburg, N.Y., U.S.	B6	109
Edinburg, Tx., U.S.	F3	120
Edinburg, Va., U.S.	B4	123
Edinburgh, Scot., U.K.	C5	10
Edinburgh, In., U.S.	F6	91
Edirne, Tur.	B6	40
Edison, Ga., U.S.	E2	87
Edison, Ne., U.S.	D6	104
Edison, Oh., U.S.	B3	112
Edison, N.J., U.S.	C4	107
Edisto, stm., S.C., U.S.	E6	117
Edisto, North Fork, stm., S.C., U.S.	D5	117
Edisto, South Fork, stm., S.C., U.S.	E5	117
Edisto Island, S.C., U.S.	F7	117
Edisto Island, i., S.C., U.S.	F7	117
Edith, Mount, mtn., Mt., U.S.	D5	103
Edithburgh, Austl.	G1	51
Edmond, Ks., U.S.	C4	93
Edmond, Ok., U.S.	B4	113
Edmonds, Wa., U.S.	B3	124
Edmondson, Ar., U.S.	B5	81
Edmondson Heights, Md., U.S.	g10	97
Edmonson, co., Ky., U.S.	C3	94
Edmonton, Ky., U.S.	D4	94
Edmonton, Alta.	C4	68
Edmore, Mi., U.S.	E5	99
Edmore, N.D., U.S.	A7	111
Edmund Lake, l., Man.	B5	70
Edmunds, co., S.D., U.S.	B6	118
Edmundston, N.B.	B1	71
Edna, Ks., U.S.	E8	93
Edna, Tx., U.S.	E4	120
Edna, W.V., U.S.	h10	125
Edolo, Italy	D9	21
Édouard, Lac, l., Que.	B5	74
Edra, Scot., U.K.	A6	13
Edremit, Tur.	C6	25
Edremit, Gulf of, b., Tur.	C6	25
Edson, Alta.	C2	68
Edson, Ks., U.S.	C2	93
Edson, Me., U.S.	D7	96
Eduardo Castex, Arg.	B4	54
Eduni, Mount, mtn., N.W. Ter.	D7	66
Edwall, Wa., U.S.	B8	124
Edward, Lake, l., Afr.	B4	48
Edward, Ont.	h13	73
Edwards, Ms., U.S.	C3	101
Edwards, N.Y., U.S.	A5	109
Edwards, co., Il., U.S.	E5	90
Edwards, co., Ks., U.S.	E4	93
Edwards, co., Tx., U.S.	E2	120
Edwards Air Force Base, mil., Ca., U.S.	E5	82
Edwardsburg, Mi., U.S.	G4	99
Edwards Butte, mtn., Or., U.S.	B3	114
Edwards Plateau, plat., Tx., U.S.	D2	120
Edwardsport, In., U.S.	G3	91
Edwardsville, Al., U.S.	B4	78
Edwardsville, Il., U.S.	E4	90
Edwardsville, Ks., U.S.	k16	93
Edwardsville, Pa., U.S.	n17	115
Edward VIII Bay, b., Ant.	C18	7
Edward VII Peninsula, pen., Ant.	B33	7

Name	Map Ref.	Page
Effingham, Il., U.S.	D5	90
Effingham, Ks., U.S.	C8	93
Effingham, N.H., U.S.	C5	106
Effingham, S.C., U.S.	C8	117
Effingham, co., Ga., U.S.	D5	87
Effingham, co., Il., U.S.	D5	90
Effingham Falls, N.H., U.S.	C4	106
Effon-Alaiye, Nig.	*E5	45
Efland, N.C., U.S.	A3	110
Eforie Nord, Rom.	C9	24
Eforie Sud (Vasile Roaită), Rom.	C9	24
Ega, stm., Spain	A4	22
Egadi Islands, is., Italy	E4	23
Egan, S.D., U.S.	D9	118
Egan Range, mts., Nv., U.S.	E7	105
Eganville, Ont.	B7	73
Egbert, Wy., U.S.	E8	127
Egedesminde, Grnld.	*C15	61
Egegik, Ak., U.S.	D8	79
Egeland, N.D., U.S.	A6	111
Egeln, E. Ger.	B6	19
Eger, Hung.	B5	24
Egersund, Nor.	H2	14
Egerton, Mount, mtn., Ant.	A28	7
Eggebek, W. Ger.	D3	15
Eggenfelden, W. Ger.	E7	19
Egg Harbor, Wi., U.S.	C6	126
Egg Harbor City, N.J., U.S.	D3	107
Egg Island Point, c., N.J., U.S.	E2	107
Egg Lake, l., Sask.	C3	75
Egilsstadir, Ice.	n25	14
Égletons, Fr.	E5	16
Eglin Air Force Base, mil., Fl., U.S.	u15	86
Eglinton Island, i., N.W. Ter.	m28	66
Eglisau, Switz.	A6	21
Egmond aan Zee, Neth.	B4	17
Egmont, Cape, c., N.Z.	M14	51
Egmont, Mount, mtn., N.Z.	M15	51
Egmont Bay, b., P.E.I.	C5	71
Egmont Channel, strt., Fl., U.S.	p10	86
Egmont Key, i., Fl., U.S.	p10	86
Egnar, Co., U.S.	D2	83
Egremont, Alta.	B3	68
Egremont, Eng., U.K.	F5	13
Egrigöz, Tur.	D8	40
Egrigoz, mtn., Tur.	C7	25
Egtved, Den.	C3	15
Egypt, Ar., U.S.	B5	81
Egypt, Ga., U.S.	D5	87
Egypt, Ma., U.S.	B6	98
Egypt, Ms., U.S.	B5	101
Egypt, ctry., Afr.	C2	38
Egypt, Lake of, res., Il., U.S.	F5	90
Egypt Lake, l., U.S.	*D4	86
Ehrenberg, Az., U.S.	D1	80
Ehrenfeld, Pa., U.S.	F4	115
Ehrhardt, S.C., U.S.	E5	117
Éibar, Spain	A4	22
Eibau, E. Ger.	C9	19
Eibenstock, E. Ger.	C7	19
Eichstätt, W. Ger.	D5	18
Eider, stm., W. Ger.	A4	18
Eidsberg, Nor.	H4	14
Eidson, Tn., U.S.	C10	119
Eidsvold, Austl.	E9	50
Eidsvoll, Nor.	G4	14
Eielson Air Force Base, mil., Ak., U.S.	C10	79
Eifel, mts., W. Ger.	C3	18
Eige, Carn, mtn., Scot., U.K.	C3	13
Eiger, mtn., Switz.	C5	21
Eigg, i., Scot., U.K.	B3	10
Eigg, Sound of, strt., Scot., U.K.	D2	13
Eightmile Creek, stm., Ks., U.S.	h12	93
Eights Coast, Ant.	B3	7
Eighty Eight, Ky., U.S.	D4	94
Eikeren, l., Nor.	p28	14
Eildon, Lake, res., Austl.	H6	51
Eileen Lake, l., N.W. Ter.	D11	66
Eilenburg, E. Ger.	C6	18
Eiler Rasmussen, Cape, c., Grnld.	A16	128
Eil Malk, i., Palau	R17	52
Einbeck, W. Ger.	C4	18
Eindhoven, Neth.	B6	16
Einsiedeln, Switz.	B4	20
Eirunepé, Braz.	C4	58
Eisenach, E. Ger.	C5	18
Eisenberg, E. Ger.	C6	19
Eisenhower, Mount, mtn., N.H., U.S.	B4	106
Eisenhüttenstadt, E. Ger.	B7	18
Eisenstadt, Aus.	E8	18
Eiserfeld, W. Ger.	C2	19
Eisfeld, E. Ger.	C5	19
Eisleben, E. Ger.	C5	18
Eita, Kir.	R18	52
Eita, i., Kir.	R18	52
Eitorf, W. Ger.	C2	19
Eitzen, Mn., U.S.	G7	100
Ejby, Den.	C3	15
Ejea de los Caballeros, Spain	A5	22
Ejeda, Madag.	h8	49
Ejigbo, Nig.	*E5	45
Ejstrup, Den.	C3	15
Ejutla de Crespo, Mex.	D5	63
Ekalaka, Mt., U.S.	E12	103
Ekenäs, Fin.	G10	14
Ekeren (part of Antwerp), Bel.	C4	17
Ekhínos, Grc.	B5	25
Ekimchan, Sov. Un.	D16	29
Ekoln, l., Swe.	t35	14
Ekron, Ky., U.S.	C3	94
Eksjö, Swe.	I6	14
Ekumakoko, Zaire	B3	48
Ekwan, stm., Ont.	F15	66
Ekwok, Ak., U.S.	D8	79
El Aaiún, W. Sah.	D2	44
Elaine, Ar., U.S.	C5	81
Elamanchili, India	I9	37
Elamton, Ky., U.S.	C6	94
Elamville, Al., U.S.	D4	78
Eland, Wi., U.S.	D4	126
El Arahal, Spain	D3	22
Elassón, Grc.	C4	25
Elat, Isr.	E6	41
Elazig, Tur.	C12	19
Elba, Al., U.S.	D3	78
Elba, Id., U.S.	G5	89
Elba, Mi., U.S.	E7	99
Elba, Mn., U.S.	F6	100
Elba, Ne., U.S.	C7	104
Elba, N.Y., U.S.	B2	109
Elba, i., Italy	C3	23
El Banco, Col.	B5	60
El Baúl, Ven.	B4	60
Elbe (Labe), stm., Eur.	B4	18
Elberfeld, In., U.S.	H3	91
Elberon, Ia., U.S.	B5	92
Elbert, Co., U.S.	B6	83
Elbert, Tx., U.S.	C3	120
Elbert, co., Co., U.S.	B6	83
Elbert, co., Ga., U.S.	B4	87
Elbert, Mount, mtn., Co., U.S.	B4	83
Elberta, Al., U.S.	E2	78
Elberta, Ga., U.S.	D3	87
Elberta, Mi., U.S.	D4	99
Elberta, Ut., U.S.	D4	121
Elberton, Ga., U.S.	B4	87
Elbeuf, Fr.	C4	16
El Beyyadh, Alg.	C5	44
El Bigenalp, Aus.	B6	20
Elbing, Ks., U.S.	f12	93
Elbistan, Tur.	C11	40
El Bluff, Nic.	E8	63
El Bolsón, Arg.	C2	54
El Bonillo, Spain	C4	22
El Bordo, Col.	C2	60
El Boulaïda (Blida), Alg.	B5	44
Elbow, Sask.	F2	75
Elbow, stm., Alta.	D3	68
Elbow Lake, Mn., U.S.	E3	100
Elbow Lake, l., Man.	B1	70
Elbridge, Tn., U.S.	A2	119
Elbrus, Mount, mtn., Sov. Un.	E7	29
Elburg, Neth.	B5	17
El Burgo de Osma, Spain	B4	22
Elburn, Il., U.S.	B5	90
Elburz Mountains, mts., Iran	B5	38
El Cajon, Ca., U.S.	F5	82
El Callao, Ven.	B5	60
El Campo, Tx., U.S.	E4	120
El Capitan, mtn., Mt., U.S.	D2	103
El Capitan Reservoir, res., Ca., U.S.	o16	82
El Carmen, Bol.	C4	55
El Carmen de Bolívar, Col.	B2	60
El Carrizo, Mex.	B3	63
El Centro, Ca., U.S.	F6	82
El Cerrito, Ca., U.S.	h8	82
El Cerro, Bol.	C3	55
El Chaparro, Ven.	B4	60
Elche, Spain	C5	22
Elcho, Wi., U.S.	C4	126
Elco, Il., U.S.	F4	90
El Cocuy, Col.	B3	60
El Cuervo Butte, mtn., N.M., U.S.	k9	108
Elda, Spain	C5	22
Elde, stm., E. Ger.	B5	18
Elderon, Wi., U.S.	D4	126
Eldersley, Sask.	E4	75
Elderton, Pa., U.S.	E3	115
El Diviso, Col.	C2	60
El Djelfa, Alg.	C5	44
El Djouf, des., Afr.	B3	45
Eldon, P.E.I.	C7	71
Eldon, Ia., U.S.	D5	92
Eldon, Mo., U.S.	C5	102
Eldora, Ia., U.S.	B4	92
Eldorado, Braz.	C3	56
Eldorado, Ont.	C7	73
Eldorado, Sask.	m7	75
El Dorado, Ar., U.S.	D3	81
Eldorado, Ga., U.S.	E3	87
El Dorado, Il., U.S.	F5	90
El Dorado, Ks., U.S.	E7	93
Eldorado, Md., U.S.	C6	97
Eldorado, N.C., U.S.	B2	110
Eldorado, Oh., U.S.	C1	112
El Dorado, Ok., U.S.	C2	113
Eldorado, Tx., U.S.	D2	120
El Dorado, Ven.	B5	60
El Dorado, co., Ca., U.S.	C3	82
Eldorado Peak, mtn., Wa., U.S.	A4	124
El Dorado Springs, Co., U.S.	B5	83
El Dorado Springs, Mo., U.S.	D3	102
Eldorendo, Ga., U.S.	E2	87
Eldoret, Kenya	A6	48
Eldred, Il., U.S.	D3	90
Eldred, Pa., U.S.	C5	115
Eldridge, Al., U.S.	B2	78
Eldridge, Ia., U.S.	C7	92
Eldridge, Mo., U.S.	D5	102
Eldridge, N.D., U.S.	C7	111
Eleanor, W.V., U.S.	C3	125
Electra, Tx., U.S.	B3	120
Electra Lake, res., Co., U.S.	D3	83
Electric Mills, Ms., U.S.	C5	101
Electric Peak, mtn., Co., U.S.	B5	83
Electric Peak, mtn., Mt., U.S.	E6	103
Elektrogorsk, Sov. Un.	n18	27
Elektrostal, Sov. Un.	n18	27
Elephant Butte, mtn., N.M., U.S.	*E4	108
Elephant Butte Reservoir, res., N.M., U.S.	D2	108
Elephant Island, i., B.A.T.	C7	7
Elephant Mountain, mtn., Me., U.S.	D2	96
El Escorial, Spain	o16	22
El Eulma, Alg.	B6	44
Eleusis see Elevsís, Grc.	g11	25
Eleuthera, i., Bah.	B5	64
Eleva, Wi., U.S.	D2	126
Eleven Mile Canyon Reservoir, res., Co., U.S.	C5	83
Eleven Point, stm., U.S.	A4	81
Elevsís (Eleusis), Grc.	g11	25
Elevsís, Gulf of, b., Grc.	g11	25
El Fasher (Al Fāshir), Sud.	C2	47
El Ferrol [del Caudillo], Spain	A1	22
Elfin Cove, Ak., U.S.	k21	79
Elfrida, Az., U.S.	F6	80
Elfros, Sask.	F4	75
El Fud, Eth.	D5	47
El Fuerte, Mex.	B3	63
El Galhak, Sud.	C3	47
El Ghazawet, Alg.	B4	44
Elgin, Man.	E1	70
Elgin, N.B.	D4	71
Elgin, Ont.	C8	73
Elgin, Scot., U.K.	D5	13
Elgin, Il., U.S.	A5	90
Elgin, Ia., U.S.	B6	92
Elgin, Ks., U.S.	E7	93
Elgin, Mn., U.S.	F6	100
Elgin, Ne., U.S.	C7	104
Elgin, N.D., U.S.	C3	111
Elgin, Or., U.S.	B9	114
Elgin, Pa., U.S.	C2	115
Elgin, S.C., U.S.	B5	117
Elgin, Tx., U.S.	D4	120
Elgin, Ut., U.S.	E5	121
Elgin, co., Ont.	E3	73
Elgol, Scot., U.K.	C2	13
Elgon, Mount, mtn., Afr.	A5	48
El Grara, Alg.	C5	44
El Grullo, Mex.	n11	63
El Huecú, Arg.	B2	54
Eli, Ne., U.S.	B4	104
Eliasville, Tx., U.S.	C3	120
Elida, N.M., U.S.	D6	108
Elida, Oh., U.S.	B1	112
Elikón Óros (Helicon), mtn., Grc.	g9	25
Elim, Ak., U.S.	C7	79
Elin, stm., Zaire	B4	48
Élisabethville see Lubumbashi, Zaire	D4	48
Elizabeth, Austl.	F6	50
Elizabeth, Co., U.S.	A3	81
Elizabeth, Co., U.S.	B6	83
Elizabeth, Il., U.S.	A3	90
Elizabeth, In., U.S.	H6	91
Elizabeth, La., U.S.	D3	95
Elizabeth, Mn., U.S.	D2	100
Elizabeth, Ms., U.S.	B3	101
Elizabeth, N.J., U.S.	B4	107
Elizabeth, W.V., U.S.	B3	125
Elizabeth, Cape, c., Wa., U.S.	B1	124
Elizabeth City, N.C., U.S.	A6	110
Elizabeth Islands, is., Ma., U.S.	D6	98
Elizabethton, Tn., U.S.	C11	119
Elizabethtown, Il., U.S.	F5	90
Elizabethtown, In., U.S.	F6	91
Elizabethtown, Ky., U.S.	C4	94
Elizabethtown, N.C., U.S.	C4	110
Elizabethtown, N.Y., U.S.	A7	109
Elizabethtown, Pa., U.S.	F8	115
Elizabethville, Pa., U.S.	E8	115
Elk, Pol.	B7	26
Elk, Ca., U.S.	C2	82
Elk, Wa., U.S.	A8	124
Elk, co., Ks., U.S.	E7	93
Elk, co., Pa., U.S.	D4	115
Elk, stm., B.C.	D10	69
Elk, stm., Al., U.S.	A2	78
Elk, stm., Co., U.S.	A4	83
Elk, stm., Ks., U.S.	E7	93
Elk, stm., W.V., U.S.	C3	125
Elk, stm., U.S.	C3	126
Elkader, Ia., U.S.	B6	92
El Kala, Alg.	F2	23
El Kairouan, Tun.	B7	44
El Kasserine, Tun.	B6	44
Elkatawa, Ky., U.S.	C6	94
Elk City, Id., U.S.	D3	89
Elk City, Ks., U.S.	E8	93
Elk City, Ne., U.S.	g12	104
Elk City, Ok., U.S.	B2	113
Elk City Lake, res., Ks., U.S.	E7	93
Elk Creek, Ca., U.S.	C2	82
Elk Creek, Ne., U.S.	D9	104
Elk Creek, Va., U.S.	D1	123
Elk Creek, stm., Ok., U.S.	B2	113
Elk Creek, stm., S.D., U.S.	C3	118
El Kef, Tun.	B6	44
El Kere, Eth.	D5	47
Elk Falls, Ks., U.S.	E7	93
Elkford, B.C.	D10	69
Elk Garden, W.V., U.S.	B5	125
Elk Grove, Ca., U.S.	C3	82
Elk Grove Village, Il., U.S.	h9	90
Elkhart, Il., U.S.	C4	90
Elkhart, In., U.S.	A6	91
Elkhart, Ks., U.S.	E2	93
Elkhart, Tx., U.S.	D5	120
Elkhart, co., In., U.S.	A6	91
Elkhart, In., U.S.	B6	91
Elkhart Lake, Wi., U.S.	E5	126
Elkhead Mountains, mts., Co., U.S.	A8	83
Elk Horn, Ia., U.S.	C2	92
Elkhorn, Man.	E1	70
Elk Horn, Ne., U.S.	g12	104
Elkhorn, W.V., U.S.	*D3	125
Elkhorn, Wi., U.S.	F5	126
Elkhorn, stm., Ne., U.S.	B7	104
Elkhorn, North Fork, stm., Ne., U.S.	B8	104
Elkhorn, South Fork, stm., Ne., U.S.	B7	104
Elkhorn City, Ky., U.S.	C7	94
Elkhorn Peaks, mts., Id., U.S.	F7	89
Elkhovo, Bul.	D8	24
Elkin, N.C., U.S.	A2	110
Elkins, Ar., U.S.	A1	81
Elkins, N.H., U.S.	D3	106
Elkins, W.V., U.S.	C5	125
Elkins Park, Pa., U.S.	F11	115
Elk Island, i., Man.	C4	70
Elk Island National Park, Alta.	C4	68
Elkland, Pa., U.S.	C7	115
Elk Mills, Md., U.S.	A6	97
Elkmont, Al., U.S.	A3	78
Elkmont, Tn., U.S.	D10	119
Elk Mound, Wi., U.S.	D2	126
Elk Mountain, Wy., U.S.	E6	127
Elk Mountain, mtn., N.M., U.S.	D1	108
Elk Mountain, mtn., Wy., U.S.	E6	127
Elk Mountains, mts., Co., U.S.	B3	83
Elko, B.C.	E10	69
Elko, Ga., U.S.	D3	87
Elko, Nv., U.S.	C6	105
Elko, S.C., U.S.	E5	117
Elko, co., Nv., U.S.	B6	105
Elk Park, N.C., U.S.	A1	110
Elk Peak, mtn., Mt., U.S.	D6	103
Elk Point, Alta.	C5	68
Elk Point, S.D., U.S.	E9	118
Elk Ranch, Ar., U.S.	B2	81
Elk Rapids, Mi., U.S.	D5	99
Elk River, Id., U.S.	C3	89
Elk River, Mn., U.S.	E5	100
Elk Springs, Co., U.S.	A2	83
Elkton, Fl., U.S.	C5	86
Elkton, Ky., U.S.	D2	94
Elkton, Md., U.S.	k14	97
Elkton, Mi., U.S.	E7	99
Elkton, Or., U.S.	D3	114
Elkton, S.D., U.S.	C9	118
Elkton, Tn., U.S.	B5	119
Elkton, Va., U.S.	B4	123
Elk Valley, Tn., U.S.	C9	119
Elkview, W.V., U.S.	m13	125
Elkville, Il., U.S.	F4	90
Ellamore, W.V., U.S.	C4	125
Ellaville, Ga., U.S.	D2	87
Ellef Ringnes Island, i., N.W. Ter.	m31	66
Ellen, Mount, mtn., Ut., U.S.	E5	121
Ellen, Mount, mtn., Vt., U.S.	C3	122
Ellenboro, N.C., U.S.	B1	110
Ellenboro, W.V., U.S.	B3	125
Ellenburg Center, N.Y., U.S.	f11	109
Ellendale, De., U.S.	E4	85
Ellendale, Mn., U.S.	G5	100
Ellendale, N.D., U.S.	C7	111
Ellensburg, Wa., U.S.	C5	124
Ellenton, Fl., U.S.	E4	86
Ellenton, Ga., U.S.	E3	87
Ellenville, N.Y., U.S.	D6	109
Ellenwood, Ga., U.S.	h8	87
Ellerbe, N.C., U.S.	B3	110
Ellerslie, N.S.	E6	71
Ellershouse, N.S.	E6	71
Ellerslie, Md., U.S.	k13	97
Ellice Islands see Tuvalu, ctry., Oc.	G10	6
Ellichpur see Achalpur, India	G6	37
Ellicott City, Md., U.S.	B4	97
Ellicottville, N.Y., U.S.	C2	109
Ellijay, Ga., U.S.	B2	87
Ellington, Ct., U.S.	B6	84
Ellington, Mo., U.S.	D7	102
Ellinwood, Ks., U.S.	D5	93
Elliot Lake, Ont.	A2	73
Elliot Lake, l., Man.	C4	70
Elliott, Il., U.S.	C5	90
Elliott, Ia., U.S.	C2	92
Elliott, Ms., U.S.	B4	101
Elliott, N.D., U.S.	C8	111
Elliott, S.C., U.S.	C7	117
Elliott, co., Ky., U.S.	B6	94
Elliott Bay, b., Wa., U.S.	e11	124
Elliott Key, i., Fl., U.S.	G6	86
Elliott Knob, mtn., Va., U.S.	B3	123
Ellis, Id., U.S.	E4	89
Ellis, Ks., U.S.	D4	93
Ellis, Ne., U.S.	D9	104
Ellis, S.D., U.S.	D9	118
Ellis, co., Ks., U.S.	D4	93
Ellis, co., Ok., U.S.	A2	113
Ellis, co., Tx., U.S.	C4	120
Ellis, stm., N.H., U.S.	B4	106
Ellisdale, N.J., U.S.	C3	107
Ellis Grove, Il., U.S.	E4	90
Ellison Bay, Wi., U.S.	C6	126
Ellis Pond, Me., U.S.	D2	96
Ellis Pond, l., Me., U.S.	D2	96
Elliston, Newf.	D5	72
Elliston, Mt., U.S.	D4	103
Elliston, Va., U.S.	C2	123
Ellistown, Ms., U.S.	A5	101
Ellisville, Il., U.S.	C3	90
Ellisville, Mo., U.S.	f12	102
Ellon, Scot., U.K.	B5	10
Ellore see Elūru, India	E7	36
Elloree, S.C., U.S.	D6	117
Elport, Pa., U.S.	E1	115
Ellrich, E. Ger.	B5	19
Ells, stm., Alta.	A4	68
Ellscott, Alta.	B4	68
Ellsinore, Mo., U.S.	E7	102
Ellsworth, Il., U.S.	C5	90
Ellsworth, Ia., U.S.	B4	92
Ellsworth, Ks., U.S.	D5	93
Ellsworth, Me., U.S.	D4	96
Ellsworth, Mi., U.S.	C5	99
Ellsworth, Mn., U.S.	G2	100
Ellsworth, Pa., U.S.	F1	115
Ellsworth, Wi., U.S.	D1	126
Ellsworth, co., Ks., U.S.	D5	93
Ellsworth Air Force Base, mil., S.D., U.S.	C2	118
Ellsworth Land, reg., Ant.	B4	7
Ellsworth Mountains, mts., Ant.	B4	7
Ellwangen, W. Ger.	D5	18
Ellwood City, Pa., U.S.	E1	115
Elm, stm., N.D., U.S.	B8	111
Elma, Ia., U.S.	A5	92
Elma, Wa., U.S.	C2	124
Elmadag, Tur.	B7	44
El Mali, Tur.	D7	25
El Manteco, Ven.	B5	60
El Menia, Alg.	C5	44
Elmer, Mo., U.S.	A5	102
Elmer, N.J., U.S.	D2	107
Elmer, Ok., U.S.	C2	113
El Metlaoui, Tun.	C6	44
El Mghayyar, Alg.	C6	44
El Milagro, Arg.	C3	54
Elmhurst, Il., U.S.	B6	90
Elmhurst, Pa., U.S.	D10	115
Elmira, Ont.	D4	73
Elmira, P.E.I.	C7	71
Elmira, In., U.S.	A7	91
Elmira, Mi., U.S.	C6	99
Elmira, Mo., U.S.	B3	102
Elmira, N.Y., U.S.	C4	109
Elmira, Or., U.S.	C3	114
Elmira, W.V., U.S.	C4	125
Elmira Heights, N.Y., U.S.	C4	109
Elmo, Ks., U.S.	D6	93
Elmo, Mo., U.S.	A2	102
Elmo, Ut., U.S.	D5	121
Elmodel, Ga., U.S.	E2	87
El Moknine, Tun.	B7	44
Elmont, Ks., U.S.	k14	93
Elmont, N.Y., U.S.	k13	109
Elmora, Pa., U.S.	E4	115
El Morro National Monument, N.M., U.S.	B1	108
El Mreiti, well, Maur.	B3	45
Elmsdale, N.B.	E6	71
Elmshorn, W. Ger.	B4	18
Elm Springs, Ar., U.S.	A1	81
Elm Springs, S.D., U.S.	C3	118
Elm Springs Colony, S.D., U.S.	C8	111
Elmsville, N.B.	D3	71
Elmvale, Ont.	C5	73
Elmville, Ct., U.S.	B8	84
Elmwood, Ont.	C3	73
Elmwood, Il., U.S.	C3	90
Elmwood, Ma., U.S.	B6	98
Elmwood, Ne., U.S.	D9	104
Elmwood, Ok., U.S.	A1	113
Elmwood, Wi., U.S.	D1	126
Elmwood Park, N.J., U.S.	h8	107
Elmwood Park, Il., U.S.	k9	90
Elmwood Place, Oh., U.S.	o13	112
Elna, Ky., U.S.	C7	94
Elne, Fr.	A5	16
El Nevado, Cerro, mtn., Arg.	B3	54
Elnora, Alta.	D4	68
Elnora, In., U.S.	G3	91
El Obeid (Al Ubayyiḍ), Sud.	C3	47
Eloise, Fl., U.S.	E5	86
Elon College, N.C., U.S.	A3	110
Elora, Ont.	D4	73
Elora, Tn., U.S.	B5	119
El Oro, prov., Ec.	B2	58
Elorza, Ven.	B4	60
El Oso, Ven.	B4	60
Eloy, Az., U.S.	E4	80
El Palmar, Ven.	B5	60
El Palmito, Mex.	D6	63
El Pao, Ven.	B5	60
El Paraíso, Hond.	D4	62
El Pardo, Spain	o17	22
El Paso, Ar., U.S.	B3	81
El Paso, Il., U.S.	C4	90
El Paso, co., Co., U.S.	C6	83
El Paso, co., Tx., U.S.	o11	120
Elphin, Ire.	D3	11
Elphinstone, Man.	D1	70
El Portal, Ca., U.S.	D4	82
El Portal, Fl., U.S.	s13	86
El Porvenir, N.M., U.S.	B4	108
El Prado, N.M., U.S.	A4	108
El Progreso, Ec.	g6	58
El Progreso, Hond.	C4	62
El Puerto de Santa María, Spain	D2	22
El Qoll, Alg.	B6	44
Elqui, stm., Chile	F1	55
Elrama, Pa., U.S.	F2	115
El Real, Pan.	F9	62
El Reno, Ok., U.S.	B4	113
El Rio, Ca., U.S.	E4	82
El Rito, N.M., U.S.	A3	108
Elrod, Al., U.S.	B2	78
El Rosa, Mn., U.S.	E4	100
Elrose, Sask.	F1	75
Elroy, Wi., U.S.	E3	126
Elsa, Yukon	D5	66
Elsa, Tx., U.S.	F4	120
Elsah, Il., U.S.	E3	90
El Salto, Mex.	C7	63
El Salvador, ctry., N.A.	E7	62
El Samán de Apure, Ven.	B4	60
El Sauce, Nic.	E7	63
Elsberry, Mo., U.S.	C7	102
El Segundo, Ca., U.S.	*n12	82
El Seibo, Dom. Rep.	E9	64
Elsie, Mi., U.S.	E6	99
Elsie, Ne., U.S.	D4	104
Elsinore see Helsingør, Den.	I5	14
Elsinore, Ca., U.S.	F5	82
Elsinore, Ut., U.S.	E3	121
Elsmere, De., U.S.	B3	85
Elsmere, Ky., U.S.	B5	94
Elsmere, Ne., U.S.	B5	104
Elsmere, N.Y., U.S.	*n15	109
El Sobrante, Ca., U.S.	*h8	82
El Sombrero, Ven.	B4	60
Elsterwerda, E. Ger.	C6	18
Elstow, Sask.	F2	75
El Tarf, Alg.	F2	23
El Tigre, Ven.	B5	60
El Tocuyo, Ven.	B4	60
El Tránsito, Chile	E1	55
El Trapiche, Col.	C2	60
El Triunfo, Hond.	D4	62
El Triunfo, Mex.	C2	63
El Tucuche, mtn., Trin.	N23	67
El Turbio, Arg.	E2	54
Eltville, W. Ger.	C3	19
Elūru (Ellore), India	E7	36
El Vado Reservoir, res., N.M., U.S.	A3	108
El Valle, Pan.	F7	62
El Valle, N.M., U.S.	*A4	108
Elvas, Port.	C3	22
Elvaston, Il., U.S.	C2	90
Elverson, Pa., U.S.	F10	115
Elverum, Nor.	G4	14
El Viejo, Nic.	E7	63
Elvins, Mo., U.S.	D7	102
El Volcán, Chile	F4	55
El Wad, Alg.	C6	44
El Wak, Kenya	A7	48
Elwell, Lake, res., Mt., U.S.	B5	103
Elwha, stm., Wa., U.S.	A2	124
Elwood, Ks., U.S.	C9	93
Elwood, In., U.S.	D6	91
Elwood, N.J., U.S.	D3	107
Elwood, Ne., U.S.	D6	104
Elwood, Ut., U.S.	B3	121
Elwood Park, Fl., U.S.	E4	86
Ely, Eng., U.K.	D7	10
Ely, Ia., U.S.	C6	92
Ely, Mn., U.S.	C7	100
Ely, Nv., U.S.	D7	105
Ely, Vt., U.S.	D4	122
Elyria, Ks., U.S.	D6	93
Elyria, Oh., U.S.	A3	112
Elysburg, Pa., U.S.	E8	115
Elysian, Mn., U.S.	F5	100
El Yunque, mtn., P.R.	B4	65
Elzach, W. Ger.	D3	18
Emāmshahr (Shāhrūd), Iran	B5	38
Emanuel, co., Ga., U.S.	D4	87
Emba, Sov. Un.	D5	28
Emba, stm., Sov. Un.	D5	28
Embarcación, Arg.	A3	55
Embarras, stm., Il., U.S.	E6	90
Embarrass, Mn., U.S.	C6	100
Embarrass, Wi., U.S.	D5	126
Embarrass, stm., Wi., U.S.	C5	126
Embden, N.D., U.S.	C8	111
Embden Pond, l., Me., U.S.	D3	96
Embetsu, Japan	D10	33
Embira, stm., Braz.	C3	58
Emblem, Wy., U.S.	B4	127
Embreeville, Tn., U.S.	C11	119
Embro, Ont.	D4	73
Embrun, Ont.	B9	73
Embrun, Fr.	E7	16
Embu, Kenya	B7	48
Embudo, N.M., U.S.	A4	108
Emden, W. Ger.	B4	18
Emden, Il., U.S.	C4	90
Emden, Mo., U.S.	B5	102
Emelle, Al., U.S.	C1	78
Emerado, N.D., U.S.	B8	111
Emerald, Austl.	D8	50
Emerald, Ne., U.S.	*D9	104
Emerson, Man.	E3	70
Emerson, Ga., U.S.	B2	87
Emerson, Ia., U.S.	C2	92
Emerson, Ne., U.S.	B9	104
Emerson, N.J., U.S.	h8	107
Emery, S.D., U.S.	D8	118
Emery, Ut., U.S.	E4	121
Emery, co., Ut., U.S.	E5	121
Emet, Tur.	C7	25
Emida, Id., U.S.	B2	89
Emigrant, Mt., U.S.	E6	103
Emigrant Gap, Ca., U.S.	C3	82
Emiliano Zapata, Mex.	D6	63
Emilia-Romagna, prov., Italy	B3	23
Emily, Mn., U.S.	D5	100
Emily, Lake, l., Mn., U.S.	E3	100
Emine, Cape, c., Bul.	D8	24
Eminence, In., U.S.	E5	91
Eminence, Ky., U.S.	B4	94
Eminence, Mo., U.S.	D6	102
Emington, Il., U.S.	C5	90
Emirau, i., Pap. N. Gui.	h13	52
Emirdağ, Tur.	C8	40
Emison, In., U.S.	G3	91
Emlenton, Pa., U.S.	D2	115
Emlyn, Ky., U.S.	D5	94
Emma, Il., U.S.	F5	90
Emma, Mo., U.S.	C4	102
Emma Lake, l., Sask.	D3	75
Emmaus, Pa., U.S.	E11	115
Emme, stm., Switz.	B4	21
Emmeline Lake, l., Sask.	C2	75
Emmen, Neth.	A7	16
Emmen, Switz.	B5	21
Emmendingen, W. Ger.	A3	20
Emmerich, W. Ger.	C3	18
Emmet, Ar., U.S.	D2	81
Emmet, Ne., U.S.	B7	104
Emmet, N.D., U.S.	B4	111
Emmet, co., Ia., U.S.	A3	92
Emmet, co., Mi., U.S.	C6	99
Emmetsburg, Ia., U.S.	A3	92
Emmett, Id., U.S.	F2	89
Emmett, Ks., U.S.	C7	93
Emmett, Mi., U.S.	E8	99
Emmitsburg, Md., U.S.	A3	97
Emmonak, Ak., U.S.	C7	79
Emmons, Mn., U.S.	G5	100
Emmons, co., N.D., U.S.	C5	111
Emory, Tx., U.S.	C5	120
Emory Peak, mtn., Tx., U.S.	E1	120
Empangeni, S. Afr.	G6	49
Empedrado, Arg.	B5	55
Empire, Al., U.S.	B2	78
Empire, Ca., U.S.	D3	82
Empire, Ga., U.S.	D3	87
Empire, La., U.S.	E6	95
Empire, Mi., U.S.	D4	99
Empire, Nv., U.S.	C2	105
Empire, Oh., U.S.	B5	112
Empoli, Italy	C3	23
Emporia, Ks., U.S.	D7	93
Emporia, Va., U.S.	D5	123
Emporium, Pa., U.S.	D5	115
Empress, Alta.	D5	68
Emptinne, Bel.	D5	17
Ems, stm., Eur.	B3	18
Emsdale, Ont.	B5	73
Emsdetten, W. Ger.	B3	18
Ems Jade Canal, W. Ger.	A7	17
Emsworth, Pa., U.S.	h13	115
Emyvale, Ire.	C5	11
Ena, Mount, mtn., Japan	n16	33
Enard Bay, b., Scot., U.K.	B3	13
Encampment, Wy., U.S.	E6	127
Encanto, Cape, c., Phil.	o13	34
Encarnación, Para.	E4	55
Encarnación de Díaz, Mex.	m12	63
Enchant, Alta.	D4	68
Enchi, Ghana	E4	45
Encinal, N.M., U.S.	*B2	108
Encinal, Tx., U.S.	E3	120
Encinitas, Ca., U.S.	F5	82
Encino, N.M., U.S.	C4	108
Encino, Tx., U.S.	F3	120
Encontrados, Ven.	B3	60
Encounter Bay, b., Austl.	G6	50
Endako, B.C.	B5	69
Endako, stm., B.C.	B5	69
Ende, Indon.	n29	34
Endeavor, Pa., U.S.	C3	115
Endeavour, Sask.	E4	75
Endelave, i., Den.	C4	15
Enderby, B.C.	D8	69
Enderby Land, reg., Ant.	C18	7
Enderlin, N.D., U.S.	C8	111
Enders Reservoir, res., Ne., U.S.	D4	104
Endiang, Alta.	D4	68
Endicott, N.Y., U.S.	C4	109
Endicott, Wa., U.S.	C8	124
Endicott Mountains, mts., Ak., U.S.	B9	79
Endwell, N.Y., U.S.	C4	109
Ene, stm., Peru	D3	58
Enebakk, Nor.	p29	14
Energetik, Sov. Un.	C5	28
Enewetak, atoll, Marsh Is.	S18	52
Enez, Tur.	B6	40
Enfield, Austl.	*F6	50
Enfield, N.S.	E6	71

Name	Map Ref.	Page
Enfield (part of London), Eng., U.K.	k12	10
Enfield, Ct., U.S.	B5	84
Enfield, Il., U.S.	E5	90
Enfield, Me., U.S.	C4	96
Enfield, N.H., U.S.	C2	106
Enfield, N.C., U.S.	A5	110
Enfield Center, N.H., U.S.	C2	106
Engadine, Mi., U.S.	B5	99
Engaño, c., Dom. Rep.	E9	64
Engaru, Japan	D11	33
Engebi, i., Marsh Is.	S18	52
En Gedi, Isr.	C7	41
Engelberg, Switz.	C4	20
Engelhard, N.C., U.S.	B7	110
Engels, Sov. Un.	F16	27
Engen, W. Ger.	A6	21
Enghien, Bel.	D4	17
Enghien, Fr.	g10	16
England, Ar., U.S.	C4	81
England, ter., U.K.	D6	10
England Air Force Base, mil., La., U.S.	C3	95
Englee, Newf.	C3	72
Englefeld, Sask.	E3	75
Engleside, Va., U.S.	g12	123
Englevale, N.D., U.S.	C8	111
Englewood, Co., U.S.	B6	83
Englewood, Fl., U.S.	F4	86
Englewood, Ks., U.S.	E4	93
Englewood, N.J., U.S.	B5	107
Englewood, Oh., U.S.	C1	112
Englewood, Tn., U.S.	D9	119
Englewood Cliffs, N.J., U.S.	h9	107
English, In., U.S.	H5	91
English Bay, b., U.S.	h16	79
English Center, Pa., U.S.	D7	115
English Channel, strt., Eur.	F5	10
English Coast, Ant.	B5	7
English Creek, N.J., U.S.	E3	107
English Harbour West, Newf.	E4	72
English Lake, In., U.S.	B4	91
Englishtown, N.J., U.S.	C4	107
Enguera, Spain	C5	22
'En Harod, Isr.	B7	41
Enid, Ms., U.S.	A4	101
Enid, Mt., U.S.	C12	103
Enid, Ok., U.S.	A4	113
Enid Lake, res., Ms., U.S.	A4	101
Enigma, Ga., U.S.	E3	87
Enilda, Alta.	B2	68
Einrik Island, i., Marsh Is.	P18	52
eNjesuthi, mtn., S. Afr.	C4	49
Enka, N.C., U.S.	f10	110
'En Kerem, Isr.	h11	41
Enkhuizen, Neth.	B5	17
Enköping, Swe.	H7	14
Enmore, Guy.	A3	59
Enna, Italy	F5	23
Ennadai Lake, l., N.W. Ter.	D12	66
Ennedi, plat., Chad	B4	46
Ennell, Lough, l., Ire.	D4	11
Enngonia, Austl.	D5	51
Ennigerloh, W. Ger.	B3	19
Enning, S.D., U.S.	C3	118
Ennis, Ire.	D2	10
Ennis, Mt., U.S.	E5	103
Ennis, Tx., U.S.	C4	120
Enniscorthy, Ire.	D3	10
Enniskillen, N. Ire., U.K.	C3	10
Ennistimon, Ire.	D2	10
Enns, Aus.	D7	18
Enns, stm., Aus.	D7	18
Ennylabegan Island, i., Marsh Is.	S17	52
Enoch, Ut., U.S.	F3	121
Enochs, Tx., U.S.	C1	120
Enola, Ar., U.S.	B3	81
Enola, Ne., U.S.	C8	104
Enola, Pa., U.S.	F8	115
Enon, Al., U.S.	C4	78
Enon, Oh., U.S.	C2	112
Enoree, S.C., U.S.	B4	117
Enoree, stm., S.C., U.S.	B3	117
Enos, In., U.S.	B3	91
Enosburg Falls, Vt., U.S.	B3	122
Enriquillo, Dom. Rep.	F8	64
Enriquillo, Lago, l., Dom. Rep.	E8	64
Enschede, Neth.	A7	16
Ensenada, Arg.	g8	54
Ensenada, Mex.	A1	62
Ensenada, N.M., U.S.	A3	108
Enshi, China	E6	31
Enshu Bay, b., Japan	I8	33
Ensign, Alta.	D4	68
Ensign, Ks., U.S.	E3	93
Ensign, Mi., U.S.	C4	99
Ensisheim, Fr.	B3	20
Ensley, Fl., U.S.	u14	86
Entebbe, Ug.	A5	48
Enterprise, Ont.	C8	73
Enterprise, Guy.	A3	59
Enterprise, Al., U.S.	D4	78
Enterprise, Fl., U.S.	D5	86
Enterprise, Ia., U.S.	e8	92
Enterprise, Ks., U.S.	D6	93
Enterprise, La., U.S.	C4	95
Enterprise, Ms., U.S.	C5	101
Enterprise, Ok., U.S.	B6	113
Enterprise, Or., U.S.	B9	114
Enterprise, Ut., U.S.	F2	121
Enterprise, W.V., U.S.	B4	125
Entiat, Wa., U.S.	B5	124
Entiat, stm., Wa., U.S.	B5	124
Entiat, Lake, l., Wa., U.S.	B5	124
Entiat Mountains, mts., Wa., U.S.	B5	124
Entrance, Alta.	C2	68
Entraygues, Fr.	E5	16
Entrée, Île d', i., Que.	B8	71
Entre Minho e Douro, hist. reg., Port.	B1	22
Entre Ríos, prov., Arg.	A5	54
Entwistle, Alta.	C3	68
Enugu, Nig.	G7	45
Enumclaw, Wa., U.S.	B4	124
Envermeu, Fr.	E9	12
Envigado, Col.	*B2	60
Enville, Tn., U.S.	B3	119
Envira, Braz.	C3	58
Enyu Channel, strt., Marsh Is.	P18	52
Enyu Island, i., Marsh Is.	P18	52
Enz, stm., W. Ger.	D4	18
Enza, stm., Italy	E6	23
Enzan, Japan	n17	33
Eola, La., U.S.	D3	95
Eola Hills, hills, Or., U.S.	h11	114
Eolia, Mo., U.S.	B6	102
Eolie Islands, is., Italy	E5	23
Eoline, Al., U.S.	C2	78
Eoscan, Ca., U.S.	D3	82
Epe, Neth.	B5	17
Epéna, Congo	A2	48
Épernay, Fr.	C5	16
Epes, Al., U.S.	C1	78

Ephesus, Ga., U.S.	C1	87
Ephesus, hist., Tur.	D6	25
Ephraim, Ut., U.S.	D4	121
Ephraim, Wi., U.S.	C6	126
Ephrata, Pa., U.S.	F9	115
Ephrata, Wa., U.S.	B6	124
Épila, Spain	C5	22
Épinac, Fr.	C7	16
Épinay [-sur-Seine], Fr.	g10	16
Epira, Guy.	E9	64
Epiphany, S.D., U.S.	D8	118
Epirus, hist. reg., Grc.	C3	25
Epoufette, Mi., U.S.	B5	99
Epping, Eng., U.K.	k13	10
Epping, N.H., U.S.	D4	106
Epping, N.D., U.S.	A2	111
Eppingen, W. Ger.	D3	19
Epps, La., U.S.	B4	95
Epsom, In., U.S.	G3	91
Epsom, N.H., U.S.	D4	106
Epsom [and Ewell], Eng., U.K.	m12	10
Epukiro, Nmb.	C2	49
Epworth, Ia., U.S.	B7	92
Eqlid, Iran	F6	39
Equality, Al., U.S.	C3	78
Equality, Il., U.S.	F5	90
Equatorial Guinea, ctry., Afr.	E1	46
Équeurdreville, Fr.	C4	12
Equinunk, Pa., U.S.	C11	115
Erath, La., U.S.	E3	95
Erath, co., Tx., U.S.	C3	120
Erba, Italy	E7	21
Erba, Jabal, mtn., Sud.	A4	47
Erbach, W. Ger.	D3	19
Erbacon, W.V., U.S.	C4	125
Erbendorf, W. Ger.	D7	19
Erciş, Tur.	C14	40
Erciyes Mountain, mtn., Tur.	C6	40
Ercsi, Hung.	B4	24
Érd, Hung.	B4	24
Erdek, Tur.	B6	25
Erdene, Mong.	C7	31
Erdene-Dzuu, Mong.	B5	31
Erdenetsagaan, Mong.	B6	32
Erdenheim, Pa., U.S.	o21	115
Erding, W. Ger.	D5	19
Erebus, Mount, mtn., Ant.	B29	7
Erechim, Braz.	D2	56
Ereğli, Tur.	D10	40
Ereğli, Tur.	B8	40
Erenhot, China	C4	32
Eresós, Grc.	C5	25
Erétria (Néa Psará), Grc.	g11	25
Erfurt, E. Ger.	C5	18
Ergene, stm., Tur.	B6	40
Erhard, Mn., U.S.	D2	100
Erial, N.J., U.S.	D2	107
Eriboll, Loch, b., Scot., U.K.	B4	13
Erice, Italy	E4	23
Ericht, Loch, l., Scot., U.K.	D4	13
Erick, Ok., U.S.	B2	113
Erickson, B.C.	E9	69
Erickson, Man.	D2	70
Ericsburg, Mn., U.S.	B5	100
Ericson, Ne., U.S.	C7	104
Erie, Co., U.S.	A5	83
Erie, Il., U.S.	B3	90
Erie, Ks., U.S.	E8	93
Erie, Mi., U.S.	G7	99
Erie, N.D., U.S.	B8	111
Erie, Pa., U.S.	B1	115
Erie, co., N.Y., U.S.	C2	109
Erie, co., Oh., U.S.	A3	112
Erie, co., Pa., U.S.	C1	115
Erie, Lake, l., N.A.	B11	76
Erieau, Ont.	E3	73
Erie Canal, N.Y., U.S.	B5	109
Eriksdale, Man.	D2	70
Érimo, Cape, c., Japan	C13	31
Erin, Ont.	D4	73
Erin, Tn., U.S.	A4	119
Erin Point, c., Trin.	O22	65
Erin Springs, Ok., U.S.	C4	113
Eriskay, i., Scot., U.K.	C1	13
Erisort, Loch, b., Scot., U.K.	B2	13
Erithraí, Grc.	C4	25
Eritrea, prov., Eth.	B4	47
Erkelenz, W. Ger.	C6	17
Erken, l., Swe.	t36	14
Erlangen, W. Ger.	D5	18
Erlanger, Ky., U.S.	A5	94
Erling, Lake, res., Ar., U.S.	D2	81
Erma, N.J., U.S.	F3	107
Ermelo, Neth.	B5	17
Ermelo, S. Afr.	C5	49
Ermenek, Tur.	D9	40
Ermont, Fr.	g10	16
Ermoúpolis (Syros), Grc.	D5	40
Erne, Upper Lough, l., Eur.	C3	10
Ernée, Fr.	C3	16
Ernest, Pa., U.S.	E3	115
Ernestina, arg.	g7	54
Ernestville, Tn., U.S.	C11	119
Ernfold, Sask.	G2	75
Erode, India	*F6	36
Eromanga, Austl.	C4	51
Eros, La., U.S.	B3	95
Errigal Mountain, mtn., Ire.	C2	10
Erris Head, c., Ire.	C1	10
Errol, N.H., U.S.	A4	106
Errol Heights, Or., U.S.	*h12	114
Erskine, Alta.	C4	68
Erskine, Mn., U.S.	C3	100
Erstein, Fr.	C7	16
Erstfeld, Switz.	C4	20
Erving, Ma., U.S.	A3	98
Erwin, N.C., U.S.	B4	110
Erwin, S.D., U.S.	C8	118
Erwin, Tn., U.S.	C11	119
Erwinville, La., U.S.	D4	95
Erwood, Sask.	E4	75
Erzincan, Tur.	C12	40
Erzurum, Tur.	C13	40
Esan, Cape, c., Japan	F10	33
Esashi, Japan	C13	31
Esashi, Japan	D11	33
Esbjerg, Den.	J3	14
Esbon, Ks., U.S.	C5	93
Escabosa, N.M., U.S.	m8	108
Escada, Braz.	k6	57
Escalante, Ut., U.S.	F4	121
Escalante, stm., Ut., U.S.	F4	121
Escalante Creek, stm., Co., U.S.	C2	83
Escalante Desert, des., Ut., U.S.	F2	121
Escalón, Mex.	B4	63
Escalon, Ca., U.S.	D3	82
Escatawpa, Ms., U.S.	B5	82
Escatawpa, Mi., U.S.	C3	99

Escanaba, stm., Mi., U.S.	B3	99
Escarpada Point, c., Phil.	B6	34
Escatawpa, Ms., U.S.	E5	101
Escatawpa, stm., U.S.	D5	101
Eschede, W. Ger.	D6	19
Eschenbach, W. Ger.	F4	15
Escholzmatt, Switz.	C4	21
Esch-sur-Alzette, Lux.	E5	17
Eschwege, W. Ger.	C5	18
Eschweiler, W. Ger.	C3	18
Escobal, Pan.	k11	62
Escocesa, Bahía, b., Dom. Rep.	E9	64
Escoheag, R.I., U.S.	E1	116
Escondida, N.M., U.S.	C3	108
Escondido, Ca., U.S.	F5	82
Escondido, stm., Nic.	D6	62
Escoumins, Rivière des, stm., Que.	A8	74
Escuinapa [de Hidalgo], Mex.	C3	63
Escuintla, Guat.	C2	62
Escuminac, Que.	A3	71
Escuminac, Point, c., N.B.	B5	71
Eséka, Cam.	E2	46
Esens, W. Ger.	A7	17
Eşfahān (Isfahan), Iran	B5	38
Esgueva, stm., Spain	B3	56
Eshimba, Zaire	C3	48
Eshkāshem, Afg.	C15	39
Eshowe, S. Afr.	C5	49
Esigodini, Zimb.	B4	49
Esk, stm., U.K.	E6	13
Esk, stm., Eng., U.K.	F5	13
Eskbank, Sask.	G2	75
Eskdale, W.V., U.S.	C3	125
Eske, Lough, l., Ire.	C3	11
Eskilstuna, Swe.	H7	14
Eskimo Lakes, l., N.W. Ter.	C6	66
Eskimo Point, N.W. Ter.	D14	66
Eskişehir, Tur.	C8	40
Esko, Mn., U.S.	D6	100
Eskridge, Ks., U.S.	D7	93
Esla, stm., Spain	B3	22
Eslāmābād, Iran	*D3	39
Eslarn, W. Ger.	D7	19
Eslava, stm., Mex.	h9	63
Eslöv, Swe.	C7	15
Eşme, Tur.	C25	25
Esmeralda, Grc.	F4	105
Esmeraldas, Ec.	A2	58
Esmeraldas, prov., Ec.	A2	58
Esmond, Il., U.S.	A5	90
Esmond, N.D., U.S.	A6	111
Esmond, R.I., U.S.	B4	116
Esmont, Va., U.S.	C4	123
Esom Hill, Ga., U.S.	C1	87
Espada, Punta, c., Col.	A3	60
Espanola, Ont.	A3	73
Espanola, Fl., U.S.	C5	86
Espanola, N.M., U.S.	B3	108
Española, Ont.	g13	124
Española, Isla (Hood), i., Ec.	g6	58
Esparto, Ca., U.S.	C2	82
Esperance, Austl.	F3	50
Esperance, Wa., U.S.	*B3	124
Esperanza, Arg.	A4	54
Esperanza, Peru	C3	58
Esperanza, Tx., U.S.	o12	120
Esperanza, stm., Pan.	k12	62
Esperanza, sci., Ant.	C7	7
Espichel, Cape, c., Port.	C1	22
Espinal, Col.	C3	60
Espinhaço, Serra do, mts., Braz.	E6	53
Espírito Santo, state, Braz.	B4	56
Espíritu Santo, i., Vanuatu	H10	6
Espita, Mex.	C7	63
Espoo, Fin.	*G11	14
Esponsede, Port.	B1	22
Espungabera, Moz.	B5	49
Espy, Pa., U.S.	D9	115
Espyville Station, Pa., U.S.	C1	115
Esquatzel Coulee, val., Wa., U.S.	C6	124
Esquel, Arg.	C2	54
Esquimalt, B.C.	E6	69
Esquina, Arg.	F4	55
Essaouira (Mogador), Mor.	C3	44
Essen, Bel.	C4	17
Essen, W. Ger.	C6	17
Essendon, Austl.	*G7	50
Essendon, Mount, mtn., Austl.	D3	50
Essequibo, stm., Guy.	B3	59
Essex, Ont.	E2	73
Essex, Ca., U.S.	E6	82
Essex, Ct., U.S.	D6	84
Essex, Il., U.S.	B5	90
Essex, Ia., U.S.	D2	92
Essex, Md., U.S.	B4	97
Essex, Ma., U.S.	A6	98
Essex, Mt., U.S.	B3	103
Essex, N.Y., U.S.	f11	109
Essex, Vt., U.S.	B2	122
Essex, co., Ont.	E2	73
Essex, co., Eng., U.K.	C8	12
Essex, co., Ma., U.S.	A5	98
Essex, co., N.J., U.S.	B4	107
Essex, co., N.Y., U.S.	B7	109
Essex, co., Vt., U.S.	C6	122
Essex, Punta, c., Ec.	g5	58
Essex Fells, N.J., U.S.	*B4	107
Essex Junction, Vt., U.S.	C2	122
Essexville, Mi., U.S.	E7	99
Es' Sider, Libya	C3	43
Esslingen, W. Ger.	D4	18
Essonne, dept., Fr.	F2	17
Es Suki, Sud.	C3	47
Est, Île de l', i., Que.	B8	71
Est, Pointe de l', c., Que.	B8	71
Estacada, Or., U.S.	B4	114
Estacado, Llano, pl., U.S.	C1	120
Estados, Isla de los, i., Arg.	h13	54
Eştahbān, Iran	G7	39
Estaire, Ont.	A4	73
Estância, Braz.	D3	57
Estancia, N.M., U.S.	C3	108
Estarreja, Port.	B1	22
Este, Italy	B3	23
Este, Punta, c., P.R.	B5	65
Esteli, Nic.	E7	63
Estella, Spain	A4	22
Estelle, La., U.S.	*E5	95
Estelline, S.D., U.S.	C9	118
Estelline, Tx., U.S.	B2	120
Estell Manor, N.J., U.S.	E3	107
Estepa, Spain	D3	22
Estepona, Spain	D3	22
Ester, Ak., U.S.	D7	127
Esterbrook, Wy., U.S.	D7	127
Esterhazy, Sask.	G5	75
Esternay, Fr.	F3	17

Esternberg, Aus.	E8	19
Estero, Fl., U.S.	F5	86
Estero Bay, b., Ca., U.S.	E3	82
Estero Bay, b., Fl., U.S.	F5	86
Estero Island, i., Fl., U.S.	F5	86
Estes Park, Co., U.S.	A5	83
Estevan, Sask.	H4	75
Estevan Group, is., B.C.	C3	69
Estevan Point, B.C.	E4	69
Esther, Alta.	D5	68
Estherville, Ia., U.S.	A3	92
Estherwood, La., U.S.	D3	95
Estill, Ms., U.S.	B3	101
Estill, S.C., U.S.	F5	117
Estill, co., Ky., U.S.	C6	94
Estillfork, Al., U.S.	A3	78
Estill Springs, Tn., U.S.	B5	119
Estlin, Sask.	G3	75
Esto, Fl., U.S.	u16	86
Estonia, state, Sov. Un.	D5	29
Estrées-Saint-Denis, Fr.	C5	16
Estrela, Braz.	C2	56
Estrela, mtn., Port.	*B2	22
Estrela, Serra da, mts., Port.	B2	22
Estrela do Norte, Braz.	A3	56
Estrela do Sul, Braz.	B3	56
Estremadura, hist. reg., Port.	C1	22
Estremadura, hist. reg., Spain	C2	22
Estremoz, Port.	C2	22
Estuary, Sask.	G1	75
Esztergom, Hung.	B4	24
Étain, Fr.	C6	16
Étables, Fr.	C5	16
Étalans, Fr.	B1	21
Étampes, Fr.	C5	16
Étang-du-Nord, Que.	B8	71
Étaples, Fr.	B4	16
Etāwah, India	C6	36
Étawney Lake, l., Austl.	A7	70
Etchojoa, Mex.	D4	62
Eten, S.D., U.S.	D8	118
Eternity Range, mts., Ant.	C6	7
Ethan, S.D., U.S.	D7	118
Ethel, Ont.	D3	73
Ethel, Ar., U.S.	C4	81
Ethel, Ms., U.S.	B4	101
Ethel, Mo., U.S.	B5	102
Ethel, W.V., U.S.	n12	125
Ethelbert, Man.	D1	70
Ethelsville, Al., U.S.	B1	78
Ethelton, Sask.	E3	75
Ether, N.C., U.S.	B3	110
Ethete, Wy., U.S.	C4	127
Ethiopia, ctry., Afr.	D4	47
Ethiopian Plateau, plat., Eth.	D4	47
Ethridge, Mt., U.S.	B5	103
Ethridge, Tn., U.S.	B4	119
Etive, Loch, l., Scot., U.K.	D3	13
Etlan, Va., U.S.	B4	123
Etna, Ca., U.S.	B2	82
Etna, Me., U.S.	D3	96
Etna, N.H., U.S.	C2	106
Etna, N.Y., U.S.	C4	109
Etna, Oh., U.S.	C3	112
Etna, Pa., U.S.	k14	115
Etna, Wy., U.S.	C1	127
Etna, Mount, mtn., Italy	F5	23
Etna Green, In., U.S.	B5	91
Etobicoke, Ont.	D5	73
Etolin Island, i., Ak., U.S.	m23	79
Etolin Strait, strt., Ak., U.S.	C6	79
Eton, Austl.	B2	87
Etoshapan, pl., Nmb.	A2	49
Etowah, Ar., U.S.	B5	81
Etowah, Tn., U.S.	D9	119
Etowah, co., Al., U.S.	A3	78
Etowah, stm., Ga., U.S.	B2	87
Étréchy, Fr.	C3	107
Étréchy, Fr.	C4	16
Étréroubles, Italy	C2	21
Étretat, Fr.	C4	16
Etta, Ms., U.S.	A4	101
Ettelbruck, Lux.	E6	17
Etten, i., Micron.	Q18	52
Etter, Tx., U.S.	B2	120
Etterbeek, Bel.	*D4	17
Etters, Pa., U.S.	F8	115
E.V. Spence Reservoir, res., Tx., U.S.	H2	75
Et Tini, hill, N. Mar. Is.	D7	52
Ettlingen, W. Ger.	E3	19
Ettrick, Va., U.S.	C5	123
Ettrick, Wi., U.S.	D2	126
Etzatlán, Mex.	m11	63
Etzikom Coulee, stm., Alta.	E5	68
Euboea see Évvoia, i., Grc.	C4	40
Eucumbene, Lake, l., Austl.	H7	51
Eudora, Ar., U.S.	D4	81
Eudora, Ks., U.S.	D8	93
Eudunda, Austl.	G2	51
Eufaula, Al., U.S.	D4	78
Eufaula, Ok., U.S.	B6	113
Eufaula Lake, res., Ok., U.S.	B6	113
Eugene, Mo., U.S.	C5	102
Eugene, Or., U.S.	C3	114
Eugenia, Punta, c., Mex.	B1	63
Eulalia, Guat.	B4	78
Euless, Tx., U.S.	*n9	120
Eulonia, Ga., U.S.	E5	87
Eunice, La., U.S.	D3	95
Eunice, N.M., U.S.	E6	108
Euphrates, stm., Asia	B3	38
Eupora, Ms., U.S.	B4	101
Eure, N.C., U.S.	A6	110
Eure, dept., Fr.	C4	16
Eure, stm., Fr.	C4	16
Eureka, Ca., U.S.	B1	82
Eureka, Il., U.S.	C4	90
Eureka, Ks., U.S.	E7	93
Eureka, Mo., U.S.	f12	102
Eureka, Mt., U.S.	B1	103
Eureka, Nv., U.S.	D6	105
Eureka, S.C., U.S.	D5	117
Eureka, S.D., U.S.	B6	118
Eureka, Ut., U.S.	D3	121
Eureka, co., Nv., U.S.	C5	105
Eureka Sound, strt., N.W. Ter.	m34	66
Eureka Springs, Ar., U.S.	A2	81
Europa, Île, i., Reu.	B7	49
Europa Point, c., Gib.	D3	22
Europe, cont.	E13	8
Euskirchen, W. Ger.	C3	18
Eustis, Fl., U.S.	D5	86
Eustis, Me., U.S.	C2	96
Eustis, Ne., U.S.	D5	104

Eutaw, Al., U.S.	C2	78
Eutawville, S.C., U.S.	E7	117
Eutin, W. Ger.	A5	18
Eutsuk Lake, l., B.C.	C4	69
Eva, Al., U.S.	A3	78
Eva, Tn., U.S.	A3	119
Evale, Ang.	E2	48
Evan, Mn., U.S.	F4	100
Evançon, stm., Italy	E4	21
Evangeline, La., U.S.	D3	95
Evangeline, co., La., U.S.	D3	95
Evans, Co., U.S.	A6	83
Evans, Ga., U.S.	C4	87
Evans, La., U.S.	C2	95
Evans, W.V., U.S.	C3	125
Evans, co., Ga., U.S.	D5	87
Evans, Lac, l., Que.	o20	73
Evans, Mount, mtn., Co., U.S.	B5	83
Evansburg, Alta.	C3	68
Evans City, Pa., U.S.	E1	115
Evansdale, Ia., U.S.	B5	92
Evans Mills, N.Y., U.S.	A5	109
Evansport, Oh., U.S.	A1	112
Evans Strait, strt., N.W. Ter.	D16	66
Evanston, Il., U.S.	A6	90
Evanston, Ky., U.S.	C6	94
Evanston, Wy., U.S.	E2	127
Evansville, Ar., U.S.	B1	81
Evansville, Il., U.S.	E4	90
Evansville, In., U.S.	D3	100
Evansville, Mn., U.S.	A3	101
Evansville, Vt., U.S.	B4	122
Evansville, Wi., U.S.	F4	126
Evansville, Wy., U.S.	D6	127
Evant, Tx., U.S.	D3	120
Evanton, Scot., U.K.	C4	13
Evarts, Ky., U.S.	D6	94
Eveleth, Mn., U.S.	C6	100
Evelyn, La., U.S.	C2	95
Evening Shade, Ar., U.S.	A4	81
Even Yehuda, Isr.	f10	41
Everard, Lake, l., Austl.	F5	50
Everest, Ks., U.S.	C8	93
Everest, Mount, mtn., Asia	C8	36
Everett, Ont.	C5	73
Everett, Pa., U.S.	F5	115
Everett, Ma., U.S.	g11	98
Everett, Wa., U.S.	B3	124
Everett, Mount, mtn., Ma., U.S.	B1	98
Everett Lake, res., N.H., U.S.	D3	106
Everettville, W.V., U.S.	h10	125
Everglades National Park, Fl., U.S.	G5	86
Evergreen, Al., U.S.	D3	78
Evergreen, Co., U.S.	B5	83
Evergreen, La., U.S.	D3	95
Evergreen, Ms., U.S.	A5	101
Evergreen, N.C., U.S.	C4	110
Evergreen, Va., U.S.	C4	123
Evergreen Park, Il., U.S.	k9	90
Everly, Ia., U.S.	A2	92
Everman, Tx., U.S.	*n9	120
Everson, Pa., U.S.	F2	115
Everson, Wa., U.S.	A3	124
Everton, Ar., U.S.	A3	81
Everton, Mo., U.S.	D4	102
Evesham, Sask.	E1	75
Evesham, Eng., U.K.	B6	12
Evian-les-Bains, Fr.	C2	20
Evinayong, Eq. Gui.	E2	46
Evington, Va., U.S.	C3	107
Evolène, Switz.	D3	21
Évora, Port.	C2	22
Évreux, Fr.	C4	16
Évros (Maritsa) (Meriç), stm., Eur.	B6	25
Evrótas, stm., Grc.	D4	25
Évvoia (Euboea), i., Grc.	C4	40
Ewa, Hi., U.S.	B3	88
Ewa Beach, Hi., U.S.	B3	88
Ewa Beach, Hi., U.S.	g9	88
Ewan, Wa., U.S.	B8	124
Ewarton, Jam.	E14	65
Ewe, Loch, b., Scot., U.K.	C3	13
Ewell, Md., U.S.	E5	97
Ewen, Mi., U.S.	m12	99
Ewing, Il., U.S.	E5	90
Ewing, Ky., U.S.	B6	94
Ewing, Mo., U.S.	A6	102
Ewing, Ne., U.S.	B7	104
Ewing, Va., U.S.	f8	123
Ewing Township, N.J., U.S.	C3	107
Ewo, Congo	B1	48
Excel, Alta.	D5	68
Excello, Mo., U.S.	B5	102
Excelsior Mountain, mtn., Ca., U.S.	C4	82
Excelsior Mountains, mts., Nv., U.S.	E3	105
Excelsior Springs, Mo., U.S.	B3	102
Exchange, Pa., U.S.	D8	115
Exchange, W.V., U.S.	C4	125
Exe, stm., Eng., U.K.	D4	12
Executive Committee Range, mts., Ant.	B36	7
Exeter, Ont.	D3	73
Exeter, Eng., U.K.	E5	10
Exeter, Ca., U.S.	D4	82
Exeter, Me., U.S.	D3	96
Exeter, Mo., U.S.	E4	102
Exeter, Ne., U.S.	D8	104
Exeter, N.H., U.S.	E5	106
Exeter, Pa., U.S.	D10	115
Exeter, R.I., U.S.	E3	116
Exeter, stm., N.H., U.S.	E5	106
Exira, Ia., U.S.	C3	92
Exline, Ia., U.S.	D5	92
Exmoor, for., Eng., U.K.	E5	10
Exmore, Va., U.S.	C7	123
Exmouth, Austl.	D1	50
Exmouth, Eng., U.K.	E5	10
Exmouth Gulf, b., Austl.	D1	50
Experiment, Ga., U.S.	C2	87
Experiment, is., Newf.	D3	72
Exploits, Bay of, b., Newf.	D4	72
Exploits, stm., Newf.	D3	72
Exshaw, Alta.	D3	68
Extension, B.C.	f12	69
Extrema, Braz.	m8	56
Exuma Sound, strt., Bah.	B5	64

Eyasi, Lake, l., Tan.	B6	48
Eyebrow, Sask.	G2	75
Eyehill Creek, stm., Can.	C5	68
Eyemouth, Scot., U.K.	C5	10
Eye Peninsula, pen., Scot., U.K.	B2	13
Eyl, Som.	D6	47
Eylar Mountain, mtn., Ca., U.S.	D3	82
Eynort, Loch, b., Scot., U.K.	C1	13
Eyota, Mn., U.S.	G6	100
Eyre, Sask.	F1	75
Eyrecourt, Ire.	D3	11
Eyre North, Lake, l., Austl.	E6	50
Eyre Peninsula, pen., Austl.	F6	50
Ezeiza, Arg.	g7	54
Ezine, Tur.	C6	40

F

Fabens, Tx., U.S.	o11	120
Faber, Va., U.S.	C4	123
Faber Lake, l., N.W. Ter.	D9	66
Fabius, N.Y., U.S.	C5	109
Fabius, stm., Mo., U.S.	A6	102
Fåborg, Den.	C4	15
Fabriano, Italy	E7	23
Fabyan, Ct., U.S.	A8	84
Facatativá, Col.	C3	60
Fachi, Niger	C7	45
Fackler, Al., U.S.	A4	78
Facpi Point, c., Guam	M9	52
Factoryville, Pa., U.S.	C10	115
Fada, Chad	B4	46
Fada Ngourma, Burkina	D5	45
Faddeya Gulf, b., Sov. Un.	B3	128
Faddey Island, i., Sov. Un.	B17	29
Fadian Point, c., Guam	L10	52
Faenza, Italy	B3	23
Faeroe Islands, ctry., Eur.	C7	8
Fafa, Mali	C5	45
Fafe, Port.	B1	22
Fafen, stm., Eth.	D5	47
Faga'alu, Am. Sam.	F13	52
Fagaitua Bay, b., Am. Sam.	G13	52
Fagaloa Bay, b., W. Sam.	F12	52
Fagamalo, W. Sam.	F11	52
Fágáras, Rom.	C7	24
Fagatogo, Am. Sam.	F13	52
Fågelbro, Swe.	t36	14
Fagernes, Nor.	G3	14
Fagersta, Swe.	G6	14
Faggo, Nig.	D6	45
Fagnano, Lago, l., S.A.	h12	54
Faguibine, Lac, l., Mali	C4	45
Fagus, Mo., U.S.	E7	102
Fahan, Ire.	B4	11
Faial, i., Port.	g8	44
Faichuk, is., Micron.	Q18	52
Fä'id, Eg.	D4	41
Faido, Switz.	D6	21
Fairacres, N.M., U.S.	E3	108
Fairbairn Reservoir, res., Austl.	A7	51
Fairbank, Az., U.S.	F5	80
Fairbank, Ia., U.S.	B5	92
Fairbanks, Ak., U.S.	C10	79
Fairbanks, Fl., U.S.	C4	86
Fairbanks, In., U.S.	F2	91
Fairbanks, Me., U.S.	D2	96
Fair Bluff, N.C., U.S.	C3	110
Fairborn, Oh., U.S.	C1	112
Fairburn, Ga., U.S.	C2	87
Fairburn, S.D., U.S.	D2	118
Fairbury, Il., U.S.	C5	90
Fairbury, Ne., U.S.	D8	104
Fairchance, Pa., U.S.	G2	115
Fairchild, Wi., U.S.	D3	126
Fairchild Air Force Base, mil., Wa., U.S.	g13	124
Fairdale, N.D., U.S.	A7	111
Fairfax, Ca., U.S.	C4	78
Fairfax, Ca., U.S.	C2	82
Fairfax, De., U.S.	A3	85
Fairfax, Mn., U.S.	F4	100
Fairfax, Mo., U.S.	A2	102
Fairfax, S.C., U.S.	F5	117
Fairfax, S.D., U.S.	D7	118
Fairfax, Vt., U.S.	B2	122
Fairfax, Va., U.S.	B5	123
Fairfax, co., Va., U.S.	B5	123
Fairfax Station, Va., U.S.	g12	123
Fairfield, Austl.	*F9	51
Fairfield, Ct., U.S.	E2	84
Fairfield, Ia., U.S.	C6	92
Fairfield, Il., U.S.	E5	90
Fairfield, Ky., U.S.	C4	94
Fairfield, Me., U.S.	D3	96
Fairfield, Mt., U.S.	C5	103
Fairfield, N.J., U.S.	*B4	107
Fairfield, N.C., U.S.	B6	110
Fairfield, Oh., U.S.	n12	112
Fairfield, Tx., U.S.	D4	120
Fairfield, Vt., U.S.	B3	122
Fairfield, co., Ct., U.S.	D2	84
Fairfield, co., Oh., U.S.	C3	112
Fairfield, co., S.C., U.S.	C5	117
Fairfield Bay, Ar., U.S.	B3	81
Fairfield Pond, l., Vt., U.S.	B3	122
Fairgrove, Mi., U.S.	E7	99
Fair Grove, Mo., U.S.	D4	102
Fair Grove, N.C., U.S.	B2	110
Fairhaven, Ma., U.S.	C6	98
Fair Haven, Mi., U.S.	F8	99
Fair Haven, N.J., U.S.	C4	107
Fair Haven, N.Y., U.S.	B4	109
Fair Haven, Vt., U.S.	D2	122
Fair Head, c., N. Ire., U.K.	B5	11
Fairholme, Sask.	D1	75
Fairhope, Al., U.S.	E2	78
Fairland, In., U.S.	E6	91
Fairland, Ok., U.S.	A7	113
Fair Lawn, N.J., U.S.	h8	107
Fairlawn, Oh., U.S.	*A4	112
Fairlawn, Va., U.S.	C2	123
Fairlee, Vt., U.S.	D4	125
Fairlee, Md., U.S.	B5	97
Fairlee, Vt., U.S.	D4	122
Fairlight, Sask.	H5	75
Fairmont, Il., U.S.	C6	90
Fairmont, Mn., U.S.	G4	100
Fairmont, N.C., U.S.	D8	104

Name	Map Ref.	Page

Fairmont, N.C., U.S. C3 110
Fairmont, Ok., U.S. A4 113
Fairmont, S.C., U.S. B3 117
Fairmont, W.V., U.S. B4 125
Fairmount, Ga., U.S. B2 87
Fairmount, Il., U.S. C6 90
Fairmount, In., U.S. D6 91
Fairmount, Ks., U.S. k16 93
Fairmount, Md., U.S. D6 97
Fairmount, N.Y., U.S. *B4 109
Fairmount, N.D., U.S. C9 111
Fairmount Heights, Md., U.S. . . f9 97
Fair Oaks, Ar., U.S. B4 81
Fair Oaks, Ca., U.S. *C3 82
Fair Oaks, Ga., U.S. h7 87
Fair Oaks, In., U.S. B3 91
Fairoaks, Pa., U.S. h13 115
Fair Plain, Mi., U.S. F4 99
Fairplain, W.V., U.S. F3 125
Fairplay, Co., U.S. B5 83
Fair Play, Md., U.S. A2 97
Fair Play, Mo., U.S. D4 102
Fair Play, S.C., U.S. B2 117
Fairpoint, Oh., U.S. B5 112
Fairpoint, S.D., U.S. C3 118
Fairport, Ia., U.S. C7 92
Fairport, Mi., U.S. C4 99
Fairport, Mo., U.S. B3 102
Fairport, N.Y., U.S. B3 109
Fair Port, U.S. C6 123
Fairport Harbor, Oh., U.S. . . A4 112
Fairton, N.J., U.S. E2 107
Fairvale, N.B. D4 71
Fairview, Alta. A1 68
Fairview, Ar., U.S. *D4 81
Fairview, Il., U.S. C3 90
Fairview, In., U.S. D7 91
Fairview, Ks., U.S. C8 93
Fairview, Ky., U.S. D2 94
Fairview, Mi., U.S. D6 99
Fairview, Mo., U.S. E3 102
Fairview, Mt., U.S. C12 103
Fairview, N.J., U.S. D3 107
Fairview, N.J., U.S. h8 107
Fairview, N.Y., U.S. *D7 109
Fairview, Ok., U.S. A3 113
Fairview, Or., U.S. *B4 114
Fairview, Pa., U.S. B1 115
Fairview, S.D., U.S. D9 118
Fairview, Tn., U.S. B4 119
Fairview, Ut., U.S. D4 121
Fairview, W.V., U.S. B4 125
Fairview, Wy., U.S. D2 127
Fairview Heights, Il., U.S. . . E3 90
Fairview Park, In., U.S. E3 91
Fairview Park, Oh., U.S. g9 112
Fairview Peak, mtn., Nv., U.S. . D3 105
Fairview Peak, mtn., Or., U.S. . D3 114
Fairview Shores, Fl., U.S. . . . *D5 86
Fair Water, Wi., U.S. E5 126
Fairway, Ks., U.S. k16 93
Fairweather, Mount, mtn., N.A. D12 79
Fairwood, Wa., U.S. *B8 124
Fairwood, W.V., U.S. *B3 125
Fairy Glen, Sask. D3 75
Faisalabad (Lyallpur), Pak. . . B5 36
Faison, N.C., U.S. B2 110
Faith, N.C., U.S. B2 110
Faith, S.D., U.S. B3 118
Faithorn, Mi., U.S. C3 99
Faizābād (Fyzabad), India . . . C7 36
Fajardo, P.R. G12 64
Fakenham, Eng., U.K. B8 12
Fakfak, Indon. F9 32
Fakse, Den. C6 15
Fakse Bugt, b., Den. C6 15
Fakse Ladeplads, Den. C6 15
Faku, China C10 32
Fal, stm., Eng., U.K. D3 12
Falaba, S.L. E2 45
Falaise, Fr. C6 16
Falalu, i., Micron. Q18 52
Fălciu, Rom. B9 24
Falcon, Ar., U.S. D2 81
Falcon, Co., U.S. C6 83
Falcon, Ms., U.S. A3 101
Falcon, N.C., U.S. B4 110
Falcón, state, Ven. A4 60
Falconer, N.Y., U.S. C1 109
Falcon Heights, Mn., U.S. . . . n12 100
Falcon Heights, Or., U.S. . . . E5 114
Falcon Lake, res., N.A. F3 120
Faléa, Mali D2 45
Falefa Harbour, b., W. Sam. . . F12 52
Falelima, W. Sam. F11 52
Falémé, stm., Afr. D2 45
Faleolo International Airport, W. Sam. F12 52
Faleshty, Sov. Un. B8 24
Falfurrias, Tx., U.S. F3 120
Falher, Alta. B2 68
Falkenberg, E. Ger. B8 19
Falkenberg, Swe. B6 15
Falkenstein, E. Ger. C7 19
Falkirk, Scot., U.K. C5 10
Falkirk, N.D., U.S. B4 111
Falkland, B.C. D8 69
Falkland Islands (Islas Malvinas), dep., S.A. I5 53
Falkner, Ms., U.S. A5 101
Falköping, Swe. H5 14
Falkville, Al., U.S. A3 78
Fall, W. Ger. B7 20
Fall, stm., Ks., U.S. E7 93
Fall Branch, Tn., U.S. C11 119
Fallbrook, Ca., U.S. F5 82
Fall City, Wa., U.S. B4 124
Fall Creek, Wi., U.S. D2 126
Fall Creek, stm., In., U.S. . . . k10 91
Fallentimber, Pa., U.S. E4 115
Falling Creek, stm., Va., U.S. . n17 123
Falling Rock Creek, stm., W.V., U.S. m13 125
Falling Water, Tn., U.S. h11 119
Falling Waters, W.V., U.S. . . . B6 125
Fallis, Ok., U.S. B4 113
Fall Mountain Lake, Ct., U.S. . C4 84
Fållnäs, Swe. u35 14
Fallon, Mt., U.S. D11 103
Fallon, Nv., U.S. D3 105
Fallon, co., Mt., U.S. D12 103
Fallon Indian Reservation, Nv., U.S. D3 105
Fallon Naval Air Station, mil., Nv., U.S. D3 105
Fall River, Ks., U.S. E7 93
Fall River, Ma., U.S. C5 98
Fallriver, Tn., U.S. B4 119
Fall River, Wi., U.S. E4 126
Fall River, co., S.D., U.S. . . . D2 118
Fall River Lake, res., Ks., U.S. E7 93
Fall River Mills, Ca., U.S. . . . B3 82
Fall Rock, Ky., U.S. C6 94
Falls, Pa., U.S. D10 115

Falls, co., Tx., U.S. D4 120
Fallsburg, Ky., U.S. B7 94
Falls Church, Va., U.S. g12 123
Falls City, Ne., U.S. D10 104
Falls City, Or., U.S. C3 114
Falls Creek, Pa., U.S. D4 115
Fallston, Md., U.S. A5 97
Fallston, N.C., U.S. B1 110
Falls Township, Pa., U.S. . . . *F12 115
Falls Village, Ct., U.S. B2 84
Falmouth, N.S. E5 71
Falmouth, Jam. E5 64
Falmouth, Eng., U.K. E4 10
Falmouth, In., U.S. E7 91
Falmouth, Ky., U.S. B5 94
Falmouth, Ma., U.S. C6 98
Falmouth, Mi., U.S. D5 99
Falmouth, Va., U.S. B5 123
Falmouth Bay, b., Eng., U.K. . D2 12
False Chipana, Punta, c., Chile D1 55
False Bay, b., S. Afr. H3 49
False Cape, c., Fl., U.S. D6 86
False Cape, c., Va., U.S. D7 123
Falso, Cabo, c., Hond. C4 64
Falster, i., Den. C6 15
Falsterbo, Swe. C6 15
Falun, Swe. G6 14
Falun, Ks., U.S. D6 93
Famagusta see Gazimağusa, N. Cyp. E9 40
Famatina, Sierra de, mts., Arg. E2 55
Family Lake, l., Man. D4 70
Fanan, i., Micron. Q18 52
Fanapanges, i., Micron. Q18 52
Fancy Farm, Ky., U.S. f9 94
Fancy Prairie, Il., U.S. D4 90
Fang, Thai. B1 34
Fangcheng, China H5 32
Fangxian, China E7 31
Fannettsburg, Pa., U.S. F6 115
Fannin, Tx., U.S. E4 120
Fannin, co., Ga., U.S. B2 87
Fannin, co., Tx., U.S. C4 120
Fanning Island see Tabuaeran Island, atoll, Kir. F12 6
Fanny, Mount, mtn., Or., U.S. B9 114
Fanny Bay, B.C. E5 69
Fannystelle, Man. E3 70
Fano, Italy C4 23
Fanø, i., Den. C2 15
Fanø Bugt, b., Den. C2 15
Fañonchuluyan, Bahia, b., N. Mar. Is. D8 52
Fan Si Pan, mtn., Viet. A5 35
Fanwood, N.J., U.S. *B4 107
Fāqūs, Eg. D3 41
Faradje, Zaire A4 48
Faradofay, Madag. h9 49
Farafangana, Madag. h9 49
Farāfirah, Al Wāḥāt al, well, Eg. C2 38
Farāh, Afg. B3 36
Farāh, stm., Afg. B3 36
Farahan, Gui. D4 45
Farasan Islands, is., Sau. Ar. . D4 38
Farber, Mo., U.S. B6 102
Fareham, Eng., U.K. D6 12
Farewell, Cape, c., N.Z. N14 51
Farge, Ga., U.S. F4 87
Fargo, N.D., U.S. C9 111
Fargo, Ok., U.S. A2 113
Far Hills, N.J., U.S. B3 107
Faribault, Mn., U.S. F5 100
Faribault, co., Mn., U.S. G4 100
Faridpur, Bngl. F12 37
Fārigh, Wādī al, val., Libya . . C1 38
Farilhões Islands, is., Port. . . C1 22
Farīmān, Iran D9 39
Farina, Austl. E2 51
Farina, Il., U.S. E5 90
Farisita, Co., U.S. D5 83
Fārskūr, Eg. C3 41
Farley, Ia., U.S. B6 92
Farley, Ma., U.S. A3 98
Farley, Mo., U.S. B3 102
Farlin, Ia., U.S. A5 108
Farmer, Oh., U.S. A1 112
Farmer, S.D., U.S. D8 118
Farmer City, Il., U.S. C5 90
Farmers, Ky., U.S. B6 94
Farmers Branch, Tx., U.S. . . . n10 120
Farmersburg, In., U.S. F3 91
Farmersburg, Ia., U.S. B6 92
Farmersville, Ca., U.S. *D4 82
Farmersville, Il., U.S. D4 90
Farmersville, Tx., U.S. C4 120
Farmerville, La., U.S. B3 95
Farmingdale, Me., U.S. D3 96
Farmingdale, N.J., U.S. *C4 107
Farmingdale, N.Y., U.S. *n15 109
Farmington, Ar., U.S. A1 81
Farmington, Ct., U.S. C4 84
Farmington, De., U.S. E3 85
Farmington, Il., U.S. C3 90
Farmington, Ia., U.S. D6 92
Farmington, Me., U.S. D2 96
Farmington, Mi., U.S. p15 99
Farmington, Mn., U.S. F5 100
Farmington, Mo., U.S. D7 102
Farmington, N.H., U.S. D4 106
Farmington, N.M., U.S. A1 108
Farmington, N.Y., U.S. *n15 109
Farmington, Pa., U.S. G2 115
Farmington, Tn., U.S. B5 119
Farmington, Wa., U.S. B8 124
Farmington, W.V., U.S. h10 125
Farmington, stm., Ct., U.S. . . B4 84
Farmington, West Branch, stm., U.S. B4 84
Farmington Hills, Mi., U.S. . . *F7 99
Farmingville, N.Y., U.S. *n15 109
Farmland, In., U.S. D7 91
Farm Pond, l., Ma., U.S. h10 98
Farmville, N.C., U.S. B5 110
Farmville, Va., U.S. C4 123
Farnam, Ne., U.S. D5 104
Farnborough, Eng., U.K. C7 12
Farne Islands, is., Eng., U.K. . C6 10
Farner, Tn., U.S. D9 119
Farnham, Que. D5 74
Farnham, Va., U.S. C6 123
Farnham, Mount, mtn., B.C. . . D9 69
Farnhamville, Ia., U.S. B3 92
Fārnigen, Switz. C6 21
Faro, Braz. C3 59
Faro, Port. D2 22
Farragut, Ia., U.S. D2 92

Farragut, Tn., U.S. *D9 119
Farrar, stm., Scot., U.K. e9 92
Farrar, stm., Scot., U.K. C4 13
Farrāshband, Iran G6 39
Farrell, Ms., U.S. A3 101
Farrell, Pa., U.S. D1 115
Farrerdale, Sask. F3 75
Farris, Ok., U.S. C6 113
Farris, i., Nor. p27 14
Farrukhābād, India C6 36
Fars, hist. reg., Iran C5 38
Farson, Ia., U.S. C5 92
Farson, Wy., U.S. D3 127
Farsund, Nor. H2 14
Fartak, Ra's, c., Yemen D5 38
Fārup, Den. B3 15
Farvel, Kap, c., Grnld. D16 61
Farwell, Mi., U.S. E6 99
Farwell, Mn., U.S. E3 100
Farwell, Ne., U.S. C7 104
Farwell, Tx., U.S. B1 120
Fasā, Iran G6 39
Fasano, Italy D6 23
Fashoda see Kodok, Sudan . . D3 47
Fassett, Que. D3 74
Fastov, Sov. Un. F7 7
Fatehpur, India C7 36
Fatsa, Tur. B11 40
Fatumafuti, Am. Sam. F13 52
Fatuosofia, Cape, c., W. Sam. F11 52
Fatu Rock, rock, Am. Sam. . . F13 52
Faucett, Mo., U.S. B3 102
Faucett, Alta. B3 68
Faulk, co., S.D., U.S. B6 118
Faulkland Heights, De., U.S. . i7 85
Faulkner, co., Ar., U.S. B3 81
Faulkton, S.D., U.S. B6 118
Faunsdale, Al., U.S. C2 78
Fauquembergues, Fr. D10 16
Fauquier, B.C. E8 69
Fauquier, co., Va., U.S. B5 123
Faust, Alta. B3 68
Favara, Italy F4 23
Faverges, Fr. D2 20
Faverney, Fr. A1 21
Faversham, Eng., U.K. *C8 12
Favorita, Fl., U.S. C5 86
Fawcett, Alta. B3 68
Fawcett Lake, l., Alta. B4 68
Fawnie Nose, mtn., B.C. C5 69
Fawnie Range, mts., B.C. . . . C5 69
Faxaflói, b., Ice. n21 14
Faxeälven, stm., Swe. F6 14
Faxon, Ok., U.S. C3 113
Faxon, Tn., U.S. A3 119
Fay, Ok., U.S. B3 113
Fayd, Sau. Ar. I14 40
Fayette, Al., U.S. B2 78
Fayette, Ia., U.S. B6 92
Fayette, Me., U.S. D2 96
Fayette, Ms., U.S. D2 101
Fayette, Mo., U.S. B5 102
Fayette, Oh., U.S. A1 112
Fayette, Ut., U.S. D4 121
Fayette, co., Al., U.S. B2 78
Fayette, co., Ga., U.S. C2 87
Fayette, co., Il., U.S. D5 90
Fayette, co., In., U.S. E7 91
Fayette, co., Ia., U.S. B6 92
Fayette, co., Ky., U.S. B5 94
Fayette, co., Oh., U.S. C2 112
Fayette, co., Pa., U.S. G2 115
Fayette, co., Tn., U.S. B2 119
Fayette, co., Tx., U.S. E4 120
Fayette, co., W.V., U.S. C3 125
Fayetteville, Al., U.S. B3 78
Fayetteville, Ar., U.S. A1 81
Fayetteville, Ga., U.S. C2 87
Fayetteville, N.C., U.S. B4 110
Fayetteville, Oh., U.S. C2 112
Fayetteville, Pa., U.S. G6 115
Fayetteville, Tn., U.S. B5 119
Fayetteville, W.V., U.S. C3 125
Faylakah, i., Kuw. C4 39
Fayville, Ma., U.S. g9 98
Fays-Billot, Fr. B1 20
Fayson, N.M., U.S. E1 108
Fazenda Nova, Braz. D2 56
Fdérik, Maur. B2 45
Fear, Cape, c., N.C., U.S. . . . D5 110
Feasterville, Pa., U.S. o21 115
Feather, stm., Ca., U.S. C3 82
Feather, Middle Fork, stm., Ca., U.S. C3 82
Feather, Mount, mtn., Ant. . . e40 7
Feather Falls, Ca., U.S. C3 82
Featherston, N.Z. N15 51
Fécamp, Fr. C4 16
Federal, Arg. A5 54
Federal Dam, Mn., U.S. *C4 100
Federal Heights, Co., U.S. . . *B6 83
Federal Point, Fl., U.S. C5 86
Federalsburg, Md., U.S. C6 97
Federal Way, Wa., U.S. *f11 124
Fedora, S.D., U.S. C8 118
Fedscreek, Ky., U.S. C7 94
Feeding Hills, Ma., U.S. B2 98
Fefan, i., Micron. Q18 52
Fegen, Swe. A7 15
Fehmarn, i., W. Ger. A5 18
Fehmarn Strait, strt., Eur. . . . A5 18
Feia, Lagoa, b., Braz. C4 56
Feijó, Braz. C3 58
Feilding, N.Z. N15 51
Feira, Port. B1 22
Feira (Luangwa), Zam. E5 48
Feira de Santana, Braz. D5 57
Fejø, i., Den. C6 15
Felanitx, Spain C7 22
Felch, Mi., U.S. C3 99
Felda, Fl., U.S. F5 86
Feldbach, Aus. E7 18
Feldberg, E. Ger. B5 19
Feldberg, mtn., W. Ger. B4 20
Feldkirch, Aus. E4 18
Felicity, Oh., U.S. D1 112
Felipe Carrillo Puerto, Mex. . C13 66
Felix, Cape, c., N.W. Ter. . . . C13 66
Felixstowe, Eng., U.K. D9 12
Felixville, La., U.S. D5 95
Fellbach, W. Ger. D5 20
Fellingsbro, Swe. t33 14
Fellowship, N.J., U.S. *D3 107
Fellsmere, Fl., U.S. E6 86
Felsenthal, Ar., U.S. D3 81
Felt, Id., U.S. F7 89
Felt, Ok., U.S. e8 113
Felton, Ca., U.S. D2 82

Felton, De., U.S. D3 85
Felton, Ga., U.S. C1 87
Felton, Mn., U.S. C2 100
Felton, Pa., U.S. G8 115
Feltre, Italy A3 23
Felts Mills, N.Y., U.S. D5 15
Femunden, l., Nor. F4 14
Fena Valley Reservoir, res., Guam M9 52
Fence, Wi., U.S. C5 126
Fence, stm., Wi., U.S. B2 99
Fence Lake, N.M., U.S. C1 108
Fence Lake, l., Wi., U.S. C4 126
Fenelon Falls, Ont. C6 73
Fengcheng, China F8 31
Fengcheng, China D11 32
Fengdu, China E6 31
Fengjie, China E6 31
Fengning, China D7 32
Fengxian, China G4 31
Fengxian, China H2 32
Fengxiang, China G2 32
Fengzhen, China D5 32
Fenimore Pass, strt., Ak., U.S. E4 79
Fenn, Id., U.S. D2 89
Fennimore, Wi., U.S. F3 126
Fennville, Mi., U.S. F4 99
Fenoarivo Atsinanana, Madag. g9 49
Fenton, Sask. D3 75
Fenton, Ia., U.S. A3 92
Fenton, La., U.S. D3 95
Fenton, Mi., U.S. F7 99
Fenton, Mo., U.S. h8 120
Fentress, Tx., U.S. C9 119
Fentress, co., Tn., U.S. C4 125
Fenwick, W.V., U.S. k11 117
Fenwick Island, De., U.S. . . . G5 85
Fenwick Island, i., S.C., U.S. . G4 75
Fenwood, Sask. D7 31
Fenyang, China I10 27
Feodosiya, Sov. Un. E4 95
Fer, Point au, c., La., U.S. . . . D4 11
Ferbane, Ire. C5 103
Ferdig, Mt., U.S. C2 89
Ferdinand, Id., U.S. H4 91
Ferdinand, In., U.S. E15 57
Ferdinand, E. Ger. B5 39
Ferdinandshof, E. Ger. F3 17
Ferdows, Iran E8 23
Fère-Champenoise, Fr. F3 17
Ferentino, Italy D2 73
Fergana, Sov. Un. E8 28
Fergana Mountains, mts., Sov. Un. D5 73
Fergus, Ont. C7 103
Fergus, Mt., U.S. C7 103
Fergus, co., Mt., U.S. D2 100
Fergus Falls, Mn., U.S. D9 69
Ferguson, B.C. C5 92
Ferguson, Ia., U.S. C5 94
Ferguson, Ky., U.S. B7 102
Ferguson, Mo., U.S. C4 68
Ferintosh, Alta. E3 45
Ferkéssédougou, I.C. E4 82
Ferme-Neuve, Que. C4 72
Ferme, Newf. C4 23
Fermo, Italy h13 74
Fermont, Que. B2 22
Fermoselle, Spain D2 10
Fermoy, Ire. C3 114
Fernandina, Isla (Narborough), i., Ec. g5 58
Fernandina Beach, Fl., U.S. . . B5 86
Fernando de Noronha, Ilha, i., Braz. B4 57
Fernandópolis, Braz. C2 56
Fernando Poo see Bioko, i., Eq. Gui. E1 46
Fernán-Núñez, Spain D3 22
Fernbank, Al., U.S. B1 78
Fern Creek, Ky., U.S. g11 94
Fern Creek, stm., Ky., U.S. . . g11 94
Ferndale, Ar., U.S. h9 81
Ferndale, Ca., U.S. B1 82
Ferndale, Ky., U.S. D6 94
Ferndale, Md., U.S. B4 97
Ferndale, Mi., U.S. P15 99
Ferndale, Pa., U.S. F4 115
Ferndale, Wa., U.S. A3 124
Ferney, S.D., U.S. B7 118
Ferney-Voltaire, Fr. E10 69
Fern Park, Fl., U.S. D2 105
Fern Ridge Lake, res., Or., U.S. C3 114
Ferns, Ire. E5 11
Fernwood, Id., U.S. B2 89
Fernwood, Ms., U.S. D3 101
Fernwood, N.Y., U.S. B4 109
Ferrara, Italy C1 22
Ferreira do Alentejo, Port. . . C1 22
Ferreira do Zêzere, Port. . . . E2 125
Ferrellsburg, W.V., U.S. E2 114
Ferrelo, Cape, c., Or., U.S. . . . E6 91
Ferreñafe, Peru A3 21
Ferrette, Fr. C4 95
Ferriday, La., U.S. E5 23
Ferriere, Italy C2 90
Ferris, Il., U.S. C4 120
Ferris, Tx., U.S. C4 122
Ferrisburg, Vt., U.S. D5 127
Ferris Mountains, mts., Wy., U.S. D5 127
Ferron, Ut., U.S. D4 121
Ferros, Braz. B4 56
Ferrum, Va., U.S. D2 123
Ferryland, Newf. E5 72
Ferry, co., Wa., U.S. A7 124
Ferry Farms, Va., U.S. B5 123
Ferry Point, c., N.J., U.S. . . . k7 107
Ferryville, Wi., U.S. E2 126
Fertile, Ia., U.S. A4 92
Fertile, Mn., U.S. C2 100
Fertilia, Italy D2 23
Fès, Mor. B3 44
Fer Mountain, Sask. H2 75
Feshi, Zaire D7 37
Fessenden, N.D., U.S. B6 111
Festus, Mo., U.S. A6 92
Festus, Mo., U.S. C7 102
Feteşti, Rom. C11 33
Fethard, Ire. D7 40
Fethiye, Tur. E4 28
Fetisovo, Sov. Un. D7 39
Fetlar, i., Scot., U.K. D6 19
Feucht, W. Ger. D5 39
Feuchtwangen, W. Ger. F2 75
Feuilles, Rivière aux, stm., Que. g12 74
Feurs, Fr. E6 16
Feversham, Ont. C4 73
Feyzābād, Afg. A5 36
Fezzan (Fazzān), hist. reg., Libya D2 43
Ffestiniog, Wales, U.K. D5 10

Fhada, Beinn, mtn., Scot., U.K. B4 10
Fiambalá, Arg. E2 55
Fianarantsoa, Madag. h9 49
Fianarantsoa, prov., Madag. . h9 49
Fianga, Chad D3 46
Fibre, Mi., U.S. B6 99
Ficarolo, Italy E7 20
Fiche, Eth. D4 47
Ficksburg, S. Afr. C4 49
Fidalgo Island, i., Wa., U.S. . . A3 124
Fidelity, Il., U.S. D3 90
Fidenza, Italy B3 23
Fidler Lake, l., Man. A3 70
Field, B.C. D3 107
Field Crest Estates, Ct., U.S. . D8 84
Fielding, Sask. E2 75
Fielding, Ut., U.S. B3 121
Fields, La., U.S. D2 95
Fields, Or., U.S. E8 114
Fields, Lake, l., La., U.S. k10 95
Fields, Lake, stm., Fl., U.S. . . B3 86
Fieldsboro, N.J., U.S. C3 107
Fieri, Alb. B2 25
Fiesch, Switz. D5 21
Fiesole, Italy C3 23
Fife, prov., Scot., U.K. D5 13
Fife Lake, Sask. H3 75
Fife Lake, Mi., U.S. D5 99
Fife Lake, l., Sask. H3 75
Fife Ness, c., Scot., U.K. B5 10
Fifteenmile Creek, stm., Wy., U.S. B4 127
Fifteen Mile Falls Reservoir, res., U.S. C5 122
Fifth Lake, l., N.Y., U.S. D10 109
Figeac, Fr. E5 16
Fig Garden, Ca., U.S. *D4 82
Figtree, Zimb. B4 49
Figueira da Foz, Port. B1 22
Figueras, Spain A7 22
Figuig, Mor. B4 44
Fiji, ctry., Oc. H10 6
Fík, Eth. D5 47
Filadelfia, Par. D4 54
Filchner Ice Shelf, ice, Ant. . . B8 7
File Lake, l., Man. B1 70
Filer, Id., U.S. G4 89
Filer City, Mi., U.S. D4 99
Filey, Eng., U.K. F8 13
Fili, Grc. g11 25
Filiatrá, Grc. D3 25
Filicudi, i., Italy E5 23
Filingué, Niger D5 45
Filisur, Switz. C8 21
Fillmore, Sask. H4 75
Fillmore, Ca., U.S. E4 82
Fillmore, Il., U.S. D4 90
Fillmore, In., U.S. E4 91
Fillmore, Mo., U.S. A3 102
Fillmore, N.Y., U.S. C2 109
Fillmore, N.D., U.S. A6 111
Fillmore, Ok., U.S. C5 113
Fillmore, Ut., U.S. E3 121
Fillmore, co., Mn., U.S. G6 100
Fillmore, co., Ne., U.S. D8 104
Fimi, stm., Zaire B2 48
Finale Emilia, Italy E7 20
Fincastle, Va., U.S. C3 123
Finch, Ont. B9 73
Finch, Scot., U.K. C5 13
Findhorn, stm., Scot., U.K. . . C5 13
Findlater, Sask. G3 75
Findlay, Il., U.S. D5 90
Findlay, Oh., U.S. A2 112
Findlay, Mount, mtn., B.C. . . D9 69
Fine, N.Y., U.S. A5 109
Finesville, N.J., U.S. B2 107
Fingal, N.D., U.S. C8 111
Finger, Tn., U.S. B3 119
Finger Lake, l., Ont. C5 70
Fingerville, S.C., U.S. A3 117
Finger, co., Il., U.S. C5 86
Finland, B.C. E10 69
Finksburg, Md., U.S. B4 97
Finland, Mn., U.S. C7 100
Finland, ctry., Eur. E12 14
Finland, Gulf of, b., Eur. H12 14
Finlay, stm., B.C. m17 69
Finlayson, Mn., U.S. D6 100
Finley, N.D., U.S. B8 111
Finley, Ok., U.S. C6 113
Finley, Tn., U.S. A2 119
Finleyson, Ga., U.S. D3 87
Finmoore, B.C. C6 69
Finningen, Alta. D3 68
Finney, co., Ks., U.S. D3 93
Finn German, Al., U.S. D3 68
Finschhafen, Pap. N. Gui. . . . k12 50
Finspång, Swe. u33 14
Finsteraarhorn, mtn., Switz. . . E14 21
Finsterwalde, E. Ger. C6 18
Fintona, N. Ire., U.K. C4 11
Fintona, Ire. C4 11
Fionn Loch, l., Scot., U.K. . . . C3 13
Fir, Isr. Occ. F10 40
Fir, stm., Sask. D5 70
Firbaugh, Ca., U.S. D3 82
Firenze, Italy B3 23
Firesteel, S.D., U.S. B4 118
Firestone, Co., U.S. A6 83
Firmat, Arg. A4 54
Firminy, Fr. E6 16
Fir Mountain, Sask. H2 75
Firozpur, India E6 36
Firozābād, India D7 36
Firsovo, Sov. Un. C11 33
First Connecticut Lake, l., N.H., U.S. f7 106
First Roach Pond, l., Me., U.S. C3 96
Firth, B.C. D9 104
Firth, Id., U.S. F6 89
Firth, Ne., U.S. D9 104
Firūzābād, Iran G6 39
Firūz Kūh, Iran B5 38
Fischot Island, i., Newf. C2 72
Fish, stm., Me., U.S. A4 96
Fish, stm., Me., U.S. B3 72
Fish Cove Point, c., Newf. . . . A3 72
Fish Creek, Wi., U.S. C6 126
Fish Creek, stm., N.J., U.S. . . g8 125
Fisheating Creek, stm., Fl., U.S. F5 86

Fisher, Ar., U.S. B5 81
Fisher, Il., U.S. C5 90
Fisher, La., U.S. C2 95
Fisher, Mn., U.S. C2 100
Fisher, Pa., U.S. D3 115
Fisher, W.V., U.S. B5 125
Fisher, co., Tx., U.S. C2 120
Fisher, stm., Man. D3 70
Fisher Bay, b., Man. D3 70
Fisher Branch, Man. D3 70
Fisher Glacier, ice, Ant. B19 7
Fisher Lake, l., N.S. E4 71
Fisher Lake, l., Va., U.S. h15 123
Fishers, In., U.S. E5 91
Fishers Island, i., N.Y., U.S. . . m16 109
Fishers Peak, mtn., Co., U.S. . D8 83
Fisher Strait, strt., N.W. Ter. . D16 61
Fishersville, Va., U.S. B4 123
Fishertown, Pa., U.S. F4 115
Fisherville, Ont. E5 73
Fishguard [and Goodwick], Wales, U.K. E4 10
Fish Haven, Id., U.S. G7 89
Fishhook, Il., U.S. D3 90
Fishing Bay, b., Md., U.S. . . . D5 97
Fishing Creek, Md., U.S. D5 97
Fishing Creek, stm., N.C., U.S. A5 110
Fishing Creek, stm., S.C., U.S. B5 117
Fishing Creek, stm., W.V., U.S. B4 125
Fishing Creek, North Fork, stm., W.V., U.S. h9 125
Fishing Creek, South Fork, stm., W.V., U.S. h9 125
Fishing Creek Reservoir, res., S.C., U.S. B6 117
Fishing Lake, l., Man. C4 70
Fishing Lake, l., Sask. F4 75
Fishkill, N.Y., U.S. D7 109
Fish Lake, l., Ut., U.S. D4 100
Fish River Lake, l., Me., U.S. . B4 96
Fish Springs Range, mts., Ut., U.S. D2 121
Fishtail, Mt., U.S. E7 103
Fishtail Point, c., Ant. f39 7
Fishtrap Lake, res., Ky., U.S. . C7 94
Fisk, Mo., U.S. E7 102
Fiskburg, Ky., U.S. B5 94
Fiskdale, Ma., U.S. B3 98
Fiske, Sask. F1 75
Fismes, Fr. E3 17
Fitch-Bay, Que. D5 74
Fitchburg, Ma., U.S. A4 98
Fitchburg, Wi., U.S. *F4 126
Fitchville, Ct., U.S. C7 84
Fithian, Il., U.S. C6 90
Fitlers, Mo., U.S. C2 101
Fittstown, Ok., U.S. C5 113
Fitzgerald, Ga., U.S. E3 87
Fitzhugh, Ok., U.S. C5 113
Fitz Hugh Sound, strt., B.C. . . D4 69
Fitzpatrick, Que. B5 74
Fitz Roy, Arg. D3 54
Fitzroy, stm., Austl. C4 50
Fitzroy, stm., Austl. D9 50
Fitzroy, Monte (Cerro Chaltel), mtn., S.A. D2 54
Fitzroy Harbour, Ont. B8 73
Fitzwilliam, N.H., U.S. E2 106
Fitzwilliam Depot, N.H., U.S. . E2 106
Fitzwilliam Island, i., Ont. . . . B3 73
Fiume see Rijeka, Yugo. . . . C2 24
Fiumicino, Italy h8 23
Five Islands, N.S. D5 71
Fivemile Creek, stm., Wy., U.S. C4 127
Fivemiletown, N. Ire., U.K. . . C4 11
Five Points, Al., U.S. B4 78
Five Points, N.M., U.S. B3 108
Fizi, Zaire B4 48
Fjärås Kyrkby, Swe. A6 15
Fjärdhundra, Swe. t34 14
Fjerritslev, Den. A3 15
Flagg Mountain, hill, Al., U.S. C3 78
Flag Knob, mtn., Ky., U.S. . . C7 94
Flagler, Co., U.S. B7 83
Flagler, co., Fl., U.S. C5 86
Flagler Beach, Fl., U.S. C5 86
Flag Pond, Tn., U.S. C11 119
Flagstaff, Az., U.S. B4 80
Flagstaff Lake, l., Or., U.S. . . E7 114
Flagtown, N.J., U.S. B3 107
Flamand, Lac, l., Que. B4 74
Flambeau, Wi., U.S. C3 126
Flambeau, South Fork, stm., Wi., U.S. C3 126
Flamborough Head, c., Eng., U.K. C6 10
Flaming Gorge Dam, Ut., U.S. C6 121
Flaming Gorge National Recreation Area, U.S. E3 127
Flaming Gorge Reservoir, res., U.S. E3 127
Flanagan, Il., U.S. C5 90
Flanders, Ont. E5 70
Flanders, Ct., U.S. *C8 84
Flanders, N.J., U.S. *B3 107
Flanders, hist. reg., Eur. C9 16
Flandreau, S.D., U.S. C9 118
Flandreau Indian Reservation, S.D., U.S. C9 118
Flannan Islands, is., Scot., U.K. A3 10
Flåren, l., Swe. A8 15
Flasher, N.D., U.S. C4 111
Flat, Ak., U.S. C7 79
Flat, Ky., U.S. C6 94
Flat, Mo., U.S. D6 102
Flat, Mi., U.S. E5 99
Flat, stm., N.C., U.S. A4 110
Flat, stm., R.I., U.S. E2 116
Flat Bay, Newf. D2 72
Flat Brook, stm., N.J., U.S. . . A3 107
Flatbrookville, N.J., U.S. B3 107
Flatbush, Alta. B3 68
Flat Creek, Tn., U.S. B5 119
Flathead, co., Mt., U.S. B2 103
Flathead, North Fork, stm., N.A. B2 103
Flathead, South Fork, stm., Mt., U.S. C3 103
Flathead Indian Reservation, Mt., U.S. C2 103
Flathead Lake, l., Mt., U.S. . . C2 103
Flathead Valley, val., Mt., U.S. C2 103
Flat Island, i., Newf. D4 72
Flat Lake, l., Alta. k9 95
Flatlands, N.B. B3 71
Flat Lick, Ky., U.S. D6 94
Flat Mountain, mtn., N.Z. . . . P11 51

Name	Map Ref.	Page
Flatonia, Tx., U.S.	E4	120
Flat River, P.E.I.	C7	71
Flat River, Mo., U.S.	D7	102
Flat River Reservoir, res., R.I., U.S.	D3	116
Flat Rock, Al., U.S.	A4	78
Flat Rock, Il., U.S.	E6	90
Flat Rock, In., U.S.	F6	91
Flat Rock, Mi., U.S.	F7	99
Flat Rock, N.C., U.S.	f10	110
Flat Rock, Oh., U.S.	A3	112
Flatrock, stm., In., U.S.	F6	91
Flatrock Lake, l., Man.	B1	70
Flattery, Cape, c., Wa., U.S.	A1	124
Flatts, Ber.	p20	64
Flatwood, Al., U.S.	C2	78
Flatwoods, Ky., U.S.	B7	94
Flatwoods, La., U.S.	C3	95
Flatwoods, Tn., U.S.	B4	119
Flatwoods, W.V., U.S.	*C4	125
Flawil, Switz.	B5	20
Flaxcombe, Sask.	F1	75
Flaxton, N.D., U.S.	A3	111
Flaxville, Mt., U.S.	B11	103
Fleet, Alta.	C5	68
Fleet, Eng., U.K.	C7	12
Fleetwood, Eng., U.K.	G5	13
Fleetwood, N.C., U.S.	A1	110
Fleetwood, Pa., U.S.	F10	115
Fleischmanns, N.Y., U.S.	C6	109
Flekkefjord, Nor.	H2	14
Fleming, Sask.	G5	75
Fleming, Co., U.S.	A8	83
Fleming, Ky., U.S.	C7	94
Fleming, Pa., U.S.	E6	115
Fleming, co., Ky., U.S.	B6	94
Fleming-Neon, Ky., U.S.	C7	94
Flemingsburg, Ky., U.S.	B6	94
Flemington, Ga., U.S.	E5	87
Flemington, Mo., U.S.	D4	102
Flemington, N.J., U.S.	B3	107
Flemington, Pa., U.S.	D7	115
Flemington, W.V., U.S.	k10	125
Flen, Swe.	t34	14
Flensburg, W. Ger.	A4	18
Flensburg, Mn., U.S.	E4	100
Flensburg Fjord, b., Eur.	D3	15
Flers, Fr.	C3	16
Flesherton, Ont.	C4	73
Fletcher, Ont.	E2	73
Fletcher, N.C., U.S.	f10	110
Fletcher, Oh., U.S.	B1	112
Fletcher, Ok., U.S.	C3	113
Fletcher, Vt., U.S.	B3	122
Fletcher Islands, is., Ant.	B7	7
Fleur-de-Lys, Newf.	C3	72
Fleurier, Switz.	C2	20
Fleurus, Bel.	C4	19
Flims, Switz.	C7	21
Flinders, stm., Austl.	C7	50
Flinders Island, i., Austl.	F5	50
Flinders Range, mts., Austl.	F6	50
Flin Flon, Man.	B1	70
Flint, Wales, U.K.	A4	12
Flint, In., U.S.	A7	91
Flint, Mi., U.S.	E7	99
Flint, stm., U.S.	E2	87
Flint City, Al., U.S.	A3	78
Flint Creek, stm., Al., U.S.	A3	78
Flint Creek Range, mts., Mt., U.S.	D3	103
Flinthill, Mo., U.S.	C7	102
Flint Hill, Va., U.S.	B4	123
Flint Hills, hills, Ks., U.S.	D7	93
Flint Island, i., Kir.	G12	6
Flinton, Sask.	H2	75
Flinton, Ont.	C7	73
Flint Run, stm., W.V., U.S.	k9	125
Flintstone, Md., U.S.	k13	97
Flintville, Tn., U.S.	B5	119
Flipper Point, c., Wake I.	A2	52
Flippin, Ar., U.S.	A3	81
Flippin, Ky., U.S.	D4	94
Flixecourt, Fr.	D2	17
Flöha, E. Ger.	C8	19
Flom, Mn., U.S.	C2	100
Flomaton, Al., U.S.	D2	78
Flomot, Tx., U.S.	B2	120
Flood Range, mts., Ant.	B35	7
Floodwood, Mn., U.S.	D6	100
Flora, Il., U.S.	E5	90
Flora, In., U.S.	C4	91
Flora, Ms., U.S.	C3	101
Flora, N.D., U.S.	B6	111
Florahome, Fl., U.S.	C5	86
Florala, Al., U.S.	D3	78
Floral City, Fl., U.S.	D4	86
Floral Park, N.Y., U.S.	*k13	109
Flora Vista, N.M., U.S.	A1	108
Florence (Firenze), Italy	C3	23
Florence, Al., U.S.	A2	78
Florence, Az., U.S.	D4	80
Florence, Ca., U.S.	*n12	82
Florence, Co., U.S.	C5	83
Florence, In., U.S.	C8	91
Florence, Ks., U.S.	D7	93
Florence, Ky., U.S.	A5	94
Florence, Ms., U.S.	C3	101
Florence, Mo., U.S.	C5	102
Florence, Mt., U.S.	D2	103
Florence, N.J., U.S.	C3	107
Florence, Or., U.S.	D2	114
Florence, S.C., U.S.	C8	117
Florence, S.D., U.S.	B8	118
Florence, Tx., U.S.	D4	120
Florence, Vt., U.S.	D2	122
Florence, Wa., U.S.	A3	124
Florence, Wi., U.S.	C5	126
Florence, co., S.C., U.S.	C8	117
Florence, co., Wi., U.S.	C5	126
Florence Junction, Az., U.S.	D4	80
Florenceville, N.B.	C2	71
Florencia, Col.	C2	60
Floreffe, Bel.	E5	17
Floresville, Bel.	D7	63
Flores, dept., Ur.	f8	54
Flores, i., Indon.	G6	34
Flores, i., Port.	g8	44
Flores Island, i., B.C.	E4	69
Flores Sea, Indon.	G5	34
Floresta, Braz.	C3	57
Floresville, Tx., U.S.	E3	120
Florham Park, N.J., U.S.	B4	107
Floriano, Braz.	C2	57
Floriano Peixoto, Braz.	C4	58
Florianópolis, Braz.	D3	56
Florida, Cuba	D4	64
Florida, Ma., U.S.	A1	98
Florida, N.M., U.S.	C3	108
Florida, N.Y., U.S.	D6	109
Florida, Oh., U.S.	A1	112
Florida, Ur.	E1	56
Florida, dept., Ur.	f8	54
Florida, state, U.S.	E5	86
Florida, Cape, c., Fl., U.S.	G6	86
Florida, Straits of, strt., N.A.	F11	76
Florida Bay, b., Fl., U.S.	H6	86
Floridablanca, Col.	*B3	60
Florida City, Fl., U.S.	G6	86
Florida Keys, is., Fl., U.S.	H6	86
Florida Mountains, mts., N.M., U.S.	E2	108
Florida State Indian Reservation, Fl., U.S.	F5	86
Florien, La., U.S.	C2	95
Florin, Ca., U.S.	*C3	82
Flórina (Phlorina), Grc.	B3	25
Florissant, Co., U.S.	C5	83
Florissant, Mo., U.S.	f13	102
Florissant Fossil Beds National Monument, Co., U.S.	C5	83
Flossmoor, Il., U.S.	k9	90
Flournoy, Ca., U.S.	C2	82
Flourtown, Pa., U.S.	o21	115
Flovilla, Ga., U.S.	C3	87
Flower Brook, stm., Vt., U.S.	E2	122
Floweree, Mt., U.S.	C5	103
Flower Hill, N.Y., U.S.	*E7	109
Flower's Cove, Newf.	C3	72
Flower Station, Ont.	B8	73
Flowery Branch, Ga., U.S.	B3	87
Flowood, Ms., U.S.	C3	101
Floyd, Ia., U.S.	A5	92
Floyd, N.M., U.S.	C6	108
Floyd, Va., U.S.	D2	123
Floyd, co., Ga., U.S.	B1	87
Floyd, co., In., U.S.	H6	91
Floyd, co., Ia., U.S.	A5	92
Floyd, co., Ky., U.S.	C7	94
Floyd, co., Tx., U.S.	B2	120
Floyd, co., Va., U.S.	D2	123
Floyd, stm., Ia., U.S.	B1	92
Floydada, Tx., U.S.	C2	120
Floyd Dale, S.C., U.S.	C9	117
Floydsburg, Ky., U.S.	g12	94
Floyds Fork, stm., Ky., U.S.	B4	94
Floyds Knobs, In., U.S.	H6	91
Fluchthorn, mtn., Eur.	C9	21
Fluessen, l., Neth.	B5	17
Flumendosa, stm., Italy	E2	23
Flums, Switz.	B7	21
Flushing, Mi., U.S.	E7	99
Flushing, Oh., U.S.	B4	112
Fluvanna, Tx., U.S.	C2	120
Fluvanna, co., Va., U.S.	C4	123
Fly, stm.	k11	50
Fly Creek, N.Y., U.S.	C6	109
Flying H, N.M., U.S.	D4	108
Flyinge, Swe.	C7	15
Foam Lake, Sask.	F4	75
Foam Lake, l., Sask.	F4	75
Foard, co., Tx., U.S.	B3	120
Foça, Tur.	C6	25
Foča, Yugo.	D4	24
Fochabers, Scot., U.K.	C5	13
Focşani, Rom.	C8	24
Foggia, Italy	D5	23
Fogland Point, c., R.I., U.S.	E6	116
Fogliano, Italy	A4	18
Fogo, Newf.	D4	72
Fogo, Cape, c., Newf.	D4	72
Fogo Island, i., Newf.	D4	72
Föhnsdorf, Aus.	E7	18
Föhr, i., W. Ger.	A4	18
Foix, Fr.	F4	16
Folcroft, Pa., U.S.	*p20	115
Foley, Al., U.S.	E2	78
Foley, Mn., U.S.	E5	100
Foley, Mo., U.S.	B7	102
Foley Island, i., N.W. Ter.	C17	66
Foligno, Italy	C4	23
Folkestone, Eng., U.K.	E7	10
Folkston, Ga., U.S.	F4	87
Folkston, N.C., U.S.	C5	110
Follansbee, W.V., U.S.	A4	125
Follett, Tx., U.S.	A2	120
Follonica, Italy	C3	23
Folly Beach, S.C., U.S.	F8	117
Folly Island, i., S.C., U.S.	*F8	117
Folly Lake, N.S.	D6	71
Folsom, Ca., U.S.	C3	82
Folsom, La., U.S.	D5	95
Folsom, N.J., U.S.	D3	107
Folsom, N.M., U.S.	A6	108
Folsom, W.V., U.S.	B4	125
Folsomville, In., U.S.	H3	91
Fomento, Cuba	C4	64
Fonda, Ia., U.S.	B3	92
Fonda, N.Y., U.S.	C6	109
Fond-du-Lac, Sask.	m7	75
Fond du Lac, Wi., U.S.	E5	126
Fond du Lac, co., Wi., U.S.	E5	126
Fond du Lac Indian Reservation, Mn., U.S.	D6	100
Fondi, Italy	D4	23
Fonsagrada, Spain	A2	22
Fonseca, Golfo de, b., N.A.	E7	63
Fontainebleau, Fr.	C5	16
Fontana, Ca., U.S.	m14	82
Fontana, Wi., U.S.	F5	126
Fontana Dam, N.C., U.S.	f9	110
Fontana Lake, res., N.C., U.S.	f9	110
Fontanelle, Ia., U.S.	C3	92
Fontanet, In., U.S.	E3	91
Fonte Boa, Braz.	D4	60
Fontenay-le-Comte, Fr.	D3	16
Fontenay [-sous-Bois], Fr.	g10	16
Fontenelle, Que.	A2	127
Fontenelle Reservoir, res., Wy., U.S.	D2	127
Foosland, Il., U.S.	C5	90
Foothill Farms, Ca., U.S.	*C3	82
Foothills, Alta.	C2	68
Footville, Wi., U.S.	F4	126
Foping, China	H2	32
Forada, Mn., U.S.	E3	100
Foraker, Oh., U.S.	B2	112
Foraker, Ok., U.S.	A5	113
Foraker, Mount, mtn., Ak.	f16	79
Forbach, Fr.	C7	16
Forbes, Austl.	F8	50
Forbes, Mn., U.S.	C6	100
Forbes, N.D., U.S.	D7	111
Forbes, Lac, l., Que.	A5	74
Forbes, Mount, mtn., Alta.	D2	68
Forcados, Nig.	F6	16
Forcalquier, Fr.	F6	16
Force, Pa., U.S.	D5	115
Forchheim, W. Ger.	D5	18
Ford, Scot., U.K.	E4	13
Ford, Ks., U.S.	E4	93
Ford, co., Il., U.S.	C5	90
Ford, co., Ks., U.S.	E3	93
Ford, stm., Mi., U.S.	C3	99
Ford City, Ca., U.S.	E4	82
Ford City, Pa., U.S.	E2	115
Fordland, Mo., U.S.	D5	102
Fordoche, La., U.S.	D4	95
Ford Ranges, mts., Ant.	B34	7
Ford River, Mi., U.S.	C3	99
Fords, N.J., U.S.	B4	107
Fords Prairie, Wa., U.S.	C2	124
Fordsville, Ky., U.S.	A8	111
Fordville, N.D., U.S.	A8	111
Fordwich, Ont.	D3	73
Fordyce, Ar., U.S.	D3	81
Fordyce, Ne., U.S.	B8	104
Forécariah, Gui.	E2	45
Foreman, Ar., U.S.	D1	81
Foremost, Alta.	E5	68
Foresman, In., U.S.	C3	91
Forest, Bel.	B6	16
Forest, Ont.	D2	73
Forest, In., U.S.	D5	91
Forest, Ms., U.S.	C4	101
Forest, Oh., U.S.	B2	112
Forest, Tx., U.S.	D5	120
Forest, Va., U.S.	C3	123
Forest, co., Pa., U.S.	C3	115
Forest, co., Wi., U.S.	C5	126
Forest, stm., N.D., U.S.	A8	111
Forest Acres, S.C., U.S.	C6	117
Forestburg, Alta.	C4	68
Forestburg, S.D., U.S.	C7	118
Forest City, Il., U.S.	C4	90
Forest City, Ia., U.S.	A4	92
Forest City, Me., U.S.	C5	96
Forest City, Mo., U.S.	B2	102
Forest City, N.C., U.S.	B1	110
Forest City, Pa., U.S.	C11	115
Forestdale, R.I., U.S.	B3	116
Forest Dale, Vt., U.S.	D2	122
Forest Glen, La., U.S.	h12	95
Forest Green, Mo., U.S.	B5	102
Forestgrove, Mt., U.S.	D7	103
Forest Grove, Or., U.S.	B3	114
Forest Hill, La., U.S.	C3	95
Forest Hill, Md., U.S.	A5	97
Forest Hill, Tx., U.S.	*n9	120
Forest Hills, Pa., U.S.	k14	115
Forest Home, Al., U.S.	D3	78
Forest Junction, Wi., U.S.	h9	126
Forest Knolls, Ca., U.S.	g7	82
Forest Lake, Mi., U.S.	B4	99
Forest Lake, Mn., U.S.	E6	100
Forest Lake, N.H., U.S.	E5	100
Foreston, Mn., U.S.	E5	100
Foreston, S.C., U.S.	D7	117
Forest Park, Ga., U.S.	h8	87
Forest Park, Il., U.S.	k9	90
Forest Park, La., U.S.	C5	95
Forest Park, Oh., U.S.	n12	112
Forestport, N.Y., U.S.	B5	109
Forest River, N.D., U.S.	A8	111
Forestville, Md., U.S.	*C4	97
Forestville, N.Y., U.S.	C1	109
Forestville, Pa., U.S.	D11	115
Forestville, Wi., U.S.	D6	126
Forfar, Scot., U.K.	E5	13
Forgan, Sask.	F2	75
Forgan, Ok., U.S.	A1	113
Forges-les-Eaux, Fr.	C4	16
Forget, Sask.	H4	75
Forge Village, Ma., U.S.	A5	98
Forillon, Parc National de, Que.	k14	74
Fork, N.C., U.S.	B2	110
Fork, S.C., U.S.	C9	117
Fork Creek, stm., W.V., U.S.	m12	125
Forked Deer, stm., Tn., U.S.	B2	119
Forked Deer, Middle Fork, stm., Tn., U.S.	D3	119
Forked Deer, North Fork, stm., Tn., U.S.	B3	119
Forked Deer, South Fork, stm., Tn., U.S.	B2	119
Forked Island, La., U.S.	E3	95
Forked River, N.J., U.S.	D4	107
Forkland, Al., U.S.	C2	78
Fork Mountain, Tn., U.S.	C9	119
Fork River, Man.	D1	70
Fork Shoals, S.C., U.S.	B3	117
Forksville, Pa., U.S.	D8	115
Fork Union, Va., U.S.	C4	123
Forkville, Ms., U.S.	C4	101
Forlì, Italy	B4	23
Forman, N.D., U.S.	C8	111
Formazza, Italy	C4	20
Formby, Eng., U.K.	A4	12
Formello, Italy	g8	23
Formentera, i., Spain	C6	22
Formiga, Braz.	E4	56
Formosa, Arg.	E4	55
Formosa, Braz.	B5	56
Formosa, Ont.	C3	73
Formosa, Ar., U.S.	B3	81
Formosa, prov., Arg.	D5	55
Formosa, Serra, plat., Braz.	E4	59
Formosa Bay, b., Kenya	B7	48
Formosa see Taiwan, ctry., Asia	G9	31
Formoso, Ks., U.S.	C6	93
Formoso, stm., Braz.	A5	56
Formoso, stm., Braz.	C5	59
Fornel-Lamy see N'Djamena, Chad	C3	46
Forney, Tx., U.S.	C4	120
Fornovo di Taro, Italy	E6	20
Forres, Scot., U.K.	D5	13
Forrest, Austl.	F4	50
Forrest, Il., U.S.	C5	90
Forrest, N.M., U.S.	C6	108
Forrest, co., Ms., U.S.	D4	101
Forrest City, Ar., U.S.	B5	81
Forrester Island, i., Ak., U.S.	n23	79
Forrest Lakes, l., Austl.	E5	50
Forreston, Il., U.S.	A4	90
Forsan, Tx., U.S.	C2	120
Forsayth, Austl.	C8	50
Forserum, Swe.	A8	15
Förslövsholm, Swe.	B7	15
Forst [Lausitz], E. Ger.	C7	18
Forsyth, Ga., U.S.	C3	87
Forsyth, Mo., U.S.	E4	102
Forsyth, Mt., U.S.	D10	103
Forsyth, co., Ga., U.S.	B2	87
Forsyth, co., N.C., U.S.	A2	110
Fort Adams, Ms., U.S.	D2	101
Fort Albany, Ont.	n19	73
Fortaleza, Braz.	B3	57
Fortaleza de Ituxi, Braz.	C4	58
Fort Ann, N.Y., U.S.	B7	109
Fort Apache, Az., U.S.	D6	80
Fort Apache Indian Reservation, Az., U.S.	D5	80
Fort-Archambault see Sarh, Chad	D4	46
Fort Ashby, W.V., U.S.	B6	125
Fort Assiniboine, Alta.	B3	68
Fort Atkinson, Wi., U.S.	F5	126
Fort Augustus, Scot., U.K.	C4	13
Fort Barnwell, N.C., U.S.	B5	110
Fort Beaufort, S. Afr.	D4	49
Fort Belknap Agency, Mt., U.S.	B8	103
Fort Belknap Indian Reservation, Mt., U.S.	B8	103
Fort Belvoir, Va., U.S.	g12	123
Fort Bend, co., Tx., U.S.	E5	120
Fort Benjamin Harrison, mil., In., U.S.	k10	91
Fort Benning, mil., Ga., U.S.	D2	87
Fort Benton, Mt., U.S.	C6	103
Fort Berthold Indian Reservation, N.D., U.S.	B3	111
Fort Bidwell, Ca., U.S.	B3	82
Fort Bidwell Indian Reservation, Ca., U.S.	B3	82
Fort Blackmore, Va., U.S.	f9	123
Fort Bliss, mil., Tx., U.S.	o11	120
Fort Bragg, Ca., U.S.	C2	82
Fort Bragg, mil., N.C., U.S.	B3	110
Fort Branch, In., U.S.	H2	91
Fort Bridger, Wy., U.S.	E2	127
Fort Calhoun, Ne., U.S.	C9	104
Fort Campbell, U.S.	A4	119
Fort Carson, mil., Co., U.S.	C6	83
Fort Chipewyan, Alta.	f8	68
Fort Clark, N.D., U.S.	B4	111
Fort Clatsop National Memorial, hist., Or., U.S.	A3	114
Fort Cobb, Ok., U.S.	B3	113
Fort Cobb Reservoir, res., Ok., U.S.	B3	113
Fort Collins, Co., U.S.	A5	83
Fort Coulonge, Que.	B8	73
Fort Covington, N.Y., U.S.	f10	109
Fort Crampel, Cen. Afr. Rep.	D3	46
Fort Davis, Al., U.S.	C4	78
Fort Davis, Tx., U.S.	o13	120
Fort Davis National Historic Site, hist., Tx., U.S.	o13	120
Fort Defiance, N.M., U.S.	B1	108
Fort-de-France, Mart.	I14	64
Fort-de-France, Baie de, b., Mart.	S10	65
Fort Deposit, Al., U.S.	D3	78
Fort Detrick, mil., Md., U.S.	B3	97
Fort Devens, mil., Ma., U.S.	f9	98
Fort Dix, mil., N.J., U.S.	C3	107
Fort Dodge, Ia., U.S.	B3	92
Fort Dodge, Ks., U.S.	D4	93
Fort Donelson National Military Park, Tn., U.S.	A4	119
Fort Duchesne, Ut., U.S.	C6	121
Forteau, Newf.	C3	72
Fort Edward, N.Y., U.S.	B7	109
Fort Erie, Ont.	E6	73
Fortescue, Mo., U.S.	A2	102
Fortescue, N.J., U.S.	E2	107
Fortescue, stm., Austl.	D2	50
Fort Eustis, mil., Va., U.S.	h14	123
Fort Fairfield, Me., U.S.	B5	96
Fort Fitzgerald, Alta.	f8	68
Fort Foureau, Cam.	C3	46
Fort-Foureau, Chad	C3	46
Fort Frances, Ont.	o16	73
Fort Fraser, B.C.	B5	69
Fort Frederica National Monument, Ga., U.S.	E5	87
Fort Gaines, Ga., U.S.	E1	87
Fort Garland, Co., U.S.	D5	83
Fort Gay, W.V., U.S.	C2	125
Fort Gibson, Ok., U.S.	B6	113
Fort Gibson Lake, res., Ok., U.S.	A6	113
Fort Good Hope, N.W. Ter.	C7	66
Fort Gordon, mil., Ga., U.S.	C4	87
Fort Grahame, B.C.	E8	66
Fort Greely, mil., Ak., U.S.	C10	79
Fort Green, Fl., U.S.	E5	86
Fort Hall, Kenya	B6	48
Fort Hall, Id., U.S.	F6	89
Fort Hall Indian Reservation, Id., U.S.	F6	89
Fort Hancock, Tx., U.S.	o12	120
Fort Hill, Pa., U.S.	G3	115
Fort Hood, mil., Tx., U.S.	D4	120
Fort Howard, Md., U.S.	B5	97
Fort Huachuca, mil., Az., U.S.	F5	80
Fortierville, Que.	C5	74
Fortine, Mt., U.S.	B2	103
Fortín Uno, Arg.	B3	54
Fort Jackson, mil., S.C., U.S.	C6	117
Fort Jefferson National Monument, Fl., U.S.	H4	86
Fort Jennings, Oh., U.S.	B1	112
Fort Jones, Ca., U.S.	B2	82
Fort Kent, Alta.	B5	68
Fort Kent, Me., U.S.	A4	96
Fort Kent Mills, Me., U.S.	A4	96
Fort Klamath, Or., U.S.	E5	114
Fort Knox, mil., Ky., U.S.	B4	94
Fort-Lamy see N'Djamena, Chad	C3	46
Fort Langley, B.C.	f13	69
Fort Laramie, Wy., U.S.	D8	127
Fort Laramie National Historic Site, hist., Wy., U.S.	D8	127
Fort Lauderdale, Fl., U.S.	F6	86
Fort Lawn, S.C., U.S.	B6	117
Fort Leavenworth, mil., Ks., U.S.	C9	93
Fort Lee, N.J., U.S.	B5	107
Fort Lee, mil., Va., U.S.	C5	123
Fort Leonard Wood, mil., Mo., U.S.	D5	102
Fort Lewis, mil., Wa., U.S.	B3	124
Fort Liard, N.W. Ter.	D8	66
Fort-Liberté, Haiti	E8	64
Fort Littleton, Pa., U.S.	F5	115
Fort Loramie, Oh., U.S.	B1	112
Fort Loudoun Lake, res., Tn., U.S.	D9	119
Fort Lupton, Co., U.S.	A6	83
Fort MacKay, Alta.	n12	68
Fort MacKay, Alta.	f8	68
Fort Macleod, Alta.	E4	68
Fort Madison, Ia., U.S.	D6	92
Fort Matanzas National Monument, Fl., U.S.	C5	86
Fort McClellan, mil., Al., U.S.	B4	78
Fort McDermitt Indian Reservation, Nv., U.S.	D5	80
Fort McDowell, Az., U.S.	k9	80
Fort McDowell Indian Reservation, Az., U.S.	D4	80
Fort McHenry National Monument And Historic Shrine, Md., U.S.	g11	97
Fort McKavett, Tx., U.S.	D2	120
Fort McKinley, Oh., U.S.	*C1	112
Fort McMurray, Alta.	A5	68
Fort McPherson, N.W. Ter.	C6	66
Fort Meade, Fl., U.S.	E5	86
Fort Meade, mil., Md., U.S.	B4	97
Fort Meadow Reservoir, res., Ma., U.S.	g9	98
Fort Mill, S.C., U.S.	A6	117
Fort Miller, N.Y., U.S.	B7	109
Fort Mitchell, Al., U.S.	C4	78
Fort Mitchell, Ky., U.S.	h13	94
Fort Mitchell, Va., U.S.	D4	123
Fort Mojave Indian Reservation, U.S.	C1	80
Fort Monmouth, mil., N.J., U.S.	C4	107
Fort Monroe, mil., Va., U.S.	h15	123
Fort Morgan, Al., U.S.	E1	78
Fort Morgan, Co., U.S.	A7	83
Fort Motte, S.C., U.S.	D6	117
Fort Myer, Va., U.S.	g12	123
Fort Myers, Fl., U.S.	F5	86
Fort Myers Beach, Fl., U.S.	F5	86
Fort Necessity, La., U.S.	B4	95
Fort Nelson, B.C.	m18	69
Fort Norman, N.W. Ter.	D7	66
Fort Ogden, Fl., U.S.	E5	86
Fort Oglethorpe, Ga., U.S.	B1	87
Fort Ord, mil., Ca., U.S.	D3	82
Fort Payne, Al., U.S.	A4	78
Fort Peck, Mt., U.S.	B10	103
Fort Peck Dam, Mt., U.S.	B10	103
Fort Peck Indian Reservation, Mt., U.S.	B11	103
Fort Peck Lake, res., Mt., U.S.	C9	103
Fort Pierce, Fl., U.S.	E6	86
Fort Pierce Inlet, b., Fl., U.S.	E6	86
Fort Pierre, S.D., U.S.	C5	118
Fort Plain, N.Y., U.S.	C6	109
Fort Polk, mil., La., U.S.	C2	95
Fort Portal, Ug.	A5	48
Fort Providence, N.W. Ter.	D9	66
Fort Qu'Appelle, Sask.	G4	75
Fort Randall Dam, S.D., U.S.	D7	118
Fort Ransom, N.D., U.S.	C8	111
Fort Recovery, Oh., U.S.	B1	112
Fort Reliance, N.W. Ter.	D11	66
Fort Resolution, N.W. Ter.	D10	66
Fort Rice, N.D., U.S.	C5	111
Fort Richardson, mil., Ak., U.S.	C10	79
Fort Riley, mil., Ks., U.S.	C7	93
Fort Ripley, Mn., U.S.	D4	100
Fort Ritchie, mil., Md., U.S.	A3	97
Fort Ritner, In., U.S.	G5	91
Fort Robinson, In., U.S.	B2	104
Fort Rock, Or., U.S.	D5	114
Fortrose, N.Z.	Q12	51
Fortrose, Scot., U.K.	C4	13
Fort Ross, N.W. Ter.	B14	66
Fort Rucker, mil., Al., U.S.	D4	78
Fort Saint James, B.C.	B5	69
Fort Saint John, B.C.	A7	69
Fort Sam Houston, mil., Tx., U.S.	k7	120
Fort Saskatchewan, Alta.	C4	68
Fort Scott, Ks., U.S.	E9	93
Fort Severn, Ont.	n18	73
Fort Shafter, mil., Hi., U.S.	g10	88
Fort Shaw, Mt., U.S.	C5	103
Fort Shawnee, Oh., U.S.	B1	112
Fort Sheridan, mil., Il., U.S.	h9	90
Fort-Shevchenko, Sov. Un.	E4	28
Fort Sibut, Cen. Afr. Rep.	D3	46
Fort Sill, mil., Ok., U.S.	C3	113
Fort Simpson, N.W. Ter.	D8	66
Fort Smith, Alta.	f8	68
Fort Smith, N.W. Ter.	D10	66
Fort Smith, Ar., U.S.	B1	81
Fort Stanton, N.M., U.S.	D4	108
Fort Steele, B.C.	E10	69
Fort Steele, Wy., U.S.	E6	127
Fort Stewart, mil., Ga., U.S.	D5	87
Fort Stockton, Tx., U.S.	D1	120
Fort Sumner, N.M., U.S.	C5	108
Fort Sumter National Monument, S.C., U.S.	k12	117
Fort Supply, Ok., U.S.	A2	113
Fort Supply Lake, res., Ok., U.S.	A2	113
Fort Thomas, Az., U.S.	D6	80
Fort Thomas, Ky., U.S.	h14	94
Fort Thompson, S.D., U.S.	C6	118
Fort Totten, N.D., U.S.	B7	111
Fort Totten Indian Reservation, N.D., U.S.	B7	111
Fort Towson, Ok., U.S.	C6	113
Fortuna, Ca., U.S.	B1	82
Fortuna, Mo., U.S.	C5	102
Fortuna Ledge (Marshall), Ak., U.S.	C7	79
Fortune, Newf.	E4	72
Fortune Bay, b., Newf.	E4	72
Fortune Harbour, Newf.	D4	72
Fort Union National Monument, N.M., U.S.	B5	108
Fort Valley, Ga., U.S.	D3	87
Fort Vermilion, Alta.	f7	68
Fortville, In., U.S.	E6	91
Fort Wainwright, mil., Ak., U.S.	C10	79
Fort Walton Beach, Fl., U.S.	u15	86
Fort Washakie, Wy., U.S.	C4	127
Fort Washington, Pa., U.S.	o21	115
Fort Washington Forest, Md., U.S.	C4	97
Fort Wayne, In., U.S.	B7	91
Fort Wellington, Guy.	A3	59
Fort White, Fl., U.S.	B4	86
Fort William, Scot., U.K.	B4	10
Fort Wingate, N.M., U.S.	B1	108
Fort Worth, Tx., U.S.	C4	120
Fort Wright, Ky., U.S.	h13	94
Fort Yates, N.D., U.S.	C5	111
Forty Fort, Pa., U.S.	D10	115
Fort Yukon, Ak., U.S.	B10	79
Fort Yuma Indian Reservation, Ca., U.S.	F6	82
Foss, Ok., U.S.	B2	113
Fossano, Italy	B1	23
Fosse, Nor.	p29	14
Fossil, Or., U.S.	B6	114
Fossil Butte National Monument, Wy., U.S.	E2	127
Fossil Lake, l., Or., U.S.	D6	114
Fossombrone, Italy	C4	23
Foss Reservoir, res., Ok., U.S.	B2	113
Fosston, Sask.	E4	75
Fosston, Mn., U.S.	C3	100
Foster, Ky., U.S.	B5	94
Foster, Mo., U.S.	C3	102
Foster, Ne., U.S.	B8	104
Foster, Or., U.S.	C4	114
Foster, R.I., U.S.	C2	116
Foster, Wi., U.S.	D2	126
Foster, co., N.D., U.S.	B6	111
Foster Brook, Pa., U.S.	C4	115
Foster City, Ca., U.S.	*h8	82
Foster City, Mi., U.S.	C3	99
Fosters, Al., U.S.	B2	78
Fosters Falls, Va., U.S.	D2	123
Fosters Pond, l., Ma., U.S.	f11	98
Foster Village, Hi., U.S.	g10	88
Fosterville, Tn., U.S.	B5	119
Fostoria, Al., U.S.	C3	78
Fostoria, Ia., U.S.	A2	92
Fostoria, Ks., U.S.	C7	93
Fostoria, Mi., U.S.	E7	99
Fostoria, Oh., U.S.	A2	112
Fougamou, Gabon	F2	46
Fougères, Fr.	C3	16
Fouke, Ar., U.S.	D2	81
Foula, i., Scot., U.K.	g9	10
Foulness Island, i., Eng., U.K.	C8	17
Foulwind, Cape, c., N.Z.	N13	51
Foumban, Cam.	D2	46
Foum el Hassane, Mor.	D6	94
Fount, Ky., U.S.	D6	94
Fountain, Co., U.S.	C6	83
Fountain, Fl., U.S.	B1	86
Fountain, Mi., U.S.	D4	99
Fountain, Mn., U.S.	G6	100
Fountain, N.C., U.S.	B5	110
Fountain, co., In., U.S.	D3	91
Fountain City, In., U.S.	E8	91
Fountain City, Wi., U.S.	D2	126
Fountain Creek, stm., Co., U.S.	C6	83
Fountain Green, Ut., U.S.	D4	121
Fountain Hill, Ar., U.S.	D4	81
Fountain Hill, Pa., U.S.	E11	115
Fountain Inn, S.C., U.S.	B3	117
Fountain Lake, Ar., U.S.	f8	81
Fountain Peak, mtn., Ca., U.S.	E6	82
Fountain Place, La., U.S.	C4	95
Fountain Run, Ky., U.S.	D4	94
Fountaintown, In., U.S.	E6	91
Fountain Valley, Ca., U.S.	*n13	82
Four Buttes, Mt., U.S.	B11	103
Fourchambault, Fr.	D5	16
Fourche, Ar., U.S.	*C3	81
Fourche Creek, stm., Ar., U.S.	k10	81
Fourche LaFave, stm., Ar., U.S.	C2	81
Fourche Maline, stm., Ok., U.S.	C6	113
Fourche Mountain, mtn., Ar., U.S.	C2	81
Fourchu, N.S.	D9	71
Four Corners, Ca., U.S.	E5	82
Four Corners, Or., U.S.	*C4	114
Four Corners, Wy., U.S.	B8	127
Four Lakes, Wa., U.S.	B8	124
Fourmies, Fr.	B6	16
Fourmile, Ky., U.S.	D6	94
Fourmile Creek, stm., Ia., U.S.	e8	92
Four Mountains, Islands of, is., Ak., U.S.	E6	79
Fournier, Ont.	B10	73
Four Oaks, N.C., U.S.	B4	110
Fouta Djallon, reg., Gui.	D2	45
Foveaux Strait, strt., N.Z.	Q11	51
Fowey, Eng., U.K.	D3	12
Fowler, Ca., U.S.	D4	82
Fowler, Co., U.S.	C6	83
Fowler, Il., U.S.	C2	90
Fowler, In., U.S.	C3	91
Fowler, Ks., U.S.	E3	93
Fowler, Mi., U.S.	E6	99
Fowlerton, In., U.S.	D6	91
Fowlerton, Tx., U.S.	E3	120
Fowlerville, Mi., U.S.	F6	99
Fowlkes, Tn., U.S.	B2	119
Fowlstown, Ga., U.S.	F2	87
Fox, Ar., U.S.	B3	81
Fox, Ok., U.S.	C4	113
Fox, Or., U.S.	C7	114
Fox, stm., Man.	B4	70
Fox, stm., U.S.	A6	102
Fox, stm., Wi., U.S.	D5	126
Foxboro, Ma., U.S.	B5	98
Foxboro, Wi., U.S.	*B1	126
Fox Chapel, Pa., U.S.	*h14	115
Fox Creek, Alta.	B2	68
Foxdale, I. of Man	F4	13
Foxe Basin, b., N.W. Ter.	C17	66
Foxe Channel, strt., N.W. Ter.	D16	66
Foxe Peninsula, pen., N.W. Ter.	C17	66
Foxford, Sask.	D3	75
Foxford, Ire.	D2	11
Fox Harbour, Newf.	E5	72
Fox Harbour, Newf.	B4	72
Foxholm, N.D., U.S.	A4	111
Fox Island, i., R.I., U.S.	E4	116
Fox Island, i., Wa., U.S.	f10	124
Fox Islands, is., Ak., U.S.	E6	79
Fox Lake, Il., U.S.	A5	90
Fox Lake, Wi., U.S.	E5	126
Fox Lake, l., Il., U.S.	h8	90
Fox Mountain, mtn., Yukon	D6	66
Fox Mountain, mtn., Nv., U.S.	B2	105
Foxpark, Wy., U.S.	E6	127
Fox Point, Wi., U.S.	E6	126
Fox River Grove, Il., U.S.	h8	90
Foxton, N.Z.	N15	51
Foxvale, Al., U.S.	B2	78
Fox Valley, Sask.	G1	75
Foxville, Il., U.S.	C4	122
Foxwarren, Man.	D1	70
Foxworth, Ms., U.S.	D4	101
Foyil, Ok., U.S.	A6	113
Foyle, stm., Eur.	C4	11
Foyle, Lough, b., Eur.	C3	10
Foynes, Ire.	D2	11
Foz do Cunene, Ang.	E1	48
Foz do Iguaçu, Braz.	D2	56
Foz do Jordão, Braz.	C2	58
Foz do Pauiní, Braz.	D2	56
Frackville, Pa., U.S.	E9	115
Fraga, Spain	B6	22
Fraile Muerto, Ur.	E2	56
Frametown, W.V., U.S.	C4	125
Framingham, Ma., U.S.	B5	98

Name	Map Ref.	Page
Framnes Mountains, mts., Ant.	C19	7
Franca, Braz.	C3	56
França, Braz.	D2	57
Française, Pointe, c., Fr. Gu.	A4	59
Francavilla Fontana, Italy	D6	23
France, ctry., Eur.	D5	16
Frances, Ky., U.S.	e9	94
Francés, Cabo, c., Cuba	D2	64
Francestown, N.H., U.S.	E3	106
Franceville, In., U.S.	C4	91
Franceville, Gabon	F2	46
Franche-Comté, hist. reg., Fr.	D6	16
Francis, Sask.	G4	75
Francis, Ok., U.S.	C5	113
Francis, Ut., U.S.	C4	121
Francis, W.V., U.S.	k10	125
Francis, Lake, l., N.H., U.S.	C3	106
Francis Case, Lake, res., S.D., U.S.	D6	118
Francisco, In., U.S.	H3	91
Francisco Sá, Braz.	B4	56
Francis Creek, Wi., U.S.	h10	126
Francistown, Bots.	B4	49
François, Newf.	E3	72
François Lake, l., B.C.	C5	69
Franconia, N.H., U.S.	B3	106
Franconia, Va., U.S.	*B5	123
Franconia Notch, N.H., U.S.	B3	106
Franconville, Fr.	g9	16
Francs Peak, mtn., Wy., U.S.	C3	127
Franeker, Neth.	A5	17
Frank, W.V., U.S.	C5	125
Frankel City, Tx., U.S.	C1	120
Frankenberg, E. Ger.	C8	19
Frankenberg [-Eder], W. Ger.	C4	18
Frankenmuth, Mi., U.S.	E7	99
Frankenthal, W. Ger.	D4	18
Frankewing, Tn., U.S.	B5	119
Frankfield, Jam.	E14	65
Frankford, Ont.	C7	73
Frankford, De., U.S.	F5	85
Frankford, Mo., U.S.	B6	102
Frankford, W.V., U.S.	D4	125
Frankford see Kilcormac, Ire.	D4	11
Frankfort, S. Afr.	C4	49
Frankfort, Il., U.S.	m9	90
Frankfort, In., U.S.	D4	91
Frankfort, Ks., U.S.	C7	93
Frankfort, Ky., U.S.	B5	94
Frankfort, Me., U.S.	D4	96
Frankfort, Mi., U.S.	D4	99
Frankfort, N.Y., U.S.	B5	109
Frankfort, Oh., U.S.	C2	112
Frankfort, S.D., U.S.	C7	118
Frankfurt [am Main], W. Ger.	C4	18
Frankfurt [an der Oder], E. Ger.	B7	18
Fränkische Saale, stm., W. Ger.	C5	19
Frank Lake, l., Alta.	D4	68
Franklin, Man.	D2	70
Franklin, Al., U.S.	D2	78
Franklin, Az., U.S.	E6	80
Franklin, Ar., U.S.	A4	81
Franklin, Ct., U.S.	C7	84
Franklin, Ga., U.S.	C1	87
Franklin, Id., U.S.	G7	89
Franklin, Il., U.S.	D3	90
Franklin, In., U.S.	F5	91
Franklin, Ia., U.S.	D6	92
Franklin, Ks., U.S.	E9	93
Franklin, Ky., U.S.	D3	94
Franklin, La., U.S.	E4	95
Franklin, Me., U.S.	D4	96
Franklin, Ma., U.S.	B5	98
Franklin, Mn., U.S.	F4	100
Franklin, Mo., U.S.	B5	102
Franklin, Ne., U.S.	D7	104
Franklin, N.H., U.S.	D3	106
Franklin, N.J., U.S.	A3	107
Franklin, N.Y., U.S.	C5	109
Franklin, N.C., U.S.	f9	110
Franklin, Oh., U.S.	C1	112
Franklin, Pa., U.S.	D2	115
Franklin, Tn., U.S.	B5	119
Franklin, Tx., U.S.	D4	120
Franklin, Va., U.S.	D6	123
Franklin, W.V., U.S.	C5	125
Franklin, Wi., U.S.	n11	126
Franklin, dept., N.W. Ter.	B15	66
Franklin, co., Al., U.S.	A2	78
Franklin, co., Ar., U.S.	B2	81
Franklin, co., Fl., U.S.	C2	86
Franklin, co., Ga., U.S.	B3	87
Franklin, co., Id., U.S.	G7	89
Franklin, co., Il., U.S.	E4	90
Franklin, co., In., U.S.	F7	91
Franklin, co., Ia., U.S.	B4	92
Franklin, co., Ks., U.S.	D8	93
Franklin, co., Ky., U.S.	B5	94
Franklin, co., La., U.S.	B4	95
Franklin, co., Me., U.S.	C2	96
Franklin, co., Ma., U.S.	A2	98
Franklin, co., Ms., U.S.	D3	101
Franklin, co., Mo., U.S.	C6	102
Franklin, co., Ne., U.S.	D7	104
Franklin, co., N.Y., U.S.	f10	109
Franklin, co., N.C., U.S.	A4	110
Franklin, co., Oh., U.S.	B2	112
Franklin, co., Pa., U.S.	G6	115
Franklin, co., Tn., U.S.	B5	119
Franklin, co., Tx., U.S.	C5	120
Franklin, co., Vt., U.S.	B2	122
Franklin, co., Va., U.S.	D3	123
Franklin, co., Wa., U.S.	C6	124
Franklin, Point, c., Ak., U.S.	A8	79
Franklin D. Roosevelt Lake, res., Wa., U.S.	B7	124
Franklin Falls Reservoir, res., N.H., U.S.	C3	106
Franklin Grove, Il., U.S.	B4	90
Franklin Island, i., Ont.	B4	73
Franklin Lake, l., N.W. Ter.	C13	66
Franklin Lake, l., Nv., U.S.	C6	105
Franklin Lakes, N.J., U.S.	*B4	107
Franklin Mine, Mi., U.S.	A2	99
Franklin Mountains, mts., N.W. Ter.	C8	66
Franklin Park, Il., U.S.	k9	90
Franklin Park, Pa., U.S.	h13	115
Franklin Square, N.Y., U.S.	*E7	109
Franklin Strait, strt., N.W. Ter.	B13	66
Franklinton, La., U.S.	D5	95
Franklinton, N.C., U.S.	A4	110
Franklinville, N.J., U.S.	D2	107
Franklinville, N.Y., U.S.	C2	109
Frankston, Austl.	*G8	50
Frankston, Tx., U.S.	C5	120
Franksville, Wi., U.S.	n12	126
Frankton, In., U.S.	D6	91
Franktown, Co., U.S.	B6	83
Frankville, N.S.	D8	71
Frankville, Al., U.S.	D1	78
Frannie, Wy., U.S.	B4	127
Franz Josef Land, is., Sov. Un.	B8	29
Frascati, Italy	D4	23
Fraser, Co., U.S.	B5	83
Fraser, Ia., U.S.	B4	92
Fraser, Mi., U.S.	*o16	99
Fraser, r., Austl.	E9	50
Fraser, stm., B.C.	E7	69
Fraser, stm., Newf.	g9	72
Fraser, Mount, mtn., Can.	C8	69
Fraserburg, S. Afr.	D3	49
Fraserburgh, Scot., U.K.	B6	10
Fraserdale, Ont.	o19	73
Fraser Lake, B.C.	B5	69
Fraser Lake, l., B.C.	B5	69
Fraser Plateau, plat., B.C.	D6	69
Fraserwood, Man.	D3	70
Frasne, Fr.	C2	20
Frauenfeld, Switz.	E4	18
Fray Bentos, Ur.	E1	56
Fray Marcos, Ur.	E1	56
Frazee, Mn., U.S.	D3	100
Frazer, Mt., U.S.	B10	103
Frazeysburg, Oh., U.S.	B3	112
Frazier Park, Ca., U.S.	E4	82
Freda, Mi., U.S.	A2	99
Frederic, Mi., U.S.	D6	99
Frederic, Wi., U.S.	C1	126
Frederica, De., U.S.	D4	85
Fredericia, Den.	J3	14
Frederick, Co., U.S.	A6	83
Frederick, Md., U.S.	B3	97
Frederick, Ok., U.S.	C3	113
Frederick, S.D., U.S.	B7	118
Frederick, co., Md., U.S.	B3	97
Frederick, co., Va., U.S.	A4	123
Frederick Hall, Va., U.S.	C5	123
Fredericksburg, In., U.S.	H5	91
Fredericksburg, Ia., U.S.	B5	92
Fredericksburg, Oh., U.S.	B4	112
Fredericksburg, Pa., U.S.	F9	115
Fredericksburg, Tx., U.S.	D3	120
Fredericksburg, Va., U.S.	B5	123
Frederick Sound, strt., Ak., U.S.	m23	79
Fredericktown, Mo., U.S.	D7	102
Fredericktown, Oh., U.S.	B3	112
Fredericktown, Pa., U.S.	F1	115
Fredericton, N.B.	D3	71
Fredericton Junction, N.B.	D3	71
Frederika, Ia., U.S.	B5	92
Frederiksberg, Den.	*J5	14
Frederiksberg, co., Den.	C6	15
Frederikshavn, Den.	I4	14
Frederikssted, Den.	C6	15
Frederiksted, V.I.U.S.	H12	64
Frederiksværk, Den.	C6	15
Frederik Willem IV Vallen, wtfl., Sur.	B3	59
Fredonia, Al., U.S.	C4	78
Fredonia, Az., U.S.	A3	80
Fredonia, In., U.S.	H5	91
Fredonia, Ks., U.S.	E8	93
Fredonia, Ky., U.S.	C1	94
Fredonia, N.Y., U.S.	C1	109
Fredonia, N.D., U.S.	C6	111
Fredonia, Tx., U.S.	D3	120
Fredonia, Wi., U.S.	E6	126
Fredrikstad, Nor.	H4	14
Freeborn, Mn., U.S.	G5	100
Freeborn, co., Mn., U.S.	G5	100
Freeburg, Il., U.S.	E4	90
Freeburg, Mo., U.S.	C6	102
Freeburg, Pa., U.S.	E8	115
Freedom, Ca., U.S.	*D3	82
Freedom, In., U.S.	F4	91
Freedom, Me., U.S.	D3	96
Freedom, N.H., U.S.	C4	106
Freedom, Ok., U.S.	A2	113
Freedom, Pa., U.S.	E1	115
Freedom, Wy., U.S.	D2	127
Freehold, N.J., U.S.	C4	107
Freeland, Mi., U.S.	E6	99
Freeland, N.C., U.S.	C4	110
Freeland, Pa., U.S.	D10	115
Freeland Park, In., U.S.	C3	91
Freelandville, In., U.S.	G3	91
Freel Peak, mtn., Ca., U.S.	C4	82
Freels, Cape, c., Newf.	E5	72
Freels, Cape, c., Newf.	D5	72
Freeman, Mo., U.S.	C3	102
Freeman, S.D., U.S.	D8	118
Freeman, Wa., U.S.	g14	124
Freeman, r., Alta.	B3	68
Freeman, Lake, l., In., U.S.	C4	91
Freemansburg, Pa., U.S.	E11	115
Freemanville, Al., U.S.	D2	78
Freemason Islands, is., La., U.S.	E7	95
Freemount, Ire.	E3	11
Freeport, Bah.	*A4	64
Freeport, N.S.	E3	71
Freeport, Fl., U.S.	u15	86
Freeport, Il., U.S.	A4	90
Freeport, Ia., U.S.	A6	92
Freeport, Ks., U.S.	E6	93
Freeport, Me., U.S.	E2	96
Freeport, Mi., U.S.	F5	99
Freeport, N.Y., U.S.	*E7	109
Freeport, Oh., U.S.	B4	112
Freeport, Pa., U.S.	E2	115
Freeport, Tx., U.S.	E5	120
Freer, Tx., U.S.	F3	120
Free Soil, Mi., U.S.	D4	99
Freestone, co., Tx., U.S.	D4	120
Freetown, P.E.I.	C6	71
Freetown, In., U.S.	G5	91
Freetown, S.L.	G3	44
Free Union, Va., U.S.	B4	123
Freeville, N.Y., U.S.	C4	109
Freezeout Mountains, mts., Wy., U.S.	D6	127
Fregenal de la Sierra, Spain	C2	22
Fregene, Italy	h8	23
Freiberg, E. Ger.	C6	18
Freiberger Mulde, stm., Eur.	B8	19
Freiburg [im Breisgau], W. Ger.	D3	18
Freienbach, Switz.	B6	21
Freirina, Chile	E1	55
Freising, W. Ger.	D5	18
Freistadt, Aus.	D7	18
Freital, E. Ger.	B8	19
Fréjus, Fr.	F7	16
Fréjus Tunnel, Eur.	D2	20
Frelighsburg, Que.	D5	74
Fremantle, Austl.	F2	50
Fremont, Ca., U.S.	D2	82
Fremont, In., U.S.	A8	91
Fremont, Ia., U.S.	C5	92
Fremont, Mi., U.S.	E5	99
Fremont, Mo., U.S.	E6	102
Fremont, Ne., U.S.	C9	104
Fremont, N.H., U.S.	E4	106
Fremont, N.C., U.S.	B5	110
Fremont, Oh., U.S.	A2	112
Fremont, Ut., U.S.	E4	121
Fremont, Wi., U.S.	D5	126
Fremont, co., Co., U.S.	C5	83
Fremont, co., Id., U.S.	E7	89
Fremont, co., Ia., U.S.	D2	92
Fremont, co., Wy., U.S.	C4	127
Fremont, stm., Ut., U.S.	E4	121
Fremont Island, i., Ut., U.S.	B3	121
Fremont Lake, l., Wy., U.S.	D3	127
Fremont Peak, mtn., Wy., U.S.	C3	127
French, stm., Ont.	A4	73
French Broad, stm., U.S.	D10	119
Frenchburg, Ky., U.S.	C6	94
French Camp, Ms., U.S.	B4	101
French Creek, W.V., U.S.	C4	125
French Creek, stm., Man.	A5	70
French Creek, stm., U.S.	C2	115
French Frigate Shoals, rf., Hi., U.S.	m14	88
Frenchglen, Or., U.S.	E8	114
French Guiana, dep., S.A.	B4	59
French Gulch, Ca., U.S.	B2	82
French Island, Wi., U.S.	*E2	126
French Lick, In., U.S.	G4	91
Frenchman, Nv., U.S.	D3	105
Frenchman, stm., N.A.	A8	103
Frenchman Bay, b., Me., U.S.	D4	96
Frenchman Butte, Sask.	D1	75
Frenchman Creek, stm., U.S.	D4	104
Frenchman Hills, hills, Wa., U.S.	C6	124
Frenchman Knob, mtn., Ky., U.S.	C4	94
Frenchman Lake, l., Nv., U.S.	G6	105
Frenchman's Cove, Newf.	D2	72
Frenchman's Cove, Newf.	E4	72
Frenchmans Island, Newf.	B4	72
Frenchpark, Ire.	D3	11
French Polynesia, dep., Oc.	H13	6
French River, Mn., U.S.	D7	100
French Settlement, La., U.S.	D5	95
French Southern and Antarctic Territories, dep., Afr.	*J1	2
Frenchton, W.V., U.S.	C4	125
Frenchtown, Mt., U.S.	C2	103
Frenchtown, N.J., U.S.	B2	107
French Village, N.S.	E6	71
Frenchville, Me., U.S.	A4	96
Frenda, Alg.	B5	44
Fresco, I.C.	E3	45
Fresco, stm., Braz.	E4	59
Freshfield, Mount, mtn., Can.	D2	68
Freshford, Ire.	E4	11
Freshwater, Eng., U.K.	D6	12
Fresnillo [de González Echeverría], Mex.	C4	63
Fresno, Ca., U.S.	D4	82
Fresno, Oh., U.S.	B4	112
Fresno, co., Ca., U.S.	D4	82
Fresno Reservoir, res., Mt., U.S.	B6	103
Freudenstadt, W. Ger.	D4	18
Frévent, Fr.	B5	16
Frewsburg, N.Y., U.S.	C1	109
Freyburg, E. Ger.	B6	19
Freycinet Peninsula, pen., Austl.	o15	50
Freyenstein, E. Ger.	E6	15
Freyming-Merlebach, Fr.	E6	15
Freyung, W. Ger.	E8	19
Fria, Gui.	D2	45
Fria, Cape, c., Nmb.	A1	49
Friant, Ca., U.S.	D4	82
Friars Point, Ms., U.S.	A3	101
Frías, Arg.	E2	55
Fribourg, Switz.	E3	18
Fribourg, state, Switz.	C3	20
Fridley, Mn., U.S.	m12	100
Friday Harbor, Wa., U.S.	A2	124
Fridtjof Nansen, Mount, mtn., Ant.	A32	7
Friedberg, W. Ger.	C4	18
Friedens, Pa., U.S.	F3	115
Friedland, E. Ger.	B6	18
Friedrichroda, E. Ger.	C5	19
Friedrichshafen, W. Ger.	E4	18
Friedrichskoog, W. Ger.	D2	15
Friedrichstadt, W. Ger.	D3	15
Friedrichsthal, W. Ger.	D2	19
Friedrichsthal, W. Ger.	D2	19
Friend, Ks., U.S.	D3	93
Friend, Ne., U.S.	D8	104
Friendship, In., U.S.	G7	91
Friendship, Me., U.S.	E3	96
Friendship, N.Y., U.S.	C2	109
Friendship, Oh., U.S.	D2	112
Friendship, Tn., U.S.	B2	119
Friendship, Wi., U.S.	E4	126
Friendsville, Md., U.S.	k12	97
Friendsville, Tn., U.S.	D9	91
Friendswood, Tx., U.S.	*r14	120
Frierson, La., U.S.	B2	95
Fries, Va., U.S.	D2	123
Friesack, E. Ger.	F6	15
Friesland, Wi., U.S.	E4	126
Friesland, prov., Neth.	A5	17
Fries Mills, N.J., U.S.	D2	107
Friesoythe, W. Ger.	A7	17
Frigate Point, c., Mid. Is.	K3	52
Frio, co., Tx., U.S.	E3	120
Frio, stm., Tx., U.S.	E3	120
Frio Draw, val., U.S.	C6	108
Friona, Tx., U.S.	A5	120
Fripps Island, i., S.C., U.S.	G7	117
Frisco, Co., U.S.	B4	83
Frisco, N.C., U.S.	B7	110
Frisco City, Al., U.S.	D2	78
Frisco Peak, mtn., Ut., U.S.	E2	121
Frissell, Mount, mtn., U.S.	A3	84
Fristoe, Mo., U.S.	C4	102
Fritch, Tx., U.S.	B2	120
Fritsla, Swe.	A6	15
Fritzlar, W. Ger.	C4	18
Friuli-Venezia Giulia, prov., Italy	C8	20
Frobisher, Sask.	H4	75
Frobisher Bay, b., N.W. Ter.	D19	66
Frobisher Lake, l., Sask.	m7	75
Frog Lake, l., Alta.	C5	68
Frogmore, La., U.S.	C4	95
Frogmore, S.C., U.S.	G6	117
Frohna, Mo., U.S.	D8	102
Frolovo, Sov. Un.	G14	27
Fromberg, Mt., U.S.	E8	103
Frome, Jam.	E12	65
Frome, Eng., U.K.	C5	12
Frome, stm., Eng., U.K.	D5	12
Frome, Lake, l., Austl.	F6	50
Frontenac, Ks., U.S.	E9	93
Frontenac, Mn., U.S.	F6	100
Frontenac, co., Ont.	C8	73
Frontenac, co., Que.	D7	74
Frontera, Mex.	D6	63
Frontier, Sask.	H1	75
Frontier, Wy., U.S.	E2	127
Frontier, co., Ne., U.S.	D5	104
Frontignan, Fr.	F5	16
Frontino, Páramo, mtn., Col.	B2	60
Front Range, mts., Co., U.S.	A5	83
Front Royal, Va., U.S.	B4	123
Frosinone, Italy	D4	23
Frost, Mn., U.S.	G5	100
Frost, Tx., U.S.	C4	120
Frostburg, Md., U.S.	k13	97
Frostproof, Fl., U.S.	E5	86
Froude, Sask.	H4	75
Frøya, i., Nor.	F3	14
Fruges, Fr.	D2	17
Fruita, Co., U.S.	B2	83
Fruitdale, Al., U.S.	D1	78
Fruitdale, S.D., U.S.	C2	118
Fruit Heights, Ut., U.S.	B4	121
Fruithurst, Al., U.S.	B4	78
Fruitland, Id., U.S.	F2	89
Fruitland, Ia., U.S.	C6	92
Fruitland, Md., U.S.	D6	97
Fruitland, Mo., U.S.	D8	102
Fruitland, N.M., U.S.	A1	108
Fruitland, Tn., U.S.	B3	119
Fruitland, Ut., U.S.	C5	121
Fruitland Park, Fl., U.S.	D5	86
Fruitland Park, Ms., U.S.	E4	101
Fruitport, Mi., U.S.	E4	99
Fruitvale, B.C.	E9	69
Fruitvale, Co., U.S.	B2	83
Fruitvale, Id., U.S.	E2	89
Fruitvale, Wa., U.S.	C5	124
Fruitville, Fl., U.S.	E4	86
Frunze, Sov. Un.	H10	27
Frutigen, Switz.	C4	21
Fryazevo, Sov. Un.	n18	27
Frye, Me., U.S.	D2	96
Fryeburg, Me., U.S.	D2	96
Frys, Sask.	H5	75
Fu'an, China	K8	32
Fuchou see Fuzhou, China	F8	31
Fuchū, Japan	*I9	33
Fuchū, Japan	K9	32
Fuencarral, Spain	p17	22
Fuente-Álamo [de Murcia], Spain	D5	22
Fuente de Cantos, Spain	C2	22
Fuente el Saz, Spain	o17	22
Fuente Obejuna, Spain	C3	22
Fuentesaúco, Spain	B3	22
Fuentes [de Andalucía], Spain	D3	22
Fuerte, stm., Mex.	B3	63
Fuerte Olimpo, Par.	D4	55
Fuerteventura, i., Spain	m14	22
Fuglebjerg, Den.	C5	15
Fugou, China	G6	32
Fuhai, China	C3	30
Fuji, Japan	n17	33
Fuji, Mount, vol., Japan	I9	33
Fujian, prov., China	F8	31
Fujimi, Japan	o17	33
Fujimi, Japan	n17	33
Fujin, China	B11	31
Fujinomiya, Japan	n17	33
Fujisawa, Japan	*I9	33
Fuji-yoshida, Japan	n17	33
Fukagawa, Japan	E10	33
Fūkah, Egypt	G6	40
Fukien see Fujian, prov., China	F8	31
Fukuchiyama, Japan	I7	33
Fukue Island, i., Japan	J4	33
Fukui, Japan	I8	33
Fukui, co., Japan	D12	31
Fukuoka, Japan	E11	31
Fukuoka, Japan	F10	33
Fukushima, Japan	I8	33
Fukushima, Japan	H10	33
Fukuyama, Japan	I6	33
Fūlādī, Kūh-e, mtn., Afg.	D13	39
Fulaga, i., Fiji	I16	52
Fulaga Passage, strt., Fiji	I16	52
Fulda, W. Ger.	C4	18
Fulda, In., U.S.	H4	91
Fulda, Mn., U.S.	G3	100
Fulda, stm., W. Ger.	B4	19
Fuling, China	J2	32
Fullarton, Ont.	D3	73
Fullerton, Ca., U.S.	n13	82
Fullerton, La., U.S.	D3	95
Fullerton, Ne., U.S.	C8	104
Fullerton, N.D., U.S.	C7	111
Fulshear, Tx., U.S.	r14	120
Fulton, Al., U.S.	D2	78
Fulton, Ar., U.S.	D1	81
Fulton, Il., U.S.	B3	90
Fulton, In., U.S.	C5	91
Fulton, Ks., U.S.	D9	93
Fulton, Ky., U.S.	f9	94
Fulton, Md., U.S.	B4	97
Fulton, Mi., U.S.	F5	99
Fulton, Ms., U.S.	A5	101
Fulton, Mo., U.S.	C6	102
Fulton, N.Y., U.S.	B4	109
Fulton, Oh., U.S.	B3	112
Fulton, S.D., U.S.	D8	118
Fulton, Tn., U.S.	A4	119
Fulton, Tx., U.S.	E4	120
Fulton, co., Ar., U.S.	A4	81
Fulton, co., Ga., U.S.	C2	87
Fulton, co., Il., U.S.	C3	90
Fulton, co., In., U.S.	B5	91
Fulton, co., Ky., U.S.	f9	94
Fulton, co., N.Y., U.S.	B6	109
Fulton, co., Oh., U.S.	A1	112
Fulton, co., Pa., U.S.	G5	115
Fultondale, Al., U.S.	f7	78
Fultonham, N.Y., U.S.	C6	109
Fultonville, N.Y., U.S.	C6	109
Fumay, Fr.	C6	16
Fumel, Fr.	D4	16
Funabashi, Japan	n19	33
Funafuti, Tuvalu	G10	6
Funchal, Port.	h12	22
Fundación, Col.	A3	60
Fundão, Braz.	B4	56
Fundão, Port.	B2	22
Fundy, Bay of, b., Can.	D4	71
Fundy National Park, N.B.	D4	71
Funhalouro, Moz.	B5	49
Funing, China	G6	31
Funing, China	H8	32
Funing Bay, b., China	K9	32
Funk, Ne., U.S.	D6	104
Funk Island, i., Newf.	D5	72
Funkley, Mn., U.S.	C4	100
Funkstown, Md., U.S.	A2	97
Funtua, Nig.	D6	45
Fuping, China	E2	32
Fuping, China	E6	32
Fuqing, China	F8	31
Fuquay-Varina, N.C., U.S.	B4	110
Fur, i., Den.	B3	15
Furancungo, Moz.	D5	48
Furano, Japan	E11	33
Fürg, Iran	C5	38
Furka Pass, Switz.	C5	21
Furley, Ks., U.S.	g12	93
Furman, Al., U.S.	C3	78
Furman, S.C., U.S.	F5	117
Furmanov, Sov. Un.	C13	27
Furmanovka, Sov. Un.	B2	54
Furnace Brook, stm., Vt., U.S.	D3	122
Furnas, co., Ne., U.S.	D6	104
Furnas, Represa de, res., Braz.	F5	57
Furneaux Group, is., Austl.	o15	50
Furness, Sask.	D1	75
Furqlus, Syria	E11	40
Fürstenau, W. Ger.	B7	17
Fürstenfeld, Aus.	E8	18
Fürstenfeldbruck, W. Ger.	A7	20
Fürstenwalde [Spree], E. Ger.	B7	18
Fürth, W. Ger.	D5	18
Fürth im Wald, W. Ger.	D7	19
Furukawa, Japan	H8	33
Furu Mountain, hill, Japan	P17	52
Fusagasugá, Col.	C2	60
Fuschl [am See], Aus.	B9	20
Fushun, China	C9	31
Fusilier, Sask.	F1	75
Fusong, China	E3	33
Füssen, W. Ger.	E5	18
Fusui, China	A7	35
Futatsune, rock, Japan	P17	52
Future City, Il., U.S.	F4	90
Fuwah, Eg.	C2	41
Fuxian, China	F3	32
Fuxian Hu, l., China	G5	31
Fuxin, China	C10	31
Fuyang, China	E8	31
Fuyang, China	E8	31
Fuyu, China	C2	33
Fuyu, China	B9	31
Fuyuan, China	B7	31
Fuzhou (Fuchou), China	F8	31
Fuzhou (Fuchou), China	J7	32
Fyffe, Al., U.S.	A4	78
Fyn, co., Den.	C4	15
Fyn, i., Den.	J4	14
Fyne, Loch, b., Scot., U.K.	B4	10

G

Name	Map Ref.	Page
Gaalkacyo, Som.	D6	47
Gaastra, Mi., U.S.	B2	99
Gabarus, N.S.	D9	71
Gabbs, Nv., U.S.	E4	105
Gabela, Ang.	D1	48
Gabès, Tun.	C7	44
Gabès, Golfe de, b., Tun.	C7	44
Gablenberg, Den.	C5	15
Gabon, ctry., Afr.	F2	46
Gaborone, Bots.	B4	49
Gabriel, Mount, hill, Ire.	F2	11
Gabriels, N.Y., U.S.	f10	109
Gabriola, B.C.	f12	69
Gabrovo, Bul.	D7	24
Gachsārān, Iran	F5	39
Gackle, N.D., U.S.	C6	111
Gacko, Yugo.	D4	24
Gadag, India	E6	36
Gadmen, Switz.	C5	21
Gadsby, Alta.	C4	68
Gadsden, Al., U.S.	A3	78
Gadsden, Az., U.S.	E1	80
Gadsden, S.C., U.S.	D6	117
Gadsden, co., Fl., U.S.	B2	86
Gadyach, Sov. Un.	F10	27
Gãeşti, Rom.	D7	24
Gaeta, Italy	D7	23
Gaeta, Gulf of, b., Italy	D4	23
Gaffney, S.C., U.S.	A4	117
Gafour, Tun.	B6	44
Gafsa, Tun.	C6	44
Gagan Island, i., Marsh Is.	S17	52
Gagarin, Sov. Un.	D10	27
Gage, Ok., U.S.	A2	113
Gage, co., Ne., U.S.	D9	104
Gage, Cape, c., P.E.I.	C5	71
Gagetown, N.B.	D3	71
Gagetown, Mi., U.S.	E7	99
Gaggenau, W. Ger.	E3	19
Gagliano del Capo, Italy	E7	23
Gagnoa, I.C.	E3	45
Gagnon, Que.	h13	74
Gagny, Fr.	g11	16
Gahanna, Oh., U.S.	k11	112
Gaibandha, Bngl.	E12	37
Gaïl, stm., Aus.	C9	20
Gail, Tx., U.S.	C2	120
Gaildorf, W. Ger.	E4	18
Gaillac, Fr.	E4	16
Gaillard, Lake, l., Ct., U.S.	D5	84
Gaillon, Fr.	C4	16
Gaines, Mi., U.S.	F7	99
Gaines, Pa., U.S.	C6	115
Gaines, co., Tx., U.S.	C1	120
Gainesboro, Tn., U.S.	C8	119
Gaines Creek, stm., Ok., U.S.	C6	113
Gainesville, Al., U.S.	C1	78
Gainesville, Fl., U.S.	C4	86
Gainesville, Ga., U.S.	B3	87
Gainesville, Mo., U.S.	E5	102
Gainesville, N.Y., U.S.	C2	109
Gainesville, Tx., U.S.	C4	120
Gainesville, Va., U.S.	g11	123
Gainsborough, Eng., U.K.	D7	13
Gainsborough, Sask.	H5	75
Gairdner, Lake, l., Austl.	F6	50
Gairloch, Scot., U.K.	B4	10
Gairloch, Loch, b., Scot., U.K.	C3	10
Gaithersburg, Md., U.S.	B3	97
Gaixian, China	C10	31
Gakona, Ak., U.S.	C10	79
Galahad, Alta.	C5	68
Galapagar, Spain	o16	22
Galápagos, ter., Ec.	g5	58
Galápagos Islands see Colón, Archipiélago de, is., Ec.	g5	58
Galashiels, Scot., U.K.	C5	10
Galata, Mt., U.S.	B5	103
Galați (Galacz), Rom.	C9	24
Galatia, Il., U.S.	F5	90
Galatia, Ks., U.S.	D5	93
Galatina, Italy	D7	23
Galátison, Grc.	*C4	25
Galawinku, Austl.	B6	50
Galax, Va., U.S.	D2	123
Galaxídhion, Grc.	C4	25
Galchutt, N.D., U.S.	C9	111
Gáldar, Spain	m14	22
Galeana, Mex.	A3	63
Galen, Tn., U.S.	C8	119
Galena, Ak., U.S.	C8	79
Galena, Il., U.S.	A3	90
Galena, Ks., U.S.	E9	93
Galena, Md., U.S.	B6	97
Galena, Mo., U.S.	E4	102
Galena, Oh., U.S.	B3	112
Galena Park, Tx., U.S.	r14	120
Galeota Point, c., Trin.	K14	64
Galera, Punta, c., Chile	B2	54
Galera, Punta, c., Ec.	A1	58
Galera Point, c., Trin.	K14	64
Galesburg, Il., U.S.	C3	90
Galesburg, Ks., U.S.	E8	93
Galesburg, Mi., U.S.	F5	99
Galesburg, N.D., U.S.	B8	111
Gales Creek, Or., U.S.	B3	114
Gales Ferry, Ct., U.S.	D7	84
Galesville, Md., U.S.	C4	97
Galesville, Wi., U.S.	D2	126
Galeton, Co., U.S.	A6	83
Galeton, Pa., U.S.	C6	115
Galetta, Ont.	B8	73
Galeville, N.Y., U.S.	*B4	109
Galgaduud, prov., Som.	D6	47
Galiano Island, i., B.C.	E6	69
Galich, Sov. Un.	C9	31
Galicia, hist. reg., Eur.	D6	26
Galicia, hist. reg., Spain	A1	22
Galien, Mi., U.S.	G4	99
Galilee, R.I., U.S.	F3	116
Galilee, hist. reg., Isr.	B7	41
Galilee, Lake, l., Austl.	D8	50
Galilee, Sea of see Kinneret, Yam, l., Isr.	B7	41
Galina Point, c., Jam.	E15	65
Galion, Oh., U.S.	B3	112
Galisteo Creek, stm., N.M., U.S.	k8	108
Galite Channel, strt., Tun.	F2	23
Galiuro Mountains, mts., Az., U.S.	E5	80
Galivants Ferry, S.C., U.S.	C9	117
Gallan Head, c., Scot., U.K.	B1	13
Gallant, Al., U.S.	B3	78
Gallarate, Italy	A4	23
Gällåryd, Swe.	A8	15
Gallatin, Mo., U.S.	B4	102
Gallatin, Tn., U.S.	A5	119
Gallatin, co., Il., U.S.	F5	90
Gallatin, co., Ky., U.S.	B5	94
Gallatin, co., Mt., U.S.	E5	103
Gallatin, stm., Mt., U.S.	E5	103
Gallatin Gateway, Mt., U.S.	E5	103
Gallatin Range, mts., Mt., U.S.	E5	103
Gallaway, Tn., U.S.	B2	119
Galle, Sri L.	G7	36
Gállego, stm., Spain	A5	22
Gallegos, stm., Arg.	E2	54
Galley Head, c., Ire.	F3	11
Gallia, co., Oh., U.S.	D3	112
Galliano, La., U.S.	E5	95
Galliate, Italy	D4	23
Gallican nel Lazio, Italy	h9	23
Gallina, N.M., U.S.	A3	108
Gallinas, Punta, c., Col.	A3	60
Gallinas Mountains, mts., N.M., U.S.	C2	108
Gallion, Al., U.S.	C2	78
Gallipoli, Italy	D7	23
Gallipoli see Gelibolu, Tur.	B6	40
Gallipoli Peninsula, pen., Tur.	B6	40
Gallipolis, Oh., U.S.	D3	112
Gallipolis Ferry, W.V., U.S.	C2	125
Gallitzin, Pa., U.S.	F4	115
Gällivare, Swe.	C14	14
Gallneukirchen, Aus.	E9	19
Gallo, stm., Spain	B4	22
Gallo Mountains, mts., N.M., U.S.	C1	108
Galloo Island, i., N.Y., U.S.	B4	109
Galloway, Oh., U.S.	m10	112
Galloway, W.V., U.S.	B4	125
Galloway, Mull of, c., Scot., U.K.	F4	13
Gällstad, Swe.	A7	15
Gallup, N.M., U.S.	B1	108
Galoa Bay, b., Fiji	H15	52
Galoa Harbour, b., Fiji	I15	52
Galt, Ca., U.S.	C3	82
Galt, Ia., U.S.	A4	92
Galten, b., Swe.	t34	14
Galtür, Aus.	C6	20
Galtymore Mountain, mtn., Ire.	E3	11
Galva, Il., U.S.	B3	90
Galva, Ks., U.S.	D6	93
Galveston, In., U.S.	C5	91
Galveston, Tx., U.S.	E5	120
Galveston, co., Tx., U.S.	E5	120
Galveston Bay, b., Tx., U.S.	E5	120
Galveston Island, i., Tx., U.S.	E5	120
Gálvez, Arg.	A4	54
Galway, Ire.	D2	11
Galway, co., Ire.	D2	11
Galway Bay, b., Ire.	D2	11
Gamaches, Fr.	E9	12
Gamagōri, Japan	n17	33
Gambaga, Ghana	F5	45
Gambela, Eth.	D3	43
Gambell, Ak., U.S.	C5	79
Gambia, ctry., Afr.	D1	45
Gambia, stm., Afr.	D2	45
Gambier, Bah.	m17	64
Gambier, Oh., U.S.	B3	112
Gambo, Newf.	D4	72
Gamboa, Pan.	k11	62
Gamboma, Congo	B2	48

Name	Map Ref.	Page
Gamboula, Cen. Afr. Rep.	E3	46
Gambrills, Md., U.S.	B4	97
Gameleira, Braz.	C3	57
Gamerco, N.M., U.S.	B1	108
Gammertingen, W. Ger.	A5	20
Gammon, stm., Can.	D4	70
Gamo Gofa, prov., Eth.	D4	47
Gamph, Slieve, mts., Ire.	C3	11
Ganado, Az., U.S.	B6	80
Ganado, Tx., U.S.	E4	120
Gananoque, Ont.	C8	73
Ganchong, China	C8	35
Ganda, Ang.	D1	48
Gandajika, Zaire	C3	48
Gandak, stm., Asia	D10	37
Gandeeville, W.V., U.S.	C3	125
Gander, Newf.	D4	72
Gander, stm., Newf.	D4	72
Gander Bay, Newf.	D4	72
Gander Lake, l., Newf.	D4	72
Gāndhinagar, India	D5	36
Gandhi Reservoir, res., India	E5	37
Gandia, Spain	C5	22
Gandy, Ne., U.S.	C5	104
Gangānagar, India	C5	36
Gangāpur, India	D6	37
Gangaw, Burma	D9	37
Gangdise Mountains, mts., China	B9	37
Ganges, B.C.	g12	69
Ganges, Fr.	F5	16
Ganges, Oh., U.S.	B3	112
Ganges, stm., Asia	D8	36
Ganges, Mouths of the, mth., Asia	D8	36
Gang Mills, N.Y., U.S.	C3	109
Gangtok, India	C8	36
Gangu, China	E6	31
Gani, Indon.	F7	34
Gan Jiang, stm., China	K6	32
Gannan, China	C1	33
Gannat, Fr.	D5	16
Gannet Islands, is., Newf.	B3	72
Gannett Peak, mtn., Wy., U.S.	C3	127
Gannon, Md., U.S.	k12	97
Gannvalley, S.D., U.S.	C7	118
Gano, Oh., U.S.	n13	112
Gans, Ok., U.S.	B7	113
Gansevoort, N.Y., U.S.	B7	109
Gansu, prov., China	D5	31
Ganta, Lib.	E3	45
Gantt, Al., U.S.	D3	78
Gantt, S.C., U.S.	B3	117
Gantt Lake, res., Al., U.S.	D3	78
Gantts Quarry, Al., U.S.	B3	78
Ganyu, China	E8	31
Ganzhou, China	F7	31
Gao, Mali	C5	45
Gao'an, China	J6	32
Gaoil, Sliabh, mtn., Scot., U.K.	E3	13
Gaoua, Burkina	D4	45
Gaoual, Gui.	D2	45
Gaoyou, China	H8	32
Gaoyou Lake, l., China	H8	32
Gap, Fr.	E7	16
Gap, Pa., U.S.	G9	115
Gapan, Phil.	o13	34
Gapland, Md., U.S.	B2	97
Gap Mills, W.V., U.S.	D4	125
Gar, China	B7	36
Gara, Lough, l., Ire.	D2	10
Garacad, Som.	D6	47
Garachiné, Pan.	F8	62
Garachiné, Punta, c., Pan.	F8	62
Garanhuns, Braz.	C3	57
Garapan, N. Mar. Is.	D7	52
Garapan, Lagunan, b., N. Mar. Is.	D7	52
Garau, Canal de, Mex.	h9	63
Garbahaarrey, Som.	E5	47
Garber, Ia., U.S.	B6	92
Garber, Ok., U.S.	A4	113
Garberville, Ca., U.S.	B2	82
Garbsen, W. Ger.	*B4	18
Garça, Braz.	C3	56
Garching [an der Alz], W. Ger.	A8	20
Garcia, Co., U.S.	D5	83
Garciasville, Tx., U.S.	F3	120
Gard, stm., Fr.	E6	16
Garda, Lake, l., Italy	B3	23
Gardanne, Fr.	F6	16
Gardar, N.D., U.S.	A8	111
Gardelegen, E. Ger.	B5	18
Garden, Mi., U.S.	C4	99
Garden, co., Ne., U.S.	C3	104
Gardena, Ca., U.S.	n12	82
Gardena, N.D., U.S.	A3	111
Garden City, Al., U.S.	A3	78
Garden City, Co., U.S.	*A6	83
Garden City, Ga., U.S.	D5	87
Garden City, Id., U.S.	F2	89
Garden City, In., U.S.	F6	91
Garden City, Ks., U.S.	E3	93
Garden City, La., U.S.	E4	95
Garden City, Mi., U.S.	p15	99
Garden City, Mn., U.S.	F4	100
Garden City, Mo., U.S.	C3	102
Garden City, N.Y., U.S.	*E7	109
Garden City, S.D., U.S.	C8	118
Garden City, Tx., U.S.	D2	120
Garden City, Ut., U.S.	B4	121
Garden City Park, N.Y., U.S.	*n15	109
Gardendale, Al., U.S.	B3	78
Gardendale, Tx., U.S.	E3	120
Garden Grove, Ca., U.S.	n13	82
Garden Grove, Ia., U.S.	D4	92
Garden Home, Or., U.S.	*B4	114
Garden Island, i., Mi., U.S.	C5	99
Garden of Gethsemane, Isr. Occ.	m14	41
Garden Plain, Ks., U.S.	E6	93
Garden Prairie, Il., U.S.	A5	90
Garden Reach, India	*D8	36
Gardenton, Man.	E3	70
Garden Valley, Id., U.S.	E3	89
Gardēz, Afg.	B4	36
Gardi, Ga., U.S.	E5	87
Gardiner, Me., U.S.	D3	96
Gardiner, Mt., U.S.	E6	103
Gardiner, Or., U.S.	D2	114
Gardiners Island, i., N.Y., U.S.	m16	109
Gardner, Ar., U.S.	D3	81
Gardner, Co., U.S.	D5	83
Gardner, Il., U.S.	B5	90
Gardner, Ks., U.S.	D9	93
Gardner, Ma., U.S.	A4	98
Gardner, N.D., U.S.	B9	111
Gardner, Tn., U.S.	A3	119
Gardner Canal, strt., B.C.	C3	69
Gardner Lake, l., Ct., U.S.	C6	84
Gardner Lake, l., Me., U.S.	D5	96
Gardner Mountain, mtn., N.H., U.S.	B3	106
Gardner Pinnacles, Hi., U.S.	k14	88
Gardnersville, Ky., U.S.	k14	94
Gardnerville, Nv., U.S.	E2	105
Gardone Riviera, Italy	D6	20
Gardone Val Trompia, Italy	D6	20
Garešnica, Yugo.	C3	24
Garfield, Ar., U.S.	A2	81
Garfield, Co., U.S.	C4	83
Garfield, Ga., U.S.	D4	87
Garfield, Ks., U.S.	D4	93
Garfield, Mn., U.S.	E3	100
Garfield, N.J., U.S.	h8	107
Garfield, N.M., U.S.	E2	108
Garfield, Wa., U.S.	B8	124
Garfield, co., Co., U.S.	B2	83
Garfield, co., Mt., U.S.	C9	103
Garfield, co., Ne., U.S.	C6	104
Garfield, co., Ok., U.S.	A4	113
Garfield, co., Ut., U.S.	F4	121
Garfield, co., Wa., U.S.	C8	124
Garfield Heights, Oh., U.S.	h9	112
Garfield Mountain, mtn., Mt., U.S.	F4	103
Garfield Park, De., U.S.	*B3	85
Garfield Peak, mtn., Wy., U.S.	D5	127
Gargaliánoi, Grc.	D3	25
Gargano Peninsula, pen., Italy	D5	23
Gargnano, Italy	D6	20
Garibaldi, Braz.	D2	56
Garibaldi, Or., U.S.	B3	114
Garibaldi, Mount, mtn., B.C.	D6	69
Garibaldi Provincial Park, B.C.	D6	69
Garies, S. Afr.	D2	49
Garissa, Kenya	B6	48
Garita, N.M., U.S.	B5	108
Garland, Al., U.S.	D3	78
Garland, Ar., U.S.	D2	81
Garland, Ks., U.S.	E9	93
Garland, Me., U.S.	C3	96
Garland, Ne., U.S.	D9	104
Garland, N.C., U.S.	C4	110
Garland, Pa., U.S.	C3	115
Garland, Tn., U.S.	B2	119
Garland, Tx., U.S.	n10	120
Garland, Ut., U.S.	B3	121
Garland, Wy., U.S.	B4	127
Garland, co., Ar., U.S.	C2	81
Garmisch-Partenkirchen, W. Ger.	E5	18
Garmouth, Scot., U.K.	C5	13
Garnavillo, Ia., U.S.	B6	92
Garnett, Ks., U.S.	D8	93
Garnett, S.C., U.S.	F5	117
Garnish, Newf.	E4	72
Garnpung, Lake, l., Austl.	F4	51
Garonne, stm., Eur.	E3	16
Garoowe, Som.	D4	47
Garou, Lac, l., Mali	C4	45
Garoua, Cam.	D2	46
Garrard, co., Ky., U.S.	C5	94
Garretson, S.D., U.S.	D9	118
Garrett, Il., U.S.	D5	90
Garrett, In., U.S.	B7	91
Garrett, Ky., U.S.	C7	94
Garrett, Pa., U.S.	G3	115
Garrett, Wy., U.S.	D7	127
Garrett, co., Md., U.S.	k12	97
Garrett Park, Md., U.S.	B3	97
Garrettsville, Oh., U.S.	A4	112
Garrick, Sask.	D3	75
Garrison, Ia., U.S.	B5	92
Garrison, Ky., U.S.	B6	94
Garrison, Md., U.S.	B4	97
Garrison, Mn., U.S.	D5	100
Garrison, Mt., U.S.	D4	103
Garrison, N.Y., U.S.	D7	109
Garrison, N.D., U.S.	B4	111
Garrison, Tx., U.S.	D5	120
Garrison, Ut., U.S.	E1	121
Garrison Dam, N.D., U.S.	B4	111
Garrisonville, Va., U.S.	B5	123
Garristown, Ire.	D5	11
Garron Point, c., N. Ire., U.K.	B6	11
Garrote, Pan.	h11	62
Garrovillas, Spain	C2	22
Garry, stm., Scot., U.K.	D5	13
Garry Lake, l., N.W. Ter.	C13	66
Garryowen, Mt., U.S.	E9	103
Garsen, Kenya	B7	48
Garson Lake, l., Can.	A5	68
Garson Quarry, Man.	D3	70
Garstang, Eng., U.K.	G6	13
Garth, Al., U.S.	A3	78
Garthby Station (Beaulac), Que.	D6	74
Gartz, E. Ger.	B6	18
Garut, Indon.	G3	34
Garvagh, N. Ire., U.K.	B5	11
Garve, Scot., U.K.	C4	13
Garvin, Mn., U.S.	F3	100
Garvin, Ok., U.S.	D7	113
Garvin, co., Ok., U.S.	C4	113
Garwin, Ia., U.S.	B5	92
Garwolin, Pol.	C6	26
Garwood, N.J., U.S.	*B4	107
Garwood, Tx., U.S.	E4	120
Gary, In., U.S.	A3	91
Gary, Mn., U.S.	C2	100
Gary, S.D., U.S.	C9	118
Gary, Tx., U.S.	C5	120
Gary, W.V., U.S.	D3	125
Garyarsa, China	B8	37
Garysburg, N.C., U.S.	A5	110
Garyville, La., U.S.	D5	95
Garza, co., Tx., U.S.	C2	120
Garza García, Mex.	*B4	63
Garza-Little Elm Reservoir, res., Tx., U.S.	*B4	63
Garzón, Col.	C2	60
Gas City, In., U.S.	D6	91
Gasconade, co., Mo., U.S.	C6	102
Gasconade, stm., Mo., U.S.	C6	102
Gasconade, Osage Fork, stm., Mo., U.S.	D5	102
Gascony, hist. reg., Fr.	E3	16
Gascoyne, N.D., U.S.	C2	111
Gascoyne, stm., Austl.	E2	50
Gashaka, Nig.	E7	45
Gasherbrum, mtn., Asia	*A6	36
Gas Hills, Wy., U.S.	D5	127
Gashua, Nig.	D7	45
Gasparilla Island, i., Fl., U.S.	F4	86
Gaspé, Que.	k14	74
Gaspé, Cap, c., Que.	G20	66
Gaspésie, Péninsule de la, pen., Que.	k13	74
Gasport, N.Y., U.S.	B2	109
Gasque, Al., U.S.	E2	78
Gassaway, Tn., U.S.	D8	119
Gassaway, W.V., U.S.	C4	125
Gassetts, Vt., U.S.	E3	122
Gassol, Nig.	E7	45
Gassville, Ar., U.S.	A3	81
Gaston, In., U.S.	D7	91
Gaston, N.C., U.S.	A5	110
Gaston, Or., U.S.	h11	114
Gaston, S.C., U.S.	D5	117
Gaston, co., N.C., U.S.	B1	110
Gaston, Lake, res., U.S.	A5	110
Gaston Dam, N.C., U.S.	A5	110
Gastonia, N.C., U.S.	B1	110
Gastre, Arg.	C3	54
Gata, Cape, c., Spain	D4	22
Gata, Sierra de, mts., Spain	B2	22
Gatas, Cape, c., Cyp.	E9	40
Gatchina, Sov. Un.	B8	27
Gate, Ok., U.S.	A1	113
Gate City, Va., U.S.	f9	123
Gatehouse of Fleet, Scot., U.K.	F4	13
Gates, Ne., U.S.	C6	104
Gates, N.Y., U.S.	B3	109
Gates, N.C., U.S.	A6	110
Gates, Or., U.S.	C4	114
Gates, Tn., U.S.	B2	119
Gates, co., N.C., U.S.	A6	110
Gateshead, Eng., U.K.	C6	10
Gates of the Arctic National Park, Ak., U.S.	B9	79
Gatesville, Ms., U.S.	D3	101
Gatesville, N.C., U.S.	A6	110
Gatesville, Tx., U.S.	D4	120
Gateway, Ar., U.S.	*A2	81
Gateway, Co., U.S.	C2	83
Gateway, Or., U.S.	C5	114
Gatineau, Que.	D2	74
Gatineau, co., Que.	C2	74
Gatineau, stm., Que.	D2	74
Gatineau, Parc de la, Que.	D2	74
Gatliff, Ky., U.S.	D5	94
Gatlinburg, Tn., U.S.	D10	119
Gato, Co., U.S.	D3	83
Gattman, Ms., U.S.	B5	101
Gatton, Austl.	C9	51
Gatún, Pan.	k11	62
Gatún, Lago, res., Pan.	k11	62
Gatun Locks, Pan.	k11	62
Gatzke, Mn., U.S.	B3	100
Gau, i., Fiji	I15	52
Gauer Lake, l., Man.	A3	70
Gauja, stm., Sov. Un.	C5	27
Gaula, stm., Nor.	F4	14
Gauley, stm., W.V., U.S.	C3	125
Gauley Bridge, W.V., U.S.	C3	125
Gauley Mills, W.V., U.S.	C4	125
Gause, Tx., U.S.	D4	120
Gautier, Ms., U.S.	f8	101
Gavá, Spain	D7	22
Gávdhos, i., Grc.	E5	40
Gāv Khūnī, Bātlāq-e, sw., Iran	E6	39
Gävlebukten, b., Swe.	G7	14
Gavrilovka, Sov. Un.	G11	27
Gavrilov Posad, Sov. Un.	C13	27
Gawler, Austl.	F6	50
Gawler Ranges, mts., Austl.	F6	50
Gay, Ga., U.S.	C2	87
Gay, Mi., U.S.	A2	99
Gaya, India	D7	36
Gaya, Niger	D5	45
Gaya, Nig.	D6	45
Gay Head, Ma., U.S.	D6	98
Gay Head, c., Ma., U.S.	D6	98
Gaylesville, Al., U.S.	A4	78
Gaylord, Ks., U.S.	C5	93
Gaylord, Mi., U.S.	C6	99
Gaylord, Mn., U.S.	F4	100
Gaylord, Or., U.S.	E2	114
Gaylordsville, Ct., U.S.	C2	84
Gayndah, Austl.	B8	51
Gays, Il., U.S.	D5	90
Gaysin, Sov. Un.	G7	27
Gays Mills, Wi., U.S.	E3	126
Gaysville, Vt., U.S.	D3	122
Gayville, S.D., U.S.	E8	118
Gaza (Ghazzah), Isr. Occ.	B3	38
Gaza, Ia., U.S.	A2	92
Gaza, dept., Moz.	B5	49
Gaza Strip, ter., Isr. Occ.	C6	41
Gaziantep, Tur.	D11	40
Gazimağusa, N. Cyp.	E9	40
Gboko, Nig.	E6	45
Gdańsk (Danzig), Pol.	A5	26
Gdov, Sov. Un.	B6	27
Gdynia, Pol.	A5	26
Gearhart, Or., U.S.	A3	114
Gearhart Mountain, mtn., Or., U.S.	E5	114
Geary, N.B.	D3	71
Geary, Ok., U.S.	B3	113
Geary, co., Ks., U.S.	D7	93
Geauga, co., Oh., U.S.	A4	112
Gebeit Mine, Sud.	A4	47
Gebze, Tur.	B7	25
Ged, La., U.S.	D2	95
Geddes, S.D., U.S.	D7	118
Gedera, Isr.	C6	41
Gedern, W. Ger.	E4	17
Gedinne, Bel.	E4	17
Gediz, Tur.	C7	40
Gediz, stm., Tur.	C6	40
Gedo, prov., Som.	B10	120
Gedser, Den.	D5	15
Geel, Bel.	D5	17
Geelong, Austl.	G7	50
Geetbets, Bel.	D5	17
Geff, Il., U.S.	E5	90
Gê'gyai, China	A8	37
Geidam, Nig.	D7	45
Geiger, Al., U.S.	C1	78
Geisenfeld, W. Ger.	E6	19
Geislingen, W. Ger.	E5	19
Geismar, La., U.S.	h9	95
Geistown, Pa., U.S.	F4	115
Geist Reservoir, res., In., U.S.	E6	91
Geita, Tan.	B5	48
Gejiu, China	G5	31
Gela, Italy	F5	23
Gelderland, prov., Neth.	B5	17
Geldermalsen, Neth.	C5	17
Geldern, W. Ger.	C6	17
Geldrop, Neth.	D5	17
Geleen, Neth.	D5	17
Gelendzhik, Sov. Un.	I11	27
Gelibolu (Gallipoli), Tur.	B6	40
Gelligaer, Wales, U.K.	C4	11
Gellinam Island, i., Marsh Is.	S17	52
Gelnhausen, W. Ger.	C4	19
Gelsenkirchen, W. Ger.	C3	18
Gelting, W. Ger.	D3	15
Gem, Alta.	D4	68
Gem, Id., U.S.	*B3	89
Gem, Ks., U.S.	C3	93
Gem, co., Id., U.S.	E2	89
Gemas, Malay.	K5	35
Gembloux, Bel.	D4	17
Gemena, Zaire	A2	48
Gemert, Neth.	C5	17
Gemla, Swe.	B8	15
Gemlik, Tur.	B7	40
Gemona del Friuli, Italy	C9	20
Gemünden, W. Ger.	C4	18
Genale (Jubba), stm., Afr.	D5	47
Genarp, Swe.	C7	15
Gene Autry, Ok., U.S.	C4	113
General Acha, Arg.	B4	54
General Alvear, Arg.	B3	54
General Alvear, Arg.	A3	54
General Belgrano, Arg.	B5	54
General Carrera, Lago (Lago Buenos Aires), l., S.A.	D2	54
General Conesa, Arg.	C5	54
General Enrique Martínez, Ur.	E2	56
General Eugenio A. Garay, Para.	D3	55
General José de San Martín Zapallar, Arg.	E4	55
General La Madrid, Arg.	B4	54
General Lavalle, Arg.	B5	54
General Martín Miguel de Güemes, Arg.	D2	55
General Paz, Arg.	E4	55
General Pico, Arg.	B4	54
General Pinedo, Arg.	E3	55
General Roca, Arg.	B3	54
General San Martín, Arg.	g7	54
General Sarmiento, Arg.	g7	54
General Tinio, Phil.	o13	34
General Toshevo, Bul.	D9	24
General Viamonte, Arg.	B4	54
General Villegas, Arg.	B4	54
Genesee, Id., U.S.	C2	89
Genesee, Mi., U.S.	E7	99
Genesee, Pa., U.S.	C6	115
Genesee, co., Mi., U.S.	E7	99
Genesee, co., N.Y., U.S.	B2	109
Genesee, stm., N.Y., U.S.	C2	109
Genesee Depot, Wi., U.S.	n11	126
Geneseo, Il., U.S.	B3	90
Geneseo, Ks., U.S.	D5	93
Geneseo, N.Y., U.S.	C3	109
Geneseo, N.D., U.S.	C8	111
Geneva (Genève), Switz.	C1	18
Geneva, Al., U.S.	D4	78
Geneva, Ga., U.S.	D2	87
Geneva, Id., U.S.	G7	89
Geneva, Il., U.S.	B5	90
Geneva, In., U.S.	C8	91
Geneva, Ne., U.S.	D8	104
Geneva, N.Y., U.S.	C4	109
Geneva, Oh., U.S.	A5	112
Geneva, co., Al., U.S.	D4	78
Geneva, Lake, l., Eur.	E3	18
Geneva, Lake, l., Wi., U.S.	F5	126
Geneva-on-the-Lake, Oh., U.S.	A5	112
Genève, state, Switz.	C2	20
Genichesk, Sov. Un.	H10	27
Genil, stm., Spain	D3	22
Génissiat, Fr.	C1	20
Genk, Bel.	D5	17
Gennep, Neth.	C5	17
Gennevilliers, Fr.	g10	16
Genoa (Genova), Italy	B2	23
Genoa, Co., U.S.	B7	83
Genoa, Il., U.S.	A5	90
Genoa, Ne., U.S.	C8	104
Genoa, Nv., U.S.	D2	105
Genoa, Oh., U.S.	A2	112
Genoa, Wi., U.S.	E2	126
Genoa, Gulf of, b., Italy	B2	23
Genoa City, Wi., U.S.	F5	126
Genola, Mn., U.S.	E4	100
Genola, Ut., U.S.	D4	121
Genolier, Switz.	D1	21
Genovesa, Isla, i., Ec.	f6	58
Gent (Ghent), Bel.	B5	16
Gentbrugge (part of Gent), Bel.	C3	17
Genthin, E. Ger.	B6	18
Gentilly, Fr.	g10	16
Gentilly, Mn., U.S.	C2	100
Gentofte, Den.	*C6	15
Gentry, Ar., U.S.	A1	81
Gentry, Mo., U.S.	A3	102
Gentry, co., Mo., U.S.	A3	102
Gentryville, In., U.S.	H3	91
Genzano di Roma, Italy	h9	23
Geographe Bay, b., Austl.	F2	50
Geographe Channel, strt., Austl.	E1	50
Geographical Society Island, i., Grnld.	B16	128
Geokchay, Sov. Un.	G18	8
George, S. Afr.	D3	49
George, Ia., U.S.	A2	92
George, co., Ms., U.S.	E5	101
George, i., Sov. Un.	B10	128
George, stm., Que.	g13	74
George, Cape, c., N.S.	D8	71
George, Lake, l., Austl.	G7	51
George, Lake, l., Fl., U.S.	C5	86
George, Lake, l., N.Y., U.S.	B7	109
George Air Force Base, mil., Ca., U.S.	E5	82
George B. Stevenson Reservoir, res., Pa., U.S.	D6	115
George Hill, mtn., Md., U.S.	k12	97
George Island, i., Newf.	A3	72
George Peak, mtn., Ut., U.S.	B2	121
Georges Mills, N.H., U.S.	D2	106
Georgesville, Oh., U.S.	m10	112
George Town, Austl.	o15	50
George Town, Bah.	C6	64
Georgetown, P.E.I.	C7	71
Georgetown, Cay. Is.	E7	64
Georgetown, Gam.	D2	45
Georgetown, Guy.	A3	59
George Town (Pinang), Malay.	K5	34
Georgetown, St. Vin.	U26	65
Georgetown, Ar., U.S.	B4	81
Georgetown, Ca., U.S.	C3	82
Georgetown, Co., U.S.	B5	83
Georgetown, Ct., U.S.	D2	84
Georgetown, De., U.S.	F4	85
Georgetown, Fl., U.S.	C5	86
Georgetown, Ga., U.S.	E1	87
Georgetown, Id., U.S.	G7	89
Georgetown, Il., U.S.	D6	90
Georgetown, In., U.S.	H6	91
Georgetown, Ky., U.S.	B5	94
Georgetown, La., U.S.	C3	95
Georgetown, Md., U.S.	B6	97
Georgetown, Ma., U.S.	A6	98
Georgetown, Mn., U.S.	C2	100
Georgetown, Ms., U.S.	D3	101
Georgetown, N.J., U.S.	C3	107
Georgetown, N.Y., U.S.	C5	109
Georgetown, Oh., U.S.	D2	112
Georgetown, S.C., U.S.	E9	117
Georgetown, Tn., U.S.	D9	119
Georgetown, Tx., U.S.	D4	120
Georgetown, co., S.C., U.S.	E9	117
George V Coast, Ant.	C28	7
Georgeville, Que.	D5	74
George VI Sound, strt., Ant.	B6	7
George Washington Birthplace National Monument, Va., U.S.	B6	123
George Washington Carver National Monument, Mo., U.S.	E3	102
George West, Tx., U.S.	E3	120
Georgia, state, Sov. Un.	E7	29
Georgia, state, U.S.	D3	87
Georgia, Strait of, strt., N.A.	E6	69
Georgia Center, Vt., U.S.	B2	122
Georgian Bay, b., Ont.	B3	73
Georgina, stm., Austl.	D6	50
Georgiu-Dez, Sov. Un.	F12	27
Georgiyevsk, Sov. Un.	G17	8
Gera, E. Ger.	C6	18
Geraardsbergen, Bel.	D3	17
Geral, Serra, clf., Braz.	D2	56
Gerald, Sask.	G5	75
Gerald, Mo., U.S.	C6	102
Geraldine, Mt., U.S.	C6	103
Geral de Goiás, Serra, clf., Braz.	D1	57
Geral do Paraná, Serra, mts., Braz.	A3	56
Geraldton, Austl.	E1	50
Geraldton, Ont.	o18	73
Gérardmer, Fr.	A2	20
Gerber, Ca., U.S.	B2	82
Gerber Reservoir, res., Or., U.S.	E5	114
Gercüş, Tur.	D13	40
Gerdau, stm., W. Ger.	F4	15
Gerdine, Mount, mtn., Ak., U.S.	C9	79
Gerede, Tur.	B9	40
Gereshk, Afg.	B3	36
Gérgal, Spain	D4	22
Gérin, Que.	C4	74
Gering, Ne., U.S.	C2	104
Gerlachovka, mtn., Czech.	D6	26
German Democratic Republic (East Germany), ctry., Eur.	B6	18
Germania, N.J., U.S.	D3	107
Germania, Pa., U.S.	C6	115
Germansen Lake, l., B.C.	B5	69
Germantown, N.B.	D5	71
Germantown, Il., U.S.	E4	90
Germantown, Ky., U.S.	B6	94
Germantown, Md., U.S.	B3	97
Germantown, Oh., U.S.	C1	112
Germantown, Tn., U.S.	B2	119
Germantown, Wi., U.S.	E5	126
Germany, Federal Republic of (West Germany), ctry., Eur.	C4	18
Germersheim, W. Ger.	D3	19
Germfask, Mi., U.S.	B5	99
Germiston, S. Afr.	C4	49
Gernrode, E. Ger.	B6	19
Gernsheim, W. Ger.	D3	19
Gero, Japan	n16	33
Gerolzhofen, W. Ger.	D5	19
Geronimo, Ok., U.S.	C3	113
Geronimo, Tx., U.S.	h8	120
Gerrardstown, W.V., U.S.	B6	125
Gersfeld, W. Ger.	C4	19
Gerstungen, E. Ger.	C5	19
Gertrudis Sánchez (part of Mexico City), Mex.	h9	63
Gerty, Ok., U.S.	C5	113
Gervais, Or., U.S.	B4	114
Gerze, Tur.	B10	40
Geseke, W. Ger.	B3	19
Gesher HaZiw, Isr.	A7	41
Gessie, In., U.S.	D3	91
Getafe, Spain	B4	22
Gethsémani, Que.	h9	72
Gettysburg, Pa., U.S.	G7	115
Gettysburg, S.D., U.S.	C6	118
Getúlio Vargas, Braz.	D2	56
Getz Ice Shelf, ice, Ant.	B36	7
Geuda Springs, Ks., U.S.	E6	93
Gevelsberg, W. Ger.	B2	19
Gex, Fr.	C2	20
Geyser, Mt., U.S.	C6	103
Geyserville, Ca., U.S.	C2	82
Geyve, Tur.	B8	40
Gézenti, Chad	A3	46
Ghabīyah, Wādī al, stm., Eg.	E5	41
Ghaggar, stm., India	C5	37
Ghaghara, stm., India	E9	37
Ghaghar Reservoir, res., India	E9	37
Ghana, ctry., Afr.	E4	44
Ghanzi, Bots.	B3	49
Ghardaïa, Alg.	C5	43
Gharyān, Libya	C2	43
Ghat, Libya	D7	43
Ghawr ash Sharqīyah, Qanāt al, Jord.	D5	41
Ghazal, Bahr al, stm., Sud.	D3	47
Ghazal, Bahr el, stm., Chad	D2	46
Ghāziābād, India	*C6	36
Ghazipur, India	E9	37
Ghaznī, Afg.	B4	36
Ghent see Gent, Bel.	B5	16
Gheorghe Gheorghiu-Dej, Rom.	B8	24
Gheorgheni, Rom.	B7	24
Gherla, Rom.	B6	24
Ghilizane, Alg.	B5	44
Ghlò, Beinn a', mtn., Scot., U.K.	D5	13
Ghūdāmis, Libya	C1	43
Ghūriān, Afg.	D10	39
Giannutri, i., Italy	C3	23
Giant Mountain, mtn., N.Y., U.S.	A7	109
Giants Neck, Ct., U.S.	D7	84
Giaveno, Italy	D3	20
Gibara, Cuba	D5	64
Gibbon, Mn., U.S.	F4	100
Gibbon, Ne., U.S.	D7	104
Gibbons, Alta.	C4	68
Gibbonsville, Id., U.S.	D5	89
Gibbs, Mo., U.S.	A5	102
Gibbstown, N.J., U.S.	D2	107
Gibeon, Nmb.	C2	49
Gibraleón, Spain	D2	22
Gibraltar, dep.	D3	22
Gibraltar, Strait of, strt.	E3	22
Gibraltar Point, c., Eng., U.K.	A8	12
Gibsland, La., U.S.	B2	95
Gibson, Ga., U.S.	C4	87
Gibson, La., U.S.	E5	95
Gibson, Ms., U.S.	B5	101
Gibson, Mo., U.S.	E7	102
Gibson, N.C., U.S.	C3	110
Gibson, Pa., U.S.	C10	115
Gibson, Tn., U.S.	B3	119
Gibson, co., In., U.S.	H2	91
Gibson, co., Tn., U.S.	A3	119
Gibsonburg, Oh., U.S.	A2	112
Gibson City, Il., U.S.	C5	90
Gibson Desert, des., Austl.	D4	50
Gibsonia, Fl., U.S.	*D5	86
Gibsonia, Pa., U.S.	h14	115
Gibson Island, i., Md., U.S.	B5	97
Gibsons, B.C.	E6	69
Gibsonton, Fl., U.S.	p11	86
Gibsonville, N.C., U.S.	A3	110
Giddings, Tx., U.S.	D4	120
Gideon, Mo., U.S.	E8	102
Gidole, Eth.	D4	47
Gien, Fr.	D5	16
Giessen, W. Ger.	C4	18
Gifford, Fl., U.S.	E6	86
Gifford, Id., U.S.	C2	89
Gifford, Il., U.S.	C5	90
Gifford, In., U.S.	B3	91
Gifford, Pa., U.S.	C4	115
Giffre, stm., Fr.	D2	21
Gifhorn, W. Ger.	F4	15
Gifu, Japan	D12	31
Giganta, Sierra de la, mts., Mex.	B2	63
Gigante, Col.	C2	60
Gigha Island, i., Scot., U.K.	E3	13
Gig Harbor, Wa., U.S.	B3	124
Giglio, i., Italy	C3	23
Gihon, stm., Vt., U.S.	B3	122
Gijón, Spain	A3	22
Gila, N.M., U.S.	E1	108
Gila, co., Az., U.S.	D5	80
Gila, stm., U.S.	D5	76
Gila Bend, Az., U.S.	E3	80
Gila Bend Indian Reservation, Az., U.S.	D3	80
Gila Bend Mountains, mts., Az., U.S.	D2	80
Gila Cliff Dwellings National Monument, N.M., U.S.	D1	108
Gila Mountains, mts., Az., U.S.	D6	80
Gila Peak, mtn., Az., U.S.	D6	80
Gila River Indian Reservation, Az., U.S.	D4	80
Gilbert, Ar., U.S.	B3	81
Gilbert, Az., U.S.	m9	80
Gilbert, Ia., U.S.	B4	92
Gilbert, La., U.S.	B4	95
Gilbert, Mn., U.S.	C6	100
Gilbert, Or., U.S.	*B4	114
Gilbert, S.C., U.S.	D5	117
Gilbert, W.V., U.S.	D3	125
Gilbert, stm., Austl.	C7	50
Gilbert, stm., Newf.	B3	72
Gilbert Islands see Kiribati, ctry., Oc.	G11	6
Gilbert Islands, is., Kir.	G10	6
Gilbert Peak, mtn., Wa., U.S.	C4	124
Gilbert Plains, Man.	D1	70
Gilbertsville, Ky., U.S.	f9	94
Gilbertsville, N.Y., U.S.	C5	109
Gilbertsville, Pa., U.S.	F10	115
Gilbertville, Ia., U.S.	B5	92
Gilbertville, Ma., U.S.	B3	98
Gilboa, Oh., U.S.	A2	112
Gilby, N.D., U.S.	A8	111
Gilchrist, Or., U.S.	D5	114
Gilchrist, co., Fl., U.S.	C4	86
Gilcrest, Co., U.S.	A6	83
Gildford, Mt., U.S.	B6	103
Gilead, Me., U.S.	D2	96
Gilead, Ne., U.S.	D8	104
Giles, co., Tn., U.S.	B4	119
Giles, co., Va., U.S.	C2	123
Gilford, N. Ire., U.K.	C5	11
Gilford Island, i., B.C.	D4	69
Gilford Park, N.J., U.S.	*D4	107
Gilgandra, Austl.	E7	51
Gilgit, Pak.	A5	36
Gil Island, i., B.C.	C3	69
Gill, Lough, l., Ire.	C3	11
Gillam, Man.	A5	70
Gilleleje, Den.	B6	15
Gillen, Lake, l., Austl.	D4	50
Gillespie, Il., U.S.	D4	90
Gillespie, co., Tx., U.S.	D3	120
Gillespie Dam, Az., U.S.	D3	80
Gillett, Ar., U.S.	C4	81
Gillett, Fl., U.S.	p10	86
Gillett, Pa., U.S.	C8	115
Gillett, Tx., U.S.	k8	120
Gillett, Wi., U.S.	D5	126
Gillette, Wy., U.S.	B7	127
Gillett Grove, Ia., U.S.	A2	92
Gilliam, La., U.S.	B2	95
Gilliam, Mo., U.S.	B4	102
Gilliam, co., Or., U.S.	B6	114
Gillingham, Eng., U.K.	C8	12
Gillis Point, N.S.	C9	71
Gilly (part of Charleroi), Bel.	B6	16
Gilman, Ct., U.S.	C7	84
Gilman, Ia., U.S.	C5	92
Gilman, Mn., U.S.	E5	100

Name	Map Ref.	Page
Gilman, Vt., U.S.	C5	122
Gilman, Wi., U.S.	C3	126
Gilman City, Mo., U.S.	A4	102
Gilmanton, N.H., U.S.	D4	106
Gilmanton, Wi., U.S.	D2	126
Gilmanton Iron Works, N.H., U.S.	D4	106
Gilmer, Tx., U.S.	C5	120
Gilmer, W.V., U.S.	C4	125
Gilmer, co., Ga., U.S.	B2	87
Gilmer, co., W.V., U.S.	C4	125
Gilmore, Ar., U.S.	B5	81
Gilmore City, Ia., U.S.	B3	92
Gilmour, Ont.	C7	73
Gilo, stm., Eth.	D3	47
Gilpin, Ky., U.S.	C5	94
Gilpin, co., Co., U.S.	B5	83
Gilroy, Sask.	G2	75
Gilroy, Ca., U.S.	D3	82
Gilson, Il., U.S.	C3	90
Gilsum, N.H., U.S.	D2	106
Gilt Edge, Tn., U.S.	B2	119
Giltner, Ne., U.S.	D7	104
Giluwe, Mount, mtn., Pap. N. Gui.	k11	50
Gimli, Man.	D3	70
Ginir, Eth.	D5	47
Ginns Corner, De., U.S.	C3	85
Ginosa, Italy	D6	23
Ginowan, Japan	O5	52
Ginzo [de Limia], Spain	A2	22
Gioia del Colle, Italy	D6	23
Gioiosa Ionica, Italy	E6	23
Girard, Ga., U.S.	C5	87
Girard, Il., U.S.	D4	90
Girard, Ks., U.S.	E9	93
Girard, La., U.S.	B4	95
Girard, Oh., U.S.	A5	112
Girard, Pa., U.S.	B1	115
Girard, Tx., U.S.	C2	120
Girardot, Col.	C3	60
Girardville, Pa., U.S.	E9	115
Girdletree, Md., U.S.	D7	97
Giresun, Tur.	B12	40
Giri, stm., Zaire	A2	48
Girīdīh, India	D8	36
Girna, stm., India	G5	37
Girne, N. Cyp.	E9	40
Giromagny, Fr.	D7	16
Girón, Ec.	B2	58
Gironde, est., Fr.	E3	16
Giroux, Man.	E3	70
Girouxville, Alta.	B2	68
Girvan, Scot., U.K.	C4	10
Girvin, Sask.	F3	75
Girvin, Tx., U.S.	D1	120
Gisborne, N.Z.	M17	51
Gisborne Lake, l., Newf.	E4	72
Giscome, B.C.	B6	69
Gisenyi, Rw.	B4	48
Gislaved, Swe.	A7	15
Gisors, Fr.	C4	16
Gitega, Bdi.	B4	48
Giulianova, Italy	C4	23
Giurgiu, Rom.	D7	24
Giv'atayim, Isr.	g10	41
Give, Den.	C3	15
Givet, Fr.	B6	16
Givhans, S.C., U.S.	E7	117
Givors, Fr.	E11	16
Givry, i., Micron.	Q18	52
Giza (Al Jīzah), Eg.	B3	38
Giza, Pyramids of, hist., Egypt	E3	41
Gīzāb, Afg.	E13	39
Gizhiga, Sov. Un.	C19	29
Gižycko, Pol.	A6	26
Gjirokastra, Alb.	B3	40
Gjoa Haven, N.W. Ter.	C13	66
Gjøvik, Nor.	G4	14
Glace Bay, N.S.	C10	71
Glacier, B.C.	D9	69
Glacier, Wa., U.S.	A4	124
Glacier, co., Mt., U.S.	B3	103
Glacier Bay, b., Ak., U.S.	k21	79
Glacier Bay National Park, Ak., U.S.	D12	79
Glacier National Park, B.C.	D9	69
Glacier National Park, U.S.	B2	103
Glacier Peak, mtn., Wa., U.S.	A4	124
Gladbeck, W. Ger.	B1	19
Gladbrook, Ia., U.S.	B5	92
Glade, Ks., U.S.	C4	93
Glade Creek, stm., Wa., U.S.	C6	124
Glade Creek, stm., W.V., U.S.	n14	125
Glade Creek, stm., W.V., U.S.	n13	125
Glade Park, Co., U.S.	B2	83
Glades, co., Fl., U.S.	F5	86
Glade Spring, Va., U.S.	f10	123
Glade Valley, N.C., U.S.	A1	110
Gladeview, Fl., U.S.	*G6	86
Gladeville, Tn., U.S.	A5	119
Gladewater, Tx., U.S.	C5	120
Gladmar, Sask.	H3	75
Gladstone, Austl.	D9	50
Gladstone, Man.	D2	70
Gladstone, Il., U.S.	C3	90
Gladstone, Mi., U.S.	C4	99
Gladstone, Mo., U.S.	h10	102
Gladstone, N.D., U.S.	D8	104
Gladstone, N.J., U.S.	B3	107
Gladstone, N.M., U.S.	A6	108
Gladstone, N.D., U.S.	C3	111
Gladstone, Or., U.S.	B4	114
Gladstone, Va., U.S.	C4	123
Glad Valley, S.D., U.S.	B4	118
Gladwin, Mi., U.S.	E6	99
Gladwin, co., Mi., U.S.	D6	99
Glady, W.V., U.S.	C5	125
Gladys, Va., U.S.	C3	123
Glåma, stm., Nor.	G5	14
Glamis, Sask.	F2	75
Glamoč, Yugo.	C3	24
Glan, l., Swe.	u33	14
Glan, stm., W. Ger.	D1	21
Gland, Switz.	C6	21
Glandorf, Oh., U.S.	A1	112
Glanshammar (part of Örebro), Swe.	t33	14
Glärnisch, mts., Switz.	C4	21
Glarus, Switz.	E4	18
Glarus, state, Switz.	B5	20
Glarus Alps, mts., Switz.	C6	21
Glasco, Ks., U.S.	C6	93
Glasco, N.Y., U.S.	C7	109
Glascock, co., Ga., U.S.	C4	87
Glasford, Il., U.S.	C4	90
Glasgo, Ct., U.S.	C8	84
Glasgow, Scot., U.K.	C4	10
Glasgow, Il., U.S.	D3	90
Glasgow, Ky., U.S.	C4	94
Glasgow, Mo., U.S.	B5	102
Glasgow, Mt., U.S.	B10	103
Glasgow, Va., U.S.	C3	123
Glasgow, W.V., U.S.	m13	125
Glasgow Village, Mo., U.S.	*f13	102
Glaslyn, Sask.	D1	75
Glasnevin, Sask.	H3	75
Glass, Tn., U.S.	A2	119
Glassboro, N.J., U.S.	D2	107
Glasscock, co., Tx., U.S.	D2	120
Glassmanor, Md., U.S.	*C4	97
Glassport, Pa., U.S.	F2	115
Glasston, N.D., U.S.	A8	111
Glastenbury Mountain, mtn., Vt., U.S.	F2	122
Glastonbury, Eng., U.K.	C5	12
Glastonbury, Ct., U.S.	C5	84
Glauchau, E. Ger.	C6	18
Glazier, Tx., U.S.	A2	120
Glazier Lake, l., Me., U.S.	A3	96
Glazov, Sov. Un.	B4	28
Glazypeau Mountain, mtn., Ar., U.S.	f7	81
Gleason, Tn., U.S.	A3	119
Gleason, Wi., U.S.	C4	126
Gleasondale, Ma., U.S.	g9	98
Gleichen, Alta.	D4	68
Gleiwitz see Gliwice, Pol.	C5	26
Glen, Mn., U.S.	D5	100
Glen, Mt., U.S.	E4	103
Glen, N.H., U.S.	B4	106
Glen, W.V., U.S.	m13	125
Glenade, Ire.	C3	11
Glen Alice, Tn., U.S.	D9	119
Glen Allan, Ms., U.S.	B2	101
Glen Allen, Al., U.S.	B2	78
Glenallen, Mo., U.S.	D7	102
Glen Allen, Va., U.S.	C5	123
Glen Alpine, N.C., U.S.	B1	110
Glenamaddy, Ire.	D3	11
Glenamoy, Ire.	C2	11
Glénan, Îles de, is., Fr.	D1	16
Glen Arbor, Mi., U.S.	D4	99
Glenarm, N. Ire., U.K.	C6	11
Glenavon, Sask.	G4	75
Glen Avon, Ca., U.S.	m14	82
Glenbain, Sask.	H2	75
Glenbar, Scot., U.K.	E3	13
Glenbeigh, Ire.	E2	11
Glenbeulah, Wi., U.S.	k9	126
Glenboro, Man.	E2	70
Glenbrook, Nv., U.S.	D2	105
Glenburn, N.D., U.S.	A4	111
Glen Burnie, Md., U.S.	B4	97
Glen Burnie Park, Md., U.S.	*B4	97
Glenbush, Sask.	D2	75
Glen Campbell, Pa., U.S.	E4	115
Glen Canyon, Ut., U.S.	F4	121
Glen Canyon, val., U.S.	G4	121
Glen Canyon Dam, Az., U.S.	A4	80
Glen Canyon National Recreation Area, U.S.	F5	121
Glencar, Ire.	E2	11
Glen Carbon, Il., U.S.	*E4	90
Glencliff, N.H., U.S.	C3	106
Glencoe, Ont.	E3	73
Glencoe, Al., U.S.	B4	78
Glencoe, Il., U.S.	A6	90
Glencoe, Ky., U.S.	B5	94
Glencoe, La., U.S.	E4	95
Glencoe, Md., U.S.	A4	97
Glencoe, Mn., U.S.	F4	100
Glencoe, Mo., U.S.	f12	102
Glencoe, N.M., U.S.	D4	108
Glencoe, Ok., U.S.	A5	113
Glencolumbkille, Ire.	C3	11
Glen Cove, N.Y., U.S.	h13	109
Glencross, S.D., U.S.	B5	118
Glendale, Az., U.S.	D3	80
Glendale, Ca., U.S.	m12	82
Glendale, Co., U.S.	*B6	83
Glendale, Fl., U.S.	v15	86
Glendale, Ky., U.S.	C4	94
Glendale, Ma., U.S.	*B1	98
Glendale, Mo., U.S.	*f13	102
Glendale, N.H., U.S.	C4	106
Glendale, Oh., U.S.	C1	112
Glendale, R.I., U.S.	E3	114
Glendale, S.C., U.S.	B4	117
Glendale, Tn., U.S.	B5	119
Glendale, Ut., U.S.	F3	121
Glendale, Wi., U.S.	m12	126
Glendale Colony, Mt., U.S.	C7	118
Glendale Heights, Il., U.S.	*k8	90
Glendale Heights, W.V., U.S.	g8	125
Glen Dean, Ky., U.S.	C3	94
Glendevey, Co., U.S.	A5	83
Glendive, Mt., U.S.	C12	103
Glendo, Wy., U.S.	D7	127
Glendora, Ca., U.S.	m13	82
Glendora, Ms., U.S.	B3	101
Glendora, N.J., U.S.	*D2	107
Glendo Reservoir, res., Wy., U.S.	D8	127
Glen Easton, W.V., U.S.	g8	125
Glen Echo, Md., U.S.	f8	97
Glen Elder, Ks., U.S.	C5	93
Glenelg, Scot., U.K.	C3	13
Glenelg, Md., U.S.	B4	97
Glenella, Man.	D2	70
Glen Ellis Falls, wtfl., N.H., U.S.	B4	106
Glen Ellyn, Il., U.S.	k8	90
Glenevis, Alta.	C3	68
Glen Ewen, Sask.	H4	75
Glenfarne, Ire.	C4	11
Glen Ferris, W.V., U.S.	*C3	125
Glenfield, N.Y., U.S.	B5	109
Glenfield, N.D., U.S.	B7	111
Glenfinnan, Scot., U.K.	D3	13
Glen Flora, Tx., U.S.	E4	120
Glen Gardner, N.J., U.S.	B3	107
Glengarriff, Ire.	F2	11
Glengarry, co., Ont.	B10	73
Glengyle, Austl.	D7	50
Glen Haven, Co., U.S.	A5	83
Glen Head, N.Y., U.S.	*h13	109
Glen Innes, Austl.	E9	50
Glen Jean, W.V., U.S.	D3	125
Glen Kerr, Sask.	G2	75
Glen Lake, l., Mi., U.S.	D5	99
Glen Lyon, Pa., U.S.	D9	115
Glenluce, Scot., U.K.	F4	13
Glenmont, Oh., U.S.	B3	112
Glenmora, La., U.S.	D3	95
Glenmorgan, Austl.	C7	51
Glenmore, Mi., U.S.	F4	99
Glenn, co., Ca., U.S.	C2	82
Glennallen, Ak., U.S.	f19	79
Glenn Dale, Md., U.S.	*C4	97
Glennie, Mi., U.S.	D7	99
Glennonville, Mo., U.S.	E7	102
Glenns Ferry, Id., U.S.	G3	89
Glennville, Ga., U.S.	E5	87
Glenolden, Pa., U.S.	p20	115
Glenoma, Wa., U.S.	C3	124
Glenorchy, Austl.	o15	50
Glenpool, Ok., U.S.	B5	113
Glen Raven, N.C., U.S.	A3	110
Glenridge, Ma., U.S.	h10	98
Glen Ridge, N.J., U.S.	h8	107
Glenrio, N.M., U.S.	B6	108
Glen Robertson, Ont.	B10	73
Glen Rock, N.J., U.S.	h8	107
Glen Rock, Pa., U.S.	G8	115
Glenrock, Wy., U.S.	D7	127
Glen Rose, Tx., U.S.	C4	120
Glenrothes, Scot., U.K.	D5	13
Glen Saint Mary, Fl., U.S.	B4	86
Glens Falls, N.Y., U.S.	B7	109
Glenshaw, Pa., U.S.	h14	115
Glenside, Sask.	F2	75
Glenside, Pa., U.S.	F11	115
Glentana, Mt., U.S.	B10	103
Glenties, Ire.	C3	11
Glentworth, Sask.	H2	75
Glen Ullin, N.D., U.S.	C4	111
Glenview, Il., U.S.	h9	90
Glenview Naval Air Station, mil., Il., U.S.	h9	90
Glenvil, Ne., U.S.	D7	104
Glenville, Ire.	E3	11
Glenville, Mn., U.S.	G5	100
Glenville, N.C., U.S.	f9	110
Glenville, W.V., U.S.	C4	125
Glen White, W.V., U.S.	D3	125
Glen Wilton, Va., U.S.	C3	123
Glenwood, Newf.	D4	72
Glenwood, Al., U.S.	D3	78
Glenwood, Ar., U.S.	C2	81
Glenwood, Fl., U.S.	C5	86
Glenwood, Ga., U.S.	D4	87
Glenwood, Il., U.S.	*k9	90
Glenwood, In., U.S.	E7	91
Glenwood, Ia., U.S.	C2	92
Glenwood, Md., U.S.	B3	97
Glenwood, Mn., U.S.	E3	100
Glenwood, Mo., U.S.	A5	102
Glenwood, N.M., U.S.	D1	108
Glenwood, Or., U.S.	B3	114
Glenwood, Ut., U.S.	E4	121
Glenwood, Wa., U.S.	C4	124
Glenwood, W.V., U.S.	C2	125
Glenwood City, Wi., U.S.	C1	126
Glenwood Farms, Va., U.S.	*C5	123
Glenwood Hills, Ga., U.S.	*C2	87
Glenwood Springs, Co., U.S.	B3	83
Glenwoodville, Alta.	E4	68
Gletsch, Switz.	C5	21
Glezen, In., U.S.	H3	91
Glidden, Sask.	F1	75
Glidden, Ia., U.S.	B3	92
Glidden, Wi., U.S.	B3	126
Glifádha, Grc.	h11	25
Glin, Ire.	E2	11
Glittertinden, mtn., Nor.	G3	14
Gliwice (Gleiwitz), Pol.	C5	26
Globe, Az., U.S.	D5	80
Globe, Ky., U.S.	B6	94
Globino, Sov. Un.	G9	27
Głogów, Pol.	C4	26
Glorenza, Italy	A3	23
Glória, Braz.	C3	57
Glória de Goitá, Braz.	k6	57
Glorieta, N.M., U.S.	B4	108
Glorieuses, Îles, is., Reu.	f9	49
Glossop, Eng., U.K.	A6	12
Glossopteris, Mount, mtn., Ant.	A1	7
Gloster, Ga., U.S.	h8	87
Gloster, La., U.S.	B2	95
Gloster, Ms., U.S.	D2	101
Glostrup, Den.	C6	15
Gloucester, Ont.	h12	73
Gloucester, Eng., U.K.	E5	10
Gloucester, Ma., U.S.	A6	98
Gloucester, N.B.	B4	71
Gloucester, co., Va., U.S.	C6	123
Gloucester, co., N.J., U.S.	D2	107
Gloucester City, N.J., U.S.	D2	107
Gloucester Point, Va., U.S.	C6	123
Gloucestershire, co., Eng., U.K.	C7	12
Glouster, Oh., U.S.	C3	112
Glover, Mo., U.S.	D7	102
Glover, Vt., U.S.	B4	122
Glover Gap, W.V., U.S.	h10	125
Glover Island, i., Newf.	D3	72
Gloversville, N.Y., U.S.	B6	109
Glovertown, Newf.	D4	72
Glowdy, S.C., U.S.	E4	117
Głubczyce, Pol.	C4	26
Głubokoye, Sov. Un.	D6	27
Głuchołazy, Pol.	C4	26
Gluck, S.C., U.S.	C2	117
Glücksburg, W. Ger.	D3	15
Glückstadt, W. Ger.	E3	15
Gluek, Mn., U.S.	E3	100
Glukhov, Sov. Un.	F9	27
Glussk, Sov. Un.	E7	27
Glyndon, Md., U.S.	B4	97
Glyndon, Mn., U.S.	D2	100
Glynco, Ga., U.S.	E5	87
Glynn, co., Ga., U.S.	E5	87
Gmunden, Aus.	E6	18
Gnadenhutten, Oh., U.S.	B4	112
Gnesta, Swe.	B4	26
Gniezno, Pol.	B4	26
Gnjilane, Yugo.	D5	24
Gnoien, E. Ger.	E6	15
Goa, state, India	D13	37
Goålpåra, India	D13	37
Goat Fell, mtn., Scot., U.K.	F3	13
Goat Island, i., R.I., U.S.	F5	116
Goat Island Point, c., Am. Sam.	F13	52
Goat Mountain, mtn., Mt., U.S.	C4	78
Goat Rock Dam, U.S.	C4	78
Goba, Eth.	D5	47
Gobabis, Nmb.	B2	49
Gobernador Gregores, Arg.	D2	54
Gobernador Udaondo, Arg.	g7	54
Gobi Desert, des., Asia	C5	31
Gobles, Mi., U.S.	F5	99
Gobō, Japan	J7	33
Goch, W. Ger.	C3	18
Gochas, Nmb.	B2	49
Godāvari, stm., India	E6	36
Godāvari, Mouths of the, mth., India	E7	36
Goddard, Ks., U.S.	E6	93
Goderich, Ont.	D3	73
Godfrey, Ont.	C8	73
Godfrey, Ga., U.S.	C3	87
Godfrey, Il., U.S.	E3	90
Godhavn, Grnld.	C15	61
Godhra, India	I5	37
Godley, Tx., U.S.	n9	120
Gods Lake, Man.	B4	70
Gods Lake, l., Man.	B4	70
Godthåb (Nuuk), Grnld.	C15	61
Godwin, N.C., U.S.	B4	110
Godwin Austen, see K2, mtn., Asia	A6	36
Goehner, Ne., U.S.	D8	104
Goéélands, Lac aux, l., Que.	g8	72
Goes, Neth.	C3	17
Goessel, Ks., U.S.	D6	93
Goff, Ks., U.S.	C8	93
Goff Creek, stm., Ok., U.S.	e9	113
Goffstown, N.H., U.S.	D3	106
Gogebic, co., Mi., U.S.	n12	99
Gogebic, Lake, l., Mi., U.S.	m12	99
Gogebic Range, hills, U.S.	B3	126
Goglio, Italy	D5	21
Gogō, Japan	o14	33
Gökçeada, i., Tur.	B5	25
Göksun, Tur.	C11	40
Gokwe, Zimb.	A4	49
Gol, Nor.	G3	14
Gola Island, i., Ire.	B3	11
Golam Head, c., Ire.	D2	11
Golan Heights, ter., Syria	A7	41
Golbāf, Iran	C5	38
Golchikha, Sov. Un.	B11	29
Golconda, Il., U.S.	F5	90
Golconda, Nv., U.S.	C4	105
Goldach, Switz.	B7	21
Gołdap, Pol.	A7	26
Goldbach, W. Ger.	C4	19
Gold Bar, Wa., U.S.	B4	124
Gold Beach, Or., U.S.	E2	114
Goldberg, E. Ger.	E6	15
Goldboro, N.S.	D8	71
Gold Bridge, B.C.	D6	69
Gold Coast see Southport, Austl.	E9	50
Gold Creek, Ak., U.S.	f17	79
Goldcreek, Mt., U.S.	D4	103
Golddust, Tn., U.S.	B2	119
Golden, B.C.	D9	69
Golden, Ire.	E4	11
Golden, Co., U.S.	B5	83
Golden, Il., U.S.	C2	90
Golden, Ms., U.S.	A5	101
Golden, Mo., U.S.	E4	102
Golden, N.M., U.S.	B3	108
Golden, Ok., U.S.	C7	113
Golden Bay, b., N.Z.	N14	51
Golden Beach, Fl., U.S.	*G6	86
Golden City, Mo., U.S.	D3	102
Goldendale, Wa., U.S.	D5	124
Golden Ears Provincial Park, B.C.	E6	69
Goldengate, Il., U.S.	E5	90
Golden Gate Bridge, Ca., U.S.	h7	82
Golden Gate National Recreation Area, Ca., U.S.	h7	82
Golden Glades, Fl., U.S.	*G6	86
Golden Hinde, mtn., B.C.	E5	69
Golden Lake, Ont.	B7	73
Golden Lake, l., Ont.	B7	73
Golden Meadow, La., U.S.	E5	95
Golden Prairie, Sask.	G1	75
Golden Spike National Historic Site, hist., Ut., U.S.	B3	121
Golden Spur, Ct., U.S.	D7	84
Golden Valley, Mn., U.S.	n12	100
Goldenvalley, N.D., U.S.	B3	111
Golden Valley, co., Mt., U.S.	D7	103
Golden Valley, co., N.D., U.S.	B2	111
Goldenville, N.S.	D7	71
Goldfield, Ia., U.S.	B4	92
Goldfield, Nv., U.S.	F4	105
Gold Hill, N.C., U.S.	B2	110
Gold Hill, Or., U.S.	E3	114
Goldonna, La., U.S.	B3	95
Goldsand Lake, l., Man.	A1	70
Goldsboro, Md., U.S.	B6	97
Goldsboro, N.C., U.S.	B5	110
Goldsby, Ok., U.S.	B4	113
Goldschmidt, Cape, c., Ant.	g40	7
Goldsmith, In., U.S.	D5	91
Goldsmith, Tx., U.S.	D1	120
Goldston, N.C., U.S.	B3	110
Goldsworthy, Austl.	D3	50
Goldthwaite, Tx., U.S.	D3	120
Goleen, Ire.	F2	11
Golela, S. Afr.	C5	49
Goleniów, Pol.	B3	26
Goleta, Ca., U.S.	E4	82
Golets-Skalistyy, Mount, mtn., Sov. Un.	D14	29
Golfito, C.R.	F6	62
Golf Manor, Oh., U.S.	o13	112
Goliad, Tx., U.S.	E4	120
Goliad, co., Tx., U.S.	E4	120
Golling [an der Salzach], Aus.	B9	20
Golmud, China	D3	31
Golo, stm., Fr.	D5	21
Golo Island, i., Phil.	p13	34
Golovin, Ak., U.S.	C7	79
Golpāyegān, Iran	B5	38
Golpilhares?		
Golspie, Scot., U.K.	A5	10
Goltry, Ok., U.S.	A3	113
Golts, Md., U.S.	B6	97
Golva, N.D., U.S.	C2	111
Golyamo Konare, Bul.	D7	24
Goma, Zaire	B5	48
Gomati, stm., India	D9	37
Gombari, Zaire	A5	48
Gombe, Nig.	D7	45
Gomel, Sov. Un.	E8	27
Gomera, i., Spain	m13	22
Gómez Palacio, Mex.	B4	60
Gommern, E. Ger.	A6	19
Gonābād, Iran	C3	38
Gonaïves, Haiti	E7	64
Gonâve, Golfe de la, b., Haiti	E7	64
Gonâve, Île de la, i., Haiti	E7	64
Gonbad-e Qābūs, Iran	C7	39
Gonda, India	E9	36
Gonder (Gondar), Eth.	C4	47
Gonder, prov., Eth.	C4	47
Gondia, India	G8	37
Gönen, Tur.	B6	40
Gonesse, Fr.	g10	16
Gongga Shan, mtn., China	F5	31
Gongola, stm., Nig.	D7	45
Goñi, Ur.	f8	54
Gonvick, Mn., U.S.	C3	100
Gonzales, Ca., U.S.	D3	82
Gonzales, La., U.S.	D5	95
Gonzales, Tx., U.S.	E4	120
Gonzales, co., Tx., U.S.	E4	120
González, Fl., U.S.	u14	86
Gonzalez Chaves, Arg.	B4	54
Goochland, Va., U.S.	C5	123
Goochland, co., Va., U.S.	C5	123
Goode, Va., U.S.	C3	123
Goode, Mount, mtn., Ak., U.S.	g18	79
Goodell, Ia., U.S.	B4	92
Gooderham, Ont.	C6	73
Goodeve, Sask.	F4	75
Goodfellow Air Force Base, mil., Tx., U.S.	D2	120
Goodfield, Il., U.S.	C4	90
Good Hart, Mi., U.S.	C5	99
Good Hope, Ga., U.S.	C3	87
Good Hope, Il., U.S.	C3	90
Good Hope, Ms., U.S.	C4	101
Good Hope, Oh., U.S.	C2	112
Good Hope, Cape of, c., S. Afr.	D2	49
Good Hope Mountain, mtn., B.C.	D5	69
Goodhue, Mn., U.S.	F6	100
Goodhue, co., Mn., U.S.	F6	100
Gooding, Id., U.S.	G4	89
Gooding, co., Id., U.S.	F4	89
Goodland, Fl., U.S.	G5	86
Goodland, In., U.S.	C3	91
Goodland, Ks., U.S.	C2	93
Goodland, Ok., U.S.	D6	113
Goodlettsville, Tn., U.S.	g10	119
Goodman, Ms., U.S.	C4	101
Goodman, Mo., U.S.	E3	102
Goodman, Wi., U.S.	C5	126
Goodnews Bay, Ak., U.S.	D7	79
Goodnight, Tx., U.S.	B2	120
Good Pine, La., U.S.	C3	95
Goodrich, Co., U.S.	A6	83
Goodrich, Ks., U.S.	D9	93
Goodrich, N.D., U.S.	B5	111
Goodrich, Tx., U.S.	D5	120
Goodridge, Mn., U.S.	B3	100
Good Spirit Lake, l., Sask.	F4	75
Good Spirit Lake Provincial Park, Sask.	F4	75
Goodspring, Tn., U.S.	B4	119
Goodsprings, Nv., U.S.	H6	105
Good Thunder, Mn., U.S.	F4	100
Goodview, Mn., U.S.	F7	100
Goodwater, Sask.	H4	75
Goodwater, Al., U.S.	B3	78
Goodwell, Ok., U.S.	e9	113
Goodwin, Ar., U.S.	C4	81
Goodwin, S.D., U.S.	C9	118
Goodyear, Az., U.S.	D3	80
Goole, Eng., U.K.	A7	12
Goondiwindi, Austl.	E9	50
Goor, Neth.	B6	17
Goose, stm., Newf.	h9	72
Goose, stm., N.D., U.S.	B8	111
Goose Bay see Happy Valley-Goose Bay, Newf.	B1	72
Gooseberry Creek, stm., Wy., U.S.	B4	127
Goose Creek, S.C., U.S.	F7	117
Goose Creek, stm., U.S.	G5	89
Goose Creek, stm., Ne., U.S.	B5	104
Goose Creek, stm., Va., U.S.	C3	123
Goose Creek Reservoir, res., S.C., U.S.	k11	117
Goose Island, i., B.C.	D3	69
Goose Lake, l., Ia., U.S.	C7	92
Goose Lake, l., Man.	B1	70
Goose Lake, l., Sask.	F2	75
Goose Lake, l., Sask.	D4	75
Goose Pond, l., N.H., U.S.	C2	106
Gopālganj, India	H11	37
Goplo Lake, l., Pol.	B5	26
Göppingen, W. Ger.	C5	18
Góra, Pol.	C4	26
Gorakhpur, India	G10	37
Gorday, India	E3	37
Goražde, Yugo.	C3	24
Gördes, Tur.	C7	25
Gordil, Cen. Afr. Rep.	D4	46
Gordo, Al., U.S.	B2	78
Gordon, Al., U.S.	D4	78
Gordon, Ga., U.S.	D3	87
Gordon, Ne., U.S.	B3	104
Gordon, Oh., U.S.	C1	112
Gordon, Tx., U.S.	C3	120
Gordon, Wi., U.S.	B2	126
Gordon, co., Ga., U.S.	B2	87
Gordon Creek, stm., Ne., U.S.	B5	104
Gordon Horne Peak, mtn., B.C.	D8	69
Gordon Lake, l., Alta.	A5	68
Gordon Lake, l., Sask.	B2	75
Gordon's Corner, N.J., U.S.	*C4	107
Gordonsville, Tn., U.S.	C8	119
Gordonsville, Va., U.S.	B4	123
Gordonville, Mo., U.S.	D8	102
Gore, Eth.	D4	47
Gore, N.Z.	Q12	51
Gore, Oh., U.S.	C3	112
Gore, Va., U.S.	A4	123
Gore Bay, Ont.	B3	73
Goree, Tx., U.S.	C3	120
Gore Point, c., Ak., U.S.	h16	79
Gore Range, mts., Co., U.S.	B4	83
Gore Springs, Ms., U.S.	B4	101
Gorey, Ire.	E6	11
Gorgān (Asterābād), Iran	C7	39
Gorgān, stm., Iran	C7	39
Gorgona, Isla, i., Col.	C2	60
Gorham, Il., U.S.	F4	90
Gorham, Ks., U.S.	D4	93
Gorham, Me., U.S.	E2	96
Gorham, N.H., U.S.	B4	106
Gorham, N.Y., U.S.	C3	109
Gori, Sov. Un.	E2	28
Gorin, Mo., U.S.	A5	102
Gorinchem, Neth.	C5	17
Goris, Sov. Un.	B3	39
Gorizia, Italy	B4	23
Gorkha, Nepal	C10	37
Gorki, Sov. Un.	D8	29
Gorkiy, Sov. Un.	D7	29
Gorkiy Reservoir, res., Sov. Un.	D7	29
Gørlev, Den.	C5	15
Gorlice, Pol.	D6	26
Görlitz, E. Ger.	C7	18
Gorlovka, Sov. Un.	G12	27
Gorm, Loch, l., Scot., U.K.	E2	13
Gorman, Md., U.S.	m12	97
Gorman, Tn., U.S.	A4	119
Gorman, Tx., U.S.	C3	120
Gormania, W.V., U.S.	B5	125
Gormley (part of Whitchurch-Stouffville), Ont.	k15	73
Gorna Oryakhovitsa, Bul.	D7	24
Gornji Milanovac, Yugo.	C5	24
Gorno-Altaysk, Sov. Un.	D11	29
Gornozavodsk, Sov. Un.	C10	33
Gorodenka, Sov. Un.	G5	27
Gorodets, Sov. Un.	D17	8
Gorodnya, Sov. Un.	F8	27
Gorodok, Sov. Un.	D7	27
Gorodok, Mong.	A5	31
Gorodok, Sov. Un.	G4	27
Gorodok, Sov. Un.	D8	27
Goroka, Pap. N. Gui.	k12	50
Goroke, Austl.	H3	51
Gorontalo, Indon.	E6	34
Gorrie, Ont.	D3	73
Gorskoye, Sov. Un.	q21	27
Gort, Ire.	D3	11
Gortahork, Ire.	B3	11
Gorum, La., U.S.	C3	95
Gorumna, i., Ire.	D2	11
Goryn, stm., Sov. Un.	F6	27
Gorzów [Wielkopolski], Pol.	B3	26
Gosford, Austl.	F8	51
Goshen, N.S.	D8	71
Goshen, Al., U.S.	D3	78
Goshen, Ct., U.S.	B3	84
Goshen, In., U.S.	A6	91
Goshen, Ky., U.S.	g11	94
Goshen, Ma., U.S.	B2	98
Goshen, N.H., U.S.	D2	106
Goshen, N.J., U.S.	E3	107
Goshen, N.Y., U.S.	D6	109
Goshen, Oh., U.S.	C1	112
Goshen, Ut., U.S.	D4	121
Goshen, Va., U.S.	C3	123
Goshen, co., Wy., U.S.	D8	127
Goshen Hole, Wy., U.S.	D8	127
Goshogawara, Japan	F10	33
Goshute Indian Reservation, U.S.	D7	105
Goshute Lake, l., Nv., U.S.	C7	105
Goshute Mountains, mts., Nv., U.S.	C7	105
Goslar, W. Ger.	C5	18
Gosnell, Ar., U.S.	*B6	81
Gosnells, Austl.	*F2	50
Gosper, co., Ne., U.S.	D6	104
Gospić, Yugo.	C2	24
Gosport, Eng., U.K.	D6	12
Gosport, Al., U.S.	D2	78
Gosport, In., U.S.	F4	91
Gossau, Switz.	B7	21
Gostivar, Yugo.	E5	24
Gostyn, Pol.	C4	26
Gostynin, Pol.	B5	26
Gostynya, stm., Pol.	g9	26
Gotebo, Ok., U.S.	B3	113
Göteborg (Gothenburg), Swe.	I4	14
Göteborg och Bohus, co., Swe.	A5	15
Gotel Mountains, mts., Afr.	D2	46
Gotemba, Japan	n18	33
Gotha, E. Ger.	C5	18
Gotham, Wi., U.S.	E3	126
Gothenburg, Ne., U.S.	D5	104
Gotland, i., Swe.	I8	14
Gotō Islands, is., Japan	J4	33
Gotse Delchev (Nevrokop), Bul.	E6	24
Göttingen, W. Ger.	C4	18
Gottwaldov (Zlín), Czech.	B8	21
Götzis, Aus.	B8	21
Goubangzi, China	D9	32
Gouda, Neth.	A6	16
Goudeau, La., U.S.	D2	95
Goudiry, Sen.	D2	45
Goudoumaria, Niger	D7	45
Goudswaard, Neth.	C4	17
Gough Island, i., St. Hel.	I9	5
Gough Lake, l., Alta.	C4	68
Gouin, Réservoir, res., Que.	k12	74
Goulburn, Austl.	F8	51
Gould, Que.	D6	74
Gould, Ar., U.S.	D4	81
Gould, Co., U.S.	A4	83
Gould, Ok., U.S.	C2	113
Gould City, Mi., U.S.	B5	99
Goulding, Fl., U.S.	u14	86
Goulding Cay, i., Bah.	m16	64
Gouldings Trading Post, Ut., U.S.	F5	121
Gould Island, i., R.I., U.S.	E5	116
Gouldsboro, Me., U.S.	D4	96
Gouldsboro, Pa., U.S.	D11	115
Gouldtown, N.J., U.S.	E2	107
Goulimine, Mor.	D7	45
Gounamitz, stm., N.B.	B2	71
Gounou Gaya, Chad	D3	46
Gouré, Niger	D7	45
Gournay-en-Bray, Fr.	C4	16
Gouro, Chad	D8	45
Gourock, Scot., U.K.	B5	10
Gouverneur, Sask.	H2	75
Gouverneur, N.Y., U.S.	f9	109
Govan, Sask.	F3	75
Govan, Scot., U.K.	C5	10
Gove, Ks., U.S.	D3	93
Gove, co., Ks., U.S.	D3	93
Govenlock, Sask.	H1	75
Governador Valadares, Braz.	D8	57
Government Camp, Or., U.S.	B5	114
Governors Harbour, Bah.	B5	64

Name	Map Ref.	Page
Govind Ballabh Pant Reservoir, res., India	F9	37
Govind Reservoir, res., India	B6	37
Gowan, stm., Man.	B4	70
Gowanda, N.Y., U.S.	C2	109
Gowen, Mi., U.S.	E5	99
Gowen, Ok., U.S.	C6	113
Gower, Mo., U.S.	B3	102
Gowna, Lough, l., Ire.	D3	10
Gowrie, Ia., U.S.	B3	92
Goya, Arg.	E4	55
Goz Beïda, Chad	C4	46
Graaff-Reinet, S. Afr.	D3	49
Grabill, In., U.S.	B8	91
Grabow, E. Ger.	E5	15
Gračac, Yugo.	C2	24
Gračanica, Yugo.	C4	24
Grace, Id., U.S.	G7	89
Grace, Ms., U.S.	C3	101
Grace, Mount, mtn., Ma., U.S.	A3	98
Grace City, N.D., U.S.	B7	111
Graceham, Md., U.S.	A3	97
Gracemont, Ok., U.S.	B3	113
Graceton, Mn., U.S.	B4	100
Graceville, Fl., U.S.	u16	86
Graceville, Mn., U.S.	E2	100
Gracewood, Ga., U.S.	C4	87
Gracey, Ky., U.S.	D2	94
Gracias, Hond.	E7	63
Graciosa, i., Port.	g9	44
Gradačac, Yugo.	C4	24
Gradizhsk, Sov. Un.	G9	27
Grado, Italy	D9	20
Grado, Spain	A2	22
Grady, Ar., U.S.	C4	81
Grady, N.M., U.S.	C6	108
Grady, Ok., U.S.	C4	113
Grady, co., Ga., U.S.	F2	87
Grady, co., Ok., U.S.	C4	113
Gradyville, Ky., U.S.	C4	94
Graettinger, Ia., U.S.	A3	92
Grafenau, W. Ger.	E8	19
Graford, Tx., U.S.	C3	120
Grafton, Austl.	E9	50
Grafton, Ont.	D6	73
Grafton, Il., U.S.	E3	90
Grafton, Ia., U.S.	A4	92
Grafton, Ma., U.S.	B4	98
Grafton, Ne., U.S.	D8	104
Grafton, N.H., U.S.	C3	106
Grafton, N.Y., U.S.	C7	109
Grafton, N.D., U.S.	A8	111
Grafton, Oh., U.S.	A3	112
Grafton, Vt., U.S.	E3	122
Grafton, Va., U.S.	h15	123
Grafton, W.V., U.S.	B4	125
Grafton, Wi., U.S.	E6	126
Grafton, co., N.H., U.S.	C3	106
Grafton Center, N.H., U.S.	C3	106
Graham, Al., U.S.	B4	78
Graham, Ca., U.S.	*n12	82
Graham, Fl., U.S.	C4	86
Graham, Ga., U.S.	E4	87
Graham, Ky., U.S.	C2	94
Graham, Mo., U.S.	A2	102
Graham, N.C., U.S.	A3	110
Graham, Ok., U.S.	C4	113
Graham, Tn., U.S.	B4	119
Graham, Tx., U.S.	C3	120
Graham, Wa., U.S.	B3	124
Graham, co., Az., U.S.	E5	80
Graham, co., Ks., U.S.	C4	93
Graham, co., N.C., U.S.	f9	110
Graham, stm., B.C.	A6	69
Graham, Lake, res., Tx., U.S.	C3	120
Graham, Mount, mtn., Az., U.S.	E6	80
Graham Bell, i., Sov. Un.	A7	128
Graham Creek, stm., In., U.S.	G6	91
Graham Island, i., B.C.	C1	69
Graham Island, i., N.W. Ter.	m33	66
Graham Lake, i., Alta.	A3	68
Graham Lake, l., Me., U.S.	D4	96
Graham Land, reg., Ant.	C6	7
Grahamstown, S. Afr.	D4	49
Grahamsville, N.Y., U.S.	D6	109
Grahamville, S.C., U.S.	G6	117
Grahn, Ky., U.S.	B6	94
Graian Alps, mts., Eur.	E7	16
Grainfield, Ks., U.S.	C3	93
Grainger, Alta.	D4	68
Grainger, co., Tn., U.S.	C10	119
Grainland, Sask.	F2	75
Grainola, Ok., U.S.	A5	113
Grainton, Ne., U.S.	D4	104
Grain Valley, Mo., U.S.	B3	102
Grajaú, Braz.	C1	57
Grajaú, stm., Braz.	B1	57
Grajewo, Pol.	B7	26
Gram, Den.	C3	15
Gramada, Bul.	D6	24
Gramalote, Col.	B3	60
Gramastetten, Aus.	E9	19
Grambling, La., U.S.	B3	95
Gramercy, La., U.S.	h10	95
Gramling, S.C., U.S.	A3	117
Grammer, In., U.S.	F6	91
Grammichele, Italy	F5	23
Grampian, Pa., U.S.	E4	115
Grampian, prov., Scot., U.K.	C6	13
Grampian Mountains, mts., Scot., U.K.	B4	10
Gramshi, Alb.	B3	25
Gramzow, E. Ger.	E8	15
Gran, Mount, mtn., Ant.	B29	7
Granada, Nic.	E7	63
Granada, Spain	D4	22
Granada, Co., U.S.	C8	83
Granada, Mn., U.S.	G4	100
Granard, Ire.	D4	11
Granbury, Tx., U.S.	C4	120
Granby, Que.	D5	74
Granby, Co., U.S.	A5	83
Granby, Ct., U.S.	B4	84
Granby, Ma., U.S.	B2	98
Granby, Mo., U.S.	E3	102
Granby, Vt., U.S.	B5	122
Granby, Lake, res., Co., U.S.	A5	83
Granby, Lake, res., Newf.	B4	72
Gran Canal del Desagüe, Mex.	g9	63
Gran Canaria, i., Spain	n14	44
Gran Chaco, pl., S.A.	D3	55
Grand, co., Co., U.S.	A4	83
Grand, co., Ut., U.S.	E6	121
Grand, stm., Ont.	D4	73
Grand, stm., Mi., U.S.	E5	99
Grand, stm., Mo., U.S.	A3	102
Grand, stm., Oh., U.S.	A4	112
Grand, stm., S.D., U.S.	B4	118
Grand, North Fork, stm., U.S.	B2	118
Grand, South Fork, stm., S.D., U.S.	B3	118
Grand Bahama, i., Bah.	A4	64
Grand Bank, Newf.	E4	72
Grand-Bassam, I.C.	E4	45
Grand Bay, N.B.	D3	71
Grand Bay, Al., U.S.	E1	78
Grand Bayou, stm., La., U.S.	f9	95
Grand Bayou, stm., La., U.S.	k10	95
Grand Bayou, stm., La., U.S.	h9	95
Grand Bend, Ont.	D3	73
Grand Blanc, Mi., U.S.	F7	99
Grand Bonhomme, mtn., St. Vin.	U26	65
Grand-Bourg, Guad.	I14	64
Grand Bruit, Newf.	E2	72
Grand Caillou, La., U.S.	E5	95
Grand Canal (Da Yunhe), China	E8	31
Grand Canal, Ire.	D4	11
Grand Cane, La., U.S.	B2	95
Grand Canyon, Az., U.S.	A3	80
Grand Canyon, val., Az., U.S.	A3	80
Grand Canyon National Park, Az., U.S.	A3	80
Grand Cayman, i., Cay. Is.	D8	63
Grand Centre, Alta.	B5	68
Grand Cess, Lib.	F3	45
Grand Chenier, La., U.S.	E3	95
Grand Codroy, stm., Newf.	E2	72
Grand Combin, mtn., Switz.	F4	20
Grand Coteau, La., U.S.	D3	95
Grand Coulee, Wa., U.S.	B6	124
Grand Coulee Dam, Wa., U.S.	B6	124
Grande, stm., Arg.	B3	54
Grande, stm., Arg.	D2	55
Grande, stm., Bol.	C3	55
Grande, stm., Braz.	B2	56
Grande, stm., Braz.	D2	57
Grande, Bahía, b., Arg.	E3	54
Grande, Boca, mth., Ven.	B5	60
Grande, Ilha, i., Braz.	h5	56
Grande, Rio, stm., N.A.	E7	76
Grande, Serra, mts., Braz.	C2	57
Grande-Anse, N.B.	B4	71
Grand Ecore, La., U.S.	C2	95
Grande de Arecibo, stm., P.R.	B2	65
Grande [de Matagalpa], stm., Nic.	E8	63
Grande de Santiago, stm., Mex.	C3	63
Grande de Tarija, stm., S.A.	C3	55
Grande-Digue, N.B.	C5	71
Grande-Ligne, Que.	D4	74
Grand-Entrée, Que.	B8	71
Grand Prairie, Alta.	B1	68
Grand Erg de Bilma, des., Niger	C7	45
Grand Erg Occidental, des., Alg.	C5	44
Grand Erg Oriental, des., Alg.	C6	44
Grande rivière de la Baleine, stm., Que.	g11	74
Grande Ronde, stm., U.S.	C8	124
Grandes, Salinas, pl., Arg.	F2	55
Grandes-Bergeronnes, Que.	A8	74
Grandes-Piles, Que.	C5	74
Grand-Étang, N.S.	C8	71
Grande-Terre, i., Guad.	Q9	65
Grande Vigie, Pointe de la, c., Guad.	P9	65
Grand Falls (Grand-Sault), N.B.	B2	71
Grand Falls, Newf.	D4	72
Grandfalls, Tx., U.S.	D1	120
Grand Falls Lake, l., N.A.	C5	96
Grandfather Mountain, mtn., N.C., U.S.	A1	110
Grandfield, Ok., U.S.	C3	113
Grand Forks, B.C.	E8	69
Grand Forks, N.D., U.S.	B8	111
Grand Forks, co., N.D., U.S.	B8	111
Grand Forks Air Force Base, mil., N.D., U.S.	B8	111
Grand Glaise, Ar., U.S.	B4	81
Grand Gorge, N.Y., U.S.	C6	109
Grand Gulf, Ms., U.S.	C2	101
Grand Harbour, N.B.	E3	71
Grand Haven, Mi., U.S.	E4	99
Grand Hogback, mtn., Co., U.S.	B3	83
Grandin, Mo., U.S.	E7	102
Grandin, N.D., U.S.	B9	111
Grand Island, Ne., U.S.	D7	104
Grand Island, i., La., U.S.	D6	95
Grand Island, i., Mi., U.S.	B4	99
Grand Isle, La., U.S.	E6	95
Grand Isle, Me., U.S.	A4	96
Grand Isle, co., Vt., U.S.	B2	122
Grand Isle, i., La., U.S.	E6	95
Grand Junction, Co., U.S.	B2	83
Grand Junction, Ia., U.S.	B3	92
Grand Junction, Mi., U.S.	F4	99
Grand Junction, Tn., U.S.	B2	119
Grand lac Bostonnais, l., Que.	B5	74
Grand-Lahou, I.C.	E3	45
Grand Lake, Co., U.S.	A5	83
Grand Lake, La., U.S.	D2	95
Grand Lake, l., N.B.	D3	71
Grand Lake, l., Newf.	B1	72
Grand Lake, l., Newf.	D3	72
Grand Lake, l., N.A.	C5	96
Grand Lake, l., La., U.S.	E6	95
Grand Lake, l., La., U.S.	E3	95
Grand Lake, l., Mi., U.S.	C7	99
Grand Lake, l., Oh., U.S.	B1	112
Grand Lake Matagamon, l., Me., U.S.	B4	96
Grand Lake Seboeis, l., Me., U.S.	B4	96
Grand Lake Stream, Me., U.S.	C5	96
Grand Ledge, Mi., U.S.	F6	99
Grand Lieu, Lac de, l., Fr.	D3	16
Grand Manan Channel, strt., N.A.	D6	96
Grand Manan Island, i., N.B.	E3	71
Grand Marais, Mi., U.S.	B5	99
Grand Marais, Mn., U.S.	k9	100
Grand Marsh, Wi., U.S.	E4	126
Grand Meadow, Mn., U.S.	G6	100
Grand-Mère, Que.	C5	74
Grand Mesa, mtn., Co., U.S.	C2	83
Grand Mound, Ia., U.S.	C7	92
Grândola, Port.	C1	22
Grand Pass, Mo., U.S.	B4	102
Grand Portage, Mn., U.S.	k10	100
Grand Portage Indian Reservation, Mn., U.S.	k10	100
Grand Portage National Monument, Mn., U.S.	h10	100
Grand Prairie, Tx., U.S.	n10	120
Grand Pré, N.S.	D5	71
Grand Rapids, Man.	D2	70
Grand Rapids, Mi., U.S.	F5	99
Grand Rapids, Mn., U.S.	C5	100
Grand Rapids, N.D., U.S.	C7	111
Grand Rapids, Oh., U.S.	f6	112
Grand Ridge, Fl., U.S.	B1	86
Grand Ridge, Il., U.S.	B5	90
Grand River, N.S.	D9	71
Grand River, Ia., U.S.	D4	92
Grand Ronde, Or., U.S.	B3	114
Grand Saline, Tx., U.S.	C5	120
Grand Santi, Fr. Gu.	B4	59
Grand Terrace, Ca., U.S.	*E5	82
Grand Terre Islands, is., La., U.S.	E6	95
Grand Teton, mtn., Wy., U.S.	C2	127
Grand Teton National Park, Wy., U.S.	C2	127
Grand Tower, Il., U.S.	F4	90
Grand Traverse, co., Mi., U.S.	D5	99
Grand Traverse Bay, b., Mi., U.S.	C5	99
Grand Traverse Bay, East Arm, b., Mi., U.S.	D5	99
Grand Traverse Bay, West Arm, b., Mi., U.S.	D5	99
Grand Valley, Ont.	D4	73
Grand Valley, Pa., U.S.	C2	115
Grand Valley, val., U.S.	B2	83
Grandview, Man.	D1	70
Grand View, Id., U.S.	G2	89
Grandview, Il., U.S.	D6	90
Grandview, In., U.S.	I4	91
Grandview, Ia., U.S.	C6	92
Grandview, Mo., U.S.	C3	102
Grandview, Oh., U.S.	C4	112
Grandview, Tn., U.S.	D9	119
Grandview, Wa., U.S.	C6	124
Grandview Heights, Oh., U.S.	m10	112
Grandville, Mi., U.S.	F5	99
Grand View, Wi., U.S.	B3	126
Grandvilliers, Fr.	E1	17
Grand Wash Cliffs, clf., Az., U.S.	B2	80
Grandy, Mn., U.S.	E5	100
Grandy, N.C., U.S.	A7	110
Grangärde (part of Ludvika), Swe.	G6	14
Grangeburg, Al., U.S.	D4	78
Grangemouth, Scot., U.K.	D5	13
Grange-over-Sands, Eng., U.K.	F6	13
Granger, Ia., U.S.	C4	92
Granger, Mo., U.S.	A6	102
Granger, Tx., U.S.	D4	120
Granger, Wa., U.S.	C5	124
Granger, Wy., U.S.	E3	127
Granges [-sur-Vologne], Fr.	A2	20
Grangeville, Id., U.S.	D2	89
Grangeville, La., U.S.	D5	95
Granisle, B.C.	B4	69
Granite, Co., U.S.	B4	83
Granite, Ok., U.S.	C2	113
Granite, Or., U.S.	C8	114
Granite, Ut., U.S.	*C4	121
Granite, co., Mt., U.S.	D3	103
Granite City, Il., U.S.	E3	90
Granite Falls, Mn., U.S.	F3	100
Granite Falls, N.C., U.S.	B1	110
Granite Falls, Wa., U.S.	A4	124
Granite Harbor, b., Ant.	e39	7
Granite Mountain, mtn., Ak., U.S.	B7	79
Granite Mountain, mtn., Ar., U.S.	k10	81
Granite Mountains, mts., Az., U.S.	E2	80
Granite Mountains, mts., Wy., U.S.	D5	127
Granite Park, Ut., U.S.	*C4	121
Granite Peak, Wy., U.S.	B5	127
Granite Peak, mtn., Mt., U.S.	E7	103
Granite Peak, mtn., Nv., U.S.	C2	105
Granite Peak, mtn., Nv., U.S.	B4	105
Granite Peak, mtn., Ut., U.S.	E3	121
Granite Peak, mtn., Ut., U.S.	C2	121
Granite Peak, mtn., Wy., U.S.	D4	127
Granite Point, c., Newf.	C3	72
Granite Quarry, N.C., U.S.	B2	110
Granite Range, mts., Nv., U.S.	C2	105
Graniteville, Ma., U.S.	f10	98
Graniteville, Mo., U.S.	D7	102
Graniteville, S.C., U.S.	D4	117
Graniteville, Vt., U.S.	C4	122
Granja, Braz.	B2	57
Granja de Torrehermosa, Spain	C3	22
Granma, prov., Cuba	D5	64
Grannis, Ar., U.S.	C1	81
Grano, N.D., U.S.	A4	111
Granollers, Spain	B7	22
Gran Paradiso, mtn., Italy	D3	20
Gransee, E. Ger.	E7	15
Grant, Al., U.S.	A3	78
Grant, Co., U.S.	B5	83
Grant, Fl., U.S.	E6	86
Grant, Ia., U.S.	C2	92
Grant, La., U.S.	D3	95
Grant, Mi., U.S.	E5	99
Grant, Mt., U.S.	E3	103
Grant, Ne., U.S.	D4	104
Grant, Ok., U.S.	D6	113
Grant, co., Ar., U.S.	C3	81
Grant, co., In., U.S.	C6	91
Grant, co., Ks., U.S.	E2	93
Grant, co., Ky., U.S.	B5	94
Grant, co., La., U.S.	C3	95
Grant, co., Mn., U.S.	E2	100
Grant, co., Ne., U.S.	C4	104
Grant, co., N.M., U.S.	E1	108
Grant, co., N.D., U.S.	C4	111
Grant, co., Ok., U.S.	A4	113
Grant, co., Or., U.S.	C7	114
Grant, co., S.D., U.S.	B8	118
Grant, co., Wa., U.S.	B6	124
Grant, co., W.V., U.S.	B5	125
Grant, co., Wi., U.S.	F3	126
Grant, Mount, mtn., Nv., U.S.	E3	105
Grant City, Mo., U.S.	A3	102
Grantham, Eng., U.K.	D6	10
Grantham, N.H., U.S.	D2	106
Granton, Ont.	D3	73
Granton, Wi., U.S.	D3	126
Grantown-on-Spey, Scot., U.K.	C5	13
Grant Park, Il., U.S.	B6	90
Grant Range, mts., Nv., U.S.	E6	105
Grants, N.M., U.S.	B2	108
Grantsboro, N.C., U.S.	B6	110
Grantsburg, Il., U.S.	F5	90
Grantsburg, Wi., U.S.	C1	126
Grantsdale, Mt., U.S.	D2	103
Grants Lick, Ky., U.S.	k14	94
Grants Pass, Or., U.S.	E3	114
Grantsville, Md., U.S.	k12	97
Grantsville, Ut., U.S.	C3	121
Grantsville, W.V., U.S.	C3	125
Grant Town, W.V., U.S.	B4	125
Grantville, Ga., U.S.	C2	87
Grantville, Ks., U.S.	k14	93
Grantville, Pa., U.S.	F8	115
Granum, Alta.	E4	68
Granville, Fr.	C3	16
Granville, Il., U.S.	B4	90
Granville, Ia., U.S.	B2	92
Granville, Ma., U.S.	B2	98
Granville, N.Y., U.S.	B7	109
Granville, N.D., U.S.	A5	111
Granville, Oh., U.S.	B3	112
Granville, Tn., U.S.	C8	119
Granville, Vt., U.S.	D3	122
Granville, W.V., U.S.	h11	125
Granville, co., N.C., U.S.	A4	110
Granville Centre, N.S.	E4	71
Granville Ferry, N.S.	E4	71
Granville Lake, l., Man.	A1	70
Grão Mogol, Braz.	B4	56
Grapeland, Tx., U.S.	D5	120
Grapeview, Wa., U.S.	B3	124
Grapevine, Tx., U.S.	C4	120
Grapevine Lake, res., Tx., U.S.	n9	120
Grapevine Peak, mtn., Nv., U.S.	G4	105
Gras, Lac de, l., N.W. Ter.	D10	66
Grasonville, Md., U.S.	C5	97
Grass, stm., Man.	B2	70
Grass, stm., N.Y., U.S.	f9	109
Grass Creek, In., U.S.	C5	91
Grass Creek, Wy., U.S.	C4	127
Grasse, Fr.	F7	16
Grasselli, Al., U.S.	B3	78
Grassflat, Pa., U.S.	D5	115
Grassington, Eng., U.K.	F7	13
Grass Lake, Il., U.S.	h8	90
Grass Lake, l., Il., U.S.	h8	90
Grass Lake, l., La., U.S.	k9	95
Grassrange, Mt., U.S.	C8	103
Grass River Provincial Park, Man.	B1	70
Grasston, Mn., U.S.	E5	100
Grass Valley, Ca., U.S.	C3	82
Grass Valley, Or., U.S.	B6	114
Grassy Brook, stm., Vt., U.S.	E3	122
Grassy Butte, N.D., U.S.	B2	111
Grassy Creek, N.C., U.S.	A1	110
Grassy Lake, Alta.	E5	68
Grassy Lake, l., La., U.S.	k9	95
Gråsten, Den.	D3	15
Grates Cove, Newf.	D5	72
Grates Point, c., Newf.	D5	72
Gratiot, Oh., U.S.	C3	112
Gratiot, co., Mi., U.S.	E6	99
Gratis, Oh., U.S.	C1	112
Gratz, Pa., U.S.	E8	115
Graubünden, state, Switz.	C5	20
Graulhet, Fr.	F4	16
Gravatá, Braz.	C3	57
Gravedona, Italy	D7	21
Gravelbourg, Sask.	H2	75
Gravelines, Fr.	D2	17
Gravelly Branch, stm., De., U.S.	F4	85
Gravelly Range, mts., Mt., U.S.	E4	103
Gravenhurst, Ont.	C5	73
Grave Peak, mtn., Id., U.S.	C4	89
Graves, Ga., U.S.	E2	87
Graves, S.C., U.S.	E9	117
Graves, co., Ky., U.S.	f9	94
Gravesend, Eng., U.K.	E7	10
Gravette, Ar., U.S.	A1	81
Gravina [in Puglia], Italy	D6	23
Gravity, Ia., U.S.	D3	92
Gravois, Pointe à, c., Haiti	E7	64
Gravois Mills, Mo., U.S.	C5	102
Grawn, Mi., U.S.	D5	99
Gray, Sask.	G3	75
Gray, Fr.	D6	16
Gray, Ga., U.S.	C3	87
Gray, Ky., U.S.	D5	94
Gray, La., U.S.	k10	95
Gray, Me., U.S.	g7	96
Gray, co., Ks., U.S.	E3	93
Gray, co., Tx., U.S.	B2	120
Grayback Mountain, mtn., Or., U.S.	E3	114
Gray Court, S.C., U.S.	B3	117
Gray Gables, Ma., U.S.	*C6	98
Gray Horse, Ok., U.S.	A5	113
Grayland, Wa., U.S.	C1	124
Grayling, Ak., U.S.	C7	79
Graylyn Crest, De., U.S.	A3	85
Graymont, Il., U.S.	B5	90
Grays, Eng., U.K.	m13	10
Grays Harbor, co., Wa., U.S.	B2	124
Grays Harbor, b., Wa., U.S.	C1	124
Grayslake, Il., U.S.	A5	90
Grays Lake, sw., Id., U.S.	F7	89
Grayson, Sask.	G4	75
Grayson, Al., U.S.	A2	78
Grayson, Ga., U.S.	C3	87
Grayson, Ky., U.S.	B7	94
Grayson, La., U.S.	B3	95
Grayson, Ok., U.S.	B6	113
Grayson, co., Ky., U.S.	C3	94
Grayson, co., Tx., U.S.	C4	120
Grayson, co., Va., U.S.	D1	123
Grayson Lake, res., Ky., U.S.	B7	94
Grays Peak, mtn., Co., U.S.	B5	83
Grays River, Wa., U.S.	C2	124
Gray Summit, Mo., U.S.	g12	102
Graysville, Al., U.S.	f7	78
Graysville, In., U.S.	F2	91
Graysville, Oh., U.S.	C4	112
Graysville, Pa., U.S.	G1	115
Graysville, Tn., U.S.	D8	119
Grayville, Il., U.S.	E5	90
Graz, Aus.	E7	18
Greasewood, Az., U.S.	B6	80
Great, stm., Jam.	E13	65
Great Abaco, i., Bah.	A5	64
Great Alföld, pl., Hung.	B5	24
Great Artesian Basin, Austl.	E7	50
Great Australian Bight, Austl.	F4	50
Great Averill, l., Vt., U.S.	B5	122
Great Barrier Island, i., N.Z.	L15	51
Great Barrier Reef, rf., Austl.	C8	50
Great Barrington, Ma., U.S.	B1	98
Great Basin National Park, Nv., U.S.	E7	105
Great Bay, b., N.H., U.S.	D5	106
Great Bay, b., N.J., U.S.	D4	107
Great Bear Lake, l., N.W. Ter.	C8	66
Great Bend, Ks., U.S.	D5	93
Great Bend, N.D., U.S.	C9	111
Great Bend, Pa., U.S.	C10	115
Great Bitter Lake, l., Eg.	D4	41
Great Blasket Island, i., Ire.	E1	11
Great Blue Hill, hill, Ma., U.S.	h12	98
Great Burnt Lake, l., Newf.	D3	72
Great Cacapon, W.V., U.S.	B6	125
Great Camanoe, i., V.I., Br.	B6	65
Great Captain Island, i., Ct., U.S.	F1	84
Great Channel, strt., Asia	G9	36
Great Deer, Sask.	E2	75
Great Dismal Swamp, sw., U.S.	D6	123
Great Divide Basin, Wy., U.S.	E4	127
Great Dividing Range, mts., Austl.	F9	50
Great Driffield, Eng., U.K.	F8	13
Great Duck Island, i., Ont.	B2	73
Great East Lake, l., U.S.	C5	106
Great Egg Harbor, stm., N.J., U.S.	D3	107
Greater Antilles, is., N.A.	H13	61
Greater Cincinnati Airport, Ky., U.S.	h13	94
Greater Khingan Range see Da Hinggan Ling, mts., China	B9	31
Greater London, co., Eng., U.K.	C7	12
Greater Manchester, co., Eng., U.K.	*A5	12
Great Exuma, i., Bah.	C6	64
Great Fall, wtfl., Guy.	A2	59
Great Falls, Man.	D3	70
Great Falls, Mt., U.S.	C5	103
Great Falls, S.C., U.S.	B6	117
Great Falls, wtfl., Md., U.S.	B3	97
Great Falls Dam, Tn., U.S.	D8	119
Great Guana Cay, i., Bah.	B5	64
Great Harbour Deep, b., Newf.	C3	72
Greathouse Peak, mtn., Mt., U.S.	D7	103
Great Inagua, i., Bah.	D7	64
Great Indian Desert (Thar Desert), des., Asia	C5	36
Great Island, spit, Ma., U.S.	C7	98
Great Island, i., N.C., U.S.	B6	110
Great Karroo, plat., S. Afr.	D3	49
Great Lake, l., Austl.	o15	50
Great Lakes Naval Training Center, mil., Il., U.S.	h9	90
Great Malvern, Eng., U.K.	B5	12
Great Miami, stm., U.S.	C1	112
Great Misery Island, i., Ma., U.S.	f12	98
Great Moose Lake, l., Me., U.S.	D3	96
Great Neck, N.Y., U.S.	h13	109
Great Neck Estates, N.Y.	*E7	109
Great Nicobar, i., India	G9	36
Great North Mountain, mtn., U.S.	C6	125
Great Ouse, stm., Eng., U.K.	D7	10
Great Pedro Bluff, c., Jam.	F13	65
Great Pee Dee, stm., U.S.	D9	117
Great Point, c., Ma., U.S.	D7	98
Great Pond, Me., U.S.	D4	96
Great Pond, l., Me., U.S.	D3	96
Great Pond, l., Ma., U.S.	h12	98
Great Pond, l., R.I., U.S.	h11	98
Great Quittacas Pond, l., Ma., U.S.	C6	98
Great Ruaha, stm., Tan.	C6	48
Great Sacandaga Lake, l., N.Y., U.S.	C6	109
Great Saint Bernard Pass, Eur.	B1	23
Great Salt Lake, l., Ut., U.S.	B3	121
Great Salt Lake Desert, des., Ut., U.S.	C2	121
Great Salt Plains Lake, res., Ok., U.S.	A3	113
Great Salt Pond, b., R.I., U.S.	h7	116
Great Salt Pond, l., Jam.	F15	65
Great Sand Dunes National Monument, Co., U.S.	D5	83
Great Sand Hills, hills, Sask.	G1	75
Great Sandy Desert, des., Austl.	D3	50
Great Sea Reef, rf., Fiji	H15	52
Great Seneca Creek, stm., Md., U.S.	B3	97
Great Skellig Island, i., Ire.	F1	11
Great Slave Lake, l., N.W. Ter.	D10	66
Great Smoky Mountains, mts., U.S.	B8	119
Great Smoky Mountains National Park, U.S.	f10	110
Great Sound, strt., Ber.	p19	64
Great Swamp, sw., R.I., U.S.	F3	116
Great Tenasserim, stm., Burma	F3	35
Great Torrington, Eng., U.K.	D3	12
Great Valley, val., U.S.	C2	123
Great Victoria Desert, des., Austl.	E4	50
Great Village, N.S.	D6	71
Great Wall, hist., China	C8	31
Great Wass Island, i., Me., U.S.	D5	96
Great Yarmouth, Eng., U.K.	D7	10
Great Zab, stm., Asia	D14	40
Gredos, Sierra de, mts., Spain	B3	22
Greece, N.Y., U.S.	B3	109
Greece, ctry., Eur.	C4	40
Greeley, Co., U.S.	A6	83
Greeley, Ia., U.S.	B6	92
Greeley, Ne., U.S.	C7	104
Greeley, Pa., U.S.	D12	115
Greeley, co., Ks., U.S.	D2	93
Greeley, co., Ne., U.S.	C7	104
Greeleyville, S.C., U.S.	D7	117
Greely Fiord, N.W. Ter.	k35	66
Green, Or., U.S.	D3	114
Green, co., Ky., U.S.	C4	94
Green, co., Wi., U.S.	F4	126
Green, stm., N.B.	B1	71
Green, stm., U.S.	C6	76
Green, stm., Il., U.S.	B4	90
Green, stm., Ky., U.S.	C2	94
Green, stm., Wa., U.S.	B4	124
Green, stm., Wy., U.S.	E3	127
Green Acres, De., U.S.	h8	85
Greenacres, Ca., U.S.	*E4	82
Greenacres, Wa., U.S.	B8	124
Greenacres City, Fl., U.S.	F6	86
Greenback, Tn., U.S.	D9	119
Greenbackville, Va., U.S.	C7	123
Green Bank, N.J., U.S.	D3	107
Green Bank, W.V., U.S.	C5	125
Green Bay, Va., U.S.	C4	123
Green Bay, Wi., U.S.	D6	126
Greenbelt, Md., U.S.	C4	97
Greenbriar, Va., U.S.	g12	123
Greenbrier, Ar., U.S.	B3	81
Greenbrier, Tn., U.S.	A5	119
Greenbrier, co., W.V., U.S.	D4	125
Greenbrier, stm., W.V., U.S.	D4	125
Green Brook, N.J., U.S.	*B4	107
Greenburr, Pa., U.S.	D7	115
Greenbush, Me., U.S.	C4	96
Greenbush, Mn., U.S.	B2	100
Greenbush, Wi., U.S.	k9	126
Green Camp, Oh., U.S.	B2	112
Greencastle, In., U.S.	E4	91
Greencastle, Mo., U.S.	A5	102
Greencastle, Pa., U.S.	G6	115
Green City, Mo., U.S.	A5	102
Green Cove Springs, Fl., U.S.	C5	86
Greencreek, Id., U.S.	C2	89
Green Creek, N.J., U.S.	E3	107
Greendale, In., U.S.	F8	91
Greendale, Ut., U.S.	*C6	121
Greendale, Wi., U.S.	F6	126
Greendell, N.J., U.S.	B3	107
Greene, Ia., U.S.	B5	92
Greene, Me., U.S.	D2	96
Greene, N.Y., U.S.	C5	109
Greene, N.D., U.S.	A4	111
Greene, co., Al., U.S.	C1	78
Greene, co., Ar., U.S.	A5	81
Greene, co., Ga., U.S.	C3	87
Greene, co., Il., U.S.	D3	90
Greene, co., In., U.S.	F4	91
Greene, co., Ia., U.S.	B3	92
Greene, co., Ms., U.S.	D5	101
Greene, co., Mo., U.S.	D4	102
Greene, co., N.Y., U.S.	C6	109
Greene, co., N.C., U.S.	B5	110
Greene, co., Oh., U.S.	C2	112
Greene, co., Pa., U.S.	G1	115
Greene, co., Tn., U.S.	C11	119
Greene, co., Va., U.S.	B4	123
Greeneville, Tn., U.S.	C11	119
Green Fall, stm., U.S.	F1	116
Greenfield, Ar., U.S.	B5	81
Greenfield, Ca., U.S.	D3	82
Greenfield, Il., U.S.	D3	90
Greenfield, In., U.S.	E6	91
Greenfield, Ia., U.S.	C3	92
Greenfield, Me., U.S.	C4	96
Greenfield, Mo., U.S.	D4	102
Greenfield, N.H., U.S.	E3	106
Greenfield, Oh., U.S.	C2	112
Greenfield, Ok., U.S.	B3	113
Greenfield, Tn., U.S.	A3	119
Greenfield Plaza, Ia., U.S.	e8	92
Green Forest, Ar., U.S.	A2	81
Green Grass, S.D., U.S.	B4	118
Green Harbor, Ma., U.S.	B6	98
Greenhill, Al., U.S.	A2	78
Greenhill, In., U.S.	D3	91
Green Hill Pond, l., R.I., U.S.	G3	116
Green Hill Pond, l., R.I., U.S.	G3	116
Greenhills, Oh., U.S.	n12	112
Greenhorn Creek, stm., Co., U.S.	D6	83
Green Island, Ia., U.S.	B7	92
Green Island, N.Y., U.S.	*C7	109
Green Isle, Mn., U.S.	F4	100
Green Lake, Ut., U.S.	*C6	121
Green Lake, Wi., U.S.	E5	126
Green Lake, co., Wi., U.S.	E4	126
Green Lake, l., B.C.	D7	69
Green Lake, l., Sask.	C2	75
Green Lake, l., Me., U.S.	D4	96
Green Lake, l., Wi., U.S.	E5	126
Greenland, Ar., U.S.	B1	81
Greenland, Mi., U.S.	B1	99
Greenland, N.H., U.S.	D5	106
Greenland (Kalaallit Nunaat), ctry., N.A.	B16	128
Greenland Sea	B15	128
Greenlaw, Scot., U.K.	E6	13
Greenlawn, N.Y., U.S.	*h13	109
Greenleaf, Ks., U.S.	C7	93
Greenleaf, Wi., U.S.	D5	126
Greenlee, co., Az., U.S.	D6	80
Green Lookout Mountain, mtn., Wa., U.S.	D3	124
Green Lowther, mtn., Scot., U.K.	E5	13
Green Manorville, Ct., U.S.	B5	84
Greenmount, Md., U.S.	A4	97
Green Mountain, l., Ia., U.S.	B5	92
Greenmountain, N.C., U.S.	f10	110
Green Mountain Falls, Co., U.S.	*C6	83
Green Mountain Reservoir, res., Co., U.S.	B4	83
Green Mountains, mts., Vt., U.S.	F2	122
Greenock, Scot., U.K.	D4	13
Greenock, Pa., U.S.	F2	115
Greenore Point, c., Ire.	E5	11
Greenough, Mt., U.S.	D3	103
Greenough Point, c., Ont.	C3	73
Green Peter Lake, res., Or., U.S.	C4	114
Green Pond, Al., U.S.	B2	78
Green Pond, S.C., U.S.	F6	117
Green Pond, N.J., U.S.	A4	107
Green Pond Mountain, mtn., N.J., U.S.	B3	107
Greenport, N.Y., U.S.	m16	109
Green Ridge, Mo., U.S.	C4	102
Green River, Ut., U.S.	E5	121
Green River, Wy., U.S.	E3	127
Green River Lake, res., Ky., U.S.	C4	94
Green River Lock and Dam, U.S.	I2	91
Green River Reservoir, Vt., U.S.	B3	122
Green Rock, Il., U.S.	B3	90
Greensboro, Al., U.S.	C2	78
Greensboro, Fl., U.S.	B2	86
Greensboro, Ga., U.S.	C3	87
Greensboro, In., U.S.	E7	91
Greensboro, Md., U.S.	C6	97

Name	Map Ref.	Page
Greensboro, N.C., U.S.	A3	110
Greensboro, Ga., U.S.	G2	115
Greensboro, Vt., U.S.	B4	122
Greensboro Bend, Vt., U.S.	B4	122
Greensburg, In., U.S.	F7	91
Greensburg, Ks., U.S.	E4	93
Greensburg, Ky., U.S.	C4	94
Greensburg, La., U.S.	D5	95
Greensburg, Pa., U.S.	F2	115
Green Sea, S.C., U.S.	C10	117
Greens Fork, In., U.S.	E7	91
Greens Peak, mtn., Az., U.S.	C6	80
Greenspond, Newf.	D5	72
Green Spring, W.V., U.S.	B6	125
Green Springs, Oh., U.S.	A2	112
Greenstone Point, c., Scot., U.K.	C3	13
Green Sulphur Springs, W.V., U.S.	D4	125
Greensville, co., Va., U.S.	D5	123
Green Swamp, sw., N.C., U.S.	C4	110
Greentop, Mo., U.S.	A5	102
Greentown, In., U.S.	D6	91
Green Tree, Pa., U.S.	*k13	115
Greenup, Il., U.S.	D5	90
Greenup, Ky., U.S.	B7	94
Greenup, co., Ky., U.S.	B7	94
Green Valley, Az., U.S.	F5	80
Green Valley, Il., U.S.	C4	90
Green Valley, Mn., U.S.	F3	100
Green Valley, Wi., U.S.	D5	126
Green Valley, val., Tx., U.S.	p13	120
Greenview, Il., U.S.	C4	90
Greenview, W.V., U.S.	n12	125
Greenville, Lib.	E3	45
Greenville, Al., U.S.	D3	78
Greenville, Ca., U.S.	B3	82
Greenville, De., U.S.	A3	85
Greenville, Fl., U.S.	B3	86
Greenville, Ga., U.S.	C2	87
Greenville, Il., U.S.	E4	90
Greenville, In., U.S.	H6	91
Greenville, Ia., U.S.	A2	92
Greenville, Ky., U.S.	C2	94
Greenville, Me., U.S.	C3	96
Greenville, Mi., U.S.	E5	99
Greenville, Ms., U.S.	B2	101
Greenville, Mo., U.S.	D7	102
Greenville, N.H., U.S.	E3	106
Greenville, N.Y., U.S.	*n15	109
Greenville, N.C., U.S.	B5	110
Greenville, Oh., U.S.	B1	112
Greenville, Pa., U.S.	D1	115
Greenville, R.I., U.S.	C3	116
Greenville, S.C., U.S.	B3	117
Greenville, Tx., U.S.	C4	120
Greenville, Ut., U.S.	E3	121
Greenville, Va., U.S.	B3	123
Greenville, W.V., U.S.	D4	125
Greenville, Wi., U.S.	h8	126
Greenville, co., S.C., U.S.	B3	117
Greenville Creek, stm., Oh., U.S.	B1	112
Greenville Junction, Me., U.S.	C3	96
Greenwald, Mn., U.S.	E4	100
Greenwater Lake Provincial Park, Sask.	E4	75
Greenway, Man.	E2	70
Greenway, Ar., U.S.	A5	81
Greenwell Springs, La., U.S.	D5	95
Greenwich (part of London), Eng., U.K.	m13	10
Greenwich, Ct., U.S.	E1	84
Greenwich, Ks., U.S.	g12	93
Greenwich, N.J., U.S.	E2	107
Greenwich, N.Y., U.S.	B7	109
Greenwich, Oh., U.S.	A3	112
Greenwich, Ut., U.S.	E4	121
Greenwich, Vt., U.S.	*B5	123
Greenwich Bay, b., R.I., U.S.	D4	116
Greenwich Hill, N.B.	D3	71
Greenwich Point, c., Ct., U.S.	E1	84
Greenwood, B.C.	E8	69
Greenwood, Ar., U.S.	B1	81
Greenwood, De., U.S.	E3	85
Greenwood, Fl., U.S.	B1	86
Greenwood, In., U.S.	E5	91
Greenwood, Ky., U.S.	D5	94
Greenwood, La., U.S.	B2	95
Greenwood, Ms., U.S.	B3	101
Greenwood, Mo., U.S.	k11	102
Greenwood, Ne., U.S.	D9	104
Greenwood, N.Y., U.S.	C3	109
Greenwood, Pa., U.S.	E5	115
Greenwood, S.C., U.S.	C3	117
Greenwood, S.D., U.S.	E7	118
Greenwood, Wi., U.S.	D3	126
Greenwood, co., Ks., U.S.	E7	93
Greenwood, co., S.C., U.S.	C3	117
Greenwood, Lake, res., In., U.S.	G4	91
Greenwood, Lake, res., S.C., U.S.	C4	117
Greenwood Lake, N.Y., U.S.	D6	109
Greenwood Lake, l., U.S.	A4	107
Greenwood Lake, l., Mn., U.S.	C7	100
Greenwood Village, Co., U.S.	*B6	83
Greer, Id., U.S.	C2	89
Greer, Mo., U.S.	E6	102
Greer, S.C., U.S.	B3	117
Greer, co., Ok., U.S.	C2	113
Greers Ferry Lake, res., Ar., U.S.	B3	81
Greeson, Lake, res., Ar., U.S.	C2	81
Greetsiel, W. Ger.	A7	17
Gregg, co., Tx., U.S.	C5	120
Gregoire Lake, l., Alta.	A5	68
Gregory, Ar., U.S.	B4	81
Gregory, Mi., U.S.	F6	99
Gregory, N.C., U.S.	A6	110
Gregory, S.D., U.S.	D6	118
Gregory, co., S.D., U.S.	D6	118
Gregory, stm., Austl.	C6	50
Gregory Lake, l., Austl.	E6	50
Gregory Bald, mtn., Tn., U.S.	D10	119
Gregory Range, mts., Austl.	C7	50
Greifswald, E. Ger.	A6	13
Greifswalder Bodden, b., E. Ger.	D7	15
Greig, N.Y., U.S.	B5	109
Greilickville, Mi., U.S.	D5	99
Grein, Aus.	D7	18
Greiz, E. Ger.	E8	15
Grelton, Oh., U.S.	A1	112
Gremyachinsk, Sov. Un.	D20	8
Grená, Den.	B4	14
Grenada, Ca., U.S.	B2	82
Grenada, Ms., U.S.	B4	101
Grenada, co., Ms., U.S.	B4	101
Grenada, ctry., N.A.	J14	64
Grenada Lake, res., Ms., U.S.	B4	101
Grenade, Fr.	F4	16
Grenadine Islands, is., N.A.	V26	65
Grenagh, Ire.	E3	11
Grenay, Fr.	D2	17
Grenchen, Switz.	B3	20
Grenen (The Skaw), spit, Den.	A4	15
Grenfell, Sask.	G4	75
Grenoble, Fr.	E6	16
Grenola, Ks., U.S.	E7	93
Grenora, N.D., U.S.	A2	111
Grenville, Que.	D3	74
Grenville, Gren.	W25	65
Grenville, N.M., U.S.	A6	108
Grenville, S.D., U.S.	B8	118
Grenville, co., Ont.	C9	73
Grenville, Cape, c., Austl.	A4	15
Grenville, Point, c., Wa., U.S.	B1	124
Grenville Channel, strt., B.C.	C3	69
Gresham, Or., U.S.	C8	104
Gresham, S.C., U.S.	B4	114
Gresham, S.C., U.S.	C3	23
Gresham, Or., U.S.	B4	114
Gresham, S.C., U.S.	D9	117
Gresham, Wi., U.S.	D5	126
Gresham Park, Ga., U.S.	*h8	87
Gretna, Man.	E3	70
Gretna, Scot., U.K.	F5	13
Gretna, Fl., U.S.	B2	86
Gretna, La., U.S.	E5	95
Gretna, Ne., U.S.	C9	104
Gretna, Va., U.S.	D3	123
Greven, W. Ger.	A2	19
Grevená, Grc.	B3	25
Grevenbroich, W. Ger.	B1	19
Grevesmühlen, E. Ger.	E5	15
Grey, co., Ont.	C4	73
Grey, stm., Newf.	E3	72
Grey, stm., N.Z.	O13	51
Greybull, Wy., U.S.	B4	127
Greybull, stm., Wy., U.S.	B4	127
Greycliff, Mt., U.S.	E7	103
Grey Eagle, Mn., U.S.	E4	100
Grey Islands, is., Newf.	C4	72
Greylock, Mount, mtn., Ma., U.S.	A1	98
Greymouth, N.Z.	O13	51
Grey Range, mts., Austl.	E7	50
Greys, stm., Wy., U.S.	C2	127
Greystone, Ct., U.S.	C3	84
Greystone, N.C., U.S.	A4	110
Greytown, S. Afr.	C5	49
Gribbell Island, i., B.C.	C3	69
Gridley, Ca., U.S.	C3	82
Gridley, Il., U.S.	C5	90
Gridley, Ks., U.S.	D8	93
Gridley Mountain, mtn., Ct., U.S.	A2	84
Griekwastad, S. Afr.	C3	49
Griesheim, W. Ger.	D3	19
Grieskirchen, Aus.	D6	18
Griffin, Sask.	H4	75
Griffin, Ga., U.S.	C2	87
Griffin, In., U.S.	H2	91
Griffiss Air Force Base, mil., N.Y., U.S.	B5	109
Griffith, Austl.	F8	50
Griffith Island, i., Ont.	C4	73
Griffithsville, W.V., U.S.	C3	125
Griffithville, Ar., U.S.	B4	81
Grifton, N.C., U.S.	B5	110
Griggs, Ok., U.S.	e8	113
Griggs, co., N.D., U.S.	B7	111
Griggstown, N.J., U.S.	C3	107
Griggsville, Il., U.S.	D3	90
Grigoriopol, Sov. Un.	B9	24
Grim, Cape, c., Austl.	o14	50
Grimari, Cen. Afr. Rep.	D4	46
Grimes, Al., U.S.	D4	78
Grimes, Ca., U.S.	C3	82
Grimes, co., Tx., U.S.	D4	120
Grimesland, N.C., U.S.	B5	110
Grimma, E. Ger.	C6	18
Grimmen, E. Ger.	D7	15
Grimmialp, Switz.	C4	21
Grimms Landing, W.V., U.S.	C3	125
Grimsby, Ont.	D5	73
Grimsby, Eng., U.K.	D6	10
Grimsey, i., Ice.	m23	11
Grimshaw, Alta.	A2	68
Grimsley, Tn., U.S.	C9	119
Grimstad, Nor.	H3	14
Grimsthorpe, Ont.	B2	73
Grindall Creek, Va., U.S.	n18	123
Grindelwald, Switz.	C5	21
Grindsted, Den.	I3	14
Grindstone, Me., U.S.	C4	96
Grind Stone City, Mi., U.S.	D8	99
Grinem, i., Marsh Is.	S18	52
Grinnell, Ia., U.S.	C5	92
Grinnell, Ks., U.S.	C3	93
Grinnell Peninsula, pen., N.W. Ter.	m32	66
Grise Fiord, N.W. Ter.	m35	66
Gris-Nez, Cap, c., Fr.	D9	12
Grissom Air Force Base, mil., In., U.S.	C5	91
Griswold, Man.	E1	70
Griswold, Ia., U.S.	C2	92
Griswoldville, Ma., U.S.	A2	98
Grizzly Mountain, mtn., Id., U.S.	B2	89
Grizzly Mountain, mtn., Or., U.S.	C6	114
Grizzly Mountain, mtn., Wa., U.S.	A7	124
Groais Island, i., Newf.	C4	72
Grodków, Pol.	C4	26
Grodno, Sov. Un.	E4	27
Grodzisk Mazowiecki, Pol.	m13	26
Grodzisk [Wielkopolski], Pol.	B4	26
Groenlo, Neth.	*B6	17
Groesbeck, Oh., U.S.	*o12	112
Groesbeck, Tx., U.S.	D4	120
Groix, Île de, i., Fr.	D2	16
Grójec, Pol.	D6	26
Grombalia, Tun.	F3	23
Gronau, W. Ger.	A2	19
Gronau, W. Ger.	A4	19
Groningen, Neth.	A3	17
Groningen, Sur.	A3	59
Groningen, prov., Neth.	A3	17
Gronlid, Sask.	D3	75
Groom, Tx., U.S.	B2	120
Groom Lake, l., Nv., U.S.	F6	105
Groom Range, mts., Nv., U.S.	F6	105
Groote Eylandt, i., Austl.	B6	50
Grootfontein, Nmb.	A2	49
Grootvloer, pl., S. Afr.	C3	49
Groscap, Mi., U.S.	C6	99
Grosio, Italy	D9	21
Groslay, Fr.	g10	16
Gros-Mécatina, Île du, i., Que.	C2	72
Gros Morne, mtn., Newf.	D3	72
Gros Morne National Park, Newf.	D3	72
Gross, Ne., U.S.	B7	104
Grossbreitenbach, E. Ger.	C6	19
Grosse Île, Mi., U.S.	*F7	99
Grosse Île, i., Que.	B8	71
Grosse Isle Naval Air Station, mil., Mi., U.S.	p15	99
Grosse Laaber, stm., W. Ger.	E7	19
Grossenhain, E. Ger.	C6	18
Grosse Pointe, Mi., U.S.	*F8	99
Grosse Pointe Farms, Mi., U.S.	p16	99
Grosse Pointe Park, Mi., U.S.	p16	99
Grosse Pointe Woods, Mi., U.S.	p16	99
Grosser Arber, mtn., W. Ger.	D8	19
Grosse Röder, stm., E. Ger.	B8	19
Grösser Plön, l., W. Ger.	D4	15
Grosser Priel, mtn., Aus.	E7	18
Grosse Tete, La., U.S.	D4	95
Grosseto, Italy	C3	23
Grossevichi, Sov. Un.	B9	33
Grosse-Gerau, W. Ger.	D3	19
Grossglockner, mtn., Aus.	E6	18
Grossmont, Ca., U.S.	o16	82
Grossostheim, W. Ger.	D4	19
Grossräschen, E. Ger.	B9	19
Grossröhrsdorf, E. Ger.	B9	19
Grosvenor Dale, Ct., U.S.	B8	84
Gros Ventre, stm., Wy., U.S.	C2	127
Gros Ventre Range, mts., Wy., U.S.	C2	127
Groswater Bay, b., Newf.	A3	72
Groton, Ct., U.S.	D7	84
Groton, Ma., U.S.	A4	98
Groton, N.H., U.S.	C3	106
Groton, N.Y., U.S.	C4	109
Groton, S.D., U.S.	B7	118
Groton, Vt., U.S.	C4	122
Groton Long Point, Ct., U.S.	D7	84
Grottaferrata, Italy	h9	23
Grottaglie, Italy	D6	23
Grottoes, Va., U.S.	B4	123
Grouard Mission, Alta.	B2	68
Grouse Creek, Ut., U.S.	B2	121
Grouse Creek, stm., Ks., U.S.	E7	93
Grouse Creek, stm., Ut., U.S.	B2	121
Grouse Creek Mountain, mtn., Id., U.S.	E5	89
Grouse Creek Mountains, mts., Ut., U.S.	B2	121
Grovania, Ga., U.S.	D3	87
Grove, Me., U.S.	C5	96
Grove, Ok., U.S.	A7	113
Grove City, Fl., U.S.	F4	86
Grove City, Mn., U.S.	E4	100
Grove City, Oh., U.S.	C2	112
Grove City, Pa., U.S.	D1	115
Grove Hill, Al., U.S.	D2	78
Groveland, Ca., U.S.	D3	82
Groveland, Fl., U.S.	D5	86
Groveland, Ma., U.S.	A5	98
Groveland, N.Y., U.S.	C3	109
Grove Mountains, mts., Ant.	B21	7
Grove Point, c., Md., U.S.	B5	97
Groveport, Oh., U.S.	C3	112
Grover, Co., U.S.	A6	83
Grover, N.C., U.S.	B1	110
Grover, Pa., U.S.	C8	115
Grover, S.C., U.S.	E6	117
Grover, Wy., U.S.	D2	127
Grover City, Ca., U.S.	E3	82
Grover Hill, Oh., U.S.	A1	112
Grovertown, In., U.S.	B4	91
Groves, Tx., U.S.	E6	120
Grovespring, Mo., U.S.	D5	102
Groveton, N.H., U.S.	A3	106
Groveton, Tx., U.S.	D5	120
Groveton, Va., U.S.	g12	123
Groveton Gardens, Va., U.S.	B5	123
Grovetown, Ga., U.S.	C4	87
Groveville, N.J., U.S.	C3	107
Growler Peak, mtn., Az., U.S.	E2	80
Groznyy, Sov. Un.	E7	29
Grubbs, Ar., U.S.	B4	81
Grudovo, Bul.	D8	24
Grudziądz, Pol.	B5	26
Gruetli-Laager, Tn., U.S.	D8	119
Gruinard Bay, b., Scot., U.K.	C3	13
Grulla, Tx., U.S.	F3	120
Grünberg, W. Ger.	C4	19
Grundy, Va., U.S.	e9	123
Grundy, co., Il., U.S.	B5	90
Grundy, co., Ia., U.S.	B5	92
Grundy, co., Mo., U.S.	A4	102
Grundy, co., Tn., U.S.	D8	119
Grundy Center, Ia., U.S.	B5	92
Grünstadt, W. Ger.	D3	19
Grünthal, Man.	E3	70
Grüsch, Switz.	C8	21
Gruver, Ia., U.S.	A3	92
Gruver, Tx., U.S.	A2	120
Gruyères, Switz.	C3	21
Gruž (part of Dubrovnik), Yugo.	D4	24
Gryazi, Sov. Un.	E13	27
Gryazovets, Sov. Un.	B13	27
Gryfice, Pol.	B3	26
Gryfino, Pol.	B2	26
Grygla, Mn., U.S.	B3	100
Gstaad, Switz.	C3	21
Guabito, Pan.	F6	62
Guacanayabo, Golfo de, b., Cuba	D5	64
Gu Achi, Az., U.S.	E3	80
Guadalajara, Mex.	G8	63
Guadalajara, Spain	B4	22
Guadalcanal, Spain	C3	22
Guadalcanal, i., Sol.Is.	G9	6
Guadalentín, stm., Spain	D5	22
Guadalhorce, stm., Spain	D4	22
Guadalmena, stm., Spain	C5	22
Guadalope, stm., Spain	B5	22
Guadalquivir, stm., Spain	D3	22
Guadalupe, Mex.	*B4	63
Guadalupe, Az., U.S.	m9	80
Guadalupe, Ca., U.S.	E3	82
Guadalupe, co., N.M., U.S.	C5	108
Guadalupe, co., Tx., U.S.	E4	120
Guadalupe, Isla de, i., Mex.	E15	6
Guadalupe, Sierra de, mts., Spain	C3	22
Guadalupe [Bravos], Mex.	A3	63
Guadalupe Mountains, mts., U.S.	E5	108
Guadalupe Mountains National Park, Tx., U.S.	o12	108
Guadalupe Peak, mtn., Tx., U.S.	o12	108
Guadalupita, N.M., U.S.	A4	108
Guadarrama, stm., Spain	p17	22
Guadarrama, Sierra de, mts., Spain	B4	22
Guadeloupe, dep., N.A.	H14	64
Guadeloupe Passage, strt., N.A.	H14	64
Guadiana, stm., Eur.	D2	22
Guadiana Menor, stm., Spain	D4	22
Guadiela, stm., Spain	B4	22
Guadilla, Bahía de, b., P.R.	B1	65
Guadix, Spain	D4	22
Guafo, Isla, i., Chile	C2	54
Guagua, Phil.	o13	34
Guaíba, dept., Col.	C4	60
Guainía, stm., S.A.	C4	60
Guaíra, dept., Para.	C2	56
Guaíra, dept., Para.	E4	55
Guajará Mirim, Braz.	C2	55
Guajira, dept., Col.	A3	60
Gualaceo, Ec.	B2	58
Gualala, Ca., U.S.	C2	82
Gualán, Guat.	D7	63
Gualaquiza, Ec.	B2	58
Gualeguay, Arg.	A5	54
Gualeguaychú, Arg.	A5	54
Guam, dep., Oc.	F8	6
Guaminí, Arg.	B4	54
Guamúchil, Mex.	B3	63
Guanacaste, Cordillera de, Cuba	E5	62
Guanahacabibes, Golfo de, b., Cuba	C1	64
Guana Island, i., V.I., Br.	B6	65
Guanajay, Cuba	C2	64
Guanajuato, Mex.	C4	63
Guanajuato, state, Mex.	C4	63
Guanambi, Braz.	A4	56
Guanare, Ven.	B4	60
Guandacol, Arg.	E2	55
Guandi, China	E4	33
Guane, Cuba	C1	64
Guang'an, China	I2	32
Guangchang, China	K7	32
Guangde, China	I8	32
Guangdong, prov., China	G7	31
Guangnan, China	G6	31
Guangxi Zhuangzu, prov., China	G6	31
Guangyuan, China	E6	31
Guangzhou (Canton), China	G7	31
Guánica, Laguna de, l., P.R.	B2	65
Guano Lake, l., Or., U.S.	E7	114
Guantánamo, Cuba	D6	64
Guantánamo, prov., Cuba	D6	64
Guanxian, China	F6	32
Guanyun, China	G8	32
Guapí, Col.	C2	60
Guapiara, Braz.	C5	56
Guápiles, C.R.	E6	62
Guaporé (Iténez), stm., S.A.	B3	55
Guaqui, Bol.	C2	55
Guará, Braz.	F1	57
Guarabira, Braz.	C3	57
Guaranda, Ec.	B2	58
Guaranésia, Braz.	k8	56
Guarapuava, Braz.	D2	56
Guaraqueçaba, Braz.	D3	56
Guararapes, Braz.	C2	56
Guaratinguetá, Braz.	C3	56
Guaratuba, Braz.	D3	56
Guaraúna, Port.	B2	22
Guárico, state, Ven.	B4	60
Guarujá, Braz.	n8	56
Guarulhos, Braz.	m8	56
Guarumo, Pan.	E6	62
Guasave, Mex.	B3	63
Guasdualito, Ven.	B3	60
Guasipati, Ven.	B5	60
Guastalla, Italy	B3	23
Guatemala, Guat.	E6	63
Guatemala, ctry., N.A.	D6	63
Guateque, Col.	C3	60
Guatimozín, Arg.	A4	54
Guatopo National Park, Ven.	A4	60
Guaviare, dept., Col.	C3	60
Guaviare, stm., Col.	C3	60
Guayabal, Cuba	D5	64
Guayaguayare, Trin.	O23	65
Guayama, P.R.	H11	64
Guayapo, stm., Ven.	B5	60
Guayaquil, Ec.	B1	58
Guayaquil, Golfo de, b., S.A.	B1	58
Guayaramerín, Bol.	B2	55
Guayas, prov., Ec.	B1	58
Guaymas, Mex.	B2	63
Guazacapán, Guat.	C2	62
Gubakha, Sov. Un.	B5	28
Gubbio, Italy	C4	23
Gubin, Pol.	B9	19
Gucheng, China	H4	32
Gúdar, Sierra de, mts., Spain	B5	22
Gudauta, Sov. Un.	A13	40
Gudená, stm., Den.	B3	15
Gudermes, Sov. Un.	E3	28
Gudhjem, Den.	C8	15
Gūdūr, India	F6	36
Guebwiller, Fr.	D7	16
Guéckédou, Gui.	E2	45
Guelma, Alg.	B6	44
Guelph, Ont.	D4	73
Guelph, N.D., U.S.	C7	111
Guénette, Que.	C2	74
Güera, W. Sah.	E1	44
Guercif, Mor.	C4	44
Guéréda, Chad	C5	46
Guéret, Fr.	D4	16
Guerette, Me., U.S.	A4	96
Guernica y Luno, Spain	A4	22
Guernsey, Wy., U.S.	D8	127
Guernsey, co., Oh., U.S.	B4	112
Guernsey, dep., Eur.	F5	10
Guernsey, i., Guernsey	F5	10
Guerra, Tx., U.S.	F3	120
Guerrero, state, Mex.	C4	63
Guest Peninsula, pen., Ant.	B34	7
Gueugnon, Fr.	D6	16
Gueydan, La., U.S.	D3	95
Guffey, Co., U.S.	C5	83
Gugegwe Island, i., Marsh Is.	S17	52
Guia Lopes da Laguna, Braz.	C1	56
Guibes, Nmb.	C2	49
Guichi, China	I5	32
Guide, China	D5	31
Guide Rock, Ne., U.S.	D7	104
Guidlong, Braz.	K5	32
Guidonia [Montecelio], Italy	D4	23
Guiglo, I.C.	E3	45
Guilarte, Monte, mtn., P.R.	B2	65
Guild, N.H., U.S.	D2	106
Guildford, Eng., U.K.	E6	10
Guildhall, Vt., U.S.	B5	122
Guilford, Ct., U.S.	D5	84
Guilford, In., U.S.	F8	91
Guilford, Me., U.S.	C3	96
Guilford, Mo., U.S.	A3	102
Guilford, N.Y., U.S.	C5	109
Guilford, Vt., U.S.	F3	122
Guilford, co., N.C., U.S.	A3	110
Guilherme Capelo, Ang.	C1	48
Guilin, China	F9	31
Guillaume-Delisle, Lac, l., Que.	E17	66
Guillestre, Fr.	E2	20
Guimarães, Braz.	B3	57
Guimarães, Port.	B1	22
Guimba, Phil.	o13	34
Guin, Al., U.S.	B2	78
Guinea, Va., U.S.	B5	123
Guinea, ctry., Afr.	D2	45
Guinea, Gulf of, b., Afr.	F6	42
Guinea-Bissau, ctry., Afr.	D1	45
Güines, Cuba	C2	64
Guines, Fr.	D11	12
Guingamp, Fr.	C2	16
Güira de Melena, Cuba	C2	64
Guiratinga, Braz.	B2	56
Güiria, Ven.	A5	60
Guisanbourg, Fr. Gu.	B4	59
Guisborough, Eng., U.K.	F7	13
Guise, Fr.	C5	16
Guist Creek, stm., Ky., U.S.	B4	94
Guitiriz, Spain	A2	22
Guixi, China	J7	32
Guixian, China	G6	31
Guiyang, China	F6	31
Guizhou, prov., China	F6	31
Gujan, Fr.	E3	16
Gujarat, state, India	D5	36
Gujrānwāla, Pak.	B5	36
Gujrāt, Pak.	*B5	36
Gulbarga, India	E6	36
Guldborg, Den.	D5	15
Gulf, N.C., U.S.	B3	110
Gulf, co., Fl., U.S.	C1	86
Gulf Breeze, Fl., U.S.	*u14	86
Gulf Gate Estates, Fl., U.S.	E4	86
Gulf Hammock, Fl., U.S.	C4	86
Gulf Islands National Seashore, U.S.	E5	101
Gulfport, Fl., U.S.	E4	86
Gulf Port, Il., U.S.	C2	90
Gulfport, Ms., U.S.	E4	101
Gulf Shores, Al., U.S.	E2	78
Gulgong, Austl.	F7	51
Gulkana, Ak., U.S.	C10	79
Gullion, Slieve, mtn., N. Ire., U.K.	C5	11
Gull Island, i., N.C., U.S.	B7	110
Gullivan Bay, b., Fl., U.S.	G5	86
Gulliver, Mi., U.S.	B5	99
Gull Lake, Sask.	G1	75
Gull Lake, l., Alta.	C4	68
Gull Lake, l., Mn., U.S.	D4	100
Güllük, Tur.	D6	40
Gully, Mn., U.S.	C3	100
Gulu, Ug.	A5	48
Gulyantsi, Bul.	D7	24
Gulyaypole, Sov. Un.	H11	27
Gumaca, Phil.	p14	34
Gumba, Zaire	A3	48
Gumboro, De., U.S.	G4	85
Gumefens, Switz.	C3	21
Gumel, Nig.	D6	45
Gummersbach, W. Ger.	B2	19
Gum Spring Mountain, mtn., Tn., U.S.	D8	119
Gum Springs, Ar., U.S.	C2	81
Gum Swamp Creek, stm., Ga., U.S.	E3	87
Gümüşhane, Tur.	B12	40
Guna, India	D6	36
Guna, India	E6	37
Guna, mtn., Eth.	F2	47
Gundelfingen, W. Ger.	E5	19
Gungu, Zaire	C2	48
Gunisao, stm., Man.	C3	70
Gunisao Lake, l., Man.	C3	70
Gunlock, Ut., U.S.	F2	121
Gunn, Ak., U.S.	C4	101
Gunnar, Sask.	m7	75
Gunnbjørn Fjeld, mtn., Grnld.	*C17	128
Gunnedah, Austl.	F9	50
Gunnison, Co., U.S.	C4	83
Gunnison, Ms., U.S.	B3	101
Gunnison, Ut., U.S.	D4	121
Gunnison, co., Co., U.S.	C3	83
Gunnison, stm., Co., U.S.	C2	83
Gunnison, Mount, mtn., Co., U.S.	C3	83
Gunnworth, Sask.	F1	75
Gunpowder Creek, stm., Ky., U.S.	k13	94
Gunpowder Neck, c., Md., U.S.	B5	97
Gunpowder River, b., Md., U.S.	B5	97
Gunter Air Force Base, mil., Al., U.S.	C3	78
Guntersville, Al., U.S.	A3	78
Guntersville Lake, res., Al., U.S.	A3	78
Gunton, Man.	D3	70
Guntown, Ms., U.S.	A5	101
Guntūr, India	E7	36
Gunungsitoli, Indon.	L2	35
Günz, stm., W. Ger.	A6	20
Günzburg, W. Ger.	H5	19
Gunzenhausen, W. Ger.	D5	19
Guoyang, China	H7	32
Gura Humorului, Rom.	B7	24
Gurdāspur, India	*B5	36
Gurdon, Ar., U.S.	D2	81
Gurguéia, stm., Braz.	B2	57
Guri, Embalse, res., Ven.	B5	60
Gurjevsk, Sov. Un.	E26	8
Gurk, stm., Aus.	E7	18
Gurley, Ne., U.S.	C3	104
Gurley, Al., U.S.	A3	78
Gurnee, Il., U.S.	h9	90
Gurnet Point, c., Ma., U.S.	B6	98
Gurney, Wi., U.S.	B3	126
Gurué, Moz.	D7	48
Gurupá, Braz.	C4	59
Gurupi, stm., Braz.	B1	57
Gurupi, Cabo, c., Braz.	B1	57
Guryev, Sov. Un.	E8	29
Gusau, Nig.	D6	45
Gusev, Sov. Un.	A7	26
Gushan, China	C6	31
Gusher, Ut., U.S.	E8	31
Gushi, China	E8	32
Gushikami, Japan	O5	52
Gushikawa, Japan	O5	52
Gusinje, Yugo.	D4	24
Gus-Khrustalnyy, Sov. Un.	D13	27
Gustavo A. Madero (part of Mexico City), Mex.	h9	63
Gustavus, Ak., U.S.	D12	79
Güsten, E. Ger.	B6	19
Gustine, Ca., U.S.	D3	82
Gustine, Tx., U.S.	D3	120
Güstrow, E. Ger.	B6	18
Gutau, Aus.	E9	19
Gütersloh, W. Ger.	C4	18
Guthrie, Ky., U.S.	D2	94
Guthrie, Mn., U.S.	C4	100
Guthrie, Ok., U.S.	B4	113
Guthrie, Tx., U.S.	C2	120
Guthrie, co., Ia., U.S.	C3	92
Guthrie Center, Ia., U.S.	C3	92
Guthrie Lake, l., Man.	B1	70
Guttenberg, Ia., U.S.	B6	92
Guttenberg, N.J., U.S.	h8	107
Gu Vo, Az., U.S.	E3	80
Guwāhāti, India	C9	36
Guy, Ar., U.S.	B3	81
Guy, Tx., U.S.	r14	120
Guyana, ctry., S.A.	A3	59
Guyandotte, stm., W.V., U.S.	C2	125
Guyandotte Mountain, mtn., W.V., U.S.	n12	125
Guyang, China	D4	32
Guyenne, hist. reg., Fr.	E4	16
Guymon, Ok., U.S.	e9	113
Guyot, Mount, mtn., U.S.	D10	119
Guyra, Austl.	E8	51
Guys, Tn., U.S.	B3	119
Guysborough, N.S.	D8	71
Guysborough, co., N.S.	D7	71
Guys Mills, Pa., U.S.	C2	115
Guyton, Ga., U.S.	D5	87
Guyuan, China	G2	32
Guyuan, China	D6	32
Guzar, Sov. Un.	B13	39
Güzelyurt, N. Cyp.	E9	40
Guzhen, China	H7	32
Gvardeysk, Sov. Un.	A6	26
Gwabegar, Austl.	E7	51
Gwādar, Pak.	C3	36
Gwai, Zimb.	A4	49
Gwalior, India	C6	36
Gwanda, Zimb.	B4	49
Gwane, Zaire	A4	48
Gwda, stm., Pol.	B4	26
Gweebarra Bay, b., Ire.	C3	11
Gweesalia, Ire.	C2	11
Gwembe, Zam.	E4	48
Gwent, co., Wales, U.K.	C5	12
Gweru, Zimb.	A4	49
Gwinhurst, De., U.S.	h8	85
Gwinn, Mi., U.S.	B3	99
Gwinner, N.D., U.S.	C8	111
Gwinnett, co., Ga., U.S.	C2	87
Gwydyr Bay, b., Ak., U.S.	A10	79
Gwynedd, co., Wales, U.K.	A3	12
Gwynn, Va., U.S.	C6	123
Gwynne, Alta.	C4	68
Gwynneville, In., U.S.	E6	91
Gwynns Falls, stm., Md., U.S.	g10	97
Gyangzê, China	C8	36
Gyaring Co, l., China	B8	36
Gyaring Hu, l., China	E4	31
Gyirong, China	C10	37
Gympie, Austl.	E9	50
Gyöngyös, Hung.	B3	24
Győr (Raab), Hung.	B3	24
Gypsera, Switz.	C3	21
Gypsum, Co., U.S.	B4	83
Gypsum, Ks., U.S.	D6	93
Gypsum, Oh., U.S.	A3	112
Gypsumville, Man.	D2	70
Gyula, Hung.	B5	24

H

Haag [in Oberbayern], W. Ger.	A8	20
Haakon, co., S.D., U.S.	C4	118
Haaksbergen, Neth.	B6	17
Haamstede, Neth.	C3	17
Haapamäki, Fin.	F11	14
Haapsalu, Sov. Un.	B4	27
Hab, stm., Pak.	H3	39
Habermehl Peak, mtn., Ant.	B13	7
Haboru, Japan	D10	33
Hachiman, Japan	n15	33
Hachinohe, Japan	F10	33
Hachiōji, Japan	I9	33
Hachita, N.M., U.S.	F1	108
Hacienda Heights, Ca., U.S.	*n13	82
Hack, Mount, mtn., Austl.	E2	51
Hackberry, Az., U.S.	B2	80
Hackberry, La., U.S.	E2	95
Hackberry Creek, stm., Ks., U.S.	D3	93
Hackensack, Mn., U.S.	D4	100
Hackensack, N.J., U.S.	B4	107
Hackensack, stm., N.J., U.S.	h8	107
Hacker Valley, W.V., U.S.	C4	125
Hackettstown, Ire.	E5	11
Hackett, Ar., U.S.	B1	81
Hackettstown, N.J., U.S.	B3	107
Hackleburg, Al., U.S.	A2	78
Hackney (part of London), Eng., U.K.	k12	10
Hack Point, Md., U.S.	B6	97
Hacoda, Micron.	Q18	52
Hacq, i., Micron.	Q18	52
Hadar, Ne., U.S.	B8	104
Ḥaḍārībah, Ra's al, c., Sud.	A4	47
Hadassah Alef Hospital, Isr.	m14	41
Haddam, Ct., U.S.	D5	84
Ḥaddam, Ra's al, c., Oman	C5	38
Haddington, Scot., U.K.	E6	13
Haddix, Ky., U.S.	C6	94
Haddock, Ga., U.S.	C3	87
Haddonfield, N.J., U.S.	D2	107
Haddon Heights, N.J., U.S.	D2	107
Hadejia, Nig.	D7	45
Hadejia, stm., Nig.	D6	45
Ḥadera, Isr.	B7	41
Haderslev, Den.	F10	11
Hadim, Tur.	D3	40
Ḥadīrah, Bi'r al, well, Eg.	D6	41
Hadley, Eng., U.K.	B8	12
Hadley, Ma., U.S.	B2	98
Hadley, Mn., U.S.	F3	100
Hadley, N.Y., U.S.	B7	109
Hadley, Pa., U.S.	D1	115

Name	Map Ref.	Page
Hadley Bay, b., N.W. Ter. . . .	B11	66
Hadley Lake, l., Me., U.S. . . .	D5	96
Hadlock, Wa., U.S.	A3	124
Hadlyme, Ct., U.S.	D6	84
Ha Dong, Viet.	A3	34
Hadramawt, reg., Yemen	D4	38
Hadsten, Den.	B4	15
Hadsund, Den.	B4	15
Haeju, N. Kor.	C10	31
Haenam, S. Kor.	I3	33
Haerhpin see Harbin, China . .	B10	31
Hafford, Sask.	E2	75
Ḥafīra, Qāʿal, Jord.	C8	41
Hafnarfjördur, Ice.	n22	14
Haft Gel, Iran	F4	39
Hafun, Ras, c., Som.	C7	47
Hagan, Ga., U.S.	D5	87
Hagari, stm., India	F6	36
Hagarstown, Il., U.S.	E4	90
Hagarville, Ar., U.S.	B2	81
Hagemeister Island, i., Ak., U.S.	D7	79
Hagen, Sask.	E3	75
Hagen, W. Ger.	C3	18
Hagenow, E. Ger.	E5	15
Hagensborg, B.C.	C4	69
Hagere Hiywet, Eth.	D4	47
Hagerman, Id., U.S.	G4	89
Hagerman, N.M., U.S.	D5	108
Hagerman Corners, Ont.	k15	73
Hagerstown, In., U.S.	E7	91
Hagerstown, Md., U.S.	A2	97
Hagersville, Ont.	E4	73
Haggart Lake, l., Ont.	D4	70
Haggin, Mount, mtn., Mt., U.S.	D3	103
Ha Giang, Viet.	A6	35
Hags Head, c., Ire.	E2	11
Hague, Sask.	E2	75
Hague, N.Y., U.S.	B7	109
Hague, N.D., U.S.	C6	111
Hague, Cap de la, c., Fr. . . .	C3	16
Haguenau, Fr.	C7	16
Hagues Peak, mtn., Co., U.S.	A5	83
Ha! Ha!, Baie des, b., Que. . .	C2	72
Ha! Ha!, Lac, l., Que.	A7	74
Hahira, Ga., U.S.	F3	87
Hahnville, La., U.S.	E5	95
Haicheng, China	G8	31
Haicheng, China	D10	32
Haichow Bay see Haizhou Bay, b., China	G8	32
Hai Duong, Viet.	B7	35
Haifa (Hefa), Isr.	B3	38
Haifa, Bay of see Ḥefa, Mifraẓ, b., Isr.	B6	41
Haigerloch, W. Ger.	A4	20
Haigler, Ne., U.S.	D4	104
Haikang, China	G6	31
Haikou, China	B4	34
Haʾil, Hi., U.S.	C5	88
Ḥaʾil, Sau. Ar.	C4	38
Hailar, China	B8	31
Haile, La., U.S.	B3	95
Hailesboro, N.Y., U.S.	f9	109
Hailey, Id., U.S.	F4	89
Haileybury, Ont.	p20	73
Haileyville, Ok., U.S.	C6	113
Hailong, China	C10	31
Hailun, China	B10	31
Haimen, China	F9	31
Haimen, China	I9	32
Hainan Island, i., China	B3	34
Hainaut, prov., Bel.	D3	17
Haines, Ak., U.S.	D12	79
Haines, Or., U.S.	C9	114
Hainesburg, N.J., U.S.	B2	107
Haines City, Fl., U.S.	D5	86
Haines Falls, N.Y., U.S.	C6	109
Hainesport, N.J., U.S.	D3	107
Hainesville, N.J., U.S.	A3	107
Hainichen, E. Ger.	C8	19
Haining, China	I9	32
Hai Phong, Viet.	A3	34
Hairy Hill, Alta.	C5	68
Haiti, ctry., N.A.	E7	64
Haiyang, China	F9	32
Haiyuan, China	F1	32
Haizhou, China	E8	31
Haizhou Bay, b., China	G8	32
Hajdúböszörmény, Hung. . . .	B5	24
Hajdúhadház, Hung.	B5	24
Hajdúnánás, Hung.	B5	24
Hajdúszoboszló, Hung.	B5	24
Hajiki, Cape, c., Japan	G9	33
Hajnówka, Pol.	B7	26
Hakalau, Hi., U.S.	D6	88
Hakkâri, Tur.	D14	40
Hakken, Mount, mtn., Japan . .	I7	33
Hakodate, Japan	C13	31
Hākra Branch, stm., Pak.	C4	37
Haku, Mount, mtn., Japan . . .	m15	33
Halabjah, Iraq	D2	39
Ḥalāʿib, Eg.	E7	43
Halaula, Hi., U.S.	C6	88
Halawa, Cape, c., Hi., U.S. . . .	B5	88
Halawa Heights, Hi., U.S. . . .	g10	88
Halberstadt, E. Ger.	C5	18
Halbrite, Sask.	H4	75
Halbur, Ia., U.S.	C3	92
Halcon, Mount, mtn., Phil. . . .	C6	34
Haldeman, Ky., U.S.	B6	94
Halden, Nor.	H4	14
Haldensleben, E. Ger.	B5	18
Haldimand, Ont.	E5	73
Haldimand, co., Ont.	E5	73
Hale, Co., U.S.	B8	83
Hale, Mi., U.S.	D7	99
Hale, Mo., U.S.	B4	102
Hale, co., Al., U.S.	C2	78
Hale, co., Tx., U.S.	B2	120
Haleakala Crater, crat., Hi., U.S.	C5	88
Haleakala National Park, Hi., U.S.	C6	88
Haleburg, Al., U.S.	D4	78
Hale Center, Tx., U.S.	B2	120
Haledon, N.J., U.S.	*B4	107
Haleiwa, Hi., U.S.	B3	88
Hales Corners, Wi., U.S.	n11	126
Halesowen, Eng., U.K.	B5	12
Halesworth, Eng., U.K.	B9	12
Halethorpe, Md., U.S.	B4	97
Haleyville, Al., U.S.	A2	78
Haleyville, N.J., U.S.	E2	107
Half Assini, Ghana	E4	44
Half Hollow Hills, N.Y., U.S. . .	*h13	109
Half-Moon Bay, N.Z.	Q12	51
Half Moon Bay, Ca., U.S.	k8	82
Halfway, Ky., U.S.	D3	94
Halfway, Md., U.S.	A2	97
Half Way, Mo., U.S.	D4	102
Halfway, Or., U.S.	C9	114
Halfway, stm., B.C.	A6	69
Halfway Nunatak, mtn., Ant. . .	f40	7
Ḥalḥūl, Isr. Occ.	C7	41
Haliburton, Ont.	B6	73
Haliburton, co., Ont.	B6	73
Halibut Point, c., Ma., U.S. . . .	A6	98
Halifax, Eng., U.K.	D6	10
Halifax, N.S.	E6	71
Halifax, Ma., U.S.	A5	110
Halifax, Pa., U.S.	F8	115
Halifax, Vt., U.S.	F3	122
Halifax, Va., U.S.	D4	123
Halifax, co., N.C., U.S.	A5	110
Halifax, co., Va., U.S.	D4	123
Halifax, co., N.S.	E6	71
Halifax Bay, b., Austl.	C8	50
Haliimaile, Hi., U.S.	C5	88
Halkirk, Alta.	C4	68
Hall, In., U.S.	E4	91
Hall, Mt., U.S.	D3	103
Hall, N.Y., U.S.	C3	109
Hall, co., Ga., U.S.	B3	87
Hall, co., Ne., U.S.	D7	104
Hall, co., Tx., U.S.	B2	120
Halla, Mount, mtn., S. Kor. . . .	J3	33
Halladale, stm., Scot., U.K. . . .	B5	11
Hallam, Ne., U.S.	D9	104
Hallam Peak, mtn., B.C.	C8	69
Halland, co., Swe.	B6	15
Hallandale, Fl., U.S.	G6	86
Hallands Väderö, i., Swe. . . .	B6	15
Hall Basin, b., N.A.	k39	66
Halle, Bel.	D4	17
Halle, E. Ger.	C5	18
Halle, W. Ger.	A3	19
Halleck, Nv., U.S.	C6	105
Hallein, Aus.	E6	18
Halle-Neustadt, E. Ger.	*C6	18
Hällestad, Swe.	u33	14
Hallett, Ok., U.S.	A5	113
Hallett, Cape, c., Ant.	B30	7
Hallettsville, Tx., U.S.	E4	120
Halley, Ar., U.S.	D4	81
Halley Bay, sci., Ant.	B10	7
Halliday, N.D., U.S.	B3	111
Hallie, Wi., U.S.	D2	126
Hallim, S. Kor.	J3	33
Hall Island, i., Ak., U.S.	C5	79
Hall Meadow Brook, stm., Ct., U.S.	B3	84
Hall Meadow Brook Reservoir, res., Ct., U.S.	B3	84
Hall Mountain, mtn., Wa., U.S.	A8	124
Hallock, Mn., U.S.	B2	100
Hallowell, Ks., U.S.	E9	93
Hallowell, Me., U.S.	D3	96
Hall Peninsula, pen., N.W. Ter.	D19	66
Halls, Ga., U.S.	B2	87
Halls, Tn., U.S.	B2	119
Halls, Tn., U.S.	*C10	119
Hallsberg, Swe.	t33	14
Hallsboro, N.C., U.S.	C4	110
Halls Creek, Austl.	C4	50
Halls Creek, stm., Ut., U.S. . .	F5	121
Halls Crossroads, Tn., U.S. . .	m14	119
Halls Harbour, N.S.	D5	71
Halls Stream, stm., N.H., U.S.	f7	106
Halls Summit, Ks., U.S.	D8	93
Hallstead, Pa., U.S.	C10	115
Hall Summit, La., U.S.	B2	95
Hallsville, Mo., U.S.	B5	102
Hallsville, Oh., U.S.	C3	112
Hallsville, Tx., U.S.	C5	120
Hall Top, mtn., Tn., U.S.	D10	119
Halltown, Mo., U.S.	D4	102
Hallville, Ct., U.S.	C7	84
Hallwood, Va., U.S.	C7	123
Hallwil Lake, l., Switz.	B4	20
Halma, Mn., U.S.	B2	100
Halmahera, i., Indon.	E7	34
Halmahera Sea, Indon.	F7	34
Halmstad, Swe.	I5	14
Hals, Den.	B4	15
Halsell, Al., U.S.	C1	78
Halsey, Ne., U.S.	C5	104
Halsey, N.J., U.S.	A3	107
Halsey, Or., U.S.	C3	114
Hälsö, i., Swe.	A5	15
Halstad, Mn., U.S.	C2	100
Halstead, Eng., U.K.	C8	12
Halstead, Ks., U.S.	E6	93
Haltern, W. Ger.	B2	19
Haltia, mtn., Eur.	C9	14
Halton, co., Ont.	D5	73
Halton, Ont.	D5	73
Halton Hills, Ont.	D5	73
Haltwhistle, Eng., U.K.	F6	13
Ham, Fr.	E3	17
Hamada, Japan	I6	33
Hamadān, Iran	D4	39
Hamah, Syria	B3	38
Hamahika Island, i., Japan . . .	O5	52
Hamamatsu, Japan	E12	31
Hamar, Nor.	G4	14
Hamar, N.D., U.S.	B7	111
Hambantota, Sri L.	G7	36
Hamber Provincial Park, B.C. .	C8	69
Hamblen, co., Tn., U.S.	C10	119
Hamburg, W. Ger.	B5	18
Hamburg, Ar., U.S.	D4	81
Hamburg, Ct., U.S.	D6	84
Hamburg, Il., U.S.	D3	90
Hamburg, Ia., U.S.	D2	92
Hamburg, Ms., U.S.	D2	101
Hamburg, N.J., U.S.	A3	107
Hamburg, N.Y., U.S.	C2	109
Hamburg, Pa., U.S.	E10	115
Hamburg, Wi., U.S.	C4	126
Hamburg, state, W. Ger.	E4	15
Hamburg Mountains, mts., N.J., U.S.	A3	107
Ḥamd, Wādī al, val., Sau. Ar. .	C3	38
Hamden, Ct., U.S.	D4	84
Hamden, N.Y., U.S.	C6	109
Hamden, Oh., U.S.	C3	112
Hamden, co., S.C., U.S.	F5	117
Hämeenlinna, Fin.	G11	14
Hamel, Mn., U.S.	m11	100
Hamhŭng, N. Kor.	G3	33
Hami, China	C3	31
Hamill, Id., U.S.	D6	92
Hamill, S.D., U.S.	D6	118
Hamilton, Austl.	G7	50
Hamilton, Ber.	p20	64
Hamilton, Ont.	D5	73
Hamilton, N.Z.	L15	51
Hamilton, Scot., U.K.	C4	10
Hamilton, Ak., U.S.	C7	79
Hamilton, Co., U.S.	A3	83
Hamilton, Ga., U.S.	D2	87
Hamilton, Il., U.S.	C2	90
Hamilton, In., U.S.	A8	91
Hamilton, Ia., U.S.	C5	92
Hamilton, Ks., U.S.	E7	93
Hamilton, Ma., U.S.	A6	98
Hamilton, Mi., U.S.	F4	99
Hamilton, Ms., U.S.	B5	101
Hamilton, Mo., U.S.	B3	102
Hamilton, Mt., U.S.	D2	103
Hamilton, N.Y., U.S.	C5	109
Hamilton, N.C., U.S.	B5	110
Hamilton, N.D., U.S.	A8	111
Hamilton, Oh., U.S.	C1	112
Hamilton, Or., U.S.	C7	114
Hamilton, R.I., U.S.	D4	116
Hamilton, Tx., U.S.	D3	120
Hamilton, Va., U.S.	A5	123
Hamilton, Wa., U.S.	A4	124
Hamilton, co., Fl., U.S.	B3	86
Hamilton, co., Il., U.S.	E5	90
Hamilton, co., In., U.S.	D5	91
Hamilton, co., Ia., U.S.	B4	92
Hamilton, co., Ks., U.S.	E2	93
Hamilton, co., Ne., U.S.	D7	104
Hamilton, co., N.Y., U.S.	B6	109
Hamilton, co., Oh., U.S.	C1	112
Hamilton, co., Tn., U.S.	D8	119
Hamilton, co., Tx., U.S.	D3	120
Hamilton, Lake, res., Ar., U.S.	C2	81
Hamilton, Mount, mtn., Ak., U.S.	C8	79
Hamilton, Mount, mtn., Ca., U.S.	k9	82
Hamilton, Mount, mtn., Nv., U.S.	D6	105
Hamilton City, Ca., U.S.	C2	82
Hamilton Dome, Wy., U.S. . . .	C4	127
Hamilton Inlet, b., Newf.	A2	72
Hamilton Mountain, mtn., N.Y., U.S.	B6	109
Hamilton Reservoir, res., Ma., U.S.	B3	98
Hamilton Sound, strt., Newf. .	D4	72
Hamilton Square, N.J., U.S. . .	C3	107
Hamiota, Man.	D1	70
Hamīrpur, India	C7	36
Hamjong-ni, N. Kor.	G2	33
Ham Lake, Mn., U.S.	*m12	100
Hamler, Oh., U.S.	A1	112
Hamlet, In., U.S.	B4	91
Hamlet, Ne., U.S.	D4	104
Hamlet, N.C., U.S.	C3	110
Hamlet, Mount, mtn., Ak., U.S.	B6	79
Hamletsburg, Il., U.S.	F5	90
Hamlin, Ks., U.S.	C8	93
Hamlin, Pa., U.S.	D11	115
Hamlin, Tx., U.S.	C2	120
Hamlin, W.V., U.S.	C2	125
Hamlin, co., S.D., U.S.	C8	118
Hamlin Lake, l., Mi., U.S. . . .	D4	99
Hammam Lif, Tun.	B7	44
Ḥammār, Hawr al, l., Iraq . . .	F3	39
Hammarby, Swe.	t35	14
Hamme, Bel.	C4	17
Hammel, Den.	B3	15
Hammelburg, W. Ger.	C4	18
Hammer, S.D., U.S.	B8	118
Hammerfest, Nor.	B10	14
Hammett, Id., U.S.	G3	89
Hammon, Ok., U.S.	B2	113
Hammonasset, stm., Ct., U.S.	D5	84
Hammonasset Point, c., Ct., U.S.	E5	84
Hammond, Il., U.S.	D5	90
Hammond, In., U.S.	A2	91
Hammond, La., U.S.	D5	95
Hammond, Mn., U.S.	F6	100
Hammond, Mt., U.S.	E12	103
Hammond, N.Y., U.S.	f9	109
Hammond, Or., U.S.	A3	114
Hammond, Wi., U.S.	D1	126
Hammond Bay, b., Mi., U.S. . .	C6	99
Hammondsport, N.Y., U.S. . . .	C3	109
Hammonton, N.J., U.S.	D3	107
Hamneda, Swe.	B7	15
Ham-Nord, Que.	D6	74
Hamoyet, Jabal, mtn., Afr. . . .	B4	47
Hampden, Newf.	D3	72
Hampden, N.Z.	P13	51
Hampden, Me., U.S.	D4	96
Hampden, Ma., U.S.	B3	98
Hampden, N.D., U.S.	A7	111
Hampden, co., Ma., U.S.	B2	98
Hampden Highlands, Me., U.S.	D4	96
Hampshire, Tn., U.S.	B4	119
Hampshire, co., Eng., U.K. . .	C6	12
Hampshire, co., Ma., U.S. . . .	B2	98
Hampshire, co., W.V., U.S. . .	B6	125
Hampstead, N.B.	D3	71
Hampstead (part of London), Eng., U.K.	k12	10
Hampstead, Md., U.S.	A4	97
Hampstead, N.H., U.S.	E4	106
Hampstead, N.C., U.S.	C5	110
Hampton, N.B.	D4	71
Hampton, Ar., U.S.	D3	81
Hampton, Ct., U.S.	B7	84
Hampton, Fl., U.S.	C4	86
Hampton, Ga., U.S.	C2	87
Hampton, Ia., U.S.	B4	92
Hampton, Ky., U.S.	e9	94
Hampton, Md., U.S.	*B4	97
Hampton, Mn., U.S.	F5	100
Hampton, Ne., U.S.	D8	104
Hampton, N.H., U.S.	E5	106
Hampton, N.J., U.S.	B3	107
Hampton, Or., U.S.	D6	114
Hampton, S.C., U.S.	F5	117
Hampton, Tn., U.S.	C11	119
Hampton, Va., U.S.	C6	123
Hampton, co., S.C., U.S.	F5	117
Hampton Bays, N.Y., U.S. . . .	n16	109
Hampton Beach, N.H., U.S. . .	E5	106
Hampton Butte, mtn., Or., U.S.	D6	114
Hampton Falls, N.H., U.S. . . .	E5	106
Hampton Roads, anch., Va., U.S.	k15	123
Hampton Roads Bridge-Tunnel, Va., U.S.	k15	123
Hams Fork, stm., Wy., U.S. . .	E2	127
Ham-Sud, Que.	D6	74
Ham Tan, Viet.	G7	35
Hamtramck, Mi., U.S.	p15	99
Hamyang, S. Kor.	I3	33
Han, stm., Asia	H4	33
Hana, Hi., U.S.	C6	88
Hanahan, S.C., U.S.	F7	117
Hanalei Bay, b., Hi., U.S.	A2	88
Hanamaki, Japan	G10	33
Hanamaulu, Hi., U.S.	B2	88
Hanapepe, Hi., U.S.	B2	88
Hanau, W. Ger.	C4	18
Hanceville, B.C.	D6	69
Hanceville, Al., U.S.	A3	78
Hancheng, China	G4	32
Hancock, Ia., U.S.	C2	92
Hancock, Md., U.S.	A1	97
Hancock, Mi., U.S.	A2	99
Hancock, Mn., U.S.	E3	100
Hancock, N.H., U.S.	E3	106
Hancock, N.Y., U.S.	D5	109
Hancock, Vt., U.S.	D3	122
Hancock, W.V., U.S.	B5	125
Hancock, Wi., U.S.	D4	126
Hancock, co., Ga., U.S.	C3	87
Hancock, co., Il., U.S.	C2	90
Hancock, co., In., U.S.	E6	91
Hancock, co., Ia., U.S.	A4	92
Hancock, co., Ky., U.S.	C3	94
Hancock, co., Me., U.S.	D4	96
Hancock, co., Ms., U.S.	E4	101
Hancock, co., Oh., U.S.	A2	112
Hancock, co., Tn., U.S.	C10	119
Hancock, co., W.V., U.S. . . .	A4	125
Hancock Pond, l., Me., U.S. . .	E2	96
Hancocks Bridge, N.J., U.S. . .	D2	107
Hand, co., S.D., U.S.	C6	118
Handa, Japan	o15	33
Handa, i., Scot., U.K.	B3	13
Handan, China	D7	31
Handaqi, China	A3	33
Handel, Sask.	E1	75
Handeni, Tan.	C6	48
Handesty, Ok., U.S.	e9	113
Handan, China see Handan . .		
Hanford, Ca., U.S.	D4	82
Hangchou see Hangzhou, China	E9	31
Hangchow Bay see Hangzhou Bay, b., China	I9	32
Hangelsberg, E. Ger.	F7	15
Hanging Rock, Oh., U.S.	D3	112
Hangingstone, stm., Alta. . . .	A5	68
Hangman Creek, stm., Wa., U.S.	B8	124
Hangö, Fin.	H10	14
Hangu, China	*D8	31
Hangzhou (Hangchou), China .	E9	31
Hangzhou Bay, b., China	I9	32
HaNiqra, Rosh, c., Asia	A7	41
Hanita, Isr.	A7	41
Hankinson, N.D., U.S.	C9	111
Hanksville, Ut., U.S.	E5	121
Hanley, Sask.	F2	75
Hanley Falls, Mn., U.S.	F3	100
Hann, Mount, mtn., Austl. . . .	C4	50
Hanna, Alta.	D5	68
Hanna, In., U.S.	B4	91
Hanna, Ok., U.S.	B6	113
Hanna, Ut., U.S.	C5	121
Hanna, Wy., U.S.	E6	127
Hanna City, Il., U.S.	C4	90
Hannaford, N.D., U.S.	B7	111
Hannah, N.D., U.S.	A7	111
Hannahville Indian Reservation, Mi., U.S.	C3	99
Hannawa Falls, N.Y., U.S. . . .	f10	109
Hannibal, Mo., U.S.	B6	102
Hannibal, N.Y., U.S.	B4	109
Hannibal, Oh., U.S.	C5	112
Hannover, W. Ger.	B4	18
Hannover, N.D., U.S.	B4	111
Hanoi (Ha Noi), Viet.	A3	34
Hanover, Ont.	C3	73
Hanover, B.C.	B3	81
Hanover, Ct., U.S.	C7	84
Hanover, Il., U.S.	A3	90
Hanover, In., U.S.	G7	91
Hanover, Ks., U.S.	C7	93
Hanover, Ma., U.S.	B6	98
Hanover, Mi., U.S.	F6	99
Hanover, Mn., U.S.	m11	100
Hanover, N.H., U.S.	C2	106
Hanover, N.M., U.S.	E1	108
Hanover, Pa., U.S.	G8	115
Hanover, Va., U.S.	C5	123
Hanover, co., Va., U.S.	C5	123
Hanover, hist. reg., W. Ger. . .	B4	18
Hanover, Isla, i., Chile	E2	54
Hanover Center, Ma., U.S. . . .	h12	98
Hanover Center, N.H., U.S. . .	C2	106
Hanover Park, Il., U.S.	k8	90
Hanoverton, Oh., U.S.	B5	112
Hanover Township, N.J., U.S. .	B4	107
Hansard, B.C.	B7	69
Hansboro, N.D., U.S.	A6	111
Hansell, Ia., U.S.	B4	92
Hansen, Id., U.S.	G4	89
Hansford, co., Tx., U.S.	A2	120
Han Shui, stm., China	E7	31
Hanska, Mn., U.S.	F4	100
Hanson, Ky., U.S.	C2	94
Hanson, Ma., U.S.	B6	98
Hanson, Ok., U.S.	B7	113
Hanson, co., S.D., U.S.	D8	118
Hansthol m (Hanstad), Den. . .	A2	15
Hantsport, N.S.	D5	71
Hants, co., N.S.	D6	71
Hants Harbour, Newf.	D5	72
Hantzmangarh, India	F5	37
Hanyin, China	E8	31
Hanzhong, China	E8	31
Hāora, India	D8	36
Haparanda, Swe.	E10	14
Hapeville, Ga., U.S.	C2	87
Happy, Tx., U.S.	B2	120
Happy Camp, Ca., U.S.	B2	82
Happy Corner, N.H., U.S. . . .	f7	106
Happy Jack, Az., U.S.	C4	80
Happyland, Ok., U.S.	C5	113
Happy Valley, N.M., U.S.	E5	108
Happy Valley-Goose Bay, Newf.	B1	72
Hapsu, N. Kor.	F4	33
Haql, Sau. Ar.	C3	38
Ḥaraḍ, Sau. Ar.	D5	38
Häradsback, Swe.	B8	15
Harahan, La., U.S.	k11	95
Haralson, co., Ga., U.S.	C1	87
Harare, Zimb.	A5	49
Ḥarash, Biʾr al, well, Libya . .	D4	43
Haraze, Chad	D4	46
Harbeson, De., U.S.	F4	85
Harbin (Haerhpin), China . . .	B10	31
Harbinger, N.C., U.S.	A7	110
Harboør, Den.	B2	15
Harbor, Or., U.S.	E2	114
Harbor Beach, Mi., U.S.	E8	99
Harborcreek, Pa., U.S.	B2	115
Harbor Springs, Mi., U.S. . . .	C6	99
Harborton, Va., U.S.	C7	123
Harbor View, Oh., U.S.	e7	112
Harbour Breton, Newf.	E4	72
Harbour Buffett, Newf.	E4	72
Harbour Deep, Newf.	C3	72
Harbour Grace, Newf.	E5	72
Harbour Mille, Newf.	E4	72
Harbourville, N.S.	D5	71
Harburg (part of Hamburg), W. Ger.	E3	15
Hårby, Den.	C4	15
Harcourt, N.B.	C4	71
Harcourt, Ia., U.S.	B3	92
Harcuvar Mountains, mts., Az., U.S.	D2	80
Harda, India	F6	37
Hardangerfjorden, Nor.	G1	14
Hardangerjøkulen, ice, Nor. . .	G2	14
Hardangervidda, plat., Nor. . .	G2	14
Hardaway, Al., U.S.	C4	78
Hardee, co., Fl., U.S.	E5	86
Hardeeville, S.C., U.S.	G5	117
Hardeman, co., Tn., U.S. . . .	B2	119
Hardeman, co., Tx., U.S. . . .	B3	120
Hardenberg, Neth.	B6	17
Hardenberg City, Ok., U.S. . .	C5	113
Harderwijk, Neth.	B5	17
Hardesty, Ok., U.S.	e9	113
Hardin, Il., U.S.	D3	90
Hardin, Ky., U.S.	f9	94
Hardin, Mo., U.S.	B4	102
Hardin, Mt., U.S.	E9	103
Hardin, co., Il., U.S.	F5	90
Hardin, co., Ia., U.S.	B4	92
Hardin, co., Ky., U.S.	C4	94
Hardin, co., Oh., U.S.	B2	112
Hardin, co., Tn., U.S.	B3	119
Hardin, co., Tx., U.S.	D5	120
Harding, Ma., U.S.	h10	98
Harding, Mn., U.S.	D5	100
Harding, W.V., U.S.	C3	125
Harding, co., N.M., U.S.	B5	108
Harding, co., S.D., U.S.	B2	118
Harding Lake, res., U.S.	C4	78
Harding Lake, l., Man.	A2	70
Hardinsburg, In., U.S.	H5	91
Hardinsburg, Ky., U.S.	C3	94
Hardinville, Il., U.S.	E6	90
Hardisty, Alta.	C5	68
Hardisty Lake, l., N.W. Ter. . .	D9	66
Hardman, Or., U.S.	B7	114
Hardoi, India	D8	37
Hardshell, U.S.	C6	94
Hardtner, Ks., U.S.	E5	93
Hardwick, Ga., U.S.	C3	87
Hardwick, Ma., U.S.	B3	98
Hardwick, Mn., U.S.	G2	100
Hardwick, Vt., U.S.	B4	122
Hardwicke, N.B.	B5	71
Hardwood Ridge, mtn., Pa., U.S.	D11	115
Hardy, Sask.	H3	75
Hardy, Ar., U.S.	A4	81
Hardy, Ia., U.S.	B3	92
Hardy, Ms., U.S.	B4	101
Hardy, Ne., U.S.	D8	104
Hardy, Ok., U.S.	A5	113
Hardy, Va., U.S.	C3	123
Hardy, co., W.V., U.S.	B6	125
Hardy Lakes, res., In., U.S. . .	G6	91
Hare Bay, Newf.	D4	72
Hare Bay, b., Newf.	C4	72
Haren, Neth.	A6	17
Harer (Harar), Eth.	D5	47
Harerge, prov., Eth.	D6	47
Harfleur, Fr.	C7	16
Harford, Pa., U.S.	C10	115
Harford, co., Md., U.S.	A5	97
Hargeysa, Som.	D5	47
Harghita, mtn., Rom.	B7	24
Hargill, Tx., U.S.	F3	120
Hargrave, Man.	E1	70
Hargrave, stm., Man.	B2	70
Hargrave Lake, l., Man.	B2	70
Hari, stm., Indon.	F2	34
Haridwār, India	C6	36
Ḥarīr, Wādī al, val., Syria . . .	B8	41
Ḥarīrūd, stm., Asia	C5	123
Harker Heights, Tx., U.S. . . .	*D4	120
Harkers Island, N.C., U.S. . . .	C6	110
Harlan, Ia., U.S.	C2	92
Harlan, Ks., U.S.	C5	93
Harlan, Ky., U.S.	D6	94
Harlan, co., Ky., U.S.	D6	94
Harlan, co., Ne., U.S.	D6	104
Harlan County Lake, res., Ne., U.S.	E6	104
Harlech, Wales, U.K.	B3	12
Harlem, Fl., U.S.	F6	86
Harlem, Ga., U.S.	C4	87
Harlem, Mt., U.S.	B8	103
Harleton, Tx., U.S.	C5	120
Harleyville, S.C., U.S.	E7	117
Harlingen, Neth.	A6	16
Harlingen, Tx., U.S.	F4	120
Harlow, Eng., U.K.	k13	10
Harlowton, Mt., U.S.	D7	103
Harlton, Va., U.S.	e9	123
Harmans, Md., U.S.	B4	97
Harmarville, Pa., U.S.	k14	115
Harmon, La., U.S.	B2	95
Harmon, Ok., U.S.	A2	113
Harmon, co., Ok., U.S.	C2	113
Harmon Creek, stm., W.V., U.S.	f8	125
Harmonsburg, Pa., U.S.	C1	115
Harmony, In., U.S.	E3	91
Harmony, Me., U.S.	D3	96
Harmony, Mn., U.S.	G6	100
Harmony, N.C., U.S.	A2	110
Harmony, Pa., U.S.	E1	115
Harmony, R.I., U.S.	B3	116
Harmony, Va., U.S.	D4	123
Harmony Grove, Ar., U.S. . . .	h15	81
Harmony Hills, De., U.S.	*B3	85
Harmonyville, Vt., U.S.	E3	122
Harms, Tn., U.S.	B5	119
Harned, Ky., U.S.	C3	94
Harnett, co., N.C., U.S.	B4	110
Harney, Md., U.S.	A3	97
Harney, co., Or., U.S.	D7	114
Harney, Lake, l., Fl., U.S. . . .	D5	86
Harney Lake, l., Or., U.S. . . .	D7	114
Harney Peak, mtn., S.D., U.S.	D2	118
Härnösand, Swe.	F8	14
Haro, Spain	A4	22
Haro, Cabo, c., Mex.	B2	63
Harold, Fl., U.S.	u15	86
Harold Pond, l., Bah.	m17	64
Haro Strait, strt., Wa., U.S. . .	A2	124
Harper, Lib.	F3	45
Harper, Ia., U.S.	C5	92
Harper, Ks., U.S.	E5	93
Harper, Or., U.S.	D9	114
Harper, Tx., U.S.	D3	120
Harper, Wa., U.S.	e10	124
Harper, co., Ks., U.S.	E5	93
Harper, co., Ok., U.S.	A2	113
Harper, Mount, mtn., Ak., U.S.	C11	79
Harpers Ferry, Ia., U.S.	A6	92
Harpers Ferry, W.V., U.S. . . .	B7	125
Harpers Ferry National Historical Park, W.V., U.S. . .	B7	125
Harpersville, Al., U.S.	B3	78
Harperville, Ms., U.S.	C4	101
Harper Woods, Mi., U.S.	*p16	99
Harpeth, stm., Tn., U.S.	A5	119
Harpster, Oh., U.S.	B2	112
Harpswell Center, Me., U.S. . .	*E3	96
Harptree, Sask.	H3	75
Harquahala Mountain, mtn., Az., U.S.	D2	80
Harquahala Mountains, mts., Az., U.S.	D2	80
Harrah, Ok., U.S.	B4	113
Harrah, Wa., U.S.	C5	124
Harray, Loch of, l., Scot., U.K.	A5	13
Harrell, Ar., U.S.	D3	81
Harricana, stm., Can.	F17	66
Harriet, Ar., U.S.	B3	81
Harrietta, Mi., U.S.	D5	99
Harriettsville, Oh., U.S.	C4	112
Harriman, Tn., U.S.	D9	119
Harriman Reservoir, res., Vt., U.S.	F3	122
Harrington, De., U.S.	E8	85
Harrington, Me., U.S.	D5	96
Harrington, Wa., U.S.	B7	124
Harrington Park, N.J., U.S. . .	h9	107
Harrington Pond, l., Me., U.S.	C3	96
Harrington Sound, strt., Ber. .	o20	64
Harriott Lake, l., Sask.	A4	75
Harris, Sask.	F2	75
Harris, Scot., U.K.	B3	10
Harris, Ia., U.S.	A2	92
Harris, Mn., U.S.	E6	100
Harris, Ok., U.S.	D7	113
Harris, R.I., U.S.	D3	116
Harris, Tn., U.S.	A3	119
Harris, co., Ga., U.S.	D1	87
Harris, co., Tx., U.S.	E5	120
Harris, Sound of, strt., Scot., U.K.	C1	13
Harrisburg, Ar., U.S.	B5	81
Harrisburg, Il., U.S.	F5	90
Harrisburg, Mo., U.S.	B5	102
Harrisburg, Ne., U.S.	C2	104
Harrisburg, Oh., U.S.	m10	112
Harrisburg, Or., U.S.	C3	114
Harrisburg, Pa., U.S.	F8	115
Harrisburg, S.D., U.S.	D9	118
Harris Grove, Va., U.S.	h15	123
Harris Hill, N.Y., U.S.	*C2	109
Harris Hill, hill, Ma., U.S. . . .	A3	98
Harrismith, S. Afr.	C4	49
Harrison, Ar., U.S.	A2	81
Harrison, Ga., U.S.	D4	87
Harrison, Id., U.S.	B2	89
Harrison, Me., U.S.	D2	96
Harrison, Mi., U.S.	E6	99
Harrison, N.J., U.S.	k8	107
Harrison, N.Y., U.S.	h13	109
Harrison, Oh., U.S.	C1	112
Harrison, S.D., U.S.	D7	118
Harrison, Tn., U.S.	h11	119
Harrison, co., In., U.S.	H5	91
Harrison, co., Ia., U.S.	C2	92
Harrison, co., Ky., U.S.	B5	94
Harrison, co., Ms., U.S.	E4	101
Harrison, co., Mo., U.S.	A3	102
Harrison, co., Oh., U.S.	B4	112
Harrison, co., Tx., U.S.	C5	120
Harrison, co., W.V., U.S. . . .	B4	125
Harrison, Cape, c., Newf. . . .	g10	72
Harrison Bay, b., Ak., U.S. . .	A9	79
Harrisonburg, La., U.S.	C4	95
Harrisonburg, Va., U.S.	B4	123
Harrison Hot Springs, B.C. . .	f14	69
Harrison Lake, l., B.C.	E7	69
Harrison Township, Mi., U.S. .	*F8	99
Harrison Valley, Pa., U.S. . . .	C6	115
Harrisonville, Mo., U.S.	C3	102
Harrisonville, N.J., U.S.	D2	107
Harrisonville, Pa., U.S.	G5	115
Harriston, Ont.	D4	73
Harriston, Ms., U.S.	D2	101
Harristown, Il., U.S.	D4	90
Harrisville, Mi., U.S.	D7	99
Harrisville, N.H., U.S.	E2	106
Harrisville, N.Y., U.S.	f9	109
Harrisville, Pa., U.S.	D1	115
Harrisville, R.I., U.S.	B2	116
Harrisville, Ut., U.S.	B4	121
Harrisville, W.V., U.S.	B3	125
Harrod, Oh., U.S.	B2	112
Harrodsburg, In., U.S.	F4	91
Harrodsburg, Ky., U.S.	C5	94
Harrods Creek, stm., Ky., U.S.	g11	94
Harrogate, Eng., U.K.	C6	12
Harrold, S.D., U.S.	C6	118
Harrop Lake, l., Man.	C4	70
Harrow, Ont.	E1	73
Harrowby, Man.	D1	70
Harrowsmith, Ont.	C8	73
Harrys, stm., Newf.	D2	72
Harry S. Truman Reservoir, res., Mo., U.S.	C4	102
Harry Strunk Lake, res., Ne., U.S.	D5	104
Harsīn, Iran	D3	39
Harstad, Nor.	C7	14
Hart, Mi., U.S.	E4	99
Hart, Tx., U.S.	B1	120
Hart, co., Ga., U.S.	B4	87

Name	Map Ref.	Page
Hart, co., Ky., U.S.	C4	94
Hart, Lake, l., Fl., U.S.	D5	86
Hartell, Alta.	D3	68
Hartfield, Va., U.S.	C6	123
Hartford, Al., U.S.	D4	78
Hartford, Ar., U.S.	B1	81
Hartford, Ct., U.S.	B5	84
Hartford, Il., U.S.	E3	90
Hartford, In., U.S.	*G8	91
Hartford, Ia., U.S.	C4	92
Hartford, Ks., U.S.	D8	93
Hartford, Ky., U.S.	C3	94
Hartford, Me., U.S.	D2	96
Hartford, Mi., U.S.	F4	99
Hartford, N.J., U.S.	D3	107
Hartford, N.Y., U.S.	B7	109
Hartford, S.D., U.S.	D9	118
Hartford, Tn., U.S.	D10	119
Hartford, Vt., U.S.	D4	122
Hartford, W.V., U.S.	C3	125
Hartford, Wi., U.S.	E5	126
Hartford, co., Ct., U.S.	B4	84
Hartford City, In., U.S.	D7	91
Hartha, E. Ger.	B7	19
Hartington, Ne., U.S.	B8	104
Hart Island, i., Md., U.S.	B5	97
Hart Lake, l., Or., U.S.	E7	114
Hartland, N.B.	C2	71
Hartland, Me., U.S.	D3	96
Hartland, Mn., U.S.	G5	100
Hartland, Vt., U.S.	D4	122
Hartland, W.V., U.S.	m13	125
Hartland, Wi., U.S.	E5	126
Hartland Four Corners, Vt., U.S.	D4	122
Hartland Point, c., Eng., U.K.	E4	10
Hartlepool, Eng., U.K.	C6	10
Hartley, Ia., U.S.	A2	92
Hartley, Tx., U.S.	B1	120
Hartley, co., Tx., U.S.	B1	120
Hartline, Wa., U.S.	B6	124
Hartly, De., U.S.	D3	85
Hartman, Ar., U.S.	B2	81
Hartman, Co., U.S.	C8	83
Hart Mountain, mtn., Man.	C1	70
Hartney, Man.	E1	70
Hartsburg, Il., U.S.	C4	90
Hartsburg, Mo., U.S.	C5	102
Hartsdale, N.Y., U.S.	*n15	109
Hartsel, Co., U.S.	B5	83
Hartselle, Al., U.S.	A3	78
Hartsfield, Ga., U.S.	E3	87
Hartshorn, Mo., U.S.	D6	102
Hartshorne, Ok., U.S.	C6	113
Hartsville, In., U.S.	F6	91
Hartsville, S.C., U.S.	C7	117
Hartsville, Tn., U.S.	A5	119
Hartuv, Isr.	h11	41
Hartville, Mo., U.S.	D5	102
Hartville, Oh., U.S.	B4	112
Hartville, Wy., U.S.	D8	127
Hartwell, Ga., U.S.	B4	87
Hartwell Lake, res., U.S.	B1	117
Hartwick, Ia., U.S.	C5	92
Hartwick, N.Y., U.S.	C5	109
Har Us Lake, l., Mong.	B3	31
Hārūt, stm., Afg.	E10	39
Harvard, Id., U.S.	C2	89
Harvard, Il., U.S.	A5	90
Harvard, Ia., U.S.	D4	92
Harvard, Ma., U.S.	B4	98
Harvard, Ne., U.S.	D7	104
Harvard, Mount, mtn., Co., U.S.	C4	83
Harvel, Il., U.S.	D4	90
Harvest, Al., U.S.	A3	78
Harvey, N.B.	D3	71
Harvey, N.B.	D5	71
Harvey, Il., U.S.	B6	90
Harvey, Ia., U.S.	C5	92
Harvey, La., U.S.	E5	95
Harvey, Mi., U.S.	B3	99
Harvey, N.D., U.S.	B6	111
Harvey, W.V., U.S.	n13	125
Harvey, co., Ks., U.S.	D6	93
Harvey Lake, res., Pa., U.S.	m16	115
Harvey Mountain, mtn., U.S.	B1	98
Harveysburg, Oh., U.S.	C1	112
Harveys Creek, stm., Pa., U.S.	n16	115
Harveyville, Ks., U.S.	D8	93
Harviell, Mo., U.S.	E7	102
Harwich, Eng., U.K.	E7	10
Harwich, Ma., U.S.	C7	98
Harwich Port, Ma., U.S.	C7	98
Harwinton, Ct., U.S.	B3	84
Harwood, Ont.	C6	73
Harwood, Md., U.S.	C4	97
Harwood, Mo., U.S.	f9	104
Harwood, Mo., U.S.	D3	102
Harwood, N.D., U.S.	C9	111
Harwood Heights, Il., U.S.	*k9	90
Haryāna, state, India	C6	36
Harzgerode, E. Ger.	B6	19
Harz Mountains, mts., Eur.	C5	18
Ḥasā, Wādī al, val., Jord.	D7	41
Ḥasanah, Bi'r, well, Eg.	D5	41
Hasan Dāği, mtn., Tur.	C10	40
Ḥasan Kīādeh, Iran	C4	39
Hasbrouck Heights, N.J., U.S.	h8	107
Hasdo, stm., India	F9	37
Hase, stm., W. Ger.	B3	18
Haselünne, W. Ger.	B3	18
Hashimoto, Japan	o14	33
Haskell, Ar., U.S.	C3	81
Haskell, Ok., U.S.	B6	113
Haskell, Tx., U.S.	C3	120
Haskell, co., Ks., U.S.	E3	93
Haskell, co., Ok., U.S.	B6	113
Haskell, co., Tx., U.S.	C3	120
Haskins, Oh., U.S.	A2	112
Haslach, Aus.	E9	19
Hasle, Den.	C8	15
Haslemere, Eng., U.K.	C7	12
Haslet, Tx., U.S.	n9	120
Haslett, Mi., U.S.	*F6	99
Haslev, Den.	C6	15
Hassan, India	F6	36
Hassayampa, stm., Az., U.S.	D3	80
Hassell, N.C., U.S.	B5	110
Hasselt, Bel.	B6	16
Hasselt, Neth.	B6	17
Hassfurt, W. Ger.	C5	19
Hassi Messaoud, Alg.	C6	44
Hassleben, E. Ger.	E7	15
Hässleholm, Swe.	I5	14
Hassloch, W. Ger.	F3	18
Hastings, Barb.	K20	65
Hastings, Ont.	C7	73
Hastings, N.Z.	M16	51
Hastings, Eng., U.K.	E7	10
Hastings, Fl., U.S.	C5	86
Hastings, Ia., U.S.	C2	92
Hastings, Mi., U.S.	F5	99
Hastings, Mn., U.S.	F6	100
Hastings, Ne., U.S.	D7	104
Hastings, N.D., U.S.	C7	111
Hastings, Ok., U.S.	C3	113
Hastings, Pa., U.S.	E4	115
Hastings, W.V., U.S.	h9	125
Hastings, co., Ont.	C7	73
Hastings-on-Hudson, N.Y., U.S.	h13	109
Hästveda, Swe.	B7	15
Hasty, Ar., U.S.	A2	81
Hasty, Co., U.S.	C8	83
Haswell, Co., U.S.	C7	83
Hatboro, Pa., U.S.	*F11	115
Hatch, N.M., U.S.	E2	108
Hatch, Ut., U.S.	F3	121
Hatchechubbee, Al., U.S.	C4	78
Hatchet Creek, stm., Al., U.S.	B3	78
Hatchet Lake, N.S.	E6	71
Hatchie, stm., Tn., U.S.	B2	119
Hatchineha, Lake, l., Fl., U.S.	D5	86
Hatchville, Ma., U.S.	C6	98
Hatch Wash, val., Ut., U.S.	E6	121
Hat Creek, stm., S.D., U.S.	E2	118
Hateg, Rom.	C6	24
Hatfield, Sask.	F3	75
Hatfield, Ar., U.S.	C1	81
Hatfield, In., U.S.	I3	91
Hatfield, Ma., U.S.	B2	98
Hatfield, Mn., U.S.	G2	100
Hatfield, Mo., U.S.	A3	102
Hatfield, Pa., U.S.	F11	115
Hathaway, Mt., U.S.	D10	103
Hāthras, India	G7	37
Ha Tien, Viet.	G6	35
Hatillo, P.R.	B2	65
Ha Tinh, Viet.	C6	35
Hatley, Ga., U.S.	E3	87
Hatley, Ms., U.S.	B5	101
Hatley, Wi., U.S.	D4	126
Hat Mountain, mtn., Az., U.S.	E3	80
Hato, Neth. Ant.	H19	65
Hato, Bocht van, b., Neth. Ant.	H19	65
Hato Mayor [del Rey], Dom. Rep.	E9	64
Hatta, India	E7	37
Hattem, Neth.	B6	17
Hatteras, N.C., U.S.	B7	110
Hatteras, Cape, c., N.C., U.S.	B7	110
Hatteras Inlet, b., N.C., U.S.	B7	110
Hattfjelldal, Nor.	E6	14
Hattiesburg, Ms., U.S.	D4	101
Hattieville, Ar., U.S.	B3	81
Hattingen, W. Ger.	*C3	18
Hatton, Sask.	G1	75
Hatton, Al., U.S.	A2	78
Hatton, Ar., U.S.	C1	81
Hatton, N.D., U.S.	B8	111
Hatvan, Hung.	B4	24
Hat Yai (Ban Hat Yai), Thai.	D2	34
Hatzic, B.C.	f13	69
Haubourdin, Fr.	D3	17
Haubstadt, In., U.S.	H2	91
Haugan, Mt., U.S.	C1	103
Haugen, Wi., U.S.	C2	126
Haugesund, Nor.	H1	14
Haughton, La., U.S.	B2	95
Haultain, stm., Sask.	A2	75
Hauppauge, N.Y., U.S.	*n15	109
Hauraki Gulf, b., N.Z.	L15	51
Hausach, W. Ger.	A4	20
Hauser, Or., U.S.	D2	114
Hauser Dam, Mt., U.S.	D5	103
Haut, Isle au, i., Me., U.S.	D4	96
Haut Atlas, mts., Mor.	C3	44
Haute-Marne, dept., Fr.	A1	20
Hauterive (part of Baie-Comeau), Que.	k13	74
Hautes-Alpes, dept., Fr.	E2	20
Haute-Saône, dept., Fr.	B2	20
Haute-Savoie, dept., Fr.	C2	20
Hautes Fagnes, mts., Eur.	D6	17
Hautmont, Fr.	B5	16
Haut-Rhin, dept., Fr.	B3	20
Hauula, Hi., U.S.	B4	88
Hauzenberg, W. Ger.	E8	19
Havana (La Habana), Cuba	C2	64
Havana, Al., U.S.	B2	78
Havana, Ar., U.S.	B2	81
Havana, Il., U.S.	C3	90
Havana, Ks., U.S.	E8	93
Havana, N.D., U.S.	D8	111
Havana Nakya, Az., U.S.	E4	80
Havasu, Lake, res., U.S.	C1	80
Havasupai Indian Reservation, Az., U.S.	A3	80
Havel, stm., W. Ger.	F6	15
Havelberg, E. Ger.	F6	15
Havelock, N.B.	D4	71
Havelock, Ont.	C7	73
Havelock, Ia., U.S.	B3	92
Havelock, N.C., U.S.	C6	110
Haven, Ks., U.S.	E6	93
Haven, Wi., U.S.	k10	126
Havensville, Ks., U.S.	C7	93
Haverford [Township], Pa., U.S.	o20	115
Haverfordwest, Wales, U.K.	C3	12
Haverhill, Eng., U.K.	B8	12
Haverhill, Ma., U.S.	A5	98
Haverhill, N.H., U.S.	C3	106
Haversham, R.I., U.S.	G2	116
Haverstraw, N.Y., U.S.	D7	109
Havertown, Pa., U.S.	G11	115
Haviland, Ks., U.S.	E4	93
Haviland, Oh., U.S.	A1	112
Havre, Mt., U.S.	B7	103
Havre-Aubert, Que.	B8	71
Havre Aubert, Île du, i., Que.	B8	71
Havre-aux-Maisons, Que.	B8	71
Havre aux Maisons, Île du, i., Que.	B8	71
Havre Boucher, N.S.	D8	71
Havre de Grace, Md., U.S.	A5	97
Havre North, Mt., U.S.	B7	103
Havre Saint Pierre, Que.	h9	72
Havza, Tur.	B10	40
Haw, stm., N.C., U.S.	B3	110
Hawaii, co., Hi., U.S.	D6	88
Hawaii, state, U.S.	C5	88
Hawaii, i., Hi., U.S.	D6	88
Hawaiian Gardens, Ca., U.S.	*n12	82
Hawaiian Islands, is., U.S.	m14	88
Hawaii Volcanoes National Park, Hi., U.S.	D6	88
Hawarden, Sask.	F2	75
Hawarden, Ia., U.S.	A1	92
Hawea, Lake, l., N.Z.	P12	51
Hawera, N.Z.	M15	51
Hawes, Eng., U.K.	F6	13
Hawesville, Ky., U.S.	C3	94
Hawi, Hi., U.S.	C6	88
Hawick, Scot., U.K.	C5	10
Hawke, stm., Newf.	B3	72
Hawke Bay, b., N.Z.	M16	51
Hawke Island, i., Newf.	B4	72
Hawker, Austl.	E2	51
Hawkes, Mount, mtn., Ant.	A7	7
Hawkesbury, Ont.	B10	73
Hawkesbury Island, i., B.C.	C3	69
Hawkestone, Ont.	C5	73
Hawkeye, Ia., U.S.	B6	92
Hawkins, Wi., U.S.	C3	126
Hawkins, co., Tn., U.S.	C11	119
Hawkinsville, Ga., U.S.	D3	87
Hawk Lake, Ont.	E5	70
Haw Knob, mtn., U.S.	D9	119
Hawk Point, Mo., U.S.	C6	102
Hawk Run, Pa., U.S.	E5	115
Hawksbill, mtn., Va., U.S.	B4	123
Hawk Springs, Wy., U.S.	E8	127
Hawley, Mn., U.S.	D2	100
Hawley, Pa., U.S.	D11	115
Hawley, Tx., U.S.	C3	120
Hawleyville, Ct., U.S.	D2	84
Haworth, N.J., U.S.	h9	107
Haworth, Ok., U.S.	D7	113
Haw River, N.C., U.S.	A3	110
Hawthorne, Ca., U.S.	n12	82
Hawthorne, Fl., U.S.	C4	86
Hawthorne, Nv., U.S.	E3	105
Hawthorne, N.J., U.S.	B4	107
Hawthorne, N.Y., U.S.	g13	109
Haxtun, Co., U.S.	A8	83
Hay, Austl.	F7	50
Hay, Wa., U.S.	C8	124
Hay, stm., Austl.	D6	50
Hay, stm., Can.	E9	66
Hayange, Fr.	C7	16
Haybes, Fr.	D4	17
Hayden, Al., U.S.	B3	78
Hayden, Az., U.S.	E5	80
Hayden, Co., U.S.	A3	83
Hayden, Ct., U.S.	B5	84
Hayden, Id., U.S.	*B2	89
Hayden, In., U.S.	G6	91
Haydenburg, Tn., U.S.	C8	119
Hayden Lake, l., Id., U.S.	B2	89
Haydenville, Ma., U.S.	B2	98
Haydenville, Oh., U.S.	C3	112
Hayes, La., U.S.	D3	95
Hayes, co., Ne., U.S.	D4	104
Hayes, stm., Man.	B4	70
Hayes, Mount, mtn., Ak., U.S.	C10	79
Hayes Center, Ne., U.S.	D4	104
Hayesville, N.C., U.S.	f9	110
Hayesville, Oh., U.S.	B3	112
Hayesville, Or., U.S.	*C4	114
Hayfield, Man.	E1	70
Hayfield, Ia., U.S.	A4	92
Hayfield, Mn., U.S.	G6	100
Hayfield, Va., U.S.	*B5	123
Hayford, Wa., U.S.	g13	124
Hayford Peak, mtn., Nv., U.S.	G6	105
Hayfork, Ca., U.S.	B2	82
Hay Island, i., Ont.	C5	73
Hay Lakes, Alta.	C4	68
Haylow, Ga., U.S.	F4	87
Haymana, Tur.	C9	40
Haymarket, Va., U.S.	B5	123
Haymock Lake, l., Me., U.S.	B3	96
Haymond, In., U.S.	F7	91
Haynes, Alta.	C4	68
Haynes, Ar., U.S.	C5	81
Haynes, N.D., U.S.	D3	111
Haynesville, La., U.S.	B2	95
Haynesville, Me., U.S.	C5	96
Hayneville, Al., U.S.	C3	78
Hay-on-Wye, Wales, U.K.	B4	12
Hay River, N.W. Ter.	D9	66
Hays, Ks., U.S.	D4	93
Hays, Mt., U.S.	C8	103
Hays, N.C., U.S.	A1	110
Hays, Yemen	C5	47
Hays, co., Tx., U.S.	D3	120
Hays Canyon Peak, mtn., Nv., U.S.	B2	105
Haysi, Va., U.S.	e9	123
Ḥaysī, Bi'r al, well, Eg.	E6	41
Hay Springs, Ne., U.S.	B3	104
Haystack Mountain, mtn., Ct., U.S.	B3	84
Haystack Mountain, mtn., Nv., U.S.	B6	105
Haysville, In., U.S.	H4	91
Haysville, Ks., U.S.	g12	93
Haysville, Tn., U.S.	D3	119
Hayter, Alta.	C5	68
Hayti, Mo., U.S.	E8	102
Hayti, S.D., U.S.	C8	118
Hayti Heights, Mo., U.S.	E8	102
Hayton, Wi., U.S.	h9	126
Hayward, Ca., U.S.	h8	82
Hayward, Wi., U.S.	A4	127
Hayward Addition, S.D., U.S.	*D8	118
Haywards Heath, Eng., U.K.	E7	12
Haywood, Man.	E2	70
Haywood, N.C., U.S.	C6	110
Haywood, Ok., U.S.	C6	113
Haywood, co., N.C., U.S.	f9	110
Haywood, co., Tn., U.S.	B2	119
Hazār, Kūh-e, mtn., Iran	G8	39
Hazard, Ky., U.S.	C6	94
Hazardville, Ct., U.S.	B5	84
Hazārībāg, India	E10	37
Hazebrouck, Fr.	B5	16
Hazel, Ky., U.S.	f9	94
Hazel, S.D., U.S.	C8	118
Hazel Dell, Il., U.S.	D5	90
Hazel Green, Al., U.S.	A3	78
Hazel Green, Ky., U.S.	C6	94
Hazel Green, Wi., U.S.	F3	126
Hazel Park, Mi., U.S.	C4	115
Hazel Patch, Ky., U.S.	C5	94
Hazel Run, Mn., U.S.	F3	100
Hazelton, B.C.	B4	69
Hazelton, Id., U.S.	G5	89
Hazelton, Ks., U.S.	E5	93
Hazelton, N.D., U.S.	C5	111
Hazelton Peak, mtn., Wy., U.S.	B5	127
Hazelwood, Mo., U.S.	*f13	102
Hazelwood, N.C., U.S.	f9	110
Hazen, Ar., U.S.	C4	81
Hazen, Nv., U.S.	D2	105
Hazen, N.D., U.S.	B4	111
Hazen Bay, b., Ak., U.S.	C6	79
Hazenmore, Sask.	H2	75
Hazen Strait, strt., N.W. Ter.	m29	66
Hazlehurst, Ga., U.S.	E4	87
Hazlehurst, Ms., U.S.	D3	101
Hazlet, Sask.	G1	75
Hazlet, N.J., U.S.	C4	107
Hazleton, Ia., U.S.	H2	91
Hazleton, Ia., U.S.	B6	92
Hazleton, Pa., U.S.	E10	115
Hazlett, Lake, l., Austl.	D4	50
Hazlettville, De., U.S.	D3	85
Ḥazōr Ashdod, Isr.	h9	41
Ḥazor HaGelilit, Isr.	B7	41
Head Bay d'Espoir (part of Milltown-Head Bay d'Espoir), Newf.	E4	72
Headford, Ire.	D2	11
Head Harbor Island, i., Me., U.S.	D5	96
Headland, Al., U.S.	D4	78
Headley, Mount, mtn., Mt., U.S.	C1	103
Head of Island, La., U.S.	h10	95
Headquarters, Id., U.S.	C3	89
Headrick, Ok., U.S.	C2	113
Heafford Junction, Wi., U.S.	C4	126
Healdsburg, Ca., U.S.	C2	82
Healdton, Ok., U.S.	C4	113
Healdville, Vt., U.S.	E3	122
Healing Springs, Va., U.S.	C3	123
Healy, Ak., U.S.	C10	79
Healy, Ks., U.S.	D3	93
Heanna, Japan	O5	52
Heard, co., Ga., U.S.	C1	87
Heard Island, i., Austl.	J1	2
Hearne, Sask.	G3	75
Hearne, Tx., U.S.	D4	120
Hearst, Ont.	o19	73
Hearst Island, i., Ant.	C6	7
Heart, stm., Alta.	A2	68
Heart, stm., N.D., U.S.	C3	111
Heart Butte, Mt., U.S.	B4	103
Heart Butte Dam, N.D., U.S.	C4	111
Hearthstone Mountain, mtn., Md., U.S.	A2	97
Heart Lake, l., U.S.	B5	68
Heart Lake, l., Wy., U.S.	B2	127
Heart's Content, Newf.	E5	72
Heartwell, Ne., U.S.	D7	104
Heaters, W.V., U.S.	C4	125
Heath, Al., U.S.	D3	78
Heath, Ma., U.S.	A2	98
Heath, Oh., U.S.	B3	112
Heatherton, N.S.	D8	71
Heath Springs, S.C., U.S.	B6	117
Heathsville, Va., U.S.	C6	123
Heaton, N.D., U.S.	B6	111
Heaundā, Nepal	D10	37
Heavener, Ok., U.S.	C7	113
Hebbronville, Tx., U.S.	F3	120
Hebei, prov., China	D8	31
Hebel, Austl.	D6	51
Heber, Az., U.S.	C5	80
Heber City, Ut., U.S.	C4	121
Heber Springs, Ar., U.S.	B3	81
Hebert, La., U.S.	B4	95
Hébertville, Que.	A6	74
Hebgen Lake, res., Mt., U.S.	F5	103
Hebi, China	*D7	31
Hebo, Or., U.S.	B3	114
Hebrides, Sea of the, Scot., U.K.	f9	72
Hebron, Newf.	f9	72
Hebron, Ct., U.S.	C6	84
Hebron, Il., U.S.	A5	90
Hebron, In., U.S.	B3	91
Hebron, Ky., U.S.	h13	94
Hebron, Me., U.S.	D2	96
Hebron, Md., U.S.	D6	97
Hebron, Ne., U.S.	D8	104
Hebron, N.H., U.S.	C3	106
Hebron, N.D., U.S.	C3	111
Hebron, Oh., U.S.	C3	112
Hebron, Pa., U.S.	m10	120
Hebron, W.V., U.S.	B3	114
Hebron (Al Khalīl), Isr. Occ.	G10	40
Heby, Swe.	t34	14
Hecate Strait, strt., B.C.	C2	69
Hecelchakán, Mex.	C6	63
Heceta Island, i., Ak., U.S.	n23	79
Hechingen, W. Ger.	A6	20
Hechtel, Bel.	C5	17
Hechuan, China	E8	31
Hecker, Il., U.S.	E4	90
Hecklingen, E. Ger.	B6	19
Hecla, Man.	D3	70
Hecla, S.D., U.S.	B7	118
Hecla Island, i., Man.	D3	70
Hectanooga, N.S.	E3	71
Hector, Ar., U.S.	B3	81
Hector, Mn., U.S.	F4	100
Hedo, Japan	N6	52
Hedo Cape, c., Japan	N6	52
Hedon, Eng., U.K.	A7	12
Hedrick, In., U.S.	D2	91
Hedrick, Ia., U.S.	C5	92
Heeia, Hi., U.S.	*B4	88
Heek, W. Ger.	A2	52
Heel Point, c., Wake I.	A2	52
Heeney, Co., U.S.	B4	83
Heerde, Neth.	B6	17
Heerenveen, Neth.	A6	16
Heerlen, Neth.	B6	16
Heessen, W. Ger.	B3	19
Ḥefa, Mifraz (Bay of Haifa), b., Isr.	B6	41
Hefei, China	E8	31
Heflin, Al., U.S.	B4	78
Heflin, La., U.S.	B2	95
Hefner, Lake, res., Ok., U.S.	B4	113
Hegang, China	B11	31
Hegins, Pa., U.S.	E9	115
Hehlen, W. Ger.	A5	19
Heidelberg, Austl.	*G8	50
Heidelberg, S. Afr.	D3	49
Heidelberg, Ms., U.S.	D5	101
Heiden, Switz.	B8	21
Heidenau, E. Ger.	C8	19
Heidenheim, W. Ger.	D5	18
Hendorābi, i., Iran	H6	39
Heihe (Aihui), China	A10	31
Heil, N.D., U.S.	C4	111
Heilbron, S. Afr.	C4	49
Heilbronn, W. Ger.	D4	18
Heiligenblut, Aus.	B8	20
Heiligenhafen, W. Ger.	D4	15
Heiligenstadt, E. Ger.	C5	18
Heilongjiang, prov., China	B10	31
Heilong Jiang (Amur), stm., Asia	B10	31
Heilungkiang see Heilongjiang, prov., China	B10	31
Heilwood, Pa., U.S.	E4	115
Heimbach, W. Ger.	D6	17
Heimdal, N.D., U.S.	B6	111
Heimenkirch, W. Ger.	A8	21
Heinola, Fin.	G12	14
Heinsberg, W. Ger.	C6	17
Heinsburg, Alta.	C5	68
Heiskell, Tn., U.S.	m13	119
Heisler, Alta.	C4	68
Heislerville, N.J., U.S.	E3	107
Heizer, Ks., U.S.	D5	93
Hejian, China	E7	32
Hekla, Mount, vol., Ice.	n23	14
Hekou, China	A5	35
Hel, Pol.	A5	26
Helagsfjället, mtn., Swe.	F5	14
Helan Shan, mts., China	D6	31
Helbra, E. Ger.	B6	19
Helena, Ar., U.S.	C5	81
Helena, Ga., U.S.	D4	87
Helena, Mo., U.S.	B3	102
Helena, Mt., U.S.	D4	103
Helena, N.Y., U.S.	f10	109
Helena, Oh., U.S.	A2	112
Helena, Ok., U.S.	A3	113
Helena, S.C., U.S.	C4	117
Helensburgh, Scot., U.K.	B4	10
Helenwood, Tn., U.S.	C9	119
Helga, å, stm., Swe.	B8	15
Helgasjön, l., Swe.	B8	15
Helgeröd, Nor.	p28	14
Helgoland, i., W. Ger.	A3	18
Helgoland Bay, b., W. Ger.	D2	15
Heli, China	C5	33
Helicon see Elikón Óros, mtn., Grc.	g9	25
Helix, Or., U.S.	B8	114
Hellam, Pa., U.S.	G8	115
Hellenthal, W. Ger.	D6	17
Hellertown, Pa., U.S.	E11	115
Hellin, Spain	C5	22
Hells Canyon, val., U.S.	B10	114
Hells Canyon National Recreation Area, U.S.	B10	114
Hell-Ville, Madag.	f9	49
Helm, Ca., U.S.	D3	82
Helmand, stm., Asia	B3	36
Helmbrechts, W. Ger.	C6	19
Helmer, Id., U.S.	*C2	89
Helmer, In., U.S.	A7	91
Helmeringhausen, Nmb.	C2	49
Helmetta, N.J., U.S.	C4	107
Helmond, Neth.	B6	16
Helmsburg, In., U.S.	F5	91
Helmsdale, Scot., U.K.	A5	10
Helmsdale, stm., Scot., U.K.	B5	13
Helmsley, Eng., U.K.	F7	13
Helmstedt, W. Ger.	B5	18
Helnæs, i., Den.	C3	15
Helotes, Tx., U.S.	h7	120
Helper, Ut., U.S.	D5	121
Helsingborg, Swe.	I5	14
Helsingör, Den.	I5	14
Helsinki, Fin.	G11	14
Helston, Eng., U.K.	D2	12
Heltonville, In., U.S.	G5	91
Helvellyn, mtn., Eng., U.K.	F6	13
Helvetia, Arg.	A4	54
Helvetia, W.V., U.S.	C4	125
Helvick Head, c., Ire.	E4	11
Hemau, W. Ger.	D6	19
Ḥemar, Naḥal, val., Isr.	C7	41
Hematite, Mo., U.S.	C7	102
Hemau, W. Ger.	D6	19
Hemel Hempstead, Eng., U.K.	k12	10
Hemford, N.S.	E5	71
Hemingford, Ne., U.S.	B2	104
Hemingway, S.C., U.S.	D9	117
Hemlock, In., U.S.	D5	91
Hemlock, Mi., U.S.	E6	99
Hemlock, N.Y., U.S.	C3	109
Hemlock Reservoir, res., Ct., U.S.	E2	84
Hemmesta, Swe.	t36	14
Hemmingford, Que.	D4	74
Hemmoor, W. Ger.	B5	18
Hemnesberget, Nor.	D6	14
Hemphill, Tx., U.S.	D6	120
Hemphill, co., Tx., U.S.	B2	120
Hemple, Mo., U.S.	B3	102
Hempstead, N.Y., U.S.	n15	109
Hempstead, Tx., U.S.	D4	120
Hempstead, co., Ar., U.S.	D2	81
Henagar, Al., U.S.	A4	78
Henan, prov., China	E8	31
Henares, stm., Spain	B4	22
Hendaye, Fr.	F3	16
Henderson, Arg.	B4	54
Henderson, Al., U.S.	D4	78
Henderson, Co., U.S.	B6	83
Henderson, Ky., U.S.	C2	94
Henderson, Md., U.S.	B6	97
Henderson, Mi., U.S.	E6	99
Henderson, Mn., U.S.	F5	100
Henderson, Ne., U.S.	D8	104
Henderson, Nv., U.S.	G7	105
Henderson, N.Y., U.S.	B4	109
Henderson, N.C., U.S.	A4	110
Henderson, Tn., U.S.	B3	119
Henderson, Tx., U.S.	C5	120
Henderson, co., Il., U.S.	C3	90
Henderson, co., Ky., U.S.	C2	94
Henderson, co., N.C., U.S.	f10	110
Henderson, co., Tn., U.S.	B3	119
Henderson, co., Tx., U.S.	C5	120
Henderson's Point, Ms., U.S.	g7	101
Hendersonville, N.C., U.S.	f10	110
Hendersonville, S.C., U.S.	A5	119
Hendersonville, Tn., U.S.	A5	119
Hendley, Ne., U.S.	D6	104
Hendon (part of London), Eng., U.K.	k12	10
Hendricks, Mn., U.S.	F2	100
Hendricks, W.V., U.S.	B5	125
Hendricks, co., In., U.S.	E4	91
Hendrik Verwoerd Dam, res., S. Afr.	D4	49
Hendrix, Ok., U.S.	D5	113
Hendrum, Mn., U.S.	C2	100
Hendry, co., Fl., U.S.	F5	86
Henefer, Ut., U.S.	C4	121
Hengelo, Neth.	A7	16
Hengshan, China	F3	32
Hengshan, China	K5	32
Hengxian, China	G6	31
Hengyang, China	F7	31
Hénin-Beaumont, Fr.	D2	17
Henlawson, W.V., U.S.	n12	125
Henley Harbour, Newf.	B4	72
Henley-on-Thames, Eng., U.K.	C7	12
Henlopen, Cape, c., De., U.S.	E5	85
Henlopen Acres, De., U.S.	F5	85
Hennebont, Fr.	E2	16
Hennef, W. Ger.	C2	19
Hennepin, Il., U.S.	B4	90
Hennepin, Ok., U.S.	C4	113
Hennepin, co., Mn., U.S.	E5	100
Hennessey, Ok., U.S.	A4	113
Henniker, N.H., U.S.	D3	106
Henning, Il., U.S.	C6	90
Henning, Mn., U.S.	D3	100
Henning, Tn., U.S.	B2	119
Henribourg, Sask.	D3	75
Henrico, co., Va., U.S.	C5	123
Henrietta, Mo., U.S.	B4	102
Henrietta, N.Y., U.S.	B3	109
Henrietta, N.C., U.S.	B1	110
Henrietta, Tx., U.S.	C3	120
Henrietta Island, i., Sov. Un.	B35	128
Henrietta Maria, Cape, c., Ont.	F4	121
Henrieville, Ut., U.S.	F4	121
Henry, Il., U.S.	B4	90
Henry, Ne., U.S.	C1	104
Henry, S.D., U.S.	C8	118
Henry, co., Al., U.S.	A3	119
Henry, co., Ga., U.S.	C2	87
Henry, co., Il., U.S.	B3	90
Henry, co., In., U.S.	E7	91
Henry, co., Ia., U.S.	C6	92
Henry, co., Ky., U.S.	C4	102
Henry, co., Mo., U.S.	C4	102
Henry, co., Oh., U.S.	A1	112
Henry, co., Tn., U.S.	A3	119
Henry, co., Va., U.S.	D3	123
Henry, Mount, mtn., Mt., U.S.	B1	103
Henryetta, Ok., U.S.	B6	113
Henry Kater, Cape, c., N.W. Ter.	C19	66
Henry Mountains, mts., Ut., U.S.	E5	121
Henry Pittier National Park, Ven.	A4	60
Henrys Fork, stm., U.S.	E2	127
Henryville, Que.	D4	74
Henryville, In., U.S.	G6	91
Henryville, Ky., U.S.	B5	94
Hensall, Ont.	D3	73
Hensel, N.D., U.S.	A8	111
Henshaw, Ky., U.S.	e9	94
Hensler, N.D., U.S.	B4	111
Hensley, Ar., U.S.	C3	81
Henson Creek, stm., Md., U.S.	f9	97
Hentiyn Mountains, mts., Mong.	B6	31
Henzada, Burma	E10	36
Hepburn, Sask.	E2	75
Hepburn, Ia., U.S.	D2	92
Hepburn, Oh., U.S.	B2	112
Hephzibah, Ga., U.S.	C4	87
Hepler, Ks., U.S.	E9	93
Heppenheim, W. Ger.	D3	19
Heppner, Or., U.S.	B7	114
Hepu, China	G9	31
Hepworth, Ont.	C3	73
Heqing, China	F5	31
Herāt, Afg.	B3	36
Herbert, Sask.	G2	75
Herbertingen, W. Ger.	A5	20
Herbert Peak, mtn., N.Z.	O14	51
Herbes, Isle aux, i., Al., U.S.	E1	78
Herb Lake, Man.	B2	70
Herblay, Fr.	g9	16
Herblet Lake, l., Man.	B2	70
Herborn, W. Ger.	C8	19
Herceg-Novi, Yugo.	D4	24
Hercegovina, hist. reg., Yugo.	D4	24
Herculaneum, Mo., U.S.	C7	102
Hercules, Ca., U.S.	*g8	177
Herdecke, W. Ger.	B2	19
Heredia, C.R.	B6	63
Hereford, Eng., U.K.	D5	10
Hereford, Az., U.S.	F5	80
Hereford, Co., U.S.	A6	83
Hereford, Md., U.S.	A4	97
Hereford, Or., U.S.	C8	114
Hereford, S.D., U.S.	C3	118
Hereford, Tx., U.S.	B1	120
Hereford and Worcester, co., Eng., U.K.	B5	12
Hereford Inlet, b., N.J., U.S.	E3	107
Hérémence, Switz.	D3	21
Herencia, Spain	C4	22
Herentals, Bel.	C4	17
Herford, Den.	C6	15
Herford, W. Ger.	B4	18
Héricourt, Fr.	B2	21
Herington, Ks., U.S.	D7	93
Herisau, Switz.	E4	18
Heritage Range, mts., Ant.	D1	7
Heritage Village, Ct., U.S.	*D3	84
Herkimer, Ks., U.S.	C6	93
Herkimer, N.Y., U.S.	B6	109
Herkimer, co., N.Y., U.S.	B6	109
Herman, Mi., U.S.	B2	99
Herman, Mn., U.S.	E2	100
Herman, Ne., U.S.	C9	104
Hermano Peak, mtn., Co., U.S.	D2	83
Hermansville, Mi., U.S.	C3	99
Hermantown, Mn., U.S.	D6	100
Hermanville, Ms., U.S.	D3	101
Hermeskeil, W. Ger.	D1	19
Herminie, Pa., U.S.	F2	115
Hermiston, Or., U.S.	B7	114
Hermitage, Newf.	E4	72
Hermitage, Ar., U.S.	D3	81
Hermitage, La., U.S.	D4	95
Hermitage, Mo., U.S.	D4	102
Hermitage, Pa., U.S.	*D1	115
Hermitage Bay, b., Newf.	E3	72
Hermitage Springs, Tn., U.S.	C2	119
Hermon, Me., U.S.	D4	96
Hermon, N.Y., U.S.	f9	109
Hermon, Mount, mtn., Asia	F11	40
Hermosa, S.D., U.S.	D2	118

Name	Map Ref.	Page
Honey Brook, Pa., U.S.	F10	115
Honey Creek, Ia., U.S.	C2	92
Honey Creek, Wi., U.S.	n11	126
Honey Grove, Tx., U.S.	C5	120
Honey Lake, l., Ca., U.S.	B3	82
Honeymoon Bay, B.C.	E5	69
Honeypot Glen, Ct., U.S.	C4	84
Honeyville, Ut., U.S.	B3	121
Honfleur, Fr.	C4	16
Høng, Den.	C5	15
Hon Gai, Viet.	B7	35
Hong'an, China	I6	32
Honga River, b., Md., U.S.	D5	97
Honghu, China	F7	31
Hongshui He, stm., China	G6	31
Hongwŏn, N. Kor.	G3	33
Hongze Hu, l., China	E8	31
Honiara, Sol.Is.	G9	6
Honichin Hural, Mong.	C3	32
Honiton, Eng., U.K.	D4	12
Hönö, l., Swe.	A5	15
Honobia, Ok., U.S.	C7	113
Honokaa, Hi., U.S.	C6	88
Honokahua, Hi., U.S.	B5	88
Honokohau, Hi., U.S.	D6	88
Honolulu, Hi., U.S.	B4	88
Honolulu, co., Hi., U.S.	B3	88
Honolulu International Airport, Hi., U.S.	g10	88
Honomu, Hi., U.S.	D6	88
Honor, Mi., U.S.	D4	99
Honoraville, Al., U.S.	D3	78
Honouliuli, Hi., U.S.	g9	88
Hon Quan, Viet.	G7	35
Honshū, i., Japan	D12	31
Honuapo Bay, b., Hi., U.S.	D6	88
Hood, co., Tx., U.S.	C4	120
Hood, Mount, mtn., Or., U.S.	B5	114
Hood Canal, b., Wa., U.S.	B2	124
Hoodoo, Tn., U.S.	B5	119
Hoodoo Peak, mtn., Wa., U.S.	A5	124
Hood Point, c., Austl.	F2	50
Hood River, Or., U.S.	B5	114
Hood River, co., Or., U.S.	B5	114
Hoodsport, Wa., U.S.	B2	124
Hoogeveen, Neth.	B6	17
Hoogezand, Neth.	A6	17
Hookena, Hi., U.S.	D6	88
Hooker, Ok., U.S.	e9	113
Hooker, S.D., U.S.	D8	118
Hooker, co., Ne., U.S.	C4	104
Hooker, Bi'r, well, Eg.	D2	41
Hooker, Mount, mtn., Can.	C8	69
Hookerton, N.C., U.S.	B5	110
Hook Head, c., Ire.	E5	11
Hooksett, N.H., U.S.	D4	106
Hoolehua, Hi., U.S.	B4	88
Hoonah, Ak., U.S.	D12	79
Hoopa Valley Indian Reservation, Ca., U.S.	B2	82
Hooper, Co., U.S.	D5	83
Hooper, Ne., U.S.	C9	104
Hooper, Ut., U.S.	B3	121
Hooper, Wa., U.S.	C7	124
Hooper Bay, Ak., U.S.	C6	79
Hooper Creek, stm., Ne., U.S.	h12	104
Hooper Islands, is., Md., U.S.	D5	97
Hooper Strait, strt., Md., U.S.	D5	97
Hoopersville, Md., U.S.	D5	97
Hoopes Reservoir, res., De., U.S.	A3	85
Hoopeston, Il., U.S.	C6	90
Hooping Harbour, Newf.	C3	72
Hoople, N.D., U.S.	A8	111
Hooppole, Il., U.S.	B4	90
Hoorn, Neth.	A6	16
Hoosac Range, mts., U.S.	A1	98
Hoosic, stm., U.S.	C7	109
Hoosick Falls, N.Y., U.S.	C7	109
Hoosier, Sask.	F1	75
Hoosuc Range, mts., U.S.	D1	96
Hoover, Al., U.S.	*g7	78
Hoover Dam, U.S.	G7	105
Hoover Reservoir, res., Oh., U.S.	B3	112
Hooverson Heights, W.V., U.S.	f8	125
Hooversville, Pa., U.S.	F4	115
Hopa, Tur.	B13	40
Hopatcong, N.J., U.S.	B3	107
Hopatcong, Lake, l., N.J., U.S.	A3	107
Hop Bottom, Pa., U.S.	C10	115
Hope, B.C.	E7	69
Hope, Ak., U.S.	C10	79
Hope, Ar., U.S.	D2	81
Hope, Id., U.S.	A2	89
Hope, In., U.S.	F6	91
Hope, Ks., U.S.	D6	93
Hope, Me., U.S.	D3	96
Hope, Mi., U.S.	E6	99
Hope, Mn., U.S.	G5	100
Hope, N.M., U.S.	E5	108
Hope, N.D., U.S.	B8	111
Hope, R.I., U.S.	D3	116
Hope, i., Nor.	B12	128
Hope, Ben, mtn., Scot., U.K.	A4	10
Hope, Loch, l., Scot., U.K.	B4	13
Hope, Point, c., Ak., U.S.	B6	79
Hopedale, Newf.	g9	72
Hopedale, Il., U.S.	C4	90
Hopedale, La., U.S.	E6	95
Hopedale, Ma., U.S.	B4	98
Hopedale, Oh., U.S.	B5	112
Hopeh see Hebei, prov., China	D8	31
Hope Hull, Al., U.S.	C3	78
Hope Island, i., B.C.	D4	69
Hope Island, i., R.I., U.S.	E5	116
Hopelawn, N.J., U.S.	k7	107
Hopelchén, Mex.	D7	63
Hope Mills, N.C., U.S.	C4	110
Hopes Advance, Cap, c., Que.	f13	74
Hopeton, Ok., U.S.	A3	113
Hopetoun, Austl.	G4	51
Hopetown, S. Afr.	C3	49
Hope Valley, R.I., U.S.	E2	116
Hopeville, Ia., U.S.	D4	92
Hopewell, N.S.	D7	71
Hopewell, Ms., U.S.	D3	101
Hopewell, N.J., U.S.	C3	107
Hopewell, Oh., U.S.	B3	112
Hopewell, Pa., U.S.	F5	115
Hopewell, Va., U.S.	C5	123
Hopewell Cape, N.B.	D5	71
Hopewell Junction, N.Y., U.S.	D7	109
Hopi Buttes, mtn., Az., U.S.	B5	80
Hopi Indian Reservation, Az., U.S.	A5	80
Hopkins, Mi., U.S.	F5	99
Hopkins, Mn., U.S.	n12	100
Hopkins, Mo., U.S.	A3	102
Hopkins, S.C., U.S.	D6	117
Hopkins, co., Ky., U.S.	C2	94
Hopkins, co., Tx., U.S.	C5	120
Hopkinsville, Ky., U.S.	D2	94
Hopkinton, Ia., U.S.	B6	92
Hopkinton, Ma., U.S.	B4	98
Hopkinton, N.H., U.S.	D3	106
Hopkinton, N.Y., U.S.	f10	109
Hopkinton, R.I., U.S.	F1	116
Hopkinton Lake, res., N.H., U.S.	D3	106
Hopland, Ca., U.S.	C2	82
Hopson, Tn., U.S.	C11	119
Hopwood, Pa., U.S.	G2	115
Hoquiam, Wa., U.S.	C2	124
Horace, Ks., U.S.	D2	93
Horace, N.D., U.S.	C9	111
Horace Mountain, mtn., Ak., U.S.	B10	79
Horatio, Ar., U.S.	D1	81
Horatio, S.C., U.S.	C6	117
Horažďovice, Czech.	D8	19
Horb, W. Ger.	E3	19
Hørby, Den.	A4	15
Hörby, Swe.	C7	15
Horconcitos, Pan.	F6	62
Hord, Il., U.S.	F5	90
Hordville, Ne., U.S.	C8	104
Horgen, Switz.	E4	18
Horicon, Wi., U.S.	E5	126
Horine, Mo., U.S.	C7	102
Horizon, Sask.	H3	75
Horle, Swe.	A7	15
Horlick Mountains, mts., Ant.	A36	7
Hormoz, i., Iran	H8	39
Hormuz, Strait of, strt., Asia	C5	38
Horn, c., Aus.	D7	18
Horn, c., Ice.	m21	14
Horn, Cape, c., Chile	k12	54
Hornavan, l., Swe.	D7	14
Hornbeak, Tn., U.S.	A2	119
Hornbeck, La., U.S.	C2	95
Hornburg, W. Ger.	A5	19
Horncastle, Eng., U.K.	A7	12
Hornell, N.Y., U.S.	C3	109
Hornerstown, N.J., U.S.	C3	107
Hornersville, Mo., U.S.	E7	102
Horn Head, c., Ire.	B4	11
Hornick, Ia., U.S.	B1	92
Horning's Mills, Ont.	C4	73
Horní Počernice, Czech.	n18	26
Horn Island, i., Ms., U.S.	E5	101
Horn Island Pass, strt., Ms., U.S.	g8	101
Horn Lake, Ms., U.S.	A3	101
Horn Mountain, mtn., Al., U.S.	B3	78
Horn Plateau, plat., N.W. Ter.	D9	66
Horn Pond, l., Ma., U.S.	g11	98
Hornsby, Tn., U.S.	B3	119
Hornsbyville, Va., U.S.	h15	123
Hornsea, Eng., U.K.	D6	10
Hornslet, Den.	B4	15
Hörnum, W. Ger.	A4	18
Hořovice, Czech.	D8	19
Horqin Youyi Qianqi, China	A10	32
Horqin Youyi Zhongqi, China	B9	32
Horqueta, Para.	D4	55
Horred, Swe.	A6	15
Horry, co., S.C., U.S.	D10	117
Horse, stm., Alta.	A5	68
Horse, stm., I., U.S.	C6	84
Horse Branch, Ky., U.S.	C3	94
Horse Cave, Ky., U.S.	C4	94
Horse Creek, Wy., U.S.	E7	127
Horse Creek, stm., U.S.	E8	127
Horse Creek, stm., Co., U.S.	C7	83
Horse Creek, stm., Mo., U.S.	A6	102
Horse Creek Reservoir, res., Co., U.S.	C7	83
Horsefly, B.C.	C7	69
Horsefly Lake, l., B.C.	C7	69
Horsehead Lake, l., N.D., U.S.	B6	111
Horseheads, N.Y., U.S.	C4	109
Horse Heaven Hills, hills, Wa., U.S.	C6	124
Horse Islands, Newf.	C4	72
Horse Mountain, mtn., N.M., U.S.	D1	108
Horsens, Den.	J3	14
Horseshoe Beach, Fl., U.S.	C3	86
Horseshoe Bend, Id., U.S.	F2	89
Horseshoe Bend National Military Park, Al., U.S.	C4	78
Horseshoe Cove, b., Fl., U.S.	C3	86
Horseshoe Lake, l., Man.	C4	70
Horseshoe Point, c., Fl., U.S.	C3	86
Horseshoe Reservoir, res., Az., U.S.	C4	80
Horse Springs, N.M., U.S.	D1	108
Horsham, Austl.	G7	50
Horsham, Eng., U.K.	C7	12
Horsham, Pa., U.S.	*F11	115
Horšovský Týn, Czech.	D7	19
Horta, Port.	g8	4
Horten, Nor.	H4	14
Hortense, Ga., U.S.	E5	87
Horton, Al., U.S.	A3	78
Horton, Ks., U.S.	C8	93
Horton, Mo., U.S.	D3	102
Horton, stm., N.W. Ter.	C8	66
Hortonia, Lake, l., Vt., U.S.	D2	122
Hortonville, Wi., U.S.	D5	126
Hørve, Den.	C5	15
Hörvik, Swe.	B8	15
Horw, Switz.	B5	21
Hoschton, Ga., U.S.	B3	87
Hoséré Vokré, mtn., Cam.	D2	46
Hosford, Fl., U.S.	B2	86
Hoshāb, Pak.	H11	39
Hoshiārpur, India	B6	36
Hoskins, Ne., U.S.	B8	104
Hoskins, Or., U.S.	C3	114
Hoskinston, Ky., U.S.	C6	94
Hosmer, B.C.	E10	69
Hosmer, S.D., U.S.	B6	118
Hospers, Ia., U.S.	A2	92
Hospital, Ire.	E3	11
Hospitalet, Spain	B7	22
Hosston, La., U.S.	B2	95
Hosta Butte, mtn., N.M., U.S.	B1	108
Hotaka, Mount, mtn., Japan	H8	36
Hotan, China	A7	36
Hotan, stm., China	A7	36
Hotchkiss, Co., U.S.	C3	83
Hotchkissville, Ct., U.S.	C3	84
Hot Coffee, Ms., U.S.	D4	101
Hot Creek Range, mts., Nv., U.S.	E5	105
Hot Creek Valley, val., Nv., U.S.	E5	105
Hötensleben, E. Ger.	A6	19
Hotevilla, Az., U.S.	B5	80
Hoting, Swe.	E7	14
Hot Spring, co., Ar., U.S.	C2	81
Hot Springs, Mt., U.S.	C2	103
Hot Springs see Truth or Consequences, N.M., U.S.	D2	108
Hot Springs, N.C., U.S.	f10	110
Hot Springs, S.D., U.S.	D2	118
Hot Springs, Va., U.S.	C3	123
Hot Springs, co., Wy., U.S.	C4	127
Hot Springs National Park, Ar., U.S.	C2	81
Hot Springs National Park, Ar., U.S.	C2	81
Hot Springs Peak, mtn., Ca., U.S.	B3	82
Hot Springs Peak, mtn., Nv., U.S.	B4	105
Hot Sulphur Springs, Co., U.S.	A4	83
Hottah Lake, l., N.W. Ter.	C9	66
Hotte, Massif de la, mts., Haiti	E7	64
Houck, Az., U.S.	B6	80
Houffalize, Bel.	D5	17
Houghton, Mi., U.S.	A2	99
Houghton, N.Y., U.S.	C2	109
Houghton, S.D., U.S.	B7	118
Houghton, co., Mi., U.S.	B2	99
Houghton Lake, Mi., U.S.	D6	99
Houghton Lake, l., Mi., U.S.	D6	99
Houghton Lake Heights, Mi., U.S.	D6	99
Houilles, Fr.	g9	16
Houlka, Ms., U.S.	A4	101
Houlton, Me., U.S.	B5	96
Houltonville, La., U.S.	h11	95
Houma, La., U.S.	E5	95
Houmt Essouk, Tun.	C7	44
Houndé, Burkina	D4	45
Hourn, Loch, b., Scot., U.K.	C13	13
Housatonic, Ma., U.S.	B1	98
Housatonic, stm., U.S.	D3	84
House, N.M., U.S.	C6	108
House, stm., Alta.	B4	68
House Range, mts., Ut., U.S.	D2	121
House Springs, Mo., U.S.	g12	102
Houston, B.C.	B4	69
Houston, Al., U.S.	A2	78
Houston, Ar., U.S.	B3	81
Houston, De., U.S.	E3	85
Houston, Mn., U.S.	G7	100
Houston, Mo., U.S.	D6	102
Houston, Oh., U.S.	B1	112
Houston, Pa., U.S.	F1	115
Houston, Tx., U.S.	E5	120
Houston, co., Al., U.S.	D4	78
Houston, co., Ga., U.S.	D3	87
Houston, co., Mn., U.S.	G7	100
Houston, co., Tn., U.S.	A4	119
Houston, co., Tx., U.S.	D5	120
Houston, stm., La., U.S.	D2	95
Houston, Lake, res., Tx., U.S.	r14	120
Houston Intercontinental Airport, Tx., U.S.	r14	120
Houtzdale, Pa., U.S.	E5	115
Hovd, Mong.	B3	31
Hovd, stm., Mong.	B3	31
Hove, Eng., U.K.	E6	10
Hövelhof, W. Ger.	B3	19
Hoven, S.D., U.S.	B6	118
Hovenweep National Monument, Ut., U.S.	F6	121
Hovland, Mn., U.S.	k10	100
Hövsgöl Lake, l., Mong.	A5	31
Howar, Wādī, val., Afr.	B2	47
Howard, Al., U.S.	B2	78
Howard, Ga., U.S.	D2	87
Howard, Ks., U.S.	E7	93
Howard, Ms., U.S.	B3	101
Howard, N.Y., U.S.	C3	109
Howard, Pa., U.S.	D6	115
Howard, S.D., U.S.	C8	118
Howard, Wi., U.S.	D5	126
Howard, co., Ar., U.S.	C2	81
Howard, co., In., U.S.	C5	91
Howard, co., Ia., U.S.	A5	92
Howard, co., Md., U.S.	B4	97
Howard, co., Mo., U.S.	B5	102
Howard, co., Ne., U.S.	C7	104
Howard, co., Tx., U.S.	C2	120
Howard City, Mi., U.S.	E5	99
Howard Hanson Reservoir, res., Wa., U.S.	B4	124
Howard Lake, Mn., U.S.	E4	100
Howard Prairie Lake, res., Or., U.S.	E4	114
Howards Grove-Millersville, Wi., U.S.	E6	126
Howardville, Mo., U.S.	E8	102
Howe, Id., U.S.	F6	89
Howe, In., U.S.	A7	91
Howe, Ok., U.S.	C7	113
Howe, Cape, c., Austl.	G9	50
Howell, Mi., U.S.	F7	99
Howell, Tn., U.S.	B5	119
Howell, co., Mo., U.S.	E6	102
Howells, Ne., U.S.	C8	104
Howes, S.D., U.S.	C3	118
Howe Sound, strt., B.C.	E6	69
Howesville, W.V., U.S.	B5	125
Howick, Que.	D4	74
Howison, Ms., U.S.	E4	101
Howland, Me., U.S.	C4	96
Howland, Oh., U.S.	*A5	112
Howland Island, i., Oc.	F11	6
Howley, Newf.	D3	72
Howley, Mount, mtn., Newf.	D2	72
Howser, B.C.	D9	69
Howson Peak, mtn., B.C.	B4	69
Howth (part of Dublin), Ire.	D5	11
Hoxie, Ar., U.S.	A5	81
Hoxie, Ks., U.S.	C3	93
Höxter, W. Ger.	B4	19
Hoy, i., Scot., U.K.	B5	13
Hoya, W. Ger.	B4	18
Hoyerswerda, E. Ger.	B4	19
Hoylake, Eng., U.K.	A4	12
Hoyleton, Il., U.S.	E4	90
Hoyo, Sierra del, mts., Spain	o17	22
Hoyt, N.B.	D3	71
Hoyt, Co., U.S.	A6	83
Hoyt, Ks., U.S.	C8	93
Hoyt, Ok., U.S.	B6	113
Hoyt Lakes, Mn., U.S.	C6	100
Hoytville, Oh., U.S.	A2	112
Hradec Králové, Czech.	E8	26
Hranice, Czech.	D5	26
Hřiňová, Czech.	D5	26
Hron, stm., Czech.	D5	26
Hrubieszów, Pol.	C7	26
Hsinchu, Tai.	G9	31
Hsipaw, Burma	A2	35
Huacho, Peru	D2	58
Huachuca City, Az., U.S.	F5	80
Huacrachuco, Peru	C2	58
Huade, China	D5	32
Huadian, China	C10	31
Hua Hin, Thai.	C1	34
Huai'an (Huaicheng), China	H8	32
Huaibei, China	*E8	31
Huaibin, China	C9	31
Huailai, China	D6	32
Huaiji, China	E8	31
Huaiyang, China	H6	32
Huaiyuan, China	H7	32
Huajuapan de León, Mex.	D5	63
Hualalai, vol., Hi., U.S.	D6	88
Hualapai Indian Reservation, Az., U.S.	B2	80
Hualapai Mountains, mts., Az., U.S.	C2	80
Hualapai Peak, mtn., Az., U.S.	B2	80
Hualgayoc, Peru	C2	58
Hualien, Tai.	G9	31
Huallaga, stm., Peru	C2	58
Huallanca, Peru	C2	58
Huamachuco, Peru	C2	58
Huamantla, Mex.	n15	63
Huambo, Ang.	D2	48
Huambo, dept., Ang.	D2	48
Huancabamba, Peru	C2	58
Huancané, Peru	E4	58
Huancavelica, Peru	D2	58
Huancavelica, dept., Peru	D2	58
Huancayo, Peru	D2	58
Huanchaca, Bol.	D5	55
Huangchuan, China	H6	32
Huanggang, China	E8	31
Huang He (Yellow), stm., China	D8	31
Huanghua, China	D6	31
Huangling, China	I6	32
Huangmei, China	I6	32
Huangshi, China	E8	31
Huangxian, China	F9	32
Huangyan, China	J9	32
Huanguyuan, China	D5	31
Huanjiang, China	G6	31
Huánuco, Peru	C2	58
Huánuco, dept., Peru	C2	58
Huanuni, Bol.	C2	55
Huara, Chile	C5	55
Huaral, Peru	D2	58
Huaráz, Peru	C2	58
Huari, Bol.	C2	55
Huariaca, Peru	C2	58
Huarina, Bol.	C2	55
Huascarán, Nevado, mtn., Peru	C2	58
Huasco, Chile	E1	55
Huasco, stm., Chile	E1	55
Huatabampo, Mex.	B3	63
Huatusco [de Chicuellar], Mex.	n15	63
Huauchinango, Mex.	m14	63
Huaxian, China	G2	32
Huayllay, Peru	D2	58
Huaytará, Peru	D2	58
Huayuan, China	J3	32
Hubbard, Sask.	F4	75
Hubbard, Ia., U.S.	B4	92
Hubbard, Mn., U.S.	D4	100
Hubbard, Oh., U.S.	A5	112
Hubbard, Or., U.S.	B4	114
Hubbard, Tx., U.S.	D4	120
Hubbard, co., Mn., U.S.	C4	100
Hubbard Creek Lake, res., Tx., U.S.	C3	120
Hubbard Lake, Mi., U.S.	D7	99
Hubbard Lake, l., Mi., U.S.	D7	99
Hubbards, N.S.	E5	71
Hubbardston, Ma., U.S.	B3	98
Hubbardston, Mi., U.S.	E6	99
Hubbardton, stm., Vt., U.S.	D2	122
Hubbell, Mi., U.S.	A2	99
Hubbell, Ne., U.S.	D8	104
Hubei, prov., China	E7	31
Huben, Aus.	C8	20
Huber, Ga., U.S.	D3	87
Huberdeau, Que.	D3	74
Huber Heights, Oh., U.S.	*C1	112
Huber Ridge, Oh., U.S.	*B3	112
Huber South, Oh., U.S.	*C1	112
Hubli-Dhārwār, India	E6	36
Huckleberry Hill, Ct., U.S.	C3	84
Huckleberry Mountain, mtn., Or., U.S.	D6	114
Huddersfield, Eng., U.K.	D6	10
Huddinge, Swe.	*H7	14
Huddleston, Va., U.S.	C3	123
Huddleston Knob, mtn., Tn., U.S.	C8	119
Hude, W. Ger.	E2	18
Hudiksvall, Swe.	F7	14
Hudson, Co., U.S.	A6	83
Hudson, Fl., U.S.	D4	86
Hudson, Il., U.S.	C5	90
Hudson, In., U.S.	A7	91
Hudson, Ia., U.S.	B5	92
Hudson, Ks., U.S.	D5	93
Hudson, Me., U.S.	C4	96
Hudson, Ma., U.S.	B4	98
Hudson, Mi., U.S.	G6	99
Hudson, N.H., U.S.	E4	106
Hudson, N.Y., U.S.	C7	109
Hudson, N.C., U.S.	B1	110
Hudson, Oh., U.S.	A4	112
Hudson, S.D., U.S.	D9	118
Hudson, Wi., U.S.	D1	126
Hudson, Wy., U.S.	D4	127
Hudson, co., N.J., U.S.	B4	107
Hudson, stm., U.S.	E7	109
Hudson, Lake, res., Ok., U.S.	A6	113
Hudson Bay, Sask.	E4	75
Hudson Bay, Can.	D15	66
Hudson Falls, N.Y., U.S.	B7	109
Hudson Hope, B.C.	A6	69
Hudson Lake, In., U.S.	A4	91
Hudson Mountains, mts., Ant.	B3	7
Hudson Strait, strt., Can.	D18	66
Hudsonville, Mi., U.S.	F5	99
Hudspeth, co., Tx., U.S.	o12	120
Hudwin Lake, l., Man.	C4	70
Hue, Viet.	B4	35
Huedin, Rom.	B6	24
Huehuetenango, Guat.	D6	63
Huejotzingo, Mex.	n14	63
Huejutla [de Reyes], Mex.	m14	63
Huelma, Spain	D4	22
Huelva, Spain	D2	22
Huércal-Overa, Spain	D5	22
Huerfano, co., Co., U.S.	D5	83
Huerfano Mountain, mtn., N.M., U.S.	A2	108
Huerta, stm., Co., U.S.	D6	83
Huesca, Spain	A5	22
Huéscar, Spain	D4	22
Huete, Spain	B4	22
Huetter, Id., U.S.	*B2	89
Hueytown, Al., U.S.	g6	78
Huffakers, Nv., U.S.	D2	105
Huff, N.D., U.S.	C5	111
Huff, S.C., U.S.	h12	117
Huggins, Mount, mtn., Ant.	B29	7
Hugh Butler Lake, res., Ne., U.S.	D5	104
Hughden, Austl.	D7	50
Hughenden, Alta.	C5	68
Hughes, Ak., U.S.	B9	79
Hughes, Ar., U.S.	C5	81
Hughes, co., Ok., U.S.	B5	113
Hughes, co., S.D., U.S.	C5	118
Hughes, Man.	A1	70
Hughes, North Fork, stm., W.V., U.S.	B3	125
Hughes, South Fork, stm., W.V., U.S.	B3	125
Hughesville, Md., U.S.	C4	97
Hughesville, Mo., U.S.	C4	102
Hughesville, N.J., U.S.	A3	107
Hughesville, Pa., U.S.	D8	115
Hughson, Sask.	F2	75
Hugli, stm., India	D8	36
Hugo, Co., U.S.	B7	83
Hugo, Mn., U.S.	m13	100
Hugo, Ok., U.S.	C6	113
Hugo Lake, res., Ok., U.S.	C6	113
Hugoton, Ks., U.S.	E2	93
Huguley, Al., U.S.	*C4	78
Huichang, China	F8	31
Huichapan, Mex.	m14	63
Hüichŏn, N. Kor.	F3	33
Huila, dept., Ang.	D2	48
Huila, dept., Col.	C2	60
Huila, Nevado de, mtn., Col.	C2	60
Huili, China	F5	31
Huimanguillo, Mex.	B1	62
Huimin, China	E4	32
Huiñaimarca, Lago de, l., S.A.	E4	58
Huinan, China	C10	31
Huitzuco [de los Figueroa], Mex.	n14	63
Huixtla, Mex.	D6	63
Huizen, Neth.	B5	17
Huizhou, China	G7	31
Hukou, China	F8	31
Hukuntsi, Bots.	B3	49
Hulan, China	B10	31
Hulbert, Mi., U.S.	B5	99
Hulbert, Ok., U.S.	B6	113
Hulen, Ky., U.S.	D6	94
Hulett, Wy., U.S.	B8	127
Hull, Que.	D2	74
Hull, Il., U.S.	D2	90
Hull, Ia., U.S.	A1	92
Hull, Ma., U.S.	B6	98
Hull, Tx., U.S.	D5	120
Hull, co., Que.	D2	74
Hull see Kingston upon Hull, Eng., U.K.	D6	10
Hulls Cove, Me., U.S.	D4	96
Huludao, China	C9	31
Hulu Hu, l., China	E3	41
Ḩulwān, Eg.	B3	41
Huma, China	A10	31
Humacao, P.R.	E14	64
Humahuaca, Arg.	A2	54
Humaitá, Braz.	E5	56
Humansdorp, S. Afr.	H4	49
Humansville, Mo., U.S.	D4	102
Humarock, Ma., U.S.	h13	98
Humbe, Ang.	E1	48
Humber, stm., Eng., U.K.	D6	10
Humberside, co., Eng., U.K.	G8	13
Humbird, Wi., U.S.	D3	126
Humble, Tx., U.S.	E5	120
Humboldt, Sask.	E3	75
Humboldt, Az., U.S.	C3	80
Humboldt, Il., U.S.	D5	90
Humboldt, Ia., U.S.	B3	92
Humboldt, Ks., U.S.	E8	93
Humboldt, Mn., U.S.	B1	100
Humboldt, Ne., U.S.	D10	104
Humboldt, Nv., U.S.	C3	105
Humboldt, Tn., U.S.	B3	119
Humboldt, co., Ca., U.S.	B2	82
Humboldt, co., Ia., U.S.	B3	92
Humboldt, co., Nv., U.S.	B3	105
Humboldt, North Fork, stm., Nv., U.S.	B6	105
Humboldt Mountains, mts., Ant.	B14	7
Humboldt Range, mts., Nv., U.S.	C3	105
Hume, Il., U.S.	D6	90
Hume, Mo., U.S.	C3	102
Hume, N.Y., U.S.	C2	109
Hume, Va., U.S.	B5	123
Hume, Lake, res., Austl.	G6	51
Humenné, Czech.	D6	26
Humeston, Ia., U.S.	D4	92
Hummels Wharf, Pa., U.S.	E8	115
Humnoke, Ar., U.S.	C4	81
Humpata, Ang.	E1	48
Humphrey, Ar., U.S.	C4	81
Humphrey, Ne., U.S.	C8	104
Humphreys, Mo., U.S.	A4	102
Humphreys, co., Ms., U.S.	B3	101
Humphreys, co., Tn., U.S.	A4	119
Humphreys, Mount, mtn., Ca., U.S.	D4	82
Humphreys Peak, mtn., Az., U.S.	B4	80
Humpolec, Czech.	D3	26
Humptulips, Wa., U.S.	C2	124
Hûn, Libya	D3	43
Hūnaflói, b., Ice.	n22	14
Hunan, prov., China	F7	31
Hunchun, China	C11	31
Hundested, Den.	C5	15
Hundred, W.V., U.S.	B4	125
Hundred Acre Pond, l., R.I., U.S.	E3	116
Hunedoara, Rom.	C6	24
Hünfeld, W. Ger.	C4	19
Hungary, ctry., Eur.	B4	24
Hungerford, Austl.	D5	51
Hüngnam, N. Kor.	D10	31
Hungry Hill, mtn., Ire.	F2	11
Hungry Horse, Mt., U.S.	B2	103
Hungry Horse Reservoir, res., Mt., U.S.	B3	103
Huningue, Fr.	D7	16
Hunish, Rubha, c., Scot., U.K.	C2	13
Hunjiang, China	C10	31
Hunn, l., Swe.	u33	14
Hunnewell, Ks., U.S.	E6	93
Hunnewell, Mo., U.S.	B6	102
Hunstanton, Eng., U.K.	B8	12
Hunt, Ar., U.S.	B2	81
Hunt, Tx., U.S.	D5	90
Hunt, co., Tx., U.S.	C4	120
Hunt, stm., R.I., U.S.	D4	116
Hunte, stm., W. Ger.	F2	15
Hunter, Ar., U.S.	B4	81
Hunter, Ks., U.S.	C5	93
Hunter, N.D., U.S.	B8	111
Hunter, Ok., U.S.	A4	113
Hunter, i., Austl.	o14	50
Hunter, Cape, c., N.W. Ter.	B18	66
Hunterdon, co., N.J., U.S.	B3	107
Hunter Island, i., B.C.	D3	69
Hunter Mountain, mtn., N.Y., U.S.	C6	109
Hunters, Wa., U.S.	A7	124
Huntersfield Mountain, mtn., N.Y., U.S.	C6	109
Huntersville, W.V., U.S.	C4	125
Huntertown, In., U.S.	B7	91
Hunting Creek, stm., Md., U.S.	C4	97
Huntingdon, Que.	D3	74
Huntingdon, Eng., U.K.	B7	12
Huntingdon, Pa., U.S.	F6	115
Huntingdon, Tn., U.S.	A3	119
Huntingdon, co., Que.	D3	74
Huntingdon, co., Pa., U.S.	F5	115
Hunting Island, i., S.C., U.S.	G7	117
Huntington, Ar., U.S.	B1	81
Huntington, In., U.S.	C7	91
Huntington, Ma., U.S.	B2	98
Huntington, N.Y., U.S.	E7	109
Huntington, Or., U.S.	C9	114
Huntington, Tx., U.S.	D5	120
Huntington, Ut., U.S.	D5	121
Huntington, Vt., U.S.	C3	122
Huntington, W.V., U.S.	C2	125
Huntington, co., In., U.S.	C6	91
Huntington Bay, N.Y., U.S.	*E7	109
Huntington Beach, Ca., U.S.	F4	82
Huntington Center, Vt., U.S.	C3	122
Huntington Creek, stm., Nv., U.S.	C6	105
Huntington Lake, res., In., U.S.	C7	91
Huntington Park, Ca., U.S.	*E4	82
Huntington Station, N.Y., U.S.	*E7	109
Huntington Woods, Mi., U.S.	p15	99
Huntland, Md., U.S.	C4	97
Huntland, Tn., U.S.	B5	119
Huntley, Il., U.S.	A5	90
Huntley, Mn., U.S.	G4	100
Huntley, Mt., U.S.	E8	103
Huntley, Ne., U.S.	D6	104
Huntley, Wy., U.S.	E8	127
Huntly, Scot., U.K.	D6	10
Hunt Mountain, mtn., Wy., U.S.	B5	127
Hunts Point, N.S.	F5	71
Huntsville, Ont.	B5	73
Huntsville, Al., U.S.	A3	78
Huntsville, Ar., U.S.	A2	81
Huntsville, Il., U.S.	C3	90
Huntsville, Ky., U.S.	C3	94
Huntsville, Mo., U.S.	B5	102
Huntsville, Oh., U.S.	B2	112
Huntsville, Tn., U.S.	C9	119
Huntsville, Tx., U.S.	D5	120
Huntsville, Ut., U.S.	B4	121
Hunucmá, Mex.	C7	63
Hunyuan, China	D7	31
Huoshan, China	I7	32
Huoxian, China	E7	31
Hupeh see Hubei, prov., China	E7	31
Hurayḍah, Wādī, val., Eg.	B3	41
Hurd, Cape, c., Ont.	B3	73
Hurdland, Mo., U.S.	A5	102
Hurdsfield, N.D., U.S.	B6	111
Hure Qi, China	C9	32
Hurley, Mo., U.S.	E4	102
Hurley, N.M., U.S.	E1	108
Hurley, N.Y., U.S.	D6	109
Hurley, S.D., U.S.	D8	118
Hurley, Va., U.S.	e9	123
Hurley, Wi., U.S.	B3	126
Hurleyville, N.Y., U.S.	D6	109
Hurliness, Scot., U.K.	B5	13
Hurlock, Md., U.S.	C6	97
Hurmägai, Pak.	G12	39
Huron, Ca., U.S.	D4	82
Huron, Ks., U.S.	C8	93
Huron, Oh., U.S.	A3	112
Huron, S.D., U.S.	C7	118
Huron, co., Mi., U.S.	E7	99
Huron, co., Oh., U.S.	A3	112
Huron, stm., Mi., U.S.	p14	99
Huron, Lake, l., N.A.	B11	76
Huron Mountains, hills, Mi., U.S.	B3	99
Hurricane, Al., U.S.	B3	99
Hurricane, Ms., U.S.	A4	101
Hurricane, Ut., U.S.	F2	121
Hurricane, W.V., U.S.	C2	125
Hurricane Cliffs, clf., U.S.	A2	80
Hurricane Creek, stm., Ar., U.S.	C3	81
Hurricane Mills, Tn., U.S.	B4	119
Hurricane Mountain, mtn., Tn., U.S.	C9	119
Hurst, Tx., U.S.	*n9	120
Hurstville, Austl.	*F9	50
Hurt, Va., U.S.	C3	123
Hürth, W. Ger.	C1	19
Hurtsboro, Al., U.S.	C4	78
Hurup, Den.	B2	15
Huşi, Rom.	B9	24

Name	Map Ref.	Page
Huskvarna (part of Jönköping), Swe.	I6	14
Huson, Mt., U.S.	C2	103
Hussar, Alta.	D4	68
Husser, La., U.S.	D5	95
Hustburg, Tn., U.S.	B4	119
Hustisford, Wi., U.S.	E5	126
Hustle, Va., U.S.	B5	123
Hustontown, Pa., U.S.	F5	115
Hustonville, Ky., U.S.	C5	94
Husum, W. Ger.	A4	18
Husum, Wa., U.S.	D4	124
Hutchins, Tx., U.S.	n10	120
Hutchinson, Ks., U.S.	D6	93
Hutchinson, Mn., U.S.	F4	100
Hutchinson, N.J., U.S.	B2	107
Hutchinson, co., S.D., U.S.	D8	118
Hutchinson, co., Tx., U.S.	B2	120
Hutchinson Island, i., Fl., U.S.	E6	86
Hutchinson Island, i., S.C., U.S.	k11	117
Hutch Mountain, mtn., Az., U.S.	C4	80
Hutsonville, Il., U.S.	D6	90
Hüttental, W. Ger.	C3	19
Huttig, Ar., U.S.	D3	81
Hutto, Tx., U.S.	D4	120
Hutton, Md., U.S.	m12	97
Huttonsville, W.V., U.S.	C5	125
Huttwil, Switz.	B4	21
Hutuo He, stm., China	E5	32
Huu, Indon.	G5	34
Ḥuwwārah, Isr. Occ.	g12	41
Ḥuwwārah, Isr. Occ.	B7	41
Huxford, Al., U.S.	D2	78
Huxley, Alta.	D4	68
Huxley, Ia., U.S.	C4	92
Huy, Bel.	B6	16
Hūzgān, Iran	F4	39
Huzhou, China	*E9	31
Hvalpsund, Den.	B3	15
Hvannadalshnúkur, mtn., Ice.	n24	14
Hvar, i., Yugo.	D3	24
Hvidbjerg, Den.	B2	15
Hvide Sande, Den.	C2	15
Hvidovre, Den.	*C6	15
Hvitsten, Nor.	p28	14
Hvittingfoss (part of Kongsberg), Nor.	p28	14
Hwange, Zimb.	A4	49
Hwang Ho see Huang He, stm., China	D8	31
Hyak, Wa., U.S.	B4	124
Hyampom, Ca., U.S.	B2	82
Hyannis, Ma., U.S.	C7	98
Hyannis, Ne., U.S.	C4	104
Hyannis Port, Ma., U.S.	C7	98
Hyargas Lake, l., Mong.	B3	31
Hyas, Sask.	F4	75
Hyatts, Oh., U.S.	B2	112
Hyattstown, Md., U.S.	B3	97
Hyattsville, Md., U.S.	C4	97
Hyattville, Wy., U.S.	B5	127
Hybart, Al., U.S.	D2	78
Hybla Valley, Va., U.S.	g12	123
Hyco, stm., Va., U.S.	D3	123
Hyco Lake, res., N.C., U.S.	A3	110
Hydaburg, Ak., U.S.	D13	79
Hyde, Pa., U.S.	D5	115
Hyde, co., N.C., U.S.	B6	110
Hyde, co., S.D., U.S.	C6	118
Hyden, Austl.	F2	50
Hyden, Ky., U.S.	C6	94
Hyde Park, Guy.	A3	59
Hyde Park, N.Y., U.S.	D7	109
Hyde Park, Ut., U.S.	B4	121
Hyde Park, Vt., U.S.	B3	122
Hyder, Ak., U.S.	D13	79
Hyderābād, India	E6	36
Hyderābād, Pak.	C4	36
Hydetown, Pa., U.S.	C2	115
Hydeville, Ct., U.S.	B6	84
Hydeville, Vt., U.S.	D2	122
Hydra see Ídhra, i., Grc.	D4	25
Hydraulic, B.C.	C7	69
Hydro, Ok., U.S.	B3	113
Hyères, Fr.	F7	16
Hyères, Îles d' is., Fr.	F7	16
Hyesan, N. Kor.	C10	31
Hygiene, Co., U.S.	A5	83
Hylo, Alta.	B4	68
Hyman, S.C., U.S.	D8	117
Hymera, In., U.S.	F3	91
Hyndman, Pa., U.S.	G4	115
Hyndman Peak, mtn., Id., U.S.	F4	89
Hyner, Pa., U.S.	D6	115
Hyŏpchŏn, S. Kor.	I4	33
Hyrum, Ut., U.S.	B4	121
Hyrynsalmi, Fin.	E13	14
Hysham, Mt., U.S.	D9	103
Hythe, Alta.	B1	68
Hythe, Eng., U.K.	C9	12
Hyvinkää, Fin.	*G11	14

I

Name	Map Ref.	Page
Iaco (Yaco), stm., S.A.	D4	58
Iaeger, W.V., U.S.	D3	125
Ialomiţa, stm., Rom.	C8	24
Iamonia, Lake, l., Fl., U.S.	B2	86
Iantha, Mo., U.S.	D3	102
Iapu, Braz.	B4	56
Iași, Rom.	B8	24
Iatan, Mo., U.S.	B3	102
Iates Point, c., Guam	L10	52
Iatt, Lake, res., La., U.S.	C3	95
Iauaretê, Braz.	C4	60
Iba, Phil.	o18	34
Ibadan, Nig.	E5	45
Ibagué, Col.	C2	60
Ibanda, Ug.	B5	48
Ibapah, Ut., U.S.	C2	121
Ibapah Peak, mtn., Ut., U.S.	D2	121
Ibar, stm., Yugo.	C4	24
Ibaraki, Japan	*I7	33
Ibarra, Ec.	A2	58
Ibb, Yemen	C5	47
Ibbenbüren, W. Ger.	A2	19
Iberá, Laguna, l., Arg.	E4	55
Iberia, Mo., U.S.	C5	102
Iberia, Oh., U.S.	B3	112
Iberia, co., La., U.S.	E4	95
Iberville, Que.	D4	74
Iberville, La., U.S.	D4	95
Iberville, co., Que.	D4	74
Iberville, co., La., U.S.	D4	95
Iberville, Mont d' (Mount Caubvick), mtn., Can.	g14	74
Ibi, Nig.	E6	45
Ibi, Nig., Japan	n15	33
Ibiá, Braz.	B3	56
Ibiapaba, Serra da, mts., Braz.	B2	57
Ibicuí, stm., Braz.	D1	56
Ibicuy, Arg.	A5	54
Ibirapuitã, stm., Braz.	E1	56
Ibitinga, Braz.	C3	56
Ibiza (Iviza), Spain	C6	22
Ibiza, i., Spain	C6	22
Ibo, Moz.	D7	48
Ibu, Japan	N6	52
Iburg, W. Ger.	A3	19
Ica, Peru	D2	58
Ica, dept., Peru	D2	58
Içá (Putumayo), stm., S.A.	D4	60
Içana, Braz.	A4	58
Içana (Isana), stm., S.A.	C4	60
İçel (Mersin), Tur.	D10	40
Icém, Braz.	C3	56
Ichikawa, Japan	n18	33
Ichinomiya, Japan	n15	33
Ichinoseki, Japan	G10	33
Ichnya, Sov. Un.	F9	27
Icicle Creek, stm., Wa., U.S.	B5	124
Ickesburg, Pa., U.S.	F7	115
Icó, Braz.	C3	57
Icy Cape, c., Ak., U.S.	A7	79
Icy Strait, strt., Ak., U.S.	k22	79
Ida, La., U.S.	A2	95
Ida, Mi., U.S.	G7	99
Ida, co., Ia., U.S.	B2	92
Ida, Lake, l., Mn., U.S.	D3	100
Ida, Mount, mtn., Grc.	E5	25
Idabel, Ok., U.S.	D7	113
Ida Grove, Ia., U.S.	B2	92
Idah, Nig.	E6	45
Idaho, co., Id., U.S.	D3	89
Idaho, state, U.S.	E3	89
Idaho City, Id., U.S.	F3	89
Idaho Falls, Id., U.S.	F6	89
Idaho Springs, Co., U.S.	B5	83
Idalia, Co., U.S.	B8	83
Idalou, Tx., U.S.	C2	120
Idamay, W.V., U.S.	k10	125
Idana, Ks., U.S.	C6	93
Idanha, Or., U.S.	C4	114
Idanha-a-Nova, Port.	C2	22
Idar-Oberstein, W. Ger.	D2	19
Idaville, In., U.S.	C4	91
Idaville, Or., U.S.	B3	114
'Idd al Ghanam, Sud.	C1	47
Iddesleigh, Alta.	D5	68
Ideal, Ga., U.S.	D2	87
Ideal, S.D., U.S.	D6	118
Idehan, des., Libya	D2	43
Ider, Al., U.S.	A4	78
Ider, stm., Mong.	B4	31
Idfīnā, Eg.	C3	38
Idfū, Eg.	C3	38
Ídhra (Hydra), i., Grc.	D4	25
Idi, Indon.	C2	41
Idiofa, Zaire	C2	48
Idkū, Eg.	C2	41
Idkū Lake, l., Eg.	C2	41
Idlewild, Mi., U.S.	E5	99
Idlewild, Tn., U.S.	A3	119
Idleyld Park, Or., U.S.	D3	114
Idlib, Syria	E11	40
Idnah, Isr. Occ.	C4	41
Idrigill Point, c., Scot., U.K.	C2	13
Idrija, Yugo.	B2	24
Idritsa, Sov. Un.	C7	27
Idro, Lake, l., Italy	D6	20
Idutywa, Transkei	D4	49
Ie Island, i., Japan	N5	52
Iepê, Braz.	C2	56
Ieper (Ypres), Bel.	B5	16
Ierápetra, Grc.	E5	40
Ierisós, Grc.	B4	25
Ife, Nig.	E5	45
Iferouâne, Niger	C6	45
Ifôghas, Adrar des, mts., Afr.	B5	45
Ifon-Oshogbo, Nig.	*E5	45
Iganga, Ug.	A5	48
Igaraçu, Braz.	C4	57
Igara Paraná, stm., Col.	D3	60
Igarapava, Braz.	C3	56
Igarapé, Açu, Braz.	B1	57
Igarapé-Miri, Braz.	C5	59
Igarka, Sov. Un.	C11	29
Igbo-Ora, Nig.	*E5	45
Igbor, Nig.	C15	40
Iğdır, Tur.	D6	44
Igharghar, Oued, val., Afr.	C6	44
Igharghar, Oued, val., Alg.	D6	44
Iglesia, Arg.	B3	54
Iglesias, Italy	E2	23
Ignacio, Co., U.S.	D3	83
Iğneada, Tur.	B6	40
Igny, Fr.	h9	16
Igoumenítsa, Grc.	C3	25
Igra, Sov. Un.	D8	28
Igreja, Morro da, mtn., Braz.	D3	56
Iguaçu, stm., S.A.	B5	54
Iguala, Mex.	D5	63
Igualada, Spain	B6	22
Iguape, Braz.	C3	56
Iguassu Falls, wtfl., S.A.	B6	54
Iguatemi, stm., Braz.	C2	56
Iguatu, Braz.	F3	57
Iguéla, Gabon	F1	46
Iguidi, 'Erg, dunes, Afr.	B3	44
Igurin, i., Marsh Is.	S18	52
Ih Bogd Mountain, mtn., Mong.	C5	31
Iheya Island, i., Japan	N5	52
Ihiala, Nig.	E6	45
Ihlen, Mn., U.S.	G2	100
Ihosy, Madag.	h9	49
Iida, Japan	l8	33
Iidaan, Som.	D6	47
Iide, Mount, mtn., Japan	H9	33
Iijima, Japan	n16	33
Iisalmi, Fin.	F12	14
Iizuka, Japan	J5	33
IJamsville, Md., U.S.	B3	97
Ijebu Igbo, Nig.	*E5	45
Ijebu Ode, Nig.	E5	45
Ijero-Ekiti, Nig.	*E6	45
IJmuiden, Neth.	B4	17
IJsselmeer (Zuider Zee), l., Neth.	A6	16
Ijuí, Braz.	D2	56
Ijuí, stm., Braz.	D2	56
Ikaalinen, Fin.	G10	14
Ikare, Nig.	*E6	45
Ikaría, i., Grc.	D6	40
Ikast, Den.	B3	15
Ike, i., Japan	O6	52
Ikeda, Japan	o14	33
Ikela, Zaire	B3	48
Ikerre, Nig.	*E6	45
Ikhtiman, Bul.	D6	24
Iki Island, i., Japan	J4	33
Ikire, Nig.	*E5	45
Ikirun, Nig.	*E5	45
Ikole, Nig.	*E6	45
Ikorodu, Nig.	*E5	45
Ikot Ekpene, Nig.	*E6	45
Ila, Nig.	E5	45
Ila, Ga., U.S.	B3	87
Ilagan, Phil.	B6	34
Ilām, Iran	E3	39
Ilanz, Switz.	E4	21
Ilasco, Mo., U.S.	B6	102
Iława, Pol.	B5	26
Ilawe-Ekiti, Nig.	*E6	45
Ilchester, Md., U.S.	B4	97
Ilderton, Ont.	D3	73
Ile-à-la-Crosse, Sask.	m7	75
Île-à-la-Crosse, Lac, l., Sask.	B2	75
Ilebo (Port-Francqui), Zaire	B3	48
Île-de-France, hist. reg., Fr.	C5	16
Ilek, stm., Sov. Un.	E20	8
Île-Perrot, Que.	q19	74
Ileret, Kenya	A6	48
Îles, Lac des, l., Sask.	B6	68
Ilesha, Nig.	E5	45
Ilfeld, N.M., U.S.	B4	108
Ilford, Man.	A4	70
Ilfracombe, Eng., U.K.	E4	10
Ilgın, Tur.	C8	40
Ilhavo, Port.	B1	22
Ilhéus, Braz.	D3	57
Ili, stm., Asia	E10	29
Iliamna, Ak., U.S.	D8	79
Iliamna Lake, l., Ak., U.S.	D8	79
Iliamna Volcano, vol., Ak., U.S.	C9	79
Iliff, Co., U.S.	A7	83
Íliki, Lake, l., Grc.	g10	25
Ilinskaya, Sov. Un.	I13	27
Iliodhrómia, i., Grc.	C4	25
Ilio Point, c., Hi., U.S.	B4	88
Ilioúpolis, Grc.	*D4	25
Ilkeston, Eng., U.K.	B6	12
Ilkley, Eng., U.K.	G7	13
Ill, stm., Aus.	E4	18
Illampu, Nevado, mtn., Bol.	C2	55
Illana Bay, b., Phil.	D6	34
Illapel, Chile	A2	54
Ille, Fr.	F5	16
Illéla, Niger	D6	45
Iller, stm., W. Ger.	D5	18
Illfurth, Fr.	A3	21
Illiers, Fr.	C4	16
Illinois, state, U.S.	C4	90
Illinois, stm., U.S.	A7	113
Illinois, stm., Il., U.S.	B5	90
Illinois, stm., Or., U.S.	E3	114
Illinois City, Il., U.S.	B3	90
Illinois Creek, stm., W.V., U.S.	k9	125
Illinois Peak, mtn., Id., U.S.	C3	89
Illiopolis, Il., U.S.	D4	90
Illizi, Alg.	C7	44
Illkirch-Graffenstaden, Fr.	F7	17
Illnau [-Effretikon], Switz.	B6	21
Illo, Nig.	D5	45
Illora, Spain	D4	22
Ilmen, Lake, l., Sov. Un.	B8	27
Ilmenau, E. Ger.	C5	18
Ilmenau, stm., W. Ger.	B5	18
Ilo, Peru	E3	58
Ilobu, Nig.	*E5	45
Iloilo, Phil.	C6	34
Ilorin, Nig.	E5	45
Ilovaysk, Sov. Un.	r21	27
Ilovlya, Sov. Un.	D2	28
Ilsenburg, E. Ger.	B5	19
Ilwaco, Wa., U.S.	C1	124
Ilža, Pol.	C6	26
Imabari, Japan	I6	33
Imabetsu, Japan	F10	33
Imambaba, Japan	C11	39
Iman, stm., Sov. Un.	B11	31
Imandra, Lake, l., Sov. Un.	*G13	14
Imatra, Fin.	n14	14
Imazu, Japan	n14	33
Imbābah (part of Giza), Eg.	D3	41
Imbabura, prov., Ec.	A2	58
Imbituba, Braz.	D3	56
Imbler, Or., U.S.	B9	114
Imboden, Ar., U.S.	A4	81
Ime, Indon., Scot., U.K.	B8	28
Imgyt Marsh, sw., Sov. Un.	B9	28
Imi, Eth.	D5	47
Imilac, Chile	D2	55
Imlay, Nv., U.S.	C3	105
Imlay City, Mi., U.S.	E7	99
Imlaystown, N.J., U.S.	C3	107
Immeln, l., Swe.	B8	15
Immenstadt, W. Ger.	E5	18
Immokalee, Fl., U.S.	F5	86
Imnaha, Or., U.S.	B10	114
Imnaha, stm., Or., U.S.	B10	114
Imogene, Ia., U.S.	D2	92
Imola, Italy	B3	23
Imotski, Yugo.	D3	24
Imperatriz, Braz.	C1	57
Imperia, Italy	C2	23
Imperial, Ca., U.S.	F6	82
Imperial, Sask.	F3	75
Imperial, Mo., U.S.	C7	102
Imperial, Ne., U.S.	D4	104
Imperial, Pa., U.S.	k13	115
Imperial, Tx., U.S.	D1	120
Imperial, co., Ca., U.S.	F6	82
Imperial Beach, Ca., U.S.	o15	82
Imperial Dam, U.S.	E1	80
Imperial Mills, Alta.	B5	68
Imperial Reservoir, res., U.S.	E1	80
Imperial Valley, val., Ca., U.S.	F6	82
Impfondo, Congo	A3	48
Imphāl, India	D9	36
Imst, Aust.	C5	18
Imwās, Isr. Occ.	h11	41
Ina, Japan	n16	33
Ina, Il., U.S.	E5	90
Ina, stm., Pol.	B3	26
I Naftan, Puntan, c., N. Mar.	E8	52
Inajá, Braz.	C3	57
I-n-Alei, well, Mali	C4	45
In Amguel, Alg.	E6	44
Inanwatan, Indon.	F9	34
Iñapari, Peru	D4	58
Inarajan, Guam	M9	52
Inarajan Bay, b., Guam	M10	52
Inari, Fin.	C12	14
Inari, l., Fin.	C12	14
Inavale, Ne., U.S.	D7	104
Inawashiro, l., Japan	H10	33
In Azaoua, well, Niger	B6	45
In Belbel, Alg.	D5	44
Inca, Spain	C7	22
Incastro, stm., Italy	h9	23
Ince, Cape, c., Tur.	A10	40
İncesu, Tur.	C10	40
Inchard, Loch, b., Scot., U.K.	B3	13
Inchelium, Wa., U.S.	A7	124
Inch'ŏn, S. Kor.	D10	31
Indaiatuba, Braz.	m8	56
Indalsälven, stm., Swe.	F7	14
Indaw, Burma	D10	36
Independence, Ca., U.S.	D4	82
Independence, In., U.S.	D3	91
Independence, Ia., U.S.	B6	92
Independence, Ks., U.S.	E8	93
Independence, Ky., U.S.	B5	94
Independence, La., U.S.	D5	95
Independence, Ms., U.S.	A4	101
Independence, Mo., U.S.	B3	102
Independence, Oh., U.S.	*h9	112
Independence, Or., U.S.	C3	114
Independence, Va., U.S.	D1	123
Independence, Wi., U.S.	D2	126
Independence, co., Ar., U.S.	B4	81
Independence, stm., N.Y., U.S.	B5	109
Independence Mountains, mts., Nv., U.S.	C5	105
Independence National Historical Park, Pa., U.S.	p21	115
Independence Rock, mtn., Wy., U.S.	D5	127
Independencia, Braz.	C2	55
Inderborskiy, Sov. Un.	D4	28
Index, Wa., U.S.	B4	124
India, ctry., Asia	D6	36
Indiahoma, Ok., U.S.	C3	113
Indian, stm., Ont.	B7	73
Indian, stm., De., U.S.	F4	85
Indian, stm., Mi., U.S.	B4	99
Indian, stm., N.Y., U.S.	A5	109
Indiana, Pa., U.S.	E3	115
Indiana, co., Pa., U.S.	E3	115
Indiana, state, U.S.	E5	91
Indiana Dunes National Lakeshore, In., U.S.	A3	91
Indian Agency, Co., U.S.	D3	83
Indianapolis, In., U.S.	E5	91
Indian Bay, b., Fl., U.S.	D4	86
Indian Beach, De., U.S.	F5	85
Indian Brook, N.S.	C9	71
Indian Cedar Swamp, sw., R.I., U.S.	F2	116
Indian Cove, Ct., U.S.	*D4	84
Indian Creek, stm., In., U.S.	H5	91
Indian Creek, stm., Md., U.S.	C4	97
Indian Creek, stm., Oh., U.S.	C1	112
Indian Creek, stm., S.D., U.S.	B2	118
Indian Creek, stm., Tn., U.S.	B3	119
Indian Creek, stm., W.V., U.S.	k9	125
Indian Creek, stm., W.V., U.S.	D4	125
Indian Grave Mountain, hill, Ga., U.S.	C2	87
Indian Harbour Beach, Fl., U.S.	*D6	86
Indian Head, Sask.	G4	75
Indian Head, Md., U.S.	C3	97
Indian Heights, In., U.S.	*D5	91
Indian Hills, Co., U.S.	*B5	83
Indian Island, i., N.C., U.S.	B6	110
Indian Lake, N.Y., U.S.	B6	109
Indian Lake, l., Mi., U.S.	C4	99
Indian Lake, l., N.Y., U.S.	B6	109
Indian Lake, l., Oh., U.S.	B2	112
Indian Lake, l., R.I., U.S.	F4	116
Indian Lake Shores, R.I., U.S.	F4	116
Indian Mound, Tn., U.S.	A4	119
Indian Mound Beach, Ma., U.S.	C6	98
Indian Mountain, mtn., Ct., U.S.	B2	84
Indian Neck, Ct., U.S.	D4	84
Indian Ocean	G2	2
Indian Orchard, Ma., U.S.	D6	90
Indianola, Ia., U.S.	C4	92
Indianola, Ms., U.S.	B3	101
Indianola, Ne., U.S.	D5	104
Indianola, Ok., U.S.	B6	113
Indianópolis, Braz.	B5	56
Indian Peak, mtn., Ut., U.S.	E2	121
Indian Peak, mtn., Wy., U.S.	B3	127
Indian Pond, l., Me., U.S.	C3	96
Indian Pond, l., Me., U.S.	C3	96
Indian Prairie Canal, Fl., U.S.	E5	86
Indian Ridge Estates, Az., U.S.	E5	80
Indian River, co., Fl., U.S.	E6	86
Indian River, De., U.S.	D5	90
Indian River, Mi., U.S.	C6	99
Indian River, co., Fl., U.S.	E6	86
Indian River, b., De., U.S.	F5	85
Indian River Bay, b., De., U.S.	F5	85
Indian Rock, mtn., Wa., U.S.	D5	124
Indian Rocks Beach, Fl., U.S.	p10	86
Indian Springs, Ga., U.S.	C3	87
Indian Springs, Nv., U.S.	G6	105
Indian Stream, stm., N.H., U.S.	f7	106
Indiantown, Fl., U.S.	E6	86
Indian Trail, N.C., U.S.	B2	110
Indian Valley, Id., U.S.	E2	89
Indian Valley, Va., U.S.	D2	123
Indian Village, Ks., U.S.	E8	93
Indian Village, La., U.S.	D2	95
Indian Wells, Az., U.S.	B5	80
Indiaópolis, Braz.	B5	56
Indigirka, stm., Sov. Un.	C17	29
Indio, Ca., U.S.	F5	82
Indispensable Reefs, rf., Oceania	k10	62
Indochina, reg., Asia	B2	35
Indonesia, ctry., Asia	F5	34
Indore, India	D6	36
Indragiri, stm., Indon.	F2	34
Indramayu, Indon.	G3	34
Indre, stm., Fr.	C4	16
Indrio, Fl., U.S.	E6	86
Indus, stm., Asia	D5	36
Indus, stm., Asia	C2	36
Industry, Il., U.S.	C3	90
Ine, Japan	n14	33
Inebolu, Tur.	B9	40
İnegöl, Tur.	*B7	40
Inez, Ky., U.S.	C7	94
Inez, Tx., U.S.	E4	120
Infanta, Phil.	o13	34
Infanta, Phil.	o12	34
Infantas, Col.	B3	60
Infiernillo, Presa del, res., Mex.	D4	63
Infiesto, Spain	A3	22
Ingá, Braz.	h6	57
Ingá Dam, Zaire	C1	48
Ingall, Niger	C6	45
Ingalls, Ar., U.S.	D3	81
Ingalls, In., U.S.	E6	91
Ingalls, Ks., U.S.	E3	93
Ingalls, Mi., U.S.	C3	99
Ingalls, Ok., U.S.	A5	113
Ingalls Park, Il., U.S.	B5	90
Ingelheim, W. Ger.	D3	19
Ingende, Zaire	B2	48
Ingeniero Jacobacci, Arg.	C3	54
Ingeniero Luiggi, Arg.	B4	54
Ingenika, stm., B.C.	A5	69
Inger, Mn., U.S.	C5	100
Ingersheim, Fr.	A3	20
Ingersoll, Ont.	D4	73
Ingersoll, Ok., U.S.	A3	113
Ingham, Austl.	C8	50
Ingham, co., Mi., U.S.	F6	99
Ingleside, Md., U.S.	B6	97
Ingleside, Tx., U.S.	F4	120
Inglewood, Ont.	D5	73
Inglewood, N.Z.	M15	51
Inglewood, Ca., U.S.	n12	82
Inglewood, Ca., U.S.	C9	104
Inglewood, Tx., U.S.	*B3	124
Inglis, Man.	D1	70
Ingoda, stm., Sov. Un.	B7	31
Ingoldsby, Ont.	C6	73
Ingolf, Ont.	E4	70
Ingolstadt, W. Ger.	D5	18
Ingomar, Ms., U.S.	A4	101
Ingomar, Mt., U.S.	D9	103
Ingonish, N.S.	C9	71
Ingonish Beach, N.S.	C9	71
Ingornachoix Bay, b., Newf.	C3	72
Ingraham, Il., U.S.	E5	90
Ingram, Pa., U.S.	k13	115
Ingram, Wi., U.S.	C3	126
Ingrid Christensen Coast, Ant.	C20	7
In Guezzam, Alg.	H9	27
Ingul, stm., Sov. Un.	H9	27
Ingulets, stm., Sov. Un.	H9	27
Inhambane, Moz.	B6	49
Inhambane, dept., Moz.	B5	49
Inhambane, Baía de, b., Moz.	D7	49
Inhambupe, Braz.	D3	57
Inhaminga, Moz.	A5	49
Inharrime, Moz.	B6	49
Inhuçu, Braz.	B2	57
Inhumas, Braz.	B3	56
Iniesta, Spain	C5	22
Inírida, stm., Col.	C4	60
Inisa, Nig.	*E5	45
Inishark, i., Ire.	D1	11
Inishbofin, i., Ire.	D1	10
Inishcrone, Ire.	C2	11
Inisheer, i., Ire.	D2	11
Inishkea Islands, is., Ire.	C1	11
Inishmaan, i., Ire.	D2	11
Inishmore, i., Ire.	D2	11
Inishmurray, i., Ire.	C3	11
Inishowen Head, c., Ire.	B5	11
Inishtooskert, i., Ire.	E1	11
Inishtrahull, rock, Ire.	C3	10
Inishturk, i., Ire.	D1	10
Inishvickillane, i., Ire.	E1	11
Inistioge, Ire.	E4	11
Injune, Austl.	B7	51
Inkerman, N.B.	B5	71
Inkom, Id., U.S.	G6	89
Inkster, Mi., U.S.	p15	99
Inkster, N.D., U.S.	A8	111
Inland, Ne., U.S.	D7	104
Inle Lake, l., Burma	B2	35
Inlet, N.Y., U.S.	B6	109
Inman, Ga., U.S.	C2	87
Inman, Ks., U.S.	D6	93
Inman, Ne., U.S.	B7	104
Inman, S.C., U.S.	A3	117
Inn, stm., Eur.	D6	18
Innamincka, Austl.	E8	50
Inner Hebrides, is., Scot., U.K.	D6	13
Innerleithen, Scot., U.K.	E5	13
Inner Mongolia (Nei Mongol), prov., China	C7	31
Inner Sound, strt., Scot., U.K.	B4	10
Innisfail, Austl.	C8	50
Innisfail, Alta.	C4	68
Innisfree, Alta.	C5	68
Innokentyevskiy, Sov. Un.	B10	33
Innsbruck, Aus.	E5	18
Inny, stm., Ire.	I3	11
Inny, stm., Ire.	J6	33
Inocência, Braz.	B2	56
Inola, Ok., U.S.	A6	113
Inongo, Zaire	B2	48
Inowrocław, Pol.	B5	26
In Salah, Alg.	D5	44
Inscription House Ruin, hist., Az., U.S.	A5	80
Insein, Burma	E10	36
Insinger, Sask.	F4	75
Inspiration, Az., U.S.	D5	80
Institute, W.V., U.S.	m12	125
Instow, Sask.	H1	75
Intercession City, Fl., U.S.	D5	86
Interior, S.D., U.S.	D4	118
Interlachen, Fl., U.S.	C5	86
Interlaken, Switz.	E4	21
Interlaken, Ma., U.S.	*B1	98
Interlaken, N.Y., U.S.	C4	109
International Falls, Mn., U.S.	B5	100
International Peace Garden, N.A.	A5	111
Intersection Mountain, mtn., Can.	C8	69
Inthanon, Mount, mtn., Thai.	B1	36
Intiyaco, Arg.	B4	54
Intracoastal City, La., U.S.	E3	95
Intracoastal Waterway, U.S.	E6	86
Introbio, Italy	E7	21
Inubō, Cape, c., Japan	I10	33
Inukjuak, N.W. Ter.	g11	66
Inútil, Bahía, b., Chile	h12	54
Inuvik, N.W. Ter.	C6	66
Inver Bay, b., Ire.	C3	11
Inverbervie, Scot., U.K.	D6	13
Invercargill, N.Z.	Q12	51
Inverell, Austl.	E9	50
Invergordon, Scot., U.K.	C4	13
Invergrove Heights, Mn., U.S.	n12	100
Invermay, Sask.	F4	75
Invermere, B.C.	D9	69
Inverness, N.S.	C8	71
Inverness, Que.	C6	74
Inverness, Scot., U.K.	B4	13
Inverness, Al., U.S.	C4	78
Inverness, Ca., U.S.	C2	82
Inverness, Fl., U.S.	D4	86
Inverness, Il., U.S.	*A5	90
Inverness, Ms., U.S.	B3	101
Inverness, Mt., U.S.	B6	103
Inverness, co., N.S.	C8	71
Inverurie, Scot., U.K.	C6	13
Invisible Mountain, mtn., Id., U.S.	F5	89
Inwood, Man.	D3	70
Inwood, Ont.	E3	73
Inwood, Fl., U.S.	*D5	86
Inwood, Ia., U.S.	A1	92
Inwood, N.Y., U.S.	k13	109
Inwood, Vt., U.S.	C4	122
Inwood, W.V., U.S.	B6	125
Inyanga, Zimb.	A5	49
Inyangani, mtn., Zimb.	A5	49
Inyan Kara Creek, stm., Wy., U.S.	B8	127
Inyan Kara Mountain, mtn., Wy., U.S.	B8	127
Inyo, co., Ca., U.S.	D5	82
Inyo, Mount, mtn., Ca., U.S.	D5	82
Inyokern, Ca., U.S.	E5	82
Inyo Mountains, mts., Ca., U.S.	D4	82
Inyonga, Tan.	C5	48
Inza, Sov. Un.	E16	27
Inzana Lake, l., B.C.	B5	69
Ioánnina, Grc.	C3	40
Ioka, kanga, Sov. Un.	D18	14
Iola, Il., U.S.	E5	90
Iola, Ks., U.S.	E8	93
Iola, Wi., U.S.	D4	126
Iona, N.S.	D9	71
Iona, Id., U.S.	F7	89
Iona, Mn., U.S.	G3	100
Iona, N.J., U.S.	D2	107
Iona, S.D., U.S.	D6	118
Iona, i., Scot., U.K.	D2	13
Ione, Ca., U.S.	C3	82
Ione, Co., U.S.	A6	83
Ione, Nv., U.S.	E4	105
Ione, Or., U.S.	B7	114
Ione, Wa., U.S.	A8	124
Ionia, Ia., U.S.	A5	92
Ionia, Ks., U.S.	C5	93
Ionia, Mi., U.S.	F5	99
Ionia, Mo., U.S.	C4	102
Ionia, co., Mi., U.S.	F5	99
Ionian Islands, is., Grc.	C3	25
Ionian Sea, Eur.	H12	8
Íos, i., Grc.	D5	40
Iosco, co., Mi., U.S.	D7	99
Iosegun, stm., Alta.	B2	68
Iota, La., U.S.	D3	95
Iowa, La., U.S.	D2	95
Iowa, co., Ia., U.S.	C5	92
Iowa, co., Wi., U.S.	E3	126
Iowa, state, U.S.	C4	92
Iowa, stm., Ia., U.S.	C6	92
Iowa, West Branch, stm., Ia., U.S.	B4	92
Iowa City, Ia., U.S.	C6	92
Iowa Falls, Ia., U.S.	B4	92
Iowa Indian Reservation, U.S.	C8	93
Iowa Lake, l., U.S.	A3	92
Iowa Park, Tx., U.S.	C3	120
Ipameri, Braz.	B3	56
Ipava, Il., U.S.	C3	90
Ipel' (Ipoly), stm., Eur.	D5	26
Iphigenia Bay, b., Ak., U.S.	n22	79
Ipiales, Col.	C2	60
Ipirá, Braz.	D3	57
Ipoh, Malay.	E2	34
Ipoly (Ipel'), stm., Eur.	D5	26
Iporá, Braz.	B2	56
Ippy, Cen. Afr. Rep.	A4	48
Ipsala, Tur.	B6	25
Ipswich, Austl.	E9	50
Ipswich, Eng., U.K.	D7	10
Ipswich, Ma., U.S.	A6	98
Ipswich, S.D., U.S.	B6	118
Ipswich, stm., Ma., U.S.	B2	57
Ipu, Braz.	B2	57
Ipueiras, Braz.	B2	57
Iqaluit, N.W. Ter.	D19	66
Iquique, Chile	D1	55
Iquitos, Peru	B3	58
Ira, Tx., U.S.	C2	120
Ira, Vt., U.S.	D2	122
Iraan, Tx., U.S.	D2	120
Iracoubo, Fr. Gu.	A4	59
Iraí, Braz.	B6	56
Iráklion (Candia), Grc.	E5	40
Iran, ctry., Asia	B5	38
Iran, Plateau of, plat., Asia	C6	38
Iran Mountains, mts., Asia	E4	34
Irānshahr, Iran	H10	39
Irapa, Ven.	A5	60
Irapuato, Mex.	C4	63
Iraq, ctry., Asia	B4	38
Irasburg, Vt., U.S.	B3	122
Irazú, Volcán, vol., C.R.	F6	62
Irbid, Jord.	B3	38
Irbil, Iraq	D4	38
Irbit, Sov. Un.	D21	8
Irebu, Zaire	B2	48
Iredell, Tx., U.S.	C3	120
Iredell, co., N.C., U.S.	B2	110
Ireland, In., U.S.	H3	91
Ireland, ctry., Eur.	D3	10
Ireland Island, i., Ber.	p19	64
Irene, S.D., U.S.	D8	118
Irene, Tx., U.S.	C4	120
Irgiz, Sov. Un.	D9	28
Irgiz, stm., Sov. Un.	D9	28
Iri, S. Kor.	I3	33
Irian Jaya, prov., Indon.	F10	34
Iriba, Chad	B4	46
Iriklinskoye Reservoir, res., Sov. Un.	C5	28
Iringa, Tan.	C6	48
Iringa, prov., Tan.	C6	48
Iriomote Island, i., Japan	g11	52
Irion, co., Tx., U.S.	D2	120
Iriona, Hond.	C4	59
Iriri, stm., Braz.	C4	59
Irish, Mount, mtn., Nv., U.S.	F6	105
Irish Sea, Eur.	E8	8
Irkutsk, Sov. Un.	D13	29
Irma, Alta.	C5	68
Irmo, S.C., U.S.	C5	117
Iron, co., Mi., U.S.	B2	99
Iron, co., Mo., U.S.	D7	102
Iron, co., Ut., U.S.	F2	121
Iron, co., Wi., U.S.	B3	126

Name	Map Ref.	Page
Iron Belt, Wi., U.S.	B3	126
Iron City, Ga., U.S.	E2	87
Iron City, Tn., U.S.	B4	119
Irondale, Al., U.S.	f7	78
Irondale, Mo., U.S.	D7	102
Irondale, Oh., U.S.	B5	112
Irondequoit, N.Y., U.S.	B3	109
Iron Gate, Va., U.S.	C3	123
Iron Gate, val., Eur.	C6	24
Iron Gate Reservoir, res., Eur.	C5	24
Iron Gate Reservoir, res., Ca., U.S.	B2	82
Ironia, N.J., U.S.	B3	107
Iron Lightning, S.D., U.S.	B4	118
Iron Mountain, Mi., U.S.	C2	99
Iron Mountain, Mo., U.S.	D7	102
Iron Mountain, mtn., Az., U.S.	D4	80
Iron Mountains, mts., U.S.	D1	123
Iron Ridge, Wi., U.S.	E5	126
Iron River, Mi., U.S.	B2	99
Iron River, Wi., U.S.	B2	126
Irons, Mi., U.S.	D5	99
Ironside, Que.	h12	73
Ironside, Or., U.S.	C9	114
Ironspot, Oh., U.S.	C3	112
Iron Springs, Az., U.S.	C3	80
Ironton, Mn., U.S.	D5	100
Ironton, Mo., U.S.	D7	102
Ironton, Oh., U.S.	D3	112
Ironwood, Mi., U.S.	n11	99
Iroquois, Ont.	C9	73
Iroquois, S.D., U.S.	C7	118
Iroquois, stm., U.S.	C8	118
Iroquois, co., Il., U.S.	C6	90
Iroquois, stm., U.S.	C6	90
Iroquois, Lake, l., Vt., U.S.	B2	122
Iroquois Falls, Ont.	o19	73
Irrawaddy see Ayeyarwady, stm., Burma	D10	36
Irricana, Alta.	D4	68
Irrigon, Or., U.S.	B7	114
Irt, stm., Eng., U.K.	F5	13
Irthing, stm., Eng., U.K.	F6	13
Irtysh, Sov. Un.	C8	28
Irtysh, stm., Sov. Un.	D9	29
Irumu, Zaire	A4	48
Irún, Spain	A5	22
Irvine, Alta.	E5	68
Irvine, Scot., U.K.	C4	10
Irvine, Ca., U.S.	n13	82
Irvine, Fl., U.S.	C4	86
Irvine, Ky., U.S.	C6	94
Irvine, Ks., U.S.	C3	115
Irvine, stm., Scot., U.K.	E4	13
Irvines Landing, B.C.	E5	69
Irving, Il., U.S.	D4	90
Irving, Tx., U.S.	n10	120
Irvington, Al., U.S.	E1	78
Irvington, Il., U.S.	E4	90
Irvington, Ky., U.S.	C3	94
Irvington, Ne., U.S.	g12	104
Irvington, N.J., U.S.	k8	107
Irvington, N.Y., U.S.	g13	109
Irvington, Va., U.S.	C6	123
Irvona, Pa., U.S.	E4	115
Irwin, Id., U.S.	F7	89
Irwin, Ia., U.S.	C2	92
Irwin, Pa., U.S.	F2	115
Irwin, co., Ga., U.S.	E3	87
Irwinton, Ga., U.S.	D3	87
Irwinville, Ga., U.S.	E3	87
Isa, Nig.	D6	45
Isaac Lake, l., B.C.	C7	69
Isaacs Harbour, N.S.	D8	71
Isabel, Ks., U.S.	E5	93
Isabel, S.D., U.S.	B4	118
Isabel, Bahía, b., Ec.	g5	58
Isabel, Mount, mtn., Wy., U.S.	D2	127
Isabela, Phil.	D6	34
Isabela, P.R.	A1	65
Isabela, Isla (Albemarle Island), i., Ec.	g5	58
Isabelia, Cordillera, mts., Nic.	D5	62
Isabella, Ga., U.S.	D1	70
Isabella, Mn., U.S.	E3	87
Isabella, Mo., U.S.	C7	100
Isabella, Ok., U.S.	E5	102
Isabella, Pa., U.S.	A3	113
Isabella, Tn., U.S.	G2	115
Isabella, co., Mi., U.S.	D9	119
Isabella Indian Reservation, Mi., U.S.	E6	99
Isabella Lake, l., Mn., U.S.	E6	99
Isaccea, Rom.	C7	100
Isachsen, N.W. Ter.	C9	24
Ísafjarðardjúp, Ice.	m31	66
Ísafjörður, Ice.	m21	14
Isahaya, Japan	m21	14
Isaka, Zaire	J5	33
Isana (Içana), stm., S.A.	B2	48
Isanga, Zaire	C4	60
Isangi, Zaire	B3	48
Isanti, Mn., U.S.	A3	48
Isanti, co., Mn., U.S.	E5	100
Isar, stm., Eur.	E5	100
Isarco, stm., Italy	D6	18
Ísawīyah, Isr. Occ.	A3	23
Ísawīyah, Sau. Ar.	m14	41
Isbergues, Fr.	G12	40
Isbister, stm., Man.	D2	17
Ischgl, Aus.	C4	70
Ischia, i., Italy	B9	21
Ischua, N.Y., U.S.	D4	23
Ise (Uji-yamada), Japan	C2	109
Ise, stm., W. Ger.	I8	33
Ise Bay, b., Japan	F4	15
Isefjord, b., Den.	o15	33
Isel, stm., Aus.	C5	15
Iselin, N.J., U.S.	E6	18
Iselin, Pa., U.S.	B4	107
Isen, stm., W. Ger.	E3	115
Isenthal, Switz.	C6	21
Iseo, Lake, l., Italy	D5	20
Isère, dept., Fr.	D1	20
Isère, stm., Fr.	E6	16
Iserlohn, W. Ger.	B2	19
Isernia, Italy	D5	23
Isesaki, Japan	H9	33
Iseyin, Nig.	E5	45
Isfahan see Eşfahān, Iran	B5	38
Ishikari Bay, b., Japan	E10	33
Ishim, Sov. Un.	D9	29
Ishim, stm., Sov. Un.	D9	29
Ishimbay, Sov. Un.	C8	28
Ishinomaki, Japan	D13	31
Ishioka, Japan	m19	33
Ishpeming, Mi., U.S.	B3	99
Isigny-sur-Mer, Fr.	C3	16
Isil-Kul', Sov. Un.	C8	28
Isinglass, stm., N.H., U.S.	D4	106
Isiolo, Kenya	A6	48
Isiro, Zaire	A4	48
Isisford, Austl.	B5	51
İskenderun (Alexandretta), Tur.	D11	40
İskilip, Tur.	B10	40
Iskitim, Sov. Un.	E25	8
Iskŭr, stm., Bul.	D6	24
Iskushuban, Som.	C7	47
Iskwatikan Lake, l., Sask.	B3	75
İslāmābād, Pak.	B5	36
Islamorada, Fl., U.S.	H6	86
Island, co., Wa., U.S.	A3	124
Island Beach, N.J., U.S.	D4	107
Island-Brook, Que.	D6	74
Island City, Or., U.S.	B8	114
Island Creek, Ma., U.S.	*B6	98
Island Falls, Sask.	B4	75
Island Falls, Me., U.S.	B4	96
Island Grove, Fl., U.S.	C4	86
Island Heights, N.J., U.S.	D4	107
Island Lake, Man.	C4	70
Island Lake, l., Man.	C4	70
Island Lake, stm., Man.	B4	70
Island Park, Id., U.S.	E7	89
Island Park, N.Y., U.S.	*E7	109
Island Park, R.I., U.S.	E6	116
Island Park Reservoir, res., Id., U.S.	E7	89
Island Pond, l., Ma., U.S.	B5	122
Island Pond, l., N.H., U.S.	E4	106
Islands, Bay of, b., Newf.	D2	72
Islands, Bay of, b., N.Z.	K15	51
Isla Vista, Ca., U.S.	E4	82
Islay, Alta.	C5	68
Islay, i., Scot., U.K.	C4	10
Islay, Sound of, strt., Scot., U.K.	E3	13
Isle, Mn., U.S.	D5	100
Isle, stm., Fr.	E4	16
Isle au Haut, Me., U.S.	D4	96
Isle-aux-Morts, Newf.	E2	72
Isle La Motte, Vt., U.S.	B2	122
Isle of Man, ctry., Eur.	C4	10
Isle of Palms, S.C., U.S.	k12	117
Isle of Wight, Va., U.S.	D6	123
Isle of Wight, co., Eng., U.K.	D6	10
Isle of Wight, co., Va., U.S.	D6	123
Isle of Wight Bay, b., Md., U.S.	D7	97
Isle Pierre, B.C.	C6	69
Isle Royale National Park, Mi., U.S.	h9	99
Islesboro, Me., U.S.	D4	96
Islesboro Island, i., Me., U.S.	D4	96
Islesford, Me., U.S.	D4	96
Isleta, N.M., U.S.	C3	108
Isleta Indian Reservation, N.M., U.S.	C3	108
Isleton, Ca., U.S.	C3	82
Islington, Ma., U.S.	h11	98
Islip, N.Y., U.S.	*n15	109
Islip Terrace, N.Y., U.S.	*n15	109
Ismael Cortinas, Ur.	f5	54
Ismailia, Eg.	B3	38
Ismā'īlīyah Canal, Eg.	D3	41
Ismay, Mt., U.S.	D12	103
Isna, Eg.	C3	38
Isny, W. Ger.	A9	21
Isoka, Zam.	D5	48
Isola, Ms., U.S.	B3	101
Isola della Scala, Italy	D7	20
Isola di Capo Rizzuto, Italy	E6	23
Isonzo, stm., Eur.	A4	23
Isparta, Tur.	D8	40
İspir, Tur.	B13	40
Israel, ctry., Asia	D3	38
Israel, stm., N.H., U.S.	B3	106
Israeli Occupied Areas, dep., Asia	B7	41
Issano, Guy.	A3	59
Issaquah, Wa., U.S.	B3	124
Issaquena, co., Ms., U.S.	C2	101
Issia, I.C.	E3	45
Issoire, Fr.	E5	16
Issoudun, Fr.	D4	16
Issus, Tan.	C5	48
Issy, Fr.	g10	16
Issyk-Kul, Lake, l., Sov. Un.	E10	29
Istachatta, Fl., U.S.	D4	86
İstädēh-ye Moqor, Āb-e, l., Afg.	B4	36
İstanbul (Constantinople) (Byzantium), Tur.	B7	40
Istiaia, Grc.	C4	25
Istmina, Col.	E3	60
Isto, Mount, mtn., Ak., U.S.	B11	79
Istokpoga, Lake, l., Fl., U.S.	E5	86
Istranca Mountains, mts., Tur.	B6	25
Istres, Fr.	F7	16
Istrian Peninsula, pen., Yugo.	C1	24
Itá, Para.	E4	55
Itabaiana, Braz.	D3	57
Itabaiana, Braz.	D3	57
Itabaianinha, Braz.	C3	57
Itaberaba, Braz.	B4	56
Itaberaí, Braz.	B4	56
Itabira, Braz.	E7	57
Itaboraí, Braz.	h6	57
Itabuna, Braz.	B4	56
Itacaiunas, stm., Braz.	D3	59
Itacaré, Braz.	B4	56
Itacoatiara, Braz.	A3	60
Itaeté, Braz.	B4	56
Itaguaçu, Braz.	B4	56
Itaguara, Braz.	h6	56
Itaguatins, Braz.	E9	57
Itaguí, Col.	*B2	60
Itaí, Braz.	A7	56
Itaituba, Braz.	C3	59
Itajá, Braz.	B3	57
Itajaí, Braz.	D3	56
Itajubá, Braz.	C3	56
Italy, Tx., U.S.	C4	120
Itamaraju, Braz.	h6	57
Itamarandiba, Braz.	D3	57
Itambacuri, Braz.	B4	56
Itambé, Braz.	B4	56
Itami, Japan	o14	33
Itanhaém, Braz.	n8	56
Itapaci, Braz.	B2	56
Itapagipe, Braz.	D3	57
Itapecuru-Mirim, Braz.	B2	56
Itapemirim, Braz.	C4	56
Itaperuna, Braz.	C4	56
Itapetinga, Braz.	C3	56
Itapetininga, stm., Braz.	m7	56
Itapeva, Braz.	C4	56
Itapicuru, stm., Braz.	D3	57
Itapipoca, Braz.	B3	57
Itapira, Braz.	m8	56
Itapiranga, Braz.	C3	59
Itapirapuã, Braz.	B2	56
Itápolis, Braz.	k7	56
Itaporã, Braz.	C2	56
Itaporanga, Braz.	C3	57
Itapúa, dept., Para.	E4	55
Itapura, Braz.	B2	56
Itaqui, Braz.	D1	56
Itararé, Braz.	C3	56
Itararé, stm., Braz.	C3	56
Itārsi, India	F6	37
Itasca, Il., U.S.	k8	90
Itasca, Tx., U.S.	C4	120
Itasca, co., Mn., U.S.	C5	100
Itasca, Lake, l., Mn., U.S.	C3	100
Itatiaia National Park, Braz.	h5	56
Itatiba, Braz.	m8	56
Itatinga, Braz.	m7	56
Itaúna, Braz.	m7	56
Itawamba, co., Ms., U.S.	A5	101
Itéa, Grc.	C4	25
Iténez (Guaporé), stm., S.A.	B3	55
Itenhém, Braz.	B4	56
Ithaca, Mi., U.S.	E6	99
Ithaca, Ne., U.S.	g11	104
Ithaca, N.Y., U.S.	C4	109
Ithaca see Itháki, i., Grc.	C3	25
Itháki, Grc.	C3	25
Itháki (Ithaca), i., Grc.	C3	25
Itigi, Tan.	C5	48
Itimbiri, stm., Zaire	A3	48
Itinga, Braz.	B4	56
Itiquira, Braz.	B2	56
Itiquira, stm., Braz.	*B1	56
Itiquira, stm., Braz.	B1	56
Itirapina, Braz.	m8	56
Itō, Japan	o18	33
Itoigawa, Japan	H8	33
Itoko, Zaire	B3	48
Itoman, Japan	O5	52
Itta Bena, Ms., U.S.	B3	101
Itu, Braz.	B2	60
Ituango, Col.	B2	60
Ituí, stm., Braz.	B3	58
Ituiutaba, Braz.	B3	56
Itumbiara, Braz.	B3	56
Ituna, Sask.	F4	75
Ituporanga, Braz.	D3	56
Iturama, Braz.	B2	56
Ituverava, Braz.	C3	56
Ituxi, stm., Braz.	C4	58
Ityäy al Bārūd, Eg.	D2	41
Itzehoe, W. Ger.	B4	18
Iuka, Il., U.S.	E5	90
Iuka, Ks., U.S.	E5	93
Iuka, Ms., U.S.	A5	101
Iva, Il., U.S.	C2	117
Iva, W. Sam.	F11	52
Ivaí, stm., Braz.	C2	56
Ivalo, Fin.	C12	14
Ivan, Ar., U.S.	D3	81
Ivangrad, Yugo.	D4	24
Ivanhoe, Austl.	F5	51
Ivanhoe, Mn., U.S.	F2	100
Ivanhoe, N.C., U.S.	C4	110
Ivanhoe, Va., U.S.	D2	123
Ivanić Grad, Yugo.	A9	21
Ivano-Frankovsk, Sov. Un.	G5	27
Ivanovichi, Sov. Un.	D7	33
Ivanovka, Sov. Un.	q21	27
Ivanovo, Sov. Un.	D7	29
Ivanteyevka, Sov. Un.	n17	27
Ivato, Madag.	g9	49
Ivaylovgrad, Bul.	E8	24
Ivdel, Sov. Un.	A6	27
Ivesdale, Il., U.S.	D5	90
Ives Estates, Fl., U.S.	*G6	86
Ivigtut, Grnld.	C19	128
Ivinheima, stm., Braz.	C2	56
Ivins, Ut., U.S.	F2	121
Ivohibe, Madag.	h9	49
Ivor, Va., U.S.	D6	123
Ivory Coast, ctry., Afr.	E3	45
Ivoryton, Ct., U.S.	D6	84
Ivösjön, l., Swe.	B8	15
Ivrea, Italy	B1	23
Ivry-Nord, Que.	C3	74
Ivry-sur-Seine, Fr.	g10	16
Ivujivik, Que.	f11	74
Ivy, Va., U.S.	B4	123
Ivydale, W.V., U.S.	C3	125
Ivyton, Ky., U.S.	C7	94
Ivywild, Co., U.S.	C6	83
Iwaki (Taira), Japan	H10	33
Iwaki, Mount, mtn., Japan	F10	33
Iwakuni, Japan	I6	33
Iwamizawa, Japan	E10	33
Iwanai, Japan	E10	33
Iwate, Mount, mtn., Japan	G10	33
Iwo, Nig.	E5	45
Iwo Jima, i., Japan	E8	6
Iwón, N. Kor.	C12	31
Ixelles (Elsene), Bel.	*D4	17
Ixiamas, Bol.	D3	57
Ixmiquilpan, Mex.	m14	63
Ixtacalco (part of Mexico City), Mex.	h9	63
Ixtapa, Punta, c., Mex.	D4	63
Ixtapalapa (part of Mexico City), Mex.	h9	63
Ixtlán de Juárez, Mex.	o15	63
Ixtlán del Río, Mex.	C4	63
Izabal, Lago de, l., Guat.	D7	63
Izamal, Mex.	C7	63
Izard, co., Ar., U.S.	A4	81
Izberbash, Sov. Un.	C7	28
Izegem, Bel.	D3	17
Izena Island, i., Japan	N5	52
Izhma, Sov. Un.	C19	8
Izmail, Sov. Un.	I7	27
İzmir (Smyrna), Tur.	C6	40
İzmit (Kocaeli) (Nicomedia), Tur.	B7	40
İznik (Nicaea), Tur.	B7	40
Izozog, Bañados de, sw., Bol.	C3	57
Izra', Syria	C7	41
Iztaccíhuatl, vol., Mex.	n14	63
Izúcar de Matamoros, Mex.	n14	63
Izuhara, Japan	I4	33
Izu Islands, is., Japan	D8	6
Izumo, Japan	I6	33
Izyum, Sov. Un.	G11	27
J		
Jabal al Awliyā', Sud.	B3	47
Jabalón, stm., Spain	C4	22
Jabalpur, India	D6	36
Jabālyah, Isr. Occ.	C6	41
Jablonec [nad Nisou], Czech.	C3	26
Jablonná, Czech.	o17	26
Jablunkov Pass, Czech.	D5	26
Jaboatão, Braz.	C4	57
Jaboticabal, Braz.	C3	56
Jabrīn, i., Iran	C5	38
Jaca, Spain	A5	22
Jacala de Ledesma, Mex.	m14	63
Jacaraci, Braz.	A4	56
Jacaré, stm., Braz.	D2	57
Jacareí, Braz.	m9	56
Jacarezinho, Braz.	C2	56
Jachin, Al., U.S.	C1	78
Jáchymov, Czech.	C2	26
Jacinto, Ms., U.S.	A5	101
Jacinto City, Tx., U.S.	r14	120
Jack, Al., U.S.	D4	78
Jack, co., Tx., U.S.	C3	120
Jackhead Harbour, Man.	D3	70
Jackman, Me., U.S.	C2	96
Jackman Station, Me., U.S.	C2	96
Jack Mountain, mtn., Mt., U.S.	D4	103
Jack Mountain, mtn., Va., U.S.	B3	123
Jack Mountain, mtn., Wa., U.S.	A5	124
Jackpot, Nv., U.S.	B7	105
Jacksboro, Tn., U.S.	C9	119
Jacksboro, Tx., U.S.	C3	120
Jacks Creek, Tn., U.S.	B3	119
Jacks Mountain, mtn., Pa., U.S.	E6	115
Jackson, Al., U.S.	D2	78
Jackson, Ca., U.S.	C3	82
Jackson, Ga., U.S.	C3	87
Jackson, Ky., U.S.	C6	94
Jackson, La., U.S.	D4	95
Jackson, Me., U.S.	D3	96
Jackson, Mi., U.S.	F6	99
Jackson, Mn., U.S.	G4	100
Jackson, Ms., U.S.	C3	101
Jackson, Mo., U.S.	D8	102
Jackson, Mt., U.S.	E3	103
Jackson, Ne., U.S.	B9	104
Jackson, N.H., U.S.	B4	106
Jackson, N.J., U.S.	C4	107
Jackson, N.C., U.S.	A5	110
Jackson, Oh., U.S.	C3	112
Jackson, S.C., U.S.	E4	117
Jackson, Tn., U.S.	B3	119
Jackson, Wi., U.S.	E5	126
Jackson, Wy., U.S.	C2	127
Jackson, co., Al., U.S.	A3	78
Jackson, co., Ar., U.S.	B4	81
Jackson, co., Co., U.S.	A4	83
Jackson, co., Fl., U.S.	B1	86
Jackson, co., Ga., U.S.	B3	87
Jackson, co., Il., U.S.	F4	90
Jackson, co., Ia., U.S.	B7	92
Jackson, co., Ks., U.S.	C8	93
Jackson, co., Ky., U.S.	C5	94
Jackson, co., La., U.S.	B3	95
Jackson, co., Mi., U.S.	F6	99
Jackson, co., Mn., U.S.	G3	100
Jackson, co., Ms., U.S.	E5	101
Jackson, co., Mo., U.S.	B3	102
Jackson, co., N.C., U.S.	f9	110
Jackson, co., Oh., U.S.	C3	112
Jackson, co., Ok., U.S.	C2	113
Jackson, co., Or., U.S.	E4	114
Jackson, co., S.D., U.S.	D4	118
Jackson, co., Tn., U.S.	C8	119
Jackson, co., Tx., U.S.	E4	120
Jackson, co., W.V., U.S.	C3	125
Jackson, co., Wi., U.S.	D3	126
Jackson, stm., Va., U.S.	C3	123
Jackson, Lake, l., Fl., U.S.	E5	86
Jackson, Lake, l., Fl., U.S.	B2	86
Jackson, Mount, mtn., N.H., U.S.	B4	106
Jackson, Port, b., Austl.	F8	51
Jacksonboro, S.C., U.S.	F7	117
Jacksonburg, W.V., U.S.	B4	125
Jackson Center, Oh., U.S.	B1	112
Jackson Center, Pa., U.S.	D1	115
Jackson Dam, Al., U.S.	D2	78
Jackson Hill, In., U.S.	F3	91
Jackson Junction, Ia., U.S.	A5	92
Jackson Lake, res., Ga., U.S.	C3	87
Jackson Lake, res., Wy., U.S.	C2	127
Jackson Mountain, mtn., Me., U.S.	D2	96
Jackson Mountains, mts., Nv., U.S.	B3	105
Jackson's Arm, Newf.	D3	72
Jacksons Gap, Al., U.S.	C4	78
Jacksonville, Al., U.S.	B4	78
Jacksonville, Ar., U.S.	C3	81
Jacksonville, Fl., U.S.	B5	86
Jacksonville, Ga., U.S.	E4	87
Jacksonville, Il., U.S.	D3	90
Jacksonville, Me., U.S.	D5	96
Jacksonville, Mo., U.S.	B5	102
Jacksonville, N.C., U.S.	C5	110
Jacksonville, Oh., U.S.	C3	112
Jacksonville, Or., U.S.	E4	114
Jacksonville, Tx., U.S.	D5	120
Jacksonville, Vt., U.S.	F3	122
Jacksonville Beach, Fl., U.S.	B5	86
Jacksonville Naval Air Station, mil., Fl., U.S.	B5	86
Jacks Peak, mtn., Ut., U.S.	E3	121
Jacktown, Ok., U.S.	B4	113
Jacmel, Haiti	E7	64
Jacob, Congo	B1	48
Jacobabad, Pak.	F2	36
Jacobina, Braz.	A3	80
Jacob Lake, Az., U.S.	A3	80
Jacobson, Mn., U.S.	D5	100
Jacobsburg, N.J., U.S.	B2	99
Jacobsville, Mi., U.S.	B2	99
Jacques-Cartier, stm., Que.	B6	74
Jacques-Cartier, Détroit de, strt., Que.	h8	72
Jacques-Cartier, Mont, mtn., Que.	G19	66
Jacquet River, N.B.	B3	71
Jacumba, Ca., U.S.	F5	82
Jacundá, stm., Braz.	D8	59
Jacupiranga, Braz.	A7	56
Jadabpur, India	*D8	36
Jade, W. Ger.	B4	18
Jade Bay, b., W. Ger.	B4	18
Jādū, Libya	C2	43
Jadwin, Mo., U.S.	D6	102
Jaegerspris, Den.	C5	15
Jaén, Peru	C2	58
Jaén, Spain	D4	22
Jaffa, Cape, c., Austl.	G6	50
Jaffa Gate, hist., Isr. Occ.	m14	41
Jaffna, Sri L.	G7	36
Jaffrey, N.H., U.S.	E2	106
Jaffrey Center, N.H., U.S.	E2	106
Jagdalpur, India	E7	36
Jagersfontein, S. Afr.	B3	56
Jaggayyapeta, India	I8	37
Jagin, stm., Iran	H9	39
Jagst, stm., W. Ger.	D4	19
Jaguarão, Braz.	E2	56
Jaguariaíva, Braz.	C2	56
Jaguaribe, stm., Braz.	A3	56
Jagüey Grande, Cuba	C3	64
Jahrom, Iran	C5	38
Jaicós, Braz.	C2	57
Jailolo, Indon.	E7	34
Jaipur, India	C6	34
Jaisalmer, India	C5	36
Jaisinghpur, India	D8	36
Jajce, Yugo.	C2	24
Jajpur, India	E12	37
Jakarta (Djakarta), Indon.	G3	34
Jakin, Ga., U.S.	E2	87
Jakobstad, Fin.	F10	14
Jal, N.M., U.S.	E6	108
Jalālābād, Afg.	B5	36
Jalālah al Baḥrīyah, Jabal, plat., Eg.	E4	41
Jalandhar, India	B6	36
Jalapa, Guat.	E6	63
Jalapa Enríquez, Mex.	D5	63
Jalaun, India	C6	36
Jalgaon, India	D8	36
Jalisco, state, Mex.	C3	63
Jālna, India	E6	36
Jalón, stm., Spain	B5	22
Jālor, India	E4	37
Jalpa, Mex.	C4	63
Jalpan, Mex.	C5	63
Jālū, Wāḥat, well, Libya	D4	43
Jalūlā, Iraq	D2	39
Jamaame, Som.	C3	47
Jamaica, In., U.S.	C3	91
Jamaica, Ia., U.S.	C3	92
Jamaica, Vt., U.S.	E3	122
Jamaica, ctry., N.A.	E5	64
Jamaica Bay, b., N.Y., U.S.	k13	109
Jamaica Channel, strt., N.A.	E6	64
Jamālpur, Bngl.	E12	37
Jamālpur, India	H13	37
Jamanxim, stm., Braz.	D3	59
Jamari, stm., Braz.	D2	59
Jambi, Indon.	F2	34
Jambuair, Cape, c., Indon.	D1	34
James, stm., Alta.	D3	68
James, stm., Mo., U.S.	E4	102
James, stm., S.D., U.S.	C5	123
James, Lake, l., In., U.S.	A7	91
James, Lake, res., N.C., U.S.	B1	110
James Bay, b., Can.	F16	66
James Branch, stm., De., U.S.	F3	85
James City, N.C., U.S.	B5	110
James City, co., Va., U.S.	C6	123
James Craik, Arg.	A4	54
James Creek, Pa., U.S.	F5	115
James Island, B.C.	g12	69
James Island, S.C., U.S.	k12	117
James Island, i., Md., U.S.	C5	97
James Island, i., S.C., U.S.	F8	117
Jameson, Mo., U.S.	A4	102
Jamesport, Mo., U.S.	B3	102
James River Bridge, Va., U.S.	k15	123
James Ross Island, i., Ant.	C7	7
James Ross Strait, strt., N.W. Ter.	C13	66
Jamestown, Austl.	F2	51
Jamestown, Ire.	D3	11
Jamestown, Al., U.S.	A4	78
Jamestown, Co., U.S.	A5	83
Jamestown, In., U.S.	E4	91
Jamestown, Ks., U.S.	C6	93
Jamestown, Ky., U.S.	D4	94
Jamestown, La., U.S.	B2	95
Jamestown, Mo., U.S.	C5	102
Jamestown, N.Y., U.S.	C1	109
Jamestown, N.C., U.S.	B3	110
Jamestown, N.D., U.S.	C7	111
Jamestown, Oh., U.S.	C2	112
Jamestown, Pa., U.S.	C1	115
Jamestown, R.I., U.S.	E5	116
Jamestown, Tn., U.S.	C9	119
Jamestown Dam, N.D., U.S.	C7	111
Jamestown Reservoir, res., N.D., U.S.	C7	111
Jamesville, N.C., U.S.	B6	110
Jamesville, Va., U.S.	C7	123
Jamieson, Or., U.S.	C9	114
Jamiltepec, Mex.	D5	63
Jamison, Pa., U.S.	F11	115
Jammerbugten, b., Den.	A3	15
Jammu and Kashmir, dep., Asia	A6	36
Jamnagar (Navanagar), India	D5	37
Jāmpur, Pak.	E3	36
Jamsah, Eg.	D2	43
Jamshedpur, India	E12	37
Jamul, Ca., U.S.	F5	82
Jamuna, stm., Bngl.	E12	37
Janaúba, Braz.	A3	56
Janaucu, Ilha de, i., Braz.	B4	59
Jandaia, Braz.	B2	56
Jandaq, Iran	B5	38
Jandiatuba, stm., Braz.	B4	58
Jándula, stm., Spain	C7	22
Jane, Mo., U.S.	E3	102
Jane Lew, W.V., U.S.	B4	125
Janesville, Ca., U.S.	B3	82
Janesville, Ia., U.S.	B5	92
Janesville, Mn., U.S.	F5	100
Janesville, Wi., U.S.	F4	126
Jangipur, India	E12	37
Janīn, Isr. Occ.	C6	41
Janos, Mex.	A3	63
Jánoshalma, Hung.	I11	26
Janow, Man.	E4	70
Janów, Pol.	C7	26
Janów Lubelski, Pol.	C7	26
Jansen, Sask.	F3	75
Jansen, Co., U.S.	D6	83
Jansen, Ne., U.S.	D8	104
Januária, Braz.	B4	56
Japan, ctry., Asia	D12	31
Japan, Sea of, Asia	C12	31
Japaratuba, Braz.	D3	57
Japim, Braz.	C3	58
Japurá (Caquetá), stm., S.A.	C4	60
Jaqué, Pan.	G8	62
Jarābulus, Syria	D12	40
Jaraguá, Braz.	B3	56
Jaraguá do Sul, Braz.	D3	56
Jaraguari, Braz.	C2	56
Jaral del Progreso, Mex.	m13	63
Jarales, N.M., U.S.	C3	108
Jarama, stm., Spain	B4	22
Jaramānah, Syria	*F11	41
Jarash, Jord.	B7	41
Jarbalo, Ks., U.S.	k15	93
Jarbidge, Nv., U.S.	B6	105
Jardim, Braz.	C1	56
Jardim de Angicos, Braz.	g6	57
Jardim do Seridó, Braz.	C3	57
Jardinah, Libya	C4	43
Jardine, Mt., U.S.	E6	103
Jardines de la Reina, Archipiélago de los, is., Cuba	D4	64
Jardinópolis, Braz.	k8	56
Järfälla, Swe.	*H7	14
Jargalang, China	C10	32
Jargalant, Mong.	B7	31
Jari, stm., Braz.	B4	59
Järlåsa (part of Uppsala), Swe.	t35	14
Järna (part of Södertälje), Swe.	t35	14
Jarnac, Fr.	E3	16
Jarny, Fr.	E5	17
Jarocin, Pol.	C4	26
Jaroměř, Czech.	C7	26
Jarosław, Pol.	C7	26
Jaroso, Co., U.S.	D5	83
Jarratt, Va., U.S.	D5	123
Jarrettsville, Md., U.S.	A5	97
Jarrow, Alta.	C5	68
Jaru, Braz.	B3	55
Jarud Qi, China	C9	31
Jarvie, Alta.	B4	68
Jarvis, Ont.	E4	73
Jarvis, i., Oc.	G12	6
Jarvisburg, N.C., U.S.	A7	110
Jasień, Pol.	B10	19
Jāsk, Iran	I8	39
Jasło, Pol.	D6	26
Jasmin, Sask.	F4	75
Jasmine Estates, Fl., U.S.	D4	86
Jason Peninsula, pen., Ant.	C6	7
Jasonville, In., U.S.	E3	91
Jasper, Alta.	C1	68
Jasper, Ont.	C9	73
Jasper, Al., U.S.	B2	78
Jasper, Ar., U.S.	B2	81
Jasper, Fl., U.S.	B3	86
Jasper, Ga., U.S.	B2	87
Jasper, In., U.S.	H4	91
Jasper, Mn., U.S.	G2	100
Jasper, Mo., U.S.	D3	102
Jasper, N.Y., U.S.	C3	109
Jasper, Oh., U.S.	C2	112
Jasper, Tn., U.S.	D8	119
Jasper, Tx., U.S.	D6	120
Jasper, co., Ga., U.S.	C3	87
Jasper, co., Il., U.S.	D5	90
Jasper, co., In., U.S.	B3	91
Jasper, co., Ia., U.S.	C4	92
Jasper, co., Ms., U.S.	C4	101
Jasper, co., Mo., U.S.	D3	102
Jasper, co., S.C., U.S.	G5	117
Jasper, co., Tx., U.S.	D6	120
Jasper Lake, l., Alta.	C1	68
Jasper National Park, Alta.	C1	68
Jastarnia, Pol.	A5	26
Jastrzebia Góra, Pol.	A5	26
Jastrzebie-Zdrój, Pol.	h9	26
Jászapáti, Hung.	B5	24
Jászberény, Hung.	B4	24
Jataí, Braz.	B2	56
Jatibonico, Cuba	D4	64
Játiva, Spain	C5	22
Jatni, India	G10	37
Jatobá, stm., Braz.	E4	59
Jaú, Braz.	C3	56
Jaú, stm., Braz.	C3	59
Jauaperi, stm., Braz.	C2	59
Jaumave, Mex.	C5	63
Jaunpur, India	H10	37
Java, S.D., U.S.	B6	118
Java (Jawa), i., Indon.	G3	34
Javari, stm., S.A.	B3	58
Java Sea, Indon.	G4	34
Jávea, Spain	C6	22
Jawhar, India	H4	37
Jawor, Pol.	C4	26
Jaworzno, Pol.	g10	26
Jay, Fl., U.S.	u14	86
Jay, La., U.S.	E5	95
Jay, Me., U.S.	D2	96
Jay, N.Y., U.S.	f11	109
Jay, Ok., U.S.	A7	113
Jay, co., In., U.S.	D7	91
Jayanca, Peru	B2	58
Jaya Peak, mtn., Indon.	F9	34
Jayapura, Indon.	F10	34
Jay Em, Wy., U.S.	D8	127
Jayess, Ms., U.S.	D3	101
Jay Peak, mtn., Vt., U.S.	B3	122
Jayton, Tx., U.S.	C2	120
Jaz Mūrīān, Hāmūn-e, l., Iran	H9	39
J. B. Thomas, Lake, res., Tx., U.S.	C2	120
Jean, Nv., U.S.	H6	105
Jeanerette, La., U.S.	E4	95
Jean Lafitte National Historical Park, La., U.S.	k12	95
Jeannette, Pa., U.S.	F2	115
Jeannette Island, i., Sov. Un.	B35	128
Jebba, Nig.	G8	45
Jeberos, Peru	C2	58
Jedburg, S.C., U.S.	h11	117
Jedburgh, Scot., U.K.	C5	10
Jeddito, Az., U.S.	B6	80
Jeddo, Mi., U.S.	E8	99
Jeddore Lake, res., Newf.	D3	72
Jedrzejów, Pol.	C6	26
Jeetze, stm., Eur.	B5	18
Jeff, Ky., U.S.	C6	94
Jeff Davis, co., Ga., U.S.	E4	87
Jeff Davis, co., Tx., U.S.	o12	120
Jeffers, Mn., U.S.	*F3	100

Name	Map Ref.	Page
Jeffers, Mt., U.S.	E5	103
Jefferson, Al., U.S.	C2	78
Jefferson, Ar., U.S.	C3	81
Jefferson, Co., U.S.	B5	83
Jefferson, Ga., U.S.	B3	87
Jefferson, In., U.S.	D4	91
Jefferson, Ia., U.S.	C3	92
Jefferson, La., U.S.	k11	95
Jefferson, Me., U.S.	D3	96
Jefferson, Md., U.S.	B2	97
Jefferson, Ma., U.S.	B4	98
Jefferson, N.H., U.S.	B4	106
Jefferson, N.J., U.S.	D2	107
Jefferson, N.Y., U.S.	C6	109
Jefferson, N.C., U.S.	A1	110
Jefferson, Oh., U.S.	A5	112
Jefferson, Ok., U.S.	A4	113
Jefferson, Or., U.S.	C3	114
Jefferson, Pa., U.S.	*F2	115
Jefferson, S.C., U.S.	B7	117
Jefferson, S.D., U.S.	E9	118
Jefferson, Tx., U.S.	C5	120
Jefferson, Wi., U.S.	E5	126
Jefferson, co., Al., U.S.	B3	78
Jefferson, co., Ar., U.S.	C3	81
Jefferson, co., Co., U.S.	B5	83
Jefferson, co., Fl., U.S.	B3	86
Jefferson, co., Ga., U.S.	C4	87
Jefferson, co., Id., U.S.	F6	89
Jefferson, co., Il., U.S.	E5	90
Jefferson, co., In., U.S.	G6	91
Jefferson, co., Ia., U.S.	C5	92
Jefferson, co., Ks., U.S.	C8	93
Jefferson, co., Ky., U.S.	B4	94
Jefferson, co., La., U.S.	E5	95
Jefferson, co., Ms., U.S.	D2	101
Jefferson, co., Mo., U.S.	C7	102
Jefferson, co., Mt., U.S.	D4	103
Jefferson, co., Ne., U.S.	D8	104
Jefferson, co., N.Y., U.S.	A5	109
Jefferson, co., Oh., U.S.	B5	112
Jefferson, co., Ok., U.S.	C4	113
Jefferson, co., Or., U.S.	C5	114
Jefferson, co., Pa., U.S.	D3	115
Jefferson, co., Tn., U.S.	C10	119
Jefferson, co., Tx., U.S.	E5	120
Jefferson, co., Wa., U.S.	B1	124
Jefferson, co., W.V., U.S.	B7	125
Jefferson, co., Wi., U.S.	E5	126
Jefferson, stm., Mt., U.S.	E5	103
Jefferson, Mount, mtn., Id., U.S.	E7	89
Jefferson, Mount, mtn., Nv., U.S.	E5	105
Jefferson, Mount, mtn., Or., U.S.	C5	114
Jefferson City, Mo., U.S.	C5	102
Jefferson City, Mt., U.S.	D5	103
Jefferson City, Tn., U.S.	C10	119
Jefferson Davis, co., La., U.S.	D3	95
Jefferson Davis, co., Ms., U.S.	D4	101
Jefferson Farms, De., U.S.	i7	85
Jefferson Hill, hill, Ky., U.S.	g11	94
Jefferson Manor, Va., U.S.	*B5	123
Jefferson Proving Ground, mil., In., U.S.	G7	91
Jefferson Valley, N.Y., U.S.	*D7	109
Jefferson Village, Va., U.S.	*B5	123
Jeffersonville, Ga., U.S.	D3	87
Jeffersonville, In., U.S.	H6	91
Jeffersonville, Ky., U.S.	C6	94
Jeffersonville, N.Y., U.S.	D6	109
Jeffersonville, Oh., U.S.	C2	112
Jeffersonville, Vt., U.S.	B3	122
Jeffrey, W.V., U.S.	D3	125
Jeffrey City, Wy., U.S.	D5	127
Jeffries Creek, stm., S.C., U.S.	C8	117
Jega, Nig.	F6	45
Jehossee Island, i., S.C., U.S.	k11	117
Jejui-Guazú, stm., Para.	D4	55
Jēkabpils, Sov. Un.	C5	27
Jekyll Island, i., Ga., U.S.	E5	87
Jelenia Góra (Hirschberg), Pol.	C3	26
Jelgava (Yelgava), Sov. Un.	C4	27
Jellico, Tn., U.S.	C9	119
Jelling, Den.	C3	15
Jelm, Wy., U.S.	E6	127
Jelm Mountain, mtn., Wy., U.S.	E7	127
Jeløya, i., Nor.	p28	14
Jemaja, i., Indon.	K6	35
Jember, Indon.	G4	34
Jemez, stm., N.M., U.S.	k7	108
Jemez Dam, N.M., U.S.	k7	108
Jemez Indian Reservation, N.M., U.S.	h7	108
Jemez Pueblo, N.M., U.S.	B3	108
Jemez Springs, N.M., U.S.	B3	108
Jemison, Al., U.S.	C3	78
Jemseg, N.B.	D3	71
Jemtland, Me., U.S.	A4	96
Jena, E. Ger.	C5	18
Jena, Fl., U.S.	C3	86
Jena, La., U.S.	C3	95
Jenaz, Switz.	C8	21
Jenbach, Aus.	B7	20
Jendouba, Tun.	F2	23
Jenera, Oh., U.S.	B2	112
Jenison, Mi., U.S.	*F5	99
Jenkins, Ky., U.S.	C7	94
Jenkins, Mn., U.S.	D4	100
Jenkins, N.J., U.S.	D3	107
Jenkins, co., Ga., U.S.	D5	87
Jenkinsburg, Ga., U.S.	C2	87
Jenkinsville, S.C., U.S.	C5	117
Jenkintown, Pa., U.S.	o21	115
Jenks, Ok., U.S.	A6	113
Jenner, Alta.	D5	68
Jenners, Pa., U.S.	F3	115
Jennie, Ar., U.S.	D4	81
Jennings, Fl., U.S.	B3	86
Jennings, Ks., U.S.	C3	93
Jennings, La., U.S.	D3	95
Jennings, Md., U.S.	k12	97
Jennings, Mi., U.S.	D5	99
Jennings, Mo., U.S.	f13	102
Jennings, Ok., U.S.	A5	113
Jennings, co., In., U.S.	G6	91
Jennings Lodge, Or., U.S.	*B4	114
Jenny Jump Mountain, mtn., N.J., U.S.	B3	107
Jenny Lind, Ar., U.S.	B1	81
Jensen, Ut., U.S.	C6	121
Jensen Beach, Fl., U.S.	E6	86
Jeptha Knob, hill, Ky., U.S.	B4	94
Jequié, Braz.	C4	56
Jequitaí, Braz.	E2	57
Jequitinhonha, Braz.	E2	57
Jequitinhonha, stm., Braz.	E2	57
Jerada, Mor.	B5	44
Jérémie, Haiti	E6	64
Jeremoabo, Braz.	D3	57
Jerez de García Salinas, Mex.	C4	63

Jerez de la Frontera, Spain	D2	22
Jerez de los Caballeros, Spain	C2	22
Jericho (Arīḥā), Isr. Occ.	C7	41
Jericho, Ar., U.S.	B5	81
Jericho, N.Y., U.S.	*E7	109
Jericho, Vt., U.S.	B3	122
Jericho Center, Vt., U.S.	C3	122
Jerico Springs, Mo., U.S.	D4	102
Jerimoth Hill, hill, R.I., U.S.	C1	116
Jermyn, Pa., U.S.	C10	115
Jermyn, Tx., U.S.	C3	120
Jerome, Ar., U.S.	D4	81
Jerome, Fl., U.S.	F5	86
Jerome, Id., U.S.	G4	89
Jerome, Ia., U.S.	D4	92
Jerome, Mi., U.S.	F6	99
Jerome, Mo., U.S.	D6	102
Jerome, Pa., U.S.	F4	115
Jerome, co., Id., U.S.	G4	89
Jeromesville, Oh., U.S.	B3	112
Jersey, co., Il., U.S.	D3	90
Jersey, dep., Eur.	F5	10
Jersey City, N.J., U.S.	B4	107
Jersey Mountain, mtn., Id., U.S.	E3	89
Jersey Shore, Pa., U.S.	D7	115
Jerseyville, Il., U.S.	D3	90
Jerumenha, Braz.	C2	57
Jerusalem, Ar., U.S.	B3	81
Jerusalem (Yerushalayim), Isr.	B3	38
Jerusalem, Ar., U.S.	B3	81
Jerusalem, Oh., U.S.	C4	112
Jervis Bay, b., Austl.	G9	50
Jervis Inlet, b., B.C.	D6	69
Jesenice Reservoir, res., Czech.	C7	19
Jesenice, Czech.	C4	26
Jessamine, co., Ky., U.S.	C5	94
Jessen, E. Ger.	B7	19
Jisr ash Shughūr, Syria	E11	40
Jessie, N.D., U.S.	B7	111
Jessieville, Ar., U.S.	C2	81
Jessnitz, E. Ger.	B7	19
Jessore, Bngl.	F12	37
Jessup, Md., U.S.	B4	97
Jessup, Pa., U.S.	m18	115
Jesterville, Md., U.S.	D6	97
Jesup, Ga., U.S.	E5	87
Jesup, Ia., U.S.	B5	92
Jesup, Lake, l., Fl., U.S.	D5	86
Jésus, Île, i., Que.	p19	74
Jesús Carranza, Mex.	D5	63
Jesús María, Arg.	A4	54
Jesús María, Arg.	*D2	54
Jesús, Peru	A3	113
Jet, Ok., U.S.	A3	113
Jetersville, Va., U.S.	C4	123
Jetmore, Ks., U.S.	D4	93
Jetson, Ky., U.S.	C3	94
Jette, Bel.	D4	17
Jeumont, Fr.	D4	17
Jever, W. Ger.	B3	18
Jewel Cave National Monument, S.D., U.S.	D2	118
Jewell, Ia., U.S.	B4	92
Jewell, Ks., U.S.	C5	93
Jewell, Oh., U.S.	A1	112
Jewell, co., Ks., U.S.	C5	93
Jewell Ridge, Va., U.S.	e10	123
Jewett, Il., U.S.	D5	90
Jewett, Oh., U.S.	B4	112
Jewett, Tx., U.S.	D4	120
Jewett City, Ct., U.S.	C8	84
Jewett Lake, l., Sask.	A3	75
Jeziorka, stm., Pol.	m14	26
Jhālāwār, India	E6	37
Jhal, Pak.	C1	37
Jhal Jhao, Pak.	C4	36
Jhang Sadar, Pak.	B4	37
Jhansi, India	C6	36
Jhawāni, Nepal	D10	37
Jhelum, Pak.	B5	36
Jhelum, stm., Asia	B5	36
Jhunjhunūn, India	C5	37
Jialing Jiang, stm., China	E6	31
Jiamusi, China	B11	31
Ji'an, China	F7	31
Ji'an, China	D12	32
Jianchang, China	D11	32
Jiande, China	J8	32
Jiangling, China	E7	31
Jiangmen, China	G7	31
Jiang'ou, China	F8	31
Jiangping, China	C8	31
Jiangshi, China	I3	32
Jiangshui, China	K8	32
Jianyang, China	E3	31
Jiaoxian, China	D9	31
Jiaozhou Bay, b., China	F9	32
Jiaozuo, China	D7	31
Jiashan, China	H8	32
Jiaxian, China	E4	32
Jiaxing, China	E9	31
Jiayu, China	I5	32
Jicarilla Indian Reservation, N.M., U.S.	A2	108
Jičín, Czech.	C3	26
Jiddah, Sau. Ar.	C3	38
Jiddī, Jabal al, mtn., Eg.	D5	41
Jidy, Bi'r al, well, Eg.	D5	41
Jiek'kevarri, mtn., Nor.	C8	14
Jiexiu, China	F4	32
Jieyang, China	G8	31
Jifnā, Isr. Occ.	h11	41
Jigger, La., U.S.	B4	95
Jiggs, Nv., U.S.	C6	105
Jihlava, Czech.	D3	26
Jihočeský, prov., Czech.	D9	19
Jijel, Alg.	B6	44
Jijia, stm., Rom.	B8	24
Jijiga, Eth.	D5	47
Jiji, Som.	E5	47
Jijona, Spain	C5	22
Jilbānah, Bi'r al, well, Eg.	D4	41
Jilib, Som.	E5	47
Jilin, China	C10	31
Jilin, prov., China	C10	31
Jiloca, stm., Spain	B5	22
Jílové u Prahy, Czech.	o18	26
Jima, Eth.	D4	47
Jimbolia, Rom.	D4	24
Jimena [de los Frontera], Spain	D3	22
Jim Falls, Wi., U.S.	C2	126
Jim Hogg, co., Tx., U.S.	F3	120
Jim Lake, res., N.D., U.S.	B7	111
Jim Thorpe, Pa., U.S.	E10	115
Jim Wells, co., Tx., U.S.	F3	120

Jināḥ, Eg.	D6	43
Jincheng, China	G5	32
Jindřichův Hradec, Czech.	A6	51
Jingbian, China	F3	32
Jingchuan, China	G2	32
Jingde, China	I8	31
Jingdezhen, China	F8	31
Jing He, stm., China	G3	32
Jinghong, China	G5	31
Jingmen, China	I5	32
Jingning, China	G1	32
Jingshan, China	I5	32
Jingxi, China	D9	32
Jingxian, China	K3	32
Jingxian, China	I8	32
Jingxing, China	A10	32
Jingziguan, China	H4	32
Jinhua, China	F8	31
Jining, China	D8	31
Jining, China	C7	31
Jinja, Ug.	A5	48
Jinniu, China	I6	32
Jinotega, Nic.	E7	63
Jinotepe, Nic.	E7	63
Jinsha Jiang, stm., China	F4	31
Jinshi, China	J4	32
Jinta, China	C4	31
Jinxi, China	*C9	31
Jinxian, China	D9	31
Jinyun, China	J9	32
Jinzhou, China	C9	31
Ji-Paraná, Braz.	B3	55
Jiparaná, stm., Braz.	D2	59
Jipijapa, Ec.	B1	58
Jiquilisco, El Sal.	D3	62
Jiquilpan de Juárez, Mex.	n12	63
Jirāfī, Wādī al (Naḥal Paran), val.	E6	41
Jirjā, Eg.	C3	38
Jirkov, Czech.	C8	19
Jiu, stm., Rom.	C6	24
Jiujiang, China	F8	31
Jiuquan, China	D4	31
Jiurongcheng, China	F10	32
Jixi, China	B11	31
Jixian, China	G6	32
Jizera, stm., Czech.	C9	19
Joaçaba, Braz.	D2	56
Joaíma, Braz.	E2	57
Joanna, S.C., U.S.	C4	117
João Belo see Xai-Xai, Moz.	E5	49
João Câmara, Braz.	g6	57
João Pessoa (Paraiba), Braz.	C4	57
João Pinheiro, Braz.	B3	56
Joaquín V. González, Arg.	E3	55
Job, Ok., U.S.	C5	113
Job Peak, mtn., Nv., U.S.	D3	105
Jobstown, N.J., U.S.	C3	107
Jocassee, Lake, res., U.S.	B1	117
Jocotepec, Mex.	m12	63
Jódar, Spain	D4	22
Jo Daviess, co., Il., U.S.	A3	90
Jodhpur, India	C5	36
Jodie, W.V., U.S.	m13	125
Jodoigne, Bel.	D4	17
Joe Batt's Arm [-Barr'd Islands-Shoal Bay], Newf.	D4	72
Joensuu, Fin.	F13	14
Joes, Co., U.S.	B8	83
Joes Brook, stm., Vt., U.S.	C4	122
Joes Creek, stm., W.V., U.S.	m12	125
Joetsu, Japan	H9	33
Jœuf, Fr.	C6	16
Joffre, Mount, mtn., Can.	D3	68
Joggins, N.S.	D5	71
Jogjakarta see Yogyakarta, Indon.	G4	34
Johannesburg, S. Afr.	C4	49
Johannesburg, Ca., U.S.	E5	82
Johannesburg, Mi., U.S.	D6	99
John, Cape, c., N.S.	D6	71
John Crow Mountains, mts., Jam.	E16	65
John Day, Or., U.S.	C8	114
John Day, stm., Or., U.S.	B6	114
John Day, North Fork, stm., Or., U.S.	C7	114
John Day Dam, U.S.	D5	124
John Day Fossil Beds National Monument, Or., U.S.	C6	114
John F. Kennedy Space Center, sci., Fl., U.S.	D6	86
John H. Kerr Dam, Va., U.S.	D4	123
John H. Kerr Reservoir, res., U.S.	D4	123
John Martin Reservoir, res., Co., U.S.	C7	83
John Muir National Historical Site, hist., Ca., U.S.	h8	82
John o'Groats, Scot., U.K.	B5	13
John Redmond Reservoir, res., Ks., U.S.	D8	93
Johnsburg, Il., U.S.	h8	90
Johnsburg, N.Y., U.S.	*B7	109
Johnsburg, Wi., U.S.	k9	126
John Sevier, Tn., U.S.	m14	119
Johns Island, S.C., U.S.	F7	117
Johns Island, i., S.C., U.S.	F7	117
Johnson, In., U.S.	A1	81
Johnson, In., U.S.	H2	91
Johnson, Ne., U.S.	D10	104
Johnson, Vt., U.S.	B3	122
Johnson, Wa., U.S.	C8	124
Johnson, co., Ar., U.S.	B2	81
Johnson, co., Ga., U.S.	D4	87
Johnson, co., Il., U.S.	F5	90
Johnson, co., In., U.S.	F5	91
Johnson, co., Ia., U.S.	C6	92
Johnson, co., Ks., U.S.	D9	93
Johnson, co., Ky., U.S.	C7	94
Johnson, co., Mo., U.S.	C4	102
Johnson, co., Ne., U.S.	D9	104
Johnson, co., Tn., U.S.	C12	119
Johnson, co., Tx., U.S.	C4	120
Johnson, co., Wy., U.S.	C6	127
Johnson, i., U.S.	E11	6
Johnson, Lake, l., Austl.	F3	50
Johnson City, Il., U.S.	F5	90
Johnson City, N.Y., U.S.	C5	109
Johnson City, Tn., U.S.	C11	119
Johnson City, Tx., U.S.	D3	120
Johnson Creek, Wi., U.S.	E5	126
Johnsondale, Ca., U.S.	E4	82
Johnsons Bayou, La., U.S.	E2	95
Johnsons Grove, Tn., U.S.	B2	119
Johnston, S.C., U.S.	D4	117
Johnston, co., N.C., U.S.	B4	110
Johnston, co., Ok., U.S.	C5	113
Johnston, i., U.S.	E11	6
Johnston, Lake, l., Austl.	F3	50
Johnston City, Il., U.S.	F5	90

Johnstone, Scot., U.K.	*E4	13
Johnstone Strait, strt., B.C.	D4	69
Johnston Key, i., Fl., U.S.	H5	86
Johnston's Point, c., Scot., U.K.	E3	13
Johnstown, Co., U.S.	A6	83
Johnstown, Ne., U.S.	B5	104
Johnstown, N.Y., U.S.	B6	109
Johnstown, N.D., U.S.	A8	111
Johnstown, Oh., U.S.	B3	112
Johnstown, Pa., U.S.	F4	115
Johntown, Tx., U.S.	C5	120
Johnville, Que.	D6	74
Johnville, Md., U.S.	A3	97
John W. Flannagan Reservoir, res., Va., U.S.	e9	123
Johor, state, Malay.	K5	35
Johor Baharu, Malay.	E2	34
Joice, Ia., U.S.	A4	92
Joigny, Fr.	D5	16
Joiner, Ar., U.S.	B5	81
Joinvile, Braz.	D3	56
Joinville, Fr.	C6	16
Joinville Island, i., Ant.	C7	7
Jojutla, Mex.	n14	63
Jokkmokk, Swe.	D8	14
Jolfā, Iran	B2	39
Joliet, Il., U.S.	B5	90
Joliet, Mt., U.S.	E8	103
Joliette, Que.	C4	74
Joliette, co., Que.	C3	74
Jolley, Ia., U.S.	B3	92
Jolo, Phil.	D6	34
Jomalig Island, i., Phil.	o14	34
Jomda, China	E4	31
Jonas Ridge, N.C., U.S.	B1	110
Jonava, Sov. Un.	A8	26
Jones, Phil.	n13	34
Jones, Al., U.S.	C3	78
Jones, Ga., U.S.	E5	87
Jones, La., U.S.	B4	95
Jones, co., Ga., U.S.	C3	87
Jones, co., Ia., U.S.	B6	92
Jones, co., Ms., U.S.	D4	101
Jones, co., N.C., U.S.	B5	110
Jones, co., S.D., U.S.	D5	118
Jones, co., Tx., U.S.	C3	120
Jonesboro, Ar., U.S.	B5	81
Jonesboro, Ga., U.S.	C2	87
Jonesboro, Il., U.S.	F4	90
Jonesboro, In., U.S.	D6	91
Jonesboro, La., U.S.	B3	95
Jonesboro, Me., U.S.	D5	96
Jonesboro, Tn., U.S.	C11	119
Jonesborough, Tn., U.S.	C11	119
Jones Creek, Tx., U.S.	s14	120
Jones Mill, Ar., U.S.	C3	81
Jones Mills, Tn., U.S.	A3	119
Jones Mills, Pa., U.S.	F3	115
Jones Mountains, mts., Ant.	B7	7
Jonesport, Me., U.S.	D5	96
Jones Sound, strt., N.W. Ter.	m34	66
Jonestown, Ms., U.S.	A3	101
Jonestown, Pa., U.S.	F9	115
Jonesville, La., U.S.	C4	95
Jonesville, Mi., U.S.	G6	99
Jonesville, N.C., U.S.	A2	110
Jonesville, S.C., U.S.	B4	117
Jonesville, Vt., U.S.	C3	122
Jonesville, Va., U.S.	f8	123
Jönköping, Swe.	I6	14
Jönköping, co., Swe.	A8	15
Jonquière, Que.	A6	74
Jonuta, Mex.	D6	63
Jonzac, Fr.	E3	16
Joplin, Mo., U.S.	D3	102
Joplin, Mt., U.S.	B6	103
Joppa, Al., U.S.	A3	78
Joppa, Il., U.S.	F5	90
Joppa, Md., U.S.	B5	97
Jordan, In., U.S.	D1	78
Jordan, Ar., U.S.	A3	81
Jordan, Ky., U.S.	f8	94
Jordan, Mn., U.S.	F5	100
Jordan, Mt., U.S.	C10	103
Jordan, N.Y., U.S.	B4	109
Jordan, ctry., Asia	B3	38
Jordan, stm., Asia	B7	41
Jordan, stm., Ut., U.S.	C4	121
Jordan Creek, stm., U.S.	E9	114
Jordan Lake, l., N.S.	E4	71
Jordan Lake, res., Al., U.S.	C3	78
Jordan Valley, Or., U.S.	D9	114
Jorhāt, India	h8	37
Jörn, Swe.	D9	14
Jornado del Muerto, des., N.M., U.S.	D3	108
Jos, Nig.	E6	45
José Battle y Ordóñez, Ur.	E1	56
José de San Martin, Arg.	C2	54
José María Blanco, Arg.	B4	54
Joseph, Or., U.S.	B9	114
Joseph, Ut., U.S.	E3	121
Joseph, Lac, l., Newf.	h8	72
Joseph Bonaparte Gulf, b., Austl.	B4	50
Joseph City, Az., U.S.	C5	80
Josephine, co., Or., U.S.	E3	114
Josephville, Mo., U.S.	f12	102
Joshua, Tx., U.S.	n9	120
Joshua Tree, Ca., U.S.	E5	82
Joshua Tree National Monument, Ca., U.S.	F6	82
Josselin, Fr.	E2	16
Jostedalsbreen, ice, Nor.	G2	14
Jost Van Dyke, i., V.I., Br.	B6	65
Jotunheimen, mts., Nor.	G3	14
Jourdanton, Tx., U.S.	E3	120
Joussard, Alta.	B3	68
Joux, Lac l., Switz.	C1	20
Jouy-en-Josas, Fr.	g9	16
Jovellanos, Cuba	C7	64
Joveyn, Afg.	B3	36
Joviânia, Braz.	B3	56
Jowhar, Som.	E6	47
Joy, Il., U.S.	B3	90
Joy, Ok., U.S.	*E4	113
Joyce, La., U.S.	C3	95
Joyce, Wa., U.S.	A2	124
Józefów, Pol.	m14	26
J. Percy Priest Lake, res., Tn., U.S.	A5	119
Juab, co., Ut., U.S.	D3	121
Juaja, Peru	D2	58
Juan Aldama, Mex.	C4	63
Juan B. Arruabarrena, Arg.	A5	54
Juan de Fuca, Strait of, strt., N.A.	A1	124

Juan Díaz (part of Panamá), Pan.	k12	62
Juan E. Barra, Arg.	B4	54
Juan Fernández, Archipiélago, is., Chile	G2	53
Juanita, N.D., U.S.	B7	111
Juanita, Wa., U.S.	*B3	124
Juan José Castelli, Arg.	*E3	55
Juanjui, Peru	C2	58
Juan L. Lacaze, Ur.	g8	54
Juárez, Mex.	B4	63
Juarez, Braz.	C2	57
Juazeiro, Braz.	C3	57
Juazeiro do Norte, Braz.	C3	57
Jubba (Genale), stm., Afr.	E5	47
Jubbada Dhexe, prov., Som.	E5	47
Jubbada Hoose, prov., Som.	E5	47
Jubbah, Sau. Ar.	I13	40
Jubilee Lake, l., Newf.	D4	72
Juby, Cap, c., Mor.	D2	44
Júcar, stm., Spain	C5	22
Juçara, Braz.	B2	56
Juchipila, Mex.	m12	63
Juchipila, stm., Mex.	m12	63
Juchitán [de Zaragoza], Mex.	D5	63
Jucuapa, El Sal.	D3	62
Juda, Wi., U.S.	F4	126
Judah, N.D., U.S.	C7	111
Judean Hills, hills, Asia	C7	41
Jude Island, i., Newf.	E4	72
Judenburg, Aus.	E7	18
Judique, N.S.	D8	71
Judith, stm., Mt., U.S.	C7	103
Judith, Point, c., R.I., U.S.	G4	85
Judith Basin, co., Mt., U.S.	C6	103
Judith Gap, Mt., U.S.	D7	103
Judith Mountains, mts., Mt., U.S.	C7	103
Judith Peak, mtn., Mt., U.S.	C7	103
Judson, In., U.S.	E3	91
Judson, Mn., U.S.	F4	100
Judson, N.D., U.S.	C4	111
Judson, Ar., U.S.	B4	81
Judyville, In., U.S.	D3	91
Juelsminde, Den.	C4	15
Jufayr, Bi'r al, well, Eg.	D4	41
Juigalpa, Nic.	D5	62
Juist, i., W. Ger.	B3	18
Juiz de Fora, Braz.	C4	56
Jujuy, prov., Arg.	D2	55
Jukkasjärvi (part of Kiruna), Swe.	D9	14
Julesburg, Co., U.S.	A8	83
Juliaca, Peru	E3	58
Juliaetta, Id., U.S.	C2	89
Julian, Ca., U.S.	F5	82
Julian, Ne., U.S.	D10	104
Julian, N.C., U.S.	B3	110
Julian, W.V., U.S.	C3	125
Juliana Top, mtn., Sur.	B3	59
Julian Alps, mts., Eur.	B3	24
Juliánehåb, Grnld.	C16	61
Jülich, W. Ger.	D6	17
Juliette, Ga., U.S.	C3	87
Julimes, Mex.	B3	63
Júlio de Castilhos, Braz.	D2	56
Julita, Swe.	t34	14
Juliustown, N.J., U.S.	C3	107
Julu, China	F6	32
Jumaʾl, Bi'r, well, Eg.	D5	41
Jumbo, Som.	F5	47
Jumbo Peak, mtn., Nv., U.S.	G7	105
Jumet (part of Charleroi), Bel.	B6	16
Jumilla, Spain	C5	22
Jump, Wi., U.S.	C3	126
Jump, North Fork, stm., Wi., U.S.	C3	126
Jump, South Fork, stm., Wi., U.S.	C3	126
Jumping Branch, W.V., U.S.	D4	125
Jumping Lake, l., Sask.	E3	75
Jūnāgadh, India	D5	36
Juncos, P.R.	B4	65
Junction, Il., U.S.	F5	90
Junction, Oh., U.S.	A1	112
Junction, Tx., U.S.	D3	120
Junction, Ut., U.S.	E3	121
Junction City, Ar., U.S.	D3	81
Junction City, Ga., U.S.	D2	87
Junction City, Ks., U.S.	C7	93
Junction City, Ky., U.S.	C5	94
Junction City, La., U.S.	A3	95
Junction City, Oh., U.S.	C3	112
Junction City, Or., U.S.	C3	114
Junction City, Wi., U.S.	D4	126
Jundiaí, Braz.	C3	56
June in Winter, Lake, l., Fl., U.S.	E5	86
June Lake, Ca., U.S.	D4	82
Juneau, Ak., U.S.	D13	79
Juneau, Wi., U.S.	E5	126
Juneau, co., Wi., U.S.	E3	126
Junee, Austl.	F8	50
Jungfrau, mtn., Switz.	E3	18
Junggar Pendi (Dzungarian Basin), China	B2	31
Junglinster, Lux.	E6	17
Juniata, Ne., U.S.	D7	104
Juniata, co., Pa., U.S.	F7	115
Juniata, stm., Pa., U.S.	F7	115
Juniata, Raystown Branch, stm., Pa., U.S.	F5	115
Juniata Terrace, Pa., U.S.	E6	115
Junín, Arg.	A4	54
Junín, Peru	D2	58
Junín, dept., Peru	C2	58
Junín, Lago, l., Peru	D2	58
Junín de los Andes, Arg.	B2	54
Junior, W.V., U.S.	C5	125
Junior Lake, l., Me., U.S.	C4	96
Juniper, N.B.	C2	71
Juniper Mountains, mts., Az., U.S.	B2	80
Junipero Serra Peak, mtn., Ca., U.S.	D3	82
Junius, S.D., U.S.	C8	118
Juno, Tx., U.S.	D2	120
Junqalī, prov., Sud.	D3	47
Juntura, Or., U.S.	D8	114
Jupiter, Fl., U.S.	F6	86
Jupiter Inlet, b., Fl., U.S.	F6	86
Jupiter Island, i., Fl., U.S.	E6	86
Juquiá, Braz.	C3	56
Juquitiba, Braz.	m8	56
Jura, state, Switz.	B3	20
Jura, dept., Fr.	C1	20
Jura, i., Scot., U.K.	C4	10
Jura, Sound of, strt., Scot., U.K.	C4	10
Jura Mountains, mts., Eur.	E3	18

Jurbarkas, Sov. Un.	A7	26
Jurf ad Darāwīsh, Jord.	G10	40
Juruá, Braz.	B4	58
Juruá, stm., S.A.	B4	58
Juruena, stm., Braz.	D3	59
Juruti, Braz.	C3	59
Jussey, Fr.	B1	20
Justice, Il., U.S.	*k9	90
Justin, Tx., U.S.	C4	120
Justiceburg, Tx., U.S.	C2	120
Justo Daract, Arg.	A3	54
Jüterbog, E. Ger.	C6	19
Jutiapa, Guat.	E7	63
Juticalpa, Hond.	E7	63
Jutland, pen., Den.	I3	14
Juventud, Isla de la (Isle of Pines), i., Cuba	D2	64
Juxian, China	G8	32
Juyongguan Pass, China	D7	32
Júzna Morava, stm., Yugo.	C5	24
Jyderup, Den.	C5	15
Jyväskylä, Fin.	F11	14

K

K2 (Godwin Austen), mtn., Asia	A6	36
Kaaawa, Hi., U.S.	f10	88
Kaala, mtn., Hi., U.S.	f9	88
Kaalualu Bay, b., Hi., U.S.	E6	88
Kaaumakua, Puu, mtn., Hi., U.S.	f10	88
Kabala, S.L.	E2	45
Kabale, Ug.	B4	48
Kabalega Falls (Murchison Falls), wtfl., Ug.	A5	48
Kabalo, Zaire	C4	48
Kabambare, Zaire	B4	48
Kabara, i., Fiji	I16	52
Kabarnet, Kenya	A6	48
Kabba, Nig.	E6	45
Kabenga, Zaire	C4	48
Kabetogama Lake, l., Mn., U.S.	B5	100
Kabinda, Zaire	C4	48
Kabompo, Zam.	D3	48
Kabīr Kūh, mts., Iran	E3	39
Kabompo, Zam.	D3	48
Kabompo, stm., Zam.	D3	48
Kabong, Malay.	C4	34
Kabongo, Zaire	C4	48
Kabul (Kābol), Afg.	B4	36
Kabul, stm., Asia	D14	39
Kabwe (Broken Hill), Zam.	D4	48
Kachchh, Gulf of (Kutch), b., India	D4	36
Kachess Lake, res., Wa., U.S.	B4	124
Kachug, Sov. Un.	D13	29
Kackley, Ks., U.S.	C6	93
Kadaň, Czech.	C2	26
Kadan, i., Burma	F3	35
Kadavu, i., Fiji	I15	52
Kade, Ghana	E4	45
Kadena, Japan	O5	52
Kadet Channel, strt., Eur.	A6	18
Kading, prov., Laos	C6	35
Kadınhanı, Tur.	D2	40
Kadiolo, Mali	D3	45
Kadiri, India	F6	36
Kadirli, Tur.	*D11	40
Kadoka, S.D., U.S.	D4	118
Kadoma, Zimb.	A4	49
Kaduna, Nig.	D6	45
Kaduna, stm., Nig.	D6	45
Kaédi, Maur.	C2	45
Kaélé, Cam.	C2	46
Kaena Point, c., Hi., U.S.	B3	88
Kaeryŏng, S. Kor.	H4	33
Kaesŏng, N. Kor.	D10	31
Käf, Sau. Ar.	B3	38
Kafanchan, Nig.	E6	45
Kaffrine, Sen.	D1	45
Kafia Kingi, Sud.	D1	47
Kafr ad Dawwār, Eg.	C2	41
Kafr ash Shaykh, Eg.	C2	41
Kafr az Zayyāt, Eg.	D2	41
Kafr Mālik, Isr. Occ.	h12	41
Kafr Qaddūm, Isr. Occ.	g11	41
Kafr Qāsim, Isr.	g10	41
Kafr Salīm, Eg.	C2	41
Kafr Saqr, Eg.	D3	41
Kafr Ţarkhān al Gharbī, Eg.	E3	41
Kafr Zībād, Isr. Occ.	g11	41
Kafue, stm., Zam.	E4	48
Kagan, Sov. Un.	B12	39
Kagawong, Ont.	B2	73
Kagera, stm., Afr.	B5	48
Kagızman, Tur.	B14	40
Kagoshima, Japan	E11	31
Kagoshima Bay, b., Japan	K5	33
Kahakuloa, Hi., U.S.	B5	88
Kahaluu, Hi., U.S.	g10	88
Kahaluu, Hi., U.S.	D6	88
Kahama, Tan.	B5	48
Kahana, Hi., U.S.	B4	88
Kahana Bay, b., Hi., U.S.	f10	88
Kahayan, stm., Indon.	F4	34
Kahemba, Zaire	C3	48
Kahla, E. Ger.	C5	124
Kahnūjī, Iran	G3	39
Kahoka, Mo., U.S.	A6	102
Kahoolawe, i., Hi., U.S.	C5	88
Kahramanmaraş, Tur.	D11	40
Kahuku, Hi., U.S.	B4	88
Kahuku Point, c., Hi., U.S.	B4	88
Kahului, Hi., U.S.	C5	88
Kahului Bay, b., Hi., U.S.	C5	88
Kaiama, Nig.	E5	45
Kahoka, Mo., U.S.	A6	102
Kaiapoi, N.Z.	O14	51
Kaibab Indian Reservation, Az., U.S.	A3	80
Kaibab Plateau, plat., Az., U.S.	A3	80
Kaibito, Az., U.S.	A4	80
Kaibito Plateau, plat., Az., U.S.	A4	80
Kaieteur Fall, wtfl., Guy.	A3	59
Kaifeng, China	E7	31
Kaihua, China	J8	32
Kai Islands, is., Indon.	B8	51
Kaikoura, N.Z.	O14	51
Kaikoura Peninsula, pen., N.Z.	O14	51
Kailahun, S.L.	E2	45
Kailas Range see Gangdisi Mountains, mts., China	B9	37
Kailu, China	C9	32
Kailua, Hi., U.S.	B4	88
Kailua Bay, b., Hi., U.S.	g11	88

Name	Map Ref.	Page
Kailua Kona, Hi., U.S.	D6	88
Kai Malino, Hi., U.S.	D6	88
Kaimana, Indon.	F8	34
Kaimu, Hi., U.S.	D7	88
Kainaliu, Hi., U.S.	D6	88
Kainan, Japan	I7	33
Kainji Dam, Nig.	E5	45
Kainji Lake, res., Nig.	D5	45
Kaipara Harbour, b., N.Z.	L15	51
Kaiparowits Plateau, plat., Ut., U.S.	F4	121
Kaipokok Bay, b., Newf.	g10	72
Kaiserslautern, W. Ger.	D3	18
Kaiserstuhl, Switz.	A5	21
Kaišiadorys, Sov. Un.	A8	26
Kaitaia, N.Z.	K14	51
Kaitangata, N.Z.	Q12	51
Kaithal, India	C6	37
Kaiwi Channel, strt., Hi., U.S.	B4	88
Kaixian, China	E6	31
Kaiyuan, China	C11	32
Kaizuka, Japan	o14	33
Kajaani, Fin.	E12	14
Kajakī, Band-e, res., Afg.	E12	39
Kajiado, Kenya	B6	48
Kajikazawa, Japan	n17	33
Kākā, Sud.	C3	47
Kakagi Lake, l., Ont.	E5	70
Kakamas, S. Afr.	C3	49
Kakamega, Kenya	A5	48
Kaka Point, c., Hi., U.S.	C5	88
Kake, Ak., U.S.	D13	79
Kakegawa, Japan	o17	33
Kakhovka, Sov. Un.	H9	27
Kakhovka Reservoir, res., Sov. Un.	E6	29
Kākināda (Cocanada), India	E7	36
Kakisa Lake, l., N.W. Ter.	D9	66
Kakogawa, Japan	*I7	33
Kakuma, Kenya	A5	48
Kakwa, stm., Can.	B1	68
Kālābagh, Pak.	B5	36
Kalabáka, Grc.	C3	25
Kalabakan, Malay.	E5	34
Kalābishah, Eg.	E6	43
Kalabo, Zam.	D3	48
Kalach, Sov. Un.	F13	27
Kalach-na-Donu, Sov. Un.	G14	27
Kaladar, Ont.	C7	73
Ka Lae, c., Hi., U.S.	E6	88
Kalahari Desert, des., Afr.	B3	49
Kalahari Gemsbok National Park, S. Afr.	C3	49
Kalaheo, Hi., U.S.	B2	88
Kalaho, Pidos, hill, N. Mar. Is.	C8	52
Kalai-Mor, Sov. Un.	D11	39
Kalama, Wa., U.S.	C3	124
Kálámai, Grc.	D4	40
Kalamaki, Tur.	D7	25
Kalamariá, Grc.	*B4	25
Kalamazoo, Mi., U.S.	F5	99
Kalamazoo, co., Mi., U.S.	F5	99
Kalamazoo, stm., Mi., U.S.	F5	99
Kalambo Falls, wtfl., Afr.	C5	48
Kalandula, Ang.	C2	48
Kalaoa Homesteads, Hi., U.S.	D6	88
Kalaotoa, i., Indon.	G6	34
Kalapana, Hi., U.S.	D7	88
Kalasin, Thai.	D5	35
Kalāt, Pak.	C4	36
Kalaupapa, Hi., U.S.	B5	88
Kalaupapa Peninsula, pen., Hi., U.S.	B5	88
Kalávrita, Grc.	C4	25
Kalawao, co., Hi., U.S.	B5	88
Kalba, Ra's al, c., Yemen	D4	38
Kalbā', U.A.E.	B9	40
Kaledik, Tur.	B9	40
Kaleden, B.C.	E8	69
Kalegauk, i., Burma	E2	35
Kalehe, Zaire	B4	48
Kaleköy, Tur.	B5	25
Kalemie (Albertville), Zaire	C4	48
Kalena, Puu, mtn., Hi., U.S.	g9	88
Kaleva, Mi., U.S.	D4	99
Kalevala, Sov. Un.	E14	14
Kalewa, Burma	D9	36
Kalgalaksha, Sov. Un.	E16	14
Kalgin Island, i., Ak., U.S.	g16	79
Kalgoorlie, Austl.	F3	50
Kalibo, Phil.	C6	34
Kalihiwai, Hi., U.S.	A2	88
Kalima, Zaire	B4	48
Kálimnos, Grc.	D6	40
Kálimnos, i., Grc.	D6	40
Kalinin, Sov. Un.	D6	29
Kaliningrad, Sov. Un.	n17	27
Kaliningrad (Königsberg), Sov. Un.	D5	29
Kalininsk, Sov. Un.	F15	27
Kalinkovichi, Sov. Un.	E7	27
Kalis, Som.	D6	47
Kāli Sindh, stm., India	E6	37
Kalispel Indian Reservation, Wa., U.S.	A8	124
Kalispell, Mt., U.S.	B2	103
Kalisz, Pol.	C5	26
Kaliua, Tan.	C5	48
Kälixälven, stm., Swe.	D10	14
Kalkaska, Mi., U.S.	D5	99
Kalkaska, co., Mi., U.S.	D5	99
Kalkfeld, Nmb.	B2	49
Kalkrand, Nmb.	B2	49
Kallithéa, Grc.	h11	25
Kallsjön, l., Swe.	F5	14
Kalmalo, Nig.	D6	45
Kalmar, Swe.	H11	14
Kalmar, co., Swe.	t35	14
Kalmarsund, strt., Swe.	I7	14
Kalmykovo, Sov. Un.	D4	28
Kalo, Ia., U.S.	B3	92
Kalocsa, Hung.	B4	24
Kalohi Channel, strt., Hi., U.S.	C4	88
Kaloli Point, c., Hi., U.S.	D7	88
Kalomo, Zam.	E4	48
Kalona, Ia., U.S.	C6	92
Kalone Peak, mtn., B.C.	C4	69
Kālpi, India	D7	37
Kalskag, Ak., U.S.	C7	79
Kaltag, Ak., U.S.	C8	79
Kaluga, Sov. Un.	G19	22
Kalulushi, Zam.	D4	48
Kalundborg, Den.	C5	15
Kalush, Sov. Un.	G5	27
Kałuszyn, Pol.	B6	26
Kalvarija, Sov. Un.	A7	26
Kalvehave, Den.	D5	15
Kalvesta, Ks., U.S.	D3	93
Kalvsjön, l., Swe.	A7	15
Kalyān, India	H4	37
Kama, Zaire	B4	48
Kama, stm., Sov. Un.	D8	29
Kamaing, Burma	C10	36
Kamaishi, Japan	D13	31
Kamakou, mtn., Hi., U.S.	B5	88
Kamakura, Japan	n18	33
Kamakwie, S.L.	E2	45
Kamananui Stream, stm., Hi., U.S.	f9	88
Kamaniskeg Lake, l., Ont.	A1	49
Kamanjab, Nmb.	A1	49
Kamaran, i., Yemen	D4	38
Kama Reservoir, res., Sov. Un.	D8	29
Kāmārhāti, India	*D8	36
Kamaria Fall, wtfl., Guy.	A3	59
Kama Rock, i., Japan	P17	52
Kamas, Ut., U.S.	C4	121
Kamatsi Lake, l., Sask.	A4	75
Kambalda, Austl.	F3	50
Kambove, Zaire	D4	48
Kamchatka Peninsula, pen., Sov. Un.	D18	29
Kamenets-Podolskiy, Sov. Un.	G6	27
Kamenjak, Cape, c., Yugo.	C1	24
Kamenka, Sov. Un.	G7	27
Kamenka, Sov. Un.	C2	28
Kamen-na-Obi, Sov. Un.	D11	29
Kamensk-Shakhtinskiy, Sov. Un.	G13	27
Kamensk-Uralskiy, Sov. Un.	D9	29
Kamenz, E. Ger.	C7	18
Kameoka, Japan	o14	33
Kāmet, mtn., Asia	B7,	37
Kamiah, Id., U.S.	C2	89
Kamiak Butte, mtn., Wa., U.S.	C8	124
Kamień Pomorski, Pol.	B3	26
Kamina, Zaire	C4	48
Kamioka, Japan	m16	33
Kamloops, B.C.	D7	69
Kammuri, Mount, mtn., Japan	I6	33
Kamo, Sov. Un.	B15	40
Kamoa Mountains, mts., Guy.	B3	59
Kamooloa, Hi., U.S.	f9	88
Kamouraska, Que.	B8	74
Kamouraska, co., Que.	B8	74
Kampala, Ug.	A5	48
Kampar, Malay.	J4	35
Kampar, stm., Indon.	E2	34
Kampen, Neth.	A6	16
Kampeska, Lake, l., S.D., U.S.	C8	118
Kamphaeng Phet, Thai.	D3	35
Kampong Cham, Camb.	C3	34
Kampong Chhnang, Camb.	C2	34
Kampong Khleang, Camb.	F6	35
Kampong Saom, Camb.	C2	34
Kampong Saom Bay, b., Camb.	C2	34
Kampong Spoe, Camb.	G6	35
Kampong Thum, Camb.	C2	34
Kampot, Camb.	C2	34
Kampsville, Il., U.S.	D3	90
Kampuchea see Cambodia, ctry., Asia	F6	34
Kamrar, Ia., U.S.	B4	92
Kamsack, Sask.	F5	75
Kamuchawie Lake, l., Can.	A4	75
Kamuela (Waimea), Hi., U.S.	C6	88
Kamuli, Ug.	A5	48
Kamyshevakha, Sov. Un.	q21	27
Kamyshin, Sov. Un.	F15	27
Kamyshlov, Sov. Un.	B6	28
Kanab, Ut., U.S.	F3	121
Kanab Creek, stm., U.S.	A3	80
Kanabec, co., Mn., U.S.	E5	100
Kanacea, i., Fiji	H16	52
Kanaga Island, i., Ak., U.S.	E4	79
Kanairiktok, stm., Newf.	g9	72
Kanakanaskis, stm., Alta.	D3	68
Kananga (Luluabourg), Zaire	C3	48
Kanapou Bay, b., Hi., U.S.	C5	88
Kanarraville, Ut., U.S.	F2	121
Kanash, Sov. Un.	D16	27
Kanata, Ont.	B9	73
Kanauga, Oh., U.S.	D3	112
Kanawha, Ia., U.S.	B4	92
Kanawha, co., W.V., U.S.	C3	125
Kanawha, stm., W.V., U.S.	C3	125
Kanayama, Japan	n16	33
Kanazawa, Japan	D12	31
Kanbe, Burma	*E10	36
Kanchanaburi, Thai.	E3	35
Kānchenjunga, mtn., Asia	C8	36
Kānchipuram (Conjeevaram), India	F7	36
Kānchrāpāra, India	*D8	37
Kandahar (Qandahār), Afg.	F7	39
Kandahar, Sask.	F3	75
Kandalaksha, Sov. Un.	C5	28
Kandangan, Indon.	F5	34
Kandel, W. Ger.	D3	19
Kandern, W. Ger.	A4	21
Kandersteg, Switz.	C3	21
Kandi, Benin	D5	45
Kandira, Tur.	B8	40
Kandiyohi, Mn., U.S.	E4	100
Kandiyohi, co., Mn., U.S.	E3	100
Kandla, India	F3	37
Kandrāch, Pak.	C4	36
Kandreho, Madag.	g9	49
Kandy, Sri L.	G7	36
Kane, Il., U.S.	D3	90
Kane, Pa., U.S.	C4	115
Kane, co., Il., U.S.	B5	90
Kane, co., Ut., U.S.	F3	121
Kane Basin, strt., N.A.	m38	66
Kaneohe, Hi., U.S.	B4	88
Kaneohe Bay, b., Hi., U.S.	g10	88
Kaneohe Bay Marine Corps Air Station, mil., Hi., U.S.	g10	88
Kanevskaya, Sov. Un.	H12	27
Kang, Bots.	B3	49
Kangaba, Mali	D3	45
Kangal, Tur.	C11	40
Kangar, Malay.	I4	35
Kangaroo, i., Austl.	G6	50
Kangbao, China	C7	31
Kangding, China	E5	31
Kāngīmnagar, India	H7	37
Kangean Islands, is., Indon.	F5	34
Kanggye, N. Kor.	C10	31
Kangiqsualujjuaq, Que.	f8	72
Kangiqsujuaq, Que.	f12	74
Kangirsuk, Que.	f12	74
Kangley, Il., U.S.	B5	90
Kangnung, S. Kor.	D10	31
Kango, Gabon	E2	46
Kangoku Rock, i., Japan	P17	52
Kangrinboqê Mountain, mtn., China	B2	37
Kani, Burma	A1	35
Kani, I.C.	E3	45
Kaniama, Zaire	C3	48
Kanimekh, Sov. Un.	A12	39
Kanin Nos, Cape, c., Sov. Un.	C7	29
Kanjiža, Yugo.	B5	24
Kankakee, Il., U.S.	B6	90
Kankakee, co., Il., U.S.	B6	90
Kankakee, stm., U.S.	B5	90
Kankan, Gui.	D3	45
Kānker, India	D7	36
Kankossa, Maur.	C2	45
Kannapolis, N.C., U.S.	B2	110
Kannauj, India	D7	37
Kano, Nig.	D6	45
Kanopolis, Ks., U.S.	D5	93
Kanopolis Lake, res., Ks., U.S.	D5	93
Kanorado, Ks., U.S.	C1	93
Kanosh, Ut., U.S.	E3	121
Kanoya, Japan	K5	33
Kānpur, India	C7	36
Kansas, Al., U.S.	B2	78
Kansas, Il., U.S.	D6	90
Kansas, Oh., U.S.	A2	112
Kansas, Ok., U.S.	A7	113
Kansas, state, U.S.	D5	93
Kansas, stm., Ks., U.S.	C7	93
Kansas City, Ks., U.S.	C9	93
Kansas City, Mo., U.S.	B3	102
Kansasville, Wi., U.S.	n11	126
Kansk, Sov. Un.	D12	29
Kansu see Gansu, prov., China	D5	31
Kantang, Thai.	D1	34
Kanton Island, i., Kir.	G11	6
Kantunilkin, Mex.	C7	63
Kanturk, Ire.	E3	11
Kanuku Mountains, mts., Guy.	B3	59
Kanuma, Japan	H9	33
Kanye, Bots.	B4	49
Kaohsiung, Tai.	G9	31
Kaoko Veld, plat., Nmb.	A1	49
Kaolack, Sen.	D1	45
Kaoma, Zam.	D3	48
Kaouar, reg., Niger	C7	45
Kapaa, Hi., U.S.	A2	88
Kapaau, Hi., U.S.	C6	88
Kapal, Sov. Un.	F24	8
Kapandrítion, Grc.	g11	25
Kapanga, Zaire	C3	48
Kapapa Island, i., Hi., U.S.	g10	88
Kaparéllion, Grc.	g10	25
Kapchagay, Sov. Un.	E9	29
Kapchagay Reservoir, res., Sov. Un.	E9	29
Kapenguria, Kenya	A6	48
Kapfenberg, Aus.	E7	18
Kapiri Mposhi, Zam.	D4	48
Kapit, Malay.	E4	34
Kaplan, La., U.S.	D3	95
Kaplice, Czech.	E9	19
Kapoeta, Sud.	E3	47
Kaposvár, Hung.	B3	24
Kaposvar Creek, stm., Sask.	G4	75
Kapowsin, Wa., U.S.	C3	124
Kappa, Il., U.S.	C4	90
Kapsan, N. Kor.	F4	33
Kapuas, stm., Indon.	C6	34
Kapulena, Hi., U.S.	C6	88
Kapuskasing, Ont.	o19	73
Kaputar, mtn., Austl.	E8	51
Kapuvár, Hung.	B3	24
Kara, Sov. Un.	C9	29
Karabash, Sov. Un.	D21	8
Kara-Bogaz-Gol, Sov. Un.	E4	28
Karabük, Tur.	*B9	40
Karachev, Sov. Un.	E10	27
Karāchi, Pak.	D4	36
Karāchi Cantonment, Pak.	*D4	36
Karaga, Zaire	D19	29
Karaganda, Sov. Un.	E10	29
Karagin Island, i., Sov. Un.	D19	29
Karaisalı, Tur.	D10	40
Karaj, Iran	D5	38
Karakas, Sov. Un.	D10	28
Karakelong, i., Indon.	E7	34
Karakoram Pass, Asia	A6	36
Karakoram Range, mts., Asia	A6	36
Karaköse see Ağrı, Tur.	C14	40
Kara-Kum, des., Sov. Un.	B8	38
Kara-Kum Canal, Sov. Un.	H21	8
Karaman, Tur.	D9	40
Karamay, China	B1	31
Karamea, N.Z.	N14	51
Karamea Bight, N.Z.	N13	51
Karamürsel, Tur.	B7	40
Karapinar, Tur.	D9	40
Karasburg, Nmb.	C3	49
Kara Sea, Sov. Un.	B9	29
Karasu, Sov. Un.	C8	40
Karasu, Tur.	B8	40
Karasuk, Sov. Un.	C9	28
Karatal, stm., Sov. Un.	D9	28
Karatas, Cape, c., Tur.	D10	40
Karatau Range, mts., Sov. Un.	E7	28
Karatobe, Sov. Un.	D4	28
Karatsu, Japan	J4	33
Karauli, India	D7	37
Karaulkeldy, Sov. Un.	D5	28
Karawanken, mts., Eur.	D5	24
Karbalā', Iraq	F15	41
Karcag, Hung.	B5	24
Karczew, Pol.	m14	26
Kardhítsa, Grc.	C3	40
Karema, Tan.	C5	48
Karesuando (part of Kiruna), Swe.	C10	14
Kargasok, Sov. Un.	D11	29
Kargat, Sov. Un.	D25	29
Kargil, India	B6	36
Kargopol, Sov. Un.	A12	51
Kargui, Niger	D7	45
Karguéri, Niger	B5	25
Kariai, Grc.	B5	25
Kariba, Zimb.	E3	48
Kariba, Lake, res., Afr.	A4	49
Karibib, Nmb.	B2	49
Karikari, Cape, c., N.Z.	K14	51
Karimata Islands, is., Indon.	F3	34
Karimata Strait, strt., Indon.	F3	34
Karimunjawa Islands, is., Indon.	F4	34
Karin, Som.	C6	47
Karisimbi, Volcán, vol., Afr.	C5	48
Káristos, Grc.	C5	40
Kariya, Japan	o15	33
Kārīz, Iran	D10	39
Karkar, i., Pap. N. Gui.	h12	50
Karkaralinsk, Sov. Un.	E10	29
Karkheh, stm., Iran	E6	38
Karkinit Gulf, b., Sov. Un.	I9	27
Karl-Marx-Stadt (Chemnitz), E. Ger.	C6	18
Karlobag, Yugo.	B4	24
Karloske, stm., Man.	B4	70
Karlovac, Yugo.	D7	24
Karlovo, Bul.	D7	24
Karlovy Vary, Czech.	E11	19
Karlshamn, Swe.	I6	14
Karlskoga, Swe.	H6	14
Karlskrona, Swe.	I6	14
Karlsruhe, W. Ger.	D4	18
Karlsruhe, N.D., U.S.	A5	111
Karlstad, Swe.	H5	14
Karlstad, Mn., U.S.	B2	100
Karlstadt, W. Ger.	D4	19
Karluk, Ak., U.S.	D9	79
Karnak, Il., U.S.	F5	90
Karnal, India	*C6	36
Karnāli, stm., Nepal	C8	37
Karnataka, state, India	F6	36
Karnes, co., Tx., U.S.	E4	120
Karnes City, Tx., U.S.	E4	120
Karnobat, Bul.	D8	24
Karns, Tn., U.S.	n13	119
Karns City, Pa., U.S.	E2	115
Kärnten, state, Aus.	C9	20
Karoi, Zimb.	A4	49
Karonga, Mwi.	C5	48
Karora, Sud.	B4	47
Karow, Zimb.	E6	15
Kárpathos, i., Grc.	E6	40
Karpenísion, Grc.	C3	25
Karratha, Austl.	D2	50
Kars, Tur.	B14	40
Karsakpay, Sov. Un.	E9	29
Karsha, Sov. Un.	D4	28
Karshi, Sov. Un.	F9	29
Karstädt, E. Ger.	E5	15
Kartal, Tur.	B8	25
Kartaly, Sov. Un.	D9	29
Kartuzy, Pol.	A5	26
Kārūn, stm., Iran	F4	39
Karup, Den.	B3	15
Karup Å, stm., Den.	B3	15
Karval, Co., U.S.	C7	83
Karvia, Fin.	F10	14
Karviná, Czech.	D5	26
Kārwār, India	F5	36
Kås, Den.	A3	15
Kaš, Sud.	C1	47
Kaş, Tur.	D7	40
Kasaan, Ak., U.S.	n23	79
Kasai, hist. reg., Zaire	B2	48
Kasai (Cassai), stm., Afr.	B2	48
Kasaji, Zaire	D3	48
Kasama, Japan	D5	48
Kasama, Zam.	C5	48
Kasane, Bots.	A4	49
Kasane, Tan.	C5	48
Kāsaragod, India	F5	36
Kasba, India	E11	37
Kasba Lake, l., N.W. Ter.	D12	66
Kasba Tadla, Mor.	C3	44
Kasempa, Zam.	C4	48
Kasenga, Zaire	D4	48
Kasese, Ug.	A5	48
Kashan, Iran	B5	38
Kashi, China	F10	29
Kashihara, Japan	o14	33
Kashima, Japan	n19	33
Kashin, Sov. Un.	D12	27
Kashirka, stm., Sov. Un.	n18	27
Kashiwazaki, Japan	H9	33
Kāshmar (Turshīz), Iran	B5	38
Kashmor, Pak.	C2	37
Kasigluk, Ut., U.S.	B4	121
Kasilof, Ak., U.S.	C9	79
Kasimov, Sov. Un.	D13	27
Kaskaskia, Il., U.S.	F4	90
Kaskaskia, stm., Il., U.S.	D5	90
Kaskö, Fin.	F9	14
Kaslo, B.C.	E9	69
Kasongo, Zaire	B4	48
Kasongo-Lunda, Zaire	C2	48
Kásos, i., Grc.	E6	40
Kasota, Mn., U.S.	F5	100
Kassalā, Sud.	B4	47
Kassalā, prov., Sud.	B4	47
Kassandra, Gulf of, b., Grc.	C4	18
Kassel (Cassel), W. Ger.	F6	100
Kasson, Mn., U.S.	B9	40
Kastamonu, Tur.	B9	40
Kastélli, Grc.	E7	52
Kastoría, Grc.	B3	40
Kástron, Grc.	g10	25
Kasukabe, Japan	n18	33
Kasulu, Tan.	B5	48
Kasumi, Japan	I7	33
Kasumiga-Ura, l., Japan	H10	33
Kasungu, Mwi.	D5	48
Kasūr, Pak.	B5	36
Katako-Kombe, Zaire	B3	48
Katanga, hist. reg., Zaire	C4	48
Katanning, Austl.	F2	50
Katano Point, c., Japan	P17	52
Katata, Japan	n14	33
Katepwa Beach, Sask.	G4	75
Katerini, Grc.	B4	40
Kates Needle, mtn., Ak., U.S.	m24	79
Katha, Burma	D10	36
Katherine, Austl.	B5	50
Kāthiāwār Peninsula, pen., India	D4	36
Kathleen, Fl., U.S.	D4	86
Kathmandu (Kāthmāndū), Nepal	C8	36
Kathryn, Alta.	D4	68
Kathryn, N.D., U.S.	C8	111
Kathua, India	A5	37
Katie, Ok., U.S.	C4	113
Katihār, India	E11	37
Katimik Lake, l., Man.	C2	70
Katiola, I.C.	E3	45
Katire, Sud.	E3	47
Katlehong, S. Afr.	*C4	49
Katmai, Mount, mtn., Ak., U.S.	D9	79
Katmai National Park, Ak., U.S.	D9	79
Katokhí, Grc.	g10	25
Katonga, Zaire	C3	48
Katoomba, Austl.	F9	50
Katrīmnagar, India	H7	37
Katowice (Stalinogród), Pol.	C5	26
Katrine, Loch, l., Scot., U.K.	D4	13
Katsina, Nig.	D6	45
Katsina Ala, stm., Afr.	H7	45
Katsuta, Japan	*H10	33
Kattakurgan, Sov. Un.	H22	8
Kattegat, strt., Eur.	B5	14
Katun, stm., Sov. Un.	E26	29
Katwijk aan Zee, Neth.	A4	16
Katy, Tx., U.S.	r14	120
Kau, Indon.	E7	34
Kauai, co., Hi., U.S.	B1	88
Kauai, i., Hi., U.S.	A2	88
Kauai Channel, strt., Hi., U.S.	B3	88
Kau Desert, des., Hi., U.S.	D6	88
Kauehi, i., Fr. Poly.	G5	53
Kaufbeuren, W. Ger.	E5	18
Kaufman, Tx., U.S.	C4	120
Kaufman, co., Tx., U.S.	C4	120
Kauhajoki, Fin.	F10	14
Kauhava, Fin.	F10	14
Kauiki Head, c., Hi., U.S.	C6	88
Kaukauna, Wi., U.S.	D5	126
Kaukau Veld, plat., Afr.	B3	49
Kaula Island, i., Hi., U.S.	m15	88
Kaulakahi Channel, strt., Hi., U.S.	A2	88
Kaumakani, Hi., U.S.	B2	88
Kaumalapau, Hi., U.S.	C5	88
Kaumalapau Harbor, Hi., U.S.	B4	88
Kauna Point, c., Hi., U.S.	D6	88
Kaunakakai, Hi., U.S.	B5	88
Kaunas, Sov. Un.	D5	29
Kauna Namoda, Nig.	D6	45
Kautokeino, Nor.	C10	14
Kavacha, Sov. Un.	C19	29
Kavála, Alb.	B2	25
Kavála, Grc.	B5	40
Kavála, Gulf of, b., Grc.	B5	25
Kāvali, India	F6	36
Kavarna, Bul.	D9	24
Kavieng, Pap. N. Gui.	h13	50
Kaw, Tur.	B14	40
Kävlinge, Swe.	C7	15
Kaw, Fr. Gu.	B4	59
Kawagama Lake, l., Ont.	B6	73
Kawagoe, Japan	n18	33
Kawaguchi, Japan	n18	33
Kawaihae, Hi., U.S.	C6	88
Kawaihae Bay, b., Hi., U.S.	D5	115
Kawaihoa Point, c., Hi., U.S.	B1	88
Kawaikini, mtn., Hi., U.S.	A2	88
Kawailoa, Hi., U.S.	f9	88
Kawailoa Beach, Hi., U.S.	f9	88
Kawakawa, N.Z.	K15	51
Kawambwa, Zam.	C4	48
Kawardha, India	F8	37
Kawasaki, Japan	D12	31
Kawela, Hi., U.S.	f9	88
Kawhia Harbour, b., N.Z.	M15	51
Kawia Peak, mtn., Nv., U.S.	F5	105
Kawich Range, mts., Nv., U.S.	F5	105
Kawkareik, Burma	D3	35
Kaw Lake, res., Ok., U.S.	A5	113
Kawm Ḥamādah, Eg.	D2	41
Kawm Ūmbū, Eg.	D4	41
Kawthaung, Burma	F10	36
Kay, co., Ok., U.S.	A4	113
Kaya, Burkina	D4	45
Kayangel Islands, is., Palau	R17	52
Kaycee, Wy., U.S.	C6	127
Kayenta, Az., U.S.	A5	80
Kayes, Congo	B1	48
Kayes, Mali	D2	45
Kayford, W.V., U.S.	C3	125
Kaylor, S.D., U.S.	D8	118
Kayō, Japan	N6	52
Kayser Gebergte, mts., Sur.	B3	59
Kayseri, Tur.	C10	40
Kaysville, Ut., U.S.	B4	121
Kayuagung, Indon.	F2	34
Kayyville, Sask.	H3	75
Kazachye, Sov. Un.	B16	29
Kazakevichevo, Sov. Un.	B7	33
Kazakh Hills, hills, Sov. Un.	D7	28
Kazakh S.S.R., state, Sov. Un.	E9	29
Kazalinsk, Sov. Un.	D6	28
Kazanlŭk, Bul.	D7	24
Kazan, stm., N.W. Ter.	D12	66
Kazan, Sov. Un.	F5	100
Kazbek, mtn., Sov. Un.	E2	28
Kazerūn, Iran	A4	28
Kazi-Magomed, Sov. Un.	A9	28
Kazimierz [Dolny], Pol.	A5	24
Kazincbarcika, Hung.	A5	24
Kazumba, Zaire	C3	48
Kazym, stm., Sov. Un.	C22	8
Kdyně, Czech.	D8	19
Kéa, i., Grc.	D5	40
Kéa, Grc.	D5	40
Keaau, Hi., U.S.	D6	88
Keahiakahoe, Puu, mtn., Hi., U.S.	g10	88
Keahole Point, c., Hi., U.S.	D5	88
Kealaikahiki Channel, strt., Hi., U.S.	C5	88
Kealaikahiki Point, c., Hi., U.S.	C5	88
Kealakekua, Hi., U.S.	D6	88
Kealia, Hi., U.S.	D6	88
Keams Canyon, Az., U.S.	B5	80
Keanapapa Point, c., Hi., U.S.	C4	88
Keansburg, N.J., U.S.	C4	107
Kearney, Ont.	B5	73
Kearney, Mo., U.S.	B3	102
Kearney, Ne., U.S.	D7	104
Kearney, co., Ne., U.S.	D7	104
Kearneysville, W.V., U.S.	B7	125
Kearns, Ut., U.S.	C4	121
Kearny, Az., U.S.	D5	80
Kearny, co., Ks., U.S.	D2	93
Kearny, N.J., U.S.	h8	107
Kearsarge, Mi., U.S.	A2	99
Kearsarge, N.H., U.S.	B4	106
Kearsarge, Mount, mtn., N.H., U.S.	D3	106
Kearsarge North, mtn., N.H., U.S.	B4	106
Keatchie, La., U.S.	B2	95
Keatley, Sask.	E2	75
Keaton, Ky., U.S.	C7	94
Keats, Ks., U.S.	C7	93
Keban Reservoir, res., Tur.	C12	40
Kebbi, Nig.	E5	45
Kebock Head, c., Scot., U.K.	C2	13
Kebri Dehar, Eth.	C7	47
Kecskemét, Hung.	B4	24
Kedainiai, Sov. Un.	A8	26
Kedges Straits, strt., Md., U.S.	D5	97
Kedgwick, N.B.	B2	71
Kédougou, Sen.	D2	45
Kedong, China	D2	33
Kedzierzyn-Koźle, Pol.	C5	26
Keefers, B.C.	D6	69
Keego Harbor, Mi., U.S.	o15	99
Keei, Hi., U.S.	D6	88
Keele Peak, mtn., Yukon	D6	66
Keeler, Sask.	G3	75
Keeler, Ca., U.S.	D5	82
Keeline, Wy., U.S.	D8	127
Keeling, Tn., U.S.	B2	119
Keeling, Va., U.S.	D3	123
Keels, Newf.	D5	72
Keelung see Chilung, Tai.	F9	31
Keene, Ont.	C6	73
Keene, Ca., U.S.	E4	82
Keene, Ky., U.S.	C5	94
Keene, N.H., U.S.	E2	106
Keene, N.Y., U.S.	A7	109
Keene, N.D., U.S.	B3	111
Keene, Oh., U.S.	B4	112
Keene, Tx., U.S.	n9	120
Keenes, Il., U.S.	E5	90
Keensburg, Co., U.S.	A6	83
Keene Valley, N.Y., U.S.	f11	109
Keeney Knob, mtn., W.V., U.S.	D4	125
Keensburg, Il., U.S.	E6	90
Keeseville, N.Y., U.S.	f11	109
Keesler Air Force Base, mil., Ms., U.S.	E5	101
Keetmanshoop, Nmb.	C2	49
Keet Seel Ruin, hist., Az., U.S.	A5	80
Keewatin, Ont.	E4	70
Keewatin, Mn., U.S.	C5	100
Keewatin, dept., N.W. Ter.	D13	66
Keewatin, stm., Man.	A1	70
Keezletown, Va., U.S.	B4	123
Kefa, prov., Eth.	D4	47
Kefallinía (Cephalonia), i., Grc.	A7	41
Kefar 'Eqron, Isr.	h10	41
Kefar Blum, Isr.	f9	88
Kefar Monash, Isr.	f10	41
Kefar Sava, Isr.	B6	41
Kefar Yona, Isr.	f10	41
Keffi, Nig.	*E6	45
Keflavík, Ice.	o21	14
Ke Ga, Cape, c., Viet.	F8	35
Kegaska, Que.	h9	72
Kegonsa, Lake, l., Wi., U.S.	F4	126
Kehl, W. Ger.	D2	15
Keho Lake, l., Alta.	E4	68
Kehsi Mansam, Burma	B2	35
Keighley, Eng., U.K.	D6	10
Keilor, Austl.	*G7	51
Keimoes, S. Afr.	C3	49
Keiser, Ar., U.S.	B5	81
Keitele, l., Fin.	F11	14
Keith, Austl.	H3	51
Keith, Scot., U.K.	B5	10
Keith, co., Ne., U.S.	C4	104
Keithley Creek, B.C.	C7	69
Keithsburg, Il., U.S.	B3	90
Keithville, La., U.S.	B2	95
Keitum, W. Ger.	D2	15
Keizer, Or., U.S.	C3	114
Kejimkujik Lake, l., N.S.	E4	71
Kejimkujik National Park, N.S.	E4	71
Kekaha, Hi., U.S.	B1	88
Kékes, mtn., Hung.	*B5	24
Kelafo, Eth.	D5	47
Kelan, China	E4	32
Kelang, Malay.	E2	34
Kelantan, state, Malay.	J4	35
Kelantan, stm., Malay.	J5	35
Keldron, S.D., U.S.	B4	118
Kelfield, Sask.	F1	75
Kelford, N.C., U.S.	A5	110
Kelheim, W. Ger.	E6	19
Kelibia, Tun.	F3	23
Kelkit, stm., Tur.	B11	40
Kell, Il., U.S.	E5	90
Kellé, Congo	B1	48
Kellenhusen, W. Ger.	D5	15
Keller, Tx., U.S.	n9	120
Keller, Va., U.S.	C7	123
Keller Lake, l., Sask.	A2	75
Kellerman, Al., U.S.	B2	78
Kellerton, Ia., U.S.	D3	92
Kellerville, Il., U.S.	D3	90
Kellett, Cape, c., N.W. Ter.	B7	66
Kellettville, Pa., U.S.	D3	115
Kelley, Ia., U.S.	C4	92
Kelleys Island, i., Oh., U.S.	A3	112
Kelleys Island, i., Oh., U.S.	A3	112
Kelliher, Sask.	F4	75
Kelliher, Mn., U.S.	C4	100
Kellmünz, W. Ger.	A6	20
Kellnersville, Wi., U.S.	D6	126
Kelloe, Man.	D1	70
Kellogg, Id., U.S.	B2	89
Kellogg, Ia., U.S.	C5	92
Kellogg, Mn., U.S.	F6	100
Kells see Ceanannus Mór, Ire.		
Kelly, La., U.S.	C3	95
Kelly, Wy., U.S.	C2	127
Kelly Air Force Base, mil., Tx., U.S.	k7	120
Kelly Brook Mountain, mtn., Me., U.S.	A3	96
Kelly Island, i., De., U.S.	D4	85
Kelly Lake, B.C.	B7	69
Kelly Lake, Mn., U.S.	C5	100
Kellyton, Al., U.S.	C3	78
Kellyville, N.H., U.S.	D2	106
Kellyville, Ok., U.S.	B5	113
Kellyville, Tx., U.S.	C5	120
Kelmä, Sov. Un.	A7	26
Kélo, Chad	D3	46
Kelowna, B.C.	E8	69
Kelsey, Alta.	C4	68
Kelsey Lake, l., Man.	A2	70
Kelseyville, Ca., U.S.	C2	82
Kelso, Sask.	H5	75
Kelso, Scot., U.K.	D5	10
Kelso, Mo., U.S.	D8	102
Kelso, Wa., U.S.	C3	124
Keltie, Mount, mtn., B.C.	I40	7
Keltonburg, Tn., U.S.	D8	119
Keluang, Malay.	E2	34
Kelvington, Sask.	E4	75
Kelwood, Man.	D2	70
Kem, stm., Sov. Un.	C15	8
Kem, Sov. Un.	D3	8
Ké Macina, Mali	D4	45
Kemano, B.C.	C4	69
Kembé, Cen. Afr. Rep.	D4	46
Kemerovo, Sov. Un.	E11	29
Kemi, Fin.	D11	14
Kemijärvi, Fin.	C12	14
Kemijoki, stm., Fin.	D11	14
Kemme, well, Libya	E3	43
Kemmerer, Wy., U.S.	E2	127
Kemnath, W. Ger.	D6	19
Kemnay, Man.	E1	70
Kemp, Ok., U.S.	D5	113
Kemp, Tx., U.S.	C4	120
Kemp, Lake, res., Tx., U.S.	C3	120

171

Name	Map Ref.	Page
Kemp Coast, Ant.	C18	7
Kempen, W. Ger.	C6	17
Kemper, S.C., U.S.	C9	117
Kemper, co., Ms., U.S.	C5	101
Kempner, In., U.S.	D4	120
Kemp Peninsula, pen., Ant.	B6	7
Kempsey, Austl.	F9	50
Kempshall Mountain, mtn., N.Y., U.S.	A6	109
Kempten [in Allgäu], W. Ger.	E5	18
Kempton, Il., U.S.	C5	90
Kempton, In., U.S.	D5	91
Kempton, N.D., U.S.	B8	111
Kemptville, Ont.	B9	73
Kenai, Ak., U.S.	C9	79
Kenai Fjords National Park, Ak., U.S.	D10	79
Kenai Mountains, mts., Ak., U.S.	h16	79
Kenai Peninsula, pen., Ak., U.S.	h16	79
Kenamu, stm., Newf.	B1	72
Kenansville, Fl., U.S.	E6	86
Kenansville, N.C., U.S.	C5	110
Kenaston, Sask.	F2	75
Kenbridge, Va., U.S.	D4	123
Ken Caryl, Co., U.S.	*B5	83
Kendal, Sask.	G4	75
Kendal, Eng., U.K.	C5	10
Kendall, Fl., U.S.	s13	86
Kendall, Ks., U.S.	E2	93
Kendall, N.Y., U.S.	B2	109
Kendall, Wi., U.S.	E3	126
Kendall, co., Il., U.S.	B5	90
Kendall, co., Tx., U.S.	E3	120
Kendall Green, Fl., U.S.	*F6	86
Kendall Park, N.J., U.S.	C3	107
Kendallville, In., U.S.	B7	91
Kendari, Indon.	F6	34
Kendrāparha, India	D8	36
Kendrick, Id., U.S.	C2	89
Kendrick, Ok., U.S.	B5	113
Kendujhargarh, India	G10	37
Kenduskeag, Me., U.S.	D4	96
Kenedy, Tx., U.S.	E4	120
Kenedy, co., Tx., U.S.	F4	120
Kenefic, Ok., U.S.	C5	113
Kenel, S.D., U.S.	B5	118
Kenema, S.L.	E2	45
Kenesaw, Ne., U.S.	D7	104
Kenge, Zaire	B2	48
Kēng Tung, Burma	D10	36
Kenhardt, S. Afr.	C3	49
Kéniéba, Mali	D2	45
Kenilworth, Il., U.S.	h9	90
Kenilworth, N.J., U.S.	*B4	107
Kenilworth, Ut., U.S.	D5	121
Kenitra, Mor.	C3	44
Kenly, N.C., U.S.	B4	110
Kenmare, Ire.	E2	10
Kenmare, N.D., U.S.	A3	111
Kenmare, River, Ire.	E1	10
Kenmore, N.Y., U.S.	C2	109
Kenmore, Wa., U.S.	*B3	124
Kenna, N.M., U.S.	D6	108
Kenna, W.V., U.S.	C3	125
Kennaday Peak, mtn., Wy., U.S.	E6	127
Kennan, Wi., U.S.	C3	126
Kennard, In., U.S.	E6	91
Kennard, Ne., U.S.	C9	104
Kennard, Tx., U.S.	D5	120
Kennebago Lake, l., Me., U.S.	C2	96
Kennebec, S.D., U.S.	D5	118
Kennebec, co., Me., U.S.	D3	96
Kennebec, stm., Me., U.S.	D3	96
Kennebunk, Me., U.S.	E2	96
Kennebunkport, Me., U.S.	E2	96
Kennedale, Tx., U.S.	n9	120
Kennedy, Sask.	G4	75
Kennedy, Al., U.S.	B2	78
Kennedy, Mn., U.S.	B2	100
Kennedy, N.Y., U.S.	C1	109
Kennedy, Mount, mtn., Yukon	D5	66
Kennedy Channel, strt., N.A.	k38	66
Kennedy Entrance, strt., Ak., U.S.	D9	79
Kennedy Heights, La., U.S.	*E5	95
Kennedy Lake, l., Sask.	D4	75
Kennedy Township, Pa., U.S.	*F1	115
Kennedyville, Md., U.S.	B6	97
Kenner, La., U.S.	E5	95
Kennesaw, Ga., U.S.	B2	87
Kennesaw Mountain, mtn., Ga., U.S.	C2	87
Kennesaw Mountain National Battlefield Park, Ga., U.S.	h7	87
Kennet, stm., Eng., U.K.	c6	12
Kennetcook, N.S.	D6	71
Kenneth, Ks., U.S.	m16	93
Kenneth, Mn., U.S.	G2	100
Kennett, Mo., U.S.	E7	102
Kennett Square, Pa., U.S.	G10	115
Kennewick, Wa., U.S.	C6	124
Kenney, Il., U.S.	C4	90
Kenney Dam, B.C.	C5	69
Kennisis Lake, l., Ont.	B6	73
Kennydale, Wa., U.S.	e11	124
Keno, Or., U.S.	E5	114
Kénogami, Que.	A6	74
Kénogami, Lac, l., Que.	A6	74
Kenora, Ont.	o16	73
Kenora, dept., Ont.	o17	73
Kenosha, Wi., U.S.	F6	126
Kenosha, co., Wi., U.S.	F5	126
Kenova, W.V., U.S.	C2	125
Ken Rock, Il., U.S.	*A4	90
Kensal, N.D., U.S.	B7	111
Kensett, Ar., U.S.	B4	81
Kensett, Ia., U.S.	A4	92
Kensico Reservoir, res., N.Y., U.S.	g13	109
Kensington, P.E.I.	C6	71
Kensington (part of London), Eng., U.K.	k12	10
Kensington, Ca., U.S.	*h8	82
Kensington, Ct., U.S.	C4	84
Kensington, Ks., U.S.	C4	93
Kensington, Mn., U.S.	E3	100
Kensington, N.H., U.S.	E5	106
Kensington, Oh., U.S.	B5	112
Kent, Al., U.S.	C4	78
Kent, Ct., U.S.	C2	84
Kent, In., U.S.	G6	91
Kent, Ia., U.S.	D3	92
Kent, Mn., U.S.	D2	100
Kent, Oh., U.S.	A4	112
Kent, Or., U.S.	C6	114
Kent, Tx., U.S.	o12	120
Kent, Wa., U.S.	B3	124
Kent, co., N.B.	C4	71
Kent, co., Eng., U.K.	C8	12
Kent, co., De., U.S.	D3	85
Kent, co., Md., U.S.	B5	97
Kent, co., Mi., U.S.	E5	99
Kent, co., R.I., U.S.	D2	116
Kent, co., Tx., U.S.	C2	120
Kent Bridge, Ont.	E2	73
Kent City, Mi., U.S.	E5	99
Kent Island, i., De., U.S.	D4	85
Kent Island, i., Md., U.S.	C5	97
Kent Junction, N.B.	C4	71
Kentland, In., U.S.	C3	91
Kenton, Man.	E1	70
Kenton, De., U.S.	D3	85
Kenton, Ky., U.S.	e9	94
Kenton, Mi., U.S.	B2	99
Kenton, Oh., U.S.	B2	112
Kenton, Ok., U.S.	e8	113
Kenton, Tn., U.S.	A2	119
Kenton, co., Ky., U.S.	B5	94
Kent Point, co., Md., U.S.	C5	97
Kentucky, state, U.S.	C4	94
Kentucky, stm., Ky., U.S.	B5	94
Kentucky, Middle Fork, stm., Ky., U.S.	C6	94
Kentucky, North Fork, stm., Ky., U.S.	C6	94
Kentucky, South Fork, stm., Ky., U.S.	C6	94
Kentucky Dam, Ky., U.S.	e9	94
Kentucky Lake, res., U.S.	C10	76
Kentucky Ridge, mtn., Ky., U.S.	D6	94
Kentville, N.S.	D5	71
Kentwood, La., U.S.	D5	95
Kentwood, Mi., U.S.	F5	99
Kenvil, N.J., U.S.	B3	107
Kenvir, Ky., U.S.	D6	94
Kenwood, Oh., U.S.	*A4	112
Kenwood, Ok., U.S.	A7	113
Kenya, ctry., Afr.	A6	48
Kenya, Mount see Kirinyaga, mtn., Kenya	B6	48
Kenyon, Mn., U.S.	F6	100
Kenyon, R.I., U.S.	F2	116
Keo, Ar., U.S.	C3	81
Keokea, Hi., U.S.	C5	88
Keokuk, Ia., U.S.	D6	92
Keokuk, co., Ia., U.S.	C5	92
Keokuk Lock and Dam, U.S.	D6	92
Keoma, Alta.	D4	68
Keosauqua, Ia., U.S.	D6	92
Keota, Co., U.S.	A6	83
Keota, Ia., U.S.	C5	92
Keota, Ok., U.S.	B7	113
Keowee, Lake, res., S.C., U.S.	B2	117
Kepno, Pol.	C5	26
Keppel, Sask.	B5	75
Kepsut, Tur.	B5	25
Kerala, state, India	F6	36
Kerang, Austl.	G7	50
Keratsínion, Grc.	*D4	25
Kerby, Or., U.S.	E3	114
Kerch, Sov. Un.	E6	29
Kerchemya, Sov. Un.	C19	8
Kerch Strait, strt., Sov. Un.	I11	27
Kerema, Pap. N. Gui.	k12	50
Keremeos, B.C.	E8	69
Kerempe, Cape, c., Tur.	A9	40
Keren, Eth.	B4	47
Kerend, Iran	D3	39
Kerens, Tx., U.S.	C4	120
Kerguélen, Îles, is., F.S.A.T.	J1	2
Kerhonkson, N.Y., U.S.	D6	109
Kericho, Kenya	B6	48
Kerinci, mtn., Indon.	F2	34
Kerkebet, Eth.	B4	47
Kerkenna, Îles, is., Tun.	C7	44
Kerkhoven, Mn., U.S.	E3	100
Kerki, Sov. Un.	H22	8
Kérkira, Grc.	C2	40
Kérkira (Corfu), i., Grc.	C2	40
Kerkrade, Neth.	B7	16
Kermadec Islands, is., N.Z.	I11	6
Kermān, Iran	B5	38
Kermānshāh see Bakhtarān, Iran	B4	38
Kerme, Gulf of, b., Tur.	D6	25
Kermit, Tx., U.S.	D1	120
Kermit, W.V., U.S.	D2	125
Kermode, Mount, mtn., B.C.	C2	69
Kern, co., Ca., U.S.	E4	82
Kern, stm., Ca., U.S.	E4	82
Kernersville, N.C., U.S.	A2	110
Kernville, Ca., U.S.	E4	82
Kérouané, Gui.	G4	45
Kerpen, W. Ger.	C1	19
Kerr, co., Tx., U.S.	E3	120
Kerr, Lake, l., Fl., U.S.	C5	86
Kerrick, Mn., U.S.	D6	100
Kerrick, Tx., U.S.	A1	120
Kerrobert, Sask.	F1	75
Kerrville, Tx., U.S.	D3	120
Kerry, co., Ire.	E2	11
Kerry Head, c., Ire.	E2	11
Kersey, Co., U.S.	A6	83
Kersey, Pa., U.S.	D4	115
Kershaw, S.C., U.S.	B6	117
Kershaw, co., S.C., U.S.	C6	117
Kersley, B.C.	C6	69
Kerteminde, Den.	C4	15
Kerulen, stm., Asia	B7	31
Kerzaz, Alg.	D4	44
Kerzers, Switz.	C3	21
Keşan, Tur.	B6	40
Kesch, Piz, mtn., Switz.	C5	20
Kesennuma, Japan	G10	33
Kesh, N. Ire., U.K.	C4	11
Keshan, China	B10	31
Keshena, Wi., U.S.	D5	126
Keshendeh, Afg.	C13	39
Kesley, Ia., U.S.	B5	92
Kestenga, Sov. Un.	E14	14
Keswick, Ont.	C5	73
Keswick, Eng., U.K.	F5	13
Keswick, Ia., U.S.	C5	92
Keswick, Va., U.S.	B4	123
Keszthely, Hung.	B3	24
Keta, Ghana	G6	45
Ketapang, Indon.	F3	34
Ketchikan, Ak., U.S.	D13	79
Ketchum, Id., U.S.	F4	89
Ketchum, Ok., U.S.	A6	113
Kete Krachi, Ghana	E4	45
Ketmen Range, mts., Asia	E10	28
Ketona, Al., U.S.	f7	78
Kétou, Benin	E5	45
Ketrzyn, Pol.	A6	26
Kettering, Eng., U.K.	D6	10
Kettering, Md., U.S.	*C4	97
Kettering, Oh., U.S.	C1	112
Kettle, stm., N.A.	E8	69
Kettle, stm., Mn., U.S.	D6	100
Kettle Creek, stm., Pa., U.S.	D6	115
Kettle Creek Lake, res., Pa., U.S.	D6	115
Kettle Falls, Wa., U.S.	A7	124
Kettleman City, Ca., U.S.	E4	82
Kettle River, Mn., U.S.	D6	100
Kettwig, W. Ger.	B1	19
Kety, Pol.	D5	26
Ketzin, E. Ger.	A7	19
Keuka Lake, l., N.Y., U.S.	C3	109
Keuterville, Id., U.S.	C2	89
Kevil, Ky., U.S.	e9	94
Kevin, Mt., U.S.	B5	103
Kewanee, Il., U.S.	B4	90
Kewanee, Ms., U.S.	C5	101
Kewanee, Mo., U.S.	E8	102
Kewanna, In., U.S.	B5	91
Kewaskum, Wi., U.S.	E5	126
Kewaunee, Wi., U.S.	D6	126
Kewaunee, co., Wi., U.S.	D6	126
Keweenaw, co., Mi., U.S.	A2	99
Keweenaw Bay, Mi., U.S.	B2	99
Keweenaw Bay, b., Mi., U.S.	B2	99
Keweenaw Peninsula, pen., Mi., U.S.	A3	99
Keweenaw Point, c., Mi., U.S.	A3	99
Key, Lough, l., Ire.	C3	11
Keyapaha, S.D., U.S.	D5	118
Keya Paha, co., Ne., U.S.	B6	104
Keya Paha, stm., U.S.	A5	104
Key Biscayne, Fl., U.S.	*G6	86
Keyes, Man.	D2	70
Keyes, Ok., U.S.	e8	113
Keyesport, Il., U.S.	E4	90
Keyhole Reservoir, res., Wy., U.S.	B8	127
Key Junction, Ont.	B4	73
Key Largo, Fl., U.S.	G6	86
Keymar, Md., U.S.	A3	97
Keynsham, Eng., U.K.	C5	12
Keyport, N.J., U.S.	C4	107
Keysburg, Ky., U.S.	D2	94
Keyser, W.V., U.S.	B6	125
Keystone, Ia., U.S.	C5	92
Keystone, Ne., U.S.	C4	104
Keystone, S.D., U.S.	D2	118
Keystone, W.V., U.S.	D3	125
Keystone, Wy., U.S.	E6	127
Keystone Heights, Fl., U.S.	C4	86
Keystone Lake, res., Ok., U.S.	A5	113
Keystone Peak, mtn., Az., U.S.	F4	80
Keysville, Ga., U.S.	C4	87
Keysville, Va., U.S.	C4	123
Keytesville, Mo., U.S.	B5	102
Key West, Fl., U.S.	H5	86
Key West, Ia., U.S.	B7	92
Key West Naval Air Station, mil., Fl., U.S.	H5	86
Kezar Falls, Me., U.S.	E2	96
Kezar Lake, l., Me., U.S.	D2	96
Kezar Pond, l., Me., U.S.	D2	96
Kezhma, Sov. Un.	D13	29
Kežmarok, Czech.	D6	26
Khabab, Syria	A8	41
Khabarovsk, Sov. Un.	E16	29
Khabīs see Shahdād, Iran	F8	39
Khachmas, Sov. Un.	E3	8
Khaidhárion, Grc.	*C4	25
Khairpur, Pak.	C4	36
Khakhea, Bots.	B3	49
Khalándrion, Grc.	*C4	25
Khálki (Chalke), i., Grc.	g11	25
Khalkidhikí Penninsula, pen., Grc.	B4	25
Khalkís, Grc.	C4	40
Khalūf, Oman	C5	38
Khambhāliya, India	D4	36
Khambhāt, India	F4	37
Khambhāt, Gulf of, b., India	D5	36
Khāmgaon, India	D6	36
Khāmgaon, India	I8	37
Khammam, India	A4	36
Khānābād, Afg.	B4	38
Khānaqīn, Iraq	D6	36
Khānderi, i., India	D6	36
Khandwa, India	D6	36
Khaniá (Canea), Grc.	E4	25
Khaniá, Gulf of, b., Grc.	C5	36
Khānpur, Pak.	A7	28
Khanty-Mansiysk, Sov. Un.	D8	36
Khapalur, India	G12	39
Khārān, Pak.	E7	39
Kharānoq, Iran	B5	38
Kharg Island, i., Iran	G5	37
Khargon, India	C3	38
Khārijah, Al Wāḥāt al, well, Eg.	D6	29
Kharkov, Sov. Un.	G6	39
Kharmān, Kūh-e, mtn., Iran	E7	24
Kharmanli, Bul.	B13	27
Kharovsk, Sov. Un.	B3	47
Khartoum (Al Khartūm), Sud.	B3	47
Khartoum North (Al Khartūm Bahrī), Sud.	q21	27
Khartsyzsk, Sov. Un.	G18	4
Khasavyurt, Sov. Un.	B3	36
Khāsh, Afg.	G10	39
Khāsh, Iran	B3	36
Khāsh, stm., Afg.	C4	47
Khashm al Qirbah, Khazzān, res., Sud.	B14	40
Khashuri, Sov. Un.	C9	36
Khasi Hills, hills, India	E7	24
Khaskovo, Bul.	B13	29
Khatanga, Sov. Un.	B13	29
Khatanga, stm., Sov. Un.	A8	37
Khavast, Sov. Un.	C3	44
Khemisset, Mor.	B5	34
Khemmarat, Thai.	B6	44
Khenchla, Alg.	C3	44
Khenifra, Mor.	H9	27
Kherson, Sov. Un.	B12	29
Kheta, stm., Sov. Un.	E4	35
Khieo Peak, mtn., Thai.	D14	29
Khilok, Sov. Un.	n17	27
Khimki, Sov. Un.	C6	40
Khíos, Grc.	C6	40
Khíos (Chios), i., Grc.	B7	41
Khirbat al Ghazālah, Syria	B7	41
Khisfīn, Isr. Occ.	E8	28
Khiva, Sov. Un.	G7	27
Khmelnik, Sov. Un.	G6	27
Khmelnitsky, Sov. Un.	H6	35
Khoai, i., Viet.	D11	40
Khodzheyli, Sov. Un.	B4	36
Kholm, Afg.	D2	10
Kholm, Sov. Un.	E17	29
Kholmsk, Sov. Un.	E5	39
Khomeyn, Iran	E5	39
Khomeynīshahr, Iran	E5	39
Khon Kaen, Thai.	B2	34
Khóra Sfakíon, Grc.	F14	27
Khor, stm., Sov. Un.	B12	31
Khordha, India	G10	37
Khorinsk, Sov. Un.	A6	31
Khorog, Sov. Un.	F10	29
Khorramābād, Iran	E4	39
Khorramshahr, Iran	B4	38
Khotin, Sov. Un.	G6	27
Khouribga, Mor.	C3	44
Khowst, Afg.	B4	36
Khrisoúpolis, Grc.	B5	25
Khromtau, Sov. Un.	C8	28
Khu Khan, Thai.	E6	35
Khulna, Bngl.	A16	40
Khunjerab Pass, Asia	A4	37
Khunzakh, Sov. Un.	A16	40
Khurr, Wādī al, val., Asia	G14	40
Khushāb, Pak.	A3	37
Khust, Sov. Un.	G4	27
Khuzdār, Pak.	C4	36
Khvāf, Iran	B6	38
Khvor, Iran	E7	39
Khvormūj, Iran	G5	39
Khvoy, Iran	B4	38
Khwae Noi, stm., Thai.	E3	35
Khyber Pass, Asia	*G6	36
Kia, i., Fiji	H15	52
Kiamichi, stm., Ok., U.S.	C6	113
Kiamika, Que.	C2	74
Kiamika, stm., Que.	C2	74
Kiana, Ak., U.S.	B7	79
Kiangarow, Mount, mtn., Austl.	C8	51
Kiangsi see Jiangxi, prov., China	F8	31
Kiangsu see Jiangsu, prov., China	E9	31
Kiantajärvi, l., Fin.	E13	14
Kiaton, Grc.	C4	25
Kiawah Island, i., S.C., U.S.	F7	117
Kibangou, Congo	B1	48
Kibau, Tan.	C6	48
Kiberege, Tan.	C6	48
Kibombo, Zaire	B4	48
Kibondo, Tan.	B5	48
Kibwezi, Kenya	B6	48
Kičevo, Yugo.	C4	24
Kickamuit, stm., R.I., U.S.	D5	116
Kickapoo, stm., Wi., U.S.	E3	126
Kickapoo, Lake, res., Tx., U.S.	C3	120
Kickapoo Creek, stm., Il., U.S.	C4	90
Kickapoo Indian Reservation, Ks., U.S.	C8	93
Kicking Horse Pass, Can.	D2	68
Kidal, Mali	C5	45
Kidder, Mo., U.S.	B3	102
Kidder, S.D., U.S.	B8	118
Kidder, co., N.D., U.S.	C6	111
Kidderminster, Eng., U.K.	D5	10
Kidira, Sen.	D2	45
Kidnappers, Cape, c., N.Z.	M16	51
Kidron, Valley of, val., Isr. Occ.	m14	41
Kidsgrove, Eng., U.K.	A5	12
Kidugallo, Tan.	C6	48
Kidwelly, Wales, U.K.	C3	12
Kief, N.D., U.S.	B5	111
Kiefer, Ok., U.S.	B5	113
Kiel, W. Ger.	A5	18
Kiel, Wi., U.S.	E5	126
Kiel Bay, b., W. Ger.	A5	18
Kiel Canal, W. Ger.	A4	18
Kielce, Pol.	C6	26
Kiester, Mn., U.S.	G5	100
Kiev, Sov. Un.	D5	29
Kiev Reservoir, res., Sov. Un.	F8	27
Kiffa, Maur.	C2	45
Kifisiá, Grc.	g11	25
Kifisós (Cephisus), stm., Grc.	g9	25
Kifisós, stm., Grc.	g11	25
Kifrī, Iraq	E15	40
Kigali, Rw.	B5	48
Kiği, Tur.	C13	40
Kigoma, Tan.	B4	48
Kigoma, prov., Tan.	B5	48
Kihei, Hi., U.S.	C5	88
Kiholo Bay, b., Hi., U.S.	D5	88
Kii Strait, strt., Japan	J7	33
Kikinda, Yugo.	C5	24
Kikongo, Zaire	B2	48
Kikori, Pap. N. Gui.	k11	50
Kikori, stm., Pap. N. Gui.	k11	50
Kikwit, Zaire	C2	48
Kila, Mt., U.S.	B2	103
Kilauea, Hi., U.S.	A2	88
Kilauea Crater, crat., Hi., U.S.	D6	88
Kilauea Point, c., Hi., U.S.	A2	88
Kilbaha, Ire.	E2	11
Kilbeggan, Ire.	D4	11
Kilbourne, Il., U.S.	C4	90
Kilbourne, La., U.S.	B4	95
Kilbourne, Oh., U.S.	B3	112
Kilbrannan Sound, strt., Scot., U.K.	E3	13
Kilburn, N.B.	C2	71
Kilcar, Ire.	C3	11
Kilchoan, Scot., U.K.	D3	13
Kilchreest, Ire.	D3	11
Kilchu, N. Kor.	F4	33
Kilcock, Ire.	D5	11
Kilconnell, Ire.	D3	11
Kilcoole, Ire.	D5	11
Kilcormac (Frankford), Ire.	D4	11
Kilcullen, Ire.	D5	11
Kildare (Saint-Ambroise-de-Kildare), Que.	C4	74
Kildare, Ire.	D5	11
Kildare, Ok., U.S.	A4	113
Kildare, co., Ire.	D5	11
Kildare, Cape, c., P.E.I.	C6	71
Kildorrery, Ire.	E3	11
Kilembe, Zaire	C3	48
Kilfenora, Ire.	E2	11
Kilfinnane, Ire.	E3	11
Kilgore, N.C., U.S.	f2	110
Kilgore, Ne., U.S.	B5	104
Kilgore, Tx., U.S.	C5	120
Kilifi, Kenya	B6	48
Kilimanjaro, prov., Tan.	B6	48
Kilimanjaro, mtn., Tan.	B6	48
Kilindoni, Tan.	C6	48
Kilingi-Nõmme, Sov. Un.	C14	27
Kilis, Tur.	F2	11
Kiliya, Sov. Un.	I7	27
Kilkeel, N. Ire., U.K.	C5	11
Kilkenny, Ire.	D3	10
Kilkenny, Mn., U.S.	F5	100
Kilkenny, co., Ire.	E4	11
Kilkerrin, Ire.	D3	11
Kilkieran, Ire.	D2	11
Kilkieran Bay, b., Ire.	D2	11
Kilkis, Grc.	B4	25
Killadoon, Ire.	D2	11
Killadysert, Ire.	E2	11
Killala, Ire.	C2	10
Killala Bay, b., Ire.	C2	11
Killaloe, Ire.	E3	11
Killaloe Station, Ont.	B7	73
Killaly, Sask.	G4	75
Killam, Alta.	C5	68
Killarney, Man.	E2	70
Killarney, Ire.	D2	10
Killarney Provincial Park, Ont.	A3	73
Killashandra, Ire.	C4	11
Killavally, Ire.	D2	11
Killbuck, Oh., U.S.	B4	112
Killdeer, Sask.	H2	75
Killdeer, N.D., U.S.	B3	111
Killdeer Mountains, mts., N.D., U.S.	B3	111
Killduff, Ia., U.S.	C5	92
Killeen, Tx., U.S.	D4	120
Killen, Al., U.S.	A2	78
Killenaule, Ire.	E4	11
Killeter, N. Ire., U.K.	C3	11
Killian, La., U.S.	h10	95
Killiecrankie, Pass of, Scot., U.K.	D5	13
Killik, stm., Ak., U.S.	B9	79
Killillan, Scot., U.K.	B4	10
Killin, Scot., U.K.	D3	11
Killingly Center, Ct., U.S.	*B8	84
Killington Peak, mtn., Vt., U.S.	D3	122
Killingworth, Ct., U.S.	D5	84
Killini, Grc.	D3	25
Killiniq Island, i., Can.	f8	72
Killona, La., U.S.	h11	95
Killorglin, Ire.	E2	11
Killucan, Ire.	D4	11
Killybegs, Ire.	C3	11
Killyleagh, N. Ire., U.K.	C6	11
Kilmacthomas, Ire.	E4	11
Kilmaine, Ire.	D2	11
Kilmallock, Ire.	E3	11
Kilmanagh, Ire.	E7	11
Kilmarnock, Scot., U.K.	C4	10
Kilmarnock, Va., U.S.	C6	123
Kilmelford, Scot., U.K.	D3	13
Kilmichael, Ms., U.S.	B4	101
Kilmore, Austl.	G6	50
Kilosa, Tan.	C6	48
Kilrea, N. Ire., U.K.	C5	11
Kilronan, Ire.	D2	10
Kilrush, Ire.	E2	10
Kilsyth, Scot., U.K.	E4	13
Kilteen, Ire.	D5	11
Kiltimagh, Ire.	D3	11
Kiltoom, Ire.	D3	11
Kilwa, Zaire	C4	48
Kilwa Kisiwani, Tan.	C6	48
Kilwa Kivinje, Tan.	C6	48
Kim, Co., U.S.	D7	83
Kimamba, Tan.	C6	48
Kimball, Mn., U.S.	E4	100
Kimball, S.D., U.S.	D7	118
Kimball, W.V., U.S.	D3	125
Kimball, co., Ne., U.S.	C2	104
Kimball, Mount, mtn., Ak., U.S.	C11	79
Kimballton, Ia., U.S.	C2	92
Kimberley, B.C.	E9	69
Kimberley, S. Afr.	G5	100
Kimberley Plateau, plat., Austl.	C4	50
Kimberlin Heights, Tn., U.S.	n14	119
Kimberly, Al., U.S.	B3	78
Kimberly, Id., U.S.	G4	89
Kimberly, Or., U.S.	C7	114
Kimberly, W.V., U.S.	m13	125
Kimberly, Wi., U.S.	h9	126
Kimble, co., Tx., U.S.	D3	120
Kimbolton, Oh., U.S.	B4	112
Kimbrough, Al., U.S.	D2	78
Kimbrough, N.M., U.S.	E6	108
Kimchaek (Sŏngjin), N. Kor.	C10	31
Kimchŏn, S. Kor.	H4	33
Kimesville, N.C., U.S.	B3	110
Kimi, Grc.	C5	25
Kimiwan Lake, l., Alta.	B2	68
Kimmell, In., U.S.	B6	91
Kimmins, Tn., U.S.	B4	119
Kimmswick, Mo., U.S.	g13	102
Kimovsk, Sov. Un.	C11	27
Kimry, Sov. Un.	B11	27
Kin, Japan	O5	52
Kinabalu, Mount, mtn., Malay.	D6	34
Kinard, Fl., U.S.	B1	86
Kinards, S.C., U.S.	C4	117
Kinbasket Lake, res., B.C.	D8	69
Kinbrace, Scot., U.K.	B5	13
Kinbrae, Mn., U.S.	G3	100
Kincaid, Sask.	H2	75
Kincaid, Il., U.S.	D4	90
Kincaid, Ks., U.S.	D8	93
Kincaid, W.V., U.S.	m13	125
Kincaid, Lake, res., Il., U.S.	D4	90
Kincardine, Ont.	C3	73
Kinchafoonee Creek, stm., Ga., U.S.	E2	87
Kincheloe Air Force Base, mil., Mi., U.S.	B6	99
Kinde, Mi., U.S.	E8	99
Kinder, La., U.S.	D3	95
Kinderhook, Il., U.S.	D2	90
Kinderhook, N.Y., U.S.	C7	109
Kinder Scout, mtn., Eng., U.K.	A6	12
Kindersley, Sask.	F1	75
Kindia, Gui.	F2	45
Kindred, N.D., U.S.	C9	111
Kineo, Mount, mtn., Me., U.S.	C3	96
Kineshma, Sov. Un.	C14	27
King, N.C., U.S.	A2	110
King, Wi., U.S.	D4	126
King, co., Tx., U.S.	C2	120
King, co., Wa., U.S.	B3	124
King, i., Austl.	G7	50
King and Queen, co., Va., U.S.	C6	123
King and Queen Court House, Va., U.S.	C6	123
King Christian IX Land, reg., Grnld.	C18	128
King Christian X Land, reg., Grnld.	B17	128
King City, Ont.	k14	73
King City, Ca., U.S.	D3	82
King City, Mo., U.S.	A3	102
King Cove, Ak., U.S.	E7	79
King David Hotel, Isr.	m14	41
King Ferry, N.Y., U.S.	C4	109
Kingfield, Me., U.S.	D2	96
Kingfisher, Ok., U.S.	B4	113
Kingfisher, co., Ok., U.S.	B3	113
King Frederik VI Coast, Grnld.	C19	128
King Frederik VIII Land, reg., Grnld.	B17	128
King George, Va., U.S.	B5	123
King George, co., Va., U.S.	B5	123
King George, Mount, mtn.	D10	69
King George Island, i., B.A.T.	C7	7
King George Sound, strt., Austl.	G2	50
King Hill, Id., U.S.	F3	89
King Island, i., B.C.	C4	69
King Lake, Ne., U.S.	*C9	104
King Lear Peak, mtn., Nv., U.S.	B3	105
King Leopold Ranges, mts., Austl.	C4	50
Kingman, Alta.	C4	68
Kingman, Az., U.S.	B1	80
Kingman, In., U.S.	E3	91
Kingman, Ks., U.S.	E5	93
Kingman, Me., U.S.	C4	96
Kingman, co., Ks., U.S.	E5	93
King Mountain, mtn., Ok., U.S.	C2	113
King Mountain, mtn., Or., U.S.	D3	114
King Mountain, mtn., Or., U.S.	F11	115
King of Prussia, Pa., U.S.	F11	115
King Peak, mtn., Ca., U.S.	B1	82
Kings, Il., U.S.	A4	90
Kings, Ms., U.S.	C3	101
Kings, co., N.B.	D4	71
Kings, co., N.S.	E5	71
Kings, co., P.E.I.	C7	71
Kings, co., Ca., U.S.	D4	82
Kings, co., N.Y., U.S.	E7	109
Kings, stm., Ar., U.S.	A2	81
Kings, stm., Ca., U.S.	D4	82
Kings, stm., Nv., U.S.	B3	105
King Salmon, Ak., U.S.	D8	79
Kingsbridge, Eng., U.K.	A4	92
Kingsburg, Ca., U.S.	D4	82
Kingsbury, In., U.S.	A4	91
Kingsbury, Tx., U.S.	h8	120
Kingsbury, co., S.D., U.S.	C8	118
Kings Canyon National Park, Ca., U.S.	D4	82
Kingsclear, N.B.	D3	71
Kings Corner, Ct., U.S.	B5	84
Kingscote, Austl.	G2	50
Kings Creek, S.C., U.S.	A5	117
Kingsdown, Ks., U.S.	E4	93
Kingsey-Falls, Que.	D5	74
Kingsford, Mi., U.S.	C2	99
Kingsgate, B.C.	E9	69
Kingsgate, Wa., U.S.	*B3	124
Kings Grant, N.C., U.S.	*C5	110
Kingsland, Ar., U.S.	D3	81
Kingsland, Ga., U.S.	F5	87
Kingsland, Tx., U.S.	D3	120
Kingsley, Ia., U.S.	B2	92
Kingsley, Mi., U.S.	D5	99
Kingsley Dam, Ne., U.S.	C4	104
King's Lynn, Eng., U.K.	D7	10
Kingsmere Lake, l., Sask.	C2	75
Kings Mill, Tx., U.S.	B2	120
Kings Mills, Oh., U.S.	C1	112
Kings Mountain, Ky., U.S.	C5	94
Kings Mountain, N.C., U.S.	B1	110
King Sound, strt., Austl.	*C3	50
Kings Park, N.Y., U.S.	*E7	109
Kings Park, Va., U.S.	*B5	123
Kings Park West, Va., U.S.	B5	123
Kings Peak, mtn., Ut., U.S.	C5	121
Kings Point, Newf.	D3	72
Kings Point, Fl., U.S.	*F6	86
Kings Point, N.Y., U.S.	*E7	109
Kingsport, Tn., U.S.	C11	119
Kingston, N.S.	E5	71
Kingston, Ont.	C8	73
Kingston, Jam.	F5	64
Kingston, N.Z.	P12	51
Kingston, Ar., U.S.	A2	81
Kingston, Ga., U.S.	B2	87
Kingston, Id., U.S.	B2	89
Kingston, Il., U.S.	A5	90
Kingston, Ma., U.S.	C6	97
Kingston, Mi., U.S.	E7	99
Kingston, Mo., U.S.	B3	102
Kingston, N.H., U.S.	E4	106
Kingston, N.Y., U.S.	D6	109
Kingston, Oh., U.S.	C3	112
Kingston, Ok., U.S.	D5	113
Kingston, Pa., U.S.	D10	115
Kingston, R.I., U.S.	F3	116
Kingston, Tn., U.S.	D9	119
Kingston, Ut., U.S.	E3	121
Kingston, W.V., U.S.	D3	125
Kingston, Wi., U.S.	E4	126
Kingston Southeast, Austl.	G2	50
Kingston Springs, Tn., U.S.	A4	119
Kingston upon Hull, Eng., U.K.	D6	10
Kingston upon Thames (part of London), Eng., U.K.	m12	10
Kingstown, St. Vin.	J14	65
Kingstown, Md., U.S.	B5	97
Kingstree, S.C., U.S.	D8	117
Kings Valley, Or., U.S.	C3	114
Kingsville, Ont.	E2	73
Kingsville, Md., U.S.	B5	97
Kingsville, Mo., U.S.	C3	102
Kingsville, Tx., U.S.	F4	120
Kingsville Naval Air Station, mil., Tx., U.S.	F4	120
Kingwood, Ky., U.S.	C5	94
Kingwood, W.V., U.S.	B5	125
Kington, Eng., U.K.	B4	12
Kingurutik Lake, l., Newf.	g9	72
Kingussie, Scot., U.K.	B4	10
King William, Va., U.S.	C5	123
King William, co., Va., U.S.	C5	123
King William Island, i., N.W. Ter.	C13	66
King William's Town, S. Afr.	H5	49
Kingwood, Tx., U.S.	*E5	120
Kinistino, Sask.	E3	75
Kinkala, Congo	B1	48
Kinkora, P.E.I.	C6	71
Kinley, Sask.	E2	75
Kin-Li-Chee, Az., U.S.	B6	80

Name	Map Ref.	Page

Kinloch, Mo., U.S. f13 102
Kinlochewe, Scot., U.K. C3 13
Kinloch Hourn, Scot., U.K. .. C3 13
Kinmount, Ont. C6 73
Kinmundy, Il., U.S. E5 90
Kinnairds Head, c., Scot., U.K. B6 13
Kinnelon, N.J., U.S. B4 107
Kinnear, Wy., U.S. C4 127
Kinneret, Yam (Sea of Galilee), l., Isr. B7 41
Kinney, co., Tx., U.S. E2 120
Kinomoto, Japan n15 33
Kinosaki, Japan I7 33
Kinross, P.E.I. C7 71
Kinross, Scot., U.K. D5 13
Kinsale, Ire. E2 10
Kinsale, Va., U.S. B6 123
Kinsella, Alta. C5 68
Kinsey, Al., U.S. D4 78
Kinsey, Mt., U.S. D11 103
Kinshasa (Léopoldville), Zaire B2 48
Kinsley, Ks., U.S. E4 93
Kinsman, Oh., U.S. A5 112
Kinston, Al., U.S. D3 78
Kinston, N.C., U.S. B5 110
Kinta, Ok., U.S. B6 113
Kintampo, Ghana E4 45
Kintinku, Tan. C6 48
Kintore, Scot., U.K. C6 13
Kintyre, N.D., U.S. C6 111
Kintyre, Mull of, c., Scot., U.K. E3 13
Kinuso, Alta. B3 68
Kinvarra, Ire. D3 11
Kinyangiri, Tan. B5 48
Kinyeti, mtn., Sud. E3 47
Kinzig, stm., W. Ger. C4 19
Kinzig, stm., W. Ger. E2 19
Kinzua, Or., U.S. C6 114
Kioa, i., Fiji H15 52
Kiona, Wa., U.S. C6 124
Kioshkokwi Lake, l., Ont. A6 73
Kiosk, Ont. A6 73
Kiowa, Co., U.S. B6 83
Kiowa, Ks., U.S. E5 93
Kiowa, co., Co., U.S. C6 113
Kiowa, co., Ks., U.S. E4 93
Kiowa, co., Ok., U.S. C2 113
Kiowa Creek, stm., Co., U.S. . B6 83
Kiowa Creek, stm., Ok., U.S. . A1 113
Kipahigan Lake, l., Can. D5 70
Kipahulu, Hi., U.S. *C5 88
Kipapa Stream, stm., Hi., U.S. g9 88
Kiparissia, Grc. D3 25
Kiparissia, Gulf of, b., Grc. .. D3 25
Kipembawe, Tan. C5 48
Kipili, Tan. C5 48
Kipini, Kenya B7 48
Kipling, Sask. G4 75
Kipling, Mi., U.S. C3 99
Kipnuk, Ak., U.S. C7 79
Kipp, Alta. E4 68
Kipp, Ks., U.S. D6 93
Kipton, Oh., U.S. A3 112
Kipushi, Zaire D4 48
Kirby, Ar., U.S. C2 81
Kirby, Tx., U.S. *E3 120
Kirby, Wy., U.S. C4 127
Kirbyville, Tx., U.S. D6 120
Kirchberg, Switz. *B7 21
Kirchdorf, E. Ger. E5 15
Kirchhain, W. Ger. C3 19
Kirchheimbolanden, W. Ger. . D2 19
Kirchheim [unter Teck], W. Ger. E4 19
Kirchhunden, W. Ger. B3 19
Kirdäsah, Eg. D3 41
Kirensk, Sov. Un. D13 29
Kirghiz S.S.R., state, Sov. Un. E10 29
Kirgiz Range, mts., Sov. Un. .. E8 28
Kiri, Zaire B2 48
Kiribati, ctry., Oc. G11 6
Kınkhan, Tur. *D11 40
Kınkkale, Tur. C9 40
Kirin see Jilin, prov., China .. C10 31
Kirinian, i., Marsh Is. S18 52
Kirinyaga (Mount Kenya), mtn., Kenya B6 48
Kiritimati Island (Christmas Island), i., Kir. F12 6
Kirk, Co., U.S. B8 83
Kirkby Lonsdale, Eng., U.K. .. F6 13
Kirkby Stephen, Eng., U.K. .. F6 13
Kirkcaldy, Alta. D4 68
Kirkcaldy, Scot., U.K. B5 10
Kirkcolm, Scot., U.K. F3 13
Kirkcudbright, Scot., U.K. ... C5 10
Kirkcudbright Bay, b., Scot., U.K. F4 13
Kirkenes, Nor. C13 14
Kirkersville, Oh., U.S. C3 112
Kirkfield, Ont. C5 73
Kirkintilloch, Scot., U.K. B5 13
Kirkland, Al., U.S. D2 78
Kirkland, Az., U.S. C3 80
Kirkland, Ga., U.S. E4 87
Kirkland, Il., U.S. A5 90
Kirkland, Tn., U.S. B5 119
Kirkland, Tx., U.S. B3 120
Kirkland, Wa., U.S. B3 124
Kirkland Lake, Ont. o19 73
Kirklareli, Tur. B6 40
Kirklin, In., U.S. D5 91
Kirkman, Ia., U.S. C2 92
Kirkmansville, Ky., U.S. D2 94
Kirkoswald, Eng., U.K. F6 13
Kirkpatrick, Mount, mtn., Ant. A29 7
Kirkpatrick Lake, l., Alta. D5 68
Kirksey, Ky., U.S. f9 94
Kirksey, S.C., U.S. C3 117
Kirksville, Ky., U.S. C5 94
Kirksville, Mo., U.S. A5 102
Kirkton, Ont. D3 73
Kirkton of Glenisla, Scot., U.K. D5 13
Kirkūk, Iraq B4 38
Kirkville, In., U.S. C5 92
Kirkwall, Scot., U.K. A5 10
Kirkwood, S. Afr. D4 49
Kirkwood, De., U.S. B3 85
Kirkwood, Ga., U.S. C3 97
Kirkwood, Mo., U.S. f13 102
Kirn, W. Ger. D3 18
Kiron, Ia., U.S. B2 92
Kirov, Sov. Un. D7 29
Kirovabad, Sov. Un. E7 29
Kirovakan, Sov. Un. B15 40
Kirov Bay, b., Sov. Un. B4 39
Kirovograd, Sov. Un. G9 27
Kirovsk, Sov. Un. C6 29
Kirovsk, Sov. Un. D5 68
Kirriemuir, Alta. D5 68
Kirriemuir, Scot., U.K. E5 13
Kirsanov, Sov. Un. E14 27
Kirşehir, Tur. C10 40

Kırthar Range, mts., Pak. C4 36
Kirtland, N.M., U.S. A1 108
Kirtland, Oh., U.S. *C1 112
Kirtland Air Force Base, mil., N.M., U.S. k7 108
Kiruna, Swe. D9 14
Kirundu, Zaire B4 48
Kirwin, Ks., U.S. C4 93
Kirwin Reservoir, res., Ks., U.S. C4 93
Kiryū, Japan H9 33
Kisaki, Tan. C6 48
Kisanga, Zaire C4 48
Kisangani (Stanleyville), Zaire A4 48
Kisarazu, Japan n18 33
Kisatchie, La., U.S. C2 95
Kisbey, Sask. H4 75
Kiselevsk, Sov. Un. C11 28
Kisengwa, Zaire C4 48
Kish, i., Iran H6 39
Kishanganj, India D11 37
Kishangarh, India C5 36
Kishi, Nig. E5 45
Kishinev, Sov. Un. E6 29
Kishiwada, Japan o14 33
Kishorganj, Bngl. D9 36
Kishwaukee, stm., Il., U.S. ... A5 90
Kisii, Kenya B5 48
Kisiju, Tan. C6 48
Kisiwa Creek, stm., Ks., U.S. . g11 93
Kisiwani, Tan. B6 48
Kiska Island, i., Ak., U.S. ... E3 79
Kiskatinaw, stm., B.C. B7 69
Kiskittogisu Lake, l., Man. ... B2 70
Kiskitto Lake, l., Man. B2 70
Kiskőrös, Hung. B4 24
Kiskundorozsma (part of Szeged), Hung. B5 24
Kiskunfélegyháza, Hung. B4 24
Kiskunhalas, Hung. B4 24
Kiskunmajsa, Hung. B4 24
Kislovodsk, Sov. Un. E2 28
Kismaayo, Som. F5 47
Kismet, Ks., U.S. E3 93
Kiso-sammyaku, mts., Japan . n16 33
Kissamos, Grc. E4 25
Kissee Mills, Mo., U.S. E4 102
Kisseynew Lake, l., Can. B1 70
Kissidougou, Gui. E2 45
Kissimmee, Fl., U.S. D5 86
Kissimmee, stm., Fl., U.S. ... E5 86
Kissimmee, Lake, l., Fl., U.S. . E5 86
Kissimmee Park, Fl., U.S. ... D5 86
Kissing, Man. B1 70
Kississing, stm., Man. B1 70
Kississing Lake, l., Man. B1 70
Kisslegg, W. Ger. A8 21
Kistefjellet, mtn., Nor. C8 14
Kistigan Lake, l., Man. B5 70
Kistler, Wy., U.S. D3 125
Kistrand, Nor. B11 14
Kisújszállás, Hung. B5 24
Kisumu, Kenya A5 48
Kisvárda, Hung. A6 24
Kita, Mali D3 45
Kita, Mount, mtn., Japan I9 33
Kita-iwo, i., Japan E8 6
Kitakyūshū, Japan E11 31
Kitale, Kenya A5 48
Kitami, Japan E11 33
Kitangari, Tan. D6 48
Kit Carson, Co., U.S. C8 83
Kit Carson, co., Co., U.S. ... C8 83
Kitchell, In., U.S. E8 91
Kitchener, Ont. D4 73
Kite, Ga., U.S. D4 87
Kitgum, Ug. A5 48
Kíthira, Grc. D4 25
Kíthira (Cythera), i., Grc. ... D4 25
Kíthnos, i., Grc. D5 40
Kitimat, B.C. B3 69
Kitridge Point, c., Barb. K21 65
Kitsap, co., Wa., U.S. B3 124
Kitscoty, Alta. C5 68
Kittanning, Pa., U.S. E2 115
Kittatinny Mountain, mtn., U.S. B2 107
Kittery, Me., U.S. E2 96
Kittery Point, Me., U.S. E2 96
Kittilä, Fin. D11 14
Kittitas, Wa., U.S. C5 124
Kittitas, co., Wa., U.S. B4 124
Kittitas Valley, val., Wa., U.S. . B5 124
Kittrell, N.C., U.S. A4 110
Kitts, Ky., U.S. D6 94
Kitts Hummock, De., U.S. ... D4 85
Kittson, co., Mn., U.S. B2 100
Kitty Hawk, N.C., U.S. A7 110
Kitty Hawk Bay, b., N.C., U.S. A7 110
Kitui, Kenya B6 48
Kitwanga, B.C. B3 69
Kitwe, Zam. D4 48
Kitzbühel, Aus. E6 18
Kitzingen, W. Ger. D5 18
Kitzmiller, Md., U.S. m12 97
Kivalina, Ak., U.S. B7 79
Kivu, hist. reg., Zaire B4 48
Kivu, Lac, l., Afr. B4 48
Kiya, stm., Sov. Un. D26 8
Kiyan, Japan O5 52
Kiyan Point, c., Japan O5 52
Kiyiköy, Tur. B7 40
Kiyiu Lake, l., Sask. F1 75
Kizel, Sov. Un. B5 29
Kizıl, stm., Tur. B10 40
Kizlyar, Sov. Un. E3 28
Kizyl-Arvat, Sov. Un. F8 29
Kjaekan, Nor. C10 14
Kjellerup, Den. B3 15
Kjelvik, Nor. B12 14
Kladno, Czech. C3 26
Klagenfurt, Aus. E7 18
Klaipeda (Memel), Sov. Un. . D3 27
Klamath, co., Or., U.S. E5 114
Klamath, stm., U.S. B2 82
Klamath Falls, Or., U.S. E5 114
Klamath Glen, Ca., U.S. B2 82
Klamath Mountains, mts., U.S. E2 114
Klarabküll, W. Ger. D2 15
Klarälven, stm., Eur. D2 26
Klatovy, Czech. D2 26
Klawer, S. Afr. D2 49
Klawock, Ak., U.S. D13 79
Kleena Kleene, B.C. D5 69
Klein, Tx., U.S. r14 120
Kleinburg, Ont. k14 73
Klemme, Ia., U.S. A4 92
Klerksdorp, S. Afr. C4 49
Kletnya, Sov. Un. E9 27
Kletsk, Sov. Un. E6 27

Kleve (Cleves), W. Ger. C3 18
Klibreck, Ben, mtn., Scot., U.K. B4 13
Klíčany, Czech. n17 26
Klickitat, Wa., U.S. D4 124
Klickitat, co., Wa., U.S. D4 124
Klickitat, stm., Wa., U.S. C4 124
Klimovsk, Sov. Un. n17 27
Klin, Sov. Un. C11 27
Klinaklini, stm., B.C. D5 69
Kline, S.C., U.S. E5 117
Klingenthal, E. Ger. C7 19
Klintsy, Sov. Un. E9 27
Klippan, Swe. B7 15
Klitmøller, Den. A2 15
Kljuc̆, Yugo. C3 24
Kłobuck, Pol. C5 26
Klock, Ont. A6 73
Kłodnica, stm., Pol. g9 26
Kłodzko, Pol. C4 26
Klondike, In., U.S. D4 91
Klondike, Tx., U.S. C5 120
Klondike Gold Rush National Historical Park, Ak., U.S. . k22 79
Klondike Region, hist. reg., Yukon D5 66
Klondyke, Az., U.S. E5 80
Klos, Alb. B3 25
Klostermansfeld, E. Ger. B6 19
Klosterneuburg, Aus. D8 18
Klosters [-Serneus], Switz. .. C8 21
Kloten, Switz. B6 21
Kloten, N.D., U.S. B7 111
Klötze, E. Ger. F5 15
Klötzsche, E. Ger. B8 19
Kluane Lake, l., Yukon D5 66
Kluane National Park, Yukon . D5 66
Kluczbork, Pol. C5 26
Klukwan, Ak., U.S. k22 79
Klutina Lake, l., Ak., U.S. ... g19 79
Klütz, E. Ger. E5 15
Klyazma, stm., Sov. Un. C13 27
Klyuchevskaya Sopka, vol., Sov. Un. D18 29
Knapp, Wi., U.S. D1 126
Knapp Creek, stm., W.V., U.S. C5 125
Knaresborough, Eng., U.K. .. F7 13
Knee Lake, l., Man. B4 70
Knee Lake, l., Sask. B2 75
Knesebeck, W. Ger. F4 15
Knesset, Isr. m14 41
Knezha, Bul. D7 24
Knickerbocker, Tx., U.S. D2 120
Knierim, Ia., U.S. B3 92
Knife, stm., N.D., U.S. B3 111
Knife River, Mn., U.S. D7 100
Knifley, Ky., U.S. C4 94
Knight Inlet, b., B.C. D5 69
Knight Island, i., Ak., U.S. .. g18 79
Knighton, Wales, U.K. B4 12
Knights Landing, Ca., U.S. .. C3 82
Knights Town, Ire. F1 11
Knightstown, In., U.S. E6 91
Knightsville, In., U.S. E3 91
Knightville Reservoir, res., Ma., U.S. B2 98
Knin, Yugo. C3 24
Knippa, Tx., U.S. E3 120
Knislinge, Swe. B8 15
Knittelfeld, Aus. E7 18
Knob Creek, stm., Ky., U.S. . g11 94
Knobel, Ar., U.S. A5 81
Knob Lick, Ky., U.S. C4 94
Knob Lick, Mo., U.S. D7 102
Knobly Mountain, mtn., W.V., U.S. B5 125
Knob Noster, Mo., U.S. C4 102
Knobsville, Pa., U.S. F6 115
Knock, Ire. C3 11
Knockadoon Head, c., Ire. .. F4 11
Knockalongy, mtn., Ire. B3 11
Knockanefune, hill, Ire. E2 11
Knockboy, mtn., Ire. F2 11
Knocklong, Ire. E3 11
Knockmealdown Mountains, mts., Ire. D2 10
Knokke [-Heist], Bel. C3 17
Knollwood, Ct., U.S. D6 84
Knollwood, W.V., U.S. m12 125
Knops Pond, l., Ma., U.S. ... f9 98
Knott, Tx., U.S. C2 120
Knott, co., Ky., U.S. C6 94
Knotts Island, N.C., U.S. ... A7 110
Knottsville, Ky., U.S. C3 94
Knowles, Ok., U.S. A1 113
Knowlton, Wi., U.S. D4 126
Knox, Austl. *G8 50
Knox, In., U.S. B4 91
Knox, N.D., U.S. A6 111
Knox, Pa., U.S. D2 115
Knox, co., Il., U.S. B3 90
Knox, co., In., U.S. G3 91
Knox, co., Ky., U.S. D6 94
Knox, co., Me., U.S. D4 96
Knox, co., Mo., U.S. A5 102
Knox, co., Ne., U.S. B8 104
Knox, co., Oh., U.S. B3 112
Knox, co., Tn., U.S. C10 119
Knox, co., Tx., U.S. C3 120
Knox, Cape, c., B.C. B1 69
Knox City, Mo., U.S. A5 102
Knox City, Tx., U.S. C3 120
Knox Coast, Ant. C23 7
Knox Dale, Pa., U.S. D3 115
Knoxville, Al., U.S. C2 78
Knoxville, Ar., U.S. B2 81
Knoxville, Ga., U.S. D3 87
Knoxville, Il., U.S. C3 90
Knoxville, Ia., U.S. C4 92
Knoxville, Md., U.S. B2 97
Knoxville, Ms., U.S. D2 101
Knoxville, Pa., U.S. C7 115
Knoxville, Tn., U.S. D10 119
Knurów, Pol. g9 26
Knysna, S. Afr. D3 49
Knyszyn, Pol. B6 26
Ko, Mount, mtn., Sov. Un. .. C8 33
Kobayashi, Japan K5 33
Kōbe, Japan E11 31
Kobelyaki, Sov. Un. G10 27
Kobenhavn, co., Den. C6 15
Koblenz (Coblence), W. Ger. . C3 18
Koboko, Ug. A5 48
Kobona, Sov. Un. r32 14
Kobrin, Sov. Un. E5 27
Kobroor, i., Indon. G8 34
Kobuk, Ak., U.S. B8 79
Kobuk, stm., Ak., U.S. B8 79
Kobuk Valley National Park, Ak., U.S. B8 79

Kobuleti, Sov. Un. B13 40
Kōca, stm., Tur. D7 25
Kočabâ, stm., Czech. o17 26
Kocaeli see İzmit, Tur. B7 40
Kočani, Yugo. E6 24
Kočevje, Yugo. C2 24
Koch Bihâr, India C8 36
Kōchi, Japan E11 31
Kochkor, Sov. Un. B7 20
Köchel, W. Ger. B7 20
Kochel Lake, l., W. Ger. B7 20
Kocher, stm., W. Ger. D4 19
Koch Peak, mtn., Mt., U.S. . E5 103
Kock, Pol. C7 26
Kodari, Nepal D10 37
Kodiak, Ak., U.S. D9 79
Kodiak Island, i., Ak., U.S. . D9 79
Kodok (Fashoda), Sud. D3 47
Koera Joeri, Neth. Ant. H18 65
Koes, Nmb. C2 49
Koettlitz Glacier, ice, Ant. .. f39 7
Kofa Mountains, mts., Az., U.S. D2 80
Koffiefontein, S. Afr. C3 49
Koforidua, Ghana E4 45
Kōfu, Japan m18 33
Koga, Japan m18 33
Kogalym, stm., Newf. g9 72
Kogalym, Den. C6 15
Kåge, Den. C6 15
Kohala Mountains, mts., Hi., U.S. C6 88
Kohât, Pak. B5 36
Kohatk, Az., U.S. E4 80
Kohima, India C9 36
Kohler, Wi., U.S. E6 126
Kohtla-Järve, Sov. Un. B6 27
Koidu, S.L. E2 45
Kōinge, Swe. A6 15
Ko Island, i., Japan F9 33
Köje Island, i., S. Kor. I4 33
Kokand, Sov. Un. E10 29
Kokanee Glacier Provincial Park, B.C. E9 69
Kokchetav, Sov. Un. D9 29
Kokkola, Fin. F10 14
Koko, Nig. D5 45
Koko Head, c., Hi., U.S. ... B4 88
Kokolik, stm., Ak., U.S. B7 79
Kokomo, Hi., U.S. C5 88
Kokomo, In., U.S. D5 91
Kokomo, Ms., U.S. D3 101
Koko Nor see Qinghai Hu, l., China D4 31
Kokopo, Pap. N. Gui. h13 50
Kokosing, stm., Oh., U.S. .. B3 112
Kokrines, Sov. Un. C9 79
Koksan, N. Kor. G3 33
Koksilah, B.C. g12 69
Koksoak, stm., Que. E19 66
Kokstad, S. Afr. D4 49
Kola, Sov. Un. C15 14
Kola Peninsula, pen., Sov. Un. C6 29
Kolâr, India F6 36
Kolâr Gold Fields, India *F6 36
Kolari, Fin. D10 14
Kolárovo, Czech. E4 26
Kolāyat, India D4 37
Kolbano, Indon. G6 34
Kolbio, Kenya B7 48
Kolbuszowa, Pol. C6 26
Kolchugino, Sov. Un. C12 27
Kolczewo, Pol. B2 26
Kolda, Sen. D2 45
Koldewey, i., Grnld. B16 128
Kolding, Den. C3 15
Kole, Zaire B4 48
Kolek, Czech. n17 26
Koleen, In., U.S. G4 91
Kolezhma, Sov. Un. E16 14
Kolguyev Island, i., Sov. Un. C7 29
Kolhâpur, India E5 36
Koliganek, Ak., U.S. D8 79
Kolimbine, stm., Afr. D3 45
Kolín, Czech. C3 26
Kolín, La., U.S. C3 95
Kölleda, E. Ger. B6 19
Kolno, Pol. B6 26
Koło, Pol. B5 26
Koloa, Hi., U.S. B2 88
Kolob Canyon, val., Ut., U.S. F2 121
Kolokani, Mali D3 45
Kolola Springs, Ms., U.S. .. B5 101
Kolomyya, Sov. Un. G5 27
Kolondiéba, Mali D3 45
Kolonia, Micron. Q17 52
Kolonodale, Indon. F6 34
Kolp, stm., Sov. Un. B10 27
Kolpashevo, Sov. Un. B10 28
Kolpino, Sov. Un. s31 14
Kolwezi, Zaire D4 48
Kolyberovo, Sov. Un. n18 27
Kolyma, stm., Sov. Un. C18 29
Kolyma Mountains, mts., Sov. Un. C18 29
Komádi, Hung. B5 24
Komandorski Islands, is., Sov. Un. D19 29
Komárno, Czech. E5 26
Komárom, Czech. D5 26
Komarno Marsh, sw., Sov. Un. B10 27
Komárom, Hung. E5 26
Komatipoort, S. Afr. C5 49
Komatke, Az., U.S. m8 80
Komatsu, Japan H8 33
Komatsushima, Japan I7 33
Komló, Hung. B4 24
Kommunarsk, Sov. Un. ... G12 27
Komodo, i., Indon. G5 34
Komoé, stm., Indon. E4 45
Komono, Congo B1 48
Komono, Congo B1 48
Komotiní, Grc. B5 40
Komrat, Sov. Un. H7 27
Komsomolets, i., Sov. Un. .. A4 128
Komsomolsk [-na-Amure], Sov. Un. D16 29
Konahuanui, Puu, mtn., Hi., U.S. g10 88
Konar, e-Khâş, Afg. D15 39
Konawa, Ok., U.S. C5 113
Kondinskoye, Sov. Un. B7 28
Kondoa, Tan. B6 48
Kondopoga, Sov. Un. F16 14
Kondūz, Afg. C14 39
Konechnaya, Sov. Un. C9 28
Konętensk, Sov. Un. D6 29
Kong, i., Camb. G5 35
Kong, stm., Asia C3 34
Kongeå, stm., Den. C2 15

Kongju, S. Kor. H3 33
Kongolo, Zaire C4 48
Kongsberg, Nor. H3 14
Kongsmark, Den. C2 15
Kongsvinger, Nor. G5 14
Königsberg see Kaliningrad, Sov. Un. D5 29
Königsbrück, E. Ger. B8 19
Königslutter, W. Ger. A5 19
Königstein, E. Ger. C9 19
Königs Wusterhausen, E. Ger. A8 19
Konin, Pol. B5 26
Konispoli, Alb. C3 40
Kónitsa, Grc. B3 25
Konjic, Yugo. C3 24
Konni, Switz. C3 21
Konnern, E. Ger. B6 19
Konolfingen, Switz. C4 21
Konomoc, Lake, res., Ct., U.S. D7 84
Konosha, Sov. Un. A13 27
Konotop, Sov. Un. F9 27
Konstancin-Jeziorna, Pol. .. m14 26
Konstantinovka, Sov. Un. .. q20 27
Konstanz (Constance), W. Ger. E4 18
Kontagora, Nig. D6 45
Kontcha, Cam. D2 46
Kontich, Bel. C4 17
Kontiomäki, Fin. E13 14
Kon Tum, Viet. C3 34
Konya, Tur. D9 40
Konyang, S. Kor. I3 33
Konzhakovskiy Kamen, mtn., Sov. Un. B5 28
Koocanusa, Lake, res., N.A. . B1 103
Koochiching, co., Mn., U.S. . B4 100
Koolau Range, mts., Hi., U.S. f10 88
Kooloonong, Austl. G4 51
Koontz Lake, In., U.S. B5 91
Koosharem, Ut., U.S. E4 121
Kooskia, Id., U.S. C3 89
Kootenai, co., Id., U.S. B2 89
Kootenai, stm., U.S. B10 69
Kootenay, co., B.C. E9 69
Kootenay Lake, l., B.C. E9 69
Kootenay National Park, B.C. E9 69
Kopervik, Nor. H1 14
Kopet Mountains, mts., Asia B8 39
Koping, Swe. H6 14
Koppány, stm., Hung. B4 24
Koppel, Pa., U.S. E1 115
Kopruvnica, Yugo. B3 24
Kopychintsy, Sov. Un. G6 27
Korahe, Eth. D5 47
Korarou, Lac, l., Mali C4 45
Korba, India D9 37
Korba, Tun. F3 23
Korbach, W. Ger. B3 18
Korea, Lua, stm., L.S. k10 95
Korea, North, ctry., Asia ... D10 31
Korea, South, ctry., Asia ... D10 31
Korea Bay, b., Asia D9 31
Korea Strait, strt., Asia E10 31
Korets, Sov. Un. F6 27
Korhogo, I.C. E3 45
Kori Creek, stm., India F2 37
Koridhallós, Grc. E5 25
Korini, Grc. g9 25
Kórinthos (Corinth), Grc. .. D4 25
Kōriyama, Japan H10 33
Korkino, Sov. Un. D8 40
Korkuteli, Tur. C3 31
Korla, China C3 31
Kórmend, Hung. B3 24
Kornat, i., Yugo. D2 24
Kornesti, Aus. D8 18
Kornwestheim, W. Ger. ... D4 19
Koro, Mali D4 45
Koro, i., Fiji H15 52
Korocha, Sov. Un. C6 48
Koror, Palau R17 52
Koror, i., Palau R17 52
Korosten, Sov. Un. F7 27
Koro Toro, Chad B3 46
Korotoyak, Sov. Un. F12 27
Korovin Volcano, vol., Ak., U.S. E5 79
Korsakov, Sov. Un. E17 29
Korsør, Den. C5 15
Kortrijk (Courtrai), Bel. D2 17
Korucam, Cape, c., N. Cyp. . E9 40
Korumburra, Austl. I5 51
Koryak Mountains, mts., Sov. Un. C19 29
Kos, Grc. D6 40
Kos (Cos), i., Grc. D6 40
Koschagyl, Sov. Un. C18 29
Košcian, Pol. C4 26
Kościerzyna, Pol. A4 26
Kosciusko, Ms., U.S. B4 101
Kosciusko, co., In., U.S. ... B6 91
Kosciusko, Mount, mtn., Austl. G8 50
Kösdag̃ı, mtn., Tur. C14 40
Koshigaya, Japan *I9 33
Koshiki Islands, is., Japan . K4 33
Koshkonong, Mo., U.S. ... E6 102
Koshkonong, Lake, l., Wi., U.S. F5 126
Košice, Czech. D6 26
Košíře (part of Prague), Czech. n17 26
Koskaecodde Lake, l., Newf. C18 72
Koslan, Sov. Un. G4 53
Kosovska Mitrovica, Yugo. . D4 24
Kosrae, i., Micron. F9 6
Kosse, Tx., U.S. D4 120
Kosslarn, W. Ger. D9 18
Kossol Passage, strt., Palau R17 52
Kossol Reef, rf., Palau R17 52
Kossuth, Ms., U.S. A5 101
Kossuth, co., Ia., U.S. A3 92
Kostajnica, Yugo. C3 24
Kostelec, Czech. o18 26
Kostroma, Sov. Un. D7 29
Kostrzyn, Pol. B3 26
Koszalin (Köslin), Pol. A4 26
Köszeg, Hung. B3 24
Kota, India D4 37
Kota Baharu, Malay. D2 34
Kotabaru, Indon. F5 34
Kotabumi, Indon. F2 34
Kotah see Kota, India D4 37
Kota Kinabalu, Malay. D5 34
Kotatengah, Indon. L4 35
Kotcho, stm., B.C. A7 69
Kotel, Bul. D8 24
Kotelnich, Sov. Un. B3 28
Kotelnikovo, Sov. Un. H14 27

Kotelny Island, i., Sov. Un. .. B16 29
Köthen, E. Ger. C5 18
Kotido, Ug. A5 48
Kotka, Fin. G12 14
Kotlas, Sov. Un. C7 29
Kotlik, Ak., U.S. C7 79
Kotonkoro, Nig. D6 45
Kotor, Yugo. D4 24
Kotor Bay, b., Yugo. D4 24
Kotor Varoš, Yugo. C3 24
Kotovsk, Sov. Un. E13 27
Kotovsk, Sov. Un. H7 27
Kotri, Pak. E2 37
Kottagüdem, India D6 37
Kotte, Sri L. *G6 36
Kotto, stm., Cen. Afr. Rep. . D4 46
Kotzebue, Ak., U.S. B7 79
Kotzebue Sound, strt., Ak., U.S. B7 79
Kötzting, W. Ger. D7 19
Kouandé, Benin D5 45
Kouango, Cen. Afr. Rep. ... D6 46
Koudougou, Burkina F2 46
Koula-Moutou, Gabon B2 48
Koulikoro, Mali D3 45
Koumra, Chad D3 46
Koungheul, Sen. D2 45
Kounradskiy, Sov. Un. D9 28
Kountze, Tx., U.S. D5 120
Koupéla, Burkina D4 45
Kouri Island, i., Japan N6 52
Kourou, Fr. Gu. A4 59
Kouroussa, Gui. D3 45
Kouts, In., U.S. B3 91
Ko Vaya, Az., U.S. E4 80
Kovel, Sov. Un. F5 27
Kovrov, Sov. Un. C13 27
Kowloon, H.K. G7 31
Köycegiz, Tur. D7 40
Koyuk, Ak., U.S. C7 79
Koyukuk, stm., Ak., U.S. .. B8 79
Kozan, Tur. D10 40
Kozáni, Grc. B3 25
Kozelsk, Sov. Un. D10 27
Kozienice, Pol. C6 26
Koźle, Pol. C5 26
Kozłoduy, Bul. D6 24
Kozuchów, Pol. C3 26
Kōzu Island, i., Japan I9 33
Kpandu, Ghana E5 45
Kra, Isthmus of, Asia C1 34
Krabi, Thai. H3 35
Kraéheh, Camb. C3 34
Kraenau, Lua, stm. k10 95
Kragerö, Nor. H3 14
Kragujevac, Yugo. D5 24
Kraków, Yugo. C5 26
Krakower, i., E. Ger. E6 15
Kraljevo, Yugo. D5 24
Královské Vinohrady (part of Prague), Czech. n17 26
Kralupy [nad Vltavou], Czech. n17 26
Králův Dvůr, Czech. o17 26
Kramatorsk, Sov. Un. G11 27
Kramer, In., U.S. D3 91
Kramer, N.D., U.S. A5 111
Kranidhion, Grc. D4 25
Kranj, Yugo. B2 24
Kranzburg, S.D., U.S. C9 118
Kraslice, Czech. C2 26
Krasnaya Polyana, Sov. Un. C7 29
Krasnik, Pol. C6 26
Krasnoarmeysk, Sov. Un. . F15 27
Krasnoarmeysk, Sov. Un. . G15 27
Krasnoarmeysk, Sov. Un. . C7 28
Krasnodar, Sov. Un. E6 29
Krasnodon, Sov. Un. q22 27
Krasnogorsk, Sov. Un. ... B11 33
Krasnograd, Sov. Un. G10 27
Krasnokamsk, Sov. Un. ... B5 28
Krasnoselkup, Sov. Un. ... B25 8
Krasnoselye, Sov. Un. ... G9 27
Krasnoslobodsk, Sov. Un. . D14 27
Krasnoslobodsk, Sov. Un. . C9 28
Krasnoturinsk, Sov. Un. .. B6 28
Krasnoufimsk, Sov. Un. ... D21 8
Krasnouralsk, Sov. Un. B5 28
Krasnovishersk, Sov. Un. .. A6 28
Krasnovodsk, Sov. Un. E8 29
Krasnoye Selo, Sov. Un. ... s31 14
Krasnoyarsk, Sov. Un. C7 28
Krasnystaw, Pol. C7 26
Krasnyy Kholm, Sov. Un. .. B11 27
Krasnyy Kut, Sov. Un. q21 27
Krasnyy Liman, Sov. Un. .. q20 27
Krasnyy Luch, Sov. Un. ... q21 27
Krasnyy Sulin, Sov. Un. ... H13 27
Krasnyy Yar, Sov. Un. F15 27
Kratovo, Yugo. D6 24
Kraul Mountains, mts., Ant. H1 7
Krawang, Indon. *G3 34
Krebs, Ok., U.S. C6 113
Krefeld, W. Ger. C3 18
Kremenchug Reservoir, res., Sov. Un. G9 27
Kremenets, Sov. Un. F5 27
Kremikovtsi, Bul. p21 27
Kremlin, Mt., U.S. A4 103
Kremling, Co., U.S. A4 83
Krems [am der Donau], Aus. D7 18
Kresgeville, Pa., U.S. E10 115
Kress, Tx., U.S. B2 120
Kreuzlingen, Switz. B6 21
Krichev, Sov. Un. E8 27
Krilon, Cape, c., Sov. Un. . D11 33
Krishna, India E6 36
Krishnagar, India F12 37
Kristiansand, Swe. I6 14
Kristiansand, co., Swe. ... B8 15
Kristinestad, Fin. F9 14
Kriva Palanka, Yugo. D5 24
Krivoy Rog, Sov. Un. H9 27
Křiževci, Yugo. B3 24
Krk, i., Yugo. C2 24
Krka, stm., Yugo. D11 33

Name · Map Ref. · Page

Krnov, Czech. C4 26
Krokeaí, Grc. D4 25
Krokstadelva, Nor. p28 14
Krolevets, Sov. Un. F9 27
Kroměříž, Czech. D4 26
Kromy, Sov. Un. E10 27
Kronach, W. Ger. C6 19
Kronau, Sask. G3 75
Kronoberg, co., Swe. B8 15
Kronshtadt, Sov. Un. B7 27
Kroonstad, S. Afr. C4 49
Kröpelin, E. Ger. D5 15
Kropotkin, Sov. Un. I13 27
Krosno, Pol. D6 26
Krosno Odrzańskie, Pol. B3 26
Krotoszyn, Pol. C4 26
Krotz Springs, La., U.S. D4 95
Krško, Yugo. C2 24
Kruger National Park, S. Afr. C5 49
Krugersdorp, S. Afr. C4 49
Kruja, Alb. B2 25
Krumbach, W. Ger. A6 20
Krumovgrad, Bul. E7 24
Kruševac, Yugo. D5 24
Kruševo, Yugo. E5 24
Kruszwica, Pol. B5 26
Kruzof Island, i., Ak., U.S. m21 79
Krydor, Sask. E2 75
Krymsk, Sov. Un. I11 27
Krynica, Pol. D6 26
Krynki, Pol. B7 26
Ksar el Kebir, Mor. B3 44
Ksar es Souk, Mor. C4 44
Kuala Kangsar, Malay. J4 35
Kualakurun, Indon. F4 34
Kuala Lipis, Malay. E2 34
Kuala Lumpur, Malay. E2 34
Kualapuu, Hi., U.S. B4 88
Kuala Terengganu, Malay. D2 34
Kuandang, Indon. E6 34
Kuandian, China D11 31
Kuantan, Malay. E2 34
Kuba, Sov. Un. E3 28
Kuban, stm., Sov. Un. I13 27
Kubitzer Bodden, b., E. Ger. D7 15
Kubokawa, Japan J6 33
Kuching, Malay. E4 34
Kuchinoerabu Island, i., Japan K5 33
Kuchino Island, i., Japan L4 33
Kuçovë see Stalin, Alb. B2 25
Küçükmenderes, stm., Tur. C6 25
Kudaka Island, i., Japan O5 52
Kudat, Malay. D5 34
Kudirkos Naumiestis, Sov. Un. A7 26
Kudus, Indon. G4 34
Kudymkar, Sov. Un. B4 28
Kuee Ruins, hist., Hi., U.S. D6 88
Kufstein, Aus. E6 18
Kuhaylī, Sud. B3 47
Kuhēsi, Alb. A3 25
Kūh Lab, Ra's-e, c., Iran I10 39
Kühpäyeh, Iran E6 39
Kuito, Ang. C2 49
Kuiu Island, i., Ak., U.S. m23 79
Kuji, Japan F10 33
Kujū, Mount, mtn., Japan J5 33
Kukaiau, Hi., U.S. C6 88
Kukawa, Nig. D7 45
Kuki, Japan m18 33
Kukuihaele, Hi., U.S. C6 88
Kukuiula, Hi., U.S. B2 88
Kuku Point, c., Wake I. A1 52
Kula, Bul. D6 24
Kula, Tur. C7 25
Kula, Hi., U.S. C5 88
Kula, Yugo. C4 24
Kula Kangri, mtn., Bhu. C6 36
Kulebaki, Sov. Un. D14 27
Kulim, Malay. J4 35
Kullorp, Swe. A7 15
Kulm, N.D., U.S. C7 111
Kulmbach, W. Ger. C5 18
Kulpmont, Pa., U.S. E9 115
Kulunda, Sov. Un. C9 28
Kulunda, Lake, l., Sov. Un. C9 28
Kulwin, Austl. G4 51
Kulyab, Sov. Un. H22 8
Kŭm, stm., S. Kor. H3 33
Kuma, stm., Sov. Un. F18 8
Kumagaya, Japan m18 33
Kumai, Indon. F4 34
Kumamoto, Japan E11 31
Kumano Bay, b., Japan J8 33
Kumanovo, Yugo. D5 24
Kumasi, Ghana E4 45
Kumba, Cam. E1 46
Kumba-konam, India F6 36
Kumbo, Cam. D2 46
Kümhwa, S. Kor. G3 33
Kumi, Ug. A5 48
Kumihama, Japan n14 33
Kumla, Swe. H6 14
Kummerower Lake, l., E. Ger. E6 15
Kumo, Nig. E7 45
Kumukahi, Cape, c., Hi., U.S. D7 88
Kuna, Id., U.S. F2 89
Kundar, stm., Asia B2 37
Kundiawa, Pap. N. Gui. k11 50
Kuneitra (Al Qunayţirah), Isr. Occ. A7 41
Kunggyü Lake, l., China B9 37
Kunghit Island, i., B.C. C2 69
Kungrad, Sov. Un. E5 28
Kungsbacka, Swe. A6 15
Kungsör, Swe. t34 14
Kungu, Zaire A2 48
Kungur, Sov. Un. B5 28
Kunia, Hi., U.S. g9 88
Kunigami, Japan N6 52
Kunimi, Mount, mtn., Japan m17 115
Kunkle, Pa., U.S. m17 115
Kunlun Shan, mts., China F11 30
Kunming, China F5 31
Kunsan, S. Kor. D10 31
Kunszentmárton, Hung. B5 24
Künzelsau, W. Ger. D13 14
Kuolayarvi, Sov. Un. D13 14
Kuop, atoll, Micron. Q18 52
Kuopio, Fin. F12 14
Kupa, stm., Yugo. C2 24
Kupang, Indon. G6 34
Kupino, Sov. Un. m23 79
Kupreanof, Ak., U.S. m23 79
Kupreanof Island, i., Ak., U.S. m23 79
Kupyansk, Sov. Un. G11 27
Kur, stm., Sov. Un. B7 33
Kura, stm., Asia E3 28
Kurashiki, Japan I6 33
Kuray, Sov. Un. E26 8
Kuraymah, Sud. B3 47
Kurayyimah, Jord. f13 41
Kurdistan, hist. reg., Asia B4 38

Kurdufān al Janūbīyah (Southern Kurdufan), prov., Sud. C2 47
Kurdufān ash Shamālīyah (Northern Kurdufan), prov., Sud. C2 47
Kürdzhali, Bul. E7 24
Kure, Japan E11 31
Kure Island, i., Hi., U.S. k12 88
Kuressaare, Sov. Un. B4 27
Kureyka, stm., Sov. Un. C12 29
Kurgaldzhinskiy, Sov. Un. C8 28
Kurgan, Sov. Un. D9 29
Kurganinsk, Sov. Un. G17 8
Kurgan-Tyube, Sov. Un. H22 8
Kuria Muria Islands (Khūryān Mūryān), is., Oman D5 38
Kurigram, Bngl. E12 37
Kuril Islands, is., Sov. Un. E17 29
Kuril Strait, strt., Sov. Un. D18 29
Kurinskaya, Cape, c., Sov. Un. H18 8
Kurmuk, Sud. C3 47
Kurnool, India E6 36
Kuro Island, i., Japan K4 33
Kuroki, Sask. F4 75
Kurovskoye, Sov. Un. n18 27
Kurow, N.Z. P13 51
Kurri Kurri, Austl. F9 50
Kuršumlija, Yugo. D5 24
Kurthwood, La., U.S. C2 95
Kurtistown, Hi., U.S. D6 88
Kurtz, In., U.S. G5 91
Kuruman, S. Afr. D3 49
Kurume, Japan E11 31
Kurunegala, Sri L. G7 36
Kuşadası, Tur. C6 25
Kusakaki Island, i., Japan K4 33
Kusatsu, Japan n14 33
Kusel, W. Ger. D2 19
Kushchevskaya, Sov. Un. H12 27
Kushimoto, Japan J7 33
Kushiro, Japan C13 31
Kushka, Sov. Un. F9 29
Kushmurun, Sov. Un. C6 28
Kushmurun, Lake, l., Sov. Un. C6 28
Kuskokwim, stm., Ak., U.S. C8 79
Kuskokwim Bay, b., Ak., U.S. D7 79
Kuskokwim Mountains, mts., Ak., U.S. C8 79
Kuş Lake, l., Tur. B6 25
Küsnacht, Switz. B6 21
Küssnacht [am Rigi], Switz. B6 21
Kustanay, Sov. Un. D9 29
Küsten Canal, W. Ger. B7 17
Küstī, Sud. C3 47
Kut, i., Thai. G5 35
Kuta, Alb. B2 25
Kutacane, Indon. K2 35
Kütahya, Tur. C7 40
Kutaisi, Sov. Un. G17 8
Kutawagan Lake, l., Sask. F3 75
Küt Barrage, Iraq E2 39
Kutina, Yugo. C3 24
Kutná Hora, Czech. D3 26
Kutno, Pol. B5 26
Kuttawa, Ky., U.S. e9 94
Kutu, Zaire B2 48
Kutum, Sud. C1 47
Kuturagha see Banda Aceh, Indon. k11 34
Kuty, Sov. Un. A7 24
Kutztown, Pa., U.S. E10 115
Kuujjuaq, Que. g13 74
Kuūm-ni, N. Kor. G2 33
Kuusamo, Fin. E13 14
Kuvandyk, Sov. Un. E20 8
Kuvango (Capelongo), Ang. D2 48
Kuwait (Al Kuwayt), Kuw. C4 38
Kuwait, ctry., Asia C4 38
Kuwait Bay, b., Kuw. G9 39
Kuwana, Japan I8 33
Kuybyshev, Sov. Un. B9 28
Kuybyshev, Sov. Un. D8 29
Kuybyshevo, Sov. Un. H12 27
Kuybyshev Reservoir, res., Sov. Un. D7 29
Kūysanjaq, Iraq D15 40
Kuyto, l., Sov. Un. E14 14
Kuznetsk, Sov. Un. E16 27
Kuznetsk Basin, Sov. Un. D25 8
Kuznetsovo, Sov. Un. C10 33
Kvarner, b., Yugo. C2 24
Kvismare Kanal, Swe. t33 14
Kvitøya, i., Nor. A11 128
Kwajalein, atoll, Marsh Is. S17 52
Kwajalein Island, i., Marsh Is. S17 52
Kwakoegron, Sur. A3 59
Kwale, Kenya B6 48
Kwa Mashu, S. Afr. *C5 49
Kwamouth, Zaire B2 48
Kwangju, S. Kor. D10 31
Kwango (Cuango), stm., Afr. C2 48
Kwangsi Chuang see Guangxi Zhuangzu, prov., China G6 31
Kwangtung see Guangdong, prov., China G7 31
Kwatisore, Indon. F8 34
Kweichow see Guizhou, prov., China F6 31
Kwekwe, Zimb. A4 49
Kwenge, stm., Afr. C2 48
Kwethluk, Ak., U.S. C7 79
Kwidzyn, Pol. B5 26
Kwigillingok, Ak., U.S. D7 79
Kwilu, stm., Afr. B2 48
Kwinana, Austl. F2 50
Kyabé, Chad D3 46
Kyabram, Austl. H5 51
Kyaiklat, Burma E10 36
Kyaikto, Burma D13 29
Kyakhta, Sov. Un. D13 29
Kyaukpadaung, Burma B1 35
Kyaukpyu, Burma E9 36
Kyaukse, Burma D10 36
Kybartai, Sov. Un. A7 26
Kyle, Czech. n18 26
Kyle, Sask. G1 75
Kyle, S.D., U.S. D3 118
Kyle, Tx., U.S. E4 120
Kyles Ford, Tn., U.S. C10 119
Kylestrome, Scot., U.K. B3 13
Kyll, stm., W. Ger. E6 17
Kyllburg, W. Ger. E6 17
Kyōga, Cape, c., Japan I7 33
Kyoga, Lake, l., Ug. A5 48
Kyōmipo see Songnim, N. Kor. G2 33
Kyonggi Bay, b., Asia H2 33
Kyŏngju, S. Kor. D10 31

Kyŏngsŏng, N. Kor. F4 33
Kyōto, Japan D12 31
Kyritz, E. Ger. B6 18
Kyrkjebö, Nor. G1 14
Kyrock, Ky., U.S. C3 94
Kyshtovka, Sov. Un. D24 8
Kyshtym, Sov. Un. B6 28
Kyuquot, B.C. D4 69
Kyuquot Sound, strt., B.C. D4 69
Kyūroku Island, i., Japan F9 33
Kyūshū, i., Japan E11 31
Kyustendil, Bul. D6 24
Kyzyl, Sov. Un. D12 29
Kyzyl-Kiya, Sov. Un. E8 28
Kyzyl-Kum, des., Sov. Un. E9 28
Kyzyltas Mountains, mts., Sov. Un. D9 28
Kzyl-Orda, Sov. Un. E9 28

L
Laa [an der Thaya], Aus. D8 18
Laage, E. Ger. E6 15
La Almunia de Doña Godina, Spain B5 22
La Araucanía, prov., Chile B2 54
Laas Caanood, Som. D6 47
La Asunción, Ven. A5 60
Laau Point, c., Hi., U.S. B4 88
Labadie, Mo., U.S. f13 102
Labadieville, La., U.S. E5 95
La Banda, Arg. B3 55
La Barca, Mex. C4 63
La Barge, Wy., U.S. D2 127
La Barge Creek, stm., Wy., U.S. D2 127
Labasa, Fiji H15 52
La Bisbal, Spain C10 22
Labo, Phil. o14 34
Labo, Mount, mtn., Phil. p14 34
La Boca, Pan. m11 62
Laboe, W. Ger. D4 15
La Bolt, S.D., U.S. *B9 118
Labouheyre, Fr. E3 16
Laboulaye, Arg. A4 54
Labrador, reg., Newf. g9 72
Labrador City, Newf. h8 72
Labrador Sea, N.A. g10 72
Lábrea, Braz. D2 59
La Brea, Trin. O22 65
La Broquerie, Man. E3 70
Labuan Island, i., Malay. D5 34
Labuha, Indon. F7 34
Labuhanbilik, Indon. K4 35
Labuk Bay, b., Malay. D5 34
Lac-à-Beauce, Que. B5 74
Lacadena, Sask. G1 75
La Calera, Chile A2 54
Lacamp, La., U.S. C3 95
La Canada Flintridge, Ca., U.S. m12 82
La Capelle [-en-Thiérache], Fr. E3 17
La Carlota, Arg. A4 54
La Carolina, Spain C4 22
Lac-aux-Brochets, Que. B5 74
Lac-aux-Sables, Que. C5 74
Lac-Baker, N.B. B1 71
Lac-Beauport, Que. n17 74
Lac-Bouchette, Que. A5 74
Lac-Brome, Que. D5 74
Laccadive, Minicoy and Amindivi Islands see Lakshadweep, ter., India *F5 36
Laccadive Islands see Lakshadweep, is., India F5 36
Lac-Carré, Que. C3 74
Lac-Chat, Que. B5 74
Lac Courte Oreilles Indian Reservation, Wi., U.S. C2 126
Lac-des-Écorces, Que. C2 74
Lac-des-Seize-Îles, Que. D3 74
Lac du Bonnet, Man. D3 70
Lac du Flambeau, Wi., U.S. C4 126
Lac du Flambeau Indian Reservation, Wi., U.S. C4 126
Lac-Édouard, Que. B5 74
La Ceiba, Hond. D7 63
La Ceiba, Ven. B3 60
La Center, Ky., U.S. e9 94
Lac-Etchemin, Que. C7 74
Lacey, Wa., U.S. B3 124
Laceys Spring, Al., U.S. A3 78
Laceyville, Pa., U.S. C9 115
Lac-Frontière, Que. C7 74
La Chambre, Fr. D7 16
Lachapelle [-sous-Rougemont], Fr. A3 21
La Charité, Fr. D5 16
La Chartre, Fr. D7 16
La Chaux-de-Fonds, Switz. E3 18
Lachay, Punta, c., Peru D2 58
Lachen, Switz. B6 21
Lachine, Que. D4 74
Lachine, Mi., U.S. C7 99
Lachlan, stm., Austl. F8 50
La Chorrera, Col. D3 60
La Chorrera, Pan. h8 62
Lachute, Que. D3 74
Laçi, Alb. B2 25
La Cienega, N.M., U.S. h8 108
La Ciotat, Fr. H5 51
La Cisa Pass, Italy B2 23
Lackawanna, co., Pa., U.S. D10 115
Lackawaxen, Pa., U.S. D12 115
Lackland Air Force Base, mil., Tx., U.S. k7 120
Lac La Belle, Mi., U.S. A2 99
Lac la Hache, B.C. D7 69
Lac la Ronge Provincial Park, Sask. B3 75
Laclede, Id., U.S. A2 89
La Clede, Il., U.S. E5 90
Laclede, Mo., U.S. B4 102
Laclede, co., Mo., U.S. D5 102
Lac-Mégantic, Que. D7 74
La Cocha, Arg. E2 54
Lacolle, Que. D4 74
La Colorada, Mex. B2 63
Lacomb, Or., U.S. C4 114

Lacombe, Alta. C4 68
Lacombe, La., U.S. D6 95
Lacombe Bayou, stm., La., U.S. h12 95
Lacon, Il., U.S. B4 90
Lacona, Ia., U.S. C4 92
Lacona, N.Y., U.S. B4 109
La Concepción, Pan. F6 62
La Conception, Que. C3 74
Laconia, In., U.S. H5 91
Laconia, N.H., U.S. C4 106
Laconia, Tn., U.S. B2 119
Laconia, Gulf of, b., Grc. D4 25
La Conner, Wa., U.S. A3 124
Lacoochee, Fl., U.S. D4 86
La Coruña, Spain A1 22
Lacota, Mi., U.S. F4 99
La Courneuve, Fr. g10 16
Lacq, Fr. F3 16
La Crescent, Mn., U.S. G7 100
La Crescenta, Ca., U.S. *m12 82
La Crete, Alta. f7 68
La Crosse, Ar., U.S. A4 81
La Crosse, Fl., U.S. C4 86
La Crosse, In., U.S. B4 91
La Crosse, Ks., U.S. D4 93
La Crosse, Va., U.S. D4 123
La Crosse, Wi., U.S. E2 126
Lacrosse, Wa., U.S. C8 124
La Crosse, co., Wi., U.S. E2 126
La Crosse, stm., Wi., U.S. E3 126
La Cruz, Col. G3 60
La Cruz, C.R. E5 62
La Cruz, Mex. C3 63
La Cruz [de Río Grande], Nic. D5 62
La Cygne, Ks., U.S. D9 93
Ladário, Braz. B1 56
Ladd, Il., U.S. B4 90
Ladder Creek, stm., Ks., U.S. D2 93
Laddonia, Mo., U.S. B6 102
Ladera Heights, Ca., U.S. *m12 82
La Désirade, i., Guad. Q9 65
Ladispoli, Italy h8 23
Ladner, S.D., U.S. B2 118
Lādnūn, India D5 37
Ladoga, Lake, l., Sov. Un. C6 29
Ladoga, In., U.S. E4 91
Ladonia, Tx., U.S. C5 120
Ladora, Ia., U.S. C5 92
La Dorada, Col. B3 60
Ladson, S.C., U.S. F7 117
Ladue, Mo., U.S. *C7 102
Ladue, Mo., U.S. f13 102
Ladybank, Scot., U.K. D5 13
Ladybrand, S. Afr. C4 49
Lady Laurier, Mount, mtn., B.C. A6 69
Ladysmith, B.C. E6 69
Ladysmith, S. Afr. C4 49
Ladysmith, Wi., U.S. C2 126
Lae, Pap. N. Gui. k12 50
Laesø, i., Den. A4 15
Lafarge, Wi., U.S. E3 126
LaFargeville, N.Y., U.S. A5 109
Lafayette, Al., U.S. C4 78
Lafayette, Ca., U.S. *h8 82
Lafayette, Co., U.S. B5 83
Lafayette, Ga., U.S. B1 87
Lafayette, In., U.S. D4 91
Lafayette, La., U.S. D3 95
Lafayette, N.J., U.S. A3 107
Lafayette, N.Y., U.S. C4 109
Lafayette, Oh., U.S. B1 112
Lafayette, Or., U.S. B3 114
Lafayette, R.I., U.S. E4 116
Lafayette, Tn., U.S. A5 119
Lafayette, co., Ar., U.S. D2 81
Lafayette, co., Fl., U.S. C3 86
Lafayette, co., La., U.S. D3 95
Lafayette, co., Ms., U.S. A4 101
Lafayette, co., Mo., U.S. B4 102
Lafayette, co., Wi., U.S. F3 126
Lafayette, Mount, mtn., N.H., U.S. B3 106
Lafayette Southwest, La., U.S. *D3 95
Lafe, Ar., U.S. A5 81
La Fère, Fr. C5 16
La Feria, Tx., U.S. F4 120
La Ferté-Bernard, Fr. C4 16
La Ferté-Macé, Fr. C3 16
La Ferté-sous-Jouarre, Fr. C5 16
Lafferty, Oh., U.S. B4 112
Lafia, Nig. E6 45
Lafiagi, Nig. E6 45
Laflèche, Sask. H2 75
La Flèche, Fr. D3 16
La Follette, Tn., U.S. C9 119
La Fontaine, In., U.S. C6 91
Lafontaine, Ks., U.S. E8 93
Lafourche, co., La., U.S. E5 95
Lafourche, Bayou, stm., La., U.S. E5 95
La France, S.C., U.S. B2 117
La Galera, stm., Italy h8 23
La Galite, i., Tun. F2 23
Lagan, Swe. I5 14
Lage, W. Ger. B3 19
Lågen, stm., Nor. G3 14
Laggan, Loch, res., Scot., U.K. D4 13
Laggan Bay, b., Scot., U.K. E2 13
Laghouat, Alg. C5 44
La Gloria, Col. B3 60
Lagny, Fr. C5 16
Lago, Mount, mtn., Wa., U.S. A5 124
Lagoa, Port. D1 22
Lagonda, La., U.S. *E4 95
Lagos, Nig. E5 45

Lagos, Port. D1 22
Lagos de Moreno, Mex. C4 63
La Goulette, Tun. *B7 44
Lago Viedma, Arg. D2 54
La Grande, Or., U.S. B8 114
La Grande, stm., Que. h11 74
La Grande Deux, Réservoir, res., Que. h11 74
La Grande Quatre, Réservoir, res., Que. F18 66
La Grange, Ar., U.S. C5 81
Lagrange, Fl., U.S. *D6 86
La Grange, Ga., U.S. C1 87
Lagrange, Il., U.S. B6 90
Lagrange, In., U.S. A7 91
La Grange, Ky., U.S. B4 94
La Grange, Me., U.S. C4 96
La Grange, Mo., U.S. A6 102
La Grange, N.C., U.S. B5 110
Lagrange, Oh., U.S. A3 112
La Grange, Tn., U.S. B2 119
La Grange, Tx., U.S. E4 120
Lagrange, co., In., U.S. A7 91
La Grange Highlands, Il., U.S. *k9 90
La Grue Bayou, stm., Ar., U.S. C4 81
La Guadeloupe (Saint-Évariste), Que. D7 74
La Guaira, Ven. A4 60
La Guardia, Spain B1 22
La Guata, Hond. C4 62
Laguna, Braz. D2 56
Laguna, N.M., U.S. B2 108
Laguna Beach, Ca., U.S. F5 82
Laguna Dam, U.S. E1 80
Laguna Hills, Ca., U.S. *n13 82
Laguna Indian Reservation, N.M., U.S. C2 108
Laguna Niguel, Ca., U.S. *F5 82
Lagunas, Peru B2 58
Lagunillas, Bol. C3 55
La Habana, prov., Cuba C2 64
La Habra, Ca., U.S. n13 82
Lahad Datu, Malay. D6 34
Lahaina, Hi., U.S. C5 88
Lahat, Indon. F3 34
La Have, N.S. E5 71
La Have, stm., N.S. E5 71
La Have Island, N.S. E5 71
Lahfān, Bi'r, well, Eg. D5 41
Lahn, stm., W. Ger. C4 18
Lahij, Yemen C5 47
Lāhīǰān, Iran E5 39
Lāhoma, Ok., U.S. A3 113
Lahore, Pak. B5 36
Lahore Cantonment, Pak. *B5 36
Lahr, W. Ger. D3 18
Lahti, Fin. G11 14
La Huaca, Peru B1 58
Laï, Chad D3 46
Lai Chau, Viet. A5 35
Laichow Bay see Laizhou Wan, b., China D8 31
Laide, Scot., U.K. C3 13
Laidon, Loch, l., Scot., U.K. D4 13
Laie, Hi., U.S. B4 88
Laifeng, China J3 32
L'Aigle, Fr. C4 16
L'Aigle Creek, stm., Ar., U.S. D3 81
Laihka, Burma B2 35
Laingsburg, S. Afr. D3 49
Laingsburg, Mi., U.S. F6 99
Laird, Ky., U.S. B5 94
Laird, Sask. E2 75
Laird, Co., U.S. A8 83
Lairg, Scot., U.K. A4 10
Laiwui, Indon. F7 34
Laiyang, China D10 31
Laiyuan, China D9 31
Laizhou Wan, b., China D8 31
La Jalca, Peru B2 58
La Jara, Co., U.S. D5 83
La Jara, N.M., U.S. A3 108
Laje Point, c., Port. f9 22
Lajeado, Braz. D2 56
Lajes, Braz. B6 56
Lajes, Braz. C3 57
La Jolla, Point, c., Ca., U.S. o15 82
La Joya, Mex. h9 63
La Joya, N.M., U.S. C3 108
La Joya, Peru E3 58
La Joya (part of Mexico City), Mex. h9 63
Lajosmizse, Hung. B4 24
La Junta, Co., U.S. D7 83
Lake, Mi., U.S. E5 99
Lake, Ms., U.S. C4 101
Lake, co., Ca., U.S. C2 82
Lake, co., Co., U.S. B4 83
Lake, co., Fl., U.S. D5 86
Lake, co., Il., U.S. A6 90
Lake, co., In., U.S. B3 91
Lake, co., Mi., U.S. E5 99
Lake, co., Mn., U.S. C7 100
Lake, co., Mt., U.S. C2 105
Lake, co., Oh., U.S. A4 112
Lake, co., Or., U.S. E6 114
Lake, co., S.D., U.S. C8 118
Lake, co., Tn., U.S. A2 119
Lake Alfred, Fl., U.S. D5 86
Lake Alma, Sask. H3 75
Lake Andes, S.D., U.S. D7 118
Lake Ariel, Pa., U.S. D11 115
Lake Arrowhead, Ca., U.S. *E5 82
Lake Arthur, La., U.S. D3 95
Lake Arthur, N.M., U.S. E5 108
Lakeba Passage, strt., Fiji H16 52
Lake Barcroft, Va., U.S. B5 123
Lake Benton, Mn., U.S. F2 100
Lake Beulah, Wi., U.S. n11 126
Lake Bluff, Il., U.S. A6 90
Lake Bonaparte, N.Y., U.S. A5 109
Lake Bronson, Mn., U.S. B2 100
Lake Bruce, In., U.S. B4 91
Lake Butler, Fl., U.S. B4 86
Lake Cargelligo, Austl. F6 51
Lake Carmel, N.Y., U.S. *E7 109
Lake Carroll, Fl., U.S. *D4 86
Lake Charles, La., U.S. D2 95
Lake Chelan National Recreation Area, Wa., U.S. A5 124

Lake City, Ar., U.S. B5 81
Lake City, Ca., U.S. B3 82
Lake City, Co., U.S. C3 83
Lake City, Fl., U.S. B4 86
Lake City, Ia., U.S. B3 92
Lake City, Ks., U.S. E5 93
Lake City, Mi., U.S. D5 99
Lake City, Mn., U.S. F6 100
Lake City, Pa., U.S. B1 115
Lake City, S.C., U.S. D8 117
Lake City, S.D., U.S. B8 118
Lake City, Tn., U.S. C9 119
Lake Clark National Park, Ak., U.S. C9 79
Lake Como, Pa., U.S. C11 115
Lake Cormorant, Ms., U.S. A3 101
Lake Cowichan, B.C. g11 69
Lakecreek, Or., U.S. E4 114
Lake Crystal, Mn., U.S. F4 100
Lake Delta, N.Y., U.S. B5 109
Lake Delton, Wi., U.S. E4 126
Lake District, reg., Eng., U.K. C5 10
Lake Elmo, Mn., U.S. *n13 100
Lake Elmore, Vt., U.S. B3 122
Lake Elsinore, Ca., U.S. F5 82
Lake Erie Beach, N.Y., U.S. C1 109
Lakefield, Ont. C6 73
Lakefield, Mn., U.S. G3 100
Lake Forest, Fl., U.S. *s13 86
Lake Forest, Il., U.S. A6 90
Lake Fork, Id., U.S. E2 89
Lake Fork, Il., U.S. D4 90
Lake Fork, stm., Ut., U.S. C5 121
Lake Geneva, Wi., U.S. F5 126
Lake George, Co., U.S. C5 83
Lake George, Mi., U.S. E6 99
Lake George, N.Y., U.S. B7 109
Lake Grove, N.J., U.S. A3 107
Lake Grove, N.Y., U.S. *E7 109
Lake Hamilton, Ar., U.S. g7 81
Lake Harbour, N.W. Ter. D19 66
Lake Havasu City, Az., U.S. C1 80
Lake Helen, Fl., U.S. D5 86
Lake Hiawatha, N.J., U.S. B4 107
Lake Hubert, Mn., U.S. D5 100
Lake Hughes, Ca., U.S. E4 82
Lake Huntington, N.Y., U.S. D5 109
Lakehurst, N.J., U.S. C4 107
Lakehurst Naval Air Station, mil., N.J., U.S. C4 107
Lake in the Hills, Il., U.S. h8 90
Lake Itasca, Mn., U.S. C3 100
Lake Jackson, Tx., U.S. r14 120
Lake Katrine, N.Y., U.S. D7 109
Lakeland, Fl., U.S. D5 86
Lakeland, Ga., U.S. E3 87
Lakeland Highlands, Fl., U.S. *E5 86
Lake Leelanau, Mi., U.S. D5 99
Lake Lenore, Sask. E3 75
Lake Lillian, Mn., U.S. F4 100
Lake Linden, Mi., U.S. A2 99
Lake Lindsey, Fl., U.S. D4 86
Lake Lorraine, Fl., U.S. *u15 86
Lake Louise, Alta. D2 68
Lake Luzerne, N.Y., U.S. B7 109
Lake Magdalene, Fl., U.S. o11 86
Lake Mary, Fl., U.S. D5 86
Lake Mcdonald, Mt., U.S. B3 105
Lake Mead National Recreation Area, U.S. H7 105
Lake Meredith National Recreation Area, Tx., U.S. B2 120
Lake Metigoshe, N.D., U.S. A5 111
Lake Mills, Ia., U.S. A4 92
Lake Mills, Wi., U.S. E5 126
Lake Minchumina, Ak., U.S. C9 79
Lakemont, Pa., U.S. F5 115
Lakemore, Oh., U.S. A4 112
Lake Mountain, mtn., Wy., U.S. E6 127
Lakenan, Mo., U.S. B5 102
Lake Nebagamon, Wi., U.S. B2 126
Lake Norden, S.D., U.S. C8 118
Lake Odessa, Mi., U.S. F5 99
Lake Of The Woods, co., Mn., U.S. B4 100
Lake Orion, Mi., U.S. F7 99
Lake Oswego, Or., U.S. B4 114
Lake Ozark, Mo., U.S. C5 102
Lake Park, Fl., U.S. F6 86
Lake Park, Ga., U.S. F3 87
Lake Park, Ia., U.S. A2 92
Lake Park, Mn., U.S. D2 100
Lake Placid, Fl., U.S. E5 86
Lake Placid, N.Y., U.S. A7 109
Lake Pleasant, N.Y., U.S. B6 109
Lake Pontchartrain Causeway, La., U.S. h11 95
Lakeport, Ca., U.S. C2 82
Lake Preston, S.D., U.S. C8 118
Lake Providence, La., U.S. B4 95
Lake Range, mts., Nv., U.S. C2 105
Lakeridge, Nv., U.S. *E2 105
Lake Ridge, Va., U.S. B5 123
Lake River, Ont. n19 73
Lake Ronkonkoma, N.Y., U.S. *n15 109
Lake Shore, Md., U.S. B5 97
Lakeshore, Mi., U.S. E4 99
Lake Shore, Ut., U.S. *C4 121
Lakeside, Az., U.S. C6 80
Lakeside, Ca., U.S. *B5 82
Lakeside, Ct., U.S. C2 84
Lakeside, Mt., U.S. B2 105
Lakeside, Oh., U.S. A3 112
Lakeside, Or., U.S. D2 114
Lakeside, Va., U.S. *C5 123
Lakeside Mountains, mts., Ut., U.S. C3 121
Lakeside Park, Ky., U.S. h13 94
Lakeside-Pinetop, Az., U.S. C6 80
Lake Station, In., U.S. A3 91
Lake Stevens, Wa., U.S. A3 124
Lake Superior Provincial Park, Ont. p18 73
Lake Swamp, stm., S.C., U.S. D8 117
Lake Tansi, Tn., U.S. D8 119
Lake Telemark, N.J., U.S. B4 107
Lake Tomahawk, Wi., U.S. C4 126
Laketon, In., U.S. B6 91
Laketown, Ut., U.S. B4 121
Lake Toxaway, N.C., U.S. f10 110
Lake Traverse, Ont. B6 73
Lake Valley, Sask. G2 75
Lake Valley, val., Nv., U.S. E7 105
Lakeview, Ga., U.S. *B1 87

Name	Map Ref.	Page
Lakeview, Id., U.S.	B2	89
Lake View, Ia., U.S.	B2	92
Lakeview, Mi., U.S.	E5	99
Lakeview, Mt., U.S.	F5	103
Lake View, N.Y., U.S.	*E7	109
Lakeview, N.Y., U.S.	C2	109
Lakeview, Oh., U.S.	B2	112
Lakeview, Or., U.S.	E6	114
Lake View, S.C., U.S.	C9	117
Lakeview, Tx., U.S.	B2	120
Lake Villa, Il., U.S.	h8	90
Lake Village, Ar., U.S.	D4	81
Lake Village, In., U.S.	B3	91
Lakeville, Ct., U.S.	B2	84
Lakeville, In., U.S.	A5	91
Lakeville, Ma., U.S.	C6	98
Lakeville, Mn., U.S.	F5	100
Lakeville, N.Y., U.S.	C3	109
Lake Waccamaw, N.C., U.S.	C4	110
Lake Wales, Fl., U.S.	E5	86
Lake Williams, N.D., U.S.	B6	111
Lake Wilson, Mn., U.S.	G3	100
Lake Winola, Pa., U.S.	m17	115
Lake Wissota, Wi., U.S.	*D2	126
Lakewood, Ca., U.S.	n12	82
Lakewood, Co., U.S.	B5	83
Lakewood, Il., U.S.	D5	90
Lakewood, La., U.S.	f8	92
Lakewood, Me., U.S.	D3	96
Lakewood, N.J., U.S.	C4	107
Lakewood, N.M., U.S.	E5	108
Lakewood, N.Y., U.S.	C1	109
Lakewood, Oh., U.S.	A4	112
Lakewood, Pa., U.S.	C10	115
Lakewood, Wa., U.S.	A3	124
Lakewood, Wi., U.S.	C5	126
Lakewood Center, Wa., U.S.	B3	124
Lake Worth, Fl., U.S.	F6	86
Lake Worth Inlet, b., Fl., U.S.	F7	86
Lake Zurich, Il., U.S.	h8	90
Lakhī, Afg.	B3	36
Lakhīmpur, India	C7	36
Lakhta (part of Leningrad), Sov. Un.	r31	14
Lakin, Ks., U.S.	E2	93
Lakota, I.C.	E3	45
Lakota, Ia., U.S.	A3	92
Lakota, N.D., U.S.	A7	111
Laksefjorden, Nor.	B12	14
Lakshadweep (Laccadive, Minicoy and Amīndīvi Islands), ter., India	*F5	36
Lakshadweep (Laccadive Islands), is., India	F5	36
La Laguna, Spain	m13	22
La Libertad, El Sal.	D3	62
La Libertad, Guat.	B2	62
La Libertad, dept., Peru	C2	58
La Ligua, Chile	A2	54
Lalín, Spain	A1	22
La Línea, Spain	D3	22
La Loche, Sask.	m7	75
La Loche, Lac, l., Sask.	A6	68
La Loma, N.M., U.S.	B4	108
La Luz, N.M., U.S.	D4	108
La Macarena, Serranía de, mts., Col.	C3	60
La Machine, Fr.	D5	16
La Maddalena, Italy	D2	23
La Madera, N.M., U.S.	A3	108
Lama-Kara, Togo	E5	45
La Malbaie, Que.	B7	74
Lamaline, Newf.	E4	72
La Mancha, reg., Spain	C4	22
Lamanibot Sanhilo, Puntan, c., N. Mar. Is.	D7	52
Lamar, Ar., U.S.	B2	81
Lamar, Co., U.S.	C8	83
Lamar, In., U.S.	H4	91
Lamar, Ms., U.S.	A4	101
Lamar, Mo., U.S.	D3	102
Lamar, Ne., U.S.	D4	104
Lamar, Ok., U.S.	B5	113
Lamar, Pa., U.S.	D7	115
Lamar, S.C., U.S.	C7	117
Lamar, co., Al., U.S.	B1	78
Lamar, co., Ga., U.S.	C2	87
Lamar, co., Ms., U.S.	D4	101
Lamar, co., Tx., U.S.	C5	120
Lamar, co., Wy., U.S.	B2	127
Lamarche, Fr.	A1	20
La Marque, Tx., U.S.	*15	120
Lamas, Peru	C2	58
Lamasco, Ky., U.S.	f10	94
La Mauricie, Parc National de, Que.	C5	74
Lamb, co., Tx., U.S.	B1	120
Lamballe, Fr.	C2	16
Lambaréné, Gabon	F2	46
Lambayeque, Peru	C2	58
Lambayeque, dept., Peru	C2	58
Lambay Island, i., Ire.	D5	11
Lambert, Ms., U.S.	A3	101
Lambert, Mt., U.S.	C12	103
Lambert, Ok., U.S.	A3	113
Lambert Glacier, ice, Ant.	B19	7
Lambert Lake, Me., U.S.	C5	96
Lamberton, Mn., U.S.	F3	100
Lambert's Bay, S. Afr.	D2	49
Lambertville, Mi., U.S.	G7	99
Lambertville, N.J., U.S.	C3	107
Lambeth, Ont.	E3	73
Lambeth (part of London), Eng., U.K.	m12	10
Lambourn, Eng., U.K.	C6	12
Lambrecht (Pfalz), W. Ger.	D3	19
Lambro, stm., Italy	D5	20
Lambrook, Ar., U.S.	C5	81
Lambsburg, Va., U.S.	D2	123
Lamb's Head, c., Ire.	F1	11
Lambton, Que.	D6	74
Lambton, co., Ont.	E2	73
Lambton, Cape, c., N.W. Ter.	B8	66
Lamdesar, Indon.	G8	34
Lame Deer, Mt., U.S.	E10	103
Lamego, Port.	B2	22
Lamèque, Chile	B5	71
Lamèque, Île, i., N.B.	B5	71
La Merced (Superí), Arg.	F5	54
La Mesa, Ca., U.S.	F5	82
La Mesa, N.M., U.S.	E3	108
Lamesa, Tx., U.S.	C2	120
Lamia, Grc.	C4	40
La Minerve, Que.	C3	74
Lamington, Mount, mtn. Pap. N. Gui.	k12	50
La Mirada, Ca., U.S.	*E4	82
Lamlam, Mount, mtn., Guam	M9	52
Lamlash, Scot., U.K.	E3	13
Lammermuir Hills, hills, Scot., U.K.	E6	13
Lammhult, Swe.	A8	15
Lamoil, i., Micron.	Q18	52
La Moille, Il., U.S.	B4	90
Lamoille, Nv., U.S.	C6	105
Lamoille, co., Vt., U.S.	B3	122
Lamoille, stm., Vt., U.S.	B3	122
Lamoille, North Branch, stm., Vt., U.S.	B3	122
La Moine, stm., Il., U.S.	C3	90
Lamona, Wa., U.S.	B7	124
Lamon Bay, b., Phil.	C6	34
L'Ange-Gardien, Que.	n17	74
Langeland, i., Den.	D4	15
Langeloth, Pa., U.S.	F1	115
Langen, W. Ger.	D3	19
Langenau, W. Ger.	E5	19
Langenburg, Sask.	G5	75
Langenselbold, W. Ger.	C4	19
Langenthal, Switz.	E3	18
Langenzenn, W. Ger.	D5	19
Langeoog, W. Ger.	A7	17
Langeoog, i., W. Ger.	B3	18
Langerak, strt., Den.	A4	15
Langesund, Nor.	H3	14
Langford, B.C.	h12	69
Langford, S.D., U.S.	B8	118
Langham, Sask.	E2	75
Länghem, Swe.	A7	15
Langholm, Scot., U.K.	E5	13
Langhorne, Pa., U.S.	F12	115
Langjökull, ice, Ice.	n22	14
Langkawi, i., Malay.	I3	35
Langlade, co., Wi., U.S.	C4	126
Langlade, i., St. P./M.	E3	72
Langley, B.C.	f13	69
Langley, Ar., U.S.	C2	81
Langley, Ky., U.S.	C7	94
Langley, Ok., U.S.	A6	113
Langley, S.C., U.S.	E4	117
Langley, Wa., U.S.	A3	124
Langley Air Force Base, mil., Va., U.S.	h15	123
Langley Park, Md., U.S.	f9	97
Langleyville, Il., U.S.	D4	90
Langlois, Or., U.S.	E2	114
Langnau [in Emmental], Switz.	E4	18
Langogne, Fr.	E5	16
Langon, Fr.	E3	16
Langøya, i., Nor.	C6	14
Langres, Fr.	E6	16
Langres, Plateau de, plat., Fr.	D6	16
Langruth, Man.	D2	70
Langsa, Indon.	E1	34
Lang Son, Viet.	B7	35
Langstaff, Ont.	k15	73
Langston, Al., U.S.	A3	78
Langston, Ok., U.S.	B4	113
Langton, Ont.	E4	73
Langtry, Tx., U.S.	E2	120
Languedoc, hist. reg., Fr.	F5	16
L'Anguille, stm., Ar., U.S.	B5	81
Langzhong, China	E6	31
Lanham, Md., U.S.	C4	97
Lanier, co., Ga., U.S.	E3	87
Lanigan, Sask.	F3	75
Lanigan Creek, stm., Sask.	F3	75
Lanín, Volcán, vol., S.A.	B2	54
Lankin, N.D., U.S.	A8	111
Lanklaar, Bel.	C5	17
Lannion, Fr.	C2	16
Lannon, Wi., U.S.	m11	126
L'Annonciation, Que.	C3	74
Lanoka Harbor, N.J., U.S.	D4	107
Lanoraie, Que.	D4	74
Lansdale, Pa., U.S.	F11	115
Lansdowne, Ont.	C8	73
Lansdowne, Md., U.S.	B4	97
Lansdowne, Pa., U.S.	*p20	115
Lansdowne House, Ont.	n18	73
L'Anse, Mi., U.S.	B2	99
L'Anse-au-Clair, Newf.	C3	72
L'Anse-au-Loup, Newf.	C3	72
L'Anse-aux-Meadows, Newf.	C4	72
L'Anse Indian Reservation, Mi., U.S.	B2	99
L'Anse-Saint-Jean, Que.	A7	74
Lansford, N.D., U.S.	A4	111
Lansford, Pa., U.S.	E10	115
Lansing, Il., U.S.	B6	90
Lansing, Ia., U.S.	A6	92
Lansing, Ks., U.S.	C9	93
Lansing, Mi., U.S.	F6	99
Lansing, N.C., U.S.	A1	110
Lansing, W.V., U.S.	m13	125
Lanslebourg, Fr.	D2	16
Lantana, Fl., U.S.	F6	86
Lantern Hill, hill, Ct., U.S.	D8	84
Lantry, S.D., U.S.	B4	118
Lanusei, Italy	E2	23
Lanuvio, Italy	h9	23
Lanxi, China	F8	31
Lanxi, China	A12	32
Lanzarote, i., Spain	m15	22
Lanzhou (Lanchou), China	D7	31
Laoag, Phil.	B6	34
Lao Cai, Viet.	A6	35
Laohekou, China	E7	31
Laoighis see Laois, co., Ire.	D4	11
Laois, co., Ire.	D4	11
Laolao, Bahia, b., N. Mar. Is.	D8	52
Laolao Kattan, Puntan, c., N. Mar. Is.	D8	52
Laon, Fr.	C5	16
Laona, Wi., U.S.	C5	126
La Oroya, Peru	D2	58
Laos, ctry., Asia	B7	35
Laotto, In., U.S.	B7	91
Lapa, Braz.	B7	56
La Palma, Pan.	F8	62
La Palma, Az., U.S.	E4	80
La Palma, Ca., U.S.	*n12	82
La Palma [del Condado], Spain	D2	22
La Paloma, Ur.	E2	56
La Pampa, prov., Arg.	B3	54
La Paragua, Ven.	B5	60
La Pasión, stm., Guat.	B2	62
La Passe, Ont.	B8	73
La Patrie, Que.	D6	74
La Paz, Arg.	A5	54
La Paz, Bol.	C2	55
La Paz, Hond.	E7	63
La Paz, Mex.	C2	63
La Paz, Mex.	A5	63
La Paz, Mex.	E7	63
La Paz, dept., Bol.	C2	55
La Paz, dept., Hond.	E7	63
La Paz, Bahía de, b., Mex.	D4	60
La Pedrera, Col.	D5	60
Lapeer, Mi., U.S.	E7	99
Lapeer, co., Mi., U.S.	E7	99
Lapel, In., U.S.	D6	91
La Perouse Strait, strt., Asia	D10	33
La Piedad [Cavadas], Mex.	m12	63
La Pine, Or., U.S.	D5	114
La Place, Il., U.S.	D5	90
La Place, La., U.S.	h11	95
Lapland, reg., Eur.	C11	14
La Plant, S.D., U.S.	B5	118
La Plata, Arg.	A5	54
La Plata, Col.	C2	60
La Plata, Md., U.S.	C4	97
La Plata, Mo., U.S.	A5	102
La Plata, N.M., U.S.	A1	108
La Plata, co., Co., U.S.	D3	83
La Plata Mountains, mts., Co., U.S.	D3	83
La Plata Peak, mtn., Co., U.S.	B4	83
La Platte, Ne., U.S.	g13	104
La Platte, stm., Vt., U.S.	C2	122
La Pobla de Lillet, Spain	A6	22
La Pocatière, Que.	B7	74
La Poile Bay, b., Newf.	E2	72
Laporte, Ut., U.S.	C6	121
La Porte, Wi., U.S.	h5	126
La Porte, Ca., U.S.	B3	126
Laporte, Co., U.S.	A5	83
La Porte, In., U.S.	A4	91
Laporte, Mn., U.S.	C4	100
Laporte, Pa., U.S.	D9	115
La Porte, Tx., U.S.	r14	120
La Porte, co., In., U.S.	A4	91
La Porte City, Ia., U.S.	B5	92
Läppe, Swe.	I33	14
Lappeenranta, Fin.	G13	14
La Prairie, Que.	D4	74
La Prairie, Mn., U.S.	C5	100
Laprairie, co., Que.	D4	74
Laprida, Arg.	B4	54
La Pryor, Tx., U.S.	E3	120
Lâpseki, Tur.	B6	40
Laptev Sea, Sov. Un.	B15	29
La Puebla, Spain	C7	22
La Puebla de Montalbán, Spain	C3	22
La Puente, Ca., U.S.	*m13	82
La Puente, N.M., U.S.	A3	108
La Purísima, Mex.	B2	63
La Push, Wa., U.S.	B1	124
Lapwai, Id., U.S.	C2	89
Laqīyat al Arba'īn, Sud.	B2	47
La Quiaca, Arg.	D2	55
L'Aquila (Aquila), Italy	C4	23
Lār, Iran	C5	38
Lara, state, Ven.	A3	60
Larache, Mor.	B3	44
Lārak, i., Iran	H8	39
Laramie, Wy., U.S.	E7	127
Laramie, co., Wy., U.S.	E8	127
Laramie, stm., U.S.	E7	127
Laramie Mountains, mts., Wy., U.S.	D7	127
Laramie Peak, mtn., Wy., U.S.	D7	127
Laranjeiras, Braz.	D3	57
Laranjeiras do Sul, Braz.	B6	56
Larantuka, Indon.	G6	34
Larap, Phil.	o14	34
Larche Pass, Eur.	E2	20
Laredo, Spain	A4	22
Laredo, Mo., U.S.	A4	102
Laredo, Tx., U.S.	F3	120
Laredo Sound, strt., B.C.	C3	69
La Réole, Fr.	E4	16
Lares, P.R.	B2	65
Largeau, Chad	E9	45
Largentière, Fr.	E6	16
Largo, Fl., U.S.	E4	86
Largo, Cañon, val., N.M., U.S.	A2	108
Largo, Cayo, i., Cuba	D3	64
Largo, Key, i., Fl., U.S.	G6	86
Largs, Scot., U.K.	E4	13
Lariat, Tx., U.S.	B1	120
La Ricamarie, Fr.	E6	16
Larimer, co., Co., U.S.	A5	83
Larimore, N.D., U.S.	B8	111
Larino, Italy	C5	23
La Rioja, Arg.	B2	55
La Rioja, Cuba	D5	64
La Rioja, prov., Arg.	C2	55
Lárisa, Grc.	C4	40
Laristan, hist. reg., Iran	C5	38
La Riviera, Ca., U.S.	*C3	82
La Rivière, Man.	E2	70
Lark, N.D., U.S.	C4	111
Lark, Ut., U.S.	C3	121
Lārkāna, Pak.	B3	36
Lark Harbour, Newf.	D2	72
Larkinsville, Al., U.S.	A3	78
Larkspur, Ca., U.S.	h7	82
Larkspur, Co., U.S.	B6	83
Larksville, Pa., U.S.	n17	115
Larnaca see Lárnax, Cyp.	E9	40
Lárnax (Larnaca), Cyp.	E9	40
Larne, N. Ire., U.K.	C4	11
Larned, Ks., U.S.	D4	93
La Robla, Spain	A3	22
La Rochelle, Fr.	D3	16
La-Roche-sur-Foron, Fr.	C2	16
La-Roche-sur-Yon, Fr.	D3	16
La Roda, Spain	C4	22
La Romana, Dom. Rep.	B3	64
La Ronge, Sask.	D3	75
La Rose, Il., U.S.	B4	90
Larose, La., U.S.	E5	95
Larrabee, Ia., U.S.	B2	92
Larrys River, N.S.	D8	71
Larsen Bay, Ak., U.S.	D9	79
Larsen Ice Shelf, ice, Ant.	C6	7
Larsmont, Mn., U.S.	D7	100
Larson, N.D., U.S.	A3	111
Larto, La., U.S.	C4	95
La Rubia, Arg.	A4	54
La Rue, Oh., U.S.	B2	112
Larue, co., Ky., U.S.	C4	94
Laruns, Fr.	F3	16
Larvik, Nor.	H3	14
Larwill, In., U.S.	B6	91
La Salle, co., Tx., U.S.	E3	120
La Sal Mountains, mts., Ut., U.S.	E6	121
Las Animas, Co., U.S.	C7	83
Las Animas, co., Co., U.S.	D6	83
La Santa, Cerro, mtn., P.R.	B3	65
La Sarre, Que.	k11	74
Lasbergr, Aus.	E9	19
Las Cabras, Chile	A2	54
Lascahobas, Haiti	E8	64
Lascano, Ur.	E2	56
Lascar, Volcán, vol., Chile	D2	55
Lascassas, Tn., U.S.	B5	119
Las Coloradas, Arg.	B2	54
Las Cruces, N.M., U.S.	E3	108
La Serena, Chile	E1	55
La Seyne [-sur-Mer], Fr.	F6	16
Las Flores, Arg.	B5	54
Lashburn, Sask.	D1	75
Lashio, Burma	D10	36
Łask, Pol.	C5	26
Las Lajas, Arg.	B2	54
Las Lajas, Pan.	F7	62
Las Lomitas, Arg.	D3	55
Las Marismas, sw., Spain	D2	22
La Solana, Spain	C4	22
Las Palmas [de Gran Canaria], Spain	m14	22
La Spezia, Italy	B2	23
Las Piedras, Ur.	E1	56
Las Piedras, Río de, stm., Peru	D3	58
Las Plumas, Arg.	C3	54
Las Rosas, Arg.	A4	54
Las Rozas de Madrid, Spain	p17	22
Lassance, Braz.	B4	56
Lassen, co., Ca., U.S.	B3	82
Lassen Peak, vol., Ca., U.S.	B3	82
Lassen Volcanic National Park, Ca., U.S.	B3	82
Lasso, hill, N. Mar. Is.	D7	52
L'Assomption, Que.	D4	74
L'Assomption, co., Que.	D4	74
Las Tablas, Pan.	G7	62
Las Tablas, N.M., U.S.	A3	108
Last Chance, Co., U.S.	B7	83
Las Termas, Arg.	A3	54
Lastoursville, Gabon	F2	46
Lastovo, i., Yugo.	D3	24
Lastrup, W. Ger.	B7	17
Lastrup, Mn., U.S.	D5	100
Las Tunas, prov., Cuba	D5	64
Las Varillas, Arg.	A4	54
Las Vegas, Nv., U.S.	G6	105
Las Vegas, N.M., U.S.	B4	108
Las Vigas, Mex.	n15	63
Latacunga, Ec.	C2	58
Latady Island, i., Ant.	B5	7
La Tagua, Col.	D3	60
Latah, Wa., U.S.	B8	124
Latah, co., Id., U.S.	C2	89
Latakia (Al Lādhiqīyah), Syria	B3	38
La Teste-de-Buch, Fr.	E3	16
Latexo, Tx., U.S.	D5	120
Latham, Il., U.S.	D4	90
Latham, Ks., U.S.	E7	93
Latham, N.Y., U.S.	*n15	109
Lathrop, Mo., U.S.	B3	102
Lathrop Wells, Nv., U.S.	G5	105
Latimer, Ia., U.S.	B4	92
Latimer, Ks., U.S.	D7	93
Latimer, co., Ok., U.S.	C6	113
Latina, Italy	D4	23
Latium (Lazio), prov., Italy	C4	23
Laton, Ca., U.S.	D4	82
Latoritsa (Latorica), stm., Sov.	D7	26
La Torrecilla, mtn., P.R.	B3	65
La Tortuga, Isla, i., Ven.	A4	60
Latour, Mo., U.S.	C3	102
La Tour-du-Pin, Fr.	E6	16
Latour Peak, mtn., Id., U.S.	B2	89
La Tremblade, Fr.	E3	16
La Trinité, Mart.	H14	64
Latrobe, Pa., U.S.	F3	115
Latrún, Isr. Occ.	C4	41
Latta, S.C., U.S.	C9	117
Lattimer Mines, Pa., U.S.	E10	115
Lattimore, N.C., U.S.	B1	110
Latty, Oh., U.S.	A1	112
La Tuque, Que.	B5	74
La Verkin, Ut., U.S.	F2	121
La Verne, Ca., U.S.	m13	82
Laverne, Ok., U.S.	A2	113
La Vernia, Tx., U.S.	E3	120
Laverton, Austl.	D4	50
La Veta, Co., U.S.	D5	83
Laviana, Spain	A3	22
La Victoria, Peru	*D2	58
La Victoria, Ven.	A4	60
Lavieille, Lake, l., Ont.	B6	73
Lavillette, N.B.	B4	71
Lavina, Mt., U.S.	D8	103
Lavinia, Braz.	C2	56
Lavinia, Tn., U.S.	B3	119
La Vista, Ga., U.S.	h8	87
La Vista, Ne., U.S.	g12	104
La Viuda, mtn., Peru	C2	58
Lavon Lake, res., Tx., U.S.	m10	120
Lavoy, Alta.	C5	68
Lavras, Braz.	C4	56
Lavras da Mangabeira, Braz.	E11	57
Lavras do Sul, Braz.	E2	56
Lávrion (Laurium), Grc.	D5	25
Lavumisa, Swaz.	C5	49
Lawai, Hi., U.S.	B2	88
Lawen, Or., U.S.	D8	114
Lawers, Ben, mtn., Scot., U.K.	D4	13
Lawit, mtn., Malay.	J5	35
Lawler, Ia., U.S.	A5	92
Lawler, Mn., U.S.	D5	100
Lawn, Newf.	E4	72
Lawn, Tx., U.S.	C3	120
Lawndale, Ca., U.S.	*E4	82
Lawndale, N.C., U.S.	B1	110
Lawnside, N.J., U.S.	*D2	107
Lawra, Ghana	D4	45
Lawrence, N.Z.	P12	51
Lawrence, In., U.S.	E5	91
Lawrence, Ks., U.S.	D8	93
Lawrence, Ma., U.S.	A5	98
Lawrence, Mi., U.S.	F4	99
Lawrence, Ms., U.S.	C4	101
Lawrence, Ne., U.S.	D7	104
Lawrence, N.Y., U.S.	k13	109
Lawrence, Pa., U.S.	F1	115
Lawrence, co., Al., U.S.	A2	78
Lawrence, co., Ar., U.S.	A4	81
Laurbjerg, Den.	B3	15
Laurel, Ont.	D4	73
Laurel, De., U.S.	F3	85
Laurel, Fl., U.S.	E4	86
Laurel, In., U.S.	F7	91
Laurel, Ia., U.S.	C5	92
Laurel, Md., U.S.	B4	97
Laurel, Ms., U.S.	D4	101
Laurel, Mt., U.S.	E8	103
Laurel, Ne., U.S.	B8	104
Laurel, Va., U.S.	C5	123
Laurel, co., Ky., U.S.	C5	94
Laurel Bay, S.C., U.S.	G6	117
Laurel Bloomery, Tn., U.S.	C12	119
Laurel Creek, stm., W.V., U.S.	n14	125
Laurel Creek, stm., W.V., U.S.	m12	125
Laureldale, N.J., U.S.	D3	107
Laureldale, Pa., U.S.	F10	115
Laureles, Ur.	E1	56
Laurel Fork, Va., U.S.	D2	123
Laurel Fork, stm., W.V., U.S.	C5	125
Laurel Hill, Fl., U.S.	u15	86
Laurel Hill, N.C., U.S.	C3	110
Laurel Mountain, mtn., W.V., U.S.	B5	125
Laurel River Lake, res., Ky., U.S.	D5	94
Laurel Run, Pa., U.S.	n17	115
Laurelton, Pa., U.S.	E7	115
Laurelville, Oh., U.S.	C3	112
Laurelwood Academy, Or., U.S.	h11	114
Laurence G. Hanscom Air Force Base, mil., Ma., U.S.	g10	98
Laurence Harbor, N.J., U.S.	C4	107
Laurencekirk, Scot., U.K.	D6	13
Laurens, Ia., U.S.	B3	92
Laurens, S.C., U.S.	C3	117
Laurens, co., Ga., U.S.	D4	87
Laurens, co., S.C., U.S.	C4	117
Laurentides, Que.	D4	74
Laurentides, Parc Provincial des, Que.	B6	74
Laurenum, hist., Italy	h8	23
Lauria, Interiore, Italy	D5	23
Laurie, stm., Man.	A1	70
Laurie Island, i., B.A.T.	C8	7
Laurie Lake, l., Can.	A1	70
Laurier, Man.	D2	70
Laurierville, Que.	C6	74
Laurin, Mt., U.S.	E4	103
Laurinburg, N.C., U.S.	C3	110
Laurium, Mt., U.S.	A2	99
Lausanne, Switz.	E3	18
Laut, i., Indon.	F5	34
Laut, i., Indon.	J8	35
Lautaro, Chile	B2	54
Lauterbach, W. Ger.	C4	19
Lauterbrunnen, Switz.	C4	21
Lauterecken, W. Ger.	D2	19
Laut Kecil Islands, is., Indon.	F5	34
Lautoka, Fiji	H14	52
Lauzon, Que.	C6	74
Lava Beds National Monument, Ca., U.S.	B3	82
Lavaca, Al., U.S.	C1	78
Lavaca, co., Tx., U.S.	E4	120
Lava Hot Springs, Id., U.S.	G6	89
Laval, Que.	D4	74
Laval, Fr.	C3	16
La Vale, Md., U.S.	k13	97
Lavalle, Arg.	A5	54
La Valle, Wi., U.S.	E3	126
Lavallette, N.J., U.S.	D4	107
La Valley, Co., U.S.	D5	83
Lavaltrie, Que.	D4	74
La Vega, Dom. Rep.	E8	64
La Vela de Coro, Ven.	A4	60
Lavelanet, Fr.	F4	16
Lavello, Italy	D5	23
L'Avenir, Que.	D5	74
La Vergne, Tn., U.S.	A5	119

Name	Map Ref.	Page
Lawrence, co., Il., U.S.	E6	90
Lawrence, co., In., U.S.	G4	91
Lawrence, co., Ky., U.S.	B7	94
Lawrence, co., Ms., U.S.	D3	101
Lawrence, co., Mo., U.S.	D4	102
Lawrence, co., Oh., U.S.	D3	112
Lawrence, co., Pa., U.S.	E1	115
Lawrence, co., S.D., U.S.	E2	32
Lawrence, co., Tn., U.S.	B4	119
Lawrenceburg, In., U.S.	F8	91
Lawrenceburg, Ky., U.S.	B5	94
Lawrenceburg, Tn., U.S.	B4	119
Lawrence Park, Pa., U.S.	B1	115
Lawrenceport, In., U.S.	G5	91
Lawrence Station, N.B.	D2	71
Lawrencetown, N.S.	E4	71
Lawrenceville, Que.	D5	74
Lawrenceville, Ga., U.S.	C3	87
Lawrenceville, Il., U.S.	E6	90
Lawrenceville, N.J., U.S.	C3	107
Lawrenceville, N.Y., U.S.	f10	109
Lawrenceville, Va., U.S.	D5	123
Lawshe, Oh., U.S.	D2	112
Lawson, Sask.	G2	75
Lawson, Ar., U.S.	D3	81
Lawson, Mo., U.S.	B3	102
Lawsonia, Md., U.S.	E6	97
Lawsonville, N.C., U.S.	A2	110
Lawtell, La., U.S.	D3	95
Lawtey, Fl., U.S.	B4	86
Lawton, Ia., U.S.	B1	92
Lawton, Ky., U.S.	B6	94
Lawton, Mi., U.S.	F5	99
Lawton, N.D., U.S.	A7	111
Lawton, Ok., U.S.	C3	113
Lawyersville, N.Y., U.S.	C6	109
Lawz, Jabal al, mtn., Sau. Ar.	H10	40
Lax Kw'alaams, B.C.	B2	69
Laxou, Fr.	C7	16
Lay, Point, c., Viet.	D7	35
Lay Dam, Al., U.S.	C3	78
Lay Lake, res., Al., U.S.	C3	78
Layland, W.V., U.S.	n14	125
Layou, St. Vin.	U26	65
Laysan Island, i., Hi., U.S.	k13	88
Laysville, Ct., U.S.	D6	84
Layton, Ut., U.S.	B4	121
Laytonsville, Md., U.S.	B3	97
Laytonville, Ca., U.S.	C2	82
Lazdijai, Sov. Un.	A7	26
Lazear, Co., U.S.	C3	83
Łaziska Górne, Pol.	g9	26
Lea, co., N.M., U.S.	D6	108
Lea, stm., Eng., U.K.	k12	10
Leach, Ok., U.S.	A7	113
Leachville, Ar., U.S.	B5	81
Leacross, Sask.	D3	75
Lead, S.D., U.S.	C2	118
Leadbetter Point, c., Wa., U.S.	C1	124
Leader, Sask.	G1	75
Lead Hill, Ar., U.S.	A3	81
Lead Hill, hill, Mo., U.S.	D5	102
Lead Mountain, mtn., Me., U.S.	D4	96
Lead Mountain Ponds, l., Me., U.S.	D4	96
Leadore, Id., U.S.	E5	89
Leadville, Co., U.S.	B4	83
Leadwood, Mo., U.S.	D7	102
Leaf, Ms., U.S.	D5	101
Leaf, stm., Ms., U.S.	D5	101
Leaf Lake, l., Sask.	E4	75
Leaf Rapids, Man.	A1	70
Leaf River, Il., U.S.	A4	90
League City, Tx., U.S.	*r14	120
Leah, Ga., U.S.	C4	87
Leake, co., Ms., U.S.	C4	101
Leakesville, Ms., U.S.	D5	101
Leakey, Tx., U.S.	E3	120
Leal, N.D., U.S.	B7	111
Lealman, Fl., U.S.	p10	86
Leamington, Ont.	E2	73
Leamington, Ut., U.S.	D3	121
Leamington see Royal Leamington Spa, Eng., U.K.	D6	10
Leane, Lough, l., Ire.	E2	11
Leapwood, Tn., U.S.	B3	119
Learned, Ms., U.S.	C3	101
Leary, Ga., U.S.	E2	87
Leasburg, Mo., U.S.	C6	102
Leasburg, N.C., U.S.	A3	110
Leaside (part of East York), Ont.	m15	73
Leask, Sask.	E2	75
Leatherhead, Eng., U.K.	m12	10
Leatherman Peak, mtn., Id., U.S.	E5	89
Leatherwood, Ky., U.S.	C6	94
L'Eau Frais Creek, stm., Ar., U.S.	C3	81
Leavenworth, In., U.S.	H5	91
Leavenworth, Ks., U.S.	C9	93
Leavenworth, Wa., U.S.	B5	124
Leavenworth, co., Ks., U.S.	C8	93
Leavittsburg, Oh., U.S.	A5	112
Leawood, Ks., U.S.	D9	93
Łeba, Pol.	A4	26
Lebam, Wa., U.S.	C2	124
Lebanon, Ct., U.S.	C7	84
Lebanon, De., U.S.	D4	85
Lebanon, Il., U.S.	E4	90
Lebanon, In., U.S.	D5	91
Lebanon, Ks., U.S.	C5	93
Lebanon, Ky., U.S.	C4	94
Lebanon, Mo., U.S.	D5	102
Lebanon, Ne., U.S.	D5	104
Lebanon, N.H., U.S.	C2	106
Lebanon, N.J., U.S.	B3	107
Lebanon, Oh., U.S.	C1	112
Lebanon, Or., U.S.	D5	113
Lebanon, Or., U.S.	C4	114
Lebanon, Pa., U.S.	F9	115
Lebanon, S.D., U.S.	B6	118
Lebanon, Tn., U.S.	A5	119
Lebanon, Va., U.S.	f9	123
Lebanon, co., Pa., U.S.	F8	115
Lebanon, ctry., Asia	B3	38
Lebanon Junction, Ky., U.S.	C4	94
Le Bardo, Tun.	*B7	44
Lebeau, La., U.S.	D4	95
Lebec, Ca., U.S.	E4	82
Lebedin, Sov. Un.	F10	27
Lebedyan, Sov. Un.	E12	27
Le Biot, Fr.	D2	21
Le Blanc, Fr.	D4	16
Le Blanc-Mesnil, Fr.	g10	16
Lebo, Ks., U.S.	D8	93
Lebo, Zaire	A3	48
Lębork, Pol.	A4	26
Le Bourg-d'Oisans, Fr.	D2	20
Le Bourget, Fr.	g10	16
Le Bouscat, Fr.	E3	16
Le Brassus, Switz.	C1	21
Lebret, Sask.	G4	75
Lebrija, Spain	D2	22
Lebu, Chile	B2	54
Lebyazhye, Sov. Un.	B7	28
Le Cateau, Fr.	B5	16
Lecce, Italy	D7	23
Lecco, Italy	B2	23
Lecco, Lake, l., Italy	E7	21
Le Center, Mn., U.S.	F5	100
Lech, stm., Eur.	E6	16
Le Chambon-Feugerolles, Fr.	E6	16
Le Château, Fr.	E3	16
Lechbruck, W. Ger.	B6	20
Le Chesnay, Fr.	g9	16
Le Chesnay, Fr.	E4	17
Leck, W. Ger.	D2	15
Le Claire, Ia., U.S.	C7	92
Leclercville, Que.	C6	74
Lecompte, La., U.S.	C3	95
Lecompton, Ks., U.S.	C8	93
Léconi, Gabon	F2	46
Leconte, Mount, mtn., Tn., U.S.	D10	119
Lecontes Mills, Pa., U.S.	D5	115
Le Coteau, Fr.	D6	16
Le Creusot, Fr.	D6	16
Le Croisic, Fr.	D2	16
Le Crotoy, Fr.	D9	12
Lectoure, Fr.	F4	16
Lecznya, Pol.	B6	26
Ledbetter, N.C., U.S.	C3	110
Ledbury, Eng., U.K.	B5	12
Lédčice, Czech.	n17	26
Ledesma, Spain	B2	22
Ledford, Il., U.S.	F5	90
Ledger, Mt., U.S.	B5	103
Ledgewood, N.J., U.S.	B3	107
Ledo, India	C10	36
Ledoux, N.M., U.S.	B4	108
Leduc, Alta.	C4	68
Ledyard, Ct., U.S.	D7	84
Ledyard, Ia., U.S.	A3	92
Lee, Fl., U.S.	B3	86
Lee, Il., U.S.	B5	90
Lee, Me., U.S.	C4	96
Lee, Ma., U.S.	B1	98
Lee, Nv., U.S.	C6	105
Lee, N.H., U.S.	D4	106
Lee, co., Al., U.S.	D8	119
Lee, co., Ar., U.S.	C5	81
Lee, co., Fl., U.S.	F5	86
Lee, co., Ga., U.S.	E2	87
Lee, co., Il., U.S.	B5	90
Lee, co., Ia., U.S.	D6	92
Lee, co., Ky., U.S.	C6	94
Lee, co., Ms., U.S.	A5	101
Lee, co., N.C., U.S.	B3	110
Lee, co., S.C., U.S.	C7	117
Lee, co., Tx., U.S.	D4	120
Lee, co., Va., U.S.	f8	123
Lee, stm., Ire.	E2	10
Lee Center, Il., U.S.	B4	90
Leechburg, Pa., U.S.	E2	115
Leech Lake, l., Sask.	F4	75
Leech Lake, l., Mn., U.S.	C4	100
Leech Lake Indian Reservation, Mn., U.S.	C4	100
Leechville, N.C., U.S.	B6	110
Lee Creek, stm., U.S.	B1	81
Leedey, Ok., U.S.	B2	113
Leedom Estates, De., U.S.	*B3	85
Leeds, Eng., U.K.	D6	10
Leeds, Al., U.S.	B3	78
Leeds, N.D., U.S.	A6	111
Leeds, S.C., U.S.	B5	117
Leeds, Ut., U.S.	F2	121
Leeds [and Grenville], co., Ont.	C8	73
Leeds Point, N.J., U.S.	E4	107
Leeds-Village, Que.	C6	74
Leek, Eng., U.K.	A5	12
Leelanau, co., Mi., U.S.	D5	99
Leelanau, Lake, l., Mi., U.S.	C5	99
Leenaun, Ire.	D2	11
Lee Park, Pa., U.S.	n17	115
Leeper, Mo., U.S.	D7	102
Leeper, Pa., U.S.	D2	115
Leer, W. Ger.	B3	18
Leesburg, Al., U.S.	A4	78
Leesburg, Fl., U.S.	D5	86
Leesburg, Ga., U.S.	E2	87
Leesburg, In., U.S.	B6	91
Leesburg, N.J., U.S.	E3	107
Leesburg, Oh., U.S.	C2	112
Leesburg, Va., U.S.	A5	123
Lees Landing, La., U.S.	h11	95
Lees Summit, Mo., U.S.	C3	102
Leesville, La., U.S.	*C6	84
Leesville, La., U.S.	C2	95
Leesville, Oh., U.S.	B4	112
Leesville, S.C., U.S.	D4	117
Leesville, Tx., U.S.	E4	120
Leesville Lake, res., Va., U.S.	C3	123
Leetes Island, Ct., U.S.	D5	84
Leeton, Austl.	G6	51
Leeton, Mo., U.S.	C4	102
Leetonia, Oh., U.S.	B5	112
Leetsdale, Pa., U.S.	h13	115
Leeuwarden, Neth.	A6	16
Leeuwin, Cape, c., Austl.	F2	50
Leeville, La., U.S.	E5	95
Lee Vining, Ca., U.S.	D4	82
Leeward Islands, is., N.A.	H13	64
Le Ferriere, Italy	h9	23
Leffingwell, Ca., U.S.	*n12	82
Leflore, Ok., U.S.	C7	113
Leflore, co., Ms., U.S.	B3	101
Le Flore, co., Ok., U.S.	C7	113
Lefor, N.D., U.S.	C3	111
Lefors, Tx., U.S.	B2	120
Le François, Mart.	I14	64
Lefroy, Ont.	C5	73
Lefroy, Lake, l., Austl.	F3	50
Leftrook Lake, l., Man.	A2	69
Legal, Alta.	C4	68
Leganés, Spain	p17	22
Legaspi, Phil.	C6	34
Leggett, Ca., U.S.	C2	82
Leghorn see Livorno, Italy	C4	23
Legionowo, Pol.	k13	26
Legnago, Italy	D7	20
Legnano, Italy	B2	23
Legnica (Liegnitz), Pol.	C4	26
Le Gore, N.D., U.S.	A3	97
Le Grand, Ca., U.S.	D3	82
Le Grand, Ia., U.S.	B5	92
Le Grand-Quevilly, Fr.	C4	16
Le Gros Cap, i., Que.	B7	71
Leh, India	B6	36
Le Havre, Fr.	C4	16
Lehi, Ut., U.S.	C4	121
Lehigh, Ia., U.S.	B3	92
Lehigh, Ks., U.S.	D6	93
Lehigh, Ok., U.S.	C5	113
Lehigh, co., Pa., U.S.	E10	115
Lehigh, stm., Pa., U.S.	E10	115
Lehigh Acres, Fl., U.S.	F5	86
Lehighton, Pa., U.S.	E10	115
Lehinch, Ire.	E2	11
Lehman, Pa., U.S.	n16	115
Lehr, N.D., U.S.	C6	111
Lehrte, W. Ger.	B4	18
Lehua Island, i., Hi., U.S.	A1	88
Leiah, Pak.	B5	36
Leibnitz, Aus.	E7	18
Leicester, Eng., U.K.	D6	10
Leicester, Ma., U.S.	B4	98
Leicester, N.Y., U.S.	C3	109
Leicester, Vt., U.S.	D2	122
Leicester Junction, Vt., U.S.	D2	122
Leicestershire, co., Eng., U.K.	B6	12
Leichhardt, Austl.	*F9	50
Leiden, Neth.	A6	16
Leigh, Ne., U.S.	C8	104
Leigh Creek, Austl.	F6	50
Leighton, Al., U.S.	A2	78
Leinan, Sask.	G2	75
Leine, stm., Eur.	B4	18
Leinster, hist. reg., Ire.	D4	11
Leinster, Mount, mtn., Ire.	D5	11
Leipalingis, Sov. Un.	A7	26
Leipers Fork, Tn., U.S.	B5	119
Leipsic, De., U.S.	D3	85
Leipsic, In., U.S.	G5	91
Leipsic, Oh., U.S.	A2	112
Leipsic, stm., De., U.S.	C3	85
Leipzig, Sask.	E1	75
Leipzig, E. Ger.	C6	18
Leiria, Port.	C1	22
Leisnig, E. Ger.	B7	19
Leiston, Eng., U.K.	B9	11
Leisure City, Fl., U.S.	s13	86
Leitches Creek, N.S.	C9	71
Leitchfield, Ky., U.S.	C3	94
Leiter, Wy., U.S.	B6	127
Leitersburg, Md., U.S.	A2	97
Leiters Ford, In., U.S.	B5	91
Leith, N.D., U.S.	C4	111
Leitha, stm., Eur.	B3	24
Leitrim, co., Ire.	C3	11
Leiva, Cerro, mtn., Col.	C3	60
Leixlip, Ire.	D5	11
Leizhou Bandao, pen., China	G7	31
Leizhou Bay, b., China	B9	35
Lejunior, Ky., U.S.	D6	94
Lek, stm., Neth.	C4	17
Leka, i., Nor.	E4	14
Lekeba, i., Fiji	I16	52
Lekoa, S. Afr.	*C4	49
Le Kreïder, Alg.	C5	44
Leksand, Swe.	E2	14
Leksula, Indon.	F7	34
Lela, Tx., U.S.	B2	120
Le Lamentin, Mart.	S10	65
Leland, Il., U.S.	B5	90
Leland, Ia., U.S.	A4	92
Leland, Mi., U.S.	C5	99
Leland, Ms., U.S.	B3	101
Leleiwi Point, c., Hi., U.S.	D7	88
Leleque, Arg.	C2	54
Lelia Lake, Tx., U.S.	B2	120
Leloaloa, Am. Sam.	F13	52
Le Locle, Switz.	E3	18
Le Lorrain, Mart.	S10	65
Leloup, Ks., U.S.	D8	93
Lelystad, Neth.	B5	17
Le Maire, Estrecho de, strt., Arg.	h12	54
Le Mans, Fr.	C4	16
Le Marin, Mart.	I14	64
Le Mars, Ia., U.S.	B1	92
Lemasters, Pa., U.S.	G6	115
Lemay, Mo., U.S.	*g13	102
Lembach, Fr.	F7	17
Lemberg, Sask.	G4	75
Lemdiyya, Alg.	B5	44
Leme, Braz.	m8	56
Lemelerveld, Neth.	B6	17
Lemery, Phil.	p13	34
Lemesós (Limassol), Cyp.	E9	40
Lemgo, W. Ger.	B4	18
Lemhi, Id., U.S.	E5	89
Lemhi, co., Id., U.S.	E4	89
Lemhi, stm., Id., U.S.	E5	89
Lemhi Pass, Id., U.S.	E5	89
Lemhi Range, mts., Id., U.S.	E5	89
Lemieux, Que.	C5	74
Lemitar, N.M., U.S.	C3	108
Lemmer, Neth.	B5	17
Lemmon, S.D., U.S.	B3	118
Lemmon, Mount, mtn., Az., U.S.	E5	80
Lemmon Valley, Nv., U.S.	D2	105
Lemnos see Límnos, i., Grc.	C5	40
Lemon, Lake, l., In., U.S.	F5	91
Lemon Fair, stm., Vt., U.S.	C2	122
Lemon Grove, Ca., U.S.	o15	82
Lemon Island, i., S.C., U.S.	G6	117
Lemons, Mo., U.S.	A4	102
Lemont, Il., U.S.	B5	90
Lemont, Pa., U.S.	E6	115
Lemonweir, stm., Wi., U.S.	D3	126
Lemoore, Ca., U.S.	D4	82
Lemoore Naval Air Station, mil., Ca., U.S.	D3	82
Lemoore Station, Ca., U.S.	*D4	82
Le Moyen, La., U.S.	D3	95
Le Moyne, Ne., U.S.	C4	104
Lemoyne, Oh., U.S.	f7	112
Lempa, stm., N.A.	D3	62
Lem Peak, mtn., Id., U.S.	E5	89
Lempster, N.H., U.S.	D2	106
Lemsford, Sask.	G1	75
Lemvig, Den.	B2	15
Lena, Il., U.S.	A4	90
Lena, La., U.S.	C3	95
Lena, Ms., U.S.	C4	101
Lena, Wi., U.S.	D5	126
Lena, stm., Sov. Un.	C15	29
Lenapah, Ok., U.S.	A6	113
Lenawee, co., Mi., U.S.	G6	99
Lençóis, Braz.	D2	57
Lend, Aus.	D7	20
Lendinara, Italy	D7	20
Lenexa, Ks., U.S.	E2	93
Leney, Sask.	E2	75
Lengby, Mn., U.S.	B3	91
Lenger, Sov. Un.	D7	28
Lengede, W. Ger.	A5	19
Lengerich, W. Ger.	A2	19
Lenghu, China	D3	31
Lengshuijiang, China	*F7	31
Lenhartsville, Pa., U.S.	E10	115
Lenin, Sov. Un.	E9	29
Leninabad, Sov. Un.	E2	28
Leninakan, Sov. Un.	E2	28
Leningrad, Sov. Un.	C6	29
Leningradskaya, sci., Ant.	C28	7
Lenino, Sov. Un.	n17	27
Leninogorsk, Sov. Un.	D11	29
Lenin Peak, mtn., Sov. Un.	*F10	29
Leninsk, Sov. Un.	G15	27
Leninsk-Kuznetskiy, Sov. Un.	D11	29
Leninskoye, Sov. Un.	C7	28
Lennox, S.D., U.S.	D9	118
Lennox and Addington, co., Ont.	C7	73
Lennoxville, Que.	D6	74
Leno, Italy	D6	20
Lenoir, N.C., U.S.	B1	110
Lenoir, co., N.C., U.S.	B5	110
Lenoir City, Tn., U.S.	D9	119
Lenora, Ks., U.S.	C4	93
Lenore, Man.	E1	70
Lenore, Id., U.S.	C2	89
Lenore Lake, l., Sask.	E3	75
Lenore Lake, l., Wa., U.S.	B6	124
Lenox, Al., U.S.	D2	78
Lenox, Ga., U.S.	E3	87
Lenox, Ia., U.S.	D3	92
Lenox, Ma., U.S.	B1	98
Lenox, Mo., U.S.	D6	102
Lenox, Tn., U.S.	A2	119
Lenox Dale, Ma., U.S.	B1	98
Lens, Fr.	B5	16
Lentner, Mo., U.S.	B5	102
Lenzburg, Switz.	S5	21
Lenzburg, Il., U.S.	E4	90
Lenzerheide, Switz.	C8	21
Leo, In., U.S.	B7	91
Leo, Burkina	D4	45
Leo, In., U.S.	A7	18
Léogâne, Haiti	E7	64
Leola, Ar., U.S.	C3	81
Leola, S.D., U.S.	B7	118
Leominster, Eng., U.K.	B5	12
Leominster, Ma., U.S.	A4	98
Leon, Nic.	A2	63
León, Spain	A4	22
Leon, In., U.S.	E7	91
Leon, Ks., U.S.	E7	93
Leon, N.Y., U.S.	C1	109
Leon, Ok., U.S.	D4	113
Leon, W.V., U.S.	C3	125
Leon, co., Fl., U.S.	B2	86
Leon, co., Tx., U.S.	D4	120
León, hist. reg., Spain	B3	22
Leona, Ks., U.S.	C8	93
Leona, Tx., U.S.	D5	120
Leonard, Mi., U.S.	F7	99
Leonard, Mo., U.S.	B5	102
Leonard, N.D., U.S.	C8	111
Leonard, Ok., U.S.	B6	113
Leonard, Tx., U.S.	C4	120
Leonardo, N.J., U.S.	C4	107
Leonardsville, N.Y., U.S.	C5	109
Leonardsville, N.B.	E3	71
Leonardville, Nmb.	B2	49
Leonardville, Ks., U.S.	C7	93
Leonberg, W. Ger.	E3	19
Leone, Am. Sam.	G13	52
Leone, Bay b., Am. Sam.	G13	52
Leonforte, Italy	F5	23
Leonia, Fl., U.S.	I5	51
Leonia, N.J., U.S.	u15	86
Leonia, N.J., U.S.	h9	107
Leonidion, Grc.	C3	40
Leonora, Austl.	C3	11
Leon Valley, Tx., U.S.	*E3	120
Leopold, In., U.S.	H4	91
Leopold and Astrid Coast, Ant.	C21	7
Leopoldina, Braz.	C4	56
Leopoldsburg, Bel.	C5	17
Léopoldville see Kinshasa, Zaire	B2	48
Leota, Mn., U.S.	G2	100
Leoti, Ks., U.S.	D2	93
Leoville, Sask.	D2	75
Leoville, Ks., U.S.	C3	93
Leovo, Sov. Un.	H7	27
Lepanto, Ar., U.S.	B5	81
Lepe, Spain	D2	22
Lepel, Sov. Un.	D7	27
Lepine, Que.	D4	74
Lepihué, Chile	C2	54
Leping, China	J7	32
L'Épiphanie, Que.	D4	74
Le-Plain-de-Coravillers, Fr.	A2	21
Le Plessis-Belleville, Fr.	E2	17
Le Plessis-Robinson, Fr.	G10	16
Le Pont, Switz.	C1	21
Lepontine Alps, mts., Eur.	A2	23
Le Portel, Fr.	D9	12
Lepreau, Point, c., N.B.	D3	71
Lepsinsk, Sov. Un.	F25	8
Lepsy, Sov. Un.	D9	28
Le Puy [-en-Velay], Fr.	E5	16
Le Quesnoy, Fr.	D3	17
Lequire, Ok., U.S.	B6	113
Le Raincy, Fr.	g11	16
Le Raysville, Pa., U.S.	C9	115
Lercara Friddi, Italy	F4	23
Léré, Chad	G9	45
Lérida, Col.	C3	60
Lérida, Spain	B6	22
Lerma, Spain	A4	22
Lerma, stm., Mex.	m13	63
Lermoos, Aus.	B6	20
Léros, i., Grc.	D6	40
Leross, Sask.	F4	75
Leroux Wash, val., Az., U.S.	B5	80
Leroy, Sask.	F3	75
Leroy, Al., U.S.	D1	78
Le Roy, Il., U.S.	C5	90
Le Roy, Ia., U.S.	D4	92
Le Roy, Ks., U.S.	D8	93
Le Roy, Mi., U.S.	D5	99
Le Roy, Mn., U.S.	G6	100
Le Roy, N.Y., U.S.	C3	109
Leroy, N.D., U.S.	A8	111
Le Roy, Pa., U.S.	C8	115
Lerum, Swe.	A6	15
Le Russey, Fr.	B2	21
Léry, Que.	q19	74
Lery, Lake, l., La., U.S.	k12	95
Les Abymes, Guad.	Q8	65
Le Saint-Esprit, Mart.	S11	65
Les Cayes, Haiti	E7	64
Les Diablerets, Switz.	C3	21
Les Éboulements, Que.	B7	74
Les Echelles, Fr.	D1	20
Les Escoumins, Que.	A8	74
Les Étroits, Que.	B9	74
Les Fonds, Que.	o16	74
Leshan, China	F5	31
Leshara, Ne., U.S.	g12	104
Les Haudères, Switz.	C3	20
Lesina, Lake, b., Italy	D5	23
Lesko, Pol.	D7	26
Leskovac, Yugo.	D5	24
Leslie, Sask.	F4	75
Leslie, Ar., U.S.	B3	81
Leslie, Ga., U.S.	E2	87
Leslie, Id., U.S.	F5	89
Leslie, Mi., U.S.	F6	99
Leslie, S.C., U.S.	B6	117
Leslie, W.V., U.S.	C4	125
Leslie, co., Ky., U.S.	C6	94
Leslieville, Alta.	C3	68
Lesneven, Fr.	C1	16
Lesnoy, Sov. Un.	B4	28
Lesogorsk, Sov. Un.	B11	33
Lesosibirsk, Sov. Un.	E16	29
Lesozavodsk, Sov. Un.	B13	29
Lesparre, Fr.	E3	16
Les Ponts-de-Cé, Fr.	D3	16
Les Rousses, Fr.	D1	21
Les Sables-d'Olonne, Fr.	D2	16
Lesser Antilles, is.	B4	53
Lesser Khing Range see Xiao Hinggan Ling, mts., China	B10	31
Lesser Slave Lake, l., Alta.	B3	68
Lesser Sunda Islands (Nusa Tenggara), is., Indon.	G5	34
Lessines, Bel.	D3	17
Lester, Ia., U.S.	A1	92
Lester, W.V., U.S.	n13	125
Lester Prairie, Mn., U.S.	F4	100
Lesterville, Mo., U.S.	D7	102
Lesterville, S.D., U.S.	D8	118
Lestock, Sask.	F3	75
Le Sueur, Mn., U.S.	F5	100
Le Sueur, co., Mn., U.S.	F5	100
Les Verrières, Switz.	C1	21
Lésvos (Lesbos), i., Grc.	C5	40
Leszno, Pol.	C4	26
Letart Falls, Oh., U.S.	C3	112
Letcher, S.D., U.S.	D7	118
Letcher, co., Ky., U.S.	C7	94
Le Teil, Fr.	E6	16
Letellier, Man.	E3	70
Letha, Id., U.S.	F2	89
Lethbridge, Alta.	E4	68
Lethbridge, Newf.	D5	72
Lethem, Guy.	B3	59
Le Thillot, Fr.	B2	21
Letiahau, stm., Bots.	B3	49
Leticia, Col.	D4	60
Leti Islands, is., Indon.	G7	34
Letohatchee, Al., U.S.	C3	78
Letona, Ar., U.S.	B4	81
Le Touquet-Paris-Plage, Fr.	D9	12
Le Tourneau, Ms., U.S.	C3	101
Le Tréport, Fr.	B4	16
Letpadan, Burma	E10	36
Letsok-Aw, i., Burma	G3	35
Letterfrack, Ire.	D2	11
Letterkenny, Ire.	C3	11
Lettermullan, Ire.	D2	11
Letts, In., U.S.	F6	91
Letts, Ia., U.S.	C6	92
Lettsworth, La., U.S.	D4	95
Leucas see Levkás, i., Grc.	C3	40
Leuchtenberg, W. Ger.	C7	19
Leuctra see Lévktra, Grc.	g10	25
Leuk, Switz.	D4	21
Leukerbad, Switz.	D4	21
Leulumoega, W. Sam.	F12	52
Leupp, Az., U.S.	B5	80
Leupp Corner, Az., U.S.	B5	80
Leuser, mtn., Indon.	m11	34
Leutkirch, W. Ger.	B6	20
Leuven (Louvain), Bel.	B6	16
Leuze, Bel.	D3	17
Levádhia, Grc.	B4	40
Levanger, Nor.	F4	14
Levanna, mtn., Eur.	E7	16
Levant, Ks., U.S.	C2	93
Levant, Me., U.S.	D4	96
Leveaux Mountain, mtn., Mn., U.S.	k9	100
Levelland, Tx., U.S.	C1	120
Leven, Scot., U.K.	B5	10
Leven, Cape, c., Austl.	C3	50
Leveque, Cape, c., Austl.	C3	50
Leverett Glacier, ice, Ant.	A32	7
Levering, Mi., U.S.	C6	99
Leverkusen, W. Ger.	B1	19
Levice, Czech.	B4	26
Levick, Mount, mtn., Ant.	B29	7
Levie, Fr.	D2	23
Levier, Fr.	C1	21
Le Vigan, Fr.	F4	16
Levin, N.Z.	N15	51
Levis, Que.	C6	74
Lévis, co., Que.	C6	74
Levisa Fork, stm., U.S.	D7	94
Levítha, i., Grc.	D6	25
Levittown, N.Y., U.S.	E7	109
Levittown, Pa., U.S.	F12	115
Levkás, i., Grc.	C3	40
Lévkas (Leucas), i., Grc.	g10	25
Lévktra (Leuctra), Grc.	g10	25
Levoča, Czech.	D6	26
Levuka, Fiji	H15	52
Levy, co., Fl., U.S.	C4	86
Lewellen, Ne., U.S.	C3	104
Lewes, Eng., U.K.	E7	10
Lewes, De., U.S.	E5	85
Lewes and Rehoboth Canal, De., U.S.	F5	85
Lewis, In., U.S.	F3	91
Lewis, Ia., U.S.	C2	92
Lewis, Ks., U.S.	E4	93
Lewis, Mo., U.S.	C4	102
Lewis, N.Y., U.S.	A7	109
Lewis, Wi., U.S.	C1	126
Lewis, co., Id., U.S.	C2	89
Lewis, co., Ky., U.S.	B6	94
Lewis, co., Mo., U.S.	A6	102
Lewis, co., N.Y., U.S.	B5	109
Lewis, co., Tn., U.S.	B4	119
Lewis, co., Wa., U.S.	C3	124
Lewis, co., W.V., U.S.	C4	125
Lewis, stm., Wy., U.S.	B2	127
Lewis, Butt of, c., Scot., U.K.	A3	10
Lewis, Isle of, i., Scot., U.K.	A3	10
Lewis, Mount, mtn., Nv., U.S.	C5	105
Lewis and Clark, co., Mt., U.S.	C4	103
Lewis and Clark Cavern, Mt., U.S.	D5	103
Lewis and Clark Lake, res., U.S.	E8	118
Lewisberry, Pa., U.S.	F8	115
Lewisburg, Ky., U.S.	D3	94
Lewisburg, La., U.S.	D3	95
Lewisburg, Oh., U.S.	C1	112
Lewisburg, Pa., U.S.	E8	115
Lewisburg, Tn., U.S.	B5	119
Lewisburg, W.V., U.S.	D4	125
Lewis Center, Oh., U.S.	B2	112
Lewis Creek, stm., Sask.	F3	75
Lewis Creek, stm., Vt., U.S.	C2	122
Lewis Hills, hills, Newf.	D2	72
Lewis Lake, l., Wy., U.S.	B2	127
Lewisport, Ky., U.S.	C3	94
Lewisporte, Newf.	D4	72
Lewis Range, mts., N.A.	C4	76
Lewis Run, Pa., U.S.	C4	115
Lewis Smith Lake, res., Al., U.S.	B2	78
Lewiston, Id., U.S.	C1	89
Lewiston, Me., U.S.	D2	96
Lewiston, Mi., U.S.	D6	99
Lewiston, Mn., U.S.	G7	100
Lewiston, Ut., U.S.	B4	121
Lewiston Peak, mtn., Ut., U.S.	C3	121
Lewiston Woodville, N.C., U.S.	A5	110
Lewistown, Il., U.S.	C3	90
Lewistown, Md., U.S.	A3	97
Lewistown, Mo., U.S.	A6	102
Lewistown, Mt., U.S.	C7	103
Lewistown, Pa., U.S.	E6	115
Lewisville, N.B.	C5	71
Lewisville, Ar., U.S.	D2	81
Lewisville, Id., U.S.	F6	89
Lewisville, In., U.S.	E7	91
Lewisville, Oh., U.S.	C4	112
Lewisville, Tx., U.S.	C4	120
Lewisville Lake, res., Tx., U.S.	C4	120
Lexa, Ar., U.S.	C5	81
Lexington, Al., U.S.	A2	78
Lexington, Ga., U.S.	C4	87
Lexington, Il., U.S.	C5	90
Lexington, In., U.S.	G6	91
Lexington, Ky., U.S.	B5	94
Lexington, Ma., U.S.	B5	98
Lexington, Mi., U.S.	E8	99
Lexington, Mo., U.S.	B4	102
Lexington, Ne., U.S.	D6	104
Lexington, N.Y., U.S.	C6	109
Lexington, N.C., U.S.	B2	110
Lexington, Oh., U.S.	B3	112
Lexington, Ok., U.S.	B4	113
Lexington, Or., U.S.	B7	114
Lexington, S.C., U.S.	D5	117
Lexington, Tn., U.S.	B3	119
Lexington, Tx., U.S.	D4	120
Lexington, Va., U.S.	C3	123
Lexington, co., S.C., U.S.	D5	117
Lexington Park, Md., U.S.	D5	97
Leyba, N.M., U.S.	B4	108
Leyburn, Eng., U.K.	F7	12
Leyond, stm., Man.	D3	70
Leysin, Switz.	D2	21
Leyte, i., Phil.	C6	34
Lezajsk, Pol.	C7	26
Lézha, Alb.	B2	40
Lézignan, Fr.	F5	16
Lgov, Sov. Un.	F10	27
Lhasa, China	F3	31
L'Haÿ-les-Roses, Fr.	g10	16
Lhazê, China	C11	37
Lhokseumawe, Indon.	k11	34
Lhoksukon, Indon.	J2	35
Liangping, China	I2	32
Lianhua, China	K5	32
Lianjiang, China	B9	35
Lianyungang, China	E8	31
Lianyungang, China	G8	32
Liaocheng, China	F6	32
Liao He, stm., China	C9	31
Liaodong Bay, b., China	C9	31
Liaotung Bay see Liaodong Bay, b., China	E9	32
Liaotung Peninsula, pen., China	D9	31
Liaoyang, China	C9	31
Liaoyuan, China	C10	31
Liard, stm., Can.	E7	66
Liart, Fr.	C5	17
Liathach, mtn., Scot., U.K.	C3	13
Líbano, Col.	C3	60
Libau, Man.	D3	70
Libby, Mt., U.S.	B1	103
Libčice [nad Vltavou], Czech.	n17	26
Libčice, Czech.	n17	26
Libenge, Zaire	A2	48
Liberal, Mo., U.S.	D3	102
Liberal, Ks., U.S.	E3	93
Liberec, Czech.	B4	26
Liberia, C.R.	D4	63
Liberia, ctry., Afr.	E3	45
Libertad, Ven.	B4	60
Libertador General Bernardo O'Higgins, prov., Chile	A2	54
Libertador General San Martín, Arg.	D3	55
Liberty, Sask.	F3	75
Liberty, Il., U.S.	G7	89
Liberty, In., U.S.	E8	91
Liberty, Ky., U.S.	C5	94
Liberty, Me., U.S.	D3	96
Liberty, Ms., U.S.	D3	101
Liberty, Mo., U.S.	h10	102
Liberty, Ne., U.S.	D9	104
Liberty, N.Y., U.S.	D6	109

Index

Name	Map Ref.	Page
Liberty, N.C., U.S.	B3	110
Liberty, Pa., U.S.	C7	115
Liberty, S.C., U.S.	B2	117
Liberty, Tn., U.S.	C8	119
Liberty, Tx., U.S.	D5	120
Liberty, Wa., U.S.	B5	124
Liberty, co., Fl., U.S.	B2	86
Liberty, co., Ga., U.S.	E5	87
Liberty, co., Mt., U.S.	B5	103
Liberty, co., Tx., U.S.	D5	120
Liberty Acres, Ca., U.S.	*n12	82
Liberty Center, In., U.S.	C7	91
Liberty Center, Ia., U.S.	C4	92
Liberty Center, Oh., U.S.	A1	112
Liberty Corner, N.J., U.S.	B3	107
Liberty Grove, Md., U.S.	A5	97
Liberty Hill, Ct., U.S.	C6	84
Liberty Hill, S.C., U.S.	C6	117
Liberty Lake, Wa., U.S.	g14	124
Liberty Lake, res., Md., U.S.	B4	97
Liberty Mills, In., U.S.	B6	91
Libertytown, Md., U.S.	B3	97
Libertyville, Il., U.S.	A6	90
Libertyville, Ia., U.S.	D5	92
Libiron, i., Marsh Is.	S18	52
Liblar, W. Ger.	C1	19
Libourne, Fr.	E3	16
Libramont, Bel.	E5	17
Libreville, Gabon	E1	46
Libuse, La., U.S.	C3	95
Libušín, Czech.	n17	26
Libya, ctry., Afr.	D3	43
Libyan Desert, des., Afr.	D4	43
Libyan Plateau, plat., Afr.	C4	43
Licantén, Chile	B2	54
Licata, Italy	F4	23
Lice, Tur.	C13	40
Licenza, Italy	g9	23
Lichfield, Eng., U.K.	B6	12
Lichinga, Moz.	D6	48
Lichtenburg, S. Afr.	C4	49
Lichtenfels, W. Ger.	C6	19
Lichtenstein, E. Ger.	C7	19
Lick Creek, stm., Tn., U.S.	C11	119
Licking, Mo., U.S.	D6	102
Licking, co., Oh., U.S.	B3	112
Licking, stm., Ky., U.S.	B6	94
Licking, North Fork, stm., Ky., U.S.	B5	94
Licking, South Fork, stm., Ky., U.S.	B5	94
Licosa, Point, c., Italy	D5	23
Licungo, stm., Moz.	A6	49
Lida, Sov. Un.	E5	27
Lida, Lake, l., Mn., U.S.	D3	100
Liddel Water, stm., U.K.	E6	13
Lidderdale, Ia., U.S.	B3	92
Lidgerwood, N.D., U.S.	C8	111
Lidhult, Swe.	B7	15
Lidice, Czech.	C3	26
Lidingö, Swe.	H8	14
Lidköping, Swe.	H5	14
Lido di Roma, Italy	h8	23
Lidzbark Warmiński, Pol.	A6	26
Liebenthal, Sask.	G1	75
Liebenthal, Ks., U.S.	D4	93
Lieberose, E. Ger.	B9	19
Liechtenstein, ctry., Eur.	E4	18
Liège (Luik), Bel.	B6	16
Liège, prov., Bel.	D5	17
Liege, stm., Alta.	A4	68
Liegnitz see Legnica, Pol.	C4	26
Lieksa, Fin.	F14	14
Lienen, W. Ger.	A2	19
Lienz, Aus.	E6	18
Liepāja, Sov. Un.	C3	27
Lier (Lierre), Bel.	B6	16
Lierneux, Bel.	D5	17
Lierre see Lier, Bel.	B6	16
Liestal, Switz.	E3	18
Liévin, Fr.	D2	17
Lièvre, Rivière du, stm., Que.	D2	74
Lièvres, Île aux, i., Que.	B8	74
Liffey, stm., Ire.	D3	10
Lifford, Fr.	C3	10
Liftwood, De., U.S.	*A3	85
Light, Ar., U.S.	A5	81
Lighthouse Inlet, b., S.C., U.S.	k12	117
Lighthouse Point, Fl., U.S.	*F6	86
Lighthouse Point, c., Fl., U.S.	C2	86
Lighthouse Point, c., La., U.S.	E3	95
Lighthouse Point, c., Mi., U.S.	C5	99
Lightning Creek, stm., Wy., U.S.	C8	127
Lightning Ridge, Austl.	D6	51
Lignite, N.D., U.S.	A3	111
Lignum, Va., U.S.	B5	123
Ligny-en-Barrois, Fr.	F5	17
Ligonha, stm., Moz.	E6	48
Ligonier, In., U.S.	B6	91
Ligonier, Pa., U.S.	F3	115
Ligovo (part of Leningrad), Sov. Un.	s31	14
Liguria, prov., Italy	E4	20
Liguria, prov., Italy	B2	23
Ligurian Apennines, mts., Italy	E4	20
Ligurian Sea, Eur.	C2	23
Lihue, Hi., U.S.	B2	88
Lijiang, China	F5	31
Lijin, China	F8	32
Likasi, Zaire	D4	48
Likely, B.C.	C7	69
Likely, Ca., U.S.	B3	82
Likhoslavl, Sov. Un.	C10	27
Likino-Dulevo, Sov. Un.	n18	27
Lilbourn, Mo., U.S.	E8	102
Lilburn, Ga., U.S.	h8	87
L'Île-Rousse, Fr.	C2	23
Liesville, N.C., U.S.	C3	110
Liling, China	K5	32
Lille, Fr.	B5	16
Lille, Me., U.S.	A4	96
Lille Bælt, strt., Den.	C3	15
Lillehammer, Nor.	G4	14
Lillers, Fr.	D2	17
Lillesand, Nor.	H3	14
Lilleström, Nor.	H4	14
Lillian, Al., U.S.	E2	78
Lillian, Tx., U.S.	n9	120
Lillie, La., U.S.	B3	95
Lillington, N.C., U.S.	B4	110
Lillinonah, Lake, l., Ct., U.S.	C2	84
Lilloet, B.C.	D7	69
Lillooet, stm., B.C.	D6	69
Lillooet Lake, l., B.C.	D6	69
Lillooet Range, mts., B.C.	E7	69
Lilly, Ga., U.S.	D3	87
Lilly Fork, stm., W.V., U.S.	m13	125
Lilly Grove, W.V., U.S.	D3	125
Lilongwe, Mwi.	D5	48
Lily, Ky., U.S.	C5	94
Lily, S.D., U.S.	B8	118
Lily, Wi., U.S.	C5	126
Lim, stm., Yugo.	D4	24
Lima, Para.	D4	55
Lima, Peru	D2	58
Lima, Il., U.S.	C2	90
Lima, Mt., U.S.	F4	103
Lima, N.Y., U.S.	C3	109
Lima, Oh., U.S.	B1	112
Lima, dept., Peru	D2	58
Lima, stm., Eur.	B1	22
Lima Duarte, Braz.	C4	56
Limanowa, Pol.	D6	26
Lima Reservoir, res., Mt., U.S.	F4	103
Limassol see Lemesós, Cyp.	E9	40
Limavady, N. Ire., U.K.	B5	11
Limay, stm., Arg.	B3	54
Limay Mahuida, Arg.	B3	54
Limbach [-Oberfrohna], E. Ger.	C7	19
Limbe, Cam.	E1	46
Limbé, Haiti	E7	64
Limburg, W. Ger.	C4	18
Limburg, prov., Bel.	D5	17
Limburg, prov., Neth.	D5	17
Lime City, Oh., U.S.	e6	112
Limedale, In., U.S.	E4	91
Limeil-Brévannes, Fr.	h10	16
Limeira, Braz.	C3	56
Limerick, Sask.	H2	75
Limerick, Ire.	D2	10
Limerick, Me., U.S.	E2	96
Limerick, co., Ire.	E3	11
Lime Rock, Ct., U.S.	B2	84
Limerock, R.I., U.S.	B4	116
Lime Springs, Ia., U.S.	A5	92
Limestone, Me., U.S.	A5	96
Limestone, Fl., U.S.	E5	86
Limestone, Me., U.S.	B5	96
Limestone, N.Y., U.S.	C2	109
Limestone, Pa., U.S.	D3	115
Limestone, Tn., U.S.	C11	119
Limestone, co., Al., U.S.	A2	78
Limestone, co., Tx., U.S.	D4	120
Limestone, co., Man.	A4	70
Limestone Bay, b., Man.	C2	70
Limestone Lake, l., Man.	A4	70
Limestone Point, pen., Man.	C2	70
Limeton, Va., U.S.	B4	123
Lime Village, Ak., U.S.	C8	79
Limfjorden, strt., Den.	B3	15
Limington, Me., U.S.	E2	96
Limmen Bight, Austl.	B6	50
Límni, Grc.	C4	25
Límnos (Lemnos), i., Grc.	C5	40
Limoeiro, Braz.	C3	57
Limoeiro do Norte, Braz.	C3	57
Limoges, Ont.	B9	73
Limoges, Fr.	E4	16
Limón, C.R.	E8	63
Limón, Hond.	D7	63
Limon, Co., U.S.	B6	83
Limón, Bahía, b., Pan.	k11	62
Limousin, hist. reg., Fr.	E4	16
Limousin Plateau, plat., Fr.	E4	16
Limoux, Fr.	F5	16
Limpopo, stm., Afr.	B5	49
Linard, mtn., Switz.	C9	21
Linares, Chile	B2	54
Linares, Col.	C2	60
Linares, Mex.	C5	63
Linares, Spain	C4	22
Linares, Braz.	E2	57
Linhe, China	D2	32
Linaro, Cape, c., Italy	g9	23
Lince, Peru	*D2	58
Linch, Wy., U.S.	C6	127
Linchuan, China	F8	31
Lincoln, Arg.	A4	54
Lincoln, Ont.	D5	73
Lincoln, Eng., U.K.	D6	10
Lincoln, Al., U.S.	B3	78
Lincoln, Ar., U.S.	B1	81
Lincoln, Ca., U.S.	C3	82
Lincoln, De., U.S.	E4	85
Lincoln, Id., U.S.	F7	89
Lincoln, Il., U.S.	C4	90
Lincoln, Ia., U.S.	C5	91
Lincoln, Ks., U.S.	C5	93
Lincoln, Me., U.S.	C4	96
Lincoln, Ma., U.S.	g10	98
Lincoln, Mi., U.S.	D7	99
Lincoln, Mo., U.S.	C4	102
Lincoln, Mt., U.S.	D4	103
Lincoln, Ne., U.S.	D9	104
Lincoln, N.M., U.S.	D4	108
Lincoln, Tn., U.S.	B5	119
Lincoln, Vt., U.S.	C3	122
Lincoln, Va., U.S.	A5	123
Lincoln, Wa., U.S.	B7	124
Lincoln, co., Ar., U.S.	D4	81
Lincoln, co., Co., U.S.	C7	83
Lincoln, co., Ga., U.S.	C4	87
Lincoln, co., Id., U.S.	G4	89
Lincoln, co., Ks., U.S.	C5	93
Lincoln, co., Ky., U.S.	C5	94
Lincoln, co., La., U.S.	B3	95
Lincoln, co., Me., U.S.	D3	96
Lincoln, co., Mn., U.S.	F2	100
Lincoln, co., Mo., U.S.	B7	102
Lincoln, co., Mt., U.S.	B1	103
Lincoln, co., Ne., U.S.	D5	104
Lincoln, co., Nv., U.S.	F6	105
Lincoln, co., N.M., U.S.	D4	108
Lincoln, co., N.C., U.S.	B1	110
Lincoln, co., Ok., U.S.	B5	113
Lincoln, co., Or., U.S.	C3	114
Lincoln, co., S.D., U.S.	D9	118
Lincoln, co., Tn., U.S.	B5	119
Lincoln, co., Wa., U.S.	B7	124
Lincoln, co., W.V., U.S.	C2	125
Lincoln, co., Wi., U.S.	C4	126
Lincoln, co., Wy., U.S.	D2	127
Lincoln, Mount, mtn., Co., U.S.	B4	83
Lincoln Acres, Ca., U.S.	o15	82
Lincoln Center, Me., U.S.	C4	96
Lincoln City, In., U.S.	H4	91
Lincoln City, Or., U.S.	C3	114
Lincoln Heights, Oh., U.S.	o13	112
Lincoln Park, Co., U.S.	C5	83
Lincoln Park, Ga., U.S.	D2	87
Lincoln Park, Mi., U.S.	p15	99
Lincoln Park, N.J., U.S.	B4	107
Lincoln Park, Nv., U.S.	*D2	105
Lincoln Sea, N.A.	A15	61
Lincoln Village, Ca., U.S.	*g10	82
Lincoln Village, Oh., U.S.	*m10	112
Lincolnshire, co., Eng., U.K.	A7	12
Lincoln Tomb State Memorial, hist., Il., U.S.	D4	90
Lincolnton, Ga., U.S.	C4	87
Lincolnton, N.C., U.S.	B1	110
Lincolnville, Ks., U.S.	D7	93
Lincolnville, Me., U.S.	D3	96
Lincolnville, S.C., U.S.	h11	117
Lincolnwood, Il., U.S.	h9	90
Lincroft, N.J., U.S.	C4	107
L'Incudine, mtn., Fr.	D2	23
Lind, Wa., U.S.	C7	124
Linda, Ca., U.S.	*C3	82
Lindale, Ga., U.S.	B1	87
Lindale, Tx., U.S.	C5	120
Lindau, W. Ger.	E4	18
Lindbergh, Alta.	C5	68
Linden, Alta.	D4	68
Linden, Al., U.S.	C2	78
Linden, In., U.S.	D4	91
Linden, Ia., U.S.	C3	92
Linden, Mi., U.S.	F7	99
Linden, N.J., U.S.	k8	107
Linden, N.C., U.S.	B4	110
Linden, Pa., U.S.	D7	115
Linden, Tn., U.S.	B4	119
Linden, Tx., U.S.	C5	120
Linden, Wi., U.S.	F3	126
Lindenhurst, Il., U.S.	h8	90
Lindenhurst, N.Y., U.S.	n15	109
Lindenwold, N.J., U.S.	D3	107
Linderöd, Swe.	C7	15
Lindesberg, Swe.	H6	14
Lindgren Acres, Fl., U.S.	*G6	86
Líndhos, Grc.	D7	40
Lindi, Tan.	C6	48
Lindi, prov., Tan.	C6	48
Lindi, stm., Zaire	A4	48
Lindian, China	A11	32
Lindlar, W. Ger.	B2	19
Lindome, Swe.	A6	15
Lindon, Co., U.S.	B7	83
Lindon, Ut., U.S.	C4	121
Lindow, E. Ger.	F6	15
Lindrith, N.M., U.S.	A2	108
Lindsay, Ont.	C6	73
Lindsay, Ca., U.S.	D4	82
Lindsay, Mt., U.S.	C11	103
Lindsay, Ne., U.S.	C8	104
Lindsay, Ok., U.S.	C4	113
Lindsborg, Ks., U.S.	D6	93
Lindstrom, Mn., U.S.	E6	100
Lindy, Ne., U.S.	B8	104
Lineboro, Md., U.S.	A4	97
Linefork, Ky., U.S.	C7	94
Linesville, Pa., U.S.	C1	115
Lineville, Al., U.S.	B4	78
Lineville, Ia., U.S.	D4	92
Linfen, China	D7	31
Linganore Creek, stm., Md., U.S.	B3	97
Lingao, China	B8	35
Lingayen, Phil.	B6	34
Lingayen Gulf, b., Phil.	n13	34
Lingen, W. Ger.	A2	18
Lingga Islands, is., Indon.	F2	34
Lingle, Wy., U.S.	D8	127
Linglestown, Pa., U.S.	F8	115
Lingling, China	F7	31
Lingo, N.M., U.S.	D6	108
Lingshan, China	G6	31
Linguère, Sen.	C1	45
Lingwu, China	E2	32
Lingyuan, China	C8	31
Linhai, China	F9	31
Linhares, Braz.	E2	57
Linhe, China	D2	32
Linh Peak, mtn., Viet.	B3	34
Linière, Que.	C7	74
Linjiang, China	F3	33
Linköping, Swe.	H6	14
Linkou, China	B11	31
Linlithgow, Scot., U.K.	E5	13
Linn, Ks., U.S.	C6	93
Linn, Mo., U.S.	C6	102
Linn, Tx., U.S.	F3	120
Linn, co., Ia., U.S.	B6	92
Linn, co., Ks., U.S.	D9	93
Linn, co., Mo., U.S.	B4	102
Linn, co., Or., U.S.	C4	114
Linn Creek, Mo., U.S.	C5	102
Linneus, Me., U.S.	B5	96
Linneus, Mo., U.S.	B4	102
Linn Grove, In., U.S.	C7	91
Linn Grove, Ia., U.S.	B2	92
Linnhe, Loch, b., Scot., U.K.	E4	13
Lino Lakes, Mn., U.S.	m12	100
Linqing, China	D8	31
Linru, China	G5	32
Lins, Braz.	C3	56
Linstead, Jam.	E14	65
Lintan, China	D5	31
Lintao, China	D5	31
Linth, stm., Switz.	C7	21
Linthal, Switz.	C7	21
Linthicum Heights, Md., U.S.	B4	97
Lintlaw, Sask.	E4	75
Linton, Que.	B5	74
Linton, In., U.S.	F3	91
Linton, N.D., U.S.	C5	111
Linville, N.C., U.S.	A1	110
Linville, Va., U.S.	B4	123
Linwood, Ont.	D4	73
Linwood, Ks., U.S.	m15	93
Linwood, Ma., U.S.	B4	98
Linwood, Mi., U.S.	E7	99
Linwood, Ne., U.S.	C9	104
Linwood, N.J., U.S.	E3	107
Linwood, N.C., U.S.	B2	110
Linworth, Oh., U.S.	k10	112
Linxi, China	C8	31
Linxia, China	D5	31
Linyi, China	D8	31
Linz, Aus.	D7	18
Lions, Gulf of, b., Fr.	F6	16
Lion's Head, Ont.	C3	73
Lionville, Pa., U.S.	F10	115
Lipa, Phil.	C6	34
Lipari, Italy	E5	23
Lipari, i., Italy	E5	23
Lipetsk, Sov. Un.	D12	27
Lipez, Cerro, mtn., Bol.	D2	55
Lipik, Yugo.	C3	24
Liping, China	F6	31
Lipkany, Sov. Un.	A8	24
Lipno, Pol.	B5	26
Lipno Reservoir, res., Czech.	E9	19
Lipova, Rom.	B5	24
Lippe, stm., W. Ger.	C2	18
Lippitt Estate, R.I., U.S.	C4	116
Lippstadt, W. Ger.	B3	18
Lipscomb, Tx., U.S.	A2	120
Lipscomb, co., Tx., U.S.	A2	120
Lipsoí, i., Grc.	D6	25
Lipton, Sask.	G4	75
Lipu, China	G7	31
Lira, Ug.	A5	48
Li Rangu, Sud.	E2	47
Lircay, Peru	D3	58
Liri, stm., Italy	D4	23
Liria, Spain	C5	22
Liro, stm., Italy	D7	21
Lisafa, Zaire	B2	48
Lisala, Zaire	A3	48
Lisbon (Lisboa), Port.	C1	22
Lisbon, Ct., U.S.	C7	84
Lisbon, Il., U.S.	B5	90
Lisbon, Ia., U.S.	C6	92
Lisbon, Me., U.S.	D2	96
Lisbon, Md., U.S.	B3	97
Lisbon, N.H., U.S.	B3	106
Lisbon, N.Y., U.S.	f9	109
Lisbon, N.D., U.S.	C8	111
Lisbon, Oh., U.S.	B5	112
Lisbon Center, Me., U.S.	f7	96
Lisbon Falls, Me., U.S.	E2	96
Lisburn, N. Ire., U.K.	C3	10
Lisburne, Cape, c., Ak., U.S.	B6	79
Liscannor Bay, b., Ire.	D2	11
Lisco, Ne., U.S.	C3	104
Liscomb, Ia., U.S.	B5	92
Lisdoonvarna, Ire.	D2	11
Lishi, China	F4	32
Lishu, China	C11	31
Lishui, China	F8	31
Lisianski Island, i., Hi., U.S.	k13	88
Lisichansk, Sov. Un.	q21	27
Lisieux, Sask.	H2	75
Lisieux, Fr.	C4	16
Liskeard, Eng., U.K.	D3	12
Lisle, Ont.	C5	73
L'Isle, Switz.	C1	21
Lisle, Il., U.S.	k8	90
L'Isle [-sur-le-Doubs], Fr.	B2	20
L'Islet, co., Que.	B7	74
L'Islet-sur-Mer, Que.	B7	74
L'Isle-Verte, Que.	A8	74
Lisman, Al., U.S.	C1	78
Lismore, Austl.	E9	50
Lismore, N.S.	D7	71
Lismore, Ire.	E4	11
Lismore, Mn., U.S.	G3	100
Lismore Island, i., Scot., U.K.	D3	13
Lisnaskea, N. Ire., U.K.	C4	11
List, W. Ger.	C2	15
Listafjorden, b., Nor.	H2	14
Lister, B.C.	E9	69
Listie, Pa., U.S.	F3	115
Listowel, Ont.	D4	73
Listowel, Ire.	D2	10
Litang, China	F5	31
Litavka, Czech.	o16	26
Litchfield, Ca., U.S.	B3	82
Litchfield, Ct., U.S.	C3	84
Litchfield, Il., U.S.	D4	90
Litchfield, Mi., U.S.	F6	99
Litchfield, Mn., U.S.	E4	100
Litchfield, Ne., U.S.	C6	104
Litchfield, N.H., U.S.	E4	106
Litchfield, co., Ct., U.S.	B2	84
Litchfield Park, Az., U.S.	m8	80
Litchville, N.D., U.S.	C7	111
Liteň, Czech.	o17	26
Literberry, Il., U.S.	D3	90
Lithgow, Austl.	F8	51
Lithia Springs, Ga., U.S.	h7	87
Líthinon, Cape, c., Grc.	E5	25
Lithonia, Ga., U.S.	C2	87
Lithuania, state, Sov. Un.	D5	27
Lititz, Pa., U.S.	F9	115
Litókhoron, Grc.	B4	25
Litoměřice, Czech.	C4	26
Litomyšl, Czech.	D4	26
Litslena, Swe.	t35	14
Littau, Switz.	B5	21
Little, stm., U.S.	D7	113
Little, stm., U.S.	C7	84
Little, stm., Ct., U.S.	C2	84
Little, stm., Ga., U.S.	C3	87
Little, stm., Ga., U.S.	C3	87
Little, stm., Ky., U.S.	D2	94
Little, stm., La., U.S.	B3	95
Little, stm., N.C., U.S.	B3	110
Little, stm., Ok., U.S.	C6	113
Little, stm., S.C., U.S.	C2	117
Little, stm., Tn., U.S.	n14	119
Little, stm., Vt., U.S.	C3	122
Little Acres, Az., U.S.	D5	80
Little Alföld, pl., Hung.	*B3	24
Little America, Wy., U.S.	*E3	127
Little Andaman, i., India	F9	36
Little Arkansas, stm., Ks., U.S.	D6	93
Little Bay Islands, Newf.	D4	72
Little Bear Lake, l., Sask.	C3	75
Little Beaver Creek, stm., Ks., U.S.	C2	93
Little Belt Mountains, mts., Mt., U.S.	D6	103
Little Bighorn, stm., U.S.	E9	103
Little Birch, W.V., U.S.	C4	125
Little Bitter Lake, l., Eg.	D4	41
Little Black, stm., Me., U.S.	A3	96
Little Blue, stm., In., U.S.	H5	91
Little Boars Head, N.H., U.S.	E5	106
Little Bow, stm., Alta.	D4	68
Little Britain, Ont.	C6	73
Little Brook, N.S.	E3	71
Little Bullhead, Man.	D3	70
Little Cacapon, stm., W.V., U.S.	B6	125
Little Cadotte, stm., Alta.	A2	68
Little Canada, Mn., U.S.	*m12	100
Little Carpathians, mts., Czech.	D4	26
Little Catalina, Newf.	D5	72
Little Cayman, i., Cay. Is.	E5	64
Little Cedar, Ia., U.S.	A5	92
Little Cedar, stm., Ia., U.S.	A5	92
Little Chief, Ok., U.S.	A5	113
Little Choptank River, b., Md., U.S.	C5	97
Little Churchill, stm., Man.	A4	70
Little Chute, Wi., U.S.	D5	126
Little Colorado, stm., Az., U.S.	A5	80
Little Compton, R.I., U.S.	E6	116
Little Creek, De., U.S.	D4	85
Little Creek Naval Amphibious Base, mil., Va., U.S.	k15	123
Little Creek Peak, mtn., Ut., U.S.	F3	121
Little Current, Ont.	B3	73
Little Deer Isle, Me., U.S.	D4	96
Little Diomede Island, i., Ak., U.S.	B6	79
Little Dry Creek, stm., Mt., U.S.	C10	103
Little Eagle, S.D., U.S.	B5	118
Little Egg Harbor, b., N.J., U.S.	D4	107
Little Egg Inlet, b., N.J., U.S.	E4	107
Little Falls, Mn., U.S.	E4	100
Little Falls, N.J., U.S.	B4	107
Little Falls, N.Y., U.S.	B6	109
Little Ferry, N.J., U.S.	h8	107
Littlefield, Az., U.S.	A2	80
Littlefield, Tx., U.S.	C1	120
Little Fishing Creek, stm., W.V., U.S.	h9	125
Littlefork, Mn., U.S.	B5	100
Little Fork, stm., Mn., U.S.	B5	100
Little Frog Mountain, mtn., Tn., U.S.	D9	119
Little Goose Creek, stm., Wy., U.S.	B5	127
Little Grand Lake, l., Newf.	D3	72
Little Gunpowder Falls, stm., Md., U.S.	A4	97
Little Harbour Deep, Newf.	C3	72
Little Hocking, Oh., U.S.	C4	112
Little Humboldt, stm., Nv., U.S.	B4	105
Little Humboldt, North Fork, stm., Nv., U.S.	B4	105
Little Humboldt, South Fork, stm., Nv., U.S.	B5	105
Little Inagua, i., Bah.	D7	64
Little Kanawha, stm., W.V., U.S.	C4	125
Little Kanawha, West Fork, stm., W.V., U.S.	B3	125
Little Lake, Mi., U.S.	B3	99
Little Lake, l., La., U.S.	E5	95
Littlelot, Tn., U.S.	B4	119
Little Lynches, stm., S.C., U.S.	C7	117
Little Manatee, stm., Fl., U.S.	p11	86
Little Manitou Lake, l., Sask.	F3	75
Little Marais, Mn., U.S.	C7	100
Little Mazarn Creek, stm., Ar., U.S.	g7	81
Little Meadows, Pa., U.S.	C9	115
Little Mecatina, stm., Can.	h9	72
Little Mexico, Tx., U.S.	D1	120
Little Miami, stm., Oh., U.S.	C1	112
Little Miami, East Fork, stm., Oh., U.S.	C1	112
Little Miami, Todd Fork, stm., Oh., U.S.	C1	112
Little Missouri, stm., U.S.	A7	76
Little Missouri, stm., Ar., U.S.	D2	81
Little Moose Mountain, mtn., N.Y., U.S.	B6	109
Little Mountain, S.C., U.S.	C5	117
Little Mountain, mtn., Wy., U.S.	E3	127
Little Muddy, stm., Il., U.S.	E4	90
Little Muddy, stm., N.D., U.S.	A2	111
Little Orleans, Md., U.S.	A1	97
Little Osage, stm., U.S.	E9	93
Little Otter Creek, stm., Vt., U.S.	C2	122
Little Owyhee, stm., U.S.	B5	105
Little Pee Dee, stm., S.C., U.S.	C9	117
Little Pigeon Creek, stm., In., U.S.	I3	91
Little Pipe Creek, stm., Md., U.S.	A3	97
Little Playgreen Lake, l., Man.	B3	70
Littleport, Ia., U.S.	B6	92
Little Powder, stm., U.S.	F11	103
Little Quill Lake, l., Sask.	F3	75
Little Rann of Kachchh, pl., India	F3	37
Little Red, stm., Ar., U.S.	B4	81
Little Red, Middle Fork, stm., Ar., U.S.	B3	81
Little River, N.S.	E3	71
Little River, Ct., U.S.	C7	84
Little River, Ks., U.S.	D5	93
Little River, S.C., U.S.	D10	117
Little River, co., Ar., U.S.	D1	81
Little River Inlet, b., S.C., U.S.	D10	117
Little Rock, Ar., U.S.	C3	81
Little Rock, Il., U.S.	B5	90
Little Rock, Ia., U.S.	A2	92
Little Rock, Ky., U.S.	B5	94
Little Rock, S.C., U.S.	C9	117
Little Rock Air Force Base, mil., Ar., U.S.	C3	81
Littlerock, Wa., U.S.	C2	124
Little Sable Point, c., Mi., U.S.	E4	99
Little Sachigo Lake, l., Ont.	B5	70
Little Saint Bernard Pass, Eur.	E7	16
Little Salt Lake, l., Ut., U.S.	F3	121
Little Sand Creek, stm., Mn., U.S.	D6	100
Little Sandy, stm., Ky., U.S.	B6	94
Little Sandy Creek, stm., Wy., U.S.	D3	127
Little Sauk, Mn., U.S.	E4	100
Little Sebago Lake, l., Me., U.S.	g7	96
Little Silver, N.J., U.S.	C4	107
Little Sioux, Ia., U.S.	C1	92
Little Sioux, stm., U.S.	B2	92
Little Sioux, West Fork, stm., Ia., U.S.	B2	92
Little Smoky, stm., Alta.	B2	68
Little Snake, stm., U.S.	A2	83
Little Southwest Miramichi, stm., N.B.	C3	71
Little Spokane, stm., Wa., U.S.	B8	124
Little Suamico, Wi., U.S.	D6	126
Little Tallapoosa, stm., U.S.	B4	78
Little Tenmile Creek, stm., W.V., U.S.	k10	125
Little Tennessee, stm., U.S.	D9	119
Littleton, Co., U.S.	B6	83
Littleton, Il., U.S.	C3	90
Littleton, Me., U.S.	B5	96
Littleton, Ma., U.S.	f10	98
Littleton, N.H., U.S.	B3	106
Littleton, N.C., U.S.	A5	110
Littleton, W.V., U.S.	B4	125
Little Tucson, Az., U.S.	F4	80
Little Valley, Ca., U.S.	B3	82
Little Valley, N.Y., U.S.	C2	109
Littleville, Al., U.S.	A2	78
Little Wabash, stm., Il., U.S.	E5	90
Little Walnut, stm., Ks., U.S.	g13	93
Little West Fork, stm., Tn., U.S.	A4	119
Little White, stm., S.D., U.S.	D5	118
Little Wolf, stm., Wi., U.S.	D4	126
Little Wood, stm., Id., U.S.	F4	89
Little York, Il., U.S.	B3	90
Little York, In., U.S.	G6	91
Little Zab, stm., Asia	E15	40
Littoria see Latina, Italy	D4	23
Litvinov, Czech.	C8	19
Liuba, China	E6	31
Liucheng, China	G6	31
Liucura, Chile	B2	54
Liuhe, China	C11	31
Liupan Mountains, mts., China	F1	32
Liuyang, China	J5	32
Liuzhou, China	G6	31
Livelong, Sask.	D1	75
Lively, Ont.	A3	73
Livengood, Ak., U.S.	B10	79
Livenza, stm., Italy	D8	20
Live Oak, Ca., U.S.	*D3	82
Live Oak, Fl., U.S.	B4	86
Live Oak, Tx., U.S.	*E3	120
Live Oak, co., Tx., U.S.	E3	120
Live Oak Manor, La., U.S.	*E5	95
Livermore, Ca., U.S.	h9	82
Livermore, Co., U.S.	A5	83
Livermore, Ia., U.S.	B3	92
Livermore, Ky., U.S.	C2	94
Livermore, Me., U.S.	D2	96
Livermore, Mount, mtn., Tx., U.S.	o12	120
Livermore Falls, Me., U.S.	D2	96
Livermore Falls, N.H., U.S.	C3	106
Liverpool, Austl.	*F9	50
Liverpool, N.S.	E5	71
Liverpool, Eng., U.K.	D5	10
Liverpool, N.Y., U.S.	B4	109
Liverpool, Tx., U.S.	r14	120
Liverpool, W.V., U.S.	C3	125
Liverpool Bay, b., N.W. Ter.	B7	66
Liverpool Range, mts., Austl.	C9	51
Livingston, Guat.	D7	63
Livingston, Al., U.S.	C1	78
Livingston, Ca., U.S.	D3	82
Livingston, Il., U.S.	E4	90
Livingston, Ky., U.S.	C5	94
Livingston, La., U.S.	D5	95
Livingston, Mt., U.S.	E6	103
Livingston, N.J., U.S.	B4	107
Livingston, N.Y., U.S.	C7	109
Livingston, S.C., U.S.	D5	117
Livingston, Tn., U.S.	C8	119
Livingston, Tx., U.S.	D5	120
Livingston, Wi., U.S.	F3	126
Livingston, co., Il., U.S.	C5	90
Livingston, co., Ky., U.S.	e9	94
Livingston, co., La., U.S.	D5	95
Livingston, co., Mi., U.S.	F7	99
Livingston, co., Mo., U.S.	B4	102
Livingston, co., N.Y., U.S.	C3	109
Livingston, Lake, res., Tx., U.S.	D5	120
Livingston, Zam.	E4	48
Livingston Cove, N.S.	D8	71
Livingstone Falls, wtfl., Afr.	*C1	48
Livingstonia, Mwi.	D5	48
Livingston Island, i., B.A.T.	C6	7
Livingston Manor, N.Y., U.S.	D6	109
Livno, Yugo.	D3	24
Livny, Sov. Un.	E11	27
Livona, N.D., U.S.	C5	111
Livonia, In., U.S.	G5	91
Livonia, La., U.S.	D4	95
Livonia, Mi., U.S.	F7	99
Livonia, Mo., U.S.	A5	102
Livonia, N.Y., U.S.	C3	109
Livorno (Leghorn), Italy	C3	23
Livramento do Brumado, Braz.	C3	56
Livry-Gargan, Fr.	g11	16
Liwale, Tan.	C6	48
Lixian, China	J4	32
Liyang, China	I8	32
Lizard Creek, stm., Ia., U.S.	B3	92
Lizard Head Pass, Co., U.S.	D3	83
Lizard Head Peak, mtn., Wy., U.S.	D3	127
Lizard Point, c., Eng., U.K.	F4	10
Lizella, Ga., U.S.	D3	87
Lizemores, W.V., U.S.	C3	125
Lizton, In., U.S.	E4	91
Ljubljana, Yugo.	B2	24
Ljubuški, Yugo.	D3	24
Ljungby, Swe.	I5	14
Ljusdal, Swe.	G7	14
Ljusterö, Swe.	t36	14
Llandeilo, Wales, U.K.	C4	12
Llandovery, Wales, U.K.	A1	12
Llandrindod Wells, Wales, U.K.	D5	10
Llandudno, Wales, U.K.	D4	10
Llanelli, Wales, U.K.	E4	10
Llanes, Spain	A3	22
Llanfyllin, Wales, U.K.	B4	12
Llangefni, Wales, U.K.	A3	12
Llangollen, Wales, U.K.	B4	12
Llanidloes Estates, De., U.S.	*B3	85
Llangynog, Wales, U.K.	B4	12
Llanidloes, Wales, U.K.	B4	12
Llano, Tx., U.S.	D3	120
Llano, co., Tx., U.S.	D3	120
Llano, stm., Tx., U.S.	D3	120
Llanos, pl., S.A.	B3	60
Llanquihue, Lago, l., Chile	C2	54
Llanrwst, Wales, U.K.	A4	12
Llata, Peru	C2	58
Llaves, N.M., U.S.	A3	108
Lleyn Peninsula, pen., Wales, U.K.	D4	10
Llico, Chile	A2	55
Llobregat, stm., Spain	B6	22
Lloyd, Fl., U.S.	B2	86
Lloyd, Ky., U.S.	B7	94
Lloyd, Mt., U.S.	B7	103
Lloyd Harbor, N.Y., U.S.	*E7	109
Lloydminster, Alta.	C5	68
Lloydminster (Alta. and Sask.), Sask.	D1	75
Lloyds, stm., Newf.	D3	72
Lluchmayor, Spain	D2	55
Llullaillaco, Volcán, vol., S.A.	B6	55
Lo, stm., Viet.	B3	34
Loa, Ut., U.S.	E4	121
Loa, stm., Chile	A2	55
Loachapoka, Al., U.S.	C4	78
Loami, Il., U.S.	D4	90
Loange, stm., Afr.	C2	48
Lobatse, Bots.	C4	49
Löbau, E. Ger.	C7	18
Lobelville, Tn., U.S.	B4	119
Lobenstein, E. Ger.	C6	19
Lobería, Arg.	B5	54
Lobito, Ang.	D1	48

Name	Map Ref.	Page
Lobnya, Sov. Un.	m17	27
Lobo, Phil.	p13	34
Lobos, Arg.	B5	54
Lobos, Cabo, c., Mex.	B2	63
Lobos, Punta, c., Mex.	B2	63
Lobos de Tierra, Isla, i., Peru	C1	58
Lobster Lake, l., Me., U.S.	C3	96
Loburg, E. Ger.	A7	19
Locarno, Switz.	E4	18
Lochaber, N.S.	D7	71
Lochcarron, Scot., U.K.	C3	13
Lochdonhead, Scot., U.K.	D3	13
Lochearnhead, Scot., U.K.	D4	13
Lochem, Neth.	B6	17
Loches, Fr.	D4	16
Lochgilphead, Scot., U.K.	D3	13
Lochinver, Scot., U.K.	B3	13
Loch Lomond, Va., U.S.	B5	123
Loch Lynn Heights, Md., U.S.	m12	97
Lochmaben, Scot., U.K.	E5	13
Lochmere, N.H., U.S.	D3	106
Lochnagar, mtn., Scot., U.K.	D5	13
Lochranza, Scot., U.K.	E3	13
Loch Raven Reservoir, res., Md., U.S.	B4	97
Lochsa, stm., Id., U.S.	C3	89
Lochy, Loch, l., Scot., U.K.	D4	13
Lockbourne, Oh., U.S.	m11	112
Locke, In., U.S.	B5	91
Locke, N.Y., U.S.	C4	109
Locke, Tn., U.S.	B1	119
Locke Mills, Me., U.S.	D2	96
Lockeport, N.S.	F4	71
Lockerbie, Scot., U.K.	E5	13
Lockesburg, Ar., U.S.	D1	81
Lockhart, Al., U.S.	D3	78
Lockhart, Fl., U.S.	*D5	86
Lockhart, Mn., U.S.	*C2	100
Lockhart, S.C., U.S.	B5	117
Lockhart, Tx., U.S.	E4	120
Lock Haven, Pa., U.S.	D7	115
Lockland, Oh., U.S.	o13	112
Lockney, Tx., U.S.	B2	120
Lockport, Man.	D3	70
Lockport, Il., U.S.	B5	90
Lockport, Ky., U.S.	B5	94
Lockport, La., U.S.	E5	95
Lockport, N.Y., U.S.	B2	109
Lockridge, Ia., U.S.	C6	92
Lock Springs, Mo., U.S.	B4	102
Lockwood, Sask.	F3	75
Lockwood, Mo., U.S.	D4	102
Lockwood, Mt., U.S.	E8	103
Lockwood, W.V., U.S.	C3	125
Loc Ninh, Viet.	G7	35
Loco, Ok., U.S.	C4	113
Loco Hills, N.M., U.S.	E6	108
Locumba, Peru	E3	58
Locust, N.J., U.S.	C4	107
Locust, N.C., U.S.	B2	110
Locust Bayou, Ar., U.S.	D3	81
Locust Creek, stm., Mo., U.S.	A4	102
Locust Fork, stm., Al., U.S.	B3	78
Locust Grove, Ga., U.S.	C2	87
Locust Grove, Md., U.S.	B2	97
Locust Grove, N.Y., U.S.	*C7	109
Locust Grove, Ok., U.S.	A6	113
Locust Hill (part of Markham), Ont.	k15	73
Lod, Isr.	G10	40
Loda, Il., U.S.	C5	90
Loděnice, stm., Czech.	n17	26
Löderup, Swe.	C8	15
Lodève, Fr.	F5	16
Lodeynoye Pole, Sov. Un.	A9	27
Lodge, Newf.	B4	72
Lodge, S.C., U.S.	E6	117
Lodge Creek, stm., N.A.	B7	103
Lodge Grass, Mt., U.S.	E9	103
Lodgepole, Alta.	C3	68
Lodge Pole, Mt., U.S.	B8	103
Lodgepole, Ne., U.S.	C3	104
Lodgepole, S.D., U.S.	B3	118
Lodgepole Creek, stm., U.S.	C13	104
Lodi, Italy	B2	23
Lodi, Ca., U.S.	C3	82
Lodi, N.J., U.S.	h8	107
Lodi, N.Y., U.S.	C4	109
Lodi, Oh., U.S.	A3	112
Lodi, Wi., U.S.	E4	126
Lodi, Zaire	B3	48
Lodja, Zaire	B3	48
Lodore, Canyon of, val., Co., U.S.	A2	83
Lods, Fr.	B2	20
Lodwar, Kenya	A6	48
Łódź, Pol.	C5	26
Loeches, Spain	p18	22
Loei, Thai.	D4	35
Loelli, l., Sud.	D3	47
Loeriesfontein, S. Afr.	D2	49
Lofer, Aus.	B8	20
Lofoten, Nor.	C5	14
Loftus, Eng., U.K.	F8	13
Loga, Niger	D5	45
Logan, Il., U.S.	F5	90
Logan, Ia., U.S.	C2	92
Logan, Ks., U.S.	C4	93
Logan, Mt., U.S.	E5	103
Logan, N.M., U.S.	B6	108
Logan, N.D., U.S.	A4	111
Logan, Oh., U.S.	C3	112
Logan, Ok., U.S.	A1	113
Logan, Ut., U.S.	B4	121
Logan, W.V., U.S.	D3	125
Logan, co., Ar., U.S.	B2	81
Logan, co., Co., U.S.	A7	83
Logan, co., Il., U.S.	C4	90
Logan, co., Ks., U.S.	D2	93
Logan, co., Ky., U.S.	D3	94
Logan, co., Ne., U.S.	C5	104
Logan, co., N.D., U.S.	C6	111
Logan, co., Oh., U.S.	B2	112
Logan, co., Ok., U.S.	B4	113
Logan, co., W.V., U.S.	D3	125
Logandale, Nv., U.S.	G7	105
Logan Lake, B.C.	D7	69
Logan Martin Lake, res., Al., U.S.	B3	78
Logan Mountains, mts., Yukon	D7	66
Logan Pass, Mt., U.S.	B2	103
Logansport, In., U.S.	C5	91
Logansport, Ky., U.S.	C3	94
Logansport, La., U.S.	C2	95
Loganton, Pa., U.S.	D7	115
Loganville, Ga., U.S.	C3	87
Loganville, Wi., U.S.	E3	126
Loge, stm., Ang.	C1	48
Loggieville, N.B.	B4	71
Log Lane Village, Co., U.S.	A7	83
Logone, stm., Afr.	C3	46
Logroño, Spain	A4	22
Logrosán, Spain	C3	22
Løgstør, Den.	B3	15
Løgumkloster, Den.	C2	15
Lohals, Den.	C4	15
Lohärdaga, India	D7	36
Lohr, W. Ger.	D4	19
Lohrville, Ia., U.S.	B3	92
Loi, mtn., Laos	B5	35
Loikaw, Burma	C2	35
Loir, stm., Fr.	D4	16
Loire, stm., Fr.	D3	16
Loíza, Lago, res., P.R.	B3	65
Loja, Ec.	B2	58
Loja, Spain	D3	22
Loja, prov., Ec.	B2	58
Lokandu, Zaire	B4	48
Lokan Reservoir, res., Fin.	C13	14
Lokeren, Bel.	C3	17
Lokhvitsa, Sov. Un.	F9	27
Lokichar, Kenya	A6	48
Lokichokio, Kenya	A5	48
Lokitaung, Kenya	A6	48
Løkken, Den.	A3	15
Lokoja, Nig.	E6	45
Lokolama, Zaire	B2	48
Lokoro, stm., Zaire	B2	48
Lokossa, Benin	E5	45
Lol, stm., Sud.	D2	47
Lola, Ky., U.S.	e9	94
Lola, Mount, mtn., Ca., U.S.	C3	82
Loliondo, Tan.	B6	48
Lolland, i., Den.	J4	14
Lollar, W. Ger.	C3	19
Lollie, stm., Ar., U.S.	D4	87
Lolo, Mt., U.S.	D2	103
Lolo Hot Springs, Mt., U.S.	D2	103
Lolo Pass, U.S.	C4	89
Lom, Bul.	D6	24
Loma, Co., U.S.	B2	83
Loma, Mt., U.S.	C6	103
Loma, Ne., U.S.	C9	104
Loma, N.D., U.S.	A7	111
Loma Linda, Ca., U.S.	*E5	82
Lomami, stm., Zaire	B5	48
Loma Mountains, mts., S.L.	E2	45
Loman, Mn., U.S.	B5	100
Lomas, Peru	E3	58
Lomas de Zamora, Arg.	A5	54
Lomax, Ca., U.S.	C3	78
Lomax, Il., U.S.	C2	90
Lombard, Il., U.S.	k8	90
Lombarda, Serra, plat., Braz.	B4	57
Lombardia, prov., Italy	D5	20
Lombardy (Lombardia), prov., Italy	B2	23
Lomblen, i., Indon.	G6	34
Lombok, i., Indon.	G5	34
Lombok Strait, strt., Indon.	G5	34
Lomé, Togo	E5	45
Lomela, Zaire	B3	48
Lomela, stm., Zaire	B3	48
Lometa, Tx., U.S.	D3	120
Lomié, Cam.	E2	46
Lomira, Wi., U.S.	E5	126
Lomita, Ca., U.S.	*E4	82
Lommel, Bel.	C5	17
Lomond, Alta.	D4	68
Lomond, Newf.	D3	72
Lomond, Loch, l., Scot., U.K.	D4	13
Lomonosov, Sov. Un.	s30	14
Lomonosovka, Sov. Un.	C7	28
Lompoc, Ca., U.S.	E3	82
Lom Sak, Thai.	D4	35
Łomża, Pol.	B7	26
Lonaconing, Md., U.S.	k13	97
Loncoche, Chile	B2	54
Londesborough, Ont.	D3	73
London, Ont.	E3	73
London, Eng., U.K.	E6	10
London, Ar., U.S.	B2	81
London, In., U.S.	E6	91
London, Ky., U.S.	C5	94
London, Oh., U.S.	C2	112
London, Tx., U.S.	D3	120
London (Heathrow) Airport, Eng., U.K.	m12	10
Londonderry, N.S.	D6	71
Londonderry (Derry), N. Ire., U.K.	C3	10
Londonderry, N.H., U.S.	E4	106
Londonderry, Oh., U.S.	C3	112
Londonderry, Vt., U.S.	E3	122
Londonderry, Cape, c., Austl.	B4	50
Londonderry, Isla, i., Chile	k11	54
London Mills, Il., U.S.	C3	90
Londontowne, Md., U.S.	*C4	97
Londrina, Braz.	C2	56
Lone Elm, Ks., U.S.	D8	93
Lone Grove, Ok., U.S.	C4	113
Lone Jack, Mo., U.S.	C3	102
Lonely Island, i., Ont.	B3	73
Lone Mountain, Tn., U.S.	C10	119
Lone Mountain, mtn., Nv., U.S.	E4	105
Lone Oak, Ky., U.S.	e9	94
Lone Oak, Tx., U.S.	C5	120
Lone Pine, Ca., U.S.	D4	82
Lonepine, Mt., U.S.	C2	103
Lone Rock, Sask.	D1	75
Lone Rock, Ia., U.S.	A3	92
Lone Rock, Wi., U.S.	E3	126
Lone Star, S.C., U.S.	D6	117
Lonetree, Wy., U.S.	E2	127
Lone Tree Creek, stm., Co., U.S.	A6	83
Lone Wolf, Ok., U.S.	C2	113
Longa, co., Ga., U.S.	E5	87
Longa, stm., Ang.	D1	48
Longá, stm., Braz.	B2	57
Longarone, Italy	C8	20
Long Bar Harbor, Md., U.S.	*B5	97
Long Bay, b., Jam.	E12	65
Long Bay, b., Jam.	F14	65
Long Beach, Ca., U.S.	F4	82
Long Beach, Md., U.S.	D5	97
Long Beach, Ms., U.S.	g7	101
Long Beach, N.Y., U.S.	E7	109
Long Beach Naval Shipyard, mil., Ca., U.S.	n12	82
Longboat Key, Fl., U.S.	q10	86
Longboat Key, i., Fl., U.S.	E4	86
Longboat Pass, strt., Fl., U.S.	q10	86
Long Bottom, Oh., U.S.	C4	112
Long Branch (part of Etobicoke), Ont.	m14	73
Long Branch, N.J., U.S.	C5	107
Long Branch, Tx., U.S.	C5	120
Longbranch, Wa., U.S.	B3	124
Long Cay, i., Bah.	m17	64
Long Creek, Or., U.S.	C7	114
Longcreek, S.C., U.S.	B1	117
Long Creek, stm., N.A.	H3	75
Long Creek Mountain, mtn., Wy., U.S.	D5	127
Longdale, Ok., U.S.	A3	113
Long Eaton, Eng., U.K.	B6	12
Long Eddy, N.Y., U.S.	D5	109
Longford, Ont.	C5	73
Longford, Ire.	D10	10
Longford, Ks., U.S.	C6	93
Longford, co., Ire.	D4	11
Long Grove, Ia., U.S.	C7	92
Long Harbour [-Mount Arlington Heights], Newf.	E5	72
Long Hill, Ct., U.S.	*D7	84
Longhua, Indon.	F5	34
Longisland, Ks., U.S.	C4	93
Longisland, N.C., U.S.	B2	110
Long Island, i., Bah.	C6	64
Long Island, i., N.C., U.S.	E3	71
Long Island, i., Me., U.S.	g7	96
Long Island, i., Ma., U.S.	g12	98
Long Island, i., N.Y., U.S.	E7	109
Long Island Sound, strt., U.S.	E7	109
Long Key, Fl., U.S.	H6	86
Long Key, i., Fl., U.S.	H6	86
Longkou, China	F9	32
Longlac, Ont.	G15	66
Long Lake, Il., U.S.	h8	90
Long Lake, Mi., U.S.	D7	99
Long Lake, N.Y., U.S.	B6	109
Longlake, S.D., U.S.	B6	118
Long Lake, Wi., U.S.	C5	126
Long Lake, l., Me., U.S.	B3	71
Long Lake, l., Me., U.S.	A4	96
Long Lake, l., Mi., U.S.	D2	96
Long Lake, l., Mi., U.S.	D5	99
Long Lake, l., Mi., U.S.	D6	99
Long Lake, l., Mn., U.S.	B6	109
Long Lake, l., N.D., U.S.	C6	111
Long Lake, l., Wa., U.S.	f10	124
Long Lake Colony, S.D., U.S.	*B7	118
Long Lane, Mo., U.S.	D5	102
Longleaf, La., U.S.	C3	95
Longlin, China	G6	31
Longmeadow, Ma., U.S.	B2	98
Longmont, Co., U.S.	A5	83
Long Mountain, mtn., Mo., U.S.	E5	102
Long Mountain, mtn., N.H., U.S.	A4	106
Long Pine, Ne., U.S.	B6	104
Long Point, N.S.	D8	71
Long Point, Ont.	E4	73
Long Point, i., Man.	C2	70
Long Point, c., Newf.	D2	72
Long Point, pen., Ont.	E4	73
Long Pond, l., Me., U.S.	C3	96
Long Pond, l., Me., U.S.	C6	96
Long Pond, l., Ma., U.S.	C6	98
Long Pond, res., Fl., U.S.	C4	86
Longport, N.J., U.S.	E3	107
Lorlie, Sask.	G4	75
Long Prairie, Mn., U.S.	E4	100
Longquan, China	F8	31
Long Range Mountains, mts., Newf.	D3	72
Longreach, Austl.	D7	50
Longridge, Eng., U.K.	G6	13
Long Run, W.V., U.S.	k9	125
Longs Peak, mtn., Co., U.S.	A5	83
Long Strait, strt., Sov. Un.	B20	29
Longstreet, La., U.S.	B2	95
Longton, Ks., U.S.	E7	93
Longtown, Eng., U.K.	E6	13
Longtown, Mo., U.S.	D8	102
Longueau, Fr.	E2	17
Longueuil, Que.	D4	74
Longuyon, Fr.	C6	16
Longvale, Ca., U.S.	C2	82
Long Valley, Az., U.S.	C4	80
Long Valley, N.J., U.S.	B3	107
Longvalley, S.D., U.S.	D4	118
Longview, Alta.	D3	68
Longview, Il., U.S.	D5	90
Long View, Ky., U.S.	C4	94
Longview, Ms., U.S.	B5	101
Long View, N.C., U.S.	B1	110
Longview, Tx., U.S.	C5	120
Longview, Wa., U.S.	C3	124
Longville, La., U.S.	D2	95
Longville, Mn., U.S.	C4	100
Longwood, Fl., U.S.	*D5	86
Longwood, N.C., U.S.	C4	110
Longwoods, Md., U.S.	C5	97
Longwy, Fr.	C6	16
Longxian, China	D8	32
Long Xuyen, Viet.	G6	35
Longyan, China	F8	31
Longyao, China	F6	32
Longzhen, China	B3	33
Longzhou, China	G6	31
Lonkin, Burma	C10	36
Lonoke, Ar., U.S.	C4	81
Lonoke, co., Ar., U.S.	C4	81
Lönsdal, Nor.	D6	14
Lonsdale, Ar., U.S.	C3	81
Lonsdale, Mn., U.S.	F5	100
Lonsdale, R.I., U.S.	B4	116
Lons-le-Saunier, Fr.	D6	16
Lontzen, Bel.	D5	17
Looe, Eng., U.K.	D3	12
Loogootee, In., U.S.	G4	91
Lookeba, Ok., U.S.	B3	113
Lookout, Ca., U.S.	B3	82
Lookout, Ky., U.S.	C7	94
Lookout, W.V., U.S.	C4	125
Lookout, Cape, c., N.C., U.S.	C6	110
Lookout, Point, c., Mi., U.S.	d7	99
Lookout Mountain, Tn., U.S.	h11	119
Lookout Mountain, mtn., U.S.	D8	119
Lookout Mountain, mtn., Or., U.S.	C6	114
Lookout Pass, U.S.	B3	89
Lookout Point Lake, res., Or., U.S.	D4	114
Loomis, Sask.	H1	75
Loomis, Ne., U.S.	D6	104
Loomis, S.D., U.S.	D7	118
Loomis, Wa., U.S.	A5	124
Loon, stm., Alta.	A3	68
Loon, stm., Alta.	A1	70
Loon Bay, Newf.	D4	72
Loon Lake, Wa., U.S.	A8	124
Loon Lake, l., Alta.	A3	68
Loon Lake, l., Can.	B1	70
Loon Lake, l., Me., U.S.	B3	96
Loon Lake Mountains, mtn., N.Y., U.S.	f10	109
Loon Straits, Man.	D3	70
Loop, Or., U.S.	C1	120
Loop Creek, stm., W.V., U.S.	m13	125
Loop Head, c., Ire.	D1	10
Loos, Fr.	D3	17
Loosahatchie, stm., Tn., U.S.	B2	119
Loose Creek, Mo., U.S.	C6	102
Looxahoma, Ms., U.S.	A4	101
Lopatka, Cape, c., Sov. Un.	D18	29
Lop Buri, Thai.	C2	34
Lopeno, Tx., U.S.	F3	120
Lopez, Pa., U.S.	D9	115
Lopez, Cap, c., Gabon	F1	46
Lopez Bay, b., Phil.	p14	34
Lopez Island, i., Wa., U.S.	A3	124
Lopori, stm., Zaire	A3	48
Lora, Hāmūn-i-, l., Asia	G12	39
Lora [del Río], Spain	D3	22
Lora, Chile	B2	54
Lorado, W.V., U.S.	D3	125
Lorain, Oh., U.S.	A3	112
Lorain, co., Oh., U.S.	A3	112
Loraine, Il., U.S.	C2	90
Loraine, N.D., U.S.	A4	111
Loraine, Tx., U.S.	C2	120
Loralai, Pak.	B2	37
Loramie, Lake, res., Oh., U.S.	B1	112
Loranger, La., U.S.	D5	95
Lorca, Spain	D5	22
Lord Howe Island, i., Austl.	I9	6
Lordsburg, N.M., U.S.	E1	108
Lords Point, Ct., U.S.	D8	84
Loreburn, Sask.	F2	75
Lore City, Oh., U.S.	C4	112
Lorena, Braz.	C5	56
Lorena, Tx., U.S.	D4	120
Lorengau, Pap. N. Gui.	h12	50
Lorentz, W.V., U.S.	C5	125
Lorenzo, Id., U.S.	F7	89
Lorenzo, Ne., U.S.	C2	104
Lorenzo, Tx., U.S.	C2	120
Lorenzo Geyres, Ur.	E1	56
Loreto, Braz.	C1	57
Loreto, Col.	D3	60
Loreto, Italy	C4	23
Loreto, Mex.	B2	63
Loreto, Para.	D4	55
Loreto, dept., Peru	B3	58
Loretta, Ks., U.S.	D4	93
Loretta, Wi., U.S.	C3	126
Lorette, Man.	E3	70
Loretteville, Que.	C6	74
Loretto, Ky., U.S.	C4	94
Loretto, Mi., U.S.	C3	99
Loretto, Ne., U.S.	C7	104
Loretto, Pa., U.S.	F4	115
Loretto, Tn., U.S.	B4	119
Lorica, Col.	B2	60
Lorida, Fl., U.S.	E5	86
Lorient, Fr.	D2	16
L'Orignal, Ont.	B10	73
Lorimor, Ia., U.S.	C3	92
Loring, Mt., U.S.	B9	103
Loring Air Force Base, mil., Me., U.S.	B5	96
Loris, S.C., U.S.	C10	117
Lorman, Ms., U.S.	D2	101
Lorn, Firth of, est., Scot., U.K.	D3	13
Lorne, N.B.	B3	71
Lorneville, Ont.	C5	73
Lorquin, Fr.	C7	16
Lörrach, W. Ger.	E3	18
Lorraine, Ks., U.S.	D5	93
Lorraine, N.Y., U.S.	B5	109
Lorraine, hist. reg., Fr.	C7	16
Lorraine Plateau, plat., Fr.	C7	16
Lorsch, W. Ger.	D3	19
Lorton, Va., U.S.	*B5	123
Lorup, W. Ger.	B7	17
Los Alamitos, Ca., U.S.	*F5	82
Los Alamos, Ca., U.S.	E3	82
Los Alamos, N.M., U.S.	B3	108
Los Alamos, co., N.M., U.S.	B3	108
Los Altos, Ca., U.S.	k8	82
Los Altos Hills, Ca., U.S.	*k8	82
Los Amates, Guat.	C7	63
Los Andes, Chile	A2	54
Los Ángeles, Chile	B2	54
Los Ángeles, Ca., U.S.	E4	82
Los Angeles, co., Ca., U.S.	E4	82
Los Angeles Aqueduct, Ca., U.S.	E4	82
Losantville, In., U.S.	D7	91
Los Banos, Ca., U.S.	D3	82
Los Blancos, Arg.	D3	55
Los Cerrillos, Arg.	A3	54
Los Ebanos, Tx., U.S.	F3	120
Los Fresnos, Tx., U.S.	F4	120
Los Gatos, Ca., U.S.	D2	82
Los Hermanos, Islas, is., Ven.	A5	60
Los Lagos, Chile	B2	54
Los Lagos, prov., Chile	B2	54
Los Lunas, N.M., U.S.	C3	108
Los Mochis, Mex.	D5	63
Los Molinos, Ca., U.S.	B2	82
Los Monjes, Islas, is., Ven.	A3	60
Los Nietos, Ca., U.S.	*n12	82
Los Ojos, N.M., U.S.	A3	108
Los Osos, Ca., U.S.	*E3	82
Los Padillas, N.M., U.S.	*B3	108
Los Palacios, Cuba	C2	64
Los Palacios [y Villafranca], Spain	D3	22
Los Peares, Spain	A2	22
Los Pinos, N.M., U.S.	A3	108
Los Pinos, stm., U.S.	A3	83
Los Ranchos de Albuquerque, N.M., U.S.	*B3	108
Los Remedios, stm., Mex.	g9	63
Los Reyes [de Salgado], Mex.	D4	63
Los Reyes la Paz, Mex.	h10	63
Los Ríos, prov., Ec.	B2	58
Los Roques, Islas, is., Ven.	A4	60
Los Santos [de Maimona], Spain	C2	22
Los Sarmientos, Arg.	E2	55
Los Sauces, Chile	B2	54
Lossiemouth, Scot., U.K.	C5	13
Lössnitz, E. Ger.	C7	19
Lost, stm., In., U.S.	G4	91
Lost, stm., Wa., U.S.	A5	124
Lost, stm., W.V., U.S.	B6	125
Lostant, Il., U.S.	B4	90
Los Taques, Ven.	A3	60
Lost City, W.V., U.S.	C6	125
Lost Creek, W.V., U.S.	B4	125
Lost Creek, stm., Ar., U.S.	C3	81
Lost Creek, stm., Wy., U.S.	D4	127
Los Teques, Ven.	A4	60
Los Testigos, Islas, is., Ven.	A5	60
Lost Hills, Ca., U.S.	E4	82
Lostine, Or., U.S.	B9	114
Lost Nation, Ia., U.S.	C7	92
Lost Peak, mtn., Ut., U.S.	F2	121
Lost Ranger Peak, mtn., Co., U.S.	A4	83
Lost River, Id., U.S.	F5	89
Lost River, Ia., U.S.	e8	92
Lost River Glacial Caverns, N.H., U.S.	B3	106
Lost River Range, mts., Id., U.S.	E5	89
Lost Springs, Ks., U.S.	D7	93
Lost Springs, Wy., U.S.	D8	127
Lost Trail Pass, U.S.	*D5	89
Los Vigiles, N.M., U.S.	*B4	108
Los Vilos, Chile	A2	54
Lot, stm., Fr.	E4	16
Lota, Chile	B2	54
Lotawana, Lake, res., Mo., U.S.	k11	102
Lotbinière, Que.	C6	74
Lotbinière, co., Que.	C6	74
Lothair, Mt., U.S.	B5	103
Lothian, prov., Scot., U.K.	E5	13
Loto, Zaire	B3	48
Lotofaga, W. Sam.	F12	52
Lötschberg Tunnel, Switz.	E3	18
Lotung, Tai.	G9	31
Loubomo, Congo	B1	48
Loudon, N.H., U.S.	D4	106
Loudon, Tn., U.S.	D9	119
Loudon, co., Tn., U.S.	D9	119
Loudonville, Oh., U.S.	B3	112
Loudoun, co., Va., U.S.	A5	123
Loudun, Fr.	D4	16
Louga, Sen.	C1	45
Loughborough, Eng., U.K.	D6	10
Lougheed, Alta.	C5	68
Lougheed Island, i., N.W. Ter.	m31	66
Loughman, Fl., U.S.	D5	86
Loughrea, Ire.	D2	10
Loughros More Bay, b., Ire.	C3	11
Louin, Ms., U.S.	C4	101
Louisa, Ky., U.S.	B7	94
Louisa, Va., U.S.	B4	123
Louisa, co., Ia., U.S.	C6	92
Louisa, co., Va., U.S.	C5	123
Louisa, Lake, l., Fl., U.S.	D5	86
Louisbourg, N.S.	D10	71
Louisburg, Ks., U.S.	D9	93
Louisburg, Mn., U.S.	E2	100
Louisburg, Mo., U.S.	D4	102
Louisburg, N.C., U.S.	A4	110
Louisburgh, Ire.	D2	11
Louisdale, N.S.	D8	71
Louise, Ms., U.S.	C3	101
Louise, Tx., U.S.	E4	120
Louise, W.V., U.S.	f8	125
Louise, Lake, l., Ak., U.S.	f18	79
Louise Island, i., B.C.	C2	69
Louiseville, Que.	C5	74
Louisiade Archipelago, is., Pap. N. Gui.	G9	6
Louisiana, Mo., U.S.	B6	102
Louisiana, state, U.S.	C3	95
Louis Trichardt, S. Afr.	B4	49
Louisville, Al., U.S.	D4	78
Louisville, Ga., U.S.	C4	87
Louisville, Il., U.S.	E5	90
Louisville, Ky., U.S.	B4	94
Louisville, Ms., U.S.	B4	101
Louisville, Ne., U.S.	D9	104
Louisville, N.Y., U.S.	f9	109
Louisville, Oh., U.S.	B4	112
Louis-XIV, Pointe, c., Que.	h11	74
Loukhi, Sov. Un.	D15	14
Loulé, Port.	D1	22
Louny, Czech.	C2	26
Loup, co., Ne., U.S.	C6	104
Loup, stm., Ne., U.S.	C8	104
Loup, Île au, i., Que.	B8	71
Loup, Rivière du, stm., Que.	C4	74
Loup, Rivière du, stm., Que.	B8	74
Loup City, Ne., U.S.	C7	104
Lourdes, Newf.	D2	72
Lourdes, Que.	C4	74
Lourdes, Fr.	F3	16
Lourenço Marques see Maputo, Moz.	C5	49
Loures, Port.	f9	22
Lousã, Port.	B1	22
Lousana, Alta.	C4	68
Louth, Ire.	D5	11
Louth, Eng., U.K.	D7	10
Louth, co., Ire.	D5	11
Loutrá Aidhipsoú, Grc.	C4	25
Loutrákion, Grc.	h9	25
Loutre, Bayou de, stm., La., U.S.	B3	95
Louvain see Leuven, Bel.	D4	17
Louvale, Ga., U.S.	D1	87
Louviers, Co., U.S.	B6	83
Louviers, Fr.	C4	16
Love, Sask.	D3	75
Love, co., Ok., U.S.	D4	113
Lovech, Bul.	D7	24
Loveland, Co., U.S.	A5	83
Loveland, Oh., U.S.	C1	112
Loveland Park, Oh., U.S.	n13	112
Loveland Pass, Co., U.S.	B5	83
Lovell, Me., U.S.	D2	96
Lovell, Wy., U.S.	B4	127
Lovells, Mi., U.S.	D6	99
Lovelock, Nv., U.S.	C3	105
Lovenia, Mount, mtn., Ut., U.S.	C5	121
Love Point, c., Md., U.S.	B5	97
Loverna, Sask.	F1	75
Loves Park, Il., U.S.	A4	90
Lovett, Ga., U.S.	D4	87
Lovett, In., U.S.	G6	91
Lovettsville, Va., U.S.	A5	123
Lovewell Pond, l., Me., U.S.		
Lovick, Al., U.S.	f7	78
Lovilia, Ia., U.S.	C5	92
Loving, N.M., U.S.	E5	108
Loving, co., Tx., U.S.	D1	120
Lovington, Il., U.S.	D5	90
Lovington, N.M., U.S.	E6	108
Lovosice, Czech.	C9	19
Low, Que.	D2	74
Low, Cape, c., N.W. Ter.	D15	66
Lowa, Zaire	B4	48
Lowa, stm., Zaire	B4	48
Lowden, Ia., U.S.	C7	92
Lowe Farm, Man.	E3	70
Lowell, Ar., U.S.	A1	81
Lowell, In., U.S.	B3	91
Lowell, Ma., U.S.	A5	98
Lowell, Mi., U.S.	F5	99
Lowell, N.C., U.S.	B1	110
Lowell, Oh., U.S.	C4	112
Lowell, Or., U.S.	D4	114
Lowell, Vt., U.S.	B4	122
Lowell, W.V., U.S.	C3	125
Lowell, Wi., U.S.	E5	126
Lowell, Lake, res., Id., U.S.	F2	89
Lowell Mountains, mts., Vt., U.S.	B4	122
Lowellville, Oh., U.S.	A5	112
Lower Arrow Lake, res., B.C.	E8	69
Lower Bank, N.J., U.S.	D3	107
Lower Brule, S.D., U.S.	C6	118
Lower Brule Indian Reservation, S.D., U.S.	C6	118
Lower Burrell, Pa., U.S.	*h15	115
Lower Cabot, Vt., U.S.	C4	122
Lower California, pen., Mex.	B2	63
Lower East Pubnico, N.S.	F4	71
Lower Hutt, N.Z.	N15	51
Lower Island Cove, Newf.	D5	72
Lower Klamath Lake, l., Ca., U.S.	B3	82
Lower Loch Erne, l., N. Ire., U.K.	C3	10
Lower Manitou Lake, l., Ont.	E5	70
Lower Marlboro, Md., U.S.	C4	97
Lower Matecumbe Key, i., Fl., U.S.	H6	86
Lower Merion Township, Pa., U.S.	*F11	115
Lower Monumental Lake, res., Wa., U.S.	C7	124
Lower Moreland Township, Pa., U.S.	*F11	115
Lower New York Bay, b., N.J., U.S.	B4	107
Lower Otay Reservoir, res., Ca., U.S.	o16	82
Lower Paia, Hi., U.S.	C5	88
Lower Peach Tree, Al., U.S.	D2	78
Lower Red Lake, l., Mn., U.S.	C3	100
Lower Rice Lake, l., Mn., U.S.	C3	100
Lower Salem, Oh., U.S.	C4	112
Lower Salmon Dam, Id., U.S.	G4	89
Lower Southampton Township, Pa., U.S.	*G11	115
Lower Village, Vt., U.S.	C3	122
Lower West Pubnico, N.S.	F4	71
Lower Wilson Pond, l., Me., U.S.	C3	96
Lower Woods Harbour, N.S.	F4	71
Lowes, Ky., U.S.	f9	94
Lowestoft, Eng., U.K.	D7	10
Lowgap, N.C., U.S.	A2	110
Łowicz, Pol.	B5	26
Lowland, N.C., U.S.	B6	110
Lowman, Id., U.S.	E3	89
Lowmansville, Ky., U.S.	C7	94
Low Moor, Ia., U.S.	C7	92
Lowmoor, Va., U.S.	C3	123
Lowndes, Mo., U.S.	D7	102
Lowndes, co., Al., U.S.	C3	78
Lowndes, co., Ga., U.S.	F3	87
Lowndes, co., Ms., U.S.	B5	101
Lowndesboro, Al., U.S.	C3	78
Lowndesville, S.C., U.S.	C2	117
Lowry, Mn., U.S.	E3	100
Lowry, S.D., U.S.	B6	118
Lowry Air Force Base, mil., Co., U.S.	B6	83
Lowry City, Mo., U.S.	C4	102
Lowrys, S.C., U.S.	B5	117
Low Tatra Mountains, mts., Czech.	D5	26
Lowville, N.Y., U.S.	B5	109
Loxley, Al., U.S.	E2	78
Loxton, Austl.	G3	51
Loyal, Ok., U.S.	B3	113
Loyal, Wi., U.S.	D3	126
Loyalist, Alta.	C5	68
Loyall, Ky., U.S.	D6	94
Loyalsock Creek, stm., Pa., U.S.	D8	115
Loyalton, Ca., U.S.	C3	82
Loyalton, S.D., U.S.	B6	118
Loyalty Islands, is., N. Cal.	H10	6
Loysburg, Pa., U.S.	F5	115
Loysville, Pa., U.S.	F7	115
Loznica, Yugo.	C4	24
Lozovaya, Sov. Un.	G9	27
Lozoya, Canal of, Spain	o17	22
Lualaba, stm., Zaire	B4	48
Luama, stm., Zaire	B5	48
Lu'an, China	I7	32
Luana, Ia., U.S.	A6	92
Luanda, Ang.	C1	48
Luanda, Braz.	C2	56
Luanda, dept., Ang.	C1	48
Luang, Thai.	D1	34
Luang Chiang Dao, mtn., Thai.	C4	35
Luanginga, stm., Afr.	D4	48
Luangwa, stm., Afr.	D5	48
Luan He, stm., China	C8	31
Luanshya, Zam.	D4	48
Luanxian, China	B7	32
Luapula, prov., Zam.	D4	48
Luarca, Spain	A2	22
Luashi, Zaire	D4	48
Luba, Eq. Gui.	E1	46
Lubaczów, Pol.	D2	26
Lubang, Phil.	p13	34
Lubang, i., Phil.	p14	34
Lubang Islands, is., Phil.	p13	34
Lubango, Ang.	D1	48
Lubartów, Pol.	C7	26
Lubawa, Pol.	B5	26
Lübbecke, W. Ger.	A3	19
Lübben, E. Ger.	C6	19

Name	Map Ref.	Page

Lübbenau, E. Ger. — B8 19
Lubbock, Tx., U.S. — C2 120
Lubbock, co., Tx., U.S. — C2 120
Lubec, Me., U.S. — D6 96
Lübeck, W. Ger. — B5 18
Lübeck Bay, b., Eur. — A5 18
Lubefu, Zaire — B3 48
Lubero, Zaire — B4 48
Lubicon Lake, l., Alta. — A3 68
Lubilash, stm., Zaire — C3 48
Lublin, Pol. — C7 26
Lublin, Wi., U.S. — C3 126
Lubliniec, Pol. — C5 26
Lubny, Sov. Un. — F9 27
Luboń, Pol. — B4 26
Lubsko, Pol. — C3 26
Lübtheen, E. Ger. — E5 15
Lubudi, Zaire — C4 48
Lubudi, stm., Zaire — C3 48
Lubue, Zaire — B2 48
Lubumbashi (Élisabethville), Zaire — D4 48
Lubutu, Zaire — B4 48
Lucama, N.C., U.S. — B4 110
Lucan, Ont. — D3 73
Lucan, Ire. — D5 11
Lucan, Mn., U.S. — F3 100
Lucania, Mount, mtn., Yukon — D4 66
Lucas, Ia., U.S. — C4 92
Lucas, Ks., U.S. — C5 93
Lucas, Ky., U.S. — D3 94
Lucas, Oh., U.S. — D5 99
Lucas, S.D., U.S. — D6 118
Lucas, co., Ia., U.S. — C4 92
Lucas, co., Oh., U.S. — A2 112
Lucasville, Oh., U.S. — D3 112
Lucca, Italy — C3 23
Lucé, Fr. — C4 16
Luce, co., Mi., U.S. — B5 99
Lucea, Jam. — E4 64
Luce Bay, b., Scot., U.K. — C4 10
Lucedale, Ms., U.S. — E5 101
Lucena, Phil. — C6 34
Lucena, Spain — D3 22
Lucena del Cid, Spain — B5 22
Lučenec, Czech. — D5 26
Lucera, Italy — D5 23
Lucerne, Co., U.S. — C2 82
Lucerne, Ca., U.S. — A6 83
Lucerne, In., U.S. — C5 91
Lucerne, Mo., U.S. — A4 102
Lucerne, Lake of, l., Switz. — E4 18
Lucernemines, Pa., U.S. — E3 115
Lucerne Valley, Ca., U.S. — E5 82
Luceville, Que. — A9 74
Lunda Norte, dept., Ang. — C2 48
Luchou see Luzhou, China — F6 31
Lüchow, W. Ger. — F5 15
Luchuan, China — A9 35
Lucien, Ms., U.S. — D3 101
Lucien, Ok., U.S. — A4 113
Lucile, Id., U.S. — D2 89
Lucille, Al., U.S. — B2 78
Lucinda, Pa., U.S. — D2 115
Lucipara Islands, is., Indon. — G7 34
Luck, Wi., U.S. — C1 126
Luçon, Fr. — D3 16
Lucrecia, Cabo, c., Cuba — D6 64
Lucy, La., U.S. — h10 95
Lucy, Tn., U.S. — B2 119
Lüda see Dalian, China — D9 31
Luda Kamchiya, stm., Bul. — D8 24
Ludden, N.D., U.S. — C7 111
Ludell, Ks., U.S. — C3 93
Lüdenscheid, W. Ger. — C3 18
Lüderitz, Nmb. — C2 49
Ludgate, Ont. — B4 73
Ludhiāna, India — B6 36
Luding, China — F5 31
Lüdinghausen, W. Ger. — B2 19
Ludington, Mi., U.S. — E4 99
Ludlow, N.B. — C3 71
Ludlow, Eng., U.K. — D5 10
Ludlow, Il., U.S. — C5 90
Ludlow, Ky., U.S. — h13 94
Ludlow, Me., U.S. — B4 96
Ludlow, Ma., U.S. — B3 98
Ludlow, Mo., U.S. — B4 102
Ludlow, Pa., U.S. — C4 115
Ludlow, S.D., U.S. — B2 118
Ludlow, Vt., U.S. — E3 122
Ludlow Falls, Oh., U.S. — B1 112
Ludlow Mountain, mtn., Vt., U.S. — E3 122
Ludowici, Ga., U.S. — E5 87
Ludvika, Swe. — G6 14
Ludwigsburg, W. Ger. — D4 18
Ludwigshafen [am Rhein], W. Ger. — D4 18
Ludwigslust, E. Ger. — B5 18
Luebo, Zaire — C3 48
Lueders, Tx., U.S. — C3 120
Luena, Ang. — D2 48
Luepa, Ven. — B5 60
Lüeyang, China — H2 32
Lufkin, Tx., U.S. — D5 120
Lufuna, Zaire — C2 48
Luga, Sov. Un. — B7 27
Luga, stm., Sov. Un. — B7 27
Lugagnano Val d'Arda, Italy — D3 21
Lugan, stm., Sov. Un. — q22 27
Luganchik, stm., Sov. Un. — q22 27
Lugano, Switz. — E4 18
Lugano, Lake, l., Eur. — E7 21
Lugau, E. Ger. — C7 19
Lugenda, stm., Moz. — D6 48
Lugnaquillia Mountain, mtn., Ire. — D3 10
Lugo, Italy — B3 23
Lugo, Spain — A2 22
Lugoff, S.C., U.S. — C6 117
Lugoj, Rom. — C5 24
Lugovoy, Sov. Un. — E8 28
Luhuo, China — E3 31
Luiana, Ang. — D3 48
Luidhorn, Neth. — A6 17
Luik see Liège, Bel. — B6 16
Luing, i., Scot., U.K. — B2 13
Luis Correia, Braz. — C3 57
Luis Gomes, Braz. — C3 57
Luis Lopez, N.M., U.S. — D3 108
Luiza, Zaire — C3 48

Lujuna Point, c., Guam — L10 52
Lukachukai, Az., U.S. — A6 80
Luke, Md., U.S. — m12 97
Luke Air Force Base, mil., Az., U.S. — D3 80
Lukenie, stm., Zaire — B2 48
Lukeville, Az., U.S. — F3 80
Lukolela, Zaire — B2 48
Lukovit, Bul. — D7 24
Lukoyanov, Sov. Un. — D15 27
Lukuga, stm., Zaire — C4 48
Łuków, Pol. — C7 26
Lukulu, Zam. — D3 48
Lula, Ga., U.S. — B3 87
Lula, Ms., U.S. — A3 101
Lula, Ok., U.S. — C5 113
Luleå, Swe. — E10 14
Luleälven, stm., Swe. — D9 14
Lüleburgaz, Tur. — B6 40
Luling, La., U.S. — k11 95
Luling, Tx., U.S. — E4 120
Lulong, China — D8 31
Lulu, Fl., U.S. — B4 86
Lulua, stm., Zaire — C3 48
Luluabourg see Kananga, Zaire — C3 48
Lum, Mi., U.S. — E7 99
Lumba, Zaire — A2 48
Lumbala N'guimbo, Ang. — D3 48
Lumber, stm., U.S. — C9 117
Lumber Bridge, N.C., U.S. — C3 110
Lumber City, Ga., U.S. — E4 87
Lumberport, W.V., U.S. — B4 125
Lumberton, Ms., U.S. — D4 101
Lumberton, N.J., U.S. — D3 107
Lumberton, N.M., U.S. — A3 108
Lumberton, N.C., U.S. — C3 110
Lumbo, Moz. — E7 48
Lumby, B.C. — D8 69
Luminao Reef, rf., Guam — L9 52
Lummi Indian Reservation, Wa., U.S. — A3 124
Lumpkin, Ga., U.S. — D2 87
Lumpkin, co., Ga., U.S. — B2 87
Lumsden, Newf. — D5 72
Lumsden, Sask. — G3 75
Lumsden, N.Z. — P12 51
Lumsden, Scot., U.K. — C6 13
Lumsden Beach, Sask. — G3 75
Luna, N.M., U.S. — D1 108
Luna, co., N.M., U.S. — E2 108
Luna Pier, Mi., U.S. — G7 99
Lund, B.C. — D5 69
Lund, Swe. — J5 14
Lund, Nv., U.S. — E6 105
Lundale, W.V., U.S. — n12 125
Lundar, Man. — D2 70
Lundazi, Zam. — D5 48
Lundbreck, Alta. — E3 68
Lundby, Den. — C5 15
Lundby, Swe. — t34 14
Lunderskov, Den. — C3 15
Lundu, Malay. — E3 34
Lundy, i., Eng., U.K. — E4 10
Lune, stm., Eng., U.K. — F6 13
Lüneburg, W. Ger. — B5 18
Lunel, Fr. — F6 16
Lünen, W. Ger. — B2 19
Lunenburg, N.S. — E5 71
Lunenburg, Ma., U.S. — A4 98
Lunenburg, Vt., U.S. — C5 122
Lunenburg, Va., U.S. — D4 123
Lunenburg, co., N.S. — E5 71
Lunenburg, co., Va., U.S. — D4 123
Lunéville, Fr. — C7 16
Lungi, S.L. — C2 45
Lungué-Bungo, stm., Afr. — D2 48
Luni, stm., India — C5 36
Lunino, Sov. Un. — E15 27
Lunsar, S.L. — C2 45
Lunyama, Zaire — C4 48
Luochuan, China — A9 35
Luohe, China — E7 31
Luoding, China — G4 32
Luoning, China — E7 31
Luoshan, China — H6 32
Luoyang, China — E7 31
Luozi, Zaire — B1 48
Lupani, Zimb. — A4 49
Lupeni, Rom. — C6 24
Lupton, Az., U.S. — B6 80
Lupton, Mi., U.S. — D6 99
Lupus, Mo., U.S. — C5 102
Luquillo, Sierra de, mts., P.R. — E4 65
Lūrah, stm., Afg. — g11 94
Luray, Ks., U.S. — C5 93
Luray, Mo., U.S. — B4 102
Luray, S.C., U.S. — F5 117
Luray, Tn., U.S. — B3 119
Luray, Va., U.S. — B4 123
Lure, Fr. — D7 16
Lure, Lake, res., N.C., U.S. — f10 110
Lurgan, N. Ire., U.K. — C3 10
Luribay, Bol. — C2 55
Lúrio, Moz. — D7 48
Lurton, Ar., U.S. — B2 81
Lusaka, Zam. — E4 48
Lusaka, prov., Zam. — E5 48
Lusako, Zaire — B4 48
Lusambo, Zaire — B3 48
Lusby, Md., U.S. — D5 97
Luscar, Alta. — C1 68
Luseland, Sask. — E1 75
Lushan, China — H5 32
Lushan, China — F8 34
Lushnja, Alb. — D3 24
Lushoto, Tan. — B6 48
Lushton, Ne., U.S. — D8 104
Lushun, China — D9 31
Lusignan, Fr. — D4 16
Lusk, Wy., U.S. — D8 127
Lustre, Mt., U.S. — B11 103
Lūt, Dasht-e, des., Iran — B5 38
Lutcher, La., U.S. — D5 95
Lutesville, Mo., U.S. — D8 102
Luther, Ia., U.S. — C4 92
Luther, Mt., U.S. — E7 103
Luther, Ok., U.S. — B4 113
Luthersburg, Pa., U.S. — D5 115
Lutherville-Timonium, Md., U.S. — B4 97
Lütjenburg, W. Ger. — A10 18
Luton, Eng., U.K. — E6 10
Luton, Ia., U.S. — B1 92
Lutong, Malay. — E4 34
Lutsen, Mn., U.S. — k9 100
Lutsk, Sov. Un. — F5 27
Luttrell, Tn., U.S. — C10 119
Lutts, Tn., U.S. — B4 119

Lutugino, Sov. Un. — q22 27
Lutz, Fl., U.S. — D4 86
Lützow-Holm Bay, b., Ant. — C16 7
Luuq, Som. — E5 47
Luverne, Al., U.S. — D3 78
Lu Verne, Ia., U.S. — B3 92
Luverne, Mn., U.S. — G2 100
Luverne, N.D., U.S. — B8 111
Luvua, stm., Zaire — C4 48
Luwingu, Zam. — D4 48
Luwuk, Indon. — F6 34
Luxapallila Creek, stm., U.S. — B5 101
Luxembourg, Lux. — C7 16
Luxembourg, prov., Bel. — E5 17
Luxembourg, ctry., Eur. — C7 16
Luxemburg, Ia., U.S. — B6 92
Luxemburg, Wi., U.S. — D6 126
Luxeuil-les-Bains, Fr. — D7 16
Luxi, China — F7 31
Luxor (Al Uqṣur), Eg. — C3 38
Luxor, hist., Egypt — D6 43
Luxora, Ar., U.S. — B6 81
Luz, Braz. — B3 56
Luza, Sov. Un. — A3 28
Luza, stm., Sov. Un. — A3 28
Lyakhov Islands, is., Sov. Un. — B15 29
Lyall, Mount, mtn., N.Z. — P11 51
Lyallpur see Faisalabad, Pak. — B5 36
Lyaskovets, Bul. — D7 24
Lybster, Scot., U.K. — B5 13
Lychen, E. Ger. — E7 15
Lycksele, Swe. — E8 14
Lycoming, N.Y., U.S. — B4 109
Lycoming, co., Pa., U.S. — D7 115
Lycoming Creek, stm., Pa., U.S. — D7 115
Lydenburg, S. Afr. — C5 49
Lydia, Mn., U.S. — F5 100
Lydia, S.C., U.S. — C7 117
Lyell, Mount, mtn., Can. — D2 68
Lyell Island, i., B.C. — C2 69
Lyerly, Ga., U.S. — B1 87
Lyford, In., U.S. — E3 91
Lyford, Tx., U.S. — F4 120
Lygnern, l., Swe. — A6 15
Lykens, Pa., U.S. — E8 115
Lyle, Mn., U.S. — G6 100
Lyle, Wa., U.S. — D4 124
Lyles, Tn., U.S. — B4 119
Lyleton, Man. — E1 70
Lyman, Ms., U.S. — E4 101
Lyman, Ne., U.S. — C1 104
Lyman, S.C., U.S. — B3 117
Lyman, Ut., U.S. — E4 121
Lyman, Wy., U.S. — E2 127
Lyman, co., S.D., U.S. — D6 118
Lyman Lake, res., Az., U.S. — C6 80
Lyme, Ct., U.S. — D6 84
Lyme, N.H., U.S. — C2 106
Lyme Bay, b., Eng., U.K. — E5 12
Lyme Center, N.H., U.S. — C2 106
Lymington, Eng., U.K. — D6 12
Łyna, stm., Eur. — B6 26
Lynbrook, N.Y., U.S. — *E7 109
Lynch, Ky., U.S. — D7 94
Lynch, Md., U.S. — B5 97
Lynch, Ne., U.S. — B7 104
Lynchburg, Oh., U.S. — C2 112
Lynchburg, S.C., U.S. — C7 117
Lynchburg, Tn., U.S. — B5 119
Lynchburg, Va., U.S. — C3 123
Lynches, stm., S.C., U.S. — D8 117
Lynch Heights, De., U.S. — E4 85
Lynch Station, Va., U.S. — C3 123
Lyncourt, N.Y., U.S. — *B4 109
Lynd, Mn., U.S. — F3 100
Lyndeborough, N.H., U.S. — E3 106
Lynden, Wa., U.S. — A3 124
Lynde Point, c., Ct., U.S. — D6 84
Lyndhurst, Ont. — C8 73
Lyndhurst, N.J., U.S. — h8 107
Lyndhurst, Oh., U.S. — g10 112
Lyndon, Il., U.S. — B4 90
Lyndon, Ks., U.S. — D8 93
Lyndon, Ky., U.S. — g11 94
Lyndon, Vt., U.S. — B4 122
Lyndon B. Johnson National Historical Site, hist., Tx., U.S. — D3 120
Lyndon B. Johnson Space Center, sci., Tx., U.S. — r14 120
Lyndon Center, Vt., U.S. — B4 122
Lyndon Station, Wi., U.S. — E4 126
Lyndonville, N.Y., U.S. — B2 109
Lyndonville, Vt., U.S. — B4 122
Lyndora, Pa., U.S. — E2 115
Lyngby [-Tårbæk], Den. — C6 15
Lynn, Al., U.S. — A2 78
Lynn, Ar., U.S. — A4 81
Lynn, In., U.S. — D8 91
Lynn, Ma., U.S. — B6 98
Lynn, Pa., U.S. — C10 115
Lynn, co., Tx., U.S. — C2 120
Lynn, Lake, res., W.V., U.S. — B5 125
Lynn Canal, b., Ak., U.S. — k22 79
Lynndyl, Ut., U.S. — D3 121
Lynne, Fl., U.S. — C5 86
Lynne Acres, Md., U.S. — B4 97
Lynnfield, Ma., U.S. — f11 98
Lynn Garden, Tn., U.S. — C11 119
Lynn Grove, Ky., U.S. — f9 94
Lynn Haven, Fl., U.S. — u16 86
Lynnhaven Roads, b., Va., U.S. — k15 123
Lynn Lake, Man. — A1 70
Lynnport, Pa., U.S. — E10 115
Lynnville, In., U.S. — H3 91
Lynnville, Ia., U.S. — C5 92
Lynnville, Tn., U.S. — B4 119
Lynnwood, Wa., U.S. — B3 124
Lynton, Eng., U.K. — E4 12
Lynville, Il., U.S. — D3 90
Lynx Lake, l., N.W. Ter. — D12 66
Lyø, i., Den. — A2 15
Lyon, Fr. — E6 16
Lyon, co., Ia., U.S. — A1 92
Lyon, co., Ks., U.S. — D7 93
Lyon, co., Ky., U.S. — C1 94

Lyon, co., Mn., U.S. — F3 100
Lyon, co., Nv., U.S. — D2 105
Lyon, stm., Scot., U.K. — D4 13
Lyon Creek, stm., Ks., U.S. — D7 93
Lyon Mountain, N.Y., U.S. — f11 109
Lyon Mountain, mtn., N.Y., U.S. — f11 109
Lyonnais, hist. reg., Fr. — E6 16
Lyons, Co., U.S. — A5 83
Lyons, Ga., U.S. — D4 87
Lyons, Il., U.S. — k9 90
Lyons, In., U.S. — G3 91
Lyons, Ks., U.S. — D5 93
Lyons, Mi., U.S. — F6 99
Lyons, Ne., U.S. — C9 104
Lyons, N.Y., U.S. — B3 109
Lyons, Oh., U.S. — A1 112
Lyons, Or., U.S. — C4 114
Lyons, S.D., U.S. — D9 118
Lyons, Tx., U.S. — D4 120
Lyons, Wi., U.S. — n11 126
Lyons Falls, N.Y., U.S. — B5 109
Lyons Plains, Ct., U.S. — E2 84
Lyracrumpane, Ire. — E2 11
Lys, stm., Eur. — D3 17
Lysá [nad Labem], Czech. — n18 26
Lysaya Gora, Sov. Un. — G8 27
Lysekil, Swe. — H4 14
Lysite, Wy., U.S. — C5 127
Lyss, Switz. — B3 21
Lyster Station, Que. — C6 74
Lysva, Sov. Un. — D8 29
Lytham Saint Anne's, Eng., U.K. — A5 12
Lytle, Oh., U.S. — C1 112
Lytle, Tx., U.S. — E3 120
Lytton, Ia., U.S. — B3 92
Lytton, B.C. — D7 69
Lyubar, Sov. Un. — G6 27
Lyubertsy, Sov. Un. — n17 27
Lyudinovo, Sov. Un. — E10 27

M

Ma, stm., Asia — A2 34
Ma'ād, Jord. — B7 41
Maalaea, Hi., U.S. — *C5 88
Maalaea Bay, b., Hi., U.S. — *C5 88
Ma'alot-Tarshīḥa, Isr. — B7 41
Maamoura, Cap, c., Tun. — A8 23
Maam Cross, Ire. — D2 11
Ma'ān, Jord. — G10 40
Ma'anshan, China — *E8 31
Ma'arrat an Nu'mān, Syria — *E11 40
Maas, Ire. — C3 11
Maas (Meuse), stm., Eur. — B6 16
Maaseik, Bel. — C5 17
Maastricht, Neth. — B6 16
Mabalacat, Phil. — o13 34
Mabana, Wa., U.S. — A3 124
Mabank, Tx., U.S. — C4 120
Mabaruma, Guy. — A3 59
Mabel, Mn., U.S. — G7 100
Mabel, Lake, l., B.C. — D8 69
Mabelvale, Ar., U.S. — k10 81
Maben, Ms., U.S. — B4 101
Maberly, Ont. — C8 73
Mableton, Ga., U.S. — h7 87
Mablethorpe, Eng., U.K. — A8 12
Mabote, Moz. — B6 49
Mabou, N.S. — C8 71
Mabrous Tafidinga, well, Niger — D3 125
Mabscott, W.V., U.S. — D3 125
Mabton, Wa., U.S. — C5 124
Macachín, Arg. — B4 54
Macaé, Braz. — C4 56
Macaíba, Braz. — g6 57
Macalelon, Phil. — p14 34
MacAlpine Lake, l., N.W. Ter. — C12 66
Macan Islands, is., Indon. — G7 31
Macao, dep., Asia — G7 31
Macapá, Braz. — B4 59
Macará, Ec. — B2 58
Macas, Ec. — B2 58
Macau, Braz. — C3 57
Macaúbas, Braz. — A4 56
Maccagno [Superiore], Italy — D6 21
Maccan, N.S. — D5 71
Maccarese, Italy — h8 23
MacClenny, Fl., U.S. — B4 86
Macclesfield, Eng., U.K. — D5 10
MacClesfield, N.C., U.S. — B5 110
Macculloch, Cape, c., N.W. Ter. — B18 66
Macdonald, Man. — D2 70
Macdonald, W.V., U.S. — D3 125
Macdonald, Lake, l., Austl. — D4 50
Macdonald Range, mts., B.C. — E10 69
Macdonaldton, Pa., U.S. — G4 115
Macdonnell Ranges, mts., Austl. — D5 50
MacDowell Reservoir, res., N.H., U.S. — E2 106
Macduff, Scot., U.K. — D5 13
Macedon, N.Y., U.S. — B3 109
Macedonia, Ct., U.S. — B2 84
Macedonia, Il., U.S. — E5 90
Macedonia, Ia., U.S. — C2 92
Macedonia, Oh., U.S. — A4 112
Macedonia, hist. reg., Eur. — B4 24
Maceió, Braz. — C3 57
Macenta, Gui. — C3 45
Macerata, Italy — *C3 23
Maces Bay, b., N.B. — D3 71
Macfarlan, W.V., U.S. — B3 125
Macgillycuddy's Reeks, mts., Ire. — E2 11
MacGregor, Man. — E2 70
Machache, Braz. — B4 56
Machachi, Ec. — B2 58
Machakos, Kenya — *B6 48
Machala, Ec. — B2 58
Machanao, Mount, hill, Guam — L10 52
Machattie, Lake, l., Austl. — D6 50
Macheng, China — *A4 90
Machesney Park, Il., U.S. — *A4 90
Machias, Me., U.S. — D5 96
Machias, N.Y., U.S. — C2 109
Machias, stm., Me., U.S. — D5 96
Machias, stm., Me., U.S. — B4 96
Machias Bay, b., Me., U.S. — D5 96
Machias Lakes, l., Me., U.S. — C5 96
Machiasport, Me., U.S. — D5 96
Machichi, stm., Man. — A6 70

Machico, Port. — h12 22
Machida, Japan — *I9 33
Machilipatnam, India — E7 36
Machiques, Ven. — A3 60
Macho, Arroyo del, val., N.M., U.S. — C4 108
Machrihanish, Scot., U.K. — E3 13
Machu Picchu, hist., Peru — D3 58
Machynlleth, Wales, U.K. — B4 12
Macia, Moz. — C5 49
Măcin, Rom. — C9 24
Macina, reg., Mali — D4 45
Macintyre, stm., Austl. — D7 51
Mack, Co., U.S. — B2 83
Mackay, Austl. — D8 50
Mackay, Id., U.S. — F5 89
Mackay, stm., Alta. — A4 68
MacKay, Lake, l., Austl. — D4 50
MacKay Lake, l., N.W. Ter. — D10 66
MacKenzie, B.C. — B6 69
Mackenzie, Guy. — A3 59
Mackenzie, dept., N.W. Ter. — D11 66
Mackenzie, co., N.W. Ter. — C6 66
Mackenzie, stm., N.W. Ter. — C6 66
MacKenzie Bay, b., Ant. — C20 7
MacKenzie Bay, b., Can. — C3 66
Mackenzie King Island, i., N.W. Ter. — m29 66
Mackenzie Mountains, mts., Can. — D7 66
Mackey, Ont. — A7 73
Mackey, In., U.S. — H3 91
Mackeys, N.C., U.S. — B6 110
Mackeyville, Pa., U.S. — D7 115
Mackinac, co., Mi., U.S. — B5 99
Mackinac, Straits of, strt., Mi., U.S. — C6 99
Mackinac Bridge, Mi., U.S. — C6 99
Mackinac Island, i., Mi., U.S. — C6 99
Mackinaw, Il., U.S. — C4 90
Mackinaw, stm., Il., U.S. — C4 90
Mackinaw City, Mi., U.S. — C6 99
Mackinnon Road, Kenya — B6 48
Macklin, Sask. — E1 75
Macksburg, Oh., U.S. — C4 112
Macks Creek, Mo., U.S. — D5 102
Macksville, Ks., U.S. — E5 93
Mackville, Ky., U.S. — C4 94
Mackville, Wi., U.S. — h9 126
Maclean, Austl. — E10 51
Maclean Strait, strt., N.W. Ter. — m31 66
Maclear, S. Afr. — D4 49
Macleod, Lake, l., Austl. — D1 50
MacNutt, Sask. — F5 75
Maco, Bol. — B2 55
Macocolo, Ang. — C2 48
Macomb, Il., U.S. — C3 90
Macomb, co., Mi., U.S. — F8 99
Mâcon, Fr. — D6 16
Macon, Ga., U.S. — D3 87
Macon, Il., U.S. — D5 90
Macon, Ms., U.S. — B5 101
Macon, Mo., U.S. — B5 102
Macon, Ne., U.S. — D7 104
Macon, N.C., U.S. — A4 110
Macon, Tn., U.S. — B2 119
Macon, co., Al., U.S. — C4 78
Macon, co., Ga., U.S. — D2 87
Macon, co., Il., U.S. — D4 90
Macon, co., Mo., U.S. — B5 102
Macon, co., N.C., U.S. — f9 110
Macon, Bayou, stm., U.S. — B4 95
Macoun, Sask. — H4 75
Macoun Lake, l., Sask. — A4 75
Macoupin, co., Il., U.S. — D3 90
Macoupin Creek, stm., Il., U.S. — D3 90
Macovane, Moz. — B6 49
Macquarie, stm., Austl. — F8 50
Macquarie Island, i., Austl. — J7 2
Macroom, Ire. — E2 11
Macrorie, Sask. — F2 75
MacTier, Ont. — B5 73
Macuelizo, Hond. — C3 60
Macujer, Col. — C3 60
Macungie, Pa., U.S. — E10 115
Macwahoc, Me., U.S. — C4 96
Macy, Ne., U.S. — B9 104
Mad, stm., Ca., U.S. — B2 82
Mad, stm., Ct., U.S. — B3 84
Mad, stm., N.H., U.S. — C3 106
Mad, stm., Oh., U.S. — C2 112
Ma'dabā, Jord. — C7 41
Madame, Isle, i., N.S. — D9 71
Madang, Pap. N. Gui. — k12 50
Madaoua, Niger — D6 45
Madawaska, Me., U.S. — A4 96
Madawaska, co., N.B. — B9 74
Madawaska, stm., Ont. — B9 74
Madawaska, stm., Can. — C7 74
Madawaska Lake, l., Me., U.S. — A4 96
Madaya, Burma — A2 35
Madbury, N.H., U.S. — D5 106
Madden, Ms., U.S. — C4 101
Maddock, N.D., U.S. — B6 111
Maddox, Md., U.S. — D4 97
Madeira, Oh., U.S. — o13 112
Madeira, stm., S.A. — D2 59
Madeira Islands, is., Port. — C1 44
Madeleine, Îles de la, is., Que. — B8 71
Madelia, Mn., U.S. — F4 100
Madeline, Ca., U.S. — B3 82
Madeline Island, i., Wi., U.S. — B3 126
Madera, Mex. — B3 63
Madera, Ca., U.S. — D4 82
Madera, Pa., U.S. — E5 115
Madera, co., Ca., U.S. — D4 82
Madgaon, India — E5 36
Madge Lake, l., Sask. — F5 75
Madhupur, India — E11 37
Madhya Pradesh, state, India — D6 36
Madill, Ok., U.S. — C5 113
Madīnat ash Sha'b, Yemen — G6 36
Madison, Al., U.S. — A3 78
Madison, Ar., U.S. — B5 81
Madison, Ct., U.S. — D5 84
Madison, Fl., U.S. — B3 86
Madison, Ga., U.S. — C3 87
Madison, Il., U.S. — E3 90
Madison, In., U.S. — G7 91
Madison, Ks., U.S. — D7 93
Madison, Me., U.S. — D3 96
Madison, Md., U.S. — C5 97
Madison, Mn., U.S. — E2 100
Madison, Mo., U.S. — B5 102
Madison, Ne., U.S. — C8 104
Madison, N.H., U.S. — C4 106
Madison, N.J., U.S. — B4 107
Madison, N.Y., U.S. — C5 109
Madison, N.C., U.S. — A3 110
Madison, Oh., U.S. — A4 112
Madison, S.C., U.S. — B1 117
Madison, S.D., U.S. — C8 118
Madison, Va., U.S. — B4 123
Madison, W.V., U.S. — C3 125
Madison, Wi., U.S. — E4 126
Madison, co., Al., U.S. — A3 78
Madison, co., Ar., U.S. — B2 81
Madison, co., Fl., U.S. — B3 86
Madison, co., Ga., U.S. — B3 87
Madison, co., Id., U.S. — F7 89
Madison, co., Il., U.S. — E4 90
Madison, co., In., U.S. — D6 91
Madison, co., Ia., U.S. — C3 92
Madison, co., Ky., U.S. — C5 94
Madison, co., La., U.S. — B4 95
Madison, co., Ms., U.S. — C4 101
Madison, co., Mo., U.S. — D7 102
Madison, co., Mt., U.S. — E5 103
Madison, co., Ne., U.S. — C8 104
Madison, co., N.Y., U.S. — C5 109
Madison, co., N.C., U.S. — f10 110
Madison, co., Oh., U.S. — C2 112
Madison, co., Tn., U.S. — B3 119
Madison, co., Tx., U.S. — D5 120
Madison, co., Va., U.S. — B4 123
Madison, stm., Mt., U.S. — E5 103
Madisonburg, Pa., U.S. — E7 115
Madison Heights, Mi., U.S. — o15 99
Madison Heights, Va., U.S. — C3 123
Madison Lake, Mn., U.S. — F5 100
Madison Range, mts., Mt., U.S. — E5 103
Madisonville, Ky., U.S. — C2 94
Madisonville, La., U.S. — D5 95
Madisonville, Tn., U.S. — D9 119
Madisonville, Tx., U.S. — D5 120
Madiun, Indon. — G4 34
Madoc, Ont. — C7 73
Madoc, Mt., U.S. — B11 103
Madon, stm., Fr. — A2 20
Madona, Sov. Un. — C6 27
Madonna di Campiglio, Italy — C6 20
Madrakah, Ra's al, c., Oman — D5 38
Madras, India — F7 36
Madras, Or., U.S. — C5 114
Madras see Tamil Nadu, state, India — G6 36
Madre, Laguna, b., Mex. — C5 63
Madre, Laguna, b., Tx., U.S. — F4 120
Madre, Sierra, mts., N.A. — D6 63
Madre, Sierra, mts., Phil. — B6 34
Madre de Dios, dept., Peru — D3 58
Madre de Dios, stm., S.A. — D4 58
Madre de Dios, Isla, i., Chile — E1 54
Madre del Sur, Sierra, mts., Mex. — D4 63
Madre Occidental, Sierra, mts., Mex. — C5 63
Madre Oriental, Sierra, mts., Mex. — C5 63
Madrid, Spain — B4 22
Madrid, Al., U.S. — D4 78
Madrid, Ia., U.S. — C4 92
Madrid, Me., U.S. — D2 96
Madrid, N.Y., U.S. — f9 109
Madridejos, Spain — C4 22
Madrūsah, Libya — E2 43
Madura, i., Indon. — G4 34
Madurai, India — G6 36
Maebashi, Japan — D12 31
Mae Hong Son, Thai. — A2 35
Maella, Spain — B6 22
Maengsan, N. Kor. — G3 33
Maeser, Ut., U.S. — C6 121
Maesteg, Wales, U.K. — C4 12
Maestra, Sierra, mts., Cuba — D5 64
Maevatanana, Madag. — g9 49
Maeystown, Il., U.S. — E3 90
Ma'fan, Libya — D2 43
Mafeking, Man. — C1 70
Mafeking see Mafikeng, S. Afr. — C4 49
Maffra, Austl. — H6 51
Mafia, i., Tan. — C6 48
Mafikeng, S. Afr. — C4 49
Mafra, Braz. — C4 56
Mafra, Port. — C1 22
Magadan, Sov. Un. — D18 29
Magadi, Kenya — B6 48
Magadi, Lake, l., Kenya — B6 48
Magaguadavic Lake, l., N.B. — D2 71
Magalia, Ca., U.S. — C3 82
Magallanes y Antártica Chilena, prov., Chile — h11 54
Maganey, Ire. — E5 11
Maganga, Zaire — A4 48
Magangué, Col. — B3 60
Magaria, Niger — D6 45
Magat, stm., Phil. — n13 34
Magazine Mountain, mtn., Ar., U.S. — B2 81
Magdalena, Arg. — B5 54
Magdalena, Bol. — B3 55
Magdalena, N.M., U.S. — C2 108
Magdalena, dept., Col. — A3 60
Magdalena, stm., Col. — B3 60
Magdalena, reg., Mex. — h9 63
Magdalena, Isla, i., Chile — C2 54
Magdalena [de Kino], Mex. — A2 63
Magdalena del Mar, Peru — *D2 58
Magdalena Mountains, mts., N.M., U.S. — D2 108
Magdeburg, E. Ger. — B5 18
Magdi'el, Isr. — g10 41
Magé, Braz. — h6 56
Magee, Ms., U.S. — D4 101
Magellan, Strait of (Estrecho de Magallanes), strt., S.A. — h11 54
Magenta, Italy — B2 23
Maggia, stm., Switz. — C4 20
Maggie Creek, stm., Nv., U.S. — C5 105
Maggiore, Lake, l., Eur. — C4 23
Maghāghah, Eg. — D6 43
Maghama, Maur. — D2 45
Maghera, N. Ire., U.K. — C5 11
Magherafelt, N. Ire., U.K. — C5 11
Magic Reservoir, res., Id., U.S. — F4 89
Magilligan Point, c., N. Ire., U.K. — C4 11
Maglaj, Yugo. — C4 24

Name	Map Ref.	Page
Maglić, Yugo.	D5	24
Maglie, Italy	D7	23
Magna, Ut., U.S.	C3	121
Magness, Ar., U.S.	B4	81
Magnet, Man.	D2	70
Magnet, Ne., U.S.	H5	91
Magnet, Ne., U.S.	B8	104
Magnetawan, Ont.	B5	73
Magnetawan, stm., Ont.	B4	73
Magnet Cove, Ar., U.S.	C3	81
Magnetic Springs, Oh., U.S.	B2	112
Magnitogorsk, Sov. Un.	D8	29
Magnolia, Ar., U.S.	D2	81
Magnolia, De., U.S.	D4	85
Magnolia, Il., U.S.	B4	90
Magnolia, Ia., U.S.	C2	92
Magnolia, Ky., U.S.	C4	94
Magnolia, Md., U.S.	B5	97
Magnolia, Mn., U.S.	G2	100
Magnolia, Ms., U.S.	D3	101
Magnolia, N.J., U.S.	*D2	107
Magnolia, N.C., U.S.	C4	110
Magnolia, Oh., U.S.	B4	112
Magnolia, Tx., U.S.	D5	120
Magnolia Springs, Al., U.S.	E2	78
Mago, i., Fiji	H16	52
Magoffin, co., Ky., U.S.	C6	94
Magog, Que.	D5	74
Magothy River, b., Md., U.S.	B4	97
Magoúla, Grc.	g11	25
Magpie, Que.	h8	72
Magpie, stm., Que.	h8	72
Magrath, Alta.	E4	68
Magruder Mountain, mtn., Nv., U.S.	F4	105
Maguari, Cabo, c., Braz.	B1	57
Magude, Moz.	B5	49
Magway, Burma	D9	36
Mahābād, Iran	B4	38
Mahabo, Madag.	h8	49
Mahaffey, Pa., U.S.	E4	115
Mahagi, Zaire	A5	48
Mahaicony Village, Guy.	A3	59
Mahajanga, Madag.	g9	49
Mahajanga, prov., Madag.	g9	49
Mahakam, stm., Indon.	F5	34
Mahalatswe, Bots.	B4	49
Mahallāt, Iran	E5	39
Mahānadi, stm., India	D7	36
Mahanoro, Madag.	g9	49
Mahanoy City, Pa., U.S.	E9	115
Mahārāshtra, state, India	D6	36
Mahaska, Ks., U.S.	C6	93
Mahaska, co., Ia., U.S.	C5	92
Maḩaṭṭat Ḍab'ah, Jord.	C8	41
Mahbūbnagar, India	E6	36
Mahenge, Tan.	C6	48
Mahesāna, India	F4	37
Mahi, stm., India	D5	36
Mahia Peninsula, pen., N.Z.	M16	51
Mahned, Ms., U.S.	D4	101
Mahnomen, Mn., U.S.	C3	100
Mahnomen, co., Mn., U.S.	C3	100
Mahoba, India	E7	37
Mahogany Mountain, mtn., Or., U.S.	D9	114
Mahomet, Il., U.S.	C5	90
Mahón, Spain	C8	22
Mahone Bay, N.S.	E5	71
Mahoning, co., Oh., U.S.	B5	112
Mahoning, stm., U.S.	A5	112
Mahoosuc Range, mts., N.H., U.S.	B4	106
Mahopac, N.Y., U.S.	D7	109
Mahto, S.D., U.S.	B5	118
Mahtowa, Mn., U.S.	D6	100
Mahuta, Tan.	D6	48
Mahuva, India	G3	37
Mahwah, N.J., U.S.	A4	107
Maîche, Fr.	B2	20
Maicurú, stm., Braz.	C4	59
Maida, N.D., U.S.	A7	111
Maiden, N.C., U.S.	B1	110
Maidenhead, Eng., U.K.	C7	12
Maiden Rock, Wi., U.S.	D1	126
Maidens, rock, N. Ire., U.K.	C6	11
Maidstone, Sask.	D1	75
Maidstone, Eng., U.K.	E7	10
Maidstone Lake, l., Vt., U.S.	B5	122
Maidsville, W.V., U.S.	B5	125
Maihar, India	D7	45
Maikala Range, mts., India	F8	37
Maiko, stm., Zaire	B4	48
Maikoor, i., Indon.	G8	34
Maili, Hi., U.S.	g9	88
Maili Point, c., Hi., U.S.	g9	88
Maillard, Que.	B7	74
Mailley-et-Chazelot, Fr.	A1	21
Main, stm., W. Ger.	D4	18
Main, stm., N. Ire., U.K.	C5	11
Main-à-Dieu, N.S.	C10	71
Mainburg, W. Ger.	E6	19
Main Centre, Sask.	G2	75
Main Channel, strt., Ont.	B3	73
Mai-Ndombe, Lac, l., Zaire	B2	48
Maine, N.Y., U.S.	C4	109
Maine, hist. reg., Fr.	C4	16
Maine, state, U.S.	C3	96
Mainesburg, Pa., U.S.	C7	115
Maïné-Soroa, Niger	D7	45
Mainland, i., Scot., U.K.	g10	10
Mainland, i., Scot., U.K.	A5	10
Mainland, i., Man.	C4	70
Main Pass, strt., La., U.S.	E6	95
Maintirano, Madag.	g8	49
Main Topsail, mtn., Newf.	D3	72
Mainz (Mayence), W. Ger.	D4	18
Maipo, Volcán, vol., S.A.	A3	54
Maipú, Arg.	B5	54
Maiquetía, Ven.	A4	60
Maira, stm., Italy	E3	20
Mairiporã, Braz.	m8	56
Maisi, Punta de, c., Cuba	D6	64
Maisonnette, N.B.	B4	71
Maisons-Laffitte, Fr.	g9	16
Maitland, Austl.	F9	50
Maitland, N.S.	D6	71
Maitland, Ont.	C9	73
Maitland, Fl., U.S.	*D5	86
Maitland, Mo., U.S.	A2	102
Maíz, Islas del, is., Nic.	H6	62
Maize, Ks., U.S.	g12	93
Maizières-lès-Vic, Fr.	E1	19
Maizuru, Japan	I7	33
Majagual, Col.	B3	60
Majene, Indon.	F5	34
Majenica, In., U.S.	C7	91
Majestic, Ky., U.S.	C7	94
Maji, Eth.	D4	47
Major, Sask.	F1	75
Major, co., Ok., U.S.	A3	113
Majuro, atoll, Marsh Is.	F10	6
Makaha, Hi., U.S.	g9	88
Makaha Point, c., Hi., U.S.	A2	88
Makah Indian Reservation, Wa., U.S.	A1	124
Makahuena Point, c., Hi., U.S.	B2	88
Makakilo City, Hi., U.S.	g9	88
Makalado, Zaire	A4	48
Makallé, Arg.	E4	55
Makālu, mtn., Asia	*C8	36
Makanda, Il., U.S.	F4	90
Makanza, Zaire	A2	48
Makapala, Hi., U.S.	C6	88
Makapuu Head, c., Hi., U.S.	B4	88
Makarov, Sov. Un.	B13	31
Makarska, Yugo.	D3	24
Makasar see Ujungpandang, Indon.	G5	34
Makassar Strait, strt., Indon.	F5	34
Makat, Sov. Un.	E8	29
Makawao, Hi., U.S.	C5	88
Makaweli, Hi., U.S.	B2	88
Makeni, S.L.	E2	45
Makeyevka, Sov. Un.	E6	29
Makgadikgadi Pans, pl., Bots.	B4	49
Makhachkala, Sov. Un.	E7	29
Makharadze, Sov. Un.	B14	40
Makhfar al Quwayrah, Jord.	E7	41
Makinak, Man.	D2	70
Makindu, Kenya	B6	48
Makinsk, Sov. Un.	C8	28
Makkinga, Neth.	B6	17
Makkovik, Newf.	g10	72
Makkum, Neth.	A5	17
Maknassy, Tun.	C6	44
Makó, Hung.		
Makogai, i., Fiji	H15	52
Makokou, Gabon	E2	46
Makoti, N.D., U.S.	A4	111
Makoua, Congo	B2	48
Maków [Mazowiecki], Pol.	B6	26
Makteïr, reg., Maur.	B2	45
Mākū, Iran	B2	39
Makumbi, Zaire	C3	48
Makurazaki, Japan	K5	33
Makurdi, Nig.	E6	45
Makushin Volcano, vol., Ak., U.S.	E6	79
Mala, Punta, c., Pan.	G8	62
Malabar, Fl., U.S.	D6	86
Malabar Coast, India	F6	36
Malabo, Eq. Gui.	E1	46
Malacca, Strait of, strt., Asia	E2	34
Malacca see Melaka, Malay.	E2	34
Malad City, Id., U.S.	G6	89
Málaga, Col.	B3	60
Malaga, Spain	D3	22
Málaga, N.J., U.S.	D2	107
Malaga, N.M., U.S.	E5	108
Málaga Bay, b., Spain	D3	22
Malagash, N.S.	D6	71
Malagón, Spain	C4	22
Malaimbandy, Madag.	h9	49
Malaita, i., Sol.Is.	G9	6
Malakāl, Sud.	D3	47
Malakoff, Fr.	g10	16
Malakoff, Tx., U.S.	C4	120
Malalbergo, Italy	E7	20
Malambo, Col.	*A3	60
Malang, Indon.	G4	34
Malange see Malanje, Ang.	C2	48
Malange, Ang.	C2	48
Malanje, dept., Ang.	C2	48
Malanville, Benin	D5	45
Malanzán, Arg.	A3	54
Maťa Panew, stm., Pol.	f9	26
Mälaren, l., Swe.	t34	14
Malargüe, Arg.	B3	54
Malartic, Que.	k11	74
Malaspina, Arg.	C3	54
Malaspina Glacier, ice, Ak., U.S.	D11	79
Malatya, Tur.	C12	40
Malawi, ctry., Afr.	D5	48
Malaya Vishera, Sov. Un.	B9	27
Malaybalay, Phil.	D7	34
Malāyer, Iran	D4	39
Malay Peninsula, pen., Asia.	D2	34
Malaysia, ctry., Asia	E4	34
Malazgirt, Tur.	C14	40
Malbaie, stm., Que.	B7	74
Mal Bay, b., Ire.	D2	10
Malbork, Pol.	A5	26
Malchin, E. Ger.	B6	18
Malchow, E. Ger.	B6	18
Malcolm, Ne., U.S.	D9	104
Malcom, Ia., U.S.	C5	92
Malden, Il., U.S.	B4	90
Malden, Ma., U.S.	B5	98
Malden, Mo., U.S.	E8	102
Malden, W.V., U.S.	m12	125
Malden Island, i., Kir.	G12	6
Maldives, ctry., Asia	G5	36
Maldon, Eng., U.K.	C8	12
Maldonado, Ur.	E2	56
Maléa, Ákra, c., Grc.	D4	40
Malegaon, India	G5	37
Malema, Moz.	D6	48
Malemba-Nkulu, Zaire	C4	48
Māler Kotla, India	B6	36
Malesherbes, Fr.	C5	16
Malesus, Tn., U.S.	B3	119
Malha Wells, Sud.	B2	47
Malin, Ire.	B4	11
Malin, Sov. Un.	F7	27
Malindi, Kenya	B7	48
Malin Beg, Ire.	C3	11
Malinau, Indon.	E5	34
Malines see Mechelen, Bel.	B6	16
Malin Head, c., Ire.	C3	10
Malino, Sov. Un.	n18	27
Malinta, Oh., U.S.	A1	112
Maliwun, Burma	F10	36
Maljamar, N.M., U.S.	E6	108
Malkara, Tur.	B6	40
Malko Tŭrnovo, Bul.	E8	24
Mallaig, Alta.	B5	68
Mallaig, Scot., U.K.	B4	10
Mallaranny, Ire.	D2	11
Mallard, Ia., U.S.	B3	92
Mallawī, Eg.	C3	38
Mallersdorf, W. Ger.	E7	19
Malles Venosta, Italy	C6	20
Mallet Creek, Oh., U.S.	A4	112
Malletts Bay, b., Vt., U.S.	B2	122
Mallorca, i., Spain	C7	22
Mallorytown, Ont.	C9	73
Mallow, Ire.	D2	10
Malmbäck, Swe.	A8	15
Malmberget, Swe.	D9	14
Malmédy, Bel.	B7	16
Malmköping, Swe.	t34	14
Malmö, Swe.	J5	14
Malmo, Ne., U.S.	C9	104
Malmöhus, co., Swe.	C7	15
Malmstrom Air Force Base, mil., Mt., U.S.	C5	103
Malmyzh, Sov. Un.	B12	31
Maloarkhangelsk, Sov. Un.	E11	27
Maloggia (Maloja), Switz.	D8	21
Maloja Pass, Switz.	C5	20
Malolo, i., Fiji	H14	52
Malolos, Phil.	o13	34
Malone, Ont.	C7	73
Malone, Fl., U.S.	B1	86
Malone, N.Y., U.S.	f10	109
Malone, Wa., U.S.	C2	124
Maloney Reservoir, res., Ne., U.S.	C5	104
Malonga, Zaire	D3	48
Malonno, Italy	D9	21
Maloton, Man.	D3	70
Malott, Wa., U.S.	A6	124
Maloy, Ia., U.S.	D3	92
Maloyaroslavets, Sov. Un.	D11	27
Malpelo, Isla de, i., Col.	C2	53
Malpeque Bay, b., P.E.I.	C6	71
Mālpura, India	D5	37
Malsch, W. Ger.	E3	19
Malta, Id., U.S.	G5	89
Malta, Il., U.S.	B5	90
Malta, Mt., U.S.	B9	103
Malta, Oh., U.S.	C4	112
Malta, ctry., Eur.	H11	8
Malta Bend, Mo., U.S.	B4	102
Maltahöhe, Nmb.	B2	49
Malton (part of Mississauga), Ont.	m14	73
Malton, Eng., U.K.	C6	10
Malung, Swe.	C7	14
Malvern, Al., U.S.	D4	78
Malvern, Ar., U.S.	C3	81
Malvern, Ia., U.S.	D2	92
Malvern, Oh., U.S.	B4	112
Malvern, Pa., U.S.	o19	115
Malverne, N.Y., U.S.	k13	109
Malvérnia, Moz.	B5	49
Malyye Karmakuly, Sov. Un.	B9	28
Malyy Uzen, stm., Sov. Un.	D8	28
Mamala Bay, b., Hi., U.S.	g10	88
Mamantel, Mex.	A2	63
Mamaroneck, N.Y., U.S.	h13	109
Mamba, Japan	m17	33
Mambasa, Zaire	A4	48
Mamberamo, stm., Indon.	F9	34
Mamelodi, S. Afr.	*C4	49
Ma-Me-O Beach, Alta.	C4	68
Mamers, Fr.	C4	16
Mamers, N.C., U.S.	B4	110
Mamfe, Cam.	D1	46
Mamie, C., U.S.	A7	110
Mamiña, Chile	D2	55
Mammern, Switz.	A6	21
Mammoth, Az., U.S.	E5	80
Mammoth, Ut., U.S.	D3	121
Mammoth, W.V., U.S.	C3	125
Mammoth Cave National Park, Ky., U.S.	C4	94
Mammoth Lakes, Ca., U.S.	D4	83
Mammoth Spring, Ar., U.S.	A4	81
Mamonovo, Sov. Un.	A5	26
Mamoré, stm., S.A.	B2	55
Mamou, Gui.	D3	45
Mamou, La., U.S.	D3	95
Mampong, Ghana	E4	45
Mamry Lake, l., Pol.	A6	26
Mamuju, Indon.	F5	34
Man, I.C.	E3	45
Man, W.V., U.S.	D3	125
Man, stm., Sask.	D4	75
Man, Isle of, i., I. of Man	C4	10
Mana, Fr. Gu.	A4	59
Mana, Hi., U.S.	A2	88
Mana, stm., Fr. Gu.	A4	59
Manabí, prov., Ec.	D2	60
Manacacías, stm., Col.	C3	60
Manacapuru, Braz.	C2	59
Manacor, Spain	C7	22
Manado, Indon.	E6	34
Mañagaha, Isleta, i., N. Mar. Is.	D7	52
Managua, Nic.	E7	63
Managua, Lago de, l., Nic.	D4	62
Manahawkin, N.J., U.S.	D4	107
Manakara, Madag.	h9	49
Manakin, Va., U.S.	C5	123
Manalapan, N.J., U.S.	C4	107
Manam, i., Pap. N. Gui.	h12	50
Manama, Bahr.	C5	39
Manana Island, i., Hi., U.S.	g11	88
Mananara, Madag.	g9	49
Mananara, stm., Madag.	h9	49
Mananjary, Madag.	h9	49
Manantenina, Madag.	h9	49
Manantico Creek, stm., N.J., U.S.	E3	107
Manapire, stm., Ven.	B4	60
Mana Point, c., Hi., U.S.	A2	88
Manas He, stm., China	B2	31
Manas Hu, l., China	B2	31
Manasquan, N.J., U.S.	C4	107
Manasquan, stm., N.J., U.S.	C4	107
Manassa, Co., U.S.	D5	83
Manassas, Va., U.S.	B5	123
Manassas National Battlefield Park, Va., U.S.	g11	123
Manassas Park, Va., U.S.	B5	123
Manatee, co., Fl., U.S.	E4	86
Manatee, stm., Fl., U.S.	E4	86
Manatí, P.R.	E5	65
Manaus, Braz.	C2	59
Manavgat, Tur.	D8	40
Manawa, Wi., U.S.	D5	126
Manawan Lake, l., Sask.	B4	75
Mancelona, Mi., U.S.	D5	99
Manchac, Bayou, stm., La., U.S.	h10	95
Mancha Real, Spain	D4	22
Manchaug, Ma., U.S.	B4	98
Manchester, Eng., U.K.	D5	10
Manchester, Ga., U.S.	D2	87
Manchester, Il., U.S.	D3	90
Manchester, Ia., U.S.	B6	92
Manchester, Ks., U.S.	C6	93
Manchester, Ky., U.S.	C6	94
Manchester, Me., U.S.	D3	96
Manchester, Md., U.S.	A4	97
Manchester, Ma., U.S.	A6	98
Manchester, Mi., U.S.	F6	99
Manchester, Mo., U.S.	f12	102
Manchester, N.H., U.S.	E4	106
Manchester, N.Y., U.S.	C3	109
Manchester, Oh., U.S.	D2	112
Manchester, Ok., U.S.	A3	113
Manchester, Pa., U.S.	F8	115
Manchester, S.D., U.S.	C8	118
Manchester, Tn., U.S.	B5	119
Manchester, Tx., U.S.	C5	120
Manchester, Vt., U.S.	E2	122
Manchester Center, Vt., U.S.	E2	122
Manchuria, hist. reg., China	B10	31
Mancos, Co., U.S.	D2	83
Mancos, stm., U.S.	D2	83
Mand, stm., Iran	G6	39
Manda, Tan.	D5	48
Mandabe, Madag.	h8	49
Mandaguari, Braz.	C2	56
Mandal, Nor.	H2	14
Mandalay, Burma	D10	36
Mandalgovĭ, Mong.	B6	31
Mandalya, Iraq	E2	39
Mandan, N.D., U.S.	C5	111
Mandara Mountains, mts., Afr.	C2	46
Mandaree, N.D., U.S.	B3	111
Mandeb, Bāb el, strt.	E10	39
Mandel, Afg.	D6	17
Mandera, Kenya	A7	48
Manderfield, Bel.	D6	17
Manderson, S.D., U.S.	D3	118
Manderson, Wy., U.S.	B5	127
Mandeure, Fr.	E2	21
Mandeville, Que.	C4	74
Mandeville, Jam.	E5	64
Mandeville, Ar., U.S.	D2	81
Mandeville, La., U.S.	D5	95
Mandidzudzure, Zimb.	A5	49
Mandimba, Moz.	D6	48
Mandø, i., Den.	C2	15
Mandsaur, India	D6	36
Mandurah, Austl.	F2	50
Manduria, Italy	D6	23
Māndvi (Cutch Māndvi), India	D4	36
Mandvi, India	C3	37
Mandya, India	F4	36
Manfalūt, Eg.	C3	38
Manfred, N.D., U.S.	B6	111
Manfredonia, Italy	D5	23
Manfredonia, Gulf of, b., Italy	D6	23
Manga, Braz.	A4	56
Manga, Phil.	B6	34
Mangalia, Rom.	D9	24
Mangalore, India	F3	36
Mangaratiba, Braz.	h5	56
Mangereva, Phil.	o13	34
Mangerton Mountain, mtn., Ire.	F2	11
Mangham, La., U.S.	B4	95
Mangkalihat, Cape, c., Indon.	E5	34
Mangoche, Mwi.	D6	48
Mangoky, stm., Madag.	h8	49
Mangole, i., Indon.	F7	34
Mangueni, Plateau de, plat., Niger	B7	45
Mangum, Ok., U.S.	C2	113
Manhasset, N.Y., U.S.	*h13	109
Manhattan, Ks., U.S.	C7	93
Manhattan, Mt., U.S.	E5	103
Manhattan, Nv., U.S.	E4	105
Manhattan Beach, Ca., U.S.	n12	82
Manhattan Island, i., N.Y., U.S.	h13	109
Manheim, Pa., U.S.	F9	115
Manhica, Moz.	B5	49
Manhuaçu, Braz.	C4	56
Maniago, Italy	C8	20
Maniamba, Moz.	D6	48
Manica, dept., Moz.	A5	49
Manicoré, stm., Braz.	D2	59
Manicouagan, stm., Que.	G19	66
Manicouagan, Réservoir, res., Que.	h13	74
Manifest, La., U.S.	C4	95
Manigotagan, Man.	D3	70
Manigotagan, stm., Can.	D3	70
Manigotagan Lake, l., Man.	D4	70
Manila, Phil.	C6	34
Manila, Ar., U.S.	B5	81
Manila, Ut., U.S.	C6	121
Manila Bay, b., Phil.	o13	34
Manilla, Austl.	E8	51
Manilla, Ia., U.S.	C2	92
Manipur, state, India	D9	36
Manisa, Tur.	C6	40
Manistee, Mi., U.S.	D4	99
Manistee, co., Mi., U.S.	D4	99
Manistee, stm., Mi., U.S.	D5	99
Manistique, Mi., U.S.	C4	99
Manistique, stm., Mi., U.S.	B4	99
Manistique Lake, l., Mi., U.S.	B5	99
Manito, Il., U.S.	C4	90
Manito, stm., Can.	C3	70
Manitoba, prov., Can.	C3	70
Manitoba, Lake, l., Man.	D2	70
Manitou, Man.	E2	70
Manitou, stm., Can.	C3	113
Manitou, stm., Ont.	E5	70
Manitou, Lake, l., Ont.	B3	73
Manitou Beach, Sask.	F3	75
Manitou Beach, Mi., U.S.	C7	99
Manitou Island, i., Mi., U.S.	A3	99
Manitou Lake, l., Ont.	A6	73
Manitou Lake, l., Sask.	E1	75
Manitoulin Island, i., Ont.	B2	73
Manitou Springs, Co., U.S.	C6	83
Manitowoc, Wi., U.S.	D6	126
Manitowoc, co., Wi., U.S.	D5	126
Manitowoc, stm., Wi., U.S.	h10	126
Manitowoc, North Branch, stm., Wi., U.S.	h9	126
Manitowoc, South Branch, stm., Wi., U.S.	k9	126
Maniwaki, Que.	C2	74
Manizales, Col.	B2	60
Manja, Madag.	h8	49
Manjacaze, Moz.	B5	49
Manjimup, Austl.	F2	50
Mānjra, stm., India	E6	36
Mankato, Ks., U.S.	C5	93
Mankato, Mn., U.S.	F5	100
Mankono, I.C.	E3	45
Mankota, Sask.	H2	75
Manley, Ne., U.S.	h12	104
Manley Hot Springs, Ak., U.S.	B9	79
Manlius, Il., U.S.	B4	90
Manlius, N.Y., U.S.	C5	109
Manlléu, Spain	A7	22
Manly, Ia., U.S.	A4	92
Manmād, India	G5	37
Mannar, Sri L.	G6	36
Mannar, Gulf of, b., Asia	G6	36
Mannboro, Va., U.S.	C5	123
Mannford, Ok., U.S.	A5	113
Mannheim, W. Ger.	D4	18
Manning, Alta.	A2	68
Manning, Ar., U.S.	C3	81
Manning, Ia., U.S.	C3	92
Manning, N.D., U.S.	B3	111
Manning, Or., U.S.	g11	114
Manning, S.C., U.S.	D7	117
Manning Provincial Park, B.C.	E7	69
Mannington, Ky., U.S.	C2	94
Mannington, W.V., U.S.	B4	125
Manns Choice, Pa., U.S.	G4	115
Manns Creek, stm., W.V., U.S.	n14	125
Manns Harbor, N.C., U.S.	B7	110
Mannsville, N.Y., U.S.	B4	109
Mannville, Alta.	C5	68
Manoa, Bol.	A2	55
Man of War Bay, b., Trin.	M24	65
Manokin, Md., U.S.	D6	97
Manokin, stm., Md., U.S.	D6	97
Manokotak, Ak., U.S.	D8	79
Manokwari, Indon.	F8	34
Manombo, Madag.	h8	49
Manomet, Ma., U.S.	C6	98
Manomet Hill, hill, Ma., U.S.	C6	98
Manomet Point, c., Ma., U.S.	C6	98
Manono, Zaire	C4	48
Manono, i., W. Sam.	F11	52
Manor, Sask.	H4	75
Manor, Ga., U.S.	E4	87
Manor, Pa., U.S.	F2	115
Manor, Tx., U.S.	D4	120
Manorhamilton, Ire.	C4	25
Manorhaven, N.Y., U.S.	*h13	109
Manorville, Pa., U.S.	E2	115
Manosque, Fr.	F6	16
Manotick, Ont.	B9	73
Manouane, Lac, l., Que.	h12	74
Manp'o, N. Kor.	F3	33
Manresa, Spain	B6	22
Mansa (Fort Rosebery), Zam.	D4	48
Mansa Konko, Gam.	D1	45
Mansel Island, i., N.W. Ter.	D17	66
Manseau, Que.	C5	74
Mansfield, Austl.	H6	51
Mansfield, Eng., U.K.	D6	10
Mansfield, Ar., U.S.	B1	81
Mansfield, Ga., U.S.	C3	87
Mansfield, Il., U.S.	C5	90
Mansfield, La., U.S.	B2	95
Mansfield, Ma., U.S.	B5	98
Mansfield, Mo., U.S.	D5	102
Mansfield, Oh., U.S.	B3	112
Mansfield, Pa., U.S.	C7	115
Mansfield, S.D., U.S.	B7	118
Mansfield, Tn., U.S.	A3	119
Mansfield, Tx., U.S.	n9	120
Mansfield, Wa., U.S.	B6	124
Mansfield, Mount, mtn., Vt., U.S.	B3	122
Mansfield Center, Ct., U.S.	B7	84
Mansfield Depot, Ct., U.S.	B7	84
Mansfield Four Corners, Ct., U.S.	B7	84
Mansfield Hollow Lake, res., Ct., U.S.	B7	84
Manso, stm., Braz.	B2	56
Manson, Ia., U.S.	B3	92
Manson, Wa., U.S.	B5	124
Manson, stm., B.C.	B5	69
Manson Creek, B.C.	B5	69
Mansonville, Que.	D5	74
Mansura, La., U.S.	C3	95
Mantachie, Ms., U.S.	A5	101
Mantador, N.D., U.S.	C9	111
Mantagao, stm., Man.	D3	70
Manteca, Ca., U.S.	D3	82
Mantee, Ms., U.S.	B4	101
Manteno, Il., U.S.	B6	90
Manteo, N.C., U.S.	B7	110
Manter, Ks., U.S.	E2	93
Mantes [-la-Jolie], Fr.	C4	16
Manti, Ut., U.S.	D4	121
Mantiqueira, Serra da, mts., Braz.	C4	56
Manton, Mi., U.S.	D5	99
Mantorville, Mn., U.S.	F6	100
Mantua (Mantova), Italy	D5	20
Mantua, Oh., U.S.	A4	112
Mantua, Ut., U.S.	B4	121
Manu, Peru	D3	58
Manuel Benavides, Mex.	B4	63
Manuel Urbano, Braz.	C4	58
Manui, i., Indon.	F6	34
Manukau Harbour, b., N.Z.	L15	51
Manumuskin, stm., N.J., U.S.	E3	107
Manus, i., Pap. N. Gui.	h12	50
Manvel, N.D., U.S.	A8	111
Manvel, Tx., U.S.	r14	120
Manville, N.J., U.S.	B3	107
Manville, R.I., U.S.	B4	116
Manville, Wy., U.S.	D8	127
Many, La., U.S.	C2	95
Many Farms, Az., U.S.	A6	80
Manyara, Lake, l., Tan.	B6	48
Manyberries, Alta.	E5	68
Manych, stm., Sov. Un.	H13	27
Manych Lake, l., Sov. Un.	H14	27
Many Island Lake, l., Can.	D5	68
Manyoni, Tan.	C5	48
Manzanares, stm., Spain	o17	22
Manzanares Canal, Spain	p17	22
Manzanillo, Cuba	D5	64
Manzanillo, Mex.	D4	63
Manzanillo, Punta, c., Pan.	F8	62
Manzano, N.M., U.S.	C3	108
Manzano Mountains, mts., N.M., U.S.	C3	108
Manzano Peak, mtn., N.M., U.S.	C3	108
Manzhouli, China	C8	31
Manziana, Italy	g8	23
Manzilah, Lake, l., Eg.	C3	41
Manzini, Swaz.	C5	49
Mao, Chad	C4	46
Mao, Dom. Rep.	E8	64
Maoke Mountains, mts., Indon.	F9	34
Maoming, China	G7	31
Mapai, Moz.	B5	49
Mapam Yumco, l., China	B7	36
Mapastepec, Mex.	D6	63
Mapaville, Mo., U.S.	C7	102
Mapes, N.D., U.S.	A7	111
Mapia Islands, is., Indon.	E8	34
Mapire, Ven.	B5	60
Mapiri, Bol.	C2	55
Maple (part of Vaughan), Ont.	k14	73
Maple, Tx., U.S.	C1	120
Maple, Wi., U.S.	B2	126
Maple, stm., U.S.	A7	118
Maple, stm., Ia., U.S.	B2	92
Maple, stm., N.D., U.S.	C8	111
Maple Bay, Mn., U.S.	C2	100
Maple Bluff, Wi., U.S.	E4	126
Maple Creek, Sask.	H1	75
Maple Creek, stm., U.S.	C9	104
Maple Falls, Wa., U.S.	A3	124
Maple Grove, Mn., U.S.	m12	100
Maple Heights, Oh., U.S.	h9	112
Maple Hill, Ks., U.S.	C7	93
Maple Island, Mn., U.S.	G5	100
Maple Lake, Mn., U.S.	E5	100
Maple Mount, Ky., U.S.	C2	94
Maple Plain, Mn., U.S.	m11	100
Maple Rapids, Mi., U.S.	E6	99
Maple Ridge, B.C.	E6	69
Maples, In., U.S.	B7	91
Maple Shade, N.J., U.S.	D2	107
Maplesville, Al., U.S.	C3	78
Mapleton, Ia., U.S.	B2	92
Mapleton, Ks., U.S.	D9	93
Mapleton, Me., U.S.	B4	96
Mapleton, Mn., U.S.	G5	100
Mapleton, N.D., U.S.	C8	111
Mapleton, Or., U.S.	C3	114
Mapleton, Ut., U.S.	C4	121
Mapleton Depot, Pa., U.S.	F6	115
Maple Valley, Wa., U.S.	f11	124
Mapleville, R.I., U.S.	B2	116
Maplewood, Mn., U.S.	n12	100
Maplewood, Mo., U.S.	f13	102
Maplewood, N.J., U.S.	B4	107
Mapuera, stm., Braz.	C3	59
Maputo (Lourenço Marques), Moz.	C5	49
Maputo, dept., Moz.	C5	49
Maqārīyūs, Dayr, hist., Eg.	D2	41
Maqellarë, Alb.	B3	25
Maqna, Sau., Ar.	D1	38
Maquela do Zombo, Ang.	C2	48
Maquinchao, Arg.	C3	54
Maquoketa, Ia., U.S.	B7	92
Maquoketa, stm., Ia., U.S.	B6	92
Maquoketa, North Fork, stm., Ia., U.S.	B7	92
Maquon, Il., U.S.	C3	90
Mar, Serra do, clf., Braz.	B5	48
Mara, prov., Tan.	B5	48
Maraã, Braz.	D2	60
Marabá, Braz.	D5	59
Maracá, Ilha de, i., Braz.	B4	59
Maracaibo, Ven.	A3	60
Maracaibo, Lago de, l., Ven.	A3	60
Maracaju, Braz.	C1	56
Maracaju, Serra de, hills, S.A.	A4	56
Maracay, Ven.	A4	60
Marādah, Libya	D3	43
Maradi, Niger	D6	45
Marāgheh, Iran	B4	38
Maragogi, Braz.	k6	57
Maragojipe, Braz.	B3	92
Marais des Cygnes, stm., U.S.	D8	93
Marajó, Baía de, b., Braz.	C5	59
Marajó, Ilha de, i., Braz.	C5	59
Maralal, Kenya	A6	48
Maramec, Ok., U.S.	A5	113
Marana, Az., U.S.	E4	80
Marand, Iran	B4	38
Maranguape, Braz.	B7	57
Maranhão, state, Braz.	B1	57
Marano, Laguna di, b., Italy	D9	20
Maranoa, stm., Austl.	E9	50
Marañon, stm., Peru	B2	58
Mărăşeşti, Rom.	C8	24
Marathon, Ont.	o18	73
Marathon, Grc.	g11	25
Marathon, Fl., U.S.	H5	86
Marathon, Ia., U.S.	B2	92
Marathon, N.Y., U.S.	C4	109
Marathon, Tx., U.S.	D1	120
Marathon, Wi., U.S.	D4	126
Marathon, co., Wi., U.S.	D4	126
Maratua, i., Indon.	E5	34
Marau, Braz.	D2	56
Maravatío de Ocampo, Mex.	n13	63
Marāwah, Libya	C4	43
Marawi, Sud.	B3	47
Marbach [am Neckar], W. Ger.	E4	19
Marbella, Spain	D3	22
Marble, Ar., U.S.	A2	81
Marble, Co., U.S.	B3	83
Marble, Mn., U.S.	C5	100
Marble, N.C., U.S.	f9	110
Marble Bar, Austl.	D2	50
Marble Canyon, Az., U.S.	A4	80
Marble Canyon, val., Az., U.S.	A4	80
Marble City, Ok., U.S.	B7	113
Marble Cliff, Oh., U.S.	m10	112
Marble Dale, Ct., U.S.	C2	84
Marble Falls, Tx., U.S.	D3	120
Marble Hall, S. Afr.	B4	49
Marblehead, Ma., U.S.	B6	98
Marblehead, Oh., U.S.	A3	112
Marblehill, Ga., U.S.	B2	87
Marble Mountain, N.S.	D8	71
Marble Rock, Ia., U.S.	B5	92
Marbleton, Que.	D6	74
Marbleton, Wy., U.S.	D2	127
Marburg, W. Ger.	C4	18
Marbury, Al., U.S.	C3	78
Marbury, Md., U.S.	C3	97
Marcala, Hond.	C3	62
Marcaria, Italy	D6	20
Marceline, Mo., U.S.	B5	102
Marcelin, Sask.	E2	75

Name	Map Ref.	Page
Marcella, Ar., U.S.	B4	81
Marcelline, Il., U.S.	C2	90
Marcellus, Mi., U.S.	F5	99
March, Eng., U.K.	B8	12
March Air Force Base, mil., Ca., U.S.	F5	82
Marchand, Man.	E3	70
Marche, hist. reg., Fr.	D4	16
Marche-en-Famenne, Bel.	D5	17
Marchena, Spain	D3	22
Marchena, Isla, i., Ec.	f5	58
Marches (Marche), prov., Italy	C4	23
Marchwell, Sask.	G5	75
Marco, Fl., U.S.	G5	86
Marco, In., U.S.	G3	91
Marcola, Or., U.S.	C4	114
Marcos Juárez, Arg.	A4	54
Marcus, Ia., U.S.	B2	92
Marcus, S.D., U.S.	C3	118
Marcus, Wa., U.S.	A7	124
Marcus Baker, Mount, mtn., Ak., U.S.	g18	79
Marcus Hook, Pa., U.S.	G11	115
Marcy, Mount, mtn. N.Y., U.S.	A7	109
Marcy Colony, S.D., U.S.	D8	118
Mardān, Pak.	B5	36
Mar de Espanha, Braz.	g6	56
Mardela Springs, Md., U.S.	D6	97
Mar del Plata, Arg.	B5	54
Mardin, Tur.	D13	40
Marechal Deodoro, Braz.	C3	57
Maree, Loch, l., Scot., U.K.	C3	13
Mareeba, Austl.	C8	50
Marenanuka, Kir.	R18	52
Marengo, Sask.	F1	75
Marengo, Il., U.S.	A5	90
Marengo, In., U.S.	H5	91
Marengo, Ia., U.S.	C5	92
Marengo, Oh., U.S.	B3	112
Marengo, Wa., U.S.	B7	124
Marengo, Wi., U.S.	B3	126
Marengo, co., Al., U.S.	C2	78
Marenisco, Mi., U.S.	n12	99
Marennes, Fr.	E3	16
Maretz, Fr.	D3	17
Mareuil-sur-Ourcq, Fr.	C5	17
Marfa, Tx., U.S.	o12	120
Marfrance, W.V., U.S.	C4	125
Margai Co, l., China	A8	36
Marganets, Sov. Un.	H10	22
Margaree, N.S.	C8	71
Margaree Harbour, N.S.	C8	71
Margaret, Man.	E2	70
Margaret, Al., U.S.	B3	78
Margaret, Tx., U.S.	B3	120
Margaretsville, N.S.	D4	71
Margaretville, N.Y., U.S.	C6	109
Margarita, Isla de, i., Ven.	A5	60
Margate, Eng. U.K.	E7	10
Margate, Fl., U.S.	F6	86
Margate, Md., U.S.	*B4	97
Margate City, N.J., U.S.	E3	107
Margerum, Al., U.S.	A1	78
Margherita Peak, mtn., Afr.	A4	48
Marghī, Afg.	D13	39
Marghūb, Kūh-e, mtn., Iran	E8	39
Margie, Mn., U.S.	B5	100
Margilan, Sov. Un.	E10	29
Margny-lès-Compiègne, Fr.	C5	17
Margo, Sask.	F4	75
Mārgow, Dasht-e, des., Afg.	F11	39
Margrethe, Lake, l., Mi., U.S.	D6	99
Marguerite Bay, b., Ant.	C6	7
Maria, Que.	A3	71
Maria, i., Austl.	o15	50
María Chiquita, Pan.	k11	62
Mariager, Den.	B3	15
Mariager Fjord, Den.	B4	15
Mariah Hill, In., U.S.	H4	91
María la Baja, Col.	A2	60
Marian, Lake, l., Fl., U.S.	E5	86
Marianna, Ar., U.S.	C5	81
Marianna, Fl., U.S.	B1	86
Mariánské Lázně, Czech.	D2	26
Mariapolis, Man.	E2	70
Marias, stm., Mt., U.S.	B4	103
Marias, Islas, is., Mex.	C3	63
Marias Pass, Mt., U.S.	B3	103
Maria Stein, Oh., U.S.	B1	112
Maria van Diemen, Cape, c., N.Z.	K14	51
Mariaville, Me., U.S.	D4	96
Maribel, N.C., U.S.	B6	110
Maribel, Wi., U.S.	h10	126
Maribo, Den.	D5	15
Maribor, Yugo.	B2	24
Maricá, Braz.	h6	56
Maricaban Island, i., Phil.	p13	34
Maricopa, Az., U.S.	E3	80
Maricopa, Ca., U.S.	E4	82
Maricopa, co., Az., U.S.	D3	80
Maricopa Mountains, mts., Az., U.S.	m7	80
Marīdī, Sud.	E2	47
Marié, stm., Braz.	D4	60
Marie Byrd Land, reg., Ant.	B1	7
Mariedamm, Swe.	u33	14
Mariefred, Swe.	t35	14
Marie-Galante, i., Guad.	I14	64
Mariehamn, Fin.	G8	14
Marie Lake, l., Alta.	B5	68
Mariembourg, Bel.	D5	17
Mariemont, Oh., U.S.	o13	112
Marienberg, E. Ger.	C8	19
Mariental, Nmb.	B2	49
Marienthal, Ks., U.S.	D2	93
Marienville, Pa., U.S.	D3	115
Marie-Reine, Alta.	A2	68
Maries, co., Mo., U.S.	C6	102
Mariestad, Swe.	H5	14
Marietta, Ga., U.S.	C2	87
Marietta, Il., U.S.	F6	91
Marietta, Mn., U.S.	E2	100
Marietta, Oh., U.S.	C4	112
Marietta, Ok., U.S.	D4	113
Marietta, S.C., U.S.	A2	117
Marietta, Wa., U.S.	A3	124
Marieville, Que.	D4	74
Mariinsk, Sov. Un.	B11	28
Marijampolė, Sov. Un.	A7	26
Mari Lake, l., Sask.	B4	75
Marília, Braz.	C2	56
Marimba, Ang.	C2	48
Marín, Spain	A1	22
Marin, co., Ca., U.S.	*D3	82
Marina, Ca., U.S.	*D3	82
Marina del Rey, Ca., U.S.	*n12	82
Marina di Ravenna, Italy	*E8	20
Marine, Il., U.S.	E4	90
Marine City, Mi., U.S.	F8	99
Marine On St. Croix, Mn., U.S.	E6	100
Marinette, Wi., U.S.	C6	126
Marinette, co., Wi., U.S.	C5	126
Maringá, Braz.	C2	56
Maringa, stm., Zaire	A3	48
Maringouin, La., U.S.	D4	95
Marinha Grande, Port.	C1	22
Marino, Italy	h9	23
Marion, Austl.	*G6	50
Marion, Al., U.S.	C2	78
Marion, Ar., U.S.	B5	81
Marion, Ct., U.S.	C4	84
Marion, Il., U.S.	F5	90
Marion, In., U.S.	C6	91
Marion, Ia., U.S.	B6	92
Marion, Ks., U.S.	D6	93
Marion, Ky., U.S.	e9	94
Marion, La., U.S.	B3	95
Marion, Ma., U.S.	C6	98
Marion, Mi., U.S.	D5	99
Marion, Ms., U.S.	C5	101
Marion, Mt., U.S.	B2	103
Marion, Ne., U.S.	D5	104
Marion, N.Y., U.S.	B3	109
Marion, N.C., U.S.	B1	110
Marion, N.D., U.S.	C7	111
Marion, Oh., U.S.	B2	112
Marion, Or., U.S.	k12	114
Marion, Pa., U.S.	G6	115
Marion, S.C., U.S.	C9	117
Marion, S.D., U.S.	D8	118
Marion, Ut., U.S.	C4	121
Marion, Va., U.S.	f10	123
Marion, Wi., U.S.	D5	126
Marion, co., Al., U.S.	A2	78
Marion, co., Ar., U.S.	A3	81
Marion, co., Fl., U.S.	C4	86
Marion, co., Ga., U.S.	D2	87
Marion, co., Il., U.S.	E4	90
Marion, co., In., U.S.	E5	91
Marion, co., Ia., U.S.	C4	92
Marion, co., Ks., U.S.	D6	93
Marion, co., Ky., U.S.	C4	94
Marion, co., Ms., U.S.	D4	101
Marion, co., Mo., U.S.	B6	102
Marion, co., Oh., U.S.	B2	112
Marion, co., Or., U.S.	C4	114
Marion, co., S.C., U.S.	C9	117
Marion, co., Tn., U.S.	D8	119
Marion, co., Tx., U.S.	C5	120
Marion, co., W.V., U.S.	B4	125
Marion Center, Pa., U.S.	E3	115
Marion Heights, In., U.S.	F3	91
Marion Junction, Al., U.S.	C2	78
Marion Station, Md., U.S.	D6	97
Marionville, Mo., U.S.	D4	102
Mariposa, Ca., U.S.	D4	82
Mariposa, co., Ca., U.S.	D3	82
Mariscal Estigarribia, Para.	D3	55
Marissa, Il., U.S.	E4	90
Maritime Alps, mts. Eur.	E7	16
Maritsa (Évros) (Meriç), stm., Eur.	A5	25
Mariupol, Sov. Un.	E6	29
Marīvān, Iran	D3	39
Mariveles, Phil.	o13	34
Marj 'Uyūn, Leb.	F10	40
Mark, Il., U.S.	B4	90
Marka, Som.	E5	47
Marka Kul, l., Sov. Un.	B2	31
Markala, Mali	D3	45
Markam, China	F4	31
Markaryd, Swe.	I5	14
Mark Center, Oh., U.S.	A1	112
Markdale, Ont.	C4	73
Marked Tree, Ar., U.S.	B5	81
Markerwaard, reg., Neth.	B5	17
Markesan, Wi., U.S.	E5	126
Market Drayton, Eng., U.K.	B5	12
Market Harborough, Eng., U.K.	B7	12
Markethill, N. Ire., U.K.	C5	11
Market Rasen, Eng., U.K.	C7	11
Market Weighton, Eng., U.K.	G8	13
Markham, Ont.	D5	73
Markham, Il., U.S.	k9	90
Markham, Tx., U.S.	E4	120
Markham, Va., U.S.	B5	123
Markham, Mount, mtn., Ant.	A29	7
Marki, Pol.	k14	26
Markinch, Sask.	G3	75
Markkleeberg, E. Ger.	B7	19
Markland, In., U.S.	G7	91
Markland Lock and Dam, U.S.	B5	94
Markle, In., U.S.	C7	91
Markleeville, Ca., U.S.	C4	82
Markleville, In., U.S.	E6	91
Markleysburg, Pa., U.S.	G3	115
Markneukirchen, E. Ger.	C7	19
Markópoulon, Grc.	h11	25
Markovka, Sov. Un.	G12	27
Markovo, Sov. Un.	C11	29
Markovo, Sov. Un.	C20	29
Markranstädt, E. Ger.	B7	19
Marks, Ms., U.S.	A3	101
Marksboro, N.J., U.S.	B3	107
Marksville, La., U.S.	C3	95
Marktheidenfeld, W. Ger.	D4	19
Marktredwitz, W. Ger.	C6	18
Markville, Ont.	*C3	18
Marl, W. Ger.	D6	100
Marland, Ok., U.S.	A4	113
Marlbank, Ont.	C7	73
Marlboro, Alta.	C2	68
Marlboro, N.J., U.S.	C4	107
Marlboro, N.Y., U.S.	D6	109
Marlboro, Vt., U.S.	F3	122
Marlboro, co., S.C., U.S.	B8	117
Marlborough, Guy.	A3	59
Marlborough, Eng., U.K.	C6	12
Marlborough, Ct., U.S.	C6	84
Marlborough, Ma., U.S.	B4	98
Marlborough, N.H., U.S.	E2	106
Marle, Fr.	*E3	17
Marlene Village, Or., U.S.	*B4	114
Marlette, Mi., U.S.	E7	99
Marley, In., U.S.	B4	97
Marlin, Wa., U.S.	B7	124
Marlinton, W.V., U.S.	C4	125
Marlow, E. Ger.	D6	15
Marlow, Al., U.S.	D5	78
Marlow, N.H., U.S.	D2	106
Marlow, Ok., U.S.	C4	113
Marlow, W.V., U.S.	B7	125
Marlow Heights, Md., U.S.	*C4	97
Marlton, N.J., U.S.	D3	107
Marly-le-Roi, Fr.	g9	17
Marmaduke, Ar., U.S.	A5	81
Marmande, Fr.	E4	16
Marmara, Sea of	C2	25
Marmara Island, i., Tur.	B6	25
Marmaris, Tur.	D7	40
Marmarth, N.D., U.S.	C2	111
Marmelos, Rio dos, stm., Braz.	D2	59
Marmet, W.V., U.S.	C3	125
Marmolada, mtn., Italy	C7	20
Marmora, Ont.	C7	73
Marmora, N.J., U.S.	E3	107
Marmore, stm., Italy	E4	21
Marnay, Fr.	B1	20
Marnaz, Fr.	D22	21
Marne, W. Ger.	E3	15
Marne, Ia., U.S.	C2	92
Marne, Mi., U.S.	E5	99
Marne, dept., Fr.	F4	17
Marne, stm., Fr.	C5	16
Marne au Rhin, Canal de la, Fr.	F4	17
Maroa, Il., U.S.	C5	90
Maroa, Ven.	C4	60
Maroantsetra, Madag.	g9	49
Maromokotro, mtn., Madag.	f9	49
Marondera, Zimb.	A5	49
Marone, Italy	E9	21
Maroni, stm., S.A.	B4	59
Maroochydore-Mooloolaba, Austl.	E9	50
Maro Reef, rf., Hi., U.S.	k13	88
Maroua, Cam.	C2	46
Marovoay, Madag.	g9	49
Marowijne, dept., Sur.	B4	59
Marquam, Or., U.S.	B4	114
Marquand, Mo., U.S.	D7	102
Marquesas Islands, is., Fr. Poly.	G13	6
Marquesas Keys, is., Fl., U.S.	H4	86
Marquette, Man.	D3	70
Marquette, Ia., U.S.	A6	92
Marquette, Ks., U.S.	D6	93
Marquette, Mi., U.S.	B3	99
Marquette, Ne., U.S.	D8	104
Marquette, co., Mi., U.S.	B3	99
Marquette, co., Wi., U.S.	E4	126
Marquette Heights, Il., U.S.	C4	90
Marquez, Tx., U.S.	D4	120
Marquis, Sask.	G3	75
Marquise, Fr.	D9	12
Marrah, Jabal, mts., Sud.	C1	47
Marrakech, Mor.	C3	44
Marree, Austl.	E6	50
Marrero, La., U.S.	E5	95
Marrickville, Austl.	*F9	50
Marriott, Ut., U.S.	*B3	121
Marromeu, Moz.	A6	49
Marrowbone, Ky., U.S.	D4	94
Marrtown, W.V., U.S.	B3	125
Mars, Pa., U.S.	E1	115
Mars, Rivière à, stm., Que.	A7	74
Marsabit, Kenya	A6	48
Marsá Burayqah, Libya	C3	43
Marsala, Italy	F4	23
Marsá Maţrūḩ, Eg.	B2	38
Marsá Sūsah, Libya	B2	43
Marsden, Sask.	E1	75
Marseillan, Fr.	F5	16
Marseille, Fr.	F6	16
Marseilles, Il., U.S.	B5	90
Marshall, Sask.	D1	75
Marshall, Lib.	E2	45
Marshall, Ar., U.S.	B3	81
Marshall, Il., U.S.	D6	90
Marshall, In., U.S.	E3	91
Marshall, Mi., U.S.	F6	99
Marshall, Mn., U.S.	F3	100
Marshall, Mo., U.S.	B4	102
Marshall, N.C., U.S.	f10	110
Marshall, N.D., U.S.	D3	111
Marshall, Ok., U.S.	A4	113
Marshall, Tx., U.S.	C5	120
Marshall, Va., U.S.	B5	123
Marshall, Wa., U.S.	g13	124
Marshall, Wi., U.S.	E4	126
Marshall, co., Al., U.S.	A3	78
Marshall, co., Il., U.S.	B4	90
Marshall, co., In., U.S.	B5	91
Marshall, co., Ia., U.S.	C4	92
Marshall, co., Ks., U.S.	C7	93
Marshall, co., Ky., U.S.	f9	94
Marshall, co., Mn., U.S.	B2	100
Marshall, co., Ms., U.S.	A4	101
Marshall, co., Ok., U.S.	D5	113
Marshall, co., S.D., U.S.	B8	118
Marshall, co., Tn., U.S.	B5	119
Marshall, co., W.V., U.S.	B4	125
Marshallberg, N.C., U.S.	C6	110
Marshall Corner, N.J., U.S.	C3	107
Marshall Islands, ter., T.T.P.I.	F10	6
Marshalls Creek, Pa., U.S.	D11	115
Marshallton, De., U.S.	A3	85
Marshallton, Pa., U.S.	F10	115
Marshallville, Ga., U.S.	D3	87
Marshallville, Oh., U.S.	B4	112
Marshes Siding, Ky., U.S.	D5	94
Marshfield, Ma., U.S.	B6	98
Marshfield, Mo., U.S.	D5	102
Marshfield, Vt., U.S.	C4	122
Marshfield, Wi., U.S.	D3	126
Marshfield Hills, Ma., U.S.	B6	98
Marsh Fork, stm., W.V., U.S.	n13	125
Marsh Harbour, Bah.	A5	64
Marsh Hill, Pa., U.S.	D8	115
Mars Hill, Me., U.S.	B5	96
Mars Hill, N.C., U.S.	f10	110
Mars Hill, mtn., Me., U.S.	B5	96
Marsh Island, i., La., U.S.	E4	95
Marsh Lake, res., Mn., U.S.	E2	100
Marsh Peak, mtn., Ut., U.S.	C6	121
Marshville, N.C., U.S.	C2	110
Marshyhope Creek, stm., Md., U.S.	C6	97
Marsing, Id., U.S.	F2	89
Marstal, Den.	D4	15
Marsteller, Pa., U.S.	E4	115
Marston, Mo., U.S.	E8	102
Marston, N.C., U.S.	C3	110
Marstons Mills, Ma., U.S.	C7	98
Mart, Tx., U.S.	D4	120
Martaban, Burma	E10	36
Martaban, Gulf of, b., Burma	E10	36
Martap, Cam.	D2	46
Martapura, Indon.	F4	34
Martel, Fl., U.S.	C4	86
Martelange, Bel.	E5	17
Martell, Ne., U.S.	D9	104
Martell, Ca., U.S.	C3	82
Martensdale, Ia., U.S.	C4	92
Martha, Ok., U.S.	C2	113
Marthasville, Mo., U.S.	C6	102
Martha's Vineyard, i., Ma., U.S.	D6	98
Marthaville, La., U.S.	C2	95
Martí, Cuba	D5	64
Martignano, Lake, l., Italy	g8	23
Martigny[-Ville], Switz.	E3	18
Martigues, Fr.	F6	16
Martin, Czech.	D5	26
Martin, Ga., U.S.	B3	87
Martin, Ky., U.S.	C7	94
Martin, La., U.S.	B2	95
Martin, Mi., U.S.	F5	99
Martin, N.D., U.S.	B5	111
Martin, Oh., U.S.	e7	112
Martin, S.C., U.S.	C5	117
Martin, S.D., U.S.	D4	118
Martin, Tn., U.S.	A3	119
Martin, Ut., U.S.	D5	121
Martin, co., Fl., U.S.	E6	86
Martin, co., In., U.S.	G4	91
Martin, co., Ky., U.S.	C7	94
Martin, co., Mn., U.S.	G4	100
Martin, co., N.C., U.S.	B5	110
Martin, co., Tx., U.S.	C2	120
Martina [Franca], Italy	D6	23
Martin City, Mt., U.S.	B3	103
Martindale, Tx., U.S.	h8	120
Martinez, Ca., U.S.	C2	82
Martinez, Ga., U.S.	C4	87
Martinique, dep., N.A.	I14	64
Martin Lake, res., Al., U.S.	C4	78
Martin Peninsula, pen., Ant.	B1	7
Martin Point, c., Ak., U.S.	A11	79
Martinsburg, In., U.S.	H5	91
Martinsburg, Mo., U.S.	B6	102
Martinsburg, Ne., U.S.	B9	104
Martinsburg, N.Y., U.S.	B5	109
Martinsburg, Oh., U.S.	B3	112
Martinsburg, Pa., U.S.	F5	115
Martinsburg, W.V., U.S.	B7	125
Martinsdale, Mt., U.S.	D6	103
Martins Ferry, Oh., U.S.	B5	112
Martins Pond, l., Ma., U.S.	f11	98
Martinsville, Il., U.S.	D6	90
Martinsville, In., U.S.	F5	91
Martinsville, Mo., U.S.	A3	102
Martinsville, Oh., U.S.	C2	112
Martinsville, Va., U.S.	D3	123
Martinville, Que.	D6	74
Martofte, Den.	C4	15
Martos, Spain	D4	22
Martre, Lac la, l., N.W. Ter.	D9	66
Martwick, Ky., U.S.	C2	94
Marty, S.D., U.S.	E7	118
Marudi, Malay.	E4	34
Maruf, Afg.	B4	36
Marugame, Japan	I6	33
Marum, Neth.	A6	17
Marvel, Co., U.S.	D3	83
Marvel, Ar., U.S.	C5	81
Marvin, S.D., U.S.	B9	118
Marvine, Mount, mtn., Ut., U.S.	E4	121
Marwayne, Alta.	C5	68
Mary, Sov. Un.	F9	29
Mary, Lake, l., Mn., U.S.	E3	100
Mary, Lake, l., Ms., U.S.	D2	101
Maryborough, Austl.	E9	50
Maryborough, Austl.	G7	50
Marydel, Md., U.S.	B6	97
Marydel, De., U.S.	C6	85
Maryfield, Sask.	H5	75
Maryland, state, U.S.	B4	97
Maryland City, Md., U.S.	B4	97
Maryland Heights, Mo., U.S.	f13	102
Maryland Line, Md., U.S.	A4	97
Maryland Point, c., Md., U.S.	D3	97
Maryport, Eng., U.K.	C5	10
Marys, stm., Nv., U.S.	B6	105
Mary's Harbour, Newf.	B4	72
Mary's Igloo, Ak., U.S.	B6	79
Marys Peak, mtn., Or., U.S.	C3	114
Marystown, Newf.	E4	72
Marysville, N.B.	D3	71
Marysville, Ca., U.S.	C3	82
Marysville, In., U.S.	H6	91
Marysville, Ks., U.S.	C7	93
Marysville, Mi., U.S.	F8	99
Marysville, Oh., U.S.	B2	112
Marysville, Pa., U.S.	F8	115
Marysville, Wa., U.S.	A3	124
Maryūt, Buḩayrat, l., Eg.	C1	41
Maryville, Mo., U.S.	A3	102
Maryville, Tn., U.S.	D10	119
Marzagão, Braz.	B3	56
Marzūq, Libya	D2	43
Marzūq, Idehan, dunes, Libya	E2	43
Mas'adah, Isr. Occ.	A7	41
Masai Steppe, pl., Tan.	B6	48
Masaka, Ug.	B5	48
Masalembu Besar, i., Indon.	F5	34
Masalok, Puntan, c., N. Mar. Is.	D7	52
Masan, S. Kor.	D10	31
Masardis, Me., U.S.	B4	96
Masaryktown, Fl., U.S.	D4	86
Masasi, Tan.	D6	48
Masatepe, Nic.	E4	62
Masaya, Nic.	E4	62
Masbate, Phil.	C6	34
Masbate, i., Phil.	C6	34
Mascara, Alg.	C2	45
Mascarene Islands, is., Afr.	H24	2
Mascoma Lake, l., N.H., U.S.	C2	106
Mascot, Tn., U.S.	C10	119
Mascota, Mex.	G7	63
Mascoutah, Il., U.S.	E4	90
Mascuspana, Mex.	B1	62
Masefield, Sask.	H2	75
Masham, Eng., U.K.	F11	13
Mashapaug Pond, l., Ct., U.S.	A7	84
Mashhad, Iran	B5	38
Mashī, Iran	G8	39
Mashkel, Hāmūn-i-, reg., Pak.	G11	39
Mashkīd, stm., Asia	H11	39
Mashpee, Ma., U.S.	C7	98
Mashra'ar Raqq, Sud.	D2	47
Masi-Manimba, Zaire	B2	48
Masindi, Ug.	A5	48
Maşīrah, i., Oman	C5	38
Maşīrah, Gulf of, b., Oman	C5	38
Masisea, Peru	C3	58
Masisi, Zaire	B4	48
Masjed-e Soleymān, Iran	B4	38
Mask, Lough, l., Ire.	D2	10
Maskanah, Syria	D12	40
Maskell, Ne., U.S.	B9	104
Maskinongé, Que.	C4	74
Maskinongé, co., Que.	C4	74
Masnières, Fr.	D3	17
Masoala, Cap, c., Madag.	g10	49
Mason, Il., U.S.	E5	90
Mason, Mi., U.S.	F6	99
Mason, Nv., U.S.	E2	105
Mason, N.H., U.S.	E3	106
Mason, Oh., U.S.	C1	112
Mason, Ok., U.S.	B5	113
Mason, Tx., U.S.	D3	120
Mason, W.V., U.S.	B2	125
Mason, Wi., U.S.	B2	126
Mason, co., Il., U.S.	C4	90
Mason, co., Ky., U.S.	B6	94
Mason, co., Mi., U.S.	D4	99
Mason, co., Tx., U.S.	D3	120
Mason, co., Wa., U.S.	B2	124
Mason, co., W.V., U.S.	C3	125
Mason City, Il., U.S.	C4	90
Mason City, Ia., U.S.	A4	92
Mason City, Ne., U.S.	C6	104
Masonhall, Tn., U.S.	A2	119
Masontown, Pa., U.S.	G2	115
Masontown, W.V., U.S.	B5	125
Masonville, Ar., U.S.	D4	81
Masonville, Co., U.S.	A5	83
Masonville, N.Y., U.S.	C5	109
Masqaţ, Oman	C5	38
Massa, Italy	B3	23
Massabesic Lake, l., N.H., U.S.	E4	106
Massac, co., Il., U.S.	F5	90
Massachusetts, state, U.S.	B4	98
Massachusetts Bay, b., Ma., U.S.	B6	98
Massacre Lake, l., Nv., U.S.	B2	105
Massaemett Mountain, mtn., Ma., U.S.	A2	98
Massafra, Italy	D6	23
Massakory, Chad	C3	46
Massa Marittima, Italy	C3	23
Massangena, Moz.	B5	49
Massanutten Mountain, mts., Va., U.S.	B4	123
Massapê, Braz.	B2	57
Massapequa, N.Y., U.S.	*E7	109
Massapequa Park, N.Y., U.S.	*E7	109
Massapoag Lake, l., Ma., U.S.	h11	98
Massasecum, Lake, l., N.H., U.S.	D3	106
Massawa (Mitsiwa), Eth.	B4	47
Massena, Ia., U.S.	C3	92
Massena, N.Y., U.S.	f10	109
Masseny, Chad	C3	46
Masset, B.C.	C1	69
Masset Inlet, b., B.C.	C1	69
Massey, Ont.	A2	73
Massey, Md., U.S.	B6	97
Massies Mill, Va., U.S.	C3	123
Massillon, Oh., U.S.	B4	112
Massinga, Moz.	B6	49
Massive, Mount, mtn., Co., U.S.	B4	83
Masson Island, i., Ant.	C22	7
Masten's Corner, De., U.S.	E3	85
Mastergeehy, Ire.	F11	11
Masterton, N.Z.	N15	51
Mastic, N.Y., U.S.	*n16	109
Mastic Beach, N.Y., U.S.	n16	109
Mastung, Pak.	C4	36
Masturah, Sau. Ar.	C3	38
Masuda, Japan	I5	33
Masuria, reg., Pol.	B6	26
Masvingo (Nyanda), Zimb.	B5	49
Mata, Zaire	C3	48
Mata Amarilla, Arg.	D2	54
Matachewan, Ont.	p19	73
Matadi, Zaire	C1	48
Matador, Sask.	G2	75
Matador, Tx., U.S.	B2	120
Matagalpa, Nic.	E7	63
Matagorda, Tx., U.S.	E5	120
Matagorda, co., Tx., U.S.	E5	120
Matagorda Bay, b., Tx., U.S.	E5	120
Matagorda Island, i., Tx., U.S.	E4	120
Matagorda Peninsula, pen., Tx., U.S.	E5	120
Matak, i., Indon.	K7	35
Matam, Sen.	C2	45
Matamata, N.Z.	N5	51
Matamoras, Pa., U.S.	D12	115
Matamoros, Mex.	B5	63
Matamoros [de la Laguna], Mex.	B4	63
Matane, Que.	A3	71
Matanuska, stm., Ak., U.S.	g18	79
Matanzas, Cuba	C3	64
Matanzas, prov., Cuba	C3	64
Matanzas Inlet, b., Fl., U.S.	C5	86
Matão, Braz.	k7	56
Matapédia, Que.	B3	71
Matara, Sri L.	G7	36
Mataram, Indon.	N15	51
Matarani, Peru	E3	58
Mataró, Spain	D4	22
Matatiele, S. Afr.	D5	49
Matáutu, W. Sam.	F12	52
Matawan, N.J., U.S.	C4	107
Matawin, stm., Que.	C4	74
Mateke Hills, Zimb.	B5	49
Mateko, Zaire	B2	48
Matera, Italy	D6	23
Matészalka, Hung.	B6	24
Mateur, Tun.	F2	23
Matewan, W.V., U.S.	D2	125
Matfield Green, Ks., U.S.	D7	93
Mather, Man.	E2	70
Mather, Pa., U.S.	G1	115
Mather Air Force Base, mil., Ca., U.S.	C3	82
Mather Peaks, mts., Wy., U.S.	B5	127
Matherville, Il., U.S.	B3	90
Matherville, Ms., U.S.	D5	101
Matheson, Co., U.S.	B6	83
Matheson, Ont.	p18	73
Matheson Island, Man.	C3	70
Mathews, Al., U.S.	C3	78
Mathews, Va., U.S.	C6	123
Mathews, co., Va., U.S.	C6	123
Mathews, Lake, l., Ca., U.S.	n14	82
Mathias, W.V., U.S.	B5	125
Mathis, Tx., U.S.	E4	120
Mathiston, Ms., U.S.	B4	101
Mathura (Muttra), India	C6	36
Mati, stm., Alb.	B2	25
Matiakoali, Burkina	D5	45
Matinenda Lake, l., Ont.	A2	73
Matinicus, Me., U.S.	E4	96
Matinicus Island, i., Me., U.S.	E3	96
Matlock, Eng., U.K.	A6	12
Matlock, Ia., U.S.	A2	92
Matoaca, Va., U.S.	n18	123
Matoaka, W.V., U.S.	D3	125
Mato Grosso, state, Braz.	B4	55
Mato Grosso, Planalto do, plat., Braz.	E5	53
Mato Grosso do Sul, state, Braz.		
Matosinhos, Port.	B1	22
Mato Verde, Braz.	A4	56
Maţraḩ, Oman	C5	38
Matrosovo, Sov. Un.	B11	33
Matsqui, B.C.	f13	69
Matsudo, Japan	*I9	33
Matsue, Japan	D11	31
Matsuida, Japan	m17	33
Matsumae, Japan	F10	33
Matsumoto, Japan	H9	33
Matsusaka, Japan	I8	33
Matsuyama, Japan	E11	31
Matsuzaki, Japan	o17	33
Mattamiscontis Lake, l., Me., U.S.	C4	96
Mattamuskeet, Lake, l., N.C., U.S.	B6	110
Mattapoisett, Ma., U.S.	C6	98
Mattaponi, stm., Va., U.S.	C5	123
Mattawa, Ont.	A6	73
Mattawamkeag, Me., U.S.	C4	96
Mattawamkeag, stm., Me., U.S.	C4	96
Mattawamkeag, East Branch, stm., Me., U.S.	C4	96
Mattawamkeag, West Branch, stm., Me., U.S.	C4	96
Mattawamkeag Lake, l., Me., U.S.	C4	96
Mattawana, Pa., U.S.	F6	115
Mattawoman Creek, stm., Md., U.S.	C3	97
Matterhorn, mtn., Eur.	B1	23
Matterhorn, mtn., Nv., U.S.	C6	105
Matterson Inlet, b., Ant.	g40	7
Matter Vispa, stm., Switz.	D4	21
Matteson, Il., U.S.	k9	90
Matthews, Ga., U.S.	C4	87
Matthews, In., U.S.	D7	91
Matthews, Mo., U.S.	E8	102
Matthews, N.C., U.S.	B2	110
Matthews Mountain, mtn., Mo., U.S.	D6	102
Matthews Ridge, Guy.	A2	59
Matthew Town, Bah.	D7	64
Mattituck, N.Y., U.S.	n16	109
Mattoon, Il., U.S.	D5	90
Mattoon, Wi., U.S.	C4	126
Mattoon, Lake, res., Il., U.S.	D5	90
Mattson, Ms., U.S.	A3	101
Mattydale, N.Y., U.S.	B4	109
Matucana, Peru	D2	58
Matuku Island, i., Fiji	I15	52
Matundu, Zaire	A3	48
Matunuck, R.I., U.S.	G3	116
Matura Bay, b., Trin.	N23	65
Maturín, Ven.	B5	60
Maúa, Moz.	A6	49
Mauban, Phil.	o13	34
Maubeuge, Fr.	B5	16
Ma-ubin, Burma	D1	35
Mauckport, In., U.S.	H5	91
Mauchline, Scot., U.K.	E4	13
Maud, Oh., U.S.	n13	112
Maud, Ok., U.S.	B5	113
Maud, Tx., U.S.	C5	120
Maudlow, Mt., U.S.	D5	103
Maués, Braz.	C3	59
Maués-Açu, stm., Braz.	C3	59
Mauganj, India	E8	37
Maugansville, Md., U.S.	A2	97
Maugerville, N.B.	D3	71
Maughold Head, c., I. of Man	F4	13
Maui, co., Hi., U.S.	B5	88
Maui, i., Hi., U.S.	C6	88
Mauk, Ga., U.S.	D2	87
Mauldin, S.C., U.S.	B3	117
Maule, prov., Chile	B2	54
Mauléon [-Licharre], Fr.	F3	16
Maumakeogh, hill, Ire.	C2	11
Maumee, Oh., U.S.	A2	112
Maumee, stm., U.S.	A2	112
Maumee Bay, b., U.S.	G7	99
Maumelle, Lake, res., Ar., U.S.	C3	81
Maun, Bots.	A3	49
Mauna Kea, vol., Hi., U.S.	D6	88
Maunaloa, Hi., U.S.	B4	88
Mauna Loa, vol., Hi., U.S.	D6	88
Maunalua Bay, b., Hi., U.S.	g10	88
Maunath Bhanjan, India	E9	37
Maunawili, Hi., U.S.	g10	88
Maungdaw, Burma	D9	36
Maunie, Il., U.S.	E5	90
Maunoir, Lac, l., N.W. Ter.	C8	66
Maupin, Or., U.S.	B5	114
Maurepas, La., U.S.	h10	95
Maurepas, Lake, l., La., U.S.	D5	95
Maurertown, Va., U.S.	B4	123
Maurice, La., U.S.	D3	95
Maurice, stm., N.J., U.S.	E2	107
Maurice, Lake, l., Austl.	E5	50
Mauritania, ctry., Afr.	C2	44
Mauritius, ctry., Afr.	H24	2
Maury, N.C., U.S.	B5	110
Maury, co., Tn., U.S.	B4	119
Maury City, Tn., U.S.	B2	119
Maury Island, pen., Wa., U.S.	f11	124
Mauston, Wi., U.S.	E3	126
Mauterndorf, Aus.	E6	18
Mauwee Peak, mtn., Ct., U.S.	B2	84
Mavinga, Ang.	B3	49
Mawchi, Burma	B1	70
Mawer, Sask.	G2	75
Mawjib, Wādī al, val., Jord.	C7	41
Mawlaik, Burma	C10	36
Mawlamyine, Burma	E10	36
Mawson, sci., Ant.	C19	7
Mawson Coast, Ant.	C19	7
Mawson Escarpment, clf., Ant.	B19	7
Mawson Glacier, ice, Ant.	e40	7
Mawson Peninsula, pen., Ant.	C28	7
Max, Ne., U.S.	D4	104
Max, N.D., U.S.	B4	111
Maxbass, N.D., U.S.	A4	111
Maxcanú, Mex.	C6	63
Maxeys, Ga., U.S.	C3	87

Name	Map Ref.	Page

Name	Ref.	Page
Maxie, La., U.S.	D3	95
Maxinkuckee, Lake, l., In., U.S.	B5	91
Maxixe, Moz.	B6	49
Max Meadows, Va., U.S.	D2	123
Maxstone, Sask.	H2	75
Maxton, N.C., U.S.	C3	110
Maxville, Ont.	B10	73
Maxville, Mt., U.S.	D3	103
Maxwell, In., U.S.	E6	91
Maxwell, Ca., U.S.	C2	82
Maxwell, Ia., U.S.	C4	92
Maxwell, Ne., U.S.	C5	104
Maxwell, N.M., U.S.	A5	108
Maxwell, Tn., U.S.	B5	119
Maxwell Acres, W.V., U.S.	g8	125
Maxwell Air Force Base, mil., Al., U.S.	C3	78
Maxwell Colony, S.D., U.S.	D8	118
May, Id., U.S.	E5	89
May, Ok., U.S.	A2	113
May, Tx., U.S.	C3	120
May, Isle of, i., Scot., U.K.	D6	13
May, Mount, mtn., Alta.	B1	68
Maya, Mesa de, mtn., Co., U.S.	D7	83
Mayaguana, i., Bah.	C7	64
Mayaguana Passage, strt., Bah.	C7	64
Mayagüez, P.R.	G11	64
Mayagüez, Bahía de b., P.R.	B11	65
Mayama, Congo	B1	48
Maya Mountains, mts., N.A.	B3	62
Mayarí, Cuba	D6	64
Mayaro Bay, b., Trin.	O24	65
Maybank, Ms., U.S.	D4	101
Maybee, Mi., U.S.	F7	99
Maybell, Co., U.S.	A2	83
Mayberry, Md., U.S.	A3	97
Maybeury, W.V., U.S.	*D3	125
Maybole, Scot., U.K.	C4	10
Maydh, Som.	C6	47
Maydī, Yemen	D4	38
Maydūm Pyramid, hist., Egypt	E3	41
Mayen, W. Ger.	C3	18
Mayence see Mainz, W. Ger.	D4	18
Mayenne, Fr.	C3	16
Mayenne, stm., Fr.	D3	16
Mayer, Az., U.S.	C3	80
Mayersville, Ms., U.S.	C2	101
Mayerthorpe, Alta.	C3	68
Mayes, co., Ok., U.S.	A6	113
Mayesville, S.C., U.S.	D7	117
Mayetta, Ks., U.S.	C8	93
Mayetta, N.J., U.S.	D4	107
Mayfair, Sask.	E2	75
Mayfield, Ks., U.S.	E6	93
Mayfield, Ky., U.S.	f9	94
Mayfield, N.Y., U.S.	B4	109
Mayfield, Ok., U.S.	B2	113
Mayfield, Pa., U.S.	C10	115
Mayfield, Ut., U.S.	D4	121
Mayfield Heights, Oh., U.S.	A4	112
Mayfield Lake, res., Wa., U.S.	C3	124
Mayflower, Ar., U.S.	C3	81
Mayflower Village, Ca., U.S.	*E4	82
Mayger, Or., U.S.	A3	114
Mayhew, Ms., U.S.	B5	101
Mayhill, N.M., U.S.	E4	108
Maykain, Sov. Un.	C9	28
Mayking, Ky., U.S.	C7	94
Maykop, Sov. Un.	G17	8
Mayland, Tn., U.S.	C8	119
Maymont, Sask.	E2	75
Maymyo, Burma	D10	36
Maynard, Ar., U.S.	A5	81
Maynard, Ia., U.S.	B6	92
Maynard, Ky., U.S.	D3	94
Maynard, Ma., U.S.	B5	98
Maynard, Mn., U.S.	F3	100
Maynardville, Tn., U.S.	C10	119
Mayne, B.C.	g12	69
Mayne Island, i., B.C.	g12	69
Maynooth, Ont.	B7	73
Maynooth, Ire.	D5	11
Mayo, Yukon	D5	66
Mayo, Fl., U.S.	B3	86
Mayo, Md., U.S.	C4	97
Mayo, S.C., U.S.	A4	117
Mayo, co., Ire.	D2	11
Mayo, stm., Arg.	D2	54
Mayodan, N.C., U.S.	A3	110
Mayo Lake, l., Yukon	D6	66
Mayon Volcano, vol., Phil.	C6	34
Mayor Pablo Lagerenza, Para.	C3	55
Mayotte, dep., Afr.	f9	49
May Park, Or., U.S.	B8	114
May Pen, Jam.	F5	64
Mayport Naval Station, mil., Fl., U.S.	B5	86
Mayreau, i., St. Vin.	V26	65
Mayrhofen, Aus.	B7	20
Mays, In., U.S.	E7	91
Mays Landing, N.J., U.S.	E3	107
Mays Lick, Ky., U.S.	B6	94
Maysville, Al., U.S.	A3	78
Maysville, Ar., U.S.	A1	81
Maysville, Ga., U.S.	B3	87
Maysville, In., U.S.	G3	91
Maysville, Ia., U.S.	g10	92
Maysville, Ky., U.S.	B6	94
Maysville, Mo., U.S.	B3	102
Maysville, N.C., U.S.	C5	110
Maysville, Ok., U.S.	C4	113
Maysville, W.V., U.S.	B5	125
Mayumba, Gabon	F2	46
Māyūram, India	F6	36
Mayview, Mo., U.S.	B4	102
Mayville, Mi., U.S.	E7	99
Mayville, N.Y., U.S.	C1	109
Mayville, N.D., U.S.	B8	111
Mayville, Or., U.S.	B6	114
Mayville, Wi., U.S.	E5	126
Maywood, Ca., U.S.	*n12	82
Maywood, Il., U.S.	k9	90
Maywood, Ne., U.S.	D5	104
Maywood, N.J., U.S.	h8	107
Maywood Park, Or., U.S.	B6	114
Maza, Arg.	B4	54
Maza, N.D., U.S.	A6	111
Mazabuka, Zam.	E4	48
Mazagão, Braz.	D7	57
Mazamet, Fr.	F5	16
Mazapil, Mex.	D5	61
Mazār-e Sharīf, Afg.	B3	36
Mazāri'an Nūbānī, Isr. Occ.	g11	41
Mazarn Creek, stm., Ar., U.S.	g7	81
Mazarredo, Arg.	D3	54
Mazarrón, Spain	D5	22
Mazaruni, stm., Guy.	A2	59
Mazaruni-Potaro, dept., Guy.	A3	59
Mazatenango, Guat.	E6	63
Mazatlán, Mex.	C3	63
Mazatzal Mountains, mts., Az., U.S.	C4	80
Mazatzal Peak, mtn., Az., U.S.	C4	80
Mažeikiai, Sov. Un.	C4	27
Mazenod, Sask.	H2	75
Mazeppa, Mn., U.S.	F6	100
Mazie, Ok., U.S.	A6	113
Mazomanie, Wi., U.S.	E4	126
Mazon, Il., U.S.	B5	90
Mazzarino, Italy	F5	23
Mbabane, Swaz.	C5	49
Mbaïki, Cen. Afr. Rep.	E3	46
Mbala (Abercorn), Zam.	C5	48
Mbale, Ug.	A5	48
Mbalmayo, Cam.	E2	46
Mbamba Bay, Tan.	D5	48
Mbandaka, Zaire	A2	48
M'banza Congo, Ang.	C1	48
Mbanza-Ngungu, Zaire	C1	48
Mbarara, Ug.	B5	48
Mbeya, Tan.	C5	48
Mbeya, prov., Tan.	C5	48
Mbinda, Congo	B1	48
Mbour, Sen.	D1	45
Mbout, Maur.	C2	45
Mbuji-Mayi, Zaire	C3	48
Mburucuyá, Arg.	E4	55
McAdam, N.B.	D2	71
McAdams, Ms., U.S.	B4	101
McAdoo, Pa., U.S.	E9	115
McAfee, Ms., U.S.	C2	120
McAfee Peak, mtn., Nv., U.S.	B6	105
McAlester, Ok., U.S.	C6	113
McAlester, Lake, res., Ok., U.S.	B6	113
McAlister, N.M., U.S.	C6	108
McAlisterville, Pa., U.S.	E7	115
McAllen, Tx., U.S.	F3	120
McAllister, Mt., U.S.	E5	103
McAlmont, Ar., U.S.	h10	81
McAlpin, Fl., U.S.	B4	86
McAlpine, Md., U.S.	B4	97
McAlpine Lock and Dam, U.S.		
McAndrews, Oh., U.S.	C7	94
McArthur, Oh., U.S.	C3	112
McAuley, Man.	D1	70
McBain, Mi., U.S.	D5	99
McBaine, Mo., U.S.	C5	102
McBee, S.C., U.S.	C7	117
McBride, B.C.	C7	69
McBride, Mo., U.S.	D8	102
McCabe, Mt., U.S.	B12	103
McCall, Id., U.S.	E2	89
McCalla, Al., U.S.	g6	78
McCall Creek, Ms., U.S.	D3	101
McCallsburg, Ia., U.S.	B4	92
McCamey, Tx., U.S.	D1	120
McCammon, Id., U.S.	G6	89
McCandless, Pa., U.S.	h13	115
McCanna, N.D., U.S.	A8	111
McCarley, Ms., U.S.	B4	101
McCarthy, Ak., U.S.	C11	79
McCartney Mountain, mtn., Mt., U.S.	E4	103
McCartys, N.M., U.S.	B2	108
McCaskill, Ar., U.S.	D2	81
McCauley Island, i., B.C.	C2	69
McCaulley, Tx., U.S.	C2	120
McCaysville, Ga., U.S.	B2	87
McChord Air Force Base, mil., Wa., U.S.	f11	124
McClain, co., Ok., U.S.	C4	113
McClave, Co., U.S.	C8	83
McCleary, Wa., U.S.	B2	124
McClellan Air Force Base, mil., Ca., U.S.	C3	82
McClelland, Ar., U.S.	B4	81
McClelland, Ia., U.S.	C2	92
McClellandville, De., U.S.	B2	85
McClellanville, S.C., U.S.	E9	117
McCleod, Mt., U.S.	E6	103
McCloud, Ca., U.S.	B2	82
McClure, Il., U.S.	F4	90
McClure, Oh., U.S.	A2	112
McClure, Pa., U.S.	E7	115
McClure Bridge, Or., U.S.	e9	114
McClure, stm., Or., U.S.	C4	114
McClusky, N.D., U.S.	B5	111
McColl, S.C., U.S.	B8	117
McComas, W.V., U.S.	D3	125
McComb, Ms., U.S.	D3	101
McComb, Oh., U.S.	A2	112
McCondy, Ms., U.S.	B5	101
McCone, co., Mt., U.S.	C11	103
McConnell, Il., U.S.	A4	90
McConnell, Tn., U.S.	A3	119
McConnell Air Force Base, mil., Ks., U.S.	g12	93
McConnells, S.C., U.S.	B5	117
McConnellsburg, Pa., U.S.	G6	115
McConnellstown, Pa., U.S.	F5	115
McConnelsville, Oh., U.S.	C4	112
McCook, Ne., U.S.	D5	104
McCook, co., S.D., U.S.	D8	118
McCook Lake, S.D., U.S.	E9	118
McCool, Ms., U.S.	B4	101
McCool Junction, Ne., U.S.	D8	104
McCord, Sask.	H2	75
McCordsville, In., U.S.	E6	91
McCormick, S.C., U.S.	D3	117
McCormick, co., S.C., U.S.	D3	117
McCoy, Co., U.S.	B4	83
McCracken, Ks., U.S.	D4	93
McCracken, co., Ky., U.S.	e9	94
McCreary, Man.	D2	70
McCreary, co., Ky., U.S.	D5	94
McCrory, Ar., U.S.	B4	81
McCulloch, co., Tx., U.S.	D3	120
McCullom Lake, Il., U.S.	h8	90
McCullough Mountain, mtn., Nv., U.S.	H6	105
McCullum, Al., U.S.	B2	78
McCune, Ks., U.S.	E8	93
McCurtain, Ok., U.S.	B7	113
McCurtain, co., Ok., U.S.	C7	113
McCutchenville, Oh., U.S.	B2	112
McDade, Tx., U.S.	D4	120
McDaniel, Md., U.S.	C5	97
McDavid, Fl., U.S.	u14	86
McDermitt, Nv., U.S.	B4	105
McDermott, Oh., U.S.	D2	112
McDonald, Ks., U.S.	C2	93
McDonald, Ms., U.S.	C4	101
McDonald, N.M., U.S.	D6	108
McDonald, Pa., U.S.	h12	115
McDonald, co., Mo., U.S.	E3	102
McDonald Creek, stm., Mt., U.S.	C8	103
McDonald Islands, is., Austl.	J1	2
McDonough, Ga., U.S.	C2	87
McDonough, N.Y., U.S.	C5	109
McDonough, co., Il., U.S.	C3	90
McDougal, Ar., U.S.	A5	81
McDougall, Mount, mtn., Wy., U.S.	D2	127
McDowell, Ky., U.S.	C7	94
McDowell, Va., U.S.	B3	123
McDowell, co., N.C., U.S.	f10	110
McDowell, co., W.V., U.S.	D3	125
McDowell Mountains, mts., Az., U.S.	k9	80
McDowell Peak, mtn., Az., U.S.	k9	80
McDuffie, co., Ga., U.S.	C4	87
McElhattan, Pa., U.S.	D7	115
McElroy Creek, stm., W.V., U.S.	k9	125
McEwen, Tn., U.S.	A4	119
McFadden, Wy., U.S.	E6	127
McFall, Mo., U.S.	A3	102
McFarlan, N.C., U.S.	C3	110
McFarland, Ca., U.S.	E4	82
McFarland, Ks., U.S.	C7	93
McFarland, Wi., U.S.	E4	126
McGaheysville, Va., U.S.	B4	123
McGee, Sask.	F1	75
McGehee, Ar., U.S.	D4	81
McGill, Nv., U.S.	D7	105
McGillivray, B.C.	D6	69
McGillivray, Lac, l., Que.	A7	73
McGivney, N.B.	C3	71
McGrady, N.C., U.S.	A1	110
McGrath, Ak., U.S.	C8	79
McGrath, Mn., U.S.	D5	100
McGraw, N.Y., U.S.	C4	109
McGraws, W.V., U.S.	D3	125
McGregor, Ia., U.S.	A6	92
McGregor, Mn., U.S.	D5	100
McGregor, N.D., U.S.	A3	111
McGregor, Tx., U.S.	D4	120
McGregor, stm., B.C.	B7	69
McGregor Lake, l., Alta.	D4	68
McGrew, Ne., U.S.	C2	104
McGuffey, Oh., U.S.	B2	112
McGuire, Mount, mtn., Id., U.S.	D4	89
McGuire Air Force Base, mil., N.J., U.S.	C3	107
McHenry, Il., U.S.	A5	90
McHenry, Ky., U.S.	C3	94
McHenry, Md., U.S.	k12	97
McHenry, Ms., U.S.	E4	101
McHenry, N.D., U.S.	B7	111
McHenry, co., Il., U.S.	A5	90
McHenry, co., N.D., U.S.	A5	111
Mchinga, Tan.	C6	48
Mchinji, Mwi.	C5	48
McHue, Ar., U.S.	B4	81
McIndoe Falls, Vt., U.S.	C4	122
McIntire, Ia., U.S.	A5	92
McIntosh, Mn., U.S.	C2	100
McIntosh, N.M., U.S.	C3	108
McIntosh, S.D., U.S.	B4	118
McIntosh, co., Ga., U.S.	E5	87
McIntosh, co., N.D., U.S.	C6	111
McIntosh, co., Ok., U.S.	B6	113
McIntosh Lake, l., Sask.	B3	75
McIntosh Run, stm., Md., U.S.	D4	97
McIntyre, Ga., U.S.	D3	87
McIntyre, Pa., U.S.	E3	115
McKague, Sask.	E4	75
McKean, co., Pa., U.S.	C4	115
McKee, Ky., U.S.	C6	94
McKee City, N.J., U.S.	E3	107
McKeesport, Pa., U.S.	F2	115
McKees Rocks, Pa., U.S.	F1	115
McKenney, Va., U.S.	D5	123
McKenzie, Al., U.S.	D3	78
McKenzie, N.D., U.S.	C5	111
McKenzie, Tn., U.S.	A3	119
McKenzie, co., N.D., U.S.	B2	111
McKenzie, stm., Or., U.S.	C4	114
McKenzie Bridge, Or., U.S.	C4	114
McKerrow, Ont.	A3	73
McKinley, co., N.M., U.S.	B1	108
McKinley, stm., Braz.	C7	51
McKinley, Mount, mtn., Ak., U.S.	C9	79
McKinley Park, Ak., U.S.	C10	79
McKinleyville, Ca., U.S.	B1	82
McKinney, Ky., U.S.	C5	94
McKinney, Tx., U.S.	C4	120
McKinney, Lake, l., Ks., U.S.	E2	93
McKinnon, Wy., U.S.	E3	127
McKittrick, Ca., U.S.	E4	82
McKittrick, Mo., U.S.	C6	102
McKittrick Summit, mtn., Ca., U.S.	E4	82
McKnight Lake, l., Man.	A1	70
McLain, Ms., U.S.	D5	101
McLaughlin, Alta.	C5	68
McLaughlin, S.D., U.S.	B5	118
McLaughlin, stm., Man.	C3	70
McLaurin, Ms., U.S.	D4	101
McLean, Sask.	G3	75
McLean, Il., U.S.	C4	90
McLean, Ne., U.S.	B8	104
McLean, Tx., U.S.	B2	120
McLean, co., Il., U.S.	C4	90
McLean, co., Ky., U.S.	C2	94
McLean, co., N.D., U.S.	B4	111
McLean, Lake, l., Sask.	A6	68
McLean Mountain, mtn., Me., U.S.	A4	96
McLeansboro, Il., U.S.	E5	90
McLemoresville, Tn., U.S.	A3	119
McLennan, Alta.	B2	68
McLennan, co., Tx., U.S.	D4	120
McLennan Lake, l., Sask.	B3	75
McLeod, N.D., U.S.	C8	111
McLeod, co., Mn., U.S.	F4	100
McLeod, stm., Alta.	C2	68
McLeod Lake, B.C.	B6	69
M'Clintock Channel, strt., N.W. Ter.	B12	66
McLoud, Ok., U.S.	B4	113
McLoughlin, Mount, mtn., Or., U.S.	D4	114
McMahon, Sask.	G2	75
McMechen, W.V., U.S.	B5	99
McMillan, Mi., U.S.	B5	99
McMillan, Lake, res., N.M., U.S.	E5	108
McMillin, Wa., U.S.	f11	124
McMinn, co., Tn., U.S.	D9	119
McMinnville, Or., U.S.	B3	114
McMinnville, Tn., U.S.	D8	119
McMorran, Sask.	F1	75
McMullen, co., Tx., U.S.	E3	120
McMurdo, sci., Ant.	B29	7
McMurdo Sound, strt., Ant.	B29	7
McNab, Ar., U.S.	D2	81
McNabb, Il., U.S.	B4	90
McNair, Ms., U.S.	D2	101
McNairy, Tn., U.S.	B3	119
McNairy, co., Tn., U.S.	B3	119
McNary, Az., U.S.	C6	80
McNary, La., U.S.	D3	95
McNary Dam, U.S.	B7	114
McNaughton Lake, res., B.C.	C8	69
McNeal, Ar., U.S.	F6	80
McNeil, Ar., U.S.	D2	81
McNeil, Tx., U.S.	D4	120
McNeil, Mount, mtn., B.C.	B2	69
McNeil Island, i., Wa., U.S.	f10	124
McNeill, Ms., U.S.	E4	101
McNulty, Or., U.S.	*B4	114
McNutts Island, i., N.S.	*F4	71
McPhail, stm., Man.	C3	70
McPherson, Ks., U.S.	D6	93
McPherson, co., Ks., U.S.	D6	93
McPherson, co., Ne., U.S.	C4	104
McPherson, co., S.D., U.S.	B6	118
McPherson Park, Ok., U.S.	C3	113
McQuady, Ky., U.S.	C3	94
McQueeney, Tx., U.S.	h7	120
McRae, Ar., U.S.	B4	81
McRae, Ga., U.S.	D4	87
McRoberts, Ky., U.S.	C7	94
McSherrystown, Pa., U.S.	G7	115
McTaggart, Sask.	H3	75
McTavish, Man.	E3	70
McVeigh, Ky., U.S.	C7	94
McVeytown, Pa., U.S.	F6	115
McVille, N.D., U.S.	B7	111
McWilliams, Al., U.S.	D2	78
Mdandu, Tan.	C5	48
Mdantsane, Ciskei	*D4	49
Me, i., Viet.	C6	35
Meacham, Or., U.S.	B8	114
Meacham, Sask.	E3	75
Mead, Co., U.S.	A6	83
Mead, Ne., U.S.	C9	104
Mead, Ok., U.S.	D5	113
Mead, Wa., U.S.	B8	124
Mead, Lake, res., U.S.	A1	80
Meade, Ks., U.S.	E3	93
Meade, co., Ks., U.S.	E3	93
Meade, co., Ky., U.S.	C3	94
Meade, co., S.D., U.S.	C3	118
Meade, stm., Ak., U.S.	A8	79
Meaden Peak, mtn., Co., U.S.	A3	83
Meade Peak, mtn., Id., U.S.	G7	89
Meadow, Ky., U.S.	D3	94
Meadow, S.D., U.S.	B3	118
Meadow, Tx., U.S.	C1	120
Meadow, Ut., U.S.	E3	121
Meadow, stm., W.V., U.S.	C4	125
Meadow Bridge, W.V., U.S.	D4	125
Meadowbrook, Fl., U.S.	*D5	86
Meadow Creek, W.V., U.S.	k10	125
Meadow Creek, stm., W.V., U.S.	n14	125
Meadow Grove, Ne., U.S.	B8	104
Meadow Lake, Sask.	n7	75
Meadowlands, Pa., U.S.	C10	100
Meadow Lands, Pa., U.S.	F1	115
Meadow Mountain, mtn., Md., U.S.	k12	97
Meadowood, De., U.S.	*B3	85
Meadows, Id., U.S.	E2	89
Meadows, N.H., U.S.	B4	106
Meadow Valley Wash, val., Nv., U.S.	F7	105
Meadowview, Va., U.S.	f10	123
Meadville, Ms., U.S.	D3	101
Meadville, Mo., U.S.	B4	102
Meadville, Pa., U.S.	C1	115
Meaford, Ont.	C4	73
Meagher, co., Mt., U.S.	D6	103
Meaghers Grant, N.S.	E6	71
Mealy Mountains, mts., Newf.	h9	72
Meandarra, Austl.	C7	51
Meander Creek Reservoir, res., Oh., U.S.	A5	112
Means, Ky., U.S.	C6	94
Means, stm., Braz.	C1	57
Mears, Mi., U.S.	E4	99
Me'a She'arim (part of Jerusalem), Isr.	m11	41
Meath, co., Ire.	C5	11
Meath Park, Sask.	D3	75
Meaux, Fr.	C5	16
Mebane, N.C., U.S.	A3	110
Mecca (Makkah), Sau. Ar.	C3	38
Mecca, Ca., U.S.	F5	82
Mecca, In., U.S.	E3	91
Mechanic Falls, Me., U.S.	D2	96
Mechanicsburg, In., U.S.	D5	91
Mechanicsburg, Oh., U.S.	B2	112
Mechanicsburg, Pa., U.S.	F7	115
Mechanicsville, Ia., U.S.	C6	92
Mechanicsville, Md., U.S.	D4	97
Mechanicsville, Vt., U.S.	C2	122
Mechanicsville, Va., U.S.	C5	123
Mechanicville, N.Y., U.S.	C7	109
Mechant, Lake, l., La., U.S.	E4	95
Mechelen (Malines), Bel.	B6	16
Mechriyya, Alg.	g12	123
Meck Island, i., Marsh Is.	S17	52
Mecklenburg, co., N.C., U.S.	B2	110
Mecklenburg, co., Va., U.S.	D4	123
Mecklenburg, hist. reg., E. Ger.	B5	18
Mecklenburg Bay, b., Eur.	D5	18
Meckling, S.D., U.S.	E8	118
Meconta, Moz.	E6	48
Mecosta, Mi., U.S.	E5	99
Mecosta, co., Mi., U.S.	E5	99
Mecúfi, Moz.	*D7	49
Medak, India	H7	37
Medan, Indon.	E1	34
Médanos, Arg.	f7	54
Medanosa, Punta, c., Arg.	D3	54
Medart, Fl., U.S.	B2	86
Medaryville, In., U.S.	B4	91
Meddybemps, Me., U.S.	C5	96
Meddybumps Lake, l., Me.	C5	96
Medeglia, Switz.	D6	21
Medellín, Col.	B2	60
Medemblik, Neth.	C5	16
Médenine, Tun.	A4	46
Mederdra, Maur.	C1	45
Medfield, Ma., U.S.	h10	98
Medford, Ma., U.S.	B5	98
Medford, Mn., U.S.	F5	100
Medford, N.J., U.S.	D3	107
Medford, N.Y., U.S.	*n15	109
Medford, Ok., U.S.	A4	113
Medford, Or., U.S.	E4	114
Medford, Wi., U.S.	C3	126
Medford Lakes, N.J., U.S.	D3	107
Medgidia, Rom.	C9	24
Media, Il., U.S.	C3	90
Media, Pa., U.S.	G11	115
Mediapolis, Ia., U.S.	C6	92
Medical Lake, Wa., U.S.	B8	124
Medicina, Italy	E7	20
Medicine Bow, Wy., U.S.	E6	127
Medicine Bow, stm., Wy., U.S.	E6	127
Medicine Bow Mountains, mts., U.S.	E6	127
Medicine Bow Peak, mtn., Wy., U.S.	E6	127
Medicine Creek, stm., Mo., U.S.	B4	102
Medicine Creek, stm., Ne., U.S.	D5	104
Medicine Hat, Alta.	D5	68
Medicine Lake, Mt., U.S.	B12	103
Medicine Lodge, Ks., U.S.	E5	93
Medicine Lodge, stm., U.S.	E4	93
Medicine Park, Ok., U.S.	C3	113
Medill, Mo., U.S.	A6	102
Medina, Braz.		
Medina, N.Y., U.S.	B2	109
Medina, N.D., U.S.	C6	111
Medina, Oh., U.S.	A4	112
Medina, Tn., U.S.	B3	119
Medina, Wa., U.S.	e11	124
Medina, co., Oh., U.S.	A4	112
Medina, co., Tx., U.S.	E3	120
Medina, stm., Tx., U.S.	k7	120
Medina (Al Madīnah), Sau. Ar.	C3	38
Medina del Campo, Spain	B3	22
Medina de Ríoseco, Spain	B3	22
Medina-Sidonia, Spain	D3	22
Medinīpur, India	D8	36
Mediterranean Sea	H12	8
Medjerda, stm., Tun.	F2	23
Medjerda, Monts de la, mts., Afr.	F2	23
Medjez el Bab, Tun.	F2	23
Mednogorsk, Sov. Un.	C5	28
Medomak, Me., U.S.	D3	96
Medon, Tn., U.S.	B3	119
Medora, Man.	E1	70
Medora, Il., U.S.	D3	90
Medora, In., U.S.	G5	91
Medora, N.D., U.S.	C2	111
Médouneu, Gabon	E2	46
Medstead, Sask.	D1	75
Meductic, N.B.	D2	71
Meduxnekeag, North Branch, stm., N.A.	B5	96
Medveditsa, Sov. Un.	F15	27
Medvedovskaya, Sov. Un.	I12	27
Medvezhi Islands, is., Sov. Un.	B19	29
Medvezhyegorsk, Sov. Un.	C6	29
Medway, Me., U.S.	C4	96
Medway, Ma., U.S.	B5	98
Medway, stm., N.S.	E5	71
Medzhibozh, Sov. Un.	G6	27
Meeker, Co., U.S.	A3	83
Meeker, co., Mn., U.S.	E4	100
Meelpaeg Lake, res., Newf.	D3	72
Meerane, E. Ger.	C6	18
Meerbusch, W. Ger.	*C3	18
Meersburg, W. Ger.	A7	21
Meerut, India	*C6	36
Meeteetse, Wy., U.S.	B4	127
Megali Canal, Grc.	g10	25
Megalópolis, Grc.	D4	25
Mégantic, co., Que.	C6	74
Mégantic, Lac, l., Que.	D7	74
Mégantic, Mont, mtn., Que.	D6	74
Megargel, Al., U.S.	D2	78
Megargel, Tx., U.S.	C3	120
Mégève, Fr.	E2	21
Meggett, S.C., U.S.	F7	117
Meghalaya, state, India	C9	36
Mehadia?		
Mehar, Pak.	C4	36
Mehekar, India	G6	37
Meherrin, Va., U.S.	C4	123
Meherrin, stm., U.S.	A4	110
Mehlville, Mo., U.S.	f13	102
Mehoopany, Pa., U.S.	C9	115
Mehrān, Iran	E3	39
Mehun-sur-Yèvre, Fr.	D5	16
Meia Ponte, stm., Braz.	B3	56
Meiganga, Cam.	E2	46
Meighen Island, i., N.W. Ter.	K32	66
Meigs, Ga., U.S.	E2	87
Meigs, co., Oh., U.S.	C3	112
Meigs, co., Tn., U.S.	D9	119
Meiktila, Burma	D10	36
Meiners Oaks, Ca., U.S.	*E4	82
Meiningen, E. Ger.	C5	18
Meiringen, Switz.	E4	18
Meissen, E. Ger.	C6	18
Meizhou, China	G8	31
Mejillones, Chile	D1	55
Mékambo, Gabon	E2	46
Mekele, Eth.	C4	47
Mékhé, Sen.	C1	45
Mekhtar, Pak.	C4	36
Mékinac, Lac, l., Que.	B5	74
Mekong, stm., Asia	H13	30
Mekoryuk, Ak., U.S.	C6	79
Meknès, Mor.	C3	44
Mékong?		
Melaka (Malacca), Malay.		
Melaka, state, Malay.	K5	35
Melalap?		
Melba, Id., U.S.	F2	89
Melber, Ky., U.S.	f9	94
Melbeta, Ne., U.S.	C2	104
Melbourne, Austl.	G8	50
Melbourne, Ont.	E3	73
Melbourne, Fl., U.S.	D6	86
Melbourne, Ia., U.S.	C4	92
Melbourne, Ky., U.S.	h14	94
Melbourne, Mo., U.S.	A4	102
Melbourne Beach, Fl., U.S.	D6	86
Melcher, Ia., U.S.	C4	92
Melder, La., U.S.	C3	95
Meldorf, W. Ger.	D3	15
Meldrim, Ga., U.S.	D5	87
Meldrum Bay, Ont.	B1	73
Meleb, Man.	D3	70
Melekeok, Palau	R17	52
Melekess, Sov. Un.	E18	8
Melenki, Sov. Un.	D13	27
Mélèzes, Rivière aux, stm., Que.	g12	74
Melfi, Chad	C3	46
Melfi, Italy	D5	23
Melfort, Sask.	E3	75
Melghir, Chott, l., Alg.	C6	44
Melilla, Sp. N. Afr.	B4	44
Melipilla, Chile	A2	54
Mélisey, Fr.	A2	21
Melito di Porto Salvo, Italy	F5	23
Melitopol, Sov. Un.	H10	27
Mella, stm., Italy	D6	20
Melle, Fr.	D3	16
Melle, W. Ger.	A3	19
Mellen, Wi., U.S.	B3	126
Mellette, S.D., U.S.	B7	118
Mellette, co., S.D., U.S.	D5	118
Mellit, Sud.	C2	47
Mellor Glacier, ice, Ant.	B19	7
Mellott, In., U.S.	D3	91
Mellow Valley, Al., U.S.	B4	78
Mellrichstadt, W. Ger.	C5	19
Mellum, i., W. Ger.	E5	15
Mellwood, Ar., U.S.	C4	81
Melmore, Oh., U.S.	A2	112
Mělník, Czech.	n18	26
Melo, Ur.	e11	54
Melocheville, Que.	q19	74
Melrose, N.B.	C6	71
Melrose, Ct., U.S.	B5	84
Melrose, Fl., U.S.	C4	86
Melrose, Ia., U.S.	C4	92
Melrose, La., U.S.	C3	95
Melrose, Ma., U.S.	B5	98
Melrose, Mn., U.S.	E4	100
Melrose, N.M., U.S.	C6	108
Melrose, Oh., U.S.	A1	112
Melrose, Wi., U.S.	D3	126
Melrose Park, Fl., U.S.	r13	86
Melrose Park, Il., U.S.	*k9	90
Mels, Switz.	B7	21
Melstone, Mt., U.S.	D9	103
Melstrand, Mi., U.S.	B4	99
Melsungen, W. Ger.	B5	19
Melton Hill Lake, res., Tn., U.S.	D9	119
Melton Mowbray, Eng., U.K.	I11	9
Melun, Fr.	C5	16
Melvaig, Scot., U.K.	C3	13
Melvern, Ks., U.S.	D8	93
Melvern Lake, res., Ks., U.S.	D8	93
Melville, Austl.	*F2	50
Melville, La., U.S.	D4	95
Melville, Mt., U.S.	D7	103
Melville, N.Y., U.S.	*n15	109
Melville, Sask.	G4	75
Melville, i., Austl.	B5	50
Melville, Cape, c., Austl.	B7	50
Melville, Lake, l., Newf.	B2	72
Melville Bugt, b., Grnld.	B14	61
Melville Hills, hills, N.W. Ter.	C8	66
Melville Island, i., N.W. Ter.	m30	66
Melville Peninsula, pen., N.W. Ter.	C16	66
Melvin, Al., U.S.	D1	78
Melvin, Il., U.S.	C5	90
Melvin, Ia., U.S.	A2	92
Melvin, Ky., U.S.	C7	94
Melvin, Tx., U.S.	D3	120
Melvin, Lough, l., Eur.	C3	11
Melvindale, Mi., U.S.	*p7	99
Melvine, Tn., U.S.	D8	119
Melvin Village, N.H., U.S.	C4	106
Memba, Moz.	D7	48
Memberamo, stm., Indon.	F4	34
Memel, E. Ger.	E5	16
Memmingen, W. Ger.	E5	19
Mempawah, Indon.	B3	34
Memphis, Fl., U.S.	p10	86
Memphis, Mi., U.S.	H6	91
Memphis, Mo., U.S.	F8	99
Memphis, Ne., U.S.	g12	104
Memphis, Tn., U.S.	B1	119
Memphis, Tx., U.S.	B2	120
Memphis, hist., Egypt	C3	38
Memphis Naval Air Station, mil., Tn., U.S.	B2	119
Memphrémagog, Lake, l., N.A.	D5	74
Memramcook, N.B.	C5	71
Mena, Ar., U.S.	C1	81
Menaggu, Mn., U.S.	D3	100
Menai Strait, strt., Wales, U.K.	A5	13
Ménaka, Mali	C5	45
Menan, Id., U.S.	F7	89
Menands, N.Y., U.S.	C7	109
Menard, Tx., U.S.	D3	120
Menard, co., Il., U.S.	C4	90
Menard, co., Tx., U.S.	D3	120
Menasha, Wi., U.S.	D5	126
Mendawai, stm., Indon.	F4	34
Mende, Fr.	E5	16
Menden, W. Ger.	B3	19
Mendenhall, Ms., U.S.	D4	101
Mendes, Ga., U.S.	D5	87
Mendham, Sask.	G1	75
Mendham, N.J., U.S.	B3	107
Mendi, Eth.	D4	47
Mendip Hills, hills, Eng., U.K.	C5	13
Mendocino, Ca., U.S.	C2	82
Mendocino, co., Ca., U.S.	C2	82
Mendon, Il., U.S.	C2	90
Mendon, Mi., U.S.	h9	99
Mendon, Mo., U.S.	F5	99
Mendon, N.Y., U.S.	B4	102
Mendon, Oh., U.S.	B1	112
Mendon, Vt., U.S.	D3	122
Mendota, Ca., U.S.	D3	82
Mendota, Il., U.S.	B4	90
Mendota Heights, Mn., U.S.	*m13	100
Mendoza, Arg.	A3	54
Mendoza, Pan.	k11	62
Mendoza, prov., Arg.	A3	54
Mendrisio, Switz.	E6	21
Mene de Mauroa, Ven.	A3	60
Mene Grande, Ven.	B3	60
Menemen, Tur.	C6	25
Menen, Bel.	D3	17
Menfi, Italy	F4	23
Mengcheng, China	E8	31
Menggala, Indon.	F3	34

Name	Map Ref.	Page
Menghai, China	B4	35
Menglian, China	G4	31
Mengzi, China	G5	31
Menifee, Ar., U.S.	B3	81
Menifee, co., Ky., U.S.	C6	94
Menihek Lakes, l., Newf.	g8	72
Menindee, Austl.	F7	50
Menindee Lake, l., Austl.	F4	51
Menlo, Ga., U.S.	B1	87
Menlo, Ia., U.S.	C3	92
Menlo, Ks., U.S.	C3	93
Menlo, Wa., U.S.	C2	124
Menlo Park, Ca., U.S.	k8	82
Menno, S.D., U.S.	D8	118
Meno, Ok., U.S.	A3	113
Menoken, N.D., U.S.	C5	111
Menominee, Mi., U.S.	C3	99
Menominee, co., Mi., U.S.	C3	99
Menominee, co., Wi., U.S.	C5	126
Menominee, stm., U.S.	C6	126
Menominee Indian Reservation, Wi., U.S.	C5	126
Menomonee, stm., Wi., U.S.	m11	126
Menomonee Falls, Wi., U.S.	E5	126
Menomonie, Wi., U.S.	D2	126
Menongue, Ang.	D2	48
Menor, Mar, b., Spain	D5	22
Menorca, i., Spain	C8	22
Mentakab, Malay.	K5	35
Mentana, Italy	g9	23
Mentawai Islands, is., Indon.	F1	34
Mentmore, N.M., U.S.	B1	108
Menton, Fr.	F7	16
Mentone, Al., U.S.	A4	78
Mentone, In., U.S.	B5	91
Mentone, Tx., U.S.	D1	120
Mentor, Ky., U.S.	k14	94
Mentor, Mn., U.S.	C2	100
Mentor, Oh., U.S.	A4	112
Mentor, Tn., U.S.	n13	119
Mentor-on-the-Lake, Oh., U.S.	A4	112
Menzel Bourguiba, Tun.	B6	44
Menzies, Mount, mtn., Ant.	B19	7
Menziken, Switz.	B5	21
Meoqui, Mex.	B3	63
Meota, Sask.	D1	75
Meppel, Neth.	A7	16
Meppen, W. Ger.	B3	18
Meqerghane, Sebkha, pl., Alg.	D5	44
Mequon, Wi., U.S.	E6	126
Merabolo, Gulf of, b., Grc.	E5	25
Meramec, stm., Mo., U.S.	C7	102
Merano, Italy	A3	23
Merasheen, Newf.	E4	72
Merasheen Island, i., Newf.	E4	72
Merate, Italy	E7	21
Merauke, Indon.	G10	34
Meraux, La., U.S.	k12	95
Mercāra, India	F6	36
Merced, Ca., U.S.	D3	82
Merced, co., Ca., U.S.	D3	82
Merced, stm., Ca., U.S.	D3	82
Mercedes, Arg.	A3	54
Mercedes, Arg.	A5	54
Mercedes, Arg.	E4	55
Mercedes, Tx., U.S.	F4	120
Mercedes, Ur.	E1	56
Mercer, Me., U.S.	D3	96
Mercer, Mo., U.S.	A4	102
Mercer, N.D., U.S.	B5	111
Mercer, Oh., U.S.	B1	112
Mercer, Pa., U.S.	D1	115
Mercer, Tn., U.S.	B2	119
Mercer, Wi., U.S.	B3	126
Mercer, co., Il., U.S.	B3	90
Mercer, co., Ky., U.S.	C5	94
Mercer, co., Mo., U.S.	A4	102
Mercer, co., N.J., U.S.	C3	107
Mercer, co., N.D., U.S.	B4	111
Mercer, co., Oh., U.S.	B1	112
Mercer, co., Pa., U.S.	D1	115
Mercer, co., W.V., U.S.	D3	125
Mercer Island, Wa., U.S.	e11	124
Mercer Island, i., Wa., U.S.	e11	124
Mercersburg, Pa., U.S.	G6	115
Mercerville, N.J., U.S.	C3	107
Mercês, Braz.	g6	56
Merchantville, N.J., U.S.	*D2	107
Mercier, Que.	D4	74
Mercier, Ks., U.S.	C8	93
Mercoal, Alta.	C2	68
Mercury Bay, b., N.Z.	L15	51
Mercury Islands, is., N.Z.	L15	51
Mercy, Cape, c. N.W. Ter.	D20	66
Meredith, Co., U.S.	B4	83
Meredith, N.H., U.S.	C3	106
Meredith, Lake, l., Co., U.S.	C7	83
Meredith, Lake, res., Tx., U.S.	B2	120
Meredith Center, N.H., U.S.	C3	106
Meredosia, Il., U.S.	D3	90
Meredosia Lake, l., Il., U.S.	D3	90
Mereeg, Som.	E6	47
Merefa, Sov. Un.	G11	27
Merepoint, Me., U.S.	g7	96
Mergui, Burma	F10	36
Mergui Archipelago, is., Burma	F10	36
Meriç (Maritsa) (Évros), stm., Eur.	B6	25
Merid, Sask.	F1	75
Mérida, Mex.	C7	63
Mérida, Spain	C2	22
Mérida, Ven.	B3	60
Mérida, state, Ven.	B3	60
Meriden, Ct., U.S.	C4	84
Meriden, Ia., U.S.	B2	92
Meriden, Ks., U.S.	C8	93
Meriden, Mn., U.S.	F5	100
Meriden, N.H., U.S.	C2	106
Meriden, Wy., U.S.	E8	127
Meridian, Id., U.S.	E3	87
Meridian, Id., U.S.	F2	89
Meridian, Ms., U.S.	C5	101
Meridian, N.Y., U.S.	B4	109
Meridian, Pa., U.S.	E2	115
Meridian, Tx., U.S.	D4	120
Meridian Hills, In., U.S.	k10	91
Meridian Naval Air Station, mil., Ms., U.S.	C5	101
Meridianville, Al., U.S.	A3	78
Mérignac, Fr.	E3	16
Merigold, Ms., U.S.	B3	101
Merigomish, N.S.	D7	71
Merikarvia, Fin.	G9	14
Meringur, Austl.	G3	51
Merino, Co., U.S.	A7	83
Meriwether, co., Ga., U.S.	C2	87
Merizo, Guam	M9	52
Merkel, Tx., U.S.	C2	120
Merkinė, Sov. Un.	A8	26
Merksem (part of Antwerp), Bel.	B6	16
Merksplas, Bel.	C4	17
Merkys, stm., Sov. Un.	D5	27
Merlin, Ont.	E2	73
Merlin, Or., U.S.	E3	114
Merlo, Arg.	g7	54
Mermentau, La., U.S.	D3	95
Mermentau, stm., La., U.S.	E3	95
Mern, Den.	C6	15
Merna, Ne., U.S.	C6	104
Merom, In., U.S.	F2	91
Meron, Mount, mtn., Isr.	A7	41
Merredin, Austl.	F2	50
Merriam, In., U.S.	B7	91
Merriam, Ks., U.S.	k16	93
Merrick, N.Y., U.S.	*n15	109
Merrick, co., Ne., U.S.	C7	104
Merrick, mtn., Scot., U.K.	E4	13
Merrick Brook, stm., Ct., U.S.	C7	84
Merrickville, Ont.	C9	73
Merricourt, N.D., U.S.	C7	111
Merrifield, Mn., U.S.	D4	100
Merrifield, Va., U.S.	*B5	123
Merrill, Ia., U.S.	B1	92
Merrill, Mi., U.S.	E6	99
Merrill, Ms., U.S.	E5	101
Merrill, Or., U.S.	E5	114
Merrill, Wi., U.S.	C4	126
Merrillan, Wi., U.S.	D3	126
Merrillville, In., U.S.	B3	91
Merrimac, Ky., U.S.	C4	94
Merrimac, Ma., U.S.	A5	98
Merrimac, Wi., U.S.	E4	126
Merrimack, N.H., U.S.	E4	106
Merrimack, co., N.H., U.S.	D3	106
Merrimack, stm., U.S.	A5	98
Merriman, Ne., U.S.	B4	104
Merrimon, N.C., U.S.	C6	110
Merritt, B.C.	D7	69
Merritt, N.C., U.S.	B6	110
Merritt Island, Fl., U.S.	D6	86
Merritt Reservoir, res., Ne., U.S.	B5	104
Merriwa, Austl.	F8	51
Merriweather, Mi., U.S.	m12	99
Merrow, Ct., U.S.	B6	84
Merry Hill, N.C., U.S.	A6	110
Merrymeeting Lake, l., N.H., U.S.	D4	106
Merry Oaks, N.C., U.S.	B3	110
Merryville, La., U.S.	D2	95
Mersa Fatma, Eth.	B5	47
Merseburg, E. Ger.	C5	18
Mersey, stm., Eng., U.K.	D5	10
Merseyside, co., Eng., U.K.	A4	12
Mershon, Ga., U.S.	E4	87
Mersing, Malay.	E2	34
Merthyr Tydfil, Wales, U.K.	E5	10
Merti, Kenya	A6	48
Mértola, Port.	D2	22
Merton, Wi., U.S.	m11	126
Mertz Glacier, ice, Ant.	C27	7
Mertzon, Tx., U.S.	D2	120
Méru, Fr.	C5	16
Meru, Kenya	A6	48
Meru, Mount, mtn., Tan.	B6	48
Mervelier, Switz.	B4	21
Merville, Fr.	D2	17
Mervin, Sask.	D1	75
Merwin, Mo., U.S.	C3	102
Merwin Lake, res., Wa., U.S.	C3	124
Méry [-sur-Seine], Fr.	F3	17
Merzifon, Tur.	B10	40
Merzig, W. Ger.	E6	17
Mesa, Az., U.S.	D4	80
Mesa, Co., U.S.	B2	83
Mesa, Id., U.S.	E2	89
Mesa, co., Co., U.S.	B2	83
Mesa Mountain, mtn., Co., U.S.	D4	83
Mesa Verde National Park, Co., U.S.	D2	83
Mescalero, N.M., U.S.	D4	108
Mescalero Indian Reservation, N.M., U.S.	D4	108
Meschede, W. Ger.	B3	19
Mesegon, i., Micron.	Q18	52
Mesena, Ga., U.S.	C4	87
Meservey, Ia., U.S.	B4	92
Meshcherskoye, Sov. Un.	n17	27
Meshchovsk, Sov. Un.	D10	27
Meshkovskaya, Sov. Un.	G13	27
Meshomasic Mountain, mtn., Ct., U.S.	C5	84
Meshoppen, Pa., U.S.	C9	115
Mesic, N.C., U.S.	B6	110
Mesick, Mi., U.S.	D5	99
Mesilla, N.M., U.S.	E3	108
Mesita, N.M., U.S.	B2	108
Mesita, Co., U.S.	D5	83
Mesocco, Switz.	C5	20
Mesolóngion, Grc.	C3	25
Mesquita, Braz.	B4	56
Mesquite, Nv., U.S.	G7	105
Mesquite, N.M., U.S.	E3	108
Mesquite, Tx., U.S.	n10	120
Messalonskee Lake, l., Me., U.S.	D3	96
Méssápion Óros, mtn., Grc.	g10	25
Messen, Switz.	B3	21
Messina, Italy	E5	23
Messina, S. Afr.	E5	49
Messina, Strait of, strt., Italy	E5	23
Messini, Grc.	D4	25
Messíni, Gulf of, b., Grc.	D4	25
Messkirch, W. Ger.	E5	18
Mesta (Néstos), stm., Eur.	B4	25
Mestghanem (Mostaganem), Alg.	B5	44
Mestre, Italy	D7	23
Mesudiye, Tur.	B11	40
Meta, Mo., U.S.	C5	102
Meta, dept., Col.	C3	60
Meta, stm., S.A.	B4	60
Métabetchouan, Que.	A6	74
Metán, Arg.	E3	55
Metapán, El Sal.	C3	62
Meta Pond, l., Newf.	D4	72
Metaponto, Italy	D6	23
Metarica, Moz.	A7	49
Métascouac, Lac, l., Que.	B6	74
Metasville, Ga., U.S.	C4	87
Metcalf, Ga., U.S.	F3	87
Metcalf, Il., U.S.	D6	90
Metcalfe, Ont.	B9	73
Metcalfe, Ms., U.S.	B2	101
Metcalfe, co., Ky., U.S.	C4	94
Metchosin, B.C.	h12	69
Metedeconk, North Branch, stm., N.J., U.S.	C4	107
Metedeconk, South Branch, stm., N.J., U.S.	C3	107
Meteghan, N.S.	E3	71
Meteghan River, N.S.	E3	71
Meteghan Station, N.S.	E3	71
Metema, Eth.	C4	47
Meteor Crater, crat., Az., U.S.	C4	80
Methow, Wa., U.S.	A5	124
Methow, stm., Wa., U.S.	A5	124
Methuen, Ma., U.S.	A5	98
Metiskow, Alta.	C5	68
Metković, Yugo.	D3	24
Metlakatla, Ak., U.S.	D13	79
Meto, Bayou, stm., Ar., U.S.	C4	81
Metolius, Or., U.S.	C5	114
Metonga, Lake, l., Wi., U.S.	C5	126
Metropolis, Il., U.S.	F5	90
Metropolitana, prov., Chile	A2	54
Métsovon, Grc.	C3	25
Mettawee, stm., U.S.	E2	122
Metten, W. Ger.	E7	19
Metter, Ga., U.S.	D4	87
Mettet, Bel.	D4	17
Mettingen, W. Ger.	B5	16
Mettmann, W. Ger.	B1	19
Metuchen, N.J., U.S.	B4	107
Metula, Isr.	A7	41
Metz, Fr.	C7	16
Metz, In., U.S.	A8	91
Metz, Mi., U.S.	C7	99
Metz, Mo., U.S.	D3	102
Metzeral, Fr.	B3	20
Metzger, Or., U.S.	h12	114
Meudon, Fr.	g9	16
Meulaboh, Indon.	m11	34
Meung, Fr.	D4	16
Meureudu, Indon.	J2	35
Meurthe, stm., Fr.	F6	17
Meurthe-et-Moselle, dept., Fr.	F6	17
Meuse, dept., Fr.	E5	17
Meuse (Maas), stm., Eur.	C6	16
Meuse, Côtes de, mtn., Fr.	C5	16
Meuselwitz, E. Ger.	B7	19
Mexia, Al., U.S.	D2	78
Mexia, Tx., U.S.	D4	120
Mexia, Lake, res., Tx., U.S.	D4	120
Mexicali, Mex.	A1	63
Mexican Hat, Ut., U.S.	F6	121
Mexican Springs, N.M., U.S.	B1	108
Mexico, In., U.S.	C5	91
Mexico, Ky., U.S.	e9	94
Mexico, Me., U.S.	D2	96
Mexico, Mo., U.S.	B6	102
Mexico, N.Y., U.S.	B4	109
Mexico, Pa., U.S.	E7	115
México, state, Mex.	D5	63
Mexico, ctry., N.A.	D5	63
Mexico, Gulf of, b., N.A.	G11	61
Mexico City, Mex.	D5	63
Meycauayan, Phil.	o13	34
Meydān-e Gel, pl., Iran	G7	39
Meydanī, Ra's-e, c., Iran	C5	38
Meyers Chuck, Ak., U.S.	n23	79
Meyersdale, Pa., U.S.	G3	115
Meyísti, i., Grc.	D7	25
Meymaneh, Afg.	A4	36
Meyrin, Switz.	D1	21
Meyrone, Sask.	H2	75
Mèze, Fr.	F5	16
Mezen, Sov. Un.	C7	29
Mezen, stm., Sov. Un.	C7	29
Mezen Bay, b., Sov. Un.	B17	8
Mézenc, Mont, mtn., Fr.	E6	16
Mezhdurechenskiy, Sov. Un.	B7	28
Meziadin Lake, l., B.C.	A3	69
Mézières, Switz.	C2	21
Mezőkövesd, Hung.	B5	24
Mezőtúr, Hung.	B5	24
Mezzana, Italy	C6	20
Mezzolombardo, Italy	C7	20
Mga, Sov. Un.	s32	14
Mga, stm., Sov. Un.	s32	14
Mglin, Sov. Un.	E9	27
Mhòr, Beinn, mtn., Scot., U.K.	C1	13
Mhòr, Loch, l., Scot., U.K.	D3	13
Mhow, India	F5	37
Miahuatlán de Porfirio Díaz, Mex.	D5	63
Miajadas, Spain	C3	22
Miami, Man.	E2	70
Miami, Az., U.S.	D5	80
Miami, Fl., U.S.	G6	86
Miami, In., U.S.	C5	91
Miami, Mo., U.S.	B4	102
Miami, N.M., U.S.	A5	108
Miami, Ok., U.S.	A7	113
Miami, Tx., U.S.	B2	120
Miami, W.V., U.S.	m13	125
Miami, co., In., U.S.	C5	91
Miami, co., Ks., U.S.	D9	93
Miami, co., Oh., U.S.	B1	112
Miami Beach, Fl., U.S.	G6	86
Miami Canal, Fl., U.S.	F6	86
Miami International Airport, Fl., U.S.	*G6	86
Miami Lakes, Fl., U.S.	*G6	86
Miamisburg, Oh., U.S.	C1	112
Miami Shores, Fl., U.S.	G6	86
Miami Springs, Fl., U.S.	s13	86
Miamitown, Oh., U.S.	o12	112
Miándoāb, Iran	C3	39
Miandrivazo, Madag.	g9	49
Miāneh, Iran	D7	34
Miangas Island, i., Indon.	D7	34
Mianning, China	F5	31
Mianus Reservoir, res., U.S.	E1	84
Mianyang, China	I5	32
Miarinarivo, Madag.	g9	49
Miass, Sov. Un.	F8	28
Miass, stm., Sov. Un.	B6	28
Miasteczko Śląskie, Pol.	f9	26
Miastko, Pol.	A4	26
Mica, Wa., U.S.	B8	124
Mica Creek, B.C.	C7	69
Mica Mountain, mtn., Az., U.S.	E5	80
Micanopy, Fl., U.S.	C4	86
Micco, Fl., U.S.	E6	86
Miccosukee, Fl., U.S.	B2	86
Miccosukee, Lake, res., Fl., U.S.	B4	86
Michael, Il., U.S.	D3	90
Michael Island, i., Newf.	A2	72
Michalovce, Czech.	D6	26
Michałów-Reginów, Pol.	k13	26
Michaud, Point, c., N.S.	D9	71
Michelson, Mount, mtn., Ak., U.S.	B11	79
Michendorf, E. Ger.	A8	19
Michichi, Alta.	D4	68
Michie, Tn., U.S.	B3	119
Michigamme, Mi., U.S.	B2	99
Michigamme, Lake, l., Mi., U.S.	B2	99
Michigamme Reservoir, res., Mi., U.S.	B2	99
Michigan, N.D., U.S.	A7	111
Michigan, state, U.S.	E6	99
Michigan, stm., Co., U.S.	A4	83
Michigan, Lake, l., U.S.	B10	76
Michigan Center, Mi., U.S.	F6	99
Michigan City, In., U.S.	A4	91
Michigan City, Ms., U.S.	A4	101
Michigan Island, i., Wi., U.S.	B3	126
Michigan Prairie, reg., Wa., U.S.	C7	124
Michigantown, In., U.S.	D5	91
Michoacán, state, Mex.	D4	63
Michurin (Tsarevo), Bul.	D8	24
Michurinsk, Sov. Un.	E13	27
Micoud, St. Luc.	J14	64
Micro, N.C., U.S.	B4	110
Micronesia, Federated States of, ter., T.T.P.I.	F9	6
Midai, i., Indon.	K7	35
Midale, Sask.	H4	75
Midas, Id., U.S.	A2	89
Middelburg, Neth.	B5	16
Middelburg, S. Afr.	D4	49
Middelfart, Den.	C3	15
Middelharnis, Neth.	C4	17
Middelkerke, Bel.	C2	17
Middle, Ia., U.S.	C6	92
Middle, stm., B.C.	B5	69
Middle, stm., Ia., U.S.	C6	92
Middle Andaman, i., India	F9	36
Middlebourne, W.V., U.S.	B4	125
Middlebranch, Oh., U.S.	B4	112
Middlebro, Man.	E4	70
Middlebrook, Va., U.S.	B3	123
Middleburg, Fl., U.S.	B5	86
Middleburg, Ky., U.S.	C5	94
Middleburg, Md., U.S.	A3	97
Middleburg, N.C., U.S.	A4	110
Middleburg, Pa., U.S.	E7	115
Middleburg Heights, Oh., U.S.	h9	112
Middleburgh, N.Y., U.S.	C6	109
Middlebury, Ct., U.S.	C3	84
Middlebury, In., U.S.	A6	91
Middlebury, Vt., U.S.	C2	122
Middlefield, Ct., U.S.	C5	84
Middlefield, Ma., U.S.	B1	98
Middlefield, Oh., U.S.	A4	112
Middle Granville, N.Y., U.S.	B7	109
Middle Ground, rf., Mid. Is.	J3	52
Middle Haddam, Ct., U.S.	C5	84
Middle Island, N.Y., U.S.	*n16	109
Middle Island Creek, stm., W.V., U.S.	B3	125
Middle Loup, stm., Ne., U.S.	C5	104
Middle Musquodoboit, N.S.	D6	71
Middle Nodaway, stm., Ia., U.S.	C3	92
Middle Park, val., Co., U.S.	A4	83
Middle Patuxent, stm., Md., U.S.	B4	97
Middle Point, Oh., U.S.	B1	112
Middleport, N.Y., U.S.	B2	109
Middleport, Oh., U.S.	C3	112
Middle Raccoon, stm., Ia., U.S.	C3	92
Middle River, Md., U.S.	B5	97
Middle River, stm., Ia., U.S.	C3	92
Middle River, Mn., U.S.	B2	100
Middlesboro, Ky., U.S.	D6	94
Middlesbrough (Teesside), Eng., U.K.	C6	10
Middlesex, Belize	D7	63
Middlesex, N.J., U.S.	B4	107
Middlesex, N.Y., U.S.	C3	109
Middlesex, N.C., U.S.	B4	110
Middlesex, Vt., U.S.	C3	122
Middlesex, co., Ct., U.S.	D5	84
Middlesex, co., Ma., U.S.	A5	98
Middlesex, co., N.J., U.S.	C4	107
Middlesex, co., Va., U.S.	C6	123
Middlesex Fells Reservation, Ma., U.S.	g11	98
Middle Stewiacke, N.S.	D6	71
Middleton, N.S.	E4	71
Middleton, Id., U.S.	F2	89
Middleton, Ma., U.S.	A5	98
Middleton, Mi., U.S.	E6	99
Middleton, Tn., U.S.	B3	119
Middleton, Wi., U.S.	E4	126
Middletown, Ca., U.S.	C2	82
Middletown, Ct., U.S.	C5	84
Middletown, De., U.S.	C3	85
Middletown, In., U.S.	D6	91
Middletown, Ky., U.S.	g11	94
Middletown, Md., U.S.	B2	97
Middletown, N.J., U.S.	C4	107
Middletown, N.Y., U.S.	D6	109
Middletown, Oh., U.S.	C1	112
Middletown, Pa., U.S.	F8	115
Middletown, R.I., U.S.	E5	116
Middletown, Va., U.S.	A4	123
Middletown Springs, Vt., U.S.	E2	122
Middletown Township, Pa., U.S.	*G11	115
Middle Valley, N.J., U.S.	B3	107
Middleville, Mi., U.S.	F5	99
Middleville, N.Y., U.S.	B6	109
Midfield, Al., U.S.	g7	78
Midgic, N.B.	D5	71
Mid Glamorgan, co., Wales, U.K.	C4	12
Midhurst, Ont.	C5	73
Midi d'Ossau, Pic du, mtn., Fr.	A3	16
Midkiff, W.V., U.S.	C2	125
Midland, Ont.	B5	73
Midland, Al., U.S.	B4	78
Midland, In., U.S.	F3	91
Midland, La., U.S.	D5	95
Midland, Md., U.S.	k13	97
Midland, Mi., U.S.	E6	99
Midland, N.C., U.S.	B2	110
Midland, Oh., U.S.	C2	112
Midland, Pa., U.S.	E1	115
Midland, S.D., U.S.	C4	118
Midland, Tx., U.S.	D1	120
Midland, Va., U.S.	B5	123
Midland, co., Mi., U.S.	E6	99
Midland, co., Tx., U.S.	D1	120
Midland Basin, Tx., U.S.	A2	83
Midland City, Al., U.S.	D4	78
Midland Park, Ks., U.S.	g12	93
Midland Park, N.J., U.S.	B4	107
Midland Park, S.C., U.S.	k11	117
Midleton, Ire.	E2	10
Midlothian, Il., U.S.	k9	90
Midlothian, Md., U.S.	k13	97
Midlothian, Tx., U.S.	C4	120
Midlothian, Va., U.S.	m17	123
Midnapore, Alta.	D3	68
Midnight, Ms., U.S.	B3	101
Midongy Sud, Madag.	h9	49
Midpines, Ca., U.S.	D4	82
Midreshet Ben Gurion, Isr.	D6	41
Midvale, Oh., U.S.	B4	112
Midvale, Ut., U.S.	C4	121
Midville, Ga., U.S.	D4	87
Midway, B.C.	E8	69
Midway, Al., U.S.	C4	78
Midway, De., U.S.	F5	85
Midway, Fl., U.S.	B2	86
Midway, Ga., U.S.	E5	87
Midway, Ky., U.S.	B5	94
Midway, Or., U.S.	*B4	114
Midway, Pa., U.S.	G7	115
Midway, stm., Ma., U.S.	h9	98
Midway, Tn., U.S.	C11	119
Midway, Ut., U.S.	C4	121
Midway Islands, dep., Oc.	E11	6
Midway Naval Station, mil., Mid. Is.	K3	52
Midway Range, mts., B.C.	E8	69
Midwest, Wy., U.S.	C6	127
Midwest City, Ok., U.S.	B4	113
Miechów, Pol.	D5	26
Międzychód, Pol.	B3	26
Międzyrzec [Podlaski], Pol.	C7	26
Międzyrzecz, Pol.	B3	26
Międzyrzecze, Pol.	g10	26
Międzyzdroje, Pol.	B3	26
Mielec, Pol.	C6	26
Mien, l., Swe.	B8	15
Mienia, stm., Pol.	m14	26
Mier, In., U.S.	C6	91
Miercurea Ciuc, Rom.	B7	24
Mieres, Spain	A3	22
Miesbach, W. Ger.	B7	20
Mieso, Eth.	D5	47
Mifflin, Pa., U.S.	E7	115
Mifflin, Tn., U.S.	B3	119
Mifflin, co., Pa., U.S.	E6	115
Mifflinburg, Pa., U.S.	E7	115
Mifflintown, Pa., U.S.	E7	115
Mifflinville, Pa., U.S.	D9	115
Migdal, Isr.	B7	41
Migennes, Fr.	D5	16
Mignon, Lake, l., Fl., U.S.	E20	74
Miguel Alemán, Presa, res., Mex.	n15	63
Miguel Alves, Braz.	B2	57
Miguel Auza, Mex.	C4	63
Mihai Viteazu, Rom.	C9	24
Mihama, Japan	o15	33
Mihara, Japan	H5	32
Mijares, stm., Spain	B5	22
Mijdahah, Yemen	F4	47
Mikado, Sask.	D7	75
Mikado, Mi., U.S.	D7	99
Mika, co., Cze.	C2	126
Mikha Tskhakaya, Sov. Un.	A14	40
Mikhaylov, Sov. Un.	D12	27
Mikhaylov, Cape, c., Ant.	C24	7
Mikhaylovgrad, Bul.	D6	24
Mikhaylovka, Sov. Un.	F14	27
Mikhaylovka, Sov. Un.	H10	27
Mikhaylovskiy, Sov. Un.	C9	28
Mikindani, Tan.	D7	48
Mikkalo, Or., U.S.	B6	114
Mikkeli, Fin.	G12	14
Mikołów, Pol.	g9	26
Mikonos, i., Grc.	D5	25
Mikulov, Czech.	D4	26
Mikumi, Tan.	C6	48
Milaca, Mn., U.S.	E5	100
Milagro, Ec.	B2	58
Milam, W.V., U.S.	C5	125
Milam, co., Tx., U.S.	D4	120
Milan (Milano), Italy	D2	23
Milan, Ga., U.S.	D3	87
Milan, Il., U.S.	B3	90
Milan, In., U.S.	F7	91
Milan, Ks., U.S.	E6	93
Milan, Mi., U.S.	F7	99
Milan, Mo., U.S.	A4	102
Milan, N.H., U.S.	B4	106
Milan, N.M., U.S.	B2	108
Milan, Oh., U.S.	A3	112
Milan, Tn., U.S.	B3	119
Milan, Wa., U.S.	B8	124
Milâs, Tur.	D6	25
Milazzo, Italy	E5	23
Milbank, S.D., U.S.	B9	118
Milbanke Sound, strt., B.C.	C3	69
Milbridge, Me., U.S.	D5	96
Milburn, Ne., U.S.	C6	104
Milburn, Ok., U.S.	C5	113
Milden, Sask.	F2	75
Mildenhall, Eng., U.K.	D7	10
Mildmay, Ont.	C3	73
Mildred, Sask.	D2	75
Mildura, Austl.	F7	50
Miles, Austl.	E9	50
Miles, Ia., U.S.	B7	92
Miles, Tx., U.S.	D2	120
Miles City, Mt., U.S.	D11	103
Miles Mountain, mtn., Az., U.S.	G3	80
Milestone, Sask.	G3	75
Miletus, hist., Tur.	D6	25
Milevsko, Czech.	D9	19
Miley, S.C., U.S.	F5	117
Milfay, Ok., U.S.	B5	113
Milford, Ca., U.S.	B3	82
Milford, Ct., U.S.	E3	84
Milford, De., U.S.	E4	85
Milford, Il., U.S.	C6	90
Milford, In., U.S.	B6	91
Milford, Ia., U.S.	A2	92
Milford, Ks., U.S.	C7	93
Milford, Ky., U.S.	B5	94
Milford, Me., U.S.	D4	96
Milford, Ma., U.S.	B4	98
Milford, Mi., U.S.	F7	99
Milford, Mo., U.S.	D3	102
Milford, Ne., U.S.	D8	104
Milford, N.H., U.S.	E3	106
Milford, N.J., U.S.	B2	107
Milford, N.Y., U.S.	C6	109
Milford, Oh., U.S.	C1	112
Milford, Pa., U.S.	D12	115
Milford, Ut., U.S.	E2	121
Milford, Va., U.S.	B5	123
Milford Center, Oh., U.S.	B2	112
Milford Haven, Wales, U.K.	E4	10
Milford Lake, res., Ks., U.S.	C6	93
Milford Sound, strt., N.Z.	P11	51
Milford Station, N.S.	D6	71
Milh, Ra's al, c., Libya	F5	40
Milicz, Pol.	C4	26
Mililani Town, Hi., U.S.	g9	88
Miling, Austl.	F2	50
Milk, stm., N.A.	B8	103
Milk Creek, stm., Co., U.S.	A3	83
Milk River, Alta.	E4	68
Milk River Ridge Reservoir, res., Alta.	E4	68
Milladore, Wi., U.S.	D4	126
Millard, Mo., U.S.	A5	102
Millard, co., Ut., U.S.	D2	121
Millars Sound, strt., Bah.	n17	64
Millarton, N.D., U.S.	C7	111
Millau, Fr.	E5	16
Millbank, Ont.	D4	73
Millboro, S.D., U.S.	D6	118
Millboro, Va., U.S.	C3	123
Millbrae, Ca., U.S.	h8	82
Millbridge, Ont.	C7	73
Millbrook, Ont.	C6	73
Millbrook, Al., U.S.	C3	78
Millbrook, Mi., U.S.	E5	99
Millbrook, N.Y., U.S.	D7	109
Mill Brook, stm., Vt., U.S.	B5	122
Millbury, Ma., U.S.	B4	98
Millbury, Oh., U.S.	e7	112
Mill City, Nv., U.S.	C3	105
Mill City, Or., U.S.	C4	114
Mill City, Pa., U.S.	m17	115
Millcreek, Il., U.S.	F4	90
Millcreek, In., U.S.	A4	91
Mill Creek, In., U.S.	A4	91
Mill Creek, Mo., U.S.	D7	102
Mill Creek, Ok., U.S.	C5	113
Mill Creek, Pa., U.S.	F6	115
Mill Creek, Ut., U.S.	C4	121
Mill Creek, W.V., U.S.	C5	125
Mill Creek, stm., In., U.S.	F4	91
Mill Creek, stm., Ks., U.S.	C7	93
Mill Creek, stm., Ks., U.S.	C6	93
Mill Creek, stm., Oh., U.S.	B2	112
Mill Creek, stm., W.V., U.S.	C3	125
Mill Creek, stm., W.V., U.S.	m13	125
Millcreek Township, Pa., U.S.	B1	115
Milldale, Ct., U.S.	C4	71
Milledge, Ga., U.S.	C3	87
Milledgeville, Ga., U.S.	C3	87
Milledgeville, Il., U.S.	B4	90
Milledgeville, Tn., U.S.	B3	119
Mille Îles, Rivière des, stm., Que.	p19	74
Mille Lacs, co., Mn., U.S.	E5	100
Mille Lacs Indian Reservation, Mn., U.S.	D5	100
Mille Lacs Lake, l., Mn., U.S.	D5	100
Millen, Ga., U.S.	D5	87
Miller, Mo., U.S.	D4	102
Miller, Ne., U.S.	D6	104
Miller, Oh., U.S.	D3	112
Miller, S.D., U.S.	C7	118
Miller, co., Ar., U.S.	D2	81
Miller, co., Ga., U.S.	E2	87
Miller, co., Mo., U.S.	C5	102
Miller, Mount, mtn., Ak., U.S.	C11	79
Miller Creek, stm., De., U.S.	C6	85
Miller Dale Colony, S.D., U.S.	C6	118
Millerovo, Sov. Un.	G13	27
Miller Peak, mtn., Az., U.S.	F5	80
Miller Place, N.Y., U.S.	*n16	109
Miller Run, stm., Vt., U.S.	B4	122
Millers, stm., Ma., U.S.	A3	98
Millersburg, Ia., U.S.	C5	92
Millersburg, Ky., U.S.	B5	94
Millersburg, Mi., U.S.	C6	99
Millersburg, Oh., U.S.	B4	112
Millersburg, Pa., U.S.	E8	115
Millers Falls, Ma., U.S.	A3	98
Millers Ferry, Al., U.S.	C2	78
Millers Ferry Dam, Al., U.S.	C2	78
Millersport, Oh., U.S.	C3	112
Millersview, Tx., U.S.	D3	120
Millersville, Pa., U.S.	F9	115
Millerton, N.B.	C4	71
Millerton, Ia., U.S.	D4	92
Millerton, N.Y., U.S.	D7	109
Millerton, Ok., U.S.	D6	113
Millerton, Pa., U.S.	C8	115
Millertown, Newf.	D3	72
Millerville, Al., U.S.	B4	78
Millerville, Mn., U.S.	D3	100
Millet, Alta.	C4	68
Millett, Tx., U.S.	E3	120
Mill Grove, In., U.S.	D7	91
Mill Grove, Mo., U.S.	A4	102
Mill Hall, Pa., U.S.	D7	115
Millhousen, In., U.S.	F7	91
Milligan, Fl., U.S.	u15	86
Milligan, Ne., U.S.	D8	104
Milligan College, Tn., U.S.	C11	119
Milliken, Co., U.S.	A6	83
Millington, Mi., U.S.	E7	99
Millington, Md., U.S.	B6	97
Millington, N.J., U.S.	B4	107
Millington, Tn., U.S.	B2	119
Millinocket, Me., U.S.	C4	96
Millinocket Lake, l., Me., U.S.	B4	96
Millinocket Lake, l., Me., U.S.	C4	96

Name	Map Ref.	Page
Mill Iron, Mt., U.S.	E12	103
Millis, Ma., U.S.	B5	98
Mill Island, i., Ant.	C23	7
Millmerran, Austl.	C8	51
Millom, Eng., U.K.	F5	13
Mill Point, W.V., U.S.	C4	125
Millport, Scot., U.K.	E4	13
Millport, Al., U.S.	B1	78
Millport, Pa., U.S.	C5	115
Millrift, Pa., U.S.	D12	115
Mill River, Ma., U.S.	B1	98
Mill Run, Pa., U.S.	G3	115
Millry, Al., U.S.	D1	78
Mills, Ne., U.S.	B6	104
Mills, N.M., U.S.	A5	108
Mills, Pa., U.S.	C6	115
Mills, Wy., U.S.	D6	127
Mills, co., Ia., U.S.	C2	92
Mills, co., Tx., U.S.	D3	120
Millsboro, De., U.S.	F4	85
Millsboro, Pa., U.S.	G1	115
Mill Shoals, Il., U.S.	E5	90
Mills Lake, l., N.W. Ter.	D9	66
Mill Spring, Mo., U.S.	D7	102
Millstadt, Il., U.S.	E3	90
Millston, Wi., U.S.	D3	126
Millstone, stm., N.J., U.S.	C4	107
Millstreet, Ire.	E2	11
Milltown, Al., U.S.	B4	78
Milltown, In., U.S.	H5	91
Milltown, Ky., U.S.	C4	94
Milltown, Mt., U.S.	D3	103
Milltown, N.J., U.S.	C4	107
Milltown, S.D., U.S.	D8	118
Milltown, Wi., U.S.	C1	126
Milltown [-Head of Bay d'Espoir], Newf.	E4	72
Milltown Malbay, Ire.	E2	11
Millvale, Pa., U.S.	k14	115
Mill Valley, Ca., U.S.	D2	82
Mill Village, N.S.	E5	71
Mill Village, Pa., U.S.	C2	115
Millville, N.B.	C2	71
Millville, De., U.S.	F5	85
Millville, Ky., U.S.	B5	94
Millville, Ma., U.S.	B4	98
Millville, N.J., U.S.	E2	107
Millville, Oh., U.S.	n12	112
Millville, Pa., U.S.	D9	115
Millville, Ut., U.S.	B4	121
Millville, W.V., U.S.	B7	125
Millville Lake, N.H., U.S.	E4	106
Millwood, Ga., U.S.	E4	87
Millwood, Oh., U.S.	B3	112
Millwood, Va., U.S.	A4	123
Millwood, Wa., U.S.	g14	124
Millwood Lake, res., Ar., U.S.	D1	81
Milmay, N.J., U.S.	E3	107
Milner, B.C.	f13	69
Milner, Co., U.S.	A3	83
Milner, Ga., U.S.	C2	87
Milner Dam, Id., U.S.	G5	89
Milner Ridge, Man.	D3	70
Milnesand, N.M., U.S.	D6	108
Milnor, N.D., U.S.	C8	111
Milo, Alta.	D4	68
Milo, Ia., U.S.	C4	92
Milo, Me., U.S.	C4	96
Milo, Mo., U.S.	D3	102
Milo, Or., U.S.	E3	114
Mililoli, Hi., U.S.	D6	88
Milos, i., Grc.	D5	40
Milparinka, Austl.	D3	51
Milpitas, Ca., U.S.	*k9	82
Milroy, In., U.S.	F7	91
Milroy, Mn., U.S.	F3	100
Milroy, Pa., U.S.	E6	115
Milstead, Al., U.S.	C4	78
Milstead, Ga., U.S.	C3	87
Miltenberg, W. Ger.	D4	19
Milton, N.S.	E5	71
Milton, Ont.	D5	73
Milton, N.Z.	Q12	51
Milton, Ct., U.S.	B2	84
Milton, De., U.S.	E4	85
Milton, Fl., U.S.	u14	86
Milton, Il., U.S.	D3	90
Milton, In., U.S.	E7	91
Milton, Ia., U.S.	D5	92
Milton, Ks., U.S.	E6	93
Milton, Ky., U.S.	B4	94
Milton, La., U.S.	D3	95
Milton, Ma., U.S.	B5	98
Milton, N.H., U.S.	D5	106
Milton, N.Y., U.S.	D7	109
Milton, N.C., U.S.	A3	110
Milton, N.D., U.S.	A7	111
Milton, Pa., U.S.	D8	115
Milton, Vt., U.S.	B2	122
Milton, Wa., U.S.	f11	124
Milton, W.V., U.S.	C2	125
Milton, Wi., U.S.	F5	126
Milton, Lake, l., Oh., U.S.	A4	112
Miltona, Mn., U.S.	D3	100
Miltona, Lake, l., Mn., U.S.	D3	100
Milton-Freewater, Or., U.S.	B8	114
Milton Keynes, Eng., U.K.	B7	12
Milton Mills, N.H., U.S.	C5	106
Milton Reservoir, res., Co., U.S.	A6	83
Miltonvale, Ks., U.S.	C6	93
Milverton, Ont.	D4	73
Milwaukee, N.C., U.S.	A5	110
Milwaukee, Wi., U.S.	E6	126
Milwaukee, co., Wi., U.S.	E6	126
Milwaukee, stm., Wi., U.S.	m12	126
Milwaukie, Or., U.S.	B4	114
Mimbres, N.M., U.S.	E2	108
Mimbres Mountains, mts., N.M., U.S.	E2	108
Mimico (part of Etobicoke), Ont.	m15	73
Mimizan, Fr.	E3	16
Mimoň, Czech.	C9	19
Mimongo, Gabon	F2	46
Mimosa Park, La., U.S.	*E5	95
Mims, Fl., U.S.	D6	86
Mina, Nv., U.S.	E3	105
Mina, S.D., U.S.	B7	118
Minā' al Aḥmadi, Kuw.	C4	38
Mīnāb, Iran	H8	39
Minago, stm., Man.	B2	70
Minaki, Ont.	E4	70
Minamata, Japan	J5	33
Minami-iwo, i., Japan	E8	6
Minami-Tori Island, i., Japan	E9	6
Minas, Cuba	D5	64
Minas, Ur.	E1	56
Minas Basin, b., N.S.	D5	71
Minas Channel, strt., N.S.	D5	71
Minas de Corrales, Ur.	E1	56
Minas de Oro, Hond.	C4	62
Minas de Ríotinto, Spain	D2	22
Minas Gerais, state, Braz.	B4	56
Minas Novas, Braz.	B4	56
Minatare, Ne., U.S.	C2	104
Minatitlán, Mex.	D6	63
Minbu, Burma	D9	36
Minburn, Alta.	C5	68
Minburn, Ia., U.S.	C3	92
Mincio, stm., Italy	D6	20
Minco, Ok., U.S.	B4	113
Mindanao, i., Phil.	D6	34
Mindel, stm., W. Ger.	A6	20
Mindelheim, W. Ger.	A6	20
Mindemoya, Ont.	B2	73
Minden, Ont.	C6	73
Minden, W. Ger.	B4	18
Minden, La., U.S.	B2	95
Minden, Ne., U.S.	D7	104
Minden, Nv., U.S.	E2	105
Minden City, Mi., U.S.	E8	99
Mindenmines, Mo., U.S.	D3	102
Mindi, Pan.	k11	62
Mindoro, i., Phil.	C6	34
Mindoro, Wi., U.S.	D2	126
Mindoro Strait, strt., Phil.	C6	34
Mine Centre, Ont.	E5	70
Minechoag Mountain, hill, Ma., U.S.	B3	98
Minehead, Eng., U.K.	E5	10
Mine Head, c., Ire.	F4	11
Mine Hill, N.J., U.S.	B3	107
Mineiros, Braz.	B2	56
Mine La Motte, Mo., U.S.	D7	102
Mineola, N.Y., U.S.	E7	109
Mineola, Tx., U.S.	C5	120
Miner, Mo., U.S.	E8	102
Miner, co., S.D., U.S.	D8	118
Mineral, Ca., U.S.	B3	82
Mineral, Il., U.S.	B4	90
Mineral, Va., U.S.	B5	123
Mineral, Wa., U.S.	C3	124
Mineral, co., Co., U.S.	D4	83
Mineral, co., Mt., U.S.	C1	103
Mineral, co., Nv., U.S.	E3	105
Mineral, co., W.V., U.S.	B6	125
Mineral City, Oh., U.S.	B4	112
Mineral del Monte, Mex.	m14	63
Mineral del Oro, Mex.	n13	63
Mineral Hills, Mi., U.S.	B2	99
Mineral Mountains, mts., Ut., U.S.	E3	121
Mineral Park, Tn., U.S.	h11	119
Mineral Point, Mo., U.S.	D7	102
Mineral Point, Wi., U.S.	F3	126
Mineral Springs, Ar., U.S.	D2	81
Mineral Wells, Ms., U.S.	A4	101
Mineral Wells, Tx., U.S.	C3	120
Minersville, Oh., U.S.	C4	112
Minersville, Pa., U.S.	E9	115
Minersville, Ut., U.S.	E3	121
Minerva, N.Y., U.S.	B7	109
Minerva, Oh., U.S.	B4	112
Minervino Murge, Italy	D6	23
Minetto, N.Y., U.S.	B4	109
Mineville, N.Y., U.S.	A7	109
Mingan, Que.	h8	72
Mingechaur, Sov. Un.	G18	8
Mingechaur Reservoir, res., Sov. Un.	E3	28
Mingenew, Austl.	E2	50
Mingo, Ia., U.S.	C4	92
Mingo, co., W.V., U.S.	D2	125
Mingo Junction, Oh., U.S.	B5	112
Mingoyo, Tan.	D6	48
Mingshui, China	C4	31
Mingshui, China	C2	33
Minho (Miño), stm., Eur.	B1	22
Minicoy Island, i., India	G5	36
Minidoka, Id., U.S.	G5	89
Minidoka, co., Id., U.S.	G5	89
Minidoka Dam, Id., U.S.	G5	89
Minier, Il., U.S.	C4	90
Miniota, Man.	D1	70
Minipi Lake, l., Newf.	h9	72
Minisink Island, i., N.J., U.S.	A3	107
Minitonas, Man.	C1	70
Minna, Nig.	E6	45
Minna Bluff, pen., Ant.	B29	7
Minneapolis, Ks., U.S.	C6	93
Minneapolis, Mn., U.S.	F5	100
Minneapolis, N.C., U.S.	e11	110
Minnedosa, Man.	D2	70
Minnedosa, stm., Man.	D1	70
Minnehaha, co., S.D., U.S.	D9	118
Minneola, Ks., U.S.	E3	93
Minneola, Mn., U.S.	F7	100
Minneota, Mn., U.S.	F3	100
Minnesota, state, U.S.	E4	100
Minnesota, stm., Mn., U.S.	F2	100
Minnesota Lake, Mn., U.S.	G5	100
Minnetonka, Mn., U.S.	n12	100
Minnetonka, Lake, l., Mn., U.S.	n11	100
Minnewanka, Lake, l., Alta.	D3	68
Minnewaska, Lake, l., Mn., U.S.	E3	100
Minnewaukan, N.D., U.S.	A6	111
Mino, Japan	n15	33
Miño (Minho), stm., Eur.	A1	22
Minocqua, Wi., U.S.	C4	126
Minokamo, Japan	n15	33
Minong, Wi., U.S.	B2	126
Minonk, Il., U.S.	C4	90
Minooka, Il., U.S.	B5	90
Minor Hill, Tn., U.S.	B4	119
Minot, Ma., U.S.	h12	98
Minot, N.D., U.S.	A4	111
Minot Air Force Base, mil., N.D., U.S.	A4	111
Minqin, China	D5	31
Minquadale, De., U.S.	i7	85
Minsen, W. Ger.	A7	17
Minsk, Sov. Un.	D5	29
Minsk Mazowiecki, Pol.	B6	26
Minster, Oh., U.S.	B1	112
Minter, Al., U.S.	C2	78
Minter City, Ms., U.S.	B3	101
Mint Hill, N.C., U.S.	B2	110
Minto, Man.	E1	70
Minto, N.B.	C3	71
Minto, Ak., U.S.	C10	79
Minto, N.D., U.S.	A8	111
Minto, Lac, l., Que.	g11	74
Minton, Sask.	H3	75
Minturn, Co., U.S.	B4	83
Minturn, S.C., U.S.	B8	117
Minturn, Me., U.S.	D4	96
Minturno, Italy	D4	23
Minūf, Eg.	D2	41
Minusinsk, Sov. Un.	D12	29
Minute Man National Historical Park, Ma., U.S.	g10	98
Minvoul, Gabon	E2	46
Minyā al Qamḥ, Eg.	D3	41
Minya Konka see Gongga Mountain, mtn., China	F5	31
Mio, Mi., U.S.	D6	99
Miquelon, i., St. P./M.	E3	72
Mira, Port.	B1	22
Mira, La., U.S.	B2	95
Mira, stm., Port.	D1	22
Mira, stm., S.A.	A2	58
Mirabel, Que.	D3	74
Miracema do Norte, Braz.	C5	59
Miracle Hot Springs, Ca., U.S.	E4	82
Mirador, Braz.	C2	57
Miraflores, Col.	C3	60
Miraflores, Peru	*D2	58
Miraflores Locks, Pan.	m11	62
Miragoâne, Haiti	E7	64
Mira Gut, N.S.	C10	71
Miraí, Braz.	g6	56
Miraj, India	E5	36
Mira Loma, Ca., U.S.	*m13	82
Miramar, Arg.	B5	54
Miramar, Fl., U.S.	s13	86
Miramar Naval Air Station, mil., Ca., U.S.	F5	82
Miramichi Bay, b., N.B.	B5	71
Miranda, Braz.	C1	56
Miranda, Col.	C2	60
Miranda, S.D., U.S.	C7	118
Miranda, state, Ven.	A4	60
Miranda, stm., Braz.	C1	56
Miranda de Ebro, Spain	A4	22
Miranda do Douro, Port.	B2	22
Mirande, Fr.	F4	16
Mirandela, Port.	B2	22
Miranda City, Tx., U.S.	F3	120
Mirandola, Italy	E7	20
Mirassol, Braz.	C3	56
Miravalles, Volcán, vol., C.R.	E5	62
Mirbāṭ, Oman	D5	38
Mirebalais, Haiti	E7	64
Mirecourt, Fr.	C7	16
Mirepoix, Fr.	F4	16
Mirgorod, Sov. Un.	G9	27
Miri, Malay.	E4	34
Miriam Vale, Austl.	D9	51
Mirim, Lagoa, b., S.A.	E2	56
Mirina, Grc.	C5	40
Mirond Lake, l., Sask.	B4	75
Mirow, E. Ger.	E6	15
Mīrpur, Bngl.	*D9	36
Mīrpur Khās, Pak.	C4	36
Mirror, Alta.	C4	68
Mirror Lake, N.H., U.S.	C4	106
Mirror Lake, l., N.H., U.S.	C4	106
Mirzāpur, India	C7	36
Misāḥah, Bi'r, well, Eg.	E5	43
Misakubo, Japan	n16	33
Misantla, Mex.	D5	63
Misburg, W. Ger.	A4	19
Miscoe Hill, hill, Ma., U.S.	h9	98
Miscou Centre, N.B.	B5	71
Miscouche, P.E.I.	C6	71
Miscou Island, i., N.B.	A5	71
Miscou Point, c., N.B.	A5	71
Misenheimer, N.C., U.S.	B2	110
Mishan, China	D6	33
Mishawaka, In., U.S.	A5	91
Misheguk Mountain, mtn., Ak., U.S.	B7	79
Mishicot, Wi., U.S.	D6	126
Mishima, Japan	I9	33
Misiones, prov., Arg.	B5	55
Misiones, dept., Para.	E4	55
Miskitos, Cayos, is., Nic.	E8	63
Miskolc, Hung.	B4	24
Mismār, Sud.	B4	47
Misool, i., Indon.	F7	34
Mispillion, stm., De., U.S.	E4	85
Misquamicut, R.I., U.S.	G1	116
Miṣr al Jadīdah (Heliopolis) (part of Cairo), Eg.	D3	41
Miṣrātah, Libya	C3	43
Missaukee, co., Mi., U.S.	D5	99
Missaukee, Lake, l., Mi., U.S.	D5	99
Missinaibi, stm., Ont.	G16	66
Mission, Ks., U.S.	m16	93
Mission, S.D., U.S.	D5	118
Mission, Tx., U.S.	F3	120
Mission City, B.C.	E6	69
Mission Hills, S.D., U.S.	E8	118
Mission Hills, Ks., U.S.	*k16	93
Mission Mountain, mtn., Ok., U.S.	A7	115
Mission Range, mts., Mt., U.S.	C3	103
Mission Ridge, S.D., U.S.	C5	118
Mission Viejo, Ca., U.S.	n13	82
Missispuskiow, stm., Sask.	D4	75
Missisquoi, co., Que.	D4	74
Missisquoi, stm., Vt., U.S.	B3	122
Missisquoi Bay, b., Vt., U.S.	A2	122
Mississauga, Ont.	D5	73
Mississinewa, stm., U.S.	D7	91
Mississinewa Lake, res., In., U.S.	C6	91
Mississippi, co., Ar., U.S.	B5	81
Mississippi, co., Mo., U.S.	E8	102
Mississippi, state, U.S.	C4	101
Mississippi, stm., U.S.	D9	76
Mississippi Delta, La., U.S.	E6	95
Mississippi Lake, l., Ont.	B8	73
Mississippi Sound, strt., U.S.	E5	101
Mississippi State, Ms., U.S.	B5	101
Missoula, Mt., U.S.	D2	103
Missoula, co., Mt., U.S.	D2	103
Missouri, Mor.	C4	44
Missouri, state, U.S.	C5	102
Missouri, stm., U.S.	B8	76
Missouri Buttes, mtn., Wy., U.S.	B8	127
Missouri City, Mo., U.S.	h11	102
Missouri City, Tx., U.S.	r14	120
Missouri Valley, Ia., U.S.	C2	92
Mistake Point, c., Newf.	E5	72
Mistassini, Que.	h12	74
Mistassini, Lac, l., Que.	h12	74
Mistastin Lake, l., Newf.	g9	72
Mistatim, Sask.	E4	75
Mistelbach [an der Zaya], Aus.	D8	18
Misti, Volcán, vol., Peru	E3	58
Mistretta, Italy	F5	23
Mita, Punta, c., Mex.	D3	63
Mitaka, Japan	*I9	33
Mitake, Japan	I8	33
Mitcham, Austl.	*F6	50
Mitchell, Austl.	D8	51
Mitchell, Ont.	D3	73
Mitchell, Il., U.S.	E3	90
Mitchell, In., U.S.	G5	91
Mitchell, Ia., U.S.	A5	92
Mitchell, La., U.S.	C2	95
Mitchell, Ne., U.S.	C2	104
Mitchell, Or., U.S.	C6	114
Mitchell, S.D., U.S.	D7	118
Mitchell, co., Ga., U.S.	E2	87
Mitchell, co., Ia., U.S.	A5	92
Mitchell, co., Ks., U.S.	C5	93
Mitchell, co., N.C., U.S.	e10	110
Mitchell, co., Tx., U.S.	C2	120
Mitchell, stm., Austl.	C7	50
Mitchell, Lake, l., Mi., U.S.	D5	99
Mitchell, Lake, res., Al., U.S.	C3	78
Mitchell, Mount, mtn., N.C., U.S.	f10	110
Mitchell Island, i., La., U.S.	E6	95
Mitchellsburg, Ky., U.S.	C5	94
Mitchellville, Ia., U.S.	C4	92
Mitchelstown, Ire.	D2	11
Mit Fāris, Eg.	C3	41
Mit Ghamr, Eg.	D3	41
Mithapur, India	D4	36
Mitilíni, Grc.	C6	40
Mitishto, stm., Man.	B2	70
Mitkof Island, i., Ak., U.S.	m23	79
Mitla Pass, Eg.	E4	41
Mito, Japan	H10	33
Mitra do Bispo, mtn., Braz.	h5	56
Mitre, mtn., N.Z.	N15	51
Mitry-Mory, Fr.	E2	17
Mitsinjo, Madag.	g9	49
Mittelland Canal, Eur.	B5	18
Mittenwald, W. Ger.	B7	20
Mittersill, Aus.	B8	20
Mitterteich, W. Ger.	B6	20
Mittweida, E. Ger.	C6	18
Mītū, Col.	C3	60
Mituruba, Monts, mts., Zaire	C4	48
Mitwaba, Zaire	C5	48
Mitzic, Gabon	E2	46
Miura, Japan	n18	33
Mixquiahuala, Mex.	m14	63
Mixteco, stm., Mex.	o14	63
Miyagi Island, i., Japan	O5	52
Miyake Island, i., Japan	I9	33
Miyako, Japan	G10	33
Miyakonojō, Japan	K5	33
Miyazaki, Japan	K5	33
Miyoshi, Japan	n14	33
Mizdah, Libya	C2	43
Mize, Ms., U.S.	D4	101
Mizen Head, c., Ire.	F2	11
Mizil, Rom.	C8	24
Mizoram, state, India	D9	36
Mizpah, Mn., U.S.	C4	100
Mizpah, N.J., U.S.	E3	107
Mizpah, stm., Mt., U.S.	E11	103
Mizpé Ramon, Isr.	G10	40
Mizque, Bol.	C2	55
Mjölby, Swe.	H6	14
Mjøsa, l., Nor.	G4	14
Mkalama, Tan.	B5	48
Mladá Boleslav, Czech.	C3	26
Mława, Pol.	B6	26
Mljet, i., Yugo.	C2	24
Mnichovo Hradiště, Czech.	C9	19
Mnyusi, Tan.	C6	48
Mo, Nor.	D6	14
Moa, i., Austl.	B7	50
Moab, Ut., U.S.	E6	121
Moala Island, i., Fiji	I15	52
Moamba, Moz.	C5	49
Moanda, Gabon	F2	46
Moapa, Nv., U.S.	G7	105
Moapa River Indian Reservation, Nv., U.S.	G7	105
Moar Lake, l., Can.	A5	70
Moate, Ire.	D4	11
Moba, Zaire	C4	48
Mobaye, Cen. Afr. Rep.	E4	46
Mobayi-Mbongo, Zaire	A3	48
Mobeetie, Tx., U.S.	B2	120
Moberly, Mo., U.S.	B5	102
Moberly, Lake, B.C.	B7	69
Moberly Lake, l., B.C.	B7	69
Mobile, Al., U.S.	E1	78
Mobile, Az., U.S.	D3	80
Mobile, co., Al., U.S.	E1	78
Mobile, stm., Al., U.S.	E1	78
Mobile Bay, b., Al., U.S.	E1	78
Mobridge, S.D., U.S.	B5	118
Mobula, Zaire	A4	48
Moca, Dom. Rep.	E8	64
Mocajuba, Braz.	C5	59
Moçambique, Moz.	D7	48
Mocanaqua, Pa., U.S.	D9	115
Moccasin, Az., U.S.	A3	80
Moccasin, Mt., U.S.	C7	103
Mocha, i., Chile	B2	54
Moc Hoa, Viet.	G6	35
Mocho Mountains, mts., Jam.	E14	65
Mochudi, Bots.	B4	49
Mocímboa da Praia, Moz.	D7	48
Möckeln, l., Swe.	B8	15
Mocksville, N.C., U.S.	B2	110
Moclips, Wa., U.S.	B1	124
Môco, Serra, mtn., Ang.	D2	48
Mocoa, Col.	C2	60
Mococa, Braz.	C5	56
Mocorito, Mex.	B3	63
Moctezuma, Mex.	B3	63
Moctezuma, stm., Mex.	m14	63
Mocuba, Moz.	A6	49
Mocúbúri, Moz.	D6	48
Modale, Ia., U.S.	C2	92
Modane, Fr.	D2	20
Model, Co., U.S.	D6	83
Model Reservoir, res., Co., U.S.	D6	83
Modena, Italy	E6	23
Modena, Mo., U.S.	A4	102
Modena, N.Y., U.S.	D6	109
Modena, Ut., U.S.	F2	121
Modena, Wi., U.S.	D2	126
Modesto, Ca., U.S.	D3	82
Modesto, Il., U.S.	D4	90
Modica, Italy	F5	23
Modigliana, Italy	E6	23
Mödling, Aus.	D8	18
Modoc, In., U.S.	D7	91
Modoc, co., Ca., U.S.	B3	82
Modoc Point, Or., U.S.	E5	114
Modřany, Czech.	o17	26
Moe, Austl.	G8	50
Moehau, mtn., N.Z.	L15	51
Moen, i., Micron.	Q18	52
Moenave, Az., U.S.	A4	80
Moengo, Sur.	A4	59
Moenkopi, Az., U.S.	A4	80
Moenkopi Plateau, plat., Az., U.S.	B4	80
Moenkopi Wash, val., Az., U.S.	A5	80
Moerbeke, Bel.	C3	17
Moers, W. Ger.	B1	19
Moesa, stm., Switz.	D7	21
Moeskroen see Mouscron, Bel.	B5	16
Moffat, Scot., U.K.	E5	13
Moffat, co., Co., U.S.	A2	83
Moffat Tunnel, Co., U.S.	B5	83
Moffett, Ok., U.S.	B7	113
Moffett Field Naval Air Station, mil., Ca., U.S.	k8	82
Moffit, N.D., U.S.	C5	111
Moga, Zaire	B4	48
Mogadishu (Muqdisho), Som.	E6	47
Mogadore, Oh., U.S.	A4	112
Mogaung, Burma	C10	36
Mogi das Cruzes, Braz.	C3	56
Mogilev, Sov. Un.	D6	29
Mogilev-Podolskiy, Sov. Un.	G6	27
Mogilno, Pol.	B4	26
Mogi-Mirim, Braz.	C3	56
Mogincual, Moz.	A7	49
Mogocha, Sov. Un.	D14	29
Mogochin, Sov. Un.	B10	28
Mogok, Burma	D10	36
Mogollon, N.M., U.S.	D1	108
Mogollon Mesa, mtn., Az., U.S.	C4	80
Mogollon Mountains, mts., N.M., U.S.	D1	108
Mogollon Rim, clf., Az., U.S.	C5	80
Mogotes, Punta, c., Arg.	B5	54
Moguer, Spain	D2	22
Mohács, Hung.	C4	24
Mohale's Hoek, Leso.	D4	49
Mohall, N.D., U.S.	A4	111
Mohammedia, Mor.	C3	44
Mohave, co., Az., U.S.	B1	80
Mohave, Lake, res., U.S.	H7	105
Mohave Mountains, mts., Az., U.S.	C1	80
Mohave Valley, Az., U.S.	C1	80
Mohawk, Mi., U.S.	A2	99
Mohawk, N.Y., U.S.	C5	109
Mohawk, stm., N.H., U.S.	g7	106
Mohawk, stm., N.Y., U.S.	C6	109
Mohawk Lake, l., N.J., U.S.	A3	107
Mohawk Mountain, mtn., Ct., U.S.	B2	84
Mohawk Mountains, mts., Az., U.S.	E2	80
Mohe, China	A9	31
Mohegan, Ct., U.S.	D7	84
Mohegan, R.I., U.S.	B2	116
Mohican, Black Fork, stm., Oh., U.S.	B3	112
Mohican, Clear Fork, stm., Oh., U.S.	B3	112
Mohill, Ire.	D4	11
Mohler, Wa., U.S.	B7	124
Mohnton, Pa., U.S.	F10	115
Mohoro, Tan.	C6	48
Moiese, Mt., U.S.	C2	103
Moineşti, Rom.	B8	24
Moinkum Desert, des., Sov. Un.	E8	28
Moira, N.Y., U.S.	f10	109
Moisie, Que.	h8	72
Moisie, stm., Que.	h8	72
Moissac, Fr.	E4	16
Moïssala, Chad	D3	46
Moita, Port.	f10	22
Mojave, Ca., U.S.	E4	82
Mojave, stm., Ca., U.S.	E5	82
Mojave Desert, des., Ca., U.S.	E5	82
Moji-Guaçu, stm., Braz.	k8	56
Mojo, Eth.	D4	47
Mojokerto, Indon.	*G4	34
Mokāma, India	E10	37
Mokane, Mo., U.S.	C6	102
Mokapu, Hi., U.S.	*B4	88
Mokapu Peninsula, pen., Hi., U.S.	g10	88
Mokapu Point, c., Hi., U.S.	g11	88
Mokelumne, stm., Ca., U.S.	C3	82
Mokelumne Hill, Ca., U.S.	C3	82
Mokena, Il., U.S.	k9	90
Mokhotlong, Leso.	C4	49
Mokochu, mtn., Thai.	E3	35
Mokolo, Cam.	C2	46
Mokp'o, S. Kor.	E10	31
Moksha, stm., Sov. Un.	D14	27
Mol, Bel.	C6	17
Mol, Yugo.	C5	24
Mola [di Bari], Italy	D6	23
Molalla, Or., U.S.	B4	114
Molanosa, Sask.	C3	75
Molat, i., Yugo.	C2	24
Moldau see Vltava, stm., Czech.	D3	26
Moldavia, state, Sov. Un.	E5	29
Moldavia, hist. reg., Rom.	B8	24
Molde, Nor.	F2	14
Moldova, stm., Rom.	B8	24
Moldoveanu, mtn., Rom.	C7	24
Molega Lake, l., N.S.	E5	71
Molena, Ga., U.S.	C2	87
Molenbeek-Saint Jean, Bel.	*D4	17
Molepolole, Bots.	B6	109
Molfetta, Italy	D6	23
Molina, Chile	B2	54
Molina de Aragón, Spain	B5	22
Molina de Segura, Spain	C5	22
Moline, Il., U.S.	B3	90
Moline, Ks., U.S.	E7	93
Moline, Mi., U.S.	F5	99
Moline, Oh., U.S.	e6	112
Molinella, Italy	E7	20
Molino, Fl., U.S.	u14	86
Molino de Rosas (part of Mexico City), Mex.	h9	63
Molinos, Arg.	B2	55
Moliro, Zaire	C5	48
Molise, prov., Italy	D5	23
Moliterno, Italy	D5	23
Möll, stm., Aus.	C9	20
Mölle, Swe.	B6	15
Mollendo, Peru	E3	58
Mollusk, Va., U.S.	C6	123
Mölndal, Swe.	I4	14
Molochansk, Sov. Un.	H10	27
Molodechno, Sov. Un.	D6	27
Molokai, i., Hi., U.S.	B5	88
Molokini, i., Hi., U.S.	C5	88
Molopo, stm., Afr.	C3	49
Moloundou, Cam.	E3	46
Molsheim, Fr.	F7	17
Molson, Man.	D3	70
Molson, Wa., U.S.	A6	124
Molson, stm., Man.	C3	70
Molson Lake, l., Man.	B3	70
Molt, Mt., U.S.	E8	103
Molteno, S. Afr.	D4	49
Moluccas (Maluku), is., Indon.	F7	34
Molucca Sea, Indon.	E7	34
Molus, Ky., U.S.	D6	94
Moma, Moz.	A6	49
Mombasa, Kenya	B6	48
Mombetsu, Japan	D11	33
Mombongo, Zaire	A3	48
Momchilgrad, Bul.	E7	24
Momence, Il., U.S.	B6	90
Momi, Japan	H14	52
Momostenango, Guat.	C2	62
Mompog Pass, strt., Phil.	p14	34
Mompono, Zaire	B3	60
Mompós, Col.	B3	60
Møn, i., Den.	I9	14
Mona, Ut., U.S.	D4	121
Mona, Isla de, i., P.R.	G11	64
Mona, Punta, c., C.R.	F6	62
Monaca, Pa., U.S.	E1	115
Monaco, ctry., Eur.	F7	16
Monadhliath Mountains, mts., Scot., U.K.	C4	13
Monadnock, Mount, mtn., N.H., U.S.	E2	106
Monadnock Mountain, mtn., Vt., U.S.	B5	122
Monagas, state, Ven.	C5	60
Monaghan, Ire.	C5	11
Monaghan, co., Ire.	C5	11
Monahans, Tx., U.S.	D1	120
Monamolin, Ire.	E5	11
Monango, N.D., U.S.	C7	111
Mona Passage, strt., N.A.	E10	64
Monarch, Alta.	E4	68
Monarch, Mt., U.S.	C5	103
Monarch Mills, S.C., U.S.	B4	117
Monarch Mountain, mtn., B.C.	D5	69
Monarch Pass, Co., U.S.	C4	83
Monashee Mountains, mts., B.C.	D8	69
Monastir, Tun.	B7	44
Monastyrshchina, Sov. Un.	D8	27
Monavatu, mtn., Fiji	H14	52
Moncalieri, Italy	B1	23
Monção, Braz.	B1	57
Monção, Port.	B1	22
Moncey, Fr.	B1	23
Monchegorsk, Sov. Un.	D15	14
Monchique, Port.	D1	22
Mönchengladbach, W. Ger.	C3	18
Monchique, Serra de, mts., Port.	D1	22
Moncks Corner, S.C., U.S.	E7	117
Monclova, Mex.	B4	63
Monclova, Oh., U.S.	e6	112
Moncton, N.B.	C5	71
Moncure, N.C., U.S.	B3	110
Mondamin, Ia., U.S.	C1	92
Mondego, stm., Port.	B1	22
Mondego, Cabo, c., Port.	B1	22
Mond Lake, l., Ont.	A2	73
Mondoñedo, Spain	A2	22
Mondorf-les-Bains, Lux.	E6	17
Mondoví, Italy	B1	23
Mondovi, Wi., U.S.	D2	126
Monee, Il., U.S.	B6	90
Monessen, Pa., U.S.	F2	115
Moneta, Va., U.S.	C3	123
Monett, Mo., U.S.	E4	102
Monetta, S.C., U.S.	D4	117
Monette, Ar., U.S.	B5	81
Money, Ms., U.S.	B3	101
Moneymore, N. Ire., U.K.	C5	11
Monfalcone, Italy	B4	23
Monforte de Lemos, Spain	A2	22
Monfort Heights, Oh., U.S.	o12	112
Monga, Zaire	A3	48
Mongaguá, Braz.	n8	56
Mongala, stm., Zaire	A3	48
Mongala, Sud.	D3	47
Mong Hsat, Burma	B3	35
Möng Mit, Burma	D10	36
Mongo, Chad	D3	46
Mongo, stm., Afr.	A7	91
Mongolia, ctry., Asia	B5	31
Mongolia, Plateau of, plat., Mong.	B6	31
Möng Pan, Burma	B3	35
Möng Yai, Burma	A2	35
Monhegan Island, i., Me., U.S.	E3	96
Mönh Hayrhan Mountain, mtn., Mong.	B4	31
Moniac, Ga., U.S.	F4	87
Moniave, Scot., U.K.	E5	13
Monico, Wi., U.S.	C4	126
Monida Pass, U.S.	E6	89
Monie, Md., U.S.	D6	97
Moninabad see Ambājogai, India	H6	37
Moniteau, co., Mo., U.S.	C5	102
Monitor, Alta.	D6	68
Monitor, Or., U.S.	h12	114
Monitor Range, mts., Nv., U.S.	E5	105
Monitor Valley, val., Nv., U.S.	D3	11
Monivea, Ire.	D3	11
Monkey Point, c., Nic.	B3	62
Monkey River, Belize	B3	62
Monkira, Austl.	B3	48
Monkoto, Zaire	B3	48
Monkton, Vt., U.S.	C2	122
Mon Louis, Al., U.S.	E1	78
Monmouth, Wales, U.K.	C5	12
Monmouth, Il., U.S.	C3	90
Monmouth, Ia., U.S.	B7	92
Monmouth, Me., U.S.	D2	96

Name	Map Ref.	Page
Monmouth, Or., U.S.	C3	114
Monmouth, co., N.J., U.S.	C4	107
Monmouth Beach, N.J., U.S.	C5	107
Monmouth Junction, N.J., U.S.	C3	107
Monmouth Mountain, mtn., B.C.	D6	69
Monnickendam, Neth.	B5	17
Monnow, stm., U.K.	C5	12
Mono, co., Ca., U.S.	D4	82
Monocacy, stm., Md., U.S.	B3	97
Mono Lake, l., Ca., U.S.	D4	82
Monomonac, Lake, l., U.S.	E3	106
Monomoy Island, i., Ma., U.S.	C7	98
Monomoy Point, c., Ma., U.S.	C7	98
Monon, In., U.S.	C4	91
Monona, Ia., U.S.	A6	92
Monona, Wi., U.S.	E4	126
Monona, co., Ia., U.S.	B1	92
Monona, Lake, l., Wi., U.S.	E4	126
Monongah, W.V., U.S.	B4	125
Monongahela, Pa., U.S.	F2	115
Monongahela, stm., U.S.	G2	115
Monongalia, co., W.V., U.S.	B4	125
Monopoli, Italy	D6	23
Monor, Hung.	B4	24
Monos Island, i., Trin.	N22	65
Monóvar, Spain	C5	22
Monoville, Tn., U.S.	C8	119
Monowi, Ne., U.S.	B7	104
Monowice, Pol.	g10	26
Monponsett, Ma., U.S.	B6	98
Monreale, Italy	E4	23
Monroe, Ar., U.S.	C4	81
Monroe, Ct., U.S.	D3	84
Monroe, Ga., U.S.	C3	87
Monroe, In., U.S.	C8	91
Monroe, Ia., U.S.	C4	92
Monroe, La., U.S.	B3	95
Monroe, Me., U.S.	D3	96
Monroe, Ne., U.S.	C8	104
Monroe, N.H., U.S.	B2	106
Monroe, N.J., U.S.	A3	107
Monroe, N.Y., U.S.	D6	109
Monroe, N.C., U.S.	C2	110
Monroe, Oh., U.S.	C1	112
Monroe, Ok., U.S.	C7	113
Monroe, Or., U.S.	C3	114
Monroe, S.D., U.S.	D8	118
Monroe, Ut., U.S.	E3	121
Monroe, Wa., U.S.	B4	124
Monroe, Wi., U.S.	F4	126
Monroe, co., Al., U.S.	D2	78
Monroe, co., Ar., U.S.	C4	81
Monroe, co., Fl., U.S.	G5	86
Monroe, co., Ga., U.S.	D3	87
Monroe, co., Il., U.S.	E3	90
Monroe, co., In., U.S.	F4	91
Monroe, co., Ia., U.S.	D5	92
Monroe, co., Ky., U.S.	D4	94
Monroe, co., Mi., U.S.	G7	99
Monroe, co., Ms., U.S.	B5	101
Monroe, co., Mo., U.S.	B5	102
Monroe, co., N.Y., U.S.	B3	109
Monroe, co., Oh., U.S.	C4	112
Monroe, co., Pa., U.S.	D11	115
Monroe, co., Tn., U.S.	D9	119
Monroe, co., W.V., U.S.	D4	125
Monroe, co., Wi., U.S.	E3	126
Monroe Bridge, Ma., U.S.	A2	98
Monroe Center, Ct., U.S.	D3	84
Monroe Center, Il., U.S.	A5	90
Monroe City, In., U.S.	G3	91
Monroe City, Mo., U.S.	B6	102
Monroe Lake, res., In., U.S.	F5	91
Monroe Park, De., U.S.	h7	85
Monroeton, Pa., U.S.	C9	115
Monroeville, Al., U.S.	D2	78
Monroeville, In., U.S.	C8	91
Monroeville, N.J., U.S.	D2	107
Monroeville, Oh., U.S.	A3	112
Monroeville, Pa., U.S.	k14	115
Monrovia, Lib.	E2	45
Monrovia, Ca., U.S.	m13	82
Monrovia, In., U.S.	E5	91
Mons (Bergen), Bel.	B5	16
Monsaràs, Ponta do, c., Braz.	E3	57
Monschau, W. Ger.	D7	17
Monselice, Italy	D7	20
Monsey, N.Y., U.S.	*m14	109
Møns Klint, clf., Den.	D6	15
Monson, Ma., U.S.	B3	98
Monson, Me., U.S.	D3	96
Montabaur, W. Ger.	C2	19
Montagnais Point, c., Newf.	B1	72
Montagnana, Italy	D7	20
Montague, P.E.I.	C7	71
Montague, Ca., U.S.	B2	82
Montague, Ma., U.S.	B2	98
Montague, Mi., U.S.	E4	99
Montague, Tx., U.S.	C4	120
Montague, co., Tx., U.S.	C4	120
Montague Island, i., Ak., U.S.	D10	79
Montague Lake, l., Sask.	H3	75
Montague Peak, mtn., Ak., U.S.	g18	79
Montague Strait, strt., Ak., U.S.	h18	79
Montalbán, Spain	B5	22
Montalegre, Port.	B2	22
Mont Alto, Pa., U.S.	G6	115
Montalto, mtn., Italy	E5	23
Montana, Ak., U.S.	g17	79
Montana, state, U.S.	D7	103
Montana-Vermala, Switz.	D3	21
Montánchez, Spain	C2	22
Montandon, Pa., U.S.	E8	115
Montargis, Fr.	D5	16
Montataire, Fr.	C5	16
Montauban, Fr.	E4	16
Montauban-les-Mines, Que.	C5	74
Montauk, N.Y., U.S.	m17	109
Montbard, Fr.	D6	16
Montbéliard, Fr.	D7	16
Mont Belvieu, Tx., U.S.	E5	120
Montblanch, Spain	B6	22
Mont Blanc Tunnel, Eur.	D7	16
Montbozon, Fr.	B1	21
Montbrison, Fr.	E6	16
Montcalm, co., Que.	C3	74
Montcalm, co., Mi., U.S.	E5	99
Mont-Carmel, Que.	B8	74
Mont Cenis Pass, Eur.	E7	16
Montcerf, Que.	C1	74
Montchanin, Fr.	D6	16
Montchanin, De., U.S.	h7	85
Montclair, N.J., U.S.	B4	107
Mont Clare, Pa., U.S.	o19	115
Montcoal, W.V., U.S.	D3	125
Montcornet, Fr.	E3	17
Mont-de-Marsan, Fr.	F3	16
Montdidier, Fr.	C5	16
Monteagle, Tn., U.S.	D8	119
Monte Alegre, Braz.	C2	56
Monte Alegre, Braz.	B4	56
Monte Alegre de Goiás, Braz.	A3	56
Monte Azul, Braz.	B4	56
Montebello, Que.	D3	74
Montebello, Ca., U.S.	m12	82
Montebello, Va., U.S.	C3	123
Montebello Islands, is., Austl.	D2	50
Montebelluna, Italy	D8	20
Monte Carmelo, Braz.	B3	56
Monte Caseros, Arg.	A5	54
Montecatini Terme, Italy	C3	23
Montecito, Ca., U.S.	*E4	82
Monte Comán, Arg.	A3	54
Monte Cristi, Dom. Rep.	B1	58
Monte Cristo, Bol.	B3	55
Montecristo, i., Italy	C3	23
Montefrío, Spain	D3	22
Montego Bay, Jam.	E5	64
Montego Bay, b., Jam.	E13	65
Monteiro, Braz.	D2	56
Monteith, Mount, mtn., B.C.	B6	69
Montelavar, Port.	f9	22
Montélimar, Fr.	E6	16
Montelindo, stm., Para.	D4	55
Montellano, Spain	D3	22
Montello, Nv., U.S.	B7	105
Montello, Wi., U.S.	E4	126
Montemayor, Meseta de, plat., Arg.	C3	54
Montemorelos, Mex.	B5	63
Montemor-o-Novo, Port.	C1	22
Montenegro, Braz.	D2	56
Montenegro, hist. reg., Yugo.	D4	24
Monte Patria, Chile	A2	54
Monte Plata, Dom. Rep.	E9	64
Monte Porzio Catone, Italy	h9	23
Montepuez, Moz.	D6	48
Montepulciano, Italy	C3	23
Monte Quemado, Arg.	E3	55
Montereau [-faut-Yonne], Fr.	C5	16
Monterey, Al., U.S.	D3	78
Monterey, Ca., U.S.	D3	82
Monterey, In., U.S.	B4	91
Monterey, Ky., U.S.	B5	94
Monterey, La., U.S.	C4	95
Monterey, Ma., U.S.	B1	98
Monterey, Tn., U.S.	C8	119
Monterey, Va., U.S.	B3	123
Monterey, co., Ca., U.S.	D3	82
Monterey Bay, b., Ca., U.S.	D2	82
Monterey Park, Ca., U.S.	m12	82
Montería, Col.	B2	60
Monteros, Arg.	E2	55
Monterotondo, Italy	g9	23
Monterrey, Mex.	B4	63
Montesano, Wa., U.S.	C2	124
Monte Sano Mountain, mtn., Al., U.S.	A3	78
Monte Sant'Angelo, Italy	D5	23
Monte Santo, Braz.	D3	57
Monte Santu, Capo di, c., Italy	D2	23
Montevallo, Al., U.S.	B3	78
Montevarchi, Italy	C3	23
Montevideo, Mn., U.S.	F3	100
Montevideo, Ur.	C5	56
Monteview, Id., U.S.	F6	89
Monte Vista, Co., U.S.	D4	83
Montezuma, Ga., U.S.	D3	87
Montezuma, In., U.S.	E3	91
Montezuma, Ia., U.S.	C5	92
Montezuma, Ks., U.S.	E3	93
Montezuma, N.M., U.S.	B4	108
Montezuma, Oh., U.S.	B1	112
Montezuma, co., Co., U.S.	D2	83
Montezuma Canyon, val., Ut., U.S.	F6	121
Montezuma Castle National Monument, Az., U.S.	C4	80
Montezuma Creek, Ut., U.S.	F6	121
Montezuma Peak, mtn., Az., U.S.	D3	80
Montfaucon, Switz.	B3	21
Montfort, Que.	D3	74
Montfort, Wi., U.S.	F3	126
Montfort-sur-Meu, Fr.	C3	16
Montgomery, Wales, U.K.	B4	12
Montgomery, Al., U.S.	C3	78
Montgomery, Ga., U.S.	E5	87
Montgomery, Il., U.S.	B5	90
Montgomery, In., U.S.	G3	91
Montgomery, La., U.S.	C3	95
Montgomery, Mi., U.S.	G6	99
Montgomery, Mn., U.S.	F5	100
Montgomery, N.Y., U.S.	D6	109
Montgomery, Oh., U.S.	o13	112
Montgomery, Pa., U.S.	D8	115
Montgomery, W.V., U.S.	C3	125
Montgomery, co., Al., U.S.	C3	78
Montgomery, co., Ar., U.S.	C2	81
Montgomery, co., Ga., U.S.	D4	87
Montgomery, co., Il., U.S.	D4	90
Montgomery, co., In., U.S.	D4	91
Montgomery, co., Ia., U.S.	C2	92
Montgomery, co., Ks., U.S.	E8	93
Montgomery, co., Ky., U.S.	B6	94
Montgomery, co., Md., U.S.	B3	97
Montgomery, co., Ms., U.S.	B4	101
Montgomery, co., Mo., U.S.	C6	102
Montgomery, co., N.Y., U.S.	C6	109
Montgomery, co., N.C., U.S.	B3	110
Montgomery, co., Oh., U.S.	C1	112
Montgomery, co., Pa., U.S.	F11	115
Montgomery, co., Tn., U.S.	A4	119
Montgomery, co., Tx., U.S.	D5	120
Montgomery, co., Va., U.S.	C2	123
Montgomery Center, Vt., U.S.	B3	122
Montgomery City, Mo., U.S.	C6	102
Montgomery Creek, Ca., U.S.	B3	82
Montgomery see Sāhīwāl, Pak.		
Montgomery Village, Md., U.S.	*B3	97
Montguyon, Fr.	E4	17
Monthey, Switz.	C2	20
Monticello, Ar., U.S.	D4	81
Monticello, Fl., U.S.	B3	86
Monticello, Ga., U.S.	C3	87
Monticello, Il., U.S.	C5	90
Monticello, In., U.S.	C4	91
Monticello, Ia., U.S.	B6	92
Monticello, Ky., U.S.	D5	94
Monticello, Me., U.S.	B5	96
Monticello, Mn., U.S.	E5	100
Monticello, Ms., U.S.	D3	101
Monticello, Mo., U.S.	A6	102
Monticello, N.M., U.S.	D2	108
Monticello, N.Y., U.S.	D6	109
Monticello, Ut., U.S.	F6	121
Monticello, Wi., U.S.	F4	126
Mont Ida, Ks., U.S.	D8	93
Montier-en-Der, Fr.	F4	17
Montiers-sur-Saulx, Fr.	F5	17
Montignac, Fr.	E4	16
Montignies [-lés-Metz], Fr.	C7	16
Montijo, Port.	C1	22
Montijo, Spain	C2	22
Montilla, Spain	D3	22
Monti Verdi, Ut., U.S.	*B4	121
Montivilliers, Fr.	C4	16
Mont-Joli, Que.	A9	74
Mont-Laurier, Que.	C2	74
Montlhéry, Fr.	D5	16
Montluçon, Fr.	F5	16
Montmagny, Que.	C7	74
Montmagny, co., Que.	C7	74
Montmartre, Sask.	G4	75
Montmédy, Fr.	E5	17
Montmélian, Fr.	D2	20
Montmirail, Fr.	F3	17
Montmorenci, In., U.S.	D3	91
Montmorenci, S.C., U.S.	D4	117
Montmorency, Fr.	g10	16
Montmorency, co., Mi., U.S.	C6	99
Montmorency, stm., Que.	B6	74
Montmorency Number One, co., Que.	B6	74
Montmorency Number Two, co., Que.	C7	74
Montmorillon, Fr.	D4	16
Montney, B.C.	A7	69
Monto, Austl.	B8	51
Montone, stm., Italy	B3	23
Montoro, Spain	C3	22
Montour, co., Pa., U.S.	D8	115
Montour Falls, N.Y., U.S.	C4	109
Montoursville, Pa., U.S.	D8	115
Montoya, N.M., U.S.	B5	108
Montpelier, Id., U.S.	G7	89
Montpelier, In., U.S.	C7	91
Montpelier, Ia., U.S.	C7	92
Montpelier, La., U.S.	D5	95
Montpelier, Ms., U.S.	B5	101
Montpelier, N.D., U.S.	C7	111
Montpelier, Oh., U.S.	A1	112
Montpelier, Vt., U.S.	C3	122
Montpelier Station, Va., U.S.	B4	123
Montpellier, Que.	D2	74
Montpellier, Fr.	F5	16
Montréal, Que.	D4	74
Montreal, Wi., U.S.	B3	126
Montreal, stm., Sask.	C3	75
Montréal, Île de l, Que.	q19	75
Montreal Lake, Sask.	C3	75
Montreal Lake, l., Sask.	C3	75
Montréal-Nord, Que.	p19	74
Montreat, N.C., U.S.	f10	110
Montreuil [-sous-Bois], Fr.	C5	16
Montreuil-sur-Mer, Fr.	B4	16
Montreux, Switz.	E3	18
Montricher, Switz.	C1	21
Mont-Rolland, Que.	D3	74
Montrose, B.C.	E9	69
Montrose, Scot., U.K.	B5	10
Montrose, Al., U.S.	E2	78
Montrose, Ar., U.S.	D4	81
Montrose, Co., U.S.	C3	83
Montrose, Ga., U.S.	D3	87
Montrose, Il., U.S.	D5	90
Montrose, Ia., U.S.	D6	92
Montrose, Ks., U.S.	C5	93
Montrose, Mi., U.S.	E7	99
Montrose, Ms., U.S.	C4	101
Montrose, Mo., U.S.	C4	102
Montrose, Pa., U.S.	C10	115
Montrose, S.D., U.S.	D8	118
Montrose, Va., U.S.	m18	123
Montrose, co., Co., U.S.	C2	83
Montross, Va., U.S.	B6	123
Montrouge, Fr.	g10	16
Mont-Royal, Que.	p19	74
Mont-Saint-Martin, Fr.	C6	16
Mont-Saint-Michel, Fr.	D4	13
Montserrat, dep., N.A.	H13	64
Montserrat, mtn., Spain	B6	22
Mont-Tremblant, Que.	C3	74
Mont-Tremblant, Parc Provincial du, Que.	C3	74
Montvale, N.J., U.S.	A4	107
Montvale, Va., U.S.	C3	123
Mont Vernon, N.H., U.S.	E3	106
Montville, Ct., U.S.	D7	84
Montville, Ma., U.S.	B1	98
Montville, N.J., U.S.	B4	107
Montz, La., U.S.	h11	95
Montzen, Bel.	D5	17
Monument, Co., U.S.	B6	83
Monument, Ks., U.S.	C2	93
Monument, N.M., U.S.	E6	108
Monument, Or., U.S.	C7	114
Monument Beach, Ma., U.S.	C6	98
Monument Heights, Va., U.S.	*C5	123
Monument Peak, mtn., Co., U.S.	B3	83
Monument Peak, mtn., Id., U.S.	G4	89
Monument Valley, Ut., U.S.	*F5	121
Monument Valley, val., Az., U.S.	A5	80
Monywa, Burma	D10	36
Monza, Italy	B2	23
Monzón, Peru	C2	58
Monzón, Spain	B6	22
Moodus, Ct., U.S.	D6	84
Moodus Reservoir, res., Ct., U.S.	C6	84
Moody, Me., U.S.	E2	96
Moody, Mo., U.S.	E6	102
Moody, Tx., U.S.	D4	120
Moody, co., S.D., U.S.	C9	118
Moody Air Force Base, mil., Ga., U.S.	F3	87
Moody Beach, Me., U.S.	E2	96
Moodys, Ok., U.S.	A7	113
Moodys Forks, N.Y., U.S.	f11	109
Moon, Ok., U.S.	D7	113
Moonachie, N.J., U.S.	*B4	107
Moonie, stm., Austl.	C7	51
Moon Lake, l., Ms., U.S.	A3	101
Moon Run, Pa., U.S.	k13	115
Moora, Austl.	F2	50
Moorabbin, Austl.	*G8	50
Moorcroft, Wy., U.S.	B8	127
Moore, Id., U.S.	F5	89
Moore, Mt., U.S.	D7	103
Moore, Ok., U.S.	B4	113
Moore, S.C., U.S.	B4	117
Moore, Tx., U.S.	E3	120
Moore, W.V., U.S.	B5	125
Moore, co., N.C., U.S.	B3	110
Moore, co., Tn., U.S.	B5	119
Moore, co., Tx., U.S.	B2	120
Moore, Lake, l., Austl.	E2	50
Moore Dam, U.S.	B3	106
Moorefield, Ky., U.S.	B6	94
Moorefield, Ne., U.S.	D5	104
Moorefield, W.V., U.S.	B6	125
Moore Haven, Fl., U.S.	F5	86
Mooreland, Ok., U.S.	A2	113
Mooreland, Id., U.S.	F6	89
Moore Mill, N.B.	D2	71
Moore Park, Man.	D2	70
Moore Reservoir, res., U.S.	B3	106
Moores Corner, Ma., U.S.	A3	98
Moores Creek National Military Park, N.C., U.S.	C4	110
Moores Hill, In., U.S.	F7	91
Mooresboro, N.C., U.S.	B1	110
Moorestown, Mi., U.S.	D5	99
Moorestown, N.J., U.S.	D3	107
Mooresville, In., U.S.	E5	91
Mooresville, Mo., U.S.	B4	102
Mooresville, N.C., U.S.	B2	110
Mooresville, Tn., U.S.	B5	119
Mooreton, N.D., U.S.	C9	111
Mooreville, Ms., U.S.	A5	101
Moorhead, Ia., U.S.	C2	92
Moorhead, Mn., U.S.	D2	100
Moorhead, Ms., U.S.	B3	101
Mooring, Tn., U.S.	A2	119
Mooringsport, La., U.S.	B2	95
Moorland, Ia., U.S.	B3	92
Moorman, Ky., U.S.	C2	94
Moorpark, Ca., U.S.	*E4	82
Moosburg, W. Ger.	E6	19
Moose, Wy., U.S.	C2	127
Moose, stm., N.H., U.S.	B4	106
Moose, stm., N.Y., U.S.	B5	109
Moose, stm., Vt., U.S.	B5	122
Moose Creek, Ont.	B10	73
Moose Factory, Ont.	F16	66
Moosehead Lake, l., Me., U.S.	C3	96
Mooseheart, Il., U.S.	B5	90
Moose Heights, B.C.	C6	69
Moose Hill, hill, Ma., U.S.	h11	98
Moosehorn, Man.	D2	70
Moose Island, i., Man.	D3	70
Moose Jaw, Sask.	G3	75
Moose Jaw, stm., Sask.	G3	75
Moose Lake, Man.	C1	70
Moose Lake, Mn., U.S.	D6	100
Moose Lake, l., B.C.	C1	68
Moose Lake, l., Wi., U.S.	B2	126
Mooseleuk Stream, stm., Me., U.S.	B4	96
Mooselookmeguntic Lake, l., Me., U.S.	D2	96
Moose Mountain, mtn., Sask.	H4	75
Moose Mountain, mtn., N.H., U.S.	C2	106
Moose Mountain Creek, stm., Sask.	H4	75
Moose Mountain Provincial Park, Sask.	H4	75
Moose Pass, Ak., U.S.	C10	79
Moose River, Me., U.S.	C2	96
Moosic, Pa., U.S.	m18	115
Moosilauke, Mount, mtn., N.H., U.S.	B3	106
Moosomin, Sask.	G5	75
Moosonee, Ont.	o19	73
Moosup, Ct., U.S.	C8	84
Moosup, stm., U.S.	C1	116
Moosup Valley, R.I., U.S.	D1	116
Mopang Lake, l., Me., U.S.	D5	96
Mopti, Mali	D4	45
Moquegua, Peru	E3	58
Moquegua, dept., Peru	E3	58
Mor, Hung.	B4	24
Mor, i., Micron.	Q18	52
Mor, Glen, val., Scot., U.K.	D4	13
Mòr, Sgùrr, mtn., Scot., U.K.	C3	13
Mora, Cam.	C4	46
Mora, Spain	C3	22
Mora, Swe.	G6	14
Mora, Ga., U.S.	E4	87
Mora, Mn., U.S.	E5	100
Mora, N.M., U.S.	B4	108
Mora, co., N.M., U.S.	A5	108
Mora, stm., N.M., U.S.	B5	108
Morača, stm., Yugo.	D4	24
Moradābād, India	C6	36
Morada Nova, Braz.	C3	57
Mora de Ebro, Spain	B6	22
Morafenobe, Madag.	g8	49
Morag, Pol.	B5	26
Moraga, Ca., U.S.	*D2	82
Moraine, Oh., U.S.	*C1	112
Morales, Guat.	C3	62
Morales, Mex.	k13	63
Moramanga, Madag.	g9	49
Moran, Ks., U.S.	D4	93
Moran, Mi., U.S.	B6	99
Moran, Tx., U.S.	C3	120
Moran, Wy., U.S.	C2	127
Morann, Pa., U.S.	E5	115
Morant Point, c., Jam.	F5	64
Morar, Loch, l., Scot., U.K.	D3	13
Morat, Lake, l., Switz.	C3	20
Morata de Tajuña, Spain	p18	22
Moratico, Va., U.S.	C6	123
Moratuwa, Sri L.	G6	36
Morava, stm., Eur.	D5	26
Moravia, Ia., U.S.	D5	92
Moravia, N.Y., U.S.	C4	109
Moravia, hist. reg., Czech.	D4	26
Moraya, Bol.	D2	55
Morawhanna, Guy.	A3	59
Moray Firth, est., Scot., U.K.	B5	10
Morbach, W. Ger.	D2	19
Morbegno, Italy	D8	21
Morbi, India	F3	37
Morden, Man.	E2	70
Morden, N.S.	D5	71
More, Ben, mtn., Scot., U.K.	E5	13
More, Ben, mtn., Scot., U.K.	D3	13
More Assynt, Ben, mtn., Scot., U.K.	A4	10
Moreau, stm., S.D., U.S.	B3	118
Moreau, North Fork, stm., S.D., U.S.	B2	118
Moreau, South Fork, stm., S.D., U.S.	B2	118
Moreau Peak, mtn., S.D., U.S.	B2	118
Moreauville, La., U.S.	C4	95
Morecambe, Eng., U.K.	F6	13
Morecambe Bay, b., Eng., U.K.	D5	10
Moree, Austl.	E8	50
Morehead, Ky., U.S.	B6	94
Morehead City, N.C., U.S.	C6	110
Morehouse, Mo., U.S.	E8	102
Morehouse, co., La., U.S.	B4	95
Mörel, Switz.	D5	21
Moreland, Ar., U.S.	B3	81
Moreland, Ga., U.S.	C2	87
Moreland, Id., U.S.	F6	89
Moreland, Ky., U.S.	C5	94
Morelia, Mex.	D4	63
Morell, P.E.I.	C7	71
Morella, Spain	B5	22
Morelos, state, Mex.	D5	63
Morena, Sierra, mts., Spain	D2	22
Morenci, Az., U.S.	D6	80
Morenci, Mi., U.S.	G6	99
Moreno Valley, Ca., U.S.	*F5	82
Moresby Island, i., B.C.	C2	69
Moreton Bay, b., Austl.	C9	51
Moreton-in-Marsh, Eng., U.K.	C6	12
Moreton Island, i., Austl.	C9	51
Moretown, Vt., U.S.	C3	122
Moreuil, Fr.	C5	16
Morewood, Ont.	B9	73
Morey, Lake, l., Vt., U.S.	C4	122
Morey Peak, mtn., Nv., U.S.	E5	105
Morez, Fr.	D7	16
Morgan, Austl.	G2	51
Morgan, Ga., U.S.	E2	87
Morgan, Ky., U.S.	B5	94
Morgan, Mn., U.S.	F4	100
Morgan, Tx., U.S.	C4	120
Morgan, Ut., U.S.	B4	121
Morgan, Vt., U.S.	B4	122
Morgan, co., Al., U.S.	A3	78
Morgan, co., Co., U.S.	A7	83
Morgan, co., Ga., U.S.	C3	87
Morgan, co., Il., U.S.	D3	90
Morgan, co., In., U.S.	F5	91
Morgan, co., Ky., U.S.	C6	94
Morgan, co., Mo., U.S.	C5	102
Morgan, co., Oh., U.S.	C4	112
Morgan, co., Tn., U.S.	C9	119
Morgan, co., Ut., U.S.	B4	121
Morgan, co., W.V., U.S.	B6	125
Morgan Center, Vt., U.S.	B5	122
Morgan City, Al., U.S.	A3	78
Morgan City, La., U.S.	E4	95
Morgan City, Ms., U.S.	B3	101
Morganfield, Ky., U.S.	C2	94
Morgan Island, i., S.C., U.S.	G6	117
Morgan Point, c., Ct., U.S.	E4	84
Morganton, Ar., U.S.	B3	81
Morganton, Ga., U.S.	B2	87
Morganton, N.C., U.S.	B1	110
Morgantown, In., U.S.	F5	91
Morgantown, Ky., U.S.	C3	94
Morgantown, Ms., U.S.	D4	101
Morgantown, Tn., U.S.	D8	119
Morgantown, W.V., U.S.	B5	125
Morganville, Ks., U.S.	C6	93
Morganville, N.J., U.S.	C4	107
Morganza, La., U.S.	D4	95
Morges, Switz.	C2	20
Morgex, Italy	D2	20
Morghāb, stm., Asia	A3	36
Morhange, Fr.	F6	17
Mori, Japan	E10	33
Moriah, Trin.	M24	65
Moriah, Mount, mtn., Nv., U.S.	D7	105
Moriah, Mount, mtn., N.H., U.S.	B4	106
Moriarty, N.M., U.S.	C3	108
Morice, stm., B.C.	B4	69
Morice Lake, l., B.C.	B4	69
Moriguchi, Japan	*I7	33
Morin-Heights, Que.	D3	74
Morinville, Alta.	C4	68
Morioka, Japan	D13	31
Morjärv, Swe.	D10	14
Morjim, stm., B.C.	C7	69
Morkill, stm., B.C.	C7	69
Morki, Sov. Un.	r32	14
Morlaix, Fr.	C2	16
Morland, Ks., U.S.	C3	93
Morley, Alta.	D3	68
Morley, Mi., U.S.	E5	99
Morley, Mo., U.S.	D8	102
Morley, N.Y., U.S.	f9	109
Mormon Lake, l., Az., U.S.	C4	80
Mormon Peak, mtn., Nv., U.S.	G7	105
Morne-à-l'Eau, Guad.	Q9	65
Morningside, S.D., U.S.	C7	118
Morning Sun, Ia., U.S.	C6	92
Morning View, Ky., U.S.	k14	94
Moro, Ar., U.S.	C5	81
Moro, Or., U.S.	B5	114
Morobay, Ar., U.S.	D3	81
Morobe, Pap. N. Gui.	k12	50
Morocco, In., U.S.	C3	91
Morocco, ctry., Afr.	C4	44
Morococha, Peru	D2	58
Moro Creek, stm., Ar., U.S.	C3	81
Morogoro, Tan.	C6	48
Morogoro, prov., Tan.	C6	48
Moro Gulf, b., Phil.	D6	34
Moroleón, Mex.	m13	63
Morombe, Madag.	h8	49
Morón, Arg.	*D2	54
Morón, Cuba	C6	64
Mörön, Mong.	B5	31
Morona, stm., Peru	B2	58
Morona-Santiago, prov., Ec.	B2	58
Morón de la Frontera, Spain	D3	22
Moroni, Com.	D8	49
Moroni, Ut., U.S.	D4	121
Morotai, i., Indon.	A5	48
Moroto, Ug.	A6	48
Morozovsk, Sov. Un.	G13	27
Morpeth, Ont.	E3	73
Morpeth, Eng., U.K.	E7	13
Morral, Oh., U.S.	B2	112
Morrill, Ne., U.S.	C2	104
Morrill, co., Ne., U.S.	C2	104
Morrilton, Ar., U.S.	B3	81
Morrin, Alta.	D4	68
Morrinhos, Braz.	B3	56
Morrinsville, N.Z.	L15	51
Morris, Man.	E3	70
Morris, Ct., U.S.	C3	84
Morris, Il., U.S.	B5	90
Morris, In., U.S.	F7	91
Morris, Mn., U.S.	E3	100
Morris, N.Y., U.S.	C5	109
Morris, Ok., U.S.	B6	113
Morris, co., Ks., U.S.	D7	93
Morris, co., N.J., U.S.	B3	107
Morris, co., Tx., U.S.	C5	120
Morris, Mount, mtn., N.Y., U.S.	A6	109
Morrisburg, Ont.	C9	73
Morris Chapel, Tn., U.S.	B3	119
Morrisdale, Pa., U.S.	E5	115
Morris Island, i., S.C., U.S.	F8	117
Morris Jesup, Kap, c., Grnld.	A17	61
Morrison, Co., U.S.	B5	83
Morrison, Il., U.S.	B4	90
Morrison, Mo., U.S.	C6	102
Morrison, Ok., U.S.	A4	113
Morrison, Tn., U.S.	D8	119
Morrison, Wi., U.S.	h10	126
Morrison, co., Mn., U.S.	D4	100
Morrison City, Tn., U.S.	C11	119
Morrisonville, Il., U.S.	D4	90
Morrisonville, N.Y., U.S.	f11	109
Morris Plains, N.J., U.S.	B4	107
Morris Run, Pa., U.S.	C7	115
Morristown, Fl., U.S.	C4	86
Morristown, Az., U.S.	D3	80
Morristown, In., U.S.	E6	91
Morristown, Mn., U.S.	F5	100
Morristown, N.J., U.S.	B4	107
Morristown, N.Y., U.S.	f9	109
Morristown, S.D., U.S.	B4	118
Morristown, Tn., U.S.	C10	119
Morristown, Vt., U.S.	B3	122
Morristown National Historical Park, N.J., U.S.	B3	107
Morrisville, Mo., U.S.	D4	102
Morrisville, N.Y., U.S.	C5	109
Morrisville, Pa., U.S.	F12	115
Morrisville, Vt., U.S.	B3	122
Morrito, Nic.	E7	63
Morro, Ec.	B1	58
Morro, Punta, c., Chile	E1	55
Morro, Punta, c., Mex.	D6	63
Morro Bay, Ca., U.S.	E3	82
Morro do Chapéu, Braz.	D2	57
Morropón, Peru	B1	58
Morrosquillo, Golfo de, b., Col.	B2	60
Morrow, Ga., U.S.	C2	87
Morrow, La., U.S.	D3	95
Morrow, Oh., U.S.	C1	112
Morrow, co., Oh., U.S.	B3	112
Morrow, co., Or., U.S.	B7	114
Morrumbene, Moz.	B6	49
Mors, i., Den.	B2	15
Morse, Sask.	G2	75
Morse, La., U.S.	D3	95
Morse, Tx., U.S.	A2	120
Morse, Wi., U.S.	B3	126
Morse Bluff, Ne., U.S.	C9	104
Morse Mill, Mo., U.S.	g12	102
Morse Reservoir, res., In., U.S.	D5	91
Morses Creek, stm., N.J., U.S.	k8	107
Morshansk, Sov. Un.	E13	27
Mortagne, Fr.	C4	16
Mortara, Italy	B2	23
Morteau, Fr.	D7	16
Mortes, Rio das, stm., Braz.	E4	59
Mortlach, Sask.	G2	75
Morton, Il., U.S.	C4	90
Morton, Mn., U.S.	F4	100
Morton, Ms., U.S.	C4	101
Morton, Tx., U.S.	C1	120
Morton, Wa., U.S.	C3	124
Morton, co., Ks., U.S.	E2	93
Morton, co., N.D., U.S.	C4	111
Morton Grove, Il., U.S.	h9	90
Morton Pass, Wy., U.S.	E7	127
Mortons Gap, Ky., U.S.	C2	94
Moruga, Trin.	O23	65
Moruya, Austl.	G8	51
Morvan Mountains, mts., Fr.	D6	16
Morven, Ga., U.S.	F3	87
Morven, N.C., U.S.	C2	110
Morven, mtn., Scot., U.K.	B5	13
Morwell, Austl.	G8	50
Moryakovskiy Zaton, Sov. Un.	B10	28
Morye, Sov. Un.	r32	14
Mosalsk, Sov. Un.	D10	27
Mosbach, W. Ger.	D4	19
Mosby, Mo., U.S.	h11	102
Mosby, Mt., U.S.	D9	103
Mosca, Co., U.S.	D5	83
Moscarello, Italy	k9	23
Moscos Islands, is., Burma	F10	36
Moscow, Id., U.S.	C2	89
Moscow, Ks., U.S.	E2	93
Moscow, Mi., U.S.	G6	99
Moscow, Oh., U.S.	D1	112
Moscow, Pa., U.S.	m18	115
Moscow, R.I., U.S.	E2	116
Moscow, Tn., U.S.	B2	119
Moscow, Vt., U.S.	C3	122
Moscow Mills, Mo., U.S.	C7	102
Moscow (Moskva), Sov. Un.	D6	29
Mosel (Moselle), stm., Eur.	D3	18
Moseley, Va., U.S.	C5	123
Moselle, Ms., U.S.	D4	101
Moselle, dept., Fr.	C7	16
Moselle (Mosel), stm., Eur.	C7	16
Moses River, N.S.	E7	71
Moses Coulee, val., Wa., U.S.	B6	124
Moses Lake, Wa., U.S.	B6	124
Moses Lake, l., Wa., U.S.	B6	124
Mosgiel, N.Z.	P13	51
Mosheim, Tn., U.S.	C11	119
Mosher, S.D., U.S.	D5	118
Mosherville, N.S.	D6	71
Moshi, Tan.	B6	48
Moshupa, Bots.	F5	49
Mosinee, Wi., U.S.	D4	126
Moskva, stm., Sov. Un.	n18	27
Mosomane (Artesia), Bots.	B4	49
Mosonmagyaróvár, Hung.	B3	24
Mosquera, Col.	C2	60
Mosquero, N.M., U.S.	B6	108
Mosquito Coast, N.A.	D6	62
Mosquito, Newf.	E5	72
Mosquito Creek, stm., Ia., U.S.	C2	92
Mosquito Creek Lake, res., Oh., U.S.	A5	112
Mosquito Lagoon, b., Fl., U.S.	D6	86
Mosquitos, Golfo de los, b., Pan.	F7	62
Moss, Nor.	H4	14

Name	Map Ref.	Page
Moss, Ms., U.S.	D4	101
Moss, Tn., U.S.	C8	119
Mossaka, Congo	B2	48
Mossbank, Sask.	H3	75
Moss Bluff, La., U.S.	D2	95
Mossburn, N.Z.		
Mossendjo, Congo	B1	48
Mossleigh, Alta.	D4	68
Mossman, Austl.	C8	50
Moss Mountain, mtn., Ar., U.S.	C3	81
Mossoró, Braz.	C3	57
Moss Point, Ms., U.S.	E5	101
Moss Vale, Austl.	G8	51
Mossy, stm., Man.	D2	70
Mossy, stm., Sask.	C4	75
Mossy Head, Fl., U.S.	u15	86
Mossyrock, Wa., U.S.	C3	124
Most, Czech.	C2	26
Mostar, Yugo.	D3	24
Mostefa, Cap, c., Tun.	F3	23
Móstoles, Spain	p17	22
Mostrim (Edgeworthstown), Ire.	D4	11
Mosul (Al Mawṣil), Iraq	B4	38
Moswansicut Pond, l., R.I., U.S.	C3	116
Motagua, stm., N.A.	E6	63
Motala, Swe.	H6	14
Motatán, Ven.	B3	60
Motherwell, Scot., U.K.	C5	10
Motīhāri, India	D10	37
Motilla del Palancar, Spain	C5	22
Motley, Mn., U.S.	D4	100
Motley, co., Tx., U.S.	B2	120
Motobu, Japan	N5	52
Motomachi, Japan	o18	33
Moto Mountain, hill, Japan	P17	52
Motril, Spain	D4	22
Motru, stm., Rom.	C6	24
Mott, N.D., U.S.	C3	111
Motueka, N.Z.	N14	51
Motul [de Felipe Carrillo Puerto], Mex.	C7	63
Motupe, Peru	C2	58
Moturiki, i., Fiji	H15	52
Mou, Den.	B4	15
Mouaskar, Alg.	B5	44
Moúdhros (Mudros), Grc.	C5	25
Moudjéria, Maur.	C2	45
Moudon, Switz.	C2	20
Mouila, Gabon	F2	46
Moulamein Billabong Creek, stm., Austl.	G5	51
Mould Bay, N.W. Ter.	m28	66
Moule, Guad.	H14	64
Moulins, Fr.	D5	16
Moulouya, Oued, stm., Mor.	C4	44
Moulton, Al., U.S.	A2	78
Moulton, Ia., U.S.	D5	92
Moultonboro, N.H., U.S.	C4	106
Moultrie, Ga., U.S.	E3	87
Moultrie, co., Il., U.S.	D5	90
Moultrie, Lake, res., S.C., U.S.	E7	117
Mound, La., U.S.	B4	95
Mound, Mn., U.S.	n11	100
Mound Bayou, Ms., U.S.	B3	101
Mound City, Il., U.S.	F4	90
Mound City, Ks., U.S.	D9	93
Mound City, Mo., U.S.	A2	102
Mound City, S.D., U.S.	B5	118
Mound City Group National Monument, Oh., U.S.	C2	112
Moundou, Chad	D3	46
Moundridge, Ks., U.S.	D6	93
Mounds, Il., U.S.	F4	90
Mounds, Ok., U.S.	B5	113
Moundsville, Mn., U.S.	m12	100
Moundsville, W.V., U.S.	B4	125
Mound Valley, Ks., U.S.	E8	93
Moundville, Al., U.S.	C2	78
Moundville, Mo., U.S.	D3	102
Mounier, Mont, mtn., Fr.	E7	16
Mountain, N.D., U.S.	A8	111
Mountain, W.V., U.S.	B4	125
Mountain, Wi., U.S.	C5	126
Mountainair, N.M., U.S.	C3	108
Mountainaire, Az., U.S.	B4	80
Mountain Ash, Ky., U.S.	D5	94
Mountainboro, Al., U.S.	A3	78
Mountain Brook, Al., U.S.	g7	78
Mountainburg, Ar., U.S.	B1	81
Mountain City, Ga., U.S.	B3	87
Mountain City, Nv., U.S.	B6	105
Mountain City, Tn., U.S.	C12	119
Mountain Dale, N.Y., U.S.	D6	109
Mountain Fork, stm., U.S.	C7	113
Mountain Grove, Ont.	C8	73
Mountain Grove, Mo., U.S.	D5	102
Mountain Home, Ar., U.S.	A3	81
Mountain Home, Id., U.S.	F3	89
Mountainhome, Pa., U.S.	D11	115
Mountain Home, Tx., U.S.	D3	120
Mountain Home, Ut., U.S.	C5	121
Mountain Home Air Force Base, mil., Id., U.S.	F3	89
Mountain Iron, Mn., U.S.	C6	100
Mountain Lake, Mn., U.S.	G4	100
Mountain Lake, l., Sask.	B3	75
Mountain Lake Park, Md., U.S.	m12	97
Mountain Lakes, N.J., U.S.	*B4	107
Mountain Nile (Al Baḥr al Jabal), stm., Sud.	D3	47
Mountain Park, Alta.	C2	68
Mountain Park, Fl., U.S.	*C2	87
Mountain Park, Ok., U.S.	C3	113
Mountain Pine, Ar., U.S.	C2	81
Mountain Point, Ak., U.S.	n24	79
Mountainside, N.J., U.S.	B4	107
Mountain Springs, Nv., U.S.	*G6	105
Mountain Valley, Alta.	E4	68
Mountain View, Ar., U.S.	B3	81
Mountain View, Ca., U.S.	k8	82
Mountain View, Co., U.S.	*B5	83
Mountain View, Co., U.S.	*A5	83
Mountainview, Hi., U.S.	*D6	88
Mountain View, Mo., U.S.	D6	102
Mountain View, N.M., U.S.	C3	108
Mountain View, Ok., U.S.	B3	113
Mountain View, Wy., U.S.	E2	127
Mountain View, Wy., U.S.	*D6	127
Mountain Village, Ak., U.S.	C7	79
Mount Airy, Ga., U.S.	B3	87
Mount Airy, Md., U.S.	B3	97
Mount Airy, N.J., U.S.	C3	107
Mount Airy, N.C., U.S.	A2	110
Mount Albert, Ont.	C5	73
Mount Angel, Or., U.S.	B4	114
Mount Arlington, N.J., U.S.	B3	107
Mount Assiniboine Provincial Park, B.C.	D10	69
Mount Athos, ter., Grc.	B5	25
Mount Auburn, Il., U.S.	D4	90
Mount Auburn, In., U.S.	B5	92
Mount Ayr, In., U.S.	C3	91
Mount Ayr, Ia., U.S.	D3	92
Mount Barker, Austl.	G2	51
Mount Bellew Bridge, Ire.	D3	11
Mount Berry, Ga., U.S.	B1	87
Mount Blanchard, Oh., U.S.	B2	112
Mount Brydges, Ont.	E3	73
Mount Calvary, Wi., U.S.	E5	126
Mount Carleton Provincial Park, N.B.	B3	71
Mount Carmel, Al., U.S.	C3	78
Mount Carmel, Il., U.S.	E6	90
Mount Carmel, In., U.S.	F8	91
Mount Carmel, N.D., U.S.	A7	111
Mount Carmel, Oh., U.S.	o13	112
Mount Carmel, Pa., U.S.	E9	115
Mount Carmel, S.C., U.S.	C2	117
Mount Carmel, Ut., U.S.	F3	121
Mount Carmel Junction, Ut., U.S.	F3	121
Mount Carmel [-Mitchell's Brook-Saint Catherine's], Newf.	E5	72
Mount Carroll, Il., U.S.	A4	90
Mount Clare, W.V., U.S.	B4	125
Mount Clemens, Mi., U.S.	F8	99
Mount Clinton, Va., U.S.	B4	123
Mount Cory, Oh., U.S.	B2	112
Mount Crawford, Va., U.S.	B4	123
Mount Croghan, S.C., U.S.	B7	117
Mount Darwin, Zimb.	A5	49
Mount Desert, Me., U.S.	*D4	96
Mount Desert Island, i., Me., U.S.	D4	96
Mount Dora, Fl., U.S.	D5	86
Mount Dora, N.M., U.S.	A6	108
Mount Eaton, Oh., U.S.	B4	112
Mount Eden, Ky., U.S.	B4	94
Mount Elgin, Ont.	E4	73
Mount Emmons, Ut., U.S.	*C5	121
Mount Enterprise, Tx., U.S.	D5	120
Mount Ephraim, N.J., U.S.	*D2	107
Mount Erie, Il., U.S.	E5	90
Mount Etna, In., U.S.	C6	91
Mount Etna, Ia., U.S.	C3	92
Mount Forest, Ont.	D4	73
Mount Forest, Mi., U.S.	E6	99
Mount Freedom, N.J., U.S.	B3	107
Mount Gambier, Austl.	G7	50
Mount Gay, W.V., U.S.	D2	125
Mount Gilead, N.C., U.S.	B3	110
Mount Gilead, Oh., U.S.	B3	112
Mount Hagen, Pap. N. Gui.	k11	50
Mount Healthy, Oh., U.S.	o12	112
Mount Hebron, Ca., U.S.	B2	82
Mount Hermon, La., U.S.	D5	95
Mount Hermon, Ma., U.S.	A3	98
Mount Heron, Va., U.S.	e9	123
Mount Holly, Ar., U.S.	D3	81
Mount Holly, N.J., U.S.	D3	107
Mount Holly, N.C., U.S.	B1	110
Mount Holly, S.C., U.S.	E7	117
Mount Holly, Vt., U.S.	E3	122
Mount Holly Springs, Pa., U.S.	F7	115
Mount Hood, Or., U.S.	B5	114
Mount Hope, Ont.	D5	73
Mount Hope, Al., U.S.	A2	78
Mount Hope, Ks., U.S.	E6	93
Mount Hope, W.V., U.S.	D3	125
Mount Hope, Wi., U.S.	F3	126
Mount Hope, stm., Ct., U.S.	B7	84
Mount Hope Bay, b., U.S.	D6	116
Mount Horeb, Wi., U.S.	E4	126
Mount Ida, Ar., U.S.	C2	81
Mount Idaho, Id., U.S.	D2	89
Mount Isa, Austl.	D6	50
Mount Jackson, Va., U.S.	B4	123
Mount Jewett, Pa., U.S.	C4	115
Mount Joy, Pa., U.S.	F9	115
Mount Judea, Ar., U.S.	B2	81
Mount Juliet, Tn., U.S.	A5	119
Mount Kisco, N.Y., U.S.	D7	109
Mountlake Terrace, Wa., U.S.	*B3	124
Mount Lebanon, Pa., U.S.	F1	115
Mount Lemmon, Az., U.S.	E5	80
Mount Lookout, W.V., U.S.	C4	125
Mount Magnet, Austl.	E3	50
Mount Meigs, Al., U.S.	C3	78
Mountmellick, Ire.	D4	11
Mount Montgomery, Nv., U.S.	F3	105
Mount Morgan, Austl.	D9	50
Mount Moriah, Mo., U.S.	A4	102
Mount Morris, Il., U.S.	A4	90
Mount Morris, Mi., U.S.	E7	99
Mount Morris, N.Y., U.S.	C3	109
Mount Morris, Pa., U.S.	G1	115
Mount of Olives, hill, Isr. Occ.	m14	41
Mount Olive, Al., U.S.	B3	78
Mount Olive, Il., U.S.	D4	90
Mount Olive, Ms., U.S.	D4	101
Mount Olive, N.C., U.S.	B4	110
Mount Olive, Tn., U.S.	n14	119
Mount Olivet, Ky., U.S.	B5	94
Mount Olympus, Ut., U.S.	*C4	121
Mount Orab, Oh., U.S.	C2	112
Mount Pearl, Newf.	E5	72
Mount Penn, Pa., U.S.	F10	115
Mount Pleasant, Fl., U.S.	B2	86
Mount Pleasant, Ga., U.S.	D6	92
Mount Pleasant, Ia., U.S.	B2	86
Mount Pleasant, Md., U.S.	E6	99
Mount Pleasant, Mi., U.S.	A4	101
Mount Pleasant, N.J., U.S.	B2	110
Mount Pleasant, N.C., U.S.	F2	115
Mount Pleasant, Pa., U.S.	F8	117
Mount Pleasant, S.C., U.S.	B4	119
Mount Pleasant, Tn., U.S.	C5	120
Mount Pleasant, Tx., U.S.	D4	121
Mount Pleasant, Ut., U.S.	D11	115
Mount Pocono, Pa., U.S.	A6	90
Mount Prospect, Il., U.S.	C4	90
Mount Pulaski, Il., U.S.	A3	111
Mountrail, co., N.D., U.S.	f9	97
Mount Rainier, Md., U.S.	C4	124
Mount Rainier National Park, Wa., U.S.	D8	69
Mount Revelstoke National Park, B.C.	C8	69
Mount Robson Provincial Park, B.C.	D1	123
Mount Rogers National Recreation Area, Va., U.S.	D2	118
Mount Rushmore National Memorial, hist., S.D., U.S.	k13	97
Mount Savage, Md., U.S.	D7	12
Mount's Bay, b., Eng., U.K.	B2	82
Mount Shasta, Ca., U.S.		
Mount Sidney, Va., U.S.	B4	123
Mount Sinai, N.Y., U.S.	*n15	109
Mount Solon, Va., U.S.	B3	123
Mount Sterling, Al., U.S.	C1	78
Mount Sterling, Il., U.S.	D3	90
Mount Sterling, Ky., U.S.	B6	94
Mount Sterling, Oh., U.S.	C2	112
Mount Stewart, P.E.I.	C7	71
Mount Storm, W.V., U.S.	B5	125
Mount Summit, In., U.S.	D7	91
Mount Sunapee, N.H., U.S.	D2	106
Mount Tabor, Vt., U.S.	E3	122
Mount Uniacke, N.S.	E6	71
Mount Union, Ia., U.S.	C6	92
Mount Union, Pa., U.S.	F6	115
Mount Upton, N.Y., U.S.	C5	109
Mount Vernon, Al., U.S.	D1	78
Mount Vernon, Ar., U.S.	B3	81
Mount Vernon, Ga., U.S.	D4	87
Mount Vernon, Il., U.S.	E5	90
Mount Vernon, In., U.S.	I2	91
Mount Vernon, Ia., U.S.	C6	92
Mount Vernon, Ky., U.S.	C5	94
Mount Vernon, Me., U.S.	D3	96
Mount Vernon, Md., U.S.	D6	97
Mount Vernon, Mo., U.S.	D4	102
Mount Vernon, N.Y., U.S.	h13	109
Mount Vernon, Oh., U.S.	B3	112
Mount Vernon, Or., U.S.	C7	114
Mount Vernon, S.D., U.S.	D7	118
Mount Vernon, Tn., U.S.	D9	119
Mount Vernon, Tx., U.S.	C5	120
Mount Vernon, Wa., U.S.	A3	124
Mount Victory, Oh., U.S.	B2	112
Mount View, R.I., U.S.	C4	116
Mount Washington, Ky., U.S.	B4	94
Mount Washington, Ma., U.S.	B1	98
Mount Wolf, Pa., U.S.	F8	115
Mount Zion, Ga., U.S.	C1	87
Mount Zion, Il., U.S.	D5	90
Moura, Austl.	D8	50
Moura, Braz.	C2	59
Moura, Port.	C2	22
Mourdi, Dépression du, depr., Chad	B4	46
Mourmelon-le-Grand, Fr.	E4	17
Mourne Mountains, mts., N. Ire., U.K.	C3	10
Mouscron (Moeskroen), Bel.	B5	16
Mousie, Ky., U.S.	C7	94
Moussoro, Chad	C3	46
Mouthe, Fr.	C1	21
Moutier, Switz.	B3	21
Moûtiers[-Tarentaise], Fr.	E7	16
Mouy, Fr.	E2	17
Moville, Ire.	B4	11
Moville, Ia., U.S.	B1	92
Moweaqua, Il., U.S.	D4	90
Mowrystown, Oh., U.S.	C2	112
Moxahala, Oh., U.S.	C3	112
Moxee City, Wa., U.S.	C5	124
Moxie Pond, l., Me., U.S.	C3	96
Moxley, Ga., U.S.	D4	87
Moy, stm., Ire.	B2	11
Moy, Cnoc, hill, Scot., U.K.	E3	13
Moyale, Eth.	A6	47
Moyale, Kenya	A6	47
Moyamba, S.L.	E2	45
Moycullen, Ire.	D2	11
Moyers, Ok., U.S.	C6	113
Moyeuvre[-Grande], Fr.	C7	16
Moyie, B.C.	E10	69
Moyie Springs, Id., U.S.	A2	89
Moynalty, Ire.	C4	11
Moyobamba, Peru	B2	58
Moyock, N.C., U.S.	A6	110
Moyuta, Guat.	C2	62
Moza, Isr.	h11	41
Mozambique, ctry., Afr.	H9	42
Mozambique Channel, strt., Afr.	H10	42
Mozart, Sask.	F3	75
Mozdok, Sov. Un.	E2	28
Mozelle, Ky., U.S.	D6	94
Mozhaysk, Sov. Un.	D11	27
Mozhga, Sov. Un.	D19	27
Mozyr, Sov. Un.	E7	27
Mpanda, Tan.	C5	48
Mpika, Zam.	D5	48
Mporokoso, Zam.	C5	48
Mpouya, Congo	B2	48
Mpraeso, Ghana	E4	45
Mpwapwa, Tan.	C6	48
Mragowo, Pol.	B7	26
Mšec, Czech.	n16	26
Mšeno[-Mělnické], Czech.	n17	26
M'Sila, Alg.	B5	44
Msta, stm., Sov. Un.	B9	27
Mstislavl, Sov. Un.	D8	27
Mtakuja, Tan.	C5	48
Mtsensk, Sov. Un.	E11	27
Mtubatuba, S. Afr.	C5	49
Mtwara, Tan.	D7	48
Mu, stm., Burma	A1	35
Mucusso, Ang.	E3	48
Mud, stm., Ky., U.S.	C3	94
Mud, stm., Mn., U.S.	B3	100
Mud, stm., W.V., U.S.	C2	125
Muda, stm., Malay.	I4	35
Mudanjiang, China	C10	31
Mudan Jiang, stm., China	C4	33
Mudanya, Tur.	B7	25
Mud Butte, S.D., U.S.	C3	118
Mud Creek, stm., Al., U.S.	g6	78
Mud Creek, stm., Co., U.S.	D8	83
Mud Creek, stm., Ia., U.S.	e9	92
Mud Creek, stm., Ne., U.S.	C6	104
Mud Creek, stm., Ok., U.S.	C3	113
Mud Creek Mountain, mtn., Ar., U.S.	C2	81
Mud Lake, l., Sask.	E1	75
Muddy, Il., U.S.	F5	90
Muddy Boggy Creek, stm., Ok., U.S.	C6	113
Muddy Creek, stm., Co., U.S.	A4	83
Muddy Creek, stm., Ks., U.S.	k14	93
Muddy Creek, stm., Ut., U.S.	E4	121
Muddy Creek, stm., Wy., U.S.	D4	127
Muddy Creek, stm., Wy., U.S.	D6	127
Muddy Creek, stm., Wy., U.S.	E5	127
Muddy Creek, stm., Wy., U.S.	E2	127
Muddy Creek Mountain, mtn., Ar., U.S.	C2	81
Muddy Lake, l., Sask.	E1	75
Muddy Mountain, mtn., Wy., U.S.	D6	127
Muddy Mountains, mts., Nv., U.S.	G7	105
Muddy Peak, mtn., Nv., U.S.	G7	105
Müden, W. Ger.	F4	15
Mudgee, Austl.	F8	51
Mudjatik, stm., Sask.	A7	75
Mud Lake, l., Id., U.S.	F6	89
Mud Lake, l., Me., U.S.	A4	96
Mud Lake, l., Nv., U.S.	F4	105
Mud Lick Creek, stm., Ky., U.S.	k13	94
Mudon, Burma	E10	36
Mudros see Moúdhros, Grc.	C5	25
Mudug, prov., Som.	D6	47
Mueda, Moz.	D6	48
Mueller, Sask.	C4	75
Mueller, Tx., U.S.	B4	120
Muff, Ire.	B4	11
Mufulira, Zam.	D4	48
Mugarripug, China	A11	37
Mugia, Spain	A1	22
Mugla, Tur.	D7	40
Mugodzhary Mountains, hills, Sov. Un.	D5	28
Muḥammad Qawl, Sud.	A4	47
Muhlacker, W. Ger.	E3	19
Mühldorf, W. Ger.	G11	19
Muhlenberg, co., Ky., U.S.	C2	94
Mühlhausen [in Thüringen], E. Ger.	C5	18
Mühlig-Hofmann Mountains, mts., Ant.	B13	7
Muhulu, Zaire	B5	48
Muhutwe, Tan.	B5	48
Mui, i., Marsh Is.	S18	52
Muine Bheag, Ire.	E5	11
Muir, Mi., U.S.	E6	99
Muirkirk, Scot., U.K.	E4	13
Muirkirk, Md., U.S.	B4	97
Muir Woods National Monument, Ca., U.S.	h7	82
Mukachevo, Sov. Un.	G4	27
Mukah, Malay.	E4	34
Mukden see Shenyang, China	C9	31
Mukilteo, Wa., U.S.	B3	124
Mukutawa, stm., Man.	C3	70
Mukwonago, Wi., U.S.	F5	126
Mula, Spain	G10	22
Mulanje, Mwi.	E6	48
Mulberry, Ar., U.S.	B1	81
Mulberry, Fl., U.S.	E4	86
Mulberry, In., U.S.	D4	91
Mulberry, Ks., U.S.	E9	93
Mulberry, N.C., U.S.	A1	110
Mulberry, Oh., U.S.	C1	112
Mulberry, Tn., U.S.	B5	119
Mulberry, stm., Ar., U.S.	B1	81
Mulberry Fork, stm., Al., U.S.	B3	78
Mulberry Grove, Il., U.S.	E4	90
Mulberry Mountain, mtn., Ar., U.S.	B3	81
Mulchén, Chile	B2	54
Mulde, stm., E. Ger.	C6	18
Muldoon, Tx., U.S.	E4	120
Muldraugh, Ky., U.S.	C4	94
Muldrow, Ok., U.S.	B7	113
Mule Creek, N.M., U.S.	D1	108
Mulegé, Mex.	B2	63
Muleshoe, Tx., U.S.	B1	120
Mulga, Al., U.S.	B3	78
Mulhall, Ok., U.S.	A4	113
Mulhacén, mtn., Spain	D4	22
Mülheim [an der Ruhr], W. Ger.	C3	18
Mulhouse, Fr.	D7	16
Muling, China	D5	33
Muling He, stm., China	D6	33
Mull, Island of, i., Scot., U.K.	C2	10
Mull, Sound of, strt., Scot., U.K.	B3	10
Mullaghcleevaun, mtn., Ire.	D5	11
Mullan, Id., U.S.	B3	89
Mullan Pass, Mt., U.S.	B4	104
Mullen, Ne., U.S.	B5	104
Mullens, W.V., U.S.	D3	125
Muller Mountains, mts., Indon.	E4	34
Mullet Key, i., Fl., U.S.	p10	86
Mullet Lake, Mi., U.S.	C6	99
Mullett Lake, l., Mi., U.S.	C6	99
Mullewa, Austl.	E2	50
Mull Head, c., Scot., U.K.	A6	13
Mullica, stm., N.J., U.S.	D3	107
Mullica Hill, N.J., U.S.	D2	107
Mulliken, Mi., U.S.	F6	99
Mullin, Tx., U.S.	D3	120
Mullinavat, Ire.	E4	11
Mullingar, Ire.	C4	11
Mullins, S.C., U.S.	C9	117
Müllrose, E. Ger.	A9	19
Müllheim, W. Ger.	E3	18
Mulroy Bay, b., Ire.	B4	11
Multan, Pak.	E4	36
Multnomah, co., Or., U.S.	B4	114
Mulurulu, Lake, l., Austl.	F4	51
Mulvane, Ks., U.S.	E6	93
Mulvihill, Man.	D2	70
Mumbwa, Zam.	D4	48
Mummy Range, mts., Co., U.S.	A5	83
Mun, stm., Thai.	B2	34
Muna, Mex.	C7	63
Münchberg, W. Ger.	C6	19
Münchenstein, Switz.	A4	21
Muncho Lake, l., B.C.	C8	69
Munchŏn, N. Kor.	G3	33
Muncie, In., U.S.	D7	91
Muncy, Pa., U.S.	D8	115
Mundare, Alta.	C4	68
Munday, Tx., U.S.	C3	120
Mundelein, Il., U.S.	A5	90
Munden, W. Ger.	C4	18
Mundford, Al., U.S.	B4	78
Munford, Tn., U.S.	B2	119
Mundfordville, Ky., U.S.	C4	94
Mungallala Creek, stm., Austl.	D6	51
Mungári, Moz.	A5	49
Mungbere, Zaire	A4	48
Munger, India	C8	36
Munger, Mi., U.S.	E7	99
Mungindi, Austl.	E8	50
Munhall, Pa., U.S.	k14	115
Munich (München), W. Ger.	D5	18
Munising, Mi., U.S.	B4	99
Munith, Mi., U.S.	F6	99
Munjor, Ks., U.S.	D4	93
Munnsville, N.Y., U.S.	C5	109
Muñoz, Phil.	o13	34
Muñoz Gamero, Península, pen., Chile	h11	54
Munro Lake, l., Man.	B4	70
Munsan-ni, S. Kor.	H3	33
Münsingen, W. Ger.	E4	19
Münsingen, Switz.	C4	21
Munson, Alta.	D4	68
Munson, Fl., U.S.	u15	86
Munson, Pa., U.S.	E5	115
Munsonville, N.H., U.S.	D2	106
Munster, Fr.	D7	16
Munster, hist. reg., Ire.	E3	11
Münster [in Westfalen], W. Ger.	C3	18
Munster, In., U.S.	A2	91
Munster, Sask.	F3	75
Munster, Tx., U.S.	C4	120
Muntenia, hist. reg., Rom.	C7	24
Muntok, Indon.	F3	34
Munuscong Lake, l., Mi., U.S.	B6	99
Muonio, Fin.	D10	14
Muonio, stm., Eur.	D10	14
Muotathal, Switz.	C6	21
Mur (Mura), stm., Eur.	B2	24
Mura (Mur), stm., Eur.	B3	24
Murakami, Japan	G9	33
Murākh, Bi'r, well, Eg.	E6	41
Murano, Italy	D8	20
Murashi, Sov. Un.	B3	28
Murat, Fr.	E5	16
Murat, mtn., Tur.	C7	25
Murat, stm., Tur.	C13	40
Murau, Aus.	E7	18
Muravera, Italy	E3	19
Muravyevo, Sov. Un.	C11	33
Mürcheh Khvort, Iran	*B5	38
Murchison, N.Z.	N14	51
Murchison, stm., Austl.	E2	50
Murchison Falls see Kabalega Falls, wtfl., Ug.	A5	48
Murcia, Spain	C5	22
Murcia, hist. reg., Spain	C5	22
Murcki, Pol.	g10	26
Murdo, S.D., U.S.	D5	118
Murdock, Fl., U.S.	E4	86
Murdock, Il., U.S.	D6	90
Murdock, Ks., U.S.	E6	93
Murdock, Mn., U.S.	E3	100
Murdock, Ne., U.S.	C9	104
Mureş, stm., Eur.	C6	24
Muret, Fr.	F7	16
Murewa, Zimb.	A5	49
Murfreesboro, Ar., U.S.	C2	81
Murfreesboro, N.C., U.S.	A5	110
Murfreesboro, Tn., U.S.	B5	119
Murgha Kibzai, Pak.	B4	36
Murgon, Austl.	E9	51
Muri, Nig.	E7	45
Muriaé, Braz.	C4	56
Muriaé, stm., Braz.	A5	56
Muriel Lake, l., Alta.	B5	68
Müritz Lake, l., E. Ger.	B6	18
Murmansk, Sov. Un.	C8	29
Murnau, W. Ger.	B7	20
Murom, Sov. Un.	D13	27
Muroran, Japan	C13	31
Muros, Spain	A1	22
Muroto, Japan	J7	33
Murphy, Ga., U.S.	E3	87
Murphy, Id., U.S.	F2	89
Murphy, Mo., U.S.	g13	102
Murphy, N.C., U.S.	f8	110
Murphy, Or., U.S.	E3	114
Murphy Island, i., S.C., U.S.	E9	117
Murphy Lake, l., B.C.	C7	69
Murphys, Ca., U.S.	C3	82
Murphysboro, Il., U.S.	F4	90
Murphy, W.V., U.S.	B3	125
Murr, Bi'r, well, Eg.	E6	41
Murray, Id., U.S.	B3	89
Murray, Ia., U.S.	C4	92
Murray, Ky., U.S.	f9	94
Murray, Ut., U.S.	D10	104
Murray, co., Ga., U.S.	B2	87
Murray, co., Mn., U.S.	F3	100
Murray, co., Ok., U.S.	C4	113
Murray, stm., Austl.	B7	50
Murray, stm., B.C.	B7	69
Murray, Lake, res., Ok., U.S.	C4	113
Murray, Lake, l., S.C., U.S.	C4	117
Murray Bridge, Austl.	G6	50
Murray Harbour, P.E.I.	C7	71
Murray Head, c., P.E.I.	C7	71
Murray Lake, l., Alta.	E5	68
Murray River, P.E.I.	C7	71
Murraysburg, S. Afr.	D3	49
Murrayville, Il., U.S.	D3	90
Murrayville, Ga., U.S.	f13	87
Murrells Inlet, S.C., U.S.	D10	117
Murrells Inlet, b., S.C., U.S.	E9	117
Mürren, Switz.	F4	21
Murrhardt, W. Ger.	E4	19
Murrieta, Ca., U.S.	F5	82
Murrumbidgee, stm., Austl.	F8	50
Murrupula, Moz.	A6	49
Murrysville, Pa., U.S.	*k15	115
Mursala, i., Indon.	K3	35
Murska Sobota, Yugo.	B3	24
Murten, Switz.	C3	21
Murtaugh, Id., U.S.	G4	89
Murtle Lake, l., B.C.	C8	69
Murud, India	D7	36
Murwāra, India	D7	36
Murwillumbah, Austl.	E9	50
Mürz, stm., Aus.	E7	18
Mürzzuschlag, Aus.	E7	18
Muş, Tur.	*C13	40
Musaid, Libya	A5	47
Musala, mtn., Bul.	D6	24
Musan, N. Kor.	C10	31
Musangoi, Zaire	C3	48
Müsā Qal'eh, Afg.	E12	39
Musashino, Japan	*I9	33
Muscat see Masqaṭ, Oman	C5	38
Muscatatuck, Vernon Fork, stm., In., U.S.	G6	91
Muscatine, Ia., U.S.	C6	92
Muscatine, co., Ia., U.S.	C6	92
Muscle Shoals, Al., U.S.	A2	78
Musclow, Mount, mtn., B.C.	C4	69
Muscoda, Wi., U.S.	E3	126
Muscogee, co., Ga., U.S.	D2	87
Musconetcong, stm., N.J., U.S.	B4	107
Musconetcong Mountain, mtn., N.J., U.S.	B2	107
Muscooten Bay, l., Il., U.S.	C3	90
Muscotah, Ks., U.S.	C8	93
Muscoy, Ca., U.S.	*E5	82
Muse, Ok., U.S.	C7	113
Muse, Pa., U.S.	F1	115
Musgrave Harbour, Newf.	D5	72
Musgrave Ranges, mts., Austl.	E5	50
Musgravetown, Newf.	D5	72
Mushie, Zaire	B2	48
Mushin, Nig.	E5	45
Mushketovo, Sov. Un.	r20	27
Musi, stm., Indon.	F2	34
Muskeg Bay, b., Mn., U.S.	B3	100
Muskeget Channel, strt., Ma., U.S.	D7	98
Muskeget Island, i., Ma., U.S.	D7	98
Muskego, Wi., U.S.	F5	126
Muskego Lake, l., Wi., U.S.	n11	126
Muskegon, Mi., U.S.	E4	99
Muskegon, co., Mi., U.S.	E4	99
Muskegon, stm., Mi., U.S.	E4	99
Muskegon Heights, Mi., U.S.	E4	99
Muskegon Lake, l., Mi., U.S.	E4	99
Muskingum, co., Oh., U.S.	B4	112
Muskingum, stm., Oh., U.S.	C4	112
Muskö, Swe.	u36	14
Muskogee, Ok., U.S.	B6	113
Muskogee, co., Ok., U.S.	B6	113
Muskoka, co., Ont.	B5	73
Muskoka, Lake, l., Ont.	C5	73
Muskrat Dam Lake, res., Ont.	C6	70
Muskwa, stm., Alta.	A3	68
Muskwa Lake, l., Alta.	A3	68
Muslimbāgh, Pak.	B4	36
Musoma, Tan.	B5	48
Musquacook Lakes, l., Me., U.S.	B3	96
Musquaro, Lac, l., Que.	h14	71
Musquash, N.B.	D3	71
Musquash Mountain, mtn., Me., U.S.	C5	96
Musquodoboit Harbour, N.S.	E6	71
Musselburgh, Scot., U.K.	C5	10
Musselshell, stm., Mt., U.S.	D9	103
Musselshell, co., Mt., U.S.	D8	103
Musselshell, stm., Mt., U.S.	D9	103
Mussende, Ang.	D2	48
Mussolinia see Arborea, Italy	E2	20
Mustafakemalpaşa, Tur.	B7	40
Mustang, Ok., U.S.	B4	113
Mustang, i., Tx., U.S.	F4	120
Mustinka, stm., Mn., U.S.	E2	100
Mustique, i., St. Vin.	V26	65
Müt, Eg.	C2	47
Mut, Tur.	D9	40
Mutá, Ponta do, c., Braz.	D5	57
Mutare, Zimb.	A5	49
Mutayyim, Yemen	B5	47
Mutena, Zaire	C3	48
Muti, i., Marsh Is.	S18	52
Mutoko, Zimb.	A5	49
Mutorashanga, Zimb.	A5	49
Mutsu, Japan	F10	33
Mutsu Bay, b., Japan	F10	33
Mutton Bay, Que.	C2	72
Mutton Mountains, mts., Or., U.S.	C5	114
Mutŭbis, Eg.	A2	41
Mutunópolis, Braz.	A3	56
Mutzig, Fr.	F7	16
Mu Us Shamo (Ordos Desert), des., China	D6	31
Muxima, Ang.	C1	48
Muyinga, Bdi.	B5	48
Muynak, Sov. Un.	E5	28
Muyula, i., Pap. N. Gui.	k13	50
Muzaffargarh, Pak.	B3	37
Muzaffarnagar, India	C6	36
Muzaffarpur, India	C8	36
Muzambinho, Braz.	k8	57
Muzhi, Sov. Un.	B21	29
Muztag, mtn., China	A8	36
Muztag, mtn., China	A7	36
Muztagata, mtn., China	F10	29
Mvuma, Zimb.	A5	49
Mwadui, Tan.	B5	48
Mwami, Zimb.	A4	49
Mwanza, Tan.	B5	48
Mwanza, prov., Tan.	B5	48
Mwaya, Tan.	C5	48
Mweelrea, mtn., Ire.	D2	11
Mweka, Zaire	B3	48
Mwene-Ditu, Zaire	C3	48
Mwenezi, Zimb.	B5	49
Mwenga, Zaire	B4	48
Mweru, Lake, l., Afr.	C4	48
Mwimba, Zaire	C3	48
Mwinilunga, Zam.	D3	48
Myājlār, India	D3	37
Myakka, stm., Fl., U.S.	E4	86
Myakka City, Fl., U.S.	E4	86
Myanaung, Burma	D1	35
Myaungmya, Burma	D1	35
Mycenae, hist., Grc.	C4	25
Myers Corner, N.Y., U.S.	*D7	109
Myerstown, Pa., U.S.	F9	115
Myersville, Md., U.S.	A2	97

Name	Map Ref.	Page
Myingyan, Burma	D10	36
Myitkyinā, Burma	C10	36
Myitnge, stm., Burma	B2	35
Myjava, Czech.	D4	26
Mylo, N.D., U.S.	A6	111
Mymensingh, Bngl.	D9	36
Mynaral, Sov. Un.	D8	28
Mynard, Ne., U.S.	h13	104
Myrick, Ms., U.S.	D5	101
Myrnam, Alta.	C5	68
Myrtle, Man.	E3	70
Myrtle, Ms., U.S.	A4	101
Myrtle, Mo., U.S.	E6	102
Myrtle Beach, S.C., U.S.	D10	117
Myrtle Beach Air Force Base, mil., S.C., U.S.	D10	117
Myrtle Creek, Or., U.S.	D3	114
Myrtle Grove, Fl., U.S.	u14	86
Myrtle Grove, La., U.S.	k12	95
Myrtle Point, Or., U.S.	D2	114
Myrtlewood, Al., U.S.	C2	78
Mysen, Nor.	p29	14
Myślenice, Pol.	D5	26
Myślibórz, Pol.	B3	26
Mysłowice, Pol.	g10	26
Mysore, India	F6	36
Mysore see Karnataka, state, India	F6	36
Mystic, Ct., U.S.	D8	84
Mystic, Ga., U.S.	E3	87
Mystic, Ia., U.S.	D5	92
Mystic Lakes, l., Ma., U.S.	g11	98
Myszków, Pol.	f10	26
My Tho, Viet.	C3	34
Mytilene see Mitilíni, Grc.	C6	40
Mytishchi, Sov. Un.	n17	27
Myton, Ut., U.S.	C5	121
Mže, stm., Czech.	D8	19
Mzimba, Mwi.	D5	48
Mzuzu, Mwi.	D5	48
N		
Naab, stm., W. Ger.	D7	19
Naalehu, Hi., U.S.	D6	88
Naamans Garden, De., U.S.	*A3	85
Na'an, Isr.	h10	41
Naantali, Fin.	G10	14
Naas, Ire.	D3	10
Nabā, Jabal (Mount Nebo), mtn., Jord.	C7	41
Nabadwīp, India	*D8	36
Nabb, In., U.S.	G6	91
Nabberu, Lake, l., Austl.	E3	50
Nabburg, W. Ger.	D7	19
Nabeina, Kir.	R18	52
Nabekavu, Fiji	H15	52
Naberezhnyye Chelny (Brezhnev), Sov. Un.	D8	29
Nabeul, Tun.	B7	44
Nabi Shuayb, Mount, mtn., Yemen	*D4	38
Nabnasset, Ma., U.S.	A5	98
Naboomspruit, S. Afr.	B4	49
Nabouwalu, Fiji	H15	52
Nabq, Eg.	H10	40
Nābulus, Isr. Occ.	B3	38
Nacala, Moz.	D7	48
Nacaome, Hond.	D4	62
Naches, Wa., U.S.	C5	124
Naches, stm., Wa., U.S.	C5	124
Nachingwea, Tan.	D6	48
Náchod, Czech.	C4	26
Nacilau Point, c., Fiji	H14	52
Nacimiento, Chile	B2	54
Nacimiento Reservoir, res., Ca., U.S.	E3	82
Nacka, Swe.	*H8	14
Nacmine, Alta.	D4	68
Naco, Az., U.S.	F6	80
Nacogdoches, Tx., U.S.	D5	120
Nacogdoches, co., Tx., U.S.	D5	120
Nacozari [de García], Mex.	A3	63
Nacula, i., Fiji	H14	52
Nadarzyn, Pol.	m13	26
Nadeau, Mi., U.S.	C3	99
Naden Harbour, b., B.C.	B1	69
Nadi, Fiji	H14	52
Nadiād, India	F4	37
Nădlac, Rom.	B5	24
Nador, Mor.	B4	44
Naduri, Fiji	H15	52
Nadvornaya, Sov. Un.	G5	27
Nadym, stm., Sov. Un.	B23	8
Næstved, Den.	J4	14
Nafada, Nig.	D7	45
Nafishah, Eg.	D4	41
Naga, Phil.	C6	34
Naga Hills, mts., Asia	C10	36
Nāgāland, state, India	*C9	36
Nagano, Japan	D12	31
Nagaoka, Japan	D12	31
Nāgappattinam, India	F6	36
Nagarote, Nic.	D4	62
Nagar Pārkar, Pak.	D5	36
Nagasaki, Japan	E10	31
Nagaur, India	D4	37
Nageezi, N.M., U.S.	A2	108
Nāgercoil, India	G6	36
Nagiba, Phil.	p13	34
Nagles Mountains, mts., Ire.	E3	11
Nago, Japan	N5	52
Nago Bay, b., Japan	N5	52
Nagog Pond, l., Ma., U.S.	f10	98
Nagold, W. Ger.	E3	19
Nagoya, Japan	D12	31
Nāgpur, India	D6	36
Nagqu, China	E3	31
Nags Head, N.C., U.S.	B7	110
Nagua, Dom. Rep.	E9	64
Naguabo, P.R.	B4	65
Nagykanizsa, Hung.	E3	24
Nagykörös, Hung.	B4	24
Naha, Japan	F10	31
Nahalat Yehuda, Isr.	h10	41
Nahanni National Park, N.W. Ter.	D7	66
Nahant, Ma., U.S.	g12	98
Nahariyya, Isr.	B7	41
Nahāvand, Iran	D4	39
Nahe, stm., W. Ger.	D3	18
Nahma, Mi., U.S.	C4	99
Nahmakanta Lake, l., Me., U.S.	C3	96
Nahuel Huapi, Arg.	C2	54
Nahuel Huapi, Lago, l., Arg.	C2	54
Nahuel Niyeu, Arg.	C3	54
Nahunta, Ga., U.S.	E5	87
Naic, Phil.	o13	34
Naicam, Sask.	E3	75
Naiguatá, Pico, mtn., Ven.	A4	60
Naihāti, India	*D8	36
Naila, W. Ger.	C6	19
Nailaga, Fiji	H14	52
Nain, Newf.	g9	72
Nā'īn, Iran	E6	39
Naini Tāl, India	C7	37
Nairai, i., Fiji	H15	52
Nairn, Scot., U.K.	B5	10
Nairn, stm., Scot., U.K.	C4	13
Nairobi, Kenya	*B6	48
Naitonitoni, Fiji	I15	52
Naivasha, Kenya	B6	48
Najafābād, Iran	E5	39
Naj Hammādī, Eg.	D6	43
Najībābād, India	C7	37
Najin, N. Kor.	C11	31
Najran, well, Sau. Ar.	D4	38
Naju, S. Kor.	I3	33
Nakadōri Island, i., Japan	J4	33
Nakagusuku Bay, b., Japan	O5	52
Nakaminato, Japan	m19	33
Nakamura, Japan	J6	33
Nakaosu, Japan	N6	52
Nakatsu, Japan	J5	33
Nakfa, Eth.	B4	47
Nakhichevan, Sov. Un.	F3	28
Nakhodka, Sov. Un.	E6	33
Nakhon Chai Si, stm., Thai.	F3	35
Nakhon Pathom, Thai.	F3	35
Nakhon Phanom, Thai.	B2	34
Nakhon Ratchasima, Thai.	C2	34
Nakhon Sawan, Thai.	B1	34
Nakhon Si Thammarat, Thai.	D2	34
Nakina, Ont.	o18	73
Nakina, N.C., U.S.	C4	110
Nakło [nad Notecią], Pol.	B4	26
Naknek, Ak., U.S.	D8	79
Naknek Lake, l., Ak., U.S.	D8	79
Nakono Island, i., Japan	L4	33
Nakskov, Den.	J4	14
Nakuru, Kenya	B6	48
Nakusp, B.C.	D9	69
Nalchik, Sov. Un.	E2	28
Nallen, W.V., U.S.	m14	125
Nalón, stm., Spain	A2	22
Nālūt, Libya	C2	43
Nam, stm., Asia	B3	35
Namacurra, Moz.	E7	48
Namak, Daryācheh-ye, l., Iran	D5	39
Namak, Kavīr-e, des., Iran	D8	39
Namaka, Alta.	D4	68
Namakan Lake, l., N.A.	B6	100
Namangan, Sov. Un.	E10	29
Namanock Island, i., N.J., U.S.	A3	107
Namanyere, Tan.	C5	48
Namapa, Moz.	D6	48
Namasagali, Ug.	A5	48
Namatanai, Pap. N. Gui.	h13	50
Nambe Pueblo, N.M., U.S.	B4	108
Nambour, Austl.	E9	50
Nam Co, l., China	E3	31
Nam Dinh, Viet.	A3	34
Nāmdö, i., Swe.	t36	14
Nam Du Islands, is., Viet.	H6	35
Namekagon, stm., Wi., U.S.	B2	126
Namekagon Lake, l., Wi., U.S.	B2	126
Namen see Namur, Bel.		
Nametil, Moz.	A6	49
Namew Lake, l., Can.	C5	75
Namib Desert, des., Afr.	B1	49
Namibe (Moçâmedes), Ang.	E1	48
Namibe, dept., Ang.	E1	48
Namibia (South West Africa), ctry., Afr.	B2	49
Namiquipa, Mex.	B3	63
Namjagbarwa Feng, mtn., China	F4	31
Namlea, Indon.	F7	34
Nam Ngum Reservoir, res., Laos	C5	35
Namoi, stm., Austl.	F8	50
Namoruputh, Kenya	A6	48
Nampa, Alta.	A2	68
Nampa, Id., U.S.	F2	89
Nampala, Mali	E3	45
Nampo (Chinnampo), N. Kor.	D10	31
Nampula, Moz.	A6	49
Nampula, dept., Moz.	D6	48
Namsen, stm., Nor.	E4	14
Namsos, Nor.	E4	14
Namu, B.C.	D4	69
Namu Island, i., Marsh Is.	P18	52
Namur (Namen), Bel.	B6	16
Namur, Que.	D3	74
Namur, prov., Bel.	D4	17
Namur Island, i., Marsh Is.	S17	52
Namutoni, Nmb.	A2	49
Namwala, Zam.	E4	48
Namwŏn, S. Kor.	I3	33
Namysłów, Pol.	C4	26
Nan, Thai.	A2	34
Nan, stm., Thai.	B2	34
Nana, stm., Cen. Afr. Rep.	D3	46
Nanafalia, Al., U.S.	C2	78
Nanaimo, B.C.	E5	69
Nanakuli, Hi., U.S.	B3	88
Nanao, Japan	H8	33
Nanatsu Island, i., Japan	H8	33
Nance, co., Ne., U.S.	C7	104
Nanchang, China	F8	31
Nancheng, China	F8	31
Nancheng, China	E6	31
Nanchong, China	E8	31
Nanchuan, China	J2	32
Nancy, Fr.	C7	16
Nancy, Ky., U.S.	C5	94
Nancy Creek, stm., Ga., U.S.	h8	87
Nanda Devi, mtn., India	B7	36
Nānded, India	H6	37
Nandurbār, India	G5	37
Nanfeng, China	K7	32
Nanga Eboko, Cam.	E2	46
Nanga Parbat, mtn., Pak.	A5	36
Nangis, Fr.	F2	17
Nangong, China	F6	32
Nang Rong, Thai.	F5	35
Nanhua, China	F3	31
Nanjemoy, Md., U.S.	D3	97
Nanjing (Nanking), China	E8	31
Nanking see Nanjing, China	E9	31
Nanning, China	G6	31
Nanoose Bay, B.C.	f11	69
Nanowin, stm., Man.	C3	70
Nanping, China	F8	31
Nansemond, stm., Va., U.S.	k14	123
Nansen Sound, strt., N.W. Ter.	k33	66
Nan Shan see Qilian Shan, mts., China	D4	31
Nansio, Tan.	B5	48
Nanson, N.D., U.S.	A6	111
Nanterre, Fr.	g9	16
Nantes, Fr.	E5	16
Nanteuil-le-Haudouin, Fr.	E2	17
Nantian, China	J9	32
Nanticoke, Ont.	E4	73
Nanticoke, Md., U.S.	D6	97
Nanticoke, Pa., U.S.	D10	115
Nanticoke, stm., U.S.	D6	97
Nanton, Alta.	D4	68
Nantong, China	E9	31
Nantua, Fr.	D6	16
Nantucket, Ma., U.S.	D7	98
Nantucket, co., Ma., U.S.	D7	98
Nantucket Island, i., Ma., U.S.	D7	98
Nantucket Sound, strt., Ma., U.S.	C7	98
Nantuxent Point, c., N.J., U.S.	E2	107
Nantwich, Eng., U.K.	A5	12
Nanty Glo, Pa., U.S.	F4	115
Nanuet, N.Y., U.S.	g12	109
Nanukuloa, Fiji	H15	52
Nanuku Passage, strt., Fiji	H16	52
Nanuku Reef, rf., Fiji	H16	52
Nanuque, Braz.	B4	56
Nanyang, China	E7	31
Nanyuki, Kenya	A6	48
Nanzhang, China	I4	32
Nao, Cape, c., Spain	C6	22
Naoli He, stm., China	C6	33
Naoma, W.V., U.S.	n13	125
Naomi Peak, mtn., Ut., U.S.	B4	121
Náousa, Grc.	B4	25
Napa, Ca., U.S.	C2	82
Napa, co., Ca., U.S.	C2	82
Napadogan, N.B.	C3	71
Napakiak, Ak., U.S.	C7	79
Napanee, Ont.	C8	73
Napanoch, N.Y., U.S.	D6	109
Napatree Point, c., R.I., U.S.	G1	116
Napavine, Wa., U.S.	C3	124
Nape, Laos	C6	35
Naper, Ne., U.S.	B6	104
Naperville, Il., U.S.	B5	90
Napetipi, stm., Can.	C2	72
Napf, mtn., Switz.	C4	21
Napier, N.Z.	M16	51
Napier Mountains, mts., Ant.	C18	7
Napierville, Que.	D4	74
Napierville, co., Que.	D4	74
Napinka, Man.	E1	70
Naples (Napoli), Italy	D5	23
Naples, Fl., U.S.	F5	86
Naples, Id., U.S.	A2	89
Naples, Il., U.S.	D3	90
Naples, Me., U.S.	E2	96
Naples, N.Y., U.S.	C3	109
Naples, S.D., U.S.	C8	118
Naples, Tx., U.S.	C5	120
Naples, Ut., U.S.	C6	121
Naples, Gulf of, b., Italy	D5	23
Naples Park, Fl., U.S.	*F5	86
Napo, prov., Ec.	B2	58
Napo, stm., S.A.	B3	58
Napoleon, Mo., U.S.	B3	102
Napoleon, N.D., U.S.	C6	111
Napoleon, Oh., U.S.	A1	112
Napoleonville, La., U.S.	E4	95
Naponee, Ne., U.S.	D6	104
Nappanee, In., U.S.	B5	91
Napton, Mo., U.S.	B4	102
Naqadeh, Iran	C4	39
Nara, Japan	o14	33
Nara, Mali	C3	45
Nāra Canal, Pak.	D2	37
Naracoorte, Austl.	G7	50
Naramata, B.C.	E8	69
Naranja, Fl., U.S.	G6	86
Narathiwat, Thai.	D2	34
Nara Visa, N.M., U.S.	B6	108
Nārāyanganj, Bngl.	D9	36
Nārāyanpet, India	I6	37
Narberth, Wales, U.K.	E3	12
Narberth, Pa., U.S.	p20	115
Narbonne, Fr.	F5	16
Narcisse, Ok., U.S.	A7	113
Narcisse, Man.	D3	70
Narcoossee, Fl., U.S.	D5	86
Nardin, Ok., U.S.	A4	113
Nardò, Italy	D7	23
Nares Strait, strt., N.A.	m37	66
Narew, stm., Eur.	B6	26
Nāřī, Jabal an, hills, Libya	E4	43
Nariño, dept., Col.	C2	60
Narita, Japan	n19	33
Narka, Ks., U.S.	C6	93
Narmada, stm., India	D6	36
Narodnaya, Mount, mtn., Sov. Un.	C9	29
Naro-Fominsk, Sov. Un.	D11	27
Narok, Kenya	B6	48
Narol, Man.	D3	70
Narrabri, Austl.	F8	50
Narragansett, R.I., U.S.	F4	116
Narragansett Bay, b., R.I., U.S.	E5	116
Narraguagus, stm., Me., U.S.	D5	96
Narran, stm., Austl.	F8	50
Narrandera, Austl.	D6	50
Narran Lake, l., Austl.	F8	50
Narromine, Austl.	F8	50
Narrows, Va., U.S.	C2	123
Narrowsburg, N.Y., U.S.	D5	109
Narsimhapur, India	F7	37
Narsipatnam, India	I9	37
Naruna, Va., U.S.	C3	123
Narva, Nor.	C7	14
Narvik, Nor.	C7	14
Naryan-Mar, Sov. Un.	C8	29
Narylico, Austl.	D3	51
Narym, Sov. Un.	D25	8
Naryn, stm., Sov. Un.	E9	28
Naryn, stm., Sov. Un.	E10	28
Narynkol, Sov. Un.	A7	35
Na Sam, Viet.	D1	34
Nasarawa, Nig.	E6	45
Nase, Japan	P13	31
Naseby, N.Z.	P13	51
Naselle, Wa., U.S.	C2	124
Nash, N.D., U.S.	A8	111
Nash, Ok., U.S.	A3	113
Nash, Tx., U.S.	C5	120
Nash, co., N.C., U.S.	A4	110
Nash Creek, N.B.	B3	71
Nashoba, Ok., U.S.	C6	113
Nashoba Hill, hill, Ma., U.S.	f10	98
Nashua, Ia., U.S.	B5	92
Nashua, Mn., U.S.	D2	100
Nashua, Mt., U.S.	B10	103
Nashua, N.H., U.S.	E4	106
Nashua, stm., U.S.	E3	106
Nashville, Ga., U.S.	E3	87
Nashville, Il., U.S.	E4	90
Nashville, In., U.S.	F5	91
Nashville, Ks., U.S.	E5	93
Nashville, Mi., U.S.	F5	99
Nashville, Mo., U.S.	D3	102
Nashville, N.C., U.S.	B5	110
Nashville, Oh., U.S.	B3	112
Nashville, Tn., U.S.	A5	119
Nashwaak, stm., N.B.	C3	71
Nashwaaksis, N.B.	D3	71
Nashwauk, Mn., U.S.	C5	100
Nasielsk, Pol.	B6	26
Nasīf, Bi'r, well, Eg.	D2	41
Nāsijärvi, l., Fin.	G10	14
Nāsik, India	B4	38
Nāsir, Sud.	D3	47
Nasiri see Ahvāz, Iran	B4	38
Naskaupi, stm., Newf.	g9	72
Nason, Il., U.S.	E5	90
Nasonville, R.I., U.S.	B3	116
Nass, stm., B.C.	E7	66
Nassau, Bah.	B5	64
Nassau, De., U.S.	E5	85
Nassau, Mn., U.S.	E2	100
Nassau, N.Y., U.S.	C7	109
Nassau, co., Fl., U.S.	B5	86
Nassau, co., N.Y., U.S.	E7	109
Nassau, co., Fl., U.S.	k8	86
Nassau, Bahía, b., Chile	k12	54
Nassau International Airport, Bah.	m17	64
Nassau Shores, N.Y., U.S.	*n15	109
Nassau Sound, b., Fl., U.S.	B5	86
Nassauville, Fl., U.S.	B5	86
Nassawadox, Va., U.S.	C7	123
Nassawango Creek, stm., Md., U.S.	D7	97
Nasser, Lake, res., Afr.	E6	43
Nässjö, Swe.	H6	14
Nasugbu, Phil.	o13	34
Nasukoin Mountain, mtn., Mt., U.S.	B2	103
Nata, Bots.	B4	49
Natá, Pan.	F7	62
Natagaima, Col.	C2	60
Natal, Braz.	C3	57
Natal, prov., S. Afr.	C5	49
Natalbany, La., U.S.	D5	95
Natalia, Tx., U.S.	E3	120
Natanes Plateau, plat., Az., U.S.	D5	80
Natashquan, Que.	h9	72
Natashquan, stm., Can.	h9	72
Natashwaun Lake, l., Man.	B3	70
Natchaug, stm., Ct., U.S.	B7	84
Natchez, Ms., U.S.	D2	101
Natchitoches, La., U.S.	C2	95
Natchitoches, co., La., U.S.	C2	95
Natewa Bay, b., Fiji	H15	52
Nathalie, Va., U.S.	D4	123
Nathrop, Co., U.S.	C4	83
Natimuk, Austl.	H3	51
Nation, stm., B.C.	B6	69
National City, Ca., U.S.	F5	82
National City, Mi., U.S.	D7	99
National Gardens, Fl., U.S.	C5	86
National Park, N.J., U.S.	*D2	107
Natitingou, Benin	D1	57
Natividade, Braz.	D1	57
Natoma, Ks., U.S.	C4	93
Natron, Lake, l., Afr.	B6	48
Natrona, Wy., U.S.	C6	127
Natrona, co., Wy., U.S.	D5	127
Natrona Heights, Pa., U.S.	E2	115
Nattarö, i., Swe.	u36	14
Nattaung, mtn., Burma	C2	35
Natural Bridge, Al., U.S.	A2	78
Natural Bridge, N.Y., U.S.	A5	109
Natural Bridge, Va., U.S.	C3	123
Natural Bridge, Ut., U.S.	F3	121
Natural Bridge, Va., U.S.	C3	123
Natural Bridges National Monument, Ut., U.S.	F6	121
Naturaliste, Cape, c., Austl.	F1	50
Natural Steps, Ar., U.S.	h10	81
Naturita, Co., U.S.	C2	83
Naubinway, Mi., U.S.	B5	99
Nauders, Aus.	E5	18
Nauen, E. Ger.	B6	18
Naugatuck, Ct., U.S.	D3	84
Naugatuck, stm., Ct., U.S.	D3	84
Naumburg, W. Ger.	B4	19
Naumburg [an der Saale], E. Ger.	C5	18
Naunhof, E. Ger.	B7	19
Naupactus see Návpaktos, Grc.	C3	25
Ñaupe, Peru	C2	58
Nauru, ctry., Oc.	G10	6
Naushon Island, i., Ma., U.S.	D6	98
Nauta, Peru	D3	58
Nautilus Park, Ct., U.S.	D7	84
Nautla, Mex.	C5	63
Nauvoo, Al., U.S.	B2	78
Nauvoo, Il., U.S.	C2	90
Nauwigewauk, N.B.	D4	71
Nava, Lake, l., Spain	A3	22
Nava del Rey, Spain	C6	22
Navahermosa, Spain	C3	22
Navajo, Az., U.S.	B6	80
Navajo, co., Az., U.S.	B5	80
Navajo Dam, N.M., U.S.	A2	108
Navajo Indian Reservation, U.S.	A4	80
Navajo Mountain, mtn., Ut., U.S.	F5	121
Navajo National Monument, U.S.	A5	80
Navajo Reservoir, res., U.S.	A2	108
Navalcarnero, Spain	B3	22
Navalmoral de la Mata, Spain	C3	22
Navan see An Uaimh, Ire.	D3	10
Navan, Cape, c., Sov. Un.	C20	29
Navarino, Isla, i., Chile	k12	54
Navarre, Fl., U.S.	u15	86
Navarre, Oh., U.S.	B4	112
Navarre, hist. reg., Spain	B5	22
Navarro, co., Tx., U.S.	C4	120
Navas de Tolosa, Spain	C4	22
Navasota, Tx., U.S.	D4	120
Navasota, stm., Tx., U.S.	D4	120
Navassa, N.C., U.S.	C4	110
Navassa Island, i., N.A.	E6	64
Navatu, rf., Fiji	I16	52
Nävekvarn, Swe.	u34	14
Naver, stm., Scot., U.K.	B4	13
Naver, Loch, l., Scot., U.K.	B4	13
Navesink, N.J., U.S.	C4	107
Navet Reservoir, res., Trin.	O23	65
Navia, Arg.	A3	54
Navia, stm., Spain	A2	22
Navidad, Chile	A2	54
Naviti, i., Fiji	H14	52
Navojoa, Mex.	B3	63
Navolato, Mex.	C3	63
Návpaktos (Naupactus), Grc.	C3	25
Návplion, Grc.	D4	25
Navrongo, Ghana	D4	45
Navsāri, India	G4	37
Nawābshāh, Pak.	C4	36
Nawāda, India	E10	37
Nawāh, Afg.	E13	39
Nawiliwili Bay, b., Hi., U.S.	B2	88
Náxos, Grc.	D5	40
Náxos, i., Grc.	D5	40
Nay, Fr.	F3	16
Nayarit, state, Mex.	C3	63
Nayau Island, i., Fiji	H16	52
Nāy Band, Iran	C5	39
Nāy Band, Iran	E8	39
Nāy Band, Kūh-e, mtn., Iran	E8	39
Nāy Band, Ra's-e, c., Iran	H6	39
Naylor, Ga., U.S.	F3	87
Naylor, Mo., U.S.	E7	102
Nayoro, Japan	D11	33
Nazaré, Braz.	D5	57
Nazaré, Port.	C1	22
Nazaré da Mata, Braz.	h6	57
Nazareth (Nazerat), Isr.	B3	38
Nazareth, Ky., U.S.	C4	94
Nazareth, Pa., U.S.	E11	115
Nazareth, Tx., U.S.	B1	120
Nazário, Braz.	B3	56
Nazas, Mex.	B4	63
Nazas, stm., Mex.	B4	63
Nazca, Peru	D3	58
Nazilli, Tur.	D7	40
Nazimovo, Sov. Un.	D27	8
Naziya, Sov. Un.	s32	17
Nazko, stm., B.C.	C6	69
Nazlini, Az., U.S.	B6	80
Nazret, Eth.	D4	47
Nazyvayevsk, Sov. Un.	B8	28
Ncheu, Mwi.	D5	48
Ndala, Tan.	B5	48
N'dalatando, Ang.	C1	48
Ndélé, Cen. Afr. Rep.	F2	46
Ndendé, Gabon	F2	46
N'Djamena (Fort-Lamy), Chad	C3	46
Ndjolé, Gabon	F2	46
Ndola, Zam.	D4	48
Neagh, Lough, l., N. Ire., U.K.	C3	10
Neah Bay, Wa., U.S.	A1	124
Neal, Ks., U.S.	E7	93
Neale, stm., Austl.	E6	50
Néa Ionía, Grc.	*C4	25
Néa Liósia, Grc.	*C4	25
Néa Páfos, Cyp.	E9	40
Néa Palátia, Grc.	g11	25
Neápolis, Grc.	D4	25
Néa Smírni, Grc.	*D4	25
Near Islands, is., Ak., U.S.	E2	79
Neath, Wales, U.K.	E4	12
Neavitt, Md., U.S.	C5	97
Neba, Japan	n16	33
Nebine Creek, stm., Austl.	E8	50
Nebo, Il., U.S.	D3	90
Nebo, Ky., U.S.	C2	94
Nebo, La., U.S.	C3	95
Nebo, Mo., U.S.	D5	102
Nebo, Mount, mtn., Ut., U.S.	D4	121
Nebo, Mount see Nabā, Jabal, mtn., Jord.	C7	41
Nebraska, In., U.S.	F7	91
Nebraska, state, U.S.	C6	104
Nebraska City, Ne., U.S.	D10	104
Nebužely, Czech.	n18	19
Necedah, Wi., U.S.	D3	126
Nechako, stm., B.C.	C5	69
Nechako Range, mts., B.C.	C5	69
Neche, N.D., U.S.	A8	111
Neches, stm., Tx., U.S.	D5	120
Nechí, Col.	B3	60
Nechí, stm., Col.	B3	60
Nechranice Reservoir, res., Czech.	C9	19
Neckar, stm., W. Ger.	C4	19
Neckarsulm, W. Ger.	D4	19
Neck City, Mo., U.S.	D3	102
Necker Island, i., Hi., U.S.	m15	88
Necochea, Arg.	C5	54
Neder Rijn, stm., Neth.	C5	17
Nedrow, N.Y., U.S.	C4	109
Needham, Ma., U.S.	g11	98
Needle Mountain, mtn., Wy., U.S.	B3	127
Needles, Ca., U.S.	E6	82
Needmore, In., U.S.	G5	91
Needmore, Pa., U.S.	G5	115
Needville, Tx., U.S.	r14	120
Neelin, Man.	E2	70
Neely, Ms., U.S.	D5	101
Neels Gap, Ga., U.S.	B3	87
Neely's Landing, Mo., U.S.	D8	102
Neelyton, Pa., U.S.	F6	115
Ñeembucú, dept., Para.	B4	54
Negro, stm., Braz.	B1	56
Negro, stm., S.A.	D4	53
Negro, stm., S.A.	E1	56
Negro Mountain, mtn., Md., U.S.	k12	97
Negros, i., Phil.	D6	34
Negru-Vodă, Rom.	D9	24
Neguac, N.B.	B4	71
Nehalem, Or., U.S.	B3	114
Nehalem, stm., Or., U.S.	A3	114
Nehawka, Ne., U.S.	D10	104
Nehbandān, Iran	F10	39
Nehe, China	B2	33
Neheim-Hüsten, W. Ger.	B3	19
Neiba, Dom. Rep.	E8	64
Neiden, Nor.	C13	14
Neidpath, Sask.	G2	75
Neihart, Mt., U.S.	D6	103
Neihuang, China	G6	32
Neijiang, China	F6	31
Neilburg, Sask.	E1	75
Neill Point, c., Wa., U.S.	f11	124
Neillsville, Wi., U.S.	D3	126
Nei Monggol see Inner Mongolia, prov., China	C7	31
Neisse, stm., Eur.	C7	18
Neiva, Col.	C2	60
Neixiang, China	E7	31
Nejd, reg., Sau. Ar.	C4	38
Nejdek, Czech.	C7	19
Nekemte, Eth.	D4	47
Nekoma, Ks., U.S.	D4	93
Nekoma, N.D., U.S.	A7	111
Nekoosa, Wi., U.S.	D4	126
Neksø, Den.	C8	15
Nelagoney, Ok., U.S.	A5	113
Nelidovo, Sov. Un.	C9	27
Neligh, Ne., U.S.	B7	104
Nellis Air Force Base, mil., Nv., U.S.	G6	105
Nell Island, i., Marsh Is.	S17	52
Nellore, India	F7	36
Nellysford, Va., U.S.	C4	123
Nelma, Sov. Un.	C9	33
Nelson, N.Z.	N14	51
Nelson, Az., U.S.	B2	80
Nelson, B.C.	E9	69
Nelson, Ga., U.S.	B2	87
Nelson, Ky., U.S.	C2	94
Nelson, Mn., U.S.	E3	100
Nelson, Mo., U.S.	B4	102
Nelson, Ne., U.S.	D7	104
Nelson, Nv., U.S.	H7	105
Nelson, Pa., U.S.	C7	115
Nelson, Wi., U.S.	D1	126
Nelson, co., Ky., U.S.	C4	94
Nelson, co., N.D., U.S.	B7	111
Nelson, co., Va., U.S.	C4	123
Nelson, stm., Man.	A4	70
Nelson, Cape, c., Austl.	I3	51
Nelson Forks, B.C.	m18	69
Nelson House, Man.	B2	70
Nelson Lake, l., Man.	B2	70
Nelsonville, Oh., U.S.	C3	112
Nelspruit, S. Afr.	B5	49
Néma, Maur.	E3	45
Nemacolin, Pa., U.S.	G2	115
Nemadji, stm., U.S.	B1	126
Nemaha, Ia., U.S.	B2	92
Nemaha, Ne., U.S.	D10	104
Nemaha, co., Ks., U.S.	C7	93
Nemaha, co., Ne., U.S.	D10	104
Nemakščiai, Sov. Un.	A7	26
Neman (Nemunas), stm., Sov. Un.	E5	27
Nembe, Nig.	F6	45
Nemeiben Lake, l., Sask.	B3	75
Nemi, Lake, l., Italy	h9	23
Nemiscau, Que.	h11	74
Nemo, S.D., U.S.	C2	118
Nemours, Fr.	C5	16
Nemunas (Neman), stm., Sov. Un.	D4	27
Nemuro, Japan	C14	31
Nemuro Strait, strt., Asia	D12	33
Nenagh, Ire.	D2	10
Nenana, Ak., U.S.	C10	79
Nendeln, Liech.	B8	21
Nene, stm., Eng., U.K.	B8	21
Nenjiang, China	B10	31
Nen (Nonni), stm., China	B9	31
Nenzel, Ne., U.S.	B4	104
Nenzing, Aus.	B8	21
Neodesha, Ks., U.S.	E8	93
Neoga, Il., U.S.	D5	90
Neola, Ia., U.S.	C2	92
Neola, Ut., U.S.	C5	121
Néon Karlovásion, Grc.	D6	25
Neopit, Wi., U.S.	D5	126
Neosho, Mo., U.S.	E3	102
Neosho, Wi., U.S.	E5	126
Neosho, co., Ks., U.S.	E8	93
Neosho, stm., U.S.	A6	113
Neosho Falls, Ks., U.S.	D8	93
Neosho Rapids, Ks., U.S.	D8	93
Neotsu, Or., U.S.	B3	114
Nepal, ctry., Asia	C7	36
Nepalganj, Nepal	C5	37
Nepaug, Ct., U.S.	*B4	84
Nepaug Reservoir, res., Ct., U.S.	B3	84
Nepean, Ont.	B9	73
Nepewassi Lake, l., Ont.	A4	73
Nephi, Ut., U.S.	D4	121
Nephton, Ont.	B7	73
Nepisiguit, stm., N.B.	B3	71
Nepisiguit Bay, b., N.B.	B4	71
Nepomuk, Czech.	D8	19
Neponset, Il., U.S.	B4	90
Neponset, stm., Ma., U.S.	h11	98
Neptune, Sask.	H3	75
Nepton, Ky., U.S.	B6	94
Neptune, N.J., U.S.	C4	107
Neptune Beach, Fl., U.S.	B5	86
Neptune City, N.J., U.S.	C4	107
Nera, stm., Italy		
Nérac, Fr.	D14	19
Nerchinsk, Sov. Un.	A8	33
Nerchinskiy Zavod, Sov. Un.	A8	33
Nerekhta, Sov. Un.	C13	27
Neretva, stm., Yugo.	D3	24
Nerinquinha, Ang.	E3	48
Neris, stm., Sov. Un.	D6	27
Nerja, Spain	D4	22
Nerpichye, Sov. Un.	B12	33
Nerstrand, Mn., U.S.	F5	100
Nerva, Spain	D2	22
Nes, Neth.		
Nesbit, Ms., U.S.	A3	101
Nesbitt, Man.	E2	70
Nesco, N.J., U.S.	D3	107
Nesconset, N.Y., U.S.	*n15	109

Name	Map Ref.	Page
Nescopeck, Pa., U.S.	D9	115
Nesebŭr, Bul.	D8	24
Neshanic, stm., N.J., U.S.	C3	107
Neshanic Station, N.J., U.S.	B3	107
Nesher, Isr.	B7	41
Neshkoro, Wi., U.S.	E4	126
Neshoba, Ms., U.S.	C4	101
Neshoba, co., Ms., U.S.	C4	101
Nesika Beach, Or., U.S.	E2	114
Neskaupstadur, Ice.	n26	14
Neskowin, Or., U.S.	B3	114
Nesle, Fr.	E2	17
Nesmith, S.C., U.S.	D8	117
Nesodden, Nor.	p28	14
Nesowadnehunk, l., Me., U.S.	B3	96
Nespelem, Wa., U.S.	A7	124
Nesquehoning, Pa., U.S.	E10	115
Ness, co., Ks., U.S.	D4	93
Ness, Loch, l., Scot., U.K.	C4	13
Ness City, Ks., U.S.	D4	93
Nesselrode, Mount, mtn., N.A.	E6	66
Nesselwang, W. Ger.	B6	20
Nesslau, Switz.	B5	20
Nessmersiel, W. Ger.	A7	17
Nesterov, Sov. Un.	C7	26
Nesterov, Sov. Un.	A7	26
Nestório, Braz.	B3	25
Nestorville, W.V., U.S.	B5	125
Néstos (Mesta), stm., Eur.	B5	25
Nesvizh, Sov. Un.	E6	27
Nes Ziyyona, Isr.	C6	41
Netanya, Isr.	B6	41
Netarts, Or., U.S.	B3	114
Netawaka, Ks., U.S.	C8	93
Netcong, N.J., U.S.	B3	107
Netherhill, Sask.	F1	75
Netherlands, ctry., Eur.	A6	16
Netherlands Antilles, ctry., N.A.	A4	60
Nether Providence Township, Pa., U.S.	*G11	115
Nethy Bridge, Scot., U.K.	C5	13
Netolice, Czech.	D9	19
Netrakona, Bngl.	E13	37
Nettie, W.V., U.S.	C4	125
Nettilling Lake, l., N.W. Ter.	C18	66
Nett Lake, Mn., U.S.	B5	100
Nett Lake, l., Mn., U.S.	B5	100
Nett Lake Indian Reservation, Mn., U.S.	B6	100
Nettleton, Ms., U.S.	A5	101
Nettleton, Mo., U.S.	B4	102
Nettuno, Italy	k9	23
Netvořice, Czech.	o18	26
Netzahualcóyotl, Mex.	h9	63
Neubeckum, W. Ger.	B3	19
Neubrandenburg, E. Ger.	B6	18
Neuburg [an der Donau], W. Ger.	D5	18
Neuchâtel, Switz.	E3	18
Neuchâtel, state, Switz.	C2	20
Neuchâtel, Lake, l., Switz.	E3	18
Neudorf, Sask.	G4	75
Neuenegg, Switz.	C3	21
Neuenkirchen, W. Ger.	A8	17
Neuenrade, W. Ger.	B2	19
Neuerburg, W. Ger.	E6	17
Neufchâteau, Bel.	E5	17
Neufchâteau, Fr.	C6	16
Neufchâtel-en-Bray, Fr.	C4	16
Neufchâtel-sur-Aisne, Fr.	E4	17
Neufelden, Aus.	D6	18
Neugersdorf, E. Ger.	C9	19
Neuharlingersiel, W. Ger.	A7	17
Neuhaus, E. Ger.	E4	15
Neuhaus, E. Ger.	C6	19
Neuilly [-sur-Seine], Fr.	g11	16
Neu-Isenburg, W. Ger.	C3	19
Neukirchen am Grossvenediger, Aus.	B8	20
Neumarkt, W. Ger.	D5	18
Neumarkt-Sankt Veit, W. Ger.	A8	20
Neumünster, W. Ger.	A4	18
Neunburg vorm Wald, W. Ger.	D7	19
Neunkirch, Switz.	A6	21
Neunkirchen, Aus.	E8	18
Neunkirchen, W. Ger.	D2	19
Neuquén, Arg.	B3	54
Neuquén, prov., Arg.	B3	54
Neuquén, stm., Arg.	B3	54
Neurara, Chile	D2	55
Neuruppin, E. Ger.	B6	18
Neuse, stm., N.C., U.S.	B6	110
Neusiedler Lake, l., Eur.	E8	18
Neuss, W. Ger.	B1	19
Neustadt, Ont.	C4	73
Neustadt, E. Ger.	B9	19
Neustadt, E. Ger.	B2	19
Neustadt, W. Ger.	E4	18
Neustadt am Rübenberge, W. Ger.	F3	19
Neustadt an der Aisch, W. Ger.	D5	18
Neustadt an der Dosse, E. Ger.	B6	18
Neustadt an der Waldnaab, W. Ger.	D7	19
Neustadt [an der Weinstrasse], W. Ger.	D4	18
Neustadt [bei Coburg], W. Ger.	C5	19
Neustadt-Glewe, E. Ger.	E5	15
Neustadt [in Holstein], W. Ger.	A5	18
Neustrelitz, E. Ger.	B6	18
Neu-Ulm, W. Ger.	D5	18
Neuville, Que.	C6	74
Neuville-lès-Dieppe, Fr.	E9	12
Neuwerk, i., W. Ger.	E2	15
Neuwied, W. Ger.	C3	18
Neva, Tn., U.S.	C12	119
Neva, stm., Sov. Un.	s31	14
Nevada, Ia., U.S.	B4	92
Nevada, Mo., U.S.	D3	102
Nevada, co., Ar., U.S.	D2	81
Nevada, co., Ca., U.S.	C3	82
Nevada, state, U.S.	D5	105
Nevada, Sierra, mts., Spain	D4	22
Nevada, Sierra, mts., U.S.	D4	82
Nevada City, Ca., U.S.	C3	82
Nevada Mills, In., U.S.	A7	91
Nevado, Cerro, mtn., Col.	C4	49
Nevel, Sov. Un.	C7	27
Nevelsk, Sov. Un.	B13	31
Nevelski, Mount, mtn., Sov. Un.	A11	33
Nevers, Fr.	D5	16
Neversink, stm., N.Y., U.S.	D6	109
Neversink Reservoir, res., N.Y., U.S.	D6	109
Nevesinje, Yugo.	D4	24
Neville, Sask.	H2	75
Neville, Fr.	E8	12
Nevils, Ga., U.S.	D5	87
Nevinnomyssk, Sov. Un.	G17	8
Nevinville, Ia., U.S.	C3	92
Nevis, i., St. C.-N.	H13	64
Nevis, Ben, mtn., Scot., U.K.	C3	13
Nevis, Loch, b., Scot., U.K.	C3	13
Nevşehir, Tur.	C10	40
New, stm., U.S.	C3	125
New, stm., Az., U.S.	k8	80
New, stm., N.C., U.S.	C5	110
Newala, Tan.	D6	48
New Albany, In., U.S.	H6	91
New Albany, Ks., U.S.	E8	93
New Albany, Ms., U.S.	A4	101
New Albany, Oh., U.S.	k11	112
New Albany, Pa., U.S.	C9	115
New Albin, Ia., U.S.	A6	92
Newald, Wi., U.S.	C5	126
New Almelo, Ks., U.S.	C3	93
New Alsace, In., U.S.	F8	91
New Amsterdam, Guy.	A3	59
Newark, Ar., U.S.	B4	81
Newark, Ca., U.S.	h8	82
Newark, De., U.S.	B3	85
Newark, Il., U.S.	B5	90
Newark, Md., U.S.	D7	97
Newark, Mo., U.S.	B6	102
Newark, N.J., U.S.	B4	107
Newark, N.Y., U.S.	B3	109
Newark, Oh., U.S.	B3	112
Newark, Tx., U.S.	m9	120
Newark Bay, b., N.J., U.S.	k8	107
Newark Lake, l., Nv., U.S.	D6	105
Newark Valley, N.Y., U.S.	C4	109
New Athens, Il., U.S.	E4	90
New Athens, Oh., U.S.	B4	112
New Auburn, Mn., U.S.	F4	100
New Auburn, Wi., U.S.	C2	126
New Augusta, Ms., U.S.	D4	101
Newaygo, Mi., U.S.	E5	99
Newaygo, co., Mi., U.S.	E5	99
New Baden, Il., U.S.	E4	90
New Baltimore, Mi., U.S.	F8	99
New Baltimore, N.Y., U.S.	C7	109
New Baltimore, Oh., U.S.	n12	112
New Baltimore, Pa., U.S.	G4	115
New Bedford, Il., U.S.	B4	90
New Bedford, Ma., U.S.	C6	98
New Bedford, Pa., U.S.	D1	115
Newberg, Or., U.S.	B4	114
New Berlin, Il., U.S.	D4	90
New Berlin, N.Y., U.S.	C5	109
New Berlin, Pa., U.S.	E7	115
New Berlin, Tx., U.S.	k7	120
New Berlin, Wi., U.S.	n11	126
New Bern, N.C., U.S.	B5	110
Newbern, Tn., U.S.	A2	119
Newberry, Fl., U.S.	C4	86
Newberry, In., U.S.	G3	91
Newberry, Mi., U.S.	B5	99
Newberry, S.C., U.S.	C4	117
Newberry, co., S.C., U.S.	C4	117
Newberry Springs, Ca., U.S.	E5	82
New Bethlehem, Pa., U.S.	D3	115
New Blaine, Ar., U.S.	B2	81
New Bloomfield, Mo., U.S.	C5	102
New Bloomfield, Pa., U.S.	F7	115
New Bloomington, Oh., U.S.	B2	112
Newborn, Ga., U.S.	C3	87
Newboro, Ont.	C8	73
New Boston, Il., U.S.	B3	90
New Boston, Ia., U.S.	D6	92
New Boston, Ma., U.S.	B1	98
New Boston, Mi., U.S.	p15	99
New Boston, N.H., U.S.	E3	106
New Boston, Oh., U.S.	D3	112
New Boston, Tx., U.S.	C5	120
New Braintree, Ma., U.S.	B3	98
New Braunfels, Tx., U.S.	E3	120
New Bremen, N.Y., U.S.	B5	109
New Bremen, Oh., U.S.	B1	112
New Bridge, Or., U.S.	C9	114
New Brigden, Alta.	D5	68
New Brighton, Mn., U.S.	m12	100
New Brighton, Pa., U.S.	E1	115
New Britain, Ct., U.S.	C4	84
New Britain, i., Pap. N. Gui.	k13	50
New Brockton, Al., U.S.	D4	78
Newbrook, Alta.	B4	68
New Brunswick, N.J., U.S.	C4	107
New Brunswick, prov., Can.	C3	71
New Buffalo, Mi., U.S.	G4	99
Newburg, Ia., U.S.	C5	92
Newburg, Ky., U.S.	*B4	94
Newburg, Md., U.S.	D4	97
Newburg, Mo., U.S.	D6	102
Newburg, N.D., U.S.	A5	111
Newburg, Pa., U.S.	F6	115
Newburg, W.V., U.S.	B5	125
Newburg, Wi., U.S.	E5	126
Newburgh, Ont.	C8	73
Newburgh, Scot., U.K.	C7	13
Newburgh, N.Y., U.S.	D6	109
Newburgh Heights, Oh., U.S.	h9	112
Newburn, Ont.	E3	73
Newbury, Eng., U.K.	E6	10
Newbury, Ma., U.S.	A6	98
Newbury, Oh., U.S.	A4	112
Newbury, Vt., U.S.	C4	122
Newburyport, Ma., U.S.	A6	98
New Caledonia, dep., Oc.	H10	6
New Cambria, Ks., U.S.	D6	93
New Cambria, Mo., U.S.	B5	102
New Canaan, Ct., U.S.	E2	84
New Canton, Il., U.S.	D2	90
New Canton, Va., U.S.	C4	123
New Carlisle, Que.	A4	71
New Carlisle, In., U.S.	A4	91
New Carlisle, Oh., U.S.	C1	112
New Carrollton, Md., U.S.	*C4	97
New Cassel, N.Y., U.S.	*n15	107
New Castle, hist. reg., Spain	C4	22
Newcastle, Austl.	F8	51
Newcastle, N.B.	C4	71
Newcastle, Ont.	D6	73
Newcastle, Ire.	E4	11
Newcastle, S. Ire., U.K.	C6	11
Newcastle, Al., U.S.	B3	78
Newcastle, Co., U.S.	B3	83
Newcastle, De., U.S.	B3	85
Newcastle, Me., U.S.	D3	96
Newcastle, Ne., U.S.	B9	104
Newcastle, Ok., U.S.	B4	113
Newcastle, Pa., U.S.	D1	115
Newcastle, Tx., U.S.	C3	120
Newcastle, Ut., U.S.	F2	121
New Castle, Va., U.S.	C2	123
Newcastle, Wy., U.S.	C8	127
Newcastle Creek, N.B.	C3	71
Newcastle Emlyn, Wales, U.K.	B3	12
Newcastle Mine, Alta.	D4	68
Newcastle-under-Lyme, Eng., U.K.	A5	12
Newcastle upon Tyne, Eng., U.K.	C6	10
Newcastle West, Ire.	E2	11
Newcestown, Ire.	F3	11
New City, N.Y., U.S.	D6	109
New Columbia, Pa., U.S.	D8	115
Newcomb, N.M., U.S.	A1	108
Newcomb, N.Y., U.S.	B6	109
Newcomb, Tn., U.S.	A7	119
Newcomerstown, Oh., U.S.	B4	112
New Concord, Ky., U.S.	f9	94
New Concord, Oh., U.S.	C4	112
New Cumberland, Pa., U.S.	F8	115
New Cumberland, W.V., U.S.	A4	125
New Cumnock, Scot., U.K.	C4	10
Newdale, Man.	D1	70
Newdale, Id., U.S.	F7	89
New Dayton, Alta.	E4	68
New Delhi, India	C6	35
New Denmark, N.B.	C2	71
New Denver, B.C.	D9	69
New Diggings, Wi., U.S.	F3	126
New Durham, N.H., U.S.	D4	106
New Edinburg, Ar., U.S.	D3	81
New Effington, S.D., U.S.	B9	118
New Egypt, N.J., U.S.	C3	107
Newell, Al., U.S.	B4	78
Newell, Ar., U.S.	D3	81
Newell, Ia., U.S.	B2	92
Newell, S.D., U.S.	C2	118
Newell, W.V., U.S.	A4	125
New Ellenton, S.C., U.S.	E4	117
Newellton, La., U.S.	B4	95
New England, N.D., U.S.	C3	111
New Enterprise, Pa., U.S.	F5	115
New Era, Mi., U.S.	E4	99
Newe Sha'anan, Isr.	m14	41
New Fairfield, Ct., U.S.	D2	84
Newfane, N.Y., U.S.	B2	109
Newfane, Vt., U.S.	F3	122
Newfield, Me., U.S.	E2	96
Newfield, N.J., U.S.	D2	107
Newfields, N.H., U.S.	D5	106
New Florence, Mo., U.S.	C6	102
New Florence, Pa., U.S.	F3	115
Newfolden, Mn., U.S.	B2	100
New Forest, for., Eng., U.K.	D6	12
Newfound Gap, U.S.	f9	110
Newfound Lake, l., N.H., U.S.	C3	106
Newfoundland, N.J., U.S.	A4	107
Newfoundland, Pa., U.S.	D11	115
Newfoundland, prov., Can.	D4	72
Newfoundland, i., Newf.	D3	72
Newfoundland Mountains, mts., Ut., U.S.	B2	121
New Franken, Wi., U.S.	D6	126
New Franklin, Mo., U.S.	B5	102
New Freedom, Pa., U.S.	G8	115
New Galilee, Pa., U.S.	E1	115
New Galloway, Scot., U.K.	C4	10
Newgate, B.C.	E10	69
New Gate, hist., Isr.	m14	41
New Germany, N.S.	E5	71
New Glarus, Wi., U.S.	F4	126
New Glasgow, N.S.	D7	71
New Gloucester, Me., U.S.	E2	96
New Goshen, In., U.S.	E2	91
New Gretna, N.J., U.S.	D4	107
New Guinea, i.	G8	6
Newhalem, Wa., U.S.	A4	124
Newhall, Ca., U.S.	E4	82
Newhall, Ia., U.S.	C6	92
Newhall, W.V., U.S.	D3	125
New Hamburg, Ont.	D4	73
New Hampshire, state, U.S.	C3	106
New Hampton, Ia., U.S.	A5	92
New Hampton, Mo., U.S.	A3	102
New Hanover, co., N.C., U.S.	C5	110
New Hanover, i., Pap. N. Gui.	h12	50
New Harbor, Me., U.S.	E3	96
New Harbour, Newf.	E5	72
New Harmony, In., U.S.	H2	91
New Harmony, Ut., U.S.	F2	121
New Hartford, Ct., U.S.	B4	84
New Hartford, Ia., U.S.	B5	92
New Haven, Ct., U.S.	D4	84
New Haven, Il., U.S.	F5	90
New Haven, In., U.S.	B7	91
New Haven, Ky., U.S.	C4	94
New Haven, Mi., U.S.	F8	99
New Haven, Mo., U.S.	C6	102
New Haven, N.Y., U.S.	B4	109
New Haven, Oh., U.S.	A3	112
New Haven, Vt., U.S.	C2	122
New Haven, W.V., U.S.	C3	125
New Haven, co., Ct., U.S.	D4	84
New Haven, stm., Vt., U.S.	C2	122
New Haven Harbor, b., Ct., U.S.	E4	84
New Hazelton, B.C.	B4	69
New Hebrides see Vanuatu, ctry., Oc.	H10	6
New Hebron, Ms., U.S.	D4	101
New Holland, Ga., U.S.	B3	87
New Holland, Il., U.S.	C4	90
New Holland, Oh., U.S.	C2	112
New Holland, Pa., U.S.	F9	115
New Holland, S.D., U.S.	D7	118
New Holstein, Wi., U.S.	E5	126
New Hope, Al., U.S.	A3	78
Newhope, Ar., U.S.	C2	81
New Hope, Ky., U.S.	C4	94
New Hope, Mn., U.S.	m12	100
New Hope, N.C., U.S.	*B4	110
New Hope, Pa., U.S.	F12	115
New Hope Mountain, mtn., Al., U.S.	g7	78
New Hradec, N.D., U.S.	B3	111
New Hudson, Mi., U.S.	o14	99
New Hyde Park, N.Y., U.S.	*E7	109
New Iberia, La., U.S.	D4	95
Newington, Ct., U.S.	C5	84
Newington, Ga., U.S.	D5	87
Newington, Va., U.S.	*B5	123
New Inlet, b., N.C., U.S.	C5	110
New Ipswich, N.H., U.S.	E3	106
New Ireland, i., Pap. N. Gui.	h13	50
New Jersey, state, U.S.	C4	107
New Johnsonville, Tn., U.S.	A4	119
New Kensington, Pa., U.S.	E2	115
New Kent, Va., U.S.	C5	123
New Kent, co., Va., U.S.	C5	123
Newkirk, N.M., U.S.	B5	108
Newkirk, Ok., U.S.	A4	113
New Knoxville, Oh., U.S.	B1	112
New Kowloon, H.K.	*G7	31
New Laguna, N.M., U.S.	B2	108
New Lake, l., N.C., U.S.	B6	110
Newland, N.C., U.S.	A1	110
New Lebanon, In., U.S.	F3	91
New Lebanon, N.Y., U.S.	C7	109
New Leipzig, N.D., U.S.	C4	111
New Lenox, Il., U.S.	B6	90
New Lexington, Oh., U.S.	C3	112
New Liberty, Ky., U.S.	B5	94
New Lima, Ok., U.S.	B5	113
New Limerick, Me., U.S.	B5	96
New Lisbon, In., U.S.	E7	91
New Lisbon, N.J., U.S.	D3	107
New Liskeard, Ont.	p20	73
Newllano, La., U.S.	C2	95
Newlon, W.V., U.S.	C4	125
New London, Ct., U.S.	D7	84
New London, Ia., U.S.	D6	92
New London, Mn., U.S.	E4	100
New London, Mo., U.S.	B6	102
New London, N.H., U.S.	D3	106
New London, N.C., U.S.	B2	110
New London, Oh., U.S.	A3	112
New London, Wi., U.S.	D5	126
New London, co., Ct., U.S.	C7	84
New London Submarine Base, mil., Ct., U.S.	D7	84
New Lothrop, Mi., U.S.	E7	99
New Lowell, Ont.	C5	73
New Madison, Oh., U.S.	C1	112
New Madrid, Mo., U.S.	E8	102
New Madrid, co., Mo., U.S.	E8	102
Newman, Austl.	D2	50
Newman, Ca., U.S.	D3	82
Newman, Il., U.S.	D6	90
Newman, Ks., U.S.	k15	93
New Manchester, W.V., U.S.	e8	125
Newman Grove, Ne., U.S.	C8	104
Newman Lake, l., Wa., U.S.	B8	124
Newmanstown, Pa., U.S.	F9	115
New Marion, In., U.S.	F7	91
Newmarket, Ont.	C5	73
New Market, Al., U.S.	A3	78
New Market, In., U.S.	E4	91
New Market, Ia., U.S.	D3	92
New Market, Md., U.S.	B3	97
New Market, Tn., U.S.	C10	119
New Market, Va., U.S.	B4	123
Newmarket, Ire.	E2	11
Newmarket, Eng., U.K.	B8	12
Newmarket on Fergus, Ire.	E3	11
New Marlboro, Ma., U.S.	B1	98
New Marshfield, Oh., U.S.	C3	112
New Martinsville, W.V., U.S.	B4	125
New Matamoras, Oh., U.S.	C4	112
New Meadows, Id., U.S.	D2	89
New Melle, Mo., U.S.	C7	102
New Mexico, state, U.S.	C3	108
New Miami, Oh., U.S.	C1	112
New Middletown, In., U.S.	H5	91
New Milford, Ct., U.S.	C2	84
New Milford, N.J., U.S.	h8	107
New Milford, Pa., U.S.	C10	115
New Mills, N.B.	B3	71
New Milton, W.V., U.S.	B4	125
New Minden, Il., U.S.	E4	90
New Munich, Mn., U.S.	E4	100
New Munster, Wi., U.S.	n11	126
New Norfolk, Austl.	o15	50
New Norway, Alta.	C4	68
New Offenburg, Mo., U.S.	D7	102
New Orleans, La., U.S.	E5	95
New Orleans Naval Air Station, mil., La., U.S.	k11	95
New Osgoode, Sask.	E4	75
New Oxford, Pa., U.S.	*G7	115
New Palestine, In., U.S.	E6	91
New Paltz, N.Y., U.S.	D6	109
New Paris, In., U.S.	A6	91
New Paris, Oh., U.S.	C1	112
New Perlican, Newf.	E5	72
New Philadelphia, Oh., U.S.	B4	112
New Philadelphia, Pa., U.S.	E9	115
New Pine Creek, Ca., U.S.	B3	82
New Pine Creek, Or., U.S.	F5	114
New Plymouth, N.Z.	M15	51
New Plymouth, Id., U.S.	F2	89
New Plymouth, Oh., U.S.	C3	112
New Point, In., U.S.	F7	91
New Point, Mo., U.S.	A2	102
New Point Comfort, c., Va., U.S.	C6	123
Newport, Ire.	E3	11
Newport, Ire.	D2	11
New Port, Neth. Ant.	H19	65
Newport, Eng., U.K.	E6	10
Newport, Eng., U.K.	E5	12
Newport, Wales, U.K.	E5	10
Newport, Ar., U.S.	B4	81
Newport, De., U.S.	B3	85
Newport, Fl., U.S.	B2	86
Newport, In., U.S.	E3	91
Newport, Ky., U.S.	A5	94
Newport, Me., U.S.	D3	96
Newport, Mi., U.S.	G7	99
Newport, Mn., U.S.	n13	100
Newport, Ne., U.S.	B6	104
Newport, N.H., U.S.	D2	106
Newport, N.C., U.S.	C6	110
Newport, Oh., U.S.	C4	112
Newport, Or., U.S.	C2	114
Newport, Pa., U.S.	F7	115
Newport, R.I., U.S.	F5	116
Newport, S.C., U.S.	B5	117
Newport, Tn., U.S.	D10	119
Newport, Tx., U.S.	C4	120
Newport, Vt., U.S.	B4	122
Newport, Va., U.S.	C2	123
Newport, Wa., U.S.	A8	124
Newport, co., R.I., U.S.	E5	116
Newport Beach, Ca., U.S.	n13	82
Newport Hills, Wa., U.S.	*e11	124
New Portland, Me., U.S.	D2	96
Newport News, Va., U.S.	D6	123
New Port Richey, Fl., U.S.	D4	86
Newport Station, N.S.	E5	71
New Prague, Mn., U.S.	F5	100
New Preston, Ct., U.S.	C2	84
New Providence, Ia., U.S.	B4	92
New Providence, N.J., U.S.	B4	107
New Providence, Pa., U.S.	G9	115
New Providence, i., Bah.	B5	64
New Quay, Wales, U.K.	B3	12
New Raymer, Co., U.S.	A7	83
New Richland, Mn., U.S.	G5	100
New Richmond, Que.	A4	71
New Richmond, In., U.S.	D4	91
New Richmond, Oh., U.S.	D1	112
New Richmond, Wi., U.S.	C1	126
New Riegel, Oh., U.S.	A2	112
New River, Az., U.S.	D3	80
New River, Tn., U.S.	C9	119
New River Gorge, val., W.V., U.S.	m13	125
New River Inlet, b., N.C., U.S.	C5	110
New River Station, N.C., U.S.	*C5	110
New Road, N.S.	E6	71
New Roads, La., U.S.	D4	95
New Rochelle, N.Y., U.S.	E7	109
New Rockford, N.D., U.S.	B6	111
New Ross, N.S.	E5	71
New Ross, Ire.	D3	10
New Ross, Ire.	E4	11
Newry, N. Ire., U.K.	C3	10
Newry, Me., U.S.	D2	96
Newry, S.C., U.S.	B2	117
New Salem, Il., U.S.	D3	90
New Salem, In., U.S.	E7	91
New Salem, Ks., U.S.	E7	93
New Salem, Ma., U.S.	A3	98
New Salem, N.D., U.S.	C4	111
New Salisbury, In., U.S.	H5	91
New Sarepta, Alta.	C4	68
New Sarpy, La., U.S.	k11	95
New Sharon, Ia., U.S.	C5	92
New Sharon, Me., U.S.	D2	96
New Sharon, N.J., U.S.	C3	107
New Siberian Islands, is., Sov. Un.	B18	29
New Site, Al., U.S.	B4	78
New Site, Ms., U.S.	A5	101
New Smyrna Beach, Fl., U.S.	C6	86
Newsoms, Va., U.S.	D5	123
New South Wales, state, Austl.	F8	50
New Straitsville, Oh., U.S.	C3	112
New Sweden, Me., U.S.	B4	96
New Tazewell, Tn., U.S.	C10	119
Newtok, Ak., U.S.	C7	79
Newton, Al., U.S.	D4	78
Newton, Ga., U.S.	E2	87
Newton, Il., U.S.	E5	90
Newton, Ia., U.S.	C4	92
Newton, Ks., U.S.	D6	93
Newton, Ma., U.S.	B5	98
Newton, Ms., U.S.	C4	101
Newton, N.H., U.S.	E4	106
Newton, N.J., U.S.	A3	107
Newton, N.C., U.S.	B1	110
Newton, Tx., U.S.	D6	120
Newton, Ut., U.S.	B4	121
Newton, W.V., U.S.	C3	125
Newton, Wi., U.S.	k10	126
Newton, co., Ar., U.S.	B2	81
Newton, co., Ga., U.S.	C3	87
Newton, co., In., U.S.	B3	91
Newton, co., Ms., U.S.	C4	101
Newton, co., Mo., U.S.	E3	102
Newton, co., Tx., U.S.	D6	120
Newton Abbot, Eng., U.K.	D4	12
Newton Aycliffe, Eng., U.K.	F7	13
Newton Falls, N.Y., U.S.	A6	109
Newton Falls, Oh., U.S.	A5	112
Newton Grove, N.C., U.S.	B4	110
Newton Hamilton, Pa., U.S.	F6	115
Newton Junction, N.H., U.S.	E4	106
Newton Stewart, Scot., U.K.	F4	13
Newtonsville, Oh., U.S.	C1	112
Newtonville, N.J., U.S.	D3	107
New Toronto (part of Etobicoke), Ont.	m14	73
Newtown, Newf.	D5	72
Newtown, Wales, U.K.	D5	10
Newtown, Ct., U.S.	D2	84
Newtown, Mo., U.S.	A4	102
Newtown, N.D., U.S.	B3	111
Newtown, Oh., U.S.	C1	112
Newtown Lake, l., Mi., U.S.	B6	99
Newtownabbey, N. Ire., U.K.	C6	11
Newtownards, N. Ire., U.K.	C4	10
Newtown Crommelin, N. Ire., U.K.	C5	11
Newtownhamilton, N. Ire., U.K.	C5	11
Newtown Mount Kennedy, Ire.	E5	11
Newtown Square, Pa., U.S.	p20	115
Newtownstewart, N. Ire., U.K.	C4	11
New Trenton, In., U.S.	F8	91
New Ulm, Mn., U.S.	F4	100
New Ulm, Tx., U.S.	E4	120
New Underwood, S.D., U.S.	C3	118
New Vienna, Ia., U.S.	B6	92
New Vienna, Oh., U.S.	C2	112
New Village, N.J., U.S.	B2	107
Newville, Al., U.S.	D4	78
Newville, Pa., U.S.	F7	115
New Vineyard, Me., U.S.	D2	96
New Virginia, Ia., U.S.	C4	92
New Washington, In., U.S.	G6	91
New Washington, Oh., U.S.	B3	112
New Washoe City, Nv., U.S.	*D2	105
New Waterford, N.S.	C9	71
New Waterford, Oh., U.S.	B5	112
New Waverly, In., U.S.	C5	91
New Waverly, Tx., U.S.	D5	120
New Westminster, B.C.	E6	69
New Whiteland, In., U.S.	E5	91
New Wilmington, Pa., U.S.	D1	115
New Windsor, Il., U.S.	B3	90
New Windsor, Md., U.S.	A3	97
New Windsor, N.Y., U.S.	D6	109
New Woodstock, N.Y., U.S.	C5	109
New World Island, i., Newf.	D4	72
New York, N.Y., U.S.	E7	109
New York, co., N.Y., U.S.	k13	109
New York, state, U.S.	C6	109
New York Mills, Mn., U.S.	D3	100
New Zealand, ctry., Oc.	N14	51
New Zion, S.C., U.S.	D7	117
Neyshābūr, Iran	B5	38
Nezhin, Sov. Un.	F8	27
Nezperce, Id., U.S.	*C2	89
Nez Perce, co., Id., U.S.	C2	89
Nez Perce Indian Reservation, Id., U.S.	C2	89
Nezpique, Bayou, stm., La., U.S.	D3	95
Ngabang, Indon.	E3	34
Ngabé, Congo	B2	48
Ngala, Nig.	D7	45
Ngami, Lake, l., Bots.	B3	49
Ngangla Ringco, l., China	B7	36
Ngangzê Lake, l., China	B11	37
Ngaoundéré, Cam.	D2	46
Ngara, Tan.	B5	48
Ngaruangl Reef, rf., Palau	R17	52
Ngaruawahia, N.Z.	L15	51
Ngatapa, N.Z.	M16	51
Ngemelis Islands, is., Palau	R17	52
Ngerekebesang, i., Palau	R17	52
Ngerkeel, Palau	R17	52
Ngermechau, Palau	R17	52
Ngeruktabel, i., Palau	R17	52
Ngetbong, Palau	R17	52
Ngidinga, Zaire	C2	48
Ngong, Kenya	B6	48
Ngoring Hu, l., China	D4	32
Ngounié, stm., Gabon	F2	46
Ngouri, Chad	C3	46
Nguigmi, Niger	D7	45
Nguru, Nig.	D7	45
Nhamundá, Braz.	C3	59
Nhamundá, stm., Braz.	C3	59
Nha Trang, Viet.	C3	34
Nhill, Austl.	H3	51
Nhulunbuy, Austl.	B6	50
Niafounké, Mali	C4	45
Niagara, N.D., U.S.	B8	111
Niagara, Wi., U.S.	C6	126
Niagara, co., N.Y., U.S.	B2	109
Niagara, stm., N.A.	B1	109
Niagara Falls, Ont.	D5	73
Niagara Falls, N.Y., U.S.	B1	109
Niagara-on-the-Lake, Ont.	D5	73
Niagara Town, N.Y., U.S.	*B2	109
Niamey, Niger	D5	45
Niamtougou, Togo	E5	45
Niangara, Zaire	A4	48
Niangua, Mo., U.S.	D5	102
Niangua, stm., Mo., U.S.	D5	102
Niantic, Ct., U.S.	D7	84
Niarada, Mt., U.S.	C2	103
Nias, i., Indon.	E1	34
Niassa, dept., Moz.	D6	48
Nibe, Den.	B3	15
Nibley, Ut., U.S.	B4	121
Nicaragua, ctry., N.A.	E7	63
Nicaragua, Lago de, l., Nic.	E7	63
Nicastro (Lamezia Terme), Italy	E6	23
Nicatous Lake, l., Me., U.S.	C4	96
Nice, Fr.	F7	16
Niceville, Fl., U.S.	u15	86
Nichican, Lac, l., Que.	h12	74
Nichinan, Japan	K5	33
Nicholas, co., Ky., U.S.	B6	94
Nicholas, co., W.V., U.S.	C4	125
Nicholas Channel, strt., N.A.	C3	64
Nicholasville, Ky., U.S.	C5	94
Nicholls, Ga., U.S.	E4	87
Nichols, Ia., U.S.	C6	92
Nichols, N.Y., U.S.	C4	109
Nichols, S.C., U.S.	C9	117
Nichols Hills, Ok., U.S.	B4	113
Nicholson, Ms., U.S.	E4	101
Nicholson, Pa., U.S.	C10	115
Nicholson, stm., Austl.	C6	50
Nicholville, N.Y., U.S.	f10	109
Nickajack Lake, res., Tn., U.S.	D8	119
Nickel Centre, Ont.	p19	73
Nickelsville, Va., U.S.	f9	123
Nickerie, dept., Sur.	B3	59
Nickerie, stm., Sur.	A3	59
Nickerson, Ks., U.S.	D5	93
Nickerson, Ne., U.S.	C9	104
Nickerson Hill, hill, Ct., U.S.	D6	84
Nicman, Que.	h10	74
Nicobar Islands, is., India	G9	36
Nicodemus, Ks., U.S.	C4	93
Nicola, B.C.	D7	69
Nicola, stm., B.C.	D7	69
Nicolet, Que.	C5	74
Nicolet, co., Que.	C5	74
Nicolet, stm., Que.	C5	74
Nicolet, Lake, l., Mi., U.S.	B6	99
Nicollet, Mn., U.S.	F4	100
Nicollet, co., Mn., U.S.	F4	100
Nicolls Town, Bah.	B4	64
Nicoma Park, Ok., U.S.	B4	113
Nicosia (Levkosía / Lefkoşa), Cyp.	E9	40
Nicosia [Sicilia], Italy	F5	23
Nicotera, Italy	E5	23
Nicoya, C.R.	E7	63
Nicoya, Golfo de, b., C.R.	F5	62
Nicoya, Península de, pen., C.R.	F7	63
Nictaux Falls, N.S.	E4	71
Nida, stm., Pol.	C6	26
Nid d l'Aigle, Cap du, c., St. P./M.	D4	78
Nidan Rock, hill, Japan	P17	52
Nidd, stm., Eng., U.K.	F7	13
Nidda, W. Ger.	C3	19
Nidda, stm., W. Ger.	C4	19
Nidwalden, state, Switz.	C4	20
Niebüll, W. Ger.	D2	15
Niederbronn-les-Bains, Fr.	F7	17
Niedermarsberg, W. Ger.	B3	19
Niedersachsen, state, W. Ger.	F3	15
Nielsville, Mn., U.S.	C2	100
Niemodlin, Pol.	C5	26
Nienburg, W. Ger.	B4	18
Nierstein, W. Ger.	D3	19
Nieszawa, Pol.	B5	26
Nietleben, E. Ger.	D7	19
Nieuw Amsterdam, Sur.	A3	59
Nieuwegein, Neth.	*B5	17
Nieuweroord, Neth.	C6	17
Nieuw Nickerie, Sur.	A3	59
Nieuwpoort, Bel.	C2	17
Niğde, Tur.	D10	40
Niger, ctry., Afr.	C6	45
Niger, stm., Afr.	E6	45
Niger Delta, Nig.	F6	45
Nigeria, ctry., Afr.	E6	45
Nigg, Scot., U.K.	C5	13

Index

Name	Map Ref.	Page
Nighthawk, Wa., U.S.	A6	124
Nigríta, Grc.	B4	25
Nihing, stm., Asia	H11	39
Nihoa, i., Hi., U.S.	m15	88
Niigata, Japan	D12	31
Niihama, Japan	J6	33
Niihau, i., Hi., U.S.	B1	88
Nii Island, i., Japan	I9	33
Niimi, Japan	I6	33
Nijar, Spain	D4	22
Nijkerk, Neth.	B5	17
Nijmegen, Neth.	B6	16
Níkaia, Grc.	*D4	25
Nikep, Md., U.S.	k13	97
Nikishka, Ak., U.S.	g16	79
Nikitinka, Sov. Un.	D9	27
Nikitovka, Sov. Un.	q21	27
Nikki, Benin	E5	45
Nikkō, Japan	D12	31
Nikolayev, Sov. Un.	E6	29
Nikolayevsk, Sov. Un.	F15	27
Nikolayevsk [-na-Amure], Sov. Un.	D17	29
Nikolsk, Sov. Un.	D8	28
Nikolski, Ak., U.S.	E6	79
Nikonovskoye, Sov. Un.	n18	27
Nikopol, Bul.	D7	24
Nikopol, Sov. Un.	H10	27
Niksar, Tur.	B11	40
Nīkshahr, Iran	H10	37
Nikšić, Yugo.	D4	24
Nile, N.Y., U.S.	C2	109
Nile, stm., Afr.	D9	42
Nilangé, Fr.		
Niles, Il., U.S.	h9	90
Niles, Ks., U.S.	D6	93
Niles, Mi., U.S.	G4	99
Niles, Oh., U.S.	A5	112
Nilvange, Fr.		
Nilwood, Il., U.S.	D4	90
Nīmach, India	E5	37
Nimba, Mont, mtn., Afr.	E3	45
Nimba Mountains, mts., Afr.	E3	45
Nîmes, Fr.	F6	16
Nimmons, Ar., U.S.	A5	81
Nimpkish, stm., B.C.	D4	69
Nimröh, Wādī, val., Jord.	h13	41
Nimrod Glacier, ice, Ant.	A29	7
Nimrod Lake, res., Ar., U.S.	C2	81
Nimule, Sud.	E3	47
Ninemile Creek, stm., Ks., U.S.	k15	93
Nine Mile Creek, stm., Ut., U.S.	D5	121
Nine Mile Falls, Wa., U.S.	g13	124
Ninemile Point, c., Mi., U.S.	C6	99
Ninette, Man.	E2	70
Ninety Mile Beach, Austl.	G8	50
Ninety Six, S.C., U.S.	C3	117
Nineveh, Pa., U.S.	G1	115
Nineveh, hist., Iraq	B4	38
Ninga, Man.	E2	70
Ning'an, China	C10	31
Ningbo, China	F9	31
Ningde, China	F8	31
Ningdu, China	K6	32
Ninghai, China	J9	32
Ninghua, China	K7	32
Ningjin, China	F6	32
Ningming, China	A7	35
Ningqiang, China	H2	32
Ningsia Hui see Ningxia Huizu, prov., China	D6	31
Ningwu, China	D7	31
Ningxia Huizu, prov., China	D6	31
Ningxian, China	D6	31
Ninh Binh, Viet.	A3	34
Niniguet Pond, l., R.I., U.S.	G2	116
Ninilchik, Ak., U.S.	C9	79
Ninnekah, Ok., U.S.	C4	113
Ninnescah, stm., Ks., U.S.	E6	93
Ninnescah, North Fork, stm., Ks., U.S.	E5	93
Ninnescah, South Fork, stm., Ks., U.S.	E5	93
Ninnis Glacier, ice, Ant.	C27	7
Ninole, Hi., U.S.	D6	88
Ninove, Bel.	D4	17
Nioaque, Braz.	C1	56
Niobe, N.D., U.S.	A3	111
Niobrara, co., Wy., U.S.	C8	127
Niobrara, stm., U.S.	B7	104
Nioki, Zaire	D3	45
Niono, Mali	E3	45
Nioro du Rip, Sen.	C3	45
Nioro du Sahel, Mali	D3	45
Niort, Fr.	F3	16
Niota, Il., U.S.	C2	90
Niota, Tn., U.S.	D9	119
Niotaze, Ks., U.S.	E7	93
Nipawin, Sask.	D4	75
Nipawin Provincial Park, Sask.	C3	75
Nipekamew Lake, l., Sask.	C3	75
Nipew Lake, l., Sask.	B3	75
Nipigon, Ont.	o17	73
Nipigon, Lake, l., Ont.	o17	73
Nipishish Lake, l., Newf.	g9	72
Nipissing, dept., Ont.	A6	73
Nipissing, Lake, l., Ont.	A5	73
Nipomo, Ca., U.S.	E3	82
Nippers Harbour, Newf.	D4	72
Nipple Mountain, mtn., Co., U.S.	D2	83
Nipton, Ca., U.S.	E6	82
Niquelândia, Braz.	A3	56
Niquero, Cuba	D5	64
Nirasaki, Japan	n17	33
Nirmal, India	H7	37
Nirmāli, India	D11	37
Niš, Yugo.	D5	24
Nisa, Port.	C2	22
Nišava, stm., Eur.	D6	24
Nishinomiya, Japan	*I7	33
Nishio, Japan	o16	33
Nísiros, i., Grc.	D6	25
Niskayuna, N.Y., U.S.	C7	109
Nisland, S.D., U.S.	C2	118
Nisqually, stm., Wa., U.S.	C3	124
Nissan, stm., Swe.	B7	15
Nissum Bredning, b., Den.	B2	15
Nissum Fjord, Den.	B2	15
Nisswa, Mn., U.S.	D4	100
Nistowiak Lake, l., Sask.	B3	75
Nisula, Mi., U.S.	B2	99
Niterói, Braz.		
Nith, stm., Scot., U.K.	E5	13
Nitra, Czech.	D5	26
Nitra, stm., Czech.	D5	26
Nitro, W.V., U.S.	C3	125
Nitta Yuma, Ms., U.S.	B3	101
Nittenau, W. Ger.	D7	19
Niue, ctry., Oc.	H11	6
Nivelles, Bel.	B6	16
Nivernais, Côtes du, hills, Fr.	D5	16
Niverville, Man.	E3	70
Nivskiy, Sov. Un.	D15	14
Niwot, Co., U.S.	A5	83
Nixa, Mo., U.S.	D4	102
Nixburg, Al., U.S.	C3	78
Nixon, Nv., U.S.	D2	105
Nixon, Tn., U.S.	B3	119
Nixon, Tx., U.S.	E4	120
Nizāmābād, India	H7	37
Nizām Sāgar, res., India	H7	37
Nizhnekamsk, Sov. Un.	*D8	29
Nizhnekolymsk, Sov. Un.	C19	29
Nizhne-Leninskoye, Sov. Un.	C6	33
Nizhneudinsk, Sov. Un.	D12	29
Nizhneye, Sov. Un.	q21	27
Nizhniy, Sov. Un.	G14	27
Nizhniy Chir, Sov. Un.	E14	27
Nizhniy Lomov, Sov. Un.	E14	27
Nizhniy Pyandzh, Sov. Un.	H22	8
Nizhniy Tagil, Sov. Un.	D9	29
Nizhnyaya Tunguska, stm., Sov. Un.	C12	29
Nizhnyaya Tura, Sov. Un.	C11	29
Nizip, Tur.	*D11	40
Nizmennyy, Cape, c., Sov. Un.	E7	33
Nizza Monferrato, Italy	E4	20
Nizzana, Isr.	D6	41
Nizzana, Nahal, val., Isr.	D6	41
Njombe, Tan.	C5	48
Njurunda, Swe.	F7	14
Nkambe, Cam.	D2	46
Nkayi, Zimb.	A4	49
Nkhata Bay, Mwi.	D5	48
Nkhota Kota, Mwi.	D5	48
Nkongsamba, Cam.	E1	46
Nnewi, Nig.	E6	45
Noākhāli, Bngl.	F13	37
Noank, Ct., U.S.	D8	84
Noasca, Italy	D3	20
Noatak, Ak., U.S.	B7	79
Noatak, stm., Ak., U.S.	B7	79
Nobeoka, Japan	J5	33
Noble, Ga., U.S.	B1	87
Noble, Il., U.S.	E5	90
Noble, La., U.S.	C2	95
Noble, Ok., U.S.	B4	113
Noble, co., In., U.S.	B7	91
Noble, co., Oh., U.S.	C4	112
Noble, co., Ok., U.S.	A4	113
Nobleboro, Me., U.S.	D3	96
Nobleford, Alta.	E4	68
Noblesville, In., U.S.	D6	91
Nobscot Hill, hill, Ma., U.S.	B5	98
Nocatee, Fl., U.S.	E5	86
Nocona, Tx., U.S.	C4	120
Nodaway, Ia., U.S.	D3	92
Nodaway, co., Mo., U.S.	A3	102
Nodaway, stm., U.S.	A2	102
Noel, Mo., U.S.	E3	102
Noel Paul's Brook, stm., Newf.	D3	72
Noelville, Ont.	A4	73
Nogal, N.M., U.S.	D4	108
Nogales, Mex.	n15	63
Nogales, Az., U.S.	F5	80
Nogara, Italy	D7	20
Nōgata, Japan	J5	33
Nogent-en-Bassigny, Fr.	C6	16
Nogent-le-Rotrou, Fr.	C4	16
Nogent [-sur-Marne], Fr.	g10	16
Nogent-sur-Seine, Fr.	C5	16
Noginsk, Sov. Un.	D12	27
Nogoa, stm., Austl.	B6	51
Nogoyá, Arg.	A5	54
Nohar, India	C5	36
Noheji, Japan	F10	33
Noirmoutier, Île de, i., Fr.	D2	16
Noisy-le-Sec, Fr.	g10	16
Nojima, Cape, c., Japan	I9	33
Nok Kundi, Pak.	F3	75
Nokesville, Va., U.S.	B5	123
Nokomis, Sask.	F3	75
Nokomis, Fl., U.S.	E4	86
Nokomis, Il., U.S.	D4	90
Nokomis, Lake, res., Wi., U.S.	C4	126
Nokou, Chad	E3	46
Nola, Cen. Afr. Rep.	E3	46
Nola, Italy	D5	23
Nolan, Tx., U.S.	D3	101
Nolan, co., Tx., U.S.	C2	120
Nolan, W.V., U.S.	D2	125
Nolanville, Tx., U.S.		
Nolichucky, stm., Tn., U.S.	C10	119
Nolin, stm., Ky., U.S.	C3	94
Nolin Lake, res., Ky., U.S.	C3	94
Nolinsk, Sov. Un.	B3	28
Noma, Fl., U.S.	u16	86
Noma, Cape, c., Japan	K5	33
Nomans Land, i., Ma., U.S.	D6	98
Nombre de Dios, Pan.	h12	62
Nome, Ak., U.S.	C6	79
Nome, N.D., U.S.	C8	111
Nomeny, Fr.		
Nomgon, Mong.	C1	32
Nominingue, Que.	C2	74
Nomoneas, is., Micron.	Q18	52
Nonacho Lake, l., N.W. Ter.	D11	66
Nonantola, Italy		
Nondalton, Ak., U.S.	C8	79
Nonesuch, stm., Me., U.S.	g7	96
Nong'an, China	C10	31
Nong Khai, Thai.	B2	34
Nongoma, S. Afr.	C5	49
Nonoava, Mex.		
Nonquit Pond, l., R.I., U.S.		
Nooksack, Wa., U.S.	A3	124
Nooksack, North Fork, stm., Wa., U.S.	A4	124
Nooksack, South Fork, stm., Wa., U.S.	A3	124
Noonan, N.D., U.S.	A2	111
Noone, N.H., U.S.	E3	106
Noordpunt, c., Neth. Ant.	H18	65
Noordwijk-Binnen, Neth.	B4	17
Noorvik, Ak., U.S.	B7	79
Nootka Island, i., B.C.	E4	69
Nootka Sound, strt., B.C.	E4	69
Nopiming Provincial Park, Man.	D4	70
No Point, Point, c., Md., U.S.	D5	97
Noquebay, Lake, l., Wi., U.S.	C6	126
Nóqui, Ang.	C1	48
Nora, Sask.	D5	105
Nora, Swe.	H6	14
Nora, Il., U.S.	A4	90
Nora Springs, Ia., U.S.	A5	92
Noranda, Que.	k11	74
Norbertville, Que.	C6	74
Norborne, Mo., U.S.	B4	102
Norcatur, Ks., U.S.	C3	93
Norco, Ca., U.S.	*n13	82
Norco, La., U.S.	D5	95
Norcross, Ga., U.S.	C2	87
Norcross, Mn., U.S.	E2	100
Nord, dept., Fr.	D2	17
Nord, Canal du, Fr.	D3	17
Nordborg, Den.	C3	15
Nordegg, Alta.	C2	68
Nordegg, stm., Alta.	C2	68
Nordenham, W. Ger.	B3	18
Nordenskjöld Archipelago, is., Sov. Un.	B4	128
Nordenskjöld Ice Tongue, ice, Ant.	e39	7
Norderney, W. Ger.	A7	17
Norderney, i., W. Ger.	B3	18
Norderstedt, W. Ger.	*B5	18
Nordfjord, Nor.	G1	14
Nordhausen, E. Ger.	C5	18
Nordhorn, W. Ger.	B3	18
Nordjylland, co., Den.	B3	15
Nordli, Wa., U.S.	A3	124
Nördlingen, W. Ger.	D5	18
Nordmaling, Swe.	F8	14
Nordman, Id., U.S.	A2	89
Nordostrundingen, c., Grnld.	A19	61
Nordreisa, Nor.	C9	14
Nordrhein-Westfalen, state, W. Ger.	B2	19
Nordstrand, i., W. Ger.	A4	18
Nore, mtn., Ire.	D3	10
Norene, Tn., U.S.	A5	119
Norfolk, Ct., U.S.	B3	84
Norfolk, Ma., U.S.	h10	98
Norfolk, Ne., U.S.	B8	104
Norfolk, N.Y., U.S.	f9	109
Norfolk, Va., U.S.	D6	123
Norfolk, co., Eng., U.K.	B8	12
Norfolk, co., Ma., U.S.	B5	98
Norfolk Island, dep., Oc.	H10	6
Norfolk Naval Base, mil., Va., U.S.	k15	123
Norfolk Naval Shipyard, mil., Va., U.S.	k15	123
Norfork, Ar., U.S.	A3	81
Norfork Dam, Ar., U.S.	A3	81
Norfork Lake, res., Ar., U.S.	A3	81
Norge, Ok., U.S.	C4	113
Norias, Tx., U.S.	F4	120
Norilsk, Sov. Un.	C11	29
Norland, Ont.	C6	73
Norland, Fl., U.S.	s13	86
Norlina, N.C., U.S.	A4	110
Norma, N.J., U.S.	E2	107
Norma, N.D., U.S.	A4	111
Norma, Tn., U.S.	C9	119
Normal, Al., U.S.	A3	78
Normal, Il., U.S.	C5	90
Norman, Ar., U.S.	C2	81
Norman, In., U.S.	G5	91
Norman, Ne., U.S.	D7	104
Norman, N.C., U.S.	B3	110
Norman, Ok., U.S.	B4	113
Norman, co., Mn., U.S.	C2	100
Norman, Lake, res., N.C., U.S.	B2	110
Normanby, stm., Austl.	B7	50
Normandy, Mo., U.S.	f13	102
Normandy, Tn., U.S.	B5	119
Normandy, hist. reg., Fr.	C3	16
Normandy, Hills of, hills, Fr.	C3	16
Normandy Beach, N.J., U.S.	C4	107
Normangee, Tx., U.S.	D4	120
Norman Island, i., V.I., Br.	E6	65
Norman Park, Ga., U.S.	E3	87
Normanton, Austl.	C8	50
Normantown, Ga., U.S.	D4	87
Norman Wells, N.W. Ter.	C7	66
Norphlet, Ar., U.S.	D3	81
Norquay, Sask.	F4	75
Norquincó, Arg.	C2	54
Norrahammar, Swe.	A8	15
Nørre Åby, Den.	C3	15
Nørre Alslev, Den.	D5	15
Nørresundby (part of Ålborg), Den.	A3	15
Norridge, Il., U.S.	k9	90
Norridgewock, Me., U.S.	D3	96
Norris, Il., U.S.	C3	90
Norris, Mt., U.S.	E5	103
Norris, S.C., U.S.	B2	117
Norris, S.D., U.S.	D4	118
Norris, Tn., U.S.	C9	119
Norris Arm, Newf.	D4	72
Norris City, Il., U.S.	F5	90
Norris Dam, Tn., U.S.	C9	119
Norris Lake, res., Tn., U.S.	C10	119
Norris Point, Newf.	D3	72
Norristown, Pa., U.S.	F11	115
Norrisville, Md., U.S.	A5	97
Norrköping, Swe.	H7	14
Norrtälje, Swe.	H8	14
Norseman, Austl.	F3	50
Norte, Cabo, c., Braz.	B5	59
Norte, Canal do, strt., Braz.	B4	59
Norte, Punta, c., Arg.	C4	54
Norte, Serra do, plat., Braz.	E3	59
Norte de Santander, dept., Col.	B3	60
Nortelândia, Braz.	A1	56
North, S.C., U.S.	D5	117
North, stm., Newf.	B3	72
North, stm., Al., U.S.	B3	72
North, stm., Ia., U.S.	f8	92
North, stm., Ma., U.S.	h12	98
North, stm., W.V., U.S.	B6	125
North, Cape, c., N.S.	B9	71
North Abington, Ma., U.S.	B6	98
North Acton, Ma., U.S.	f10	98
North Adams, Ma., U.S.	A1	98
North Adams, Mi., U.S.	G6	99
North Albany, Or., U.S.	k11	114
North Amherst, Ma., U.S.	B2	98
North America, cont.		
North Amity, Me., U.S.	D2	96
North Amityville, N.Y., U.S.	*n15	109
Northam, Austl.	F2	50
Northampton, Eng., U.K.	D6	12
Northampton, Ma., U.S.	B2	98
Northampton, Pa., U.S.	E11	115
Northampton, co., N.C., U.S.	A4	110
Northampton, co., Pa., U.S.	E11	115
Northampton, co., Va., U.S.	C7	123
Northamptonshire, co., Eng., U.K.	B7	12
North Andaman, i., India	F9	36
North and Bent Pyramids, hist., Egypt	E3	41
North Andover, Ma., U.S.	A5	98
North Andrews Gardens, Fl., U.S.	r13	86
North Anna, stm., Va., U.S.	B5	123
North Anson, Me., U.S.	D3	96
North Apollo, Pa., U.S.	E2	115
North Arapaho Peak, mtn., Co., U.S.	A5	83
North Arlington, N.J., U.S.	h8	107
North Atlanta, Ga., U.S.	h8	87
North Attleboro, Ma., U.S.	C5	98
North Auburn, Ca., U.S.	*C3	82
North Augusta, Ont.	C9	73
North Augusta, S.C., U.S.	D4	117
North Aulatsivik Island, i., Newf.	f9	72
North Aurora, Il., U.S.	k8	90
North Avondale, Co., U.S.	C6	83
North Babylon, N.Y., U.S.	*n15	109
North Baltimore, Oh., U.S.	A2	112
North Bangor, N.Y., U.S.	f10	109
North Battleford, Sask.	E1	75
North Bay, Ont.	A5	73
North Bay Shore, N.Y., U.S.	*n15	109
North Beach, Md., U.S.	C4	97
North Belgrade, Me., U.S.	D3	96
North Bellmore, N.Y., U.S.	*n15	109
North Bellport, N.Y., U.S.	*n16	109
North Belmont, N.C., U.S.	B1	110
North Bend, B.C.	E7	69
North Bend, Ne., U.S.	C9	104
North Bend, Oh., U.S.	o12	112
North Bend, Or., U.S.	D2	114
North Bend, Pa., U.S.	D6	115
North Bend, Wa., U.S.	B4	124
North Bend, Wi., U.S.	D2	126
North Bennington, Vt., U.S.	F2	122
North Bergen, N.J., U.S.	h8	107
North Berwick, Scot., U.K.	D6	13
North Berwick, Me., U.S.	E2	96
North Billerica, Ma., U.S.	A5	98
North Bloomfield, Oh., U.S.	A5	112
North Bonneville, Wa., U.S.	D4	124
Northboro, Ia., U.S.	D2	92
Northborough, Ma., U.S.	B4	98
North Brabant (Noord-Brabant), prov., Neth.	C4	17
North Braddock, Pa., U.S.	*k14	115
North Bradford, Me., U.S.	C4	96
North Bradley, Mi., U.S.	E6	99
North Branch, Mi., U.S.	E7	99
North Branch, Mn., U.S.	E6	100
North Branch, N.H., U.S.	D3	106
North Branch, N.J., U.S.	B3	107
North Branford, Ct., U.S.	D4	84
North Breakers, rf., Mid. Is.	J3	52
North Bridgton, Me., U.S.	D2	96
Northbridge, Ma., U.S.	B4	98
North Brookfield, Ma., U.S.	B3	98
North Brookfield, Me., U.S.	D3	96
North Brother, Me., U.S.	C4	96
North Brunswick, N.J., U.S.	C4	107
North Buena Vista, Ia., U.S.	B7	92
North Caldwell, N.J., U.S.	B4	107
North Canadian, stm., Ok., U.S.	A5	113
North Canton, Ct., U.S.	B4	84
North Canton, Ga., U.S.	B2	87
North Canton, Oh., U.S.	B4	112
North Cape, c., P.E.I.	B6	71
North Cape, c., Nor.	B11	14
North Cape May, N.J., U.S.	F3	107
North Carolina, state, U.S.	B3	110
North Carrollton, Ms., U.S.	B4	101
North Carver, Ma., U.S.	C6	98
North Cascades National Park, Wa., U.S.	A4	124
North Cay, i., Bah.	m17	64
North Channel, strt., Ont.	A2	73
North Channel, strt., U.K.	C3	10
North Charleston, S.C., U.S.	F8	117
North Charlestown, N.H., U.S.	D2	106
North Chatham, N.H., U.S.	B4	106
North Chicago, Il., U.S.	A6	90
North Chichester, N.H., U.S.	D4	106
North Clarendon, Vt., U.S.	D3	122
Northcliffe, Austl.	F2	50
North Cohasset, Ma., U.S.	g12	98
North Cohocton, N.Y., U.S.	C3	109
North College Hill, Oh., U.S.	o12	112
North Collins, N.Y., U.S.	C2	109
North Concord, Vt., U.S.	C5	122
North Conway, N.H., U.S.	B4	106
North Corbin, Ky., U.S.	D5	94
Northcote, Austl.	*G8	50
North Creek, N.Y., U.S.	B7	109
North Crossett, Ar., U.S.	D4	81
North Crows Nest, In., U.S.	k10	91
North Dakota, state, U.S.	B5	111
North Danville, Vt., U.S.	C4	122
North Dartmouth, Ma., U.S.	C6	98
North Decatur, Ga., U.S.	*h8	87
North Dighton, Ma., U.S.	C5	98
North Dixmont, Me., U.S.	D3	96
North Downs, plat., Eng., U.K.	E7	10
North Druid Hills, Ga., U.S.	h8	87
North Eagle Butte, S.D., U.S.	B4	118
North East, Md., U.S.	A6	97
North East, Pa., U.S.	B2	115
Northeast, stm., Md., U.S.	A6	97
Northeast Cape, c., Ak., U.S.	C6	79
Northeast Cape Fear, stm., N.C., U.S.	C5	110
North East Carry, Me., U.S.	C3	96
North Eastham, Ma., U.S.	C8	98
North Eastern, prov., Kenya	A6	48
Northeast Henrietta, N.Y., U.S.	*B3	109
Northeast Point, c., Newf.	B4	72
Northeast Polder, Neth.	B5	17
Northeast Pond, l., N.H., U.S.	D5	106
North Edisto, stm., S.C., U.S.	k11	117
North Egremont, Ma., U.S.	B1	98
North English, Ia., U.S.	C5	92
North English, stm., Ia., U.S.	C5	92
Northeim, W. Ger.	C4	18
North Enid, Ok., U.S.	A4	113
Northern, prov., Mwi.	D5	48
Northern, prov., Zam.	D5	48
Northern Arm, Newf.	D4	72
Northern Cheyenne Indian Reservation, Mt., U.S.	E10	103
Northern Donets, stm., Sov. Un.	G13	27
Northern Dvina, stm., Sov. Un.	C7	29
Northern Head, c., N.B.	E3	71
Northern Indian Lake, l., Man.	A3	70
Northern Ireland, ter., U.K.	C3	10
Northern Mariana Islands, ter., T.T.P.I.	E8	6
Northern Range, mts., Trin.	N23	65
Northern Sporades, is., Grc.	C5	25
Northern Territory, ter., Austl.	C5	50
North Esk, stm., Scot., U.K.	D6	13
North Fairfield, Oh., U.S.	A3	112
North Fair Oaks, Ca., U.S.	*k8	82
North Falmouth, Ma., U.S.	C6	98
North Ferrisburg, Vt., U.S.	C2	122
Northfield, B.C.	f12	69
Northfield, Ct., U.S.	C3	84
Northfield, Il., U.S.	*h9	90
Northfield, Me., U.S.	D5	96
Northfield, Mn., U.S.	F5	100
Northfield, N.H., U.S.	D3	106
Northfield, N.J., U.S.	E3	107
Northfield, Oh., U.S.	h9	112
Northfield, Tx., U.S.	B2	120
Northfield, Vt., U.S.	C3	122
Northfield, Wi., U.S.	D2	126
Northfield Center, Vt., U.S.	C3	122
Northfield Falls, Vt., U.S.	C3	122
Northfield Mountains, mts., Vt., U.S.	C3	122
North Fond du Lac, Wi., U.S.	E5	126
North Foreland, c., Eng., U.K.	E7	10
North Fork, Ca., U.S.	D4	82
North Fork, Id., U.S.	D5	89
North Fork Reservoir, res., Or., U.S.	C4	114
North Fort Myers, Fl., U.S.	F5	86
North Fox Island, i., Mi., U.S.	C5	99
North Franklin, Ct., U.S.	C7	84
North Freedom, Wi., U.S.	E4	126
North Friesian Islands, is., Eur.	A4	18
North Fryeburg, Me., U.S.	D2	96
North Galiano, B.C.	f12	69
Northgate, Sask.	H4	75
Northgate, N.D., U.S.	A3	111
Northglenn, Co., U.S.	B6	83
North Gorham, Me., U.S.	g7	96
North Gower, Ont.	B9	73
North Grafton, Ma., U.S.	B4	98
North Granby, Ct., U.S.	B5	84
North Great River, N.Y., U.S.	*n18	109
North Grosvenordale, Ct., U.S.	B8	84
North Gulfport, Ms., U.S.	E4	101
North Halawa Stream, stm., Hi., U.S.	g10	88
North Haledon, N.J., U.S.	B4	107
North Hampton, N.H., U.S.	E5	106
North Hanover, Ma., U.S.	h12	98
North Harpswell, Me., U.S.	g8	96
North Hartland, Vt., U.S.	D4	122
North Hartland Reservoir, res., Vt., U.S.	D4	122
North Hatley, Que.	D6	74
North Haven, Ct., U.S.	D4	84
North Haven, Me., U.S.	D4	96
North Haverhill, N.H., U.S.	B2	106
North Head, N.B.	E3	71
North Henderson, Il., U.S.	B3	90
North Hero, Vt., U.S.	B2	122
North Hero Island, i., Vt., U.S.	B2	122
North Highlands, Ca., U.S.	*C3	82
North Hill, Wa., U.S.	*B3	124
North Holland (Noord-Holland), prov., Neth.	B4	17
North Holston, Va., U.S.	f10	123
North Horn Lake, l., Tn., U.S.	e8	119
North Horr, Kenya	A6	48
North Houston, Tx., U.S.	*E5	120
North Hudson, N.Y., U.S.	B7	109
North Hudson, Wi., U.S.	*C1	126
North Hyde Park, Vt., U.S.	B3	122
North Industry, Oh., U.S.	B4	112
North Inlet, b., S.C., U.S.	E9	117
North Island, i., N.Z.	M15	51
North Island Naval Air Station, mil., Ca., U.S.	o15	82
North Islands, is., La., U.S.	E7	95
North Java, N.Y., U.S.	C2	109
North Jay, Me., U.S.	D2	96
North Kansas City, Mo., U.S.	h10	102
North Kingstown, R.I., U.S.	E4	116
North Kingsville, Oh., U.S.	A5	112
North Komelik, Az., U.S.	E4	80
North La Junta, Co., U.S.	C7	83
North Lake, Il., U.S.	k9	90
North Lake, Wi., U.S.	m11	126
North Laramie, stm., Wy., U.S.	D7	127
North Las Vegas, Nv., U.S.	G6	105
North Lauderdale, Fl., U.S.	*r13	86
North La Veta Pass, Co., U.S.	D5	83
North Lawrence, N.Y., U.S.	f10	109
North Lemmon, N.D., U.S.	D3	111
North Liberty, In., U.S.	A5	91
North Liberty, Ia., U.S.	C6	92
North Lima, Oh., U.S.	B5	112
North Lindenhurst, N.Y., U.S.	*n15	109
North Little Rock, Ar., U.S.	C3	81
North Logan, Ut., U.S.	B4	121
North Long Beach, Ms., U.S.	*E4	101
North Loon Mountain, mtn., Id., U.S.	D3	89
North Loup, Ne., U.S.	C7	104
North Loup, stm., Ne., U.S.	C5	104
North Lubec, Me., U.S.	D5	96
North Madison, Oh., U.S.	*A4	112
North Mamm Peak, mtn., Co., U.S.	B3	83
North Manchester, In., U.S.	C6	91
North Manitou Island, i., Mi., U.S.	C4	99
North Mankato, Mn., U.S.	F4	100
North Marshfield, Ma., U.S.	h12	98
North Massapequa, N.Y., U.S.	*E7	109
North Merrick, N.Y., U.S.	*n15	109
North Merrydale, La., U.S.	*D4	95
North Miami, Fl., U.S.	G6	86
North Miami, Ok., U.S.	A7	113
North Miami Beach, Fl., U.S.	s13	86
North Middleboro, Ma., U.S.	C6	98
North Middletown, Ky., U.S.	B5	94
North Monmouth, Me., U.S.	D2	96
North Montpelier, Vt., U.S.	C4	122
Northmoor, Mo., U.S.	h10	102
North Moose Lake, l., Man.	B1	70
North Mountain, mtn., Pa., U.S.	D9	115
North Muskegon, Mi., U.S.	E4	99
North Myrtle Beach, S.C., U.S.	D10	117
North Naples, Fl., U.S.	F5	86
North Negril Point, c., Jam.	E12	65
North Newcastle, Me., U.S.	D3	96
North New Hyde Park, N.Y., U.S.	*E7	109
North Newport, Ct., U.S.	D2	106
North New Portland, Me., U.S.	D2	96
North New River Canal, Fl., U.S.	F6	86
North Norwich, N.Y., U.S.	C5	109
North Ogden, Ut., U.S.	B4	121
North Olmsted, Oh., U.S.	h9	112
North Omaha, Ne., U.S.	g13	104
Northome, Mn., U.S.	C4	100
North Orange, Ma., U.S.	A3	98
North Oxford, Ma., U.S.	B4	98
North Palisade, mtn., Ca., U.S.	D4	82
North Palm Beach, Fl., U.S.	*F6	86
North Park, Il., U.S.	A4	90
North Park, val., Co., U.S.	A4	83
North Parsonfield, Me., U.S.	E2	96
North Pass, strt., La., U.S.	E7	95
North Patchogue, N.Y., U.S.	*n15	109
North Pembroke, Ma., U.S.	B6	98
North Pitcher, N.Y., U.S.	C5	109
North Plainfield, N.J., U.S.	B4	107
North Plains, Or., U.S.	B4	114
North Plains, pl., N.M., U.S.	C1	108
North Platte, Ne., U.S.	C5	104
North Platte, stm., U.S.	B6	76
North Point, c., Barb.	K20	65
North Point, c., Md., U.S.	B5	97
North Point, c., Md., U.S.	C5	97
North Point, c., Mi., U.S.	C7	99
North Pole	A1	128
North Pomfret, Vt., U.S.	D4	122
North Pond, l., Me., U.S.	D3	96
North Pond, l., Me., U.S.	h9	96
North Port, Al., U.S.	B2	78
North Port, Fl., U.S.	*D4	86
Northport, Mi., U.S.	C5	99
Northport, Ne., U.S.	C2	104
Northport, N.Y., U.S.	*n15	109
Northport, Wa., U.S.	A8	124
North Portal, Sask.	H4	75
North Powder, Or., U.S.	B9	114
North Pownal, Me., U.S.	g7	96
North Pownal, Vt., U.S.	F2	122
North Prairie, Wi., U.S.	F5	126
North Providence, R.I., U.S.	C4	116
North Raccoon, stm., Ia., U.S.	C3	92
North Range Corner, N.S.	E4	71
North Reading, Ma., U.S.	f11	98
North Richland Hills, Tx., U.S.	n9	120
Northridge, Oh., U.S.	C2	112
Northridge, Oh., U.S.	*C1	112
North Ridgeville, Oh., U.S.	A3	112
North Rim, Az., U.S.	A3	80
North River Bridge, N.S.	C9	71
North Riverside, Il., U.S.	*k9	90
North Robinson, Oh., U.S.	B3	112
North Ronaldsay, i., Scot., U.K.	A5	10
Northrop, Mn., U.S.	G4	100
North Rose, N.Y., U.S.	B4	109
North Royalton, Oh., U.S.	h9	112
North Rustico, P.E.I.	C6	71
North Salem, In., U.S.	E4	91
North Salem, N.H., U.S.	E4	106
North Salt Lake, Ut., U.S.	C4	121
North Sanbornton, N.H., U.S.	C3	106
North Sandwich, N.H., U.S.	C4	106
North Santee, stm., S.C., U.S.	E9	117
North Saskatchewan, stm., Can.	F10	66
North Schell Peak, mtn., Nv., U.S.	D7	105
North Scituate, Ma., U.S.	h12	98
North Scituate, R.I., U.S.	C3	116
North Sea, Eur.	D9	8
Norths Highland, plat., Ant.	C25	7
North Shores, De., U.S.	F5	85
North Shoshone Peak, mtn., Nv., U.S.	D4	105
North Shrewsbury, Vt., U.S.	D3	122
North Sioux City, S.D., U.S.	E9	118
North Skunk, stm., Ia., U.S.	C5	92
North Sound, strt., Ire.		
North Sound, strt., Scot., U.K.	A6	13
North Spicer Island, i., N.W. Ter.	C17	66
North Springfield, Or., U.S.	*C3	114
North Springfield, Vt., U.S.	E3	122
North Springfield, Va., U.S.	*B5	123
North Springfield Reservoir, res., Vt., U.S.	E4	122
North Star, De., U.S.	A3	85
North Star, Mi., U.S.	E6	99
North Star, Oh., U.S.	B1	112
North Stonington, Ct., U.S.	D8	84
North Stradbroke, i., Austl.	E9	50
North Stratford, N.H., U.S.	A3	106
North Sudbury, Ma., U.S.	g10	98
North Sutton, N.H., U.S.	D3	106
North Swansea, Ma., U.S.	C5	98
North Swanzey, N.H., U.S.	E2	106
North Sydney, Austl.	*F9	50
North Sydney, N.S.	C9	71
North Syracuse, N.Y., U.S.	B4	109
North Taranaki Bight, N.Z.	M15	51
North Tarrytown, N.Y., U.S.	D7	109
North Tea Lake, l., Ont.	B5	73
North Terre Haute, In., U.S.	E3	91
North Tewksbury, Ma., U.S.	A5	98
North Thetford, Vt., U.S.	D4	122
North Thompson, stm., B.C.	D8	69
North Tolsta, Scot., U.K.	C6	13
North Tonawanda, N.Y., U.S.	B2	109
North Trenton, N.J., U.S.	*C6	112
North Troy, Vt., U.S.	A4	122
North Truro, Ma., U.S.	*B7	98
North Tunbridge, Vt., U.S.	D4	122
North Turner Mountain, mtn., Me., U.S.	C4	96
North Twin Lake, l., Newf.	D4	72
North Twin Lake, l., Wi., U.S.	C4	126
North Tyne, stm., Eng., U.K.	E6	13
North Uist, i., Scot., U.K.	C6	13
Northumberland, N.H., U.S.	A3	106
Northumberland, Pa., U.S.	E8	115
Northumberland, co., N.B.	C6	71
Northumberland, co., Va., U.S.	C6	123
Northumberland, co., Eng., U.K.	E6	13

Northumberland, co., Pa., U.S. D8 115
Northumberland, co., Va., U.S. C6 123
Northumberland Isles, is., Austl. D9 50
Northumberland Strait, strt., Can. C6 71
North Umpqua, stm., Or., U.S. D3 114
North Uxbridge, Ma., U.S. B4 98
Northvale, N.J., U.S. g9 107
North Valley Stream, N.Y., U.S. *n15 109
North Vancouver, B.C. E6 69
North Vassalboro, Me., U.S. D3 96
North Vernon, In., U.S. F6 91
North Versailles, Pa., U.S. *k14 115
Northview, Mi., U.S. *E5 99
Northview, Mo., U.S. D4 102
Northview, Oh., U.S. *C1 112
North Village, N.H., U.S. E3 106
Northville, Ct., U.S. C2 84
Northville, Mi., U.S. p15 99
Northville, N.Y., U.S. B6 109
Northville, S.D., U.S. B7 118
North Wabasca Lake, l., Alta. A4 68
North Waldoboro, Me., U.S. D3 96
North Wales, Pa., U.S. F11 115
North Walpole, N.H., U.S. D2 106
North Walsham, Eng., U.K. D7 10
North Wantagh, N.Y., U.S. *n15 109
North Warren, Pa., U.S. C3 115
North Waterford, Me., U.S. D2 96
Northway, Ak., U.S. C11 79
North Webster, In., U.S. B6 91
North West, dept., Guy. A3 59
North West Cape, c., Austl. D1 50
North Westchester, Ct., U.S. C6 84
North-Western, prov., Zam. D4 48
North West Highlands, plat., Scot., U.K. B4 10
North Westminster, Vt., U.S. E4 122
Northwest Miramichi, stm., N.B. B3 71
Northwest Polder, reg., Neth. B5 17
Northwest Providence Channel, strt., Bah. A4 64
North West River, Newf. B1 72
Northwest Territories, prov., Can. C13 66
Northwest Upsalquitch, stm., N.B. B2 71
Northwich, Eng., U.K. A5 12
North Wildwood, N.J., U.S. E3 107
North Wilkesboro, N.C., U.S. A1 110
North Wilmington, Ma., U.S. f11 98
North Windham, Ct., U.S. C7 84
North Windham, Me., U.S. E2 96
Northwood, Ia., U.S. A4 92
Northwood, N.H., U.S. D4 106
Northwood, N.D., U.S. B8 111
Northwood, Oh., U.S. *c7 112
Northwood Center, N.H., U.S. D4 106
Northwood Ridge, N.H., U.S. D4 106
Northwoods, Mo., U.S. *f13 102
North Woodstock, N.H., U.S. B3 106
North Yarmouth, Me., U.S. g7 96
North York, Ont. D5 73
North York, Pa., U.S. G8 115
North York Moors, hills, Eng., U.K. C6 10
North Yorkshire, co., Eng., U.K. F7 13
North Zulch, Tx., U.S. D4 120
Norton, N.B. D4 71
Norton, Eng., U.K. F8 13
Norton, Ks., U.S. C4 93
Norton, Ma., U.S. C5 98
Norton, Oh., U.S. A4 112
Norton, Tx., U.S. D2 120
Norton, Va., U.S. f9 123
Norton, W.V., U.S. C5 125
Norton, co., Ks., U.S. C4 93
Norton Air Force Base, mil., Ca., U.S. E5 82
Norton Bay, b., Ak., U.S. C7 79
Norton Creek, stm., Al., U.S. B1 78
Norton Pond, l., Vt., U.S. B5 122
Norton Reservoir, res., Ks., U.S. C3 93
Nortons Corner, Az., U.S. D4 80
Norton Shores, Mi., U.S. E4 99
Norton Sound, strt., Ak., U.S. C6 79
Nortonville, Ks., U.S. C8 93
Nortonville, Ky., U.S. C2 94
Nortonville, N.D., U.S. C7 111
Nortorf, W. Ger. D3 15
Norvegia, Cape, c., Ant. B11 7
Norwalk, Ca., U.S. n12 82
Norwalk, Ct., U.S. E2 84
Norwalk, Ia., U.S. C4 92
Norwalk, Oh., U.S. A3 112
Norwalk, Wi., U.S. E3 126
Norwalk, stm., Ct., U.S. E2 84
Norwalk Islands, is., Ct., U.S. E2 84
Norway, Ca., U.S. C4 91
Norway, Ia., U.S. C6 92
Norway, Ks., U.S. C6 93
Norway, Me., U.S. D2 96
Norway, Mi., U.S. C3 99
Norway, Or., U.S. D2 114
Norway, S.C., U.S. E5 117
Norway, ctry., Eur. F4 14
Norway House, Man. C3 70
Norway Lake, l., Mn., U.S. E3 100
Norwegian Bay, b., N.W. Ter. m33 66
Norwegian Sea, Eur. C14 128
Norwell, Ma., U.S. h12 98
Norwich, Ont. E4 73
Norwich, Eng., U.K. D7 10
Norwich, Ct., U.S. C7 84
Norwich, Ks., U.S. E6 93
Norwich, N.Y., U.S. C5 109
Norwich, N.D., U.S. A5 111
Norwich, Vt., U.S. D4 122
Norwood, Ont. C7 73
Norwood, Co., U.S. C2 83
Norwood, Ga., U.S. C4 87
Norwood, La., U.S. D4 95
Norwood, Ma., U.S. B5 98
Norwood, Mn., U.S. F5 100
Norwood, Mo., U.S. D5 102
Norwood, N.J., U.S. h9 107
Norwood, N.Y., U.S. f10 109
Norwood, N.C., U.S. B2 110
Norwood, Oh., U.S. o13 112
Norwood, Pa., U.S. p20 115
Norwoodville, Ia., U.S. e8 92
Norwottock, Mount, mtn., Ma., U.S. B3 98
Nosbonsing, Lake, l., Ont. A5 73
Noshiro, Japan F9 33
Nösjön, l., Swe. A6 15
Nossa Senhora das Dores, Braz. D3 57
Nossen, E. Ger. B8 19
Noss Head, c., Scot., U.K. B5 13

Nossob, stm., Afr. C3 49
Nosy Varika, Madag. h9 49
Notasulga, Al., U.S. C4 78
Notch Hill, B.C. D8 69
Notch Mountain, mtn., Ma., U.S. A3 98
Notch Peak, mtn., Ut., U.S. D3 121
Noteć, stm., Pol. B3 26
Notikewin, Alta. A2 68
Notikewin, stm., Alta. A1 68
Noto, Italy F5 23
Noto, Gulf of, b., Italy F5 23
Notodden, Nor. H3 14
Noto Island, i., Japan H8 33
Noto Peninsula, pen., Japan D12 31
Notouse, Kir. R18 52
Notre-Dame, N.B. C5 71
Notre Dame, Monts, mts., Que. k13 74
Notre Dame Bay, b., Newf. D4 72
Notre Dame de Lourdes, Man. E2 70
Notre-Dame-de-Montauban, Que. C5 74
Notre-Dame-des-Bois, Que. D6 74
Notre-Dame-du-Lac, Que. B9 74
Notre-Dame-du-Laus, Que. C2 74
Nottawa, Ont. C4 73
Nottawasaga Bay, b., Ont. C4 73
Nottaway, stm., Que. h11 74
Nottely Lake, res., Ga., U.S. B2 87
Nottingham, Eng., U.K. D6 10
Nottingham, N.H., U.S. D4 106
Nottingham Island, i., N.W. Ter. D17 66
Nottinghamshire, co., Eng., U.K. A7 12
Nottoway, Va., U.S. C4 123
Nottoway, co., Va., U.S. C4 123
Nottoway, stm., Va., U.S. D5 123
Notukeu Creek, stm., Sask. H2 75
Notus, Id., U.S. F2 89
Nouadhibou, Maur. B1 45
Nouakchott, Maur. C1 45
Nouamrhar, Maur. C1 45
Nouméa, N. Cal. H10 6
Nouna, Burkina D4 45
Noupoort, S. Afr. D3 49
Noutonice, Czech. n17 26
Nouvelle-France, Cap de la, Que. D18 66
Nouzonville, Fr. C6 16
Nova, Oh., U.S. A3 112
Nova Caipemba, Ang. C1 48
Nova Cruz, Braz. C3 57
Nova Friburgo, Braz. C4 56
Nova Iguaçu, Braz. h6 56
Nova Lima, Braz. C4 56
Nova Londrina, Braz. C2 56
Nova Lusitânia, Moz. A5 49
Nova Mambone, Moz. B6 49
Nova Olinda do Norte, Braz. C3 59
Nova Ponte, Braz. B3 56
Nova Prata, Braz. D2 56
Novar, Ont. B5 73
Novara, Italy B2 23
Nova Roma, Braz. A3 56
Nova Russas, Braz. B2 57
Nova Sofala, Moz. B5 49
Nova Soure, Braz. B3 57
Novate Mezzola, Italy D7 21
Novato, Ca., U.S. C2 82
Nova Varoš, Yugo. D4 24
Nova Venécia, Braz. B4 56
Nova Vida, Braz. B3 55
Novaya Astrakhan, Sov. Un. p21 27
Novaya Kazanka, Sov. Un. F18 8
Novaya Ladoga, Sov. Un. A9 27
Novaya Lyalya, Sov. Un. D9 29
Novaya Odessa, Sov. Un. H8 27
Novaya Sibir Island, i., Sov. Un. B17 29
Novaya Zemlya, is., Sov. Un. B8 29
Nova Zagora, Bul. D8 24
Novelda, Spain C5 22
Novelty, Mo., U.S. A5 102
Nové Město [nad Váhom], Czech. D4 26
Nové Strášeci, Czech. C8 19
Nové Zámky, Czech. E5 26
Novgorod, Sov. Un. D6 29
Novgorod-Severskiy, Sov. Un. E9 27
Novi, Mi., U.S. p15 99
Novice, Tx., U.S. D3 120
Novigrad, Yugo. C2 24
Novi Ligure, Italy B2 23
Novinger, Mo., U.S. A5 102
Novi Pazar, Bul. D8 24
Novi Pazar, Yugo. D5 24
Novi Sad, Yugo. C4 24
Novo, stm., Braz. g6 56
Novo Airão, Braz. C2 59
Novoaltaysk, Sov. Un. E25 8
Novoanninskiy, Sov. Un. C2 28
Novo Aripuanã, Braz. D2 59
Novoaydar, Sov. Un. G12 27
Novocherkassk, Sov. Un. H13 27
Novoekonomicheskoye, Sov. Un. q20 27
Novograd-Volynskiy, Sov. Un. F6 27
Novogrudok, Sov. Un. E5 27
Novokazalinsk, Sov. Un. E9 29
Novokuybyshevsk, Sov. Un. *D7 29
Novokuznetsk, Sov. Un. D11 29
Novomirgorod, Sov. Un. G8 27
Novomoskovsk, Sov. Un. G10 27
Novomoskovsk, Sov. Un. D6 29
Novopokrovskaya, Sov. Un. I13 27
Novo-Selo, Bul. E6 29
Novoshakhtinsk, Sov. Un. H12 27
Novosibirsk, Sov. Un. D11 29
Novosibirsk Reservoir, res., Sov. Un. C10 28
Novosil, Sov. Un. E11 27
Novotroitsk, Sov. Un. C5 28
Novoukrainka, Sov. Un. G8 27
Novouzensk, Sov. Un. C3 28
Novovoronezhskiy, Sov. Un. B11 33
Novozybkov, Sov. Un. E9 27
Nový Bohumín, Czech. D5 26
Nový Bydžov, Czech. C2 24
Nový Jičín, Czech. D5 26
Novyye Senzhary, Sov. Un. G10 27
Novyy Oskol, Sov. Un. F11 27
Novyy Port, Sov. Un. C10 29
Novyy Urengoy, Sov. Un. C10 29
Novyy Uzen, Sov. Un. G19 8
Novyy Vasyugan, Sov. Un. B9 28
Nowagród, Pol. B10 19
Nowa Ruda, Pol. C4 26
Nowa Sól, Pol. C3 26

Nowata, Ok., U.S. A6 113
Nowata, co., Ok., U.S. A6 113
Nowood, stm., Wy., U.S. B5 127
Nowra-Bomaderry, Austl. G8 51
Nowshāk, mtn., Asia k17 39
Nowy Dwór [Mazowiecki], Pol. k13 26
Nowy Sacz, Pol. D6 26
Nowy Targ, Pol. D6 26
Nowy Tomyśl, Pol. B3 26
Noxapater, Ms., U.S. C4 101
Noxen, Pa., U.S. D9 115
Noxon, Mt., U.S. C1 103
Noxon Reservoir, res., Mt., U.S. C1 103
Noxontown Lake, res., De., U.S. C3 85
Noxubee, co., Ms., U.S. B5 101
Noxubee, stm., U.S. B5 101
Noya, Spain A1 22
Noyes, Mn., U.S. B1 100
Noyes Island, i., Ak., U.S. n22 79
Noyon, Fr. C5 16
Nozeroy, Fr. C7 21
Nsanje, Mwi. E6 48
Nsawam, Ghana E4 45
Nsukka, Nig. E6 45
Ntem, stm., Afr. E2 46
Nuatabu, Kir. R18 52
Nubanusit Lake, l., N.H., U.S. E2 106
Nūbārīyah, Tur'at an, Eg. D2 41
Nuberg, Ga., U.S. B4 87
Nubian Desert, des., Sud. A3 47
Nuckolls, co., Ne., U.S. D7 104
Nucla, Co., U.S. C2 83
Nueces, co., Tx., U.S. F4 120
Nueces, stm., Tx., U.S. E3 120
Nueltin Lake, l., Can. D13 66
Nueva, Isla, i., Chile k12 54
Nueva Antioquia, Col. B4 60
Nueva Asunción, dept., Para. D3 55
Nueva Casas Grandes, Mex. A3 63
Nueva Esparta, state, Ven. A5 60
Nueva Gerona, Cuba D2 64
Nueva Imperial, Chile B2 54
Nueva Lubecka, Arg. B2 54
Nueva Ocotepeque, Hond. C3 62
Nueva Palmira, Ur. E1 56
Nueva Providencia, Pan. k11 64
Nueva Rosita, Mex. B4 63
Nueva San Salvador, El Sal. D3 62
Nueve de Julio, Arg. B4 54
Nuevitas, Cuba D5 64
Nuevo, Golfo, b., Arg. C3 54
Nuevo Emperador, Pan. m11 64
Nuevo Laredo, Mex. B5 63
Nuevo León, state, Mex. B5 63
Nuevo San Juan, Pan. k11 62
Nugaal, prov., Som. D6 47
Nühь, Rās, c., Pak. I11 39
Nuits, Fr. D6 16
Nukhayb, Iraq G14 40
Nuku'alofa, Tonga H11 6
Nukus, Sov. Un. E5 28
Nulato, Ak., U.S. C8 79
Nules, Spain C5 22
Nulhegan, stm., Vt., U.S. B5 122
Nullagine, Austl. D3 50
Nullarbor Plain, pl., Austl. F4 50
Numa, Ia., U.S. D5 92
Numan, Nig. E7 45
Numazu, Japan I9 33
Numfoor, i., Indon. F8 34
Numila, Hi., U.S. B2 88
Nu Mine, Pa., U.S. E3 115
Nunawading, Austl. *G8 50
Nunda, N.Y., U.S. C3 109
Nunda, S.D., U.S. C8 118
Nuneaton, Eng., U.K. B6 12
Nunez, Ga., U.S. D4 87
Nunica, Mi., U.S. E4 99
Nunivak Island, i., Ak., U.S. D6 79
Nunn, Co., U.S. A6 83
Nunnelly, Tn., U.S. B4 119
Nuoro, Italy D2 23
Nuquí, Col. B2 60
Nura, stm., Sov. Un. E23 8
Nuremberg, Pa., U.S. E9 115
Nuremberg see Nürnberg, W. Ger.
Nuri, Mex. B5 63
Nurmes, Fin. F13 14
Nürnberg (Nuremberg), W. Ger. D5 18
Nursery, Tx., U.S. E4 120
Nürtingen, W. Ger. E4 19
Nus, Italy E3 21
Nusaybin, Tur. D13 40
Nushki, Pak. C5 43
Nusle (part of Prague), Czech. n17 26
Nuthe, stm., E. Ger. A8 19
Nutley, N.J., U.S. B4 107
Nut Mountain, Sask. E4 75
Nutrioso, Az., U.S. D6 80
Nutter Fort, W.V., U.S. k10 125
Nutting Lake, Ma., U.S. f10 98
Nutwood, Il., U.S. D3 90
Nuuanu Pali, Hi., U.S. g10 88
Nu'utele Island, i., W. Sam. G12 52
Nuutoi, Cape, c., W. Sam. G12 52
Nuwara-Eliya, Sri L. G7 36
Nuyaka, Ok., U.S. B5 113
Nūzvīd, India I8 37
Nyac, Ak., U.S. C8 79
Nyack, N.Y., U.S. D7 109
Nyala, Sud. C1 47
Nyamandhlovu, Zimb. A4 49
Nyamtumbo, Tan. D6 48
Nyandoma, Sov. Un. C7 29
Nyanza, Rw. B4 48
Nyanza, prov., Kenya B5 48
Nyasa, Lake, l., Afr. D5 48
Nyborg, Den. C4 15
Nybro, Swe. I6 14
Nye, Mt., U.S. E7 103
Nye, co., Nv., U.S. E5 105
Nyeri, Kenya B6 48
Nyilumba, Tan. D7 48
Nyimba, Zam. D5 48
Nyíregyháza, Hung. B5 24
Nykøbing Falster, Den. D5 15
Nykøbing Sjælland, Den. C5 15
Nyköping, Swe. H7 14
Nylstroom, S. Afr. B4 49
Nymagee, Austl. F6 51
Nymburk, Czech. C6 26
Nymindegab, Den. C2 15
Nynäshamn, Swe. H8 14

Nyngan, Austl. F8 50
Nyon, Switz. E3 18
Nyong, stm., Cam. E2 46
Nýřany, Czech. D2 26
Nýrsko, Czech. D8 19
Nysa, Pol. C4 26
Nyssa, Or., U.S. D9 114
Nysted, Den. D5 15
Nyunzu, Zaire C4 48
Nzega, Tan. B5 48
Nzérékoré, Gui. E3 45
N'zeto, Ang. C1 48
Nzwani, i., Com. f8 49

O

Oacoma, S.D., U.S. D6 118
Oahe, Lake, res., U.S. A7 76
Oahe Dam, S.D., U.S. C5 118
Oahu, i., Hi., U.S. B4 88
Oakalla, Tx., U.S. D4 120
Oak, Ne., U.S. D8 104
Oak, Ar., U.S. B2 81
Oak Bay, B.C. h12 69
Oak Bay, N.B. D2 71
Oak Bluffs, Ma., U.S. D6 98
Oakboro, N.C., U.S. B2 110
Oak Brook, Il., U.S. *k9 90
Oakburn, Man. D1 70
Oak City, N.C., U.S. B5 110
Oak City, Ut., U.S. D3 121
Oak Creek, Co., U.S. A4 83
Oak Creek, Wi., U.S. n12 126
Oakdale, Ca., U.S. D3 82
Oakdale, Ct., U.S. D7 84
Oakdale, Il., U.S. E4 90
Oakdale, La., U.S. D3 95
Oakdale, Ma., U.S. h8 84
Oakdale, Mn., U.S. *n13 100
Oakdale, Ne., U.S. B8 104
Oakdale, N.Y., U.S. *n15 109
Oakdale, Pa., U.S. k13 115
Oakdale, Tn., U.S. D9 119
Oakengates, Eng., U.K. B5 12
Oakes, N.D., U.S. C8 111
Oakesdale, Wa., U.S. B8 124
Oakey, Austl. E9 51
Oakfield, Ga., U.S. E3 87
Oakfield, Me., U.S. B4 96
Oakfield, N.Y., U.S. B2 109
Oakfield, Wi., U.S. E5 126
Oakford, Il., U.S. C4 90
Oakford, In., U.S. D5 91
Oak Forest, Il., U.S. k9 90
Oak Grove, Ar., U.S. A2 81
Oak Grove, Ky., U.S. D2 94
Oak Grove, La., U.S. B4 95
Oak Grove, Or., U.S. B4 114
Oak Grove, S.C., U.S. *D5 117
Oakham, Eng., U.K. B7 12
Oakham, Ma., U.S. B3 98
Oak Harbor, Oh., U.S. A2 112
Oak Harbor, Wa., U.S. A3 124
Oak Hill, De., U.S. *B3 85
Oak Hill, Fl., U.S. D6 86
Oak Hill, Ks., U.S. *C6 93
Oak Hill, Oh., U.S. D3 112
Oak Hill, W.V., U.S. D3 125
Oak Hill, mtn., Ma., U.S. f9 98
Oak Island, i., Wi., U.S. B3 126
Oakhurst, N.J., U.S. C4 107
Oakhurst, Ok., U.S. A5 113
Oak Lake, Man. E1 70
Oak Lake, l., Man. E1 70
Oakland, Ont. D4 73
Oakland, Al., U.S. A2 78
Oakland, Ar., U.S. A3 81
Oakland, Ca., U.S. D2 82
Oakland, Fl., U.S. *D5 86
Oakland, Il., U.S. D5 90
Oakland, Ia., U.S. C2 92
Oakland, Ky., U.S. C3 94
Oakland, Md., U.S. m12 97
Oakland, Ms., U.S. A4 101
Oakland, Ne., U.S. C9 104
Oakland, N.J., U.S. A4 107
Oakland, Ok., U.S. C5 113
Oakland, Or., U.S. D3 114
Oakland, Pa., U.S. C10 115
Oakland, R.I., U.S. B2 116
Oakland, Tn., U.S. B2 119
Oakland, co., Mi., U.S. F7 99
Oakland City, In., U.S. H3 91
Oakland Gardens, Ct., U.S. C5 84
Oakland Park, Fl., U.S. r13 86
Oak Lawn Manor, De., U.S. *A3 85
Oak Lawn, Il., U.S. B6 90
Oaklawn, Ks., U.S. g12 93
Oakleigh, Austl. *G8 50
Oakley, Ca., U.S. G5 89
Oakley, Id., U.S. G5 89
Oakley, Ks., U.S. C3 93
Oakley, Mi., U.S. E6 99
Oakley, Ms., U.S. C3 101
Oakley, S.C., U.S. E7 117
Oakley, Ut., U.S. C4 121
Oaklyn, N.J., U.S. *D4 107
Oakman, Al., U.S. B2 78
Oakman, Ga., U.S. B2 87
Oakmont, Pa., U.S. E2 115
Oak Mountain, mtn., Ga., U.S. B2 87
Oak Mountain, mtn., Tn., U.S. h11 119
Oak Orchard, De., U.S. F5 85
Oak Park, Ca., U.S. *E5 82
Oak Park, Ga., U.S. A2 92
Oak Park, Il., U.S. B6 90
Oak Park, Mi., U.S. p15 99
Oak Point, Man. D3 70
Oak Ridge, Fl., U.S. *D5 86
Oak Ridge, La., U.S. B4 95
Oak Ridge, Mo., U.S. D8 102
Oak Ridge, N.C., U.S. A3 110
Oak Ridge, Pa., U.S. E3 115
Oak Ridge, Tn., U.S. C9 119
Oak Ridge Reservoir, res., N.J., U.S. A3 107
Oak Ridges (part of Richmond Hill), Ont. k15 73
Oak River, Man. D1 70
Oaks, Ok., U.S. A7 113
Oaks, Pa., U.S. o20 115
Oakton, Ky., U.S. f8 94
Oakton, Va., U.S. g12 123
Oaktown, In., U.S. G3 91
Oak Vale, Ms., U.S. D4 101

Oakvale, W.V., U.S. *D4 125
Oak Valley, N.J., U.S. *D2 107
Oakville, Man. E2 70
Oakville, Ont. D5 73
Oakville, Ct., U.S. C3 84
Oakville, In., U.S. D7 91
Oakville, Ia., U.S. C6 92
Oakville, Mo., U.S. *g13 102
Oakville, Wa., U.S. C2 124
Oakway, S.C., U.S. B1 117
Oakwood, Ga., U.S. B3 87
Oakwood, Il., U.S. C6 90
Oakwood, Ne., U.S. C6 104
Oakwood, N.D., U.S. A8 111
Oakwood, Oh., U.S. A1 112
Oakwood, Oh., U.S. C1 112
Oakwood, Tx., U.S. D5 120
Oakwood, Va., U.S. e9 123
Oakwood Beach, N.J., U.S. D1 107
Oamaru, N.Z. P13 51
Ōamishirasato, Japan n19 33
Oark, Ar., U.S. B2 81
Oasis, Ut., U.S. D3 121
Oatman, Az., U.S. C1 80
Oats, S.C., U.S. C7 117
Oaxaca, state, Mex. D5 63
Oaxaca [de Juárez], Mex. D5 63
Ob, stm., Sov. Un. C9 29
Oba, Ont. G16 66
Obama, Japan n14 33
Oban, Sask. E1 75
Oban, Scot., U.K. B4 10
Ob Bay, b., Sov. Un. C10 29
Obed, Alta. C2 68
Obed, stm., Tn., U.S. C9 119
Oberá, Arg. E4 55
Oberammergau, W. Ger. B7 20
Oberdrauburg, Aus. C8 20
Oberhausen, W. Ger. C3 18
Oberkirch, W. Ger. E3 19
Oberlin, Ks., U.S. C3 93
Oberlin, La., U.S. D3 95
Oberlin, Oh., U.S. A3 112
Obernai, Fr. C7 16
Obernburg [am Main], W. Ger. E3 19
Oberon, N.D., U.S. B6 111
Oberösterreich, state, Aus. E9 19
Oberstaufen, W. Ger. B6 20
Oberstdorf, W. Ger. E5 18
Obersursel, W. Ger. C3 19
Oberwald, Switz. C4 20
Obetz, Oh., U.S. C3 112
Obihiro, Japan C13 31
Obi Islands, is., Indon. F7 34
Obion, Tn., U.S. A2 119
Obion, co., Tn., U.S. A2 119
Obion, stm., Tn., U.S. A2 119
Obion, Middle Fork, stm., Tn., U.S. A3 119
Obion, Rutherford Fork, stm., Tn., U.S. A3 119
Obion, South Fork, stm., Tn., U.S. A3 119
Obion Creek, stm., Ky., U.S. f9 94
Oblachnaya, Mount, mtn., Sov. Un. E7 33
Oblong, Il., U.S. D6 90
Obo, Cen. Afr. Rep. D5 46
Obluchye, Sov. Un. E16 29
Obock, Dji. C5 47
Oborniki, Pol. B4 26
Oboyan, Sov. Un. F11 27
O'Brien, Fl., U.S. B4 86
O'Brien, Or., U.S. E3 114
O'Brien, co., Ia., U.S. A2 92
Observation Peak, mtn., Ca., U.S. B3 82
Obuasi, Ghana E4 45
Obwalden, state, Switz. C4 20
Ocala, Fl., U.S. C4 86
Ocampo, Mex. B3 63
Ocaña, Col. B3 60
Ocaña, Spain C4 22
Ocate, N.M., U.S. A5 108
Occidental, Cordillera, mts., Col. C2 60
Occidental, Cordillera, mts., Peru D3 58
Occidental, Cordillera, mts., S.A. C2 55
Occoquan, Va., U.S. B5 123
Ocean, co., N.J., U.S. D4 107
Ocean, W.V., U.S. D3 125
Oceana, W.V., U.S. D3 125
Oceana, co., Mi., U.S. E4 99
Oceana Naval Air Station, mil., Va., U.S. k15 123
Ocean Bluff, Ma., U.S. B6 98
Ocean City, Fl., U.S. u15 86
Ocean City, Md., U.S. D7 97
Ocean City, N.J., U.S. E3 107
Ocean Falls, B.C. C4 69
Ocean Gate, N.J., U.S. D4 107
Ocean Grove, Ma., U.S. C5 98
Ocean Grove, N.J., U.S. C4 107
Ocean Heights, N.J., U.S. D6 98
Ocean Park, Wa., U.S. C1 124
Ocean Port, N.J., U.S. C4 107
Oceanside, Ca., U.S. F5 82
Oceanside, N.Y., U.S. *E7 109
Ocean Springs, Ms., U.S. E5 101
Ocean View (Township), N.J., U.S. E3 107
Ocean View, De., U.S. F5 85
Oceanville, N.J., U.S. E4 107
Ochamchira, Sov. Un. A13 40
Ocheda Lake, l., Mn., U.S. G3 100
Ochelata, Ok., U.S. A6 113
Ocheyedan, Ia., U.S. A2 92
Ocheyedan, stm., Ia., U.S. A2 92
Ochil Hills, hills, Scot., U.K. p15 99
Ochiltree, co., Tx., U.S. A2 120
Ochlockonee, Ga., U.S. F2 87
Ochlockonee, stm., Fl., U.S. B2 86
Ochoco Lake, res., Or., U.S. C6 114
Ochopee, Fl., U.S. G5 86
Ochre River, Man. D2 70
Ochsenfurt, W. Ger. A3 19
Ochtrup, W. Ger. A2 19
Ocilla, Ga., U.S. E3 87
Ockelbo, Swe. G7 14
Öckerö, l., Swe. A5 15
Ockley, In., U.S. C4 91
Ocmulgee, stm., Ga., U.S. D3 87
Ocmulgee National Monument, Ga., U.S. D3 87
Ocna-Sibiului, Rom. C7 24
Ocnele Mari, Rom. C7 24

Ocoee, Tn., U.S. D9 119
Ocoee, Lake, res., Tn., U.S. D9 119
Ocotlán, Mex. C4 63
Ocoña, Peru E3 58
Oconee, Ga., U.S. D4 87
Oconee, co., Ga., U.S. C3 87
Oconee, co., S.C., U.S. B1 117
Oconee, stm., Ga., U.S. C3 87
Oconee, Lake, res., Ga., U.S. C3 87
Oconomowoc, Wi., U.S. E5 126
Oconto, Ne., U.S. C6 104
Oconto, Wi., U.S. D6 126
Oconto, co., Wi., U.S. D5 126
Oconto Falls, Wi., U.S. D5 126
Ocós, Guat. C1 62
Ocotal, Nic. E7 63
Ocotillo, Az., U.S. m9 80
Ocracoke, N.C., U.S. B7 110
Ocracoke Inlet, b., N.C., U.S. B6 110
Ocracoke Island, i., N.C., U.S. B7 110
Ocros, Peru D2 58
Octavia, Ne., U.S. C8 104
Octavia, Ok., U.S. C7 113
Octeville, Fr. C3 16
October Revolution Island, i., Sov. Un. B4 29
Octoraro Creek, stm., U.S. A5 97
Ocumare del Tuy, Ven. A4 60
Oda, Ghana E4 45
Odanah, Wi., U.S. B3 126
Ōdate, Japan F10 33
Odawara, Japan n18 33
Odd, W.V., U.S. *D3 125
Odda, Nor. G2 14
Odder, Den. C4 15
Odebolt, Ia., U.S. B2 92
Odell, Il., U.S. B5 90
Odell, Ne., U.S. D9 104
Odell, Or., U.S. B5 114
Odell, Tx., U.S. B3 120
Odell Lake, l., Or., U.S. E5 114
Odem, Tx., U.S. F4 120
Odemira, Port. D2 22
Ödemiş, Tur. C7 40
Ödendaalsrus, S. Afr. C4 49
Odensala, Swe. t35 14
Odense, Den. J4 14
Odensbacken (part of Örebro), Swe. t33 14
Odense Å, stm., Den. C4 15
Odenton, Md., U.S. B4 97
Odenville, Al., U.S. B3 78
Odenwald, mts., W. Ger. D3 19
Oder (Odra), stm., Eur. B3 26
Oder Spree Canal, E. Ger. A9 19
Odessa, Ont. C8 73
Odessa, Sov. Un. G4 27
Odessa, Fl., U.S. *D4 86
Odessa, Mn., U.S. E2 100
Odessa, Mo., U.S. C4 102
Odessa, N.Y., U.S. C4 109
Odessa, Tx., U.S. D1 120
Odessa, Wa., U.S. B7 124
Odiel, stm., Spain D2 22
Odienné, I.C. E3 45
Odin, Il., U.S. E4 90
Odin, Ks., U.S. D5 93
Odin, Mn., U.S. G4 100
Odin, Mount, mtn., B.C. D8 69
Odivelas, Port. f9 22
Odobeşti, Rom. C8 24
Ododи? O'Donnell, Tx., U.S. C2 120
Odorheiu Secuiesc, Rom. B7 24
Odra (Oder), stm., Eur. B3 26
Odum, Ga., U.S. E4 87
Odzi, Zimb. A5 49
Oeiras, Braz. C2 57
Oeiras, Port. f9 22
Oelde, W. Ger. B3 19
Oelsnitz [im Erzgebirge], E. Ger. C6 18
Oelsnitz [im Vogtland], E. Ger. C7 19
Oelwein, Ia., U.S. B6 92
Oensingen, Switz. B4 21
Oesede, W. Ger. A3 19
Oettingen [in Bayern], W. Ger. E5 19
Oeyón Island, i., S. Kor. H2 33
Ofahoma, Ms., U.S. C4 101
O'Fallon, Il., U.S. E4 90
O'Fallon, Mo., U.S. f12 102
O'Fallon Creek, stm., Mt., U.S. D12 103
Ofanto, stm., Italy D5 23
Ofaqim, Isr. D1 41
Offa, Nig. *E5 45
Offaly, co., Ire. C4 18
Offenbach [am Main], W. Ger. C4 18
Offenburg, W. Ger. E3 19
Offence, Mount of, hist., Isr. m14 41

Oficina Pedro de Valdivia, Chile D2 55
Ōfunato, Japan G10 33
Oga, Japan G9 33
Ōgaki, Japan I8 33
Ogallah, Ks., U.S. C4 93
Ogallala, Ne., U.S. C4 104
Oga Peninsula, pen., Japan G10 33
Ogbomosho, Nig. E5 45
Ogden, Ar., U.S. D1 81
Ogden, Ia., U.S. B3 92
Ogden, Ks., U.S. C7 93
Ogden, Ut., U.S. B4 121
Ogden, Mount, mtn., Ak., U.S. k23 79
Ogdensburg, N.J., U.S. A3 107
Ogdensburg, N.Y., U.S. f9 109
Ogdensburg, Wi., U.S. D5 126
Ogeechee, stm., Ga., U.S. D5 87
Ogema, Sask. H3 75
Ogema, Mn., U.S. C3 100
Ogema, Wi., U.S. C3 126
Ogemaw, Ar., U.S. D2 81
Ogemaw, co., Mi., U.S. D6 99
Ogilvie, Mn., U.S. E5 100
Ogilvie Mountains, mts., Yukon D5 66
Ogle, co., Il., U.S. A4 90
Oglesby, Il., U.S. B4 90
Oglesby, Ok., U.S. A6 113

Name	Map Ref.	Page
Oglethorpe, Ga., U.S.	D2	87
Oglethorpe, co., Ga., U.S.	C3	87
Oglethorpe, Mount, mtn., Ga., U.S.	B2	87
Oglio, stm., Italy	B3	23
Ognon, stm., Fr.	B1	20
Ogoamas, mtn., Indon.	E6	34
Ogoja, Nig.	E6	45
Ogoki, stm., Ont.	o18	73
Ogooué, stm., Afr.	F2	46
Ogosta, stm., Bul.	D6	24
Ogrodzieniec, Pol.	g11	26
Ogulin, Yugo.	C2	24
Ogunquit, Me., U.S.	E2	96
Ogurchinskiy Island, i., Sov. Un.	B6	39
Ohakune, N.Z.	M15	51
Ohanet, Alg.	D6	44
O'Hanly, stm., Man.	D4	70
Ōhara, Japan	n19	33
Ohatchee, Al., U.S.	B3	78
Ohaton, Alta.	C4	68
O'Higgins, Lago (Lago San Martín), l., S.A.	D2	54
Ohio, Co., U.S.	C4	83
Ohio, Il., U.S.	B4	90
Ohio, N.Y., U.S.	B6	109
Ohio, co., In., U.S.	G7	91
Ohio, co., Ky., U.S.	C3	94
Ohio, co., W.V., U.S.	A4	125
Ohio, state, U.S.	B3	112
Ohio, stm., U.S.	C11	76
Ohio Brush Creek, stm., Oh., U.S.	D2	112
Ohio City, Oh., U.S.	B1	112
Ohio Peak, mtn., Co., U.S.	C3	83
Ohiopyle, Pa., U.S.	G3	115
Ohioville, Pa., U.S.	E1	115
Ohiowa, Ne., U.S.	D8	104
Ohlman, Il., U.S.	D4	90
Ohoopee, Al., U.S.	D4	87
Ohoopee, stm., Ga., U.S.	D4	87
Ohre, stm., Eur.	C2	26
Ohrdruf, E. Ger.	C5	19
Ohrid, Yugo.	D6	24
Ohrid, Lake, l., Eur.	E5	24
Ohrigstad, S. Afr.	B5	49
Öhringen, W. Ger.	D4	19
Oiapoque, Braz.	B4	59
Oiapoque (Oyapock), stm., S.A.	B4	59
Oies, Île aux, i., Que.	B7	74
Oikull, Palau	R17	52
Oil Center, N.M., U.S.	E6	108
Oil City, La., U.S.	B2	95
Oil City, Ms., U.S.	C3	101
Oil City, Pa., U.S.	D2	115
Oil Creek, stm., Pa., U.S.	C2	115
Oildale, Ca., U.S.	E4	82
Oilmont, Mt., U.S.	B5	103
Oil Springs, Ont.	E2	73
Oilton, Ok., U.S.	A5	113
Oilton, Tx., U.S.	F3	120
Oil Trough, Ar., U.S.	B4	81
Oir, Beinn an, mtn., Scot., U.K.	E3	13
Oise, dept., Fr.	E2	17
Oise, stm., Eur.	C5	16
Oiseau, stm., Can.	D4	70
Oisemont, Fr.	E9	12
Ō Island, i., Japan	F9	33
Ō Island, i., Japan	I9	33
Oita, Japan	J5	33
Oiticica, Braz.	C2	57
Ojai, Ca., U.S.	E4	82
Ojinaga, Mex.	B4	63
Ojocaliente, Mex.	C4	63
Ojo Caliente, N.M., U.S.	A3	108
Ojo Feliz, N.M., U.S.	A4	108
Ojo Sarco, N.M., U.S.	A4	108
Ojos del Salado, Nevado, mtn., S.A.	E2	55
Oka, Que.	D3	74
Oka, Nig.	E6	45
Oka, stm., Sov. Un.	C14	27
Okaba, Indon.	G9	34
Okabena, Mn., U.S.	G3	100
Okahandja, Nmb.	B2	49
Okak Islands, is., Newf.	g9	72
Okaloosa, co., Fl., U.S.	u15	86
Okamanpeedan Lake, l., U.S.	A3	92
Okanagan Centre, B.C.	D8	69
Okanagan Falls, B.C.	E8	69
Okanagan Lake, l., B.C.	D8	69
Okanagan Landing, B.C.	D8	69
Okanagan Range, mts., N.A.	E7	69
Okanogan, Wa., U.S.	A6	124
Okanogan, co., Wa., U.S.	A5	124
Okanogan, stm., N.A.	A6	124
Okapilco Creek, stm., Ga., U.S.	E3	87
Okāra, Pak.	B4	37
Okarche, Ok., U.S.	B4	113
Okatibbee Reservoir, res., Ms., U.S.	C5	101
Okatoma Creek, stm., Ms., U.S.	D4	101
Okaton, S.D., U.S.	D5	118
Okauchee, Wi., U.S.	*E5	126
Okauchee Lake, Wi., U.S.	E5	126
Okaukuejo, Nmb.	A2	49
Okavango, stm., Afr.	H7	42
Okavango Swamps, sw., Bots.	A3	49
Okawville, Il., U.S.	E4	90
Okay, Ok., U.S.	B6	113
Okaya, Japan	H8	33
Okayama, Japan	E11	31
Okazaki, Japan	o16	33
O'Kean, Ar., U.S.	A5	81
Okeana, Oh., U.S.	n12	112
Okecie (part of Warsaw), Pol.	m13	26
Okeechobee, Fl., U.S.	E6	86
Okeechobee, co., Fl., U.S.	E6	86
Okeechobee, Lake, l., Fl., U.S.	F6	86
Okeene, Ok., U.S.	A3	113
Okefenokee Swamp, sw., U.S.	F4	87
Okehampton, Eng., U.K.	E4	11
Okemah, Ok., U.S.	B5	113
Okemos, Mi., U.S.	*F6	99
Oker, stm., W. Ger.	F4	15
Okesa, Ok., U.S.	A5	113
Oketo, Ks., U.S.	C7	93
Okfuskee, co., Ok., U.S.	B5	113
Okha, Sov. Un.	D17	29
Okhotsk, Sov. Un.	D17	29
Okhotsk, Sea of, Asia	D17	29
Okiep, S. Afr.	C2	49
Oki Islands, is., Japan	D11	31
Okinawa Island, i., Japan	F10	31
Oklahoma, co., Ok., U.S.	B4	113
Oklahoma, state, U.S.	B4	113
Oklahoma City, Ok., U.S.	B4	113
Oklawaha, Fl., U.S.	C5	86
Oklawaha, stm., Fl., U.S.	C5	86
Oklawaha, Lake, res., Fl., U.S.	C5	86
Oklee, Mn., U.S.	C3	100
Okmulgee, Ok., U.S.	B6	113
Okmulgee, co., Ok., U.S.	B5	113
Okoboji, Ia., U.S.	A2	92
Okobojo Creek, stm., S.D., U.S.	C5	118
Okolona, Ar., U.S.	D2	81
Okolona, Ky., U.S.	g11	94
Okolona, Ms., U.S.	B5	101
Okondja, Gabon	F2	46
Okotoks, Alta.	D4	68
Okreek, S.D., U.S.	D5	118
Oktaha, Ok., U.S.	B6	113
Oktibbeha, co., Ms., U.S.	B5	101
Oktyabrsk, Sov. Un.	D5	28
Oktyabrskiy, Sov. Un.	C4	28
Okulovka, Sov. Un.	B9	27
Okuma Bay, b., Ant.	B32	7
Okuniew, Pol.	k14	26
Okushiri, Japan	E9	33
Okushiri Island, i., Japan	E9	33
Ola, Ar., U.S.	B2	81
Ólafsfjördur, Ice.	m23	14
Ólafsvík, Ice.	n21	14
Olalla, Wa., U.S.	f10	124
Olamon, Me., U.S.	C4	96
Olancha, Ca., U.S.	D5	82
Olancha Peak, mtn., Ca., U.S.	D5	82
Olanchito, Hond.	C4	62
Öland, i., Swe.	I7	14
Olanta, Pa., U.S.	E4	115
Olanta, S.C., U.S.	D8	117
Olar, S.C., U.S.	E5	117
Olascoaga, Arg.	B4	54
Olathe, Co., U.S.	C3	83
Olathe, Ks., U.S.	D9	93
Olavarría, Arg.	B4	54
Olazagutia, Spain	A4	22
Olberg, Az., U.S.	D4	80
Olbernhau, E. Ger.	C8	19
Olbia, Italy	D2	23
Olcott, N.Y., U.S.	B2	109
Olcott, N.Y., U.S.	C3	125
Old Bahama Channel, strt., N.A.	C4	64
Old Bennington, Vt., U.S.	F2	122
Old Bethpage, N.Y., U.S.	*n15	109
Old Bight, Bah.	B6	64
Old Bridge, N.J., U.S.	C4	107
Old Castle, hist. reg., Spain	B4	22
Oldcastle, Ire.	D4	11
Old Crow, Yukon	C5	66
Oldeani, Tan.	B6	48
Olden, Tx., U.S.	C3	120
Oldenburg, W. Ger.	B4	15
Oldenburg, In., U.S.	F7	91
Oldenburg [in Holstein], W. Ger.	A5	15
Oldenzaal, Neth.	B6	17
Old Faithful Geyser, Wy., U.S.	B2	127
Old Forge, N.Y., U.S.	B6	109
Old Forge, Pa., U.S.	D10	115
Old Fort, N.C., U.S.	f10	110
Old Fort, Oh., U.S.	A2	112
Old Fort Bay, Que.	C3	72
Oldham, Eng., U.K.	D5	10
Oldham, S.D., U.S.	C8	118
Oldham, co., Ky., U.S.	B4	94
Oldham, co., Tx., U.S.	B1	120
Oldham Village, Ma., U.S.	*B6	98
Old Harbor, Ak., U.S.	D9	79
Old Harbour Bay, Jam.	F14	65
Old Head of Kinsale, c., Ire.	E2	10
Old Hickory Lake, res., Tn., U.S.	A5	119
Old Lyme, Ct., U.S.	D6	84
Oldman, stm., Alta.	E4	68
Old Man Mountain, mtn., Newf.	D3	72
Old Man of the Mountain, N.H., U.S.	B3	106
Oldmans Creek, stm., N.J., U.S.	D2	107
Oldmeldrum, Scot., U.K.	C6	13
Old Mkushi, Zam.	D4	48
Old Monroe, Mo., U.S.	C7	102
Old Mystic, Ct., U.S.	D8	84
Old Northwood, N.H., U.S.	D4	106
Old Orchard Beach, Me., U.S.	E2	96
Old Perlican, Newf.	D5	72
Old Point Comfort, c., Va., U.S.	h15	123
Old Rhodes Key, i., Fl., U.S.	G6	86
Old Ripley, Il., U.S.	E4	90
Old River Lake, l., Ar., U.S.	k10	81
Olds, Alta.	D3	68
Olds, Ia., U.S.	C6	92
Old Saybrook, Ct., U.S.	D6	84
Oldsmar, Fl., U.S.	o10	86
Old Speck Mountain, mtn., Me., U.S.	D2	96
Old Tampa Bay, b., Fl., U.S.	p10	86
Old Tappan, N.J., U.S.	g9	107
Old Tate, Bots.	B4	49
Old Topsail Inlet, b., N.C., U.S.	C5	110
Old Town, Fl., U.S.	C3	86
Old Town, Id., U.S.	A1	89
Old Town, Me., U.S.	C4	96
Oldtown, Md., U.S.	k13	97
Old Village, N.Y., U.S.	*E7	109
Old Washington, Oh., U.S.	B4	112
Oldwick, N.J., U.S.	B3	107
Old Wives, Sask.	G2	75
Old Wives Lake, l., Sask.	G2	75
Olean, Mo., U.S.	C5	102
Olean, N.Y., U.S.	C2	109
O'Leary, P.E.I.	C5	71
Olecko, Pol.	A7	26
Oleiros, Spain	A1	22
Olekma, stm., Sov. Un.	D15	29
Olekminsk, Sov. Un.	C15	29
Olenek, stm., Sov. Un.	C14	29
Olentangy, stm., Oh., U.S.	B3	112
Oléron, Île d', i., Fr.	C4	20
Oleśnica (Oels), Pol.	C4	26
Olesno, Pol.	C5	26
Oleta, Ok., U.S.	C6	113
Oley, Pa., U.S.	F10	115
Olga, Sov. Un.	C12	31
Olga, Mount, mtn., Vt., U.S.	F3	122
Ólgiy, Mong.	B2	31
Ølgod, Den.	D3	15
Olgopol, Sov. Un.	G7	27
Olhão, Port.	I9	33
Olifants, stm., Afr.	B5	49
Ólimbos, mtn., Cyp.	B3	40
Olímpia, Braz.	C3	56
Olin, Ia., U.S.	B6	92
Olinda, Braz.	C4	57
Oliononó, Cape, c., W. Sam.	F12	52
Olite, Spain	A5	22
Oliva, Spain	C5	22
Oliva de la Frontera, Spain	C2	22
Olivais, Port.	f9	22
Olive, Mt., U.S.	E11	103
Olive, Ok., U.S.	A5	113
Olive Branch, Il., U.S.	F4	90
Olive Branch, Ms., U.S.	A4	101
Olive Hill, Ky., U.S.	B6	94
Olivehill, Tn., U.S.	B3	119
Olivehurst, Ca., U.S.	C3	82
Oliveira, Braz.	C4	56
Olivenza, Spain	C2	22
Oliver, B.C.	E8	69
Oliver, Al., U.S.	A2	78
Oliver, Il., U.S.	D5	87
Oliver, Pa., U.S.	G2	115
Oliver, Wi., U.S.	B1	126
Oliver, co., N.D., U.S.	B4	111
Oliver Dam, U.S.	C5	78
Oliver Springs, Tn., U.S.	C9	119
Olivet, Il., U.S.	D6	90
Olivet, Ks., U.S.	D8	93
Olivet, Md., U.S.	D5	97
Olivet, Mi., U.S.	F6	99
Olivet, S.D., U.S.	D8	118
Olivette, Mo., U.S.	*f13	102
Olivia, Mn., U.S.	F4	100
Olivia, N.C., U.S.	B3	110
Olivone, Switz.	C4	20
Öljaren, l., Swe.	t34	14
Olkusz, Pol.	g11	26
Olla, La., U.S.	C3	95
Ollagüe, Chile	C16	58
Ollei, Palau	R17	52
Olmito, Tx., U.S.	F4	120
Olmitz, Ks., U.S.	D5	93
Olmos, Peru	C2	58
Olmos Park, Tx., U.S.	k7	120
Olmstead, Ky., U.S.	D2	94
Olmsted, Ut., U.S.	*C4	121
Olmsted, Il., U.S.	F4	90
Olmsted, co., Mn., U.S.	G6	100
Olmsted Falls, Oh., U.S.	h9	112
Olmstedville, N.Y., U.S.	B7	109
Olney, Il., U.S.	E5	90
Olney, Md., U.S.	B3	97
Olney, Mo., U.S.	B6	102
Olney, Mt., U.S.	B2	103
Olney, Tx., U.S.	C3	120
Olney Springs, Co., U.S.	C7	83
Olofström, Swe.	B8	15
Olomouc, Czech.	D4	26
Olongapo, Phil.	o13	34
Oloron, Gave d', stm., Fr.	F3	16
Oloron-Sainte-Marie, Fr.	F3	16
Olot, Spain	A7	22
Olowalu, Hi., U.S.	C5	88
Olpe, W. Ger.	B2	19
Olpe, Ks., U.S.	D7	93
Olsburg, Ks., U.S.	C7	93
Olše, stm., Eur.	h9	26
Olshany, Sov. Un.	F10	27
Olst, Neth.	B6	17
Olsztyn (Allenstein), Pol.	B6	26
Olt, stm., Rom.	C7	24
Olten, Switz.	E3	18
Oltenia, hist. reg., Rom.	C6	24
Oltenița, Rom.	C8	24
Oltet, stm., Rom.	C6	24
Oltu, Tur.	B13	40
Olupona, Nig.	*E5	45
Olustee, Fl., U.S.	B4	86
Olustee, Ok., U.S.	C2	113
Olvenstedt, E. Ger.	A6	19
Olvera, Spain	D3	22
Olvey, Ar., U.S.	A3	81
Olympia, Ky., U.S.	B6	94
Olympia, Wa., U.S.	B3	124
Olympia, hist., Grc.	B6	40
Olympia Heights, Fl., U.S.	*s13	86
Olympic Mountains, mts., Wa., U.S.	B2	124
Olympic National Park, Wa., U.S.	B2	124
Olympus, Mount, mtn., Grc.	B4	40
Olympus, Mount, mtn., Ky., U.S.	B6	94
Olympus, Mount, mtn., Wa., U.S.	B2	124
Olyphant, Ar., U.S.	B4	81
Olyphant, Pa., U.S.	D10	115
Olyutorski, Cape, c., Sov. Un.	D20	29
Oma, Ar., U.S.	A3	81
Oma, stm., Sov. Un.	g7	81
Omae, Cape, c., Japan	o17	33
Omagh, N. Ire., U.K.	C3	10
Omaguas, Peru	B3	58
Omaha, Ar., U.S.	A2	81
Omaha, Ga., U.S.	D1	87
Omaha, Il., U.S.	F5	90
Omaha, Ne., U.S.	C10	104
Omaha Indian Reservation, Ne., U.S.	B9	104
Omak, Wa., U.S.	A6	124
Omak Lake, l., Wa., U.S.	A6	124
Oman, ctry., Asia	C5	38
Oman, Gulf of, b., Asia	C6	38
Omar, W.V., U.S.	D3	125
Omaruru, Nmb.	B2	49
Omas, Peru	D2	58
Omboué, Gabon	F1	46
Omdurman (Umm Durmān), Sud.	B3	47
Omega, Ga., U.S.	E3	87
Omega, N.M., U.S.	C1	108
Omega, Oh., U.S.	C3	112
Omegna, Italy	D3	23
Omemee, N.D., U.S.	A5	111
Omemee, Ont.	C6	73
Omer, Mi., U.S.	D7	99
Omerville, Que.	D5	74
Ometepe, Isla de, i., Nic.	C5	62
Ometepec, Mex.	D5	63
Om Hajer, Eth.	C4	47
Omineca, stm., B.C.	B5	69
Omineca Mountains, mts., B.C.	A4	69
Ōmiya, Japan	o15	33
Ōmiya, Japan	I9	33
Ommaney, Cape, c., Ak., U.S.	D12	79
Ommen, Neth.	B6	17
Omo, Den.	C5	15
Omo, stm., Eth.	D4	47
Omolon, stm., Sov. Un.	C18	29
Ompompanoosuc, stm., Vt., U.S.	D4	122
Ompompanoosuc, West Branch, stm., Vt., U.S.	D4	122
Omro, Wi., U.S.	D5	126
Omsk, Sov. Un.	D10	29
Ōmuta, Japan	J5	33
Omutninsk, Sov. Un.	D19	8
Onaga, Ks., U.S.	C7	93
Onaka, S.D., U.S.	B6	118
Onalaska, Wa., U.S.	C3	124
Onalaska, Wi., U.S.	E2	126
Onamia, Mn., U.S.	D5	100
Onancock, Va., U.S.	C7	123
Onanole, Man.	D2	70
Onao, l., Micron.	Q18	52
Onarga, Il., U.S.	C6	90
Onawa, Ia., U.S.	B1	92
Onawa, Me., U.S.	C3	96
Onawa, Lake, l., Me., U.S.	C3	96
Onaway, Id., U.S.	*C2	89
Onaway, Mi., U.S.	C6	99
Onchiota, N.Y., U.S.	f10	109
Oncativo, Arg.	C3	54
Onda, Spain	C5	22
Ondangua, Nmb.	A2	49
Ondas, stm., Czech.	D6	26
Ondjiva (Ngiva), Ang.	E2	48
Ondo, Nig.	E5	45
Öndörhaan, Mong.	B7	31
Oneco, Ct., U.S.	C8	84
Oneco, Fl., U.S.	E4	86
Onega, Sov. Un.	C6	29
Onega, stm., Sov. Un.	C16	8
Onega, Lake, l., Sov. Un.	C6	29
One Hundred Fifty Mile House, B.C.	C7	69
One Hundred Mile House, B.C.	D7	69
Oneida, Ar., U.S.	C5	81
Oneida, Il., U.S.	B3	90
Oneida, Ia., U.S.	B6	92
Oneida, Ks., U.S.	C8	93
Oneida, Ky., U.S.	C6	94
Oneida, N.Y., U.S.	B5	109
Oneida, Oh., U.S.	C1	112
Oneida, Tn., U.S.	C9	119
Oneida, Vt., U.S.	B4	123
Oneida, co., Id., U.S.	G6	89
Oneida, co., N.Y., U.S.	B5	109
Oneida, co., Wi., U.S.	C4	126
Oneida Lake, l., N.Y., U.S.	B5	109
O'Neill, Ne., U.S.	B7	104
Onekama, Mi., U.S.	D4	99
Onemak Island, i., Marsh Is.	S17	52
Oneonta, Al., U.S.	B3	78
Oneonta, N.Y., U.S.	C5	109
Ongea Levu, i., Fiji	I16	52
Ongiin Hiid, Mong.	B5	31
Ongiyn, stm., Mong.	B5	31
Ongjin, N. Kor.	H2	33
Onida, S.D., U.S.	C5	118
Onilahy, stm., Madag.	h8	49
Oniotto Island, i., Marsh Is.	S17	52
Onitsha, Nig.	E6	45
Only, Tn., U.S.	B4	119
Onley, Va., U.S.	C7	123
Onna, Fl., U.S.	O5	52
Ōno, Japan	n15	33
Ono, i., Fiji	I15	52
Ono Channel, strt., Fiji	I15	52
Onomichi, Japan	I6	33
Onondaga, Mi., U.S.	F6	99
Onondaga, co., N.Y., U.S.	C4	109
Onondaga Indian Reservation, N.Y., U.S.	C4	109
Onota Lake, l., Ma., U.S.	B1	98
Onoway, Alta.	C3	68
Onset, Ma., U.S.	C6	98
Onslow, Austl.	D2	50
Onslow, co., N.C., U.S.	C5	110
Onslow Bay, b., N.C., U.S.	C5	110
Onsong, N. Kor.	E4	33
Onsted, Mi., U.S.	F6	99
Ontake, Mount, mtn., Japan	n16	33
Ontario, In., U.S.	A7	91
Ontario, N.Y., U.S.	B3	109
Ontario, Oh., U.S.	B3	112
Ontario, Or., U.S.	C10	114
Ontario, co., N.Y., U.S.	C3	109
Ontario, prov., Can.	C6	73
Ontario, Lake, l., N.A.	B12	76
Onteniente, Spain	C5	22
Ontonagon, Mi., U.S.	m12	99
Ontonagon, co., Mi., U.S.	m12	99
Ontonagon Indian Reservation, Mi., U.S.	B1	99
Onward, In., U.S.	C5	91
Oodnadatta, Austl.	E6	50
Ood Weyne, Som.	D6	47
Ooka, Hi., U.S.	C6	88
Oolitic, In., U.S.	G4	91
Oologah, Ok., U.S.	A6	113
Oologah Lake, res., Ok., U.S.	A6	113
Ooltewah, Tn., U.S.	D8	119
Ooltgensplaat, Neth.	C4	17
Oostburg, Neth.	C3	17
Oostburg, Wi., U.S.	E6	126
Oostende (Ostende), Bel.	B5	16
Oosterend, Neth.	A5	17
Oosterend, Neth.	A4	17
Oosterhout, Neth.	C4	17
Oosterschelde, b., Neth.	C3	17
Oosterschelde, Bel.	B5	16
Oostmahorn, Neth.	A6	17
Oostpunt, c., Neth. Ant.	H19	65
Oost-Vlieland, Neth.	A5	17
Oostvoorne, Neth.	C4	17
Ootsa Lake, B.C.	C4	69
Ootsa Lake, l., B.C.	C4	69
Opal, Alta.	C4	68
Opal, S.D., U.S.	C3	118
Opal, Wy., U.S.	E2	127
Opala, Zaire	B4	48
Opa-Locka, Fl., U.S.	s13	86
Opalenica, Austl.	A4	51
Opava, Czech.	D4	26
Opdyke, Il., U.S.	E5	90
Opelika, Al., U.S.	C4	78
Opelousas, La., U.S.	D3	95
Opeongo, stm., Ont.	B6	73
Opeongo Lake, l., Ont.	B6	73
Opequon Creek, stm., W.V., U.S.	B6	125
Opheim, Mt., U.S.	B10	103
Ophir, Mt., U.S.	C7	114
Ophir, Ut., U.S.	C3	121
Ophir, Mount, mtn., Indon.	E1	34
Opihikao, Hi., U.S.	D7	88
Opiscóteo, Lac, l., Que.	F19	66
Opobo, Nig.	F6	45
Opochka, Sov. Un.	C7	27
Opoczno, Pol.	C6	26
Opole, Pol.	C4	26
Opole Lubelskie, Pol.	C7	26
Oporto see Porto, Port.	B1	22
Opotiki, N.Z.	M16	51
Opp, Al., U.S.	D3	78
Oppdal, Nor.	F3	14
Oppelo, Ar., U.S.	B3	81
Opportunity, Wa., U.S.	B8	124
Optic Lake, Man.	B1	70
Optima, Ok., U.S.	e9	113
Optima Reservoir, res., Ok., U.S.	e9	113
Opyan, Puntan, c., N. Mar. Is.	D7	52
Oquawka, Il., U.S.	C3	90
Oquossoc, Me., U.S.	D2	96
Ora, Italy	C7	20
Ora, In., U.S.	B4	91
Ora, Ms., U.S.	D4	101
Ora, S.C., U.S.	B4	117
Oracle, Az., U.S.	E5	80
Oradea, Rom.	B5	24
Oradell, N.J., U.S.	h8	107
Oradell Reservoir, res., N.J., U.S.	h9	107
Orai, India	E7	37
Oraibi, Az., U.S.	B5	80
Oraibi Wash, val., Az., U.S.	A5	80
Oral, S.D., U.S.	D2	118
Oran (Wahran), Alg.	B4	44
Oran, Mo., U.S.	D8	102
Orange, Austl.	F8	50
Orange, Fr.	E6	16
Orange, Ca., U.S.	n13	82
Orange, Ct., U.S.	D3	84
Orange, In., U.S.	E7	91
Orange, Ma., U.S.	A3	98
Orange, N.H., U.S.	C3	106
Orange, N.J., U.S.	B4	107
Orange, Tx., U.S.	D6	120
Orange, Vt., U.S.	C4	122
Orange, Va., U.S.	B4	123
Orange, co., Ca., U.S.	F5	82
Orange, co., Fl., U.S.	D5	86
Orange, co., In., U.S.	G4	91
Orange, co., N.Y., U.S.	D6	109
Orange, co., N.C., U.S.	A3	110
Orange, co., Tx., U.S.	D6	120
Orange, co., Vt., U.S.	C3	122
Orange, co., Va., U.S.	B4	123
Orange, Cabo, c., Braz.	B4	59
Orange Beach, Al., U.S.	E2	78
Orangeburg, S.C., U.S.	E6	117
Orangeburg, co., S.C., U.S.	E6	117
Orange City, Fl., U.S.	D5	86
Orange City, Ia., U.S.	B1	92
Orangedale, N.S.	D8	71
Orange Free State, prov., S. Afr.	C4	49
Orange Grove, Ms., U.S.	E5	101
Orange Grove, Tx., U.S.	F4	120
Orange Lake, Fl., U.S.	C4	86
Orange Lake, l., Fl., U.S.	C4	86
Orange Park, Fl., U.S.	B5	86
Orangevale, Ca., U.S.	*C3	82
Orangeville, Il., U.S.	A4	90
Orangeville, Ut., U.S.	D4	121
Orange Walk, Belize	D7	63
Orani, Phil.	o13	34
Oranienbaum, E. Ger.	B7	19
Oranienburg, E. Ger.	B6	18
Oranje Gebergte, mts., Sur.	C2	49
Oranjemund, Nmb.	C2	49
Oranjestad, Aruba	G17	65
Oranmore, Ire.	D3	11
Or 'Aqiva, Isr.	B6	41
Orăștie, Rom.	C6	24
Oravița, Rom.	C5	24
Orba, stm., Italy	E4	20
Orbe, Switz.	C2	21
Orbetello, Italy	C3	23
Orbey, Fr.	A3	20
Orbigo, stm., Spain	A3	22
Orbisonia, Pa., U.S.	F6	115
Orbost, Austl.	H7	51
Orby, Swe.	A6	15
Orcas Island, i., Wa., U.S.	A3	124
Orchard, Co., U.S.	A6	83
Orchard, Ne., U.S.	B7	104
Orchard City, Co., U.S.	C3	83
Orchard Farm, Mo., U.S.	f13	102
Orchard Homes, Mt., U.S.	D2	103
Orchard Mesa, Co., U.S.	*B2	83
Orchard Park, N.Y., U.S.	C2	109
Orchards, Wa., U.S.	D3	124
Orchard Valley, Wy., U.S.	E8	127
Orchies, Fr.	A5	16
Orchila, Isla, i., Ven.	A4	60
Orcotuna, Peru	D2	58
Orcutt, Ca., U.S.	E3	82
Orcutts, Ct., U.S.	C5	84
Ord, Ne., U.S.	C7	104
Ord, Mount, mtn., Austl.	C4	50
Ordale, Sask.	D2	75
Ordenes, Spain	A1	22
Orderville, Ut., U.S.	F3	121
Ording, W. Ger.	D2	15
Ordos Desert see Mu Us Shamo, des., China	D6	31
Ordot, Guam	L10	52
Ordu, Tur.	B11	40
Orduña, Spain	A4	22
Ordzhonikidze (Dzaudzhikau), Sov. Un.	C7	83
Oreana, Il., U.S.	D5	90
Oreba Island, i., Marsh Is.	S17	52
Oregon, Il., U.S.	A4	90
Oregon, Mo., U.S.	A2	102
Oregon, Oh., U.S.	A2	112
Oregon, Wi., U.S.	F4	126
Oregon, co., Mo., U.S.	E6	102
Oregon, state, U.S.	C6	114
Oregon Caves National Monument, Or., U.S.	E2	114
Oregon City, Or., U.S.	B4	114
Oregon Inlet, b., N.C., U.S.	B7	110
Øregrund, Swe.	G8	14
Orehoved, Den.	D5	15
Orekhov, Sov. Un.	H10	27
Orekhovo, Bul.	D6	24
Orekhovo-Zuyevo, Sov. Un.	D12	27
Orel, Sov. Un.	D6	29
Orem, Ut., U.S.	C4	121
Ore Mountains, mts., Eur.	C6	18
Orenburg, Sov. Un.	D8	29
Orense, Spain	A2	22
Orestes, In., U.S.	D6	91
Orestiás, Grc.	B6	40
Øresund (The Sound), strt., Eur.	J5	14
Oreti, stm., N.Z.	P12	51
Oretta, La., U.S.	D2	95
Orford, N.H., U.S.	C2	106
Orford, Mont, mtn., Que.	D5	74
Orford Ness, c., Eng., U.K.	B9	11
Orfordville, N.H., U.S.	C2	106
Orfordville, Wi., U.S.	F4	126
Organ, N.M., U.S.	E3	108
Organ Cave, W.V., U.S.	D4	125
Organ Mountains, mts., N.M., U.S.	E3	108
Organ Pipe Cactus National Monument, Az., U.S.	E3	80
Orgas, W.V., U.S.	m12	125
Orgaz, Spain	C4	22
Orgelet, Fr.	C1	20
Orgeyev, Sov. Un.	H7	27
Orgún, Afg.	B4	36
Orhon, stm., Mong.	B5	31
Orick, Ca., U.S.	B1	82
Orient, Il., U.S.	F5	90
Orient, Ia., U.S.	C3	92
Orient, Me., U.S.	C5	96
Orient, N.Y., U.S.	m16	109
Orient, Oh., U.S.	C2	112
Orient, S.D., U.S.	C6	118
Orient, Wa., U.S.	A7	124
Oriental, N.C., U.S.	B6	110
Oriental, Cordillera, mts., Col.	C3	60
Orihuela, Spain	C5	22
Orillia, Ont.	C5	73
Orinda, Ca., U.S.	*h8	82
Orinoco, stm., S.A.	B5	60
Oriole, Md., U.S.	D6	97
Orion, Alta.	E5	68
Orion, Phil.	o13	34
Orion, Il., U.S.	B3	90
Oriska, N.D., U.S.	C8	111
Oriskany, N.Y., U.S.	B5	109
Oriskany, stm., N.Y., U.S.	C3	123
Oriskany Falls, N.Y., U.S.	C5	109
Orissa, state, India	E7	36
Oristano, Italy	E2	23
Oristano, Gulf of, b., Italy	E2	23
Orivesi, l., Fin.	F13	14
Oriximiná, Braz.	C3	59
Orizaba, Mex.	D5	63
Orizaba, Pico de (Citlaltépetl), vol., Mex.	n15	63
Orizona, Braz.	B3	56
Ørkanger, Nor.	F3	14
Orkelljunga, Swe.	B7	15
Orkla, stm., Nor.	F4	14
Orkney, Sask.	H2	75
Orkney, prov., Scot., U.K.	A5	13
Orkney Islands, is., Scot., U.K.	A5	13
Orla, Tx., U.S.	o13	120
Orland, Ca., U.S.	C2	82
Orland, In., U.S.	A7	91
Orland, Me., U.S.	D4	96
Orlando, Fl., U.S.	D5	86
Orland Park, Il., U.S.	k9	90
Orléans, Braz.	D3	56
Orléans, Fr.	D8	16
Orleans, Ca., U.S.	B2	82
Orleans, In., U.S.	G5	91
Orleans, Ia., U.S.	A2	92
Orleans, Ma., U.S.	C7	98
Orleans, Ne., U.S.	D6	104
Orleans, Vt., U.S.	B4	122
Orleans, co., La., U.S.	E6	95
Orleans, co., N.Y., U.S.	B2	109
Orleans, co., Vt., U.S.	B4	122
Orléans, Île d', i., Que.	h12	73
Orlík Reservoir, res., Czech.	D9	19
Orlinda, Tn., U.S.	A5	119
Orlová, Czech.	*D5	26
Orlovista, Fl., U.S.	*D5	86
Orly, Fr.	h10	16
Orlyak, Bul.	D8	24
Orman Dam, S.D., U.S.	C2	118
Ormāra, Pak.	C3	36
Ormāra, Rās, c., Pak.	I12	39
Ormiston, Sask.	H3	75
Ormond Beach, Fl., U.S.	C5	86
Ormond By The Sea, Fl., U.S.	*C5	86
Ormsby, Ont.	C7	73
Ormsby, Mn., U.S.	G4	100
Ormskirk, Eng., U.K.	D5	12
Ormstown, Que.	D3	74
Ornans, Fr.	B2	20
Orne, stm., Fr.	C6	16
Orneta, Pol.	A6	26
Örnö, i., Swe.	t36	14
Örnsköldsvik, Swe.	F8	14
Orø, i., Den.	C5	15
Orocué, Col.	C3	60
Orodara, Burkina	F4	45
Orofino, Id., U.S.	C2	89
Oro Grande, Ca., U.S.	E5	82
Orograde, N.M., U.S.	B4	54
Orohena, mtn., Fr. Poly.	*H13	6
Oromocto, N.B.	D3	71
Oromocto Lake, l., N.B.	D2	71
Oron, Nig.	F6	45
Oron-la-Ville, Switz.	C2	21
Orono, Ont.	D6	73
Orono, Me., U.S.	D4	96
Oronoco, Mn., U.S.	*n11	100
Oronoco, Mn., U.S.	F6	100
Oronogo, Mo., U.S.	D3	102
Oronsay, i., Scot., U.K.	D2	13
Oropuche, stm., Trin.	O23	65
Oroquieta, Phil.	D6	34
Orós, Braz.	D2	57
Orosei, Gulf of, b., Italy	D2	23
Oroshaza, Hung.	B4	24
Orote Peninsula, pen., Guam	L9	52
Orovada, Nv., U.S.	C4	105
Oroville, Ca., U.S.	C3	82
Oroville, Wa., U.S.	A6	124
Oroville, Lake, res., Ca., U.S.	C3	82
Orpington (part of London), Eng., U.K.	m13	10
Orr, Mn., U.S.	B6	100
Orrick, Mo., U.S.	B3	102
Orrin, N.D., U.S.	A5	111

Orrington, Me., U.S. — D4 96
Orr Lake, l., Man. — A3 70
Orrs Island, Me., U.S. — E3 96
Orrstown, Pa., U.S. — F6 115
Orrum, N.C., U.S. — C4 110
Orrville, Ont. — B5 73
Orrville, Al., U.S. — C2 78
Orrville, Oh., U.S. — B4 112
Orsa, Swe. — G6 14
Orsay, Fr. — F2 17
Orsha, Sov. Un. — D8 27
Orsières, Switz. — C3 20
Orsk, Sov. Un. — D8 22
Orson, Pa., U.S. — C11 115
Orşova, Rom. — C6 24
Ørsted, Den. — B4 15
Örsundsbro, Swe. — t35 14
Orta, Lake, l., Italy — D4 20
Ortaca, Tur. — D7 25
Orta [San Giulio], Italy — E5 21
Ortegal, Cape, c., Spain — A2 22
Orthez, Fr. — F3 16
Ortigueira, Spain — A2 22
Orting, Wa., U.S. — B3 124
Ortisei, Italy — C7 20
Ortiz, Mex. — B2 63
Ortiz, Co., U.S. — D4 83
Ortiz Mountain, mtn., N.M., U.S. — k8 108
Ortley, S.D., U.S. — B8 118
Ortoire, stm., Trin. — O23 65
Ortona, Italy — C5 23
Ortonville, Mi., U.S. — F7 99
Ortonville, Mn., U.S. — E2 100
Orūmīyeh (Urmia), Iran — B4 38
Oruro, Bol. — C2 55
Oruro, dept., Bol. — C2 55
Orvieto, Italy — C4 23
Orviston, Pa., U.S. — D6 115
Orwell, N.Y., U.S. — B4 109
Orwell, Oh., U.S. — A5 112
Orwell, Vt., U.S. — D2 122
Orwigsburg, Pa., U.S. — E9 115
Or Yehuda, Isr. — g10 41
Orysa, Tn., U.S. — B2 119
Orzesze, Pol. — g9 26
Osa, Peninsula de, pen., C.R. — F6 62
Osage, Ia., U.S. — A5 92
Osage, Mn., U.S. — D3 100
Osage, Ok., U.S. — A5 113
Osage, Wy., U.S. — C8 127
Osage, co., Ks., U.S. — D8 93
Osage, co., Mo., U.S. — C6 102
Osage, co., Ok., U.S. — A5 113
Osage, stm., Mo., U.S. — C3 102
Osage Beach, Mo., U.S. — C5 102
Osage City, Ks., U.S. — D8 93
Osage Creek, stm., Ar., U.S. — A2 81
Ōsaka, Japan — E12 31
Osaka, Japan — n16 33
Ōsaka Bay, b., Japan — o14 33
Osaka Mountain, hill, Japan — P17 52
Osakis, Mn., U.S. — E3 100
Osakis, Lake, l., Mn., U.S. — E3 100
Osawatomie, Ks., U.S. — D9 93
Osborn, Mo., U.S. — B3 102
Osborne, Ks., U.S. — C5 93
Osborne, co., Ks., U.S. — C5 93
Osbornsville, N.J., U.S. — C4 107
Osburn, Id., U.S. — B3 89
Osby, Swe. — B8 15
Oscar, La., U.S. — D4 95
Oscar, Ok., U.S. — D4 113
Osceola, Ar., U.S. — B6 81
Osceola, In., U.S. — A5 91
Osceola, Ia., U.S. — C4 92
Osceola, Mo., U.S. — C4 102
Osceola, Ne., U.S. — C8 104
Osceola, Pa., U.S. — C7 115
Osceola, S.D., U.S. — C8 118
Osceola, Tx., U.S. — C4 120
Osceola, Wi., U.S. — C1 126
Osceola, co., Fl., U.S. — E5 86
Osceola, co., Ia., U.S. — A2 92
Osceola, co., Mi., U.S. — E5 99
Osceola Mills, Pa., U.S. — E5 115
Oschatz, E. Ger. — C6 18
Oschersleben, E. Ger. — B5 18
Oscoda, Mi., U.S. — D7 99
Oscoda, co., Mi., U.S. — D6 99
Oscura Mountains, mts., N.M., U.S. — D3 108
Osek, Czech. — C3 19
Oselki, Sov. Un. — r31 14
Osgood, In., U.S. — F7 91
Osgood, Mo., U.S. — A4 102
Osgood, Oh., U.S. — B1 112
Osgoode, Ont. — B9 73
Osh, Sov. Un. — E10 29
Oshamambe, Japan — E10 31
Oshawa, Ont. — D6 73
Oshkosh, Ne., U.S. — C3 104
Oshkosh, Wi., U.S. — D5 126
Oshnovīyeh, Iran — C2 39
Oshogbo, Nig. — E5 45
Oshoto, Wy., U.S. — B8 127
Oshtorān Kūh, mtn., Iran — E4 39
Oshwe, Zaire — B2 48
Osijek, Yugo. — C4 24
Osilinka, stm., B.C. — A5 69
Osinniki, Sov. Un. — E26 8
Osipovichi, Sov. Un. — E7 27
Oskaloosa, Ia., U.S. — C5 92
Oskaloosa, Ks., U.S. — C8 93
Oskaloosa, Mo., U.S. — D3 102
Oskarshamn, Swe. — I7 14
Oskol, stm., Sov. Un. — G11 27
Oskü, Iran — C2 39
Osler, Sask. — E2 75
Oslo, Nor. — H4 14
Oslo, Mn., U.S. — B1 100
Oslofjorden, Nor. — H4 14
Osma, Spain — C17 66
Osmānābād, India — H6 37
Osmancık, Tur. — B10 40
Osmaneli, Tur. — B7 25
Osmond, Ne., U.S. — B8 104
Osnabrock, N.D., U.S. — A7 111
Osnabrück, W. Ger. — B4 18
Osório, Braz. — D2 56
Osorno, Chile — C2 54
Osoyoos, B.C. — E8 69
Osoyoos Lake, l., Wa., U.S. — A6 124
Ospika, stm., B.C. — A6 69
Osprey, Fl., U.S. — E4 86
Oss, Neth. — B6 16
Ossa, Mount, mtn., Austl. — o15 50
Ossabaw Island, i., Ga., U.S. — E5 87
Ossabaw Sound, strt., Ga., U.S. — E6 87
Osseo, Mn., U.S. — m12 100

Osseo, Wi., U.S. — D2 126
Ossian, In., U.S. — C7 91
Ossian, Ia., U.S. — A6 92
Ossineke, Mi., U.S. — D7 99
Ossining, N.Y., U.S. — D7 109
Ossipee, N.H., U.S. — C4 106
Ossipee, stm., U.S. — C5 106
Ossipee Lake, l., N.H., U.S. — C4 106
Ossipee Mountains, mts., N.H., U.S. — C4 106
Ossokmanuan Lake, l., Newf. — h8 72
Ossora, Sov. Un. — D34 128
Östanå, Swe. — t36 14
Ostashkov, Sov. Un. — C9 27
Osteen, Fl., U.S. — D5 86
Ostende see Oostende, Bel. — B5 16
Osterburg, E. Ger. — F5 15
Osterburg, Pa., U.S. — F4 115
Osterode, W. Ger. — B5 19
Östersund, Swe. — F6 14
Osterville, Ma., U.S. — C7 98
Osterwieck, E. Ger. — B5 19
Ostia Antica, Italy — h8 23
Ostiglia, Italy — D7 20
Ostrach, W. Ger. — B5 20
Ostrander, Mn., U.S. — G6 100
Ostrander, Oh., U.S. — B2 112
Ostrava, Czech. — D5 26
Ostróda, Pol. — B5 26
Ostrog, Sov. Un. — F6 27
Ostrogozhsk, Sov. Un. — F12 27
Ostrołęka, Pol. — B6 26
Ostrov, Czech. — C2 26
Ostrov, Rom. — C8 24
Ostrov, Sov. Un. — C7 27
Ostrowiec 95Świętokrzyski], Pol. — C6 26
Ostrów Lubelski, Pol. — C7 26
Ostrów Mazowiecka, Pol. — B6 26
Ostrów Wielkopolski, Pol. — C4 26
Ostrzeszów, Pol. — C4 26
Ostseebad Graal-Müritz, E. Ger. — D6 15
Ostuni, Italy — D6 23
Ōsuka, Japan — o16 33
Osum, stm., Bul. — D7 24
Ōsumi, stm., Alb. — B3 25
Ōsumi Islands, is., Japan — E11 31
Ōsumi Strait, strt., Japan — K5 33
Osuna, Spain — D3 22
Osvaldo Cruz, Braz. — C2 56
Oswayo, Pa., U.S. — C5 115
Oswegatchie, Ct., U.S. — *D7 84
Oswegatchie, stm., N.Y., U.S. — f9 109
Oswego, Il., U.S. — B5 90
Oswego, Ks., U.S. — E9 93
Oswego, Mt., U.S. — B11 103
Oswego, N.Y., U.S. — B4 109
Oswego, S.C., U.S. — C7 117
Oswego, co., N.Y., U.S. — B4 109
Oswego, stm., N.J., U.S. — D4 107
Oswego, stm., N.Y., U.S. — B4 109
Oswestry, Eng., U.K. — D5 10
Oświęcim (Auschwitz), Pol. — C5 26
Osyka, Ms., U.S. — D3 101
Ōta, Japan — *H9 33
Otago Peninsula, pen., N.Z. — P13 51
Otaki, Japan — n19 33
Otar, Sov. Un. — E9 28
Otaru, Japan — C13 31
Otava, stm., Czech. — D8 19
Otavalo, Ec. — A2 58
Otavi, Nmb. — A2 49
Otchinjau, Ang. — E1 48
Otego, N.Y., U.S. — C5 109
Otero, co., Co., U.S. — D7 83
Otero, co., N.M., U.S. — E3 108
Othello, Wa., U.S. — C6 124
Otho, Ia., U.S. — B3 92
Othonoí, i., Grc. — C2 25
Óthris Mountains, mts., Grc. — C4 25
Oti, stm., Afr. — E5 45
Otis, In., U.S. — A4 91
Otis, Ks., U.S. — D4 93
Otis, Ma., U.S. — B1 98
Otisco, In., U.S. — G6 91
Otisco, Mn., U.S. — G5 100
Otisco Lake, l., N.Y., U.S. — C4 109
Otis Orchards, Wa., U.S. — g14 124
Otis Reservoir, res., Ma., U.S. — B1 98
Otisville, Mi., U.S. — E7 99
Otjiwarongo, Nmb. — B2 49
Otley, Ia., U.S. — C4 92
Oto, Ia., U.S. — B2 92
Otočac, Yugo. — C2 24
Otoe, Ne., U.S. — D9 104
Otoe, co., Ne., U.S. — D9 104
Otra, stm., Nor. — H2 14
Otradnoye, Sov. Un. — s31 14
Otranto, Italy — D7 23
Otranto, Strait of, strt., Eur. — D2 40
Otsego, Mi., U.S. — F5 99
Otsego, co., Mi., U.S. — C6 99
Otsego, co., N.Y., U.S. — C5 109
Otsego Lake, l., Mi., U.S. — D6 99
Otsego Lake, l., N.Y., U.S. — C6 109
Ōtsu, Japan — o14 33
Ōtsuki, Japan — n17 33
Ottauquechee, stm., Vt., U.S. — D4 122
Ottawa, Ont. — B9 73
Ottawa, Il., U.S. — B5 90
Ottawa, Ks., U.S. — D8 93
Ottawa, Oh., U.S. — A1 112
Ottawa, W.Va., U.S. — n12 125
Ottawa, co., Ks., U.S. — C6 93
Ottawa, co., Mi., U.S. — F4 99
Ottawa, co., Oh., U.S. — A2 112
Ottawa, co., Ok., U.S. — A7 113
Ottawa, stm., Can. — G17 66
Ottawa, stm., Oh., U.S. — A1 112
Ottawa-Carleton, co., Ont. — B9 73
Ottawa Hills, Oh., U.S. — e6 112
Ottawa Islands, is., N.W. Ter. — E16 66
Ottawa Lake, Mi., U.S. — G7 99
Otter, Mt., U.S. — E10 103
Otter, stm., Alta. — D4 68
Otter, stm., Eng., U.K. — D4 12
Otterbein, In., U.S. — D3 91
Otterburn, Eng., U.K. — F6 10
Otterburne, Man. — E3 70
Otter Brook, stm., N.H., U.S. — E2 106
Otter Brook Lake, res., N.H., U.S. — E2 106
Otter Creek, Fl., U.S. — C4 86
Otter Creek, Me., U.S. — D4 96
Otter Creek, stm., Ut., U.S. — E4 121
Otter Creek, stm., Vt., U.S. — C2 122
Otter Creek Reservoir, res., Ut., U.S. — E4 121

Otter Islands, is., S.C., U.S. — m11 117
Otter Lake, Mi., U.S. — E7 99
Otter Lake, N.Y., U.S. — B5 109
Otter Lake, l., Sask. — B3 75
Otterndorf, W. Ger. — E2 15
Otter River, Ma., U.S. — A3 98
Ottersberg, W. Ger. — E3 15
Ottersleben, E. Ger. — A6 19
Otter Tail, co., Mn., U.S. — D3 100
Otter Tail, stm., Mn., U.S. — D3 100
Otter Tail Lake, l., Mn., U.S. — D3 100
Otterup, Den. — C4 15
Otterville, Ont. — E4 73
Otterville, Il., U.S. — D3 90
Otterville, Mo., U.S. — C4 102
Otthon, Sask. — F4 75
Ottignies, Bel. — D4 17
Otto, Wy., U.S. — B4 127
Ottokee, Oh., U.S. — A1 112
Ottone, Italy — E5 20
Ottosen, Ia., U.S. — B3 92
Ottoville, Oh., U.S. — B1 112
Ottumwa, Ia., U.S. — C5 92
Ottumwa, S.D., U.S. — C4 118
Otway, N.C., U.S. — C6 110
Otway, Cape, c., Austl. — G7 50
Otway, Seno, b., Chile — h11 54
Otwell, In., U.S. — H3 91
Otwock, Pol. — m14 26
Ōtztal Alps, mts., Eur. — C6 20
Ōtztaler Ach, stm., Aus. — B6 20
Ou, stm., Laos — B5 35
Ouachita, co., Ar., U.S. — D3 81
Ouachita, co., La., U.S. — B3 95
Ouachita, Lake, res., Ar., U.S. — C2 81
Ouachita Mountains, mts., U.S. — D9 76
Ouadane, Maur. — B2 45
Ouaddaï, hist. reg., Chad — C4 46
Ouagadougou, Burkina — D4 45
Ouahigouya, Burkina — D4 45
Ouaka, stm., Cen. Afr. Rep. — C3 46
Oualâta, Maur. — C3 45
Ouallam, Niger — D5 45
Ouallene, Alg. — E5 44
Ouanary, Fr. Gu. — B4 59
Ouanda Djallé, Cen. Afr. Rep. — D4 46
Ouarane, reg., Maur. — B3 45
Ouarzazate, Mor. — C3 44
Oubangui (Ubangi), stm., Afr. — A2 48
Ouddorp, Neth. — D3 17
Oudenaarde, Bel. — A7 17
Oude-Pekela, Neth. — A7 17
Oudtshoorn, S. Afr. — H4 49
Oued Zem, Mor. — *C3 44
Ouellé, I.C. — E4 45
Ouémé, stm., Benin — E5 45
Ouesso, Congo — A3 48
Ouest, Pointe de l', Que. — k8 72
Ouest, Pointe du, c., St. P./M. — E3 72
Ouezzane, Mor. — B3 44
Ouham, stm., Afr. — A2 46
Oughter, Lough, l., Ire. — D2 11
Oughterard, Ire. — D2 11
Ouidah, Benin — E5 45
Oujda, Mor. — E4 44
Oullins, Fr. — E6 16
Oulu, Fin. — E11 14
Oulujärvi, l., Fin. — E12 14
Oum Chalouba, Chad — B4 46
Oum Hadjer, Chad — C3 46
Ounâne, Bîr, well, Mali — B4 45
Ounasjoki, stm., Fin. — D11 14
Ounianga Kébir, Chad — B4 46
Ouray, Co., U.S. — C3 83
Ouray, Ut., U.S. — C6 121
Ouray, co., Co., U.S. — C3 83
Ouray, Mount, mtn., Co., U.S. — C4 83
Ouri, Chad — A3 46
Ouricuri, Braz. — E11 57
Ourinhos, Braz. — C3 56
Ourique, Port. — D1 22
Ouro Fino, Braz. — C3 56
Ouro Prêto, Braz. — C4 56
Ourthe, stm., Bel. — D5 17
Ouse, stm., Eng., U.K. — D6 10
Outagamie, co., Wi., U.S. — D5 126
Outardes Quatre, Réservoir, res., Que. — h13 74
Outer Hebrides, is., Scot., U.K. — B3 10
Outer Island, i., Wi., U.S. — A3 126
Outer Santa Barbara Passage, strt., Ca., U.S. — F4 82
Outing, Mn., U.S. — D5 100
Outjo, Nmb. — B2 49
Outlook, Sask. — F2 75
Outlook, Mt., U.S. — B12 103
Outlook, Wa., U.S. — C5 124
Outpost Mountain, mtn., Ak., U.S. — B9 79
Outreau, Fr. — B4 16
Outremont, Que. — p19 74
Ouville-la-Rivière, Fr. — E8 12
Ouzinkie, Ak., U.S. — D9 79
Ovada, Italy — B2 23
Ovalau, i., Fiji — H15 52
Ovalle, Chile — A2 54
Ovana, Cerro, mtn., Ven. — C4 60
Ovando, Mt., U.S. — C3 103
Ovar, Port. — B1 22
Overath, W. Ger. — D2 19
Overbrook, Ks., U.S. — D8 93
Overbrook, Ok., U.S. — D4 113
Overflowing, stm., Can. — D5 73
Overgaard, Az., U.S. — C5 80
Overijse, Bel. — D4 17
Overijssel, prov., Neth. — C6 16
Overisel, Mi., U.S. — F4 99
Overland, Mo., U.S. — f13 102
Overland Park, Ks., U.S. — m16 93
Overlea, Md., U.S. — B5 97
Overlook, Oh., U.S. — *C1 112
Overly, N.D., U.S. — A5 111
Overstreet, Fl., U.S. — B1 86
Overton, Ne., U.S. — D6 104
Overton, Nv., U.S. — G7 105
Overton, Tx., U.S. — C5 120
Overton, co., Tn., U.S. — C8 119
Övertorneå, Swe. — D10 14
Ovett, Ms., U.S. — D4 101
Ovid, Co., U.S. — A8 83
Ovid, Mi., U.S. — E6 99

Ovid, N.Y., U.S. — C4 109
Oviedo, Spain — A3 22
Ovruch, Sov. Un. — F7 27
Owando, Congo — B2 48
Owaneco, Il., U.S. — D4 90
Owanka, S.D., U.S. — C3 118
Owasco Lake, l., N.Y., U.S. — C4 109
Owasso, Ok., U.S. — A6 113
Owatonna, Mn., U.S. — F5 100
Owbeh, Afg. — D11 39
Owego, N.Y., U.S. — C4 109
Owen, Wi., U.S. — D3 126
Owen, co., In., U.S. — F4 91
Owen, co., Ky., U.S. — B5 94
Owen, Lake, l., Wi., U.S. — B2 126
Owen, Mount, mtn., N.Z. — N14 51
Owen, Mount, mtn., Co., U.S. — C3 83
Owendale, Mi., U.S. — E7 99
Owens, stm., Ca., U.S. — D4 82
Owensboro, Ky., U.S. — C2 94
Owensburg, In., U.S. — G4 91
Owens Creek, stm., Md., U.S. — A3 97
Owens Cross Roads, Al., U.S. — A3 78
Owens Lake, l., Ca., U.S. — D5 82
Owen Sound, Ont. — C4 73
Owen Sound, b., Ont. — C4 73
Owen Stanley Range, mts., Pap. N. Gui. — k12 50a
Owensville, In., U.S. — H2 91
Owensville, Mo., U.S. — C6 102
Owensville, Oh., U.S. — C1 112
Owenton, Ky., U.S. — B5 94
Owerri, Nig. — E6 45
Owey Island, i., Ire. — B3 11
Owikeno Lake, l., B.C. — D4 69
Owings, Md., U.S. — C4 97
Owings Mills, Md., U.S. — B4 97
Owingsville, Ky., U.S. — B6 94
Owl Creek, stm., Wy., U.S. — C4 127
Owl Creek Mountains, mts., Wy., U.S. — C4 127
Owls Head, Me., U.S. — D3 96
Owo, Nig. — E6 45
Owosso, Mi., U.S. — E6 99
Owsley, co., Ky., U.S. — C6 94
Owyhee, Nv., U.S. — B5 105
Owyhee, co., Id., U.S. — G2 89
Owyhee, stm., U.S. — E9 114
Owyhee, Lake, res., Or., U.S. — D9 114
Owyhee, North Fork, stm., U.S. — E9 114
Owyhee, South Fork, stm., U.S. — G2 89
Owyhee Dam, Or., U.S. — D9 114
Owyhee Mountains, mts., U.S. — G2 89
Öxabäck, Swe. — A6 15
Oxbow, Sask. — H4 75
Oxbow, Me., U.S. — B4 96
Oxbow, Or., U.S. — B10 114
Oxbow Dam, U.S. — E2 89
Oxelösund, Swe. — u35 14
Oxford, N.S. — D6 71
Oxford, Eng., U.K. — E6 10
Oxford, Al., U.S. — B4 78
Oxford, Ct., U.S. — D3 84
Oxford, Fl., U.S. — D4 86
Oxford, Ga., U.S. — C3 87
Oxford, In., U.S. — C3 91
Oxford, Ia., U.S. — C6 92
Oxford, Ks., U.S. — E6 93
Oxford, Me., U.S. — D2 96
Oxford, Md., U.S. — C5 97
Oxford, Ma., U.S. — B4 98
Oxford, Mi., U.S. — F7 99
Oxford, Ms., U.S. — A4 101
Oxford, Ne., U.S. — D6 104
Oxford, N.J., U.S. — B3 107
Oxford, N.Y., U.S. — C5 109
Oxford, N.C., U.S. — A4 110
Oxford, Oh., U.S. — C1 112
Oxford, Pa., U.S. — G10 115
Oxford, Wi., U.S. — E4 126
Oxford, co., Me., U.S. — D2 96
Oxford, co., Ont. — D4 73
Oxford House, Man. — B4 70
Oxford Junction, Ia., U.S. — C7 92
Oxford Lake, l., Man. — B4 70
Oxford Peak, mtn., Id., U.S. — G6 89
Oxfordshire, co., Eng., U.K. — C6 12
Oxly, Mo., U.S. — E7 102
Oxnard, Ca., U.S. — E4 82
Oxon Hill, Md., U.S. — f9 97
Oyace, Italy — E3 21
Oyama, B.C. — D8 69
Oyama, Japan — m18 33
Oyapock (Oiapoque), stm., S.A. — B4 59
Oyat, stm., Sov. Un. — A10 27
Oyem, Gabon — A2 48
Oyen, Alta. — D5 68
Oyens, Ia., U.S. — B1 92
Öyeren, l., Nor. — p29 14
Oykel, stm., Scot., U.K. — C4 13
Oykel Bridge, Scot., U.K. — C17 29
Oymyakon, Sov. Un. — E5 45
Oyo, Nig. — E5 45
Oyonnax, Fr. — E7 16
Oyster Bay, N.Y., U.S. — E7 109
Oyster Keys, is., Fl., U.S. — G6 86
Oyster Ridge, mtn., Wy., U.S. — E2 127
Ozamiz, Phil. — D6 34
Ozan, Ar., U.S. — D2 81
Ozark, Al., U.S. — D4 78
Ozark, Ar., U.S. — B2 81
Ozark, Mo., U.S. — D4 102
Ozark, co., Mo., U.S. — E5 102
Ozark Escarpment, clf., U.S. — B9 76
Ozark Plateau, plat., U.S. — C5 102
Ozark Reservoir, res., Ar., U.S. — B1 81
Ozarks, Lake of the, res., Mo., U.S. — C5 102
Ożarowice, co., Wi., U.S. — g10 126
Ozaukee, co., Wi., U.S. — E6 126
Ozawkie, Ks., U.S. — k15 93
Ózd, Hung. — A5 24
Ozernyy, Sov. Un. — G11 27
Ozette Lake, l., Wa., U.S. — A1 124
Ozieri, Italy — D2 23
Ozona, Fl., U.S. — o10 86
Ozona, Tx., U.S. — D2 120
Ozone, Ar., U.S. — B2 81
Ozorków, Pol. — C5 26
Ōzu, Japan — J6 33

Ozuluama, Mex. — C5 63

P

Paar, stm., W. Ger. — E6 19
Paarl, S. Afr. — D2 49
Paauhau, Hi., U.S. — C6 88
Paauilo, Hi., U.S. — C6 88
Pabbay, i., Scot., U.K. — C1 13
Pabianice, Pol. — C5 26
Pablo, Mt., U.S. — C2 103
Pābna, Bngl. — D8 36
Pacaás Novos, Serra dos, mts., Braz. — E2 59
Pacajá, stm., Braz. — C4 59
Pacasmayo, Peru — C2 58
Pace, Fl., U.S. — u14 86
Pace, Ms., U.S. — B3 101
Pachaug Pond, l., Ct., U.S. — C8 84
Pachmarhi, India — F7 37
Pachuca [de Soto], Mex. — C5 63
Pachuta, Ms., U.S. — C5 101
Pacific, B.C. — B3 69
Pacific, Mo., U.S. — C7 102
Pacific, Wa., U.S. — f11 124
Pacific, co., Wa., U.S. — C2 124
Pacifica, Ca., U.S. — h8 82
Pacific Beach, Wa., U.S. — B1 124
Pacific City, Or., U.S. — B3 114
Pacific Creek, stm., Wy., U.S. — D3 127
Pacific Grove, Ca., U.S. — D3 82
Pacific Islands, Trust Territory of the, dep., Oc. — F9 6
Pacific Junction, Ia., U.S. — C2 92
Pacific Ocean — E11 6
Pacific Palisades, Hi., U.S. — g10 88
Pacific Ranges, mts., B.C. — D4 69
Pacific Rim National Park, B.C. — E5 69
Packard Mountain, hill, Ma., U.S. — B3 98
Pack Monadnock Mountain, mtn., N.H., U.S. — E3 106
Packwaukee, Wi., U.S. — E4 126
Packwood, Ia., U.S. — C5 92
Packwood, Wa., U.S. — C4 124
Pacolet, S.C., U.S. — B4 117
Pacolet, stm., S.C., U.S. — A4 117
Pacolet Mills, S.C., U.S. — B4 117
Pacora, Pan. — k12 62
Pacora, stm., Pan. — k12 62
Pacov, Czech. — D9 19
Pacquet, Newf. — D3 72
Pactola Reservoir, res., S.D., U.S. — C2 118
Pactolus, N.C., U.S. — B5 110
Paczków, Pol. — C4 26
Padang, Indon. — F2 34
Padang, i., Indon. — L5 35
Padang Endau, Malay. — K5 35
Padangpanjang, Indon. — F2 34
Padangsidempuan, Indon. — E1 34
Padauiri, stm., Braz. — B2 59
Paddle Prairie, Alta. — f7 68
Paddling Lake, l., Sask. — D1 75
Paddock Lake, Wi., U.S. — n11 126
Paddockwood, Sask. — D3 75
Paddy Knob, mtn., U.S. — C5 125
Paden, Ok., U.S. — B5 113
Paden City, W.Va., U.S. — B4 125
Paderborn, W. Ger. — C4 18
Padova (Padua), Italy — D6 20
Padre Island, i., Tx., U.S. — F4 120
Padre Island National Seashore, Tx., U.S. — F4 120
Padroni, Co., U.S. — A7 83
Padstow, Eng., U.K. — D3 12
Paducah, Ky., U.S. — e9 94
Paducah, Tx., U.S. — B2 120
Paektu, Mount, mtn., Asia — F4 33
Paepae'olei'a, Cape, c., W. Sam. — F11 52
Paeroa, N.Z. — L15 51
Paestum, hist., Italy — D5 23
Pag, i., Yugo. — C2 24
Pagai Selatan, i., Indon. — F2 34
Pagai Utara, i., Indon. — F2 34
Pagasitikós Kólpos (Gulf of Vólos), b., Grc. — C4 40
Pagatan, Indon. — F4 34
Pagato, stm., Sask. — A4 75
Page, Az., U.S. — A4 80
Page, Ne., U.S. — B7 104
Page, N.D., U.S. — B8 111
Page, W.Va., U.S. — m13 125
Page, co., Ia., U.S. — D2 92
Page, co., Va., U.S. — B4 123
Pageland, S.C., U.S. — B7 117
Page Manor, Oh., U.S. — *C1 112
Paglia, mtn., Switz. — D5 17?
Pago Bay, b., Guam — M10 52
Pagoda Peak, mtn., Co., U.S. — A3 83
Pagoda Point, c., Burma — E9 36
Pago Pago, Am. Sam. — G13 52
Pago Pago Harbor, b., Am. Sam. — F13 52
Pago Point, c., Guam — M10 52
Pagosa Springs, Co., U.S. — D3 83
Paguate, N.M., U.S. — B2 108
Pahala, Hi., U.S. — D6 88
Pahang, state, Malay. — K5 35
Pahang, stm., Malay. — K5 35
Pahaska, Wy., U.S. — B3 127
Pahoa, Hi., U.S. — D7 88
Pahokee, Fl., U.S. — F6 86
Pahrump, Nv., U.S. — G6 105
Pahute Mesa, mtn., Nv., U.S. — F5 105
Paignton, Eng., U.K. — D4 12
Päijänne, l., Fin. — G11 14
Pailin, Tn., U.S. — D8 119
Pailolo Channel, strt., Hi., U.S. — C5 88
Paincourt, Ont. — E2 73
Paincourtville, La., U.S. — k9 95
Painesdale, Mi., U.S. — A2 99
Painesville, Oh., U.S. — A4 112
Paint, stm., Mi., U.S. — B2 99
Paint Bank, Va., U.S. — C2 123
Paint Creek, stm., Oh., U.S. — C2 112
Paint Creek, North Fork, stm., Oh., U.S. — C2 112
Paint Creek Lake, res., Oh., U.S. — C2 112
Painted Desert, des., Az., U.S. — B4 80
Painted Post, N.Y., U.S. — C3 109

Painted Rock Reservoir, res., Az., U.S. — D3 80
Painter, Va., U.S. — C7 123
Paint Lake, l., Man. — B3 70
Paint Lick, Ky., U.S. — C5 94
Paint Mountain, mtn., W.V., U.S. — n13 125
Paint Rock, Al., U.S. — A3 78
Paint Rock, Tx., U.S. — D3 120
Paintsville, Ky., U.S. — C7 94
Paisley, Ont. — C3 73
Paisley, Scot., U.K. — C4 10
Paisley, Fl., U.S. — D5 86
Paisley, Or., U.S. — E6 114
Paita, Peru — C1 58
Pajala, Swe. — D10 14
Pajarito, N.M., U.S. — *B3 108
Pajaros Point, c., V.I., Br. — A7 65
Pajon Point, c., Guam — L10 52
Pakenham, Ont. — B8 73
Pakistan, ctry., Asia — C4 36
Pakokku, Burma — D9 36
Pakowki Lake, l., Alta. — E5 68
Pakra, stm., Yugo. — C3 24
Paks, Hung. — B4 24
Pakse, Laos — B3 34
Pala, Chad — D2 46
Palacios, Tx., U.S. — E4 120
Palafrugell, Spain — B7 22
Palagruža, is., Yugo. — D3 24
Palaiokhóra, Grc. — E4 25
Palaión Fáliron, Grc. — h11 25
Palamás, Grc. — C4 25
Palamós, Spain — B7 22
Palana, Sov. Un. — D3 27
Palanga, Sov. Un. — D3 27
Palangkaraya, Indon. — F4 34
Pālanpur, India — D5 36
Palaoa Point, c., Hi., U.S. — C4 88
Palapye, Bots. — B4 49
Palas del Rey, Spain — A2 22
Palatine, Il., U.S. — A5 90
Palatka, Fl., U.S. — C5 86
Palau (Belau), ter., T.T.P.I. — F8 6
Palauig, Phil. — o12 34
Palauig Point, c., Phil. — o12 34
Palauli (Vailoa), W. Sam. — F11 52
Palauli Bay, b., W. Sam. — F11 52
Palawan, i., Phil. — C5 34
Palazzolo Acreide, Italy — F5 23
Palco, Ks., U.S. — C4 93
Palembang, Indon. — F2 34
Palena, stm., S.A. — C2 54
Palencia, Spain — A3 22
Palenque, hist., Mex. — B2 62
Palenville, N.Y., U.S. — C6 109
Palermo, Italy — E4 23
Palermo, Me., U.S. — D3 96
Palermo, N.J., U.S. — E3 107
Palermo, N.D., U.S. — A3 111
Palestine, Ar., U.S. — *C5 81
Palestine, Ct., U.S. — *D2 84
Palestine, Il., U.S. — D6 90
Palestine, Oh., U.S. — B1 112
Palestine, Tx., U.S. — D5 120
Palestine, W.V., U.S. — B3 125
Palestine, hist. reg., Asia — G10 40
Palestine, Lake, res., Tx., U.S. — C5 120
Palestrina, Italy — h9 23
Paletwa, Burma — D9 36
Pālghāt, India — F6 36
Palhoça, Braz. — D3 56
Palidoro (Baebiana), Italy — h8 23
Palikea Point, c., Micron. — Q17 52
Paliker Point, c., Micron. — Q17 52
Palikea, Togo — E5 45
Pall Mall, Tn., U.S. — C9 119
Palma, Moz. — D7 48
Palma del Río, Spain — D3 22
Palma [de Mallorca], Spain — C7 22
Palmar Sur, C.R. — F6 62
Palmares, Braz. — D2 56
Palmas, Braz. — D2 56
Palmas, Cape, c., Lib. — F3 45
Palmas de Monte Alto, Braz. — A4 56
Palma Sola, Fl., U.S. — *E4 86
Palma Soriano, Cuba — D5 64
Palm Bay, Fl., U.S. — D6 86
Palm Beach, Fl., U.S. — F6 86
Palm Beach, co., Fl., U.S. — F6 86
Palm Beach Gardens, Fl., U.S. — E4 82
Palmdale, Ca., U.S. — E4 82
Palmdale, Fl., U.S. — F5 86
Palm Desert, Ca., U.S. — *F5 82
Palmeira, Braz. — D2 56
Palmeira d'Oeste, Braz. — C2 56
Palmeira dos Indios, Braz. — C3 57
Palmeirais, Ponta das, Ang. — C1 48
Palmer, Sask. — H2 75
Palmer, Il., U.S. — D4 90
Palmer, Ia., U.S. — B3 92
Palmer, Ks., U.S. — C6 93
Palmer, Ma., U.S. — B3 98
Palmer, Mi., U.S. — B3 99
Palmer, Ne., U.S. — C7 104
Palmer, Tn., U.S. — D8 119
Palmer, Tx., U.S. — n10 120
Palmer Land, reg., Ant. — B6 7
Palmer Park, Md., U.S. — *C4 97
Palmerston, Ont. — D4 73
Palmerston, N.Z. — P13 51
Palmerston North, N.Z. — N15 51
Palmerton, Pa., U.S. — E10 115
Palmetto, Fl., U.S. — E4 86
Palmetto, Ga., U.S. — C2 87
Palmetto Estates, Fl., U.S. — *G6 86
Palm Harbor, Fl., U.S. — o10 86

Name	Map Ref.	Page

Palmi, Italy — E5 — 23
Palmira, Col. — C2 — 60
Palmira, Cuba — C3 — 64
Palmira, Ec. — B2 — 58
Palmitas, Ur. — f8 — 54
Palms, Mi., U.S. — E8 — 99
Palms, Isle of, i., S.C., U.S. — F8 — 117
Palm Springs, Ca., U.S. — F5 — 82
Palm Springs, Fl., U.S. — F6 — 86
Palm Valley, Fl., U.S. — m9 — 86
Palmyra, Il., U.S. — D4 — 90
Palmyra, In., U.S. — H5 — 91
Palmyra, Ia., U.S. — f9 — 92
Palmyra, Me., U.S. — D3 — 96
Palmyra, Mo., U.S. — B6 — 102
Palmyra, Ne., U.S. — D9 — 104
Palmyra, N.J., U.S. — C2 — 107
Palmyra, N.Y., U.S. — B3 — 109
Palmyra, N.C., U.S. — A5 — 110
Palmyra, Pa., U.S. — F8 — 115
Palmyra, Tn., U.S. — A4 — 119
Palmyra, Va., U.S. — C4 — 123
Palmyra, Wi., U.S. — F5 — 126
Palmyra, atoll, Oc. — F12 — 6
Palmyras Point, c., India — G11 — 37
Palo (Alsium), Italy — h8 — 23
Palo, Italy — E6 — 23
Palo, Ia., U.S. — B6 — 92
Palo, Ks., U.S. — E9 — 93
Palo Alto, Ca., U.S. — D2 — 82
Palo Alto, co., Ca., U.S. — A3 — 92
Palo Duro Canyon, val., Tx., U.S. — B2 — 120
Paloich, Sud. — C3 — 47
Palomar Mountain, mtn., Ca., U.S. — F5 — 82
Palomas Mountains, mts., Az., U.S. — D2 — 80
Palombara Sabina, Italy — g9 — 23
Palo Negro, Col. — C3 — 60
Palo Pinto, Tx., U.S. — C3 — 120
Palo Pinto, co., Tx., U.S. — C3 — 120
Palopo, Indon. — F6 — 34
Palos, Cape, c., Spain — D5 — 22
Palos Heights, Il., U.S. — *k9 — 90
Palos Hills, Il., U.S. — *k9 — 90
Palos Park, Il., U.S. — k9 — 90
Palos Verdes Estates, Ca., U.S. — n12 — 82
Palourde, Lake, l., La., U.S. — k9 — 95
Palouse, Wa., U.S. — C8 — 124
Palouse, stm., Wa., U.S. — C7 — 124
Palo Verde, Az., U.S. — D3 — 80
Palo Verde, Ca., U.S. — F6 — 82
Palpa, Peru — D3 — 58
Pålsboda, Swe. — t33 — 14
Palu, Indon. — *F5 — 34
Palvār, Kūh-e, mtn., Iran — F8 — 39
Pama, Burkina — D5 — 45
Pamamaroo Lake, l., Austl. — F4 — 51
Pambrun, Sask. — H2 — 75
Pamekasan, Indon. — G4 — 34
Pamiers, Fr. — F4 — 16
Pamir, mts., Asia — F10 — 29
Pamlico, co., N.C., U.S. — B6 — 110
Pamlico, stm., N.C., U.S. — B6 — 110
Pamlico Sound, strt., N.C., U.S. — B6 — 110
Pampa, Tx., U.S. — B2 — 120
Pampa, reg., Arg. — G4 — 53
Pampa Grande, Bol. — C3 — 55
Pampanga, stm., Phil. — o13 — 34
Pampas, Peru — D3 — 58
Pampilhosa do Botão, Port. — B1 — 22
Pamplico, S.C., U.S. — D8 — 117
Pamplin, Va., U.S. — C4 — 123
Pamplona, Col. — B3 — 60
Pamplona, Spain — A5 — 22
Pamunkey, stm., Va., U.S. — C5 — 123
Pana, Il., U.S. — D4 — 90
Panaca, Nv., U.S. — F7 — 105
Panacea, Fl., U.S. — B2 — 86
Panache, Lake, l., Ont. — A3 — 73
Panagyurishte, Bul. — D7 — 24
Panaitan, i., Indon. — G3 — 34
Panaji, India — E3 — 37
Panamá, Braz. — B3 — 56
Panama, Pan. — F8 — 62
Panama, Il., U.S. — D4 — 90
Panama, Ne., U.S. — D9 — 104
Panama, N.Y., U.S. — C1 — 109
Panama, Ok., U.S. — B7 — 113
Panama, ctry., N.A. — F8 — 62
Panamá, Bahia de, b., Pan. — F8 — 62
Panamá, Golfo de, b., Pan. — F8 — 62
Panama Canal, Pan. — k11 — 62
Panama City, Fl., U.S. — u16 — 86
Panama City Beach, Fl., U.S. — u16 — 86
Panambi, Braz. — D2 — 56
Panamint Range, mts., Ca., U.S. — D5 — 82
Panao, Peru — C2 — 58
Panarea, i., Italy — E5 — 23
Panaro, stm., Italy — B3 — 23
Panay, i., Phil. — C6 — 34
Pancake Range, mts., Nv., U.S. — E6 — 105
Pančevo, Yugo. — C5 — 24
Panch'iao (T'aipeihsien), Tai. — *F9 — 31
Pancoastburg, Oh., U.S. — C2 — 112
Panda, Moz. — B5 — 49
Pandharpur, India — E6 — 36
Pāndhurna, India — G7 — 37
Pando, Ur. — E1 — 56
Pando, dept., Bol. — A3 — 59
Pandora, Oh., U.S. — B2 — 112
Pandora, Tx., U.S. — E4 — 120
Pandu, Zaire — A2 — 48
Panelas, Braz. — k5 — 57
Panet, Que. — C7 — 74
Panevežys, Sov. Un. — D5 — 27
Pangala, Congo — B1 — 48
Pangani, Tan. — C6 — 48
Pangburn, Ar., U.S. — B4 — 81
Pangi, Zaire — B4 — 48
Pangkalanbuun, Indon. — F4 — 34
Pangkalpinang, Indon. — F3 — 34
Pangman, Sask. — H3 — 75
Pangnirtung, N.W. Ter. — C19 — 66
Pangsau Pass, Asia — C10 — 36
Panguipulli, Chile — B2 — 54
Panguitch, Ut., U.S. — F3 — 121
Panhandle, Tx., U.S. — B2 — 120
Paniau, mtn., Hi., U.S. — B1 — 88
Panié, Mont, mtn., N. Cal. — *H10 — 6
Pānihāti, India — *D8 — 36
Panipat, India — D6 — 37
Paniqui, Phil. — o13 — 34
Panj, stm., Asia — k17 — 39
Panjāb, Afg. — C2 — 36
Panjgūr, Pak. — C3 — 36
Panjim see Panaji, India — —
Panjnad, Pak. — E5 — 36
Panjpāi, Pak. — G13 — 39

Pankey, Ar., U.S. — h10 — 81
Pankeyville, Il., U.S. — F5 — 90
Pankshin, Nig. — E6 — 45
Panmunjŏm, N. Kor. — H3 — 33
Panna, India — D7 — 36
Panola, Al., U.S. — C1 — 78
Panola, co., Ms., U.S. — A3 — 101
Panola, co., Tx., U.S. — C5 — 120
Panora, Ia., U.S. — C3 — 92
Panorama, Braz. — C2 — 56
Panruti, India — G5 — 37
Pansey, Al., U.S. — D4 — 78
Panshan, China — D9 — 32
Panshi, China — C11 — 32
Pantar, i., Indon. — G6 — 34
Pantego, N.C., U.S. — B6 — 110
Pantelleria, Italy — F3 — 23
Pantelleria, i., Italy — F4 — 23
Panthersville, Ga., U.S. — *h8 — 87
Pantin, Fr. — g10 — 16
Panton, Vt., U.S. — C2 — 122
Pánuco, Mex. — C5 — 63
Pánuco, stm., Mex. — k14 — 63
Panulcillo, Chile — F1 — 55
Panzi, Zaire — C2 — 48
Panzós, Guat. — D7 — 63
Pão de Açúcar, Braz. — C3 — 57
Paola, Italy — E6 — 23
Paola, Ks., U.S. — D9 — 93
Paoli, Co., U.S. — A8 — 83
Paoli, In., U.S. — G5 — 91
Paoli, Ok., U.S. — C4 — 113
Paoli, Pa., U.S. — o20 — 115
Paonia, Co., U.S. — C3 — 83
Paoua, Cen. Afr. Rep. — D3 — 46
Paoy Pet, Camb. — F5 — 35
Pápa, Hung. — B3 — 24
Papaaloa, Hi., U.S. — D6 — 88
Papagayo, Golfo de b., C.R. — E7 — 63
Papago Indian Reservation, Az., U.S. — E3 — 80
Papaikou, Hi., U.S. — D6 — 88
Papantla [de Olarte], Mex. — C5 — 63
Papawai Point, c., Hi., U.S. — C5 — 88
Papeete, Fr. Poly. — H13 — 6
Papenburg, W. Ger. — B3 — 18
Paper Mill Village, Vt., U.S. — F2 — 122
Papillion, Ne., U.S. — C9 — 104
Papineau, Il., U.S. — C6 — 90
Papineau, co., Que. — D2 — 74
Papineau Lake, l., Ont. — B7 — 73
Papineauville, Que. — D2 — 74
Paposo, Chile — E1 — 55
Papua, Gulf of, b., Pap. N. Gui. — k11 — 50
Papua New Guinea, ctry., Oc. — G8 — 6
Papudo, Chile — A2 — 54
Papun, Burma — E10 — 36
Paquette, Que. — D6 — 74
Paquetville, N.B. — B4 — 71
Pará, state, Braz. — C4 — 59
Para, dept., Sur. — A3 — 59
Pará, stm., Braz. — C5 — 59
Parabel, Sov. Un. — B10 — 28
Paracale, Phil. — o14 — 34
Paracatu, Braz. — B3 — 56
Paracatu, stm., Braz. — B3 — 56
Paracel Islands, is., Asia — B4 — 34
Parachute, Co., U.S. — B2 — 83
Paracuru, Braz. — B3 — 57
Paradis, La., U.S. — k11 — 95
Paradise, Ca., U.S. — C3 — 82
Paradise, Ks., U.S. — C5 — 93
Paradise, Mi., U.S. — B5 — 99
Paradise, Mt., U.S. — C2 — 103
Paradise, Nv., U.S. — G6 — 105
Paradise, Ut., U.S. — B4 — 121
Paradise, stm., Newf. — B3 — 72
Paradise Hill, Sask. — D1 — 75
Paradise Hills, N.M., U.S. — B3 — 108
Paradise Island, i., Bah. — m18 — 64
Paradise River, Newf. — B3 — 72
Paradise Valley, Alta. — C5 — 68
Paradise Valley, Az., U.S. — k9 — 80
Paradise Valley, Nv., U.S. — B4 — 105
Paradise Valley, Wy., U.S. — D6 — 127
Paradox, Co., U.S. — C2 — 83
Paragon, In., U.S. — F4 — 91
Paragonah, Ut., U.S. — F3 — 121
Paragould, Ar., U.S. — A5 — 81
Paraguá, stm., Ven. — B5 — 60
Paraguaçu, stm., Braz. — D3 — 57
Paraguaçu Paulista, Braz. — C2 — 56
Paraguai (Paraguay), stm., S.A. — D4 — 55
Paraguaná, Península de, pen., Ven. — A4 — 60
Paraguari, Para. — E4 — 55
Paraguari, dept., Para. — E4 — 55
Paraguay, ctry., S.A. — D4 — 55
Paraguay (Paraguai), stm., S.A. — D4 — 55
Paraíba, state, Braz. — C3 — 57
Paraíba, stm., Braz. — h6 — 57
Paraíba do Sul, Braz. — h6 — 56
Paraíba do Sul, stm., Braz. — g6 — 56
Paraisópolis, Braz. — G6 — 56
Paraíso, Pan. — k11 — 62
Paraíso, Braz. — C3 — 56
Parakou, Benin — E5 — 45
Paralomar, Ar., U.S. — D1 — 81
Paramaribo, Sur. — A3 — 59
Paramirim, Braz. — A4 — 56
Paramithía, Grc. — C3 — 25
Paramonga, Peru — D2 — 58
Paramount, Ca., U.S. — *n12 — 82
Paramount, Md., U.S. — A2 — 97
Paramus, N.J., U.S. — h8 — 107
Paraná, Arg. — A4 — 54
Paraná, Braz. — D1 — 57
Paraná, state, Braz. — C2 — 56
Paraná, stm., Braz. — D1 — 57
Paraná, stm., S.A. — G5 — 53
Paranaguá, Braz. — D3 — 56
Paranaíba, Braz. — B2 — 56
Paranaíba, stm., Braz. — B2 — 56
Paranaiguara, Braz. — B2 — 56
Paranapanema, stm., Braz. — C2 — 56
Paranapiacaba, Serra do, mts., Braz. — m8 — 56
Paranavaí, Braz. — C2 — 56
Paraopeba, Braz. — C3 — 56
Paraopeba, stm., Braz. — E2 — 57
Parapeti, stm., Bol. — C3 — 55
Parati, Braz. — D2 — 57
Paratinga, Braz. — D1 — 57
Paraúna, Braz. — B2 — 56
Paray-le-Monial, Fr. — D6 — 16
Pārbati, stm., India — E6 — 36
Parbhani, India — H6 — 37

Parchim, E. Ger. — B5 — 18
Parchment, Mi., U.S. — F5 — 99
Parczew, Pol. — C7 — 26
Pardee, Va., U.S. — e9 — 123
Pardeeville, Wi., U.S. — E4 — 126
Pardes Hanna-Karkur, Isr. — B6 — 41
Pardo, stm., Braz. — C2 — 56
Pardo, stm., Braz. — C3 — 56
Pardo, stm., Braz. — E2 — 57
Pardoe, Pa., U.S. — D1 — 115
Pardubice, Czech. — C3 — 26
Parecis, Chapada dos, mts., Braz. — B4 — 55
Paredes de Nava, Spain — A3 — 22
Parem, i., Micron. — Q18 — 52
Parempec, i., Micron. — Q17 — 52
Parent, Que. — k12 — 74
Parepare, Indon. — F5 — 34
Párga, Grc. — C3 — 40
Pargo, Ponta do, c., Port. — h11 — 22
Pargolovo, Sov. Un. — r31 — 14
Paria, stm., — A4 — 80
Paria, Gulf of, b., — A5 — 60
Paria, Península de, pen., Ven. — A5 — 60
Pariaguán, Ven. — n12 — 63
Paria Plateau, plat., Az., U.S. — A4 — 80
Paricutín, vol., Mex. — n12 — 63
Parigi, Indon. — F6 — 34
Parika, Guy. — A3 — 59
Parima, Serra, mts., S.A. — B2 — 59
Parima, Sierra (Serra Parima), mts., S.A. — C5 — 60
Pariñas, Punta, c., Peru — B1 — 58
Parintins, Braz. — C3 — 59
Paris, Ont. — D4 — 73
Paris, Fr. — C5 — 16
Paris, Ar., U.S. — B2 — 81
Paris, Id., U.S. — G7 — 89
Paris, Il., U.S. — D6 — 90
Paris, Ky., U.S. — B5 — 94
Paris, Me., U.S. — D2 — 96
Paris, Mi., U.S. — E5 — 99
Paris, Ms., U.S. — A4 — 101
Paris, Mo., U.S. — B5 — 102
Paris, Tn., U.S. — A3 — 119
Paris, Tx., U.S. — C5 — 120
Paris, Va., U.S. — A5 — 123
Paris Crossing, In., U.S. — G6 — 91
Parish, N.Y., U.S. — B4 — 109
Parishville, N.Y., U.S. — f10 — 109
Paris Peak, mtn., Id., U.S. — G7 — 89
Parisville, Que. — C5 — 74
Park, Ks., U.S. — C3 — 93
Park, co., Co., U.S. — B5 — 83
Park, co., Mt., U.S. — E6 — 103
Park, co., Wy., U.S. — B3 — 127
Parkbeg, Sask. — G2 — 75
Park City, Ks., U.S. — g12 — 93
Park City, Ky., U.S. — C3 — 94
Park City, Mt., U.S. — E8 — 103
Park City, Ut., U.S. — C4 — 121
Parkdale, P.E.I. — C6 — 71
Parkdale, Ar., U.S. — D4 — 81
Parkdale, Mi., U.S. — D4 — 99
Parkdale, Or., U.S. — B5 — 114
Parke, co., In., U.S. — E3 — 91
Parker, Az., U.S. — C1 — 80
Parker, Co., U.S. — B6 — 83
Parker, Fl., U.S. — u16 — 86
Parker, Id., U.S. — F7 — 89
Parker, Ks., U.S. — D9 — 93
Parker, Pa., U.S. — D2 — 115
Parker, S.D., U.S. — D8 — 118
Parker, Wa., U.S. — C5 — 124
Parker, co., Tx., U.S. — C4 — 120
Parker City, In., U.S. — D7 — 91
Parker Dam, Ca., U.S. — E6 — 82
Parker Dam, U.S. — C1 — 80
Parker Peak, mtn., S.D., U.S. — F2 — 118
Parkersburg, Il., U.S. — E5 — 90
Parkersburg, Ia., U.S. — B5 — 92
Parkersburg, W.V., U.S. — B3 — 125
Parkers Prairie, Mn., U.S. — D3 — 100
Parkertown, N.J., U.S. — D4 — 107
Parkerview, Sask. — F4 — 75
Parkes, Austl. — F8 — 50
Parkesburg, Pa., U.S. — G10 — 115
Park Falls, Wi., U.S. — C3 — 126
Park Forest, Il., U.S. — *B6 — 90
Park Forest South, Il., U.S. — *B6 — 90
Park Hall, Md., U.S. — D5 — 97
Park Head, Ont. — C3 — 73
Parkhill, Ont. — D3 — 73
Park Hill, Ok., U.S. — B7 — 113
Park Hills, Ky., U.S. — h13 — 94
Parkin, Ar., U.S. — B5 — 81
Parkland, Wa., U.S. — B3 — 124
Parkland, Alta. — f11 — 124
Park Layne, Oh., U.S. — C1 — 112
Parkman, Sask. — H5 — 75
Parkman, Me., U.S. — C3 — 96
Parkman, Oh., U.S. — A4 — 112
Parkman, Wy., U.S. — B5 — 127
Park Place, Or., U.S. — h12 — 114
Park Plateau, plat., Co., U.S. — D6 — 83
Park Range, mts., Co., U.S. — A4 — 83
Park Rapids, Mn., U.S. — D3 — 100
Park Ridge, Il., U.S. — B6 — 90
Park Ridge, N.J., U.S. — g8 — 107
Park River, N.D., U.S. — A8 — 111
Parkrose, Or., U.S. — B4 — 114
Parks, Ar., U.S. — C2 — 81
Parks, La., U.S. — D4 — 95
Parks, Ne., U.S. — D4 — 104
Parkside, Sask. — D2 — 75
Parksley, Va., U.S. — C7 — 123
Parkston, S.D., U.S. — D8 — 118
Parksville, B.C. — E5 — 69
Parksville, N.Y., U.S. — D6 — 109
Parksville, S.C., U.S. — D3 — 117
Parkton, Md., U.S. — A5 — 97
Parkton, N.C., U.S. — C3 — 110
Parkville, Mo., U.S. — B3 — 102
Park Valley, Ut., U.S. — B2 — 121
Parkwater, Wa., U.S. — g14 — 124
Parkway, Ca., U.S. — *C3 — 82
Parkwood, N.C., U.S. — B4 — 110
Parlākimidi, India — H10 — 37
Parle, Lac qui, l., Mn., U.S. — E3 — 100
Parlier, Ca., U.S. — D4 — 82
Parlin, Co., U.S. — C4 — 83
Parma, Italy — E3 — 23
Parma, Id., U.S. — F2 — 89
Parma, Mi., U.S. — F6 — 99
Parma, Mo., U.S. — E8 — 102
Parma, Oh., U.S. — A4 — 112
Parma, stm., Italy — E6 — 20
Parma Heights, Oh., U.S. — h9 — 112

Parmele, N.C., U.S. — B5 — 110
Parmelee, S.D., U.S. — D4 — 118
Parmer, co., Tx., U.S. — B1 — 120
Parnaguá, Braz. — D2 — 57
Parnaíba, Braz. — B2 — 57
Parnaíba, stm., Braz. — B2 — 57
Parnassós, mtn., Grc. — C4 — 25
Parnell, Ia., U.S. — C6 — 92
Parnell, Mo., U.S. — A3 — 102
Párnis Óros, mtn., Grc. — g11 — 25
Pärnu, Sov. Un. — B5 — 27
Paro, Bhu. — C8 — 36
Paron, Ar., U.S. — C3 — 81
Paroo, stm., Austl. — F7 — 50
Páros, Grc. — D5 — 25
Páros, i., Grc. — D5 — 40
Parowan, Ut., U.S. — F3 — 121
Par Pond, res., S.C., U.S. — D5 — 117
Parr, In., U.S. — C4 — 91
Parral, Chile — B2 — 54
Parramatta, Austl. — *F9 — 50
Parramore Island, i., Va., U.S. — C7 — 123
Parras de la Fuente, Mex. — B4 — 63
Parrett, stm., Eng., U.K. — C5 — 12
Parrish, Al., U.S. — B2 — 78
Parrish, Fl., U.S. — E4 — 86
Parrish, Wi., U.S. — C4 — 126
Parris Island, S.C., U.S. — *G6 — 117
Parrott, Ga., U.S. — E2 — 87
Parrott, Va., U.S. — C2 — 123
Parrottsville, Tn., U.S. — C10 — 119
Parrsboro, N.S. — D5 — 71
Parry, Cape, c., N.W. Ter. — B8 — 66
Parry, Mount, mtn., B.C. — C3 — 69
Parry Island, i., Marsh Is. — S18 — 52
Parry Islands, is., N.W. Ter. — m29 — 66
Parry Sound, Ont. — B4 — 73
Parry Sound, dept., Ont. — B5 — 73
Parseta, stm., Pol. — A3 — 26
Parshall, Co., U.S. — A4 — 83
Parshall, N.D., U.S. — B3 — 111
Parsippany, N.J., U.S. — B4 — 107
Parsnip, stm., B.C. — B6 — 69
Parsons, Ks., U.S. — E8 — 93
Parsons, Tn., U.S. — B3 — 119
Parsons, W.V., U.S. — B5 — 125
Parsonsburg, Md., U.S. — D7 — 97
Parson's Pond, Newf. — C3 — 72
Partenen, Aus. — C6 — 20
Parthenay, Fr. — D3 — 16
Parthenon, Ar., U.S. — B2 — 81
Partinico, Italy — E4 — 23
Partlow, Va., U.S. — B5 — 123
Partridge, Ks., U.S. — E5 — 93
Partridge Point, c., Newf. — C3 — 72
Partry, Ire. — D2 — 11
Paru, stm., Braz. — C4 — 59
Paru de Oeste, stm., Braz. — C3 — 59
Parys, S. Afr. — G5 — 49
Pasadena, Newf. — D3 — 72
Pasadena, Ca., U.S. — E4 — 82
Pasadena, Md., U.S. — B4 — 97
Pasadena, Tx., U.S. — r14 — 120
Pasado, Cabo, c., Ec. — B1 — 58
Pasaje, Ec. — B2 — 58
Pa Sak, stm., Thai. — D4 — 35
Pasay, Phil. — C6 — 34
Pascagoula, Ms., U.S. — E5 — 101
Pascagoula, stm., Ms., U.S. — D5 — 101
Pascagoula Bay, b., Ms., U.S. — f8 — 101
Pascani, Rom. — B8 — 24
Pasco, Wa., U.S. — C6 — 124
Pasco, dept., Peru — D2 — 58
Pasco, co., Fl., U.S. — D4 — 86
Pascoag, R.I., U.S. — B2 — 116
Pascoag Reservoir, res., R.I., U.S. — B2 — 116
Pascola, Mo., U.S. — E8 — 102
Pascua, Isla de (Easter Island), i., Chile — H15 — 6
Pas-de-Calais, dept., Fr. — B9 — 16
Pasewalk, E. Ger. — B7 — 18
Pashkovo, Sov. Un. — B11 — 31
Pasig, Phil. — o13 — 34
Pasni, Pak. — C3 — 36
Paso de Indios, Arg. — C3 — 54
Paso de los Libres, Arg. — E4 — 55
Paso de los Toros, Ur. — E1 — 55
Paso Limay, Arg. — C2 — 54
Paso Robles, Ca., U.S. — E3 — 82
Pasqua, Sask. — G3 — 75
Pasque Island, i., Ma., U.S. — D6 — 98
Pasquia, stm., Sask. — D4 — 75
Pasquia Hills, hills, Sask. — D4 — 75
Pasquotank, co., N.C., U.S. — A6 — 110
Pasrūr, Pak. — D5 — 36
Passaconaway, Mount, mtn., N.H., U.S. — C4 — 106
Passadumkeag, Me., U.S. — C4 — 96
Passadumkeag Mountain, mtn., Me., U.S. — C4 — 96
Passage East, Ire. — E5 — 11
Passage West, Ire. — F3 — 11
Passaic, N.J., U.S. — B4 — 107
Passaic, co., N.J., U.S. — A4 — 107
Passaic, stm., N.J., U.S. — h8 — 107
Passamaquoddy Bay, b., Me., U.S. — C6 — 96
Passau, W. Ger. — D6 — 18
Pass Christian, Ms., U.S. — E4 — 101
Passekeag, N.B. — D4 — 71
Passero, Cape, c., Italy — F5 — 23
Passo Fundo, Braz. — D2 — 56
Passos, Braz. — C3 — 56
Passumpsic, Vt., U.S. — C4 — 122
Passumpsic, stm., Vt., U.S. — C4 — 122
Passy, Fr. — E2 — 21
Pastaza, prov., Ec. — B2 — 58
Pastaza, stm., S.A. — B2 — 58
Pasto, Col. — C2 — 60
Pastora Peak, mtn., Az., U.S. — A6 — 80
Pastura, N.M., U.S. — C5 — 108
Pasuruan, Indon. — G4 — 34
Paswegin, Sask. — F3 — 75
Patagonia, Az., U.S. — F5 — 80
Patagonia, reg., Arg. — D3 — 54
Pătan, India — p17 — 22
Patan see Lalitpur, Nepal — C8 — 36
Patapedia, stm., Can. — A4 — 71
Patapsco, Md., U.S. — A4 — 97
Patapsco, stm., Md., U.S. — B4 — 97
Patapsco, North Branch, stm., Md., U.S. — A4 — 97
Patargān, Daqq-e, sw., Asia — E10 — 39
Pataskala, Oh., U.S. — C3 — 112
Pataz, Peru — C2 — 58
Patchet Brook Reservoir, res., R.I., U.S. — B3 — 116
Patchogue, N.Y., U.S. — n15 — 109

Pat Cleburne, Lake, res., Tx., U.S. — C4 — 120
Patea, N.Z. — M15 — 51
Patéras Óros, mtn., Grc. — g10 — 25
Paternò, Italy — F5 — 23
Pateros, Wa., U.S. — A6 — 124
Paterson, N.J., U.S. — B4 — 107
Paterson, Wa., U.S. — D6 — 124
Pathein, Burma — E9 — 36
Pathānkot, India — D6 — 36
Pathfinder Reservoir, res., Wy., U.S. — D6 — 127
Pathfork, Ky., U.S. — D6 — 94
Pathlow, Sask. — E3 — 75
Patía, stm., Col. — C2 — 60
Patiāla, India — D6 — 36
Patience Island, i., R.I., U.S. — D5 — 116
Pati Point, c., Guam — L10 — 52
Patman, Lake, res., Tx., U.S. — C5 — 120
Patmos, Ar., U.S. — D2 — 81
Pátmos, i., Grc. — D6 — 40
Patna, India — C8 — 36
Patnanongan Island, i., Phil. — o14 — 34
Patoka, Il., U.S. — E4 — 90
Patoka, In., U.S. — H2 — 91
Patoka, stm., In., U.S. — H2 — 91
Patoka Lake, res., In., U.S. — H4 — 91
Paton, Ia., U.S. — B3 — 92
Patos, Braz. — C3 — 57
Patos, Lagoa dos, b., Braz. — C6 — 56
Patos de Minas, Braz. — B3 — 56
Patosi, Braz. — B2 — 55
Patquía, Arg. — F2 — 55
Patrai (Patras), Grc. — C3 — 40
Pátrai, Gulf of see Patraïkós Kólpos, b., Grc. — C3 — 40
Patraïkós Kólpos (Gulf of Pátrai), b., Grc. — C3 — 40
Patras see Pátrai, Grc. — C3 — 40
Patricia, Alta. — D5 — 68
Patricia, Tx., U.S. — C1 — 120
Patrick, S.C., U.S. — B7 — 117
Patrick, co., Va., U.S. — D2 — 123
Patrick Air Force Base, mil., Fl., U.S. — D6 — 86
Patricksburg, In., U.S. — F4 — 91
Patrick Springs, Va., U.S. — D2 — 123
Patrocínio, Braz. — B3 — 56
Patsaliga Creek, stm., Al., U.S. — D3 — 78
Patsville, Nv., U.S. — B6 — 105
Patten, Me., U.S. — C4 — 96
Pattenburg, N.J., U.S. — B2 — 107
Patterson, Ar., U.S. — B4 — 81
Patterson, Ca., U.S. — D3 — 82
Patterson, Ga., U.S. — E4 — 87
Patterson, Id., U.S. — E5 — 89
Patterson, Il., U.S. — D3 — 90
Patterson, La., U.S. — E4 — 95
Patterson, Mo., U.S. — D7 — 102
Patterson, N.Y., U.S. — D7 — 109
Patterson, Oh., U.S. — B2 — 112
Patterson Creek, stm., W.V., U.S. — B5 — 125
Pattison, Ms., U.S. — D3 — 101
Patton, Mo., U.S. — D7 — 102
Patton, Pa., U.S. — E4 — 115
Pattonsburg, Mo., U.S. — A3 — 102
Pattullo, Mount, mtn., B.C. — A3 — 69
Patuākhāli, Bngl. — F13 — 37
Patuca, stm., Hond. — D8 — 63
Patuca, Punta, c., Hond. — D8 — 63
Patuxent, stm., Md., U.S. — C4 — 97
Patuxent River Naval Air Test Center, mil., Md., U.S. — D5 — 97
Pátzcuaro, Mex. — D4 — 63
Pátzcuaro, Lago de, l., Mex. — n13 — 63
Patzicía, Guat. — C2 — 64
Patzún, Guat. — C2 — 64
Pau, Fr. — F3 — 16
Pau, Gave de, stm., Fr. — F3 — 16
Paucarbamba, Peru — D2 — 58
Paudalho, Braz. — k6 — 57
Pau dos Ferros, Braz. — C3 — 57
Pauillac, Fr. — D3 — 16
Pauini, Braz. — C4 — 58
Pauk, Burma — D9 — 36
Paul, Id., U.S. — G5 — 89
Paula, stm., Hond. — C5 — 62
Paulden, Az., U.S. — C3 — 80
Paulding, Mi., U.S. — n12 — 99
Paulding, Oh., U.S. — A1 — 112
Paulding, co., Ga., U.S. — C2 — 87
Paulding, co., Oh., U.S. — A1 — 112
Paulette, La., U.S. — h10 — 95
Paulina, La., U.S. — h10 — 95
Paulina, N.J., U.S. — B3 — 107
Paulina Mountains, mts., Or., U.S. — D5 — 114
Paulina Peak, mtn., Or., U.S. — E5 — 114
Pauline, S.C., U.S. — B4 — 117
Pauline, Mount, mtn., Can. — C1 — 68
Paulins Kill, stm., N.J., U.S. — A3 — 107
Paul Island, i., Newf. — g9 — 72
Paulista, Braz. — k6 — 57
Paull, stm., Sask. — B3 — 75
Paullina, Ia., U.S. — B2 — 92
Paul Lake, l., Sask. — A3 — 75
Paulo Afonso, Cachoeira de, wtfl., Braz. — D4 — 57

Pavlovskaya, Sov. Un. — H13 — 27
Pavlovskiy Posad, Sov. Un. — n18 — 27
Pavo, Ga., U.S. — F3 — 87
Pavón, Col. — C3 — 60
Pawcatuck, Ct., U.S. — D8 — 84
Pawcatuck, stm., R.I., U.S. — G11 — 116
Paw Creek, N.C., U.S. — B2 — 110
Pawhuska, Ok., U.S. — A5 — 113
Pawlet, Vt., U.S. — E2 — 122
Pawleys Island, S.C., U.S. — E9 — 117
Pawling, N.Y., U.S. — D7 — 109
Pawnee, Il., U.S. — D4 — 90
Pawnee, Ok., U.S. — A5 — 113
Pawnee, Tx., U.S. — E4 — 120
Pawnee, co., Ks., U.S. — D4 — 93
Pawnee, co., Ne., U.S. — D9 — 104
Pawnee, co., Ok., U.S. — A5 — 113
Pawnee, stm., Ks., U.S. — D3 — 93
Pawnee City, Ne., U.S. — D9 — 104
Pawnee Creek, stm., Co., U.S. — A7 — 83
Pawnee Rock, Ks., U.S. — D5 — 93
Paw Paw, Il., U.S. — B5 — 90
Paw Paw, Mi., U.S. — F5 — 99
Paw Paw, W.V., U.S. — B6 — 125
Pawpaw, Il., U.S. — F4 — 99
Pawpaw Creek, stm., W.V., U.S. — h10 — 125
Pawtuckaway Pond, l., N.H., U.S. — D4 — 106
Pawtucket, R.I., U.S. — C4 — 116
Pawtuxet, R.I., U.S. — C4 — 116
Pawtuxet, North Branch, stm., R.I., U.S. — D3 — 116
Pawtuxet, South Branch, stm., R.I., U.S. — D3 — 116
Pax, W.V., U.S. — n13 — 125
Paxico, Ks., U.S. — C7 — 93
Paxoí, i., Grc. — C3 — 25
Paxton, Fl., U.S. — u15 — 86
Paxton, Il., U.S. — C5 — 90
Paxton, In., U.S. — F3 — 91
Paxton, Ma., U.S. — B4 — 98
Paxton, Ne., U.S. — C4 — 104
Paxtonville, Pa., U.S. — E7 — 115
Payakumbuh, Indon. — *F2 — 34
Payerne, Switz. — C2 — 21
Payette, Id., U.S. — E2 — 89
Payette, co., Id., U.S. — E2 — 89
Payette, North Fork, stm., Id., U.S. — E2 — 89
Payette, South Fork, stm., Id., U.S. — E2 — 89
Payette Lake, res., Id., U.S. — E3 — 89
Payne, Ga., U.S. — D3 — 87
Payne, Oh., U.S. — A1 — 112
Payne, co., Ok., U.S. — A4 — 113
Payne, Lac, l., Que. — g12 — 74
Paynes, Ms., U.S. — B3 — 101
Paynes Creek, Ca., U.S. — B3 — 82
Paynesville, Mn., U.S. — E4 — 100
Paynesville, Mo., U.S. — B7 — 102
Paynesville, Ky., U.S. — C3 — 94
Paynton, Sask. — D1 — 75
Paysandú, Ur. — E1 — 56
Payson, Az., U.S. — C4 — 80
Payson, Il., U.S. — D2 — 90
Payson, Ok., U.S. — B5 — 113
Payson, Ut., U.S. — C4 — 121
Pazarbaşi, Cape, c., Tur. — B8 — 40
Pazardzhik, Bul. — D7 — 24
Pazin, Yugo. — C1 — 24
Pea, stm., Al., U.S. — D3 — 78
Peabody, Ks., U.S. — D6 — 93
Peabody, Ma., U.S. — A6 — 98
Peabody, N.H., U.S. — B4 — 106
Peace, stm., Can. — E9 — 66
Peace, stm., Fl., U.S. — E5 — 86
Peace Dale, R.I., U.S. — F3 — 116
Peace River, Alta. — A2 — 68
Peacham, Vt., U.S. — C4 — 122
Peacham Pond, res., Vt., U.S. — C4 — 122
Peach Creek, W.V., U.S. — D5 — 125
Peachland, B.C. — E8 — 69
Peachland, N.C., U.S. — C2 — 110
Peach Orchard, Ar., U.S. — A5 — 81
Peach Orchard, Ga., U.S. — *C4 — 87
Peach Orchard Knob, mtn., Ky., U.S. — C3 — 94
Peach Point, c., Ma., U.S. — f12 — 98
Peach Springs, Az., U.S. — B2 — 80
Peachtree City, Ga., U.S. — *C2 — 87
Peacock, Mi., U.S. — D5 — 99
Peacock Hills, hills, N.W. Ter. — C10 — 66
Peacock Point, c., Wake I. — B2 — 7
Peacock Sound, strt., Ant. — B2 — 7
Peaima Fall, wtfl., Guy. — A2 — 59
Peak, Ca., U.S. — C5 — 117
Peaked Mountain, mtn., Me., U.S. — B4 — 96
Peaks Island, i., Me., U.S. — g7 — 96
Peale, Mount, mtn., Ut., U.S. — E6 — 121
Peale Island, i., Wake I. — A2 — 52
Pea Patch Island, i., De., U.S. — B3 — 85
Pearcy, Ar., U.S. — C2 — 81
Pea Ridge National Military Park, Ar., U.S. — A1 — 81
Pearisburg, Va., U.S. — C2 — 123
Pearl, Il., U.S. — D3 — 90
Pearl, Ms., U.S. — C3 — 101
Pearl, stm., U.S. — D3 — 101
Pearland, Tx., U.S. — r14 — 120
Pearl and Hermes Reef, rf., Hi. — k12 — 88
Pearl City, Hi., U.S. — B4 — 88
Pearl City, Il., U.S. — A4 — 90
Pearl Harbor, b., Hi., U.S. — B3 — 88
Pearl Harbor Naval Station, mil., Hi., U.S. — g10 — 88
Pearlington, Ms., U.S. — E4 — 101
Pearl River, N.Y., U.S. — g12 — 109
Pearl River, co., Ms., U.S. — E4 — 101
Pearl River, stm., U.S. — E3 — 120
Pearsall, Tx., U.S. — E3 — 120
Pearsoll Peak, mtn., Or., U.S. — E3 — 114
Pearson, Ga., U.S. — E4 — 87
Pearson Channel, strt., N.W. Ter. — m30 — 66
Peary Land, reg., Grnld. — A18 — 128
Pease, Mn., U.S. — E5 — 100
Pease, stm., Tx., U.S. — B3 — 120
Pease Air Force Base, mil., N.H., U.S. — D5 — 106
Pebane, Moz. — A6 — 49
Pebas, Peru — C3 — 58
Pebworth, W.V., U.S. — C6 — 94
Peça nha, Braz. — B4 — 56
Pecatonica, Il., U.S. — A4 — 90

Name	Map Ref.	Page

Pecatonica, stm., U.S. — A4 90
Pecatonica, East Branch, stm., Wi., U.S. — F4 126
Pechenga, Sov. Un. — C6 29
Pechora, Sov. Un. — C8 29
Pechora, Sov. Un. — B20 8
Pechora Bay, b., Sov. Un. — B19 8
Peck, Id., U.S. — C2 89
Peck, Ks., U.S. — E6 93
Peck, Mi., U.S. — E8 99
Peckerwood Lake, res., Ar., U.S. — C4 81
Peckham, Ok., U.S. — A4 113
Pecos, N.M., U.S. — B4 108
Pecos, Tx., U.S. — D1 120
Pecos, co., Tx., U.S. — D1 120
Pecos, stm., U.S. — D7 76
Pecos National Monument, N.M., U.S. — B4 108
Pécs, Hung. — B4 24
Peculiar, Mo., U.S. — C3 102
Pedasí, Pan. — G7 62
Peddocks Island, i., Ma., U.S. — g12 98
Pedernales, Ven. — B5 60
Pedra Azul, Braz. — B4 56
Pedregal (part of Panamá), Pan. — k12 62
Pedregal, Pan. — F6 62
Pedregal, Pan. — B2 57
Pedreiras, Braz. — B2 57
Pedricktown, N.J., U.S. — D2 107
Pedro Afonso, Braz. — C1 57
Pedro Antonio Santos, Mex. — A3 62
Pedro Avelino, Braz. — C3 57
Pedro Juan Caballero, Para. — B4 55
Pedro Luro, Arg. — D4 54
Pedro Miguel, Pan. — k11 62
Pedro R. Fernández (Manuel F. Mantilla), Arg. — E4 55
Pedro Velho, Braz. — h6 57
Peebinga, Austl. — G3 51
Peebles, Sask. — G4 75
Peebles, Scot., U.K. — C5 10
Peebles, Oh., U.S. — D2 112
Peebles, Wi., U.S. — k9 126
Peekaboo Mountain, hill, Me., U.S. — C5 96
Peekskill, N.Y., U.S. — D7 109
Peel, N.B. — C2 71
Peel, I. of Man — F4 13
Peel, co., Ont. — D5 73
Peel, stm., Can. — C5 66
Peel Fell, mtn., U.K. — E6 13
Pe Ell, Wa., U.S. — C2 124
Peel Sound, strt., N.W. Ter. — B13 66
Peene, stm., E. Ger. — B6 18
Peer, Bel. — C5 17
Peerless, Mt., U.S. — B11 103
Peerless Lake, l., Alta. — A3 68
Peers, Alta. — C3 68
Peesane, Sask. — E4 75
Peetz, Co., U.S. — A7 83
Peever, S.D., U.S. — B9 118
Pefferlaw, Ont. — C5 73
Pegan Hill, hill, Ma., U.S. — g10 98
Pegasus Bay, b., N.Z. — O14 51
Pegau, E. Ger. — B7 19
Peggs, Ok., U.S. — A6 113
Peggy, Tx., U.S. — E3 120
Pegnitz, W. Ger. — D6 19
Pegnitz, stm., W. Ger. — D5 18
Pego, Spain — C5 22
Pegram, Tn., U.S. — A4 119
Pegu Yoma, mts., Burma — C1 35
Pehčevo, Yugo. — E6 24
Pehuajó, Arg. — B4 54
Peine, W. Ger. — B5 18
Peiping see Beijing, China — D6 31
Peipus, Lake, l., Sov. Un. — D1 29
Peixe, Braz. — D1 57
Peixian, China — G7 32
Peixian, China — G7 32
Pejepscot, Me., U.S. — E2 96
Pekalongan, Indon. — G3 34
Pekan, Malay. — L7 35
Pekanbaru, Indon. — N6 35
Pekin, Il., U.S. — C4 90
Pekin, In., U.S. — G5 91
Pekin, N.D., U.S. — B7 111
Peking see Beijing, China — D6 31
Pelabuhan Kelang, Malay. — K4 35
Pélagos, i., Grc. — C5 25
Pelahatchie, Ms., U.S. — C4 101
Pelaihari, Indon. — F4 34
Pelat, Mont, mtn., Fr. — E7 16
Pelée, Montagne, mtn., Mart. — I14 64
Pelee Island, i., Ont. — F2 73
Peleliu, i., Palau — R17 52
Pelham, Ont. — D5 73
Pelham, Al., U.S. — B3 78
Pelham, Ga., U.S. — E2 87
Pelham, Ma., U.S. — B3 98
Pelham, N.H., U.S. — E4 106
Pelham, N.Y., U.S. — *h13 109
Pelham, N.C., U.S. — A3 110
Pelham, Tn., U.S. — D8 119
Pelham Manor, N.Y., U.S. — h13 109
Pelhřimov, Czech. — D3 26
Pelican, Ak., U.S. — m21 79
Pelican, La., U.S. — C2 95
Pelican, N.D., U.S. — A6 111
Pelican Bay, b., Man. — C1 70
Pelican Lake, Wi., U.S. — C4 126
Pelican Lake, l., Alta. — B4 68
Pelican Lake, l., Man. — C1 70
Pelican Lake, l., Sask. — B4 75
Pelican Lake, l., Mn., U.S. — D4 100
Pelican Lake, l., Mn., U.S. — E5 100
Pelican Lake, l., Mn., U.S. — B6 100
Pelican Lake, l., Mn., U.S. — D3 100
Pelican Lake, l., Wi., U.S. — C4 126
Pelican Mountain, mtn., Alta. — B4 68
Pelican Narrows, Sask. — C4 75
Pelican Rapids, Man. — C1 70
Pelican Rapids, Mn., U.S. — D2 100
Pélican, Lac de, res., Haiti — E8 64
Pelion, S.C., U.S. — D5 117
Pella, Ia., U.S. — C5 92
Pell City, Al., U.S. — B3 78
Pellice, stm., Italy — E3 20
Pell Lake, Wi., U.S. — n11 126
Pellston, Mi., U.S. — C6 99
Pellville, Ky., U.S. — C3 94
Pellworm, i., W. Ger. — A4 18
Pelly, Sask. — F5 75
Pelly, stm., Yukon — D6 66
Pelly Crossing, Yukon — D5 66
Pelly Lake, l., N.W. Ter. — C12 66
Pelly Mountains, mts., Yukon — D6 66
Peloncillo Mountains, mts., U.S. —
Peloponnesos, hist. reg., Grc. — D4 25
Pelotas, Braz. — E2 56
Pelotas, stm., Braz. — D2 56
Pel'ovo, Bul. — D7 24

Pelton, Lake, l., La., U.S. — E5 95
Pelusium, hist., Eg. — C4 41
Pelusium Bay, b., Eg. — C4 41
Pelzer, S.C., U.S. — B3 117
Pemadumcook Lake, l., Me., U.S. — C3 96
Pemalang, Indon. — *G3 34
Pemanggil, i., Malay. — K6 35
Pemaquid, Me., U.S. — E3 96
Pematangsiantar, Indon. — m11 34
Pemba, Moz. — D7 48
Pemba, Zam. — E4 48
Pemba, prov., Tan. — C6 48
Pemba, i., Tan. — C6 48
Pemberton, B.C. — D6 69
Pemberton, N.J., U.S. — D3 107
Pemberton, Oh., U.S. — B1 112
Pemberville, Oh., U.S. — A2 112
Pembina, N.D., U.S. — A8 111
Pembina, co., N.D., U.S. — A8 111
Pembina, stm., Alta. — C3 68
Pembina, stm., N.A. — E2 70
Pembina Mountains, mts., N.A. — A7 111
Pembine, Wi., U.S. — C6 126
Pembroke, Wales, U.K. — E4 10
Pembroke, Ga., U.S. — D5 87
Pembroke, Ky., U.S. — D2 94
Pembroke, Ma., U.S. — B6 98
Pembroke, N.Y., U.S. — B2 109
Pembroke, N.C., U.S. — C3 110
Pembroke, Va., U.S. — C2 123
Pembroke Park, Fl., U.S. — *G6 86
Pembroke Pines, Fl., U.S. — r13 86
Pembuang, stm., Indon. — F4 34
Pemigewasset, stm., N.H., U.S. — C3 106
Pemigewasset, East Branch, stm., N.H., U.S. — B3 106
Pemiscot, co., Mo., U.S. — E8 102
Pemmican Portage, Sask. — D4 75
Pemuco, Chile — B2 54
Pena Blanca, N.M., U.S. — B3 108
Penafiel, Port. — B1 22
Peñafiel, Spain — C3 22
Peñalara, mtn., Spain — B4 22
Penalosa, Ks., U.S. — E5 93
Penamacor, Port. — B2 22
Penápolis, Braz. — C2 56
Peñaranda de Bracamonte, Spain — B3 22
Pen Argyl, Pa., U.S. — E11 115
Peñarroya-Pueblonuevo, Spain — C3 22
Peñas, Cape, c., Spain — A3 22
Penas, Golfo de, b., Chile — D2 54
Penasco, N.M., U.S. — A4 108
Peñasco, Rio, stm., N.M., U.S. — E4 108
Penbrook, Pa., U.S. — F8 115
Pence, In., U.S. — D2 91
Pencer, Mn., U.S. — B3 100
Penck Trough, val., Ant. — B12 7
Pendembu, S.L. — E2 45
Pender, Ne., U.S. — B9 104
Pender, co., N.C., U.S. — C4 110
Pender Island, B.C. — g12 69
Pendergrass, Ga., U.S. — B3 87
Pendleton, In., U.S. — E6 91
Pendleton, Or., U.S. — B8 114
Pendleton, S.C., U.S. — B2 117
Pendleton, co., Ky., U.S. — B5 94
Pendleton, co., W.V., U.S. — C5 125
Pendley Hills, Ga., U.S. — h8 87
Pend Oreille, co., Wa., U.S. — A8 124
Pend Oreille, stm., N.A. — A8 124
Pend Oreille, Lake, l., Id., U.S. — A2 89
Pend Oreille, Mount, mtn., Id., U.S. — A2 89
Pendroy, Mt., U.S. — B4 103
Penedo, Braz. — D3 57
Penetanguishene, Ont. — C5 73
Peneus see Piniós, stm., Grc. — C4 40
Penfield, Ga., U.S. — C3 87
Penfield, Il., U.S. — C6 90
Penfield, N.Y., U.S. — *B3 109
Penfield, Pa., U.S. — D5 115
Peng'an, China — I2 32
Penganga, stm., India — H6 37
Penge, Zaire — C5 48
Pengibu, i., Indon. — L7 35
Penglai, China — F9 32
Pengshui, China — J3 32
Penguin Islands, is., Newf. — E3 72
Penha, Braz. — D3 56
Penhold, Alta. — C4 68
Penhook, Va., U.S. — D3 123
Peniche, Port. — C1 22
Penicuik, Scot., U.K. — E5 13
Peninsula, Oh., U.S. — A4 112
Peninsular Malaysia, hist. reg., Malay. — E2 34
Penitas, Tx., U.S. — F3 120
Penitente, Serra do, hills, Braz. — C1 57
Penitentiary Mountain, hill, Al., U.S. — A2 78
Pénjamo, Mex. — m13 63
Penn, Sask. — D2 75
Penn, N.D., U.S. — A6 111
Penn Acres, De., U.S. — *B3 85
Pennant Point, c., N.S. — E6 71
Pennant Station, Sask. — G1 75
Pennask Mountain, mtn., B.C. — E7 69
Penne, Italy — C4 23
Pennell, Mount, mtn., Ut., U.S. — F5 121
Pennellville, N.Y., U.S. — B4 109
Penner, stm., India — F6 36
Penneshaw, Austl. — G1 51
Penney Farms, Fl., U.S. — C5 86
Pennfield, N.B. — D3 71
Penn Hills, Pa., U.S. — k14 115
Penniac, N.B. — C3 71
Pennington, Al., U.S. — C1 78
Pennington, N.J., U.S. — C3 107
Pennington, co., Mn., U.S. — B2 100
Pennington, co., S.D., U.S. — D2 118
Pennington Gap, Va., U.S. — f8 123
Pennock, Mn., U.S. — E3 100
Pennsauken, N.J., U.S. — D2 107
Pennsboro, W.V., U.S. — B4 125
Pennsburg, Pa., U.S. — F11 115
Penns Grove, N.J., U.S. — D2 107
Pennsuco, Fl., U.S. — s13 86
Pennsville, N.J., U.S. — D1 107
Pennsville, Oh., U.S. — C4 112
Pennsylvania, state, U.S. — E7 115
Penn Valley, Pa., U.S. — o20 115
Pennville, In., U.S. — D7 91
Penny, Tx., U.S. — C5 120
Penn Yan, N.Y., U.S. — C3 109
Pennycutaway, stm., Man. — A5 70

Penobscot, Me., U.S. — D4 96
Penobscot, co., Me., U.S. — C4 96
Penobscot, stm., Me., U.S. — C4 96
Penobscot, East Branch, stm., Me., U.S. — C4 96
Penobscot, North Branch, stm., Me., U.S. — B2 96
Penobscot, West Branch, stm., Me., U.S. — C3 96
Penobscot Bay, b., Me., U.S. — D3 96
Penobscot Lake, l., Me., U.S. — C2 96
Penobsquis, N.B. — D4 71
Penokee, Ks., U.S. — C3 93
Penong, Austl. — F5 50
Penonomé, Pan. — F7 62
Penrhyn, Cape, c., N.W. Ter. — C16 66
Penrith, Austl. — *F9 50
Penrith, Eng., U.K. — E4 10
Pensacola, Fl., U.S. — u14 86
Pensacola, Ok., U.S. — A6 113
Pensacola Bay, b., Fl., U.S. — u14 86
Pensacola Dam, Ok., U.S. — A6 113
Pensacola Mountains, mts., Ant. — A6 7
Pensacola Naval Air Station, mil., Fl., U.S. — u14 86
Pensaukee, Wi., U.S. — D6 126
Pense, Sask. — G3 75
Pentagon Mountain, mtn., Mt., U.S. — C3 103
Pentecostes, Braz. — B3 57
Pentelicus see Pendéli, mtn., Grc. — g11 25
Penticton, B.C. — E8 69
Pentland Firth, strt., Scot., U.K. — A5 10
Pentland Hills, hills, Scot., U.K. — E5 13
Penton, N.J., U.S. — D2 107
Pentwater, Mi., U.S. — E4 99
Penwell, Tx., U.S. — D1 120
Penza, Sov. Un. — D7 29
Penzance, Sask. — F3 75
Penzance, Eng., U.K. — E4 10
Penzberg, W. Ger. — E5 18
Penzlin, E. Ger. — B7 15
Peoa, Ut., U.S. — C4 121
Peonan Point, c., Man. — D2 70
Peoples, Ky., U.S. — C5 94
Peoria, Az., U.S. — D3 80
Peoria, Il., U.S. — C4 90
Peoria, Oh., U.S. — B2 112
Peoria, co., Il., U.S. — C4 90
Peoria Heights, Il., U.S. — C4 90
Peotone, Il., U.S. — B6 90
Pepacton Reservoir, res., N.Y., U.S. — C6 109
Pepeekeo, Hi., U.S. — D6 88
Pepin, Wi., U.S. — D1 126
Pepin, co., Wi., U.S. — D2 126
Pepin, Lake, l., U.S. — D1 126
Pepper Creek, stm., De., U.S. — F5 85
Pepper Pike, Oh., U.S. — *h10 112
Peqin, Alb. — B2 25
Pequabuck, Ct., U.S. — C4 84
Pequannock, N.J., U.S. — B4 107
Pequeá, stm., Pan. — k12 62
Pequea, stm., Pa., U.S. — G9 115
Pequop Mountains, mts., Nv., U.S. — C7 105
Pequot Lakes, Mn., U.S. — D4 100
Perabumulih, Indon. — F2 34
Perak, state, Malay. — J4 35
Perak, stm., Malay. — J4 35
Perakhóra, Grc. — g9 25
Perales de Tajuña, Spain — p18 22
Peralta, N.M., U.S. — k7 108
Pérama, Grc. — h11 25
Percival, La., U.S. — C2 95
Percy, Il., U.S. — E4 90
Percy, N.H., U.S. — A4 106
Perdido, Al., U.S. — D2 78
Perdido, mtn., Spain — A6 22
Perdido, stm., U.S. — E2 78
Perdido Bay, b., Al., U.S. — E2 78
Perdizes, Braz. — B5 56
Perdue, Sask. — E2 75
Perea, N.M., U.S. — B1 108
Pereira, Col. — E4 60
Pereira Barreto, Braz. — C2 56
Perekop, Sov. Un. — H9 27
Père Marquette, stm., Mi., U.S. — E4 99
Peremennyy, Cape, c., Ant. — C23 7
Perené, stm., Peru — D3 58
Pereslavl-Zalesskiy, Sov. Un. — C12 27
Pereyaslav-Khmelnitskiy, Sov. Un. — F8 27
Pergamino, Arg. — A4 54
Pergine Valsugana, Italy — A3 23
Perham, Me., U.S. — B4 96
Perham, Mn., U.S. — D3 100
Péribonca, Que. — A5 74
Peridot, Az., U.S. — D5 80
Périgueux, Fr. — E4 16
Périjá, Sierra de, mts., S.A. — B3 60
Perim, i., Yemen — D4 38
Peristérion, Grc. — g11 25
Perito Moreno, Arg. — D2 54
Perkasie, Pa., U.S. — F11 115
Perkins, Que. — D2 74
Perkins, Ga., U.S. — D5 87
Perkins, Mi., U.S. — C3 99
Perkins, Ok., U.S. — B4 113
Perkins, co., Ne., U.S. — D4 104
Perkins, co., S.D., U.S. — B3 118
Perkinston, Ms., U.S. — E4 101
Perkinsville, Wi., U.S. — C3 126
Perkinsville, Vt., U.S. — E3 122
Perkiomen, stm., Pa., U.S. — F10 115
Perl-Mack, Co., U.S. — *B6 83
Perm, Sov. Un. — D9 29
Pérmet, Alb. — C2 25
Pernambuco, state, Braz. — C3 57
Pernell, Ok., U.S. — C4 113
Pernik, Bul. — D6 24
Péronne, Fr. — C5 16
Perote, Al., U.S. — D4 78
Perpignan, Fr. — F5 16
Perquimans, co., N.C., U.S. — A6 110
Perrin, Tx., U.S. — C3 120
Perrine, Fl., U.S. — G6 86
Perrineville, N.J., U.S. — C4 107

Perris, Ca., U.S. — F5 82
Perro, Laguna del, l., N.M., U.S. — C4 108
Perronville, Mi., U.S. — C3 99
Perros-Guirec, Fr. — C2 16
Perrot, Île, i., Que. — q19 74
Perry, Ar., U.S. — B3 81
Perry, Fl., U.S. — B3 86
Perry, Ga., U.S. — D3 87
Perry, Ia., U.S. — C3 92
Perry, Ks., U.S. — C8 93
Perry, La., U.S. — E3 95
Perry, Me., U.S. — D5 96
Perry, Mi., U.S. — F6 99
Perry, Mo., U.S. — B6 102
Perry, N.Y., U.S. — C2 109
Perry, Oh., U.S. — A4 112
Perry, Ok., U.S. — A4 113
Perry, Ut., U.S. — B3 121
Perry, co., Al., U.S. — C2 78
Perry, co., Ar., U.S. — C3 81
Perry, co., Il., U.S. — E4 90
Perry, co., In., U.S. — H4 91
Perry, co., Ky., U.S. — C6 94
Perry, co., Ms., U.S. — D4 101
Perry, co., Mo., U.S. — D8 102
Perry, co., Oh., U.S. — C3 112
Perry, co., Pa., U.S. — F7 115
Perry, co., Tn., U.S. — B4 119
Perry Hall, Md., U.S. — B5 97
Perry Heights, Oh., U.S. — *B4 112
Perry Lake, res., Ks., U.S. — C8 93
Perryman, Md., U.S. — B5 97
Perry Peak, mtn., Ma., U.S. — B1 98
Perry Point, Md., U.S. — A5 97
Perrysburg, N.Y., U.S. — C1 109
Perrysburg, Oh., U.S. — A2 112
Perrysburg Heights, Oh., U.S. — e6 112
Perry Stream, stm., N.H., U.S. — f7 106
Perry's Victory and International Peace Memorial, hist., Oh., U.S. — A2 112
Perrysville, In., U.S. — D3 91
Perrysville, Oh., U.S. — B3 112
Perrysville, Pa., U.S. — h13 115
Perryton, Tx., U.S. — A2 120
Perryvale, Alta. — B4 68
Perryville, Ak., U.S. — D8 79
Perryville, Ky., U.S. — C5 94
Perryville, La., U.S. — B4 95
Perryville, Md., U.S. — A5 97
Perryville, Mo., U.S. — D8 102
Perryville, R.I., U.S. — F3 116
Perryville, Tn., U.S. — B3 119
Persberg, Swe. — B7 15
Persepolis, hist., Iran — G6 39
Perseverance, Bol. — B3 55
Pershing, In., U.S. — E7 91
Pershing, Mo., U.S. — C6 102
Pershing, co., Nv., U.S. — C3 105
Persia, Ia., U.S. — C2 92
Persian Gulf, b., Asia — C5 38
Persimmon Grove, Ky., U.S. — k14 94
Person, co., N.C., U.S. — A3 110
Pertek, Tur. — C12 40
Perth, Austl. — F2 50
Perth, Ont. — C8 73
Perth, Scot., U.K. — B5 10
Perth, Ks., U.S. — E6 93
Perth, N.D., U.S. — A6 111
Perth, co., Ont. — D3 73
Perth Amboy, N.J., U.S. — B4 107
Perth-Andover, N.B. — B2 71
Perthshire, Ms., U.S. — B3 101
Pertuis, Fr. — F6 16
Peru, Il., U.S. — B4 90
Peru, In., U.S. — C5 91
Peru, Me., U.S. — D2 96
Peru, Ne., U.S. — D10 104
Peru, N.Y., U.S. — f11 109
Peru, Vt., U.S. — E3 122
Peru, ctry., S.A. — C2 58
Perugia, Italy — C4 23
Peruíbe, Braz. — C3 56
Peruque, Mo., U.S. — f12 102
Pervomaysk, Sov. Un. — q21 27
Pervomaysk, Sov. Un. — G8 27
Pervouralsk, Sov. Un. — D8 29
Pesaro, Italy — C4 23
Pescadero, Ca., U.S. — D2 82
Pescara, Italy — C5 23
Pescara, stm., Italy — C4 23
Peschanyy, Cape, c., Sov. Un. — G19 29
Peschanyy, Cape, c., Sov. Un. — B10 33
Peski, Sov. Un. — F14 27
Peski, Sov. Un. — n18 27
Peski, Sov. Un. — C7 28
Pesotum, Il., U.S. — C5 90
Pesqueira, Braz. — C3 57
Pessac, Fr. — E3 16
Petacas, Cerro, mtn., Col. — C2 60
Petal, Ms., U.S. — D4 101
Petaling Jaya, Malay. — K4 35
Petaluma, Ca., U.S. — C2 82
Petatlán, Mex. — D4 63
Petauke, Zam. — D5 48
Petawawa, Ont. — B7 73
Petén Itzá, Lago, l., Guat. — B3 62
Petenwell Lake, res., Wi., U.S. — D4 126
Peterborough, Austl. — F6 50
Peterborough, Eng., U.K. — D6 10
Peterborough, N.H., U.S. — E3 106
Peterborough, Ont. — C6 73
Peterborough, co., Ont. — C6 73
Peter Dana Point, Me., U.S. — C5 96
Peterhead, Scot., U.K. — B6 10
Peter I Island, i., Ant. — C3 7
Peterlee, Eng., U.K. — F7 13
Peter Lougheed Provincial Park, Alta. — D3 68
Peterman, Al., U.S. — D2 78

Petermann Ranges, mts., Austl. — E4 50
Peter Pond Lake, l., Sask. — m7 75
Petersburg, Ak., U.S. — D13 79
Petersburg, De., U.S. — D3 85
Petersburg, Il., U.S. — C4 90
Petersburg, In., U.S. — H3 91
Petersburg, Ky., U.S. — h13 94
Petersburg, Mi., U.S. — G7 99
Petersburg, Ne., U.S. — C7 104
Petersburg, N.J., U.S. — E3 107
Petersburg, N.Y., U.S. — C7 109
Petersburg, N.D., U.S. — A8 111
Petersburg, Oh., U.S. — B5 112
Petersburg, Pa., U.S. — E5 115
Petersburg, Tn., U.S. — B5 119
Petersburg, Tx., U.S. — C2 120
Petersburg, Va., U.S. — C5 123
Petersburg, W.V., U.S. — B5 125
Petersburg Naval Shipyard, mil., Pa., U.S. — P21 115
Petersdorf, W. Ger. — D5 15
Petersfield, Eng., U.K. — C7 12
Petersham, Ma., U.S. — B3 98
Peters Landing, Tn., U.S. — D4 125
Peterson, Al., U.S. — B2 78
Peterson, Ia., U.S. — B2 92
Peterson, Mn., U.S. — G7 100
Peterson, Ut., U.S. — B4 121
Peterson Field, mil., Co., U.S. — C6 83
Peterstown, W.V., U.S. — D4 125
Petersville, Ky., U.S. — B6 94
Peter the Great Bay, b., Sov. Un. — C11 31
Petilia Policastro, Italy — E6 23
Pétionville, Haiti — E7 64
Petit Bois Island, i., Ms., U.S. — E5 101
Petitcodiac, N.B. — D4 71
Petitcodiac, stm., N.B. — C5 71
Petit-de-Grat, N.S. — D9 71
Petite Amite, stm., La., U.S. — h10 95
Petite Rivière, N.S. — E5 71
Petite-Rivière-de-l'Artibonite, Haiti — E7 64
Petite-Rivière-de-l'Île, N.B. — B5 71
Petit-Étang, N.S. — C8 71
Petit-Goâve, Haiti — E7 64
Petit Jean, stm., Ar., U.S. — B2 81
Petit Jean Mountain, mtn., Ar., U.S. — C2 81
Petit Lac Des Allemands, l., La., U.S. — k11 95
Petit Lake, l., La., U.S. — k12 95
Petit-Mécatina, Île du, i., Que. — C2 72
Petit-Rocher, N.B. — B4 71
Petitsikapau Lake, l., Newf. — g8 72
Peto, Mex. — C7 63
Petorca, Chile — A2 54
Petoskey, Mi., U.S. — C6 99
Petra, hist., Jord. — D7 41
Petras, Mount, mtn., Ant. — B36 7
Petrey, Al., U.S. — D3 78
Petrich, Bul. — E6 24
Petrified Forest National Park, Az., U.S. — B6 80
Petrikov, Sov. Un. — E7 27
Petrila, Rom. — C6 24
Petrinja, Yugo. — C3 24
Petrodvorets, Sov. Un. — s30 19
Petrohué, Chile — C2 54
Petrokrepost, Sov. Un. — F2 50
Petrolândia, Braz. — C3 57
Petroleum, In., U.S. — C7 91
Petroleum, co., Mt., U.S. — C8 103
Petrolia, Ont. — E2 73
Petrolia, Il., U.S. — E6 90
Petrolia, Pa., U.S. — D2 115
Petrolia, Tx., U.S. — B3 120
Petrolina, Braz. — C3 57
Petropavlovsk, Sov. Un. — D9 29
Petropavlovsk-[Kamchatskiy], Sov. Un. — D18 29
Petrópolis, Braz. — C6 56
Petros, Tn., U.S. — C9 119
Petroşani, Rom. — C6 24
Petrovgrad see Zrenjanin, Yugo. — C5 24
Petrovsk, Sov. Un. — E15 27
Petrovsk-Zabaykalskiy, Sov. Un. — D13 29
Petrozavodsk, Sov. Un. — C6 29
Pettaquamscutt Lake Shores, R.I., U.S. — F4 116
Pettibone, N.D., U.S. — B6 111
Pettigo, Ire. — C4 11
Pettigrew, Ar., U.S. — B2 81
Pettingell Peak, mtn., Co., U.S. — B5 83
Pettis, co., Mo., U.S. — C4 102
Pettisville, Oh., U.S. — A1 112
Pettneu, Aus. — B9 19
Pettus, Tx., U.S. — E4 120
Petukhovo, Sov. Un. — D7 28
Pevek, Sov. Un. — C33 128
Pevely, Mo., U.S. — g13 102
Pewamo, Mi., U.S. — E6 99
Pewaukee, Wi., U.S. — *E5 126
Pewaukee Lake, l., Wi., U.S. — m11 126
Pewee Valley, Ky., U.S. — g11 94
Peyton, Co., U.S. — B6 83
Pézenas, Fr. — F5 16
Pezinok, Czech. — G17 19
Pfaffenhofen [an der Ilm], W. Ger. — D6 19
Pfäffikon, Switz. — B6 21
Pfarrkirchen, W. Ger. — D6 19
Pfeifer, Ks., U.S. — D4 93
Pforzheim, W. Ger. — D4 19
Pfunds, Aus. — C6 20
Pfungstadt, W. Ger. — D4 19
Phalodi, India — C5 36
Phaltan, India — C3 36
Phangan, i., Thai. — H4 35
Phangnga, Thai. — H3 35
Phanom Dongrak Range, mts., Asia — E5 35
Phan Rang, Viet. — C3 34
Phan Thiet, Viet. — C3 34
Pharaoh, Ok., U.S. — B5 113
Pharr, Tx., U.S. — F3 120
Pharsalus see Fársala, Grc. — C4 25
Phatthalung, Thai. — C3 35
Phayao, Thai. — B3 35
Pheba, Ms., U.S. — B5 101
Phelan, Ca., U.S. — E5 82
Phelps, Ky., U.S. — C7 94
Phelps, N.Y., U.S. — C3 109
Phelps, Wi., U.S. — B4 126
Phelps, co., Mo., U.S. — D5 102
Phelps, co., Ne., U.S. — D6 104
Phelps Lake, l., N.C., U.S. — B6 110
Phenix, Va., U.S. — C4 123
Phenix City, Al., U.S. — C4 78

Phetchabun, Thai. — B2 34
Phetchabun Range, mts., Thai. — E4 35
Phetchaburi, Thai. — C1 34
Phichit, Thai. — B2 35
Philadelphia, Il., U.S. — C4 90
Philadelphia, Ms., U.S. — C4 101
Philadelphia, Mo., U.S. — B6 102
Philadelphia, N.Y., U.S. — A5 109
Philadelphia, Pa., U.S. — G11 115
Philadelphia, Tn., U.S. — D9 119
Philadelphia, co., Pa., U.S. — G12 115
Philadelphia Naval Shipyard, mil., Pa., U.S. — P21 115
Phil Campbell, Al., U.S. — A2 78
Philip, S.D., U.S. — C3 118
Philipp, Ms., U.S. — B3 101
Philippeville see Skikda, Alg. — B6 44
Philippeville, Bel. — D4 17
Philippi, W.V., U.S. — B4 125
Philippi Glacier, ice, Ant. — C21 7
Philippines, ctry., Asia — C6 34
Philippine Sea — E7 6
Philipsburg, Que. — D4 74
Philipsburg, Mt., U.S. — D3 103
Philipsburg, Pa., U.S. — E5 115
Philipsville, Ont. — C8 73
Philleo Lake, l., Wa., U.S. — h14 124
Phillip Island, i., Austl. — I5 51
Phillippy, Tn., U.S. — A2 119
Phillips, Me., U.S. — D2 96
Phillips, Ne., U.S. — D7 104
Phillips, Ok., U.S. — C5 113
Phillips, Tx., U.S. — B2 120
Phillips, Wi., U.S. — C3 126
Phillips, co., Ar., U.S. — C5 81
Phillips, co., Co., U.S. — A8 83
Phillips, co., Ks., U.S. — C4 93
Phillips, co., Mt., U.S. — B8 103
Phillips Brook, stm., N.H., U.S. — A4 106
Phillipsburg, Ks., U.S. — C4 93
Phillipsburg, Mo., U.S. — D5 102
Phillipsburg, N.J., U.S. — B2 107
Phillipston, Ma., U.S. — A3 98
Philmont, N.Y., U.S. — C7 109
Philo, Il., U.S. — C5 90
Philo, Oh., U.S. — C4 112
Philomath, Ga., U.S. — C4 87
Philomath, Or., U.S. — C3 114
Philpott Reservoir, res., Va., U.S. — D2 123
Phippen, Sask. — E1 75
Phippsburg, Co., U.S. — A4 83
Phippsburg, Me., U.S. — g8 96
Phitsanulok, Thai. — B2 34
Phlorina see Flórina, Grc. — B3 25
Phlox, Wi., U.S. — C4 126
Phnum Penh (Phnom Penh), Camb. — C2 34
Phoenicia, N.Y., U.S. — C6 109
Phoenix, Az., U.S. — D3 80
Phoenix, Il., U.S. — k9 90
Phoenix, Md., U.S. — A4 97
Phoenix, Mi., U.S. — A2 99
Phoenix, N.Y., U.S. — B4 109
Phoenix, Or., U.S. — E4 114
Phoenix Islands, is., Kir. — G11 6
Phoenixville, Pa., U.S. — F10 115
Phong, stm., Thai. — D5 35
Phongsali, Laos — B3 34
Phrae, Thai. — B2 35
Phra Nakhon Si Ayutthaya, Thai. — E4 35
Phuket, Thai. — D1 34
Phuket, i., Thai. — I3 35
Phumi Samraong, Camb. — G5 35
Phu Quoc, i., Viet. — G5 35
Phu Tho, Viet. — B6 35
Phutthaisong, Thai. — E5 35
Piaanu Pass, strt., Micron. — Q18 52
Piacenza, Italy — B3 23
Pialba, Austl. — B9 51
Pianguan, China — D9 32
Pianosa, i., Italy — C3 23
Pianosa Island, i., Italy — C5 23
Piapot, Sask. — H1 75
Piaseczno, Pol. — m14 27
Piastów, Pol. — m13 26
Piatra-Neamț, Rom. — B8 24
Piatt, co., Il., U.S. — D5 90
Piauí, state, Braz. — C2 57
Piauí, stm., Braz. — C2 57
Piave, stm., Italy — A4 23
Piazza Armerina, Italy — F5 23
Pibor, stm., Afr. — D3 48
Pibor Post, Sud. — D3 17
Pibroch, Alta. — B4 68
Picabo, Id., U.S. — F4 89
Picacho, Az., U.S. — E4 80
Picacho, N.M., U.S. — D4 108
Picard, Que. — B8 74
Picardy, hist. reg., Fr. — C5 16
Picayune, Ms., U.S. — E4 101
Piccadilly, Newf. — D2 72
Piceance Creek, stm., Co., U.S. — B2 83
Pichanal, Arg. — D3 55
Picher, Ok., U.S. — A7 113
Pichilemu, Chile — A2 54
Pichincha, prov., Ec. — B2 58
Pickardville, Alta. — B4 68
Pickaway, co., Oh., U.S. — C2 112
Pick City, N.D., U.S. — B4 111
Pickens, Ar., U.S. — D4 81
Pickens, Ms., U.S. — C4 101
Pickens, Ok., U.S. — C6 113
Pickens, S.C., U.S. — B2 117
Pickens, W.V., U.S. — C4 125
Pickens, co., Al., U.S. — B1 78
Pickens, co., Ga., U.S. — B2 87
Pickens, co., S.C., U.S. — B2 117
Pickensville, Al., U.S. — B1 78
Pickerel, Ont. — B4 73
Pickerel, stm., Ont. — B4 73
Pickerel Lake, l., Wi., U.S. — D5 73
Pickering, Ont. — D5 73
Pickering, Eng., U.K. — D6 10
Pickering, Mo., U.S. — A3 102
Pickerington, Oh., U.S. — C3 112
Pickett, co., Tn., U.S. — C8 119
Pickford, Mi., U.S. — B6 99
Pickrell, Ne., U.S. — D9 104
Pickstown, S.D., U.S. — E7 118
Pickwick Dam, Tn., U.S. — B3 119
Pickwick Lake, res., U.S. — A6 101
Pickworth Point, c., Ma., U.S. — f12 98
Pico, i., Port. — g8 44
Pico, Ponta do, mtn., Port. — *g8 44
Pico Rivera, Ca., U.S. — n12 82
Picos, Braz. — C2 57
Picton, Ont. — D7 73
Picton, N.Z. — N14 51
Pictou, N.S. — D7 71

Name	Map Ref.	Page

Pictou, co., N.S. — D7 71
Pictou Island, i., N.S. — D7 71
Pictou Landing, N.S. — D7 71
Picture Butte, Alta. — E4 68
Pictured Rocks National Lakeshore, Mi., U.S. — B4 99
Picture Rocks, Pa., U.S. — D8 115
Picuí, Braz. — h5 57
Picún Leufú, Arg. — B3 54
Pidálion, Akrotírion, c., Cyp. — E10 40
Pidurutalagala, mtn., Sri L. — G7 36
Piedade, Braz. — m8 56
Piedal, stm., Mex. — h9 63
Piedmont, Que. — D3 74
Piedmont, Al., U.S. — B4 78
Piedmont, Ca., U.S. — h8 82
Piedmont, Ks., U.S. — E7 93
Piedmont, Mo., U.S. — D7 102
Piedmont, Ok., U.S. — B4 113
Piedmont, S.C., U.S. — B3 117
Piedmont, S.D., U.S. — C2 118
Piedmont, W.V., U.S. — B5 125
Piedmont (Piemonte), prov., Italy — B1 23
Piedmont Lake, res., Oh., U.S. — B4 112
Piedra, Ca., U.S. — D4 82
Piedra, stm., Co., U.S. — D3 83
Piedrabuena, Spain — C3 22
Piedras, stm., Pan. — k12 62
Piedras, stm., Pan. — k11 62
Piedras, Punta, c., Arg. — B5 54
Piedras, Punta, c., Ven. — A5 60
Piedras Blancas, Point, c., Ca., U.S. — E3 82
Piedras Negras, Guat. — D6 63
Piedras Negras, Mex. — B4 63
Piedra Sola, Ur. — E1 56
Piekary Śląskie, Pol. — g9 26
Pieksämäki, Fin. — F12 14
Pielinen, l., Fin. — F13 14
Piemonte, prov., Italy — D3 20
Piendamó, Col. — C2 60
Pierce, Co., U.S. — A6 83
Pierce, Fl., U.S. — E5 86
Pierce, Id., U.S. — C3 89
Pierce, Ne., U.S. — B8 104
Pierce, Tn., U.S. — A3 119
Pierce, co., Ga., U.S. — E4 87
Pierce, co., Ne., U.S. — B8 104
Pierce, co., N.D., U.S. — A5 111
Pierce, co., Wa., U.S. — C3 124
Pierce, co., Wi., U.S. — D1 126
Pierce, Lake, l., Fl., U.S. — E5 86
Pierce City, Mo., U.S. — E3 102
Piercefield, N.Y., U.S. — A6 109
Pierce Lake, l., Can. — B5 70
Pierce Pond, l., Me., U.S. — C2 96
Pierces Point, N.J., U.S. — E3 107
Pierceton, In., U.S. — B6 91
Pierceville, In., U.S. — F7 91
Pierceville, Ks., U.S. — E3 93
Piercy, Ca., U.S. — C2 82
Piermont, N.H., U.S. — C2 106
Pierowall, Scot., U.K. — A6 13
Pierpont, Oh., U.S. — A5 112
Pierpont, S.D., U.S. — B8 118
Pierre, S.D., U.S. — C5 118
Pierre, Bayou, stm., Ms., U.S. — D3 101
Pierrefitte, Fr. — g10 16
Pierrefitte-sur-Aire, Fr. — F5 17
Pierrefonds, Que. — q19 74
Pierre Part, La., U.S. — k9 95
Pierreville, Que. — C5 74
Pierron, Il., U.S. — E4 90
Pierson, Man. — E1 70
Pierson, Fl., U.S. — C5 86
Pierson, Ia., U.S. — B2 92
Pierz, Mn., U.S. — E4 100
Piešťany, Czech. — D4 26
Pietermaritzburg, S. Afr. — C5 49
Pietersburg, S. Afr. — B4 49
Pie Town, N.M., U.S. — C1 108
Pietrasanta, Italy — C3 23
Piet Retief, S. Afr. — C5 49
Pietrosu, mtn., Rom. — B7 24
Pietrosul, mtn., Rom. — B7 24
Pieve di Cadore, Italy — A4 23
Pigeon, Mi., U.S. — E7 99
Pigeon, stm., Man. — C3 70
Pigeon, stm., U.S. — f9 110
Pigeon, stm., In., U.S. — A6 91
Pigeon, stm., Mn., U.S. — h10 100
Pigeon, stm., Wi., U.S. — k10 126
Pigeon Bay, b., Man. — C3 70
Pigeon Cove, Ma., U.S. — A6 98
Pigeon Creek, stm., Al., U.S. — D3 78
Pigeon Creek, stm., In., U.S. — H3 91
Pigeon Falls, Wi., U.S. — D2 126
Pigeon Forge, Tn., U.S. — D10 119
Pigeon Lake, l., Alta. — C3 68
Pigeon Mountain, mtn., U.S. — B1 87
Pigeon Point, c., Mn., U.S. — h10 100
Pigg, stm., Va., U.S. — D3 123
Piggott, Ar., U.S. — A5 81
Pigüé, Arg. — B4 54
Piiraí, i., Marsh Is. — S18 52
Pijijiapan, Mex. — D6 63
Pike, N.H., U.S. — B2 106
Pike, co., Al., U.S. — D4 78
Pike, co., Ar., U.S. — C2 81
Pike, co., Ga., U.S. — C2 87
Pike, co., Il., U.S. — D2 90
Pike, co., In., U.S. — H3 91
Pike, co., Ky., U.S. — C7 94
Pike, co., Ms., U.S. — D3 101
Pike, co., Mo., U.S. — B6 102
Pike, co., Oh., U.S. — C2 112
Pike, co., Pa., U.S. — D11 115
Pike, stm., Wi., U.S. — C6 126
Pike City, Ar., U.S. — C2 81
Pike Island Dam, U.S. — f8 125
Pike Lake, Mn., U.S. — D6 100
Pike Road, N.C., U.S. — B6 110
Pikes Peak, mtn., Co., U.S. — C5 83
Pikes Rocks, mtn., Pa., U.S. — C3 115
Pikesville, Md., U.S. — B4 97
Piketberg, S. Afr. — D2 49
Piketon, Oh., U.S. — C2 112
Pikeville, Ky., U.S. — C7 94
Pikeville, N.C., U.S. — B5 110
Pikeville, Tn., U.S. — D8 119
Pikou, China — E10 32
Pikwitonei, Man. — B3 70
Piła, Pol. — B4 26
Pilar, Braz. — C3 57
Pilar, Para. — E4 55
Pilar, N.M., U.S. — A4 108
Pilar de Goiás, Braz. — A3 56
Pilar do Sul, Braz. — m8 56
Pilatus, mtn., Switz. — C4 20
Pilcomayo, stm., S.A. — D4 55
Pilger, Sask. — E3 75
Pilger, Ne., U.S. — B8 104
Pilgrams Knob, Va., U.S. — e10 123

Pilgrim, Ky., U.S. — C7 94
Pilibhit, India — C7 37
Pilica, stm., Pol. — C5 26
Pillaro, Ec. — B2 58
Pillager, Mn., U.S. — D4 100
Pillar Point, c., Ca., U.S. — k7 82
Pilley's Island, Newf. — D4 72
Pillow, Pa., U.S. — E6 115
Pillsbury, N.D., U.S. — B8 111
Pilos, Grc. — D3 25
Pilot Butte, Sask. — G3 75
Pilot Grove, Mo., U.S. — C5 102
Pilot Knob, Mo., U.S. — D7 102
Pilot Knob, mtn., Ar., U.S. — B2 81
Pilot Knob, mtn., Id., U.S. — C1 81
Pilot Knob, mtn., Id., U.S. — D3 89
Pilot Mound, Man. — E2 70
Pilot Mound, Ia., U.S. — B3 92
Pilot Mountain, N.C., U.S. — A2 110
Pilot Peak, mtn., Nv., U.S. — B7 105
Pilot Peak, mtn., Nv., U.S. — E4 105
Pilot Peak, mtn., Wy., U.S. — B3 127
Pilot Point, Ak., U.S. — D8 79
Pilot Point, Tx., U.S. — C4 120
Pilot Range, mts., Nv., U.S. — B7 105
Pilot Range, mts., N.H., U.S. — A4 106
Pilot Rock, Or., U.S. — B7 114
Pilot Station, Ak., U.S. — C7 79
Pilottown, La., U.S. — E6 95
Pilsen, Wi., U.S. — h10 126
Pilvo, Sov. Un. — A11 33
Pima, Az., U.S. — E6 80
Pima, co., Az., U.S. — E3 80
Pimmit Hills, Va., U.S. — g12 123
Pimpri-Chinchwad, India — *E5 36
Piña, Pan. — k10 62
Pinal, co., Az., U.S. — E4 80
Pinaleno Mountains, mts., Az., U.S. — E5 80
Pinal Mountains, mts., Az., U.S. — D5 80
Pinang see George Town, Malay. — D2 34
Pinang, state, Malay. — J4 35
Pinang, i., Malay. — D2 34
Pinarbaşı, Tur. — C11 40
Pinar del Río, Cuba — C2 64
Pinar del Río, prov., Cuba — C2 64
Pinardville, N.H., U.S. — E3 106
Pinás, Arg. — A3 54
Pinatubo, Mount, mtn., Phil. — o13 34
Pinawa, Man. — D4 70
Pincher Creek, Alta. — E4 68
Pincher Station, Alta. — E4 68
Pinckard, Al., U.S. — D4 78
Pinckney, Mi., U.S. — F7 99
Pinckney Island, i., S.C., U.S. — G6 117
Pinckneyville, Il., U.S. — E4 90
Pinconning, Mi., U.S. — E7 99
Pińczów, Pol. — C6 26
Pindall, Ar., U.S. — A3 81
Pindamonhangaba, Braz. — C3 56
Pindaré, stm., Braz. — B1 57
Pindiga, Nig. — *E7 44
Pindus Mountains, mts., Grc. — C3 40
Pine, Az., U.S. — C4 80
Pine, Co., U.S. — B5 83
Pine, co., Mn., U.S. — D5 100
Pine, stm., B.C. — B6 69
Pine, stm., Man. — D1 70
Pine, stm., Mi., U.S. — D7 99
Pine, stm., Mi., U.S. — D5 99
Pine, stm., N.H., U.S. — C4 106
Pine, stm., Wi., U.S. — C5 126
Pine, stm., Wi., U.S. — C4 126
Pine Apple, Al., U.S. — D3 78
Pine Bank, Pa., U.S. — G1 115
Pine Barrens, reg., N.J., U.S. — D3 107
Pine Bluff, Ar., U.S. — C3 81
Pinebluff, N.C., U.S. — B3 110
Pine Bluffs, Wy., U.S. — E8 127
Pine Bridge, Ct., U.S. — D3 84
Pinebur, Ms., U.S. — D4 101
Pine Bush, N.Y., U.S. — D6 109
Pine Castle, Fl., U.S. — D5 86
Pine City, Mn., U.S. — E6 100
Pine City, Wa., U.S. — B8 124
Pine Creek, Austl. — B5 50
Pine Creek, stm., Nv., U.S. — C5 105
Pine Creek, stm., Pa., U.S. — C6 115
Pine Creek, stm., Wa., U.S. — B8 124
Pine Creek Lake, res., Ok., U.S. — C6 113
Pinecrest, Ca., U.S. — C4 82
Pinedale, Al., U.S. — C3 78
Pinedale, Az., U.S. — C5 80
Pinedale, Wy., U.S. — D3 127
Pine Falls, Man. — D3 70
Pine Forest Range, mts., Nv., U.S. — B3 105
Pine Grove, Ga., U.S. — E4 87
Pine Grove, La., U.S. — D5 95
Pine Grove, N.J., U.S. — D3 107
Pine Grove, Pa., U.S. — E9 115
Pine Grove, W.V., U.S. — B4 125
Pine Grove Mills, Pa., U.S. — E6 115
Pine Hall, N.C., U.S. — A2 110
Pine Hill, Austl. — A6 51
Pine Hill, Al., U.S. — D2 78
Pine Hill, Ky., U.S. — C5 94
Pine Hill, N.J., U.S. — D3 107
Pine Hills, Fl., U.S. — D5 86
Pine Island, Mn., U.S. — F6 100
Pine Island, N.Y., U.S. — D6 109
Pine Island, i., Fl., U.S. — F4 86
Pine Island Bay, b., Ant. — B2 7
Pine Island Sound, strt., Fl., U.S. — F4 86
Pine Key, i., Fl., U.S. — p10 86
Pine Knot, Ky., U.S. — D5 94
Pine Lake, Ga., U.S. — h8 87
Pine Lake, l., Ga., U.S. — g10 98
Pine Lake, l., In., U.S. — A4 91
Pine Lake, l., Wi., U.S. — C5 126
Pineland, S.C., U.S. — F5 117
Pine Lawn, Mo., U.S. — f13 102
Pine Level, N.C., U.S. — B4 110
Pine Level, Al., U.S. — C3 78
Pinellas, co., Fl., U.S. — E4 86
Pinellas Point, c., Fl., U.S. — p10 86
Pinellas Park, Fl., U.S. — E4 86
Pine Meadow, Ct., U.S. — B4 84
Pine Mountain, Ga., U.S. — D2 87
Pine Mountain, mtn., U.S. — D6 94

Pine Mountain, mtn., Ct., U.S. — B4 84
Pine Mountain, mtn., Ga., U.S. — D2 87
Pine Mountain, mtn., Tn., U.S. — C9 119
Pine Mountain, mtn., Or., U.S. — E3 127
Pine Mountain, hills, Ok., U.S. — C6 113
Pineora, Ga., U.S. — D5 87
Pine Orchard, Ct., U.S. — D4 84
Pine Park, Ga., U.S. — F2 87
Pine Plains, N.Y., U.S. — D7 109
Pine Point, N.W. Ter. — D10 66
Pine Point, Me., U.S. — E2 96
Pine Prairie, La., U.S. — D3 95
Piner Bay, b., Ant. — C27 7
Pine Rest, Ma., U.S. — g10 98
Pine Ridge, Ar., U.S. — C2 81
Pine Ridge, Ms., U.S. — D2 101
Pine Ridge, S.D., U.S. — D3 118
Pine Ridge, mtn., Ne., U.S. — B2 104
Pine Ridge Indian Reservation, S.D., U.S. — D3 118
Pine River, Man. — D1 70
Pine River, Mn., U.S. — D4 100
Pinerolo, Italy — B1 23
Pines, Isle of see Juventud, Isla de la, i., Cuba — D2 64
Pines, Lake o' the, res., Tx., U.S. — C5 120
Pinesdale, Mt., U.S. — D2 103
Pine Stump Junction, Mi., U.S. — B5 99
Pine Swamp Knob, mtn., W.V., U.S. — B5 125
Pinetops, N.C., U.S. — B5 110
Pinetown, N.C., U.S. — B6 110
Pine Tree Corners, De., U.S. — C3 85
Pinetta, Fl., U.S. — B3 86
Pine Valley, Ca., U.S. — F5 82
Pine Valley, N.H., U.S. — E3 106
Pine Valley, Ut., U.S. — F2 121
Pine Valley, val., Ut., U.S. — E2 121
Pine Valley Mountains, mts., Ut., U.S. — F2 121
Pineview, Ga., U.S. — D3 87
Pine Village, In., U.S. — D3 91
Pineville, Ky., U.S. — D6 94
Pineville, La., U.S. — C3 95
Pineville, Mo., U.S. — E3 102
Pineville, N.C., U.S. — B2 110
Pineville, W.V., U.S. — D3 125
Pinewald, N.J., U.S. — D4 107
Pinewood, Fl., U.S. — s13 86
Pinewood, Mn., U.S. — C3 100
Pinewood, S.C., U.S. — D7 117
Pinewood Park, Fl., U.S. — *G6 86
Piney, Man. — E4 70
Piney Creek, stm., W.V., U.S. — n13 125
Piney Flats, Tn., U.S. — C11 119
Piney Fork, Oh., U.S. — B5 112
Piney Fork, stm., W.V., U.S. — h9 125
Piney Point, Md., U.S. — D4 97
Piney View, W.V., U.S. — n13 125
Piney Woods, Ms., U.S. — C3 101
Ping, stm., Thai. — B1 34
Pingding, China — F5 32
Pingdingshan, China — D8 31
Pingdu, China — D5 32
Pingjiang, China — J5 32
Pingle, China — G7 31
Pingli, China — D6 31
Pingliang, China — E2 32
Pingnan, China — G7 31
Pingquan, China — D8 32
Pingree, Id., U.S. — F6 89
Pingree, N.D., U.S. — B7 111
Pingwu, China — E5 31
Pingxiang, China — F7 31
Pingxiang, China — G6 31
Pinhal, Braz. — C3 56
Pinhal Novo, Port. — f10 22
Pinheiro, Braz. — B1 57
Pinhel, Port. — B2 22
Pini, i., Indon. — D6 34
Piniós (Peneus), stm., Grc. — C4 40
Pink Cliffs, clf., Ut., U.S. — F3 121
Pinkham Notch, N.H., U.S. — B4 106
Pink Hill, N.C., U.S. — B5 110
Pinkstaff, Il., U.S. — E6 90
Pinnacle, Ar., U.S. — C3 81
Pinnacle, N.C., U.S. — A2 110
Pinnacle, mtn., N.Y., U.S. — B6 109
Pinnacle Buttes, mtn., Wy., U.S. — C3 127
Pinnacles National Monument, Ca., U.S. — D3 82
Pinnaroo, Austl. — G3 51
Pinneberg, W. Ger. — B5 18
Pinnebog, Mi., U.S. — E7 99
Pinola, Ms., U.S. — D4 101
Pinole, Ca., U.S. — h8 82
Pinon, Fr. — E3 17
Pinon, Az., U.S. — A5 80
Pinon, N.M., U.S. — E4 108
Pinopolis, S.C., U.S. — E7 117
Pinopolis Dam, S.C., U.S. — E8 117
Pinos, Mex. — C4 63
Pinos, Mount, mtn., Ca., U.S. — E4 82
Pinos, Point, c., Ca., U.S. — D2 82
Pinos Altos, N.M., U.S. — E1 108
Pinoso, Spain — C5 22
Pinos-Puente, Spain — B2 22
Pins, Pointe aux, c., Ont. — E3 73
Pinsk, Sov. Un. — E6 27
Pinsk Marshes, sw., Sov. Un. — E6 27
Pinson, Al., U.S. — f7 78
Pinson, Tn., U.S. — B3 119
Pinta, Isla, i., Ec. — f5 58
Pinta, Sierra, mts., Az., U.S. — E2 80
Pintados, Chile — D2 55
Pinto, Spain — p17 22
Pinto, Md., U.S. — k13 97
Pinto Butte, mtn., Sask. — H2 75
Pinto Creek, stm., Sask. — H2 75
Pintura, Braz. — F2 121

Piove di Sacco, Italy — D8 20
Pipe, Wi., U.S. — k9 126
Pipe Creek, stm., In., U.S. — D6 91
Piper, Ks., U.S. — k16 93
Piper City, Il., U.S. — C5 90
Pipéri, i., Grc. — C5 25
Piperville, Ont. — h12 73
Pipe Spring National Monument, Az., U.S. — A3 80
Pipestem, W.V., U.S. — D4 125
Pipestem Creek, stm., N.D., U.S. — B6 111
Pipestone, Man. — E1 70
Pipestone, Mn., U.S. — G2 100
Pipestone, co., Mn., U.S. — F2 100
Pipestone Creek, stm., Can. — E1 70
Pipestone National Monument, Mn., U.S. — G2 100
Pipestone Pass, Mt., U.S. — E4 103
Pipinas, Arg. — B5 54
Pipmuacan, Réservoir, res., Que. — k12 74
Piqua, Ks., U.S. — E8 93
Piqua, Oh., U.S. — B1 112
Piquiri, stm., Braz. — C2 56
Plácido de Castro, Braz. — D4 58
Piracanjuba, Braz. — B3 56
Piracicaba, Braz. — G6 56
Piracicaba, stm., Braz. — m8 56
Piracuruca, Braz. — B2 57
Piraeus see Piraiévs, Grc. — D4 40
Piraiévs (Piraeus), Grc. — D4 40
Piraju, Braz. — C3 56
Pirajuí, Braz. — B3 56
Piramida, Mount, mtn., Sov. Un. — D12 29
Piran, Yugo. — C1 24
Pirané, Arg. — E4 55
Piranhas, Braz. — C3 57
Piranhas, stm., Braz. — C3 57
Pirapora, Braz. — B4 56
Pirassununga, Braz. — C3 56
Piratini, Braz. — E2 56
Piratininga, Braz. — C3 56
Pírgos, Grc. — D3 40
Piriápolis, Ur. — E1 56
Pirin Mountains, mts., Bul. — E6 24
Piripiri, Braz. — B2 57
Pirmasens, W. Ger. — D3 18
Pirna, E. Ger. — C6 18
Pirot, Yugo. — D6 24
Pirovskoye, Sov. Un. — D27 3
Pirtleville, Az., U.S. — F6 80
Piryatin, Sov. Un. — F9 27
Piru, Indon. — F7 34
Pisa, Italy — C3 23
Pisac, hist., Peru — D3 58
Pisagua, Chile — C1 55
Piscataqua, stm., N.H., U.S. — D5 106
Piscataquis, co., Me., U.S. — C3 96
Piscataquis, stm., Me., U.S. — C3 96
Piscataquog, stm., N.H., U.S. — D3 106
Piscataway, N.J., U.S. — B4 107
Piscataway Creek, stm., Md., U.S. — C4 97
Pisciotta, Italy — D5 23
Pisco, Peru — D2 58
Piseco Lake, l., N.Y., U.S. — B6 109
Písek, Czech. — D3 26
Pisek, N.D., U.S. — A8 111
Pisgah, Al., U.S. — A4 78
Pisgah, Ia., U.S. — C2 92
Pisgah, Md., U.S. — C3 97
Pisgah, Oh., U.S. — n13 112
Pisgah, Mount, mtn., Ct., U.S. — B3 84
Pisgah, Mount, mtn., Vt., U.S. — B5 122
Pisgah, Mount, mtn., Wy., U.S. — C3 127
Pisgah Forest, N.C., U.S. — f10 110
Pishin, Pak. — B4 36
Pishin Lora, stm., Asia — C4 36
Pisinemo, Az., U.S. — E3 80
Pismo Beach, Ca., U.S. — E3 82
Pissis, Monte, mtn., Arg. — E2 55
Pisticci, Italy — D6 23
Pistoia, Italy — C3 23
Pistol River, Or., U.S. — E2 114
Pisuerga, stm., Spain — A3 22
Pisz, Pol. — B6 26
Pit, stm., Ca., U.S. — B3 82
Pita, Gui. — C2 45
Pital, Col. — *C3 62? C2 60
Pital, Cerro el, mtn., N.A. — *C3 62
Pitanga, Braz. — C2 56
Pitangui, Braz. — E6 56
Pitcairn, Pa., U.S. — k14 115
Pitcairn, dep., Oc. — H14 6
Pitcher Hill, N.Y., U.S. — *B4 109
Piteå, Swe. — E9 14
Piteälven, stm., Swe. — D9 14
Piteşti, Rom. — C7 24
Pithiviers, Fr. — C5 16
Piti, Guam — L9 52
Pitkin, La., U.S. — D3 95
Pitkin, co., Co., U.S. — B4 83
Pitlochry, Scot., U.K. — B5 13
Pitman, N.J., U.S. — D2 107
Pitsburg, Oh., U.S. — C1 112
Pitt, Mn., U.S. — B4 100
Pitt, co., N.C., U.S. — B5 110
Pitt Island, i., B.C. — C3 69
Pittman Center, Tn., U.S. — D10 119
Pittsboro, In., U.S. — E5 91
Pittsboro, Ms., U.S. — B4 101
Pittsboro, N.C., U.S. — B3 110
Pittsburg, Ca., U.S. — g9 82
Pittsburg, Ks., U.S. — E9 93
Pittsburg, Ok., U.S. — C6 113
Pittsburg, Tx., U.S. — C5 120
Pittsburg, co., Ok., U.S. — C6 113
Pittsburg, Pa., U.S. — F1 115
Pittsfield, Il., U.S. — D3 90
Pittsfield, Ma., U.S. — B1 98
Pittsfield, N.H., U.S. — D4 106
Pittsfield, Me., U.S. — D3 96
Pittsfield, Vt., U.S. — D2 122
Pittsford, Mi., U.S. — G6 99
Pittsford, Vt., U.S. — D2 122
Pittston, Pa., U.S. — D10 115
Pittsview, Al., U.S. — C4 78
Pittsville, Md., U.S. — D7 97
Pittsville, Wi., U.S. — D3 126

Pittsylvania, co., Va., U.S. — D3 123
Piui, Braz. — C3 56
Piura, Peru — C1 58
Piura, dept., Peru — C1 58
Piute Peak, mtn., Ca., U.S. — E4 82
Piute Reservoir, res., Ut., U.S. — E3 121
Piuthan, Nepal — C9 37
Piva, stm., Yugo. — D4 24
Pixley, Ca., U.S. — E4 82
Pizzo, Italy — E6 23
P. K. le Roux Dam, res., S. Afr. — D3 49
Placentia, Newf. — E5 72
Placentia, Ca., U.S. — n13 82
Placentia Bay, b., Newf. — *E4 72
Placer, co., Ca., U.S. — C3 82
Placerville, Ca., U.S. — C3 82
Placerville, Co., U.S. — C3 83
Placetas, Cuba — C4 64
Placid, Lake, l., Fl., U.S. — E5 86
Placid, Lake, l., N.Y., U.S. — f11 109
Placida, Fl., U.S. — F4 86
Plácido de Castro, Braz. — D4 58
Placitas, N.M., U.S. — B3 108
Plaffeien, Switz. — C3 21
Plain, Wi., U.S. — E3 126
Plain City, Oh., U.S. — B2 112
Plain City, Ut., U.S. — B3 121
Plain Dealing, La., U.S. — B2 95
Plainedge, N.Y., U.S. — *E7 109
Plainfield, Ct., U.S. — C8 84
Plainfield, Il., U.S. — B5 90
Plainfield, In., U.S. — E5 91
Plainfield, Ma., U.S. — A2 98
Plainfield, N.H., U.S. — C2 106
Plainfield, N.J., U.S. — B4 107
Plainfield, Oh., U.S. — B3 112
Plainfield, Vt., U.S. — C4 122
Plainfield, Wi., U.S. — D4 126
Plainfield Heights, Mi., U.S. — E5 99
Plains, Ga., U.S. — D2 87
Plains, Ks., U.S. — E3 93
Plains, Mt., U.S. — C2 103
Plains, Pa., U.S. — n17 115
Plains, Tx., U.S. — C1 120
Plainsboro, N.J., U.S. — C3 107
Plainview, Ar., U.S. — C2 81
Plainview, Mn., U.S. — F6 100
Plainview, Ne., U.S. — B8 104
Plainview, N.Y., U.S. — *E7 109
Plainview, Tx., U.S. — B2 120
Plainville, Ct., U.S. — C4 84
Plainville, In., U.S. — G3 91
Plainville, Ks., U.S. — C4 93
Plainville, Ma., U.S. — B5 98
Plainwell, Mi., U.S. — F5 99
Plaisance, Que. — D2 74
Plaisance, Haiti — E7 64
Plaisance, Baie de b., Que. — B8 71
Plaisance-du-Gers, Fr. — F4 16
Plaisted, Me., U.S. — A4 96
Plaistow, N.H., U.S. — E4 106
Plamondon, Alta. — B4 68
Planá, Czech. — D7 19
Planalto, Braz. — B3 56
Plankinton, S.D., U.S. — D7 118
Plano, Il., U.S. — B5 90
Plano, Ia., U.S. — D4 92
Plano, Tx., U.S. — D12 103? C4 120
Plantagenet, Ont. — B9 73
Plantation, Fl., U.S. — r13 86
Plant City, Fl., U.S. — D4 86
Plantersville, Ms., U.S. — A5 101
Plantersville, S.C., U.S. — D9 117
Plantsite, Az., U.S. — D6 80
Plantsville, Ct., U.S. — C4 84
Plaquemine, La., U.S. — D4 95
Plaquemines, co., La., U.S. — E6 95
Plasencia, Spain — B2 22
Plaster Rock, N.B. — C2 71
Plastun, Sov. Un. — D8 33
Plasy, Czech. — D2 19
Plata, Río de la, est., S.A. — B5 54
Plateau, N.S. — C8 71
Plateau City, Co., U.S. — B3 83
Plateau Creek, stm., Co., U.S. — B3 83
Plate Cove West, Newf. — D5 72
Platina, Ca., U.S. — B2 82
Platinum, Ak., U.S. — D7 79
Platner, Co., U.S. — A7 83
Plato, Col. — B5 60
Plato, Mo., U.S. — D5 102
Plato Sánchez, Mex. — m14 63
Platte, S.D., U.S. — D7 118
Platte, co., Mo., U.S. — B3 102
Platte, co., Ne., U.S. — C8 104
Platte, co., Wy., U.S. — D7 127
Platte, stm., U.S. — B3 102
Platte, stm., Ne., U.S. — D6 104
Platte, stm., Mi., U.S. — D4 99
Platte Center, Ne., U.S. — C8 104
Platte City, Mo., U.S. — B3 102
Platteville, Co., U.S. — A6 83
Platteville, Wi., U.S. — F3 126
Plattling, W. Ger. — E7 19
Plattsburg, Mo., U.S. — B3 102
Plattsburgh, N.Y., U.S. — f11 109
Plattsburgh Air Force Base, mil., N.Y., U.S. — f11 109
Plattsmouth, Ne., U.S. — D10 104
Plauchville, La., U.S. — D3 95
Plauen, E. Ger. — C6 18
Play Cu, Viet. — H9 35
Playgreen Lake, l., Man. — B2 70
Playas Lake, l., N.M., U.S. — F1 108
Plaza, N.D., U.S. — A4 111
Pleasant, Lake, res., Az., U.S. — D3 80
Pleasant, Mount, mtn., Va., U.S. — C3 123
Pleasant Bay, N.S. — C9 71
Pleasant City, Oh., U.S. — C4 112
Pleasantdale, Sask. — E3 75
Pleasant Dale, Ne., U.S. — D9 104
Pleasant Garden, N.C., U.S. — B3 110
Pleasant Grove, Al., U.S. — g7 78

Pleasant Grove, Ms., U.S. — A3 101
Pleasant Grove, Ut., U.S. — C4 121
Pleasant Hill, Al., U.S. — C3 78
Pleasant Hill, Ca., U.S. — h8 82
Pleasant Hill, Il., U.S. — D3 90
Pleasant Hill, Ia., U.S. — e8 92
Pleasant Hill, La., U.S. — C2 95
Pleasant Hill, Me., U.S. — g7 96
Pleasant Hill, Mo., U.S. — C3 102
Pleasant Hill, Ms., U.S. — A4 101
Pleasant Hill, Oh., U.S. — B1 112
Pleasant Hill, Ok., U.S. — D7 113
Pleasant Hill, S.C., U.S. — B6 117
Pleasant Hills, Pa., U.S. — *k14 115
Pleasant Hope, Mo., U.S. — D4 102
Pleasant Lake, In., U.S. — A7 91
Pleasant Lake, Ma., U.S. — C7 98
Pleasant Lake, l., N.D., U.S. — A6 111
Pleasant Lake, l., Me., U.S. — C5 96
Pleasant Lake, l., N.H., U.S. — D4 106
Pleasant Mills, In., U.S. — C8 91
Pleasant Mount, Pa., U.S. — C11 115
Pleasanton, Ca., U.S. — h9 82
Pleasanton, Ia., U.S. — D4 92
Pleasanton, Ks., U.S. — D9 93
Pleasanton, Ne., U.S. — D6 104
Pleasanton, N.M., U.S. — D1 108
Pleasanton, Tx., U.S. — E3 120
Pleasant Plain, Ia., U.S. — C6 92
Pleasant Plains, Ar., U.S. — B4 81
Pleasant Plains, Il., U.S. — D4 90
Pleasant Pond, l., Me., U.S. — C3 96
Pleasant Prairie, Wi., U.S. — n12 126
Pleasants, co., W.V., U.S. — B3 125
Pleasant Shade, Tn., U.S. — C8 119
Pleasant Valley, Ct., U.S. — B4 84
Pleasant Valley, Ia., U.S. — g11 92
Pleasant Valley, Md., U.S. — A3 97
Pleasant Valley, Mo., U.S. — h11 102
Pleasant Valley, Nv., U.S. — *D2 105
Pleasant Valley, N.Y., U.S. — D7 109
Pleasant View, Co., U.S. — *B5 83
Pleasant View, Tn., U.S. — A4 119
Pleasant View, Ut., U.S. — B3 121
Pleasant View, Wi., U.S. — D5 94
Pleasantville, In., U.S. — G3 91
Pleasantville, Ia., U.S. — C4 92
Pleasantville, N.J., U.S. — E3 107
Pleasantville, N.Y., U.S. — D7 109
Pleasantville, Oh., U.S. — C3 112
Pleasantville, Pa., U.S. — C2 115
Pleasure Beach, Ct., U.S. — D7 84
Pleasure Ridge Park, Ky., U.S. — g11 94
Pleasureville, Ky., U.S. — B4 94
Pledger, Tx., U.S. — r14 120
Pleebo, Lib. — F3 45
Plenița, Rom. — C6 24
Plenty, Sask. — F1 75
Plenty, Bay of, b., N.Z. — L16 51
Plentywood, Mt., U.S. — B12 103
Plérin, Fr. — C2 16
Plesetsk, Sov. Un. — C7 29
Plessis, N.Y., U.S. — A5 109
Plessisville, Que. — C6 74
Pleszew, Pol. — C4 26
Plétipi, Lac, l., Que. — h12 74
Plettenberg, W. Ger. — B2 19
Pleven, Bul. — D7 24
Plevna, Mo., U.S. — E5 102
Plevna, Mt., U.S. — D12 103
Pliny Range, mts., N.H., U.S. — B4 106
Pljevlja, Yugo. — D3 24
Plochingen, W. Ger. — E4 19
Płock, Pol. — C5 26
Ploërmel, Fr. — D2 16
Ploiești, Rom. — C8 24
Plomárion, Grc. — C6 25
Plomb du Cantal, mtn., Fr. — E5 16
Plombières-les-Bains, Fr. — B2 20
Plomosa Mountains, mts., Az., U.S. — D1 80
Plön, W. Ger. — A5 18
Plonge, Lac la, l., Sask. — B2 75
Płońsk, Pol. — B6 26
Plougastel, Fr. — C1 16
Plovdiv, Bul. — D7 24
Plover, Ia., U.S. — B3 92
Plover, Wi., U.S. — D4 126
Plover, stm., Wi., U.S. — D4 126
Plum, Pa., U.S. — k14 115
Pluma, S.D., U.S. — C2 118
Plumas, Man. — D2 70
Plumas, co., Ca., U.S. — B3 82
Plum Bayou, stm., Ar., U.S. — k10 81
Plum Beach, R.I., U.S. — E4 116
Plum Branch, S.C., U.S. — D3 117
Plumbridge, N. Ire., U.K. — C4 11
Plum City, Wi., U.S. — D1 126
Plum Coulee, Man. — E3 70
Plum Island, i., Ma., U.S. — A6 98
Plummer, Id., U.S. — B2 89
Plummer, Mn., U.S. — C2 100
Plum Point, R.I., U.S. — E4 116
Plumsteadville, Pa., U.S. — F11 115
Plumtree, Zimb. — B4 49
Plunkett, Sask. — E3 75
Plunkettville, Ok., U.S. — C7 113
Plush, Or., U.S. — E7 114
Plymouth, Monts. — H13 64
Plymouth, Eng., U.K. — E4 10
Plymouth, Ca., U.S. — C3 82
Plymouth, Ct., U.S. — C4 84
Plymouth, Fl., U.S. — D5 86
Plymouth, Il., U.S. — C3 90
Plymouth, In., U.S. — B5 91
Plymouth, Ia., U.S. — A4 92
Plymouth, Ks., U.S. — D7 93
Plymouth, Me., U.S. — D3 96
Plymouth, Ma., U.S. — C6 98
Plymouth, Mi., U.S. — p15 99
Plymouth, Mn., U.S. — m12 100
Plymouth, N.H., U.S. — C3 106
Plymouth, N.C., U.S. — B6 110
Plymouth, Oh., U.S. — A3 112
Plymouth, Pa., U.S. — D10 115
Plymouth, Ut., U.S. — B3 121
Plymouth, Wi., U.S. — E6 126
Plymouth, W.V., U.S. — C3 125
Plymouth, co., Ia., U.S. — B1 92
Plymouth, co., Ma., U.S. — C6 98
Plymouth Bay, b., Ma., U.S. — C6 98
Plymouth Township, Pa., U.S. — *F11 115
Plympton, Ma., U.S. — C6 98
Plzeň, Czech. — D2 26
Pô, Burkina — D4 45

Name	Map Ref.	Page
Po, stm., Italy	B3	23
Po, stm., Va., U.S.	B5	123
Po, Mouths of the, mth., Italy	B4	23
Poamoho Stream, stm., Hi., U.S.	f9	88
Pobé, Benin	E5	45
Pobeda, Mount, mtn., Sov. Un.	C36	128
Pobedino, Sov. Un.	B11	33
Pobedy, Peak, mtn., Asia	E11	29
Poca, W.V., U.S.	*C3	125
Pocahontas, Ar., U.S.	A5	81
Pocahontas, Il., U.S.	E4	90
Pocahontas, Ia., U.S.	B3	92
Pocahontas, Tn., U.S.	B3	119
Pocahontas, Va., U.S.	e10	123
Pocahontas, co., Ia., U.S.	B3	92
Pocahontas, co., W.V., U.S.	C4	125
Pocasset, Ma., U.S.	C6	98
Pocasset, Ok., U.S.	B4	113
Pocatalico, W.V., U.S.	C3	125
Pocatalico, stm., W.V., U.S.	C3	125
Pocatello, Id., U.S.	G6	89
Pochep, Sov. Un.	E9	27
Pochutla, Mex.	D5	63
Pocola, Ok., U.S.	B7	113
Pocomoke, stm., Md., U.S.	D7	97
Pocomoke City, Md., U.S.	D6	97
Pocomoke Sound, strt., Md., U.S.	E6	97
Poconé, Braz.	B1	56
Pocono Mountains, hills, Pa., U.S.	E11	115
Pocono Pines, Pa., U.S.	D11	115
Poços de Caldas, Braz.	C3	56
Pocotopaug Lake, res., Ct., U.S.	C6	84
Pocri, Pan.	G7	62
Pocumtuck Mountain, mtn., Ma., U.S.	A2	98
Podbořany, Czech.	C8	19
Podgornoye, Sov. Un.	D25	8
Podgorze, Sov. Un.	n17	26
Podhořany, Czech.		
Podkamennaya Tunguska, Sov. Un.	C27	8
Podkamennaya Tunguska, stm., Sov. Un.	C12	29
Podolsk, Sov. Un.	D11	27
Podor, Sen.	C2	45
Podporozhye, Sov. Un.	G16	14
Poe, In., U.S.	C7	91
Poel, i., E. Ger.	E5	15
Pofadder, S. Afr.	C2	49
Poge, Cape, c., Ma., U.S.	D7	98
Poggibonsi, Italy	C3	23
Pöggstall, Aus.	D7	18
Pogradeci, Alb.	B3	25
Pogranichnoye, Sov. Un.	A11	33
Pogranichnyy, Sov. Un.	D5	33
Pohang, S. Kor.	D10	31
Pohénégamook, Que.	B8	74
Pohnpei, i., Micron.	F9	6
Pohue Bay, b., Hi., U.S.	E6	88
Poinsett, Cape, c., Ant.	C24	7
Poinsett, Lake, l., S.D., U.S.	C8	118
Point Arena, Ca., U.S.	C2	82
Point Baker, Ak., U.S.	D13	79
Point Blue, La., U.S.	D3	95
Point Cedar, Ar., U.S.	C2	81
Point Clear, Al., U.S.	E2	78
Pointe à la Hache, La., U.S.	E6	95
Pointe-à-Pierre, Trin.	O23	65
Pointe-à-Pitre, Guad.	H14	64
Pointe au Baril Station, Ont.	B4	73
Pointe-au-Pic, Que.	B7	74
Pointe-aux-Trembles (part of Montréal), Que.	p20	74
Pointe-Bleue, Que.	A5	74
Pointe-Calumet, Que.	p19	74
Pointe-Claire, Que.	D4	74
Pointe-des-Cascades, Que.	q19	74
Pointe du Bois, Man.	D4	70
Pointe-du-Chêne, N.B.	C5	71
Pointe-du-Lac, Que.	C5	74
Point Edward, Ont.	D2	73
Pointe-Noire, Congo	B1	48
Pointe-Noire, Guad.	Q8	65
Pointers, N.J., U.S.	D2	107
Pointe-Verte, N.B.	A4	71
Point Fortin, Trin.	O22	65
Point Hope, Ak., U.S.	B6	79
Point Imperial, mtn., Az., U.S.	A4	80
Point Independence, Ma., U.S.	*C6	98
Point Judith, R.I., U.S.	G4	116
Point Judith Pond, l., R.I., U.S.	F4	116
Point Lake, l., N.W. Ter.	C10	66
Point Leamington, Newf.	D4	72
Point Lookout, Md., U.S.	D5	97
Point Lookout, Mo., U.S.	E4	102
Point Marion, Pa., U.S.	G2	115
Point Mugu Naval Air Station, mil., Ca., U.S.	E4	82
Point of Rocks, Md., U.S.	B2	97
Point of Rocks, Wy., U.S.	E4	127
Point Pelee National Park, Ont.	F2	73
Point Pleasant, N.J., U.S.	C4	107
Point Pleasant, W.V., U.S.	C2	125
Point Pleasant Beach, N.J., U.S.	C4	107
Point Reyes National Seashore, Ca., U.S.	C2	82
Point Roberts, Wa., U.S.	A2	124
Point Sapin, N.B.	C5	71
Point Washington, Fl., U.S.	u15	86
Poipu, Hi., U.S.	B2	88
Poirino, Italy	E3	20
Poison Creek, stm., Wy., U.S.	C5	127
Poisson Blanc, Lac du, res., Que.	C2	74
Poissy, Fr.	C5	16
Poitiers, Fr.	D4	16
Poitou, hist. reg., Fr.	D3	16
Poix, Fr.	E1	17
Pojo, Bol.	C3	55
Pojoaque Valley, N.M., U.S.	B3	108
Pokaran, India	C5	36
Pokataroo, Austl.	D7	51
Pokegama Lake, l., Mn., U.S.	C5	100
Pokegama Lake, l., Wi., U.S.	C2	126
Pokharā, Nepal	C9	36
Pokkye-ri, N. Kor.	G3	33
Poko, Zaire	A4	48
Poko Mountain, mtn., Ak., U.S.	B7	79
Pokrov, Sov. Un.	n19	27
Pokrovskoye, Sov. Un.	H12	27
Polacca, Az., U.S.	B5	80
Polān, Iran	C6	38
Poland, In., U.S.	F4	91
Poland, Me., U.S.	*D2	96
Poland, N.Y., U.S.	B5	109
Poland, ctry., Eur.	C5	26
Poland Spring, Me., U.S.	D2	96
Polar, Wi., U.S.	C5	126
Polar Bear Provincial Park, Ont.	n18	73
Polaris, Mt., U.S.	E3	103
Polar Record Glacier, ice, Ant.	C20	7
Polar Times Glacier, ice, Ant.	C20	7
Polathane see Akçaabat, Tur.	B12	40
Polatlı, Tur.	*C9	40
Polbain, Scot., U.K.	B3	13
Polch, W. Ger.	C2	19
Polcura, Chile	B2	54
Polebridge, Mt., U.S.	B2	103
Polesella, Italy	E7	20
Polessk, Sov. Un.	A6	26
Polevskoy, Sov. Un.	D21	8
Polgár, Hung.	B5	24
Poli, Cam.	D2	46
Policastro, Gulf of, b., Italy	E5	23
Police, Pol.	B3	26
Poligny, Fr.	D6	16
Polikhnítos, Grc.	C6	25
Polillo, Phil.	o13	34
Polillo Islands, is., Phil.	B6	34
Polillo Strait, strt., Phil.	o13	34
Pólis, Cyp.	E9	40
Polish Mountain, mtn., U.S.	k13	97
Políyiros, Grc.	B4	25
Polk, Ne., U.S.	C8	104
Polk, Oh., U.S.	B3	112
Polk, Pa., U.S.	D2	115
Polk, Tn., U.S.	A2	119
Polk, co., Ar., U.S.	C1	81
Polk, co., Fl., U.S.	E5	86
Polk, co., Ga., U.S.	C1	87
Polk, co., Ia., U.S.	C4	92
Polk, co., Mn., U.S.	C2	100
Polk, co., Mo., U.S.	D4	102
Polk, co., Ne., U.S.	C8	104
Polk, co., N.C., U.S.	f10	110
Polk, co., Or., U.S.	C3	114
Polk, co., Tn., U.S.	D9	119
Polk, co., Tx., U.S.	D5	120
Polk, co., Wi., U.S.	C1	126
Polk City, Fl., U.S.	D5	86
Polk City, Ia., U.S.	C4	92
Polkton, N.C., U.S.	B2	110
Polkville, Ms., U.S.	C4	101
Pollard, Al., U.S.	D2	78
Pollard, Ar., U.S.	A5	81
Pollards Point, Newf.	D3	72
Pollensa, Spain	C7	22
Pollock, Id., U.S.	C20	17
Pollock, La., U.S.	C3	95
Pollock, Mo., U.S.	A4	102
Pollock, S.D., U.S.	B5	118
Pollockville, N.C., U.S.	B5	110
Pollockville, Alta.	D5	68
Polo, Il., U.S.	B4	90
Polo, Mo., U.S.	B3	102
Polochic, stm., Guat.	C3	62
Pologi, Sov. Un.	H11	27
Polonnoye, Sov. Un.	F6	27
Polotsk, Sov. Un.	D7	27
Polson, Mt., U.S.	C2	103
Poltava, Sov. Un.	E6	29
Poltimore, Que.	D2	74
Polunochnoye, Sov. Un.	A6	28
Polvadera, N.M., U.S.	C3	108
Polwarth, Sask.	D2	75
Polyarnyy, Sov. Un.	C15	14
Pomabamba, Peru	C2	58
Pomarão, Port.	D2	22
Pomaria, S.C., U.S.	C5	117
Pomba, stm., Braz.	g6	56
Pombal, Braz.	C3	57
Pombal, Port.	C1	22
Pomerania, hist. reg., Pol.	B4	26
Pomeranian Bay, b., Eur.	D8	15
Pomerene, Az., U.S.	E5	80
Pomeroy, N. Ire., U.K.	C5	11
Pomeroy, Ia., U.S.	B3	92
Pomeroy, Oh., U.S.	C3	112
Pomeroy, Wa., U.S.	C8	124
Pomezia, Italy	h9	23
Pomfret, Ct., U.S.	B8	84
Pomfret, Md., U.S.	C3	97
Pomfret, Vt., U.S.	D3	122
Pomfret Center, Ct., U.S.	B8	84
Pomme de Terre, stm., Mn., U.S.	E3	100
Pomme de Terre, stm., Mo., U.S.	D4	102
Pomme de Terre Lake, res., Mo., U.S.	D4	102
Pomoho, Hi., U.S.	f9	88
Pomona, Ca., U.S.	E5	82
Pomona, Ks., U.S.	D8	93
Pomona, Mo., U.S.	E6	102
Pomona Lake, res., Ks., U.S.	D7	93
Pomorie, Bul.	D8	24
Pompano Beach, Fl., U.S.	*F6	86
Pompano Beach Highlands, Fl., U.S.	*F6	86
Pompeii, hist., Italy	D5	23
Pompeyevka, Sov. Un.	B5	33
Pompeys Pillar, Mt., U.S.	E9	103
Pompton Lakes, N.J., U.S.	A4	107
Pomquet, N.S.	D8	71
Ponaganset, stm., R.I., U.S.	C2	116
Ponaganset Reservoir, res., R.I., U.S.	C2	116
Ponape International Airport, Micron.	Q17	52
Ponask Lake, l., Ont.	B5	70
Ponass Lakes, l., Sask.	E3	75
Ponca, Ar., U.S.	A2	81
Ponca, Ne., U.S.	B9	104
Ponca City, Ok., U.S.	A4	113
Ponca Creek, stm., U.S.	A6	104
Ponca Indian Reservation, Ne., U.S.	B7	104
Ponce, P.R.	H11	64
Ponce de Leon, Fl., U.S.	u16	86
Ponce de Leon Bay, b., Fl., U.S.	G5	86
Ponce de Leon Inlet, b., Fl., U.S.	C6	86
Poncha Pass, Co., U.S.	C4	83
Poncha Springs, Co., U.S.	C4	83
Ponchatoula, La., U.S.	D5	95
Pond, stm., Ky., U.S.	C2	94
Pond, West Fork, stm., Ky., U.S.	C2	94
Pond Creek, Ok., U.S.	A3	113
Pond Creek, stm., Co., U.S.	*C7	83
Pond Creek, stm., Ky., U.S.	g11	94
Pondera, co., Mt., U.S.	B4	103
Ponder, Id., U.S.	A2	89
Ponderosa, N.M., U.S.	B3	108
Pond Fork, stm., W.V., U.S.	D3	125
Pond Fork, West Fork, stm., W.V., U.S.	n12	125
Pondicherry, India	F6	36
Pondicherry, ter., India	*F6	36
Pond Inlet, N.W. Ter.	B17	66
Ponds, Island of, i., Newf.	B4	72
Pone Island, i., Md., U.S.	D5	97
Poneloya, Nic.	D4	62
Ponemah, Mn., U.S.	B4	100
Poneto, In., U.S.	C7	91
Ponferrada, Spain	A2	22
Pongoma, Sov. Un.	E16	14
Ponhook Lake, l., N.S.	E5	71
Ponkapog Pond, l., Ma., U.S.	h11	98
Ponoka, Alta.	C4	68
Ponoy, Sov. Un.	D19	14
Ponoy, stm., Sov. Un.	B16	8
Pons, Fr.	E3	16
Ponsford, Mn., U.S.	D3	100
Ponta Delgada, Port.	h9	44
Ponta de Pedras, Braz.	C5	59
Ponta Grossa, Braz.	D2	56
Pontal, Braz.	k7	56
Pontalina, Braz.	B3	56
Pont-à-Mousson, Fr.	C7	16
Ponta Porã, Braz.	C1	56
Pontarlier, Fr.	D7	16
Pontchartrain, Lake, l., La., U.S.	D5	95
Pont-de-Roide, Fr.	B2	20
Pontedera, Italy	C3	23
Ponte de Sor, Port.	C2	22
Ponte di Legno, Italy	C5	20
Pontefract, Eng., U.K.	A6	12
Ponte Nova, Braz.	H2	75
Pontevedra, Spain	A1	22
Ponte Vedra Beach, Fl., U.S.	B5	86
Pontfaverger-Moronvilliers, Fr.	E4	17
Pontiac, Il., U.S.	C5	90
Pontiac, Mi., U.S.	F7	99
Pontiac, co., Que.	C6	117
Pontianak, Indon.	F3	34
Pontic Mountains, mts., Tur.	B11	40
Pontivy, Fr.	C2	16
Pont-l'Abbé, Fr.	D1	16
Pontoise, Fr.	C5	16
Pontoosuc Lake, l., Ma., U.S.	B1	98
Pontotoc, Ms., U.S.	A4	101
Pontotoc, Tx., U.S.	D3	120
Pontotoc, co., Ms., U.S.	A4	101
Pontotoc, co., Ok., U.S.	C5	113
Pontremoli, Italy	B2	23
Pontresina, Switz.	C5	20
Pontrilas, Sask.	D3	75
Pont-Rouge, Que.	C6	74
Pont-Sainte-Maxence, Fr.	E2	17
Pontypool, Ont.	C6	73
Pontypool, Wales, U.K.	C4	12
Pontypridd (Taff-Ely), Wales, U.K.	C4	12
Pony, Mt., U.S.	E5	103
Ponza, i., Italy	D4	23
Ponziane Islands, is., Italy	D4	23
Poole, Eng., U.K.	E5	10
Poole, Ky., U.S.	C2	94
Poole, Ne., U.S.	D7	104
Pooler, Ga., U.S.	E5	87
Pooles Island, i., Md., U.S.	B5	97
Poolesville, Md., U.S.	B3	97
Pooleville, Ok., U.S.	C4	113
Poolewe, Scot., U.K.	B3	13
Pooley Island, i., B.C.	C3	69
Poolville, Tx., U.S.	C4	120
Poona see Pune, India	E3	36
Poopó, Bol.	C2	55
Poopó, Lago, l., Bol.	C2	55
Poor Knights Islands, is., N.Z.	K15	51
Pootatuck Park, Ct., U.S.	*D2	84
Popanaya, Sov. Un.	q21	27
Popayán, Col.	C2	60
Pope, Man.	D1	70
Pope, Ms., U.S.	A4	101
Pope, co., Ar., U.S.	B2	81
Pope, co., Il., U.S.	F5	90
Pope, co., Mn., U.S.	E3	100
Pope Air Force Base, mil., N.C., U.S.	B3	110
Popejoy, Ia., U.S.	B4	92
Poperinge, Bel.	D2	17
Popham Beach, Me., U.S.	E3	96
Popham Point, c., Ont.	B3	73
Poplar, Mt., U.S.	B11	103
Poplar, N.C., U.S.	e10	110
Poplar, Wi., U.S.	B2	126
Poplar, stm., Can.	C3	70
Poplar, stm., N.A.	B11	103
Poplar, West Fork, stm., U.S.	B11	103
Poplar Bluff, Mo., U.S.	E7	102
Poplar Branch, N.C., U.S.	A7	110
Poplar Creek, Ms., U.S.	B4	101
Poplarfield, Man.	D3	70
Poplar Grove, Ar., U.S.	C5	81
Poplar Grove, Il., U.S.	A5	90
Poplar Island, i., Md., U.S.	C5	97
Poplar Mountain, mtn., Ky., U.S.	B6	94
Poplar Plains, Ky., U.S.	B6	94
Poplar Point, Man.	D3	70
Poplarville, Ms., U.S.	E4	101
Popocatépetl, Volcán, vol., Mex.	n14	63
Popokabaka, Zaire	C2	48
Popomanaseu, Mount, mtn., Sol. Is.	A11	50
Popondetta, Pap. N. Gui.	k12	50
Popovo, Bul.	D8	24
Poppel, Bel.	C5	17
Popple, stm., Wi., U.S.	C5	126
Poprad, Czech.	*D6	26
Poquonock, Ct., U.S.	B5	84
Poquonock Bridge, Ct., U.S.	D7	84
Poquoson, Va., U.S.	C6	123
Porali, stm., Pak.	H13	37
Porangatu, Braz.	A3	56
Porbandar, India	D4	36
Porcher Island, i., B.C.	C2	69
Porcuna, Spain	D3	22
Porcupine, S.D., U.S.	D3	118
Porcupine, stm., N.A.	B11	79
Porcupine, Cape, c., Newf.	B2	72
Porcupine Hills, hills, Can.	E5	75
Porcupine Mountains, mts., Mi., U.S.	m12	99
Porcupine Plain, Sask.	E4	75
Pordenone, Italy	C4	23
Poreč, Yugo.	*C1	24
Pori, Fin.	G9	14
Porirua, N.Z.	N15	51
Porjus, Swe.	D8	14
Porkhov, Sov. Un.	C7	27
Porkkala, Fin.	G11	14
Porlamar, Ven.	A5	60
Porlezza, Italy	D7	21
Pornic, Fr.	D2	16
Poroma, Bol.	C2	55
Poronaysk, Sov. Un.	E17	29
Poroshiri, Mount, mtn., Japan	E11	33
Porpoise Bay, b., Ant.	C25	7
Porrentruy, Switz.	E3	18
Porsangen, Nor.	B12	14
Porsgrunn, Nor.	p27	14
Portachuelo, Bol.	C3	55
Portacloy, Ire.	C2	11
Portadown, N. Ire., U.K.	C6	11
Portaferry, N. Ire., U.K.	C6	11
Portage, P.E.I.	C5	71
Portage, In., U.S.	A3	91
Portage, Me., U.S.	B4	96
Portage, Mi., U.S.	F5	99
Portage, Pa., U.S.	B3	121
Portage, Ut., U.S.	B3	121
Portage, Wi., U.S.	E4	126
Portage, co., Oh., U.S.	A4	112
Portage, co., Wi., U.S.	D4	126
Portage, stm., Oh., U.S.	B2	112
Portage, North Branch, stm., Oh., U.S.	f7	112
Portage Bay, b., Man.	D2	70
Portage Des Sioux, Mo., U.S.	f13	102
Portage Head, c., Wa., U.S.	A1	124
Portage Island, i., N.B.	B4	71
Portage Lake, l., Me., U.S.	B4	96
Portage Lakes, Oh., U.S.	B4	112
Portage la Prairie, Man.	E2	70
Portageville, Mo., U.S.	E8	102
Portageville, N.Y., U.S.	C2	109
Portal, Az., U.S.	F6	80
Portal, Ga., U.S.	D5	87
Portal, N.D., U.S.	A3	111
Portal, Or., U.S.	B4	114
Port-Alfred, Que.	A7	74
Port Alfred (Kowie), S. Afr.	D4	49
Port Alice, B.C.	D4	69
Port Allegany, Pa., U.S.	C5	115
Port Allen, La., U.S.	D4	95
Port Amherst, W.V., U.S.	m12	125
Port Angeles, Wa., U.S.	A2	124
Port Anson, Newf.	D4	72
Port Antonio, Jam.	E5	64
Port Aransas, Tx., U.S.	F4	120
Port Arthur, see Lüshun, China	D9	31
Port Arthur, Tx., U.S.	E6	120
Port Askaig, Scot., U.K.	E2	13
Port Augusta, Austl.	F6	50
Port au Port Bay, b., Newf.	D2	72
Port au Port [West-Aguathuna-Felix Cove], Newf.	D2	72
Port-au-Prince, Haiti	E7	64
Port au Prince Peninsula, pen., Newf.	D2	72
Port Austin, Mi., U.S.	D7	99
Port Barre, La., U.S.	D4	95
Port-Bergé, Madag.	g9	49
Port Birmingham, Al., U.S.	B2	78
Port Blair, India	H2	36
Port Blakely, Wa., U.S.	e10	124
Port Blandford, Newf.	D4	72
Port Bolivar, Tx., U.S.	E5	120
Port Borden, P.E.I.	C6	71
Port Burwell, Ont.	E4	73
Port Byron, Il., U.S.	B3	90
Port Byron, N.Y., U.S.	B4	109
Port Canning, India	F12	37
Port Carbon, Pa., U.S.	E9	115
Port Carling, Ont.	B5	73
Port-Cartier-Ouest, Que.	k13	74
Port Chalmers, N.Z.	P13	51
Port Charlotte, Fl., U.S.	F4	86
Port Chester, N.Y., U.S.	E7	109
Port Clements, B.C.	C1	69
Port Clinton, Oh., U.S.	A3	112
Port Clyde, N.S.	F4	71
Port Clyde, Me., U.S.	E3	96
Port Colborne, Ont.	E5	73
Port Coquitlam, B.C.	E6	69
Port Credit, Ont.	D5	73
Port-Daniel, Que.	A5	71
Port-de-Bouc, Fr.	F6	16
Port-de-Paix, Haiti	E7	64
Port Deposit, Md., U.S.	A5	97
Port Dickinson, N.Y., U.S.	C5	109
Port Dickson, Malay.	E2	34
Port Dover, Ont.	E4	73
Port Eads, La., U.S.	E6	95
Port Edward, B.C.	B2	69
Port Edwards, Wi., U.S.	D4	126
Porteirinha, Braz.	B4	56
Portel, Braz.	C4	59
Port Elgin, N.B.	C5	71
Port Elgin, Ont.	C3	73
Port Elizabeth, S. Afr.	D4	49
Port Elizabeth, N.J., U.S.	E3	107
Port Ellen, Scot., U.K.	E2	13
Porteña, Arg.	A4	54
Porter, Al., U.S.	B2	78
Porter, In., U.S.	A3	91
Porter, Me., U.S.	E2	96
Porter, Mn., U.S.	F2	100
Porter, Ok., U.S.	B6	113
Porter, Tx., U.S.	D5	120
Porter, co., In., U.S.	B3	91
Porter Corners, N.Y., U.S.	B7	109
Porter Creek, stm., W.V., U.S.	m13	125
Porterdale, Ga., U.S.	C3	87
Port Erin, I. of Man	F4	13
Porter Lake, l., Sask.	m7	75
Porterville, Ca., U.S.	D4	82
Porterville, Ms., U.S.	C5	101
Portersville, Pa., U.S.	E1	115
Port Essington, B.C.	B2	69
Port Ewen, N.Y., U.S.	D7	109
Port Fairy, Austl.	I4	51
Port Gamble, Wa., U.S.	B3	124
Port Gamble Indian Reservation, Wa., U.S.	B3	124
Port-Gentil, Gabon	F1	46
Port George, N.S.	C4	71
Port Gibson, Ms., U.S.	D3	101
Port Glasgow, Scot., U.K.	C4	13
Portglenone, N. Ire., U.K.	C5	11
Port Graham, Ak., U.S.	D9	79
Port Harcourt, Nig.	F6	45
Port Hardy, B.C.	D4	69
Port Hastings, N.S.	D8	71
Port Hawkesbury, N.S.	D8	71
Port Hedland, Austl.	D2	50
Port Heiden, Ak., U.S.	D7	79
Port Henry, N.Y., U.S.	A7	109
Port Hill, P.E.I.	C6	71
Port Hood, N.S.	C8	71
Port Hope, Ont.	D6	73
Port Hope, Mi., U.S.	E8	99
Port Hope Simpson, Newf.	B3	72
Port Hueneme, Ca., U.S.	E4	82
Port Huron, Mi., U.S.	F8	99
Portia, Ar., U.S.	A4	81
Portici, Italy	D1	22
Portimão, Port.	C5	93
Portis, Ks., U.S.	C5	93
Port Isabel, Tx., U.S.	F4	120
Port Jefferson, N.Y., U.S.	n15	109
Port Jefferson Station, N.Y., U.S.	*n15	109
Port Jervis, N.Y., U.S.	D6	109
Port Keats, Austl.	B5	50
Port Kent, N.Y., U.S.	f11	109
Portland, Austl.	G7	50
Portland, Ar., U.S.	D4	81
Portland, Ct., U.S.	C5	84
Portland, Fl., U.S.	u15	86
Portland, In., U.S.	D8	91
Portland, Me., U.S.	E2	96
Portland, Mi., U.S.	F6	99
Portland, Mo., U.S.	C6	102
Portland, N.Y., U.S.	C1	109
Portland, N.D., U.S.	B8	111
Portland, Or., U.S.	B4	114
Portland, Pa., U.S.	E11	115
Portland, Tn., U.S.	A5	119
Portland, Tx., U.S.	F4	120
Portland, Bill of, c., Eng., U.K.	E5	10
Portland Bight, Jam.	F14	65
Portland Canal, b., N.A.	A2	69
Portland Creek Pond, l., Newf.	C3	72
Portland Inlet, b., B.C.	B2	69
Portland Mills, Pa., U.S.	D4	115
Portland Point, c., Jam.	F14	65
Portlandville, N.Y., U.S.	C6	109
Port Laoise, Ire.	D3	10
Port Lavaca, Tx., U.S.	E4	120
Portlaw, Ire.	E4	11
Port Leyden, N.Y., U.S.	B5	109
Port Lincoln, Austl.	F6	50
Port Lions, Ak., U.S.	D9	79
Port Loko, S.L.	G3	45
Port Loring, Ont.	B4	73
Port-Louis, Fr.	D2	16
Port-Louis, Guad.	Q8	65
Port Louis, Mrts.	H24	2
Port Ludlow, Wa., U.S.	B3	124
Port Macquarie, Austl.	F9	50
Port Madison Indian Reservation, Wa., U.S.	B3	124
Portmagee, Ire.	F1	11
Portmahomack, Scot., U.K.	C5	13
Port Maitland, N.S.	F3	71
Port Maitland (part of Dunnville), Ont.	E5	73
Port Maria, Jam.	E5	64
Port Matilda, Pa., U.S.	E5	115
Port Mayaca, Fl., U.S.	F6	86
Port McNeil, B.C.	D4	69
Port McNicoll, Ont.	C5	73
Port Medway, N.S.	E5	71
Port Mellon, B.C.	E6	69
Port-Menier, Que.	k8	72
Port Moller, Ak., U.S.	D7	79
Port Monmouth, N.J., U.S.	C4	107
Port Morant, Jam.	F5	64
Portmore, Jam.	*F15	65
Port Moresby, Pap. N. Gui.	k12	50
Port Morien, N.S.	C10	71
Port Morris, N.J., U.S.	B3	107
Port Mouton, N.S.	F5	71
Port Mouton Island, i., N.S.	F5	71
Port Murray, N.J., U.S.	B3	107
Port Neches, Tx., U.S.	E6	120
Portnahaven, Scot., U.K.	E2	13
Port Nolloth, S. Afr.	C2	49
Port Norris, N.J., U.S.	E2	107
Porto (Oporto), Port.	B1	22
Porto Acre, Braz.	C4	58
Porto Alegre, Braz.	E2	56
Porto Alexandre see Tombua, Ang.	E1	48
Porto Amboim, Ang.	D1	48
Porto Belo, Braz.	D3	56
Portobelo, Pan.	F8	62
Porto Calvo, Braz.	C7	57
Porto de Mós, Port.	C1	22
Pôrto de Moz, Braz.	C4	59
Porto Esperança, Braz.	B1	56
Porto Feliz, Braz.	C3	56
Portoferraio, Italy	C3	23
Portofino, Italy	B2	23
Porto Garibaldi, Italy	E8	20
Porto Grande, Braz.	C4	59
Portogruaro, Italy	C4	23
Portola, Ca., U.S.	C3	82
Porto Lucena, Braz.	D1	56
Portomaggiore, Italy	E8	20
Porto Mendes, Braz.	C1	56
Porto Murtinho, Braz.	D4	55
Porto Nacional, Braz.	D1	59
Porto-Novo, Benin	E5	45
Porto Orange, Braz.	C6	86
Porto Santana, Braz.	C4	59
Porto Seguro, Braz.	D3	57
Porto Torres, Italy	D2	23
Porto União, Braz.	D2	56
Porto-Vecchio, Fr.	D2	23
Porto Velho, Braz.	B5	58
Portoviejo, Ec.	B1	58
Portpatrick, Scot., U.K.	D3	13
Port Penn, De., U.S.	B3	85
Port Perry, Ont.	C6	73
Port Phillip Bay, b., Austl.	G7	50
Port Pirie, Austl.	F6	50
Port Radium, N.W. Ter.	C9	66
Port Reading, N.J., U.S.	k8	107
Port Rexton, Newf.	D5	72
Portree, Scot., U.K.	C2	13
Portreeve, Sask.	G1	75
Port Renfrew, B.C.	E5	69
Port Republic, N.J., U.S.	D4	107
Port Republic, Va., U.S.	B4	123
Port Rexton, Newf.	D5	72
Port Richey, Fl., U.S.	D4	86
Port Rowan, Ont.	E4	73
Port Royal, Ky., U.S.	B4	94
Port Royal, Pa., U.S.	F7	115
Port Royal, S.C., U.S.	G6	117
Port Royal, Va., U.S.	A4	119
Port Royal, Va., U.S.	B5	123
Port Royal Island, i., S.C., U.S.	G6	117
Port Royal Sound, strt., S.C., U.S.	G6	117
Portrush, N. Ire., U.K.	B5	11
Port Said (Būr Saʿīd), Eg.	B3	47
Port Saint Joe, Fl., U.S.	C1	86
Port Saint Johns, Transkei	D4	49
Port-Saint-Louis [-du-Rhône], Fr.	F6	16
Port Saint Lucie, Fl., U.S.	E6	86
Port Salerno, Fl., U.S.	E6	86
Portsalon, Ire.	B4	11
Port Sanilac, Mi., U.S.	E8	99
Port Saunders, Newf.	C3	72
Port Sewall, Fl., U.S.	E6	86
Port Shepstone, S. Afr.	D5	49
Portsmouth, Dom.	I14	64
Portsmouth, Eng., U.K.	E6	10
Portsmouth, Ia., U.S.	C2	92
Portsmouth, N.H., U.S.	D5	106
Portsmouth, Oh., U.S.	D3	112
Portsmouth, R.I., U.S.	E6	116
Portsmouth, Va., U.S.	D6	123
Portsmouth Naval Shipyard, mil., Me., U.S.	D5	106
Portsoy, Scot., U.K.	C6	13
Port Stanley, Ont.	E3	73
Port Sudan (Būr Sūdān), Sud.	A7	47
Port Sulphur, La., U.S.	E6	95
Port-sur-Saône, Fr.	D2	16
Port Talbot (Afan), Wales, U.K.	C4	12
Porttipahdan Reservoir, res., Fin.	C12	14
Port Tobacco Village, Md., U.S.	C3	97
Port Townsend, Wa., U.S.	A3	124
Portugal, ctry., Eur.	C1	22
Portugal Cove South, Newf.	E5	72
Portugalete, Spain	A4	22
Portuguesa, state, Ven.	B4	60
Portuguesa, stm., Ven.	B4	60
Portumna, Ire.	D3	11
Port Union, Newf.	D5	72
Port Union, Oh., U.S.	n13	112
Port-Vendres, Fr.	F5	16
Port-Vila, Vanuatu	H10	6
Portville, N.Y., U.S.	C2	109
Port Vincent, La., U.S.	*D5	95
Port Vue, Pa., U.S.	*k14	115
Port Wakefield, Austl.	G2	51
Port Washington, N.Y., U.S.	h13	109
Port Washington, Oh., U.S.	B4	112
Port Washington, Wi., U.S.	E6	126
Port Wentworth, Ga., U.S.	D5	87
Port William, Scot., U.K.	F4	13
Port William, Oh., U.S.	C2	112
Port Wing, Wi., U.S.	B2	126
Porum, Ok., U.S.	B6	113
Porvenir, Chile	h11	54
Porz, W. Ger.	C2	19
Posadas, Arg.	E4	55
Posadas, Spain	D3	22
Poschiavo, Switz.	D9	21
Posen, Il., U.S.	k9	90
Posen, Mi., U.S.	C7	99
Posey, co., In., U.S.	H2	91
Poseyville, In., U.S.	H2	91
Poshekhonye-Volodarsk, Sov. Un.	B12	27
Poso, Indon.	F6	34
Poso, Lake, l., Indon.	F6	34
Posong, S. Kor.	I3	33
Posse, Braz.	A3	56
Pössneck, E. Ger.	C6	19
Post, Or., U.S.	C6	114
Post, Tx., U.S.	C2	120
Poste-de-la-Baleine, Que.	g11	74
Post Falls, Id., U.S.	B2	89
Post Mills, Vt., U.S.	C4	122
Postojna, Yugo.	C1	24
Poston, S.C., U.S.	D9	117
Postville, Newf.	g10	72
Postville, Ia., U.S.	A6	92
Potaro Landing, Guy.	A3	59
Potato Creek, S.D., U.S.	D3	118
Potawatomi Indian Reservation, Ks., U.S.	C8	93
Potchefstroom, S. Afr.	C4	49
Poteau, Ok., U.S.	B7	113
Poteau, stm., U.S.	B7	113
Poteau Mountain, mtn., U.S.	C1	81
Poteet, Tx., U.S.	E3	120
Potenza, Italy	D5	23
Potenza, stm., Italy	A4	23
Potgietersrus, S. Afr.	B4	49
Poth, Tx., U.S.	E3	120
Potholes Reservoir, res., Wa., U.S.	B6	124
Poti, Sov. Un.	G17	8
Poti, stm., Braz.	D7	57
Potiskum, Nig.	D7	45
Potlatch, Id., U.S.	C2	89
Potomac, Il., U.S.	C6	90
Potomac, Md., U.S.	C3	97
Potomac, Mt., U.S.	D3	103
Potomac, stm., U.S.	D4	97
Potomac, North Branch, stm., U.S.	m12	97
Potomac, South Branch, stm., U.S.	B6	125
Potomac, South Branch, North Fork, stm., U.S.	C5	125
Potomac, South Branch, South Fork, stm., U.S.	B6	125
Potomac Heights, Md., U.S.	C3	97
Potomac Park, Md., U.S.	k13	97
Potosí, Bol.	C2	55
Potosi, Wi., U.S.	F3	126
Potosi, dept., Bol.	D2	55
Potrerillos, Chile	E2	53
Potrerillos, Hond.	C4	62
Potro, Cerro el, mtn., S.A.	E2	53
Potsdam, E. Ger.	C6	19
Potsdam, N.Y., U.S.	f10	109
Pottawatomie, co., Ks., U.S.	C7	93
Pottawatomie, co., Ok., U.S.	B4	113
Pottawatomie Creek, stm., Ks., U.S.	D8	93
Pottawattamie, co., Ia., U.S.	C1	92
Potter, Ar., U.S.	C1	81

Index

Name	Map Ref.	Page

Potter, Ks., U.S. — C8 93
Potter, Ne., U.S. — C2 104
Potter, Wi., U.S. — h9 126
Potter, co., Pa., U.S. — C6 115
Potter, co., S.D., U.S. — B6 118
Potter, co., Tx., U.S. — B2 120
Potter Hill, R.I., U.S. — F1 116
Potter Place, N.H., U.S. — D3 106
Potters Mills, Pa., U.S. — E6 115
Pottersville, Mo., U.S. — E5 102
Pottersville, N.J., U.S. — B3 107
Pottersville, N.Y., U.S. — B7 109
Potter Valley, Ca., U.S. — C2 82
Potterville, Ga., U.S. — D2 87
Potts Camp, Ms., U.S. — A4 101
Potts Creek, stm., U.S. — C2 123
Pottstown, Pa., U.S. — F10 115
Pottsville, Ar., U.S. — B2 81
Pottsville, Pa., U.S. — E9 115
Pottsville, Tx., U.S. — D3 120
Potwin, Ks., U.S. — E6 93
Pouce Coupe, B.C. — B7 69
Pouch Cove, Newf. — E5 72
Poughkeepsie, Ar., U.S. — A4 81
Poughkeepsie, N.Y., U.S. — D7 109
Poulan, Ga., U.S. — E3 87
Poulsbo, Wa., U.S. — B3 124
Poultney, Vt., U.S. — D2 122
Poultney, stm., Vt., U.S. — D2 122
Pound, Va., U.S. — e9 123
Pound, Wi., U.S. — C5 126
Pound Gap, U.S. — C7 94
Pouso Alegre, Braz. — C3 56
Poutasi, W. Sam. — G12 52
Pouthisat, Camb. — C2 34
Pouxeux, Fr. — D13 16
Považská Bystrica, Czech. — *D5 26
Povenets, Sov. Un. — C16 8
Poverty Bay, b., N.Z. — M16 51
Póvoa de Varzim, Port. — B1 22
Povorino, Sov. Un. — C2 28
Povorotnyy, Cape, c., Sov. Un. — E6 33
Povungnituk, Que. — f11 74
Powassan, Ont. — A5 73
Poway, Ca., U.S. — F5 82
Powder, stm., U.S. — A6 76
Powder, stm., Or., U.S. — C9 114
Powder, Middle Fork, stm., Wy., U.S. — C6 127
Powder, North Fork, stm., Wy., U.S. — C6 127
Powder, South Fork, stm., Wy., U.S. — C6 127
Powderhorn, Co., U.S. — C3 83
Powder River, Wy., U.S. — A6 76
Powder River, co., Mt., U.S. — E11 103
Powder River Pass, Wy., U.S. — B5 127
Powder Springs, Ga., U.S. — h8 87
Powderville, Mt., U.S. — E11 103
Powder Wash, Co., U.S. — A2 83
Powe, Mo., U.S. — E7 102
Powell, Mo., U.S. — E3 102
Powell, Oh., U.S. — B2 112
Powell, Pa., U.S. — C9 115
Powell, Tn., U.S. — m13 119
Powell, Wy., U.S. — B4 127
Powell, co., Ky., U.S. — C6 94
Powell, co., Mt., U.S. — D4 103
Powell, stm., U.S. — C10 119
Powell, Lake, res., U.S. — F5 121
Powell, Mount, mtn., Co., U.S. — B4 83
Powell Butte, Or., U.S. — C5 114
Powellhurst, Or., U.S. — *B4 114
Powell Mountain, mtn., U.S. — C10 119
Powell Mountain, mtn., N.M., U.S. — B1 108
Powell Park, reg., Co., U.S. — A2 83
Powell River, B.C. — E5 69
Powellsville, N.C., U.S. — A6 110
Powellville, Md., U.S. — D7 97
Powelton, Ga., U.S. — C4 87
Power, Mt., U.S. — C5 103
Power, co., Id., U.S. — G5 89
Power Head, c., Ire. — F3 11
Powers, Mi., U.S. — C3 99
Powers, Or., U.S. — E2 114
Powers Lake, N.D., U.S. — A3 111
Powersville, Mo., U.S. — A4 102
Powerview, Man. — D3 70
Poweshiek, co., Ia., U.S. — C5 92
Powhatan, Al., U.S. — B2 78
Powhatan, Ar., U.S. — A4 81
Powhatan, La., U.S. — C2 95
Powhatan, co., Va., U.S. — C5 123
Powhatan, co., Va., U.S. — C5 123
Powhatan Point, Oh., U.S. — C5 112
Powhattan, Ks., U.S. — C8 93
Pownal, Me., U.S. — g7 96
Pownal, Vt., U.S. — F2 122
Pownal Center, Me., U.S. — g7 96
Pownal Center, Vt., U.S. — F2 122
Powys, co., Wales, U.K. — B4 12
Poxoréo, Braz. — B2 56
Poyang Hu, l., China — F8 31
Poyarkovo, Sov. Un. — B4 33
Poydras, La., U.S. — *E6 95
Poygan, Lake, l., Wi., U.S. — D5 126
Poynette, Wi., U.S. — E4 126
Poynor, Mo., U.S. — E7 102
Poyntzpass, N. Ire., U.K. — C5 11
Poy Sippi, Wi., U.S. — D4 126
Požarevac, Yugo. — C5 24
Poza Rica de Hidalgo, Mex. — m15 63
Poznań, Pol. — B4 26
Pozo Almonte, Chile — D2 55
Pozoblanco, Spain — C3 22
Pozo Colorado, Para. — D4 55
Pozo Redondo Mountains, mts., Az., U.S. — E3 80
Pozos, Mex. — m13 63
Pozuelo de Alarcón, Spain — p17 22
Pozuelos, Ven. — A5 60
Pozuzo, Peru — D2 58
Pozzallo, Italy — F5 23
Pozzuoli, Italy — D5 23
Prachatice, Czech. — E9 19
Prachin Buri, Thai. — C2 34
Prachuap Khiri Khan, Thai. — G3 35
Praco, Al., U.S. — f6 78
Prácticos, Punta de c., Cuba — D5 64
Prades, Fr. — F5 16
Prado Flood Control Basin, Ca., U.S. — n13 82
Præstø, Den. — I8 14
Praga (part of Warsaw), Pol. — k14 26
Prague (Praha), Czech. — C3 26
Prague, Ne., U.S. — C9 104
Prague, Ok., U.S. — B5 113
Prainha, Braz. — C4 59
Prairie, Al., U.S. — C2 78
Prairie, Ms., U.S. — B5 101

Prairie, co., Ar., U.S. — C4 81
Prairie, co., Mt., U.S. — D11 103
Prairie, stm., Wi., U.S. — C5 100
Prairie, stm., Wi., U.S. — C4 126
Prairie Bayou, stm., Ar., U.S. — g7 81
Prairie City, Il., U.S. — C3 90
Prairie City, Ia., U.S. — C4 92
Prairie City, Or., U.S. — C8 114
Prairie City, S.D., U.S. — B3 118
Prairie Creek, In., U.S. — F3 91
Prairie Creek Reservoir, res., In., U.S. — D7 91
Prairie Dog Creek, stm., U.S. — C3 93
Prairie du Chien, Wi., U.S. — E2 126
Prairie Du Rocher, Il., U.S. — E3 90
Prairie du Sac, Wi., U.S. — E4 126
Prairie Farm, Wi., U.S. — C2 126
Prairie Grove, Ar., U.S. — B1 81
Prairie Hill, Mo., U.S. — B5 102
Prairie Home, Mo., U.S. — C5 102
Prairie Home, Ne., U.S. — h11 104
Prairie Point, Ms., U.S. — B5 101
Prairie River, Sask. — E4 75
Prairies, Lake of the, res., Can. — F5 75
Prairies, Rivière des, stm., Que. — p19 74
Prairieton, In., U.S. — F3 91
Prairie View, Ar., U.S. — B2 81
Prairie View, Ks., U.S. — C4 93
Prairie View, Tx., U.S. — D5 120
Prairie Village, Ks., U.S. — m16 93
Prairieville, La., U.S. — h10 95
Pralognan-la-Vanoise, Fr. — D2 20
Pran Buri, Thai. — C2 34
Praszka, Pol. — C5 26
Prata, Braz. — B3 56
Pratāpgarh, India — E5 37
Prato, Italy — C3 23
Prats-de-Mollo, Fr. — F5 16
Pratt, Ks., U.S. — E5 93
Pratt, W.V., U.S. — *C3 125
Pratt, co., Ks., U.S. — E5 93
Pratteln, Switz. — A4 21
Prattsburg, N.Y., U.S. — C3 109
Prattsville, Ar., U.S. — C3 81
Prattsville, N.Y., U.S. — C6 109
Prattville, Al., U.S. — C3 78
Prattville, Mi., U.S. — G6 99
Pravdinsk, Sov. Un. — A6 26
Pravia, Spain — A2 22
Preble, In., U.S. — C7 91
Preble, co., Oh., U.S. — C1 112
Predazzo, Italy — C7 20
Preeceville, Sask. — F4 75
Preetz, W. Ger. — D4 15
Pregel, stm., Sov. Un. — D3 27
Pregnall, S.C., U.S. — E7 117
Pregolya, stm., Sov. Un. — A6 26
Prelate, Sask. — G1 75
Premana, Italy — D7 21
Premont, Tx., U.S. — F3 120
Prémontré, Fr. — E3 17
Premosello, Italy — D5 21
Prenjasi, Alb. — B3 25
Prenter, W.V., U.S. — C3 125
Prentice, Wi., U.S. — C3 126
Prentiss, Me., U.S. — C4 96
Prentiss, Ms., U.S. — D4 101
Prentiss, co., Ms., U.S. — A5 101
Prenzlau, E. Ger. — B6 18
Přerov, Czech. — D4 26
Prescott, Ont. — C9 73
Prescott, Az., U.S. — C3 80
Prescott, Ar., U.S. — D2 81
Prescott, Ia., U.S. — C3 92
Prescott, Ks., U.S. — D9 93
Prescott, Mi., U.S. — D7 99
Prescott, Wa., U.S. — A4 114
Prescott, Wa., U.S. — C7 124
Prescott, co., Ont. — B10 73
Presho, S.D., U.S. — D5 118
Presidencia Roque Sáenz Peña, Arg. — E3 55
Presidente Epitácio, Braz. — E3 55
Presidente Hayes, dept., Para. — D4 55
Presidente Olegário, Braz. — B3 56
Presidente Prudente, Braz. — C2 56
Presidential Range, mts., N.H., U.S. — B4 106
Presidents Island, i., Tn., U.S. — e8 119
Presidio, Tx., U.S. — p12 120
Presidio, co., Tx., U.S. — o12 120
Presidio of San Francisco, mil., Ca., U.S. — h8 82
Preslav, Bul. — D8 24
Prešov, Czech. — D6 26
Prespa, Lake, l., Eur. — E5 24
Presque Isle, Me., U.S. — B5 96
Presque Isle, Mi., U.S. — C7 99
Presque Isle, co., Mi., U.S. — C6 99
Pressath, W. Ger. — D6 19
Prestatyn, Wales, U.K. — A4 12
Presteigne, Wales, U.K. — B4 12
Přeštice, Czech. — D8 19
Preston, Austl. — *G8 50
Preston, Eng., U.K. — C4 12
Preston, Ct., U.S. — C8 84
Preston, Ga., U.S. — D2 87
Preston, Id., U.S. — G7 89
Preston, Ia., U.S. — B7 92
Preston, Ks., U.S. — E5 93
Preston, Ky., U.S. — B6 94
Preston, Md., U.S. — C6 97
Preston, Mn., U.S. — G6 100
Preston, Ms., U.S. — C5 101
Preston, Ok., U.S. — B5 113
Preston, co., W.V., U.S. — B5 125
Preston Peak, mtn., Ca., U.S. — B2 82
Prestonsburg, Ky., U.S. — C7 94
Prestonville, Ky., U.S. — B4 94
Prestrud Inlet, b., Ant. — B33 7
Prestwick, Scot., U.K. — D2 11
Prestwick, Al., U.S. — D2 78
Presumpscot, stm., Me., U.S. — g7 96
Preti, mtn., Italy — C8 20
Pretoria, S. Afr. — C4 49
Prêto, stm., Braz. — D2 57
Prêto do Igapó-Açu, stm., Braz. — D2 59
Prettyboy Reservoir, res., Md., U.S. — A4 97
Pretty Prairie, Ks., U.S. — E5 93
Préveza, Grc. — C3 40
Prewitt, N.M., U.S. — B1 108
Prewitt Reservoir, res., Co., U.S. — A7 83

Prey Veng, Camb. — G6 35
Pribilof Islands, is., Ak., U.S. — D5 79
Priboj, Yugo. — D4 24
Příbram, Czech. — D3 26
Price, Md., U.S. — B6 97
Price, Tx., U.S. — C5 120
Price, Ut., U.S. — D5 121
Price, co., Wi., U.S. — C3 126
Price, stm., Ut., U.S. — D5 121
Pricedale, Ms., U.S. — D3 101
Price Inlet, b., S.C., U.S. — k12 117
Price Island, i., B.C. — C3 69
Priceville, Ont. — C4 73
Prichard, Al., U.S. — E1 78
Prichard, W.V., U.S. — C2 125
Priddy, Tx., U.S. — D3 120
Priego [de Córdoba], Spain — D3 22
Prien, La., U.S. — *D2 95
Prienai, Sov. Un. — A7 26
Prieska, S. Afr. — C3 49
Priest, Lake, l., Id., U.S. — A2 89
Priestley, Mount, mtn., B.C. — B3 69
Priest Rapids Dam, Wa., U.S. — C6 124
Priest Rapids Lake, res., Wa., U.S. — C6 124
Priest River, Id., U.S. — A2 89
Prievidza, Czech. — *D5 26
Prijedor, Yugo. — C4 24
Prijepolje, Yugo. — D4 24
Prikumsk, Sov. Un. — E2 28
Prilep, Yugo. — E5 24
Prilly, Switz. — C2 21
Priluki, Sov. Un. — F9 27
Prim, Point, c., P.E.I. — C6 71
Primate, Sask. — E1 75
Primero, stm., Arg. — A4 54
Primghar, Ia., U.S. — A2 92
Primorsk, Sov. Un. — D7 20
Primorsk, Sov. Un. — A6 26
Primorsk, Sov. Un. — A7 27
Primorsko-Akhtarsk, Sov. Un. — H12 27
Primrose, Ne., U.S. — C7 104
Primrose, R.I., U.S. — B3 116
Primrose Lake, l., Can. — B6 68
Prince, Sask. — E1 75
Prince, co., P.E.I. — C5 71
Prince, Lake, res., Va., U.S. — k14 123
Prince Albert, Sask. — D3 75
Prince Albert Mountains, mts., Ant. — B29 7
Prince Albert National Park, Sask. — C2 75
Prince Albert Sound, strt., N.W. Ter. — B9 66
Prince Alfred, Cape, c., N.W. Ter. — B8 66
Prince Charles Foreland, i., Nor. — B14 128
Prince Charles Island, i., N.W. Ter. — C17 66
Prince Charles Mountains, mts., Ant. — B19 7
Prince Edward, co., Ont. — C7 73
Prince Edward, co., Va., U.S. — C4 123
Prince Edward Island, prov., Can. — C6 71
Prince Edward Island National Park, P.E.I. — C6 71
Prince Edward Islands, is., S. Afr. — J23 2
Prince Frederick, Md., U.S. — C4 97
Prince George, B.C. — C6 69
Prince George, Va., U.S. — C5 123
Prince George, co., Va., U.S. — C5 123
Prince Georges, co., Md., U.S. — C4 97
Prince of Wales, i., Austl. — B7 50
Prince of Wales, Cape, c., Ak., U.S. — B6 79
Prince of Wales Island, i., N.W. Ter. — B13 66
Prince of Wales Island, i., Ak., U.S. — n23 79
Prince of Wales Strait, strt., N.W. Ter. — B9 66
Prince Olav Coast, Ant. — C17 7
Prince Patrick Island, i., N.W. Ter. — m27 66
Prince Regent Inlet, b., N.W. Ter. — B14 66
Prince Rupert, B.C. — B2 69
Princesa Isabel, Braz. — C3 57
Princes Lakes, In., U.S. — F5 91
Princes Risborough, Eng., U.K. — C7 12
Princess Anne, Md., U.S. — D6 97
Princess Astrid Coast, Ant. — B14 7
Princess Charlotte Bay, b., Austl. — B7 50
Princess Martha Coast, Ant. — B11 7
Princess Ragnhild Coast, Ant. — B15 7
Princess Royal Channel, strt., B.C. — C3 69
Princess Royal Island, i., B.C. — C3 69
Princes Town, Trin. — O23 65
Princeton, B.C. — E7 69
Princeton, Newf. — D5 72
Princeton, Ont. — D4 73
Princeton, Al., U.S. — A3 78
Princeton, Ar., U.S. — D3 81
Princeton, Ca., U.S. — C2 82
Princeton, Fl., U.S. — G6 86
Princeton, Il., U.S. — B4 90
Princeton, In., U.S. — H2 91
Princeton, Ia., U.S. — C7 92
Princeton, Ky., U.S. — C2 94
Princeton, Me., U.S. — C5 96
Princeton, Mn., U.S. — E5 100
Princeton, Mo., U.S. — A4 102
Princeton, N.J., U.S. — C3 107
Princeton, N.C., U.S. — B4 110
Princeton, W.V., U.S. — D3 125
Princeton, Wi., U.S. — E4 126
Princeton, Mount, mtn., Co., U.S. — C4 83
Princeton Junction, N.J., U.S. — C3 107
Princeville, Que. — C6 74
Princeville, Il., U.S. — C4 90
Princeville, N.C., U.S. — B5 110
Prince William, N.B. — C2 71
Prince William, co., Va., U.S. — B5 123
Prince William Sound, strt., Ak., U.S. — g18 79
Príncipe, is., S. Tom./P. — E1 46
Príncipe Channel, strt., B.C. — C3 69
Prineville, Or., U.S. — C6 114
Prineville Reservoir, res., Or., U.S. — C6 114
Pringle, S.D., U.S. — D2 118

Prinsburg, Mn., U.S. — F3 100
Prinzapolka, Nic. — E8 63
Prinzapolka, stm., Nic. — D6 62
Prior Lake, Mn., U.S. — F5 100
Priozersk, Sov. Un. — A8 27
Pripyat, Sov. Un. — F7 27
Pripyat (Pripet), stm., Sov. Un. — E7 27
Prishib, Sov. Un. — B4 39
Priština, Yugo. — D5 24
Pritchards Island, i., S.C., U.S. — G6 117
Pritchett, Co., U.S. — D8 83
Pritchett, Tx., U.S. — C5 120
Pritzerbe, E. Ger. — F6 15
Pritzwalk, E. Ger. — B6 18
Privas, Fr. — E6 16
Privert, Lac, l., Que. — g8 72
Privolnoye, Sov. Un. — H9 27
Prizren, Yugo. — D5 24
Prizzi, Italy — F4 23
Probolinggo, Indon. — G4 34
Procious, W.V., U.S. — m13 125
Procter, B.C. — E9 69
Procter, Mn., U.S. — D6 100
Proctor, Mt., U.S. — C2 103
Proctor, Ok., U.S. — B7 113
Proctor, Tx., U.S. — D3 120
Proctor, Vt., U.S. — D2 122
Proctor, W.V., U.S. — g8 125
Proctor Lake, res., Tx., U.S. — C3 120
Proctorsville, Vt., U.S. — E3 122
Proctorville, N.C., U.S. — C3 110
Proctorville, Oh., U.S. — D3 112
Proença-a-Nova, Port. — C2 22
Progreso, Mex. — C7 63
Prokhladnyy, Sov. Un. — E2 28
Prokopyevsk, Sov. Un. — D11 29
Prokuplje, Yugo. — D5 24
Prole, Ia., U.S. — f8 92
Proletarsk, Sov. Un. — H13 27
Proletarsk, Sov. Un. — q21 27
Prome (Pye), Burma — E10 36
Promise City, Ia., U.S. — D4 92
Promissão, Braz. — C3 56
Promontory Mountains, mts., Ut., U.S. — B3 121
Pronsfeld, W. Ger. — D6 17
Prophetstown, Il., U.S. — B4 90
Propriá, Braz. — D3 57
Prorer Wiek, b., E. Ger. — D7 15
Prorva, Sov. Un. — D4 28
Proserpine, Austl. — D8 50
Prosna, stm., Pol. — C5 26
Prosotsáni, Grc. — B5 25
Prospect, N.S. — E6 71
Prospect, Ct., U.S. — C4 84
Prospect, In., U.S. — C6 91
Prospect, Oh., U.S. — B2 112
Prospect, Or., U.S. — E4 114
Prospect, Pa., U.S. — E1 115
Prospect, Tn., U.S. — B4 119
Prospect Harbor, Me., U.S. — D4 96
Prospect Heights, Il., U.S. — *C5 83
Prospect Heights, Il., U.S. — *h9 90
Prospect Hill, mtn., Or., U.S. — k11 114
Prospect Hill, hill, Ma., U.S. — D6 98
Prospect Hill, hill, Ma., U.S. — g10 98
Prospect Park, N.J., U.S. — B4 107
Prospect Park, Pa., U.S. — p20 115
Prospect Plains, N.J., U.S. — C4 107
Prosperity, S.C., U.S. — C4 117
Prosperity, W.V., U.S. — n13 125
Prosser, Ne., U.S. — D7 104
Prosser, Wa., U.S. — C6 124
Prostějov, Czech. — D4 26
Prostki, Pol. — B7 26
Protection, Ks., U.S. — E4 93
Proton, Mo., U.S. — E5 102
Protivin, Ia., U.S. — A5 92
Proton Station, Ont. — C4 73
Prouts Neck, Me., U.S. — g7 96
Provadiya, Bul. — D8 24
Provadiyska, stm., Bul. — D8 24
Provençal, La., U.S. — C2 95
Provence, hist. reg., Fr. — F7 16
Providence, Fl., U.S. — C4 86
Providence, Ky., U.S. — C2 94
Providence, R.I., U.S. — C4 116
Providence, co., R.I., U.S. — B4 116
Providence, co., R.I., U.S. — C2 116
Providence Bay, Ont. — B2 73
Providence Forge, Va., U.S. — C5 123
Providence Point, c., R.I., U.S. — C5 116
Providencia, Isla de i., Col. — D7 62
Province Lake, l., N.H., U.S. — C5 106
Provincetown, Ma., U.S. — B7 98
Provins, Fr. — E5 16
Provo, Ar., U.S. — C1 81
Provo, S.D., U.S. — D2 118
Provo, Ut., U.S. — C4 121
Provo, stm., Ut., U.S. — C4 121
Provost, Alta. — D5 68
Prowers, co., Co., U.S. — D8 83
Prozor, Yugo. — D3 24
Pruden, Tn., U.S. — C10 119
Prudence Island, i., R.I., U.S. — E5 116
Prudence Island, i., R.I., U.S. — C5 116
Prudenville, Mi., U.S. — D6 99
Prudentópolis, Braz. — B6 56
Prudhoe Bay, Ak., U.S. — A10 79
Prudhoe Bay, b., Ak., U.S. — A10 79
Prud'homme, Sask. — E3 75
Prudnik, Pol. — C4 26
Prue, Ok., U.S. — A5 113
Prüm, W. Ger. — C6 17
Pruszków, Pol. — B6 26
Prut, stm., Eur. — B9 24
Pruzhany, Sov. Un. — E6 27
Prydz Bay, b., Ant. — C20 7
Pryor, Co., U.S. — D6 83
Pryor, Mt., U.S. — E8 103
Pryor, Ok., U.S. — A6 113
Pryor Mountains, mts., Mt., U.S. — E8 103
Przasnysz, Pol. — B6 26
Przeborz, Pol. — C6 26
Przemyśl, Pol. — D7 26
Przeworsk, Pol. — C7 26
Przewóz, Pol. — B9 19
Przhevalsk, Sov. Un. — E9 29
Psakhná, Grc. — C4 25
Psará, i., Grc. — C5 40
Psary, Pol. — g10 19
Psel, stm., Sov. Un. — G9 27
Pskov, Sov. Un. — D5 29
Pskov, Lake, l., Sov. Un. — B7 27
Pszczyna, Pol. — D5 26
Pszczyna, stm., Pol. — h10 26
Ptich, stm., Sov. Un. — E7 27
Ptolemaís, Grc. — B3 25
Ptuj, Yugo. — B2 24

Puako, Hi., U.S. — D6 88
Puán, Arg. — B4 54
Pu'apu'a, W. Sam. — F11 52
Pucallpa, Peru — C3 58
Pucheng, China — K8 32
Pucheng, China — G6 32
Puchón, S. Kor. — *H3 33
Puck, Pol. — A5 26
Puckaway Lake, l., Wi., U.S. — E4 126
Puckett, Ms., U.S. — C4 101
Pudasjärvi, Fin. — E12 14
Pudozh, Sov. Un. — A11 27
Puebla, state, Mex. — D5 63
Puebla de Don Fadrique, Spain — D4 22
Puebla del Caramiñal, Spain — A1 22
Puebla [de Zaragoza], Mex. — D5 63
Pueblo, Co., U.S. — C6 83
Pueblo, co., Co., U.S. — C6 83
Pueblo Colorado Wash, val., Az., U.S. — B6 80
Pueblo Hundido, Chile — E1 55
Pueblo Libre, Peru — *D2 58
Pueblo Mountain, mtn., Or., U.S. — E8 114
Pueblo Mountains, mts., Or., U.S. — E8 114
Pueblo Nuevo (part of Panamá), Pan. — k11 62
Pueblo Nuevo, Ven. — A4 60
Pueblo Reservoir, res., Co., U.S. — C6 83
Puebloviejo, Ec. — C2 58
Puente-Ceso, Spain — A1 22
Puentedeume, Spain — A1 22
Puente-Genil, Spain — D3 22
Pueo Point, c., Hi., U.S. — B1 88
Puer, China — G5 31
Puerco, Punta, c., P.R. — B4 65
Puerco, stm., U.S. — C6 80
Puerco, Rio, stm., N.M., U.S. — C2 108
Puerto Acosta, Bol. — C2 55
Puerto Aisén, Chile — D2 54
Puerto Alegre, Bol. — B3 55
Puerto Armuelles, Pan. — F6 62
Puerto Asís, Col. — C2 60
Puerto Ayacucho, Ven. — C3 60
Puerto Baquerizo Moreno, Ec. — g6 58
Puerto Barrios, Guat. — D7 63
Puerto Belgrano, Arg. — B4 54
Puerto Bermúdez, Peru — D3 58
Puerto Berrío, Col. — B2 60
Puerto Bolívar, Ec. — C1 58
Puerto Cabello, Ven. — A4 60
Puerto Cabezas, Nic. — E8 63
Puerto Carreño, Col. — B4 60
Puerto Casado, Para. — D4 55
Puerto Chicama, Peru — C2 58
Puerto Colombia, Col. — A3 60
Puerto Constanza, Arg. — f7 54
Puerto Cortés, Hond. — D7 63
Puerto Cumarebo, Ven. — A4 60
Puerto de la Cruz, Arg. — A3 54
Puerto del Rosario, Spain — m15 22
Puerto del Son, Spain — A1 22
Puerto de Luna, N.M., U.S. — C5 108
Puerto Deseado, Arg. — D3 54
Puerto Eten, Peru — C2 58
Puerto Francisco de Orellana, Ec. — B2 58
Puerto Guaraní, Para. — D4 55
Puerto Heath, Bol. — B2 55
Puerto Inírida, Col. — C4 60
Puerto Jiménez, C.R. — F6 62
Puerto la Cruz, Ven. — A5 60
Puerto Leguízamo, Col. — D3 60
Puerto Limón, Col. — C3 60
Puertollano, Spain — C3 22
Puerto Lobos, Arg. — C3 54
Puerto López, Col. — C3 60
Puerto Madryn, Arg. — C3 54
Puerto Maldonado, Peru — D4 58
Puerto México see Coatzacoalcos, Mex. — D6 63
Puerto Mineral, Arg. — E4 55
Puerto Montt, Chile — C2 54
Puerto Morazán, Nic. — D4 62
Puerto Nariño, Col. — C4 60
Puerto Natales, Chile — D2 54
Puerto Padre, Cuba — D5 64
Puerto Páez, Ven. — C4 60
Puerto Peñasco, Mex. — A2 63
Puerto Pilón, Pan. — k11 62
Puerto Pinasco, Para. — D4 55
Puerto Pirámides, Arg. — C3 54
Puerto Plata, Dom. Rep. — E8 64
Puerto Portillo, Peru — C3 58
Puerto Princesa, Phil. — D5 34
Puerto Real, Spain — D2 22
Puerto Rico, ctry., N.A. — G11 64
Puerto Saavedra, Chile — C2 54
Puerto Sastre, Para. — D4 55
Puerto Siles, Bol. — B2 55
Puerto Suárez, Bol. — C4 55
Puerto Supe, Peru — D2 58
Puerto Tejada, Col. — C2 60
Puerto Toledo, Col. — C3 60
Puerto Vallarta, Mex. — C3 63
Puerto Varas, Chile — C2 54
Puerto Victoria, Peru — C3 58
Puerto Viejo, C.R. — F6 62
Puerto Villamizar, Col. — B3 60
Puerto Visser, Arg. — D3 54
Puerto Wilches, Col. — B3 60
Pugachev, Sov. Un. — C3 28
Puget Sound, strt., Wa., U.S. — B3 124
Puget Sound Naval Shipyard, mil., Wa., U.S. — e10 124
Puget-Théniers, Fr. — F7 16
Pugwash, N.S. — D6 71
Puhi, Hi., U.S. — B2 88
Puhja, China — H8 32
Puigcerdá, Spain — A6 22
Pujili, Ec. — C2 58
Pujiang, China — E8 32
Pukalani, Hi., U.S. — C5 88
Pukaskwa National Park, Ont. — o18 73
Pukchŏng, N. Kor. — C12 31
Pukeashun Mountain, mtn., B.C. — D8 69
Pukekohe, N.Z. — L15 51
Pukhan, stm., Asia — H3 33
Pukou, China — H8 32
Puksubaek, Mount, mtn., N. Kor. — F3 33
Pukwana, S.D., U.S. — D6 118
Pula, Italy — E2 23
Pula, Alb. — A2 25
Pulaski, Hi., U.S. — C8 88

Pulaski, In., U.S. — C4 91
Pulaski, Ia., U.S. — D5 92
Pulaski, Ms., U.S. — C4 101
Pulaski, N.Y., U.S. — B4 109
Pulaski, Tn., U.S. — B4 119
Pulaski, Va., U.S. — C2 123
Pulaski, Wi., U.S. — D5 126
Pulaski, co., Ar., U.S. — C3 81
Pulaski, co., Ga., U.S. — D3 87
Pulaski, co., Il., U.S. — F4 90
Pulaski, co., In., U.S. — B4 91
Pulaski, co., Ky., U.S. — C5 94
Pulaski, co., Mo., U.S. — D5 102
Pulaski, co., Va., U.S. — C2 123
Pulaski, co., ... — C6 26
Pulheim, W. Ger. — *C3 18
Pullman, Mi., U.S. — F4 99
Pullman, Wa., U.S. — C8 124
Pullman, Wa., U.S. — B4 125
Pulog, Mount, mtn., Phil. — B6 34
Pulozero, Sov. Un. — C15 14
Pułtusk, Pol. — B6 26
Pumo Lake, l., China — C13 37
Pumphrey, Md., U.S. — h11 97
Pumpkin Buttes, mtn., Wy., U.S. — C7 127
Pumpkin Creek, stm., Mt., U.S. — E11 103
Pumpkin Creek, stm., Ne., U.S. — C2 104
Pumpville, Tx., U.S. — E2 120
Puná, Bol. — C2 55
Puná, Isla, i., Ec. — C1 58
Punakha, Bhu. — C8 36
Punat, Yugo. — C2 24
Punata, Bol. — C2 55
Punchaw, B.C. — C6 69
Pune, India — E5 36
Pungo, India — B6 110
Pungsan, N. Kor. — F4 33
Punia, Zaire — B4 48
Punjab, state, India — B5 36
Punjab, prov., Pak. — B5 36
Punnichy, Sask. — F3 75
Puno, Peru — E3 58
Puno, dept., Peru — F4 58
Punta Alta, Arg. — B4 54
Punta Arenas, Chile — h11 54
Punta de Díaz, Chile — E1 55
Punta del Este, Ur. — E2 56
Punta de Piedras, Ven. — A5 60
Punta de Vacas, Arg. — A3 54
Punta Gorda, Belize — D7 63
Punta Gorda, Fl., U.S. — F4 86
Punta Gorda, Bahía de, b., Nic. — E8 63
Punta Moreno, Peru — C2 58
Puntarenas, C.R. — E5 62
Punto Fijo, Ven. — A3 60
Puntzi Lake, l., B.C. — C5 69
Punxsutawney, Pa., U.S. — E4 115
Puposky, Mn., U.S. — C4 100
Puquio, Peru — D3 58
Pur, stm., Sov. Un. — C10 29
Puranpur, India — C8 37
Purari, stm., Pap. N. Gui. — k11 50
Purcell, Mo., U.S. — D3 102
Purcell, Ok., U.S. — B4 113
Purcell Mountains, mts., N.A. — D9 69
Purcellville, Va., U.S. — A5 123
Purdham Hill, mtn., Ar., U.S. — h10 81
Purdum, Ne., U.S. — B5 104
Purdy, Mo., U.S. — E4 102
Purépero, Mex. — n12 63
Purgatoire, stm., Co., U.S. — D7 83
Purgatoire Peak, mtn., Co., U.S. — D5 83
Puri, India — E8 36
Purmerend, Neth. — B4 17
Pürnia, stm., India — H6 37
Pürnia, India — E8 36
Purple Springs, Alta. — E5 68
Purus, stm., S.A. — D4 53
Puruliya, India — m13 37
Purus, stm., S.A. — D5 53
Purwakarta, Indon. — *G3 34
Purworkerto, Indon. — *G3 34
Puryear, Tn., U.S. — A3 119
Puryŏng-dong, N. Kor. — F4 33
Pusan, S. Kor. — D10 31
Pushaw Lake, l., Me., U.S. — D4 96
Pushkin, Sov. Un. — D6 29
Pushkino, Sov. Un. — C11 27
Pushmataha, Al., U.S. — C1 78
Pushmataha, co., Ok., U.S. — C6 113
Pushthrough, Newf. — E3 72
Pusiano, Lago di, l., Italy — E7 21
Püspökladány, Hung. — B5 24
Pustelnik, Pol. — k14 26
Pustynnaya, Sov. Un. — B8 28
Putao, Burma — C10 36
Puteaux, Fr. — g9 16
Putian, China — I8 32
Putilovo, Sov. Un. — s32 14
Puting, Cape, c., Indon. — F4 34
Putivl, Sov. Un. — F9 27
Putlitz, E. Ger. — E6 15
Putnam, Al., U.S. — C1 78
Putnam, Ct., U.S. — B8 84
Putnam, Ok., U.S. — B3 113
Putnam, Tx., U.S. — C3 120
Putnam, co., Fl., U.S. — C5 86
Putnam, co., Ga., U.S. — C3 87
Putnam, co., Il., U.S. — B4 90
Putnam, co., In., U.S. — E4 91
Putnam, co., Mo., U.S. — A4 102
Putnam, co., N.Y., U.S. — D7 109
Putnam, co., Oh., U.S. — B1 112
Putnam, co., Tn., U.S. — C8 119
Putnam, co., W.V., U.S. — C3 125
Putnam Station, N.Y., U.S. — B7 109
Putnamville, In., U.S. — E4 91
Putney, Ga., U.S. — E2 87
Putney, Vt., U.S. — F3 122
Putney, S.D., U.S. — B7 118
Putorana, Gory, mts., Sov. Un. — C12 29
Puttalam, Sri L. — C6 38
Putte, Neth. — C4 17
Püttlingen, W. Ger. — D1 19
Putumayo, dept., Col. — C2 60
Putumayo (Içá), stm., S.A. — C12 40
Putre, Chile — C2 55
Puukohola Heiau National Historic Site, hist., Hi., U.S. — D6 88
Puukolii, Hi., U.S. — C5 88
Puulavesi, l., Fin. — G12 14
Puunene, Hi., U.S. — C5 88
Puurs, Bel. — C4 17
Puxico, Mo., U.S. — E7 102
Puyallup, Wa., U.S. — B3 124

Name	Map Ref.	Page
Puyallup, stm., Wa., U.S.	C3	124
Puyang, China	G6	32
Puyehue, Chile	C2	54
Puyo, Ec.	B2	58
Pūzak, Hāmūn-e, l., Afg.	F10	39
Pwani, prov., Tan.	C6	48
Pweto, Zaire	C4	48
Pwllheli, Wales, U.K.	D4	10
Pyaozero, l., Sov. Un.	D14	14
Pyapon, Burma	E10	36
Pyasina, stm., Sov. Un.	B12	29
Pyatigorsk, Sov. Un.	E2	28
Pyatt, Ar., U.S.	A3	81
Pyhäjärvi, l., Fin.	G10	14
Pyinmana, Burma	E10	36
Pyland, Ms., U.S.	B4	101
Pyles Fork, stm., W.V., U.S.	h10	125
Pymatuning Reservoir, res., U.S.	C1	115
Pyŏngchang, S. Kor.	H4	33
Pyŏngtaek, S. Kor.	H3	33
Pyŏngyang, N. Kor.	D10	31
Pyote, Tx., U.S.	D1	120
Pyramid Lake, l., Nv., U.S.	C2	105
Pyramid Lake Indian Reservation, Nv., U.S.	D2	105
Pyramid Mountains, mts., N.M., U.S.	E1	108
Pyramid Peak, mtn., N.M., U.S.	E1	108
Pyramid Peak, mtn., Wy., U.S.	C2	127
Pyramids, hist., Eg.	C3	38
Pyrenees, mts., Eur.	A6	22
Pyrites, N.Y., U.S.	f9	109
Pyrmont, In., U.S.	D4	91
Pyrzyce, Pol.	B3	26
Pyskowice, Pol.	g9	26
Pytalovo, Sov. Un.	C6	27
Pyu, Burma	E10	36
Q		
Qabātiyah, Isr. Occ.	B7	41
Qā'emshahr, Iran	C6	39
Qā'en, Iran	E9	39
Qahar Youyi Zhongqi, China	D5	32
Qaidam Pendi (Tsaidam Basin), China	D3	31
Qalamshāh, Eg.	H8	40
Qalāt, Afg.	B4	36
Qal'at Bīshah, Sau. Ar.	C4	38
Qal'at Şāliḩ, Iraq	F3	39
Qal'at Sukkar, Iraq	F3	39
Qal'eh-ye Now, Afg.	D11	39
Qallābāt, Sud.	C4	47
Qalqīliya, Isr. Occ.	B6	41
Qalyūb, Eg.	D3	41
Qamdo, China	E4	31
Qamea, i., Fiji	H16	52
Qamīnis, Libya	C4	43
Qānā, Leb.	A7	41
Qandahār see Kandahar, Afg.	B4	36
Qandala, Som.	C6	47
Qārah, Egypt	H6	40
Qardho, Som.	D6	47
Qareh, stm., Iran	D5	39
Qārūn, Birkat, l., Eg.	D6	43
Qaryat Abu Nujaym, Libya	C3	43
Qaşr al Farāfirah, Eg.	C2	38
Qaşr Banī Walīd, Libya	C2	43
Qasr el Boukhari, Alg.	B5	44
Qaşr-e Shīrīn, Iran	D2	39
Qa'ţabah, Yemen	D4	38
Qatar, ctry., Asia	C5	38
Qattara Depression, depr., Eg.	B4	47
Qawz Rajab, Sud.	B4	38
Qazvīn, Iran	B4	38
Qeshm, Iran	H8	39
Qeshm, i., Iran	C5	38
Qezel Owzan, stm., Iran	D8	32
Qian'an, China	J3	32
Qianjiang, China	J3	32
Qianshan, China	I7	32
Qiantang Jiang, stm., China	J8	32
Qianxian, China	G3	32
Qianyang, China	F7	31
Qiaojia, China	F5	31
Qichun, China	I6	32
Qiemo, China	A8	36
Qijiang, China	J2	32
Qila Lādgasht, Pak.	C3	36
Qila Saifullāh, Pak.	B2	37
Qilian Shan, mts., China	D4	31
Qimen, China	J7	32
Qinā, Eg.	C3	38
Qing'an, China	C3	33
Qingdao (Tsingtao), China	D9	31
Qinghai Hu, l., China	D4	31
Qingjian, China	D7	31
Qingjiang, China	J6	32
Qingliu, China	F8	31
Qingpu, China	E9	31
Qingyang, China	D6	31
Qingyuan, China	C11	32
Qingyun, China	F7	32
Qing Zang Gaoyuan (Plateau of Tibet), plat., China	G11	30
Qin He, stm., China	G5	32
Qinhuangdao, China	D8	31
Qin Ling (Tsinling Shan), mts., China	E6	31
Qinxian, China	F5	32
Qinyang, China	G5	32
Qinzhou, China	B8	35
Qiongshan, China	B4	34
Qiongzhou Haixia, strt., China	B8	35
Qiqian, China	A9	31
Qiqihar (Tsitsihar), China	B9	31
Qiryat Ata, Isr.	B7	41
Qiryat Gat, Isr.	C6	41
Qiryat Mal'akhi, Isr.	C6	41
Qiryat Ono, Isr.	g10	41
Qiryat Shemona, Isr.	B7	41
Qiryat Yam, Isr.	B7	41
Qishn, Yemen	D6	38
Qishon, stm., Isr.	B7	41
Qitai, China	C2	31
Qitaihe, China	*B11	31
Qiyang, China	F7	31
Qīzān, Sau. Ar.	D4	38
Qnadsa, Alg.	C4	44
Qom, Iran	B5	38
Qom, stm., Iran	E5	39
Qomemiyyut (Talbiya) (part of Jerusalem), Isr.	m14	41
Qomsheh, Iran	E5	39
Quabbin Reservoir, res., Ma., U.S.	B3	98
Quaco Head, c., N.B.	D4	71
Quaddick, Ct., U.S.	B8	84
Quaddick Reservoir, res., Ct., U.S.	B8	84
Quail Oaks, Va., U.S.	n18	123
Quakenbrück, W. Ger.	B3	18
Quaker City, Oh., U.S.	C4	112
Quaker Hill, Ct., U.S.	D7	84
Quakertown, N.J., U.S.	B3	107
Quakertown, Pa., U.S.	F11	115
Qualicum Beach, B.C.	E5	69
Quality, Ky., U.S.	C3	94
Quamba, Mn., U.S.	E5	100
Quanah, Tx., U.S.	B3	120
Quang Ngai, Viet.	B3	34
Quang Trach, Viet.	D7	35
Quang Tri, Viet.	B3	34
Quannapowitt, Lake, l., Ma., U.S.	f11	98
Quantico, Md., U.S.	D6	97
Quantico, Va., U.S.	B5	123
Quantico Marine Corps Air Station, mil., Va., U.S.	B5	123
Quantico Station, Va., U.S.	*B5	123
Quanzhou, China	F7	31
Quanzhou, China	G8	31
Quapaw, Ok., U.S.	A7	113
Qu'Appelle, Sask.	G4	75
Qu'Appelle, stm., Can.	G4	75
Quarai, Braz.	E1	56
Quarai, stm., S.A.	E1	56
Quarles Mountains, mts., Indon.	F5	34
Quarryville, N.B.	C4	71
Quarryville, Ct., U.S.	B6	84
Quarryville, Pa., U.S.	G9	115
Quartu Sant' Elena, Italy	E2	23
Quartz Hill, Ca., U.S.	*E4	82
Quartz Mountain, mtn., Or., U.S.	D4	114
Quartzsite, Az., U.S.	D1	80
Quasqueton, Ia., U.S.	B6	92
Quassapaug, Lake, l., Ct., U.S.	C3	84
Quatre, Isle, i., St. Vin.	V26	65
Quatsino Sound, strt., B.C.	D3	69
Quay, N.M., U.S.	C6	108
Quay, Ok., U.S.	A5	113
Quay, co., N.M., U.S.	C6	108
Qūchān, Iran	B5	38
Quealy, Wy., U.S.	E3	127
Québec, Que.	C6	74
Quebec, co., Que.	B5	74
Quebec, prov., Can.	C5	74
Quebeck, Tn., U.S.	D8	119
Quechee, Vt., U.S.	D4	122
Quechee Gorge, val., Vt., U.S.	D4	122
Quecreek, Pa., U.S.	F3	115
Quedlinburg, E. Ger.	C5	18
Queen, stm., R.I., U.S.	E2	116
Queen, Cape, c., N.W. Ter.	D17	66
Queen Alexandra Range, mts., Ant.	A29	7
Queen Anne, Md., U.S.	B5	97
Queen Annes, co., Md., U.S.	B5	97
Queen Bess, Mount, mtn., B.C.	D5	69
Queenborough [-in-Sheppey], Eng., U.K.	E7	10
Queen Charlotte, B.C.	C1	69
Queen Charlotte Islands, is., B.C.	C1	69
Queen Charlotte Mountains, mts., B.C.	C1	69
Queen Charlotte Sound, strt., B.C.	n17	69
Queen Charlotte Strait, strt., B.C.	D4	69
Queen City, Mo., U.S.	A5	102
Queen City, Tx., U.S.	C5	120
Queen Creek, Az., U.S.	m9	80
Queen Elizabeth Islands, is., N.W. Ter.	k30	66
Queen Fabiola Mountains, mts., Ant.	B16	7
Queen Mary Coast, Ant.	C22	7
Queen Maud Gulf, b., N.W. Ter.	C12	66
Queen Maud Land, reg., Ant.	B15	7
Queen Maud Mountains, mts., Ant.	A31	7
Queens, co., N.B.	D4	71
Queens, co., P.E.I.	C6	71
Queens, co., N.Y., U.S.	E7	109
Queensborough, Ont.	C7	73
Queensborough, Wa., U.S.	*B3	124
Queensferry see South Queensferry, Scot., U.K.	E5	13
Queen Shoals, W.V., U.S.	C3	125
Queensland, state, Austl.	E3	87
Queensland, Ga., U.S.	E3	87
Queensport, N.S.	D8	71
Queens Sound, strt., B.C.	C3	69
Queenstown, Austl.	o15	50
Queenstown, Alta.	D4	68
Queenstown, N.B.	D3	71
Queenstown, N.Z.	F2	51
Queenstown, S. Afr.	D4	49
Queenstown, Md., U.S.	C5	97
Queen Victoria Sea, Eur.	A5	29
Queets, Wa., U.S.	B1	124
Queguay Grande, stm., Ur.	E1	56
Queimadas, Braz.	B2	57
Queimadinhas, Braz.	A4	56
Queixada, Braz.	B4	56
Quela, Ang.	C2	48
Quelelevu, i., Fiji	H16	52
Quelimane, Moz.	A6	49
Quemado, N.M., U.S.	C1	108
Quemado, Tx., U.S.	E2	120
Quemado de Güines, Cuba	C6	64
Quemú Quemú, Arg.	B4	54
Quenemo, Ks., U.S.	D8	93
Quentin, Ms., U.S.	D3	101
Quepos, C.R.	F5	62
Quequén, Arg.	B5	54
Querétaro, Mex.	C4	63
Querétaro, state, Mex.	C5	63
Querfurt, E. Ger.	B6	19
Quers, Fr.	A1	21
Quesada, Spain	D4	22
Queshan, China	H6	32
Quesnel, B.C.	C6	69
Quesnel, stm., B.C.	C7	69
Quesnel Lake, l., B.C.	C7	69
Questa, N.M., U.S.	A4	108
Quetena, Bol.	D2	55
Quetico Provincial Park, Ont.	o17	73
Quetta, Pak.	B4	36
Quevedo, Ec.	B2	58
Quezaltenango, Guat.	E6	63
Quezaltepeque, El Sal.	C6	63
Quezon City, Phil.	C6	34
Quibala, Ang.	D1	48
Quibdó, Col.	B2	60
Quiberon, Fr.	D2	16
Quiberon Peninsula, pen., Fr.	E6	16
Quicksburg, Va., U.S.	B4	123
Quidnessett, R.I., U.S.	E4	116
Quidnick, R.I., U.S.	D3	116
Quidnick Reservoir, res., R.I., U.S.	D2	116
Quiindy, Para.	E4	55
Quilá, Mex.	C3	63
Quilcene, Wa., U.S.	B3	124
Quilengues, Ang.	D1	48
Quileute Indian Reservation, Wa., U.S.	B1	124
Quilino, Arg.	F3	55
Quillagua, Chile	D2	55
Quillan, Fr.	F5	16
Quill Lake, Sask.	E3	75
Quillota, Chile	A2	54
Quilmes, Arg.	g7	54
Quilon, India	G6	36
Quilpie, Austl.	E7	50
Quilpué, Chile	A2	54
Quilty, Ire.	E2	11
Quimbele, Ang.	C2	48
Quimby, Ia., U.S.	B2	92
Quimby, Me., U.S.	B4	96
Quimilí, Arg.	E3	55
Quimper, Fr.	C1	16
Quimperlé, Fr.	D2	16
Quinaby, Or., U.S.	B4	114
Quinault, stm., Wa., U.S.	B1	124
Quinault, Lake, l., Wa., U.S.	B1	124
Quinault Indian Reservation, Wa., U.S.	B1	124
Quince Orchard, Md., U.S.	*B3	97
Quincy, Ca., U.S.	C3	82
Quincy, Fl., U.S.	B2	86
Quincy, Il., U.S.	D2	90
Quincy, In., U.S.	F4	91
Quincy, Ks., U.S.	E8	93
Quincy, Ky., U.S.	B6	94
Quincy, Ma., U.S.	B5	98
Quincy, Mi., U.S.	G6	99
Quincy, Mo., U.S.	C5	102
Quincy, Oh., U.S.	B2	112
Quincy, Or., U.S.	A3	114
Quincy, Wa., U.S.	B6	124
Quincy Bay, b., Ma., U.S.	g12	98
Quindío, dept., Col.	C2	60
Quinebaug, Ct., U.S.	A8	84
Quinebaug, stm., Ct., U.S.	C8	84
Quines, Arg.	A3	54
Quinga, Moz.	A7	49
Quinhagak, Ak., U.S.	D7	79
Qui Nhon, Viet.	C4	34
Quinlan, Ok., U.S.	A2	113
Quinlan, Tx., U.S.	C4	120
Quinn, S.D., U.S.	D3	118
Quinn, stm., Nv., U.S.	B3	105
Quinn Canyon Range, mts., Nv., U.S.	F6	105
Quinnesec, Mi., U.S.	C3	99
Quinnipiac, stm., Ct., U.S.	D4	84
Quinnville, R.I., U.S.	B4	116
Quintana de la Serena, Spain	C4	22
Quintanar [de la Orden], Spain	C4	22
Quintana Roo, state, Mex.	D7	63
Quinter, Ks., U.S.	C3	93
Quintero, Chile	A2	54
Quinton, Sask.	F3	75
Quinton, Ky., U.S.	D5	94
Quinton, N.J., U.S.	D2	107
Quinton, Ok., U.S.	B6	113
Quinwood, W.V., U.S.	C4	125
Quipapá, Braz.	C3	57
Quipungo, Ang.	D1	48
Quirauk Mountain, mtn., Md., U.S.	A2	97
Quirindi, Austl.	E8	51
Quirinópolis, Braz.	B5	56
Quiroga, Ven.	B5	60
Quiroga, Spain	A2	22
Quirpon Island, i., Newf.	C4	72
Quissanga, Moz.	D7	48
Quitaque, Tx., U.S.	B2	120
Quita Sueño Bank, Col.	C7	62
Quitman, Ar., U.S.	B3	81
Quitman, Ga., U.S.	F3	87
Quitman, La., U.S.	B3	95
Quitman, Ms., U.S.	C5	101
Quitman, Mo., U.S.	A2	102
Quitman, Tx., U.S.	C5	120
Quitman, co., Ga., U.S.	E1	87
Quitman, co., Ms., U.S.	A3	101
Quitman Mountains, mts., Tx., U.S.	o12	120
Quito, Ec.	B2	58
Quixadá, Braz.	C3	57
Quixeramobim, Braz.	C3	57
Qulin, Mo., U.S.	E7	102
Quoi, i., Micron.	Q18	52
Quonnipaug Lake, l., Ct., U.S.	D5	84
Quonochontaug, R.I., U.S.	G2	116
Quonochontaug Pond, l., R.I., U.S.	G2	116
Quonset Point, c., R.I., U.S.	E4	116
Quorn, Austl.	F2	51
Qurayyah, Wādī, val., Eg.	D6	41
Qūs, Eg.	C3	38
Qusṛah, Isr. Occ.	g12	41
Quthing, Leso.	D4	49
Quxian, China	E7	31
Quxian, China	F8	31
Quzhou, China	*F8	31
R		
Raab (Rába), stm., Eur.	B2	24
Raabs [an der Thaya], Aus.	D7	18
Raahe, Fin.	E11	14
Raalte, Neth.	B6	17
Ra'ananna, Isr.	g10	41
Raasay, i., Scot., U.K.	C2	13
Rab, i., Yugo.	C2	24
Raba, Indon.	G6	34
Rába (Raab), stm., Eur.	B3	24
Rabastens, Fr.	F4	16
Rabat, Mor.	B3	44
Rabaul, Pap. N. Gui.	h13	50
Rabbit Creek, stm., S.D., U.S.	B3	118
Rabbit Ears Pass, Co., U.S.	A4	83
Rabbit Hash, Ky., U.S.	k13	94
Rabbit Lake, Sask.	D2	75
Rabi, i., Fiji	H16	52
Rābigh, Sau. Ar.	C3	38
Rabun, Al., U.S.	D2	78
Rabun, co., Ga., U.S.	B3	87
Rabun Bald, mtn., Ga., U.S.	B3	87
Rača, Yugo.	C5	24
Raccoon Creek, stm., Oh., U.S.	D3	112
Raccourci Island, i., La., U.S.	D4	95
Race, Cape, c., Newf.	E5	72
Raceland, Ky., U.S.	B7	94
Raceland, La., U.S.	E5	95
Race Point, c., Ma., U.S.	B7	98
Race Pond, Ga., U.S.	F4	87
Rach Gia, Viet.	C4	34
Raciborz, Pol.	C5	26
Racine, Mn., U.S.	G6	100
Racine, Mo., U.S.	E3	102
Racine, Oh., U.S.	D4	112
Racine, Pa., U.S.	D8	115
Racine, Wi., U.S.	F6	126
Racine, co., Wi., U.S.	F5	126
Radbuza, stm., Czech.	D8	19
Råde, Nor.	p28	14
Radeberg, E. Ger.	C6	18
Radebeul, E. Ger.	B8	19
Radersburg, Mt., U.S.	D5	103
Radford, Va., U.S.	C2	123
Radhanpur, India	F3	37
Radisson, Sask.	E2	75
Radisson, Wi., U.S.	C3	126
Radium, Ks., U.S.	D5	93
Radium, Mn., U.S.	B2	100
Radium Hot Springs, B.C.	D9	69
Radium Springs, N.M., U.S.	E3	108
Radnice, Czech.	D8	19
Radnor, Oh., U.S.	B2	112
Radnor Township, Pa., U.S.	*F11	115
Radom, Pol.	C6	26
Radom, Il., U.S.	E4	90
Radomsko, Pol.	C5	26
Radomyshl, Sov. Un.	F7	27
Radoviš, Yugo.	E6	24
Radstadt, Aus.	E6	18
Radville, Sask.	H3	75
Radway, Alta.	B4	68
Radzionków, Pol.	g9	26
Radzymin, Pol.	k14	26
Radzyń [Podlaski], Pol.	C7	26
Rae, N.W. Ter.	D9	66
Rae Bareli, India	C7	36
Rāe Lakes, l., Ire.	E3	50
Raeford, N.C., U.S.	C3	110
Raeside, Lake, l., Austl.	E3	50
Rae Strait, strt., N.W. Ter.	C14	66
Rafaela, Arg.	A4	54
Rafaï, Cen. Afr. Rep.	D4	46
Rafah, Isr. Occ.	G10	41
Rafhā', Sau. Ar.	C4	38
Rafsanjān, Iran	F8	39
Raft, stm., Id., U.S.	G5	89
Raft River Mountains, mts., Ut., U.S.	B2	121
Raga, Sud.	D2	47
Ragan, Ne., U.S.	D6	104
Ragay, Phil.	p14	34
Ragay Gulf, b., Phil.	p14	34
Ragged Island, i., Me., U.S.	E4	96
Ragged Island Range, is., Bah.	C6	64
Ragged Lake, l., Me., U.S.	C3	96
Ragged Top Mountain, mtn., Wy., U.S.	E7	127
Raghza, Pak.	B4	36
Raglan, N.Z.	B3	78
Raglesville, In., U.S.	G4	91
Ragley, La., U.S.	D2	95
Rago, Ks., U.S.	E5	93
Ragsdale, Tn., U.S.	G3	91
Ragunda, Swe.	F7	14
Ragusa, Italy	F5	23
Rahad al Bardi, Sud.	C1	47
Rahden, W. Ger.	F2	15
Rahīmyār Khān, Pak.	C5	36
Rahway, N.J., U.S.	B4	107
Rahway, stm., N.J., U.S.	k7	107
Rāichūr, India	E6	36
Raiford, Fl., U.S.	B4	86
Raigarh, India	D7	36
Railroad Valley, val., Nv., U.S.	E6	105
Raimbault, stm., Que.	A5	74
Rainbow Bridge National Monument, Ut., U.S.	F5	121
Rainbow City, Pan.	k11	62
Rainbow City, Al., U.S.	*A3	78
Rainbow Falls, wtfl., Tn., U.S.	D10	119
Rainbow Flowage, res., Wi., U.S.	C4	126
Rainbow Lake, l., Me., U.S.	C3	96
Rainelle, W.V., U.S.	D4	125
Raines, Or., U.S.	E3	87
Rainier, Or., U.S.	A4	114
Rainier, Wa., U.S.	C3	124
Rainier, Mount, mtn., Wa., U.S.	C4	124
Rains, Tx., U.S.	C5	120
Rains, co., Tx., U.S.	C5	120
Rainsboro, Oh., U.S.	C2	112
Rainsville, Al., U.S.	A4	78
Rainy, stm., N.A.	B4	100
Rainy Lake, l., Mn., U.S.	B5	100
Rainy Lake, l., Mn., U.S.	B5	100
Rainy River, Ont.	o16	73
Rainy River, dept., Ont.	o16	73
Raipur, India	D7	36
Ra'īs, Sau. Ar.	C3	38
Raismes, Fr.	D3	17
Raja, Cape, c., Indon.	K2	35
Rājahmundry, India	D7	36
Rajang, stm., Malay.	E4	34
Rājapālaiyam, India	*G6	36
Rājasthan, state, India	G4	37
Rajin, N. Kor.	D5	31
Rājpipla, India	D5	37
Rājpura, India	D3	122
Rāka Zangbo, stm., China	C11	30
Rakaia, stm., N.Z.	O13	51
Rake, Ia., U.S.	A4	92
Rakhov, Sov. Un.	A7	24
Rakkestad, Nor.	p29	14
Rakovník, Czech.	B6	27
Rakvere, Sov. Un.	B6	27
Raleigh, Newf.	C4	72
Raleigh, Fl., U.S.	C4	86
Raleigh, Il., U.S.	F5	90
Raleigh, In., U.S.	E7	91
Raleigh, Ms., U.S.	C4	101
Raleigh, N.C., U.S.	B4	110
Raleigh, N.D., U.S.	C4	111
Raleigh, W.V., U.S.	n13	125
Raleigh, co., W.V., U.S.	D3	125
Raleigh Bay, b., N.C., U.S.	C6	110
Raleigh Hills, Or., U.S.	*B4	114
Ralls, Tx., U.S.	C2	120
Ralls, co., Mo., U.S.	B6	102
Ralph, Al., U.S.	B2	78
Ralph, Mi., U.S.	B3	99
Ralph, W.V., U.S.	n13	125
Ralston, Ia., U.S.	B3	92
Ralston, Ne., U.S.	g12	104
Ralston, Ok., U.S.	A5	113
Ralston, Pa., U.S.	D8	115
Ralston, Tn., U.S.	A3	119
Ralston, Wa., U.S.	B4	124
Ralston Valley, val., Nv., U.S.	E4	105
Ram, stm., Alta.	C3	68
Rama, Sask.	F4	75
Rama, Isr.	B7	41
Rama, Nic.	E8	63
Ramādi Barrage, Iraq	F14	40
Ramah, Co., U.S.	B6	83
Ramah, N.M., U.S.	B1	108
Ramah Indian Reservation, N.M., U.S.	C1	108
Ramapo, stm., N.J., U.S.	A4	107
Ramapo Mountains, mts., N.J., U.S.	A4	107
Ramat Gan, Isr.	B6	41
Ramat ḤaKovesh, Isr.	g10	41
Ramat HaSharon, Isr.	C7	16
Rambervillers, Fr.	*B3	85
Rambleton Acres, De., U.S.	D3	107
Ramblewood, N.J., U.S.	C4	16
Rambouillet, Fr.	E3	72
Ramea, Newf.	E3	72
Ramea Islands, is., Newf.	D12	27
Ramenskoye, Sov. Un.	C3	78
Ramer, Al., U.S.	B3	119
Ramer, Tn., U.S.	F3	120
Ramirez, Tx., U.S.	C6	41
Ramla, Isr.	H10	41
Ramm, Jabal, mtn., Jord.	t34	14
Ramnäs, Swe.	D6	41
Ramon, Har, mtn., Isr.	D6	41
Ramon, Naḥal, val., Isr.	F5	82
Ramona, Ca., U.S.	D6	93
Ramona, Ks., U.S.	A6	113
Ramona, Ok., U.S.	C8	118
Ramona, S.D., U.S.	C4	11
Ramor, Lough, l., Ire.	B9	79
Rampart, Ak., U.S.	B5	83
Rampart Range, mts., Co., U.S.	C6	36
Rāmpur, India	n12	99
Ramsay, Mi., U.S.	h12	73
Ramsayville, Ont.	B3	110
Ramseur, N.C., U.S.	B7	12
Ramsey, Eng., U.K.	C4	10
Ramsey, I. of Man	D4	90
Ramsey, Il., U.S.	E5	100
Ramsey, Mn., U.S.	A4	107
Ramsey, N.J., U.S.	E5	100
Ramsey, co., Mn., U.S.	A7	111
Ramsey, co., N.D., U.S.	E7	10
Ramsgate, Eng., U.K.	E5	103
Ramshorn Peak, mtn., Mt., U.S.	C3	127
Ramshorn Peak, mtn., Wy., U.S.	k11	50
Ramu, stm., Pap. N. Gui.	F12	37
Ranāghāt, India	F2	34
Ranau, Lake, l., Indon.	B4	78
Ranburne, Al., U.S.	A2	54
Rancagua, Chile	C2	56
Rancharia, Braz.		
Rancheria Rock, mtn., Or., U.S.	C6	114
Ranchester, Wy., U.S.	B5	127
Rānchi, India	D8	36
Ranchito, N.M., U.S.	A4	108
Rancho Cordova, Ca., U.S.	*C3	82
Rancho Mirage, Ca., U.S.	*F5	82
Rancho Palos Verdes, Ca., U.S.	n12	82
Rancho Rinconado, Ca., U.S.	*k8	82
Rancho Santa Fe, Ca., U.S.	F5	82
Ranchos de Taos, N.M., U.S.	A4	108
Ranco, Lago, l., Chile	C2	54
Rancocas, N.J., U.S.	D3	107
Rancocas Creek, stm., N.J., U.S.	C3	107
Rancocas Creek, South Branch, stm., N.J., U.S.	D3	107
Rancocas Woods, N.J., U.S.	D3	107
Rand, Co., U.S.	A4	83
Rand, W.V., U.S.	C3	125
Randalia, Ia., U.S.	B6	92
Randall, Ks., U.S.	C5	93
Randall, Mn., U.S.	D4	100
Randall, co., Tx., U.S.	B2	120
Randallstown, Md., U.S.	B4	97
Randers, Den.	I4	14
Randle, Wa., U.S.	C4	124
Randleman, N.C., U.S.	B3	110
Randlett, Ok., U.S.	D8	102
Randlett, Ut., U.S.	C6	121
Randolph, Al., U.S.	C3	78
Randolph, Az., U.S.	E4	80
Randolph, Ks., U.S.	C7	93
Randolph, Me., U.S.	D3	96
Randolph, Ma., U.S.	B5	98
Randolph, Ne., U.S.	B8	104
Randolph, N.H., U.S.	B4	106
Randolph, N.Y., U.S.	C2	109
Randolph, Oh., U.S.	A4	112
Randolph, Vt., U.S.	D3	122
Randolph, Wi., U.S.	E4	126
Randolph, co., Al., U.S.	B4	78
Randolph, co., Ar., U.S.	A4	81
Randolph, co., Ga., U.S.	E2	87
Randolph, co., Il., U.S.	E4	90
Randolph, co., In., U.S.	D7	91
Randolph, co., Mo., U.S.	B5	102
Randolph, co., N.C., U.S.	B3	110
Randolph, co., W.V., U.S.	C5	125
Randolph Air Force Base, mil., Tx., U.S.	h7	120
Randolph Center, Vt., U.S.	D3	122
Randolph Hills, Md., U.S.	B3	97
Random Island, i., Newf.	D5	72
Random Lake, Wi., U.S.	E6	126
Rangoon (Yangon), Burma	E10	36
Randsburg, Ca., U.S.	E5	82
Ranfurly, Alta.	C5	68
Ranfurly, N.Z.	F2	51
Rangaunu Bay, b., N.Z.	K14	51
Rangeley, Me., U.S.	D2	96
Rangeley Lake, l., Me., U.S.	D2	96
Rangely, Co., U.S.	A2	83
Ranger, Ga., U.S.	B2	87
Ranger, Tx., U.S.	C3	120
Ranger, W.V., U.S.	C2	125
Ranger Lake, l., N.M., U.S.	D6	108
Rangiora, N.Z.	O14	51
Rangitata, stm., N.Z.	O13	51
Rangpur, Bngl.	C8	36
Rāniganj, India	D8	36
Rankin, Pa., U.S.	k14	115
Rankin, Tx., U.S.	D2	120
Rankin, co., Ms., U.S.	C4	101
Rannoch, Loch, res., Scot., U.K.	D4	13
Ranong, Thai.	H3	35
Ransom, Il., U.S.	B5	90
Ransom, Ks., U.S.	D3	93
Ransom, Pa., U.S.	m17	115
Ransom, co., N.D., U.S.	C8	111
Ransomville, N.Y., U.S.	B2	109
Ranson, W.V., U.S.	B7	125
Rantauprapat, Indon.	E3	34
Rantekombola, mtn., Indon.	F6	34
Rantoul, Il., U.S.	C5	90
Rantowles, S.C., U.S.	k11	117
Ranum, Den.	B8	15
Raon-l'Étape, Fr.	A2	20
Raoui, Erg er, des., Alg.	D4	44
Raoul, Ga., U.S.	B3	87
Rapallo, Italy	B2	23
Rāpch, stm., Iran	I9	39
Rapelje, Mt., U.S.	E7	103
Raphine, Va., U.S.	C3	123
Raphoe, Ire.	C4	11
Rapid, stm., Mn., U.S.	B4	100
Rapid, North Branch, stm., Mn., U.S.	B4	100
Rapidan, Va., U.S.	B4	123
Rapid City, Man.	D1	70
Rapid City, Mi., U.S.	D5	99
Rapid City, S.D., U.S.	C2	118
Rapides, co., La., U.S.	C3	95
Rapid River, Mi., U.S.	C4	99
Rapids City, Il., U.S.	B3	90
Rappahannock, co., Va., U.S.	B4	123
Rappahannock, stm., Va., U.S.	B5	123
Rappahannock Academy, Va., U.S.	B5	123
Rapperswil, Switz.	B6	21
Rāpti, stm., Asia	D9	37
Raquette, stm., N.Y., U.S.	f10	109
Raquette Lake, N.Y., U.S.	B6	109
Raquette Lake, l., N.Y., U.S.	B6	109
Rarden, Oh., U.S.	D2	112
Raritan, Il., U.S.	C3	90
Raritan, N.J., U.S.	B3	107
Raritan, stm., N.J., U.S.	C4	107
Raritan, South Branch, stm., N.J., U.S.	B3	107
Raritan Bay, b., N.J., U.S.	C4	107
Ra's al 'Ayn, Syria	D13	39
Ra's al Khaymah, U.A.E.	C5	38
Ra's al Unūf, Libya	C3	43
Ra's al 'Ushsh, Eg.	C4	41
Ra's an Naqb, Jord.	C3	38
Ra's Dashen Terara, mtn., Eth.	C4	47
Raseiniai, Sov. Un.	A7	26
Ra's Gharib, Eg.	D6	43
Rashād, Sud.	C3	47
Rāshayyā, Leb.	F10	40
Rashid (Rosetta), Eg.	B3	38
Rāshidah, Ma'ṭan, well, Libya	H3	40
Rashkov, Sov. Un.	B9	24
Rasht, Iran	B4	38
Raška, Yugo.	D5	24
Raška, stm., Yugo.	D5	24
Raso, Cabo, c., Arg.	C3	54
Raspberry Peak, mtn., Ar., U.S.	C1	81
Rasskazovo, Sov. Un.	E13	27
Ra's Tannūrah, Sau. Ar.	C5	38
Rastatt, W. Ger.	D4	18
Rastede, W. Ger.	A8	18
Rastibonne Monastery, Isr.	m14	41
Raszyn, Pol.	m13	26
Rat, stm., Man.	E3	70
Rat, stm., Man.	E3	70
Ratchaburi, Thai.	C1	34
Ratcliff, Ar., U.S.	B2	81
Ratekau, W. Ger.	B5	15
Rathbun, Ia., U.S.	D5	92
Rathbun Lake, res., Ia., U.S.	D5	92
Rathdrum, Id., U.S.	B2	89
Rathdrum, Ire.	E5	11
Rathenow, E. Ger.	B6	18
Rathfriland, N. Ire., U.K.	C5	11
Rathkeale, Ire.	E4	11
Rathlin Island, i., N. Ire., U.K.	C3	10
Rathlin Sound, strt., N. Ire., U.K.	B5	11
Ráth Luirc, Ire.	E4	11
Rathmelton, Ire.	B4	11
Rathmore, Ire.	E2	11
Rathmullen, Ire.	B4	11
Rathnew, Ire.	E5	11
Rathowen, Ire.	C4	11
Rathwell, Man.	E2	70
Ratingen, W. Ger.	C5	81
Ratio, Ar., U.S.	B5	81
Rat Islands, is., Ak.	E3	79
Rat Lake, l., Man.	A2	70
Rat Lake, l., Man.	F5	37
Ratlām, India	D3	36
Ratnāgiri, India	D3	75
Ratner, Sask.	A5	108
Raton, N.M., U.S.	A5	108
Raton Pass, N.M., U.S.	C6	113
Rattan, Ok., U.S.	E5	18
Rattenberg, Aus.	E4	93
Rattlesnake Creek, stm., Ks., U.S.	E4	93
Rattlesnake Creek, stm., Oh., U.S.	C2	112
Rattlesnake Flat, pl., Wa., U.S.	C6	124
Rattlesnake Hills, hills, Wa., U.S.	C6	124
Rattlesnake Hills, hills, Wy., U.S.	D5	127
Rattlesnake Mountain, mtn., Ct., U.S.	C4	84
Rattling Brook, Newf.	D3	72
Rattray Head, c., Scot., U.K.	C7	13
Rättvik, Swe.	G6	14
Ratzeburg, W. Ger.	E4	15

Name	Map Ref.	Page
Ratzeburger, I., Eur.	E4	15
Raub, Malay.	K4	35
Raub, In., U.S.	C3	91
Raub, N.D., U.S.	B3	111
Rauch, Arg.	B5	54
Rauer, i., Nor.	p28	14
Raufarhöfn, Ice.	m25	14
Raukumara, mtn., N.Z.	L17	51
Rauland, Nor.	H2	14
Rauma, Fin.	G9	14
Raurkela, India	F10	37
Rausu, Mount, mtn., Japan	D12	33
Rautalampi, Fin.	F12	14
Ravalli, Mt., U.S.	C2	103
Ravalli, co., Mt., U.S.	D2	103
Ravanna, Ar., U.S.	D1	81
Ravanna, Ne., U.S.	A4	102
Rāvar, Iran	B5	38
Rava-Russkaya, Sov. Un.	F4	27
Raven, Va., U.S.	e10	123
Ravena, N.Y., U.S.	C7	109
Ravendale, Ca., U.S.	B3	82
Ravenden, Ar., U.S.	A4	81
Ravenden Springs, Ar., U.S.	A4	81
Ravenel, S.C., U.S.	k11	117
Ravenglass, Eng., U.K.	F5	13
Ravenna, Italy	B4	23
Ravenna, Ky., U.S.	C6	94
Ravenna, Mi., U.S.	E5	99
Ravenna, Ne., U.S.	C7	104
Ravenna, Oh., U.S.	A4	112
Raven Park, reg., Co., U.S.	A2	83
Raven Rock, N.J., U.S.	C2	107
Ravensburg, W. Ger.	E4	18
Ravenscrag, Sask.	H1	75
Ravenscroft, Tn., U.S.	D8	119
Ravensdale, Wa., U.S.	f12	124
Ravensthorpe, Austl.	F3	50
Ravenswood, In., U.S.	k10	91
Ravenswood, W.V., U.S.	C3	125
Ravensworth, Ont.	B5	73
Ravenwood, Mo., U.S.	A3	102
Rāvi, stm., Asia	B4	37
Ravia, Ok., U.S.	C5	113
Ravinia, S.D., U.S.	D7	118
Rāwalpindi, Pak.	B5	36
Rāwalpindi Cantonment, Pak.	*B5	36
Rawa Mazowiecka, Pol.	C6	26
Rawāndūz, Iraq	D15	40
Rawdon, Que.	C4	74
Rawḍ Sālim, Bi'r, well, Eg.	D5	41
Rawhide Creek, stm., Wy., U.S.	D8	127
Rawicz, Pol.	C4	26
Rawlings, Md., U.S.	k13	97
Rawlings, Va., U.S.	D5	123
Rawlinna, Austl.	F4	50
Rawlins, Wy., U.S.	E5	127
Rawlins, co., Ks., U.S.	C2	93
Rawson, Arg.	C3	54
Rawson, Arg.	g6	54
Rawson, N.D., U.S.	B2	111
Rawson, Oh., U.S.	B2	112
Rawsonville, Vt., U.S.	E3	122
Ray, In., U.S.	A8	91
Ray, Mn., U.S.	B5	100
Ray, N.D., U.S.	A2	111
Ray, co., Mo., U.S.	B3	102
Ray, Cape, c., Newf.	E2	72
Raya, mtn., Indon.	F4	34
Raya, i., Indon.	J1	35
Rāyagarha, India	H9	37
Raychikhinsk, Sov. Un.	B4	33
Ray City, Ga., U.S.	E3	87
Raygorodka, Sov. Un.	q22	27
Rayle, Ga., U.S.	C4	87
Raymond, Alta.	E4	68
Raymond, Ca., U.S.	D4	82
Raymond, Ga., U.S.	C2	87
Raymond, Il., U.S.	D4	90
Raymond, In., U.S.	F7	91
Raymond, Ks., U.S.	D5	93
Raymond, Me., U.S.	E2	96
Raymond, Mn., U.S.	E3	100
Raymond, Ms., U.S.	C3	101
Raymond, Mt., U.S.	B12	103
Raymond, Ne., U.S.	D9	104
Raymond, N.H., U.S.	D4	106
Raymond, S.D., U.S.	C8	118
Raymond, Wa., U.S.	C2	124
Raymond Terrace, Austl.	F8	51
Raymondville, Mo., U.S.	D6	102
Raymondville, N.Y., U.S.	f10	109
Raymondville, Tx., U.S.	F4	120
Raymore, Sask.	F3	75
Raymore, Mo., U.S.	C3	102
Rayne, La., U.S.	D3	95
Rayner Glacier, ice, Ant.	C17	7
Raynesford, Mt., U.S.	C6	103
Raynham, Ma., U.S.	C5	98
Raynham Center, Ma., U.S.	C5	98
Rayón, Mex.	B2	63
Rayong, Thai.	F4	35
Rayside-Balfour, Ont.	*p19	73
Raytown, Mo., U.S.	h11	102
Rayville, La., U.S.	B4	95
Rayville, Mo., U.S.	B3	102
Razan, Iran	D4	39
Razgrad, Bul.	D8	24
Razlog, Bul.	D6	24
Razorback Mountain, mtn., B.C.	D5	69
Re, i., Viet.	E8	35
Ré, Île de i., Fr.	D3	16
Rea, Mo., U.S.	A3	102
Rea, Lough, l., Ire.	D3	11
Reader, Ar., U.S.	D2	81
Reader, W.V., U.S.	B4	125
Reader Lake, l., Man.	C1	70
Readfield, Me., U.S.	D3	96
Reading, Eng., U.K.	E6	10
Reading, Ks., U.S.	D8	93
Reading, Ma., U.S.	A5	98
Reading, Mi., U.S.	G6	99
Reading, Oh., U.S.	C1	112
Reading, Pa., U.S.	F10	115
Reading, Vt., U.S.	E3	122
Reading Center, N.Y., U.S.	C4	109
Readland, Ar., U.S.	D4	81
Readlyn, Sask.	H3	75
Readlyn, Ia., U.S.	B5	92
Readsboro, Vt., U.S.	F3	122
Readstown, Wi., U.S.	E3	126
Readyville, Tn., U.S.	B5	119
Reagan, Tn., U.S.	B3	119
Reagan, co., Tx., U.S.	D2	120
Real, co., Tx., U.S.	E3	120
Real, Cordillera, mts., S.A.	C2	55
Realicó, Arg.	B4	54
Realitos, Tx., U.S.	F3	120
Reamstown, Pa., U.S.	F9	115
Reardan, Wa., U.S.	B8	124
Reasnor, Ia., U.S.	C4	92
Reata, Mex.	B4	63
Reaville, N.J., U.S.	C3	107
Reay, Scot., U.K.	B5	13
Rebecca, Ga., U.S.	E3	87
Rebersburg, Pa., U.S.	E7	115
Rebiana, well, Libya	E4	43
Rebiana Sand Sea, des., Libya	E3	43
Reboly, Sov. Un.	F14	14
Rebun Island, i., Japan	D10	33
Recalde, Arg.	B4	54
Recanati, Italy	C4	23
Recherche, Archipelago of the, is., Austl.	F3	50
Rechitsa, Sov. Un.	E8	27
Recife, Braz.	C4	57
Recinto, Chile	B2	54
Recklinghausen, W. Ger.	C3	18
Recluse, Wy., U.S.	B7	127
Recogne, Bel.	E5	17
Reconquista, Arg.	A5	54
Recovery, Ga., U.S.	F2	87
Recreo, Arg.	E2	55
Rector, Ar., U.S.	A5	81
Red, stm., N.A.	A8	76
Red, stm., N.A.	D9	76
Red, stm., Ky., U.S.	C6	94
Red, stm., Tn., U.S.	A4	119
Red, Elm Fork, stm., U.S.	B2	113
Red, North Fork, stm., U.S.	B1	113
Red, Salt Fork, stm., U.S.	C2	113
Red, South Fork, stm., U.S.	A5	119
Red, West Fork, stm., U.S.	A4	119
Redang, i., Malay.	J5	35
Redange, Lux.	E5	17
Red Bank, N.J., U.S.	C4	107
Red Bank, S.C., U.S.	D5	117
Red Bank, Tn., U.S.	D8	119
Red Banks, Ms., U.S.	A4	101
Red Bay, Newf.	C3	72
Red Bay, Al., U.S.	A1	78
Redbay, Fl., U.S.	u16	86
Red Bay, b., N. Ire., U.K.	B6	11
Redberry Lake, l., Sask.	E2	75
Redbird, Oh., U.S.	A4	112
Redbird, Ok., U.S.	B6	113
Red Bird, stm., Ky., U.S.	C6	94
Red Bluff, Ca., U.S.	B2	82
Red Bluff Lake, res., U.S.	o12	120
Red Boiling Springs, Tn., U.S.	C8	119
Redby, Mn., U.S.	C4	100
Redcar, Eng., U.K.	F7	13
Red Cedar, stm., Wi., U.S.	C2	126
Red Cedar Lake, l., Wi., U.S.	C2	126
Redcliff, Alta.	D5	68
Redcliff, Co., U.S.	B4	83
Red Cliff, Wi., U.S.	B3	126
Redcliffe, Austl.	E9	50
Red Cliff Indian Reservation, Wi., U.S.	B2	126
Red Cloud, Ne., U.S.	D7	104
Redcloud Peak, mtn., Co., U.S.	D3	83
Red Creek, N.Y., U.S.	B4	109
Red Creek, stm., Ms., U.S.	E4	101
Red Deer, Alta.	C4	68
Red Deer, stm., Can.	D4	68
Red Deer, stm., Can.	E4	75
Red Deer Lake, l., Man.	C1	70
Reddell, La., U.S.	D3	95
Red Desert, Wy., U.S.	E4	127
Reddick, Fl., U.S.	C4	86
Reddick, Il., U.S.	B5	90
Redding, Ca., U.S.	B2	82
Redding, Ct., U.S.	D2	84
Redding, Ia., U.S.	D3	92
Redding Ridge, Ct., U.S.	D2	84
Reddish Knob, mtn., U.S.	C5	125
Redditch, Eng., U.K.	B6	12
Redditt, Ont.	E4	70
Red Earth Lake, l., Sask.	D4	75
Redenção, Braz.	B3	57
Redeye, stm., Mn., U.S.	D3	100
Red Feather Lakes, Co., U.S.	A5	83
Redfield, Ar., U.S.	C3	81
Redfield, Ia., U.S.	C3	92
Redfield, Ks., U.S.	E9	93
Redfield, N.Y., U.S.	B5	109
Redfield, S.D., U.S.	C7	118
Redford, Mi., U.S.	F7	99
Redford, N.Y., U.S.	f11	109
Redgranite, Wi., U.S.	D4	126
Redhill, Eng., U.K.	m12	10
Red Hook, N.Y., U.S.	C7	109
Redhouse, Ky., U.S.	C6	94
Red House, Va., U.S.	C4	123
Redig, S.D., U.S.	B2	118
Red Indian Lake, l., Newf.	D3	72
Red Island, i., Newf.	E4	72
Red Jacket, W.V., U.S.	D2	125
Redkey, In., U.S.	D7	91
Red Lake, Ont.	o16	73
Redlake, Mn., U.S.	C3	100
Red Lake, co., Mn., U.S.	C2	100
Red Lake, l., Az., U.S.	B1	80
Red Lake, l., Mn., U.S.	C2	100
Red Lake Falls, Mn., U.S.	C2	100
Red Lake Indian Reservation, Mn., U.S.	B3	100
Redlands, Ca., U.S.	E5	82
Red Level, Al., U.S.	D3	78
Red Lick, Ms., U.S.	D3	101
Red Lion, Pa., U.S.	G8	115
Red Lodge, Mt., U.S.	E7	103
Red Mill Pond, l., De., U.S.	F5	85
Redmon, Il., U.S.	D6	90
Redmond, Or., U.S.	C5	114
Redmond, Wa., U.S.	e11	124
Red Mountain, Ca., U.S.	E5	82
Red Mountain, mtn., Al., U.S.	B3	78
Red Mountain, mtn., Ca., U.S.	A4	103
Red Mountain Pass, Co., U.S.	D3	83
Rednitz, stm., W. Ger.	D5	18
Red Oak, Ga., U.S.	h7	87
Red Oak, Ia., U.S.	D2	92
Red Oak, N.C., U.S.	A5	110
Red Oak, Ok., U.S.	C6	113
Red Oak, Tx., U.S.	n10	120
Red Oak Mill, N.Y., U.S.	*D7	109
Red Oaks, La., U.S.	h9	95
Redon, Fr.	D2	16
Redonda Islands, is., B.C.	D4	69
Redondela, Spain	A1	22
Redondo, Port.	C2	22
Redondo, Wa., U.S.	f11	124
Redondo Beach, Ca., U.S.	n12	82
Redoubt Volcano, vol., Ak., U.S.	g15	79
Redowl, S.D., U.S.	C3	118
Red Pass, B.C.	C8	69
Red Peak, mtn., Co., U.S.	B4	83
Red Pheasant, Sask.	E1	75
Red Rapids, N.B.	C2	71
Red River, N.M., U.S.	A4	108
Red River, co., La., U.S.	B2	95
Red River, co., Tx., U.S.	C5	120
Red Rock, B.C.	C6	69
Red Rock, Az., U.S.	E4	80
Redrock, N.M., U.S.	E1	108
Red Rock, Ok., U.S.	A4	113
Red Rock, Tx., U.S.	E4	120
Red Rock, stm., Mt., U.S.	F4	103
Red Rock, Lake, res., Ia., U.S.	C4	92
Red Scaffold, S.D., U.S.	C4	118
Red Sea	C3	38
Red Shirt, S.D., U.S.	D3	118
Red Springs, N.C., U.S.	C3	110
Redstone, B.C.	C6	69
Redstone, Co., U.S.	B3	83
Redstone, Mt., U.S.	B12	103
Red Sucker, stm., U.S.	B4	106
Red Sucker Lake, l., Man.	B5	70
Red Table Mountain, mts., Co., U.S.	B4	83
Redvale, Co., U.S.	C2	83
Redvers, Sask.	H5	75
Redwater, Alta.	C4	68
Redwater, stm., Mt., U.S.	C11	103
Red Willow, Alta.	C4	68
Red Willow, co., Ne., U.S.	D5	104
Redwillow, stm., Can.	B7	69
Red Willow Creek, stm., Ne., U.S.	D5	104
Redwine, Ky., U.S.	B6	94
Red Wing, Co., U.S.	D5	83
Red Wing, Mn., U.S.	F6	100
Redwood, Ms., U.S.	C3	101
Redwood, N.Y., U.S.	A5	109
Redwood, Ut., U.S.	*C4	121
Redwood, co., Mn., U.S.	F3	100
Redwood, stm., Mn., U.S.	F3	100
Redwood City, Ca., U.S.	D2	82
Redwood Falls, Mn., U.S.	F3	100
Redwood National Park, Ca., U.S.	B2	82
Redwood Valley, Ca., U.S.	C2	82
Red see Yuan Jiang, stm., Asia	G5	36
Ree, Lough, l., Ire.	D2	10
Reece, Ks., U.S.	E7	93
Reece City, Al., U.S.	A3	78
Reed, Ok., U.S.	C2	113
Reed City, Mi., U.S.	E5	99
Reeder, N.D., U.S.	C3	111
Reed Lake, l., Man.	B1	70
Reed Lake, l., Sask.	G2	75
Reedley, Ca., U.S.	D4	82
Reedpoint, Mt., U.S.	E7	103
Reeds Beach, N.J., U.S.	E3	107
Reedsburg, Wi., U.S.	E3	126
Reeds Peak, mtn., N.M., U.S.	D2	108
Reedsport, Or., U.S.	D2	114
Reeds Spring, Mo., U.S.	E4	102
Reedsville, Oh., U.S.	C4	112
Reedsville, Pa., U.S.	E6	115
Reedsville, W.V., U.S.	B5	125
Reedurban, Oh., U.S.	*B4	112
Reedville, Va., U.S.	C6	123
Reedy, W.V., U.S.	C3	125
Reedy Lake, l., Fl., U.S.	E5	86
Reefton, N.Z.	O13	51
Ree Heights, S.D., U.S.	C6	118
Reelsville, In., U.S.	E4	91
Reere Island, i., Marsh Is.	P18	52
Reese, Mi., U.S.	E7	99
Reese, stm., Nv., U.S.	C4	105
Reese Air Force Base, mil., Tx., U.S.	C1	120
Reese Station, Oh., U.S.	m11	112
Reeseville, Wi., U.S.	E5	126
Reesville, Oh., U.S.	C2	112
Reeth, Eng., U.K.	F7	13
Reeves, La., U.S.	D2	95
Reeves, co., Tx., U.S.	o13	120
Reevesville, Il., U.S.	F5	90
Reevesville, S.C., U.S.	E6	117
Reform, Al., U.S.	B1	78
Reform, Ms., U.S.	B4	101
Refresco, Chile	E2	55
Reftele, Swe.	A7	15
Refuge Cove, B.C.	D5	69
Refugio, Tx., U.S.	E4	120
Refugio, co., Tx., U.S.	E4	120
Rega, stm., Pol.	B3	26
Regan, N.D., U.S.	B5	111
Regen, W. Ger.	E8	19
Regen, stm., W. Ger.	D6	18
Regensburg, W. Ger.	D6	18
Regent, Man.	E1	70
Regent, N.D., U.S.	C3	111
Reger, Mo., U.S.	A4	102
Reggane, Alg.	D5	44
Reggio di Calabria, Italy	E5	23
Reggio nell'Emilia, Italy	B3	23
Reghin, Rom.	B7	24
Regina, Sask.	G3	75
Régina, Fr. Gu.	B4	59
Regina, Mt., U.S.	C9	103
Regina Beach, Sask.	G3	75
Register, Ga., U.S.	D5	87
Regna, Swe.	u33	14
Regnitz, stm., W. Ger.	D5	19
Reguengos de Monsaraz, Port.	C2	22
Rehau, W. Ger.	C7	19
Rehavya (part of Jerusalem), Isr.	m14	41
Rehna, E. Ger.	E5	15
Rehoboth, Nmb.	B2	49
Rehoboth, Ma., U.S.	C5	98
Rehoboth, N.M., U.S.	B1	108
Rehoboth Bay, b., De., U.S.	F5	85
Rehoboth Beach, De., U.S.	F5	85
Rehovot, Isr.	C6	41
Reichenbach, E. Ger.	E6	15
Reichenbach, W. Ger.	A4	20
Reid, stm., Austl.	n24	79
Reid, Mount, mtn., Ak., U.S.	n24	79
Reid Lake, res., Sask.	G1	75
Reidland, Ky., U.S.	e9	94
Reids Grove, Md., U.S.	C6	97
Reidsville, Ga., U.S.	D4	87
Reidsville, N.C., U.S.	A3	110
Reidville, S.C., U.S.	B3	117
Reigate, Eng., U.K.	C6	10
Reims, Fr.	C6	16
Reina Adelaida, Archipiélago, is., Chile	E2	54
Reinbeck, Ia., U.S.	B5	92
Reindeer, stm., Sask.	B4	75
Reindeer Island, i., Man.	C3	70
Reindeer Lake, l., Can.	m8	75
Reinersville, Oh., U.S.	C4	112
Reinholds, W. Ger.	E4	15
Reinosa, Spain	A3	22
Reisterstown, Md., U.S.	B4	97
Reit im Winkl, W. Ger.	B8	20
Reitz, S. Afr.	C4	49
Rekarne, Swe.	t34	14
Reliance, De., U.S.	F3	85
Reliance, S.D., U.S.	D6	118
Reliance, Tn., U.S.	D9	119
Reliance, Wy., U.S.	E3	127
Remada, Tun.	C7	44
Remagen, W. Ger.	C2	19
Remanso, Braz.	C2	57
Rembert, S.C., U.S.	C6	117
Rembertów (part of Warsaw), Pol.	k14	26
Remedios, Cuba	C4	64
Remedios, Pan.	F7	62
Remer, Mn., U.S.	C5	100
Remerton, Ga., U.S.	F3	87
Remeshk, Iran	H9	39
Remington, In., U.S.	C3	91
Remington, Va., U.S.	B5	123
Remiremont, Fr.	C7	16
Rémire, Fr. Gu.	B4	59
Remlap, Al., U.S.	B3	78
Remmel Dam, Ar., U.S.	g8	81
Remscheid, W. Ger.	C3	18
Remsen, Ia., U.S.	B2	92
Remsen, N.Y., U.S.	B5	109
Remus, Mi., U.S.	E5	99
Rena Lara, Ms., U.S.	A3	101
Renault, Il., U.S.	E4	90
Renco, Ks., U.S.	k15	93
Rend Lake, res., Il., U.S.	E5	90
Rendsburg, W. Ger.	A4	18
Rendville, Oh., U.S.	C3	112
Renedo, Spain	A2	22
Renens, Switz.	C1	21
Renews [-Cappahayden], Newf.	E5	72
Renfrew, Ont.	B8	73
Renfrew, S.C., U.S.	B3	117
Renfrew, co., Ont.	B7	73
Renfrew, Ok., U.S.	A4	113
Rengo, Chile	A2	54
Reni, Sov. Un.	C9	24
Renick, Mo., U.S.	B5	102
Renick, W.V., U.S.	C4	125
Renish Point, c., Scot., U.K.	C2	13
Renmark, Austl.	F7	50
Renner, S.D., U.S.	D9	118
Rennerod, W. Ger.	C3	19
Rennert, N.C., U.S.	C3	110
Rennes, Fr.	C3	16
Rennick Bay, b., Ant.	C29	7
Rennick Glacier, ice, Ant.	B29	7
Rennie, Man.	E4	70
Reno, Nv., U.S.	D2	105
Reno, Oh., U.S.	C4	112
Reno, co., Ks., U.S.	E5	93
Reno, stm., Italy	B3	23
Reno Hill, mtn., Wy., U.S.	D6	127
Renous, N.B.	C4	71
Renovo, Pa., U.S.	D6	115
Rensselaer, In., U.S.	C3	91
Rensselaer, N.Y., U.S.	C7	109
Rensselaer, co., N.Y., U.S.	C7	109
Rensselaer Falls, N.Y., U.S.	f9	109
Rensselaerville, N.Y., U.S.	C6	109
Rentiesville, Ok., U.S.	B6	113
Renton, Wa., U.S.	B3	124
Rentz, Ga., U.S.	D4	87
Renville, Mn., U.S.	F4	100
Renville, co., Mn., U.S.	F4	100
Renville, co., N.D., U.S.	A4	111
Renwick, Ia., U.S.	B4	92
Repentigny, Que.	D4	74
Repton, Al., U.S.	D2	78
Republic, Mi., U.S.	B3	99
Republic, Mo., U.S.	D4	102
Republic, Oh., U.S.	A2	112
Republic, Wa., U.S.	A7	124
Republic, co., Ks., U.S.	C6	93
Republican, stm., U.S.	C6	93
Republican, North Fork, stm., U.S.	A8	83
Republican, South Fork, stm., U.S.	E4	104
Republican City, Ne., U.S.	D6	104
Repulse Bay, N.W. Ter.	C15	66
Repulse Bay, b., Austl.	D8	50
Requena, Spain	C5	22
Reşadiye, Tur.	B11	40
Resang, Cape, c., Malay.	E2	34
Rescue, Va., U.S.	k14	123
Reserve, Sask.	C5	75
Reserve, Ks., U.S.	C8	93
Reserve, La., U.S.	h10	95
Reserve, Mt., U.S.	B12	103
Reserve, N.M., U.S.	D1	108
Reserve, Wi., U.S.	C2	126
Reservoir Pond, l., Ma., U.S.	h11	98
Resistencia, Arg.	B5	54
Reşiţa, Rom.	C5	24
Resko, Pol.	B2	26
Resolute, N.W. Ter.	n32	66
Resolution Island, i., N.W. Ter.	D20	66
Resplendor, Braz.	E8	57
Resthaven Mountain, mtn., Alta.	C1	68
Restigouche, stm., Can.	B2	71
Restigué, Punta, c., Pan.	G7	62
Reston, Man.	E1	70
Reston, Va., U.S.	B5	123
Retalhuleu, Guat.	G2	63
Retamito, Arg.	A3	54
Rethel, Fr.	C5	16
Réthimnon, Grc.	E5	41
Retie, Bel.	C5	17
Retlaw, Alta.	D4	68
Retsof, N.Y., U.S.	C3	109
Reubens, Id., U.S.	*C2	89
Reuland, Bel.	D6	17
Reunion, dep., Afr.	H24	2
Reus, Spain	B6	22
Reuss, stm., Switz.	B5	21
Reuterstadt Stavenhagen, E. Ger.	E6	15
Reutlingen, W. Ger.	D4	18
Reutte, Aus.	E5	18
Revda, Sov. Un.	B2	118
Revel, Fr.	F5	16
Revelo, Ky., U.S.	D5	94
Revelstoke, B.C.	D8	69
Revelstoke Lake, res., B.C.	D8	69
Reventazón, Peru	C1	58
Revere, Ma., U.S.	g11	98
Revere, Mn., U.S.	F3	100
Revere, Mo., U.S.	A6	102
Reverie, Tn., U.S.	B2	119
Revigny [-sur-Ornain], Fr.	F4	17
Revillagigedo, Islas, is., Mex.	D2	63
Revillagigedo Island, i., Ak., U.S.	n24	79
Revillo, S.D., U.S.	B9	118
Revin, Fr.	C6	16
Revloc, Pa., U.S.	F4	115
Řevnice, Czech.	o17	26
Rewa, India	D7	36
Reward, Sask.	E1	75
Rewari, India	C6	36
Rewey, Wi., U.S.	F3	126
Rex, Ga., U.S.	h8	87
Rex, Mount, mtn., Ant.	B5	7
Rexburg, Id., U.S.	F7	89
Rexford, Ks., U.S.	C3	93
Rexford, Mt., U.S.	B1	103
Rexham, Ma., U.S.	h13	98
Rexton, N.B.	C5	71
Rey, Iran	D2	46
Rey Bouba, Cam.	D2	46
Reydell, Ar., U.S.	C4	81
Reydon, Ok., U.S.	B2	113
Reyes, Point, c., Ca., U.S.	C2	82
Reykjavík, Ice.	n22	14
Reynaud, Sask.	E3	75
Reyno, Ar., U.S.	A5	81
Reynolds, Ga., U.S.	D2	87
Reynolds, Il., U.S.	B3	90
Reynolds, In., U.S.	C4	91
Reynolds, Mo., U.S.	D6	102
Reynolds, Ne., U.S.	D8	104
Reynolds, N.D., U.S.	B8	111
Reynolds, co., Mo., U.S.	D6	102
Reynoldsville, Pa., U.S.	D4	115
Reynoldsburg, Oh., U.S.	C3	112
Reynosa (Reinosa), Mex.	B5	63
Rezā'īyeh see Orūmīyeh, Iran	B4	38
Rezé, Fr.	D3	16
Rezekne, Sov. Un.	C6	27
Rezeny, Sov. Un.	B9	24
Rhaetian Alps, mts., Eur.	A3	23
Rhame, N.D., U.S.	C2	111
Rheims see Reims, Fr.	C6	16
Rheda-Wiedenbrück, W. Ger.	B3	19
Rheden, Neth.	A7	16
Rhein, Sask.	F4	75
Rheine, W. Ger.	B3	18
Rheinfelden, Switz.	A4	21
Rheinhausen, W. Ger.	B1	19
Rheinland, hist. reg., W. Ger.	C2	18
Rheinland-Pfalz, state, W. Ger.	C2	19
Rheinsberg, E. Ger.	B12	16
Rheinwaldhorn, mtn., Switz.	C5	20
Rhenen, Neth.	C5	17
Rheydt, W. Ger.	C6	17
Rhiana, Fr.	A3	20
Rhin Canal, E. Ger.	F6	15
Rhine, Ga., U.S.	E3	87
Rhine, stm., Eur.	C3	18
Rhinelander, Wi., U.S.	C4	126
Rhineland, Mo., U.S.	C6	102
Rhinow, E. Ger.	F6	15
Rhir, Cap, c., Mor.	C3	44
Rhode Island, state, U.S.	D3	116
Rhode Island, i., R.I., U.S.	E5	116
Rhode Island Sound, strt., U.S.	F5	116
Rhodell, W.V., U.S.	D3	125
Rhodes, Ia., U.S.	C4	92
Rhodes, Mi., U.S.	E6	99
Rhodes see Ródhos, i., Grc.	D7	40
Rhodesia see Zimbabwe, ctry., Afr.	A5	49
Rhodes Peak, mtn., Id., U.S.	C4	89
Rhodes Point, Md., U.S.	E5	97
Rhodhiss, N.C., U.S.	B1	110
Rhodope Mountains, mts., Eur.	E7	24
Rhondda, Wales, U.K.	J9	13
Rhône, stm., Eur.		
Rhône au Rhin, Canal du, Fr.	A3	20
Rhum, i., Scot., U.K.	D6	12
Rhum, Sound of, strt., Scot.	D2	13
Rhyl, Wales, U.K.	D5	10
Rhymney, Wales, U.K.	C4	12
Riacho de Santana, Braz.	A3	56
Rialma, Braz.	C4	57
Rialto, Ca., U.S.	m14	82
Rianjo, Spain	C5	123
Riau Islands, is., Indon.	E2	34
Ribadavia, Spain	A1	22
Ribadeo, Spain	A2	22
Ribadesella, Spain	A3	22
Ribas do Rio Pardo, Braz.	C2	56
Ribauè, Moz.	D7	48
Ribble, stm., Eng., U.K.	G6	13
Ribe, Den.	C2	15
Ribe, co., Den.	C2	15
Ribeauvillé, Fr.	C3	20
Ribeira, Braz.	C3	56
Ribeira, stm., Braz.	C3	56
Ribeira do Pombal, Braz.	D3	57
Ribeirão Bonito, Braz.	m7	56
Ribeirão Branco, Braz.	n7	56
Ribeirão Prêto, Braz.	B2	56
Ribera, Italy	F4	23
Ribera, N.M., U.S.	B4	108
Ribérac, Fr.	E4	16
Ribnica, Bol.	B5	7
Rib Lake, Wi., U.S.	C3	126
Rib Mountain, mtn., Wi., U.S.	D6	126
Ribnitz-Damgarten, E. Ger.	A6	26
Ricardo, Arg.	A3	54
Riccione, Italy	B4	23
Řičany, Czech.	o18	26
Rice, Mn., U.S.	E4	100
Rice, Va., U.S.	C4	123
Rice, co., Ks., U.S.	D5	93
Rice, co., Mn., U.S.	F5	100
Rice Creek, stm., Mn., U.S.	m12	100
Rice Lake, Wi., U.S.	C2	126
Rice Lake, l., Ont.	C6	73
Rice Lake, l., Mn., U.S.	D5	100
Rice Lake, l., Ont.	C6	73
Rices Landing, Pa., U.S.	G1	115
Riceton, Sask.	G3	75
Riceville, Ia., U.S.	A5	92
Riceville, Tn., U.S.	D9	119
Rich, Ms., U.S.	A3	101
Rich, co., Ut., U.S.	B4	121
Rich, Cape, c., Ont.	C4	73
Richard, Sask.	E2	75
Richard City, Tn., U.S.	D8	119
Richards, Mo., U.S.	D3	102
Richards, Tx., U.S.	D5	120
Richards-Gebaur Air Force Base, mil., Mo., U.S.	C3	102
Richard's Harbour, Newf.	E3	72
Richardson, Sask.	G3	75
Richardson, Ky., U.S.	C7	94
Richardson, Tx., U.S.	n10	120
Richardson, co., Ne., U.S.	D10	104
Richardson Lakes, l., Me., U.S.	D2	96
Richardson Mountains, mts., Can.	C5	66
Richardson Park, De., U.S.	*B3	85
Richards Spur, Ok., U.S.	C3	113
Richardton, N.D., U.S.	C3	111
Richboro, Pa., U.S.	*F11	115
Richburg, N.Y., U.S.	C2	109
Richburg, S.C., U.S.	B5	117
Rich Creek, Va., U.S.	C2	123
Richdale, Alta.	D5	68
Riche, Pointe, c., Newf.	C3	72
Richelieu, co., Que.	D4	74
Richelieu, stm., Que.	D4	74
Richer, Man.	E3	70
Richey, Mt., U.S.	C11	103
Richfield, Id., U.S.	F4	89
Richfield, Ks., U.S.	E2	93
Richfield, Mn., U.S.	F5	100
Richfield, Ne., U.S.	g12	104
Richfield, N.C., U.S.	B2	110
Richfield, Ut., U.S.	E3	121
Richfield, Wi., U.S.	m11	126
Richfield Springs, N.Y., U.S.	C5	109
Richford, N.Y., U.S.	C4	109
Richford, Vt., U.S.	B3	122
Rich Fountain, Mo., U.S.	C6	102
Rich Hill, Mo., U.S.	C3	102
Richibucto, N.B.	C5	71
Rich Lake, Alta.	B5	68
Richland, Ga., U.S.	D2	87
Richland, In., U.S.	I3	91
Richland, Ia., U.S.	C6	92
Richland, Mi., U.S.	F5	99
Richland, Mo., U.S.	D5	102
Richland, Mt., U.S.	B10	103
Richland, co., Il., U.S.	E5	90
Richland, co., La., U.S.	B4	95
Richland, co., Mt., U.S.	C12	103
Richland, co., N.D., U.S.	C8	111
Richland, co., Oh., U.S.	B3	112
Richland, co., S.C., U.S.	C6	117
Richland, co., Wi., U.S.	E3	126
Richland Balsam, mtn., N.C., U.S.	f10	110
Richland Center, Wi., U.S.	E3	126
Richland Creek, stm., Tn., U.S.	B5	119
Richland Hills, Tx., U.S.	*C4	120
Richlands, N.C., U.S.	C5	110
Richlands, Va., U.S.	e10	123
Richland Springs, Tx., U.S.	D3	120
Richlandtown, Pa., U.S.	F11	115
Richlea, Sask.	F1	75
Richmond, Austl.	D7	50
Richmond, B.C.	E6	69
Richmond, Ont.	B9	73
Richmond, P.E.I.	C6	71
Richmond, Que.	D5	74
Richmond, N.Z.	N14	51
Richmond, S. Afr.	C5	49
Richmond, S. Afr.	D3	49
Richmond (part of London), Eng., U.K.	C7	12
Richmond, Eng., U.K.	F7	13
Richmond, Ca., U.S.	D2	82
Richmond, Il., U.S.	A5	90
Richmond, In., U.S.	E8	91
Richmond, Ia., U.S.	C6	92
Richmond, Ky., U.S.	C5	94
Richmond, Me., U.S.	D3	96
Richmond, Ma., U.S.	B1	98
Richmond, Mi., U.S.	F8	99
Richmond, Mo., U.S.	B4	102
Richmond, Tx., U.S.	E5	120
Richmond, Ut., U.S.	B4	121
Richmond, Va., U.S.	C5	123
Richmond, Vt., U.S.	B3	124
Richmond, co., Ga., U.S.	C4	87
Richmond, co., N.Y., U.S.	E6	109
Richmond, co., N.C., U.S.	C3	110
Richmond, co., Va., U.S.	C6	123
Richmond Beach, Wa., U.S.	B3	124
Richmond Dale, Oh., U.S.	C3	112
Richmond Heights, Fl., U.S.	s13	86
Richmond Heights, Mo., U.S.	f13	102
Richmond Heights, Oh., U.S.	*g9	112
Richmond Highlands, Wa., U.S.	B3	124
Richmond Hill, Ont.	D5	73
Richmond Hill, Ga., U.S.	E5	87
Richmond National Battlefield Park, Va., U.S.	n18	123
Richmond Park, Pa., U.S.	m12	10
Richmondville, N.Y., U.S.	C6	109
Richmound, Sask.	G1	75
Rich Mountain, mtn., Ar.	C1	81
Rich Mountain, mtn., U.S.	C1	123
Rich Mountain, mtn., W.V., U.S.	C4	125
Rich Square, N.C., U.S.	A5	110
Richthofen, Mount, mtn., Co., U.S.	A5	83
Richton, Ms., U.S.	D5	101
Richton Park, Il., U.S.	*m9	90
Richvalley, In., U.S.	*C6	91

Name	Map Ref.	Page
Richview, Il., U.S.	E4	90
Richville, Mi., U.S.	E7	99
Richville, Mn., U.S.	D7	100
Richville, N.Y., U.S.	f9	109
Richwood, Ky., U.S.	k13	94
Richwood, Oh., U.S.	B2	112
Richwood, W.V., U.S.	C4	125
Richwoods, Mo., U.S.	C7	102
Rickenbacker Air Force Base, mil., U.S.	m11	112
Ricketts, Ia., U.S.	B2	92
Rickman, Tn., U.S.	C8	119
Rickmansworth, Eng., U.K.	k12	10
Rickreall, Or., U.S.	C3	114
Rico, Co., U.S.	D2	83
Riddle, Id., U.S.	G2	89
Riddle, N.C., U.S.	A6	110
Riddle, Or., U.S.	E3	114
Riddle Mountain, mtn., Or., U.S.	D8	114
Riddlesburg, Pa., U.S.	F5	115
Rideau, stm., Ont.	B9	73
Riderwood, Al., U.S.	C1	78
Ridge, N.Y., U.S.	*n16	109
Ridgebury, Ct., U.S.	D1	84
Ridgecrest, Ca., U.S.	E5	82
Ridgecrest, N.C., U.S.	f10	110
Ridgecrest, Wa., U.S.	*B3	124
Ridgedale, Sask.	D3	75
Ridgedale, Mo., U.S.	E4	102
Ridge Farm, Il., U.S.	D6	90
Ridgefield, Ct., U.S.	D2	84
Ridgefield, N.J., U.S.	h8	107
Ridgefield, Wa., U.S.	D3	124
Ridgefield Park, N.J., U.S.	B4	107
Ridgeland, Ms., U.S.	C3	101
Ridgeland, S.C., U.S.	G6	117
Ridgeland, Wi., U.S.	C2	126
Ridgeley, W.V., U.S.	B6	125
Ridgely, Md., U.S.	C6	97
Ridgely, Tn., U.S.	A2	119
Ridgeside, Tn., U.S.	h11	119
Ridgetop, Tn., U.S.	A5	119
Ridgetown, Ont.	E3	73
Ridgeview, S.D., U.S.	B5	118
Ridgeview, W.V., U.S.	C3	125
Ridgeville, Man.	E3	70
Ridgeville, Ga., U.S.	E5	87
Ridgeville, In., U.S.	D7	91
Ridgeville, S.C., U.S.	E7	117
Ridgeville Corners, Oh., U.S.	A1	112
Ridgeway, Ia., U.S.	A6	92
Ridgeway, Mi., U.S.	F7	99
Ridgeway, Mo., U.S.	A4	102
Ridgeway, Oh., U.S.	B2	112
Ridgeway, S.C., U.S.	C6	117
Ridgeway, Va., U.S.	D3	123
Ridgeway, Wi., U.S.	E4	126
Ridgewood, N.J., U.S.	B4	107
Ridgewood Park, Ct., U.S.	D7	84
Ridgway, Co., U.S.	C3	83
Ridgway, Il., U.S.	F5	90
Ridgway, Pa., U.S.	D4	115
Riding Mountain, hills, Man.	D1	70
Riding Mountain National Park, Man.	D1	70
Ridley Park, Pa., U.S.	p20	115
Ridley Township, Pa., U.S.	*G11	115
Ridott, Il., U.S.	A4	90
Ried [im Innkreis], Aus.	D6	18
Riehen, Switz.	A4	21
Rienza, stm., Italy	C7	20
Rienzi, Ms., U.S.	A5	101
Riesa, E. Ger.	C6	18
Riesco, Isla, i., Chile	h11	54
Riesel, Tx., U.S.	D4	120
Rieth, Or., U.S.	B8	114
Rieti, Italy	C4	23
Riffe Lake, res., Wa., U.S.	C3	124
Rifle, Co., U.S.	B3	83
Rifle, stm., Mi., U.S.	D6	99
Rift Valley, prov., Kenya	A6	48
Rift Valley, val., Afr.	*F9	42
Riga, Sov. Un.	D5	29
Riga, Gulf of, b., Sov. Un.	C4	27
Rigan, Iran	C5	38
Rigan, Iran	G9	39
Rigaud, Que.	D3	74
Rigby, Id., U.S.	F7	89
Rigestan, reg., Afg.	B4	36
Riggins, Id., U.S.	D2	89
Riggisberg, Switz.	C3	21
Rigi, mtn., Switz.	B4	20
Rigil, i., Marsh Is.	S18	52
Rigney, Fr.	B1	21
Rigo, Pap. N. Gui.	k12	50
Rigolet, Newf.	A2	72
Riihimäki, Fin.	G11	14
Riiser-Larsen Peninsula, pen., Ant.	C16	7
Rijeka (Fiume), Yugo.	C2	24
Rijssen, Neth.	B6	17
Riley, In., U.S.	F3	91
Riley, Ks., U.S.	C7	93
Riley, Ky., U.S.	C4	94
Riley, Or., U.S.	D7	114
Riley, co., Ks., U.S.	C7	93
Riley, Mount, mtn., N.M., U.S.	F2	108
Rillito, Az., U.S.	E4	80
Rilly-la-Montagne, Fr.	E1	17
Rimac, Peru	*D2	58
Rimavská Sobota, Czech.	D6	26
Rimbey, Alta.	C3	68
Rimbo, Swe.	t36	14
Rimella, Italy	E5	21
Rimersburg, Pa., U.S.	D3	115
Rimini, Italy	B4	23
Rîmnicu-Sărat, Rom.	C8	24
Rîmnicu-Vîlcea, Rom.	C7	24
Rimouski, Que.	A9	74
Rimouski, co., Que.	A9	74
Rimouski, stm., Que.	A9	74
Rimouski-Est, Que.	A9	74
Rimrock, Az., U.S.	C4	80
Rimrock Lake, res., Wa., U.S.	C4	124
Rinard, Il., U.S.	E5	90
Rinard, Ia., U.S.	B3	92
Rincon, Ga., U.S.	D5	87
Rincon, N.M., U.S.	E2	108
Rincón, Bahía de b., P.R.	C3	65
Rinconada, Arg.	D2	55
Rincón del Bonete, Lago Artificial de, res., Ur.	E1	56
Rincón de Romos, Mex.	k12	63
Rincon Mountains, mts., Az., U.S.	E5	80
Rindge, N.H., U.S.	E2	106
Riner, Va., U.S.	C2	123
Rineyville, Ky., U.S.	C4	94
Ringas, India	D5	37
Ringe, Den.	D5	15
Ringelheim, W. Ger.	A5	19
Ringel Spitze, mtn., Switz.	C7	21
Ringerike, Nor.	*G4	14
Ringgold, La., U.S.	B2	95
Ringgold, Md., U.S.	A2	97
Ringgold, Ne., U.S.	C5	104
Ringgold, Tx., U.S.	C4	120
Ringgold, Va., U.S.	D3	123
Ringgold, co., Ia., U.S.	D3	92
Ringgold Isles, is., Fiji	H16	52
Ringim, Nig.	D6	45
Ringkøbing, Den.	I3	14
Ringkøbing, co., Den.	B2	15
Ringkøbing Fjord, Den.	B2	15
Ringling, Mt., U.S.	D6	103
Ringling, Ok., U.S.	C4	113
Ringoes, N.J., U.S.	C3	107
Ringold, Ok., U.S.	C6	113
Ringos Mills, Ky., U.S.	B6	94
Ringsaker, Nor.	G4	14
Ringsjön, l., Swe.	C7	15
Ringsön, i., Swe.	u35	14
Ringsted, Den.	C5	15
Ringsted, Ia., U.S.	A3	92
Ringville, Ire.	E4	11
Ringwood, Il., U.S.	A4	90
Ringwood, N.J., U.S.	A4	107
Ringwood, Ok., U.S.	A3	113
Riñihue, Chile	B2	54
Rinjani, mtn., Indon.	G5	34
Rinnes, Ben, mtn., Scot., U.K.	C5	13
Rinns Point, c., Scot., U.K.	E2	13
Rinteln, W. Ger.	A4	19
Rio, Fl., U.S.	E6	86
Rio, Il., U.S.	B3	90
Rio, W.V., U.S.	B6	125
Rio, Wi., U.S.	E4	126
Río Arriba, co., N.M., U.S.	A2	108
Riobamba, Ec.	B2	58
Río Benito, Eq. Gui.	E1	46
Río Blanco, Co., Co., U.S.	B2	83
Río Blanco, Braz.	A2	55
Río Branco, Ur.	E2	56
Río Branco do Sul, Braz.	D3	56
Río Brilhante, Braz.	D2	56
Río Bueno, Chile	C2	54
Río Caribe, Ven.	A5	60
Río Chico, Ven.	A4	60
Río Claro, Braz.	C3	56
Río Claro, Trin.	O23	65
Río Colorado, Arg.	B4	54
Río Cuarto, Arg.	A4	54
Rio de Janeiro, Braz.	C4	56
Rio de Janeiro, state, Braz.	C4	56
Río de Jesús, Pan.	G7	62
Rio Dell, Ca., U.S.	B1	82
Rio Del Mar, Ca., U.S.	*D3	82
Río de Oro, Col.	B3	60
Rio do Prado, Braz.	B4	56
Rio do Sul, Braz.	D3	56
Río Gallegos, Arg.	E3	54
Rio Grande, Arg.	h12	54
Rio Grande, Braz.	E2	56
Rio Grande, Mex.	C4	63
Rio Grande, N.J., U.S.	E3	107
Rio Grande, Oh., U.S.	D3	112
Rio Grande, co., Co., U.S.	D4	83
Rio Grande City, Tx., U.S.	F3	120
Rio Grande do Norte, state, Braz.	C3	57
Rio Grande do Sul, state, Braz.	D2	56
Rio Grande Reservoir, res., Co., U.S.	D3	83
Ríohacha, Col.	A3	60
Río Hato, Pan.	F7	62
Rio Hondo, Tx., U.S.	F4	120
Rio Hondo, Mex.	h9	63
Rioja, Peru	C2	58
Riolândia, Braz.	B3	56
Rio Linda, Ca., U.S.	*C3	82
Riom, Fr.	C1	16
Rio Maior, Port.	C1	22
Río Mayo, Arg.	D2	54
Río Mulatos, Bol.	C2	55
Río Muni, prov., Eq. Gui.	E2	46
Rion, S.C., U.S.	C5	117
Riondel, B.C.	E9	69
Río Negro, Braz.	D3	56
Río Negro, prov., Arg.	C3	54
Rionero in Vulture, Italy	D5	23
Rio Pardo, Braz.	D2	56
Rio Pardo de Minas, Braz.	B4	56
Rio Pomba, Braz.	g6	56
Rio Preto da Eva, Braz.	C3	59
Río Primero, Arg.	A4	54
Rio Rancho, N.M., U.S.	B3	108
Ríosucio, Col.	B2	60
Ríosucio, Col.	B2	60
Río Tercero, Arg.	A4	54
Ríoverde, Mex.	m13	63
Rioverde, Ec.	B2	58
Rio Verde, Braz.	B2	56
Rio Verde de Mato Grosso, Braz.	B2	56
Rio Vermelho, Braz.	B4	56
Rio Vista, Ca., U.S.	C3	82
Rioz, Fr.	B1	21
Ripley, Ont.	C3	73
Ripley, Eng., U.K.	A6	12
Ripley, Ca., U.S.	F6	82
Ripley, Il., U.S.	C3	90
Ripley, Me., U.S.	D3	96
Ripley, Ms., U.S.	A5	101
Ripley, N.Y., U.S.	C1	109
Ripley, Oh., U.S.	D2	112
Ripley, Ok., U.S.	A5	113
Ripley, Tn., U.S.	B2	119
Ripley, W.V., U.S.	C3	125
Ripley, co., In., U.S.	F7	91
Ripley, co., Mo., U.S.	E7	102
Ripon, Que.	D2	74
Ripon, Eng., U.K.	C6	10
Ripon, Ca., U.S.	D3	82
Ripon, Wi., U.S.	E5	126
Rippey, Ia., U.S.	C3	92
Rippon, W.V., U.S.	B7	125
Rippowam, stm., Ct., U.S.	E1	84
Ripton, Vt., U.S.	D2	122
Risaralda, dept., Col.	B2	60
Risco, Mo., U.S.	E8	102
Rishiri Island, i., Japan	D10	33
Rishon LeZiyyon, Isr.	C4	41
Rising City, Ne., U.S.	C8	104
Rising Star, Tx., U.S.	C3	120
Rising Sun, In., U.S.	G8	91
Rising Sun, Ia., U.S.	e9	92
Rising Sun, Md., U.S.	A5	97
Risingsun, Oh., U.S.	A2	112
Risle, stm., Fr.	C4	16
Rison, Ar., U.S.	D3	81
Rison, Md., U.S.	C3	97
Risör, Nor.	H3	14
Ritchey, Mo., U.S.	E3	102
Ritchie, co., W.V., U.S.	B3	125
Ritidian Point, c., Guam	L10	52
Ritscher Upland, plat., Ant.	B12	7
Ritter, Or., U.S.	C7	114
Ritter, Mount, mtn., Ca., U.S.	D4	82
Rittman, Oh., U.S.	B4	112
Ritzville, Wa., U.S.	B7	124
Riva [del Garda], Italy	B3	23
Rivadavia, Arg.	A3	54
Rivadavia, Arg.	B4	54
Rivadavia, Arg.	D3	55
Rivadavia, Chile	E1	55
Rivare, In., U.S.	C8	91
Rivas, Nic.	E4	63
Rive-de-Gier, Fr.	E6	16
Rivera, Arg.	B4	54
Rivera, Ur.	E1	56
Rivera, Ca., U.S.	*C2	87
Rivera, Tn., U.S.	C9	119
Riverbank, Ca., U.S.	D3	82
Riverbank, Ca., U.S.	m12	124
Riverbinston, Me., U.S.	C5	96
River Bourgeois, N.S.	D9	71
River Cess, Lib.	E3	45
Riverdale, Ca., U.S.	D4	82
Riverdale, Ga., U.S.	*C2	87
Riverdale, Il., U.S.	k9	90
Riverdale, Ia., U.S.	g11	92
Riverdale, Ks., U.S.	E6	93
Riverdale, Md., U.S.	C4	97
Riverdale, Ne., U.S.	D6	104
Riverdale, N.J., U.S.	B4	107
Riverdale, N.D., U.S.	B4	111
Riverdale, Ut., U.S.	*B3	121
Riverdale, stm., Ga., U.S.	C5	90
River Edge, N.J., U.S.	h8	107
River Falls, Al., U.S.	D3	78
River Falls, Wi., U.S.	D1	126
River Forest, Il., U.S.	k9	90
River Grove, Il., U.S.	k9	90
Riverhaven, In., U.S.	B7	91
River Hebert, N.S.	D5	71
Riverhead, N.Y., U.S.	n16	109
River Heights, Ut., U.S.	B4	121
Riverhurst, Sask.	G2	75
Riverina, reg., Austl.	F7	50
River John, N.S.	D6	71
River Jordan, B.C.	h11	69
River Oaks, Tx., U.S.	*n9	120
River of Ponds, Newf.	C3	72
River Pines, Il., U.S.	f10	98
Riverport, N.S.	E5	71
River Ridge, La., U.S.	k11	95
River Road, Or., U.S.	C3	114
River Rouge, Mi., U.S.	p15	99
Rivers, Man.	D1	70
Rivers, Lake of the, l., Sask.	H3	75
Riverside, N.S.	D6	71
Riverside, Al., U.S.	B3	78
Riverside, Ca., U.S.	F5	82
Riverside, Ct., U.S.	E1	84
Riverside, Ga., U.S.	E3	87
Riverside, Il., U.S.	k9	90
Riverside, Ia., U.S.	C6	92
Riverside, Ma., U.S.	*A2	98
Riverside, N.J., U.S.	C3	107
Riverside, N.C., U.S.	D8	114
Riverside, Or., U.S.	D8	114
Riverside, Pa., U.S.	E8	115
Riverside, Ut., U.S.	B3	121
Riverside, Wa., U.S.	A6	124
Riverside, Wy., U.S.	E6	127
Riverside, co., Ca., U.S.	F5	82
Riverside-Albert, N.B.	D5	71
Riverside Reservoir, res., Co., U.S.	A6	83
Rivers Inlet, b., B.C.	D4	69
River Sioux, Ia., U.S.	C1	92
Riverton, Man.	D3	70
Riverton, N.Z.	Q12	51
Riverton, Ct., U.S.	B3	84
Riverton, Il., U.S.	D4	90
Riverton, Ia., U.S.	D2	92
Riverton, Ks., U.S.	E9	93
Riverton, La., U.S.	B3	95
Riverton, Mn., U.S.	D4	100
Riverton, Ne., U.S.	D7	104
Riverton, N.J., U.S.	C3	107
Riverton, Or., U.S.	D2	114
Riverton, Ut., U.S.	C4	121
Riverton, Vt., U.S.	C3	122
Riverton, Va., U.S.	B4	123
Riverton, W.V., U.S.	C5	125
Riverton, Wy., U.S.	C5	127
Riverton Heights, Wa., U.S.	f11	124
River Vale, N.J., U.S.	h8	107
River View, Al., U.S.	C4	78
Riverview, Fl., U.S.	p11	86
Riverview, Mi., U.S.	p15	99
Rives, Mo., U.S.	E7	102
Rives, Tn., U.S.	A2	119
Rivesaltes, Fr.	F5	16
Rivesville, W.V., U.S.	B4	125
Riviera, Az., U.S.	B1	80
Riviera, Tx., U.S.	F4	120
Riviera Beach, Fl., U.S.	F6	86
Riviera Beach, Md., U.S.	B4	97
Riviera Beach, N.J., U.S.	C4	107
Rivière-à-Pierre, Que.	B5	74
Rivière-Bleue, Que.	B8	74
Rivière-du-Loup, Que.	B8	74
Rivière-du-Loup, co., Que.	B8	74
Rivière-Ouelle, Que.	B7	74
Rivière-Trois-Pistoles, Que.	A8	74
Rivière-Verte, N.B.	B1	71
Rivière-Verte, Que.	B8	74
Rivoli, Italy	D2	103
Rixford, Pa., U.S.	C4	115
Rixe's, Nv., U.S.	*C5	105
Riyadh (Ar Riyāḍ), Sau. Ar.	C5	38
Rize, Tur.	B13	40
Rizhao, China	D8	31
Rizzuto, Cape, c., Italy	F7	23
Rjukan, Nor.	H3	14
Roachdale, In., U.S.	E4	91
Roads, Oh., U.S.	D3	112
Roadstown, N.J., U.S.	D2	107
Road Town, V.I., Br.	G12	64
Roan Cliffs, clf., U.S.	B2	83
Roan Creek, stm., Co., U.S.	B2	83
Roane, co., Tn., U.S.	D9	119
Roane, co., W.V., U.S.	C3	125
Roann, In., U.S.	C6	91
Roan Mountain, Tn., U.S.	C11	119
Roanne, Fr.	D6	16
Roanoke, Al., U.S.	B4	78
Roanoke, Il., U.S.	C4	90
Roanoke, In., U.S.	C7	91
Roanoke, La., U.S.	D3	95
Roanoke, Tx., U.S.	C4	120
Roanoke, Va., U.S.	C3	123
Roanoke, W.V., U.S.	C4	125
Roanoke, co., Va., U.S.	C2	123
Roanoke, stm., U.S.	A5	110
Roanoke Island, i., N.C., U.S.	B7	110
Roanoke Rapids, N.C., U.S.	A5	110
Roanoke Rapids Lake, res., U.S.	A5	110
Roan Plateau, plat., U.S.	B2	83
Roaring Branch, Pa., U.S.	C8	115
Roaring Fork, stm., Co., U.S.	C4	83
Roaring Spring, Pa., U.S.	F5	115
Roaring Springs, Tx., U.S.	C2	120
Roaringwater Bay, b., Ire.	F2	11
Roark, Ky., U.S.	C6	94
Roatán, Hond.	D7	63
Roba, stm., Va., U.S.	C4	78
Robards, Ky., U.S.	C2	94
Robb, Alta.	C2	68
Robbins, Il., U.S.	k9	90
Robbins, N.C., U.S.	B3	110
Robbins, Tn., U.S.	C9	119
Robbinsdale, Mn., U.S.	m12	100
Robbinston, Me., U.S.	C5	96
Robbinsville, N.J., U.S.	C3	107
Robbinsville, N.C., U.S.	f9	110
Robbs, Il., U.S.	F5	90
Robe, stm., Ire.	D2	11
Robeline, La., U.S.	C2	95
Robersonville, N.C., U.S.	B5	110
Roberta, Ga., U.S.	D2	87
Roberta Mills, N.C., U.S.	B2	110
Robert Lee, Tx., U.S.	D2	120
Roberts, Id., U.S.	F6	89
Roberts, Il., U.S.	C5	90
Roberts, Mt., U.S.	E7	103
Roberts, Wi., U.S.	C1	126
Roberts, co., S.D., U.S.	B8	118
Roberts, co., Tx., U.S.	B2	120
Roberts, Cape, c., Ont.	A7	73
Robert's Arm, Newf.	D4	72
Roberts Creek Mountain, mtn., Nv., U.S.	D5	105
Robertsdale, Al., U.S.	E2	78
Robertsdale, Pa., U.S.	F5	115
Roberts Mountain, mtn., Ak., U.S.	C6	79
Roberts Mountain, mtn., Wy., U.S.	D3	127
Robertson, S. Afr.	D3	49
Robertson, Wy., U.S.	E2	127
Robertson, co., Ky., U.S.	B5	94
Robertson, co., Tn., U.S.	A5	119
Robertson, co., Tx., U.S.	D4	120
Robertson, Lac, l., Que.	C7	72
Robertson Bay, b., Ant.	B29	7
Robertsonville, Que.	C6	74
Roberts Peak, mtn., B.C.	F8	66
Robertsport, Lib.	E2	45
Robertstown, Ga., U.S.	B3	87
Robertsville, N.J., U.S.	*C4	107
Robertville, N.B.	B4	71
Robeson, co., N.C., U.S.	C3	110
Robesonia, Pa., U.S.	F9	115
Robin Hood's Bay, Eng., U.K.	F8	13
Robinhood, Ky., U.S.	D5	94
Robins, Ia., U.S.	B6	92
Robins, Oh., U.S.	C4	112
Robins Air Force Base, mil., Ga., U.S.	D3	87
Robinson, Ks., U.S.	C8	93
Robinson, N.D., U.S.	B6	111
Robinson, Pa., U.S.	B7	113
Robinson, Tx., U.S.	*n10	120
Robinson Crusoe, Isla, i., Chile	g3	53
Robinson Fork, stm., W.V., U.S.	k9	125
Robinson Fork, stm., W.V., U.S.	m14	125
Robinson Mountain, mtn., Ar., U.S.	A1	81
Robinsons, Newf.	D2	72
Robinsonville, Ms., U.S.	A3	101
Robinvale, Austl.	F7	50
Roblin, Man.	D1	70
Roblin, Man.	A5	70
Roborė, Bol.	C4	55
Robsart, Sask.	H1	75
Robson, B.C.	E9	69
Robson, Mount, mtn., B.C.	C8	69
Robstown, Tx., U.S.	F4	120
Roby, Mo., U.S.	D5	102
Roby, Tx., U.S.	C2	120
Roca, Ne., U.S.	h11	104
Roca, Cape, c., Port.	f9	22
Rocafuerte, Ec.	B1	58
Rocafuerte, Peru	B2	58
Rocanville, Sask.	G5	75
Rocas, Átol das, atoll, Braz.	A7	57
Rocca Massima, Italy	h9	23
Roccastrada, Italy	C3	23
Rochdale, Eng., U.K.	D5	10
Rochdale, Ma., U.S.	B4	98
Rochdale, N.J., U.S.	C4	107
Rochechouart, Fr.	E4	16
Rochedo, Braz.	B2	56
Rochefort, Bel.	B6	16
Rochefort, Fr.	E3	16
Roche Harbor, Wa., U.S.	A2	124
Rochelle, Ga., U.S.	E3	87
Rochelle, Il., U.S.	B4	90
Rochelle, Tx., U.S.	D3	120
Rochelle Park, N.J., U.S.	h8	107
Roche-Percée, Sask.	H4	75
Rochepont, Mo., U.S.	C5	102
Rochester, Alta.	B4	68
Rochester, Eng., U.K.	E7	10
Rochester, Il., U.S.	D4	90
Rochester, In., U.S.	B5	91
Rochester, Ky., U.S.	C3	94
Rochester, Ma., U.S.	C6	98
Rochester, Mi., U.S.	F7	99
Rochester, Mn., U.S.	F6	100
Rochester, N.H., U.S.	D5	106
Rochester, N.Y., U.S.	B3	109
Rochester, Pa., U.S.	E1	115
Rochester, Tx., U.S.	C3	120
Rochester, Vt., U.S.	D3	122
Rochester, Wa., U.S.	C2	124
Rochester Hills, Mi., U.S.	*F7	99
Rochester Mountain, mtn., Vt., U.S.	D3	122
Rochford, S.D., U.S.	C2	118
Rochfort Bridge, Alta.	C3	68
Rochfortbridge, Ire.	C4	11
Rochikarai Island, i., Marsh Is.	P18	52
Rochlitz, E. Ger.	B7	19
Rociada, N.M., U.S.	B4	108
Rock, Ks., U.S.	E7	93
Rock, Ma., U.S.	*C6	98
Rock, Mi., U.S.	B3	99
Rock, co., Mn., U.S.	G2	100
Rock, co., Ne., U.S.	B6	104
Rock, co., Wi., U.S.	F4	126
Rock, stm., U.S.	A1	92
Rock, stm., U.S.	A1	92
Rock Bay, B.C.	D5	69
Rock Bluff, Fl., U.S.	B2	86
Rockbridge, Il., U.S.	D3	90
Rockbridge, Oh., U.S.	C3	112
Rockbridge, co., Va., U.S.	C3	123
Rockcastle, co., Ky., U.S.	C5	94
Rockcastle, stm., Ky., U.S.	C5	94
Rock Creek, B.C.	E8	69
Rock Creek, Ks., U.S.	k14	93
Rock Creek, Mn., U.S.	E6	100
Rock Creek, Oh., U.S.	A5	112
Rock Creek, stm., N.A.	H2	75
Rock Creek, stm., U.S.	B3	97
Rock Creek, stm., Ia., U.S.	h14	124
Rock Creek, stm., Ks., U.S.	g10	93
Rock Creek, stm., Ne., U.S.	g11	104
Rock Creek, stm., Nv., U.S.	C5	105
Rock Creek, stm., Or., U.S.	B6	114
Rock Creek, stm., Wa., U.S.	B8	124
Rock Creek, stm., Wa., U.S.	D5	124
Rock Creek, stm., Wy., U.S.	E6	127
Rock Creek Butte, mtn., Or., U.S.	C8	114
Rockdale, Austl.	*F9	50
Rockdale, Il., U.S.	*B5	90
Rockdale, Md., U.S.	B4	97
Rockdale, Tn., U.S.	D8	119
Rockdale, Tx., U.S.	D4	120
Rockdale, co., Ga., U.S.	C3	87
Rock Elm, Wi., U.S.	D1	126
Rockfall, Ct., U.S.	C5	84
Rock Falls, Il., U.S.	B4	90
Rock Falls, Ia., U.S.	A4	92
Rockfield, In., U.S.	C4	91
Rockfield, Ky., U.S.	D3	94
Rockfield, Wi., U.S.	m11	126
Rockford, Al., U.S.	C3	78
Rockford, Il., U.S.	A4	90
Rockford, Ia., U.S.	A5	92
Rockford, Mn., U.S.	E5	100
Rockford, Oh., U.S.	B1	112
Rockford, Tn., U.S.	D10	119
Rockford, Wa., U.S.	B8	124
Rock Hall, Md., U.S.	B5	97
Rockham, S.D., U.S.	C7	118
Rockhampton, Austl.	D9	50
Rockhaven, Sask.	E1	75
Rock Hill, Mo., U.S.	*f13	102
Rock Hill, S.C., U.S.	B5	117
Rockhill Furnace, Pa., U.S.	F6	115
Rockholds, Ky., U.S.	D5	94
Rockingham, Austl.	E4	87
Rockingham, N.C., U.S.	C3	110
Rockingham, Vt., U.S.	E4	122
Rockingham, co., N.H., U.S.	D4	106
Rockingham, co., N.C., U.S.	A3	110
Rockingham, co., Va., U.S.	B4	123
Rock Island, Il., U.S.	B3	90
Rock Island, Ok., U.S.	B7	113
Rock Island, Pa., U.S.	B5	124
Rock Island, Tx., U.S.	*n10	120
Rock Island, i., Fl., U.S.	C3	86
Rock Island, co., Il., U.S.	B3	90
Rock Island, i., Wi., U.S.	C7	126
Rocklake, N.D., U.S.	A6	111
Rock Lake, l., Man.	E2	70
Rock Lake, l., Wa., U.S.	B8	124
Rockland, Ont.	B9	73
Rockland, Id., U.S.	G6	89
Rockland, Ma., U.S.	B6	98
Rockland, Me., U.S.	D3	96
Rockland, Mi., U.S.	m12	99
Rockland, N.Y., U.S.	D6	109
Rockland, co., N.Y., U.S.	D6	109
Rocklands Reservoir, res., Austl.	H3	51
Rockledge, Fl., U.S.	D6	86
Rockledge, Ga., U.S.	D4	87
Rockledge, Pa., U.S.	o20	115
Rockleigh, N.J., U.S.	g9	107
Rockmart, Ga., U.S.	B1	87
Rock Mountain, mtn., Al., U.S.	B2	78
Rock Mountain, mtn., Co., U.S.	D3	83
Rock Point, Az., U.S.	A6	80
Rock Point, Md., U.S.	D4	97
Rockport, Ar., U.S.	g8	81
Rockport, Il., U.S.	D2	90
Rockport, In., U.S.	I3	91
Rockport, Ky., U.S.	C3	94
Rockport, Me., U.S.	D3	96
Rockport, Ma., U.S.	A6	98
Rock Port, Mo., U.S.	A2	102
Rockport, Tx., U.S.	E4	120
Rockport, Wa., U.S.	A4	124
Rock Rapids, Ia., U.S.	A1	92
Rock River, Wy., U.S.	E7	127
Rock Run, Al., U.S.	A4	78
Rock Springs, Mt., U.S.	D10	103
Rock Springs, Tx., U.S.	D2	120
Rock Springs, Wi., U.S.	E3	126
Rock Springs, Wy., U.S.	E3	127
Rockstone, Guy.	A3	59
Rock Valley, Ia., U.S.	A1	92
Rockville, Ct., U.S.	B6	84
Rockville, In., U.S.	E3	91
Rockville, Md., U.S.	B3	97
Rockville, Mn., U.S.	E4	100
Rockville, Ne., U.S.	C7	104
Rockville, R.I., U.S.	F1	116
Rockville, Ut., U.S.	F2	121
Rockville, Va., U.S.	C5	123
Rockville Centre, N.Y., U.S.	n15	109
Rockwall, Tx., U.S.	C4	120
Rockwall, co., Tx., U.S.	C4	120
Rockwell, Ia., U.S.	B4	92
Rockwell, N.C., U.S.	B2	110
Rockwell City, Ia., U.S.	B3	92
Rockwell Park, N.C., U.S.	B2	110
Rockwood, Ont.	D4	73
Rockwood, Al., U.S.	A2	78
Rockwood, Il., U.S.	F4	90
Rockwood, Me., U.S.	C3	96
Rockwood, Mi., U.S.	F7	99
Rockwood, Or., U.S.	*B4	114
Rockwood, Pa., U.S.	G3	115
Rockwood, Tn., U.S.	D9	119
Rockwood, Tx., U.S.	D3	120
Rocky, Ok., U.S.	B2	113
Rocky, stm., Alta.	C2	68
Rocky, stm., N.C., U.S.	B2	110
Rocky, stm., S.C., U.S.	C2	117
Rocky, East Branch, stm., Oh., U.S.	h9	112
Rocky, West Branch, stm., Oh., U.S.	h9	112
Rocky Bay, b., Newf.	B4	72
Rocky Boys Indian Reservation, Mt., U.S.	B7	103
Rocky Comfort, Mo., U.S.	E3	102
Rocky Coulee, stm., Wa., U.S.	B6	124
Rocky Creek, Fl., U.S.	*o10	86
Rocky Ford, Co., U.S.	C7	83
Rocky Ford, Ga., U.S.	D5	87
Rocky Fork Lake, l., Oh., U.S.	C2	112
Rocky Gap, Va., U.S.	C1	123
Rocky Harbour, Newf.	D3	72
Rocky Hill, Ct., U.S.	C5	84
Rocky Hill, Ky., U.S.	C3	94
Rocky Hill, N.J., U.S.	C3	107
Rocky Lake, l., Man.	B1	70
Rocky Lake, l., Me., U.S.	D5	96
Rocky Mount, N.C., U.S.	B5	110
Rocky Mount, Va., U.S.	D3	123
Rocky Mountain, mtn., Mt., U.S.	C4	103
Rocky Mountain House, Alta.	C3	68
Rocky Mountain National Park, Co., U.S.	A5	83
Rocky Mountains, mts., N.A.	E9	61
Rocky Point, N.Y., U.S.	*n16	109
Rocky Point, c., Wa., U.S.	C5	110
Rocky Ripple, In., U.S.	k10	91
Rocky River, Oh., U.S.	A4	112
Rocky Top, mtn., Or., U.S.	C4	114
Rocroi, Fr.	E4	17
Roda, Va., U.S.	f9	123
Rodach, W. Ger.	C5	19
Rodanthe, N.C., U.S.	B7	110
Rodarte, N.M., U.S.	*A4	108
Rødby, Den.	D5	15
Rødbyhavn, Den.	D5	15
Rødding, Den.	C3	15
Rødding, Den.	C3	15
Roddickton, Newf.	C3	72
Roddy, Tn., U.S.	D9	119
Rødekro, Den.	C3	15
Rodeo, Ca., U.S.	*g8	82
Rodeo, N.M., U.S.	F1	108
Roderfield, W.V., U.S.	D3	125
Roderick Island, i., B.C.	C3	69
Rodessa, La., U.S.	B2	95
Rodewisch, E. Ger.	C7	19
Rodey, N.M., U.S.	E2	108
Rodez, Fr.	E5	16
Ródhos, Grc.	D7	40
Ródhos (Rhodes), i., Grc.	D7	40
Roding, W. Ger.	D6	19
Rodman, Ia., U.S.	A3	92
Rodney, Ont.	E3	73
Rodney, Ms., U.S.	D2	101
Rodney, Cape, c., Ak., U.S.	C6	79
Rodney Pond, l., Newf.	D3	72
Rodney Village, De., U.S.	D3	85
Roduco, N.C., U.S.	A6	110
Roe, Ar., U.S.	C4	81
Roebling, N.J., U.S.	C3	107
Roebourne, Austl.	D2	50
Roebuck, S.C., U.S.	B4	117
Roebuck Bay, b., Austl.	C3	50
Roeland Park, Ks., U.S.	k16	93
Roermond, Neth.	B6	17
Roeselare (Roulers), Bel.	B5	16
Roessleville, N.Y., U.S.	*C7	109
Roes Welcome Sound, strt., N.W. Ter.	D15	66
Roetgen, W. Ger.	D6	17
Roff, Ok., U.S.	C5	113
Rogachev, Sov. Un.	E2	27
Rogagua, Laguna, l., Bol.	B2	55
Rogáguado, Laguna, l., Bol.	B2	55
Roganville, Tx., U.S.	D6	120
Rogatica, Yugo.	D4	24
Roger Mills, co., Ok., U.S.	B2	113
Rogers, Ar., U.S.	A1	81
Rogers, Ct., U.S.	B8	84
Rogers, Mn., U.S.	E5	100
Rogers, Ne., U.S.	C9	104
Rogers, N.M., U.S.	D6	108
Rogers, Oh., U.S.	B5	112
Rogers, Tx., U.S.	D4	120
Rogers, co., Ok., U.S.	A6	113
Rogers, Mount, mtn., Va., U.S.	f10	123
Rogers City, Mi., U.S.	C7	99
Rogers Lake, res., Ct., U.S.	D6	84
Rogerson, Id., U.S.	G4	89
Rogers Pass, Mt., U.S.	C4	103
Rogersville, Al., U.S.	A2	78
Rogersville, Mo., U.S.	G1	115
Rogersville, Tn., U.S.	C10	119
Roggen, Co., U.S.	A6	83
Rogoźno, Pol.	B4	26
Rogue, stm., Or., U.S.	E3	114
Rogue River, Or., U.S.	E3	114
Rohnert Park, Ca., U.S.	*C2	82
Rohrersville, Md., U.S.	B2	97
Rohri Canal, Pak.	G3	37
Rohtak, India	C6	37
Roi Et, Thai.	B2	34
Roissy-en-France, Fr.	g11	16
Rojas, Arg.	A4	54
Rojo, Cabo, c., Mex.	m15	63
Rojo, Cabo, c., P.R.	H11	64
Rokan, stm., Indon.	L4	35
Rokeby, Sask.	F4	75
Rokel, stm., S.L.	E2	45
Rokiškis, Sov. Un.	C7	14
Rokycany, Czech.	D2	26
Roland, Man.	E3	70
Roland, Ar., U.S.	*C3	81
Roland, Ia., U.S.	B4	92
Roland, Ok., U.S.	B7	113
Roland, Lake, res., Md., U.S.	g11	97
Rolesville, N.C., U.S.	B4	110
Rolette, N.D., U.S.	A6	111
Rolette, co., N.D., U.S.	A6	111
Rolfe, Ia., U.S.	B3	92

Name	Map Ref.	Page
Roll, Az., U.S.	E2	80
Roll, In., U.S.	C7	91
Roll, Ok., U.S.	B2	113
Rolla, B.C.	B7	69
Rolla, Al., U.S.	C3	81
Rolla, Ks., U.S.	E2	93
Rolla, Mo., U.S.	D6	102
Rolla, N.D., U.S.	A6	111
Rolle, Switz.	E3	18
Rolleville, Bah.	C6	64
Rollingbay, Wa., U.S.	e10	124
Rolling Fork, Ms., U.S.	C3	101
Rolling Fork, stm., Ar., U.S.	C1	81
Rolling Fork, stm., Ky., U.S.	C4	94
Rolling Hills Estates, Ca., U.S.	*n12	82
Rolling Meadows, Il., U.S.	h8	90
Rollingstone, Mn., U.S.	F7	100
Rollins, Mt., U.S.	C2	103
Rollinsford, N.H., U.S.	D5	106
Rolvsøya, i., Nor.	B10	14
Roma, Austl.	E8	50
Roma, Alta.	A2	68
Roma, Tx., U.S.	F3	120
Romain, Cape, c., S.C., U.S.	F9	117
Romaine, stm., Can.	h9	72
Roman, Rom.	B8	24
Romania, ctry., Eur.	C7	24
Roman Nose Mountain, mtn., Md., U.S.	m12	97
Roman Nose Mountain, mtn., Or., U.S.	D3	114
Romano, Cape, c., Fl., U.S.	G5	86
Romano, Cayo, i., Cuba	C5	64
Romanshorn, Switz.	A7	21
Romans [-sur-Isère], Fr.	E6	16
Romanzof, Cape, c., Ak., U.S.	C6	79
Romanzof Mountains, mts., Ak., U.S.	B11	79
Romayor, Tx., U.S.	D5	120
Rombauer, Mo., U.S.	E7	102
Rome (Roma), Italy	D4	23
Rome, Ga., U.S.	B1	87
Rome, Il., U.S.	C4	90
Rome, In., U.S.	I4	91
Rome, Ia., U.S.	D6	92
Rome, Ms., U.S.	B3	101
Rome, N.Y., U.S.	B5	109
Rome, Oh., U.S.	D3	112
Rome, Pa., U.S.	C9	115
Rome City, In., U.S.	B7	91
Romema (part of Jerusalem), Isr.	m14	41
Romeo, Co., U.S.	D4	83
Romeo, Mi., U.S.	F7	99
Romeoville, Il., U.S.	k8	90
Romeville, La., U.S.	h10	95
Romford (part of London), Eng., U.K.	k13	10
Romilly, Fr.	C5	16
Romita, Mex.	m13	63
Romney, In., U.S.	D4	91
Romney, W.V., U.S.	B6	125
Romny, Sov. Un.	F9	27
Rømø, i., Den.	C2	15
Romona, Il., U.S.	F4	91
Romont, Switz.	C2	21
Romorantin, Fr.	D4	16
Rompin, stm., Malay.	K5	35
Romsey, Eng., U.K.	D6	12
Romulus, Mi., U.S.	p15	99
Romulus, N.Y., U.S.	C4	109
Romunum, i., Micron.	Q18	52
Romurikku Island, i., Marsh Is.	P18	52
Ron, Viet.	D7	35
Ron, Cape, c., Viet.	C7	35
Rona, i., Scot., U.K.	C3	13
Rona, i., Scot., U.K.	A3	13
Ronald, Wa., U.S.	B4	124
Ronan, Mt., U.S.	C2	103
Roncador, Serra do, plat., Braz.	E4	59
Roncador Bank, Col.	D7	62
Ronceverte, W.V., U.S.	D4	125
Ronciglione, Italy	C4	23
Ronda, Spain	D3	22
Ronda, N.C., U.S.	A2	110
Rønde, Den.	B4	15
Ronde Island, i., Gren.	W25	65
Rondo, Ar., U.S.	C5	81
Rondônia, state, Braz.	E5	56
Rondonópolis, Braz.	B2	56
Roneys Point, W.V., U.S.	f8	125
Ronge, Lac la, l., Sask.	B3	75
Rongjiang, China	L3	32
Rongxian, China	G7	31
Ronkiti Harbor, b., Micron.	Q17	52
Ronkonkoma, N.Y., U.S.	*n15	109
Rønne, Den.	J6	14
Rönne, stm., Swe.	B6	15
Ronneburg, E. Ger.	C7	19
Ronne Entrance, b., Ant.	B5	7
Ronnemark, Alta.	D4	68
Ronse, Bel.	B5	16
Ronuro, stm., Braz.	E4	59
Roodepoort-Maraisburg, S. Afr.	*C4	49
Roodeschool, Neth.	A6	17
Roodhouse, Il., U.S.	D3	90
Roof Butte, mtn., Az., U.S.	A6	80
Rooks, co., Ks., U.S.	C4	93
Roopville, Ga., U.S.	C1	87
Roosendaal, Neth.	B6	16
Roosevelt, Mn., U.S.	B3	100
Roosevelt, N.J., U.S.	C3	107
Roosevelt, N.Y., U.S.	*n15	109
Roosevelt, Ok., U.S.	C2	113
Roosevelt, Tx., U.S.	D2	120
Roosevelt, Ut., U.S.	C5	121
Roosevelt, Wa., U.S.	D5	124
Roosevelt, co., Mt., U.S.	B11	103
Roosevelt, co., N.M., U.S.	C6	108
Roosevelt, stm., Braz.	D2	59
Roosevelt Campobello International Park, N.A.	E3	71
Roosevelt Island, i., Ant.	B32	7
Roosevelt Park, Mi., U.S.	E4	99
Root, stm., Mn., U.S.	G7	100
Root, stm., Wi., U.S.	n12	126
Rootstown, Oh., U.S.	A4	112
Ropczyce, Pol.	E6	26
Roper, N.C., U.S.	B6	110
Roper, stm., Austl.	B6	50
Ropesville, Tx., U.S.	C1	120
Roque Bluffs, Me., U.S.	D5	96
Roquefort, Fr.	E3	16
Roquetas, Spain	B6	22
Rora Head, c., Scot., U.K.	B5	13
Roraima, ter., Braz.	C7	56
Roraima, Mount, mtn., S.A.	A2	59
Rorke Lake, l., Can.	D2	70
Rorketon, Man.	D2	70
Røros, Nor.	F4	14
Rorschach, Switz.	E4	18
Rosa, La., U.S.	D3	95
Rosa, Monte, mtn., Eur.	B1	23
Rosa, Punta, c., Mex.	B3	63
Rosales, Phil.	o13	34
Rosalia, Ks., U.S.	E7	93
Rosalia, Wa., U.S.	B8	124
Rosalind, Alta.	C4	68
Rosamond, Ca., U.S.	E4	82
Rosamond, Il., U.S.	D4	90
Rosamorada, Mex.	k11	63
Rosario, Arg.	A4	54
Rosario, Braz.	B2	57
Rosario, Mex.	C3	63
Rosario, Para.	D4	55
Rosario, Ur.	E1	56
Rosario, [Villa del], Ven.	A3	60
Rosario de la Frontera, Arg.	E3	55
Rosario del Tala, Arg.	A5	54
Rosário Oeste, Braz.	A1	56
Rosati, Mo., U.S.	C6	102
Rosburg, Wa., U.S.	C2	124
Roscoe, Il., U.S.	A5	90
Roscoe, Mn., U.S.	E4	100
Roscoe, Mo., U.S.	D4	102
Roscoe, Ne., U.S.	E7	104
Roscoe, N.Y., U.S.	D6	109
Roscoe, Pa., U.S.	F2	115
Roscoe, S.D., U.S.	B6	118
Roscoe, Tx., U.S.	C2	120
Roscoe Glacier, ice, Ant.	C22	7
Roscommon, Ire.	D2	10
Roscommon, Mi., U.S.	D6	99
Roscommon, co., Ire.	D3	11
Roscommon, co., Mi., U.S.	D6	99
Roscrea, Ire.	D3	10
Rose, Ne., U.S.	B6	104
Rose, Ok., U.S.	A6	113
Rose, Mount, mtn., Nv., U.S.	D2	105
Roseau, Dom.	I14	64
Roseau, Mn., U.S.	B3	100
Roseau, co., Mn., U.S.	B3	100
Roseau, stm., N.A.	E3	70
Roseau, South Fork, stm., Mn., U.S.	B3	100
Rosebery, B.C.	D9	69
Rose-Blanche [-Harbour le Cou], Newf.	E2	72
Roseboro, N.C., U.S.	C4	110
Rosebud, Alta.	D4	68
Rose Bud, Ar., U.S.	B3	81
Rosebud, Mo., U.S.	C6	102
Rosebud, S.D., U.S.	D5	118
Rosebud, Tx., U.S.	D4	120
Rosebud, co., Mt., U.S.	D10	103
Rosebud, stm., Alta.	D4	68
Rosebud Creek, stm., Mt., U.S.	E10	103
Rosebud Indian Reservation, S.D., U.S.	D5	118
Roseburg, Or., U.S.	D3	114
Rosebush, Mi., U.S.	E6	99
Rose City, Mi., U.S.	D6	99
Rose Creek, Mn., U.S.	G6	100
Rosedale, Alta.	D4	68
Rosedale, B.C.	f14	69
Rosedale, In., U.S.	E3	91
Rosedale, Md., U.S.	g11	97
Rosedale, Ms., U.S.	B2	101
Rosedale, Ok., U.S.	C4	113
Rosedale, Tn., U.S.	C9	119
Rosedale, Wa., U.S.	f10	124
Rosedale Colony, S.D., U.S.	*D8	118
Rose Farm, Oh., U.S.	C3	112
Rosegen, N.D., U.S.	B4	111
Rosehearty, Scot., U.K.	C6	13
Rose Hill, Il., U.S.	D5	90
Rose Hill, Ks., U.S.	E6	93
Rose Hill, Ms., U.S.	C4	101
Rose Hill, N.C., U.S.	C4	110
Rose Hill, Va., U.S.	*B5	123
Rose Hill, Va., U.S.	f8	123
Roseisle, Man.	E2	70
Roseland, Ca., U.S.	*C2	82
Roseland, Fl., U.S.	E6	86
Roseland, In., U.S.	A5	91
Roseland, La., U.S.	D5	95
Roseland, Ne., U.S.	D7	104
Roseland, N.J., U.S.	*B4	107
Roseland, Oh., U.S.	B3	112
Roselawn, In., U.S.	B3	91
Roselle, Il., U.S.	k8	90
Roselle, N.J., U.S.	k7	107
Roselle Park, N.J., U.S.	k7	107
Rose Lynn, Alta.	D5	68
Rosemark, Tn., U.S.	B2	119
Rosemary, Alta.	D4	68
Rosemead, Ca., U.S.	*m15	82
Rosemère, Que.	p19	74
Rosemont, Ca., U.S.	*C3	82
Rosemont, N.J., U.S.	C3	107
Rosemont, W.V., U.S.	k10	125
Rosemount, Mn., U.S.	F5	100
Rosenberg, Tx., U.S.	E5	120
Rosendale, Mo., U.S.	A3	102
Rosendale, Wi., U.S.	E5	126
Rosenfeld, Man.	E3	70
Rosenhayn, N.J., U.S.	E2	107
Rosenheim, W. Ger.	E6	18
Rose Peak, mtn., Az., U.S.	D6	80
Rosepine, La., U.S.	D2	95
Rose Point, c., B.C.	B2	69
Rose Prairie, B.C.	A7	69
Roseray, Sask.	G1	75
Roseville, Ca., U.S.	C3	82
Roseville, Il., U.S.	C3	90
Roseville, Mi., U.S.	o16	99
Roseville, Mn., U.S.	m12	100
Roseville, Oh., U.S.	C3	112
Roseville, Pa., U.S.	C8	115
Rosewood, Oh., U.S.	B2	112
Rosewood Heights, Il., U.S.	E3	90
Rosharon, Tx., U.S.	r14	120
Rosheim, Fr.	F7	17
Rosh Ha' Ayin, Isr.	B6	41
Rosh Pinna, Isr.	B7	41
Rosholt, S.D., U.S.	B9	118
Rosholt, Wi., U.S.	D4	126
Rosiclare, Il., U.S.	F5	90
Rosie, Ar., U.S.	B4	81
Rosier, Ga., U.S.	D4	87
Rosières-en-Santerre, Fr.	E2	17
Rosignano Marittimo, Italy	C3	23
Rosignol, Guy.	A3	59
Roșiorii de Vede, Rom.	C7	24
Roskilde, Den.	C6	15
Roskilde, co., Den.	C6	15
Roslavl, Sov. Un.	E9	27
Roslyn, Pa., U.S.	o21	115
Roslyn, S.D., U.S.	B8	118
Roslyn, Wa., U.S.	B4	124
Roslyn Heights, N.Y., U.S.	h13	109
Rosman, N.C., U.S.	f10	110
Ross, N.Z.	O13	51
Ross, Mn., U.S.	B3	100
Ross, N.D., U.S.	A3	111
Ross, co., Oh., U.S.	C2	112
Ross, Mount, mtn., N.Z.	N15	51
Rossa, Switz.	D7	21
Rossano, Italy	E6	23
Ross Barnett Reservoir, res., Ms., U.S.	C3	101
Rossburg, Oh., U.S.	B1	112
Rossburn, Man.	D1	70
Ross Carbery, Ire.	F2	11
Ross Dam, Wa., U.S.	A4	124
Rosseau, Ont.	B5	73
Rossendale, Man.	E2	70
Rosser, Tx., U.S.	n10	120
Rosses Bay, b., Ire.	B3	11
Rosses Point, Ire.	C3	11
Ross Ice Shelf, ice, Ant.	A31	7
Ross Island, i., Ant.	B29	7
Ross Island, i., Man.	B3	70
Rossiter, Pa., U.S.	E4	115
Ross Lake, res., N.A.	A4	124
Ross Lake National Recreation Area, Wa., U.S.	A5	124
Rossland, B.C.	E9	69
Rosslare, Ire.	E5	11
Rosslau, E. Ger.	B7	19
Rossmoor, Ca., U.S.	*n12	82
Rossmoor, Ca., U.S.	C1	45
Ross-on-Wye, Eng., U.K.	C5	12
Rossosh, Sov. Un.	F12	27
Ross River, Yukon	D6	66
Ross Sea, Ant.	B31	7
Rosston, Ar., U.S.	D2	81
Rosston, Ok., U.S.	A2	113
Ross Township, Pa., U.S.	*E1	115
Rossville, Ga., U.S.	B1	87
Rossville, Il., U.S.	C6	90
Rossville, In., U.S.	D4	91
Rossville, Ks., U.S.	C8	93
Rossville, Ok., U.S.	B5	113
Rossville, Tn., U.S.	B2	119
Rostock, E. Ger.	A6	18
Rostov, Sov. Un.	C12	27
Rostov-na-Donu, Sov. Un.	E6	29
Roșul Pass, Rom.	C7	24
Roswell, Ga., U.S.	B2	87
Roswell, Id., U.S.	F2	89
Roswell, N.M., U.S.	D5	108
Roswell, S.D., U.S.	C8	118
Rota, Spain	D2	22
Rotan, Tx., U.S.	C2	120
Rothaar Mountains, mts., W. Ger.	C4	18
Rothbury, Eng., U.K.	E7	13
Röthenbach [bei Sankt Wolfgang], W. Ger.	D6	19
Röthenbach im Emmental, Switz.	C4	21
Rothenburg, E. Ger.	B9	19
Rothenburg [ob der Tauber], W. Ger.	D5	18
Rothenthurm, Switz.	B6	21
Rother, stm., Eng., U.K.	D8	12
Rotherham, Eng., U.K.	A6	12
Rothesay, N.B.	D4	71
Rothesay, Scot., U.K.	C4	10
Rothsay, Mn., U.S.	D2	100
Rothschild, Wi., U.S.	D4	126
Rothville, Mo., U.S.	B4	102
Rothwell, N.B.	C3	71
Roto, Austl.	F5	51
Rotondella, Italy	D6	23
Rotondo, Monte, mtn., Fr.	C2	23
Rotorua, N.Z.	M16	51
Rott, stm., W. Ger.	D6	19
Rottenburg, W. Ger.	E3	19
Rottenmann, Aus.	E7	18
Rotterdam, Neth.	B6	16
Rotterdam, N.Y., U.S.	C6	109
Rottumeroog, i., Neth.	A6	17
Rottweil, W. Ger.	D4	18
Roubaix, Fr.	B5	16
Roubideau Creek, stm., Co., U.S.	C2	83
Roudnice [nad Labem], Czech.	n17	26
Rouen, Fr.	C4	16
Rouge, stm., Que.	D3	74
Rougemont, Fr.	B2	20
Rougemont, N.C., U.S.	A4	110
Rough, stm., Ky., U.S.	C3	94
Rough River Lake, res., Ky., U.S.	C3	94
Rougon, La., U.S.	D4	95
Rouleau, Sask.	G3	75
Roulette, Pa., U.S.	C5	115
Round Harbour, Newf.	D4	72
Roundhead, Oh., U.S.	B2	112
Round Hill, Alta.	C4	68
Round Hill, Va., U.S.	A5	123
Round Island, i., Ms., U.S.	g8	101
Round Island Passage, strt., Fiji	H14	52
Round Lake, Mn., U.S.	G3	100
Roundlake, Ms., U.S.	A3	101
Round Lake, N.Y., U.S.	C7	109
Round Lake, l., Ont.	B7	73
Round Lake, l., Sask.	G4	75
Round Lake Beach, Il., U.S.	h8	90
Round Mound, hill, Ks., U.S.	D4	93
Round Mountain, Nv., U.S.	E4	105
Round Mountain, Tx., U.S.	D3	120
Round Mountain, mtn., Austl.	F9	50
Round Oak, Ga., U.S.	C3	87
Round Pond, Ar., U.S.	B5	81
Round Pond, Me., U.S.	E3	96
Round Pond, l., Newf.	D4	72
Round Rock, Az., U.S.	A6	80
Round Rock, Tx., U.S.	D4	120
Round Spring, Mo., U.S.	D6	102
Roundstone, Ire.	D2	11
Round Top Hill, mtn., Ma., U.S.	B2	98
Roundup, Mt., U.S.	D8	103
Round Valley Indian Reservation, Ca., U.S.	C2	82
Round Valley Reservoir, res., N.J., U.S.	B3	107
Roura, Fr. Gu.	B4	59
Rousay, i., Scot., U.K.	A5	10
Rouses Point, N.Y., U.S.	f11	109
Rouseville, Pa., U.S.	D2	115
Routon, Tn., U.S.	A3	119
Routt, co., Co., U.S.	A3	83
Rouville, co., Que.	D4	74
Rouyn, Que.	k11	74
Rouzerville, Pa., U.S.	G6	115
Rovaniemi, Fin.	D11	14
Rovato, Italy	B2	23
Rovenki, Sov. Un.	G12	27
Rovenki, Sov. Un.	G12	27
Rover, Ar., U.S.	C2	81
Rover, Tn., U.S.	B5	119
Roveredo, Switz.	D7	21
Rovereto, Italy	B3	23
Rovigo, Italy	B3	23
Rovinj, Yugo.	C1	24
Rovno, Sov. Un.	D5	29
Rovnoye, Sov. Un.	F16	27
Rowan, Ia., U.S.	B4	92
Rowan, co., Ky., U.S.	B6	94
Rowan, co., N.C., U.S.	B2	110
Rowena, S.D., U.S.	D9	118
Rowena, Tx., U.S.	D2	120
Rowesville, S.C., U.S.	E6	117
Rowland, Ky., U.S.	C5	94
Rowland, N.C., U.S.	C3	110
Rowland, Ok., U.S.	D11	115
Rowland Heights, Ca., U.S.	*n13	82
Rowlesburg, W.V., U.S.	B5	125
Rowlett, Tx., U.S.	*n9	120
Rowletts, Ky., U.S.	C4	94
Rowley, Alta.	D4	68
Rowley, Ma., U.S.	A6	98
Rowley Shoals, rf., Austl.	C2	50
Rowan's Ravine Provincial Park, Sask.	G3	75
Roxana, De., U.S.	G5	85
Roxas (Capiz), Phil.	C6	34
Roxboro, N.C., U.S.	A4	110
Roxbury, Ct., U.S.	C2	84
Roxbury, Ks., U.S.	D6	93
Roxbury, Me., U.S.	D2	96
Roxbury, N.Y., U.S.	C6	109
Roxbury, Vt., U.S.	C3	122
Roxie, Ms., U.S.	D2	101
Roxobel, N.C., U.S.	A5	110
Roxton, Tx., U.S.	C5	120
Roxton Falls, Que.	D5	74
Roxton Pond, Que.	D5	74
Roy, La., U.S.	B2	95
Roy, Mt., U.S.	C8	103
Roy, N.M., U.S.	B5	108
Roy, Ut., U.S.	B3	121
Roy, Wa., U.S.	C3	124
Roya, Peña, mtn., Spain	B5	22
Royal, Ia., U.S.	A2	92
Royal, Ne., U.S.	B7	104
Royal, N.C., U.S.	B6	110
Royal, Tn., U.S.	B5	119
Royal, stm., Me., U.S.	g7	96
Royal Canal, Ire.	D4	11
Royal Center, In., U.S.	C4	91
Royale, Isle, i., Mi., U.S.	h9	99
Royal Gorge, val., Co., U.S.	C5	83
Royal Leamington Spa, Eng., U.K.	D6	10
Royal Oak, B.C.	h12	69
Royal Oak, Md., U.S.	C5	97
Royal Oak, Mi., U.S.	*F7	99
Royal Pines, N.C., U.S.	f10	110
Royalston, Ma., U.S.	A3	98
Royalton, Il., U.S.	F4	90
Royalton, In., U.S.	k9	91
Royalton, Ky., U.S.	C6	94
Royalton, Mn., U.S.	E4	100
Royalton, Vt., U.S.	D3	122
Royal Tunbridge Wells, Eng., U.K.	E7	10
Royalty, Tx., U.S.	D1	120
Roye, Fr.	C5	16
Royersford, Pa., U.S.	F10	115
Royerton, In., U.S.	D7	91
Royse City, Tx., U.S.	*C4	120
Royston, B.C.	E5	69
Royston, Ga., U.S.	B3	87
Royston, Eng., U.K.	D7	12
Rozay-en-Brie, Fr.	F2	17
Rozel, Ks., U.S.	D4	93
Rozet, Wy., U.S.	B7	127
Rožňava, Czech.	E14	27
Rtishchevo, Sov. Un.	E14	27
Rub' al Khali, des., Sau. Ar.	C5	38
Rubiataba, Braz.	B3	57
Rubidoux, Ca., U.S.	n14	82
Rubim, Braz.	D8	57
Rubonia, Fl., U.S.	p10	86
Rubottom, Ok., U.S.	C4	113
Ruby, Ak., U.S.	C8	79
Ruby, La., U.S.	C3	95
Ruby, S.C., U.S.	B7	117
Ruby Dome, mtn., Nv., U.S.	C6	105
Ruby Lake, l., Nv., U.S.	C6	105
Ruby Mountains, mts., Nv., U.S.	C6	105
Ruby Range, mts., Co., U.S.	C3	83
Ruby Range, mts., Mt., U.S.	E4	103
Rubys Inn, Ut., U.S.	F3	121
Ruby Valley, Nv., U.S.	C6	105
Ruch, i., Marsh Is.	S18	52
Rucker, Tn., U.S.	B5	119
Ruda, stm., Pol.	g9	26
Ruda Śląska, Pol.	g9	26
Rūdbār, Afg.	B3	36
Rudd, Ia., U.S.	A5	92
Ruddell, Sask.	E2	75
Ruddels Mills, Ky., U.S.	B5	94
Rüdesheim, W. Ger.	C3	18
Rudkøbing, Den.	D4	15
Rudnichnyy, Sov. Un.	B4	28
Rudnyy, Sov. Un.	*D9	29
Rudolf, Lake, l., Afr.	H6	47
Rudolph, Oh., U.S.	A2	112
Rudolph, i., Sov. Un.		
Rudolstadt, E. Ger.	C5	18
Rūdsar, Iran	B5	38
Rudy, Ar., U.S.	*B1	81
Rudyard, Mi., U.S.	B6	99
Rudyard, Mt., U.S.	B6	103
Rue, Fr.	B4	16
Rueil-Malmaison, Fr.	g9	16
Ruelle, Fr.	D4	16
Rueun, Switz.	C7	21
Rufā'ah, Sud.	C3	47
Rufe, Ok., U.S.	C6	113
Ruffec, Fr.	D4	16
Ruffin, N.C., U.S.	A3	110
Ruffin, S.C., U.S.	E6	117
Rufiji, stm., Tan.	C6	48
Rufino, Arg.	A4	54
Rufisque, Sen.	D1	45
Rufus Woods Lake, res., Wa., U.S.	A6	124
Rugao, China	H9	32
Rugby, Eng., U.K.	A6	12
Rugby, N.D., U.S.	A6	111
Rugeley, Eng., U.K.	D6	10
Rügen, i., E. Ger.	A6	18
Rugged Mountain, mtn., B.C.	D4	69
Rugozero, Sov. Un.	E15	14
Ruhengeri, Rw.	B4	48
Ruhla, E. Ger.	C5	19
Ruhland, E. Ger.	B8	19
Ruhr, stm., W. Ger.	C4	18
Rui'an, China	F9	31
Ruidosa, Tx., U.S.	p12	120
Ruidoso, N.M., U.S.	D4	108
Ruidoso Downs, N.M., U.S.	D4	108
Ruiz, Mex.	m11	63
Rujiyoru, i., Marsh Is.	S18	52
Rukaji Island, i., Marsh Is.	P18	52
Rukoji Pass, strt., Marsh Is.	P18	52
Rukuruku Bay, b., Fiji	H15	52
Rukwa, prov., Tan.	C5	48
Rukwa, Lake, l., Tan.	C5	48
Rule, Tx., U.S.	C3	120
Rule Creek, stm., Co., U.S.	D7	83
Ruleville, Ms., U.S.	B3	101
Rulo, Ne., U.S.	D10	104
Rum, stm., Mn., U.S.	D5	100
Ruma, Yugo.	C4	24
Rumbek, Sud.	D2	47
Rumbley, Md., U.S.	D6	97
Rumburk, Czech.	C9	19
Rum Cay, i., Bah.	C6	64
Rum Creek, stm., W.V., U.S.	n12	125
Rumely, Mi., U.S.	B3	99
Rumford, Me., U.S.	D2	96
Rumilly, Fr.	D1	20
Rummah, Wādī ar, val., Sau. Ar.	C4	38
Rummānah, Eg.	C4	41
Rumney, N.H., U.S.	C3	106
Rumney Depot, N.H., U.S.	C3	106
Rumoi, Japan	E10	33
Rumphi, Mwi.	D5	49
Rump Mountain, mtn., Me., U.S.	C1	96
Rumsey, Alta.	D4	68
Rumsey, Ca., U.S.	C2	82
Rumson, N.J., U.S.	C5	107
Rumstick Point, c., R.I., U.S.	D5	116
Runan, China	H6	32
Runcorn, Eng., U.K.	A5	12
Rung, i., Camb.	I3	35
Runge, Tx., U.S.	E4	120
Rungwa, Tan.	C5	48
Runit Island, i., Marsh Is.	S18	52
Runnells, Ia., U.S.	C4	92
Runnels, co., Tx., U.S.	D3	120
Runnemede, N.J., U.S.	D2	107
Runnymede, Sask.	F5	75
Runtu, Nmb.	A2	49
Ruoqiang, China	D2	31
Ruo Shui, stm., China	C5	31
Rupanco, Chile	C2	54
Rupat, i., Indon.	L4	35
Rupert, Id., U.S.	G5	89
Rupert, Vt., U.S.	E2	122
Rupert, W.V., U.S.	D4	125
Rupert, Rivière de, stm., Que.	h11	74
Rupununi, dept., Guy.	B3	59
Rupununi, stm., Guy.	B3	59
Rur, stm., Eur.	C1	18
Rural Hall, N.C., U.S.	A2	110
Rural Retreat, Va., U.S.	D1	123
Rurrenabaque, Bol.	D1	56
Rusagonis, Sask.	D3	71
Rusape, Zimb.	A5	49
Ruşayriş, Khazzān ar, res., Afr.	E7	10
Ruse, Bul.	D7	24
Rush, Ire.	D3	10
Rush, Ky., U.S.	B7	94
Rush, co., In., U.S.	E6	91
Rush, co., Ks., U.S.	D4	93
Rush, stm., Mn., U.S.	F4	100
Rush, stm., Wi., U.S.	D1	126
Rush Center, Ks., U.S.	D4	93
Rush City, Mn., U.S.	E6	100
Rush Creek, stm., Co., U.S.	C7	83
Rush Creek, stm., Ne., U.S.	C3	104
Rush Creek, stm., Oh., U.S.	B2	112
Rush Creek, stm., Ok., U.S.	C4	113
Rushden, Eng., U.K.	B7	12
Rushford, Mn., U.S.	G7	100
Rushford, N.Y., U.S.	C2	109
Rush Hill, Mo., U.S.	B6	102
Rush Lake, Sask.	G2	75
Rush Lake, l., Mn., U.S.	E5	100
Rush Lake, l., Wi., U.S.	E5	126
Rushmere, Va., U.S.	h14	123
Rushmore, Mn., U.S.	G3	100
Rush Springs, Ok., U.S.	C4	113
Rushsylvania, Oh., U.S.	B2	112
Rush Valley, Ut., U.S.	C3	121
Rushville, Il., U.S.	C3	90
Rushville, In., U.S.	E7	91
Rushville, Mo., U.S.	B2	102
Rushville, Ne., U.S.	B3	104
Rushville, N.Y., U.S.	C3	109
Rusk, Tx., U.S.	D5	120
Rusk, co., Tx., U.S.	C5	120
Rusk, co., Wi., U.S.	C2	126
Ruskin, Fl., U.S.	E4	86
Ruskin, Ne., U.S.	D8	104
Ruso, N.D., U.S.	B5	111
Russas, Braz.	B3	57
Russell, Man.	D1	70
Russell, Ont.	B9	73
Russell, Ar., U.S.	B4	81
Russell, Fl., U.S.	m8	86
Russell, Ia., U.S.	D4	92
Russell, Ks., U.S.	D5	93
Russell, Ky., U.S.	B7	94
Russell, Ma., U.S.	B2	98
Russell, Mn., U.S.	F3	100
Russell, N.Y., U.S.	f9	109
Russell, N.D., U.S.	A5	111
Russell, Pa., U.S.	C3	115
Russell, co., Al., U.S.	C4	78
Russell, co., Ks., U.S.	D5	93
Russell, co., Ky., U.S.	D4	94
Russell, co., Va., U.S.	f9	123
Russell, Mount, mtn., Ak., U.S.	f16	79
Russell Cave National Monument, Al., U.S.	A4	78
Russell Fork, stm., U.S.	C7	94
Russellkonda, India	H10	37
Russell Lake, l., Man.	A3	68
Russell Lake, l., Man.	A1	70
Russell Springs, Ks., U.S.	D2	93
Russell Springs, Ky., U.S.	C4	94
Russellville, Al., U.S.	A2	78
Russellville, Ar., U.S.	B2	81
Russellville, Il., U.S.	E6	90
Russellville, In., U.S.	E4	91
Russellville, Ky., U.S.	D3	94
Russellville, Mo., U.S.	C5	102
Russellville, Oh., U.S.	D2	112
Russellville, Or., U.S.	*B4	114
Russellville, S.C., U.S.	E8	117
Russellville, Tn., U.S.	C10	119
Rüsselsheim, W. Ger.	D3	19
Russia, Oh., U.S.	B1	112
Russian, stm., Ca., U.S.	C2	82
Russian Soviet Federative Socialist Republic, state, Sov. Un.	C12	29
Russiaville, In., U.S.	D5	91
Russum, Ms., U.S.	D2	101
Rustad, Mn., U.S.	D2	100
Rustavi, Sov. Un.	B15	40
Rustburg, Va., U.S.	C3	123
Rustenburg, S. Afr.	C4	49
Ruston, La., U.S.	B3	95
Ruston, Wa., U.S.	B3	124
Ruswil, Switz.	B5	21
Ruszów, Pol.	B10	19
Rutana, Bdi.	B4	48
Rute, Spain	D3	22
Ruteng, Indon.	G6	34
Ruth, Mi., U.S.	E8	99
Ruth, Nv., U.S.	D6	105
Ruth, N.C., U.S.	f11	110
Ruth, W.V., U.S.	m12	125
Rutherford, N.J., U.S.	B4	107
Rutherford, Tn., U.S.	A3	119
Rutherford, co., N.C., U.S.	B1	110
Rutherford, co., Tn., U.S.	B5	119
Rutherfordton, N.C., U.S.	B1	110
Rutherglen, Ont.	A5	73
Rutherglen, Scot., U.K.	E4	13
Ruthilda, Sask.	F1	75
Ruthin, Wales, U.K.	A4	12
Ruthton, Mn., U.S.	F2	100
Ruthven, Ia., U.S.	A3	92
Rüti, Switz.	B4	20
Rutland, B.C.	E8	69
Rutland, Il., U.S.	C4	90
Rutland, Ma., U.S.	B4	98
Rutland, N.D., U.S.	C8	111
Rutland, Oh., U.S.	C3	112
Rutland, S.D., U.S.	C9	118
Rutland, Vt., U.S.	D2	122
Rutland, co., Vt., U.S.	D2	122
Rutland Station, Sask.	E1	75
Rutledge, Al., U.S.	D3	78
Rutledge, Ga., U.S.	C3	87
Rutledge, Mn., U.S.	D6	100
Rutledge, Mo., U.S.	A5	102
Rutledge, Tn., U.S.	C10	119
Rutog, China	B6	36
Rutshuru, Zaire	B4	48
Rutter, Ont.	A4	73
Ruvo [di Puglia], Italy	D6	23
Ruvu, Tan.	C6	48
Ruvuma, prov., Tan.	D6	48
Ruvuma, stm., Afr.	A4	48
Ruwenzori, mts., Afr.	A4	48
Ruza, Sov. Un.	D11	27
Ruzayevka, Sov. Un.	D15	27
Ružomberok, Czech.	D5	26
Rwanda, ctry., Afr.	B5	48
Ry, Den.	B3	15
Ryā, stm., Den.	A3	15
Ryan, Ia., U.S.	B6	92
Ryan, Ok., U.S.	C4	113
Ryan Creek, stm., Al., U.S.	A3	78
Ryan Park, Wy., U.S.	E6	127
Ryan Peak, mtn., Id., U.S.	F4	89
Ryazan, Sov. Un.	D6	29
Ryazhsk, Sov. Un.	E13	27
Rybache, Sov. Un.	E9	28
Rybatskoye (part of Leningrad), Sov. Un.	s31	14
Rybinsk see Andropov, Sov. Un.	D6	29
Rybinsk Reservoir, res., Sov. Un.	C5	29
Rybnik, Pol.	C5	26
Rybnitsa, Sov. Un.	B9	24
Rychnov [nad Kněžnou], Czech.		
Rycroft, Alta.	B1	68
Ryde, Austl.	*F9	50
Ryde, Eng., U.K.	B4	111
Ryder, N.D., U.S.	B4	111
Ryderwood, Wa., U.S.	C2	124
Rye, Co., U.S.	D6	83
Rye, N.H., U.S.	E5	106
Rye, N.Y., U.S.	h13	109
Rye Beach, N.H., U.S.	D5	106
Rye Brook, N.Y., U.S.	*D7	103
Ryegate, Mt., U.S.	D7	103
Ryegate, Vt., U.S.	C4	122
Rye Patch Dam, Nv., U.S.	C3	105
Rye Patch Reservoir, res., Nv., U.S.	C3	105
Ryerson, Sask.	H5	75
Rygge, Nor.	p28	14

Index

Name	Map Ref.	Page
Ryley, Alta.	C4	68
Rylsk, Sov. Un.	F10	27
Rynda, Sov. Un.	C17	14
Ryomgård, Den.	B4	15
Ryōtsu, Japan	G9	33
Rypin, Pol.	B5	26
Rysy, mtn., Eur.	*D6	26
Ryukyu Islands, is., Japan	F10	31
Rzadza, stm., Pol.	k14	26
Rzepin, Pol.	B3	26
Rzeszów, Pol.	C6	26
Rzhev, Sov. Un.	C10	27
S		
Saale, stm., Eur.	C5	18
Saaler Bodden, b., E. Ger.	D6	15
Saalfeld, E. Ger.	C5	18
Saalfelden, Aus.	B8	20
Saanen, Switz.	D3	21
Saar, hist. reg., W. Ger.	D3	18
Saar, stm., Eur.	E6	17
Saarbrücken, W. Ger.	D3	18
Saaremaa, i., Sov. Un.	B4	27
Saarland, state, W. Ger.	E6	17
Saarlouis, W. Ger.	D3	18
Saas-Almagell, Switz.	D4	21
Saas-Fee, Switz.	D4	21
Saavedra, Arg.	B4	54
Saba, i., Neth. Ant.	H13	64
Šabac, Yugo.	C4	24
Sabadell, Spain	B7	22
Sabae, Japan	n15	33
Sabael, N.Y., U.S.	B6	109
Sabah (North Borneo), state, Malay.	D5	34
Sa'bah, Qārat as, mtn., Libya	D3	43
Sabana, Archipiélago de, is., Cuba	C3	64
Sabana de la Mar, Dom. Rep.	E9	64
Sabanagrande, Hond.	D4	62
Sabanalarga, Col.	A3	60
Sabaneta, Puntan, c., N. Mar. Is.	C8	52
Sabang, Indon.	k11	34
Sabará, Braz.	B4	56
Sābarmati, stm., India	D5	36
Sabastīyah, Isr. Occ.	f11	41
Sabattus, Me., U.S.	D2	96
Sabaudia, Italy	D4	23
Sabbathday Pond, l., Me., U.S.	g7	96
Sabetha, Ks., U.S.	C8	93
Sabhah, Libya	D2	43
Sabillasville, Md., U.S.	A3	97
Sabin, Mn., U.S.	D2	100
Sabina, Oh., U.S.	C2	112
Sabinal, Tx., U.S.	E3	120
Sabinas, Mex.	B4	63
Sabinas Hidalgo, Mex.	B4	63
Sabine, W.V., U.S.	D3	125
Sabine, co., La., U.S.	C2	95
Sabine, co., Tx., U.S.	D6	120
Sabine, stm., U.S.	D6	120
Sabine, Mount, mtn., Ant.	B29	7
Sabine Lake, l., U.S.	E2	95
Sabine Pass, Tx., U.S.	E6	120
Sabine Pass, strt., U.S.	E2	95
Sabinópolis, Braz.	B4	56
Sabinsville, Pa., U.S.	C7	115
Sablé, Fr.	D3	16
Sable, Cape, c., N.S.	H19	66
Sable, Cape, c., Fl., U.S.	G5	86
Sable Island, i., N.S.	F10	71
Sable River, N.S.	F9	71
Sabon Birni, Nig.	D6	45
Sabor, stm., Port.	B2	22
Şabrātah, Libya	*C2	43
Sabrina Coast, Ant.	C25	7
Sabula, Ia., U.S.	B7	92
Sabula, Mo., U.S.	D7	102
Sabzevār, Iran	B5	38
Sac, co., Ia., U.S.	B2	92
Sac, stm., Mo., U.S.	D4	102
Sacaba, Bol.	C2	55
Sacajawea, Lake, res., Wa., U.S.	C7	124
Sacajawea Peak, mtn., Or., U.S.	B9	114
Sacandaga Lake, l., N.Y., U.S.	B6	109
Sac and Fox Indian Reservation, Ia., U.S.	C5	92
Sacaton, Az., U.S.	D4	80
Sacavém, Port.	f9	22
Sac City, Ia., U.S.	B2	92
Săcele, Rom.	C7	24
Sachem Head, Ct., U.S.	E5	84
Sachigo Lake, l., Ont.		
Sachse, Tx., U.S.	n10	120
Sachs Harbour, N.W. Ter.	B8	66
Sachuest Point, c., R.I., U.S.	F6	116
Sacile, Italy	D8	20
Sackets Harbor, N.Y., U.S.	B4	109
Säckingen, W. Ger.	A4	21
Sackville, N.B.	D5	71
Saclay, Fr.	h9	16
Saco, Al., U.S.	D4	78
Saco, Me., U.S.	E2	96
Saco, Mt., U.S.	B9	103
Saco, stm., U.S.	E2	96
Saco, East Branch, stm., N.H., U.S.	B4	106
Sacramento, Ca., U.S.	C3	82
Sacramento, Ky., U.S.	C2	94
Sacramento, N.M., U.S.	E4	108
Sacramento, co., Ca., U.S.	C3	82
Sacramento, stm., Ca., U.S.	C3	82
Sacramento, stm., N.M., U.S.	E4	108
Sacramento Mountains, mts., N.M., U.S.	D4	108
Sacramento Valley, val., Az., U.S.	B1	80
Sacramento Valley, val., Ca., U.S.	C2	82
Sacré-Coeur-Saguenay, Que.	A8	74
Sacred Heart, Mn., U.S.	F3	100
Sacrofano, Italy	g8	23
Sacul, Tx., U.S.	D5	120
Şa'dah, Yemen	C3	38
Sadani, Tan.	C6	48
Saddle (Burnt), mtn., Alta.	B1	68
Saddle, Mtn., N.J., U.S.	h8	107
Saddleback Mountain, mtn., Az., U.S.	k8	80
Saddleback Mountain, mtn., Me., U.S.	D2	96
Saddleback Mountain, mtn., Me., U.S.	B4	96
Saddle Ball Mountain, mtn., Ma., U.S.	A1	98
Saddle Brook, N.J., U.S.	h8	107
Saddlebunch Keys, is., Fl., U.S.	H5	86
Saddle Mountain, mtn., Or., U.S.	B3	114
Saddle Mountains, mts., Wa., U.S.	C5	124
Saddle River, N.J., U.S.	A4	107
Saddlestring, Wy., U.S.	B6	127
Sadieville, Ky., U.S.	B5	94
Sadiya, India	C10	36
Sado, stm., Port.	C1	22
Sado Island, i., Japan	D12	31
Sadorus, Il., U.S.	D5	90
Sadská, Czech.	n18	26
Saeby, Den.	A4	15
Saegertown, Pa., U.S.	C1	115
Safājah, Bûr, well, Egypt	H9	40
Safety Harbor, Fl., U.S.	E4	86
Saffell, Ar., U.S.	B4	81
Safford, Al., U.S.	C2	78
Safford, Az., U.S.	E6	80
Saffron Walden, Eng., U.K.	B8	12
Safi, Mor.	C3	44
Safīd Kūh (Selseleh-ye, mts.), Afg.	D12	39
Safonovo, Sov. Un.	D9	27
Safranbolu, Tur.	B8	41
Safune Bay, b., W. Sam.	F11	52
Saga, China	C8	36
Saga, Japan	J5	33
Sagaing, Burma	D10	36
Sagamihara, Japan	*I9	33
Sagami Sea, b., Japan	n18	33
Sagamore, Ma., U.S.	C6	98
Sagamore, Pa., U.S.	E2	115
Sagamore Beach, Ma., U.S.	*C6	98
Sagamore Hills, Oh., U.S.	h9	112
Sagån, stm., Swe.	t34	14
Saganaga Lake, l., Mn., U.S.	B7	100
Sāgar, India	D6	36
Sagara, Japan	o17	33
Sage, Ar., U.S.	A4	81
Saggart, Ire.	D5	11
Sag Harbor, N.Y., U.S.	m16	109
Saginaw, Al., U.S.	B3	78
Saginaw, Mi., U.S.	E7	99
Saginaw, Or., U.S.	D3	114
Saginaw, Tx., U.S.	n9	120
Saginaw, co., Mi., U.S.	E6	99
Saginaw Bay, b., Mi., U.S.	E7	99
Sagiz, Sov. Un.	D4	28
Sagiz, stm., Sov. Un.	D5	28
Sagle, Id., U.S.	A2	89
Sagleipie, Lib.	E3	45
Saglek Bay, b., Newf.	f9	72
Sagola, Mi., U.S.	B2	99
Saguache, Co., U.S.	C4	83
Saguache, co., Co., U.S.	C4	83
Saguache Creek, stm., Co., U.S.	C4	83
Sagua de Tánamo, Cuba	D6	64
Sagua la Grande, Cuba	C3	64
Saguaro National Monument, Az., U.S.	E5	80
Saguaro National Monument (Tucson Mountain Section), Az., U.S.	E4	80
Saguenay, co., Que.	A8	74
Saguenay, stm., Que.	A7	74
Sagunto, Spain	C5	22
Sahāb, Jord.	C8	41
Sahagún, Col.	B2	60
Sahand, Kūh-e, mtn., Iran	C3	39
Sahara, des., Afr.	D6	42
Sahāranpur, India	C6	36
Sahiwal (Montgomery), Pak.	B5	36
Şahrajat al Kubrá, Eg.	D3	41
Şahuaripa, Mex.	B3	63
Sahuarita, Az., U.S.	F5	80
Sahuayo [de Díaz], Mex.	m12	63
Said, Sov. Un.	E6	28
Saïda, Alg.	C5	44
Saïdu, Bngl.	C8	36
Saigō, Japan	H6	33
Saigon see Ho Chi Minh City, Viet.	C3	34
Saiki, Japan	J5	33
Sailor Springs, Il., U.S.	E5	90
Saimaa, l., Fin.	G13	14
Saint Abb's Head, c., Scot., U.K.	E6	13
Saint-Adelphe, Que.	C5	74
Saint-Adolphe, Man.	E3	70
Saint-Affrique, Fr.	F5	16
Saint-Agapit, Que.	C6	74
Saint Agatha, Me., U.S.	A4	96
Saint Agatha, Man.	E3	70
Sainte-Agathe-des-Monts, Que.	C3	74
Sainte-Agnès-de-Dundee, Que.	D3	74
Saint-Aimé (Massueville), Que.	D5	74
Saint-Alban's, Newf.	E4	72
Saint-Alban, Que.	C5	74
Saint Albans, Eng., U.K.	E6	10
Saint Albans, Me., U.S.	D3	96
Saint Albans, Vt., U.S.	B2	122
Saint Albans, W.V., U.S.	C3	125
Saint Albans Bay, Vt., U.S.	B2	122
Saint Albans Bay, b., Vt., U.S.	B2	122
Saint Albert, Alta.	C4	68
Saint Aldhelm's Head, c., Eng., U.K.	E6	10
Saint-Alexandre, Que.	D4	74
Saint-Alexandre [de-Kamouraska], Que.	B8	74
Saint-Alexis-des-Monts, Que.	C4	74
Saint-Alphonse [-de-Granby], Que.	D5	74
Saint-Amand-les-Eaux, Fr.	D3	17
Saint-Amand-Mont-Rond, Fr.	D5	16
Saint Amant, La., U.S.	h10	95
Saint-Amarin, Fr.	B3	20
Saint-Ambroise, Que.	A6	74
Saint-Anaclet, Que.	A9	74
Saint-André, Cap., c., Madag.	g8	49
Saint-André-Avellin, Que.	D2	74
Saint-André-Est, Que.	D3	74
Saint Andrew Bay, b., Fl., U.S.	u16	86
Saint Andrews, Newf.	E2	72
Saint Andrews, Scot., U.K.	B5	10
Saint Andrews, S.C., U.S.	F7	117
Saint Andrews, S.C., U.S.	C5	117
Saint Andrews, Tn., U.S.	D8	119
Saint Andrews Bay, b., Scot., U.K.	D6	13
Saint Andrew Sound, strt., Ga., U.S.	F5	87
Sainte-Angèle [-de-Monnoir], Que.	D4	74
Saint-Anicet, Que.	D3	74
Saint Ann, Mo., U.S.	*f13	102
Saint Anna, Mo., U.S.	k9	126
Sainte-Anne, Guad.	H14	64
Saint Anne, Il., U.S.	B6	90
Sainte-Anne, stm., Que.	B6	74
Sainte-Anne-de-Beaupré, Que.	B7	74
Sainte-Anne [-de-Bellevue], Que.	q19	74
Sainte-Anne-de-la-Pérade, Que.	C5	74
Sainte Anne-de-Madawaska, N.B.	B1	71
Sainte-Anne-des-Chênes, Man.	E3	70
Sainte-Anne [-des-Plaines], Que.	D4	74
Sainte-Anne-du-Lac, Que.	k11	74
Sainte-Anne du Nord, stm., Que.	B7	74
Saint Anns, N.S.	C9	71
Saint Ann's Bay, Jam.	E9	64
Saint Anns Peak, mtn., Trin.	N23	65
Saint-Anselme, Que.	C7	74
Saint Ansgar, Ia., U.S.	A5	92
Saint Anthony, Newf.	C4	72
Saint Anthony, Id., U.S.	F7	89
Saint Anthony, In., U.S.	H4	91
Saint Anthony, Ia., U.S.	B4	92
Saint Anthony, N.D., U.S.	*E5	100
Saint Antoine, N.B.	C5	71
Saint-Antoine [-de-Tilly], Que.	C6	74
Saint-Antoine [-sur-Richelieu], Que.	D4	74
Saint-Antonin, Que.	B8	74
Saint-Apollinaire, Que.	C6	74
Saint-Apolline, Que.	C7	74
Saint Arnaud, Austl.	H4	51
Saint-Arsène, Que.	B8	74
Saint Arthur, N.B.	B3	71
Saint-Athanase, Que.	B8	74
Saint-Aubert, Que.	B7	74
Saint-Augustin, Que.	o17	74
Saint-Augustin, stm., Can.	C2	72
Saint-Augustin-Deux-Montagnes, Que.	p19	74
Saint Augustine, Fla., U.S.	C5	86
Saint-Augustin-Nord-Ouest, stm., Que.	C2	72
Saint Augustin-Saguenay, Que.	C2	72
Saint Austell, Eng., U.K.	D3	12
Saint-Avold, Fr.	C7	16
Saint-Barbe, Que.	D3	74
Saint-Barnabé, Que.	C5	74
Saint-Barnabé-Nord, Que.	C5	74
Saint-Barthélemy, Que.	C4	74
Saint-Barthélemy, i., Guad.	H13	64
Saint Basile, N.B.	B1	71
Saint Basile [-Sud], Que.	C6	74
Saint-Béatrix, Que.	C4	74
Saint Bees Head, c., Eng., U.K.	C5	10
Saint Benedict, Sask.	E3	75
Saint Benedict, Ks., U.S.	C7	93
Saint-Benoît-Labre, Que.	C7	74
Saint-Bernard, Que.	C6	74
Saint Bernard, Al., U.S.	A3	78
Saint Bernard, La., U.S.	E6	95
Saint Bernard, Ne., U.S.	C8	104
Saint Bernard, Oh., U.S.	o13	112
Saint Bernard, co., La., U.S.	E6	95
Saint Bernice, In., U.S.	E2	91
Saint Bethlehem, Tn., U.S.	A4	119
Sainte-Blandine, Que.	A9	74
Saint-Bonaventure, Que.	D5	74
Saint Boswells, Sask.	G2	75
Saint Brendan's, Newf.	D5	72
Saint Bride, Mount, mtn., Alta.		
Saint Bride's, Newf.	E4	72
Saint Brides Bay, b., Wales, U.K.	E4	10
Saint-Brieuc, Fr.	C2	16
Saint Brieux, Sask.	E3	75
Sainte-Brigide [-d'Iberville], Que.	D4	74
Sainte-Brigitte [-des-Saults], Que.	C5	74
Saint-Bruno, Que.	A6	74
Saint-Calais, Fr.	D4	16
Saint-Calixte, Que.	D4	74
Saint-Camille, Que.	D6	74
Saint-Camille [-de-Bellechasse], Que.	C7	74
Saint-Casimir, Que.	C5	74
Saint Catharine, Ky., U.S.	C4	94
Saint Catharines, Ont.	D5	73
Saint-Catherine, Que.	C4	74
Saint Catherine, Lake, l., Vt., U.S.	E2	122
Saint Catherine, Mount, mtn., Gren.	W25	65
Saint Catherines Island, i., Ga., U.S.	E5	87
Saint Catherine's Point, c., Eng., U.K.	D6	12
Saint Catherines Sound, strt., Ga., U.S.	E5	87
Sainte-Cécile [-de-Frontenac], Que.	C7	74
Saint-Célestin (Annaville), Que.	C5	74
Saint-Césaire, Que.	D4	74
Saint-Chamond, Fr.	E6	16
Saint-Charles, Que.	C7	74
Saint Charles, Ar., U.S.	C4	81
Saint Charles, Id., U.S.	G7	89
Saint Charles, Il., U.S.	B5	90
Saint Charles, Ky., U.S.	C2	94
Saint Charles, Md., U.S.	*C4	97
Saint Charles, Mi., U.S.	E6	99
Saint Charles, Mn., U.S.	G6	100
Saint Charles, Mo., U.S.	C7	102
Saint Charles, S.D., U.S.	D6	118
Saint Charles, Va., U.S.	f8	123
Saint Charles, co., Mo., U.S.	C7	102
Saint Charles, Cape, c., Newf.	B4	72
Saint Charles Mesa, Co., U.S.	*D6	83
Saint-Chély-d'Apcher, Fr.	E5	16
Saint-François-Xavier [-de-Brompton], Que.	D5	74
Saint Christopher (Saint Kitts)-Nevis, ctry., N.A.	H13	64
Saint-Chrysostome, Que.	D4	74
Saint Clair, Mi., U.S.	F8	99
Saint Clair, Mn., U.S.	F5	100
Saint Clair, Mo., U.S.	C6	102
Saint Clair, Pa., U.S.	E9	115
Saint Clair, co., Al., U.S.	B3	78
Saint Clair, co., Il., U.S.	E3	90
Saint Clair, co., Mi., U.S.	F8	99
Saint Clair, co., Mo., U.S.	C4	102
Saint Clair, stm., N.A.	E2	99
Saint Clair, Lake, l., N.A.	E2	73
Saint-Claire, Que.	C7	74
Saint Clair Shores, Mi., U.S.	p16	99
Saint Clairsville, Oh., U.S.	B5	112
Saint Claude, Man.	E2	70
Saint-Claude, Que.	D6	74
Saint-Claude, Fr.	D6	16
Saint-Clément, Que.	B8	74
Saint Clements Creek, stm., Md., U.S.	D4	97
Sainte-Clothilde, Que.	D5	74
Saint-Cloud, Fr.	g9	16
Saint Cloud, Fl., U.S.	D5	86
Saint Cloud, Mn., U.S.	E4	100
Saint Cloud, Wi., U.S.	E5	126
Saint-Coeur-de-Marie, Que.	A6	74
Saint-Côme, Que.	C4	74
Saint-Constant, Que.	q19	74
Saint Croix, N.B.	D2	71
Sainte-Croix, Switz.	C2	20
Sainte-Croix, Que.	C6	74
Saint Croix, In., U.S.	H4	91
Saint Croix, co., Wi., U.S.	C1	126
Saint Croix, i., V.I.U.S.	H12	64
Saint Croix, i., N.A.	C5	96
Saint Croix, stm., N.A.	C1	126
Saint Croix, Lake, l., U.S.	C1	126
Saint Croix Falls, Wi., U.S.	C1	126
Saint Croix Stream, stm., Me., U.S.	B4	96
Saint-Cuthbert, Que.	C4	74
Saint-Cyrille [-de-L'Islet], Que.	B7	74
Saint-Cyrille [-de-Wendover], Que.	D5	74
Saint-Cyr [-sur-Loire], Fr.	D4	16
Saint-Damase, Que.	D4	74
Saint-Damase-des-Aulnaies, Que.	B7	74
Saint-Damien-de-Brandon, Que.	C4	74
Saint-Damien [-de-Buckland], Que.	C7	74
Saint David, Az., U.S.	F5	80
Saint David, Me., U.S.	A4	96
Saint-David-de-l'Auberivière, Que.	n17	74
Saint-David [-d'Yamaska], Que.	D5	74
Saint David's, Newf.	D2	72
Saint David's, Wales, U.K.	C2	12
Saint David's Head, c., Wales, U.K.	E4	10
Saint David's Island, i., Ber.	o21	64
Saint-Denis, Que.	D4	74
Saint-Denis, Fr.	C5	16
Saint-Denis, Reu.	H24	2
Saint-Denis [de-la-Bouteillerie], Que.	B8	74
Sainte-Didace, Que.	C4	74
Saint-Dié, Fr.	C7	16
Saint-Dizier, Fr.	D6	16
Saint-Dominique, Que.	D5	74
Saint-Dominique, Que.	q18	74
Saint-Donat [-de-Montcalm], Que.	C3	74
Saint Donatus, Ia., U.S.	B7	92
Saint-Édouard [-de-Napierville], Que.	q19	74
Saint Edward, Ne., U.S.	C8	104
Saint-Edwidge, Que.	D6	74
Saint Eleanor, P.E.I.	C6	71
Saint Elias, Cape, c., Ak., U.S.	D11	79
Saint Elias Mountains, mts., N.A.	C11	79
Saint-Élie, Fr. Gu.	B4	59
Saint-Élisabeth, Que.	C4	74
Saint Elizabeth, Mo., U.S.	C5	102
Saint Elmo, Al., U.S.	E1	78
Saint Elmo, Il., U.S.	D5	90
Saint-Éloi, Que.	A8	74
Sainte-Émélie-de-l'Énergie, Que.	C4	74
Saint-Émile [-de-Suffolk], Que.	D3	74
Saint-Éphrem [-de-Tring], Que.	C7	74
Saint-Esprit, Que.	D4	74
Saint-Étienne, Fr.	E6	16
Saint-Étienne [de-Beauharnois], Que.	q19	74
Sainte-Eulalie, Que.	C5	74
Sainte-Euphémie, Que.	C7	74
Saint-Eusèbe, Que.	B9	74
Saint-Eustache, Que.	D4	74
Saint-Fabien, Que.	A9	74
Sainte-Famille, Que.	C7	74
Sainte-Famille-d'Aumond, Que.	C2	74
Saint-Faustin, Que.	C3	74
Saint-Félicien, Que.	A5	74
Saint-Félix-de-Valois, Que.	C4	74
Saint-Ferdinand (Bernierville), Que.	C6	74
Saint-Ferréol [-les-Neiges], Que.	B7	74
Saint-Fidèle, Que.	B7	74
Saintfield, N. Ire., U.K.	C6	11
Saint Fintan's, Newf.	D2	72
Saint-Flavien, Que.	C6	74
Saint-Florent, Fr.	D5	16
Saint Florian, Al., U.S.	A2	78
Saint-Flour, Fr.	E5	16
Sainte-Fortunat, Que.	D6	74
Sainte-Foy, Que.	n17	74
Sainte-Foy-la-Grande, Fr.	E4	16
Saint Francis, Ar., U.S.	A5	81
Saint Francis, Ks., U.S.	C2	93
Saint Francis, Me., U.S.	A4	96
Saint Francis, Mn., U.S.	E5	100
Saint Francis, S.D., U.S.	D5	118
Saint Francis, Wi., U.S.	n12	126
Saint Francis, co., Ar., U.S.	B5	81
Saint Francis, stm., N.A.	A5	81
Saint Francis, Cape, c., Newf.	E5	72
Saint Francisville, Il., U.S.	E6	90
Saint Francisville, La., U.S.	D4	95
Saint-François, Guad.	Q9	65
Saint-François, co., Mo., U.S.	D7	102
Saint-François, stm., Que.	D5	74
Saint-François, Lac, l., Que.	A8	74
Saint François Mountains, hills, Mo., U.S.	D7	102
Saint-Frédéric, Que.	C7	74
Saint Froid Lake, l., Me., U.S.	B4	96
Saint-Fulgence, Que.	A7	74
Saint-Gabriel, Que.	C4	74
Saint-Gabriel, La., U.S.	h9	95
Saint-Gaudens, Fr.	F4	16
Saint-Gédéon, Que.	D5	74
Sainte-Geneviève, Mo., U.S.	D7	102
Sainte-Geneviève, co., Mo., U.S.	D7	102
Sainte-Geneviève-de-Batiscan, Que.	C5	74
Saint George, Austl.	E8	50
Saint George, Ber.	o20	64
Saint George, N.B.	D3	71
Saint George, Ont.	D4	73
Saint George, Ga., U.S.	F4	87
Saint George, Ks., U.S.	C7	93
Saint George, Me., U.S.	D3	96
Saint George, S.C., U.S.	E6	117
Saint George, Ut., U.S.	F2	121
Saint George, co., N.B.	D3	71
Saint George, i., V.I.U.S.	G12	64
Saint George, i., U.S.	G19	66
Saint George, Cape, c., Newf.	D4	72
Saint George, Cape, c., Fl., U.S.	C1	86
Saint George Island, Md., U.S.	D4	97
Saint George Island, i., Ak., U.S.	D6	79
Saint George Island, i., Fl., U.S.	C2	86
Saint-Georges, Bel.	D5	17
Saint-Georges, Que.	C5	74
Saint-Georges, Fr. Gu.	J14	64
Saint Georges, Gren.	J14	64
Saint Georges, De., U.S.	B3	85
Saint Georges Bay, b., Newf.	D2	72
Saint Georges Bay, b., N.S.	D8	71
Saint George's Cathedral, Isr. Occ.		
Saint George's Channel, strt., Eur.	E3	10
Saint-Georges [-de-Windsor], Que.	D6	74
Saint-Georges-Ouest, Que.	C7	74
Saint-Gérard, Que.	D6	74
Saint-Germain, Forêt de, Fr.	g9	16
Saint-Germain-de-Kamouraska, Que.	B8	74
Saint-Germain-en-Laye, Fr.	g9	16
Saint-Gervais, Que.	C7	74
Saint-Gervais-les-Bains, Fr.	D2	20
Saint-Gilles (Sint-Gillis), Bel.	*D4	17
Saint-Gilles, Que.	C6	74
Saint-Gilles-Croix-de-Vie, Fr.	D3	16
Saint-Gilles-du-Gard, Fr.	F6	16
Saint-Golngolph, Switz.	D2	21
Saint-Grégoire (Larochelle), Que.	C5	74
Saint Gregor, Sask.	E3	75
Saint Gregory, Mount, mtn., Newf.	D2	72
Saint-Guillaume-d'Upton, Que.	D5	74
Saint Helen, Lake, l., Mi., U.S.	D6	99
Saint Helena, Ca., U.S.	C2	82
Saint Helena, Ne., U.S.	B8	104
Saint Helena, co., La., U.S.	D5	95
Saint Helena Island, i., S.C.		
Saint Helena Sound, strt., S.C., U.S.	G7	117
Sainte-Hélène [-de-Kamouraska], Que.	B8	74
Saint Helens, Eng., U.K.	A5	12
Saint Helens, Or., U.S.	B4	114
Saint Helens, Mount, vol., Wa., U.S.	C3	124
Saint Helier, Jersey	F5	10
Saint-Henri [-de-Lévis], Que.	C6	74
Saint Henry, Oh., U.S.	B1	112
Saint-Herménegilde, Que.	D6	74
Saint Hilaire, Mn., U.S.	B2	100
Saint-Hilaire-de-Dorset, Que.	D7	74
Saint-Hilarion, Que.	B7	74
Saint-Hippolyte, Fr.	B2	21
Saint-Honoré, Que.	D7	74
Saint-Honoré-de-Témiscouata, Que.	B8	74
Saint-Hubert, Bel.	D5	17
Saint-Hubert, Que.	q20	74
Saint-Hubert-de-Témiscouata, Que.	B8	74
Saint-Hugues, Que.	D5	74
Sainte-Hyacinthe, Que.	D5	74
Saint-Hyacinthe, co., Que.	D4	74
Saint Ignace, N.B.	C4	71
Saint Ignace, Mi., U.S.	C6	99
Saint Ignatius, Guy.	B3	59
Saint Ignatius, Mt., U.S.	C2	103
Saint-Imier, Switz.	B3	21
Saint Inigoes, Md., U.S.	D5	97
Saint Isidore, N.B.	B4	71
Saint-Isidore, Que.	q19	74
Saint-Isidore-d'Auckland, Que.	D6	74
Saint Isidore de Prescott, Ont.	B10	73
Saint Ives, Eng., U.K.	B7	12
Saint Ives, Eng., U.K.	D2	12
Saint Jacob, Il., U.S.	E4	90
Saint Jacobs, Ont.	D4	73
Saint-Jacques, N.B.	B1	71
Saint-Jacques, Que.	D4	74
Saint-Jacques-le-Mineur, Que.	q20	74
Saint James, Ar., U.S.	B4	81
Saint James, Mi., U.S.	C5	99
Saint James, Mn., U.S.	G4	100
Saint James, Mo., U.S.	D6	102
Saint James, N.Y., U.S.	*n15	109
Saint James, co., La., U.S.	D5	95
Saint James, Cape, c., B.C.	D2	69
Saint James City, Fl., U.S.	F4	86
Saint-Jean, stm., Que.	A7	74
Saint-Jean, Lac, l., Que.	A5	74
Saint Jean Baptiste, Man.	E3	70
Saint-Jean-Chrysostome, Que.	o17	74
Saint-Jean-d'Angély, Fr.	D3	16
Saint-Jean-de-Dieu, Que.	A8	74
Saint-Jean-de-Luz, Fr.	F3	16
Saint-Jean-de-Matha, Que.	C4	74
Saint-Jean-de-Maurienne, Fr.	D2	20
Saint-Jean-Port-Joli, Que.	B7	74
Saint-Jean-sur-Richelieu, Que.	D4	74
Saint-Jérôme, Que.	D3	74
Saint Jo, Tx., U.S.	C4	120
Saint-Joachim, Que.	B7	74
Saint-Joachim [-de-Courval], Que.	D5	74
Saint Joe, Ar., U.S.	A3	81
Saint Joe, In., U.S.	B8	91
Saint Joe, stm., Id., U.S.	B3	89
Saint John, N.B.	D3	71
Saint John, Ks., U.S.	D5	93
Saint John, Me., U.S.	A4	96
Saint John, N.D., U.S.	A6	111
Saint John, Wa., U.S.	B8	124
Saint John, co., N.B.	D3	71
Saint John, i., V.I.U.S.	G12	64
Saint John, N.A.	G19	66
Saint John, Cape, c., Newf.	D4	72
Saint John, Southeast Branch, stm., N.A.	B2	96
Saint John Bay, b., Newf.	C3	72
Saint John Island, i., Newf.	C3	72
Saint John's, Antig.	H14	64
Saint John's, Newf.	E5	72
Saint Johns, Az., U.S.	C6	80
Saint Johns, Il., U.S.	E4	90
Saint Johns, Mi., U.S.	F6	99
Saint Johns, Mo., U.S.	*f13	102
Saint Johns, Oh., U.S.	B1	112
Saint Johns, co., Fl., U.S.	C5	86
Saint Johns, stm., Fl., U.S.	B5	86
Saint Johnsbury, Vt., U.S.	C4	122
Saint Johnsbury Center, Vt., U.S.	C4	122
Saint John's Point, c., Ire.	C3	11
Saint John's Point, c., N. Ire., U.K.	C6	11
Saint Johnsville, N.Y., U.S.	B6	109
Saint John the Baptist, co., La., U.S.	D5	95
Saint Jones, stm., De., U.S.	D4	85
Saint Joseph, N.B.	D5	71
Saint Joseph, Dom.	I14	64
Saint Joseph, La., U.S.	C4	95
Saint Joseph, Mi., U.S.	F4	99
Saint Joseph, Mo., U.S.	B3	102
Saint Joseph, Tn., U.S.	B4	119
Saint Joseph, co., In., U.S.	A5	91
Saint Joseph, co., Mi., U.S.	G5	99
Saint-Joseph, Lac, l., Que.	n16	74
Saint-Joseph, Lake, l., Ont.	o17	73
Saint-Joseph-de-Beauce, Que.	C7	74
Saint-Joseph-de-la-Rive, Que.	B7	74
Saint-Joseph-du-Lac, Que.	p18	74
Saint Joseph Point, c., Fl., U.S.	v16	86
Saint Joseph's, Newf.	E5	72
Saint Joseph Sound, strt., Fl., U.S.	o10	86
Saint-Jovite, Que.	C3	74
Saint-Jude, Que.	D5	74
Saint-Julien [-en-Genevois], Fr.	D1	21
Sainte-Julienne, Que.	D4	74
Sainte-Julie-Station, Que.	C6	74
Saint-Junien, Fr.	E4	16
Saint Just, Eng., U.K.	D2	12
Saint-Just-en-Chaussée, Fr.	E2	17
Sainte-Justine [-de-Newton], Que.	D3	74
Sainte-Justine, Que.	C7	74
Saint-Lambert [-de-Lévis], Que.	C6	74
Saint-Lambert, Que.	p19	74
Saint Landry, La., U.S.	D3	95
Saint Landry, co., La., U.S.	D3	95
Saint Laurent, Man.	D3	70
Saint-Laurent, Que.	p19	74
Saint-Laurent-Blangy, Fr.	D2	17
Saint-Laurent-de-la-Salanque, Fr.	F5	16
Saint-Laurent [du-Maroni], Fr. Gu.	B4	59
Saint Laurent [du Maroni], ter., Fr. Gu.	B4	59
Saint-Laurent-en-Grandvaux, Fr.	C1	20
Saint Lawrence, Austl.	D8	50
Saint Lawrence, Newf.	E4	72
Saint Lawrence, S.D., U.S.	C7	118
Saint Lawrence, co., N.Y., U.S.	A5	109
Saint Lawrence, stm., N.A.	G19	66
Saint Lawrence, Cape, c., N.S.	B9	71
Saint Lawrence, Gulf of, b., Can.	G20	66
Saint Lawrence Island, i., Ak., U.S.	C5	79
Saint Lawrence Islands National Park, Ont.	C9	73
Saint Lazare, Man.	D1	70
Saint Lazare, Que.	q18	74
Saint Leo, Fl., U.S.	D4	86
Saint-Léon, Que.	C5	74
Saint-Léonard, N.B.	B2	71
Saint-Léonard, Fr.	E4	16
Saint-Léonard-d'Aston, Que.	C5	74
Saint Leonard, Md., U.S.	C4	97
Saint-Léonard-de-Portneuf, Que.	C6	74
Saint Lewis, stm., Newf.	B3	72
Saint Lewis Sound, strt., Newf.	B4	72
Saint Libory, Il., U.S.	E4	90
Saint Libory, Ne., U.S.	C7	104
Saint-Lô, Fr.	C5	16
Saint Louis, P.E.I.	C6	71
Saint Louis, Sask.	E3	75
Saint Louis, Guad.	R9	65
Saint Louis, Sen.	C1	45
Saint Louis, Mi., U.S.	E6	99
Saint Louis, Mo., U.S.	C7	102
Saint Louis, Ok., U.S.	B5	113
Saint Louis, co., Mn., U.S.	C6	100
Saint Louis, co., Mo., U.S.	C7	102
Saint Louis, Lac, l., Que.	q19	74
Saint Louis Bay, b., Ms., U.S.	f7	101
Saint Louis Crossing, In., U.S.	F6	91
Saint-Louis [-de-Bonsecours], Que.	D5	74
Saint-Louis-de-Gonzague, Que.	D3	74
Saint-Louis-du-Ha! Ha!, Que.	B8	74
Sainte-Louise, Que.	B7	74
Saint Louis Park, Mn., U.S.	n12	100
Saint-Loup-sur-Semouse, Fr.	B2	20
Saint-Luc, Que.	D4	74
Saint-Luc, Switz.	D4	21
Saint Lucas, Ia., U.S.	A6	92
Saint Lucia, ctry., N.A.	J14	64
Saint Lucia, Cape, c., S. Afr.	C5	49
Saint Lucia, Lake, l., S. Afr.	C5	49
Saint Lucia Channel, strt., N.A.	I14	64
Saint Lucie, co., Fl., U.S.	E6	86
Saint Lucie Canal, Fl., U.S.	F6	86
Sainte-Lucie-de-Beauregard, Que.	C7	74
Saint Lucie Inlet, b., Fl., U.S.	E6	86

Name	Map Ref.	Page

Saint-Ludger, Que. — D7 74
Sainte-Madeleine, Que. — D4 74
Saint-Magloire, Que. — C7 74
Saint Magnus Bay, b., Scot., U.K. — g10 10
Saint-Maixent-l'École, Fr. — D3 16
Saint-Malachie, Que. — C7 74
Saint Malo, Man. — E3 70
Saint Malo, Fr. — C2 16
Saint Malo, Gulf of, b., Fr. — C2 16
Saint-Mandé, Fr. — g10 16
Saint-Marc, Que. — D4 74
Saint-Marc, Haiti — E7 64
Saint-Marc [-des-Carrières], Que. — C5 74
Saint-Marcel-de-L'Islet, Que. — C7 74
Saint-Marcellin, Fr. — E6 16
Saint Margaret Bay, b., Newf. — C3 72
Saint Margaret's Hope, Scot., U.K. — B6 13
Sainte-Marguerite, stm., Que. — h8 74
Sainte-Marguerite, stm., Que. — A7 74
Sainte-Marguerite-de-Dorchester, Que. — C7 74
Sainte-Marguerite Nord-Est, stm., Que. — A7 74
Sainte-Marie, Que. — C5 74
Sainte-Marie, Que. — C6 74
Sainte-Marie, Mart. — S11 65
Sainte Marie, Il., U.S. — E5 90
Sainte-Marie, Cap, c., Madag. — i8 49
Sainte-Marie-aux-Mines, Fr. — A3 20
Sainte Maries, Id. — B2 89
Sainte Marie-sur-Mer, N.B. — B5 71
Saint Mark, Ks., U.S. — g11 93
Saint Marks, Fl., U.S. — B2 86
Sainte-Marthe, Que. — D3 74
Saint-Martin, co., La., U.S. — D4 95
Saint Martin, i., N.A. — G13 64
Saint Martin, i., La., Man. — — 2
Saint Martin, stm., Md., U.S. — D7 97
Saint Martin, stm., La., Man. — — 2
Saint-Martin-Boulogne, Fr. — D9 12
Sainte-Martine, Que. — D4 74
Saint Martin Island, i., Mi., U.S. — C4 99
Saint Martins, N.B. — D4 71
Saint Martin Station, Man. — D2 70
Saint Martinville, La., U.S. — D4 95
Saint-Martory, Fr. — F4 16
Saint Mary, Ky., U.S. — C4 94
Saint Mary, Mo., U.S. — D8 102
Saint Mary, co., La., U.S. — E4 95
Saint Mary, stm., B.C. — E2 68
Saint Mary, stm., N.A. — E4 68
Saint Mary-of-the-Woods, In., U.S. — E3 91
Saint Mary Peak, mtn., Austl. — F6 50
Saint Mary Reservoir, res., Alta. — E4 68
Saint Mary's, Newf. — E5 72
Saint Mary's, Ont. — D3 73
Saint Marys, Ak., U.S. — C7 79
Saint Marys, Ga., U.S. — F5 87
Saint Marys, In., U.S. — A5 91
Saint Marys, Ks., U.S. — C7 93
Saint Marys, Oh., U.S. — B1 112
Saint Marys, Pa., U.S. — D4 115
Saint Marys, W.V., U.S. — B3 125
Saint Marys, co., Md., U.S. — D4 97
Saint Marys, stm., N.S. — D8 71
Saint Marys, stm., U.S. — F5 87
Saint Marys, stm., U.S. — C8 91
Saint Marys, stm., Md., U.S. — D5 97
Saint Mary's, Cape, c., Newf. — E4 72
Saint Mary's Bay, b., Newf. — E5 72
Saint Marys Bay, b., N.S. — E3 71
Saint Marys City, Md., U.S. — D5 97
Saint Marys Entrance, strt., Ga., U.S. — F5 87
Saint-Mathieu, Que. — q19 74
Sainte-Mathieu, Que. — A9 74
Saint Matthew Island, i., Ak., U.S. — C5 79
Saint Matthews, Ky., U.S. — B4 94
Saint Matthews, S.C., U.S. — D6 117
Saint-Maur-des-Fossés, Fr. — g10 16
Saint-Maurice, Que. — C5 74
Saint-Maurice, Switz. — C3 20
Saint Maurice, La., U.S. — C3 95
Saint-Maurice, co., Que. — C4 74
Saint-Maurice, stm., Que. — C4 74
Saint Meinrad, In., U.S. — H4 91
Sainte-Mélanie, Que. — C4 74
Saint-Memmie, Fr. — F4 17
Sainte-Menehould, Fr. — C6 16
Saint-Méthode [-de-Frontenac], Que. — C6 74
Saint Michael, Alta. — C4 68
Saint Michael, Ak., U.S. — C7 79
Saint Michael, Mn., U.S. — E5 100
Saint Michael, N.D., U.S. — B7 111
Saint Michaels, Az., U.S. — B6 80
Saint Michaels, Md., U.S. — C5 97
Saint Michaels Bay, b., Newf. — B4 72
Saint-Michel, Fr. — E4 17
Saint-Michel, Fr. — D2 20
Saint-Michel [-de-Bellechasse], Que. — C7 74
Saint-Michel-de-Napierville, Que. — q19 74
Saint-Michel-des-Saints, Que. — C4 74
Saint-Mihiel, Fr. — C6 16
Saint-Modeste, Que. — B8 74
Sainte-Monique [-de-Nicolet], Que. — C5 74
Saint-Nazaire, Que. — D5 74
Saint-Nazaire [-de-Buckland], Que. — C7 74
Saint-Nazaire-de-Chicoutimi, Que. — A6 74
Saint Nazianz, Wi., U.S. — D6 126
Saint Neots, Eng., U.K. — B7 12
Saint-Nérée, Que. — C7 74
Saint-Nicolas, Que. — o17 74
Saint-Nicolas see Sint-Niklaas, Bel. — B6 16
Saint-Odilon, Que. — C7 74
Saint Olaf, Ia., U.S. — B6 92
Saint-Omer, Fr. — B5 16
Saint Onge, S.D., U.S. — C2 118
Saintonge, hist. reg., Fr. — E3 16
Saint-Ouen, Fr. — g10 16
Saint-Ours, Que. — D4 74
Saint-Pacôme, Que. — B8 74
Saint-Pamphile, Que. — C8 74
Saint Paris, Oh., U.S. — B2 112
Saint-Pascal, Que. — B8 74
Saint Patrice, Lac, l., Que. — A8 73
Saint Paul, Alta. — B5 68
Saint Paul, Ak., U.S. — D5 79
Saint Paul, Ar., U.S. — B2 81

Saint Paul, In., U.S. — F6 91
Saint Paul, Ks., U.S. — E8 93
Saint Paul, Mn., U.S. — F5 100
Saint Paul, Mo., U.S. — f12 102
Saint Paul, Ne., U.S. — C7 104
Saint Paul, Or., U.S. — h12 114
Saint Paul, S.C., U.S. — D7 117
Saint Paul, Va., U.S. — f9 123
Saint-Paul, stm., Can. — C3 72
Saint-Paul, stm., Lib. — E2 45
Saint-Paul, Île, i., F.S.A.T. — I2 2
Saint-Paul-de-Chester, Que. — D6 74
Saint-Paul-de-la-Croix, Que. — B8 74
Saint-Paul-du-Montminy, Que. — C7 74
Saint-Paul-du-Nord, Que. — A8 74
Saint Paul Island, i., N.S. — B9 71
Saint Paul Island, i., Ak., U.S. — D5 79
Saint Paul Park, Mn., U.S. — n12 100
Saint Pauls, N.C., U.S. — C4 110
Sainte-Perpétue-de-L'Islet, Que. — B8 74
Saint Peter, Il., U.S. — E5 90
Saint Peter, Ks., U.S. — C3 93
Saint Peter, Mn., U.S. — F5 100
Saint Peter Port, Guernsey — F5 10
Saint Peters, N.S. — D9 71
Saint Peters, In., U.S. — F7 91
Saint Peters, Mo., U.S. — C7 102
Saint Peters Bay, P.E.I. — C7 71
Saint Petersburg, Fl., U.S. — E4 86
Saint Petersburg, Pa., U.S. — D2 115
Saint Petersburg Beach, Fl., U.S. — p10 86
Saint-Philémon, Que. — C7 74
Saint Philip, In., U.S. — I2 91
Saint-Philippe [-de-Laprairie], Que. — D4 74
Saint-Philippe-de-Néri, Que. — B8 74
Saint Phillips Island, i, S.C., U.S. — G6 117
Saint-Pie, Que. — D5 74
Saint-Pierre, Mart. — I14 64
Saint-Pierre, St. P./M. — E3 72
Saint-Pierre, i., St. P./M. — E3 72
Saint-Pierre, Lac, l., Que. — C5 74
Saint Pierre and Miquelon, dep., N.A. — E3 72
Saint-Pierre-d'Albigny, Fr. — D2 20
Saint-Pierre-en-Port, Fr. — C4 16
Saint-Pierre-Jolys, Man. — E3 70
Saint-Pierre-Montmagny, Que. — C7 74
Saint-Placide, Que. — p18 74
Saint-Pol-de-Léon, Fr. — C2 16
Saint-Pol-sur-Mer, Fr. — C2 17
Saint-Pol [-sur-Ternoise], Fr. — B5 16
Saint-Pourçain, Fr. — D5 16
Saint-Prime, Que. — A5 74
Saint-Prosper, Que. — C5 74
Saint-Prosper-de-Dorchester, Que. — C7 74
Saint Quentin, N.B. — B2 71
Saint-Quentin, Fr. — C5 16
Saint-Raphaël, Que. — C7 74
Saint-Raphaël, Fr. — F7 16
Saint-Raphaël-sur-Mer, N.B. — B5 71
Saint-Raymond, Que. — C6 74
Saint-Rédempteur, Que. — o17 74
Saint Regis, Mt., U.S. — C1 103
Saint Regis, stm., N.A. — f10 109
Saint Regis, West Branch, stm., N.Y., U.S. — f10 109
Saint Regis Falls, N.Y., U.S. — f10 109
Saint-Rémi, Que. — D4 74
Saint-Rémi-d'Amherst, Que. — C3 74
Saint-Rémi [-de-Tingwick], Que. — D6 74
Saint-Roch [-de-Richelieu], Que. — D4 74
Saint-Roch-des-Aulnaies, Que. — B7 74
Saint-Romuald, Que. — C6 74
Sainte-Rose, Guad. — H14 64
Sainte Rose, La., U.S. — k11 95
Sainte Rose du Lac, Man. — D2 70
Saintes, Fr. — E3 16
Saintes, Île des, is., Guad. — R8 65
Sainte-Sabine-de-Bellechasse, Que. — C7 74
Saint Samuel, Que. — D7 74
Saint Sanford, Man. — E3 70
Saint Sauveur, N.B. — B4 71
Saint-Sauveur-des-Monts, Que. — D3 74
Sainte-Savine, Fr. — C6 16
Saint-Sébastien, Que. — D7 74
Saint-Sébastien, Cap, c., Madag. — f9 49
Saint-Sébastien [-sur-Loire], Fr. — E5 16
Saint-Sever, Fr. — F3 16
Saint-Séverin-de-Beauce, Que. — C6 74
Saint Shotts, Newf. — E5 72
Saint-Siméon, Que. — B8 74
Saint-Siméon, Fr. — F3 17
Saint-Simon-de-Rimouski, Que. — A8 74
Saint Simons Island, Ga., U.S. — E5 87
Saint Simons Island, i., Ga., U.S. — E5 87
Saint Simons Sound, strt., Ga., U.S. — I6 51
Saint-Sixte, Que. — D2 74
Sainte-Sophie [-de-Lévrard], Que. — C5 74
Sainte-Sophie [-de-Mégantic], Que. — C6 74
Saint Stephen, N.B. — D2 71
Saint Stephen, S.C., U.S. — E8 117
Saint Stephens, Al., U.S. — D1 78
Saint Stephens, N.C., U.S. — *B1 110
Saint Stephen's Church, Isr. Occ. — m14 41
Saint Stephen's Gate, hist., Isr. Occ. — m14 41
Saint-Sylvère, Que. — C5 74
Saint-Sylvestre, Que. — C6 74
Sainte-Thècle, Que. — C5 74
Sainte-Théophile, Que. — D7 74
Sainte-Thérèse, Que. — D4 74
Saint Thomas, Ont. — E3 73
Saint Thomas, Mo., U.S. — C5 102
Saint Thomas, N.D., U.S. — A8 111
Saint Thomas, Pa., U.S. — G6 115
Saint Thomas, i., V.I.U.S. — G12 64
Saint-Thomas [-de-Joliette], Que. — D4 74
Saint Timothée, Que. — q18 74
Saint-Tite, Que. — C5 74
Saint-Tite-des-Caps, Que. — B7 74
Saint-Tropez, Fr. — F7 16
Saint-Ubalde, Que. — C5 74
Saint-Urbain-de-Charlevoix, Que. — B7 74

Saint-Urbain [-de-Châteauguay], Que. — q19 74
Saint-Valérien, Que. — D5 74
Saint-Valérien, Que. — C5 74
Saint-Valéry-en-Caux, Fr. — E8 12
Saint-Valéry-sur-Somme, Fr. — B4 16
Saint-Vallier, Que. — C7 74
Saint-Vallier, Fr. — E6 16
Sainte-Véronique, Que. — C3 74
Saint-Victor, Que. — C7 74
Saint Vincent, i., St. Vin. — U26 65
Saint Vincent, Cape, c., Madag. — h8 49
Saint Vincent, Cape, c., Port. — D1 22
Saint Vincent and the Grenadines, ctry., N.A. — J14 64
Saint Vincent Island, i., Fl., N.A. — C1 86
Saint Vincent Passage, strt., N.A. — J14 64
Saint Vincent's [-Saint Stephens-Peter's River], Newf. — E5 72
Saint-Vith, Bel. — D6 17
Saint Vrain, N.M., U.S. — C6 108
Saint Walburg, Sask. — D1 75
Saint Wendells, In., U.S. — H2 91
Saint Williams, Ont. — E4 73
Saint-Yrieix-la-Perche, Fr. — E4 16
Saint-Zacharie, Que. — C7 74
Saint-Zéphirin, Que. — C5 74
Saipan, i., N. Mar. Is. — E8 6
Saipan Channel, strt., N. Mar. Is. — D7 52
Saipan International Airport, N. Mar. Is. — D7 52
Sairecábur, Cerro, mtn., S.A. — D2 55
Sa Yok, Thai. — E3 35
Sajama, Nevado, mtn., Bol. — C2 55
Sakai, Kenya — B6 48
Sa Kaeo, Thai. — F5 35
Sakai, Japan — o14 33
Sakākah, Sau. Ar. — C4 38
Sakakawea, Lake, res., N.D., U.S. — B3 111
Sakami, Lac, l., Que. — F17 66
Sakania, Zaire — D4 48
Sakaraha, Madag. — h8 49
Sakarya, stm., Tur. — B8 40
Sakashita, Japan — n16 33
Sakata, Japan — D12 31
Sakchu, N. Kor. — F2 33
Sakishima Islands, is., Japan — G9 31
Sakmara, stm., Sov. Un. — C5 28
Sakon Nakhon, Thai. — B2 34
Sakonnet, R.I., U.S. — F6 116
Sakonnet, stm., R.I., U.S. — E6 116
Sakonnet Point, c., R.I., U.S. — F6 116
Sakskøbing, Den. — D5 15
Sakti, India — H2 36
Sal, stm., Sov. Un. — H14 27
Sal, Point, c., Ca., U.S. — E3 82
Sala, Swe. — H7 14
Sala-y-Gómez, Isla, i., Chile — H15 6
Salaberry-de-Valleyfield, Que. — D3 74
Sala Consilina, Italy — D5 23
Salado, Arg. — B5 54
Saladillo, Arg. — B5 54
Salado, stm., Arg. — B3 54
Salado, stm., Arg. — F3 55
Salado, stm., Mex. — B4 63
Salado, Arroyo, stm., Arg. — C3 54
Salado, Río, stm., N.M., U.S. — C2 108
Salaga, Ghana — A4 45
Sala ilua, W. Sam. — F11 52
Sala'ilua Bay, b., W. Sam. — F11 52
Salālah, Oman — D5 38
Salamá, Guat. — C2 62
Salamá, Hond. — E7 63
Salamanca, Chile — A2 54
Salamanca, Mex. — m13 63
Salamanca, Spain — B3 22
Salamanca, N.Y., U.S. — C2 109
Salamat, Bahr, stm., Chad — C3 46
Salamaua, Pap. N. Gui. — k12 50
Salamina, Col. — B2 60
Salamís, Grc. — D4 25
Salamís, i., Grc. — h10 25
Salamonia, In., U.S. — D8 91
Salamonie, stm., In., U.S. — C6 91
Salamonie Lake, res., In., U.S. — C6 91
Salani, W. Sam. — G12 52
Salar de Pocitos, Arg. — D2 55
Salas, Spain — A2 22
Salatiga, Indon. — *G4 34
Salavat, Sov. Un. — C5 28
Salaverry, Peru — C2 58
Salavina, Arg. — E3 55
Salawati, i., Indon. — F8 34
Sala y Gómez, Isla, i., Chile — H15 6
Salbris, Fr. — D5 16
Salcedo, Ec. — B2 58
Saldanha, S. Afr. — D2 49
Saldus, Sov. Un. — C4 27
Sale, Austl. — I6 51
Salé, Mor. — C3 44
Sale City, Ga., U.S. — E2 87
Sale Creek, Tn., U.S. — D8 119
Salée, Rivière, strt., Guad. — Q8 65
Salekhard, Sov. Un. — C9 29
Salem, India — F6 36
Salem, Al., U.S. — C4 78
Salem, Ar., U.S. — A4 81
Salem, Ct., U.S. — D6 84
Salem, Fl., U.S. — C3 86
Salem, Il., U.S. — E5 90
Salem, In., U.S. — G8 91
Salem, Ia., U.S. — D6 92
Salem, Ky., U.S. — e9 94
Salem, Ma., U.S. — A6 98
Salem, Mi., U.S. — p14 99
Salem, Mo., U.S. — D6 102
Salem, Ne., U.S. — D10 104
Salem, N.H., U.S. — E4 106
Salem, N.J., U.S. — D2 107
Salem, N.M., U.S. — E2 108
Salem, N.Y., U.S. — B7 109
Salem, Or., U.S. — C4 114
Salem, S.C., U.S. — B2 117
Salem, S.D., U.S. — D8 118
Salem, Ut., U.S. — C4 121
Salem, Va., U.S. — C2 123
Salem, W.V., U.S. — B4 125
Salem, Wi., U.S. — n11 126
Salem, co., N.J., U.S. — D2 107
Salem, stm., N.J., U.S. — D2 107
Salem, Lake, l., Vt., U.S. — B4 122
Salemburg, N.C., U.S. — B4 110

Salemi, Italy — F4 23
Salen, Scot., U.K. — D3 13
Salen, Scot., U.K. — D3 13
Salerno, Italy — D5 23
Salerno, Gulf of, b., Italy — D5 23
Salfit, Isr. Occ. — B7 41
Salford, Eng., U.K. — D10 10
Salgótarján, Hung. — A4 24
Salgueiro, Braz. — C3 57
Salida, Co., U.S. — C5 83
Salies-de-Béarn, Fr. — F3 16
Salihli, Tur. — C7 25
Salima, Mwi. — D5 48
Salīmah, Wāḥat, well, Sud. — A2 47
Salin, Burma — B1 35
Salina, Az., U.S. — A6 80
Salina, Ks., U.S. — D6 93
Salina, Ok., U.S. — A6 113
Salina, Ut., U.S. — E4 121
Salina, i., Italy — E5 23
Salina Cruz, Mex. — D5 63
Salinas, Braz. — B4 56
Salinas, Ca., U.S. — D3 82
Salinas, Ec. — B1 58
Salinas, stm., Ca., U.S. — D3 82
Salinas, Cape, c., Spain — C7 22
Salinas, Pampa de las, pl., Arg. — A3 54
Salinas de Garci Mendoza, Bol. — C2 55
Salinas National Monument, N.M., U.S. — C3 108
Salinas Peak, mtn., N.M., U.S. — D3 108
Saline, La., U.S. — B3 95
Saline, Mi., U.S. — F7 99
Saline, co., Ar., U.S. — C3 81
Saline, co., Il., U.S. — F5 90
Saline, co., Ks., U.S. — D6 93
Saline, co., Mo., U.S. — B4 102
Saline, co., Ne., U.S. — D8 104
Saline, stm., Ar., U.S. — C1 81
Saline, stm., Ar., U.S. — D4 81
Saline, stm., Ks., U.S. — C3 93
Saline, North Fork, stm., Il., U.S. — F5 90
Saline, South Fork, stm., Ar., U.S. — f8 81
Saline Bayou, stm., La., U.S. — B3 95
Saline Lake, res., La., U.S. — C3 95
Salineno, Tx., U.S. — F3 120
Salines, Point, c., Gren. — W25 65
Salines, Pointe des, c., Mart. — T11 65
Salinópolis, Braz. — B1 57
Salins-les-Bains, Fr. — E6 16
Salisbury, Austl. — *F6 50
Salisbury, N.B. — C4 71
Salisbury, Eng., U.K. — E6 10
Salisbury, Ct., U.S. — B2 84
Salisbury, Md., U.S. — D6 97
Salisbury, Ma., U.S. — A6 98
Salisbury, Mo., U.S. — B5 102
Salisbury, N.H., U.S. — D3 106
Salisbury, N.C., U.S. — B2 110
Salisbury, Pa., U.S. — G3 115
Salisbury, Vt., U.S. — D2 122
Salisbury Center, N.Y., U.S. — B6 109
Salisbury see Harare, Zimb. — A5 49
Salisbury Heights, N.H., U.S. — D3 106
Salisbury Island, i., N.W. Ter. — D17 66
Salisbury Plain, pl., Eng., U.K. — C6 12
Salitpa, Al., U.S. — D1 78
Salix, Ia., U.S. — B1 92
Salkehatchie, stm., S.C., U.S. — E5 117
Salkum, Wa., U.S. — C3 124
Salladasburg, Pa., U.S. — D7 115
Sallanches, Fr. — D2 20
Salley, S.C., U.S. — D5 117
Saliqueló, Arg. — B4 54
Sallis, Ms., U.S. — B4 101
Sallisaw, Ok., U.S. — B7 113
Sallūm, Khalīj as, b., Afr. — G5 40
Salm, i., Sov. Un. — B9 28
Salmās, Iran — B2 39
Salmo, B.C. — E9 69
Salmon, Id., U.S. — D5 89
Salmon, stm., B.C. — B6 69
Salmon, stm., N.B. — C4 71
Salmon, stm., N.B. — B2 71
Salmon, stm., N.B. — f10 109
Salmon, stm., N.B. — D3 69
Salmon, Middle Fork, stm., Id., U.S. — E4 89
Salmon, South Fork, stm., Id., U.S. — E3 89
Salmon Arm, B.C. — D8 69
Salmon-Bay, Que. — C3 72
Salmon Creek, Wa., U.S. — D3 124
Salmon Creek Reservoir, res., Id., U.S. — G4 89
Salmon Falls, stm., U.S. — D5 106
Salmon Falls Creek, stm., U.S. — G4 89
Salmon Mountain, mtn., N.H., U.S. — f7 106
Salmon Mountains, mts., Ca., U.S. — B2 82
Salmon Peak, mtn., Tx., U.S. — E2 120
Salmon Point, c., Ont. — D7 73
Salmon River Mountains, mts., Id., U.S. — E3 89
Salmon River Reservoir, res., N.Y., U.S. — B5 109
Salmon Valley, B.C. — B6 69
Salo, Fin. — G10 14
Salò, Italy — D6 20
Salol, Mn., U.S. — B3 100
Salome, Az., U.S. — D2 80
Salon-de-Provence, Fr. — F6 16
Salonika see Thessaloniki, Grc. — B4 40
Salonika, Gulf of see Thermaïkós Kólpos, b., Grc. — B5 40
Salonta, Rom. — A3 54
Salsacate, Arg. — A3 54
Salsk, Sov. Un. — H13 27
Salsomaggiore Terme, Italy — B2 23
Salt, stm., Az., U.S. — D4 80
Salt, stm., Ky., U.S. — C4 94
Salt, stm., Mo., U.S. — B6 102
Salt, Middle Fork, stm., Mo., U.S. — B5 102
Salt, North Fork, stm., Mo., U.S. — B5 102
Salt, South Fork, stm., Mo., U.S. — B5 102
Salta, Arg. — D2 55
Salta, prov., Arg. — A3 54
Saltash, Eng., U.K. — D3 12
Saltburn-by-the-Sea, Eng., U.K. — F8 13

Salt Cay, i., Bah. — m18 64
Saltcoats, Sask. — F4 75
Saltcoats, Scot., U.K. — E4 13
Salt Creek, stm., Il., U.S. — C4 90
Salt Creek, stm., Ks., U.S. — f10 93
Salt Creek, stm., Ne., U.S. — h11 104
Salt Creek, stm., N.M., U.S. — D5 108
Salt Creek, stm., Oh., U.S. — C3 112
Salt Creek, stm., Wy., U.S. — C6 127
Salt Fork, Ok., U.S. — A4 113
Salt Fork Lake, res., Oh., U.S. — B4 112
Saltholm, i., Den. — C6 15
Saltillo, Mex. — B4 63
Saltillo, In., U.S. — G5 91
Saltillo, Ms., U.S. — A5 101
Saltillo, Tn., U.S. — B3 119
Salt Lake, co., Ut., U.S. — C3 121
Salt Lake, l., Hi., U.S. — g10 88
Salt Lake, l., N.M., U.S. — E6 108
Salt Lake City, Ut., U.S. — C4 121
Salt Lick, Ky., U.S. — B6 94
Salto, Braz. — m8 56
Salto, Ur. — E1 56
Salto Grande, Braz. — C3 56
Salton Sea, l., Ca., U.S. — F5 82
Saltonstall, Lake, l., Ct., U.S. — D4 84
Salt Point, c., Ca., U.S. — C2 82
Saltpond, Ghana — E4 45
Salt River Indian Reservation, Az., U.S. — k9 80
Salt River Range, mts., Wy., U.S. — D2 127
Salt Rock, W.V., U.S. — C2 125
Saltsburg, Pa., U.S. — F3 115
Saltsjöbaden (part of Nacka), Swe. — t36 14
Saltspring Island, i., B.C. — E6 69
Salt Springs, Fl., U.S. — C5 86
Saltville, Va., U.S. — f10 123
Saltwater, Wa., U.S. — *B3 124
Salt Wells Creek, stm., Wy., U.S. — E4 127
Salud, Pan. — k10 62
Saluda, N.C., U.S. — f10 110
Saluda, S.C., U.S. — C4 117
Saluda, Va., U.S. — C6 123
Saluda, co., S.C., U.S. — C4 117
Saluda, stm., S.C., U.S. — C4 117
Saluda Dam, S.C., U.S. — C5 117
Salūr, India — E7 36
Salus, Ar., U.S. — B2 81
Saluvia, Pa., U.S. — F5 115
Saluzzo, Italy — B1 23
Salvador, Braz. — D3 57
Salvador, Sask. — E1 75
Salvador, Lake, l., La., U.S. — E5 95
Salvage, Newf. — D5 72
Salvatierra, Mex. — m13 63
Salvisa, Ky., U.S. — C5 94
Salwa Bay, b., Asia — I5 39
Salween (Thanlwin), stm., Asia — D10 36
Salyān, Nepal — C9 37
Salyany, Sov. Un. — I9 27
Salyer, Ca., U.S. — B2 82
Salyersville, Ky., U.S. — C6 94
Salym Marsh, sw., Sov. Un. — B8 28
Salzach, stm., Eur. — E6 18
Salzburg, Aus. — E6 18
Salzburg, state, Aus. — E6 18
Salzgitter, W. Ger. — B5 18
Salzwedel, E. Ger. — B5 18
Sama [de Langreo], Spain — A3 22
Samaipata, Bol. — C5 55
Samalá, stm., Guat. — C2 62
Samālūt, Eg. — D6 43
Samaná, Dom. Rep. — E9 64
Samana Cay, i., Bah. — C7 64
Samandağ, Tur. — D10 40
Samani, Japan — E11 33
Samaniego, Col. — C2 60
Samannūd, Eg. — D3 41
Samar, Isr. — E6 41
Samar, i., Phil. — C7 34
Samara, Sov. Un. — C4 28
Samarai, Pap. N. Gui. — m13 50
Samarga, Sov. Un. — G6 29
Samaria, Id., U.S. — G6 89
Samariapo, Ven. — F5 60
Samarkand, Sov. Un. — I11 28
Sāmarrā', Iraq — B4 38
Sāmarrā Barrage, Iraq — E14 40
Samataita, W. Sam. — F11 52
Samatan, Fr. — F4 16
Samawāri, Pak. — C1 37
Sambalpur, India — J11 36
Sambar, Cape, c., Indon. — F4 34
Sambas, Indon. — E3 34
Sambava, Madag. — f10 49
Sambhal, India — F8 36
Sambhar, India — D5 37
Sambor, Sov. Un. — C4 27
Samborombón, Bahía, b., Arg. — B5 54
Sambre, stm., Eur. — B2 16
Samburg, Tn., U.S. — A2 119
Samch'ŏk, S. Kor. — H4 33
Samch'ŏnpo, S. Kor. — I4 33
Same, Tan. — B7 48
Samedan, Switz. — C5 20
Sammamish Lake, l., Wa., U.S. — e11 124
Samnū, Libya — D2 43
Samoa, i., Phil. — B1 82
Samokov, Bul. — D6 24
Samoset, Fl., U.S. — q10 86
Samosir, i., Indon. — E1 34
Sámos, i., Grc. — D6 40
Samoth, Il., U.S. — B5 90
Samothrace see Samothráki, i., Grc. — B5 40
Samothráki (Samothrace), i., Grc. — B5 40
Sampacho, Arg. — A4 54
Sampaloc Point, c., Phil. — o13 34
Sampit, Indon. — F4 34
Sampit, stm., S.C., U.S. — E9 117
Sampson, co., N.C., U.S. — B4 110
Sampwe, Zaire — C4 48
Sam Rayburn Reservoir, res., Tx., U.S. — D5 120
Samsang, China — C9 37
Samsø, i., Den. — D3 15
Samsø Bælt, strt., Den. — D3 15
Samson, Al., U.S. — D3 78
Samsun, Tur. — B11 40
Samtown, La., U.S. — *C3 95

Samtredia, Sov. Un. — A14 40
Samuels, Id., U.S. — A2 89
Samui, i., Thai. — H4 35
Samus, Sov. Un. — D25 8
Samut Sakhon, Thai. — C2 34
San, Mali — D4 45
San, stm., Asia — F7 35
San, stm., Eur. — C7 26
Ṣan'ā', Yemen — C6 47
Sanaag, prov., Som. — C6 47
San Acacia, N.M., U.S. — C3 108
San Acacio, Co., U.S. — D5 83
Sanaga, stm., Cam. — E2 46
San Agustín, Col. — C2 60
San Agustín, Plains of, pl., N.M., U.S. — C2 108
San Agustín de Valle Fértil, Arg. — A3 54
Sanak Islands, is., Ak., U.S. — E7 79
San Ambrosio, Isla, i., Chile — F3 53
Sanana, i., Indon. — F7 34
Sanandaj, Iran — C3 82
San Andreas, Ca., U.S. — C3 82
San Andrés, Col. — D7 62
San Andrés, Isla de, i., Col. — g7 64
San Andres Mountains, mts., N.M., U.S. — E3 108
San Andres Peak, mtn., N.M., U.S. — E3 108
San Andrés Tetepilco (part of Mexico City), Mex. — h9 63
San Andrés Tuxtla, Mex. — D5 63
San Andrés y Providencia, dept., Col. — *D7 62
San Angelo, Tx., U.S. — D2 120
San Anselmo, Ca., U.S. — h7 82
San Antonio, Arg. — A2 54
San Antonio, Chile — E2 55
San Antonio, Chile — A2 54
San Antonio, N. Mar. Is. — D7 52
San Antonio, Phil. — o13 34
San Antonio, Fl., U.S. — D4 86
San Antonio, N.M., U.S. — k8 108
San Antonio, Tx., U.S. — E3 120
San Antonio, Cabo, c., Arg. — B5 54
San Antonio, Cabo, c., Cuba — D1 64
San Antonio Abad, Spain — C6 22
San Antonio Bay, b., Tx., U.S. — E4 120
San Antonio de Areco, Arg. — g7 54
San Antonio de los Baños, Cuba — C2 64
San Antonio de los Cobres, Arg. — D2 55
San Antonio Mountain, mtn., N.M., U.S. — A3 108
San Antonio Oeste, Arg. — C4 54
Sanarate, Guat. — C2 62
San Ardo, Ca., U.S. — D3 82
Sanatorium, Ms., U.S. — D4 101
San Augustine, Tx., U.S. — D5 120
San Augustine, co., Tx., U.S. — D5 120
San Bartolomeo [in Galdo], Italy — D5 23
San Benedetto del Tronto, Italy — C4 23
San Benito, Tx., U.S. — F4 120
San Benito, co., Ca., U.S. — D3 82
San Benito Mountain, mtn., Ca., U.S. — D3 82
San Bernardino, Switz. — D7 21
San Bernardino, Ca., U.S. — E5 82
San Bernardino, co., Ca., U.S. — E5 82
San Bernardo, Chile — A2 54
San Blas, Mex. — m11 63
San Blas, Cape, c., Fl., U.S. — v16 86
San Blas, Cordillera de, mts., Pan. — F8 62
San Bonifacio, Italy — D7 20
San Borja, Bol. — B2 55
San Borja, stm., Mex. — h9 63
San Borja, Mex. — A2 92
San Bruno, Ca., U.S. — D2 82
San Candido, Italy — C8 20
San Carlos, Arg. — A3 54
San Carlos, Chile — B2 54
San Carlos, Nic. — E8 64
San Carlos, Phil. — o13 34
San Carlos, Ur. — D5 56
San Carlos, Ven. — B4 60
San Carlos de Bariloche, Arg. — C2 54
San Carlos del Zulia, Ven. — B3 60
San Carlos de Río Negro, Ven. — C4 60
San Carlos Indian Reservation, Az., U.S. — D5 80
San Carlos Lake, res., Az., U.S. — D5 80
San Cataldo, Italy — F4 23
Sancerre, Fr. — E9 16
Sánchez, Dom. Rep. — E9 64
Sanch'ung, Tai. — *F9 31
San Ciro de Acosta, Mex. — m14 63
San Clemente, Spain — C4 22
San Clemente, Ca., U.S. — F5 82
San Clemente Island, i., Ca., U.S. — *F4 82
San Cristóbal, Dom. Rep. — E8 64
San Cristóbal, Ven. — B3 60
San Cristóbal, i., Sol. Is. — A4 108
San Cristóbal, i., Sol. Is. — G9 6
San Cristóbal, Isla (Chatham), i., Ec. — g6 58
San Cristóbal, Volcán, vol., Nic. — D4 62
San Cristóbal de las Casas, Mex. — D6 63
Sancti-Spíritus, Cuba — D4 64
Sancti-Spíritus, prov., Cuba — C4 64
Sanctuary, Sask. — G1 75
Sancy, Puy de, mtn., Fr. — E5 16
Sanda, Japan — o14 33
Sanda Island, i., Scot., U.K. — E3 13
Sandakan, Malay. — D5 34
Sandalfoot Cove, Fl., U.S. — *F6 86
San Daniele del Friuli, Italy — D7 20
Sandaré, Mali — D2 45
Sanday, i., Scot., U.K. — A5 13
Sanday Sound, strt., Scot., U.K. — A6 13
Sandborn, In., U.S. — G3 91
Sand Brook, N.J., U.S. — *C3 107

Name	Map Ref.	Page
Sand Coulee, Mt., U.S.	C5	103
Sand Creek, Wi., U.S.	C2	126
Sand Creek, stm., In., U.S.	F6	91
Sand Creek, stm., Ks., U.S.	g12	93
Sand Creek, stm., Wy., U.S.	C7	127
Sand Draw, Wy., U.S.	*D4	127
Sande, Nor.	p28	14
Sandefjord, Nor.	p28	14
Sanders, Az., U.S.	B6	80
Sanders, Ky., U.S.	B5	94
Sanders, Mt., U.S.	D9	103
Sanders, co., Mt., U.S.	C1	103
Sanderson, Tx., U.S.	D1	120
Sandersville, Ga., U.S.	D4	87
Sandersville, Ms., U.S.	D4	101
Sandfly Lake, l., Sask.	B2	75
Sandford, In., U.S.	E2	91
Sand Fork, W.V., U.S.	C4	125
Sandhammaren, c., Swe.	C8	15
Sand Hill, Ma., U.S.	h13	98
Sand Hill, Ms., U.S.	D5	101
Sand Hill, Ms., U.S.	C4	101
Sand Hill, stm., Newf.	B3	72
Sand Hill, stm., Mn., U.S.	C2	100
Sandi, India	C7	36
Sandia, Peru	D4	58
Sandia, N.M., U.S.	*B3	109
Sandia, Tx., U.S.	E4	120
Sandia Crest, mtn., N.M., U.S.	k8	108
Sandia Indian Reservation, N.M., U.S.	k7	108
Sandia Mountains, mts., N.M., U.S.	k8	108
Sandia Park, N.M., U.S.	k8	108
San Diego, Ca., U.S.	F5	82
San Diego, Tx., U.S.	F3	120
San Diego, co., Ca., U.S.	o15	82
San Diego, stm., Ca., U.S.	o15	82
San Diego, Cabo, c., Arg.	h12	54
San Diego Naval Station, mil., Ca., U.S.	o15	82
San Diego Naval Training Center, mil., Ca., U.S.	o15	82
Sandikli, Tur.	C8	40
Sandilands, Man.	E3	70
San Dimas, Mex.	C3	63
San Dimas, Ca., U.S.	*m13	82
Sand Island, i., Mid. Is.	K3	52
Sand Island, i., Mid. Is.	g10	16
Sand Island, i., Wi., U.S.	B3	126
Sand Islet, i., U.S.	J3	52
Sand Key, i., Fl., U.S.	E4	86
Sand Lake, Mi., U.S.	E5	99
Sandlick Creek, stm., W.V., U.S.	n13	125
Sand Mountain, mtn., U.S.	A3	78
Sandnes, Nor.	H1	14
Sandoa, Zaire	C3	48
Sandomierz, Pol.	C6	26
Sandon, B.C.	D9	69
Sandoná, Col.	C2	60
San Donà di Piave, Italy	B4	23
Sandoval, Il., U.S.	E4	90
Sandoval, co., N.M., U.S.	B2	108
Sandover, stm., Austl.	D6	50
Sandoway, Burma	E9	36
Sandown, Eng., U.K.	D6	12
Sandown, N.H., U.S.	E4	106
Sand Point, Ont.	B8	73
Sand Point, Ak., U.S.	D7	79
Sandpoint, Id., U.S.	A2	89
Sands, Mi., U.S.	B3	99
Sands Key, i., Fl., U.S.	s3	86
Sandspit, B.C.	C2	69
Sand Springs, Mt., U.S.	C9	103
Sand Springs, Ok., U.S.	A5	113
Sandston, Va., U.S.	m18	123
Sandstone, Austl.	E2	50
Sandstone, Mn., U.S.	D6	100
Sandstone, W.V., U.S.	D4	125
Sandtown, De., U.S.	D3	85
Sandusky, Mi., U.S.	E8	99
Sandusky, N.Y., U.S.	C2	109
Sandusky, Oh., U.S.	A3	112
Sandusky, co., Oh., U.S.	A2	112
Sandusky, stm., Oh., U.S.	B2	112
Sandusky Bay, b., Oh., U.S.	A3	112
Sandvig (part of Allinge-Sandvig), Den.	C8	15
Sandviken, Swe.	G7	14
Sandwich, Il., U.S.	B5	90
Sandwich, Ma., U.S.	C7	98
Sandwich, N.H., U.S.	C4	106
Sandwich Bay, b., Newf.	B3	72
Sandwich Range, mts., N.H., U.S.	C3	106
Sandwick, B.C.	E5	69
Sandwith, Sask.	D1	75
Sandy, Or., U.S.	B4	114
Sandy, Ut., U.S.	C4	121
Sandy, stm., Me., U.S.	D2	96
Sandy Bay Mountain, mtn., Me., U.S.	C2	96
Sandy Brook, stm., Ct., U.S.	A3	84
Sandy Cape, c., Austl.	D9	50
Sandy Creek, N.Y., U.S.	B4	109
Sandy Creek, stm., Oh., U.S.	B4	112
Sandy Creek, stm., Ok., U.S.	C2	113
Sandy Hook, Ct., U.S.	D2	84
Sandy Hook, Ky., U.S.	B6	94
Sandy Hook, Md., U.S.	B2	97
Sandy Hook, Ms., U.S.	D4	101
Sandy Hook, spit, N.J., U.S.	C5	107
Sandy Island, i., S.C., U.S.	D9	117
Sandy Lake, Man.	D1	70
Sandy Lake, Pa., U.S.	D1	115
Sandy Lake, l., Newf.	D3	72
Sandy Lake, l., Ont.	n16	73
Sandy Lake, l., Sask.	B2	75
Sandy Neck, pen., Ma., U.S.	C7	98
Sandy Point, Me., U.S.	D4	96
Sandy Point, c., Trin.	M24	65
Sandy Point, c., V.I.U.S.	h7	116
Sandy Pond, l., Ma., U.S.	g10	98
Sandy Ridge, Al., U.S.	C3	78
Sandy Ridge, N.C., U.S.	A2	110
Sandy Ridge, Pa., U.S.	E5	115
Sandy Ridge, mtn., Va., U.S.	e9	123
Sandy Springs, Ga., U.S.	h8	87
Sandy Springs, S.C., U.S.	B2	117
Sandyville, Md., U.S.	A4	97
Sandyville, W.V., U.S.	C3	125
San Elizario, Tx., U.S.	o11	120
San Enrique, Arg.	B4	54
San Estanislao, Para.	D4	55
San Esteban, Hond.	D7	63
San Felice sul Panaro, Italy	E7	20
San Felipe, Chile	A2	54
San Felipe, Col.	C4	60
San Felipe, Mex.	m13	63
San Felipe, Ven.	A4	60
San Felipe, Punta, c., Mex.	A2	63
San Felipe Indian Reservation, N.M., U.S.	k8	108
San Felipe Pueblo, N.M., U.S.	B3	108
San Feliu de Guixols, Spain	B7	22
San Félix, Isla, i., Chile	F2	53
San Fernando, Arg.	A5	54
San Fernando, Chile	A2	54
San Fernando, Mex.	C5	63
San Fernando, Phil.	B6	34
San Fernando, Phil.	o13	34
San Fernando, Trin.	K14	64
San Fernando, Ca., U.S.	m12	82
San Fernando de Apure, Ven.	B4	60
San Fernando de Atabapo, Ven.	C4	60
San Fernando de Henares, Spain	p17	22
San Fidel, N.M., U.S.	B2	108
Sânfjället, mtn., Swe.	F5	14
Sânfjället National Park, Swe.	F5	14
Sanford, Co., U.S.	D5	83
Sanford, Fl., U.S.	D5	86
Sanford, Me., U.S.	E2	96
Sanford, Mi., U.S.	E6	99
Sanford, Ms., U.S.	D4	101
Sanford, N.C., U.S.	B3	110
Sanford, Tx., U.S.	B2	120
Sanford, Mount, mtn., Ak., U.S.	C11	79
San Francisco, Arg.	A4	54
San Francisco, Col.	C2	60
San Francisco, co., Ca., U.S.	D2	82
San Francisco, Ca., U.S.	D2	82
San Francisco, Paso de, S.A.	E2	55
San Francisco Bay, b., Ca., U.S.	h8	82
San Francisco de Borja, Mex.	B3	63
San Francisco del Oro, Mex.	B3	63
San Francisco del Rincón, Mex.	m13	63
San Francisco de Macorís, Dom. Rep.	E8	64
San Francisco Gotera, El Sal.	D3	62
San Francisco Mountains, mts., Ut., U.S.	E2	121
San Francisco Solano, Punta, c., Col.	B2	60
San Gabriel, Ec.	A2	58
San Gabriel, Ca., U.S.	m12	82
San Gabriel, Punta, c., Mex.	B2	63
San Gabriel Chilac, Mex.	D5	63
San Gabriel Mountains, mts., Ca., U.S.	m12	82
San Gallan, Isla, i., Peru	D2	58
Sangamner, India	H5	37
Sangamon, co., Il., U.S.	D4	90
Sangamon, stm., Il., U.S.	C3	90
Sangatte, Fr.	D9	12
Sangay, Volcán, vol., Ec.	B2	58
Sang-e Mãsheh, Afg.	E13	39
Sanger, Ca., U.S.	D4	82
Sanger, Tx., U.S.	C4	120
Sangerhausen, E. Ger.	C5	18
Sangerville, Me., U.S.	C3	96
Sanggau, Indon.	E4	34
Sangha, stm., Afr.	E3	46
San Giacomo Pass, Eur.	D5	21
Sanghe, i., Indon.	E7	34
San Gil, Col.	B3	60
San Gimignano, Italy	C3	23
San Giovanni in Fiore, Italy	E6	23
San Giovanni in Persiceto, Italy	E7	20
Sangju, S. Kor.	H4	33
Sangli, India	*E5	36
Sangmélima, Cam.	E2	46
San Gorgonio Mountain, mtn., Ca., U.S.	E5	82
Sangre de Cristo Mountains, mts., U.S.	C6	76
San Gregorio, Ca., U.S.	k8	82
San Gregorio, Ur.	E1	56
Sangre Grande, Trin.	N23	64
Sangro, stm., Italy	D5	23
Sangrūr, India	B5	37
Sangudo, Alta.	C3	68
Sangue, Rio do, stm., Braz.	B4	55
Sangüesa, Spain	A5	22
Sanguinetto, Italy	h8	23
Sanhedriyya (part of Jerusalem), Isr.	m14	41
Sanibel, Fl., U.S.	F4	86
Sanibel Island, i., Fl., U.S.	F4	86
San Ignacio, Belize	B3	62
San Ignacio, Bol.	B2	55
San Ignacio, Bol.	C3	55
San Ignacio, Para.	E4	55
Sanilac, co., Mi., U.S.	E8	99
San Ildefonso, Cape, c., Phil.	B6	34
San Ildefonso [o la Granja], Spain	B3	22
San Ildefonso Peninsula, pen., Phil.	n14	34
Sanish, N.D., U.S.	B3	111
San Isidro, Arg.	g7	54
San Isidro, Peru	*D2	58
San Isidro [del General], C.R.	F6	62
San Jacinto, Ca., U.S.	F5	82
San Jacinto, co., Tx., U.S.	D5	120
San Jacinto, stm., Tx., U.S.	r14	120
San Jacinto Peak, mtn., Ca., U.S.	F5	82
San Javier, Arg.	A4	54
San Javier, Bol.	C3	55
San Javier, Arg.	F3	55
San Javier [de Loncomilla], Chile	B2	54
San Jerónimo, Serranía de, mts., Col.	B2	60
San Jerónimo Lidice (part of Mexico City), Mex.	h9	63
Sanjiang, China	L3	30
Sanjō, Japan	H9	33
San Joaquin, Arg.	D4	55
San Joaquin, co., Ca., U.S.	D3	82
San Joaquin, stm., Ca., U.S.	D3	82
San Joaquin Valley, val., Ca., U.S.	D3	82
San Jon, N.M., U.S.	B6	108
San Jorge, Golfo, b., Arg.	D3	54
San José, Belize	B3	62
San José, C.R.	F8	63
San José, Guat.	E6	63
San Jose, N. Mar. Is.	E7	52
San Jose, N. Mar. Is.	D7	52
San Jose, Phil.	C6	34
San Jose, Phil.	B6	34
San Jose, Az., U.S.	E6	80
San Jose, Il., U.S.	C4	90
San Jose, N.M., U.S.	B4	108
San José, dept., Ur.	g8	54
San Jose, stm., B.C.	D7	69
San José, stm., Ur.	g8	54
San José, Isla, i., Mex.	B2	63
San José [de Chiquitos], Bol.	C3	55
San José de Feliciano, Arg.	A5	54
San José de Guanipa (El Tigrito), Ven.	B5	60
San José de Jachal, Arg.	F2	55
San José del Boquerón, Arg.	E3	55
San José del Cabo, Mex.	F5	63
San José del Guaviare, Col.	C3	60
San José de los Molinos, Peru	D2	58
San José de Mayo, Ur.	E1	56
San José de Ocuné, Col.	C3	60
San Jose Island, i., Tx., U.S.	E4	120
San Juan, Arg.	A3	55
San Juan, Phil.	p13	34
San Juan, Phil.	n13	34
San Juan, P.R.	G11	64
San Juan, Co., U.S.	D6	83
San Juan, Tx., U.S.	F3	120
San Juan, prov., Arg.	A3	54
San Juan, co., Co., U.S.	D3	83
San Juan, co., N.M., U.S.	A1	108
San Juan, co., Ut., U.S.	F5	121
San Juan, co., Wa., U.S.	A2	124
San Juan, stm., Arg.	A3	54
San Juan, stm., B.C.	g11	69
San Juan, stm., Col.	C2	60
San Juan, stm., N.A.	E8	63
San Juan, stm., U.S.	C6	76
San Juan, Cabezas de, c., P.R.	B4	65
San Juan Bautista, Para.	E4	55
San Juan Capistrano, Ca., U.S.	F5	82
San Juan de Aragón (part of Mexico City), Mex.	h9	63
San Juan de Colón, Ven.	B3	60
San Juan [de la Maguana], Dom. Rep.	E8	64
San Juan de Lima, Punta, c., Mex.	D4	63
San Juan del Norte, Nic.	E8	63
San Juan de los Cayos, Ven.	A4	60
San Juan de los Morros, Ven.	B4	60
San Juan de los Lagos, Mex.	m12	63
San Juan del Río, Mex.	m13	63
San Juan del Sur, Nic.	E7	63
San Juan Mountains, mts., Co., U.S.	D3	83
San Juan Nepomuceno, Col.	B2	60
San Juan Pueblo, N.M., U.S.	*A3	108
San Juan y Martínez, Cuba	C2	64
San Julián, Arg.	D3	54
San Justo, Arg.	A4	54
Sankarani, stm., Afr.	D3	45
Sankt Anton [am Arlberg], Aus.	B6	20
Sankt Blasien, W. Ger.	B4	20
Sankt Gallen, Switz.	E4	18
Sankt Gallen, state, Switz.	B5	20
Sankt Gallenkirch, Aus.	B8	21
Sankt Georgen [im Attergau], Aus.	B9	20
Sankt Goarshausen, W. Ger.	C2	19
Sankt Johann [in Tirol], Aus.	B8	20
Sankt Margrethen, Switz.	B8	21
Sankt Michaelisdonn, W. Ger.	E3	15
Sankt Moritz, Switz.	E4	18
Sankt Olof, Swe.	C8	15
Sankt Pölten, Aus.	E7	20
Sankt Veit [an der Glan], Aus.	E7	18
Sankt Wendel, W. Ger.	D2	19
Sankuru, stm., Zaire	B3	48
San Leandro, Ca., U.S.	h8	82
San Lorenzo, Arg.	A4	54
San Lorenzo, Ec.	A2	58
San Lorenzo, Hond.	D4	62
San Lorenzo, P.R.	B4	65
San Lorenzo, N.M., U.S.	E2	108
San Lorenzo, Cerro, mtn., S.A.	D2	54
San Lorenzo de El Escorial, Spain	B3	22
Sanlúcar [de Barrameda], Spain	D2	22
San Lucas, Bol.	D2	55
San Lucas, Mex.	C2	63
San Lucas, Cabo, c., Mex.	C3	63
San Lucas, Serranía de, mts., Col.	B3	60
San Luis, Arg.	A3	54
San Luis, Cuba	D6	64
San Luis, Guat.	D7	63
San Luis, Az., U.S.	E3	80
San Luis, Co., U.S.	D5	83
San Luis, prov., Arg.	A3	54
San Luis, stm., Mex.	h9	63
San Luis, Point, c., Ca., U.S.	E3	82
San Luis Creek, stm., Co., U.S.	C5	83
San Luis de la Paz, Mex.	m13	63
San Luis Jilotepeque, Guat.	C3	62
San Luis Obispo, Ca., U.S.	E3	82
San Luis Obispo, co., Ca., U.S.	E3	82
San Luis Peak, mtn., Co., U.S.	D4	83
San Luis Potosí, Mex.	F5	62
San Luis Potosí, state, Mex.	C4	63
San Luis Río Colorado, Mex.	A2	63
San Luis Valley, val., Co., U.S.	D4	83
San Manuel, Az., U.S.	E5	80
San Marco [in Lamis], Italy	D5	23
San Marcos, Col.	B2	60
San Marcos, Guat.	C2	62
San Marcos, Tx., U.S.	E4	120
San Marcos, Tx., U.S.	h8	120
San Marcos de Colón, Hond.	D4	62
San Marino, Ca., U.S.	m12	82
San Marino, ctry., Eur.	C4	23
San Marino, Italy	C4	23
San Martín, Arg.	A3	54
San Martín, Col.	C3	60
San Martín, dept., Peru	B2	58
San Martín, stm., Bol.	B3	55
San Martín, Lago (Lago O'Higgins), l., S.A.	D2	54
San Martín de la Vega, Spain	p17	22
San Martín de los Andes, Arg.	D2	54
San Martino di Castrozza, Italy	D7	20
San Mateo, Spain	B6	22
San Mateo, Ca., U.S.	D2	82
San Mateo, Fl., U.S.	C5	86
San Mateo, N.M., U.S.	B2	108
San Mateo, co., Ca., U.S.	D2	82
San Mateo Mountains, mts., N.M., U.S.	D2	108
San Mateo Mountains, mts., N.M., U.S.	B2	108
San Matías, Bol.	C4	55
San Matías, Golfo, b., Arg.	C4	54
Sanmen Bay, b., China	J9	32
Sanmenxia, China	E7	31
San Miguel, El Sal.	E7	63
San Miguel, Az., U.S.	F4	80
San Miguel, N.M., U.S.	E3	108
San Miguel, co., Co., U.S.	D2	83
San Miguel, co., N.M., U.S.	B5	108
San Miguel, stm., Bol.	C3	55
San Miguel, stm., S.A.	C2	58
San Miguel, stm., Co., U.S.	C2	83
San Miguel, Golfo de, b., Pan.	F8	62
San Miguel de Allende, Mex.	m13	63
San Miguel de Tucumán, Arg.	E2	55
San Miguel Island, i., Ca., U.S.	E3	82
San Miguelito, Pan.	*F8	62
San Miguel Mountains, mts., Co., U.S.	D2	83
Sanming, China	K7	32
Sannår, Sud.	C3	47
San Narciso, Phil.	o13	34
San Narciso, Phil.	p14	34
Sannar Dam, Sud.	C3	47
San Nicolás [de los Arroyos], Arg.	A4	54
San Nicolás de los Garzas, Mex.	*B4	63
San Nicolas Island, i., Ca., U.S.	F4	82
Sanniquellie, Lib.	E3	45
Sannois, Fr.	g10	16
Sano, Japan	m18	33
Sanok, Pol.	D7	26
San Onofre, Col.	B2	60
San Pablo, Phil.	o13	34
San Pablo, Co., U.S.	*h8	82
San Pablo, Co., U.S.	D5	83
San Pablo, Bol.	C3	55
San Pablo, Punta, c., Mex.	B2	63
San Pablo Bay, b., Ca., U.S.	g8	82
San Patricio, N.M., U.S.	D4	108
San Patricio, co., Tx., U.S.	E4	120
San Patricio, Bayou, stm., La., U.S.	C2	95
San Pedrillo, Punta, c., C.R.	F6	62
San Pedro, Arg.	D3	54
San Pedro, Bol.	B3	55
San Pedro, Chile	D2	55
San Pedro, Para.	D4	55
San Pedro, N.M., U.S.	*B3	108
San Pedro, dept., Para.	D5	55
San Pedro, stm., Mex.	k11	63
San Pedro, stm., N.A.	B2	62
San Pedro, stm., Az., U.S.	E5	80
San Pedro Bay, b., Ca., U.S.	n12	82
San Pedro, Punta, c., Chile	E1	55
San Pedro de Atacama, Chile	A2	54
San Pedro [de Buena Vista], Bol.	C2	55
San Pedro de las Colonias, Mex.	B4	63
San Pedro de Lloc, Peru	B2	58
San Pedro de Macorís, Dom. Rep.	E9	64
San Pedro Mártir, Sierra, mts., Mex.	A1	63
San Pedro Peaks, mts., N.M., U.S.	A3	108
San Pedro Sula, Hond.	D3	108
San Pedro Tlaquepaque see Tlaquepaque, Mex.	m12	63
Sanpete, co., Ut., U.S.	D4	121
San Pierre, In., U.S.	B4	91
San Pitch Mountains, mts., Ut., U.S.	D4	121
Sanpoil, stm., Wa., U.S.	A7	124
Sanpoil, West Fork, stm., Wa., U.S.	A7	124
Sanquhar, Scot., U.K.	E5	13
San Quintín, Phil.	o13	34
San Quintín, Cabo, c., Mex.	A1	63
San Rafael, Arg.	A3	54
San Rafael, Ca., U.S.	D2	82
San Rafael, N.M., U.S.	B2	108
San Rafael, stm., Ut., U.S.	D5	121
San Rafael del Norte, Nic.	E7	63
San Rafael Desert, des., Ut., U.S.	E5	121
San Rafael Knob, mtn., Ut., U.S.	E5	121
San Rafael Mountains, mts., Ca., U.S.	E4	82
San Rafael Swell, plat., Ut., U.S.	E5	121
San Ramón, Peru	D2	58
San Ramon, Ca., U.S.	h9	82
San Ramón, Ur.	g9	54
San Ramón de la Nueva Orán, Arg.	A3	54
San Remo, Italy	C1	23
San Remo, N.Y., U.S.	*n15	109
San Román, Spain	D3	22
San Roque, Mar. Is.	D8	22
San Roque, Spain	D3	22
San Rosendo, Chile	D2	54
San Saba, Tx., U.S.	D3	120
San Saba, co., Tx., U.S.	D3	120
San Saba, stm., Tx., U.S.	D3	120
San Salvador, Arg.	A5	54
San Salvador, El Sal.	E7	63
San Salvador (Watling Island), i., Bah.	B6	64
San Salvador, Isla (James), i., Ec.	g5	58
San Salvador de Jujuy, Arg.	D2	55
Sansanné-Mango, Togo	D5	45
Sans Bois Mountains, mts., Ok., U.S.	B6	113
San Sebastián (part of San José), C.R.	F5	62
San Sebastián, Spain	A4	22
San Sebastián, Cabo, c., Arg.	h12	54
San Sebastián de los Reyes, Spain	o17	22
Sansepolcro, Italy	C4	23
San Severo, Italy	D5	23
San Simeon, Ca., U.S.	E3	82
San Simon, stm., Az., U.S.	E6	80
Sans Souci, S.C., U.S.	*B3	117
Santa, Peru	C2	58
Santa, Id., U.S.	B2	89
Santa, stm., Peru	C2	58
Santa Ana, Bol.	C2	55
Santa Ana, Bol.	B2	55
Santa Ana, El Sal.	E7	63
Santa Ana, Mex.	A3	63
Santa Ana, Peru	D3	58
Santa Ana, Ca., U.S.	F5	82
Santa Ana, Ven.	B5	60
Santa Ana, stm., Ca., U.S.	n13	82
Santa Ana Indian Reservation, N.M., U.S.	h7	108
Santa Ana Mountains, mts., Ca., U.S.	n13	82
Santa Ana Pueblo, N.M., U.S.	B3	108
Santa Anita (part of Mexico City), Mex.	h9	63
Santa Anna, Tx., U.S.	D3	120
Santa Bárbara, Chile	B2	54
Santa Bárbara, Hond.	C3	62
Santa Bárbara, Mex.	B3	63
Santa Barbara, co., Ca., U.S.	E3	82
Santa Barbara Channel, strt., Ca., U.S.	E3	82
Santa Bárbara d'Oeste, Braz.	m8	56
Santa Barbara Island, i., Ca., U.S.	F4	82
Santa Catalina, Arg.	D2	55
Santa Catalina, Gulf of, b., Ca., U.S.	F5	82
Santa Catalina Island, i., Ca., U.S.	F4	82
Santa Catalina Mountains, mts., Az., U.S.	E5	80
Santa Catarina, Mex.	*B4	63
Santa Catarina, state, Braz.	D2	56
Santa Catarina, Ilha de, i., Braz.	D3	56
Santa Clara, Cuba	D2	64
Santa Clara, Ca., U.S.	D2	82
Santa Clara, N.Y., U.S.	f10	109
Santa Clara, Or., U.S.	*C3	114
Santa Clara, Ut., U.S.	F2	121
Santa Clara, co., Ca., U.S.	D3	82
Santa Clara, stm., Ca., U.S.	E4	82
Santa Clara Pueblo, N.M., U.S.	*B3	108
Santa Claus, In., U.S.	H4	91
Santa Clotilde, Peru	D3	58
Santa Coloma de Farnés, Spain	B7	22
Santa Coloma [de Gramanet], Spain	B7	22
Santa Croce, Cape, c., Italy	F5	23
Santa Cruz, Arg.	E3	54
Santa Cruz, Bol.	C3	55
Santa Cruz, Braz.	C3	57
Santa Cruz, Chile	A2	54
Santa Cruz, C.R.	F4	62
Santa Cruz, N.M., U.S.	B3	108
Santa Cruz, Phil.	p13	34
Santa Cruz, Phil.	o13	34
Santa Cruz, Phil.	o12	34
Santa Cruz, N.M., U.S.	B3	108
Santa Cruz, prov., Arg.	D3	54
Santa Cruz, dept., Bol.	C3	55
Santa Cruz, co., Az., U.S.	F5	80
Santa Cruz, co., Ca., U.S.	D2	82
Santa Cruz, stm., Arg.	E3	54
Santa Cruz, stm., Az., U.S.	E4	80
Santa Cruz, Isla (Indefatigable Island), i., Ec.	g5	58
Santa Cruz de la Palma, Spain	m13	22
Santa Cruz del Quiché, Guat.	C2	62
Santa Cruz del Sur, Cuba	D5	64
Santa Cruz de Tenerife, Spain	m13	22
Santa Cruz do Rio Pardo, Braz.	C3	56
Santa Cruz do Sul, Braz.	D2	56
Santa Cruz Island, i., Ca., U.S.	F4	82
Santa Cruz Islands, is., Sol. Is.	G10	6
Santa Cruz Mountains, mts., Jam.	F13	65
Santa Elena, Ec.	A2	58
Santa Elena, Tx., U.S.	F3	120
Santa Elena, Bahía de, b., Ec.	A2	58
Santa Elena, Cabo, c., C.R.	E7	63
Santa Elena, Punta, c., Ec.	B1	58
Santa Elena de Uairén, Ven.	C5	60
Santa Eugenia, Spain	A1	22
Santa Eulalia del Río, Spain	C6	22
Santa Fe, Arg.	A4	54
Santa Fé, Spain	D3	22
Santa Fe (part of Mexico City), Mex.	h9	63
Santa Fe, Pan.	F7	63
Santa Fe, N.M., U.S.	B4	108
Santa Fe, Oh., U.S.	B1	112
Santa Fe, Tn., U.S.	B4	119
Santa Fe, Tx., U.S.	r14	120
Santa Fe, prov., Arg.	A4	54
Santa Fe, co., N.M., U.S.	h8	108
Santa Fe, stm., Fl., U.S.	C4	86
Santa Fe Baldy, mtn., N.M., U.S.	B4	108
Santa Fe Springs, Ca., U.S.	*n12	82
Santa Filomena, Braz.	E6	57
Santai, China	E6	31
Santa Inés, Isla, i., Chile	h11	54
Santa Inés Ahuatempan, Mex.	n14	63
Santa Isabel, Arg.	B3	54
Santa Isabel, P.R.	C3	65
Santa Isabel, Pico de, mtn., Eq. Gui.	*E1	46
Santa Isabel de Sihuas, Peru	D3	58
Santa Isabel do Rio Negro, Braz.	C2	59
Santa Isabel see Malabo, Eq. Gui.	E1	46
Santa Lucía, Cuba	D6	64
Santa Lucía, Ur.	E1	56
Santa Lucia, Ur.	g8	54
Santa Lucia Range, mts., Ca., U.S.	E3	82
Santa Magdalena, Isla, i., Mex.	C2	63
Santa Margarita, Isla, i., Mex.	C2	63
Santa María, Braz.	D2	56
Santa María, Mex.	B3	63
Santa María, stm., Mex.	m14	63
Santa María, i., Port.	h9	44
Santa María, Isla, i., Ec.	g5	58
Santa Maria [Capua Vetere], Italy	D5	23
Santa Maria, Az., U.S.	C3	80
Santa Maria, Ca., U.S.	E3	82
Santa Marta, Spain	C2	22
Santa Marta Grande, Cabo de, c., Braz.	D3	56
Santa Monica, Ca., U.S.	m12	82
Santana, Az., U.S.	m9	80
Santana, Braz.	D2	57
Santana, Braz.	h12	57
Santana, Coxilha de, hills, S.A.	E2	56
Santana do Cariri, Braz.	C3	57
Santana do Ipanema, Braz.	C3	57
Santana do Livramento, Braz.	E1	56
Santander, Col.	C2	60
Santander, Spain	A4	22
Santander, dept., Col.	B3	60
Santander Jiménez, Mex.	C5	63
Sant'Angelo Romano, Italy	g9	23
Santanilla, Islas, is., Hond.	B6	62
Santanoni Peak, mtn., N.Y., U.S.	A6	109
Sant'Antioco, i., Italy	E2	23
Santañy, Spain	C7	22
Santa Paula, Ca., U.S.	E4	82
Santaquin, Ut., U.S.	D4	121
Santa Quitéria, Braz.	B2	57
Santarém, Braz.	C4	59
Santarém, Port.	C1	22
Santa Rita, Braz.	C4	57
Santa Rita, Guam	M9	52
Santa Rita, Mt., U.S.	B4	103
Santa Rita, Ven.	A3	60
Santa Rita do Weil, Braz.	B4	58
Santa Rita Park, Ca., U.S.	D3	82
Santa Rosa, Arg.	A3	54
Santa Rosa, Arg.	B4	54
Santa Rosa, Arg.	A3	54
Santa Rosa, Bol.	B2	55
Santa Rosa, Braz.	D2	56
Santa Rosa, Ec.	A2	58
Santa Rosa, Ec.	B2	58
Santa Rosa, Ca., U.S.	C2	82
Santa Rosa, Mo., U.S.	B3	102
Santa Rosa, N.M., U.S.	C5	108
Santa Rosa, co., Fl., U.S.	u14	86
Santa Rosa, Mount, hill, Guam	L10	52
Santa Rosa Beach, Fl., U.S.	u15	86
Santa Rosa de Aguán, Hond.	C5	62
Santa Rosa de Copán, Hond.	C3	62
Santa Rosa de Osos, Col.	B2	60
Santa Rosa [de Río Primero], Arg.	A4	54
Santa Rosa Island, i., Ca., U.S.	F3	82
Santa Rosa Island, i., Fl., U.S.	u14	86
Santa Rosalía, Mex.	C3	63
Santa Rosa Range, mts., Nv., U.S.	B4	105
Santa Teresa Gallura, Italy	D2	23
Santa Ursúla Coapa (part of Mexico City), Mex.	h9	63
Santa Venetia, Ca., U.S.	*D2	82
Santa Vittoria do Palmar, Braz.	E2	56
Santa Ynez, Ca., U.S.	E3	82
Santee, Ca., U.S.	o16	82
Santee, Ne., U.S.	B8	104
Santee, stm., S.C., U.S.	E8	117
Santee Dam, S.C., U.S.	E7	117
Santee Indian Reservation, Ne., U.S.	B8	104
Sant'Eufemia, Gulf of, b., Italy	E6	23
Santiago, Braz.	D2	56
Santiago, Chile	A2	54
Santiago, Mex.	C3	63
Santiago, Pan.	F7	62
Santiago, Para.	E4	55
Santiago, Phil.	n13	34
Santiago, stm., S.A.	B2	58
Santiago, Cape, c., Phil.	p13	34
Santiago [de Compostela], Spain	A1	22
Santiago de Cuba, Cuba	E6	64
Santiago de Cuba, prov., Cuba	D6	64
Santiago del Estero, Arg.	E3	55
Santiago del Estero, prov., Arg.	E3	55
Santiago de los Caballeros, Dom. Rep.	E8	64
Santiago de Machaca, Bol.	C2	55
Santiago Island, i., Phil.	n12	34
Santiago Ixcuintla, Mex.	C3	63
Santiago Papasquiaro, Mex.	B3	63
Santiago Peak, mtn., Ca., U.S.	n13	82
Santiago Reservoir, res., Ca., U.S.	n13	82
Santiam Pass, Or., U.S.	C4	114
Säntis, mtn., Switz.	B7	21
Santisteban del Puerto, Spain	C4	22
Santo Amaro, Braz.	D3	57
Santo Amaro, Ilha de, i., Braz.	m8	56
Santo Anastácio, Braz.	D2	56
Santo Antônio, Braz.	C3	57
Santo Antônio, Ponta de, c., Braz.	E3	57
Santo Antônio de Jesus, Braz.	D3	57
Santo Antônio do Içá, Braz.	D4	60
Santo Corazón, Bol.	C4	55
Santo Domingo, Dom. Rep.	E9	64
Santo Domingo, Nic.	E8	63
Santo Domingo, stm., Mex.	n15	63
Santo Domingo de la Calzada, Spain	A4	22
Santo Domingo de los Colorados, Ec.	B2	58
Santo Domingo Indian Reservation, N.M., U.S.	h8	108
Santo Domingo Pueblo, N.M., U.S.	B3	108
Santoña, Spain	A4	22
Santorini see Thíra, i., Grc.	D5	25
Santos, Braz.	m8	56
Santos Dumont, Braz.	C4	57
Santo Tomás, Nic.	E8	63
Santo Tomás, Peru	D3	58
Santo Tomás, Ven.	B5	60
Santo Tomé, Arg.	B5	54
Santuit, Ma., U.S.	*C7	98
San Valentín, Cerro, mtn., Chile	D2	54
San Vicente, El Sal.	E7	63
San Vicente, N. Mar. Is.	D7	52
San Vicente de Alcántara, Spain	C2	22
San Vicente de Cañete, Peru	D2	58
San Vicente de la Barquera, Spain	A3	22
San Vicente del Caguán, Col.	C3	60
San Vicente Reservoir, res., Ca., U.S.	o16	82
San Vito al Tagliamento, Italy	B4	23
San Xavier Indian Reservation, Az., U.S.	E4	80

Name	Map Ref.	Page
San Ygnacio, Tx., U.S.	F3	120
San Ysidro, N.M., U.S.	B3	108
Sanza Pombo, Ang.	C2	48
Sanzhan, China	B3	33
São Bento do Sul, Braz.	D3	56
São Bento do Una, Braz.	k5	57
São Bernardo do Campo, Braz.	C3	56
São Borja, Braz.	D1	56
São Carlos, Braz.	C3	56
São Cristóvão, Braz.	D3	57
São Domingos, Braz.	A3	56
São Félix do Araguaia, Braz.	E4	59
São Félix do Xingu, Braz.	D4	59
São Fidélis, Braz.	C4	56
São Francisco, Braz.	B4	56
São Francisco, stm., Braz.	C3	57
São Francisco do Sul, Braz.	D3	56
São Gabriel, Braz.	E2	56
São Gabriel da Cachoeira, Braz.	D4	60
São Gotardo, Braz.	B3	56
Sao Hill, Tan.	C6	48
São Jerônimo, Braz.	E2	56
São Jerônimo, Serra de, plat., Braz.	B2	56
São João da Barra, Braz.	C4	56
São João da Boa Vista, Braz.	C3	56
São João da Ponte, Braz.	B4	56
São João das Lampas, Port.	f9	22
São João del Rei, Braz.	C4	56
São João do Cariri, Braz.	h5	57
São João do Piauí, Braz.	C2	57
São João Nepomuceno, Braz.	C4	56
São Joaquim, Braz.	D3	56
São Joaquim National Park, Braz.	D2	56
São Jorge, i., Port.	g8	44
São José de Mipibu, Braz.	h6	57
São José do Barreiro, Braz.	h5	56
São José do Rio Pardo, Braz.	k8	56
São José do Rio Preto, Braz.	C3	56
São José dos Campos, Braz.	C3	56
São José dos Pinhais, Braz.	D3	56
São Leopoldo, Braz.	D2	56
São Lourenço, Braz.	C3	56
São Lourenço, stm., Braz.	B1	56
São Lourenço do Sul, Braz.	E2	56
São Luís, Braz.	B2	57
São Luís de Quitunde, Braz.	k6	57
São Luís Gonzaga, Braz.	D2	56
São Manuel, Braz.	C3	56
São Manuel, stm., Braz.	D3	59
São Mateus, Braz.	E3	57
São Miguel, i., Port.	h9	44
São Miguel Arcanjo, Braz.	m7	56
São Miguel dos Campos, Braz.	k5	57
Saona, Isla, i., Dom. Rep.	E9	64
Saône, stm., Fr.	D6	16
São Paulo, Braz.	C3	56
São Paulo, state, Braz.	C3	56
São Paulo de Olivença, Braz.	D4	60
São Pedro, Braz.	m8	56
São Pedro do Piauí, Braz.	C2	57
São Raimundo Nonato, Braz.	C2	57
São Romão, Braz.	B3	56
São Roque, Braz.	m8	56
São Roque, Cabo de, c., Braz.	C3	57
Saorre, Mount, mtn., N.W. Ter.	D16	66
São Sebastião, Ilha de, i., Braz.	C3	56
São Sebastião, Ponta, c., Moz.	B6	49
São Sebastião do Caí, Braz.	D2	56
São Sebastião do Paraíso, Braz.	C3	56
São Sepé, Braz.	E2	56
São Simão, Braz.	C3	56
São Tomé, S. Tom./P.	E1	46
São Tomé, i., S. Tom./P.	E1	46
São Tomé, Cabo de, c., Braz.	C4	56
São Tomé, Pico de, mtn., S. Tom./P.	*E1	46
Sao Tome and Principe, ctry., Afr.	E1	46
Saoura, Oued, val., Alg.	D4	44
São Vicente, Braz.	C3	56
São Vicente, Port.	h11	22
São Vicente do Sul, Braz.	D2	56
Sápai, Grc.	B5	25
Sapele, Nig.	E6	45
Sapello, N.M., U.S.	B4	108
Sapelo Island, i., Ga., U.S.	E5	87
Sapelo Sound, strt., Ga., U.S.	E5	87
Sapinero, Co., U.S.	C3	83
Sapitwa, mtn., Mwi.	E6	48
Saposoa, Peru	C2	58
Sapozhok, Sov. Un.	E13	27
Sappa Creek, stm., U.S.	E5	104
Sappa Creek, Middle Fork, stm., U.S.	C2	93
Sappa Creek, South Fork, stm., Ks., U.S.	C3	93
Sappemeer (part of Hoogezand), Neth.	A6	17
Sapphire Mountains, mts., Mt., U.S.	D3	103
Sappington, Mo., U.S.	f13	102
Sapporo, Japan	C13	31
Sapri, Italy	D5	23
Sapulpa, Ok., U.S.	B5	113
Saqqârah, Eg.	E3	41
Saqqez, Iran	C3	39
Saquarema, Braz.	C4	56
Saquena, Peru	B3	58
Sarāb, Iran	C3	39
Sarābiyūm, Eg.	D4	41
Saraburi, Thai.	E4	35
Saragosa, Tx., U.S.	D1	120
Saragossa, Al., U.S.	B2	78
Saragossa, Es.	B2	58
Saraguro, Ec.	A3	101
Sarah, Ms., U.S.	A3	101
Sarajevo, Yugo.	C10	24
Sarakhs, Iran	C10	39
Saraktash, Sov. Un.	E20	8
Saraland, Al., U.S.	E1	78
Saramacca, dept., Sur.	B3	59
Saranac, Mi., U.S.	F5	99
Saranac, N.Y., U.S.	f11	109
Saranac Inn, N.Y., U.S.	F11	109
Saranac Lake, N.Y., U.S.	f10	109
Saranac Lakes, l., N.Y., U.S.	f10	109
Saranda, Alb.	C3	40
Sarandí, Braz.	D2	56
Sarandí del Yi, Ur.	E1	54
Sarangani Bay, b., Phil.	D8	34
Sārangpur, India	F6	37
Saranley, Som.	A5	47
Saransk, Sov. Un.	D7	29
Sarapuí, Braz.	m8	56
Sarapul, Sov. Un.	B4	28
Sarasota, Fl., U.S.	E4	86
Sarasota, co., Fl., U.S.	E4	86
Sarasota Bay, b., Fl., U.S.	E4	86
Sarata, Sov. Un.	B9	24
Saratoga, Ar., U.S.	D2	81
Saratoga, Ca., U.S.	k8	82
Saratoga, In., U.S.	D8	91
Saratoga, Ia., U.S.	A5	92
Saratoga, N.C., U.S.	B5	110
Saratoga, Tx., U.S.	D5	120
Saratoga, Wy., U.S.	E6	127
Saratoga, co., N.Y., U.S.	B7	109
Saratoga Lake, l., N.Y., U.S.	C7	109
Saratoga National Historical Park, N.Y., U.S.	B7	109
Saratoga Springs, Fl., U.S.	*E4	86
Saratoga Springs, N.Y., U.S.	B7	109
Saratov, Sov. Un.	D7	29
Sārāvān, Iran	H11	39
Saravan, Laos	E7	35
Sarawak, state, Malay.	E4	34
Saray, Tur.	D7	40
Sarayköy, Tur.	D7	40
Sarbāz, Iran	C6	38
Sárbogárd, Hung.	B4	24
Sarca, stm., Italy	D6	20
Sarcelles, Fr.	g10	16
Sarcoxie, Mo., U.S.	D3	102
Sārda, stm., Asia	C8	37
Sardalas, Libya	D2	43
Sardina, Col.	C4	60
Sardinia, In., U.S.	F6	91
Sardinia, Oh., U.S.	C2	112
Sardinia, i., Italy	D2	23
Sardis, B.C.	f14	69
Sardis, Al., U.S.	C2	78
Sardis, Ga., U.S.	D5	87
Sardis, Ky., U.S.	B6	94
Sardis, Ms., U.S.	A4	101
Sardis, Oh., U.S.	C5	112
Sardis, Ok., U.S.	C6	113
Sardis, Tn., U.S.	B3	119
Sardis Lake, res., Ms., U.S.	A4	101
Sarektjåkkå, mtn., Swe.	D7	14
Sar-e Pol, Afg.	C12	39
Sarepta, La., U.S.	B2	95
Sarepta, Ms., U.S.	A4	101
Sargans, Switz.	B5	20
Sargent, Mn., U.S.	G6	100
Sargent, Ne., U.S.	C6	104
Sargent, co., N.D., U.S.	C8	111
Sargents, Co., U.S.	C4	83
Sargodha, Pak.	*B5	36
Sarh (Fort-Archambault), Chad	D3	46
Sārī, Iran	C6	39
Saría, i., Grc.	E6	25
Sarıkamış, Tur.	B14	40
Sarina, Austl.	D8	50
Sarine, stm., Switz.	C3	20
Sariñena, Spain	B5	22
Sarita, Tx., U.S.	F4	120
Sariwŏn, N. Kor.	G2	33
Sark, i., Guernsey	F5	10
Sarkand, Sov. Un.	F24	8
Sarkışla, Tur.	C11	40
Sarköy, Tur.	B6	40
Sarlat, Fr.	E4	16
Sarles, N.D., U.S.	A6	111
Sarmiento, Arg.	D3	54
Sarmiento, Cerro, mtn., Chile	h11	54
Särna, Swe.	G5	14
Sarnen, Switz.	C4	20
Sarnen, Lake, l., Switz.	C4	20
Sarnia, Ont.	E2	73
Sarny, Sov. Un.	F6	27
Särö, Swe.	A5	15
Sarona, Wi., U.S.	C2	126
Saronic Gulf, b., Grc.	D4	25
Saronno, Italy	B3	23
Saronville, Ne., U.S.	D8	104
Saros, Gulf of, b., Tur.	B6	40
Sárospatak, Hung.	A5	24
Sarova, Sov. Un.	D14	27
Šar Planina, mts., Yugo.	E5	24
Sarpsborg, Nor.	p29	14
Sarpy, co., Ne., U.S.	C9	104
Sarrebourg, Fr.	F7	17
Sarreguemines, Fr.	F7	17
Sarre-Union, Fr.	F7	17
Sarria, Spain	A2	22
Sarsfield, Ont.	h13	73
Sarstedt, W. Ger.	A4	19
Sarstún, stm., N.A.	C3	62
Sartell, Mn., U.S.	E4	100
Sartène, Fr.	D2	23
Sarthe, stm., Fr.	D3	16
Sartrouville, Fr.	g9	16
Sarufutsu, Japan	D11	31
Sárvár, Hung.	B3	24
Sarvestān, Iran	G6	39
Sary-Ishikotrau Desert, des., Sov. Un.	D9	28
Sary-Ozek, Sov. Un.	E9	28
Sarysu, stm., Sov. Un.	D7	28
Sarzana, Italy	B2	23
Sasabe, Az., U.S.	F4	80
Sasaginnigak Lake, l., Man.	D4	70
Sasakwa, Ok., U.S.	C5	113
Sāsarām, India	D7	36
Sasebo, Japan	E10	31
Sashemene, Eth.	D4	47
Saskatchewan, prov., Can.	E3	75
Saskatchewan, stm., Can.	F12	66
Saskatoon, Sask.	E2	75
Sasovo, Sov. Un.	D13	27
Saspamco, Tx., U.S.	k7	120
Sassafras, stm., Md., U.S.	B5	97
Sassafras Mountain, mtn., U.S.	A2	117
Sassandra, I.C.	F3	45
Sassandra, stm., I.C.	E3	45
Sassari, Italy	D2	23
Sassenberg, W.Ger.	B3	19
Sasser, Ga., U.S.	E2	87
Sassnitz, E. Ger.	A6	18
Sasso Marconi, Italy	E7	20
Sassuolo, Italy	E6	20
Sastown, Lib.	F3	45
Sastre, Arg.	A4	54
Sasu-ri, N. Kor.	D10	33
Satah Mountain, mtn., B.C.	C5	69
Satanta, Ks., U.S.	E3	93
Sātāra, India	I4	37
Satartia, Ms., U.S.	C3	101
Sataua, W. Sam.	F11	52
Satellite Beach, Fl., U.S.	*D6	86
Satilla, stm., Ga., U.S.	E5	87
Satipo, Peru	D3	58
Satırlar, Tur.	D7	28
Satka, Sov. Un.	D8	29
Sātmāla Range, mts., India	H7	37
Satna, India	E8	37
Sátoraljaújhely, Hung.	A5	24
Sätpura Range, mts., India	D6	36
Sátrabrunn, Swe.	t34	14
Satrup, W. Ger.	D13	15
Satsop, Wa., U.S.	B2	124
Satsuma, Al., U.S.	E1	78
Satsuma, Fl., U.S.	C5	86
Sattahip, Thai.	F4	35
Sattler, Tx., U.S.	h7	120
Satu Mare, Rom.	B6	24
Satun, Thai.	I4	35
Satupa'itea, W. Sam.	F11	52
Saturna Island, i., B.C.	E6	69
Satus Creek, stm., Wa., U.S.	C5	124
Sauce, Arg.	A5	54
Sauceda Mountains, mts., Az., U.S.	E3	80
Saucier, Ms., U.S.	E4	101
Sucillo, Mex.	B3	63
Sauda, Nor.	H2	14
Saudi Arabia, ctry., Asia	C4	38
Sauêruiná, stm., Braz.	B4	56
Saufley Field Naval Air Station, mil., Fl., U.S.	u14	86
Saugatuck, Mi., U.S.	F4	99
Saugatuck, stm., Ct., U.S.	D2	84
Saugatucket, stm., R.I., U.S.	F4	116
Saugatuck Reservoir, res., Ct., U.S.	D2	84
Saugerties, N.Y., U.S.	C7	109
Saugus, Ca., U.S.	*E4	82
Saugus, Ma., U.S.	B5	98
Saugus, stm., Ma., U.S.	g11	98
Sauk, co., Wi., U.S.	E4	126
Sauk, stm., Mn., U.S.	E4	100
Sauk Centre, Mn., U.S.	E4	100
Sauk City, Wi., U.S.	E4	126
Sauk Rapids, Mn., U.S.	E4	100
Sauk Village, Il., U.S.	*m9	90
Saukville, Wi., U.S.	E6	126
Saül, Fr. Gu.	B7	59
Saulgrub, W. Ger.	H11	19
Saulnierville, N.S.	E3	71
Saulsbury, Tn., U.S.	B2	119
Saulston, N.C., U.S.	B5	110
Sault-au-Mouton, Que.	A8	74
Sault Sainte Marie, Ont.	p18	73
Sault Sainte Marie, Mi., U.S.	B6	99
Saulx [-de-Vesoul], Fr.	A1	21
Saumâtre, Étang, l., Haiti	E7	64
Saumlaki, Indon.	G8	34
Saunders, co., Ne., U.S.	C9	104
Saunderstown, R.I., U.S.	E4	116
Saunemin, Il., U.S.	C5	90
Saurimo, Ang.	C4	48
Sausalito, Ca., U.S.	D2	82
Sauveterre, Fr.	E5	16
Savá, Hond.	C4	62
Sava, stm., Yugo.	C4	24
Savage, Md., U.S.	B4	97
Savage, Mn., U.S.	*F5	100
Savage, Mt., U.S.	C12	103
Savage, stm., Md., U.S.	k12	97
Savai'i, i., W. Sam.	G11	6
Savalou, Benin	E5	45
Savanna, Il., U.S.	A3	90
Savanna, Ok., U.S.	C6	113
Savannah, Ga., U.S.	D5	87
Savannah, Mo., U.S.	B3	102
Savannah, N.Y., U.S.	B4	109
Savannah, Oh., U.S.	B3	112
Savannah, Tn., U.S.	B3	119
Savannah, stm., U.S.	F5	117
Savannah River Plant, sci., S.C., U.S.	E4	117
Savannakhet, Laos	D7	35
Savanna-la-Mar, Jam.	E4	64
Savanna-la-Mar, Jam.	B5	92
Savanur, India	E3	37
Sāveh, Iran	D5	39
Săveni, Rom.	B8	24
Saverne, Fr.	C7	16
Savery, Wy., U.S.	E2	127
Savigliano, Italy	B1	23
Savigny [-sur-Orge], Fr.	F2	17
Saville Dam, Ct., U.S.	B4	84
Savoie, dept., Fr.	D7	16
Savona, B.C.	D7	69
Savona, Italy	E3	20
Savonburg, Ks., U.S.	E8	93
Savonlinna, Fin.	G13	14
Savoonga, Ak., U.S.	C5	79
Savoy, Il., U.S.	C5	90
Savoy, Ma., U.S.	A1	98
Savran, Sov. Un.	G8	27
Sävsjö, Swe.	A8	15
Savur, Tur.	D13	40
Savusavu Bay, b., Fiji	H15	52
Savu Sea, Indon.	G6	34
Sawahlunto, Indon.	F2	34
Sawākin (part of Port Sudan), Sud.	B4	47
Sawankhalok, Thai.	B1	35
Sawatch Range, mts., Co., U.S.	B4	83
Sawdā', Jabal as, hills, Libya	D3	43
Sawel Mountain, mtn., N. Ire., U.K.	C4	11
Sawhāj, Eg.	D6	43
Sawknah, Libya	D3	43
Sawl, Eg.	E3	41
Sawmill, Az., U.S.	B6	80
Sawnee Mountain, mtn., Ga., U.S.	B2	87
Sawpit, Co., U.S.	D3	83
Sawtooth Mountains, mts., Id., U.S.	F4	89
Sawtooth National Recreation Area, Id., U.S.	E3	89
Sawtooth Ridge, mtn., Wa., U.S.	A5	124
Sawyer, Ks., U.S.	E5	93
Sawyer, Mi., U.S.	G4	99
Sawyer, Mn., U.S.	D6	100
Sawyer, N.D., U.S.	A4	111
Sawyer, Ok., U.S.	C6	113
Sawyer, co., Wi., U.S.	C2	126
Sawyerville, Que.	D6	74
Sawyers Hill, mtn., Newf.	E5	72
Sawyerville, N.C., U.S.	B3	110
Saxapahaw, N.C., U.S.	B3	110
Saxe, Va., U.S.	D4	123
Saxis, Va., U.S.	C7	123
Saxmundham, Eng., U.K.	B9	12
Saxon, W.V., U.S.	n13	125
Saxon, Wi., U.S.	B3	126
Saxonburg, Pa., U.S.	E2	115
Saxony, hist. reg., E. Ger.	C6	18
Saxony-Anhalt, hist. reg., E. Ger.	B6	19
Saxton, Ky., U.S.	D5	94
Saxton, Pa., U.S.	F5	115
Saxtons, stm., Vt., U.S.	E3	122
Saxtons River, Vt., U.S.	E3	122
Say, Niger	D5	45
Sayan, Peru	D2	58
Sayan Mountains, mts., Asia	D12	29
Saybrook, Il., U.S.	C5	90
Saybrook Manor, Ct., U.S.	D6	84
Saybrook Point, Ct., U.S.	D6	84
Saydā (Sidon), Leb.	B3	38
Şaydā, Yemen	D5	38
Sayhūt, Yemen	D5	38
Saylesville, R.I., U.S.	B4	116
Saylorsburg, Pa., U.S.	E11	115
Saylorville, Ia., U.S.	e8	92
Saylorville Lake, res., Ia., U.S.	C4	92
Sayner, Wi., U.S.	B4	126
Saynshand, Mong.	C7	31
Sayre, Al., U.S.	B3	78
Sayre, Ok., U.S.	B2	113
Sayre, Pa., U.S.	C8	115
Sayreton, Al., U.S.	B3	78
Sayreville, N.J., U.S.	C4	107
Sayula, Mex.	D4	63
Sayula, Laguna de, l., Mex.	m12	63
Say'ün, Yemen	D4	38
Sayville, N.Y., U.S.	n15	109
Sayward, B.C.	D5	69
Sazanit, i., Alb.	B2	25
Sázava, Czech.	o18	26
Sázava, stm., Czech.	D3	26
Sazliyka, stm., Bul.	D7	24
Scafell Pikes, mtn., Eng., U.K.	F5	13
Scales Mound, Il., U.S.	A3	90
Scalp Level, Pa., U.S.	F4	115
Scaly Mountain, N.C., U.S.	f9	110
Scammon, Ks., U.S.	E9	93
Scammon Bay, Ak., U.S.	C6	79
Scandia, Alta.	D4	68
Scandia, Ks., U.S.	C6	93
Scandicci, Italy	C3	23
Scandinavia, Wi., U.S.	D4	126
Scanlon, Mn., U.S.	D6	100
Scansano, Italy	C3	23
Scanterbury, Man.	D3	70
Scantic, Ct., U.S.	B5	84
Scanzano, Italy	D6	23
Scapa Flow, b., Scot., U.K.	A5	11
Scapegoat Mountain, mtn., Mt., U.S.	C3	103
Scappoose, Or., U.S.	B4	114
Scarba, i., Scot., U.K.	D3	13
Scarboro, Me., U.S.	E2	96
Scarborough, Ont.	m15	73
Scarborough, Eng., U.K.	K14	64
Scarborough, Me., U.S.	E2	96
Scarbro, W.V., U.S.	n13	125
Scariff Island, i., Ire.	F11	11
Scarriff, Ire.	E3	11
Scarsdale, N.Y., U.S.	h13	109
Scartaglin, Ire.	E2	11
Scarth, Man.	E1	70
Science Hill, Ky., U.S.	C5	94
Scarville, Ia., U.S.	A4	92
Scena, Italy	F4	23
Sceaux, Fr.	g10	16
Scenic, S.D., U.S.	D3	118
Sceptre, Sask.	G1	75
Schaal, I., Eur.	A4	19
Schaefferstown, Pa., U.S.	F9	115
Schaerbeek (Schaarbeek), Bel.	*D4	17
Schaffer, Mi., U.S.	C3	99
Schaffhausen, Switz.	A4	20
Schaffhausen, state, Switz.	B4	20
Schagen, Neth.	B4	17
Schaghticoke, N.Y., U.S.	C7	109
Schaller, Ia., U.S.	B2	92
Schangnau, Switz.	C4	21
Schärding, Aus.	E8	19
Scharnhorn, i., W. Ger.	E2	15
Schaumburg, Il., U.S.	h8	90
Schell City, Mo., U.S.	C3	102
Schell Creek Range, mts., Nv., U.S.	D7	105
Schellsburg, Pa., U.S.	F4	115
Schenectady, N.Y., U.S.	C7	109
Schenectady, co., N.Y., U.S.	C6	109
Schenefeld, W. Ger.	D3	15
Schenevus, N.Y., U.S.	C6	109
Scherer, Lake, res., Ga., U.S.	C3	87
Schererville, In., U.S.	B3	91
Scherfede, W. Ger.	B4	19
Schertz, Tx., U.S.	h7	120
Scheveningen (part of The Hague), Neth.	B4	17
Schiedam, Neth.	B6	16
Schiermonnikoog, i., Neth.	A6	17
Schifferstadt, W. Ger.	D3	19
Schilpario, Italy	C6	20
Schiltigheim, Fr.	C7	16
Schio, Italy	B3	23
Schkeuditz, E. Ger.	B7	18
Schladming, Aus.	E6	18
Schlater, Ms., U.S.	B3	101
Schlei, W. Ger.	D3	15
Schleicher, co., Tx., U.S.	D2	120
Schleiden, Sud.	C2	47
Schleiz, E. Ger.	C6	18
Schleswig, W. Ger.	A4	18
Schleswig, Ia., U.S.	B2	92
Schleswig-Holstein, state, W. Ger.	D3	15
Schleswig-Holstein, hist. reg., W. Ger.	A4	18
Schley, co., Ga., U.S.	D2	87
Schley, Va., U.S.	B5	123
Schlitz, W. Ger.	C4	19
Schloss Neuhaus, W. Ger.	B4	19
Schlüchtern, W. Ger.	C4	19
Schmalkalden, E. Ger.	C5	18
Schmallenberg, W. Ger.	B3	19
Schmelz, W. Ger.	D2	19
Schmölln, E. Ger.	C7	18
Schöneck, E. Ger.	C7	19
Schongau, W. Ger.	E5	18
Schöningen, W. Ger.	A5	19
Schoodic Lake, l., Me., U.S.	C4	96
Schoolcraft, Mi., U.S.	F5	99
Schoolcraft, co., Mi., U.S.	B4	99
Schooleys Mountain, mtn., N.J., U.S.	B3	107
Schoonhoven, Neth.	C4	17
Schopfheim, W. Ger.	B3	20
Schorndorf, W. Ger.	E4	19
Schoten, Bel.	C4	17
Schötmar, W. Ger.	A3	19
Schouten Islands, is., Indon.	F9	34
Schramberg, W. Ger.	D4	18
Schram City, Il., U.S.	D4	90
Schriever, La., U.S.	E5	95
Schrobenhausen, W. Ger.	D5	18
Schroeder, Mn., U.S.	C8	100
Schroon Lake, N.Y., U.S.	B7	109
Schroon Lake, l., N.Y., U.S.	B7	109
Schuchk, Az., U.S.	E4	80
Schuchuli, Az., U.S.	E3	80
Schulenburg, Tx., U.S.	E4	120
Schuler, Alta.	D5	68
Schulte, Ks., U.S.	g12	93
Schulter, Ok., U.S.	B6	113
Schulzpheim, Switz.	B5	21
Schurz, Nv., U.S.	E3	105
Schussen, stm., W. Ger.	E5	18
Schüttorf, W. Ger.	A2	19
Schuyler, Ne., U.S.	C8	104
Schuyler, Va., U.S.	C4	123
Schuyler, co., Il., U.S.	C3	90
Schuyler, co., Mo., U.S.	A5	102
Schuyler, co., N.Y., U.S.	C4	109
Schuyler Lake, N.Y., U.S.	C5	109
Schuylerville, N.Y., U.S.	B7	109
Schuylkill, co., Pa., U.S.	E9	115
Schuylkill, stm., Pa., U.S.	F10	115
Schuylkill Haven, Pa., U.S.	E9	115
Schwabach, W. Ger.	D5	18
Schwäbische Alb, mts., W. Ger.	D4	19
Schwäbisch Gmünd, W. Ger.	D4	19
Schwäbisch Hall, W. Ger.	D4	19
Schwabmünchen, W. Ger.	A6	20
Schwanden, Switz.	B4	20
Schwandorf, W. Ger.	D6	18
Schwaner Mountains, mts., Indon.	F4	34
Schwarmstedt, W. Ger.	F3	15
Schwarza, stm., W. Ger.	A5	21
Schwarze Elster, stm., E. Ger.	B8	19
Schwarzenbach [an der Saale], W. Ger.	C6	19
Schwarzenbek, W. Ger.	C7	19
Schwarzenberg, E. Ger.	C7	19
Schwarzenfeld, W. Ger.	D7	19
Schwarzheide, E. Ger.	B8	19
Schwaz, Aus.	E5	18
Schwedt, E. Ger.	E2	15
Schweinfurt, W. Ger.	C5	18
Schwerin, E. Ger.	B5	18
Schwerin, Lake, l., E. Ger.	B5	18
Schwetzingen, W. Ger.	D4	18
Schwyz, Switz.	E4	18
Schwyz, state, Switz.	F4	23
Sciacca, Italy	F4	23
Science Hill, Ky., U.S.	E1	70
Scilly, Isles of, is., Eng., U.K.	F3	10
Scio, Oh., U.S.	B4	112
Scio, Or., U.S.	C4	114
Scioto, co., Oh., U.S.	D3	112
Scioto, stm., Oh., U.S.	B2	112
Scioto Furnace, Oh., U.S.	D3	112
Scipio, In., U.S.	F6	91
Scipio, Ut., U.S.	E4	121
Scirentville?	D5	91
Scituate, Ma., U.S.	B6	98
Scituate Reservoir, res., R.I., U.S.	C3	116
Sciuëref, Libya	D2	43
Scobey, Mt., U.S.	B11	103
Scofield, Ut., U.S.	D4	121
Scofield Reservoir, res., Ut., U.S.	D4	121
Scollard, Alta.	D4	68
Scone, Austl.	F8	51
Scooba, Ms., U.S.	C5	101
Scopus, Mount, mtn., Isr.	m14	41
Scoresbysund, Grnld.	B17	128
Scotch Plains, N.J., U.S.	B4	107
Scotchtown, N.Y., U.S.	*D6	109
Scotia, Ca., U.S.	B1	82
Scotia, Ne., U.S.	C7	104
Scotia, N.Y., U.S.	C7	109
Scotia, S.C., U.S.	F5	117
Scotland, Ont.	D4	73
Scotland, Ar., U.S.	B3	81
Scotland, Ct., U.S.	C7	84
Scotland, In., U.S.	G4	91
Scotland, Pa., U.S.	G6	115
Scotland, S.C., U.S.	D8	118
Scotland, co., Mo., U.S.	A5	102
Scotland, co., N.C., U.S.	C3	110
Scotland, ter., U.K.	B4	10
Scotland Neck, N.C., U.S.	A5	110
Scotlandville, La., U.S.	D4	95
Scotrun, Pa., U.S.	D11	115
Scotsburn, N.S.	D7	71
Scotsguard, Sask.	H1	75
Scotstown, Que.	D6	74
Scott, Sask.	E1	75
Scott, Ar., U.S.	C3	81
Scott, La., U.S.	D3	95
Scott, Ms., U.S.	C2	101
Scott, Oh., U.S.	B1	112
Scott, co., Ar., U.S.	C1	81
Scott, co., Il., U.S.	D3	90
Scott, co., In., U.S.	G6	91
Scott, co., Ia., U.S.	C7	92
Scott, co., Ks., U.S.	D3	93
Scott, co., Ky., U.S.	B5	94
Scott, co., Mn., U.S.	F5	100
Scott, co., Mo., U.S.	D8	102
Scott, co., Tn., U.S.	C9	119
Scott, co., Va., U.S.	f9	123
Scott, sci., Ant.	B29	7
Scott, Cape, c., B.C.	B5	73
Scott, Mount, mtn., Ok., U.S.	C3	113
Scott Air Force Base, mil., Il., U.S.	E4	90
Scott City, Ks., U.S.	D3	93
Scott City, Mo., U.S.	D8	102
Scottdale, Ga., U.S.	h8	87
Scottdale, Pa., U.S.	F2	115
Scott Glacier, ice, Ant.	C23	7
Scott Glacier, ice, Ant.	A33	7
Scott Islands, is., B.C.	D3	69
Scott Lake, Fl., U.S.	*G6	86
Scott Mountain, mtn., Id., U.S.	E3	89
Scott Peak, mtn., Id., U.S.	E6	89
Scott Reef, rf., Austl.	B3	50
Scott Reservoir, res., N.C., U.S.	A1	110
Scotts, Mi., U.S.	F5	99
Scottsbluff, Ne., U.S.	C2	104
Scotts Bluff, co., Ne., U.S.	C2	104
Scotts Bluff National Monument, Ne., U.S.	C2	104
Scottsboro, Al., U.S.	A3	78
Scottsburg, In., U.S.	G6	91
Scottsburg, Or., U.S.	D3	114
Scottsburg, Va., U.S.	D4	123
Scottsdale, Az., U.S.	D4	80
Scotts Hill, N.C., U.S.	C5	110
Scotts Hill, Tn., U.S.	B3	119
Scotts Mills, Or., U.S.	B4	114
Scotts Mountain, mtn., N.J., U.S.	B2	107
Scotts Valley, Ca., U.S.	*D2	82
Scottsville, Ky., U.S.	D3	94
Scottsville, Ks., U.S.	C6	93
Scottsville, N.Y., U.S.	B3	109
Scottsville, Va., U.S.	C4	123
Scott Township, Pa., U.S.	*k13	115
Scottville, Il., U.S.	D3	90
Scottville, Mi., U.S.	E4	99
Scourie, Scot., U.K.	H3	13
Scout Lake, Sask.	H3	75
Scow Bay, Ak., U.S.	m23	79
Scraggly Lake, l., Me., U.S.	B4	96
Scranton, Ar., U.S.	B2	81
Scranton, Ia., U.S.	B3	92
Scranton, Ks., U.S.	D8	93
Scranton, Ky., U.S.	C6	94
Scranton, N.D., U.S.	D2	111
Scranton, Pa., U.S.	D10	115
Scranton, S.C., U.S.	D8	117
Screven, Ga., U.S.	E4	87
Screven, co., Ga., U.S.	D5	87
Scribner, Ne., U.S.	C9	104
Scridain, Loch, b., Scot., U.K.	D2	13
Scrivia, stm., Italy	E4	20
Scugog, Lake, l., Ont.	C6	73
Scullville, N.J., U.S.	E3	107
Scunthorpe, Eng., U.K.	D6	10
Scuol (Schuls), Switz.	E5	18
Scurry, co., Tx., U.S.	C2	120
Scutari, Lake, l., Eur.	D4	24
Scutari see Shkodra, Alb.	A2	40
Scyrene, Al., U.S.	D2	78
Scyros see Skíros, i., Grc.	C5	40
Seaboard, N.C., U.S.	A5	110
Seabreeze, De., U.S.	F5	85
Sea Bright, N.J., U.S.	*C4	107
Seabrook, Md., U.S.	C4	97
Seabrook, N.H., U.S.	E5	106
Seabrook, N.J., U.S.	E2	107
Seabrook, Tx., U.S.	r14	120
Seabrook Beach, N.H., U.S.	E5	106
Seabrook Island, i., S.C., U.S.	F7	117
Sea City, N.J., U.S.	*E7	109
Seadrift, Tx., U.S.	E4	120
Seaford, De., U.S.	F3	85
Seaford, N.Y., U.S.	*E7	109
Seaford, Va., U.S.	h15	123
Seaforth, Ont.	D3	73
Seaforth, Mn., U.S.	F3	100
Sea Girt, N.J., U.S.	C4	107
Seagoville, Tx., U.S.	n10	120
Seagram Lakes, l., Sask.	E1	75
Seagrave, Ont.	C6	73
Seagraves, Tx., U.S.	C1	120
Seagrove, N.C., U.S.	B3	110
Seaham, Eng., U.K.	F7	13
Seahouses, Eng., U.K.	E7	13
Sea Isle City, N.J., U.S.	E3	107
Seal, stm., Man.	f8	70
Seal Bay, b., Ant.	B11	7
Seal Beach, Ca., U.S.	*n12	82
Seal Cove, N.B.	E3	71
Seal Cove, Newf.	D3	72
Seal Cove, Newf.	D4	96
Seale, Al., U.S.	C4	78
Sealevel, N.C., U.S.	C6	110
Seal Harbor, Me., U.S.	D4	96
Seal Lake, l., Newf.	g9	72
Seal Point, c., P.E.I.	C5	71
Seal Rock, Or., U.S.	C2	114
Sealston, Va., U.S.	B5	123
Sealy, Tx., U.S.	E4	120
Seama, N.M., U.S.	B2	108
Seaman, Oh., U.S.	D2	112
Seaman Range, mts., Nv., U.S.	F6	105
Seanor, Pa., U.S.	F4	115
Searchlight, Nv., U.S.	H7	105
Searcy, Ar., U.S.	B4	81
Searcy, co., Ar., U.S.	B3	81
Searight, Al., U.S.	D3	78
Searing, Al., U.S.	B2	78
Searles, Al., U.S.	E5	82
Searles Lake, l., Ca., U.S.	E5	82
Sears, Mi., U.S.	E5	99
Searsboro, Ia., U.S.	C5	92
Searsburg, Vt., U.S.	F3	122
Sears Falls, wtfl., Ne., U.S.	B5	104
Searsmont, Me., U.S.	D3	96
Searsport, Me., U.S.	D4	96
Seaside, Ca., U.S.	*D3	82
Seaside, Or., U.S.	B3	114
Seaside Heights, N.J., U.S.	D4	107
Seaside Park, N.J., U.S.	D4	107
Seat Pleasant, Md., U.S.	C4	97
Seattle, Wa., U.S.	B3	124
Seattle-Tacoma International Airport, Wa., U.S.	f11	124
Sea View, Wa., U.S.	*H13	41
Seaview, Wa., U.S.	C1	124
Seaward Roads, strt., Mid. Is.	J3	52
Seba Beach, Alta.	D3	68
Sébaco, Nic.	D4	62
Sebago Lake, Me., U.S.	E2	96
Sebasco Estates, Me., U.S.	g8	96
Sebastian, Fl., U.S.	E6	86
Sebastian, co., Ar., U.S.	B1	81
Sebastian, Cape, c., Or., U.S.	E2	114
Sebastian Inlet, b., Fl., U.S.	E6	86
Sebastián Vizcaíno, Bahía, b., Mex.	B2	63

Name — Map Ref. — Page

Sebasticook Lake, l., Me., U.S. — D3 96
Sebastopol, Ca., U.S. — C2 82
Sebastopol, Ms., U.S. — C4 101
Sebatik Island, i., Asia — E5 34
Sebderat, Eth. — B4 47
Sebec, Me., U.S. — C3 96
Sebec Lake, l., Me., U.S. — C3 96
Sebeka, Mn., U.S. — D3 100
Sebewaing, Mi., U.S. — B7 99
Sebeş, Rom. — C6 24
Şebinkarahisar, Tur. — B12 40
Šebnitz, E. Ger. — C7 18
Seboeis, Me., U.S. — C4 96
Seboeis, stm., Me., U.S. — B4 96
Seboeis Lake, l., Me., U.S. — C4 96
Sebomook Lake, l., Me., U.S. — C3 96
Seboyeta, N.M., U.S. — B2 108
Sebree, Ky., U.S. — C2 94
Sebrell, Va., U.S. — D5 123
Sebring, Fl., U.S. — E5 86
Sebring, Oh., U.S. — B4 112
Sebringville, Ont. — D3 73
Secaucus, N.J., U.S. — h8 107
Secchia, stm., Italy — B3 23
Sechelt, B.C. — E6 69
Sechura, Peru — C1 58
Sechura, Bahía de, b., Peru — C1 58
Sechura, Desierto de, des., Peru — C1 58
Seclin, Fr. — D3 17
Seco, Ky., U.S. — C7 94
Second Lake, l., N.H., U.S. — f7 106
Second Mesa, Az., U.S. — B5 80
Secor, Il., U.S. — C4 90
Secretan, Sask. — G2 75
Secretary, Md., U.S. — C6 97
Secretary Island, i., N.Z. — P11 51
Secret Lake, l., R.I., U.S. — E4 116
Section, Al., U.S. — A4 78
Sector Popular (part of Mexico City), Mex. — h9 63
Security, Co., U.S. — C6 83
Sedalia, Alta. — D5 68
Sedalia, Co., U.S. — B6 83
Sedalia, In., U.S. — D4 91
Sedalia, Ky., U.S. — f9 94
Sedalia, Mo., U.S. — C4 102
Sedalia, Oh., U.S. — C2 112
Sedan, Fr. — C6 16
Sedan, Ks., U.S. — E7 93
Sedan, Mn., U.S. — E3 100
Sedan, N.M., U.S. — A6 108
Sedberg, Eng., U.K. — F6 13
Sederot, Isr. — C6 41
Sedgewick, Alta. — C5 68
Sedgewick, Mount, mtn., N.M., U.S. — B1 108
Sedgewickville, Mo., U.S. — D8 102
Sedgwick, Ar., U.S. — B5 81
Sedgwick, Co., U.S. — A8 83
Sedgwick, Ks., U.S. — E6 93
Sedgwick, Me., U.S. — D4 96
Sedgwick, co., Co., U.S. — A8 83
Sedgwick, co., Ks., U.S. — E6 93
Sédhiou, Sen. — D1 45
Sedillo Hill, N.M., U.S. — k8 108
Sedlčany, Czech. — D9 19
Sedley, Sask. — G3 75
Sedley, Va., U.S. — D6 123
Sedom, Isr. — C7 41
Sedona, Az., U.S. — C4 80
Sedot Yam, Isr. — B6 41
Sedro Woolley, Wa., U.S. — A3 124
Sedrun, Switz. — C6 21
Seebe, Alta. — D3 68
Seeber, stm., Can. — C5 70
Seebert, W.V., U.S. — C4 125
Seehausen, E. Ger. — F5 15
Seeheim, Nmb. — C2 49
Seeis, Nmb. — B2 49
Seekonk, Ma., U.S. — C5 98
Seekonk, stm., R.I., U.S. — C4 116
Seeley, Ca., U.S. — F6 82
Seeley Lake, Mt., U.S. — C3 103
Seeleys Bay, Ont. — C8 73
Seelow, E. Ger. — F8 15
Seelyville, In., U.S. — F3 91
Seelyville, Pa., U.S. — C11 115
Sées, Fr. — C4 16
Seesen, W. Ger. — B5 19
Seez, stm., Switz. — C7 21
Sefadu, S.L. — E2 45
Seferihisar, Tur. — C2 40
Sefid, stm., Iran — C4 39
Sefid Ābeh, Iran — F10 39
Segamat, Malay. — K5 35
Segbwema, S.L. — E2 45
Segesta, hist., Italy — F4 23
Segezha, Sov. Un. — F16 14
Segorbe, Spain — C5 22
Segovia, Spain — B3 22
Segozero, l., Sov. Un. — F15 14
Segré, Fr. — D3 16
Segre, stm., Eur. — B6 22
Segreganset, Ma., U.S. — C5 98
Seguam Island, i., Ak., U.S. — E5 79
Seguam Pass, strt., Ak., U.S. — E5 79
Séguédine, Niger — B7 45
Séguéla, I.C. — E3 45
Seguin, Tx., U.S. — E4 120
Seguin Falls, Ont. — B5 73
Segundo, Co., U.S. — D6 83
Segura, stm., Spain — C5 22
Sehnkwehn, Lib. — E3 45
Sehore, India — F6 37
Sehwän, Pak. — D1 37
Seibert, Co., U.S. — B8 83
Seiling, Ok., U.S. — A3 113
Seille, stm., Fr. — C6 16
Seinäjoki, Fin. — F10 14
Seine, stm., Fr. — C4 16
Seine, Bay of the, est., Fr. — C3 16
Seine-et-Marne, dept., Fr. — F3 17
Seixal, Port. — f9 22
Sejerby, Den. — C5 15
Sejerø, i., Den. — C5 15
Sejerø Bugt, b., Den. — C5 15
Sekenke, Tan. — B5 48
Seki, Japan — o15 33
Sekiu, Wa., U.S. — A1 124
Sekondi-Takoradi, Ghana — F4 45
Sekota, Eth. — C4 47
Selah, Wa., U.S. — C5 124
Selangor, state, Malay. — K4 35
Selanovtsi, Bul. — D7 24
Selaru, i., Indon. — G8 34
Selatan, Cape, c., Indon. — F4 34
Selatpanjang, Indon. — L5 35
Selawik, Ak., U.S. — B7 79
Selawik Lake, l., Ak., U.S. — B7 79
Selayar, i., Indon. — G6 34
Selb, W. Ger. — C6 18
Selbourne, Cape, c., Ant. — g40 7

Selbu, Nor. — F4 14
Selby, Eng., U.K. — A6 12
Selby, S.D., U.S. — B5 118
Selbyville, De., U.S. — G5 85
Selbyville, W.V., U.S. — C4 125
Selde, Den. — B3 15
Selden, N.Y., U.S. — *n15 109
Seldovia, Ak., U.S. — D9 79
Selenge, stm., Asia — B5 31
Selenica, Alb. — B2 25
Selenter l., W. Ger. — D4 15
Sélestat, Fr. — C7 16
Seletyteniz, Lake, l., Sov. Un. — C8 28
Sélibaby, Maur. — C2 45
Seligenstadt, W. Ger. — C3 19
Seliger, Lake, l., Sov. Un. — C9 27
Seligman, Az., U.S. — B3 80
Seligman, Mo., U.S. — E4 102
Selinsgrove, Pa., U.S. — E8 115
Selinunte, hist., Italy — F4 23
Selizharovo, Sov. Un. — C9 27
Selkirk, Man. — D3 70
Selkirk, Ont. — E5 73
Selkirk, Scot., U.K. — C5 10
Selkirk Mountains, mts., N.A. — D9 69
Selle, Pic la, mtn., Haiti — E8 64
Selleck, Wa., U.S. — B4 124
Sellers, Al., U.S. — C3 78
Sellers, S.C., U.S. — C9 117
Sellersburg, In., U.S. — H6 91
Sellersville, Pa., U.S. — F11 115
Sells, Az., U.S. — F4 80
Selm, W. Ger. — B2 19
Selma, N.S. — D6 71
Selma, Al., U.S. — C2 78
Selma, Ar., U.S. — D4 81
Selma, Ca., U.S. — D4 82
Selma, In., U.S. — D7 91
Selma, N.C., U.S. — B4 110
Selma, Ok., U.S. — E3 114
Selmer, Tn., U.S. — B3 119
Selsey, Eng., U.K. — D7 12
Selsey Bill, c., Eng., U.K. — D7 12
Selva, Arg. — E3 55
Selvagens, Ilhas, is., Port. — m14 22
Selvas, for., Braz. — D4 53
Selvin, Ky., U.S. — H3 91
Selway, stm., Id., U.S. — C3 89
Selwyn, Mount, mtn., B.C. — A6 69
Selwyn Lake, l., Can. — k8 75
Selwyn Mountains, mts., Can. — D6 66
Selz, N.D., U.S. — B6 111
Seman, Al., U.S. — C3 78
Semani, stm., Alb. — B2 25
Semans, Sask. — F3 75
Semara, W. Sah. — D2 44
Semarang, Indon. — G4 34
Semenovka, Sov. Un. — E9 27
Semeru, mtn., Indon. — G4 34
Seminary, Ms., U.S. — D4 101
Seminoe Dam, Wy., U.S. — D6 127
Seminoe Mountains, mts., Wy., U.S. — D6 127
Seminoe Reservoir, res., Wy., U.S. — D6 127
Seminole, Al., U.S. — E2 78
Seminole, Ok., U.S. — B5 113
Seminole, Tx., U.S. — C1 120
Seminole, co., Fl., U.S. — D5 86
Seminole, co., Ga., U.S. — F2 87
Seminole, co., Ok., U.S. — B5 113
Seminole, Lake, res., U.S. — F2 87
Seminole Park, Fl., U.S. — *p10 86
Semipalatinsk, Sov. Un. — D11 29
Semisopochnoi Island, i., Ak., U.S. — E3 79
Semitau, Indon. — E4 34
Semiyarskoye, Sov. Un. — C9 28
Semliki, stm., Afr. — A5 48
Semmens Lake, l., Man. — B4 70
Semmering Pass, Aus. — E7 18
Semmes, Al., U.S. — E1 78
Semnān, Iran — B5 38
Semois, stm., Eur. — C6 16
Semonov, Sov. Un. — D17 8
Semora, N.C., U.S. — A3 110
Sempach, Switz. — B5 21
Sempacher Lake, l., Switz. — B5 21
Semur-en-Auxois, Fr. — D6 16
Sen, stm., Camb. — F6 35
Sena, N.M., U.S. — B4 108
Senachwine Lake, l., Il., U.S. — B4 90
Senador Pompeu, Braz. — C3 57
Sena Madureira, Braz. — C4 58
Senanga, Zam. — E3 48
Senate, Sask. — H1 75
Senath, Mo., U.S. — E7 102
Senatobia, Ms., U.S. — A4 101
Sendai, Japan — K5 33
Sendai, Japan — D13 31
Sendai Bay, b., Japan — G10 33
Seneca, Il., U.S. — B5 90
Seneca, Ks., U.S. — C7 93
Seneca, Mo., U.S. — E3 102
Seneca, N.M., U.S. — A6 108
Seneca, Or., U.S. — C8 114
Seneca, Pa., U.S. — D2 115
Seneca, S.C., U.S. — B2 117
Seneca, S.D., U.S. — B6 118
Seneca, co., N.Y., U.S. — C4 109
Seneca, co., Oh., U.S. — A2 112
Seneca Falls, N.Y., U.S. — C4 109
Seneca Lake, l., N.Y., U.S. — C4 109
Senecaville, Oh., U.S. — C4 112
Senecaville Lake, l., Oh., U.S. — C4 112
Seneffe, Bel. — D4 17
Senegal, ctry., Afr. — D2 45
Senegal, stm., Afr. — C2 45
Senetosa, Point, c., Italy — D2 23
Seney, Mi., U.S. — B5 99
Senftenberg, E. Ger. — C6 18
Senga Hill, Zam. — C5 48
Sênggê Zangbo, stm., China — B7 36
Senhor do Bonfim, Braz. — D2 57
Senigallia, Italy — C4 23
Senj, Yugo. — C2 24
Senja, i., Nor. — C7 14
Senlac, Sask. — E1 75
Senlis, Fr. — C5 16
Senneterre, Que. — k11 74
Sens, Fr. — C5 16
Senta, Yugo. — C5 24
Sentery, Zaire — C4 48

Sentinel, Ok., U.S. — B2 113
Sentinel Butte, N.D., U.S. — C2 111
Sentinel Butte, mtn., N.D., U.S. — C2 111
Sentinel Peak, mtn., B.C. — B6 69
Sentinel Range, mts., Ant. — B4 7
Senzu, Japan — n17 33
Seo de Urgel, Spain — A6 22
Seongnam, S. Kor. — *H3 31
Seoni, India — F7 37
Seoul (Sŏul), S. Kor. — D10 31
Sepik, stm., Pap. N. Gui. — h11 50
Sępólno [Krajeńskie], Pol. — B4 26
Sept-Îles (Seven Islands), Que. — h13 74
Sepulga, stm., Al., U.S. — D3 78
Sequatchie, Tn., U.S. — D8 119
Sequatchie, co., Tn., U.S. — D8 119
Sequatchie, stm., Tn., U.S. — D8 119
Sequim, Wa., U.S. — A2 124
Sequoia National Park, Ca., U.S. — D4 82
Sequoia National Park, Ca., U.S. — D4 82
Sequoyah, co., Ok., U.S. — B7 113
Serafimovich, Sov. Un. — G14 27
Serafina, N.M., U.S. — B4 108
Seraing, Bel. — B6 16
Serang, Indon. — G3 34
Serasan, i., Indon. — k8 35
Serbia, hist. reg., Yugo. — D5 24
Serdo, Eth. — C5 47
Serdobsk, Sov. Un. — E15 27
Sered', Czech. — D4 26
Şereflikoçhisar, Tur. — C9 40
Seremban, Malay. — E2 34
Serengeti Plain, pl., Tan. — B5 48
Serenje, Zam. — D5 48
Sergeant, Pa., U.S. — C4 115
Sergeant Bluff, Ia., U.S. — B1 92
Sergeantsville, N.J., U.S. — C3 107
Sergino, Sov. Un. — C22 8
Sergipe, state, Braz. — D3 57
Seria, Bru. — E4 34
Sérifos, Grc. — D5 25
Sérifos, i., Grc. — D5 25
Serina, Italy — E8 21
Seringapatam Reef, rf., Austl. — B3 50
Serinhaém, Braz. — k6 57
Serio, stm., Italy — E8 21
Serles, Tn., U.S. — B3 119
Sermaize [-les-Bains], Fr. — F4 17
Sernyy Zavod, Sov. Un. — B9 39
Serón, Spain — D4 22
Serov, Sov. Un. — D9 29
Serowe, Bots. — B4 49
Serpa, Port. — D2 22
Serpentine Lakes, l., Austl. — E4 50
Serpents Mouth, strt. — K14 64
Serpukhov, Sov. Un. — D6 27
Serra dos Órgãos National Park, Braz. — h6 56
Sérrai, Grc. — B4 40
Serrana Bank, Col. — C7 62
Serra Negra, Braz. — m8 56
Serranilla Bank, Col. — C8 62
Serranópolis, Braz. — B2 56
Serra Talhada, Braz. — C3 57
Serres, Fr. — E1 20
Serrinha, Braz. — D3 57
Serrezuela, Arg. — A3 54
Sêrro, Braz. — B4 56
Sertã, Port. — C1 22
Sertânia, Braz. — C3 57
Sertãozinho, Braz. — k8 56
Serua, i., Indon. — G8 34
Serui, Indon. — F9 34
Serule, Bots. — B4 49
Sérvia, Grc. — B4 25
Servia, In., U.S. — C6 91
Sêrxü, China — E4 31
Sese Islands, is., Ug. — B5 48
Sesfontein, Nmb. — A1 49
Sesheke, Zam. — E3 48
Sesia, stm., Italy — B2 23
Sesser, Il., U.S. — E4 90
Sessums, Ms., U.S. — B5 101
Sesto [Fiorentino], Italy — C3 23
Seštokai, Sov. Un. — A7 26
Sesto San Giovanni, Italy — D5 20
Sestri Levante, Italy — B3 23
Sestriere, Italy — B1 23
Sestri Ponente, Italy — B3 23
Sestroretsk, Sov. Un. — A8 27
Setana, Japan — E9 33
Sète, Fr. — F5 16
Sete Guedas National Park, Braz. — C2 56
Sete Lagoas, Braz. — D2 57
Seth, W.V., U.S. — C3 125
Seto, Japan — l8 33
Seton Portage, B.C. — D6 69
Seto Sea, Japan — H6 33
Settat, Mor. — C3 44
Sette Cama, Gabon — F1 46
Settee Lake, l., Sask. — B3 75
Setting Lake, l., Man. — B2 70
Settle, Eng., U.K. — F6 13
Setúbal, Port. — C1 22
Setúbal, Bay of, b., Port. — C1 22
Seul, Lac, l., Ont. — o16 73
Seul Choix Point, c., Mi., U.S. — C5 99
Sevan, Lake, l., Sov. Un. — A5 39
Sevastopol, Sov. Un. — E6 29
Seven Devils Lake, res., Ar., U.S. — D4 81
Seven Devils Mountains, mts., Id., U.S. — D2 89
Seven Heads, c., Ire. — F3 11
Seven Hills, Oh., U.S. — h9 112
Seven Islands Bay, b., Newf. — f9 72
Seven Mile, Oh., U.S. — C1 112
Seven Mile Beach, N.J., U.S. — E3 107
Sevenoaks, Eng., U.K. — m13 11
Seven Oaks, Pa., U.S. — *C5 117
Seven Persons, Alta. — E5 68
Seven Sisters Peaks, mts., B.C. — B3 69
Seven Springs, N.C., U.S. — B5 110
Seventy Mile House, B.C. — D7 69
Severance, Co., U.S. — A6 83
Severance, Ks., U.S. — C8 93
Severance, N.H., U.S. — D4 106
Severka, stm., Sov. Un. — n18 27
Severn, Md., U.S. — B4 97
Severn, N.C., U.S. — A5 110
Severn, stm., Ont. — n17 73
Severn, stm., U.K. — D5 10
Severn, Mouth of the, mth., U.K. — C5 11
Severna Park, Md., U.S. — B4 97
Severnaya Zemlya, is., Sov. Un. — B11 29
Severn River, b., Md. — B4 97
Severočeský, prov., Czech. — C9 19
Severodonetsk, Sov. Un. — q21 27

Severodvinsk, Sov. Un. — C16 8
Severomorsk, Sov. Un. — C15 14
Severouralsk, Sov. Un. — C21 8
Severy, Ks., U.S. — E7 93
Sevier, Ut., U.S. — E3 121
Sevier, co., Ar., U.S. — D1 81
Sevier, co., Tn., U.S. — D10 119
Sevier, co., Ut., U.S. — E4 121
Sevier, stm., Ut., U.S. — D3 121
Sevier, East Fork, stm., Ut., U.S. — F3 121
Sevier Bridge Reservoir, res., Ut., U.S. — D4 121
Sevier Desert, des., Ut., U.S. — D3 121
Sevier Lake, l., Ut., U.S. — E2 121
Sevierville, Tn., U.S. — D10 119
Sevilla, Col. — C2 60
Sevilla, Spain — D3 22
Seville, Fl., U.S. — C5 86
Seville, Ga., U.S. — E3 87
Seville, Oh., U.S. — A4 112
Sevlievo, Bul. — D7 24
Sevran, Fr. — g11 16
Sèvre, stm., Fr. — D3 16
Sèvre Niortaise, stm., Fr. — D3 16
Sèvres, Fr. — g9 16
Sewanee, Tn., U.S. — D8 119
Seward, Ak., U.S. — C10 79
Seward, Ks., U.S. — D5 93
Seward, Ne., U.S. — D8 104
Seward, N.Y., U.S. — C6 109
Seward, Ok., U.S. — B4 113
Seward, Pa., U.S. — F3 115
Seward, co., Ks., U.S. — E3 93
Seward, co., Ne., U.S. — D8 104
Seward Peninsula, pen., Ak., U.S. — B7 79
Sewaren, N.J., U.S. — k7 107
Sewell, Chile — A2 54
Sewell, N.J., U.S. — D2 107
Sewen, Fr. — A2 21
Sewickley, Pa., U.S. — E1 115
Sexsmith, Alta. — B1 68
Sextonville, Wi., U.S. — E3 126
Seychelles, ctry., Afr. — G24 2
Seydişehir, Tur. — D8 40
Seydisfjördur, Ice. — n26 14
Seyhan (Sarus), stm., Tur. — C10 40
Seylac, Som. — C5 47
Seym, stm., Sov. Un. — F9 27
Seymchan, Sov. Un. — C18 29
Seymour, Austl. — H5 51
Seymour, Ct., U.S. — D3 84
Seymour, Il., U.S. — C5 90
Seymour, In., U.S. — G6 91
Seymour, Ia., U.S. — D4 92
Seymour, Mo., U.S. — D5 102
Seymour, Tn., U.S. — D10 119
Seymour, Tx., U.S. — C3 120
Seymour, Wi., U.S. — D5 126
Seymour Inlet, b., B.C. — D4 69
Seymour Johnson Air Force Base, mil., N.C., U.S. — B5 110
Seymour Lake, l., Vt., U.S. — B4 122
Seymourville, La., U.S. — h9 95
Sézanne, Fr. — C5 16
Sezimbra, Port. — C1 22
Sezze, Italy — D4 23
Sfax, Tun. — C7 44
Shaanxi, prov., China — D6 31
Shabbona, Il., U.S. — B5 90
Shabeellaha Dhexe, prov., Som. — E6 47
Shabeellaha Hoose, prov., Som. — E5 47
Shabeelle (Shebele), stm., Afr. — E5 47
Shabogamo Lake, l., Newf. — h8 72
Shabunda, Zaire — B5 48
Shabwah, Yemen — B6 47
Shache, China — F10 29
Shackelford, co., Tx., U.S. — C3 120
Shackleton, Sask. — G1 75
Shackleton Glacier, ice, Ant. — A31 7
Shackleton Ice Shelf, ice, Ant. — C23 7
Shackleton Range, mts., Ant. — A10 7
Shadehill, S.D., U.S. — B3 118
Shadehill Dam, S.D., U.S. — B3 118
Shadehill Reservoir, res., S.D., U.S. — B3 118
Shades Creek, stm., Al., U.S. — g7 78
Shades Mountain, mtn., Al., U.S. — g7 78
Shadow Mountain National Recreation Area, Co., U.S. — A4 83
Shadrinsk, Sov. Un. — B6 28
Shady Cove, Or., U.S. — E4 114
Shady Dale, Ga., U.S. — C3 87
Shady Grove, Al., U.S. — D3 78
Shady Grove, Fl., U.S. — B3 86
Shady Grove, Ky., U.S. — e10 94
Shady Grove, Pa., U.S. — G6 115
Shady Rest, Ct., U.S. — *D2 84
Shady Point, Ok., U.S. — B7 113
Shady Side, Md., U.S. — C4 97
Shadyside, Oh., U.S. — C5 112
Shady Spring, W.V., U.S. — D3 125
Shady Valley, Tn., U.S. — C12 119
Shafer, Lake, l., In., U.S. — C4 91
Shafer Butte, mtn., Id., U.S. — F2 89
Shafter, Ca., U.S. — E4 82
Shafter, Nv., U.S. — C7 105
Shafter, Tx., U.S. — p12 120
Shaftesbury, Eng., U.K. — C5 12
Shaftsbury, Vt., U.S. — E2 122
Shaftsbury Center, Vt., U.S. — *E2 122
Shagamu, Nig. — *E5 45
Shageluk, Ak., U.S. — C8 79
Shag Harbour, N.S. — F4 71
Shaguotun, China — B5 32
Shah Alam, Malay. — *K4 35
Shahbanou Farah Dam, Iran — C4 39
Shähdädkot, Pak. — D1 37
Shahdol, India — F8 37
Shähgarh, India — C4 36
Shahhāt, Libya — C4 43
Shāhī, i., Iran — C2 61
Shahjahänpur, India — D8 37
Shähpur, Pak. — C4 36
Shāhpura, India — I6 37
Shahrak, Afg. — D12 39
Shahr-e Bäbak, Iran — E5 39
Shahr-e Kord, Iran — E5 39
Shährüd, stm., Iran — B5 38
Shährüd see Emämshahr, Iran —
Shakawe, Bots. — A3 49
Shaker Heights, Oh., U.S. — A4 112
Shakhrisyabz, Sov. Un. — B13 39
Shakhty, Sov. Un. — E7 29
Shakhunya, Sov. Un. — D12 27
Shaki, Nig. — E5 45
Shakopee, Mn., U.S. — F5 100

Shakotan, Cape, c., Japan — E10 33
Shaktoolik, Ak., U.S. — C7 79
Shala, Lake, l., Eth. — D4 47
Shalath, B.C. — D6 69
Shalkar, Lake, l., Sov. Un. — C4 28
Shallmar, Md., U.S. — m12 97
Shallotte, N.C., U.S. — D4 110
Shallotte Inlet, b., N.C., U.S. — D4 110
Shallow Lake, Ont. — C3 73
Shallow Water, Ks., U.S. — D3 93
Shallowater, Tx., U.S. — C2 120
Shamattawa, Man. — B5 70
Shambat, Sud. — B3 47
Shambaugh, Ia., U.S. — D2 92
Shambe, Sud. — D3 47
Shamīl, Iran — H8 39
Shamokin, Pa., U.S. — E8 115
Shamokin Dam, Pa., U.S. — E8 115
Shamrock, Sask. — G2 75
Shamrock, Fl., U.S. — C3 86
Shamrock, Ok., U.S. — B5 113
Shamrock, Tx., U.S. — B2 120
Shamva, Zimb. — A5 49
Shandaken, N.Y., U.S. — C6 109
Shandī, Sud. — B3 47
Shandon, Ca., U.S. — E3 82
Shandon, Oh., U.S. — n12 112
Shandong, prov., China — D8 31
Shandong Bandao, pen., China — D9 31
Shangdu, China — D5 32
Shanghai, China — E9 31
Shangnan, China — H4 32
Shangqiu, China — E8 31
Shangrao, China — F8 31
Shangshui, China — E8 31
Shangsi, China — A7 35
Shangxian, China — H4 32
Shangzhi, China — D4 33
Shanhaiguan, China — C8 31
Shaniko, Or., U.S. — B6 114
Shannock, R.I., U.S. — F2 116
Shannon, Ga., U.S. — B1 87
Shannon, Il., U.S. — A4 90
Shannon, Ms., U.S. — A5 101
Shannon, co., Mo., U.S. — D6 102
Shannon, co., S.D., U.S. — D3 118
Shannon, i., Grnld. — B16 128
Shannon, stm., Ire. — D2 11
Shannon, Lake, l., Wa., U.S. — A4 124
Shannon Airport, Ire. — E3 11
Shannon City, Ia., U.S. — D3 92
Shannontown, S.C., U.S. — D7 117
Shanshan, China — C3 31
Shantar Islands, is., Sov. Un. — D16 29
Shantou (Swatow), China — G8 31
Shantung see Shandong, China —
Shantung Peninsula see Shandong Bandao, pen., China — D9 31
Shanwa, Tan. — B5 48
Shaobo, China — H8 32
Shaodong, China — G7 31
Shaoguan, China — K7 32
Shaowu, China — K3 33
Shaoxing, China — F9 31
Shaoyang, China — F7 31
Shap, Eng., U.K. — F6 13
Shapinsay, i., Scot., U.K. — A6 13
Shapio Lake, l., Newf. — g9 72
Shapki, Sov. Un. — s32 14
Shapleigh, Me., U.S. — *E2 96
Shaqqah, Bi'r ash, well, Egypt — G5 40
Sharafkhäneh, Iran — B5 38
Sharangad, Mong. — B2 32
Sharbatät, Ra's ash-, c., Oman — D5 38
Sharbot Lake, Ont. — C8 73
Sharhulsan, Mong. — E12 33
Shari, Japan — E13 33
Sharīţah, Ra's, c., Oman — H8 39
Shark Bay, b., Austl. — E1 50
Sharkey, co., Ms., U.S. — C3 101
Shark Point, c., Fl., U.S. — H5 86
Sharktooth Mountain, mtn., B.C. — E7 66
Sharm ash Shaykh, Eg. — D6 43
Sharon, Ct., U.S. — B2 84
Sharon, Ga., U.S. — C4 87
Sharon, Ks., U.S. — E5 93
Sharon, Ma., U.S. — B5 98
Sharon, N.H., U.S. — E3 106
Sharon, N.D., U.S. — B8 111
Sharon, Ok., U.S. — A2 113
Sharon, Pa., U.S. — D1 115
Sharon, S.C., U.S. — A5 117
Sharon, Tn., U.S. — A3 119
Sharon, Vt., U.S. — D4 122
Sharon, W.V., U.S. — m13 125
Sharon, Wi., U.S. — F5 126
Sharon Grove, Ky., U.S. — D2 94
Sharon Hill, Pa., U.S. — p20 115
Sharon Park, Oh., U.S. — n12 112
Sharon Springs, Ks., U.S. — D2 93
Sharon Springs, N.Y., U.S. — C6 109
Sharon Valley, Ct., U.S. — B2 84
Sharonville, Oh., U.S. — n13 112
Sharp, co., Ar., U.S. — A4 81
Sharpe, Lake, res., S.D., U.S. — C6 118
Sharpe Lake, l., Man. — B5 70
Sharples, W.V., U.S. — D3 125
Sharpley, De., U.S. — h7 85
Sharpsburg, Ia., U.S. — D3 92
Sharpsburg, Ky., U.S. — B6 94
Sharpsburg, Md., U.S. — B2 97
Sharpsburg, N.C., U.S. — B5 110
Sharpsburg, Pa., U.S. — k14 115
Sharps Chapel, Tn., U.S. — C10 119
Sharpsville, In., U.S. — D5 91
Sharpsville, Pa., U.S. — D1 115
Sharptown, Md., U.S. — C6 97
Sharptown, N.J., U.S. — D2 107
Sharya, Sov. Un. — D13 27
Shasha, China — E7 31
Shashi, stm., Afr. — B4 49
Shasta, co., Ca., U.S. — B2 82
Shasta, Mount, vol., Ca., U.S. — B2 82
Shasta Lake, res., Ca., U.S. — B2 82
Shatney Mountain, mtn., N.H., U.S. — f7 106
Shattuck, Ok., U.S. — A2 113
Shattuckville, Ma., U.S. — A2 98
Shatura, Sov. Un. — D12 27
Shaunavon, Sask. — H1 75
Shaw, Ms., U.S. — B3 101

Shaw, Or., U.S. — k12 114
Shaw Air Force Base, mil., S.C., U.S. — D7 117
Shawanaga, Ont. — B4 73
Shawangunk Mountains, mts., N.Y., U.S. — D6 109
Shawano, Wi., U.S. — D5 126
Shawano, co., Wi., U.S. — D5 126
Shawano Lake, l., Wi., U.S. — D5 126
Shawboro, N.C., U.S. — A6 110
Shawbridge, Que. — D3 74
Shawhan, Ky., U.S. — B5 94
Shawinigan, Que. — C5 74
Shawinigan Lake, B.C. — g12 69
Shawinigan-Sud, Que. — C5 74
Shawmut, Al., U.S. — C4 78
Shawmut, Mt., U.S. — D7 103
Shawnee, Co., U.S. — B5 83
Shawnee, Ga., U.S. — D5 87
Shawnee, Ks., U.S. — k16 93
Shawnee, Oh., U.S. — C3 112
Shawnee, Ok., U.S. — B5 113
Shawnee, Wy., U.S. — D7 127
Shawnee, co., Ks., U.S. — D8 93
Shawnee Hills, Oh., U.S. — B2 112
Shawneetown, Il., U.S. — F5 90
Shawsheen, stm., Ma., U.S. — f11 98
Shawsville, Md., U.S. — A4 97
Shawsville, Va., U.S. — C2 123
Shawville, Que. — B8 73
Shaxian, China — F8 31
Shayang, China — I5 32
Shay Gap, Austl. — D3 50
Shaykh Miskīn, Syria — B8 41
Shchekino, Sov. Un. — D11 27
Shchelkovo, Sov. Un. — n18 27
Shchetovo, Sov. Un. — q22 27
Shchigry, Sov. Un. — F11 27
Shchors, Sov. Un. — F9 27
Shchuchinsk, Sov. Un. — C8 28
Shchurovo, Sov. Un. — n18 27
Shebele (Shabeelle), stm., Afr. — D5 47
Sheberghän, Afg. — A4 36
Sheboygan, Wi., U.S. — E6 126
Sheboygan, co., Wi., U.S. — E6 126
Sheboygan, stm., Wi., U.S. — k10 126
Sheboygan Falls, Wi., U.S. — E6 126
Shedd, Or., U.S. — C3 114
Shedden, Ont. — E3 73
Shediac, N.B. — C5 71
Sheekh, Som. — D6 47
Sheelin, Lough, l., Ire. — D3 10
Sheenjek, stm., Ak., U.S. — B11 79
Sheep Creek, stm., Alta. — C1 68
Sheep Haven, b., Ire. — B4 11
Sheep Mountain, mtn., Az., U.S. — E1 80
Sheep Mountain, mtn., Wy., U.S. — C2 127
Sheep Mountain, mtn., Wy., U.S. — B5 127
Sheep Peak, mtn., Nv., U.S. — G6 105
Sheep Range, mts., Nv., U.S. — G6 105
Sheep's Head, c., Ire. — F2 11
Sheeps Heaven Mountain, mtn., Ma., U.S. — A1 98
Sheerness, Alta. — D5 68
Sheerness, Eng., U.K. — C8 12
Sheet Harbour, N.S. — E7 71
Shefar'am, Isr. — B7 41
Shefayim, Isr. — g10 41
Sheffield, N.Z. — O14 51
Sheffield, Eng., U.K. — D6 10
Sheffield, Al., U.S. — A2 78
Sheffield, Il., U.S. — B4 90
Sheffield, Ia., U.S. — B4 92
Sheffield, Ma., U.S. — B1 98
Sheffield, Pa., U.S. — C3 115
Sheffield, Tx., U.S. — D2 120
Sheffield, Vt., U.S. — B4 122
Sheffield Lake, Oh., U.S. — A3 112
Sheffield Lake, l., Newf. — D3 72
Shefford, co., Que. — D5 74
Sheho, Sask. — F4 75
Shehuen, stm., Arg. — D2 54
Sheila, N.B. — B5 71
Shekhüpura, Pak. — E6 39
Shelagski, Cape, c., Sov. Un. — B33 128
Shelagyote Peak, mtn., B.C. — B4 69
Shelbiana, Ky., U.S. — C7 94
Shelbina, Mo., U.S. — B5 102
Shelburn, In., U.S. — F3 91
Shelburne, N.S. — F4 71
Shelburne, Ont. — C4 73
Shelburne, Ma., U.S. — A2 98
Shelburne, Vt., U.S. — C2 122
Shelburne, co., N.S. — F4 71
Shelburne Falls, Ma., U.S. — A2 98
Shelburne Pond, l., Vt., U.S. — C2 122
Shelby, Al., U.S. — B3 78
Shelby, Ia., U.S. — C2 92
Shelby, Mi., U.S. — E4 99
Shelby, Ms., U.S. — B3 101
Shelby, Mt., U.S. — B5 103
Shelby, N.C., U.S. — B1 110
Shelby, Ne., U.S. — C8 104
Shelby, Oh., U.S. — B3 112
Shelby, co., Al., U.S. — B3 78
Shelby, co., Il., U.S. — D5 90
Shelby, co., In., U.S. — E6 91
Shelby, co., Ia., U.S. — C2 92
Shelby, co., Ky., U.S. — B4 94
Shelby, co., Mo., U.S. — B5 102
Shelby, co., Oh., U.S. — B1 112
Shelby, co., Tn., U.S. — B2 119
Shelby, co., Tx., U.S. — D5 120
Shelbyville, Il., U.S. — D5 90
Shelbyville, In., U.S. — F6 91
Shelbyville, Ky., U.S. — B4 94
Shelbyville, Mo., U.S. — B5 102
Shelbyville, Tn., U.S. — B5 119
Shelbyville, Lake, res., Il., U.S. — D5 90
Sheldahl, Ia., U.S. — e8 92
Sheldon, Il., U.S. — C6 90
Sheldon, Ia., U.S. — A2 92
Sheldon, Mo., U.S. — D3 102
Sheldon, N.D., U.S. — C8 111
Sheldon, S.C., U.S. — F6 117
Sheldon, Vt., U.S. — B3 122
Sheldon, Wi., U.S. — r14 120
Sheldon Springs, Vt., U.S. — B3 122
Shelekhov, Gulf of, b., Sov. Un. — C18 29
Shelikof Strait, strt., Ak., U.S. — D9 79
Shell, Wy., U.S. — B5 127
Shell, stm., Man. — D1 70
Shell, Loch, b., Scot., U.K. — C2 13
Shellbrook, Sask. — D2 75
Shell Creek, Tn., U.S. — C11 119

Name	Map Ref.	Page
Shell Creek, stm., U.S.	A2	83
Shell Creek, stm., Wy., U.S.	B5	127
Shelley, B.C.	C6	69
Shelley, Id., U.S.	F6	89
Shellharbour, Austl.	G8	51
Shell Lake, Sask.	D2	75
Shell Lake, Wi., U.S.	C2	126
Shell Lake, l., Mn., U.S.	D3	100
Shell Lake, l., Wi., U.S.	C2	126
Shellman, Ga., U.S.	E2	87
Shellman Bluff, Ga., U.S.	E5	87
Shellmouth, Man.	D1	70
Shellpot Creek, stm., De., U.S.	h7	85
Shell Rock, Ia., U.S.	B5	92
Shell Rock, stm., Ia., U.S.	B5	92
Shell Rock, West Fork, stm., Ia., U.S.	B5	92
Shellsburg, Ia., U.S.	B6	92
Shelly, Mn., U.S.	C2	100
Shelly Mountain, mtn., Id., U.S.	F5	89
Shelter Harbor, R.I., U.S.	G2	116
Shelter Island, N.Y., U.S.	m16	109
Shelton, Ct., U.S.	D3	84
Shelton, Ne., U.S.	D7	104
Shelton, Wa., U.S.	B2	124
Shemogue, N.B.	C5	71
Shemya Air Force Base, mil., Ak., U.S.	E2	79
Shenandoah, Ia., U.S.	D2	92
Shenandoah, Pa., U.S.	E9	115
Shenandoah, Va., U.S.	B4	123
Shenandoah, co., Va., U.S.	B4	123
Shenandoah, stm., U.S.	A5	123
Shenandoah, North Fork, stm., Va., U.S.	B4	123
Shenandoah, South Fork, stm., Va., U.S.	B4	123
Shenandoah Mountain, mtn., U.S.	B3	123
Shenandoah National Park, Va., U.S.	B4	123
Shenandoah Valley, val., U.S.	B4	123
Shenango River Lake, res., U.S.	D1	115
Shengxian, China	J9	32
Shenipsit Lake, l., Ct., U.S.	B6	84
Shenmu, China	D7	31
Shenqiu, China	H6	32
Shensi see Shaanxi, prov., China	D6	31
Shenyang, China	C9	31
Sheopur, India	E6	37
Shepard, Alta.	D4	68
Shepard Island, i., Ant.	B35	7
Shepardsville, In., U.S.	E3	91
Shepaug, stm., Ct., U.S.	C2	84
Shepaug Dam, Ct., U.S.	D2	84
Shepaug Reservoir, res., Ct., U.S.	C2	84
Shepetovka, Sov. Un.	F6	22
Shepherd, Mi., U.S.	E6	99
Shepherd, Mt., U.S.	E8	103
Shepherd, Tx., U.S.	D5	120
Shepherdstown, W.V., U.S.	B7	123
Shepherdsville, Ky., U.S.	C4	94
Sheppard Air Force Base, mil., Tx., U.S.	C3	120
Shepparton, Austl.	G8	50
Sheppey, Isle of, i., Eng., U.K.	C8	12
Sheppton, Pa., U.S.	E9	115
Shepton Mallet, Eng., U.K.	C5	12
Sheqi, China	H5	32
Sherabad, Sov. Un.	C13	39
Sherard, Ms., U.S.	A3	101
Sherborn, Ma., U.S.	h10	98
Sherborne, Eng., U.K.	D5	12
Sherbro Island, i., S.L.	E2	45
Sherbrooke, N.S.	D8	71
Sherbrooke, Que.	D6	74
Sherbrooke, co., Que.	D5	74
Sherbrooke Lake, l., N.S.	E5	71
Sherburn, Mn., U.S.	G4	100
Sherburne, N.Y., U.S.	C5	109
Sherburne, co., Mn., U.S.	E5	100
Shercock, Ire.	C5	11
Shereshevo, Sov. Un.	B8	26
Sheridan, Ar., U.S.	C3	81
Sheridan, Co., U.S.	*B6	83
Sheridan, Il., U.S.	B5	90
Sheridan, In., U.S.	D5	91
Sheridan, Ky., U.S.	e9	94
Sheridan, Me., U.S.	B4	96
Sheridan, Mi., U.S.	E5	99
Sheridan, Mo., U.S.	A3	102
Sheridan, Mt., U.S.	E4	103
Sheridan, Or., U.S.	B3	114
Sheridan, Wy., U.S.	B6	127
Sheridan, co., Ks., U.S.	C3	93
Sheridan, co., Mt., U.S.	B12	103
Sheridan, co., Ne., U.S.	B3	104
Sheridan, co., N.D., U.S.	B5	111
Sheridan, co., Wy., U.S.	B5	127
Sheridan, Mount, mtn., Wy., U.S.	B2	127
Sheridan Beach, Wa., U.S.	*B3	124
Sheridan Gardens, Wy., U.S.	*B6	127
Sheridan Lake, Co., U.S.	C8	83
Sheringham, Eng., U.K.	D7	10
Sherman, Ct., U.S.	C2	84
Sherman, Me., U.S.	C4	96
Sherman, Ms., U.S.	A5	101
Sherman, Mo., U.S.	f12	102
Sherman, N.Y., U.S.	C1	109
Sherman, S.D., U.S.	D9	118
Sherman, Tx., U.S.	C4	120
Sherman, co., Ks., U.S.	C2	93
Sherman, co., Ne., U.S.	C6	104
Sherman, co., Or., U.S.	B6	114
Sherman, co., Tx., U.S.	A2	120
Sherman Mills, Me., U.S.	C4	96
Sherman Mountain, mtn., Ar., U.S.	A2	81
Sherman Reservoir, res., Ne., U.S.	C7	104
Sherman Station, Me., U.S.	C4	96
Sherpur, Bngl.	E12	37
Sherrard, Il., U.S.	B3	90
Sherrelwood, Co., U.S.	B6	83
Sherridon, Man.	B1	70
Sherrill, Ia., U.S.	B7	92
Sherrill, N.Y., U.S.	B5	109
Sherrodsville, Oh., U.S.	B4	112
's Hertogenbosch, Neth.	B6	16
Sherwood, P.E.I.	C6	71
Sherwood, Ar., U.S.	C3	81
Sherwood, Ms., U.S.	B4	101
Sherwood, N.D., U.S.	A4	111
Sherwood, Oh., U.S.	A1	112
Sherwood, Or., U.S.	h12	114
Sherwood, Tn., U.S.	D8	119
Sherwood, Wi., U.S.	h9	126
Sherwood Manor, Ct., U.S.	A5	84
Sherwood Park, Alta.	C4	68
Sherwood Park, De., U.S.	i7	85
Shetek, Lake, l., Mn., U.S.	G3	100
Shetland Islands, is., Scot., U.K.	g10	10
Shetucket, stm., Ct., U.S.	C7	84
Shevchenko, Sov. Un.	E8	29
Shevlin, Mn., U.S.	C3	100
Shevut 'Am, Isr.	f10	41
Shewa, prov., Eth.	D4	47
Shewa Gimira, Eth.	D4	47
Shexian, China	J8	32
Sheyenne, N.D., U.S.	B6	111
Sheyenne, stm., N.D., U.S.	C8	111
Sheyenne Lake, res., N.D., U.S.	B5	111
Sheykhābād, Afg.	D14	39
Shiant Islands, is., Scot., U.K.	C2	13
Shiawassee, co., Mi., U.S.	F6	99
Shibām, Yemen	D4	38
Shibata, Japan	H9	33
Shibecha, Japan	E12	33
Shibetsu, Japan	D11	33
Shibetsu, Japan	E12	33
Shibīn al Kawm, Eg.	D3	41
Shibīn al Qanāṭir, Eg.	D3	41
Shicheng, China	K7	32
Shickley, Ne., U.S.	D8	104
Shickshinny, Pa., U.S.	D9	115
Shidao, China	F10	32
Shideler, In., U.S.	D7	91
Shiderty, stm., Sov. Un.	C8	28
Shidler, Ok., U.S.	A5	113
Shiel, Loch, l., Scot., U.K.	D3	13
Shieldaig, Scot., U.K.	C3	13
Shields, Ks., U.S.	D3	93
Shields, N.D., U.S.	C4	111
Shihezi, China	C2	31
Shijiazhuang, China	D7	31
Shikārpur, Pak.	C4	36
Shikohābād, India	D7	37
Shikoku, i., Japan	E11	33
Shiliguri, India	C8	36
Shilka, Sov. Un.	D14	29
Shilka, Sov. Un.	A8	31
Shilka, stm., Sov. Un.	D14	29
Shillington, Pa., U.S.	F10	115
Shillong, India	C9	36
Shiloh, Ga., U.S.	D2	87
Shiloh, N.J., U.S.	E2	107
Shiloh, N.C., U.S.	A6	110
Shiloh, Oh., U.S.	B3	112
Shiloh, Pa., U.S.	*G8	115
Shiloh, Tn., U.S.	B3	119
Shiloh National Military Park, Tn., U.S.	B3	119
Shimabara, Japan	J5	33
Shimada, Japan	o17	33
Shimanovsk, Sov. Un.	D15	29
Shimber Berris, mtn., Som.	C6	47
Shimen, China	F7	31
Shimizu, Japan	I9	33
Shimla, India	B6	36
Shimoda, Japan	o17	33
Shimodate, Japan	m19	33
Shimoga, India	F6	36
Shimo Island, i., Japan	J4	33
Shimonoseki, Japan	E11	33
Shimotsuma, Japan	m18	33
Shin, Loch, l., Scot., U.K.	A4	10
Shinano, stm., Japan	H9	33
Shīndand, Afg.	B3	36
Shingbwiyang, Burma	C10	36
Shinglehouse, Pa., U.S.	C5	115
Shingū, Japan	J8	33
Shinjō, Japan	G10	33
Shinkolobwe, Zaire	D4	48
Shinnston, W.V., U.S.	B4	125
Shin Pond, Me., U.S.	B4	96
Shinshiro, Japan	o16	33
Shinyanga, Tan.	B5	48
Shinyanga, prov., Tan.	B5	48
Shiocton, Wi., U.S.	D5	126
Shiogama, Japan	G10	33
Shiojiri, Japan	m16	33
Shioya, Cape, c., Japan	H10	33
Ship Bottom, N.J., U.S.	D4	107
Ship Cove, Newf.	E4	72
Ship Harbour, N.S.	E7	71
Ship Island, i., Ms., U.S.	E5	101
Ship Island Pass, strt., Ms., U.S.	g7	101
Shipka Pass, Bul.	D7	24
Shipki Pass, India	B7	37
Shipley, Eng., U.K.	G7	13
Shipman, Sask.	D3	75
Shipman, Il., U.S.	D4	90
Shipman, Va., U.S.	C4	123
Shippegan, N.B.	B5	71
Shippensburg, Pa., U.S.	F6	115
Shippenville, Pa., U.S.	D2	115
Shiprock, N.M., U.S.	A1	108
Ship Rock, mtn., N.M., U.S.	A1	108
Shipshewana, In., U.S.	A6	91
Shipyard, Belize	D7	63
Shiquan, China	E6	31
Shirane, Mount, mtn., Japan	F7	33
Shirase Glacier, ice, Ant.	B16	7
Shīrāz, Iran	C5	38
Shirbīn, Eg.	C3	41
Shire, stm., Afr.	E5	48
Shiretoko, Cape, c., Japan	D12	33
Shiribetsu, Mount, mtn., Japan	E10	33
Shiriya, Cape, c., Japan	F10	33
Shīr Kūh, mtn., Iran	F7	39
Shirley, In., U.S.	E6	91
Shirley, Ma., U.S.	A4	98
Shirley, N.Y., U.S.	*n16	109
Shirley, W.V., U.S.	k9	125
Shirley Basin, Wy., U.S.	D6	127
Shirley Center, Ma., U.S.	A4	98
Shirley Mills, Me., U.S.	C3	96
Shirley Mountains, mts., Wy., U.S.	D6	127
Shirleysburg, Pa., U.S.	F6	115
Shiroishi, Japan	H10	33
Shirotori, Japan	n15	33
Shirvān, Iran	C8	39
Shishaldin Volcano, vol., Ak., U.S.	E7	79
Shishmaref, Ak., U.S.	B6	79
Shishou, China	J5	32
Shitara, Japan	n16	33
Shively, Ky., U.S.	B4	94
Shivpuri, India	E6	37
Shivwits, Ut., U.S.	F2	121
Shivwits Plateau, plat., Az., U.S.	A2	80
Shiyan, China	*E7	31
Shizuishan, China	D6	31
Shizuoka, Japan	E12	31
Shkhara, Mount, mtn., Sov. Un.	*E7	29
Shkodra (Scutari), Alb.	A2	40
Shkotovo, Sov. Un.	E6	33
Shoal, stm., Man.	C1	70
Shoal Creek, stm., U.S.	B4	119
Shoal Harbour, Newf.	D4	72
Shoal Lake, Man.	D1	70
Shoal Lake, l., Can.	C8	75
Shoals, In., U.S.	G4	91
Shoals, Isles of, is., Me., U.S.	E2	96
Shoalwater, Cape, c., Wa., U.S.	C1	124
Shobonier, Il., U.S.	E4	90
Shoe Cove, Newf.	D4	72
Shoemakersville, Pa., U.S.	F10	115
Sholes, Ne., U.S.	B8	104
Shomolu, Nig.	*E5	45
Shongaloo, La., U.S.	B2	95
Shongopovi, Az., U.S.	B5	80
Shonkin, Mt., U.S.	C6	103
Shonto, Az., U.S.	A5	80
Shooting Creek, N.C., U.S.	f9	110
Shop Springs, Tn., U.S.	A5	119
Shoreacres, B.C.	E9	69
Shore Acres, Ma., U.S.	h13	98
Shore Acres, N.J., U.S.	C4	107
Shore Acres, R.I., U.S.	E4	116
Shoreham, Mi., U.S.	F4	99
Shoreham, Vt., U.S.	D2	122
Shoreview, Mn., U.S.	m12	100
Shorewood, Il., U.S.	k8	90
Shorewood, Wi., U.S.	n11	126
Shorewood Hills, Wi., U.S.	*E4	126
Short Beach, Ct., U.S.	D4	84
Shorter, Al., U.S.	C4	78
Shorterville, Al., U.S.	D4	78
Short Falls, N.H., U.S.	D4	106
Short Mountain, mtn., Tn., U.S.	D8	119
Shortsville, N.Y., U.S.	C3	109
Shoshone, Ca., U.S.	E5	82
Shoshone, Id., U.S.	G4	89
Shoshone, co., Id., U.S.	B2	89
Shoshone, stm., Wy., U.S.	B4	127
Shoshone, North Fork, stm., Wy., U.S.	B3	127
Shoshone, South Fork, stm., Wy., U.S.	B3	127
Shoshone Falls, wtfl., Id., U.S.	G4	89
Shoshone Lake, l., Wy., U.S.	B2	127
Shoshone Mountains, mts., Nv., U.S.	E4	105
Shoshone Peak, mtn., Nv., U.S.	G5	105
Shoshone Range, mts., Nv., U.S.	C5	105
Shoshong, Bots.	B4	49
Shoshoni, Wy., U.S.	C4	127
Shostka, Sov. Un.	F9	22
Shouldice, Alta.	D4	68
Shouns, Tn., U.S.	C12	119
Shoup, Id., U.S.	D4	89
Showell, Md., U.S.	D7	97
Show Low, Az., U.S.	C5	80
Shpola, Sov. Un.	G8	27
Shreve, Oh., U.S.	B3	112
Shreveport, La., U.S.	B2	95
Shrewsbury, Eng., U.K.	D5	10
Shrewsbury, Ma., U.S.	B4	98
Shrewsbury, Mo., U.S.	*f13	102
Shrewsbury, N.J., U.S.	C4	107
Shrewsbury, Pa., U.S.	G8	115
Shrīrangapattana, India	F6	36
Shropshire (Salop) co., Eng., U.K.	B5	12
Shrule, Ire.	D2	11
Shuangcheng, China	B10	31
Shuangjiang, China	G6	31
Shuangliao, China	C9	31
Shuangshan, China	C10	32
Shuangyang, China	C11	32
Shuangyashan, China	B11	31
Shubenacadie, N.S.	D6	71
Shubenacadie Lake, l., N.S.	E6	71
Shubert, Ne., U.S.	D10	104
Shubrā al Khaymah, Eg.	C6	43
Shubrā Khīt, Eg.	C2	41
Shubuta, Ms., U.S.	D5	101
Shucheng, China	I7	32
Shueib Dam, Jord.	h13	41
Shu'fāṭ, Isr. Occ.	h11	41
Shujāābād, Pak.	C3	37
Shuksan, Mount, mtn., Wa., U.S.	A4	124
Shulan, China	D3	33
Shulaps Peak, mtn., B.C.	D6	69
Shule He, stm., China	D5	31
Shulerville, S.C., U.S.	E8	117
Shullsburg, Wi., U.S.	F3	126
Shumagin Islands, is., Ak., U.S.	E7	79
Shumaykh, Libya	C3	43
Shumen, Bul.	D8	24
Shumerlya, Sov. Un.	D16	27
Shumikha, Sov. Un.	B6	28
Shumway, Il., U.S.	D5	90
Shūnat Nimrīn, Jord.	h13	41
Shunchang, China	K7	32
Shungnak, Ak., U.S.	B8	79
Shuoxian, China	H7	32
Shuozhou, China	D3	33
Shuqrah, Yemen	E4	38
Shuqualak, Ms., U.S.	C5	101
Shūr, stm., Iran	D5	39
Shūr, stm., Iran	F7	39
Shuri, Japan	O5	33
Shurugwi, Zimb.	B9	49
Shushan, N.Y., U.S.	B7	109
Shūshat al Maghārah, mtn., Eg.	D5	41
Shūshtar, Iran	B4	38
Shuswap, stm., B.C.	D8	69
Shuswap Lake, l., B.C.	D8	69
Shutesbury, Ma., U.S.	B3	98
Shuwak, Sud.	C4	47
Shuwaykah, Isr. Occ.	f11	41
Shuya, Japan	N6	52
Shuya, Sov. Un.	C13	27
Shwebo, Burma	D10	36
Shwegyin, Burma	D2	35
Siālkot, Pak.	B5	36
Siam, Gulf of see Thailand, Gulf of, b., Asia	C2	34
Siam see Thailand, ctry., Asia	B2	34
Sian see Xi'an, China	E6	31
Siantan, i., Indon.	K7	35
Siasconset, Ma., U.S.	D8	98
Siátista, Grc.	B3	25
Siau, i., Indon.	E7	34
Šiauliai, Sov. Un.	C4	27
Sibay, Sov. Un.	C5	28
Sibbald, Alta.	D5	68
Šibenik, Yugo.	D2	24
Siberia, In., U.S.	H4	91
Siberia, reg., Sov. Un.	C13	29
Sibert, Ky., U.S.	C6	94
Siʿīr, Isr. Occ.	C7	41
Sibi, Pak.	C4	36
Sibiryakov, i., Sov. Un.	B7	128
Sibiti, Congo	B1	48
Sibiu, Rom.	C7	24
Sibley, Il., U.S.	C5	90
Sibley, Ia., U.S.	A2	92
Sibley, La., U.S.	B2	95
Sibley, Ms., U.S.	D2	101
Sibley, Mo., U.S.	h11	102
Sibley, N.D., U.S.	B8	111
Sibley, co., Mn., U.S.	F4	100
Sibolga, Indon.	E1	34
Sibsāgar, India	C9	36
Sibu, Malay.	E4	34
Sibuan, mtn., Indon.	K3	35
Sibuco, Phil.	E5	34
Sibutu Island, i., Phil.	E5	34
Sibutu Passage, strt., Asia	E5	34
Sibuyan Sea, Phil.	C6	34
Sicamous, B.C.	D8	69
Si Chang, i., Thai.	F4	35
Sichomovi, Az., U.S.	B5	80
Sichuan, prov., China	E5	31
Sicily, i., Italy	F4	23
Sicily Island, La., U.S.	C4	95
Sicklerville, N.J., U.S.	D3	107
Sicuani, Peru	D3	58
Sidamo, prov., Eth.	E4	47
Sidlaw Hills, hills, Scot., U.K.	D5	13
Sidell, Il., U.S.	D6	90
Siderno Marina, Italy	E6	23
Sidheros, Ákra, c., Grc.	E6	40
Sidhirókastron, Grc.	B4	40
Sidi Barrānī, Eg.	C5	43
Sidi bel Abbès, Alg.	B4	44
Sidi Bennour, Mor.	C3	44
Sidi Ifni, Mor.	D2	44
Sidi Kacem, Mor.	*C3	44
Sidikalang, Indon.	m11	34
Sīdī Muḥammad, 'Ayn, well, Libya	H3	40
Sīdī Sālim, Eg.	C2	41
Sidi Slimane, Mor.	*C3	44
Sidley, Mount, mtn., Ant.	B36	7
Sidmouth, Eng., U.K.	D4	12
Sidnaw, Mi., U.S.	B2	99
Sidney, B.C.	E6	69
Sidney, Man.	E2	70
Sidney, Ar., U.S.	A4	81
Sidney, Il., U.S.	C5	90
Sidney, In., U.S.	B6	91
Sidney, Ia., U.S.	D2	92
Sidney, Mt., U.S.	C12	103
Sidney, Ne., U.S.	C3	104
Sidney, N.J., U.S.	B3	107
Sidney, N.Y., U.S.	C5	109
Sidney, Oh., U.S.	B1	112
Sidney, S.D., U.S.	C5	109
Sidney Center, N.Y., U.S.	C5	109
Sidney Lanier, Lake, res., Ga., U.S.	B2	87
Sidon, Ms., U.S.	B3	101
Sidon, Tn., U.S.	A3	119
Sidon see Ṣaydā, Leb.	B3	38
Sidorovka, Sov. Un.	D25	8
Sidra, Gulf of (Khalīj Surt), b., Libya	C3	43
Sidrolândia, Braz.	C2	56
Siedlce, Pol.	B7	26
Sieg, stm., W. Ger.	C3	18
Siegburg, W. Ger.	C3	18
Siegen, W. Ger.	C2	19
Siemianowice Śląskie, Pol.	g10	26
Siemiatycze, Pol.	B7	26
Siemreab, Camb.	C2	34
Siena, Italy	C3	23
Sieper, La., U.S.	C3	95
Sieradz, Pol.	C5	26
Sierentz, Fr.	A3	21
Siero, Spain	A3	22
Sierpc, Pol.	B5	26
Sierra, co., Ca., U.S.	C3	82
Sierra, co., N.M., U.S.	D2	108
Sierra Blanca, Tx., U.S.	o12	120
Sierra Blanca Peak, mtn., N.M., U.S.	D4	108
Sierra City, Ca., U.S.	C3	82
Sierra Colorada, Arg.	C3	54
Sierra Estrella, mts., Az., U.S.	m8	80
Sierra Gorda, Chile	D2	55
Sierra Leone, ctry., Afr.	E2	45
Sierra Madre, Ca., U.S.	m12	82
Sierra Mojada, Mex.	B4	63
Sierra Nevada (Simón Bolívar) National Park, Ven.	B3	60
Sierraville, Ca., U.S.	C3	82
Sierra Vista, Az., U.S.	F5	80
Sieste, Switz.	F13	21
Siesta Key, Fl., U.S.	*E4	86
Siesta Key, i., Fl., U.S.	E4	86
Siewierz, Pol.	g10	26
Sífnos, i., Grc.	D5	40
Sifton, Man.	D1	70
Sigatoka, Fiji	I14	52
Sigean, Fr.	F5	16
Sigel, Pa., U.S.	D3	115
Sighetu Marmaţiei, Rom.	B6	24
Sighişoara, Rom.	B7	24
Sighty Crag, mtn., Eng., U.K.	F5	16
Sigli, Indon.	k11	34
Siglufjörður, Ice.	m23	14
Sigmaringen, W. Ger.	D5	19
Signachi, Sov. Un.	E7	29
Signal Hill, Ca., U.S.	*n12	82
Signal Mountain, Tn., U.S.	D8	119
Signal Mountain, mtn., Tn., U.S.	C9	119
Signal Mountain, mtn., Vt., U.S.	C4	122
Signal Mountain, mtn., Va., U.S.	g11	123
Signal Peak, mtn., Az., U.S.	D1	80
Signal Peak, mtn., Ut., U.S.	F2	121
Signau, Switz.	C4	21
Signy-l'Abbaye, Fr.	E4	17
Sigourney, Ia., U.S.	C5	92
Sigsbee, Ga., U.S.	E3	87
Sigtuna, Swe.	t35	14
Siguatepeque, Hond.	C4	62
Sigüenza, Spain	B4	22
Siguiri, Gui.	D3	45
Sigurd, Ut., U.S.	E4	121
Sihabuhabu, mtn., Indon.	K3	35
Sihanoukville see Kampong Saom, Camb.	C2	34
Sihl Lake, l., Switz.	B6	21
Sihuas, Peru	C2	58
Si'īr, Isr. Occ.	C7	41
Siirt, Tur.	D13	40
Siis, i., Micron.	Q18	52
Sikasso, Mali	D3	45
Sikeston, Mo., U.S.	E8	102
Sikhote-Alin Mountains, mts., Sov. Un.	E16	29
Sikiá, Grc.	C5	40
Sikinos, i., Grc.	D5	40
Sikkim, state, India	C8	36
Siklós, Hung.	C4	24
Silandro, Italy	A3	23
Silang, Phil.	o13	34
Silao, Mex.	m13	63
Silat Az Ẓahr, Isr. Occ.	f11	41
Silchar, India	D9	36
Šile, Tur.	B7	40
Siler City, N.C., U.S.	B3	110
Silerton, Tn., U.S.	B3	119
Silesia, hist. reg., Pol.	C4	26
Silesia, Or., U.S.	C3	114
Silex, Mo., U.S.	B6	102
Silgarhi-Doti, Nepal	C8	36
Silica, Oh., U.S.	e6	112
Siling Co, l., China	D9	40
Silistra, Bul.	D8	24
Siljan, l., Swe.	G6	14
Silkeborg, Den.	B3	15
Sillery, Que.	n17	74
Silloth, Eng., U.K.	F5	13
Sil Nakaya, Az., U.S.	E4	80
Siloam, Ga., U.S.	C3	87
Siloam Springs, Ar., U.S.	A1	81
Silsbee, Tx., U.S.	D5	120
Silsby Lake, l., Man.	B4	70
Silt, Co., U.S.	B3	83
Sils im Domleschg, Switz.	D8	21
Siltcoos Lake, l., Or., U.S.	D2	114
Šilutė, Sov. Un.	A6	26
Silva, Mo., U.S.	D7	102
Silva, N.D., U.S.	A6	111
Silva Jardim, Braz.	h6	56
Silvânia, Braz.	B3	56
Silver Bay, Mn., U.S.	C7	100
Silver Bow, co., Mt., U.S.	E4	103
Silver City, Ia., U.S.	C2	92
Silver City, Ms., U.S.	B3	101
Silver City, Ne., U.S.	C3	104
Silver City, Nv., U.S.	D2	105
Silver City, N.M., U.S.	E1	108
Silver City, S.D., U.S.	C2	118
Silver Cliff, Co., U.S.	C5	83
Silver Creek, Ga., U.S.	B1	87
Silver Creek, Ms., U.S.	D3	101
Silver Creek, Ne., U.S.	C8	104
Silver Creek, N.Y., U.S.	C1	109
Silver Creek, stm., In., U.S.	H6	91
Silver Creek, stm., Ne., U.S.	g11	104
Silver Creek, stm., Or., U.S.	D7	114
Silver Fork, Ut., U.S.	*C4	121
Silver Gate, Mt., U.S.	E7	103
Silver Grove, Ky., U.S.	h14	94
Silverhill, Al., U.S.	E2	78
Silver Hill, Md., U.S.	f9	97
Silver Island Mountains, mts., Ut., U.S.	C2	121
Silver Lake, Ks., U.S.	C8	93
Silver Lake, Ma., U.S.	f11	98
Silver Lake, Mn., U.S.	F4	100
Silver Lake, N.H., U.S.	C4	106
Silver Lake, Or., U.S.	D5	114
Silver Lake, Wi., U.S.	F5	126
Silverlake, Wa., U.S.	C3	124
Silver Lake, l., De., U.S.	D3	85
Silver Lake, l., Ia., U.S.	A3	92
Silver Lake, l., Me., U.S.	D2	96
Silver Lake, l., N.H., U.S.	E2	106
Silver Lake, l., Or., U.S.	D7	114
Silver Plume, Co., U.S.	*B5	83
Silver Point, Tn., U.S.	C8	119
Silver Run, Md., U.S.	A3	97
Silver Spring, Md., U.S.	C3	97
Silver Springs, Fl., U.S.	C4	86
Silver Springs, Nv., U.S.	D2	105
Silver Springs, N.Y., U.S.	C2	109
Silver Star, Mt., U.S.	E4	103
Silver Star Mountain, mtn., Wa., U.S.	A5	124
Silverstreet, S.C., U.S.	C4	117
Silverthrone Mountain, mtn., B.C.	D4	69
Silvertip Mountain, mtn., Mt., U.S.	C3	103
Silverton, B.C.	E9	69
Silverton, Co., U.S.	D3	83
Silverton, Oh., U.S.	o13	112
Silverton, Tx., U.S.	B2	120
Silverville, In., U.S.	G4	91
Silvia, Col.	C2	60
Silvies, stm., Or., U.S.	D7	114
Silview, De., U.S.	B3	85
Silwān (part of Jerusalem), Isr. Occ.	h11	41
Simanggang, Malay.	E4	34
Simao, China	G5	31
Simav, Tur.	B7	40
Simav, stm., Tur.	B3	40
Simcoe, Ont.	E4	73
Simcoe, co., Ont.	C4	73
Simcoe, Lake, l., Ont.	C5	73
Simdega, India	F10	37
Simeulue, i., Indon.	m11	34
Simferopol, Sov. Un.	E6	29
Sími, i., Grc.	D6	40
Simi, i., Grc.	D6	40
Similan Islands, is., Thai.	H2	35
Similkameen, stm., N.A.	E7	69
Simití, Col.	B3	60
Simi Valley, Ca., U.S.	E4	82
Simla, Co., U.S.	B6	83
Şimleu Silvaniei, Rom.	B6	24
Simme, stm., Switz.	C3	21
Simmern, W. Ger.	C2	19
Simmesport, La., U.S.	D4	95
Simmie, Sask.	H1	75
Simmons, Mo., U.S.	D5	102
Simms, Mt., U.S.	C5	103
Simms Point, c., Bah.	m16	64
Simms Stream, stm., N.H., U.S.	g7	106
Simonette, stm., Alta.	B1	68
Simonhouse Lake, l., Man.	B1	70
Simonstorp (part of Norrköping), Swe.	u34	14
Simonstown (Simonstad), S. Afr.	D2	49
Simonsville, Vt., U.S.	E3	122
Simoom Sound, B.C.	D4	69
Simpang-kiri, stm., Indon.	K2	35
Simplicio Mendes, Braz.	C2	57
Simplon Pass, Switz.	C4	20
Simplon Tunnel, Eur.	A2	23
Simpson, Sask.	F3	75
Simpson, Il., U.S.	F5	90
Simpson, Ks., U.S.	C6	93
Simpson, La., U.S.	C3	95
Simpson, Mn., U.S.	G6	100
Simpson, N.C., U.S.	B5	110
Simpson, Ok., U.S.	C5	113
Simpson, Pa., U.S.	C11	115
Simpson, W.V., U.S.	k10	125
Simpson, co., Ky., U.S.	D3	94
Simpson, co., Ms., U.S.	D3	101
Simpson Creek, stm., W.V., U.S.	k10	125
Simpson Desert, des., Austl.	E6	50
Simpson Peninsula, pen., N.W. Ter.	C15	66
Simpsonville, Ky., U.S.	B4	94
Simpsonville, S.C., U.S.	B3	117
Simrishamn, Swe.	J6	14
Sims, Ar., U.S.	C2	81
Sims, Il., U.S.	E5	90
Sims, In., U.S.	D5	91
Sims, N.C., U.S.	B4	110
Simsboro, La., U.S.	B3	95
Simsbury, Ct., U.S.	B4	84
Sims Chapel, Al., U.S.	D1	78
Simson, Sask.	G3	75
Simunjan, Malay.	E4	34
Sinabang, Indon.	K2	35
Sinai, S.D., U.S.	C8	118
Sinaia, Rom.	C7	24
Sinai Peninsula, pen., Eg.	C3	43
Sinajana, Guam	L10	52
Sinaloa, state, Mex.	B3	63
Sinaloa [de Leyva], Mex.	B3	63
Sinan, China	F6	31
Sīnārū, Eg.	E2	41
Sīnāwan, Libya	C2	43
Sincan, Tur.	*C9	40
Sinçé, Col.	B2	60
Sincelejo, Col.	B2	60
Sinclair, Man.	E1	70
Sinclair, Me., U.S.	A4	96
Sinclair, Wy., U.S.	E5	127
Sinclair, Lake, res., Ga., U.S.	C3	87
Sinclair's Bay, b., Scot., U.K.	B5	13
Sinclairville, N.Y., U.S.	C1	109
Sind, prov., Pak.	C4	36
Sind, stm., India	D7	37
Sindal, Den.	A4	15
Sindara, Gabon	F2	46
Sindelfingen, W. Ger.	E3	19
Sindirgi, Tur.	C7	40
Sinelnikovo, Sov. Un.	G10	27
Sines, Port.	D1	22
Sinfra, I.C.	E3	45
Singapore, Sing.	E2	34
Singapore, ctry., Asia	E2	34
Singapore Strait, strt., Asia	L5	35
Singaraja, Indon.	G5	34
Singen (Hohentwiel), W. Ger.	B4	20
Singer, La., U.S.	D2	95
Singhampton, Ont.	C4	73
Singida, Tan.	B5	48
Singida, prov., Tan.	B5	48
Singitic Gulf, b., Grc.	B4	25
Singkang, Indon.	F6	34
Singkep, i., Indon.	F2	34
Singkil, Indon.	E1	34
Singleton, Austl.	F8	51
Sinhung, N. Kor.	D12	33
Siniscola, Italy	D2	23
Sinj, Yugo.	D2	24
Sinjah, Sud.	C3	47
Sinjil, Isr. Occ.	g12	41
Sinkāt, Sud.	B4	47
Sinkiang see Xinjiang Uygur, prov., China	C2	31
Sinking Creek, stm., Ky., U.S.	C2	94
Sinking Spring, Oh., U.S.	C2	112
Sinks Grove, W.V., U.S.	D4	125
Sinnamahoning, Pa., U.S.	D5	115
Sinnamary, Fr. Gu.	A4	59
Sinnemahoning Creek, stm., Pa., U.S.	D5	115
Sinnemahoning Creek, First Fork, stm., Pa., U.S.	D5	115
Sînnicolau Mare, Rom.	B5	24
Sinnūris, Eg.	E2	41
Sinop, Tur.	A10	40
Sinpo, N. Kor.	F4	33
Sintaluta, Sask.	G4	75
Sint-Amandsberg (part of Gent), Bel.	C3	17
Sintang, Indon.	E4	34
Sint Christoffelberg, hill, Neth. Ant.	H18	64
Sint Eustatius, i., Neth. Ant.	H13	64
Sint Helenabaai, b., S. Afr.	D2	49
Sint Jacobiparochie, Neth.	A5	17
Sint Kruis, Neth. Ant.	H18	64
Sint-Lenaarts, Bel.	C4	17
Sint Marie, Kaap, c., Neth. Ant.	H18	64
Sint Nicolaas, Neth. Ant.	H17	64
Sint-Niklaas (Saint-Nicolas), Bel.	B6	16
Sinton, Tx., U.S.	E4	120
Sintra, Port.	f9	22
Sint-Truiden, Bel.	D5	17
Sinú, stm., Col.	B2	60
Sinúju, N. Kor.	C12	33
Sinyavino, Sov. Un.	s32	14
Sinzig, W. Ger.	C3	18
Sion, Switz.	E3	18
Sioux, co., Ia., U.S.	A1	92
Sioux, co., Ne., U.S.	B2	104
Sioux, co., N.D., U.S.	C4	111
Sioux Center, Ia., U.S.	A1	92
Sioux City, Ia., U.S.	B1	92

Name	Map Ref.	Page
Sioux Falls, S.D., U.S.	D9	118
Sioux Lookout, Ont.	o17	73
Sioux Rapids, Ia., U.S.	B2	92
Sipanok Channel, mth., Sask.	D4	75
Siparia, Trin.	O22	65
Siping, China	C9	31
Sipiwesk Lake, l., Man.	B3	70
Siple, sci., Ant.	B4	7
Siple, Mount, mtn., Ant.	B36	7
Siple Coast, Ant.	A33	7
Sipsey, Al., U.S.	B2	78
Sipsey, stm., Al., U.S.	B2	78
Sipsey Fork, stm., Al., U.S.	A2	78
Sipura, i., Indon.	F1	34
Siquirres, C.R.	E6	62
Siquisique, Ven.	A4	60
Şīr Abū Nu'Ayr, i., U.A.E.	I7	39
Siracusa (Syracuse), Italy	F5	23
Sirājganj, Bngl.	D8	36
Sir Alexander, Mount, mtn., B.C.	C7	69
Sirdar, B.C.	E9	69
Sir Douglas, Mount, mtn., Can.	D3	68
Sir Edward Pellew Group, is., Austl.	C6	50
Siren, Wi., U.S.	C1	126
Siret, Rom.	B8	24
Siret, stm., Eur.	B8	24
Sirhān, Wādī as, val., Asia	C7	43
Sirik, Cape, c., Malay.	E4	34
Sirina, i., Grc.	D6	25
Sir James MacBrien, Mount, mtn., N.W. Ter.	D7	66
Sīrjān, Iran	G7	39
Sirmans, Fl., U.S.	B3	86
Sirmione, Italy	D6	20
Sironj, India	E6	37
Síros, i., Grc.	D5	25
Sirpur, India	H7	37
Sirr, Mushāsh as, well, Eg.	D5	41
Sīrrī, i., Iran	I7	39
Sirsa, India	C6	36
Sir Sandford, Mount, mtn., B.C.	D9	69
Širvintos, Sov. Un.	A8	26
Sir-Wilfrid, Mont, mtn., Que.	C2	74
Sir Wilfrid Laurier, Mount, mtn., B.C.	C8	69
Sisak, Yugo.	C3	24
Si Sa Ket, Thai.	B2	34
Sishui, China	G7	32
Sisib Lake, l., Man.	C2	70
Siskiyou, co., Ca., U.S.	B2	82
Siskiyou Mountains, mts., U.S.	F3	114
Siskiyou Pass, Or., U.S.	E4	114
Sisquoc, stm., Ca., U.S.	E3	82
Sissach, Switz.	B4	21
Sisseton, S.D., U.S.	B8	118
Sisseton Indian Reservation, U.S.	B8	118
Sissiboo, stm., N.S.	E4	71
Sisson Branch Reservoir, res., N.B.	B2	71
Sissonville, W.V., U.S.	C3	125
Sisteron, Fr.	E6	16
Sisters, Or., U.S.	C5	114
Sisterdale, Tx., U.S.	E3	120
Sistersville, W.V., U.S.	B4	125
Sītāpur, India	C7	36
Sitía, Grc.	E6	40
Sítio da Abadia, Braz.	A3	56
Sitionuevo, Col.	A3	60
Sitka, Ak., U.S.	D12	79
Sitka National Historical Park, Ak., U.S.	m22	79
Sitka Sound, strt., Ak., U.S.	m22	79
Sittard, Neth.	D5	17
Sittoung, stm., Burma	E10	36
Sittwe (Akyab), Burma	D9	36
Siuna, Nic.	D5	62
Siuri, India	D8	36
Sivas, Tur.	C11	40
Siverek, Tur.	D12	40
Siwah, Eg.	C2	38
Siwalik Range, mts., India	B6	36
Six-Fours-la-Plage, Fr.	F6	16
Sixian, China	H7	32
Si see Xi Jiang, stm., China	G7	31
Six Mile, S.C., U.S.	B2	117
Sixmile Creek, stm., Fl., U.S.	n8	86
Sixmilecross, N. Ire., U.K.	C4	11
Sixt, Fr.	D2	21
Sizhan, China	B2	33
Sjælland, i., Den.	J4	14
Sjællands Odde, pen., Den.	B5	15
Sjenica, Yugo.	D5	24
Sjöbo, Swe.	C7	15
Skælskør, Den.	C5	15
Skagen, Den.	A4	15
Skagerrak, strt., Eur.	I3	14
Skagit, co., Wa., U.S.	A4	124
Skagit, stm., N.A.	A3	69
Skagway, Ak., U.S.	D12	79
Skälderviken, b., Swe.	B6	15
Skalka Reservoir, res., Czech.	C7	19
Skamania, Wa., U.S.	D3	124
Skamania, co., Wa., U.S.	D3	124
Skamokawa, Wa., U.S.	C2	124
Skanderborg, Den.	B3	15
Skaneateles, N.Y., U.S.	C4	109
Skaneateles Lake, l., N.Y., U.S.	C4	109
Skanee, Mi., U.S.	B2	99
Skånes-Fagerhult, Swe.	B7	15
Skänör, Swe.	C6	15
Skántzoura, i., Grc.	C5	25
Skara, Swe.	H5	14
Skarven, l., Swe.	t35	14
Skarzysko-Kamienna, Pol.	C6	26
Skawa, stm., Pol.	h11	26
Skawina, Pol.	D5	26
Skedee, Ok., U.S.	A5	113
Skeena, stm., B.C.	F7	66
Skeena Mountains, mts., B.C.	E7	66
Skegness, Eng., U.K.	D7	10
Skeldon, Guy.	A3	59
Skeleton Lake, l., Ont.	B5	73
Skellefteå, Swe.	E9	14
Skellefteälven, stm., Swe.	E8	14
Skellytown, Tx., U.S.	B2	120
Skelton, W.V., U.S.	n13	125
Skelton Glacier, ice, Ant.	f40	7
Skene, Ms., U.S.	B3	101
Skerries, Ire.	D5	11
Skerry, Stack, rock, Scot., U.K.	A4	13
Skhimatárion, Grc.	g11	25
Skiathos, Grc.	C4	25
Skíathos, i., Grc.	C4	25
Skiatook, Ok., U.S.	A5	113
Skiatook Reservoir, res., Ok., U.S.	A5	113
Skibbereen, Ire.	E2	10
Skibby, Den.	C5	15
Skiddaw, mtn., Eng., U.K.	F5	13
Skidegate, B.C.	C2	69
Skidegate Inlet, b., B.C.	C2	69
Skidmore, Mo., U.S.	A2	102
Skidmore, Tx., U.S.	E4	120
Skien, Nor.	H3	14
Skierniewice, Pol.	C6	26
Skiff, Alta.	E5	68
Skihist Mountain, mtn., B.C.	D7	69
Skikda (Philippeville), Alg.	B6	44
Skillet Fork, stm., Il., U.S.	E5	90
Skillman, N.J., U.S.	C3	107
Skipperville, Al., U.S.	D4	78
Skipton, Eng., U.K.	G7	13
Skíros, Grc.	C5	40
Skíros (Scyros), i., Grc.	C5	40
Skive, Den.	B3	15
Skjern, Den.	C2	15
Skjern Å, stm., Den.	C2	15
Skoczów, Pol.	h9	26
Škofja Loka, Yugo.	B2	24
Skokie, Il., U.S.	A6	90
Skokomish Indian Reservation, Wa., U.S.	B2	124
Skole, Sov. Un.	D7	26
Skopin, Sov. Un.	C4	40
Skopje, Yugo.	E12	27
Skopje, Yugo.	D5	24
Skørping, Den.	B3	15
Skotovataya, Sov. Un.	q20	27
Skotselv, Nor.	p27	14
Skövde, Swe.	H5	14
Skovorodino, Sov. Un.	D15	29
Skowhegan, Me., U.S.	D3	96
Skownan, Man.	D2	70
Skradin, Yugo.	D2	24
Skreen, Ire.	C3	11
Skull Valley, Az., U.S.	C3	80
Skull Valley, val., Ut., U.S.	C3	121
Skull Valley Indian Reservation, Ut., U.S.	C3	121
Skuna, stm., Ms., U.S.	B4	101
Skunk, stm., Ia., U.S.	D6	92
Skurup, Swe.	C7	15
Skvira, Sov. Un.	G7	27
Skwentna, Ak., U.S.	g16	79
Skwentna, stm., Ak., U.S.	g15	79
Skwierzyna (Schwerin), Pol.	B3	26
Skye, Island of, i., Scot., U.K.	B3	10
Skykomish, Wa., U.S.	B4	124
Skykomish, stm., Wa., U.S.	B4	124
Sky Lake, Fl., U.S.	*D5	86
Skyland, Nv., U.S.	D2	105
Skyland, N.C., U.S.	f10	110
Skylight, Ky., U.S.	g11	94
Skylight Mountain, mtn., Ar., U.S.	B1	81
Skyline, Al., U.S.	A3	78
Skyring, Seno, strt., Chile	h11	54
Skyway, Co., U.S.	C6	83
Skyway, Wa., U.S.	*f11	124
Slade, Ky., U.S.	C6	94
Slagelse, Den.	C5	15
Slagle, La., U.S.	C2	95
Slamet, mtn., Indon.	G3	34
Slane, Ire.	D5	11
Slaney, stm., Ire.	E5	11
Slangerup, Den.	C6	15
Slánic, Rom.	C7	24
Slaný, Czech.	n17	26
Slapy, Czech.	o17	26
Slapy Reservoir, res., Czech.	D9	19
Slater, Co., U.S.	A3	83
Slater, Ia., U.S.	C4	92
Slater, Mo., U.S.	B4	102
Slater, S.C., U.S.	A3	117
Slatersville, R.I., U.S.	A3	116
Slatersville Reservoir, res., R.I., U.S.	B3	116
Slate Spring, Ms., U.S.	B4	101
Slatina, Rom.	C7	24
Slatington, Pa., U.S.	E10	115
Slaton, Tx., U.S.	C2	120
Slaughter, La., U.S.	D4	95
Slaughter Beach, De., U.S.	E4	85
Slaughters, Ky., U.S.	C2	94
Slave, stm., Can.	D10	66
Slave Lake, Alta.	B3	68
Slavgorod, Sov. Un.	D10	29
Slavonia, hist. reg., Yugo.	C3	24
Slavonska Požega, Yugo.	C3	24
Slavonski Brod, Yugo.	C4	24
Slavsk, Sov. Un.	A6	26
Slavyanoserbsk, Sov. Un.	q21	27
Slavyansk, Sov. Un.	G11	27
Slavyansk-na-Kubani, Sov. Un.	I12	27
Sławno, Pol.	A4	26
Slayden, Ms., U.S.	A4	101
Slayton, Mn., U.S.	G3	100
Slaytonville, De., U.S.	E3	85
Sleaford, Eng., U.K.	A7	12
Slea Head, c., Ire.	E1	11
Sleat, Point of, c., Scot., U.K.	C2	13
Sleat, Sound of, strt., Scot., U.K.	C3	13
Sledge, Ms., U.S.	A3	101
Sled Lake, l., Sask.	C2	75
Sleepers, stm., Vt., U.S.	D5	102
Sleeping Bear Dunes National Lakeshore, Mi., U.S.	D4	99
Sleeping Bear Point, c., Mi., U.S.	D4	99
Sleepy Creek, W.V., U.S.	B6	125
Sleepy Eye, Mn., U.S.	F4	100
Sleepy Point, c., Fiji	H15	52
Sleetmute, Ak., U.S.	C8	79
Slemp, Ky., U.S.	C6	94
Slick, Ok., U.S.	B5	113
Slick Rock, Co., U.S.	C2	83
Slickville, Pa., U.S.	F2	115
Slidell, La., U.S.	D6	95
Slide Mountain, mtn., N.Y., U.S.	D6	109
Sliderock Mountain, mtn., Mt., U.S.	D3	103
Slieve Aughty Mountains, mts., Ire.	D3	11
Slievecallan, hill, Ire.	E2	11
Slievekimalta, mtn., Ire.	E3	11
Slieve Mish Mountains, mts., Ire.	E2	11
Slievenamon, mtn., Ire.	E4	11
Sligo, Ire.	C3	11
Sligo, Pa., U.S.	D3	115
Sligo, co., Ire.	C3	11
Sligo Bay, b., Ire.	C2	10
Slim Buttes, mtn., S.D., U.S.	B2	118
Slinger, Wi., U.S.	E5	126
Slippery Rock, Pa., U.S.	D1	115
Sliven, Bul.	D8	24
Slivenec, Czech.	n17	26
Sloan, Ia., U.S.	B1	92
Sloan, Nv., U.S.	H6	105
Sloan, N.Y., U.S.	C2	109
Sloans Valley, Ky., U.S.	D5	94
Sloat, Ca., U.S.	C3	82
Sloatsburg, N.Y., U.S.	*D6	109
Slobodskoy, Sov. Un.	B4	28
Slobozia, Rom.	C8	24
Slocan, B.C.	E9	69
Slocan Lake, l., B.C.	E9	69
Slocomb, Al., U.S.	D4	78
Slocum, R.I., U.S.	C3	116
Slonim, Sov. Un.	E5	27
Slope, co., N.D., U.S.	C2	111
Slough, Eng., U.K.	k11	10
Slovak, Ar., U.S.	C4	81
Slovakia, hist. reg., Czech.	D5	26
Slovan, Pa., U.S.	F1	115
Slovenia, hist. reg., Yugo.	C2	24
Słubice, Pol.	A9	19
Sluch, stm., Sov. Un.	F6	27
Slunj, Yugo.	B4	24
Slupca, Pol.	B4	26
Słupsk, Pol.	A4	26
Slutsk, Sov. Un.	E6	27
Slyne Head, c., Ire.	D1	10
Slyudyanka, Sov. Un.	D13	29
Smackover, Ar., U.S.	D3	81
Smackover Creek, stm., Ar., U.S.	D3	81
Smålandsfarvandet, strt., Den.	C5	15
Small Point, Me., U.S.	g8	96
Small Point, c., Me., U.S.	g8	96
Smallwood Reservoir, res., Newf.	g8	72
Smarr, Ga., U.S.	D3	87
Smarts Mountain, mtn., N.H., U.S.	C2	106
Smartt, Tn., U.S.	D8	119
Smeaton, Sask.	D7	75
Smečno, Czech.	n17	26
Smederevo, Yugo.	C5	24
Smela, Sov. Un.	G8	27
Smelterville, Id., U.S.	B2	89
Smethport, Pa., U.S.	C5	115
Smethwick (Warley), Eng., U.K.	D5	10
Smíchov (part of Prague), Czech.	n17	26
Smicksburg, Pa., U.S.	E3	115
Smidovich, Sov. Un.	B6	33
Smiley, Sask.	F1	75
Smiley, Tx., U.S.	E4	120
Smirnov, Sov. Un.	H11	27
Smirnykh, Sov. Un.	H20	33
Smith, Alta.	B3	68
Smith, Nv., U.S.	E2	105
Smith, co., Ks., U.S.	C5	93
Smith, co., Ms., U.S.	C4	101
Smith, co., Tn., U.S.	A5	119
Smith, co., Tx., U.S.	C5	120
Smith, stm., U.S.	D3	123
Smith, stm., Mt., U.S.	D5	103
Smith, Cape, c., Ont.	B3	73
Smith and Sayles Reservoir, res., R.I., U.S.	B2	116
Smith Bay, b., Ak., U.S.	A9	79
Smithboro, Il., U.S.	E4	90
Smithburg, W.V., U.S.	B4	125
Smith Canyon, val., Co., U.S.	D7	83
Smith Center, Ks., U.S.	C5	93
Smithdale, Ms., U.S.	D3	101
Smithers, B.C.	B4	69
Smithers, W.V., U.S.	C3	125
Smithfield, Il., U.S.	C3	90
Smithfield, Me., U.S.	D3	96
Smithfield, Ne., U.S.	D6	104
Smithfield, N.C., U.S.	B4	110
Smithfield, Oh., U.S.	B5	112
Smithfield, Pa., U.S.	G2	115
Smithfield, Ut., U.S.	B4	121
Smithfield, Va., U.S.	D6	123
Smithfield, W.V., U.S.	k9	125
Smith Island, i., B.A.T.	C6	7
Smith Island, i., Md., U.S.	D5	97
Smith Island, i., Va., U.S.	C7	123
Smithland, Ia., U.S.	B2	92
Smithland, Ky., U.S.	e9	94
Smithmill, Pa., U.S.	E5	115
Smith Mills, Ky., U.S.	C2	94
Smith Mountain Lake, res., Va., U.S.	C3	123
Smith Peak, mtn., Wa., U.S.	A2	89
Smith Peninsula, pen., Ant.	B7	7
Smith Point, c., N.S.	D4	71
Smith Point, c., Ma., U.S.	D7	98
Smith Point, c., Va., U.S.	C6	123
Smith River, Ca., U.S.	B1	82
Smiths, Al., U.S.	C4	78
Smithsburg, Md., U.S.	A2	97
Smiths Cove, N.S.	E4	71
Smiths Falls, Ont.	C8	73
Smiths Ferry, Id., U.S.	E2	89
Smiths Grove, Ky., U.S.	C3	94
Smithshire, Il., U.S.	C2	90
Smithsonia, Al., U.S.	A2	78
Smith Sound, strt., B.C.	C3	69
Smithton, Austl.	o15	50
Smithton, Il., U.S.	E4	90
Smithton, Mo., U.S.	C4	102
Smith Town, Ky., U.S.	D5	94
Smithtown, N.Y., U.S.	n15	109
Smithville, Ga., U.S.	E2	87
Smithville, In., U.S.	F4	91
Smithville, Ms., U.S.	A5	101
Smithville, Mo., U.S.	B3	102
Smithville, N.J., U.S.	E3	107
Smithville, Oh., U.S.	B4	112
Smithville, Ok., U.S.	C7	113
Smithville, Tn., U.S.	D8	119
Smithville, Tx., U.S.	D4	120
Smithville, W.V., U.S.	B3	125
Smithville Flats, N.Y., U.S.	C5	109
Smithwick, S.D., U.S.	D2	118
Smoaks, S.C., U.S.	E6	117
Smoke Creek Desert, des., Nv., U.S.	C2	105
Smokerun, Pa., U.S.	E5	115
Smokey, Cape, c., N.S.	C9	71
Smokey Dome, mtn., Id., U.S.	F4	89
Smoky, stm., Alta.	B1	68
Smoky Cape, c., Austl.	E9	51
Smoky Hill, Ks., U.S.	D5	93
Smoky Hill, North Fork, stm., U.S.	C9	119
Smoky Junction, Tn., U.S.	C9	119
Smoky Lake, Alta.	B4	68
Smoky Mountains, mts., Id., U.S.	F4	89
Smela, i., Nor.	F2	14
Smolan, Ks., U.S.	D6	93
Smolensk, Sov. Un.	D6	29
Smolyan, Bul.	E7	24
Smoot, Wy., U.S.	D2	127
Smooth Rock Falls, Ont.	o19	73
Smoothstone, stm., Sask.	B2	75
Smoothstone Lake, l., Sask.	C2	75
Smoots Creek, stm., Ks., U.S.	g11	93
Smyadovo, Bul.	D8	24
Smygehamn, Swe.	C7	15
Smyrna, De., U.S.	C3	85
Smyrna, Ga., U.S.	C2	87
Smyrna, N.Y., U.S.	C5	109
Smyrna, S.C., U.S.	A5	117
Smyrna, Tn., U.S.	B5	119
Smyrna, stm., De., U.S.	C3	85
Smyrna see İzmir, Tur.	C6	40
Smyrna Mills, Me., U.S.	B4	96
Smyth, co., Va., U.S.	f10	123
Smythe, Mount, mtn., B.C.	E8	66
Snaefell, mtn., I. of Man	F4	13
Snake, stm., U.S.	A4	76
Snake, stm., Mn., U.S.	D5	100
Snake, stm., Ne., U.S.	B4	104
Snake Creek, stm., U.S.	B2	104
Snake Falls, wtfl., Ne., U.S.	B5	104
Snake Indian, stm., Alta.	C1	68
Snake Mountain, mtn., U.S.	A10	119
Snake Mountain, mtn., Vt., U.S.	C2	122
Snake Range, mts., U.S.	E7	105
Snake River Plain, pl., Id., U.S.	F2	89
Snake River Range, mts., U.S.	C2	127
Snake Valley, val., U.S.	D2	121
Snares Islands, is., N.Z.	R11	51
Sneads, Fl., U.S.	B2	86
Sneads Ferry, N.C., U.S.	C5	110
Snedsted, Den.	B2	15
Sneedville, Tn., U.S.	C10	119
Sneek, Neth.	A6	16
Sneem, Ire.	F2	11
Snelling, S.C., U.S.	E5	117
Snellville, Ga., U.S.	*h8	87
Snezhnoye, Sov. Un.	q21	27
Śniardwy, Jezioro, l., Pol.	B6	26
Snipe Keys, is., Fl., U.S.	H5	86
Snipe Lake, l., Alta.	B2	68
Snizort, Loch, b., Scot., U.K.	C2	13
Snøhetta, mtn., Nor.	F3	14
Snohomish, Wa., U.S.	B3	124
Snohomish, co., Wa., U.S.	A4	124
Snoqualmie, Wa., U.S.	B4	124
Snoqualmie, stm., Wa., U.S.	B4	124
Snoqualmie Pass, Wa., U.S.	B4	124
Snøtinden, mtn., Nor.	D5	14
Snov, stm., Sov. Un.	F8	27
Snow, Ok., U.S.	C6	113
Snowbank Lake, l., Mn., U.S.	B7	100
Snow Camp, N.C., U.S.	B3	110
Snowden, Sask.	D3	75
Snowdon, mtn., Wales, U.K.	D4	10
Snowflake, Man.	E2	70
Snowflake, Az., U.S.	C5	80
Snow Hill, Al., U.S.	D3	78
Snow Hill, Md., U.S.	D7	97
Snow Hill, N.C., U.S.	B5	110
Snowking Mountain, mtn., Wa., U.S.	A4	124
Snow Lake, Man.	B1	70
Snow Lake, Ar., U.S.	C4	81
Snowmass, Co., U.S.	B4	83
Snowmass Mountain, mtn., Co., U.S.	B3	83
Snow Peak, mtn., Wa., U.S.	A7	124
Snow Road Station, Ont.	C8	73
Snow Shoe, Pa., U.S.	D6	115
Snowshoe Lake, l., Me., U.S.	B4	96
Snowshoe Peak, mtn., Mt.	B1	103
Snow Water Lake, l., Nv., U.S.	C7	105
Snowville, N.H., U.S.	C4	106
Snowville, Va., U.S.	*C2	123
Snowy, stm., Austl.	H7	51
Snowy Mountain, mtn., N.Y., U.S.	B6	109
Snowy Mountains, mts., Austl.	G8	50
Snyatyn, Sov. Un.	A7	24
Snyder, Co., U.S.	A7	83
Snyder, Ne., U.S.	C9	104
Snyder, Ok., U.S.	C3	113
Snyder, Tx., U.S.	C2	120
Snyder, co., Pa., U.S.	E7	115
Snyder Knob, mtn., W.V., U.S.	C5	125
Soacha, Col.	*C3	60
Soalala, Madag.	g9	49
Soap Lake, Wa., U.S.	B6	124
Soar, stm., Eng., U.K.	B6	12
Soata, Col.	B3	60
Soay, i., Scot., U.K.	C1	13
Sobat, stm., Sud.	D3	47
Soběslav, Czech.	D9	19
Sobieski, Mn., U.S.	D4	100
Sobinka, Sov. Un.	D13	27
Sobral, Braz.	B2	57
Sobti, well, Mali	B4	45
Søby, Den.	C2	15
Socastee, S.C., U.S.	D9	117
Sochaczew, Pol.	B4	26
Sochaux, Fr.	A2	21
Social Circle, Ga., U.S.	C3	87
Social Hill, Ar., U.S.	C3	81
Society Hill, S.C., U.S.	C8	117
Society Islands, is., Fr. Poly.	H12	6
Socompa, Paso de, S.A.	m8	56
Socorro, Col.	B3	60
Socorro, N.M., U.S.	C3	108
Socorro, co., N.M., U.S.	D2	108
Socotra (Suquţrā), i., Yemen	D5	38
Soc Trang, Viet.	D3	34
Socuéllamos, Spain	C4	22
Soda Creek, B.C.	C6	69
Sodankylä, Fin.	D12	14
Soda Springs, Id., U.S.	G7	89
Sodaville, Or., U.S.	C4	114
Soddy-Daisy, Tn., U.S.	D8	119
Söderala, Swe.	F7	14
Söderhamn, Swe.	H7	14
Södertälje, Swe.	t35	14
Sodo, Eth.	D4	47
Sodus, N.Y., U.S.	B3	109
Sodus Point, N.Y., U.S.	B4	109
Soest, W. Ger.	C4	18
Sofádhes, Grc.	B5	25
Sofala, dept., Moz.	D6	49
Sofia (Sofiya), Bul.	E7	24
Sofia, stm., Madag.	g9	49
Sofiyevka, Sov. Un.	H16	27
Sogamoso, Col.	B3	60
Sogamoso, stm., Col.	B7	17
Sogndal, Nor.	C8	25
Sognefjorden, Nor.	C8	25
Söğüt, Tur.	B4	108
Soham, Eng., U.K.	D4	17
Son, stm., India	D7	36
Soná, Pan.	F7	62
Sŏnchŏn, N. Kor.	G2	33
Soncino, Italy	D5	20
Sønder, stm., Den.	D3	15
Sønderborg, Den.	C5	16
Sønderho, Den.	D3	15
Sønderjylland, co., Den.	C3	15
Sønder Omme, Den.	C2	15
Sondershausen, E. Ger.	C5	18
Søndervig, Den.	B2	15
Sondheimer, La., U.S.	B4	95
Sondrio, Italy	A2	23
Sonepur, India	D7	36
Sonestown, Pa., U.S.	D8	115
Song, Nig.	E7	45
Song Cau, Viet.	F8	35
Songhua Jiang, stm., China	B10	31
Songjin see Kimchaek, N. Kor.	C10	31
Songkan, China	E9	31
Songkhla, Thai.	D2	34
Songnim (Kyōmipo), N. Kor.	G2	33
Songololo, Zaire	C1	48
Songtao, China	J3	32
Sonid Youqi, China	C5	32
Sonid Zuoqi, China	C5	32
Son La, Viet.	B5	35
Sonmiāni, Pak.	C4	36
Sonmiāni Bay, b., Pak.	I13	39
Sonneberg, E. Ger.	C6	18
Sonnette, Mt., U.S.	E11	103
Sonningdale, Sask.	E2	75
Sono, Rio do, stm., Braz.	C1	57
Sonobe, Japan	n14	13
Sonoita, Mex.	A2	63
Sonoita, Mex.	A2	63
Sonoma, Ca., U.S.	C2	82
Sonoma, co., Ca., U.S.	C2	82
Sonoma Peak, mtn., Nv., U.S.	C4	105
Sonoma Range, mts., Nv., U.S.	C4	105
Sonora, Ca., U.S.	D3	82
Sonora, Ky., U.S.	C4	94
Sonora, Oh., U.S.	C4	112
Sonora, Tx., U.S.	D2	120
Sonora, state, Mex.	B2	63
Sonora, co., Mex.	B2	63
Sonqor, Iran	D3	39
Sonsón, Col.	B2	60
Sonsonate, El Sal.	E7	63
Son Tay, Viet.	A3	34
Sonthofen, W. Ger.	A9	21
Sontra, W. Ger.	C3	109
Sooke, B.C.	E6	69
Soo Locks, N.A.	B6	99
Sopchoppy, Fl., U.S.	B2	86
Soper, Ok., U.S.	C6	113
Soperton, Ga., U.S.	D4	87
Sophia, N.C., U.S.	B3	110
Sophia, W.V., U.S.	D3	125
Sopot, Pol.	A5	26
Soquel, Ca., U.S.	*D3	82
Sor, stm., Port.	C1	22
Sŏrak, Mount, mtn., S. Kor.	G4	33
Sorata, Bol.	D4	22
Sorbas, Spain	D4	22
Sorel, Que.	C4	74
Sorell, Cape, c., Austl.	o15	50
Soreq, stm., Isr.	h10	41
Soresina, Italy	B3	23
Soria, Spain	B4	22
Soriano, Col.	f7	54
Soriano, dept., Ur.	f8	54
Sorocaba, Braz.	C3	56
Sorochinsk, Sov. Un.	C4	28
Soroki, Sov. Un.	G7	27
Sorong, Indon.	F8	34
Sorø, Den.	A5	48
Sorøya, i., Nor.	B10	14
Sorraia, stm., Port.	C1	22
Sorrento, Italy	D5	23
Sorrento, Fl., U.S.	D5	86
Sorrento, La., U.S.	D5	95
Sorris Sorris, Nmb.	B1	49
Sør Rondane Mountains, mts., Ant.	B15	7
Sorsogon, Phil.	C6	34
Sortavala, Sov. Un.	A8	27
Sørumsand, Nor.	p29	14
Sŏsan, S. Kor.	H3	33
Sosnogorsk, Sov. Un.	C19	9
Sosnovka, Sov. Un.	E13	27
Sosnowiec, Pol.	C5	26
Soso, Ms., U.S.	C5	101
Sosva, Sov. Un.	C21	9
Sottern, l., Swe.	t33	14
Sotteville-lès-Rouen, Fr.	C4	16
Souanké, Congo	A1	48
Soubré, I.C.	E3	45
Soucook, stm., N.H., U.S.	C6	100
Soudan, Mn., U.S.	C6	100
Souderton, Pa., U.S.	F11	115
Souflion, Grc.	B6	25
Soufrière, mtn., Guad.	Q8	65
Soufrière, mtn., St. Vin.	U26	65
Soughegan, stm., N.H., U.S.	E3	106
Soulac, Fr.	G6	16
Soulanges, co., Que.	q19	74
Sound Beach, N.Y., U.S.	*n16	109
Sounding Creek, stm., Alta.	D5	68
Sounding Lake, l., Alta.	C5	68
Sound View, Ct., U.S.	D6	84
Sources, Mount aux, mtn., Afr.	C4	49
Soure, Braz.	C5	59
Soure, Port.	B1	22
Souris, Man.	E1	70
Souris, stm., N.A.	A5	111
Souris, N.D., U.S.	A5	111
Souris, stm., N.A.	A7	18
Souris, P.E.I.	C2	92
Sous, Oued, val., Mor.	C3	44
Sousa, Braz.	C3	57

Name	Map Ref.	Page
Sousse, Tun.	B7	44
Soustons, Fr.	F3	16
South, stm., Ont.	B5	73
South, stm., Ga., U.S.	h8	87
South, stm., In., U.S.	C4	92
South, stm., N.C. U.S.	C4	110
South Acton, Ma., U.S.	g10	98
South Acworth, N.H., U.S.	D2	106
South Addison, Me., U.S.	D5	96
South Africa, ctry., Afr.	C4	49
South Amboy, N.J., U.S.	C4	107
South America, cont.	E5	53
South Amherst, Ma., U.S.	B2	98
South Amherst, Oh., U.S.	A3	112
Southampton, N.B.	D2	71
Southampton, Ont.	C3	73
Southampton, Eng., U.K.	E6	10
Southampton, Ma., U.S.	B2	98
Southampton, N.Y., U.S.	n16	109
Southampton, co., Va., U.S.	D5	123
Southampton, Cape, c., N.W. Ter.	D16	66
Southampton Island, i., N.W. Ter.	D16	66
South Andaman, i., India	F9	36
South Anna, stm., Va., U.S.	C5	123
Southard, Ok., U.S.	A3	113
South Ashburnham, Ma., U.S.	A4	98
South Ashfield, Ma., U.S.	A2	98
South Aulatsivik Island, i., Newf.	g9	72
South Australia, state, Austl.	E5	50
Southaven, Ms., U.S.	A3	101
South Bald Mountain, mtn., Co., U.S.	A5	83
South Baldy, mtn., N.M., U.S.	D2	108
Southbank, B.C.	C5	69
South Barnstead, N.H., U.S.	D4	106
South Barre, Ma., U.S.	B3	98
South Barre, Vt., U.S.	C3	122
South Barrule, hill, I. of Man	F4	13
South Bay, Fl., U.S.	F6	86
South Bay, b., Ont.	B3	73
Southbeach, Or., U.S.	C2	114
South Belmar, N.J., U.S.	C4	107
South Beloit, Il., U.S.	A4	90
South Bend, In., U.S.	A5	91
South Bend, Ne., U.S.	h12	104
South Bend, Tx., U.S.	C3	120
South Bend, Wa., U.S.	C2	124
South Bentinck Arm, b., B.C.	C4	69
South Berwick, Me., U.S.	E2	96
South Bethany, De., U.S.	F5	85
South Bethlehem, N.Y., U.S.	C7	109
South Bloomfield, Oh., U.S.	C3	112
South Boardman, Mi., U.S.	D5	99
South Bolton, Que.	D5	74
Southborough, Ma., U.S.	B4	98
South Boston, Va., U.S.	D4	123
South Bound Brook, N.J., U.S.	B3	107
South Bradenton, Fl., U.S.	*E4	86
South Branch, Newf.	E2	72
South Branch, stm., U.S.	D7	99
South Branch Lake, l., Me., U.S.	C4	96
South Branch Mountain, mtn., W.V., U.S.	B6	125
Southbridge, Ma., U.S.	B3	98
South Bristol, Me., U.S.	E3	96
South Britain, Ct., U.S.	D3	84
South Broadway, Wa., U.S.	C5	124
South Brookfield, N.S.	E5	71
South Bruny, i., Austl.	o15	50
South Burlington, Vt., U.S.	C2	122
Southbury, Ct., U.S.	D3	84
South Byfield, Ma., U.S.	A6	98
South Byron, N.Y., U.S.	B2	109
South Canaan, Pa., U.S.	D11	115
South Cape, c., Nor.	B13	128
South Carolina, state, U.S.	D6	117
South Carver, Ma., U.S.	C6	98
South Channel, strt., Marsh Is.	S18	52
South Charleston, Oh., U.S.	C2	112
South Charleston, W.V., U.S.	C3	125
South Charlestown, N.H., U.S.	D2	106
South Chatham, Ma., U.S.	C7	98
South Chatham, N.H., U.S.	B4	106
South Chicago Heights, Il., U.S.	m9	90
South China, Me., U.S.	D3	96
South China Sea, Asia	H14	30
South Cle Elum, Wa., U.S.	B5	124
South Coffeyville, Ok., U.S.	A6	113
South Colby, Wa., U.S.	e10	124
South Colton, N.Y., U.S.	f10	109
South Congaree, S.C., U.S.	D5	117
South Connellsville, Pa., U.S.	G2	115
South Corning, N.Y., U.S.	C3	109
South Cottonwood, Ut., U.S.	*C4	121
South Dakota, state, U.S.	C5	118
South Danville, N.H., U.S.	E4	106
South Dartmouth, Ma., U.S.	C6	98
South Dayton, N.Y., U.S.	C1	109
South Daytona, Fl., U.S.	C5	86
South Decatur, Ga., U.S.	*h8	87
South Deerfield, Ma., U.S.	B2	98
South Deerfield, N.H., U.S.	D4	106
South Deer Isle, Me., U.S.	D4	96
South Dennis, Ma., U.S.	C7	98
South Dennis, N.J., U.S.	E3	107
South Dorset, Vt., U.S.	E2	122
South Dos Palos, Ca., U.S.	D3	82
South Downs, plat., Eng., U.K.	E6	10
South Dum Dum, India	F12	37
South Duxbury, Ma., U.S.	B6	98
Southeast Cape, c., Ak., U.S.	C6	79
South Easton, Ma., U.S.	B5	98
Southeast Pass, strt., La., U.S.	E7	95
Southeast Point, c., R.I., U.S.	h7	116
South Effingham, N.H., U.S.	C5	106
South Egremont, Ma., U.S.	B1	98
South Elgin, Il., U.S.	B5	90
South El Monte, Ca., U.S.	*m12	82
South Fallsburg, N.Y., U.S.	D6	109
South Farmingdale, N.Y., U.S.	*n15	109
Southfield, Ma., U.S.	B1	98
Southfield, Mi., U.S.	o15	99
South Flevoland, reg., Neth.	B5	17
South Fork, Sask.	H1	75
South Fork, Co., U.S.	D4	83
South Fork, Pa., U.S.	F4	115
South Fort George, B.C.	C6	69
South Foster, R.I., U.S.	C2	116
South Fox Island, i., Mi., U.S.	C5	99
South Freeport, Me., U.S.	g7	96
South Fulton, Tn., U.S.	A3	119
South Gastonia, N.C., U.S.	B1	110
South Gate, Ca., U.S.	n12	82
Southgate, Fl., U.S.	*E4	86
Southgate, Ky., U.S.	h14	94
South Gate, Md., U.S.	*B4	97
Southgate, Mi., U.S.	p15	99
South Gifford, Mo., U.S.	A5	102
South Glamorgan, co., Wales, U.K.	C4	12
South Glastonbury, Ct., U.S.	C5	84
Southglenn, Co., U.S.	*B6	83
South Glens Falls, N.Y., U.S.	B7	109
South Grafton, Ma., U.S.	B4	98
South Grand, stm., Mo., U.S.	C3	102
South Greenfield, Mo., U.S.	D4	102
South Gulf of Évvoia, b., Grc.	g11	25
South Hackensack, N.J., U.S.	*B4	107
South Hadley, Ma., U.S.	B2	98
South Hadley Falls, Ma., U.S.	B2	98
South Hamilton, Ma., U.S.	A6	98
South Hampton, N.H., U.S.	E5	106
South Hanover, Ma., U.S.	h12	98
South Harpswell, Me., U.S.	g7	96
South Harwich, Ma., U.S.	C7	98
South Haven, In., U.S.	A3	91
South Haven, Ks., U.S.	E6	93
South Haven, Mi., U.S.	F4	99
South Heart, N.D., U.S.	C3	111
South Heart, stm., Alta.	B2	68
South Hero, Vt., U.S.	B2	122
South Hero Island, i., Vt., U.S.	B2	122
South Hill, N.Y., U.S.	*C4	109
South Hill, Va., U.S.	D4	123
South Hingham, Ma., U.S.	h12	98
South Holland, Il., U.S.	k9	90
South Holland (Zuid-Holland), prov., Neth.	B4	17
South Holston Lake, res., U.S.	A9	119
South Hooksett, N.H., U.S.	D4	106
South Hopkinton, R.I., U.S.	F1	116
South Houston, Tx., U.S.	r14	120
South Huntington, N.Y., U.S.	*n15	109
South Hutchinson, Ks., U.S.	f11	93
South Indian Lake, Man.	A2	70
Southington, Ct., U.S.	C4	84
South International Falls, Mn., U.S.	B5	100
South Island, i., Micron.	Q18	52
South Island, i., N.Z.	O13	51
South Island, i., S.C., U.S.	E9	117
South Jacksonville, Il., U.S.	D3	90
South Jordan, Ut., U.S.	C3	121
South Junction, Man.	E4	70
South Kenosha, Wi., U.S.	F6	126
South Kensington, Md., U.S.	*B3	97
South Kent, Ct., U.S.	C2	84
South Killingly, Ct., U.S.	B8	84
South Komelik, Az., U.S.	F4	80
South Laguna, Ca., U.S.	*F5	82
South Lake Tahoe, Ca., U.S.	C4	82
South Lancaster, Ma., U.S.	B4	98
South Laramie, Wy., U.S.	*E7	127
South Laurel, Md., U.S.	*B4	97
South Lebanon, Me., U.S.	E2	96
South Lebanon, Oh., U.S.	C1	112
South Lee, Ma., U.S.	B1	98
South Lincoln, Vt., U.S.	C3	122
South Londonderry, Vt., U.S.	E3	122
South Loup, stm., Ne., U.S.	C6	104
South Lunenburg, Vt., U.S.	C5	122
South Lyme, Ct., U.S.	D6	84
South Lyndeborough, N.H., U.S.	E3	106
South Lyon, Mi., U.S.	F7	99
South Magnetawan, Ont.	B4	73
South Magnetic Pole, Ant.	C26	7
South Manitou Island, i., Mi., U.S.	C4	99
South Mansfield, La., U.S.	B2	95
South Marsh Island, i., Md., U.S.	D5	97
South Medford, Or., U.S.	E4	114
South Merrimack, N.H., U.S.	E3	106
South Miami, Fl., U.S.	G6	86
South Miami Heights, Fl., U.S.	s13	86
South Middleboro, Ma., U.S.	C6	98
South Milford, In., U.S.	A7	91
South Mills, N.C., U.S.	A6	110
South Milwaukee, Wi., U.S.	F6	126
Southminster, Eng., U.K.	C8	12
South Modesto, Ca., U.S.	*D3	82
South Molton, Eng., U.K.	C4	12
Southmont, N.C., U.S.	B2	110
South Montrose, Pa., U.S.	C10	115
South Moose Lake, l., Man.	C1	70
South Mountain, Pa., U.S.	G7	115
South Mountain, mtn., Id., U.S.	B2	97
South Mountain, mtn., Id., U.S.	G2	89
South Mountain, mtn., N.M., U.S.	k8	108
South Mountains, mts., Az., U.S.	m8	80
South Mountains, mts., N.C., U.S.	B1	110
South Naknek, Ak., U.S.	D8	79
South Negril Point, c., Jam.	E4	64
South New Berlin, N.Y., U.S.	C5	109
South Newbury, N.H., U.S.	D3	106
South Newbury, Vt., U.S.	C4	122
South Newfane, Vt., U.S.	F3	122
South New River Canal, Fl., U.S.	r13	86
South Northfield, Vt., U.S.	C3	122
South Nyack, N.Y., U.S.	*D7	109
South Ogden, Ut., U.S.	B4	121
South Orange, N.J., U.S.	B4	107
South Orkney Islands, is., B.A.T.	C8	7
South Orrington, Me., U.S.	D4	96
South Otselic, N.Y., U.S.	C5	109
South Paris, Me., U.S.	D2	96
South Park, val., Co., U.S.	B5	83
South Pasadena, Ca., U.S.	*m12	82
South Pass, Wy., U.S.	D4	127
South Pass, strt., La., U.S.	E6	95
South Pass, strt., Marsh Is.	S17	52
South Pass City, Wy., U.S.	D4	127
South Patrick Shores, Fl., U.S.	D6	86
South Peacham, Vt., U.S.	C4	122
South Pekin, Il., U.S.	C4	90
South Pittsburg, Tn., U.S.	D8	119
South Plainfield, N.J., U.S.	B4	107
South Platte, stm., U.S.	B7	76
South Point, c., Austl.	I6	51
South Point, c., Barb.	K20	65
South Point, c., Newf.	C4	72
South Point, c., Mi., U.S.	D7	99
South Pole, Ant.	A7	7
South Pomfret, Vt., U.S.	D3	122
Southport (Gold Coast), Austl.	E9	50
Southport, Eng., U.K.	D5	10
Southport, Fl., U.S.	u16	86
Southport, In., U.S.	E5	91
Southport, N.Y., U.S.	C4	109
Southport, N.C., U.S.	D4	110
South Portland, Me., U.S.	E2	96
South Poultney, Vt., U.S.	E2	122
South Prairie, Wa., U.S.	B3	124
South Range, Mi., U.S.	A2	99
South Range, Wi., U.S.	B2	126
South Reading, Vt., U.S.	E3	122
South Renovo, Pa., U.S.	D6	115
South Revelstoke, B.C.	D8	69
South River, Ont.	B5	73
South River, N.J., U.S.	C4	107
South River, b., Md., U.S.	C4	97
South Ronaldsay, i., Scot., U.K.	A5	10
South Royalston, Ma., U.S.	A3	98
South Royalton, Vt., U.S.	D3	122
South Rustico, P.E.I.	C6	71
South Ryegate, Vt., U.S.	C4	122
South Salem, Oh., U.S.	C2	112
South Salt Lake, Ut., U.S.	*C4	121
South Sandwich Islands, is., S.A.	D10	7
South San Francisco, Ca., U.S.	h8	82
South San Gabriel, Ca., U.S.	*m12	82
South San Jose Hills, Ca., U.S.	*m13	82
South Saskatchewan, stm., Can.	F11	66
South Seaville, N.J., U.S.	E3	107
South Setauket, N.Y., U.S.	*n15	109
South Shetland Islands, is., B.A.T.	C7	7
South Shields, Eng., U.K.	C6	10
South Shore, Mo., U.S.	f12	102
South Shore, S.D., U.S.	B9	118
Southside, Al., U.S.	B3	78
Southside, N.C., U.S.	B1	110
Southside, Tn., U.S.	A4	119
Southside Place, Tx., U.S.	r14	120
South Sioux City, Ne., U.S.	B9	104
South Skunk, stm., Ia., U.S.	C4	92
South Slocan, B.C.	E9	69
South Solon, Oh., U.S.	C2	112
South Sound, strt., Ire.	D2	11
South Spicer Island, i., N.W. Ter.	C17	66
South Sterling, Pa., U.S.	D11	115
South Stony Brook, N.Y., U.S.	n15	109
South St. Paul, Mn., U.S.	n12	100
South Strafford, Vt., U.S.	D4	122
South Streator, Il., U.S.	B5	90
South Sumter, S.C., U.S.	*D7	117
South Superior, Wy., U.S.	E4	127
South Sutton, N.H., U.S.	D3	106
South Swansea, Ma., U.S.	C5	98
South Tamworth, N.H., U.S.	C4	106
South Taranaki Bight, N.Z.	M15	51
South Toms River, N.J., U.S.	D4	107
South Torrington, Wy., U.S.	D8	127
South Tucson, Az., U.S.	E5	80
South Tunnel, Tn., U.S.	A5	119
South Twin Lake, l., Newf.	D4	72
South Twin Mountain, mtn., N.H., U.S.	B3	106
South Tyne, stm., Eng., U.K.	F6	i3
South Uist, i., Scot., U.K.	B3	10
South Valley Stream, N.Y., U.S.	n15	109
South Van Buren, Mo., U.S.	E6	102
South Venice, Fl., U.S.	E4	86
South Ventana Cone, vol., Ca., U.S.	D3	82
South Vienna, Oh., U.S.	C2	112
South Wabasca Lake, l., Alta.	B4	68
South Wadesboro, N.C., U.S.	C2	110
South Wallingford, Vt., U.S.	E3	122
South Walpole, Ma., U.S.	h10	98
South Waterford, Me., U.S.	D2	96
South Waverly, Pa., U.S.	C8	115
South Wayne, Wi., U.S.	F4	126
South Weare, N.H., U.S.	D3	106
South Webster, Oh., U.S.	D3	112
South Wellfleet, Ma., U.S.	C8	98
South Wellington, B.C.	f12	69
Southwest, Pa., U.S.	F3	115
South West Africa see Namibia, dep., Afr.		
South West Bay, b., Bah.	n16	64
South Westbury, N.Y., U.S.	n15	109
South West Cape, c., Austl.	o15	50
Southwest Cape, c., N.Z.	Q11	51
Southwest Channel, strt., Fl., U.S.	E4	86
South West City, Mo., U.S.	E3	102
Southwest Harbor, Me., U.S.	D4	96
Southwest Head, c., N.B.	E3	71
Southwest Miramichi, stm., N.B.	C3	71
Southwest Mountains, mts., Va., U.S.	B4	123
Southwest Pass, strt., La., U.S.	E3	95
Southwest Pass, strt., La., U.S.	F6	95
Southwest Passage, strt., Marsh Is.	S18	52
Southwest Point, c., R.I., U.S.	h7	116
South Weymouth Naval Air Station, mil., Ma., U.S.	B6	98
South Whitley, In., U.S.	B6	91
South Whittier, Ca., U.S.	*n13	82
Southwick, Id., U.S.	C2	89
Southwick, Ma., U.S.	B2	98
South Williamson, Ky., U.S.	C7	94
South Williamsport, Pa., U.S.	D7	115
South Willington, Ct., U.S.	B6	84
South Windham, Me., U.S.	E2	96
South Windsor, Ct., U.S.	B5	84
Southwold, Eng., U.K.	C9	12
South Wolfeboro, N.H., U.S.	C4	106
South Wolf Island, i., Newf.	B4	72
Southwood, Co., U.S.	D6	83
Southwood Acres, Ct., U.S.	A5	84
Spiceland, In., U.S.	E7	91
Spicer, Mn., U.S.	E4	100
Spickard, Mo., U.S.	A4	102
Spider Lake, l., Wi., U.S.	B2	126
Spiekeroog, W. Ger.	A7	17
South Yorkshire, co., Eng., U.K.	A6	12
South Yuba City, Ca., U.S.	*C3	82
South Zanesville, Oh., U.S.	C3	112
Soverato, Italy	E6	23
Sovereign, Sask.	F2	75
Soveria, Italy	E6	23
Sovetsk (Tilsit), Sov. Un.	D3	27
Sovetskaya Gavan, Sov. Un.	E16	29
Sovetskaya Gavan, Sov. Un.	B10	33
Soviet Union, ctry., Asia	D11	29
Soweto, S. Afr.	C4	49
Soyo, Ang.	C1	48
Sōya, Cape, c., Japan	D10	33
Sozh, stm., Sov. Un.	E8	27
Sozopol, Bul.	D8	24
Spa, Bel.	B6	16
Spain, ctry., Eur.	B4	22
Spalding, Austl.	F2	51
Spalding, Sask.	E3	75
Spalding, Eng., U.K.	D6	10
Spalding, Id., U.S.	C2	89
Spalding, Ne., U.S.	C7	104
Spalding, co., Ga., U.S.	C2	87
Spangle, Wa., U.S.	B8	124
Spangler, Pa., U.S.	E4	115
Spaniard's Bay, Newf.	E5	72
Spanish, stm., Ont.	A2	73
Spanishburg, W.V., U.S.	D3	125
Spanish Fork, Ut., U.S.	C4	121
Spanish Fort, Al., U.S.	E2	78
Spanish Lake, Mo., U.S.	f13	102
Spanish North Africa, dep., Afr.	*B4	44
Spanish Peak, mtn., Or., U.S.	C7	114
Spanish Ranch, Ca., U.S.	C3	82
Spanish Town, Jam.	F5	64
Sparkman, Ar., U.S.	D3	81
Sparks, Ga., U.S.	E3	87
Sparks, Ne., U.S.	B5	104
Sparks, Nv., U.S.	D2	105
Sparks, Ok., U.S.	B5	113
Sparksville, Ky., U.S.	C4	94
Sparland, Il., U.S.	B4	90
Sparreholm, Swe.	t34	14
Sparrows Point, Md., U.S.	B5	97
Sparta see Spárti, Grc.	D4	40
Sparta, Ga., U.S.	C4	87
Sparta, Il., U.S.	E4	90
Sparta, Ky., U.S.	B5	94
Sparta, Mi., U.S.	E5	99
Sparta, Mo., U.S.	D4	102
Sparta, N.J., U.S.	A3	107
Sparta, N.C., U.S.	A1	110
Sparta, Oh., U.S.	B3	112
Sparta, Tn., U.S.	D8	119
Sparta, Wi., U.S.	E3	126
Sparta Mountains, mts., N.J., U.S.	B3	107
Spartanburg, In., U.S.	D8	91
Spartanburg, S.C., U.S.	B4	117
Spartanburg, co., S.C., U.S.	B3	117
Spartansburg, Pa., U.S.	C2	115
Spárti (Sparta), Grc.	D4	40
Spartivento, Cape, c., Italy	F6	23
Spartivento, Cape, c., Italy	E2	23
Spas-Demensk, Sov. Un.	D10	27
Spassk-Dalniy, Sov. Un.	E16	29
Spassk-Ryazanskiy, Sov. Un.	D13	27
Spáta, Grc.	h11	25
Spátha, Ákra, c., Grc.	E4	40
Spavinaw, Ok., U.S.	A6	113
Spavinaw Creek, stm., Ok., U.S.	A7	113
Spear, Cape, c., Newf.	E5	72
Spearfish, S.D., U.S.	C2	118
Spearhill, Man.	D2	70
Spearman, Tx., U.S.	A2	120
Spearville, Ks., U.S.	E4	93
Spearville, La., U.S.	B3	95
Speculator, N.Y., U.S.	B6	109
Speed, In., U.S.	H6	91
Speed, Ks., U.S.	C4	93
Speed, N.C., U.S.	B5	110
Speed, W.V., U.S.	C3	125
Speedway, In., U.S.	E5	91
Speedwell, Tn., U.S.	C10	119
Speedwell, Va., U.S.	D1	123
Speers, Sask.	E2	75
Speigner, Al., U.S.	C3	78
Speight, Ky., U.S.	C7	94
Spelter, W.V., U.S.	k10	125
Spenard (part of Anchorage), Ak., U.S.	g17	79
Spencer, Id., U.S.	E6	89
Spencer, In., U.S.	F4	91
Spencer, Ia., U.S.	A2	92
Spencer, Ma., U.S.	B3	98
Spencer, Ne., U.S.	B7	104
Spencer, N.Y., U.S.	C4	109
Spencer, N.C., U.S.	B2	110
Spencer, Oh., U.S.	A3	112
Spencer, S.D., U.S.	D8	118
Spencer, Tn., U.S.	D8	119
Spencer, Va., U.S.	D2	123
Spencer, Wi., U.S.	D3	126
Spencer, W.V., U.S.	C3	125
Spencer, co., In., U.S.	H4	91
Spencer, co., Ky., U.S.	B4	94
Spencer, Cape, c., Ak., U.S.	k21	79
Spencer Gulf, b., Austl.	F6	50
Spencer Lake, l., Me., U.S.	C2	96
Spencerport, N.Y., U.S.	B3	109
Spencers Island, N.S.	D5	71
Spencerville, In., U.S.	B8	91
Spencerville, Md., U.S.	*B4	97
Spencerville, Oh., U.S.	B1	112
Spencerville, Ok., U.S.	C6	113
Spences Bridge, B.C.	D7	69
Spennymoor, Eng., U.K.	F7	13
Sperkhiós, stm., Grc.	C4	25
Sperrin Mountains, mts., N. Ire., U.K.		
Sperry, Ia., U.S.	D6	92
Sperryville, Va., U.S.	B4	123
Spešutie Island, i., Md., U.S.	B5	97
Spey, stm., Scot., U.K.	C4	10
Speyer, W. Ger.	D4	18
Sphinx, hist., Eg.	E3	41
Spiceland, In., U.S.	E7	91
Spiekeroog, i., W. Ger.	B3	18
Spiez, Switz.	C4	21
Spigno Monferrato, Italy	E4	20
Spijkenisse, Neth.	*C4	17
Spilamberto, Italy	E5	20
Spilsby, Eng., U.K.	D7	10
Spinazzola, Italy	D6	23
Spindale, N.C., U.S.	B1	110
Spink, S.D., U.S.	E9	118
Spink, co., S.D., U.S.	C7	118
Spink Colony, S.D., U.S.	C7	118
Spirit Lake, Id., U.S.	B2	89
Spirit Lake, Ia., U.S.	A2	92
Spirit Lake, l., Ia., U.S.	A2	92
Spirit Lake, l., Wa., U.S.	C3	124
Spirit River, Alta.	B1	68
Spirit River Flowage, res., Wi., U.S.	C4	126
Spiritwood, N.D., U.S.	C7	111
Spiro, Ok., U.S.	B7	113
Spišská Nová Ves, Czech.	D6	26
Spitsbergen, i., Nor.	B13	128
Spittal, Aus.	E6	18
Spivey, Ks., U.S.	E5	93
Split, Yugo.	D3	24
Split, Cape, c., N.S.	D5	71
Split Lake, l., Man.	A4	70
Split Rock Creek, stm., U.S.	G2	100
Splügen, Switz.	C5	20
Splügen Pass, Eur.	C5	20
Spofford, N.H., U.S.	E2	106
Spofford, Tx., U.S.	E2	120
Spofford Lake, l., N.H., U.S.	E2	106
Spokane, La., U.S.	C4	95
Spokane, Wa., U.S.	B8	124
Spokane, co., Wa., U.S.	B8	124
Spokane, stm., U.S.	B8	124
Spokane, Mount, mtn., Wa., U.S.	B8	124
Spokane Indian Reservation, Wa., U.S.	B8	124
Spöl, stm., Eur.	C9	21
Spoleto, Italy	C4	23
Spondin, Alta.	D5	68
Spoon, stm., Il., U.S.	C3	90
Spooner, Wi., U.S.	C2	126
Spooner Lake, l., Wi., U.S.	C2	126
Spotswood, N.J., U.S.	C4	107
Spotsylvania, Va., U.S.	B5	123
Spotsylvania, co., Va., U.S.	B5	123
Spotted Island, i., Newf.	B4	72
Spottsville, Ky., U.S.	C2	94
Spragge, Ont.	A2	73
Sprague, Man.	E4	70
Sprague, Ne., U.S.	D9	104
Sprague, Wa., U.S.	B8	124
Sprague, W.V., U.S.	n13	125
Sprague, stm., Or., U.S.	E5	114
Sprague Lake, l., Wa., U.S.	B7	124
Sprague River, Or., U.S.	E5	114
Spragueville, Ia., U.S.	B7	92
Spragueville, N.Y., U.S.	A5	109
Spragueville, R.I., U.S.	B3	116
Spray, Or., U.S.	C7	114
Spread Eagle, Wi., U.S.	C5	126
Spreckelsville, Hi., U.S.	*C5	88
Spree, stm., E. Ger.	B7	18
Spremberg, E. Ger.	C7	18
Sprigg, W.V., U.S.	D2	125
Spring, Tx., U.S.	q14	120
Spring, stm., Ar., U.S.	A4	81
Spring, South Fork, stm., U.S.	A4	81
Spring Arbor, Mi., U.S.	F6	99
Spring Bay, b., Ut., U.S.	B3	121
Springbok, S. Afr.	C2	49
Springboro, Oh., U.S.	C1	112
Springboro, Pa., U.S.	C1	115
Springbrook, Ia., U.S.	B7	92
Spring Brook, N.D., U.S.	A2	111
Springbrook, Wi., U.S.	C2	126
Spring Brook, stm., Pa., U.S.	n18	115
Spring City, Pa., U.S.	F10	115
Spring City, Tn., U.S.	D9	119
Spring City, Ut., U.S.	D4	121
Spring Coulee, Alta.	E4	68
Spring Creek, Pa., U.S.	C2	115
Spring Creek, Tn., U.S.	B3	119
Spring Creek, stm., U.S.	B8	104
Spring Creek, stm., Co., U.S.	B8	83
Spring Creek, stm., Ga., U.S.	E2	87
Spring Creek, stm., Nv., U.S.	C4	105
Spring Creek Colony, S.D., U.S.	D3	118
Springdale, Newf.	D3	72
Springdale, Ar., U.S.	A1	81
Springdale, Mt., U.S.	E6	103
Springdale, Oh., U.S.	n13	112
Springdale, Or., U.S.	B4	114
Springdale, Pa., U.S.	E2	115
Springdale, S.C., U.S.	D5	117
Springdale, Ut., U.S.	F3	121
Springdale, Wa., U.S.	A8	124
Springdell, Ut., U.S.	*C4	121
Springe, W. Ger.	A4	19
Springer, N.M., U.S.	A5	108
Springer, Ok., U.S.	C4	113
Springerton, Il., U.S.	E5	90
Springerville, Az., U.S.	C6	80
Springfield, N.B.	D4	71
Springfield, Ont.	E4	73
Springfield, Co., U.S.	D8	83
Springfield, Fl., U.S.	u16	86
Springfield, Ga., U.S.	D5	87
Springfield, Il., U.S.	D4	90
Springfield, Ky., U.S.	C4	94
Springfield, La., U.S.	D5	95
Springfield, Ma., U.S.	B2	98
Springfield, Mn., U.S.	F4	100
Springfield, Mo., U.S.	D4	102
Springfield, Ne., U.S.	C9	104
Springfield, N.H., U.S.	D3	106
Springfield, N.J., U.S.	B4	107
Springfield, Oh., U.S.	C2	112
Springfield, Or., U.S.	C4	114
Springfield, Pa., U.S.	p20	115
Springfield, S.C., U.S.	E5	117
Springfield, S.D., U.S.	E8	118
Springfield, Tn., U.S.	A5	119
Springfield, Vt., U.S.	E4	122
Springfield, Va., U.S.	*B5	123
Springfield, W.V., U.S.	B6	125
Springfield, Lake, res., Il., U.S.	D4	90
Springfield Township, Pa., U.S.	*F11	115
Springfontein, S. Afr.	D4	49
Spring Garden, Al., U.S.	B4	78
Spring Garden, Pa., U.S.	*G8	115
Spring Glen, Ut., U.S.	D5	121
Spring Green, Wi., U.S.	E3	126
Spring Grove, Il., U.S.	h8	90
Spring Grove, Mn., U.S.	G7	100
Spring Grove, Pa., U.S.	G8	115
Springhill, Al., U.S.	D4	78
Spring Hill, Ar., U.S.	D2	81
Spring Hill, Ct., U.S.	B7	84
Spring Hill, Fl., U.S.	D4	86
Spring Hill, Ia., U.S.	k10	91
Spring Hill, Ks., U.S.	f8	93
Spring Hill, Tn., U.S.	B5	119
Springhill Junction, N.S.	D5	71
Spring Hope, N.C., U.S.	B4	110
Springhouse, B.C.	D6	69
Spring Island, i., S.C., U.S.	G6	117
Spring Lake, Fl., U.S.	D4	86
Spring Lake, Mi., U.S.	E4	99
Spring Lake, N.J., U.S.	C4	107
Spring Lake, N.C., U.S.	B4	110
Spring Lake, l., Me., U.S.	C2	96
Spring Lake, res., l., S.	B3	90
Spring Lake Heights, N.J., U.S.	C4	107
Spring Lake Park, Mn., U.S.	*E5	100
Spring Lick, Ky., U.S.	C3	94
Spring Mills, Pa., U.S.	E6	115
Spring Mountains, mts., Nv., U.S.	G6	105
Spring Place, Ga., U.S.	B2	87
Springport, In., U.S.	D7	91
Springport, Mi., U.S.	F6	99
Springs, S. Afr.	C4	49
Springside, Sask.	F4	75
Springsure, Austl.	D8	50
Springvale, Austl.	A3	51
Springvale, Me., U.S.	E2	96
Spring Valley, Sask.	H3	75
Spring Valley, Al., U.S.	A2	78
Spring Valley, Ca., U.S.	o16	82
Spring Valley, Il., U.S.	B4	90
Spring Valley, Mn., U.S.	G6	100
Spring Valley, N.Y., U.S.	g12	109
Spring Valley, Oh., U.S.	C1	112
Spring Valley, Wi., U.S.	D1	126
Springview, Ne., U.S.	B6	104
Springville, Al., U.S.	B3	78
Springville, Ca., U.S.	D4	82
Springville, Ia., U.S.	B6	92
Springville, Ms., U.S.	A4	101
Springville, N.Y., U.S.	C2	109
Springville, Pa., U.S.	C10	115
Springville, Tn., U.S.	A3	119
Springville, Ut., U.S.	C4	121
Springwater, Sask.	F1	75
Springwater, N.Y., U.S.	C3	109
Spruce, Mi., U.S.	D7	99
Spruce, stm., Sask.	D3	75
Spruce Brook, Newf.	D2	72
Spruce Creek, Pa., U.S.	E5	115
Sprucedale, Ont.	B5	73
Spruce Fork, stm., W.V., U.S.	m12	125
Spruce Knob, mtn., W.V., U.S.	C6	125
Spruce Knob-Seneca Rocks National Recreation Area, W.V., U.S.	C5	125
Spruce Lake, Sask.	D1	75
Spruce Mountain, mtn., Az., U.S.	C3	80
Spruce Mountain, mtn., Nv., U.S.	C7	105
Spruce Pine, Al., U.S.	A2	78
Spruce Pine, N.C., U.S.	f10	110
Spruce Run Reservoir, res., N.J., U.S.	B3	107
Spruga, Switz.	D6	21
Spur, Tx., U.S.	C2	120
Spurfield, Alta.	B3	68
Spurgeon, In., U.S.	H3	91
Spurn Head, c., Eng., U.K.	A8	12
Spurr, Mount, mtn., Ak., U.S.	g15	79
Spy Hill, Sask.	G5	75
Squamish, B.C.	E6	69
Squam Lake, l., N.H., U.S.	C4	106
Squam Mountains, mts., N.H., U.S.	C3	106
Squapan Lake, l., Me., U.S.	B4	96
Square Islands, Newf.	B4	72
Square Lake, l., Me., U.S.	A4	96
Squatec, Que.	B9	74
Squaw Cap Mountain, mtn., N.B.	B3	71
Squaw Harbor, Ak., U.S.	D7	79
Squaw Hill, Wy., U.S.	C4	127
Squaw Lake, Mn., U.S.	C4	100
Squaw Peak, mtn., Mt., U.S.	C2	103
Squaw Rapids, Sask.	D4	75
Squibnocket Point, c., Ma., U.S.	D6	98
Squillace, Gulf of, b., Italy	E6	23
Squire, W.V., U.S.	D3	125
Squires, Mo., U.S.	E5	102
Squirrel, Id., U.S.	E7	89
Srbobran, Yugo.	C4	24
Srednekolymsk, Sov. Un.	C18	29
Sredniy Vasyugan, Sov. Un.	D24	8
Śrem, Pol.	B7	19
Sremska Mitrovica, Yugo.	C4	24
Sremski Karlovci, Yugo.	C4	24
Srepok, stm., Asia	C4	34
Sretensk, Sov. Un.	D14	29
Sri Lanka, ctry., Asia	B5	36
Srinagar, India	B5	36
Środa Śląska, Pol.	B6	19
Środa [Wielkopolska], Pol.	B4	19
Staatsburg, N.Y., U.S.	D7	109
Stab, Ky., U.S.	C5	94
Stack Reservoir, res., R.I., U.S.	C3	116
Stack's Mountains, mts., Ire.	E2	11
Stacy, Ar., U.S.	B5	81
Stacy, N.C., U.S.	C6	110
Stacyville, Ia., U.S.	A5	92
Stacyville, Me., U.S.	C4	96
Stade, W. Ger.	B4	18
Stadskanaal, Neth.	A6	17
Stadthagen, W. Ger.	A4	19
Stadtkyll, W. Ger.	C2	18
Stadtlohn, W. Ger.	B1	19
Stadtroda, E. Ger.	C6	19

Name	Map Ref.	Page
Stäfa, Switz.	B6	21
Staffa, i., Scot., U.K.	D2	13
Stafford, Eng., U.K.	D5	10
Stafford, Ct., U.S.	B6	84
Stafford, Ks., U.S.	E5	93
Stafford, N.Y., U.S.	C2	109
Stafford, Oh., U.S.	C4	112
Stafford, Ok., U.S.	B2	113
Stafford, Va., U.S.	B5	123
Stafford, co., Ks., U.S.	D5	93
Stafford, co., Va., U.S.	B5	123
Stafford Pond, l., R.I., U.S.	D6	116
Staffordshire, co., Eng., U.K.	B5	12
Stafford Springs, Ct., U.S.	B6	84
Staffordville, Ct., U.S.	B6	84
Staffordville, N.J., U.S.	D4	107
Staines, Eng., U.K.	m11	10
Stains, Fr.	g10	16
Stairs Mountain, mtn., N.H., U.S.	B4	106
Stakhanov, Sov. Un.	G12	27
Stålboga, Swe.	t34	14
Stalden, Switz.	D4	21
Staley, N.C., U.S.	B3	110
Stalin (Kuçovë), Alb.	B2	25
Stalingrad see Volgograd, Sov. Un.	E7	29
Stalingród see Katowice, Pol.		
Stall Lake, Man.	F13	66
Stallworthy, Cape, c., N.W. Ter.	k33	66
Stalowa Wola, Pol.	C7	26
Stalwart, Sask.	F3	75
Stalwart, Mi., U.S.	B6	99
Stambaugh, Mi., U.S.	B2	99
Stamford, Eng., U.K.	B7	12
Stamford, Ct., U.S.	E1	84
Stamford, Ne., U.S.	D6	104
Stamford, N.Y., U.S.	C6	109
Stamford, Tx., U.S.	C3	120
Stamford, Vt., U.S.	F2	122
Stamford, Lake, res., Tx., U.S.	C3	120
Stamping Ground, Ky., U.S.	B5	94
Stampriet, Nmb.	B2	49
Stamps, Ar., U.S.	D2	81
Stanaford, W.V., U.S.	D3	125
Stanardsville, Va., U.S.	B4	123
Stanberry, Mo., U.S.	A3	102
Stanchfield, Mn., U.S.	E5	100
Standard, Alta.	D4	68
Standard, Il., U.S.	B4	90
Standard, La., U.S.	C3	95
Standerton, S. Afr.	C4	49
Standing Rock, N.C., U.S.	B4	78
Standing Rock, N.M., U.S.	B1	108
Standing Rock Indian Reservation, U.S.	B4	118
Standish, Me., U.S.	E2	96
Standish, Mi., U.S.	E7	99
Standish, N.Y., U.S.	f11	109
Stanfield, Az., U.S.	E3	80
Stanfield, Or., U.S.	B7	114
Stanford, Ca., U.S.	*k8	82
Stanford, Il., U.S.	C4	90
Stanford, Ky., U.S.	C5	94
Stanford, Mt., U.S.	C6	103
Stangeville, Wi., U.S.	D6	126
Stanger, S. Afr.	C5	49
Stanhope, Que.	D6	74
Stanhope, Eng., U.K.	F6	13
Stanhope, Ia., U.S.	B4	92
Stanhope, N.J., U.S.	B3	107
Staniard Creek, Bah.	B5	64
Stanislaus, co., Ca., U.S.	D3	82
Stanisławów, Pol.	k15	26
Stanke Dimitrov (Dupnitsa), Bul.	D6	24
Stanley, N.B.	C3	71
Stanley, Falk. Is.	I5	53
Stanley, Id., U.S.	E4	89
Stanley, Ks., U.S.	D9	93
Stanley, Ky., U.S.	C2	94
Stanley, La., U.S.	C2	95
Stanley, N.M., U.S.	B4	108
Stanley, N.C., U.S.	B1	110
Stanley, N.D., U.S.	A3	111
Stanley, Va., U.S.	B4	123
Stanley, Wi., U.S.	D3	126
Stanley, co., S.D., U.S.	C5	118
Stanley Falls see Boyoma Falls, wtfl., Zaire	A4	48
Stanleytown, Va., U.S.	D3	123
Stanleyville, N.C., U.S.	A2	110
Stanleyville see Kisangani, Zaire	A4	48
Stanly, co., N.C., U.S.	B2	110
Stanmore, Alta.	D5	68
Stann Creek, Belize	D7	63
Stans, Switz.	C4	20
Stansbury Mountains, mts., Ut., U.S.	C3	121
Stansbury Park, Ut., U.S.	*C3	121
Stanstead, Que.	D5	74
Stanstead, co., Que.	D5	74
Stanthorpe, Austl.	E9	50
Stanton, Ca., U.S.	*n13	82
Stanton, Ia., U.S.	D2	92
Stanton, Ky., U.S.	C6	94
Stanton, Mi., U.S.	E5	99
Stanton, Mo., U.S.	C6	102
Stanton, Ne., U.S.	C8	104
Stanton, N.J., U.S.	B3	107
Stanton, N.D., U.S.	B4	111
Stanton, Tn., U.S.	B2	119
Stanton, Tx., U.S.	C2	120
Stanton, co., Ks., U.S.	E2	93
Stanton, co., Ne., U.S.	C8	104
Stantonsburg, N.C., U.S.	B5	110
Stantonville, Tn., U.S.	B3	119
Stanwood, Ia., U.S.	C6	92
Stanwood, Mi., U.S.	E5	99
Stanwood, Wa., U.S.	A3	124
Staplehurst, Ne., U.S.	D8	104
Staples, Mn., U.S.	D4	100
Staples, Tx., U.S.	H8	120
Stapleton, Al., U.S.	E2	78
Stapleton, Ga., U.S.	C4	87
Stapleton, Ne., U.S.	C5	104
Star, Id., U.S.	F2	89
Star, Ms., U.S.	C3	101
Star, N.C., U.S.	B3	110
Star, Tx., U.S.	D3	120
Starachowice, Pol.	C6	26
Staráya Russa, Sov. Un.	C8	27
Stará Zagora, Bul.	D7	24
Starbuck, Man.	E3	70
Starbuck, Mn., U.S.	E3	100
Starbuck, Wa., U.S.	C7	124
Starbuck Island, i., Kir.	G12	6
Star City, Sask.	E3	75
Star City, Ar., U.S.	D4	81
Star City, In., U.S.	C4	91
Star City, W.V., U.S.	B5	125
Starford, Pa., U.S.	E4	115
Stargard [Szczeciński], Pol.	B3	26
Stargo, Az., U.S.	D6	80
Staritsa, Sov. Un.	C10	27
Stark, Ks., U.S.	E8	93
Stark, N.H., U.S.	A4	106
Stark, co., Il., U.S.	B4	90
Stark, co., N.D., U.S.	C3	111
Stark, co., Oh., U.S.	B4	112
Starke, Fl., U.S.	C4	86
Starke, co., In., U.S.	B4	91
Starkey, Va., U.S.	C3	123
Starks, La., U.S.	D2	95
Starks, Me., U.S.	D3	96
Starksboro, Vt., U.S.	C2	122
Starkville, Co., U.S.	D6	83
Starkville, Ms., U.S.	B5	101
Starkville, N.Y., U.S.	C6	109
Starkweather, N.D., U.S.	A7	111
Star Lake, l., Mn., U.S.	D3	100
Starlight, Pa., U.S.	C11	115
Starnberg, W. Ger.	D6	18
Starnberg Lake, l., W. Ger.	E5	18
Starobelsk, Sov. Un.	G12	27
Starodub, Sov. Un.	E9	27
Starogard [Gdański], Pol.	B5	26
Starokonstantinov, Sov. Un.	G6	27
Starominskaya, Sov. Un.	H12	27
Star Peak, mtn., Nv., U.S.	C3	105
Star Prairie, Wi., U.S.	C1	126
Starr, S.C., U.S.	C2	117
Starr, co., Tx., U.S.	F3	120
Starr Mountain, mtn., Tn., U.S.	D9	119
Starrucca, Pa., U.S.	C11	115
Start Bay, b., Eng., U.K.	D4	12
Startex, S.C., U.S.	B3	117
Start Point, c., Eng., U.K.	E5	10
Startup, Wa., U.S.	B4	124
Starý Plzenec, Czech.	D8	19
Staryy Oskol, Sov. Un.	F11	27
Stassfurt, E. Ger.	C5	18
Staszów, Pol.	C6	26
State Center, Ia., U.S.	B4	92
State College, Pa., U.S.	E6	115
State Line, In., U.S.	D2	91
State Line, Ma., U.S.	B1	98
State Line, Ms., U.S.	D5	101
State Line, Pa., U.S.	G6	115
Stateline, Nv., U.S.	E2	105
Staten Island, i., N.Y., U.S.	k12	109
Statenville, Ga., U.S.	F4	87
State Road, N.C., U.S.	A2	110
Statesboro, Ga., U.S.	D5	87
Statesville, N.C., U.S.	B2	110
Statham, Ga., U.S.	C3	87
Statue of Liberty National Monument, N.J., U.S.	k8	107
Staufen, W. Ger.	B3	20
Staunton, Il., U.S.	D4	90
Staunton, In., U.S.	F3	91
Staunton, Va., U.S.	B3	123
Stavanger, Nor.	H1	14
Stave Lake, l., B.C.	f13	69
Staveley, Eng., U.K.	A6	12
Stavelot, Bel.	D5	17
Stavely, Alta.	D4	68
Staveren, Neth.	C4	17
Stavropol, Sov. Un.	E7	29
Stawell, Austl.	H4	51
Stayner, Ont.	C4	73
Stayton, Or., U.S.	C4	114
Stead, N.M., U.S.	A6	108
Steamboat Canyon, Az., U.S.	B6	80
Steamboat Mountain, mtn., Mt., U.S.	C4	103
Steamboat Mountain, mtn., Wy., U.S.	E4	127
Steamboat Rock, Ia., U.S.	B4	92
Steamboat Springs, Co., U.S.	A4	83
Stearns, Ky., U.S.	D5	94
Stearns, co., Mn., U.S.	E4	100
Stearns Brook, stm., N.H., U.S.	A4	106
Stebbins, Ak., U.S.	C7	79
Steblev, Sov. Un.	G8	27
Štěchovice, Czech.	o17	26
Štěchovice, Czech.	o17	26
Stecker, Ok., U.S.	C3	113
Stecoah, N.C., U.S.	f9	110
Steele, Al., U.S.	B3	78
Steele, Mo., U.S.	E8	102
Steele, N.D., U.S.	C6	111
Steele, co., Mn., U.S.	F5	100
Steele, co., N.D., U.S.	B8	111
Steele, Mount, mtn., Wy., U.S.	E6	127
Steele City, Ne., U.S.	D8	104
Steeleville, Il., U.S.	E4	90
Steelton, Pa., U.S.	F8	115
Steelville, Mo., U.S.	D6	102
Steen, Mn., U.S.	G2	100
Steenbergen, Neth.	C4	17
Steens, Ms., U.S.	B5	101
Steens Mountain, mts., Or., U.S.	E8	114
Steenwijk, Neth.	B6	17
Steep Falls, Me., U.S.	E2	96
Steephill Lake, l., Sask.	B4	75
Steep Point, c., Austl.	E1	50
Steep Rock, Man.	D2	70
Steep Rock Lake, Ont.	o17	73
Ştefăneşti, Rom.	B8	24
Stefanie, Lake, l., Afr.	E4	47
Stefansson Island, i., N.W. Ter.	B11	66
Steffisburg, Switz.	C4	21
Stege, Den.	D6	15
Steger, Il., U.S.	B6	90
Stehekin, Wa., U.S.	A5	124
Steilacoom, Wa., U.S.	f10	124
Stein, W. Ger.	D5	19
Steinach, Aus.	B7	20
Stein [am Rhein], Switz.	E4	18
Steinbach, Man.	E3	70
Steinauer, Ne., U.S.	D9	104
Steinbach-Hallenberg, E. Ger.	E5	17
Steinfort, Lux.	E5	17
Steinhatchee, Fl., U.S.	C3	86
Steinhatchee, stm., Fl., U.S.	C3	86
Steinhausen, Nmb.	B2	49
Steinhuder, l., W. Ger.	F3	15
Steinkjer, Nor.	E4	14
Stella, Ont.	C8	73
Stella, Ky., U.S.	f9	94
Stella, Mo., U.S.	E3	102
Stella, Ne., U.S.	D10	104
Stella, mtn., Italy	C5	20
Stellarton, N.S.	D7	71
Stem, N.C., U.S.	A4	110
Stendal, E. Ger.	B5	18
Stendal, In., U.S.	H3	91
Stenen, Sask.	F4	75
Stenness, Loch of, l., Scot., U.K.	A5	13
Stepanakert, Sov. Un.	F3	28
Stepenitz, stm., E. Ger.	E6	15
Stephan, S.D., U.S.	C6	118
Stephen, Mn., U.S.	B2	100
Stephens, Ar., U.S.	D2	81
Stephens, Ga., U.S.	C3	87
Stephens, co., Ga., U.S.	B3	87
Stephens, co., Ok., U.S.	C4	113
Stephens, co., Tx., U.S.	C3	120
Stephens, Port, b., Austl.	F9	51
Stephens City, Va., U.S.	A4	123
Stephens Knob, hill, Ky., U.S.	D5	94
Stephens Lake, res., Man.	A4	70
Stephenson, Mi., U.S.	C3	99
Stephenson, co., Il., U.S.	A4	90
Stephenson, Mount, mtn., Ant.	C19	7
Stephens Passage, strt., Ak., U.S.	m23	79
Stephensport, Ky., U.S.	C3	94
Stephenville, Newf.	D2	72
Stephenville, Tx., U.S.	C3	120
Stephenville Crossing, Newf.	D2	72
Stepnica, Pol.	B3	15
Stepnyak, Sov. Un.	C8	28
Steppes, plat., Sov. Un.	C8	28
Step Pyramid, hist., Egypt	E3	41
Steps Point, c., Am. Sam.	G13	52
Steptoe, Nv., U.S.	D7	105
Steptoe, Wa., U.S.	B8	124
Sterkstroom, S. Afr.	D4	49
Sterling, Ak., U.S.	g16	79
Sterling, Co., U.S.	A7	83
Sterling, Ct., U.S.	C8	84
Sterling, Il., U.S.	B4	90
Sterling, Ks., U.S.	D5	93
Sterling, Ma., U.S.	B4	98
Sterling, Mi., U.S.	D6	99
Sterling, Ne., U.S.	D9	104
Sterling, N.D., U.S.	C5	111
Sterling, Ok., U.S.	C3	113
Sterling, Ut., U.S.	D4	121
Sterling, Va., U.S.	A5	123
Sterling, co., Tx., U.S.	D2	120
Sterling City, Tx., U.S.	D2	120
Sterling Heights, Mi., U.S.	o15	99
Sterling Reservoir, res., Co., U.S.	A6	83
Sterling Run, Pa., U.S.	D5	115
Sterlington, La., U.S.	B3	95
Sterlitamak, Sov. Un.	D8	29
Sternberg, E. Ger.	E5	15
Šternberk, Czech.	D4	26
Sterrett, Al., U.S.	B3	78
Štěti, Czech.	C9	19
Stetson, Me., U.S.	D3	96
Stetson Mountain, mtn., Me., U.S.	C4	96
Stetsonville, Wi., U.S.	C3	126
Stettin Lagoon, b., Eur.	B7	18
Stettin see Szczecin, Pol.		
Stettler, Alta.	C4	68
Steuben, Me., U.S.	D5	96
Steuben, Mi., U.S.	B3	99
Steuben, Wi., U.S.	E3	126
Steuben, co., In., U.S.	A7	91
Steuben, co., N.Y., U.S.	C3	109
Steubenville, Oh., U.S.	B5	112
Stevenage, Eng., U.K.	F7	12
Stevens, N.J., U.S.	C3	107
Stevens, co., Ks., U.S.	E2	93
Stevens, co., Mn., U.S.	E2	100
Stevens, co., Wa., U.S.	A7	124
Stevens Creek Dam, U.S.	A4	78
Stevenson, Al., U.S.	A4	78
Stevenson, Ct., U.S.	D3	84
Stevenson, Wa., U.S.	D4	124
Stevenson, stm., Man.	C4	70
Stevenson Lake, l., Man.	C4	70
Stevenson Mountain, mtn., Ar., U.S.	B1	81
Stevens Pass, Wa., U.S.	B4	124
Stevens Peak, mtn., Id., U.S.	B3	89
Stevens Point, Wi., U.S.	D4	126
Stevens Pottery, Ga., U.S.	D3	87
Stevens Village, Ak., U.S.	B10	79
Stevensville, Md., U.S.	C5	97
Stevensville, Mi., U.S.	F4	99
Stevensville, Pa., U.S.	C9	115
Steward, Il., U.S.	B4	90
Stewardson, Il., U.S.	D5	90
Stewart, B.C.	B3	69
Stewart, Al., U.S.	C2	78
Stewart, Mn., U.S.	F4	100
Stewart, Ms., U.S.	B4	101
Stewart, Tn., U.S.	A4	119
Stewart, co., Ga., U.S.	D2	87
Stewart, co., Tn., U.S.	A4	119
Stewart, stm., Yukon	D5	66
Stewart Island, i., N.Z.	Q11	51
Stewart Mountain, mtn., U.S.	k9	80
Stewarton, Scot., U.K.	E4	13
Stewarts Point, Nv., U.S.	G7	105
Stewartstown, N. Ire., U.K.	C5	11
Stewartstown, N.H., U.S.	f6	106
Stewartstown, Pa., U.S.	G8	115
Stewartstown Hollow, N.H., U.S.	g7	106
Stewartsville, Al., U.S.	A3	78
Stewartsville, In., U.S.	H2	91
Stewartsville, Mo., U.S.	B3	102
Stewartsville, N.J., U.S.	B2	107
Stewart Valley, Sask.	G2	75
Stewartville, Mn., U.S.	G6	100
Stewiacke, N.S.	D6	71
Steynsburg, S. Afr.	D4	49
Steyr, Aus.	D7	18
Stickney, Il., U.S.	*k9	90
Stickney, S.D., U.S.	D7	118
Stif (Sétif), Alg.	B6	44
Stigler, Ok., U.S.	B6	113
Stikine, stm., N.A.	E6	66
Stikine, stm., Ak., U.S.	D13	79
Stilesville, In., U.S.	E4	91
Stilis, Grc.	C4	25
Still, stm., Ct., U.S.	B3	84
Stillaguamish, North Fork, stm., Wa., U.S.	A4	124
Stillaguamish, South Fork, stm., Wa., U.S.	A4	124
Stillhouse Hollow Lake, res., Tx., U.S.	D4	120
Stillman Valley, Il., U.S.	A4	90
Still Pond, Md., U.S.	B5	97
Still River, Ma., U.S.	f10	98
Stillwater, B.C.	E5	69
Stillwater, Mn., U.S.	E6	100
Stillwater, N.Y., U.S.	C7	109
Stillwater, Ok., U.S.	A4	113
Stillwater, Pa., U.S.	D9	115
Stillwater, co., Mt., U.S.	E7	103
Stillwater Range, mts., Nv., U.S.	D3	105
Stillwater Reservoir, res., N.Y., U.S.	B5	109
Stillwater Reservoir, res., R.I., U.S.	B3	116
Stillwell, Ga., U.S.	D5	87
Stillwell, In., U.S.	A4	91
Stilson, Ga., U.S.	D5	87
Stilwell, Ks., U.S.	D9	93
Stilwell, Ok., U.S.	B7	113
Stimson, Mount, mtn., Mt., U.S.	B3	103
Stinear Nunataks, mts., Ant.	C19	7
Stine Mountain, mtn., Mt., U.S.	E3	103
Stinesville, In., U.S.	F4	91
Stinking Lake, l., N.M., U.S.	A3	108
Stinnett, Tx., U.S.	B2	120
Stinson Lake, N.H., U.S.	C3	106
Štip, Yugo.	E6	24
Stirling, Austl.	F2	50
Stirling, Alta.	E4	68
Stirling, Ont.	C7	73
Stirling, Scot., U.K.	B5	10
Stirling, N.J., U.S.	B4	107
Stirling City, Ca., U.S.	C3	82
Stirrat, W.V., U.S.	D3	125
Stites, Id., U.S.	C3	89
Stittsville, Ont.	B9	73
Stjördalshalsen, Nor.	F4	14
Stockach, W. Ger.	A7	21
Stockbridge, Ga., U.S.	C2	87
Stockbridge, Ma., U.S.	B1	98
Stockbridge, Mi., U.S.	F6	99
Stockbridge, Vt., U.S.	D3	122
Stockbridge, Wi., U.S.	D5	126
Stockbridge-Munsee Indian Reservation, Wi., U.S.	D5	126
Stockdale, Oh., U.S.	D3	112
Stockdale, Tx., U.S.	E4	120
Stockertown, Pa., U.S.	E11	115
Stockett, Mt., U.S.	C5	103
Stockham, Ne., U.S.	D8	104
Stockholm, Sask.	G4	75
Stockholm, Swe.	H8	14
Stockholm, Me., U.S.	A4	96
Stockholm, N.J., U.S.	A4	107
Stockholm, S.D., U.S.	B9	118
Stockholm, Wi., U.S.	D1	126
Stockhorn, mtn., Switz.	C3	20
Stockton, Il., U.S.	A4	90
Stockley, De., U.S.	F4	85
Stockport, Eng., U.K.	D5	10
Stockport, Oh., U.S.	C4	112
Stockton, Man.	E2	70
Stockton, Ca., U.S.	D3	82
Stockton, Ga., U.S.	F4	87
Stockton, Il., U.S.	A4	90
Stockton, Ks., U.S.	C4	93
Stockton, Mo., U.S.	D7	102
Stockton, N.J., U.S.	C3	107
Stockton, N.Y., U.S.	C1	109
Stockton, Ut., U.S.	C3	121
Stockton Island, i., Wi., U.S.	B3	126
Stockton Lake, res., Mo., U.S.	D4	102
Stockton-on-Tees, Eng., U.K.	F7	13
Stockton Plateau, plat., Tx., U.S.	D1	120
Stockton Springs, Me., U.S.	D4	96
Stockville, Ne., U.S.	D5	104
Stockwell, In., U.S.	D4	91
Stod, Czech.	D8	19
Stoddard, N.H., U.S.	E2	106
Stoddard, Wi., U.S.	E2	126
Stoddard, co., Mo., U.S.	E8	102
Stoeckl, Mount, mtn., N.A.	A2	69
Stoeng Treng, Camb.	D3	34
Stoer, Point of, c., Scot., U.K.	B3	13
Stoke-Centre, Que.	D6	74
Stoke-on-Trent, Eng., U.K.	B5	10
Stokes, Sc., U.S.	A2	110
Stokes, co., N.C., U.S.	A2	110
Stokes, Mount, mtn., N.Z.	N15	51
Stokesdale, N.C., U.S.	A3	110
Stokesley, Eng., U.K.	F7	13
Stokke, Nor.	p28	14
Stolac, Yugo.	D3	24
Stolberg, W. Ger.	C3	18
Stolbovaya, Sov. Un.	n17	27
Stolbovoy, i., Sov. Un.	B1	128
Stolberg, E. Ger.	C7	19
Stollings, W.V., U.S.	n12	125
Stolzenau, W. Ger.	F3	15
Stone, Eng., U.K.	B5	12
Stone, Id., U.S.	G6	89
Stone, co., Ar., U.S.	B3	81
Stone, co., Ms., U.S.	E4	101
Stone, co., Mo., U.S.	E4	102
Stonebluff, In., U.S.	D3	91
Stoneboro, Pa., U.S.	D1	115
Stone City, Ia., U.S.	B6	92
Stone Corral Lake, l., Or., U.S.	E7	114
Stonefort, Il., U.S.	F5	90
Stonega, Va., U.S.	f9	123
Stoneham, Co., U.S.	A7	83
Stoneham, Ma., U.S.	g11	98
Stone Harbor, N.J., U.S.	E3	107
Stonehaven, N.B.	B4	71
Stonehaven, Scot., U.K.	B5	10
Stonehenge, Austl.	B4	51
Stone Lake, Wi., U.S.	C2	126
Stone Mountain, mtn., Ga., U.S.	C2	87
Stone Mountain, mtn., Vt., U.S.	B5	122
Stone Mountains, mts., U.S.	A1	110
Stoner, B.C.	C6	69
Stoner, Co., U.S.	D2	83
Stones River National Battlefield, hist., Tn., U.S.	B4	119
Stoneville, Ms., U.S.	B3	101
Stoneville, N.C., U.S.	A3	110
Stonewall, Man.	D3	70
Stonewall, Ga., U.S.	C2	87
Stonewall, La., U.S.	B2	95
Stonewall, Ms., U.S.	C5	101
Stonewall, Tx., U.S.	D3	120
Stonewall, co., Tx., U.S.	C2	120
Stonewood, W.V., U.S.	k10	125
Stoney Creek, Ont.	D5	73
Stonington, Co., U.S.	D8	83
Stonington, Ct., U.S.	D8	84
Stonington, Il., U.S.	D4	90
Stonington, Me., U.S.	D4	96
Stonington, Mn., U.S.	B2	100
Stono, stm., S.C., U.S.	k11	117
Stono Inlet, b., S.C., U.S.	F8	117
Stony Beach, Sask.	G3	75
Stony Brook, N.Y., U.S.	n15	109
Stony Brook, stm., N.J., U.S.	C3	107
Stony Creek, Ct., U.S.	D5	84
Stony Creek, N.Y., U.S.	B7	109
Stony Creek, Va., U.S.	D5	123
Stony Creek, stm., Va., U.S.	C5	123
Stony Island, i., Newf.	B4	72
Stony Lake, l., Ont.	C6	73
Stony Mountain, Man.	D3	70
Stony Plain, Alta.	C3	68
Stony Point, N.Y., U.S.	*D7	109
Stony Point, N.C., U.S.	B1	110
Stony Rapids, Sask.	m7	75
Stony Ridge, Oh., U.S.	e6	112
Stör, stm., W. Ger.	B4	18
Stora Lulevatten, l., Swe.	D8	14
Stora Sundby, Swe.	t34	14
Storden, Mn., U.S.	F3	100
Store Bælt, strt., Den.	C4	15
Store Heddinge, Den.	J5	14
Storey, co., Nv., U.S.	D2	105
Storkow, E. Ger.	A8	19
Storla, S.D., U.S.	D7	118
Storlien, Swe.	E7	14
Storm Lake, Ia., U.S.	B2	92
Storm Lake, l., Ia., U.S.	B2	92
Storm Mountain, mtn., Ak., U.S.	h16	79
Stormont, co., Ont.	B10	73
Stornoway, Sask.	F4	75
Stornoway, Scot., U.K.	A3	10
Storozhinets, Sov. Un.	G5	27
Storrs, Ct., U.S.	B7	84
Storsjö, Swe.	F5	14
Storsjön, l., Swe.	E8	14
Storsjön, l., Swe.	F6	14
Storstrøm, co., Den.	D5	15
Storthoaks, Sask.	H5	75
Storuman, Swe.	E7	14
Storuman, l., Swe.	E7	14
Story, Ar., U.S.	C2	81
Story, Wy., U.S.	B6	127
Story, co., Ia., U.S.	B4	92
Story City, Ia., U.S.	B4	92
Stotesbury, Mo., U.S.	D3	102
Stotts City, Mo., U.S.	D4	102
Stottville, N.Y., U.S.	C7	109
Stoughton, Sask.	H4	75
Stoughton, Ma., U.S.	B5	98
Stoughton, Wi., U.S.	F4	126
Stour, stm., Eng., U.K.	E7	10
Stour, stm., Eng., U.K.	E6	10
Stourbridge, Eng., U.K.	B5	12
Stourport-on-Severn, Eng., U.K.	B5	12
Stout, Oh., U.S.	D2	112
Stoutland, Mo., U.S.	D5	102
Stoutsville, Mo., U.S.	B6	102
Stoutsville, Oh., U.S.	C3	112
Stovall, Ga., U.S.	D2	87
Stovall, Ms., U.S.	A3	101
Stovall, N.C., U.S.	A4	110
Stover, Mo., U.S.	C5	102
Stow, Me., U.S.	D2	96
Stow, Ma., U.S.	B4	98
Stow, Oh., U.S.	A4	112
Stowe, Pa., U.S.	F10	115
Stowe, Vt., U.S.	C3	122
Stowe Township, Pa., U.S.	*k13	115
Stowmarket, Eng., U.K.	B8	12
Stoy, Il., U.S.	E6	90
Stoystown, Pa., U.S.	F4	115
Strabane, N. Ire., U.K.	C3	11
Strabane, Pa., U.S.	F1	115
Strachur, Scot., U.K.	D3	13
Stradbally, Ire.	D4	11
Stradone, Ire.	D4	11
Strafford, Mo., U.S.	D4	102
Strafford, N.H., U.S.	D4	106
Strafford, Vt., U.S.	D4	122
Strafford, co., N.H., U.S.	D4	106
Straffordville, Ont.	E4	73
Straight, Ok., U.S.	e9	113
Strakonice, Czech.	D2	26
Stralsund, E. Ger.	A6	18
Strand, S. Afr.	D2	49
Strandburg, S.D., U.S.	B9	118
Strandby, Den.	A4	15
Strandhill, Ire.	C3	11
Strandquist, Mn., U.S.	B2	100
Strang, Ne., U.S.	D8	104
Strang, Ok., U.S.	A5	113
Strängnäs, Swe.	t35	14
Stranorlar, Ire.	C4	11
Stranraer, Sask.	F1	75
Stranraer, Scot., U.K.	C4	10
Strasbourg, Sask.	F3	75
Strasbourg, Fr.	C7	16
Strasburg, E. Ger.	E7	15
Strasburg, Il., U.S.	D5	90
Strasburg, Mo., U.S.	C3	102
Strasburg, N.D., U.S.	C5	111
Strasburg, Oh., U.S.	B4	112
Strasburg, Pa., U.S.	G9	115
Strasburg, Va., U.S.	B4	123
Strasswalchen, Aus.	B9	20
Stratford, Ont.	D4	73
Stratford, N.Z.	M15	51
Stratford, Ct., U.S.	E3	84
Stratford, Ia., U.S.	B4	92
Stratford, N.H., U.S.	A3	106
Stratford, Ok., U.S.	C5	113
Stratford, S.D., U.S.	B7	118
Stratford, Tx., U.S.	A1	120
Stratford, Wi., U.S.	D3	126
Stratford Centre, Que.	D6	74
Stratford Landing, Va., U.S.	*B5	123
Stratford Point, c., Ct., U.S.	E3	84
Stratford-upon-Avon, Eng., U.K.	D6	10
Strathaven, Scot., U.K.	E4	13
Strathclair, Man.	D1	70
Strathclyde, prov., Scot., U.K.	E4	13
Strathcona, Ont.	C8	73
Strathcona, Mn., U.S.	B2	100
Strathcona Provincial Park, B.C.	E5	69
Strathlorne, N.S.	C8	71
Strathmere, N.J., U.S.	E3	107
Strathmore, Alta.	D4	68
Strathmore, Ca., U.S.	D4	82
Strathmore, Va., U.S.	C4	107
Strathroy, Ont.	E3	73
Strathy Point, c., Scot., U.K.	B4	13
Strattanville, Pa., U.S.	D3	115
Stratton, Co., U.S.	B8	83
Stratton, Me., U.S.	C2	96
Stratton, Ne., U.S.	D4	104
Stratton, Oh., U.S.	B5	112
Stratton Meadows, Co., U.S.	B6	83
Stratton Mountain, mtn., Vt., U.S.	E3	122
Straubing, W. Ger.	D6	18
Straubville, N.D., U.S.	C8	111
Straughn, In., U.S.	E7	91
Strausberg, E. Ger.	F7	15
Strausstown, Pa., U.S.	F9	115
Strawberry, Ar., U.S.	B4	81
Strawberry, stm., Ar., U.S.	A4	81
Strawberry, stm., Ut., U.S.	C5	121
Strawberry Mountain, mtn., Or., U.S.	C8	114
Strawberry Plains, Tn., U.S.	C10	119
Strawberry Point, Ia., U.S.	B6	92
Strawberry Point, c., Ma., U.S.	B6	98
Strawberry Range, mts., Or., U.S.	C8	114
Strawberry Reservoir, res., Ut., U.S.	C4	121
Strawn, Il., U.S.	C5	90
Strawn, Ks., U.S.	D8	93
Strawn, Tx., U.S.	C3	120
Strážnice, Czech.	D4	26
Streamstown, Alta.	C5	68
Streamwood, Il., U.S.	*h8	90
Streator, Il., U.S.	B5	90
Středočeský, prov., Czech.	D9	19
Streeter, N.D., U.S.	C6	111
Streetman, Tx., U.S.	D4	120
Streetsboro, Oh., U.S.	*A4	112
Streetsville, Ont.	m14	73
Strehaia, Rom.	C6	24
Strelka, Sov. Un.	D27	8
Strelka-Chunya, Sov. Un.	C13	29
Stresa, Italy	D4	20
Stříbro, Czech.	D8	19
Strimón (Struma), stm., Eur.	B4	25
Strimón, Gulf of, b., Grc.	B4	25
Stringer, Ms., U.S.	D4	101
Stringtown, Co., U.S.	B4	83
Stringtown, Ky., U.S.	B5	94
Stringtown, Ms., U.S.	B3	101
Stringtown, Ok., U.S.	C5	113
Strofádhes, is., Grc.	D3	25
Stroh, In., U.S.	A7	91
Stromboli, i., Italy	E5	23
Strome, Alta.	C4	68
Stromeferry, Scot., U.K.	C3	13
Stromness, Scot., U.K.	B5	13
Stromsburg, Ne., U.S.	C8	104
Stronach, Mi., U.S.	D4	99
Strong, Ar., U.S.	D3	81
Strong, Me., U.S.	D2	96
Strong, Ms., U.S.	C4	101
Strong City, Ks., U.S.	D7	93
Strong City, Ok., U.S.	B2	113
Strongfield, Sask.	F2	75
Stronghurst, Il., U.S.	C3	90
Strongs, Mi., U.S.	B6	99
Strongsville, Oh., U.S.	A4	112
Stronsay, i., Scot., U.K.	A5	10
Stronsay Firth, sirt., Scot., U.K.	A6	13
Strontian, Scot., U.K.	D3	13
Stroud, Eng., U.K.	C5	12
Stroud, Ok., U.S.	B5	113
Stroudsburg, Pa., U.S.	E11	115
Stroudwater, stm., Me., U.S.	g7	96
Struble, Ia., U.S.	B1	92
Struer, Den.	I3	14
Struga, Yugo.	E5	24
Strule, stm., N. Ire., U.K.	C4	11
Struma (Strimón), stm., Eur.	B2	12
Strumble Head, c., Wales, U.K.	B2	12
Strumica, Yugo.	E6	24
Strunk, Ky., U.S.	D5	94
Struthers, Oh., U.S.	A5	112
Stryama, stm., Bul.	D7	24
Stryker, Mt., U.S.	B2	103
Stryker, Oh., U.S.	A1	112
Strykersville, N.Y., U.S.	C2	109
Stryy, Sov. Un.	G4	27
Stryy, stm., Sov. Un.	D7	26
Strzegom, Pol.	D3	26
Strzelce Krajeńskie, Pol.	C3	26
Strzelce [Opolskie], Pol.	C5	26
Strzelecki Creek, stm., Austl.	E7	50
Strzelin, Pol.	C4	26
Strzelno, Pol.	B5	26
Strzemieszyce, Pol.	g10	26
Stuart, Fl., U.S.	E6	86
Stuart, Ia., U.S.	C3	92
Stuart, Ne., U.S.	B6	104
Stuart, Ok., U.S.	C5	113
Stuart, Va., U.S.	D2	123
Stuart, stm., B.C.	B5	69
Stuart, Mount, mtn., Wa., U.S.	B5	124
Stuart Draft, Va., U.S.	B3	123
Stuart Lake, l., B.C.	B5	69
Stubbekøbing, Den.	D6	15
Stub Hill, mtn., N.H., U.S.	f7	106
Stühlingen, W. Ger.	A5	21
Stull, Can.	B5	70
Stull, stm., Can.	B5	70
Stump Creek, Pa., U.S.	D4	115
Stump Pond, res., R.I., U.S.	D2	116
Stumptown, W.V., U.S.	C4	125
Stumpy Point, N.C., U.S.	B7	110
Stupino, Sov. Un.	D11	27
Sturbridge, Ma., U.S.	B3	98
Sturgeon, Mo., U.S.	B5	102
Sturgeon, stm., Mi., U.S.	B2	99
Sturgeon, stm., Mi., U.S.	B4	99
Sturgeon Bay, Wi., U.S.	D6	126
Sturgeon Bay, b., Man.	C3	70
Sturgeon Falls, Ont.	A5	73
Sturgeon Lake, l., Ont.	C6	73
Sturgeon Lake, l., Ont.	D6	100
Sturgeon Lake, l., Sask.	D2	75

Name	Map Ref.	Page
Sturgeon Landing, Sask.	C5	75
Sturgeon-weir, stm., Sask.	C4	75
Sturgis, Sask.	F4	75
Sturgis, Ky., U.S.	e10	94
Sturgis, Mi., U.S.	G5	99
Sturgis, Ms., U.S.	B4	101
Sturgis, S.D., U.S.	C2	118
Sturt Creek, stm., Austl.	C4	50
Sturt Desert, des., Austl.	D3	51
Sturtevant, Wi., U.S.	F6	126
Stutsman, co., N.D., U.S.	B6	111
Stutterheim, S. Afr.	D4	49
Stuttgart, W. Ger.	D4	18
Stuttgart, Ar., U.S.	C4	81
Stuttgart, Ks., U.S.	C4	93
Styr, stm., Sov. Un.	F5	27
Styria, hist. reg., Aus.	E7	18
Subarnarekha, stm., India	F11	37
Subi, i., Indon.	K8	34
Subiaco, Ar., U.S.	B2	81
Subic, Phil.	o13	34
Subic Bay, b., Phil.	o13	34
Sublette, Il., U.S.	B4	90
Sublette, Ks., U.S.	E3	93
Sublette, co., Wy., U.S.	D2	127
Sublett Range, mts., Id., U.S.	G6	89
Sublimity, Or., U.S.	C4	114
Subotica, Yugo.	B4	24
Sucarnoochee, stm., Al., U.S.	C1	78
Succasunna, N.J., U.S.	B3	107
Success, Sask.	G1	75
Success, Ar., U.S.	A5	81
Success, Mo., U.S.	D5	102
Success, Mount, mtn., N.H., U.S.	B4	106
Suceava, Rom.	B8	24
Suceava, stm., Rom.	B8	24
Sucha [Beskidzka], Pol.	D5	26
Suchdol, Czech.	n17	26
Suches, Ga., U.S.	B2	87
Suchitoto, El Sal.	D3	62
Süchow see Xuzhou, China	E8	31
Suck, stm., Ire.	D2	10
Sucre, Bol.	C2	55
Sucre, state, Ven.	A5	60
Sucre, dept., Col.	C4	60
Sucuaro, Col.	C4	60
Sucuriú, stm., Braz.	C2	56
Sucy-en-Brie, Fr.	g11	16
Sudan, Tx., U.S.	B1	120
Sudan, ctry., Afr.	C2	47
Sudan, reg., Afr.	E7	42
Sudbury, Ont.	A4	73
Sudbury, Eng., U.K.	B8	12
Sudbury, Ma., U.S.	B5	98
Sudbury, Vt., U.S.	D2	122
Sudbury, dept., Ont.	p19	73
Sudbury, stm., Ma., U.S.	B5	98
Sudbury Center, Ma., U.S.	g10	98
Sudbury Reservoir, res., Ma., U.S.	g10	98
Suddie, Guy.	A3	59
Süderbrarup, W. Ger.	D3	15
Suderburg, W. Ger.	B5	18
Sudetes, mts., Eur.	C4	26
Sudlersville, Md., U.S.	B6	97
Süd-Nord Canal, W. Ger.	B7	17
Sudogda, Sov. Un.	D13	29
Sudr, 'Ayn, well, Eg.	E5	41
Sudzha, Sov. Un.	F10	27
Sue, stm., Sud.	D2	47
Sueca, Spain	C5	22
Suez (As Suways), Eg.	C3	38
Suez, Gulf of, b., Eg.	C3	38
Suez Canal, Eg.	B3	38
Suffern, N.Y., U.S.	D6	109
Suffield, Alta.	D5	68
Suffield, Ct., U.S.	B5	84
Suffolk, Va., U.S.	C7	103
Suffolk, co., Eng., U.K.	D6	123
Suffolk, co., Eng., U.K.	B8	12
Suffolk, co., Ma., U.S.	B5	98
Suffolk, co., N.Y., U.S.	n15	109
Sugar, stm., U.S.	F4	126
Sugar, stm., N.H., U.S.	D2	106
Sugar, North Branch, stm., N.H., U.S.	B3	106
Sugar City, Co., U.S.	C7	83
Sugar City, Id., U.S.	F7	89
Sugar Creek, Mo., U.S.	h11	102
Sugarcreek, Pa., U.S.	D2	115
Sugar Creek, stm., In., U.S.	F6	91
Sugar Creek, stm., In., U.S.	E3	91
Sugar Creek, stm., Oh., U.S.	C2	112
Sugar Grove, Pa., U.S.	C8	115
Sugar Grove, N.C., U.S.	A1	110
Sugar Grove, Oh., U.S.	C3	112
Sugargrove, Pa., U.S.	C3	115
Sugar Grove, Va., U.S.	D1	123
Sugar Grove, W.V., U.S.	C5	125
Sugar Hill, Ga., U.S.	B2	87
Sugar Hill, N.H., U.S.	B3	106
Sugar Island, i., Mi., U.S.	B6	99
Sugar Land, Tx., U.S.	E5	120
Sugarland Run, Va., U.S.	A5	123
Sugar Loaf, Ar., U.S.	C3	123
Sugar Loaf, mtn., Braz.	h6	56
Sugarloaf, mtn., N.H., U.S.	A4	106
Sugarloaf, hill, Oh., U.S.	A4	112
Sugarloaf Mountain, mtn., Me., U.S.	C2	96
Sugar Loaf Mountain, mtn., Md., U.S.	B3	97
Sugarloaf Mountain, mtn., Mt., U.S.	C4	103
Sugar Loaf Mountain, mtn., Ok., U.S.	B7	113
Sugarloaf Point, c., Austl.	F9	51
Sugar Mountain, mtn., Mi., U.S.	k9	99
Sugar Notch, Pa., U.S.	n17	115
Sugartown, La., U.S.	D2	95
Sugar Valley, Ga., U.S.	B1	87
Sugden, Ok., U.S.	C4	113
Suggi Lake, l., Sask.	C4	75
Suggsville, Al., U.S.	D2	78
Şuḩār, Oman	C6	38
Sühbaatar, Mong.	A6	31
Suhl, E. Ger.	C5	18
Suiattle, stm., Wa., U.S.	A4	124
Suibin, China	C5	33
Suichuan, China	F3	31
Suide, China	D7	31
Suifenhe, China	C11	33
Suihua, China	B10	31
Suijiang, China	F5	31
Suileng, China	C3	33
Suining, China	E6	31
Suipacha, Arg.	g7	54
Suipacha, Bol.	D2	55
Suippes, Fr.	E4	17
Suir, stm., Ire.	D3	10
Suisun City, Ca., U.S.	*C2	82
Suita, Japan	*I7	33
Suitland, Md., U.S.	C4	97
Suixian, China	E7	31
Suixian, China	G6	32
Suizhong, China	D9	32
Sukabumi, Indon.	G3	34
Sukadana, Indon.	F3	34
Sukaraja, Indon.	F4	34
Sukarnapura see Jayapura, Indon.	F10	34
Sukhaya Tunguska, Sov. Un.	B26	8
Sukhobuzimskoye, Sov. Un.	D27	8
Sukhona, stm., Sov. Un.	C7	29
Sukhothai, Thai.	B1	34
Sukhumi, Sov. Un.	G17	27
Sukkur, Pak.	C4	36
Sukumo, Japan	J6	33
Sukunka, stm., B.C.	B7	69
Sul, Canal do, strt., Braz.	C5	59
Sula, Mt., U.S.	E3	103
Sula, stm., Sov. Un.	F9	27
Sulaco, stm., Hond.	C4	62
Sulaimān Range, mts., Pak.	C4	36
Sula Islands, is., Indon.	F7	34
Sula Sgeir, i., Scot., U.K.	A2	13
Sulecin, Pol.	B3	26
Sulejówek, Pol.	m14	26
Sule Skerry, rock, Scot., U.K.	A4	13
Sulina, Rom.	C9	24
Sulingen, W. Ger.	F2	15
Sulitelma, mtn., Eur.	D7	14
Sullana, Peru	B1	58
Sulligent, Al., U.S.	B1	78
Sullivan, Il., U.S.	D5	90
Sullivan, In., U.S.	F3	91
Sullivan, Ky., U.S.	C2	94
Sullivan, Mo., U.S.	C6	102
Sullivan, N.H., U.S.	D2	106
Sullivan, Oh., U.S.	A3	112
Sullivan, Wi., U.S.	E5	126
Sullivan, co., In., U.S.	F3	91
Sullivan, co., Mo., U.S.	A4	102
Sullivan, co., N.H., U.S.	D2	106
Sullivan, co., N.Y., U.S.	D6	109
Sullivan, co., Pa., U.S.	D9	115
Sullivan, co., Tn., U.S.	C11	119
Sullivan Lake, l., Alta.	D5	68
Sullivans Island, S.C., U.S.	k12	117
Sully, Ia., U.S.	C5	92
Sully, co., S.D., U.S.	C5	118
Sulmona, Italy	C7	23
Sulphide, Ont.	C7	73
Sulphur, Ky., U.S.	B4	94
Sulphur, La., U.S.	D2	95
Sulphur, Ok., U.S.	C5	113
Sulphur, stm., Alta.	C1	68
Sulphur, stm., U.S.	D2	81
Sulphur Rock, Ar., U.S.	B4	81
Sulphur Spring Range, mts., Nv., U.S.	C5	105
Sulphur Springs, In., U.S.	D7	91
Sulphur Springs, Mo., U.S.	g13	102
Sulphur Springs, Oh., U.S.	B3	112
Sulphur Springs, Tx., U.S.	C5	120
Sulphur Springs Valley, val., Az., U.S.	E6	80
Sultan, Wa., U.S.	B4	124
Sultānpur, India	D9	37
Sulu Archipelago, is., Phil.	D6	34
Sulūq, Libya	C4	43
Sulu Sea, Asia	D5	34
Sulzbach, W. Ger.	C4	19
Sulzbach-Rosenberg, W. Ger.	D6	19
Sulzberger Bay, b., Ant.	B33	7
Sumas, Wa., U.S.	A3	124
Sumatra, Fl., U.S.	B2	86
Sumatra, Mt., U.S.	D9	103
Sumatra (Sumatera), i., Indon.	F2	34
Sumava Resorts, In., U.S.	B3	91
Sumba, i., Indon.	G6	34
Sumbar, stm., Sov. Un.	B7	39
Sumbawa, i., Indon.	G5	34
Sumbawa Besar, Indon.	G5	34
Sumbawanga, Tan.	C5	48
Sumbe, Peru	E3	58
Sumbe (Ngunza), Ang.	D1	48
Sumburgh Head, c., Scot., U.K.	h10	10
Sümeg, Hung.	B3	24
Sumenep, Indon.	G4	34
Sumgait, Sov. Un.	A4	39
Sumiswald, Switz.	B4	21
Sumiton, Al., U.S.	B2	78
Summerberry, Sask.	G4	75
Summerdale, Al., U.S.	E2	78
Summerfield, Fl., U.S.	C4	86
Summerfield, Ks., U.S.	C7	93
Summerfield, La., U.S.	B3	95
Summerfield, Mo., U.S.	C6	102
Summerfield, N.C., U.S.	A3	110
Summerfield, Oh., U.S.	C4	112
Summerford, Newf.	D4	72
Summerhill, Ire.	D5	11
Summer Hill, Il., U.S.	D3	90
Summer Island, i., Mi., U.S.	C3	99
Summer Lake, l., Or., U.S.	E6	114
Summer Lake, l., Or., U.S.	E6	114
Summerland, B.C.	E8	69
Summerland Key, Fl., U.S.	H5	86
Summers, co., W.V., U.S.	D4	125
Summer Shade, Ky., U.S.	D4	94
Summerside, P.E.I.	C6	71
Summersville, Ky., U.S.	C4	94
Summersville, Mo., U.S.	D6	102
Summersville, W.V., U.S.	C4	125
Summersville Lake, res., W.V., U.S.	C4	125
Summerton, S.C., U.S.	D7	117
Summertown, Ga., U.S.	D4	87
Summertown, Tn., U.S.	B4	119
Summerville, Ga., U.S.	B1	87
Summerville, Or., U.S.	B8	114
Summerville, Pa., U.S.	D3	115
Summerville, S.C., U.S.	E7	117
Summit, Ar., U.S.	A3	81
Summit, Il., U.S.	k9	90
Summit, Ms., U.S.	D3	101
Summit, N.J., U.S.	B4	107
Summit, Ok., U.S.	B6	113
Summit, R.I., U.S.	D2	116
Summit, S.D., U.S.	B8	118
Summit, Tn., U.S.	h11	119
Summit, Ut., U.S.	F3	121
Summit, co., Co., U.S.	B4	83
Summit, co., Oh., U.S.	A4	112
Summit, co., Ut., U.S.	C5	121
Summit, mtn., N.Z.	N16	51
Summit Grove, In., U.S.	E4	91
Summit Hill, Pa., U.S.	E10	115
Summit Lake, l., Ia., U.S.	C3	92
Summit Lake Indian Reservation, Nv., U.S.	B2	105
Summit Mountain, mtn., Nv., U.S.	D5	105
Summit Peak, mtn., Co., U.S.	D4	83
Summit Point, W.V., U.S.	B7	125
Summit Station, Oh., U.S.	k11	112
Summitville, Co., U.S.	D4	83
Summitville, In., U.S.	D6	91
Summitville, Tn., U.S.	D8	119
Summum, Il., U.S.	C3	90
Sumner, Ga., U.S.	E3	87
Sumner, Il., U.S.	E6	90
Sumner, Ia., U.S.	B5	92
Sumner, Ms., U.S.	B3	101
Sumner, Mo., U.S.	B4	102
Sumner, Ne., U.S.	D6	104
Sumner, Ok., U.S.	A4	113
Sumner, Wa., U.S.	B3	124
Sumner, co., Ks., U.S.	E6	93
Sumner, co., Tn., U.S.	A5	119
Sumner, Lake, res., N.M., U.S.	C5	108
Sumner Strait, strt., Ak., U.S.	m23	79
Sumoto, Japan	I7	33
Šumperk, Czech.	D4	26
Sumpter, Or., U.S.	C8	114
Sumrall, Ms., U.S.	D4	101
Sumter, S.C., U.S.	D7	117
Sumter, co., Al., U.S.	C1	78
Sumter, co., Fl., U.S.	D4	86
Sumter, co., Ga., U.S.	D2	87
Sumter, co., S.C., U.S.	D7	117
Sumterville, Al., U.S.	C1	78
Sumy, Sov. Un.	D6	29
Sun, La., U.S.	D6	95
Sun, stm., Mt., U.S.	C4	103
Sunapee, N.H., U.S.	D2	106
Sunapee Lake, l., N.H., U.S.	D2	106
Sunapee Mountain, mtn., N.H., U.S.	D2	106
Sunart, Loch, l., Scot., U.K.	D3	13
Sunbright, Tn., U.S.	C9	119
Sunburg, Mn., U.S.	E3	100
Sunburst, Mt., U.S.	B5	103
Sunbury, N.C., U.S.	A6	110
Sunbury, Oh., U.S.	B3	112
Sunbury, Pa., U.S.	E8	115
Suncho Corral, Arg.	B4	54
Sunchales, Arg.	E4	55
Sunchon, N. Kor.	G2	33
Sunchon, S. Kor.	I3	33
Sun City, Ca., U.S.	*F5	82
Sun City, Fl., U.S.	p10	86
Sun City, Ks., U.S.	E5	93
Sun City Center, Fl., U.S.	*E4	86
Suncook, N.H., U.S.	D4	106
Suncook Lakes, l., N.H., U.S.	D4	106
Sundance, Wy., U.S.	B8	127
Sundance Mountain, mtn., Wy., U.S.	B8	127
Sundarbans, reg., Asia	D8	36
Sunda Strait, strt., Indon.	G3	34
Sunday Strait, strt., Austl.	C3	50
Sundbyberg, Swe.	t35	14
Sunderland, Ont.	C5	73
Sunderland, Eng., U.K.	C6	10
Sunderland, Md., U.S.	C4	97
Sunderland, Ma., U.S.	B2	98
Sunderland, Vt., U.S.	E2	122
Sundown, Man.	E3	70
Sundown, Tx., U.S.	C1	120
Sundre, Alta.	D3	68
Sundridge, Ont.	B5	73
Sunds, Den.	B3	15
Sundsvall, Swe.	F7	14
Sunfield, Mi., U.S.	F5	99
Sunflower, Ms., U.S.	B3	101
Sunflower, co., Ms., U.S.	B3	101
Sunflower, Mount, mtn., Ks., U.S.	C2	93
Sungaiguntung, Indon.	E2	34
Sungaipenuh, Indon.	F2	34
Sungai Petani, Malay.	J4	35
Sungari Reservoir, res., China	E3	33
Sungari see Songhua Jiang, stm., China	B10	31
Sungurlu, Tur.	B10	40
Sunland Park, N.M., U.S.	F3	108
Sunlight Creek, stm., Wy., U.S.	B3	127
Sunman, In., U.S.	F7	91
Sunne, Swe.	H5	14
Sunny Brook, Alta.	C3	68
Sunny Isles, Fl., U.S.	*G6	86
Sunnyland, Fl., U.S.	q11	86
Sunnymead, Ca., U.S.	*F5	82
Sunnynook, Alta.	E5	72
Sunnyside, Newf.	E5	72
Sunnyside, Ca., U.S.	*D4	82
Sunnyside, Ut., U.S.	D5	121
Sunnyside, Wa., U.S.	C5	124
Sunny South, Al., U.S.	D2	78
Sunnyvale, Ca., U.S.	k8	82
Sunnyvale, S.D., U.S.	C9	118
Sunol, Ca., U.S.	h9	82
Sunol, Ne., U.S.	C3	104
Sun Prairie, Wi., U.S.	E4	126
Sunray, Tx., U.S.	A2	120
Sunrise, Fl., U.S.	*r13	86
Sunrise Manor, Nv., U.S.	G6	105
Sunrise Mountain, mtn., N.J., U.S.	A3	107
Sun River, Mt., U.S.	C4	103
Sunset, Fl., U.S.	*G6	86
Sunset, La., U.S.	D3	95
Sunset, Me., U.S.	D4	96
Sunset, Ut., U.S.	B4	121
Sunset Beach, Hi., U.S.	f9	88
Sunset Crater National Monument, Az., U.S.	B4	80
Sunset Hill, hill, Ct., U.S.	B7	84
Sunshine, Austl.	f16	79
Sunshine, Me., U.S.	D4	96
Sunshine, Mt., U.S.	D4	96
Sunspot, N.M., U.S.	E4	108
Suntar, Sov. Un.	C14	29
Suntrana, Ak., U.S.	C10	79
Sun Valley, Id., U.S.	F4	89
Sun Valley, Nv., U.S.	D2	105
Suo Sea, Japan	J5	33
Suoyarvi, Sov. Un.	F15	14
Superb, Sask.	F1	75
Superior, Az., U.S.	o15	80
Superior, Ca., U.S.	D4	82
Superior, Co., U.S.	B5	83
Superior, Ia., U.S.	A3	92
Superior, Mt., U.S.	C2	103
Superior, Ne., U.S.	D7	104
Superior, Wi., U.S.	B1	126
Superior, Lake, l., N.A.	A10	76
Superstition Mountains, mts., Az., U.S.	m10	80
Supai, Az., U.S.	A3	80
Suphan Buri, Thai.	B1	34
Supi Oidak, Az., U.S.	F4	80
Supreme, La., U.S.	k9	95
Supung Reservoir, res., Asia	F2	33
Sūq ash Shuyūkh, Iraq	F3	39
Suquamish, Wa., U.S.	B3	124
Sur, Point, c., Ca., U.S.	D3	82
Sur, stm., Sov. Un.	D16	27
Surabaya, Indon.	G4	34
Surakarta, Indon.	G4	34
Surakhany, Sov. Un.	E4	28
Šurany, Czech.	D5	26
Surat, Austl.	C7	51
Surat, India	D5	36
Sūratgarh, India	C4	37
Surat Thani, Thai.	D1	34
Surazh, Sov. Un.	E9	27
Şūr Bāhir, Isr. Occ.	k11	41
Surco, Peru	*D2	58
Surendranagar, India	F3	37
Suresnes, Fr.	g9	16
Surette Island, N.S.	E4	71
Surf City, N.J., U.S.	D4	107
Surfside, Fl., U.S.	s13	86
Surfside Beach, S.C., U.S.	D10	117
Surgères, Fr.	D3	16
Surgoinsville, Tn., U.S.	C11	119
Surgut, Sov. Un.	C4	28
Suriāpet, India	I7	37
Suribachi, Mount, hill, Japan	P17	52
Surigao, Phil.	D7	34
Suring, Wi., U.S.	D5	126
Suriname, ctry., S.A.	B3	59
Suriname, dept., Sur.	A3	59
Surkhan Darya, stm., Sov. Un.	C13	39
Surprise, Az., U.S.	k8	80
Surprise, Ne., U.S.	C8	104
Surrency, Ga., U.S.	D4	87
Surrey, co., Eng., U.K.	C7	12
Surrey, Me., U.S.	D4	96
Surry, N.H., U.S.	D2	106
Surry, Va., U.S.	C6	123
Surry, co., N.C., U.S.	A2	110
Surry, co., Va., U.S.	C6	123
Surry Mountain Lake, res., N.H., U.S.	D2	106
Sursee, Switz.	B5	21
Surt, Libya	C3	43
Sürüç, Tur.	D12	40
Suruga Bay, b., Japan	o17	33
Suryān'ī, Dayr as, hist., Eg.	D2	41
Susa, Italy	B1	23
Sušak, i., Yugo.	D3	24
Sušac, i., Yugo.	C2	24
Susak (part of Rijeka), Yugo.	C2	24
Susanino, Sov. Un.	s31	14
Susank, Ks., U.S.	D5	93
Susanville, Ca., U.S.	B3	82
Susitna, stm., Ak., U.S.	C10	79
Susoh, Indon.	K2	35
Susong, China	I7	32
Susquehanna, Pa., U.S.	C10	115
Susquehanna, co., Pa., U.S.	C10	115
Susquehanna, stm., U.S.	A5	97
Susquehanna, West Branch, stm., Pa., U.S.	D5	115
Susques, Arg.	D2	55
Sussex, N.B.	D4	71
Sussex, N.J., U.S.	A3	107
Sussex, Va., U.S.	D5	123
Sussex, Wi., U.S.	m11	126
Sussex, co., De., U.S.	F4	85
Sussex, co., N.J., U.S.	A3	107
Sussex, co., Va., U.S.	D5	123
Sussex Shores, De., U.S.	F5	85
Susurluk, Tur.	C7	40
Sutcliffe, Nv., U.S.	D2	105
Sutherland, S. Afr.	D3	49
Sutherland, Ia., U.S.	B2	92
Sutherland, Ne., U.S.	C4	104
Sutherland, Ut., U.S.	D2	121
Sutherland, Va., U.S.	C5	123
Sutherlin, Or., U.S.	D3	114
Sutlej (Langqên Zangbo), stm., Asia	B6	36
Sutter, co., Ca., U.S.	C3	82
Sutter Creek, Ca., U.S.	C3	82
Sutton, Que.	D5	74
Sutton, Ak., U.S.	g17	79
Sutton, Ma., U.S.	*B4	98
Sutton, Ne., U.S.	D8	104
Sutton, N.H., U.S.	D3	106
Sutton, N.D., U.S.	*B7	111
Sutton, Vt., U.S.	B4	122
Sutton, W.V., U.S.	C4	125
Sutton, co., Tx., U.S.	D2	120
Sutton Coldfield, Eng., U.K.	B6	12
Sutton in Ashfield, Eng., U.K.	D6	10
Sutton Lake, res., W.V., U.S.	C4	125
Sutton Park, N.J., U.S.	A3	107
Sutton West, Ont.	C5	73
Suttsu, Japan	E10	33
Sutwik Island, i., Ak., U.S.	D8	79
Suva, Fiji	I15	52
Suva Harbour, b., Fiji	I15	52
Suwa, Japan	m17	33
Suwałki, Pol.	A7	26
Suwannee, Ga., U.S.	B2	87
Suwannee, co., Fl., U.S.	B3	86
Suwannee, stm., U.S.	C3	86
Suwannee Lake, l., Man.	A1	70
Suwannee Sound, strt., Fl., U.S.	C3	86
Suwaylih, Jord.	B7	41
Suwaymah, Thamīlat, well, Eg.	D6	41
Suwaymah, Jord.	h13	41
Suwŏn, S. Kor.	H3	33
Suxian, China	H7	32
Suyo, Peru	B1	58
Suzaka, Japan	o15	33
Suzhou, China	E9	31
Suzu, Cape, c., Japan	H8	33
Suzu, Japan	o15	33
Suzzara, Italy	E6	20
Svalbard, ter., Nor.	B13	128
Svaneke, Den.	C8	15
Svärtagård, Swe.	u35	14
Svartån, stm., Swe.	t34	14
Svatovo, Sov. Un.	G12	27
Svay Rieng, Camb.	C3	34
Svedala, Swe.	C7	15
Svedrup, i., Sov. Un.	B7	128
Sveg, Swe.	F6	14
Svelvik, Nor.	p27	14
Svendborg, Den.	C4	15
Svenljunga, Swe.	A7	15
Svensen, Or., U.S.	A3	114
Svenstrup, Den.	B3	15
Sverdlovsk, Sov. Un.	q22	27
Sverdlovsk, Sov. Un.	D9	29
Sverdrup Islands, is., N.W. Ter.	m32	66
Svetlaya, Sov. Un.	C9	33
Svetlograd, Sov. Un.	I14	27
Svetlyy, Sov. Un.	D8	26
Svetozarevo, Yugo.	C5	24
Svilajnac, Yugo.	C5	24
Svilengrad, Bul.	E8	24
Svindal, Nor.	p29	14
Świnoujście, Pol.	B3	26
Svir, stm., Sov. Un.	A10	27
Svirstroy, Sov. Un.	A9	27
Svishtov, Bul.	D7	24
Svitavy, Czech.	D4	26
Svobodnyy, Sov. Un.	D15	29
Svobodnyy, Cape, c., Sov. Un.	C11	33
Svyatoy Nos, Cape, c., Sov. Un.	B16	29
Swadlincote, Eng., U.K.	B6	12
Swaffham, Eng., U.K.	B8	12
Swain, co., N.C., U.S.	f9	110
Swain Mountain, mtn., Ar., U.S.	A2	81
Swainsboro, Ga., U.S.	D4	87
Swakopmund, Nmb.	B1	49
Swale, stm., Eng., U.K.	C6	10
Swaledale, Ia., U.S.	B4	92
Swallwell, Alta.	D4	68
Swampscott, Ma., U.S.	B6	98
Swan, stm., Alta.	B3	68
Swan, stm., Can.	C1	70
Swan Creek, Il., U.S.	C3	90
Swan Creek, stm., Oh., U.S.	e6	112
Swandale, W.V., U.S.	m14	125
Swan Falls, wtfl., Id., U.S.	F2	89
Swan Hill, Austl.	G7	50
Swan Hills, Alta.	B3	68
Swan Hills, hills, Alta.	B3	68
Swan Lake, Man.	E2	70
Swanlake, Id., U.S.	G6	89
Swan Lake, Ms., U.S.	B3	101
Swan Lake, Mt., U.S.	C3	103
Swan Lake, l., Man.	C1	70
Swan Lake, l., Me., U.S.	C4	96
Swan Lake, l., Ne., U.S.	C3	104
Swannanoa, N.C., U.S.	f10	110
Swan Peak, mtn., Mt., U.S.	C3	103
Swanquarter, N.C., U.S.	B6	110
Swan Range, mts., Mt., U.S.	C3	103
Swan River, Man.	C1	70
Swan River, Mn., U.S.	C5	100
Swansboro, N.C., U.S.	C5	110
Swansea, Wales, U.K.	E4	10
Swansea, Il., U.S.	E4	90
Swansea, Ma., U.S.	C5	98
Swansea, S.C., U.S.	D5	117
Swansea Bay, b., Wales, U.K.	C4	12
Swansea Center, Ma., U.S.	C5	98
Swans Island, Me., U.S.	D4	96
Swanson, Sask.	F2	75
Swanson Lake, res., Ne., U.S.	D5	104
Swanton, Md., U.S.	m12	97
Swanton, Oh., U.S.	A2	112
Swanton, Vt., U.S.	B2	122
Swan Valley, Id., U.S.	F7	89
Swanville, Mn., U.S.	E4	100
Swanwick, Il., U.S.	E4	90
Swanwyck Estates, De., U.S.	*B3	85
Swanzey Center, N.H., U.S.	E2	106
Swarthmore, Pa., U.S.	p20	115
Swartswood, N.J., U.S.	A3	107
Swartswood Lake, l., N.J., U.S.	A3	107
Swartz, La., U.S.	B4	95
Swartz Creek, Mi., U.S.	F7	99
Swatara, Mn., U.S.	D5	100
Swatara Township, Pa., U.S.	*F8	115
Swatow see Shantou, China	F8	31
Swayzee, In., U.S.	C6	91
Swaziland, ctry., Afr.	C5	49
Swea City, Ia., U.S.	A3	92
Sweatman, Ms., U.S.	B4	101
Swedeborg, Mo., U.S.	D5	102
Sweden, ctry., Eur.	F6	14
Swedesboro, N.J., U.S.	D2	107
Sweeny, Tx., U.S.	r14	120
Sweet, Id., U.S.	F2	89
Sweet Briar, Va., U.S.	C3	123
Sweetgrass, Mt., U.S.	B5	103
Sweet Grass, co., Mt., U.S.	E7	103
Sweet Home, Or., U.S.	C4	114
Sweet Home, Tx., U.S.	E4	120
Sweetser, In., U.S.	C6	91
Sweet Springs, Mo., U.S.	C4	102
Sweet Springs, W.V., U.S.	D4	125
Sweet Valley, Pa., U.S.	D9	115
Sweet Water, Al., U.S.	C2	78
Sweetwater, Fl., U.S.	*G6	86
Sweetwater, Ok., U.S.	B2	113
Sweetwater, Tn., U.S.	D9	119
Sweetwater, Tx., U.S.	C2	120
Sweetwater, co., Wy., U.S.	E3	127
Sweetwater, stm., Wy., U.S.	D4	127
Sweetwater Creek, Fl., U.S.	p10	86
Sweetwater Creek, stm., Ok., U.S.	B1	113
Sweetwater Station, Wy., U.S.	D4	127
Swellendam, S. Afr.	D3	49
Swenson, Tx., U.S.	C2	120
Swepsonville, N.C., U.S.	A3	110
Świdnica, Pol.	C4	26
Świdnik, Pol.	B8	26
Świebodzice, Pol.	C4	26
Świebodzin, Pol.	B3	26
Świecie, Pol.	B5	26
Świętochłowice, Pol.	g9	26
Świętokrzyskie, Góry, mts., Pol.	C6	26
Swift, Mn., U.S.	B3	100
Swift, co., Mn., U.S.	E3	100
Swift, stm., N.H., U.S.	B4	106
Swift Creek, stm., N.C., U.S.	B5	110
Swift Creek, stm., Va., U.S.	n17	123
Swift Creek Reservoir, res., Wa., U.S.	C3	124
Swift Current, Sask.	G2	75
Swiftcurrent Creek, stm., Sask.	H1	75
Swift Diamond, stm., N.H., U.S.	g7	106
Swifton, Ar., U.S.	B4	81
Swiftown, Ms., U.S.	B3	101
Swiftwater, N.H., U.S.	B3	106
Swilly, Lough, b., Ire.	B4	11
Swinburne, Cape, c., N.W. Ter.	B13	66
Swindle Island, i., B.C.	C3	69
Swindon, Eng., U.K.	E6	10
Swinford, Ire.	D3	11
Swink, Co., U.S.	C7	83
Swink, Ok., U.S.	C6	113
Swinomish Indian Reservation, Wa., U.S.	A3	124
Swisher, Ia., U.S.	C6	92
Swisher, co., Tx., U.S.	B2	120
Swiss, W.V., U.S.	C3	125
Swisshome, Or., U.S.	C3	114
Swissvale, Pa., U.S.	I 14	115
Switz City, In., U.S.	F3	91
Switzer, W.V., U.S.	D3	125
Switzerland, Fl., U.S.	m8	86
Switzerland, S.C., U.S.	G5	117
Switzerland, co., In., U.S.	G7	91
Switzerland, ctry., Eur.	E4	18
Swords, Ire.	D5	11
Swords, Ga., U.S.	C3	87
Swoyerville, Pa., U.S.	D10	115
Sycamore, Al., U.S.	B3	78
Sycamore, Ga., U.S.	E3	87
Sycamore, Il., U.S.	B5	90
Sycamore, Ks., U.S.	E8	93
Sycamore, Mo., U.S.	E5	102
Sycamore, Oh., U.S.	B2	112
Sycamore, S.C., U.S.	E5	117
Sycamore Creek, stm., Tn., U.S.	A4	119
Sycamore Creek, stm., W.V., U.S.	m13	125
Sychevka, Sov. Un.	D10	27
Syców, Pol.	C4	26
Sydenham, Ont.	C8	73
Sydney, Austl.	F9	50
Sydney, N.S.	C9	71
Sydney Mines, N.S.	C9	71
Sykeston, N.D., U.S.	B6	111
Sykesville, Md., U.S.	B4	97
Sykesville, Pa., U.S.	D4	115
Sykkylven, Nor.	p28	14
Syktyvkar, Sov. Un.	C8	29
Sylacauga, Al., U.S.	B3	78
Sylamore, Ar., U.S.	B3	81
Sylhet, Bngl.	D9	36
Sylling, Nor.	p28	14
Sylt, i., W. Ger.	A4	18
Sylva, N.C., U.S.	f9	110
Sylvan, Pa., U.S.	G6	115
Sylvan Grove, Ks., U.S.	C5	93
Sylvan Hills, Ar., U.S.	h10	81
Sylvania, Sask.	E3	75
Sylvania, Al., U.S.	A4	78
Sylvania, Ga., U.S.	D5	87
Sylvania, Oh., U.S.	A2	112
Sylvania, Pa., U.S.	C8	115
Sylvan Lake, Alta.	C3	68
Sylvan Lake, Mi., U.S.	o15	99
Sylvan Lake, l., In., U.S.	B7	91
Sylvan Pass, Wy., U.S.	B2	127
Sylvarena, Ms., U.S.	C4	101
Sylvester, Ga., U.S.	E3	87
Sylvester, Tx., U.S.	C2	120
Sylvester, Mount, hill, Newf.	D4	72
Sylvia, Ks., U.S.	E5	93
Sylvia, Tn., U.S.	A4	119
Sym, stm., Sov. Un.	C26	8
Symmes Creek, stm., Oh., U.S.	D3	112
Symsonia, Ky., U.S.	f9	94
Syosset, N.Y., U.S.	*E7	109
Syracuse, In., U.S.	B6	91
Syracuse, Ks., U.S.	E2	93
Syracuse, Mo., U.S.	C5	102
Syracuse, Ne., U.S.	D9	104
Syracuse, N.Y., U.S.	B4	109
Syracuse, Ut., U.S.	B3	121
Syr Darya, stm., Asia	E9	29
Syria, ctry., Asia	B3	38
Syria, hist. reg., Asia	D2	35
Syriam, Burma	D2	35
Syrian Desert, des., Asia	A3	92
Syros see Ermoúpolis, Grc.	D5	40
Sysladobsis Lake, l., Me., U.S.	C4	96
Sysola, stm., Sov. Un.	C19	8
Syurkum, Cape, c., Sov. Un.	A10	33
Syzran, Sov. Un.	D7	29
Szabadszállás, Hung.	B4	24
Szamos (Someş), stm., Eur.	B6	24
Szamotuły, Pol.	B4	26
Szarvas, Hung.	B5	24
Szczakowa (part of Jaworzno), Pol.	g10	26
Szczebrzeszyn, Pol.	C7	26
Szczecin (Stettin), Pol.	B3	26
Szczecinek, Pol.	B4	26
Szczuczyn, Pol.	B7	26
Szczytno, Pol.	B6	26
Szechwan see Sichuan, prov., China	E5	31
Szeged, Hung.	B5	24
Székesfehérvár, Hung.	B4	24
Szekszárd, Hung.	B4	24
Szentendre, Hung.	B4	24
Szentes, Hung.	B5	24
Szigetvár, Hung.	B3	24
Szolnok, Hung.	B5	24
Szombathely, Hung.	B3	24
Szprotawa, Pol.	C3	26
Sztum, Pol.	B5	26
Szydłowiec, Pol.	C6	26
Szypliszki, Pol.	m12	26

T

Name	Map Ref.	Page
Taal, Phil.	p13	34
Taal, Lake, l., Phil.	p13	34
Tab, In., U.S.	D3	91
Tabar Islands, is., Pap. N. Gui.	h13	50
Tabarka, Tun.	F2	23
Tabas, Iran	E8	39
Tabasco, state, Mex.	D6	63
Tābas Masīnā, Iran	E10	39
Tabatinga, Braz.	k7	56

Name	Map Ref.	Page

Tabayin, Burma — A1 35
Tabbys Peak, mtn., Ut., U.S. — C3 121
Tabelbala, Alg. — D4 44
Taber, Alta. — E4 68
Tabernacle, N.J., U.S. — D3 107
Tabernas, Spain — D4 22
Tabernash, Co., U.S. — B5 83
Taberville, Mo., U.S. — C4 102
Tabik Island, i., Marsh Is. — S17 52
Tabiona, Ut., U.S. — C5 121
Tabiteuea, Kir. — R18 52
Tabla, Cerro de la, mtn., P.R. — B3 65
Tablas, Cabo, c., Chile — A2 54
Tablas Island, i., Phil. — C6 34
Table Bay, b., S. Afr. — D2 49
Table Bay, b., Newf. — B3 72
Table Grove, Il., U.S. — C3 90
Table Head, c., Newf. — B4 72
Table Mountain, mtn., Newf. — E2 72
Table Mountain, mtn., Az., U.S. — E5 80
Table Rock, Ne., U.S. — D9 104
Table Rock Lake, res., U.S. — E4 102
Table Top, mtn., Az., U.S. — E3 80
Taboada, Spain — A2 22
Tábor, Czech. — D3 26
Tabor, Ia., U.S. — D2 92
Tabor, Mn., U.S. — B2 100
Tabor, S.D., U.S. — E8 118
Tabor, Mount, mtn., Isr. — B7 41
Tabora, Tan. — C5 48
Tabora, prov., Tan. — C5 48
Tabor City, N.C., U.S. — C4 110
Tabou, I.C. — F3 45
Tabrīz, Iran — B4 38
Tabuaeran Island (Fanning Island), atoll, Kir. — F12 6
Tabūk, Sau. Ar. — C3 38
Tabusintac, stm., N.B. — B4 71
Täby, Swe. — *H8 14
Tacámbaro de Codallos, Mex. — n13 63
Tacheng, China — B1 31
Tachie, stm., B.C. — B5 69
Tachiiwa Point, c., Japan — P17 52
Tachikawa, Japan — n18 33
Táchira, state, Ven. — B3 60
Tachov, Czech. — D2 26
Tacloban, Phil. — C7 34
Tacna, Peru — E3 58
Tacna, Az., U.S. — E1 80
Tacna, dept., Peru — E3 58
Tacoma, Wa., U.S. — D3 83
Tacoma, Wa., U.S. — B3 124
Taconic, Ct., U.S. — A2 84
Taconic Range, mts., U.S. — A1 98
Taconite, Mn., U.S. — C5 100
Tacoronte, Spain — m13 22
Tacuarembó, Ur. — E1 56
Tacuatí, Para. — D4 55
Tad, W.V., U.S. — m13 125
Tademaït, Plateau du, plat., Alg. — D5 44
Tadjoura, Dji. — C5 47
Tadoule Lake, l., Man. — f8 70
Tadoussac, Que. — A8 74
T'aebaek-Sanmaek, mts., Asia — H4 33
Taegu, S. Kor. — D10 31
Taejon, S. Kor. — D10 31
Taeyu-dong, N. Kor. — F2 33
Tafalla, Spain — A5 22
Tafi Viejo, Arg. — E2 55
Tafo, Ghana — *E4 45
Taft, Ca., U.S. — E4 82
Taft, La., U.S. — k11 95
Taft, Ok., U.S. — B6 113
Taft, Tn., U.S. — B5 119
Taft, Tx., U.S. — F4 120
Taftān, Kūh-e, mtn., Iran — G10 39
Taftsville, Vt., U.S. — D4 122
Tafuna International Airport, Am. Sam. — G13 52
Taganrog, Sov. Un. — H12 27
Taganrog, Gulf of, b., Sov. Un. — H12 27
Tagaytay, Phil. — o13 34
Tagbilaran, Phil. — D6 34
Taghmon, Ire. — E5 11
Taghrīfat, Libya — D3 43
Tagliamento, stm., Italy — C8 20
Tagolo Point, c., Phil. — D6 34
Taguan Point, c., Guam — L10 52
Taguatinga, Braz. — D1 57
Tagus (Tejo) (Tajo), stm., Eur. — C1 22
Tahan, mtn., Malay. — E2 34
Tahat, mtn., Alg. — E6 44
Tahgong, Puntan, c., N. Mar. Is. — D7 52
Tahiti, i., Fr. Poly. — H13 6
Tahlequah, Ok., U.S. — B7 113
Ţaḥmā wa Minshāt 'Abd as Sayyid, Eg. — E3 41
Tahoe, Lake, l., U.S. — E1 105
Tahoe City, Ca., U.S. — C3 82
Tahoka, Tx., U.S. — C2 120
Taholah, Wa., U.S. — B1 124
Tahoma, Ca., U.S. — C3 82
Tahoua, Niger — D6 45
Tahquamenon, stm., Mi., U.S. — B5 99
Tahsis, B.C. — E4 69
Ţaḥţā, Eg. — C3 38
Tahtsa Lake, l., B.C. — C4 69
Tahtsa Peak, mtn., B.C. — C4 69
Tahuya, Wa., U.S. — B2 124
Taï, I.C. — E3 45
Tai'an, China — D10 32
Tai'an, China — F7 32
Taiban, N.M., U.S. — C5 108
Taibus Qi, China — D6 32
T'aichung, Tai. — G9 31
Taigu, China — F5 32
Taihape, N.Z. — M15 51
Taiho, Japan — N6 52
Tai Hu, l., China — E8 31
Tailai, China — A10 32
Tailem Bend, Austl. — G8 50
Tailevu Point, c., Fiji — H15 52
Tain, Scot., U.K. — B4 10
T'ainan, Tai. — G9 31
Taínaron, Ákra, c., Grc. — D4 40
Taining, China — K7 32
Taiobeiras, Braz. — B4 56
Taipei, Tai. — G9 31
Taiping, Malay. — E2 34
Taipu, Braz. — g6 57
Taira see Iwaki, Japan — H10 33
Taishun, China — K8 32
Taitao, Península de, pen., Chile — D2 54
T'aitung, Tai. — G9 31
Taivalkoski, Fin. — E13 14
Taiwan, ctry., Asia — G9 31
Taiwan Strait, strt., Asia — G8 31
Taiyiba, Isr. — B7 41
Taiyuan, China — D7 31

Taizhao, China — E3 31
Taizhou, China — H8 32
Ta'izz, Yemen — D4 38
Tajarhī, Libya — E2 43
Tajik S.S.R., state, Sov. Un. — F9 29
Tajimi, Japan — I8 33
Tajique, N.M., U.S. — C3 108
Tajumulco, Volcán, vol., Guat. — C2 62
Tajuña, stm., Spain — B4 22
Tājūrā', Libya — C2 43
Tak, Thai. — B1 34
Takabanare Island, i., Japan — O6 52
Takahe, Mount, mtn., Ant. — B1 7
Takaka, N.Z. — N14 51
Takamatsu, Japan — E11 31
Takanabe, Japan — H8 33
Takaoka, Japan — H8 33
Takapuna, N.Z. — L15 51
Takara Island, i., Japan — L4 33
Takasaki, Japan — H9 33
Takashippu, Japan — O5 52
Takatō, Japan — n17 33
Takatsuki, Japan — o14 33
Takaw, Burma — B3 35
Takayama, Japan — H8 33
Takefu, Japan — n15 33
Takengon, Indon. — J2 35
Tākestān, Iran — C4 39
Takev, Camb. — G6 35
Takhta-Bazar, Sov. Un. — D11 39
Takhtakupyr, Sov. Un. — E6 28
Takigawa, Japan — E10 33
Takijuq Lake, l., N.W. Ter. — C10 66
Takpocha, Okso, mtn., N. Mar. Is. — D7 52
Takishiri Island, i., Japan — D10 33
Takla Lake, l., B.C. — B5 69
Taklamakan Shamo, des., China — F11 29
Takoma Park, Md., U.S. — f8 97
Takotna, Ak., U.S. — C8 79
Takut, Burma — A3 35
Taku, stm., N.A. — k23 79
Takua Pa, Thai. — H3 35
Taku Glacier, ice, Ak., U.S. — k22 79
Takum, Nig. — G7 45
Talā, Eg. — D2 41
Tala, Mex. — m12 63
Tala, Ur. — E1 56
Talagante, Chile — A2 54
Talakan, Sov. Un. — B6 33
Talala, Ok., U.S. — A6 113
Talara, Peru — B1 58
Talas, Sov. Un. — E8 28
Talasea, Pap. N. Gui. — k13 50
Talata Mafara, Nig. — D6 45
Talaud Islands, is., Indon. — E7 34
Talavera de la Reina, Spain — C3 22
Talawdī, Sud. — C3 47
Talbert, Ky., U.S. — C6 94
Talbot, In., U.S. — D3 91
Talbot, co., Ga., U.S. — D2 87
Talbot, co., Md., U.S. — C5 97
Talbot Island, i., Fl., U.S. — B5 86
Talbot Lake, l., Man. — B2 70
Talbotton, Ga., U.S. — D2 87
Talca, Chile — B2 54
Talcahuano, Chile — B2 54
Tålcher, India — D8 36
Talco, Tx., U.S. — C5 120
Talcott, W.V., U.S. — D4 125
Talcottville, N.Y., U.S. — B5 109
Taldy-Kurgan, Sov. Un. — D9 28
Tālesh, Iran — C4 39
Taliabu, i., Indon. — F6 34
Taliaferro, co., Ga., U.S. — C4 87
Talica, Sov. Un. — B6 28
Talihina, Ok., U.S. — C6 113
Talim Island, i., Phil. — o13 34
Tali Post, Sud. — D3 47
Talisay, Phil. — o14 34
Talisheek, La., U.S. — D6 95
Talish Mountains, mts., Asia — C4 39
Talkeetna, Ak., U.S. — C10 79
Talkeetna Mountains, mts., Ak., U.S. — f17 79
Talkhā, Eg. — C3 41
Talking Rock, Ga., U.S. — B2 87
Tall, Isr. Occ. — g11 41
Talla Bena, La., U.S. — B4 95
Talladega, Al., U.S. — B3 78
Talladega, co., Al., U.S. — B3 78
Talladega, stm., Al., U.S. — B3 78
Talladega Springs, Al., U.S. — B3 78
Tallahala Creek, stm., Ms., U.S. — D4 101
Tallahassee, Fl., U.S. — B2 86
Tallahatchie, co., Ms., U.S. — B3 101
Tallahatchie, stm., Ms., U.S. — B3 101
Tall al Abyaḍ, Syria — B3 38
Tallangatta, Austl. — H6 51
Tallant, Ok., U.S. — A5 113
Tallapoosa, Ga., U.S. — C1 87
Tallapoosa, Mo., U.S. — E8 102
Tallapoosa, co., Al., U.S. — C4 78
Tallapoosa, stm., Al., U.S. — C3 78
Tallard, Fr. — E2 20
Tallassee, Al., U.S. — C4 78
Talleyville, De., U.S. — A3 85
Tallinn, Est. — D5 27
Tallmadge, Oh., U.S. — A4 112
Tallow, Ire. — E3 11
Tallulah, Il., U.S. — D4 90
Tallulah, La., U.S. — B4 95
Tallulah Falls, Ga., U.S. — B2 87
Talma, Isr. Occ. — f12 41
Talmage, Sask. — H4 75
Talmage, Ks., U.S. — C6 93
Talmage, Ne., U.S. — D9 104
Talnoye, Sov. Un. — G8 27
Taloga, Ok., U.S. — A3 113
Talofofo, Guam — M10 52
Talofofo Bay, b., Guam — M10 52
Talon, Lake, l., Ont. — A5 73
Talowah, Ms., U.S. — D4 101
Talpa, Tx., U.S. — D3 120
Talpa de Allende, Mex. — m11 63
Talquin, Lake, res., Fl., U.S. — B2 86
Talsi, Sov. Un. — E1 114
Taltal, Chile — E1 55
Tama, Ia., U.S. — C5 92
Tama, co., Ia., U.S. — B5 92
Tamacuarí, Pico, mtn., S.A. — B7 60
Tamaha, Ok., U.S. — B7 113
Tamalameque, Col. — B6 60
Tamale, Ghana — E4 45
Tamalpais, Mount, mtn., Ca., U.S. — h7 82

Tamalpais Valley, Ca., U.S. — *D2 82
Taman, Sov. Un. — I11 27
Tamana, Mount, hill, Trin. — O23 65
Tamana, Mor. — C3 44
Tamanar, Mor. — C3 44
Tamano, Japan — I6 33
Tamaqua, Pa., U.S. — E10 115
Tamar, stm., Eng., U.K. — D3 12
Tamarac, Fl., U.S. — *r13 86
Tamarack, Mn., U.S. — D5 100
Tamarite [de Litera], Spain — B6 22
Tamaroa, Il., U.S. — E4 90
Tamassee, S.C., U.S. — B1 117
Tamaulipas, state, Mex. — C5 63
Tamazula de Gordiano, Mex. — n12 63
Tamazulapan [del Progreso], Mex. — o15 63
Tamazunchale, Mex. — A6 48
Tambach, Kenya — A6 48
Tambacounda, Sen. — D2 45
Tambaú, Braz. — k8 56
També, Braz. — C3 57
Tambelan Besar, i., Indon. — L7 35
Tambelan Islands, is., Indon. — E3 34
Tambo, Austl. — B6 51
Tambo, stm., Peru — F5 58
Tambo, stm., Peru — D3 58
Tambo Grande, Peru — B1 58
Tambohorano, Madag. — g8 49
Tambov, Sov. Un. — D6 28
Tambre, stm., Spain — A1 22
Tambura, Sud. — D2 47
Tamchaket, Maur. — C2 45
Tamdybulak, Sov. Un. — B12 29
Tame, Col. — B3 60
Tamega, stm., Port. — B2 22
Tamel Aike, Arg. — D2 54
Tamenghest, Alg. — B5 44
Tamenghest, Oued, val., Alg. — E5 44
Tamgué, Massif du, mts., Gui. — B3 59
Tamiahua, Mex. — C5 63
Tamiahua, Laguna de, b., Mex. — C5 63
Tamiami, Fl., U.S. — *G6 86
Tamiami Canal, Fl., U.S. — G6 86
Tamil Nadu (Madras), state, India — G6 36
Tamina, Tx., U.S. — D5 120
Tamins, Switz. — C7 21
Tamiš, stm., Eur. — C5 24
Tam Ky, Viet. — E8 35
Tamms, Il., U.S. — F4 90
Tamo, Ar., U.S. — C4 81
Tamora, Ne., U.S. — D8 104
Tampa, Fl., U.S. — E4 86
Tampa, Ks., U.S. — D6 93
Tampa Bay, b., Fl., U.S. — E4 86
Tampere, Fin. — G10 14
Tampico, Mex. — C5 63
Tampico, Il., U.S. — B4 90
Tampico, Mt., U.S. — B10 103
Tams, W.V., U.S. — D3 125
Tamsagbulag, Mong. — B8 31
Tamshiyacu, Peru — B3 58
Tamuning, Guam — L10 52
Tamworth, Austl. — F9 50
Tamworth, Ont. — C8 73
Tamworth, Eng., U.K. — B6 12
Tamworth, N.H., U.S. — C4 106
Tana, stm., Eur. — B12 14
Tana, stm., Kenya — B7 48
Tana, Lake, l., Eth. — C4 47
Tanabe, Japan — J7 33
Tanabi, Braz. — C3 56
Tanacross, Ak., U.S. — C11 79
Tanafjorden, Nor. — B13 14
Tanaga Island, i., Ak., U.S. — E4 79
Tanahbala, i., Indon. — F1 34
Tanahgrogot, Indon. — F5 34
Tanahmasa, i., Indon. — F1 34
Tanakpur, India — C4 50
Tanami, Austl. — C4 50
Tan An, Viet. — G7 35
Tanana, Ak., U.S. — B9 79
Tanana, stm., Ak., U.S. — C10 79
Tanana, atoll, Kir. — F10 6
Tananarive see Antananarivo, Madag. — g9 49
Tanapag, N. Mar. Is. — D8 52
Tanapag, Lagunan, b., N. Mar. Is. — D7 52
Tanaro, stm., Italy — B2 23
Tanaunella, Italy — D2 23
Tanavuso Point, c., Fiji — H15 52
Tancheng, China — G8 32
Tanchon, N. Kor. — F4 33
Tancook Island, N.S. — E5 71
Tānda, India — D9 37
Tandaltī, Sud. — C8 24
Tāndārei, Rom. — C8 24
Tandil, Arg. — B5 54
Tando Ādam, Pak. — E2 37
Tandou Lake, l., Austl. — E4 51
Tanega Island, i., Japan — *E11 31
Tanegashima Strait, strt., Japan — K5 33
Taney, co., Mo., U.S. — E4 102
Taneycomo, Lake, res., Mo., U.S. — E4 102
Taneytown, Md., U.S. — A3 97
Taneyville, Mo., U.S. — E4 102
Tanezrouft, des., Afr. — E4 44
Tanga, Tan. — C6 48
Tanga, prov., Tan. — B6 48
Tanganyika, Lake, l., Afr. — C4 48
Tangent, Or., U.S. — C3 114
Tangermünde, E. Ger. — B5 18
Tanggula Shan, mts., China — E7 31
Tanghe, China — E7 31
Tangier, N.S. — E7 71
Tangier (Tanger), Mor. — B3 44
Tangier, In., U.S. — E3 91
Tangier, Va., U.S. — C7 123
Tangier Island, i., Va., U.S. — C6 123
Tangier Sound, strt., Md., U.S. — D6 97
Tangipahoa, co., La., U.S. — D5 95
Tangipahoa, stm., La., U.S. — D5 95
Tanglewood, Fl., U.S. — *F5 86
Tangra Yumco, l., China — E12 31
Tangshan, China — D10 32
Tanguiéta, Benin — D5 45
Tanguisson Point, c., Guam — L10 52
Tangwang He, stm., China — B10 31
Tangyuan, China — B8 31
Tanimbar Islands, is., Indon. — G8 34
Taninges, Fr. — F7 20
Tanjore see Thanjāvūr, India — F6 36
Tanjung, Indon. — F5 34
Tanjungbalai, Indon. — E1 34
Tanjungkarang-Telukbetung, Indon. — G3 34

Tanjungpandan, Indon. — F3 34
Tanjungselor, Indon. — E5 34
Tānk, Pak. — B5 36
Tānnås, Swe. — F5 14
Tanner, Al., U.S. — A3 78
Tanner, W.V., U.S. — C4 125
Tanner, Mount, mtn., B.C. — E8 69
Tannersville, N.Y., U.S. — C6 109
Tannis Bugt, b., Den. — A4 15
Tannu-Ola Mountains, mts., Asia — A3 31
Tânout, Niger — C6 45
Tanpok, stm., Fr. Gu. — B4 59
Tanque Verde, Az., U.S. — E5 80
Tantā, Eg. — C3 38
Tantallon, Sask. — G5 75
Tantani, Peru — C5 58
Tantoyuca, Mex. — m14 63
Tanzania, ctry., Afr. — C5 48
Tao, i., Thai. — G3 35
Tao'an, China — B9 31
Tao'er He, stm., China — B9 31
Taopi, Mn., U.S. — G6 100
Taormina, Italy — F5 23
Taos, Mo., U.S. — C5 102
Taos, N.M., U.S. — A4 108
Taos, co., N.M., U.S. — A4 108
Taos Pueblo, N.M., U.S. — A4 108
Taoudenni, Mali — B4 45
Taoyuan, China — J4 32
Tapachula, Mex. — C6 63
Tapaga, Cape, c., W. Sam. — G12 52
Tapajós, stm., Braz. — C3 59
Tapaktuan, Indon. — m11 34
Tapalquén, Arg. — B5 54
Tapanahony, stm., Sur. — B3 59
Tapanui, N.Z. — P12 51
Tapauá, Braz. — D2 59
Tapauá, stm., Braz. — C3 59
Tapejara, Braz. — D2 56
Taperoá, Braz. — h5 57
Tāpi, stm., India — D5 36
Tapirapé, stm., Braz. — E4 59
Tapoco, N.C., U.S. — f9 110
Tappahannock, Va., U.S. — C6 123
Tappan, N.Y., U.S. — g13 109
Tappan Lake, res., N.J., U.S. — g9 107
Tappan Lake, res., Oh., U.S. — B4 112
Tappen, N.D., U.S. — C6 111
Tapuaenuku, mtn., N.Z. — N14 51
Taputapu, Cape, c., Am. Sam. — G13 52
Taqāṭu' Ḥayyā, Sud. — B4 47
Taquara, Braz. — D2 56
Taquari, stm., Braz. — B1 56
Taquari, stm., Braz. — k7 56
Taquaritinga do Norte, Braz. — h5 57
Tar, stm., N.C., U.S. — B5 110
Tara, Ont. — C3 73
Tara, Sov. Un. — D10 29
Tara, stm., Sov. Un. — B9 28
Tara, stm., Yugo. — D4 24
Tara, Hill of, hist., Ire. — D5 11
Tarabai, Braz. — C2 56
Tarata, Bol. — C2 55
Tarata, Peru — E3 58
Tarauacá, Braz. — C3 58
Tarauacá, stm., Braz. — C3 58
Tarawa, atoll, Kir. — F10 6
Tarawera, N.Z. — M16 51
Tarazit, Massif de, mts., Niger — B7 45
Tarazona, Spain — B5 22
Tarazona [de la Mancha], Spain — C5 22
Tarbagatay Range, mts., Asia — D10 28
Tarbat Ness, c., Scot., U.K. — B5 10
Tarbellville, Vt., U.S. — D3 122
Tarbert, Ire. — E2 11
Tarbert, Scot., U.K. — C2 13
Tarbert, Scot., U.K. — E3 13
Tarbes, Fr. — F4 16
Tarbet, Scot., U.K. — E4 13
Tarboro, Ga., U.S. — E3 87
Tarboro, N.C., U.S. — B5 110
Tarbū, Libya — D3 43
Tarcenay, Fr. — B1 21
Tarcento, Italy — C9 20
Tarcoola, Austl. — F5 50
Tardoki-Yani, Mount, mtn., Sov. Un. — B9 33
Taree, Austl. — F9 50
Tarentum, Pa., U.S. — E2 115
Tarfawi, Bi'r, well, Sud. — A3 47
Tarfaya, Mor. — C2 44
Tarfside, Scot., U.K. — D6 13
Targhee Pass, U.S. — E7 89
Tarhūnah, Libya — C2 43
Tarifa, Spain — D3 22
Tarifa, Point, c., Spain — D3 22
Tariffville, Ct., U.S. — B4 84
Taritg Point, c., Phil. — n14 34
Tarija, Bol. — D3 55
Tarija, dept., Bol. — D3 55
Tarim He, stm., China — E11 29
Tarim Pendi, des., China — E11 29
Tarkastad, S. Afr. — D4 49
Tarkiln, R.I., U.S. — B3 116
Tarkiln Hill, Me., U.S. — g7 96
Tarkio, Mo., U.S. — A2 102
Tarko-Sale, Sov. Un. — C24 8
Tarkwa, Ghana — E4 45
Tarland, Scot., U.K. — B6 13
Tarlton, Oh., U.S. — C3 112
Tārn, stm., Fr. — F4 16
Tarm, Den. — C2 15
Tarnobrzeg, Pol. — C5 19
Tarnopol, Sask. — E3 75
Tarnów, Pol. — C6 19
Tarnowskie Góry, Pol. — B5 19
Taro, stm., Italy — B2 23
Taroom, Austl. — B7 51
Taroudant, Mor. — C3 44
Tarp, W. Ger. — D3 15
Tarpey, Ca., U.S. — D4 82

Tarpley, Tx., U.S. — E3 120
Tarpon, Lake, l., Fl., U.S. — o10 86
Tarpon Springs, Fl., U.S. — D4 86
Tarqui, Peru — B2 58
Tarquinia, Italy — C3 23
Tarragona, Spain — B6 22
Tarrant, co., Tx., U.S. — C4 120
Tarrant City, Al., U.S. — B3 78
Tarrasa, Spain — B7 22
Tarrega, Spain — B6 22
Tarry, Ar., U.S. — C4 81
Tarryall Creek, stm., Co., U.S. — B5 83
Tarryall Mountains, mts., Co., U.S. — B5 83
Tarrytown, Fl., U.S. — D4 86
Tarrytown, Ga., U.S. — D4 87
Tarrytown, N.Y., U.S. — D7 109
Tārs, Den. — A4 15
Tarsus, Tur. — D10 40
Tartagal, Arg. — D3 55
Tartas, Fr. — F4 16
Tartu, Sov. Un. — D5 29
Tartuguan Point, c., Guam — M10 52
Tarțūs, Syria — E10 40
Tārūt, i., Sau. Ar. — H5 39
Tarutung, Indon. — L3 35
Tarver, Ga., U.S. — F4 87
Tarves, Scot., U.K. — C6 13
Tasaral, Sov. Un. — D8 28
Tasäwah, Libya — D2 43
Taseko, stm., B.C. — D6 69
Taseko Lakes, l., B.C. — D6 69
Taseko Mountain, mtn., B.C. — D6 69
Tashauz, Sov. Un. — E5 28
Tashkent, Sov. Un. — E9 29
Tasikmalaya, Indon. — G3 34
Tåsinge, i., Den. — C4 15
Taskan, Sov. Un. — C18 29
Taşköprü, Tur. — B10 40
Tasman Bay, b., N.Z. — N14 51
Tasmania, state, Austl. — o15 50
Tasman Peninsula, pen., Austl. — o15 50
Tasman Sea, Oc. — I9 6
Tasso, Tn., U.S. — D9 119
Taswell, In., U.S. — H4 91
Tatabánya, Hung. — B4 24
Tatamagouche, N.S. — D6 71
Tatar Strait, strt., Sov. Un. — D17 29
Tate, Sask. — F3 75
Tate, co., Ms., U.S. — A4 101
Tateville, Ky., U.S. — D5 94
Tatitlek, Ak., U.S. — C10 79
Tatla Lake, l., B.C. — C5 69
Tatlayoko Lake, l., B.C. — D5 69
Tatnam, Cape, c., Man. — f9 70
Tattershall, Eng., U.K. — A7 12
Tattnall, co., Ga., U.S. — D4 87
Tatuí, Braz. — C3 56
Tatum, N.M., U.S. — D6 108
Tatum, S.C., U.S. — B8 117
Tatumville, Tn., U.S. — A2 119
Tatvan, Tur. — C14 40
Tauá, Braz. — C2 57
Taubaté, Braz. — C3 56
Tauber, stm., W. Ger. — B7 19
Tauberbischofsheim, W. Ger. — B7 19
Taucha, E. Ger. — B7 19
Tauern Tunnel, Aus. — C9 20
Taughmaconnell, Ire. — D3 11
Taumarunui, N.Z. — L15 51
Taum Sauk Mountain, mtn., Mo., U.S. — D6 102
Taung, Boph. — C3 49
Taungdwingyi, Burma — D10 36
Taunggyi, Burma — D10 36
Taunton, Eng., U.K. — E5 10
Taunton, Ma., U.S. — C5 98
Taunton, Mn., U.S. — F2 100
Taunton, stm., Ma., U.S. — C5 98
Taunton Lakes, N.J., U.S. — D3 107
Taunus, mts., W. Ger. — E7 18
Taupo, Lake, l., N.Z. — M15 51
Tauragè, Sov. Un. — C4 27
Tauranga, N.Z. — L16 51
Taureau, Réservoir, res., Que. — C4 74
Taurianova, Italy — E6 23
Taurus Mountains, mts., Tur. — D8 40
Taus, Spain — B3 22
Tauste, Spain — B5 22
Tauves, Fr. — E4 16
Tavannes, Switz. — B3 21
Tavares, Fl., U.S. — D5 86
Tavas, Tur. — D7 25
Tavda, Sov. Un. — D9 29
Tavda, stm., Sov. Un. — D9 29
Tavernier, Fl., U.S. — G6 86
Taveuni, i., Fiji — H16 52
Tavira, Port. — D2 22
Tavistock, Ont. — D4 73
Tavistock, Eng., U.K. — D3 12
Tavoy Point, c., Burma — F2 35
Tavolzhan, Sov. Un. — C9 28
Tavoy, Burma — C7 40
Tawakoni, Lake, res., Tx., U.S. — C4 120
Tawas City, Mi., U.S. — D7 99
Tawas Point, c., Mi., U.S. — D7 99
Tawatinaw, Alta. — B4 68
Tawau, Malay. — E5 34
Tawitawi Group, is., Phil. — D6 34
Tawi-Tawi Island, i., Phil. — D5 34
Tawkar, Sud. — B4 47
Tawny, Ire. — B4 11
Tāwurghā', Libya — C3 43
Taxco de Alarcón, Mex. — n14 63
Tay, stm., Scot., U.K. — B5 10
Tay, Firth of, est., Scot., U.K. — B5 10
Tay, Loch, l., Scot., U.K. — B4 10
Tayabamba, Peru — n14 63
Tayasheh, Isr. Occ. — f12 41
Taycheedah, Wi., U.S. — C8 103
Tayga, Sov. Un. — B11 28
Taylor, B.C. — A7 69
Taylor, Az., U.S. — C5 80
Taylor, Mi., U.S. — p15 99
Taylor, Ms., U.S. — A4 101
Taylor, Ne., U.S. — C6 104
Taylor, N.D., U.S. — C3 111
Taylor, Pa., U.S. — D10 115
Taylor, Tx., U.S. — D4 120
Taylor, Wi., U.S. — D2 126
Taylor, co., Fl., U.S. — B3 86
Taylor, co., Ga., U.S. — D2 87
Taylor, co., Ia., U.S. — D3 92
Taylor, co., Ky., U.S. — C4 94
Taylor, co., Tx., U.S. — C3 120

Taylor, co., W.V., U.S. — B4 125
Taylor, co., Wi., U.S. — C3 126
Taylor, co., Man. — B2 70
Taylor, stm., Co., U.S. — C4 83
Taylor, Mount, mtn., N.Z. — O13 51
Taylor, Mount, mtn., N.M., U.S. — B2 108
Taylor Knob, hill, Tn., U.S. — G10 119
Taylor Mill, Ky., U.S. — k14 94
Taylor Mountain, mtn., Id., U.S. — E4 89
Taylor Park Reservoir, res., Co., U.S. — C4 83
Taylor Ridge, mtn., Ga., U.S. — B1 87
Taylors, S.C., U.S. — B3 117
Taylors Bridge, De., U.S. — C3 85
Taylors Falls, Mn., U.S. — E6 100
Taylors Island, Md., U.S. — D5 97
Taylor Springs, Il., U.S. — D4 90
Taylorsport, Ky., U.S. — h13 94
Taylorsville, Ga., U.S. — B2 87
Taylorsville, In., U.S. — F6 91
Taylorsville, Ky., U.S. — B4 94
Taylorsville, Ms., U.S. — D4 101
Taylorsville, N.C., U.S. — B1 110
Taylorsville, Ut., U.S. — *C4 121
Taylorville, Il., U.S. — D4 90
Taymā', Sau. Ar. — D7 43
Taymouth, N.B. — C3 71
Taymyr Lake, l., Sov. Un. — B13 29
Taymyr Peninsula, pen., Sov. Un. — B12 29
Tay Ninh, Viet. — G7 35
Tayport, Scot., U.K. — D6 13
Tayshet, Sov. Un. — D12 29
Tayside, prov., Scot., U.K. — D5 13
Taytay, Phil. — C5 34
Taytsy, Sov. Un. — s31 14
Taz, stm., Sov. Un. — C11 29
Taz, Mor. — C4 44
Taz Bay, b., Sov. Un. — C7 128
Tazewell, Ga., U.S. — D2 87
Tazewell, Tn., U.S. — C10 119
Tazewell, Va., U.S. — e10 123
Tazewell, co., Il., U.S. — C4 90
Tazewell, co., Va., U.S. — e10 123
Tazrouk, Alg. — E6 44
Tbessa, Alg. — B6 44
Tbilisi, Sov. Un. — E7 29
Tchefuncta, stm., La., U.S. — D5 95
Tchibanga, Gabon — F2 46
Tchien, Lib. — E3 45
Tczew, Pol. — A5 26
Tea, S.D., U.S. — D9 118
Teacapán, Mex. — D4 60
Teachey, N.C., U.S. — C4 110
Tea Creek, stm., Sask. — C2 75
Teague, Tx., U.S. — D4 120
Teanaue Butte, mtn., Id., U.S. — C2 89
Te Anau, Lake, l., N.Z. — P11 51
Teaneck, N.J., U.S. — h8 107
Teangue, Scot., U.K. — C3 13
Tearaght, i., Ire. — E1 11
Tearinibai, Kir. — R18 52
Teasdale, Ut., U.S. — E4 121
Teaticket, Ma., U.S. — C7 98
Te Awamutu, N.Z. — M15 51
Tebbetts, Mo., U.S. — C6 102
Tebicuary, stm., Para. — E4 55
Tebingtinggi, Indon. — E1 34
Tecalitlán, Mex. — n12 63
Teche, Bayou, stm., La., U.S. — D4 95
Techirghiol, Rom. — C9 24
Tecka, Arg. — C2 54
Tecolote, N.M., U.S. — B4 108
Tecolotito, N.M., U.S. — k9 108
Tecolutla, stm., Mex. — m15 63
Tecomán, Mex. — D4 63
Tecopa, Ca., U.S. — E5 82
Tecpan de Galeana, Mex. — D4 63
Tecuala, Mex. — C3 63
Tecucí, Rom. — C8 24
Tecumseh, Ont. — E2 73
Tecumseh, Ks., U.S. — k14 93
Tecumseh, Mi., U.S. — G7 99
Tecumseh, Ne., U.S. — D9 104
Tecumseh, Ok., U.S. — B5 113
Tecumseh, Mount, mtn., N.H., U.S. — C3 106
Ted Ceidaar Dabole, Som. — A11 112
Tedrow, Oh., U.S. — A1 112
Tedzhen, Sov. Un. — C10 39
Teec Nos Pos, Az., U.S. — A6 80
Teeswater, Ont. — C3 73
Teeside see Middlesbrough, Eng., U.K. — C6 10
Tees, stm., Eng., U.K. — C6 10
Tefé, Braz. — C2 59
Tefé, stm., Braz. — C2 59
Tefé, Lago de, l., Braz. — C2 59
Tefenni, Tur. — D7 25
Tefft, In., U.S. — B4 91
Tegal, Indon. — G3 34
Tegelen, Neth. — C6 17
Tegernsee, W. Ger. — B7 19
Teglio, Italy — D9 21
Tegucigalpa, Hond. — C2 62
Teguise, Spain — m15 22
Tehachapi, Ca., U.S. — E4 82
Tehachapi Mountains, mts., Ca., U.S. — E4 82
Tehama, co., Ca., U.S. — B2 82
Tehrān, Iran — B5 38
Tehri, India — E7 37
Tehuacán, Mex. — D5 63
Tehuantepec, Mex. — D6 63
Tehuantepec, Golfo de, b., Mex. — D6 63
Tehuitzingo, Mex. — n14 63
Teifi, stm., Wales, U.K. — D3 12
Teignmouth, Eng., U.K. — D4 12
Teiteiripucchi, i., Marsh Is. — S18 52
Tekamah, Ne., U.S. — C9 104
Tekax de Álvaro Obregón, Mex. — C7 63
Tekeli, Sov. Un. — E9 28
Tekezē, stm., Afr. — C4 47
Tekirdağ, Tur. — H10 37
Tekkali, India — B8 124
Tekonsha, Mi., U.S. — F5 99
Tekro, well, Chad — C6 46
Te Kuiti, N.Z. — M15 51
Tel, stm., India — D7 36
Tela, Hond. — D7 63

Name	Map Ref.	Page
Telavi, Sov. Un.	E3	28
Tel Aviv-Yafo (Tel Aviv-Jaffa), Isr.	B3	38
Telde, Spain	m14	22
Telegraph Creek, B.C.	m16	69
Telén, Arg.	B3	54
Teleneshty, Sov. Un.	B9	24
Teleorman, stm., Rom.	C7	24
Telephone, Tx., U.S.	C4	120
Télérthéba, Djebel, mtn., Alg.	E6	44
Telescope Peak, mtn., Ca., U.S.	D5	82
Telfair, co., Ga., U.S.	E4	87
Telford, Eng., U.K.	B5	12
Telford, Pa., U.S.	F11	115
Telford, Tn., U.S.	C11	119
Telfs, Aus.	B7	20
Télimélé, Gui.	D2	45
Telkwa, B.C.	B4	69
Tell, Tx., U.S.	B2	120
Tell City, In., U.S.	I4	91
Teller, Ak., U.S.	B6	79
Teller, co., Co., U.S.	C5	83
Tellico Plains, Tn., U.S.	D9	119
Telluride, Co., U.S.	D3	83
Tel Mond, Isr.	B6	41
Telogia, Fl., U.S.	B2	86
Telok Anson (Teluk Intan), Malay.	E2	34
Teloloapan, Mex.	D5	63
Telos Lake, l., Me., U.S.	B3	96
Telsen, Arg.	C3	54
Tema, Ghana	E5	45
Temax, Mex.	C7	63
Tembo, Zaire	C2	48
Temecula, Ca., U.S.	F5	82
Temelli, Tur.	C8	40
Temirtau, Sov. Un.	E26	8
Temirtau, Sov. Un.	D10	29
Témiscaming, Que.	G17	66
Témiscouata, co., Que.	B9	74
Témiscouata, Lac, l., Que.	B9	74
Te-Moak Indian Reservation, Nv., U.S.	C6	105
Temora, Austl.	G6	51
Temósachic, Mex.	B3	63
Tempe, Az., U.S.	D4	80
Tempe Downs, Austl.	D5	50
Temperance, Mi., U.S.	G7	99
Temperance, stm., Mn., U.S.	C8	100
Temperanceville, Va., U.S.	C7	123
Tempio Pausania, Italy	D2	23
Temple, Mi., U.S.	D5	99
Temple, N.H., U.S.	E3	106
Temple, Ok., U.S.	C3	113
Temple, Pa., U.S.	F10	115
Temple, Tx., U.S.	D4	120
Temple City, Ca., U.S.	*m12	82
Temple Hill, Ky., U.S.	D4	94
Templemore, Ire.	E4	11
Temple Terrace, Fl., U.S.	o11	86
Templeton, In., U.S.	C3	91
Templeton, Ia., U.S.	C3	92
Templeton, Ma., U.S.	A3	98
Templeton, Pa., U.S.	E3	115
Templeville, Md., U.S.	B6	97
Templin, E. Ger.	B6	18
Tempoal, stm., Mex.	m14	63
Temryuk, Sov. Un.	I11	27
Temuco, Chile	B2	54
Temuka, N.Z.	P13	51
Temwen, i., Micron.	Q17	51
Tena, Ec.	B2	58
Tenafly, N.J., U.S.	B5	107
Tenaha, Tx., U.S.	D5	120
Tenakee Springs, Ak., U.S.	D12	79
Tenāli, India	*E7	36
Tenancingo [de Degollado], Mex.	D5	63
Tenango del Valle, Mex.	n14	63
Tenant Mountain, mtn., N.Y., U.S.	B6	109
Tenants Harbor, Me., U.S.	E3	96
Tenasserim, Burma	F10	36
Tenay, Fr.	E6	16
Tenby, Wales, U.K.	C3	12
Tendaho, Eth.	C5	47
Tende, Fr.	E7	16
Ten Degree Channel, strt., India	G9	36
Tendoy, Id., U.S.	E5	89
Tendre, Mont, mtn., Switz.	C2	20
Ténéré, des., Niger	C7	45
Tenerife, i., Spain	m13	22
Ténès, Alg.	B5	44
Teng, stm., Burma	D5	36
Tengah Islands, is., Indon.	G5	34
Tengchong, China	F4	31
Tengiz, Lake, l., Sov. Un.	D9	29
Tengxian, China	G7	32
Tenino, Wa., U.S.	C3	124
Tenke, Zaire	D4	48
Tenkiller Ferry Lake, res., Ok., U.S.	B6	113
Tenkodogo, Burkina	D4	45
Ten Mile, Tn., U.S.	D9	119
Tenmile, stm., U.S.	B5	116
Tenmile Creek, stm., W.V., U.S.	k10	125
Ten Mile Lake, l., Newf.	C3	72
Tenmile Lake, l., Mn., U.S.	D4	100
Tennant, Ia., U.S.	C2	92
Tennant Creek, Austl.	C5	50
Tennent, N.J., U.S.	C4	107
Tennessee, Il., U.S.	C3	90
Tennessee, state, U.S.	B5	119
Tennessee, stm., U.S.	D10	76
Tennessee City, Tn., U.S.	A4	119
Tennessee Pass, Co., U.S.	B4	83
Tennessee Ridge, Tn., U.S.	A4	119
Tennga, Ga., U.S.	B2	87
Tennille, Ga., U.S.	D4	87
Tennyson, In., U.S.	H3	91
Tenosique [de Pino Suárez], Mex.	D6	63
Tenryū, stm., Japan	n16	33
Tensas, co., La., U.S.	B4	95
Tensas, stm., La., U.S.	B4	95
Tensaw, stm., Al., U.S.	E2	78
Tensed, Id., U.S.	B2	89
Ten Sleep, Wy., U.S.	B5	127
Tenstrike, Mn., U.S.	C4	100
Tenterfield, Austl.	E9	51
Ten Thousand Islands, is., Fl., U.S.	G5	86
Teocaltiche, Mex.	C4	63
Teófilo Otoni, Braz.	E8	57
Tepa, Indon.	G7	34
Tepalcatepec, Mex.	n12	63
Tepalcatepec, stm., Mex.	n12	63
Tepatitlán [de Morelos], Mex.	C4	63
Tepeji del Río, Mex.	n14	63
Tepelena, Alb.	B2	25
Tepepan (part of Mexico City), Mex.	h9	63
Tepic, Mex.	C4	63
Teplice, Czech.	C2	26
Tepoca, Cabo, c., Mex.	A2	63
Tequila, Mex.	m12	63
Ter, stm., Spain	A7	22
Téra, Niger	D5	45
Teraina Island (Washington Island), i., Kir.	F12	6
Teramo, Italy	C4	23
Ter Apel, Neth.	B7	17
Tercan, Tur.	C13	40
Terceira, i., Port.	g9	44
Tercero, stm., Arg.	A4	54
Terebovlya, Sov. Un.	G5	27
Terek, stm., Sov. Un.	G18	8
Terek Pass, Sov. Un.	G23	8
Terekty, Sov. Un.	D7	28
Terence Bay, N.S.	E6	71
Terengganu, state, Malay.	J5	35
Terenos, Braz.	C2	56
Teresina, Braz.	C2	57
Teresinha, Braz.	B4	59
Teresópolis, Braz.	C4	56
Tergnier, Fr.	E3	17
Terhune, In., U.S.	D5	91
Teriberka, Sov. Un.	C16	14
Terlingua, Tx., U.S.	D1	120
Terlton, Ok., U.S.	A5	113
Termez, Sov. Un.	F9	29
Termini Imerese, Italy	F4	23
Términos, Laguna de b., Mex.	D6	63
Termoli, Italy	C5	23
Ternate, Indon.	E7	34
Ternate, i., Indon.	E7	34
Terneuzen, Neth.	B5	16
Terney, Sov. Un.	D8	33
Terni, Italy	C4	23
Ternopol, Sov. Un.	G5	27
Terpeniya Bay, b., Sov. Un.	B11	33
Terpeniye, Cape, c., Sov. Un.	B12	33
Terra Alta, W.V., U.S.	B5	125
Terrace, B.C.	B3	69
Terrace, Mn., U.S.	E3	100
Terrace Bay, Ont.	G15	66
Terracina, Italy	D4	23
Terral, Ok., U.S.	D4	113
Terra Nova, Newf.	D4	72
Terra Nova National Park, Newf.	D4	72
Terra Rica, Braz.	C2	56
Terrasson, Fr.	E4	16
Terrebonne, Bayou, stm., La., U.S.	k10	95
Terrebonne, Que.	D4	74
Terrebonne, Or., U.S.	C5	114
Terrebonne, co., Que.	C3	74
Terrebonne, co., Que.	C3	74
Terrebonne Bay, b., La., U.S.	E5	95
Terre Haute, In., U.S.	C3	90
Terre Haute, In., U.S.	F3	91
Terre Hill, Pa., U.S.	F9	115
Terrell, N.C., U.S.	B2	110
Terrell, Tx., U.S.	C4	120
Terrell, co., Ga., U.S.	E2	87
Terrell, co., Tx., U.S.	D1	120
Terrell Hills, Tx., U.S.	k7	120
Terrenceville, Newf.	E4	72
Terreton, Id., U.S.	F6	89
Terri, Mont, mtn., Switz.	A3	20
Terril, Ia., U.S.	A3	92
Terror, Mount, mtn., Ant.	e38	7
Terry, Ms., U.S.	C3	101
Terry, Mt., U.S.	D11	103
Terry, co., Tx., U.S.	C1	120
Terry Peak, mtn., S.D., U.S.	C2	118
Terrytown, La., U.S.	*E5	95
Terrytown, Ne., U.S.	C2	104
Terryville, Ct., U.S.	C3	84
Terryville, N.Y., U.S.	*n15	109
Tersakkan, stm., Sov. Un.	C7	28
Terschelling, i., Neth.	A6	16
Terskey-Alatau Range, mts., Sov. Un.	E9	28
Teruel, Col.	C5	60
Teruel, Spain	B5	22
Terutao, i., Thai.	I3	35
Terwagne, Bel.	D5	17
Tešanj, Yugo.	C3	24
Tescott, Ks., U.S.	C6	93
Teseney, Eth.	B4	47
Teshekpuk Lake, l., Ak., U.S.	A9	79
Teshie, Ghana	*E5	45
Teshio, Japan	D10	33
Tesiyn, stm., Asia	B4	31
Teslin, Yukon	D6	66
Teslin Lake, l., Can.	D6	66
Tessalit, Mali	B5	45
Tessier, Sask.	F2	75
Tessin, E. Ger.	D5	15
Test, stm., Eng., U.K.	E6	10
Tesuque, N.M., U.S.	B4	108
Tesuque Pueblo, N.M., U.S.	B4	108
Tetachuck Lake, l., B.C.	C5	69
Tetagouche, stm., N.B.	B3	71
Tetas, Punta, c., Chile	F3	53
Tetbury, Eng., U.K.	C5	12
Tete, Moz.	A5	49
Tete, dept., Moz.	A5	49
Tête-à-la-Baleine, Que.	C2	72
Tête Jaune Cache, B.C.	C8	69
Teterow, E. Ger.	B6	18
Teteven, Bul.	D7	24
Tetlin, Ak., U.S.	C11	79
Teton, Id., U.S.	F7	89
Teton, co., Id., U.S.	F7	89
Teton, co., Mt., U.S.	C4	103
Teton, co., Wy., U.S.	C2	127
Tetonia, Id., U.S.	F7	89
Teton Pass, Wy., U.S.	C2	127
Teton Range, mts., Wy., U.S.	C2	127
Teton Village, Wy., U.S.	C2	127
Tétouan, Mor.	B3	44
Tetovo, Yugo.	E5	24
Tettnang, W. Ger.	A8	21
Tetu Lake, l., Ont.	D4	70
Teuchern, E. Ger.	B7	19
Teuco, stm., Arg.	D3	53
Teufen, Switz.	B7	21
Teulada, Italy	E2	23
Teúl de González Ortega, Mex.	m12	63
Teupitz, E. Ger.	D3	70
Teutopolis, Il., U.S.	D5	90
Teviot, stm., Scot., U.K.	F6	13
Tevriz, Sov. Un.	D8	28
Te Waewae Bay, b., N.Z.	Q11	51
Tewantin-Noosa, Austl.	E9	50
Tewkesbury, Eng., U.K.	C5	12
Tewksbury, Ma., U.S.	A5	98
Texada Island, i., B.C.	E5	69
Texanna, Ok., U.S.	B6	113
Texarkana, Ar., U.S.	D1	81
Texarkana, Tx., U.S.	C5	120
Texas, co., Mo., U.S.	D5	102
Texas, co., Ok., U.S.	e9	113
Texas, state, U.S.	D3	120
Texcaltitlán, Mex.	n14	63
Texcoco, Lago de, l., Mex.	g10	63
Texcoco [de Mora], Mex.	n14	63
Texel, i., Neth.	A6	16
Texhoma, Ok., U.S.	e9	113
Texhoma, Tx., U.S.	A2	120
Texico, N.M., U.S.	C6	108
Texline, Tx., U.S.	A1	120
Texoma, Lake, res., U.S.	D5	113
Texon, Tx., U.S.	D2	120
Teywarah, Afg.	E12	39
Teziutlán, Mex.	D5	63
Tezpur, India	C9	36
Tezzeron Lake, l., B.C.	B5	69
Thabana Ntlenyana, mtn., Leso.	C4	49
Thacker, W.V., U.S.	D2	125
Thackeray, Il., U.S.	E5	90
Thackerville, Ok., U.S.	D4	113
Thai Binh, Viet.	B7	35
Thailand, ctry., Asia	B2	34
Thailand, Gulf of, b., Asia	C2	34
Thai Nguyen, Viet.	B6	35
Thal, Pak.	B5	36
Thale, E. Ger.	B6	19
Thale Luang, b., Thai.	I4	35
Thalia, Tx., U.S.	C3	120
Thame, Eng., U.K.	C7	12
Thames, N.Z.	L15	51
Thames, stm., Ont.	E3	73
Thames, stm., Eng., U.K.	E6	10
Thames, stm., Ct., U.S.	C7	84
Thames, Firth of, b., N.Z.	L15	51
Thamesville, Ont.	E3	73
Thāna, India	H4	37
Thanh Hoa, Viet.	C6	35
Thanjāvūr, India	F6	36
Thann, Fr.	D7	16
Thannhausen, W. Ger.	A6	20
Thaon[-les-Vosges], Fr.	C7	16
Tharād, India	E3	37
Thar Desert (Great Indian Desert), des., Asia	D2	37
Tharrawaddy, Burma	E10	36
Thásos, Grc.	B5	25
Thásos, i., Grc.	B5	40
Thatcher, Az., U.S.	E6	80
Thatcher, Id., U.S.	G7	89
Thaton, Burma	E10	36
Thawville, Il., U.S.	C5	90
Thaxton, Ms., U.S.	A4	101
Thayer, Il., U.S.	D4	90
Thayer, In., U.S.	B3	91
Thayer, Ia., U.S.	C3	92
Thayer, Ks., U.S.	E8	93
Thayer, Mo., U.S.	E6	102
Thayer, Ne., U.S.	D8	104
Thayer, co., Ne., U.S.	D8	104
Thayer, W.V., U.S.	n13	125
Thayetmyo, Burma	C1	35
Thayne, Wy., U.S.	D1	127
Thazi, Burma	B2	35
Thealka, Ky., U.S.	C7	94
Theba, Az., U.S.	E3	80
The Backway, b., Newf.	A2	72
The Barrens, plat., Tn., U.S.	B5	119
Thebes, Il., U.S.	F4	90
Thebes, hist., Eg.	C3	47
Thebes see Thívai, Grc.	C4	25
The Bight, Bah.	B6	64
The Cheviot, mtn., Eng., U.K.	C5	10
The Cheviot Hills, hills, U.K.	C5	10
The Colony, Tx., U.S.	C4	120
The Coteau, hills, Sask.	F2	75
The Dalles, Or., U.S.	B5	114
The Dells, val., Wi., U.S.	E4	126
Thedford, Ont.	D3	73
Thedford, Ne., U.S.	C5	104
The Dome, mtn., Vt., U.S.	F2	122
The Entrance, Austl.	F8	51
The Everglades, sw., Fl., U.S.	G6	86
The Father, mtn., Pap. N. Gui.	k13	50
The Fens, sw., Eng., U.K.	B8	12
The Fishing Lake, l., Sask.	G3	75
The Flat Tops, mts., Co., U.S.	B3	83
The Flume, wtfl., N.H., U.S.	B3	106
The Graves, is., Ma., U.S.	g12	98
The Hague ('s Gravenhage), Neth.	A6	16
The Heads, c., Or., U.S.	E2	114
The Hummocks, R.I., U.S.	D6	116
The Landes, reg., Fr.	E6	10
The Little Minch, strt., Scot., U.K.	B3	10
Thelma, N.C., U.S.	A5	110
Thelon, stm., N.W. Ter.	D12	66
The Minch, strt., Scot., U.K.	A4	10
The Narrows, strt., Wa., U.S.	f10	124
The Naze, i., Nor.	I2	14
The Naze, c., Eng., U.K.	C9	12
The Oa, pen., Scot., U.K.	E2	13
Theodore, Austl.	D9	50
Theodore, Sask.	F4	75
Theodore, Al., U.S.	E1	78
Theodore Roosevelt Lake, res., Az., U.S.	D4	80
Theodore Roosevelt National Park (South Unit), N.D., U.S.	C2	111
Theodore Roosevelt National Park (North Unit), N.D., U.S.	B2	111
Theodosia, Mo., U.S.	E5	102
Theológos, Grc.	C7	25
The Palisades, clf., N.J., U.S.	h9	107
The Pas, Man.	C1	70
The Peak, mtn., N.C., U.S.	A1	110
The Pinnacle, hill, Ct., U.S.	B4	84
The Pinnacle, hill, Mo., U.S.	B5	102
The Plains, Oh., U.S.	C3	112
The Plains, Va., U.S.	B5	123
Thérain, stm., Fr.	C9	16
The Range, N.B.	C4	71
The Raven Point, c., Ire.	E5	11
Theresa, N.Y., U.S.	A5	109
Theresa, Wi., U.S.	E5	126
Therien, Alta.	B5	68
Thermaïkós Kólpos (Gulf of Salonika), b., Grc.	B4	40
Thérmon, Grc.	D3	25
Thermopolis, Wy., U.S.	C4	127
Thermopylae, hist., Grc.	C4	25
The Rock, Wi., U.S.	D3	126
The Rockies, mts., Wa., U.S.	C3	124
Theron Mountains, mts., Ant.	B10	7
The Solent, strt., Eng., U.K.	D6	12
The Sound see Øresund, strt.,	J5	14
Thessalon, Ont.	p19	73
Thessaloniki (Salonika), Grc.	B4	40
Thessaly, hist. reg., Grc.	C4	25
The Storr, mtn., Scot., U.K.	C2	13
Theta, Tn., U.S.	B4	119
Thetford, Eng., U.K.	D7	10
Thetford, Vt., U.S.	D4	122
Thetford Center, Vt., U.S.	D4	122
Thetford Mines, Que.	C6	74
The Thimbles, is., Ct., U.S.	E5	84
The Village, Ok., U.S.	B4	113
The Village of India, Oh., U.S.	*C1	112
The Wash, b., Eng., U.K.	D7	10
The Wolds, hills, Eng., U.K.	D6	10
The Woodlands, Tx., U.S.	*E5	120
Thibar, Tun.	F2	23
Thibaudeau, Man.	A4	70
Thibodaux, La., U.S.	E5	95
Thicket Portage, Man.	B3	70
Thickwood Hills, hills, Sask.	E2	75
Thida, Ar., U.S.	B4	81
Thief, stm., Mn., U.S.	B2	100
Thief Lake, l., Mn., U.S.	B3	100
Thief River Falls, Mn., U.S.	B2	100
Thiel Mountains, mts., Ant.	A2	7
Thielsen, Mount, mtn., Or., U.S.	D4	114
Thiene, Italy	D7	20
Thiensville, Wi., U.S.	E6	126
Thiers, Fr.	E5	16
Thiès, Sen.	D1	45
Thika, Kenya	B6	48
Thimbu see Thimphu, Bhu.	C8	36
Thimphu (Thimbu), Bhu.	C8	36
Thingangyun, Burma	*E10	36
Thionville, Fr.	C7	16
Thíra, i., Grc.	D5	40
Third Lake, l., N.H., U.S.	f7	106
Thirsk, Eng., U.K.	F7	13
Thisted, Den.	B2	15
Thívai (Thebes), Grc.	C4	25
Tho Chu, is., Viet.	H5	35
Tholen, Neth.	C4	17
Thomas, Wa., U.S.	f11	124
Thomas, W.V., U.S.	B5	125
Thomas, co., Ga., U.S.	F3	87
Thomas, co., Ks., U.S.	C2	93
Thomas, co., Ne., U.S.	C5	104
Thomasboro, Il., U.S.	C5	90
Thomas Creek, stm., Fl., U.S.	k8	86
Thomas Mountains, mts., Ant.	B5	7
Thomaston, Al., U.S.	C2	78
Thomaston, Ct., U.S.	C3	84
Thomaston, Ga., U.S.	D2	87
Thomaston, Me., U.S.	D3	96
Thomaston, Tx., U.S.	E4	120
Thomaston Reservoir, res., Ct., U.S.	C3	84
Thomastown, Ire.	E4	11
Thomastown, Ms., U.S.	C4	101
Thomasville, Al., U.S.	D2	78
Thomasville, Ga., U.S.	F3	87
Thomasville, Mo., U.S.	E6	102
Thomasville, N.C., U.S.	B2	110
Thomasville, Tn., U.S.	A4	119
Thomlinson, Mount, mtn., B.C.	B4	69
Thompson, Man.	B3	70
Thompson, Ct., U.S.	B8	84
Thompson, Ia., U.S.	A4	92
Thompson, Mi., U.S.	C4	99
Thompson, Mo., U.S.	B6	102
Thompson, N.D., U.S.	B8	111
Thompson, Oh., U.S.	A4	112
Thompson, Pa., U.S.	C10	115
Thompson, Ut., U.S.	E6	121
Thompson, stm., B.C.	D7	69
Thompson, stm., U.S.	A4	102
Thompson Creek, stm., Ms., U.S.	D5	101
Thompson Falls, Mt., U.S.	C1	103
Thompson Island, i., Ma., U.S.	g11	98
Thompson Lake, l., U.S.	D2	96
Thompson Peak, mtn., Ca., U.S.	B2	82
Thompson Peak, mtn., N.M., U.S.	h9	108
Thompson Reservoir, res., Or., U.S.	E5	114
Thompsons Station, Tn., U.S.	B5	119
Thompsontown, Pa., U.S.	E7	115
Thompsonville, Il., U.S.	F5	90
Thompsonville, Mi., U.S.	D5	99
Thomson, Ga., U.S.	C4	87
Thomson, Il., U.S.	B3	90
Thomson, Mn., U.S.	D6	100
Thomson, stm., Austl.	D7	50
Thomson's Falls, Kenya	A6	48
Thônes, Fr.	E1	21
Thonon-les-Bains, Fr.	C2	20
Thonotosassa, Fl., U.S.	D4	86
Thor, Ia., U.S.	B3	92
Thorburn, N.S.	D7	71
Thoreau, N.M., U.S.	B1	108
Thorhild, Alta.	B4	68
Thornburg, Ar., U.S.	C3	81
Thornbury, Ont.	C4	73
Thorndale, Ont.	D3	73
Thorndale, Tx., U.S.	D4	120
Thorndike, Me., U.S.	D3	96
Thorndike, Ma., U.S.	B3	98
Thornfield, Mo., U.S.	E5	102
Thornhill, Man.	k15	73
Thornhill, Scot., U.K.	E5	13
Thornton, Ont.	C5	73
Thornton, Ar., U.S.	D3	81
Thornton, Co., U.S.	*B6	83
Thornton, Ia., U.S.	B4	92
Thornton, Il., U.S.	k9	90
Thornton, N.H., U.S.	C3	106
Thornton, Tx., U.S.	D4	120
Thornton, Wa., U.S.	B8	124
Thornton Gap, Va., U.S.	B4	123
Thorntonville, Tx., U.S.	D1	120
Thorntown, In., U.S.	D4	91
Thornville, Oh., U.S.	C3	112
Thornwood, N.Y., U.S.	*m15	109
Thornwood, W.V., U.S.	C5	125
Thorny Mountain, mtn., Mo., U.S.	D6	102
Thorofare, N.J., U.S.	D2	107
Thorold, Ont.	D5	73
Thorp, Wa., U.S.	B5	124
Thorp, Wi., U.S.	D3	126
Thorpe, Wy., U.S.	C4	127
Thorsby, Alta.	C3	68
Thorsby, Al., U.S.	C3	78
Thouars, Fr.	E3	16
Thousand Islands, is., N.Y., U.S.	A4	109
Thousand Lake Mountain, mtn., Ut., U.S.	E4	121
Thousand Oaks, Ca., U.S.	*E4	82
Thousand Springs Creek, stm., U.S.	B7	105
Thrace, hist. reg., Eur.	B6	25
Thrapston, Eng., U.K.	B7	12
Thrashers, Ms., U.S.	A5	101
Three Bridges, N.J., U.S.	B3	107
Three Fingered Jack, mtn., Or.	C5	114
Three Forks, Mt., U.S.	E5	103
Three Hills, Alta.	D4	68
Three Kings Islands, is., N.Z.	K14	51
Three Lakes, Wi., U.S.	C4	126
Three Mile Bay, N.Y., U.S.	A4	109
Three Mile Plains, N.S.	E5	71
Three Nunataks, mtn., Ant.	g41	7
Three Oaks, Mi., U.S.	G4	99
Threepoint Lake, l., Man.	B2	70
Three Points, Cape, c., Ghana	F4	45
Three Rivers, Ma., U.S.	B3	98
Three Rivers, Mi., U.S.	G5	99
Three Rivers, N.M., U.S.	E3	108
Three Rivers, Tx., U.S.	E3	120
Three Rock Cove, Newf.	D2	72
Three Sisters, mtn., Or., U.S.	C5	114
Three Springs, Pa., U.S.	F6	115
Throckmorton, Tx., U.S.	C3	120
Throckmorton, co., Tx., U.S.	C3	120
Throop, Pa., U.S.	m18	115
Thu Dau Mot, Viet.	G7	35
Thuin, Viet.	G8	35
Thuir, Fr.	F5	16
Thu (Qaanaaq), Grnld.	B14	61
Thun, Switz.	E3	18
Thun, Lake, l., Switz.	E3	18
Thunder Bay, Ont.	o17	73
Thunder Bay, dept., Ont.	o17	73
Thunder Bay, b., Mi., U.S.	D7	99
Thunder Bay, stm., Mi., U.S.	D6	99
Thunder Bay, North Branch, stm., Mi., U.S.	C6	99
Thunderbird, Lake, res., Ok., U.S.	B4	113
Thunderbolt, Ga., U.S.	D5	87
Thunder Butte, S.D., U.S.	B4	118
Thunder Butte, mtn., S.D.,	B4	118
Thunder Butte Creek, stm., S.D., U.S.	B3	118
Thunder Hawk, S.D., U.S.	B4	118
Thunder Hills, hills, Sask.	C2	75
Thung Song, Thai.	H3	35
Thur, stm., Switz.	A6	21
Thurgau, state, Switz.	B5	20
Thüringer Wald, mts., E. Ger.	C5	18
Thuringia, hist. reg., E. Ger.	C5	18
Thurles, Ire.	D3	10
Thurlow Dam, Al., U.S.	C4	78
Thurman, Ia., U.S.	D2	92
Thurman, Oh., U.S.	D3	112
Thurmont, Md., U.S.	A3	97
Thurø, i., Den.	C4	15
Thursday Island, Austl.	B7	50
Thurso, Que.	D2	74
Thurso, Scot., U.K.	A5	10
Thurso, stm., Scot., U.K.	B5	13
Thurston, Ne., U.S.	B9	104
Thurston, co., Ne., U.S.	B9	104
Thurston, co., Wa., U.S.	C2	124
Thurston Island, i., Ant.	B3	7
Thusis, Switz.	E4	18
Thuvu, Fiji	I14	52
Thwaites Iceburg Tongue, ice, Ant.	B2	7
Thyborøn, Den.	B2	15
Thyborøn Kanal, strt., Den.	B2	15
Tiahuanaco, Bol.	C2	55
Tianjin (Tientsin), China	D8	31
Tianjun, China	D4	31
Tianmen, China	I5	32
Tianshui, China	E6	31
Tianzhen, China	D6	32
Tiawah, Ok., U.S.	A6	113
Tibagi, Braz.	C2	56
Tibagi, stm., Braz.	C2	56
Tibati, Cam.	D2	46
Tibé, Pic de, mtn., Gui.	E3	45
Tiber (Tevere), stm., Italy	C4	23
Tiberias (Teverya), Isr.	F10	40
Tibesti, mts., Chad	A3	46
Tibet (Xizang), prov., China	E3	31
Tibiri, Niger	D6	45
Tibooburra, Austl.	E7	50
Tiburón, Isla, i., Mex.	B2	63
Tice, Fl., U.S.	F5	86
Tichborne, Ont.	C8	73
Tichfield, Sask.	F2	75
Tichît, Maur.	C3	45
Ticino, state, Switz.	C4	20
Ticino, stm., Eur.	B2	23
Tickfaw, La., U.S.	D5	95
Tickfaw, stm., La., U.S.	C5	95
Ticomán (part of Mexico City), Mex.	g9	63
Ticonderoga, N.Y., U.S.	B7	109
Ticul, Mex.	C7	63
Tide Head, N.B.	B3	71
Tidikelt, pl., Alg.	D5	44
Tidioute, Pa., U.S.	C3	115
Tidjikdja, Maur.	C3	45
Tidra, Île, i., Maur.	C1	45
Tiel, Neth.	C5	17
Tieli, China	B12	31
Tieling, China	C11	31
Tielmes de Tajuña, Spain	p18	22
Tielt, Bel.	D3	17
Tienen, Bel.	B6	16
Tien Shan, mts., Asia	E10	30
Tientsin see Tianjin, China	D8	31
Tien Yen, Viet.	B6	35
Tie Plant, Ms., U.S.	B4	101
Tierp, Swe.	K16	14
Tierra Amarilla, Chile	E1	55
Tierra Amarilla, N.M., U.S.	A3	108
Tierra Blanca, Mex.	D5	63
Tierra del Fuego, Antártida e Islas del Atlántico Sur, ter.	h12	54
Tierra del Fuego, Isla Grande de, i., S.A.	h12	54
Tie Siding, Wy., U.S.	E7	127
Tiétar, stm., Spain	C5	22
Tietê, Braz.	C3	56
Tietê, stm., Braz.	C3	56
Tieton, Wa., U.S.	C5	124
Tieton, stm., Wa., U.S.	C4	124
Tieton Dam, Wa., U.S.	C4	124
Tiffany Mountain, mtn., Wa., U.S.	A6	124
Tiff City, Mo., U.S.	E3	102
Tiffin, Ia., U.S.	C6	92
Tiffin, Oh., U.S.	A2	112
Tiffin, stm., Oh., U.S.	A1	112
Tiflis see Tbilisi, Sov. Un.	I7	27
Tift, co., Ga., U.S.	E3	87
Tifton, Ga., U.S.	E3	87
Tigard, Or., U.S.	h12	114
Tiger, Ga., U.S.	B3	87
Tigerton, Wi., U.S.	D4	126
Tigerville, S.C., U.S.	A3	117
Tighnabruaich, Scot., U.K.	E3	13
Tigil, Sov. Un.	D18	29
Tignall, Ga., U.S.	C4	87
Tignère, Cam.	D2	46
Tignish, P.E.I.	C5	71
Tigray (Tigre), prov., Eth.	A5	47
Tigre, Arg.	g7	54
Tigre, stm., Peru	B3	58
Tigre, stm., Ven.	B5	60
Tigris (Dicle), stm., Asia	B4	38
Tiguabos, Cuba	D6	64
Tiguentourine, Alg.	D6	44
Tih, Jabal at plat., Eg.	E5	41
Tihert, Alg.	B5	44
Tihuatlán, Mex.	m15	63
Tijeras, N.M., U.S.	B3	108
Tiji, Libya	C2	43
Tijuana, Mex.	A1	63
Tijucas, Braz.	D3	56
Tikal, hist., Guat.	D7	63
Tikamgarh, India	H8	37
Tikhoretsk, Sov. Un.	I13	27
Tikhvin, Sov. Un.	B9	27
Tiko, Cam.	E1	46
Tikrīt, Iraq	E14	40
Tiksi, Sov. Un.	B15	29
Tilamuta, Indon.	E6	34
Tilarán, C.R.	E5	62
Tilburg, Neth.	B6	16
Tilbury, Ont.	E2	73
Tilbury, Eng., U.K.	m13	10
Tilcara, Arg.	D2	55
Tilden, Ne., U.S.	B8	104
Tilden, Tx., U.S.	E3	120
Tilemsés, Niger	C5	45
Tilemsi, Vallée du, val., Mali	C5	45
Tilford, S.D., U.S.	C2	118
Tilghman, Md., U.S.	C5	97
Tilghman Island, i., Md., U.S.	C5	97
Tilimsen (Tlemcen), Alg.	C4	44
Till, stm., Eng., U.K.	e9	13
Tillamook, Or., U.S.	B3	114
Tillamook, co., Or., U.S.	B3	114
Tillar, Ar., U.S.	D4	81
Tillatoba, Ms., U.S.	B4	101
Tillberga (part of Västerås), Swe.	t34	14
Tiller, Or., U.S.	E4	114
Tillery, Lake, res., N.C., U.S.	B2	110
Tilley, Alta.	D5	68
Tillman, S.C., U.S.	G5	117
Tillman, co., Ok., U.S.	C2	113
Tillmans Corner, Al., U.S.	E1	78
Tillson, N.Y., U.S.	D6	109
Tillsonburg, Ont.	E4	73
Tilly, Ar., U.S.	B3	81
Tilpa, Austl.	E5	51
Tilrhemt, Alg.	C5	44
Tilston, Man.	E1	70
Tilton, Ga., U.S.	B2	87
Tilton, Il., U.S.	C6	90
Tilton, N.H., U.S.	D3	106
Tiltonsville, Oh., U.S.	B5	112
Timaná, Col.	F4	60
Timaru, N.Z.	P13	51
Timashevsk, Sov. Un.	I12	27
Timbalier Bay, b., La., U.S.	E5	95
Timbalier Island, i., La., U.S.	E5	95
Timbaúba, Braz.	h6	57
Timber, Or., U.S.	B3	114
Timbered Knob, mtn., Mo., U.S.	E5	102
Timberlake, N.C., U.S.	A4	110
Timberlake, Va., U.S.	C3	123
Timberville, Va., U.S.	B4	123
Timbo, Ar., U.S.	B3	81
Timbuktu see Tombouctou, Mali	C4	45
Timerzit, Mor.	C4	44
Timewell, Il., U.S.	C3	90
Timimoun, Alg.	C5	44
Timiris, Cap, c., Maur.	C1	45
Timiskaming, dept., Ont.	o19	73
Timişoara, Rom.	C5	24
Timken, Ks., U.S.	D4	93
Timmendorfer Strand, W. Ger.	B6	15
Timmins, Ont.	o19	73
Timmonsville, S.C., U.S.	C8	117
Timms Hill, Wi., U.S.	C3	126
Timnath, Co., U.S.	A5	83
Timok, stm., Eur.	C5	24
Timor, i., Indon.	G6	34
Timor Sea	B4	50
Timpanogos Cave National Monument, Ut., U.S.	C4	121
Timpas Creek, stm., Co., U.S.	D7	83
Timrå, Swe.	F7	14
Timsâh, lake, l., Eg.	D4	41
Tims Ford Lake, res., Tn., U.S.	B5	119
Tin, Ra's at, c., Libya	B4	43
Tina, Mo., U.S.	B4	102
Tinaca Point, c., Phil.	D7	34
Tinahely, Ire.	E5	11
Tinaquillo, Ven.	B4	60
Tindouf, Alg.	C3	44
Tineo, Spain	A2	22
Tinghert, Hammādāt, plat.,	D2	43
Tinghert, Plateau du (Hammādāt Tinghert), plat., Afr.	D6	44
Tingley, Den.	D3	15
Tingley, Ia., U.S.	D3	92
Tingmerkpuk Mountain, mtn., Ak., U.S.	B7	79
Tingo María, Peru	C2	58
Tingréla, I.C.	D3	45
Tingrì, China	C11	37

Name	Map Ref.	Page
Tingsryd, Swe.	B8	15
Tinguipaya, Bol.	C2	55
Tingwick, Que.	D6	74
Tinian, i., N. Mar. Is.	F8	6
Tinian Harbor, b., N. Mar. Is.	E7	52
Tinizong, Switz.	C8	21
Tinker Air Force Base, mil., Ok., U.S.	B4	113
Tinkerville, N.H., U.S.	B3	106
Tinkisso, stm., Gui.	D2	45
Tinley Park, Il., U.S.	k9	90
Tinnie, N.M., U.S.	D4	108
Tinniswood, Mount, mtn., B.C.	D6	69
Tinogasta, Arg.	E2	55
Tinos, Grc.	D5	40
Tínos, i., Grc.	D5	40
Tinqueux, Fr.	E3	17
Tinsley, Ms., U.S.	C3	101
Tinsman, Ar., U.S.	D3	81
Tinsukia, India	C10	28
Tintah, Mn., U.S.	D2	100
Tintigny, Bel.	E5	17
Tintina, Arg.	E3	55
Tintinara, Austl.	G3	51
Tinton Falls, N.J., U.S.	C4	107
Ti-n-Zaouatene, Alg.	E5	44
Tio, Eth.	C5	47
Tioga, Il., U.S.	C2	90
Tioga, La., U.S.	C3	95
Tioga, N.D., U.S.	A3	111
Tioga, Pa., U.S.	C7	115
Tioga, W.V., U.S.	C4	125
Tioga, co., N.Y., U.S.	C4	109
Tioga, co., Pa., U.S.	C7	115
Tioga, stm., Pa., U.S.	B7	115
Tiogue Lake, res., R.I., U.S.	D3	116
Tioman, i., Malay.	K6	35
Tiona, Va., U.S.	C3	115
Tione di Trento, Italy	C6	20
Tionesta, Pa., U.S.	D3	115
Tionesta Creek, stm., Pa., U.S.	C3	115
Tionesta Lake, res., Pa., U.S.	D3	115
Tioughnioga, stm., N.Y., U.S.	C4	109
Tipler, Wi., U.S.	C5	126
Tiplersville, Ms., U.S.	A5	101
Tippah, co., Ms., U.S.	A5	101
Tippah, stm., Ms., U.S.	A4	101
Tipp City, Oh., U.S.	C1	112
Tippecanoe, In., U.S.	B5	91
Tippecanoe, co., In., U.S.	D4	91
Tippecanoe, stm., In., U.S.	C4	91
Tipperary, Ire.	D2	10
Tipperary, co., Ire.	E4	11
Tippo, Ms., U.S.	B3	101
Tipton, Ca., U.S.	D4	82
Tipton, In., U.S.	D5	91
Tipton, Ia., U.S.	C6	92
Tipton, Ks., U.S.	C5	93
Tipton, Mo., U.S.	C5	102
Tipton, Ok., U.S.	C2	113
Tipton, Tn., U.S.	B2	119
Tipton, co., In., U.S.	D5	91
Tipton, co., Tn., U.S.	B2	119
Tipton, Mount, mtn., Az., U.S.	B1	80
Tiptonville, Tn., U.S.	A2	119
Tip Top, Ky., U.S.	C6	94
Tiptop, Va., U.S.	C1	123
Tip Top Mountain, mtn., Ont.	o18	73
Tiquisate, Guat.	C2	62
Tira, Isr.	B6	41
Tīrān, Jazīrat, i., Sau. Ar.	I10	40
Tirana (Tiranë), Alb.	B2	40
Tiranë see Tirana, Alb.	B2	40
Tirano, Italy	A3	23
Tiraque, Bol.	C2	55
Tiraspol, Sov. Un.	H7	27
Tirat Karmel, Isr.	B7	41
Tirat Zevi, Isr.	B7	41
Tire, Tur.	C6	40
Tirebolu, Tur.	B12	40
Tiree, i., Scot., U.K.	B3	10
Tire Hill, Pa., U.S.	F4	115
Tîrgoviște, Rom.	C7	24
Tîrgu-Frumos, Rom.	B8	24
Tîrgu-Jiu, Rom.	C6	24
Tîrgu-Neamț, Rom.	B8	24
Tîrgu-Ocna, Rom.	B8	24
Tîrgu-Secuiesc, Rom.	B8	24
Tirich Mīr, mtn., Pak.	A5	36
Tiriro, Gui.	D3	45
Tirlyanskiy, Sov. Un.	E20	8
Tîrnava Mică, stm., Rom.	B7	24
Tîrnăveni, Rom.	B7	24
Tîrnavos, Grc.	C4	25
Tiro, Oh., U.S.	B3	112
Tirol (Tyrol), state, Aus.	B7	20
Tirol, hist. reg., Aus.	E5	18
Tiros, Braz.	B3	56
Tirschenreuth, W. Ger.	D7	19
Tirso, stm., Italy	D2	23
Tirstrup, Den.	B4	15
Tiruchchirāppalli (Trichinopoly), India	F6	36
Tirunelveli (Tinnevelly), India	G6	36
Tiruppur, India	*F6	36
Tisa (Tisza), stm., Eur.	C5	24
Tisaren, I., Swe.	I33	14
Tisch Mills, Wi., U.S.	h10	126
Tisdale, Sask.	E3	75
Tishomingo, Ms., U.S.	A5	101
Tishomingo, Ok., U.S.	C5	113
Tishomingo, co., Ms., U.S.	A5	101
Tiskilwa, Il., U.S.	B4	90
Tisnaren, I., Swe.	u33	14
Tissemsilt, Alg.	B5	44
Tista, stm., Asia	D12	37
Tisvildeleje, Den.	B6	15
Tisza (Tisa), stm., Eur.	B5	24
Tiszafüred, Hung.	B5	24
Tiszakécske, Hung.	B5	24
Titicaca, Lago, I., S.A.	E4	58
Titograd, Yugo.	D4	24
Titonka, Ia., U.S.	A3	92
Titovo Užice, Yugo.	D4	24
Titov Veles, Yugo.	E5	24
Titule, Zaire	A4	48
Titus, co., Tx., U.S.	C5	120
Titusville, Fl., U.S.	D6	86
Titusville, N.J., U.S.	C3	107
Titusville, Pa., U.S.	C2	115
Tivaouane, Sen.	C1	45
Tiverton, N.S.	E3	71
Tiverton, Ont.	C3	73
Tiverton, Eng., U.K.	E5	10
Tiverton, R.I., U.S.	D6	116
Tiverton Four Corners, R.I., U.S.	E6	116
Tivoli, Italy	D4	23
Tivoli, N.Y., U.S.	C7	109
Tivoli, Tx., U.S.	E4	120
Tixtla [de Guerrero], Mex.	o14	63
Tizapán (part of Mexico City), Mex.	h9	63
Tizard Bank, atoll, Asia	C4	34
Tizimín, Mex.	C7	63
Tōkyō, Japan	D12	31
Tizi-Ouzou, Alg.	B5	44
Tiznit, Mor.	D3	44
Tjeukemeer, I., Neth.	B5	17
Tlacolula [de Matamoros], Mex.	D5	63
Tlacotalpan, Mex.	D5	63
Tlacotepec, Mex.	o13	63
Tláhuac (part of Mexico City), Mex.	h9	63
Tlahualilo de Zaragoza, Mex.	B4	63
Tlalnepantla, stm., Mex.	g9	63
Tlalnepantla [de Comonfort], Mex.	g9	63
Tlalpan (part of Mexico City), Mex.	h9	63
Tlalpujahua, Mex.	n13	63
Tlaltenango [de Sánchez Román], Mex.	C4	63
Tlaltenco (part of Mexico City), Mex.	h9	63
Tlapa, Mex.	o14	63
Tlapacoyan, Mex.	n15	63
Tlapaneco, stm., Mex.	o14	63
Tlaquepaque (San Pedro Tlaquepaque), Mex.	m12	63
Tlaxcala, state, Mex.	D5	63
Tlaxcala [de Xicohténcatl], Mex.	D5	63
Tlaxco [de Morelos], Mex.	n14	63
Tlaxiaco, Mex.	D5	63
Tłuszcz, Pol.	k14	26
Tmassah, Libya	D3	43
Toadlena, N.M., U.S.	A1	108
Toamasina, Madag.	g9	49
Toamasina, prov., Madag.	g9	49
Toano, Va., U.S.	C6	123
Toano Range, mts., Nv., U.S.	C7	105
Toast, N.C., U.S.	A2	110
Toay, Arg.	B4	54
Toba, Japan	o15	33
Toba, stm., B.C.	D5	69
Toba, Danau, I., Indon.	E1	34
Tobacco Root Mountains, mts., Mt., U.S.	E5	103
Tobago, i., Trin.	K14	64
Tobago Cays, is., St. Vin.	V26	65
Toba Inlet, b., B.C.	D5	69
Tobarra, Spain	C5	22
Tobaru, Japan	O5	52
Tobercurry, Ire.	C3	11
Tobermory, Ont.	B3	73
Tobermory, Scot., U.K.	D2	13
Tobias, Ne., U.S.	D8	104
Tobiishi Point, c., Japan	P17	52
Tobi Island, i., Japan	G9	33
Tobin, Mount, mtn., Nv., U.S.	C4	105
Tobin Lake, I., Austl.	D4	50
Tobin Lake, I., Sask.	D4	75
Tobin Range, mts., Nv., U.S.	C4	105
Tobins Harbor, Mi., U.S.	h10	99
Tobique, stm., N.B.	B2	71
Tobol, Sov. Un.	C6	28
Tobol, stm., Sov. Un.	D9	28
Tobolsk, Sov. Un.	D9	29
Tobruk see Ţubruq, Libya	C4	43
Toby, Mount, mtn., Ma., U.S.	B2	98
Tobyhanna, Pa., U.S.	D11	115
Tocantinópolis, Braz.	C1	57
Tocantins, stm., Braz.	D6	53
Tocantins National Park, Braz.	A3	56
Toccoa, Ga., U.S.	B3	87
Toccoa, stm., Ga., U.S.	B2	87
Toccoa Falls, Ga., U.S.	B3	87
Toccopola, Ms., U.S.	A4	101
Toce, stm., Italy	C4	23
Tochcha Lake, I., B.C.	B5	69
Tochigi, Japan	H9	33
Toco, Trin.	N24	65
Tocoa, Hond.	C4	62
Tocopilla, Chile	A1	54
Tocsin, In., U.S.	C7	91
Tocumen, Pan.	F8	62
Tocumwal, Austl.	G5	51
Tocuyo, stm., Ven.	A4	60
Todd, N.C., U.S.	A1	110
Todd, co., Ky., U.S.	D3	94
Todd, co., Mn., U.S.	D4	100
Todd, co., S.D., U.S.	D5	118
Todd Estates, De., U.S.	*B3	85
Toddville, Md., U.S.	D5	97
Toddy Pond, I., Me., U.S.	D4	96
Tödi, mtn., Switz.	C4	20
Todoga, Cape, c., Japan	G11	33
Todos os Santos, Baía de, b., Braz.	D7	57
Todos Santos, Bol.	C2	55
Todos Santos, Mex.	C2	63
Todtnau, W. Ger.	B3	20
Toe Head, c., Ire.	F2	11
Toe Head, c., Scot., U.K.	C1	13
Tofield, Alta.	C4	68
Tofino, B.C.	E5	69
Tofte, Mn., U.S.	C8	100
Toftlund, Den.	C3	15
Togdheer, prov., Som.	D6	47
Togiak, Ak., U.S.	D7	79
Togian Islands, is., Indon.	F6	34
Togo, Sask.	F5	75
Togo, ctry., Afr.	F5	45
Togtoh, China	D4	32
Togwotee Pass, Wy., U.S.	C2	127
Tohakum Peak, mtn., Nv., U.S.	C2	105
Tohatchi, N.M., U.S.	B1	108
Tohopekaliga, Lake, I., Fl., U.S.	D5	86
Toi, Cape, c., Japan	K5	33
To Island, i., Japan	I9	33
Toivola, Mi., U.S.	B2	99
Toivola, Mn., U.S.	C6	100
Tok, Ak., U.S.	C11	79
Tokaj, Hung.	A5	24
Tokara Islands, is., Japan	F10	31
Tokara Strait, strt., Japan	K5	33
Tokat, Tur.	B11	40
Tōkchŏn, N. Kor.	G3	33
Tokelau, dep., Oc.	G11	6
Tokio, N.D., U.S.	B7	111
Tokio, Tx., U.S.	C1	120
Toki Point, c., Wake I.	A1	52
Tok Islands (Take Islands), is., Asia	H5	33
Tokmak, Sov. Un.	H10	27
Tokmak, Sov. Un.	E9	28
Tokoroa, N.Z.	M15	51
Tokuno Island, i., Japan	F10	31
Tokushima, Japan	E11	31
Tokuyama, Japan	J5	33
Tōkyō, Japan	D12	31
Tōkyō Bay, b., Japan	n18	31
Tokzār, Afg.	D13	39
Tol, i., Micron.	Q18	52
Tolar, N.M., U.S.	C6	108
Tolbukhin (Dobrich), Bul.	D8	24
Toleak Point, c., Wa., U.S.	B1	124
Toledo, Braz.	C2	56
Toledo, Ont.	C8	73
Toledo, Spain	C3	22
Toledo, Il., U.S.	D5	90
Toledo, Ia., U.S.	B5	92
Toledo, Oh., U.S.	A2	112
Toledo, Or., U.S.	C3	114
Toledo, Wa., U.S.	C3	124
Toledo, Montes de, mts., Spain	C3	22
Toledo Bend Reservoir, res., U.S.	C2	95
Toler, Ky., U.S.	C7	94
Tolga, Alg.	C6	44
Toliara, Madag.	h8	49
Toliara, prov., Madag.	h8	49
Tolima, dept., Col.	C2	60
Tolima, Nevado del, mtn., Col.	C2	60
Tolimán, Mex.	m14	63
Tolitoli, Indon.	E6	34
Tolken, I., Swe.	A6	15
Tolland, Ct., U.S.	B6	84
Tolland, co., Ct., U.S.	B6	84
Tollense, I., E. Ger.	E7	15
Tollense, stm., E. Ger.	E7	15
Tollesboro, Ky., U.S.	B6	94
Tolleson, Az., U.S.	m8	80
Tollette, Ar., U.S.	D2	81
Tolley, N.D., U.S.	A4	111
Tollhouse, Ca., U.S.	D4	82
Tolloche, Arg.	E3	55
Tolmezzo, Italy	C4	23
Tolmin, Yugo.	C4	24
Tolna, Hung.	B4	24
Tolna, N.D., U.S.	B7	111
Tolo, Gulf of, b., Indon.	F6	34
Tolono, Il., U.S.	D5	90
Tolosa, Spain	A4	22
Tolovana Park, Or., U.S.	B3	114
Tolsta Head, c., Scot., U.K.	B2	13
Tolstoi, Man.	E3	70
Tolstoy, S.D., U.S.	B6	118
Toltén, Chile	D2	54
Tolt Reservoir, res., Wa., U.S.	B4	124
Tolú, Col.	B2	60
Tolu, Ky., U.S.	e9	94
Toluca, Il., U.S.	B4	90
Toluca, Nevado de, vol., Mex.	n14	63
Toluca [de Lerdo], Mex.	D5	63
Tolyatti, Sov. Un.	C3	28
Tom, Ok., U.S.	D7	113
Tom, Mount, hill, Ct., U.S.	C2	84
Tomah, Wi., U.S.	E3	126
Tomahawk, Wi., U.S.	C4	126
Tomahawk Lake, I., Wi., U.S.	C4	126
Tomakomai, Japan	E10	31
Tomakovka, Sov. Un.	H10	27
Tomanivi, mtn., Fiji	H15	52
Tomar, Port.	C1	22
Tomari, Sov. Un.	E17	29
Tomaszów Lubelski, Pol.	C7	26
Tomaszów Mazowiecki, Pol.	C6	26
Tomatlán, Mex.	D3	63
Tomato, Ar., U.S.	B6	81
Tomave, Bol.	C2	55
Tombador, Serra do, plat., Braz.	B4	56
Tomball, Tx., U.S.	D5	120
Tombigbee, stm., U.S.	D1	78
Tomboco, Ang.	C1	48
Tombouctou (Timbuktu), Mali	E4	45
Tombstone, Az., U.S.	F5	80
Tombstone Mountain, mtn., Yukon	D5	66
Tombua (Porto Alexandre), Ang.	E1	48
Tomé, Chile	D2	54
Tome, N.M., U.S.	C3	108
Tomelilla, Swe.	C7	15
Tomelloso, Spain	C4	22
Tom Green, co., Tx., U.S.	D2	120
Tomichi Creek, stm., Co., U.S.	C4	83
Tomini, Gulf of, b., Indon.	E6	34
Tominian, Mali	F4	45
Tomintoul, Scot., U.K.	C5	13
Tomkins Cove, N.Y., U.S.	D6	109
Tommot, Sov. Un.	D15	29
Tom Nevers Head, c., Ma., U.S.	D8	98
Tomnolen, Ms., U.S.	B4	101
Tomo, stm., Col.	B4	60
Tomobe, Japan	m19	33
Tomori, Japan	O5	52
Tonalá, Mex.	D6	63
Tonalá, stm., Mex.	D6	63
Tonantins, Braz.	D5	60
Tonasket, Wa., U.S.	A6	124
Tonate, Fr. Gu.	B4	59
Tonawanda, N.Y., U.S.	B2	109
Tonbridge, Eng., U.K.	C8	12
Tondano, Indon.	E6	34
Tønder, Den.	D2	15
Tone, stm., Japan	n19	33
Tonekābon, Iran	B5	38
Toney, Al., U.S.	A3	78
Tonga, ctry., Oc.	H11	6
Tonganoxie, Ks., U.S.	C8	93
Tongbei, China	B3	32
Tongcheng, China	i7	32
Tongchuan, China	G3	32
Tongeren, Bel.	D7	17
Tonghe, China	C10	31
Tonghua, China	C10	31
Tongjiang, China	B4	32
Tongjiang, China	C6	33
Tongjosŏn Bay, b., N. Kor.	G3	33
Tongliao, China	C9	31
Tongling, China	E8	31
Tongoy, Chile	F1	55
Tongren, China	G3	32
Tongue, Scot., U.K.	B4	13
Tongue, stm., Mt., U.S.	E10	103
Tongue, stm., Tx., U.S.	p13	120
Tongue, Kyle of, b., Scot., U.K.	B4	13
Tongyu, China	B10	32
Tongzi, China	J2	32
Tónichi, Mex.	B3	63
Tonj, Sud.	D2	47
Tonk, India	C6	36
Tonkawa, Ok., U.S.	A4	113
Tonkin, hist. reg., Viet.	B6	35
Tonkin, Gulf of, b., Asia	B3	34
Tonle Sap, I., Camb.	C2	34
Tonneins, Fr.	E4	16
Tonnerre, Fr.	D5	16
Tönning, W. Ger.	D2	15
Tonopah, Az., U.S.	D3	80
Tonopah, Nv., U.S.	E4	105
Tonosí, Pan.	G7	62
Tønsberg, Nor.	H4	14
Tontitown, Ar., U.S.	A1	81
Tonto, stm., Mex.	n15	63
Tonto Basin, Az., U.S.	D4	80
Tontogany, Oh., U.S.	f6	112
Tonto National Monument, Az., U.S.	D4	80
Tonto Natural Bridge, Az., U.S.	C4	80
Tony, Wi., U.S.	C3	126
Tooele, Ut., U.S.	C3	121
Tooele, co., Ut., U.S.	C2	121
Toole, co., Mt., U.S.	B5	103
Toombs, co., Ga., U.S.	D4	87
Toomsboro, Ga., U.S.	D3	87
Toomsuba, Ms., U.S.	C5	101
Toomyvara, Ire.	E3	11
Toone, Tn., U.S.	B3	119
Toowoomba, Austl.	E9	50
Topawa, Az., U.S.	F4	80
Topaz, Ca., U.S.	C4	82
Topeka, In., U.S.	A6	91
Topeka, Ks., U.S.	C8	93
Topinabee, Mi., U.S.	C6	99
Topki, Sov. Un.	B11	28
Topley, B.C.	B4	69
Toplica, stm., Yugo.	D5	24
Topocalma, Punta, c., Chile	A2	54
Topock, Az., U.S.	C1	80
Topol'čany, Czech.	D5	26
Topolnitsa, stm., Bul.	D7	24
Topolobampo, Mex.	B3	63
Topolovgrad, Bul.	D8	24
Toponas, Co., U.S.	A4	83
Topozero, I., Sov. Un.	E14	14
Toppenish, Wa., U.S.	C5	124
Toppenish Ridge, mtn., Wa., U.S.	C5	124
Top Pond, I., Newf.	E3	72
Topsfield, Me., U.S.	C5	96
Topsfield, Ma., U.S.	A6	98
Topsham, Me., U.S.	E3	96
Topsham, Vt., U.S.	C4	122
Topton, N.C., U.S.	f9	110
Topton, Pa., U.S.	F10	115
Toquerville, Ut., U.S.	F2	121
Toquima Range, mts., Nv., U.S.	E5	105
Torbalı, Tur.	C6	25
Torbat-e Ḩeydarīyeh, Iran	D9	39
Torbat-e Jām, Iran	D10	39
Torbay, Newf.	E5	72
Tor Bay, b., Eng., U.K.	D4	12
Torbert, Mount, mtn., Ak., U.S.	g15	79
Torbrook, N.S.	E5	71
Torcello, Italy	D8	20
Torch, stm., Sask.	D4	75
Torch Lake, I., Mi., U.S.	D5	99
Torekov, Swe.	B6	15
Torez, Sov. Un.	q21	27
Torgau, E. Ger.	C6	18
Toride, Japan	n19	33
Tori Island, i., Japan	J4	33
Torit, Sud.	E3	47
Tormes, stm., Spain	B2	22
Tornado Mountain, mtn., Can.	E3	68
Torneälven, stm., Eur.	D10	14
Torneträsk, I., Swe.	C9	14
Torngat Mountains, mts., Can.	f8	72
Tornillo, Tx., U.S.	o11	120
Tornio, Fin.	E11	14
Tornquist, Arg.	B4	54
Toro, Spain	B3	22
Torö, Swe.	u35	14
Törökszentmiklós, Hung.	B5	24
Toronto, Ont.	D5	73
Toronto, Ks., U.S.	E8	93
Toronto, Oh., U.S.	B5	112
Toronto, co., N.Y., U.S.	C9	118
Toronto Lake, res., Ks., U.S.	E7	93
Toro Peak, mtn., Ca., U.S.	F5	82
Toropets, Sov. Un.	C8	27
Tororo, Ug.	A6	48
Toro Rumi, mtn., Peru	D3	58
Torote, stm., Spain	o18	22
Torpbruk, Swe.	A8	15
Torquay, Sask.	H4	75
Torquay, Eng., U.K.	E5	10
Torrance, Ca., U.S.	n12	82
Torrance, co., N.M., U.S.	C3	108
Torre Annunziata, Italy	D5	23
Torre de Cerredo, mtn., Spain	A3	22
Torre del Greco, Italy	D5	23
Torredonjimeno, Spain	D3	22
Torrelavega, Spain	A3	22
Torremaggiore, Italy	D5	23
Torrens, Lake, I., Austl.	F6	50
Torrente, Spain	C5	22
Torreón, Mex.	B4	63
Torres, Braz.	D6	57
Torres Novas, Port.	C1	22
Torres Strait, strt., Austl.	A7	50
Torres Vedras, Port.	C1	22
Torrevieja, Spain	D5	22
Torrey, Ut., U.S.	E4	121
Torridge, stm., Eng., U.K.	E4	12
Torridon, Loch, b., Scot., U.K.	C3	13
Torriglia, Italy	E5	23
Tørring, Den.	C3	15
Torrington, Alta.	D4	68
Torrington, Ct., U.S.	B3	84
Torrington, Wy., U.S.	D8	127
Torrinha, Braz.	m7	56
Torrox, Spain	D4	22
Tors Cove, Newf.	E5	72
Torshälla (part of Eskilstuna), Swe.	t34	14
Tórshavn, Faer. Is.	C7	8
Tortilla Flat, Az., U.S.	D4	80
Tortola, i., V.I., Br.	G12	64
Tortona, Italy	B2	23
Tortosa, Spain	B6	22
Tortosa, Cape, c., Spain	B6	22
Tortue, Île de la, i., Haiti	D7	64
Tortugas, Golfo, b., Col.	C2	60
Toruń, Pol.	B5	26
Torup, Swe.	B7	15
Torysa, stm., Czech.	C6	26
Torzhok, Sov. Un.	C10	27
Torzym, Pol.	A10	19
Tosa-shimizu, Japan	J6	33
Tosno, Sov. Un.	B8	27
Tostado, Arg.	E3	55
Toston, Mt., U.S.	D5	103
Tosya, Tur.	B10	40
Toszek, Pol.	g9	26
Totagatic, stm., Wi., U.S.	B2	126
Totana, Spain	D5	22
Toteng, Bots.	B5	49
Totness, Sur.	A3	59
Totonicapán, Guat.	C2	62
Totora Palca, Bol.	C2	55
Totowa, N.J., U.S.	B4	107
Totoya Island, i., Fiji	I16	52
Totson Mountain, mtn., Ak., U.S.	C8	79
Tottenham, Austl.	F6	51
Tottenham, Ont.	C5	73
Tottenham (part of London), Eng., U.K.	k12	12
Tottori, Japan	D11	31
Touba, I.C.	E3	45
Touba, Sen.	D1	45
Toubkal, Jbel, mtn., Mor.	C3	44
Touchet, stm., Wa., U.S.	C7	124
Touchwood Lake, I., Man.	B4	70
Tougan, Burkina	E4	45
Touggourt, Alg.	C6	44
Touho, Gui.	D2	45
Touhy, Ne., U.S.	C9	104
Touisset, Ma., U.S.	C5	98
Toul, Fr.	C6	16
Touléplu, I.C.	E3	45
Toulon, Fr.	F6	16
Toulon, Il., U.S.	B4	90
Toulouse, Fr.	F4	16
Toungoo, Burma	E10	36
Touraine, hist. reg., Fr.	D4	16
Tourlaville, Fr.	C3	16
Tournai (Doornik), Bel.	D3	17
Tournon, Fr.	E6	16
Tournus, Fr.	D6	16
Touros, Braz.	C3	57
Tourville, Que.	B8	74
Touside, Pic, mtn., Chad.	A3	46
Toussaint Creek, stm., Oh., U.S.	f7	112
Toutle, North Fork, stm., Wa., U.S.	C3	124
Tovar, Ven.	B3	60
Tovarkovskiy, Sov. Un.	E12	27
Tovey, Il., U.S.	D4	90
Tow, Tx., U.S.	D3	120
Towada, I., Japan	F10	33
Towanda, Il., U.S.	C5	90
Towanda, Ks., U.S.	E7	93
Towanda, Pa., U.S.	C8	115
Towanda Creek, stm., Pa., U.S.	C8	115
Towaoc, Co., U.S.	D2	83
Tower, Mi., U.S.	C6	99
Tower, Mn., U.S.	C6	100
Tower City, N.D., U.S.	C8	111
Tower City, Pa., U.S.	E8	115
Tower Hill, Il., U.S.	D5	90
Town and Country, Wa., U.S.	*B8	124
Town Creek, Al., U.S.	A2	78
Town Creek Manor, Md., U.S.	D5	97
Towner, Co., U.S.	C8	83
Towner, N.D., U.S.	A5	111
Towner, co., N.D., U.S.	A6	111
Town Hill, Ct., U.S.	B3	84
Town Hill, hill, Ber.	p20	64
Townley, Al., U.S.	B2	78
Town 'n Country, Fl., U.S.	*E4	86
Towns, co., Ga., U.S.	B3	87
Townsend, De., U.S.	C3	85
Townsend, Ma., U.S.	A4	98
Townsend, Mt., U.S.	D6	103
Townsend, Tn., U.S.	D10	119
Townsend, Va., U.S.	C7	123
Townsend, Vt., U.S.	E3	122
Townshend Reservoir, res., Vt., U.S.	E3	122
Townsville, Austl.	C8	50
Townville, N.C., U.S.	A4	110
Townville, S.C., U.S.	B2	117
Townville, Pa., U.S.	C2	115
Towson, Md., U.S.	B4	97
Towuti, Lake, I., Indon.	F6	34
Toxey, Al., U.S.	D1	78
Toyah, Tx., U.S.	o13	120
Toyahvale, Tx., U.S.	o13	120
Toyama, Japan	F10	33
Toyama Bay, b., Japan	H8	33
Toyohashi, Japan	H9	33
Toyokawa, Japan	*I8	33
Toyonaka, Japan	o14	33
Toyota, Japan	n16	33
Tracy, Que.	C4	74
Tracy, Ca., U.S.	D3	82
Tracy, Ia., U.S.	C5	92
Tracy, Mn., U.S.	F3	100
Tracy, Mo., U.S.	B3	102
Tracy City, Tn., U.S.	D8	119
Tracys Creek, stm., Md., U.S.	C4	97
Tracyton, Wa., U.S.	e10	124
Tradate, Italy	E6	21
Trade Lake, I., Sask.	B4	75
Tradewater, stm., Ky., U.S.	C2	94
Trading Post, Ks., U.S.	D9	93
Traer, Ia., U.S.	B5	92
Traer, Ks., U.S.	C3	93
Trafalgar, In., U.S.	F5	91
Trafalgar, Cape, c., Spain	D2	22
Trafford, Pa., U.S.	k14	115
Trafford, Lake, l., Fl., U.S.	F5	86
Traiguén, Chile	B2	54
Trail, B.C.	E9	69
Trail, Mn., U.S.	C3	100
Trail, Or., U.S.	E4	114
Trail City, S.D., U.S.	B5	118
Trail Creek, In., U.S.	A4	91
Traill, i., Grnld.	B16	128
Traill, co., N.D., U.S.	B8	111
Trail Ridge, mtn., U.S.	F4	87
Traipu, Braz.	C3	57
Trairi, stm., Braz.	h6	57
Tralee, Ire.	D2	10
Tralee Bay, b., Ire.	E2	11
Tramelan [-Dessus], Switz.	B3	21
Trammel, Va., U.S.	e9	123
Tramore, Ire.		
Trampas, N.M., U.S.	A4	108
Tramping Lake, Sask.	E1	75
Tramping Lake, l., Sask.	E1	75
Tranås, Swe.	H6	14
Trancão, stm., Port.	f9	22
Trancas, Arg.	E2	55
Troncoso, Port.	B2	22
Tranebjerg, Den.	C4	15
Tranemo, Swe.	A7	15
Trang, Thai.	D1	34
Trangan, i., Indon.	G8	34
Trani, Italy	D6	23
Tranninh, Plateau du, plat., Laos	C5	35
Tranquility, N.J., U.S.	B3	107
Tranquility, Ca., U.S.	D3	82
Transfer, Pa., U.S.	D1	115
Transkei, ctry., Afr.	D4	49
Transvaal, prov., S. Afr.	B4	49
Transylvania, co., N.C., U.S.	f10	110
Transylvania, hist. reg., Rom.	B6	24
Transylvanian Alps, mts., Rom.	C7	24
Trapani, Italy	E4	23
Trap Mountain, mtn., Ar., U.S.	g7	81
Trappe, Md., U.S.	C5	97
Trapper Creek, stm., Md., U.S.	C5	97
Trapper Peak, mtn., Mt., U.S.	E2	103
Traralgon, Austl.	G8	50
Traryd, Swe.	B7	15
Trasimeno, Lake, I., Italy	C4	23
Trask, Mo., U.S.	E6	102
Traskwood, Ar., U.S.	C3	81
Tras-os-Montes, hist. reg., Port.	B2	22
Trat, Thai.	C2	34
Traun, stm., Aus.	D7	18
Traunik, Mi., U.S.	B4	99
Traunstein, W. Ger.	E4	19
Travelers Rest, S.C., U.S.	B3	117
Travers, Alta.	D4	68
Travers, Switz.	C2	21
Traverse, co., Mn., U.S.	E2	100
Traverse, Lake, I., U.S.	B9	118
Traverse City, Mi., U.S.	D5	99
Traverspine, stm., Newf.	B1	72
Travers Reservoir, res., Alta.	D4	68
Travis, co., Tx., U.S.	D4	120
Travis Air Force Base, mil., Ca., U.S.	C2	82
Travnik, Yugo.	C3	24
Tray Mountain, mtn., Ga., U.S.	B3	87
Treadway, Tn., U.S.	C10	119
Treasure, co., Mt., U.S.	D9	103
Treasure Island, Fl., U.S.	*p10	86
Treasure Island Naval Station, Ca., U.S.	h8	82
Trebbia, stm., Italy	E5	23
Trebel, stm., E. Ger.	E6	15
Třebíč, Czech.	D3	26
Trebinje, Yugo.	D4	24
Trebišov, Czech.	D6	26
Treble Mountain, mtn., B.C.	B3	69
Trebloc, Ms., U.S.	B5	101
Třeboň, Czech.	D3	26
Trece Martires, Phil.	o13	34
Trees, Ks., U.S.	E9	93
Trees, La., U.S.	B1	95
Tregaron, Wales, U.K.	D5	10
Trego, Mt., U.S.	B2	103
Trego, Wi., U.S.	C2	126
Trego, co., Ks., U.S.	D4	93
Treguier, Fr.	C2	16
Treherne, Man.	E2	70
Treig, Loch, res., Scot., U.K.	D4	13
Treinta y Tres, Ur.	C6	54
Treinta y Tres, dept., Ur.	E2	56
Trélazé, Fr.	D3	16
Trelew, Arg.	C3	54
Trelleborg, Swe.	J5	14
Tremadog Bay, b., Wales, U.K.	D4	10
Tremblay, Fr.	g11	16
Trembleur Lake, l., B.C.	B5	69
Trementina, N.M., U.S.	B5	108
Tremiti Islands, is., Italy	C5	23
Tremont, Il., U.S.	C4	90
Tremont, Ms., U.S.	A5	101
Tremont, Pa., U.S.	E9	115
Tremonton, Ut., U.S.	B3	121
Tremont City, Oh., U.S.	B2	112
Tremp, Spain	A6	22
Trempealeau, Wi., U.S.	D2	126
Trempealeau, co., Wi., U.S.	D2	126
Trempealeau, stm., Wi., U.S.	D2	126
Trenary, Mi., U.S.	B4	99
Trenche, stm., Que.	B5	74
Trenčín, Czech.	D5	26
Trenque Lauquen, Arg.	B4	54
Trent, E. Ger.	A5	19
Trent, S.D., U.S.	D9	118
Trent, Tx., U.S.	C2	120
Trent, stm., Eng., U.K.	D6	10

Name	Map Ref.	Page
Trent, stm., N.C., U.S.	B5	110
Trente et un Milles, Lac des, l., Que.	C2	74
Trentino-Alto Adige, prov., Italy	C7	20
Trento (Trent), Italy	A3	23
Trenton, N.S.	D7	71
Trenton, Ont.	C7	73
Trenton, Al., U.S.	A3	78
Trenton, Fl., U.S.	C4	86
Trenton, Ga., U.S.	B1	87
Trenton, Il., U.S.	E4	90
Trenton, Ky., U.S.	D2	94
Trenton, Mi., U.S.	F7	99
Trenton, Mo., U.S.	A4	102
Trenton, Ne., U.S.	D4	104
Trenton, N.J., U.S.	C3	107
Trenton, N.C., U.S.	B5	110
Trenton, N.D., U.S.	A2	111
Trenton, Oh., U.S.	C1	112
Trenton, S.C., U.S.	D4	117
Trenton, Tn., U.S.	B3	119
Trenton, Tx., U.S.	C4	120
Trenton, Ut., U.S.	B4	121
Trepassey, Newf.	E5	72
Trepassey Bay, b., Newf.	E5	72
Tres Algarrobos, Arg.	B4	54
Tres Árboles, Ur.	E1	56
Tres Arroyos, Arg.	B4	54
Tres Cerros, Arg.	D3	54
Tresckow, Pa., U.S.	E10	115
Três Corações, Braz.	C3	56
Tres Esquinas, Col.	C2	60
Treshnish Point, c., Scot., U.K.	D2	13
Tres Irmãos, Serra dos, hills, Braz.	D2	59
Treska, stm., Yugo.	E5	24
Três Lagoas, Braz.	C2	56
Três Marias, Represa, res., Braz.	B3	56
Tres Piedras, N.M., U.S.	A4	108
Tres Puntas, Cabo, c., Arg.	D3	54
Três Rios, Braz.	h6	56
Tres Ritos, N.M., U.S.	A4	108
Trestle Creek, Id., U.S.	A2	89
Treuchtlingen, W. Ger.	F5	19
Treuenbrietzen, E. Ger.	A7	19
Treutlen, co., Ga., U.S.	D4	87
Treviglio, Italy	B2	23
Trévillers, Fr.	B2	21
Treviño, Spain	A4	22
Treviso, Italy	B4	23
Trevlac, In., U.S.	F5	91
Trevor, Wi., U.S.	n11	126
Trevorton, Pa., U.S.	E8	115
Trevose, Pa., U.S.	o22	115
Trevose Head, c., Eng., U.K.	D2	12
Treynor, Ia., U.S.	C2	92
Treysa, W. Ger.	C4	19
Trezevant, Tn., U.S.	A3	119
Trhové Sviny, Czech.	E9	19
Triadelphia, W.V., U.S.	A4	125
Triadelphia Reservoir, res., Md., U.S.	B3	97
Triánda, Grc.	D7	25
Triangle, Va., U.S.	B5	123
Triaucourt [-en-Argonne], Fr.	F5	17
Tribbett, Ms., U.S.	B3	101
Tribbey, Ok., U.S.	B4	113
Tribune, Sask.	H4	75
Tribune, Ks., U.S.	D2	93
Trichinopoly see Tiruchchirāppalli, India	F6	36
Trichūr, India	F6	36
Tri City, Or., U.S.	E3	114
Tridell, Ut., U.S.	C6	121
Trident, Mt., U.S.	E5	103
Trident Peak, mtn., Nv., U.S.	B3	105
Trier, W. Ger.	D3	18
Trieste, Italy	B4	23
Trieste, Gulf of, b., Eur.	B4	23
Trigg, co., Ky., U.S.	D2	94
Triglav, mtn., Yugo.	B1	24
Trigo Mountains, mts., Az., U.S.	D1	80
Trigueros, Spain	D2	22
Trikala, Grc.	C3	40
Trikhonís, Lake, l., Grc.	C3	25
Trikora Peak, mtn., Indon.	F9	34
Tri Lakes, In., U.S.	B7	91
Trilby, Fl., U.S.	D4	86
Trilla, Il., U.S.	D5	90
Trillick, N. Ire., U.K.	C4	11
Trim, Ire.	H5	11
Trimble, Mo., U.S.	B3	102
Trimble, Tn., U.S.	A2	119
Trimble, co., Ky., U.S.	B4	94
Trimont, Mn., U.S.	G4	100
Trimountain, Mi., U.S.	A2	99
Trinchera, Co., U.S.	D6	83
Trinchera Creek, stm., Co., U.S.	D5	83
Trincomalee, Sri L.	G7	36
Trindade, i., Braz.	H8	5
Třinec, Czech.	*D5	26
Tring Jonction, Que.	C6	74
Trinidad, Bol.	B3	55
Trinidad, Col.	B3	60
Trinidad, Cuba	D4	64
Trinidad, Co., U.S.	D6	83
Trinidad, Tx., U.S.	C4	120
Trinidad, Ur.	E1	56
Trinidad, i., Trin.	K14	64
Trinidad, Bahía, b., Pan.	k11	62
Trinidad, Isla, i., Arg.	B4	54
Trinidad and Tobago, ctry., N.A.	K14	64
Trinidad Head, c., Ca., U.S.	B1	82
Trinity, Newf.	D5	72
Trinity, Al., U.S.	A2	78
Trinity, N.C., U.S.	*B3	110
Trinity, Tx., U.S.	D5	120
Trinity, co., Ca., U.S.	B2	82
Trinity, co., Tx., U.S.	D5	120
Trinity, stm., Ca., U.S.	B2	82
Trinity, stm., Tx., U.S.	D5	120
Trinity, East Fork, stm., Tx., U.S.	n10	120
Trinity, Elm Fork, stm., Tx., U.S.	m10	120
Trinity, South Fork, stm., Ca., U.S.	B2	82
Trinity, West Fork, stm., Tx., U.S.	n9	120
Trinity Bay, b., Newf.	D5	72
Trinity Center, Ca., U.S.	B2	82
Trinity Islands, is., Ak., U.S.	D9	79
Trinity Mountain, mtn., Id., U.S.	F3	89
Trinity Mountains, mts., Ca., U.S.	B2	82
Trinity Peak, mtn., Nv., U.S.	C3	105
Trinity Range, mts., Nv., U.S.	C3	105
Trinity Springs, In., U.S.	G4	91
Trino, Italy	B2	23
Trinway, Oh., U.S.	B3	112
Trio, S.C., U.S.	E8	117
Trion, Ga., U.S.	B1	87
Tripoli (Ṭarābulus), Leb.	B3	38
Tripoli (Ṭarābulus), Libya	C2	43
Tripoli, Ia., U.S.	B5	92
Tripoli, Wi., U.S.	C4	126
Tripolis, Grc.	D4	40
Tripolitania (Ṭarābulus), hist. reg., Libya	C3	43
Tripp, S.D., U.S.	D8	118
Tripp, co., S.D., U.S.	D6	118
Tripura, state, India	D9	36
Trisanna, stm., Aus.	B9	21
Trischen, i., W. Ger.	A4	18
Tristan da Cunha, is., St. Hel.	I9	5
Triste, Golfo, b., Ven.	A4	60
Triune, Tn., U.S.	B5	119
Triunfo, Braz.	C5	57
Trivandrum, India	G6	36
Trnava, Czech.	G7	27
Trobriand Islands, is., Pap. N. Gui.	k13	50
Trochu, Alta.	D4	68
Trogir, Yugo.	E5	24
Trögstad, Nor.	p29	14
Troisdorf, W. Ger.	C2	19
Trois-Pistoles, Que.	A8	74
Trois-Rivières, Que.	C5	74
Trois-Rivières-Ouest, Que.	C5	74
Trois-Saumons, Que.	B7	74
Troitsk, Sov. Un.	D9	29
Troitskoye, Sov. Un.	B8	33
Trolldalen, Nor.	p28	14
Trollhättan, Swe.	H5	14
Trombetas, stm., Braz.	C3	59
Trombly, Mi., U.S.	B3	99
Tromper Wiek, b., E. Ger.	D7	15
Tromsö, Nor.	C14	14
Trona, Ca., U.S.	E5	82
Tronador, Monte, mtn., S.A.	C2	54
Trondheim, Nor.	F4	14
Trondheimsfjorden, Nor.	F3	14
Troon, Scot., U.K.	E4	13
Trooper, Pa., U.S.	*F11	115
Tropea, Italy	E5	23
Trophy Mountain, mtn., B.C.	D8	69
Tropic, Ut., U.S.	F3	121
Tropoja, Swe.	u35	14
Trosky, Mn., U.S.	G2	100
Trossachs, Sask.	H3	75
Trostan, mtn., N. Ire., U.K.	B5	11
Trotters, N.D., U.S.	B2	111
Trotwood, Oh., U.S.	C1	112
Troup, Tx., U.S.	C5	120
Troup, co., Ga., U.S.	C1	87
Trousdale, Ks., U.S.	E4	93
Trousdale, co., Tn., U.S.	A5	119
Trousers Lake, l., N.B.	B3	71
Trout, La., U.S.	C3	95
Trout, stm., Alta.	A3	68
Trout, stm., Fl., U.S.	m8	86
Trout, stm., Vt., U.S.	B3	122
Trout Creek, Ont.	B5	73
Trout Creek, Mi., U.S.	n12	99
Trout Creek, Mt., U.S.	C1	103
Trout Creek, Ut., U.S.	D2	121
Trout Creek Pass, Co., U.S.	C5	83
Troutdale, Me., U.S.	C5	96
Troutdale, Or., U.S.	*B4	114
Trout Dale, Va., U.S.	D1	123
Trout Lake, B.C.	D9	69
Trout Lake, Mi., U.S.	B6	99
Trout Lake, Wa., U.S.	D4	124
Trout Lake, l., B.C.	D9	69
Trout Lake, l., N.W. Ter.	D8	66
Trout Lake, l., Ont.	A5	73
Trout Lake, l., Ont.	o16	73
Trout Lake, l., Mn., U.S.	B6	100
Trout Lake, l., Wi., U.S.	n15	126
Troutman, N.C., U.S.	B2	110
Trout Peak, mtn., Wy., U.S.	B3	127
Trout River, Newf.	D2	72
Trout Run, Pa., U.S.	D7	115
Troutville, Va., U.S.	C3	123
Trouville [-sur-Mer], Fr.	C4	16
Trowbridge, Eng., U.K.	E5	10
Troy, Al., U.S.	D4	78
Troy, Id., U.S.	C2	89
Troy, Il., U.S.	E4	90
Troy, In., U.S.	H4	91
Troy, Ks., U.S.	C8	93
Troy, Mi., U.S.	o15	99
Troy, Mo., U.S.	C7	102
Troy, Mt., U.S.	B1	103
Troy, N.H., U.S.	E2	106
Troy, N.Y., U.S.	C7	109
Troy, N.C., U.S.	B3	110
Troy, Oh., U.S.	B1	112
Troy, Ok., U.S.	C5	113
Troy, Pa., U.S.	C8	115
Troy, S.C., U.S.	D3	117
Troy, S.D., U.S.	B9	118
Troy, Tn., U.S.	A2	119
Troy, Vt., U.S.	B4	122
Troy, W.V., U.S.	B4	125
Troy (Ilion), hist., Tur.	C6	25
Troy Grove, Il., U.S.	B4	90
Troy Mills, Ia., U.S.	B6	92
Truax, Sask.	H3	75
Trubchevsk, Sov. Un.	E9	27
Trubschachen, Switz.	C4	21
Truchas, N.M., U.S.	A4	108
Truchas Peak, mtn., N.M., U.S.	B4	108
Truckee, Ca., U.S.	C3	82
Truckee, stm., U.S.	D7	63
Trujillo, Hond.	G5	62
Trujillo, Peru	B2	58
Trujillo, Spain	C3	22
Trujillo, Ven.	B3	60
Trujillo, state, Ven.	B3	60
Truk, Micron.	F9	6
Truk International Airport, Micron.	Q18	52
Truman, Mn., U.S.	G4	100
Trumann, Ar., U.S.	B5	81
Trumansburg, N.Y., U.S.	C4	109
Trumbull, Ct., U.S.	E3	84
Trumbull, Ne., U.S.	D7	104
Trumbull, co., Oh., U.S.	A5	112
Trumbull, Mount, mtn., U.S.	A2	80
Trün, Bul.	D6	24
Truro, N.S.	D6	71
Truro, Eng., U.K.	E4	10
Truro, Ia., U.S.	C4	92
Truro, Ma., U.S.	C7	98
Truscott, Tx., U.S.	C3	120
Truskmore, mtn., Ire.	C3	11
Trussville, Al., U.S.	B3	78
Trustom Pond, l., R.I., U.S.	G3	116
Trust Territory of the Pacific Islands see Pacific Islands, Trust Territory of the, dep., Oc.	F9	6
Truth or Consequences (Hot Springs), N.M., U.S.	D2	108
Trutnov, Czech.	C3	26
Truxton, Az., U.S.	B2	80
Truxton, Mo., U.S.	B6	102
Truxton, N.Y., U.S.	C4	109
Tryon, Ne., U.S.	C5	104
Tryon, N.C., U.S.	f10	110
Tryon, Ok., U.S.	B5	113
Trysil, Nor.	G5	14
Trzcianka, Pol.	B4	26
Trzebiatów, Pol.	A3	26
Trzebinia, Pol.	C5	26
Trzebnica, Pol.	C4	26
Tsagaan Tologoy Hiid, Mong.	C2	32
Tsaidam Basin see Qaidam Pendi, China	D3	31
Tsakir, Sov. Un.	A5	31
Tsala Apopka Lake, l., Fl., U.S.	D4	86
Tsaratanana, Madag.	g9	49
Tsast Bogd Mountain, mtn., Mong.	B3	31
Tsau, Bots.	B3	49
Tsavo, Kenya	B6	48
Tschetter Colony, S.D., U.S.	D8	118
Tschida, Lake, res., N.D., U.S.	C4	111
Tselinograd, Sov. Un.	D10	29
Tsentralnyy, Sov. Un.	D26	8
Tsetserleg, Mong.	B5	31
Tshabong, Bots.	C3	49
Tshane, Bots.	B3	49
Tshela, Zaire	B1	48
Tshikapa, Zaire	C3	48
Tshilongo, Zaire	D4	48
Tshimbo, Zaire	C4	48
Tshofa, Zaire	C4	48
Tshuapa, stm., Zaire	B3	48
Tshukudu, Bots.	B3	49
Tshwaane, Bots.	B3	49
Tsiafajavona, mtn., Madag.	g9	49
Tsihombe, Madag.	i9	49
Tsimlyansk Reservoir, res., Sov. Un.	E7	29
Tsin Barrel see Jinan, China	D8	31
Tsinghai see Qinghai, prov., China	D4	31
Tsingtao see Qingdao, China	D9	31
Tsining Shan see Qin Ling, mts., China	E6	31
Tsintsabis, Nmb.	A2	49
Tsiroanomandidy, Madag.	g9	49
Tsitsihar see Qiqihar, China	B9	31
Tsivory, Madag.	h9	49
Tskhinvali, Sov. Un.	E2	28
Tsodilo Hill, hill, Bots.	A3	49
Tsogttsetsiy, Mong.	C1	32
Tsu, Japan	I8	33
Tsuchiura, Japan	H10	33
Tsugaru Strait, strt., Japan	F10	33
Tsuken Island, i., Japan	O5	52
Tsulukidze, Sov. Un.	A14	40
Tsumeb, Nmb.	A2	49
Tsumis Park, Nmb.	B2	49
Tsun Wan, H.K.	*G7	31
Tsuruga, Japan	I8	33
Tsurugi, Mount, mtn., Japan	J7	33
Tsuruoka, Japan	G9	33
Tsushima, Japan	n15	33
Tsu Shima, is., Japan	E10	31
Tsuyama, Japan	I6	33
Ttsu, stm., Port.	G2	22
Tual, Indon.	G8	34
Tualatin, Or., U.S.	*h12	114
Tualatin, stm., Or., U.S.	h11	114
Tuam, Ire.	H3	11
Tuamotu Archipelago, is., Fr. Poly.	H13	6
Tuangku, i., Indon.	K2	35
Tuapse, Sov. Un.	G16	8
Tuasivi, W. Sam.	F11	52
Tuasivi, Cape, c., W. Sam.	F11	52
Tuatapere, N.Z.	Q11	51
Tuba City, Az., U.S.	A4	80
Tubarão, Braz.	D3	56
Tubas, Isr. Occ.	B7	41
Tuberose, Sask.	G1	75
Tubize, Italy	D6	20
Tubruq (Tobruk), Libya	C4	43
Tubuai Islands, is., Fr. Poly.	H13	6
Tucacas, Ven.	A4	60
Tucano, Braz.	D3	57
Tuchola, Pol.	B4	26
Tuckahoe, N.J., U.S.	E3	107
Tuckahoe, N.Y., U.S.	h13	109
Tuckahoe, stm., N.J., U.S.	E3	107
Tuckahoe Creek, stm., Md., U.S.	C6	97
Tucker, Ar., U.S.	C4	81
Tucker, Ga., U.S.	h8	87
Tucker, Tx., U.S.	D5	120
Tucker, co., W.V., U.S.	B5	125
Tucker Island, i., N.J., U.S.	E4	107
Tuckerman, Ar., U.S.	B4	81
Tuckernuck Island, i., Ma., U.S.	D7	98
Tuckers Crossing, Ms., U.S.	D4	101
Tuckerton, N.J., U.S.	D4	107
Tucson, Az., U.S.	E5	80
Tucumán, prov., Arg.	B3	54
Tucumcari, N.M., U.S.	B6	108
Tucumcari Mountain, mtn., N.M., U.S.	B6	108
Tucunuí, Braz.	B5	60
Tucupido, Ven.	C5	59
Tucupita, Ven.	C11	60
Tucuruí, Braz.	g10	26
Tudela, Spain	A5	22
Tudmur (Palmyra), Syria	E12	40
Tufi, Pap. N. Gui.	k12	50
Tuftonboro, N.H., U.S.	C4	106
Tugaloo Lake, l., U.S.	B1	117
Tug Fork, stm., U.S.	C2	125
Tuguegarao, Phil.	B6	34
Tuira, stm., Pan.	G9	62
Tukangbesi Islands, is., Indon.	G6	34
Tükrah, Libya	C4	43
Tuktoyaktuk, N.W. Ter.	C6	66
Tukums, Sov. Un.	C4	27
Tukuyu, Tan.	C5	48
Tukwila, Wa., U.S.	f11	124
Tula, Mex.	C5	63
Tula, Sov. Un.	D6	29
Tula, Ms., U.S.	A4	101
Tula de Allende, Mex.	m14	63
Tulalip Indian Reservation, Wa., U.S.	A3	124
Tulancingo, Mex.	C5	63
Tulare, Ca., U.S.	D4	82
Tulare, S.D., U.S.	C7	118
Tulare, co., Ca., U.S.	D4	82
Tulare Lake, l., Ca., U.S.	D4	82
Tularosa, N.M., U.S.	D3	108
Tularosa Mountains, mts., N.M., U.S.	D1	108
Tularosa Valley, val., N.M., U.S.	E3	108
Tulbagh, S. Afr.	D2	49
Tulcán, Ec.	A2	58
Tulcea, Rom.	C9	24
Tulchin, Sov. Un.	G7	27
Tulelake, Ca., U.S.	B3	82
Tulelake, Sw., U.S.	B3	82
Tule Lake Sump, sw., Ca., U.S.	E4	82
Tule River Indian Reservation, Ca., U.S.	E4	82
Tuletta, Tx., U.S.	E4	120
Tule Valley, val., Ut., U.S.	D2	121
Tuli, Zimb.	B4	49
Tülkarm, Isr. Occ.	B7	41
Tullahassee, Ok., U.S.	B6	113
Tullahoma, Tn., U.S.	B5	119
Tullamore, Ire.	D3	10
Tulle, Fr.	E4	16
Tullins, Fr.	E6	16
Tulln, Aus.	D8	18
Tullos, La., U.S.	C3	95
Tullow, Ire.	E5	11
Tully, Austl.	C8	50
Tully, N.Y., U.S.	C4	109
Tulsa, Ok., U.S.	A6	113
Tulsa, co., Ok., U.S.	B6	113
Tulsequah, B.C.	E6	66
Tulsk, Ire.	D3	11
Tuluá, Col.	C2	60
Tulun, Sov. Un.	D13	29
Tulungagung, Indon.	G4	34
Tulu Welel, mtn., Eth.	D3	47
Tuma, stm., Nic.	D5	62
Tumacacori National Monument, Az., U.S.	F4	80
Tumaco, Col.	C2	60
Tumaco, Ensenada de, b., Col.	C2	60
Tumalo, Or., U.S.	C5	114
Tumatumari, Guy.	A3	59
Tumba, Swe.	t35	14
Tumba, Lac, l., Zaire	B2	48
Tumbarumba, Austl.	G7	51
Tumbaya, Arg.	D2	55
Tumbes, Peru	B1	58
Tumbes, dept., Peru	B1	58
Tumble Mountain, mtn., Mt., U.S.	E7	103
Tumbler Ridge, B.C.	B7	69
Tumbling Shoals, Ar., U.S.	B3	81
Tumen, China	C10	31
Tumen Jiang, stm., Asia	E4	33
Tumeremo, Ven.	B5	60
Tumkūr, India	F6	36
Tumnin, stm., Sov. Un.	A10	33
Tumon Bay, b., Guam	L10	52
Tumtum, Wa., U.S.	B8	124
Tumu, Ghana	D4	45
Tumuc-Humac Mountains, mts., S.A.	B3	59
Tumut, Austl.	G7	51
Tumwater, Wa., U.S.	B3	124
Tunapuna, Trin.	N23	65
Tunas de Zaza, Cuba	D4	64
Tunaycha, i., Sov. Un.	C11	33
Tunbridge, Vt., U.S.	D4	122
Tunbridge Wells see Royal Tunbridge Wells, Eng., U.K.	E7	10
Tunduru, Tan.	D6	48
Tundzha, stm., Eur.	D8	24
Tunga, stm., India	F6	36
Tungla, Nic.	D5	62
Tungurahua, prov., Ec.	B2	58
Tuni, India	I9	37
Tunica, La., U.S.	D4	95
Tunica, Ms., U.S.	A3	101
Tunica, co., Ms., U.S.	A3	101
Tunis, Tun.	B7	44
Tunis, Gulf of, b., Tun.	F3	23
Tunis Mills, Md., U.S.	C5	97
Tunisia, ctry., Afr.	C6	44
Tunja, Col.	B3	60
Tunkhannock, Pa., U.S.	C10	115
Tunk Lake, l., Me., U.S.	D4	96
Tunnel Hill, Ga., U.S.	B1	87
Tunnel Springs, Al., U.S.	D2	78
Tunnelton, In., U.S.	G5	91
Tunnelton, W.V., U.S.	B5	125
Tunø, i., Den.	C4	15
Tunp Range, mts., Wy., U.S.	D2	127
Tunungayualok Island, i., Newf.	g9	72
Tunuyán, Arg.	A3	54
Tunuyán, stm., Arg.	A3	54
Tunxi, China	F8	31
Tuolumne, Ca., U.S.	D3	82
Tuolumne, co., Ca., U.S.	C4	82
Tuolumne, stm., Ca., U.S.	D3	82
Tuolumne Meadows, Ca., U.S.	D4	82
Tupã, Braz.	D2	56
Tupaciretã, Braz.	D2	56
Tupelo, Ar., U.S.	B4	81
Tupelo, Ms., U.S.	A5	101
Tupelo, Ok., U.S.	C5	113
Tupiza, Bol.	D2	55
Tupman, Ca., U.S.	E4	82
Tupper, B.C.	B7	69
Tupper Lake, N.Y., U.S.	A6	109
Tupper Lake, l., N.Y., U.S.	A6	109
Tuppers Plains, Oh., U.S.	C4	112
Tupperville, Ont.	E2	73
Tupungato, Arg.	A3	54
Tupungato, Cerro, mtn., S.A.	A3	54
Tuquan, China	B9	31
Túquerres, Col.	C2	60
Tura, India	E13	37
Tura, Sov. Un.	C13	29
Tura, stm., Sov. Un.	B6	28
Turan Lowland, pl., Sov. Un.	E5	28
Turayf, Sau. Ar.	B3	38
Turbaco, Col.	A2	60
Turbat, Pak.	C3	36
Turbenthal, Switz.	B6	21
Turbeville, S.C., U.S.	D7	117
Turbo, Col.	B2	60
Turbotville, Pa., U.S.	D8	115
Turda, Rom.	B6	24
Turek, Pol.	B5	26
Turgay, Sov. Un.	E9	29
Turgay, stm., Sov. Un.	D8	28
Türgen Mountain, mtn., Mong.	B3	31
Türgovishte, Bul.	D8	24
Turgutlu, Tur.	C6	40
Turhal, Tur.	*B11	40
Turia, stm., Spain	C5	22
Turiaçu, Braz.	B1	57
Turiaçu, stm., Braz.	B1	57
Turimiquire, Cerro, mtn., Ven.	A5	60
Turin, Alta.	E4	68
Turin (Torino), Italy	B1	23
Turin, Ga., U.S.	C2	87
Turin, Ia., U.S.	B2	92
Turin, N.Y., U.S.	B5	109
Turinsk, Sov. Un.	B6	28
Turiy Rog, Sov. Un.	D5	33
Turka, Sov. Un.	G4	27
Turkestan, Sov. Un.	E9	29
Túrkeve, Hung.	B5	24
Turkey, N.C., U.S.	C4	110
Turkey, Tx., U.S.	B2	120
Turkey, ctry., Asia	C10	40
Turkey, stm., Ia., U.S.	B6	92
Turkey Creek, La., U.S.	D3	95
Turkey Creek, stm., Ne., U.S.	D8	104
Turkey Creek, stm., Ok., U.S.	A3	113
Turkey Point, c., Md., U.S.	B5	97
Turkmen S.S.R., state, Sov. Un.	F8	29
Turks and Caicos Islands, dep., N.A.	D8	64
Turks Island Passage, strt., T./C. Is.	D8	64
Turks Islands, is., T./C. Is.	D8	64
Turku (Åbo), Fin.	G10	14
Turkwel, stm., Kenya	A6	48
Turley, Ok., U.S.	A6	113
Turlock, Ca., U.S.	D3	82
Turmalina, Braz.	A6	56
Turmus ʻAyyā, Isr. Occ.	B7	41
Turnbull, Mount, mtn., Az., U.S.	D5	80
Turneffe Islands, is., Belize	D7	63
Turner, Ar., U.S.	C4	81
Turner, Me., U.S.	D2	96
Turner, Mt., U.S.	B8	103
Turner, Or., U.S.	C4	114
Turner, co., Ga., U.S.	E3	87
Turner, co., S.D., U.S.	D8	118
Turner Mountain, hill, Ct., U.S.	C1	84
Turners Falls, Ma., U.S.	A2	98
Turner Valley, Alta.	D3	68
Turney, Mo., U.S.	B3	102
Turnhout, Bel.	B6	16
Turnor Lake, l., Sask.	m7	75
Turnov, Czech.	C3	26
Turnu-Măgurele, Rom.	D7	24
Turochak, Sov. Un.	E26	8
Turon, Ks., U.S.	E5	93
Turpan, China	C2	31
Turpan Pendi, China	C2	31
Turpin, Ok., U.S.	e10	113
Turquino, Pico, mtn., Cuba	E5	64
Turrell, Ar., U.S.	B5	81
Turret Peak, mtn., Az., U.S.	C4	80
Turriff, Scot., U.K.	D6	13
Turshiz see Kāshmar, Iran	B5	38
Turtkul, Sov. Un.	E9	29
Turtle, stm., Ont.	o16	73
Turtle Creek, N.B.	D5	71
Turtle Creek, Pa., U.S.	k14	115
Turtle Flambeau Flowage, res., Wi., U.S.	B3	126
Turtleford, Sask.	D1	75
Turtle Lake, N.D., U.S.	B5	111
Turtle Lake, Wi., U.S.	C1	126
Turtle Lake, l., Sask.	D1	75
Turtle Mountain Indian Reservation, N.D., U.S.	A6	111
Turtle Mountains, hills, N.A.	A5	111
Turton, S.D., U.S.	B7	118
Turukhansk, Sov. Un.	C11	29
Turya, stm., Sov. Un.	F5	27
Tuscaloosa, Al., U.S.	B2	78
Tuscaloosa, co., Al., U.S.	B2	78
Tuscarawas, Oh., U.S.	B4	112
Tuscarawas, co., Oh., U.S.	B4	112
Tuscarawas, stm., Oh., U.S.	B4	112
Tuscarora, Nv., U.S.	B5	105
Tuscarora Indian Reservation, N.Y., U.S.	B2	109
Tuscarora Mountain, mtn., Pa., U.S.	F6	115
Tuscarora Mountains, mts., Nv., U.S.	B5	105
Tuscola, Il., U.S.	D5	90
Tuscola, Ms., U.S.	C4	101
Tuscola, Tx., U.S.	C3	120
Tuscola, co., Mi., U.S.	E7	99
Tusculum, hist., Italy	h9	23
Tuscumbia, Al., U.S.	A2	78
Tuscumbia, Mo., U.S.	C5	102
Tushka, Ok., U.S.	C6	113
Tuskahoma, Ok., U.S.	C6	113
Tuskegee, Al., U.S.	C4	78
Tusket, N.S.	F4	71
Tusket, N.S.	E4	71
Tustin, Ca., U.S.	*n13	82
Tustin, Mi., U.S.	D5	99
Tustumena Lake, l., Ak., U.S.	g16	79
Tuszyn, Pol.	B5	26
Tutayev, Sov. Un.	C6	28
Tuticorin, India	G6	36
Tutrakan, Bul.	D8	24
Tuttle, N.D., U.S.	B6	111
Tuttle, Ok., U.S.	B4	113
Tuttle Creek Dam, U.S.	C7	93
Tuttle Creek Lake, res., Ks., U.S.	C7	93
Tuttlingen, W. Ger.	E4	19
Tutuala, Indon.	G8	34
Tutuila, i., Am. Sam.	G13	52
Tutupaca, Volcán, vol., Peru	E3	58
Tututalak Mountain, mtn., Ak., U.S.	B7	79
Tutwiler, Ms., U.S.	A3	101
Tuvalu, ctry., Oc.	G10	6
Tuve, Swe.	k2	14
Tuvuca, i., Fiji	H16	52
Tuwayq, Jabal, mts., Sau. Ar.	C4	38
Tuxedo, N.C., U.S.	f10	110
Tuxedo Park, De., U.S.	i7	85
Tuxford, Sask.	G3	75
Tuxpan, Mex.	n12	63
Tuxpan, Mex.	C3	63
Tuxpan, Mex.	m15	63
Tuxpan de Rodríguez Cano, Mex.	C5	63
Tuxtepec, Mex.	n15	63
Tuxtla Gutiérrez, Mex.	D6	63
Túy, Spain	A1	22
Tuyen Quang, Viet.	B8	35
Tuy Hoa, Viet.	F8	35
Tuymazy, Sov. Un.	C4	28
Tüysärkān, Iran	C9	40
Tuz, Lake, l., Tur.	C9	40
Tuzigoot National Monument, Az., U.S.	C4	80
Tūz Khurmātū, Iraq	E15	40
Tuzla, Yugo.	C4	24
Tweed, Ont.	C7	73
Tweed, stm., U.K.	C5	10
Tweedsmuir Provincial Park, B.C.	C4	69
Tweedy Mountain, mtn., Mt., U.S.	E4	103
Twelve Mile, In., U.S.	C5	91
Twelve Mile Lake, l., Sask.	H2	75
Twelvepole Creek, stm., W.V., U.S.	C2	125
Twelvepole Creek, East Fork, stm., W.V., U.S.	C2	125
Twelvepole Creek, West Fork, stm., W.V., U.S.	C2	125
Twentymile Creek, stm., U.S.	C3	125
Twentynine Palms, Ca., U.S.	E5	82
Twentynine Palms Base, Ca., U.S.	*E5	82
Twentynine Palms Marine Corps Base, mil., Ca., U.S.	E5	82
Twig, Mn., U.S.	D6	100
Twiggs, co., Ga., U.S.	D3	87
Twillingate, Newf.	D4	72
Twin Bridges, Mt., U.S.	E4	103
Twin Brooks, S.D., U.S.	B9	118
Twin Buttes, mtn., Or., U.S.	C4	114
Twin Buttes Reservoir, res., Tx., U.S.	D2	120
Twin City, Ga., U.S.	D4	87
Twin Creek, stm., Oh., U.S.	C1	112
Twin Falls, Id., U.S.	G4	89
Twin Falls, co., Id., U.S.	G4	89
Twining, Mi., U.S.	D7	99
Twin Knolls, Az., U.S.	m9	80
Twin Lakes, Co., U.S.	B4	83
Twin Lakes, Wi., U.S.	F3	87
Twin Lakes, In., U.S.	B5	91
Twin Lakes, Wi., U.S.	F5	126
Twin Lakes, l., Ct., U.S.	A2	84
Twin Lakes, l., Me., U.S.	B3	92
Twin Lakes, l., Me., U.S.	C4	96
Twin Lakes Mountain, mtn., N.Y., U.S.	B6	109
Twin Mountain, N.H., U.S.	B3	106
Twin Mountains, mts., Wy., U.S.	E7	127
Twin Peaks, mts., Id., U.S.	E4	89
Twin Rivers, N.J., U.S.	C4	107
Twin Rocks, Pa., U.S.	F4	115
Twinsburg, Oh., U.S.	A4	112
Twinton, Tn., U.S.	C8	119
Twin Valley, Mn., U.S.	C2	100
Twisp, Wa., U.S.	A5	124
Twist, Ar., U.S.	B5	81
Two Butte Creek, stm., Co., U.S.	D8	83
Two Buttes, Co., U.S.	D8	83
Two Creeks, Man.	D1	70
Twodot, Mt., U.S.	D6	103
Twoforks, stm., U.S.	C2	75
Two Harbors, Mn., U.S.	C7	100
Two Hills, Alta.	C5	68
Two Mile Beach, N.J., U.S.	F3	107
Two Prairie, Bayou, stm., Ar., U.S.	h11	81
Two Rivers, Wi., U.S.	D6	126
Two Rivers, North Branch, stm., Mn., U.S.	B2	100
Two Rivers, South Branch, stm., Mn., U.S.	B2	100
Tyachev, Sov. Un.	D7	26
Tyaskin, Md., U.S.	D6	97
Tybee Island, Ga., U.S.	D6	87
Tychy, Pol.	g9	26
Tye River, Va., U.S.	C4	123
Tygart Lake, res., W.V., U.S.	B5	125
Tygart River, Falls of the, wtfl., W.V., U.S.	k10	125
Tygarts Creek, stm., Ky., U.S.	B7	94
Tygart Valley, stm., W.V., U.S.	B4	125
Tyger, stm., S.C., U.S.	B4	117
Tyler, Al., U.S.	C3	78
Tyler, Mn., U.S.	F2	100
Tyler, Pa., U.S.	D4	115
Tyler, Tx., U.S.	C5	120
Tyler, co., Tx., U.S.	D5	120
Tyler, co., W.V., U.S.	B4	125
Tyler, Lake, res., Tx., U.S.	C5	120
Tyler Branch, stm., Vt., U.S.	B3	122
Tyler Heights, W.V., U.S.	C3	125
Tylersburg, Pa., U.S.	D3	115
Tylersville, Pa., U.S.	E7	115
Tylerton, Md., U.S.	E5	97
Tylertown, Ms., U.S.	D3	101
Tym, stm., Sov. Un.	C25	8
Tymochtee Creek, stm., Oh., U.S.	B2	112
Tynagh, Ire.	D3	11
Tyndall, Man.	D3	70
Tyndall, S.D., U.S.	D8	118
Tyndall Air Force Base, mil., Fl., U.S.	u16	86
Tyndrum, Scot., U.K.	D4	13
Tyne, stm., Eng., U.K.	C5	10
Tyne, stm., Scot., U.K.	E6	13
Tyne and Wear, co., Eng., U.K.	E7	13
Tynec, Czech.	o18	26
Tynemouth, Eng., U.K.	C6	10
Tyner, Ky., U.S.	C6	94
Tyner, Sask.	G1	75
Tyner, In., U.S.	B5	91
Tyner, N.C., U.S.	A6	110
Tyne Valley, P.E.I.	C6	71
Tyngsboro, Ma., U.S.	A5	98
Tyn nad Vltavou, Czech.	D9	19
Tynset, Nor.	F4	14
Tyonek, Ak., U.S.	C9	79
Tyre (Şūr), Leb.	B3	38
Tyringham, Ma., U.S.	B1	98
Tyrma, Sov. Un.	A6	33
Tyro, Ks., U.S.	E8	93

215

Name	Map Ref.	Page
Tyrone, Ky., U.S.	B5	94
Tyrone, N.M., U.S.	E1	108
Tyrone, Ok., U.S.	e9	113
Tyrone, Pa., U.S.	E5	115
Tyronza, Ar., U.S.	B5	81
Tyrrell, co., U.S.	B6	110
Tyrrell, Lake, l., Austl.	G4	51
Tyrrhenian Sea, Eur.	D3	23
Tysons Corner, Va., U.S.	*B5	123
Ty Ty, Ga., U.S.	E3	87
Ty Ty Creek, stm., Ga., U.S.	E3	87
Tyub-Karagan Peninsula, pen., Sov. Un.	E4	28
Tyukalinsk, Sov. Un.	D9	28
Tyuleniy Island, i., Sov. Un.	B12	33
Tyumen, Sov. Un.	D9	29
Tyuratam, Sov. Un.	D6	28
Tyvan, Sask.	G4	75
Tywyn, Wales, U.K.	B3	12
Tzaneen, S. Afr.	B5	49

U

Name	Map Ref.	Page
Uatumã, stm., Braz.	C3	59
Uaupés (Vaupés), stm., S.A.	C4	60
Ubá, Braz.	C4	56
Ubaira, Braz.	D3	57
Ubaitaba, Braz.	D3	57
Ubangi (Oubangui), stm., Afr.	A2	48
Ubaye, stm., Fr.	E2	20
Ubayyiḍ, Wādī al, val., Asia	B4	38
Ube, Japan	E11	31
Úbeda, Spain	C4	22
Uberaba, Braz.	B3	56
Uberlândia, Braz.	B3	56
Überlingen, W. Ger.	E4	18
Ubiaja, Nig.	E6	45
Ubombo, S. Afr.	C5	49
Uborka, Sov. Un.	D7	33
Ubort, stm., Sov. Un.	F6	27
Ubrique, Spain	D2	22
Ubundu (Ponthierville), Zaire	B4	48
Ucayali, dept., Peru	*C3	58
Ucayali, stm., Peru	C3	58
Uccle, Bel.	B6	16
Ucharal, Sov. Un.	D10	28
Uchiura Bay, b., Japan	E10	33
Uchiza, Peru	C2	58
Uchoa, Braz.	C3	56
Uckange, Fr.	E6	17
Ucluelet, B.C.	E5	69
Ucon, Id., U.S.	F7	89
Udagamandalam, India	F6	36
Udaipur, India	D5	36
Udall, Ks., U.S.	E6	93
Udall, Mo., U.S.	E5	102
Udaquiola, Arg.	B5	54
Uddevalla, Swe.	H4	14
Uden, Neth.	C5	17
Udgīr, India	H6	37
Udhampur, India	B6	36
Udine, Italy	A4	23
Udon Thani, Thai.	B2	34
Udot, i., Micron.	Q18	52
Udu Point, c., Fiji	H16	52
Uecker, stm., Ger.	B6	18
Ueckermünde, E. Ger.	B6	18
Ueda, Japan	H9	33
Uehling, Ne., U.S.	C9	104
Uele, stm., Zaire	A3	48
Uelen, Sov. Un.	C21	29
Uelkal, Sov. Un.	C21	29
Uelsen, W. Ger.	B6	17
Uelzen, W. Ger.	B5	18
Ueno, Japan	o15	33
Uere, stm., Zaire	A4	48
Uesslingen, Switz.	A6	21
Uetendorf, Switz.	C4	21
Uetersen, W. Ger.	E3	15
Ufa, Sov. Un.	D8	29
Ufa, stm., Sov. Un.	B5	28
Uffenheim, W. Ger.	D5	19
Ugab, stm., Nmb.	B2	49
Ugalla, stm., Tan.	C5	48
Uganda, ctry., Afr.	A5	48
Ugashik, Ak., U.S.	D8	79
Ugashik Lakes, l., Ak., U.S.	D8	79
Ugep, Nig.	E6	45
Ugine, Fr.	D7	20
Uglegorsk, Sov. Un.	B13	31
Uglich, Sov. Un.	C12	27
Ugra, stm., Sov. Un.	D10	27
Ugürchin, Bul.	D7	24
Uh, stm., Eur.	D7	26
Uherské Hradiště, Czech.	D4	26
Úhlava, stm., Czech.	D8	19
Ühlingen, W. Ger.	A5	21
Uhlman Lake, l., Man.	A2	70
Uhrichsville, Oh., U.S.	B4	112
Uhříněves, Czech.	n18	26
Uig, Scot., U.K.	B2	13
Uig, Scot., U.K.	C2	13
Uíge, Ang.	C2	48
Uíge, dept., Ang.	C2	48
Uijeongbu, S. Kor.	H3	33
Uiju, N. Kor.	C9	31
Uil, Sov. Un.	D4	28
Uil, stm., Sov. Un.	D4	28
Uinkaret Plateau, plat., Az., U.S.	A2	80
Uinta, co., Wy., U.S.	E2	127
Uinta, stm., Ut., U.S.	C5	121
Uintah, Ut., U.S.	*B4	121
Uintah, co., Ut., U.S.	D6	121
Uintah and Ouray Indian Reservation, Ut., U.S.	C5	121
Uinta Mountains, mts., Ut., U.S.	C5	121
Uitenhage, S. Afr.	D4	49
Uithuizen, Neth.	A6	17
Uivak, Cape, c., Newf.	f9	72
Uji Islands, is., Japan	K4	33
Ujiji, Tan.	B4	48
Uji-yamada see Ise, Japan	I8	33
Ujjain, India	D6	36
Ujungpandang (Makasar), Indon.	G5	34
Uka, Sov. Un.	D19	29
Uka, stm., Sov. Un.	D19	29
Ukerewe, i., Tan.	B5	48
Ukhta, Sov. Un.	C8	29
Ukiah, Ca., U.S.	C2	82
Ukiah, Or., U.S.	B8	114
Ukmergė, Sov. Un.	D5	27
Ukraine, state, Sov. Un.	E5	29
Uku, Ang.	D1	48
Ulaangom, Mong.	B3	31
Ulak Island, i., Ak., U.S.	E4	79
Ulan Bator (Ulaanbaatar), Mong.	B6	31
Ulan-Ude, Sov. Un.	D13	29
Ulba, Sov. Un.	E25	8
Ulchin, S. Kor.	H4	33
Ulcinj, Yugo.	E4	24
Uldza, stm., Asia	B7	31
Ulen, In., U.S.	D5	91
Ulen, Mn., U.S.	C2	100
Uleta, Fl., U.S.	*s13	86
Ulhāsnagar, India	*E5	36
Uliastay, Mong.	B4	31
Ulindi, stm., Zaire	B4	48
Ulla, Sov. Un.	D7	27
Ulla, stm., Spain	A1	22
Ulladulla, Austl.	G8	51
Ullapool, Scot., U.K.	B4	10
Ullared, Swe.	A6	15
Ullin, Il., U.S.	F4	90
Ullswater, l., Eng., U.K.	F6	13
Ullung Island, i., S. Kor.	H5	33
Ulm, W. Ger.	D4	18
Ulm, Ar., U.S.	C4	81
Ulm, Mt., U.S.	C5	103
Ulman, Mo., U.S.	C5	102
Ulongué, Moz.	D5	48
Ulricehamn, Swe.	I5	14
Ulsan, S. Kor.	I4	33
Ulster, Pa., U.S.	C9	115
Ulster, co., N.Y., U.S.	D6	109
Ulster, hist. reg., Eur.	C4	11
Ulúa, stm., Hond.	C3	62
Ulubat Lake, l., Tur.	B7	25
Uluborlu, Tur.	C8	40
Uludağ, mtn., Tur.	B7	40
Ulukışla, Tur.	D10	40
Ulungur He, stm., China	B2	31
Ulva, i., Scot., U.K.	D2	13
Ulverston, Eng., U.K.	F6	13
Ulverstone, Austl.	o15	50
Ulyanovka, Sov. Un.	s31	14
Ulyanovsk, Sov. Un.	D7	29
Ulysses, Ks., U.S.	E2	93
Ulysses, Ne., U.S.	C8	104
Ulysses, Pa., U.S.	C6	115
Ulzburg, W. Ger.	E3	15
Uman, Sov. Un.	G8	27
Uman, i., Micron.	Q18	52
Umarkot, Pak.	C4	36
Umatac, Guam	M9	52
Umatac Bay, b., Guam	M9	52
Umatilla, Fl., U.S.	D5	86
Umatilla, co., Or., U.S.	B7	114
Umatilla, Or., U.S.	B8	114
Umatilla, stm., Or., U.S.	B7	114
Umatilla Indian Reservation, Or., U.S.	B8	114
Umba, Sov. Un.	D16	14
Umbagog Lake, l., U.S.	A4	106
Umboi, i., Pap. N. Gui.	k12	50
Umbrail Pass, Eur.	C9	21
Umbria, prov., Italy	C4	23
Umbuzeiro, Braz.	C3	57
Umcolcus Lake, l., Me., U.S.	B4	96
Umeå, Swe.	F9	14
Umeälven, stm., Swe.	E8	14
Umhausen, Aus.	B6	20
Umlazi, S. Afr.	B7	49
Umm el Faḥm, Isr.	B7	41
Umm Kaddādah, Sud.	C2	47
Umm Lajj, Sau. Ar.	C3	38
Umm Ruwābah, Sud.	C3	47
Umnak Island, i., Ak., U.S.	E6	79
Umniati, stm., Zimb.	A4	49
Umpire, Ar., U.S.	C1	81
Umpqua, Or., U.S.	D3	114
Umpqua, stm., Or., U.S.	D3	114
Umrān, Yemen	B5	47
Umsaskis Lake, l., Me., U.S.	B3	96
Umtanum Ridge, mtn., Wa., U.S.	C5	124
Umtata, Transkei	D4	49
Umuahia, Nig.	E6	45
Umzinto, S. Afr.	D5	49
Una, stm., Braz.	k6	57
Una, stm., Yugo.	C2	24
Unadilla, Ga., U.S.	D3	87
Unadilla, N.Y., U.S.	C5	109
Unadilla, stm., N.Y., U.S.	C5	109
Unaí, Braz.	B3	56
Unalakleet, Ak., U.S.	C7	79
Unalaska Island, i., Ak., U.S.	E6	79
'Unayzah, Sau. Ar.	C4	38
Uncasville, Ct., U.S.	D7	84
Uncia, Bol.	C2	55
Uncompahgre Butte, mtn., Co., U.S.	C2	83
Uncompahgre Mountains, mts., Co., U.S.	C3	83
Uncompahgre Peak, mtn., Co., U.S.	C3	83
Uncompahgre Plateau, plat., Co., U.S.	C2	83
Underhill, Vt., U.S.	B3	122
Underhill Center, Vt., U.S.	B3	122
Underwood, Al., U.S.	B3	78
Underwood, Ia., U.S.	G6	91
Underwood, In., U.S.	C2	92
Underwood, Mn., U.S.	D3	100
Underwood, N.D., U.S.	B4	111
Underwood, Wa., U.S.	D4	124
Unecha, Sov. Un.	E9	27
Uneiuxi, stm., Braz.	D6	45
Unezhma, Sov. Un.	F17	14
Ungava, Austl.	F6	51
Ungava, Péninsule d', pen., Que.	g12	74
Ungava Bay, b., Can.	E19	66
Unggi, N. Kor.	C11	31
Unhošt', Czech.	n17	26
União da Victória, Braz.	D2	56
União dos Palmares, Braz.	C3	57
Unicoi, Tn., U.S.	C11	119
Unicoi, co., Tn., U.S.	C11	119
Unicoi Mountains, mts., U.S.	D9	119
Unije, i., Yugo.	C2	24
Unimak Island, i., Ak., U.S.	D7	79
Unimak Pass, strt., Ak., U.S.	E6	79
Unión, Arg.	B3	54
Union, Ct., U.S.	B7	84
Union, Il., U.S.	A5	90
Union, In., U.S.	H3	91
Union, Ky., U.S.	k13	94
Union, La., U.S.	h10	95
Union, Me., U.S.	D3	96
Union, Ms., U.S.	C4	101
Union, Mo., U.S.	C6	102
Union, Ne., U.S.	D10	104
Union, N.H., U.S.	D4	106
Union, N.J., U.S.	*B4	107
Union, N.C., U.S.	A5	110
Union, N.D., U.S.	A8	111
Union, Oh., U.S.	*C1	112
Union, Or., U.S.	B9	114
Union, S.C., U.S.	B4	117
Union, Ut., U.S.	*C4	121
Union, Wa., U.S.	B2	124
Union, W.V., U.S.	D4	125
Union, co., Ar., U.S.	D3	81
Union, co., Fl., U.S.	B4	86
Union, co., Ga., U.S.	B2	87
Union, co., Il., U.S.	F4	90
Union, co., In., U.S.	E8	91
Union, co., Ia., U.S.	C3	92
Union, co., Ky., U.S.	C2	94
Union, co., La., U.S.	B3	95
Union, co., Ms., U.S.	A4	101
Union, co., N.J., U.S.	B4	107
Union, co., N.M., U.S.	A6	108
Union, co., N.C., U.S.	B2	110
Union, co., Oh., U.S.	B2	112
Union, co., Or., U.S.	B8	114
Union, co., Pa., U.S.	E7	115
Union, co., S.C., U.S.	B4	117
Union, co., S.D., U.S.	E9	118
Union, co., Tn., U.S.	C10	119
Union, West Branch, stm., Me., U.S.	D4	96
Union Bay, B.C.	E5	69
Union Beach, N.J., U.S.	C4	107
Union Bridge, Md., U.S.	A3	97
Union Center, S.D., U.S.	C3	118
Union Center, Wi., U.S.	E3	126
Union Church, Ms., U.S.	D3	101
Union City, Ca., U.S.	h8	82
Union City, Ga., U.S.	C2	87
Union City, In., U.S.	D8	91
Union City, Mi., U.S.	F5	99
Union City, N.J., U.S.	h8	107
Union City, Oh., U.S.	B1	112
Union City, Ok., U.S.	B4	113
Union City, Pa., U.S.	C2	115
Union City, Tn., U.S.	A2	119
Union Creek, Or., U.S.	E4	114
Union Dale, Pa., U.S.	C10	115
Unión de Reyes, Cuba	C3	64
Unión de Tula, Mex.	n11	63
Union Flat Creek, stm., Wa., U.S.	C8	124
Union Furnace, Oh., U.S.	C3	112
Union Gap, Wa., U.S.	C5	124
Union Grove, Wi., U.S.	F5	126
Union Hall, Va., U.S.	C3	123
Union Island, i., St. Vin.	V26	65
Union Lake, Mi., U.S.	*o15	99
Union Lake, l., N.J., U.S.	E2	107
Union Mill, Vie., U.S.	C6	88
Union Mills, In., U.S.	B4	91
Union Mills, Md., U.S.	A3	97
Union of Soviet Socialist Republics see Soviet Union, ctry., Asia	D11	29
Union Park, Fl., U.S.	*D5	86
Union Pier, Mi., U.S.	G4	99
Union Point, Ga., U.S.	C3	87
Union Springs, Al., U.S.	C4	78
Union Springs, N.Y., U.S.	C4	109
Union Star, Mo., U.S.	B3	102
Uniontown, Al., U.S.	C2	78
Uniontown, Ks., U.S.	E9	93
Uniontown, Ky., U.S.	C2	94
Uniontown, Md., U.S.	A3	97
Uniontown, Oh., U.S.	B4	112
Uniontown, Pa., U.S.	G2	115
Uniontown, Wa., U.S.	C8	124
Unionville, Ont.	k15	73
Unionville, Ct., U.S.	B4	84
Unionville, Il., U.S.	F5	90
Unionville, In., U.S.	F5	91
Unionville, Ia., U.S.	D5	92
Unionville, Me., U.S.	D5	96
Unionville, Mo., U.S.	A4	102
Unionville, Nv., U.S.	C3	105
Unionville, N.C., U.S.	B2	110
Unionville, Oh., U.S.	A5	112
Unionville, Tn., U.S.	B5	119
Unionville, Va., U.S.	B5	123
Unionville Center, Oh., U.S.	B2	112
Unisan, Phil.	p13	34
United Arab Emirates, ctry., Asia	C5	38
United Kingdom, ctry., Eur.	C5	10
United Nations Headquarters, N.Y., U.S.	h12	109
United Pueblos Indian Reservations, N.M., U.S.	A3	108
United States, ctry., N.A.	C8	76
United States Air Force Academy, mil., Co., U.S.	B6	83
United States Military Academy, mil., N.Y., U.S.	C6	109
United States Naval Academy, mil., Md., U.S.	C4	97
Unity, Sask.	E1	75
Unity, Il., U.S.	F4	90
Unity, Me., U.S.	D3	96
Unity, N.H., U.S.	D2	106
Unity, Or., U.S.	C8	114
Unity Pond, l., Me., U.S.	D3	96
Unity Reservoir, res., Or., U.S.	C8	114
Unityville, S.D., U.S.	D8	118
Universal, In., U.S.	E3	91
Universal City, Tx., U.S.	*E3	120
University, Fl., U.S.	*D4	86
University City, Mo., U.S.	C7	102
University Gardens, N.Y., U.S.	*n15	109
University Heights, Ia., U.S.	C6	92
University Heights, Oh., U.S.	h9	112
University Park, Ia., U.S.	C5	92
University Park, N.M., U.S.	E3	108
University Park, Tx., U.S.	n10	120
University Place, Wa., U.S.	f10	124
Unna, W. Ger.	A5	20
Unnen, l., Swe.	B7	15
Unst, i., Scot., U.K.	g10	10
Unstrut, stm., E. Ger.	B6	19
Unterwasser, Switz.	B7	21
Unuk, stm., N.A.	A2	69
Unwhao, hill, N.Z.	K14	51
Unwin, Sask.	E1	75
Unye, Tur.	B11	40
Unzha, stm., Sov. Un.	B2	29
Uozu, Japan	H8	33
Upata, Ven.	B5	60
Upatoi Creek, stm., Ga., U.S.	D2	87
Upemba, Lac, l., Zaire	C4	48
Upernavik, Grnld.	B15	61
Upham, N.D., U.S.	A5	111
Upia, stm., Col.	C3	60
Upington, S. Afr.	C3	49
Upland, Ca., U.S.	E5	82
Upland, In., U.S.	D7	91
Upland, Ne., U.S.	D7	104
Upolu, i., W. Sam.	G11	6
Upolu Point, c., Hi., U.S.	C6	88
Upper, prov., Ghana	D4	45
Upper Ammonoosuc, stm., N.H.	A4	106
Upper Arlington, Oh., U.S.	B2	112
Upper Arrow Lake, res., B.C.	D9	69
Upper Black Eddy, Pa., U.S.	E11	115
Upper Blackville, N.B.	C4	71
Upper Chichester Township, Pa., U.S.	*G11	115
Upperco, Md., U.S.	A4	97
Upper Darby, Pa., U.S.	G11	115
Upper Dublin Township, Pa., U.S.	*F11	115
Upper Fairmount, Md., U.S.	D6	97
Upper Fraser, B.C.	B7	69
Upper Frenchville, Me., U.S.	A4	96
Upper Gagetown, N.B.	D3	71
Upper Ganges Canal, India	C6	37
Upper Gloucester, Me., U.S.	E2	96
Upper Graniteville, Vt., U.S.	C4	122
Upper Greenwood Lake, N.J., U.S.	A4	107
Upper Humber, stm., Newf.	D3	72
Upper Indian Pond, l., Newf.	D3	72
Upper Iowa, stm., Ia., U.S.	A5	92
Upper Island Cove, Newf.	E5	72
Upper Jay, N.Y., U.S.	f11	109
Upper Kapuas Mountains, mts., Asia	E4	34
Upper Kent, N.B.	C2	71
Upper Klamath Lake, l., Or., U.S.	E4	114
Upper Manitou Lake, l., Ont.	E5	70
Upper Marlboro, Md., U.S.	C4	97
Upper Merion Township, Pa., U.S.	*F11	115
Upper Moreland Township, Pa., U.S.	*F11	115
Upper Musquodoboit, N.S.	D7	71
Upper New York Bay, b., U.S.	k8	107
Upper Providence Township, Pa., U.S.	*G11	115
Upper Red Lake, l., Mn., U.S.	B4	100
Upper Saddle River, N.J., U.S.	A4	107
Upper Saint Clair, Pa., U.S.	*F1	115
Upper Sandusky, Oh., U.S.	B2	112
Upper Sheila, N.B.	B5	71
Upper Silesia, hist. reg., Pol.	g9	26
Upper Southampton Township, Pa., U.S.	*F11	115
Upper Strasburg, Pa., U.S.	F6	115
Upper Tract, W.V., U.S.	C5	125
Upperville, Va., U.S.	B5	123
Upper Volta see Burkina Faso, ctry., Afr.	D4	45
Upper Wilson Pond, l., Me., U.S.	C3	96
Upper Woods Harbour, N.S.	F4	71
Uppsala, Swe.	H7	14
Upright, Cape, c., Ak., U.S.	C5	79
Upsala, Mn., U.S.	E4	100
Upsalquitch, N.B.	B3	71
Upshur, co., Tx., U.S.	C5	120
Upshur, co., W.V., U.S.	C4	125
Upson, Wi., U.S.	B3	126
Upson, co., Ga., U.S.	D2	87
Upton, Que.	D5	74
Upton, Ky., U.S.	C4	94
Upton, Me., U.S.	D1	96
Upton, Ma., U.S.	B4	98
Upton, Wy., U.S.	B8	127
Upton, co., Tx., U.S.	D2	120
Urabá, Golfo de, b., Col.	B2	60
Uracoa, Ven.	C5	60
Urad Qianqi, China	D3	32
Ural, stm., Sov. Un.	D8	29
Ural Mountains, mts., Sov. Un.	D8	29
Uralsk, Sov. Un.	D8	29
Urandi, Braz.	A4	56
Urania, La., U.S.	C3	95
Uranium City, Sask.	m7	75
Uraricoera, Braz.	B2	59
Uraricoera, stm., Braz.	B2	59
Urasoe, Japan	O5	52
Ura-Tyube, Sov. Un.	H22	8
Uravan, Co., U.S.	C2	83
Urawa, Japan	I9	33
Urbana, Ar., U.S.	D3	81
Urbana, Il., U.S.	C5	90
Urbana, Ia., U.S.	B6	92
Urbana, Md., U.S.	B3	97
Urbana, Mo., U.S.	D4	102
Urbana, Oh., U.S.	B2	112
Urbancrest, Oh., U.S.	m10	112
Urbandale, Ia., U.S.	C4	92
Urbank, Mn., U.S.	D3	100
Urbanna, Va., U.S.	C6	123
Urbino, Italy	C4	23
Urcos, Peru	D3	58
Urdaneta, Phil.	o13	34
Urdzhar, Sov. Un.	D10	28
Ure, stm., Eng., U.K.	F7	13
Ures, Mex.	B2	63
Urfa, Tur.	D12	40
Urga, Sov. Un.	E5	28
Uri, state, Switz.	C4	20
Uria, stm., Col.	A3	60
Urich, Mo., U.S.	C4	102
Urique, Mex.	B3	63
Urla, Tur.	A1	38
Urmi, stm., Sov. Un.	B6	31
Urmia, Lake, l., Iran	B4	38
Urmia see Orūmīyeh, Iran	B4	38
Uroyán, Montañas de, mts., P.R.	B2	65
Urubamba, stm., Peru	D3	58
Urubu, stm., Braz.	C3	59
Urucará, Braz.	C3	59
Uruçuí, Braz.	C2	57
Urucurituba, Braz.	C3	59
Uruguaiana, Braz.	D1	56
Uruguay, ctry., S.A.	E1	56
Uruguay (Uruguai), stm., S.A.	E1	56
Urumchi see Ürümqi, China	C2	31
Ürümqi (Urumchi), China	C2	31
Uruno Point, c., Guam	L10	52
Urusha, Sov. Un.	D15	29
Urutaí, Braz.	B2	56
Uryu, stm., Japan	D11	33
Uryupinsk, Sov. Un.	F14	27
Urziceni, Rom.	C8	24
Usa, stm., Sov. Un.	B20	29
Uşak, Tur.	C7	40
Usakos, Nmb.	B2	49
Usedom, E. Ger.	A7	18
Usedom, i., Eur.	E8	15
Ushaki, Sov. Un.	s32	14
Ushibuka, Japan	J4	33
Ushtobe, Sov. Un.	D9	28
Ushuaia, Arg.	h12	54
Usingen, W. Ger.	C3	19
Usk, B.C.	B3	69
Usk, Wa., U.S.	A8	124
Uslar, W. Ger.	B4	19
Usolye-Sibirskoye, Sov. Un.	D13	29
Uspenskiy, Sov. Un.	D8	28
Usquepaug, R.I., U.S.	F3	116
Ussel, Fr.	E5	16
Ussuri (Wusuli), stm., Asia	B11	31
Ussuriysk, Sov. Un.	E16	29
Ust-Bolsheretsk, Sov. Un.	D18	29
Uster, Switz.	B4	20
Ustica, i., Italy	E4	23
Ústí nad Labem, Czech.	C3	26
Ustinov see Izhevsk, Sov. Un.	D8	29
Ust-Ishim, Sov. Un.	B8	28
Ust-Kamchatsk, Sov. Un.	D19	29
Ust-Kamenogorsk, Sov. Un.	E11	29
Ust-Kut, Sov. Un.	D13	29
Ust-Maya, Sov. Un.	C16	29
Ust-Olenek, Sov. Un.	B14	29
Ust-Shchugor, Sov. Un.	C9	28
Ust-Srednekan, Sov. Un.	C18	29
Ust-Tsilma, Sov. Un.	C8	29
Ust-Tym, Sov. Un.	B9	29
Ust-Urt Plateau, plat., Sov. Un.	E8	29
Ust-Usa, Sov. Un.	C8	29
Ustyuzhna, Sov. Un.	B11	27
Usu, China	C1	31
Usulután, El Sal.	E7	63
Usumacinta, stm., N.A.	D6	63
Utah, co., Ut., U.S.	C4	121
Utah, state, U.S.	D4	121
Utah Lake, l., Ut., U.S.	C4	121
Utajärvi, Fin.	E12	14
Ute, Ia., U.S.	B2	92
Ute Creek, stm., N.M., U.S.	A6	108
Ute Mountain Indian Reservation, U.S.	D2	83
Ute Park, N.M., U.S.	A4	108
Ute Reservoir, res., N.M., U.S.	B6	108
Utete, Tan.	C6	48
Uthai Thani, Thai.	B1	34
Utica, Il., U.S.	B5	90
Utica, In., U.S.	H6	91
Utica, Ks., U.S.	D3	93
Utica, Ky., U.S.	C2	94
Utica, Ms., U.S.	C3	101
Utica, Mo., U.S.	B4	102
Utica, N.Y., U.S.	B5	109
Utica, Oh., U.S.	B3	112
Utica, Pa., U.S.	D2	115
Utica, S.D., U.S.	E8	118
Utiel, Spain	C5	22
Utikuma Lake, l., Alta.	B3	68
Utö, i., Swe.	u36	14
Utopia, Tx., U.S.	E3	120
Utopia, Lake, l., N.B.	D3	71
Utrania, stm., Pol.	m13	26
Utrecht, Neth.	A6	16
Utrecht, prov., Neth.	B5	17
Utrera, Spain	D3	22
Utsjoki, Fin.	C12	14
Utsunomiya, Japan	D12	31
Uttaradit, Thai.	B2	34
Uttar Pradesh, state, India	C6	36
Uttoxeter, Eng., U.K.	B6	12
Utuado, P.R.	B2	65
Utulei, Am. Sam.	F13	52
Utva, stm., Sov. Un.	D8	28
Uusikaupunki, Fin.	G9	14
Uvá, Col.	C3	60
Uvalda, Ga., U.S.	D4	87
Uvalde, Tx., U.S.	E3	120
Uvalde, co., Tx., U.S.	E3	120
Úvaly, Czech.	n18	26
Uvarovo, Sov. Un.	E14	27
Uvat, Sov. Un.	D8	28
Uverito Point, c., Fiji	H14	52
Uvinza, Tan.	C5	48
Uvira, Zaire	B4	48
Uvs Lake, l., Asia	A3	31
Uwajima, Japan	J6	33
Uwayl, Sud.	D2	47
'Uwaynāt, Jabal al, mtn., Afr.	E4	43
Uwharrie, stm., N.C., U.S.	B3	110
Uxbridge, Ont.	C5	73
Uxbridge (part of London), Eng., U.K.	k12	10
Uxbridge, Ma., U.S.	B4	98
Uxmal, hist., Mex.	C7	63
Uyar, Sov. Un.	D27	9
Uyo, Nig.	*E6	45
Uyuni, Bol.	D2	55
Uyuni, Salar de, pl., Bol.	D2	55
Uzbek S.S.R., state, Sov. Un.	E9	28
Uzès, Fr.	E6	16
Uzh, stm., Sov. Un.	D7	26
Uzhgorod, Sov. Un.	G4	27
Uzlovaya, Sov. Un.	E11	27
Uzunköprü, Tur.	B6	40
Uzwil, Switz.	B7	21

V

Name	Map Ref.	Page
Vaal, stm., S. Afr.	C4	49
Vaals, Neth.	D5	17
Vaasa, Fin.	F9	14
Vác, Hung.	B4	24
Vaca Key, i., Fl., U.S.	H5	86
Vacaria, Braz.	D2	56
Vacaville, Ca., U.S.	C3	82
Vacha, E. Ger.	C5	19
Vacherie, La., U.S.	h10	95
Vader, Wa., U.S.	C3	124
Vadis, V.I., U.S.	B4	125
Vadito, N.M., U.S.	A4	108
Vadnais Heights, Mn., U.S.	*m12	100
Vado, N.M., U.S.	E3	108
Vadodara, India	D5	36
Vadsø, Nor.	B13	14
Vaduz, Liech.	E4	18
Vagay, Sov. Un.	B7	28
Vaggeryd, Swe.	A8	15
Vagney, Fr.	E6	17
Vagnhärad, Swe.	u35	14
Vagos, Port.	B1	22
Váh, stm., Czech.	D4	26
Vahsel Bay, b., Ant.	B9	7
Vaiden, Ms., U.S.	B4	101
Vaigai, stm., India	G6	36
Vaihingen, W. Ger.	E3	19
Vail, Az., U.S.	E5	80
Vail, Co., U.S.	B4	83
Vail Homes, N.J., U.S.	*C4	107
Vailala see Palauli, W. Sam.	F11	52
Vails, N.J., U.S.	B2	107
Vaitele Bay, b., W. Sam.	F12	52
Vakh, stm., Sov. Un.	C25	8
Vākhān, reg., Afg.	k17	39
Vakhrushev, Sov. Un.	B11	33
Valais, state, Switz.	C3	20
Valatie, N.Y., U.S.	C7	109
Val-Barrette, Que.	n17	74
Val-Bélair, Que.	C6	74
Valcheta, Arg.	C3	54
Val-David, Que.	C3	74
Valcourt, Que.	D5	74
Valdagno, Italy	D7	20
Valdai Hills, hills, Sov. Un.	C9	27
Valdemarsvik, Swe.	H7	14
Valdemorillo, Spain	o16	22
Valdepeñas, Spain	C4	22
Valderaduey, stm., Spain	A3	22
Valders, Wi., U.S.	D6	126
Valdés, Península, pen., Arg.	C4	54
Valdese, N.C., U.S.	B1	110
Valdez, Ak., U.S.	C10	79
Valdez, N.M., U.S.	A4	108
Valdilecha, Spain	p18	22
Valdivia, Chile	B2	54
Valdivia, Col.	B2	60
Valdobbiadene, Italy	D7	20
Val-d'Or, Que.	k11	74
Valdosta, Ga., U.S.	F3	87
Vale, Or., U.S.	D9	114
Vale, S.D., U.S.	C2	118
Vale, Tn., U.S.	A3	119
Valemount, B.C.	C8	69
Valença, Braz.	D3	57
Valença do Piauí, Braz.	C2	57
Valence, Fr.	E6	16
Valencia, Spain	C5	22
Valencia, Ven.	A4	60
Valencia, co., N.M., U.S.	C3	108
Valencia, hist. reg., Spain	C5	22
Valencia [de Alcántara], Spain	C2	22
Valencia Heights, S.C., U.S.	D6	117
Valencia Island, i., Ire.	E1	10
Valenciennes, Fr.	B5	16
Valentigney, Fr.	D7	16
Valentine, Ne., U.S.	B5	104
Valentine, Tx., U.S.	o12	120
Valera, Ven.	B3	60
Valhalla, N.Y., U.S.	D7	109
Valhermoso Springs, Al., U.S.	A3	78
Valiente, Punta, c., Pan.	F7	62
Valier, Il., U.S.	E4	90
Valier, Mt., U.S.	B4	103
Valier, Pa., U.S.	E3	115
Valinda, Ca., U.S.	*m13	82
Val-Jalbert, Que.	A5	74
Valjevo, Yugo.	C4	24
Valka, Sov. Un.	C8	27
Valkeakoski, Fin.	G11	14
Valkenswaard, Neth.	C5	17
Valki, Sov. Un.	G10	27
Valladolid, Mex.	C7	63
Valladolid, Spain	B3	22
Vallåkra, Swe.	C6	15
Vall de Uxó, Spain	C5	22
Vallecas, Spain	B4	22
Vallecito, Co., U.S.	D3	83
Vallecito Reservoir, res., Co., U.S.	D3	83
Vallecitos, N.M., U.S.	A3	108
Valle d'Aosta, prov., Italy	D2	20
Valle de la Pascua, Ven.	B4	60
Valle del Cauca, dept., Col.	C2	60
Valle de Santiago, Mex.	m13	63
Valledupar, Col.	A3	60
Vallée-Jonction, Que.	C7	74
Vallegrande, Bol.	C3	55
Vallenar, Chile	E1	56
Valletta, Malta	H11	8
Valley, co., Id., U.S.	E3	89
Valley, co., Mt., U.S.	B10	103
Valley, co., Ne., U.S.	C7	104
Valley, stm., Man.	D1	70
Valley, Wa., U.S.	A8	124
Valley, Ne., U.S.	C9	104
Valley Bend, W.V., U.S.	C5	125
Valley Center, Ks., U.S.	E6	93
Valley Centre, Sask.	F2	75
Valley City, Il., U.S.	D3	90
Valley City, N.D., U.S.	C8	111
Valley City, Oh., U.S.	A4	112
Valley Cottage, N.Y., U.S.	g13	109
Valley Creek, stm., Al., U.S.	g6	78
Valley East, Ont.	p19	73
Valley Falls, Ks., U.S.	C8	93
Valley Falls, Or., U.S.	E6	114
Valley Falls, R.I., U.S.	B4	116
Valley Farms, Az., U.S.	E4	80
Valleyfield (part of Badger's Quay-Valleyfield-Pool's Island), Newf.	D5	72

Name	Map Ref.	Page
Valleyford, Wa., U.S.	B8	124
Valley Forge, Pa., U.S.	o20	115
Valley Grove, W.V., U.S.	A4	125
Valley Head, Al., U.S.	A4	78
Valley Head, W.V., U.S.	C4	125
Valley Lee, Md., U.S.	D4	97
Valley Mills, Tx., U.S.	D4	120
Valley Park, Ms., U.S.	C3	101
Valley Park, Mo., U.S.	f12	102
Valley Ridge, Wa., U.S.	*B3	124
Valley Springs, Ar., U.S.	A3	81
Valley Springs, S.D., U.S.	D9	118
Valley Station, Ky., U.S.	g11	94
Valley Stream, N.Y., U.S.	n15	109
Valleyview, Alta.	B2	68
Valley View, Ky., U.S.	C5	94
Valley View, Pa., U.S.	E8	115
Valley View, Tx., U.S.	C4	120
Valliant, Ok., U.S.	D6	113
Vallo della Lucania, Italy	D5	23
Vallonia, In., U.S.	G5	91
Vallorbe, Switz.	E3	18
Valls, Spain	B6	22
Vallscreek, W.V., U.S.	D3	125
Val Marie, Sask.	H2	75
Valmeyer, Il., U.S.	E3	90
Valmiera, Sov. Un.	C5	27
Valmont, Que.	C5	74
Valmontone, Italy	h9	23
Valmora, N.M., U.S.	B5	108
Val-Morin, Que.	C3	74
Valmy, Nv., U.S.	C4	105
Valognes, Fr.	C3	16
Valois, N.Y., U.S.	C4	109
Valona see Vlora, Alb.	B2	40
Valparaíso, Sask.	H2	75
Valparaíso, Chile	A2	54
Valparaíso, Mex.	C4	63
Valparaiso, Fl., U.S.	u15	86
Valparaiso, In., U.S.	B3	91
Valparaiso, Ne., U.S.	C9	104
Valparaíso, prov., Chile	A2	54
Val-Racine, Que.	D6	74
Valréas, Fr.	E6	16
Vals, Cape, c., Indon.	G9	34
Val-Saint-Michel, Que.	n17	74
Valsetz, Or., U.S.	C3	114
Vals Platz, Switz.	C7	21
Valtournanche, Italy	E4	21
Valuyki, Sov. Un.	F12	27
Val Verda, Ut., U.S.	C4	121
Val Verde, co., Tx., U.S.	E2	120
Valverde del Camino, Spain	D2	22
Vamdrup, Den.	C3	15
Vamori, Az., U.S.	F4	80
Van, Tur.	C14	40
Van, Tx., U.S.	C5	120
Van, W.V., U.S.	n12	125
Van, Lake, l., Tur.	C14	40
Vanadium, N.M., U.S.	E1	108
Van Alstyne, Tx., U.S.	C4	120
Vananda, Sask.	E5	69
Van-Bruyssel, Que.	B5	74
Van Buren, Ar., U.S.	B1	81
Van Buren, In., U.S.	C6	91
Van Buren, Me., U.S.	A5	96
Van Buren, Mo., U.S.	E6	102
Van Buren, co., Ar., U.S.	A2	112
Van Buren, co., Ia., U.S.	D6	92
Van Buren, co., Mi., U.S.	F4	99
Van Buren, co., Tn., U.S.	D8	119
Vance, Ms., U.S.	A3	101
Vance, S.C., U.S.	E7	117
Vance, co., N.C., U.S.	A4	110
Vance Air Force Base, mil., Ok., U.S.	A3	113
Vanceboro, Me., U.S.	C5	96
Vanceboro, N.C., U.S.	B5	110
Vanceburg, Ky., U.S.	B6	94
Vancleave, Ms., U.S.	E5	101
Vancleve, Ky., U.S.	C6	94
Vancorum, Co., U.S.	C2	83
Vancouver, B.C.	E6	69
Vancouver Island, i., B.C.	E4	69
Vancouver Island Ranges, mts., B.C.	D4	69
Vandalia, Il., U.S.	E4	90
Vandalia, Mo., U.S.	B6	102
Vandalia, Mt., U.S.	B10	103
Vandalia, Oh., U.S.	*C1	112
Vandemere, N.C., U.S.	B6	110
Vandenberg Air Force Base, mil., Ca., U.S.	E3	82
Vandenberg Village, Ca., U.S.	*E3	82
Vander, N.C., U.S.	B4	110
Vanderbilt, Mi., U.S.	C6	99
Vanderbilt, Pa., U.S.	F2	115
Vanderbilt, Tx., U.S.	E4	120
Vanderbilt Peak, mtn., N.M., U.S.	E1	108
Vanderburgh, co., In., U.S.	H2	91
Vanderhoof, B.C.	C5	69
Vandergrift, Pa., U.S.	E2	115
Vanderhoof, B.C.	C5	69
Vanderpool, Tx., U.S.	E3	120
Vandervoort, Ar., U.S.	C1	81
Vanderwagen, N.M., U.S.	B1	108
Van Diemen, Cape, c., Austl.	B5	50
Van Diemen Gulf, b., Austl.	B5	50
Vandiver, Al., U.S.	B3	78
Vandling, Pa., U.S.	C11	115
Vanduser, Mo., U.S.	E8	102
Vandyne, Wi., U.S.	k9	126
Vanegas, Mex.	C4	63
Vänern, l., Swe.	H5	14
Vänersborg, Swe.	H5	14
Van Etten, N.Y., U.S.	C4	109
Vang, Mount, mtn., Ant.	B6	7
Vanga, Kenya	B6	48
Vangaindrano, Madag.	h9	49
Vanguard, Sask.	H2	75
Van Horn, Tx., U.S.	o12	120
Van Horne, Ia., U.S.	B5	92
Vanier, Ont.	h12	73
Vankleek Hill, Ont.	B10	73
Van Kull, Kill, stm., N.J., U.S.	k8	107
Van Lear, Ky., U.S.	C7	94
Vanleer, Tn., U.S.	A4	119
Vanlue, Oh., U.S.	B2	112
Van Meter, Ia., U.S.	C4	92
Vanna, Nor.	B3	14
Vanndale, Ar., U.S.	B5	81
Vannes, Fr.	E3	16
Vanoss, Ok., U.S.	C5	113
Van Phong Bay, b., Viet.	F8	35
Van Rees Mountains, mts., Indon.	F9	34
Vanrhynsdorp, S. Afr.	D2	49
Vansant, Va., U.S.	e9	123
Vanscoy, Sask.	E2	75
Vantaa (Vanda), Fin.	*G11	14
Vantage, Sask.	H2	75
Van Tassell, Wy., U.S.	D8	127
Vanua Balavu, i., Fiji	H16	52
Vanua Levu, i., Fiji	H15	52
Vanuatu, ctry., Oc.	H10	6
Vanua Vatu, i., Fiji	I16	52
Vanves, Fr.	g10	16
Van Vleck, Tx., U.S.	r14	120
Van Vleet, Ms., U.S.	B5	101
Van Wert, Ga., U.S.	C1	87
Van Wert, Ia., U.S.	D4	92
Van Wert, Oh., U.S.	B1	112
Van Wert, co., Oh., U.S.	B1	112
Van Wyck, S.C., U.S.	B6	117
Vanzant, Mo., U.S.	E5	102
Varallo, Italy	D4	20
Varāmīn, Iran	D5	39
Vārānasi (Benares), India	C7	36
Varangerfjorden, Nor.	B14	14
Varano, Lake, b., Italy	D5	23
Varazze, Italy	B2	23
Varberg, Swe.	I5	14
Vardaman, Ms., U.S.	B4	101
Vardar (Axiós), stm., Eur.	B4	40
Varde, Den.	C2	15
Varde Å, stm., Den.	C2	15
Vardenis, Sov. Un.	B15	40
Vardø, Nor.	B14	14
Varel, W. Ger.	B4	18
Varennes, Sov. Un.	A8	26
Varennes, Que.	D4	74
Varennes, Fr.	D5	16
Vareš, Yugo.	C4	24
Varese, Italy	B2	23
Varese, Lake, l., Italy	E6	21
Varginha, Braz.	C3	56
Vári, Grc.	h11	25
Varina, Ia., U.S.	B3	92
Varina, Va., U.S.	C5	123
Varkaus, Fin.	F12	14
Varkhān, mtn., Afg.	E12	39
Varna (Stalin), Bul.	D8	24
Varna, Ont.	D3	73
Varna, Il., U.S.	B4	90
Värnamo, Swe.	I6	14
Varney, Ont.	C4	73
Varnsdorf, Czech.	C3	26
Varnville, S.C., U.S.	F5	117
Värö, Swe.	A6	15
Várpalota, Hung.	B4	24
Vars, Ont.	h13	73
Varysburg, N.Y., U.S.	C2	109
Várzea, stm., Braz.	D2	56
Várzea da Palma, Braz.	D2	56
Várzea Grande, Braz.	B1	56
Varzi, Italy	E5	20
Varzuga, stm., Sov. Un.	D17	14
Vashon, Wa., U.S.	B3	124
Vashon, Point, c., Wa., U.S.	E11	124
Vashon Island, i., Wa., U.S.	f11	124
Vasilkov, Sov. Un.	F8	27
Vaslui, Rom.	B8	24
Vass, N.C., U.S.	B3	110
Vassalboro, Me., U.S.	*D3	96
Vassar, Man.	E4	70
Vassar, Ks., U.S.	D8	93
Vassar, Mi., U.S.	E7	99
Vassouras, Braz.	h6	56
Västerås, Swe.	H7	14
Västerhaninge, Swe.	t36	14
Västervik, Swe.	I7	14
Vasto, Italy	C5	23
Vasyugan, stm., Sov. Un.	B9	28
Vaternish Point, c., Scot., U.K.	C2	13
Vatican City, ctry., Eur.	D4	23
Vaticano, Cape, c., Italy	E5	23
Vatnajökull, ice, Ice.	n24	14
Vatomandry, Madag.	g9	49
Vatra Dornei, Rom.	B7	24
Vättern, l., Swe.	H6	14
Vatulele, i., Fiji	I14	52
Vatu Vara, i., Fiji	H16	52
Vaucluse, S.C., U.S.	D4	117
Vaucouleurs, Fr.	F5	17
Vaud, State, Switz.	C2	21
Vaudreuil, Que.	D3	74
Vaudreuil, co., Que.	D3	74
Vaughan, Ont.	D5	73
Vaughan, Ms., U.S.	C3	101
Vaughan, N.C., U.S.	A4	110
Vaughan, W.V., U.S.	m13	125
Vaughn, Mt., U.S.	C5	103
Vaughn, N.M., U.S.	C4	108
Vaughn, Or., U.S.	C3	114
Vaughnsville, Oh., U.S.	B1	112
Vaupés, dept., Col.	C3	60
Vaupés (Uaupés), stm., S.A.	C3	60
Vauvillers, Fr.	B2	20
Vauxhall, Alta.	D4	68
Vawn, Sask.	D1	75
Vaxholm, Swe.	t36	14
Växjö, Swe.	I6	14
Växtorp, Swe.	B7	15
Vaygach Island, i., Sov. Un.	C8	29
Váyia, Grc.	g10	25
Vazante, Braz.	B3	56
Veadeiros, Braz.	C2	56
Veazie, Me., U.S.	D4	96
Veblen, S.D., U.S.	B8	118
Vechta, W. Ger.	F2	15
Vechte, stm., Eur.	A7	16
Veckholm, Swe.	t35	14
Vecsés, Hung.	B4	24
Veddige, Swe.	A6	15
Vedea, stm., Rom.	C7	24
Vedia, Arg.	A4	54
Veedersburg, In., U.S.	D3	91
Veendam, Neth.	A6	17
Vega, Tx., U.S.	B1	120
Vega, i., Nor.	E4	14
Vega Alta, P.R.	B3	65
Vega Baja, P.R.	B3	65
Veguita, N.M., U.S.	C3	108
Veimandu Channel, strt., Mald.	B2	36
Veinticinco de Mayo, Arg.	A3	54
Veinticinco de Mayo, Arg.	B4	54
Vejen, Den.	C3	15
Vejer [de la Frontera], Spain	D3	22
Vejle, Den.	J3	14
Vejle, co., Den.	C3	15
Ve勤prém, Czech.	C2	26
Vela, Cabo de la, c., Col.	A3	60
Velarde, N.M., U.S.	A4	108
Velas, Cabo, c., C.R.	E5	62
Velbert, W. Ger.	B2	19
Velda Rose Estates, Az., U.S.	D4	80
Velden, W. Ger.	A8	20
Velebit Mountains, mts., Yugo.	C2	24
Velestínon, Grc.	C4	25
Vélez, Col.	B3	60
Vélez Blanco, Spain	D4	22
Vélez-Málaga, Spain	D3	22
Vélez Rubio, Spain	D4	22
Velgast, E. Ger.	D6	15
Velhas, Rio das, stm., Braz.	B4	56
Velikaya, stm., Sov. Un.	C5	27
Velikaya Lepetikha, Sov. Un.	H10	27
Velikiye Luki, Sov. Un.	C8	27
Velikiy Ustyug, Sov. Un.	C7	29
Veliko Türnovo, Bul.	D7	24
Vélingara, Sen.	D2	45
Vélingara, Sen.	D2	45
Velizh, Sov. Un.	D8	27
Velletri, Italy	D4	23
Vellinge, Swe.	C7	15
Vellore, India	F6	36
Velpen, In., U.S.	H3	91
Velsen (part of IJmuiden), Neth.	B4	17
Velsk, Sov. Un.	C7	29
Veltrusy, Czech.	n17	26
Velva, N.D., U.S.	A5	111
Velvary, Czech.	n17	26
Vemb, Den.	B2	15
Ven, i., Swe.	C6	15
Venaco, Fr.	C2	23
Venado Tuerto, Arg.	A4	54
Venango, Ne., U.S.	D3	104
Venango, Pa., U.S.	C1	115
Venango, co., Pa., U.S.	D2	115
Venceslau Brás, Braz.	A5	56
Venda, ctry., Afr.	B5	49
Vendôme, Fr.	D4	16
Vendrell, Spain	B6	22
Venedocia, Oh., U.S.	B1	112
Venedy, Il., U.S.	E4	90
Veneta, Or., U.S.	C3	114
Veneta, Laguna, b., Italy	D8	20
Venetia (Veneto), prov., Italy	A3	23
Venetie, Ak., U.S.	B10	79
Veneto, prov., Italy	D7	20
Venezuela, ctry., S.A.	B4	60
Venezuela, Golfo de, b., S.A.	A3	60
Veniaminof, Mount, mtn., Ak., U.S.	D8	79
Venice, Alta.	B4	68
Venice (Venezia), Italy	B4	23
Venice, Fl., U.S.	E4	86
Venice, Il., U.S.	E3	90
Venice, La., U.S.	E6	95
Venice, Ne., U.S.	g12	104
Venice, Ut., U.S.	E4	121
Venice, Gulf of, b., Eur.	B4	23
Venice Gardens, Fl., U.S.	*E4	86
Venissieux, Fr.	E6	16
Venn Bridge, P.E.I.	C7	71
Vernon Center, Mn., U.S.	G4	100
Vennachar, Ont.	B7	73
Veno, i., Den.	B2	15
Venlo, Neth.	B7	16
Vent, Aus.	C6	20
Venta, stm., Sov. Un.	C3	27
Ventana, Az., U.S.	E3	80
Ventimiglia, Italy	C1	23
Ventnor, Ont.	C9	73
Ventnor, Eng., U.K.	D6	12
Ventnor City, N.J., U.S.	E4	107
Venton, Md., U.S.	D6	97
Ventoux, Mont, mtn., Fr.	E6	16
Ventry, Ire.	E1	11
Ventspils, Sov. Un.	C3	27
Venturi, stm., Ven.	C4	60
Ventura (San Buenaventura), Ca., U.S.	E4	82
Ventura, Ia., U.S.	A4	92
Ventura, co., Ca., U.S.	E4	82
Ventura, N.D., U.S.	D6	111
Verónica, Arg.	g8	54
Venus, Fl., U.S.	E5	86
Venus, Pa., U.S.	D2	115
Venus, Tx., U.S.	n9	120
Vera, Arg.	E3	55
Vera, Spain	D5	22
Veracruz, Mex.	D5	63
Vera, Ok., U.S.	A6	113
Vera, Tx., U.S.	C3	120
Vera Cruz, In., U.S.	C7	91
Veracruz, state, Mex.	C5	63
Veracruz [Llave], Mex.	D5	63
Veradale, Wa., U.S.	*B8	124
Veranópolis, Braz.	C3	56
Verbania, Italy	D4	20
Verbena, Al., U.S.	C3	78
Vercel, Fr.	B1	21
Vercelli, Italy	B2	23
Verchères, Que.	D4	74
Verchères, co., Que.	D4	74
Verda, Ky., U.S.	D6	94
Verde, stm., Braz.	B4	56
Verde, stm., Braz.	H3	75
Verwood, Sask.	B2	56
Verde, stm., Braz.	B2	56
Verde, stm., Mex.	m14	63
Verde, stm., Mex.	m12	63
Verde, stm., Para.	D4	55
Verde, stm., Az., U.S.	C4	80
Verde, Point, c., Newf.	E4	72
Verde Island, i., Phil.	p13	34
Verde Island Passage, strt., Phil.	p13	34
Verdel, Ne., U.S.	B7	104
Verden, W. Ger.	B4	18
Verden, Ok., U.S.	B3	113
Verdi, Mn., U.S.	F2	100
Verdi Peak, mtn., Nv., U.S.	C6	105
Verdigre, Ne., U.S.	B7	104
Verdigris, Ok., U.S.	A6	113
Verdigris, stm., U.S.	A6	113
Verdon, Ne., U.S.	D10	104
Verdun, Que.	q19	74
Verdun, Fr.	E4	16
Verdunville, W.V., U.S.	*D2	125
Vereeniging, S. Afr.	C4	49
Vereshchagino, Sov. Un.	D19	31
Verghereto, Italy	E7	20
Vergara, Ur.	E2	55
Vergara, Sp.	A4	22
Vergennes, Il., U.S.	F4	90
Vergennes, Vt., U.S.	C2	122
Veríssimo Sarmento see Camissombo, Ang.	C3	48
Verkhneimbatsk, Sov. Un.	C26	31
Verkhnekolymsk, Sov. Un.	C18	29
Verkhneuralsk, Sov. Un.	E20	31
Verkhneusinskoye, Sov. Un.	E27	8
Verkhniy Baskunchak, Sov. Un.	D3	28
Verkhniy Ufaley, Sov. Un.	B6	28
Verkhnyaya Tura, Sov. Un.	D21	8
Verkhoyansk, Sov. Un.	C16	29
Verkhoyansk Mountains, mts., Sov. Un.	C15	29
Verlo, Sask.	G1	75
Vermilion, Alta.	C5	68
Vermilion, Il., U.S.	D6	90
Vermilion, Oh., U.S.	A3	112
Vermilion, co., Il., U.S.	C6	90
Vermilion, co., La., U.S.	E3	95
Vermilion, stm., Alta.	C5	68
Vermilion, stm., Il., U.S.	C5	90
Vermilion, stm., La., U.S.	E3	95
Vermilion, stm., Mn., U.S.	B6	100
Vermilion, stm., Oh., U.S.	A3	112
Vermilion Bay, Ont.	E5	70
Vermilion Bay, b., La., U.S.	E3	95
Vermilion Lake, l., Mn., U.S.	C6	100
Vermilion Pass, Can.	D2	68
Vermilion Range, hills, Mn., U.S.	C7	100
Vermillion, Ks., U.S.	C7	93
Vermillion, S.D., U.S.	E9	118
Vermillion, co., In., U.S.	E2	91
Vermillion, East Fork, stm., S.D., U.S.	D8	118
Vermillion Bluffs, cliff, Co., U.S.	A2	83
Vermillion Creek, stm., Co., U.S.	A2	83
Vermont, Il., U.S.	C3	90
Vermont, state, U.S.	D3	122
Vermontville, Mi., U.S.	F5	99
Vernal, Ut., U.S.	C6	121
Vernalis, Ca., U.S.	h10	82
Verndale, Mn., U.S.	D3	100
Verner, Ont.	A4	73
Verneuil, Fr.	C4	16
Verneukpan, pl., S. Afr.	D3	49
Vernon, B.C.	D8	69
Vernon, Fr.	C4	16
Vernon, Al., U.S.	B1	78
Vernon, Az., U.S.	C6	80
Vernon, Co., U.S.	B1	83
Vernon, Ct., U.S.	B6	84
Vernon, Fl., U.S.	u16	86
Vernon, Il., U.S.	E4	90
Vernon, In., U.S.	G6	91
Vernon, Ok., U.S.	B6	113
Vernon, Tn., U.S.	B4	119
Vernon, Tx., U.S.	B3	120
Vernon, Ut., U.S.	C3	121
Vernon, Vt., U.S.	F3	122
Vernon, co., La., U.S.	C2	95
Vernon, co., Mo., U.S.	D3	102
Vernon, co., Wi., U.S.	E3	126
Vernon, Lake, l., Ont.	B5	73
Vernon Bridge, P.E.I.	C7	71
Vernon Hill, Va., U.S.	D3	123
Vernon Hills, Il., U.S.	h9	90
Vernonia, Or., U.S.	B3	114
Vernon River, P.E.I.	C7	71
Vero Beach, Fl., U.S.	E6	86
Verona, Ont.	C8	73
Verona, Italy	B3	23
Verona, Il., U.S.	B5	90
Verona, Ky., U.S.	k13	94
Verona, Ms., U.S.	A5	101
Verona, Mo., U.S.	E4	102
Verona, N.J., U.S.	B4	107
Verona, N.C., U.S.	C5	110
Verona, N.D., U.S.	C7	111
Verona, Oh., U.S.	C1	112
Verona, Pa., U.S.	k14	115
Verona, Tn., U.S.	B5	119
Verona, Wi., U.S.	F4	126
Verret, Lake, l., La., U.S.	E4	95
Verret, N.B.	B1	71
Versailles, Fr.	C5	16
Versailles, Ct., U.S.	C7	84
Versailles, In., U.S.	F7	91
Versailles, Ky., U.S.	B5	94
Versailles, Mo., U.S.	C5	102
Versailles, Oh., U.S.	B1	112
Vershire, Vt., U.S.	D4	122
Versmold, W. Ger.	A3	19
Versoix, Switz.	C2	21
Vert, Cap, c., Sen.	E4	42
Verte, stm., Que.	B8	74
Verte, Île, i., Que.	A8	74
Verton, Fr.	D9	12
Vertou, Fr.	D3	16
Vertus, Fr.	F4	17
Verviers, Bel.	B6	16
Vervins, Fr.	C5	16
Verwall Group, mts., Aus.	B9	21
Verwood, Sask.	H3	75
Verzasca, stm., Switz.	D6	21
Verzenay, Fr.	k14	17
Veselovskiy, N.D., U.S.	A8	111
Veselí nad Lužnicí, Czech.	D9	19
Veseloye, Sov. Un.	H10	27
Vesoul, Fr.	A1	21
Vesper, Ks., U.S.	C5	93
Vesper, Wi., U.S.	D4	126
Vesta, C.R.	F6	62
Vesta, Mn., U.S.	F3	100
Vestaburg, Mi., U.S.	E6	99
Vestal, N.Y., U.S.	C4	109
Vestavia Hills, Al., U.S.	g7	78
Vestby, Nor.	p28	14
Vesterålen, i., Nor.	C6	14
Vesterø Havn, Den.	A4	15
Vesterøya, i., Nor.	p28	14
Vestfjorden, Nor.	D5	14
Vestmanna Islands, i., Ice.	o22	14
Vestsjælland, co., Den.	C5	15
Vesuvius, vol., Italy	D5	23
Veszprém, Hung.	B3	24
Vésztő, Hung.	B5	24
Vetal, S.D., U.S.	D4	118
Veteran, Wy., U.S.	E8	127
Vetlanda, Swe.	I6	14
Vetluga, stm., Sov. Un.	B3	28
Vetluzhskiy, Sov. Un.	C6	28
Vetovo, Bul.	D8	24
Vetren, Bul.	D7	24
Veurne, Bel.	C2	17
Veun, Ind.	G7	91
Vevay, In., U.S.	G7	91
Vevey, Switz.	E3	18
Veynes, Fr.	E6	16
Veyo, Ut., U.S.	F2	121
Veyrier-du-Lac, Fr.	E1	21
Vézère, stm., Fr.	E4	16
Vezirköprü, Tur.	B10	40
Viacha, Bol.	C2	55
Viadana, Italy	B3	23
Viamonte, Arg.	A4	54
Vian, Ok., U.S.	B7	113
Viana, Braz.	B2	57
Viana do Bollo, Spain	A2	22
Viana do Alentejo, Port.	C1	22
Viana do Castelo, Port.	B1	22
Vianen, Neth.	C5	17
Viangchan (Vientiane), Laos	B3	56
Vianópolis, Braz.	B3	56
Viar, stm., Spain	D3	22
Viareggio, Italy	C3	23
Vibank, Sask.	G4	75
Vijayawāda (Bezwada), India	E7	36
Vík, Ice.	o23	14
Vikersund, Nor.	p27	14
Viking, Alta.	C5	68
Viking, Mn., U.S.	B2	100
Viburnum, Mo., U.S.	D6	102
Vila Alferes Chamusca, Moz.	B5	49
Vila Bela de Santissima Trinidade, Braz.	B4	55
Vila da Maganja, Moz.	A6	49
Vila de Manica, Moz.	A5	49
Vila de Rei, Port.	C1	22
Vila de Sena, Moz.	A6	49
Vila do Conde, Port.	B1	22
Vila Fontes, Moz.	A6	49
Vilafranca del Penedés, Spain	B6	22
Vila Franca de Xira, Port.	C1	22
Vilaine, stm., Fr.	D2	16
Vilanculos, Moz.	B6	49
Vila Nova de Foz Côa, Port.	B2	22
Vila Nova de Gaia, Port.	B1	22
Vila Nova de Milfontes, Port.	D1	22
Vila Real, Port.	B2	22
Vila Real de Santo António, Port.	D2	22
Vilas, Co., U.S.	D8	83
Vilas, S.D., U.S.	C8	118
Vilas, co., Wi., U.S.	B4	126
Vila São Luís, Braz.	B3	59
Vila Vasco da Gama, Moz.	A5	49
Vila Velha, Braz.	C4	56
Vila Viçosa, Port.	C2	22
Vilcabamba, Peru	...	...
Vicálvaro, Spain	p17	22
Vicco, Ky., U.S.	C6	94
Vicente, Point, c., Ca., U.S.	n12	82
Vicenza, Italy	B3	23
Viceroy, Sask.	H3	75
Vich, Spain	B7	22
Vichada, dept., Col.	C4	60
Vichada, stm., Col.	C4	60
Vichuga, Sov. Un.	C13	27
Vichuquén, Chile	A2	54
Vichy, Fr.	D5	16
Vichy, Mo., U.S.	C6	102
Vici, Ok., U.S.	A2	113
Vick, Ar., U.S.	D3	81
Vick, La., U.S.	C3	95
Vickery, Oh., U.S.	A3	112
Vicksburg, In., U.S.	F3	91
Vicksburg, Mi., U.S.	F5	99
Vicksburg, Ms., U.S.	C3	101
Vicksburg National Military Park, Ms., U.S.	C3	101
Viçosa, Braz.	C4	56
Viçosa, Braz.	C3	57
Viçosa do Ceará, Braz.	B2	57
Vicosoprano, Switz.	D8	21
Vicovaro, Italy	g9	23
Vic [-sur-Seille], Fr.	F6	17
Victor, Co., U.S.	C5	83
Victor, Id., U.S.	F7	89
Victor, Ia., U.S.	C5	92
Victor, Mt., U.S.	D2	103
Victor, N.Y., U.S.	C3	109
Victor, S.D., U.S.	D9	118
Victor Harbor, Austl.	G6	50
Victoria, Arg.	A4	54
Victoria, B.C.	E6	69
Victoria, Newf.	E5	72
Victoria, P.E.I.	C6	71
Victoria, Chile	A2	54
Victoria, Gren.	W25	65
Victoria (Hong Kong), H.K.	G7	31
Victoria, Malay.	D5	34
Victoria, Phil.	o13	34
Victoria, Il., U.S.	B3	90
Victoria, Ks., U.S.	D4	93
Victoria, Mo., U.S.	C7	102
Victoria, Tn., U.S.	D8	119
Victoria, Tx., U.S.	E4	120
Victoria, Va., U.S.	D4	123
Victoria, state, Austl.	G7	50
Victoria, co., N.B.	B2	71
Victoria, co., N.S.	C9	71
Victoria, co., Tx., U.S.	E4	120
Victoria, stm., Austl.	C5	50
Victoria, stm., Newf.	D3	72
Victoria, Lake, l., Afr.	B5	48
Victoria, Lake, l., Austl.	F3	51
Victoria, Mount, mtn., Pap. N. Gui.	k12	50
Victoria Beach, Man.	D3	70
Victoria de Durango see Durango, Mex.	C4	63
Victoria de las Tunas, Cuba	D7	64
Victoria Falls, Zimb.	A4	49
Victoria Falls, wtfl., Afr.	A4	49
Victoria Harbour, Ont.	C5	73
Victoria Island, i., N.W. Ter.	B10	66
Victoria Lake, res., Newf.	D3	72
Victoria Land, reg., Ant.	B28	7
Victoria Peak, mtn., Belize	B3	62
Victoria Road, Ont.	C6	73
Victoria Strait, strt., N.W. Ter.	C12	66
Victoria West, S. Afr.	D3	49
Victorica, Arg.	C4	60
Victorino, Ven.	C4	60
Victorino de la Plaza, Arg.	B4	54
Victorville, Ca., U.S.	E5	82
Victory, Ok., U.S.	C2	113
Victory, Wi., U.S.	E3	126
Vicuña, Chile	E2	55
Vida, Mt., U.S.	C11	103
Vidal, Ca., U.S.	E6	82
Vidalia, Ga., U.S.	D4	87
Vidalia, La., U.S.	C4	95
Vidette, Ga., U.S.	D4	87
Vidin, Bul.	C5	24
Vidisha, India	D6	36
Vidor, Tx., U.S.	D6	120
Vidora, Sask.	H1	75
Viechtach, W. Ger.	D7	19
Viedma, Arg.	E3	55
Viedma, Lago, l., Arg.	...	...
Vieja, Sierra, mts., Tx., U.S.	o12	120
Viejo, Cerro el, mtn., Col.	D5	60
Vielsalm, Bel.	B6	17
Vienenburg, W. Ger.	B5	19
Vienna (Wien), Aus.	D8	19
Vienna, Ont.	E4	73
Vienna, Ga., U.S.	D3	87
Vienna, Il., U.S.	F5	90
Vienna, Md., U.S.	D6	97
Vienna, Mo., U.S.	C6	102
Vienna, N.J., U.S.	B3	107
Vienna, S.D., U.S.	C8	118
Vienna, Va., U.S.	B5	123
Vienna, W.V., U.S.	B3	125
Vienne, Fr.	E6	16
Vienne, stm., Fr.	D4	16
Vieques, P.R.	B5	65
Vieques, Isla de, i., P.R.	B5	65
Vieques, Pasaje de, strt., P.R.	B5	65
Vieques, Sonda de, strt., P.R.	B5	65
Vierheim, W. Ger.	D3	19
Viersen, W. Ger.	C6	17
Vierzon, Fr.	D5	16
Viesca, Mex.	B4	63
Vieste, Italy	D6	23
Vietnam, ctry., Asia	B3	34
Vieux Desert, Lac, l., Wi., U.S.	...	...
Vieux Fort, St. Luc.	J14	64
Vieux-Fort, Pointe du, c., Guad.	R8	65
View Park, Ca., U.S.	*m12	82
Vigan, Phil.	B6	34
Vigevano, Italy	B2	23
Vignola, Italy	E6	20
Vigo, Spain	A1	22
Vigo, co., In., U.S.	F3	91
Vigsø Bugt, b., Den.	A2	15
Vihowa, Pak.	B5	36
Vilafamés, Spain	B2	22
Vila Frontera, Moz.	B4	49
Vila García, Mex.	k13	63
Villagarcía, Spain	A1	22
Village, Va., U.S.	C6	123
Village Creek, stm., Al., U.S.	f7	78
Village Springs, Al., U.S.	B3	78
Villa González, Mex.	C5	63
Villa Grove, Co., U.S.	C5	83
Villa Grove, Il., U.S.	D5	90
Villaguay, Arg.	A5	54
Villa Hayes, Para.	E1	55
Villahermosa, Mex.	D6	63
Villa Hills, Ky., U.S.	*A5	94
Villa Huidobro, Arg.	A4	54
Villa Iris, Arg.	...	...
Villajoyosa, Spain	C5	22
Villalba, Spain	A2	22
Villalonga, Arg.	...	...
Villalpando, Spain	A3	22
Villa María, Arg.	A4	54
Villa María Grande, Arg.	...	...
Villamartín, Spain	D3	22
Villa Mazán, Arg.	E2	55
Villamil, Ec.	g5	58
Villa Montes, Bol.	D3	55
Villanueva, Hond.	...	...
Villanueva, N.M., U.S.	B4	108
Villanueva de Córdoba, Spain	C3	22
Villanueva del Arzobispo, Spain	C4	22
Villanueva de la Serana, Spain	C3	22
Villanueva de los Infantes, Spain	C4	22
Villanueva y Geltrú, Spain	B6	22
Villa Obregón (part of Mexico City), Mex.	h9	63
Villa Ocampo, Arg.	E3	55
Villa Ojo de Agua, Arg.	E2	55
Villa Oliva, Para.	...	...
Villa Park, Ca., U.S.	*n13	82
Villa Park, Il., U.S.	k8	90
Villaputzu, Italy	...	...
Villard, Mn., U.S.	E3	100
Villard-Bonnot, Fr.	E6	16
Villa Rica, Ga., U.S.	C2	87
Villa Ridge, Il., U.S.	A4	90
Villa Ridge, Mo., U.S.	C7	102
Villarreal, Spain	C5	22
Villarrica, Chile	B2	54
Villarrica, Para.	E1	55
Villarrobledo, Spain	C4	22
Villarrubia [de los Ojos], Spain	C4	22
Villars-le-Terroir, Switz.	J13	21
Villa Rica, Ga., U.S.	C2	87
Villa San Martín (Loreto), Arg.	E3	55
Villa Unión, Arg.	E2	55

Index

Name	Map Ref.	Page
Villa Unión, Mex.	B4	63
Villa Unión, Mex.	C3	63
Villa Valeria, Arg.	A4	54
Villaverde, Spain	p17	22
Villavicencio, Col.	C3	60
Villaviciosa, Spain	A3	22
Villefranche, Fr.	E5	16
Villefranche [-sur-Saône], Fr.	D6	16
Villegreen, Co., U.S.	D7	83
Villejuif, Fr.	g10	16
Ville Marie, Que.	G17	66
Villemomble, Fr.	g11	16
Villena, Spain	C5	22
Villenauxe-la-Grande, Fr.	F3	17
Villeneuve-d'Ascq, Fr.	*B5	16
Villeneuve-le-Roi, Fr.	h10	16
Villeneuve [-lès-Avignon], Fr.	F6	16
Villeneuve-Saint-Georges, Fr.	h10	16
Villeneuve-sur-Lot, Fr.	E4	16
Villeneuve-sur-Yonne, Fr.	E4	16
Villepinte, Fr.	g11	16
Ville Platte, La., U.S.	D3	95
Villeroy, Que.	C6	74
Villers-Bretonneux, Fr.	E2	17
Villers-Cotterêts, Fr.	C5	16
Villersexel, Fr.	A1	21
Villers-Outréaux, Fr.	D3	17
Villers-Semeuse, Fr.	E4	17
Villerupt, Fr.	C6	16
Ville Saint-Georges, Que.	C7	74
Villeta, Para.	E4	55
Villeurbanne, Fr.	E6	16
Villingen-Schwenningen, W. Ger.	D4	18
Villisca, Ia., U.S.	D3	92
Vilna, Alta.	B5	68
Vilonia, Ar., U.S.	B3	81
Vilppula, Fin.	F11	14
Vils, stm., W. Ger.	E7	19
Vils, stm., W. Ger.	D6	19
Vilsbiburg, W. Ger.	E7	19
Vilseck, W. Ger.	D6	19
Vilshofen, W. Ger.	E8	19
Vilvoorde, Bel.	B6	16
Vilyuy, Sov. Un.	C15	29
Vilyuysk, Sov. Un.	C15	29
Vimianzo, Spain	A1	22
Vimmerby, Swe.	I6	14
Vimperk, Czech.	D2	26
Vimy Ridge, Ar., U.S.	k10	81
Vina, Al., U.S.	A1	78
Vina, Ca., U.S.	C2	82
Viña del Mar, Chile	A2	54
Vinalhaven, Me., U.S.	D4	96
Vinalhaven Island, i., Me., U.S.	D4	96
Vinaroz, Spain	B6	22
Vincennes, Fr.	g10	16
Vincennes, In., U.S.	G2	91
Vincennes Bay, b., Ant.	C23	7
Vincent, Al., U.S.	B3	78
Vincent, Ia., U.S.	B3	92
Vincent, Oh., U.S.	C4	112
Vincent, Tx., U.S.	C2	100
Vincentown, N.J., U.S.	D3	107
Vinces, Ec.	B2	58
Vinchina, Arg.	E2	55
Vinchina, stm., Arg.	E2	55
Vinco, Ok., U.S.	B4	113
Vindelälven, stm., Swe.	E8	14
Vindeln, Swe.	E8	14
Vinderup, Den.	B2	15
Vindhya Range, mts., India	D6	36
Vine Brook, stm., Ma., U.S.	g11	98
Vinegar Hill, mtn., Or., U.S.	C8	114
Vine Grove, Ky., U.S.	C4	94
Vineland, N.J., U.S.	E2	107
Vinemont, Al., U.S.	A3	78
Vineyard Haven, Ma., U.S.	D6	98
Vineyard Sound, strt., Ma., U.S.	D6	98
Vingåker, Swe.	t33	14
Vinh, Viet.	B3	34
Vinhais, Port.	B2	22
Vinh Long, Viet.	C3	34
Vining, Ks., U.S.	C6	93
Vining, Mn., U.S.	D3	100
Vinita, Ok., U.S.	A6	113
Vinkovci, Yugo.	C4	24
Vinland, Ks., U.S.	m15	93
Vinnitsa, Sov. Un.	E5	29
Vinson, Ok., U.S.	C2	113
Vinson Massif, mtn., Ant.	B4	7
Vinton, Ia., U.S.	B5	92
Vinton, La., U.S.	D2	95
Vinton, Oh., U.S.	D3	112
Vinton, Va., U.S.	C3	123
Vinton, co., Oh., U.S.	C3	112
Vintondale, Pa., U.S.	F4	115
Viola, Ar., U.S.	A4	81
Viola, De., U.S.	D3	85
Viola, Id., U.S.	C1	89
Viola, Il., U.S.	B3	90
Viola, Ks., U.S.	E6	93
Viola, N.Y., U.S.	*D6	109
Viola, Tn., U.S.	D8	119
Viola, Wi., U.S.	E3	126
Violet, La., U.S.	k12	95
Vipiteno, Italy	C7	20
Virden, Man.	E1	70
Virden, Il., U.S.	D4	90
Virden, N.M., U.S.	E1	108
Vire, Fr.	C3	16
Vire, stm., Fr.	C3	16
Viren, i., Swe.	t34	14
Virgem da Lapa, Braz.	B4	56
Vírgenes, Cabo, c., S.A.	E3	54
Virgil, Ks., U.S.	E7	93
Virgil, N.Y., U.S.	C4	109
Virgil, S.D., U.S.	C7	118
Virgilina, Va., U.S.	D4	123
Virgin, Ut., U.S.	F2	121
Virgin, stm., U.S.	G8	105
Virgin Gorda, i., V.I., Br.	G12	64
Virginia, Ire.	D4	11
Virginia, S. Afr.	C4	49
Virginia, Al., U.S.	g6	78
Virginia, Il., U.S.	D3	90
Virginia, Mn., U.S.	C6	100
Virginia, Ne., U.S.	D9	104
Virginia, state, U.S.	C4	123
Virginia Beach, Va., U.S.	D7	123
Virginia City, Mt., U.S.	E5	103
Virginia City, Nv., U.S.	D2	105
Virginia Peak, mtn., Nv., U.S.	D2	105
Virgin Islands, dep., N.A.	G12	64
Virgin Islands, is., N.A.	B6	65
Virgin Mountains, mts., U.S.	A1	80
Virginópolis, Braz.	B4	56
Virgin Passage, strt., N.A.	*D2	65
Virgolândia, Braz.	B4	56
Virochey, Camb.	C3	34
Viroflay, Fr.	g9	16
Viron, Grc.	*	
Viroqua, Wi., U.S.	E3	126
Virovitica, Yugo.	C3	24
Virpazar, Yugo.	D4	24
Virrat, Fin.	F10	14
Virserum, Swe.	I6	14
Virton, Bel.	E5	17
Virú, Peru	C2	58
Vis, i., Yugo.	D3	24
Vis, i., Yugo.	D3	24
Visalia, Ca., U.S.	D4	82
Visalia, Ky., U.S.	k14	94
Visayan Sea, Phil.	C6	34
Visby, Swe.	I8	14
Visconde do Rio Branco, Braz.	C4	56
Viscount, Sask.	F3	75
Viscount Melville Sound, strt., N.W. Ter.	B11	66
Visé, Bel.	D5	17
Višegrad, Yugo.	D4	24
Viseu, Braz.	B1	57
Viseu, Port.	B2	22
Vishakhapatnam (Vizagapatam), India	E7	36
Vishera, stm., Sov. Un.	A5	28
Viskan, stm., Swe.	A6	15
Vislanda, Swe.	B8	15
Viso, Mount, mtn., Italy	B1	23
Visoko, Yugo.	D4	24
Visp, Switz.	E3	18
Vista, Man.	D1	70
Vista, Ca., U.S.	F5	82
Vista, Mo., U.S.	D4	102
Vista, Nv., U.S.	*D2	105
Vista Alegre, Braz.	C4	60
Vistonís, Lake, l., Grc.	B5	25
Vistula, In., U.S.	A6	91
Vistula Lagoon, b., Eur.	A5	26
Vistula see Wisła, stm., Pol.	B5	26
Vit, stm., Bul.	D7	24
Vita, Man.	E3	70
Vitanovac, Yugo.	D5	24
Vitarte, Peru	D2	58
Vitebsk, Sov. Un.	D6	29
Viterbo, Italy	C4	23
Vitichi, Bol.	D2	55
Viti Levu, i., Fiji	H14	52
Viti Levu Bay, b., Fiji	H15	52
Vitim, Sov. Un.	D14	29
Vitim, stm., Sov. Un.	D14	29
Vítor, Peru	E3	58
Vitória, Braz.	C4	56
Vitória, Braz.	C4	59
Vitória, Spain	A4	22
Vitória da Conquista, Braz.	A4	56
Vitória [de Santo Antão], Braz.	B2	57
Vitória do Mearim, Braz.	B2	57
Vitória Quebrangulo, Braz.	k5	57
Vitré, Fr.	C3	16
Vitry [-sur-Seine], Fr.	g10	16
Vittel, Fr.	C6	16
Vittoria, Ont.	E4	73
Vittoria, Italy	F5	23
Vittorio Veneto, Italy	B4	23
Vivero, Spain	A2	22
Vivian, La., U.S.	B2	95
Vivian, S.D., U.S.	D5	118
Vivian Park, Ut., U.S.	C4	121
Vivorată, Arg.	B5	54
Viwa, i., Fiji	H14	52
Vize, Tur.	B6	40
Vizianagaram, India	E7	36
Vizille, Fr.	E6	16
Viziru, Rom.	C8	24
Vizzini, Italy	F5	23
Vjosa, stm., Eur.	B3	25
Vlaardingen, Neth.	B6	16
Vladimir, Sov. Un.	D7	29
Vladimiro-Aleksandrovskoye, Sov. Un.	C11	31
Vladimirovo, Sov. Un.	B12	33
Vladimir-Volynskiy, Sov. Un.	F5	27
Vladivostok, Sov. Un.	E16	29
Vlasenica, Yugo.	C4	24
Vlašim, Czech.	D9	26
Vlasotince, Yugo.	D6	24
Vličany, Czech.	n18	26
Vlieland, i., Neth.	A6	16
Vlissingen, Neth.	B5	16
Vlkava, Czech.	n18	26
Vlkava, stm., Czech.	n18	26
Vlora (Valona), Alb.	B2	40
Vlotho, W. Ger.	A3	19
Vltava, stm., Czech.	D3	26
Voca, Tx., U.S.	D3	120
Vodňany, Czech.	D9	19
Vodlozero, l., Sov. Un.	F17	14
Voerde, W. Ger.	D1	19
Voghera, Italy	D3	23
Vohenstrauss, W. Ger.	D7	19
Vohibinany, Madag.	g9	49
Vohimarina, Madag.	f9	49
Vohipeno, Madag.	h9	49
Voi, Kenya	B6	48
Void, Fr.	F5	17
Voil, Loch, l., Scot., U.K.	D4	13
Voinjama, Lib.	E3	45
Voiron, Fr.	E6	16
Voitsberg, Aus.	E7	18
Vojens, Den.	C3	15
Vokhma, Sov. Un.	B3	28
Volary, Czech.	E8	19
Volcano, Mt., U.S.	E11	103
Volcano, Hi., U.S.	D6	88
Volcano Island, i., Phil.	o13	34
Volcano Islands, is., Japan	E8	6
Volchansk, Sov. Un.	F11	27
Volchya, stm., Sov. Un.	B7	33
Volga, Ia., U.S.	B6	92
Volga, S.D., U.S.	C9	118
Volga, W.V., U.S.	B4	125
Volga, stm., Sov. Un.	E7	29
Volga Plateau, plat., Sov. Un.	C3	28
Volgodonsk, Sov. Un.	H13	27
Volgograd (Stalingrad), Sov. Un.	E7	29
Volgograd Reservoir, res., Sov. Un.	D7	29
Volin, S.D., U.S.	E8	118
Volkach, W. Ger.	D5	19
Volkhov, Sov. Un.	B9	27
Volkhov, stm., Sov. Un.	B8	27
Völklingen, W. Ger.	D1	19
Volkovysk, Sov. Un.	E5	27
Vollenhove, Neth.	B5	17
Volney, Va., U.S.	D1	123
Volnovakha, Sov. Un.	H11	27
Volo, Il., U.S.	h8	90
Volochayevka Vtoraya, Sov. Un.	B7	33
Volochisk, Sov. Un.	G6	27
Volodarskiy (part of Leningrad), Sov. Un.	s31	14
Volodarskoye, Sov. Un.	C7	28
Vologda, Sov. Un.	D7	29
Vólos, Grc.	C4	40
Vólos, Gulf of see Pagasitikós Kólpos, b., Grc.	C4	40
Volsk, Sov. Un.	C3	28
Volta, prov., Ghana	E5	45
Volta, Lake, res., Ghana	E5	45
Voltaire, N.D., U.S.	A5	111
Volta Redonda, Braz.	C4	56
Volta Noire (Black Volta), stm., Afr.	D4	45
Volterra, Italy	C3	23
Voltri, Italy	B2	23
Volturno, stm., Italy	D5	23
Voluntown, Ct., U.S.	C8	84
Volusia, co., Fl., U.S.	C5	86
Volzhskiy, Sov. Un.	G15	27
Vombsjön, l., Swe.	C7	15
Vona, Co., U.S.	B8	83
Vonda, Sask.	E2	75
Von Frank Mountain, mtn., Ak., U.S.	C9	79
Vónitsa, Grc.	C3	25
Vonore, Tn., U.S.	D9	119
Von Ormy, Tx., U.S.	k7	120
Voqnafjördur, Ice.	n25	14
Vorarlberg, state, Aus.	B5	20
Vorderrhein, stm., Switz.	C7	21
Vorderthal, Switz.	B6	21
Vordingborg, Den.	C5	15
Vorkuta, Sov. Un.	C9	29
Vorona, stm., Sov. Un.	E14	27
Voronezh, Sov. Un.	D6	29
Voronezh, stm., Sov. Un.	E12	27
Voronya, stm., Sov. Un.	C16	14
Voroshilovgrad, Sov. Un.	E6	29
Vorskla, stm., Sov. Un.	G10	27
Vørterkaka Nunatak, mtn., Ant.	B15	7
Vosburg, S. Afr.	D3	49
Vosges, dept., Fr.	A2	20
Vosges, mts., Fr.	C7	16
Voskresensk, Sov. Un.	n18	27
Voss, Nor.	G2	14
Voss, N.D., U.S.	A8	111
Vossburg, Ms., U.S.	D5	101
Vostochnyy, Sov. Un.	B11	33
Vostok, sci., Ant.	B23	7
Vostok Island, i., Kir.	G12	6
Votaw, Tx., U.S.	D5	120
Votice, Czech.	D9	19
Votkinsk, Sov. Un.	B4	28
Vouga, stm., Port.	B1	22
Vouliagméni, Grc.	h11	25
Vouvray, Fr.	D4	16
Vouziers, Fr.	C6	16
Voyageurs National Park, Mn., U.S.	B5	100
Voyeykov Ice Shelf, ice, Ant.	C25	7
Vozhega, Sov. Un.	A13	27
Voznesensk, Sov. Un.	H8	27
Voznesenskoye, Sov. Un.	A8	33
Voznesenye, Sov. Un.	A10	27
Vrå, Den.	A3	15
Vranje, Yugo.	D5	24
Vratsa, Bul.	D6	24
Vrbas, Yugo.	C4	24
Vrbas, stm., Yugo.	C3	24
Vrchlabí, Czech.	C3	26
Vrede, S. Afr.	C5	49
Vreden, W. Ger.	A1	19
Vredenburgh, Al., U.S.	D2	78
Vreed en Hoop, Guy.	A3	59
Vrena, Swe.	u34	14
Vriezenveen, Neth.	B6	17
Vrigstad, Swe.	A8	15
Vrin, Switz.	C7	21
Vršac, Yugo.	C5	24
Vršovice (part of Prague), Czech.	n17	26
Vrútky, Czech.	D5	26
Vryburg, S. Afr.	C3	49
Vryheid, S. Afr.	C5	49
Všetaty, Czech.	n18	26
Vsetín, Czech.	D5	26
Vsevolozhsk, Sov. Un.	r31	14
Vuaqava, i., Fiji	I16	52
Vúcha, stm., Bul.	E7	24
Vuda Point, c., Fiji	H14	52
Vukovar, Yugo.	C4	24
Vulcan, Alta.	D4	68
Vulcan, Mi., U.S.	C3	99
Vulcan, Mo., U.S.	D7	102
Vulcano, i., Italy	E5	23
Vúlchedrúma, Bul.	D6	24
Vung Tau, Viet.	G7	35
Vung Tau, Cape, c., Viet.	G7	35
Vunidawa, Fiji	H15	52
Vuolvojarvi, Sov. Un.	r31	14
Vuoxa, stm., Fiji	H15	52
Vuya Point, c., Fiji	H14	52
Vyatka, stm., Sov. Un.	D7	29
Vyatskiye Polyany, Sov. Un.	C7	33
Vyazemskiy, Sov. Un.	C7	33
Vyazma, Sov. Un.	D10	27
Vyazniki, Sov. Un.	C14	27
Vyborg, Sov. Un.	A5	29
Vychegda, stm., Sov. Un.	C18	8
Vygozero, l., Sov. Un.	F16	14
Vyksa, Sov. Un.	D14	27
Vym, Sov. Un.	s31	14
Výrovka, stm., Czech.	n19	26
Vyshniy Volochek, Sov. Un.	C10	27
Vyškov, Czech.	D4	26
Vysočany (part of Prague), Czech.	n17	26
Vysoká, Czech.	n18	26
Vysoké Mýto, Czech.	D4	26
Vyšší Brod, Czech.	E9	19
Vytegra, Sov. Un.	C6	29

W

Name	Map Ref.	Page
Wa, Ghana	D4	45
Waal, stm., Neth.	B6	16
Waalwijk, Neth.	B6	16
Waawaa, Puu, mtn., Hi., U.S.	D6	88
Wabamun, Alta.	C3	68
Wabamun Lake, l., Alta.	C3	68
Wabana (Bell Island), Newf.	E5	72
Wabasca, Alta.	B4	68
Wabasca, stm., Alta.	f11	68
Wabash, Ar., U.S.	C5	81
Wabash, In., U.S.	C6	91
Wabash, Ne., U.S.	h12	104
Wabash, co., In., U.S.	C6	91
Wabash, co., Il., U.S.	E6	90
Wabasha, Mn., U.S.	F6	100
Wabasha, co., Mn., U.S.	F6	100
Wabasso, Fl., U.S.	E6	86
Wabasso, Mn., U.S.	F4	100
Wabaunsee, Ks., U.S.	C7	93
Wabaunsee, co., Ks., U.S.	D7	93
Wabeno, Wi., U.S.	C5	126
Wabigoon, Ont.	E5	70
Wabigoon Lake, l., Ont.	E5	70
Wabowden, Man.	B2	70
Wabrzeźno, Pol.	B5	26
Wabush, Newf.	h8	72
Wabuska, Nv., U.S.	D2	105
Waccamaw, stm., U.S.	D9	117
Waccamaw, Lake, l., N.C., U.S.	C4	110
Waccasassa Bay, b., Fl., U.S.	C4	86
Wachapreague, Va., U.S.	C7	123
Wachusett Mountain, mtn., Ma., U.S.	B4	98
Wachusett Reservoir, res., Ma., U.S.	B4	98
Wacissa, Fl., U.S.	B3	86
Wacker, Il., U.S.	C1	87
Waco, Ga., U.S.	g12	87
Waco, Ne., U.S.	D8	104
Waco, N.C., U.S.	B1	110
Waco, Tx., U.S.	D4	120
Waco Lake, res., Tx., U.S.	D4	120
Waconda Lake, res., Ks., U.S.	C5	93
Waconia, Mn., U.S.	F5	100
Waddān, Libya	D3	43
Waddān, Jabal, mtn., Libya	D3	43
Waddell, Az., U.S.	D3	80
Wadden Zee, Neth.	A6	16
Waddington, N.Y., U.S.	f9	109
Waddington, Mount, mtn., B.C.	D5	69
Waddy, Ky., U.S.	B4	94
Wade, N.C., U.S.	B4	110
Wade, Ok., U.S.	D5	113
Wade, Mount, mtn., Ant.	A32	7
Wade Hampton, S.C., U.S.	*B3	117
Wadena, Sask.	F4	75
Wadena, In., U.S.	C3	91
Wadena, Ia., U.S.	B6	92
Wadena, Mn., U.S.	D3	100
Wadena, co., Mn., U.S.	D4	100
Wädenswil, Switz.	B4	20
Wadesboro, N.C., U.S.	C2	110
Wadesville, In., U.S.	H2	91
Wadham Islands, is., Newf.	D5	72
Wadhwān see Surendranagar, India	F3	37
Wādī al Jayb (Ha Arava), val., Asia	G10	40
Wādī al Jōz (part of Jerusalem), Isr. Occ.	m14	41
Wading, stm., N.J., U.S.	D3	107
Wading, West Branch, stm., N.J., U.S.	C3	107
Wading River, N.J., U.S.	D4	107
Wading River, N.Y., U.S.	n16	109
Wadley, Al., U.S.	B4	78
Wadley, Ga., U.S.	D4	87
Wad Madani, Sud.	C3	47
Wadmalaw Island, i., S.C., U.S.	F7	117
Wadowice, Pol.	D5	26
Wadsworth, Al., U.S.	C3	78
Wadsworth, Il., U.S.	h9	90
Wadsworth, Nv., U.S.	D2	105
Wadsworth, Oh., U.S.	A4	112
Waelder, Tx., U.S.	E4	120
Wagarville, Al., U.S.	D1	78
Wagener, S.C., U.S.	D5	117
Wageningen, Sur.	A3	59
Wager Bay, b., N.W. Ter.	C15	66
Wagga, Sud.	B4	47
Wagga Wagga, Austl.	G8	50
Waggoner, Il., U.S.	D4	90
Waging [am See], W. Ger.	E6	18
Waginger Lake, l., W. Ger.	E6	18
Wägital Lake, l., Switz.	B6	21
Wagner, Mt., U.S.	B8	103
Wagner, S.D., U.S.	D7	118
Wagners Lake, Ne., U.S.	*C8	104
Wagoner, Ok., U.S.	B6	113
Wagoner, co., Ok., U.S.	B6	113
Wagon Mound, N.M., U.S.	A5	108
Wagontire Mountain, mtn., Or., U.S.	D7	114
Wagram, N.C., U.S.	C3	110
Wagrowiec, Pol.	B4	26
Waha, Libya	D3	43
Wahai, Indon.	F7	34
Wah Cantonment, Pak.	*B5	36
Wahiawa, Hi., U.S.	B3	88
Wahiawa Reservoir, res., Hi., U.S.	g9	88
Wahkiakum, co., Wa., U.S.	C2	124
Wahkon, Mn., U.S.	D5	100
Wahlern, Switz.	C3	21
Wahoo, Ne., U.S.	C9	104
Wahoo Creek, stm., Ne., U.S.	g11	104
Wahpeton, N.D., U.S.	C9	111
Wah Wah Mountains, mts., Ut., U.S.	E2	121
Wahweap Creek, stm., Ut., U.S.	F4	121
Waialua, Hi., U.S.	B3	88
Waialua Bay, b., Hi., U.S.	B3	88
Waianae, Hi., U.S.	B3	88
Waianae Range, mts., Hi., U.S.	f9	88
Waiau, stm., N.Z.	O14	51
Waiawa Stream, stm., Hi., U.S.	g10	88
Waiblingen, W. Ger.	E4	19
Waidhofen [an der Thaya], Aus.	D7	18
Waigeo, i., Indon.	F8	34
Wai Islands, is., Camb.	H5	35
Waikabubak, Indon.	G5	34
Waikari, N.Z.	O14	51
Waikato, stm., N.Z.	L15	51
Waikawa, N.Z.	Q12	51
Waikelo, Indon.	G5	34
Waikerie, Austl.	G2	51
Waikiki Beach, Hi., U.S.	g10	88
Wailagi Lala, i., Fiji	H16	52
Wailea, Hi., U.S.	D6	88
Wailua, Hi., U.S.	A2	88
Wailuku, Hi., U.S.	C5	88
Wailuku, stm., Hi., U.S.	D6	88
Waimanalo, Hi., U.S.	B4	88
Waimanalo Bay, b., Hi., U.S.	g11	88
Waimate, N.Z.	P13	51
Waimea, Hi., U.S.	A2	88
Waimea, Hi., U.S.	C5	88
Wainganga, stm., India	G6	34
Waini Point, c., Guy.	A3	59
Wainunu Bay, b., Fiji	H15	52
Wainwright, Alta.	C5	68
Wainwright, Ak., U.S.	A8	79
Wainwright, Oh., U.S.	B4	112
Wainwright, Ok., U.S.	B6	113
Waiohinu, Hi., U.S.	D6	88
Waipahu, Hi., U.S.	B3	88
Waipara, N.Z.	O14	51
Waipawa, N.Z.	M16	51
Waipio Acres, Hi., U.S.	g9	88
Waipio Peninsula, pen., Hi., U.S.	g10	88
Waipukurau, N.Z.	N16	51
Wairau, stm., N.Z.	N14	51
Wairoa, N.Z.	M16	51
Waitaki, stm., N.Z.	P13	51
Waitara, N.Z.	M15	51
Waite, Me., U.S.	C5	96
Waite Park, Mn., U.S.	E4	100
Waiteville, W.V., U.S.	D4	125
Waits, stm., Vt., U.S.	C4	122
Waits River, Vt., U.S.	C4	122
Waitsburg, Wa., U.S.	C7	124
Waitsfield, Vt., U.S.	C3	122
Waiwo, Indon.	F8	34
Wajima, Japan	H8	33
Wajir, Kenya	A7	48
Waka, Eth.	D4	47
Waka, Tx., U.S.	A2	120
Waka, Zaire	A3	48
Wakarusa, In., U.S.	A5	91
Wakarusa, Ks., U.S.	D8	93
Wakarusa, stm., Ks., U.S.	D8	93
Wakasa Bay, b., Japan	I7	33
Wakatipu, Lake, l., N.Z.	P12	51
Wakatomika Creek, stm., Oh., U.S.	B3	112
Wakaw, Sask.	E3	75
Wakayama, Japan	E12	31
Wakaya, i., Fiji	H15	52
Wake, co., N.C., U.S.	B4	110
Wa Keeney, Ks., U.S.	C4	93
Wakefield, Que.	D2	74
Wakefield, Eng., U.K.	A6	12
Wakefield, Ks., U.S.	C6	93
Wakefield, La., U.S.	D4	95
Wakefield, Ma., U.S.	B5	98
Wakefield, Mi., U.S.	n12	99
Wakefield, Ne., U.S.	B9	104
Wakefield, N.H., U.S.	C4	106
Wakefield, Oh., U.S.	D2	112
Wakefield, R.I., U.S.	F3	116
Wakefield, Va., U.S.	D6	123
Wake Forest, N.C., U.S.	B4	110
Wake Island, dep., Oc.	E10	6
Wake Island Air Force Base, mil., Wake I.	B2	52
Wake Lagoon, b., Wake I.	B2	52
Wakeman, Oh., U.S.	A3	112
Wakenda, Mo., U.S.	B4	102
Wakerstroom, S. Afr.	C5	49
Wakita, Ok., U.S.	A4	113
Wakkanai, Japan	B13	31
Wakonda, S.D., U.S.	D8	118
Wakopa, Man.	E2	70
Wakpala, S.D., U.S.	B5	118
Wakuach, Lac, l., Que.	g8	72
Waku Kungo, Ang.	D2	48
Wakulla, Fl., U.S.	B2	86
Wakulla, co., Fl., U.S.	B2	86
Walachia, hist. reg., Rom.	C7	24
Walbridge, Oh., U.S.	e6	112
Walbrzych (Waldenburg), Pol.	C4	26
Walchen Lake, l., W. Ger.	B7	20
Walcott, Ia., U.S.	C7	92
Walcott, N.D., U.S.	C9	111
Walcott, Wy., U.S.	E6	127
Walcott, Lake, res., Id., U.S.	G5	89
Walden, Co., U.S.	A4	83
Walden, N.Y., U.S.	D6	109
Walden Pond, l., Ma., U.S.	g10	98
Walden Ridge, mtn., Tn., U.S.	D8	119
Waldheim, Sask.	E2	75
Waldheim, E. Ger.	B8	19
Waldkappel, W. Ger.	C4	19
Waldkirchen, W. Ger.	E8	19
Waldmünchen, W. Ger.	D7	19
Waldnaab, stm., W. Ger.	D7	19
Waldo, B.C.	E10	69
Waldo, Ar., U.S.	D2	81
Waldo, Fl., U.S.	C4	86
Waldo, Ks., U.S.	C5	93
Waldo, Me., U.S.	D3	96
Waldo, Oh., U.S.	B2	112
Waldo, co., Me., U.S.	D3	96
Waldo Lake, l., Or., U.S.	D4	114
Waldorf, Md., U.S.	C4	97
Waldport, Or., U.S.	C2	114
Waldron, Sask.	G4	75
Waldron, Ar., U.S.	C1	81
Waldron, In., U.S.	F6	91
Waldron, Ks., U.S.	E5	93
Waldron, Mi., U.S.	G6	99
Waldron, Mo., U.S.	h10	102
Waldsassen, W. Ger.	C7	19
Waldshut, W. Ger.	E4	18
Waldwick, N.J., U.S.	A4	107
Walen, l., Switz.	B5	20
Wales, Ak., U.S.	B6	79
Wales, N.D., U.S.	A7	111
Wales, Ut., U.S.	D4	121
Wales, ter., U.K.	D5	10
Waleska, Ga., U.S.	B2	87
Walford Station, Ont.	A2	73
Walgett, Austl.	E8	50
Walgreen Coast, Ant.	B2	7
Walhalla, N.D., U.S.	A8	111
Walhalla, S.C., U.S.	B1	117
Walhonding, stm., Oh., U.S.	B3	112
Walikale, Zaire	B5	48
Walker, La., U.S.	g10	95
Walker, Mn., U.S.	C4	100
Walker, Mo., U.S.	D3	102
Walker, S.D., U.S.	C5	91
Walker, co., Al., U.S.	B2	78
Walker, co., Ga., U.S.	B1	87
Walker, co., Tx., U.S.	D5	120
Walker, stm., Nv., U.S.	D3	105
Walker Lake, l., Man.	B3	70
Walker Lake, l., Nv., U.S.	E3	105
Walker Mill, Md., U.S.	*C4	97
Walker Mountain, mtn., Ga., U.S.	g9	87
Walker Mountain, mtn., Va., U.S.	C1	123
Walker River Indian Reservation, Nv., U.S.	D3	105
Walkersville, Md., U.S.	B3	97
Walkersville, W.V., U.S.	C4	125
Walkerton, Ont.	C3	73
Walkerton, In., U.S.	B5	91
Walkertown, N.C., U.S.	A2	110
Walkerville, Mi., U.S.	E4	99
Walkerville, Mt., U.S.	D4	103
Wall, S.D., U.S.	D3	118
Wallace, N.S.	D6	71
Wallace, Id., U.S.	B3	89
Wallace, Ks., U.S.	D2	93
Wallace, Mi., U.S.	C3	99
Wallace, N.Y., U.S.	C3	109
Wallace, N.C., U.S.	C5	110
Wallace, S.D., U.S.	B8	118
Wallace, Va., U.S.	f9	123
Wallace, W.V., U.S.	B4	125
Wallace, co., Ks., U.S.	D2	93
Wallaceburg, Ont.	E2	73
Wallacetown, Ont.	E3	73
Wallagrass, Me., U.S.	A4	96
Wallal, Tn., U.S.	D10	119
Wallaroo, Austl.	F6	50
Wallasey, Eng., U.K.	D5	10
Walled Lake, Mi., U.S.	o15	99
Wallen, In., U.S.	B7	91
Wallenpaupack, Lake, l., Pa., U.S.	D11	115
Wallen Ridge, mtn., Tn., U.S.	C10	119
Waller, Tx., U.S.	q14	120
Waller, co., Tx., U.S.	E4	120
Wallingford, Eng., U.K.	C6	12
Wallingford, Ct., U.S.	D4	84
Wallingford, Vt., U.S.	E3	122
Walling Mountain, mtn., Ma., U.S.	B1	98
Wallington, N.J., U.S.	h8	107
Wallis, Tx., U.S.	E4	120
Wallis and Futuna, dep., Oc.	G11	6
Wallis Sands, N.H., U.S.	D5	106
Wallkill, N.Y., U.S.	D6	109
Wallkill, stm., N.Y., U.S.	D6	109
Wall Lake, Ia., U.S.	B2	92
Walloomsac, stm., U.S.	F2	122
Walloon Lake, l., Mi., U.S.	C6	99
Wallowa, Or., U.S.	B9	114
Wallowa, co., Or., U.S.	B9	114
Wallowa Mountains, mts., Or., U.S.	B9	114
Wallpack Center, N.J., U.S.	A3	107
Walls, Ms., U.S.	A3	101
Wallsburg, Ut., U.S.	C4	121
Wallsend, Eng., U.K.	C6	10
Wallula, Wa., U.S.	C7	124
Wallula, Lake, res., U.S.	C7	124
Wallum Lake, l., U.S.	A1	116
Walney, Isle of, i., Eng., U.K.	C5	10
Walnut, Il., U.S.	B4	90
Walnut, Ia., U.S.	C2	92
Walnut, Ks., U.S.	E8	93
Walnut, Ms., U.S.	A5	101
Walnut, N.C., U.S.	f10	110
Walnut, stm., Ks., U.S.	E6	93
Walnut Bottom, Pa., U.S.	F7	115
Walnut Canyon National Monument, Az., U.S.	B4	80
Walnut Cove, N.C., U.S.	A2	110
Walnut Creek, Ca., U.S.	h8	82
Walnut Creek, stm., Ks., U.S.	D4	93
Walnut Creek West, Ca., U.S.	*D2	82
Walnut Grove, Al., U.S.	A3	78
Walnut Grove, Mn., U.S.	F3	100
Walnut Grove, Mo., U.S.	D4	102
Walnut Hill, Fl., U.S.	u14	86
Walnut Hill, Ma., U.S.	g7	98
Walnut Hill, hill, Ct., U.S.	B3	84
Walnut Park, Ca., U.S.	*n12	82
Walnut Ridge, Ar., U.S.	A5	81
Walnutport, Pa., U.S.	E10	115
Walpole, N.H., U.S.	D2	106
Walpole, Ma., U.S.	B5	98
Walsall, Eng., U.K.	D6	10
Walsenburg, Co., U.S.	D6	83
Walsh, Alta.	E5	68
Walsh, Co., U.S.	D8	83
Walsh, co., N.D., U.S.	A8	111
Walsingham, Cape, c., N.W. Ter.	C20	66
Walsrode, W. Ger.	B3	15
Walter Bathurst, Cape, c., N.W. Ter.	B17	66
Walterboro, S.C., U.S.	F6	117
Walter F. George Dam, U.S.	D4	78
Walter F. George Lake, res., U.S.	D4	78
Walterhill, Tn., U.S.	B5	119
Walters, La., U.S.	C4	95
Walters, Mn., U.S.	G5	100
Walters, Ok., U.S.	C3	113
Walters, Va., U.S.	D6	123
Walters Falls, Ont.	C4	73
Waltershausen, E. Ger.	C5	19
Walterville, Or., U.S.	C4	114
Walthall, Ms., U.S.	B4	101
Walthall, co., Ms., U.S.	D3	101
Waltham, Me., U.S.	D4	96
Waltham, Ma., U.S.	B5	98
Waltham Station, Que.	B8	73
Walthourville, Ga., U.S.	E5	87
Walton, Ont.	D3	73
Walton, In., U.S.	C5	91

Name	Map Ref.	Page
Walton, Ks., U.S.	D6	93
Walton, Ky., U.S.	B5	94
Walton, Ne., U.S.	h11	104
Walton, N.Y., U.S.	C5	109
Walton, W.V., U.S.	C3	125
Walton, co., Fl., U.S.	u15	86
Walton, co., Ga., U.S.	C3	87
Waltonville, Il., U.S.	E4	90
Walvisbaai (Walvis Bay), S. Afr.	B1	49
Walvis Bay see Walvisbaai, S. Afr.	B1	49
Walworth, N.Y., U.S.	B3	109
Walworth, Wi., U.S.	F5	126
Walworth, co., S.D., U.S.	B5	118
Walworth, co., Wi., U.S.	F5	126
Wamac, Il., U.S.	E4	90
Wamba, Nig.	E6	45
Wamba, Zaire	A4	48
Wamba, stm., Afr.	C2	48
Wamego, Ks., U.S.	C7	93
Wamesit, Ma., U.S.	A5	98
Wami, stm., Tan.	C6	48
Wamic, Or., U.S.	B5	114
Wampsville, N.Y., U.S.	B5	109
Wampum, Pa., U.S.	E1	115
Wamsutter, Wy., U.S.	E5	127
Wāna, Pak.	B4	36
Wanaka, N.Z.	P12	51
Wanaka, Lake, l., N.Z.	P12	51
Wanakena, N.Y., U.S.	A6	109
Wanamie, Pa., U.S.	D9	115
Wanamingo, Mn., U.S.	F6	100
Wan'an, China	K6	32
Wanapitei, l., Ont.	A4	73
Wanapum Dam, Wa., U.S.	C6	124
Wanapum Lake, res., Wa., U.S.	B6	124
Wanaque, N.J., U.S.	A4	107
Wanaque Reservoir, res., N.J., U.S.	A4	107
Wanatah, In., U.S.	B4	91
Wanblee, S.D., U.S.	D4	118
Wanchese, N.C., U.S.	B7	110
Wanda, Mn., U.S.	F3	100
Wandering River, Alta.	B4	68
Wando, S. Kor.	I3	33
Wando, S.C., U.S.	F8	117
Wando, stm., S.C., U.S.	F8	117
Wandoan, Austl.	C7	51
Wando Woods, S.C., U.S.	k11	117
Wandsworth (part of London), Eng., U.K.	m12	10
Wanette, Ok., U.S.	C4	113
Wang, stm., Thai.	D3	35
Wanganui, N.Z.	M15	51
Wangaratta, Austl.	G8	50
Wangen [im Allgäu], W. Ger.	B5	20
Wangerooge, i., W. Ger.	B3	18
Wangkui, China	A12	32
Wangqing, China	C10	31
Wanham, Alta.	B1	68
Wanilla, Ms., U.S.	D3	101
Wanipigow, stm., Can.	D4	70
Wankie National Park, Zimb.	A4	49
Wann, Ne., U.S.	g12	104
Wann, Ok., U.S.	A6	113
Wannaska, Mn., U.S.	B3	100
Wanship, Ut., U.S.	C4	121
Wantage, Eng., U.K.	C6	12
Wantagh, N.Y., U.S.	*E7	109
Wanup, Ont.	A4	73
Wanxian, China	E6	31
Wanzai, China	J6	32
Wapakoneta, Oh., U.S.	B1	112
Wapanucka, Ok., U.S.	C5	113
Wapato, Wa., U.S.	C5	124
Wapawekka Hills, hills, Sask.	C3	75
Wapawekka Lake, l., Sask.	C3	75
Wapella, Sask.	G5	75
Wapella, Il., U.S.	C5	90
Wapello, Ia., U.S.	C6	92
Wapello, co., Ia., U.S.	C5	92
Wapisu Lake, l., Man.	B2	70
Wapiti, Wy., U.S.	B3	127
Wapiti, stm., Can.	B1	68
Wapiti Ridge, mtn., Wy., U.S.	B3	127
Wappapello, Mo., U.S.	E7	102
Wappapello, Lake, res., Mo., U.S.	D7	102
Wappingers Falls, N.Y., U.S.	D7	109
Wapsipinicon, stm., Ia., U.S.	B6	92
Wapske, N.B.	C2	71
Wapus Lake, l., Sask.	A4	75
Wapwallopen, Pa., U.S.	D9	115
Wāqid, Eg.	D2	41
Waqqāş, Jord.	B7	41
Waquoit, Ma., U.S.	C6	98
War, W.V., U.S.	D3	125
Waramaug, Lake, l., Ct., U.S.	C2	84
Warangal, India	E6	36
Warba, Mn., U.S.	C5	100
Warburg, Alta.	C3	68
Warburg, W. Ger.	B4	19
Warburton, Austl.	H5	51
Warburton Creek, stm., Austl.	E6	50
Ward, Al., U.S.	C1	78
Ward, Ar., U.S.	B4	81
Ward, co., U.S.	*A5	83
Ward, S.C., U.S.	D4	117
Ward, S.D., U.S.	C9	118
Ward, co., N.D., U.S.	A4	111
Ward, co., Tx., U.S.	D1	120
Ward, Mount, mtn., Ant.	B6	7
Wardell, Mo., U.S.	E8	102
Warden, Alta.	C4	68
Warden, Que.	D5	74
Warden, Wa., U.S.	B4	95
Warden, Wa., U.S.	C6	124
Wardensville, W.V., U.S.	B6	125
Warder, l., W. Ger.	E4	15
Wardha, India	D6	36
Wardha, stm., India	D6	36
Ward Hill, hill, Scot., U.K.	B5	13
Wardlow, Alta.	D5	68
Ward Mountain, mtn., Mt., U.S.	D2	103
Wardner, B.C.	E10	69
Wardner, Id., U.S.	B2	89
Wardsboro, Vt., U.S.	E3	122
Wardsville, Ont.	E3	73
Wardville, Ok., U.S.	C5	113
Ware, Ma., U.S.	B3	98
Ware, co., Ga., U.S.	E4	87
Ware, stm., Ma., U.S.	B3	98
War Eagle, W.V., U.S.	D3	125
War Eagle Creek, stm., Ar., U.S.	A2	81
War Eagle Mountain, mtn., Id., U.S.	G2	89
Wareham, Eng., U.K.	D5	12
Wareham, Ma., U.S.	C6	98
Warehouse Point, Ct., U.S.	B5	84
Waren, E. Ger.	B6	18
Waren, Indon.	F9	34
Warendorf, W. Ger.	B2	19
Waresboro, Ga., U.S.	E4	87
Ware Shoals, S.C., U.S.	C3	117
Waretown, N.J., U.S.	D4	107
Warfield, B.C.	E9	69
Warfield, Ky., U.S.	C7	94
Warfield, Va., U.S.	D5	123
Warfordsburg, Pa., U.S.	G5	115
Warin, Alg.	C6	44
Warin, E. Ger.	E5	15
Waring, Tx., U.S.	E3	120
Wark, Eng., U.K.	E6	13
Warkworth, Ont.	C7	73
Warkworth, N.Z.	L15	51
Warley see Smethwick, Eng., U.K.	D5	10
Warman, Sask.	E2	75
Warmbad, Nmb.	C2	49
Warm Beach, Wa., U.S.	A3	124
Warminster, Eng., U.K.	C5	12
Warminster, Pa., U.S.	F11	115
Warm Lake, Id., U.S.	E3	89
Warm River, Id., U.S.	E7	89
Warm Springs, Ar., U.S.	A4	81
Warm Springs, Ga., U.S.	D2	87
Warm Springs, Nv., U.S.	E5	105
Warm Springs, Va., U.S.	B3	123
Warm Springs Indian Reservation, Or., U.S.	C5	114
Warm Springs Reservoir, res., Or., U.S.	D8	114
Warner, Alta.	E4	68
Warner, N.H., U.S.	D3	106
Warner, Oh., U.S.	C4	112
Warner, Ok., U.S.	B6	113
Warner, S.D., U.S.	B7	118
Warner, stm., N.H., U.S.	D3	106
Warner Mountain, mtn., Ma., U.S.	B1	98
Warner Mountains, mts., Ca., U.S.	B3	82
Warner Peak, mtn., Or., U.S.	E7	114
Warner Robins, Ga., U.S.	D3	87
Warner Springs, Ca., U.S.	F5	82
Warnes, Bol.	C3	55
Warnow, stm., E. Ger.	B5	18
Warracknabeal, Austl.	H4	51
Warragul, Austl.	I5	51
Warrego, stm., Austl.	E8	50
Warren, Austl.	E6	51
Warren, Ont.	A4	73
Warren, Ct., U.S.	C2	84
Warren, Id., U.S.	D3	89
Warren, Il., U.S.	A4	90
Warren, In., U.S.	C7	91
Warren, Me., U.S.	D3	96
Warren, Ma., U.S.	B3	98
Warren, Mi., U.S.	F7	99
Warren, Mn., U.S.	B2	100
Warren, N.H., U.S.	C3	106
Warren, Oh., U.S.	A5	112
Warren, Ok., U.S.	C2	113
Warren, Or., U.S.	B4	114
Warren, Pa., U.S.	C3	115
Warren, R.I., U.S.	D5	116
Warren, Tx., U.S.	D5	120
Warren, Vt., U.S.	C3	122
Warren, co., Ga., U.S.	C4	87
Warren, co., Il., U.S.	C3	90
Warren, co., In., U.S.	D3	91
Warren, co., Ia., U.S.	C4	92
Warren, co., Ky., U.S.	C3	94
Warren, co., Ms., U.S.	C3	101
Warren, co., Mo., U.S.	C6	102
Warren, co., N.J., U.S.	B3	107
Warren, co., N.Y., U.S.	B7	109
Warren, co., N.C., U.S.	A4	110
Warren, co., Oh., U.S.	C1	112
Warren, co., Pa., U.S.	C3	115
Warren, co., Tn., U.S.	D8	119
Warren, co., Va., U.S.	B4	123
Warren, stm., U.S.	D5	116
Warren Center, Pa., U.S.	C9	115
Warrendale, Pa., U.S.	h13	115
Warren Park, In., U.S.	k10	91
Warren Peaks, mts., Wy., U.S.	B8	127
Warrenpoint, N. Ire., U.K.	C5	11
Warren Point, R.I., U.S.	F6	116
Warrens, Wi., U.S.	D3	126
Warrensburg, Il., U.S.	D4	90
Warrensburg, Mo., U.S.	C4	102
Warrensburg, N.Y., U.S.	B7	109
Warrensburg, Tn., U.S.	C10	119
Warrensville, Pa., U.S.	D8	115
Warrensville Heights, Oh., U.S.	h9	112
Warrenton, S. Afr.	C3	49
Warrenton, Ga., U.S.	C4	87
Warrenton, Mo., U.S.	C6	102
Warrenton, N.C., U.S.	A4	110
Warrenton, Or., U.S.	A3	114
Warrenton, Va., U.S.	B5	123
Warrenville, Ct., U.S.	B7	84
Warrenville, Il., U.S.	k8	90
Warrenville, S.C., U.S.	D4	117
Warri, Nig.	E6	45
Warrick, co., In., U.S.	H3	91
Warrington, Eng., U.K.	D5	10
Warrington, Fl., U.S.	u14	86
Warrior, Al., U.S.	B3	78
Warrior Mountain, mtn., Md., U.S.	k13	97
Warrior Reservoir, res., Al., U.S.	C2	78
Warriors Mark, Pa., U.S.	E5	115
Warrnambool, Austl.	G7	50
Warroad, Mn., U.S.	B3	100
Warsaw (Warszawa), Pol.	B6	26
Warsaw, Il., U.S.	C2	90
Warsaw, In., U.S.	B6	91
Warsaw, Ky., U.S.	B5	94
Warsaw, Mo., U.S.	C4	102
Warsaw, N.Y., U.S.	C2	109
Warsaw, N.C., U.S.	B4	110
Warsaw, Oh., U.S.	B3	112
Warsaw, Va., U.S.	C6	123
Warspite, Alta.	B4	68
Warstein, W. Ger.	B3	19
Warta, Pol.	C5	26
Warta, stm., Pol.	B3	26
Wartburg, Tn., U.S.	C9	119
Warth, Aus.	B6	20
Warthen, Ga., U.S.	C4	87
Wartime, Sask.	F1	75
Wartrace, Tn., U.S.	B5	119
Warwick, Austl.	D8	51
Warwick, Ont.	D3	73
Warwick, Que.	D6	74
Warwick, Eng., U.K.	D6	10
Warwick, Ga., U.S.	E3	87
Warwick, Md., U.S.	B6	97
Warwick, N.Y., U.S.	D6	109
Warwick, N.D., U.S.	B7	111
Warwick, R.I., U.S.	D4	116
Warwick, Pa., U.S.	F10	115
Warwick Dam, Ga., U.S.	E3	87
Warwickshire, co., Eng., U.K.	B6	12
Wasaga Beach, Ont.	C4	73
Wasatch, co., Ut., U.S.	C4	121
Wasatch Plateau, plat., Ut., U.S.	D4	121
Wasatch Range, mts., U.S.	B5	76
Wascana Creek, stm., Sask.	G3	75
Wasco, Ca., U.S.	E4	82
Wasco, Or., U.S.	B5	114
Wasco, co., Or., U.S.	B5	114
Waseca, Sask.	D1	75
Waseca, Mn., U.S.	F5	100
Waseca, co., Mn., U.S.	F5	100
Washago, Ont.	C5	73
Washakie, co., Wy., U.S.	C4	127
Washakie Needles, mts., Wy., U.S.	C3	127
Washburn, Il., U.S.	C4	90
Washburn, Ia., U.S.	B5	92
Washburn, Me., U.S.	B4	96
Washburn, Mo., U.S.	E4	102
Washburn, N.D., U.S.	B5	111
Washburn, Tn., U.S.	C10	119
Washburn, Wi., U.S.	B3	126
Washburn, co., Wi., U.S.	C2	126
Washburn, Mount, mtn., Wy., U.S.	B2	127
Wāshīm, India	G6	37
Washington, Ar., U.S.	D2	81
Washington, Ct., U.S.	C2	84
Washington, D.C., U.S.	C3	97
Washington, Ga., U.S.	C4	87
Washington, Il., U.S.	C4	90
Washington, In., U.S.	G3	91
Washington, Ia., U.S.	C6	92
Washington, Ks., U.S.	C6	93
Washington, Ky., U.S.	B6	94
Washington, La., U.S.	D3	95
Washington, Ma., U.S.	B1	98
Washington, Ms., U.S.	D2	101
Washington, Mo., U.S.	C6	102
Washington, Ne., U.S.	g12	104
Washington, N.H., U.S.	D2	106
Washington, N.J., U.S.	B3	107
Washington, N.C., U.S.	B5	110
Washington, Ok., U.S.	B4	113
Washington, Pa., U.S.	F1	115
Washington, Tn., U.S.	D9	119
Washington, Ut., U.S.	F2	121
Washington, Vt., U.S.	C4	122
Washington, Va., U.S.	B4	123
Washington, W.V., U.S.	B3	125
Washington, co., Al., U.S.	D1	78
Washington, co., Ar., U.S.	A1	81
Washington, co., Co., U.S.	B7	83
Washington, co., Fl., U.S.	u16	86
Washington, co., Ga., U.S.	C4	87
Washington, co., Id., U.S.	E2	89
Washington, co., Il., U.S.	E4	90
Washington, co., In., U.S.	G5	91
Washington, co., Ia., U.S.	C6	92
Washington, co., Ks., U.S.	C6	93
Washington, co., Ky., U.S.	C4	94
Washington, co., La., U.S.	D5	95
Washington, co., Me., U.S.	D5	96
Washington, co., Md., U.S.	A2	97
Washington, co., Mn., U.S.	E6	100
Washington, co., Ms., U.S.	B3	101
Washington, co., Mo., U.S.	D7	102
Washington, co., Ne., U.S.	C9	104
Washington, co., N.Y., U.S.	B7	109
Washington, co., N.C., U.S.	B6	110
Washington, co., Oh., U.S.	C4	112
Washington, co., Ok., U.S.	A6	113
Washington, co., Or., U.S.	B3	114
Washington, co., Pa., U.S.	F1	115
Washington, co., R.I., U.S.	E2	116
Washington, co., Tn., U.S.	C11	119
Washington, co., Tx., U.S.	D4	120
Washington, co., Ut., U.S.	F2	121
Washington, co., Vt., U.S.	C3	122
Washington, co., Va., U.S.	f9	123
Washington, co., Wi., U.S.	E5	126
Washington, state, U.S.	B5	124
Washington, Cape, c., Fiji	I14	52
Washington, Lake, l., Fl., U.S.	D6	86
Washington, Lake, l., Mn., U.S.	E4	100
Washington, Lake, l., Ms., U.S.	B3	101
Washington, Lake, l., Wa., U.S.	e11	124
Washington, Mount, mtn., N.H., U.S.	B4	106
Washington Court House, Oh., U.S.	C2	112
Washington Crossing, N.J., U.S.	C3	107
Washington Depot, Ct., U.S.	C2	84
Washington Island, i., Wi., U.S.	C7	126
Washington Island see Teraina Island, i., Kir.	F12	6
Washington Park, Fl., U.S.	*F6	86
Washington Park, Il., U.S.	E3	90
Washington Terrace, Ut., U.S.	B4	121
Washington Township, N.J., U.S.	*B4	107
Washingtonville, Pa., U.S.	D8	115
Washingtonville, Oh., U.S.	B5	112
Washita, co., Ok., U.S.	B2	113
Washita, stm., Ok., U.S.	C4	113
Washoe, co., Nv., U.S.	C2	105
Washoe City, Nv., U.S.	D2	105
Washougal, Wa., U.S.	D3	124
Washow Bay, b., Man.	D3	70
Washta, Ia., U.S.	B2	92
Washtenaw, co., Mi., U.S.	F7	99
Washtucna, Wa., U.S.	C7	124
Wasque Point, c., Ma., U.S.	D7	98
Wassaw Sound, strt., Ga., U.S.	E6	87
Wassenaar, Neth.	B4	17
Wasseralfingen [am Inn], W. Ger.	E5	19
Wasserburg [am Inn], W. Ger.	D6	18
Wasserkuppe, mtn., W. Ger.	C3	18
Wass Lake, l., Man.	C4	70
Wasson, Il., U.S.	F5	90
Wassookeag, Lake, l., Me., U.S.	C3	96
Wassuk Range, mts., Nv., U.S.	E3	105
Wassy-sur-Blaise, Fr.	F4	17
Wasta, S.D., U.S.	C3	118
Waswanipi, Que.	o20	73
Wataga, Il., U.S.	B3	90
Watampone, Indon.	F6	34
Watapi Lake, l., Sask.	B6	68
Watatic, Mount, mtn., Ma., U.S.	A4	98
Watauga, S.D., U.S.	B4	118
Watauga, Tn., U.S.	C11	119
Watauga, Tx., U.S.	*n9	120
Watauga, co., N.C., U.S.	A1	110
Watauga, stm., Tn., U.S.	C12	119
Watauga Lake, res., Tn., U.S.	C12	119
Watchaug Pond, l., R.I., U.S.	F2	116
Watchet, Eng., U.K.	C4	12
Watch Hill, R.I., U.S.	G1	116
Watch Hill Point, c., R.I., U.S.	G1	116
Watchung, N.J., U.S.	B4	107
Waterboro, Me., U.S.	E2	96
Waterbury, Ct., U.S.	C3	84
Waterbury, Ne., U.S.	B9	104
Waterbury, Vt., U.S.	C3	122
Waterbury Center, Vt., U.S.	C3	122
Waterbury Reservoir, res., Vt., U.S.	C3	122
Waterdown, Ont.	D5	73
Wateree, stm., S.C., U.S.	D6	117
Wateree Lake, res., S.C., U.S.	C6	117
Waterfall, Ak., U.S.	n23	79
Waterflow, N.M., U.S.	A1	108
Waterford, Ont.	E4	73
Waterford, Ire.	D3	10
Waterford, Ct., U.S.	D7	84
Waterford, Ire.	I5	11
Waterford, Mi., U.S.	*F7	99
Waterford, Ms., U.S.	A4	101
Waterford, N.Y., U.S.	C7	109
Waterford, Oh., U.S.	C4	112
Waterford, Pa., U.S.	C2	115
Waterford, Va., U.S.	A5	123
Waterford, Wi., U.S.	F5	126
Waterford, co., Ire.	I5	11
Waterford Harbour, b., Ire.	I6	11
Waterford Mills, In., U.S.	A6	91
Waterford Works, N.J., U.S.	D3	107
Watergrasshill, Ire.	E3	11
Waterhen Lake, l., Man.	C2	70
Waterloo, Bel.	D4	17
Waterloo, Ont.	D4	73
Waterloo, Que.	D5	74
Waterloo, S.L.	E2	45
Waterloo, Al., U.S.	A1	78
Waterloo, Ar., U.S.	D2	81
Waterloo, Il., U.S.	E3	90
Waterloo, In., U.S.	B7	91
Waterloo, Ia., U.S.	B5	92
Waterloo, Ks., U.S.	g11	93
Waterloo, Mt., U.S.	E4	103
Waterloo, Ne., U.S.	g12	104
Waterloo, N.Y., U.S.	C4	109
Waterloo, Or., U.S.	C4	114
Waterloo, S.C., U.S.	C3	117
Waterloo, Wi., U.S.	E5	126
Waterloo, co., Ont.	D4	73
Waterman, Il., U.S.	B5	90
Waterman Four Corners, R.I., U.S.	C3	116
Waterman Reservoir, res., R.I., U.S.	B3	116
Waterproof, La., U.S.	C4	95
Waters, Mi., U.S.	D6	99
Watersmeet, Mi., U.S.	n12	99
Waterton, stm., N.A.	E4	68
Waterton-Glacier International Peace Park, N.A.	B3	103
Waterton Lakes National Park, Alta.	E3	68
Waterton Park, Alta.	E3	68
Watertown, Ct., U.S.	C3	84
Watertown, Fl., U.S.	B4	86
Watertown, Ma., U.S.	g11	98
Watertown, N.Y., U.S.	B5	109
Watertown, S.D., U.S.	C8	118
Watertown, Tn., U.S.	A5	119
Watertown, Wi., U.S.	E5	126
Water Valley, Ky., U.S.	f9	94
Water Valley, Ms., U.S.	A4	101
Water Valley, Tx., U.S.	D2	120
Water View, Va., U.S.	C6	123
Water Village, N.H., U.S.	C4	106
Waterville, N.S.	D5	71
Waterville, Ire.	F1	11
Waterville, Ia., U.S.	A6	92
Waterville, Ks., U.S.	C7	93
Waterville, Me., U.S.	D3	96
Waterville, Mn., U.S.	F5	100
Waterville, N.Y., U.S.	C5	109
Waterville, Oh., U.S.	A2	112
Waterville, Pa., U.S.	D7	115
Waterville, Vt., U.S.	B3	122
Waterville, Wa., U.S.	B5	124
Waterville Valley, N.H., U.S.	C3	106
Watervliet, Bel.	C3	17
Watervliet, Mi., U.S.	F4	99
Watervliet, N.Y., U.S.	C7	109
Watford, Eng., U.K.	k12	10
Watford City, N.D., U.S.	B2	111
Watha, N.C., U.S.	C4	110
Wathena, Ks., U.S.	C9	93
Watino, Alta.	B2	68
Watkins, Co., U.S.	*B6	83
Watkins, Mn., U.S.	E4	100
Watkins Glen, N.Y., U.S.	C4	109
Watkinsville, Ga., U.S.	C3	87
Watonga, Ok., U.S.	B3	113
Watonwan, co., Mn., U.S.	F4	100
Watonwan, stm., Mn., U.S.	G4	100
Watou, Bel.	D2	17
Watova, Ok., U.S.	A6	113
Watrous, Sask.	F3	75
Watrous, N.M., U.S.	A5	108
Watsa, Zaire	A4	48
Watseka, Il., U.S.	C6	90
Watson, Sask.	E3	75
Watson, Ar., U.S.	D4	81
Watson, Il., U.S.	D5	90
Watson, In., U.S.	H6	91
Watson, Mn., U.S.	E3	100
Watson, Mo., U.S.	A2	102
Watson, Ok., U.S.	C7	113
Watson Chapel, Ar., U.S.	C3	81
Watson Lake, Yukon	D7	66
Watsontown, Pa., U.S.	D8	115
Watsonville, Ca., U.S.	D3	82
Watten, Fr.	D10	17
Watten, Fr.	D2	17
Watten, Loch, l., Scot., U.K.	B5	13
Wattenberg, Co., U.S.	A6	83
Wattensaw Bayou, stm., Ar., U.S.	C4	81
Watton, Mi., U.S.	B2	99
Wattrelos, Fr.	B5	16
Watts, Ok., U.S.	A7	113
Watts (part of Los Angeles), Ca., U.S.	n12	82
Watts Bar Dam, Tn., U.S.	D9	119
Watts Bar Lake, res., Tn., U.S.	D9	119
Wattsburg, Pa., U.S.	B2	115
Wattsville, Al., U.S.	B3	78
Wattsville, S.C., U.S.	B4	117
Wattwil, Switz.	E9	21
Watu, Zaire	B3	48
Watubela Islands, is., Indon.	F8	34
Watupa Pond, l., Ma., U.S.	C5	98
Waubamik, Ont.	B4	73
Waubaushene, Ont.	C5	73
Waubay, S.D., U.S.	B8	118
Waubay Lake, l., S.D., U.S.	B8	118
Waubun, Mn., U.S.	C3	100
Wauchope, Austl.	E9	51
Wauchope, Sask.	H5	75
Wauchula, Fl., U.S.	E5	86
Waucoma, Ia., U.S.	A5	92
Wauconda, Il., U.S.	h8	90
Wauconda, Wa., U.S.	A6	124
Waugh, Man.	E4	70
Waugh Mountain, mtn., Id., U.S.	D4	89
Waukau, Wi., U.S.	E5	126
Waukee, Ia., U.S.	C4	92
Waukegan, Il., U.S.	A6	90
Waukesha, Wi., U.S.	F5	126
Waukesha, co., Wi., U.S.	E5	126
Waukewan, Lake, l., N.H., U.S.	C3	106
Waukomis, Ok., U.S.	A4	113
Waukon, Ia., U.S.	A6	92
Wauna, Wa., U.S.	f10	124
Wauneta, Ne., U.S.	D4	104
Waupaca, Wi., U.S.	D5	126
Waupaca, co., Wi., U.S.	D5	126
Waupun, Wi., U.S.	E5	126
Wauregan, Ct., U.S.	C8	84
Waurika, Ok., U.S.	C4	113
Waurika Lake, res., Ok., U.S.	C3	113
Wausa, Ne., U.S.	B8	104
Wausau, Fl., U.S.	u16	86
Wausau, Wi., U.S.	D4	126
Wausau, Lake, res., Wi., U.S.	D4	126
Wausaukee, Wi., U.S.	C6	126
Wauseon, Oh., U.S.	A1	112
Waushara, co., Wi., U.S.	D4	126
Wautoma, Wi., U.S.	D4	126
Wauwatosa, Wi., U.S.	m12	126
Wauzeka, Wi., U.S.	E3	126
Waveland, In., U.S.	E3	91
Waveland, Ms., U.S.	E4	101
Waveney, stm., Eng., U.K.	D7	10
Waverley, Austl.	*F9	50
Waverley, Austl.	*G8	50
Waverley, Austl.	E6	71
Waverly, Al., U.S.	C4	78
Waverly, Il., U.S.	D4	90
Waverly, In., U.S.	E5	91
Waverly, Ia., U.S.	B5	92
Waverly, Ks., U.S.	D8	93
Waverly, Ky., U.S.	C2	94
Waverly, Mi., U.S.	*F6	99
Waverly, Mo., U.S.	B4	102
Waverly, Ne., U.S.	D9	104
Waverly, N.Y., U.S.	C4	109
Waverly, Oh., U.S.	C3	112
Waverly, Tn., U.S.	A4	119
Waverly, Va., U.S.	C5	123
Waverly, W.V., U.S.	B3	125
Waverly Hall, Ga., U.S.	D2	87
Wavre, Bel.	D4	17
Wāw, Sud.	D2	47
Wawa, Ont.	o18	73
Wawa, Nig.	E5	45
Wawa, stm., Nic.	C6	62
Wawaka, In., U.S.	B7	91
Wāw al Kabīr, Libya	C6	16
Wawanesa, Man.	E2	70
Wawasee, Lake, l., In., U.S.	B6	91
Wawayanda Lake, l., N.J., U.S.	A4	107
Wawayanda Mountain, mtn., Ne., U.S.	A4	107
Waweig, N.B.	D2	71
Wawota, Sask.	H4	75
Waxahachie, Tx., U.S.	C4	120
Waxhaw, N.C., U.S.	B2	110
Waxweiler, W. Ger.	D6	17
Waya, i., Fiji	H14	52
Wayagamac, Lac, l., Que.	B5	74
Wayan, Id., U.S.	G7	89
Waycross, Ga., U.S.	E4	87
Wayland, Ia., U.S.	C6	92
Wayland, Ky., U.S.	C7	94
Wayland, Ma., U.S.	g10	98
Wayland, Mi., U.S.	F5	99
Wayland, Mo., U.S.	A6	102
Wayland, N.Y., U.S.	C3	109
Wayland Springs, Tn., U.S.	B4	119
Waylyn, S.C., U.S.	k12	117
Waymart, Pa., U.S.	C11	115
Wayne, Alta.	D4	68
Wayne, Mi., U.S.	p15	99
Wayne, Ne., U.S.	B8	104
Wayne, N.J., U.S.	B4	107
Wayne, N.Y., U.S.	C3	109
Wayne, Oh., U.S.	A2	112
Wayne, Pa., U.S.	F11	115
Wayne, W.V., U.S.	C2	125
Wayne, co., Ga., U.S.	E5	87
Wayne, co., Il., U.S.	E5	90
Wayne, co., In., U.S.	E7	91
Wayne, co., Ia., U.S.	D4	92
Wayne, co., Ky., U.S.	D5	94
Wayne, co., Mi., U.S.	F7	99
Wayne, co., Ms., U.S.	D5	101
Wayne, co., Mo., U.S.	D7	102
Wayne, co., Ne., U.S.	B8	104
Wayne, co., N.Y., U.S.	B3	109
Wayne, co., N.C., U.S.	B4	110
Wayne, co., Oh., U.S.	B4	112
Wayne, co., Pa., U.S.	C11	115
Wayne, co., Tn., U.S.	B4	119
Wayne, co., Ut., U.S.	E4	121
Wayne, co., W.V., U.S.	C2	125
Wayne City, Il., U.S.	E5	90
Waynesboro, Ga., U.S.	C4	87
Waynesboro, Ms., U.S.	D5	101
Waynesboro, Pa., U.S.	G6	115
Waynesboro, Tn., U.S.	B4	119
Waynesboro, Va., U.S.	B4	123
Waynesburg, Ky., U.S.	C5	94
Waynesburg, Oh., U.S.	B4	112
Waynesburg, Pa., U.S.	G1	115
Waynesville, Il., U.S.	C4	90
Waynesville, Mo., U.S.	D5	102
Waynesville, N.C., U.S.	f10	110
Waynesville, Oh., U.S.	C1	112
Waynetown, In., U.S.	D3	91
Waynewood, Va., U.S.	g12	123
Waynoka, Ok., U.S.	A3	113
Wayside, Ks., U.S.	E8	93
Wayside, Ms., U.S.	B2	101
Wayside, Tx., U.S.	B2	120
Wayside, Wi., U.S.	h10	126
Wayzata, Mn., U.S.	n11	100
We, i., Indon.	J1	35
Weakley, co., Tn., U.S.	A3	119
Weare, N.H., U.S.	D3	106
Weatherby, Mo., U.S.	B3	102
Weatherford, Ok., U.S.	B3	113
Weatherford, Tx., U.S.	C4	120
Weatherly, Pa., U.S.	E10	115
Weatogue, Ct., U.S.	B4	84
Weaubleau, Mo., U.S.	D4	102
Weaver, Al., U.S.	B4	78
Weaver Lake, l., Man.	C3	70
Weaver Mountains, mts., Az., U.S.	C3	80
Weaverville, Ca., U.S.	B2	82
Weaverville, N.C., U.S.	f10	110
Webb, Sask.	G1	75
Webb, Al., U.S.	D4	78
Webb, Ms., U.S.	B3	101
Webb, co., Tx., U.S.	F3	120
Webb Air Force Base, mil., Tx., U.S.	C2	120
Webb City, Mo., U.S.	D3	102
Webb City, Ok., U.S.	A5	113
Webber, Ks., U.S.	C5	93
Webber Lake, l., Man.	B5	70
Webbers Falls, Ok., U.S.	B6	113
Webberville, Mi., U.S.	F6	99
Webb Hill, hill, Ma., U.S.	B3	98
Webb Lake, l., Me., U.S.	D2	96
Webbwood, Ont.	A3	73
Weber, co., Ut., U.S.	B4	121
Weber, Mount, mtn., B.C.	B3	69
Webster, Fl., U.S.	D4	86
Webster, In., U.S.	E8	91
Webster, Ma., U.S.	B4	98
Webster, Mn., U.S.	F5	100
Webster, N.H., U.S.	D3	106
Webster, N.Y., U.S.	B3	109
Webster, N.D., U.S.	A7	111
Webster, Oh., U.S.	B1	112
Webster, Pa., U.S.	F2	115
Webster, S.D., U.S.	B8	118
Webster, Tx., U.S.	r14	120
Webster, Wi., U.S.	C1	126
Webster, co., Ga., U.S.	D2	87
Webster, co., Ia., U.S.	B3	92
Webster, co., Ky., U.S.	C2	94
Webster, co., La., U.S.	B2	95
Webster, co., Ms., U.S.	B4	101
Webster, co., Mo., U.S.	D5	102
Webster, co., Ne., U.S.	D7	104
Webster, co., W.V., U.S.	C4	125
Webster City, Ia., U.S.	B4	92
Webster Groves, Mo., U.S.	f13	102
Webster Mills, Pa., U.S.	G5	115
Webster Reservoir, res., Ks., U.S.	C4	93
Webster Springs, W.V., U.S.	C4	125
Webstervile, Vt., U.S.	C4	122
Wecota, S.D., U.S.	B6	118
Weda, Indon.	E7	34
Weddell Sea, Ant.	C9	7
Wedderburn, Or., U.S.	E2	114
Wedgefield, S.C., U.S.	D6	117
Wedgeport, N.S.	F4	71
Wedgewood, Mo., U.S.	f13	102
Wedowee, Al., U.S.	B4	78
Wedron, Il., U.S.	B5	90
Weed, Ca., U.S.	B2	82
Weed, N.M., U.S.	E4	108
Weed Heights, Nv., U.S.	E2	105
Weedon, Que.	D6	74
Weed Patch Hill, hill, In., U.S.	F5	91
Weedsport, N.Y., U.S.	B4	109
Weedville, Pa., U.S.	D5	115
Weehawken, N.J., U.S.	h8	107
Weekapaug, R.I., U.S.	G1	116
Weekes, Sask.	E4	75
Weeksbury, Ky., U.S.	C7	94
Weekstown, N.J., U.S.	D3	107
Weeksville, N.C., U.S.	A6	110
Weems, Va., U.S.	C6	123
Weener, W. Ger.	A7	17
Weeping Water, Ne., U.S.	D9	104
Weeping Water Creek, stm., Ne., U.S.	h12	104
Weert, Neth.	B6	16
Weesen, Switz.	B7	21
Weesp, Neth.	B5	17
Weferlingen, E. Ger.	A6	19
Wegdahl, Mn., U.S.	F3	100
Weggis, Switz.	B5	21
Węgorzewo, Pol.	B7	26
Wegrów, Pol.	B7	26
Wehr, W. Ger.	A4	21
Weichang, China	C8	31
Weiden, E. Ger.	D6	18
Weidman, Mi., U.S.	E6	99
Weifang, China	D8	31
Weigelstown, Pa., U.S.	*G8	115
Weihai, China	D9	31
Wei He, stm., China	E6	31
Weilburg, W. Ger.	C3	19
Weiler, W. Ger.	A8	21
Weilheim, W. Ger.	E5	20

Name	Map Ref.	Page
Weimar, E. Ger.	C5	18
Weimar, Tx., U.S.	E4	120
Weinan, China	E6	31
Weinböhla, E. Ger.	B8	19
Weiner, W. Ger.	B5	81
Weinert, Tx., U.S.	C3	120
Weinfelden, Switz.	A7	21
Weingarten, W. Ger.	D3	19
Weingarten, W. Ger.	A8	21
Weinheim, W. Ger.	D4	18
Weining, China	F5	31
Weinsberg, W. Ger.	D4	19
Weipa, Austl.	B7	50
Weippe, Id., U.S.	D3	89
Weir, Que.	D3	74
Weir, Ks., U.S.	E9	93
Weir, Ky., U.S.	C2	94
Weir, Ms., U.S.	B4	101
Weir, stm., Man.	A4	70
Weir, Lake, l., Fl., U.S.	C5	86
Weirdale, Sask.	D3	75
Weir River, Man.	A4	70
Weirsdale, Fl., U.S.	D5	86
Weirton, W.V., U.S.	A4	125
Weisburg, In., U.S.	F7	91
Weiser, Id., U.S.	E2	89
Weiser, stm., Id., U.S.	E2	89
Weishan Lake, l., China	G7	32
Weishi, China	G6	32
Weisner Mountain, hill, Al., U.S.	A4	78
Weisse Elster, stm., E. Ger.	B7	19
Weissenburg, W. Ger.	D5	18
Weissenburg, Switz.	C3	21
Weissenfels, E. Ger.	B6	19
Weissenhorn, W. Ger.	A6	20
Weissen Lake, l., Aus.	C9	20
Weissert, Ne., U.S.	C6	104
Weisshorn, mtn., Switz.	C3	20
Weiss Lake, res., U.S.	A4	78
Weisswasser, E. Ger.	B9	19
Weitra, Aus.	E9	19
Weixi, China	F4	31
Weizhou Dao, i., China	B8	35
Wejherowo, Pol.	A4	18
Wekiva Springs, Fl., U.S.	*D5	86
Wekusko Lake, l., Man.	B2	70
Welaka, Fl., U.S.	C5	86
Welch, Ok., U.S.	A6	113
Welch, Tx., U.S.	C1	120
Welch, W.V., U.S.	D3	125
Welches, Or., U.S.	B5	114
Welcome, In., U.S.	h10	91
Welcome, Mn., U.S.	G4	100
Welcome, S.C., U.S.	B3	117
Weld, co., Co., U.S.	A6	83
Welda, Ks., U.S.	D8	93
Welden, W. Ger.	B5	19
Weldon, Sask.	D3	75
Weldon, Ar., U.S.	B4	81
Weldon, Il., U.S.	C5	90
Weldon, Ia., U.S.	D4	92
Weldon, N.C., U.S.	A5	110
Weldon, U.S.	D5	120
Weldona, Co., U.S.	A7	83
Weldon Spring, Mo., U.S.	f12	102
Weleetka, Ok., U.S.	B5	113
Welega, prov., Eth.	D4	47
Welkom, S. Afr.	C4	49
Welland, Ont.	E5	73
Welland, stm., Eng., U.K.	D6	10
Wellandport, Ont.	D5	73
Wellborn, Fl., U.S.	B4	86
Wellborn, Tx., U.S.	D4	120
Wellersburg, Pa., U.S.	G4	115
Welles Harbor, b., Mid. Is.	K3	52
Wellesley, Ont.	D4	73
Wellesley, Ma., U.S.	B5	98
Wellesley Islands, is., Austl.	C6	50
Wellfleet, Ma., U.S.	C7	98
Wellfleet, Ne., U.S.	D5	104
Wellford, S.C., U.S.	B3	117
Wellin, Bel.	D5	17
Welling, Ok., U.S.	B7	113
Wellingborough, Eng., U.K.	B7	12
Wellington, Austl.	F7	51
Wellington, B.C.	f11	69
Wellington, Ont.	D7	73
Wellington, N.Z.	N15	51
Wellington, S. Afr.	D2	49
Wellington, Eng., U.K.	B5	12
Wellington, Eng., U.K.	C4	12
Wellington, Al., U.S.	B4	78
Wellington, Co., U.S.	A5	83
Wellington, Il., U.S.	C6	90
Wellington, Ks., U.S.	E6	93
Wellington, Me., U.S.	C3	96
Wellington, Mo., U.S.	B4	102
Wellington, Nv., U.S.	E2	105
Wellington, Oh., U.S.	A3	112
Wellington, Tx., U.S.	B2	120
Wellington, Ut., U.S.	D5	121
Wellington, co., Ont.	D4	73
Wellington, Isla, i., Chile	D2	54
Wellington Channel, strt., N.W. Ter.	m33	66
Wellington Station, N.S.	E6	71
Wellington Station, P.E.I.	C5	71
Wellman, Ia., U.S.	C6	92
Wellman, Tx., U.S.	C1	120
Wellpinit, Wa., U.S.	B8	124
Wells, B.C.	C7	69
Wells, Eng., U.K.	C5	12
Wells, Ks., U.S.	C6	93
Wells, Me., U.S.	E2	96
Wells, Mi., U.S.	C3	99
Wells, Mn., U.S.	G5	100
Wells, Nv., U.S.	B7	105
Wells, N.Y., U.S.	B6	109
Wells, Tx., U.S.	D5	120
Wells, Vt., U.S.	E2	122
Wells, co., In., U.S.	C7	91
Wells, co., N.D., U.S.	B6	111
Wells, stm., Vt., U.S.	D3	122
Wells, Lake, l., Austl.	E3	50
Wells Beach, Me., U.S.	E2	96
Wellsboro, In., U.S.	B4	91
Wellsboro, Pa., U.S.	C7	115
Wellsburg, Ia., U.S.	B5	92
Wellsburg, N.Y., U.S.	C4	109
Wellsford, Ks., U.S.	E4	93
Wells Gray Provincial Park, B.C.	C8	69
Wells Lake, l., Man.	A1	70
Wells-next-the-Sea, Eng., U.K.	D7	10
Wells River, Vt., U.S.	C4	122
Wells Tannery, Pa., U.S.	F5	115
Wellston, Mi., U.S.	D5	99
Wellston, Oh., U.S.	C3	112
Wellston, Ok., U.S.	B4	113
Wellsville, Ks., U.S.	D8	93
Wellsville, Mo., U.S.	B6	102
Wellsville, N.Y., U.S.	C3	109
Wellsville, Oh., U.S.	B5	112
Wellsville, Pa., U.S.	F8	115
Wellsville, Ut., U.S.	B4	121
Wells see Wells-next-the-Sea, Eng., U.K.	D7	10
Wellton, Az., U.S.	E1	80
Wellwood, Man.	D2	70
Welo, prov., Eth.	C5	47
Wels, Aus.	D7	18
Welsford, N.B.	D3	71
Welsh, La., U.S.	D3	95
Welshpool, Wales, U.K.	C7	10
Welton, Ia., U.S.	C7	92
Welty, Ok., U.S.	B5	113
Welwitschia, Nmb.	B1	49
Welwyn, Sask.	G5	75
Welwyn Garden City, Eng., U.K.	k12	10
Welzow, E. Ger.	B9	19
Wem, Eng., U.K.	B5	12
Wema, Zaire	B3	48
Wembere, stm., Tan.	B5	48
Wembley, Alta.	B1	68
Wemding, W. Ger.	E5	19
Wemme, Or., U.S.	B5	114
Wenasoga, Ms., U.S.	A5	101
Wenatchee, Wa., U.S.	B5	124
Wenatchee, stm., Wa., U.S.	B5	124
Wenatchee Lake, l., Wa., U.S.	B5	124
Wenatchee Mountains, mts., Wa., U.S.	B5	124
Wenchang, China	C9	35
Wenchi, Ghana	E4	45
Wenchow see Wenzhou, China	F9	31
Wendel, Ca., U.S.	B3	82
Wendell, Id., U.S.	G4	89
Wendell, Ma., U.S.	A3	98
Wendell, Mn., U.S.	D2	100
Wendell, N.H., U.S.	D2	106
Wendell, N.C., U.S.	B4	110
Wenden, Az., U.S.	D2	80
Wendeng, China	F10	32
Wendo, Eth.	D4	47
Wendover, Nv., U.S.	C7	105
Wendover, Ut., U.S.	C1	121
Wenham, Ma., U.S.	A6	98
Wenham Lake, l., Ma., U.S.	f12	98
Wenham Swamp, sw., Ma., U.S.	f12	98
Wenji Gefersa, Eth.	*D4	47
Wenlock, stm., Austl.	B7	50
Wenona, Il., U.S.	B4	90
Wenona, Md., U.S.	D6	97
Wenonah, N.J., U.S.	D2	107
Wenshan, China	G5	31
West Carthage, N.Y., U.S.	B5	109
Wentworth, Austl.	F4	51
Wentworth, N.S.	D6	71
Wentworth, N.H., U.S.	C3	106
Wentworth, N.C., U.S.	A3	110
Wentworth, S.D., U.S.	C8	118
Wentworth, Wi., U.S.	B2	126
Wentworth, co., Ont.	D4	73
Wentworth, Lake, l., N.H.	C4	106
Wentzville, Mo., U.S.	C7	102
Weohyakapka, Lake, l., Fl., U.S.	E5	86
Weott, Ca., U.S.	B2	82
Wepener, S. Afr.	C4	49
Wequetequock, Ct., U.S.	D8	84
Werbomont, Bel.	D5	17
Werdau, E. Ger.	C6	18
Werder, E. Ger.	A7	19
Werdohl, W. Ger.	B2	19
Werfen, Aus.	E6	18
Werl, W. Ger.	B2	19
Wernberg, W. Ger.	D6	18
Werne, W. Ger.	B2	19
Werneuchen, E. Ger.	B6	18
Wernigerode, E. Ger.	C5	18
Werra, stm., Eur.	C4	18
Wertach, stm., W. Ger.	D5	18
Wertheim, W. Ger.	D4	19
Wertingen, W. Ger.	E5	19
Wervik, Bel.	D3	17
Wesco, Mo., U.S.	D6	102
Wesel, W. Ger.	C3	18
Weskan, Ks., U.S.	D2	93
Weslaco, Tx., U.S.	F4	120
Weslemkoon Lake, l., Ont.	C7	73
Wesley, Ar., U.S.	A2	81
Wesley, Ia., U.S.	A4	92
Wesley, Me., U.S.	D5	96
Wesleyville, Newf.	D5	72
Wesleyville, Pa., U.S.	B2	115
Wesselburen, W. Ger.	D2	15
Wessel Islands, is., Austl.	B6	50
Wesserunsett Lake, l., Me.	D3	96
Wessington, S.D., U.S.	C7	118
Wessington Springs, S.D., U.S.	C7	118
Wesson, Ar., U.S.	D3	81
Wesson, Ms., U.S.	D3	101
West, Ms., U.S.	B4	101
West, Tx., U.S.	D4	120
West, stm., P.E.I.	C6	71
West, stm., Ct., U.S.	D5	84
West, stm., U.S.	h9	98
West, stm., Ct., U.S.	E3	122
West Abington, Ma., U.S.	h12	98
West Acton, Ma., U.S.	g10	98
West Alexander, Pa., U.S.	F1	115
West Alexandria, Oh., U.S.	C1	112
West Allis, Wi., U.S.	m11	126
Westalton, Mo., U.S.	f13	102
West Alton, N.H., U.S.	C4	106
West Amityville, N.Y., U.S.	n15	109
West Andover, Ma., U.S.	A5	98
West Arichat, N.S.	D8	71
West Athens, Ca., U.S.	*n12	82
West Athens, Me., U.S.	D3	96
West Augusta, Va., U.S.	B3	123
West Babylon, N.Y., U.S.	*E7	109
West Baden Springs, In., U.S.	G4	91
West Baldwin, Me., U.S.	E2	96
Westbank, B.C.	D8	69
West Bank, ter.: Isr. Occ.	B7	41
West Barnet, Vt., U.S.	C4	122
West Barnstable, Ma., U.S.	C7	98
West Barrington, R.I., U.S.	C5	116
West Baton Rouge, co., La., U.S.	D4	95
West Bay, Newf.	A3	72
West Bay, N.S.	D5	71
West Bay, Fl., U.S.	u16	86
West Bay, b., Fl., U.S.	u16	86
West Bay, b., N.C., U.S.	B6	110
West Bay, b., Tx., U.S.	r15	120
West Bay Shore, N.Y., U.S.	*n15	109
West Bend, Sask.	F4	75
West Bend, Ia., U.S.	B3	92
West Bend, Wi., U.S.	E5	126
West Bengal, state, India	F11	37
West Berkshire, Vt., U.S.	B3	122
West Berlin, N.J., U.S.	D3	107
West Berlin see Berlin (West), W. Ger.	B6	18
West Bethel, Me., U.S.	D2	96
West Billerica, Ma., U.S.	f10	98
West Blocton, Al., U.S.	B2	78
West Bloomfield, N.Y., U.S.	C3	109
West Bloomfield Township, Mi., U.S.	*F7	99
Westboro, Mo., U.S.	A2	102
Westboro, Wi., U.S.	C3	126
Westborough, Ma., U.S.	B4	98
West Bountiful, Ut., U.S.	C4	121
Westbourne, Man.	D2	70
West Bowdoin, Me., U.S.	f7	96
West Boylston, Ma., U.S.	B4	98
West Bradenton, Fl., U.S.	*E4	86
West Branch, Ia., U.S.	C6	92
West Branch, Mi., U.S.	D6	99
West Branch Reservoir, res., Ct., U.S.	B3	84
West Brentwood, N.Y., U.S.	*n15	109
West Bridgewater, Ma., U.S.	B5	98
West Bridgewater, Vt., U.S.	D3	122
West Bromwich, Eng., U.K.	D6	10
West Brookfield, Ma., U.S.	B3	98
West Brooklyn, Il., U.S.	B4	90
Westbrook, Ct., U.S.	D6	84
Westbrook, Me., U.S.	E2	96
Westbrook, Mn., U.S.	F3	100
Westbrook, Tx., U.S.	C2	120
Westbrookville, N.Y., U.S.	D6	109
West Burke, Vt., U.S.	B5	122
West Burlington, Ia., U.S.	D6	92
Westbury, N.Y., U.S.	*n15	109
West Butte, mtn., Mt., U.S.	B5	103
West Buxton, Me., U.S.	E2	96
Westby, Mt., U.S.	B12	103
Westby, Wi., U.S.	E3	126
West Cache Creek, stm., Ok., U.S.	C3	113
West Caldwell, N.J., U.S.	B4	107
West Campton, N.H., U.S.	C3	106
West Canaan, N.H., U.S.	C2	106
West Canada Creek, stm., N.Y., U.S.	B6	109
West Cape Howe, c., Austl.	G2	50
West Cape May, N.J., U.S.	F3	107
West Carroll, co., La., U.S.	B4	95
West Carrollton, Oh., U.S.	C1	112
West Carry Pond, l., Me., U.S.	C2	96
West Carson, Ca., U.S.	*n12	82
West Carthage, N.Y., U.S.	B5	109
West Castleton, Vt., U.S.	D2	122
West Charleston, Vt., U.S.	B4	122
West Chatham, Ma., U.S.	C8	98
West Chazy, N.Y., U.S.	f11	109
Westchester, Fl., U.S.	*s13	86
Westchester, Il., U.S.	k9	90
West Chester, Ia., U.S.	C6	92
West Chester, Oh., U.S.	n13	112
West Chester, Pa., U.S.	G10	115
West Chesterfield, N.H., U.S.	E1	106
Westchester Station, N.S.	D6	71
West Chicago, Il., U.S.	k8	90
West Chop, c., Ma., U.S.	D6	98
West City, Il., U.S.	F5	90
Westcliffe, Co., U.S.	C5	83
West Coffeyville, Ks., U.S.	E8	93
West College Corner, In., U.S.	E8	91
West Columbia, S.C., U.S.	D5	117
West Columbia, Tx., U.S.	E5	120
West Compton, Ca., U.S.	*F4	82
West Concord, Ma., U.S.	B5	98
West Concord, Mn., U.S.	F6	100
West Concord, N.C., U.S.	B2	110
Westconnaug Reservoir, res., R.I., U.S.	C2	116
West Cornwall, Ct., U.S.	B2	84
West Cote Blanche Bay, b., La., U.S.	E4	95
West Covina, Ca., U.S.	m13	82
West Creek, N.J., U.S.	D4	107
West Crossett, Ar., U.S.	D4	81
West Cumberland, Me., U.S.	E2	96
West Cummington, Ma., U.S.	B2	98
West Danby, N.Y., U.S.	C4	109
West Danville, Vt., U.S.	C4	122
West Decatur, Pa., U.S.	E5	115
West Dennis, Ma., U.S.	C7	98
West Des Moines, Ia., U.S.	C4	92
West Dover, Vt., U.S.	F3	122
West Dudley, Ma., U.S.	B4	98
West Dummerston, Vt., U.S.	F3	122
West Elk Mountains, mts., Co., U.S.	C3	83
West Elk Peak, mtn., Co., U.S.	C3	83
West Elkton, Oh., U.S.	C1	112
West Elmira, N.Y., U.S.	*C4	109
West Elwood, In., U.S.	D6	91
West Eminence, Mo., U.S.	D6	102
West Emma Creek, stm., Ks., U.S.	D6	93
West End, Bah.	A4	64
Westend, Ca., U.S.	E5	82
West End, N.C., U.S.	B3	110
West Enfield, Me., U.S.	C4	96
West Epping, N.H., U.S.	D4	106
Westerkappeln, W. Ger.	A2	19
Westerland, W. Ger.	A4	18
Westerly, R.I., U.S.	F1	116
Western, Ne., U.S.	D8	104
Western, prov., Ghana	E4	45
Western, prov., Kenya	A5	48
Western, prov., Zam.	E4	48
Western Australia, state, Austl.	D3	50
Western Channel, strt., Asia	I4	33
Western Desert, des., Eg.		C2
Western Dvina (Daugava), stm., Sov. Un.	D7	27
Western Ghāts, mts., India	E5	36
Western Grove, Ar., U.S.	A3	81
Western Head, c., Newf.		E4
Western Head, c., N.S.	F5	71
Western Hills, Co., U.S.	*B6	83
Western Island, l., Newf.		C4
Western Isles, prov., Scot., U.K.	B2	13
Westernport, Md., U.S.	m12	97
Westernport Reservoir, res., Md., U.S.	k12	97
Western Sahara, dep., Afr.	D2	44
Western Samoa, ctry., Oc.	G11	6
Western Shore, N.S.	E5	71
Western Springs, Il., U.S.	k9	90
Westerschelde, est., Neth.	B5	16
Westerstede, W. Ger.	A7	17
Westervelt, Il., U.S.	D5	90
Westerville, Ne., U.S.	C6	104
Westerville, Oh., U.S.	B3	112
Westerwald, mts., W. Ger.	C4	18
West Fairlee, Vt., U.S.	D4	122
West Fairview, Pa., U.S.	*F8	115
West Falmouth, Ma., U.S.	C6	98
West Fargo, N.D., U.S.	C9	111
West Farmington, Me., U.S.	D2	96
West Farmington, Oh., U.S.	A5	112
West Feliciana, co., La., U.S.	D4	95
Westfield, In., U.S.	D5	91
Westfield, Il., U.S.	D6	90
Westfield, Ia., U.S.	B1	92
Westfield, Me., U.S.	B5	96
Westfield, Ma., U.S.	B2	98
Westfield, N.J., U.S.	B4	107
Westfield, N.Y., U.S.	C1	109
Westfield, N.C., U.S.	A2	110
Westfield, N.D., U.S.	C5	111
Westfield, Pa., U.S.	C6	115
Westfield, Vt., U.S.	B4	122
Westfield, Wi., U.S.	E4	126
Westfield, stm., Ma., U.S.	B2	98
Westfield Center, Oh., U.S.	A4	112
Westfir, Or., U.S.	D4	114
West Flanders, prov., Bel.	C3	17
Westford, Ct., U.S.	B7	84
Westford, Ma., U.S.	f10	98
Westford, Vt., U.S.	B3	122
West Fork, Ar., U.S.	B1	81
West Fork, W.V., U.S.	B3	125
West Frankfort, Il., U.S.	F5	90
West Freehold, N.J., U.S.	C4	107
West Friendship, Md., U.S.	B4	97
West Frisian Islands, is., Neth.	A6	16
Westgate, Fl., U.S.	F6	86
Westgate, Ia., U.S.	B6	92
West Gate, Va., U.S.	*B5	123
West Gate of Lomond, Va., U.S.	*B5	123
West Germany see Germany, Federal Republic of, ctry., Eur.	C4	18
West Glacier, Mt., U.S.	B3	103
West Glamorgan, co., Wales, U.K.	C4	12
West Glens Falls, N.Y., U.S.	*B7	109
West Glocester, R.I., U.S.	B1	116
West Glover, Vt., U.S.	B4	122
West Gorham, Me., U.S.	g7	96
West Goshen, Ct., U.S.	B4	84
West Gouldsboro, Me., U.S.	D4	96
West Granby, Ct., U.S.	B4	84
West Grand Lake, l., Me., U.S.	C5	96
West Granville, Ma., U.S.	B2	98
West Green, Ga., U.S.	E4	87
West Greene, Al., U.S.	C1	78
West Greenville, R.I., U.S.	B3	116
West Groton, Ma., U.S.	A4	98
West Grove, Ia., U.S.	D5	92
West Grove, Pa., U.S.	G10	115
West Halifax, Vt., U.S.	F3	122
West Hamlin, W.V., U.S.	C2	125
West Hampstead, N.H., U.S.	E4	106
West Hampton, Ma., U.S.	B2	98
West Hanover, Ma., U.S.	h12	98
West Harrison, In., U.S.	F8	91
West Hartford, Ct., U.S.	B4	84
West Hartford, Vt., U.S.	D4	122
West Hartland, Ct., U.S.	A4	84
West Hatfield, Ma., U.S.	B2	98
West Haven, Ct., U.S.	D4	84
West Haven, Or., U.S.	*B4	114
West Haverstraw, N.Y., U.S.	*D7	109
West Hazleton, Pa., U.S.	E9	115
West Helena, Ar., U.S.	C5	81
West Hempstead, N.Y., U.S.	*k13	109
West Hickory, Pa., U.S.	C3	115
West Hill Reservoir, res., Ma., U.S.	B4	98
Westhoff, Tx., U.S.	E4	120
West Hollywood, Ca., U.S.	*m12	82
West Hopkinton, N.H., U.S.	D3	106
West Huntington, N.Y., U.S.	*n15	109
West Hyannisport, Ma., U.S.	C7	98
West Ice Shelf, ice, Ant.	C21	7
West Indies, is.	A3	53
West Island, i., Austl.		A3
West Islip, N.Y., U.S.	*E7	109
West Jefferson, N.C., U.S.	A1	110
West Jefferson, Oh., U.S.	C2	112
West Jersey, Il., U.S.	B4	90
West Jordan, Ut., U.S.	C4	121
Westkapelle (part of Knokke-Heist), Bel.	C3	17
Westkapelle, Neth.	C3	17
West Kennebunk, Me., U.S.	E2	96
West Kingston, R.I., U.S.	F3	116
West Lafayette, In., U.S.	D4	91
West Lafayette, Oh., U.S.	B4	112
West Lake, l., Me., U.S.	C4	96
Westlake, La., U.S.	D2	95
Westlake, Oh., U.S.	h9	112
Westlake, Or., U.S.	D2	114
Westlake Village, Ca., U.S.	*E4	82
Westland, Mi., U.S.	F7	99
West Laramie, Wy., U.S.	E7	127
West Lawn, Pa., U.S.	F10	115
West Lebanon, In., U.S.	D3	91
West Lebanon, N.H., U.S.	D2	106
West Lebanon, Me., U.S.	E2	96
West Leisenring, Pa., U.S.	G2	115
West Leyden, N.Y., U.S.	B5	109
West Liberty, Ia., U.S.	C6	92
West Liberty, Ky., U.S.	C6	94
West Liberty, Oh., U.S.	B2	112
West Liberty, W.V., U.S.	f8	125
West Lima, Wi., U.S.	E3	126
West Lincoln, Vt., U.S.	C2	122
Westline, Pa., U.S.	C4	115
West Linn, Or., U.S.	B4	114
West Medway, Ma., U.S.	B5	98
West Melbourne, Fl., U.S.	*D6	86
West Memphis, Ar., U.S.	B5	81
West Miami, Fl., U.S.	s13	86
West Middlesex, Pa., U.S.	D1	115
West Middleton, In., U.S.	D5	91
West Midlands, co., Eng., U.K.	*B6	12
West Mifflin, Pa., U.S.	F2	115
West Milan, N.H., U.S.	A4	106
West Milford, N.J., U.S.	A4	107
West Milton, Oh., U.S.	C1	112
West Milton, Pa., U.S.	D8	115
West Milwaukee, Wi., U.S.	m12	126
West Mineral, Ks., U.S.	E9	93
West Modesto, Ca., U.S.	*D3	82
West Monroe, La., U.S.	B3	95
Westmont, Ca., U.S.	n12	82
Westmont, Il., U.S.	k9	90
Westmont, N.J., U.S.	D2	107
Westmont, Pa., U.S.	F4	115
West Monterey, Pa., U.S.	D2	115
Westmoreland, Ks., U.S.	C7	93
Westmoreland, N.H., U.S.	E2	106
Westmoreland, Tn., U.S.	A5	119
Westmoreland, co., Pa., U.S.	F2	115
Westmoreland, co., Va., U.S.	B6	123
Westmorland, co., N.B.	C4	71
Westmorland, Ca., U.S.	F6	82
West Mountain, mtn., Me., U.S.	f7	81
West Mountain, mtn., N.Y., U.S.	B6	109
West Mountain, mtn., Vt., U.S.	B5	122
West Muncie, In., U.S.	D7	91
West Musquash Lake, l., Me., U.S.	C5	96
West Mystic, Ct., U.S.	D8	84
West Newbury, Ma., U.S.	A6	98
West Newbury, Vt., U.S.	C4	122
West Newfield, Me., U.S.	E2	96
West Newton, Pa., U.S.	F2	115
New York, N.J., U.S.	h8	107
West Nicholson, Zimb.	B4	49
West Nishnabotna, stm., Ia., U.S.	C2	92
West Norriton, Pa., U.S.	o20	115
West Nottingham, N.H., U.S.	D4	106
West Nyack, N.Y., U.S.	*D7	109
West Olive, Mi., U.S.	F7	99
Weston, Co., U.S.	D6	83
Weston (part of York), Ont.	m14	73
Weston, Ct., U.S.	E2	84
Weston, Ga., U.S.	E2	87
Weston, Id., U.S.	G7	89
Weston, Il., U.S.	C5	90
Weston, Ma., U.S.	B5	98
Weston, Me., U.S.	C5	96
Weston, Ne., U.S.	C9	104
Weston, Oh., U.S.	A2	112
Weston, Or., U.S.	B8	114
Weston, W.V., U.S.	B4	125
Weston, Wi., U.S.	D4	126
Weston, Wy., U.S.	B7	127
Weston, co., Wy., U.S.	C8	127
Weston-super-Mare, Eng., U.K.	E5	10
West Orange, N.J., U.S.	B4	107
West Ossipee, N.H., U.S.	C4	106
Westover, Al., U.S.	B3	78
Westover, Md., U.S.	D6	97
Westover, Pa., U.S.	E4	115
Westover, Tn., U.S.	B3	119
Westover, W.V., U.S.	B5	125
Westover Air Force Base, mil., Ma., U.S.	B4	98
West Palm Beach, Fl., U.S.	F6	86
West Paris, Me., U.S.	D2	96
West Park, N.Y., U.S.	D7	109
West Pasco, Wa., U.S.	*C6	124
West Paterson, N.J., U.S.	*B4	107
West Pawlet, Vt., U.S.	E2	122
West Pearl, stm., La., U.S.	D6	95
West Pelham, Ma., U.S.	*B2	98
West Pelzer, S.C., U.S.	B3	117
West Pembroke, Me., U.S.	D5	96
West Pensacola, Fl., U.S.	u14	86
West Peoria, Il., U.S.	C4	90
West Peru, Me., U.S.	D2	96
West Peterborough, N.H., U.S.	E3	106
Westphalia, In., U.S.	G3	91
Westphalia, Ks., U.S.	D8	93
Westphalia, Mi., U.S.	F6	99
Westphalia, Mo., U.S.	C5	102
Westphalia, hist. reg., W. Ger.	C3	18
West Pittsburg, Ca., U.S.	*g9	82
West Pittsburg, Pa., U.S.	E1	115
West Pittston, Pa., U.S.	m17	115
West Plains, Mo., U.S.	E6	102
West Plymouth, N.H., U.S.	C3	106
West Point, Ar., U.S.	B4	81
West Point, Ca., U.S.	C3	82
West Point, Ga., U.S.	D1	87
West Point, Il., U.S.	C2	90
West Point, Ia., U.S.	D6	92
West Point, Ky., U.S.	C4	94
West Point, Ms., U.S.	B5	101
West Point, Ne., U.S.	C9	104
West Point, N.Y., U.S.	D7	109
West Point, Oh., U.S.	B5	112
West Point, Ut., U.S.	*B3	121
West Point, Va., U.S.	C6	123
West Point, l., Ak., U.S.	C11	79
West Point Lake, res., U.S.	C1	87
West Poland, Me., U.S.	D2	96
West Portsmouth, Oh., U.S.	D2	112
West Prairie, stm., Alta.	B2	68
West Pubnico, N.S.	F4	71
West Puente Valley, Ca., U.S.	*m13	82
West Quoddy Head, c., Me., U.S.	D6	96
Westray, i., Scot., U.K.	A5	10
Westray Firth, strt., Scot., U.K.	A5	13
West Reading, Pa., U.S.	F10	115
West Redding, Ct., U.S.	D2	84
Westrhauderfehn, W. Ger.	A7	17
West Ridge, N.H., U.S.	E2	106
West River, Md., U.S.	C4	97
West Road, stm., B.C.	C5	69
West Rumney, N.H., U.S.	C3	106
West Rupert, Vt., U.S.	E2	122
West Rutland, Vt., U.S.	D2	122
West Rye, N.H., U.S.	D5	106
West Sacramento, Ca., U.S.	*C3	82
West Saint Modeste, Newf.	C3	72
West Saint Paul, Mn., U.S.	n12	100
West Salem, Il., U.S.	E5	90
West Salem, Oh., U.S.	B3	112
West Salem, Wi., U.S.	E2	126
West Salt Creek, stm., Co., U.S.	B2	83
West Sayville, N.Y., U.S.	*n15	109
West Scarborough, Me., U.S.	E2	96
West Seneca, N.Y., U.S.	C2	109
West Siberian Lowland, pl., Sov. Un.	C10	29
Westside, Ia., U.S.	B2	92
West Simsbury, Ct., U.S.	B4	84
West Slope, Or., U.S.	g12	114
West Spanish Peak, mtn., Co., U.S.	D6	83
West Spit, spit, Marsh Is.	S18	52
West Springfield, Ma., U.S.	B2	98
West Springfield, N.H., U.S.	D2	106
West Springfield, Va., U.S.	g12	123
West Stafford, Ct., U.S.	B6	84
West Stockbridge, Ma., U.S.	B1	98
West Suffield, Ct., U.S.	A5	84
West Sullivan, Me., U.S.	D4	96
West Sumner, Me., U.S.	D2	96
West Sunbury, Pa., U.S.	D2	115
West Sussex, co., Eng., U.K.	D7	12
West Swanzey, N.H., U.S.	E2	106
West Terre Haute, In., U.S.	F3	91
West Thornton, N.H., U.S.	C3	106
West Tisbury, Ma., U.S.	D6	98
West Topsham, Vt., U.S.	C4	122
West Townsend, Ma., U.S.	A4	98
West Townsend, Vt., U.S.	E3	122
West Union, Il., U.S.	D6	90
West Union, Ia., U.S.	B6	92
West Union, Oh., U.S.	D2	112
West Union, S.C., U.S.	B1	117
West Union, W.V., U.S.	B4	125
West Unity, Oh., U.S.	A1	112
West University Place, Tx., U.S.	r14	120
West Upton, Ma., U.S.	B4	98
Westvale, N.Y., U.S.	*B4	109
West Valley, N.Y., U.S.	C2	109
West Valley City, Ut., U.S.	C4	121
West Vancouver, B.C.	f12	69
West Van Lear, Ky., U.S.	C7	94
Westview, Fl., U.S.	*G6	86
West View, Pa., U.S.	h13	115
Westville, In., U.S.	A4	91
Westville, Fl., U.S.	u16	86
Westville, Il., U.S.	C6	90
Westville, In., U.S.	A4	91
Westville, N.H., U.S.	E4	106
Westville, N.J., U.S.	D2	107
Westville, Ok., U.S.	A7	113
Westville, S.C., U.S.	C6	117
Westville Lake, res., Ma., U.S.	B3	98
West Virginia, state, U.S.	C4	125
West Walker, stm., U.S.	E2	105
West Wardsboro, Vt., U.S.	E3	122
West Wareham, Ma., U.S.	C6	98
West Warren, Ma., U.S.	B3	98
West Warwick, R.I., U.S.	*D3	116
West Webster, N.Y., U.S.	*B3	109
Westwego, La., U.S.	k11	95
West Whittier, Ca., U.S.	*n12	82
West Willington, Ct., U.S.	B6	84
West Willow, Mi., U.S.	*F7	99
West Wilton, N.H., U.S.	E3	106
West Winfield, N.Y., U.S.	C5	109
Westwold, B.C.	D8	69
Westwood, Ca., U.S.	B3	82
Westwood, Ky., U.S.	B7	94
Westwood, Ma., U.S.	B5	98
Westwood, Mi., U.S.	*F5	99
Westwood, N.J., U.S.	A4	107
Westwood Lakes, Fl., U.S.	s13	86
West Woodstock, Ct., U.S.	B8	84
West Wyalong, Austl.	F8	50
West Wyoming, Pa., U.S.	n17	115
West Yarmouth, Ma., U.S.	C7	98
West Yellowstone, Mt., U.S.	F5	103
West York, Il., U.S.	D6	90
West York, Pa., U.S.	G8	115
West Yorkshire, co., Eng., U.K.	*G7	13
Wetar, i., Indon.	G7	34
Wetaskiwin, Alta.	C4	68
Wete, Tan.	C6	48
Wethersfield, Ct., U.S.	C5	84
Wetmore, Co., U.S.	C5	83
Wetmore, Ks., U.S.	C8	93
Wetmore, Mi., U.S.	B4	99
Wetonka, S.D., U.S.	B7	118
Wettingen, Switz.	B5	20
Wetumka, Ok., U.S.	B5	113
Wetumpka, Al., U.S.	C4	78
Wetzel, co., W.V., U.S.	B4	125
Wetzikon, Switz.	B5	20
Wetzlar, W. Ger.	C4	18
Wever, Ia., U.S.	D6	92
Wewahitchka, Fl., U.S.	C1	86
Wewak, Pap. N. Gui.	h11	50
Wewoka, Ok., U.S.	B5	113
Wexford, co., Ire.	E5	11
Wexford, Ire.	E5	11
Wexford Harbour, b., Ire.	E5	11
Weyakwin Lake, l., Sask.	C3	75
Weyanoke, La., U.S.	D4	95
Weyauwega, Wi., U.S.	D5	126

Name	Map Ref.	Page
Weybridge, Eng., U.K.	m12	10
Weyburn, Sask.	H4	75
Weyerhaeuser, Wi., U.S.	C2	126
Weyers Cave, Va., U.S.	B4	123
Weymouth, N.S.	E4	71
Weymouth, Ma., U.S.	B6	98
Weymouth, Ma., U.S.	D3	107
Weymouth [and Melcombe Regis], Eng., U.K.		
Weymouth Bay, b., Eng., U.K.	D5	12
Whakatane, N.Z.	L16	51
Whalan, Mn., U.S.	G7	100
Whales, Bay of, b., Ant.	B32	7
Whaleysville, Md., U.S.	D7	97
Whalom, Ma., U.S.	A4	98
Whangarei, N.Z.	K15	51
Wharfe, stm., Eng., U.K.	D6	10
Wharton, N.J., U.S.	B3	107
Wharton, Oh., U.S.	B2	112
Wharton, Tx., U.S.	E4	120
Wharton, W.V., U.S.	n12	125
Wharton, co., Tx., U.S.	E4	120
Whataroa, N.Z.	O13	51
What Cheer, Ia., U.S.	C5	92
Whatcom, co., Wa., U.S.	A4	124
Whatcom, Lake, l., Wa., U.S.	A3	124
Whately, Ma., U.S.	B2	98
Whatley, Al., U.S.	D2	78
Wheatcroft, Ky., U.S.	C2	94
Wheatfield, In., U.S.	B3	91
Wheatland, Ca., U.S.	C3	82
Wheatland, In., U.S.	G3	91
Wheatland, Ia., U.S.	C7	92
Wheatland, Mo., U.S.	D4	102
Wheatland, N.D., U.S.	C8	111
Wheatland, Pa., U.S.	D1	115
Wheatland, Wy., U.S.	D8	127
Wheatland, co., Mt., U.S.	D7	103
Wheatland Reservoir, res., Wy., U.S.	E7	127
Wheatley, Ont.	E2	73
Wheatley, Ar., U.S.	C4	81
Wheaton, Il., U.S.	B5	90
Wheaton, Ks., U.S.	C7	93
Wheaton, Md., U.S.	B3	97
Wheaton, Mn., U.S.	E2	100
Wheat Ridge, Co., U.S.	B5	83
Wheelbarrow Peak, mtn., Nv., U.S.	F5	105
Wheeler, Al., U.S.	A2	78
Wheeler, Ar., U.S.	A1	81
Wheeler, Il., U.S.	D5	90
Wheeler, In., U.S.	B3	91
Wheeler, Ks., U.S.	C2	93
Wheeler, Ms., U.S.	A5	101
Wheeler, Or., U.S.	B3	114
Wheeler, Tx., U.S.	B2	120
Wheeler, Wi., U.S.	C2	126
Wheeler, co., Ga., U.S.	D4	87
Wheeler, co., Ne., U.S.	C7	104
Wheeler, co., Or., U.S.	C6	114
Wheeler, co., Tx., U.S.	B2	120
Wheeler Air Force Base, mil., Hi., U.S.	g9	88
Wheeler Dam, Al., U.S.	A2	78
Wheeler Lake, res., Al., U.S.	A2	78
Wheeler Peak, mtn., Ca., U.S.	C4	82
Wheeler Peak, mtn., Nv., U.S.	E7	105
Wheeler Peak, mtn., N.M., U.S.	A4	108
Wheelersburg, Oh., U.S.	D3	112
Wheeling, Il., U.S.	h9	90
Wheeling, Mo., U.S.	B4	102
Wheeling, W.V., U.S.	A4	125
Wheeling Creek, stm., W.V., U.S.	f8	125
Wheelock, N.D., U.S.	A2	111
Wheelock, Vt., U.S.	B4	122
Wheelock Mountain, mtn., Vt., U.S.	B4	122
Wheelockville, Ma., U.S.	*B4	98
Wheelon, Ut., U.S.	*B3	121
Wheelwright, Ky., U.S.	C7	94
Wheelwright, Ma., U.S.	B3	98
Whelen Springs, Ar., U.S.	D2	81
Whernside, mtn., Eng., U.K.	F6	13
Whetstone, stm., U.S.	E2	100
Whickham, Eng., U.K.	F7	13
Whidbey Island, i., Wa., U.S.	A3	124
Whidbey Island Naval Air Station, mil., Wa., U.S.	A3	124
Whigham, Ga., U.S.	F2	87
Whigville, Ct., U.S.	C4	84
Whipholt, Mn., U.S.	C4	100
Whipple, W.V., U.S.	n13	125
Whiskey Gap, Alta.	E4	68
Whiskey Peak, mtn., Wy., U.S.	D5	127
Whiskeytown-Shasta-Trinity National Recreation Area, Ca., U.S.	B2	82
Whisky Chitto Creek, stm., La., U.S.	C2	95
Whistler, B.C.	D6	69
Whitacres, Ct., U.S.	A5	84
Whitakers, N.C., U.S.	A5	110
Whitbourne, Newf.	E5	72
Whitby, Ont.	D6	73
Whitby, Eng., U.K.	C6	10
Whitchurch, Eng., U.K.	B5	12
Whitchurch-Stouffville, Ont.	D5	73
Whitcombe, Mount, mtn., N.Z.	O13	51
Whitcomb Mountain, mtn., N.H., U.S.	A4	106
White, S.D., U.S.	C9	118
White, co., Ar., U.S.	B4	81
White, co., Ga., U.S.	B3	87
White, co., Il., U.S.	E5	90
White, co., In., U.S.	C4	91
White, co., Tn., U.S.	D8	119
White, stm., B.C.	D3	68
White, stm., U.S.	C4	81
White, stm., U.S.	C7	121
White, stm., Az., U.S.	D5	80
White, stm., In., U.S.	H2	91
White, stm., Mi., U.S.	E4	99
White, stm., Nv., U.S.	E6	105
White, stm., Vt., U.S.	D4	122
White, stm., Wa., U.S.	B4	124
White, East Fork, stm., In., U.S.	G5	91
White, Lake, l., Austl.	D4	50
White Bay, b., Newf.	D3	72
White Bear, Sask.	G1	75
White Bear, stm., Newf.	E3	72
White Bear Islands, is., Newf.	A3	72
White Bear Lake, Mn., U.S.	A5	100
White Bear Lake, l., Newf.	A2	72
White Bear Lake, l., Sask.	H4	75
White Bird, Id., U.S.	D2	89
White Bluff, Tn., U.S.	A4	119
White Breast Creek, stm., Ia., U.S.	C4	92
White Butte, mtn., N.D., U.S.	C2	111
White Cap Mountain, mtn., Me., U.S.	C3	96
White Carpathians, mts., Czech.	D4	26
White Castle, La., U.S.	D4	95
White Center, Wa., U.S.	e11	124
White City, Fl., U.S.	C1	86
White City, Ks., U.S.	D7	93
White City, Or., U.S.	E4	114
White City, Ut., U.S.	*C4	121
White Clay Creek, stm., U.S.	A3	104
White Clay Creek, stm., De., U.S.	B3	85
White Cliffs, Austl.	E4	51
White Cloud, Ks., U.S.	C8	93
White Cloud, Mi., U.S.	E5	99
White Coomb, mtn., Scot., U.K.	C5	10
White Creek, stm., U.S.	E2	122
Whiteday, stm., W.V., U.S.	h10	125
White Deer, Pa., U.S.	D8	115
White Deer, Tx., U.S.	B2	120
White Earth, Mn., U.S.	C3	100
White Earth, N.D., U.S.	A3	111
White Earth Indian Reservation, Mn., U.S.	C3	100
White Earth Lake, l., Mn., U.S.	C3	100
Whiteface, Tx., U.S.	C1	120
Whiteface, Mn., U.S.	C6	100
Whiteface Mountain, mtn., N.Y., U.S.	f10	109
White Face Mountain, mtn., Vt., U.S.	B3	122
White Fathers, N.Y., U.S.	f10	109
Whitefield, Me., U.S.	*D3	96
Whitefield, N.H., U.S.	*B3	106
Whitefield, Ok., U.S.	B6	113
Whitefish, Mt., U.S.	B2	103
Whitefish Bay, Wi., U.S.	m12	126
Whitefish Bay, b., Mi., U.S.	B6	99
Whitefish Falls, Ont.	A3	73
Whitefish Lake, l., Alta.	B4	68
Whitefish Lake, l., Mn., U.S.	D4	100
Whitefish Point, Mi., U.S.	B6	99
Whitefish Range, mts., Mt., U.S.	B2	103
White Fox, Sask.	D3	75
White Fox, stm., Sask.	D3	75
White Gull Creek, stm., Sask.	D3	75
Whitehall, Ire.	E4	11
White Hall, Al., U.S.	C3	78
White Hall, Ar., U.S.	C3	81
White Hall, Ga., U.S.	B3	87
White Hall, Il., U.S.	D3	90
White Hall, La., U.S.	D5	95
White Hall, Md., U.S.	A4	97
Whitehall, Mi., U.S.	E4	99
Whitehall, Mt., U.S.	E4	103
Whitehall, N.Y., U.S.	B7	109
Whitehall, Oh., U.S.	m11	112
Whitehall, Pa., U.S.	*E11	115
Whitehall, Pa., U.S.	*k14	115
Whitehall, S.C., U.S.	F6	117
Whitehall, Wi., U.S.	D2	126
Whitehall Reservoir, res., Ma., U.S.	h9	98
Whitehaven, Eng., U.K.	C5	10
Whitehaven, Md., U.S.	D6	97
White Haven, Pa., U.S.	D10	115
Whitehead, N. Ire., U.K.	C6	11
White Heath, Il., U.S.	C5	90
Whitehorn, Point, c., Wa., U.S.	A3	124
White Horse, Yukon	D5	66
White Horse, N.J., U.S.	C3	107
Whitehorse, S.D., U.S.	B5	118
White Horse Beach, Ma., U.S.	C6	98
Whitehouse, Oh., U.S.	A2	112
White House, Tn., U.S.	A5	119
White House Station, N.J., U.S.	B3	107
White Island, i., Ant.	C17	7
White Island, i., Ant.	f38	7
White Island Shores, Ma., U.S.	C6	98
White Knob Mountains, mts., Id., U.S.	F5	89
White Lake, Ont.	B8	73
White Lake, S.D., U.S.	D7	118
White Lake, Wi., U.S.	C5	126
White Lake, l., Ont.	B8	73
White Lake, l., La., U.S.	E3	95
Whitelaw, Alta.	A1	68
Whitelaw, Wi., U.S.	h10	126
Whiteman Air Force Base, mil., Mo., U.S.	C4	102
Whitemarsh Township, Pa., U.S.	*F11	115
White Meadow Lake, N.J., U.S.	B3	107
White Mesa Natural Bridge, Az., U.S.	A4	80
White Mills, Pa., U.S.	C11	115
White Mountain, Ak., U.S.	C7	79
White Mountain Peak, mtn., Ca., U.S.	D4	82
White Mountains, mts., U.S.	D4	82
White Mountains, mts., N.H., U.S.	B3	106
Whitemouth, Man.	E4	70
Whitemouth Lake, l., Man.	E4	70
Whitemud, stm., Alta.	A2	68
White Nile (Al Baḥr al Abyaḍ), stm., Sud.	C3	47
White Nile Dam, Sud.	B3	47
White Oak, Ga., U.S.	E5	87
White Oak, N.C., U.S.	C4	110
White Oak, Oh., U.S.	o12	112
White Oak, Pa., U.S.	*k14	115
White Oak, S.C., U.S.	C5	117
White Oak Creek, stm., Oh., U.S.	D2	112
Whiteoak Creek, stm., Tn., U.S.	A4	119
White Oak Lake, res., Ar., U.S.	D2	81
White Oak Mountain, mtn., Ar., U.S.	C2	81
White Owl, S.D., U.S.	C3	118
White Pass, N.A.	D12	79
White Pigeon, Mi., U.S.	G5	99
White Pine, Mi., U.S.	m12	99
White Pine, Tn., U.S.	C10	119
White Pine, co., Nv., U.S.	D6	105
White Plains, Ga., U.S.	C3	87
White Plains, Ky., U.S.	C2	94
White Plains, Md., U.S.	C4	97
White Plains, N.Y., U.S.	D7	109
White Plains, N.C., U.S.	A2	110
White Pond, S.C., U.S.	E5	117
Whiteriver, Az., U.S.	D6	80
White River, S.D., U.S.	D5	118
White River Junction, Vt., U.S.	D4	122
White River Plateau, plat., Co., U.S.	B3	83
White Rock, B.C.	E6	69
White Rock, N.M., U.S.	*B3	108
White Rock, R.I., U.S.	F1	116
White Rock, S.C., U.S.	C5	117
White Rock, S.D., U.S.	B9	118
White Rock Creek, stm., Ks., U.S.	C5	93
Whiterocks, Ut., U.S.	C6	121
White Rocks, mtn., Ky., U.S.	D6	94
White Russia, see Byelorussia, state, Sov. Un.	D5	29
Whitesail Lake, l., B.C.	C4	69
White Salmon, Wa., U.S.	D4	124
White Salmon, stm., Wa., U.S.	D4	124
Whitesand, stm., Sask.	F4	75
Whitesboro, N.J., U.S.	E3	107
Whitesboro, N.Y., U.S.	B5	109
Whitesboro, Ok., U.S.	C7	113
Whitesboro, Tx., U.S.	C4	120
Whitesburg, Ga., U.S.	C2	87
Whitesburg, Ky., U.S.	C7	94
Whites City, N.M., U.S.	E5	108
Whites Creek, stm., Tn., U.S.	g10	119
White Sea, Sov. Un.	C6	29
White Settlement, Tx., U.S.	*n9	120
Whiteshell Provincial Park, Man.	D4	70
Whiteshore Lake, l., Sask.	E1	75
Whiteside, Mo., U.S.	B6	102
Whiteside, Tn., U.S.	D8	119
Whiteside, co., Il., U.S.	B3	90
Whitestone, Or., U.S.	B3	114
Whitestone, Ga., U.S.	B2	87
White Stone, Va., U.S.	C6	123
White Stone Lake, l., Man.	A3	70
Whitestown, In., U.S.	C5	91
White Sulphur Springs, Mt., U.S.	D6	103
White Sulphur Springs, W.V., U.S.	D4	125
Whitesville, De., U.S.	G4	85
Whitesville, Ky., U.S.	C3	94
Whitesville, N.Y., U.S.	C3	109
Whitesville, W.V., U.S.	D3	125
White Swan, Wa., U.S.	C5	124
Whiteswan Lakes, l., Sask.	C3	75
Whitetail, Mt., U.S.	B11	103
White Tank Mountains, mts., Az., U.S.	k7	80
Whiteville, N.C., U.S.	C4	110
Whiteville, Tn., U.S.	B2	119
White Volta, stm., Afr.	D4	45
Whitewater, Man.	E1	70
Whitewater, Co., U.S.	C2	83
Whitewater, Ks., U.S.	E6	93
Whitewater, Mo., U.S.	D8	102
Whitewater, Wi., U.S.	F5	126
Whitewater, stm., U.S.	F7	91
Whitewater, stm., Ks., U.S.	E6	93
Whitewater, East Fork, stm., U.S.	E8	91
Whitewater, West Branch, stm., Ks., U.S.	g12	93
Whitewater Baldy, mtn., N.M., U.S.	D1	108
Whitewater Bay, b., Fl., U.S.	G6	86
White Woman Creek, stm., Ks., U.S.	D2	93
Whitewood, Sask.	G4	75
Whitewood, S.D., U.S.	C2	118
Whitewright, Tx., U.S.	C4	120
Whitfield, Al., U.S.	C1	78
Whitfield, co., Ga., U.S.	B2	87
Whitfield Estates, Fl., U.S.	q10	86
Whithorn, Scot., U.K.	C4	10
Whiting, In., U.S.	A3	91
Whiting, Ia., U.S.	B1	92
Whiting, Ks., U.S.	C8	93
Whiting, Me., U.S.	D5	96
Whiting, N.J., U.S.	C4	107
Whiting, Vt., U.S.	D2	122
Whiting, Wi., U.S.	D4	126
Whitingham, Vt., U.S.	F3	122
Whitinsville, Ma., U.S.	B4	98
Whiting Field Naval Air Station, mil., Fl., U.S.	u14	86
Whitlash, Mt., U.S.	B5	103
Whitley, co., In., U.S.	B6	91
Whitley, co., Ky., U.S.	D5	94
Whitley City, Ky., U.S.	D5	94
Whitlock, Tn., U.S.	A3	119
Whitman, Ma., U.S.	B6	98
Whitman, Ne., U.S.	B4	104
Whitman, N.D., U.S.	A7	111
Whitman, W.V., U.S.	D2	125
Whitman, co., Wa., U.S.	C8	124
Whitmans Pond, l., Ma., U.S.	h12	98
Whitman Square, N.J., U.S.	D2	107
Whitmell, Va., U.S.	D3	123
Whitmire, S.C., U.S.	C4	117
Whitmore Lake, Mi., U.S.	p14	99
Whitmore Mountains, mts., Ant.	A2	7
Whitmore Village, Hi., U.S.	f9	88
Whitney, Ont.	B6	73
Whitney, Id., U.S.	G7	89
Whitney, Pa., U.S.	F3	115
Whitney, Tx., U.S.	D4	120
Whitney, Lake, res., Tx., U.S.	D4	120
Whitney, Mount, mtn., Ca., U.S.	D4	82
Whitney Point, N.Y., U.S.	C5	109
Whitney Point Lake, res., N.Y., U.S.	C5	109
Whitsett, N.C., U.S.	A3	110
Whitstable, Eng., U.K.	C9	12
Whitt, Tx., U.S.	C3	120
Whittemore, Ia., U.S.	A3	92
Whittemore, Mi., U.S.	D7	99
Whitten, Ia., U.S.	B4	92
Whittier, Ak., U.S.	C10	79
Whittier, Ca., U.S.	F4	82
Whittier, N.H., U.S.	C4	106
Whittier, N.C., U.S.	f9	110
Whittlesey, Eng., U.K.	B7	12
Whittlesey, Mount, hill, Wi., U.S.	B3	126
Whitwell, Tn., U.S.	D8	119
Wholdaia Lake, l., N.W. Ter.	D12	66
Whyalla, Austl.	F6	50
Whycocomagh, N.S.	D8	71
Wiarton, Ont.	C3	73
Wiau Lake, l., Alta.	B5	68
Wibaux, Mt., U.S.	D12	103
Wibaux, co., Mt., U.S.	D12	103
Wichita, Ks., U.S.	E6	93
Wichita, co., Ks., U.S.	D2	93
Wichita, co., Tx., U.S.	B3	120
Wichita Falls, Tx., U.S.	C3	120
Wichita Mountains, mts., Ok., U.S.	C3	113
Wick, Scot., U.K.	A5	10
Wickatunk, N.J., U.S.	C4	107
Wickenburg, Az., U.S.	D3	80
Wickes, Ar., U.S.	C1	81
Wickes, Mt., U.S.	D4	103
Wickett, Tx., U.S.	D1	120
Wickham, Que.	D5	74
Wickiup Reservoir, res., Or., U.S.	E5	114
Wickliffe, Ky., U.S.	f8	94
Wickliffe, Oh., U.S.	*A5	112
Wicklow, Ire.	D3	10
Wicklow, co., Ire.	E5	11
Wicklow Head, c., Ire.	E6	11
Wicklow Mountains, mts., Ire.	D3	10
Wicomico, co., Md., U.S.	D6	97
Wicomico, co., Md., U.S.	D6	97
Wiconisco, Pa., U.S.	E8	115
Widefield, Co., U.S.	C6	83
Widen, W.V., U.S.	C4	125
Widener, Ar., U.S.	B5	81
Wide Ruins, Az., U.S.	B6	80
Widgeon, Eng., U.K.	A5	12
Wiebelskirchen, W. Ger.	D2	19
Wieliczka, Pol.	C6	26
Wieluń, Pol.	C5	26
Wiener Neustadt, Aus.	E8	18
Wiergate, Tx., U.S.	D6	120
Wieprz, stm., Pol.	C7	26
Wieprzanka, stm., Pol.	h10	26
Wiesau, W. Ger.	D7	19
Wiesbaden, W. Ger.	C4	18
Wiese, stm., W. Ger.	A4	21
Wiesenburg, E. Ger.	A7	19
Wiesental, W. Ger.	D3	19
Wiesloch, W. Ger.	D3	19
Wigan, Eng., U.K.	A5	12
Wiggins, Co., U.S.	A6	83
Wiggins, Ms., U.S.	E4	101
Wight, Isle of, i., Eng., U.K.	E6	10
Wigston, Eng., U.K.	F5	13
Wigtown, Scot., U.K.	C4	10
Wijhe, Neth.	B6	17
Wikieup, Az., U.S.	C2	80
Wikwemikong, Ont.	B3	73
Wil, Switz.	B5	20
Wilayah Persekutuan (Federal Territory), ter., Malay.	*K4	35
Wilbar, N.C., U.S.	A1	110
Wilbarger, co., Tx., U.S.	B3	120
Wilber, Ne., U.S.	D9	104
Wilberforce, Ont.	B6	73
Wilberforce, Oh., U.S.	C2	112
Wilbraham, Ma., U.S.	B3	98
Wilbur, Or., U.S.	D3	114
Wilbur, Wa., U.S.	B7	124
Wilburton, Ok., U.S.	C6	113
Wilcannia, Austl.	F7	50
Wilcox, Sask.	G3	75
Wilcox, Ne., U.S.	D6	104
Wilcox, Pa., U.S.	C4	115
Wilcox, co., Al., U.S.	D2	78
Wilcox, co., Ga., U.S.	E3	87
Wilczek, i., Sov. Un.	A8	128
Wild Ammonoosuc, stm., N.H., U.S.	B3	106
Wildbad [im Schwarzwald], W. Ger.	E3	19
Wild Branch, stm., Vt., U.S.	B4	122
Wildcat Creek, stm., In., U.S.	D4	91
Wildcat Hill, hill, Sask.	D4	75
Wildcat Top, mtn., Tn., U.S.	D10	119
Wilder, Id., U.S.	F2	89
Wilder, Vt., U.S.	D4	122
Wilder Dam, U.S.	C2	106
Wildervank (part of Veendam), Neth.	A7	16
Wilderville, Or., U.S.	E3	114
Wildeshausen, W. Ger.	F2	15
Wildhay, stm., Alta.	C2	68
Wildhaus, Switz.	B7	21
Wildhorn, mtn., Switz.	D3	21
Wild Horse, Co., U.S.	C7	83
Wildhorse Creek, stm., Ok., U.S.	C4	113
Wild Horse Reservoir, res., Nv., U.S.	B6	105
Wildhorst Lake, l., Sask.	C4	75
Wildorado, Tx., U.S.	B1	120
Wild Rice, stm., Mn., U.S.	C2	100
Wild Rice, stm., N.D., U.S.	C8	111
Wild Rice, South Branch, stm., Mn., U.S.	C2	100
Wild Rose, Wi., U.S.	D4	126
Wildrose, N.D., U.S.	A2	111
Wildsville, La., U.S.	C4	95
Wildwood, Alta.	C3	68
Wildwood, Fl., U.S.	D4	86
Wildwood, Il., U.S.	h9	90
Wildwood, N.J., U.S.	F3	107
Wildwood, Ut., U.S.	*C4	121
Wildwood Crest, N.J., U.S.	F3	107
Wiley, Co., U.S.	C8	83
Wiley, Wa., U.S.	C5	124
Wilhelm, Mount, mtn., Pap. N. Gui.	k12	50
Wilhelmina Gebergte, mts., Sur.	B3	59
Wilhelm-Pieck-Stadt Guben, E. Ger.	C7	18
Wilhelmshaven, W. Ger.	B4	18
Wilhoit, Az., U.S.	C3	80
Wilkau [-Hasslau], E. Ger.	C7	19
Wilkes, co., Ga., U.S.	C4	87
Wilkes, co., N.C., U.S.	A1	110
Wilkes-Barre, Pa., U.S.	D10	115
Wilkesboro, N.C., U.S.	A1	110
Wilkes Island, i., Wake I.	A1	52
Wilkes Land, reg., Ant.	B25	7
Wilkeson, Wa., U.S.	B3	124
Wilkie, Sask.	E1	75
Wilkin, co., Mn., U.S.	D2	100
Wilkinsburg, Pa., U.S.	F2	115
Wilkinson, In., U.S.	E6	91
Wilkinson, Ms., U.S.	D2	101
Wilkinson, W.V., U.S.	D3	125
Wilkinson, co., Ga., U.S.	D3	87
Wilkinson, co., Ms., U.S.	D2	101
Will, co., Il., U.S.	B6	90
Willacoochee, Ga., U.S.	E3	87
Willacy, co., Tx., U.S.	F4	120
Willamette, stm., Or., U.S.	C3	114
Willamette, Middle Fork, stm., Or., U.S.	D4	114
Willamette Pass, Or., U.S.	D4	114
Willamina, Or., U.S.	B3	114
Willangee, Austl.	E3	51
Willapa, Wa., U.S.	C2	124
Willapa Bay, b., Wa., U.S.	C1	124
Willard, Ks., U.S.	C8	93
Willard, Ky., U.S.	B7	94
Willard, Mo., U.S.	D4	102
Willard, Mt., U.S.	D12	103
Willard, N.M., U.S.	C3	108
Willard, N.Y., U.S.	C4	109
Willard, N.C., U.S.	C5	110
Willard, Oh., U.S.	A3	112
Willard, Ut., U.S.	B3	121
Willard, Wi., U.S.	D3	126
Willard Bay, b., Ut., U.S.	C3	121
Willards, Md., U.S.	D7	97
Willard Stream, stm., Vt., U.S.	B5	122
Willcox, Az., U.S.	E6	80
Willcox Playa, l., Az., U.S.	E5	80
Willemstad, Neth.	C4	17
Willemstad, Neth. Ant.	H19	65
Willet, N.Y., U.S.	C5	109
Willette, Tn., U.S.	C8	119
William "Bill" Dannelly Reservoir, res., Al., U.S.	C2	78
William Lake, l., Man.	C2	70
William P. Lane, Jr. Memorial Bridge, Md., U.S.	B5	97
Williams, Az., U.S.	B3	80
Williams, Ca., U.S.	C2	82
Williams, In., U.S.	G4	91
Williams, Ia., U.S.	B4	92
Williams, Mn., U.S.	B4	100
Williams, S.C., U.S.	E6	117
Williams, co., N.D., U.S.	A2	111
Williams, co., Oh., U.S.	A1	112
Williams, stm., Vt., U.S.	E3	122
Williams, stm., W.V., U.S.	C4	125
Williams, Cape, c., Ant.	B29	7
Williams Air Force Base, mil., Az., U.S.	D4	80
Williams Bay, Wi., U.S.	F5	126
Williamsburg, Ont.	C9	73
Williamsburg, Co., U.S.	*C5	83
Williamsburg, In., U.S.	E8	91
Williamsburg, Ia., U.S.	C5	92
Williamsburg, Ky., U.S.	D5	94
Williamsburg, Mi., U.S.	D5	99
Williamsburg, Oh., U.S.	C1	112
Williamsburg, Pa., U.S.	F5	115
Williamsburg, Va., U.S.	C6	123
Williamsburg, co., S.C., U.S.	D8	117
Williamsfield, Il., U.S.	B4	90
Williams Fork, stm., Co., U.S.	A3	83
Williams Harbour, Newf.	B4	72
Williams Lake, B.C.	C6	69
Williams Mountain, mtn., Ok., U.S.	C7	113
Williamson, Ga., U.S.	C2	87
Williamson, Ia., U.S.	C4	92
Williamson, N.Y., U.S.	B3	109
Williamson, W.V., U.S.	D2	125
Williamson, co., Il., U.S.	F4	90
Williamson, co., Tn., U.S.	B5	119
Williamson, co., Tx., U.S.	D4	120
Williamson, Mount, mtn., Ca., U.S.	D4	82
Williamsport, Newf.	C3	72
Williamsport, In., U.S.	D3	91
Williamsport, Md., U.S.	A2	97
Williamsport, Oh., U.S.	C2	112
Williamsport, Pa., U.S.	D7	115
Williamsport, Tn., U.S.	B4	119
Williamston, Mi., U.S.	F6	99
Williamston, N.C., U.S.	B5	110
Williamston, S.C., U.S.	B3	117
Williamstown, Ont.	B10	73
Williamstown, Ky., U.S.	B5	94
Williamstown, Ma., U.S.	A1	98
Williamstown, Mo., U.S.	A6	102
Williamstown, N.J., U.S.	D3	107
Williamstown, N.Y., U.S.	B5	109
Williamstown, Pa., U.S.	E8	115
Williamstown, Vt., U.S.	C3	122
Williamstown, W.V., U.S.	B3	125
Williamsville, Il., U.S.	D4	90
Williamsville, Mo., U.S.	D7	102
Williamsville, N.Y., U.S.	C2	109
Williford, Ar., U.S.	A4	81
Willimantic, Ct., U.S.	C7	84
Willimantic, stm., Ct., U.S.	B6	84
Willimantic Reservoir, res., Ct., U.S.	C7	84
Willingboro, N.J., U.S.	C3	107
Willis, Ks., U.S.	C8	93
Willis, Tx., U.S.	D5	120
Willis, Va., U.S.	D5	123
Willisburg, Ky., U.S.	C4	94
Willis Island, i., Newf.	D5	72
Williston, N.D., U.S.	A2	111
Williston, S.C., U.S.	E5	117
Williston, Tn., U.S.	B2	119
Williston, Vt., U.S.	C2	122
Williston Basin, U.S.	B2	111
Williston Lake, res., B.C.	B6	69
Williston Park, N.Y., U.S.	*E7	109
Willisville, Ar., U.S.	D2	81
Willisville, Il., U.S.	F4	90
Willis Wharf, Va., U.S.	C7	123
Willits, Ca., U.S.	C2	82
Willmar, Sask.	H4	75
Willmar, Mn., U.S.	E3	100
Willmore Wilderness Park, Alta.	C1	68
Willoughby, Austl.	*F9	51
Willoughby, Oh., U.S.	A4	112
Willoughby, Lake, l., Vt., U.S.	B4	122
Willoughby Hills, Oh., U.S.	A4	112
Willow, Ak., U.S.	g17	79
Willow, Ar., U.S.	C3	81
Willow, Ok., U.S.	B2	113
Willow, stm., B.C.	C6	69
Willow Branch, In., U.S.	E6	91
Willowbrook, Sask.	F4	75
Willow Brook, Ca., U.S.	*n12	82
Willowbrook, Il., U.S.	*B6	89
Willow Bunch, Sask.	H3	75
Willow Bunch Lake, l., Sask.	H3	75
Willow City, N.D., U.S.	A5	111
Willow City, Tx., U.S.	D3	120
Willow Creek, Mt., U.S.	E5	103
Willow Creek, stm., Alta.	E3	68
Willow Creek, stm., Nv., U.S.	E5	105
Willow Creek, stm., Ut., U.S.	C6	121
Willow Creek, stm., Wy., U.S.	D4	127
Willow Glen, La., U.S.	C3	95
Willow Grove, De., U.S.	D3	85
Willow Grove, Pa., U.S.	F11	115
Willow Grove Naval Air Station, mil., Pa., U.S.	F11	115
Willow Hill, Il., U.S.	E5	90
Willow Hill, Pa., U.S.	F6	115
Willowick, Oh., U.S.	A4	112
Willow Lake, Ne., U.S.	D5	104
Willow Lake, S.D., U.S.	C8	118
Willow Reservoir, res., Wi., U.S.	C3	126
Willow River, B.C.	C6	69
Willow River, Mn., U.S.	D6	100
Willow Run, De., U.S.	i7	85
Willow Run, Mi., U.S.	p14	99
Willows, Sask.	H3	75
Willows, Ca., U.S.	C2	82
Willow Springs, Il., U.S.	k9	90
Willow Springs, Mo., U.S.	E6	102
Willsboro, N.Y., U.S.	f11	109
Wills Hill, hill, Ma., U.S.	f11	98
Willshire, Oh., U.S.	B1	112
Wills Mountain, mtn., U.S.	k13	97
Willston, Va., U.S.	B5	123
Wilmar, Ar., U.S.	D4	81
Wilmer, Al., U.S.	E1	78
Wilmer, Tx., U.S.	n10	120
Wilmerding, Pa., U.S.	k14	115
Wilmersdorf, E. Ger.	E7	15
Wilmette, Il., U.S.	A6	90
Wilmington, Austl.	F2	51
Wilmington, De., U.S.	B3	85
Wilmington, Il., U.S.	B5	90
Wilmington, Ma., U.S.	A5	98
Wilmington, N.Y., U.S.	f11	109
Wilmington, N.C., U.S.	C5	110
Wilmington, Oh., U.S.	C2	112
Wilmington, Vt., U.S.	F3	122
Wilmington Island, Ga., U.S.	*E5	87
Wilmington Manor, De., U.S.	i7	85
Wilmington Manor Gardens, De., U.S.	*B3	85
Wilmont, Mn., U.S.	G3	100
Wilmore, Ks., U.S.	E4	93
Wilmore, Ky., U.S.	C5	94
Wilmot, N.S.	E4	71
Wilmot, Ar., U.S.	D4	81
Wilmot, N.H., U.S.	D3	106
Wilmot, Oh., U.S.	B4	112
Wilmot, S.D., U.S.	B9	118
Wilmot Flat, N.H., U.S.	D3	106
Wilmslow, Eng., U.K.	A5	12
Wilno, Ont.	B7	73
Wilsall, Mt., U.S.	E6	103
Wilsey, Ks., U.S.	D7	93
Wilson, Ar., U.S.	B5	81
Wilson, Ks., U.S.	D5	93
Wilson, La., U.S.	D4	95
Wilson, Mi., U.S.	C3	99
Wilson, N.Y., U.S.	B2	109
Wilson, N.C., U.S.	B5	110
Wilson, Ok., U.S.	C4	113
Wilson, Pa., U.S.	E11	115
Wilson, Tx., U.S.	C2	120
Wilson, Tx., U.S.	B3	121
Wilson, Wy., U.S.	C2	127
Wilson, co., Ks., U.S.	E8	93
Wilson, co., N.C., U.S.	B5	110
Wilson, co., Tn., U.S.	A5	119
Wilson, co., Tx., U.S.	E3	120
Wilson, Mount, mtn., Austl.	C4	51
Wilson, Mount, mtn., Az., U.S.	B1	80
Wilson, Mount, mtn., Ca., U.S.	m12	82
Wilson, Mount, mtn., Co., U.S.	D2	83
Wilson, Mount, mtn., Nv., U.S.	E7	105
Wilson, Mount, mtn., Or., U.S.	B5	114
Wilson Creek, Wa., U.S.	B6	124
Wilson Creek, stm., Wa., U.S.	B6	124
Wilson Dam, Al., U.S.	A2	78
Wilson Lake, l., Al., U.S.	A2	78
Wilson Lake, res., Ks., U.S.	D4	93
Wilson Piedmont Glacier, ice, Ant.	e39	7
Wilsons, Va., U.S.	C5	123
Wilsons Beach, N.B.	E3	71
Wilsons Mills, Me., U.S.	D1	96
Wilsons Mills, N.C., U.S.	B4	110
Wilsons Promontory, c., Austl.	G8	50
Wilsonville, Al., U.S.	B3	78
Wilsonville, Il., U.S.	A8	90
Wilsonville, Ne., U.S.	D5	104
Wilstedt, W. Ger.	E3	15
Wilster, W. Ger.	B3	15
Wilton, Al., U.S.	B3	78
Wilton, Ct., U.S.	D1	81
Wilton, Ia., U.S.	C6	92
Wilton, Me., U.S.	D2	96
Wilton, Mn., U.S.	D4	95
Wilton, N.H., U.S.	E3	106
Wilton, N.Y., U.S.	B7	109
Wilton, N.C., U.S.	A4	110
Wilton, N.D., U.S.	B5	111

Name	Map Ref.	Page
Wilton, Wi., U.S.	E3	126
Wilton Center, N.H., U.S.	E3	106
Wilton Manors, Fl., U.S.	*r13	86
Wiltshire, co., Eng., U.K.	C6	12
Wiltz, Lux.	C6	16
Wiluna, Austl.	E3	50
Wimapedi, stm., Man.	B2	70
Wimauma, Fl., U.S.	E4	86
Wimbledon (part of London), Eng., U.K.	m12	10
Wimbledon, N.D., U.S.	B7	111
Wimborne, Alta.	D4	68
Wimborne Minster, Eng., U.K.	D6	12
Wimico, Lake, l., Fl., U.S.	C1	86
Winagami Lake, l., Alta.	B2	68
Winamac, In., U.S.	B4	91
Winburg, S. Afr.	C4	49
Winburne, Pa., U.S.	E5	115
Wincheck Pond, l., R.I., U.S.	E1	116
Winchell Mountain, mtn., Ma., U.S.	B2	98
Winchendon, Ma., U.S.	A3	98
Winchendon Springs, Ma., U.S.	A3	98
Winchester, Ont.	B9	73
Winchester, Eng., U.K.	E6	10
Winchester, Ar., U.S.	D4	81
Winchester, Id., U.S.	C2	89
Winchester, Il., U.S.	D3	90
Winchester, In., U.S.	D8	91
Winchester, Ks., U.S.	k15	93
Winchester, Ky., U.S.	C5	94
Winchester, Ma., U.S.	g11	98
Winchester, Ms., U.S.	D5	101
Winchester, Mo., U.S.	A6	102
Winchester, Nv., U.S.	G6	105
Winchester, N.H., U.S.	E2	106
Winchester, Oh., U.S.	D2	112
Winchester, Tn., U.S.	B5	119
Winchester, Va., U.S.	A4	123
Winchester Bay, Or., U.S.	D2	114
Winchester Center, Ct., U.S.	B3	84
Wind, stm., Wa., U.S.	D4	124
Wind, stm., Wy., U.S.	C4	127
Windber, Pa., U.S.	F4	115
Wind Cave National Park, S.D., U.S.	D2	118
Wind Creek, stm., Wy., U.S.	C7	127
Windcrest, Tx., U.S.	*E3	120
Winder, Ga., U.S.	C3	87
Windermere, B.C.	D10	69
Windermere, Ont.	B5	73
Windermere, l., Eng., U.K.	F6	13
Windfall, Alta.	B2	68
Windfall, In., U.S.	D6	91
Windgap, Pa., U.S.	E11	115
Windham, Ct., U.S.	C7	84
Windham, Mt., U.S.	C6	103
Windham, N.Y., U.S.	C6	109
Windham, Oh., U.S.	A4	112
Windham, co., Ct., U.S.	B7	84
Windham, co., Vt., U.S.	F3	122
Windham Center, Me., U.S.	*E2	96
Windhoek, Nmb.	B2	49
Windigo, stm., Que.	B4	74
Winding Stair Mountain, mts., Ok., U.S.	C6	113
Wind Lake, Wi., U.S.	F5	126
Wind Lake, l., Wi., U.S.	n11	126
Windmill Point, c., Va., U.S.	C6	123
Windom, Ks., U.S.	D6	93
Windom, Mn., U.S.	G3	100
Windom Peak, mtn., Co., U.S.	D3	83
Window Rock, Az., U.S.	B6	80
Wind Point, Wi., U.S.	n12	126
Wind Ridge, Pa., U.S.	G1	115
Wind River Indian Reservation, Wy., U.S.	C4	127
Wind River Peak, mtn., Wy., U.S.	D3	127
Wind River Range, mts., Wy., U.S.	C3	127
Windsbach, W. Ger.	D5	19
Windsor, Newf.	D4	72
Windsor, N.S.	E5	71
Windsor, Ont.	E1	73
Windsor, Que.	D5	74
Windsor (New Windsor), Eng., U.K.	E6	10
Windsor, Co., U.S.	A6	83
Windsor, Ct., U.S.	B5	84
Windsor, Il., U.S.	D5	90
Windsor, Ma., U.S.	A1	98
Windsor, Mo., U.S.	C4	102
Windsor, N.J., U.S.	C3	107
Windsor, N.C., U.S.	B6	110
Windsor, N.D., U.S.	C6	111
Windsor, Pa., U.S.	G8	115
Windsor, S.C., U.S.	E4	117
Windsor, Vt., U.S.	E4	122
Windsor, Va., U.S.	D6	123
Windsor, co., Vt., U.S.	D3	122
Windsor Heights, Ia., U.S.	e8	92
Windsor Hills, Ca., U.S.	*n12	82
Windsor Locks, Ct., U.S.	B5	84
Windsorville, Ct., U.S.	B5	84
Windthorst, Sask.	G4	75
Windthorst, Tx., U.S.	C3	120
Windward Islands, is., N.A.	I14	64
Windward Passage, strt., N.A.	E7	64
Windygates, Man.	E2	70
Windy Hill, S.C., U.S.	C8	117
Windy Lake, l., Sask.	C4	75
Windy Peak, mtn., Wa., U.S.	A6	124
Windy Point, c., Newf.	C4	72
Winefred, stm., Alta.	B5	68
Winefred Lake, l., Alta.	B5	68
Winfall, N.C., U.S.	A6	110
Winfield, Alta.	C3	68
Winfield, Al., U.S.	B2	78
Winfield, Ia., U.S.	C6	92
Winfield, Ks., U.S.	E7	93
Winfield, Md., U.S.	B3	97
Winfield, Mo., U.S.	C7	102
Winfield, N.J., U.S.	k7	107
Winfield, Pa., U.S.	E8	115
Winfield, Tn., U.S.	C9	119
Winfield, W.V., U.S.	C3	125
Winfred, S.D., U.S.	D8	118
Wing, Al., U.S.	D3	78
Wing, Ar., U.S.	C2	81
Wing, N.D., U.S.	B5	111
Wing, stm., Mn., U.S.	D3	100
Wingate, In., U.S.	D4	91
Wingate, Md., U.S.	D5	97
Wingate, N.C., U.S.	C2	110
Winger, Mn., U.S.	C3	100
Wingham, Ont.	D3	73
Wingo, Ky., U.S.	f9	94
Winifred, Mt., U.S.	C7	103
Winifreda, Arg.	B4	54
Winifrede, W.V., U.S.	m12	125
Winigan, Mo., U.S.	A5	102
Winisk, Ont.	n18	73
Winisk, stm., Ont.	n18	73
Winisk Lake, l., Ont.	n18	73
Wink, Tx., U.S.	D1	120
Winkelman, Az., U.S.	E5	80
Winkler, Man.	E3	70
Winkler, co., Tx., U.S.	D1	120
Winlaw, B.C.	E9	69
Winlock, Wa., U.S.	C3	124
Winn, Me., U.S.	C4	96
Winn, Mi., U.S.	E6	99
Winn, co., La., U.S.	C3	95
Winnabow, N.C., U.S.	C4	110
Winnebago, Il., U.S.	A4	90
Winnebago, Mn., U.S.	G4	100
Winnebago, Ne., U.S.	B9	104
Winnebago, Wi., U.S.	h8	126
Winnebago, co., Il., U.S.	A4	90
Winnebago, co., Ia., U.S.	A4	92
Winnebago, co., Wi., U.S.	D5	126
Winnebago, stm., Ia., U.S.	A4	92
Winnebago, Lake, l., Wi., U.S.	E5	126
Winnebago Indian Reservation, Ne., U.S.	B9	104
Winneconne, Wi., U.S.	D5	126
Winnemucca, Nv., U.S.	C4	105
Winnemucca Lake, l., Nv., U.S.	C2	105
Winner, S.D., U.S.	D6	118
Winneshiek, co., Ia., U.S.	A6	92
Winnetka, Il., U.S.	A6	90
Winnetoon, Ne., U.S.	B8	104
Winnett, Mt., U.S.	C8	103
Winnfield, La., U.S.	C3	95
Winnibigoshish, Lake, l., Mn., U.S.	C4	100
Winnifred, Alta.	E5	68
Winnipeg, Man.	E3	70
Winnipeg, stm., Can.	D4	70
Winnipeg, Lake, l., Man.	C3	70
Winnipeg Beach, Man.	D3	70
Winnipegosis, Man.	D2	70
Winnipegosis, Lake, l., Man.	C2	70
Winnipesaukee, N.H., U.S.	C4	106
Winnipesaukee, Lake, l., N.H., U.S.	C4	106
Winnsboro, La., U.S.	B4	95
Winnsboro, S.C., U.S.	C5	117
Winnsboro, Tx., U.S.	C5	120
Winnsboro Mills, S.C., U.S.	C5	117
Winona, Ks., U.S.	C2	93
Winona, Mn., U.S.	F7	100
Winona, Ms., U.S.	B4	101
Winona, Mo., U.S.	D6	102
Winona, N.H., U.S.	C3	106
Winona, W.V., U.S.	C4	125
Winona, co., Mn., U.S.	F7	100
Winona Lake, In., U.S.	B6	91
Winona Lake, l., Vt., U.S.	C2	122
Winooski, Vt., U.S.	C2	122
Winooski, stm., Vt., U.S.	C3	122
Winooski, North Branch, stm., Vt., U.S.	C3	122
Winschoten, Neth.	A7	16
Vinsen, W. Ger.	E4	15
Winsford, Eng., U.K.	A5	12
Winside, Ne., U.S.	B8	104
Winslow, Az., U.S.	C5	80
Winslow, Ar., U.S.	B1	81
Winslow, Il., U.S.	A4	90
Winslow, In., U.S.	H3	91
Winslow, Me., U.S.	D3	96
Winslow, Ne., U.S.	C9	104
Winslow, N.J., U.S.	D3	107
Winston, co., Al., U.S.	A2	78
Winston, co., Ms., U.S.	B4	101
Winston-Salem, N.C., U.S.	A2	110
Winstonville, Ms., U.S.	B3	101
Winsum, Neth.	A6	17
Winter, Wi., U.S.	C2	126
Winter Beach, Fl., U.S.	E6	86
Winterberg, W. Ger.	B3	19
Winter Garden, Fl., U.S.	D5	86
Winter Harbor, Me., U.S.	D4	96
Winter Harbour, B.C.	D3	69
Winter Haven, Fl., U.S.	D5	86
Wintering Lake, l., Man.	B3	70
Winter Park, Co., U.S.	B5	83
Winter Park, Fl., U.S.	D5	86
Winter Park, N.C., U.S.	C5	110
Winterpock, Va., U.S.	C5	123
Winterport, Me., U.S.	D4	96
Winter Ridge, mtn., Or., U.S.	E6	114
Winters, Ca., U.S.	C2	82
Winters, Tx., U.S.	D3	120
Winterset, Ia., U.S.	C4	92
Winter Springs, Fl., U.S.	*D5	86
Wintersville, Oh., U.S.	B5	112
Winterswijk, Neth.	C6	17
Winterthur, Switz.	E4	18
Winterton, Newf.	E5	72
Winterville, Ga., U.S.	C3	87
Winterville, Me., U.S.	B4	96
Winterville, Ms., U.S.	B2	101
Winterville, N.C., U.S.	B5	110
Winthrop, Ar., U.S.	D1	81
Winthrop, Ct., U.S.	D5	84
Winthrop, Ia., U.S.	B6	92
Winthrop, Me., U.S.	D3	96
Winthrop, Ma., U.S.	B6	98
Winthrop, Mn., U.S.	F4	100
Winthrop, Mo., U.S.	B2	102
Winthrop, Wa., U.S.	A5	124
Winthrop Harbor, Il., U.S.	A6	90
Winton, Austl.	D8	50
Winton, Bah.	m18	64
Winton, Mn., U.S.	C7	100
Winton, N.C., U.S.	A6	110
Winton Lake, res., Oh., U.S.	o12	113
Wintzenheim, Fr.	A3	20
Winyah Bay, b., S.C., U.S.	E9	117
Wiota, Ia., U.S.	C3	92
Wirātnagar, Nepal	C8	36
Wirral, N.B.	D3	71
Wirt, Mn., U.S.	C5	100
Wirt, co., W.V., U.S.	B3	125
Wirtz, Va., U.S.	C3	123
Wisbech, Eng., U.K.	D7	10
Wiscasset, Me., U.S.	D3	96
Wisconsin, state, U.S.	D4	126
Wisconsin, stm., Wi., U.S.	E3	126
Wisconsin, Lake, res., Wi., U.S.	E4	126
Wisconsin Dells, Wi., U.S.	E4	126
Wisconsin Rapids, Wi., U.S.	D4	126
Wisdom, Mt., U.S.	E3	103
Wise, N.C., U.S.	A4	110
Wise, Va., U.S.	f9	123
Wise, co., Tx., U.S.	C4	120
Wise, co., Va., U.S.	e9	123
Wiseman, Ak., U.S.	B9	79
Wise River, Mt., U.S.	E4	103
Wiseton, Sask.	F2	75
Wishart, Sask.	F3	75
Wishart, Mo., U.S.	D4	102
Wishaw, Scot., U.K.	E5	13
Wishek, N.D., U.S.	C6	111
Wishram, Wa., U.S.	D4	124
Wisła (Vistula), stm., Pol.	B5	26
Wisłok, stm., Pol.	C7	26
Wisłoka, stm., Pol.	D6	26
Wismar, E. Ger.	B5	18
Wismar Bucht, b., E. Ger.	D5	15
Wisner, La., U.S.	C4	95
Wisner, Ne., U.S.	C9	104
Wissant, Fr.	D9	12
Wissembourg, Fr.	C7	16
Wissota, Lake, res., Wi., U.S.	D2	126
Wister, Ok., U.S.	C7	113
Wister Lake, res., Ok., U.S.	C7	113
Witbank, S. Afr.	C4	49
Witchekan Lake, l., Sask.	D2	75
Witch Lake, Mi., U.S.	B3	99
Witham, Eng., U.K.	C8	12
Witham, stm., Eng., U.K.	A7	12
Withee, Wi., U.S.	D3	126
Witherbee, N.Y., U.S.	A7	109
Witherspoon, Mount, mtn., Ak., U.S.	g18	79
Withlacoochee, stm., U.S.	B3	86
Withlacoochee, stm., Fl., U.S.	C4	86
Withrow, Wa., U.S.	B6	124
Witless Bay, Newf.	E5	72
Witney, Eng., U.K.	C6	12
Witry-lès-Reims, Fr.	E4	17
Witt, Il., U.S.	D4	90
Witten, W. Ger.	B2	19
Witten, S.D., U.S.	D5	118
Witten, l., W. Ger.	D3	15
Wittenberg, E. Ger.	C6	18
Wittenberg, Wi., U.S.	D4	126
Wittenberge, E. Ger.	B5	18
Wittenheim, Fr.	B3	20
Wittingen, W. Ger.	B3	18
Wittlich, W. Ger.	D3	18
Wittman, Md., U.S.	C5	97
Wittmann, Az., U.S.	D3	80
Wittmund, W. Ger.	A7	17
Wittstock, E. Ger.	B6	18
Witu Islands, is., Pap. N. Gui.	h12	50
Witvlei, Nmb.	B2	49
Witzenhausen, W. Ger.	B4	19
Wiveliscombe, Eng., U.K.	C4	12
Wiwŏn, N. Kor.	F3	33
Wixom, Mi., U.S.	o14	99
Wixom Lake, res., Mi., U.S.	E6	99
Wkra, stm., Pol.	B6	26
Władysławowo, Pol.	A5	26
Włocławek, Pol.	B5	26
Włodawa, Pol.	C7	26
Włoszczowa, Pol.	C5	26
Woburn, Que.	D7	74
Woburn, Ma., U.S.	B5	98
Woden, Ia., U.S.	A4	92
Wodzisław Śląski, Pol.	*C5	26
Woerden, Neth.	B4	17
Wohlen, Switz.	B5	21
Wohlthat Mountains, mts., Ant.	B14	7
Woito, Ont.	B7	73
Wokam, i., Indon.	G8	34
Woking, Alta.	B1	68
Woking, Eng., U.K.	m11	10
Wokingham, Eng., U.K.	C7	12
Wolbach, Ne., U.S.	C7	104
Wolcott, Co., U.S.	B4	83
Wolcott, Ct., U.S.	C3	84
Wolcott, In., U.S.	C3	91
Wolcott, N.Y., U.S.	B4	109
Wolcott, Vt., U.S.	B4	122
Wolcottville, In., U.S.	A7	91
Woldegk, E. Ger.	B7	15
Wolf, Wy., U.S.	B5	127
Wolf, stm., Ms., U.S.	E4	101
Wolf, stm., Tn., U.S.	e9	119
Wolf, stm., Wi., U.S.	C5	126
Wolf, Isla, i., Ec.	f5	58
Wolf, North Fork, stm., Tn., U.S.	B2	119
Wolf, Volcán, vol., Ec.	f5	58
Wolf Creek, Mt., U.S.	C4	103
Wolf Creek, Or., U.S.	E3	114
Wolf Creek, stm., U.S.	A2	113
Wolf Creek, stm., Mi., U.S.	B5	92
Wolf Creek, stm., Mi., U.S.	D7	99
Wolf Creek, stm., W.V., U.S.	m13	125
Wolf Creek Pass, Co., U.S.	D3	83
Wolfe, co., Que.	D6	74
Wolfe, co., Ky., U.S.	C6	94
Wolfeboro, N.H., U.S.	C4	106
Wolfeboro Falls, N.H., U.S.	C4	106
Wolfe City, Tx., U.S.	C4	120
Wolfegg, W. Ger.	A8	21
Wolfen, E. Ger.	B7	19
Wolfenbüttel, W. Ger.	B5	18
Wolfenschiessen, Switz.	C5	21
Wolfhagen, W. Ger.	B4	19
Wolf Island, Mo., U.S.	E8	102
Wolf Lake, Il., U.S.	F4	90
Wolf Lake, l., In., U.S.	B7	91
Wolf Lake, l., Mi., U.S.	D3	99
Wolf Lake, l., Mn., U.S.	B3	100
Wolf Lake, l., Alta.	B5	68
Wolf Lake, l., Il., U.S.	k9	90
Wolf Mountain, mtn., Ak., U.S.	B9	79
Wolf Point, Mt., U.S.	B11	103
Wolfratshausen, W. Ger.	D5	20
Wolfsberg, Aus.	E7	18
Wolfsburg, W. Ger.	B5	18
Wolfsville, Md., U.S.	A2	97
Wolf Swamp, sw., N.C., U.S.	C5	110
Wolf Trap, Va., U.S.	*B5	123
Wolfville, N.S.	D5	71
Wolgast, E. Ger.	A6	18
Wolhusen, Switz.	B4	20
Wolin, Pol.	B8	15
Wolin, i., Pol.	E8	15
Wollaston, Cape, c., N.W. Ter.	B9	66
Wollaston, Islas, is., Chile	k12	54
Wollaston Lake, l., Sask.	m8	75
Wollongong, Austl.	F9	50
Wolmaransstad, S. Afr.	C4	49
Wolmirstedt, E. Ger.	A6	19
Wołomin, Pol.	k14	26
Wołów, Pol.	B4	26
Wolseley, Sask.	G4	75
Wolsey, S.D., U.S.	C7	118
Wolstenholme, Austl.	I6	51
Wolsztyn, Pol.	B4	26
Wolverhampton, Eng., U.K.	C5	10
Wolverine, Mi., U.S.	C6	99
Wolverton, Eng., U.K.	B7	12
Wolverton, Mn., U.S.	D2	100
Womack Hill, Al., U.S.	D1	78
Woman Lake, l., Mn., U.S.	D4	100
Womelsdorf, Pa., U.S.	F9	115
Wonalancet, N.H., U.S.	C4	106
Wonder Lake, Il., U.S.	A5	90
Wonderland, Ca., U.S.	B3	82
Wonewoc, Wi., U.S.	E3	126
Wŏnju, S. Kor.	H3	33
Wonotobo Vallen, wtfl., Sur.	B7	69
Wonowon, B.C.	A7	69
Wŏnsan, N. Kor.	D10	31
Wonthaggi, Austl.	G8	50
Wood, N.C., U.S.	A4	110
Wood, Pa., U.S.	F5	115
Wood, S.D., U.S.	D5	118
Wood, co., Oh., U.S.	A2	112
Wood, co., Tx., U.S.	C5	120
Wood, co., W.V., U.S.	B3	125
Wood, co., Wi., U.S.	D3	126
Wood, stm., B.C.	C8	69
Wood, stm., Sask.	H2	75
Wood, stm., R.I., U.S.	F2	116
Wood, stm., Wy., U.S.	C3	127
Wood, Mount, mtn., Mt., U.S.	E7	103
Woodall Mountain, mtn., Ms., U.S.	A5	101
Woodberry, Ar., U.S.	D3	81
Woodbine, Ga., U.S.	F5	87
Woodbine, Il., U.S.	A3	90
Woodbine, Ia., U.S.	C2	92
Woodbine, Ks., U.S.	D7	93
Woodbine, Ky., U.S.	D5	94
Woodbine, Md., U.S.	B3	97
Woodbine, N.J., U.S.	E3	107
Woodbourne, N.Y., U.S.	D6	109
Woodbridge, Eng., U.K.	B9	12
Woodbridge, Va., U.S.	B5	123
Woodbridge [Township], N.J., U.S.	B4	107
Wood Buffalo National Park, Can.	E10	66
Woodburn, In., U.S.	B8	91
Woodburn, Ia., U.S.	C4	92
Woodburn, Ky., U.S.	D3	94
Woodburn, Or., U.S.	B4	114
Woodbury, Ct., U.S.	C3	84
Woodbury, Ga., U.S.	D2	87
Woodbury, Ky., U.S.	C3	94
Woodbury, Mn., U.S.	F6	100
Woodbury, N.J., U.S.	D2	107
Woodbury, N.Y., U.S.	*E7	109
Woodbury, Tn., U.S.	B5	119
Woodbury, Vt., U.S.	C4	122
Woodbury, co., Ia., U.S.	B1	92
Woodbury Mountain, mtn., Vt., U.S.	C4	122
Woodcliff, Ga., U.S.	D5	87
Woodcliff Lake, N.J., U.S.	g8	107
Woodcliff Lake, l., N.J., U.S.	g8	107
Wood Dale, Il., U.S.	k9	90
Wood End, spit, Ma., U.S.	B7	98
Woodenhawk, De., U.S.	E3	85
Woodfibre, B.C.	E6	69
Woodfield, S.C., U.S.	C6	117
Woodford, Ire.	D3	11
Woodford, S.C., U.S.	D5	117
Woodford, co., Il., U.S.	C4	90
Woodford, co., Ky., U.S.	B5	94
Woodfords, Ca., U.S.	C4	82
Woodhaven, Mi., U.S.	*F7	99
Woodhull, Il., U.S.	B3	90
Woodhull, N.Y., U.S.	C3	109
Woodlake, Ca., U.S.	D4	82
Wood Lake, Ne., U.S.	B5	104
Woodlake, Tx., U.S.	D5	120
Wood Lake, l., Sask.	H4	75
Woodland, Al., U.S.	B4	78
Woodland, Ca., U.S.	C3	82
Woodland, Ga., U.S.	D2	87
Woodland, Il., U.S.	C6	90
Woodland, Me., U.S.	C5	96
Woodland, Ms., U.S.	B4	101
Woodland, Pa., U.S.	E5	115
Woodland, Wa., U.S.	D3	124
Woodland Acres, Co., U.S.	D6	83
Woodland Beach, De., U.S.	C4	85
Woodland Mills, Tn., U.S.	A2	119
Woodland Park, Co., U.S.	C5	83
Woodlawn, Ont.	h11	73
Woodlawn, Il., U.S.	E4	90
Woodlawn, Ky., U.S.	e9	94
Woodlawn, Md., U.S.	*C4	97
Woodlawn, Oh., U.S.	n13	112
Woodlawn, Va., U.S.	D2	123
Woodleaf, N.C., U.S.	B2	110
Woodlynne, N.J., U.S.	*D2	107
Woodman, Wi., U.S.	E3	126
Woodmere, N.Y., U.S.	*k13	109
Woodmont, Ct., U.S.	E4	84
Woodmoor, Md., U.S.	B4	97
Wood Mountain, Sask.	H2	75
Woodport, N.J., U.S.	B3	107
Woodridge, Man.	E3	70
Wood-Ridge, N.J., U.S.	h8	107
Wood River, Il., U.S.	E3	90
Wood River, Ne., U.S.	D7	104
Wood River Junction, R.I., U.S.	F2	116
Woodrow, Sask.	H2	75
Woodruff, Az., U.S.	C5	80
Woodruff, S.C., U.S.	B3	117
Woodruff, Ut., U.S.	B4	121
Woodruff, co., Ar., U.S.	B4	81
Woods, co., Ok., U.S.	A3	113
Woods, Lake, l., Austl.	C5	50
Woods, Lake, res., Tn., U.S.	B5	119
Woods, Lake of the, l., N.A.	E4	70
Woodsboro, Md., U.S.	A3	97
Woodsboro, Tx., U.S.	E4	120
Woods Cross, Ut., U.S.	C4	121
Woodsdale, N.C., U.S.	A4	110
Woodsfield, Oh., U.S.	C4	112
Woods Hole, Ma., U.S.	C6	98
Woodside, Austl.	I6	51
Woodside, Ca., U.S.	*k8	82
Woodside, De., U.S.	D3	85
Wood's Island, Newf.	D2	72
Woodson, Ar., U.S.	C3	81
Woodson, Il., U.S.	D3	90
Woodson, Tx., U.S.	C3	120
Woodson, co., Ks., U.S.	E8	93
Woodstock, N.B.	C2	71
Woodstock, Ont.	D4	73
Woodstock, Al., U.S.	B2	78
Woodstock, Ct., U.S.	B8	84
Woodstock, Ga., U.S.	B2	87
Woodstock, Il., U.S.	A5	90
Woodstock, Md., U.S.	B4	97
Woodstock, N.H., U.S.	C3	106
Woodstock, N.Y., U.S.	C6	109
Woodstock, Oh., U.S.	B2	112
Woodstock, Vt., U.S.	D3	122
Woodstock, Va., U.S.	B4	123
Woodstock Valley, Ct., U.S.	B7	84
Woodstown, N.J., U.S.	D2	107
Woodville, Ont.	C5	73
Woodville, Austl.	*F6	50
Woodville, N.Z.	N15	51
Woodville, Fl., U.S.	B2	86
Woodville, Ga., U.S.	C3	87
Woodville, Id., U.S.	F6	89
Woodville, Ky., U.S.	e9	94
Woodville, Ma., U.S.	h9	98
Woodville, Mi., U.S.	E5	99
Woodville, Ms., U.S.	D2	101
Woodville, Oh., U.S.	A2	112
Woodville, Ok., U.S.	D5	113
Woodville, R.I., U.S.	F2	116
Woodville, Tx., U.S.	D5	120
Woodville, Wi., U.S.	D1	126
Woodward, Al., U.S.	B3	78
Woodward, Ok., U.S.	A2	113
Woodward, co., Ok., U.S.	A2	113
Woodwards Cove, N.B.	E3	71
Woodway, Tx., U.S.	*D4	120
Woodway, Va., U.S.	f9	123
Woodworth, La., U.S.	C3	95
Woodworth, N.D., U.S.	B6	111
Woody, Can.	C1	70
Wooldridge, Mo., U.S.	C5	102
Wooler, Eng., U.K.	E6	13
Woolford, Md., U.S.	C5	97
Woollahra, Austl.	*F9	50
Woolmarket, Ms., U.S.	E5	101
Woolper Creek, stm., Ky., U.S.	h13	94
Woolrich, Pa., U.S.	D7	115
Woolsey Peak, mtn., Az., U.S.	D3	80
Woolstock, Ia., U.S.	B4	92
Woolwich, Me., U.S.	g8	96
Woomera, Austl.	F6	50
Woonsocket, R.I., U.S.	A3	116
Woonsocket, S.D., U.S.	C7	118
Woonsocket Reservoir Number Three, res., R.I., U.S.	B3	116
Wooster, Ar., U.S.	B3	81
Wooster, Oh., U.S.	B4	112
Woosung, Il., U.S.	B4	90
Woqooyi Galbeed, prov., Som.	C5	47
Worb, Switz.	C4	21
Worbis, E. Ger.	B5	19
Worcester, S. Afr.	D2	49
Worcester, Eng., U.K.	D5	10
Worcester, Ma., U.S.	B4	98
Worcester, N.Y., U.S.	C6	109
Worcester, Vt., U.S.	C3	122
Worcester, co., Md., U.S.	D7	97
Worcester, co., Ma., U.S.	A3	98
Worcester Mountains, mts., Vt., U.S.	C3	122
Worden, Il., U.S.	E4	90
Worden, Mt., U.S.	E8	103
Worden, Or., U.S.	E5	114
Worden Pond, l., R.I., U.S.	F3	116
Wordsworth, Sask.	H4	75
Workington, Eng., U.K.	C5	10
Worksop, Eng., U.K.	B7	12
Workum, Neth.	B5	17
Worland, Wy., U.S.	B5	127
Worley, Id., U.S.	B2	89
Wormerveer, Neth.	B4	17
Worms, W. Ger.	C4	18
Worms, Ne., U.S.	C7	104
Worms Head, c., Wales, U.K.	C3	12
Woronoco, Ma., U.S.	B2	98
Worth, Mo., U.S.	A3	102
Worth, co., Ga., U.S.	E3	87
Worth, co., Ia., U.S.	A4	92
Worth, co., Mo., U.S.	A3	102
Wortham, Tx., U.S.	D4	120
Worthing, Eng., U.K.	E7	10
Worthing, S.D., U.S.	D9	118
Worthington, Ia., U.S.	B6	92
Worthington, In., U.S.	F4	91
Worthington, Ky., U.S.	B7	94
Worthington, Ma., U.S.	B2	98
Worthington, Mn., U.S.	G3	100
Worthington, Oh., U.S.	B2	112
Worthington, Pa., U.S.	E2	115
Worthington, W.V., U.S.	k10	125
Worthington Knob, mtn., Tn., U.S.	D8	119
Worthington Peak, mtn., Nv., U.S.	F6	105
Worthington Springs, Fl., U.S.	C4	86
Worthville, Ky., U.S.	B4	94
Worthville, N.C., U.S.	B3	110
Worton, Md., U.S.	B5	97
Wostok, Alta.	C4	68
Wotton, Que.	D5	74
Wounded Knee, S.D., U.S.	D3	118
Wouwani, Nic.	E8	63
Wowoni, i., Indon.	F6	34
Woy Woy, Austl.	f10	50
Woźniki, Pol.	E6	26
Wrangel Island, i., Sov. Un.	B21	29
Wrangell, Ak., U.S.	D13	79
Wrangell, Mount, mtn., Ak., U.S.	f19	79
Wrangell Island, i., Ak., U.S.	m24	79
Wrangell Mountains, mts., N.A.	D4	66
Wrangell Mountains, mts., Ak., U.S.	C11	79
Wrangell-Saint Elias National Park, Ak., U.S.	C11	79
Wrath, Cape, c., Scot., U.K.	A4	10
Wray, Co., U.S.	A8	83
Wray, Ga., U.S.	E3	87
Wren, Oh., U.S.	B1	112
Wrens, Ga., U.S.	C4	87
Wrenshall, Mn., U.S.	D6	100
Wrentham, Alta.	E4	68
Wrentham, Ma., U.S.	B5	98
Wrexham, Wales, U.K.	D5	10
Wriezen, E. Ger.	B7	18
Wright, Al., U.S.	A2	78
Wright, Fl., U.S.	*u15	86
Wright, Ia., U.S.	C5	92
Wright, Ks., U.S.	E4	93
Wright, Wy., U.S.	D5	100
Wright, co., Ia., U.S.	B4	92
Wright, co., Mn., U.S.	E4	100
Wright, co., Mo., U.S.	D5	102
Wright, Mount, mtn., Mt., U.S.	C4	103
Wright Brothers National Memorial, hist., N.C., U.S.	A7	110
Wright City, Mo., U.S.	C8	102
Wright City, Ok., U.S.	C6	113
Wright-Patterson Air Force Base, mil., Oh., U.S.	C1	112
Wrightson, Mount, mtn., Az., U.S.	F5	80
Wrightstown, N.J., U.S.	C3	107
Wrightstown, Wi., U.S.	D5	126
Wrightsville, Ar., U.S.	C3	81
Wrightsville, Ga., U.S.	D4	87
Wrightsville, Pa., U.S.	F8	115
Wrightsville Beach, N.C., U.S.	C5	110
Wrightsville Reservoir, res., Vt., U.S.	C3	122
Wrightwood, Ca., U.S.	E5	82
Wrigley, N.W. Ter.	D8	66
Wrigley, Tn., U.S.	B4	119
Wrigley Gulf, b., Ant.	B36	7
Wrocław (Breslau), Pol.	C4	26
Wrong Lake, l., Man.	C3	70
Wroxeter, Ont.	D3	73
Wroxham, Eng., U.K.	B9	12
Wroxton, Sask.	F5	75
Września, Pol.	B4	26
Wschowa, Pol.	C4	26
Wuchang, China	D3	33
Wuchou see Wuzhou, China	G7	31
Wuchuan, China	J3	32
Wuchuan, China	I7	32
Wuchuan, China	B9	35
Wuda, China	D6	31
Wudaoliang, China	D3	31
Wudu, China	E6	31
Wufeng, China	I4	32
Wugang, China	F7	31
Wuhai, China	E2	32
Wuhan, China	E7	31
Wuhe, China	H7	32
Wuhu, China	E8	31
Wu Jiang, stm., China	F6	31
Wukari, Nig.	E6	45
Wum, Cam.	D2	46
Wümme, stm., W. Ger.	E3	15
Wunnummin Lake, l., Ont.	C6	19
Wunsiedel, W. Ger.	C6	19
Wunstorf, W. Ger.	A4	19
Wupatki National Monument, Az., U.S.	B4	80
Wuppertal, W. Ger.	C3	18
Wurtsboro, N.Y., U.S.	D6	109
Wurtsmith Air Force Base, mil., Mi., U.S.	D7	99
Württemberg, hist. reg., W. Ger.	D4	18
Würzburg, W. Ger.	D4	18
Wurzen, E. Ger.	C6	18
Wushan, China	B2	70
Wushan, China	E2	32
Wuskwatim Lake, l., Man.	B2	70
Wusong, China	I9	32
Wusuli (Ussuri), stm., Asia	B11	35
Wutongqiao, China	F5	31
Wuwei, China	D5	31
Wuwei, China	I7	32
Wuxi, China	E9	31
Wuyi, China	F6	32
Wuyi, China	B10	31
Wuyiling, China	C6	31
Wuyuan, China	C6	31
Wuzhi Peak, mtn., China	B3	34
Wuzhong, China	E2	32
Wuzhou (Wuchou), China	G7	31
Wyaconda, Mo., U.S.	A6	102
Wyaconda, stm., Mo., U.S.	A6	102
Wyalusing, Pa., U.S.	C9	115
Wyandot, co., Oh., U.S.	B2	112
Wyandotte, Mi., U.S.	F7	99
Wyandotte, Ok., U.S.	A7	113
Wyandotte, co., Ks., U.S.	C9	93
Wyandra, Austl.	C6	51
Wyanet, Il., U.S.	B4	90
Wyarno, Wy., U.S.	B6	127
Wyatt, In., U.S.	A5	91
Wyatt, Mo., U.S.	E8	102
Wyckoff, N.J., U.S.	*A4	107
Wyco, W.V., U.S.	D3	125
Wye, stm., U.K.	C5	12
Wyebridge, Ont.	C5	73
Wye Mills, Md., U.S.	C5	97
Wyevale, Ont.	C5	73
Wyeville, Wi., U.S.	D3	126
Wykoff, Mn., U.S.	G6	100
Wylie, Lake, res., U.S.	A5	117
Wyliesburg, Va., U.S.	D4	123
Wyman Lake, res., Me., U.S.	C3	96
Wymark, Sask.	G2	75
Wymondham, Eng., U.K.	B9	12
Wymore, Ne., U.S.	D9	104
Wyndham, Austl.	C4	50
Wynne, N.D., U.S.	C8	111
Wynnburg, Tn., U.S.	A2	119
Wynne, Ar., U.S.	B5	81
Wynnewood, Ok., U.S.	C4	113
Wynona, Ok., U.S.	A5	113
Wynot, Ne., U.S.	B8	104
Wynyard, Sask.	F3	75
Wyocena, Wi., U.S.	E4	126
Wyodak, Wy., U.S.	B7	127
Wyola, Mt., U.S.	E8	103
Wyoming, Ont.	E2	73
Wyoming, De., U.S.	D3	85
Wyoming, Il., U.S.	B4	90
Wyoming, Ia., U.S.	B6	92
Wyoming, Mi., U.S.	F5	99
Wyoming, Mn., U.S.	E6	100

Name	Map Ref.	Page
Wyoming, N.Y., U.S.	C2	109
Wyoming, Oh., U.S.	o13	112
Wyoming, Pa., U.S.	n17	115
Wyoming, R.I., U.S.	E2	116
Wyoming, co., N.Y., U.S.	C2	109
Wyoming, co., Pa., U.S.	D9	115
Wyoming, co., W.V., U.S.	D3	125
Wyoming, state, U.S.	C5	127
Wyoming Peak, mtn., Wy., U.S.	D2	127
Wyoming Range, mts., Wy., U.S.	D2	127
Wyomissing, Pa., U.S.	F10	115
Wyrzysk, Pol.	B4	26
Wysocking Bay, b., N.C., U.S.	B7	110
Wysokie Mazowieckie, Pol.	B7	26
Wyszków, Pol.	B6	26
Wythe, co., Va., U.S.	D1	123
Wytheville, Va., U.S.	D1	123
Wytopitlock, Me., U.S.	C4	96
Wyvis, Ben, mtn., Scot., U.K.	C4	13

X

Name	Map Ref.	Page
Xaafuun, Som.	C7	47
Xainza, China	B8	36
Xai-Xai (João Belo), Moz.	C5	49
Xalin, Som.	D6	47
Xambioá, Braz.	D5	59
Xam Nua, Laos	A2	34
Xangongo, Ang.	E1	48
Xánthi, Grc.	B5	40
Xapecó, stm., Braz.	D2	56
Xapuri, Braz.	E2	55
Xarardheere, Som.	E6	47
Xau, l., Bots.	B3	49
Xbonil, Mex.	D6	63
Xcalak, Mex.	D7	63
Xenia, Il., U.S.	E5	90
Xenia, Oh., U.S.	C2	112
Xiaguan, China	F5	31
Xiajiang, China	F8	31
Xiajin, China	F6	32
Xiamen (Amoy), China	G8	31
Xi'an (Sian), China	E6	31
Xiangfan, China	E7	31
Xiang Jiang, stm., China	J5	32
Xiangkhoang, Laos	B2	34
Xiangtan, China	F7	31
Xiangxiang, China	K5	32
Xianning, China	J6	32
Xianyang, China	E6	31
Xianyou, China	F8	31
Xiao Hinggan Ling (Lesser Khingan Range), mts., China	B10	31
Xiapu, China	F9	31
Xichang, China	F5	31
Xifeng, China	C11	32
Xigazê, China	C8	36
Xi Jiang, stm., China	G7	31
Xilitla, Mex.	m14	63
Xin Barag Zuoqi, China	B8	31
Xinbin, China	D11	32
Xincai, China	H6	32
Xingcheng, China	D9	32
Xinghua, China	H8	32
Xingkai Hu (Lake Khanka), l., Asia	B11	31
Xingtai, China	D7	31
Xingu, stm., Braz.	C4	59
Xinhua, China	K4	32
Xining, China	D5	31
Xinjiang, China	G4	32
Xinjiang Uygur, prov., China	C2	31
Xinjin, China	D9	31
Xinmin, China	C9	31
Xinning, China	K4	32
Xintai, China	*D8	31
Xinwen, China	G7	32
Xinxian, China	D7	31
Xinxiang, China	D7	31
Xinyang, China	E7	31
Xinye, China	H5	32
Xinyi He, stm., China	G8	32
Xinzhou, China	C8	35
Xique-Xique, Braz.	D2	57
Xishui, China	I6	32
Xi Ujimqin Qi, China	B7	32
Xiushui, China	J6	32
Xixabangma Mountain, mtn., Asia	C8	36
Xixian, China	F4	32
Xizang see Tibet, prov., China	E3	31
Xochimilco (part of Mexico City), Mex.	h9	63
Xuancheng, China	I8	32
Xuanhua, China	C8	31
Xuchang, China	E7	31
Xuddun, Som.	D6	47
Xuddur, Som.	E5	47
Xuguit Qi (Yakeshi), China	*B9	31
Xunhe, China	B4	33
Xunke, China	B4	33
Xupu, China	K4	32
Xuwen, China	B9	35
Xuyi, China	H8	32
Xuy Nong, is., Viet.	B7	35
Xuyong, China	F6	31
Xuzhou (Süchow), China	E8	31

Y

Name	Map Ref.	Page
Ya'an, China	F5	31
Ya'bad, Isr. Occ.	B7	41
Yabassi, Cam.	E2	46
Yabbenohr Island, i., Marsh Is.	S17	52
Yablis, Nic.	C6	62
Yablonovy Mountains, mts., Sov. Un.	D14	29
Yabu, Japan	N5	52
Yabucoa, P.R.	B4	65
Yacata, i., Fiji	H16	52
Yachats, Or., U.S.	C2	114
Yacheng, China	B3	34
Yaco (Iaco), stm., S.A.	D3	58
Yacolt, Wa., U.S.	D3	124
Yacuiba, Bol.	D3	55
Yad Eli'ezer, Isr.	h10	41
Yadkin, co., N.C., U.S.	A2	110
Yadkin, stm., N.C., U.S.	B2	110
Yadkinville, N.C., U.S.	A2	110
Yad Mordekhay, Isr.	C6	41
Yadong, China	D12	37
Yadua, i., Fiji	H15	52
Yagasa Cluster, is., Fiji	I16	52
Yagoua, Cam.	C3	46
Yaguajay, Cuba	C4	64
Yaguas, stm., Peru	B3	58
Yahk, B.C.	E9	69
Yahuma, Zaire	A3	48
Yainax Butte, mtn., Or., U.S.	E5	114
Yaizu, Japan	o17	33
Yakima, Wa., U.S.	C5	124
Yakima, co., Wa., U.S.	C4	124
Yakima, stm., Wa., U.S.	C6	124
Yakima Indian Reservation, Wa., U.S.	C5	124
Yakima Ridge, mtn., Wa., U.S.	C5	124
Yakima Valley, val., Wa., U.S.	C5	124
Yako, Burkina	D4	45
Yakobi Island, i., Ak., U.S.	m21	79
Yakoma, Zaire	A3	48
Yaku Island, i., Japan	E11	31
Yakutat, Ak., U.S.	D12	79
Yakutat Bay, b., Ak., U.S.	D11	79
Yakutsk, Sov. Un.	C15	29
Yala, Thai.	D2	34
Yalaha, Fl., U.S.	D5	86
Yale, B.C.	E7	69
Yale, Il., U.S.	D5	90
Yale, Ia., U.S.	C3	92
Yale, Mi., U.S.	E8	99
Yale, Ok., U.S.	A5	113
Yale, S.D., U.S.	C8	118
Yale, Va., U.S.	D5	123
Yale, Mount, mtn., Co., U.S.	C5	83
Yale Lake, res., Wa., U.S.	D3	124
Yalinga, Cen. Afr. Rep.	D4	46
Yallahs Hill, hill, Jam.	F15	65
Yalobusha, co., Ms., U.S.	A4	101
Yalobusha, stm., Ms., U.S.	B4	101
Yalong Jiang, stm., China	E5	31
Yalova, Tur.	B7	40
Yalta, Sov. Un.	I10	27
Yalu, China	B9	31
Yalu Jiang, stm., Asia	C9	31
Yalutorovsk, Sov. Un.	B7	28
Yalvaç, Tur.	C8	40
Yama, Sov. Un.	q21	27
Yamachiche, Que.	C5	74
Yamagata, Japan	D13	31
Yamaguchi, Japan	I5	33
Yamal Peninsula, pen., Sov. Un.	B9	29
Yamantau, Mount, mtn., Sov. Un.	D8	29
Yamaska (Saint-Michel), Que.	C5	74
Yamaska, co., Que.	C5	74
Yambio, Sud.	E2	47
Yambol, Bul.	D8	24
Yamdena, i., Indon.	G8	34
Yamethin, Burma	D10	36
Yamhill, Or., U.S.	h11	114
Yamhill, co., Or., U.S.	B3	114
Yamkino, Sov. Un.	n18	27
Yamma Yamma, Lake, l., Austl.	E7	50
Yamoussoukro, I.C.	E3	45
Yampa, Co., U.S.	A4	83
Yampa, stm., Co., U.S.	A2	83
Yampa Plateau, plat., U.S.	A1	83
Yamparáez, Bol.	C2	55
Yamsay Mountain, mtn., Or., U.S.	E5	114
Yamsk, Sov. Un.	D18	29
Yamuna, stm., India	C7	36
Yamzho Yumco, l., China	C9	36
Yana, stm., Sov. Un.	C16	29
Yanac, Austl.	H3	51
Yanam, India	E7	36
Yan'an, China	D6	31
Yanaoca, Peru	D3	58
Yanaul, Sov. Un.	D20	8
Yanbu' al Baḩr, Sau. Ar.	C3	38
Yancey, co., N.C., U.S.	f10	110
Yanceyville, N.C., U.S.	A3	110
Yancheng, China	*E9	31
Yancheng, China	H9	32
Yancheng, China	H5	32
Yanfolila, Mali	D3	45
Yangambi, Zaire	A3	48
Yangbajain, China	B13	37
Yangchou see Yangzhou, China	E8	31
Yangchun, China	G7	31
Yangdŏk, N. Kor.	G3	33
Yangiyul, Sov. Un.	G22	8
Yangjiang, China	G7	31
Yangquan, China	D7	31
Yangtze (Chang Jiang), stm., China	E8	31
Yangxian, China	H2	32
Yangyang, S. Kor.	G4	33
Yangzhou (Yangchou), China	E8	31
Yanji, China	C10	31
Yankeetown, Fl., U.S.	C4	86
Yankeetown, In., U.S.	I3	91
Yankton, S.D., U.S.	E8	118
Yankton, co., S.D., U.S.	D8	118
Yanonge, Zaire	A3	48
Yanqi, China	C2	31
Yanshan, China	E7	32
Yanshi, China	G5	32
Yanshou, China	D4	33
Yantai, China	D9	31
Yantic, stm., Ct., U.S.	C7	84
Yantley, Al., U.S.	C1	78
Yantra, stm., Bul.	D7	24
Yanush, Ok., U.S.	C6	113
Yanzhou, China	D8	31
Yao, Chad	C3	46
Yao, Japan	*I7	33
Yaosca, Nic.	D5	62
Yaoundé, Cam.	E2	46
Yap, i., Micron.	F8	6
Yapen, i., Indon.	F9	34
Yaphank, N.Y., U.S.	*n16	109
Yaqeta, i., Fiji	H14	52
Yaque del Norte, stm., Dom. Rep.	E8	64
Yaqui, stm., Mex.	B3	63
Yar, Sov. Un.	B4	28
Yaracuy, state, Ven.	A4	60
Yaraka, Austl.	D7	50
Yardley, Pa., U.S.	F12	115
Yardville, N.J., U.S.	C3	107
Yarensk, Sov. Un.	C18	8
Yarí, stm., Col.	C3	60
Yarīm, Yemen	C5	47
Yaritagua, Ven.	A4	60
Yarker, Ont.	C8	73
Yarkovo, Sov. Un.	B7	28
Yarmouth, N.S.	F3	71
Yarmouth, Ia., U.S.	C6	92
Yarmouth, Me., U.S.	E2	96
Yarmouth, Ma., U.S.	C7	98
Yarmouth, co., N.S.	F4	71
Yarmouth Port, Ma., U.S.	*C7	98
Yarmūk, Nahr al, stm., Asia	B7	41
Yarnell, Az., U.S.	C3	80
Yarnema, Sov. Un.	F18	14
Yaroslavl, Sov. Un.	D6	29
Yarovskoye Marsh, sw., Sov. Un.	B8	28
Yarqah, Mayyat, well, Eg.	E5	41
Yarqon, stm., Isr.	B6	41
Yarram, Austl.	I6	51
Yarrow, B.C.	f13	69
Yarrowsburg, Md., U.S.	B2	97
Yartsevo, Sov. Un.	C27	8
Yartsevo, Sov. Un.	D9	27
Yarumal, Col.	B2	60
Yasawa, i., Fiji	H14	52
Yasawa Group, is., Fiji	H14	52
Yashi, Nig.	D6	45
Yasinovataya, Sov. Un.	q20	27
Yasinya, Sov. Un.	A7	24
Yasothon, Thai.	E6	35
Yass, Austl.	F8	50
Yata, Bol.	B2	55
Yates, co., N.Y., U.S.	C3	109
Yatesboro, Pa., U.S.	E3	115
Yates Center, Ks., U.S.	E8	93
Yates City, Il., U.S.	C3	90
Yatesville, Ga., U.S.	D2	87
Yathkyed Lake, l., N.W. Ter.	D13	66
Yatsuga, Mount, mtn., Japan	n17	33
Yatsushiro, Japan	J5	33
Yatsushiro Sea, Japan	J4	33
Yaṭṭah, Isr. Occ.	C7	41
Yauca, Peru	E3	58
Yauco, P.R.	B2	65
Yauco, Embalse de, res., P.R.	B2	65
Yauli, Peru	D2	58
Yaupi, Ec.	B2	58
Yauri, Peru	D3	58
Yautepec, Mex.	n14	63
Yauyos, Peru	D2	58
Yavapai, co., Az., U.S.	C3	80
Yavarí (Javari), stm., S.A.	B3	58
Yavatmāl, India	G7	37
Yaví, Cerro, mtn., Ven.	B4	60
Yaviza, Pan.	F9	62
Yavne, Isr.	C6	41
Yavorov, Sov. Un.	G4	27
Yawatahama, Japan	J6	33
Yawgoog Pond, l., R.I., U.S.	E1	116
Yaxian, China	B3	34
Yazd (Yezd), Iran	B5	38
Yazoo, co., Ms., U.S.	C3	101
Yazoo, stm., Ms., U.S.	C3	101
Yazoo City, Ms., U.S.	C3	101
Ybbs, stm., Aus.	D7	18
Yding Skovhøj, hill, Den.	B3	15
Ye, Burma	E10	36
Yeadon, Pa., U.S.	p21	115
Yeager, Ok., U.S.	B5	113
Yeagertown, Pa., U.S.	E6	115
Yebbi Bou, Chad	A3	46
Yecla, Spain	C5	22
Yeddo, In., U.S.	D3	91
Yefremov, Sov. Un.	E12	27
Yegindybulak, Sov. Un.	D9	28
Yegoryevsk, Sov. Un.	D12	27
Yeguas, Punta, c., P.R.	B4	65
Yehud, Isr.	g10	41
Yei, Sud.	E3	47
Yekaterinoslavka, Sov. Un.	A4	33
Yelabuga, Sov. Un.	D19	8
Yelabuga, Sov. Un.	B7	33
Yelan, Sov. Un.	F14	27
Yelan-Kolenovskiy, Sov. Un.	F13	27
Yelanskoye, Sov. Un.	C15	29
Yelets, Sov. Un.	D6	29
Yélimané, Mali	C2	45
Yell, co., Ar., U.S.	B2	81
Yell, i., Scot., U.K.	g10	10
Yellandu, India	I8	37
Yellow, stm., U.S.	u15	86
Yellow, stm., Ga., U.S.	h8	87
Yellow, stm., In., U.S.	B4	91
Yellow, stm., Wi., U.S.	D3	126
Yellow, stm., Wi., U.S.	C3	126
Yellow Creek, Sask.	E3	75
Yellow Creek, stm., Tn., U.S.	A4	119
Yellow Grass, Sask.	H3	75
Yellowhead Pass, Can.	C1	68
Yellow see Huang He, stm., China	D8	31
Yellow Jacket, Co., U.S.	D2	83
Yellowjacket Mountains, mts., Id., U.S.	D4	89
Yellowknife, N.W. Ter.	D10	66
Yellow Lake, l., Wi., U.S.	C1	126
Yellow Medicine, co., Mn., U.S.	F2	100
Yellow Pine, Al., U.S.	D1	78
Yellow Pine, Id., U.S.	E3	89
Yellow Sea, Asia	D9	31
Yellow Springs, Md., U.S.	B3	97
Yellow Springs, Oh., U.S.	C2	112
Yellowstone, co., Mt., U.S.	D8	103
Yellowstone, stm., U.S.	D10	103
Yellowstone, Clarks Fork, stm., U.S.	F7	103
Yellowstone Lake, l., Wy., U.S.	B2	127
Yellowstone National Park, Wy., U.S.	B2	127
Yellowstone National Park, co., Mt., U.S.	E6	103
Yellowstone National Park, U.S.	B2	127
Yellville, Ar., U.S.	A3	81
Yelm, Wa., U.S.	C3	124
Yelnya, Sov. Un.	D9	27
Yeltes, stm., Spain	B2	22
Yelverton Bay, b., N.W. Ter.	k35	66
Yelvington, Ky., U.S.	C3	94
Yelwa, Nig.	D5	45
Yemanzhelinsk, Sov. Un.	C6	28
Yemassee, S.C., U.S.	F6	117
Yemen, ctry., Asia	D4	38
Yena, Sov. Un.	D14	14
Yenakiyevo, Sov. Un.	G12	27
Yenangyat, Burma	B1	35
Yenangyaung, Burma	B1	35
Yenashimskiy Polkan, Mount, mtn., Sov. Un.	D12	29
Yen Bai, Viet.	B6	35
Yendéré, Burkina	D4	45
Yendi, Ghana	E4	45
Yenice, stm., Tur.	B9	40
Yenisey, stm., Sov. Un.	C11	29
Yenisey Ridge, mts., Sov. Un.	D27	8
Yeniseysk, Sov. Un.	D12	29
Yentna, stm., Ak., U.S.	f16	79
Yeo Lake, l., Austl.	E3	50
Yeoman, In., U.S.	C4	91
Yeotmal see Yavatmāl, India	G7	37
Yeovil, Eng., U.K.	E5	10
Yeppoon, Austl.	D9	50
Yeránia Óri, mts., Grc.	g10	25
Yerba Buena, Chile	E1	55
Yerevan, Sov. Un.	E7	29
Yerington, Nv., U.S.	E2	105
Yerington Indian Reservation, Nv., U.S.	D2	105
Yermakovskoye, Sov. Un.	E27	8
Yermentau, Sov. Un.	C8	28
Yermo, Ca., U.S.	E5	82
Yermolayevo, Sov. Un.	C5	28
Yerres, Fr.	h10	16
Yerres, stm., Fr.	F2	17
Yerseke, Neth.	C4	17
Yershov, Sov. Un.	C3	28
Yerupaja, Nevado, mtn., Peru	D2	58
Yeso, N.M., U.S.	C5	108
Yessentuki, Sov. Un.	G17	8
Yessey, Sov. Un.	C13	29
Yeste, Spain	C4	22
Yetter, Ia., U.S.	B3	92
Yeu, Île d', i., Fr.	D2	16
Yevlach, Sov. Un.	E3	28
Yevpatoriya, Sov. Un.	I9	27
Yexian, China	F8	32
Yeya, stm., Sov. Un.	H12	27
Yeysk, Sov. Un.	H12	27
Yezd see Yazd, Iran	B5	38
Yi, stm., Ur.	E1	56
Yiannitsá, Grc.	B4	25
Yíaros, i., Grc.	D5	25
Yibin, China	F5	31
Yichang, China	E7	31
Yicheng, China	I5	32
Yichuan, China	D7	31
Yichun, China	B10	31
Yichun, China	K6	32
Yidu, China	I4	32
Yidu, China	F8	32
Yigo, Guam	L10	52
Yilan, China	B10	31
Yiliang, China	G5	31
Yimianpo, China	D4	33
Yinchuan, China	D6	31
Yingde, China	G7	31
Ying He, stm., China	E8	31
Yingkou, China	C9	31
Yingshang, China	H7	32
Yingxian, China	E5	32
Yining, China	E11	29
Yin Mountains, mts., China	D4	32
Yioúra, i., Grc.	C5	25
Yirga Alem, Eth.	D4	47
Yirol, Sud.	D3	47
Yishan, China	G6	31
Yíthion, Grc.	D4	40
Yitong, China	C11	32
Yixian, China	D9	32
Yixing, China	I8	32
Yiyang, China	F7	31
Ylig Bay, b., Guam	M10	52
Ylikitka, l., Fin.	D13	14
Ymers, i., Grnld.	B16	128
Ymir, B.C.	E9	69
Yoakum, Tx., U.S.	E4	120
Yoakum, co., Tx., U.S.	C1	120
Yockanookany, stm., Ms., U.S.	C4	101
Yocona, stm., Ms., U.S.	A4	101
Yoder, In., U.S.	C7	91
Yoder, Ks., U.S.	g11	93
Yoder, Wy., U.S.	E8	127
Yogyakarta, Indon.	G4	34
Yoho National Park, B.C.	D9	69
Yoichi, Japan	E10	33
Yojoa, Lago de, l., Hond.	C3	62
Yokadouma, Cam.	E2	46
Yokkaichi, Japan	E12	31
Yoko, Cam.	D2	46
Yokoate Island, i., Japan	L4	33
Yokohama, Japan	D12	31
Yokoshiba, Japan	n19	33
Yokosuka, Japan	D12	31
Yokote, Japan	G10	33
Yokum Seat, mtn., Ma., U.S.	B1	98
Yola, Nig.	E7	45
Yolo, co., Ca., U.S.	C2	82
Yolyn, W.V., U.S.	n12	125
Yom, stm., Thai.	B1	34
Yomba Indian Reservation, Nv., U.S.	D4	105
Yona, Guam	M10	52
Yonabaru, Japan	O5	52
Yonago, Japan	I6	33
Yonaha Mountain, hill, Japan	N6	52
Yoncalla, Or., U.S.	D3	114
Yonezawa, Japan	H10	33
Yong'an, China	F8	31
Yŏngan, N. Kor.	F4	33
Yonges Island, S.C., U.S.	F7	117
Yonghŭng, N. Kor.	G3	33
Yŏngil Bay, b., S. Kor.	H4	33
Yongji, China	G4	32
Yongnian, China	F6	32
Yongshou, China	G2	32
Yongshun, China	F6	31
Yongxiu, China	J6	32
Yonkers, N.Y., U.S.	E7	109
Yonne, stm., Fr.	D5	16
Yopal, Col.	B3	60
Yorba Linda, Ca., U.S.	*n13	82
York, Austl.	F2	50
York, Ont.	D5	73
York, Eng., U.K.	D6	10
York, Al., U.S.	C1	78
York, Il., U.S.	D6	90
York, In., U.S.	A8	91
York, Me., U.S.	E2	96
York, Ne., U.S.	D8	104
York, N.D., U.S.	A6	111
York, Pa., U.S.	G8	115
York, S.C., U.S.	B5	117
York, co., N.B.	C3	71
York, co., Ont.	D5	73
York, co., Me., U.S.	E2	96
York, co., Ne., U.S.	D8	104
York, co., Pa., U.S.	G8	115
York, co., S.C., U.S.	A5	117
York, co., Va., U.S.	C6	123
York, stm., Ont.	B7	73
York, stm., Va., U.S.	C6	123
York, Cape, c., Austl.	B7	50
York, Kap, c., Grnld.	B14	61
York Beach, Me., U.S.	E2	96
Yorke Peninsuia, pen., Austl.	F6	50
Yorketown, N.J., U.S.	*C4	107
York Factory, Man.	A5	70
York Harbor, Me., U.S.	E2	96
York Haven, Pa., U.S.	F8	115
Yorklyn, De., U.S.	A3	85
York Point, c., Newf.	C4	72
Yorkshire, N.Y., U.S.	C2	109
York Springs, Pa., U.S.	F7	115
Yorkton, Sask.	F4	75
Yorktown, Ar., U.S.	C4	81
Yorktown, In., U.S.	D7	91
Yorktown, Ia., U.S.	D2	92
Yorktown, N.J., U.S.	D2	107
Yorktown, N.Y., U.S.	*D7	109
Yorktown, Tx., U.S.	E4	120
Yorktown, Va., U.S.	C6	123
Yorktown Heights, N.Y., U.S.	*D7	109
Yorktown Manor, R.I., U.S.	C3	116
Yorkville, Il., U.S.	B5	90
Yorkville, N.Y., U.S.	B5	109
Yorkville, Oh., U.S.	B5	112
Yorkville, Tn., U.S.	A2	119
Yoro, Hond.	C4	62
Yorosso, Mali	D4	45
Yoseki, Zaire	A3	48
Yosemite, Ky., U.S.	C5	94
Yosemite National Park, Ca., U.S.	D4	82
Yosemite National Park, Ca., U.S.	D4	82
Yoshkar-Ola, Sov. Un.	B3	28
Yos Sudarsa Islands, i., Indon.	G9	34
Yost, Ut., U.S.	B2	121
Yost Lake, Ok., U.S.	A5	113
Yŏsu, S. Kor.	I3	33
Yotala, Bol.	C2	55
Yotvata, Isr.	E7	41
Youbou, B.C.	g11	69
Youghal, Ire.	D2	10
Youghal Bay, b., Ire.	E3	10
Youghiogheny, stm., U.S.	F2	115
Youghiogheny River Lake, res., U.S.	G3	115
You Jiang, stm., China	G6	31
Youkounkoun, Gui.	D2	45
Young, Austl.	G7	51
Young, Sask.	F3	75
Young, Az., U.S.	C5	80
Young, Ur.	E1	56
Young, co., Tx., U.S.	C3	120
Young America, In., U.S.	C5	91
Young Harris, Ga., U.S.	B3	87
Youngs, Lake, l., Wa., U.S.	f11	124
Youngs Creek, In., U.S.	H4	91
Youngs Point, Ont.	C6	73
Youngstown, Alta.	D5	68
Youngstown, Fl., U.S.	B1	86
Youngstown, In., U.S.	F3	91
Youngstown, N.Y., U.S.	B1	109
Youngstown, Oh., U.S.	A5	112
Youngsville, La., U.S.	D3	95
Youngsville, N.M., U.S.	A3	108
Youngsville, N.C., U.S.	A4	110
Youngsville, Pa., U.S.	C3	115
Youngtown, Az., U.S.	k8	80
Youngwood, Pa., U.S.	F2	115
Youssoufia, Mor.	C3	44
Youxi, China	K8	32
Youyang, China	J3	32
Youyu, China	C7	31
Yozgat, Tur.	C10	40
Ypacaraí, Para.	E4	55
Ypané, stm., Para.	D4	55
Ypres see Ieper, Bel.	B5	16
Ypsilanti, Mi., U.S.	F7	99
Ypsilanti, N.D., U.S.	C7	111
Yreka, Ca., U.S.	B2	82
Yssingeaux, Fr.	E6	16
Ystad, Swe.	J5	14
Ythan, stm., Scot., U.K.	C6	13
Yu'alliq, Jabal, mtn., Eg.	D5	41
Yuan'an, China	I4	32
Yuanjiang, China	G5	31
Yuan Jiang (Red), stm., Asia	G5	31
Yuan Jiang (Red), stm., Asia	G5	36
Yuan Jiang, stm., China	F7	31
Yuanling, China	F7	31
Yuanping, China	E5	32
Yuanshi, China	F6	32
Yuba, Ok., U.S.	D5	113
Yuba, co., Ca., U.S.	C3	82
Yuba, stm., Ca., U.S.	C3	82
Yuba City, Ca., U.S.	C3	82
Yūbari, Japan	E10	33
Yucaipa, Ca., U.S.	*E5	82
Yucatán, state, Mex.	C7	63
Yucatan Channel, strt., N.A.	C7	63
Yucca, Az., U.S.	C1	80
Yucca Lake, l., Nv., U.S.	F5	105
Yucca Mountain, mtn., Nv., U.S.	G5	105
Yucca Valley, Ca., U.S.	*E5	82
Yucheng, China	F7	32
Yuci, China	F5	32
Yudu, China	F8	31
Yueqing, China	F9	31
Yueyang, China	F7	31
Yug, stm., Sov. Un.	A3	28
Yugoslavia, ctry., Eur.	C4	24
Yuhuan, China	J9	32
Yukhnov, Sov. Un.	D10	27
Yukon, Ok., U.S.	B4	113
Yukon, W.V., U.S.	D3	125
Yukon, prov., Can.	D5	66
Yukon, stm., N.A.	C9	79
Yule Bay, b., Ant.	B29	7
Yulee, Fl., U.S.	B5	86
Yuli, Nig.	E7	45
Yulin, China	G7	31
Yulin, China	D6	31
Yulin, China	G7	31
Yulin, China	B3	34
Yuma, Az., U.S.	E1	80
Yuma, Co., U.S.	A8	83
Yuma, Mi., U.S.	D5	99
Yuma, co., Az., U.S.	E1	80
Yuma, co., Co., U.S.	A8	83
Yuma Desert, des., N.A.	E1	80
Yuma Marine Corps Air Station, mil., Az., U.S.	E1	80
Yumbi, Zaire	B4	48
Yumen, China	D4	31
Yumenzhen, China	C4	31
Yuna, Japan	N6	52
Yuna, stm., Dom. Rep.	E8	64
Yuncheng, China	D7	31
Yungas, reg., Bol.	C2	55
Yungay, Chile	B2	54
Yungay, Peru	C2	58
Yun Gui Plateau, plat., China	F5	31
Yunhe, China	J8	32
Yunnan, prov., China	G5	31
Yunnan Plateau see Yun Gui Plateau, plat., China	F5	31
Yunta, Austl.	F2	51
Yunxian, China	G5	31
Yunxian, China	E7	31
Yurécuaro, Mex.	m12	63
Yurga, Sov. Un.	D25	8
Yurimaguas, Peru	C2	58
Yurino, Sov. Un.	C16	27
Yuriria, Mex.	m13	63
Yurochi Island, i., Marsh Is.	P18	52
Yuryevets, Sov. Un.	C14	27
Yuryev-Polskiy, Sov. Un.	C12	27
Yuscarán, Hond.	E7	63
Yushan, China	J8	32
Yü Shan, mtn., Tai.	G9	31
Yushkozero, Sov. Un.	E15	14
Yushu, China	E4	31
Yutan, Ne., U.S.	C9	104
Yutian, China	E7	32
Yuty, Para.	E4	55
Yuwang, China	F2	32
Yuxian, China	E6	32
Yuyao, China	I9	32
Yuzha, Sov. Un.	C13	27
Yuzhno-Sakhalinsk, Sov. Un.	E17	29
Yuzhnoye, Sov. Un.	C11	33
Yverdon, Switz.	E3	18
Yvetot, Fr.	C4	16
Yvonand, Switz.	C2	21
Yzeure, Fr.	D5	16

Z

Name	Map Ref.	Page
Zaanstad, Neth.	A6	16
Zabīd, Yemen	D4	38
Ząbki, Pol.	k14	26
Ząbkowice, Pol.	g10	26
Ząbkowice 95Śląskie], Pol.	C4	26
Zābol, Iran	B6	38
Zābolī, Iran	H10	39
Zabré, Burkina	D4	45
Zabrze, Pol.	C5	26
Zacapa, Guat.	E7	63
Zacapu, Mex.	n13	63
Zacatecas, Mex.	C4	63
Zacatecas, state, Mex.	C4	63
Zacatecoluca, El Sal.	D3	62
Zachary, La., U.S.	D4	95
Zacoalco [de Torres], Mex.	C4	63
Zacualpan, Mex.	m14	63
Zacualtipán, Mex.	m14	63
Zadar, Yugo.	C2	24
Zadetkale, i., Burma	G3	35
Zadetkyi, i., Burma	H3	35
Zadonsk, Sov. Un.	E12	27
Zafer, Cape, c., N. Cyp.	E10	40
Zafra, Spain	C2	22
Zafra, Ok., U.S.	C7	113
Żagań, Pol.	C3	26
Zaghouan, Tun.	B7	44
Zagorá, Grc.	C4	25
Zagora, Mor.	C3	44
Zagorsk, Sov. Un.	C12	27
Zagreb, Yugo.	C2	24
Zagros Mountains, mts., Iran	E3	39
Zagyva, stm., Hung.	B5	24
Zāhedān, Iran	C6	38
Zahl, N.D., U.S.	A2	111
Zaḩlah, Leb.	F10	40
Zahna, E. Ger.	B7	19
Zailiyskiy Alatau Mountains, mts., Sov. Un.	E9	28
Zaire, dept., Ang.	C1	48
Zaire, ctry., Afr.	B3	48
Zaire Basin (Congo Basin), Afr.	B3	48
Zaječar, Yugo.	D6	24
Zaka, Zimb.	B5	49
Zakataly, Sov. Un.	B16	40
Zākhū, Iraq	D14	40
Zákinthos, Grc.	D3	40
Zákinthos (Zante), i., Grc.	D3	40
Zakopane, Pol.	D5	26
Zakroczym, Pol.	B6	26
Zala, stm., Hung.	B3	24
Zalaegerszeg, Hung.	B3	24
Zalamea de la Serana, Spain	C3	22
Zalamea la Real, Spain	D2	22
Zalău, Rom.	B6	24
Zaleski, Oh., U.S.	C3	112
Zalewo, Pol.	B5	26
Zalingei, Sud.	C1	47
Zalma, Mo., U.S.	D7	102
Zaltbommel, Neth.	C5	17
Zama, Ms., U.S.	C4	101
Zambales Mountains, mts., Phil.	o13	34
Zambezi (Balovale), Zam.	D3	48
Zambezi, stm., Afr.	H8	42
Zambézia, dept., Moz.	A6	49
Zambia, ctry., Afr.	D4	48
Zamboanga, Phil.	D6	34
Zambrano, Col.	B3	60
Zambrów, Pol.	B7	26
Zamora, Ec.	B2	58
Zamora, Spain	B3	22
Zamora, stm., Ec.	B2	58
Zamora-Chinchipe, prov., Ec.	B2	58
Zamora de Hidalgo, Mex.	D4	63
Zamość, Pol.	C7	26
Zamzam, Wādī, val., Libya	C2	43
Zanaga, Congo	B1	48
Zandvoort, Neth.	B4	17
Zanesville, In., U.S.	C7	91
Zanesville, Oh., U.S.	C4	112
Zanjān, Iran	B4	38
Zanpa Cape, c., Japan	O5	52
Zante see Zákinthos, i., Grc.	D3	40
Zanzibar, Tan.	C6	48
Zanzibar, i., Tan.	C6	48
Zaozhuang, China	G7	32
Zap, N.D., U.S.	B4	111
Zapadna Morava, stm., Yugo.	D5	24
Západočeský, prov., Czech.	D8	19
Zapala, Arg.	B2	54
Zapata, Tx., U.S.	F3	120
Zapata, co., Tx., U.S.	F3	120
Zapata, Península de, pen., Cuba	C3	64
Zapatoca, Col.	B3	60
Zapopan, Mex.	m12	63
Zaporozhye, Sov. Un.	E6	29
Zapotillo, Ec.	B1	58
Zara, Tur.	C11	40
Zaragoza, Col.	B3	60
Zaragoza, Mex.	B4	63
Zaragoza, Mex.	k13	63
Zaragoza, Spain	B5	22
Zarand, Iran	F8	39
Zárate, Arg.	A5	54
Zaraysk, Sov. Un.	D12	27
Zaraza, Ven.	B4	60
Zard Kūh, mtn., Iran	E5	39
Zarembo Island, i., Ak., U.S.	m23	79
Zarephath, N.J., U.S.	B3	107
Zaria, Nig.	D6	45
Zarnekow, E. Ger.	E7	15
Zarqā', Nahr az, stm., Jord.	B7	41
Zarrentin, E. Ger.	E4	15
Zarrīn Shahr, Iran	E5	39
Zaruma, Ec.	B2	58
Zarumilla, Peru	B1	58
Żary, Pol.	C3	26
Zarzal, Col.	C2	60
Zarzis, Tun.	C7	44
Zasenbeck, W. Ger.	F4	15
Zasieki, Pol.	C3	26
Zásmuky, Czech.	o19	26
Zastavna, Sov. Un.	A7	24
Zastron, S. Afr.	D4	49
Žatec, Czech.	C2	26
Zator, Pol.	h10	26
Zavala, co., Tx., U.S.	E3	120
Zavalla, Tx., U.S.	D5	120
Zavitinsk, Sov. Un.	D15	29
Zavodo-Petrovskiy, Sov. Un.	B7	28
Zawiercie, Pol.	C5	26
Zawīlah, Libya	D3	43

Name	Map Ref.	Page
Zāwiyat Masūs, Libya	C4	43
Zawr, Ra's az, c., Sau. Ar.	H4	39
Zaysan, Sov. Un.	E11	29
Zaysan, Lake, l., Sov. Un.	E11	29
Zaza, stm., Cuba	C4	64
Zbraslav, Czech.	o17	26
Žd'ár [nad Sazavou], Czech.	D3	26
Zdice, Czech.	o16	26
Zdolbunov, Sov. Un.	F6	27
Zduńska Wola, Pol.	C5	26
Zealandia, Sask.	F2	75
Zearing, Ia., U.S.	B4	92
Zeballos, B.C.	D4	69
Zebla, mtn., Tun.	F2	23
Zebrzydowice, Pol.	h9	26
Zebulon, Ga., U.S.	C2	87
Zebulon, Ky., U.S.	C7	94
Zebulon, N.C., U.S.	B4	110
Zeebrugge (part of Brugge), Bel.	B5	16
Zeeland, Mi., U.S.	F5	99
Zeeland, N.D., U.S.	D6	111
Zeeland, prov., Neth.	C3	17
Zeerust, S. Afr.	C4	49
Zefat (Safad), Isr.	F10	40
Zegrze, Pol.	k14	26
Zehdenick, E. Ger.	B6	18
Zeigler, Il., U.S.	F4	90
Zeil, Mount, mtn., Austl.	D5	50
Zeist, Neth.	A6	16
Zeitz, E. Ger.	C6	18
Zekiah Swamp Run, stm., Md., U.S.	D4	97
Żelechów, Pol.	C6	26
Zelenodolsk, Sov. Un.	B3	28
Zelenogorsk, Sov. Un.	A7	27
Zelenograd, Sov. Un.	C11	27
Železná Ruda, Czech.	D8	19
Zelienople, Pa., U.S.	E1	115
Zell, S.D., U.S.	C7	118
Zella-Mehlis, E. Ger.	C5	18
Zell am Ziller, Aus.	B7	20
Zeller Lake, l., Aus.	B8	20
Zelma, Sask.	F3	75
Zelzate, Bel.	C3	17
Zembra, i., Tun.	F3	23
Zemetchino, Sov. Un.	E14	27
Zemio, Cen. Afr. Rep.	D5	46
Zenda, Ks., U.S.	E5	93
Zendeh Jān, Afg.	D10	39
Zenica, Yugo.	C3	24
Zenith, Ks., U.S.	E5	93
Zenith, Wa., U.S.	f11	124
Zenon Park, Sask.	D4	75
Zenobia Peak, mtn., Co., U.S.	A2	83
Zeona, S.D., U.S.	B3	118
Zepče, Yugo.	C4	24
Zephyr, Tx., U.S.	D3	120
Zephyr Cove, Nv., U.S.	E2	105
Zephyrhills, Fl., U.S.	D4	86
Zerbst, E. Ger.	C6	18
Zereh, Gowd-e, depr., Afg.	C3	36
Zernez, Switz.	C6	20
Zermatt, Switz.	C3	20
Zeta, stm., Yugo.	D4	24
Zeulenroda, E. Ger.	C6	19
Zeven, W. Ger.	E3	15
Zevenaar, Neth.	C6	17
Zevgolation, Grc.	D3	25
Zeya, Sov. Un.	D15	29
Zeya, stm., Sov. Un.	D15	29
Zeya Reservoir, res., Sov. Un.	D15	29
Zgierz, Pol.	C5	26
Zgorzelec, Pol.	C3	26
Zhanatas, Sov. Un.	E7	28
Zhangbei, China	D6	32
Zhangiztobe, Sov. Un.	D10	28
Zhangjiakou, China	C7	31
Zhangwu, China	C10	32
Zhangye, China	D5	31
Zhangzhou (Changchou), China	G8	31
Zhanjiang, China	G7	31
Zhanyu, China	B10	32
Zhao'an, China	G8	31
Zhaodong, China	A11	32
Zhaoqing, China	G7	31
Zhaotong, China	F5	31
Zhaoxing, China	C5	33
Zhaoyuan, China	B11	32
Zhaozhou, China	D2	33
Zhari Namco, l., China	B8	36
Zharkamys, Sov. Un.	D5	28
Zhashui, China	H3	32
Zhaxigang, China	A7	37
Zhdanov see Mariupol, Sov. Un.	E6	29
Zhecheng, China	G6	32
Zhejiang, prov., China	F9	31
Zhelaniya, Cape, c., Sov. Un.	B9	29
Zhen'an, China	H3	32
Zhenba, China	H2	32
Zheng'an, China	J2	32
Zhenglan Qi, China	C6	32
Zhengyangguan, China	H7	32
Zhengzhou (Chengchou), China	E7	31
Zhenjiang, China	E8	31
Zhenlai, China	B10	32
Zhenping, China	I3	32
Zhenyuan, China	K3	32
Zhidachov, Sov. Un.	D8	26
Zhidan, China	D6	31
Zhigansk, Sov. Un.	C15	29
Zhijiang, China	K3	32
Zhilaya Kosa, Sov. Un.	D4	28
Zhilevo, Sov. Un.	o18	27
Zhitomir, Sov. Un.	D5	29
Zhizdra, Sov. Un.	E10	27
Zhmerinka, Sov. Un.	G7	27
Zhob, Pak.	B4	36
Zhob, stm., Pak.	B2	37
Zhongba, China	C7	36
Zhongdian, China	F5	31
Zhongwei, China	D6	31
Zhongxian, China	E6	31
Zhongxiang, China	I5	32
Zhoukou, China	*E7	32
Zhoushan Qundao, is., China	E9	31
Zhuanghe, China	E10	32
Zhucheng, China	F8	32
Zhuji, China	J9	32
Zhukovskiy, Sov. Un.	n18	27
Zhumadian, China	H6	32
Zhuoxian, China	E6	32
Zhuzhou, China	E7	31
Zhuzhou, China	F7	31
Zia Indian Reservation, N.M., U.S.	h7	108
Zia Pueblo, N.M., U.S.	*B3	108
Zibo, China	D8	31
Ziebach, co., S.D., U.S.	C4	118
Zielona Góra, Pol.	C3	26
Zierikzee, Neth.	C3	17
Ziesar, E. Ger.	A7	19
Ziftā, Eg.	D3	41
Zigazinskiy, Sov. Un.	C5	28
Zigey, Chad	C3	46
Zigong, China	F5	31
Zigui, China	E7	31
Ziguinchor, Sen.	D1	45
Zikhron Ya'aqov, Isr.	B6	41
Zile, Tur.	B10	40
Zillah, Libya	C5	124
Zillah, Wa., U.S.	D3	43
Ziller, stm., Aus.	B7	20
Zilwaukee, Mi., U.S.	E7	99
Zima, Sov. Un.	D13	29
Zimapán, Mex.	C5	63
Zimba, Zam.	E4	48
Zimbabwe, ctry., Afr.	A5	49
Zimmerman, Mn., U.S.	E5	100
Zimnicea, Rom.	D7	24
Zin, Naḥal, val., Isr.	D7	41
Zinal, Switz.	D4	21
Zinc, Ar., U.S.	A3	81
Zincville, Ok., U.S.	A7	113
Zinder, Niger	D6	45
Zingst, E. Ger.	D6	15
Zion, Il., U.S.	A6	90
Zion, N.J., U.S.	C3	107
Zion, S.C., U.S.	C9	117
Zion Gate, hist., Isr. Occ.	m14	41
Zion National Park, Ut., U.S.	F3	121
Zion Reservoir, res., Az., U.S.	C6	80
Zionsville, In., U.S.	E5	91
Zionville, N.C., U.S.	A1	110
Zirándaro, Mex.	n13	63
Zirkel, Mount, mtn., Co., U.S.	A4	83
Zirndorf, W. Ger.	D5	19
Zistersdorf, Aus.	D8	18
Zitácuaro, Mex.	n13	63
Zittau, E. Ger.	C7	18
Ziway, Lake, l., Eth.	D4	47
Ziyang, China	E6	31
Ziyuan, China	K4	32
Žižkov (part of Prague), Czech.	n17	26
Zlatograd, Bul.	E7	24
Zlatoust, Sov. Un.	D9	29
Złoczew, Pol.	C5	26
Zlonice, Czech.	n17	26
Złotoryja, Pol.	C3	26
Złotów, Pol.	B4	26
Zlynka, Sov. Un.	E8	27
Zmeinogorsk, Sov. Un.	C10	28
Znamenka, Sov. Un.	G9	27
Żnin, Pol.	B4	26
Znojmo, Czech.	D4	26
Žilina, Czech.	D5	26
Zoetermeer, Neth.	*B4	17
Zofingen, Switz.	B4	21
Zogno, Italy	E8	21
Zohreh, stm., Iran	F5	39
Zollikofen, Switz.	B3	21
Zollikon, Switz.	B6	21
Zolochev, Sov. Un.	G5	27
Zolfo Springs, Fl., U.S.	E5	86
Zolotonosha, Sov. Un.	G9	27
Zolotoy, Cape, c., Sov. Un.	B12	31
Zomba, Mwi.	E6	48
Zomergem, Bel.	C3	17
Zongo, Zaire	A2	48
Zonguldak, Tur.	B8	40
Zörbig, E. Ger.	B7	19
Zorita, Spain	C3	22
Zorritos, Peru	B1	58
Zortman, Mt., U.S.	C8	103
Zossen, E. Ger.	B6	18
Zottegem, Bel.	D3	17
Zouar, Chad	A3	46
Zoutkamp, Neth.	A6	17
Zreigat, Bir, well, Maur.	B3	45
Zrenjanin (Petrovgrad), Yugo.	C5	24
Zrmanja, stm., Yugo.	C2	24
Zschopau, E. Ger.	C5	19
Zuata, stm., Ven.	B4	60
Zубtsov, Sov. Un.	C10	27
Zuénoula, I.C.	E3	45
Zuera, Spain	B5	22
Zug, Switz.	E4	18
Zug, W. Sah.	E2	44
Zug, Lake, l., Switz.	E4	18
Zug, state, Switz.	B4	20
Zugdidi, Sov. Un.	A13	40
Zugspitze, mtn., Eur.	B6	20
Zuider Zee see IJsselmeer, l., Neth.	A6	16
Zulia, state, Ven.	B3	60
Zülpich, W. Ger.	C1	19
Zumbi, Ponta do, c., Braz.	B2	57
Zumbo, Moz.	A5	49
Zumbro, stm., Mn., U.S.	F6	100
Zumbro Falls, Mn., U.S.	F6	100
Zumbrota, Mn., U.S.	F6	100
Zumpango, Mex.	n14	63
Zungeru, Nig.	E6	45
Zunhua, China	C8	31
Zuni, N.M., U.S.	B1	108
Zuni, Va., U.S.	k14	123
Zuni, stm., U.S.	C6	80
Zuni Indian Reservation, N.M., U.S.	B1	108
Zuni Mountains, mts., N.M., U.S.	B1	108
Zunyi, China	F6	31
Zuoquan, China	F5	32
Zuqar, i., Yemen	C5	47
Zurich, Ont.	D3	73
Zuri, N.M., U.S.	E4	18
Zurich, Ks., U.S.	C4	93
Zürich, Switz.	E4	18
Zurich, Mt., U.S.	B7	103
Zürich, state, Switz.	B4	20
Zürich, Lake, l., Switz.	E4	18
Zusam, stm., W. Ger.	E5	19
Zussdorf, W. Ger.	A7	21
Zutphen, Neth.	A7	16
Zuwārah, Libya	C7	41
Zuwayzā, Jord.	C7	41
Zuyevka, Sov. Un.	G8	27
Zuzenhausen, W. Ger.	B4	28
Zvishavane, Zimb.	B5	49
Zvolen, Czech.	D5	26
Zvornik, Yugo.	C4	24
Zwartsluis, Neth.	B6	17
Zweibrücken, W. Ger.	D3	18
Zweisimmen, Switz.	C3	20
Zwenkau, E. Ger.	B7	19
Zwettl, Aus.	D7	18
Zwickau, E. Ger.	C6	18
Zwickauer Mulde, stm., E. Ger.	C7	19
Zwiesel, W. Ger.	D8	19
Zwingle, Ia., U.S.	B7	92
Zwischenahn, W. Ger.	A7	17
Zwolle, Neth.	A6	16
Zwolle, La., U.S.	C2	95
Zyljks, La., U.S.	A1	95
Żyrardów, Pol.	B6	26
Zyryanovsk, Sov. Un.	D10	28
Żywiec, Pol.	D5	26